Encyclopedia of the Third World

Fourth Edition

Volume II
(Guinea to Pakistan)

Edited by George Thomas Kurian

Facts On File
New York • Oxford

Encyclopedia of the Third World, Fourth Edition

Facts On File, Inc.
460 Park Avenue South
New York, NY 10016
USA

Facts On File Limited
Collins Street
Oxford OX4 1XJ
United Kingdom

Library of Congress Cataloging in Publication Data

Kurian, George Thomas.
Encyclopedia of the Third World / by George Thomas Kurian. — 4th ed.
p. cm.
Includes bibliographical references (p.) and index.
Contents: v. 1. Afghanistan to Guinea
ISBN 0-8160-2261-5 3 Vol. Set
ISBN 0-8160-2262-3 Vol. 1
ISBN 0-8160-2263-1 Vol. 2
ISBN 0-8160-2264-X Vol. 3
1. Developing countries—Encyclopedias. I. Title.
HC59.7.K87 1992
909'.09724—dc20 92-3544

A British CIP catalogue record for this book is available from the British Library.

Facts On File books are available at special discounts when purchased in bulk quantities for businesses, associations, institutions or sales promotions. Please call our Special Sales Department in New York at 212/683-2244 (dial 800/322-8755 except in NY, AK or HI) or in Oxford at 865/728399.

Composition and manufacturing by
the Maple-Vail Book Manufacturing Group

Printed in the United States of America

10 9 8 7 6 5 4 3 2 1

This book is printed on acid-free paper.

Encyclopedia of the Third World

Fourth Edition

Volume II

(Guinea to Pakistan)

TRAVAIL
JUSTICE
SOLIDARITE

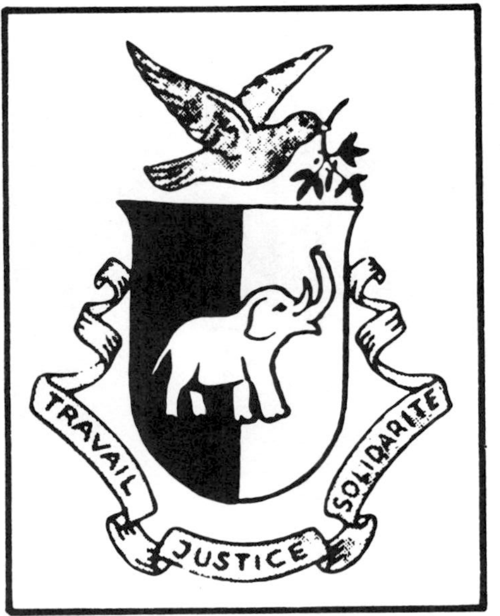

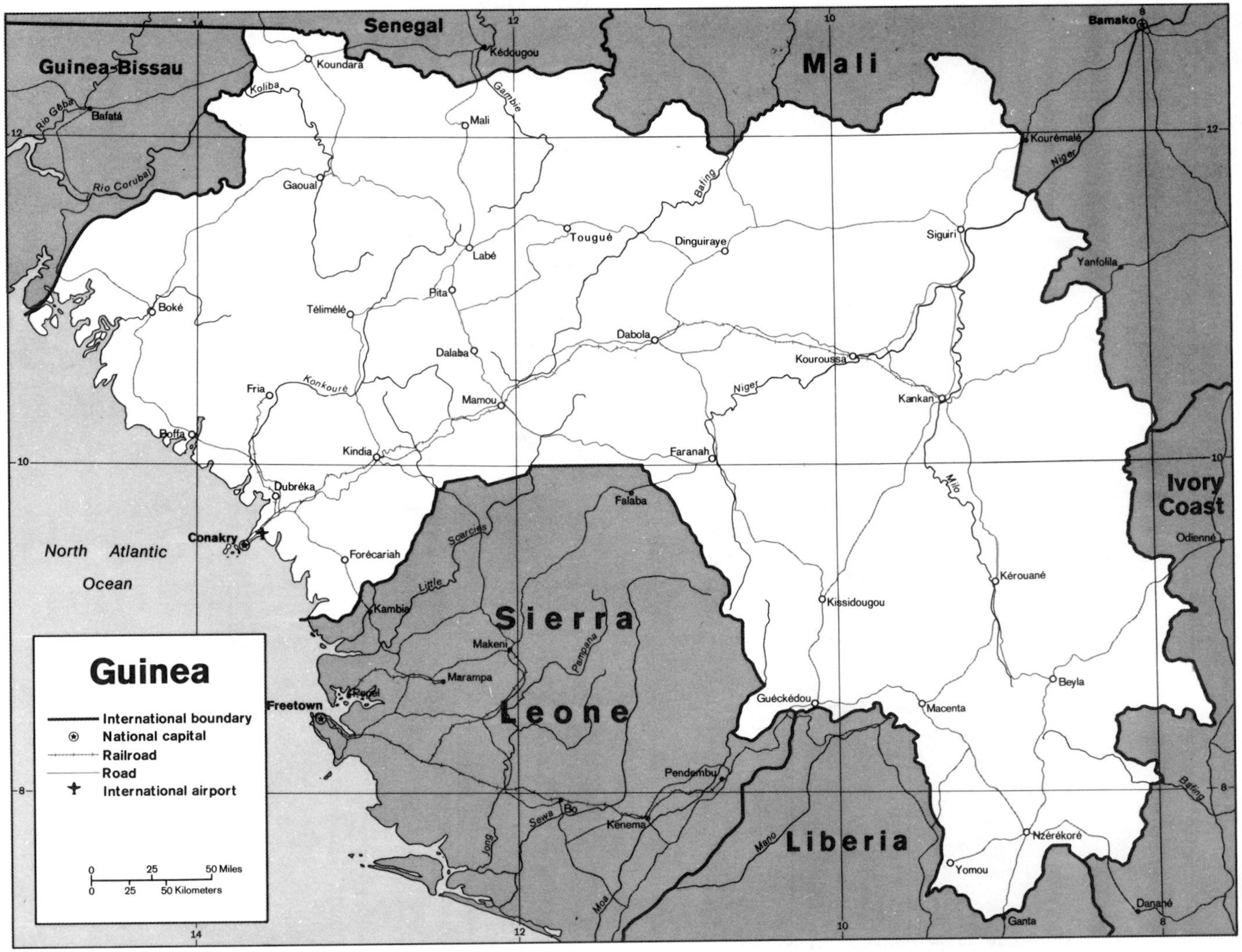
Guinea
International boundary
National capital
Railroad
Road
International airport
0 25 50 Miles
0 25 50 Kilometers
Senegal
Guinea-Bissau
Mali
Ivory Coast
Sierra Leone
Liberia
North Atlantic Ocean
Bamako
Koundara
Kédougou
Bafatá
Rio Gêba
Rio Corubal
Koliba
Gambie
Mali
Gaoual
Labé
Tougué
Dinguiraye
Bafing
Kourémalé
Niger
Siguiri
Yanfolila
Boké
Télimélé
Pita
Dalaba
Dabola
Kouroussa
Kankan
Fria
Konkouré
Mamou
Niger
Boffa
Kindia
Faranah
Dubréka
Conakry
Forécariah
Falaba
Scarcies
Little
Kambia
Makeni
Marampa
Pampana
Freetown
Pepel
Kissidougou
Kérouané
Milo
Odienné
Beyla
Guéckédou
Macenta
Pendembu
Kenema
Bo
Sewa
Jong
Moa
Mano
Nzérékoré
Yomou
Ganta
Danané
Bafing

GUINEA

BASIC FACT SHEET

OFFICIAL NAME: Republic of Guinea (République de Guinée)

ABBREVIATION: GV

CAPITAL: Conakry

HEAD OF STATE: President Gen. Lansana Conté (from 1984)

NATURE OF GOVERNMENT: Military dictatorship

POPULATION: 7,269,240

AREA: 245,857 sq. km. (94,926 sq. mi.)

ETHNIC MAJORITY: Fulani (Peul), Malinké and Soussou

LANGUAGES: French (official) and eight national languages

RELIGIONS: Islam, Christianity and animism

UNIT OF CURRENCY: Guinea franc (G.F.)

NATIONAL FLAG: Tricolor of red, green and yellow vertical stripes

NATIONAL EMBLEM: The principal elements of the national emblem are a dove with an olive branch; the elephant (the national animal); and *Travail, Justice, Solidarité* in French on a scroll under a heraldic shield

NATIONAL ANTHEM: "Liberty"

NATIONAL HOLIDAYS: October 2 (Independence Day, National Day); January 1 (New Year's Day); May 1 (Labor Day); September 28 (Referendum Day); November 1 (Army Day); various Christian festivals, such as Assumption, All Saints' Day, Christmas and Easter Monday, as well as variable Islamic festivals

NATIONAL CALENDAR: Gregorian

PHYSICAL QUALITY OF LIFE INDEX: 25

DATE OF INDEPENDENCE: October 2, 1958

DATE OF CONSTITUTION: None

WEIGHTS & MEASURES: Metric

GEOGRAPHICAL FEATURES

Guinea is located in southwestern West Africa, in an arc curving over Sierra Leone and Liberia. Guinea's total land area of 245,857 sq. km. (94,925 sq. mi.) extends 831 km. (516 mi.) southeast to northwest and 493 km. (306 mi.) northeast to southwest. Its Atlantic coastline stretches for 352 km. (219 mi.).

Guinea's total international land boundary of 3,468 km. (2,155 mi.) is shared with six countries: Guinea-Bissau (386 km.; 240 mi.); Senegal (330 km.; 205 mi.); Mali (932 km.; 579 mi.); Ivory Coast (605 km.; 376 mi.); Liberia (563 km.; 350 mi.); and Sierra Leone (652 km.; 405 mi.). The border with Guinea-Bissau is based on the 1886 convention between France and Portugal and was demarcated in 1905; the border with Liberia is based on the 1892 convention between France and Liberia and was demarcated in 1911; the border with Sierra Leone is based on Anglo-French agreements of the 1890s. The borders with the three remaining countries—Mali, Senegal and Ivory Coast—were administrative boundaries of former French West Africa. Physical borders have little meaning to the inhabitants of these countries, and herders and smugglers cross borders freely. There are no current border disputes.

The capital is Conakry, with a 1983 population of 656,000. The other major urban centers are Kankan (278,000), N'Zérékoré (290,743), Siguiri (253,758) and Labé (273,000).

Guinea's varied terrain is divided topographically into four regions: Lower, or Maritime Guinea; Middle Guinea, including the Fouta Djallon Highlands; Upper Guinea savannas; and the Forest Region of southeastern Guinea.

Lower Guinea stretches from the coastal swamps across an alluvial plain 50 to 90 km. (30 to 55 mi.) broad crossed by winding tidal rivers. About 50 km. (30 mi.) inland of Kakoulima Massif rises to 1,124 m. (3,688 ft.). Lower Guinea also comprises the Kaloum Peninsula: the island of Tombo, on which Conakry stands; and the Los islands. Middle Guinea, formed by the Fouta Djallon Massif, consists of a stepped plateau with an average elevation of 900 m. (3,000 ft.), deeply cut in many places by narrow valleys. Upper Guinea, in the northeast, is a region of grassy plains and savannas. The Forest Region, in the southeast, reaches its highest elevation in Mt. Nimba (1,850 m.; 6,069 ft.). The Forest Region's major feature is the Guinea Highlands, although areas around Beyla and N'Zérékoré consist of rolling plains once covered by rain forest.

Over one-third of the country is drained by the Niger River, which rises in the Guinea Highlands. Lower Guinea is crisscrossed by numerous short rivers, the most important of which are Rio Nuñez, Fatala, Melikhouré, Konkouré, Cogon and Rio Kapatchez. Only the first three are used for navigation. Guinea also is the source of the principal rivers of West Africa, including the Gambia, the Senegal and the Bafing rivers.

CLIMATE & WEATHER

Guinea has a tropical climate with two distinct seasons. Although there are seasonal variations, the wet season generally lasts from April-May to October-November, with the heaviest rainfall during July and August. The dry season lasts from November to April. April is the hottest month.

Lower Guinea has an average rainfall of 2,400 mm. (95 in.) annually, although in some places, such as Conakry, the rainfall may exceed 4,300 mm. (169 in.) in most years. Toward the interior the rainfall diminishes in volume but is more evenly distributed. The mean average varies from 2,540 mm. (100 in.) in southern Fouta Djallon to 1,830 mm. (72 in.) in the savannas of Upper Guinea.

Temperatures and humidity are high. Conakry has an annual average maximum of 29°C (85°F) and an annual average minimum of 23°C (74°F). In Upper Guinea the temperature range is 18°C to 40°C (64°F to 104°F). Temperatures are lower in the Fouta Djallon region, with daily mean temperatures between 12.2°C (54°F) and 34.4°C (94°F) in the dry period and 18.3°C (65°F) to 26.7°C (80°F) in the wet period.

The prevailing wind systems are the southwestern monsoons and the northeastern harmattan, the latter a dry, scorching wind from the Sahara. Tornadoes and thunderstorms are common in coastal areas.

VITAL STATISTICS

Crude birth rate (/1,000): 48 (1988); 46 (1965)
Crude death rate (/1,000): 22 (1988); 29 (1965)
Infant mortality rate (/1,000 live births): 147 (1990)
Life expectancy (yrs.) at birth: males, 40; females, 44 (1990)
Gross reproduction rate (/woman) (1980–85): 3.05
Total fertility rate (/woman): 6.1 (1990)
Rate of natural increase (/1,000) (1985–90): 24.7
Average household size: 4.7

POPULATION

The population of Guinea was estimated in 1990 at 7,269,240.

The most densely populated regions are Labe and Pita in Fouta Djallon; Gueckedou and N'Zérékoré in the Forest Region; and Dubreka and Fria in Lower Guinea. Upper Guinea, encompassing two-fifths of the land area, has the lowest density of population, with 10 persons per sq. km. (26 persons per sq. mi.).

The urban population in towns of over 5,000 constituted 22.19% of the total population in 1984, up from 9.6% in 1960. All towns have shared in this increase, particularly Conakry, which grew from 78,000 in 1959 to 656,000 in 1984 and now accounts for 80% of the urban population. However, urbanization has not become a matter for official concern, and the rate of urban growth has remained steady at about 5.4% since 1985.

Migration is a major phenomenon, but most of it is seasonal and restricted to farmers and cattle herders, who move across borders at will. Large-scale politically motivated emigration took place during the 1960s and early 1970s as émigrés from the Touré regime took refuge in neighboring countries. Immigration is restricted by a 1965 decree requiring all aliens to obtain special residence permits.

Immediately on taking over the government in 1984, the ruling CMRN invited refugees and those who had left for economic reasons to return to Guinea. Of an estimated 1.5 million Guineans living in other countries, some 200,000 have returned since Sekou Touré's death, adding a heavy burden on the economy. The government estimates that at least 250,000 in all will eventually return and, to meet the emergency, was granted $1 million in supplies and medicines by the U.N. high commissioner for refugees for the remainder of 1984.

Women in Guinea have enjoyed a special status as a result of the important political role they played prior to independence. Guinean women are represented in all professions, from civil engineering to the national police and armed forces. An Office of Women's Affairs has been established in the Ministry of Social Affairs. The majority of students enrolled in the National Medical College have been women. The government's health-care policies have stressed prevention and child and mother care, but the quality of care has been low, owing to inadequate facilities and med-

DEMOGRAPHIC INDICATORS

Population (millions): 7.269 (1990)
Year of last census: 1983
Sex distribution (% at last census): males, 48.6; females: 51.4
Population estimates and projections (millions)

1950: 3.245	1980: 5.407	2010: 11.451
1960: 3.660	1990: 7.269	
1970: 4.388	2000: 8.879	

Age profile (% at last census)

0–14: 43.1	30–44: 16.3	60–74: 4.2
15–29: 26.2	45–59: 9.6	75 and over: 0.7

Median age (yrs.): 18.4 (1985)
Youth population (% age 15–24): 18.9 (1985); 18.8 (2000)
Total dependency ratio: 85.2 (1985)
Annual growth rate (%)

1950–55: 1.03	1975–1980: 2.17	2000–2005: 2.58
1955–60: 1.38	1980–1985: 2.33	2005–2010: 2.57
1960–65: 1.68	1985–1990: 2.45	2010–2015: 2.37
1965–70: 1.95	1990–1995: 2.54	2015–2020: 2.15
1970–75: 2.01	1995–2000: 2.57	2020–2025: 1.81

Hypothetical size of stationary population (millions): 34
Assumed year of reaching net reproduction rate of 1: 2050
Urban population (millions): 1.348 (1985)
Urban population (%): 24 (1988); 12 (1965)
Annual urban population growth rate (%, 1985–90): 5.36
Annual rural population growth rate (%, 1985–90): 1.57
Percentage of urban population in largest city: 80 (1980)
Percentage of urban population in
cities of population over 500,000: 80 (1980)
Number of cities of population over 500,000: 1 (1980)
Population density per sq. km. (per sq. mi.): 28.0 (72.4) (latest)

STATUS OF WOMEN INDICATORS

Number of women (millions): 2.895 (1985)
Women of childbearing age (15–49) (% of pop.): 46 (1987)
Women's literacy rate (%): 17 (1985)
Women in labor force (%): 59 (1985)
Total fertility rate (/woman): 6.1 (1990)

ical supplies. Improvement of the national health sector also is one of the CMRN's priorities.

Guinea has no official birth control programs or policies.

ETHNIC COMPOSITION

Guinea's ethnic composition conforms to the general African pattern of numerous tribal groups with no single group in the majority, although four groups together are numerically dominant. Guinea's ethnic groups number nearly 24. Of these, three groups constitute 75% of the total, each with its own geographical niche. The Malinké and the Peul (also known as the Fulani, Fulbé or Foulah) each account for about 30% of the population and the Soussou for 16.1%. The Soussou are most numerous in Lower Guinea, the Peul in Middle Guinea and the Malinké in Upper Guinea. The earliest settlers in Guinea are believed to have been the Baga. Later came the Soussou, a group related to the Malinké, who drove the Baga to the coast. Last of all came the Fulani, who established a kingdom in Fouta Djallon in the 16th century. The forest groups together make up 18% of the population. Ethnic affiliations, however, are fluid, and the smaller groups tend to be subject to a constant process of assimilation within the larger ones. Though ethnic loyalties tend to be pervasive and persistent, ethnic differences are less crucial in Guinea than in most other African countries.

Besides the Soussou, the major ethnic groups in Lower Guinea are the Baga, who live scattered along the coast; the Baga Foré, who live in the coastal swamps around Monchon; the Nalou, who live on the lower Rio Nuñez and the Kogan River and on the Tristão Islands; the Landouma, who live along the Guinea-Bissau border between the Rio Nuñez and the Fatala River; and the Mmani, who live between the Kolenté and the Forecariah rivers. Besides the Peul, the major ethnic groups in Middle Guinea are the Dialonké, native to southern and central Fouta Djallon; the Diakhanké, concentrated in Gaoul; and the Tenda, who live in the northern part of Middle Guinea. Besides the Malinké, the only major group in Upper Guinea is the Ouassoulounké, who are related to the Peul and live near the Mali border. The three major forest groups are the Kissi, the Toma and the Guerzé.

Since independence the government has sought to break down ethnic barriers and to deethnicize politics. The process of national integration has been accelerated by the fact that the tribal groups no longer have access to the traditional machinery of keeping alive historic cultural and emotional ties among their members. The government also has encouraged mixed marriages to build up a new community without clear-cut ethnic affiliations. People are encouraged to identify themselves as Guineans rather than as members of a tribe.

Among the foreign community, Russians, Cubans, Czechs, Yugoslavs and Chinese are most numerous. The Lebanese and the Syrians constitute a special category because many of them have adopted Guinean citizenship. The number of Frenchmen does not exceed 100. Over 107 Americans were reported in the country in 1976, of whom 80 were private citizens.

Under the leadership of Sekou Touré, Guineans turned their backs on the West and were isolated periodically from Western contacts. Thus Guinean attitudes toward foreigners are colored by official indoctrination, which categorizes all Western influences as forms of neocolonialism and suspects all Western activities as directed to the subversion and overthrow of the Republic of Guinea.

LANGUAGES

Guinea has one official language, French, and eight national languages, the country's eight major vernaculars: Poular, Malinke, Soussou, Kissi, Guerzé, Toma, Coniagui and Bassari. Because these vernaculars do not have their own script, they are transcribed into a modified Latin alphabet. Among Guinea's vernaculars Baga, Landouma, Mmani, Nalou, Poular, Badyaranké, Kissi, Coniagui and Bassari belong to the West Atlantic family of languages, Soussou, Mikhifore, Dialonké, Diakhanké, Malinké, Ouassoulounké, Guerzé, Toma, Mano, Kono, Konianké, Kouranko and Toma-Manian belong to the Mande family of languages. Of these, Soussou and Malinké serve as lingua francas over large areas. Poular, using Arabic script, has an extensive literature.

French is understood by about 20% of the literate population.

RELIGIONS

Guinea is a secular state, but Islam is the religion of the majority of the people, cutting across ethnic lines. Slightly more than one-third adhere to traditional African beliefs, and less than 2% are Christian. But even within the framework of Islam or Christianity, traditional beliefs and practices have survived, if in a modified form. Islam is believed to be growing at the expense of other faiths. At the same time, in the process of being adopted by the majority of Guineans, Islam has assumed a specifically local quality.

The Christian community is overwhelmingly Catholic and is concentrated in Lower Guinea. The Roman Catholic Church in Guinea is presided over by the archbishop of Conakry, and two bishops, at Kankan and N'Zérékoré. Church-state relations have deteriorated since 1967, when President Touré ordered that only Guinean nationals be allowed to serve in the Roman Catholic priesthood. Four years later the archbishop of Conakry was sentenced to life imprisonment at hard labor for allegedly plotting against the state. All Catholic mission schools were nationalized in 1961. However, there is no overt persecution of Christians.

As before the April 1984 coup, all religions have the right to establish places of worship and maintain contacts with coreligionists in other countries. The former cabinet included a Ministry of Islamic Affairs, even though Islam is not the official religion of the state. The present government has restructured that ministry, naming it the Ministry of Religious Affairs, and created the Christian Affairs Department. The minister is a Muslim leader. The government also has invited Christian organizations in Guinea to reestablish the private schools that had been forced to close by the previous regime.

The Marxist-oriented government began a campaign against religious superstitions in the 1960s. The campaign was directed particularly against fetishes, initiation rites and sacrifices in traditional religions, but the government also has criticized what it sees as retrogressive trends in Islam.

HISTORICAL BACKGROUND

Effective French colonial rule in Guinea began in 1898, with the capture of Malinke adventurer Samory Touré, who had overrun Upper Guinea by late 1870s. Guinea was part of French West Africa until 1958, when it became the first and only state in Francophone Africa to vote against the French Community concept proposed by President Charles de Gaulle.

French rule revolved around the central concept of assimilation as the instrument of a civilizing mission to extend France's language, institutions, laws and customs to Africa. Under the influence of this concept, all existing political and legal institutions were dismantled and replaced by French ones with little or no modification. However, the process of Frenchification became counterproductive by the end of World War II, as it created a class of labor leaders and teachers deeply influenced by Marxism of the French school and hostile to all forms of colonialism.

On independence the break with France was complete and decisive. France showed its displeasure at Guinea's opting out of the French Community by suspending aid, withdrawing administrative personnel and rescinding the favored-nation status of Guinean exports to France. Guinea retaliated by de-Westernizing education and administration. Relations between the two countries were suspended from 1965 to 1975. Anti-French feelings were very strong in the Touré administration. French, however, is retained, for pragmatic reasons, as the official language. The legal system also continues to operate within a French framework.

At independence on October 2, 1958, Ahmed Sekou Touré, leader of the dominant Parti Démocratique de Guinée (PDG), became president. The following month, he established the PDG as the sole party, eliminated all opposition and instituted a program of economic and political centralization. In principle, Touré's policies were directed toward building "scientific socialism," but in practice they were a reflection of party corruption and the president's desire to maintain power.

Touré's administration was dominated by political unrest and attempted coups, with Touré developing a siege mentality that resulted in imprisonment, torture and execution of those thought to oppose him. There is evidence that the French planned to overthrow him in 1960 and allegations that the Soviet Union, the United States, Germany and Portugal were at one time or another involved in coup attempts. In 1970 Portuguese troops and dissident Guineans attempted an invasion. The coup failed, but in response Touré unleashed a reign of terror against any suspected enemies. In 1976 Touré's minister of justice, Diallo Telli, was arrested on charges of conspiracy against the government and executed while awaiting trial.

Touré died in March 1984 while undergoing heart surgery, and Prime Minister Lansana Beavogui assumed office as acting president. Several days later, the military staged a successful coup, forming a Comite Militaire de Redressement National (CMRN). The committee installed Col. Lansana Conté as president and Col. Diarra Traoré as prime minister. The CMRN immediately acted to reduce political repression. It released more than 1,000 political prisoners, lifted censorship and restored freedom of speech and internal

GOVERNMENT LIST
(July/August 1991)

President	Conté, Lansana, *Gen.*
Minister Secretary General at the Presidency of the Republic	Gomez, Alseny Rene
Minister at the Presidency of the Republic for Economic & Financial Control	Foulah, Henry, *Maj.*
Minister at the Presidency of the Republic for Information, Culture & Tourism	Bargoura, Herve Vincent
Minister at the Presidency of the Republic for National Defense & Security	Diallo, Abdourahmane, *Maj.*
Minister Resident for Forest Region	Diallo, Ibrahima Sory, *Maj.*
Minister Resident for Guinea Maritime	Tofani, Henri, *Lt. Col.*
Minister Resident for Middle Guinea	Camara, Abou, *Lt. Col.*
Minister Resident for Upper Guinea	Camara, Kissi, *Maj.*
Minister of Administration Reform & Public Service	Bangoura, Mamouna
Minister of Agriculture & Animal Resources	Kourouma, Aboubacar Koly
Minister of Economy & Finance	Benjamin, Edouard
Minister of Foreign Affairs	Traoré, Jean, *Maj.*
Minister of Industry, Commerce & Crafts	Sylla, Ousmane
Minister of Interior & Decentralization	Conde, Alhassane
Minister of Justice & Keeper of the Seals	Touré, Faciné, *Maj.*
Minister of National Education in Charge of Higher Education & Scientific Research	Diawara, Mamadi
Minister of Natural Resources & Environment	Traore, Mohamed Lamine
Minister of Planning & International Cooperation	Sylla, Ibrahima
Minister of Post & Telecommunications	Kourouma, Fassou Jean-Claude, *Capt.*
Minister of Public Health & Population	Fofana, Madigbe, *M.D.*
Minister of Social Affairs & Employment	Barry, Basirou
Minister of Town Planning & Housing	Sidibé, Bahna
Minister of Transport & Public Works	Diallo, Ibrahima, *Maj.*
Minister of Youth, Sports & Art	Zoumanigui, Joseph Gbagbo, *Capt.*
Secretary of State at the Ministery of Agriculture & Animal Resources in Charge of Fisheries	Barry, Mamadou Boye
Secretary of State at the Ministery of Information, Culture & Tourism in Charge of Tourism & Hostellery	Camara, Nantenin
Secretary of State at the Ministery of Interior & Decentralization in Charge of Decentralization	Sow, Ibrahima Sory
Secretary of State at the Minister of National Education in Charge of Pre-University Education	Bah, Diallo Aicha
Secretary of State at the Ministery of Natural Resources & Environment in Charge of Energy	Sacko, Toumani Dakoum
Governor, Central Bank	Yansane, Kerfalla

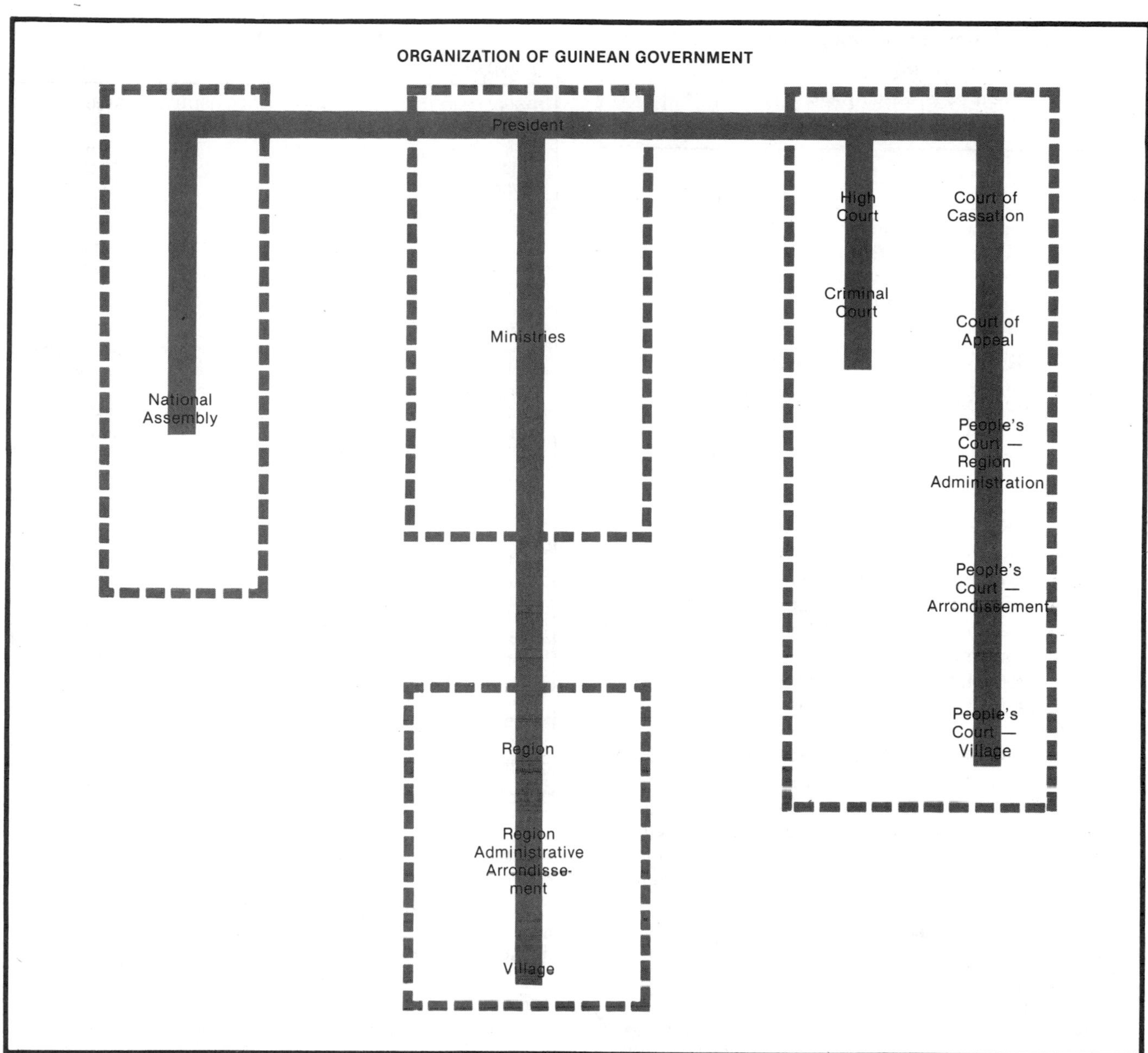

travel. It also promised to liberalize the economy and to return property confiscated in Touré's drive toward centralization. As a result some of the two million Guineans who had fled Touré returned.

In the following months, Conté consolidated his power by abolishing the office of prime minister and demoting Traoré to education minister. Traoré in 1985 led an unsuccessful coup that was crushed by troops loyal to Conté. Traoré was arrested and executed without trial.

Following the coup, Conté continued to press for economic reform and the implementation of austerity programs demanded by the World Bank and the IMF before foreign aid was granted. These measures, together with serious inflation, prompted civil unrest in 1988. The following year Conté promised a return to a two-party system and a transitional government, composed of military and civilians, that would oversee the transition to democracy.

CONSTITUTION & GOVERNMENT

Guinea is ruled by a 20-person Military Committee for National Redressment (CMRN). On seizing power April 3, 1984, the CMRN abolished Sékou Touré's Democratic Party of Guinea (Parti Démocratique de Guinée, PDG) and the Constitution and named a president (Lansana Conté), as head of state; a prime minister (Diarra Traoré); and a cabinet of 33 military personnel and eight civilians. (In a reorganization on December 18, 1984, the office of the prime minister was abolished and the cabinet and the CMRN were reduced in numbers.) Members of the various armed forces were named to principal offices at the regional and subregional levels. Citizens subsequently have been invited to organize representative councils at the local level.

The country's original name was restored in 1984, replacing the Popular and Revolutionary Republic of Guinea adopted in 1978.

RULERS OF GUINEA (from 1958)

Presidents

October 1958–April 1984: Sékou Touré
April 1984– : Lansana Conté

ADMINISTRATIVE REGIONS

Region	Capital
Beyla	Beyla
Boffa	Boffa
Boké	Boké
Conakry	Conakry
Coyah	Coyah
Dabola	Dabola
Dalaba	Dalaba
Dinguiraye	Dinguiraye
Faranah	Faranah
Forécariah	Forécariah
Fria	Fria
Gaoual	Gaoual
Guéckédou	Guéckédou
Kankan	Kankan
Kerouané	Kerouané
Kindia	Kindia
Kissidougou	Kissidougou
Koubia	Koubia
Koundara	Koundara
Kourassa	Kourassa
Labé	Labé
Lelouma	Lelouma
Lola	Lola
Macenta	Macenta
Mali	Mali
Mamou	Mamou
Mandiana	Mandiana
N'Zérékoré	N'Zérékoré
Pita	Pita
Siguiri	Siguiri
Telimelé	Telimelé
Tongué	Tongué
Yomou	Yomou

In 1989 President Conté promised a return to a two-party system as well as the democratic election of the president and assembly after a transitional period supervised by a National Recovery Council composed of military personnel and civilians.

FREEDOM & HUMAN RIGHTS

In terms of political and civil rights, Guinea is classified as a partly free country.

The previous regime had imprisoned without trial and executed many Guineans over a period of years, including up to the time of the coup. Torture of prisoners was commonplace, and thousands simply disappeared. Toward the end, Touré had begun to relax controls on several aspects of Guinea's political and social life, beginning in the late 1970s. A general amnesty of all Guinean exiles had been declared in July 1977, and thousands of emigrants returned to Guinea. However, immediately after the coup, the military government released 250 political prisoners, mainly from Camp Boiro, the principal political detention center, and permitted reporters to describe the heinous conditions and practices, including standard tiny concrete cells and the "black diet" (total deprivation of food and water). The new military government invited Amnesty International to interview former political detainees in the early fall, and signed an instrument of adherence by the Republic of Guinea to the Geneva Conventions of August 12, 1949 (plus additional protocols), on Civil and Political Rights. It also announced its intent to adhere to the Universal Declaration of Human Rights.

However, following Traoré's unsuccessful coup in 1985, the military began a purge of suspected followers. Traoré was executed immediately, and 60 other officers were sentenced to death following a secret trial.

CIVIL SERVICE

No information is available on the codes, structure or size of the Guinean civil service.

LOCAL GOVERNMENT

For administrative purposes Guinea is divided into four tiers. At the apex are the four regions corresponding to the four geographic regions: Lower Guinea, Middle Guinea, Upper Guinea and the Forest Region, each headed by a minister delegate or super governor. At the next level are 33 administrative regions *(régions administratives)*, under the authority of a governor appointed by the president. Each administrative region has a popularly elected 40-member general council. The third tier is the district *(arrondissement administrative)*, of which there are 175. The commandant, or the executive head of a district is responsible to the governor of the administrative region. The basic village-level unit of government is the local revolutionary authority *(pouvoir révolutionnaire local*, PRL), numbering 7,800 and combining local administrative organs.

No separate municipal forms of administration exist, although Conakry is classified as an administrative region by itself.

FOREIGN POLICY

Guinea's foreign policy has fluctuated since independence between an outward-looking pan-Africanism and a defensive isolationism, between ideological fervor and pragmatism, and between calls for cooperation and paranoid suspicion. Guinea once was hailed as a model of political and economic development, but its influence in African affairs has declined over the years because of Sékou Touré's frequent policy reversals, virulent attacks on leaders of other countries and false charges regarding alleged plots against Guinea.

Despite its heavy ideological content, Touré's foreign policy was rife with obvious inconsistencies and contradictions. Although verbally supporting African unity, he dissociated Guinea from regional and continental organizations working for African unity. He fostered trade with "neocolonialist" countries even while condemning them. Although personally involved in formulation of foreign policy at all levels, Touré showed a marked reluctance, for security reasons, to travel abroad to promote his policies.

Among neighboring states, Guinea's relations are closest with Sierra Leone, Gambia and Guinea-Bissau. Ties with Sierra Leone were strengthened by a mutual defense treaty signed in 1971. Guinea's long-standing support for Partido Africano da Independencia da Guiné e Cabo Verde (PAIGC) paid off when Guinea-Bissau became independent in 1974, with the PAIGC taking power.

On the other hand, relations with Senegal, Ivory Coast, Mali and Ghana have been plagued by ideological and economic issues. Both Senegal and Ivory Coast have served as havens for Guinean refugees fleeing the Touré regime and as bases of operations for Guinean exile groups. The frequent temperamental clashes between Touré and the heads of state of these countries led on a number of occasions to the closing of their respective embassies. Relations with Ghana were on a war footing from the fall of Nkrumah to his death in 1972. As a member of the Economic Community of West African States, Guinea was involved in the effort to end Liberia's civil war. In August 1990 it agreed to become part of a multinational peacekeeping force whose stated goals were to enforce a truce and establish an interim administration that would organize free elections. The establishment of the 3,000-strong military force marked the first time that African nations had organized a cooperative military intervention into the affairs of another African state.

Guinea's departure from the French Community in 1958 was accompanied by a wave of anti-French sentiment, which was carried over into the early years of independence. Bitterness against the French was manifested in constant denunciations by all sections of the population. In 1965 France was accused of being involved in an anti-Touré plot, and diplomatic relations between the two countries were suspended. Since then a number of Frenchmen have been jailed in Guinea and French businesses have been expropriated. Diplomatic ties were resumed in 1975 through the mediation of U.N. secretary general Kurt Waldheim.

Diplomatic relations with the United Kingdom were suspended over the Rhodesian question but were restored in 1968. Diplomatic relations with West Germany were broken in 1971, and were resumed in 1975. Relations with the United States have been maintained on a low level, with occasional irritants, such as the expulsion of the Peace Corps in 1966. U.S. private investments have provided the main connection between the two countries.

Relations with the communist bloc have remained the most successful area of Guinean foreign policy. Initially the Soviet Union stepped in to fill the void caused by the French departure, in the belief that Guinea could become a showcase of socialist development in Africa. However, as events in Guinea belied these expectations, Soviet influence and aid began to decline, reaching a nadir under Khrushchev, when the Soviet ambassador was forced to leave Guinea. Soviet aid resumed, though at a lower level, after the fall of Khrushchev. The Chinese communists began to compete with the Soviet Union for influence in Conakry, and Chinese-aided projects multiplied in number, particularly after 1970. Although it is difficult to measure the actual influence of the Soviet Union and China on Guinean foreign affairs, both of them had greater influence than the Western nations in the country under Touré.

During 1978 and 1979 Touré made a number of efforts to break out of the isolation to which his policies had led Guinea. In 1978 he came to an understanding with his old enemies Presidents Houphouet-Boigny of Ivory Coast and Léopold Senghor of Senegal, at a "summit of reconciliation" in Monrovia. In the same year President Giscard d'Estaing of France made the first visit of a French president to independent Guinea and received a warm welcome. In 1979 the Guinea president made one of his rare visits overseas, to Washington D.C., to meet President Carter. All these events pointed to a new direction in Guinean foreign policy based on Guinea's practical needs rather than on Marxist rhetoric.

The 1984 coup restored Guinea to the community of pro-Western nations in Africa after a long interregnum. Immediate response to the coup was positive from almost all Western capitals.

The United States and Guinea are parties to 14 treaties and agreements covering agricultural commodities, cultural relations, defense, economic and technical cooperation, information media guarantees, investment guarantees, the Peace Corps and telecommunications.

Guinea joined the United Nations in 1958. Guinea is a member of 11 U.N. organizations and 12 other international organizations.

PARLIAMENT

The National Assembly was dissolved by the CMRN in April 1984. The former legislature was elected for five-year terms by universal suffrage from a single slate of candidates selected by the PDG. Under the constitutional changes of 1974, the National Assembly became the "nation's third legislative body," after the PDG and the National Council for the Revolution. Deputies did not represent constituencies but were drawn from the country at large. Ninety of the members were selected by PDG regional organs; 48 by the National Political Bureau; and four each by the party's women's, labor and youth organizations.

Under the Constitution the National Assembly had extensive powers of investigative and fiscal control. The National Assembly had the sole right to legislate, and the president was responsible to it for the policies of his cabinet. A body known as the Permanent Commission functioned when the National Assembly was not in session. However, with the growth of the revolutionary character of the regime, the powers of the National Assembly had been whittled down. Its rights to question the executive and challenge its acts had fallen into disuse. The National Assembly had become a rubber stamp, ratifying the acts and decisions of the president and the PDG. Nearly one-fifth of its membership consisted of technocrats or officials or directors of state enterprises.

POLITICAL PARTIES

The Democratic Party of Guinea (Parti Démocratique de Guinée, PDG), the republic's founding party, was dissolved by the CMRN in 1984. Founded in 1947 as a section of the Rassemblement Démocratique Africain (RDA), the PDG owed much of its initial strength to Communist-backed labor union movements.

In his dual role as secretary general of the PDG and president of the republic, Touré had impressed his own philosophies on the ideology and goals of the party. Touré had described the rule of the PDG as a popular dictatorship based on the will of the whole people, as opposed to the class struggles of the orthodox Marxist states. However, the PDG borrowed its organization, discipline and intolerance of opposition from Soviet and East European models. But the PDG was Marxist more in form than in philosophy. Labeled "African socialism" or "democratic centralism," PDG ideology shared with Marxism its hostility toward capitalism and insistence on total independence from foreign control. But it differed from Marxism in its rejection of the concept of class struggle and its concern for national unity to bind together the country's ethnically diverse peoples. Membership in the party was open to anyone willing to purchase a membership card, although party posts were restricted to the militants. In a curious mixture of democracy and dictatorship, party members could express opinions on any issue within the party, but once a decision was made by the party's central leadership, all disagreements were supposed to cease and the central directives were to be unquestioningly obeyed by the party members and the general population. Such obedience was enforced through state agencies. Neither civil rights nor individualism were relevant to PDG ideology, which, in the African tradition, placed collective good above that of the individual good. All Guineans, particularly students and civil servants, were constantly indoctrinated in PDG ideology through the media and the Ministry of Ideology, created in 1972.

The exile group Organisation Unifiée pour la Libération de la Guinée is based on the Ivory Coast.

ECONOMY

Guinea is a nation rich in natural resources with considerable potential for agricultural development. It is the world's second largest producer of bauxite and has valuable deposits of iron ore, gold, diamonds, uranium and oil. Despite its resources, Guinea is one of the low-income countries of the world and one of the least developed. Its per capita GNP was $430 in 1989. The economy's poor performance reflects a policy of rigid socialism that prevailed until the end of the 1970s.

In 1979, the country's rigidly socialist approach was modified through major reforms in the liberalization of private commerce and the opening of investment opportunities in small and medium-size enterprises. The minerals sector continued to dominate the economy, but growth in foreign exchange receipts slowed as bauxite mines produced at near-capacity levels. Despite good potential, agriculture still was hampered by an unrealistic state farm policy and by inadequate incentives; production continued to stagnate. Prospects for near-term growth are complicated by a serious foreign-debt problem, by lack of effective planning mechanisms and by the country's limited absorptive capacity.

Guinea has had a centrally planned economy using two basic forms of business organization; wholly government-owned, semiautonomous state enterprises; and mixed enterprises—foreign investment in joint ventures with the government of Guinea. In addition, the government granted permission for some private Guineans to set up joint ventures with foreign firms. The government-owned enterprises generally had a monopoly in their respective fields and ranged from manufacturing firms (e.g., cigarettes and cloth) to trading firms (e.g., food distribution). The agricultural sector also was controlled by the government, which fixes producer prices, import prices and consumer prices.

Following the CMRN takeover, Conté announced a policy of economic liberalization and privatization. In 1986 the government implemented a series of reforms

PRINCIPAL ECONOMIC INDICATORS

Gross National Product (U.S. $ billions): 2.372 (1989)
GNP per capita (U.S. $): 430 (1989)
GNP per capita average annual growth rate (%, 1987–89): −0.3

GROSS DOMESTIC PRODUCT

GDP nominal (G.F. billions): 857.4 (1986)
GDP per capita (U.S. $): 350 (1988)
Average annual growth rate of GDP (%, 1985–88): 4.2
GDP by type of expenditure (%) 1986
- Consumption
  - Private: 75
  - Government: 8
- Gross domestic investment: 13
- Gross domestic saving: 19
- Foreign trade
  - Exports: 32
  - Imports: −28

Sectoral origin of GDP (%) 1986
- Primary
  - Agriculture: 45
  - Mining: 23
- Secondary
  - Manufacturing: 1
  - Construction: 3
  - Public utilities: 1
- Tertiary
  - Transportation & communications: 2
  - Trade: 19
  - Finance: 3
  - Other services & government: 7

necessary to receive IMF aid. These included devaluation of the currency, privatization or closure of state corporations, reduction of the civil service and reform of financial practices.

Guinea's extraordinary mineral and agricultural resources give the country a much brighter long-term outlook, especially if the government accelerates development of policies aimed at economic liberalization.

PUBLIC FINANCE

The Guinean fiscal year runs from October 1 through September 30. No consolidated budget is published for the public sector, and separate budgets are prepared for the central government, the 33 administrative regions, the 220 *arrondissements* and the more than 70 public enterprises. The central budget is divided into an ordinary budget and a capital budget.

CENTRAL GOVERNMENT REVENUES, 1983

% of total current revenues
- Taxes on income, profit & capital gain: 22.2
- Social security contributions: 0.0
- Domestic taxes on goods & services: 1.4
- Taxes on international trade & transactions: 37.6
- Other taxes: 0.0
- Current nontax revenue: 34.5

Total current revenue as % of GNP:
General government consumption as % of GDP: 10 (1988)

Guinea's first development plan was drawn up with the assistance of a French team of Marxist professors. It was characterized by inadequate statistical planning and inadequate administrative coordination. It placed primary emphasis on industry and showcase projects. Succeeding plans shifted the emphasis to mining, infrastructure and agriculture. Throughout its history, Guinea has received substantial amounts of foreign capital and aid from Western and communist governments.

FOREIGN AID

Total foreign aid (U.S. $ millions): 468.4
- Bilateral: 269.9
- Multilateral: 198.5

The best estimates on foreign aid to Guinea place it at $1.2 billion through 1974, including $300 million to $400 million in foreign exchange or equipment received for the bauxite mining projects. It is not known how much of this aid was in the form of grants and how much in the form of soft or hard loans. The largest amounts were received from the Communist bloc. From 1954 through 1976, Guinea received $201 million from the USSR, making it the second-largest recipient of Soviet aid in Africa after Algeria. Aid from East European countries amounted to $77 million and aid from China to $105 million in the same period. By the mid-1970s Guinea had become less exclusively reliant on Communist aid and more receptive to private direct investment from the West. In 1974 Guinea also became eligible to receive aid from the U.N. Emergency Operation for countries hardest hit by the rise in oil prices. Under the U.N. Development Program Guinea was allocated $23.4 million through 1978. Wealthy Arab nations entered the ranks of foreign aid donors in 1975.

CURRENCY & BANKING

The Guinean unit of currency is the Guinea franc (G.F.) reintroduced in 1986. The Guinea franc had been replaced by the syli in 1972. Notes are issued in denominations of 25, 50, 100, 500, 1,000 and 5,000 Guinea francs. The June 1991 exchange rate was $1 = GF715.0.

Guinea withdrew from the franc zone in 1960 and established the Central Bank of the Republic of Guinea (Banque Centrale de la République de Guinée) as the central bank and bank of issue. By 1961 all private banks were nationalized and taken over by the central bank, but the banking system was decentralized the next year through the establishment of four state-owned banks: the National Credit Bank for Commerce, Industry and Housing; the Guinean Foreign Trade Bank;

FINANCIAL INDICATORS, 1989

Money supply 1986
- Stock (nat. currency billions): 22.5
- M1 per capita: 3,660

External debt 1988
- Total (U.S. $ billions): 2.563
  - of which public (U.S. $ billions): 2.312
  - of which private (U.S. $ billions): 0
- Debt service (long term)
  - Total (U.S. $ millions): 143
  - Repayment
    - Principal (%): 78.3
    - Interest (%): 21.7
- Debt service ratio (%): 21.9
- External public debt as % of GNP: 94.7
- Debt service as % of GNP: 5.9
- Debt service as % of exports: 21.9
- Terms of public borrowing
  - Commitments (U.S. $ millions): 271
  - Average interest rate (%): 1.4
  - Average maturity (yrs.): 30
- Net flow of publicly guaranteed external capital (U.S. $ millions): 197
- Net direct private investment (U.S. $ millions): 57 (1987)

GROWTH PROFILE
(Annual Growth Rates, %)

Projected population (1988–2000): 2.6
Projected crude birth rate (/1,000) (1990–95): 45.5
Projected crude death rate (/1,000) (1990–95): 20.2
Urban population (1980–88): 5.36
Labor force (1985–2000): 1.8
GNP per capita (1987–89): −0.3
GDP (1985–88): 4.2
Energy production (1980–88): 1.5
Energy consumption (1980–99): 1.1

the National Agricultural Development Bank and the National Bank of Credit.

As part of the economic reforms of 1985–86, all state-owned banks were liquidated and replaced by joint-venture banks. Guinea currently has four commercial banks: Banque Internationale pour l'Afrique en Guinée, Banque Internationale pour le Commerce et l'Industrie de la Guinée; Société Générale de Banques en Guinée and Union Internationale de Banque en Guinée. It also has an Islamic bank: Banque Islamique de Guinée.

AGRICULTURE

President Touré described agriculture as the cornerstone of the nation's development strategy. Of the total land area of 24,585,700 ha. (60,726,679 ac.), roughly 18% is considered arable.

Although the share of public investment devoted to agriculture has increased in recent years, almost all of these funds have been spent on collectivized production programs. At the same time, the 500,000 Guinean families who occupy 80% of the cultivated land and achieve yields twice as high as collective farms have had little or no access to government credit or to agricultural research and extension facilities.

Guinea is unable to feed itself despite relatively good soils, generally adequate rainfall and a number of favorable climatic zones, enabling the country to produce a wide range of crops. More than 1 million ha. (2.47 million ac.) are under cultivation, but yields are low. For example, yields for rice range from .7 to 1 ton per hectare (.3 to .4 ton per acre), compared with several tons per hectare or per acre in neighboring countries.

Since independence, Guinea has changed from a net exporter to a net importer of food. In 1983 a total of 112,000 metric tons of cereals had to be imported above 25,000 tons of food aid. Drought, smuggling and a lack of price incentives have combined to make agriculture the weakest link in the economy. Furthermore, development plans have tended to emphasize industry and mining over agriculture. In 1975 the Ministry of Agriculture was replaced by seven Ministries of Rural Development, at Conakry, Boké, Kindia, Faranah, Labé, N'Zérékoré and Kankan. The PDG-controlled Pouvoirs Révolutionnaires Locaux (PRLs) were given responsibility for growing and marketing all agricultural products; 434 mechanized production brigades, manned by students and officials, were sent out into rural areas. However, the scheme proved ineffective, and Conté abolished it.

In many regions the traditional slash-and-burn system of cultivation is practiced. Fertilizers and pesticides are rarely used. Improved techniques, such as transplanting rice seedlings from nursery seedbeds and crop rotation sequences, are being introduced only gradually. Mechanization has made little headway.

Under the traditional land tenure system, land belongs to the community, and disposal rights are held by the lineage elders, even though the rights to use the land belong to the farmer. This system still prevails in large measure, but it has been modified to assert the right of the state to reallocate vacant lands and to acquire insufficiently improved land. Some lands belonging to the tribal chiefs also have been nationalized.

Touré also focused agricultural efforts on FAPAs (*fermes agro-pastorales d'arrondissement*), state farms at the district level. Two hundred fifty such farms were to be established, with an initial government investment in the form of machinery and personnel. The FAPAs are designed to carry out experimental and intensive crop and livestock production as well as to provide extension services to small farmers. FACs (*fermes agricoles communales*) were at the village level and consisted of mechanized and/or animal traction production brigades. Low producer prices coupled with favorable trading opportunities on the local parallel market and in neighboring countries have led to a situation in which only a small amount of Guinea's agricultural production actually passes through the state distribution system. As a result, the government had to import rice to provide for urban dwellers, the army and others dependent on the official food distribution system. The Conté government abolished the agricultural collective farms and is investigating the possibility of returning some of the state-owned enterprises to the private sector.

The principal food crops are manioc, cassava, corn, rice, millet, sweet potatoes and sorghum. Cash crops include bananas, peanuts, palm kernels, coffee and

AGRICULTURAL INDICATORS

Agriculture's share of GDP (%): 30 (1989)
Value added in agriculture (U.S. $ millions): 761 (1988)
Cereal imports (000 metric tons): 222 (1988)
Index of agricultural production (1979 – 81 = 100): 108 (1986)
Index of food production per capita (1979 – 81 = 100): 93 (1986–88)
Number of tractors: 180 (1986)
Total fertilizer consumption (000 metric tons): 0.4 (1985–86)
Fertilizer consumption (g./ha., hundreds): 6 (1987–88)
Land use % 1985–87
- Cropland: 6
- Pasture: 12
- Forest: 41
- Other: 40

Yields (kg./ha.) 1989
- Grains: 999
- Roots & tubers: 5,488
- Legumes: 769
- Milk (kg./animal): 185

Production 1989
- Fruits (000 metric tons): 696
- Vegetables (000 metric tons): 420

Livestock (000)
- Cattle: 1,800
- Horses: 1 (1986)
- Sheep: 506
- Pigs: 33

Forestry 1988
- Production of roundwood (million cubic meters): 4.559
  - of which industrial roundwood (%): 14.0
- Value of exports (U.S. $ 000): 800

Fishing 1988
- Total catch (000 metric tons): 34.0
  - of which marine (%): 91.2
- Value of exports (U.S. $ 000): 0.0

citrus fruits. Marketing of export crops is the monopoly of the state-owned Guinexport.

Two-thirds of the country's livestock are raised by the Peul and the Malinké in Fouta Djallon and the savanna lands. Almost all the cattle are the small, humpless N'dama variety. Guinea's national herd has been steadily declining in numbers since the 1960s.

Forests cover 4% of the land area, or 1.5 million ha. (3.7 million ac.), of which the primary forests are mainly in N'Zérékoré and Seredou. The main timber species are teak, ebony and acacia.

Fishing in the coastal and inland waters is a major activity for Guinea's estimated 10,000 traditional fishermen, using crudely built dugouts and barks. A state company operates a fleet of fishing vessels and handles distribution and sales. More recently, coventures have been established with United States and French interests. However, fishing remains largely undeveloped.

Agricultural credit is provided by the National Agricultural Development Bank.

MANUFACTURING

Constraints on industrial expansion include shortages of foreign exchange and skilled workers, and bad planning. Most of the established industries are aimed at import substitution. Manufacturing activity is dominated by the public sector, which accounts for nearly 90% of the output. Principal public enterprises include the alumina plant at Fria, the cannery at Mamou, a sawmill, a textile factory and a sugar complex. Beginning in 1963, a policy of encouraging coventures with foreign partners was initiated. Private enterprise was legalized in 1979, but businessmen are required to pay $6,000 before starting operations. The National Investment Code of 1984 removed restrictions on foreign investors, including control by the central bank over their foreign currency receipts and state participation in management. The principal industrial centers are Conakry, Fria, Mamou, Kankan, Macenta, Kassa, Beyla, Dabola and Agola.

MANUFACTURING INDICATORS, 1987

Share of GDP (%): 5 (1988)
Labor force economically active in manufacturing (% est.): 9.4
Value added in manufacturing (U.S. $ millions): 117

In 1975 Touré created a National Economic Council, presided over by himself, for bringing all aspects of the national economy under total state control. By 1977 the state had monopolized domestic and foreign trade, diamond mining, forestry, trawling, banking, insurance, manufacturing, telecommunications, transportation, the media and electric power. The number of public enterprises is reported to have increased to 125. In 1975 three holding companies were created to manage all state-sector companies: Coficom in the commercial sector; Ocofi in the industrial and energy sectors; and Secafi in the agriculture and livestock, transportation and services sectors. Persistent dissatisfaction over the mediocre performance of these companies causes constant changes in their functions, nomenclature and organization.

MINING

Mining is the largest sector of the Guinean economy, accounting for 75% of foreign exchange earnings and 23% of the GDP. Mining also plays a large role in the government's development plans. The two most important minerals are bauxite and iron. Bauxite reserves are estimated at 8 billion tons, or two-thirds of the world's known reserves. Guinea is expected to produce 25 million tons annually, making it the world's largest producer. Of the country's five or six major deposits, only those at Fria, Sangaredi and Kindia are being mined. The deposits at Dabola and Tongué are being explored by investors. Guinea also is one of the founding members of the International Bauxite Association, with headquarters at Kingston, Jamaica.

The Fria deposits are worked by an international consortium, known as Friguia, in which Guinea holds 49% of the shares. The other 51% is divided among French (26.5%), Canadian (48.5%), British (10%), Swiss (10%) and West German (5%) interests. Each partner receives a quota of alumina exports. The Guinean government takes in 65% of the net taxable profits after depreciation and debt servicing.

The Sangaredi deposits at Boké are worked by the Bauxite Company of Guinea, in which the government holds 49% of the shares. The other 51% is held by an international consortium known as HALCO, in which three American companies, Alcan, Alcoa and Martin Marietta, hold 74%; France has 10%; West Germany holds 10%; and Italy has 6%. The company also operates a 136-km. (85-mi.) railway and the port of Kamsar.

The Debele deposits, near Kindia, are worked by the Kindia Bauxite Office with Soviet backing. Swiss and Yugoslav bauxite companies have joined to form the Society for the Development of the Alumina Industry of Tougué-Dabola, in which the Guinean government holds a half share, to develop a mining and processing complex at Dabola and Tougué in central Guinea. The Guinea-Arab Alumina Company was formed in 1976 to exploit reserves estimated at 500 million tons at Ayékoyé in northwestern Guinea. New projects in this sector include the $1 billion Akékoyé aluminum smelter and the 155,000-ton aluminum smelter associated with the Korkouré hydroelectric project. The government's policy is to obtain a greater voice over prices and destinations of exports and to establish more processing plants near the bauxite deposits. Production has been steadily rising since 1973, when it was 13.9 million tons.

Iron was mined at Kaloum until 1967. Interest now centers on richer deposits in the Mount Nimba and Simandou Mountain areas near the Liberian border. The reserves are estimated at 300 million to 600 million tons at Mount Nimba and from 450 million to 1 billion tons at Simandou, both with about 65% iron content. In 1974 the Mifergui-Simandou and the Mifergui-Nimba mining companies were formed, with the government holding 50% of the shares and the balance being held by Nigeria, Algeria, Liberia, Yugoslavia, Japan, Romania, Switzerland and Spain.

Diamond mining is the monopoly of the state-owned Guinean Diamond Exploitation Enterprise. Official production in 1983 was 40,000 carats, but there is considerable illicit production.

ENERGY

Guinea possesses no known deposits of fossil fuels, but the government established a joint venture with a U.S. company, Butte Resources, to explore for offshore petroleum. The nation has great potential for hydroelectric power. Since Guinea's independence several plants have been built, primarily to supply mining enterprises.

ENERGY INDICATORS

Average annual energy production growth rate (%, 1980–87): 1.5
Energy consumption per capita (kg. oil equivalent): 78 (1988)
Average annual growth rate of energy consumption (%, 1980–88): 1.1
Electricity 1988
  Installed capacity (000 kw.): 176
  Production (million kw.-hr.): 512
    % fossil fuel: 66.8
    %hydro: 33.2
  Consumption per capita (kw.-hr.): 78
Natural gas
  Proved reserves (billion cu. m.): 24 (1990)
Petroleum
  Production (million bbl.): 0 (1989)
  Consumption (million bbl.): 0 (1988)
  Refining capacity (000 bbl./day): 0 (1990)

LABOR

Only 6% of the labor force is believed to be wage- or salary-earning workers in the modern monetary economy, mostly in public administration and mining. Guinea is one of the few African nations where Africanization programs have been totally and effectively enforced.

Except in the civil service, workers do not receive fringe benefits such as health care, training and Social Security.

LABOR INDICATORS, 1985

Total economically active population (millions): 2.846
  % working-age (15–64): 76.2
  % female: 40.8
Activity rate (%)
  Total: 46.8
  Male: 56.1
  Female: 40.0
Sectoral employment of economically active (%)
  Agriculture, forestry, fishing: 78.6
  Construction, manufacturing, mining, quarrying, public utilities: 9.4
  Trade, hotels, restaurants, transportation, communications, finance, real estate & services: 12.0
Average annual growth rate of labor force (%, 1980–2000): 1.8

There are about 10,000 members in the country's sole trade union, the National Federation of Guinean Workers (Confédération National des Travailleurs Guinéens, CNTG), which has 19 federations and 32 local administrative offices. Strikes are not permitted.

FOREIGN COMMERCE

Guinea's major imports are food, machinery, transportation equipment, petroleum, building materials and textiles from the EEC, the United States and the Soviet Union. The major exports are bauxite, alumina, coffee, pineapples, bananas and palm kernels to the United States, France, Germany, the Soviet Union and Spain.

Export-import trade is a state monopoly.

FOREIGN TRADE INDICATORS, 1988

Exports (U.S. $ millions): 553
Imports (U.S. $ millions): 509
Balance of trade (U.S. $ millions): 44

Direction of Trade (%), 1988 (est.)

	Imports	Exports
European Community	62.1	48.5
United States	7.8	23.1
U.S.S.R. & Eastern European economies	7.1	20.4
Japan	2.2	0.2

Composition of Trade (%), 1980

	Imports	Exports
Food, agricultural raw materials, and mineral ores & concentrates	10.0	99.8
Fuels and other energy	30.3	0.0
Manufactured goods	59.7	0.2
of which chemicals	3.0	0.0
of which machinery	39.8	0.0

TRANSPORTATION & COMMUNICATIONS

The rail system consists of two parts: the aged state-owned single-track railroad from Conakry to Kankan, and the ore-transport lines from Fria to Conakry, from Sangaredi to Kamsar and from Conakry to Kindia. Work has been started on a $555 million, 1,200-km. (746-mi.) railroad linking Conakry and the iron mines of Simandou and Nimba near the Liberian border.

Most of the country's rivers are navigable for short distances only. The Niger is navigable from July to November from Kouroussa to Bamako in Mali. Milo, the largest tributary of the Niger, is navigable by shallow barges as far as Kankan. Traffic is limited to poled barges and canoes on other rivers. The total length of inland waterways is 1,295 km. (805 mi.).

Although subject to silting, Conakry Harbor is one of the finest in West Africa and has 2,450 m. (8,038 ft.) of quays, with nine berths for oceangoing vessels. A new deep-water ore port has been built at Kamsar, and there are lesser ports at Kassar, Benty and Kakandé.

The country's roads are in an advanced state of disrepair, and only about one-third of the motor vehi-

TRANSPORTATION INDICATORS

Roads (latest)
Length, km. (mi.): 28,400 (17,648)
Paved (%): 4
Motor vehicles (latest)
Automobiles: 12,000
Trucks and buses: 12,000
Persons per vehicle: 259
Railroads (latest)
Track, km. (mi.): 662 (411)
Merchant marine
Vessels (over 100 tons): 22 (1989)
Total deadweight tonnage (000): 2.8 (1989)
Ports (pre-1986)
Cargo loaded (million metric tons): 10.106
Cargo unloaded (000 metric tons): 489
Air
Passenger-km. (passenger-mi.) (millions): 28.8 (17.9) (latest)
Freight, metric ton-km. (short ton-mi.) (millions): 2.5 (1.7) (latest)
Airports with scheduled flights: 1 (1990)
Inland waterways (latest)
Length, km. (mi.): 1,295 (805)

COMMUNICATION INDICATORS, 1983

Telephones
Total (000): 16 (1981)
Persons per telephone: 310 (1981)
Post office
Pieces of mail handled (millions): 14,897 (1987)
Telegraph
Total traffic (000 calls): 50
National: 21
International: 29
Telex
Subscriber lines: 195
Telecommunications 1990
Satellite stations: 1

cles are actually operating. Guinea has implemented a program of rehabilitation and maintenance financed by a loan from the International Development Association. A road linking Conakry to Mamou was completed in 1988. That year the government announced that 10,000 km. (6,200 mi.) of road were to be improved.

The national airline is Air Guinée, with a fleet of 10 aircraft. The principal international airport is at Conakry.

No information is available on the number of tourists visiting Guinea.

DEFENSE

The defense establishment is headed by the president as commander in chief. The line of command runs through the minister of the People's Army to the Combined Armed Forces General Staff.

Military manpower is provided by voluntary enlistment. A conscription law created by ordinance in 1959 makes all able-bodied male citizens liable for military service between the ages of 19 and 49, but it has never been enforced. Military personnel are liable to reserve duty after release.

The total strength of the armed forces is 9,900.

Army

Personnel: 8,500

Organization: 1 armored battalion; 5 infantry battalions; 1 artillery battalion; 1 engineer battalion; 1 commando battalion; 1 special force battalion; 1 air defense battalion

Equipment: 53 tanks; 20 light tanks; 25 combat vehicles; 40 armored personnel carriers; 26 guns; 20 mortars; antitank guns; air defense guns; SAM

Navy

Personnel: 600

Units: 6 fast attack craft; 16 patrol craft; 2 landing craft

Naval bases: Conakry and Kakandé

Air Force

Personnel: 800

Equipment: 6 combat aircraft; 6 fighters; 4 transports; 2 trainers; 4 helicopters

The Guinean army had been completely politicized over the years through indoctrination in PDG ideology and through periodic purges of potential dissidents. The PDG had maintained tight control over the army, which it regarded as a functional and subordinate entity. The soldiers have been integrated into the civil service since 1970. It was therefore all the more surprising that the army threw off its ideological shackles so easily and dissolved the PDG after the 1984 coup.

Guinea's armed forces have never been tested in battle, and their combat-worthiness and deterrent capability are largely undetermined. Military leadership, constantly decimated in political purges, is notoriously unprofessional. Tactical equipment, mostly of Soviet origin, is unsuited to Guinean conditions.

Guinea is completely dependent on foreign sources for equipment and ammunition. The main suppliers since independence have been the Soviet Union, China, Cuba and Czechoslovakia. Soviet military aid through 1970 was $25 million. Aid from the West includes $902,000 from United States and $2.5 million from West Germany. Arms purchases in 1982 totaled $5 million.

EDUCATION

Guinea has introduced free, universal and compulsory education for six years, from ages seven to 13. However, this has had little effect on school enrollment rates, which remain low: 36% in the primary age group (five to 14) and 16% in the secondary age group (15 to 19), for a combined enrollment rate of 26%.

Schooling consists of 12 years, divided into six years of primary school, three years of the first cycle of secondary school and three years of the second cycle of the secondary school. French curricula and degrees have been retained, but under Touré history and social studies were Africanized. Primary studies are nonspecialized, and secondary studies consist of 40% general course work, 20% vocational instruction and 40% productive activities.

The academic year runs from September to July. The medium of instruction is French, but eight vernaculars have been added to the curriculum below the fourth grade.

In 1966 the government introduced a new type of rural secondary school known until 1968 as *collège d'enseignement rural* and from 1968 as *centre d'education révolutionnaire* (CER). CERs, which number over 84, are designed as productive units that ultimately become the nuclei of agricultural cooperatives.

The school system suffers from a shortage of teachers. Primary-level teachers are trained at six primary normal schools, and secondary-level teachers are trained at four higher normal schools. The teaching staff has been almost completely Africanized since 1960. The teacher–pupil ratio is 1:36 at the primary level, 1:25 at the secondary level and 1:10 at the postsecondary level.

Technical and vocational courses are included in the curricula of all secondary schools. More intensive training is provided by technical schools, and agricultural training at specialized agricultural schools. About 6% of secondary students were enrolled in the vocational stream in 1987.

All schools other than Koranic schools were nationalized and secularized in 1961. All Catholic mission schools have been absorbed into the public school system.

With assistance from France and neighboring countries, the CMRN over a six-year period reorganized the entire education system to eliminate ideology based on the writings and declarations of former president Sékou Touré and to upgrade the quality of the system. The reorganization involved a complete overhaul of administration, infrastructure, curricula, textbooks, and qualifications for teaching. Public education is free and universal, and private schools are allowed. French was being restored as the language of instruction in primary schools.

The educational system is under the overall control of the education and culture domain in the cabinet and is divided between two ministries: the Ministry of Pre-University Education and Literacy, and the Ministry of Advanced Education and Scientific Research. Teachers' salaries, current expenditures and maintenance of postsecondary institutions are covered by the national budget, and maintenance of primary and secondary schools is the responsibility of regional administrations.

Guinea has no university, but there are three institutions of higher learning, including two polytechnics and the Higher School of Administration.

EDUCATION INDICATORS, 1987

Literacy
- Total (%): 28.3
- Male (%): 29.7
- Female (%): 17.2

First level
- Schools: 2,204
- Students: 270,140
- Teachers: 7,493
- Student/teacher ratio: 36.0
- Net enrollment ratio: 23

Second level
- Schools: 225
- Students: 76,493
- Teachers: 3,577
- Student/teacher ratio: 21.4
- Net enrollment ratio: 7 (1985)

Vocational
- Schools: 31
- Students: 4,929
- Teachers: 758
- Student/teacher ratio: 6.5

Third level (postsecondary)
- Institutions: 23
- Students: 7,470
- Teachers: 946
- Student/teacher ratio: 7.9
- Gross enrollment ratio: 1.1
- Student (/100,000 pop.): 93

Foreign study
- Foreign students in national universities: 50 (1988)
- Students abroad: 1,129
  - of whom in
    - United States: 50 (1988)
    - France: 337 (1988)
    - Federal Republic of Germany: 43 (1988)
    - United Kingdom: 4 (1987)

Public expenditure
- Total (G.F. 000): 19,743
- % of GNP: 3.3
- % of national budget: 21.5
- % of current: 77.6

GRADUATES, 1986

Total: 1,129
Education: 156
Humanities & religion: 0
Fine & applied arts: 0
Law: 0
Social & behavioral sciences: 0
Commerce & business: 107
Mass communication: 0
Home economics: 0
Service trades: 0
Natural sciences: 129
Mathematics & computer science: 0
Medicine: 0
Engineering: 0
Architecture: 19
Industrial programs: 44
Transportation & communications: 0
Agriculture, forestry, fisheries: 674
Other: 0

LEGAL SYSTEM

Despite frequent attempts to Guineanize the legal system, French commercial and civil codes have been retained almost intact. A new Penal Code was introduced in 1965 and a new Code of Criminal Procedure in the following year.

The court system was reorganized in 1973; people's courts were created in villages and city wards and presided over by the mayor. The other two members of these courts also are elected party members. People's courts also exist at the *arrondissement* and the administrative region levels; but only at the latter level are they headed by magistrates. Criminal courts and courts of appeal are at Conakry and at the four regional headquarters. The seven members of these courts consist of three professional judges and four officials. At the apex of the court system is the Superior Court of Cassation, composed of three magistrates and two people's judges. Outside of the regular court system are the High Court of Justice, which hears cases concerning state security; the Special Court, which tries crimes concerning external commerce; and the Supreme Revolutionary Tribunal.

The reorganized judicial system is independent, with courts of first instance at the subprefecture and prefecture levels, courts of appeal at the provincial level and the Supreme Court at the national level. There also are to be juvenile courts, a Labor Court and a Military Tribunal. Judges are to be appointed on the basis of their qualifications instead of political credentials, as was the previous practice. Private legal practice has been restored, and legal assistance is to be provided to the poor to ensure that everyone will have the benefit of a fair trial. The government also is revising various legal codes.

The corrections system includes the Camayeene Central Prison in Conakry, local prisons in each administrative region and lockups in each district. Political prisoners are incarcerated in three "camps." All prisoners are subjected to penal labor.

LAW ENFORCEMENT

The national police consists of three units: the Sûreté Nationale (National Police), the gendarmerie and the Garde Républicaine (Republican Guard), all under the General Directorate of Security Services.

The Sûreté Nationale is the civil police force in towns and cities and is under the General Directorate of Police Services. Although the Sûreté Nationale is under the overall administrative supervision of the central government, it is, at the same time, under the operational control of the governors of the administrative regions. Each administrative region has its chief of police, and larger towns have police commissioners. The strength of Sûreté Nationale is estimated at 1,000 officers and men.

The gendarmerie is a paramilitary force, with ranks and grades corresponding to those of the army, and is organized into four types of brigades, each under a lieutenant: administrative region brigades, frontier brigades, mobile brigades and criminal brigades. The gendarmerie's strength is estimated at 900.

The Garde Républicaine also is a paramilitary force, of some 1,600 officers and men, with one section guarding the president and another the political prisoner camps.

No criminal statistics have been published since independence. However, the most serious law enforcement problems, based on reports in the government-controlled press, are smuggling, black-marketing and illegal currency transactions. Most of these illicit activities are conducted by, or with the support of, influential government and party officials.

HEALTH

Principal health problems are malaria, venereal diseases, tuberculosis, leprosy, schistosomiasis and filariasis.

HEALTH INDICATORS

Health personnel, 1988
- Physicians: 635
  - persons per: 10,300
- Dentists: 22
- Nurses: 243
- Pharmacists: 261
- Midwives: 343

Hospitals, 1988
- Number: 38
- Number of beds (/10,000): 6

Type of hospitals (%), 1988
- Government: 100.0
- Private nonprofit: 0
- Private profit: 0

Public health expenditures (latest)
- Per capita (U.S. $): 3.10

Vital statistics
- Crude death rate (/1,000): 22 (1990)
- Life expectancy at birth 1990
- Males: 40
- Females: 44
- Infant mortality rate (/1,000 live births): 147 (1990)
- Child mortality rate under 5 yrs. (/1,000 live births) (1985–90): 249
- Population with access to safe water (%): 19 (latest)

FOOD & NUTRITION

Rice is the staple element of the Guinean diet. It is generally eaten in the form of a porridge along with a hot and spicy sauce. Where rice is not available, fonio (a variety of millet), corn, cassava, taro and sweet potatoes form the staples. Consumption of fish is limited to the coast and riverine areas. Meat and eggs are rarely consumed. Milk is used only by the livestock-breeding tribes, such as the Peul.

Dietary patterns vary with the season. The hungry season lasts from April to September and the abundant season from October to February or March. Because of this unevenness of food supplies and because of dietary taboos against some foods, there is widespread nutritional inadequacy. Daily per capita intake of food is 1,987 calories (86% of requirements).

MEDIA & CULTURE

There are three monthlies with an aggregate circulation of 18,500. Other periodicals include an official gazette and a trade union journal. Until April 1984, criticism of the government was rarely allowed, and journalists generally confined their reporting to accounts of government activities and development issues. Foreign books, newspapers and journals were rarely available in Guinea, and censorship of printed material existed. Since April 1984 the government has been vigorously engaged in promoting freedom of speech and press. However, given the nature of the government and the lack of tradition in Guinea for freely ventilating opposition viewpoints, inhibitions still appear to exist in this area. In regard to criticism of the government, CMRN members have asked for "constructive" criticism by Guinean citizens. Films, as well as publications distributed by diplomatic missions in Guinea, continue to be censored.

The national news agency is Agence Guinéenne de Presse. Xinhua, Novosti Xinhua News Agency and Tass are represented in Conakry.

The only significant book publisher is the Government Printer. Guinea does not adhere to any copyright convention.

The official broadcasting service, Radiodiffusion Télévision de Guinéenne, broadcasts in French, English, Arabic, Portuguese and local dialects.

Guinea has a growing film industry, with a number of recognized film producers and a limited production of feature films, some of which have won prizes at international film festivals. Most of the theaters are owned by the state, and film distribution is a state monopoly.

The only library is the National Library at Conakry, with 12,000 volumes.

MEDIA INDICATORS

Newspapers
- Number of dailies: 0 (latest)
- Circulation (000): 0 (latest)
- Per 1,000 pop.: 0 (latest)

Radio
- Number of transmitters: 9 (latest)
- Number of persons per radio receiver: 34 (1989)

Television
- Television transmitters: 1 (latest)
- Number of persons per T.V. receiver: 134 (1989)

Cinema
- Number of fixed cinemas: 29 (latest)
- Seating capacity (000): 61.2 (latest)
  - Seats (/1,000 pop.): 10.1 (1985)
- Annual attendance (millions): 2.6 (latest)

Films
- Production of long films: 1 (latest)
- Import of long films: 231 (1985)
  - % from United States: 48.1
  - % from India: 15.2
  - % from Hong Kong: 11.3
  - % from Soviet Union: 9.5

CULTURAL & ENVIRONMENTAL INDICATORS

Libraries (pre-1986)
- Number: 1
- Volumes (000): 12

Museums (pre-1986)
- Annual attendance (000): 21
- Attendance (/1,000 pop.): 4

Nature reserves (latest)
- Number of facilities: 2

SOCIAL WELFARE

The National Social Security Fund administers a limited Social Security and welfare program. It provides benefits for old age, family allowances for children and maternity benefits for women. However, primary welfare aid is available for the vast majority from extended families or kinship groups only.

GLOSSARY

domain: superministries in the Guinean cabinet.

fonio: a variety of millet grown in Guinea.

pouvoir révolutionnaire local: the basic village unit of local government interlocking party and government administration.

region administrative: subdivision of a region, headed by a governor.

CHRONOLOGY (from 1958)

1958— Republic of Guinea is proclaimed as Guineans overwhelmingly reject the French Community in national referendum. . . . New Constitution is promulgated.

1959— Guinea launches human investment project utilizing unpaid voluntary labor. . . . Guinea begins to receive aid from the Communist bloc.

1960— Guinea withdraws from the franc zone, establishes the Central Bank of the Republic of Guinea (Banque Centrale de la République de Guinée) and introduces the Guinean franc as the national currency.

1961— The Guinean school system is secularized and nationalized. . . . A teachers' union strike is put down, and the Soviet ambassador is expelled for alleged complicity in the strike.

1964— The Democratic Party of Guinea (Parti Démocratique de Guinée) becomes a cadre party.

1965— Diplomatic relations with France are suspended over French support for Guinean dissidents.

1966— The U.S. Peace Corps is expelled, and the American embassy in Conakry is attacked. . . . Kwame Nkrumah is named copresident of Guinea following his overthrow in Ghana.

1967— Diplomatic relations with the United Kingdom are suspended over Rhodesia.

1968— "Cultural Revolution" is launched, and de-Westernization programs are intensified. . . . Sékou Touré is reelected president.

1969— Over 1,000 Guineans, including three cabinet ministers, are arrested in the so-called Labé plot.

1970— Portuguese-backed Guinean dissidents mount a seaborne invasion of Conakry; the invasion is foiled. In the aftermath of the invasion, mass purges are ordered by Touré; over 100 persons are sentenced to death; over 250 are convicted and sentenced to life imprisonment, including the Roman Catholic archbishop of Conakry; nearly 10,000 are arrested.

1971— Defense treaty is concluded with Sierra Leone. Diplomatic relations with West Germany are broken.

1972— Office of the prime minister is created, and Louis Lansana Beavogui is named to the post. . . . Syli is introduced as the national currency.

1973— Local revolutionary authority *(pouvoir révolutionnaire local)* is created as the basic unit of village-level administration.

1974— In extensive constitutional changes, the PDG is elevated as the supreme state organ. . . . Touré is reelected to a third seven-year term.

1975— Diplomatic relations with France are restored. . . . Guinea signs the Lomé Convention. . . . Private trading is abolished.

1976— Justice minister and former secretary general of the OAU Diallo Telli is arrested and later dies of poisoning in jail.

1978— At a meeting in Monrovia, Liberia, Guinea and five other nations—Senegal, Ivory Coast, Liberia, Togo and Gambia—sign a treaty of nonaggression and mutual assistance. Touré meets with Léopold Senghor of Senegal and Felix Houphouet-Boigny of Ivory Coast in a Summit of Reconciliation at Monrovia; diplomatic relations with Senegal are reestablished. . . . The country is renamed the Popular and Revolutionary Republic of Guinea. . . . President Giscard d'Estaing of France visits Guinea and receives a warm welcome.

1979— Private enterprise is legalized; ten ministers are dismissed in a government reshuffle. . . . In legislative elections voters approve list of 210 candidates to the National Assembly. Touré visits the United States for the first time and meets with President Carter. . . . Two hundred political prisoners are released out of the more than 2,000 believed to be held in Guinean jails.

1984— President Touré dies. . . . Before PDG names a successor, the army seizes power and installs the Military Committee for National Redressment (CMRN), with Col. Lansana Conté as head. . . . The CMRN dissolves the PDG, suspends the Constitution and the National Assembly and releases all political detainees. . . . The office of prime minister is abolished.

1985— Diarra Traoré leads an unsuccessful coup. He is arrested and immediately executed.

1989— Conté promises a return to a two-party system.

1990— Guinea sends troops to Liberia as part of a peacekeeping force under the auspices of the Economic Community of West African States.

1991— The U.N. estimates that there are 400,000 Liberian refugees in Guinea. Guinea deploys troops into Sierra Leone to help repulse an incursion by rebels from neighboring Liberia.

BIBLIOGRAPHY

BOOKS

Adamolekun, Lapido. *Sékou Touré's Guinea.* London, 1976.

Charles, Bernard. *La République de Guinée.* Paris, 1972.

Derman, William and Louise. *Serfs, Peasants and Socialists: A Former Serf Village in the Republic of Guinea.* Berkeley, Calif., 1973.

Economist Intelligence Unit, The. *Country Profile. Guinea, Mali, Mauritania.* (London, 1986).

Rivière, Claude. *Guinea: The Mobilization of a People.* (Ithaca, N.Y., 1977).

Sure-Canale, Jean. *La République de Guinée.* Paris, 1970.

Toole, Thomas. *Historical Dictionary of Guinea.* Metuchen, N.J., 1978.

Touré, Sékou. *Permanent Struggle.* Palo Alto, Calif., 1976.

UNIDADE
LUTA
PROGRESSO

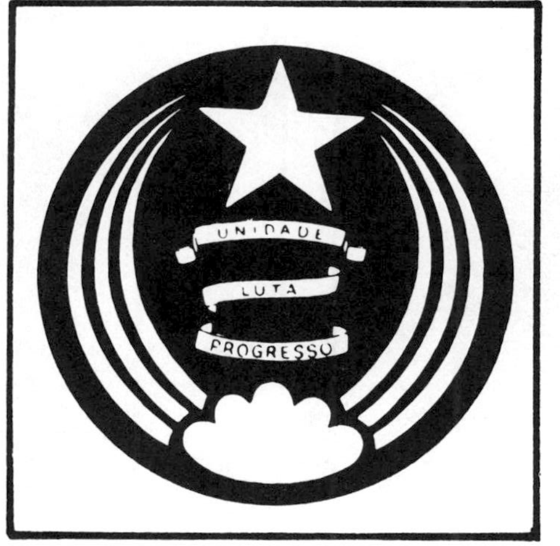

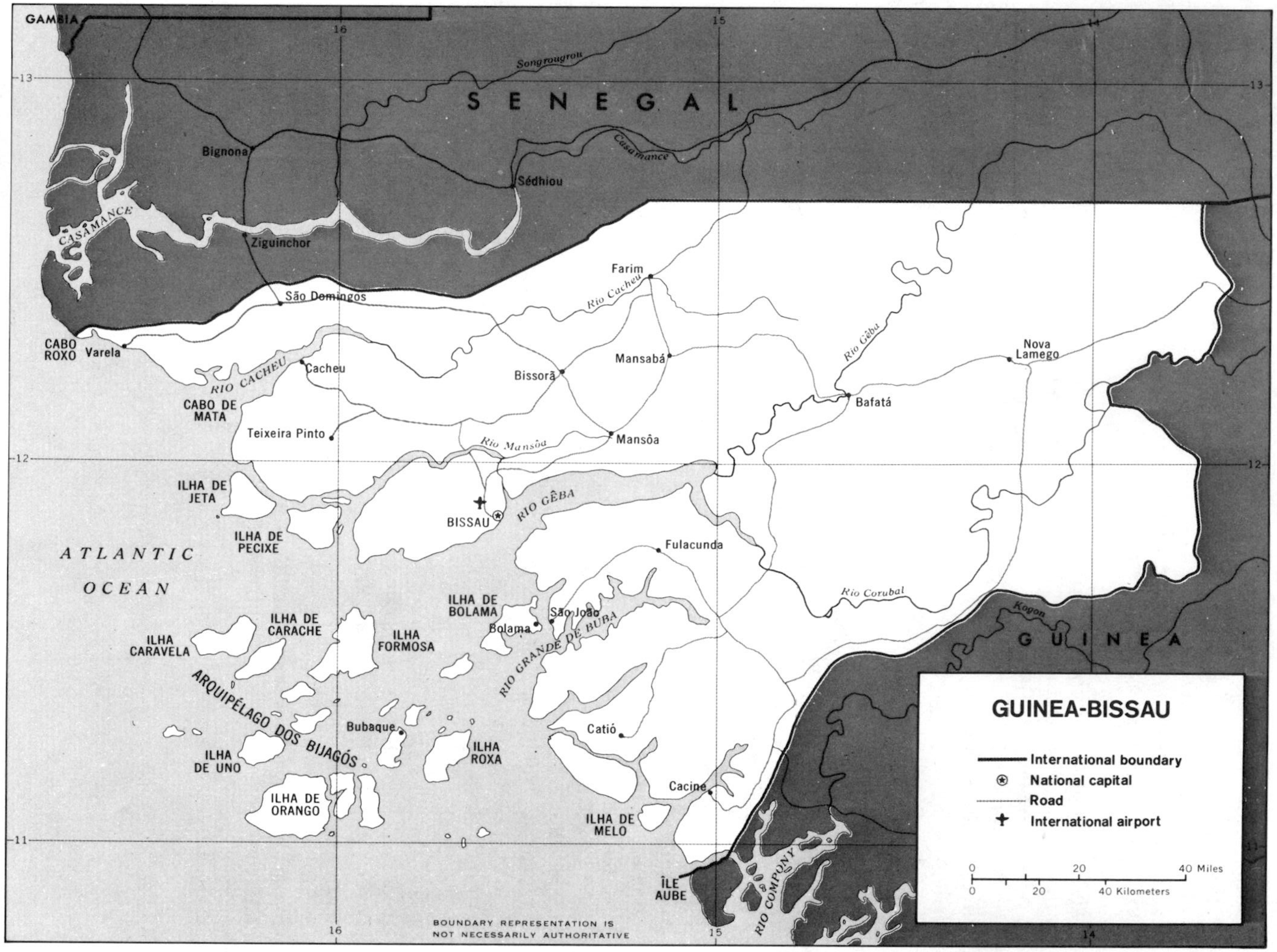
GUINEA-BISSAU
International boundary
National capital
Road
International airport
0 20 40 Miles
0 20 40 Kilometers
GAMBIA
SENEGAL
GUINEA
Songrougrou
Casamance
CASAMANCE
Bignona
Sédhiou
Ziguinchor
São Domingos
Farim
Rio Cacheu
CABO ROXO
Varela
Cacheu
RIO CACHEU
CABO DE MATA
Teixeira Pinto
Bissorã
Mansabá
Mansôa
Rio Mansôa
Rio Gêba
Bafatá
Nova Lamego
ILHA DE JETA
BISSAU
RIO GÊBA
ILHA DE PECIXE
ATLANTIC OCEAN
Fulacunda
Rio Corubal
Kogon
ILHA DE BOLAMA
São João
Bolama
RIO GRANDE DE BUBA
ILHA DE CARACHE
ILHA FORMOSA
ILHA CARAVELA
ARQUIPÉLAGO DOS BIJAGÓS
Bubaque
ILHA ROXA
ILHA DE UNO
Catió
Cacine
ILHA DE ORANGO
ILHA DE MELO
ÎLE AUBE
RIO COMPONY
BOUNDARY REPRESENTATION IS NOT NECESSARILY AUTHORITATIVE
16
15
14
13
12
11

GUINEA-BISSAU

BASIC FACT SHEET

OFFICIAL NAME: Republic of Guinea-Bissau (República da Guiné-Bissau)

ABBREVIATION: GB

CAPITALS: Bissau (administrative); Madina do Boe (de jure)

HEAD OF STATE & HEAD OF GOVERNMENT: President of the Council of State João Bernardo Vieira (from 1980)

NATURE OF GOVERNMENT: One-party civilian dictatorship

POPULATION: 998,963 (1990)

AREA: 36,125 sq. km. (13,948 sq. mi.)

ETHNIC MAJORITY: Balante, Fulani and Malinke

LANGUAGE: Portuguese (official)

RELIGIONS: Animism, Islam and Christianity

UNIT OF CURRENCY: Guinean peso (P.G.)

NATIONAL FLAG: Three stripes, two horizontal of yellow over green in the fly and a red vertical at the hoist with a black star in the center of the red stripe

NATIONAL EMBLEM: Three curved hornlike stripes on the left and right flanking a star in the top and the national motto *Unidade, Luta, Progresso* (Unity, Struggle, Progress) in the center

NATIONAL ANTHEM: "This Is Our Well-Beloved Land"

NATIONAL HOLIDAYS: September 24 (Independence Day); also variable Christian festivals

NATIONAL CALENDAR: Gregorian

PHYSICAL QUALITY OF LIFE INDEX: 29

DATE OF INDEPENDENCE: September 24, 1973 (de facto), September 10, 1974 (de jure)

DATE OF CONSTITUTION: May 16, 1984

WEIGHTS & MEASURES: Metric

GEOGRAPHICAL FEATURES

Guinea-Bissau is on the coast of West Africa and occupies a total land area of 36,125 sq. km. (13,948 sq. mi.), including land under water during high tides. The country extends 336 km. (209 mi.) north to south and 203 km. (126 mi.) east to west. Its Atlantic coastline stretches 398 km. (247 mi.).

Guinea-Bissau shares its total international land boundary of 724 km. (450 mi.) with two countries: Senegal (338 km.; 210 mi.) and Guinea (386 km.; 240 mi.). The borders with these two countries were delimited in 1886 by a formal treaty, and they were demarcated by a joint commission in 1905. There are no current border disputes.

The administrative capital is Bissau, although Madina do Boe is designated as the de jure capital. Bissau had an estimated population of 105,273 in 1980. Other major urban centers are Bafata (13,429), Bolama, Gabu (7,803), Farim, Teixeira Pinto, Mansoa (5,390), Nova Lamego, Catio (5,179) and Bissora.

Guinea-Bissau consists of a mainland; the Bijagos Archipelago; and various coastal islands, such as Jeta, Bolama, Melo, Pecixe, Bissau, Areicas and Como. The Bijagos Archipelago consists of over 18 islands, among them Caravela, Caraxe, Formosa, Uno, Orango, Orangozinho, Bubaque and Roxa. The mainland relief consists of a coastal plain and a transition plateau forming the Planalto de Bafata in the center and the Planalto de Gabu abutting on the Fouta Djallon. The highest elevation is 244 m. (80 ft.), in the Southeast.

The country is drained by a number of meandering rivers flowing into the Atlantic through wide estuaries. The main rivers are Cacheu, also known as Farim for part of its course; the Mansoa; the Geba; the Corubal; the Rio Grande and, on the southern border with Guinea, the Cacine. These rivers provide the principal means of transportation. Oceangoing vessels of shallow draught can reach most of the main towns, and flat-bottomed tugs and barges can reach smaller settlements, except those in the Northeast.

CLIMATE & WEATHER

Guinea-Bissau has a typical tropical climate with two seasons: a dry season from December to May and a rainy season from June to November. April and May are the hottest months; December and January are the coolest; August is the rainiest. Rainfall is abundant and exceeds 1,980 mm. (78 in.) in the north. The maximum temperature is 30°C (86°F) and the minimum about 25°C (77°F). During the dry season the prevailing wind is the hot, dry harmattan blowing from the desert to the west.

POPULATION

The population of Guinea-Bissau was 998,963 in 1990, based on the last official census, in 1979, when the population was 767,739.

The population is fairly evenly distributed. Nearly 27% of the population is urbanized, but the towns themselves are small, and only Bissau has a population of over 50,000. A total of 87% of the population lives in communal villages *(tabancas)*, which are the country's basic economic and social units. The remaining 13% of the population is concentrated largely in and around the administrative capital city of Bissau.

DEMOGRAPHIC INDICATORS

Population (000): 973 (1990)
Year of last census: 1979
Sex distribution (% at last census): males, 48.2; females, 51.8
Population estimates and projections (000)

1940: 341	1970: 653	2000: 1,200
1950: 411	1980: 787	2010: 1,480
1960: 520	1990: 970	

Age profile (% at 1985 est.)

0–14: 44.3	30–44: 15.1	60–74: 4.7
15–29: 25.5	45–59: 8.2	75 and over: 2.2

Median age (yrs.): 19.9 (1985)
Youth population (% age 15–24): 17.8 (1985); 19.0 (2000)
Total dependency ratio: 81.8 (1985)
Annual growth rate (%)

1950–55: 0.60	1975–1980: 5.04	2000–2005: 2.44
1955–60: 0.73	1980–1985: 1.91	2005–2010: 2.30
1960–65: −0.56	1985–1990: 2.08	2010–2015: 2.28
1965–70: 0.06	1990–1995: 2.25	2015–2020: 2.20
1970–75: 3.55	1995–2000: 2.44	2020–2025: 1.86

Urban population (000): 24 (1985)
Annual urban population growth rate (%, 1985–90): 4.60
Annual rural population growth rate (%, 1985–90): 1.06
Population density per sq. km. (per sq. mi.): 26.9 (69.8) (latest)

VITAL STATISTICS

Crude birth rate (/1,000: 43 (1990)
Crude death rate (/1,000): 19 (1990)
Infant mortality rate (/1,000 live births): 127 (1990)
Maternal mortality rate (/1,000 live births) (1980–1984): 140
Life expectancy (yrs.) at birth: males, 44; females, 48 (1990)
Gross reproduction rate (/woman) (1980–85): 2.65
Total fertility rate (/woman): 5.9 (1990)
Rate of natural increase (/1,000) (1985–90): 20.8
Average household size: 4.1 (latest)
Legitimate births (%): 11.3 (latest)

Seventeen years of civil and military turmoil in the country led to a mass exodus from the country of two opposing groups: the pro-Portuguese Guineans fleeing from the guerrillas and the proindependence Guineans fleeing from the Portuguese. Over 90,000 Guineans have returned to Guinea-Bissau from Senegal and Gambia since the end of the war. Pro-Portuguese elements remain in Senegal and Portugal.

There is no government or party discrimination against women. The National Women's Movement, a party organization, is active nationally. Women hold some senior government and party positions. Political activity by women is officially encouraged at all levels. By statute, party organizations must have a stated proportion of women officeholders. Official discrimination against women in the modern sector of society does not take place. In most rural sectors, however, traditional male-dominant sociological practices prevail, imposing attendant limitations on women. The president of the National Assembly and the mayor of Bissau are both women.

Guinea-Bissau has no official birth control policies or programs.

STATUS OF WOMEN INDICATORS

Number of women (000): 398 (1979)
Women in labor force %: 41.2 (1988)
Total fertility rate (/woman): 5.9 (1990)

ETHNIC COMPOSITION

Guineans may be broadly divided ethnically into *mesticos*, or half-breeds; *assimilados*, of Guinean stock; and *indígenas*, or Africans proper, who constitute 95% of the population. There are at least five principal African ethnic groups: the Balante of the central region (30%), the Fulani of the north (20%), the Malinke of the north-central region (13%), the Mandyako (14%) and the Pepel (7%) of the coastal area.

The *mesticos*, Cape Verdean mulattoes and the *assimilados* constitute the most important ethnic minorities, accounting for about 2% of the total population. Guinea-Bissau never was intensively settled by the Portuguese, and following the repatriation of the Portuguese in 1974 the number of whites has declined to a few hundred. Some Cape Verdeans also have left for independent Cape Verde. The small foreign community consists mainly of Lebanese and Syrian traders and Cuban advisers, who have been temporarily assigned from Cuba to help in the reconstruction of the country. No Americans are known to be resident permanently in the country.

LANGUAGES

The official language is Portuguese, but the lingua franca and trade language is Crioulo, an Africanized Portuguese patois.

RELIGIONS

Guinea-Bissau is a predominantly animist country where over 65% of the population adhere to traditional religious beliefs. Nearly 30% of the population is Muslim, mainly Malinke and Fulani tribesmen. Catholics account for only 0.5% of the population, and their influence is marginal. There is an apostolic prefecture at Bissau.

HISTORICAL BACKGROUND

Guinea-Bissau was under Portuguese rule from 1879, when it was made a Portuguese dependency subordinate to Cape Verde Island, to 1974, when the country won its independence after a 17-year underground struggle. Guinea-Bissau was not a settler colony. Moreover, Portuguese influence on the interior, which was not effectively occupied until 1920, was nominal. Guinea-Bissau became a Portuguese overseas province in 1951, but five years later a group of dissident Cape Verdeans

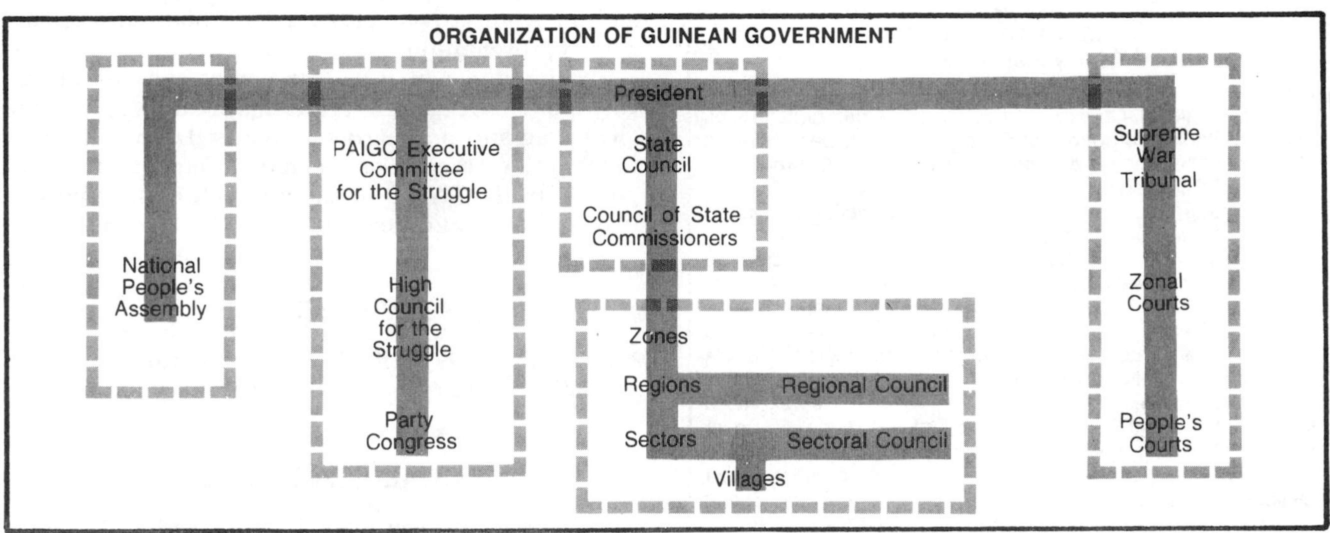

founded an underground movement known as Partido Africano da Independencia do Guiné e Cabo Verde (PAIGC), with Amilcar Cabral as secretary general. The long struggle that followed took a heavy toll in men and matériel and undermined the Portuguese administrative apparatus. By 1973 PAIGC was in virtual control of the country, and its unilateral declaration of independence was accepted by the United Nations. When Portugal finally granted de jure independence in 1974, it represented not so much an act of statesmanship as one of capitulation.

At independence Luiz Cabral, brother of Amilcar, became president. He was reelected in 1977, and João Bernardo Vieira was designated vice president. Vieira became prime minister the following year. PAIGC became the sole political party and was synonymous with the state. However, the armed forces exercise decisive political influence.

In November 1980 Cabral was overthrown in a coup led by Vieira. Cabral was placed under house arrest and later exiled to Cuba. The coup stemmed from a long-standing struggle between the blacks of Guinea-Bissau and the mulattoes of Guinea-Bissau's sister republic Cape Verde. Although both were Marxist-leaning countries and former Portuguese colonies, there were splits between the two because of racial animosities and the issue of unification. Cabral is a mulatto from Cape Verde, and Vieira is a black from the mainland. A special party conference in 1981 legitimized the new regime and reaffirmed its socialist orientation.

Guinean politics during the 1980s were characterized by instability with frequent changes of ministers, constitutional changes and several attempted coups. In 1984 Prime Minister Victor Sáude Maria was dismissed, the office of prime minister abolished, and the presidency strengthened. The following year Paulo Correia, the first vice-president and minister of justice was accused of plotting a coup against Vieira. He was executed after a trial in 1986.

Beginning in 1983 Vieira initiated a plan of economic liberalization designed to reduce state controls over trade and the economy. In 1990 he announced that Guinea-Bissau would start the process of creating a multiparty state.

CONSTITUTION & GOVERNMENT

The Republic of Guinea-Bissau returned to a form of constitutional government in 1984. In May the armed forces-dominated Revolutionary Council, which had ruled the country since the 1980 coup d'etat, was abolished. Following legislative elections controlled by the country's only legal political party—the African Party for the Independence of Guinea and Cape Verde—the 150-member National People's Assembly reconvened for the first time since 1980. It approved a new Constitution, elected General João Bernardo Vieira to a five-year term as president of the Council of State and chose the 14 other members of the Council. Despite these changes, effective political power remains concentrated in the hands of the Council and President Vieira who currently serves as head of state, head of government, armed forces commander-in-chief, and secretary general of the party. The Council includes seven military men and five former members of the now defunct Revolutionary Council. All Council of State members also are members of the party's Political and/or Central Committee.

Opposition political activity is not permitted. Under the May 1984 Constitution, the party is "the guiding political force of Guinea-Bissau society and the state." Elections at the district, regional and national levels are controlled by the party.

The armed forces remain the dominant element in state security. The military's role in the maintenance of internal security and public order is specifically mandated in the new Constitution. The creation of special tribunals is constitutionally prohibited except with respect to military courts established to deal with military offenses.

The Regional Council is responsible for public order and defense of the rights of citizens. It is comprised of representatives from each sector of a region. The

GOVERNMENT LIST
(July/August 1991)

President	Vieira, João Bernardo, *Brig. Gen.*
1st Vice President, Council of State	Camara, Iafai, *Col.*
2nd Vice President, Council of State	Cabral, Vasco
Minister of Civil Service & Labor	Cabral, Mario
Minister of Commerce, Tourism & Handicrafts	Sanca, Luis Oliveira
Minister of Education, Sports & Culture	Furtado, Alexandre Brito
Minister of Fisheries	Monteiro, Victor Freire
Minister of Foreign Affairs	Semedo, Julio
Minister of Health	Gomes, Henriqueta Godhino
Minister of Information & Telecommunications	Djassi, Moussa
Minister of International Cooperation	Cardoso, Bernardino
Minister of Justice	Cabral, Vasco
Minister of National Security & Public Order	Balde, Abubacar
Minister of Natural Resources & Industry	Barros, Filinto de
Minister of Public Works	Gomes, Alberto Lima
Minister of State at the Presidency	D'Almada, Fidelis Cabral
Minister of State for Armed Forces	Camara, Iafai, *Col.*
Minister of State for Economy & Finance	Santos, Manuel Maria dos
Minister of State for Rural Development & Agriculture	Correia, Carlos
Minister of State for Social Affairs	Pereira, Carmen
Minister of Transportation	da Silva, Avito José, *Maj.*
Minister of Women's Affairs	Pereira, Francisca
Minister Resident for Eastern Province	Correia, Mario Mendes
Minister Resident for Northern Province	Martins, Zeca
Minister Resident for Southern Province	Correia, Vasco Salvador
Secretary of State for Administration Reform	Rosario, Osvaldo
Secretary of State for Agriculture	Mane, Samba Lamine
Secretary of State for Defense	Vieira, Jose Marques
Secretary of State for Foreign Affairs	Lima, Marcelino
Secretary of State for Health	Costa, Celestino
Secretary of State for Information	Regala, Agnelo
Secretary of State for Natural Resources	Cardosa, Joao
Secretary of State for Planning	Mane, Ansumane
Secretary of State for Social Affairs	Ribeiro, Luis Candido
Secretary of State for Tourism	Turpin, Joseph
Secretary of State for Treasury	Fernandes, Eduardo
Secretary of State for Veterans	Furtado, Joaquim
President, Supreme Court of Justice	Pinto, Joao Aurigema Cruz
Attorney General	Lopes, Mario Semedo
Minister-Governor, Central Bank	Gomes, Pedro Godhino

Regional Council elects a Regional State Committee and sector state committees.

FREEDOM & HUMAN RIGHTS

In terms of political and civil rights Guinea-Bissau is classified as a not-free country.

The government of Guinea-Bissau has accused the regime of former president Luiz Cabral of responsibility for hundreds of executions of political opponents during his six-year rule. There have been no reports of such occurrences since the 1980 coup. However, Article 22 of the Constitution denies political rights and fundamental liberties to those who encourage "colonialism, imperialism, racism or tribalism." The number of political prisoners is not believed to be large. Trials generally are fair, but there are no private attorneys, and the state provides lawyers for those who require legal representation.

The freedoms of press, assembly and speech are very limited. Occasional criticisms are directed toward local programs and parochial issues. Despite the new Constitution, there has been no dimunition of the powers of the PAIGC or the concentration of powers in a select group of leaders.

CIVIL SERVICE

No information is available on the structure, governing regulations or size of the civil service in Guinea-Bissau.

LOCAL GOVERNMENT

For purposes of local administration Guinea-Bissau is divided into three provinces, each subdivided into regions, sectors and villages. Party committees are organized at each level. The eight regions are Cacheu, Bissora-Mansoa, Farim, Bijagos, Gabu, Bafata, Fulacunda and Catio. Each region has a regional council consisting of elected representatives from its sectors. There are sector state committees at the sectoral level. The lowest unit of administration is the *tabanca* (village). In addition, there are nine municipalities also administered by party committees.

FOREIGN POLICY

The foreign policy of Guinea-Bissau is defined as one of "positive neutrality," but as in other former Portuguese colonies, the government has set the country on a socialist path. Cultural and other agreements have been entered into with the socialist government of Portugal, and the relations between the two countries have been recast on an equal and friendly footing. The government also is sympathetic to countries such as the Soviet Union, Cuba and the People's Republic of China, from whom the PAIGC received military and other assistance during the guerrilla struggle. As the first Portuguese colony in Africa to achieve independence, Guinea-Bissau cherishes its reputation as a leader in the struggle against colonialism. It also has a natural affinity with other Portuguese-speaking countries such as Angola, Mozambique and Brazil. A union of Guinea-Bissau and Cape Verde, a basic tenet of President Cabral, appears to have been permanently shelved following his ouster. However, both Cape Verde and Guinea-Bissau leaders meet periodically at summits of former Portuguese African colonies, and there are a number of interministerial commissions in which these five Lusophone states participate. Guinea-Bissau maintains a special relationship with Guinea, which provided a haven for PAIGC leaders during the struggle for independence. A controversy between Senegal and Guinea-Bissau erupted in 1984 over offshore borders drawn during the colonial period. The matter was later assigned to an ad hoc international tribunal. Guinea-Bissau and the United States are parties to one agreement covering economic and technical cooperation. The interest of the United States in Guinea-Bissau is purely humanitarian, and U.S. assistance to date includes a grant for resettlement of refugees returning to Guinea-Bissau at the close of the war with Portugual.

The overthrow of President Cabral signified the end of Soviet influence in Guinea-Bissau as well as in most of West Africa. President João Bernardo Vieira in 1982 replaced two strongly pro-Soviet cabinet ministers with Western technocrats and initiated appeals for Western developmental aid.

Guinea-Bissau joined the United Nation in 1974. It is a member of six U.N. organizations and the organization of African Unity.

PARLIAMENT

The national legislature is the National People's Assembly, a unicameral body of 150 members, elected or appointed for a term of five years. It meets at least once a year. All members belong to the sole legal political party, the PAIGC.

The Constitution provides for universal adult suffrage over 15. The country's first election was held on May 14, 1984.

POLITICAL PARTIES

The sole legal party is the PAIGC (African Party for the Independence of Guinea and Cape Verde, Partido Africano da Independencia do Guine e Cabo Verde), which was founded in 1956 by Amilcar Cabral and which led the armed struggle against Portugual starting in 1963. The party is acknowledged in the Constitution of 1973 as "the supreme expression of the sovereign will of the people." The party's ideology is defined as democratic centralism, which means in effect that the party controls the state. The party's High Council for the Struggle, equivalent to a central committee, has 85 members and ordinarily is convened once a year by the Executive Committee for the Struggle, a 24-member body that is the PAIGC's political bureau. The PAIGC's Party Congress meets once every three years. In 1990 Vieira announced a move toward a multiparty system.

ECONOMY

Guinea-Bissau is one of the low-income countries of the world and one of the least-developed countries. The country is in the process of rebuilding an economy seriously disrupted by the extended conflict from 1963 to 1974.

Guinea-Bissau has a centrally planned socialist economy in which the dominant sector is public.

Agriculture and fishing are the main economic activities. The former was seriously disrupted by the civil war; cultivated areas are less than a third of what they were before the war. Agricultural output made some recovery in the late 1970s, but was badly hit by drought and plagues of locusts during the 1980s.

Exploitation of mineral resources is currently unlikely because of poor infrastructure and the high cost of development.

PRINCIPAL ECONOMIC INDICATORS

Gross National Product (U.S. $ millions): 173 (1989)
GNP per capita (U.S. $): 180 (1989)
GNP average annual growth rate (%, 1980–89): 3.3
GNP per capita average annual growth rate (%, 1987–89): 2.4

GROSS DOMESTIC PRODUCT

GDP nominal (P.G. billions): 21.2 (1985)
GDP per capita (U.S. $): 160 (1988)
Average annual growth rate of GDP (%, 1975–85): 1.7
GDP by type of expenditure (%) 1987
- Consumption
  - Private: 89
  - Government: 12
- Gross domestic investment: 24
- Foreign trade
  - Exports: 15
  - Imports: −39

Sectoral origin of GDP (%) 1986
- Primary
  - Agriculture: 51
- Secondary
  - Manufacturing & mining: 1
  - Construction: 2
  - Public utilities: 2
- Tertiary
  - Transportation & communications: 18
  - Finance: 4
  - Other services: 5
  - Government: 16

PUBLIC FINANCE

The Guinean fiscal year is the calendar year.

In 1989, the last year for which figures are available, indirect taxes made up almost half of all revenues. Another 25% came from direct taxes.

Economic Services accounted for 40% of expenditures in 1987, general public services 25%, agriculture 20%, social security and housing nine and eight percent respectively. Education accounted for 2.7% and health for 1.4% of expenditures in 1989.

Guinea-Bissau's development programs have emphasized rural development and agriculture.

From 1970 to 1988 the nation received $46 million in aid from the United States, $519 million in aid from other Western nations, $68 million from communist countries and $41 million from OPEC.

FOREIGN AID, 1989

Total foreign aid (U.S. $ millions): 201.4
- Bilateral: 73.7
- Multilateral: 127.7

CENTRAL GOVERNMENT EXPENDITURES, 1989

% of total expenditures
- Defense: 4.2
- Education: 2.7
- Health: 1.4
- Housing, social security, welfare: 17.1 (1987)
- Economic services: 40.0 (1987)

Total expenditures as % of GDP: 108.61
Overall surplus or deficit as % of GDP: −22.0 (1986)

CENTRAL GOVERNMENT REVENUES, 1988

% of total current revenues
- Taxes on income, profit & capital gain: 5.5
- Social security contributions: 0.9
- Domestic taxes on goods & services: 24.7
- Taxes on international trade & transactions: 37.1
- Other taxes: 3.8 (1989)
- Current nontax revenue: 63.9 (1989)

Total current revenue as % of GNP: 11.2 (1986)
General government consumption as % of GDP: 33 (1985)

CURRENCY & BANKING

The Guinean unit of currency is the peso, introduced in 1976 and replacing the Guinean escudo at par. Both currencies are at par with the Portuguese escudo. The peso, like the escudo, is divided into 100 centavos. Coins are issued in denominations of 10, 20 and 50 centavos; notes are issued in denominations of 50, 100 and 500 centavos.

In June 1991 the dollar exchange rate was $1 = P3,313.

FINANCIAL INDICATORS, 1988

External debt 1988
- Debt service (long term)
  - Total (U.S. $ millions): 7.0
  - Repayment
    - Principal (%): 28.6
    - Interest (%): 71.4
  - Debt service ratio (%): 27.1

GROWTH PROFILE
(Annual Growth Rates, %)

GNP (1980–89): 3.4
GNP per capital (1987–89): 2.4

The central bank and the bank of issue for the peso is Banco Nacional da Guiné-Bissau, founded in 1976 when Guinea-Bissau left the escudo monetary area. Commercial banking is conducted by Portuguese banking institutions.

AGRICULTURE

Severe droughts and plagues of locusts reduced agricultural earnings in the late 1970s and early 1980s and resulted in a sharp increase in imported foodstuffs to make up for the deficit in production. Rice is imported by the state-owned Armazens do Povo (People's Stores) and is almost wholly financed or donated by foreign governments and distributed and sold by government outlets.

The country is divided into three major zones on the basis of water availability and soil features. The palm-tree zone covers the river estuaries and coastal areas. Rice is cultivated in the intermediate marshy areas, and peanuts are grown in the sandy tracts of the interior. All the farms are now owned by Africans following the expropriation of all properties owned by nonnationals by the PAIGC government after independence. Mechanization has made little headway, and there were only 25 tractors in the country in 1982.

The staple crop is rice, though the output of cassava exceeds that of rice. The major cash crops are peanuts and palm kernels.

AGRICULTURAL INDICATORS

Agriculture's share of GDP (%): 4.7 (1989)
Index of agricultural production (1979–81 = 100): 148 (1986)
Index of food production (1979–81 = 100): 148 (1986)
Number of farms (000): 87 (1961)
Average size of holding (ha.): 3.0 (1961)
Size class (%), 1961
- Below 1 ha. (below 2.47 ac.): 13.4
- 1–5 ha. (2.47–12.35 ac.): 73.3
- 5–10 ha. (12.35–24.7 ac.): 10.0
- 10–20 ha. (24.7–49.4 ac.): 3.0
- 20–50 ha. (49.4–123.5 ac.): 0.3
- 50–200 ha. (123.5–494 ac.): 0.0
- Over 200 ha. (over 494 ac.): 0.0

Land use % 1985–87
- Cropland: 12
- Pasture: 38
- Forest: 38
- Other: 12
- Yields (kg./ha.) 1989
  - Grains: 1,029
  - Roots & tubers: 6,154
  - Legumes: 567
  - Milk (kg./animal): 170
- Production 1989
  - Fruits (000 metric tons): 42
  - Vegetables (000 metric tons): 20
- Livestock (000) 1987
  - Cattle: 340
  - Sheep: 205
  - Pigs: 290
- Forestry 1988
  - Production of roundwood (000 cubic meters): 565
    - of which industrial roundwood (%): 25.3
  - Value of exports (U.S. $ 000): 350
- Fishing 1988
  - Total catch (000 metric tons): 3.5
    - of which marine (%): 100.0
  - Value of exports (U.S. $ millions): 1.500

The Fulani and Balante tribes are herders and, despite the incidence of the tsetse fly, livestock constitutes a substantial portion of the national wealth.

Timber has become a leading export.

Guinea-Bissau's rivers and coastal waters have enormous potential to sustain a viable fishing industry. A fishing fleet is being built up with vessels supplied by the Soviet Union. Significant exports of fish and shrimp began only in 1976.

MANUFACTURING

Manufacturing is the smallest economic sector. In 1987 only 1.5 of the labor force was engaged in manufacturing. Industry is underdeveloped in Guinea-Bissau due to fundamental deficiencies in the human and physical infrastructure, and a small internal market. What industry exists is geared toward import substitution, with some exports. Industry ownership is divided into the private, mixed and public sectors.

The government has a pragmatic approach to the small, private industrial sector, avoiding bureaucratic or ideological harassment. There is a demand for privately produced local products with an expansion potential. This also is true for the mixed sector, particularly the beer and fishing industries.

The public sector is the largest sector in industry. The government places great emphasis on public industry for eventual growth. All public firms are given extensive and costly protection by the government. An example of this is the Cumere Agro-Industrial Complex, which eventually will process 70,000 tons of groundnuts and 50,000 tons of rice.

MINING

Guinea-Bissau's mineral resources include deposits of about 200 million tons of bauxite. There is as yet no mineral production.

ENERGY

Guinea-Bissau does not produce any form of mineral energy and suffers chronic power shortages. A diesel power plant is being built with aid from the Soviet Union, and there is great potential for the development of hydroelectric power.

ENERGY INDICATORS

Electricity 1988
- Installed capacity (000 kw.): 7
- Production (million kw.-hr.): 15
  - % fossil fuel: 100.0
  - % hydro: 0.0
  - % nuclear: 0.0
- Consumption per capita (kw.-hr.): 16

Petroleum
- Production (million bbl.): 0 (1989)
- Consumption (million bbl.): 0 (1988)
- Refining capacity (000 bbl./day): 0 (1990)

LABOR

About 72% of the total labor force is engaged in agriculture, forestry and fishing. 1.9% in manufacturing, 0.9% in construction, 2.6% in trade, 0.1% in public utilities, 1.2% in transportation and communications, 0.1% in finance, 13.8% in public administration and defense and 0.5 in other.

The established labor union, the United National Workers of Guinea-Bissau, is a member of the Organization of African Trade Union Unity and is a "mass action" organ of the PAIGC. The union claims 20,000 members. It is forbidden to organize public employees—a prohibition dating from colonial days. Strikes, although not formally illegal, have not taken place, and the vast majority of salaried workers are employees of the state.

LABOR INDICATORS, 1988

Total economically active population (000): 279
- % working-age (15–64): 41.0
- % female: 3.3

Activity rate (%)
- Total: 30.0
- Male: 60.1
- Female: 1.9

Sectoral employment of economically active (%)
- Agriculture, forestry, fishing: 71.9
- Construction, manufacturing, mining, quarrying, public utilities: 1.5
- Trade, hotels, restaurants: 2.4
- Transportation, communications: 1.1
- Finance, real estate: 0.1
- Services: 12.3

FOREIGN COMMERCE

Guinea-Bissau's most important exports are cashews, fish, peanuts and palm kernels. Its major imports are capital equipment, consumer goods, semiprocessed goods, foods and petroleum. Portugal, Spain, the European Community, the Soviet Union and the United States are its principal trading partners.

FOREIGN TRADE INDICATORS, 1987

Exports (U.S. $ millions): 15
Imports (U.S. $ millions): 49
Balance of trade (U.S. $ millions): −34

Direction of Trade (%), 1984

	Imports	Exports
European Community	51.9	64.4
United States	8.8	0.0
U.S.S.R. & Eastern European economies	15.2	0.0
Japan	0.2	0.0

Composition of Trade (%), 1980

	Imports	Exports
Food and agricultural raw materials	20.1	87.1
Fuels & other energy	6.2	0.0
Mineral ores & concentrates	2.2	0.3
Manufactured goods	71.5	12.6
of which chemicals	5.6	0.0
of which machinery	36.4	0.0

TRANSPORTATION & COMMUNICATIONS

Guinea-Bissau has no railroads, but it is well served by an extensive system of inland waterways with a total length of 1,600 km. (994 mi.). All rivers are navigable by tugs and barges and some by oceangoing vessels of shallow draft. Bissau is the principal port for international shipping. There are two other minor ports, for coastal shipping.

TRANSPORTATION INDICATORS

Road (latest)
  Length, km. (mi.): 5,058 (3,143)
  Paved (%): 8
Motor vehicles (latest)
  Automobiles: 3,000
  Trucks and buses: 2,000
  Persons per vehicle: 179
Merchant marine
  Vessels (over 100 tons): 17 (1989)
  Total deadweight tonnage (000): 1.8 (1989)
Ports (pre 1986)
  Cargo loaded (000 metric tons): 33
  Cargo unloaded (000 metric tons): 129
Air
  Km. (mi.) flown (millions): 1.0 (0.7) (1985)
  Passenger-km. (passenger-mi.) (millions): 9 (6) (pre-1986)
  Freight, metric ton-km. (short ton-mi.) (millions): 1.0 (0.7) (pre-1986)
  Airports with scheduled flights: 2 (1990)

COMMUNICATION INDICATORS, 1986

Telephones
  Total (000): 3.0
  Persons per telephone: 297
Telecommunications 1990
  Satellite stations: 1

More than half of the total road length is accounted for by narrow tracks in the interior. The main highways connect Bissau with Varela and with the border post of Buruntuma, and Enchude with Catio.

The national airline is Transportes Aereos da Guiné-Bissau, which operates internal flights with two planes. The main international airport is at Bissau (Bissalanca), with a runway of over 2,500 m. (8,000 ft.).

DEFENSE

The Guinean armed forces, known as the People's Revolutionary Armed Forces (FARP), are headed by the president, and the line of command runs through the state commissioner for the armed forces. The FARP is manned mainly by Balanta and Nalu tribesmen. Guinea-Bissau has a defense treaty with Senegal, apparently directed against Guinea, which claims two of the Piolau Islands in southwestern Guinea-Bissau. The FARP has grown since independence to 7,200 men.

Army

Personnel: 6,800

Organization: 1 armored battalion; 5 infantry battalions; 1 reconnaissance squadron; 1 engineer company; 1 artillery battalion

Equipment: 30 tanks; 10 combat vehicles; 55 armored personnel carriers; 18 guns; 8 mortars; 28 air defense guns; SAM

Navy

Personnel: 300

Units: 11 patrol craft; 4 landing craft

Air Force

Personnel: 100; 2 transports; 1 helicopter

EDUCATION

The national adult literacy rate is 31.4% (46.2% for males and 17.3% for females).

Guinea-Bissau has introduced universal, free and compulsory education, in principle, from ages seven to 13.

EDUCATION INDICATORS

Literacy
  Total (%): 31.4
  Male (%): 46.2
  Female (%): 17.3
First level
  Schools: 668
  Students: 81,444
  Teachers: 3,158
  Student/teacher ratio: 25.8
  Net enrollment ratio: 42 (1986)
Second level
  Schools: 12
  Students: 11,710
  Teachers: 650
  Student/teacher ratio: 18.0
  Net enrollment ratio: 3 (1983)
Vocational
  Schools: 4
  Students: 1,027
  Teachers: 107
  Student/teacher ratio: 9.6
Foreign study
  Students abroad: 502
    of whom in
      United States: 25 (1988)
      France: 20 (1988)
      Federal Republic of Germany: 6 (1988)
Public expenditure, 1987
  Total (P.G. 000):
  % of GNP: 2.8
  % of current: 97.6

Schooling consists of 11 years, divided into six years for the basic first cycle, three years for the basic second cycle and two years for the secondary cycle. The curriculum has been completely Africanized, but shortages of textbooks and educational materials plague the system. The academic year runs from October to July. The medium of instruction is Portuguese.

In 1985 there were 3,910 teachers, compared with 30 in 1962. Mass literacy campaigns have been launched by the PAIGC youth organization, Juventude Africana Amilcar Cabral (JAAC).

Guinea-Bissau has no institution of higher learning.

LEGAL SYSTEM

The judicial system is headed by the Supreme War Tribunal, to which appeals come from two subordinate levels of courts: zonal courts and people's courts. People's courts are elected in each region. The judiciary is subordinate to both the executive and the PAIGC.

There is no published civil or criminal code. Habeas corpus based on the Portuguese Penal Code exists in urban areas but generally is not observed in rural areas, where traditional law prevails. There are no bail procedures. In rural areas, nonpolitical offenders in other than the most important criminal and civil cases are often tried outside the formal court system, under traditional law. The private practice of law is prohibited. Defendants are assigned legal assistants from the Ministry of Justice when available. The judiciary is not independent. The civilian court system is essentially a continuation of that which existed under Portuguese colonial rule. The Supreme Court is the highest civilian court of appeal. Regional military courts have jurisdiction over military, militia and security personnel on military missions. The Supreme Court has jurisdiction over more serious crimes such as acts against state security, attempts against the lives of party members, treason and piracy. It also is an appeal court for the regional military courts. The interval between arrest and trial may be lengthy.

No information is available on correctional facilities or the penal system in Guinea-Bissau.

LAW ENFORCEMENT

The national law enforcement force is the Polícia de Leguranca Pública, under the Ministry of National Security and Public Order. The structure of the police force is a carryover from colonial days, but other details are lacking.

No information is available on the incidence and nature of crime in the country.

HEALTH

Medical services are limited because of shortages of personnel and facilities. The government hopes to establish a hospital in each of the eight regions. In 1987 the government introduced a program to improve primary health care. However, in 1989 it announced that hospital treatment would no longer be provided free of charge.

Such tropical diseases as malaria, yaws, and sleeping sickness are prevalent.

HEALTH INDICATORS

Health personnel 1985
- Physicians: 122
  - persons per: 7,164
- Dentists: 2 (1980)
- Nurses: 674
- Pharmacists: 3 (1980)
- Midwives: 111

Hospitals 1981
- Number: 17
- Number of beds (/10,000): 19 (1983)
- Admissions/discharges (/10,000): 326
- Bed occupancy rate (%): 57.5
- Average length of stay (days): 11

Type of hospitals (%) 1981
- Government: 100.0
- Private nonprofit: 0.0
- Private profit: 0.0

Public health expenditures (latest)
- As % of national budget: 5.4
- Per capita (U.S. $): 4.30

Vital statistics
- Crude death rate (/1,000): 19 (1990)
- Life expectancy at birth 1990
  - Males: 44
  - Females: 48
- Infant mortality rate (/1,000 live births): 127 (1990)
- Child mortality rate under 5 yrs. (/1,000) (1985–90): 223
- Maternal mortality rate (/100,000 live births) (1980–84): 140 (est.)
- Population with access to safe water (%): 31 (latest)

FOOD & NUTRITION

The staple food is rice, supplemented by sweet potatoes, cassava and corn. The per capital daily intake of food is 2,357 calories.

MEDIA & CULTURE

Only two daily newspapers are published in the country: *No Pintcha*, which became a daily in 1990 and has a circulation of 6,000, and *Voz da Guine*, which also has a circulation of 6,000. Both are published in Bissau in Portuguese.

The newspaper and all periodicals are controlled by the PAIGC.

Guinea-Bissau has no national news agency. No books are published in the country.

Radiodifusão Nacional, the official station, broadcasts on shortwave, medium-wave and FM. The domestic program is on the air for about 15 hours a day. An experimental television station was introduced in mid-1988.

MEDIA INDICATORS, 1987

Newspapers
- Number of dailies: 2
- Circulation (000): 6
- Per 1,000 pop.: 7

Newsprint consumption 1988
- Total metric tons: 200
- Per 1,000 pop. (kg.): 211

Radio
- Number of transmitters: 2 (1989)
- Number of persons per radio receiver: 27 (1989)

Cinema
- Number of fixed cinemas: 4
- Seating capacity (000): 1.0

SOCIAL WELFARE

Until independence social welfare was administered by the Administrative Commission of the Development and Welfare Fund. No information is available on the postindependence period.

GLOSSARY

assimilado: Guinean who has assimilated Portuguese culture and has been alienated from traditional African society.

circunscricoes: circumscriptions, former units of local administration.
concelho: a religion consisting of a number of circumscriptions.
crioulo: an Africanized Portuguese patois, used as lingua franca in Guinea-Bissau.
mestico: a person of mixed African and Portuguese descent.
tabanca: village, as a unit of local administration.

CHRONOLOGY (from 1956)

1956— African Party for the Independence of Guinea and Cape Verde (PAIGC) is founded.

1973— Amilcar Cabral is assassinated; Aristides Pereira takes over leadership of the movement. . . . PAIGC unilaterally proclaims the establishment of the Republic of Guinea-Bissau. . . . United Nations "welcomes" the proclamation by 97 votes to 30. . . . New nation adopts for itself a new Constitution.

1974— Military coup in Portugal is followed by ceasefire in Guinea-Bissau, ending the 17-year insurrection; negotiations follow with rebel leaders. . . . By formal agreement Portugal acknowledges independence of Guinea-Bissau and withdraws all Portuguese troops from the territory.

1975— Aid agreements are signed with Portugal, France, the Soviet Union, China, Senegal and other countries. . . . National People's Assembly passes legislation nationalizing most lands and domestic and foreign trade.

1976— Protocol is signed with Cape Verde providing for integration of the judicial systems of the two countries as a prelude to political union.

1977— Guinea-Bissau attends France-Africa summit at Dakar, Senegal.

1980— President Cabral is ousted in a coup led by Prime Minister (Principal Commissioner) João Bernardo Vieira; new Revolutionary Council is set up; relations with Cape Verde are broken, and the foreseeable prospect of a union between the two countries is shattered.

1984— A new Constitution is promulgated, civilianizing the military administration. . . . President Vieira is elected as president for a five-year term. . . . Prime Minister Victor Sáude Maria is ousted along with other left-wingers in the cabinet.

1985— Col. Paulo Alexandre Nunes Correia and a number of other prominent military and civilian officials are accused of attempting to overthrow the government.

1986— Correia and five of his associates are executed.

1990— Vieira announces movement toward a multiparty system.

BIBLIOGRAPHY (from 1965)

BOOKS

Abshire, David M., and Michael A. Samuels. *Portuguese Africa: A Handbook.* New York, 1969.
Cabral, Amilcar. *Revolution in Guinea.* London, 1969.
———. *Return to the Source.* New York, 1974.
Chaliand, Gerard. *Armed Struggle in Africa: With the Guerrillas in Portuguese Guinea.* New York, 1969.
Chilcote, Ronald. *Portuguese Africa.* Englewood Cliffs, N.J., 1967.
Davidson, Basil. *The Liberation of Guinea.* Baltimore, Md., 1969.
Galli, Rosemary. *Guinea-Bissua: Politics, Economics, and Society.* Boulder, Colo., 1987.
Gibson, Richard. *African Liberation Movements.* New York, 1972.
Lobban, Richard. *Historical Dictionary of the Republics of Guinea-Bissau and Cape Verde.* Metuchen, N.J., 1979.
McCarthy, Joseph M. *Guinea-Bissau and Cape Verde: A Comprehensive Bibliography.* New York, 1977.
Minter, William. *Portuguese Africa and the West.* New York, 1973.
Rodney, Walter. *A History of Upper Guinea Coast, 1545–1800.* New York, 1980.
Rudebeck, Lars. *Guinea-Bissau: A Study of Political Mobilization.* New York, 1975.
Sarrazin, Chantal, and Ole Gjerstad. *Sowing the First Harvest: Reconstruction in Guinea-Bissau.* Oakland, Calif., 1978.
Urdang, Stephanie. *Fighting Two Colonialisms: Women in Guinea-Bissau.* New York, 1980.

GUYANA

BASIC FACT SHEET

OFFICIAL NAME: Cooperative Republic of Guyana

ABBREVIATION: GY

CAPITAL: Georgetown

HEAD OF STATE: President Hugh Desmond Hoyte (from 1985)

HEAD OF GOVERNMENT: Prime Minister Hamilton Green (from 1985)

NATURE OF GOVERNMENT: Partial democracy

POPULATION: 764,649 (1990)

AREA: 214,970 sq. km. (83,000 sq. mi.)

ETHNIC MAJORITY: East Indian (For this country the term East Indian is used to denote descendants of settlers from the Indian subcontinent and the term Amerindian is used to denote indigenous Indians of the Americas.)

LANGUAGE: English (official)

RELIGIONS: Christianity, Hinduism and Islam

UNIT OF CURRENCY: Guyana dollar (G. $)

NATIONAL FLAG: Green field with a red triangle edged with black superimposed on a yellow triangle edged with white both pointing toward the fly

NATIONAL EMBLEM: A white shield flanked by prancing gold and black indigenous jaguars, one holding a sugercane stalk and the other a miner's pickax. The shield is divided by three wavy blue lines. The upper half displays the Victoria Regina lily, the national flower, and the lower half the *canje* pheasant, with red feathers and white breast. The design is crested by a golden helmet mantled in blue and white bearing a candy-striped wreath and a blue feathered headdress of an Amerindian chief witih two diamonds in the headband. Beneath the emblem is the national motto, "One People, One Nation, One Destiny," on a red and gold riband.

NATIONAL ANTHEM: "Dear Land of Guyana, of Rivers and Plains"

NATIONAL HOLIDAYS: February 23 (Republic Day, National Day); January 1 (New Year's Day); May 1 (Labor Day); First Monday in July (Caribbean Day); August 1 (Commonwealth Day); October 24 (U.N. Day); Christian festivals include Christmas, Boxing Day, Easter Monday and Good Friday; Hindu and Islamic festivals also are celebrated.

NATIONAL CALENDAR: Gregorian

PHYSICAL QUALITY OF LIFE INDEX: 86

DATE OF INDEPENDENCE: May 26, 1966

DATE OF CONSTITUTION: October 6, 1980

WEIGHTS & MEASURES: Metric, but imperial measures are still in general use.

GEOGRAPHICAL FEATURES

Guyana, on the northeastern coast of South America, has an area of 214,970 sq. km. (83,000 sq. mi.), extending 807 km. (501 mi.) north to south and 436 km. (271 mi.) east to west. The length of the Altantic coastline is 430 km. (267 mi.).

Guyana shares its total international boundary of 2,584 km. (1,606 mi.) with three countries: Brazil, (1,208 km.; 751 mi.), Venezuela (650 km., 404 mi.) and Suriname (726 km.; 451 mi.). Guyana has unresolved boundary disputes with both Venezuela and Suriname. The border with Venezuela was delimited by the Paris Award of 1899 and established by a British-Venezuelan commission from 1902 to 1905. Venezuela disputes the entire Paris Award and claims everything west of the Essequibo River, or 137,270 sq. km. (53,000 sq. mi.), representing five-eighths of Guyana's territory. The Venezuelans have seized and fortified Anakoko Island on the Cuyuni River, half of which belongs to Guyana by the 1899 award. The dispute with Suriname relates to the territory between the Corentyne River and the New River, or about 15,540 sq. km. (6,000 sq. mi.). The disputed territory is under Guyanese control but is largely uninhabited. The capital is Georgetown, with a 1976 population of 167,078. The only other major town is New Amsterdam, with a population of 15,000.

Guyana is divided into three major geographical zones: a coastal plain, a forest zone and a grass-covered savanna. The coastal plain, about 15 to 65 km. (10 to 40 mi.) wide, is made up of alluvial mud from the Amazon River, but much of the plain is below sea level by as much as 1.2 to 1.5 m. (4 to 5 ft.) at high tide. A barrier of swamps divides the plain from the interior forest zone, which occupies 85% of the land area. Geologically the zone consists of an eroded plateau from which hill ranges known as the Pakaraima Mountains and the Kaieteurian Plateau rise. The savanna zone includes the Rupununi valley in the extreme southwestern part and an intermediate savanna about 95 km. (60 mi.) inland from the Berbice coast.

The four principal rivers from east to west are the Corentyne, Berbice, Demerara and Essequibo. Between these major rivers are several smaller rivers, such as the Canje, Mahaicomy, Abary and Mahaica. The largest of the rivers is the Essequibo, over 965 km. (600 mi.) long, which drains more than half of the country. It has four main tributaries: the Mazaruni, Cuyuni, Potaro and Rupununi. The Essequibo is navigable for 65 km. (40 mi.) upstream, the Demerara and the Corentyne

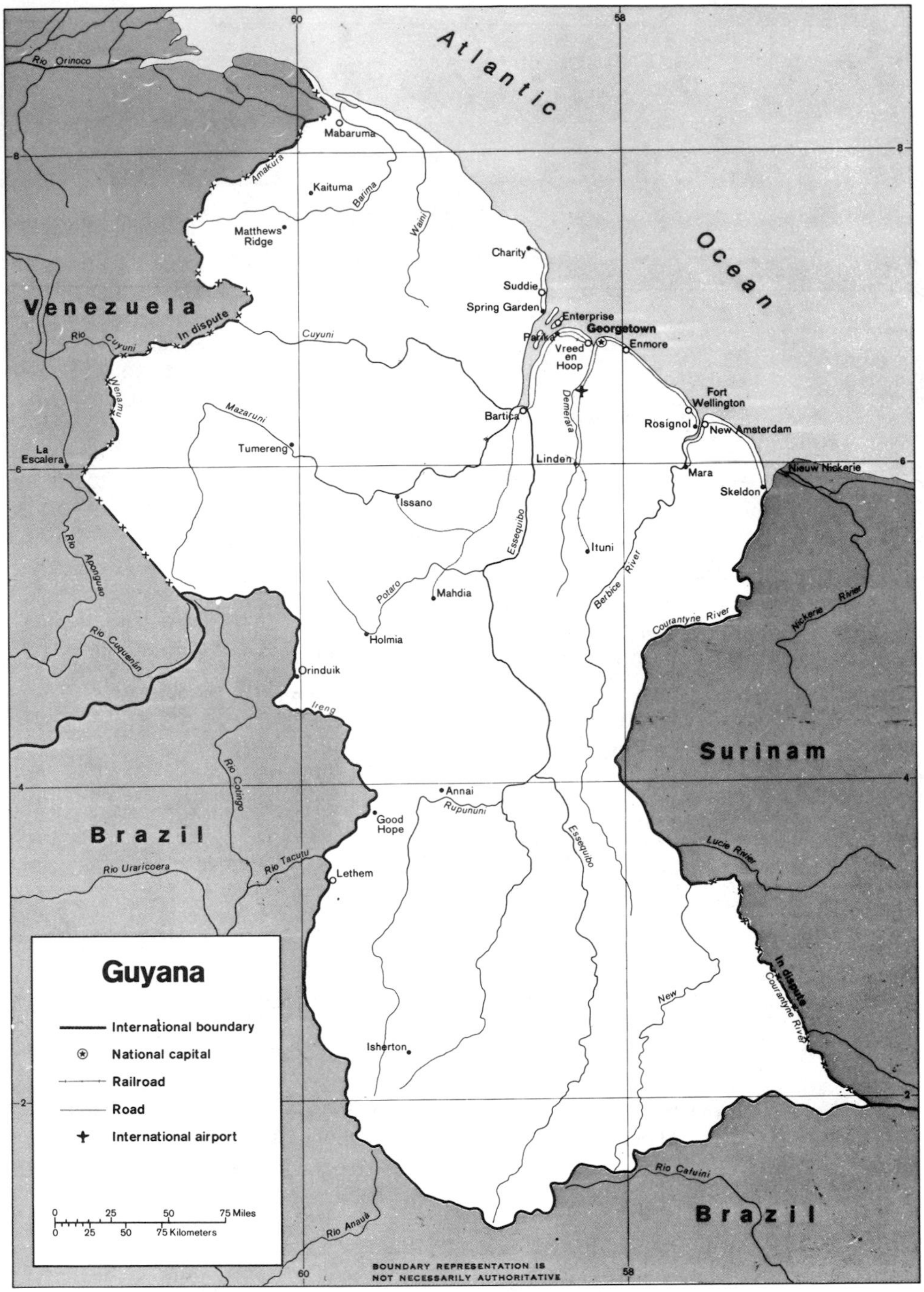
Guyana
International boundary
National capital
Railroad
Road
International airport
0 25 50 75 Miles
0 25 50 75 Kilometers
BOUNDARY REPRESENTATION IS NOT NECESSARILY AUTHORITATIVE
Atlantic
Ocean
Venezuela
Brazil
Brazil
Surinam
In dispute
In dispute
Rio Orinoco
Amakura
Barima
Waini
Rio Cuyuni
Cuyuni
Wenamu
Mazaruni
Potaro
Essequibo
Demerara
Berbice River
Courantyne River
Nickerie River
Lucie River
Courantyne River
New
Rio Aponguao
Rio Cuquenán
Ireng
Rio Cotingo
Rio Uraricoera
Rio Tacutu
Rupununi
Rio Anauá
Rio Cafuini
Mabaruma
Kaituma
Matthews Ridge
Charity
Suddie
Spring Garden
Enterprise
Parika
Georgetown
Vreed en Hoop
Enmore
Fort Wellington
Rosignol
New Amsterdam
Nieuw Nickerie
Mara
Skeldon
Bartica
Linden
Ituni
Tumereng
La Escalera
Issano
Mahdia
Holmia
Orinduik
Annai
Good Hope
Lethem
Isherton
60
58
8
6
4
2

ONE PEOPLE
ONE NATION
ONE DESTINY

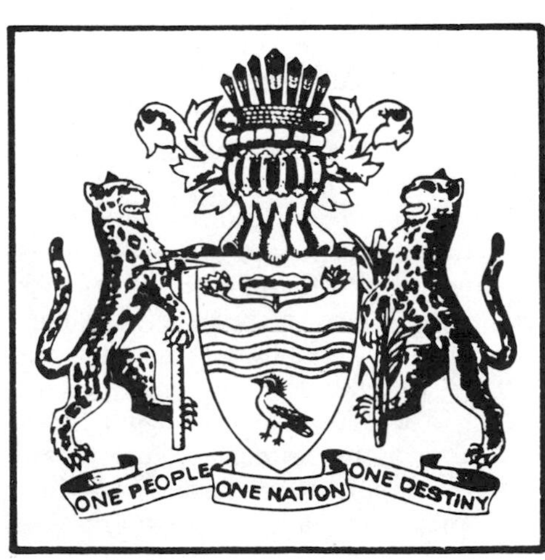

for 95 km. (60 mi.) and the Berbice for 160 km. (100 mi.). Because of low gradients the drainage is poor, and there are periodic floods, resulting in extensive swamps. Tides aggravate coastal drainage problems.

CLIMATE & WEATHER

Guyana has a subtropical climate with two rainy and two dry seasons. Although there are high temperature ranges in the interior mountains, nowhere are they extreme and, in general, temperatures are moderated by sea breezes throughout the year. Georgetown's mean temperature is 26.6°C (80°F), with a daily range of less than 11°C (20°F). Temperatures in the Rupununi River Valley range from 18.9°C (66°F) to 39.4°C (103°F), with the higher range common during the long dry season from August to May.

The coastal rainy seasons are from April to July and from November to January; in most years rain falls for 200 days. The amount of rainfall increases as one moves up the coast, from an average of 2,280 mm. (90 in.) in Georgetown to 3,560 mm. (140 in.) in the forest zone. Humidity is high throughout the year.

Guyana is to the south of the hurricane belt and thus escapes the Caribbean storms.

POPULATION

The population of Guyana was estimated at 764,649 in 1990, based on the last official census, in 1980, when the population was 701,885.

Over 90% of the population is concentrated on 4% of the available land. Vast areas of the interior are virtually uninhabited. The urban-rural distribution is closely related to the nation's ethnic composition. Although East Indians form a numerical majority in the nation, they account for less than one-fourth of the urban population, while the Afro-Guyanese constitute over 70%. Nearly 45% of the Afro-Guyanese are concentrated in the cities of Georgetown and New Amsterdam. Two-thirds of the Europeans and Chinese also reside in these cities.

Since the suspension of East Indian immigration in 1917, immigration and emigration have had no significant influence on population growth. The annual net gain through immigration and emigration is estimated at less than 2,000. Internal migration also has been relatively insignificant.

The Burnham and Hoyte regimes have been generally supportive of women's rights. In 1983 the government passed legislation to erase the stigma of illegitimacy and accord legal rights to children of unwed mothers. Women serve in many high government and business positions, and Afro-Guyanese women form the core of People's National Congress.

Guyana has no official birth control policies or programs.

DEMOGRAPHIC INDICATORS

Population (000): 765 (1990)
Year of last census: 1980
Sex distribution (% at last census): males, 49.5; females, 50.5
Population estimates and projections (000)

1930: 309	1960: 560	1990: 765
1940: 344	1970: 702	2000: 811
1950: 423	1980: 759	

Age profile (% at last census)

0–14: 40.8	30–44: 14	60–74: 4.4
15–29: 30.5	45–59: 8.8	75 and over: 1.2

Median age (yrs.): 20.9 (1985)
Youth population (% aged 15–24): 22.4 (1985), 19.5 (2000)
Total dependency ratio: 69.1 (1985)
Annual growth rate (%)

1950–55: 2.78	1975–80: 2.07	2000–2005: 1.22
1955–60: 3.14	1980–85: 1.95	2005–2010: 1.23
1960–65: 2.52	1985–90: 1.74	2010–2015: 1.13
1965–70: 1.90	1990–95: 1.46	2015–2020: 1.00
1970–75: 1.89	1995–2000: 1.34	2020–2025: 0.86

Urban population (000): 307 (1985)
Urban population (%): 30.5 (1980 est.)
Annual urban population growth rate (%, 1985–90): 3.19
Annual rural population growth rate (%, 1985–90): 1.01
Population density per sq. km. (per sq. mi.): 3.5 (9.1) (latest)

VITAL STATISTICS

Crude birth rate (/1,000): 24 (1990)
Crude death rate (/1,000): 6 (1990)
Infant mortality rate (/1,000 live births): 40 (1990)
Maternal mortality rate (/100,000 live births): 104 (1980–84)
Life expectancy (yrs.) at birth: males, 65; females, 70 (1990)
Gross reproduction rate (/woman) (1980–85): 1.59
Total fertility rate (/woman): 2.7 (1990)
Rate of natural increase (/1,000): 19 (1989)
Marriage rate (/1,000): 4.2 (1968)
Average household size: 5.1 (latest)
Legitimate births (%): 61.4 (latest)

STATUS OF WOMEN INDICATORS

Number of women (000): 489 (1985)
% women literate: 95 (1987)
% women in labor force: 24.9 (1988)
Total fertility rate (/woman): 2.7 (1990)
% women in national legislatures: 22 (1984)

ETHNIC COMPOSITION

Guyana has a varied ethnic composition, with seven definable groups. Ethnicity is an important element in the nation's political, economic and cultural life.

Most of the East Indians came to Guyana between 1844 and 1917 under what was known as the indenture system. During this period 238,960 East Indians, mostly from the United Provinces of the Indian Empire, were imported to work on the sugar plantations. Although working conditions of these coolies were almost as severe as those of slaves, they had no masters, enjoyed certain civil rights, and were free to return to India at the expiration of their contract period. Over one-third of the East Indians returned to their native land; the rest continued to live in rural areas. Nearly 84% of these were Hindus, with most of the rest being Muslims. Of the Hindus, only 10% belong to the high

PRINCIPAL ETHNIC GROUPS OF GUYANA	
Ethnic Group	Percent
East Indians	50.16
Afro-Guyanese	30.00
Mixed (or colored)	13.20
Amerindians	4.60
Portuguese	1.00
Chinese	0.60
British and other whites	0.40

Brahman caste; the others belong to a number of lower castes. Unlike the Africans, the East Indians were permitted to retain their cultural, religious and linguistic traditions. Their cultural isolation was reinforced by the compulsory education law of 1871, which exempted them from attending Christian schools. Bound by strong kinship and family ties, the East Indians have developed into a cohesive community with few attachments other than to their land. Most of the East Indians live in rural villages as farmers and have avoided participation in politics, government service and social activities. Their resistance to assimilation poses the gravest threat to national integration.

The Afro-Guyanese, who form the largest minority, are descendants of slaves imported from the Guinea coast of West Africa. They form the most mobile sector of the population and the predominant working class in the larger towns and cities. They are actively involved in politics and occupy the most important positions in the national government. The mixed or colored group forms the second-largest minority in Guyana. Formerly this group held a privileged position in society, and the mulattoes often are better educated and wealthier. The small Chinese minority has been completely assimilated as a result of frequent intermarriages with Africans. Most of Chinese have converted to evangelical Christianity and retain few of the traditional bonds of overseas Chinese. The Amerindians, the original inhabitants of the land, form three linguistic families: Warrau, Arawak and Carib. There are six Carib-speaking groups—Carib, Akawaio, Patamona, Arekuna, Makusi and Waiwai—most of whom live in the interior.

Permanent Western communities include British and Portuguese nationals, who generally do not identify themselves with the Guyanese.

The ethnic composition of Guyana has been shifting over the years in favor of the East Indians because of their sustained high rate of fertility. As the crude death and infant mortality rates dropped, the East Indian rate of increase became even more significant: 3.6% between 1946 and 1960 as against 2.7% for the Afro-Guyanese and 0.5% for the Chinese and caucasians. Whereas the East Indians represented 43% of the population in 1946, they accounted for 50.2% by 1964.

The ethnic polarization of Guyanese society is reflected not only in politics but also in the economy and in the occupational distribution of the labor force. Certain occupations are monopolized by each ethnic group, and ownership and employment in these sectors follow ethnic lines.

LANGUAGES

English is the official language. A number of vernaculars, such as Hindustani, Hindi, Urdu, Portguese and Chinese, used by the older immigrants, are being displaced by English. Amerindians speak languages belonging to three linguistic families: Warrau, Arawak and Carib.

RELIGIONS

The religious affiliations of the Guyanese correspond to the ethnic pattern. At the time of the 1970 census, 57% declared themselves as Christian, 33% as Hindu and 9% as Muslim. The largest Christian denomination is the Anglican Church of the West Indies, claiming over 170,000 members. The Roman Catholics, numbering 100,000, are mostly drawn from the Amerindian and Portuguese population. Christian values predominate in Guyana, although they are coming into conflict with the traditions of the East Indians. There also is a natural tendency to split along ethnic and religious lines and to find solidarity and identity as members of religious groups rather than as members of the Guyanese nation.

HISTORICAL BACKGROUND

The first European settlers in Guyana were the Dutch, who founded the settlement of Kijkorveral in 1616. In 1621 the colony was placed under the direction of the West Indian Company of the Netherlands, which administered it for the next 170 years. The British began migrating to the colony in large numbers and by 1760 constituted a majority of the population of Demerara. The British occupied the colony in 1796 and again in 1803 and gained formal possession in 1814. The two most important events in the early years of the British administration were the abolition of slavery in 1837 and the institution of the indenture system, under which thousands of coolies were imported from India from 1844 through 1917.

The colony was granted full self-government in 1961 and final independence in 1966.

Guyanese politics has been characterized by conflicts between the urbanized Africans and rural East Indians. In the years before independence, this was reflected in the conflict between the People's Progressive Party (PPP), led by Cheddi B. Jagan, and the People's National Congress (PNC), led by Forbes Burnham. The former was backed primarily by East Indians, the latter by Africans. The PPP won the general elections of 1957 and 1961 but was defeated in 1964 following the introduction of a system of proportional representation that made possible the formation of a coalition government composed of the PNC and the more conservative United Force (UF). Burnham remained in office through independence within the Commonwealth in 1966 and the adoption of a republican government in 1970. His government won reelection in 1968 and 1973 amid charges of fraud and the withdrawal of the UF from the coalition.

Following the end of the coalition, Burnham pushed for measures to bring about a transition to socialism, beginning with the change to Cooperative Republic status in 1970 and followed in succeeding years by nationalization of all bauxite and major sugar-producing operations. At the same time, the PNC increasingly attempted to present itself and the government as synonymous.

In 1980 a new Constitution was declared in effect. It replaced the largely ceremonial office of the president with a powerful office of the same name that combined responsibilities of head of state, chief executive and commander-in-chief of the armed forces. Forbes Burnham, for which the office was tailor-made, declared himself president. That year the PNC was credited with an overwhelming majority in elections considered fraudulent by international observers.

Incompetence and corruption, along with adverse economic conditions, brought Guyana to virtual bankruptcy in 1982. Burnham's government lost popular support and legitimacy, and it used repressive military and police force to maintain control despite popular disaffection.

In 1985 Forbes Burnham died and was succeeded by Vice President Hugh Desmond Hoyte. The general elections held in December of that year gave Hoyte a five-year mandate amid reports of widespread fraud. Hoyte made revitalization of the economy his chief priority, and in 1987 he announced the "roll-back of cooperative socialism." During the late 1980s, Hoyte, in return for IMF assistance, was forced to implement a stringent IMF-sponsored austerity plan that resulted in social unrest and industrial disruption. His government was also buffeted by increasing demands for electoral reform. However, presidential and parliamentary elections promised for early 1991 did not take place.

CONSTITUTION & GOVERNMENT

The Constitution of 1980 established Guyana as a cooperative republic within the Commonwealth. The Constitution is the supreme law of Guyana and prevails over all other laws. It includes a bill of rights based on the 1950 European Convention for the Protection of Human Rights and Fundamental Freedoms and the U.N. Covenant on Human Rights. The Constitution secures a citizen's political and legal rights and guarantees freedom of property; freedom of religion; freedom of expression, association and assembly; freedom of movement; and freedom from discrimination. The constitution also spells out the social and educational rights of citizens as well as the rights of workers. Special protection is extended to the Amerindians.

Under the 1980 Constitution, the largely ceremonial office of president was replaced by an executive presidency, which combined the responsibilities of head of state, head of government and commander-in-chief of the armed forces. The office of prime minister, which was retained, was made subsidiary to the presidency, as were other cabinet positions, including a number of vice presidencies. Appointments to cabinet positions, including prime minister and vice presidents, are made by the president. The president is chosen from the party with the largest number of votes in legislative elections.

Legislative power is vested in a unicameral National Assembly elected by universal suffrage in a system of proportional representation. The constitution provides for a Supreme Court of Judicature, consisting of the Court of Appeal and the High Court.

GOVERNMENT LIST
(July/August 1991)

President (Responsible for Home Affairs)	Hoyte, Hugh Desmond
1st Vice President (Health & Housing, Youth & Sport)	Green, Hamilton
Vice President (Culture & Social Development	
Vice President (Office of President)	Chandisingh, Ranji
Prime Minister	Green, Hamilton
Deputy Prime Minister	Murray, Winston
Deputy Prime Minister	Chandisingh, Ranji
Deputy Prime Minister (Planning & Development)	
Deputy Prime Minister (Public Works, Communication & Transportation)	Corbin Robert
Senior Minister	Kranenburg, Jules Richard
Minister of Agriculture	McKenzie, Pat
Minister of Education and Cultural Development	Bernhard, Deryck
Minister of Finance	Greenidge, Carl
Minister of Foreign Affairs	Hoyte, Hugh Desmond
Minister of Health	Green, Hamilton
Minister of Labor, Human Services, and Social Security	Ali-Kahn, Rabbian
Minister of Legal Affairs	Massiah, Keith
Minister of Trade & Tourism	Sawh, Oharamded
Attorney General	Massiah, Keith
Governor, Bank of Guyana	Matthews, Patrick

FREEDOM & HUMAN RIGHTS

In terms of civil and political rights Guyana is ranked as a partly free country.

President Hugh Hoyte and a small group of senior officials rule Guyana, meeting in cabinet sessions or in closed meetings of the People's National Congress (PNC) inner circle. In almost all matters, the president himself makes the final decision. The PNC government has ruled Guyana for some 25 years, preserving the facade of parliamentary democracy without the substance. The party has employed government apparatuses to advance its aims and to maintain political power in the hands of a ruling elite. Party loyalty is the road to advancement. Since the public sector employs over half the work force in Guyana, civil servants are reluctant to criticize the government publicly, although most Guyanese freely voice their opinions in private. Guyanese who are not members of the ruling party elite have been effectively denied meaningful participation in the decision-making processes of the state. Every election since 1964 has been marred by fraud and intimidation of the opponents of the People's National Congress. Opposition parties are able, albeit with some difficulty, to hold public political rallies, to organize and to publish their newspapers.

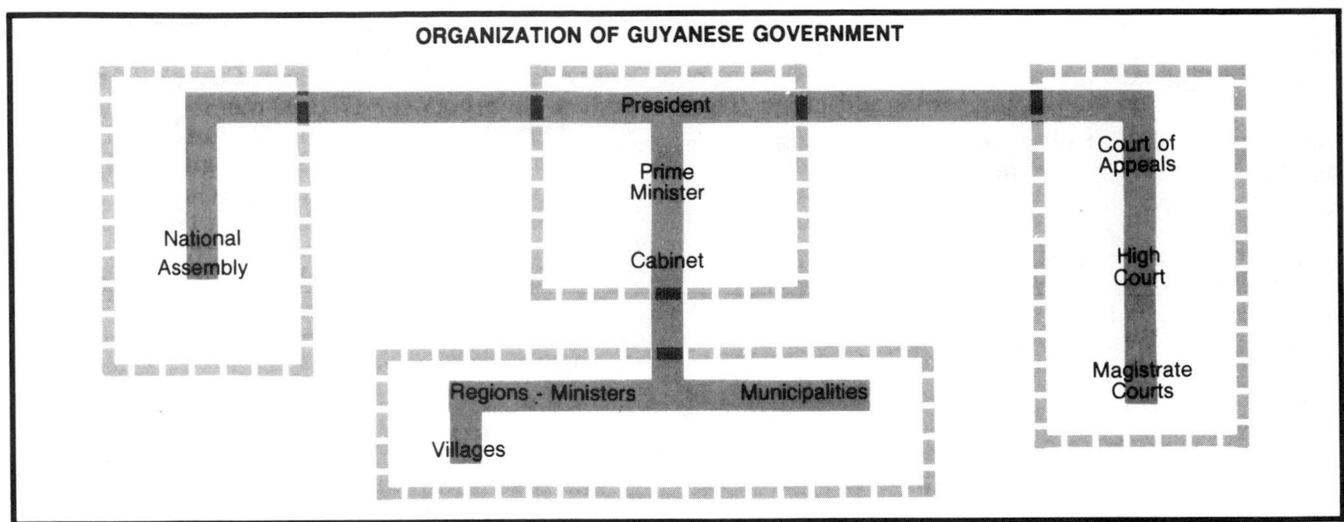

The human rights situation in Guyana deteriorated as President Forbes Burnham manipulated the Constitution and the political system to ensure the continued dominance of his party. Although the People's National Congress was returned in 1985 with a 84% majority, international observers have charged that the elections were conducted fraudulently.

There are allegations that opposition activists are subjected to physical abuse and cruel and inhuman treatment. There has been increasing use of excessive force by the police, and two members of a radical socialist group known as Working People's Alliance were killed in a confrontation with the police. Persons suspected of links with the opposition have been detained for short period without charge under the National Security Act. The opposition also has charged that the government has failed to respect the independence of the judiciary and the integrity of the judicial process in cases relating to political crimes. The Security Act allows the police to search for and seize illegal weapons, ammunitions and explosives without a warrant; sometimes these raids have led to the seizure of "subversive" literature.

The late 1970s witnessed a significant erosion in the constitutionally guaranteed freedoms of speech and press. The daily press is owned by the government or the PNC. The country's only national radio network was purchased in 1979 by the government. The only nongovernment and non-PNC organs, the *Mirror*, owned by the opposition pro-Moscow People's Progressive Party, and the *Catholic Standard*, appear in reduced format because of the government's refusal to allow them access to newsprint. In 1980 the government announced that local radio stations would no longer carry the BBC World News Service, and the state-owned press also canceled its contract with the Caribbean News Agency. However, outside sources of information remain freely available.

Wiretaps, mail interception and physical surveillance are used to monitor and intimidate political opponents of the government. Public-sector employees, who constitute nearly 64% of the work force, are frequently required to attend certain PNC functions and allegedly are coerced into working at Hope Estate, a government-owned coconut plantation, to keep their jobs. The government's emphasis on agriculture in the schools has led to small schoolchildren doing physical labor in school agricultural plots.

The government has used the religious sect known as the House of Israel (founded by an American fugitive from justice) to harass the Catholic Church. The opposition has accused the government of employing "hit men" from the sect to murder those in official disfavor and to break strikes and opposition meetings.

The government record on academic freedom is mixed. Several opposition Working People's Alliance leaders teach at the University of Guyana, and opposition parties have organized student groups there. However, some teachers critical of the government's educational policies have been summarily fired without explanation.

The Guyana Human Rights Association was founded in 1980. The government has not interfered with the activities of this organization.

CIVIL SERVICE

Guyana inherited a politically neutral civil service manned by a corps of trained civil servants at the time of independence. Although the power and influence of the higher cadres of civil servants were diluted under Burnham, their integrity and efficiency did not suffer greatly in the process. Recruitment is controlled by the Public Service Commission, a constitutional body set up in 1966. Racial balance in the civil service is enforced by the ombudsman.

LOCAL GOVERNMENT

For purpose of local government, Guyana is divided into 10 administrative regions, each administered by a chairman and council.

There are five municipalities—Georgetown, New Amsterdam, Linden, Rose Hall and Corriverton—each

ADMINISTRATIVE REGIONS

Barima-Waini
Cuyuni-Mazaruni
Demerara-Mahaica
East Berbice-Corentyne
Essequibo Islands-West Demerara
Mahaica-Berbice
Pomeroon-Supenaam
Potaro-Siparuni
Upper Demerara-Berbice
Upper Takutu-Upper Essequibo

administered by a mayor and a town council. The strength of the council varies according to the population, but their functions are more or less similar. Villages are of three types: those with elected village councils; those with no local government; and plantation and industrial communities on private estates. Village local councils are subject to the authority of the Local Government Board. However, villages have not proved to be viable administrative units, and in many cases they are too small to provide efficient government.

FOREIGN POLICY

Because Guyana was a British colony for over 150 years, its foreign policy is oriented away from Latin America and toward Great Britain, Europe, India and Africa. Border disputes with Suriname and Venezuela have further complicated Guyana's relations with its immediate neighbors and made it unsure of its standing in the South American community. In 1977 eight Guyanese troops died in a border clash with Brazilian forces in the Roraima area. The principal goal and the most active facet of Guyanese foreign policy is closer economic association with Commonwealth Caribbean countries. The second priority in foreign policy is the fostering of a special relationship with Great Britain; all major political parties are committed to the maintenance of close links with the British crown as head of the Commonwealth. Guyana also maintains close relations with Canada and with India.

Guyana condemned the United States-led invasion of Grenada in October 1983, a move that, although popular in Guyana, led to a rapid deterioration in relations with the United States. These relations had worsened after the U.S. government had vetoed anticipated loans to Guyana in September. Guyana's decision to dispense with seeking IMF financial support further compounded the country's increasing isolation among Western nations. In response, Guyana sought to improve relations with socialist countries such as Cuba, Libya, North Korea and Yugoslavia to compensate for the decline in Western aid. In 1983 President Burnham made official visits to Bulgaria and the People's Republic of China to negotiate aid agreements.

Following Hoyte's assumption of the presidency, he sought to improve relations with the United States and other Western nations and to develop relations within CARICOM.

In the broader international field, Guyana identifies itself with the nonaligned group at the United Nations. In recent years it has established diplomatic relations with the Soviet Union, China and Cuba and sought to strengthen ties with nations of sub-Saharan Africa.

Guyana and the United States are parties to 20 treaties and agreements covering agricultural commodities, aviation, consuls, defense, economic and technical cooperation, extradition, investment guarantees, mutual security, the Peace Corps, postal matters, property, telecommunications, trademarks and visas.

Guyana joined the United Nations in 1966. It is a member of 14 U.N. organizations and a number of regional organizations, including CARICOM and SELA. It has observer status at the OAS.

PARLIAMENT

The unicameral National Assembly consists of 53 members elected for five-year terms under a system of proportional representation. The National Assembly may make laws "for the peace, order and good government" of Guyana. It also may amend the Constitution subject to certain constitutional provisions. Any member may introduce a bill.

Suffrage is universal over age 18. Members of the National Assembly are elected by a system of proportional representation, with each voter casting his vote in favor of a list rather than a candidate. The seats are allocated among the lists in proportion to the popular vote, but there is no minimum percentage that a party must receive to ensure representation. Elections are conducted by the Elections Commission.

Following the 1985 elections the party position in the Assembly was as follows: People's National Congress, 42; People's Progressive Party, 8; United Force 2; and Working People's Alliance, 1.

POLITICAL PARTIES

Since Independence Guyana has been dominated by the People's National Congress (PNC), founded by Prime Minister Forbes Burnham in 1955 after breaking away from Cheddi Jagan's People's Progressive Party. The PNC is the main voice for the African community. Burnham's moderate racial policies have been able to break the solid East Indian voting bloc and to turn some East Indians away from the more radical Jagan policies. Initially the PNC advocated a policy of middle-of-the-road capitalism but has increasingly moved to the left. In the Declaration of Sophia, published on the 100th anniversary of his prime ministership, in 1974, Burnham referred to the PNC as a socialist party committed to government control over all sectors of the economy and also the nationalization of foreign business interests. With this declaration the PNC moved closer to the main opposition party, the People's Progressive Party, on most domestic issues, but substantial differences remained on foreign issues. The PNC draws much of its support from overseas Guyanese, who were enfranchised in 1968.

The People's Progressive Party (PPP), founded by East Indian dentist Cheddi Jagan and his American wife, Janet, has come to represent almost exclusively the East Indian constituency, but its ideology is orthodox communism, with state ownership of industry as the principal plank. Over the years Jagan has become more open in his espousal of Marxist-Leninist principles, and in 1969 he proclaimed the PPP to be a Communist party and expressed his admiration for Che Guevara's tactics of violent insurrection. The PPP's major effort is toward maintaining a solid East Indian voting bloc through appeals to the ethnic vote epitomized by the slogan *Apanjaht* (Vote for Your Own Kind). More recently the PPP has been plagued by internal squabbles and serious challenges to Jagan's leadership. Its militant pro-Peking youth wing, the Progressive Youth Organization, led by Moses Bhagwan, has openly broken with the party leadership on crucial issues.

Of the smaller parties, the most important is the United Force (UF), founded by Peter D'Aguliar, a wealthy Portuguese businessman. The UF represents conservative business and other interests and draws its support from white, Amerindian and other minority groups who are opposed to communism, socialism and racialism. From 1964 through 1968 the UF was a member of the government coalition, and D'Aguilar served as finance minister from 1964 to 1967. The UF withdrew from the government coalition in 1968 to protest the enfranchisement of overseas voters. It won two seats in the 1985 elections to the National Assembly. The Working People's Alliance, an alliance of left-wing groups, has emerged as the most vocal of the opposition groups, appealing to both African and East Indian constituencies. It won one seat in the 1985 elections to the National Assembly.

Other parties include the Democratic Labour Movement and the People's Democratic Movement, both centrist parties, the National Democratic Front, the Berbice Progressive Party and the Liberator Party.

Following the 1985 elections, five political parties, the People's Progressive Party, the Working People's Alliance, the Democratic Labour Movement, the People's Democratic Movement and the National Democratic Front, organized the Patriotic Coalition for Democracy to end alleged electoral malpractices.

ECONOMY

Guyana is a lower-middle-income country and also is one of the 45 countries considered by the United Nations to be most seriously affected by the adverse economic conditions in the 1980s. Until 1970 Guyana had a totally free-market economy with a dominant private sector. In that year the country was proclaimed a cooperative republic, and the government embarked on a policy of nationalization of the means of production and distribution and of transforming the economy into a centrally planned one.

Guyana's economy is highly dependent on foreign trade, with exports and imports each averaging 60% of the GNP. Two commodities, sugar and bauxite, account for 80% of exports and set the pace for economic activity in general. In recent years the economy has been hard hit by price increases for oil and other imports, as well as the low world price for sugar. The government, which had pursued ambitious social and public-investment programs in its drive to create a socialist state, initiated an austerity program to adjust the budget deficit and the balance of payments. Nationalization of foreign firms had discouraged private investment and magnified the foreign debt burden. The state corporations, which now dominate the economy, had not generated sufficient cash flow to finance capital investment and had increased their foreign debt exposure. The government has scored some impressive successes, including a reduction in commercial arrears and a buildup of international reserves. Nevertheless, reviving the economy has only begun, and success will depend on finding ways to increase production while maintaining a policy of financial viability.

Guyana faces a bleak period of economic adjustment and austerity, which will include tight foreign exchange restraints. Declining production, obsolete plant and equipment, emigration of skilled personnel, deteriorating social services and the government's tight control of the economy along with its self-proclaimed socialist policies all have contributed to the current economic malaise. According to estimates by the World Bank, Guyana's GNP declined at an average annual rate of 6% between 1980 and 1989. The country's GDP decreased by an average annual rate of 2.0% between 1985 and 1988. Lower world market prices for Guyana's principal exports, relatively higher prices for essential imported goods such as petroleum, adverse weather conditions affecting rice and sugar production, and ineffective management have resulted in a continuing decline of Guyana's foreign-exchange earnings and a reduction of the standard of living for most Guyanese. Guyana's dwindling foreign-exchange earnings will de-

PRINCIPAL ECONOMIC INDICATORS

Gross National Product (U.S. $ millions): 248 (1989)
GNP per capita (U.S. $): 310 (1989)
GNP averge annual growth rate (%, 1980–89): −6.0
GNP per capita average annual growth rate (%, 1987–89): −2.5

BALANCE OF PAYMENTS, 1985
(U.S. $ million)

Current account balance: −96.6
Merchandise exports: 214.0
Merchandise imports: −209.1
Trade balance: 4.9
Other goods, services & income +: 48.0
Other goods, services & income −: −144.3
Other goods, services & income net: −96.3
Private unrequited transfers: −2.0
Official unrequited transfers: −3.2
Capital other than reserves: −38
Net errors & omissions: −4.3
Counterpart items: −10.9
Total change in reserves: 6.4

GROSS DOMESTIC PRODUCT

GDP nominal (G. $ billions): 3.600 (1988)
GDP per capita (U.S. $): 420 (1988)
Average annual growth rate of GDP % (1985–88): −2.0
GDP by type of expenditure (%) 1987
- Consumption
  - Private: 55
  - Government: 31
- Gross domestic investment: 36
- Foreign trade
  - Exports: 91
  - Imports: −114

Cost components of GDP (%) 1987
- Net indirect taxes: 15
- Consumption of fixed capital: 4
- Compensation of employees: } 81
- Net operating surplus: }

Sectoral origin of GDP (%) 1988
- Primary
  - Agriculture: 26
  - Mining: 9
- Secondary
  - Manufacturing and public utilities: 8
  - Construction: 6
- Tertiary
  - Transportation & communications: 6
  - Trade: 7
  - Finance: 6
  - Other services: 3
  - Government, public utilities: 15

CENTRAL GOVERNMENT EXPENDITURES, 1981

% of total expenditures
- Defense: 6
- Education: 10.2
- Health: 5.7
- Housing, Social Security, Welfare: 3.2
- Total expenditures as % of GDP: 65.7
- Overall surplus or deficit as % of GDP: −28.4

CENTRAL GOVERNMENT REVENUES, 1985

% of total current revenues
- Taxes on income, profit & capital gain: 33.1
- Social Security contributions: 12.1
- Domestic taxes on goods & services: 30.3
- Taxes on international trade & transactions: 9.0
- Other taxes: .7 (1981)
- Current nontax revenue: 13.8 (1981)
- Total current revenue as % of GDP: 47.3

General government consumption as % of GDP: 31 (1987)

FOREIGN AID, 1989

Total foreign aid (U.S. $ millions): 166.7
- Bilateral: 110.1
- Multilateral: 56.6

crease the country's capacity to import necessary raw materials, equipment, spare parts, fertilizers and insecticides, thereby further reducing production. In addition, business credit facilities have been closed off to local businessmen as commercial and official debts remain unserviced.

The government is taking various actions to cope with the severe economic crisis. It has instituted a system of foreign exchange allocations whereby certain private and public corporations can retain a portion of their hard-currency earnings to purchase raw materials and equipment. During 1984 the government devalued the Guyana dollar twice and announced that in the future it would use the exchange rate more flexibly as an instrument of economic policy. Negotiations to reach an agreement with the International Monetary Fund on a standby facility have occurred intermittently without success.

PUBLIC FINANCE

The Guyanese fiscal year is the calendar year. The public budget is divided into current and capital budgets, with the former reflecting consumption expenditures, transfer payments, subsidies and interest payments, and the latter reflecting investment expenditures, scholarships and contributions to international organizations.

The official economic priorities are the modernization of the agricultural sector and the diversification of the economy. The chief aims of development plans were to improve living standards; reduce the nation's dependence on sugar, bauxite and rice; and reduce disparities in national income.

CURRENCY & BANKING

The Guyanese unit of currency is the Guyana dollar, divided into 100 cents. Coins are issued in denominations of 1, 5, 10, 25 and 50 cents; notes are issued in denominations of 1, 5, 10 and 20 dollars.

The Guyana dollar was introduced in 1965, replacing the West Indian dollar at par. When the British currency was floated in 1972, the Guyana dollar floated along with it until 1975, when a new dollar rate at U.S. $1 = G. $2.55/G. $1 = $0.39215 was established. The June 1991 exchange rate was $1 = G. $119.5.

The central bank and the bank of issue is the Bank of Guyana, with assets of G. $3.771 billion. The Bank of Guyana is the fiscal agent of the government and the official depository of all public funds. Other specialized credit and development finance institutions are the Guyana Agricultural Cooperative Development Bank, the Guyana Cooperative Mortgage Finance Bank and the Guyana National Cooperative Bank.

During 1984 the government devalued the Guyana dollar twice and announced that in the future it would use the exchange rate more flexibly as an instrument of economic policy.

AGRICULTURE

The country is divided into three agricultural zones: the coastal strip, the forests and the savanna. Agriculture is at present limited to the coastal plain between the Essequibo and the Corentyne rivers, but even here most of the land lies in part below the high-tide mark of the sea and rivers. Agricultural expansion therefore requires heavy expenditures on dikes and dams.

Existing freehold properties are those granted by the British crown prior to 1931. No grants of absolute

FINANCIAL INDICATORS, 1989

Total reserves minus gold: 3 (1988)
  SDR's (millions)L 0.0
  Reserve position in IMF (SDR's millions): 0.0
Ratio of external debt to total reserves: 224 (1988)
Central bank 1989
  Assets %
    Foreign assets: 5.7
    Claims on government: 94.3
    Claims on banks: 0.0
    Claims on private sector: 0.0
  Liabilities %
    Reserve money: 31.4
    Government deposits: 0.0
    Foreign liabilites: 219.4
    Capital accounts: 11.0
Money supply 1988
Stock (G. $ billions): 2.095
M[1] per capita: 2,780
Private banks 1989
  Assets %
    Loans to government: 33.8
    Loans to private sector: 39.7
    Reserves: 18.8
    Foreign assets: 7.7
  Liabilities: %
    deposits (G. $ billions): 9.924
    of which %
      Demand deposits: 14.2
      Savings deposits: 51.5
      Government deposits: 0.0
      Foreign liabilities: 1.9
External debt 1988
  Debt service (long-term)
    total (U.S. $ millions): 19
    Repayment
      Principal (%): 42.1
      Interest (%): 57.9
  Debt service ratio (%): 4.0

GROWTH PROFILE
(Annual Growth Rates, %)

Projected crude birth rate (/1,000) (1990–95): 21.6
Projected crude death rate (/1,000) (1990–95): 5.2
Urban population (1985–90): 3.19
Labor force (1985–2000): −2.4

property rights have been made since, only leases for 21 to 25 years. Leasehold tenure is secure for all good cultivators, but the right of occupancy does not pass automatically to heirs and descendants. Traditional smallholdings and modern plantations coexist in the agricultural sector, but with differing scales of efficiency.

Mechanization and the use of fertilizers are limited to the plantations.

Guyana has a two-crop economy but the sugar plantations also produce bananas, and the rice farmers also produce coconuts, coffee, cocoa and citrus fruits. Sugar production is dominated by the Booker Sugar Estates, nationalized in 1976. In areas with good irrigation and drainage, two rice crops are common.

Livestock has been decreasing in numbers because of a shortage of pasture and a reduced demand for draft animals.

AGRICULTURAL INDICATORS

Agriculture's share of GDP (%): 26 (latest)
Index of Agricultural Production (1979–81 = 100): 91 (1986)
Index of Food Production (1979–81 = 100): 91 (1986)
Number of tractors: 3,560 (1986)
Number of harvester-threshers: 418 (1986)
Total fertilizer consumption (000 metric tons): 12.3 (1985–86)
Farms as % of total land area: 26.2 (1964)
Land use (%) (1964)
  Meadows & pastures: 91.6
Yields (kg./ha.) 1989
  Grains: 2,012
  Roots & tubers: 7,045
  Legumes: 600
  Fruits (000 metric tons): 47
  Vegetables (000 metric tons): 12
  Milk (kg./animal): 828
Livestock (000) 1989
  Cattle: 210
  Horses: 2 (1986)
  Sheep: 120
  Pigs: 185
Forestry 1988
  Production of roundwood (000 cu. m.): 228
    of which industrial roundwood (%): 91.7
  Value of exports (U.S. $ millions): 8.000
Fishing, 1988
  Total catch (000 metric tons): 41.7
    of which marine (%): 98.1
  Value of exports (U.S. $ millions): 15.260

Forests cover much of the land area, but only 20% of the land area is accessible to commercial exploitation. Most of the forest stands consist of hardwoods, especially greenheart, which is exported.

Coastal and inland waters are rich in a wide variety of fish, especially shrimp, which is exported.

Agricultural credit is provided by the Guyana Agricultural Cooperative Development Bank.

MANUFACTURING

In 1980 manufacturing employed 11.7% of the work force. With the nationalization of the Booker Sugar Estates in 1976, the government became the largest industrial employer in the country. The processing of raw sugar is Guyana's largest industry. Booker also produces rum and gin; operates a coastal fleet; manufactures drugs and stockfeeds; processes shrimp; markets petroleum, drugs, agricultural vehicles, motor vehicles, hardware and electrical goods; and is engaged in printing and boxmaking.

The secondary manufacturing sector is limited to the processing of food and beverages and is small in terms of employment and value added.

With the advent of the cooperative republic and the nationalization (with compensation) of foreign enterprises, foreign-investment capital flow into Guyana has dried up. The government continues to welcome foreign private investment but insists on Guyanese majority control. In an effort to stimulate domestic private investment, the government announced in 1979 the Private Investment Code, to consolidate various existing and proposed investment incentive laws into one piece of legislation.

MINING

Mining is the second-largest sector of the economy. Mineral activity centers around the production of bauxite, of which Guyana is the fifth-largest producer in the world. Bauxite mining is under complete state control, the Demerara Bauxite Company, owned by Aluminum Company of Canada, having been nationalized in 1971 and the Reynolds Guyana Mines, owned by the U.S. Reynolds Metals, having been nationalized in 1975. Some gold, diamonds and asbestos also are mined. In recent years the bauxite industry has emphasized production of calcined bauxite (used to manufacture refractory bricks for the steel industry), in which Guyana has a virtual monopoly. The industry suffered significantly from the fall in world bauxite prices during the early 1980s, a lack of investment and labor disturbances during the last years of the decade. It has been estimated that less than 25% of the gold and diamonds that are mined in Guyana are declared and sold to the government, the sole legal buyer. In 1984 an IMF report claimed that the country was losing $1.7 million per week through the smuggling of gold and diamonds. Seventeen mines in the Essequibo region were closed in an attempt to halt the flow of minerals out of the country.

ENERGY

Guyana produces no form of mineral energy. Energy requirements are met by importing petroleum. Frequent interruptions in power, as a result of aging equipment and lack of capacity, have hindered economic growth. There is considerable potential for hydroelectric power. The 750-mw. hydroelectric project on the Upper Mazaruni River, completed in 1985, was the first of several projects designed to exploit this resource.

ENERGY INDICATORS

Electricity, 1988
- Installed capacity (000 kw.): 168
- Production (million kw.-hr.): 385
  - % fossil fuel: 98.7
  - % hydro: 1.3
  - % nuclear: 0.0
- Consumption per capita (kw.-hr.): 382

LABOR

One of the most interesting characteristics of the Guyanese labor force is the division of occupations along ethnic lines. The Portuguese and the Chinese are predominantly in business, while the East Indians are peasants or agricultural laborers. The Afro-Guyanese, on the other hand, are the dominant working class in the towns and cities as well as in industries and mining. The labor unions also are split along ethnic lines.

Despite a high literacy rate, the bulk of the labor force is unskilled, and skills are in short supply. Competition for skilled workers is acute. Government efforts are being directed toward expansion of technical training programs both in an academic setting and on the job.

LABOR INDICATORS, 1987

Total economically active population (000): 270
- % working-age population (15–64): 60.4
- % female: 29.9

Activity rate (%)
- Total: 35.7
- Male: 50.9
- Female: 21.0

Employment status (%) 1980
- Employers & self-employed: 14.3
- Employees: 63.8
- Unpaid family workers: 1.9
- Other: 20.0

Sectoral employment (%) 1980
- Agriculture, forestry, fishing: 20.4
- Construction: 2.8
- Manufacturing, mining, quarrying, public utilities: 16.8
- Trade, hotels, restaurants: 6.2
- Transport, communications: 3.8
- Finance, real estate: 1.2
- Services: 11.9

Unemployment (000): 9 (1987)
Labor under 20 years (%): 14.8 (1987)
Earnings in manufacturing (G. $) (wk): 94.63 (1983)
Hours of work, 1979
- Manufacturing (/wk.): 48.4

Although the government can prescribe wages for any occupation or industry by the Wages Council Ordinance of 1956, they are determined more often by collective bargaining. Minimum wages are set by legislation for only certain categories of workers who are not effectively organized. Workers in the bauxite industry receive the highest wages. Fringe benefits include annual bonuses, and (for workers on the sugar estates and in bauxite mines and plants) free housing, schools, recreational facilities, hospitalization and medical services, subsidized electricity and interest-free home-building loans. Under the National Social Security Scheme introduced in 1968, workers receive old-age pensions of 20% to 60% of their average registered earnings and injury payments and sickness benefits at 60% of normal pay.

Working conditions and work hours are governed by the Labor Ordinance of 1942. The average workweek consists of 48.8 hours, but 44-hour workweeks are common for all administrative positions. All blue-collar workers receive time and a half for overtime, but night work is prohibited for most establishments, for women and for children under 18. Legislation also covers paid holidays, annual vacations, annual pay increases and health and safety regulations. The labor laws are enforced through a corps of inspectors with powers of prosecution.

Official policy is to encourage settlement of industrial disputes by collective bargaining and to intervene through conciliators only if direct negotiations fail. Nearly all major economic sectors are governed by collective agreements between management and labor, which usually are valid for two years. Industrial relations also are moderated by the paternalistic attitudes of employers, the ethnic factor and the oversupply of labor. However, a great many strikes occur each year, including stormy wildcat strikes and unofficial work stoppages. Although government has the right to declare any strike illegal, it has not done so for many years.

Nearly 34% of the labor force is unionized, in 22 trade unions. The largest are the Trades Union Congress (TUC), the Manpower Citizen's Association and the Guyana Labor Union. The Trades Union Congress, as the umbrella labor organization, has the sole responsibility for collective bargaining. Until 1984, the TUC was progovernment, but in that year independent and opposition labor leaders defeated the progovernment slate of candidates and elected their own men to key positions. The 1984 Labor Amendment Act makes collective agreements binding in law. The act also excludes wages from the definition of fundamental property rights protected by the Constitution, thus taking wages out of judicial purview.

FOREIGN COMMERCE

Guyana's primary exports are bauxite, sugar, rice, shrimp, gold, molasses, timber and rum, which it sends primarily to the United Kingdom, United States and Canada. Its primary imports are fuels, capital goods and food, most of which it receives from Trinidad and Tobago, the United States, Barbados, Venezuela and the United Kingdom.

Guyana is a member of CARICOM and the International Bauxite Association.

State corporations are the major importers and exporters in Guyana. Private commission agents have had increasing difficulty obtaining import licenses. The government is studying the feasibility of consolidating all imports under a centralized importing agency.

Under the umbrella of the Guyana State Corporation (GUYSTAC), a state holding company, public trading entities are divided into two groups. Trading Group 1, which includes Guyana National Trading Corporation, Guyana Gajraj and Guyana Wrefords Ltd., imports consumer goods, hardware, automotive parts, agricultural machinery and fertilizers. Trading Group 2, which includes Guyana Stores Ltd., Guyana Pharmaceutical Corp., Guyana National Shipping Corporation and Guyana Lithographic Ltd., imports consumer goods, hardware, printing supplies and equipment, automotive supplies, marine supplies and chemicals.

FOREIGN TRADE INDICATORS, 1988

Exports (U.S. $ millions): 215
Imports (U.S. $ millions): 216
Balance of trade (U.S. $ millions): −1
Import Price Index (1980 = 100): 91.2 (1986)
Export Price Index (1980 = 100): 63.1 (1986)

Direction of Trade (%), 1985

	Imports	Exports
European Community	20.1	43.4
United States	16.4	23.0
U.S.S.R. & Eastern European economies	1.9	2.6
Japan	3.7	8.9

Composition of Trade (%), 1983

	Imports	Exports
Food and agricultural raw materials	5.6	52.9
Fuels and other energy	43.2	0.2
Mineral ores and concentrates	0.5	36.4
Manufactured goods	50.7	10.5
of which chemicals	9.4	2.7
of which machinery	23.2	3.4

TRANSPORTATION & COMMUNICATIONS

Guyana has no public railway system, the two government-owned lines having been scrapped in the early 1970s.

There are 6,000 km. (3,728 mi.) of inland waterways. River transportation on the Essequibo and Berbice rivers is handled by the government-owned Guyana Transport Services, while service between Georgetown

TRANSPORTATION INDICATORS

Roads (latest)
- length, km. (mi.): 8,890 (5,524)
- Paved (%): 9

Motor vehicles (latest)
- Automobiles: 33,000
- Trucks and buses: 12,500
- Persons per vehicle: 17

Railroads (latest)
- Track, km. (mi.): 88 (55)

Merchant marine
- Vessels: 75 (1989)
- Total deadweight tonnage (000): 11.0 (1989)

Ports (latest)
- Cargo loaded (million metric tons): 1.548
- Cargo unloaded (000 metric tons): 636

Air (latest)
- Passenger-km. (passenger-mi.) (millions): 185 (115)
- Freight, ton-km. (ton-mi.) (millions): 2.6 (1.8)
- Airports with scheduled flights: 1 (1990)

Inland Waterways
- Length, km. (mi.): 6,000 (3,728) (latest)

COMMUNICATION INDICATORS, 1986

Telephones
- Total (000): 30 (1987)
- Persons per telephone: 25 (1987)

Phone traffic (000 calls)
- Combined national: 88,458 (pulses) (1985)
- International: 311 (1987)

Post office
- Number of post offices: 131
- Pieces of mail handled (millions): 32.272

Telex
- Subscriber lines: 142
- Traffic (000 minutes): 365 (calls)

Telecommunications 1990
- 1 satellite station

TOURISM & TRAVEL INDICATORS, 1986

Total tourist receipts (U.S. $ millions): 30 (1988)
Expenditures by nationals abroad (U.S. $ millions): 11 (1983)
Number of hotel beds (000): 1 1987

and Linden (formerly Mackenzie) is provided by a private company.

The principal ports are Georgetown and New Amsterdam, while Springlands, on the Corentyne River, is the main port serving traffic with Suriname.

The length of the highway system is 7,650 km. (4,750 mi.), of which 550 km. (341 mi.) are paved. Most of the unpaved roads are in poor condition, and interior roads are only little better than trails.

The national airline is Guyana Airways Corporation, with six aircraft operating internal services and scheduled services to the Caribbean, Brazil, Suriname and the United States. The principal airport is Timehri, 37 km. (23 mi.) from Georgetown.

DEFENSE

The defense structure is headed by the president as head of state. Command and administration of the defense forces are vested in the Defense Board. Military manpower is provided by voluntary enlistment.

The total strength of the armed forces is 5,850.

Army

Personnel: 5,300

Organization: 3 infantry battalions; 1 guard battalion; 1 artillery battalion; 1 engineer company

Equipment: 8 armored vehicles; 32 mortars; 6 guns

Navy

Personnel: 250

Equipment: 11 patrol craft; 1 landing craft

Air Force

Personnel: 300

Equipment: 6 transports; 5 helicopters

The Guyanese armed forces are maintained more for prestige than for any pressing military or defense needs. The army has no significant military traditions, and its combat-worthiness never has been tested in the field. Its mission seems to be to help preserve law and order.

Guyana has received no military assistance in recent years from the United Kingdom or the United States.

EDUCATION

Education is free, universal and compulsory, in principle, for eight years, between ages six and 14. Schooling lasts for 12 years, divided into six years of primary school, four years of lower secondary school and two years of upper secondary school. Schooling culminates in the College of Preceptors' "O"-level examination. Pupils are permitted to choose their courses at the end of the third year in secondary schools. The curriculum emphasizes Guyanese and Caribbean history, science and commercial subjects.

The government has been accused of politicizing education, which critics cite as a principal cause of declining educational standards. In a December 1984 edition of the *Guyana Chronicle* titled "Moulding Students from an Early Age," the most important objectives of the future President's College were cited as

EDUCATION INDICATORS, 1987

Literacy
- Total (%): 95.9
- Male (%): 97.0
- Female (%): 94.8

First level
- Schools: 425
- Students: 112,501
- Teachers: 3,948
- Student/teacher ratio: 28.5
- Net enrollment ratio: 90 (1981)

Second level
- Schools: 92
- Students: 73,418
- Teachers: 2,700
- Student/teacher ratio: 27.2

Vocational
- Schools: 7
- Students: 4,647 (1980)
- Teachers: 348 (1980)
- Student/teacher ratio: 13.4 (1980)

Third level
- Institutions: 1
- Students: 1,023
- Teachers: 258 (1986)
- Student/teacher ratio: 6.3 (1986)
- Gross enrollment ratio: 2.1 (1984)
- Students (/100,000 pop.): 244
- % of population over 24 with postsecondary education: 1.8

Foreign study
- Foreign students in national universities: 20 (1985)
- Students abroad: 643
  - of whom in
    - United States: 403 (1988)
    - France: 7 (1988)
    - Federal Republic of Germany: 4 (1988)
    - United Kingdom: 86 (1987)

Public expenditures, 1987
- Total G $: 231,664
- % of GNP: 9.6
- % of national budget: 8.1
- % of current expenditure: 76.2

GRADUATES, 1985

Total: 711
Education: 156
Humanities & religion: 29
Fine & applied arts: 0
Law: 0
Social & behavioral sciences: 47
Commerce & business: 44
Mass communication: 7
Home economics: 0
Service trades: 1
Natural sciences: 29
Mathematics & computer science: 10
Medicine: 36
Engineering: 64
Architecture: 1
Industrial programs: 0
Transportation & communications: 0
Agriculture, forestry, fisheries: 129
Other: 158

"productive work habits, the cooperative ethic and an ideological commitment to socialism." Some teachers already selected to work at the school will undergo "special orientation and training" in Cuba.

The academic year runs from September to August. The medium of instruction is English throughout.

Vocational training is provided in 7 schools, of which the Technical Institute in Georgetown is the best known. In 1976 Burnham announced that the government intended to take over all denominational schools.

Public education is administered by the Directorate of Education assisted by the statutory Education Committee.

The University of Guyana, founded in 1963, is the only institution of higher learning in the country.

LEGAL SYSTEM

The legal system is based on English common law with some elements of Roman-Dutch law. The judicial structure of Guyana comprises the Supreme Court of Judicature, consisting of the Court of Appeal and the High Court as the superior courts, and a number of subordinate courts of summary jurisdiction.

The Court of Appeal consists of the chancellor as president, the chief justice, and a varying number of justices of appeal as prescribed by the National Assembly. The High Court consists of the chief justice and nine puisne judges. The lower courts are presided over by magistrates. Criminal cases always are tried by a jury of 12 persons.

The Constitution established the judiciary as an independent branch of government with the right of judicial review. The chancellor and the chief justice are appointed on the advice of the prime minister and after consultation with the leader of the opposition. The other judges and magistrates are appointed by the Judicial Service Commission. The Constitution also provides for security of tenure for all members of the judiciary.

As a former British colony, Guyana maintains a British common law system and legal procedures, and almost all the members of the Guyanese judiciary were trained in the United Kingdom. Guyana has a functioning bail system, and defendants are accorded fair public trials and are represented by counsel. Timely charges usually are presented, and appeals can be made to higher courts. There are no special courts for political security cases, nor any political prisoners. In general, judges of high personal integrity sit on the bench. Despite insinuations by the opposition about the independence of the judiciary, less partisan lawyers regard the judiciary as fairly independent. It is possible to win in court against the government. Opponents of the government complain that some magistrates have been too zealous in enforcing the government's economic policies, particularly those involving banned food imports. They charge that magistrates often hand out harsher sentences to individuals found guilty of these "economic crimes" than to individuals guilty of violent crimes against persons or property. Magistrate Vernon Persaud was dismissed for refusing to sentence persons guilty of possessing contraband wheat flour. (Wheat is not grown in Guyana, and by law it cannot be commercially imported.)

Correctional facilities are administered by the Prisons and Probation Department. The three main prisons are at Mazaruni, Georgetown and New Amsterdam.

LAW ENFORCEMENT

The Guyana Police Service is an armed semimilitary unit administered by a commissioner of police under the Ministry of Home Affairs. In addition to the regular force, there are supernumerary, special and rural constables who perform minor duties. The force has been modernized in the past decade with the construction of a training school and the acquisition of aircraft and boats for patrolling remote areas.

The largest categories of reported crime are murder, larceny and arson, with the sharpest increase in juvenile delinquency. Much of the increase may be attributable to the growing unemployment among youth.

HEALTH

Nationwide disease eradication and health education programs have helped eliminate malaria as a major problem, but filariasis, enteric fever, heminthiasis, venereal diseases and yellow fever remain constant threats.

FOOD & NUTRITION

The staple foods are rice and potatoes. Fish is the major source of protein. East Indian workers eat traditional rice and curry, while the affluent East Indians have adopted Western food customs.

The per capita daily intake of food is 2,483 calories.

HEALTH INDICATORS

Health personnel, 1989
- Physicians: 111
  - persons per: 6,809
- Dentists: 15
- Nurses: 854
- Pharmacists: 29
- Midwives: 172

Hospitals, 1979
- Number: 55
- Number of beds (/10,000): 49 (1985)

Type of hospitals (%) 1979
- Government: 87.3
- Private nonprofit: 3.6
- Private profit: 9.1

Public health expenditures (latest)
- As % of national budget: 7.7
- Per capita (U.S. $): 23.10

Vital statistics
- Crude death rate (/1,000): 6 (1990)
- Life expectancy at birth, 1990
  - Males: 65
  - Females: 70
- Infant mortality rate per 1,000 live births: 40 (1990)
- Child mortality rate under 5 yrs. (/1,000) (1985–90): 37
- Maternal mortality rate (/100,000 live births) (1986–87): 104.0

Population with access to safe water (%): 77 (latest)

MEDIA & CULTURE

The only daily is the government owned *Guyana Chronicle* with a circulation of 60,000. Eleven other weeklies and periodicals are published.

The British tradition of free speech and press persists but has been eroded in recent years. Under ordinary conditions all restraints on the media, excluding films, are voluntary. The constitutional guarantee of freedom of speech may be revoked only after the declaration of a state of public emergency. However, under the Hoyte government the media are largely progovernment, and a true opposition press does not exist.

Constitutionally the government affirms freedom of speech and press, but in fact it controls the media both directly through ownership and indirectly through control of the importation of newsprint. The government presents its view in the government-owned *Guyana Chronicle*, and the PNC's *New Nation*. Opposition viewpoints are freely expressed without prior censorship in the several weekly papers published by opponents of the Hoyte government. However, the government allocates to its papers a disproportionate amount of the scarce newsprint imported into the country and disallows increased importation of paper, even if no foreign exchange is required. It also has used libel suits against opposition newspapers; these suits are drawn out over an extended period to intimidate the papers.

MEDIA INDICATORS

Newspapers
- Number of dailies: 1 (latest)
- Circulation (000): 58 (latest)
- Per 1,000 pop.: 77 (latest)
- Newsprint consumption: (1988)
- Total metric tons: 500
- Per 1,000 pop. (kg.): 497

Book publishing
- Number of titles: 16 (post-1984)

Radio
- Number of transmitters: 5 (1989)
- Number of persons per radio receiver: 2.5 (1989)
- Total program hours: 13,500 (1987)

Television
- Total program hours: 16,950 (1987)

Cinema
- Number of fixed cinemas: 50 (pre-1986)
- Seating capacity (000): 40 (pre-1986)
- Annual attendance (millions): 13.3 (pre-1986)

Films
- Production of long films: 4 (pre-1986)

CULTURAL & ENVIRONMENTAL INDICATORS (latest)

Libraries
- Number: 1
- Volumes (000): 10

Museums
- Annual attendance (000): 97
- Attendance (/1,000 pop.): 130

Nature reserves
- Number of facilities: 1

Guyanese can receive printed materials from abroad, but foreign exchange generally is not available for subscriptions to foreign publications. The *Caribbean Contact*, a monthly regional newspaper which is published in Barbados and which generally is hostile to the Hoyte government, is sold locally without any restrictions.

The government owns the country's only national radio network, the Guyana Broadcasting Corporation, which canceled the BBC World News Service in 1980. It also owns the Guyana Television Corporation. Foreign stations can be heard on shortwave or mediumwave. Some radio interview programs allow public criticism of the government.

The government asserts that state-owned media should serve "developmental" needs. As a result, the government media seldom run items unfavorable to it, and news-gathering efforts are limited by journalistic self-censorship. Objective reporting has occasionally cost journalists jobs within the government-owned media. The Guyana News Agency (GNA) edits items that the government media receive from wire services. However, since the Soviet news agency TASS installed a teletype machine at the headquarters of the *Guyana Chronicle* and GNA, much of what has appeared in the government-owned press has been actual TASS and Cuban Prensa Latina wire service articles. This extends even to articles about U.S. domestic affairs.

Tha national news agency is the Guyana News Agency (GNA). TASS and Presna Latina are represented in Georgetown.

There are four medium-wave and three shortwave stations, and one FM station, operated by the official Guyana Broadcasting Corporation (GBC). The GBC is on the air for 236 hours a week.

There is one small publisher in Greater Georgetown, Guyana National Printers Ltd, which is owned by the government.

The largest library in the country is the Free Public Library in Georgetown.

There are two public museums.

SOCIAL WELFARE

Under the National Social Insurance Scheme, covered workers receive workmen's compensation, maternity and health insurance, death benefits and old-age pensions. Traditionally, East Indians and Africans have conducted their own welfare activities, the former through kinship groups and the latter through mutual benefit associations.

GLOSSARY

apanjaht: literally, vote for your own kind. Ethnic voting appeal or slogan introduced by the PPP.

creolization: process of acquiring Western cultural characteristics.

taki-taki: a pidgin English dialect used by the lower classes.

CHRONOLOGY

1966— Guyana becomes a self-governing dominion within the Commonwealth, with Forbes Burnham as prime minister. . . . Venezuela occupies Anakoka Island and asserts claim to land west of Essequibo River.

1968— Burnham's People's National Congress (PNC) wins electoral victory following the controversial enfranchisement of overseas Guyanese. . . . United Force (UF) leaves coalition, protesting irregularities in the elections.

1969— National Social Insurance Scheme is introduced. . . . Government suppresses Rupununi rebels trying to establish an independent state. . . . Border clashes with Suriname revive old border dispute.

1970— Guyana is proclaimed a cooperative republic; post of governor-general is abolished; Supreme Court justice Arthur Chung is elected president.

1971— Demerara Bauxite Company is nationalized.

1973— Legislation is passed permitting preventive detention without trial and restricting freedom of movement.

1974— By the Declaration of Sophia, the PNC is transformed into a socialist party committed to nationalization of all foreign enterprises and redistribution of land.

1975— Reynolds Guyana Mines are nationalized.

1976— Booker Sugar Estates are nationalized. . . . Government announces plans to nationalize the school system. . . . Guyana permits Cuban planes to refuel on their way to Angola; U.S.-Guyana relations deteriorate.

1977— CIA reports illegal payments to Burnham. . . . Burnham rejects plan of Cheddi Jagan, leader of the opposition People's Progressive Party (PPP), for a national coalition government. . . . Strike by sugar workers becomes stormy and violent as the government uses the police to break it.

1978— Government wins constitutional referendum extending term of the National Assembly. . . . Guyana signs the eight-nation Amazon Pact. . . . Jonestown in Guyana is the scene of a bizarre and grisly suicide-murder of over 900 members of the People's Temple Commune led by a U.S. cultist, Jim Jones.

1979— Burnham postpones national elections because of the dislocations caused by the Jonestown tragedy and industrial strikes. . . . Minister of Education Vincent Teekah is slain.

1980— Guyana adopts presidential form of government as new Constitution is approved; Burnham becomes the first president under the Constitution, and Ptolemy Reid, his longtime aide, is named prime minister.

1985— Burnham dies and is succeeded in office by Hugh Hoyte, who promises to continue Burnham's leftist policies. . . . In national elections Hoyte is elected president and the PNC wins predictably with a massive majority. . . . Hamilton Green is named prime minister.

1988— The IMF begins negotiations for economic assistance to Guyana.

1990— Guyana accepts the IMF conditions and begins receiving assistance; the World Bank and the Caribbean Development Bank also resume lending.

1991— Guyana becomes a member of the Organization of American States (OAS).

BIBLIOGRAPHY

BOOKS

Baber, Colin, and Henry B. Jeffre. *The Cooperative Republic of Guyana: Politics, Economics and Society.* Boulder, Colo., 1986.

Braveboy-Wagner, Jacqueline. *The Venezuela-Guyana Border Dispute: Britain's Colonial Legacy in Latin America.* Boulder, Colo., 1984.

Burnham, Forbes. *A Destiny to Mould.* London, 1970.

Burrowes, Reynold. *The Wild Coast: An Account of Politics in Guyana.* Cambridge, Mass., 1984.

Chambers, Frances. *Guyana.* Santa Barbara, Calif., 1989.

Daly, P. H. *From Revolution to Republic.* Georgetown, Guyana, 1970.

Glasgow, Roy Arthur. *Guyana: Race and Politics Among Africans and East Indians.* The Hague, 1970.

Hintzen, Percy C. *The Costs of Regime Survival: Racial Mobilization, Elite Domination, and Control of the State in Guyana and Trinidad.* New York, 1989.

Hope, Kempe R. *Development Policy in Guyana: Planning, Financing and Administration.* Boulder, Colo., 1984.

Ince, Basil A. *Guyana's Struggle for Independence.* Cambridge, Mass., 1974.

Irving, Brian. *Guyana: A Composite Monograph.* Culver City, Calif., 1972.

Jagan, Cheddi. *The West on Trial.* East Berlin, 1972.

Jeffrey, Henry B. *Guyana: Politics, Economics, and Society: Beyond the Burnham Era.* Boulder, Colo., 1986.

Manley, Robert. *Guyana Emergent: The Post-Independence Struggle for Nondependent Development.* Boston, 1979.

Pierce, Paulette. *Noncapitalist Development: The Struggle to Nationalize the Guyanese Sugar Industry.* Totowa, N.J., 1984.

Reviere, Peter. *Individual and Society in Guyana: A Comparative Study of Amerindian Social Organization.* New York, 1984.

Sanders, Ron. *Broadcasting in Guyana.* London, 1978.

Sukdeo, Iris D. *The Emergence of a Multiracial Society: The Sociology of Multiracism with Reference to Guyana.* Pompano Beach, Fla., 1981.

UNESCO. *Cultural Policy in Guyana.* Paris, 1980.

HAITI

BASIC FACT SHEET

OFFICIAL NAME: Republic of Haiti (République d'Haiti)

ABBREVIATION: HT

CAPITAL: Port-au-Prince

HEAD OF STATE & HEAD OF GOVERNMENT: Interim President Joseph Nerette (from 1991)

NATURE OF GOVERNMENT: Republic

POPULATION: 6,142,141 (1990)

AREA: 27,750 sq. km. (10,714 sq. mi.)

ETHNIC MAJORITY: Black

LANGUAGE: French (official), Creole

RELIGION: Roman Catholicism (official)

UNIT OF CURRENCY: Gourde

NATIONAL FLAG: Two horizontal stripes, blue at the top and red at the bottom, with the Haitian coat of arms in a white rectangular center panel.

NATIONAL EMBLEM: Six blue and red national flags and six rifles with fixed bayonets guarding a tall, indigenous palm tree, above which flies a blue and red national flag. In the front are two gold cannons on red caissons with gold cannon balls. At the base of the palm is a gold drum, and nearby are golden fouled anchors. Over the horizon are two hauled-down warships with pennants flying and in the foreground is a white scroll with the national motto: *L'Union Fait la Force* (Union Makes Strength).

NATIONAL ANTHEM: "Song of Dessalines"

NATIONAL HOLIDAYS: January 1 (Independence Day, National Day); January 2 (Heroes of Independence Day); April 14 (Pan American Day); May 1 (Labor and Agriculture Day); May 18 (Flag and University Day); May 22 (National Sovereignty Day); June 22 (President's Day); October 22 (United Nations Day); November 18 (Battle of Vertières and Armed Forces Day); December 5 (Discovery of Haiti Day); also all major Catholic festivals

NATIONAL CALENDAR: Gregorian

PHYSICAL QUALITY OF LIFE INDEX: 48

DATE OF INDEPENDENCE: January 1, 1804

DATE OF CONSTITUTION: March 1987

WEIGHTS & MEASURES: Metric

GEOGRAPHICAL FEATURES

Haiti occupies the western third of the Island of Hispaniola, the second-largest island in the Caribbean. Haiti's total land area of 27,750 sq. km. (10,714 sq. mi.) includes the islands of Gonave, Tortuga (Île de la Tortue), Vache, Les Cayemites and Navassa. The mainland extends 485 km. (301 mi.) east-northeast to west-southwest and 386 km. (240 mi.) south-southeast to north-northwest. The total length of the coastline is 1,040 km. (646 mi.).

Haiti has only one land neighbor, the Dominican Republic, with which it shares a border of 360 km. (224 mi.). The frontier was agreed on in a treaty signed in 1929, and certain disputed sections were settled by a protocol in 1936. Because of the pressures of illegal emigration across the border, Haiti has closed the border and banned the construction of homes within 1 km. (0.62 mi.) of the border. There are no current border disputes.

The capital is Port-au-Prince, with a 1983 population of 719,000. Other major urban centers are Cap-Haïtien (64,406), Les Cayes (34,090), Gonaïves (34,209) and Pétionville (35,333).

Covering three-fourths of the land area are five mountain ranges that meet one another to form a continuous highland. The most extensive of the ranges is the Massif du Nord, which forms part of the Caribbean Antillean system that extends from Puerto Rico and the Virgin Islands westward to Cuba. To the southwest is the Montagnes Noires, separated by the Artibonite River from another range, the Chaîne de Mateaux, which extends into the Dominican Republic as the Sierra de Neiba. To the far south is a system that extends the full length of the peninsula. To the west it is known as Massif de la Hotte and to the east as Massif de la Selle. The latter range contains the country's highest peak, Morne de la Selle (2,680 m.; 8,793 ft.).

Lowlands cover about one-quarter of the country's territory. The largest of the country's four major flatlands is the central plateau, which extends eastward from the Montagnes Noires. The northern plain is between the Atlantic Ocean and the Massif du Nord. The Artibonite Plain is to the north of the Chaîne de Mateaux. The Cul-de-Sac between the Chaîne de Mateaux and the Massif de la Selle is the fourth. There are 16 smaller valleys and plains.

Haiti has more than 100 small rivers, all flowing into the Gulf of Gonaïves and the Caribbean Sea. The largest are the Artibonite; Trois Rivières; Grande Anse; the Massacre River, also known as Río Djabon; and

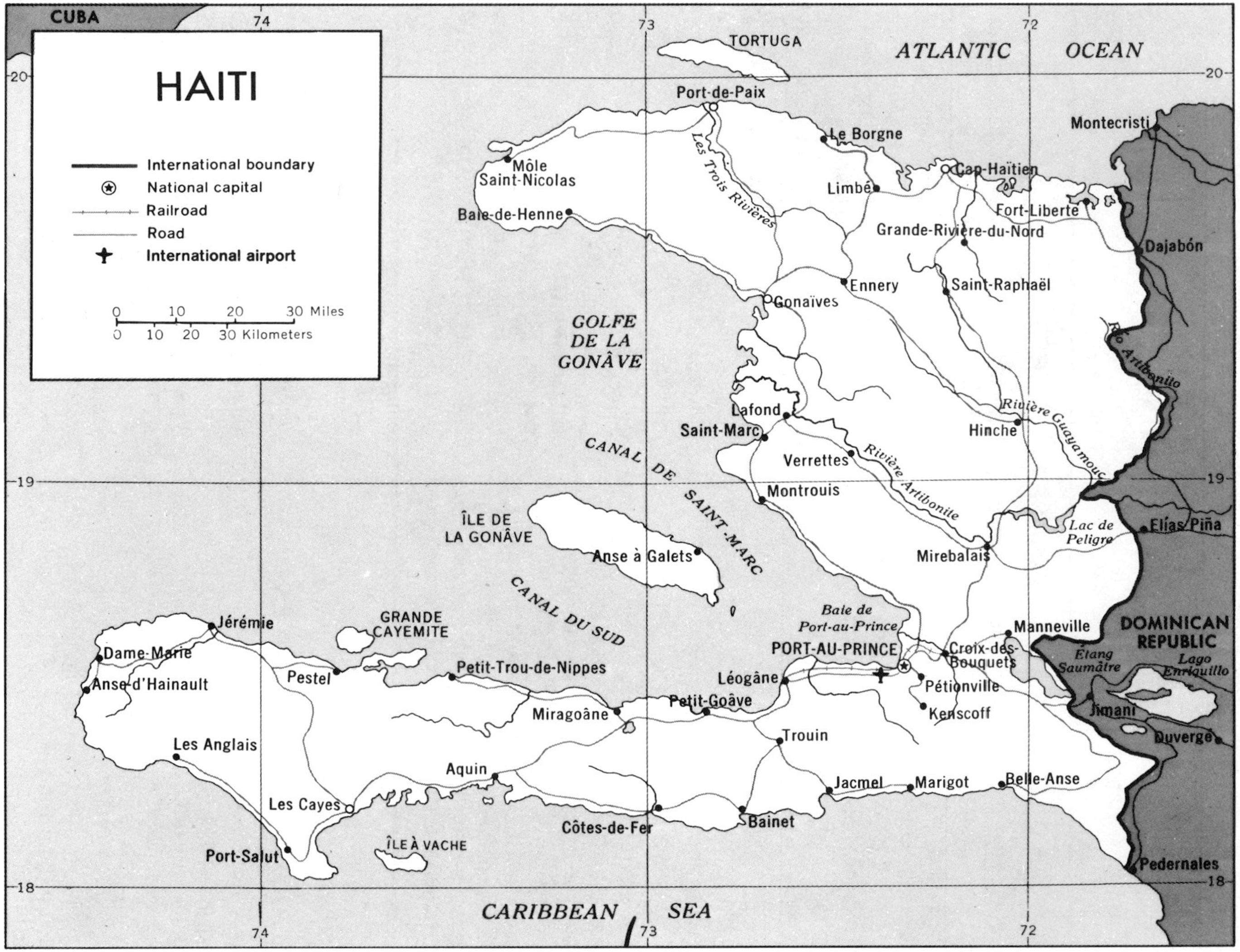

HAITI

International boundary
National capital
Railroad
Road
International airport

0 10 20 30 Miles
0 10 20 30 Kilometers

CUBA
ATLANTIC OCEAN
TORTUGA
Port-de-Paix
Le Borgne
Môle Saint-Nicolas
Les Trois Rivières
Cap-Haïtien
Limbé
Fort-Liberté
Montecristi
Baie-de-Henne
Grande-Rivière-du-Nord
Dajabón
Ennery
Saint-Raphaël
Gonaïves
GOLFE DE LA GONÂVE
Río Artibonito
Lafond
Saint-Marc
Rivière Guayamouc
Hinche
Verrettes
Rivière Artibonite
CANAL DE SAINT-MARC
Montrouis
ÎLE DE LA GONÂVE
Anse à Galets
Lac de Peligre
Elías Piña
Mirebalais
CANAL DU SUD
Baie de Port-au-Prince
Manneville
DOMINICAN REPUBLIC
Jérémie
GRANDE CAYEMITE
PORT-AU-PRINCE
Croix-des-Bouquets
Étang Saumâtre
Lago Enriquillo
Dame-Marie
Pestel
Petit-Trou-de-Nippes
Léogâne
Pétionville
Anse-d'Hainault
Jimaní
Miragoâne
Petit-Goâve
Kenscoff
Duvergé
Trouin
Les Anglais
Aquin
Jacmel
Marigot
Belle-Anse
Les Cayes
Côtes-de-Fer
Bainet
ÎLE À VACHE
Port-Salut
Pedernales
CARIBBEAN SEA
20 19 18
74 73 72

the Pedernales River. None of the rivers is navigable, but they are used for irrigation.

There are large lakes in the southern half of the island, the Étang Saumatre and the Étang de Miragoâne, the former salty and the latter fresh.

CLIMATE & WEATHER

Although the climate is tropical, the country is generally semiarid because the mountains in the middle of the island cut off the moist trade winds. The temperatures in the main population centers tend to be warm, ranging from 20°C to 34°C (68°F to 94°F). The differential between summer and winter temperatures is only 4.4°C to 5.6°C (8°F to 10°F). The highest temperatures are recorded from June through September and the lowest from February through April.

Most of the country lies in a rain shadow, and the heaviest rainfall received in the North is no more than 2,540 mm. (100 in.). Port-au-Prince has two rainy seasons, April through June and August through November, during which it receives 1,370 mm. (54 in.).

Haiti lies in the Caribbean hurricane belt, but the main paths of maximum hurricane frequency pass to the north and to the south of the island. Thunderstorms are common and sometimes destructive.

POPULATION

The population of Haiti was estimated in 1990 at 6,142,141 on the basis of the last official census, in 1982, when the population was 5,053,792.

DEMOGRAPHIC INDICATORS

Population (million): 6.142 (1990)
Year of last census: 1982
Sex distribution (% at last census): males, 48.5; females, 51.5
Population estimates and projections (million)

1940: 2.827	1970: 4.234	2000: 7.052
1950: 3.097	1980: 4.922	2010: 8.351
1960: 3.723	1990: 5.862	

Age profile (% at last census)

0–14: 39.2	30–44: 15.6	60–74: 5.4
15–29: 26.9	45–59: 10.0	75 and over: 2.9

Median age (yrs.): 19.4 (1985)
Youth population (% age 15–24): 20.5 (1985); 19.5 (2000)
Total dependency ratio: 78.5 (1985)
Annual growth rate (%)

1950–55: 1.59	1975–80: 1.76	2000–2005: 1.76
1955–60: 1.83	1980–85: 1.80	2005–2010: 1.65
1960–65: 1.93	1985–90: 1.88	2010–2015: 1.54
1965–70: 2.12	1990–1995: 1.89	2015–2020: 1.44
1970–75: 1.94	1995–2000: 1.84	2020–2025: 1.34

Hypothetical size of stationary population (millions): 17
Assumed year of reaching net reproduction rate of 1: 2025
Urban population (000): 1,613 (1985)
Urban population (%): 29 (1988); 18 (1965)
Annual urban population growth rate (%, 1985–90): 3.98
Annual rural population growth rate (%, 1985–90): 1.03
Percentage of urban population in largest city: 56 (1980)
Percentage of urban population in cities of population over 500,000: 56 (1980)
Number of cities of population over 500,000: 1 (1980)
Population density per sq. km. (per sq. mi.): 213.9 (554.1) (latest)

VITAL STATISTICS

Crude birth rate (/1,000): 45 (1990); 43 (1965)
Crude death rate (/1,000): 16 (1990); 20 (1965)
Infant mortality rate (/1,000 live births): 107 (1990)
Maternal mortality rate (/100,000 live births): 38 (1986–87)
Life expectancy (yrs.) at birth: males, 52; females, 55 (1990)
Gross reproduction rate (/woman) (1980–85): 2.46
Total fertility rate (/woman): 6.4 (1990)
Rate of natural increase (/1,000): 19.0 (1989)
Marriage rate (/1,000): 0.7 (1980)
Average household size: 4.4 (latest)

Haiti is densely populated and is rapidly reaching the limits of usable land. The density in agricultural areas reaches 340.7 per sq. km. (882 per sq. mi.). The most densely populated departments are Department of the West, Department of the North, Department of the South, Department of the Artibonite and Department of the Northwest, in that order.

The push-and-pull process of urbanization, which has caused an urban explosion in most developing countries, has not been demographically significant in Haiti because Haitian cities have few jobs or other opportunities to offer migrants. The pace of urbanization has been a modest 4%, and 71% of the population still lives in rurual areas. Port-au-Prince accounts for 56% of the urban population.

Emigration is triggered by a number of constant factors: the despotic Duvalier regimes, periodic droughts, population pressures on land, lack of jobs and the lure of relatively affluent neighbors. The net loss through emigration is estimated at over 20,000 per year. Substantial numbers emigrate annually to the United States through Puerto Rico and Guantánamo by both legal and illegal means. Faced with a mounting and uncontrollable emigration of Haitians to the United States, the two countries signed a Bilateral Agreement on Migrant Interdiction by which illegal aliens are returned to Haiti by the U.S. Coast Guard. An average of 3,000 illegals are returned to Haiti annually under this accord. Other common destinations are the Bahamas and the Dominican Republic, in both of which Haitian emigration has become a sensitive political issue. Haitian colonies also are reported in Venezuela and Cuba. The total Haitian diaspora is estimated at more than 500,000.

STATUS OF WOMEN INDICATORS

Number of women (million): 3.337 (1985)
Women of childbearing age (15–49) (% of pop.): 49 (1988)
Married women of childbearing age (15–49) using contraception (%): 5 (1986)
Women's literacy rate (%): 29 (1985)
Women in labor force (%): 42.1 (1988)
Total fertility rate (/woman): 6.4 (1990)

The role of women in Haitian society is limited by the nation's traditionalism. Since 1982 there has been no legal discrimination against women as compared to men. Women enjoy full rights to education and property ownership and such social rights as divorce.

Nevertheless, especially among the peasantry, women are limited to traditional domestic occupations. Middle-class women quite often work, but generally out of economic necessity. Women comprise a large part of the assembly work force. Secretarial, teaching and nursing positions are dominated by women. Few women, however, rise to prominent positions in the Haitian business world. As a rule, greater opportunities are available to women in the civilian government bureaucracy. Women are not permitted in the armed forces, except as nurses.

Haiti has adopted family planning as an official policy, and the Department of Family Planning Services has been set up under the Division of Family Hygiene. A number of United States-sponsored private programs, including the Church World Service, the Planned Parenthood Foundation and World Neighbors, operate in the country.

ETHNIC COMPOSITION

The population is relatively homogeneous, with blacks constituting 90% and mulattoes the balance. Until the 20th century the mulattoes were the elite class and much of Haiti's turbulent history may be explained by the rivalry between blacks and mulattoes. Mulattoes are categorized according to their parentage, within 10 major and 200 minor blood divisions. Blacks have held power continuously since 1946.

The white community is concentrated in the capital and includes French, Danish, German, Syrian, Lebanese and Corsican residents.

LANGUAGES

Haiti is the only republic in the Western Hemisphere where French is the official language. However, true French is spoken by only 10% of the people, the rest speak Creole, which is almost unintelligible to those who speak only French. Approximately 7% of the population is bilingual. In 1969 a law was passed granting legal status to Creole and permitting its use in the legislature and law courts but not in schools.

Until recently Creole was classified as pidgin French, using West African grammar. Linguistic theories now assign a higher status to Creole as a separate language influenced by both French and West African languages and as a lingua franca used by both whites and blacks. Creole literature made its first appearance in the 1920s.

English is used in the capital and provincial cities, and a Spanish Creole is spoken along the Dominican Republic border.

RELIGIONS

The official religion of the state is Roman Catholicism, which is nominally practiced by 90% of the population. Relations with the church are governed by the Concordat of 1860. Ecclesiastically the church is organized under the archdiocese of Haiti, headed by an indigenous archbishop, and six suffragan bishoprics. Almost all members of the clergy are native Haitians.

Despite its official status, Roman Catholicism has little influence outside the urban areas, where its place is taken by the folk religion of Haiti, voodooism. The Haitian peasant regards Catholicism and voodooism as inseparably one and considers himself a member of both religions, giving rise to the proverb "Haiti is 90% Catholic and 100% voodoo." Moreover, black nationalists favored and emphasized voodooism in opposition to the Western value systems represented by the Catholic church. President François Duvalier himself openly encouraged and reputedly practiced voodoo, retained voodoo priests as advisers and had a running battle with the Roman Catholic clergy.

Voodoo is an amalgam of African beliefs and Roman Catholic practices. It is an informal religion with no set theology, scriptures or clergy. Its principal elements are dance, music, magical invocation and rites and cults of the dead. Priestly functions are exercised by *houngans* (medicine men), *mambos* (priestesses) and *bocors* (sorcerers).

Protestantism, particularly Anglicanism, has had considerable success in recent years. The success of Protestant efforts is explained by their emphasis on education and social welfare, their use of Creole rather than French and active missionary work in rural areas. Most of the Protestant clergy are indigenous Haitians. There is no significant discrimination against Protestants.

HISTORICAL BACKGROUND

Haiti's colonial experience began in 1492 with the Spanish conquest of the Taino Indians on Hispaniola, but the Spanish period had little political or cultural significance. Colonization technically began only with the arrival of the French planters and their African slaves in the middle of the 17th century. A successful uprising by African-descended slaves between 1791 and 1803 established Haiti as an independent country in 1804, ruled by Jean-Jacques Dessalines. Although the French presence in Haiti was of very short duration—shorter, in fact, than that of any other colonial power in the New World—its impact was much greater and more durable. French legacies included racism and capitalism on the one hand and Roman Catholicism, education and culture on the other. Haiti accepted these legacies and value systems wholeheartedly and has never seriously attempted to shake them off. The French actually left three nations in Haiti: the white elite; the mulatto, who may aspire to some position in society through wealth or education or power; and the black slave masses. Racial strife among these three groups led to the slave revolt and the establishment of the Republic of Haiti in 1804.

Haiti's third colonial period was the U.S. occupation from 1915 to 1934. Although the Americans supported the mulattoes, U.S. policies tended to create and strengthen a strong black middle class and reinforce black consciousness among the educated classes.

Mulatto presidents retained power until 1946, when Dusmarsis Estimé, a black, was elected. He was overthrown by a military coup in 1950, led by another black, Gen. Paul Magloire. Magloire was forced to resign in 1956, and in 1957, Dr. François Duvalier was elected president.

Duvalier quickly became a dictator, who maintained his power through the means of a private army that used extortion and intimidation to quell all opposition.

Duvalier's son, Jean-Claude, became president upon his father's death in 1971. The younger Duvalier's regime was slightly more humane than his father's. He released political prisoners and appointed more moderate cabinet ministers. However, a new law was introduced in 1979 that banned all criticism of the president or government officials and any media activities deemed subversive.

The first municipal elections in 25 years were held in 1983–84. President Duvalier had promised that these would be free and democratic, but because no opposition candidates were allowed, Duvalier's party won all the Assembly seats.

Uprisings to protest widespread poverty and government corruption began in 1984, and despite Duvalier's attempts to calm the unrest by introducing humanitarian reforms, he was forced to flee the country in 1986. He was replaced as president by Gen. Henri Namphy.

Unrest continued in 1986, to protest the inclusion of pro-Duvalier officials in the new government, and continued into 1987 to protest the government's attempt to dissolve Haiti's principal trade union, the Centrale Autonome des Travailleurs Haïtiens (CATH).

Concurrent legislative and municipal elections were held in January 1988, and Leslie Manigat was elected president. Manigat did not include any pro-Duvalier members in his cabinet, which initiated protests by Duvalier supporters. In June 1988 Manigat was ousted by disaffected army members and was replaced by Gen. Henri Namphy, who reinstated Duvalier's violent policies.

Gen. Namphy was overthrown in a coup in September 1988, and was replaced by Brig.-Gen. Prosper Avril. Avril introduced radical reforms, purged the armed forces of pro-Duvalier members, and promised to hold democratic elections. The Avril government withstood two coup attempts in March 1989.

In September 1989, Avril released a timetable for elections. The president came under increasing criticism for mismanagement of the economy and for failing to put an end to a wave of robberies and killings believed to have been carried out in many instances by soldiers. During the fall of 1989 Haiti experienced a series of general strikes in response to increased taxation that was part of Avril's economic reform program. To prevent the continuation of anti-government protests and restore order, Avril, in January 1990, imposed a 30-day state of siege. He also announced that all political exiles were to be permitted to return to Haiti in preparation for elections. At the same time he announced the release of all political prisoners. In the face of growing anti-government protests Avril resigned in March. He was immediately succeeded by acting army chief, Maj. Gen. Harard Abraham, who turned power over to civilian Ertha Pascal-Trouillot, a Supreme Court Justice chosen by a coalition of opposition leaders, the Group of 12. Her appointment marked the first time since Duvalier's overthrow that Haitian civilians had taken power for themselves and chosen their own leader. Pascal-Trouillot was to rule with a Council of State until elections.

Relations between the president and the Council began to deteriorate almost immediately as the two clashed over handling Duvalier supporters. Pascal-Trouillot favored conciliation and the Council demanded exclusion of the Duvalierists from political activity. Relations worsened in August when the Council passed a motion of censure, accusing the government of corruption and incompetence.

The presidential and legislative elections took place, as scheduled, in December 1990. Jean-Bertrand Aristide, a left-wing Catholic priest who was the candidate of the Front National pour le Changement et le Democratie, won by an overwhelming margin. One month before Aristide was to be inaugurated, Roger Lafontant, a former head of Duvalier's private militia, led armed supporters in the seizure of the presidential palace. He forced the resignation of Pascal-Trouillot, but loyalist army forces crushed the coup the following day. Aristide was inaugurated in February. He immediately sought the extradition of Duvalier from France and undertook the reform of the armed forces. In April former President Pascal-Trouillot was arrested and charged as an accomplice in the coup that had tried to overthrow her government in January. Lafontant had reportedly told investigators that Trouillot had willingly handed over the presidency.

Aristide was overthrown Sept 30, 1991 in a coup staged by the nation's powerful military. The coup leaders established a three-man junta, headed by Gen. Raoul Cedras, to lead the country. In early October, under pressure from the military, the National Assembly declared the presidency vacant and, as mandated in the Constitution, swore in Supreme Court Justice Joseph Nerette as interim president.

CONSTITUTION & GOVERNMENT

Haiti is the oldest black republic in the world and the second-oldest republic in the Western Hemisphere after the United States. Haiti has had more than 20 constitutions, the first of which was drawn up in 1801 by Toussaint L'Ouverture and the last in 1987. However, most of the chief executives of Haiti during its turbulent history have ruled with virtually absolute authority as dictators. The title of president-for-life was first created in 1807, abolished in 1843, reintroduced in 1868, again abolished in 1870 and re-created in 1964. Another remarkable feature of Haitian constitutional history is the existence of constitutions that are constantly ignored but not suspended by the chief executives.

Haiti's most recent Constitution was approved by the electorate in 1987. Under its provisions, executive power is vested in a president who is elected by universal adult suffrage. The president may not serve two consecutive five-year terms. The president selects a prime minister from the controlling party in the

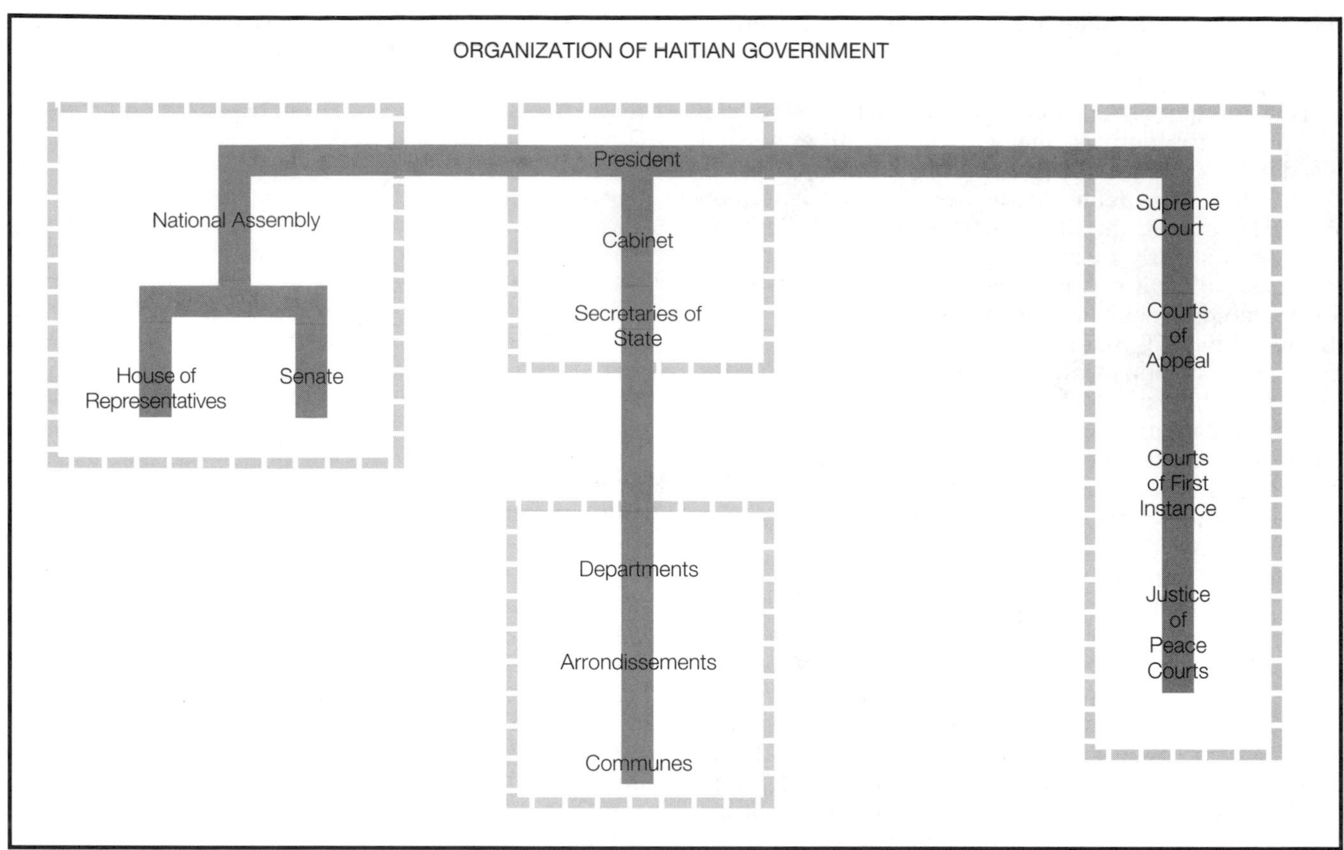

GOVERNMENT LIST
(July/August 1991)

President	Aristide, Jean-Bertrand*
Prime Minister	Preval, René
Minister of Agriculture, Natural Resources & Rural Development	Severin, François
Minister of Commerce & Industry	Chamblain, Jean-François
Minister of Finance & Economy	Rey, Marie-Michelle
Minister of Foreign Affairs	Jean-Louis, Marie-Denise, *M.D.*
Minister of Information, Coordination & Culture	Lassegue, Marie Jocelyn
Minister of Interior	Preval, René
Minister of Justice	Auguste, Karl
Minister of National Defense	Preval, René
Minister of National Education, Youth & Sports	Voltaire, Leslie
Minister of Planning, External Cooperation & Public Administration	Bernardin, Renaud
Minister of Public Health & Population	Henrys, Daniel, *M.D.*
Minister of Public Works, Transport & Communications	Verella, Frantz
Minister of Social Affairs	Celestin, Myrtha
Governor, Central Bank	Perodin, Roger

*Aristide was overthrown in a military coup 9/30/91 and the office of the presidency declared vacant. As required in the Constitution, Supreme Court Justice Joseph Nerette was sworn in as interim president in October.

legislature, who in turn selects a cabinet after consulting the president.

Legislative power is vested in bicameral legislature consisting of a 77-member Chamber of Deputies and a 27-member Senate.

The Constitution was annulled in June 1988 following a military coup. It was partially restored in March 1989.

RULERS OF HAITI (from 1941)

Presidents (Presidents-for-Life, 1964–86)

April 1941–January 1946: Elie Lescot
January 1946–August 1946: Frank Lauaud
August 1946–May 1950: Dumarsis Estimé
May–December 1950: Frank Lauaud
December 1950–December 1956: Paul Eugène Magloire
December 1956–January 1957: Joseph Nemours Pierre Louis
February–April 1957: François Sylvain
April–May 1957: Executive under military
May 1957: Léon Cantave
May 1957: Daniel Fignolé
June–October 1957: Antoine Kebreau
October 1957–April 1971: François Duvalier
April 1971–February 1986: Jean-Claude Duvalier
February 1986–February 1988: Lt. Gen. Henri Namphy
February 1988–June 1988: Leslie Manigat
June 1988–September 1988: Henri Namphy
September 1988–March 1990: Prosper Avril
March 1990–February 1991: Ertha Pascal-Trouillot
February 1991– : Jean-Bertrand Aristide

FREEDOM & HUMAN RIGHTS

In terms of political and civil rights Haiti is ranked as a not-free nation.

Haiti has had a long and troubled history of authoritarian rule characterized by serious human rights abuses. Nominally a republic, it is run more like a monarchy, with the president wielding all actual power for life. During the eight months that the president rules by decree, the Legislative chamber is in recess, and during the other four months the Legislative chamber simply rubber-stamps his decrees. In 1980, in response to growing press criticism, the government began to get tough, arresting the head of the Haitian Christian Democratic Party and later his daughter without charges. Later the government arrested and held without charges at least 40 journalists, opposition leaders and human rights activists. Some of those arrested were exiled. Jean-Claude Duvalier released political prisoners when he came to power in 1971. In 1989, following a major uprising, President Avril had more than 50 politicians arrested and had several opposition leaders deported. However, 10 days later the deported leaders were permitted to return to Haiti to participate in the forthcoming elections. It was announced at the same time that all political prisoners had been released. Beatings continue to be administered almost routinely in connection with the interrogation of suspects and incarceration of prisoners. Family members rarely are informed of an individual's arrest. Despite clear constitutional guarantees against arbitrary arrest and imprisonment, these measures are routinely used against political opponents. Similarly, the provision for a fair public trial is more honored in the breach, and defendants often languish in the jails for months without trial. Persons detained for political or security reasons are seldom charged or brought to trial. Some have been held for years. Searches without warrants are routine. The courts are not only dependent on the executive but also seem willing to follow government directions in sensitive cases.

The new press law promulgated in 1980, while milder than the 1979 code, retains serious restrictions on the media: a formal requirement (impossible in the case of daily newspapers) that all publications be submitted to the censors 72 hours in advance, the licensing of journalists by the Ministry of the Interior and the prohibition of material critical of the president and his family. Because prescreening is difficult in practice, publishers issue newspapers and journals at their own risk.

In 1980 the government established the Division of Human Rights within the Ministry of Foreign Affairs. The League of Human Rights also has been allowed to function without interference.

CIVIL SERVICE

No current information is available on the civil service in Haiti.

LOCAL GOVERNMENT

For purpose of local government Haiti is divided into nine departments: Artibonite, Centre, Grand' Anse, Nord, Nord-Est, Nord-Ouest, Ouest, Sud, and Sud-Est. Each department is headed by prefects appointed by the central government.

At the secondary level there are 27 arrondissements, and at the third level there are 112 communes. Each commune has an elected mayor.

FOREIGN POLICY

Because of the brutality associated with the Duvalier regimes, Haiti has been considered a pariah in international councils and has been outside the mainstream of hemispheric relations. The only two relationships Haiti has been historically preoccupied with are those with the Dominican Republic and the United States. Relations with the former have been strained by the activities of political exiles, and the border between the two countries is periodically closed. Relations with the United States have been alternately cordial and cool. U.S. economic and military aid was suspended briefly in 1963 but was resumed during the 1965 Dominican crisis, when Haiti's OAS vote was found to be crucial. The United States was one of the prime targets of Jean-Claude Duvalier's efforts to improve his country's image after the death of the elder Duvalier, but by 1977 Haiti had again fallen afoul of President Carter's policy toward regimes that systematically violate human rights. The United States resumed aid to Haiti in 1989 in recognition of Avril's cooperation in combatting drug-smuggling and in light of its progress toward democratic elections. Haiti's relations with Cuba have been tense from the advent of Fidel Castro's regime.

Haiti and the United States are parties to 21 treaties and agreements covering agricultural commodities, customs, defense, economic and technical cooperation, extradition, investment guarantees, maritime matters, nationality, pacific settlement of disputes, postal matters, property, publications, relief supplies and packages, telecommunications, and trade and commerce.

Haiti joined the United Nations in 1945. It is a member of 16 U.N. organizations and 25 other international organizations. Haiti has applied to become a member of the Caribbean Community (CARICOM). However, although representatives of CARICOM have expressed support for the restoration of democracy, they gave no commitment to support the application.

PARLIAMENT

Legislative power is vested in bicameral legislature consisting of a 83-member Chamber of Deputies whose members serve four year terms and a 27-member Senate whose members serve six year terms. Haiti held the first round of legislative elections in December 1990. In that election, the Front National pour le Changement et la Democratie (FNCD) won five of the 27 seats in the Senate and 18 of the 83 seats in the Chamber of Deputies. The Alliance Nationale pour la Democratie et le Progress (ANDP) won 16 seats in the lower house while seven other seats in the Chamber of Deputies were distributed among other parties. In the second round of elections, held in January 1991, the FNCD won 13 seats in the Senate and 27 seats in the Chamber of Deputies. The ANDP elected six senators and 17 deputies.

POLITICAL PARTIES

Under the dictatorship of Jean-Claude Duvalier the sole legal political party was the Party of National Unity whose only ideology was loyalty to Duvalier. Following Duvalier's downfall in 1986, many political opponents returned from exile. In August 1986 the National Council of Government granted legal status to political parties that had at least 20 founding members and 2,000 sponsors. Among the leading parties are the Front National pour le changement et la Democratie (National Front for Change and Democracy), whose leader, Jean-Bertrand Aristide is president, Mouvement pour l'Instillation de la Democratie en Haiti (Movement for the Installation of Democracy in Haiti), and the Alliance Nationale pour la Democratie et le Progress (National Alliance for Democracy and Progress). Other parties include: the Haitian Christian Democratic Party; the Haitian Social Christian Party; the National Alliance Front; the National Agricultural and Industrial Party; the Congress of Democratic Movements, the National Progressive Revolutionary Party; the National Patriotic Movement of November 28; the Movement for the Organization of the Country; and, the Mobilization for National Development.

ECONOMY

Haiti is the poorest country in the Western Hemisphere, with 85% of the population living in absolute poverty. And its economic problems are aggravated by drought, diplomatic isolation, political repression, emigration of skilled personnel, inflation and hurricanes. To shore up its declining balance of trade, Haiti has been selling blood plasma to the United States and offering nationals of other countries quick divorces. Political instability led to further economic deterioration in the 1980s exacerbated by the suspension of U.S. aid until the end of the decade.

Haiti has a free-market economy in which the dominant sector is private. Agriculture is mainly small-scale subsistence farming and employs 50% of the work force.

PUBLIC FINANCE

The Haitian fiscal year runs from October 1 through September 30. The published budget of the central government excludes the budgets of autonomous agencies, which are never published. Certain nonfiscal accounts also are excluded from the budget. Operating and development budgets are shown separately.

Of current government revenues, about one-tenth come from excises, one-fifth from import duties and approximately two-fifths from general sales taxes. Almost 12% comes from income taxes.

The national planning council is the Conseil National de Developpement et de Planification (CONADEP), an autonomous agency headed by the president. CONA-

PRINCIPAL ECONOMIC INDICATORS

Gross National Product (U.S. $ billions): 2.556 (1989)
GNP per capita (U.S. $): 400 (1989)
GNP average annual growth rate (%, 1980–89): 1.1
GNP per capita average annual growth rate (%, 1978–89): 1.9
Average annual rate of inflation (%, 1980–88): 7.9
Consumer price index (1980 = 100) 1986
- All Items: 159
- Food: 154

Average annual growth rate (%, 1980–88)
- General government consumption: −1.4
- Private consumption: 0.4
- Gross domestic investment: −5.1

BALANCE OF PAYMENTS, 1988 (U.S. $ millions)

Current account balance: −53.9
Merchandise exports: 156.1
Merchandise imports: −283.9
Trade balance: −127.8
Other goods, services & income + : 100.7
Other goods, services & income − : 219.7
Other goods, services & income net: −119.0
Private unrequited transfers: 63.4
Official unrequited transfers: 129.5
Capital other than reserves: 50
Net errors & omissions: −1.3
Counterpart items: −1.9
Liabilities constituting foreign authorities reserves: 0.0
Total change in reserves; −23.4

GROSS DOMESTIC PRODUCT

GDP nominal (G. billions): 9.752 (1987)
GDP per capita (U.S. $): 380 (1988 est.)
Average annual growth rate of GDP (%, 1980–88): −0.2
GDP by type of expenditure (%) 1987
- Consumption
  - Private: } 94
  - Government: }
- Gross domestic investment: 15
- Gross domestic saving: 4 (1988)
- Foreign trade
  - Exports: 21
  - Imports: −31

Cost components of GDP (%) 1982
- Net indirect taxes: 10
- Consumption of fixed capital: 3
- Compensation of employees: } 87
- Net operating surplus: }

Sectoral origin of GDP (%) 1986
- Primary
  - Agriculture: 33
- Secondary
  - Manufacturing: 15
  - Construction: 6
  - Public utilities: 1
- Tertiary
  - Transportation & communications: 2
  - Trade: 17
  - Finance: 10
  - Other services: 12
  - Government: 4

CENTRAL GOVERNMENT EXPENDITURES, 1982

% of total expenditures
- Defense: 9.9
- Education: 7.3
- Health: 7.4
- Housing, social security, welfare: 3.1
- Economic services: 14.5
- Other: 5.4

Total expenditures as % of GNP: 18.2
Overall surplus or deficit as % of GDP: −3.2

CENTRAL GOVERNMENT REVENUES, 1988

% of total current revenues
- Taxes on income, profit & capital gain: 11.8
- Social security contributions: 0.0
- Domestic taxes on goods & services: 42.2
- Taxes on international trade & transactions: 21.4
- Other taxes: 10.3
- Current nontax revenue: 14.3

Total current revenue as % of GNP: 10.8
General government consumption as % of GDP: 11 (1988)
Average annual growth rate of general government consumption (%, 1980–88): −1.4

DEP's development plans have focused on agriculture, social welfare services, human resources and public administration.

Haiti is a major beneficiary of international aid organizations, and up to 75% of its budget is financed by foreign donors. Since 1981 disbursement of aid has been increasingly accompanied by demands for an end to administrative corruption and for improvement in social and political conditions. Food aid is constantly supplied by the FAO, and some "food for work" programs have been introduced. The World Bank approved a 50-year credit of $19.1 million to continue a rural development project in northern Haiti to benefit small farmers. The credit was to be interest-free, and a 10-year grace period was included.

FOREIGN AID, 1989

Total foreign aid (U.S. $ millions): 268.9
- Bilateral: 159.0
- Multilateral: 110.0

During 1970–88, Haiti received $638 million in U.S. aid and $627 million from other Western countries and international organizations. In 1983–84, U.S. aid represented 24% of Haiti's budget.

Haiti has one of the lowest public debt burdens in Latin America because of substantial aid flow.

CURRENCY & BANKING

The Haitian unit of currency is the gourde, divided into 100 centimes. Notes are issued in denominations of 1, 2, 5, 10, 50, 100, 250 and 500 gourdes; coins are issued in denominations of 5, 10, 20 and 50 centimes.

The dollar exchange rate of the gourde is fixed at $1 = G5/G1 = $0.20; this rate has remained in effect despite the devaluations of the dollar.

Haiti has no exchange controls or restrictions, and U.S. dollars circulate alongside gourdes. In 1979 extensive changes in the banking laws split the national bank into a central and a commercial bank, and further changes are under consideration. During 1980, interest rates and reserve requirements were changed to help the outflow of interest-sensitive capital and to provide better control over monetary policy.

The central bank and the bank of issue is Banque de la République d'Haiti, formerly Banque Nationale. Banque de la République d'Haiti is both a central bank and a commercial bank, and it is the only banking service available outside the capital. The bank also participates in nonbanking ventures, such as the na-

FINANCIAL INDICATORS, 1989

Total reserves minus gold (SDRs millions): 10
SDRs (millions): 0
Reserve position in IMF (SDRs millions): 0
Foreign exchange (SDRs millions): 9
Gold (fine troy oz. millions): .02
Ratio of external debt to total reserves: 50.8 (1988)
Central bank 1987
- Assets (%)
  - Foreign assets: 5.0
  - Claims on government: 83.5
  - Claims on banks: 2.2
  - Claims on private sector: 9.3
- Liabilities (%)
  - Reserve money: 60.8
  - Government deposits: 11.7
  - Foreign liabilities: 31.5
  - Capital accounts: 5.9
- Money supply 1987
  - Stock (G billions): 2.098
  - M1 per capita: 390
- Private banks 1987
- Assets (%)
  - Loans to government: 0.9
  - Loans to private sector: 50.4
  - Reserves: 42.5
  - Foreign assets: 6.2
- Liabilities
  - Deposits (G billions): 1.900
  - of which %
    - Demand deposits: 34.7
    - Savings deposits: 62.3
    - Government deposits: 0.0
    - Foreign liabilities: 0.4

External debt 1988
- Total (U.S. $ millions): 823
  - of which public (U.S. $ millions): 683
  - of which private (U.S. $ millions): 0
- Debt service (long term)
  - Total (U.S. $ millions): 23
  - Repayment
    - Principal (%): 65.2
    - Interest (%): 34.8
- Debt service ratio (%): 6.0
- External public debt as % of GNP: 27.7
- Debt service as % of GNP: 0.9
- Debt service as % of exports: 8.8
- Terms of public borrowing 1987
  - Commitments (U.S. $ millions): 182
    - Average interest rate (%): 1.4
    - Average maturity (yrs.): 37
- Net flow of publicly guaranteed external capital (U.S. $ millions): 80 (1987)
- Receipt of workers' remittances (U.S. $ millions): 64 (1988)
- Net direct private investment (U.S. $ millions): 10 (1988)

GROWTH PROFILE
(Annual Growth Rates, %)

Projected population (1988–2000): 1.9
Projected crude birth rate (/1,000) (1990–95): 33.1
Projected crude death rate (/1,000) (1990–95): 11.6
Urban population (1985–90): 3.98
Labor force (1985–2000): 2.2
GNP (1980–89): 1.1
GNP per capita (1987–89): 1.9
GDP (1980–88): −0.2
Inflation (1980–88): 7.9
Manufacturing earnings per employee (1980–87): 3.4
Energy production (1980–88): 4.3
Energy consumption (1980–88): 1.6
Exports (1980–88): −2.6
Imports (1980–88): −2.4
General government consumption (1980–88): −1.4
Private consumption (1980–88): 0.4
Gross domestic investment (1980–88): −5.1

tional lottery, the national printing office and plant, and the tobacco and sugar monopolies. Of the 12 commercial banks in operation, eight are Haitian, two are United States-owned, one is Canadian, and one is French. Development finance is provided by Institut de Développement Agricole et Industriel.

AGRICULTURE

Of the total land area of 2,775,000 ha. (6,857,025 ac.), 31% is considered farmland.

It is estimated that there are over 560,000 farms in the country of an average size of about 1.4 ha. (3.4 ac.). Approximately 67% of the farms are cultivated by owners and their families: 25% are sharecropped, held by squatters or operated by managers called gerants; and 8% are mechanized sugarcane plantations or hand-cultivated sisal plantations. Because the large plantations were broken up in the 19th century, the vast bulk of the farms are smaller than 5 ha. (12 ac.). Only 4% are 5 to 10 ha. (12 to 25 ac.). Furthermore, many farms consist of noncontiguous plots on which different crops are raised.

Most small farmers use simple hand tools; the plow or animal power is used only occasionally. Mechanization is limited to the few plantations or state experimental stations. Fertilizers are used by few farmers. Fallowing is widely practiced as a soil conservation method. Planting more than one crop in the same field also is common, and usually a long-season crop is planted with a short-season one. The main irrigational facility is the Artibonite River Dam, which irrigates 36,421 ha. (90,000 ac.).

The most important export crop is coffee, which is grown on the humid mountain slopes and which constitutes 33% of Haitian exports. Other export and cash crops are sugarcane, sisal, cotton and tobacco. Rice is the leading food crop, followed by corn, manioc (cassava), bananas, sorghum and millet.

There are few cattle ranches in the country, and livestock-raising is a supplemental activity for most farmers. The national herd is of the Spanish criollo stock, upgraded by interbreeding with imported cattle.

AGRICULTURAL INDICATORS

Agriculture's share of GDP (%): 31 (1989)
Value added in agriculture (U.S. $ millions): 782 (1988)
Cereal imports (000 metric tons): 205 (1988)
Index of agricultural production (1979–81 = 100): 110 (1986)
Index of food production (1979–81 = 100): 110 (1986)
Index of food production per capita (1979–81 = 100): 95 (1986–88)
Number of tractors: 570 (1986)
Total fertilizer consumption (000 metric tons): 3.2 (1985–86)
Fertilizer consumption (g./ha., hundreds): 25 (1987–88)
Number of farms (000): 617 (1971)
Average size of holding (ha.): 1.4 (1971)
Size class (%) 1971
- Below 1 ha. (below 2.47 ac.): 58.7
- 1–5 ha. (2.47–12.35 ac.): 37.5
- 5–10 ha. (12.35–24.7 ac.): } 3.8
- 10–20 ha. (24.7–49.4 ac.): } 3.8
- 20–50 ha. (49.4–123.5 ac.): 0.0
- 50–200 ha. (123.5–494 ac.): 0.0
- Over 200 ha. (over 494 ac.): 0.0

Tenure (%) 1971
- Owner-operated: 66.6
- Rented: 25.0
- Other: 8.4

Land use (%)
- Cropland: 33
- Pasture: 18
- Forest: 2
- Other: 47

Yields (kg/ha.) 1989
- Grains 1,060
- Roots & tubers: 4,075
- Legumes: 496
- Milk (kg/animal): 237

Production 1989
- Fruits (000 metric tons): 1.009
- Vegetables (000 metric tons): 294

Livestock (000) 1989
- Cattle: 1,550
- Horses: 425 (1986)
- Sheep: 95
- Pigs: 950

Forestry 1988
- Production of roundwood (million cubic meters): 5.629
  - of which industrial roundwood (%): 4.2

Fishing 1988
- Total catch (000 metric tons): 8.1
  - of which marine (%): 46.3
- Value of exports (U.S. $ million): 2.160

Forests and wooded areas cover about 251,723 ha. (622,000 ac.). The largest stands are pine, mahogany, oak, cedar, rosewood, lavan, narra, tindalo and ipil. The export of mahogany is restricted.

Haitian coastal waters are rich in fish such as tuna, marlin, bonito and sardines, but the commercial fishing industry is underdeveloped. Exports, mainly spiny lobsters, have been dropping in value. Most of the domestic demand is met by freshwater fish, such as carp and tertar, a native fish.

Agricultural credit is provided by Institut de Développement Agricole et Industriel.

MANUFACTURING

Small shops and artisan workshops account for a large percentage of the total manufacturing production. Known as petite industry, this sector produces such products as mahogany masks and carvings and woven sisal.

Since the late 1960s the light-industry sector has become prominent. This sector consists of small assembly plants processing components for U.S. firms for reexport to the United States. Many of the products of this sector require considerable hand labor, such as baseballs, belts, boots, gloves, handbags, hairpieces, toys, wallets, shirts and sandals.

MANUFACTURING INDICATORS, 1987

Share of GDP (%): 15 (1988)
Labor force economically active in manufacturing (% est.): 5.7 (1983)
Earnings per employee in manufacturing 1987
  Growth rate (%, 1980–87): 3.4
  Index (1980 = 100): 153

Taking advantage of U.S. Code sections 806 and 807 and the Caribbean Basin Initiative (CBI), over 300 companies have been sending United States-made parts to Haiti for assembly and return to the United States. This has created more than 60,000 jobs with the requirement of a minimum of capital expenditure. This is attributable primarily to favorable government investment policy, high labor productivity, and a low minimum daily wage, which have attracted foreign businessmen either for direct investment or for subcontracting of assembly operations. Spurred by a growing U.S. economy, which receives more than 90% of the total output of the assembly industry, and the benefits of duty-free entry into the United States for many products under the Caribbean Basin Initiative, the assembly industry is expected to grow rapidly. An industrial zone has been built outside Port-au-Prince for assembly industries.

Domestic demand for industrial products is limited, and therefore manufacturing is largely devoted to processing agricultural and forestry products. The four main products of this sector are cement, sugar, cotton fabric and cigarettes. A small steel plant is in operation.

The government welcomes foreign investments in industries not competing with local production. Such enterprises are exempt from export and import duties for the first five years and enjoy a 50% tax reduction in the first year of operation. U.S. investments in the country are estimated at over $50 million.

The government is considering a new investment code that would consolidate many of the provisions already in place, including tax holidays, duty-free entry of goods that are to be reexported, guaranteed repatriation of a percentage of profits, import protection for industries satisfying 75% of the local demand and meeting certain quality and pricing requirements, and discrimination-free status for foreign firms. The National Office for Investment Promotion (ONAPI) is trying actively to promote investment in Haiti.

MINING

Production of bauxite, estimated at 400,000 to 700,000 metric tons annually, ceased in 1983 owing to low international demand. Bauxite was Haiti's third most valuable export, after coffee and sugar. The second most valuable mineral is copper, but production figures have not been reported since 1971.

ENERGY

The use of charcoal as the country's main energy source is rapidly causing the deforestation of mountainsides, leading to serious problems of soil erosion. Two hydroelectric dams have been built in the Artibonite River Valley, but they supply electricity to Port-au-Prince only.

ENERGY INDICATORS

Average annual energy production growth rate (%, 1980–88): 4.3
Energy consumption per capita (kg. oil equivalent): 57 (1988)
Energy imports as % of merchandise exports: 13 (1988)
Average annual growth rate of energy consumption (%, 1980–88): 1.6
Electricity 1988
  Installed capacity (000 kw.): 146
  Production (million kw.–hr.): 445
    % fossil fuel: 28.1
    % hydro: 71.9
  Consumption per capita (kw.–hr.): 71
Petroleum
  Production (million bbl.): 0 (1989)
  Consumption (million bbl.): 0 (1988)
  Refining capacity (000 bbl./day): 0 (1990)
Coal
  Reserves (million metric tons): 13 (latest)

LABOR

One half of Haiti's labor force is employed in agriculture. Some 51% of the labor force is self-employed; 14% are wage or salary earners, 9% are unpaid family workers and 25% are unclassified.

Statutory minimum-wage laws are in force, but their implementation is limited. In 1980 the minimum wage was $2.20 per day. The workweek consists of 48 hours, or eight hours per day. Two-week annual paid vacations are standard for nonagricultural workers.

Available estimates on the unemployment rate range from 2% to 33% and must be treated with caution. Actual unemployment is estimated at close to 12.2% and underemployment at 25%.

The government took a number of important steps in 1984 to improve the situation of labor in Haiti. A federation of union workers of Haiti was founded January 12, 1984, with nine active unions in Port-au-Prince as charter members. The federation has assumed the leading role in union activity in Haiti. Under the sponsorship of the federation, representatives from its nine affiliates develop joint resolutions to union problems and coordinate assistance to workers throughout Haiti who request aid in forming new unions. The government has publicly stated that it does not object to international labor organizations visiting Haiti.

In March 1984 the government revised the Labor Code by making it easier for employees to form unions, protecting the right of Haitians who work abroad and revising provisions on forced labor to comply with International Labor Organization conventions on forced labor. In May federation and union officials met with members of the ILO delegation and discussed the possibilities of international assistance. In June, for the first time in many years, the president of the federation traveled to the ILO conference in Geneva as the labor union representative of the official Haitian delegation.

LABOR INDICATORS, 1988

Total economically active population (million): 2.350
- % working-age (15–64): 66.3
- % female: 40.9

Activity rate (%)
- Total: 42.2
- Male: 51.4
- Female: 33.6

Employment status (%)
- Employers & self-employed: 51.6
- Employees: 14.3
- Unpaid family workers: 9.1
- Other: 25.1

Sectoral employment of economically active (%)
- Agriculture, forestry, fishing: 50.4
- Construction: 1.0
- Manufacturing, mining, quarrying, public utilities: 5.8
- Trade, hotels, restaurants: 11.1
- Transportation, communications: 0.7
- Finance, real estate: 0.2
- Services: 4.9

Average annual growth rate of labor force (%, 1980–2000): 2.2
Labor under 20 years (%): 15.9 (1988)

Less than 1% of the labor force has been organized, and the labor movement is very weak. The largest unions are Union Nationale des Ouvriers d'Haiti and Fédération Haitienne de Syndicats Chrétiens.

FOREIGN COMMERCE

Haiti's most important exports are light manufactures, coffee and other agricultural products. Its major imports are machines and manufactures, food and beverages, petroleum products and chemicals. The major import sources are the United States, Netherlands Antilles, Japan, France and Canada. The major export destinations are: the United States, France, Italy, and Germany.

A substantial but undetermined percentage of the labor force emigrates to neighboring countries, especially the United States, every year. Their remittances, estimated at $60 million a year, help the nation's foreign reserves.

Because of its relative political and economic isolation, Haiti is not a member of any trade grouping.

FOREIGN TRADE INDICATORS, 1988

Exports (U.S. $ millions): 215 (est.)
Imports (U.S. $ millions): 216 (est.)
Balance of trade (U.S. $ millions): −1 (est.)
Annual growth rate (1980–88), exports (%): −2.6
Annual growth rate (1980–88), imports (%): −2.4
International reserves in terms of months of imports covered: 0.5
Terms of trade (1980=100): 101
Import price index (1980=100): 84.9 (1986)
Export price index (1980=100): 105.4 (1986)

Direction of Trade (%), 1987

	Imports	Exports
European Community	16.8	37.9
United States	45.6	52.7
U.S.S.R. & eastern European economies	0.3	0.1
Japan	6.9	0.5

Composition of Trade (%), 1987

	Imports	Exports
Food & agricultural raw materials, mineral ores & concentrates	32.3	37.1
Fuels & other energy	11.7	10.5
Manufactured goods	56.0	62.9
of which chemicals	10.3	3.2
of which machinery	18.3	0.0

TRANSPORTATION & COMMUNICATIONS

Passenger railways no longer exist in Haiti; an 80 km. (50 mi.) railway for the transportation of sugarcane still operates. The length of navigable inland waterways is 100 km. (62 mi.).

There are about 14 seaports open to international commerce, of which Port-au-Prince handles about 90% of all imports and about 60% of all exports by volume. The balance of foreign trade is handled by six other ports: Cap-Haïtien, Gonaïves, Jacmel, Les Cayes, Petit-Goâve and Jérémie.

The road system, consisting of 4,000 km. (2,485 mi.) of main roads, of which about 600 km. (960 mi.) are paved, is in a chronic state of disrepair. Most of the unpaved roads are impassable in the rainy season, and there are few bridges.

TRANSPORTATION INDICATORS

Roads (latest)
- Length, km. (mi.): 4,000 (2,485)
- Paved (%): 15

Motor vehicles (latest)
- Automobiles: 35,000
- Trucks and buses: 12,000
- Persons per vehicle: 115

Railroads (latest)
- Track, km. (mi.): 0.0
- Passenger-km. (passenger-mi.) (millions): 0.0
- Freight, metric ton-km. (short ton-mi.) (millions): 0.0

Merchant marine
- Vessels (over 100 tons): 3 (1989)

Total deadweight tonnage (000): 0.4 (1989)

Ports (pre-1986)
- Cargo loaded (000 metric tons): 169
- Cargo unloaded (000 metric tons): 680

Air
- Airports with scheduled flights: 2 (1990)

Inland waterways (latest)
- Length, km. (mi.): 100 (62)

The national airline is the privately owned Air Haiti, which operates two aircraft on internal and external routes. The largest airport, and the only one with a runway over 2,500 m. (8,200 ft.), is François Duvalier International Airport at Port-au-Prince.

COMMUNICATION INDICATORS, 1988

Telephones
  Total (000): 50
  Persons per telephone: 114
Phone traffic (000 calls) 1987
  Local: 41,137
  Long distance: 1,293
  Combined national: 42,530
  International: 1,960
Post office
  Number of post offices: 92
  Pieces of mail handled (billion): 1.046 (1977)
Telecommunications 1990
  Satellite stations: 1

TOURISM & TRAVEL INDICATORS, 1986

Total tourist receipts (U.S. $ millions): 74 (1988)
Expenditures by nationals abroad (U.S. $ millions): 35 (1988)
Number of hotel beds (000): 4
Average length of stay (nights): 8

Tourism was once Haiti's second-largest source of foreign exchange. However, the number of visitors has dropped as a result of political instability. In 1985–86 the number of visitors totaled 208,092; in 1988–89 it was only 184,737.

DEFENSE

The defense structure is headed by the president of the republic. The line of command runs through the secretary of state for interior and national defense to the chief of the general staff. Both François and Jean-Claude Duvalier exercised personal control over the armed forces by appointing only trustworthy supporters to positions of command, periodically reshuffling commanders and storing the army's ordnance in the basement of the presidential palace.

Military manpower is provided by voluntary enlistment. Conscription has never been necessary because of the pay, prestige and power attached to a military career.

The total strength of the armed forces was estimated at 7,550 men in June 1989. This figure included the Dessalines batallion and the counterinsurgency unit, the Leopards, that were disbanded in November 1989.

Army

Personnel: 7000

Organization: Presidential Guard (1 infantry battalion, 1 armored squadron); 1 infantry battalion; 1 special forces battalion; 1 artillery group

Equipment: 6 tanks; 11 armored personnel carriers; 6 howitzers; 36 mortars; 20 antitank guns; 8 rocket launchers; 16 air defense guns

Navy

Personnel: 250

Equipment: 14 patrol craft

Air Force

Personnel: 300

Equipment: 7 combat aircraft; 11 transports; 15 training aircraft; 8 helicopters

The armed forces only have the capability of maintaining internal security and are not equipped to provide defense against external attack. Haiti faces no serious threats from its only land neighbor, the Dominican Republic, and therefore considerations of defense are not of paramount importance. The training and equipment levels of the armed forces have improved since Haiti was again placed on the list of countries eligible for U.S. military assistance, in 1972.

EDUCATION

According to 1985 UNESCO estimates, the average rate of adult illiteracy was 62.4%, the highest national level in the Western hemisphere. By 1989, the literacy rate had risen slightly to 41.5% of the population. Of the population over 25 years, 83.5% have had no schooling.

Technically, education is free, universal and compulsory for six years, from ages six to twelve.

Schooling lasts for 12 years, divided into six years of primary school and six years of secondary school. Primary schooling is divided into three cycles (preparatory, elementary and intermediate), and secondary schooling is divided into two cycles of three and four years, known as basic and upper, respectively. Secondary schools are almost entirely in urban areas. Students who complete the first six years receive a certificate; those who complete nine years receive a *brevet;* and those who complete 13 years receive the *baccalauréat.* Dropout rates are high.

The academic year runs from October through July. The medium of instruction is French throughout, but the study of English is required at the last grade of the upper cycle of secondary school.

Primary-school teachers are graduates of normal schools, and secondary-level teachers are graduates of the University of Haiti. Women outnumber men on primary-school staffs, while the ratio is reversed on secondary-school staffs. A large proportion at both levels are members of Roman Catholic orders or are Protestant missionaries. Salaries are low and attrition rates are high.

The principal adult education agency is the Office National d'Alphabetisation et d'Action Communitaire (ONAAC), which has taught over 200,000 Haitians to read and write.

Private schools play an important role in the school system. Over half of primary-school enrollment and 75% of secondary-school enrollment are in private schools. Private schools are of two types: those supported by the state, and those supported by tuition charges and contributions. The bulk of the schools in both categories are affiliated either with Roman Catholic orders or Protestant missions.

Vocational training is provided in three-year professional schools known as *écoles professionelles.* These schools are all public, whereas most commercial schools are private.

Urban education is under the control of the Secretariat of State for National Education, while rural education is under the control of the Secretariat of State for Agiculture, Natural Resources and Rural Development. The country is divided into 36 school districts (32 urban, four rural), each under an inspector.

EDUCATION INDICATORS, 1989

Literacy
- Total (%): 41.5
- Male (%): 44.0
- Female (%): 39.2

First level
- Schools: 4,799 (1988)
- Students: 889,500
- Teachers: 24,900
- Student/teacher ratio: 35.7
- Net enrollment ratio: 55 (1985)

Second level
- Schools: 503
  - Students: 182,400
  - Teachers: 6,106
  - Student/teacher ratio: 17.9
- Vocational
  - Schools: 36 (1986)
  - Students: 14,437 (1986)

Third level/postsecondary
- Institutions: 1
- Students: 4,600
- Teachers: 330
- Student/teacher ratio: 13.9
- Gross enrollment ratio: 1.2 (1984)
- Students (/100,000 pop.): 112
- % of population age 25 and over with postsecondary education: 0.7

Foreign study
- Students abroad: 1,791
  - of whom in
    - United States: 1,297 (1988)
    - France: 253 (1988)
    - Federal Republic of Germany: 38 (1988)
    - United Kingdom: 5 (1987)

Public expenditure 1987
- Total (G. 000): 207,723
- % of GNP: 1.9
- % of national budget: 20.6
- % of current: 99.2

Higher education is provided by the University of Haiti.

LEGAL SYSTEM

The judiciary is headed by the Court of Cassation, composed of a president, a vice president and 10 judges. Usually it functions in two chambers of five judges each. The second tier of the judiciary consists of four courts of appeal, in Port-au-Prince, Las Cayes, Gonaives and Cap Haitien; the court in the capital has a president and five judges. Courts of first instance are of two types: civil tribunals and criminal tribunals. Justice of the peace courts, in each of the country's 124 communes are each presided over by a single judge.

GRADUATES, 1982

Total: 831
Education: 68
Humanities & religion: 0
Fine & applied arts: 0
Law: 108
Social & behavioral sciences: 116
Commerce & business: 0
Mass communication: 0
Home economics: 0
Service trades: 0
Natural sciences: 33
Mathematics & computer science: 0
Medicine: 264
Engineering: 200
Architecture: 0.0
Transportation & communications: 0
Agriculture, forestry, fisheries: 42
Other: 0

All judges are appointed by the president.

Under the Haitian legal system, arrests must be based on a charge of violation of a law. A warrant is legally, though not in practice, necessary for arrest. Once a person has been taken into custody, the arresting authority is required by law to obtain a ruling on the validity of the arrest from a judge within 48 hours. Although this procedure is open to considerable abuse, there are indications that the government has begun to adhere to it, at least in nonsecurity, nonpolitical cases. Haitian law requires that charges against arrested persons be filed at least two weeks before a trial. In practice this is often not the case. The law allows legal counsel for defendants. However, a client sometimes is not allowed to meet with counsel until immediately before the trial. There is no system of bail, though "provisional liberty" can be obtained in some cases. The accused are permitted to know the charges against them. Both juries and judicial tribunals are permitted to hear cases, render decisions and impose sentences.

There are two major penitentiaries: the notorious Fort Dimanche; and the National Penitentiary, where the enemies of the Duvaliers usually were incarcerated without trial.

LAW ENFORCEMENT

Under the Duvaliers there is no real distinctions among the police force; the military; and the organs of terror created by François Duvalier, such as the Tontons Macoutes, the National Security Volunteers and the Secret Police. The combination of these units under the Ministry of the Interior was quite formidable as a deterrent to enemies of the state. Under the Constitution approved by referendum in 1987, the army and the police were no longer to be a combined force.

Statistics on crime are not published, but based on newspaper reports the incidence of crime is serious enough to cause official concern. Most of the crimes are in urban areas. In the early 1980s the national arrest rate was 33 per 1,000 inhabitants.

HEALTH

The major national health problems are malaria, tuberculosis, dermatosis, parasite worms and respiratory ailments. Yaws, once a major hazard, has been virtually eliminated (it was the campaign to eliminate yaws that brought François Duvalier, a physician, to national prominence in the mid-1950s). In the late 1980s the AIDS virus reached epidemic proportions. According to the WHO, there were 2,337 reported AIDS cases by December 1989. Only 38% of the population have access to safe water.

HEALTH INDICATORS

Health personnel 1989
- Physicians: 944
  - persons per: 6,087
- Dentists: 98
- Nurses: 657
- Pharmacists: 6
- Midwives: 100

Hospitals 1989
- Number: 87
- Number of beds (/10,000): 8
- Admissions/discharges (/10,000): 123

Type of hospitals (%) 1989
- Government: 61.1
- Private nonprofit: } 38.9
- Private profit: }

Public health expenditures (latest)
- Per capita (U.S. $): 3.60

Vital statistics
- Crude death rate (/1,000): 16 (1990)
- Life expectancy at birth 1990
  - Males: 52
  - Females: 55
- Infant mortality rate (/1,000 live births): 107 (1990)
- Child mortality rate under 5 yrs. (/1,000 live births) (1985–90): 156
- Maternal mortality rate (/100,000 live births) (1986–87): 38
- Population with access to safe water (%): 38 (latest)

FOOD & NUTRITION

The staple elements of the Haitian diet are corn, millet, manioc, rice, bananas and fruit. Meat, fish, eggs and poultry appear only rarely in the diet. However, the Creole cuisine, combining French, Spanish and African dishes, is noted for its variety and elegance.

The daily per capita intake of food is 1,903 calories (84% of requirements).

MEDIA & CULTURE

In 1991, eight daily newspapers were published in the country, most from Port-au-Prince.

Under the Duvaliers the media were under the complete control of the regime. In addition to direct censorship, newspapers were compelled to publish officially prepared editorials, to accept progovernment staff writers and to submit to newsprint quotas based on political loyalty. The plants of opposition papers usually were bombed by the Tontons Macoutes.

The press was governed by the 1980 Press Code, which required that all publications be submitted for governmental review 72 hours prior to publication and that all journalists (including foreigners) be accredited by the Ministry of Information. It also required that no material critical of the Duvalier family be published. While the first two of these requirements were not always enforced, the spirit of the Press Code and governmental actions serve to restrict freedom of the press.

Following the downfall of the Duvaliers in 1986, a number of new newspapers were established. Currently, there are no restrictions on the press.

The national news agency is the Haitian News Service, founded in 1981. UPI, AP, AFP and Efe are represented in Port-au-Prince.

There are two small book publishers in the capital, with an average annual output of fewer than 30 titles. Haiti adheres to the Universal Copyright Convention.

There are 25 commercial and four noncommercial radio stations, all privately owned, broadcasting in French and Creole for up to 18 hours daily.

Television services is operated by Télé-Haiti, a private commercial company, and Télévision Nationale d'Haiti. Télé-Haiti broadcasts on two channels, one in English and the other in French.

MEDIA INDICATORS

Newspapers
- Number of dailies: 8 (1991)
- Circulation (000): 45 (latest)
- Per 1,000 pop.: 8 (latest)
- Newsprint consumption, 1988
  - Total metric tons: 400
  - Per 1,000 pop. (kg.): 64

Radio 1989
- Number of transmitters: 37
- Number of persons per radio receiver: 41

Television 1989
- Television transmitters: 4
- Number of persons per T.V. receiver: 221

Cinema (pre-1986)
- Number of fixed cinemas: 28
- Seating capacity (000): 14
- Annual attendance (millions): 2.1

CULTURAL & ENVIRONMENTAL INDICATORS

Libraries (latest)
- Number: 2
- Volumes (000): 12

Museums (pre-1986)
- Annual attendance (000): 73
- Attendance (/1,000 pop.): 16

Nature reserves
- Number of facilities: 2 (latest)

The largest libraries are the Bibliothèque Nationale and the Library of the Brothers of St. Louis de Gonzaga.

SOCIAL WELFARE

The only significant Social Security program is the old-age pension, limited to a small group of mostly public personnel. Other public social welfare programs are financed through the national lottery. There are a number of private voluntary welfare agencies, such as CARE, and mutual help societies, such as the Congo Society of Cap Rouge.

GLOSSARY

arrondissement: a subdivision of a departement.
chef de section: a sheriff or rural administrator.
commune: a subdivision of an arrondissement.
département: major unit of local government, equivalent to a province.
houngan: voodoo priest.
negritude: glorification of Afro-Haitian heritage adopted by François Duvalier as official policy.
tontons macoutes: licensed thugs drawn from the core of Duvalier supporters whose principal function is to terrorize the citizens.
ville de province: provincial town.

CHRONOLOGY (from 1946)

1946— With the backing of the Haitian Guard, Dumarsis Estime elected president.
1950— The army deposes Estime, forestalling his attempt to amend the Constitution to enable him to run for another term; Col. Paul E. Magloire becomes president, supported by both mulattoes and blacks.
1956— Magloire is reinstated at the end of his constitutional term. . . . Nationwide strike forces Magloire to step down; Joseph Nemours Pierre Louis is named interim president.
1957— François Sylvain is elected president but is arrested after 53 days and replaced by an Executive Council. . . . Riots erupt nationwide and civil liberties are suspended; army commander Léon Cantave takes over. . . . Following a near-civil war, Daniel Fignole inaugurated as president. . . . The army arrests and deports Fignole. . . . The army revolts under Antoine Kebreau. . . . In nationwide elections under Kebreau's auspices François Duvalier, a black physician, is elected president.
1960— Clément Barbot, the chief of the security services, arrested. . . . Roman Catholic archbishop François Poirier exiled.
1961— Duvalier has himself elected for another six years by an electoral ruse.
1964— Duvalier sponsors new Constitution under which he is made president-for-life.
1971— In failing health, Duvalier has Constitution amended to enable him to name successor and to lower the age of induction to the presidency to 18; Duvalier names his son Jean-Claude (Baby Doc) as successor; Duvalier dies and is succeeded by Jean-Claude at age 19.
1972— Duvalier succeeds in dismissing strongman Luckner Cambronne, head of the Tontons Macoutes.
1977— Following the Carter administration's criticism of Haiti's violations of human rights, Duvalier releases a few political prisoners.
1978— Gen. Roger St. Albin named chief of staff and Jean Valme chief of police in a major government reshuffle.
1980— Mass exodus of Haitian refugees is reported. . . . Hurricane Allen kills over 200 and destroys the nation's coffee crop. . . . Duvalier reshuffles cabinet for the fifth time in two years in an effort to consolidate his power vis-à-vis his mother, Simone Duvalier.
1981— United States and Haiti reach agreement on forcible repatriation of Haitian immigrants to Haiti.
1986— President-for-Life Jean-Claude Duvalier flees Haiti, leaving the government in the hands of a clique of old Duvalier cronies, with the Chief of Staff Henri Namphy as provisional head.
1987— A new Constitution is approved by 99.8% of the voters. Two presidential candidates are murdered and 12 barred from running because of their connections with Duvalier. Presidential elections are cancelled three hours after voting begins because of violence.
1988— Leslie Manigat wins the January presidential elections. Manigat's government is overthrown by Gen. Henri Namphy and disaffected members of the army. Namphy dissolves the legislature and formally abrogates the Constitution of 1987. . . . Gen. Namphy is ousted in a coup led by Gen. Prosper Avril. Duvalier's supporters within the armed forces are purged. . . .
1989— Avril partially restores the Constitution. . . . The government survives two coup attempts by the Leopard Corps and the Dessalines battalion. General strikes occur during the fall to protest tax increases.
1990— Avril resigns and is replaced by Ertha Pascal-Trouillot as interim president. . . . Jean-Bertrand Aristide wins the December presidential elections.
1991— Roger Lafontant, former head of Duvalier's private militia, leads an unsuccessful coup against Pascal-Trouillot. Aristide is inaugurated in February. . . . The military overthrows Aristide in September.

BIBLIOGRAPHY

BOOKS & FILMS

Chambers, Frances. *Haiti* (World Bibliography Series). Santa Barbara, Calif., 1983.
Diedrich, Bernard, and Al Burt. *Papa Doc: The Truth About Haiti Today.* New York, 1969.
Foster, Charles R., and Albert Valdman. *Haiti Today and Tomorrow: An Interdisciplinary Study.* Lanham, Md., 1985.
Haiti. B&W film, 30 min. National Film Board of Canada.
Haiti. Color film, 22 min. Producer: N.A.
Healy, David. *Gunboat Diplomacy in the Wilson Era: The U.S. Navy in Haiti, 1915–16.* Madison, Wis., 1976.
Heinl, Robert D., and Nancy G. Heinl. *Written in Blood: The Story of the Haitian People.* Boston, Mass., 1978.
Introduction to Haiti. Color film, 10 min. Producer: N.A.
Levilain, Guy V. *Cultural Identity, Negritude and De-*

colonization: A Study of the Haitian Situation. New York, 1978.
Leyburn, James S. *The Haitian People.* New Haven, Conn., 1966.
Life in Haiti. Color film, 20 min. Pat Dowling Pictures.
Lundahl, Mats. *The Haitian Economy: Man, Land and Markets.* New York, 1983.
———. *Peasants and Poverty.* New York, 1979.
Moore, O. Ernest. *Haiti: Its Stagnant Society and Shackled Economy.* New York, 1972.
Nicholls, David. *From Dessalines to Duvalier: Race, Color and National Independence in Haiti.* New York, 1979.
———. *Haiti in the Caribbean Context: Ethnicity, Economy and Revolt.* New York, 1985.
Ott, Thomas O. *The Haitian Revolution.* Knoxville, Tenn., 1973.
Perusse, Roland I. *Historical Dictionary of Haiti.* Metuchen, N.J., 1977.
Portrait of Haiti. Color film, 14 min. Producer: N.A.
Rodman, Selden. *Haiti: The Black Republic.* Greenwich, Conn., 1984.
Rotberg, Robert. *Haiti: The Politics of Squalor.* Boston, 1971.
Schmidt, Hans R. *The United States Occupation of Haiti, 1915–34.* New Brunswick, N.J., 1971.
Tata, Robert J. *Haiti: Land of Poverty.* Lanham, Md., 1982.
Three Brothers in Haiti. Color film, 15 min. Producer: N.A.
Weinstein, Brian, and Aaron Segal. *Haiti: Political Failures, Cultural Successes.* New York, 1984.

OFFICIAL PUBLICATIONS

Central Bank. *Comptes Courants Secteur Public* (Public Sector Currency Accounts).
———. *Rapports Comptes Fiscaux et Non-Fiscaux* (Reports on Tax and Nontax Accounts).
———. *Rapport Dette Publique du Secteur Administration Publique* (Report on the Public Debt of the Government Sector).
———. *Rapport Ventilation des Recettes Fiscales* (Detailed Report on Tax Revenues).
———. *Sommaire des Comptes de la Banque Nationale de la République d'Haiti* (Summary of the Accounts of the National Bank of the Republic of Haiti).
Treasury. *État des Recettes Douanières et Recettes Internes* (Statement of Customs Revenues and Internal Revenues).

HONDURAS, LIBRE, - SOBERANA, INDEPENDIENTE

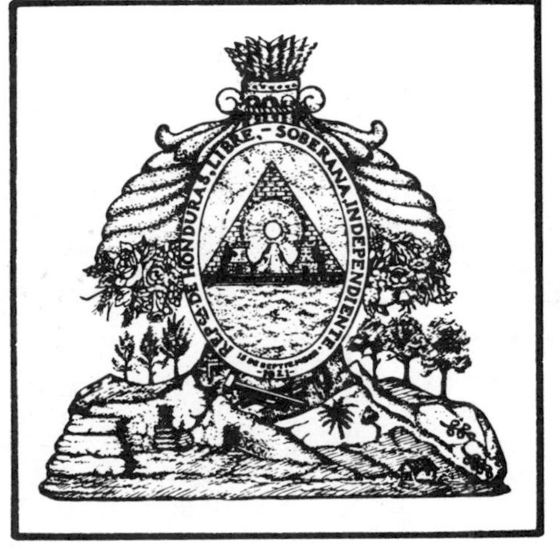

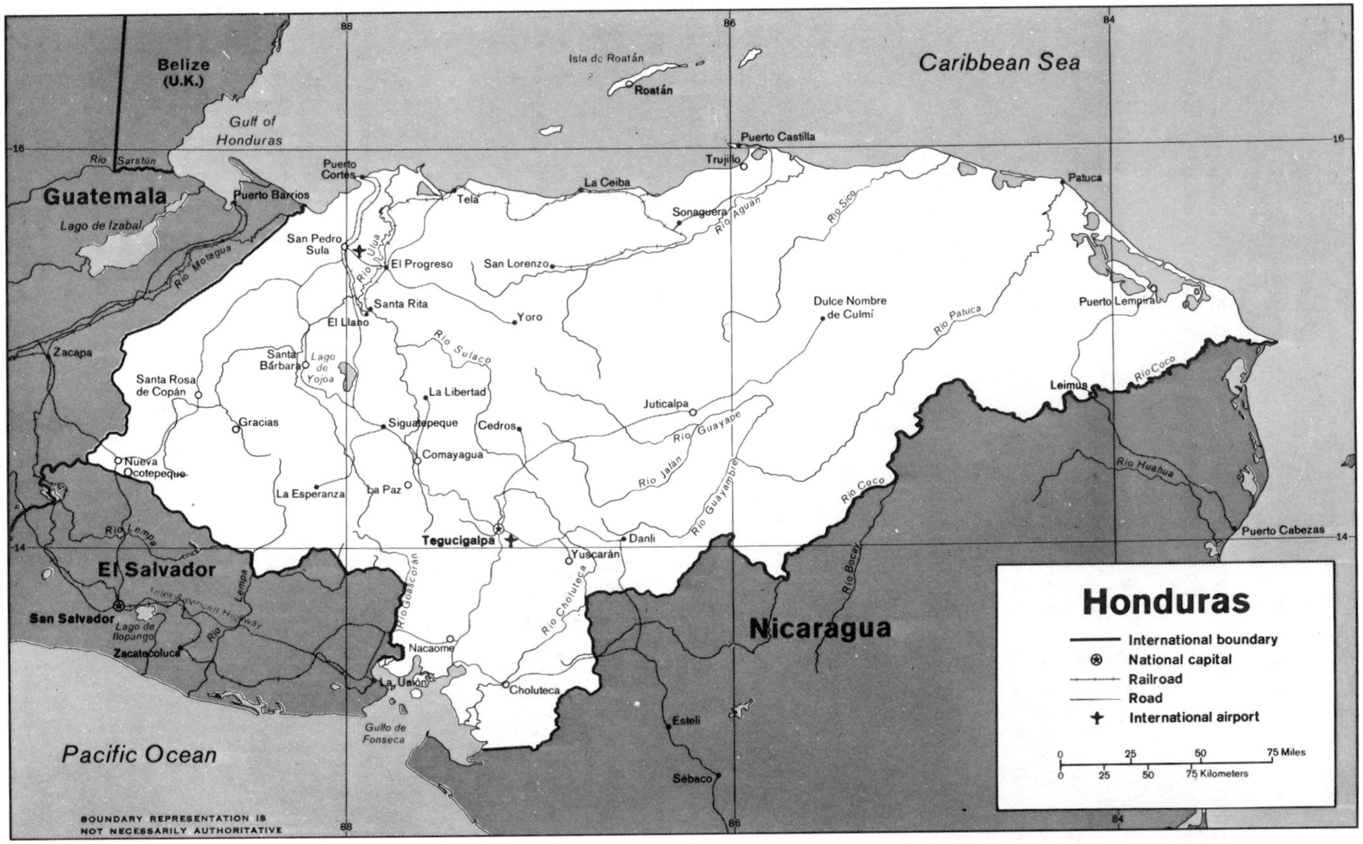
Honduras
International boundary
National capital
Railroad
Road
International airport
0 25 50 75 Miles
0 25 50 75 Kilometers
Caribbean Sea
Pacific Ocean
Gulf of Honduras
Golfo de Fonseca
Belize (U.K.)
Guatemala
El Salvador
Nicaragua
Isla de Roatán
Roatán
Puerto Castilla
Trujillo
La Ceiba
Tela
Puerto Cortés
Puerto Barrios
San Pedro Sula
El Progreso
San Lorenzo
Sonaguera
Patuca
Puerto Lempira
Leimus
Puerto Cabezas
Dulce Nombre de Culmí
Juticalpa
Yoro
Santa Rita
El Llano
Santa Bárbara
Lago de Yojoa
Santa Rosa de Copán
Gracias
Nueva Ocotepeque
La Esperanza
La Paz
Siguatepeque
Comayagua
La Libertad
Cedros
Tegucigalpa
Danlí
Yuscarán
Nacaome
La Unión
Choluteca
Zacapa
Lago de Izabal
San Salvador
Lago de Ilopango
Zacatecoluca
Estelí
Sébaco
Río Sarstún
Río Motagua
Río Ulúa
Río Sulaco
Río Aguán
Río Sico
Río Patuca
Río Coco
Río Guayape
Río Jalán
Río Guayambre
Río Choluteca
Río Goascorán
Río Lempa
Río Bocay
Río Huahua
Inter-American Highway
88
86
84
16
14
BOUNDARY REPRESENTATION IS NOT NECESSARILY AUTHORITATIVE

HONDURAS

BASIC FACT SHEET

OFFICIAL NAME: Republic of Honduras (República de Honduras)

ABBREVIATION: HO

CAPITAL: Tegucigalpa

HEAD OF STATE & HEAD OF GOVERNMENT: President Rafael Leonardo Callejas (from 1990)

NATURE OF GOVERNMENT: Constitutional democracy

POPULATION: 5,259,699 (1990)

AREA: 112,088 sq. km. (43,277 sq. mi.)

ETHNIC MAJORITY: Mestizos

LANGUAGE: Spanish

RELIGION: Roman Catholicism

UNIT OF CURRENCY: Lempira

NATIONAL FLAG: Tricolor consisting of a white horizontal stripe between two blue horizontal stripes with five blue stars on the white stripe

NATIONAL EMBLEM: The central feature of the emblem is an oval shield with a massive stone pyramid surrounded by blue skies and a blue sea. The shield is bordered with a white band inscribed with the name of the country, "Rep'ca de Honduras," the date of independence from Spain, "15 de Septiembre 1821," and the national motto, "Libre, Soberana e Independiente" ("Free, Sovereign and Independent"). The oval shield is embraced by two cornucopias spilling roses with a quiver of arrows at the crest. The emblem rests on a brown mound on which are shown a farmhouse, farm tools and trees.

NATIONAL ANTHEM: "Thy Flag Is a Floating Heavenly Light"

NATIONAL HOLIDAYS: September 15 (Independence Day, National Day); January 1 (New Year's Day); April 14 (Pan American Day); May 1 (Labor Day); October 3 (Birthday of Francisco Morazán); October 12 (Columbus Day); October 21 (Army Day); December 18 (King Alfonso's Decision Day). Also all major Roman Catholic feast days, December 24 and 25 (Christmas) and December 31.

NATIONAL CALENDAR: Gregorian

PHYSICAL QUALITY OF LIFE INDEX: 67

DATE OF INDEPENDENCE: September 15, 1821

DATE OF CONSTITUTION: January 1982

WEIGHTS & MEASURES: Both metric and Spanish systems are used.

GEOGRAPHICAL FEATURES

Honduras is in the Central American isthmus and occupies a land area of 112,088 sq. km. (43,277 sq. mi.) extending 663 km. (412 mi.) east-northeast to west-northwest and 317 km. (197 mi.) north-northwest to south-southeast. The coastline on the Gulf of Fonseca in the Southwest runs 74 km. (46 mi.), while the Caribbean coastline runs 591 km. (367 mi.).

Honduras shares its total international land boundary of 1,505 km. (935 mi.) with three countries: Nicaragua (922 km., 573 mi.), El Salvador (335 km., 208 mi.) and Guatemala 248 km., 154 mi.). The borders with Guatemala and Nicaragua have been delimited through arbitration. The border with Guatemala was settled in 1933 and has not been disputed since then. The Mosquito Coast (called after the Miskito Indian tribe) on the Caribbean between the Patuca and Segovia rivers was claimed by Nicaragua until the 1960s. The region was awarded to Honduras by King Alfonso XIII of Spain on December 18, 1906 (a date now celebrated as a national holiday) and, following border clashes, again by the International Court of Justice in 1960. The southwestern border with El Salvador is largely undefined and is the subject of recurrent disputes and border clashes. The undefined area extends from the tripoint in the Southwest along the Sumpul and Lempa rivers to the Goascorán River.

Offshore territories include the Bay Islands (Roatán, Guanaja and Utila); the Swan Islands, ceded by the United States in the 1970s, both in the Caribbean; and three islands in the Pacific (Tigre, Grand Zacate and Gueguensi). Port Amapala is on Tigre, and the Bay Islands form one of the 18 national departments.

The capital is Tegucigalpa, with a 1986 population of 604,600. Other major urban centers are: San Pedro Sula (399,700), La Ceiba (63,800), Choluteca (60,700), El Progreso (58,300), Puerto Cortés (40,900), Comayagua (30,100), Tela (27,200), Siguatepeque (25,200), Santa Rosa de Copán (20,000), Danli (18,800), Juticalpa (13,900) and Olanchito (13,000).

With the exception of the Ulúa and Aguán River valleys on the Caribbean coast and the southern coastal area, both nowhere wider than 120 km. (75 mi.), Honduras is generally mountainous. Two series of mountain ranges divided the country in half. The northern ranges, known as the Central American Cordillera, are an extension of a mountain chain that runs from Mexico to Nicaragua. The southern ranges are called the Volcanic Highlands and contain the country's two highest peaks, both over 2,750 m. (9,000 ft.).

The country is drained by an extensive river system. In the North, from west to east, are the Chamelecon, Ulúa, Aguán, Sico, Paulaya, Sicre, Patuca and Segovia rivers. In the South, from west to east, are the Lempa, Sumpul, Goascorán, Nacaome and Choluteca rivers flowing into the Gulf of Fonseca. Lake Yojoa in the West and Caratasca Lagoon in the Northwest are other important geographical features.

CLIMATE & WEATHER

The coastal regions have a wet, tropical climate, and the interior has a dry, cool climate. Both areas have a wet season from April to October and a dry season from November to March. Because most of the land lies inland between 750 and 2,200 m. (2,500 and 7,000 ft.), the country's climate may be described as temperate.

In the coastal lowlands the annual temperature averages 31°C (88°F); the intermontane valleys average 29.4°C (85°F) and the higher elevations average 23°C (73°F). In the northern coastal regions the rainfall varies between 1,770 mm. and 2,540 mm. (70 in. and 100 in.), while on the Pacific coastal plains rainfall is less, between 1,520 mm. and 2,030 mm. (60 in. and 80 in.). The capital city receives only 840 mm (33 in.).

From October to April the country receives the northerners, a moderately cold wind that tempers the heat. Hurricanes are common. The most destructive of these hurricanes was Hurricane Fifi in 1974, which took 12,000 lives, rendered 150,000 homeless, destroyed 90% of the banana plantations and caused damage estimated at $1.8 billion.

POPULATION

The population of Honduras was estimated in 1990 at 5,259,699, based on the last official census, held in 1974, when the population was 2,656,948.

In terms of density, the country is divided into three zones: western, central and eastern. The western zone, containing 27.3% of the land area, has 50.5% of the population; the central zone, with 28.2% of the land area, has 40.6% of the population; the eastern zone, with 44.5% of the land area, has only 8.9% of the population. The two most densely populated departments are Cortés and Valley in the western zone, with 50.5 per sq. km. (131 per sq. mi.) and 51.6 per sq. km. (133.9 per sq. mi.), respectively. The least populated area is Gracias a Dios Department, with 0.6 inhabitants per sq. km. (1.7 inhabitants per sq. mi.). Francisco Morazán Department contains 15.1% of the population, and Cortés Department contains 10.6% of the population. Population pressures in the southern departments have resulted from the influx of Salvadoran immigrants.

Cities with more than 10,000 inhabitants contain 63% of the urban population. The two largest cities, Tegucigalpa and San Pedro Sula, account for half of the entire urban population, and Tegucigalpa alone for 33%.

DEMOGRAPHIC INDICATORS

Population (millions): 5.259 (1990)
Year of last census: 1974
Sex distribution (% at last census): males, 49.5; females, 50.5
Population estimates and projections (millions)

1940: 1.146	1970: 2.553	2000: 6.203
1950: 1.390	1980: 3.316	2010: 7.828
1960: 1.873	1990: 4.674	

Age profile (% at last census)

0–14: 48.1	30–44: 13.9	60–74: 3.6
15–29: 25.8	45–59: 7.8	75 and over: 0.9

Median age (yrs.): 16.6 (1985)
Youth population (% age 15–24): 19.9 (1985); 20.4 (2000)
Total dependency ratio: 98.5 (1985)
Annual growth rate (%)

1950–55: 3.15	1975–1980: 3.46	2000–2005: 2.48
1955–60: 3.31	1980–1985: 3.59	2005–2010: 2.24
1960–65: 3.40	1985–1990: 3.18	2010–2015: 2.06
1965–70: 2.71	1990–1995: 3.00	2015–2020: 1.89
1970–75: 3.19	1995–2000: 2.75	2020–2025: 1.73

Hypothetical size of stationary population (millions): 18
Assumed year of reaching net reproduction rate of 1: 2025
Urban population (millions): 1.739 (1985)
Urban population (%): 42 (1988); 26 (1965)
Annual urban population growth rate (%, 1985–90): 5.06
Annual rural population growth rate (%, 1985–90): 1.84
Percentage of urban population in largest city: 33 (1980)
Number of cities of population over 500,000: 0 (1980)
Population density per sq. km. (per sq. mi.): 41.7 (108.0) (latest)

VITAL STATISTICS

Crude birth rate (/1,000): 37 (1990); 51 (1965)
Crude death rate (/1,000): 7 (1990); 17 (1965)
Infant mortality rate (/1,000 live births): 62 (1990)
Maternal mortality rate (/100,000 live births): 82 (1986–1987 est.)
Life expectancy (yrs.) at birth: males, 64; females, 67 (1990)
Gross reproduction rate (/woman) (1980–85): 3.00
Total fertility rate (/woman): 4.8 (1990)
Rate of natural increase (/1,000): 31.0 (1989)
Marriage rate (/1,000): 4.9 (1983)
Average household size: 5.7 (latest)

Honduras hosts United Nations-sponsored refugees from El Salvador, Nicaragua and Guatemala as well as nonsponsored refugees, the latter mostly Nicaraguan. As there is considerable evidence that Salvadoran guerrillas use the camps near the border as sanctuaries, these refugees are largely restricted to camps. Reception, care and protection of refugees by the Honduran government, however, is excellent.

Immigration from neighboring countries, particularly El Salvador, was significant until the Soccer War of 1969, when a law was passed severely limiting all immigration. There are U.S. communities in the Bay Islands, which are being developed as resorts. Many Hondurans immigrating to the United States are unskilled domestics.

Women are formally protected from discrimination under Honduran law. In practice, however, much depends on economic and social position. Education is equally available to men and women, and statistics

STATUS OF WOMEN INDICATORS
Number of women (million): 2.181 (1985)
Women of childbearing age (15–49) (% of pop.): 45 (1988)
Married women of childbearing age (15–49) using contraception (%): 41 (latest)
Women's literacy rate (%): 58.4 (1988)
Women in labor force (%): 18.3 (1988)
Total fertility rate (/woman): 4.8 (1990)
Women in national legislatures (%): 7 (1984)

reveal almost equal school attendance by males and females at all levels. Although women occupy judgeships and there are several respected women doctors, lawyers and other professionals, there are relatively few women in high government positions and fewer still in responsible positions in the private sector. In practice there remains some discrimination against women, especially in domestic cases. Ethnic minorities, concentrated on the northern coast, enjoy social and legal equality.

Family planning is supported officially both as a human right and as a social necessity. In addition to government programs, the private Honduran Association of Family Planning operates family planning services and clinics.

ETHNIC COMPOSITION

The predominant ethnic group is known as ladino (a broad term meaning all non-Indians), or more properly as mestizo (mixed Indian and Spanish). Ladinos constitute about 90% of the population. The remaining 10% is made up of 7% pure Indians, 2% blacks and 1% Caucasians.

Honduran society is the product of racial mixture, and though the term "mestizo" is applied to all persons of mixed stock, the precise degrees of mixture are indicated by specific terms:

Child	Father	Mother
Mestizo	Spaniard	Indian
Castiso	Spaniard	Mestiza
Españolo	Castiso	Spanish
Mulato	Negro	Spanish
Morisco	Spaniard	Mulata
Albino	Morisco	Spanish
Tornatras	Albino	Spanish
Tente en el Aire	Tornatras	Spanish
Lobo	Negro	Indian
Caribujo	Lobo	Indian
Barsino	Lobo	Mulata
Grifo	Lobo	Negro
Chaniso	Indian	Mestiza

There are two general groups of Indians: the settled agricultural Indians of the West, and the aboriginal Indians of the northern lowlands. Of the former group, the most important tribe is the Lenca, who have been systematically acculturated over the centuries. Though almost all of them speak Spanish, they still retain cultural and religious traits that set them apart from ladinos. The so-called Forest Indians of the northern lowlands are related to the South American rain forest peoples. These aboriginals, numbering over 35,000, belong to the Miskito, Payas, Sumo and Xicaque tribes. Isolated within their highlands, they have successfully resisted the inroads of Spanish language and culture.

The largest nonindigenous ethnic minority consists of black Caribs (also known as Garif or Morenos), descendants of runaway African slaves who intermarried with the Carib Indians of St. Vincent Island and who later were invited by the Spanish to migrate to the mainland. The Bay Islands have a more varied ethnic composition. The main settlements on the island of Roatán are predominantly black, the island of Utila is predominantly white and Guanaja is mixed. There are also small Mediterranean groups known as Sirios.

The resident alien population numbers about 50,000, of whom about 75% are Salvadorans and 10% are Guatemalans. There are flourishing Western communities in the capital and on the Caribbean coast.

LANGUAGE

Spanish is the official language spoken by all ladinos and the vast majority of Indians. English is spoken by a few Bay Islanders and blacks. The major Indian languages and their affiliations are as follows: Lenca (Chibchan group), Xicaque (Hokan-Siouan group), Chorti (Mayan group), Carib (Ge-Pano-Carib group), Miskito (Macro-Chibchan group) and Sumo (Macro-Chibchan group).

RELIGION

Honduras considers itself a Roman Catholic nation, and the church claims 97% of the population as nominal communicants. Catholicism is deeply rooted in Honduran traditions, and all Catholic feast days are celebrated with great ceremony. However, the Constitution guarantees religious freedom and retains the separation of church and state and the prohibition of political activities by the clergy that was introduced in 1880 and reaffirmed in the 1936 Constitution. Church schools receive government subsidies, and religious instruction is part of the school curriculum. The government and the Holy See maintain diplomatic relations. Church property and income are tax-free.

The church is ecclesiastically organized into the Archdiocese of Tegucigalpa, three dioceses (San Pedro Sula, Santa Rosa de Copán and Comayagua) and two prelatures (Choluteca and Olancho). There are 101 parishes served by 160 priests, of whom 80% are non-Hondurans. The church is faced with a severe shortage of priests; per capita there is one priest for 18,000 parishioners. The church also faces an internal division between an extremely conservative hierarchy and a socially active clergy.

Protestant missions have been active in Honduras since the 19th century. Generally their efforts have been successful, and the number of Protestants is rapidly growing. The largest Protestant denominations belong to the Methodists, the Church of God, the

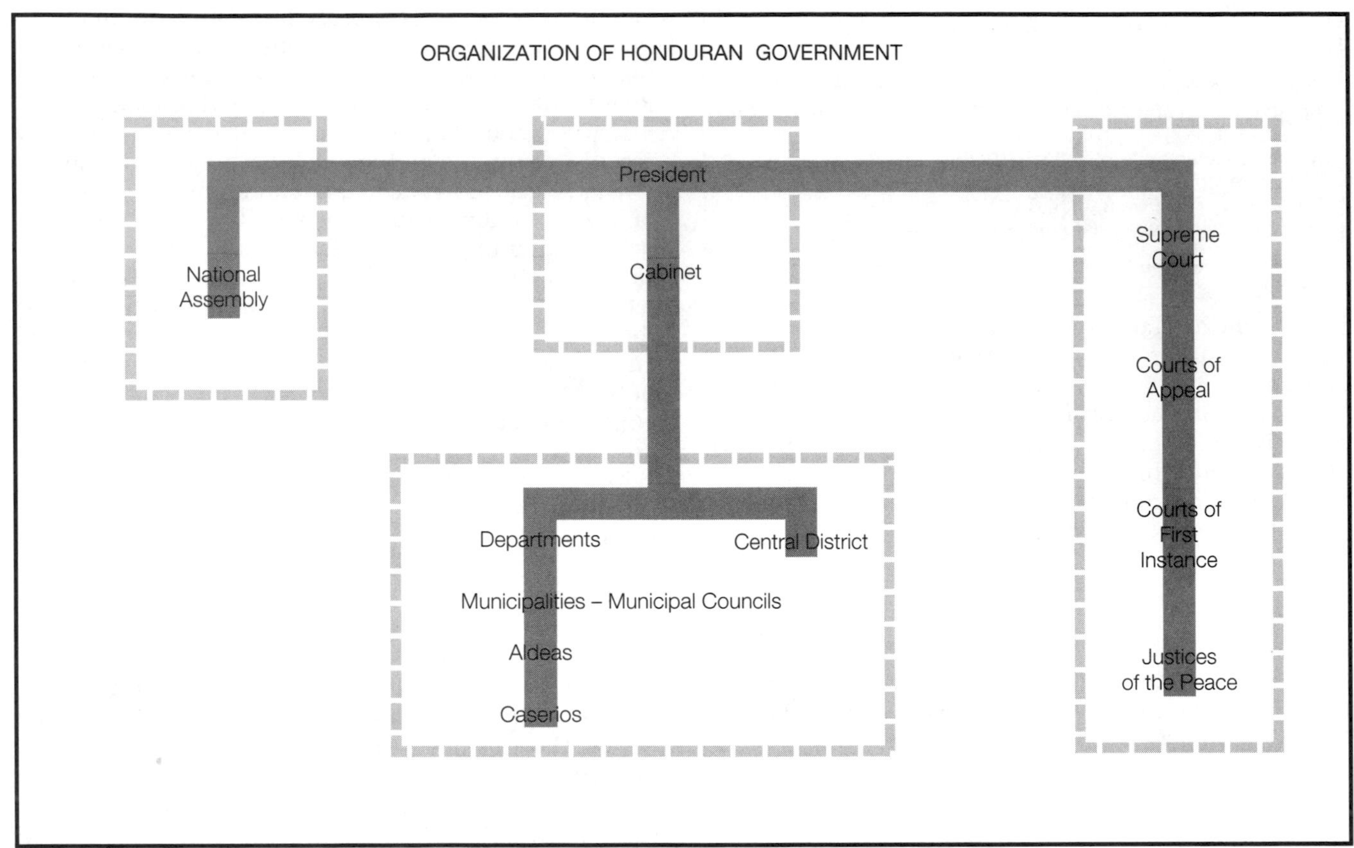

Seventh-Day Adventists and the Assemblies of God. Although the Protestant communities claim less than 100,000 members, they have more churches and more clergymen than the Catholic Church. The only concentration of Protestants is on the Bay Islands, where the population is almost entirely Protestant. Though vestiges of traditional beliefs and practices survive among Indians, no Indian religion is practiced in its original form. Jews number a few hundred, mostly in the capital.

HISTORICAL BACKGROUND

Honduras joined other provinces of Central America in declaring its independence from Spain in 1821. It was part of the Mexican empire of Agustín de Iturbide from 1822 to 1823 and a member of United Provinces of Central America from 1824 to 1838.

Honduras has a long history of political instability, revolution and military rule caused by the nation's chronically troubled economy, regional rivalries, lack of a strong sense of nationalism, flexible political morality and the enmity of neighboring countries. By the mid-1980s the nation had had 16 constitutions, 126 governments and over 380 armed rebellions. Between 1855 and 1932 Honduras had 67 different heads of state as power swung between relatively weak conservative and liberal governments. The greatest political influence was in the hands of foreign fruit companies, particularly United Fruit Co.

A measure of internal stability was achieved under the presidencies of Gen. Tiburcio Carias Andino and his successor Juan Manuel Galvez (1932–54). The election of Andino marked the political ascendancy of the military which Andino used to maintain power. From 1954 to 1982 the army held political power through a series of military coups in 1956, 1963, 1972 and 1978. Under pressure from the United States, the military returned the government to civilian hands in 1982 with the election of Roberto Suazo Córdova. However, the commander in chief of the army, Gen. Gustavo Adolfo Alvarez Martinez maintained considerable power until his removal in 1985. In November 1985 José Azcona Hoyt was elected president and assumed office the following January. His inauguration marked the first time an elected government was peacefully succeeded by another since 1929. Hoyt was succeeded by Rafael Leonardo Callejas in 1990.

CONSTITUTION & GOVERNMENT

Between 1825 and 1982 Honduras had 16 constitutions, all of them short-lived. Many of these constitutions had little political impact because they were regarded as statements of ideals rather than as legal instruments of practical government. The most recent Constitution, that of 1982, is longer than all previous ones.

The 1982 Constitution established a unitary and democratic republic with a president elected for a four-year term by the political party gaining the most votes in the national elections. Its individual and social guarantees include the right of habeas corpus (or *amparo*); freedom of expression, religion and assembly; the right of asylum for political refugees; prohibition of capital punishment, freedom from arbitrary arrest and detention; a ban on expropriation of private property without prior compensation; the right to civil marriage and divorce; and the right of free movement. Under one of its more important clauses the president, who also is the head of state, ceased to be the commander in chief. He may not succeed himself in office. The Constitution provides for a unicameral legislature whose members serve a four-year term concurrent with that of the chief executive. The military has the power of veto over ministerial appointments.

GOVERNMENT LIST
(July/August 1991)

President	Callejas, Rafael Leonardo
Minister of Communications, Public Works & Transport	Membreno, Mauro
Minister of Economy & Commerce	Medina Luna, Ramón
Minister of Finance & Public Credit	Villanueva, Benjamin
Minister of Foreign Affairs	Carias Zapata, Mario
Minister of Government & Justice	Cardona Arguelles, José Francisco
Minister of Labor & Social Security	Rosales Abella, Rodolfo
Minister of National Defense & Public Security	Romero Salgado, Alvaro Antonio, *Col.*
Minister of National Resources	Nufio Gamero, Mario
Minister of Planning, Coordination & Budget	Martínez Cantor, Manlio
Minister of Public Education	Martínez Guzman, Jaime
Minister of Public Health & Social Aid	Castellanos, César
Attorney General	Matute Murillo, Leonardo
President, Central Bank	Maduro, Ricardo

RULERS OF HONDURAS (from 1945)

February 1933–January 1949: Tiburcio Carlas Andlno
January 1949–December 1954: Juan Manuel Galvez
December 1954–October 1956: Julio Lozano Díaz
October 1956–December 1957: Roque I. Rodriguez
December 1957–October 1963: José Ramón Villeda Morales
October 1963–June 1971: Osvaldo López Arellano
June 1971–December 1972: Ramón Cruz Ucles
December 1972–April 1975: Osvaldo López Arellano
April 1975–August 1978: Juan Melgar Castro
August 1978–January 1982: Policarpo Paz García
January 1982–January 1986: Roberto Suazo Córdova
January 1986–January 1990: José Azcona Hoyo
January 1990– : Rafael Leonardo Callejas

FREEDOM & HUMAN RIGHTS

In terms of political and civil rights, Honduras is classified as a partly free country.

There are no political prisoners in Honduras. However, agrarian unrest plagues rural areas, leading to illegal land occupations and sporadic tensions. The government is anxious to avoid political activism among the peasants and has, in the past, resorted to intimidation and harassment for this purpose.

Late in 1982 political dissension was followed by arrests of left-wing sympathizers and the reported appearance of "death squads." In the same year the presence of 35,000 refugees from neighboring countries created further tensions and it was reported that the Honduran army killed several hundred Salvadoran refugees. Gen. Gustavo Alvarez who was thought to be responsible for these human rights violations was killed by left-wing guerrillas in January 1989. Amnesty International reported early in 1988 increased human rights violations by the army and right-wing "death squads." In February three human rights activists were murdered. One Honduran human rights organization reported 263 extra government executions in 1987 had been carried out by the military. Furthermore, the Honduran Government was ordered by the Inter-American Court of Human Rights to pay compensation to families whose members had "disappeared" between 1981 and 1984.

Freedom of the press, assembly and speech are respected. The press is free of state control, and in spite of occasional government expressions of annoyance, government programs come under rigorous scrutiny. The most common expression of government displeasure is the withholding of state advertising. Public demonstrations are held without interference. Although no parties have been banned, only those legally recognized can appear on the ballot. This rule was responsible for initially excluding the Christian Democratic Party because it was unable to overcome legal obstacles to its registration. However, in August 1980 it was formally recognized by the national electoral tribunal. The Honduran Communist Party, however, is still not registered. A massive voter census and registration process enrolled over 1.2 million persons, and the actual turnout of 82% was unprecedented in Honduran history.

CIVIL SERVICE

No current information is available on the Honduran civil service.

LOCAL GOVERNMENT

For purposes of local government, the country is divided into 18 departments.

Each department is headed by a governor appointed by the president. The 18 departments are divided into 282 municipalities, of which 63 are urban centers. Municipalities are further subdivided into units called *aldeas*, which are villages or hamlets. Settlements smaller than *aldeas* are known as *caserios*. There is also a central district, which consists of the capital city of Tegucigalpa and the department of Comayagua.

Municipalities are governed by popularly elected councils consisting of a mayor *(alcade)* and elected non-salaried officials known as *regidores*. Municipalities are technically autonomous and have wide powers of legislation and taxation. One of the most important functions of the municipal councils is the distribution of municipal lands to landless peasants under the *ejido* system.

FOREIGN POLICY

The principal event in the history of Honduran foreign relations from World War II to the 1980s was the so-called Soccer War with El Salvador in 1969, leading to strained relations between the two countries that persist to this day. Although the OAS mediated the dispute and arranged the withdrawal of Salvadoran troops, diplomatic relations remained broken and tensions remained high. The most severe aftereffects of the war were economic. Honduras has refused to trade with El Salvador or permit Salvadoran goods to pass through Honduran territory. Renewed hostilities broke out in 1976, and in 1986 the presidents of the two countries referred their various border disputes to the International Court of Justice. In 1988 Honduras and El Salvador allowed free passage of goods to their respective ports on the Atlantic and Pacific Oceans.

Relations with Guatemala have remained cordial since the border agreement of 1933.

The United States has had unbroken and close relations with Honduras since the mid-19th century. A 40-year Honduran claim was settled in 1972 when the United States acknowledged Honduran sovereignty over the Swan Islands. Honduras inclines toward a conservative position in inter-American and world affairs. In the 1980s Honduras emerged as the strongest ally of the United States in Central America, especially vis-à-vis Nicaragua. Although the dismissal of Gen. Gustavo Alvarez Martínez meant the loss of the most vociferous spokesman of open hostilities with Nicaragua, his policies have never been openly repudiated. In 1982 Honduras joined with Guatemala, Costa Rica and El Salvador in establishing the Central American Democratic Community (Communidad Democrática Centroamericana, CDC), in which the United States, Venezuela and Colombia serve as observers.

Relations with Nicaragua have been colored by a simmering dispute over the southeastern border. The dispute was settled through the mediations of the Inter-American Peace Committee of the OAS. However, after the takeover of Nicaragua by the Sandinistas, Honduran relations with that country were determined to a great extent by U.S. policy and by the Contras, Nicaragua's counter-revolutionaries, who controlled bases within Honduras. Opposition to the Sandinistas led the U.S., starting in 1983, to build permanent military bases in Honduras. The CIA was involved with both covert and overt operations against the Nicaraguan Government. In 1984 with the ouster of Gen. Alvarez, the Government re-examined U.S. military presence. The training of Salvadoran troops by U.S. advisers was suspended until an agreement was made with El Salvador over border disputes. In 1985 the U.S. administration refused to enter into a security pact with Honduras but promised protection from "Communist aggression."

By 1986 Honduras decided to repel Nicaraguan border violations. The revelation of the U.S. Iran-Contra misdealings created fears of withdrawal of U.S. support and led to President Azcona's request for the removal of the Contras from his country. Nevertheless, Honduras remained the U.S.'s strongest ally in the region.

The Esquipulas Agreement was a peace plan signed by Costa Rica, El Salvador, Guatemala, Honduras and Nicaragua in August 1987. Honduras only partially honored the stipulation that made it illegal for rebel forces to be encamped in foreign countries.

Following an invasion of Nicaraguan troops into the Bocay Valley in March 1988, President Azcona requested U.S. aid. Thirty-two hundred U.S. troops were airlifted to Honduras. But incursions of Nicaraguan troops into Honduras continued. In November the Honduran president ordered all Contras to leave.

An agreement in Tela, Honduras in August 1989 among the Central American Presidents improved conditions for demobilizing the Contras. But, the Tela Agreement was jeopardized in November 1989 when the Nicaraguan Government began a new offensive against the Contras and the Contras held their position in Honduras beyond the December deadline. The Nicaraguan government which had entered an action against Honduras at the International Court of Justice for illegally harboring rebels, suspended the action and hoped for an out-of-court settlement.

Honduras and the United States are parties to 35 treaties and agreements covering agricultural commodities, agriculture, aviation, defense, economic and technical cooperation, extradition, highways, investment guarantees, mapping, air force missions, army missions, nationality, the Peace Corps, postal matters, publications, relief supplies and packages, telecommunications, territorial sovereignty, trade and commerce, visas and weather stations.

Honduras joined the United Nations in 1945. It is a member of 15 U.N. organizations and 28 other international organizations.

PARLIAMENT

According to the Constitution, the national legislative body is the Asamblea Nacional (National Assembly), a 134-member body that replaced the former Congress of Deputies. It meets annually for a 100-day session. The National Assembly possesses broad constitutional powers designed to prevent absolute presidential rule, although in practice it is a tame appendage of the presidency. Besides its legislative powers, the National Assembly elects the justices of the Supreme Court, the attorney general, the comptroller general and, in cases of deadlocked elections, the president. The National Assembly could also impeach the president, declare war and make peace, and amend the Constitution. Following the 1989 elections, the Liberal Party won 71 seats and the National Party 55. The remaining seats went to the National Innovation and Unity Party.

POLITICAL PARTIES

Honduras functions under an essentially two-party system with the National Party (PN) and the Liberal Party (PL) the nation's dominant political groups.

The PN, founded in 1923, has held power for most periods in recent years. It is a close-knit organization with ties to the military and with a clearly defined program stressing modest social reforms, strict observance of the Constitution, free elections, financial reform, and protection of capital and labor. Its current leader is President Rafael Leonardo Callejas. The PL, on the other hand, is closely identified with the cause of social reform, and its strength lies mainly in the urban areas and with labor groups. It is currently led by Roberto Suazo Córdova, a former president. Both parties are dominated by personalities rather than ideologies, and factional splits are common.

The Liberal Party is split into a number of factions, and these factions into subfactions. The left wing of the party consists of the Popular Liberal Alliance (Alianza Liberal del Pueblo, Alipo) including an antimilitary and a pro-business faction. The old guard of the Liberal Party, the Rodistas, are antimilitary conservatives, while the right-wing technocrats (Suazocordovistas) are pro-army and pro-business.

The National Party is also riven by factions, of which the *oficialistas* are predominant.

Other legal parties include the National Innovation and Unity Party, the Christian Democratic Party, the Democratic Action Party and the Honduran Social Democratic Party.

The principal leftist coalition is the Honduran Patriotic Front of the Honduran Revolutionary Movement, an alliance of some 30 groups including the Communist Party, Cinchonero Popular Liberation Movement, Morazanista Front of Honduran Liberation, Lorenzo Zelaya People's Revolutionary Front, Revolutionary Party of Central American Workers, and Movement of Revolutionary Unity. Paramilitary right-wing groups include the White Hand and the Honduran Anti-Communist Movement.

PRINCIPAL ECONOMIC INDICATORS

Gross National Product (U.S. $ billions): 4.495 (1989)
GNP per capita (U.S. $): 900 (1989)
GNP average annual growth rate (%, 1980–89): 2.3
GNP per capita average annual growth rate (%, 1987–89): 0.3
Average annual rate of inflation (%, 1980–88): 4.7
Consumer price index (1980 = 100) 1986
- All items: 144
- Food: 126

Average annual growth rate (%, 1980–88)
- General government consumption: 4.9
- Private consumption: 1.9
- Gross domestic investment: −0.6

BALANCE OF PAYMENTS, 1988
(U.S. $ millions)

Current account balance: −319.0
Merchandise exports: 893.0
Merchandise imports: −916.7
Trade balance: −23.7
Other goods, services & income +: 135.8
Other goods, services & income −: −476.1
Other goods, services & income net: −340.3
Private unrequited transfers: 175
Official unrequited transfers: 27.5
Capital other than reserves: 95
Net errors & omissions: 120.9
Counterpart items: −32.7
Liabilities constituting foreign authorities reserves: −10.5
Total change in reserves: 14.2

GROSS DOMESTIC PRODUCT

GDP nominal (L. billions): 9.770
GDP per capita (U.S. $): 890 (1988)
Average annual growth rate of GDP (%, 1980–88): 1.7
GDP by type of expenditure (%) 1987
- Consumption:
  - Private: 72
  - Government: 17
- Gross domestic investment: 15
- Gross domestic saving: 11 (1988)
- Foreign trade
  - Exports: 23
  - Imports: 27

Cost components of GDP (%) 1987
- Net indirect taxes: 12
- Consumption of fixed capital: 3
- Compensation of employees and net operating surplus: 84

Sectoral origin of GDP (%) 1987
- Primary
  - Agriculture: 19
  - Mining: 1
- Secondary
  - Manufacturing: 13
  - Construction: 5
  - Public utilities: 2
- Tertiary
  - Transportation & communications: 6
  - Trade: 12
  - Finance: 13
  - Other services: 12
  - Government: 5

Average annual sectoral growth rates (%, 1980–88)
- Agriculture: 1.1
- Industry: 0.8
- Manufacturing: 1.9
- Services: 2.4

ECONOMY

Honduras is one of the world's lower-middle-income countries. Honduras is one of the poorest Central American states. Honduras has a free-market economy in which the dominant sector is private. The economy is based primarily on agriculture, which employs almost two-thirds of the labor force and produces two-thirds of export income. The nation is one of the largest exporters of bananas in the world.

The economy suffers from several basic problems: a high population growth rate; a lack of basic services; an inefficient public sector; and dependency on two crops, coffee and bananas, whose prices have been extremely volatile. During the 1980s the economy also was disrupted by hurricanes, border conflicts and the cost of accommodating the Nicaragua Contras.

PUBLIC FINANCE

The Honduran fiscal year is the calendar year. The government follows a conservative budgetary policy, and in most years there is a surplus on the current account.

Of the 1986 revenue of 3.04 billion lempira over one-tenth comes from tax on production and internal trade, less than a fifth from import duties and individual income tax, over a third from development revenue and over a fifth from non-tax revenue. Of the 3.19 billion lempira expenditure, wages and salaries made up almost a third, about one-fifth went to development and less than a fifth was applied to debt servicing.

Since the early 1970s the government has played an increasing role in the management of the economy. Government capital expenditures have increased 65% during the early 1980s while expenditures increased only 34% during the same period. Autonomous institutions now absorb more than 40% of the government budget, and this share is growing.

Beginning in 1955 various development plans were launched, all directed toward four main goals: agricultural development, infrastructure development, industrial development and development of human resources. Although heavy investments were made, the targets were not met—less because of the lack of financing than because of a shortage of qualified personnel. Overall responsibility for economic planning rests with the National Superior Planning Council, headed by the minister of economy.

Honduras has been a major recipient of foreign aid, almost all of it in the form of loans. From 1970 to 1987, the U.S. committed $1.1 billion in aid while other Western nations, the ADA and OF committed $690 million.

CENTRAL GOVERNMENT EXPENDITURES, 1972

% of total expenditures
- Defense: 12.4
- Education: 22.3
- Health: 10.2
- Housing, social security, welfare: 8.7
- Economic services: 28.3
- Other: 18.1

Total expenditures as % of GNP: 16.1
Overall surplus or deficit as % of GNP: −2.9

CENTRAL GOVERNMENT REVENUES, 1972

% of total current revenues
- Taxes on income, profit & capital gain: 19.2
- Social security contributions: 3.0
- Domestic taxes on goods & services: 33.8
- Taxes on international trade & transactions: 28.2
- Other taxes: 2.3
- Current nontax revenue: 13.5

Total current revenue as % of GNP: 13.2
General government consumption as % of GDP: 17 (1988)
Average annual growth rate of general government consumption (%, 1980–88): 4.9

FOREIGN AID, 1987

Total foreign aid (U.S. $ millions): 231.2
- Bilateral: 204.4
- Multilateral: 26.9

CURRENCY & BANKING

The Honduran unit of currency is the lempira, divided into 100 centavos. Coins are issued in denominations of one, two, five, 10, 20 and 50 centavos; notes are issued in denominations of one, five, 10, 20, 50 and 100 lempiras.

The March, 1991 exchange value of lempira is $1 = L5.480.

The banking system consists of a central bank, 11 commercial banks, two savings banks and six development banks. The central bank, Banco Central de Honduras, is the sole bank of issue and the government's fiscal agent. The Banco Nacional de Fomento is the principal government development bank. Of the commercial banks, the largest is the Atlantida Bank, which is affiliated with Chase Manhattan Bank of New York. The second-largest is the Banco de Honduras, which is affiliated with Citibank of New York.

Interest rates are set by the Central Bank.

FINANCIAL INDICATORS, 1989

Total reserves minus gold (SDRs millions): 16
SDRs (millions): 0
Reserve position in IMF (SDRs millions): 0
Foreign exchange (SDRs millions): 16
Gold (fine troy oz. millions): .02
Ratio of external debt to total reserves: 49.6 (1988)
Central bank 1989
- Assets (%)
  - Foreign assets: 3.6
  - Claims on government: 57.0
  - Claims on banks: 39.4
  - Claims on private sector: 0.0
- Liabilities (%)
  - Reserve money: 35.2
  - Government deposits: 16.6
  - Foreign liabilities: 50.9
  - Capital accounts: 18.2

Money supply 1989
- Stock (L. billions): 1.524
- M1 per capita: 330

Private banks 1989
- Assets (%)
  - Loans to government: 23.3
  - Loans to private sector: 68.6
  - Reserves: 7.3
  - Foreign assets: 0.8
- Liabilities
  - Deposits (L. billions): 3.838
  - of which %
    - Demand deposits: 20.2
    - Savings deposits: 45.3
    - Government deposits: 9.1
    - Foreign liabilities: 1.3

External debt 1988
- Total (U.S. $ billions): 3.318
  - of which public (U.S. $ billions): 2.739
  - of which private (U.S. $ millions): 98
- Debt service (long-term)
  - Total (U.S. $ millions): 265
  - Repayment
    - Principal (%): 54.3
    - Interest (%): 45.7
- Debt service ratio (%): 25.4
- External public debt as % of GNP: 65.9
- Debt service as % of GNP: 6.4
- Debt service as % of exports: 25.5
- Terms of public borrowing
  - Commitments (U.S. $ millions): 251
  - Average interest rate (%): 7.3
  - Average maturity (yrs.): 17
- Net flow of publicly guaranteed external capital (U.S. $ millions): 146
- Net direct private investment (U.S. $ millions): 47

GROWTH PROFILE
(Annual Growth Rates, %)

Projected population (1988–2000): 2.9
Projected crude birth rate (/1,000) (1990–95): 37.1
Projected crude death rate (/1,000) (1990–95): 7.2
Urban population (1980–88): 5.6
Labor force (1985–88): 3.9
GNP (1980–89): 2.3
GNP per capita (1987–89): 0.3
GDP (1980–88): 1.7
Inflation (1980–88): 4.7
Agriculture (1980–88): 1.1
Industry (1980–88) 0.8
Manufacturing (1980–88): 1.9 (latest)
Services (1980–88): 2.4
Money holdings (1980–88): 11.7
Manufacturing earnings per employee (1980–86): −0.4
Energy production (1980–88): 6.7
Energy consumption (1980–88): 3.2
Exports (1980–88): 2.8
Imports (1980–88): −0.3
General government consumption (1980–88): 4.9
Private consumption (1980–88): 1.9
Gross domestic investment (1980–88): −0.6

AGRICULTURE

Of the total land area of 112,088 sq. km. (43,277 sq. mi.), 38% is considered to be potentially arable land, or 0.01 sq. km. (1.33 ha.) per capita.

Land tenure is characterized by great disparities. Of the estimated 195,000 farms, 75% are under 0.1 sq. km. (10.1 ha.) in size, and some 27,000 farms are less than 0.01 sq. km. (1.2 ha.) in size. About 60% of the arable land is in the hands of the government and two United States-owned firms, United Brands and Standard Fruit. Another 27% of farmland is owned by 667 large landowners.

About 21% of the farms are worked by owners; the average size of these farms is 0.4 sq. km. (36.4 ha.). Another 34% are worked by *ejidatarios*, or farmers who work municipal lands called *ejido*, which comprise 17% of all arable land. The average size plot cultivated by each *ejidatario* is 0.1 sq. km. (12.1 ha.). Another 11% of the farms are cultivated by squatters; 13% by sharecroppers and tenants; and 4% by *colonos*, or workers who are permitted to farm a part of the employers' land for themselves as part of their wages. The balance of 17% is cultivated by a mixed group of tenants. Farms under the mixed tenancy average 0.2 sq. km. (18.2 ha.), while the *colonos* and the sharecroppers work an average of only 0.02 sq. km. (2 ha.). Landless laborers number 138,000.

Irrigation is limited to large plantations growing bananas, sugar and cotton. The use of mechanization and fertilizers is not widespread. Farming methods are inefficient, and yields are low. Hand tools are used on almost all the farms. Crop rotation is not generally practiced, and when the yields fall, the land is allowed to remain fallow.

Land reform has been an important political issue since 1829, when the first law was passed providing for the sale of lands belonging to the Spanish crown. In 1962 the National Agrarian Institute was created to sponsor land reform and resettlement schemes. In 1965 plans were made for distribution 6,000 sq. km. (600,000 ha.) among 100,000 families over a five-year period. The peasants' lobby, the National Front of United Peasants, has been pressing vigorously for implementation of this reform.

The most important export crops are bananas and coffee. The major food crops are corn, rice and sorghum. Bananas, benefiting from higher yields and better prices, are the leading export, with 30% of total exports, narrowly edging out coffee.

Beef cattle are raised in all departments, but the largest herds are in Choluteca and Francisco Morazán, and the best herds in Cortés, Yoro, Olancho and El Paraiso. The national herd consists primarily of two

AGRICULTURAL INDICATORS

Agriculture's share of GDP (%): 21 (1989)
Average annual growth rate (%, 1980–88): 1.1
Value added in agriculture (U.S. $ millions): 956 (1988)
Cereal imports (000 metric tons): 144 (1988)
Index of agricultural production (1979–81 = 100): 108 (1986)
Index of food production per capita (1979–81 = 100): 76 (1986–88)
Number of tractors: 3,370 (1986)
Total fertilizer consumption (000 metric tons): 22.7 (1985–86)
Fertilizer consumption (g./ha., hundreds): 190 (1987–88)
Number of farms (000): 195 (1974)
Average size of holding (ha.): 13.5 (1974)
Size class (%) (1974)
  Below 1 ha. (below 2.47 ac.): 17.3
  1–5 ha. (2.47–12.35 ac.): 46.6
  5–10 ha. (12.35–24.7 ac.): 14.5
  10–20 ha. (24.7–49.4 ac.): 9.8
  20– 50 ha. (49.4–123.5 ac.): 7.8
  50–200 ha. (123.5–494 ac.): 3.3
  Over 200 ha. (over 494 ac.): 0.8
Tenure (%) 1974
  Owner-operated: 99.8
  Rented: 0.0
  Other: 0.2
Farms as % of total land area: 23.5 (1974)
Land use (%) 1985–87
  Cropland: 16
  Pasture: 23
  Forest: 32
  Other: 30
Yields (kg./ha.) 1989
  Grains: 990
  Roots & tubers: 7,557
  Legumes: 508
  Milk (kg./animal): 895
Production 1989
  Fruits (million metric tons): 1.408
  Vegetables (000 metric tons): 142
Livestock (000) 1989
  Cattle: 2,601
  Horses: 170 (1986)
  Sheep: 7
  Pigs: 600
Forestry 1988
  Production of roundwood (million cubic meters): 5.957
    of which industrial roundwood (%): 15.8
  Value of exports (U.S. $ millions): 31.528
Fishing 1988
  Total catch (000 metric tons): 25.5
    of which marine (%): 88.7
  Value of exports (U.S. $ millions): 56.130

breeds called *chino* and *barroso*. Both United Brands and Standard Fruit have large cattle ranches.

Forests cover 45% of the total land area and include hardwoods and softwoods. The main stands are mahogany, *granadino*, *guayacán*, walnut, rosewood, cedar and pine. The development of forest resources is the responsibility of the National Corporation for Forestry Development. Wood is the fourth-largest export.

Only small-scale fishing is done on the Pacific Coast, in the Gulf of Fonseca. The main fishing grounds lie near the Bay Islands. Of the total catch of 10,572 tons in 1988, a total of 5,495 tons were shrimp. Almost all of the shrimp production is exported. Freshwater fishing is done in the many rivers and in Lake Yojoa.

Agricultural credit is provided by Banco Nacional de Fomento.

MANUFACTURING

Although the rate of industrial growth was the highest among all sectors—5.5% during 1973–83—Honduran industry is the least developed in Central America. The sector has suffered from insufficient investment, lack of spare parts, and depressed overall demand from the Central American Market (CACM). Its contribution to the GDP in 1987 was only 24%, down from previous years.

In the mid-1980s there were 849 manufacturing establishments each employing more than five workers. In 1982 a total of 87 factories closed, and the remainder were working at 50% capacity. Sawmills constitute the largest single subsector, accounting for 18% of the total number of plants, followed by furniture shops (12%) and brick and tile makers (9%). Over 70% of all plants are family-owned. Some 90% of the establishments are in the departments of Atlantida, Cortés and Francisco Morazán, and 75% are concentrated around the city of San Pedro Sula. By value of production, the largest sectors are food processing, lumber, beverages, chemicals, clothing and cement.

MANUFACTURING INDICATORS, 1987

Average annual growth rate: 1.9 (latest)
Share of GDP (%): 13 (latest)
Labor force economically active in manufacturing (% est.): 14.1 (1984)
Value added in manufacturing (U.S. $ millions): 515
  Food & tobacco (%): 56 (1986)
  Textiles & clothing (%): 10 (1986)
  Machinery & transport equipment (%): 1 (1986)
  Chemicals (%): 4 (1986)
Earnings per employee in manufacturing 1987
  Growth rate (%, 1980–86): −0.4
Total earnings as % of value added: 38

Food processing, pharmaceuticals, beauty aids, woodworking and textiles are particularly expansive sectors, as are individual enterprises with significant support by or participation with government agencies, of note being CONADI (a state investment/venture capital corporation), FONDEI (industrial development fund), INA (agrarian reform institute), COHDEFOR (state forest products corporation) and CORFINO (state Olancho forest reserve development corporation). The principal industrial development organization is Corporación Nacional de Inversiones (CONADI), and industrial credit is provided by Financiera Centroamerica and Banco Financiera Hondurena.

Honduras encourages foreign investment participation in industry, mining and agriculture. U.S. investment in Honduras was estimated at $265 million in 1984, the bulk of which was accounted for by United Brands and Standard Fruit. The former was involved in an international bribe scandal in which it admitted paying $1.25 million to President Osvaldo López Arellano for a reduction in taxes. Following the 1975 minicoup, President Melgar announced the suspension of the privileges of the two U.S. firms pending eventual nationalization.

Four of the five largest corporations in Honduras are United States-owned. Foreign capital is given the same treatment and protection as domestic capital. There are no restrictions on repatriation of profits, dividends, interest or capital. However, firms in the distribution and lumber industries must have 51% Honduran ownership. Also, foreign construction firms must have a Honduran partner, as no foreign firm is known to have successfully registered with the College of Engineers. In recent years Honduras has attracted new foreign investment in petroleum exploration, mining, pharmaceuticals, wood products, tourism, pineapples, tobacco, shrimp farming, cement, clothing and textiles. This open-door policy is at times made ineffective by lack of coordination and conflicting goals among relevant government agencies. The underdeveloped state of the Honduran bureaucracy can represent a source of frustration for foreign investors. This is particularly true of foreign investors without a well-connected local partner.

Events in the neighboring countries of Nicaragua and El Salvador have had an adverse effect on capital inflows as investors became wary and international banks cut back by imposing country loan limits on Honduras. Also, the regional situation has contributed to a certain amount of capital flight, particularly during stress periods such as the time of the fall of the Somoza regime in Nicaragua and the fall of the Romero government in El Salvador.

MINING

The mining sector is small, but because most of the production is exported, it makes an important contribution to the economy. Until 1954 the largest mining company was the New York and Honduras Rosario Mining Company, which produced from 1882 until 1954 over $60 million worth of gold and silver. By 1977 gold production had declined to 77 kg. (170 lbs.). In 1985 mineral production included 8,584 tons of lead, 21,334 tons of zinc and 44 tons of silver.

ENERGY

In 1982 Honduras consumed nearly nine times the amount of coal it produced, so that much of its energy production was reliant on mineral imports (12.3% of the value of total 1988 imports). Hydroelectric power is expanding and wood continues as a primary source of domestic energy.

ENERGY INDICATORS

Average annual energy production growth rate (%, 1980–88): 6.7
Energy consumption per capita (kg. oil equivalent): 203 (1988)
Energy imports as % of merchandise exports: 14 (1988)
Average annual growth rate of energy consumption (%, 1980–88): 3.2
Electricity 1988
  Installed capacity (000 kw.): 290
  Production (billion kw.-hr.): 1.090
    % fossil fuel: 19.3
    % hydro: 80.7
  Consumption per capita (kw.-hr.): 258
Natural gas
  Proved reserves (billion cu. m.): 0 (1990)
  Production (million cu. m.): 0 (1989)
  Consumption (million cu. m.): 0 (1988)
Petroleum
  Production (million bbl.): 0 (1989)
  Consumption (million bbl.): 2 (1988)
  Refining capacity (000 bbl./day): 14 (1990)
Coal
  Reserves (million metric tons): 21 (latest est.)

LABOR

Wages and working conditions are governed by legislation, particularly the Labor Code of 1970. The basic workweek is 48 hours, with overtime pay ranging from 25% to 75% of base pay. Workers are also entitled to 11 paid holidays during the year, double pay for work on holidays, paid vacation and severance pay. In certain sectors employers must also provide free schools, medical care and housing facilities. Mandatory minimum wage rates were first set in 1967 and are periodically revised. In 1982 weekly wages in manufacturing were L197.84. There are three government bodies concerned with labor. The director general of labor collects statistics, registers labor unions and handles labor contracts. The inspector general of labor enforces the Labor Code and ensures compliance. The director general of Social Security coordinates welfare programs.

LABOR INDICATORS, 1984

Total economically active population (millions): 1.256
  % working-age (15–64): 53.6
  % female: 16.7
Activity rate (%)
    Total: 29.7
    Male: 49.3
    Female: 9.9
Sectoral employment of economically active (%)
  Agricultural, forestry, fishing: 57.2
  Construction: 3.5
  Manufacturing, mining, quarrying, public utilities: 14.1
  Trade, hotels, restaurants: 8.5
  Transportation, communications: 3.0
  Finance, real estate: 1.0
  Services: 12.8
Average annual growth rate of labor force (%, 1985–2000): 3.9
Unemployment (000): 254 (1983)
Labor under 20 years (%): 22.4 (1984)
Earnings in manufacturing (/worker) (/wk) (L.): 107.10 (1985)

Some 7% to 10% of the labor force is estimated to be unionized. Most of the unions belong to one of four national labor federations: the Workers' Confederation of Honduras, comprising three federations and 150,000 members; the General Confederation of Labor; the Federation of Southern Workers; and the National Front of United Peasants. The Institute of Central American Trade Union Studies is in Honduras.

The Labor Code provides for conciliation, mediation and arbitration machinery. Only 10% to 20% of industrial disputes reach the labor courts.

FOREIGN COMMERCE

In 1987 estimated imports of $969 million and exports of $863 million left an unfavorable balance of $106 million. Of the imports over one-quarter was machinery and transportation equipment; less than a quarter was basic manufactures; chemical products and mineral fuels made up almost one-third; and food products made up almost a tenth. Coffee and bananas make up the bulk of this country's exports with lesser percentages of shrimp and lobster, wood, and lead and zinc being exported. The major import and export country is the U.S. To a much lesser degree Japan, Venezuela, Mexico and Guatemala are import sources. Export destinations in order of importance are Germany, Japan, Italy and Belgium.

Honduras is a member of the Central American Common Market, but because of the war with El Salvador has suspended participation in the group indefinitely.

FOREIGN TRADE INDICATORS, 1988

Exports (U.S. $ billions): 1.0
Imports (U.S. $ billions): 1.4
Balance of trade (U.S. $ billions): −0.4
Annual growth rate (1980–88), exports (%): 2.8
Annual growth rate (1980–88), imports (%): −0.3
International reserves in terms of months of imports covered: 0.5
Terms of trade (1980 = 100): 102
Import price index (1980 = 100): 95.7 (1986)
Export price index (1980 = 100): 96.1 (1986)

Direction of Trade (%), 1985

	Imports	Exports
European Community	12.9	26.6
United States	32.9	48.9
U.S.S.R. & Eastern European economies	0.3	3.9
Japan	5.9	6.7

Composition of Trade (%), 1986

	Imports	Exports
Food and agricultural raw materials	9.7	90.8
Fuels & other energy	25.9	0.9
Mineral ores & concentrates	0.3	4.5
Manufactured goods	64.2	3.9
of which chemicals	17.6	1.1
of which machinery	21.4	0.1

TRANSPORTATION & COMMUNICATIONS

The government-owned Ferrocarril Nacional has track linking Potrerillos with Puerto and La Ceiba. The capital, Tegucigalpa, is not serviced by rail links. Tela Railroad, owned by United Brands, and the Vaccaro

Line, owned by Standard Fruit, operate 340 km. (211 mi.) of track, but in 1975 the government announced steps to nationalize these lines.

Most of the rivers are short, but small craft can navigate 465 km. (289 mi.) of inland waterways.

There are five ports on the Atlantic for international commerce and 17 for coastal shipping. The five major ones are Puerto Cortés (the third-busiest in Central America), La Ceiba, Tela, Roatán and Trujillo. Tela is operated by United Brands and La Ceiba by Standard Fruit. The only port on the Pacific is Amapala, on Tigre Island.

TRANSPORTATION INDICATORS

Roads (latest)
- Length, km. (mi.): 18,494 (11,492)
- Paved (%): 12

Motor vehicles (latest)
- Automobiles: 78,080
- Trucks and buses: 24,142
- Persons per vehicle: 43

Railroads (latest)
- Track, km. (mi.): 996 (619)

Merchant marine
- Vessels (over 100 tons): 677 (1989)
- Total deadweight tonnage (000): 981.7 (1989)
- Oil tankers (000 GRT): 51 (1985)

Ports (pre-1986)
- Cargo loaded (million metric tons): 1.392
- Cargo unloaded (million metric tons): 1.138

Air
- Km. (mi.) flown (millions): 9.8 (6.1) (1985)
- Passenger-km. (passenger-mi.) (millions): 483.8 (300.6) (latest)
- Freight, metric ton-km. (short ton-mi.) (millions): 15.9 (10.9) (latest)
- Mail, metric ton-km. (short ton-mi.) (millions): 0.1 (0.07) (1987)
- Airports with scheduled flights: 9 (1990)

Inland waterways (latest)
- Length, km. (mi.): 465 (289)

COMMUNICATION INDICATORS, 1988

Telephones
- Total (000): 69
- Persons per telephone: 64

Phone traffic (million minutes)
- Local: 293.600
- Long distance: 212.700
- Combined national: 506.300
- International: 21.000

Post office 1978
- Number of post offices: 508
- Pieces of mail handled (millions): 60.689

Telegraph 1988
- Total traffic (000 calls): 859
  - National: 845
  - International: 14

Telex
- Subscriber lines: 854
- Traffic (million minutes): 3.198

Telecommunications 1990
- Satellite stations: 2

TOURISM & TRAVEL INDICATORS, 1986

Total tourist receipts (U.S. $ millions): 28 (1988)
Expenditures by nationals abroad (U.S. $ millions): 28 (1988)
Number of hotel beds (000): 8
Average length of stay (nights): 4

The Inter-Ocean Highway links the Pacific and the Caribbean, passing through both Tegucigalpa and San Pedro Sula.

The national airline is SAHSA (Servicio Aéreo de Honduras), which operates six aircraft on internal and external routes. There are two other private airlines: TAN (Transportes Aéreos Nacionales) and LANSA (Lineas Aéreas Nacionales). The major international airport is Toncontín, 6.5 km. (4.0 mi.) from Tegucigalpa, with a runway of over 2,500 m. (8,000 ft.). There are two other international airports, and a new air strip was opened at Roatán in 1988. A new airport at Tegucigalpa is under construction with aid from the Spanish government.

Tourism centers around the Mayan ruins and the fishing and boating facilities in Trujillo Bay and Lake Yojoa.

DEFENSE

The defense structure is headed by the president, who is also a military officer. The line of command runs through the secretary of defense, the Department of Defense and the Superior Council of National Defense. The Council may be said to be the most powerful body in the country—it is the arena where all the top commanders debate and decide national policy. In recent history it has installed and removed presidents at will. There are 10 military zones.

Under the Constitution, military service is compulsory for all male adults, but during peacetime, the armed forces are composed mainly of volunteers. The liability for military service is theoretically for 18 months between the ages of 18 and 32 but, on an average, each recruit spends only eight months on active service. From 1957 officers are recruited directly from the Francisco Morazán Military School in the capital which admits cadets after a stiff competitive examination for a five-year course. Graduates spend an additional year in training abroad, usually at the U.S. Army School of the Americas in the Panama Canal Zone. Air Force cadets receive additional training at the Military Aviation School at Toncontin.

Reserves are estimated at 50,000 but they are not organized into units.

The total strength of the armed forces is 19,200.

Army

Personnel: 15,400

Organization: 10 military zones; 3 infantry brigades, each 2 infantry and 1 artillery battalions; 5 independent infantry battalions; 1 engineer battalion; 1 special forces battalion; 1 presidential guard

Equipment: 12 tanks; 82 combat vehicles; 24 howitzers; 30 mortars

Navy

Personnel: 1,200 (Coast Guard)

Units: 13 patrol craft

Naval bases: Puerto Cortés, Amapala

Air Force

Personnel: 2,200

Organization: 25 combat aircraft; 1 fighter squadron; 1 counterinsurgency squadron; 1 transport squadron; 1 support squadron; 1 helicopter squadron; 19 trainers

Air bases: Tegucigalpa and San Pedro Sula

The Honduran forces performed badly against El Salvador in 1969 and again in 1976. Military effectiveness is undermined by inadequate training, discipline and equipment. The armed forces are particularly handicapped by the lack of an effective navy. The most effective combat element is the air force, which is unusually large and well-equipped.

EDUCATION

The national literacy rate is 59.5% (60.7% for males and 58.4% for females) in 1988.

Education is free, universal and compulsory, in theory, for six years from the ages of seven to 13. Schooling lasts for 11 or 12 years, divided into six years of primary school, three years of the first cycle of secondary school (a program of general education) and two or three years of the second cycle of secondary school (a program of specialized education) leading to the *baccaloreat* (baccalaureate). In 1983 there were 6,264 primary and elementary schools and 307 secondary and normal schools in the school system. Dropout rates are high, particularly in primary schools. The education system suffers from a shortage of textbooks, from unqualified teachers and from the fact that over 70% of primary schools offer only partial programs.

The academic year runs from February through November. The medium of instruction is Spanish. Some English-language private schools serve the English-speaking community in the Bay Islands.

Teachers in public schools are civil servants with tenure. Primary-level teachers are trained in secondary schools, known as normal schools, and secondary-school teachers are trained in teacher training schools and colleges.

Literacy campaigns are sponsored in rural areas by government and private organizations. In addition, two types of schools provide special adult education courses: *escuela suplementaria* (supplementary school), offering a three-year program of basic education for adults with no schooling; and *escuela complementaria* (complementary school), offering a two-year program of more advanced training.

Vocational instruction is built into the secondary school curricula. Advanced technical education is available at two-year technical institutes. Vocational students account for 28% of secondary school enrollment.

Private schools meeting state requirements and submitting to regular inspections receive government subsidies. The Catholic Church maintains over 61 schools. Private schools account for 6% of enrollment in primary schools.

The school system is directly administered by the Ministry of Education.

EDUCATION INDICATORS, 1988

Literacy
- Total (%): 59.5
- Male (%): 60.7
- Female (%): 58.4

First level
- Schools: 7,335
- Students: 878,020
- Teachers: 24,234
- Student/teacher ratio: 36.2
- Net enrollment ratio: 91 (1986)

Second level
- Schools: 474
- Students: 136,205
- Teachers: 8,110
- Student/teacher ratio: 16.8
- Net enrollment ratio: 21 (1986)

Vocational
- Students: 48,138
- Teachers: 2,488

Third level (postsecondary)
- Institutions: 8
- Students: 38,372
- Teachers: 3,138
- Student/teacher ratio: 12.2
- Gross enrollment ratio: 8.8 (1987)
- Students (/100,000 pop.): 800
- % of population age 25 and over with post-secondary education: 3.3

Foreign study
- Foreign students in national universities: 612 (1987)
- Students abroad: 1,304
  - of whom in
    - United States: 1,196 (1988)
    - France: 29 (1988)
    - Federal Republic of Germany: 16 (1988)
    - United Kingdom: 3 (1987)

Public expenditure
- Total (L. million): 376.097
- % of GNP: 4.9
- % of national budget: 19.5
- % of current expenditure: 98.3

GRADUATES, 1987

Total: 1,719
Education: 284
Humanities & religion: 6
Fine & applied arts: 1
Law: 81
Social & behavioral sciences: 198
Commerce & business: 226
Mass communication: 3
Home economics: 0
Service trades: 4
Natural sciences: 19
Mathematics & computer science: 18
Medicine: 449
Engineering: 171
Architecture: 1
Industrial programs: 1
Transportation & communications: 0
Agriculture, forestry, fisheries: 241
Other: 16

The National University, founded in 1847, is an autonomous institution with two branch campuses in San Pedro Sula and La Ceiba and a total enrollment of 27,925.

LEGAL SYSTEM

The legal system is based on Roman and Spanish civil law influenced by English common law. The judicial system consists of the Supreme Court, five courts of appeals, 32 courts of first instance and 350 local judges. The Supreme Court consists of seven judges, elected until 1972 by the Congress of Deputies and since 1972 appointed by the president. The Constitution grants the Supreme Court the right to appoint lower court judges, to declare laws unconstitutional and to censure ministers, but these powers have rarely been exercised. The five courts of appeal are composed of three judges each. Two are in Tegucigalpa and one each in San Pedro Sula, Comayagua and Santa Barbara. Original jurisdiction in criminal cases lies with the 32 courts of first instance, each presided over by a single judge. Justices of the peace have broad but undefined powers.

Although slow and at times cumbersome, the judicial system does allow for fair trial. There are no secret tribunals. Delays almost always result from administrative inadequacy and not from deliberate action. Persons are tried for criminal acts and not for political beliefs, although social and economic status are factors in obtaining adequate access to legal process. There have been cases where it appears persons may have been arrested and held for a limited time because of political beliefs. They are invariably released if they have committed no crime. There are no political prisoners.

The Constitution provides for judicial independence. Supreme Court justices are appointed for four-year terms by the National Congress and lower court judges by the Supreme Court. The executive office also exercises considerable control over the judiciary.

No information is available on the number of correctional institutions or on the penal system.

LAW ENFORCEMENT

The national law enforcement force is known as Cuerpo Especial de Seguridad (Special Security Corps, CES) under the operational control of a director general. The organizational structure of the CES is similar to that of the defense forces. Specialized branches include the National Investigation Corps and frontier and rural units. The total strength of the police force is 2,500, or one policeman for every 1,149 inhabitants. Most of this force is stationed in the cities, and there is only a sprinkling of policemen in rural areas.

Although criminal statistics are not available, violence and serious crimes are reported more often in the larger cities, such as Tegucigalpa.

HEALTH

According to the Pan American Health Organization, health conditions in Honduras are among the worst in the Western Hemisphere. The major health problems are gastritis, enteritis and tuberculosis. About 50% of the population have access to safe water.

HEALTH INDICATORS

Health personnel 1988
- Physicians: 2,418
  - persons per: 1,724
- Dentists: 459
- Nurses: 1,001
- Pharmacists: 792

Hospitals 1988
- Number: 46
- Number of beds (/10,000): 14
- Admissions/discharges (/10,000): 429 (1980)
- Bed occupancy rate (%): 70.2
- Average length of stay (days): 8

Type of hospital (%) 1988
- Government: 45.7
- Private nonprofit & private profit: 54.3

Public health expenditures (latest)
- As % of national budget: 8.0
- Per capita (U.S. $): 10.90

Vital statistics
- Crude death rate (/1,000): 7 (1990)
- Life expectancy at birth 1990
  - Males: 64
  - Females: 67
- Infant mortality rate (/1,000 live births): 62 (1990)
- Child mortality rate under 5 yrs. (/1,000 live births) (1985–90): 106
- Maternal mortality rate (/100,000 live births) (1986–87): 82 (est.)
- Population with access to safe water (%): 50 (latest)

FOOD & NUTRITION

The dietary staple is corn, eaten in the form of either tortillas (corn pancakes) or tamales (ground corncakes). Other staples are sorghum, rice, beans and wheat. Little meat is consumed, but fish is popular on the Caribbean Coast. The national drink is coffee.

Per capita daily intake of food is 2,156 calories (95% of requirements).

MEDIA & CULTURE

Seven daily newspapers are published in Honduras, all in Spanish. Four are published in Tegucigalpa, two in San Pedro Sula and one in Puerto Cortes. The most influential daily is *La Prensa* which has a circulation of 40,000 copies. The left-of-center *El Tiempo* has a circulation of 70,000 while the independent morning daily, *La Tribuna*, has a circulation of 50,000 copies.

The media are relatively free. The Constitution prohibits the closing down of any medium of information or attempting to influence it through state subsidies. The only restriction is that the media must be owned—and, in the case of newspapers, edited—by Honduran nationals.

Honduras has no national news agency. The only news bureaus in Tegucigalpa are Efe, ANPA and dpa (Deutsche Press-Agentur).

Six book publishers are active in the capital, and their combined output is about 30 titles. Two of these houses are owned by the government. Honduras adheres to the Buenos Aires Copyright Convention.

MEDIA INDICATORS
Newspapers
Number of dailies: 7 (latest)
Circulation (000): 218 (latest)
Per 1,000 pop.: 51 (latest)
Newsprint consumption 1988
Total metric tons: 4,900
Per 1,000 pop. (kg.): 1,015
Broadcasting 1985
Annual expenditures (L. millions): 17.0
Radio
Number of transmitters: 184 (1989)
Number of persons per radio receiver: 2.5 (1989)
Total program hours: 1,287,720 (1985)
Television
Television transmitters: 39 (1989)
Number of persons per T.V. receiver: 32 (1989)
Total program hours: 39,593 (1985)

The majority of the 209 broadcasting stations are owned and operated by 84 licensed private broadcasting enterprises. All broadcasts are in Spanish, but 10 stations carry some English-language broadcasts as well. All but four stations are commercially operated, and the four noncommercial stations are run by religious denominations.

CULTURAL & ENVIRONMENTAL INDICATORS
Libraries (pre-1986)
Number: 1
Volumes (000): 20
Loans (/1,000 pop.): 5
Museums (pre-1986)
Annual attendance (000): 22
Attendance (/1,000 pop.): 7
Nature reserves (latest)
Number of facilities: 15

Television, introduced in 1959, now reaches 60% of the population. The main television network is operated by a private company, Compania Televisora Hondurena, with transmitters at Tegucigalpa and San Pedro Sula and a repeater at Siguatepeque. The station is on the air for 72 hours a week. There are four other stations.

Honduras has no national film industry.

The largest library in the country is the National Library at Tegucigalpa, with close to 100,000 volumes.

SOCIAL WELFARE

Social Security services are administered by the Social Security Institute and are financed by a Social Security tax on salaries, with 50% of costs borne by employers, 25% by the government and 25% by employees. Effective coverage is limited to maternity, sickness and work injuries.

Private social welfare organizations, including five Catholic charities, are also active in the field of relief. The Charter of Social Guarantees of 1957 enumerates specific social rights, such as the rights of illegitimate children.

GLOSSARY

alcalde: mayor.
aldea: a village or hamlet, subdivision of a municipality.
caserio: a rural settlement smaller than a hamlet.
colono: a plantation worker who is permitted to farm a part of the estate in lieu of his wages.
ejido: land held in common by a village or municipality.
ladino: a person of mixed descent who has been acculturated into Hispano-American society. Also applied broadly to all non-Indians, including Caucasians.
mestizo: a person of mixed white and Indian descent.
municipio: municipality.
regidor: an elected councilman of a municipal council.

CHRONOLOGY (from 1945)

1948— President Tiburcio Carias Andino steps down after a 16-year rule; Juan Manuel Galvez is elected president.

1954— Following controversial and inconclusive presidential elections, Vice President Julio Lozano Díaz seizes power. . . . Nation's first and worst general strike paralyzes the economy.

1956— The armed forces issue proclamation against the president; army junta, led by Roque I. Rodriguez, expels Lozano and assumes power.

1957— José Ramón Villeda Morales is elected president, the first liberal in 25 years. . . . National Assembly drafts new Constitution. . . . A new labor code and Social Security law are adopted.

1963— A few weeks before the end of his six-year term, Villeda is turned out of office by an army coup led by Osvaldo López Arellano.

1965— A new Constitution is promulgated to replace the 1957 Constitution.

1969— Riots sparked by the World Cup soccer match between Honduras and El Salvador lead to a four-day war; under the auspices of the OAS, a compromise settlement is arranged, and the two nations accept a seven-point peace plan. Honduras suspends participation in the Central American Common Market.

1971— López initiates a Pact of National Unity under which seats in the National Assembly are to be divided equally between the National and Liberal parties. . . . López steps down and Ramón Ernesto Cruz Ucles is elected president.

1972— Cruz is deposed and López returns to power. . . . United States acknowledges Honduran sovereignty over Swan Islands.

1974— Hurricane Fifi strikes Honduras, leaving 12,000 dead and 150,000 homeless.

1975— Bribe scandal rocks the government as United Brands admits paying "high Honduran official" (by implication, President López) $1.25 million for reduction in banana export taxes. . . . In a minicoup,

López is overthrown and is replaced by Juan Alberto Melgar Castro.

1976— Renewed border conflicts with El Salvador lead to OAS intervention.

1978— New electoral law permits political parties to resume activities. . . . Melgar legitimizes two more political parties, including the Christian Democratic Party. . . . Melgar is ousted after charges that he was associated with a $30 million drug ring; a three-man military junta is set up, with Gen. Policarpo Paz García as president; Paz promises to keep Melgar's promise of a return to constitutional rule and to hold elections in 1980.

1980— In elections to National Assembly, Liberal Party, led by Robert Suazo Córdova, wins upset victory; Paz hands over power to National Assembly but remains as interim president until national elections in 1981.

1981— Liberal Party wins conclusively in general elections, and its leader, Roberto Suazo Córdova, is sworn in as president. But real power remains in the hands of the military, especially the chief of staff, Gen. Gustavo Alvarez, who retains the right to veto cabinet appointments.

1982— Gen. Alvarez instigates an amendment of the Constitution whereby the president is stripped of his authority as commander in chief. . . . The new Constitution is promulgated.

1984— Gen. Alvarez is ousted and sent into exile by a group of junior army officers. In his place, Gen. Walter López Reyes is named commander in chief.

1985— In national elections, José Azcona Hoyo of the Liberal Party wins the presidency even though he polled less than 30% of the vote; his rival Rafel Leonardo Callejas of the National Party polled 44%.

1986— Honduras and Nicaragua renew border fighting as Honduras attempts to curb border violations by Nicaraguan government forces waging war against Contras in Honduran territory. Following the Iran-Contra scandal, President Azcona requests the removal of the Contras.

1987— Honduras is a signatory to the Central American peace plan for the region.

1988— At the request of the Honduran government, the U.S. airlifts 3,200 troops into Honduras following the incursion of Nicaraguan troops. Amnesty International and the Inter-American Court of Human Rights report human rights violations in Honduras. The International Court of Justice considers Nicaragua's complaint that Honduras is allowing Contras to operate within its territory against international law.

1989— Honduras and Nicaragua negotiate amnesty terms offered the Contras within Honduras. Rafael Leonardo Callejas wins the presidential election. Central American nations meet to create new initiatives to demobilize Contras in Honduras.

BIBLIOGRAPHY (from 1960)

BOOKS

Acker, Alison. *Honduras: The Making of a Banana Republic.* Boston: South End Press, 1988.

Amnesty International. *Honduras: Civilian Authority—Military Power: Human Rights Violations in the 1980s.* London, 1988.

Anderson, Thomas P. *The War of the Dispossessed: Honduras and El Salvador.* Omaha, NE, 1981.

Berryman, Phillip. *Inside Central America: Essential Facts Past and Present on El Salvador, Nicaragua, Honduras and Guatemala.* New York, 1985.

Lapper, Richard. *Honduras: State for Sale.* New York, 1985.

MacCameron, Robert. *Bananas, Labor and Politics in Honduras.* Syracuse, NY, 1983.

Meyer, Harvey K. *Historical Dictionary of Honduras.* Metuchen, NJ, 1976.

Parker, Franklin P. *The Central American Republics.* London, 1964.

Rosenberg, Mark B., and Philip L. Shepherd. *Honduras Confronts Its Future: Contending Perspectives on Critical Issues.* Boulder, CO, 1985.

Stokes, William S. *Honduras: An Area Study in Government.* Westport, CT, 1974.

UNESCO. *Toward a Cultural Policy for Honduras.* Paris, 1979.

West, R. C., and J. P. Angelli. *Middle America: Its Lands and Peoples.* Englewood Cliffs, NJ, 1966.

INDIA

BASIC FACTS

OFFICIAL NAME: Republic of India (Bharat Ganarajya)

ABBREVIATION: II

CAPITAL: New Delhi

HEAD OF STATE: President Ramaswamy Iyer. Venkataraman (from 1987)

HEAD OF GOVERNMENT: Prime Minister P. V. Narsimha Rao (from 1991)

NATURE OF GOVERNMENT: Socialist secular parliamentary democracy

POPULATION: 849,746,001

AREA: 3,287,263 sq km (1,269,219 sq mi)

ETHNIC MAJORITY: Indo-Aryans

LANGUAGES: Hindi, English and 14 official languages

RELIGIONS Hinduism, Islam, Christianity, Sikhism, Buddhism, Jainism, and Zoroastrianism

UNIT OF CURRENCY: Rupee

NATIONAL FLAG: Tricolor of deep saffron, white and green horizontal stripes with a blue dharma chakra (wheel of the law, a Buddhist emblem) in the center of the white stripe. The wheel appears on the abacus of Asoka's lion capital built at Sarnath in Uttar Pradesh in 250 B.C.

NATIONAL EMBLEM: Three imperial lions standing back to back as they appear on the stone pillar erected by Emperor Asoka at Sarnath. On the base is a dharma chakra, flanked by a bull and a horse. Beneath the emblem is the national motto, "Satyameva Jayate" ("Truth Alone Triumphs"), in Devanagiri script.

NATIONAL ANTHEM: "Thou Art the Ruler of the Minds of All People" written by Nobel-Prize-winning poet Rabindranath Tagore. Two other songs—"I Bow to Thee, Mother" and "Bankim Chandra Chatterji" are accorded equal status in public functions.

NATIONAL HOLIDAYS: January 26 (Republic Day); January 1 (New Year's Day); August 15 (Independence Day); October 2 (Mahatma Gandhi's birthday). The festivals of all of India's major religions are observed in the country, many of them nationally, and others regionally. The chief of these festivals are the Hindu festivals of Rath Yatra, Janmashtami, Durga Puja, Dussehra, Diwali, Pongal, Holi, Ram Navami, Baisakhi, Raksha Bandan, Ganesh Chaturthi and Onam; the Islamic festivals of Id-ul-Fitr, Muharram, Id-uz-Zuha and Id-il-Milad; the Christian festivals of Christmas and Good Friday; the Sikh festival of Guru Nanak Jayanti; as well as the Buddha Jayanti (Buddhism), Mahavir Jayanti (Jainism) and Jamshed Navroz (Zoroastrianism).

NATIONAL CALENDAR: Gregorian and Saka. The Saka calendar, named after a North Indian dynasty of the 1st century A.D., is used only in official publications. It was adopted on March 22, 1957, which corresponded to new year's day of 1879, Saka Era.

PHYSICAL QUALITY OF LIFE INDEX: 55

DATE OF INDEPENDENCE: August 15, 1947

DATE OF CONSTITUTION: January 26, 1950

WEIGHTS & MEASURES: The metric system is official but hundreds of traditional measures and units are used in various parts of the country. Some of the more common units are: tola (11.66 grams, 4.11 oz.); seer (933.1 grams, 329.3 oz); maund (37.32 kg, 82.29 lb), and bigha (0.25 hectare, 0.625 acre). Two numerical units, unfamiliar in the West, are commonly and officially used: lakh (100,000) and crore (100 lakhs, or 10 million).

LOCATION & AREA

India, the second largest country in Asia, is located in the Indian subcontinent in South Asia. Including the Andaman and Nicobar Islands in the Bay of Bengal and Lakshadweep (formerly, the Laccadive, Minicoy and Amindivi Islands), the total land area is 3,287,263 sq km (1,269,219 sq mi), extending 3,214 km (1,997 mi) N to S and 2,933 km (1,822 mi) E to W. The length of the total coastline on the Bay of Bengal, Arabian Sea and the Indian Ocean is 5,110 km (3,175 mi).

India shares its total international land boundary of 9,988 km (6,202 mi) with six neighbors: China, excluding the Pakistani-controlled portion of Kashmir, 1,893 km, (1,176 mi); Nepal (1,508 km, 937 mi); Bhutan (573 km, 356 mi); Myanmar (1,403 km, 872 mi); Bangladesh (2,583 km, 1,605 mi); and Pakistan (2,028 km, 1,260 mi). The borders with Pakistan and Bangladesh are based on the Radcliffe Award and are perhaps the only boundaries in the world delimited by religious considerations. There are serious and long-standing border disputes with Pakistan over Jammu and Kashmir, where the present border follows the ceasefire line of 1949. Neither country recognizes the legal presence of the other in Kashmir, but three wars have failed to change the status quo. A boundary dispute in the Rann of Kutch over which India and Pakistan went to war in 1965 was settled by an international tribunal in 1968.

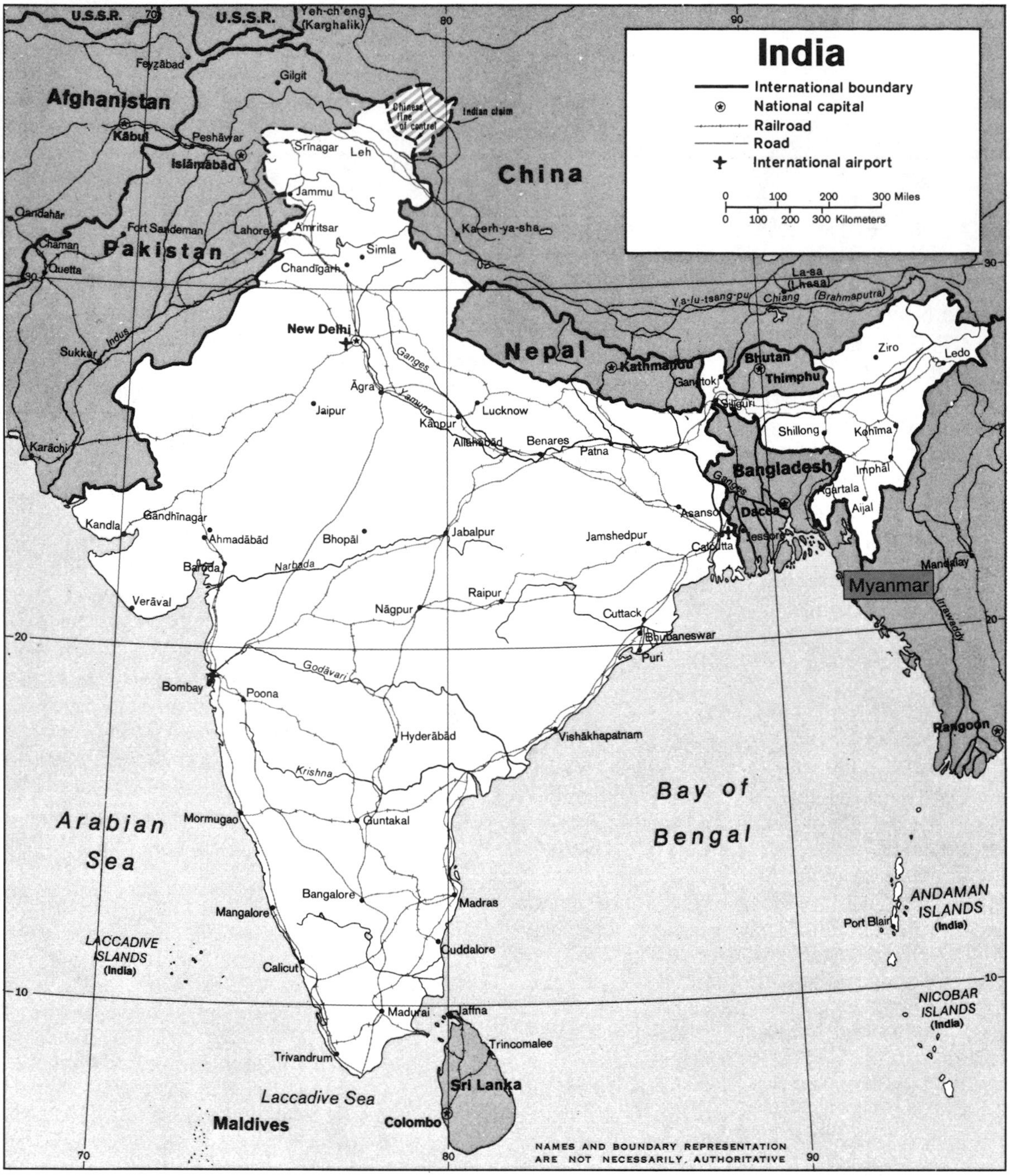

India

- International boundary
- National capital
- Railroad
- Road
- International airport

0 100 200 300 Miles
0 100 200 300 Kilometers

U.S.S.R.
U.S.S.R.
Yeh-ch'eng (Karghalik)
Feyzābad
Gilgit
Afghanistan
Kābul
Peshāwar
Islāmābād
Chinese line of control
Indian claim
Srīnagar
Leh
China
Jammu
Qandahār
Fort Sandeman
Lahore
Amritsar
Chaman
Pakistan
Ka-erh-ya-sha
Quetta
Simla
Chandīgarh
La-sa (Lhasa)
Ya-lu-tsang-pu Chiang (Brahmaputra)
Sukkur
Indus
New Delhi
Ganges
Nepal
Kathmandu
Bhutan
Thimphu
Ziro
Ledo
Gangtok
Āgra
Yamuna
Jaipur
Lucknow
Kānpur
Siliguri
Shillong
Kohīma
Karāchi
Allahābād
Benares
Patna
Bangladesh
Imphāl
Agartala
Aijal
Dacca
Asansol
Kandla
Gāndhīnagar
Ahmadābād
Bhopāl
Jabalpur
Jamshedpur
Calcutta
Jessore
Mandalay
Baroda
Narbada
Myanmar
Raipur
Irrawaddy
Verāval
Nāgpur
Cuttack
Bhubaneswar
Puri
Bombay
Godāvari
Poona
Rangoon
Hyderābād
Vishākhapatnam
Krishna
Bay of Bengal
Arabian Sea
Mormugao
Guntakal
Bangalore
Madras
ANDAMAN ISLANDS (India)
Mangalore
Port Blair
LACCADIVE ISLANDS (India)
Cuddalore
Calicut
NICOBAR ISLANDS (India)
Madurai
Jaffna
Trincomalee
Trivandrum
Sri Lanka
Laccadive Sea
Maldives
Colombo
70 80 90
30 20 10

NAMES AND BOUNDARY REPRESENTATION ARE NOT NECESSARILY AUTHORITATIVE

Of Pakistan's original claim of 9,065 sq km (3,500 sq mi), it was awarded only 777 sq km (300 sq mi). The border with China, divided into western and eastern sectors, has been the subject of conflicting claims since the 19th century. India maintains that the border is the 1914 MacMahon Line, which follows the crest of the Himalayas. Chinese territorial claims, which disregard the MacMahon Line, have resulted in the military occupation of 38,850 sq km (15,000 sq mi) of Ladakh area in eastern Kashmir and 82,880 sq km (32,000 sq mi) of North East Frontier Agency area in NE India.

The border with Myanmar also has never been clearly demarcated, and delimitation began in 1968 with a 1,100-man team.

The capital is New Delhi, built by the British architect Sir Edwin Luytens in the early years of the 20th century. Like most Indian cities, New Delhi is located cheek by jowl with an older city, Delhi, the second largest city and the ancient capital of India. The largest city is Greater Bombay, the most cosmopolitan of all of India's urban centers. The third largest city is Calcutta, which was also the capital of the Indian Empire until 1912. With its teeming millions Calcutta has become a vast slum bursting at the seams. The fourth largest city is Madras, capital of Tamil Nadu on the east coast and the center of Tamil culture. All four cities are essentially British creations: Calcutta, Bombay and Madras were founded as factories (settlements) of the English East India Company.

PRINCIPAL TOWNS
(population at 1981 census*)

Greater Bombay	8,243,405	Hubli-Dharwar	527,108
Delhi	4,884,234	Cochin	551,567
Calcutta	3,305,006	Sholapur	514,860
Madras	3,276,622	Jodhpur	506,345
Bangalore	2,628,593	Ranchi	489,626
Hyderabad	2,187,262	Trivandrum	499,531
Ahmedabad	2,159,127	Jamshedpur	457,061
Kanpur (Cawnpore)	1,486,522	Vijaywada (Vljayavada)	461,772
Nagpur	1,219,461		
Pune (Poona)	1,203,351	Rajkot	445,076
Jaipur (Jeypore)	977,165	Mysore	479,081
Lucknow	916,954	Meerut	417,395
Indore	829,327	Jalandhar	408,196
Madurai	820,891	Kozhikode (Calicut)	394,447
Surat	776,876		
Patna	813,963	Bareilly	394,938
Howrah	744,429	Chandigarh	379,660
Vadodara (Baroda)	734,473	Ajmer	375,593
Varanasi (Banaras)	720,755	Guntur	367,699
Coimbatore	704,514	Tiruchirapalli	362,045
Agra	694,191	Salem	361,394
Bhopal	671,018	Kota	358,241
Allahabad	619,628	Kolhapur	340,625
Jabalpur (Jubbulpore)	649,085	Raipur	338,245
Ludhiana	607,052	Faridabad	330,864
Amritsar	(594,844)	Moradabad	330,051
Srinagar	(594,775)	Aligarh	320,861
Visakhapatnam	584,166	Bhilainagar	(319,450)
Gwalior	539,015	Durgapur	311,798
		Thane	309,897
		Bhaunagar	(308,642)
		Gorakhpur	(307,501)

*Figures refer to the city proper in each case.

At the time of the 1981 census there were 60 cities with populations of over 300,000.

Mainland India comprises four well-defined regions: the northern mountain zone, or the Himalayas, the Indo-Gangetic Plain, the desert region and the southern region, including a narrow coastal plain along the Arabian Sea and a broader one along the Bay of Bengal.

The Himalayas (literally, the abode of snow) comprise three parallel ranges interspersed with large plateaus and valleys, like the Kashmir and Kulu Valleys. The Greater Himalayas, with an average height of 6,700 meters (20,000 ft), include such famous peaks as Mount Everest (8,847 meters, 29,028 ft) and Mount Kanchenjunga (8,597 meters, 28,208 ft). The peaks of the Lesser Himalayas range between 1,500 meters (5,000 ft) and 3,650 meters (12,000 ft). The Outer Himalayas form a system of low foothills. The high altitude limits travel to a few passes, such as the Jelep La and Natu La, NE of Darjeeling and Shipki La in the Sutlej Valley. The mountain wall extends over a distance of 2,400 km (1,490 mi) with a depth varying from 240 to 320 km (150 to 200 mi). The hill ranges are much lower in the east where the Garo, Khasi, Jaintia and Naga hills join the chain of Lushai and Arakan Hills in Burma.

The Indo-Gangetic Plain, about 2,400 km (1,500 mi) long and 240 to 320 km (140 to 200 mi) broad, is formed by the basins of three river systems: the Ganges, the Indus and the Brahmaputra. The plain is the product of millennia-long deposits of soil in what was once a gulf between the peninsula and the Himalayas. There is hardly any variation in relief, and between Delhi and the Bay of Bengal there is a drop of only 200 meters (656 ft) in elevation.

The desert region is divided into the great desert extending northward from the Rann of Kutch and the little desert extending northward from the Luni River. The absence of surface water makes the region completely sterile.

Separated from the Indo-Gengetic Plain by a mass of mountain ranges and scarped plateaus is the Indian (or Deccan) Peninsula flanked on one side by the Eastern Ghats with an average elevation of 610 meters (2,000 ft) and on the other by the Western Ghats (910 to 1,220 meters, 2,985 ft to 4,000 ft) rising in places to 2,440 meters (8,000 ft). The interior plateau between these Ghats (or mountain ranges), called the Deccan, is actually a series of plateaus intersected by many rivers. The southern point of the plateau is formed by the Nilgiri Hills and the Cardamom Hills, while toward the north, in what is called Central India, are a complex of three mountain ranges, the Aravalli, the Vindhya and the Satpura, and two plateaus, the Malwa and the Chota Nagpur. The narrow alluvial plains on the west and the east of the Peninsula vary considerably. The western coast is a narrow strip divided into three sections: the Gujarat Coast, the Konkan Coast and the Malabar Coast. The broader eastern, or Coromandel Coast, is composed of alternating delta plains and hills.

The rivers of India are generally divided into Himalayan rivers and peninsular rivers. Of the Himalayan rivers the longest—and also the holiest—is the Ganges. The Ganges basin receives waters from an area constituting one-quarter of the total land area. The Ganges has two main headwaters in the Himalayas, the Bhagirathi and the Alaknanda, the former rising from the Gangotri glacier and the latter from the Alakapuri glacier. It enters the plains at the sacred city of Hardwar and joins with its major tributary, the Jumna, at Allahabad. During the rest of its course the Ganges is joined by a number of other Himalayan rivers, such as the Yamuna, Ghaghra, Gandak and Kosi, and Central Indian rivers, such as the Chambi, Betwa and Son. After the creation of Pakistan in 1947 the Indus and the Brahmaputra river systems have become less important as they flow only part of their course through Indian territory.

Four of the six major rivers of the Deccan Peninsula—the Mahanadi, Godavari, Krishna, and Cauvery—flow into the Bay of Bengal and two—the Narbada and Tapti—flow into the Arabian Sea. The Deccan rivers are generally rain-fed and therefore fluctuate in volumes. For a country of its size, India has very few natural lakes. But there are a number of man-made reservoirs, such as the Rihand Reservoir, the Govind Sagar, and the Tungabhadra Reservoir.

WEATHER

India is a tropical country but is subject to a wide range of climates, from subfreezing Himalayan winters to 50°C (122°F) in the shade in the Indo-Gangetic Plain, from the highest annual rainfall in the world (1,096 cm, 428 in.) in Cherrapunji in Meghalaya to almost permanent drought in the Thar Desert. Four fairly distinct seasons are common to all regions: a relatively cool winter monsoon season, a hot and rainless transitional season, a rainy monsoon season, and a humid season during the retreating monsoon. Although the duration of the seasons varies according to the region, the northeast monsoon lasts from December to March, the transitional hot weather from April to May, the rainy southwest monsoon from June to September, and the transitional humid season from October to November.

Based on rainfall and temperature India may be divided into seven climatic zones as follows:

The Himalayan region with three temperature levels, 18.3°C (65°F) at 2,150 meters (7,000 ft), freezing temperatures at 4,600 meters (15,000 ft) and up to 37.8°C (100°F) in the valleys. The Eastern Himalayas have from 127 to 233 cm (50 to 80 in.) of rainfall and the Western Himalayas from 76 to 101 cm (30 to 40 in.).

Assam and West Bengal have humid and rainy weather, Assam has torrential rainfall and moderately high temperatures, while West Bengal has rainfall between 127 and 152 cm (50 to 60 in.) and an average annual temperature between 18.3°C and 29.4°C (65°F and 85°F).

In the Indo-Gangetic Plain temperatures run as high as 50°C (122°F) and as low as −2.2°C (28°F). The monsoon becomes weaker as it moves north: Patna receives 119 cm (47 in.), Delhi 71 cm (28 in.) and the Rajasthan deserts less than 25 cm (10 in.) per year.

The western coastal region receives high rainfall ranging from 190 to 305 cm (75 to 120 in.) in Mangalore and Bombay to 648 cm (255 in.) in Mahabaleshwar. Kerala in the south receives heavy rainfall during both the southwest and northeast monsoons. The temperature is fairly uniform at about 26.7°C (80°F).

The Peninsular interior has a high average annual temperature reaching 37.8°C (100°F) during April, May and June. Rainfall varies from 76 cm (30 in.) in Madhya Pradesh to between 101 and 152 cm (40 to 60 in.) in southern Uttar Pradesh and 101 and 177 cm (40 to 70 in.) in Orissa.

Northern Deccan has summer temperature maximums exceeding 37.8°C (100°F)and January minimums below 15.6°C (60°F). Most of the region is in a rain shadow and gets barely 51 to 101 cm (20 to 40 in.) of rain per year.

The east coast receives 84 to 127 cm (35 to 50 in.) of rainfall. During the summer temperatures exceed 37.8°C (100°F) on most days.

Because of the erratic nature of the monsoons both droughts and floods are common in most parts of India. The daily temperature range varies from 2°C to 3°C (4°F to 5°F) in Kerala to 33°C to 39°C (60°F to 70°F) in Rajasthan.

Tropical hurricanes and cyclones strike the coastal areas in most years between April and June and between September and December.

POPULATION

The population of India was estimated in 1990 at 849,746,001 on the basis of the last official census held in 1981 when the population was 685,184,692. With 14% of the world's population, India ranks second only to China in size of population.

Although there has been a slight decline in birth rate, the overall growth rate is still high.

India ranks among the top 20 countries in the world in overall density. Nearly 40% of the population is concentrated in the Ganges Basin states of West Bengal, Bihar, Uttar Pradesh, Punjab and Haryana. The highest density is recorded in the southern state of Kerala. States with lower population densities include Rajasthan, Himachel Pradesh and Sikkim. The northeastern states of Manipur, Meghalya and Nagaland have a low density because of their mountainous terrain.

The percentage of urban population has grown every year since 1921 (when it was 11.2%) but is still only 27%. Indian towns are different from Western towns in that few of them have separate residential and business districts; almost all of them have slums in which the majority lives and special quarters for trades and castes. The urban component of the population varies according to states. It is highest in Tamil Nadu, Gujarat, Maharashtra, West Bengal and Mysore. It is lowest in Bihar, Assam, Orissa and Nagaland. The growth rate of the cities was most marked between 1951 and 1961 but has since slowed. About two-thirds of the urban population increase occurred in large cities. As a result of deep-rooted ties to land and

DEMOGRAPHIC INDICATORS

Population (million): 849.746 (1990)
Year of last census: 1981
Sex distribution (% at last census): males, 50.3; females, 49.7
Population estimates and projections (000)

1940: 317,000	1970: 543,132	2000: 1,042,530
1950: 352,664	1980: 687,057	2010: 1,225,305
1960: 427,802	1990: 853,373	

Age profile (% at last census)

0–14: 39.5	30–44: 17.4	
15–29: 25.9	45–59: 10.7	60 and over: 6.5

Median age (yrs.): 21.1 (1985)
Youth population (% age 15–24): 19.4 (1985); 18.6 (2000)
Total dependency ratio: 72.1 (1985)
Annual growth rate (%)

1950–55: 2.00	1975–80: 2.08	2000–2005: 1.72
1955–60: 2.26	1980–85: 2.21	2005–2010: 1.51
1960–65: 2.26	1985–90: 2.08	2010–2015: 1.28
1965–70: 2.28	1990–95: 2.09	2015–2020: 1.02
1970–75: 2.24	1995–2000: 1.92	2020–2025: 1.01

Hypothetical size of stationary population (millions): 1,862
Assumed year of reaching net reproduction rate of 1: 2015
Urban population (000): 196,228 (1985)
Urban population (%): 27 (1988); 19 (1965)
Annual urban population growth rate (%, 1985–90): 3.94
Annual rural population growth rate (%, 1985–90): 1.40
Percentage of urban population in largest city: 6 (1980)
Percentage of urban population in cities of population over 500,000: 39 (1980)
Number of cities of population over 500,000: 36 (1980)
Population density per sq. km. (per sq. mi.): 269.5 (698.0) (latest)

VITAL STATISTICS

Crude birth rate (/1,000): 32 (1990); 45 (1965)
Crude death rate (/1,000): 11 (1990); 21 (1965)
Infant mortality rate (/1,000 live births): 89 (1990)
Maternal mortality rate (/100,000 live births): 500 (1980)
Life expectancy (yrs.) at birth: males, 57; females, 59 (1990)
Gross reproduction rate (/woman) (1980–85): 2.32
Total fertility rate (/woman): 3.8 (1990)
Rate of natural increase (/1,000): 20.7 (1988)
Average household size: 5.5 (latest)

community, most of the rural population is not mobile. Almost two-thirds of the population live in the same district as at birth.

There are regional variations in the sex ratio, but only one state—Kerala—reports more females than males. The proportion of women in the population decreases in the north and west and, unlike in most developing countries, men outnumber women in all major cities. Part of this imbalance may be due to deliberate underreporting of teen-age girls and widows, to whom certain Hindu social taboos apply. The female infant mortality rate is higher than that of males, reflecting the greater economic value associated with males, especially in northern India, and consequent nutritional and health-care neglect of females in poorer homes.

During the partition of India in 1947 and the civil war in East Pakistan in 1971, India witnessed some of the most massive migrations in history, followed by severe economic disruption and widespread suffering. Although the actual numbers are variously reported, it is estimated that 15 million people crossed the borders in both directions in 1947. The majority of the refugees who fled to India from Bangladesh in the year preceding independence have returned home. In the early 1980s, India admitted Tamil refugees from Sri Lanka and Afghans from Afghanistan. There has also been some exodus of Bengali-speaking peoples from Assam into West Bengal.

External voluntary migration is an older phenomenon. Between 1834 and 1934 about 30 million persons are believed to have left India, mostly as indentured laborers for other colonies of the British Empire. Although 24 million of these migrants returned to India at the end of their term, the descendants of those that remained, described as Overseas Indians, constitute one of the largest diasporas in the world: 1.1 million in Sri Lanka, 900,000 in Malaysia, 500,000 in South Africa, 500,000 in Mauritius, 300,000 in Guyana and 250,000 in Kenya. Hundreds of thousands have been repatriated from Sri Lanka, Uganda and Myanmar. In three foreign countries Indians actually constitute a majority: Mauritius, Fiji and Guyana, although they wield political control only in Mauritius.

A second wave of emigration followed after independence. Unlike the earlier migrants, the new emigres were skilled personnel, such as physicians and scientists, and their destinations were the United Kingdom and other advanced countries of the West. During the 30 years since independence, India has become one of the largest contributors to the brain drain to the West.

STATUS OF WOMEN INDICATORS

Number of women (millions): 363,238 (1985)
Women of childbearing age (15–49) (% of pop.): 49 (1988)
Married women of childbearing age (15–49) using contraception (%): 35 (latest)
Women's literacy rate (%): 29 (1988)
Women in labor force (%): 14.2 (1988)
Total fertility rate (/woman): 3.8 (1990)
Women in national legislatures (%): 7 (1984)

Although women are guaranteed equal rights and protection under the law in India, in practice long-standing cultural biases cause them to have fewer educational and career opportunities. During the 1980s, attention has focused on "dowry deaths," the death under suspicious circumstances of women whose parents have been unable to pay a supplementary dowry demanded by the husband's family after marriage. In New Delhi, which is perhaps the worst affected area, 690 women reportedly died of burns under suspicious circumstances in 1984. Most reported cases of "dowry deaths" have been in northern India, and most are in lower middle-class urban families. In 1984 Parliament passed a bill to amend the Dowry Abolition Act of 1961, but many women's organizations maintain that the changes are inadequate.

There are no legal barriers to female candidates, although their numbers have remained small since independence. The late Prime Minister, Indira Gandhi, was a woman.

Family planning was adopted as an official program in 1952 and has been pursued vigorously since; a Department of Family Planning was created in 1966. At the national level the program is coordinated by the Central Family Planning Council. The government has also launched a family planning Mass Education and Motivation Program through the press, radio, film and television. Sex education is being introduced in the school curriculum and in literacy classes.

Some of the measures adopted under Indira Gandhi to promote family planning were severe and draconian. Two-year prison sentences were imposed on those failing to sterilize within six months of the birth of the third child unless all the three children were of the same sex. Ration cards for purchase of food grains in fair-price shops were issued to parents only for three children. The civil service rules were also amended to provide for the dismissal of any employee with more than three children. Resistance to these measures, especially in rural areas, is cited as one of the reasons for the electoral defeat of Mrs. Gandhi in 1977.

In 1977, the population policy was modified to eliminate all forms of compulsion in the family planning program and to make it a family welfare program embracing all aspects of family welfare and, in particular, maternal and child health, nutrition, female education and women's rights. In 1978, a law was enacted fixing the minimum age for marriage as 21 years for males and 18 years for females.

ETHNIC COMPOSITION

Ethnically, India is one of the great mixtures of the world, and its racial diversity is perhaps the most complex to be found anywhere outside of Africa. From prehistoric times the subcontinent has absorbed several waves of conquering peoples. On its basic racial stock, a Caucasoid people who moved into the Indus (from which the name India has been derived) Valley from Central Asia and established a flourishing civilization around 2500 B.C., there has been grafted Proto-Mongoloid, Australoid and Negrito elements. The great majority of the population belongs to the Caucasoid family. The Dravidians of South India are believed to be the descendants of the Alpines, the Mediterranean branch of the Caucasoids, while most North Indians are believed to be Indo-Nordics. The former constitute 25% of the population and the latter 72%.

The aboriginal inhabitants of India have survived in geographic pockets in isolated hilly regions, constituting today 3% of the population. These tribes are concentrated in three zones, known as scheduled areas: the northeast, (in the states of Mizoram, Manipur, Nagaland, Meghalaya, Assam and Arunachal Pradesh), the hills of Central India (in the states of Madhya Pradesh and Orissa), and in the southern part of the Peninsula (in the states of Kerala and Tamil Nadu).

The tribes of the northeast are Mongoloid peoples, speaking Sino-Tibetan languages. The largest of these groups in states outside Arunachal Pradesh are the Khasi of United Khasi and Jaintia Hills, the Lushai, also called the Mizo (with three subtribes, Chutiya, Ladung and Moran), the Garo Kuki, Meithei and the Naga. The Nagas are the most Christianized and educated of all tribes. The tribes of Arunachal Pradesh (formerly the North East Frontier Agency) are more numerous and include the Wancho, who were at one time headhunters, the Singpho and the Khampti who are Buddhists, the Tangsa, the Mishmi, Adi, Gallong, Bori, Dafla, Apa Tani, Miri, Ramo, Pailibo, Aka, Sherdukpen, Monpa, Menba, Khamba and Sulung. The tribes of south India are believed to be either Negrito or Proto-Australoid and are among the most primitive in India. They include the Koyas of Andhra Pradesh, the Kadars of Kerala, the Todas of Nilgiris and the Irulas of Karnataka.

Scheduled castes (including the so-called untouchables or harijans) make up 15% of the population. The tribal people are an estimated 7%. The government has met only modest success in its efforts to improve the positions of these groups.

There are three ethnic alien groups, which, although numerically insignificant, are prominent in national life. The Parsis are descendants of refugees who fled Muslim persecution in Persia in the 8th century. Literate, wealthy and socially advanced, they dominate the economic life of Bombay and its environs. The Jews, whose numbers are being depleted every year through immigration to Israel, are a much older community, dating back to the 1st century A.D. The Anglo-Indians, descendants of marriages between Europeans and Indians, receive special protection as a minority in the Constitution. Most of them are well integrated with the other Indian communities.

Every large Indian city has substantial Western communities. For many years India has been a haven for members of the Western counterculture.

LANGUAGE

In India, 1,652 languages and dialects are spoken. Of these, 15 are recognized in the Constitution as regional languages and one, Hindi, written in the Devanagiri script, is designated as the official language. Linguistic loyalties run deep, and political boundaries of the 25 states follow, for the most part, linguistic boundaries.

The 15 languages specified in the Constitution, spoken by 91% of the population, are broadly divided into Indo-European and Dravidian. Almost 75% of the population speak one of the Indo-European languages, while 25% speak Dravidian languages.

Hindi, together with its numerous dialectal forms, such as Western Hindi, Eastern Hindi, Bihari and Pahari, is the almost exclusive language of the Indo-Gangetic Plain, and its use is growing in other parts of India. It is taught as the primary or second language throughout India. Through the Central Hindi Directorate, the government runs several programs for the enrichment and spread of Hindi. Some of these measures have met with considerable resistance in Dravidian language areas as well as in Bengal, leading to language riots.

Urdu, the language of urban Muslims, differs from Hindi in being written in Arabic–Persian script and also in the large admixture of Arabic and Persian

MAJOR LANGUAGES OF INDIA		
Language	Region	Percentage
Indo-European Family:		
Hindi	North	30.37
Sanskrit	Used mainly by Brahmin priests	N.A.
Sindhi	North	0.3
Urdu	North	5.3
Punjabi	Punjab	2.49
Assamese	Assam	1.54
Bengali	West Bengal	7.71
Gujarati	Gujarat	4.6
Kashmiri	Kashmir	0.4
Marathi	Maharashtra	7.5
Oriya	Orissa	3.5
Bihari	Bihar	3.8
Rajasthani	Rajasthan	3.39
Dravidian Family:		
Kannada or Kanarese	Karnataka	3.9
Tamil	Tamil Nadu	6.9
Malayalam	Kerala	3.8
Telugu	Andhra Pradesh	8.5

words. The spoken dialect from which both Hindi and Urdu are derived is called Hindustani, or Khari Bol. Hindustani has spread from its original home in the New Delhi-Meerut area to all bazaar towns and administrative centers and is therefore sometimes called Bazaar Hindustani. Linguistically, Assamese, Kashmiri, Bengali, Marathi, Punjabi and Gujarati are descended from Prakrit, a demotic form of Sanskrit, which was the spoken language of the people of northern India during the invasion of Alexander the Great (323 B.C.)

Whereas the Indo-European languages of the north are mutually intelligible and shade into one another, the Dravidian languages of the south are not only separate but are also mutually unintelligible. Tamil has the longest literary tradition and is also the language most removed from the pervasive influence of Sanskrit, while Malayalam is closest to Sanskrit of all the Dravidian languages. All these languages have highly developed literatures.

Linguistic heterogeneity and complexity are staggering at the dialectal level. It took Sir George Grierson 11 volumes to complete a linguistic survey of India that listed all the dialects and dialectal variations at the local level. Almost every village and every caste has its own dialect. Most of the tribal people speak languages of the Austro–Asiatic and Sino–Tibetan families.

Although English is the mother tongue only of the Anglo–Indians, it is spoken by more than 15 million persons in India with some degree of proficiency. It is accorded the position of an associate official language in the Constitution, but for practical purposes it is the official language of India, the principal medium of communication among the educated classes.

RELIGION

Almost all the major religions of the world are represented in India and four of them have originated in the country: Buddhism, Jainism, Sikhism and Hinduism.

MAJOR RELIGIONS OF INDIA (1985)			
Religion	Population	Percentage	Growth Rate (%) 1970–80
Hinduism	547,123,500	78.8 m	2.34
Islam	80,540,000	11.6 m	2.81
Christianity	27,078,000	3.9 m	3.46
Sikhism	13,886,000	2.0 m	3.0
Buddhism	5,554,000	0.8 m	1.86
Jainism	3,200,000	0.5 m	1.99
Tribals	10,415,000	1.5 m	1.21
Atheists	4,166,000	0.6 m	7.06
Parsis	115,000	(.) m	
Jews	11,500	(.) m	

Hindus form the majority of the population in all areas except Jammu and Kashmir (where Muslims are dominant) and Nagaland (where Christians are in the majority). Hinduism is less a monolithic creed than a conglomeration of loosely related but interwoven cults and traditions. It has no unifying creed or priesthood, no founder, no ecclesiastical organization and no concept of heresy. Relatively tolerant, it encompasses differing theologies and spans the religious spectrum from monism to polytheism and from atheism and animism.

Caste is the basis of Hindu social structure and determines into which one of the four hierarchical social groups each Hindu is born. These four groups, called varnas, are the Brahmin, or the priestly caste, the Kshatriyas, or the warrior caste, the Vaisyas, or trading caste, and the Sudras, or the artisan caste. The rigidity of the caste system has been mitigated since independence not only because of a constitutional prohibition against discrimination on the basis of caste, but also because of the leveling effects of urbanization, industrialization, education and the numerical superiority of the lower castes at the polls.

Religion is a pervasive influence in India, permeating all aspects of national life. Even political and economic movements have religious overtones. Hinduism particularly serves as the principal unifying force in the country. Hindu-Muslim riots are among the many deplorable features of the Indian religious scene and occur with almost predictable regularity.

Muslims are the largest religious minority and constitute the majority in Jammu and Kashmir and the second largest religious group in 12 other states.

There are two main groups of Christians in India. The older of these, known variously as the Christians of St. Thomas, Syrian Christians dating back to the 1st century and the Indian Christians from the late 16th century.

The Sikh religion was founded by Guru Nanak in the 15th century as an attempt to reconcile Hinduism and Islam, but it evolved into a warrior sect bitterly opposed to Islam. The chief temple of the Sikhs is at Amritsar, where the Sikh scripture, the Adi Granth, is enshrined.

Jainism is often considered not as a separate religion but as a sect within the Hindu fold. It was founded by Mahavira in the 6th century B.C. as a reform movement stressing self-mortification as a means to nirvana. Jains are among the most prosperous and urban communities in India and are prominent in banking, business and the professions.

Buddhism is no longer an active religious force in India, where it is confined to small groups in the Himalayas and scattered converts from the untouchable class. Among the smaller religious minorities are the Jews and Zoroastrians. The latter, who are also known as Parsis, worship the god Ahura Mazda and the sacred elements, especially fire.

India has not adopted a state religion and the Constitution guarantees every citizen the right to freedom of worship. Despite pressures from Hindu extremists, there is no discrimination against any faith or creed.

HISTORICAL BACKGROUND

The first British settlement was erected in Surat on the west coast in 1612 by the English East India Company under charter from the Mughal Emperor Jahangir. By 1857 when the company's Indian territories were taken over by the crown, its writ ran from the Himalayas to Cape Comorin and from Burma to Afghanistan. Despite many glaring inadequacies, the British must be credited with the introduction of a modern system of education, public health, public works, the railroad and road systems, banking and public finance, the judicial system, social welfare and the media. Although reluctant, they also laid the foundations of a parliamentary system of government. Above all, they welded hundreds of feudal princedoms into the modern political entity known as India, giving the country a political unity it never previously possessed within its present borders. Unlike many other former British colonies, India has not turned its back on the principal British legacies, although many of them have been Indianized in form. Much good will toward the British seems to survive, and India has retained its membership in the Commonwealth unbroken since independence.

India achieved independence in August 1947 when Great Britain put into effect the Indian Independence Act. The Act divided the subcontinent into two states based on religious majority: India (Hindu) and Pakistan (Muslim). The partition resulted in inter-communal conflict that led to more than half a million deaths and the mass migration of 13 million as Hindus and Sikhs fled as refugees from Pakistan to northern India and Muslims fled to Pakistan. In 1948 the two nations went to war over Kashmir, a Muslim-majority state whose Hindu ruler had decided to accede to India. Fighting ended in 1949 when the United Nations negotiated a cease fire that divided the region between the two combatants. Both India and Pakistan have since claimed the entire region.

In 1950 India adopted a Constitution that declared the country a republic and a federal union with a parliamentary system of government. Jawaharlal Nehru, prime minister since independence, continued as prime minister. Under Nehru the nation pursued policies of non-alignment in foreign affairs and socialism at home. Nehru focused on industrialization to spur development. However, the nation's size, growing population, refugee problems and continued tension with Pakistan all hindered economic growth. During Nehru's tenure, India constitutionally annexed Kashmir and Jammu into the Union in 1957, annexed Goa and other Portuguese possessions in 1961 and fought a limited war with China over disputed border areas in 1962.

Nehru died in 1964 and was succeeded by Lal Bahadur Shastri, who led the nation into another war with Pakistan in 1965 over the disputed regions of Jammu and Kashmir. The war ended without territorial gains for either side. Shastri died in 1966 and Indira Gandhi (Nehru's daughter) became prime minister. India again went to war with Pakistan in 1971, supporting East Pakistan's bid for independence from West Pakistan. The conflict resulted in the creation of Bangladesh.

Gandhi's tenure was marked by a decline in the political ascendancy of the Indian National Congress, the party that had dominated Indian politics since before independence. Foreign policy problems and food shortages contributed to the loss of 80 parliamentary seats in the 1967 election. In an effort to maintain her power in the legislature, Gandhi moved to form an alliance with the radical wing of the party. The right wing, led by Morarji Desai, opposed the move and the party split in 1969. In 1975, following food riots, charges of government corruption and her conviction for election law violations, Gandhi declared a state of emergency. She suspended civil liberties and postponed elections scheduled for 1976. She also sponsored legislation that retroactively cleared her of the election violations. Gandhi's actions met with widespread disapproval and when elections were held in 1977 the Congress Party suffered an overwhelming defeat, losing more than half its seats. A new government was formed under Morarji Desai, the compromise choice of the winning five-party Janata coalition. The government failed to develop a coherent set of policies and the coalition was wracked by factionalism. In 1979 Desai resigned as prime minister and was briefly succeeded by Charan Singh.

Gandhi returned to power in 1980 following an overwhelming victory by her newly reorganized Congress—Indira party. Gandhi's tenure was marked by an increase in ethnic violence. In 1983 at least 3,000 persons were killed when Hindu mobs in Assam attacked Muslim immigrants. That same year serious unrest developed in the Punjab over Sikh demands for regional autonomy. In an effort to supress Sikh militants who had organized the murder of political opponents, Gandhi, in June 1984, sent the army to assault the holiest of Sikh shrines, the Golden Temple of Amritsar, from which the militants were operating. The militants were routed but Sikhs were deeply offended by the operation. In October, Gandhi was assassinated by two of her Sikh bodyguards in retaliation. Her death led to a terrible outbreak of violence in which approximately 2,500 Sikhs were massacred. The Congress Party chose Gandhi's son, Rajiv, as her successor. He called elections for December 1984, in which he and the Congress

Party won the largest parliamentary victory in India's history.

Despite the victory, Gandhi's popularity declined dramatically. He was unable to solve the sectarian problems in the Punjab or to cleanse Indian politics of its pervasive corruption. In 1987 Gandhi sent troops to Sri Lanka to disarm the Tamil separatists. The operation proved difficult, and the last of the troops were withdrawn in March 1990.

Elections held in 1989 resulted in the defeat of Gandhi's Congress Party and victory of a National Front coalition led by the Janata Dal. V. P. Singh was sworn in as prime minister to head a minority government. Singh's tenure in office was short. In the wake of caste violence and renewed violence between Hindus and Muslims, the Singh government overwhelmingly lost a vote of confidence in November 1990 and immediately resigned. Chandra Shekhar, head of a dissident faction of the Janata Dal, became prime minister. Shekhar's government was shortlived; in March 1991 he resigned following the withdrawal of support for his minority government by the Congress (I) led by Gandhi. Gandhi was assassinated in 1991 by Tamil extremists during the election campaign that followed. In June of that year, P. V. Narasimha Rao, who had been elected head of Congress (I) following Gandhi's death, was sworn in as prime minister.

CONSTITUTION & GOVERNMENT

The Constitution of 1950, the longest constitution in the world consisting of 397 articles and nine schedules, proclaims India as a sovereign democratic, socialist, and secular republic with a parliamentary system of government. The Constitution is federal in structure with unitary features.

The Constitution also lays down certain Directive Principles of State Policy to be applied as standards in legislation. Among these are social justice, equitable distribution of ownership and control of material resources to prevent concentration of wealth, free and compulsory education.

The Constitution is flexible in character and a simple process of amendment has been adopted. The ordinary process requires a two-thirds majority of the members of each house present and voting and a simple majority in terms of total membership and the president's assent. Numerous amendments have been adopted to the Constitution dealing with various emergency measures, balance between the people and parliament, and the state and the center.

The division of powers between the union and the states is secured by demarcating the areas of legislation into three divisions: a Union List, a Concurrent List and a State List. Union parliament has exclusive powers to make laws pertaining to defense, foreign affairs, communications, interstate commerce and transportation. It can also make laws concurrently with state legislatures for 47 subjects on the Concurrent List, including marriage and divorce, trade unions, criminal law and procedure, social security, planning, price control, factories and newspapers. In case of

GOVERNMENT LIST
(July/August 1991)

President	Venkataraman, Ramaswamy Iyer
Vice President	Sharma, Shankar Dayal
Prime Minister	Rao, P. V. Narasimha
Minister of Agriculture	Jakhar, Balram
Minister of Atomic Energy & Space	
Minister of Civil Aviation & Tourism	Scindia, Madhav Rao
Minister of Civil Supplies	
Minister of Commerce,	
Minister of Communications	
Minister of Defense	Pawar, Sharad
Minister of Environment & Forests	
Minister of External Affairs	Solanki, Madhav Singh
Minister of Finance	Singh, Manmohan
Minister of Food Processing Industries	
Minister of Health & Family Welfare	Fotedar, M. L.
Minister of Home Affairs	Chavan, S. B.
Minister of Human Resource Development	Singh, Arjun
Minister of Industry	Rao, P. V. Narasimha
Minister of Information & Broadcasting	
Minister of Labor	
Minister of Law, Justice & Company Affairs	Reddy, K. Bhaskar
Minister of Parliamentary Affairs	Azad, Ghulam Nabi
Minister of Personnel, Public Grievances & Pensions	
Minister of Petroleum & Natural Gas	Shankaranand, B.
Minister of Planning & Program Implementation	
Minister of Power & Non-Conventional Energy	
Minister of Railways	Sharif, Jaffar
Minister of Science & Technology	
Minister of Steel & Mines	
Minister of Surface Transport	
Minister of Textiles	
Minister of Urban Development	Kaul, Sheila
Minister of Water Resources	Shukla, Vidya Charan
Minister of Welfare	Kesari, Sitaram
Minister of State with Independent Charge for Atomic Energy & Space	Rao, P. V. Narasimha
Minister of State with Independent Charge for Chemicals & Fertilizers	Rao, P. V. Narasimha
Minister of State with Independent Charge for Civil Supplies & Public Distribution	Rao, P. V. Narasimha
Minister of State with Independent Charge for Coal	Sangma, P. A.
Minister of State with Independent Charge for Commerce	Chidambaram, P.
Minister of State with Independent Charge for Communications	Pilot, Rajesh
Minister of State with Independent Charge for Electronics	Rao, P. V. Narasimha
Minister of State with Independent Charge for Environment & Forests	Nath, Kamal
Minister of State with Independent Charge for Food	Gagol, Tarun
Minister of State with Independent Charge for Food Processing Industries	Gomengo, Girdhar
Minister of State with Independent Charge for Information & Broadcasting	Panja, Ajit Kumar
Minister of State with Independent Charge for Labor	Ramamurthy, K.
Minister of State with Independent Charge for Mines	Yadav, Balramsingh
Minister of State with Independent Charge for Ocean Development	Rao, P. V. Narasimha
Minister of State with Independent Charge for Personnel, Public Grievances & Pensions	Rao, P. V. Narasimha
Minister of State with Independent Charge for Planning & Program Implementation	Bhardwaj, H. R.
Minister of State with Independent Charge for Power & Non-Conventional Energy	Rai, Kalpanath

GOVERNMENT LIST
(July/August 1991)

Minister of State with Independent Charge for Rural Development	Rao, P. V. Narasimha
Minister of State with Independent Charge for Science & Technology	Rao, P. V. Narasimha
Minister of State with Independent Charge for Steel	Dev, Santosh Mohan
Minister of State with Independent Charge for Surface Transport	Tytler, Jagdish
Minister of State with Independent Charge for Textiles	Gehlot, Ashok
Minister of State for Agriculture	Lenka, K. C.
Minister of State for Agriculture	Ramachandaran, M.
Minister of State for Chemicals & Fertilizers	Chintamohan
Minister of State for Civil Aviation & Tourism	Farooq, M. O. H.
Minister of State for Civil Supplies & Public Distribution	Ahmed, Kamaluddin
Minister of State for Defense	Krishnakumar, S.
Minister of State for External Affairs	Faleiro, Eduardo
Minister of State for Finance	Porthuke, Shantaram
Minister of State for Finance	Singh, M. Dalbir
Minister of State for Finance	Thakur, Rameshwar
Minister of State for Health and Family Welfare	Devi, D. K. Tara
Minister of State for Home & Parliamentary Affairs	Jacob, M. M.
Minister of State for Human Resource Development	Banerji, Mamata
Minister of State for Industry	Kurien, P. J.
Minister of State for Industry	Thungan, P. K.
Minister of State for Law & Justice	Kumaramangalam, R.
Minister of State for Parliamentary Affairs	Kumaramangalam, R.
Minister of State for Personnel, Public Grievances & Pensions	Alva, Margaret
Minister of State for Petroleum & Natural Gas	Krishnakumar, S.
Minister of State for Railways	Mallikarjun
Minister of State for Rural Development	Patel, Uttambhai H.
Minister of State for Rural Development	Venkataswamy, G.
Minister of State for Urban Development	Arunachalam, M.
Minister of State for Women & Child Welfare	Banerji, Mamata
Minister of State for Youth Affairs & Sports	Banerji, Mamata
Governor, Reserve Bank	Venkitaramanan, S.

conflict between state laws and union laws, the union laws prevail. The State List includes education, public health, local government, land revenues and irrigation.

The executive consists of a president, a vice president and a Council of Ministers headed by a prime minister. The president is elected for a renewable term of five years by an electoral college consisting of the elected members of both houses of the Union parliament and of the legislative assemblies of the states. He may be removed from office by parliament through impeachment. Although vested with broad powers, the president is a largely ceremonial figure acting solely on the advice of his prime minister and the cabinet. Among his constitutional powers are the power to promulgate ordinances, to veto state and union bills, to declare emergencies, to summon and dissolve parliament, and to appoint the prime minister, members of the Council of Ministers, the attorney general, state governors, chief justice and justices of the Supreme Court and ambassadors.

Effective executive power rests with the prime minister and the Council of Ministers. The council comprises ministers who are members of the cabinet, ministers of state and deputy ministers. The ministers are collectively and individually responsible to the Lok Sabha. At the administrative head of each ministry is a secretary. The department of cabinet affairs under the cabinet secretariat operates under the direction of the prime minister.

The governmental machinery of the states closely resembles that of the Union. Each state has a governor appointed by the president for a term of five years. The governor acts only on the advice of a Council of Ministers headed by a chief minister.

The seven Union territories are administered by the president through administrators. The administrators of Delhi, Goa, Daman and Diu, and Pondicherry are designated as lieutenant governors, while the administrators of the Andaman and Nicobar Islands and Chandigarh are designated as chief commissioners.

The highest judicial power rests with the Supreme Court. It has exclusive jurisdiction in any dispute between the union and the states.

Suffrage is universal over age 18. Parliamentary elections are normally held every five years, and the last elections were held in 1991. India is the largest democratic electorate in the world. Elections are supervised by a statutory body known as the Election Commission, headed by a chief election commissioner appointed by the president. Since some 70% of the voters are illiterate, symbols are assigned to each party and each independent candidate and are printed on the ballot papers. Election expenses are controlled, and Indian elections are generally considered fair and free.

PRIME MINISTERS OF INDIA

August 1947 to May 1964 Jawaharlal Nehru
May 1964 to January 1966 Lal Bahadur Shastri
January 1966 to March 1977 Indira Gandhi
March 1977 to July 1979 Morarji Desai
July 1979 to January 1980 Chaudhury Charan Singh (Caretaker government)
January 1980 to October 1984 Indira Gandhi
October 1984 to December 1989 Rajiv Gandhi
December 1989 to November 1990 Vishwanath Pratap Singh
November 1990 to March 1991 Chandra Shekhar
March 1991 to June 1991 Chandra Shekhar, Interim Prime Minister
June 1991–: P. V. Narsimha Rao

FREEDOM & HUMAN RIGHTS

India is a multiparty democracy with its external democratic framework still intact after 44 years of independence. It exhibits all the characteristics of a sound democracy: an independent judiciary, a nonpolitical military, a free press, regular elections, and unfettered voting rights for all citizens. Some internal strains were visible toward the end of the 1970s with ethnic and religious conflicts, disharmony between states and be-

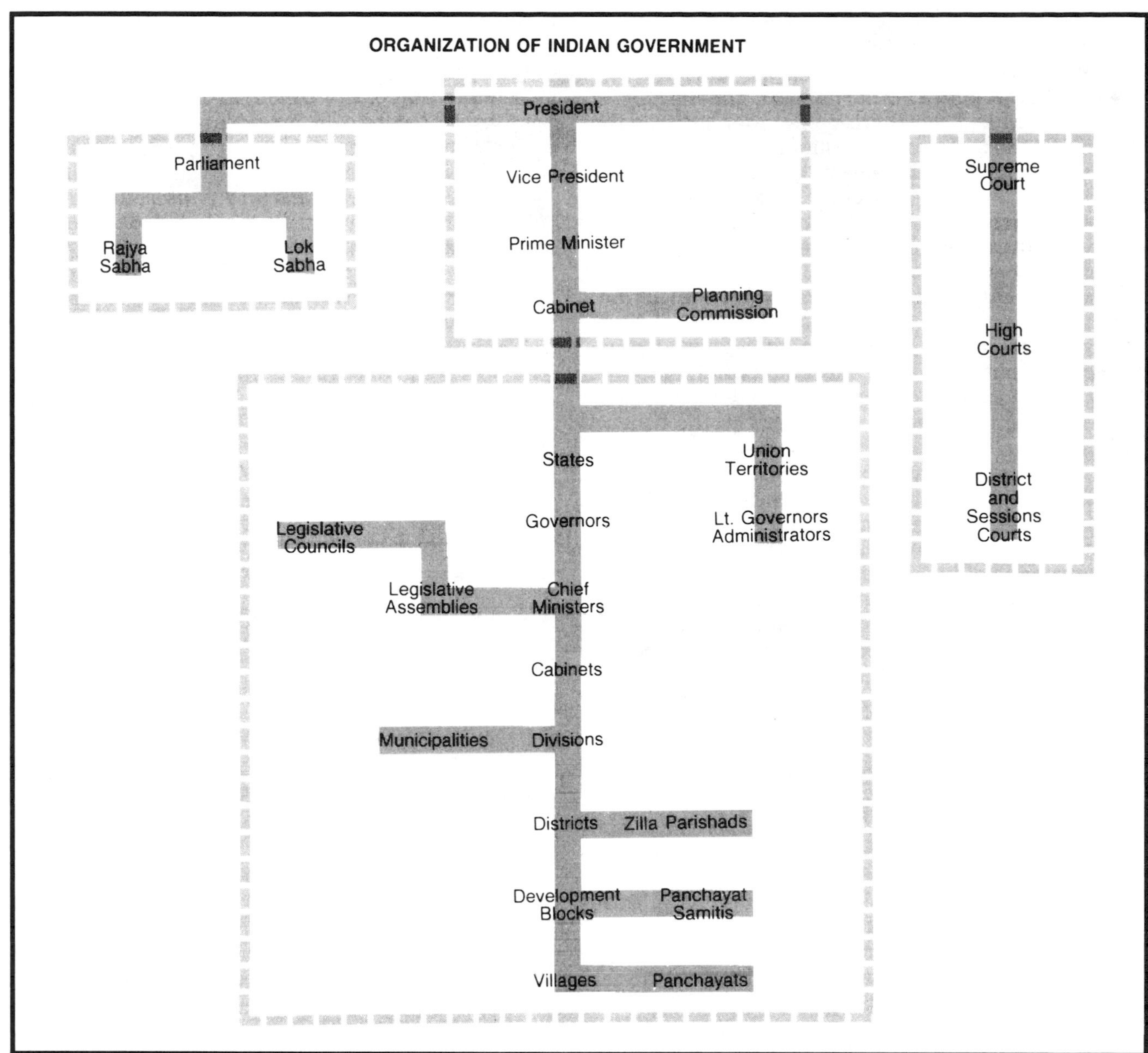

tween the federal government and the states, and police excesses.

The situation in the Punjab was the major issue of human rights concern in India in the mid-1980s. Sikh political agitation, complicated by a concurrent escalation of terrorism in the Punjab, came to a crisis in early June 1984 when the government sent army units into the Golden Temple, the Sikhs' most holy shrine. Heavy fighting with the armed extremists inside the temple complex resulted in 574 deaths, according to government figures.

Prime Minister Indira Gandhi's assassination on October 31, 1984 by two of her Sikh bodyguards triggered anti-Sikh rioting in New Delhi and elsewhere in northern India, resulting in the deaths of more than 1,200 persons. Following his appointment as prime minister, Rajiv Gandhi appealed for an end to the anti-Sikh violence and ordered deployment of the army and other security forces to quell the disturbances.

Acts of sabotage and terrorism occurred in the Punjab through the late 1980s. In October 1990 the government, reacting to the continuing violence, extended direct rule in the Punjab for an 8th term. Violence reached an unprecedented level in 1990, with the Indian press reporting about 4,000 deaths in that year. Sikh terrorists killed about 80 people in a train bombing in the Punjab in June 1991. The Punjab remains closed to foreign visitors without special permission to enter.

Incidents of communal violence have increased during the last decade. There have been clashes both between religious communities (usually Hindu–Muslim) and between castes of different economic levels, particularly attacks on untouchables by higher-caste Hindus.

There is widespread circumstantial evidence that torture by the police does occur. Amnesty International cited reports that third degree methods were used in many cases of police custody in West Bengal, and there were other reports of police torture in the Punjab, Bihar and Haryana.

While there are effective legal safeguards to ensure fair trial, the problem of prisoners awaiting trials severely vitiates the quality of justice.

In February 1980 parliament ratified a preventive detention ordinance permitting the arrest of suspected economic offenders. Later, following a Hindu–Muslim riot, a National Security Ordinance was adopted authorizing the central and state governments to order detention of individuals "to prevent action prejudicial to the defense or security of India, or to the maintenance of public order or the availability of supplies and services essential to the community." The Act has built-in safeguards against possible abuse such as a requirement for a written notification about the reason for detention within five days of arrest, access to legal counsel for the accused, and the institution of review boards.

The freedoms of press and speech are among the strongest characteristics of Indian democracy at work. The Indian press is believed to be among the freest in Asia and there is no censorship of the printed word. Electronic media, however, are entirely state controlled. Films are subject to a film censorship board where censors are more concerned with moral content than with politics. Trade unions operate without restrictions on their rights to organize, negotiate and strike.

There is universal adult suffrage that permits citizens to participate fully in the political processes and periodic elections at all levels. Elections are free and impartially administered, and supervised by an election commissioner. Every group is free to organize, agitate, publish, recruit, and to seek judicial redress in the case of perceived injustice.

CIVIL SERVICE

The administrative structure is made up of three types of civil services: all-India services, Union services and state services. Of the first category, the most prestigious are the Indian Foreign Service (IFS), the Indian Administrative Service (IAS) and the Indian Police Service (IPS), but there are also a number of minor services such as the Indian Railways Service, the Indian Audit and Accounts Service and the Indian Customs Service.

The Constitution provides for the establishment of Union and individual State Public Service Commissions to hold examinations for the civil service. The chairman and other members of the Union Public Service Commission are appointed by the president, and the chairman and members of the State Public Service Commissions are appointed by the governor of the state concerned.

LOCAL GOVERNMENT

The Republic of India is a union of 25 states and 7 Union territories:

STATES OF INDIA

State	Capital	Area Sq Km	Population	Territorial Units
Andhra Pradesh	Hyderabad	276,754	53,549,673	21 Districts
Arunchal	Pradesh	83,578	631,839	5 Districts
Assam	Dispur	78,523	19,896,843	10 Districts
Bihar	Patna	173,876	69,914,734	5 Divisions 23 Districts
Gujarat	Gandhinagar	195,984	34,085,799	19 Districts
Haryana	Chandigarh	44,222	12,922,618	7 Districts
Himachal Pradesh	Simla	55,673	420,818	12 Districts
Jammu & Kashmir	Srinager, Jammu	138,995	5,987,389	10 Districts
Karnataka	Bangalore	191,773	37,135,714	4 Divisions 19 Districts
Kerala	Trivandrum	38,864	25,453,680	11 Districts
Madhya Pradesh	Bhopal	442,841	52,178,844	43 Districts 190 Tehsils 160 municipalities
Maharashtra	Bombay	307,762	62,784,171	26 Districts
Manipur	Imphal	22,356	1,420,953	5 Districts
Meghalaya	Shillong	22,489	1,335,819	2 Districts
Mizoram	Aizwal	21,087	493,757	None
Nagaland	Kohima	16,527	774,930	7 Districts
Orissa	Bhubaneswar	155,842	26,370,271	17 Districts
Punjab	Chandigarh	50,362	16,788,915	12 Districts
Rajasthan	Jaipur	342,214	34,261,862	26 Districts
Sikkim	Gangtok	7,107	316,385	4 Districts
Tamil Nadu	Madras	130,069	48,408,077	14 Districts
Tripura	Agartala	10,477	2,053,058	1 District
Uttar Pradesh	Lucknow	294,413	110,862,013	11 Divisions 54 Districts
West Bengal	Calcutta	87,853	54,580,647	2 Divisions 15 Districts

The states and Union territories are grouped into four zones: Northern, Western, Central and Southern. Each level has a high-level advisory body known as the zonal council. The northeastern states have a Northeastern Council similar to a zonal council.

The principal subdivision within a state is the district (although some states have divisions comprising several districts), each headed by a district collector. Municipal bodies in smaller towns have less autonomy and financial resources and are more closely controlled by appointed executive officers. Municipal functions include roads, water supply, drainage, public health, education and parks.

TERRITORIES OF INDIA

State	Capital	Area Sq Km	Population	Territorial Units
Andaman & Nicobar Islands	Port Blair	8,293	188,741	2 Districts
Chandigarh	Chandigarh	114	451,610	1 District
Dadra & Nagar Haveli	Silvassa	491	103,676	None
Delhi	Delhi	1,485	6,220,406	None
Goa, Daman & Diu	Panjim	3,813	1,086,730	None
Lakshadweep	Kavaratti	32	40,249	None
Pondicherry	Pondicherry	480	604,471	None

For rural areas there is a three-tier system of panchayati raj at the village, block, and district level. Although there is some variation in the powers and structure of the panchayats (literally, the councils of five, the traditional village councils), the basic units of the panchayati raj, the general framework is the same. Elected directly by and from among villagers, the panchayats are responsible for agricultural production, rural industries, medical relief, grazing grounds, village roads, tanks and wells and sanitation.

FOREIGN POLICY

The goals of Indian foreign policy were set by Prime Minister Jawaharlal Nehru, who also headed the ministry of foreign affairs for 17 years until 1964. By proposing nonalignment as a viable alternative for developing and newly independent nations, Nehru was able to assume the role of spokesman for the Third World and to translate, with considerable success, his concepts into an instrument of mediatory diplomacy. During the 1950s and 1960s India made important contributions to peacekeeping operations in Korea, the Gaza Strip, the Congo and Cyprus. In addition, India also served as the chair of the International Control Commissions that were established in Laos, Vietnam and Cambodia under the 1954 and 1962 Geneva Agreements.

Much of this initiative has been lost since the death of Nehru in 1964, and India never regained its influence in international councils or found its proper role in the new power alignments that have emerged since the beginning of the 1970s. Indeed, during the past decade Indian foreign policy has been on the defensive and has been reduced to mending relations rather than providing new or significant leadership on international issues.

The five most crucial areas of Indian foreign policy are its relations with Pakistan, China, the United States, the United Kingdom and the Soviet Union. Other important areas are its relations with Myanmar, Nepal, Bhutan, Sri Lanka, Japan, Indonesia, the Middle East, Africa and Bangladesh.

Since 1947 India and Pakistan have lived in a state of permanent hostility ranging in intensity from verbal duels in international forums to three wars, in 1947, 1965 and 1971. Their mutual antagonism has been nurtured by a number of issues, including the unresolved dispute over Kashmir. India also accused Pakistan of training and aiding Kashmiri Muslim terrorist groups, who demand an independent Kashmir or unification with Pakistan. Although normal relations between the two countries were resumed by 1976 on the basis of the Simla Accord of 1972, little progress has been made since then. Despite tensions generated by massive U.S. aid grants and military sales to Pakistan in 1981–82, the two nations agreed to establish a permanent joint commission to discuss economic, educational, cultural and technical cooperation in 1982. In 1986 the nations agreed to formulate measures aimed at controlling drug traffic.

An equally disturbing stalemate prevails with respect to relations with China. Border tensions erupted into war in October 1962. Although the two countries exchanged ambassadors in 1976 after a break of nearly 14 years, there is little indication that the two nations' border disputes will be easily resolved. At the center of the conflict is territory in the Aksai Chin area of Kashmir and portions of Arunachal Pradesh occupied by China before the 1962 war. The two nations held inconclusive talks during the 1980s and in 1988 agreed to establish a group to facilitate settlement through peaceful consultation.

The most encouraging development during the 1980s was the marked improvement in Indo–U.S. relations, strained since 1971 over a reported U.S. tilt toward Pakistan. These relations had received further setbacks following India's explosion of an atomic device in 1974 and its subsequent refusal to permit inspection under the terms of the 1978 Nuclear Non-Proliferation Treaty. The dispute was resolved in 1982 when both parties took steps to skirt the issue.

Since India's independence in 1947, the relations between India and the United Kingdom have remained close. Although the Commonwealth has undergone radical changes during this period, India has derived considerable benefits from its membership in this organization.

India's relations with the Soviet Union have been cordial, in part reflecting similar attitudes about international problems, in part in response to Soviet economic aid. This friendship was cemented by a Treaty of Peace, Friendship and Cooperation signed by the two countries in 1971.

Relations with Nepal deteriorated in late 1989 when India closed most of the roads into Nepal in a trade dispute with its landlocked neighbor. However, the issue was settled in 1990.

Traditionally, relations with Bangladesh have been close despite continuing disputes over the sharing of the Ganges waters and conflicting claims to newly formed islands in the Bay of Bengal. In 1988 the two nations established a joint working committee to examine methods of averting the annual devastating floods in the Ganges delta.

During the late 1980s India became increasingly involved in the ethnic conflict in Sir Lanka, where the Tamil minority was attempting to establish an autonomous state. Tamils in the south Indian state of Tamil Nadu had traditionally supported their compatriots in Sri Lanka, and it was not until 1985 that the Indian government reversed its stand, coming out in opposition to the Tamil state. In 1987 India reached an agreement with Sri Lanka that permitted Indian troops to occupy parts of the island in an effort to quell the rebellion and implement a package of political concessions. The operation proved difficult with the dissidents putting up strong opposition and the majority Senhalese becoming increasingly hostile to the Indian presence. The Indian force was finally withdrawn in March 1990.

India and the United States are parties to some 60 agreements and treaties covering agricultural commodities, atomic energy, aviation, consuls, copyright, defense, economic and technical cooperation, education, extradition, finance, highways, Indian Ocean Expedition, investment guarantees, judicial assistance, lend-lease, meteorology, Peace Corps, postal matters, property, publications, relief supplies and packages, remote sensing, satellites, scientific cooperation, surplus property, taxation, telecommunication, trade and commerce, trademarks and visas.

India joined the United Nations in 1945. It is a member of 16 U.N. organizations and 42 other international organizations.

PARLIAMENT

The Indian parliament is a bicameral body consisting of an indirectly elected upper chamber, the Council of States (Rajya Sabha), and a directly elected lower chamber, the House of the People (Lok Sabha). The Council of States has a maximum membership of 250, all but 12 of whom are elected by state legislatures for six-year terms, with one-third retiring every two years. The 12 nonelected members are appointed by the president on the basis of their intellectual preeminence. The House of the People has 543 elective seats and two seats filled by nominations. Out of the elective seats, 530 are from the states and 13 from the union territories. Members are directly elected by universal suffrage for five-year terms, subject to dissolution. The president may nominate additional members if he is convinced that certain minorities, such as Anglo–Indians, are not adequately represented. The House has a normal term of five years unless dissolved earlier.

Legislation requires the consent of both houses of parliament. All financial legislation must be recommended by the president, and the Lok Sabha alone has the power to authorize appropriations and approve proposals for taxation. The president cannot withhold his assent from a money bill, but he may send back other bills to parliament for reconsideration; if both houses pass them again, the president must approve them.

Parliament must meet at intervals of at least six months, and it usually holds three sessions a year. Each daily session of the Lok Sabha begins with a questioning period, and the Rajya Sabha holds questioning periods four days a week. Parliamentary debates are often lively and vigorous.

Every state also has a legislature; Andhra Pradesh, Jammu and Kashmir, Karnataka, Bihar, Maharashtra, Tamil Nadu and Uttar Pradesh have bicameral legislatures with an upper chamber known as the Legislative Council (Vidhan Parishad) and a lower chamber known as the Legislative Assembly (Vidhan Sabha); other states have unicameral Legislative Assemblies. The Legislative Assembly is chosen by direct election from territorial constituencies. Unless dissolved earlier, it serves for five years. State Legislative Councils are permanent bodies with one-third of the membership retiring every year. At least five-sixths of Legislative Councils are elected, and the rest are named by the governor. The functions and powers of state legislatures parallel those of the Union Parliament, except that the governor may reserve any bill for the consideration of the president.

In the 1991 elections for the Lok Sabah, the Congress Party won 226 seats, the Bharatiya Janata Party 119 seats, Janata Dal 56 seats, Communist Party (M) 35 seats, Communist Party of India 13 seats, Telugu Desam Party 13 seats, and All-India Anna Dravida Munnetra Kazhagam 11 seats. Smaller parties and independents won 34 seats. Elections were postponed in the state of Punjab because of the potential for violence. The smaller parliamentary membership also made it easier for Prime Minister P. V. Narasimha Rao to form a governing coalition.

POLITICAL PARTIES

No fewer than 85 political parties contested India's first general elections in 1952, most of them splinter parties and regional parties. The very multiplicity of parties assured continued Congress successes at the polls until 1977. Parties that poll 3% or more of the vote in the previous general elections are classified as all-India parties at the national level and regional parties at the local level. Only these recognized parties are entitled to the exclusive use of certain voting symbols.

The Indian National Congress (INC), founded in 1885 by an Englishman, Allan Octavian Hume, was a monolithic party when it led India to independence. It was the ruling party of India for 30 years from 1947 to 1977. As an umbrella organization focused on independence, the Congress Party sought to unite disparate ideologies and personalities in the fight for self rule. With independence, ideological and personal differences loomed larger and led to defections from the party. In 1969 the INC split into two groups, the ruling (Gandhi) faction and the conservative, anti-Gandhi Indian National Congress (Opposition). The latter became the nation's first recognized opposition party. The INC was weakened further in 1977 when dissidents broke away to form the Congress for Democracy. In 1978 Indira Gandhi's faction was expelled from the party, and she and her followers formed a new party, called the Indian National Congress–Indira (INC–I) or Congress–I. In 1981 the party again split when the Indian National Congress–Socialist (Congress–S) was formed. That year the Supreme Court ruled that the INC–I was the real Congress Party. However, by late 1982 the anti-Gandhi Congress had disintegrated. In December 1986 Congress–S split, the majority voting to rejoin Congress–I while the remaining members decided to continue as Congress–S.

The Janata Party was formed in 1977 as a coalition of the Jana Sangh, the Bharatiya Lok Dal, the Socialists and the Congress (O). The Congress for Democracy later joined this group. The party ruled India from 1977 to 1979. Although each of these groups was supposed to submerge its separate identity into the new party, the entire period of Janata rule was characterized by factional infighting. After the Janata government collapsed, various elements and individuals left to form or reform separate parties. The Rashtriya Sanjay Manch and the Lok Dal (A) merged with the Janata Party in 1988. The party aims to achieve a socialist society free from social, political and economic exploitation.

The Bharatiya Janata Party was founded in 1980 as a breakaway group from the Janata Party. It is a radical ring-wing Hindu party.

The Communist Party of India, formed in 1925, worked with the Congress for independence in the 1930s but broke with the party during World War II. The Communists advocated collaboration with the British in the "anti-fascist war," while the Congress launched an anti-British noncooperation movement and demanded immediate independence. With the coming of independence, the Communists were divided over the appropriate approach to parliamentary democracy and to the Congress government. In 1964 the party split over this issue with the moderates advocating opposition to the Congress only on domestic issues and, then, without intent to bring down the government. The radicals, the Communist Party of India (Marxist), argued for implacable opposition to the Congress.

The All-India Anna Dravida Munnetra Kazhagam is a Tamil party founded in 1972 in a break from the Dravida Munnetra Kazhagam, an anti-Brahmin regional party dedicated to the promotion of Tamil interests.

ECONOMY

India is one of the low-income countries of the world. India has a mixed economy in which the dominant sector is public.

India's economy is a mixture of traditional village farming and handicrafts, modern agriculture, old and new industries, and a multitude of support services. It presents both the entrepreneurial skills and drives of the capitalist system and widespread government intervention of the socialist mold. Annual growth of 4-to-5% in the 1980s has softened the impact of population growth on unemployment, social tranquility and the environment. Agricultural output has continued to expand, reflecting both the greater use of modern farming techniques and improved seed that have helped to make India self-sufficient in food grains and a net agricultural exporter. Industry has benefited from a liberalization of controls. The growth rate of the service sector has also been strong.

Despite India's achievements, 40-to-50% of the people at the bottom of India's economy have been neglected and have fallen further into poverty, even using the government's austerely defined official poverty line.

From the time of the first Five-Year Plan, India's politicians tried to attain a modern economy through industrialization, concentrating on import substitution with a bias toward capital goods. The belief was that the benefits of this program would somehow automatically filter down and assure jobs and prosperity throughout the whole economy and population. What in fact happened was that pressure on scarce resources encouraged protection for infant Indian industries. The distortions thus induced were accentuated by bureaucratic controls that encouraged slowness and inefficiency, so that Indian prices were often higher than those of its competitors. This led to pressure for further controls to prevent imports of non-capital goods that might eat up scarce foreign resources. However, as Indian manufacturers were on the whole less efficient than their competitors, there was no export culture and capacity utilization was also low. For a time, new factories, new products and new jobs were created. In some of them India's performance was impressive and rivaled that of any country in the world. But then, the economy slowed.

International economic studies have tended to show that total economic growth of more than 5.5% a year is necessary before a country can begin to eliminate poverty. Also, deliberate policies are needed to distribute the growth evenly and to prevent the benefits from accruing only to the already rich. Since independence India by no means has achieved the necessary growth rate. There were land reforms, but those with useful political connections found a way around them. There was a big upsurge in education. Far more Indian children go to school today than ever before, although the very poor still cannot afford to send their children to school. The largest banks were nationalized in 1970 and more were taken into the public sector when Mrs. Gandhi returned to power in 1980, but credit remained largely in the cities or townships or went to the larger landowners.

PRINCIPAL ECONOMIC INDICATORS

Gross National Product (U.S. $ billions): 287.383 (1989)
GNP per capita (U.S. $): 350 (1989)
GNP average annual growth rate (%, 1980–89): 5.4
GNP per capita average annual growth rate (%, 1987–89): 4.9
Income distribution (%, household income) 1983
  Lowest 20%: 8.1
  Highest 10%: 26.7
Average annual rate of Inflation (%, 1980–88): 7.4
Consumer price index (1980 = 100) 1986
  All items: 170
  Food: 169
Wholesale price index (1980 = 100): 142 (1985)
Average annual growth rate (%, 1980–88)
  General government consumption: 8.8
  Private consumption: 5.8
  Gross domestic investment: 4.3

BALANCE OF PAYMENTS, 1987
(U.S. $ millions)

Current account balance: −5,192
Merchandise exports: 11,884
Merchandise imports: −17,661
Trade balance: −5,777
Other goods, services & income + : 3,813
Other goods, services & income − : −6,235
Other goods, services & income net: −2,422
Private unrequited transfers: 2,636
Official unrequited transfers: 370
Capital other than reserves: 5,325
Net errors & omissions: −409
Counterpart items: 165
Liabilities constituting foreign authorities reserves:
Total change in reserves: −318

GROSS DOMESTIC PRODUCT

GDP nominal (Re. trillions): 3.911
GDP per capita (U.S. $): 400 (1989)
Average annual growth rate of GDP (%, 1980–88): 5.2
GDP by type of expenditure (%) 1987
- Consumption
  - Private: 67
  - Government: 13
- Gross domestic investment: 23
- Gross domestic saving: 21 (1988)
- Foreign trade
  - Exports: 7 (1985)
  - Imports: −9 (1985)

Cost components of GDP (%) 1987
- Net indirect taxes: 11
- Consumption of fixed capital: 10
- Compensation of employees: }79
- Net operating surplus: }

Sectoral origin of GDP (%) 1987
- Primary
  - Agriculture: 32
  - Mining: 2
- Secondary
  - Manufacturing: 19
  - Construction: 6
  - Public utilities: 1
- Tertiary
  - Transportation & communications: 5
  - Trade: 14
  - Finance: 8
  - Other services: 6
  - Government: 6

Average annual sectoral growth rates (%, 1980–88)
- Agriculture: 2.3
- Industry: 7.6
- Manufacturing: 8.3
- Services: 6.1

Some economists have spoken or written as if there were a dualistic economy in India: one for the rich and the ruling classes in towns and another for the poor in the villages. In reality there are interlocking factors between the towns and the villages and there are seepages from the market economy. There are links between the rich in the towns and in the countryside, and the poor in both towns and villages are, in a sense, the victims of this interlocking system. Nor is there an easy dichotomy between the market economy and the subsistence economy. Some of the poor, though only a few, filter from the villages to the towns and the education system encourages the development of urban values.

PUBLIC FINANCE

The Indian fiscal year runs from April 1 through March 31. The public finance system follows the British model. Both the Union and the state governments, which maintain separate budgets, have two kinds of budgets: current, or ordinary, also known as budgets on revenue account, and capital budgets. No taxes may be levied and no expenditures from public accounts, known as the consolidated fund of India, may be made without the authorization of the Lok Sabha. Parliament also audits all government accounts to ensure that funds were legally authorized and properly spent. The railroads and the posts and telegraphs department have their own budgets presented separately to parliament. The budgets of the state governments are prepared by the state ministries of finance in consultation with the Union government. Although primary control over state finances rests with the state legislative assemblies, they are supervised by the central government through its comptroller and auditor general. Proposals for new taxes or expenditures may be initiated only by the executive at the national and state levels.

The main features of the Indian revenue system are its regressiveness and limited effect on agricultural income.

The principal sources of government revenue are customs and excise duties and domestic taxes on goods and services. Major items of expenditure are defense, grants to states and territories, interest payments on the national debt and economic, social and community services.

CENTRAL GOVERNMENT EXPENDITURES, 1988

% of total expenditures
- Defense: 19.3
- Education: 2.9
- Health: 1.8
- Housing, Social Security, Welfare: 5.4
- Economic services: 21.7
- Other: 49.0

Total expenditures as % of GNP: 17.8
Overall surplus or deficit as % of GNP: −7.9

CENTRAL GOVERNMENT REVENUES, 1988

% of total current revenues
- Taxes on income, profit & capital gain: 14.6
- Social Security contributions: 0.0
- Domestic taxes on goods & services: 35.3
- Taxes on international trade & transactions: 30.3
- Other taxes: 0.3
- Current nontax revenue: 19.5

Total current revenue as % of GNP: 14.0
General government consumption as % of GDP: 12
Average annual growth rate of general government consumption (%, 1980–88): 8.8

Planning is both a constitutional function of government and an economic necessity. Three years after independence the government set up the Planning Commission as an autonomous body responsible only to the prime minister. Because of its role in devising the basic economic strategy of both the public and private sectors, it has been described as the fourth branch of government. The Planning Commission arranges priorities, balances the needs of different sectors and the different ministries, and determines the direction and nature of state intervention in each sector. The Commission drafts five-year plans on the basis of proposals submitted by state and Union governments. The plans are designed to extend the economic base, develop basic industry, strengthen the public sector, incorporate private sector investment in overall development policy, refine a vast array of restraints and controls, and achieve self-sufficiency in various sectors. Although many of the plans were skillfully organized, several external factors have combined to neutralize and distort the development process. These include uncontrolled population growth, a series of natural catastrophes, four wars, one with China and three with Pakistan, and higher oil prices.

The emphasis of the five-year plans has been on industrial output, manufacturing, agriculture, rural development and employment. The Planning Commission was dissolved in 1980 and the Indira Gandhi government decided to terminate the 1978–83 plan as well as the "rolling plan" concept introduced by the previous Janata government. A new Planning Commission was later formed.

Foreign economic assistance has been built into every development plan since 1952. The principal channel of aid is the Aid-India Consortium formed in 1958 under the sponsorship of the World Bank with 12 members: Austria, Belgium, Canada, Denmark, France, Great Britain, Italy, Japan, the Netherlands, the United States, former West Germany and IBRD/IDA.

India was squeezed during the 1980s by cutbacks in funds from the World Bank's "soft-loan window," the International Development Association (IDA), as the Reagan administration took a tougher line. Increasingly India's aid from the Bank came from the harder-loan World Bank "window." India also suffered a rebuff in its attempts to borrow for the first time from the Asia Development Fund. Again, the United States played a role in denying India needed loans. Consequently, India was forced to expand its commercial borrowings, increasing the repayment burden.

From 1970 to 1988, the United States commitments to India, including Ex-Im, totalled $4.2 billion. Other Western countries and ODA and OOF bilateral aid totalled $18.6 in 1980–87. OPEC bilateral aid during the decade 1979–89 amounted to $10 billion. Assistance from Eastern Europe totalled $105 million in 1970–88.

FOREIGN AID, 1989

Total foreign aid (U.S. $ millions): 7,568.3
- Bilateral: 3,583.9
- Multilateral: 3,984.4

FINANCIAL INDICATORS, 1989

Total reserves minus gold (SDRs billions): 2.936
SDRs (millions): 86
Reserve position in IMF (SDRs millions): 487
Foreign exchange (SDRs billions): 2.363
Gold (fine troy oz. millions): 10.45
Ratio of external debt to total reserves: 9.2 (1988)
Central bank 1989
- Assets (%)
  - Foreign assets: 7.3
  - Claims on government: 80.9
  - Claims on banks: 11.8
  - Claims on private sector: 0.0
- Liabilities (%)
  - Reserve money: 75.9
  - Government deposits: 0.1
  - Foreign liabilities: 3.2
  - Capital accounts: 6.8
- Money supply 1988
- Stock (Re billions): 632.8
- M1 per capita: 760

Private banks 1989
- Assets (%)
  - Loans to government: 22.2
  - Loans to private sector: 63.6
  - Reserves: 14.2
  - Foreign assets: 0.0
- Liabilities
  - Deposits (nat. Re trillions): 1.867
  - of which %
    - Demand deposits: 15.6
    - Savings deposits: 71.1
    - Government deposits: 0.0
    - Foreign liabilities: 0.0

External debt 1988
- Total (U.S. $ billions): 57.513
  - of which public (U.S. $ billions): 49.695
  - of which private (U.S. $ billions): 1.473
- Debt service (long-term)
  - Total (U.S. $ billions): 4.088
  - Repayment
    - Principal (%): 41.0
    - Interest (%): 59.0
- Debt service ratio (%): 18.9
- External public debt as % of GNP: 18.7
- Debt service as % of GNP: 1.5
- Debt service as % of exports: 21.8
- Terms of public borrowing
  - Commitments (U.S. $ billions): 7.984
  - Average interest rate (%): 6.3
  - Average maturity (yrs.): 20
- Net flow of publicly guaranteed external capital (U.S. $ billions): 4.269
- Receipt of workers' remittances (U.S. $ billions): 2.850
- Net direct private investment (U.S. $ millions): 280

CURRENCY & BANKING

The Indian unit of currency is the rupee divided into 100 paise (singular: paisa). Coins are issued in denominations of 1, 2, 3, 5, 10, 20, 25 and 50 paise and 1 rupee; notes are issued in denominations of 1, 2, 5, 10, 20, 50, 100, and 500 rupees.

The central exchange rate of the rupee was fixed at £=Rs18.9677 in 1971. This rate was maintained until 1975, allowing the rupee to float in relation to non-sterling currencies. Since September 1975 the rupee has been pegged to a basket of currencies of India's principal trading partners. In June 1991 the dollar exchange rate was $1=Rs20.77.

The banking system, headed by the Reserve Bank of India, which functions as the central bank and the bank of issue, consists of scheduled and non-scheduled commercial banks and development finance organizations. Most of the scheduled banks, which account for 99.9% of aggregate banking business in the country, are in the public sector. The public sector banks occupy a dominant position, their share of the entire banking system being 91%, following the nationalization of six more banks in 1980. Among the public sector banks, the State Bank is the largest unit. Together with seven other associated subsidiaries, it accounts for some one-third of the aggregate banking business. The other banks in the public sector are known as the nationalized banks and are administered

GROWTH PROFILE
(Annual Growth Rates, %)

Projected population (1988–2000): 1.8
Projected crude birth rate (/1,000) (1990–95): 31.1
Projected crude death rate (/1,000) (1990–95): 10.2
Urban population (1985–90): 3.94
Labor force (1985–2000): 1.8
GNP (1980–89): 5.4
GNP per capita (1987–89): 4.9
GDP (1980–88): 5.2
Inflation (1980–88): 7.4
Agriculture (1980–88): 2.3
Industry (1980–88): 7.6
Manufacturing (1980–88): 8.3
Services (1980–88): 6.1
Money holdings (1980–88): 17.0 (latest)
Manufacturing earnings per employee (1980–87): 4.9
Energy production (1980–88): 6.9
Energy consumption (1980–88): 5.4
Exports (1980–88): 4.7
Imports (1980–88): 5.4
General government consumption (1980–88): 8.8
Private consumption (1980–88): 5.8
Gross domestic investment (1980–88): 4.3

by boards of directors headed by a custodian or chairman. Since nationalization, the number of bank branches has grown from 8,262 (in 1969) to 59,698 (in 1990). There are also state cooperative banks and district cooperative banks. Private scheduled banks include branches of prominent foreign banks, including two U.S. banks. Accounts of up to Rs10,000 per depositor are insured by the Deposit Insurance Corporation. Indian commercial banks also operate overseas, mainly in countries with large Indian populations. In 1975 five regional rural banks were established to supply the credit requirements of rural areas hitherto met by moneylenders.

The banking system is supplemented by an array of development finance organizations. These include the Agricultural Finance Corporation, the Agricultural Refinance Corporation, Credit Guarantee Corporation, Export Credit and Guarantee Corporation, the Industrial Development Bank, the Industrial Finance Corporation and the Industrial Credit and Investment Corporation.

A new institution, the Export–Import Bank of India was established in 1982 to finance credit for the exporting of goods and services. The major stock exchanges are located in Calcutta, Bombay and Madras.

Both scheduled and nonscheduled banks adhere to a conservative lending policy and maintain high security requirements. Despite this, there has been a continuous upward trend in bank credit. A program of differential interest rates has been in operation since 1972 under which certain categories of borrowers in backward districts receive loans from public sector banks at a concessional rate of 4%. The banks also provide export credit at concessional rates.

AGRICULTURE

Some 57% area is under cultivation. Agriculture employs a little less than 67% of the total labor force. About 80% of total agricultural output is food crops (rice, wheat, jowar, maize, and peanuts). About 20% area is given over to commercial crops. India also produces opium poppy for the pharmaceutical trade, but some finds its way into the international drug markets.

According to the nation's first agricultural census conducted in 1970–71, there were 70.5 million farms in India. At present slightly less than 10% of India's rural households own no land, and another 68% own less than 2 hectares of agricultural land. The average size of a holding is 2.0 hectares (4.94 acres). More than half of all holdings are less than one hectare (2.47 acres). There are three main crop seasons: the kharif, the rabi and summer. The kharif season lasts from July to September or October, when rice, jowar, bajra, corn,

AGRICULTURAL INDICATORS

Agriculture's share of GDP (%): 32 (1989)
Average annual growth rate (%, 1980–88): 2.3
Value added in agriculture (U.S. $ millions): 76.618 (1988)
Cereal imports (000 metric tons): 2,985 (1988)
Index of agricultural production (1979–81 = 100): 123 (1986)
Index of food production (1979–81 = 100): 124 (1986)
Index of food production per capita (1979–81 = 100): 105 (1986–88)
Number of tractors: 648,932 (1986)
Number of harvester-threshers: 2,756 (1986)
Total fertilizer consumption (000 metric tons): 8,675.5 (1985–86)
Fertilizer consumption (g./ha., hundreds) 517 (1987–88)
Number of farms (000): 81,569 (1976–77)
Average size of holding (ha.): 2.0 (1976–77)
Size class (%) 1976–77
 Below 1 ha. (below 2.47 ac.): 54.6
 1–5 ha. (2.47–12.35 ac.): 35.8
 5–10 ha. (12.35–24.7 ac.): 6.6
 10–20 ha. (24.7–49.4 ac.): 2.4
 20–50 ha. (49.4–123.5 ac.): 0.5
 50–200 ha. (123.5–494 ac.): } 0.1
 Over 200 ha. (over 494 ac.): }
Tenure (%) 1976–77
 Owner-operated: 92.7
 Rented: 1.2
 Other: 6.1
Land use (%)
 Cropland: 51
 Pasture: 4
 Forest: 37
 Other: 8
Yields (kg./ha.) 1989
 Grains: 1,851
 Roots & tubers: 15,538
 Legumes: 571
 Milk (kg./animal): 793
Production 1989
 Fruits (000 metric tons): 25,822
 Vegetables (000 metric tons): 49,626
Livestock (000) 1989
 Cattle: 195,000
 Horses: 910 (1986)
 Sheep: 53,486
 Pigs: 10,300
Forestry 1988
 Production of roundwood (000 cubic meters): 264,412
  of which industrial roundwood (%): 9.2
 Value of exports (U.S. $ 000): 16,337
Fishing 1988
 Total catch (000 metric tons): 3,145.7
  of which marine (%): 57.3
 Value of exports (U.S. $ 000): 430,570

sugarcane, sesame and peanuts are grown. The rabi season lasts from October to March when wheat, jowar, barley, gram, linseed, rapeseed and mustard are grown. Rice, corn and peanuts are grown in the summer also.

Agricultural yields are among the lowest in the world. Despite the introduction of high-yielding strains as part of the Green Revolution in the late 1960s, rice and wheat yields are about two-thirds the world average. Contributing to the poor yields are the fragmentation of landholdings, low mechanization, low rates of fertilizer and pesticide application, high illiteracy in rural areas and the fickleness of the monsoons. The level of mechanization in Indian agriculture differs vastly on regional basis. Fertilizers, tractors, and harvester-thrashers are common in the northern states of Punjab and Haryana where farms also tend to be larger than in the south.

Between 1947 and 1957 a vast body of land reform laws were enacted, which have effectively eliminated the various forms of land tenure under the British and princely rule, such as zamindari, malguzari and jagirdari, all of which were semi-feudal systems in which large landowners acted as intermediaries between the government and the peasant. The tenancy provisions of the law have been framed to benefit only tenants who do physical field labor. Legislation has also imposed ceilings on agricultural holdings that vary among states, regions and classes of land. At the same time, in an effort to safeguard efficiently managed farms, the government has exempted from ceilings certain categories of farms, such as plantations and ranches. A ceiling has also been imposed on rents payable by tenants. To restrain fragmentation under Hindu and Muslim inheritance laws, measures have been enacted in most states for consolidation on a voluntary basis, while in some states laws provide for compulsory consolidation.

In two parallel voluntary movements, known as gramdan (donation of villages) and bhoodan (donation of land), sponsored by Acharya Vinoba Bhave, landlords voluntarily handed over villages and land to peasants.

About one-third of the total cultivated area is under irrigation. With more irrigation, large areas may be able to produce at least two crops per year. Since independence a number of vast multipurpose projects have been undertaken. These include: the Bhakra-Nangal on the Sutlej River, irrigating areas in the Punjab, Rajasthan and Haryana; the Hirakud Dam spanning the Mahanadi River in Orissa, the Damodar Valley Project in West Bengal and Bihar, the Nagarjunasagar Dam on the Krishna River in Andhra Pradesh, and the Kosi Dam in Bihar. India's long-term strategy is to double the irrigated area to 92.13 million hectares (2.27 million acres) in 1992–93, which works out roughly to 81% of maximum potential irrigated area based on presently known reserves of surface and ground water.

India is one of the world's largest producers of rice, jute, sugar, spices, rape, sesame and castor seed. It ranks first in the world in production of peanuts and tea and has a virtual monopoly in the production of lac. All these products, however, face problems: sugar from overproduction, international quota restrictions and insufficient domestic demand; tea from competition from China, Kenya and Indonesia; and jute from competition from synthetics. Tea, coffee and rubber contribute significantly to the economy, although they account for less than 1% of the agricultural land. Tea, grown in Assam, West Bengal and Kerala, is the most important plantation crop and is a major contributor to foreign exchange.

Indian agriculture is dominated by food production, and in the 1980s this sector witnessed an extraordinary performance that turned the country from a net importer to an exporter. According to experts, India could feed a population about three times its present size (about 2.4 billion people) if full use were made of the land. Indian planners have predicted that the total annual output of food grains could easily reach over 200 million tons by the end of the century. Only one-fifth of the net area cultivated presently yields more than one crop. While the performance of high-yielding varieties of wheat has been generally successful, that of rice has not. Wheat is also able to benefit more from irrigation because it is grown in the spring, or rabi, season while rice is grown mainly in the monsoon, or kharif, season. This affects Indian agriculture negatively because rice accounts for 40% of the total food-grain production.

Statutory rationing of food grains, especially wheat and rice, is in force in major cities. To stabilize the country's food economy, the government has built up a buffer stock of food grains. The Food Corporation of India, set up in 1965, functions as the sole official agency for procurement, import, distribution, storage and sale of food grains. Minimum support prices and procurement prices for agricultural products are fixed by the Agricultural Prices Commission. The National Commission on Agriculture periodically examines the progress of agriculture and makes recommendations for its improvement and modernization.

Animal husbandry is underdeveloped, primarily because of Hindu belief about the sanctity of the cow, poor breeding and lack of fodder. Under the Intensive Cattle Development Program, some 100 projects have been set up in different parts of the country, including a Central Frozen Semen Bank near Bangalore and Central Herd Registration Scheme. Five central cattle breeding farms have been established for raising high quality bulls of the Red Sindhi, Tharparkar and Jersey breeds of cattle and the Murrah and Surti breeds of water-buffalo. In addition to a central sheep breeding farm at Hissar, several regional farms have been set up. There are also regional pig-breeding stations.

Forests cover about 22% of the land area, mostly in the foothills of the Himalayas, Assam, Central India, the Western Ghats and the Andaman Islands. More than 90% of the forests are owned by the government and are known as Reserved Forests. Nearly 2.5 million hectares are man-made forests.

India's forests are generally broad-leaved; less than 10% are coniferous. Almost 25% of forest land is inaccessible. Major forest by-products are bamboo, cane, fiber, floss, gums and resins, medicinal herbs, tanning bark, and lac.

India ranks third in the world in production of roundwood after Brazil and Indonesia. Per hectare production is, however, low (almost 25% of the United States, and 10% of Japan). The logging industry is not mechanized and relies extensively on elephants for transport, especially in the south.

India's vast fishing grounds cover 5,110 km (3,175 mi) of coastline, 27,353 km (7,000 mi) of inland rivers, 112,630 km (70,000 mi) of canals, in addition to lakes, ponds and reservoirs. Two hundred deep-sea fishing vessels were introduced during the late 1970s. There are major fishing harbors at Madras, Roychowk, Cochin, Vishakapatnam, Calcutta, Karwar, Port Blair, Tuticorin and Vizhinjam. The Exploratory Fisheries Project at Bombay has 11 bases under its control. The Central Fisheries Corporation has a network of cold-storage plants and refrigerated rail vans.

Indian farmers chronically suffer from agricultural indebtedness. Institutional lenders consist of agricultural credit societies, state cooperative banks and central cooperative banks. Grain banks also play a significant role in providing short-term and medium-term credit. Long-term credit is extended through land-mortgage banks, the Agricultural Finance Corporation and the Agricultural Refinance Corporation. The State Bank of India has opened more than 200 agricultural development branches.

MANUFACTURING

Manufacturing employs some 11% of the labor force. Chief manufacturing sectors are agro-based products, textiles and clothing, machinery and transport equipment, and chemicals. Nine states—Maharashtra, West Bengal, Tamil Nadu, Gujarat, Uttar Pradesh, Bihar, Andhra Pradesh, Karnataka and Madhya Pradesh—account for three-fourths of the manufacturing output. Of the 10 dominant industrial groups, the largest is textiles. The other principal industries are jute, sugar, paper and paper board, photo paper and films, iron and steel, engineering and machine tools, drugs and pharmaceuticals and petrochemicals. In terms of absolute value of output, India ranks among the 10 largest industrial countries of the non-Communist world, but it is among the least productive in terms of per capita industrial output.

The manufacturing sector is divided into an organized sector and an unorganized sector. The organized sector is subdivided into large-scale and small-scale industries. The unorganized sector consists of cottage industries, handicrafts and most service industries.

Over the last two decades the public sector has emerged as a major factor in the country's economic growth.

The central government's public undertakings represent over 50% of the value in large-scale manufacturing.

Power shortages, a thin, overburdened infrastructure, labor unrest, under-capacity of plant and personnel, high capital-output and capital-labor and shortages of essential industrial inputs are the chief causes of industrial stagnation; the iron and steel, cement, paper, sugar and cotton textiles industries witnessed a slowdown in the mid-1980s. Procrastination and indecision on the part of the Indian bureaucracy delayed implementation of large-scale projects in both the private and public sectors and were contributing factors to poor performance in the industrial area. Marginal improvements in production were reported by the leather, footwear, rubber and machine tool industries.

MANUFACTURING INDICATORS, 1987

Average annual growth rate (%, 1980–88): 8.3
Share of GDP (%): 19 (1988)
Labor force economically active in manufacturing (%): 11.1 (1981)
Value added in manufacturing (U.S. $ billions): 43.331
- Food & tobacco (%): 12
- Textiles & clothing (%): 15
- Machinery & transport equipment (%): 26
- Chemicals (%): 15

Earnings per employee in manufacturing 1987
- Growth rate (%, 1980–87): 4.9
- Index (1980 = 100): 138

Total earnings as % of value added: 48
Gross output per employee (1980 = 100): 174
Index of manufacturing production: 174 (1988)

At the same time, the Indian press continues to decry poor performance of public sector industries. Of the investment in public sector corporations, steel and coal alone accounted for some 30%. The public sector accounts for 40% of the industrial output.

Labor problems, too, were a significant contributing factor depressing India's industrial output in the 1980s. The jute and cotton textile industries, Calcutta port, and engineering industries were the most seriously affected. Increased labor unrest was largely attributable to the rapid rise in cost of living. Trade and industry sources, however, believe that with the advent of the new government under P. V. Narsimha Rao the prospects for industrial peace will improve.

Official policy toward foreign investment is determined by both the need for overseas development capital and domestic pressure to Indianize the economy. There are no restrictions on the repatriation of foreign capital, and in cases of nationalization full and equitable compensation is guaranteed. Under U.S. Public Law 480, loans in Indian rupees are available to U.S. investors if their venture has official approval. These loans carry low rates of interest. There is also no ceiling on royalties in central essential industries, and in others the ceiling ranges from 3% to 5%. As a rule, effective control of an undertaking is required to be in Indian hands. Under the Foreign Exchange Regulation Act (FERA) of 1973, foreign investors are required to restrict their shareholding to 74%, 51% or 40%, depending on their line of business and export capacity. In 1977 multinationals like Coca Cola and IBM were required to close their operations in India because of their unwillingness to conform to this regulation. The principal foreign investors are the United Kingdom, the United States, Germany and Japan.

The process of decreasing foreign shareholdings in the Indian corporate sector under the Foreign Exchange Regulation Act of 1973 was completed during

1979. Consequently, almost all 760 companies in which foreigners held shares in varying proportions (out of a total of 51,000 companies in the country) had acquired Indian registration and had become Indian companies before the law. No longer dubbed foreign companies, many of them now hope to have more opportunities for expansion and diversification. What worried them, however, was the question of whether the government would ask them to further dilute foreign holdings, which stood at 40% for most of these companies (and up to 100% for some others, depending on their lines of business).

An important objective of industrial policy is to prevent the emergence of private monopolies and concentration of economic power. All industries listed in the first schedule of the Industries (Development and Regulation) Act of 1951 are required to be licensed. The act authorizes the government to take over any mismanaged industrial undertaking. Under the Monopolies and Restrictive Trade Practices Act of 1969, large industrial houses are restricted to the production of 19 groups of products; all other products are reserved for the small-scale sector.

Institutional finance for industries is provided by the Industrial Finance Corporation of India, the Industrial Development Bank, the Industrial Credit and Investment Corporation, the Industrial Reconstruction Corporation, the National Industrial Development Corporation, the Unit Trust of India and several state financial corporations.

In December 1984, Bhopal in India was the scene of one of history's worst industrial accidents when the Union Carbide chemical plant leaked poisonous gas. Over 2,000 persons are believed to have died and several thousands more critically injured as a result of the accident. The resulting litigation is likely to be protracted. All claims have been consolidated, with the government of India as the principal suer.

MINING

India is relatively well endowed in mineral wealth. Proved reserves include hematite ore and magnetite ore, manganese, bauxite, coal, chromite, copper, ilmenite, lead, zinc, nickel and gypsum. India has the 4th largest coal reserves in the world.

Chief minerals produced are coal, bauxite, dolomite, limestone, iron ore, mica, gold, diamonds, manganese, chromium, lead, phosphate and zinc.

ENERGY

Some 76% of total energy is produced by fossil fuels, 22% by hydroelectricity, and 2% by nuclear fuel. India is developing an integrated power generation and transmission system, and rural electrification has grown steadily in recent years. Under the Department of Science and Technology research programs in biogas and biomass have been established.

India has reserves of 4.5 billion barrels of petroleum (enough to last 20 years at current rate of extraction) and 1,100 billion cubic meters of natural gas.

ENERGY INDICATORS

Average annual energy production growth rate (%, 1980–88): 6.9
Energy consumption per capita (kg. oil equivalent): 211 (1988)
Energy imports as % of merchandise exports: 20 (1988)
Average annual growth rate of energy consumption (%, 1980–88): 5.4
Electricity 1988
- Installed capacity (million kw.): 63.233
- Production (billion kw.-hr.): 237.800
  - % fossil fuel: 75.9
  - % hydro; 21.8
  - % nuclear: 2.3
- Consumption per capita (kw.-hr.): 291

Natural gas
- Proved reserves (trillion cu. m.): 1,100 (1990)
- Production (billion cu. m.): 10.620 (1989)
- Consumption (billion cu. m.): 6.909 (1988)

Petroleum
- Proved reserves (billion bbl.): 4.345 (1990)
- Years to exhaust proved reserves: 17 (1990)
- Production (million bbl.): 256 (1989)
- Consumption (million bbl.): 358 (1988)
- Refining capacity (million bbl./day): 1,080 (1990)

Coal
- Reserves (billion metric tons): 62.548 (latest)
- Production (million metric tons): 197.565 (1988)
- Consumption (million metric tons): 198.010 (1988)

There are 10 refineries, eight in the public sector and two in the private sector. With the nationalization of Exxon in 1974 and the Burmah–Shell refinery in 1976, the government controls 95% of total production and marketing of petroleum. The two principal organizations engaged in the exploration and production of crude oil are the Oil and Natural Gas Commission and Oil India Ltd., the latter a joint undertaking in which the government and Burmah–Shell have equal shares. A subsidiary, Hydrocarbons India Ltd., explores for oil in foreign countries. Marketing and distribution is the virtual monopoly of the Indian Oil Corporation, a state-owned company. Five off-shore oilfields have been discovered in the Western continental shelf off the Maharashtra coast. The first of these, called Bombay High, began commercial production in 1976 and produces 10 million metric tons annually.

Inshore deposits of petroleum have been found in Assam, Gujarat and Nagaland, and offshore oilfields have been discovered in the Western continental shelf off the Maharashtra coast, in the Cauvery basin and in the Bay of Bengal. In 1980 India announced that foreign oil companies would be allowed to explore for petroleum, both onshore and offshore. The Bassei offshore gas field is one of the largest in the world.

Petroleum from India's own resources plays a growing role in the economy. India produced about 73% of its petroleum requirements in 1984, compared with 50% in 1983 and 34% in 1980. As a result of increased production, imports (in value terms) of crude petroleum and petroleum products declined by around 25% in the fiscal year 1984. However, it is still necessary to import petroleum to ensure sufficient supplies. In 1989, imports of mineral fuels comprised approximately 15% of the estimated cost of total imports.

India is developing an integrated power generation and transmission system. Rural electrification has grown steadily and almost all major towns and cities have electricity. Nevertheless, severe power shortages are common throughout the country.

India has made considerable progress in the development of nuclear energy. The Bhabha Atomic Research Center at Trombay in Bombay is the national center for research and development of nuclear energy for peaceful uses. The research center has five research reactors. There are four atomic power stations at Kalpakkam in Amil Nadu, Kota in Rajasthan, Tarapur in Maharashtra and Narora in Uttar Pradesh. Three nuclear power stations are being built in Narora, Kakrapar, Kaiga and Rawatbhata. India has six heavy-water plants in operation. A nuclear fuel complex in Hyderabad produces the fuel required by the nuclear power stations. India successfully exploded an underground nuclear device in 1974.

LABOR

India's economically active population is estimated at 260,275 million; 26% of the labor force is female. By occupational sectors (from highest to lowest) the labor force is occupied in agriculture, manufacturing and mining, services, trade, transportation, and construction.

Wages and working conditions are governed by law. Conditions of work in the wage sector are limited to nine hours per day, with a maximum of 45 hours per week. A minimum of 10 days of yearly vacation is required, but this may go up to one day for each 20 days of actual employment. Days off ("casual" leave) of up to 10 days per year are also provided.

LABOR INDICATORS, 1981

Total economically active population (000): 260,275
- % working-age (15–64): 60.7
- % female: 26.0

Activity rate (%)
- Total: 39.1
- Male: 55.2
- Female: 21.9

Employment status (%)
- Employers & self-employed: 8.8
- Employees: 16.3
- Unpaid family workers: 3.6
- Other: 71.3

Sectoral employment of economically active (%)
- Agriculture, forestry, fishing: 66.4
- Construction: 1.5
- Manufacturing, mining, quarrying, public utilities: 11.1
- Trade, hotels, restaurants: 4.9
- Transportation, communications: 2.4
- Finance, real estate: 0.7
- Services: 7.1

Average annual growth rate of labor force (%, 1980–2000): 1.8
Unemployment (000): 30,542 (1987)
Labor under 20 years (%): 16.2
Earnings in manufacturing per worker (/) (nat. currency): 622.5 (1982)

Children below 14 may not be employed, and those between 14 and 18 must obtain a fitness certificate before being employed. Exception is made for family-run businesses, an important factor in some cottage industries. Overtime is limited to one hour per day, and a maximum of 50 hours in any three-month period, compensation being double time. Under the Industrial Employment (Standing Orders) Act of 1946, establishments employing 100 or more workers are required to adopt certified standing orders governing working conditions. Works committees, joint management councils and workers' representation on management boards have been introduced in certain types of establishments. Since 1956, annual bonuses have become mandatory regardless of whether the company made a profit. Bonuses range between 20% and 40% of total wages. The normal retirement age for wage earners is 58. Discrimination in employment against women was made illegal in 1975.

The number of unemployed has increased in recent years and millions are seriously underemployed. Official studies suggest that 32% of the rural labor force and about 20% of the urban labor force do not have stable or adequate employment. The Indian educational system produces more liberal arts graduates each year than the economy can absorb, leading to a massive wastage of human resources and skills as well as social dislocations. Emigration of skilled labor to the Middle East, Africa and Southeast Asia has acted for a long time as a safety valve. Next to overpopulation, unemployment is considered by many economists to be India's major problem.

India does not encourage immigration, especially of workers. Work permits are required for foreigners, and government policy encourages foreign corporations to employ Indians.

The lack of employment opportunities for skilled and educated Indians, on the other hand, has resulted in the emigration of many, who, in the view of Indian authorities, could help in the country's development. On balance, the government believes more benefit is derived from the repatriation of the foreign earnings of most categories of Indian workers who have gone abroad. These remittances, largely from the Middle East, help India's balance of payments. Thus, concurrently with an oversupply of unskilled workers and of persons educated through high school and college but without technical or needed professional skills, there are shortages in some occupations and professions where attractive outside opportunities exist.

Bonded labor is proscribed by law but nevertheless persists. Estimates of the number of affected laborers vary between 500,000 and 2.5 million, depending partly on the definition used. There has been considerable parliamentary and press debate over this practice, widely criticized in India as an unfortunate legacy of feudalism and poverty. Most vulnerable are landless, unemployed rural workers hired by small enterprises, particularly in the construction industry. The workers are placed in debt and kept there indefinitely by revolving loans from employers. In recent years the

Supreme Court has taken a particularly active role in pressing responsible state and central government agencies to enforce protections against bonded servitude.

Nearly 5% of the labor force is unionized. In the absence of compulsory registration and the need to file returns, a precise estimate of aggregate trades-union membership in India is difficult to make. More than half the unions have less than 300 members, and only 15 have more than 15,000 members. The majority of the unions do not have full-time officials or shop stewards. Union control over the workers is weak, the membership is unstable, and wildcat strikes are common. But they represent one of the largest organized groups in the country and serve as the base for many of the political parties. Occasionally they become the focal point for militant political action that can have great impact on the economy. The most powerful labor unions are the Congress-affiliated Indian National Trade Union Congress, with 4,408 affiliated unions and a total membership of 5,180,000, and the Communist-dominated All India Trade Union Congress, with 4,000 affiliated unions and 3,400,000 members. Other leading labor unions include the Hind Mazdoor Sabha (2,800,000 members) the United Trades Union Congress, the Beijing oriented Center of Indian Trade Unions with 963,000 members, the Confederation of Central Government Employees' Unions and National Federation of Indian Railwaymen. The overall low proportion of trade union membership hides pockets of considerably greater strength in specific economic sectors and geographic areas. Bombay, Madras, and Calcutta are three labor strongholds, and trade unions have effective strength in the railroads, in the mines, and in the engineering, plantations, oil, chemicals, textiles, and steel manufacturing sectors.

Like most developing societies, India's labor force is relatively weak in self-organization and requires the protection of laws and regulations. India's long leadership role in the ILO and the consistent prolabor stance of its government have served to emphasize this situation. Thus, a variety of labor laws has been enacted by either national or state legislatures.

Even before independence, legislation had been enacted governing workmen's compensation, wage payment regulation, and trade union rights.

With independence, laws followed that covered investigation and settling of industrial disputes including those resulting in strikes and lockouts; insurance benefits for sick and disabled industrial workers, as well as death benefits for survivors; minimum wages; safety and health standards; provident (social security) funds for factory and some other workers; mine safety; maternity benefits; bonuses (wage supplements); and many other labor standards.

Most of these laws cover only a small percentage of workers. Enforcement of these laws is another matter because the country is so large, enforcement so costly, and the staff so small. Many feel that the economy cannot really afford strict enforcement of all regulations. Nevertheless, the existence of legislation provides some measure of protection and represents a declaration of governmental policy that is useful in discouraging exploitation.

The Essential Services Maintenance Act (ESMA) of 1981 permits government intervention to ban strikes and to immediately institute conciliation in essential industries.

Industrial disputes are governed by the Industrial Disputes Act of 1947 and the Code of Discipline of 1958. Collective bargaining between employers and unions is uncommon because of the presence of rival unions within a plant and the financial weakness of unions. Most work stoppages are brief and protracted strikes are rare.

Employees of factories with 20 or more workers receive a variety of benefits under the Employees' State Insurance program. Employees of establishments with more than 50 workers are covered by the Employees' Provident Fund. Legislation also provides for maternity allowance, workmen's compensation, family pensions and death relief.

FOREIGN TRADE

India suffers from chronic trade deficits. Except for a rare surplus recorded in 1976–77, the trade deficit has been on the rise. The principal imports are petroleum and petroleum products, nonelectrical machinery, iron and steel, fertilizer, edible oils, chemicals, and nonferrous metals. The major exports are engineering goods, cotton apparel, leather and leather goods, tea, iron ore, gems and jewelry, chemicals, cotton fabrics and fish and fish preparations.

The major importers are the United States, Iran, the Soviet Union, Japan, Germany, the United Kingdom, Belgium, Iraq, Canada and Kuwait. The major export destinations are the Soviet Union, the United States,

FOREIGN TRADE INDICATORS, 1988

Exports (U.S. $ billions): 17.2 (1989)
Imports (U.S. $ billions): 24.7 (1989)
Balance of trade (U.S. $ billions): −7.5 (1989)
Annual growth rate (1980–88), exports (%): 4.7
Annual growth rate (1980–88), imports (%): 5.4
International reserves in terms of months of imports covered: 3.8
Terms of trade (1980 = 100): 119
Import price index (1980 = 100): 90.3 (1986)
Export price index (1980 = 100): 107.2 (1986)

Direction of Trade (%), 1987

	Imports	Exports
European Community	32.6	22.0
United States	9.4	18.7
U.S.S.R. & eastern European economies	7.1	18.6
Japan	12.9	10.7

Composition of Trade (%), 1987

	Imports	Exports
Food & agricultural raw materials	10.7	27.9
Fuels & other energy	15.1	3.4
Mineral ores & concentrates	11.9	21.8
Manufactured goods	62.4	47.0
of which chemicals	13.1	3.9
of which machinery	31.2	6.7

Japan, the United Kingdom, Germany, Belgium, the Netherlands, France, Kuwait and Iraq.

India has yet to develop an export culture like South Korea and Singapore where foreign trade is the engine of growth. Early emphasis on import substitution, the existence of a large subsistence sector outside the market economy, poor technology management, and an ideological association with the Soviet bloc, all contributed to depress export earnings. But, during the late 1970s, some positive features emerged: the cultivation of Middle East markets, the fall in food and petroleum imports, and growing technological skills all contributed to vigorous profits and healthy balance of trade figures. For example, India has become the world's largest exporter of cut diamonds, outdistancing both Belgium and Israel.

State trading policy is designed to bring in foreign trade under the control of state trading agencies, of which the largest is the State Trading Corporation. There are also several specialized organizations for export promotion, such as Board of Trade, the Trade Development Authority, Export Promotion Councils, Commodity Boards, the Indian Institute of Foreign Trade, the Directorate of Exhibitions and Commercial Publicity and the Export Inspection Council.

TRANSPORTATION & COMMUNICATIONS

India's rail system is the largest in Asia and the fourth largest in the world. It is also the biggest enterprise in the public sector. Of the total length, some 10% is electrified and 20% is double track. The rail system is state-owned and is operated by the Railway Board with nine operational zones. The railway budget is kept separate from the general budget, and the railroads pay an interest-dividend on the total investment. India's first underground railway is under construction in Calcutta. When completed, it is expected to carry more than one million people daily.

The length of navigable waterways in India is 16,180 km (10,054 mi), of which about one-fifth is navigable by steamers. The most important of the navigable rivers are the Ganges and the Brahmaputra and their tributaries, the Krishna and the Godavari, the backwaters and canals of Kerala, the Buckingham Canal in Andhra Pradesh and Tamil Nadu, and the Mandovi and Zuari Rivers in Goa. The Central Inland Water Transport Corporation operates river services between Bangladesh and northeast Indian states.

The major ports are Bombay, Calcutta, Cochin, Kandla, Madras, Mangalore, Haldia, Kochi, Marmagoa, Paradip, Tuticorin and Vishakapatnam. Of these, Bombay is the largest port. Marmagoa near Goa enjoys the second position in total traffic tonnage and Calcutta and Madras the third place. Cochin is one of the finest natural harbors in the world. A free trade zone was created in Kandla in 1965. In addition, there are over 160 intermediate and minor ports serving coastal traffic. Another new port has been built at Nhava Sheva to relieve the congestion at Bombay. Container traffic passing through Indian ports has doubled in the last few years but is still a tiny amount compared with the numbers handled in more modern Asian countries to the east. Major ports are administered by statutory port trusts and minor ports by the state governments. Port congestion tied up movement on the waterfront. The waiting period for ships before unloading cargo, however, has been brought down from 40 days to 15–20 days at Bombay and at Madras from 30 to 15 days. Calcutta, beset by labor problems, continues to be bad, with a waiting period of 30–35 days.

India is the second largest ship-owning country in Asia and ranks among the top 20 in the world. There are 55 shipping companies, of which the Shipping Corporation of India is the largest in the public sector. There are four major ship-building yards at Vishakapatnam, Calcutta, Bombay and Cochin.

Some 47% of Indian roads are paved. The central government is directly responsible for the national highway system, while state highways and district and rural roads are the responsibility of state governments. The National Highway System is a complex of 55 highways connecting all state capitals and major ports. The Border Roads Development Board has constructed new roads in the north and northeast border areas. Except for three Union territories, most of the states and Union territories have nationalized passenger transport in varying degrees. Goods transport, on the other hand, continues to be almost exclusively in the

TRANSPORTATION INDICATORS

Roads (latest)
- Length, km. (mi.): 1,773,000 (1,101,742)
- Paved (%): 47

Motor vehicles (latest)
- Automobiles: 2,284,000
- Trucks and buses: 1,433,000
- Persons per vehicle: 225
- Road freight, metric ton-km. (short ton-mi.) (billions): 81,000 (55,477) (pre–1986)

Railroads (latest)
- Track, km. (mi.): 61,812 (38,410)
- Passenger-km. (passenger-mi.) (billions): 263,400 (163,677)
- Freight, metric ton-km. (short ton-mi.) (billions): 226,600 (155,198)

Merchant marine
- Vessels (over 100 tons): 834 (1989)
- Total deadweight tonnage (millions): 10.206 (1989)
- Oil tankers (million GRT): 1.717 (1985)

Ports (pre–1986)
- Cargo loaded (million metric tons): 24.668
- Cargo unloaded (million metric tons): 39.490

Air
- Km. (mi.) flown (millions): 9.8 (6.1) (1985)
- Passenger-km. (passenger-mi.) (billions): 18.012 (11.193) (latest)
- Freight, metric ton-km. (short ton-mi.) (millions): 672.6 (460.7) (latest)
- Mail, metric ton-km. (short ton-mi.) (millions): 33.1 (22.7) (1985)
- Airports with scheduled flights: 99 (1990)

Pipelines 1990
- Refined, km. (mi.): 1,703 (1,058)
- Natural gas, km. (mi.): 902 (568)

Inland waterways (latest)
- Length, km. (mi.): 16,180 (10,054)

COMMUNICATION INDICATORS, 1988

Telephones
- Total (000): 4,371
- Persons per telephone: 189

Phone traffic (million calls) 1987
- Local: 16,484 (pulses)
- Long distance: 229.300
- International: 2.410

Post office
- Number of post offices: 144,829
- Pieces of mail handled (000): 13,543,157

Telegraph 1987
- Total traffic (000 calls): 62,131
  - National: 60,861
  - International: 1,270

Telex 1987
- Subscriber lines: 34,044

Telecommunications 1990
- Satellite stations: 3
- Submarine cables: 3

TOURISM & TRAVEL INDICATORS, 1986

Total tourist receipts (U.S. $ millions): 1,500 (1988)
Expenditures by nationals abroad (U.S. $ millions): 400 (1988)
Number of hotel beds (000): 60
Average length of stay (nights): 30
Number of tourists (000): 1,259 (1985)
- of whom from United States: 95.9
- United Kingdom: 119.5
- Germany, Fed. Rep.: 44.8
- France: 44.1

private sector. Roads carry about one-third of the freight and roughly 60% of passenger traffic.

The international flag carrier is Air India, which operates a fleet of 10 Boeings to 24 countries on five continents. It is one of the few international airlines that have consistently shown a profit.

The domestic airline is Indian Airlines, which provides domestic flights and flights to and from Afghanistan, Sri Lanka, Nepal and Bangladesh. Its subsidiary, Vayudoot Private Ltd., provides air links to smaller towns in northeastern India. In September 1983 an Indian commercial earth satellite was launched by the U.S. space shuttle "Challenger." It was hoped that the satellite would improve telecommunications, so that the area of India with access to television would be extended to cover 75% of the population. The four main international airports are Santa Cruz (Bombay), Dum Dum (Calcutta), Indira Gandhi (New Delhi) and Meenambakkam, (Madras).

No description of India's transport system would be complete without mention of the traditional means of transportation used in villages and cities by people too poor to afford even bus transport. These include bullock carts, tongas (horse-drawn carts) and rickshaws.

Indian National Department of Tourism maintains tourist information offices at home and abroad. India's distinctive tourist attractions include its scenery, music, dance, festivals, its historical monuments and its rich variety of wild life. Big-game-hunting is banned. In 1984 the government tightened visa regulations for foreigners coming to India and those traveling to "sensitive" areas are required to obtain special travel permits.

DEFENSE

The defense structure is headed by the president. Responsibility for national defense rests with the parliament and the cabinet. At the cabinet level there is a standing National Defense Council with the prime minister as chairman. The three chiefs of staff are equal and independent. The army is divided into five commands: Southern, Eastern, Central and Western with headquarters at Poona, Calcutta, Lucknow and Simla. The fifth command is called Northern but its headquarters remain undisclosed. The bulk of the army is deployed on the Pakistani and Chinese borders. The navy is organized into three commands—Western, Eastern and Southern—and two fleets—Eastern and Western. The air force is organized into five commands: Western, Central and Eastern and two operational commands, Training Command and Maintenance Command.

Military manpower is provided by voluntary enlistment. Since the days of the British Raj, the bulk of the recruitment is from the so-called martial races: the Rajputs, Sikhs, Gogras, Marathas, Jats and Punjabis as well as the Gurkhas, although the latter are Nepali citizens. Paramilitary forces include the territorial army, and the Lok Sahayak Sena, or the national volunteer force.

The total strength of the armed forces is 1,262,000.

Army

Personnel: 1,100,000

Organization: 5 regional commands; 8 corps HQ; 2 armored divisions; 1 mechanized division; 19 infantry divisions; 10 mountain divisions; 7 independent armored brigades; 10 independent infantry brigades; 1 mountain brigade; 1 parachute brigade; 8 independent artillery brigades; 3 independent engineer brigades

Equipment: 2,500 heavy tanks; 150 light tanks; 350 combat vehicles; 500 armored personnel carriers; 850 artillery guns; 500 mortars; howitzers; surface-to-surface missiles; antitank guns; rocket launchers; 500 air defense guns; 180 SAM

Navy

Personnel: 50,000 (including 1,500 naval air personnel)

Units: 8 submarines; 1 aircraft carrier; 1 cruiser; 3 destroyers; 23 frigates; 3 corvettes; 14 fast attack craft; 8 patrol craft; 19 mine countermeasures vessels; 13 amphibious vehicles

Naval Air Force: 2,000

36 combat aircraft; 36 combat helicopters; 1 attack squadron; 1 antisubmarine warfare squadron; 2 maritime reconnaissance squadrons; 1 communications squadron; 1 search and rescue helicopter squadron; 2 training squadrons

Naval Bases: Bombay, Cochin, Calcutta, Goa, Port Blair, Vishakapatnam, Lonavala and Jamnagar

Air Force

Personnel: 110,000

Organization: 846 combat aircraft; some 60 armored helicopters; 5 air commands; 3 bomber squadrons; 12 fighter squadrons; 20 air defense squadrons; 2 reconnaissance squadrons; 11 transport squadrons; 1 communications squadron; 16 liaison aircraft; 7 helicopter squadrons; 3 training and conversion squadrons; air-to-air missiles; air-to-surface missiles; SAM 30 battalions

Air Bases: Bangalore, New Delhi, Shillong, Hyderabad, Bamrauli and Allahabad

India's defeat by China in 1962 was a turning point in Indian military history. It led to a rapid buildup of defense capability through increased military expenditures. There has also been a greater national willingness to employ force and to mobilize productive capacities and resources for military purposes. This policy paid off when Indian forces won their first decisive victory over Pakistan in 1971. This victory radically altered the military balance of power on the Indian subcontinent in India's favor. The army has been building a flexibility that will enable it to operate under a variety of terrains—jungles, mountains and deserts. The explosion of a nuclear device in 1974 has added a new dimension to the nation's military strength—particularly in relation to Asia's other nuclear power, China.

India has developed a substantial defense production capability, including small arms and armaments, tanks, frigates and submarines, aerospace equipment, helicopters, trainers, radar and radio systems, air and ground defense electronics, machine guns, heavy mortars and anti-tank guided weapons.

EDUCATION INDICATORS, 1988

Literacy
- Total (%): 43.5
- Male (%): 57.0
- Female (%): 29.0

First level
- Schools: 543,677
- Students: 92,943,556
- Teachers: 1,616,685
- Student/teacher ratio: 57.5
- Net enrollment ratio: 92 (1986)

Second level
- Schools: 207,871
- Students: 45,412,377
- Teachers: 2,256,985
- Student/teacher ratio: 20.1
- Net enrollment ratio: 41 (1986)

Vocational 1986
- Schools: 5,494
- Students: 3,196,963

Third level (postsecondary)
- Gross enrollment ratio: 8.9 (1983)
- Students (/100,000 pop.): 776
- % of population age 25 and over with postsecondary education: 2.5

Foreign study
- Foreign students in national universities: 11,039 (1985)
- Students abroad: 24,850
  - of whom in
    - United States: 20,252 (1988)
    - France: 214 (1988)
    - Federal Republic of Germany: 604 (1988)
    - United Kingdom: 922 (1987)

Public expenditure 1987
- Total (nat. currency 000): 106,434,000
- % of GNP: 3.3
- % of national budget: 8.5
- % of current: 98.5

EDUCATION

Education, in theory, is free, universal and compulsory (in most states) for five years from the age of 6.

Schooling consists of six years of primary school, three years of lower secondary school and three years of upper secondary school, for a total of 12 years. The pattern, however, varies from state to state, with some states having eight years of integrated elementary education followed by three years of secondary education and others having seven years of elementary education followed by four years of secondary school. A national pattern of 12 years of schooling followed by three years of college has been adopted by the majority of the states. The culmination of secondary school studies is the secondary school leaving certificate examination, which is both a diploma in itself and a passport to the university. Elementary schools vary widely in curriculum facilities and in quality of instruction. A new pedagogical approach called basic education was introduced in the 1960s. The curriculum of basic schools is activity-oriented and correlates teaching with the social and physical environment of the child. The dropout rate is high, particularly in the first grade where it approaches 26%, and most of the dropouts revert to illiteracy.

The academic year runs from April to March. The medium of instruction varies from state to state and between public schools and private schools. In general, English is the medium of instruction in most private schools; Hindi or the dominant state language is the medium of instruction in primary grades in public schools, but the medium shifts to English either in the upper secondary school or early in college. Many universities, however, offer examinations in Hindi or regional languages. All students are required to be bilingual and some trilingual (in Hindi, English and their mother tongue).

Primary school teachers are trained in normal schools and secondary school teachers in special colleges of education. Nearly 70% of primary school teachers are fully qualified.

A few private schools (called public schools on the British model) cater to the wealthy. These schools receive no subsidy, but the quality of the teaching staff is generally high and the medium of instruction is English. Schools run by religious denominations, both Christian and non-Christian, also operate within the school system.

The main thrust of adult education is the eradication of illiteracy. Although the literacy rate has increased, the number of illiterates has also increased. In general, literacy is higher in urban areas and along the coast than in rural areas in the interior. It is two times higher among males than among females, higher among Brahmins, Parsis, Jains and Christians than among other castes and classes, and higher in the south than in the north. The highest literacy is recorded in Kerala (90%) and the lowest in Bihar (38.5%). In recent years the emphasis in adult education programs has shifted from literacy to functional education. These programs include Farmers' Functional Literacy Program, Polyvalent Adult Education Centers and Non-Formal Education Programs for those between 15 and 25.

About 6% of the secondary school enrollment is in the vocational stream. Vocational and technical education is provided in junior technical schools and industrial institutes.

According to the Constitution, education was a state subject, but by an amendment in 1977 it moved onto the Concurrent List. Education is funded mainly by state governments and administered by the state ministries of education and the municipal and district school boards. The Union government provides and funds support services and educational development schemes, particularly in the areas of vocational education, basic education, adult education, propagation of Hindi, textbook research and audio-visual education.

Higher education is provided in some 130 universities. Of these, 77 have been established since independence. Most universities have affiliated undergraduate colleges. The most prestigious are the universities of Calcutta, Bombay, Madras and Delhi. The University Grants Commission promotes and coordinates university education and determines and maintains standards of teaching, examinations and research. It also advises on the establishment of new universities.

LEGAL SYSTEM

The legal system is based on English common law.

The judicial system is headed by the Supreme Court, consisting of a chief justice and not more than 25 judges. The chief justice is appointed by the president and the other judges are appointed by the president after consultation with the chief justice. These appointments do not require the concurrence of parliament, but judges may be removed by the president only after a parliamentary impeachment. The Supreme Court has original, appellate and advisory jurisdiction. It exercises exclusive jurisdiction in disputes between the Union and the states and between states and is the ultimate interpreter of the Constitution and all laws.

There are 18 high courts, 17 of which are located in states and one of which is located in Delhi. Two high courts have jurisdiction over more than one state. Goa, Daman and Diu share a judicial commissioner, while the other five Union territories come under the jurisdiction of the nearest high courts. Each high court is headed by a chief justice, who is appointed by the president in consultation with the governor of the state and the chief justice of India. The number of judges on a high court bench varies from state to state, ranging from a minimum of three to a maximum of 33. High courts are not subject to the control of the state legislatures or executives; judges may be removed only in the same manner as judges of the supreme court.

Each state is divided into a number of judicial districts. Under the Code of Criminal Procedure of 1973, there are separate sets of district magistrates for the discharge of executive and judicial functions. Executive magistrates are under the control of the state governments, while judicial magistrates are under the control of the High Courts. Under the district magistrate are first- , second- and third-class magistrates, who try criminal offenses not tryable by sessions courts. At the village level, nyaya (justice) panchayats try cases involving minor offenses.

The Constitution permits the enactment of preventive detention laws against threats to the public welfare and to the national security. Such laws provide for limits on the length of detention, generally not to exceed 12 months, and for review of such detention. Two preventive detention laws are currently in force. One, used less frequently, permits the arrest of suspected "economic offenders." The other is the National Security Act, which the government amended to make its provisions more stringent. Now the courts, in order to release a detainee held under this act, must determine that all grounds for detention are invalid, rather than any one of them as before. The amended act also provides for detention for 24 months in the Punjab and Chandigarh.

The new Terrorist Affected Areas Act of 1984 empowers the government to declare any part of the country as "terrorist affected" and set up special courts which can hold trials in camera. The whole of the Punjab was so declared following the unrest in that state.

There is no constitutional guarantee of public trial. The criminal procedure code provides for open trial but permits the judiciary to close the proceedings under relatively narrow circumstances where the evidence would be prejudicial to the state. Warrants are required for searches but police are permitted to institute searches without warrant if otherwise there would be undue delay.

The judiciary is completely separate from the executive and is highly esteemed for its independence, competence and impartiality. It retained its integrity even under the pressures of Mrs. Gandhi's state of emergency. Judges of the state high court and Supreme Court are selected by the law ministry on the recommendations of the chief justice of the Supreme Court. Since 1983, state chief justices are required to be non-state residents.

Each state has an inspector general of prisons in charge of correctional facilities, which usually include a central prison and smaller district jails. Some states have model prisons without walls for those convicted of minor offenses.

According to a classification system dating from the colonial period, prison authorities grant different privileges to prisoners of different social status. Foreign nationals and political prisoners are entitled to larger or less crowded cells, better food, and other amenities than ordinary prisoners; some middle-class prisoners are segregated from other prisoners and given more privileges. This system enjoys wide support in India.

LAW ENFORCEMENT

Until 1977, when police became a Union subject, each state had its own police force under an inspector general of police. All senior officers of the state police forces belong to the all-India service, known as the Indian Police Service. Each district has a district superintendent of police, who supervises a number of thanas, or precincts. At the national level the police function is the responsibility of the Ministry of Home Affairs, which provides an array of specialized services to state police forces and also offers police training. The principal law enforcement arm of the Union government is the Central Bureau of Investigation (CBI) with powers similar to the U.S. Federal Bureau of Investigation. The Ministry of Home Affairs also maintains the Central Reserve Police Force (CRP) as the nucleus of a federal police force, the Railway Protection Force and the Border Security Force.

The crime rate is increasing but has still not reached alarming proportions. Most crimes are minor offenses related to poverty. Types of offenses showing the greatest percentage of growth are counterfeiting, criminal breach of trust, riots, theft and robberies. The most serious law enforcement problem is, perhaps, smuggling, which has become an extensive industry.

HEALTH

Health is primarily the responsibility of the state governments. The Union government sponsors national programs for disease prevention and control. The major health problems are malaria, filaria, tuberculosis, leprosy, venereal diseases, trachoma and cancer.

There are thousands of unregistered medical practitioners, herb compounders and registered practitioners following Ayurvedic (ancient Hindu system of medicine) and Unani (traditional Muslim) systems. More than 100 colleges and schools teach the Ayurvedic and Unani systems, and some 70 teach homeopathy. Various national health programs aim to combat leprosy, malaria and tuberculosis. Smallpox was declared eradicated in 1977. Plague has not been reported since 1967. A new approach to family planning was introduced in 1986 through Family Welfare Centers, so that the population does not exceed one billion by the year 2000.

FOOD

Despite the stereotype of Indian food as consisting of only rice and curry, the Indian diet is characterized by considerable variety and range. In general, diet varies from caste to caste, from region to region, and between the coastal regions and the interior. The staple food in the north is wheat, usually in the form of chapathies and poories, and northern cuisine has been influenced by that of Iran, resulting in a combination of Hindu and Muslim styles. The southern diet is rice-based and consists of light and easily digested dishes. Meat is excluded from the diet of Brahmins and high-caste Hindus and pork from the diet of Muslims. The basic source of protein is milk and milk products. Most Indians have conservative food habits and resist unfamiliar foods even when they go abroad.

The daily per capita intake of food is 2,043 calories (93% of requirements).

HEALTH INDICATORS

Health personnel 1986
- Physicians: 318,000
  - persons per: 2,471
- Dentists: 9,598 (1984)
- Nurses: 165,000 (1985)
- Pharmacists: 155,621 (1981)
- Midwives: 168,493 (1984)

Hospitals
- Number: 25,452
- Number of beds (/10,000): 8/1986)

Type of hospitals (%) 1981
- Government: 71.6
- Private nonprofit: } 28.4
- Private profit: }

Public health expenditures (latest)
- As % of national budget: 1.8
- Per capita (U.S. $): 1.10

Vital statistics
- Crude death rate (/1,000): 11 (1990)
- Life expectancy at birth 1990
  - Males: 57
  - Females: 59
- Infant mortality rate (/1,000 live births): 89 (1990)
- Child mortality rate under 5 yrs. (/1,000 live births) (1985–90): 148
- Maternal mortality rate (/100,000 live births) (1986–87): 500.0
- Population with access to safe water (%): 57 (latest)

MEDIA & CULTURE

About 1,082 daily newspapers and over 21,500 non-dailies are published in India with aggregate circulations of 59,195,000. In addition, the periodical press consists of some 10,000 titles. By state, Maharashtra has the largest number of newspapers, followed by Uttar Pradesh, Delhi, West Bengal, Tamil Nadu, Andhra Pradesh, Rajasthan, Kerala, Karnataka, Madhya Pradesh and Gujarat. By language, the largest number of newspapers is published in Hindi, followed by English, Urdu, Bengali, Marathi, Gujarati, Tamil, Malayalam, Telugu, Kannada and Punjabi. There are about 1,000 bilingual newspapers. Both the circulations and the number of newspapers have significantly decreased since the 1970s. The overwhelming majority (95.5%) of papers have circulations of less than 15,000 each. The majority of the newspapers are owned by individuals; the rest are owned by societies and associations and by central and state governments. The allocation of newsprint is determined by the Newsprint Advisory Committee.

The main characteristics of the Indian press are the dominance of the English-language press, the shortage of newsprint, 73% of which must be imported annually at the expense of foreign currency reserves, and the difficulty of adapting Indian scripts other than Bengali, Tamil and Hindi to linotype machines. Most Indian language newspapers are manually composed. In the case of papers in Urdu, for which no typeface has been developed, all texts are handwritten by calligraphers for lithographic reproduction.

Principal Dailies

Daily	Circulation
Indian Express, English	715,027
Statesman, English	399,000
Times of India, English	1,115,924
Hindu, English	378,825
Hindustan Times, English	267,647
Malayala Manorama, Malayalam	530,691
Ananda Bazar Patrika, Bengali	400,359
Nav Bharat Times, Hindi	372,027
Mathrubhumi, Malayalam	390,062
Jugantar, Bengali	319,682
Daily Thanthi, Tamil	320,343
Lok Satta, Marathi	207,915
Hindustan, Hindi	160,969
Maharashtra Times, Marathi	192,382

The quality of the press varies. There is little investigative reporting and too great a reliance on press releases from the government and foreign embassies. The vernacular press has to spend time and expense translating news stories from the English.

Freedom of the press is upheld in the Constitution and periodically reaffirmed by court decisions. The state of emergency proclaimed in 1975 imposed stringent censorship that was designed to prevent the publication of matter considered objectionable by the government, especially news or comments likely to excite opposition to the government, or create disharmony among different sections of society. During the emergency, all foreign correspondents were required to clear their stories with the Press Information Bureau and those who failed to do so were expelled. With the lifting of the emergency in 1977, the press has become once again the only news medium outside government control and ownership. In March 1979 a Press Council was set up to uphold the freedom of the press. In 1980 a second Press Commission was appointed to inquire into the growth and status of the press.

The national news agencies are: the Press Trust of India Ltd., United News of India, Hindustan Samachar and Samachar Bharati. They had been forced to merge under the first Gandhi administration under the name Samachar but were permitted to re-establish as separate entities in 1978. There are smaller news-feature agencies such as Indian News and Feature Alliance, India Press Agency, the Eastern India News Agency and 12 feature agencies including News Features of India. Foreign news bureaus include ANSA, APF, AP, DPA, UPI, Reuters, Tass and Middle East News Agency.

In terms of annual title output in English, India is one of the largest publishers in the world, ranking fourth in the world after the United States, the United Kingdom and Canada. More than 10,000 publishers are listed in the Directory of Indian Publishers. A number of official organizations are active in the field of publishing, such as the Sahitya Akademi, founded in 1954 for the development of Indian letters, the National Book Development Board, the National Book Trust, the Children's Book Trust and the Publications Division of the Union Ministry of Information and Broadcasting. An annual book fair is held in New Delhi. India adheres to the Universal, Berne and Buenos Aires Copyright Conventions.

MEDIA INDICATORS

Newspapers
- Number of dailies: 1,802 (latest)
- Circulation (000): 16,731 (latest)
- Per 1,000 pop.: 23 (latest)
- Number of nondailies: 21,638 (1986)
- Circulation (000): 42,464 (1986)
- Per 1,000 pop.: 54 (1986)
- Newsprint consumption 1988
  - Total metric tons: 505,000
  - Per 1,000 pop. (kg.): 617

Book publishing
- Number of titles: 14,219 (latest)

Radio
- Number of transmitters: 220 (latest)
- Number of persons per radio receiver: 15 (1989)

Television
- Television transmitters: 174 (latest)
- Number of persons per T.V. receiver: 42 (1989)

Cinema
- Number of fixed cinemas: 12,732 (latest)
- Seating capacity (000): 6,030 (latest)
  - Seats (/1,000 pop.): 7.6 (1987)
- Annual attendance (millions): 4,920.0 (latest)
- Gross box office receipts (millions): 6,400 (1987)

Films
- Number of long films produced: 806 (latest)
- Number of long films imported: 222 (1987)
  - % from
    - United States: 55.0
    - United Kingdom: 10.8
    - Italy: 8.1
    - France: 4.1

The All India Radio is the largest radio network in Asia with over 70 stations grouped into four zones. The programs cover some 80% of the population and about three-fourths of the geographical area. Radio programs are dedicated to information, education, culture, religion, commercials and entertainment. In addition, a self-contained all-India entertainment service, known as Vividh Bharati, is broadcast with popular music and commercial advertising. The home service is broadcast in all the principal languages and also in 51 local languages and 82 tribal dialects. The external service programs are broadcast in 16 foreign languages and eight Indian languages. The News Services Division broadcasts bulletins every day in 24 languages and 36 dialects.

Television, introduced in 1959, is now operated by Doordarshan India, from more than 20 centers. Color television began in 1981. Television broadcasting became independent of All India Radio in 1976 under the name Doordarshan India. To maximize broadcasting coverage, the government installs and maintains radio and television sets in community centers. Some 94% program hours are produced domestically dedicated to information, education and to entertainment. In August 1990 a bill was unanimously passed in Lok Sabha, which granted autonomy to the state-operated national radio and television networks.

India is the largest film producer in the world with an annual output of 806 films, nearly half in color. Madras, Bombay and Calcutta are the most important film-producing centers. The majority of the films produced are in Hindi, followed by Tamil, Telugu, Malayalam, Bengali, Kannada and other regional languages. Several foreign feature films are imported annually, largely from the United States and the United Kingdom. Films may be exhibited only after they have been certified by the Central Board of Film Censors, who may grant either an A certificate for restricted exhibition or U certificate for unrestricted exhibition. The government actively supports the film industry through film festivals, national awards for films and grants and loans through the Film Finance Corporation.

The largest library is the National Library at Calcutta with 1.8 million volumes.

CULTURAL & ENVIRONMENTAL INDICATORS

Libraries (pre-1986)
  Number: 17,024
Nature reserves (latest)
  Number of facilities: 325

SOCIAL WELFARE

Social welfare services are administered by the Union Department of Social Welfare through the Central Social Welfare Board and State Social Welfare Advisory Boards. The bulk of the programs are directed toward children, women, the handicapped, juvenile delinquents, prostitutes, convicts, displaced persons, scheduled castes and tribes, beggars and those affected by drought, floods, earthquakes and other disasters. In addition, 6,000 private voluntary organizations are engaged in social work. There is, as yet, no comprehensive social security program, but there is a limited health insurance program covering workers in large factories.

GLOSSARY

abkari: tax or excise duty on the sale and production of alcoholic liquors.
bhoodan: movement launched by Acharya Vinoba Bhave in the 1950s for redistributing land by gifts of individual holdings to landless peasants.
communalism: particularism based religious, ethnic and linguistic loyalties.
dharma: moral code of conduct comprising ritual obligations of one's caste, family, community and profession.
kharif: crop sown at the beginning of the rainy season.
kist: any of the installments in which land revenue is paid into the treasury.
Lok Sabha: the House of the People, the lower chamber of the Indian parliament.
panchayat: literally, council of five. Basic unit of local government.
Panch Shila: literally, five principles. Guiding principles of Indian foreign policy enunciated by Prime Minister Jawaharlal Nehru.
rabi: crop sown after the rains, such as wheat.
raj: sovereignty or paramount power, as in British Raj.
Rajya Sabha: the Council of States, the upper chamber of the Indian parliament.
rashtrapathi: title of the president of India.
ryot: a peasant or cultivator considered as an element of the land tenure system.
scheduled castes: official designation for economically and socially backward castes who suffer disabilities under the traditional caste system.
swadeshi: literally, of one's own country. Campaign (associated with Mahatma Gandhi) for economic self-sufficiency and promotion of cottage industries.
taluk: a subdivision of a district, presided over by a tahsildar.
untouchable: a Hindu who falls outside the traditional four castes.
Vidhan Parishad: state Legislative Council.
Vidhan Sabha: state Legislative Assembly.
zamindari: former system of land tenure in which landlords, called zamindars, also functioned as tax collectors.

CHRONOLOGY (from 1947)

1947— Under the Independence of India Act, British parliament grants full independence to India and Pakistan; Indo-Pakistani borders are delimited under the Cyril Radcliffe Award; both nations are plunged into communal violence; amid scenes of carnage 11–to–16 million Hindus, Muslims and Sikhs flee across the borders; an estimated 1 million die in post-partition violence; Lord Mountbatten, the last crown representative, becomes the first governor general of the Dominion of India and Jawaharlal Nehru its first prime minister. . . . Indian armed forces occupy Junagadh, a Hindu state whose Muslim nawab, or ruler, had acceded to Pakistan. . . . The Hindu maharaja of Jammu and Kashmir, a Muslim state, accedes to India; Pakistani irregulars invade Kashmir and occupy the NW portion of the state.
1948— Mahatma Gandhi is assassinated by a Hindu fanatic. . . . C. Rajagopalachari is named the first Indian governor general. . . . India forcibly annexes the state of Hyderabad into the Indian Union.
1949— The Indian Constitution Act is enacted. . . . A ceasefire is arranged in Jammu and Kashmir under U.N. auspices.
1950— Under the new Constitution, India proclaims itself a republic within the commonwealth. . . . Rajendra Prasad is named first president of India. . . . The integration of former princely states is completed.

1952— India holds first general elections and Nehru's Congress Party wins predictable victory.

1953— Andhra Pradesh is formed as the first linguistic state.

1956— Under the States Reorganization Act, state boundaries are redrawn on linguistic basis. . . . France cedes her Indian territories to India.

1957— In the nation's second general election, Communists win heavily in Kerala and form India's first Communist state government. . . . Decimal coinage is introduced with the naye paise replacing the former anna.

1958— Aid-India Consortium is formed by a number of donor nations.

1960— India and Pakistan sign the Indus Waters Agreement under World Bank auspices. . . . Bombay is bifurcated into Maharashtra and Gujarat states.

1961— Goa and other Portuguese territories are "liberated" and merged into the Indian Union.

1962— India holds third general elections. . . . Nagaland is formed as a separate state. . . . Chinese troops occupy disputed border areas in Ladakh (Kashmir) and Northeast India and expel Indian troops; Defense Minister V. K. Krishna Menon resigns in the wake of this defeat.

1964— Nehru dies; Lal Bahadur Shastri elected prime minister.

1965— Three-week Indo-Pakistani war over disputed areas in the Rann of Kutch ended inconclusively by the Tashkent Accord under Soviet auspices.

1966— Shastri dies at Tashkent; Nehru's daughter, Indira Gandhi, elected prime minister.

1967— Parliament authorizes continued use of English as the official language in view of southern opposition to Hindi.

1969— Power struggle breaks out in the Congress Party between Indira Gandhi's faction and the old guard; the party splits into the New Congress and the Old Congress.

1971— India intervenes in force in the civil war in East Pakistan on the side of the rebels; Indian Army occupies East Pakistan in the third conflict between India and Pakistan in 24 years; the state of Bangladesh is proclaimed. . . . Indira Gandhi wins landslide victory in general elections. . . . Titles and privileges of maharajas abolished. . . . Under the North East Areas Act of 1971 Meghalaya, Manipur and Tripura become states, and Mizoram and Arunachal Pradesh become Union territories. . . . India and the Soviet Union sign a 20-year Peace, Friendship and Cooperation Treaty.

1974— India joins the nuclear club by exploding a nuclear device in Rajasthan.

1975— Following the abolition of the monarchy by the Sikkim Assembly, Sikkim becomes India's 22nd state. . . . Indira Gandhi responds to nationwide unrest against her rule by proclaiming a state of emergency, suspending civil liberties, arresting opposition political leaders and imposing press censorship. . . . Government launches 20-point economic program.

1976— India and China exchange ambassadors after 14 years.

1977— Indira Gandhi calls surprise national elections; her Congress Party suffers serious election reverses and loses majority in parliament to a coalition of opposition parties known as Janata Party; Janata leader Morarji Desai forms government. . . . Emergency is lifted and civil rights are restored.

1978— President Jimmy Carter visits India. . . . Indira Gandhi expelled from the Congress Party; she forms a new party, also called Congress Party, with her supporters. . . . Gandhi's faction wins surprising victories in state elections. . . . Indira Gandhi elected to parliament, but is condemned by a parliamentary commission, ousted and jailed; five persons are killed in pro-Gandhi riots.

1979— Charan Singh, influential Uttar Pradeshi leader, quits Desai government but is wooed back as deputy prime minister; Janata coalition begins to break up as its factions are unable to settle on a unified policy; Desai resigns office of prime minister and leader of the Janata coalition; Charan Singh named prime minister but is unable to form government and win parliamentary majority. . . . Mother Teresa of Calcutta wins Nobel Peace Prize.

1980— Indira Gandhi leads her Congress Party to victory in parliamentary elections in January and is installed as prime minister; in one of her first official acts, recognizes the Vietnamese puppet government of Cambodia. . . . Leonid Brezhnev visits India and promises lavish Soviet military and economic aid. . . . Indira Congress Party wins majority in eight state legislatures. . . . Sanjay Gandhi, Indira Gandhi's son and prospective successor, killed in plane crash.

1983— Sikhs restive over the rejection of their separatist demands, storm parliament building . . . New Delhi hosts nonaligned nations conference.

1984— U.S. multinational Union Carbide's chemical plant in Bhopal leaks poisonous gas that kills more than 2,000 people. . . . Indian cosmonaut joins the Soviet Soyuz. . . . Indira Gandhi assassinated by Sikh revanchists. Her son, Rajiv Gandhi, nominated as prime minister; Rajiv Gandhi's Congress Party wins overwhelming majority in parliamentary elections.

1985— India joins other nations of the Indian subcontinent in forming the South Asia Regional Conference.

1986— Mizo National Front signs peace agreement with Prime Minister Rajiv Gandhi.

1987— The Union Territories of Arunachal Pradesh, Mizoram and Goa become States of the Indian Republic.

1988— Guidelines for the Eighth Five-Year Plan (1990–95) approved; four major centrist parties form a coalition National Front to oppose Congress (I) at the next general election.

1989— General elections held except in Assam; V.P. Singh sworn in as new prime minister.

1990— Widespread violent demonstrations held in many north Indian states to oppose government's stand on increasing quota of reserved jobs for lower castes; violent clashes occur between Hindus and Muslims about the disputed site of a 16th-century mosque in the Hindu holy town of Ayodhya; V.P. Singh loses prime ministership in a vote of no confidence.

1991— Chandar Shekhar resigns as prime minister, but accepts the offer to head the interim government; former Prime Minister Rajiv Gandhi assassinated; P.V. Narsimha Rao sworn in as India's 9th prime minister in June.

BIBLIOGRAPHY (from 1970)

BOOKS

Agarwala, P.N. *History of Indian Business.* New York, 1985.

Apte, M.L. *Mass Culture, Language & Arts in India.* Mystic, Conn., 1979.

Balasubramanya, V.N. *The Economy of India.* Boulder, Colo., 1985.

Baljit, Singh. *India's Foreign Policy: An Analysis.* New York, 1976.

Banerjee, A.C. *Constitutional History of India.* Columbia, Mo., 1977.

Barnett, M.R. *The Politics of Cultural Nationalism in South India.* Princeton, N.J., 1976.

Behari, Bepin and Madhuri Behari. *Indian Economy Since Independence: Chronology of Events.* New York, 1983.

Benner, Jeffrey. *The Indian Foreign Policy Bureaucracy.* Boulder, Colo., 1985.

Bhagwati, Jagdish N., and Padma Desai. *India: Planning for Industrialization: Industrialization & Trade Policies Since 1951.* New York, 1979.

Bhargava, B.S. *Indian Local Government: A Study.* Columbia, Mo., 1978.

Bhatia, H.L. *Center-State Financial Relations in India.* Columbia, Mo., 1979.

Bhatia, H.S. *Political, Legal and Military History of India.* Highland Park, N.J., 1984.

Bhatia, Shyam. *India's Nuclear Bomb.* New York, 1980.

Bindra, S.S. *India and Her Neighbors.* Highland Park, N.J., 1984.

Biria Institute of Scientific Research. *India 2001.* Mystic, Conn., 1978.

Bose, Ashish. *Studies in India's Urbanization.* Columbia, Mo., 1978.

———. *Population Statistics in India.* Columbia, Mo., 1977.

Brands, H.W. *India and the United States: the Cold Peace.* Boston, 1990.

Breman, Jan. *Of Peasants, Paupers and Migrants.* New York, 1985.

Bueno De Mesquita, Bruce and Richard L. Park. *India's Political System.* Englewood Cliffs, N.J., 1979.

Cambridge Economic History of India, 3 vols. New York, 1982/83.

Carras, Mary C. *Indira Gandhi in the Crucible of Leadership.* Boston, 1979.

Cassen, R.H. *India: Population, Economy, Society.* New York, 1978.

Chandra, Bipin. *Nationalism & Colonialism in Modern India.* Columbia, Mo., 1979.

Charak, Sukhdev. *Encyclopedia of Indian History and Culture.* Highland Park, N.J., 1981.

Chaudhuri, Asim. *Private Economic Power in India: A Study in Genesis and Concentration.* Columbia, Mo., 1976.

Chaudhuri, Pramit. *The Indian Economy: Poverty & Development.* New York, 1979.

Chesney, George T. *Indian Polity.* Columbia, Mo., 1976.

Chowhuri, S.R. *Leftist Movements in India (1917–1947).* Columbia, Mo., 1976.

Cohen, Stephen P., and Richard L. Park. *India: Emergent Power?* New York, 1978.

Das, B.C. *The President of India.* Mystic, Conn., 1977.

Dayal, Ishwar. *District Administration in India.* Columbia, Mo., 1976.

De Souza, Alfred. *The Indian City: Poverty, Ecology, & Urban Development.* Columbia, Mo., 1970.

DeSouza, Anthony. *The Politics of Change & Leadership Development: New Leaders in India and Africa.* Columbia, Mo., 1978.

Dumont, Louis. *Homo Hierarchicus: The Caste System and Its Implications.* Chicago, 1981.

Dutt, Subima. *With Nehru in the Foreign Office.* Columbia, Mo., 1977.

Dutt, V.P. *India's Foreign Policy.* New York, 1984.

Dwivedy, Surendranath. *Quest for Socialism: Fifty Years of Struggle in India.* London, 1987.

Eldersveld, Samuel, and Bashiruddin Ahmed. *Citizens & Politics: Mass Political Behavior in India.* Chicago, 1978.

Fadia, Babula. *Pressure Groups in Indian Politics.* Highland Park, N.J., 1980.

Fishlock, Trevor. *Gandhi's Children.* New York, 1983.

Gangrade, K.D. *Social Legislation in India.* Columbia, Mo., 1978.

Gapta, Giri R. *Cohesion & Conflict in Modern India.* Durham, N.C., 1978.

Gautam, Om P. *The Indian National Congress.* New York, 1984.

Gerber, William. *The Mind of India.* Carbondale, Ill., 1977.

Gokhale, B.G. *Bharatvarsha: A Political and Cultural History of India.* Highland Park, N.J., 1982.

Ghose, Sankar. *Changing India.* New York, 1978.

Gordon, A.D. *Businessmen & Politics: Rising Nationalism & Modernizing Economy in Bombay 1918–1933.* Columbia, Mo., 1978.

Gujral, M.L. *Economic Failures of Nehru & Indira Gandhi.* New York, 1980.

Gupta, Brijen and K. Dutta. *India.* (World Bibliographical Series) Santa Barbara, Calif., 1984.

Gupte, Pranay. *Vengeance: India after the Assassination of Indira Gandhi.* New York, 1985.

Hardgrave, Robert L. *India: Government and Politics in a Developing Nation.* Orlando, Fla., 1985.

Harry, Henry C. *Indira Gandhi Today.* New York, 1977.

Hazari, Bharat. *Structure of Indian Economy.* Columbia, Mo., 1981.

Hicks, John and M. Mukherjee. *The Framework of Indian Economics.* New York, 1984.

Hiro, Dilip. *Inside India Today.* New York, 1977.
Jaisingh, Hari. *India and the Nonaligned World: Search for a New Order.* New York, 1983.
Jeffrey, Robin. *People, Princes & Paramount Power: Society & Politics in the Indian Princely States.* New York, 1979.
Jha, Dayadhar. *State Legislature in India.* Columbia, Mo., 1977.
Jha, P. *Political Representation in India.* Columbia, Mo., 1976.
Jha, Shiva Chandra. *Indian Party Politics: Structure, Leadership, Programmes.* New Delhi, 1989.
Johnson, B.L. *India: Resources & Development.* New York, 1979.
Joshi, P.C. *Land Reforms in India.* Bombay, 1975.
Joshi, Ram. *Indian Constitution & Its Working.* Columbia, Mo., 1977.
Kamal, K.L. and Ralph C. Meyer. *Democratic Politics in India.* Mystic, Conn., 1977.
Kapur, J.C. *India: An Uncommitted Society.* New York, 1982.
Karkhanis, Sharad. *Indian Politics & the Role of the Press.* New York, 1980.
Karunakaran, K.P. *Democracy in India.* Columbia, Mo., 1978.
Kaul, B.N. *India and Super Powers.* New Delhi, 1989.
Khan, M.Y. *Indian Financial System.* New York, 1980.
Kothari, Ranji. *Democratic Policy & Social Change in India.* Columbia, Mo., 1976.
Krishna, Prasad. *Religious Freedom Under Indian Constitution.* Columbia, Mo., 1976.
Kumar, Satish. *Documents on India's Foreign Policy.* Columbia, Mo., 1978.
Kurian, George Thomas. *A Historical and Cultural Dictionary of India.* Metuchen, N.J., 1976.
Labor Bureau. *Indian Labor Statistics.* Simla, Annual.
———. *Indian Labor Yearbook.* Simla, Annual.
Lall, Arthur. *The Emergence of Modern India.* New York, 1981.
Lamb, Beatrice. *India: A World in Transition.* New York, 1975.
Mahajan, V. *Constitutional History of India.* Bombay, 1982.
Maheshwari, S.R. *State Governments in India.* Columbia, Mo., 1980.
———. *President's Rule in India.* Columbia, Mo., 1977.
Majumdar, R.C., and P.N. Chopra. *Main Currents of Indian History.* New York, 1980.
Malik, S.C. *Dissent, Protest & Reform in Indian Civilization.* Columbia, Mo., 1977.
Mehta, D.S. *Mass Communication & Journalism in India.* Beverly Hills, Calif., 1980.
Mejta, Ved. *India Portrait of India.* New York, 1978.
———. *The New India.* New York, 1978.
———. *A Family Affair: India under Three Prime Ministers.* New York, 1982.
Mellor, John W. *India: A Rising Middle Power.* Boulder, Co., 1979.
———. *The New Economics of Growth: A Strategy for India and the Developing World.* Ithaca, N.Y., 1980.
Mishra, Jagannath. *India's Economic Development.* New York, 1984.
Mitra, Asok. *India's Population: Aspects of Quality & Control.* Columbia, Mo., 1978.
Mohan, K.T. *Independence to Indira and After.* Mystic, Conn., 1978.
Moorhouse, Geoffrey. *India Britannica.* New York, 1983.
Morris Jones, W.H. *Politics Mainly Indian.* Columbia, Mo., 1978.
Nafziger, W. Wayne. *Class, Caste & Entrepreneurship: A Study of Indian Industrialists.* Honolulu, Hi., 1978.
Naipaul, V.S. *India: A Wounded Civilization.* New York, 1977.
Nanda, B.R. *Indian Foreign Policy: The Nehru Years.* Honolulu, Hi., 1976.
———. *Gandhi & Nehru.* New York, 1979.
Nandal, B.R. *India's Foreign Policy: The Nehru Years.* New York, 1976.
Nasenko, Yuri. *Jawaharlal Nehru and India's Foreign Policy.* Mystic, Conn., 1977.
Nayar, Baldev R. *Violence & Crime in India.* Columbia, Mo., 1975.
Neale, Walter C., and John Adams. *India: The Search for Unity, Democracy, and Process.* New York, 1976.
Noble, Allen G., and Ashok K. Dutt. *Indian Urbanization & Planning: Vehicles of Modernization.* New York, 1977.
O'Malley, L.S. *India's Social Heritage.* New York, 1976.
Operations Research Group. *India in Perspective: Development Issues.* Mystic, Conn., 1978.
Pant, S.C. *Indian Labor Problems.* Allahabad, India, 1970.
Pantham, Thomas. *Political Parties & Democratic Consensus: India.* Columbia, Mo., 1976.
Pylee, M.V. *Constitutional Government in India.* New York, 1972.
Ramroop, Govinda, V. *The Voices of India.* New York, 1980.
Rastogi, S.R. *Wage Regulation in India.* Mystic, Conn., 1979.
Rice, Edward. *Mother India's Children.* New York, 1971.
Robb, Peter. *The Government of India and Reform.* New York, 1977.
Rosenthal, Donald. *The Expansive Elite: District Politics and State Policy Making in India.* Berkeley, Calif., 1977.
———. *Urban Politics in India.* Columbia, Mo., 1976.
Rothermund, Dietmar. *Indian Economy under the British.* New York, 1983.
Rudolph, Lloyd. *Cultural Policy in India.* Columbia, Mo., 1984.
Saiyidain, K.G. *Facets of Indian Education.* New Delhi, 1977.
Schermerhorn, R.A. *Ethnic Plurality in India.* Tempe, Ariz., 1978.
Sen, Gautam. *India's Defense Policy: An Analysis.* New York, 1985.
Shah, Giri R. *India Rediscovered.* Columbia, Mo., 1975.
Sharma, B.N. *Festivals of India.* Columbia, Mo., 1978.
Sharma, Jagdish S. *Encyclopaedia Indica.* New Delhi, 1975.

———. *The National Geographical Dictionary of India.* New Delhi, 1972.

Sharma, L.N. *The Indian Prime Minister: The Office, Its Functions & Powers.* Columbia, Mo., 1976.

Sharma, M.P. *Local Self-Government in India.* Columbia, Mo., 1978.

Sharma, R.K. *Foreign Aid to India: An Economic Study.* Columbia, Mo., 1979.

Sharma, Ram N. *Indian Society and Social Institutions.* Highland Park, N.J., 1981.

Sharma, S.S. *Rural Elites in India.* New York, 1979.

Sharma, Shri Ram. *India's Foreign Policy.* New York, 1977.

Sharma, Surya P. *India's Boundary and Territorial Disputes.* New York, 1971.

Singh, A.K. *Economic Policy and Planning in India.* New York, 1985.

———. *Impact of American Aid on Indian Economy.* Mystic, Conn., 1974.

Singh, Baljit. *Indian Foreign Policy: An Analysis.* New York, 1976.

Singh, Sukhwant. *India's Wars Since Independence.* New York, 1980.

Singh, Tarlok. *India's Development Experience.* Delhi, 1974.

Singh, Yogendra. *Essays on Modernization in India.* Columbia, Mo., 1978.

Sinha, R. *Income Distribution, Growth & Basic Needs in India.* New York, 1979.

Sinha, Raghuvir. *Social Change in Indian Society.* Columbia, Mo., 1978.

Spate, Oskar H. *India, Pakistan, and Ceylon: The Regions.* New York, 1972.

Spear, Percival. *India: A Modern History.* Ann Arbor, Mich., 1972.

Srivastava, Meera. *Constitutional Crisis in the States in India.* New York, 1980.

Srivastava, V. *Cultural Contours of India.* Highland Park, N.J., 1981.

Steel, Flora. *India.* New York, 1983.

Stokes, E.T. *The Peasant and the Raj.* New York, 1980.

Suri, Surindar. *Political Change in India: 1977: Elections & the Emergency Aftermath.* Columbia, Mo., 1980.

Thakur, Janardhan. *Indira Gandhi & Her Power Game.* New York, 1980.

Thapar, Romesh. *Change & Conflict in India.* Columbia, Mo., 1978.

Tharyan, P. *India: The Critical Decade After Nehru.* Mystic, Conn., 1975.

Thomas, Richard. *India's Emergence as an Industrial Power.* London, 1982.

Uppal, J.S. *Indian Economic Planning.* Bombay, 1985.

Veit, Lawrence A. *India's Second Revolution.* New York, 1976.

Venkatalchalam, V. and R.K. Singh. *The Political, Economic and Labor Climate in India.* Pittsburgh, Pa., 1982.

Venkateswaran, R.J. *Rajiv Gandhi, Economic Perspective Towards 21st Century.* Bombay, 1989.

Webster, John C. *History and Contemporary India.* New York, 1972.

Weiner, Myron. *India at the Polls, 1980: A Study of the Parliamentary Elections.* Washington, D.C., 1983.

———. *The Indian Paradox: Essays in Indian Politics.* Newbury Park, Calif., 1989.

Wolpert, Stanley. *A New History of India.* New York, 1977.

———. *Tilak & Gokhale: Revolution & Reform in the Making of Modern India.* Berkeley, Calif., 1977.

Wood, John R. *State Politics in Indira Gandhi's India: Continuity or Crisis.* Boulder, Colo., 1985.

FILMS

Assignment India. B&W film, 56 min. NBC.

Calcutta. Color film, 79 min. Twyman Films.

Changing Face of India. B&W film, 12 min. Producer: not available.

Family Krishnappa. Color film, 25 min. Benchmark.

Family Life in India: Ten of Us. Color film, 12 min. Contemporary Films.

Family of India. Color film, 12 min. Contemporary Films.

Farmers of India. Color film, 13 min. Roger Wade.

Farm Village of India: The Struggle with Tradition. Color film, 22 min. Coronet.

Fifty Miles from Poona. B&W film, 19 min. National Film Board of Canada.

Gandhi. B&W film, 25 min. CBS.

Gandhi: A Profile in Power. Color film, 25 min. Learning Corp of America.

Gandhi's India. B&W film, 58 min. BBC.

Ganges: A Sacred River. Color film, 27 min. NBC.

Harvest of Mercy. B&W film, 41 min. CBS.

India. Color film, 24 min. Gateway.

India. Color film, 19 min. Canadian Broadcasting Corp.

India. B&W film, 13 min. March of Time.

India: Customs in the Village. Color film, 11 min. Encyclopaedia Britannica.

India: A Better Tomorrow. Color film, 16 min. BFA.

India and her Food Problem. Color film, 16 min. Producer: not available.

India and Pakistan. Color film, 13 min. Coronet.

India: Asia's New Voice. B&W film, 18 min. March of Time.

India: Asia's Subcontinent. Color film, 17 min. Paul Hoefler.

India: Eastern Neighbors. B&W film, 60 min. Modern Talking Picture Service.

India: Introduction to its History. Color/B&W film, 16 min. Encyclopaedia Britannica.

India: Nation on the Move. Color film, 20 min. Associated Film Service.

India: Pakistan and the Union of India. B&W film, 17 min. Encyclopaedia Britannica.

India: People in Transition. Color film, 17 min. Paul Hoefler.

India: Ramu of Ganapatty Street. Color film, 21 min. Universal Studios.

India: Subcontinent of Asia. Color film, 18 min. Universal Studies.

India: The Land and the People. Color film, 11 min. International Film Bureau.

India: The Struggle for Food. Color film, 19 min. Contemporary Films.

India: Urban Conditions. Color film, 19 min. Contemporary Films.

India: Writings on the Sand. Color/B&W film, 59 min. National Educational Television.

Indira Gandhi of India. Color film, 60 min. BBC.

India's Historic Twin Cities: Old Delhi and New Delhi. Color film, 16 min. Mar-Chuck Films.

India's History: British Colony to Independence. Color/B&W film, 11 min. Coronet.

India's History: Early Civilizations. Color/B&W film, 11 min. Coronet.

India's History: Mogul Empire to European Colonization. Color/B&W film, 11 min. Coronet.

Land Divided: India and Pakistan at War. B&W film, 15 min. Producer: not available.

Mahatma Gandhi. B&W film, 26 min. Encyclopaedia Britannica.

Nehru: Man of Two Worlds. B&W film, 24 min. CBS.

Nehru on Better World Relations. B&W film, 27 min. CBS.

New India's People. B&W film, 26 min. March of Time.

Sikh Politician: Between Substance and Spirit. Color film, 20 min. Producer: not available.

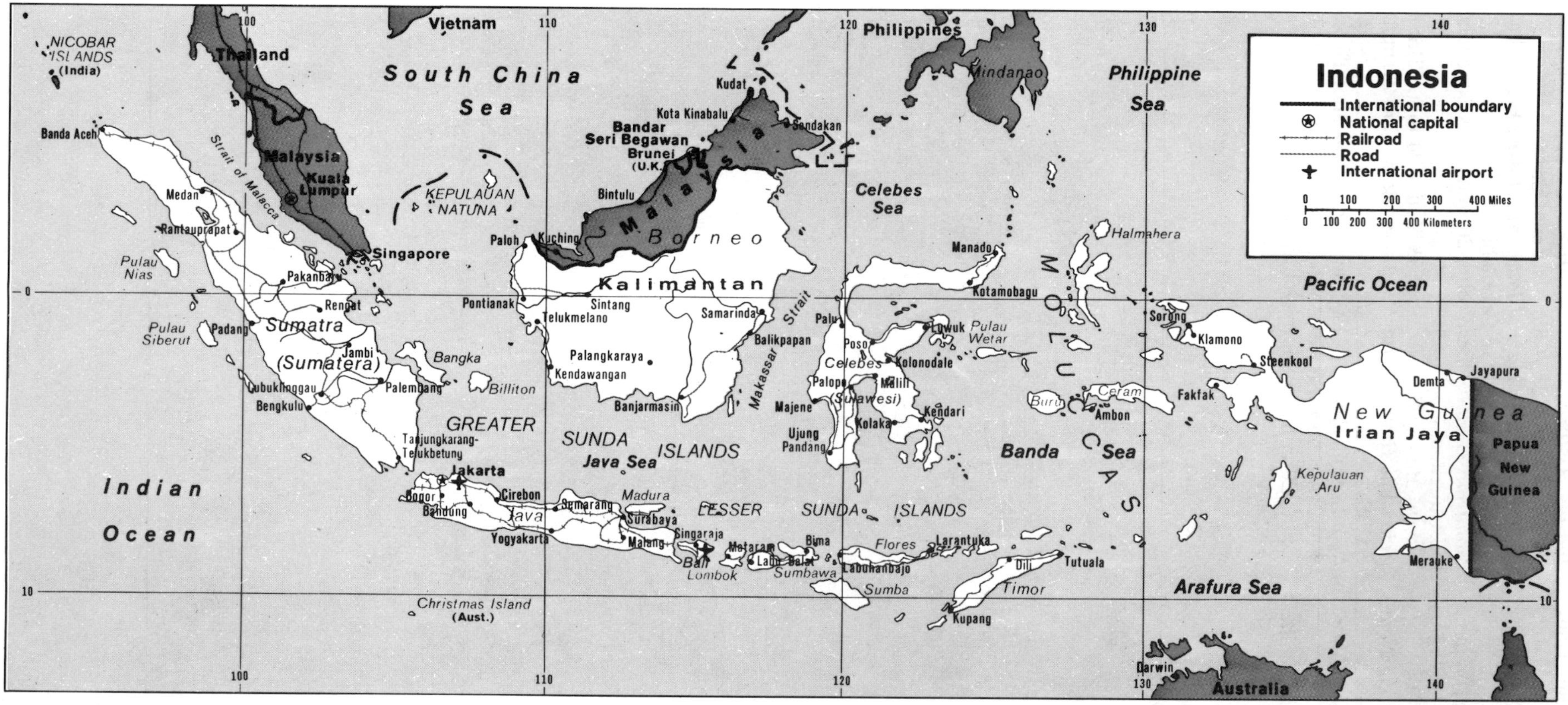
Indonesia
International boundary
National capital
Railroad
Road
International airport
0 100 200 300 400 Miles
0 100 200 300 400 Kilometers
South China Sea
Philippine Sea
Celebes Sea
Pacific Ocean
Indian Ocean
Java Sea
Banda Sea
Arafura Sea
Strait of Malacca
Makassar Strait
Vietnam
Thailand
Malaysia
Kuala Lumpur
Singapore
Philippines
Mindanao
Brunei (U.K.)
Bandar Seri Begawan
Kota Kinabalu
Kudat
Sandakan
Bintulu
Kuching
Borneo
Kalimantan
NICOBAR ISLANDS (India)
Banda Aceh
Medan
Rantauprapat
Pulau Nias
Pulau Siberut
Padang
Pakanbaru
Rengat
Sumatra (Sumatera)
Jambi
Lubuklinggau
Bengkulu
Palembang
Bangka
Billiton
Tanjungkarang-Telukbetung
KEPULAUAN NATUNA
Paloh
Pontianak
Sintang
Telukmelano
Palangkaraya
Kendawangan
Banjarmasin
Samarinda
Balikpapan
GREATER SUNDA ISLANDS
LESSER SUNDA ISLANDS
Jakarta
Bogor
Bandung
Cirebon
Java
Semarang
Yogyakarta
Madura
Surabaya
Malang
Singaraja
Bali
Lombok
Mataram
Sumbawa
Bima
Flores
Larantuka
Labuhanbajo
Sumba
Timor
Dili
Kupang
Tutuala
Christmas Island (Aust.)
Celebes (Sulawesi)
Manado
Kotamobagu
Palu
Poso
Luwuk
Kolonodale
Malili
Palopo
Majene
Ujung Pandang
Kolaka
Kendari
Pulau Wetar
MOLUCCAS
Halmahera
Buru
Ceram
Ambon
Sorong
Klamono
Steenkool
Fakfak
Kepulauan Aru
New Guinea
Irian Jaya
Demta
Jayapura
Merauke
Papua New Guinea
Darwin
Australia
100
110
120
130
140
0
10

BHINNEKA TUNGGAL IKA

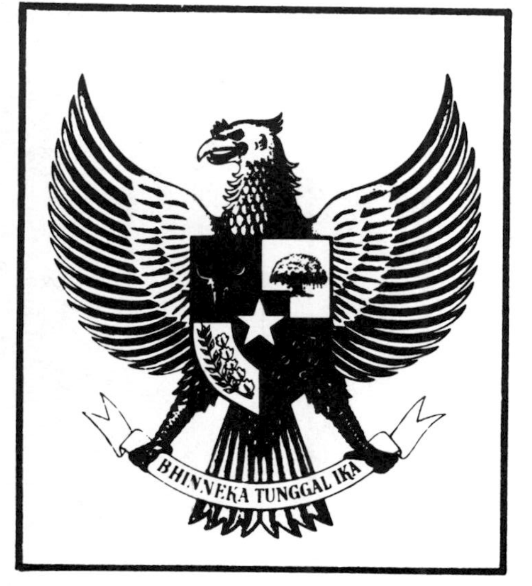

INDONESIA

BASIC FACT SHEET

OFFICIAL NAME: Republic of Indonesia (Republik Indonesia)

ABBREVIATION: IO

CAPITAL: Jakarta

HEAD OF STATE & HEAD OF GOVERNMENT: General Suharto (from March 1968)

NATURE OF GOVERNMENT: Republic

POPULATION: 190,136,221 (1990)

AREA: 1,903,650 sq. km. (735,000 sq. mi.)

ETHNIC MAJORITY: Atjehnese, Bataks and Minangkabaus in Sumatra; Javanese and Sundanese in Java; Madurese in Madura; Balinese in Bali; Sasaks in Lombok; Menadonese and Buginese in Sulawesi; Dayaks in Borneo; Irianese in Irian Jaya; Ambonese in the Moluccas

LANGUAGE: Bahasa Indonesia (official); over 25 languages belonging to Malayo-Polynesian, North Halmaheran and Papuan families.

RELIGION: Sunni Islam

UNIT OF CURRENCY: Ruplah (Rp.)

NATIONAL FLAG: Divided horizontally with the top half red and the bottom half white

NATIONAL EMBLEM: A shield with five symbols; a star (God) in the center field, a golden chain (humanity), a banyan tree (nationalism), a head of a buffalo (democracy) and rice and cotton (social justice). The shield hangs from the neck of an outstretched eagle. Clutched in its talons is a white scroll bearing the national motto in Indonesian in black letters: *Bhinneka Tunggal Ika* (Unity Through Diversity).

NATIONAL ANTHEM: "Great Indonesia"

NATIONAL HOLIDAYS: August 17 (Indonesian National Day), January 1, Good Friday, Ascension Day, Christmas; also variable Islamic festivals

NATIONAL CALENDAR: Gregorian; the orthodox Muslims or Santri use the Islamic calendar, while the Balinese use a 210-day Balinese calendar

PHYSICAL QUALITY OF LIFE INDEX: 58

DATE OF INDEPENDENCE: August 17, 1945

DATE OF CONSTITUTION: August 17, 1945

WEIGHTS & MEASURES: Metric

GEOGRAPHICAL FEATURES

Indonesia is the largest archipelago nation in the world and the third-largest country in Asia. Superimposed on a map of the conterminous United States, the island chain would overlap both New York and San Francisco. The islands lie on both sides of the equator and are divided by the Wallace Line. The total land area is 1,903,650 sq. km. (735,000 sq. mi.). The country consists of 13,667 islands, not all of which have names and only about 1,000 of which are inhabited. Five of the islands—Java, Sumatra, Sulawesi, Kalimantan and Irian Jaya—account for 90% of the land area. The total length of the coastline is 36,616 km. (22,753 mi.). The greatest east-to-west distance is 5,271 km. (3,275 mi.); the greatest north-to-south distance is 2,210 km. (1,373 mi.).

Land boundaries are shared with two countries: Malaysia (1,496 km.; 930 mi.) and Papua New Guinea (777 km.; 483 mi.). There are no current border disputes.

Jakarta is the capital as well as the center *(pusat)* of national life. Its population in 1983 was 7,636,000. The other major urban centers are: Surabaya (2,289,000), Bandung (1,602,000), Semarang (1,269,000), Malang (560,000), Semarang (1,269,000), Malang (560,000), Tjirebon (273,000), Bogor (274,000), Medan (1,966,000), Palembang (903,000), Ujungpandang (888,000), Padang (726,000), Yogyakarta (428,000), Pontianak (365,000) and Banjarmasin (437,000). Of all the islands, Irian Jaya and Sulawesi are the most mountainous, but each island has its own coastal and mountainous regions. The highest peak is Puntjak Jaya, at 5,029 m. (16,500 ft.). Indonesia is the most highly volcanic region in the world, with over 100 active volcanoes.

Indonesia has three time zones (East, Central and West), each with a one-hour time differential.

Most of Indonesia's numerous rivers are short and useful principally for irrigation. Some are navigable in parts. The largest is Mamberamo, in Irian Jaya.

CLIMATE & WEATHER

Because of its location straddling the equator, Indonesia has no seasons as understood in the Northern and Southern hemispheres; the days and nights are always 12 hours long, the humidity averages 80% year-round and there is a bare two-degree variation between the mean temperatures of the warmest and the coolest months. In the lowland areas the daily maximums and minimums range between 31.1°C and 18.9°C (88°F and 66°F). Rainfall never falls below 965 mm. (38 in.) a year, even in the driest areas. In the equatorial high-rainfall belt extending from northern Sumatra to southern and southeastern Sulawesi, Maluku and Irian Jaya, average annual rainfall exceeds 1,980 mm. (78 in.), although up to 3,810 mm. (150 in.) has been recorded in the highlands. Northern and eastern Java, Madura and northern Sulawesi have annual averages of 1,520 to 1,980 mm. (60 to 78 in.), while the Nusa Tenggara Islands have the lowest average, of 1,020 to 1,520 mm. (40 to 60 in.). Thunderstorms are frequent; the average number of storm days is 100 a year.

Indonesia has two seasons, wet and dry, determined by the monsoons. The dry monsoon season lasts from June to September and the wet monsoon season from November to March. The monsoons regulate agricultural activity.

POPULATION

The population of Indonesia in 1990 was estimated at 190,136,221. The last official census was held in 1980, when the population was 147,490,298. The population however, is unevenly distributed. Java, with only 7% of the land area, has 61.5% of the population. The government has launched a program known as transmigration to reverse migration to Java and to encourage Javanese to settle in the outer islands.

Indonesia has one of the highest population densities in Southeast Asia. In Java and Madura the average exceeds 540 per sq. km. (1,400 per sq. mi.), but in Irian Jaya it is 1.9 per sq. km. (4.0 per sq. mi.).

The population still is overwhelmingly rural, with only 26.2% living in urban areas. However, the trend toward increased urbanization is reflected in the number and population of cities. In 1930 there were only seven cities over 100,000 in population; in 1971 there were 27 cities in this category, with 9.7% of the population. There are nine cities with over 500,000 inhabitants, and they account for 50% of the urban population, with Jakarta alone claiming 23%. As in most other developing countries, slums and squatter settlements house at least 25% of the populations of all major Indonesian cities. The proportion is relatively uniform: 27% in Bandung, 26% in Jakarta and 33% in Makasari.

There is very little immigration. Emigration has been chiefly to Malaysia, Singapore and the Philippines. Since the coup of 1965 some Chinese have been repatriated to mainland China. Under its humane refugee policy, Indonesia has given first asylum to over 88,000 Indochinese refugees since 1975. In cooperation with the U.N. high commissioner for refugees, the government of Indonesia also has provided one of the region's two refugee processing centers.

A five-year family-planning program (1971–76) was implemented by the National Family Planning Coordinating Board, formed in 1970. Over 1,850 family-planning clinics are in operation. The long-term plan was to reduce fertility levels by 50% by the year 2000. The activities of the Indonesian Planned Parenthood Association are officially encouraged. It is estimated that 45% of married women practice birth control.

Indonesian women generally enjoy a high degree of economic and social freedom, and there is significant cultural latitude for women's participation in public life. Women occupy important midlevel positions in the civil service, educational institutions, labor unions, the military, the professions, private business and the parliament. The cabinet named in 1983 included two women: the minister of state for women's affairs and the minister for social affairs. Although legislation guarantees women equal treatment, they seldom receive equal pay for equal work. In addition to government-sponsored women's organizations in which mem-

VITAL STATISTICS

Crude birth rate (/1,000): 27 (1990); 43 (1965)
Crude death rate (/1,000): 9 (1990); 20 (1965)
Infant mortality rate (/1,000 live births): 75 (1990)
Maternal mortality rate (/100,000 live births): 800 (1980)
Life expectancy (yrs.) at birth: males, 58; females, 63 (1990)
Gross reproduction rate (/woman) (1980–85): 2.0
Total fertility rate (/woman): 3.1 (1990)
Rate of natural increase (/1,000): 16.1 (1988)
Marriage rate (/1,000) (1986–87): 7.3
Average household size: 4.9 (latest)

DEMOGRAPHIC INDICATORS

Population (millions): 190.136 (1990)
Year of last census: 1980
Sex distribution (% at last census): males, 49.7; females, 50.3
Population estimates and projections (millions)

1940: 70.500	1970: 119.467	2000: 180.763
1950: 75.449	1980: 146.449	2010: 214.410
1960: 92.701	1990: 183.457	

Age profile (% at last census)

0–14: 40.8	30–44: 16.4	60–74: 4.5
15–29: 27.0	45–59: 10.2	75 and over: 1.1

Median age (yrs.): 20.2 (1985)
Youth population (% age 15–24): 20.2 (1985); 19.9 (2000)
Total dependency ratio: 73.0 (1985)
Annual growth rate (%)

1950–55: 1.69	1975–80: 2.14	2000–2005: 1.14
1955–60: 2.11	1980–85: 1.96	2005–2010: 1.01
1960–65: 2.14	1985–90: 1.62	2010–2015: 0.93
1965–70: 2.33	1990–1995: 1.52	2015–2020: 0.85
1970–75: 2.41	1995–2000: 1.34	2020–2025: 0.75

Hypothetical size of stationary population (millions): 370
Assumed year of reaching net reproduction rate of 1: 2005
Urban population (millions): 42.170 (1985)
Urban population (%): 27 (1988); 16 (1965)
Annual urban population growth rate (%, 1985–90): 4.18
Annual rural population growth rate (%, 1985–90): 0.67
Percentage of urban population in largest city: 23 (1980)
Percentage of urban population in cities of population over 500,000: 50 (1980)
Number of cities of population over 500,000: 9 (1980)
Population density per sq. km. (per sq. mi.): 92.8 (240.2) (latest)

STATUS OF WOMEN INDICATORS

Number of women (millions): 80.727 (1985)
Women of childbearing age (15–49) (% of pop.): 51 (1988)
Married women of childbearing age (15–49) using contraception (%): 45 (latest)
Women's literacy rate (%): 66 (1985)
Women in labor force (%): 31.2 (1988)
Total fertility rate (/woman): 3.1 (1990)
Women in national legislatures (%): 9 (1984)

bership and participation are mandatory, several voluntary, private groups work to advance women's legal, economic and political rights. Chief among these is Kowani (Congress of Indonesian Women), an umbrella for some 55 women's groups.

Ethnic Chinese are pressured to adopt Indonesian customs and take Indonesian names. Although they are also encouraged to become citizens, some Chinese find legal avenues to citizenship blocked or are discouraged by the time-consuming and expensive task of obtaining citizenship documents. Government regulations prohibit the operation of all-Chinese schools and institutions of higher learning, teaching in Chinese languages, the formation of exclusively Chinese cultural groups in trade associations and the use of Chinese characters on signboards or in publications. However, social and religious groups that are, in effect, all-Chinese are not proscribed and do exist.

ETHNIC COMPOSITION

Indonesia is a pluralistic society, with over 300 ethnic groups speaking almost as many languages. Most of these groups belong to the Malay stock.

The Kalimantan and Irian Jaya are primitive tribes with rudimentary material cultures. Most of them follow animist beliefs and practiced headhunting, at least until recently.

The principal ethnic minority group is the Chinese, who number over 3.5 million. Their conspicuous insularity, wealth and resistance to assimilation have contributed to widespread resentment against them. During the 1970s they were restricted and harassed with increasing severity, deprived of their school system, prohibited from engaging in certain trades and forced to relocate. The Chinese are overwhelmingly urban, due partly to official policies and partly to their mercantile interests. The community is divided into the foreign Chinese Totoks and locally rooted Chinese (Peranakan Tionghoa). The majority of the Chinese are Hokkiens, who were the first to immigrate to Indonesia in large numbers, but Cantonese, Teochius and Hakkas also are represented. Ethnic aliens include Arabs and Indian Muslims, who have been assimilated into Indonesian society without difficulty. Most of the Dutch left in 1958.

LANGUAGES

An estimated 25 languages and more than 250 dialects are spoken in Indonesia. These languages belong to three language families: Malayo-Polynesian, North Halmaheran and Papuan. The Malayo-Polynesian consists of 17 groups including nearly 100 dialects. The groups are: Sumatran, Javanese, Bornean, Loinang, Banggai, Bungku-Laki, South Celebes, Muna-Butung, Bima-Sumba, Balinese-Sasak, Philippine, Gorontalo, Tomini, Toradja, Ambon-Timur, Sula-Batjan and South Halmaheran. Javanese is spoken by 40% to 50% of the population, Sundanese by 15%, Madurese by 5% to 10% and Malay by 5% to 10%.

The official language is Bahasa Indonesia, derived from trade Malay or Malay Pasar and used as a lingua franca throughout the Indonesian islands. Bahasa Indonesia differs little from standard Malay and is principally distinguished by its large vocabulary of borrowed words from European languages, Arabic and Sanskrit. Considerable efforts have been made to modernize and standardize its orthography, and in 1974 the Institute of National Language was established for this purpose. However, standard or literary Bahasa Indonesian is being displaced in government and educational institutions by colloquial Indonesian. Most Indonesians are trilingual or bilingual. The native mother tongue is spoken at home; the language of the dominant ethnic group is spoken in public; and Bahasa Indonesia is used for education and government and intergroup communication.

Despite centuries of Dutch rule, few Indonesians speak Dutch. English is officially the second language of Indonesia and is taught in schools from the senior secondary level.

RELIGION

Eight of 10 Indonesians are Muslims; Indonesia has the largest Muslim population in the world. But Indonesian Islam is deeply divided by a cleavage between the *santri* (orthodox) and the *abangan* (nominal) Muslims. The *santri*, who became an organized force with the founding of the Muhammadijah movement in central Java in 1912, are distinguished by strict observance of the Five Pillars of the Muslim faith and the Shari'a. The *abangan*, who are in the vast majority, follow an amalgam of animistic, Hindu and Muslim beliefs, rituals and institutions.

Christians form a sizable and influential minority in Indonesia and in 1987 numbered more than 7 million. The more important Christian ethnic groups are the Bataks in Sumatra, the Minahasans in Sulawesi, the Ibans in Kalimantan and the Moluccans. Smoldering hostility against Christians among *santri* Muslims erupted into anti-Christian riots in 1962, 1964 and 1967, but both Catholics and Protestants have strong political representation. The other religious minorities include the Hindus of Bali, numbering over 3.5 million in 1984; and Buddhists, Taoists and Confucianists, numbering about 1 million among Chinese Indonesians.

Indonesia's independence as defined in the preamble to the constitution is based on *Pancasila*, which is made up of five principles, the first of which is belief in the one supreme God. Because of this atheism is forbidden. Some animists in remote parts of Indonesia reportedly have been pressured to convert to Islam or Christianity to fulfill the requirement of belief in a supreme being. At the same time, mystic sects and beliefs are followed by many in the Indonesian elite. Several small Muslim sects and certain other religious groups accused of contravening widely accepted moral standards are banned by the Department of Religion. There are no legal bars to religious conversion, and conversions between faiths are common. However, a significant event in 1978 was the handing down of government decrees 70 and 77. These two edicts are having a strong impact on the Christian community. Officially, the decrees were designed to discourage overt proselytising by any religion. This is partly the result of religious tension in many areas of Indonesia, and the government's concern that these tensions could contribute to political and economic instability. In effect, the Christians see the decrees as powerful measures to curtail their missionary efforts among Indonesians of other faiths, Muslims in particular. Decree 70 declares that everyone is entitled to his own faith, and overt attempts to convert anyone from his or her religion to another is unlawful. Tract distribution, open-air evangelism and house-to-house evangelism have been officially prohibited. Decree 77 deals specifically with foreign missionaries, declaring that they are to train Indonesians to take over their tasks. Time limits for this training are mentioned, though not in specific terms.

HISTORICAL BACKGROUND

Indonesia was under the rule of the Dutch East India Company from the mid-17th century to 1800 and under the Dutch crown from 1800 to 1949 except for a brief period under Japanese occupation (1942–45). When the Japanese had withdrawn, Indonesian nationalists assumed power and proclaimed the independent Republic of Indonesia on August 17, 1945. The Netherlands government officially recognized the new republic on December 27, 1949. It was at that time the United States of Indonesia.

Dr. Sukarno, who had been a leader of the nationalist movement since the 1920s, served as president of the new nation from the time of its self-proclaimed independence, and he continued in that role after the country became legally independent. The first constitution provided for limited self-government of the 16 constituent regions. The federation was dissolved in August 1950, and the nation emerged as the unitary Republic of Indonesia. West New Guinea, which had been excluded from the 1949 independence accord, continued to be governed by the Dutch until October 1962. It was then briefly administered by the U.N. after which it was transferred to Indonesia in May 1963. It is now known as Irian Jaya.

Sukarno's presidency was marked by extreme nationalism and increasing authoritarianism. In foreign policy the People's Republic was a close ally, although the country was active in the Nonaligned Movement. Inflation and rampant corruption eventually led to open opposition in the form of an abortive military coup in September–October 1965. The Indonesian Communist Party (PKI) was suspected of initiating the attempted takeover, and a mass slaughter of party members followed. By March 1966 Sukarno conferred emergency executive powers on the military under the command of General Suharto, chief of staff of the army. Suharto outlawed the PKI. In February 1967 Suharto assumed full executive power, and in March, after Sukarno had been dismissed from office by the People's Consultative Assembly, he was appointed acting president. He assumed the position of prime minister in October 1967 and in March 1968 was inaugurated president following election by the Assembly. The first general election since 1955 was held in July 1971. The government-backed Sekretariat Bersama Golongan Karya (Joint Secretariat of Functional Groups), or the Sekber Golkar, achieved a majority victory in the House of Representatives, and in 1973 Suharto was reelected to a second term as president.

Political power was concentrated in a small group of army officers through the imposition of Suharto's "New Order." This inner circle, along with the internal security organization, Kopkamtib, suppressed left-wing movements and enforced a liberal economic policy. The general election of May 1977 produced another majority in the legislature for Golkar, and Suharto was reelected (unopposed) in March 1978. Golkar won an even greater majority in the May 1982 elections despite growing popular discontent with the government. Once again, having run unopposed, Suharto was reelected in March 1983.

In 1984 Suharto introduced legislation requiring all religious and social and political associations to accept Pancasila (the official state philosophy) as their sole ideology. This provoked intense rioting, bombings and arson, allegedly the work of Muslim opponents. Many Muslims were tried and imprisoned as a result. By July 1985 all political parties had adopted Pancasila. Criticism of Suharto's regime resurfaced in 1986 and 1987, both within the country and outside. Corruption on the part of the Suharto family and allegations of human rights abuse in East Timor were the key complaints. Despite discontent, the April 1987 general election produced another victory for Golkar, with the government party winning 299 of the 500 seats in the House of Representatives and an unprecedented victory in each of the country's 27 provinces.

Since February 1988 there has been a shift away from concentration of power solely among the military elite and a gradual trend toward empowering an emerging bureaucratic elite. Legislation enacted at that time reemphasized the dual role of the Indonesian Armed Forces (ABRI) in military and socioeconomic spheres. This was followed by General L. B. Murdani's appointment as commander-in-chief of the armed forces. Suharto was reelected unopposed as president in March. It was the subsequent vice-presidential election that pointed the way toward the new trend. In contrast to the usual procedure, Suharto did not name a preferred candidate but rather asked the People's Consultative Assembly to select one. However, when two were nominated, Suharto was forced to choose, opting for Lieutenant-General Sudharmono, chairman of Golkar. The choice was later questioned by Brigadier-General Ibrahim Salim, a senior member of ABRI primarily because of unhappiness about the trend away from military dominance. Salim later lost his seat in the People's Consultative Assembly. In a cabinet reshuffle in March, 19 ministers were replaced.

Military power was further weakened in September when Kopkamtib, under the leadership of General Murdani was replaced by the Coordinating Board for the Development of National Stability (Bakorstanas) led by General Sutrisno. Unlike Kopkamtib, some of the representatives to Bakorstanas came from the Cabinet and nonmilitary government areas. Its primary role was to expose corruption rather than to suppress left-wing movements. General Wahono was named chairman of Golkar in October following the resignation of Sudharmono. Both ABRI and the new bureaucratic group found Wahono an acceptable choice.

Land disputes in three areas of Java and on Sumbawa led to social unrest in early 1989. Between 30 and 100 people were killed when angry villagers confronted armed forces in southern Sumatra. Student protests, the first since 1978, over government's expropriation of land were unopposed by the military, leading some to question the continued leadership of Suharto. In 1990 a rebellion broke out in the province of Aceh when a group called the National Liberation Front Aceh Sumatra, reflecting traditional Acehnese hostility towards central government, demanded independence. The government launched a major offensive against the rebels during the summer, and by the end of the year between 5,000 and 12,000 troops were stationed in the area.

Although there has been speculation about a successor to Suharto, it seems probable that he would once again seek election to a sixth term as president in 1993.

CONSTITUTION & GOVERNMENT

The government of Indonesia is based on the constitution of 1945, which was supplemented by the General Elections law of 1945. It is a short, broadly phrased document that defines the national ideology, or Pancasila, but does not spell out the details of its application. Pancasila are the five principles that form the basis of the Indonesian state: belief in one supreme God, just and civilized humanity, Indonesian unity, democracy and social justice.

The Constitution provides for a strong executive form of government in which the real power is vested in the president, who is head of state and head of government.

The president is the chief executive and the supreme commander of the armed forces. He is elected indirectly for a term of five years by the MPR and may run for reelection any number of times. In the event of his death, removal or disability, the vice president succeeds him. The president is assisted by a number of executive agencies, including the cabinet, the Supreme Advisory Council (Dewan Pertimbangan Agung), the National Development Council and the National Security and Political Stabilization Board. General Suharto's cabinet ministers have substantial authority to run their departments, and a significant number of them are former university deans or professors.

The people exercise their sovereignty through the Majelis Permusyawaratan Rakyat (MPR), the People's Consultative Assembly, which is considered the embodiment of the whole Indonesian people. It is the highest authority of the state, and since 1987 has had 1,000 members. It includes all members of the Dewan Perwakilan Rakyat (DPR), House of Representatives plus regional delegates, members of political organizations and representatives of other groups. It meets at least once every five years with its role being interpretation of the Constitution and general policy of the state and government. It is responsible for electing the president and vice president who in turn implement government policy. Traditionally all decisions of the MPR are unanimous.

GOVERNMENT LIST
(July/August 1991)

President	Suharto, *Gen. (Ret.)*
Vice President	Sudharmono, *Lt. Gen. (Ret.)*
Coordinating Minister for Economics, Finance, Industry & Development Supervision	Prawiro, Radius
Coordinating Minister for Political Affairs & Security	Sudomo, *Adm. (Ret.)*
Coordinating Minister for Public Welfare	Soeparjo Roestam, *Lt. Gen. (Ret.)*
Minister of Agriculture	Wardoyo
Minister of Communications	Azwar Anas, *Maj. Gen. (Ret.)*
Minister of Cooperatives	Arifin, Bustanil, *Maj. Gen. (Ret.)*
Minister of Defense & Security	Moerdani, Leonardus B., *Gen. (Ret.)*
Minister of Education & Culture	Hassan, Fuad
Minister of Finance	Sumarlin, Johannes B.
Minister of Foreign Affairs	Alatas, Ali Abdullah
Minister of Forestry	Harahap, Harsul
Minister of Health	Adhyatma, M., *M.D.*
Minister of Home Affairs	Rudini, *Gen. (Ret.)*
Minister of Industry	Hartarto
Minister of Information	Harmoko
Minister of Justice	Saleh, Ismail, *Lt. Gen. (Ret.)*
Minister of Manpower	Batubara, Cosmas
Minister of Mining & Energy	Ginandjar Kartasasmita, *Air VMar.*
Minister of Public Works	Mochtar, Radinal
Minister of Religion	Munawir Sjadzali
Minister of Social Affairs	Soebadio, Haryati
Minister of Tourism, Post & Telecommunications	Soesilo Soedarman, *Lt. Gen. (Ret.)*
Minister of Trade	Siregar, Arfin M.
Minister of Transmigration	Soegiarto, *Lt. Gen.*
Minister of State & State Secretary	Moerdiono, *Maj. Gen.*
Minister of State for Administrative Reform	Sarwono Kusuma-atmadja
Minister of State for National Development Planning	Afiff, Saleh
Minister of State for People's Housing	Siswono Yudohusodo
Minister of State for Population & Environment	Salim, Emil
Minister of State for Research & Technology	Habibie, Bacharuddin J.
Minister of State for Role of Women	Murpratomo, A. Sulasikin
Minister of State for Youth & Sports	Tanjung, Akbar
Junior Minister & Cabinet Secretary	Mursjid Saadillah
Junior Minister for Agriculture	Sjarifudin Baharsyah
Junior Minister for Finance	Nasruddin Sumintapura
Junior Minister for Industry	Ariwibowo, Tunky
Junior Minister for National Development Planning	Muljana, Benny S.
Junior Minister for Trade	Soedradjat Djiwandono
Attorney General	Singgih
Commander, Armed Forces	Sutrisno, Try, *Gen.*
Governor, Bank Indonesia	Mooy, Adrianus

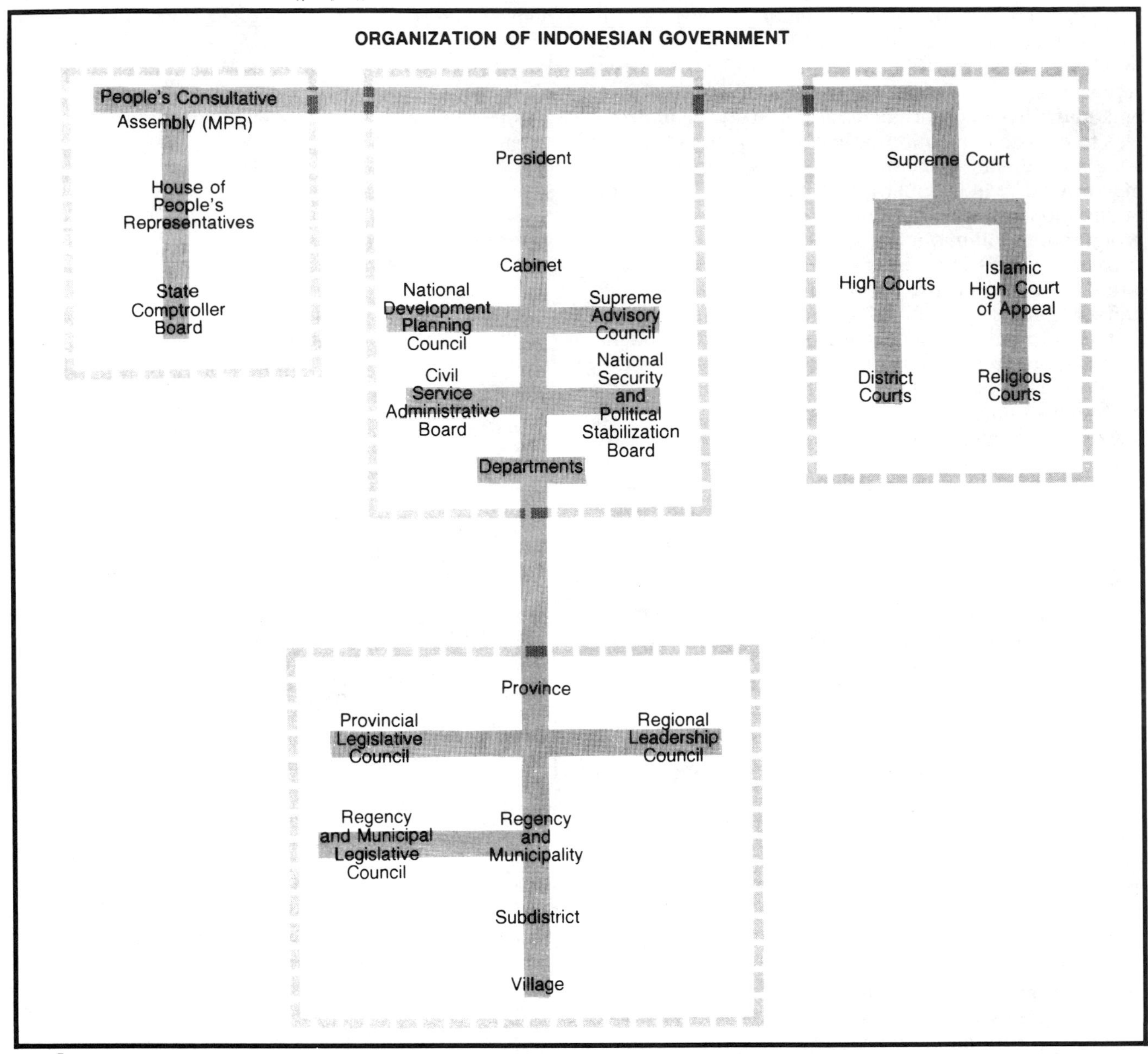

The House of Representatives is the legislative branch of the government and since 1987 has had 500 members, 100 of whom are nominated and 400 of whom are directly elected. It sits at least once each year and must approve every law. Members may submit draft bills, which must be ratified by the president. The president may enact laws during times of emergency, but these must be ratified by the House of Representatives during the next session or be revoked.

The judicial branch of government includes the Supreme Court (Mahkamah Agung), high courts and district courts. The Supreme Court is the final court of appeal. High courts located in Jakarta, Surabaya, Medan, Ujungpandang, Banda Aceh, Padang, Palembang, Bandung, Semarang, Banjarmasin, Menado, Denpasar, Ambon and Jayapura hear appeals from the district courts. District courts hear cases related to marriage, divorce and reconciliation. All courts of law exercise their judicial powers independently of the executive.

Indonesia has enjoyed a stable government since 1966 when Sukarno transferred emergency executive powers to military leaders led by General Suharto, but it also has a tradition of violent civil dissension and disorder.

RULERS OF INDONESIA (from 1945)
Presidents

August 1945–July 1966: Sukarno
July 1966– : Suharto

FREEDOM & HUMAN RIGHTS

In terms of civil and political rights Indonesia is classified as a partially free country.

Significant human rights developments in Indonesia in the 1980s include the mushrooming of private groups focusing public attention on civil and human rights.

These groups believe that there has been a trend toward better treatment of prisoners and greater leniency toward dissenters. An informal opposition group formed in 1980 and known as the Petition of 50 Group, consisting of retired military officers, some prominent Muslims and former student activists, continues its efforts to exert political influence by circulating "statements of concern" and "white papers" critical of government actions and leaders. In a related area, sermon-givers in mosques are permitted to criticize government policies in their sermons as long as they do not encourage disruption of public order. Some of the older detention centers have been closed. Charges of brutality related for the most part to prisoners held for alleged terrorist acts, affiliation with subversive Muslim groups in Sumatra and disappearances and other violations in East Timor. One human rights group has charged that over 175 individuals have been held without charge by security forces for as long as three years without notification of their families. Amnesty International has compiled a list of 22 persons who reportedly disappeared in East Timor after surrender to or capture by Indonesian forces.

Martial law, declared in 1957, has never been lifted. Under special emergency provisions instituted in 1966, a military organization, the Command for the Restoration of Security and Order (Kopkamtib), was given wide powers to detain and interrogate persons thought to endanger national security. These special arrest powers superseded the Kuhap protections and applied particularly to cases of suspected subversion, sabotage, secession or corruption. In mid-1984 the minister of justice ordered the release of 69 vagrants illegally detained in Jakarta's Pondok Bambu facility. The minister claimed Kopkamtib had no authority to arrest and detain persons whose offenses were, at worst, misdemeanors. In September 1988 Kopkamtib was replaced by the coordinating Board for the Development of National Stability (Bakorstanas). Although Kopkamtib had functioned as a military organization whose role was the suppression of left-wing movements, Bakorstanas was composed of cabinet representatives and members of nonmilitary departments whose function was to expose corruption.

Following the release of over 30,000 Class B detainees associated with or sympathetic to the Communist-inspired 1965 upheaval, there remained only 23 Class A prisoners (persons charged with serious crimes, such as murder). The trials of all but one of these have been concluded; they received varying sentences, and the majority have been released. However, Amnesty International listed 657 Class A prisoners still in prison. Few, if any, of those released have been reintegrated into society because of an official ban on their employment. For security and subversion cases there is no legal time limit for detention and no habeas corpus. Under regular criminal law, police may detain and investigate suspects for 20 days, prosecutors may detain and investigate suspects for 30 days and the court may authorize extension of this period by 30-day increments for up to one year. Major groups against whom this law was applied include student activists arrested in connection with the 1978 antigovernment demonstrations, Muslim extremists, Aceh Merdeka (a North Sumatra secessionist movement) leaders and those associated with the FRETILIN liberation movement in East Timor.

Although precise estimates of the number of persons detained without trial are unavailable, human rights observers believe there may be as many as 500 throughout Indonesia. Many of those detained for subversion are suspected Muslim extremists believed to have instigated or participated in illegal antigovernment acts. In addition, others have been detained in connection with civil unrest, including riots, bombings and circulation of antigovernment pamphlets. Most of these are charged with Criminal Code violations, although a dozen or more well-known Muslim preachers being held near Jakarta are charged with subversion.

Since 1981, Indonesian authorities have used Atauro Island off the coast of mainland East Timor as a detention facility for Timorese suspected of supporting, or of having family members fighting with, FRETILIN. The number of Timorese detained on Atauro peaked at about 4,000 in the second half of 1982. Beginning in late 1982 and continuing through 1984, the provincial government has resettled detainees on the main island. Several hundred persons were resettled to their homes.

The judiciary is not constitutionally independent because judges and prosecutors are civil servants responsible to the minister of justice. Nevertheless, there have been clear examples of judges turning down government charges and acquitting Class A detainees in the face of government pressure. Suspects are invariably provided with legal counsel (although there is no obligatory right to counsel under current law except in the case of capital offenses, and no habeas corpus), and there are Legal Aid societies in most cities. The main constraint appears to be a paucity of lawyers; there are only 500 attorneys registered with the bar in a population of over 183 million.

The press is carefully controlled. Stories of political opposition activities in 1980 prompted the government to refuse to renew the stay permits of two foreign journalists and to apply more strictly an earlier rule against dissemination of foreign news agency stories without prior clearance. The licenses of two antigovernment university papers also were revoked in 1980 on the ground that they did not abide by government rules. The government exercises regular censorship over foreign films and publications. Thus readers occasionally find portions inked out of magazines and newspapers from abroad. Despite limits on freedoms of assembly and speech, peaceful demonstrations sometimes are held. In 1980 there was a violent confrontation between students and the police.

Certain types of trade union activities are permitted. The partial right to strike and to lock out exists in private sectors. There is no official discrimination against non-Islamic minorities, and members of minority religions rank high in government circles. However, traditional tensions between Muslim extremists and other religious communities frequently surface, leading President Suharto to affirm publicly, in 1980, the government's guarantee of religious freedom.

Exit permits are required of persons leaving the country, and there has been criticism of alleged government denial of such permits to leading members of opposition groups. The government also requires permits to change residence, to control the further movement of population from rural areas into the already overcrowded cities. Former detainees are required to notify authorities of travel outside their home areas. Charges of forced resettlement have been made concerning East Timor, where large numbers of natives have been moved to resettlement centers. Restrictions on internal movement in East Timor have eased considerably as the security situation has eased. Following the integration of East Timor into Indonesia, 1,565 Portuguese were repatriated to their homes in Portugal, and 305 Timorese, with relations in Australia, were repatriated to that country. The president issued two decrees in 1980 giving ethnic Chinese and holders of foreign passports the right to opt for Indonesian citizenship; nearly 500,000 Chinese applied. The Indochinese refugee camp on Galang Island has been developed into an excellent refugee facility for transient refugees pending their resettlement in third countries. Although Indonesia has not accepted any Vietnamese for permanent settlement, neither have they been pushed off Indonesian shores.

The government discourages political activism outside of the government-supported Golkar and the two small officially sanctioned opposition parties. An informal 50-man opposition group submitted a petition critical of government leadership to the Parliament in 1980. The government responded by terminating the employment of those with official positions, withdrawing their right to travel abroad and cutting off their access to government contracts. However, this group, as well as other similar opposition groups, remain active through privately distributed tracts and private meetings.

For the past nine years a Jakarta-based Legal Aid institute, LBH, has contested human rights violations by defending or representing aggrieved parties in open court and through stimulating public discussion. It issues an annual report on human rights in Indonesia. A Human Rights Day was observed throughout the country in 1979.

CIVIL SERVICE

The civil service is governed by the Civil Service Administrative Board, under the office of the president. In 1970 there were 542,000 civil servants, of whom 30% were in the Department of Education and Culture and 30% in the Department of Religious Affairs. The civil service enjoys great social prestige but is plagued by overstaffing, lack of training and corruption.

LOCAL GOVERNMENT

Indonesia is divided into 27 first-level *propinsi* (provinces), each headed by a governor. The second tier consists of *kabupatens* (regencies), administered by *bupats* (regents), and *kota* (munipalities), administered by *walis* (mayors). There were 281 *kabupatens* in 1974. The third tier consists of *desa* (villages) administered by *lurahs* (chiefs). Each *desa* is a collection of *dukuhans* (hamlets), which are under the charge of *kamituas.* Between the *desa* and the *kabupatens* there is in some places an intermediate division known as a *ketjamaten* (subdistrict), headed by a *tjamat.*

In a reorganization of regional government in 1967, General Suharto created the Regional Leadership Council as a new advisory body to assist the *kepala daerah* (local executive chief) at the provincial, regency and municipal levels. Though there is some popular representation in regional governments, the mayors, regents and governors are all centrally appointed officials whose primary responsibility is to the central government.

The 27 provinces with their capitals are: Aceh (Banda Aceh), North Sumatra (Medan), West Sumatra (Padang), Riau (Pakan Baru), Jambi (Jambi), South Sumatra (Palembang), West Java (Bandung), Central Java (Semarang), East Java (Surabaya), West Kalimantan (Pontianak), South Kalimantan (Banjarmasin), East Kalimantan (Samarinda), Central Kalimantan (Palangka Raja), North Sulawesi (Menado), South Sulawesi (Ujung Pandang), Bali (Den Pasar), West Nusa Tenggara (Mataram), East Nusa Tenggara (Kupang), Maluku (Ambon), Irian Jaya (Jajapura), Bengkulu (Bengkulu), Lampung (Tandjungkarang Telukbetung), Jakarta Capital Region (Jakarta), Jogjakarta (Jogjakarta), Southeast Sulawesi (Kendari) and Central Sulawesi (Palu). Following the outbreak of the civil war in Portuguese Timor in 1975, Indonesia directly intervened and set up a provisional government and later integrated East Timor as the 27th province of Indonesia with Dili as it capital.

FOREIGN POLICY

Early during his regime General Suharto rejected the leftward direction and ideological base of Sukarno's foreign policy and revived the original nonaligned foreign policy of Indonesia's first decade. In 1966 Indonesia rejoined the United Nations; in the following years it reestablished close relations with those nations whom Sukarno's hostile postures had antagonized: the United States, Malaysia, India, Australia, the Netherlands, other Western European countries and Japan. Indonesia maintains correct diplomatic relations with the Soviet Union but suspended relations with Communist China in 1967. A three-year confrontation with Malaysia was terminated in 1966.

The most dramatic shift was in relations with the Netherlands. In 1970 General Suharto visited the Netherlands, and in 1971 Queen Juliana visited Indonesia, where she was warmly received. The United States replaced the Soviet Union and the People's Republic of China as the principal supplier of military hardware and economic aid.

An important and particularly intractable issue involving relations with the Netherlands is the South

Moluccan struggle for independence. Although the South Moluccan Islands reserved the right of secession when they were incorporated into Indonesia in 1949, resistance to Indonesian rule has been suppressed. South Moluccan guerrillas have waged an unrelenting terror campaign in the Netherlands, culminating in the hijacking of a train in 1975.

In 1976 Indonesia completed its takeover of the former Portuguese dependency of East Timor, in defiance of a U.N. Security Council resolution calling for Indonesian withdrawal.

There are periodic demonstrations against Japanese economic "imperialism" and Japanese collaboration with ethnic Chinese Indonesians in business ventures. Relations with Australia worsened after the accession of the Labor Party with its tilt toward the East Timor guerrillas.

Indochina has dominated Indonesian foreign policy since 1978. By the end of 1979 Indonesia had 43,000 boat people on its territory. Like its fellow ASEAN (Association of Southeast Asian Nations) members, Indonesia supports Cambodia and expressed its displeasure with Vietnam and the Soviet Union over their military intervention in that country.

Indonesia and the United States are parties to 48 agreements and treaties covering agricultural commodities, atomic energy, aviation, customs, defense, economic and technical cooperation, finance, health, informational media guarantees, investment guarantees, mapping, narcotics, the Peace Corps, postal matters, publications, satellites, scientific cooperation, surplus property, telecommunications, and trade and commerce.

Indonesia is one of the charter members of the Association of Southeast Asian Nations, founded in 1967. It is a member of 12 U.N. organizations and 19 other international organizations. It joined the United Nations in 1950, withdrew in 1965 and rejoined in 1966.

PARLIAMENT

The Indonesian parliament consists of two bodies: the People's Consultative Assembly (Majelis Permusyawaratan Rakyat, MPR) and the House of Representatives (Dewan Perwakilan Rakyat, DPR).

The membership of the MPR is 1,000. It includes the 500 members of the DPR, government appointees, 147 members elected by regional legislatures, members allocated to Golkar and the political parties in proportion to their representation in the DPR, and two seats set apart for parties that have no seats in the DPR. The MPR meets once every five years, but a standing committee of 45 is in regular session. Its principal functions are to set broad policy guidelines and to elect the president and vice president.

The DPR is the principal legislative organ of the state. Of its 500 members, 400 are elected directly and 100 are appointed by the government to represent the armed forces (75) and nonmilitary professional groups (25). The DPR meets every year. Its powers are circumscribed by the presidential right to issue ordinances in lieu of law in times of national emergencies, which may remain in force without parliamentary ratification for as long as a year. The president also can veto bills, which may not be resubmitted to the DPR during the same session. Bills are adopted in the DPR through consensus rather than through voting.

Since independence in 1945 Indonesia has had six elections: two in 1955, one in 1955, one in 1971, one in 1977, one in 1982, and one in 1987. Elections are supervised by the General Elections Institute. Members of the former PKI (Partai Komunis Indonesia) are disenfranchised. The country is divided into 26 electoral districts. Suffrage is universal over age 17, and the age for running for office is 21.

POLITICAL PARTIES

The transition to the New Order of General Suharto was marked by a restructuring of the political system and reform of the political parties. Its task was to maintain the processes and channels of popular participation in politics without restoring the multiparty system to the center of political life. In 1970 Suharto ordered that the 1971 elections be contested under two labels: two political parties and the nonpolitical Golkar. Golkar is an army-sponsored group whose mission is "to engage in politics to suppress politics." It embraces all civilian interest groups not linked to parties and claims to represent 270 affiliated groups from all walks of life. It is organized from above with unlimited access to government resources, and Suharto is its president and chairman of the advisory board. In an effort to broaden its popular base, it established the Federation of All Indonesian Workers, the Indonesian Farmers Association and the National Committee of Indonesian Youth. Golkar is directed by a 17-member advisory board and a 17-member central board, both of which are responsible to a higher organ called the National Conference. The two political parties are themselves forced mergers of diverse groups. The United Development Party (Partai Persatuan Pembangunan, PPP) is a fusion of four Muslim groups. Though extremist on all religious issues, it supports the government on other matters. It is led by Jailani Naro. The Indonesian Democratic Party (Partai Demokrasi Indonesia, PDI) is a merger of five minority parties: the Indonesian Nationalist Party, the Upholders of Indonesian Independence, the Catholic Party, the (Protestant) Christian Party and the People's Party. Its leader is Suryadi.

Because of its multiethnic racial composition, Indonesia is particular vulnerable to secessionist movements. The most active of these is the Frente Revolucionário de Este Timor Independente (FRETILIN, Revolutionary Front for an Independent East Timor). In West Papua, now Irian Jaya, the Organisasi Papua Merdeka (OPM, Free Papua Organization) operates through its armed wing, Tentara Nasional Papua (TNP). Another secessionist movement is the National Liberation Front of Aceh (NFLA) in northern Sumatra.

The Communist Party is officially banned.

ECONOMY

Indonesia is a nation of extensive natural wealth, including tropical rainforests covering two-thirds of the land surface and minerals such as crude oil, natural gas, metals and coal. However, because of its large and rapidly growing population, it remains a relatively poor nation.

Agriculture, which includes forestry and fishing is a major sector of the economy, contributing 26% to GDP and employing 54% of the labor force. Rice is the staple crop, and the country is currently almost self-sufficient in that grain. Most farming is done either at subsistence level or on smallholder or plantation farms. Other crops include sugarcane, cassava, coconuts and maize. Cannabis is illegally produced for the international drug trade. Indonesia is the world's second largest producer of rubber, which along with palm oil, is actively encouraged as a plantation crop, both to create jobs and to expand exports. Timber is an important natural resource and forest products accounted for 13.6% of total exports for 1987.

Industry, which includes mining, manufacturing, construction and power, is the other major sector of the economy, contributing 33% to GDP in 1987. Indonesia's rich natural resources of crude oil, natural gas, metals and coal provide the basis for the industrial sector. Indonesia is the main oil producer in the Far East, and the country relies heavily on it for government revenue. Although decreases in world oil prices after 1982 had an adverse effect on export revenues and led to increased diversification into non-oil and gas products, in 1987 oil still dominated external trade providing more than 60% of government revenues and over 50% of export revenues. Indonesia is also the world's leading exporter of liquified natural gas. Other significant industries include textiles, cement, chemical fertilizers, agroprocessing and rubber processing. Other than petroleum, important mineral resources are nickel, bauxite, copper, iron, tin, silver, gold and coal.

PRINCIPAL ECONOMIC INDICATORS

Gross National Product (U.S. $ billions): 87.936 (1989)
GNP per capita (U.S. $): 490 (1989)
GNP average annual growth rate (%, 1980–89): 5.7
GNP per capita average annual growth rate (%, 1987–89): 4.6
Income distribution (% household income) 1987
- Lowest 20%: 8.8
- Highest 10%: 26.5

Average annual rate of inflation (%, 1980–88): 8.5
Consumer price index (1980 = 100) 1986
- All items: 168
- Food: 162

Wholesale price index (1980 = 100): 163 (1985)
Average annual growth rate (%, 1980–88)
- General government consumption: 2.9
- Private consumption: 7.2
- Gross domestic investment: 1.9

BALANCE OF PAYMENTS, 1989 (U.S. $ millions)

Current account balance: −1,368
Merchandise exports: 22,688
Merchandise imports: −16,275
Trade balance: 6,413
Other goods, services & income +: 2,397
Other goods, services & income −: −10,475
Other goods, services & income net: −8,078
Private unrequited transfers: 125
Official unrequited transfers: 172
Capital other than reserves: 1,818
Net errors & omissions: −888
Counterpart items: −30
Total change in reserves: −420

GROSS DOMESTIC PRODUCT

GDP nominal (Rp. billions): 139.452 (1988)
Average annual growth rate of GDP (%, 1980–88): 5.1
GDP by type of expenditure (%) 1987
- Consumption
  - Private: 58
  - Government: 9
- Gross domestic investment: 31
- Gross domestic saving: 25 (1988)
- Foreign trade
  - Exports: 24
  - Imports: −22

Cost components of GDP (%) 1987
- Net indirect taxes: 4
- Consumption of fixed capital: 5
- Compensation of employees & net operating surplus: 91

Sectoral origin of GDP (%) 1987
- Primary
  - Agriculture: 26
  - Mining: 13
- Secondary
  - Manufacturing: 14
  - Construction: 5
  - Public utilities: 1
- Tertiary
  - Transportation & communications: 6
  - Trade: 17
  - Finance: 6
  - Other services: 4
  - Government: 8

Average annual sectoral growth rates (%, 1980–88)
- Agriculture: 3.1
- Industry: 5.1
- Manufacturing: 13.1
- Services: 6.4

PUBLIC FINANCE

The Indonesian fiscal year runs from April 1 through March 31.

The national budget is divided into an ordinary budget and a development budget. Of central government revenues, more than half generally comes from taxes on income, profit and capital gain and about 25% from domestic taxes on goods and services. Of total current expenditures in 1987, 8.3% goes to defense; 10% to education; 1.8% to health; 1.7% to housing, Social Security and welfare; 23.5% to economic services; and 78.2% to other areas.

Overall responsibility for economic development planning rests with the National Development Planning Council, established in 1969. Centralized planning for the economy has been in effect since 1964, when the

CENTRAL GOVERNMENT EXPENDITURES, 1988

% of total expenditures
- Defense: 8.3
- Education: 10.0
- Health: 1.8
- Housing, social security, welfare: 1.7
- Economic services: 23.5 (1987)
- Other: 54.7

Total expenditures as % of GNP: 22.7
Overall surplus or deficit as % of GNP: −3.3

CENTRAL GOVERNMENT REVENUES, 1988

% of total current revenues
- Taxes on income, profit & capital gain: 55.9
- Social security contributions: 0.0
- Domestic taxes on goods & services: 24.5
- Taxes on international trade & transactions: 5.6
- Other taxes: 3.0
- Current nontax revenue: 11.0

Total current revenue as % of GNP: 19.2
General government consumption as % of GDP: 9
Average annual growth rate of general government consumption (%, 1980–88): 2.9

first five-year development plan (Repelita) was initiated. The first plan emphasized general economic rehabilitation, and the second plan placed priority on meeting pressing social needs through construction, consumer goods production and employment. The third plan focused on food production, employment and income distribution. The 1984–89 plan had three major (in many ways, conflicting) objectives: to create sufficient employment to absorb 9.3 million new workers; to continue expansion of the "strategic" industries of mineral and timber processing and engineering; and to boost nonpetroleum exports. This emphasis did in fact result in a 31.4% increase in nonoil exports by 1988. Additionally, the government is continuing its attempts at economic restructuring, which includes reforms aimed at promoting the private sector.

From 1970 to 1988 the United States committed $4.2 billion in aid to Indonesia, and Communist countries sent $175 million. Other Western nations contributed $19.8 billion from 1970 to 1987 and OPEC $213 million from 1979 to 1989.

FOREIGN AID, 1989

Total foreign aid (U.S. $ millions): 6487.4
- Bilateral: 3611.5
- Multilateral: 2875.9

CURRENCY & BANKING

The Indonesian unit of currency is the rupiah (Rp.), divided into 100 sen. Coins are issued in denominations of 5, 10, 25, 50 and 100 rupiahs, and notes are issued in denominations of 100, 500, 1,000, 5,000 and 10,000 rupiahs. In surprise moves, the government devalued the rupiah by 33.6% in 1978 and by 27.6% in 1983.

The June 1991 rate of exchange was U.S. $ 1 = Rp. 1,940.

The Indonesian banking system consists of Bank Indonesia, the central bank; five specialized state banks; six finance corporations; and 88 private commercial banks, including 11 foreign banks. The specialized banks are the major institutional mechanisms for channeling state funds into investment financing, but their activities greatly overlap. They include Bank Bumi Daya (plantation and forestry), Bank Expor Impor Indonesia (export and import), Bank Rakyat Indonesia (rural credit), Bank Negara Indonesia (industry), Bank Tabungan Negara (savings) and Bank Dagang Negara (mining). Development banks play a limited role and account for only 4% of the assets of all financial institutions. Bank Pembangunan Indonesia and the Indonesian Development Finance Company are the largest of such banks. The credit market also includes small

FINANCIAL INDICATORS, 1989

Total reserves minus gold (SDRs billions): 4.150
SDRs (millions): 1
Reserve position in IMF (SDRs millions): 72
Foreign exchange (SDRs billions): 4.077
Gold (fine troy oz. millions): 3.11
Ratio of external debt to total reserves: 7.9 (1988)
Central bank 1989
- Assets (%)
  - Foreign assets: 34.8
  - Claims on government: 13.7
  - Claims on banks: 47.7
  - Claims on private sector: 3.8
- Liabilities (%)
  - Reserve money: 31.7
  - Government deposits: 31.0
  - Foreign liabilities: 20.0
  - Capital accounts: 11.2
- Money supply 1989
  - Stock (Rp. billions): 20.559
  - M1 per capita: 115,000
- Private banks 1989
- Assets (%)
  - Loans to government: 10.4
  - Loans to private sector: 70.1
  - Reserves: 6.7
  - Foreign assets: 12.8
- Liabilities
  - Deposits (Rp. billions): 83.686
  - of which %
    - Demand deposits: 14.9
    - Savings deposits: 45.4
    - Government deposits: 4.7
    - Foreign liabilities: 3.8

External debt 1988
- Total (U.S. $ billions): 52,600
  - of which public (U.S. $ billions): 41.258
    - of which private (U.S. $ billions): 4.397
- Debt service (long term)
  - Total (U.S. $ billions): 7.302
  - Repayment
    - Principal (%): 64.5
    - Interest (%): 34.6
- Debt service ratio (%): 33.9
- External public debt as % of GNP: 55.7
- Debt service as % of GNP: 9.9
- Debt service as % of exports: 34.1
- Terms of public borrowing
  - Commitments (U.S. $ billions): 5.740
  - Average interest rate (%): 5.2
  - Average maturity (yrs.): 21
- Net flow of publicly guaranteed external capital (U.S. $ billions): 1.530
- Receipt of workers' remittances (U.S. $ millions): 99
- Net direct private investment (U.S. $ millions): 542

savings banks, paddy banks (which use rice crops as collateral) and 18,377 cooperative societies with a total membership of 6.8 million.

The five state banks control about 80% of banking assets and are responsible for funding the creation of a *pribumi* (entrepreneurial) class. Like public and private local banks, they suffer from corruption: Over the 1969–79 decade, they were involved in fraud involving a possible write-off of $1.700 billion (33% of outstanding bank credit). The 28 development banks—including 27 regional banks owned or partly owned by provincial governments—channel official credit (in five- to 15-year loans) to industries with priority under the current five-year plan. In 1986 there were 69 private commercial banks, with about 11% of banking assets.

GROWTH PROFILE
(Annual Growth Rates, %)

Projected population (1988–2000): 1.7
Projected crude birth rate (/1,000) (1990–95): 25.4
Projected crude death rate (/1,000) (1990–95): 10.1
Urban population (1985–90): 4.18
Labor force (1985–2000): 2.2
GNP (1980–89): 5.7
GNP per capita (1987–89): 4.6
GDP (1980–88): 5.1
Inflation (1980–88): 8.5
Agriculture (1980–88): 3.1
Industry (1980–88): 5.1
Manufacturing (1980–88): 13.1
Services (1980–88): 6.4
Money holdings (1980–88): 23.8
Manufacturing earnings per employee (1980–87): 6.0
Energy production (1980–88): 1.0
Energy consumption (1980–88): 4.5
Exports (1980–88): 2.9
Imports (1980–88): −2.1
General government consumption (1980–88): 2.9
Private consumption (1980–88): 7.2
Gross domestic investment (1980–88): 1.9

AGRICULTURE

The Indonesian economy still is predominantly agricultural, but agriculture is not a growth sector, and relative to other sectors it declined during the 1980s. Agricultural land constitutes 25.3% of the total land area of 190,365,000 ha. (470,391,550 ac.). Fifty-four percent of the labor force is employed in agriculture, which contributes 24% to the GDP and 16.6% of export earnings.

Of the total agricultural land, 11.5% are arable areas under crops. About 20% of the cultivated land is served by some form of irrigation.

There have been marked gains in total rice production and substantial improvement in productivity per hectare. Due to new varieties, rehabilitation of irrigation systems and increased fertilizer consumption, Indonesia's productivity is the second largest in Southeast Asia after Malaysia. Formerly the world's largest importer of rice, Indonesia is currently almost self-sufficient.

A variety of government extension and other efforts that had until now focused mainly on rice are gradually being extended to other basic food crops. Corn, cassava, soybeans and peanut production could be increased substantially if appropriate price and other incentives and improved marketing opportunities were available. Marginal lands in the rice-growing areas and a large proportion of the lightly populated outer islands often are more suitable for certain nontraditional crops as well as livestock and a variety of tree crops. Government efforts are under way, and aid donors are seeking ways to accentuate these programs. Indonesia already has experienced considerable expansion in plantation development and associated processing industries. State plantations in palm oil (mainly in northern Sumatra) and sugar are expanding, and there are new projects for increased smallholder production of rubber and other tree crops.

AGRICULTURAL INDICATORS

Agriculture's share of GDP (%): 24 (latest)
Average annual growth rate (%, 1980–88): 3.1
Value added in agriculture (U.S. $ billions): 20.05 (1988)
Cereal imports (million metric tons): 1.702 (1988)
Index of agricultural production (1979–81 = 100): 133 (1986)
Index of food production (1979–81 = 100): 134 (1986)
Index of food production per capita (1979–81 = 100): 117 (1986–88)
Number of tractors: 12,500 (1986)
Number of harvester-threshers: 16,500 (1986)
Total fertilizer consumption (000 metric tons): 1,971.8 (1985–86)
Fertilizer consumption (g./ha., hundreds): 1,068 (1987–88)
Number of farms (million): 19.501 (1983)
Average size of holding (ha.): 1.0 (1983)
Size class (%) 1983
  Below 1 ha. (below 2.47 ac.): 70.7
  1–200 ha. (over 494 ac.): 29.3
Tenure (%) 1973
  Owner-operated: 74.8
  Rented: 3.2
  Other: 22.1
Activity (%) 1973
  Mainly crops: 86.8
  Mainly livestock: 0.0
  Mixed: 13.2
Farms as % of total land area: 25.3 (1987)
Land use % 1985–87
  Cropland: 12
  Pasture: 26
  Forest: 11
  Other: 51
Yields (kg./ha.) 1989
  Grains: 3,750
  Roots & tubers: 11,647
  Legumes: 820
  Milk (kg./animal): 988
Production 1989
  Fruits (000 metric tons): 6,212
  Vegetables (000 metric tons): 3,343
Livestock (000) 1989
  Cattle: 10,050
  Horses: .702 (1986)
  Sheep: 5,500
  Pigs: 6,700
Forestry 1988
  Production of roundwood (000 cubic meters): 173,598
    of which industrial roundwood (%): 22.8
  Value of exports (U.S. $ billion): 2.872
Fishing 1988
  Total catch (million metric tons): 2.703
    of which marine (%): 73.6
  Value of exports (U.S. $ million): 664.483

In terms of land use there are major differences between Java and the outer islands. On Java agriculture is intensive, worked mostly as smallholdings; the dominant crop is rice; and irrigation is widely used. On the outer islands land is worked in large estates as well as in smallholdings, the products are diversified and irrigation is less significant. The range of agricultural techniques include wet-rice cultivation on *sawah* (irrigated land), usually double-cropped; dry-field farming on *tegalan* (unirrigated fields); *ladang* (intermittent cultivation on land planted in perennial tree crops); and *swidden* (slash-and-burn cultivation in which land is allowed to lie fallow for five to 20 years after being cultivated for three or four years).

To extend the area under intensive cropping, the government has used the two key programs of BIMAS (Bimbingan Massa or Mass Guidance) and INMAS (Intensifikasi Massa or Mass Intensification). The first provides cheap credit from Bank Rakyat Indonesia (the State People's Bank) for essential inputs such as pesticides, seeds and fertilizers. The second distributes essential agricultural equipment to more well-off farmers. Both programs are serviced within an organizational structure comprising BUUD (Badan Usaha Unit Desa, Hamlet Unit Enterprise Body) and KUUD (Koperasi Usaha Unit Desa, Hamlet Unit Enterprise Cooperative), which are the focal points of agricultural development. The State Procurement Agency (BULOG) is responsible for collecting surplus grain, stockpiling it and keeping the rice price stable. This role is politically crucial, given the 10% to 17% weightage of rice in the cost-of-living index.

Major problems in this arrangement are corruption in the extension of credit, and the conflict between a low rice price for the urban population and a fair return for farmers. The farm price is kept down and the retail price of rice is subsidized. By suppressing farm prices, the government has discouraged rural development and penalized the already indebted farmer and even more so the tenant or sharecropper. BULOG normally buys only 5% of the domestic crop; most of the crop is sold to private buyers who also are usurious lenders who often collect their debts at below floor prices.

In the late 1970s BIMAS was largely replaced by the INSUS (Intensifikasi Khusus) program, a voluntary cooperative program that facilitates distribution of subsidized inputs such as fertilizers, guarantees floor prices and coordinates extension services.

Under the *ijon kereja* (work through debt bondage) system there is a high concentration of land ownership. Technology usually bypasses the smallholder and benefits the wealthy.

Despite an impressive growth in aggregate agricultural production, there are persisting problems in distribution and storage. Although BULOG has a warehousing capability of 2.75 million tons, postharvest losses amount to 12% to 22% of the crop. The weather also is a problem. A dry spell can reduce the crop by several million tons.

The increase in rice production, although politically popular, has been achieved at the expense of other food crops, which have declined by 3.5% in acreage and 3.4% in output. The qualitative change in farming has had two main long-term effects: The average rural diet has become more starchy and less nutritious than it was in 1968, and the total nonrice staple food production per capita has fallen.

Smallholdings account for almost all food production and a major part of estate crops or export crops. About 70% of all farms are less than 1 ha. (2.5 ac.); the average is lower on Java and Madura, at 0.64 ha. (1.6 ac.). However, most of the land is held by comparatively few landowners. One-third of the land is leased, and over 60% of all farmers are sharecroppers. The large Dutch plantations were nationalized in 1959.

Forests cover two-thirds of the land surface representing 35% of the world's total tropical forest reserves and 70% of the world's hardwood stands. However, only 20 million ha. (49 million ac.) are exploitable commercially. Timber is Indonesia's second most important export earner and was estimated at about 10% of total earnings in 1988. Export of logs was banned in 1981, and an annual quota of 4 million cu. m. (141 million cu. ft.) was established to stimulate domestic wood processing. As a result, export of timber has declined since 1980 by 30.3%. A program of expansion for the plywood industry, which increased the number of plywood mills to 60 in 1985, raised the annual output of plywood to 6 million cu. m. (212 million cu. ft.), of which half was exported.

Fishing is one of the poorest sectors of the economy.

Agricultural credit is provided by the Indonesian People's Bank and over 18,000 cooperative societies.

MANUFACTURING

The contribution of manufacturing to the GDP was 19% in 1988. Manufacturing employed only 8.4% of the labor force. In 1981 7,942 industrial units employed 20 or more workers, but only 11% were classified as large industries employing more than 300 people. Most large industries are state-owned or partly foreign-owned. The industrial sector supplies only a small part of the demand for manufactured goods and is, moreover, heavily dependent on machinery, equipment and spare parts imported from abroad. In terms of capital invested, the largest industries are food processing, tex-

MANUFACTURING INDICATORS, 1987

Average annual growth rate (%, 1980–88): 13.1
Share of GDP (%): 19 (1988)
Labor force economically active in manufacturing (% est.): 8.4 (1988)
Value added in manufacturing (U.S.$ millions): 12,876
  Food & tobacco (%): 22 (latest)
  Textiles & clothing (%): 13 (latest)
  Machinery & transport equipment (%): 8 (latest)
  Chemicals (%): 9 (latest)
Earnings per employee in manufacturing 1986
  Growth rate (%, 1980–87): 6.0
  Index (1980 = 100): 144
Total earnings as % of value added: 19
Gross output per employee (1980 = 100): 156
Index of manufacturing production: 121 (1988)

tiles, rubber products, chemicals, tobacco, beverages and paper.

The four Repelitas (development plans) were designed to promote top-heavy industrialization by utilizing oil revenues and foreign investment. Total investment in the five-year plans heavily favored industry, which received 46%, whereas agriculture received 10.2% and infrastructure 24.8%. There are a number of significant implications in this pattern of investment. First, it hindered creation of a sound, stable and diversified rural base for progress. Second, given the generous provisions of the 1967 Foreign Investment Law and the high profitability of mining, forestry and oil, the most lucrative sectors of the economy are subject to high repatriation of capital and an accelerated rundown of resources. It also is for the most part capital-intensive in a country where there is considerable unemployment. Investment in the extractive sector, where 66% of foreign investment is concentrated, creates few jobs. Although manufacturing creates jobs, it is disproportionately concentrated in and around Jakarta in Java. Industry is characterized by a historic reluctance to decentralize or move into the outer islands. Even in Java, three factors limit job creation: the high degree of capital intensity, the decline of traditional occupations, and the preference for expatriate workers in foreign-run industries. Although the job market is growing by 1.5 million new entrants annually, only 55,000 jobs are being created on average each year.

Of increasing importance to industrial growth are the free trade zones geared almost wholly to the export markets. These "export platforms" make good use of cheap, nonunionized local labor, but little linkage exists with the rest of the manufacturing economy and there is relatively little emphasis on import substitution. (The Indonesian market for consumer goods is smaller than that of South Korea, which has one-fourth the population of Indonesia.)

There is no clear demarcation between public and private sectors in Indonesia, and the former has steadily grown over the years through investment and expropriation. The state owns and operates the railroads; the highways, seaports and airports; the telecommunications system; electric power facilities; air transportation; oil distribution; agricultural estates; mining enterprises; and factories producing cement, fertilizer, textiles, paper, tires, cigarettes and glass. Salt is a government monopoly. Nearly 70% of all government employees at the national level are employees of state enterprises. Before 1969, state companies could be identified through the use of the prefix P.N. (Perusahaan Negara—state enterprise) before the company name. Unless special circumstances applied, P.N.'s were wholly owned by the government and operated under a government department.

In accordance with Decree 1 of 1969, however, state enterprises are gradually being consolidated and reorganized into three basic categories: (1) departmental agencies, with their capital to be determined annually through the state budget (these are of a public service nature and are designated Perusahaan Jawatan, or PERJAN); (2) public companies established as entities separate from the departments, with their capital separate from the state budget (these are of a public service nature also operating as businesses and are designated Perusahaan Umum, or PERUM [examples are Perum Telekomunikasi in telecommunications and Perum Listrik Negara in electric power]); and (3) public corporations with limited liability, or P.T.'s. P.T.'s are subject to the same rules and regulations as private corporations and are designated as Perusahaan Perseroan, or PERSERO, but actually bear the same prefix as the private limited liability corporations, or P.T.'s (Perseroan Terbatas). However, all or part of the shares of a P.T. must be owned by the government (national or provincial), while the remaining shares may be sold to private parties. The government has been encouraging and, in some cases, requiring state enterprises to become P.T.'s. The policy intent is to make them into profitable enterprises so their shares can eventually be sold to private (including foreign) investors, thus reducing public sector involvement.

As of 1982 there were reported to be 113 government-owned limited liability companies subject to the same commercial codes, taxes and other laws applicable to private enterprise.

Foreign investment in Indonesian industries is regulated by the Capital Investment Coordinating Board. The government has enacted legislation offering foreign private investment specific advantages in regard to taxation and repatriation. At the same time the government has required increasing participation of indigenous non-Chinese Indonesians in joint ventures. Foreign investors are avoiding Indonesia largely because of the surge of nationalism, alleged government demands for payoffs, and the financial scandal caused by the collapse of the giant Pertamina. Between 1974 and 1983 foreign investment was erratic, slumping from a 1983 high of $1.392 billion to $489 million in 1980 but rising to $2.520 billion in 1983. Indonesia is reputed to be most profitable country in the world for U.S. companies. However, there still is concern over the servicing of foreign investments and an increase in regulations. Since 1975 the government has moved to control equity, technology transfers, employment of foreign workers and the distribution and influence of foreign investment and to promote a *pribumi* (indigenous) entrepreneurial elite. For example, a foreign company must have 51% Indonesian equity after 10 years, even though the management is foreign. This law, however, applies only to the nonpetroleum sectors. In 1980 another law stipulated that *pribumi* companies must be given preference in government contracts. In addition, local businesses are protected through quotas, subsidies and tariffs, all designed to boost the economic role of politically favored Indonesians.

During 1983 and 1984 the government made a series of moves to ease controls over private investment, to increase its efficiency and to help boost the contribution of private to total investment during Repelita IV from 45% to 49%. In 1983 three steps were taken in credit reform: Bank credit "ceilings" were abandoned, state banks were given the right to set competing interest rates and "discount window" facilities were opened. In view of the free convertibility of the rupiah, such free-market fiscal policy might encourage funds to remain in the country, but it does not necessarily make borrowing any easier—and it tends to limit the amount of credit available to low-income borrowers.

A second major change in investment policy involved tax reform—partly to boost the contribution to the GDP of nonpetroleum taxes from their extremely low 8%. A value added tax of 10% came into force in July 1983, some excise taxes were extended and all income is now taxed (on the basis of self-assessment) at three different rates: those with incomes up to Rp. 10 million per year pay 15%; those earning 10 million to Rp. 50 million pay 25%; and those receiving more than Rp. 50 million pay 35% (down from 45%).

In addition to such fiscal reform, the government has committed itself to removing most of the complicated, inefficient and corrupt procedures for approval and licensing of investment, which impede free movement of domestic and foreign private investment. Net direct private investment in 1983 was $289 million.

MINING

Indonesia is one of the world's richest countries in mineral wealth. Nonoil minerals continue as the fourth-largest foreign-exchange earner after petroleum/gas timber/wood products and rubber. Currently the world's fourth-largest tin producer, Indonesia has considerable potential for growth due to its extensive reserves. However, only about 5% of the total land area has been geologically mapped in detail, and 20% is totally unexplored. Known major resources include copper, bauxite, tin and nickel as well as oil. All large-scale mining enterprises are in the hands of state corporations.

Nickel is mined in Sulawesi, with reserves estimated at 40 million tons; copper is produced in the Ertsberg Mountains of Irian Jaya; bauxite on Bintan island in the Riau archipelago: tin on the islands of Banka, Belitung and Singkep; and coal in southern Sumatra and Kalimantan.

ENERGY

Indonesia is almost totally dependent on oil for its power. In 1980 only 3.8% of its energy requirements were met by coal and hydroelectric generation. Only 10% of the population have access to electricity. A major development will be the $2 billion Bukit Assam power project, the first of 18 coal-powered power stations providing 12,000 mw. by 2006.

Indonesia has 16 billion bbl. of recoverable reserves of petroleum and 34.7 trillion cu. m. (1.225 quadrillion cu. ft.) or recoverable reserves of natural gas. With a prospective onshore area of 1.5 million sq. km. (579,000 sq. mi.), Indonesia has an area for potential exploitation of petroleum 10 times the size of the North Sea, with many sedimentary areas not tested. Indonesia is the site of the region's most comprehensive exploration program. In 1982 a total of 232 exploration wells were drilled, with a relatively high 54% success rate, at an estimated cost of $4.2 billion. Much of this activity is being undertaken by U.S. corporations, which have invested more than $5 billion in the industry and pump 90% of all crude petroleum. However, most of the oil fields are small and have a relatively short productive life. Indonesia's annual output of crude in 1988 was 484 million bbl., of which domestic consumption took 32%; of the rest, 70% was exported to Japan and 10% to the United States. At the current rate of extraction, Indonesian supplies will run out in 35 years for petroleum and 50 years for natural gas. Natural gas from the gas fields in the South China Sea may outpace petroleum as the most profitable export in the coming decades. In 1982 Indonesia exported 10.2 million tons of LNG, all to Japan, making Indonesia the world's largest exporter of LNG. Production of LNG is concentrated at the Arun plant in Aceh, Sumatra, and the Badak plant in Kalimantan.

ENERGY INDICATORS

Average annual energy production growth rate (%, 1980–88): 1.0
Energy consumption per capita (kg. oil equivalent): 22.9 (1988)
Energy imports as % of merchandise exports: 14 (1988)
Average annual growth rate of energy consumption (%, 1980–88): 4.5
Electricity 1988
  Installed capacity (million kw.): 10.680
  Production (billion kw.-hr.): 37.010
    % fossil fuel: 78.3
    % hydro: 21.1
  Consumption per capita (kw.-hr.): 212
Natural gas
  Proved reserves (trillion cu. m.): 2.423 (1990)
  Production (billion cu. m.): 40.340 (1989)
  Consumption (billion cu. m.): 11.294 (1988)
Petroleum
  Proved reserves (billion bbl.): 11.970 (1990)
  Years to exhaust proved reserves: 16 (1990)
  Production (million bbl.): 514 (1989)
  Consumption (million bbl.): 260 (1988)
  Refining capacity (000 bbl./day): 714 (1990)
Coal
  Reserves (billion metric tons): 3.000 (latest)
  Production (million metric tons): 2.741 (1988)
  Consumption (million metric tons): 2.341 (1988)

Since 1983, most oil companies, including Caltex, which pumps nearly 50% of Indonesia's crude, have operated under a production-sharing formula that leaves resource ownership with the government while the company acts as the contractor and supplies the capital. The new 18-year contract between Caltex and the state, for example, stipulates an 88:12 split in production, with 100% allowances for depreciation, investment credits for all new exploration and favorable terms for purchases of petroleum by the government.

Pertamina (Perusahaan Negara Pertambangan Minjak dan Gas Sumi Nasional, National Oil Mining and Natural Gas Company) is responsible for all petroleum activities, from exploration to marketing. Pertamina coordinates the operations of some 30 foreign concessionaires, controls all domestic marketing of petroleum and owns eight refineries. In addition, it has undertaken a number of enterprises not related to petroleum—automobile rentals, motels and restaurants (one in New York), insurance, airlines, rice milling, machine tools and steel. It also operates a large fleet of tugs, barges and tankers, and it conducts its own oil exploration.

LABOR

Employment is extremely elastic, influenced by seasonal demands in agriculture. According to a World Bank estimate, it fluctuates roughly 20% between peak and slack agricultural seasons.

National legislation provides for a seven-hour workday and a 40-hour workweek, with a 30-minute break after every four hours of continuous work. Overtime pay must be one and a half times the basic wage, while work on Sundays and holidays must pay double the usual wage. There are provisions for a rest day each week as well as special regulations regarding employment of women. The government has not adopted a minimum wage law for the country. However, in different geographic areas it has established recommended minimum wages that are paid to government laborers and that are expected to be followed by private industry employers. The minimum wages are arrived at by utilizing a formula that takes into account the local prevailing wages. Since the minimum wages rely on government persuasion rather than law for enforcement, they often are ignored.

The low income levels prevailing in Indonesia are evidenced by the high amount of per capita income spent on food. An International Labor Organization study based on 1976 data indicates that about 75% of per capita expenditures in Indonesia are used for food. For the Philippines, Thailand and Malaysia, per capita expenditures for food are in the 50% to 60% range. In developed countries the percentage spent on food is as low as 20%.

Conditions of work are regulated by the Labor Code of 1948. Occupational injuries are covered by the Labor Accident Law of 1951.

The national labor federation is the All-Indonesia Union of Workers (SPSI), with 10 national unions, 8,000 locals and a membership of 3 million. The SPSI is the only trade union legally permitted in Indonesia. Political activity by the SPSI is forbidden, as is organizing civil servants or workers in government-owned enterprises and in major sectors of the economy declared as vital, such as air transportation and oil. However, some professional organizations, such as those for teachers, act as unions in some respects. Most expenses of the SPSI are met by the government, although a checkoff of union dues was authorized in 1977. There are a number of smaller trade unions, some of them affiliated to the political parties.

Although the right to strike is guaranteed by law, it is greatly circumscribed in practice. Strikes are prohibited in "vital industries," a large category in a developing nation. To be legal, strikes must be sanctioned by regional labor courts and by the National Labor Court, which are tripartite organizations of representatives of management, government and labor. Strikes are forbidden while a court is seeking a solution through arbitration or conciliation.

FOREIGN COMMERCE

Indonesia's principal imports are machinery, chemical products and manufactured goods. Its major exports are petroleum and liquefied gas, timber, textiles, rubber and coffee. Japan and the United States are its most important trading partners.

Nine state trading companies handle a significant share of the foreign trade. Licensing of imports has been abolished, but imports may be undertaken only by or through Indonesian-owned companies.

LABOR INDICATORS, 1988

Total economically active population (million): 74.923
- % working-age (15–64): 68.4
- % female: 40.2

Activity rate (%)
- Total: 42.5
- Male: 50.6
- Female: 34.3

Employment status (%)
- Employers & self-employed: 42.7
- Employees: 25.0
- Unpaid family workers: 29.1
- Other: 3.2

Sectoral employment of economically active (%)
- Agriculture, forestry, fishing: 54.0
- Construction: 3.3
- Manufacturing, mining, quarrying, public utilities: 9.8 (1985)
- Trade, hotels, restaurants: 14.6 (1985)
- Transportation, communications: 3.1 (1985)
- Finance, real estate: 0.4 (1985)
- Services: 13.0 (1985)

Average annual growth rate of labor force (%, 1980–2000): 2.2
Unemployment (million): 1.017
Labor under 20 years (%): 14.0 (1986)

FOREIGN TRADE INDICATORS, 1988

Exports (U.S. $ billions): 21.0 (1989 est.)
Imports (U.S. $ millions): 13.2 (1989 est.)
Balance of trade (U.S. $ millions): 7.8
Annual growth rate (1980–88), exports (%): 2.9
Annual growth rate (1980–88), imports (%): −2.1
International reserves in terms of months of imports covered: 3.3
Terms of trade (1980 = 100): 70
Import price index (1980 = 100): 87.9 (1986)
Export price index (1980 = 100): 57.0 (1986)

Direction of Trade (%), 1989

	Imports	Exports
European Community	15.7	10.6
United States	13.6	15.8
U.S.S.R. and eastern European economies	1.0	0.8
Japan	23.0	42.1

Composition of Trade (%), 1989

	Imports	Exports
Food and agricultural raw materials	13.0	21.2
Fuels and other energy	7.7	39.5
Mineral ores and concentrates	3.9	3.4
Manufactured goods	75.4	35.9
of which chemicals	17.6	2.3
of which machinery	37.8	0.9

TRANSPORTATION & COMMUNICATIONS

The state-owned railways system consists of 6,583 km. (4,090 mi.) of track, of which more than 90% is of a 1.067-m. (42-in.) gauge. Nearly 70% of the track is in an interconnecting network serving all of Java.

Indonesia has an extensive port system of 392 registered ports. Of these, 16 can accommodate ocean-going ships and about 100 can accommodate interisland shipping vessels. Tanjung Priok, serving the Jakarta area, is by far the largest port for general cargo, although the port of Dumai in Sumatra, where the large Caltex oil fields are located, handled the largest volume of exports in 1978. Other major seaports in Indonesia are Tanjung Perak, the port for Surabaya; Cirebon and Cilacap in Java; Belawan, Pangkalan Susu and Palembang in Sumatra; Banjarmasin and Pontianak in Kalimantan; Ujung Pandang and Bitung in Sulawesi; Ambon in the Moluccas; and Sorong in Irian Jaya.

Ocean shipping, interisland shipping and coastal shipping are the three main divisions of the Indonesian merchant marine. The national shipping company, Pelajaran Nasional Indonesia, has a fleet of 312 vessels; Pertamina, the mining company, has its own fleet of tankers, with a GRT of 318,000. The country's merchant fleet numbers 1,722 vessels. Barely 25% of the country's foreign trade (and 10% of its oil) is carried by Indonesian ships. In 1982 the government ordered that all government-controlled exports and imports must be carried by domestic lines. The interisland fleet consisted in the early 1970s of some 350 ships totaling 450,000 gross registered tons, and coastal shipping consisted of over 17,000 vessels and small motorized craft. Both coastal and interisland navigation are reserved for Indonesian-owned vessels.

There are 21,579 km. (13,409 mi.) of inland waterways: 5,471 km. (3,399 mi.) in Sumatra, 830 km. (518 mi.) in Java, 10,460 km. (6,500 mi.) in Borneo, 241 km. (150 mi.) in Celebes and 4,587 km. (2,850 mi.) in Irian Jaya.

Most of the roads are in Java and are unpaved. Major new highways include the 1,800-km. (1,118-mi.) Trans-Sumatra Highway and the 1,900-km. (1,180-mi.) Trans-Sulawesi Highway.

The international airline is PT Garuda Indonesia, which operates regular services to cities in over 20 foreign countries in Asia, Europe and North America. PT Merpati Nusantara Airlines, a subsidiary of PT Garuda Indonesia, operates domestic and international services to Australia and Malaysia services. In addition, there are 45 private air carriers. Together these carriers operate 150 aircraft. Sukarno-Hatta Airport, the main international airport, near Jakarta, at Cengkareng, is served by 19 international airlines.

Through the Djatiluhar earth satellite station, Indonesia is directly linked to Australia, Japan, Europe and major cities in Asia. Indonesia's communications capability has improved substantially in recent years. For international communications, Indonesia established its first satellite earth station in 1969. Major communications projects recently scheduled include expansion of the domestic satellite program, telex and telegram projects and a project for telephone exchanges. The aggregate foreign exchange cost of these latter projects is about U.S. $780 million (the financing for most of this has already been arranged), and the domestic costs are equivalent to U.S. $386 million. The most dramatic addition to Indonesia's communications capabilities was the inauguration in August 1976 of its Domestic Satellite System, consisting of two satellites, Palapa A1 and A2. The system operates with 50 earth stations, 10 of which were added in Repelita II, and links Jakarta with 26 provincial capitals and 14 other major points. The satellite system enables Indonesia to achieve rapid expansion of telephone and broadcast facilities and gives it the capacity of extending multiple channels of television and radio broadcasts to all its provinces. Direct communication facilities between Jakarta and Ujung Pandang were established in 1978, when the East Indonesia microwave network began operation. The East Indonesia network joins other established microwave networks already working in Indonesia. The Java–Bali microwave network connects Jakarta, Bandung, Semarang, Jogjakata and Surabaya in Java with Denpasar in Bali. The Trans-Sumatra microwave network operates between Telukbetung in southern Sumatra and Jakarta.

In 1988 a total of 1,357,244 tourists visited Indonesia. Drawn by the volcanic scenery and temples of Java, as well as the religious festivals and traditional dancing of Bali, tourists arrived primarily from Australia, Japan,

TRANSPORTATION INDICATORS

Roads (latest)
- Length, km. (mi.): 219, 791 (136,578)
- Paved (%): 39

Motor vehicles (latest)
- Automobiles: 1,124,824
- Trucks and buses: 1,345,538
- Persons per vehicle: 72
- Road freight, metric ton-km. (short ton-mi.) (billions): 25.000 (17.122) (pre-1986)

Railroads (latest)
- Track, km. (mi.): 6,583 (4,090)
- Passenger-km. (passenger-mi.) (billions): 7.898 (4.908)
- Freight, metric ton-km. (short ton-mi.) (billions): 1.808 (1.238)

Merchant marine
- Vessels (over 100 tons): 1,722 (1989)
- Total deadweight tonnage (000): 2,742.3 (1989)
- Oil tankers (000 GRT): 491 (1985)

Ports (pre-1986)
- Cargo loaded (million metric tons): 147.552
- Cargo unloaded (million metric tons): 40.596

Air
- Km. (mi.) flown (millions): 122.4 (76.1) (1985)
- Passenger-km. (passenger-mi.) (billions): 8.940 (5.555) (latest)
- Freight, metric ton-km. (short ton-mi.) (millions): 288.7 (197.7) (latest)
- Mail, metric ton-km. (short ton-mi.) (millions): 9.8 (6.7) (1985)
- Airports with scheduled flights: 134 (1990)

Pipelines 1990
- Refined, km. (mi.): 456 (283)
- Natural gas, km. (mi.): 1,703 (1,058)

Inland waterways (latest)
- Length, km. (mi.) 21,579 (13,409)
- Freight, metric ton-km. (short ton-mi.) (billions): 25.000 (17.122) (pre-1986)

COMMUNICATION INDICATORS, 1988

Telephones
  Total (000): 938
  Persons per telephone: 187
Phone traffic (million calls)
  Combined national (pulses): 8,081.7
  International: 43.156
Post office
  Number of post offices: 20,361
  Pieces of mail handled (million): 496.6
Telegraph
  Total traffic (000 calls): 11,731
    National: 11,668
    International: 63
Telex
  Subscriber lines: 15,441
Telecommunications 1990
  Satellite stations: 3

TOURISM & TRAVEL INDICATORS, 1986

Total tourist receipts (U.S. $ millions): 1,028 (1988)
Expenditures by nationals abroad (U.S. $ millions): 489 (1988)
Number of hotel beds (000): 193
Average length of stay (nights): 12
Number of tourists (000): 700.9 (1984)
  of whom from United States: 60.1
  Australia: 95.6
  Japan: 92.4
  United Kingdom: 59.1

the United States, Singapore, the United Kingdom, the Netherlands, West Germany and France.

DEFENSE

The defense structure is headed by the president of the republic, who also is the defense minister and commander of the armed forces. Under him is the minister of defense and security, to whom the chiefs of the army, navy and air force report as their immediate superior. The armed forces are organized under a territorial system. There are four regional commands, known as *kowilhan:* Kowilhan I—Sumatra and northwestern Kalimantan; Kowilhan II—Java, Madura and the Lesser Sunda Islands; Kowilhan III—Sulawesi and the remainder of Kalimantan; and Kowilhan IV—the Moluccas and Irian Joya. The first three are commanded by generals and the last by an admiral. All services are combined in the *kowilhan* headquarters, but each service has a separate organization beneath this level. In the case of the army there are 17 *daerah* military commands *(kodam)*, each headed by a major general. Under *kodams* are *koream* (in Java) or *kodim* (outside of Java) at the district *(kabupaten)* level and *koramil* at the subdistrict *(ketjamaten)* level. These commands at the lower level also are actively involved in community affairs as well as in political direction. The relative divisions are called *kodaeral* in the navy and *kodva* in the air force. Separate from these commands is the Strategic Reserve Command, known as Kostrad. At any given time, almost a third of the army personnel are believed to be involved in civil or nonmilitary duties.

A selective service system and volunteers provide the manpower for the armed forces.

The military also is deeply involved in the national economy under the *dwifungsi* (double function) principle. Military manpower and managerial skills play a significant role in economic development plans. The military runs a number of enterprises, such as Pertamina, and is engaged in transportation, road and building construction, rice milling and timber concessions. It also participates actively in political life through regional leadership councils and through membership in both houses of the parliament. A *kekaryaan* (civilian) section at Hankam (Department of Defense and Security) is concerned with placing armed forces personnel in civilian life.

The strength of the armed forces in 1989 was 282,000, including the 20,000-member Police Mobile Brigade. They constitute 1.7 armed personnel per 1,000 inhabitants.

Army

Personnel: 215,000

Organization: 10 military area commands; 2 infantry divisions; 1 armored cavalry brigade; 3 infantry brigades; 2 airborne infantry brigades; 2 field artillery regiments; 1 AA artillery regiment; 1 field engineer regiment; 4 special warfare groups; 7 independent cavalry battalions; 63 independent infantry battalions; 4 independent airborne infantry battalions; 8 independent field artillery battalions; 7 independent AA artillery battalions; 4 independent batteries; 4 construction engineer battalions

Equipment: 152 tanks; 114 combat vehicles; 200 mechanized combat vehicles; 196 armored personnel carriers; 200 howitzers; 480 mortars; 480 rocket launchers; 311 air defense guns

Army aviation: 1 composite squadron; 1 helicopter squadron; 21 amphibious vehicles

Deployment: 20 infantry battalions in East Timor

Navy

Personnel: 43,000, including 12,000 marine corps

Units: 2 fleets; 2 submarines; 13 frigates; 45 patrol vessels; 10 fast attack craft; 2 minesweepers; 2 support ships; 18 landing craft; 11 support ships

Naval air: 19 combat aircraft; 14 helicopters; 10 antisubmarine warfare aircraft; 13 maritime reconnaissance aircraft

Marines: 5 regiments; 30 tanks; 40 combat vehicles; 57 armored personnel carriers; 40 howitzers; air defense guns

Naval bases: Surabaya, Kemajaran (Jakarta), Gorontalo

Air Force

Personnel: 24,000

Organization and equipment: 68 combat aircraft; 2 air operations areas; 2 fighter squadrons; 1 interceptor squadron; 1 counterinsurgency squadron; 1 maritime reconnaissance squadron; 4 transport squadrons; 3 helicopter squadrons; 3 training squadrons

Quick reaction forces: 5 battalions; 6 support vessels

Air bases: Medan, Palembang, Jakarta, Bandung, Iswahjudi, Denpasar, Semerang, Lombok, Balikpapan and Amboina

Defense expenditure in 1987–88 was Rp. 2,188,000

The Indonesian armed forces are one of the largest and best equipped in Asia. The average soldier is noted for loyalty, discipline and endurance. Because the military control both the government and the economy, the armed forces receive priority in budgetary allocations. Although Indonesia has not been involved in external combat since independence, the nation has witnessed more internal violence and civil wars than any other Asian nation outside of Indochina.

Indonesia received $1.2 billion in military aid from 1958 through 1965 from the Soviet Union, and $538.2 million from the United States from 1946 through 1983. Arms purchases from 1973 through 1983 totaled $1.720 billion, of which $270 million was supplied by the United States.

EDUCATION

Indonesia has an above-average literacy rate, with over 74% of its population literate (83% for males and 65.4% for females).

Schooling is technically free and in 1987 it was made compulsory for six years, between ages seven and 13, but fees are charged in many areas in addition to charges for uniforms, lunches and transportation. Under the regulations of 1972, primary schooling is six years, junior secondary school three years and senior secondary school three years for a total of 12 years.

Vocational training is provided in secondary schools. There were 1,419,773 students in the vocational track in 1989. There also is an extensive private-school system in which are included Islamic schools *(madrasahs)*, Catholic and Protestant schools and the intensely nationalist Taman Siswa school system. Private schools that meet government standards receive state subsidies. In the mid-1980s 13% of students in the primary level and 60% of students in the secondary level were enrolled in private schools.

The academic year runs from January to December, and the school year consists of three terms of 13 weeks each. All regular schools are coeducational. The language of instruction is Bahasa Indonesia, but English is taught at the senior secondary level.

National educational budgetary and policy decisions are made by the Ministry of Education and Culture.

Indonesia has 48 state universities and teacher-training colleges and 25 private universities with a total student strength in 1987–88 of 1,297,533.

In 1984 there were 13 learned societies in Indonesia, of which the oldest is the Institute of Indonesian Culture, founded in 1778. Indonesia's contribution to world scientific authorship is 0.0080%; its world rank in this respect is 42nd. In 1982 there were 17,287 scientists engaged in research and development.

EDUCATION INDICATORS, 1989

Literacy
- Total (%): 74.1
- Male: (%): 83.0
- Female (%): 65.4

First level
- Schools: 145,571
- Students: 26,725,364
- Teachers: 1,134,089
- Student/teacher ratio: 23.6
- Net enrollment ratio: 98 (1984)

Second level
- Schools: 27,396
- Students: 8,946,113
- Teachers: 604,918
- Student/teacher ratio: 14.8
- Net enrollment ratio: 36 (1984)

Vocational
- Schools: 3,620
- Students: 1,419,773
- Teachers: 99,081
- Student/teacher ratio: 14.3

Third level (postsecondary)
- Institutions: 792 (1988)
- Students: 1,179,489
- Teachers: 115,359
- Student/teacher ratio: 10.2
- Gross enrollment ratio: 6.5 (1984)
- Students (/100,000 pop.): 600
- % of population age 25 and over with postsecondary education: 0.8

Foreign study
- Foreign students in national universities: 258 (1985)
- Students abroad: 14,550
  - of whom in
    - United States: 7,565 (1988)
    - France: 398 (1988)
    - Federal Republic of Germany: 2,143 (1988)
    - United Kingdom: 515 (1987)

Public expenditure 1988
- Total (Rp. billion): 1,238
- % of GNP: 1.0
- % of national budget: 4.3
- % of current: 88.5

GRADUATES, 1984

Total: 73,627
Education: 30,000
Humanities & religion: 1,711
Fine & applied arts: 87
Law: 7,531
Social & behavioral sciences: 13,616
Commerce & business: 7,199
Mass communication: 307
Home economics: 138
Service trades: 152
Natural sciences: 913
Mathematics & computer science: 140
Medicine: 2,385
Engineering: 4,495
Architecture: 505
Industrial programs: 54
Transportation & communications: 6
Agriculture, forestry, fisheries: 4,264
Other: 124

LEGAL SYSTEM

Three systems of law are prevalent in Indonesia: the Criminal Code based on the Dutch Criminal Code; the

Code of Civil Law, which is applied to all non-Indonesians; and the customary law *(hukum adat)*, which is uncodified and varies from region to region.

The Indonesian court system has four branches: the general courts, the religious courts, the military courts and the administrative courts. Within the general court structure the court of first instance is the district court *(pengadilan negeri)*. Above it are the high courts *(pengadilan tinggi)* in at least 14 provinces. At the apex is the Supreme Court *(mahkamah agung)*, consisting of a chairman, a vice chairman and four members. The principle of the independence of the judiciary has been reaffirmed by the Suharto regime, but in practice the courts are subordinate to the government.

Indonesia's criminal justice system lacks the number of courts, judges, prosecutors and police needed to cope with the increase in crime in recent years. Accordingly, sometimes there are lengthy delays in scheduling trials. Trials are conducted by a three-judge panel that hears evidence, decides guilt or innocence and assesses punishment. Although the right of appeal is not absolute, it is observed in most cases; most court sessions are open, and most defendants have access to counsel.

It is widely believed that political interference and corruption exist in the Indonesian legal system. In criminal proceedings, sometimes defendants can buy their way out of prosecution at various stages of the proceedings. In civil cases court decisions sometimes are influenced by the payment of bribes. In response to these abuses, the attorney general and the minister of justice have directed that disciplinary action be taken against officials involved in corrupt activities and have sought to increase salaries and benefits for judicial officials, with the aim of reducing the incentive for corruption.

The penal system consists of at least 335 prisons, including a penal colony at Buru Island.

LAW ENFORCEMENT

Indonesia has a national police force, Kepolisian Republik Indonesia, one of the four services of the armed forces of the republic. There are no local police forces. The strength of the police is about 110,000. The commander of the national police is called chief. Under his headquarters at Jakarta are four staff sections and 17 districts. The primary police unit is the *kampung* (precinct). A special force, the Mobile Brigade, is maintained at the national headquarters for emergency duties. The standard police weapon is the pistol.

The Indonesian equivalent of an intelligence organization in the national security field is the KOPKAMTIB, which was founded in 1965 to counter Communist subversion. Little is known about its organization, but it is believed to possess broad inquisitorial powers, and its name still evokes terror. It serves as an instrument in the enforcement of official ideology. In 1974 Suharto assumed personal command of KOPKAMTIB.

Juvenile delinquency and prostitution are significant law enforcement problems.

HEALTH

The major health problems are tuberculosis, malaria, dysentery, cholera and plague. Only 38% of the population have access to safe water.

HEALTH INDICATORS

Health personnel 1988
- Physicians: 23,084
  - persons per: 7,512
- Dentists: 2,304 (1982)
- Nurses: 64,087 (1982)
- Pharmacists: 3,587 (1982)
- Midwives: 16,928 (1982)

Hospitals 1987
- Number: 1,436
- Number of beds (/10,000): 7
- Admissions/discharges (/10,000): 66 (1978)
- Bed occupancy rate (%): 55.1
- Average length of stay (days): 9

Type of hospitals (%) 1978
- Government: 30.2
- Private nonprofit: 23.0
- Private profit: 46.8

Public health expenditures (latest)
- As % of national budget: 1.8
- Per capita (U.S. $): 1.70

Vital statistics
- Crude death rate (/1,000): 9 (1990)
- Life expectancy at birth 1990
  - Males: 58
  - Females: 63
- Infant mortality rate (/1,000 live births): 75 (1990)
- Child mortality rate under 5 yrs. (/1,000 live births) 1985–90): 117
- Maternal mortality rate (/100,000 live births) (1986–87): 800
- Population with access to safe water (%): 38 (latest)

FOOD & NUTRITION

Rice is the staple diet, supplemented by corn, sago, sweet potatoes and coconuts. Most of the protein is provided by fish. Per capita food intake is 2,504 calories (110% of requirements).

MEDIA & CULTURE

Ninety-seven newspapers are published in the country.

Publishing is concentrated in the large cities. Jakarta alone has 24 dailies, with half the total national circulation. All of these are published in Bahasa Indonesia, except for two in English and one in Chinese. Menado has 15 dailies, Medan 12 and Surabaya nine. The provincial press is poor in quality. Two military newspapers function as official organs of the administration: *Harian Umum*, with a circulation of 80,000 and *Berita Yuddha* with a circulation of 55,000. Weekly newspapers and other magazines number about 1,545, with a total circulation of 7 million, of which weekly newspapers account for half. The press is largely privately owned.

Control of the press is based on the press law of 1966, as modified by the press regulations of 1969, which govern issuance of publishing permits. Under the Suharto regime the press enjoyed relative freedom

PRINCIPAL DAILIES (1985)

Daily	Circulation
Kompas (liberal Catholic)	415,000
Merdeka (independent)	130,000
Pikiran Rakyat (independent)	150,000
Indonesia Times	35,000
Indonesia Observer	25,000
Berita Buana	150,000
Pos Kota	250,000
Surabaya Post	85,000

until 1974, when the Jakarta riots triggered a crackdown in which the army closed a dozen newspapers. Though there is no explicit censorship, the government has the right to silence any publication that publishes material contrary to the Pancasila. The very vagueness of these restrictions makes them a grave threat to press freedom.

The national news agency is Antara (Lembaga Kantorberita Nasional Antara), which is under the direct control of the president of the republic. Antara has domestic bureaus in all provincial capitals and six foreign bureaus. Kantor Berita Nacional Indonesia is an independent news agency.

Indonesia has a healthy book publishing industry. Indonesia adheres to no copyright conventions.

Radio Republik Indonesia (RRI), a government department under the Ministry of Information, operates 138 transmitters, with studios in 45 towns throughout the country. Jakarta has 18 transmitters. Two national programs from Jakarta are on the air for 124 hours a week. For the most part, regional stations originate their own programs. In addition, there is an air force radio station in Jakarta and more than 500 small commercial stations. The external broadcasting service, Voice of Indonesia, operates five short wave transmitters.

Television was introduced in 1962. Televisi Republik Indonesia (TVRI) is a state-owned service with five main and seven relay transmitters covering Java, northern and southern Sumatra and southern Sulawesi. TVRI is on the air for five or six hours a day and includes educational programs and commercials. Indonesia's first private commericial television station began broadcasting in March 1989 to the Jakarta area.

Film distribution and production are in private hands but remain closely regulated by the government through the Film Council, established in 1969. The Film Censor Board is in charge of film censorship.

The nation's largest library is the Library of the Central Museum, with more than 350,000 volumes.

MEDIA INDICATORS

Newspapers
- Number of dailies: 97 (latest)
- Circulation (000): 3,049 (latest)
- Per 1,000 pop.: 18 (latest)
- Number of nondailies: 89 (1988)
- Circulation (000): 3,445 (1988)
- Per 1,000 pop.: 20 (1988)
- Number of periodicals: 1,456 (1988)
- Circulation (000): 3,622 (1988)
- Newsprint consumption 1988
  - Total metric tons: 133,800
  - Per 1,000 pop. (kg.): 765

Book publishing
- Number of titles: 2,052 (latest)

Radio
- Number of transmitters: 745 (latest)
- Number of persons per radio receiver: 8.0 (1989)
- Total program hours (/yr.): 405,210 (1987)

Television
- Television transmitters: 207 (latest)
- Number of persons per T.V. receiver: 89 (1989)
- Total program hours (/yr.): 8,579 (1985)

Cinema
- Number of fixed cinemas: 1,833 (latest)
- Seating capacity (000): 959 (latest)
  - Seats (/1,000 pop.): 5.8 (1985)
- Annual attendance (millions): 144.9 (pre-1986)

Films
- Number of long films produced: 63 (latest)
- Number of long films imported: 186 (1985)
  - % from United States: 39.8
    - Hong Kong: 30.1
    - India: 13.4
    - Italy: 3.2

CULTURAL & ENVIRONMENTAL INDICATORS

Libraries (pre-1986)
- Number: 275
- Volumes (000): 486
- Registered borrowers (million): 2.768

Museums (pre-1986)
- Annual attendance (million): 7.171
- Attendance (/1,000 pop.): 45

Performing arts (latest)
- Number of performances: 20,695
- Annual attendance (million): 2.084
- Attendance (/1,000 pop.): 12

Nature reserves (latest)
- Number of facilities: 141

SOCIAL WELFARE

The Ministry of Social Affairs is the principal state agency concerned with social welfare. Its work is supplemented by a number of private and religious organizations, such as the Indonesian Red Cross Society; the Congress of Indonesian Women; and the Muhammadijah, a Muslim social service. Indonesia does not have a comprehensive system of social insurance or Social Security.

GLOSSARY

abangan: nominal Indonesian Muslims who continue to practice a number of pre-Islamic rituals and hold Hindu and animist beliefs.

adat: traditional Indonesian law and custom having the force of law in Indonesian courts.

aliran: literally, stream; an ideological or sociocultural group.

Aspri: acronym of Asisten Pribadi; the inner circle of

presidential advisers who serve as the presidential assistants.

bupati: chief executive of a *kabupaten*, division of a province.

desa: a village.

dukuhan: a hamlet.

gogol: land tenure system by which a few families held traditional rights over village lands.

gotong-rojong: mutual aid and cooperation for the welfare of the community: by extension, traditional unpaid labor by an individual for the village.

Guided Democracy: Sukarno's label for his type of authoritarianism.

halus: refined aesthetic values associated with the elite.

kabupaten: administrative division of a province, formerly regency.

kamitua: head of a dukuhan or hamlet.

kampung: an urban quarter or neighborhood inhabited by a particular ethnic group.

kelurahan: a group of several villages.

ketjamaten: an intermediate administrative division between a desa and a kabupaten.

konfrontasi: Indonesia's hostile confrontation with Malaysia, 1963–65.

kota: municipality.

ladang: intermittently cultivated dry land.

Lebaran: the most important Indonesian religious festival marking the end of Ramadan.

lurah: headman of a *kelurahan* or *kampung*.

madrasah: a Muslim school teaching both religious and secular subjects.

merdeka: freedom; hence Merdeka Day, Indonesian's national day.

Muhammadijah: an orthodox Muslim reform movement launched in 1912.

mupakat: consensus among competing groups, especially as a political process.

musjawarat: search for *mupakat* through discussion, reconciliation and synthesis.

New Order: term used to describe Suharto's policies based on realism, political unity and economic growth; *Orde Baru* or *Orba* in Indonesian.

Old Order: official term used to describe the policies of the Sukarno era.

Pancsila: the Five Principles or Ideals on which the constitution of 1945 is based: belief in one supreme god, just and civilized humanity, nationalism, democracy and social justice.

pamong pradja: central government administrators constituting the core of the civil service.

peranakan: Indonesian-born and Indonesianized Chinese who have adopted Indonesian language and customs.

pondok: a rural Islamic boarding school attached to a mosque.

prijaji: the upper social elite of Javanese society including the bureaucracy and the intellectuals.

rukun tetangga: a group of 40 to 50 households.

santri: orthodox Muslims considered as a homogeneous social and political group, as opposed to the abangan.

sawah: irrigated ricefield; also the mode of rice cultivation on irrigated lands.

tegalan: unirrigated lands; also, cultivation of unirrigated lands.

totok: Ethnic Chinese born in China or oriented to Chinese culture.

transmigration: migration from Java to the outer islands.

CHRONOLOGY (from 1949)

1949— The Federal Republic of the United States of Indonesia is established; Sukarno is elected president and Mohammad Hatta becomes prime minister.

1950— Unitary Republic of Indonesia is established. Eight hundred rebels under Captain Paul "Turk" Westerling attack Bandung. . . . Revolts occur in Makassar and South Muluccas and are suppressed. . . . Hatta steps down; Mohammed Natsir is appointed prime minister. . . . Indonesia joins the United Nations.

1951— Natsir resigns and is succeeded by Soekiman as prime minister. . . . Separatist movements are active in Sumatra and Celebes.

1952— Wilopo forms new cabinet. . . . Army mutinies lead to resignation of the minster of defense, Sultan Hamengku Buwono IX, and the chief of staff, Abdul Harris Nasution. . . . State of internal war is lifted.

1953— Dar-ul-Islam revolt is quelled in Atjeh. . . . Wilopo cabinet falls; Ali Sastroamidjojo becomes prime minister. . . . Central Bank is established.

1954— Northern Sumatra rebellion is broken. . . . Indonesia ends union with the Netherlands.

1955— Afro-Asian conference is held at Bandung. . . . Sastroamidjojo quits in army dispute; Harahap forms cabinet. . . . First national elections are held; the Indonesian Nationalist Party and the Masjumi emerge as winners, followed by the Muslim Scholars' Party and the Communists.

1956— Sastroamidjojo forms new cabinet. . . . Sukarno introduces concept of guided democracy to replace parliamentary democracy. . . . Hatta resigns.

1957— Revolts occur in Sumatra, Sulawesi and Borneo; Sukarno declares state of war and siege. . . . Sastroamidjojo resigns; Djuanda Kartawidjaja forms government. . . . Peoples' Consultative Assembly meets.

1958— Sukarno launches anti-Dutch campaign over West Irian (now Irian Jaya) dispute. . . . Sjafruddin Prawiranegara leads rebellion in Sumatra; rebel government is proclaimed.

1959— People's Consultative Assembly is dissolved. . . . Sukarno appoints himself president, with Djuanda as prime minister. . . . Rebellion is quelled. . . . Dutch plantations are seized and nationalized.

1960— All political parties are banned.

1961— Rebel soldiers surrender and swear allegiance to the republic.

1962— Television is introduced. . . . Sukarno escapes two assassination attempts. . . . Conflict with the Netherlands over West Irian escalates.

1963— Sukarno is named president for life. . . . Confrontation begins with Malaysia.

1964— Indonesia is barred from Olympic Games; later is it readmitted, but withdraws.

1965— Indonesia withdraws from the United Nations. . . . Abortive Communist coup is staged, and six generals are killed; the army, under Gen. Suharto seizes power; mass slaughter of Communists and anti-Chinese riots mark the army's triumph.

1966— Indonesian membership in the United Nations is restored. . . . Confrontation with Malaysia ends. . . . Indonesian Communist Party is outlawed. Sukarno, faced with army ultimatum and student demonstrations, yields power to Suharto and is stripped of all powers and titles. . . . A total of 100,000 are reported slain in anti-Communist purges.

1967— Sukarno cedes executive powers to Suharto and is barred from presidential palace; Suharto becomes acting president. . . . Indonesia joins Association of Southeast Asian Nations (ASEAN) as charter member. . . . Relations with the People's Republic of China are suspended.

1968— Suharto is elected president.

1969— Indonesia participates in the Islamic summit at Rabat, Morocco. . . . West Irian, in a "free" plebiscite, votes for union with Indonesia.

1970— Sukarno dies. . . . Boundary treaty with Malaysia is concluded, declaring the Strait of Malacca as joint territory with only limited international rights of passage. . . . Basic Law on Judicial Procedures is passed, making judiciary independent. . . . Suharto visits the Netherlands.

1971— Second national elections are held; Golkar wins landslide victory.

1972— Pertamina, the state petroleum organization, is founded.

1973— Suharto is reelected president for a second five-year term.

1974— Aspri, the presidential inner cabinet, is disbanded. . . . Anti-Japanese demonstrations are held. . . . Chinese business activities are curbed.

1975— Portuguese Timor, a 14,925-sq.-km. (5,761-sq.-mi.) enclave, is incorporated into Indonesia.

1976— Prisoners from 1965 coup are freed. . . . Pertamina goes bankrupt.

1977— High government officials are charged with accepting large payoffs from U.S. firms, particularly Hughes Aircraft. . . . Golkar wins 65% of vote in parliamentary elections.

1978— Student unrest and demonstrations force the Suharto government to invoke repressive measures. . . . Suharto is reelected president for a third term. . . . A total of 1,324 prisoners are released.

1982— Golkar wins handily in the general elections.

1983— Golkar Congress is held. . . . Guerilla movements in Irian Jaya and Timor escalate in violence. . . . As oil prices drop, development projects are shelved.

1986— Suharto proposes austerity budget as oil revenues plummet.

1987— Nine former PKI members are executed. In April general election Golkar wins 299 of 500 House of Representatives seats and for the first time claims majority of seats in all 27 provinces.

1988— Suharto is reelected unopposed as president. Indonesia fails to win chairmanship of the Nonaligned Movement. Indonesia officially recognizes the state of Palestine.

1989— Three senior officials are expelled from Golkar and two former armed forces members are executed. Land disputes lead to social unrest in three regions of Java, the most serious of which results in the deaths of 30 to 100 people. Pope visits East Timor and pleads for Indonesian government halt to human rights violations.

1990— A group of 58 prominent Indonesians demand greater democracy and Suharto's retirement at the end of his current term. Rebellion breaks out in the province of Aceh.

BIBLIOGRAPHY

BOOKS

Anderson, Benedict, and Audrey Kahin. *Interpreting Indonesian Politics.* Ithaca, N.Y., 1983.

Aveling, Harry, *The Development of Indonesian Society.* New York, 1980.

Bandyopadhyaya, Kalyani. *Burma and Indonesia: Comparative Study of Political Economy and Foreign Policy.* Atlantic Highlands, N.J., 1983.

Carlson, Sevinc. *Indonesia's Oil.* Boulder, Colo., 1977.

Crouch, Harold. *The Army and Politics in Indonesia.* Ithaca, N.Y., 1978.

Dalton, Bill. *Indonesian Handbook.* Rutland, Vt., 1978.

Donner, Wolf. *Land Use and Environment in Indonesia.* Hawaii, 1987.

Douglas, Stephen A. *Political Socialization and Student Activism in Indonesia.* Urbana, Ill., 1970.

Emmerson, Donald K. *Indonesia's Elite: Political Culture and Cultural Policies.* Ithaca, N.Y., 1976.

Feith, Herbert, and Lance Castles. *Indonesian Political Thinking, 1945–65.* Ithaca, N.Y., 1970.

Fox, J. J. *Indonesia: The Making of a Culture.* Canberra, Austral., 1981.

Fryer, D. W., and James C. Jackson. *Indonesia.* Boulder, Colo., 1976.

George, Margaret L. *Australia and Indonesian Revolution.* Melbourne, Austral., 1980.

Ghoshal, Baladas. *Indonesian Politics, 1955–59: The Emergence of Guided Democracy.* Columbia, Mo., 1983.

Glassburner, Bruce. *Economy of Indonesia: Selected Readings.* Ithaca, N.Y., 1971.

Hanna, Willard, A. *Indonesian Banda: Colonialism and its Aftermath in the Nutmeg Islands.* Philadelphia, 1978.

Hardjono, Joan. *Transmigration in Indonesia.* New York, 1977.

Harsono, Ganis. *Recollections of an Indonesian Diplomat in the Sukarno Era.* Brisbane, Austral. 1977.
Holt, Claire. *Culture and Politics in Indonesia.* Ithaca, N.Y., 1972.
Hugo, Graeme J. *The Demographic Dimension in Indonesian Development.* New York, 1987.
Ingleson, John. *Road to Exile: Indonesian Nationalist Movement.* London, 1979.
Jackson, Karl D. *Traditional Authority, Islam and Rebellion: A Study of Indonesian Political Behavior.* Berkeley, Calif., 1980.
———, and Lucian W. Pye. *Political Power and Communications in Indonesia.* Berkeley, Calif., 1978.
Kahin, Audrey. *Regional Dynamics of the Indonesian Revolution.* Honolulu, Hawaii, 1985.
King, Dwight Y. *Interest Groups and Political Linkage in Indonesia.* DeKalb, Ill., 1982.
Knowles, Ruth S. *Indonesia Today: The Nation That Helps Itself.* Plainview, N.Y., 1973.
Koch, Kurt E. *Revival in Indonesia.* Grand Rapids, Mich., 1972.
Koentjaraningrat, R. M. *Introduction to the Peoples and Cultures of Indonesia and Malaysia.* Menlo Park, Calif., 1975.
Lagerberg, Kees. *West Irian and Jakarta Imperialism.* New York, 1980.
Leifer, M. *Malacca, Singapore and Indonesia.* The Hague, 1978.
———. *Indonesia's Foreign Policy.* London, 1983.
Liddle, R. William. *Ethnicity, Party and National Integration: An Indonesian Case Study.* New Haven, Conn., 1970.
Mackie, J. A. *The Chinese in Indonesia.* Honolulu, Hawaii, 1976.
———. *Indonesia: The Making of a Nation.* Canberra, Austral., 1981.
May, Brian. *The Indonesian Tragedy.* London, 1978.
McCawley, Peter. *Industrialization in Indonesia.* Canberra, Austral., 1980.
Mears, Leon A. *The New Rice Economy of Indonesia.* Athens, Ohio, 1981.
Mortimer, Rex. *Indonesian Communism Under Sukarno: Ideology and Politics.* Ithaca, N.Y., 1974.
Mrazek, Rudolf. *United States and the Indonesian Military, 1945–65.* New York, 1979.
Nasution, Anwar. *Financial Institutions and Policies in Indonesia.* London, 1984.
Neill, Wilfred T. *Twentieth-Century Indonesia.* New York, 1973.
Nishihara, Masashi. *Golkar and the Indonesian Elections of 1971.* Ithaca, N.Y., 1971.
———. *Japanese and Sukarno's Indonesia: Tokyo-Jakarta Relations, 1951–66.* Honolulu, Hawaii, 1976.
Oey, Hong Lee. *Indonesia After the 1971 Elections.* New York, 1974.
Osborne, Robin. *Indonesia's Secret War: The Guerrilla Struggle in Irian Jaya.* London, 1985.
Palmer, Ingrid. *The Indonesian Economy Since 1965.* Totowa, N.J., 1978.
Palmier, Leslie. *Understanding Indonesia.* London, 1985.
Pananek, Gustav F. *The Indonesian Economy.* New York, 1980.
———. *The Indonesian Economy.* New York, 1981.
Parente, William J. *Politics in Indonesia.* New York, 1980.
Park, Jae Kyu, and Jusuf Wanandi. *Korea and Indonesia in the Year 2000.* Boulder, Colo., 1985.
Penders, L. N. *Indonesia: Selected Documents on Colonialism and Nationalism, 1830–1942.* Brisbane, Austral., 1977.
Pringle, Robert, *Indonesia and the Philippines.* New York, 1980.
Reeve, David. *Golkar of Indonesia: An Alternative to the Party System.* New York, 1985.
Reid, Anthony. *The Indonesian National Revolution, 1945–50.* New York, 1974.
Ricklefs, M.C.A. *History of Modern Indonesia.* Bloomington, Ind., 1981.
Sievers, Allen M. *Mystical World of Indonesia: Culture and Economic Development in Conflict.* Baltimore, 1975.
Soebadio, H., and C. Sarvaas. *Dynamics of Indonesian History.* New York, 1978.
Southwood, Julie, and Patrick Flanagan. *Indonesia: Law, Propaganda and Terror.* London, 1983.
Suryadinata, Leo. *Political Thinking of the Indonesian Chinese, 1900–77.* Athens, Ohio, 1980.
———. *Indonesia's 1982 Geneal Election.* London, 1982.
Tairas, J. N. *A Bibliography of Bibliographies.* New York, 1975.
Tas, S. *Indonesia: The Underdeveloped Freedom.* Indianapolis, Ind., 1974.
UNESCO. *Cultural Policy in Indonesia.* Paris, 1974.
UNFPA. *Indonesia: Population Profile.* New York, 1980.
Weilhelm, Donald. *Emerging Indonesia.* New York, 1980.
Weinstein, Franklin B. *Indonesian Foreign Policy and the Dilemma of Dependence: From Sukarno to Suharto.* Ithaca, N.Y., 1976.
Widjojo, Nitisastro. *Population Trends in Indonesia.* Ithaca, N.Y., 1970.

FILMS

East Indies (Java). B&W film, 22 min. Universal Studios.

Faith in Revolution. Color film, 28 min. National Council of Churches.

Indonesia: A Time to Grow Color film, 20 min. Contemporary Films.

Indonesia: An Empire's Problem. B&W film, 19 min. March of Time.

Indonesia: A New Nation of Asia. Color film, 16 min. Encyclopaedia Britannica.

Indonesia: An Island Nation's Progress. Color film, 15 min. Universal Studios.

Indonesia: The Land and the People. Color/B&W film, 13 min. Coronet.

Indonesia: Time of Transition. Color film, 29 min. Julien Bryan.

Letter from Indonesia. Color film, 16 min. Producer: N.A.
Tropical Mountain Island: Java. B&W film, 20 min. Universal.
Wet Earth and Warm People. Color film, 58 min. Films, Inc.

OFFICIAL PUBLICATIONS

Finance Ministry. *Central Government Budget (semiannual).*
———. *Report of Directorate General of Budget* (quarterly).
———. *Report of Directorate General of Customs and Excises* (quarterly).
———. *Report of Directorate General of Monetary Affairs* (quarterly).
———. *Report of Directorate General of Taxation* (quarterly).
———. *Revenue and Expenditure Books* (quarterly).
Indonesian Bank. *Indonesian Financial Statistics* (monthly; Indonesian and English).

Emblem not available

IRAN

BASIC FACT SHEET

OFFICIAL NAME: Islamic Republic of Iran (Jomhori-e-Islami-e-Iran)

ABBREVIATION: IR

CAPITAL: Teheran

WALI FAQIH: Ayatollah Sayed Ali Khamenei
Note: *Faqih* means spiritual leader

HEAD OF STATE: President Hojatoleslam Ali Akbar Hashemi Rafsanjani (from 1989)

NATURE OF GOVERNMENT: Theocratic Republic

POPULATION: 55,647,000 (1990)

AREA: 1,648,000 sq. km. (636,296 sq. mi.)

ETHNIC MAJORITY: Iranians (Persians)

LANGUAGE: Persian (or Farsi)

RELIGION: Shia Muslim

UNIT OF CURRENCY: Rial

NATIONAL FLAG: Three horizontal stripes of green, white and red, with the emblem of the Islamic Republic centrally positioned in red with the words *Allaho Akbar* (God is Great) repeated 11 times along each of the green and red stripes.

NATIONAL EMBLEM: The creed of the Revolutionary (Islamic) Government in Persian.

NATIONAL ANTHEM: N.A.

NATIONAL HOLIDAYS: In addition to all principal Islamic festival days, there are five national holidays of which three are called Revolution Days, falling on June 5, February 11 and April 2, commemorating the various stages of the clergy-led revolution that overthrew the shah. Also, April 1 (Islamic Republic Day) and March 20 (Oil Nationalization Day).

NATIONAL CALENDAR: The national calendar, adopted in 1925, is a solar year of 365 days that begins on the first day of spring and dates from A.D. 622.

PHYSICAL QUALITY OF LIFE INDEX: 59

DATE OF INDEPENDENCE: Islamic Republic of Iran proclaimed on April 1, 1979

DATE OF CONSTITUTION: December 2–3, 1979; revised 1989

WEIGHTS & MEASURES: Metric

GEOGRAPHICAL FEATURES

Iran is located in southwestern Asia between the Persian Gulf and the Caspian Sea and shares borders with the USSR, Afghanistan, Pakistan, Turkey and Iraq. The total land area is 1,648,000 sq. km. (636,296 sq. mi.), which makes it larger than all the nine countries of the European Economic Community combined. The longest distance northwest to southeast is 2,250 km. (1,400 mi.) and northeast to southwest is 1,400 km. (870 mi.).

The kingdom shares its total international border of 5,492 km (3,413 mi.) with five countries: the Soviet Union (1,690 km., 1,050 mi.); Afghanistan (936 km., 582 mi.); Pakistan (909 km., 565 mi); Iraq (1,458 km., 906 mi); and Turkey (499 km., 310 mi.).

Teheran is the capital as well as the largest urban center, with a 1986 population of 6,042,584. The other main cities and towns are: Isfahan (988,753), Meshed (1,463,508), Tabriz (971,482), Shiraz (848,289), Ahwaz (579,826), Bakhtaran (Kermanshah) (560,514), Orumiyeh (300,746), Qazvin (248,591), Kerman (257,284), Ardebil (281,973), Yazd (230,483), Karaj (275,100), Qom (543,139), Rasht (290,897) and Hamadan (273,499).

Iran has four natural geographic regions. Of these the central, interior plateau is a barren, largely uninhabited area occupying a series of closed basins with elevations of 600 to 900 m. (2,000 to 3,000 ft.) and is completely surrounded by mountains. The plateau is covered partly by salt swamps, known as *kavirs*, and partly by salt flats, called *dashts*. Because of its forbidding nature, this region is known as the dead heart of Iran. The second region is the Zagros mountain range that originates in the Armenian Knot near the Soviet Union and extends 965 km. (600 mi.) along the Persian Gulf and the Gulf of Oman and joins the Markran range near Pakistan. In the northwestern part this region includes the fertile Azerbaijan and in the southern part the coastal plain of Khuzistan. The highest elevation in this region is 3,960 m. (13,000 ft.). The third region consists of the Elburz and Talish mountains and the Caspian lowlands. The Elburz range extends to Afghanistan along the southern side of the Soviet border, with elevations between 2,100 and 3,000 m. (7,000 and 10,000 ft.). The fourth region consists of the eastern mountains along the Pakistani and Afghan border with barren ranges and fertile valleys and elevations between 1,200 and 2,750 m. (4,000 and 9,000 ft.).

The 828-km. (515-mi.) long Karun River is the country's only navigable river and only for about 160 km. (100 mi.) of its length. The largest body of water is Lake Rezaiyeh, formerly Lake Urmia, 145 km. (90 mi.) long and 48 km. (30 mi.) wide.

CLIMATE & WEATHER

The climate of Iran is one of great extremes. Temperatures vary from −27.8°C (−18°F) to 55.6°C (132°F) in parts of the central plateau, where some of the highest temperatures in the world have been recorded. Most of Iran is arid except the northwest and the Caspian coast, which receive over 2,000 mm. (78 in.) of rainfall annually and are the most densely populated regions in the country. Generally rain falls from October to May with the heaviest concentration from December to March. Desert areas receive less than 50.8 mm. (2 in.) a year, while the Persian Gulf region receives between 200 mm. and 508 mm. (8 and 20 in.) a year. In the coastal areas humidity is high throughout the year. Two strong summer winds, the shamal in the northwest and the "Wind of 120 Days" in the southeast, blowing with destructive velocities of up to 160 km. per hour (99 mph.), intensify the heat and erode the soil.

VITAL STATISTICS

Crude birth rate (/1,000): 45 (1990); 46 (1965)
Crude death rate (/1,000): 10 (1990); 18 (1965)
Infant mortality rate (/1,000 live births): 91 (1990)
Life expectancy (yrs.) at birth: males, 62; females, 63 (1990)
Gross reproduction rate (/woman) (1980–85): 2.75
Total fertility rate (/woman): 6.3 (1990)
Rate of natural increase (/1,000): 34.0 (1989)
Marriage rate (/1,000): 8.9 (1984–85)
Average household size: 5.1 (latest)

STATUS OF WOMEN INDICATORS

Number of women (million): 21.828 (1985)
Women of childbearing age (15–49) (% of pop.): 47 (1988)
Women's literacy rate (%): 52.1 (1987)
Women in labor force (%): 14 (1985)
Total fertility rate (/woman): 6.3 (1990)

POPULATION

The population of Iran in 1990 was estimated at 55,647,000. The last official census was held in 1986 when the population was 49,857,384.

DEMOGRAPHIC INDICATORS

Population (millions): 55.647 (1990)
Year of last census: 1986
Sex distribution (% at last census): males, 51.1; females, 48.9
Population estimates and projections (millions)

1940: 14.000	1970: 28.359	2000: 73.801
1950: 16.913	1980: 38.783	2010: 93.553
1960: 21.554	1990: 56.293	

Age profile (% at 1976 census)
0–14: 45.5
15–59: 51.5
60 and over: 3.0
Median age (yrs.): 18.2 (1985)
Youth population (% age 15–24): 19.8 (1985); 19.2 (2000)
Total dependency ratio: 86.7 (1985)
Annual growth rate (%)

1950–55: 3.66	1975–1980: 3.08	2000–2005: 2.56
1955–60: 3.48	1980–1985: 4.05	2005–2010: 2.24
1960–65: 3.41	1985–1990: 3.45	2010–2015: 1.94
1965–70: 3.30	1990–1995: 2.63	2015–2020: 1.69
1970–75: 3.21	1995–2000: 2.86	2020–2025: 1.49

Hypothetical size of stationary population (millions): 247
Assumed year of reaching net reproduction rate of 1: 2040
Urban population (millions): 24.719 (1985)
Urban population (%): 54 (1988); 37 (1965)
Annual urban population growth rate (%, 1985–90): 4.57
Annual rural population growth rate (%, 1985–90): 2.16
Percentage of urban population in largest city: 28 (1980)
Percentage of urban population in
cities of population over 500,000: 47 (1980)
Number of cities of population over 500,000: 6 (1980)
Population density per sq. km. (per sq. mi.): 34.2 (88.5) (latest)

The heaviest concentration of population occurs along the Caspian Sea and in the Azerbaijan provinces. Four provinces and one governorate, all in the north and northwest, have densities of over 39 per sq. km. (100 per sq. mi.).

The national male/female ratio is 107 men to 100 women, which is considered excessive and may result from the usual under-reporting of women in Muslim countries.

The urban component of the population is estimated at 54% (1988). Nearly 17.4% of the population lives in large metropolitan areas.

Ultraconservative dress, entirely hiding the hair and all of the body except the face and hands, is now an absolute requirement for all women, regardless of their religion, national origin, citizenship or diplomatic status. Women are harassed, detained or physically attacked if they appear in public in clothing which official or self-appointed guardians of public morality deem insufficiently modest or if they wear makeup. There have also been incidents in which men have been attacked on the streets of Tehran for dressing in "un-Islamic" fashion, such as wearing short-sleeved shirts or failing to button all their shirt buttons. Employment opportunities for women are more restricted than was the case under the shah. Women are legally barred from being judges. Although there are cultural barriers making employment in professional level positions difficult to obtain and maintain, women do work as lawyers, physicians and statisticians, and in other professions in both the public and private sectors. Several women serve as deputies in the Majlis.

The Family Protection Act, passed under the shah, was revoked by the Islamic government, and replaced by a civil code reflecting Islamic law. A bill passed in mid-1983 did, however, give women the right to divorce their husbands, and regulations announced in 1984 substantially broadened, to 12, the number of grounds for which a woman may seek divorce. A husband may still obtain a divorce without having to state a reason or go to court. The new marriage regulations provide for improved financial settlements for wives whose husbands divorce them.

Family planning is an official policy, coordinated by the Ministry of Health, the Family Health Guidance Association, the Family Planning Association and other agencies. Legislation has been enacted to fix the age of marriage at 18–20 for males and 16–18 for females.

ETHNIC COMPOSITION

About two-thirds of the population consists of people of Aryan origin, of whom the Persians, or Farsi, are predominant. The Gilanis and the Mazandaranis are closely related to the Persians but speak a different dialect and have lower cultural levels. The Kurds, who form the fourth largest ethnic group in the Middle East, are concentrated in the Zagros mountain area from Khuzistan to the Soviet border. They are distinguished from the Persians by their religion (being mostly Sunni Muslims), by their physical appearance, by their ethnic origin, in their social organization and in their language. They retain a tribal type of social structure and are divided into over 40 tribes. Fiercely independent, they have made intermittent efforts to establish a Kurdish republic. South of the Kurds live two related ethnic groups, the Lurs and the Bakhtiari, each with nomadic and sedentary branches. Perhaps the poorest and least advanced people in Iran are the Baluchis, numbering about half a million, who are found in greater numbers in Pakistan and Afghanistan. About one-third of the population consists of various Turkic-speaking ethnic groups of whom the Azerbaijani in the northwest and the Qashqai in the highlands between Shiraz and Isfahan, are the most numerous. Minor turkic groups include the Shahsavans and the Qajars as well as the Afshars, who form ethnic islands in the southwest.

Ethnic minorities include the Muslim Arabs in Khuzistan province and along the Persian Gulf, who regard themselves as part of the Sunni Muslim community of Iraq and greater Arabia, the Christian Armenians, and the Assyrians. Most of the 60,000 Jews, an ancient community concentrated in urban centers, fled Iran on the establishment of the Islamic Republic. Not included in any of these ethnic groupings are about 800,000 nomads whose ethnic affiliations have not been established.

There are relatively large Western communities in Teheran, along the Caspian coast and in the booming oil towns of the south.

LANGUAGE

The official national language is Persian, or Farsi, which is spoken by about 50% of the population. Some dialects of Persian, such as Gilani and Mazandarani, are so different from pure Persian as to be virtually unintelligible to a person from Teheran or Shiraz. Other Indo-Iranian languages include Kurdish, itself divided into a number of dialects, Luri and Baluchi, each spoken by the ethnic group of that name. Turkic languages, Armenian, Assyrian, and Arabic are minority languages. Most of the languages including Farsi, Azerbaijani and Kurdish are written in the Arabic script with some modifications and additional consonants. An attempt under Reza Shah in the 1930s to romanize written Persian was dropped because of the opposition of religious leaders.

For many decades French, and to some extent German, enjoyed great prestige as the languages of the elite. English, however, has been displacing French in diplomacy and commerce.

RELIGION

Iran terms itself an Islamic republic, and religion is closely intertwined with government. Ayatollah Sayed Ali Khamenei is recognized as the supreme leader, and this position is viewed as holding something akin to divine sanction. The president and many other top officials are *mullahs* (religious leaders), as are the Speaker of the Majlis, and roughly half of the Majlis deputies. Ninety-three percent of Iranians are Shi'a, and five percent are Sunni Muslims, but the Sunnis tend to be located in tribal areas remote from Teheran. Their political influence is nearly nil. The Constitution declares that "the official religion of Iran is Islam and the sect followed is Ja'fari Shi'ism," but it also states that "other Islamic denominations shall enjoy complete respect." Although Sunnis have encountered religious discrimination on the local level, and in many cases persecution based on ethnic origin, the regime has made efforts to reduce Shi'a-Sunni antagonism.

The 1979 Constitution also states that no enactment of the National Assembly can be at variance with the "sacred" precepts of Islam. The government is required to promote the Shi'a doctrines of Islam, and all cabinet members and military commanders are required to be Muslims. Films and printed materials opposing Islam are prohibited, while the government officially finances the printing of Korans and the building of mosques. The highest religious authority in the country is the present Ayatollah, Khamenei. His predecessor, Ayatollah Khomeini, died on June 3, 1989. Other Ayatollah al ozma (great Ayatollahs) include Hossein Ali Montazeri of Teheran, Muhammad Reza Golpayeghani, Shahaboldin Marashi-Najafi and Abolgassem Khoi.

Tests of Islamic knowledge and orthodoxy, required in the early postrevolutionary years for public or semipublic employment and enrollment in higher education, have been dropped on the grounds that they conflict with the constitutional provision that "the interrogation of people regarding their beliefs is forbidden." This provision is ignored, however, in the treatment of members of the Baha'i faith.

The Baha'i religion is not recognized in Iran and Baha'is have suffered severe persecution since the revolution. This is mainly government-directed and aimed at the religious leadership, although there were some instances earlier of mob action against Baha'is. Baha'i property has been confiscated, shrines demolished, businesses disbanded or confiscated, and known Baha'is denied employment by the government. These measures effectively deny employment to most urban Baha'is. Much of the Baha'i religious leadership has been arrested, as have many ordinary Baha'is. Charges are vague: "crimes against God," "corruption on earth," "warring against God" and "Zionism" are among the most frequent. The real reason for the arrests seems to be advocacy of Baha'ism.

In August 1983, the Prosecutor General issued an order that effectively banned all Baha'i religious activity, and provided the legal foundation on which virtually all members of the faith could be charged with crimes: participation in social welfare organizations is forbidden, as are the business corporations the Baha'i operated; and teaching of the faith, even by parents to children in the home, is not permitted. Although the Baha'i national leaders dissolved the community's organizations in obedience to the Prosecutor General's edict, they were subsequently arrested, and at least some were executed.

There are small Christian, Jewish and Zoroastrian (the pre-Islamic religion of Iran) populations, concentrated mainly in urban areas. These religions are recognized by the Constitution, and they elect representatives to seats reserved for them in the Majlis. They are permitted to practice their religions, to instruct their children and in some cases to maintain schools. There have been reports of religious persecution of these minorities, particularly in the early stages of the revolution. They continue to have problems with the regime over religious practice, and some members of all three groups suffer officially sanctioned job discrimination. Jewish groups report fewer such problems because the language spoken in Jewish homes and informally among Jews is Farsi. In parts of Iran, Zoroastrians reportedly are considered "unclean" and are required to warn barbers, launderers and restaurant owners that their service will be for "unclean" people, so that they can decide whether to serve such clients.

A 1983 article in an Armenian-language publication complained about the regime's interference in Armenian schools, and the fact that the regime insisted that Armenian girls wear Islamic clothing. Although the article cited abuses, it is significant that it appeared at all. The Constitution states that recognized religious minorities shall be free in matters related to teaching and that the teaching of ethnic-language literature is permitted. Nevertheless, all Armenian schools were closed during much of 1984 due to the government's insistence that no courses could be taught in the Armenian language, that Armenian schools could not use Armenian-language bibles to teach classes on Christianity and that the Armenian schools would have to teach Christianity on the basis of Farsi texts provided by the government. Armenian schools reopened in October after an informal compromise was reached, but their status remains precarious.

In February 1989 Ayatollah Khomeini issued a death sentence against British writer Salman Rushdie for perceived blasphemies against Islam in his novel *The Satanic Verses*. This forced Rushdie to go into hiding. It also prompted a break in relations between Iran and the United Kingdom in March 1989. However, in September 1990, after the British Government accepted that the book had caused offence to Muslims, and stated that it had no wish to insult Islam, Iran and the U.K. restored full diplomatic relations.

HISTORICAL BACKGROUND

The history of Iran (known as Persia until 1935) dates from the 6th century B.C. The Medes and the Persians were united in 633 B.C. by Cyrus the Great, leading to the foundation of the first Persian Empire. The Empire was overthrown in 331 B.C. by Alexander the Great and, upon his death, was divided among his generals. The Seleucid dynasty was in power until 247 B.C., followed by the Parthian Empire of the Arsacids who ruled for 500 years. The last Empire of the Sassanids (A.D. 33–637) was defeated by Muslim Arabs in A.D. 637.

By the late 16th century, with the rise of the Safavids under Ismail Safavi, Persia re-emerged with the same general boundaries which exist today. Shi'ism was declared the state religion. The Safavids ruled until 1750 and after a short interregnum under Karim Khan Zand, the Qajar dynasty assumed and remained in power until the beginning of the 20th century. The country adopted its first imperial Constitution in 1906. In 1921 Reza Khan, a Cossack officer, staged a military coup and became minister of war. In 1923 he became prime minister and in 1925 the Majlis (Islamic Consultative Assembly) deposed the Shah and handed full power to Reza Khan. He was subsequently elected shah, taking the title Reza Shah Pahlevi. During the Second World War, Reza Shah favored Nazi Germany. British and Soviet forces entered Iran in 1941, forcing the Shah to abdicate in favor of his son, Muhammad Reza Pahlavi.

After the war, British and U.S. forces left Iran, although Soviet forces remained in Azerbaijan until 1946. The Majlis approved the nationalization of the petroleum industry in March 1951. The leading advocate of this measure was Dr. Mohammad Mossadeq, leader of the National Front, who became prime minister in April 1951. The Shah assumed full control of the government in 1963, when he began a program of land reform and social and economic modernization known as the White Revolution. The period was marked with some success as party politics functioned and elections were held in 1967, 1971 and 1975. Opposition to the increasing Westernization and secularization of Iranian society was articulated by Islamic clergy, notably Ayatollah Khomeini, exiled to Turkey and then Iraq after 1964.

In March 1975, the Shah introduced a single-party system based on the Iran National Resurgence Party. Opposition grew, however, and during 1977 and 1978, demonstrations against the Shah and his secret police (SAVAK) rose to crisis level. The most effective opposition came from Ayatollah Khomeini, who conducted his campaign from France where he had arrived in October 1978 after 14 years in exile in Iraq. Khomeini demanded a return to the principles of Islam, and the response to this call in Iran was so great that the Shah felt compelled to leave the country in January 1979. Khomeini arrived in Teheran shortly afterwards and effectively took power on February 11. A 15-member Islamic Revolutionary Council (IRC) was formed. Khomeini declared Iran an Islamic Republic on April 1, 1979, and introduced a Constitution which vested

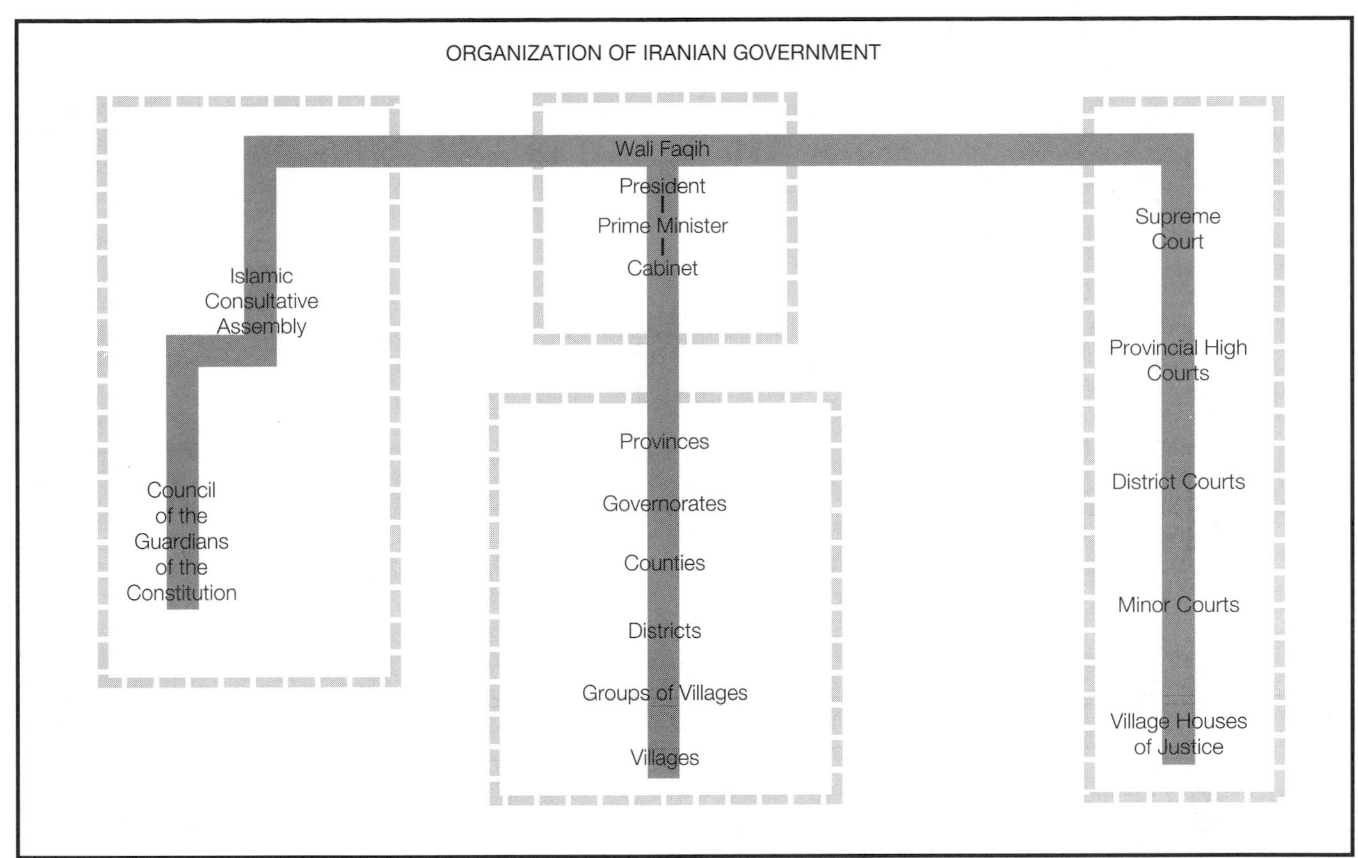

supreme authority in the Wali Faqih (religious leader), initially Khomeini. A presidential election in January 1980 resulted in a win for Abolhassan Bani-Sadr, who received about 75% of the votes. Election to the 270-seat Majlis followed and resulted in a clear win for the Islamic Republic Party (IRP).

In June 1981, proceedings on the grounds of incompetence were instituted against Bani-Sadr in the Majlis and Khomeini ordered his dismissal. He was succeeded by Mohammad Ali Rajai in July 1981. The following month, however, Rajai and his prime minister, Mohammad Javad Bahonar, were the victims of a bomb attack mounted by the Mujahidin e-Khalq, an opposition group. In October, Hojatoleslam Ali Khamenei was elected president and Mir Hosein Musavi-Khamenei was elected prime minister. Both Ali Khamenei and Musavi-Khamenei were reelected in the elections of 1985.

Ayatollah Khomeini died in June 1989. The Council of Experts elected President Khamenei to succeed Khomeini as the Wali Faqih. In the presidential election of July 1989, Hojatoleslam Hashemi Rafsanjani commanded a total of 95.9% of the votes. He was sworn in as president in August 1989.

CONSTITUTION & GOVERNMENT

A draft Constitution was published in mid-June 1979 and a 75-member "Council of Experts" was elected to debate the various clauses and propose amendments. The amended Constitution was put to a referendum in early December 1979 and easily gained the approval of the electorate. In 1989, the most important amendments to the Constitution were the elevation of the president to the government's chief executive and the abolition of the post of prime minister.

The Constitution states that the form of government of Iran is that of an Islamic republic, and that the spirituality and ethics of Islam are to be the basis for political, social and economic relations. Persians, Turks, Kurds, Arabs, Baluchis, Turkomans and others will enjoy completely equal rights.

The Constitution provides for a popularly-elected president for a term of four years and a popularly-elected Majlis (Islamic Consultative Assembly) of 270 members for a term of four years. Provision is made for the representation of Zoroastrians, Jews and Christians (but not Baha'is).

All legislation passed by the Islamic Consultative Assembly must be sent to the Council of Guardians (Article 94), which will ensure that it is in accordance with the Constitution and Islam. The Council of Guardians consists of six religious lawyers appointed by the Faqih and six lawyers appointed by the High Council of the Judiciary and approved by the Islamic Consultative Assembly. Articles 19–42 deal with the basic rights of individuals, and provide for equality of men and women before the law and for equal human, political, economic, social and cultural rights for both sexes. The Committee to Determine the Expediency of the Islamic Order, created in February 1988 and formally adopted into the Constitution in July 1989, rules on legal and theological disputes between the Majlis and the Council of Guardians.

RULERS OF IRAN

September 1941–January 1979: Shahanshah Aryamehr Muhammad Reza Pahlavi
January 1979–June 1989: Ayatollah Khomeini (Faqih)
June 1989– : Ayatollah Khamenei (Faqih)

Presidents

January 1980–July 1981: Abolhassan Bani-Sadr
July–August 1981: Mohammad Ali Rajai (assassinated)
October 1981–August 1989: Sayed Ali Khamenei
August 1989– : Hojatoleslam Ali Akbar Hashemi Rafsanjani

Prime Ministers

December 1978–February 1979: Shahpur Bakhtiar
February 1979–November 1979: Mehdi Bazargan
August 1980–August 1981: Mohammad Ali Rajai
August 1981: Hojatoleslam Mohammad Javad Bahonar (assassinated)
September 1981–October 1981: Mohammad Reza MahdaviKani
October 1981–July 1989: Mir Hosein Musavi-Khamenei

GOVERNMENT LIST (July/August 1991)

Leader of the Islamic Revolution	Khamenei, Ali Hoseini-
President	Hashemi Rafsanjani, Ali Akbar
1st Vice President	Habibi, Hasan Ebrahim
Deputy President for Atomic Energy	Amrollahi, Reza
Deputy President for Civil Service	Razavi, Mansur
Deputy President for Environmental Protection	Manafi, Hadi, *M.D.*
Deputy President for Executive Affairs	Mirzadeh, Hamid
Deputy President for Legal & Parliamentary Affairs	Mohajerani, Ataollah
Deputy President for Physical Training	Qafuri-Fard, Hasan
Deputy President for Plan & Budget	Roqani-Zanjani, Masud
Minister of Agriculture & Rural Development	Kalantari, Isa
Minister of Commerce	Vahaji, Abdol Hosein
Minister of Construction Jihad	Foruzesh, Qolam Reza
Minister of Culture & Higher Education	Moin-Najafabadi, Mostafa, *M.D.*
Minister of Defense & Armed Forces Logistics	Torkan, Akbar
Minister of Economic Affairs & Finance	Nurbakhsh, Mohsen
Minister of Education & Training	Najafi, Mohammad Ali
Minister of Energy	Namdar-Zangeneh, Bijan
Minister of Foreign Affairs	Velayati, Ali Akbar, *M.D.*
Minister of Health, Treatment & Medical Education	Malekzadeh, Reza, *M.D.*
Minister of Heavy Industries	Nejad-Hoseinian, Mohammad Hadi
Minister of Housing & Urban Development	Kazeruni, Seraj-ed-Din
Minister of Industries	Nematzadeh, Mohammad Reza
Minister of Intelligence & Security	Fallahian-Khuzestani, Ali
Minister of Interior	Nuri-Hoseinabadi, Abdollah Hamid
Minister of Islamic Culture & Guidance	Khatami-Ardakani, Ali Mohammad
Minister of Justice	Shoshtari, Mohammad Esmail
Minister of Labor & Social Affairs	Kamali, Hosein
Minister of Mines & Metals	Mahlujchi, Mohammad Hosein
Minister of Petroleum	Aqazadeh-Khoi, Qolam Reza
Minister of Post, Telegraph & Telephone	Qarazi, Mohammad
Minister of Roads & Transport	Saidi-Kia, Mohammad
Head of the Judiciary Branch	Yazdi, Mohammad Ali
Speaker of the Islamic Consultative Assembly (Majles)	Mahdavi-Karubi, Mehdi
Governor, Central Bank	Adeli, Mohammad Hosein

The amended Constitution provides for a Wali Faqih (religious leader) who, in the absence of the Imam Mehdi (the hidden Twelfth Imam), carries the burden of leadership. According to Article 57 the executive, legislative and judicial branches of state power are under the authority of the *Faqih*. Among the extensive powers reserved to the *Faqih* is the right to appoint half the members of the Council of Guardians. He is also Supreme Commander of the Armed Forces and can appoint the Joint Chiefs of Staff and the Head of the Revolutionary Guard. He appoints four of the seven members of the National Defence Council and, on their recommendation, appoints the senior commanders of the armed forces. He also has power to declare war and make peace on the recommendation of the National Defence Council. The first *Faqih* has the right to approve all candidates for the presidency (a right which was exercised by Ayatollah Khomeini). The *Faqih* can also dismiss the president on the basis of a Supreme Court decision or a vote of no confidence by the Islamic Consultative Assembly.

Elections are supervised by election supervisory councils. Suffrage is universal over age 20. Those excluded from voting are criminals, converts from Islam, and members of the armed forces and the gendarmerie. In 1963 suffrage was opened to women. The last presidential election was held in 1989. This election, which had originally been scheduled to take place in August, was brought forward to July. The election was contested only by Hojatoleslam Ali Akbar Hashemi Rafsanjani and Abbas Sheibani, a former minister, who was widely regarded as a "token candidate." According to official figures, 95.9% of the votes were for Rafsanjani, and 3.9% were for Sheibani. Rafsanjani was sworn in as President in August 1989.

FREEDOM & HUMAN RIGHTS

In terms of civil and political rights, Iran is classified as a not-free country.

The Khomeini regime set new records for disregard of human rights; the very statistics are staggering. It had imprisoned over 15,000 Iranians for alleged association with the regime of the former shah, executed over 700 through firing squads and held 51 U.S. diplomats as hostages for over a year. In Iran, torture of prisoners is routine; trials are conducted with no regard for due process, and often at night. Accused persons are not afforded the right of counsel or the right of appeal.

The new press law promulgated in August 1980 established severe penalties for criticisms of religious and political leaders. At that time, 41 newspapers were closed and 18 foreign correspondents were expelled. Persons whose names are found in an official black list of 20,000 are banned from leaving the country.

While Iran's human rights record continued to show serious abuses, there has been improvement, particularly after December 1982 when Ayatollah Khomeini made a highly publicized eight-point statement, much of which focused on human rights issues. His speech decreed that censorship of mails and telephones was to cease, entry into private homes without a search warrant was forbidden except in cases involving suspected opposition hideouts, the right to travel outside Iran was extended to most Iranians and the tests designed to measure bureaucrats' loyalty to Islam were to be discontinued. A Headquarters for the Enforcement of the Imam's Decree, headed by the chief justice of the Supreme Court, was established with branch offices in most provincial cities. Thousands of complaints were received and a number of local officials removed. Although many abuses continue, conditions have improved over the immediate postrevolutionary period, and the institutional framework to correct some human rights abuses is in place.

Arrests for expression of views critical or different from those of the government are quite common. They have decreased, however, largely because of the widespread fear of arrest. If there is a formal accusation, the charge is usually subversion, anti-regime activities or treason. There is also evidence that many persons are arrested on trumped-up criminal charges (for example, on drug charges) when their actual "offenses" are political; the lack of fair trials and other procedural safeguards encourages such a practice. Political arrests are usually made by members of the Revolutionary Guard. Arrests by Komiteh members were common, but the Revolutionary Guards have increasingly assumed this role. In political cases, there normally are no warrants for arrest. There is no judicial determination of the legality of detention in Iranian law, nor are there any other legal protections. Detainees are frequently held for long periods without charge, and in some cases have been tortured, only to have the mullah who supervises the prison apologize subsequently for the mistake. For political crimes, no access to a lawyer is permitted. Cases are heard, if at all, by the revolutionary judiciary. Bail is not legally permitted.

Amnesty International's 1984 annual report recorded an estimated 5,447 executions in Iran between February 1979 and the end of 1983; the report noted, however, that "the total number of executions was certainly much higher, with hundreds of executions reportedly taking place unannounced." A report by the U.N. Human Rights Commission, published in February 1987, estimated the number of executions by the Government at a minimum of 7,000 between 1979 and 1985. The Mujahidin-e-Khalq (the most prominent opposition guerrilla group in Iran) assesses the number of executions at more than 70,000 since June 1981. In October 1989, Amnesty International claimed that at least 1,200 people had been executed in Iran during the previous 12 months. In January 1990, a delegation from the U.N. Human Rights Commission visited Iran to investigate the alleged abuse of human rights. This was subsequently confirmed in two reports by a special representative of the U.N. A highly condemnatory report, published in December 1990 by Amnesty International, added further weight to their conclusion, and, in the same month, the U.N. Human Rights Commission drafted a resolution criticizing Iran's human rights accord.

CIVIL SERVICE

The civil service is governed by the civil service codes of 1922 and 1966, which introduced a single system of grades with seven basic grades, each having 15 in-grade steps. The number of civil servants is estimated at over 700,000. Recruitment is based on entrance examinations.

LOCAL GOVERNMENT

Iran is divided into 24 *ostans*, or provinces. The provinces are administered by *ostandars*. The powers of provincial councils, called *anjumans*, are being enlarged gradually. The second tier of local government consists of 472 *shahrestans*, or counties, under junior *farmandars*. The third tier of 499 *bakhshes*, or districts, are under *bakhshadars;* the fourth tier of *dehistans*, or groups of villages, are under *dehdars*. At the base are the villages, which are in the charge of *kadkhodas*, or headmen. Towns and cities have municipal governments with mayors and councils either elected or designated by the Ministry of Interior.

FOREIGN POLICY

Islamic Iran's foreign relations revolve around its hostility to two countries: the United States and Iraq.

The United States is the archenemy of the Islamic republic. As befits a theocratic dictatorship, it describes the United States in theological terms: often as satan and the power of evil and darkness.

In November 1979, Iranian students seized 63 hostages in the U.S. Embassy in Teheran. The original purpose of the seizure was to give support to a demand for the return of the Shah (then in the U.S.A.) to Iran to face trial. The problem was not resolved by the death of the Shah in Egypt in July 1980, as the Iranians made other demands, the most important of which was for a U.S. undertaking not to interfere in the affairs of Iran. Intense diplomatic activity finally resulted in the release of the 52 remaining U.S. hostages in January 1981. In November 1986 it emerged that the U.S., despite its discouragement of arms sales to Iran by other countries, had been conducting secret negotiations with the Islamic Republic since July 1985 and had made three shipments of weapons and spare parts to Iran through Israeli intermediaries, in September 1985 and July and October 1986. These were allegedly in exchange for Iranian assistance in releasing American hostages who had been detained by Shi'ite groups in Lebanon, and an Iranian undertaking to relinquish involvement in international terrorism. The late U.S. Republican Senator John Tower, in a new memoir in November 1990, had charged that former U.S. President Ronald Reagan had misled investigators in order to cover up White House involvement in the Iran-contra affair. In May 1990, a previously undisclosed meeting between former White House aid Oliver L. North and then-Vice President George Bush was revealed in North's notebook. The meeting had taken place in August 1986; the subject of the meeting was not revealed in the notebook. In June, former U.S. national security adviser, John M. Poindexter, was sentenced to six months in prison for lying to Congress about his involvement in the Iran-contra arms scandal.

War broke out with Iraq in September 1980, when Iraq invaded Iran over a front of 500 km. (300 mi.) after a border dispute. In October 1983, Iran staged a series of offensives across its northern border with Iraq, threatening the only remaining outlet for Iraqi petroleum exports through the Kirkuk pipeline. In February and March 1984, a further Iranian offensive led to the capture of marshlands around the Majnoun Islands in southern Iraq. The U.N. had painstakingly engineered an agreement between Iran and Iraq in June 1984, halting attacks on civilian targets, but after the failure of an Iranian offensive in March 1985, Iraq declared Iranian airspace a war zone and resumed the bombardment of Iranian cities. In February 1986 Iran began the Wal-Fajr (Dawn) 8 offensive, so called to commemorate the month of Ayatollah Khomeini's return to Iran in 1979. Iranian forces crossed the Shatt al-Arab waterway and occupied the Iraqi port of Faw on the Persian Gulf. Iraq launched a counter-offensive on Faw in mid-February. During 1986 and 1987 the waters of the Gulf increasingly became the focus of international attention. Iran had begun to attack Kuwaiti and neutral shipping because of Kuwait's support for Iraq. In July 1987 the U.N. Security Council adopted Resolution 598, urging an immediate cease-fire, the withdrawal of military troops within international boundaries, and the co-operation of Iran and Iraq to achieve a peace settlement. A cease-fire came into force on August 20, 1988. Negotiations between Iran and Iraq for a comprehensive peace settlement began in Geneva on August 25, under the aegis of the U.N. However the negotiations soon became deadlocked in disputes concerning sovereignty over the Shatt al-Arab waterway, the exchange of prisoners of war, and the withdrawal of troops to international borders. By the end of 1989, the cease-fire remained the only element of Resolution 598 to have been successfully implemented.

On August 16, 1990 Saddam Hussein sought an immediate, formal peace with Iran, accepting all the claims that Iran had pursued since the declaration of a cease-fire (including the reinstatement of the Algiers agreement of 1975, dividing the Shatt al-Arab). In January 1991, an Iraqi delegation visited Teheran, and negotiations are reported to have culminated in the conclusion of agreements concerning, among other things, arrangements for the exchange of remaining prisoners of war and the creation of a demilitarized zone along the Iran-Iraq border.

Iran consistently opposed Iraq's occupation of Kuwait and repeatedly demanded that Iraqi troops be withdrawn from that state. In December 1990, following a meeting of the National Security Council, the Government of Iran declared that it would remain neutral in the event of military conflict. At the outbreak of hostilities between the multinational forces (acting in accordance with the resolutions of the U.N. Security Council) and Iraq on January 16, 1991, there was no indication of any change in the Iranian policy of neutrality.

In June 1989, President Rafsanjani visited the USSR, where he and the Soviet leader, Mikhail Gorbachev, signed a "declaration on the principles of relations" between Iran and the USSR. In January 1990, the Soviet authorities agreed to allow greater freedom of movement for ethnic Azerbaijanis between northern Iran and the Azerbaijani enclave of Nakhichevan in the USSR. In the same month, however, tension developed between Iran and the USSR, when the USSR used force in an attempt to subdue Azeri separatism in the Azerbaijani SSR.

Relations between Iran and Saudi Arabia became increasingly strained after an incident in Mecca in July 1987, when 402 people, including 275 Iranian pilgrims, lost their lives. In late 1989 there were signs of an incipient "proxy" war between Iran and Saudi Arabia in Lebanon, when a Saudi Arabian embassy employee was assassinated by members of the pro-Iranian *Islamic Jihad* in west Beirut. There have been indications of an improvement in relations since Iraq occupied Kuwait in August 1990. In September, Iran and Saudi Arabia issued a joint communique condemning the occupation. In January 1991, Jordan announced its intention to re-establish diplomatic relations with Iran, after an 11-year rift. Iran has also sought to achieve a common stance with Syria over the crisis in the Gulf.

In March 1989, Iran severed diplomatic relations with the United Kingdom, as a result of *The Satanic Verses* (Salman Rushdie) controversy. In September 1990, full diplomatic relations were restored.

Iran was a founding member of OPEC (Organization of Petroleum Exporting Countries), in which it has been one of the strongest advocates of higher oil prices. Iran is a member of 15 U.N. agencies and 18 other international organizations. It joined the U.N. in 1948.

PARLIAMENT

The 1979 Constitution replaced the former bicameral parliament with the unicameral Islamic Consultative Assembly (Majlis-e-Shura-e-Islami) elected by popular vote for four-year terms. The first election to the Assembly, held in two stages in 1979 and 1980, resulted in an absolute majority for the mullah-dominated Islamic Republican Party. The ruling Revolutionary Council's legislative power was transferred to parliament in July when Ayatollah Hashemi Rafsanjani was elected speaker.

Beginning a year after the shah's departure, the revolutionary regime has held elections at fairly regular intervals for president, Majlis deputies, members of the Council of Experts (responsible for choosing Khomeini's successor), and members of local government councils. All candidates must be approved by the Interior Ministry, however, and only those meeting with the approval of the government may run. In practice, only supporters of the theocratic state are accepted. There has, however, been considerable diversity of opinion among candidates on economic and social questions.

Elections to the third Majlis took place in two rounds, on April 8 and May 13, 1988. These were the first elections not to be contested by political parties. The Islamic Republican Party, which had won a clear majority of seats in the elections to the Majlis, was disbanded in June 1987. In the 1988 elections, the 270 seats were contested by some 1,600 candidates, recommended by political groups and approved by local screening committees.

The Majlis hold genuine debates and normally broadcast live on radio, on a wide variety of issues. In some cases, laws proposed by the government have been voted down. Five cabinet ministers lost their posts in August 1983 when, following heated debate on the performance of the cabinet, they failed to win votes of confidence, and on several occasions during the year the prime minister's nominees to fill ministerial vacancies were rejected. Rejections of bills and officials by the Majlis is accepted by the executive branch.

Iran's Constitution provides for a Council of Guardians composed of 12 members, 6 clerics unilaterally appointed by the Faqih and 6 lay members who are well grounded in Islamic law and who are nominated by the head of the Judicial Council subject to the approval of the Majlis. The Council of Guardians must certify all bills passed by the Majlis as being in accordance with Islamic law and the Constitution. If bills fail to be certified, they are sent back to the Majlis for revision. They cannot become law until the Council has certified them. The Council of Guardians has rejected various important bills and portions of bills passed by the Majlis, including legislation on land reform, nationalization of foreign trade and reform of Iran's civil code.

POLITICAL PARTIES

The Islamic Republican Party (IRP) was founded in 1978 to bring about the Islamic Revolution under the leadership of Ayatollah Khomeini. After the revolution, the IRP became the ruling party. In June 1987, the Ayatollah dismissed the IRP at the request of party leaders. Other political parties include:

• Liberation Movement of Iran (Nehzat-e-Azad-e-Iran) founded by Mehdi Bazargan, former prime minister, and its militant affiliate known as Holy Warriors. Bazargan has turned into one of the regime's most outspoken critics still tolerated by the mullahs. The Liberation Movement boycotted the 1984 elections to the second Majlis.

• Union of National Front Forces (Jebhe-e-Melli) founded by Shahpur Bakhtiar. Boycotted the 1984 presidential election. It comprises Iran Nationalist Party, Iranian Party and Society of Iranian Students.

• National Democratic Front (Jebhe-e-Democratic-e-Melli) founded by Hedayatollah Matine-Daftari, a grandson of Mohammad Mossadeq. It protested the curtailment of civil liberties and the establishment of a religious dictatorship and boycotted the constituent assembly.

• Muslim People's Republican Party (Hezb-e-Jamhori-e-Khalq-e-Mosalman) founded by followers of Ayatollah Shariat Madari favors a strong but secular government.

• Party of the Masses (Hezb-e-Tudeh), pro-Soviet Communist Party, banned in 1983.

• Communist Party of Iran (Hezb-e-Kommunist-e-Iran) Independent Communist group.

• Party of the Toilers (Hezb-e-Kumelah), an anti-Khomeini Kurdish party.

• Kurdish Democratic Party (Hezb Democrat Kurdistan), outlawed in 1979.

• Mujahidin-e-Khalq is a terrorist organization sometimes known as the People's Mujahidin Organization of Iran. Although now supported by many Iranians who are seeking any alternative to the current regime, the Mujahidin have carried out numerous political killings directed against the shah's government, against the U.S. government, and, after breaking in mid-1981 with their policy of fervent support for Ayatollah Khomeini and the Islamic Revolution, against the present regime.

• Other terrorist and guerrilla organizations include the Warriors of the People (Fedayin-e-Khalq), the Forghan Group (Grouh-e-Forghan) with some Marxist connections, and Black Wednesday (Chaharshanbeh-e-Siah) an Arab rebel force which engages in sabotage in Khuzestan.

ECONOMY

The revolutionary government inherited an economy which was already badly disrupted, shattered by pre-Revolution strikes and concessions to workers. Industry, apart from the generally strike-exempt food and pharmaceutical sectors, was virtually moribund. The oil sector was barely meeting domestic requirements. Agriculture alone appeared to be little affected by the traumatic events. But, unlike most of the other revolutionary benchmarks, Iran's new leaders inherited a good foreign exchange reserve, low public debt and the hard currency earning power of the easily-resumed oil sector.

The banks, petroleum industry, transportation, utilities and mining have since been nationalized but the new Five-Year Development Plan (1990/91–1994/95) calls for the transfer of many government-controlled enterprises to the private sector. The Iranian economy has been hard hit by the war with Iraq, not only because of the diversion of men and materials but also because of the periodic Iraqi attacks on Kharg terminal. Although petroleum production rebounded by 1985 (after falling to 400,000 barrels per day in 1982/83), there has been serious damage to wells, refineries and terminals as well as losses from attacks on tankers in the Gulf. War-related disruptions, massive corruption, mismanagement, demographic pressures and ideological rigidities have kept economic growth at depressed levels. A combination of war damage and low oil prices brought a 2% drop in GNP in 1988. GNP probably rose slightly in 1989, considerably short of the 3.4% population growth rate in 1989.

President Rafsanjani sought to reduce Iran's military burden and broaden its international contacts so the nation could concentrate on building its war-shattered economy. Although he faced resistance from hard-liners within his government, his hand had reportedly been strengthened by the assistance that had poured into Iran from many foreign countries—including Iraq—after an earthquake in June 1990.

The outbreak of military conflict in the Gulf in January 1991 raised questions regarding the potential effect of the hostilities on the international petroleum market, on Iranian domestic politics and on Iran's relations with the Western countries participating in the war against Iraq, all of which will influence Iran's future economic reconstruction. Sustained, reliable earnings are the most important factor in Iran's future economic success.

PRINCIPAL ECONOMIC INDICATORS

Average annual growth rate (%, 1965–80)
  General government consumption: 14.6
  Private consumption: 10.1
  Gross domestic investment: 11.5

BALANCE OF PAYMENTS, 1984
(U.S. $ millions)

Current account balance: −414
Merchandise exports: 17,087
Merchandise imports: −14,729
Trade balance: 2,358
Other goods, services & income + : 1,069
Other goods, services & income − : −3,841
Other goods, services & income net: −2,772
Private unrequited transfers: −1 (1975)
Official unrequited transfers: −2 (1980)
Capital other than reserves: −3,722
Net errors & omissions: −904
Counterpart items: −28
Total change in reserves: 4,164

GROSS DOMESTIC PRODUCT

GDP nominal (RL trillions): 21.270
Average annual growth rate of GDP (%, 1985–88): −0.2
GDP by type of expenditure (%) 1985
  Consumption
    Private: 55
    Government: 16
  Gross domestic investment: 29
  Foreign trade
    Exports: 8
    Imports: −9
Cost components of GDP (%) 1986
    Net indirect taxes: 2
    Consumption of fixed capital: 7
    Compensation of employees and net operating surplus: 91
Sectoral origin of GDP (%) 1986
  Primary
    Agriculture: 19
    Mining: 10
  Secondary
    Manufacturing: 8
    Construction: 7
    Public utilities: 1
  Tertiary
    Transportation & communications: 8
    Trade: 20
    Finance: 2
    Other services: 18
    Government: 9

PUBLIC FINANCE

The Iranian fiscal year runs from March 21 through March 20. The national budget comprises two parts: the general budget and the development budget. For the financial year ending March 20, 1992 the Government drafted a budget which provided for expenditures of RL 8,188,000 m., and for revenues of RL 7,088,000 m. Main items of expenditure are education, housing and welfare, and defense. Major revenue sources are income taxation and oil sales.

The Islamic Republic's first Five-Year Development Plan was unveiled in August 1983. It was intended as the first step toward quadrupling the Gross Domestic Product between 1982/83 and 2002/03. This plan, covering the years 1983/83–1987/88 gave priority to the development of the agricultural sector. The Five-Year Development Plan of 1990/91–1994/95 seeks to reinvigorate the Iranian economy by increasing the role of the private sector, boosting non-oil income and securing foreign loans. The plan is overly ambitious but probably will generate some short-term relief.

From 1970–80 the United States contributed $1 billion in aid. Other Western nations gave $1.5 billion between 1970–87. Communist aid between 1970–88 totaled $976 million. Aid fell sharply following the 1979 revolution.

CENTRAL GOVERNMENT EXPENDITURES (latest)
(% of total expenditures)

  Defense: 14.2
  Education: 19.6
  Health: 6.0
  Housing, social security, welfare: 17.4
  Economic services: 15.7
  Other: 27.1
Total expenditures as % of GDP: 18.6 (1987)
Overall surplus or deficit as % of GNP: −6.7 (1987)

CENTRAL GOVERNMENT REVENUES (latest)
(% of total current revenues)

  Taxes on income, profit & capital gain: 13.4
  Social security contributions: 9.5
  Domestic taxes on goods & services: 8.0
  Taxes on international trade & transactions: 9.0
  Other taxes: 5.6
  Current nontax revenue: 54.4
Total current revenue as % of GNP: 19.4
General government consumption as % of GDP: 16 (1987)
Average annual growth rate
  of general government consumption (%, 1965–80): 14.6

FOREIGN AID, 1989

Total foreign aid (U.S. $ millions): 2,052.1
  Bilateral: 2,020.7
  Multilateral: 31.5

CURRENCY & BANKING

The Iranian unit of currency is the rial divided into 100 dinars. Coins are issued in denominations of 1, 2, 5, 10, 20 and 50 rials, while notes are issued in denominations of 100, 200, 500, 1,000, 2,000, 5,000 and 10,000 rials. Domestic figures are generally referred to in terms of the toman (plural: tomans), which equal 10 rials. As of June 1991, the official exchange rate was US $1 = 71.00 rials and £1 sterling = 119.75 rials. The exchange rates refer to the official rate of the Central Bank, applicable to all foreign exchange transactions since December 1984 and to almost all transactions prior to that date. Since May 22, 1990, this valuation of the Iranian rial has been linked to the IMF's Special Drawing Right (SDR). Prior to December 1984, a system of multiple exchange rates was in operation, with a preferential rate applicable to proceeds from non-oil exports, and another rate applicable to sales of foreign exchange for tourism.

FINANCIAL INDICATORS, 1989

Total reserves minus gold (SDRs millions): 0
SDRs (millions): 305
Reserve position in IMF (SDRs millions): 71 (1987)
Foreign exchange (SDRs millions): 4.792
Gold (fine troy oz. millions): 5.92 (1982)
Central bank 1983
- Assets (%)
  - Foreign assets: 12.8
  - Claims on government: 85.0
  - Claims on banks: 2.1
  - Claims on private sector: 0.0
- Liabilities (%)
  - Reserve money: 68.2
  - Government deposits: 17.9
  - Foreign liabilities: 1.6
  - Capital accounts: 3.9

Money supply 1987
- Stock (RL trillions): 3.922
- M1 per capita: 89,400

Private banks 1984
- Assets (%)
  - Loans to government: 19.3
  - Loans to private sector: 44.6
  - Reserves: 33.6
  - Foreign assets: 2.5
- Liabilities
  - Deposits (RL trillions): 6.117
  - of which %
    - Demand deposits: 37.5
    - Savings deposits: 48.8
    - Government deposits: 0.0
    - Foreign liabilities: 1.0

External debt 1985
- Debt service (long term)
  - Total (U.S. $ millions): 953 (1987)
  - Repayment
    - Principal (%): 88.6 (1987)
    - Interest (%): 11.4 (1987)
- Debt service ratio (%): 6.2 (1985)
- Net direct private investment (U.S. $ millions): 24 (1970)

Banking is one of the areas most seriously affected by the Islamic Revolution. The health of banks was uneven prior to the June 1979 nationalization with about 15 banks highly liquid and about six deposit banks in substantial foreign arrearages. Banks reopened after the revolution on a regular basis but with erratic service; the foreign exchange market has been particularly chaotic, with Central Bank regulations changed almost completely May 5, 1979, and revised often since. Bank management, as elsewhere in the economy, was shattered. Revolutionary Committees often controlled even the most routine transactions. An amnesty on payment of commercial instruments was granted through June 21, at which time all except penalty fees and interest were due. In 1979 the banking system was reorganized and nationalized and the number of banks was reduced to eight. Of these, Bank Melli Iran (The National Bank of Iran), Bank Sepah (Army Bank) and Bank Saderat Iran (The Export Bank of Iran) retained their old identity while two new banks, Bank Tejarat and Bank Mellat, were the result of the mergers of the remaining banks. In accordance with Islamic law interest has been abolished and replaced with a 4% commission on loans. One bank, the Islamic Bank (now Islamic Economy Organization), set up in May 1979, was exempt from nationalization. Although the number of foreign banks in Iran has fallen since the revolution, some 30 are still represented. Since the exclusion of French banks from the Iranian market since the end of 1983, German, Swiss, Japanese and British banks have been responsible for about 30% of total trade financing.

GROWTH PROFILE
(Annual Growth Rates, %)

Projected population (1988–2000): 3.1
Projected crude birth rate (/1,000) (1990–95): 39.0
Projected crude death rate (/1,000) (1990–95): 6.9
Urban population (1980–88): 4.1
Labor force (1985–2000): 3.2
GDP (1985–88): −0.2
Money holdings (1965–80): 28.6
Energy production (1980–88): 5.1
Energy consumption (1980–88): 2.7
General government consumption (1965–80): 14.6
Private consumption (1965–80): 10.1
Gross domestic investment (1965–80): 11.5

AGRICULTURE

Agriculture is a very widespread economic activity in Iran, though its importance relative to the other sectors has been declining. The principal cash crop is fresh and dried fruit. The principal subsistence crops are wheat, barley, sugar beet and sugar cane. Production of beef, mutton and lamb is also important. Other principal products are rice, cotton, dairy products, wool and caviar. Iran is an illicit producer of opium poppy for the domestic and international drug trade. The country is not self-sufficient in food. Cigarette tobacco is grown mainly in Hormozgan, Bushehr and West Azerbaijan *ostans*. It is purchased by the Tobacco Monopoly and manufactured in the government factory at Teheran.

The Shah of Iran, in 1963, launched an extensive land program in three phases, despite opposition from the landlords. This program was known as the White Revolution and is an important landmark in the modernization of the country's economic system.

Livestock and animal breeding are significant sources of income in rural areas. Animal products, such as wool and leather, are chiefly produced by nomadic herdsmen. The Caspian Fisheries Company (Shilat) is a government monopoly. Agricultural credit is provided through the Bank Keshavarzi (Agricultural Bank), formed in 1979 as a merger of the Agricultural Development Bank of Iran and the Agricultural Co-operative Bank of Iran.

AGRICULTURAL INDICATORS

Cereal imports (million metric tons): 4.644 (1988)
Index of agricultural production (1979–81 = 100): 117 (1986)
Index of food production (1979–81 = 100): 117 (1986)
Index of food production per capita (1979–81 = 100): 99 (1985–88)
Number of tractors: 112,000 (1986)
Number of harvester-threshers: 2,900 (1986)
Total fertilizer consumption (000 mertic tons): 902.6 (1985–86)
Fertilizer consumption (g./ha., hundreds): 659 (1987–88)
Farms as % of total land area: 12.3 (1982)
Land use % 1985–87
  Cropland: 28
  Pasture: 8
  Forest: 4
  Other: 61
Yields (kg./ha.) 1989
  Grains: 1,078
  Roots & tubers: 13,334
  Legumes: 701
  Milk (kg./animal): 750
Production 1989
  Fruits (million metric tons): 3.415
  Vegetables (million metric tons): 4.265
Livestock (000) 1989
  Cattle: 8,000
  Horses: 316 (1986)
  Sheep: 34,000
Forestry 1988
  Production of roundwood (million cubic meters): 6.817
    of which industrial roundwood (%): 64.2
  Value of exports (U.S. $ 000): 38 (1984)
Fishing 1988
  Total catch (000 metric tons): 156.0
    of which marine (%): 80.8
  Value of exports (U.S. $ million): 18

MANUFACTURING

Industry is the fastest growing sector of the national economy.

MANUFACTURING INDICATORS

Average annual growth rate (%, 1965–80): 10.0
Share of GDP (%): 12 (1965)
Value added in manufacturing (U.S. $ billions): 1.501 (1970)
  Food & tobacco (%): 13 (latest)
  Textiles & clothing (%): 22 (latest)
  Machinery & transport equipment (%): 22 (latest)
  Chemicals (%): 7 (latest)
Earnings per employee in manufacturing (1970)
Total earnings as % of value added: 25
Gross output per employee (1980 = 100): 85

Teheran is the main industrial center with over 50% of the factories; Isfahan and Tabriz are other growth centers. By the industrial policy laid down in 1970 the government sold some of its industrial holdings to private investors. The state no longer participates in new industrial ventures on the basis of total investment. Industrial development is guided by the Iran Industries Reconstruction and Expansion Organization. Financial assistance is provided through the Bank Sanat va Madan (Bank of Industry and Mines) formed in 1979 as a merger of the Industrial Credit Bank, Industrial and Mining Development Bank of Iran, Development and Investment Bank of Iran, and Iranian Bankers Investment Company.

The three most important consumer-oriented industries are textiles, food processing and construction materials. Persian carpet production is controlled by the Iranian Carpet Society. Other major industries include pharmaceuticals, petroleum refining, petrochemicals, electrical engineering, machine tools and paper products.

MINING

Mining is a state monopoly. The major known mineral resources are coal, iron, lead, copper, bauxite, chromite, phosphates and turquoise. Iran is the world's largest producer of turquoise and the fifth largest producer of zinc.

ENERGY

Iran is one of the two leading oil exporters and producers in the world with proved reserves of petroleum at 62.500 billion barrels in 1990.

Oil accounts for 90% of all export earnings. The National Iranian Oil Company (NIOC), a state organi-

ENERGY INDICATORS

Average annual energy production growth rate (%, 1980–88): 5.1
Energy consumption per capita (kg. oil equivalent): 875 (1988)
Average annual growth rate of energy consumption (%, 1980–88): 2.7
Electricity 1988
  Installed capacity (million kw.): 13.404
  Production (billion kw.-hr.): 38.770
    % fossil fuel: 83.4
    % hydro: 16.6
  Consumption per capita (kw.-hr.): 730
Natural gas
  Proved reserves (trillion cu. m.): 17.000 (1990)
  Production (billion cu. m.): 22.200 (1989)
  Consumption (billion cu. m.): 14.986 (1988)
Petroleum
  Proved reserves (billion bbl.): 62.500 (1990)
  Years to exhaust proved reserves: 58 (1990)
  Production (billion bbl.): 1.077 (1989)
  Consumption (million bbl.): 256 (1988)
  Refining capacity (000 bbl./day): 530 (1990)
Coal
  Reserves (million metric tons): 193 (latest)
  Production (million metric tons): 1.260 (1988)
  Consumption (million metric tons): 1.460 (1988)

zation controlling all petroleum, petrochemical and natural gas operations in Iran, was incorporated in April 1951. In September 1979, the Ministry of Oil took over control of NIOC.

Iran is a member of OPEC.

There are four major refineries at Abadan, Teheran, Kermanshah and Shiraz. The Abadan refinery was, until it was destroyed by Iraqis, the largest exporting refinery in the world.

Iran's natural gas reserves are the second largest in the world after those of the USSR. Exploitation is controlled by National Iranian Gas Company. The Atomic Energy Organization of Iran was originally set up in 1973 to produce nuclear power to provide for the base load electricity needs of the country. Its main aim now is the exploration and exploitation of uranium and to work on a Bushehr nuclear power plant, among other things.

LABOR

There are critical shortages of skilled workers, technicians and middle-level managers in Iran.

Working conditions are governed by the Labor Law of 1959, the Worker's Social Insurance Law of 1960, and the Labor Profit-sharing Law of 1963. The workweek consists of six eight-hour working days, with four hours of authorized overtime. In addition to wages, most workers receive traditional Now Ruz bonuses, cash bonuses on occasions of marriage, birth and death, and incentive bonuses for completion of literacy courses. Profit-sharing was introduced by legislation in 1963 calling for at least 20% of net profits to be distributed to workers. All workers are covered by social insurance.

LABOR INDICATORS 1986

Total economically active population (millions): 12.820
- % working-age (15–64): 50.2 (1976)
- % female: 10.2

Activity rate (%)
- Total: 25.9
- Male: 45.5
- Female: 5.4

Employment status (%)
- Employers & self-employed: 36.9
- Employees: 41.6
- Unpaid family workers: 3.8
- Other: 17.8

Sectoral employment of economically active (%)
- Agriculture, forestry, fishing: 24.9
- Construction: 9.4
- Manufacturing, mining, quarrying, public utilities: 12.3
- Trade, hotels, restaurants: 6.8
- Transportation, communications: 4.9
- Finance, real estate: 0.9
- Services: 23.8

Average annual growth rate of labor force (%, 1985–2000): 3.2
Labor under 20 years (%): 10.8 (1982)

Unemployment is perhaps Iran's greatest economic and political problem. Its magnitude is disguised by the present policy of voluntary or involuntary employment at previous levels regardless of need. Many wonder when the cushions of personal savings and societal relief will run out for the several million unemployed and millions more underemployed. These are found particularly in the depressed construction and transportation sectors, with slackness in industry and private services also contributing to the problem. The costs of compensation for little or no work will eventually have to be paid by the economy. In commerce, employers maintain staffs out of their pockets, awaiting an upturn in business. Government bureaucracy, like private, is still preoccupied with political and organizational concerns. Ironically, Iran's new labor movement, having successfully flexed its muscles during the political upheavals of the late 1970s, faces a depressed economy and urgings from the revolutionary leadership to forsake material goods and sacrifice for the revolution. Indeed, in 1981, the government established a special force to regulate labor and put down worker interference in operations. The government's fiscal program is said to include job creation in the rural areas, which it hopes will induce migration from the urban centers.

The basic unit of labor organization is the syndicate. A union consists of a number of syndicates and a confederation of a number of unions. In 1963 all trade unions were dissolved and syndicates were required to be registered with the government and prohibited from participating in politics. There are 67 approved syndicates, of which the largest is the National Iranian Oil Company Workers' Syndicate. It is believed that there are "Islamic workers councils" in some factories. These, however, are more instruments of government control than bodies that represent workers' interests. Several short-lived strikes in 1984 were dealt with severely. The leaders of a soft-drink plant workers' strike were reportedly arrested and executed.

FOREIGN COMMERCE

Following the seizure of the U.S. embassy in Teheran the United States imposed a trade embargo on Iran and worked to persuade U.S. allies to follow suit. The embargo remained in effect even after the release of hostages in 1981. A growing feature of Iranian foreign trade is the use of barter by which Iran is able to contract for needed capital goods in return for natural gas or petroleum.

The principal source of imports is Germany, which is also the principal market for exports. Other major trading partners are Japan, Brazil, the United Kingdom, Italy and the United Arab Emirates. Principal imports are machinery and motor vehicles, iron and steel, military supplies and foodstuffs. Principal exports are petroleum products, carpets, fruit and nuts.

There was speculation that Iran's observance of the economic sanctions imposed by the U.N. in August 1990 (when it could have done much to undermine them) was partly responsible for the United States' decision, in late 1990, to end its ban on imports of Iranian petroleum.

The most important Iranian trade fair is the Asian International Trade Fair held annually at Teheran.

FOREIGN TRADE INDICATORS 1988

Exports (U.S. $ billions): 12.3
Imports (U.S. $ billions): 12.0
Balance of trade (U.S. $ billions): 0.3

Direction of Trade (%), 1985 est.

	Imports	Exports
European Economic Community	38.5	35.5
United States	0.7	5.2
U.S.S.R. & eastern European economies	7.2	5.2
Japan	12.9	17.2

Composition of Trade (%), 1985

	Imports	Exports
Food, agricultural raw materials, mineral ores & concentrates	20.9	0.0
Fuels & other energy	2.1	98.0
Manufactured goods	77.1	0.0
of which chemicals	12.8	
of which machinery	37.6	

TRANSPORTATION & COMMUNICATIONS

The state-owned rail system consists of 11 major lines, of which the most important is the Trans-Iranian Railway which runs for 1,392 km. (864 mi.), from Bandar Turkman on the Caspian Sea in the north, through Teheran, and south to the Bandar Imam Khomeini on the Persian Gulf. Two other major lines connect Teheran and Tabriz (736 km., 457 mi.) and Garmsar and Meshed (812 km., 504 mi.).

Construction of a subway in Teheran began during 1978 but the project was suspended after the revolution in 1979. Work on two of the four lines which were to have been built resumed in September 1986 and is due to be completed in mid-1992, when work on the remaining two lines will begin.

In the Persian Gulf, the main oil terminal is at Kharg Island. The principal commercial non-oil ports are Bandar Shahid Rajai, Bandar Khomeini, Bushehr, Bandar Abbas and Chah Bahar. Khorramshshr, Iran's biggest port, was put out of action in the war with Iraq, and Bushehr and Bandar Khomeini also sustained war damage, which has restricted their use. During 1988 Iran signed a contract with the USSR for two cargo ships which will provide the basis of a new shipping line between the ports of Bandar Anzali and Bandar Nowshahr (the principal ports in the Caspian Sea), and Baku, in the USSR.

The state airline, Iran Air (Airline of the Islamic Republic of Iran) provides international services and Iran Asseman Airlines provides domestic services. The two main international airports are Mehrabad (Teheran) and Abadan. In April 1990, Lucas Aerospace, a leading British defense and aviation company, had been invited by Iran to tender a contract to overhaul two Boeing 747 jetliners for Iran Air. Lucas Industries, the parent firm, denied knowledge of any link between the potential contract and the hostage issue.

Tourism in Iran has been adversely affected by political upheaval since the revolution. Iran's chief attraction for tourists is its wealth of historical sites, notably Isfahan, Tabriz and Rasht.

TRANSPORTATION INDICATORS

Roads (latest)
- Length, km. (mi.): 139,368 (86,599)
- Paved (%): 48

Motor vehicles (pre-1986)
- Automobiles: 2,246,143
- Trucks and buses: 434,944
- Persons per vehicle: 17
- Road freight, metric ton-km. (short ton-mi.) (billions): 68.250 (46.750)

Railroads
- Track, km. (mi.): 4,601 (2,859) (latest)
- Passenger-km. (passenger-mi.) (billions): 2.526 (1.570) (pre-1986)
- Freight, metric ton-km. (short ton-mi.) (billions): 3.861 (2.645) (pre-1986)

Merchant marine
- Vessels (over 100 tons): 386 (1989)
- Total deadweight tonnage (000): 8,685.3 (1989)
- Oil tankers (000 GRT): 918 (1985)

Ports (pre-1986)
- Cargo loaded (000 metric tons): 78,667
- Cargo unloaded (000 metric tons): 12,205

Air
- Km. (mi.) flown (millions): 25.9 (16.1) (1985)
- Passenger-km. (passenger-mi.) (millions): 4,525 (2,812) (latest)
- Freight, metric ton-km. (short ton-mi.) (millions): 92 (63) (latest)
- Mail, metric ton-km. (short ton-mi.) (millions): 10.2 (7) (1985)
- Airports with scheduled flights: 24 (1990)

Pipelines 1990
- Refined, km. (mi.): 3,900 (2,423)
- Natural gas, km. (mi.): 3,300 (2,051)

Inland waterways (latest)
- Length, km. (mi.): 904 (562)

COMMUNICATION INDICATORS, 1988

Telephones
- Total (millions): 2.104
- Persons per telephone: 25

Phone traffic (million calls)
- Local: 11,340.148 (1986)
- Long distance: 276.970 (1986)
- Combined national: 11,617.118 (1986)
- International: 5.716 (1986)

Post office
- Number of post offices: 3,815 (1985)
- Pieces of mail handled (millions): 256.751 (1985)

Telegraph
- Total traffic (000 calls): 5,956
  - National: 5,872
  - International: 84

Telex
- Subscriber lines: 5,942
- Traffic (million minutes): 4.022

Telecommunications 1990
- Satellite stations: 2

TOURISM & TRAVEL INDICATORS, 1986

Total tourist receipts (U.S. $ millions): 25 (1988)
Expenditures by nationals abroad (U.S. $ millions): 396 (1988)
Number of hotel beds (000): 33
Average length of stay (nights): 5
Tourist nights (000): 280
Number of tourists (000): 89.4 (1985)
- of whom from United States: 0.1
- Turkey: 5.9
- India and Federal Republic of Germany: 5.6
- Japan: 3.7

DEFENSE

The defense structure is headed by the Faqih, Ayatollah Khamenei, who, as the supreme commander of the armed forces, exercises operational control through a joint staff organization. Soon after the outbreak of the war with Iraq, Ayatollah Khomeini handed over his military powers to then president, Bani-Sadr. The minister of war is outside the actual chain of command.

Much of Iran's military might has disintegrated following the Islamic Revolution. Because of U.S. embargo the sophisticated U.S.-supplied military equipment lacks parts and maintenance. Finally, the war with Iraq and the early reverses suffered in that war have reduced both the inventory and the morale of the troops to their lowest levels in decades.

Conscription provides the main source of military manpower. Every Iranian citizen becomes eligible for military service at the age of 19 for a period of two years. There is no organized reserve.

The strength of the armed forces is 504,000.

Army

Personnel: 305,000

Organization: Three army HQ; 4 mechanized divisions, each consisting of three brigades; 6 infantry divisions; 1 airborne brigade; and auxiliary units.

Equipment: T-54/-55/-62, T-72, 300 chieftan, M-47/-48 and M-60A1 main battle tanks.

Revolutionary Guard Corps (Pasdaran): 150,000

Navy

Personnel: 14,500

Organization: 2 fleets: the Northern or Caspian Sea and the Southern or Persian Gulf; 3 destroyers; 5 frigates; 2 corvettes; 8 fast attack craft; 7 patrol craft; 2 inshore minesweepers; 4 landing craft; 3 Marine battalions

Naval Bases: Khorramshahr, Bandar Pahlavi, Bushehr, Kharg Island, Bandar Abbas, Chah Bahar and Hengham Island.

Air Force

Personnel: 35,000

Equipment: 100 serviceable combat aircraft, including F-14 Tomcat, F-5E Tiger II, MiG-19/Chinese-built F-6 fighter bombers; transport aircraft; training aircraft.

Air Bases: Teheran, Hamadan, Dezful, Doshen-Tappeh, Mehrabad, Galeh-Marghi, Zahidan, Shiraz, Ahwaz, Isfahan, Tabriz, Faharabad, Chah Bahar, Meshed and Bushehr

The principal training institutions are the Military College, the Army Staff College, the War Academy and the National Defense University.

EDUCATION

Education is officially compulsory for eight years, between six and 14 years of age, but this has not been fully implemented in rural areas. Primary education, which is free, begins at the age of six and lasts for five years. Secondary education, from the age of 11, lasts for up to seven years.

The academic year runs from September to June. The language of instruction is Persian but both English

EDUCATION INDICATORS, 1987

Literacy
- Total (%): 61.8
- Male (%): 71.0
- Female (%): 52.1

First level
- Schools: 53,039
- Students: 7,356,257
- Teachers: 282,296
- Student/teacher ratio: 26.1
- Net enrollment ratio: 94

Second level
- Schools: 14,894
- Students: 3,376,272
- Teachers (includes vocational): 206,345
- Student/teacher ratio: 17.4 (1986)

Vocational
- Schools: 1,045
- Students: 252,620
- Student/teacher ratio: 13.4 (1986)

Third level (postsecondary)
- Institutions: 116
- Students: 167,971
- Teachers: 14,341
- Student/teacher ratio: 11.7
- Gross enrollment ratio: 4.9
- Students (/100,000 pop.): 445

Foreign study
- Foreign students in national universities: 117 (1988)
- Students abroad: 33,565
  - of whom in
    - United States: 7,759 (1988)
    - France: 3,953 (1988)
    - Federal Republic of Germany: 9,511 (1988)
    - United Kingdom: 1,165 (1987)

Public expenditure
- Total (RL 000): 729,912,000
- % of national budget: 18.1
- % of current: 91.8

GRADUATES, 1986

Total 28,868
Education: 4,447
Humanities & religion: 2,101
Fine & applied arts: 78
Law: 515
Social & behavioral sciences: 2,208
Commerce & business: 1,568
Mass communication: 190
Home economies: 0
Service trades: 0
Natural sciences: 1,871
Mathematics & computer science: 710
Medicine: 6,325
Engineering: 5,754
Architecture: 253
Industrial programs: 63
Transportation & communications: 0
Agriculture, forestry, fisheries: 2,785
Other: 0

and French are taught as second languages. There is an acute shortage of teachers at both the primary and secondary levels. Teaching staffs in primary schools are supplemented by the Literacy Corps.

Educational administration, modeled on the French system, is highly centralized under the Ministry of Education. The ministry establishes curricula, hires and trains teachers, administers examinations and prepares textbooks. The state encourages private schools and subsidizes equipment and salaries.

Christian and secular French private schools attract the best students.

Iran has eight universities, three in Teheran and the others in Shiraz, Tabriz, Ahwaz, Meshed and Isfahan. The universities are: the University of Azarabadegan (Tabriz), the University of Ferdowzi (Meshed), University of Isfahan (Isfahan), Jundi-Shahpur University (Ahwaz), University of Shiraz, National University of Iran (Teheran), University of Teheran (Teheran) and University of Technology (Teheran).

LEGAL SYSTEM

In August 1982 the Supreme Court revoked all laws dating from the previous regime which did not conform to Islam. In October 1982 all courts set up prior to the Islamic Revolution were abolished. In June 1987, Ayatollah Khomeini ordered the creation of clerical courts to try members of the clergy opposed to government policy. Islamic codes of correction were introduced in 1983, including the dismembering of a hand for theft, flogging for fornication and violations of the strict dress code for women, and stoning for adultery. One hundred and nine offenses may be punished by the death penalty. The new Supreme Court has 16 branches.

LAW ENFORCEMENT

There are three law enforcement organizations: the Imperial Iranian Gendarmerie, the National Police and the Resistance Forces. The Gendarmerie, under the Ministry of Interior, is responsible for law enforcement in rural areas and small towns of less than 5,000 persons, areas which constitute 80% of the nation. It consists of 40,000 men organized into 33 regiments, three battalions, one light aircraft battalion and one naval battalion. In wartime the Gendarmerie comes under the Ministry of War. The gendarmes are stationed in over 2,000 posts connected directly with Teheran by radio. The National Police, with a strength of 25,000, are responsible for law enforcement in towns of more than 5,000. It functions under the chief of national police. Both the Gendarmerie and the police are well-disciplined and efficient organizations. The National Resistance Forces is a paramilitary organization of about 40,000 to 50,000 civilians trained to use arms and assist the armed forces in times of war and internal unrest.

Violence is relatively rare in the cities and women and children are safe on the streets. Brigandage has not been entirely eliminated in rural areas. The main law enforcement concern is politically motivated disturbances of the left and right.

HEALTH

Iran's major health problems are typhoid, trachoma, dysentery, malaria, tuberculosis and venereal diseases. Under Article 29 of the 1979 Constitution, the Government has a duty to provide every citizen with insurance benefits covering illness.

HEALTH INDICATORS

Health personnel 1987
- Physicians: 16,918
  - persons per: 2,992
- Dentists: 2,488
- Nurses: 43,291
- Pharmacists: 2,650
- Midwives: 2,202

Hospitals 1982
- Number: 581
- Number of beds (/10,000): 16

Type of hospitals (%) 1982
- Government: 66.4
- Private nonprofit: 13.9
- Private profit: 19.7

Public health expenditures (latest)
- As % of national budget: 6.0
- Per capita (U.S. $): 54.10

Vital statistics
- Crude death rate (/1,000): 10 (1990)
- Life expectancy at birth 1990
  - Males: 62
  - Females: 63
- Infant mortality rate (/1,000 lives births): 91 (1990)
- Child mortality rate under 5 years. (/1,000 live births) (1985–90): 155
- Population with access to safe water (%): 76 (latest)

FOOD & NUTRITION

The staple diet consists of bread and meat. Per capita food intake is 2,855 calories (119% of requirements).

MEDIA & CULTURE

Teheran dominates the press scene as many of the daily papers are published there and the bi-weekly, weekly and less frequent publications in the provinces generally depend on the major metropolitan dailies as a source of news.

PRINCIPAL DAILIES

Title	Circulation
Kayhan	350,000
Ettela'at	250,000
Khorassan	40,000

The Constitution states that pre-publication censorship is forbidden and that no publications may be banned without a court order. The press law of 1979 governs the legal status of the press. They established educational and financial criteria for publishers and a licensing system under which only one license in one category may be issued to a person. While criticism of the bureaucracy is permitted, prohibited materials include articles against Islam and state policies. Minimum circulation figures are prescribed for all categories. Iran ranks 68th among the nations of the world in press freedom in which it is scaled at −1.02 (on an index with +4 as the maximum and −4 as the minimum).

MEDIA INDICATORS

Newspapers
- Number of dailies: 17 (latest)
- Newsprint consumption 1988
  - Total metric tons: 10,000
  - Per 1,000 pop. (kg.): 140

Book publishing
- Number of titles: 2,794 (latest)

Broadcasting 1987
- Annual expenditures (RL billions): 19,923.0

Radio
- Number of transmitters: 349 (1989)
- Number of persons per radio receiver: 4.7 (1989)
- Total program hours (/yr.): 48,768 (1987)

Television
- Television transmitters: 585 (1989)
- Number of persons per T.V. receiver: 24 (1989)
- Total program hours (/yr.): 10,913 (1987)

Cinema
- Number of fixed cinemas: 253 (latest)
- Seating capacity (000): 154 (latest)
  - Seats (/1,000 pop.): 3.5 (1985)
- Annual attendance (millions): 78 (latest)
- Gross box office receipts (RL millions): 2.273

Films
- Number of long films produced: 42 (latest)
- Number of long films imported: 96 (1983)
- % from
  - U.S.S.R.: 26.0
  - Italy: 22.9
  - United States: 13.5
  - United Kingdom: 10.4

The most outspoken of the opposition newspapers, *Ayandegan*, was closed down in 1979 along with 22 other opposition papers. Drastic curbs were also imposed through a new press law on foreign journalists, including a ban on unsupervised interviews with government officials and a requirement that reporters renew their press cards every three months.

The official national news agency is IRNA (Islamic Republic News Agency), operated by the Ministry of Information's General Department of Publications.

Iran has an extensive book publishing industry. Teheran is the main publishing center. The American Franklin Book Program was active until the early 1970s in the field of translation and reprints. Iran does not adhere to any copyright convention.

Broadcasting is a state activity operated by Voice of the Islamic Republic of Iran, an administratively independent body under the Ministry of Information. There are three national radio channels: Radio Networks 1 and 2, and Radio Quran, which broadcasts recitals of the Quran (Koran) and other programs related to it. Domestic programs are broadcast in Persian, Arabic, Turkmen, Kurdish, Azerbaijani, Assyrian, Armenian, Baluchi and Urdu. The foreign service, with short wave transmitters in Teheran and Kamalabad, is known as the Voice of Iran and reaches half of Europe and the whole of Asia and Africa.

Television was introduced in 1958 and is now operated by Vision of the Islamic Republic of Iran, which provides two national channels and also caters to local TV channels. The Ministry of Education owns one channel with three hours of telecasts of lectures a week for high school students. Color television was introduced in 1975. No license fee is required.

All films shown in Iran are subject to state censorship.

CULTURAL & ENVIRONMENTAL INDICATORS

Libraries (latest)
- Number: 507
- Volumes (millions): 3.332
- Registered borrowers (millions): 7.062
- Loans (/1,000 pop.): 77

Performing arts (pre-1986)
- Number of performances: 84

Nature reserves (latest)
- Number of facilities: 30

The largest library in Iran is the National Library at Teheran.

SOCIAL WELFARE

The government has a duty to provide every citizen with insurance benefits covering illness, unemployment and retirement.

Private social welfare agencies include The Red Lion and Sun Society, the Pahlavi Foundation, the Farah Pahlavi Charity Organization and the Imperial Organization for Social Services.

GLOSSARY

agha: title of respect and distinction conferred on a man in authority.

Aryamehr: literally, Light of the Aryans. Title conferred on Reza Shah by the Iranian parliament in 1965.

ayatollah: spiritual leader of the Shia Muslims in Iran.

bakhsh: subdivision of a *shahrestan*, corresponding to a district.

bigari: unpaid labor exacted from peasants or sharecroppers by landlords, now illegal.

dasht: a salt flat in the central plateau.

dehistan: a group of villages constituting a subdivision of a *bakhsh*.

dowreh: literally, a circle. Traditional discussion groups that function as the primary social unit outside the family.

Faqih: supreme spiritual leader under the 1979 Constitution.
farmandari kol: a governorate.
farsakh: traditional unit of linear measurement equal to 6.24 km. (3.88 mi.).
imam: (in the Shi'a branch of Islam) one of the 12 successors of Muhammad.
Jafari Doctrine: Official religious doctrine of Iran, from Jafar, the sixth *imam.*
kadkhoda: headman of a village, formerly the landlord's agent and now the state administrative official at the village level.
kavir: a salt crest in the central plateau.
maktab: an Islamic primary school, usually attached to a mosque.
Majlis: the lower house of Iranian parliament.
mujtahid: an authority on Islamic teachings and practices.
ostan: a province.
Pahlavi: dynastic name of the ruling house of Iran from 1925.
qanat: a shaft sunk to intercept an underground canal that taps ground water.
shahrestan: an administrative unit corresponding to a county.
tayefeh: a clan or group of related families.
urf: secular law.
White Revolution: comprehensive program of social, economic and political reforms initiated by the Shah in 1963.

CHRONOLOGY (from 1945)

1945— Iran joins U.N.
1946— British and Russian occupation troops leave Iran. . . . Ahmad Qavam al-Sultaneh becomes prime minister. . . . Azerbaijani dissidents establish independent republic; Iranian troops move into the province and put an end to the republic. . . . Nationalist Kurds rebel with Soviet encouragement; Kurdish republic of Mahabad is proclaimed; republic is suppressed by Iranian troops.
1947— Qavam resigns; Ibrahim Hakimi is appointed premier.
1948— Hakimi is succeeded by Abdul Hussein Hajir as premier; Hajir cabinet falls within months; Mohammad Maraghei Said is named premier.
1949— Constituent Assembly meets and ratifies amendment to the Constitution.
1950— Gen. Ali Razmara becomes premier. . . . Kurds revolt again.
1951— Razmara is assassinated; Hosein Ala becomes premier; Ala yields to Mohammad Mossadeq who enjoys Communist and right-wing support.
1952— Anglo-Iranian Oil Company is nationalized; relations with Great Britain are broken. . . . Shah dismisses Mossadeq and replaces him with Qavam but is forced to reinstate him; Mossadeq assumes absolute control over government.
1953— Mossadeq attempts to suppress political opposition, adopts increasingly repressive measures, loses support in the majlis, calls for referendum to abolish majlis and is dismissed by Shah; he defies dismissal and announces deposition of the Shah who flees the country; in a countercoup, Gen. Fazlollah Zahedi rallies army behind the Shah, arrests Mossadeq and supporters, assumes premiership; Shah returns to capital; Mossadeq is sentenced to three years of solitary confinement for treason.
1954— New oil agreement is reached with a consortium of western oil companies.
1955— Iran joins CENTO. . . . Zahedi resigns; Hosein Ala becomes new premier.
1957— Hosein Ala yields office to Manuchehr Eqbal.
1958— Television is introduced.
1960— Jafar Sharif Imami is named new premier. . . . Israel is recognized; Egypt breaks diplomatic relations over recognition.
1961— Imami resigns and Ali Amini becomes premier. . . . Pahlavi Foundation is established.
1962— Amini steps down and Asadollah Alam becomes premier.
1963— Shah launches "White revolution"; land reforms are approved by nationwide referendum; women are granted suffrage; Literacy Corps is organized.
1964— Iran joins the Regional Cooperation for Development (RCD) with Pakistan and Turkey as comembers. . . . Hasan Ali Mansur becomes premier.
1965— Mansur is assassinated and Amir Abbas Hovyeda becomes premier. . . . Majlis confers title of Aryamehr on the Shah.
1967— Coronation of the Shah held at Teheran.
1969— Dispute with Iraq over Shatt al-Arab erupts into open conflict.
1970— Iran accepts U.N. mediation on claim to Bahrain.
1971— 2,500th anniversary of the Persian monarchy is celebrated with pomp and splendor at Persepolis.
1973— Oil industry is nationalized; agreement with the Consortium is renegotiated to provide full ownership; Iran joins OPEC oil price hike.
1975— Rial's link with the dollar is broken; exchange rate is tied to the IMF Special Drawing Right. . . . Iran is declared a one-party state with the Restakhiz as the sole political party.
1976— Police gunfights with purported Marxist terrorists and guerrillas during the year result in the deaths of at least 25 guerrillas and the capture of many others.
1977— Premier Hoveida resigns at Shah's request and is replaced by Jamshid Amuzegar. . . . Maj. Gen. Ahmed Moqarrebi is executed after being convicted of spying for the USSR.
1978— Nationwide anti-Shah demonstrations and strikes, inspired by the exiled Ayatollah, Khomeini, paralyze the country. . . . Shah names Shahpur Bakhtiar as prime minister to conciliate the dissidents.
1979— Shah leaves the country; Khomeini returns from exile as Bahktiar is ousted. . . . An Islamic Republic

is proclaimed with Mehdi Bazargan as prime minister but Ayatollah Khomeini as the strongman; hundreds of pro-Shah officials and soldiers are executed by firing squads under orders of summary Islamic Revolutionary Courts; banks, insurance companies and key industries are nationalized; secessionist movements in Azerbaijan and Kurdish provinces are suppressed; national referendum approves new constitution establishing an Islamic government with Ayatollah Khomeini as Faqih or spiritual leader and with the president and prime minister as head of state and government respectively; Council of Guardians is established to monitor the Koranic acceptability of legislation; Islamic militants take over the U.S. embassy in Teheran and hold nearly 60 diplomatic personnel as captives; Iranian government sides with the militants; United States retaliates by freezing Iranian assets.

1980— Abolhassan Bani-Sadr is elected president under the new Constitution; in a two-stage election to parliament, the hard-line Islamic Republic Party gains absolute majority; Mohammed Ali Rajai is named prime minister; the Revolutionary Council disbands itself as the Bani-Sadr cabinet takes office. . . . The former Shah dies in Cairo after a long bout with cancer. . . . Iraq revokes the Shatt al-Arab agreements concluded with the former Imperial government of Iran and sends in troops to occupy territory that it had renounced under that agreement; Iran suffers early reversals and loses Khurramshahr. . . . U.S. attempt to rescue the hostages through a secret commando-style mission fails.

1981— The Muslim clergy accuse President Bani-Sadr of inept leadership. . . . Following long and torturous negotiations Iran releases U.S. embassy personnel in return for release of frozen Iranian assets in the United States. . . . Bani-Sadr is ousted as president. . . . Ayatollah Mohammad Hossein Beheshti, 4 government ministers, 6 deputy ministers, 27 majlis members and 34 others are killed in bomb explosion at Islamic Republican Party headquarters. . . . Prime minister Mohammad Ali Rajai is named president and Mohammad Javad Bahonar prime minister. . . . Rajai and Bahonar are killed in bomb blast. . . . Sayed Ali Khameini is named president and Mohammad Reza Mahdavi-Kani as prime minister. . . . Madhavi-Kani resigns and is succeeded in office by Mir Hosein Musavi-Khameini.

1983— Communist (Tudeh) Party is banned.

1984— In parliamentary elections, the clerical party retains control of the Islamic Consultative Assembly.

1985— Ali Khameini is reelected president. . . . Hussein Ali Montezeri is chosen as eventual successor to Ayatollah Khomeini.

1986— Iran begins the Wal-Fajr (Dawn) 8 offensive. The U.S. is reported to have been selling arms to Iran in exchange for Iranian assistance in releasing American hostages in Lebanon.

1987— The U.N. Security Council adopts Resolution 598, urging an immediate cease-fire between Iran and Iraq.

1988— Iran Air Airbus A300 B is accidentally shot down by the *USS Vincennes* over the Strait of Hormuz. Iran announces its acceptance of Resolution 598.

1989— Ayatollah Khomeini dies. Then-President Ali Khamenei is elected as Khomeini's successor. Rafsanjani is elected President.

1990— Iran and the United Kingdom restore diplomatic relations. The U.S. ends ban on imports of Iranian petroleum.

1991— Khamenei expresses hope for "an Islamic and truly popular government" in Iraq.

BIBLIOGRAPHY

BOOKS AND FILMS

Abdulghani, Jasim. *Iraq and Iran: The Years of Crisis.* Baltimore, MD, 1984.

Abrahamian, Ervand. *Iran Between Two Revolutions.* Princeton, NJ, 1982.

Afkhami, Ghulam R. *The Iranian Revolution: Thanatos on a National Scale.* Washington, D.C., 1985.

Ahmad, Ishtiag. *Anglo-Iranian Relations, 1905–1919.* New York, 1974.

Akhavi, Shahrough. *Religion and Politics in Contemporary Iran.* Albany, NY, 1980.

Albert, David H. *Tell the American People: Perspectives on the Iranian Revolution.* Berkeley, CA, 1984.

Amirsadeghi, Hossein. *Twentieth Century Iran.* New York, 1977.

Aresvik, Odduar. *Agricultural Development of Iran.* New York, 1976.

Armajani, Yahya. *Iran.* Englewood Cliffs, NJ, 1972.

Bakhash, Shaul. *The Politics of Oil and Revolution in Iran.* Washington, D.C., 1982.

Bashiriyeh, Hossein. *The State and Revolution in Iran.* New York, 1984.

Baraheni, Reza. *The Crowned Cannibals: Writings on Repression in Iran.* New York, 1977.

Batra, Ravi. *Muslim Civilization and the Crisis in Iran.* Dallas, TX, 1981.

Benham, Djamchid. *Cultural Policy in Iran.* New York, 1973.

Bharier, Julian. *Economic Development in Iran, 1900–1970.* New York, 1971.

Bill, James A. *The Politics of Iran: Groups, Classes, and Modernization.* Columbus, OH, 1972.

Bonine, Michael E. and Nikki R. Keddie. *Continuity and Change in Modern Iran.* Albany, NY, 1981.

Chubin, Shahram and Sepehr Zabih. *The Foreign Relations of Iran.* Berkeley, CA, 1975.

Cottam, Richard W. *Nationalism in Iran.* Pittsburgh, PA, 1979.

Cottrell, Alvin J., and James E. Dougherty. *Iran's Quest for Security: U.S. Arms Transfer and the Nuclear Option.* Cambridge, MA, 1977.

Farazmand, Ali. *The State, Bureaucracy, and Revolution in Modern Iran: Agrarian Reforms and Regime Politics.* New York, 1989.

Crisis in Iran. B&W film, 17 min. March of Time.

Fesharaki, Fereidun. *Development of the Iranian Oil Industry.* New York, 1976.

———. *Iran Almanac and Book of Facts.* New York, 1976.

Forbis, William H. *Fall of the Peacock Throne: The Story of Iran.* New York, 1980.

Ghirshman, R. *Iran.* New York, 1978.

Gitisetan, Dariush. *Iran: Politics and Government under the Pahlavis. An Annotated Bibliography.* Metuchen, NJ, 1985.

Graham, Robert. *Iran.* New York, 1978.

———. *Iran: The Illusion of Power.* New York, 1980.

Grayson, Benson. *United States-Iranian Revolution.* Baltimore, MD, 1981.

Halliday, Fred. *Iran: Dictatorship and Development.* New York, 1979.

Heikal, Mohamed. *Iran: The Untold Story.* New York, 1982.

Hickman, William F. *Ravaged and Reborn: The Iranian Military, 1979–1982.* Washington, D.C., 1983.

Hiro, Dilip. *Iran under the Ayatollahs.* Boston, 1985.

Hooglund, Eric J. *Land and Revolution in Iran, 1960–1980.* Austin, TX, 1982.

Hoveyda, Fereydour. *The Last Days of the Shah.* New York, 1980.

Inlow, E. Burke. *Shahanshah: A Study of the Monarchy of Iran.* Livingstone, NJ, 1979.

Iran. Color film, 22 min. Films, Inc.

Iran. Color film, 18 min. Producer: not available.

Iran: Between Two Worlds. Color/B&W film, 15 min. Encyclopaedia Britannica.

Iran: Landmarks in the Desert. Color film, 28 min. Centron Educational Films.

Iran: The Struggle to Industrialize. Color film, 17 min. ABC.

Irfani, Suroosh. *Iran's Islamic Revolution: Popular Liberation or Religious Dictatorship?* London, 1983.

Ismael, Tareq Y. *Iraq and Iran: Roots of Conflict.* Syracuse, NY, 1982.

Issawi, Charles. *The Economic History of Iran, 1800–1919.* Chicago, 1972.

Jazani, Bizhan. *Capitalism and Revolution in Iran.* New York, 1980.

Johnson, Gail. *High-Level Manpower in Iran: From Hidden Conflict to Crisis.* New York, 1980.

Kamrava, Mehran. *Revolution in Iran: the Roots of Turmoil.* New York, 1990.

Katouzina, Homa. *The Political Economy of Modern Iran: Despostism and Pseudo-Modernism 1926–1979.* New York, 1980.

Keddie, Nikki. *Iran: Religion Politics and Society.* Totowa, NJ, 1980.

——— and Eric Hooglund. *The Iranian Revolution and the Islamic Republic.* Boulder, CO, 1985.

——— and Yann Richard. *Roots of Revolution: An Interpretive History of Modern Iran.* New Haven, CT, 1981.

Kedourie, Elie, and Sylvia G. Haim. *Iran: Towards Modern Studies in Thought, Politics and Society.* Totowa, NJ, 1980.

Koury, Enver M. and Charles MacDonald. *Iran: A Reappraisal.* Hyattsville, MD, 1982.

Kuniholm, Bruce R. *Origins of the Cold War in the Middle East.* Princeton, NJ, 1980.

Lencowski, George C. *Iran Under the Pahlavis.* Stanford, CA, 1978.

Limbert, John W. *Iran.* Boulder, CO, 1985.

Looney, Robert E. *Economic Origins of the Iranian Revolution.* Elmsford, NY, 1981.

———, and Laina M. Farhat. *Iran at the End of the Century: A Hegelian Forecast.* Lexington, MA, 1977.

Nima, Ramy. *The Wrath of Allah: Islamic Revolution and Reaction in Iran.* New York, 1983.

Oil: The Story of Iran. B&W film, 14 min. Sterling Educational Films.

Pahlavi, Ashraf. *Faces in a Mirror.* Englewood Cliffs, NJ, 1980.

Peress, Gilles. *In the Name of the Revolution.* New York, 1984.

Ramazani, Rouhollah K. *Foreign Policy of Iran 1500–1941. A Developing Nation in World Affairs.* Charlottesville, VA, 1976.

———. *Iran's Foreign Policy, 1941–1973.* Charlottesville, VA, 1975.

———. *The Persian Gulf: Iran's Role.* Charlottesville, VA, 1972.

———. *The United States and Iran: The Patterns of Influence.* New York, 1982.

Roosevelt, Kermit. *Countercoup: Struggle for the Control of Iran.* New York, 1979.

Rubin, Barry. *Paved with Good Intentions: The American Experience in Iran.* New York, 1981.

Saibel, Bob. *Iran: A People in Revolution.* Chicago, IL, 1980.

Sansarian, Elizabeth. *Women's Rights Movement in Iran.* New York, 1982.

Stempel, John D. *Inside the Iranian Revolution.* Bloomington, IN, 1981.

Sullivan, William H. *Mission to Iran.* New York, 1981.

Tahir-Kheli. *The Iran-Iraq War: Old Conflicts: New Weapons.* New York, 1983.

United Nations University. *Aspects of the Iranian Revolution.* Tokyo, 1980.

Wead, R. Douglas. *The Iran Crisis.* Plainfield, NJ, 1980.

Wilbur, Donald. *Iran: Past and Present.* Princeton, NJ, 1975.

Wright, Robin B. *In the Name of God: the Khomeini Decade.* New York, 1989.

Yar-Shater, Ehsan. *Iran Faces the Seventies.* New York, 1971.

———. *Encyclopedia Iranica 3 vols.* London, 1983.

Zabih, Sepehr. *Iran Since the Revolution.* Baltimore, MD, 1982.

———. *Iran's Revolutionary Upheaval: An Interpretive Essay.* San Francisco, CA, 1979.

———. *The Mossadegh Era: Roots of the Iranian Revolution.* Chicago, IL, 1982.

Zoakas, C. *Who's Behind the Mad Khomeini?* Brooklyn, NY, 1980.

Zonis, Marvin. *Political Elite of Iran.* Princeton, NJ, 1971.

OFFICIAL PUBLICATIONS

Economic Affairs & Finance Ministry. *Liquidation Budget.*

Markazi Bank. *Annual Report & Balance Sheet.* (Persian and English)

Plan & Budget Organization. *Budget of the Government of Iran.* (Persian and English)

Social Insurance Organization. *Budget Estimates.*

Treasury. *Development Plan Credits and Payments.* (monthly)

———. *Retirement Funds Accounts.* (unpublished)

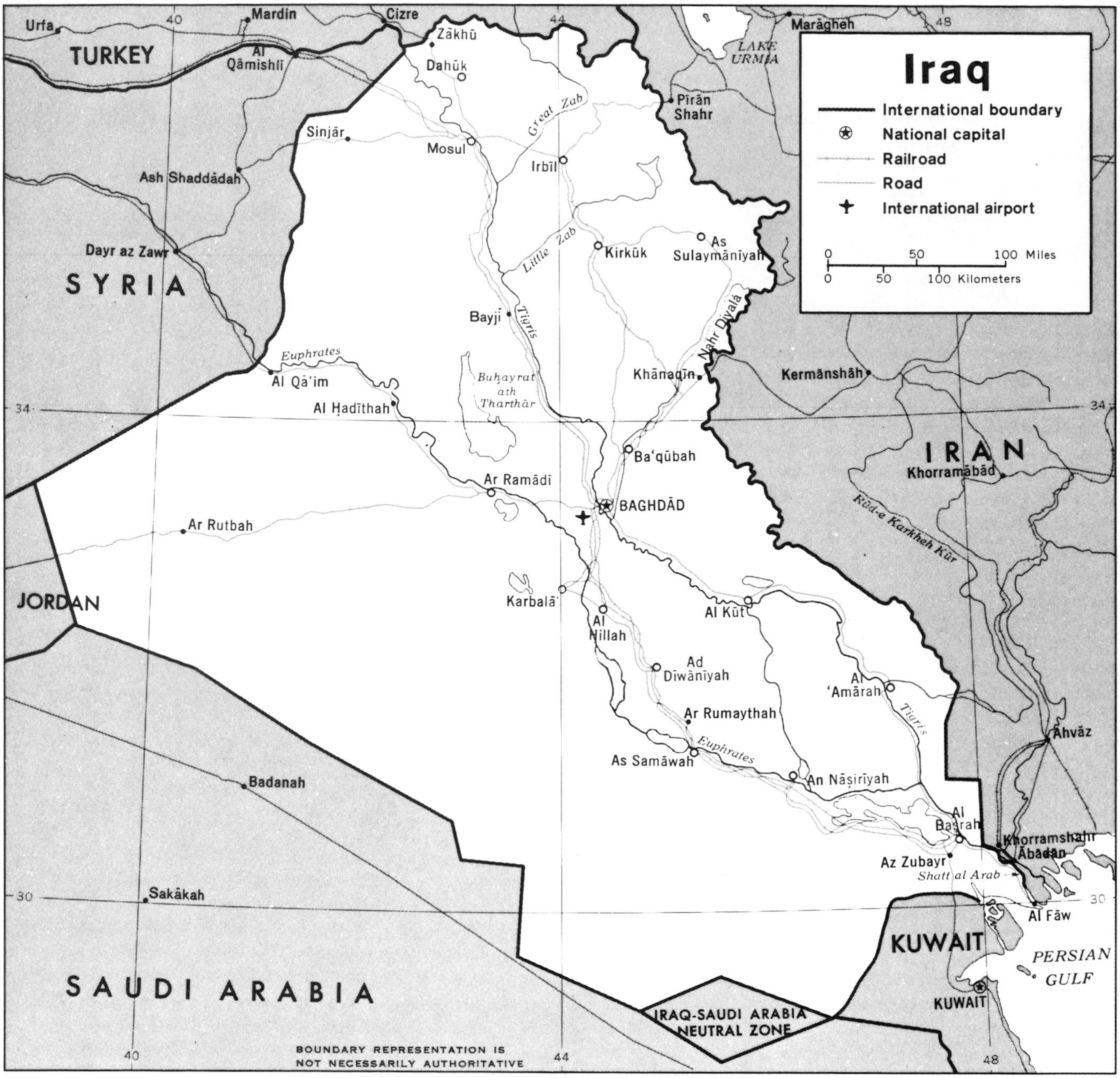
Iraq
International boundary
National capital
Railroad
Road
International airport
0 50 100 Miles
0 50 100 Kilometers
TURKEY
SYRIA
JORDAN
SAUDI ARABIA
IRAN
KUWAIT
PERSIAN GULF
IRAQ-SAUDI ARABIA NEUTRAL ZONE
Urfa
Mardin
Cizre
Al Qāmishlī
Zākhū
Dahūk
Sinjār
Mosul
Irbīl
Great Zab
Little Zab
Ash Shaddādah
Dayr az Zawr
Kirkūk
As Sulaymānīyah
Pīrān Shahr
Marāgheh
LAKE URMIA
Bayjī
Tigris
Euphrates
Al Qā'im
Al Ḥadīthah
Buḥayrat ath Tharthār
Khānaqīn
Nahr Diyālā
Kermānshāh
Ba'qūbah
Ar Ramādī
BAGHDĀD
Ar Rutbah
Khorramābād
Rūd-e Karkheh Kūr
Karbalā'
Al Ḥillah
Al Kūt
Ad Dīwānīyah
Al 'Amārah
Ar Rumaythah
As Samāwah
An Nāṣirīyah
Ahvāz
Al Baṣrah
Khorramshahr
Ābādān
Az Zubayr
Shatt al Arab
Al Fāw
Badanah
Sakākah
KUWAIT
40
44
48
34
30
BOUNDARY REPRESENTATION IS NOT NECESSARILY AUTHORITATIVE

الجمهورية العراقية

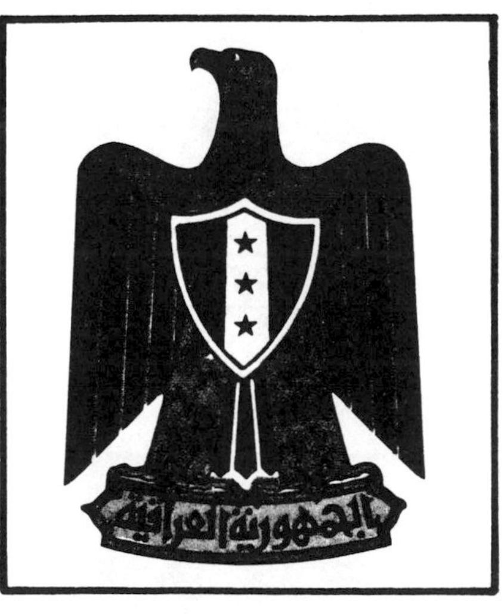

IRAQ

BASIC FACT SHEET

OFFICIAL NAME: Republic of Iraq (Al Jumhouriiyya al-Iraqiyya)

ABBREVIATION: IQ

CAPITAL: Baghdad

HEAD OF STATE & HEAD OF GOVERNMENT President, Prime Minister and Chairman of the Revolutionary Command Council Saddam Hussein Abd-al-Majid al-Tikriti (from 1979)

NATURE OF GOVERNMENT: Military dictatorship

POPULATION 18,781,770 (July 1990)

AREA: 438,446 sq. km. (169,284 sq. mi.)

ETHNIC MAJORITY: Arabs

LANGUAGE: Arabic

RELIGION: Islam

UNIT OF CURRENCY: Iraqi Dinar ($1 = DO.311, August, 1985)

NATIONAL FLAG: Tricolor of red, white and black horizontal stripes with three five-pointed stars in green in the center of the white stripe.

NATIONAL EMBLEM: An Arab eagle with a shield engraved on its breast with red, white and black stripes running vertically and green stars placed vertically on the center white stripe. It stands on a base on which is written, in Kufi Arabic script, "Republic of Iraq."

NATIONAL ANTHEM: "Hymn of the Republic"

NATIONAL HOLIDAYS: July 14 (National Day, Republic Day); January 1; January 6 (Army Day); February 8 (Baathist Revolution Day); May 1 (Labor Day); July 17 (Peaceful Revolution Day); Also variable Islamic festivals.

NATIONAL CALENDAR: Islamic and Gregorian

PHYSICAL QUALITY OF LIFE INDEX: 62

DATE OF INDEPENDENCE: 1932

DATE OF CONSTITUTION: 1958 (As amended in 1964, 1968 and 1972)

WEIGHTS & MEASURES: The metric system prevails except for *meshara* or *dunum,* a unit of land measurement equal to 2,500 sq. m. (0.62 ac.).

GEOGRAPHICAL FEATURES

Iraq is situated in the Fertile Crescent of West Asia and has an area of 438,446 sq. km. (169,284 sq. mi.). The greatest distance south-southeast to north-northwest is 984 km. (611 mi.) and east-northeast to west-southwest 730 km. (454 mi.). The coastline on the Persian Gulf runs 19 km. (12 mi.). Iraq has international boundaries with six countries with a total length of 3,719 km. (2,311 mi.), of which the longest is with Iran (1,515 km., 941 mi.). The other boundaries are with Turkey (305 km., 190 mi.), Kuwait (254 km., 158 mi.), Saudi Arabia (895 km., 556 mi), Jordan (147 km., 91 mi.) and Syria (603 km., 375 mi.). The boundary dispute with Iran was settled in 1975 by restoring the border to the Thalweg Line in the middle of the channel in the Shatt al-Arab estuary. The rhomboidal Neutral Zone with Saudi Arabia has no clearly demarcated boundaries.

The capital is Baghdad, the historic center of the country, with a 1977 population of 3,236,000, or 24% of the country's total population. The other major urban centers are Basra, in the south, and Mosul, in the north, both of which have populations over one million.

The country is divided into four main topographical regions. The north eastern highlands are dominated by the Zagros Mountains rising to 3,650 m. (12,000 ft.) near the Iranian and Turkish borders. This region is the homeland of the Iraqi Kurds and the site of the major oil fields. The upland between the Tigris north of Samarra and the Euphrates north of Hit is known as Al Jazirah. Much of this region is desert. Southeast of Baghdad the Euphrates and the Tigris meander through a broad, flat delta interlaced by numerous irrigation channels and shallow lakes fed by the rivers in flood. A large area just above the confluence of the two rivers at Qurnah is a permanent marshland. In the south and west are extensive and barren sandy and rocky deserts, part of the great Arabian and Syrian deserts. This desert constitutes 38% of the total land area.

Both the Euphrates and the Tigris have defined the location and growth of human settlements in Iraq. The Euphrates (2,350 km., 1,460 mi.) rises in Turkey and first flows through Syria and enters Iraq in the northwest. The Tigris (1,850 km., 1,150 mi.) also rises in Turkey and is joined by large and numerous tributaries, among them the Khabur, the Great Zab, the Little Zab and the Uzaym, before joining the Euphrates at Qurnah to form the Shatt al-Arab which flows 185 km. (115 mi.) into the Persian Gulf. In many places the stream beds, being higher than the surrounding flood plains, must be contained by levees. Both the rivers often change their courses. Navigation is difficult in the middle and upper reaches, and the rivers are not significant traffic routes. They have no hydroelectric potential. Highwater periods extend from March through June, when the snows melt in the spring in the Armenian Plateau. Floods of up to 10 m. (33 ft.) are not uncommon and vast stretches of villages and roads are regularly inundated. Irrigation and periodic flooding cause large quantities of silty loam to be deposited in the delta area. Facilities along both rivers were heavily damaged in the Persian Gulf War of 1991.

CLIMATE & WEATHER

Iraq has hot, dry summers lasting from May to October and cold winters from December to March. Temperatures in the summer often go over 49° C (120° F) especially during July and August. The mean minimum temperatures in the summer range from 22° C (72° F) to 28° C (82° F), with the lower end of the scale prevailing in Mosul and the upper end in Basra. Mean minimum temperatures in the winter range from −14° C (6° F) at Rutbah in the western desert to 4.4° D (40° F) in the plains, while mean winter maximums range from 10° C (50° F) in the west and northeast to 15.6° C (60° F) in the south.

Most of the rainfall occurs from December through March. Mean annual rainfall ranges between 102 mm. (4 in.) to 178 mm. (7 in.) in the cultivable areas of the south. Rainfall is more abundant in the mountains, where it may reach 1,000 mm. (40 in.) annually. The foothills and steppes receive no more than 380 mm. (15 in.) a year.

The prevailing winds are the northwesterly *shamal*, a dry, cool wind, and the southeasterly *sharqi*, or *sirocco*, a dry, dusty wind that may last for several days and is often accompanied by duststorms.

POPULATION

The population of Iraq in 1990 was estimated at 18,781,770 on the basis of the last official census held in 1977 when the population was 1,200,497. Over 75% of this population lives in the flood plains that constitute only 25% of the land area. The area of maximum population concentration lies in the center of the country defined by the Euphrates, Tigris and Diyala Rivers. The distribution of human settlements in this area has been determined for centuries by changes in the course of the rivers and the productivity of the land.

There are significant variations in density not only between settled and desert areas but also within provinces. Some subdistricts of Diyala Province have an average density of 5 per sq. km. (12.9 per sq. mi.), while other subdistricts in the same province have a density of 647 per sq. km. (1,675 per sq. mi.). Baghdad Province has the highest density (691 per sq. km., 1,789 per sq. mi.), while Ramadi Province has the lowest (15 per sq. km., 38.8 per sq. mi.).

Migration is not significant as a demographic factor in Iraq. An undetermined number of Arab Beduin nomads who are not included in census tabulations live in the mountains and in the vast deserts south and southwest of the Euphrates. They annually cross the borders without let or hindrance into Syria, Jordan and Saudi Arabia. Emigration is negligible and is limited to young men who go to Kuwait to find employment in the oil fields.

Since its founding outside Iraq in 1947, the Ba'ath Party has been committed to the equality of the sexes. The Ba'ath Party's Ninth Party Congress report of 1983 reiterated that the emancipation of women is a "natural and human right," and an "essential condition for economic, social, and cultural development." A series of laws since the Ba'ath Party came to power in 1968 has steadily improved the status of women. Such laws have protected women from exploitation in the workplace; granted subsidized maternity leave; permitted

DEMOGRAPHIC INDICATORS

Population (millions): 18.781 (1990)
Year of last census: 1987
Sex distribution (% at last census): males, 51.5; females, 48.5
Population estimates and projections (millions)

1940: 3.745	1970: 9.356	2000: 24.023
1950: 5.180	1980: 13.043	2010: 30.932
1960: 6.847	1990: 17.754	

Age profile (% at 1977 census)

0–14: 48.9	30–44: 12.3	60–74: 4.2
15–29: 24.5	45–59: 8.2	75 and over: 1.9

Median age (yrs.): 16.5
Youth population (% age 15–24): 19.0 (1985); 20.2 (2000)
Total dependency ratio: 98.4 (1985)
Annual growth rate (%)

1950–55: 2.72	1975–80: 3.75	2000–2005: 3.05
1955–60: 2.94	1980–85: 3.58	2005–2010: 2.82
1960–65: 3.05	1985–90: 3.48	2010–2015: 2.57
1965–70: 3.19	1990–1995: 3.39	2015–2020: 2.30
1970–75: 3.27	1995–2000: 3.23	2020–2025: 2.07

Hypothetical size of stationary population (millions): 90
Assumed year of reaching net reproduction rate of 1: 2035
Urban population (millions): 11.228 (1985)
Urban population (%): 73 (1988); 51 (1965)
Annual urban population growth rate (%, 1985–90): 4.46
Annual rural population growth rate (%, 1985–90): 0.90
Percentage of urban population in largest city: 55 (1980)
Percentage of urban population in cities of population over 500,000: 70 (1980)
Number of cities of population over 500,000: 3 (1980)
Population density per sq. km. (per sq. mi.): 40.8 (105.7) (latest)

VITAL STATISTICS

Crude birth rate (/1,000): 46 (1990); 49 (1965)
Crude death rate (/1,000): 7 (1990): 18 (1965)
Infant mortality rate (/1,000 live births): 67 (1990)
Life expectancy (yrs.) at birth: males, 66; females, 68 (1990)
Gross reproduction rate (/woman) (1980–85): 3.25
Total fertility rate (/woman): 7.3 (1990)
Rate of natural increase (/1,000): 37.0 (1989)
Marriage rate (/1,000): 4.0 (1982)
Average household size: 6.9 (latest)

STATUS OF WOMEN INDICATORS

Number of women (millions): 7.623 (1985)
Women of childbearing age (15–49) (% of pop.): 44 (1988)
Women's literacy rate (%): 26 (1989)
Women in labor force (%): 4 (1985)
Total fertility rate (/woman): 7.3 (1990)
Women in national legislatures (%): 6 (1984)

women to join the regular army, Popular Army and police forces; and equalized women's rights on divorce, land ownership, taxation, suffrage and election to the National Assembly. In the 1970s, the government imposed legal penalties on families who opposed sending their women to literacy schools, and on men who were seen harassing women.

Women represent about 47% of agricultural workers and about 25% of the total work force. They account for about one-third of the professionals in education and health care. In 1984 elections for the National Assembly, 32% of the seats were won by female candidates. The war with Iran from 1980–88 accelerated the government's drive to elevate the status of women, and some Iraqis believe that it has permanently broken cultural barriers to acceptance of women in traditional male roles. With official encouragement, women have become increasingly visible as architects, construction engineers, oil engineers, air traffic controllers, factory and farm managers, and Air Force pilots. Some 40,000 women reportedly were volunteers in the Popular Army in 1982.

The General Federation of Iraqi Women (GFIW) was established in 1969, the regime's first year in power, to promote the government's policies toward women. Membership in the GFIW does not require affiliation with the Ba'ath Party. The GFIW organizes conferences on women's issues, establishes training courses for women, implements programs to eradicate illiteracy, undertakes civilian war relief activities and administers nurseries. It drew up a four-year plan (1983–86) to encourage women to work outside the home, and has opened four employment offices in Baghdad for women graduates.

The government does not officially sponsor or encourage birth control programs, partly because of religious sentiments and partly because it does not consider Iraq's population excessive in relation to its physical size.

ETHNIC COMPOSITION

Ethnicity is defined in Iraq, as in other Middle Eastern countries, by religion, language and race, with these distinctions coinciding in some cases but not in others. Arabs constitute about 80% of the population. Within the Arab group are two relatively unassimilated ethnic groups: the Beduins, the nomads of the desert, and the sedentary Marsh Arabs, or Madans, of the lower Tigris and Euphrates Delta. The Kurds, the largest ethnic minority, comprise at least 15% of the population and live in the northern mountains where they retain their tribal organization. Intermittent efforts by these fiercely independent peoples to wrest some measure of autonomy from the central government at Baghdad have resulted in inconclusive civil wars followed by truces. The 1958 Constitution declared that Iraq was composed of two nationalities, Arab and Kurd, and Kurdish was made a co-official language and medium of instruction in Kurdish areas. Iraqi Kurds are divided into three groups: the Badinan, the Suran and the Baban. Although nomads by tradition, the majority of the Kurds are now settled agriculturalists or herdsmen but increasing numbers have moved to cities such as Mosul, Kirkuk, Sulaimanya and Baghdad.

Smaller ethnic minorities account for less than 5% of the population. They include Turkomans, Persians, Lurs, Assyrians, Armenians, Yazidis, Shabaks, Sabaeans (or Mandaeans) and Sarliyahs. The once prosperous Jewish community, numbering over 100,000 in the 1930s, has now dwindled to around 2,500.

Certain ethnic and religious groups within Iraq traditionally reside in particular areas of the country. Kurds, for example, have strong roots in the north. The government has sometimes tried to force changes in settlement patterns. Mass relocations of Kurds took place in the mid-1970s. More recently families and villages of the Barzani tribe were forcibly resettled following the participation by tribe leaders and members in Iran's 1983 invasion of northern Iraq.

Over 30,000 Iranians and Iraqis of alleged Iranian descent were summarily expelled to Iran in April 1980 and tens of thousands more were reported expelled subsequently. While such deportations have ceased, those remaining live under the fear of deportation or incarceration. Many "Iranian" families have been in Iraq for generations. Some say their forebears were not from Iran but claimed the nationality to evade Ottoman military conscription. Citizens considered to be of Iranian origin bear special identification, which often precludes desirable employment or impedes advancement.

In the mid-1970s there were an estimated 30,000 alien residents in Iraq, of whom about 40% were Iranians and the balance mostly Jordanians, Syrians and Pakistanis. In the late 1980s an economic development program lured laborers from other Arab countries. There are only negligible numbers of Westerners in the country, most of them resident in Kirkuk and Baghdad.

In terms of ethnic and linguistic homogeneity, Iraq ranks 66th among the nations of the world with 64% homogeneity (on an ascending scale in which North and South Korea are ranked 135th with 100% homogeneity and Tanzania first with 7% homogeneity).

Iraqis have a long tradition of hostility toward Westerners dating back to the Crusades. This hostility was reinforced by two decades of British rule and Western support for the state of Israel. The Gulf War of 1991 against an American-led allied coalition exacerbated this hostility.

LANGUAGE

Arabic is the official language of Iraq and the mother tongue of about four-fifths of the people. As in other Middle Eastern countries, Arabic exists in three forms. The classical Arabic is used for religious purposes; Modern Standard Arabic is used for writing and in the media, political communication and education; and spoken Arabic, described as the Mesopotamian dialect with its two subdialects, *qeltu* and *gelet*, is used by the common people.

Kurdish, a co-official language since 1966, is spoken by 16% of the population including Kurds, Shabaks, Sarliyahs and Yezidis. Kurdish exists in two dialects, Kurdi and Kermanji. Aramaic, the pre-Islamic language of Mesopotamia, still survives in speech islands among the Assyrians and as the liturgical language of the Chaldeans and the Jacobites. An Aramaic dialect is the sacred language of the Mandaeans. Some of the smaller ethnic groups retain their own vernaculars, although using Arabic for intergroup communication. These vernaculars include Turkmanic, Lur, Persian and Armenian.

French is the official second language, although English is the most common European language used by the educated elite. English is employed in institutions of higher learning and in scientific publications.

As part of its general Arabization policies, the government favors the use of Arabic to the exclusion of all other languages.

RELIGION

Islam is the state religion, adhered to by about 95% of the population, including Arabs, Kurds, Lurs and Turkomans. But Islam, far from being a monolithic structure, is deeply divided between the Sunnis and the Shi'as. Iraq is the only Arab country in which Shi'as form a majority of the population. With the addition of non-Arabs, such as Turkomans, Iranians and others, the Shi'as comprise about 65% of the population; among the Arabs themselves they constitute from two-thirds to three-fourths. Most Shi'as are farmers, and few have achieved prominence in national life. The Sunnis, with a higher literacy rate than the Shi'as, dominate the government and the bureaucracy. Almost all the members of the revolutionary governments since 1958 have been Sunnis. The non-Arab Kurds are also Sunnis, although their religious practices differ in some respects from those of the Arab Sunnis.

The position of the non-Muslim minorities has always been a precarious one.

Iraq is an ethnically and religiously diverse society. Many non-Muslims, principally Jews and Christians, left Iraq under previous regimes. Members of religious minorities have expressed fear that they would again face persecution if Iran were to impose an Islamic regime in Baghdad. Ba'athism emphasizes the importance of secular government, but it is an anti-Communist ideology which acknowledges the central role of religion in Arab culture. Since its rise to power in 1968, the Ba'athist government has enforced tolerance of religious diversity, seeking to submerge religious differences in the promotion of secular nationalism. However, the government also works to unify the populace by attempting to hasten cultural assimilation. In some past instances, this has taken the form of trying to wean groups away from aspects of their cultural traditions, ethnic identities, and ways of life. The Sunni Muslim-dominated government has relaxed implementation of this policy in most cases, and has more actively sought the support of ethnic and religious minorities and the underrepresented Shi'ite majority. President Hussein has included Christians and Shi'as in his ruling circles in pursuit of this policy.

A 1981 law gave the Ministry of Endowments and Religious Affairs the authority to promulgate laws and regulations governing places of worship, appointment of clergy, religious literature, and participation in religious councils and meetings. However, while the government has assumed much greater authority in Islamic religious affairs since 1981, the law has not been invoked against Iraq's Christian sects. Religious leaders operate under close government supervision. Muslim leaders are considered government employees and receive their salaries through the government. The government administers the principal Muslim shrines and mosques and has increased allotments to refurbish and maintain them in an apparent attempt to win support from the devout.

The Shi'a, who make up roughly three-fifths of the population, historically have been economically, politically and socially disadvantaged. The government has a declared policy to raise their living standards and equalize opportunities for economic and professional advancement. In recent years, the government and party have promoted Shi'a into prominent positions, and the economic and social status of the Shi'a has improved markedly. Nevertheless, the government maintains a close watch against Iranian attempts to exploit dissatisfaction among Iraqi Shi'a, who share the same branch of Islam prevalent in Iran. Inspired by Iran, the Shi'a, concentrated in southern Iraq, took advantage of the confusion caused by Iraq's defeat in the Gulf War of 1991 and undertook a largescale rebellion. The central government, however, retained enough resources to ruthlessly crush the uprising.

Christians constitute about 3% of the population. Their freedom of worship in churches of established denominations is legally protected, but they are not permitted to proselytize or to hold meetings outside church premises. Convents and monasteries exist and some new churches are constructed, in some cases with government financial support. Although Christians sometimes allege discrimination in education and jobs, adherence to their religion has not prevented many from obtaining wealth and professional advancement. Tariq 'Aziz, the deputy prime minister and, until 1991 the foreign minister, a Chaldean Christian, represented Iraq at the meeting of foreign ministers of the Organization of the Islamic Conference. Other Christians hold important official and private positions. Many are successful business people. Christians are divided into a number of denominations, of whom the principal ones are: the Chaldean Church, formerly Nestorian and now Uniate, with a patriarch at Mosul; the Monophysite Orthodox Syrian, or Jacobite Church; the Gregorian Armenian Church; the Nestorian Assyrian Church; the Uniate Syrian and Armenian Churches; and Latin Catholic and Protestant Churches. Christians live in widely scattered localities with a major concentration in Mosul.

Though insignificant in numbers, three other religious groups add to the religious diversity of the country. The Yazidis are a Kurdish-speaking group calling themselves Dasnayi. They have achieved some notoriety as devil-worshipers since their rites propitiate satan in the form of a peacock. The Sabaeans or Mandaeans, also known as Christians of St. John, follow an eclectric creed borrowed from many religions. Since their tenets stress regular immersion in water they always dwell near river banks. They also have a reputation as silversmiths. The Jews, who once dominated the professions and commerce, have all but disappeared under the pressures of the Arab-Israeli conflict.

HISTORICAL BACKGROUND

Muslim armies from Arabia conquered the area of modern Iraq in 637 A.D. and converted most of the population to Islam. Absorbed by the Ottoman Sultan Sulayman in 1534, Iraq remained part of the Ottoman Empire until the end of World War I.

England established a consulate in Baghdad in 1802, and wielded considerable influence throughout the 19th century. In the First World War, when the Ottoman Empire sided with Germany, the British occupied much of southern Iraq, including Basra and Baghdad. A nationalist movement blossomed during and after the war, but the San Remo Conference of 1920 made Iraq a British mandate, with virtual colonial status. In August 1921 Amir Faisal ibn Ausayn, son of a Mecca royal figure, became King of Iraq.

Over nationalist opposition, an Anglo-Iraqi treaty was signed in October 1922, and renewed in 1930. In 1932, the mandate ended and Iraq entered the League of Nations.

Relations with England deteriorated in the 1930s, largely because of what was perceived as Britain's pro-Zionist position. German influence increased, notably through the fascist officers' group, Golden Square. A military coup in 1941 led to a brief pro-Nazi regime, but English forces occupied Basra and Baghdad in May 1941, holding those areas until the end of the war. Cooperating with the Allies, Iraq declared war on the Axis powers in 1943.

Iraq's post-World War II history has been marked by nationalism, pan-Arabism, efforts to expand territorially and a variety of domestic factors. These include almost constant conflict between the central government and the Kurds in the north, attempts to secure and enlarge petroleum exports, the mainstay of the economy, and autocratic, centralized governments. Nuri as-Said, a corrupt, pro-British prime minister, governed from 1945 to 1958. He was swept aside by a growing, educated, nationalist elite component. Nuri and the Royal family were assassinated in July 1958.

The new government was headed by the Free Officers under General Abd al-Karim al-Qasim. But a split arose between nationalists who backed Egyptian leader Gamal Nasser's pan-Arabism and Communists who opposed it. In a February 1963 coup, nationalists and pan-Arab Ba'athists took control, and violently purged the left. They also undertook a five-year campaign against Kurdish separatists. Another coup in July 1968 by Ba'athist officers led by Ahmed Hasan al-Bakr turned towards the Soviet Union, due partly to U.S. support of Israel in 1967.

The Kurds, under General Mustafa al-Barzani, resisted most Baghdad governments from 1945 to 1965, and, with Iranian help, were intermittently in revolt from 1961 to 1975. A 1970 settlement which included Kurdish autonomy broke down over the distribution of petroleum revenue and the exclusion of Kirkuk from Kurdistan.

In July 1979 Bakr resigned from both party and government offices. He was succeeded by Saddam Hussein who had generally been considered the strongman of the regime. Hussein launched an invasion of Iran in September 1980, beginning a war which dominated Iraqi life through 1988. Among the reasons for the conflict were the climate of confusion in Tehran in the wake of the Islamic revolution and the perceived weakness in Iran's recently purged army. Iraq also attacked as a response to Iran's announced goal of exporting its revolution.

The war was intended as a short campaign which would wrest territory from Iran, giving Iraq, among other things, increased access to the Persian Gulf. But it became a devastating eight-year conflict, causing about one million casualties on each side. Early Iraqi incursions were halted, and Iran was on the offensive for most of the war. By 1988 Iraq regained the momentum, and in the summer of that year Iran agreed to a U.N. cease-fire, although permanent peace was not established until 1991. In the end, Iraq gained no territory and was left with a $60 billion war debt.

Within the Arab world, Jordan, Kuwait and eventually Egypt were Iraq's chief allies and suppliers in the war. Beginning in 1984, the U.S. and Soviet Union, both officially neutral, began supporting Iraq. By late 1987, the Soviets had given Iraq an estimated $10 billion in military aid. Restoring diplomatic ties with Baghdad after a 17-year lapse, the Americans gave funds for construction of petroleum pipelines and commodity credits totaling $2.5 billion.

Kurdish forces cooperated with Iran during the war. At one point they claimed to control a liberated zone of 10,000 square miles. But, in a development to be repeated at the end of the Gulf War of 1991, Hussein cracked down on Kurdish aspirations as the Iranian war wound down. Government counter-attacks in 1988, which included the use of chemical weapons, crushed Kurdish guerillas and forced nearly 100,000 to flee to Turkey and Iran.

Domestically, the war hurt Iraq in several ways. The disruption in Gulf oil exports reversed an economic upsurge of the 1970's due largely to petroleum sales. To retain some exporting capacity, the government undertook such projects as expanding an existing oil pipeline through Turkey and constructing two pipelines through Saudi Arabia. Austerity measures were enacted and much expenditure was channelled to war costs.

Iraq invaded and conquered Kuwait on August 2, 1990, touching off a series of events that would have major ramifications for the country. Eventually these would include largescale destruction of the Iraqi infrastructure, revolts by both the Kurds in the north and the Shi'a in the south, and the surprising survival of the Hussein regime.

The invasion of the tiny emirate seems to have been motivated by an array of factors, which in retrospect included miscalculations of international response. President Hussein was angry at Kuwait's refusal to forgive the multi-billion dollar debt Iraq ran up during the Iranian war. He also apparently hoped to turn Iraq into a regional superpower with economic might to match its military clout. Iraq and Kuwait together would control 20% of the world's oil supply.

Led by the U.S., much of the world community, under the aegis of the U.N., responded quickly to the invasion. Originally intended as a defense against a possible Iraqi move on the oil fields of Saudi Arabia, the Allies by January 1991 had an offensive force of about 500,000 troops and 2,000 tanks stationed in the region. While the U.S. accounted for the bulk of the force, 28 countries participated. These included the major Western nations and Egypt, Syria, Morrocco, Saudi Arabia, Bahrain and the United Arab Emirates.

On August 8, Hussein decreed the annexation of Kuwait as Iraq's 19th province and stationed large portions of the army there. He also used Western citizens trapped in Iraq and Kuwait as hostages against possible allied attacks. Perhaps 2,000 such people were held as "human shields" at vital installations, although all foreigners were permitted to leave by December. Hussein's effort to link occupation of Kuwait with Israeli occupation of the West Bank and Gaza drew some support in the Arab world, notably in Jordan. Diplomatic efforts to solve the crisis floundered, mostly because Iraq would not leave Kuwait.

From August to November 1990, the U.N., at the behest of the U.S., passed a series of resolutions aimed at achieving the withdrawal of Iraqi forces from Kuwait. Among these were strict economic sanctions against the Baghdad regime. On November 29, the Security Council authorized the use of force after January 15, 1991 to evict Iraqi forces from Kuwait.

The Allies launched an air war against Iraq and occupied Kuwait on January 16–17. Before the war ended on February 28, about 110,000 missions were flown, dropping 88,500 tons of munitions. Among the types of facilities destroyed were military, petroleum, industrial, transportation, communcations, power and water. A U.N. survey conducted in the immediate aftermath of the war called the damage "near apocalyptic." It was estimated that it would take 15 years and billions of dollars to rebuild the Iraqi infrastructure. There were also thousands of civilian casualties.

The Iraqi military was overwhelmed. Its major response was Scud, surface-to-surface, missile attacks against Saudi Arabia and Israel, launched at the latter in an attempt to pry the Arab members away from the coalition. While Iraq launched a total of 72 Scuds, most were destroyed by American anti-missiles, and those that fell caused little damage. They also failed to draw Israel into the conflict.

From February 24 to 28, the Allies launched a major ground offensive which succeeded in forcing Iraqi troops to retreat from Kuwait. The Allies also drove deep into central Iraq and destroyed several divisions of the Republican Guard, the elite units. On April 6 Iraq accepted formal U.N. peace terms. These included the payment of reparations to Kuwait and the Allies, as well as supervised destruction of chemical, biological and nuclear weapons.

Uprisings by Kurds and Shi'a began within days of the Allied victory. In the south, Shi'a fighters had the initial edge in Basra, Najaf and Karbala, but troops loyal to Hussein crushed the rebellion by mid-March. Kurdish guerillas claimed by March 13 that they controlled three-fourths of Kurdistan with 90,000 soldiers. But government forces successfully counter-attacked, and by early April hundreds of thousands of Kurds were in flight to Turkey and Iran. The Allies and then the U.N. set up "safe zones" for Kurds in the north. By early June 1991, despite much friction, the refugees seemed to be returning.

Internally, Hussein made certain moves following the defeat by the Allies to preserve the regime. These included promises of democratic reforms and the appointment as Premier of Saddun Hammadi, a Shiite who served as foreign minister from 1974 to 1981. Beyond that, the President fell back on his usual policy of placing relatives in key posts. His cousin, Ali Hassan al-Majid, was made Interior Minister and Hussein Kamel al-Majid, the President's son-in-law, took over as Minister of Defense.

Threats to Hussein's power, it seemed, might only come from outside. The rebuilding process following the Gulf War is enormous, and when oil exportation resumes, Iraq must give a substantial portion of the proceeds to a U.N.-mandated reparations fund. Damaged relationships with former creditors, especially Kuwait and Saudi Arabia, will make it difficult to secure loans for reconstruction. Those factors could serve to destabilize Hussein's hold on the Ba'ath party.

CONSTITUTION & GOVERNMENT

The basis of Iraqi government is the Constitution of 1958 as amended in 1964, 1968 and 1972. The Constitution defines Iraq as a popular, democratic and Islamic state founded on socialism. The supreme authority in the state is vested in the Council of Command of the Revolution, which legislates by decree. In early 1991, the Council, chaired by Hussein, had eight members. In 1973 President Ahmed al-Bakr announced a National Charter that envisaged the establishment of a national legislature and local governing councils.

Under Saddam Hussein the presidency has become the locus of power with all the principal state offices being held by him. Since taking power in 1979, Hussein has usually held the posts of president and head of state, prime minister, defense minister, commander-in-chief, chairman of the Revolutionary Command Council and secretary-general of the ruling Ba'ath Party. Under the Constitution the president and the vice president are elected by a two-thirds majority of the Revolutionary Command Council (RCC). The president appoints and removes—at his own discretion—the prime minister and members of the cabinet who constitute the council of ministers. He may also rule by decree with the nominal consent of the Council of Ministers and proclaim a state of emergency in case of actual or probable threat to national security.

The responsibility for the formulation and implementation of executive policies is vested in the Council of Ministers. Each ministry consists of a number of directorates general subdivided into sections. All officials above the rank of an undersecretary are directly appointed by the president.

In theory, legislative power is shared between the RCC and the National Assembly. However, the Assembly has no real power. Official duties of the Assembly include ratification of the budget and international treaties; the right to question and relieve any cabinet minister of his post; the debate of domestic and foreign policies; the proposal and enactment of laws; and the supervision of state institutions.

Iraq, like Syria, was long a byword in the Middle East for political instability. Cabinets are reshuffled regularly, but none are based on true parliamentary representation. During the same period the country has suffered four successful coups and a number of unsuccessful ones. As of June 1991, Hussein's Ba'athist regime faced few internal threats. The government's survival of the crushing defeat in the Gulf War of 1991 was a testament to its durability. The only other political group permitted to operate is the Communist Party but its activities are closely watched. It belongs to the National Progressive Front but has few members in the cabinet and none on the Revolutionary Command Council. Local communists who step out of line are executed. There have been no coup attempts since 1973. The army is an exclusively Ba'ath preserve.

The real source of stability in Iraq is not so much ideology (although pan-Arabism is officially touted as one) but an alliance formed between officers and civilians who are linked by ties of blood or locality. This phenomenon may best be described in the nickname, the "Tikriti Gang" which has been given to the Ba'athist regime. Tikrit is a small town, about 100 miles north of Baghdad; it is the birthplace of the former President al-Bakr, and the present President Saddam Hussein al-Tikriti. The Tikriti faction has its own internal quarrels (in 1970 Vice President Hardan al-Tikriti attempted a coup, but failed and was later murdered) but in general they have demonstrated an enormous ability to present a common front against other factions.

On a broader national front, the present regime has a narrow power base; being an exclusively Sunni government its ability to survive depends on its ruthless suppression of other racial and religious groups.

This was most evident in the crushing of revolts by both the Shi'a and the Kurds in the aftermath of the 1991 war. Hundreds of thousands of Kurdish refugees were driven into the mountains on the Turkish border and into Iran. With the help of the U.S. and the U.N., many Kurdish families were returning to their villages by June 1991, although plans for some form of autonomy were still unresolved.

RULERS OF IRAQ (from 1945)

Kings

April 1939–July 1958: Faisal II (Regent: Abdul Illahi from April 1939–May 1953)

Military Dictator

July 1958–February 1963: Abdul Karim Qassim (Muhammed Nibib ar-Rubai as Head of Council of State)

Presidents

February 1963–April 1966: Abdul Salim Muhammad Arif
April 1966–July 1968: Abdul Rahman Muhammad Arif
July 1968–July 1979: Said Ahmad Hasan al-Bakr
July 1979– : Saddam Hussein Abdal-Majid al-Tikriti

GOVERNMENT LIST (July/August 1991)

President	Husayn, SADDAM
Vice President	Ma'ruf, Taha Muhyi al-Din
Vice President	Ramadan, Taha Yasin
Prime Minister	Hammadi, Sa'dun
Department Prime Minister	'Aziz, Tariq Mikha'il
Department Prime Minister	Zubaydi, Muhammad Hamza al-
Minister of Agriculture & Irrigation	Sabbagh, 'Abd al-Wahab Mahmud 'Abdallah
Minister of Awqaf & Religious Affairs	'Abbas, 'Abdallah Fadil
Minister of Culture & Information	Hamada, Hamid Yusuf al-
Minister of Defense	Majid, Husayn Kamil Hasan al-
Minister of Education	Bazzaz, Hikmat Ibrahim al-
Minister of Finance	'Abd al-Jafar, Majid
Minister of Foreign Affairs	Samarra'i, Ahmad Husayn Khudayir al-
Minister of Health	Sa'id, 'Abd Al-Salam Muhammad
Minister of Higher Education & Scientific Research	Hashimi, 'Abd al-Razzaq Qasim al-
Minister of Housing & Reconstruction	Ahmad, Mahmud Dhiyab al-
Minister of Industry & Military Industries	Sa'di, Amir Hammudah
Minister of Interior	Majid, 'Ali Hasan al-
Minister of Justice	Maliki, Shadid Lazim al-
Minister of Labor & Social Affairs	Mubarak, Umid Midhat
Minister of Oil (Acting)	Sa'di, Amir Hammudah
Minister of Planning	Faraj, Samal Majid
Minister of Trade	Salih, Muhammad Mahdi al-
Minister of Transport & Communications	Ma'ini, 'Abd al-Sattar Ahmad al-
Minister of State	Zibari, Arshad Muhammad Ahmad al-
Minister of State for Foreign Affairs	Sahhaf, Muhammad Sa'id al-
Minister of State for Military Affairs	Shanshal, 'Abd al-Jabbar Khalil, *Staff Gen.*
Minister of State for Oil Affairs	Ifi, 'Usamah 'Abd al-Razzaq Hummadi al-
Adviser to the President for Military Affairs	Jabburi, Sa'di Tuma 'Abbas al-
Governor, Central Bank	Franjul, Subhi Nadhim

FREEDOM & HUMAN RIGHTS

In terms of civil and political rights the country is ranked as a not-free state.

Iraq is an authoritarian state, where there are few dependable sources of information about the quality of human and political rights, and it would be reasonable to surmise that there are few such rights enjoyed

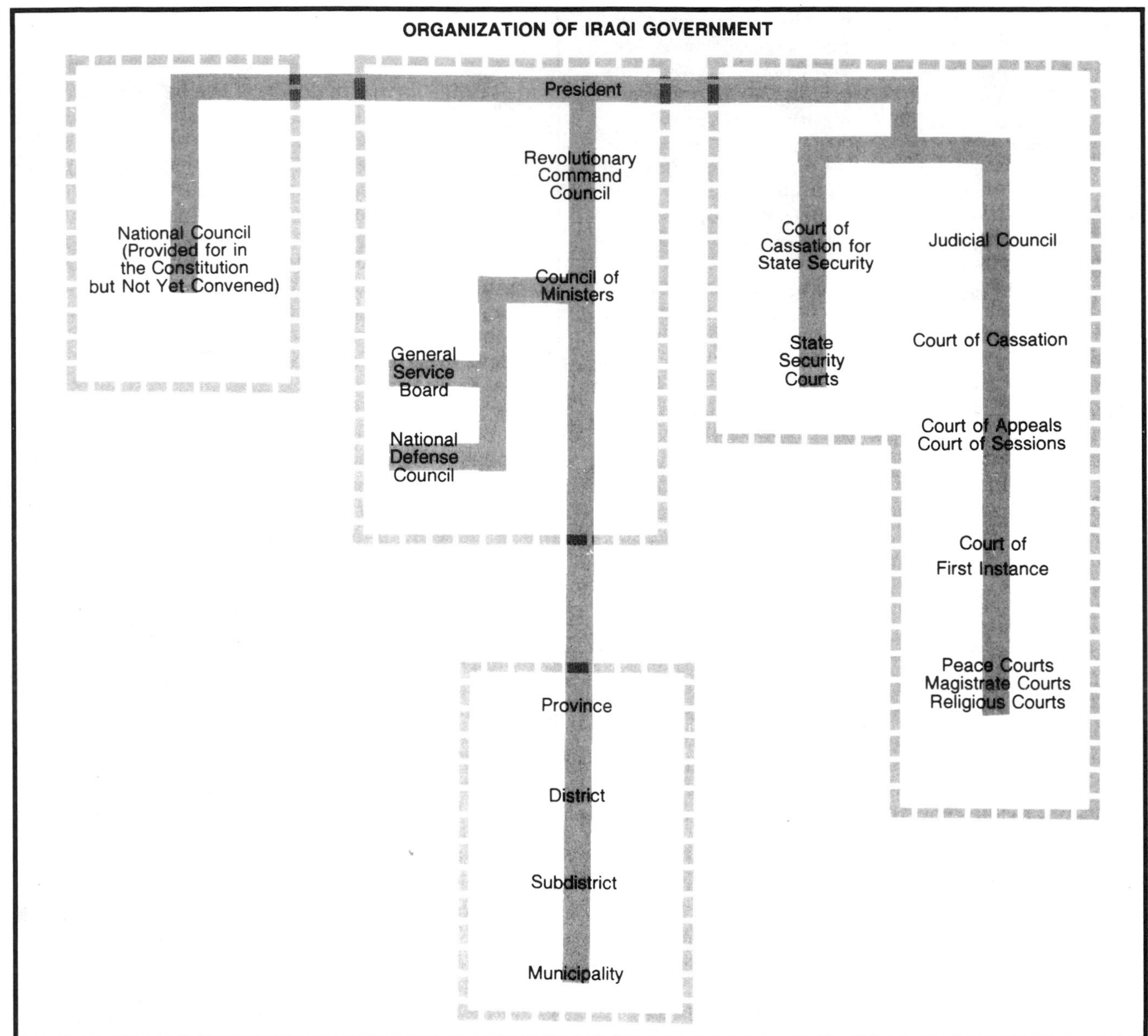

by Iraqis. Amnesty International has expressed its concern about the routine and systematic torture of political detainees. Physical and psychological torture used during interrogations include: beatings with rubber hoses or planks, suspension from a ceiling fan, electric shock treatment, threatening prisoners with loaded weapons; playing tape recordings of torture sessions and threatening members of a prisoner's family with dire consequences in his presence. Some prisoners have reportedly died under torture. Execution has been an established method for dealing with perceived political and military opponents of the government, particularly members of the outlawed Da'wa Party (fundamentalist Shi'a Muslim) and the Communist Party. In October 1983, Amnesty International stated that it had the names of 520 political prisoners reported to have been executed since 1978. Members of the political elite have also been executed as a result of factional conflict.

There were reports that Hussein ordered the executions of top Air Force commanders for ineffective performances in the 1991 Gulf War. Disappearances are frequently the result of secret executions, a fate that must have befallen Iraq's leading Shiite clergyman, Ayatollah Baqr Sadr, two prominent scientists associated with the Thuwaitha Nuclear Research Center, and others. Iraq's representative to the U.N. Human Rights Commission's Committee on Disappeared Persons himself disappeared after his return to Baghdad in 1980. Trials in civil, criminal and religious courts are open, while closed trials are the rule in revolutionary courts, and special courts constituted by the Revolutionary Command Council.

All forms of dissent are viewed as threats and this means that the exercise of the freedoms of press, speech and assembly is an anathema. The media are government controlled and foreign periodicals, movies and books are censored before distribution.

Iraq's Christian minority exists under severe disabilities, but nevertheless enjoys freedom of worship. Recently, some new church construction has been permitted. An effort to institute obligatory Koranic studies for all students, including non-Muslims, was withdrawn after protests from the Christian groups within and without the country.

In keeping with Ba'ath ideology, opposition groups are not tolerated and in fact are severely repressed. The outlawed Da'wa Party bore the brunt of the regime's persecution in 1980. The Communist Party fared little better having been removed from the ruling Progressive National Front and outlawed in 1979.

Until 1983, terrorists or their associates who resided in or transited Iraq with the apparent acquiescence of the government carried out assassinations and assassination attempts abroad. Two such groups were the Black June Organization led by Sabri al-Banna or "Abu Nidal," and the May 15 Organization under Husayn Mohammed Al-Umari, or "Abu Ibrahim." However, Iraq evidently had withdrawn its support for these groups in or by 1983. In an October 1983 interview with French journalists, President Hussein said Iraq had ceased all financial and other assistance to Abu Nidal, among others. The Black June group was expelled from Iraq the following month. Likewise, the May 15 Organization has remained out of sight since late 1982, although it may have attempted an unsuccessful operation in 1983. It reportedly was suppressed by mid-1984.

The Iraqis themselves have been the victims of terrorism supported by Syria and Iran. Iranian-backed terrorists bombed the Air Force headquarters and a broadcasting station in Baghdad in April 1983, attempted to hijack an Iraqi Airways passenger flight from Cyprus in September 1984 and bombed Iraqi diplomats' cars in Athens and a busy commercial district in Baghdad in December 1984. Iraq also reported that it prevented or broke up other planned terrorist attacks.

CIVIL SERVICE

The civil service is governed by the Civil Service Law and the Cadre Law, both enacted in 1962. Civil servants are divided into two categories: officials, holding one of nine grades in government departments, and employees of semi-government bodies. The Ministry of Interior has the largest group of officials. The civil service is administered by the General Service Board, which regulates recruitment, promotion and discipline. The Ministry of Finance is responsible for fixing the quota of civil servants in each ministry, transfer of officials and investigations of official misconduct. Recruitment is based on competitive examinations open to all Iraqi citizens over 18 years of age.

LOCAL GOVERNMENT

The country is divided into 18 governorates *(liwa* or *muhafaazat)*, each administered by a governor *(mutasarrif)* assisted by a Provincial Council. The governorates are:

Anbar	Diyala	Qadisiya
Arbil	Kerbela	Salaheddin
Babylon	Missan	Sulaimanya
Baghdad	Mulhanna	Tamin
Basra	Najaf	Thi-Qar
Dhok	Ninevah	Wasit

The desert areas are divided into three separate districts, or territories, each under a director: the Jazirah Desert (Badiyat al-Jazirah), the Northern Desert (al-Badiyah al-Shamaliyah) and the Southern Desert (al-Badiyah al-Janubiyah).

Each province is divided into a number of districts *(aqdiya)*, each under a deputy governor, or district officer *(qaimmaqam)*. Districts number 75. They are further subdivided into subdistricts, or *nawahin*, of which there are over 180, each administered by a subdistrict officer, or *mudir*. Though the mudir is the lowest official in local government, the final link is provided by the *mukhtar*, the leader of a village *(qarya)* or town quarter *(mahalla)*.

Cities and towns *(madina* or *balad)* are administered by municipal councils *(baladiyat)*, each presided over by a mayor *(rais al baladiyah)*, who is an official appointed by the Ministry of Interior. The 231 cities and towns are divided into five classes: superior (Basra, Mosul and Kirkuk), first (11), second (12), third (47) and fourth (147).

Baghdad enjoys special status as the national capital and is administered by an authority known as governorate of the capital *(amanat al asimah)* presided over by a mayor known as the guardian of the capital *(amin al asimah)*. Unlike territorial units, municipalities levy their own taxes.

FOREIGN POLICY

The foreign policy of Iraq is determined by the Ba'athist ideology of its government. The central principles of this ideology are hostility to Israel, fidelity to the ideal of Pan-Arabism, opposition to "Western imperialism" and adherence to the broad concept of positive nonalignment, which in the Iraqi case means support of the Soviet Union.

Despite common goals, Iraq's relations with other Arab states and its northern neighbors reveal the persistence of traditional rivalries and suspicions. Relations with Egypt are complicated by rival claims to leadership of the Arab world. Attempts during the regime of the Aref brothers to achieve formal unity with Egypt yielded no practical results, and relations with Egypt deteriorated after the Ba'athists became ascendant in 1968. Syria and Iraq, sharing a Ba'athist ideology, came near to union in 1963 but have been drifting apart since then. Contributing to the antagonism have been a number of conflicting economic issues, including transit royalties on Iraqi oil piped across Syria to Banias and Tripoli and Iraqi claims that Syria has been diverting excessive quantities of water from the Euphrates since the completion of a new dam at Taqba. The two Ba'ath-led nations made their last try at reconciliation in 1979 when Presidents al-Bakr and Assad declared that their goal was a unified state with one president, one government and one party (the Ba'ath). But the subsequent replacement of al-Bakr by Saddam Hussein—whom the Syrians disliked intensely—and Hussein's accusations regarding Syrian involvement in the 1979 coup attempts against him have served to reopen the old hostilities. In the Iraqi-Iranian war Syria openly espoused the Iranian side, although there were some shift towards a middle ground in 1987.

Iraq's relations with Iran were characterized by increasing tensions from 1959, when Iraq left the Baghdad Pact, to 1975. The two nations came to the brink of war in 1970 over Iranian support for Kurdish insurgents and Iran's abrogation of the 1937 border treaty with Iraq providing for exclusive Iraqi control of navigation on the Shatt al-Arab. On March 6, 1975 the two countries concluded an agreement by which Iraq made certain border concessions in return for Iran's renunciation of its support for the Kurds. It was followed in 1976 by amplifying agreements on remaining issues.

The Iran-Iraqi War, known as the Gulf War, began on September 16, 1980 with Iraqi advances along a 500 km. (300 mi.) front and the capture of the important city of Khorramshahr. Fierce Iranian resistance brought about a stalemate which lasted until the spring of 1982 when Iranian counteroffensives led to the retaking of Khorramshahr in May and the withdrawal of Iraqi troops from the territory which they had taken in 1980. In July 1982 the Iranian army crossed into Iraq. The struggle soon deteriorated into a war of attrition with neither side apparently able to stage a decisive offensive. When Iran launched a series of attacks across its northern border with Iraq in October 1983, threatening the last outlet for Iraqi exports of petroleum through the Kirkuk pipeline, Iraq intensified missile attacks and bombing raids against Iranian towns and petroleum installations. During the fall of 1983, Iraq took delivery of five French-built Super-Etendard fighter aircraft. With these and the Exocet missiles which it already possessed, Iraq threatened to destroy Iran's oil industry, centered on Kharg Island in the gulf. Iran, in turn, threatened to block the gulf at the Straits of Hormuz to all traffic if Iraqi military action makes it impossible to export its oil by that route.

In February 1984, a further Iranian offensive resulted in the capture of marshlands around the southern Iraqi island of Majnoon, the site of rich petroleum deposits. Iraq failed to recapture the territory and was censured internationally for its use of mustard gas against Iranian forces. By 1984, the balance of military power moved in Iraq's favor, and its financial position improved as both the United States and the Soviet Union provided aid. An estimated two-thirds of Iraq's total armaments and much of its ammunition was of Soviet origin as well as its SS-12 missiles. Egypt provided ammunition and hardware worth $1.3 billion and Brazil and Chile sold arms to Iraq. The delivery of eight French Mirage F-1 EQ5 fighter aircraft in October 1984 brought the Iranian Levan Island oil terminal within Iraq's range. A substantial portion of the Iraqi war budget was borne by Saudi Arabia and the smaller Gulf States. Jordan supplied a volunteer brigade to fight alongside the Iraqis.

As the military edge moved to the Iraqi side, Iran delayed its long-planned massive offensive against the port of Basra. Lacking airpower, the Iranian offensive would lack air cover while on the ground; Iraq's tank force is superior in numbers and sophistication. As the Iranians delayed, Iraq constructed a formidable defense network along the southern front. In 1984, Iraq accepted a U.N.-sponsored cease-fire and declared a week-long unilateral cease-fire, but Iran rejected the gesture, and insisted on nothing less than the removal of Saddam Hussein and $160 billion in war reparations.

By 1985, 125,000 Iraqi soldiers were POW's in Iran and 10,000 Iranian soldiers were POW's in Iraq. Many of these prisoners of war have been grossly mistreated and some have been killed in violation of the Geneva Convention.

Iran's failed siege of Basra, and internal conflicts in Tehran, led the Ayatollah Khomeini to call for a cease-fire on July 18, 1988. Immediately after that, Iraq drove Iranian forces back to the 1980 border. A U.N.-sponsored cease-fire went into effect August 20. Despite no territorial gains and a $60 billion war debt, President Hussein claimed victory in the war and ordered three days of national celebration. Both sides suffered about one million casualties in the eight-year conflict.

Negotiations on a formal peace were stalled through 1990, due mostly to Iraq's refusal to abandon the Shatt al-Arab waterway and Iran's demand for reparations. The invasion of Kuwait in August 1990, and subsequent international response, stirred Hussein to seek immediate peace with Tehran. Iraq accepted all Iranian claims, including the division of the Shatt al-Arab, and exchanges of prisoners of war began August 17.

Opposition to the United States was a major feature of Iraqi foreign policy from 1959 when Iraq withdrew from the Baghdad Pact until the Gulf War. This opposition was tied to U.S. support for Israel. Diplomatic relations between the two countries, severed in 1967, were resumed in November 1984. They were cut again during the Gulf War of 1991. Diplomatic relations with Great Britain, suspended in 1967, were resumed in 1968. France has replaced Great Britain as the major Western supplier of military hardware and economic aid. France's pro-Arab posture in the Middle East crisis substantially enhanced French influence in the region; French is now the official second language, and France is Iraq's second largest trading partner.

Until the Gulf War, Iraq was one of the two major allies of the Soviet Union in the Middle East—the other being Syria. The Iraqi Army is equipped largely with Soviet arms and Russian technical and economic assistance, first begun in 1958, has assumed massive proportions. Despite minor irritants, such as Soviet support for the Kurds and Iraqi opposition to Communist ideology, the two nations have reaffirmed and strengthened their ties. While Iraq is tied to the Soviet Union for its military supplies and has reaped immense benefits from its 1972 15-Year Friendship and Cooperation Treaty with that country, it has not hesitated to oppose Soviet policies where its own interests are concerned: over the issue of Kurdish autonomy, Soviet presence in the Horn of Africa, and its treatment of Iraqi Communists. The development of domestic military power and rising oil revenues have emboldened the Ba'ath regime to adopt a more independent stance on most international issues without reference to the known policies of its allies or neighbors. Relations with the People's Republic of China have been only of marginal significance.

Despite its opposition to Syria, Iraq joined with the hard-line Arab states opposed to President Sadat's peace initiatives in the Middle East and efforts to achieve a negotiated settlement with Israel. It participated in the Tripoli meeting of Arab nations in December 1977 but its representative walked out of the meeting before it closed, calling for a stronger stand against Egypt and Israel than that contained in the Tripoli Declaration. Relations with Libya and Syria were broken in 1980 with the onset of the Gulf War.

Iraq's relations with the West and with other Gulf Arab states were deteriorating in 1989–90, even before the August 2, 1990 invasion of Kuwait. The September 1989 explosion at an Iraqi defense industry complex, presumably a missile development site, focused Western concern on Hussein's military buildup. A good deal of that buildup was financed by Western powers. Much of the world was also outraged by Iraq's execution in early 1990 of Iranian-born British journalist Farzad Bazoff.

In April 1990, U.S. President George Bush publicly urged Iraq to abandon manufacturing chemical weapons. In late July the American Congress barred sales of military equipment to Baghdad. As Western condemnation of Hussein increased, Iraq's prestige rose in the Arab world. Hussein's reference, for instance, to chemical weapons as a deterrence against Israeli nuclear weapons drew praise even from Syria.

The decision to invade Kuwait was apparently motivated by economic and military concerns, as well as Hussein's personal desire for expansion. Iraq was confident there was no credible regional opposition to its armed forces. Further, Hussein hoped to grab a greater share of Middle East oil reserves and force conquered Kuwait to accept the debt forgiveness he had been seeking. He also desired greater access to the Gulf. Iraq also put forward a dubious historical claim to the emirate. When Kuwait received independence from the British in 1961, Iraq claimed the area. As a result, the emirate was put under the protection of British and Arab League troops until 1963, when Iraq formally recognized Kuwait's independence and sovereignty.

In late July, on the eve of an OPEC meeting, Iraq said it might take military actions against countries which ignored the cartel's quotas, and accused Kuwait of violating the border to steal Iraqi oil reserves. The government also called for a waiver of Iraq's large debt to Kuwait, accumulated during the Iranian war, and placed two armored divisions on the border. At the OPEC meeting of July 25, prices were raised to $21 from $18 per barrel, and Kuwait and the United Arab Emirates agreed to cut production. Those developments, in conjunction with the intervention of Egyptian President Hosni Mubarak, appeared to defuse the tense situation.

But negotiations between Iraq and Kuwait on the border dispute collapsed August 1, and the next day Iraq invaded and overran the tiny oil-rich emirate. There was little evidence to support Hussein's claim Iraq moved to support Kuwaiti insurgents. Quickly, the U.N. demanded Iraqi withdrawal, the U.S. sent troops to stall a possible march on the Saudi Arabian oil fields. Hussein declared the annexation of Kuwait as Iraq's 19th province. On August 28 Iraq announced the renaming of Kuwait City as Kadhima, the name under the Ottoman Empire.

The Arab League met August 3, condemning the invasion and demanding immediate Iraqi departure. Jordan, Yemen and the Palestine Liberation Organization (PLO) were among those voting against the resolution. A week later Arab heads of state met in Cairo, and 12 of the 20 nations at the conference agreed to send troops to join the multi-national force protecting Saudi Arabia. That force, which included more than 500,000 troops by January 1991, was led by the U.S., under the aegis of the U.N. It was composed of personnel from 28 countries.

Iraq's chief allies throughout the crises were Jordan and the PLO. One reason for this was Hussein's introduction on August 12 of the concept of linkage. He demanded Israeli withdrawal from the West Bank and Gaza in exchange for Iraqi departure from Kuwait, or at least an international conference on the Palestinian issue. The American-led coalition rejected those proposals. Hussein's further efforts to induce other Arab members to leave the coalition proved ineffective.

From August through November the U.N. passed several more resolutions on the crisis. While shaped by the U.S., the anti-Iraq resolves drew almost unanimous support. One of these imposed a trade embargo on Iraq, which produced serious hardships by the end of the year. On November 29, the Security Council voted to authorize member states to use force to evict Iraq if troops had not left by January 15, 1991. It was the U.N.'s first sanction of the use of force since the Korean War.

Diplomatically, unless it was willing to leave Kuwait, Iraq had little room for maneuver. In August and September, Hussein held Western citizens at strategic sites as "human shields" against possible attacks, but they were released by December. In September, the Iraqi President threatened to attack both Israel and Saudi Arabia if Iraq was strangled by economic sanctions. Foreign Minister Tariq 'Aziz failed to reach a settlement in a six-hour meeting in Geneva January 9, 1991 with U.S. Secretary of State James Baker. During the war, the Iraqis tried unsuccessfully to use the auspices of the Soviet Union to achieve an accord.

The American-led Allies launched a massive, two-part campaign January 16, which forced Iraq to withdraw from Kuwait by February 28. The first part was a series of almost continuous air strikes against various sites and troops in southern Iraq and occupied Kuwait. The second phase was a ground assault of February 24 to 28 which forced the Iraqi army to retreat from

Kuwait, and defeated eight of the elite Republican Guard divisions.

Iraq had little military response to the Allied assault. In January, Iraqi planes began flying to Iran, seeking safety from Allied fighter attacks. For some reason, Iraq did not implement the threat to use chemical or nuclear weapons against civilians or troops. Scud missile attacks against Israel and Saudi Arabia produced little damage, although considerable harm was done to property in Kuwait, especially the burning of about 600 oil wells.

Iraqi forces in southern Iraq and Kuwait totaled more than 510,000 troops and 400 tanks. But, aside from a brief attack in late January at Khafji in northern Saudi Arabia, the Iraqi command did not undertake offensive operations. Shortages of supplies and relentless pounding from Allied bombing produced low morale and many desertions among ground troops. The air attacks also disrupted communications and killed thousands of soldiers. By the time Allied ground forces attacked in late February, the Iraqi army was largely defeated. About 80,000 surrendered and at least 100,000 were killed in the six-week war.

On April 6, Iraq accepted U.N. peace terms, formally ending the conflict. They included the supervised destruction of Iraqi chemical and nuclear weapons, as well as reparation payments to Kuwait and other Allies.

Iraq joined the U.N. in 1945. It is a member of 14 U.N. organizations and 12 other international organizations, including the Arab League, OPEC and OAPEC.

PARLIAMENT

The National Assembly (Majlis al-Umma) is a 250-member body elected by universal suffrage for four year terms. Elections were held most recently in 1989. It does not enjoy any substantial legislative powers.

Hussein's announcement in January 1989 permitting opposition groups to run in April elections for seats in the National Assembly was deceptive. In fact, all candidates had to be approved by an RCC Election Committee. The elections, which drew a 75% turnout of eligible voters, resulted in the ruling Ba'ath party claiming more than one-half of the 250 seats. The National Progressive Patriotic Front, a three-party coalition led by the Ba'ath, won contests for all the openings.

The Kurdish Legislative Council is a 57-member regional assembly representing the northern autonomous regions of Arbil, D'hok and Sulaimaniyah.

POLITICAL PARTIES

Iraq is a one-party state with the Arab Ba'ath Socialist Party, founded in 1947, as the dominant political institution in the state. Ba'athist ideology is a mixture of socialism and ultra-Arab nationalism; its power base is the minority Sunni community. Its organizational structure is built on small cells and its active membership is estimated at 25,000 although the party reportedly has 1.5 million adherents. Its limited membership reflects the elitist character of the movement. Saddam Hussein is the secretary general of the party.

Established in 1973, in accordance with the provisions of the National Action Charter, the National Progressive Front consists of the Ba'ath Party, the Marxist rump of the Kurdistan Democratic Party, and the Kurdistan Revolutionary Party. Communists consisting of some 2,000 hard-core members, led by Aziz Muhammad, withdrew from the National Front (which it had joined in 1973) in 1979. In 1978 the government executed 21 Communists and purged the others. Most Communist leaders are now in exile. In 1982 the government gave amnesty to Iraqi Communists. Kurdish interests are represented by the Barzani, non-Marxist faction of the Democratic Party of Kurdistan, the political wing of the Pesh Merga, and the Patriotic Union of Kurdistan, based in Damascus.

The outlawed, Iranian-supported Da'wa (Islamic Call) Party has been a major target of persecution. It has claimed violent acts against the government in Iraq and abroad, and was implicated in the December 1983 truck bombing of the U.S. Embassy and other U.S., French and Kuwaiti targets in Kuwait. Other Shi'a opposition groups are the Holy Warriors and Organization for Islamic Action.

ECONOMY

Prior to the Gulf War of 1991, Iraq was classified as an upper middle-income country, with a socialist, centrally planned economy. Production and exportation of petroleum is the most important sector of the economy. It accounts for about one-half of GNP. Before the Gulf War Iraq was OPEC's second largest exporter of oil.

Despite high priority by the government, even before the Gulf War of 1991, Iraq's industrial sector remained underdeveloped. Money was invested in industries which rely on local raw materials for import substitution or foreign exchange earnings. Aside from petroleum, the top industries are textiles, construction materials and food processing. Iraq's agriculture was privatized in 1987, but still suffers dislocation from earlier experiments with land reform and collectivization.

Increased revenue from oil sales made the 1970's a period of growth for the Iraqi economy, but the Iranian war altered that picture. Destruction of Gulf terminals and closure of the pipeline through Syria cut revenue from petroleum exports in half in 1981, and reduced GDP by 30%. From 1980 to 1988 real GDP fell at an average annual rate of 1.5%.

Projects were undertaken to retain petroleum exporting capacity. These included upgrading the pipeline from Kirkuk through Turkey, and constructing two additional lines through Saudi Arabia. As a result, output was up to two million barrels a day by late 1985. By 1988, the total value of Iraqi exports, mostly in oil, was $12.5 billion. Production of petroleum that year totaled 141 million tons, and GDP grew by 10%, the first real growth of the decade.

The sanctions of the Gulf War devastated the nation's economy. The value of imports, for example, declined from $260 million in July 1990 to $700,000 in September. Most of Iraq's petroleum infrastructure was

BALANCE OF PAYMENTS, 1977
(U.S. $ millions)

Current account balance: 2,990
Merchandise exports: 10,838
Merchandise imports: −5,867
Trade balance: 4,971
Other goods, services & income + : 761
Other goods, services & income − : −2,707
Other goods, services & income net: −1,946
Private unrequited transfers: 1 (1975)
Official unrequited transfers: −35
Capital other than reserves: −517
Net errors & omissions: −510
Counterpart items: −79
Liabilities constituting foreign authorities reserves: −214 (1975)
Total change in reserves: −2,394

GROSS DOMESTIC PRODUCT

GDP nominal (I.D. billions): 14.547 (1985)
Average annual growth rate of GDP (%, 1975–85): 3.0
GDP by type of expenditure (%) 1986
- Consumption
  - Private and government: 79
- Gross domestic investment: 29
- Foreign trade
  - Exports: 20
  - Imports: −28

Cost components of GDP (%) 1985
- Net indirect taxes: 2
- Consumption of fixed capital: 10
- Compensation of employees: 32
- Net operating surplus: 56

Sectoral origin of GDP (%) 1985
- Primary
  - Agriculture: 18
  - Mining: 28
- Secondary
  - Manufacturing: 10
  - Construction: 9
  - Public utilities: 2
- Tertiary
  - Transportation & communications: 8
  - Trade: 14
  - Finance: 12

destroyed or damaged in the conflict. It was estimated that it would take three years and $10 to $20 billion to restore pre-war capacity. Iraq's industrial and transportation systems also received damage, and derailed a development program in effect since the conclusion of the Iranian war in 1988. A U.N. report in the spring of 1991 said Allied bombing had reduced Iraq "to the pre-industrial age."

PUBLIC FINANCE

The Iraqi fiscal year is the calendar year. The national budget consists of a set of five budgets: the Ordinary Budget, the Economic Plan Budget, the Supplementary Budget for Semi-Autonomous Government Agencies (including Ports Administration, Iraqi Railways, Telephone, Telegraph, and Postal Services and Atomic Energy Commission), the Supplementary Budget for Autonomous Government Agencies (such as the Iraqi News Agency and the Administration of Theater and Cinema) and the Supplementary Budget for Public Sector Economic Organizations (including those concerned with banking, transportation, oil refining, manufacturing and insurance).

Of central government revenues, nearly 90% comes from oil and public enterprises. On expenditures, economic services claims about 45% and defense about 25%.

On the even of the Gulf War of 1991, Iraq's foreign debt was nearly $80 billion, with more than one-half of that owed to Gulf Arab states. After the war, required reparations payments raised the debt to approximately $200 billion.

Long-term economic planning was introduced in 1961. The bulk of financing comes from oil revenues supplemented by net profits from government agencies and external loans. The major goals of the five-year plans included a massive extension and intensification of agriculture; industrial diversification; and expansion of infrastructure, transport and communications as well as development of a skilled workforce to meet the growing need for skilled manpower without importing large amounts of foreign labor.

The 1991 Gulf War severely damaged the Iraqi economy. It has been estimated that it may take 15 years to restore development to pre-war levels. Recovery is dependent on the length of time the U.N. sanctions remain in force and on reconstruction assistance. However, little foreign assistance has been made available.

FOREIGN AID, 1989

Total foreign aid (U.S. $ millions): 132.9
- Bilateral: 61.8
- Multilateral: 71.1

Most of the foreign aid received since 1958 has been from OPEC and from the Soviet Union and East European countries. From 1980 to 1989 OPEC contributed $37.2 billion in bilateral aid. Communist countries committed $3.9 billion in aid from 1970–88.

CURRENCY & BANKING

The Iraqi unit of currency is the Iraqi dinar divided into 20 dirhams and 1,000 fils. Coins are issued in denominations of 1, 5, 10, 25, 50 and 100 fils and notes in denominations of 250 and 500 fils and 1, 5 and 10 dinars. The official exchange rate in 1991 was U.S. $1 = ID .3100.

The banking system, which was completely nationalized in 1964, comprises the Central Bank, one state-owned commercial bank, the Rafidain Bank, and five state-owned specialized banks (The Agricultural Bank, the Industrial Bank, the Estate Bank, the Mortgage Bank and the Cooperative Bank). The Central Bank manages the national currency and controls the banking system and foreign exchange transactions. The Rafidain Bank handles government accounts, including oil revenues.

FINANCIAL INDICATORS

External debt 1985
- Total (U.S. $ billions): 7.150
- Debt service (long-term)
  - Total (U.S. $ billions): 1.982
  - Repayment
    - Principal (%): 75.7
    - Interest (%): 24.3
- Debt service ratio (%): 13.2
- Net direct private investment (U.S. $ millions): 25 (1970)

GROWTH PROFILE
(Annual Growth Rates, %)

Projected population (1988–2000): 3.4
Projected crude birth rate (/1,000) (1990–95): 40.5
Projected crude death rate (/1,000) (1990–95): 6.7
Urban population (1980–88): 4.8
Labor force (1985–2000): 4.0
GDP (1975–85): 3.0
Energy production (1980–88): 5.3
Energy consumption (1980–88): 5.3

AGRICULTURE

Of the total land area of 43,844,600 ha. (108,338,520 ac.), only 21% is arable and per capita agricultural land is only 0.81 ha. (2 ac.).

Agriculture accounts for less than 10% of GNP, although it occupies about one-third of the labor force. In the 1980's agricultural production rose at an annual average rate of 3.5%. The sector is hampered by labor shortages, salinization and destabilization from past experiments with land reform and collectivization.

The government invested about $1.25 billion in agriculture from 1975 to 1981 in an effort to achieve sufficiency in food, but Iraq still imports about 60% of food requirements. Most agriculture was privatized in 1987. The principal export crop is dates. In 1987, Iraq produced 1,102 tons of dates, and provided about 80% of the world's demand for them.

The Agrarian Reform Law of 1958 provided for the breakup of large estates and their redistribution to new peasant owners. The law set a maximum of 1,000 *dunums* (1 dunum = 0.25 hectare, 0.618 acre) of irrigated land and twice that limit for rain-fed holdings. Excess lands confiscated by the government were to be allotted to farmers in holdings of a maximum of 60 to 120 dunums (15 to 30 ha.). The administration of confiscated lands and their distribution was placed in the hands of the Higher Committee for Agrarian Reform. The law also called for the formation of cooperatives to take over management, credit and marketing services. The implementation of the reforms proceeded slowly but it was virtually completed by 1975 when 24,141 sq. km. (9,318 sq. mi.) of agricultural land had been sequestrated and 14,657 sq. km. (5,685 sq. mi.) had been distributed to 157,862 farmers. The government had also organized 1,360 agricultural cooperatives with 214,488 members, 72 collective farms with 11,253 members, and 8 state farms.

Despite recent changes the most common form of farm operation remains sharecropping. Sharecroppers receive 43% of the harvest for their seed and labor in irrigated land and 53% in rain-fed land.

Cultivation is limited to two zones—the northern and northeastern rain-fed zone and the irrigated zone of the plain in central and southern Iraq. The extension of arable land is possible only through expansion of the area under irrigation. The main irrigation systems are now based on the Euphrates (750,000 ha., 1,853,289 ac.), the Tigris (425,000 ha., 1,050,175 ac.), the Diyala River and the lesser Zab River. The current development plan proposes a number of major irrigation projects, including the Kirkuk, Lower Khalis, Diwaniyah-Dalmaj, Abu Gharab, Al Ishaqi, Duja Ila and Nahr Saad. The standard practice is to leave half the cropland

AGRICULTURAL INDICATORS

Cereal imports (million metric tons): 4.442 (1988)
Index of agricultural production (1979–81 = 100): 147 (1986)
Index of food production per capita (1979–81 = 100): 147 (1986)
Index of food production per capita (1979–81 = 100): 105 (1985–88)
Number of tractors: 40,915 (1986)
Number of harvester-threshers: 3,032 (1986)
Total fertilizer consumption (000 metric tons): 176.9 (1985–86)
Fertilizer consumption (g./ha., hundreds): 397 (1987–88)
Number of farms (000): 591 (1971)
Average size of holding (ha.): 9.7 (1971)
Size class (%) 1971
- Below 1 ha. (below 2.47 ac.): 20.2
- 1–5 ha. (2.47–12.35 ac.): 29.3
- 5–10 ha. (12.35–24.7 ac.): 21.4
- 10–20 ha. (24.7–49.4 ac.): 18.5
- 20–50 ha. (49.4–123.5 ac.): 9.0
- 50–200 ha. (123.5–494 ac.): 1.3
- Over 200 ha. (over 494 ac.): 0.3

Tenure (%) 1971
- Owner-operated: 52.5
- Rented: 40.9
- Other: 6.6

Activity (%) 1971
- Mainly crops: 87.9
- Mainly livestock: 11.2
- Mixed: 0.8

Farms as % of total land area: 13.1 (1971)
Land use (%) 1985–87
- Cropland: 77
- Pasture: 12
- Forest: 2
- Other: 10

Yields (kg./ha.) 1989
- Grains: 1,044
- Roots & tubers: 16,000
- Legumes: 951
- Milk (kg./animal): 749

Production 1989
- Fruits (million metric tons): 1.359
- Vegetables (million metric tons): 3.117

Livestock (000) 1989
- Cattle: 1,650
- Horses: 53 (1986)
- Sheep: 9,500

Forestry 1988
- Production of roundwood (000 cubic meters): 149
  - of which industrial roundwood (%): 33.6

Fishing 1988
- Total catch (000 metric tons): 18.0
  - of which marine (%): 27.7

fallow, to restore fertility, reduce salinity levels and store moisture. Most cropland is planted and harvested only once a year with only vegetables double cropped. There are two classes of annual crops: those planted in winter are called *shitwi* and those planted in summer are called *saifi*. Mechanization is limited to the southern plains region.

Wheat and barley are the principal staple crops and both are planted in winter. Both wheat and barley are grown in almost every province in the north and south, although Mosul Province accounts for nearly 45% of the total wheat crop. Rice and sugar beets are the major summer crops. Iraq produces some of the world's best dates, which are, after oil, one of the biggest export commodities. The chief cash crops are tobacco and, to a lesser extent, cotton.

PRINCIPAL CROP PRODUCTION (1982)

	Area (000 dunums)	Production (000 tons)
Wheat	3,430.0	965
Barley	2,143.5	902
Lentils	25.5	9
Broad beans	69.5	17
Sorghum	—	6
Rice	253.9	163
Sesame	36.7	9
Sugarcane	—	260
Tobacco	—	12
Corn	126.3	90
Dates	578.0	400
Cotton	79.3	5
Potatoes	—	110
Dry beans	—	7

Livestock is important in the rural economy, although only a relatively small number of Iraqis are full-time herders. Livestock products in the mid-1980s accounted for one-sixth of Iraq's non-oil exports.

Forests cover only 16,800 sq. km. (6,486 sq. mi.) in the northern provinces. Much of the highland timber is oak and Aleppo pine with some mixed stands of walnut and poplar. Timber cutting has been prohibited since 1954 and a substantial replanting program is under way.

Fishing is a negligible activity and fish are not significant in the Iraqi diet.

Agricultural credit is provided by the Agricultural bank.

MANUFACTURING

Despite high priority by the government, Iraq's industrial sector was underdeveloped, even prior to the destruction of the Gulf War of 1991. Resources were invested in industries which relied on local raw materials to serve as import substitutes or to generate foreign exchange earnings. Aside from petroleum, leading industries are textiles, construction materials, food processing, coal, rubber, plastic products and chemicals.

MANUFACTURING INDICATORS, 1987

Share of GDP (%): 10 (1985)
Labor force economically active in manufacturing (% est.): 8.8
Value added in manufacturing (U.S. $ millions): 325 (1970)
  Food & tobacco (%): 26 (1970)
  Textiles & clothing (%): 14 (1970)
  Machinery & transport equipment (%): 7 (1970)
  Chemicals (%): 3 (1970)
Total earnings as % of value added: 25

Industry expanded under a pair of five-year national development plans in the 1970s. Among the heavy industrial construction projects of that period were petrochemical, steel, aluminim and phosphate plants. By 1980 Iraq had the beginnings of an industrial core, but development was curtailed in the 1980s due to reallocation of resources to the Iranian war effort. The Gulf War of 1991 crippled Iraq's industrial capacity.

Since 1958 there has been increasing state intervention in industrial activities; by mid-1970s all important branches of industrial production were under government ownership or were subject to extensive government control. The culmination of the new industrial policy was the nationalization of the largest industrial and commercial firms and all banks and insurance companies in 1964. The nationalized enterprises were placed under the control of the High Council for Public Organizations with four subsidiary groups concerned with industry, banks, commerce and insurance. The emphasis on the public sector has not precluded support of private enterprise in small- or medium-sized industrial undertakings in the food and consumer products field.

Industrial policies and programs are laid down by the State Industrial Organization, which also supervises the public sector industrial enterprises. Prior to the war of 1991, industrial units were heavily concentrated in the cities of Baghdad, Basra and Mosul. Baghdad alone accounted for 50% of large enterprises employing 70% of the industrial labor force. The average public enterprise was six times larger than the average private enterprise in terms of the number of workers employed.

Relatively new public sector industrial establishments functioning before the 1991 war included a sulfur plant at Kirkuk, a fertilizer plant at Basra, an antibiotics factory at Samarra, an agricultural implements factory at Iskandriyah, an electrical equipment factory at Baghdad, a sugar mill at Maisan and an aluminum smelter at Basra.

The larger projects were carried out with the financial and technical assistance of Eastern bloc countries, particularly the USSR, Hungary, Czechoslovakia, Bulgaria and Poland. Soviet assistance has included both the financing and actual construction of over 11 factories, including a steel mill, an oil refinery, a fertilizer plant and a tractor plant.

Foreign investment is discouraged by limitation of foreign participation to 40% of share capital and limitations on repatriation of earnings.

Industrial credit is provided by the Industrial Bank.

MINING

Iraq's mineral resources, other than oil, are limited. Production of sulfur from the Mishraq field is expected to reach one million tons a year. Production in 1983 was 340,000 tons.

ENERGY

Iraq's energy sector is dominated by petroleum. Prior to the Gulf War, Iraq was OPEC's second largest exporter of oil, behind only Saudi Arabia. Sales of petroleum provide 95% of the country's foreign exchange earnings, and dominate the economy. In 1988, Iraq produced 141 million tons of crude petroleum. The oil sector, fully nationalized, is administered by the Iraq National Oil Company. Oil was discovered in the 1920s both near the Iranian border and at the major fields near Kirkuk. Other smaller deposits were uncovered in the 1950s.

The Iranian war caused considerable damage to oil facilities, and by 1988 Iraq was almost totally reliant on the pipeline from Kirkuk to the Mediterranean Sea through Turkey. Oil production had peaked in 1979 at 3.45 million barrels per day, with revenues at $21.2 billion. In 1981, for example, production fell to 900,000 barrels per day, and revenue slumped to $10.4 billion. While production remained basically at that level through 1990, the decrease of OPEC prices caused revenue to fall further. The Gulf War of 1991, at least in the short run, decimated the nation's petroleum industry.

The most important oil fields are at Kirkuk, with lesser fields at Naft Khaneh, Ayn Zalah, Butmah, al-Zubayr and Rumailah. From Kirkuk the oil was piped to Mediterranean terminals at Tripoli and Banias through Syria and Lebanon. The transit agreement with Syria and Lebanon lapsed in 1975 and lengthy negotiations to renew it resulted in a stalemate. With the outbreak of the Gulf War, pro-Teheran Syria closed the pipeline. A new strategic pipeline with a total capacity of 160 million tons annually was thereupon built between Al Hadithah in the north to the port of Fao on the Gulf Coast. This pipeline also became nonoperative as a result of Iranian attacks. Prior to the Gulf War of 1991, Iraqi efforts were concentrated on expanding its pipeline capacity away from the vulnerable gulf and Syrian territory. A new pipeline was being built parallel to the existing one from Kirkuk to Yumurtalik in Turkey at a cost of $550 million, along with a refinery to process crude at the Turkish end. Another pipeline was planned with a capacity of 500,000 barrels per day to connect with Saudi Arabia's Petroline. A second stage of this project involved an independent Iraqi pipeline parallel to the Saudi line, terminating at Yanbu on the Red Sea. A third project was a joint venture with Jordan to build a 1,650-km. (1,024-mi.) pipeline from western Iraq to Aqaba on the Red Sea with a capacity of 1 million barrels per day and at a cost of $950 million. Two-thirds of the cost of the project were to be borne by Jordan.

The Iraq National Oil Company's activities now extend beyond exploration and production of crude oil. It has built up a tanker fleet with a total tonnage of 1,141,000 in 1982. It has also moved into downstream operations with petrochemical plants, refineries and an LPG plant. It has concluded a number of oil-for-technology sales contracts with France, Japan and Eastern bloc countries.

Iraq's production of natural gas in 1983 was 578 million cubic meters.

Before the onset of Allied bombings in January 1991, Iraq had six oil refineries with a total capacity of 169,000 barrels per day, all managed by the Oil Refineries Administration. The refineries, located at Baghdad, Basra, Qayarah, Al Hadithah, Kirkuk and Khanaquin, had a total capacity of 180,000 barrels per day. There was also a sulfur recovery plant at Kirkuk producing sulfur, natural gas and liquid gas. Oil Products Distribution Administration is responsible for marketing of oil-based products all over Iraq.

Iraq has two atomic reactors, an IRT-2000 built with Soviet aid at Tuwaitha near Baghdad in 1968, and a 600 MW reactor supplied by France at Osirak. The latter was bombed by Israeli warplanes in June 1981. Both reactors are operated by the Atomic Energy Commission. In the aftermath of the war, it was not clear what atomic capacity Iraq retained.

ENERGY INDICATORS

Average annual energy production growth rate (%, 1980–88): 5.3
Energy consumption per capita (kg. oil equivalent): 781 (1988)
Average annual growth rate of energy consumption (%, 1980–88): 5.3
Electricity 1986
- Installed capacity (million kw.): 3.700
- Production (billion kw.-hr.): 23.450
  - % fossil fuel: 97.4
  - % hydro: 2.6
- Consumption per capita (kw.-hr.): 1,328

Natural gas
- Proved reserves (trillion cu. m.): 3.115 (1990)
- Production (billion cu. m.): 6.100 (1989)
- Consumption (million cu. m.): 900 (1988)

Petroleum
- Proved reserves (billion bbl.): 100 (1990)
- Years to exhaust proved reserves: 95 (1990)
- Production (billion bbl.): 1.055 (1989)
- Consumption (million bbl.): 126 (1988)
- Refining capacity (000 bbl./day): 319 (1990)

Coal
- Production (000 metric tons): 0 (1988)
- Consumption (000 metric tons): 0 (1988)

LABOR

In 1984, the labor force consisted of 3.4 million workers. Of those, 39% were employed in the service sector, 33% in agriculture and 28% in industry. Less than one-tenth of the labor force is organized. Women comprise one-quarter of the paid work force, and 47% of those employed in agriculture. One-third of the professionals in education and health care are female. In 1989, there was a foreign work force of one million, mostly from Arab countries.

The employment of children is common, although children under 12 years of age are barred from industrial establishments. Over two-thirds of the economically active population work as unpaid helpers or are self-employed.

Two striking characteristics of the labor force are its high mobility and the occupational specialization associated with each ethnic and religious community and each locality. Groups of rural workers are always on the move looking for seasonal jobs, particularly in the larger towns and cities. There are also social and ethnic factors that influence recruitment and training of workers. There is a critical shortage of skilled workers and of managers with professional qualifications. Vocational training facilities are generally inadequate, and most Iraqis tend to look down on manual labor. Until 1958 Iraq relied heavily on foreign technicians, experts and advisers, but legislation passed in that year substantially restricted their employment.

Working conditions are governed by the Labor Law of 1958 and its amendments. The law provides for an eight-hour working day and a 48-hour workweek, except during the month of Ramadan when the workday is seven hours. In practice, the workweek varies with institutions. It is 35 hours in government and 42 hours in the oilfields. Friday is the weekly restday. Overtime is limited to two hours a day or ten hours a week.

The law also governs terms of recruitment and dismissal. All workers are required to have an identity book and a discharge certificate. All foreigners must possess work permits, issued by the Directorate General of Labor, which are valid for a maximum of three years. Every termination of employment must be approved by the District Workers' Discharge and Termination Committee.

Minimum wages are determined for every industry and occupation by the Wage Board. The basic minimum wage is 270 fils (91¢) a day but there is considerable differential between wages for skilled and unskilled labor and between wages for men and women. Children receive two-thirds of the basic minimum wage. Office workers receive a minimum monthly salary of 30 dinars (about $100). A cost-of-living escalator is built into the wage structure. Workers in industrial establishments receive either an annual bonus or a share of the profits.

The Social Security Law of 1965 provides a wide range of workers' benefits, covering work-related injuries, sickness and disability. Men are eligible for old-age pensions from the age of 60 and women from the age of 55. The Program is administered by the Social Security Administration. Oil workers receive further benefits, such as low-cost housing, medical care and free transportation.

The unemployment rate is variously reported from 0.3% to 9.03% depending on whether seasonal workers are included. Under-employment is more serious, affecting perhaps half of the country's working population. Growing concern with unemployment has led to the creation of a National Employment Service.

The principal labor organization is the General Confederation of Trade Unions, which in the mid-1980s had 154 affiliated unions and 859,639 workers as members. The Confederation operates under close government surveillance. Agricultural workers are organized into farmers' societies, affiliated to the General Federation of Peasant Societies. The General Confederation of Trade Unions is affiliated with the Communist-inspired World Federation of Trade Unions and the Confederation of Arab Trade Unions.

Union workers do not represent a significant part of the total work force, comprised mostly of agricultural workers, shopkeepers and government employees. Industrial workers, the most unionized, are only a small portion of the work force. Unions may operate only under officially approved guidelines. Elections are held for union executive councils, which in turn select officers from among the council membership. Nominees are mainly party members. Workers legally have the right to strike after providing notice to the Labor Ministry, but no strikes have been reported since 1968. The unions initiate grievances, but a primary union function is to indoctrinate members with Ba'athist ideology. Union membership is a prerequisite for employment in some sectors.

Strikes and lockouts are legal but, for political reasons, rare.

LABOR INDICATORS, 1987

Total economically active population (millions): 3.956
- % working-age (15–64): 43.1
- % female: 11.6

Activity rate (%)
- Total: 24.2
- Male: 41.6
- Female: 5.8

Employment status (%)
- Employers & self-employed: 25.4 (1977)
- Employees: 59.5 (1977)
- Unpaid family workers: 11.4 (1977)
- Other: 3.7 (1977)

Sectoral employment of economically active (%)
Agriculture, forestry, fishing: 12.5
- Construction: 8.6
- Manufacturing, mining, quarrying, public utilities: 8.8
- Trade, hotels, restaurants: 5.4
- Transportation, communications: 5.7
- Finance, real estate: 0.7
- Services: 49.4

Average annual growth rate of labor force (%, 1985–2000): 4.0
Unemployment (000): 10 (1977)
Labor under 20 years (%): 13.3 (1977)

FOREIGN COMMERCE

Iraq's trade surplus in 1988 was $2.3 billion. The total value of exports was $12.5 billion, consisting mostly of crude oil. Other exports were dates, machinery and chemicals. Imports, in value, were $10.2 billion. Most came in the areas of food and manufactured goods. The largest recipient of exports was Turkey. Other buyers of Iraqi goods were the U.S., Brazil, Soviet Union, Italy, France, Japan and Yugoslavia. Japan sold more items to Iraq than other nations. Additional sources of Iraqi imports included Turkey, U.S., Britain, Germany, France, Romania and Yugoslavia.

FOREIGN TRADE INDICATORS, 1988

Exports (U.S. $ billions): 12.5
Imports (U.S. $ billions): 10.2
Balance of trade (U.S. $ billions): 2.3

Direction of Trade (%), 1986

	Imports	Exports
European Community	31.4	37.4
United States	5.7	5.7
U.S.S.R. & eastern European economies	3.4	0.2
Japan	20.4	11.7

Composition of Trade (%), 1986

	Imports	Exports
Food & agricultural raw materials	17.6	0.4
Fuels & other energy	0.3	99.6 (est.)
Mineral ores & concentrates	0.2	0.0
Manufactured goods	81.9	0.0
of which chemicals	7.5	0.0
of which machinery	39.8	0.0

The Gulf War of 1991 caused extensive damage to Iraq's foreign commerce.

Foreign trade is the virtual monopoly of the State Organization for Trade with six subsidiaries, specializing in automobiles, food products, cement, agricultural chemicals and machinery, canned products, tires and tubes, and drugs. The government also controls foreign trade through strict foreign exchange controls. All capital, service and mercantile transactions involving foreign exchange are required to be approved by the Central Bank. Iraq has trade agreements with some 30 countries. These include preferential agreements with Arab countries and barter and bilateral payment agreements with Eastern bloc countries, France, Sri Lanka and the People's Republic of China.

The principal trade exposition is the Baghdad International Fair held annually.

TRANSPORTATION & COMMUNICATIONS

Prior to the Gulf War of 1991 the Iraqi rail system consisted of 2,962 km. of domestic lines. In 1982 the railway traffic consisted of 797 million passenger kilometers and 2,254 million net ton kilometers of freight.

The ports of Basra and Um Qasr are the gateways of the country. In 1982 these two ports handled 99,754,000 tons of goods. Fao and Khoral Amya are the new terminals for oil tankers. Iraq's new merchant fleet consists of 181 vessels with a gross registered tonnage of 2,694,500 of which oil tankers account for 1,141,000 GRT. The national shipping company is the Iraqi Maritime Transport Company. The ports are administered by the State Organization of Iraqi Ports, which also controls river transport. River traffic is handled by 1,036 river craft, 48 motor vessels and 105 motor boats. The 1,015 km. (630 mi.) Shatt al-Arab, navigable for about 104 km. (64 mi.), has been closed since September 1980 because of the Gulf War.

The country has about 25,000 km. of highways. The national highways are Baghdad—Mosul—Tel Kotchuk (on the Syrian border), Baghdad—Kirkuk—Arbil-Zakho (on the Turkish border), Baghdad—Amara—Basra—Safwan (on the Kuwaiti border) and Kirkuk—Sulaimanya. An extensive program of road construction has been undertaken under the five-year plans. In 1983 there were 229,530 passenger cars and 152,768 commercial vehicles in the country. Per capita vehicle ownership is 14.8 per 1,000.

TRANSPORTATION INDICATORS

Roads (latest)
  Length, km. (mi.): 45,554 (28,305)
  Paved (%): 84
Motor vehicles (latest)
  Automobiles: 672,205
  Trucks and buses: 368,525
  Persons per vehicle: 17
Railroads (latest)
  Track, km. (mi.): 2,457 (1,527)
  Passenger-km. (passenger-mi.) (billions): 1.570 (.975)
  Freight, metric ton-km. (short ton-mi.) (billions): 2.079 (1.424)
Merchant marine
  Vessels (over 100 tons): 141 (1989)
  Total deadweight tonnage (million): 1.8127 (1989)
  Oil tankers (000 GRT): 747 (1985)
Ports (pre-1986)
  Cargo loaded (million metric tons): 97.830
  Cargo unloaded (million metric tons): 8.638
Air
  Km. (mi.) flown (millions): 15.1 (9.4) (1985)
  Passenger-km. (passenger-mi.) (billions): 1.570 (.976) (pre-1986)
  Freight, metric ton-km. (short ton-mi.) (millions): 54.6 (37.4) (pre-1986)
  Mail, metric ton-km. (short ton-mi.) (millions): 52 (36) (1985)
  Airports with scheduled flights: 3 (1990)
Pipelines 1990
  Refined, km. (mi.): 725 (450)
  Natural gas, km. (mi.): 1,360 (845)
Inland waterways (latest)
  Length, km. (mi.): 1,015 (631)

COMMUNICATION INDICATORS, 1988

Telephones
  Total (000): 937 (1987)
  Persons per telephone: 18 (1987)
Phone traffic (millions)
  Combined national: 5,339.151 (pulses)
  International: 10.329 (minutes) (1985)
Post office
  Number of post offices: 343
  Pieces of mail handled (millions): 128.526
Telegraph
  National: 844 (1983)
  International: 426 (1985)
Telex 1985
  Subscriber lines: 2,187
  Traffic (million minutes): 7.668
Telecommunications 1990
  Satellite stations: 3
  Submarine cable: 1

TOURISM & TRAVEL INDICATORS, 1986

Total tourist receipts (U.S. $ millions): 61 (1988)
Number of tourists (000): 1,811.5 (1984)
  of whom from
  Yugoslavia: 45.7
  India: 33.5
  Saudi Arabia: 28.3

The national airline is Iraqi Airways which operates a fleet of 16 aircraft flying to 39 foreign cities. In 1982 Iraqi Airways flew 13.3 million km. (8.2 million mi.) and carried 481,000 passengers. The main international airports are at Baghdad, Basra and Mosul.

Like most aspects of the Iraqi infrastructure, rails, roads and airports were heavily damaged in the Gulf War of 1991.

There are two major pipelines, both closed in the wake of the Gulf wars. A 16-inch pipeline, built in 1949 and 1952, carried Iraqi crude from Kirkuk to Tripoli in Lebanon and Baniyas. A 28-inch pipeline built in 1976 extends from Al-Hadithah to Fao on the Persian Gulf. The length of the crude oil pipeline is 3,281 km. (2,037 mi.), that of the refined products pipeline 725 km. (450 mi.) and that of the natural gas pipeline 1,360 km. (844 mi.)

DEFENSE

The defense structure is headed by the president who is also the minister of defense and the commander in chief. Each of the three services is represented on the Revolutionary Command Council. A National Defense Council advises the president on military policy issues.

The armed forces have two roles: one is to defend the regime and the second is to defend the country. The first goal is achieved through the Baghdad garrison and the general reserve which is directly under the command of the president. The general reserve, commanded by officers most loyal to the regime, is stationed at Tikrit, 100 miles north of Baghdad, the power base of the ruling faction. All other army formations are kept well away from the capital and may be even routed around it when moving from one part of the country to another. Prior to the Gulf War of 1991, about half of the remaining troops were stationed in the north on the Syrian and Iranian borders, especially at Mosul and Kirkuk. Two divisions were stationed in the south around Basra—covering the Kuwaiti and southern Iranian border.

Manpower is provided by compulsory military service for two years required of all male citizens over the age of 18. Liability for service continues through age 40. Over 70,000 males reach military age annually while conscriptable males in the population number over two million.

In July 1990, total armed forces personnel was about one million, with 650,000 reservists.

Iraqi armed forces do not constitute a balanced force. Combat effectiveness is limited by the preponderance of the army in relation to the navy and air force, and excessive reliance on infantry.

Army

Personnel: 955,000 (includes regulars and reserves)

Organization: 4 Corps HQ; 6 armored divisions; 5 mechanized infantry divisions; 5 infantry divisions; 4 mountain divisions; 1 presidential guard division; 2 special forces division; 9 reserve brigades; 15 People's Army volunteer infantry brigades

Equipment: Tanks 4,500; 3,000 combat vehicles; 500 motorized infantry combat vehicles; 4,500 guns; 150 howitzers; mortars; rocket launchers; surface-to-surface missiles

Army Aviation: 45 helicopters; Exocet missiles; 4,000 air defense guns; captured Iranian equipment in service

Navy

Personnel: 5,000 (Reserves: 3,000)

Units: 5 frigates; 15 fast attack craft; 38 patrol craft; 5 minesweepers; 3 landing craft; 1 support ship

Bases: Basra, Um Qasr

Air Force

Personnel: 40,000 (Reserves: 18,000)

Organization: 500 combat aircraft; 100 armored helicopters; 2 bomber squadrons; 11 fighter squadrons with MiG 23-BMs, super Etendards, and Mirage F-1 EQ5s; 5 interceptor squadrons; 1 reconnaissance squadron; 2 transport squadrons; 154 trainers; air-to-air and air-to-surface missiles

Air Bases: Habbaniya, Shaiba, Kirkuk, Raschid, Basra and Mosul

Until 1958 the Iraqi Army was largely British-trained and equipped, but after the coup of that year the Russians displaced the British as the principal suppliers of military hardware and training programs. Soviet military aid has totaled over $700 million. Iraq also received $46.7 million from the United States through the Military Assistance Program through 1968. Recently, France has become a major arms supplier to Iraq.

In the Iran-Iraq War, military experts gave Iraq the edge over Iran in hardware and sophisticated technological weaponry. Iraq's Air Force was far superior to that of Iran while the tank force was more than a match for that of Iran. Iraq, however, lost more men (over 125,000) as prisoners of war compared to 10,000 for Iran. Along the southern front, Iraq constructed a formidable defensive "Maginot Line." Unlike Iran, Iraq had the support of virtually all the superpowers including the United States, France, the Soviet Union and the United Kingdom.

Iraq has no defense production. Arms purchases abroad during 1975–83 totaled $23.325 billion of which $7.2 billion was supplied by the Soviet Union, $3.8 billion by France and $1.5 billion by China.

In the invasion and subjugation of Kuwait on August 2, 1990, Iraq's military affirmed a reputation as the Gulf area's major power. But the crushing defeat by the American-led coalition in 1991 showed the limits of that power. One factor which stood out was Iraq's inability to defend against or counter the well-trained, technologically sophisticated American air force. Allied planes flew almost uncontested over targets in southern Iraq and occupied Kuwait. Republican Guard divisions, the elite of the Iraqi army, were pounded for weeks before the ground war of late February. By then, American, British and French units were able to outflank and defeat Guard divisions rather easily.

EDUCATION

Education in Iraq is compulsory for those aged six to 12, and free for citizens between the ages of six and 18. In 1981, the country had 10,800 primary schools, 1600 secondary schools and 160 vocational schools. There were also six universities, over 60 teacher-training colleges and 15 other institutions of higher education. In 1984, half of those aged 12 to 17 were enrolled in secondary schools. Primary school enrollment declined from nearly 100% of the relevant age group in 1978 to 84% in 1988. Adult literacy in 1989 was estimated at 45%.

Iraq underwent a major overhaul of education in 1974–5. All schooling from nursery to the university level was made free, and private education was largely abolished. Most such schools were converted to government control.

Schooling consists of 12 years, divided into six years of primary school and six years of secondary school, which consists of a three-year intermediate course and a three-year college preparatory course. Primary schools are coeducational while secondary schools are segregated by sex.

The academic year runs from September to June. The medium of instruction is Arabic with a provision for the use of Kurdish in Kurdish areas. French is the official second language, while English is taught from grades 5 and 6 on. Classes are held six days a week for an average of five hours daily. Friday is the weekly holiday.

The curriculum in primary schools includes religion, Arabic language, arithmetic and social studies. English and general science are introduced in the secondary-intermediate level. At the secondary preparatory grade students are divided into a science stream and a humanities stream, although science subjects are also offered in the latter course. Examinations are held at the end of the primary school stage, the secondary-intermediate stage, and the secondary-preparatory stage. The difficulty of these examinations is reflected in the high attrition rates, often as high as 70%.

The majority of the schools are run by the government, but, despite the reforms of the mid-1970s, private schools continue to function at both primary and secondary levels. Most of the private primary schools are operated by Muslim religious organizations; their share of primary school enrollment was 1% in 1983. Private secondary schools, most of them maintained by Christian religious denominations, had, on the other hand, a 24% share of secondary school enrollment. The private school curricula conform to government standards. Some subjects are required to be taught by teachers appointed by the ministry of education.

Female education has made rapid strides in recent years and in the mid-1980s girls accounted for 46% of the enrollment at the first level, 35% at the second level and 32% at the third level.

Teacher training is provided in a number of institutions, including Baghdad University's two colleges of education. Unlike many other Arab countries, Iraq has no shortage of primary school teachers and, possibly, a small surplus since Iraq exported teachers to both Saudi Arabia and Yemen.

Most vocational institutions offer six-year courses at the intermediate-secondary level, while others provide two-year commercial courses. Despite massive shortages of technical workers, enrollment in vocational schools in the mid-1980s was nominal because of a general dislike of manual labor.

Adult education is offered in literacy schools and fundamental education centers. Night schools offering instruction in basic skills exist in all the major cities. Fundamental education centers offer instruction in the three Rs and vocational subjects such as health care and agriculture.

Educational administration is centralized in the Ministry of Education. The ministry's eight departments, each headed by a director general, are concerned with general education, research, inspection, vocational education, administration, cultural relations, Kurdish studies and physical education. The Council on Social and Educational Development functions as a consultative body within the ministry. The country is divided

EDUCATION INDICATORS, 1989

Literacy
- Total (%): 45.9
- Male (%): 65.9
- Female (%): 26.0

First level
- Schools: 7,930
- Students: 3,012,028
- Teachers: 122,089
- Student/teacher ratio: 24.7
- Net enrollment ratio: 86 (1987)

Second level
- Schools: 2,387
- Students: 981,409
- Teachers: 42,829
- Student/teacher ratio: 22.9
- Net enrollment ratio: 41 (1987)

Vocational
- Schools: 258
- Students: 153,647
- Teachers: 9,323
- Student/teacher ratio: 16.5

Third level (post-secondary)
- Institutions: 25 (1987)
- Students: 142,496 (1987)
- Teachers: 8,327 (1987)
- Student/teacher ratio: 17.1 (1987)
- Gross enrollment ratio: 12.5 (1987)
- Students (/100,000 pop.): 1,076

Foreign study
- Foreign students in national universities: 4,476 (1975)
- Students abroad: 5,185
  - of whom in
    - United States: 691 (1988)
    - France: 368 (1988)
    - Federal Republic of Germany: 385 (1988)
    - United Kingdom: 1,214 (1987)

Public expenditure
- Total (I.D. million): 690.134
- % of national budget: 6.4 (1987)
- % of current expenditure: 90.6

into 15 educational districts, each under a director. Construction and maintenance of schools are the responsibilities of the provincial governors.

Higher education is provided by eight universities.

LEGAL SYSTEM

The legal system is based on the Baghdad Penal Codes formulated by the British but drawing on Ottoman and French sources. These codes have been amended but never superseded. A moderate interpretation of Islamic law gives women equal rights in divorce, land ownership and suffrage.

The judiciary consists of three types of courts: civil, religious and special. The jurisdiction of the civil courts extends to all civil, commercial and criminal cases. The Courts of First Instance, distributed throughout the country in administrative centers, are of two kinds: those with limited competence and those with unlimited jurisdiction, both presided over by a single judge. Peace courts, also with a single judge, function wherever there is a court of first instance. Judges of the courts of first instance also preside over magistrate, or penal, courts with original, but limited, jurisdiction in criminal cases. More serious cases are heard by a court of sessions with three judges presided over by the president of the court of appeal in the district. Courts of sessions are located in each of the country's five judicial districts: Baghdad, Basra, Kirkuk, Hilla and Mosul. Each of these districts also contains a court of appeals consisting of a president and three vice presidents. The court of last resort is the court of cassation, consisting of a president and not less than 15 members. The court is divided into four benches: general, civil and commercial, criminal and personal status.

Cases affecting the personal status of Muslims are dealt with in the Shari'a courts, presided over by a *qadi*, and established wherever there is a court of first instance. Cases affecting the personal status of Christians and other religious minorities are heard by the spiritual, or communal, councils of each community.

Trials in civil, criminal and religious courts are open. Defendants are entitled to counsel. A lawyer is provided if a defendant cannot afford one. Charges and evidence are available for review. Appellate courts hear cases not under the jurisdiction of the revolutionary courts. The revolutionary courts, which usually hold closed trials, hear such crimes as espionage, treason, smuggling and drug trafficking. The right of defense in such courts reportedly is severely restricted. The "special courts" constituted by the Revolutionary Command Council for specific incidents, such as the reported conspiracy against the regime in 1979, are also closed. These special tribunals are apparently exempt from constitutional safeguards of defendants' rights. The right of defense is proscribed; defendants are held incommunicado, and confessions extracted by torture are used against the defendants. Appeals can be taken only to the chairman of the Revolutionary Command Council, the president. However, the availability of this appeal may be ineffective, since there are reports that executions take place shortly after trial.

The judiciary is supervised by the Ministry of Justice and a Judicial Council headed by the president of the court of cassation.

The correctional system is administered by the director general of prisons. The four major prisons are at Baghdad, Mosul, Basra and Hilla. There are numerous centers of detention in each province.

LAW ENFORCEMENT

The national police force is organized into a regular police, or civil police, including the Mobile Force, and the desert police. Both are directly controlled by the director general of police. The regular police are stationed in each of the 18 provinces under police commandants who are answerable to provincial governors. The Mobile Force is called upon only in times of serious disorders. The camel-mounted desert police operate in the desert and border regions on the west and northwest.

Statistics on crime are not released by the government, but homicide is believed to rank high among serious crimes. Smuggling and blackmarketeering are major law enforcement problems and specialized police units have been assigned to combat them.

The Iraqi secret police is the Security Directorate which is charged with suppression of crimes against the state and is vested with broad, inquisitorial powers.

HEALTH

Health care in Iraq is free. In the 1980s, despite the Iranian war, the government undertook a major expansion of health facilities. By 1986, through spending of $1.5 billion, 30 new hospitals had been constructed. Most physicians, however, practice in the large cities, with about half concentrated in Baghdad metropolis. Almost all hospitals are state run.

The major health problems and the chief causes of death and debility are parasitic diseases, malaria, tuberculosis, trachoma, dysentery, typhus and venereal diseases. Health and sanitation standards are low. Nutritional deficiencies are also responsible for the high incidence of diseases. Bombing damage inflicted on Iraq in the 1991 war has led to an array of health problems and a dramatic decline in the quality of health care.

FOOD & NUTRITION

Wheat bread is the staple food, often supplemented by rice. Lamb is the preferred meat. Yogurt and tea are consumed several times a day. Vegetables, fresh fruits and dates are other important staples.

MEDIA & CULTURE

Iraqi media are owned and controlled by the state despite the provision in the 1968 Constitution for free-

HEALTH INDICATORS

Health personnel 1984
  Physicians: 4,428
    persons per: 3,324
  Dentists: 984
  Nurses: 6,082 (1982)
  Pharmacists: 952
  Midwives: 2,267 (1982)
Hospitals 1982
  Number: 230 (1985)
  Number of beds (/10,000): 18
  Admissions/discharges (/10,000): 592
  Bed occupancy rate (%): 60.3
  Average length of stay (days): 6
Type of hospitals (%) 1982
  Government: 95.7
  Private nonprofit: 0.0
  Private profit: 4.3
Public health expenditures (latest)
  As % of national budget: 4.6
  Per capita (U.S. $): 15.20
Vital statistics
  Crude death rate (/1,000): 7 (1990)
Life expectancy at birth 1990
  Males: 66
  Females: 68
Infant mortality rate (/1,000 live births): 67 (1990)
Child mortality rate under 5 years. (/1,000 live births) (1985–90): 94
Population with access to safe water (%): 87 (latest)

dom of the press. All privately owned newspapers ceased publication in 1967, and the right to issue newspapers became the monopoly of the state-owned Press and Printing Organization established under the supervision of the Ministry of Culture and Guidance. Six dailies and 22 non-daily newspapers are published, of which *Ath-Thawra* (Revolution) enjoys the largest circulation (250,000). Total newspaper circulation is 262,000, or 14 per 1,000 inhabitants. All the newspapers are published in Baghdad; five are published in Arabic, one in English, the *Baghdad Observer*, and one in

MEDIA INDICATORS

Newspapers
  Number of dailies: 6 (latest)
  Circulation (000): 328 (latest)
  Per 1,000 pop.: 21 (latest)
  Number of nondailies: 22 (1986)
  Number of periodicals: 314 (1986)
  Newsprint consumption (1988)
    Total metric tons: 34,000
    Per 1,000 pop. (kg.): 1,925
Book publishing
  Number of titles: 82 (pre-1986)
Radio
  Number of transmitters: 39 (1989)
  Number of persons per radio receiver: 4.9 (1989)
Television
  Television transmitters: 35 (1989)
  Number of persons per T.V. receiver: 17 (1989)
Cinema
  Number of fixed cinemas: 84 (pre-1986)
  Seating capacity (000): 65 (pre-1986)
Films
  Number of long films produced: 1 (latest)

Kurdish. Most of the nearly 320 periodicals are published generally by community or special interest groups.

Censorship is based on the Press Law of 1964, which empowers the Minister of Culture and Guidance to impose fines and jail sentences on editors of newspapers or periodicals publishing offensive materials and to revoke the license of the publication. Criticism not directly affecting the government is tolerated, and the degree of censorship varies with the issues.

CULTURAL & ENVIRONMENTAL INDICATORS

Libraries (pre-1986)
  Number: 15
  Volumes (000): 240
  Registered borrowers (000): 17
Museums (pre-1986)
  Annual attendance (000): 63
  Attendance (/1,000 pop.): 4
Performing arts (latest)
  Number of performances: 60
  Annual attendance (000): 204
  Attendance (/1,000 pop.): 16

The national news agency is the Iraqi News Agency with five bureaus abroad. Foreign news agencies represented in Baghdad include ADN, AFP, AP, dpa, Hsinhua, MENA, Reuters, Tass and Novosti.

Book publishing is a minor activity limited to Baghdad. The principal publisher and distributor is the state-owned National House for Publication, Distribution and Advertisement. In 1982 182 titles were published. Iraq does not adhere to any copyright convention.

Broadcasting is controlled by the Broadcasting Service of the Republic of Iran which operates 14 medium-wave and short wave transmitters at Salman Pak, near Baghdad, and at Abu Ghuraib, and four medium-wave transmitters at Basra and Kirkuk. The home service program is on the air for about 150 hours a week broadcasting in Arabic, Kurdish, Syriac, and Turkmanic. The foreign service is on the air for 7 hours a day. No license fee is payable. Most of the radio broadcasting hours are devoted to entertainment, information and education.

Television was introduced in 1956. The state-owned Baghdad Television has a main station at Baghdad and 14 other sites, covering about three-fourths of the population. Weekly broadcasting time is about 49 hours. About half the programs are of local origin. Imported programs come from other Arab countries, the U.K., the USSR, France, Germany and the United States. No license fee is payable. In the mid-1980s, programs of entertainment, information and culture accounted for most broadcasting hours. There is no educational television.

The country's only film producer is the Cinema and Theater Administration Service of the Ministry of Culture and Guidance.

The largest library is the Central Library of the University of Baghdad with over 200,000 volumes. The National Library, founded in 1963, has over 60,000 volumes.

SOCIAL WELFARE

Organized state-sponsored social welfare is a comparatively new phenomenon in Iraq. The Social Security Law of 1965 covers all establishments employing more than 30 workers and provides a wide range of benefits, including sickness, disability, unemployment and death payments and old-age pensions. The program is administered by the State Organization for Workers' Pensions and Social Security and is financed by contributions from workers, employers and the government.

GLOSSARY

amanah: directorate.
agha: Kurdish tribal leader.
asimah: capital, as in amanat al-asimah, governorate of the capital (of Iraq).
balad (pl. bilad): town or city.
baladiyah (pl. baladiyat): municipality.
dunum: unit of area equal to 0.25 ha. or 0.618 ac. See also *mishara.*
fatwa: legal opinion on a point of Muslim religious law, issued by a *mufti.*
liwa: province.
madina: a city quarter inhabited by a particular ethnic group.
mahalla: a city quarter, as an administrative unit.
miri sirf: government land.
mishara: a unit of area equal to 0.25 ha. or 0.618 ac. See also *dunum.*
mudir: a subdistrict administrative office.
muhafaaza (pl. muhafaazat): governorate.
mujtahid: an interpreter of Islamic religious law, especially a Shi'a scholar whose judgments on legal and religious issues are accepted by the community.
mukhtar: village headman.
mutasarrif: governor.
nahiyah (pl. nawahin): county.
qada (pl. aqdiya): district.
qadi: a Muslim religious judge.
quaimmaqam: deputy governor, chief administrative officer of a qada.
qarya: precinct of a town or a village.
rais: mayor or head of a municipality or similar organization.
saifi: summer crop.
sarifah: a one-room hut made of reed matting in urban slums.
sarraf: a local money lender.
shitwi: winter crop.

CHRONOLOGY (from 1945)

1945— Iraq joins the Arab League and the United Nations.
1946— Tewfik Suweidy, Arshad al Umary, and Nuri al Said head brief governments.
1947— Salif Jabr forms new cabinet. . . . British forces are withdrawn from Iraq.
1948— Mohammed al Sadr and Muzazim al Pachachi head brief governments.
1949— Nuri al Said and Jawdat al Ayubi head brief governments. . . . Forced emigration of Jews from Iraq begins.
1950— Tewfik Suweidy and Nuri al Said head brief governments.
1952— Mustapha al Umari and Nuruddin Mahmoud head brief governments.
1953— Faisal II ascends the throne. . . . Jamil al Madfai and Fadhil Jumali head brief governments.
1954— Arshad al Umari and Nuri al Said head brief governments.
1955— Iraq joins the Baghdad Pact.
1957— Ali Jawdat and Abdul Waham Marjan head brief governments.
1958— Ahmed Mukhtar Baban heads new cabinet. . . . Iraq and Jordan unite to form the Arab Federation. . . . In swift army coup Abdul Karim Qasim, Abdul Salam Arif and other army officers seize power; Faisal II, Crown Prince Abdul Illah and Nuri al Said are executed; Arif is later dismissed from post as prime minister and arrested. . . . Agrarian reform law is passed. . . . New constitution is promulgated.
1959— Iraq withdraws from the Baghdad Pact and the Arab Federation. . . . Revolt by a military contingent in Mosul is suppressed.
1961— Kurds launch revolt under Mustafa al-Barzani.
1963— Qasim is overthrown and executed in a Ba'athist-inspired coup led by Abdul Salam Arif and Ahmed Hasan al-Bakr. . . . National Council of Revolutionary Command is formed as supreme state body. . . . Ba'athists are ousted from government after an internal power struggle.
1964— New provisional constitution is promulgated. . . . An uncertain cease-fire is arranged with the Kurds. . . . Iraqi Arab Socialist Union is formed as the country's sole political party. . . . All banks and major industries are nationalized.
1965— Arif Abd-al-Razzak is named premier and is later replaced by Rahman al Bazzaz. . . . Razzak stages two pro-Nasser coups, both unsuccessful.
1966— Arif is killed in helicopter crash with 10 aides; his brother, Abdul Rahman Mohammad Arif, is chosen to succeed to the presidency.
1967— Iraq breaks with the United States and the United Kingdom following Arab-Israeli War. . . . Television is introduced. . . . Tahir Yahya is named premier.
1968— Ahmed Hasan al-Bakr topples Arif regime and forms new Ba'athist-dominated government; Arif is exiled and Yahya is imprisoned.
1970— Iraq and Iran come to the brink of war following Iran's demand for a revision of the Shatt al-Arab border between the two countries.
1973— A National Progressive Front is formed with the Ba'ath Party and the Communist Party as partners in a ruling coalition. . . . Security chief Nazim Kazzar leads abortive coup.
1975— Iraq nationalizes the Iraq Petroleum Company and its subsidiaries. . . .

1976— Kurds in fresh uprisings against the government call for more autonomy. . . . Iran and Iraq sign treaty of reconciliation resolving the border dispute.

1977— The Revolutionary Command Council is expanded from five members to 22.

1978— The Communist Party, accused of subversion, is withdrawn from the National Progressive Front; 21 Communists are executed for engaging in political activities with the armed forces.

1979— President Ahmad Hasan al-Bakr steps down for reasons of health and is succeeded in office by his second in command, Gen. Saddam Hussein al-Tikriti. . . . Five high-ranking members of the Revolutionary Command Council are arrested and executed for plotting against the Saddam regime; Syria is identified as the foreign power behind the plotters. . . . Iraq and the Soviet Union fall out over Soviet policies toward Ethiopia and Israel.

1980— Iraq revokes agreement with Iran over the Shatt al-Arab and launches all-out attack against its Shiite neighbor; in swift thrust captures Khorramshahr and establishes credible military supremacy in the region.

1981— Iran retakes Khorramshahr. Relations with Syria and Libya are broken over their support for Iran in the Iran-Iraq War.

1983— Kurds renew their insurgency under the leadership of the sons of Mullah Barzani.

1984— Iraq restores diplomatic ties with the United States after 17 years. . . . Elections are held to the National Assembly. . . . Iran crosses border and takes oil rich Magnoon Island. Iraq retaliates with attacks on Kharg Island oil terminal and gulf shipping. . . . Iraq accepts U.N. call for ceasefire which Iran rejects. . . . Iraq enters into agreement with Turkey and Saudi Arabia for new pipeline projects that will bypass the gulf.

1986— At Ba'ath congress, Saddam Hussein strengthens position as party leader.

1987— At an Arab League meeting, Iraq and other Arab countries re-establish relations with Egypt.

1988— Iraq regains the offensive initiative in Iranian war—taking Faw peninsula, Shalamcheh area, Magnoon Island—and expels Iranian troops from Kurdistan. Iran accepts U.N. cease-fire terms in August. Iraq puts down a Kurdish revolt, forces thousands to flee to Turkey and Iran.

1989— Talks with Iran on a permanent peace are stalled over disputes on the border and on the Shatt al-Arab waterway. Elections for National Assembly draw 75% voter turnout; ruling National Progressive Patriotic Front, three-party coalition led by Ba'ath, takes all 250 seats. Explosion at Iraqi defensive industry complex, presumably a missile development site, focuses Western concern on Iraq's military buildup.

1990— Permanent peace concluded with Iran in mid-August. Iraq accepts all Iranian claims, including dividing Shatt al-Arab. Iraq invades and conquers Kuwait on August 2, declaring the tiny emirate annexed, and Iraq's 19th province, on August 8. Led by United States, a multi-national coalition, under the aegis of the U.N., responds diplomatically and militarily to Iraqi invasion. U.N. passes resolutions calling on Iraq to withdraw, imposing economic sanctions and authorizing member states to evict Iraqi forces from the occupied emirate.

1991— Thirty-member coalition, led by U.S., defeats and forces Iraq to withdraw from Kuwait, in air and ground military assault, from mid-January to late February. Iraq accepts U.N. peace terms, calling for billions in reparation payments. Allied bombing campaign inflicts massive damage on all parts of the Iraqi infrastructure. Regime of Saddam Hussein puts down revolts by Shi'as in southern Iraq and by Kurds in the north undertaken in aftermath of defeat in Gulf War.

BIBLIOGRAPHY (from 1970)

BOOKS

Abdulghani, Jasim. *Iraq and Iran: The Years of Crisis.* Baltimore, MD, 1984.

Abdul Rahman, A. J. *Iraq* (World Bibliographical Series). Boulder, CO, 1984.

Al-Arif, Ismail. *Iraq Reborn: A Firsthand Account of the 1958 Revolution and After.* New York, 1982.

Al-Eyd, Kadhim A. *Oil Revenues and Accelerated Growth.* New York, 1979.

Annual Abstracts of Statistics (Baghdad, 1973).

Attiyah, Ghassan R. *Iraq, 1908–1921: A Socio-Political Study.* Portland, OR, 1975.

Axelgard, Fred. *U.S.-Arab Relations: The Iraqi Dimension.* Washington, D.C., 1985.

El Azhary, M. S. *The Iran-Iraq War: Historical, Economic and Political Analysis.* New York, 1984.

Gabbay, Rony. *Communism and Agrarian Reform in Iraq.* Totowa, NJ, 1978.

Ghareeb, Edmund. *The Kurdish Question in Iraq.* Syracuse, NY, 1981.

Helms, Christine M. *Iraq: Eastern Flank of the Arab World.* Washington, D.C., 1984.

Hussein, Saddam. *Social and Foreign Affairs in Iraq.* Totowa, NJ, 1979.

Ireland, P. U. *Iraq: A Study in Political Development.* New York, 1970.

Ismael, Tareq Y. *Iraq and Iran: Roots of Conflict.* Syracuse, NY, 1982.

Jalal, Ferhang. *The Role of Government in the Industrialization of Iraq, 1950–65.* London, 1972.

Karsh, Efraim (editor). *The Iran-Iraq War: Impact and Implications.* London, 1989.

Kelidar, Abbas. *Integration of Modern Iraq.* New York, 1979.

Khadduri, Majid. *Republican Iraq: A Study of Iraqi Politics since the Revolution of 1958.* New York, 1970.

———. *Socialist Iraq: A Study in Iraqi Politics since 1968.* Washington, D.C., 1978.

Kimball, Lorenzo Kent. *The Changing Patterns of Political Power in Iraq, 1958–1971.* New York, 1972.

Levy, Victor C. *Aspects of Efficiency in a Socialist Developing Country.* New York, 1985.

McLaurin, R. D. *Foreign Policy Making in the Middle East, Domestic Influences on Foreign Policy in Egypt, Iraq, Israel and Syria.* New York, 1977.

Niblock, Tim. *Iraq: The Contemporary State.* New York, 1982.

Nieuwenhus, Tom. *Politics and Society in Early Modern Iraq.* Boston, MA, 1982.

O'Ballance, Edgar. *The Kurdish Revolt, 1961–1970.* Hamden, CT, 1970.

Penrose, Edith, and E. F. Penrose. *Iraq: Economics, Oil and Politics.* Boulder, CO, 1978.

Souresrafil, Behrouz. *The Iran-Iraq War.* Plainview, N.Y., 1989.

Tarbush, Mohammed. *The Role of the Military in Politics: A Case Study of Iraq to 1941.* Boston, MA, 1983.

UNESCO. *Aspects of Iraqi Cultural Policy.* Paris, 1980.

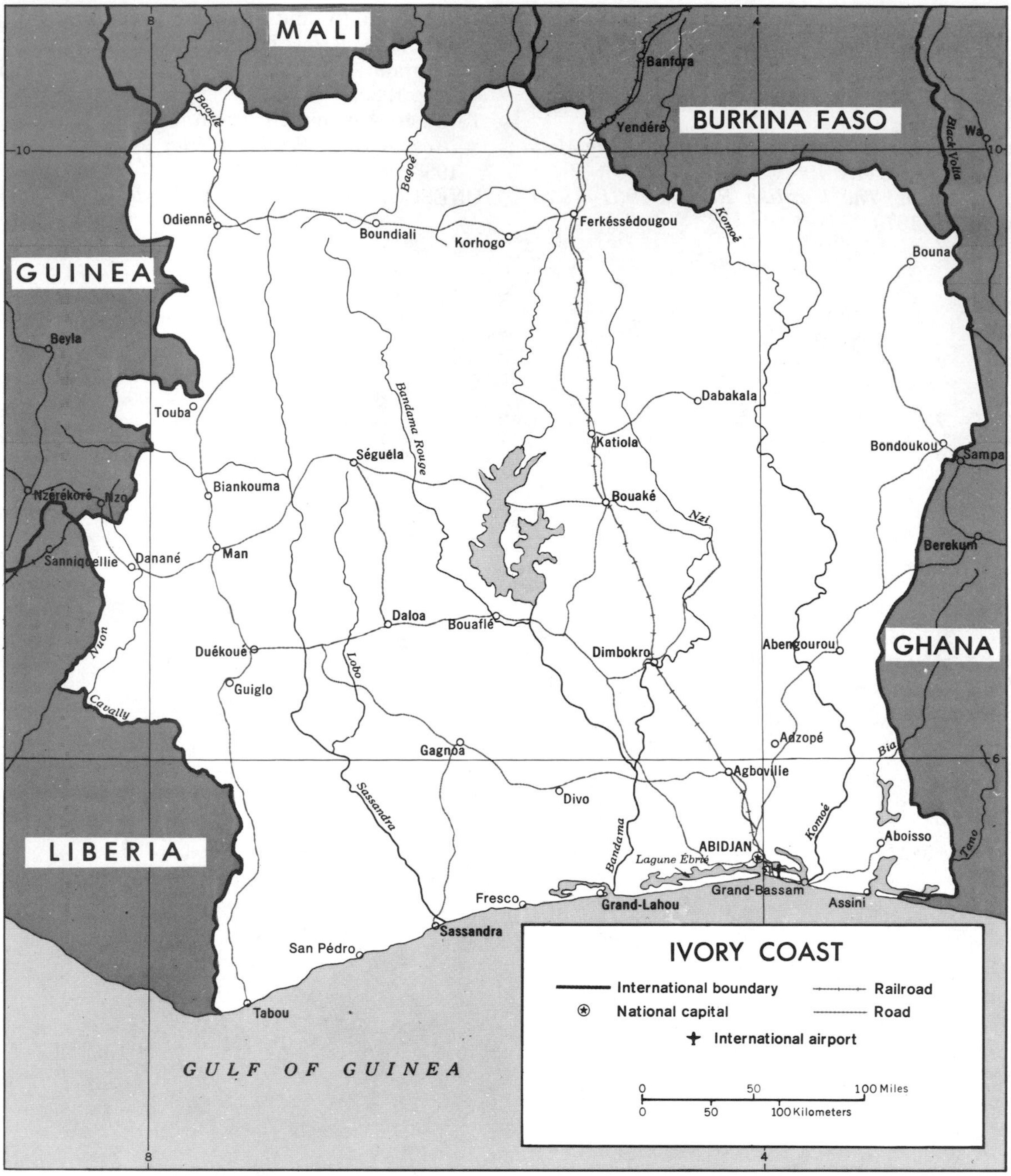

MALI
BURKINA FASO
GUINEA
GHANA
LIBERIA
GULF OF GUINEA
Banfora
Yendéré
Wa
Black Volta
Baoulé
Bagoé
Odienné
Boundiali
Korhogo
Ferkéssédougou
Komoé
Bouna
Beyla
Touba
Bandama Rouge
Dabakala
Katiola
Bondoukou
Sampa
Séguéla
Biankouma
Nzérékoré
Nzo
Bouaké
Nzi
Berekum
Sanniquellie
Danané
Man
Daloa
Bouaflé
Nuon
Duékoué
Dimbokro
Abengourou
Lobo
Guiglo
Cavally
Adzopé
Gagnoa
Bia
Agboville
Sassandra
Divo
Bandama
Komoé
Aboisso
Tano
ABIDJAN
Lagune Ébrié
Grand-Bassam
Fresco
Grand-Lahou
Assini
Sassandra
San Pédro
Tabou
IVORY COAST
International boundary
National capital
International airport
Railroad
Road
0 50 100 Miles
0 50 100 Kilometers
10
8
4
6

IVORY COAST REPUBLIC

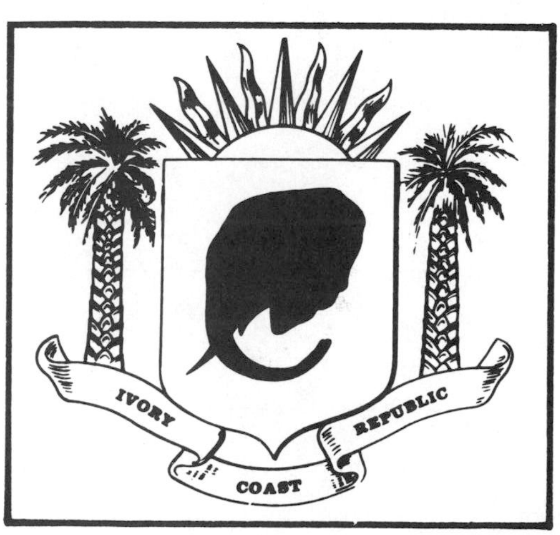

IVORY COAST

BASIC FACT SHEET

OFFICIAL NAME: Republic of Ivory Coast (République de Côte d'Ivoire)

ABBREVIATION: IV

CAPITAL: Abidjan

HEAD OF STATE & HEAD OF GOVERNMENT: President Felix Houphouet-Boigny (from 1960)

NATURE OF GOVERNMENT: Multiparty parliamentary system.

POPULATION: 12,478,024 (1990)

AREA: 322,463 sq. km. (124,503 sq. mi.)

ETHNIC MAJORITY: Akan, Lagoon, Krou, Mande, Senoufo and Lobi

LANGUAGE: French (official)

RELIGIONS: Animism, Islam and Christianity

UNIT OF CURRENCY: Communauté Financíère Africaine franc (C.F.A.F.)

NATIONAL FLAG: Tricolor of orange, white and green vertical stripes

NATIONAL EMBLEM: A shield displaying an elephant's head in profile flanked by two palm trees with the rising sun above and a scroll bearing the legend "République de Côte D'Ivoire" beneath

NATIONAL ANTHEM: "Hail, Hospitable Land of Hope"

NATIONAL HOLIDAYS: August 7 (Independence Day, National Day); January 1 (New Year's Day); Christian festivals include Assumption, All Saints' Day, Good Friday, Easter Monday, Ascension, Pentecostal Monday and Christmas; also, variable Islamic festivals are observed

NATIONAL CALENDAR: Gregorian

PHYSICAL QUALITY OF LIFE INDEX: 40 on

DATE OF INDEPENDENCE: August 7, 1960

DATE OF CONSTITUTION: November 3, 1960

WEIGHTS & MEASURES: Metric

GEOGRAPHICAL FEATURES

Ivory Coast, on the southern coast of West Africa, is roughly square in shape, with an area of 322,463 sq. km. (124,503 sq. mi.). It extends 808 km. (502 mi.) southeast to northwest and 780 km. (485 mi.) northeast to southwest. Its Gulf of Guinea coastline is 507 km. (315 mi.) long. Ivory Coast's total international boundary of 3,035 km. (1,886 mi.) is shared with five countries: Mali (515 km.; 320 mi.); Burkina Faso (531 km.; 330 mi.); Ghana (668 km.; 415 mi.); Liberia (716 km.; 445 mi.); and Guinea (605 km.; 376 mi.). The border with Ghana is based on the Anglo-French Agreement of 1893 and that with Liberia on the Franco-Liberian Accord of 1907. Other borders follow the administrative boundaries of French West Africa. There are no current border disputes.

The capital is Abidjan, with a 1980 population of 1,686,100. Other major urban centers are Bouaké (175,264), Man (50,288), Daloa (60,837) and Korhoga (45,250).

Topographically the whole country is a vast plateau sloping southward, with no major natural divisions or barriers. However, three regions and vegetation zones are commonly recognized. The lagoon region, a narrow coastal belt extending from the Ghana border to Fresco on the Sassandra River, is fringed by sandy islands or sandbars and lagoons. The lagoons run parallel to the coast and are linked to one another by small canals. On the true continental shore, plantations and woodlands extend 8 to 24 km. (5 to 10 mi.) inland. The second region is the central forest belt, which covers roughly a third of the country and varies from 150 to 300 km. (93 to 186 mi.) wide. Between Fresco and the mouth of Cavally River the forest reaches the Gulf of Guinea, in many cases to the water's edge. At the northern limits some of the higher mountains rise over 914 m. (3,000 ft.) high. The northern limit of the central forest region is marked by an irregular transition to grassy woodlands, which constitute the third region. The northern part of this region is a typical Sudanese savanna of grass and shrubs. The only mountain in this region is the continuation of the eastern slopes of the Guinea Highlands along the Guinea border.

Ivory Coast is drained by four major rivers, running roughly parallel from north to south: the Comoé, the Bandama, the Sassandra and the Cavally. They are navigable only for about 48 km. (30 mi.) inland, even for vessels of light draft, except for the Sassandra, which is navigable for about 80 km. (50 mi.). All of them are subject to flooding in the rainy season and are sluggish in the summer.

CLIMATE & WEATHER

Ivory Coast has a tropical climate, with four seasons in the South and in the central forest region and two seasons in the northern savanna region. In the coastal region the long dry season lasts from December to mid-May, followed by the great rainy season from mid-May to mid-July, then the short dry season from mid-

July to October, and finally the little rainy season from October to November. In the central forest region the short dry season from November to mid-March is followed by the short wet season from mid-March to mid-May, the short dry season from mid-May to mid-July and the long rainy season from mid-July to mid-November. In the North there is a long wet season from June to October and a dry season for the rest of the year.

The coastal region receives an average annual rainfall of 2,030 to 3,040 mm. (80 to 120 in.). The rainfall decreases to 1,340 to 2,540 mm. (53 to 100 in.) in the central forest region and to 500 mm. (20 in.) in the northern region. The temperatures are related inversely to the rainfall and progress from an annual average of 23°C to 26.6°C (73°F to 80°F) in the coastal region to 32°C to 34.4°C (90°F to 94°F) in the northern areas. Humidity corresponds to the rainfall and is highest in the South during the rainy season.

The prevailing wind systems are the southwestern monsoons and the northeastern harmattan, a dry, scorching wind from the Sahara. Tornadoes are common at the beginning and end of rainy seasons.

POPULATION

The population of Ivory Coast in 1990 was 12,478,024, based on the last official census, in 1975, when the population was 6,670,913.

The population is unevenly distributed, with heavy concentrations in the south-central and southeastern areas. The northeastern and southwestern parts of the country remain virtually uninhabited. The average density of population in 1990 was estimated at 39.5 per sq. km. (102.2 per sq. mi.); it was 120 per sq. km. (311 per sq. mi.) in agricultural areas in the mid-1980s.

The bulk of the people live in small, scattered settlements or villages, but the prevailing population movement is toward cities. The urban population is growing at an average annual rate of 6.21%. Abidjan is said to be growing at the rate of 10,000 people a year and now accounts for 33% of the urban population. However, 60% of the population of Abidjan live in slums or squatter settlements.

Ivory Coast is one of the few African countries without serious restrictions on immigration. Over the years the flow of immigrants has added nearly 1 million to 1.5 million persons, mostly male workers, to the population. Of these, some 750,000 to 1 million are Burkinabe, 50,000 to 100,000 are Malians, 200,000 are Ghanaians and 250,000 are Guineans. Non-Ivorians make up nearly half the population of Abidjan and 80% of the rural wage-earning labor force. The great majority of migrants are seasonal workers who usually return to their homeland after several years. Ivory Coast also has one of the largest non-African communities in West Africa, including 100,000 Lebanese, 37,000 Frenchmen, and large numbers of Syrians and Indians. Very few Ivorians emigrate, except for members of the Krou tribe, known as kroomen, who are noted as sailors and cargo handlers.

DEMOGRAPHIC INDICATORS

Population (millions): 12.478 (1990)
Year of last census: 1975
Sex distribution (% at last census): males, 51.8; females, 48.2
Population estimates and projections (millions)

1930: 2,075	1960: 3,865	1990: 12,657
1940: 2,350	1970: 5,550	2000: 19,289
1950: 2,775	1980: 8,320	

Age profile (% at last census)

0–14: 44.5	30–44: 16.7	60–74: 2.8
15–29: 27.0	45–59: 7.8	75 and over: 1.2

Median age (yrs.): 15.6 (1985)
Youth population (% aged 15–24): (1985) 18.3; (2000) 19.0
Total dependency rate, 1985: 104.5
Annual growth rate (%)

1950–55: 2.97	1975–80: 4.19	2000–2005: 3.67
1955–60: 3.21	1980–85: 4.16	2005–10: 3.46
1960–65: 3.49	1985–90: 4.12	2010–15: 3.09
1965–70: 4.05	1990–95: 3.91	2015–20: 2.72
1970–75: 4.07	1995–2000: 3.83	2020–25: 2.36

Hypothetical size of stationary population (millions): 94
Assumed year of reaching net reproduction rate of 1: 2050
Urban population (000): 4,302 (1985)
Urban population (%): (1988) 45; (1965) 23
Annual urban population growth rate (%, 1985–90): 6.21
Annual rural population growth rate (%, 1985–90): 2.45
Percentage of urban population in largest city: 34 (1980)
Percentage of urban population in cities of population over 500,000: 34 (1980)
Number of cities of population over 500,000: 1 (1980)
Population density per sq. km. (per sq. mi.): 39.5 (102.2) (1990)

VITAL STATISTICS

Crude birth rate (/1,000): 48 (1990); 52 (1965)
Crude death rate (/1,000): 13 (1990); 22 (1965)
Infant mortality rate (/1,000 live births): 100 (1990)
Life expectancy (yrs.) at birth: males, 52; females, 56 (1990)
Gross reproduction rate (/woman) (1980–85): 3.65
Total fertility rate (/woman): 6.9 (1990)
Rate of natural increase (/1,000): 33.0 (1989)
Average household size: 4.5 (latest)

STATUS OF WOMEN INDICATORS

Number of women (000): 4,578 (1985)
% women of childbearing age (15–49): 44 (1987)
% women literate: 34.4 (1985)
% women in labor force: 34.4 (1988)
Total fertility rate (/woman): 6.9 (1985)
% women in national legislature: 5 (1984)

Although males clearly play the preponderant role overall, some Ivorian traditional societies accord women considerable political and economic power. In rural areas tribal customs dictate the division of tasks, and sometimes these fall heavily on women. Female circumcision continues to be practiced among elements of the Ivorian population, although it is rare in urban populations. Official party policy is to encourage full participation by women in social, economic and political life. The government has a Ministry of Women's Affairs for this purpose. Women remain very lightly represented at the higher levels of government and the ruling PDCI.

Ivory Coast has no official birth control programs or policies and views population growth as an acceptable phenomenon. There has been no decline in the birth rate since 1960.

ETHNIC COMPOSITION

There has never been an ethnic census of Ivory Coast, and the composition and strength of more than 60 ethnic groups are based on estimates. No single ethnic group dominates the country or comprises more than 15% of the population. Most of these groups are smaller units of larger families who are found in greater numbers in neighboring countries. Some of them form the majority in certain geographical regions, such as the Akan do in the Southeast, the Krou and the Mande in the Southwest, the Malinké in the Northwest and the Senoufo and the Koulango in the Northeast. None of these groups is believed to be indigenous to Ivory Coast.

The Akan are the most numerous and the Agni the most modernized. Most of the Lagoon cluster tribes are sailors or farmers. The Senoufo and Mandingo are farmers. Until the Nationality Code was promulgated in 1961, all citizens of French West Africa could move freely into Ivory Coast and receive Ivorian citizenship. Though Ivory Coast law now discriminates between nationals and aliens, its liberal immigration policies have encouraged over 1 million other West Africans to settle in the country. In 1969 aliens constituted nearly one-fourth of the national population and nearly one-half of the population in Abidjan. The total non-Ivorian African population is estimated to be increasing at the rate of 1% a year. Most of the aliens are unskilled laborers seeking work in the relatively affluent Ivory Coast, but many Guineans have been political refugees fleeing from Sékou Touré's regime. The largest alien group consists of Burkinabe, followed by Malians, Ghanaians and Guineans.

There are small Lebanese merchant communities in all large towns. Though less conspicuous in Ivory Coast than elsewhere in West Africa, they enjoy more relative freedom from African harassment. Estimates of the Lebanese population in the late 1980s ranged from 100,000 to 300,000. The Ivory Coast has one of the largest French communities in West Africa, and the number of French citizens resident in the country quadrupled since independence to 60,000 in 1975 although that figure had fallen to 30,000 by 1989. They hold most managerial and senior technical positions and also are in middle-level positions. French colonists have played an active part in the political life of the country in cooperation with the ruling PDCI. In 1976 there were 913 U.S. citizens in the country, of whom 682 were private citizens. There also is a sprinkling of Belgians, Swiss and Spaniards. Though social contacts between Westerners and Ivorians usually are limited, there is growing resentment toward Western dominance in the economy. French citizens in lower-level positions are the usual targets of hostility. Feelings against non-Ivorians culminated in riots in 1969.

ETHNIC COMPOSITION OF IVORY COAST (000)

Group	Number
Akan cluster:	
Baoulé	765
Agni	185
Abrou	50
Abouré	25
Ethotile	4
Nzima	4
Lagoon cluster:	
Ahidji	N.A.
Atia	160
Abbé	85
Adioukrou	30
Alladian	10
Ebrié	N.A.
Mbato	N.A.
Senoufo cluster	465
Lobi cluster	35
Krou cluster:	
Beté	325
Dida	115
Gueré	100
Krou	N.A.
Neyho	N.A.
Ouobé	30
Nuclear Mande cluster:	
Bambara	N.A.
Dioula	N.A.
Mahou	N.A.
Mandingo	665
Peripheral Mande cluster:	
Dan	245
Gagou	N.A.
Gouro	105

LANGUAGES

The official language of Ivory Coast is French, which is the exclusive language of the media, education and the administration. The quality of written and spoken French corresponds very closely to that of France. The number of African languages spoken in the country is estimated at 60, including four major branches of the Niger-Congo family of languages. Agni, Baoulé, Senoufo and Malinke-Bambara-Dioula are the most important of these languages in terms of the number of speakers. A variant of the last, known as Kangbé, is the lingua franca in the southern markets. The government has made an effort to adapt Latin phonetic script to some of the more widely spoken languages. No newspapers are published in the vernaculars. Most Africans are, by necessity, multilingual, and some are proficient in five or six languages. English has made little headway in the country.

RELIGIONS

Ivory Coast is a secular state, and the Constitution provides for religious freedom. In statistical terms, about 65% of Ivorians follow African traditional beliefs, 23% are Muslim and about 12% Christian. Historically, Christianity has taken firm root among the southeastern peoples, especially the Agni, while Islam is concentrated among the Mandingo groups of the Northwest, especially the Dioula. Both Islam and Christianity are urban religions. The tradiational religions vary from group to group, although there are some common, basic elements.

Though a minority religion, Christianity is well established in the country. Since independence the dominant political group has been drawn from the Christian minority. Western Christian values have supplanted African traditional values in urban areas. The Catholic Church is organized under the metropolitan archdiocese of Abidjan and seven suffragan dioceses. There are numerous Protestant bodies, including local syncretic cults of doubtful orthodoxy. Among these the best known is the Harrist-methodist Church, founded by an African prophet named William Wade Harris who, until he was exiled to Liberia, led the life of a simple, itinerant preacher. Other cults also flourish—inspired in varying degrees by Christianity—as messianic movements focusing around a strong personality and seeking the reaffirmation and renewal of African traditional values.

HISTORICAL BACKGROUND

The first French posts were established in Ivory Coast in 1843. In 1893 the territory was formally named Ivory Coast and placed under a French governor. Sixty-five years later, in 1958, Ivory Coast accepted the new French Constitution and opted for the status of an autonomous state within the French Community. In 1960 the Republic of Ivory Coast proclaimed its complete independence.

Ivory Coast gained independence with hardly a murmur, let alone bloodshed. The peaceful departure of the French was, in part, a reflection of the deep pro-French sentiments of the people. Twenty-nine years after independence, Ivory Coast remains the most Francophone of West African states. French economic conservatism—not African nationalism—dominates the country's economic and foreign policies. Both capital and management of industry are largely in the hands of private French citizens. The French educational, administrative and judicial systems have been retained with little change. A significant portion of Ivory Coast's foreign trade is with France. Daily newspapers from Paris are more widely read than local newspapers in Abidjan. French is the country's sole official language.

Ivory Coast's French connection, which is perhaps the key to its political stability, is determined by two factors. One is the almost mystical Francophilism of the Ivorian leaders, including Houphouet-Boigny. The second is the pragmatic benefit of French association for the country's economic development. Ivory Coast's phenomenal economic progress through the mid-1980s was in no small part due to France's role.

Felix Houphouet-Boigny has been the main political leader since the 1940s, when he organized an international political party to fight colonialism. He became president of the autonomous republic in 1959 and has been president since elections following independence. He is responsible for the nation's political character and development. Houphouet-Boigney's administration has been characterized by moderation and a constant search for consensus and dialogue instead of political confrontation. Most potential opposition was defused and their members even absorbed into the ruling party. The government did not show undue concern for its internal security nor did it enact extraordinary legislation directed against the opposition. Largely as a result of the president's skillful management, until 1990 the stability of the central government was the most striking feature of Ivory Coast.

Political unrest has been sporadic and hampered by weak leadership. In 1963 two coup plots were discovered. One was conceived by a young group of radicals and the other by Northerners resentful of control of the government by southern Ivorians. The president responded by cutting the size of the army to reduce the chance of intervention by the armed forces, introducing a regional development plan and setting up more management of businesses by indigenes.

The government has at various times faced charges of corruption. In 1977, to deal with those allegations, Houphouet-Boigny removed ministers from three key departments—Finance, Economic Planning and Foreign Affairs—and passed legislation designed to prevent high-level corruption. Additional anticorruption measures were approved in 1984, and former housing officials were imprisoned for misconduct.

In the 1980s economic austerity led to more unrest, as well as political liberalization. Strikes and demonstrations, staged mostly by students and professionals, occurred frequently from late 1980 to mid-1983. The longest was held in the spring of 1983 by teachers protesting the withdrawal of free housing rights. The strike was aided by sympathetic doctors. It was ended through a presidential back-to-work edict. A degree of political openness was introduced in 1980 with the first free elections for seats in the National Assembly, which was expanded from 80 to 147 members. More than 600 people ran for office, and only 27 of the previous 80 incumbents were returned to the chamber. The National Assembly was later expanded to 175 members.

Massive protests by students, teachers, farmers and professionals flared again in 1990 in response to the government's decision to cut salaries and increase taxes. Growing political pressure forced Houphouet-Boigny to legalize opposition parties and run in the country's first contested election since independence. Amid charges of electoral fraud, Houphouet-Boigny won with 85% of the vote. The ruling Democratic Party won 165 seats in the 175-member parliament in the nation's first multiparty parliamentary elections. The Ivorian Popular Front won nine seats and the Ivorian Worker's Party won one seat.

CONSTITUTION & GOVERNMENT

The basis for Ivorian government is the Constitution of 1960, which established a secular, democratic and social republic with a strong presidential form of gov-

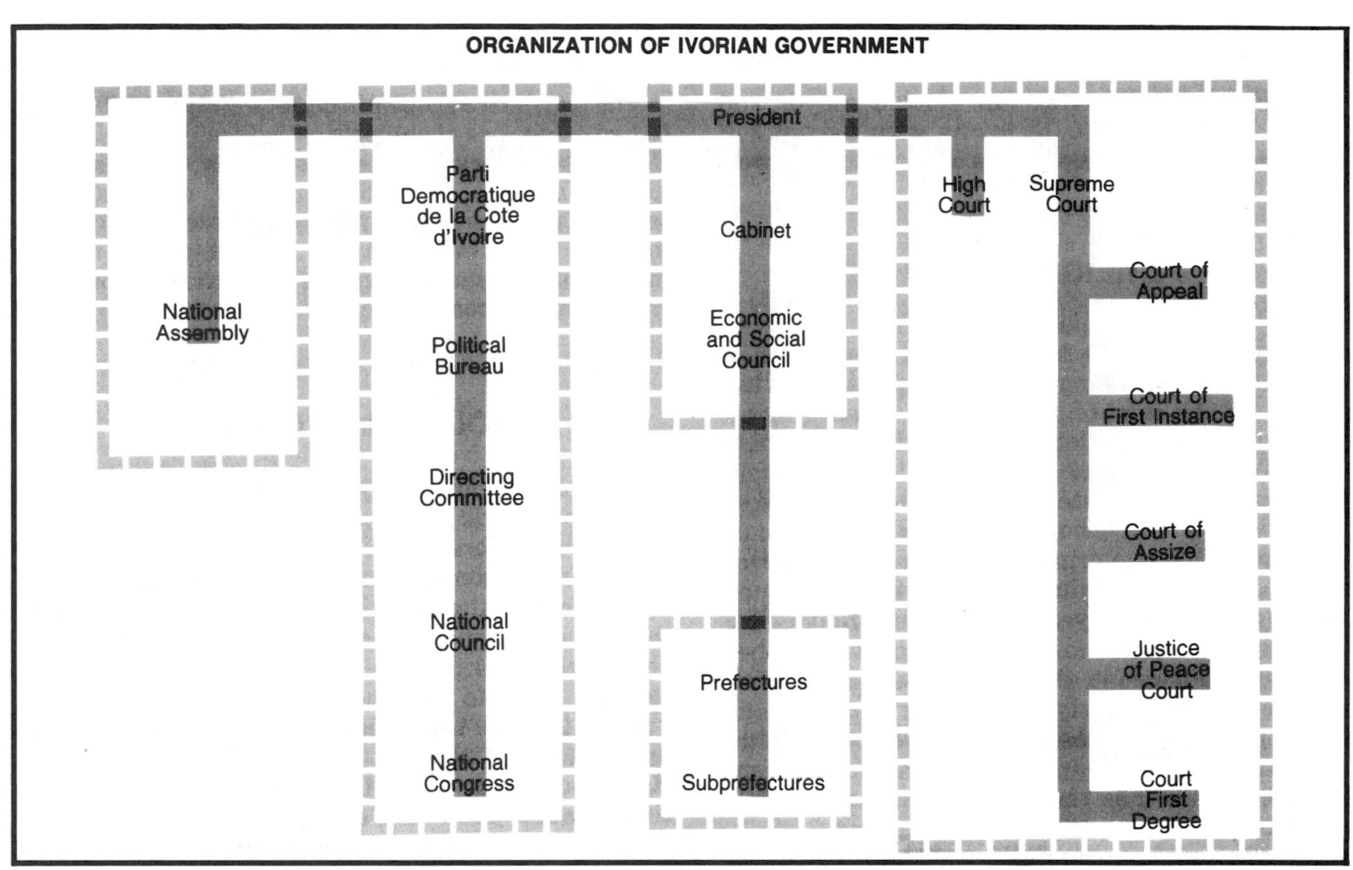

CABINET LIST
(July/August 1991)

President	Houphouet-Boigny, Félix
Prime Minister	Ouattara, Alassane
Minister of Agriculture & Animal Resources	Konan, Lambert Kouassi
Minister of Communications & Government Spokesman	Miremont, Auguste
Minister of Culture	Diabate, Henriette
Minister of Defense	Koffi, Léon Konan
Minister of Economy & Finance	Ouattara, Alassane
Minister of Employment & Civil Service	Kouame, Patrice
Minister of Environment, Construction & Urbanism	Akele, Ezan
Minister of Equipment, Transport & Tourism	Coulibaly, Adams
Minister of Foreign Affairs	Essy, Amara
Minister of Health & Social Protection	Ekra, Alain Frederic Francois
Minister of Industry, Mines & Energy	Angoran, Yed Essaie
Minister of Interior & Internal Security	Bombet, Emile
Minister of Justice	Lohoues-Oble, Jacqueline
Minister of National Education	Bamba, Vamoussa
Minister of Posts & Telecommunications	Akon, Yao Nicolas Kouassi
Minister of Promotion of Women	Grah, Claire Therese Elisabeth
Minister of Scientific Research, Professional Training & Technical Education	N'Diaye, Alhassane Salif
Minister of Youth & Sports	Diby, Rene
Minister Delegate for Economy, Finance, Plan & Commerce	Duncan, Kablan Daniel
Minister Delegate for Raw Materials	Gauze, Guy Alain Emmanuel
National Director, Central Bank	Banny, Charles Konan

ernment. The Constitution affirms the adherence of the government to the rights of man and democracy.

The Constitution provides for separation of powers by restricting the National Assembly's legislative powers to specific subjects, called *domaine de la loi.* All other matters fall within the purview of the executive, to be dealth with by decrees. The executive also shares the Assembly's legislative initiative through government bills, called *projets de loi,* as distinguished from private members' bills, or *propositions de loi.*

The president, whose powers are explicitly set out in the Constitution, is the head of state, the head of government, the prime minister, the commander in chief and the guarantor of judicial independence. He appoints and dismisses ministers, who are solely his agents. His is elected for five-year terms by direct and universal suffrage and is eligible for reelection. The president, Felix Houphouet-Boigny, enjoys in practice even more power than the Constitution grants him. His prestige, as the founding father of the Republic of Ivory Coast, is enormous. To most Ivorians he symbolizes the state itself. According to one Ivorian publication, "the government is an agency in the service of the president, who determines and directs the policy of the nation under his sole authority."

Members of the cabinet are selected from outside the legislature; members of the National Assembly who are appointed to the cabinet are required to resign their seats. In successive cabinets President Houphouet-Boigny has demonstrated his concern for consensus by including opposition and nonparty leaders in them. Thus most of the cabinets have been coalitions in which all shades of public opinion are represented; even dissident elements are absorbed and assimilated.

The Constitution also has established the Economic and Social Council, an advisory body whose function is to associate "the productive economic and social forces of the nation with the administration of affairs." It advises the president on bills, ordinances and decrees and draws his attention to desirable reforms. It also is a channel for pressure groups not otherwise represented in government.

According to the Constitution, suffrage is universal for citizens 21 years of age or older. Voters cast their ballots for a whole slate rather than for individuals, and the slate is prepared by a nominating committee. Campaigns are relatively short and are strictly regulated.

The Constitution has been amended four times, with the issue of the vice presidency the major concern. An amendment in 1986 abolished the post of first vice president of the National Assembly, and mandated that the president of the National Assembly become interim ruler in the event of a presidential vacancy.

FREEDOM & HUMAN RIGHTS

In terms of civil and political rights, Ivory Coast is classified as a partly free nation.

Ivory Coast is among the most Francophile of African states, and it has designed its human rights support system on the French model. No violations of basic human rights have been reported in recent years. There are no known political prisoners and no pending charges by human rights groups relating to such prisoners.

Within the framework of a one-party state there is a large measure of freedom of speech and complete freedom of religion. Most news media are owned or controlled by the Ministry of Information and are designed to play "positive" roles in promoting national unity and development. However, foreign publications are readily available, and are not seized even when they criticize the government.

Unions function under a government-sponsored umbrella union, leaders of which occupy important positions in the top echelons of the ruling PDCI. The right to strike exists in theory, but strikes are discouraged in practice. The government also makes an effort to bring professional groups under its tutelage to ensure that their activities are consonant with party directives.

Although political participation is limited to the ruling PDCI, there is intense competition for party posts. Opposition candidates outside the party have contested municipal and national legislative elections.

Ivory Coast has remained a nonoppressive country in recent years, although on occasion the government has taken coercive steps. In 1987, for instance, 11 members of a teachers' union were sent to reeducation camps as an outgrowth of an internal dispute over union leadership. Laurent Gbagbo, head of the opposition movement Front Populaire Ivorien, was imprisoned and held for a short time in September 1988. Gbagbo had just returned to Ivory Coast after six years of exile in Paris. Sporadic friction between indigenes and foreigners has led the government to reduce the number of outsiders in the country. By 1989, for example, only 1,600 French citizens worked in Ivory Coast, compared with 4,000 in 1980.

CIVIL SERVICE

The senior positions in the Ivorian civil service still are held by Frenchmen assigned temporarily from the French government. However, the service is being Ivorianized as rapidly as possible, according to the availability of qualified civil servants. Centre de Perfectionnement de la Fonction Publique has been established to provide accelerated training for civil servants.

LOCAL GOVERNMENT

For administrative purposes Ivory Coast is divided into 26 prefectures, each of which has an elected council. They are: Abengourou, Abidjan, Aboisso, Adzope, Agboville, Biankouma, Bondoukou, Bouaflé, Bouaké, Bouna, Boundiali, Dabakala, Dalao, Danané, Dimbakro, Divo, Ferkessédougou, Gagnoa, Guiglo, Katiola, Korhogo, Man, Odienné, Sassandra, Séguéla and Touba.

The prefectures are subdivided into 115 subprefectures, each headed by a subprefect.

There also are three self-governing municipalities Abidjan, Bouaké and Grand Bassam—each with an elected mayor and council. In addition, there are 13 towns with partial self-government under subprefects who act as mayor-adminstrators.

FOREIGN POLICY

As the elder statesman of West Africa, Felix Houphouet-Boigny has played a key role in the evolution of regional alliances among former French African territories. The Council of Entente was essentially his creation; it brought together Benin, Ivory Coast, Niger, Togo and Burkina Faso in a loose economic federation. The Entente has provided Houphouet-Boigny with a framework within which he could work toward his two primary goals: economic development and strengthening associations with France.

Houphouet-Boigny has championed a host of lost causes: Moise Tshombe's secessionst movement; the Biafran secession in Nigeria; and, most recently, a policy of dialogue with South Africa. On all these issues he went against the main currents of African thinking and nationalism. Therefore Ivory Coast has been charged with hostile behavior by many African nations.

Another issue on which Houphouet-Boigny has taken a strong stand has been the Communist presence in Africa. Often he has characterized the Soviet Union and China as threats to the independence of Africa. Relations with the Soviet Union, established in 1967, were broken off in 1970. Ivory Coast has also defied the Arab world by maintaining active relations with Israel. Relations with the United States are close but mainly economic.

In 1986 Ivory Coast resumed diplomatic relations with Israel, broken off in 1973. Official ties with the Soviet Union and other eastern European nations were renewed in 1986–87. Continuing his dialogue with South Africa, President Houphouet-Boigny hosted President Botha in 1988 and President de Klerk in 1989. In late 1989 Liberia charged Ivory Coast with aiding forces that sought to overthrow the government, but Houphouet-Boigny denied those allegations.

PARLIAMENT

The National Assembly is a unicameral legislature of 175 members elected by universal and direct suffrage from a single slate of the ruling PDCI. The term of the National Assembly is five years. It holds two sessions a year. The president of the National Assembly ranks next to the president in precedence. Much of the legislative work is done by three standing committees of 23 members each.

The legislative scope of the National Assembly is restricted to two categories of subjects, called *domaine de la loi*. The first category includes nationality, the criminal and judicial systems, taxation, currency, the electoral system and public administration. The second category includes areas in which the National Assembly only determines policies, such as defense, education, labor, and transportation and communications.

In the 1980 legislative, municipal and local party elections, any citizen could present himself as a candidate, and approximately 650 individuals ran for election to the National Assembly. The ruling PDCI played no role in choosing candidates or administering the elections. Intense competition took place in all three elections, in which all citizens were eligible to vote. About 50% of top local party officials were voted out of office, and only 27 incumbent deputies were reelected to the National Assembly.

In 1990 political unrest forced Houphouet-Boigny to allow opposition parties to run in the nation's first multiparty elections. The ruling Democratic Party won 165 seats in the 175-member chamber. The Ivorian Popular Front won nine seats and the Ivorian Worker's Party won one seat.

POLITICAL PARTIES

Until recently the sole political party in the Ivory Coast was the Parti Démocratique de la Côte d'Ivoire (PDCI), described as the fourth branch of government. The PDCI is not named in the Constitution, nor are there provisions barring other political parties, but the PDCI's historic ascendancy has been ensured by a number of simple electoral devices, such as prohibitively high security deposits for candidates.

The PDCI is one of the oldest political parties in Africa and is a direct offshoot of the African Democratic Rally, founded in 1946. Despite an increasing identity between party and state, the PDCI does not enjoy the preeminence enjoyed by similar sole parties in many other African countries. The PDCI has no clearly defined ideology other than what is generally described as Houphouetism, whose elements are national unity and cohesion, social justice and fraternity, tolerance, stability, dialogue and peace.

The principal party organs are the National Congress, the National Council, the Directing or Guiding Committee of 100 members, the Political Bureau of 60 members and the Executive Committee of 13 members. At election time the PDCI runs a list of candidates called the Union List. This list often includes nonparty members and even opposition leaders, in accordance with the PDCI policy of absorbing, rather than suppressing, critics. Because of the success of this policy, opposition has remained sporadic and unorganized until 1990, when political unrest forced Houphouet-Boigny to allow opposition parties to run in the nation's first multiparty elections. The two opposition parties that won seats were the Ivorian Popular Front and the Ivorian Worker's Party, both formed in 1990.

ECONOMY

The economy of Ivory Coast is primarily agricultural. National wealth is based largely on exporting agricultural products, especially cocoa, coffee and timber. As a result, changes in world prices for those products can have a significant impact on economic health. In the late 1980s Ivory Coast was the world's leading exporter of cocoa and one of the top producers of coffee. The small manufacturing sector focuses on processing agricultural goods. Mining in the country is insignificant, and the professional sector is small.

Classified by the United Nations as a lower-middle-income nation, Ivory Coast experienced rapid economic growth during the 1960s and early 1970s, outstanding by world as well as by African standards. Thus despite a high rate of population growth, Sahelian drought, increased oil prices and a slowdown in the world economy, the economy had an average annual growth rate of 7% during the 1970s. The real GDP per capita, the highest in West Africa, increased during this period at an annual rate of 2%. This growth was due to the increased diversification of the economy, sustained foreign demand and rising private consumption. Though often criticized as growth without development, Ivory Coast's economic progress was achieved with minimum state controls and within a framework of relative economic freedom. The private sector remains dominant in the free-market economy of Ivory Coast.

Ivorian economic strategy has been remarkably consistent since independence. The country's economic planners have concentrated on exploiting Ivory Coast's comparative advantage in coffee and cocoa production while developing new agricultural products for export. Helped by exceptionally high coffee and cocoa prices and increasing access to world financial centers, the Ivorian economy boomed in 1976–78 as the authorities unveiled a massive \$6.6 billion investment program. This investment spurt substantially increased foreign indebtedness and overheated the economy. By early

1978 Ivorian authorities were acting to slow the economy's growth and to improve the country's debt profile.

Institutional changes that aim at paring back the parastatal sector were introduced in 1979. The 1981–85 economic and social development plan called for restraint on foreign borrowing and increased emphasis on the role of the private sector in the creation of jobs and export growth. A revision of the Ivorian Investment Code provides greater fiscal incentives to firms investing in the interior and to investments undertaken for export. While the state may be prepared to invest sizable amounts of capital in these ventures, direct government ownership and operation will be deemphasized in the years ahead. After a period of major public-sector involvement in the economy, the pendulum now seems to be shifting toward greater emphasis on private-sector investment and initiative.

Falling global prices for cocoa and coffee led to slow economic growth in the 1980s. For the period 1980–89 the GNP rose at an annual average rate of only 0.9%, while GNP per capita actually declined, reaching −6.5% from 1987 to 1989. In 1989 the government attempted to raise international prices for cocoa through a temporary embargo on sales. But the effort failed, and official prices paid to producers of cocoa were reduced.

In a broad sense, Ivorian economic policy up to 1975 was mainly concerned with maximizing the rate of growth, with less attention paid to questions of regional disparities and income distribution. While World Bank studies show that the Ivorian distribution of income is the most equitable in sub-Saharan Africa, regional variations continue to be striking. All the major cash crops and products that have fueled the economy—coffee, cocoa, palm oil, pineapples, rubber, bananas and tropical hardwoods—are cultivated in the tropical rain forest that covers the southern half of the country.

Economic development has been as a result more rapid—and incomes considerably higher—in the South. Mindful of the need to promote meaningful progress in the poorer North, the government embarked on an extensive program to create new employment possibilities in poorer regions and to slow the tide of immigration to cities from these areas. The commercialization of cotton to support a major textile industry was undertaken with this goal in mind, and more recently six integrated sugar complexes were established in the North.

GROSS DOMESTIC PRODUCT

GDP nominal (C.F.A.F. billions): 3,244.3 (1986)
GDP per capita (U.S. $): 900 (1988)
Average annual growth rate of GDP (%, 1980–87): 2.2
GDP by type of expenditure (%), 1986
- Consumption
  - Private: 62
  - Government: 15
- Gross domestic investment: 13
- Gross domestic saving: 22 (1988)
- Foreign trade
  - Exports: 39
  - Imports: −27

Cost components of GDP (%), 1982
- Net indirect taxes: 19
- Consumption of fixed capital: 8
- Compensation of employees: 35
- Net operating surplus: 38

Sectoral origin of GDP (%), 1984
- Primary
  - Agriculture: 31 (1988)
  - Mining: 3
- Secondary
  - Manufacturing: 12
  - Construction: 2
  - Public utilities: 1
- Tertiary
  - Transportation & communications: 7
  - Trade, finance, other services, government: 49 (1988)

Average annual sectoral growth rate (%, 1980–87)
- Agriculture: 1.6
- Industry: −2.4
- Manufacturing: 8.2 (latest)
- Services: 4.2

PRINCIPAL ECONOMIC INDICATORS

Gross National Product (U.S. $ billions): 9.305 (1989)
GNP per capita (U.S. $): 790 (1989)
GNP average annual growth rate (%, 1980–89): 0.9
GNP per capita average annual growth rate (%, 1987–89): −6.5
Income distribution (%, household income) (1986)
- Lowest 20%: 5.0
- Highest 10%: 36.3

Average annual rate of inflation (%, 1980–88): 3.8
Consumer Price Index (1980–100) 1986
- All items: 144
- Food: 140

Average annual growth rate %, 1980–88
- General government consumption: −2.6
- Private consumption: 1.9
- Gross domestic investment: −11.4

BALANCE OF PAYMENTS, 1988
(U.S. $ millions)

Current account balance: −1,280.0
Merchandise exports: 2,354.2
Merchandise imports: −1,538.7
Trade balance: 815.5
Other goods, services & income +: 641.6
Other goods, services & income −: −2,312.3
Other goods, services & income net: 1,670.7
Private unrequited transfers: −480.1
Official unrequited transfers: 55.2
Capital other than reserves: −206
Net errors & omissions: 4.8
Counterpart items: 370.1
Liabilities constituting foreign authorities reserves: 9.0 (1987)
Total change in reserves: −60.0

PUBLIC FINANCE

The Ivorian fiscal year is the calendar year. The national budget is divided into three parts: the recurrent budget, the equipment and investment budget and the scheduled budget. The scheduled budget includes estimates for autonomous state agencies and state corporations. The recurrent and scheduled budgets are financed from domestic resources.

In the mid-1980s, taxes on international trade and transactions accounted for about two-fifths of government revenue. Other important sources of government income included domestic taxes on goods and services and taxes on net income and profit. At the same time, the major areas of public spending were capital expenditures, general public services and education.

The 1971–75 development plan projected a total outlay of C.F.A.F. 600 billion, with emphasis on road development and town planning. The five-year development and investment plan of 1975–80 allocated C.F.A.F. 1.4 trillion to economic development.

The flow of foreign economic and technical aid has played a key role in Ivory Coast's economic growth. Two-thirds of the investment budgets have been financed from foreign sources. French aid has declined since 1973, but private investment continues at a high level.

While not as severe as in other developing countries, Ivory Coast experienced foreign debt problems in the late 1980s. This was closely related to decline in income from exports. In 1988 the nation's external debt was $14.1 billion, and in 1989 the government rescheduled some foreign debt payments.

FOREIGN AID, 1989

Total foreign aid, million U.S. $: 841.1
- Bilateral: 278.5
- Multilateral: 562.9

CENTRAL GOVERNMENT EXPENDITURES, 1984

% of total expenditures
- Defense: 3.9
- Education: 20.5
- Health: 4.0
- Housing, Social Security, welfare: 5.4
- Economic services: 31.5
- Other: 34.7
- Total expenditures as % of GDP: 31.6
- Overall surplus or deficit as % of GDP: −3.1

CENTRAL GOVERNMENT REVENUES, 1984

% of total current revenues
- Taxes on income, profit & capital gain: 11.4
- Social Security contributions: 4.4
- Domestic taxes on goods & services: 15.7
- Taxes on international trade & transactions: 26.7
- Current nontax revenue: 29.6
- Total current revenue as % of GDP: 28.5
- General government consumption as % of GDP: 19 (1988)

Annual growth rate of general government consumption (%, 1980–87): −2.6

CURRENCY & BANKING

The Ivorian unit of currency is the C.F.A. (Communauté Financière Africaine) franc. Coins are issued in denominations of C.F.A.F. 1, 2, 5, 10, 25, 50 and 100; notes are issued in denominations of C.F.A.F. 100, 500, 1,000 and 5,000. The C.F.A.F., introduced in 1946, is guaranteed by the French Treasury. The June 1991 dollar exchange rate was $1 = C.F.A.F. 290.5.

The functions of a central bank in the member states of the monetary union created by the French Community in 1958 are performed by Banque Centrale des États de l'Afrique de l'Ouest (BCEAO), which has monetary jurisdiction over the Ivory Coast, Senegal,

FINANCIAL INDICATORS, 1989

Total reserves minus gold (SDR's millions): 11
SDR's (millions): 4
Reserve position in IMF (SDR's millions): 0.0
Foreign exchange (SDR's millions): 7
Gold (fine troy oz. millions): .04
Ratio of external debt to total reserves: 667.8 (1988)
Central bank, 1989
- Assets %
  - Foreign assets: 0.6
  - Claims on government: 34.5
  - Claims on banks: 64.9
  - Claims on private sector: 0.0
- Liabilities %
  - Reserve money: 39.1
  - Government deposits: 0.4
  - Foreign liabilities: 56.4
  - Capital accounts: 0.0

Money supply 1989
Stock (C.F.A.F. billions): 511.2
M^1 per capita: 41,200
Private banks 1989
- Assets %
  - Loans to government: 6.6
  - Loans to private sector: 87.9
  - Reserves: 2.2
  - Foreign assets: 3.3
- Liabilities
  - deposits (C.F.A.F. billions): 1,228.8
  - of which %
    - Demand deposits: 20.8
    - Savings deposits: 29.0
    - Government deposits: 6.6
    - Foreign liabilities: 16.2

External debt, 1988
- Total (U.S. $ millions): 14,125
- Debt service, total (long-term) (U.S. $ millions): 448
  - Repayment
    - Principal (%): 50.9
    - Interest (%): 49.1
- Debt service ratio (%): 13.2
- External public debt as % of GNP: 92.7
- Debt service as % of GNP: 5.1
- Debt service as % of exports: 13.0

GROWTH PROFILE
(Annual Growth Rates, %)

Projected population (1988–2000): 3.8
Projected crude birth rate (/1,000) (1990–95): 50.2
Projected crude death rate (/1,000) (1990–95): 12.9
Urban population (1980–88): 6.6
Labor force (1985–2000): 2.6
GNP (1980–89): 0.9
GNP per capita (1987–89): −6.5
GDP (1980–87): 2.2
Inflation (1980–88): 3.8
Agriculture (1980–87): 1.6
Industry (1980–87): −2.4
Manufacturing (1980–87): 8.2
Services (1980–87): 4.2
Money holdings (1980–88): 7.1
Exports (1980–87): 1.5
Imports (1980–87): −2.2
General government consumption (1980–88): −2.6
Private consumption (1980–88): 1.9
Gross domestic investment, (1980–88): −11.4

Benin, Niger, Burkina Faso, Mali and Mauritania. BCEAO maintains the internal and external acceptability of the C.F.A.F., controls the volume of currency in circulation and regulates credit by commercial banks.

The commercial banking sector consists of 13 banks, many of them French affiliates and subsidiaries. Specialized credit institutions and development banks include the National Agricultural Development Bank and the Ivorian Industrial Development Bank. The multinational African Development Bank has its headquarters in Abidjan. In 1984 the commercial banking sector had C.F.A.F. 39.2 billion in reserves, C.F.A.F. 70.3 billion in foreign assets, C.F.A.F. 290.6 billion in demand deposits and C.F.A.F. 215.5 billion in time deposits. The prime discount rate was 10.50% in 1984.

AGRICULTURE

Of the total land area of 32,246,300 ha. (799,680,607 ac.), 52% is considered agricultural land. In 1989 agriculture, including forestry and fishing, accounted for approximately 46% of the GDP, and by 1988 about three-fifths of the work force was employed in agriculture. About 90% of the nation's export trade consists of agricultural products. Cocoa and coffee were the chief exports.

The country is divided into two broad agricultural belts. The southern belt, known as the manioc zone, grows all the export and industrial crops, such as coffee, cocoa, pineapples, bananas and rubber. The northern belt, also known as the millet zone, produces most of the food crops, including rice, millet and Indian corn.

Though land tenure systems differ in detail among the various ethnic groups, all are based on the concept of communal ownership. However, each family is granted rights to cultivate a specific area, and these rights entail some form of inheritance within the family. However, unused lands revert to the community. In 1902 the French introduced legal land ownership by individuals or corporations with exclusive titles, but this law had little impact in the rural areas.

The prevailing system of cultivation is known as shifting, or bush fallow, in which fields normally are kept under crops for three or four years, after which they are left fallow for up to 10 years, until their fertility is renewed. Nearly all farm work is done by hand without the aid of animals or mechanization. In 1982 there were 3,200 tractors and 40 harvester-threshers in the country, most of them on the larger estates. Under the 1976–78 development plan, CFAF76 billion was allocated for construction of a dam on the Bandama River at Tabou and another on the Sassandra River at Buyo for irrigation. Annual consumption of fertilizers in 1982 was 51,800 tons, or 8.5 kg. (18.7 lb.) per hectare.

There is little direct intervention and control by the state in the agricultural sector other than prescribing quality standards and maintaining the price stability of export products. The government also has resisted local pressures for nationalization of French-owned estates and similar measures initiated by almost all other governments in Africa. However, some of the larger holdings are operated by the government through public corporations. A notable example of government efforts in this field is Motoragri, a mechanized farm that was formed in 1964 through Israeli collaboration. Land ownership has been restricted to Ivorian nationals since independence, and government policies favor the smallholder. The average size of a farm is 3.6 ha. (9.0 ac.).

The principal food crops are yams, bananas, manioc, rice and corn. In terms of cash crops, in 1987 Ivory Coast was the world's leading producer of cocoa and third-largest exporter of coffee. Others are palm oil and rubber. Coffee and cocoa farming is almost entirely in the private sector; the state-owned SODE-PALM and SOCATEI corporations dominate the production of palm oil and rubber, respectively.

Natural rubber production is viewed by many experts as the most viable of Ivory Coast's new cash crops. A major investment program involving participation of internationally prominent rubber companies

AGRICULTURAL INDICATORS

Agriculture's share of GDP (%): 46 (1989)
Average annual growth rate (% 1980–88): 1.6 (latest)
Value added in agriculture (U.S. $ millions): 2,728 (latest)
Cereal imports (000 metric tons): 494 (1988)
Index of Agricultural Production (1979–81 = 100): 118 (1986)
Index of Food Production (1979–81 = 100): 122 (1986)
Index of Food Production per Capita (1979–81 = 100): 104 (1986–88)
Number of tractors: 3,350 (1986)
Number of harvester-threshers: 53 (1986)
Total fertilizer consumption: 41.5 (000 metric tons) (1985–86)
Fertilizer consumption (g./ha., hundreds): 90 (1987–88)
Number of farms (000): 550 (1975)
Average size of holding, ha. (ac.): 5.0 (12.4) (1975)
Size class (%) (1975)
- Below 1 ha. (below 2.47 ac.): 9.5
- 1–5 ha. (2.47–12.35 ac.): 54.4
- 5–10 ha. (12.35–24.7 ac.): 24.9
- 10–20 ha. (24.7–49.4 ac.): 9.4
- 20–50 ha. (49.4–123.5 ac.): 1.7
- 50–200 ha. (123.5–494 ac.): 0.1
- Over 200 ha. (over 494 ac.): 0.0

Farms as % of total land area: 8.6 (1975)
Land use (%) (1975)
- Permanent crops: 65.9
- Temporary crops: 34.1

Yields, kg./ha. 1989
- Grains: 831
- Roots & tubers: 5,717
- Legumes: 667
- Fruits (000 metric tons): 1,457
- Vegetables (000 metric tons): 439
- Milk, kg. (lb.)/animal: 122

Livestock (000) 1989
- Cattle: 991
- Horses: 1 (1986)
- Sheep: 1,500
- Pigs: 450

Forestry, 1988
- Production of roundwood, 000 cu. m.: 12,813 (419,012)
  - of which industrial roundwood (%): 20.7
- Value of exports (U.S. $ 000): 236,147

Fishing, 1988
- Total catch (000 metric tons): 88.8
  - of which marine (%): 68.5
- Value of exports (U.S. $ millions): 126.906

was undertaken in the mid-1980s, with considerable success; 30,000 ha. (74,100 ac.) of rubber plantings are in place, and production rose to 47,000 tons in 1985. Marketing conditions for natural rubber are considered excellent, and the continued upsurge in petroleum prices steadily enhances the competitiveness of natural rubber over synthetic substitutes.

Because there are few pastoral groups in Ivory Coast, the livestock population is relatively small, and production of livestock products is insufficient to meet the country's domestic needs. The national herd consists mainly of the small, humpless N'dama breed.

Ivory Coast's tropical forests cover 5.5 million ha. (13.6 million ac.), mainly in the southern half of the country. They are rich in over 200 species of hardwoods and softwoods, of which 25 types are now utilized commercially. Forest exploitation is controlled by concessions and permits. Roughly half of production is mahoganies and a softwood known as samba. Reforestation is undertaken by SODERFOR, a state corporation. The value of exports of timber and timber products has been steadily increasing since the 1960s and by the mid-1980s exceeded that of both coffee and cocoa. Logging is the first, largest and most profitable industry in Ivory Coast. The wood-processing industry produces not only timber but also furniture, plywood and prefabricated houses.

Although lumbering activity has clearly peaked in Ivory Coast, the lumbering industry remains a major contributor to the Ivorian economy and exports. In recent years Ivorian authorities have taken a number of measures to increase local processing of logs, particularly by linking log exports to deliveries to local sawmills and wood processors. Conservation efforts have slowed depletion of timber reserves; 3.5 million ha. (8.6 million ac.) of forest have been declared a permanent reserve, and reforestation efforts have been stepped up, while cuttings have been reduced. Experts believe rising prices of timber and processed wood will offset the decline in volume.

Commercial fishing is carried on in the Gulf of Guinea, which is rich in sardines and tuna. Abidjan has a fishing wharf with modern processing facilities.

Agricultural credit is provided by the National Agricultural Development Bank.

MANUFACTURING

Manufacturing in Ivory Coast is dominated by such agriculturally related industries as processing cocoa, coffee, cotton and pineapples. A relatively insignificant sector of the economy, manufacturing accounted for only 16% of the GDP in 1987. Industry, including manufacturing, construction, mining and power, made up one-fourth of the GDP in 1987.

Although manufacturing facilities have been expanded in recent years, they have been confined to Abidjan and Bouake.

Because of the small range of natural resources, most of the industrial units are food processing plants. Heavy industry is a more recent development and consists of a motor vehicle plant and a petroleum refinery. There also is a small textile industry, utilizing domestic cotton.

The government's industrial policy favors private enterprise or, at most, mixed enterprises, in which the government participates in businesses only in areas where private enterprise has been unwilling, or does not possess the capability, to take the risks. Nevertheless, the share of state corporations in the manufacturing sector grew by 35% between 1973 and 1975.

The state is now being forced to go into an ever wider range of enterprises in an effort to restructure and diversify the economy. This is necessary if the industrial sector is to grow. However, Ivorian civil servants in the 1970s did not show themselves to be well adapted to running profitable state enterprises. A succession of government reports were written on the ills of the state sector, complaining of the low level of profitability of state firms, the overuse of foreign finance, mismanagement, corruption and general lack of managerial flair. The losses made by the 36 parastatal companies became so serious that President Houphouet-Boigny decided in 1980 to abolish some, reform others and return many to the private sector. Altogether the parastatals were responsible for 40% of the Ivory Coast's foreign debt.

MANUFACTURING INDICATORS

Average annual growth rate (%, 1980–88): 8.2 (latest)
Share of GDP (%): 16 (latest)
Value added in manufacturing (U.S. $ millions): 1,191 (latest)
  Food and agriculture (%): 27
  Textiles (%): 16
  Machinery (%): 10
  Chemicals (%): 5
Earnings per employee in manufacturing 1970
  Growth rate (%, 1970–80): −0.9
Total earnings as % of value added: 27
Gross output per employee (1980 = 100): 52

Ivory Coast's investment policy offers generous incentives to foreign investors. Besides tax exemptions and reductions on customs duties, transfer of capital and profits within the franc zone is free; transfer to the monetary zones is subject to limited control only. However, all businesses that do not reinvest at least 20% of their profits in the country must pay the government an additional 10% tax. Preferential treatment is given to foreign interest in the mining, energy and manufacturing sectors. Employment of qualified foreigners also is encouraged.

Ivorian investment laws are among the most liberal in the Third World. Virtually any foreign firm can qualify to do business simply by registration. Prior approval is required only in the case of a few restricted fields (e.g., certain foodstuffs, processing of agricultural commodities, finance, transportation and public utilities), or if the benefits of duty and tax concessions are being sought by the investor. With greater emphasis on private-sector involvement, companies hoping to win major industrial contracts have been encouraged to make equity investments in the projects. The new Investment Code provides greater incentives for export-oriented industries and for firms that establish plants in the country's interior.

In the mid-1980s book value of U.S. direct investment in Ivory Coast exceeded $150 million and was concentrated largely in petroleum distribution and exploration, with some representation also in banking, business equipment, textiles, consumer goods and chemicals. Abidjan's emergence as the leading commercial and financial center in West Africa, coupled with its excellent port and communications facilities, has induced more than 80 U.S. companies to establish local and regional offices there.

MINING

Mining in Ivory Coast is meager, accounting for only 1.5% of the GDP in 1986, although more activity is expected in the years ahead. Development of gold deposits at Ity was expected to begin in 1990, and an energy program was announced in late 1989 to exploit reserves of natural gas, partly to reduce dependence on imported energy. Deposits of iron ore and nickel remain unexploited. The only other important mineral product is diamonds. Diamond output reached 19,000 carats of industrial diamonds and 22,000 carats of gems in 1977, but no production has been reported since then. The manganese mines of Grand Lahou were closed in 1970. Other minerals known to exist in commercial quantities are gold, colombo-tantalite and ilmenite.

ENERGY

Ivory Coast embarked on a major program to tap its considerable hydroelectric potential in the early 1970s. A 176-mw. hydrofacility was commissioned in 1973 at Kossou on the Bandama River, and a second dam, with a capacity of 210 mw., was constructed downstream at Tabou and brought into production in early 1979. While Kossou's performance was considerably less than anticipated, a return to more normal rainfall levels in 1979 boosted hydrogeneration significantly and permitted a cutback in oil-fired thermal output. With the commissioning of the 165-mw. Buyo Dam on the Sassandra River in the developing Southwest, hydroelectricity accounts for 58.6% of total power generated up from only 12% in 1978.

Offshore petroleum prospects also are promising. The Esso/Shell/Petroci consortium has completed more than 25 offshore test holes, and production began in August 1980 at the Belier oil deposit, 15 km. (9.3 mi.) off Grand Bassam. Daily production peaked at 8,000 to 10,000 bd. Proved reserves are estimated at 100 million bbl., and 1989 production was 700,000 bbl. Relatively modest, the production covers only about one-quarter of Ivory Coast's net crude consumption. A second and considerably more promising find was declared by the Phillips/Agip/Petroci consortium in late April 1980. The tests of the Phillips deposit, in 457 m. (1,500 ft.) of water offshore from Jacqueville, produced a flow that should result in a peak output of at least 24,000 bd.

ENERGY INDICATORS

Energy imports as % of merchandise exports: 12 (1988)
Electricity 1988
  Installed capacity (millions kw.): 2.210
  Production (billions kw.-hr.): 1.817
    % fossil fuel: 41.4
    % hydro: 58.6
    % nuclear: 0.0
  Consumption per capita (kw.-hr.): 190
Natural gas
  Proved reserves (billion cu. m.): 100 (1990)
Petroleum
  Proved reserves (million bbl.): 100 (1990)
  Years to exhaust proved reserves: 171 (1990)
  Production (million bbl.): 0.7 (1989)
  Consumption (million bbl.): 13 (1988)
  Refining capacity (bbl./day): 69 (1990)

The Vridi oil refinery, with a capacity of 1.9 million tons a year, was completed in 1965.

LABOR

The vast majority of the working population of Ivory Coast were engaged in agriculture, forestry or livestock-raising in the late 1980s. About one-tenth of the labor force are wage earners, half of those in agriculture and the rest in government, industry, commerce or the professions. In 1985 over 70% of the population was of working age, and about one-fifth of the wage earners were enrolled in unions. In the early 1980s unskilled workers constituted 80% of the labor force, skilled workers 15% and professional workers 5%.

Non-Africans dominate the managerial and professional cadres. Among the country's 300 biggest companies, Ivorians occupy only about three in ten top management posts. In addition, many Europeans are employed in the secondary sector as mechanics, technicians and shopkeepers. The labor pool also includes nearly 1 million non-Ivorian Africans, especially Burkinabe, whose numbers are swollen every year by some 90,000 to 150,000 new additions. These foreign Africans constitute nearly 80% of the rural unskilled labor.

Though Ivorization of employment has been accepted by the government as a desirable, if long-term, goal, it has never been pushed at the expense of efficiency. Most Ivorization programs in commerce and industry are voluntary, and though the pace of Ivorization has accelerated in recent years, the campaign has neither disrupted the economy nor reduced the flow of necessary skills into the country. The labor force is characterized by high mobility among regions and also among occupational sectors. This mobility explains in part the lack of training and skills among Ivorian workers. The mobility among the skilled labor force at times results in temporary labor shortages in certain sectors.

Ivory Coast is one of the few African countries that has always enjoyed a favorable trade balance. In 1988, for example, the country's trade surplus was $900 million. Top imports in the late 1980s were machinery

LABOR INDICATORS, 1985

Total economically active population (000): 4,053
  % working-age population (15–64): 71.4
  % female: 34.7
Activity rate (%)
  Total: 41.3
  Male: 52.8
  Female: 29.3
Sectoral employment (%)
  Agriculture, forestry, fishing: 60.5
  Manufacturing, mining, quarrying, public utilities, construction: 10.1
  Trade, hotels, restaurants, transport, communications, finance, real estate, services: 29.4
Average annual growth rate of labor force, 1980–2000 (%): 2.6
Unemployment (000): 69 (1984)
Labor under 20 years (%): 95.1 (1975)

and transportation equipment, while the leading exports were cocoa, coffee and timber. France was the principal source of imports, accounting for roughly one-third of goods received. The Netherlands was the leading market for Ivorian exports. Other important trading partners were Italy, West Germany, the United States, the United Kingdom, Nigeria and Japan.

Wages and working conditions are regulated by the Labor Code of 1952. Ivory Coast has a system of guaranteed minimum wage rates, consisting of the Salaire Minimum Agricole Garanti (SMAG) for agricultural workers and the Salaire Minimum Interprofessional Garanti (SMIG). The SMIG minimum wage is presently C.F.A. 920 francs per eight-hour day, and the SMAG is about to be raised retroactively from the present C.F.A. 240 francs per eight-hour day. The maximum work period is fixed at 40 hours a week for nonagricultural labor and 2,400 hours a year for agricultural labor. The Labor Code also regulates paid holidays, sick leave, medical care and hiring and firing. Provision is made for collective agreements between employees and trade unions. There are special courts for settlement of industrial disputes.

The largest labor union is Union Générale des Travailleurs de Côte d'Ivoire, with 200,000 members.

Data are not available on the number of industrial disputes in the country.

FOREIGN COMMERCE

The government imposes few regulations on external trade. All imports are controlled by license. The export prices of coffee and cocoa also are regulated in accordance with international agreements.

Among the trade groupings to which Ivory Coast belongs are the Council of the Entente (a customs union of Burkina Faso, Benin, Niger, Togo and Ivory Coast) and the Cocoa Producers' Council.

TRANSPORTATION & COMMUNICATIONS

The only rail line is the Abidjan–Ouagadougou link, of which 549 km. (341 mi.) are in Ivory Coast. The line is administered by Régie du Chemin de fer Abidjan–Niger, controlled by a board of directors composed of representatives of Burkina Faso and Ivory Coast.

Because of shoals and rapids, navigation on the inland waterways is possible only by small canoes beyond short distances. From the Ghana border to Fresco there is a continuous chain of coastal lagoons supporting commercial traffic by barges and lighters. The total length of inland waterways is 980 km. (609 mi.). Both Abidjan and San Pedro are major ports of call, while Tabou and Sassandra can handle cargo from ship to shore by lighter.

FOREIGN TRADE INDICATORS, 1988

Exports (U.S. $ billions): 2.2
Imports (U.S. $ billions): 1.3
Balance of trade (U.S. $ millions): 900
Annual growth rate, 1980–88, exports (%): 1.5
Annual growth rate, 1980–88, imports (%): −2.2
International reserves in terms of months of imports
Terms of trade (1980=100): 92
Import Price Index (1980=100): 86.9 (1986)
Export Price Index (1980=100): 89.9 (1986)

Direction of Trade (%), 1985

	Imports	Exports
European Community	54.1	57.5
U.S.	6.9	12.6
U.S.S.R. & Eastern European economies	1.1	5.8
Japan	5.0	1.1

Composition of Trade (%), 1985

	Imports	Exports
Food and agricultural raw materials	18.2	79.8
Fuels and other energy	22.0	9.7
Mineral ores and concentrates	0.7	0.1
Manufactured goods	59.1	10.3
of which chemicals	12.8	2.5
of which machinery	22.2	1.8

TRANSPORTATION INDICATORS

Roads (latest)
  Length, km. (mi.): 55,000 (34,175)
  Paved (%): 9
Motor vehicles (latest)
  Automobiles: 182,956
  Trucks and buses: 52,491
  Persons per vehicle: 41
  Road freight, ton-km. (ton-mi) (billions): 1.630 (1.116)
Railroads (latest)
  Track, km. (mi.): 549 (341)
  Passenger-km. (passenger-mi.) (billions): .858 (.533)
  Freight, ton-km. (ton-mi.) (billions): .530 (.363)
Merchant marine
  Vessels: 52 (1989)
  Total deadweight tonnage (000): 100.4 (1989)
Ports (pre-1986)
  Cargo loaded (000 metric tons): 4,658
  Cargo unloaded (000 metric tons): 4,874
Air (latest)
  Km. (mi.) flown (millions): 3.2 (2.0) (1985)
  Passenger-km. (passenger-mi.) (millions): 458.4 (284.8)
  Freight-km. (freight-mi.) (millions): 44.7 (30.6)
  Mail ton-km (millions): (ton-mi.): 0.7 (0.3) (1985)
  Airports with scheduled flights: 13 (1990)
Inland waterways (latest)
  Length, km. (mi.): 980 (609)

COMMUNICATION INDICATORS, 1986

Telephones
  Total (000): 88 (1980)
  Persons per telephone: 97 (1980)
Post office
  Number of post offices: 1,148
  Pieces of mail handled (000): 95,807
Telegraph
  Total traffic (000 calls): 581 (1980)
  National: 508 (1980)
  International: 73 (1980)
Telex
  Subscriber lines: 1,821 (1985)
Telecommunications 1990
  2 satellite stations, 2 coaxial submarine cables

TOURISM & TRAVEL INDICATORS, 1986

Total tourist receipts (U.S. $ millions): 53 (1988)
Expenditures by nationals abroad (U.S. $ millions): 164 (1988)
Number of hotel beds (000): 24
Average length of stay: 3 nights
Tourist nights (000): 509

The national road system totals 55,000 km. (34,175 mi.), of which 9% are paved. All the paved highways radiate from Abidjan. Commercial cargo and passenger transportation by road are handled by private enterprise. In 1989 the number of passenger cars was 182,956 and trucks and buses 52,491.

The national airlines are Air Ivoire (in which the government holds 60%) and Air Afrique (in which the government holds 7%). The national civil air fleet consists of 25 aircraft. The major airport is Abidjan-Bouet, which can handle jumbo jets.

In 1981 a total of 195,600 tourists visited Ivory Coast, of whom 63,900 were from France, 8,900 from the United States, 8,000 from Italy, 3,800 from West Germany, 8,300 from the United Kingdom, 3,600 from Belgium and 1,600 from Canada. Total tourist receipts in 1988 were $53 million.

DEFENSE

The defense establishment is headed by the president, who is assisted by the Ministerial Defense council and the Military Defense Council made up of the chief of staff and the inspector general of the armed forces. The line of command runs through the minister of defense to the service commanders.

Military manpower is provided by conscription, established by law in 1961. The service obligation lasts 25 years, two of which are on active duty and the balance in reserves.

France remains critical to Ivorian defense matters. It supplies equipment to Ivorian forces, trains soldiers and maintains a contingent of several hundred in the country. In June 1989, manpower of the Ivory Coast defense forces stood at 7,100. There also was a paramilitary force of 7,800.

Army

Personnel: 5,500

Organization: 4 military regions; 3 infantry battalions; 1 armored squadron; 1 artillery battery; 1 AA artillery battery; 1 engineer company; 1 headquarters company; 1 support company; 1 parachute company

Equipment: 5 light tanks; 7 combat vehicles; 16 armored personnel carriers; 4 howitzers; 16 mortars; antitank rocket launchers; air defense guns

Navy

Personnel: 700

Naval bases: Abidjan, Sassandra, Tabou and San Pedro

Units: 2 fast attack craft; 8 patrol craft; 1 landing craft; 13 assault boats; 1 training ship

Air Force

Personnel: 900

Organization: 6 combat aircraft; 1 fighter squadron; 1 transport squadron; 3 VIP aircraft; helicopters

Air bases: Port-Bouet (Abidjan), Bouaké, Man, Daloa, Sassandra, Korhogo, Tabou and Odienné

Though Ivory Coast has no martial traditions, the combat-worthiness of the Ivorian soldier has been tested in numerous campaigns under the French in North Africa and Asia. The Ivorian soldier fights effectively and demonstrates outstanding qualities of loyalty and endurance. Only the army possesses combat capabilities; the navy and the air force are designed to serve as support forces only. Their capability to sustain offensive operations against their neighbors or to defend Ivory Coast against outside attack is limited and uncertain. The only favorable factors in any military situation are the difficult nature of the terrain, the certainty of French assistance in the case of an external invasion, and the limited strength of all its neighbors. The United States and Israel have provided military assistance.

EDUCATION

Education in Ivory Coast is free at all levels, although compulsory education has not been introduced. Youngsters attend primary school from ages seven to 13. Secondary education, which could last as long as seven years, starts at age 13. The national university is the University of Abidjan, while many students also attend French universities. The primary course is divided into three stages: preparatory, elementary and intermediate. Most primary schools are overcrowded, and not all children who wish to attend school are accepted. The secondary course is divided into two cycles: the first of four years and the second of three years. The first two years of the course consist of a general program; specialization begins only in the third year. Examinations, both oral and written, are given in the sixth and seventh years of secondary school. Africanization of the curricula has proceeded slowly because of the lack of suitable textbooks. The secondary course is offered by colleges administered by the central government, *lycées* administered by the municipal governments and secondary schools administered by religious agencies.

EDUCATION INDICATORS, 1984

Literacy
  Total (%): 57.3
  Females (%): 31.0 (1985)
First level
  Schools: 5,976
  Students: 1,179,456
  Teachers: 28,561
  Student/teacher ratio: 41.3
Second level
  Schools: 218 (1980)
  Students: 245,043
  Teachers: 4,569 (1980)
  Student/teacher ratio: 53.6
Vocational
  Schools: 38 (1980)
  Students: 21,758
  Teachers: 1,947 (1981)
  Student/teacher ratio: 11.2
Third level
  Institution: 1 (1980)
  Students: 19,660
  Teachers: 1,204 (1982)
  Student/teacher ratio: 16.3
  Gross enrollment ratio: 2.4
  Students (/100,000 pop.): 200
Foreign study
  Foreign students in national universities: 1,422 (1985)
  Students abroad: 3,778
    of whom in
      U.S.: 295 (1988)
      France: 2,714 (1988)
      Federal Republic of Germany: 63 (1988)
      U.K.: 2 (1987)
Public expenditures, 1981
  Total (C.F.A.F.): 147,478,300
  % of GNP: 6.9
  % of current expenditure: 83.5

In form and content, Ivorian education has changed little since colonial times.

The academic year runs from September to June and is divided into three terms. The average school week consists of 30 hours, with half days on Thursdays and Saturdays. The medium of instruction is French throughout.

Private schools are allowed to operate freely and receive government subsidies if they follow the standard government curriculum. The Council for Private Education coordinates public and private education, sets standards of teaching and personnel and recommends subsidies. Over 90% of private-school enrollment is accounted for by Catholic schools. Teachers are divided into five classes: professors, assistant professors, *instituteurs* (teachers), *instituteurs-adjoint* (associate teachers) and monitors. Teachers are trained in normal schools and associate teachers in pedagogic institutes. Monitors receive no special training. Almost all primary-school teachers are Ivorian, while almost all secondary-school teachers are French.

In 1984 the 21,758 students enrolled in the vocational stream made up only 9% of the secondary-school population. Vocational training is generally disfavored, but the vocational content of the curricula has increased since the creation of the Ministry of Technical and Professional Training in 1970. Apart from an educational television network, there are few adult education or literacy programs.

LEGAL SYSTEM

The court system consists of two levels. The Supreme Court, the High Court of Justice and the State Security Court constitute the higher level; the Court of Appeal, the courts of first instance, the courts of assize, the justice of peace courts and the courts of first degree constitute the lower level. The Supreme Court has four sections: constitutional, administrative, judicial and audit control. The High Court of Justice is composed of deputies chosen by the National Assembly from among its own members. It is competent to impeach the president for high treason. The Superior Council of the Judiciary assists the president in maintaining judicial independence. Among the lower courts, the Court of Appeals with its headquarters in Abidjan and eight separate tribunals, is the highest. The courts of assize try only criminal cases, and courts of first degree try only cases involving customary law.

Ivorian law establishes the right to a fair public trail. This provision is generally respected in urban centers. In rural areas justice often is administered at the village level through traditional institutions. The judiciary is independent of the executive and military. Defendants have the right to legal counsel, and the judicial system provides for court-appointed attorneys for indigent defendants. In practice, however, such attorneys are not readily available. The Court of Appeals hears appeals of verdicts of civilian courts. Civilians are not tried by military courts. There is no structure of appeals courts within the military justice system. Persons convicted by a military tribunal occasionally request the Supreme Court to set aside the tribunal's verdict and order a retrial. There are no known political prisoners in Ivory Coast. Under the Ivorian Penal Code, a public prosecutor can detain a suspect for up to 48 hours without bringing charges. During the anticrime campaign of 1983, several thousand individuals were detained under this provision for identity checks, and apparently many were held beyond the legal maximum. The identity checks continued during 1984, but on a smaller scale. The code dictates that further detention be ordered by a magistrate, who can authorize periods of up to four months but who must provide the minister of justice with a monthly written explanation of why detention should be continued.

Over half the judicial corps still is French because of the shortage of Ivorian judges. Although the independence of the judiciary is not specifically guaranteed, the rule of law is generally respected by the government, and the judiciary is noted for its integrity and fairness.

No information is available on the corrections system in Ivory Coast.

LAW ENFORCEMENT

The national police force consists of two organizations: the National Gendarmerie and the Sûreté Nationale.

The Sûreté Nationale, headed by a director, is the main police force. The Central Préfecture de Police, also headed by a director, is the centralized command of police operations. The principal operational arm of the Central Préfecture is the Service de Police, also called Police d'État. Its uniformed members are called *gardiens de la paix* (peace officers), and its officers are called *officers de la paix;* both ranks are under Officiers de Police. The two major components of the Service de Police are the Corps Urbains and the Postes du Territoire. The Corps Urbains consist of companies of urban policemen headed by an inspector or commissioner. Postes du Territoire consist of brigades of rural policemen, many of them fully motorized. The Police Auxilaire, another branch of the central prefecture, is composed of small specialist units, such as airport, traffic, sanitation and border police. The Criminal Investigation Department, working directly out of the national headquarters, is known as Corps des Agents de la Sûreté.

The National Gendarmerie is an elite, paramilitary corps that serves as part of both the armed forces and the police force. It is designated as the country's senior service and consists of over 1,500 well-disciplined officers and enlisted men. The operational unit of the National Gendarmerie is the legion, commanded by a commandant. Each prefecture is assigned one legion. Each legion is composed of a varying number of brigades forming departmental companies, which are charged with routine patrol and investigation. Mobile squadrons of the legions, made up of a number of platoons, are employed to quell public riots.

Crimes of all kinds appear to be rising. The major law enforcement problems are theft and drug use.

HEALTH

The government provides universal free medical care.

The most serious health problems are malaria, smallpox, yellow fever and measles. A total of 19% of the population have access to safe water.

HEALTH INDICATORS

Health personnel, 1982
- Physicians: 502
  - Persons per: 17,847
- Dentists: 36 (1978)
- Nurses: 3,052 (1978)
- Pharmacists: 76 (1978)
- Midwives: 615

Hospitals
- Number: 61 (1975)
- Number of beds (/10,000): 9 (1988)
- Admissions/discharges (/10,000): 171 (1975)

Type of hospitals (%), 1978
- Government: 98.4
- Private non-profit, private for profit: 1.6

Public health expenditures, (latest)
- % national budget: 4.0
- Per capita (U.S. $): 7.90

Vital statistics
- Crude death rate (/1,000 pop.): 13 (1990)
- Life expectancy at birth, 1990
  - Males: 52
  - Females: 56
- Infant mortality rate (/1,000 live births): 100 (1990)
- Child mortality rate under 5 yrs. (1985–90) (/1,000): 148

Population with access to safe water (%): 19 (latest)

FOOD & NUTRITION

The staple food are yams, manioc, plantain, millet, Indian corn and rice. Most of the food is highly seasoned. Meat is rarely consumed, although fish and eggs are popular.

The per capita intake of food in the mid-1980s was 2,652 calories (115% of requirements).

MEDIA & CULTURE

Ivory Coast has two daily newspapers, both produced by the Ministry of Information. The major paper is *Fraternité Matin.* Founded in 1964, it is the official organ of the ruling PDCI, and it had a circulation in the late 1980s of 80,000. *Ivoire Soir,* published in color, was introduced in May 1987 to complement *Fraternité Matin.* There also are several weekly and monthly publications. *Le Journal des Jeunes Chrétiens,* published five times a year by Inter-Afrique Press, was founded in 1974. It has a circulation of 5,500. Newspapers and magazines, imported from France by air, enjoy wide readership. Periodicals number 37 titles. All newspapers and periodicals are published in French.

Though there is no overt censorship, criticism of the government is considered irresponsible. Publication of "false" news bringing into disregard the laws of the country or its political institutions or injuring the morals of the population is punishable with imprisonment, fine or expulsion.

The national press agency, Agence Ivoirienne de Presse, was established in 1961. The AFP maintains a permanent bureau in Abidjan.

Ivory Coast has a small but growing book publishing industry. Centre d'Édition et de Diffusion Africaines issues schoolbooks, while the University of Abidjan Press and Institute Africain pour la Développement Économique et Social issue scholarly works. Hachette and other French publishers maintain warehouses in Abidjan. In 1989 a total of 46 titles were published in the country. Ivory Coast adheres to the Berne and Florence conventions.

The official broadcasting organization is Radiodiffusion Télévision Ivoirienne (RTI), established in 1962. The domestic network is on the air for 144 hours a week, broadcasting in French and 10 vernaculars. The international network is on the air for 48 hours a week, broadcasting in French and vernaculars. Abidjan has four shortwave transmitters and two medium-wave transmitters; Bouaké has one medium-wave transmitter. Almost two-thirds of the programming is devoted to information and education.

Television, introduced in 1961, reaches more than half of the national territory. Television Ivoirienne broadcasts in French; programs totaled 40 hours a week in the late 1980s. There has been a color network

MEDIA INDICATORS

Newspapers
 Number of dailies: 2 (latest)
 Circulation (000): 130 (latest)
 Per 000 persons: 11 (latest)
 Number of periodicals: 37 (latest)
 Newsprint consumption: (1988)
 Total metric tons: 2,200
 Per 1,000 pop. (kg.): 190
Book publishing
 Number of titles: 46 (pre-1986)
Radio
 Number of transmitters: 17 (latest)
 Number of persons per radio receiver: 8.1 (1989)
Television
 Television transmitters: 13 (latest)
 Number of persons per TV receiver: 18 (1989)
Cinema
 Number of fixed cinemas: 72 (pre-1986)
 Seating capacity (000): 42 (pre-1986)
 Annual attendance (million): 7.0 (pre-1986)
Films
 Production of long films: 2 (pre-1986)

CULTURAL & ENVIRONMENTAL INDICATORS (latest)

Libraries
 Volumes (000): 25 (pre-1986)
 Registered borrowers (000): 2 (pre-1986)
 Loans (/1,000 pop.): 3 (pre-1986)
Nature reserves
 Number of facilities: 10

since 1973. More than half of television programming is dedicated to education, while information, education and culture also are common topics.

Ivory Coast has a small film industry, which produces occasional feature films. Documentaries are produced by the Société Ivoirienne de Cinéma.

The largest libraries are the Municipal Library at Abidjan, with 50,000 volumes; the University of Abidjan Library, with 30,000 volumes; and the National Library, with 7,000 volumes.

The Ivory Coast has only one museum.

SOCIAL WELFARE

Existing Social Security legislation provides workmen's compensation, retirement benefits and family allowances to wage-earning families. However, these benefits cover less than 6% of Ivorians. The Social Security programs are financed by employers; the government and the workers do not contribute any share. Private welfare activities are coordinated by a social welfare service.

GLOSSARY

abou-san: a form of share-cropping in which land rights are divided into three parts and shared by the owner and tenant.

coutume: rent formerly paid to native chiefs for settlement and trading rights.

domaine de la loi: subjects of legislation reserved to the Assembly by the constitution.

prefecture: largest unit of local administration in the Ivory Coast.

projet de loi: a bill sponsored in the Assembly by the government.

proposition de loi: a bill sponsored in the Assembly by a private member.

service civique: mandatory public service by the army or unemployed workers.

subprefecture: a subdivision of a prefecture headed by a subprefect.

CHRONOLOGY (from 1960)

1960— Republic of Ivory Coast is proclaimed, with Felix Houphouet-Boigny as president. . . . New Constitution is adopted.

1961— New agreement is signed with France providing for extensive military and economic aid and strengthened ties.

1963— The University of Abidjan is founded. . . . Plot against the government is uncovered: hundreds are arrested as conspirators, including members of the National Assembly and cabinet members. . . . State Security Court is set up to try plotters.

1964— In far-reaching social reforms, polygamy, bride price and matrilineal inheritance are abolished.

1969— Street clashes between Ivorian workers and aliens are followed by student demonstrations. . . . Diplomatic relations with the Soviet Union are broken.

1970— The government restricts immigration of alien workers. . . . In the so-called Gagnoa affair, the government suppresses a group of Beté rebels led by Gnagbe Opadjele. . . . Prefectures replace departments as units of local administration.

1971— Houphouet-Boigny calls for dialogue with South Africa as an alternative to confrontation.

1973— Coup attempt by 12 army officers is foiled. . . . Agreement with France is renegotiated.

1974— Prime Minister Johannes Vorster of South Africa visits Ivory Coast.

1975— Five thousand political prisoners are granted amnesty. . . . Houphouet-Boigny is reelected for a fourth five-year term as president.

1976— United States increases aid to Ivory Coast following latter's support for U.S. positions at the United Nations on such issues as Zionism, Korea and Puerto Rican independence.

1977— Ivorian cabinet is completely overhauled and enlarged from 30 to 36 ministers.

1979— The deposed ruler of Central African Republic, Jean-Bedel Bokassa, is granted asylum in Ivory Coast. . . . Instances of violence against the French community are reported in Abidjan.

1983— Plans are announced for the gradual transfer of the national capital from Abidjan to Yamoussourko.

1985— In national elections, the president is reelected, but only 50% of the sitting members in the National Assembly are returned.

1990— Houphouet-Boigny legalizes opposition parties;

the nation's first multiparty elections are held; Houphouet-Boigny is reelected president.

1991— Ivory Coast hosts the first-ever summit of African and African-American leaders in Abidjan.

BIBLIOGRAPHY

BOOKS

Clignet, Remi, and Philip Foster. *The Fortunate Few: A Study of Secondary Schools and Students in the Ivory Coast.* Evanston, Ill., 1974.

Cohen, Michael A. *Urban Policy and Political Conflict in Africa: A Study of the Ivory Coast.* Chicago, 1974.

Foster, Philip, and Aristide R. Zolberg. *Ghana and the Ivory Coast.* Chicago, 1971.

Goreux, Louis M. *Interdependence in Planning: Multilevel Programming studies of the Ivory Coast.* Baltimore, Md., 1978.

Guyer, David. *Ghana and the Ivory Coast: The Impact of Colonialism in an African Setting.* New York, 1971.

Harshe, Rajen. *Pervasive Entente: France and Ivory Coast in African Affairs.* Atlantic Highlands, N.J., 1984.

Joshi, Heather. *Abidjan: Urban Development and Employment in the Ivory Coast.* Geneva, 1976.

Masini, Jean. *Multinationals in Africa: A Case Study of the Ivory Coast.* New York, 1978.

Mundt, Robert J. *Historical Dictionary of the Ivory Coast.* Metuchen, N.J., 1987.

Priovolos, Theophilos. *Coffee and the Ivory Coast: An Econometric Study.* Lexington, Mass., 1981.

Richter, Dolores. *Art, Economics and Change: The Kulebele of Northern Ivory Coast.* La Jolla, Calif., 1980.

Thompson, Virginia. *West Africa's Council of the Entente.* Ithaca, N.Y., 1970.

Weiskel, Timothy C. *French Colonial Rule and the Baule Peoples: Resistance and Cooperation, 1889–1911.* New York, 1980.

Zartman, William, I., and Christopher L. Delgado. *The Political Economy of the Ivory Coast.* New York, 1984.

OFFICIAL PUBLICATIONS

Treasury. *Balance des Comptes du Trésor* (Treasury Accounts Balance Sheets) (monthly).

JAMAICA

BASIC FACT SHEET

OFFICIAL NAME: Jamaica

ABBREVIATION: JM

CAPITAL: Kingston

HEAD OF STATE: Queen Elizabeth II, represented by Governor General Howard Cooke

HEAD OF GOVERNMENT: Prime Minister Michael N. Manley (from 1989)

NATURE OF GOVERNMENT: Parliamentary democracy in the commonwealth recognizing Elizabeth II as chief of state.

POPULATION: 2,390,000 (1990)

AREA: 11,424 sq. km. (4,411 sq. mi.)

ETHNIC MAJORITY: Black

LANGUAGE: English

RELIGION: Christianity

UNIT OF CURRENCY: Jamaican dollar (J. $)

NATIONAL FLAG: Two diagonal yellow gold bars forming a saltire divide the flag into four triangular panels, the top and bottom green and the two sides black.

NATIONAL EMBLEM: A male Indian standing on the right and a female Indian standing on the left of a shield that bears a red cross with five golden pineapples superimposed on it. The crest is a Jamaican crocodile surmounting the royal helmet and mantling. On a scroll beneath the device appears the national motto "Out of Many, One People," a translation of the Latin motto *Indus Uterque Serviet Uni* in the original armorial bearings granted to the island in 1662.

NATIONAL ANTHEM: "Eternal Father, Bless Our Land"

NATIONAL HOLIDAYS: First Monday in August (Independence Day, National Day); January 1 (New Year's Day); May 23 (Labor Day); June 2 (Queen's Birthday); Christian festivals, including Christmas, Boxing Day, Ash Wednesday, Good Friday and Easter Monday

NATIONAL CALENDAR: Gregorian

PHYSICAL QUALITY OF LIFE INDEX: 91

DATE OF INDEPENDENCE: August 6, 1962

DATE OF CONSTITUTION: August 6, 1962

WEIGHTS & MEASURES: Imperial

GEOGRAPHICAL FEATURES

Jamaica, in the Caribbean Sea north of the eastern extremity of Cuba and separated form it by 145 km. (90 mi.), has a total land area of 11,424 sq. km. (4,411 sq. mi.) and extends 235 km. (146 mi.) north to south and 82 km. (51 mi.) east to west. Its coastline stretches 518 km. (322 mi.).

The capital is Kingston, with an estimated population of 100,637 in the 1982 official census. The other principal urban centers are Spanish Town (81,416) and Montego Bay (51,614).

The topography consists mainly of coastal plains around the island divided by the Blue Mountains to the east and the hills and limestone plateaus that occupy the central and western areas of the interior. The Blue Mountains have an average elevation of 1,800 m. (6,000 ft.), with Blue Mountain peak reaching a height of 2,256 m. (7,402 ft.).

The rivers are numerous, and many rise only a few miles from the coast. Many are narrow and fast-flowing. The principal rivers are Plantain Garden, Hope, Yallahs, Rio Pedro, Rio Minho, Milk, Cabaritta, Rio Grande, Wag Water, White, Martha Brae, Montego, Great and Black. The last-named has been described as the finest river in the island and is navigable by boats of considerable size.

CLIMATE & WEATHER

The island has a tropical climate at sea level and a temperate climate in the uplands. There are four seasons, distinguished mainly by differences in rainfall: two rainy seasons, from May to June and from September to November; and two dry seasons, from July to August and from December to April. There is relatively little seasonal variation in temperature from its lowest point in January or February to a peak in July or August. The winter mean is about 24°C (75°F) and the summer mean 27°C (80°F). The temperature maximums are 32.8°C (91°F) at Kingston on the coast and 26.7°C (80°F) in the highlands.

The annual average precipitation is 1,950 mm. (77 in.), with the highest rainfall, 5,030 mm. (200 in.), recorded on the northeastern coast and on Blue Mountain, and the lowest, 840 mm. (33 in.), around Kingston, in the southwest.

The island is subject to hurricanes from late August to November.

POPULATION

The population of Jamaica was estimated in 1990 at 2,390,000, on the basis of the last official census, in 1982, when the population was 2,095,878.

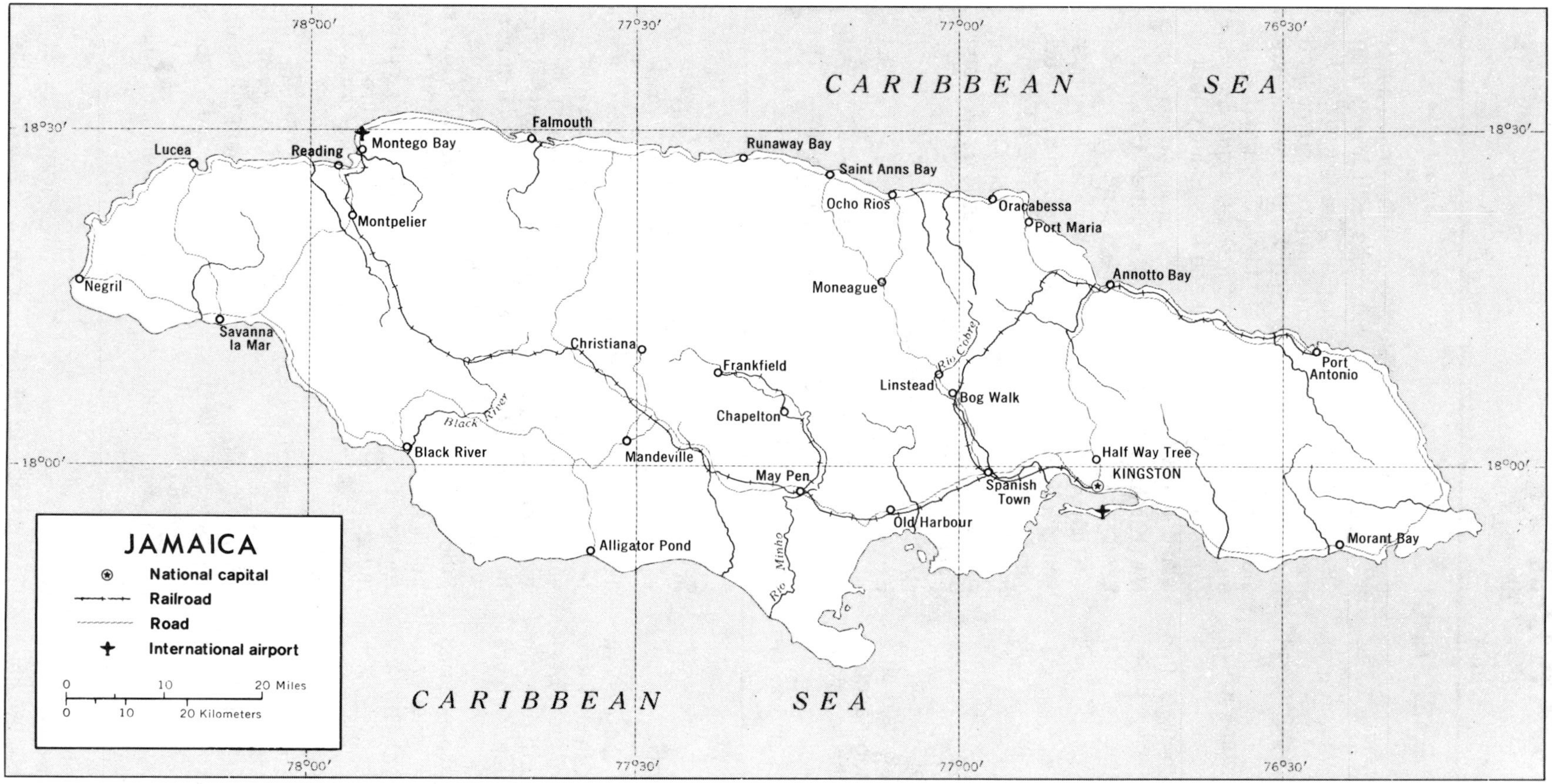
JAMAICA
National capital
Railroad
Road
International airport
0 10 20 Miles
0 10 20 Kilometers
CARIBBEAN SEA
CARIBBEAN SEA
78°00′
77°30′
77°00′
76°30′
18°30′
18°00′
Negril
Lucea
Reading
Montego Bay
Falmouth
Montpelier
Savanna la Mar
Black River
Christiana
Mandeville
Alligator Pond
Runaway Bay
Saint Anns Bay
Ocho Rios
Oracabessa
Port Maria
Moneague
Frankfield
Chapelton
May Pen
Linstead
Bog Walk
Spanish Town
Old Harbour
Annotto Bay
Half Way Tree
KINGSTON
Port Antonio
Morant Bay
Black River
Rio Cobre
Rio Minho

OUT OF MANY ONE PEOPLE

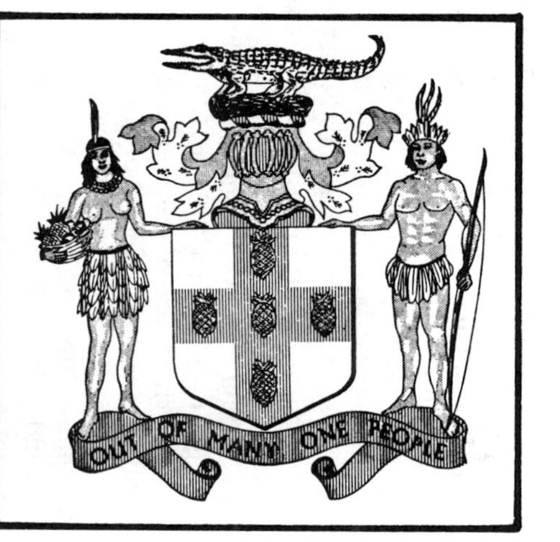

DEMOGRAPHIC INDICATORS

Population (millions): 2.39 (1990)
Year of last census: 1982
Sex distribution (% at last census): males, 49.1; females, 50.9
Population estimates and projections (millions)
1930: 1.009 1960: 1.629 1990: 2.391
1940: 1.212 1970: 1.891 2000: 2.560
1950: 1.403 1980: 2.133
Age profile (% at last census)
0–14: 38.4 30–44: 13.8 60–74: 6.9
15–29: 28.8 45–59: 9.4 75 and over: 2.6
Median age (yrs.): 20.4 (1985)
Youth population (% aged 15–24): (1985) 24.4; (2000) 18.5
Total dependency ratio, 1985: 74.7
Annual growth rate (%)
1950–55: 1.89 1975–80: 1.24 2000–2005: 1.17
1955–60: 1.10 1980–85: 1.45 2005–2010: 1.07
1960–65: 1.55 1985–90: 1.52 2010–2015: 1.05
1965–70: 1.20 1990–95: 1.42 2015–2020: 1.02
1970–75: 1.78 1995–2000: 1.29 2020–2025: 0.98
Hypothetical size of stationary population (millions): 4
Assumed year of reaching net reproduction rate of 1: 1995
Urban population (millions): 1.155 (1985)
Urban population (%): (1988) 51; (1965) 38
Annual urban population growth rate (%, 1985–90): 2.65
Annual rural population growth rate (%, 1985–90): 0.34
Percentage of urban population in largest city: 66 (1980)
Percentage of urban population in cities of population over 500,000: 66 (1980)
Number of cities of population over 500,000: 1 (1980)
Population density per sq. km. (per sq. mi.): 217.5 (563.4) (1990)

VITAL STATISTICS

Crude birth rate (/1,000): 21 (1990); 38 (1965)
Crude death rate (/1,000): 5 (1990); 9 (1965)
Infant mortality rate (/1,000 live births): 16 (1990)
Maternal mortality rate (/100,000 live births): 100 (1980)
Life expectancy (yrs.) at birth: males, 75; females, 79 (1990)
Gross reproduction rate (/woman) 1980–85: 1.65
Total fertility rate (/woman): 2.3 (1990)
Rate of natural increase (/1,000): 18.9 (1989)
Marriage rate (/1,000): 4.7 (1989)
Average household size: 4.3 (latest)
Legitimate births (%): 14.9 (latest)

STATUS OF WOMEN INDICATORS, 1985

Number of women (millions): 1.199
% childbearing age, 15–49: 50 (1988)
% married women using contraception: 52
% literate: 89.1 (1989)
% in labor force: 45.8 (1988)
Total fertility rate (/woman): 2.3 (1990)

Jamaica's reported overall and agricultural area densities are 212 per sq. km. (549 per sq. mi.) and 462 per sq. km. (1,196 per sq. mi.), respectively. The most densely populated parish is St. Andrew and the least is Clarendon.

Jamaica ranks high in urbanization, with an urban component of 51% and an urban growth rate of 2.65%. There are six cities with populations of over 10,000.

Emigration is a constant demographic factor. Since the introduction of restrictions on immigration from Commonwealth countries to the United Kingdom in 1962, the principal destination of Jamaican emigrants has been Canada.

Jamaican women are accorded full equality under the Constitution, and the Employment Act of 1975 guarantees equal pay for equal work. The legal status of women is reflected in the number of influential positions they hold in the civil service and the government, including minister of education, director of the Jamaica Information Service and president of the Senate. Nevertheless, because of cultural and social values, women often suffer economic discrimination. This discrimination frequently occurs in hiring practices. Access to higher-paying jobs and to jobs outside traditional "female" areas is limited. Reportedly, women have no choice but to settle for accepted "woman's work" in service fields such as teaching, health-care work and commercial work (e.g., as produce vendors, sales clerks, secretaries or office clerks). The higher-paying senior-level positions in commercial areas still are predominantly held by men. The 1975 act has helped to narrow the gap between men's and women's salaries, although disparities remain.

The country's economic problems tend to affect women first, because generally they work in the service sector.

The government has a number of programs to help women with the problems they face. Primary-health-care clinics provide prenatal and postnatal care for mothers and their children. The National Family Planning Board organizes education programs in family planning, population and family life. A new food-stamp program includes special provisions for pregnant and lactating women and for women whose income is below $50 a month. The Women's Bureau, established in 1974 in the Ministry of Youth and Community Development, sponsors agricultural and technical training projects and centers to provide continuing education for pregnant women. The government has announced plans to establish a national advisory committee for women's affairs.

In 1966 a family planning unit was established in the Ministry of Health, and in 1967 the semiautonomous National Family Planning Board was created. With the passage of the National Family Planning Act of 1970, the board was vested with full statutory responsibility for family planning. A commercial contraceptive program started in 1975 with assistance from the U.S. AID makes oral contraceptives and condoms available through pharmacies without prescription at nominal cost. In 1985 a total of 52% of married women of childbearing age used some form of birth control device.

ETHNIC COMPOSITION

Nearly 91.4% of the population is of African descent. Of this ethnic majority, 76.3% is of pure black origin and 15.1% is of mixed black and white origin. Of the minorities, Chinese and Afro-Chinese constitute 1.2%, East Indians and Afro-East Indians 3.4%, whites 3.2% and others 0.8%. Africans were imported to work as slaves in the plantations. When the slave trade was abolished in 1807, East Indians and Chinese were imported in lieu of black laborers.

Although relations among the ethnic groups are notably free of tensions, black racial consciousness, called black power, is a powerful social and political force. There are occasional antiwhite riots. Nevertheless, large British and American communities are resident on the island.

In terms of ethnic and linguistic homogeneity, Jamaica ranks 115th in the world, with 95% homogeneity (on an ascending scale in which North and South Korea are ranked 135th with 100% homogeneity and Tanzania is ranked first with 7% homogeneity).

LANGUAGE

The official language is English. British English is the received standard, but recent decades have been marked by the growth of a patois known as Jamaican English, whose main characteristics are the incorporation of archaic English and African words and certain peculiarities of word order and pronunciation. A formal dictionary of Jamaican English was published in 1966.

RELIGIONS

There is no established church, but Christianity is the religion followed by the vast majority of the inhabitants. Over 100 denominations are represented on the island, of which the largest are the Anglicans with 317,600 members, followed by the Baptists, the Church of God, Roman Catholics, Methodists, Presbyterians, Seventh-Day Adventists, Moravians, Congregationalists, Pentecostalists, Plymouth Brethren and the Salvation Army. Non-Christian groups include Jews, Hindus and followers of an African folk religion called Pocomania.

HISTORICAL BACKGROUND

Jamaica was discovered by Christopher Columbus in 1494 and was settled by the Spanish in the 16th century. The indigenous Arawak Indians were exterminated by the 17th century, when the Spanish themselves were expelled from the island by the British. The island was formally ceded by Spain to England in 1670. The English developed a flourishing plantation economy with slave labor brought from West Africa, but the abolition of the slave trade in 1807 and of slavery in 1834, the U.S. Civil War and the removal of tariff protection for Jamaican produce in Great Britain destroyed the basis of this economy and led to a black uprising in Morant Bay in 1865. Parliament established a crown colony government in 1866, and the administration and economy were gradually rebuilt. Jamaica achieved a measure of internal self-government in 1944 and full internal government in 1959. It joined with other British Caribbean states in 1958 to form the Federation of the West Indies but withdrew three years later.

In the decades prior to independence, Jamaica had developed a stable two-party system under the leadership of Norman W. Manley, founder of the people's National Party (PNP), and Sir Alexander Bustamante, founder of the Jamaica Labour Party (JLP). At independence in 1962, the JLP became the governing party with Bustamante assuming the post of prime minister. Bustamente retired in 1967 and was succeeded by Donald Sangster, who died shortly after assuming office. He, in turn, was succeeded by Hugh L. Shearer, who continued as prime minister until 1972 when the PNP achieved a majority. Led by Michael Norman Manley, son of the party's founder, the PNP remained in power until 1980. Manley, an advocate of democratic socialism, headed a government that emphasized economic independence and social reform.

The 1970s were a period of political unrest generated by a declining economy and high unemployment. Street violence and gang warfare erupted in 1976, prompting the government to declare a state of emergency that lasted six months. Violence again erupted in 1979.

The JLP was returned to power in 1980 in the bloodiest election campaign in Jamaica's history. Under the leadership of Edward Seaga, it governed the country until 1989. In 1983 the JLP called early elections. With only four days permitted to nominate candidates, the PNP refused to participate in the elections, and the JLP won the election unopposed, forming a one-party legislature.

Civil unrest, fanned by government economic policies that withdrew food subsidies and devalued the dollar, continued throughout the 1980s. Crime, particularly drug-related violence, increased rapidly. In this atmosphere, elections were held in early 1989, and Manley was returned to office. In local elections held in 1990, the PNP won control of 12 of the 13 municipal councils.

CONSTITUTION & GOVERNMENT

The Constitution of Jamaica is the Jamaica (Constitution) Order in Council of 1962. Under the Constitution Jamaica is a titular monarchy, with the queen of England as the head of state, represented on the island by a governor-general. The executive consists of a prime minister, the head of government, and at least 11 cabinet ministers appointed by the governor-general. All cabinet members, excluding the justice minister, must be members of Parliament. The governor-general is assisted by the Privy Council, whose six

RULERS OF JAMAICA

Queen

February 1952– : Elizabeth II

Prime Ministers

August 1962–February 1967: Sir William Alexander Bustamante
February 1967–April 1967: Sir Donald Burns Sangster (acting)
April 1967–March 1972: Hugh Lawson Shearer
March 1972–November 1980: Michael N. Manley
November 1980–February 1989: Edward Philip George Seaga
February 1989– : Michael N. Manley

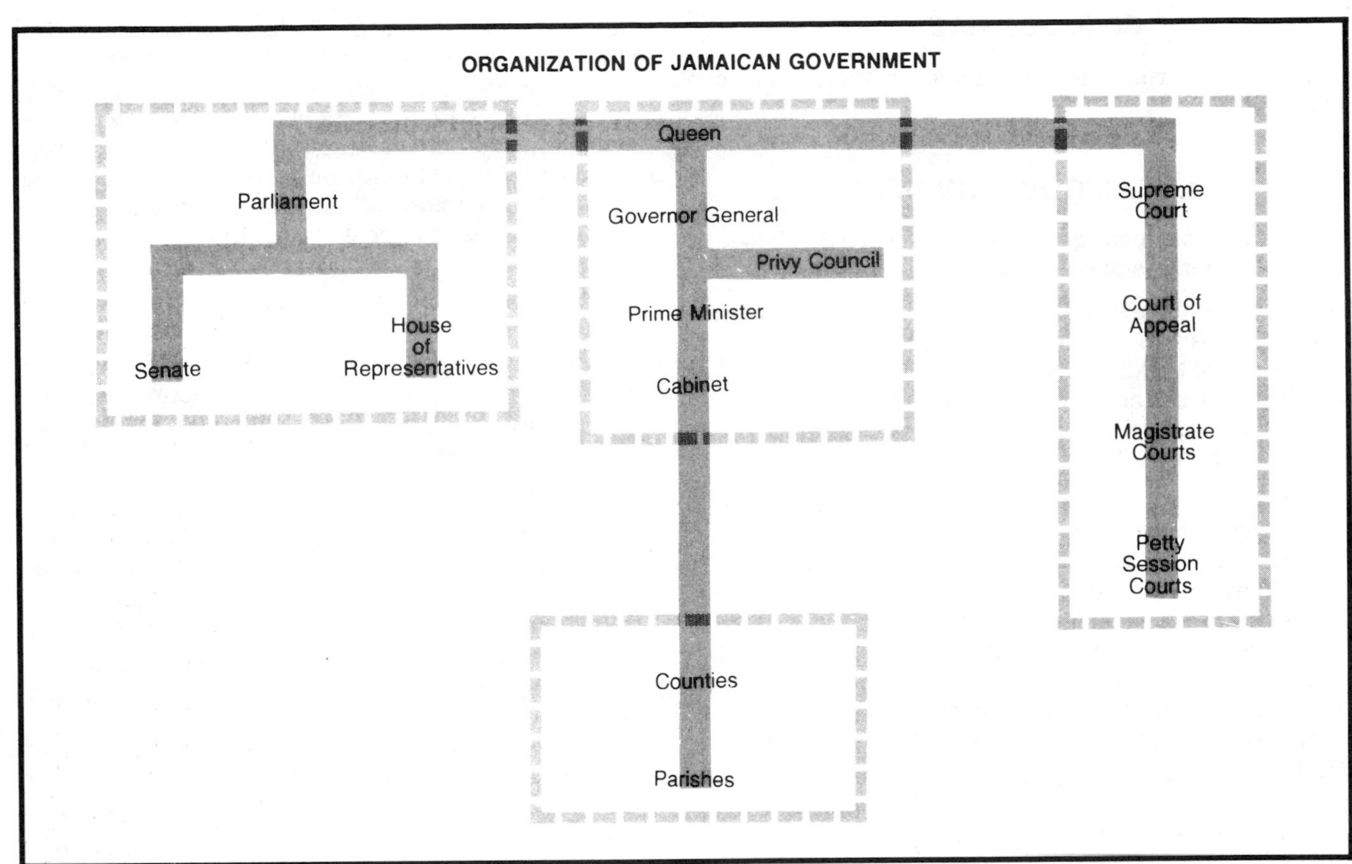

GOVERNMENT LIST
(July/August 1991)

Governor General	Cooke, Howard
Prime Minister	Manley, Michael
Deputy Prime Minister	Patterson, P. J.
Minister of Agriculture	Mullings, Seymour
Minister of Construction	Ramatallie, O. D.
Minister of Defense	Manley, Michael
Minister of Education	Dunkley, Caryle
Minister of Finance & Planning	Patterson, P. J.
Minister of Fogeign Affairs & Foreign Trade	Coore, David
Minister of Health	Douglas, Easton
Minister of Information	Robertson, Paul
Minister of Industry & Commerce	Small, Hugh
Minister of Justice	Rattray, Carl
Minister of Labor, Welfare & Sports	Simpson, Portia
Minister of Local Government	Brown, Ralph
Minister of Mining & Energy	Clarke, Horace
Minister of National Security	Knight, K. D.
Minister of Parliamentary Affairs	McNeill, Kenneth, *M.D.*
Minister of Public Service	McNeill, Kenneth, *M.D.*
Minister of Public Utilities & Transport	Pickersgill, Bobby
Minister of State	Phillips, Peter David
Minister of Tourism	Pringle, Frank
Minister of Youth, Community Development & Culture	Manley, Douglas
Attorney General	Rattray, Carl
Speaker of the House	McNeill, Kenneth, *M.D.*
Governor, Central Bank	Brown, G. Arthur

members are appointed on the advice of the prime minister.

Legislative power is vested in a bicameral Parliament with a appointed Upper House and an elected Lower House. The judicial system is comprised of the Supreme Court, which has both primary and appellate jurisdiction, a court of appeals and minor courts.

Jamaica has had a stable political system headed by a succession of vigorous leaders and backed by sound institutions. There are no extraparliamentary threats to the present government. The racial violence with which the island seethed in recent years seems to have subsided.

FREEDOM & HUMAN RIGHTS

Jamaica continues to function as a parliamentary democracy within a constitutional monarchy despite the violence and partisan fervor of its elections. The 1980 elections were one of the most violent in Jamaican history, and charges of physical abuse by members of the security forces were frequently made. There are no political prisoners. The legal system, following British common law, provides for a fair trail and ensures protection of the rights of defendants.

There is no censorship, and although most of the media are government-owned, the privately owned paper, the *Daily Gleaner* contributes to the maintenance of a free press. The *Daily Gleaner* has been highly critical of present and past Jamaican governments.

Jamaica has a strong organized labor movement; in fact, the major political parties are offshoots of two of the three major unions, the Bustamante Industrial Trade Union and the National Workers' Union.

CIVIL SERVICE

No current information is available on the Jamaican civil service.

LOCAL GOVERNMENT

For purposes of local government Jamaica is divided into three counties and 14 parishes, as follows:

- County of Cornwall: Parishes of Hanover, St. James, Trelawney, Westmoreland and St. Elizabeth
- County of Middlesex: Parishes of St. Ann, St. Mary, Manchester, Clarendon and St. Catherine
- County of Surrey: Parishes of Portland, Kingston, St. Andrew and St. Thomas

Of the 14 parishes, two—Kingston and St. Andrew—are amalgamated and administered by the Kingston and St. Andrew Corporation. In the other parishes, local affairs are administered by parish councils, consisting of 13 to 21 members elected every three years on the basis of universal adult suffrage. Members of the House of Representatives hold ex officio seats on the councils of their respective parishes. The chairman of the parish council is known as the mayor. Each parish has a *custos rotulorum*, who is the chief magistrate and also representative of the governor-general. Parish revenues are derived from central government loans and taxes.

FOREIGN POLICY

Within the Caribbean, Jamaica exercises disproportionate influence because of its traditional economic and political weight. Jamaica also is the focus of black power movements in the Caribbean, elements of which are found on every island in the West Indies. Nevertheless, relations with the United Kingdom have been surprisingly good. Relations with the United States, cordial until Michael Manley's assumption of the prime minister's office in 1972, have been marred by Jamaica's support for Cuban intervention in Angola in 1975 and by subsequent allegations of CIA involvement in attempts to overthrow Manley. Manley visited Havana in 1975, and Castro returned the visit in 1977.

The United States and other Western powers welcomed the return of the Jamaican Labor Party to power in 1980 under Edward Seaga. Manley's electoral rout then was interpreted as a setback for Cuban influence in the West Indies. On assuming office Seaga promised a return to a more balanced foreign policy and an avoidance of coattails diplomacy. Seaga was the prime mover behind the Reagan administration's Caribbean Basin Initiative (CBI), and ties to Washington were further strengthened by Jamaica's participation in the United States-led invasion of Grenada in 1983. Relations between the two governments remained cordial following Manley's return to office in 1989. His government has worked with the United States in attacking drug smuggling into the United States via Jamaica.

Jamaica and the United States are parties to 30 treaties and agreements covering agricultural commodities, aviation, consuls, defense, economic and technical cooperation, extradition, investment guarantees, property, publications, taxation, narcotic drugs, the Peace Corps, postal matters, property, publications, taxation, telecommunications, trade and commerce, trademarks, visas and weather stations.

PARLIAMENT

Under the Constitution, the bicameral Parliament consists of the Senate and the House of Representatives.

The Senate has 21 members, appointed by the governor-general. Thirteen of the senators are appointed on the advice of the prime minister and eight on the advice of the leader of the opposition. The House of Representatives consists of 60 members, the constitutional limit, elected for five-year terms. Bills may originate in either body; the Senate also is the reviewing body for legislation submitted to it by the House of Representatives. The Senate cannot delay money bills for more than one month and other bills for more than seven months.

On the British model, the governor-general appoints as leader of the opposition the member of the House of Representatives best able to command the support of the majority of members opposed to the government.

The Seaga government began a reform of the electoral system through compilation of new electoral rolls in 1985. However, before the new rolls were completed, the government called an early surprise election in 1983. Only four days were allowed for the nomination of candidates. The PNP, unable to put up candidates at such short notice, boycotted the elections. As a result, the JLP won all the seats in the House of Representatives.

Suffrage is universal over age 18. Parliamentary elections normally are held every five years. Elections are free and open. The integrity of the electoral process is monitored by the Electoral Commission. Electoral participation is high.

POLITICAL PARTIES

Jamaica has an effective two-party system. The People's National Party (PNP), founded by Norman W. Manley in 1938, was in power from 1955 to 1962 and from 1972 to 1980 and has been in power since 1989. The Jamaican Labor Party (JLP), founded by Alexander Bustamante in 1943, was in power from 1945 to 1955, from 1962 to 1972 and from 1980 to 1989. Both parties have their roots in labor unions, and both are well organized and well financed.

The People's National Party, now headed by Michael N. Manley, son of its founder, draws its support from middle-class, intellectual and urban voters. It is committed to a program of democratic socialism, Jamaicanization and friendship with Cuba. In 1983 the PNP broke off its association with the Communist-led Workers' Party in an effort to win moderates' support.

The Jamaican Labor Party also is committed to a broad program of social reform and welfare but has been suspected of being tied to foreign business interests. The JLP draws its heaviest support from rural voters. It is generally pro-West in orientation but also identifies closely with black African and other Third World nations. The JLP leader, Edward Seaga, became prime minister following the 1980 elections.

There are several minor parties, none of which holds legislative seats. The Workers's Party is a pro-Soviet Communist group that rejected Marxist-Leninism in 1990. The African Comprehensive Party, formed in 1988 as a political arm of the Rastafarians, opposes foreign aid and advocates the legalization of marijuana. The Jamaica American Party, founded in 1986, supports U.S. statehood for Jamaica.

In the 1980 elections, the JLP gained 57% of the popular vote, the highest in the party's history. It won all 60 seats in the House of Representatives in 1983 because the PNP boycotted the elections. In the 1989 elections, the PNP gained 56.7% of the popular vote and 45 of the 60 seats.

ECONOMY

Jamaica has a free-market economy based on sugar, bauxite and tourism. The economy, which declined during the 1980s (real GNP is estimated to have fallen 2.1% annually from 1980–1988), is undergoing a process of serious economic adjustment. A steep decline in bauxite earnings coupled with escalating oil import cost generated high rates of unemployment (over 18% in 1989) and inflation (16% in 1989) as well as a decline in the GNP. Compounding the problem is a foreign debt of more than $4.5 billion in 1989—one of the highest per capita in the Western Hemisphere—and a trade deficit of $395 million in 1988.

A $240 million loan, to be drawn over a period of three years, was extended by the IMF in 1977. The loan was renegotiated in 1978. The new agreement resulted in the establishment of the Extended Fund Facility (EFF) agreement, which was initially to provide balance-of-payment support of approximately U.S. $80 million per year for three years. As a condition of the agreement, the government of Jamaica adopted an economic policy designed to reduce the balance-of payments deficit. This policy had three main features: (1) abolition of the existing dual exchange rate system and establishment of a new exchange rate at U.S. $1 =J. $1.55, followed by a series of monthly mini-devaluations that ceased in May 1979, at U.S. $1=J. $1.78; (2) a series of quantitative goals imposed on Jamaica's fiscal and monetary performance, including ceilings on net foreign and domestic assets of the Bank of Jamaica, net bank credit to the public sector and arrears on foreign exchange; (3) a strong income policy aimed at reducing the level of real wages by holding wage increases to 15% while prices climbed by 40%.

PRINCIPAL ECONOMIC INDICATORS

Gross National Product (U.S. $ billions): 3.011 (1989)
GNP per capita (U.S. $): 1,260 (1989)
GNP average annual growth rate (%, 1980–88): −0.4
GNP per capita average annual growth rate (%, 1987–89): 0.7
Average annual rate of inflation (%, 1980–88): 18.7
Consumer Price Index (1980=100) 1986
  All items: 246
  Food: 249
Average annual growth rate (%, 1980–88)
  General government consumption: −1.5
  Private consumption: 2.4
  Gross domestic investment: −1.2

BALANCE OF PAYMENTS, 1988 (U.S. $ millions)

Current account balance: 76.1
Merchandise exports: 833.5
Merchandise imports: 1,228.5
Trade balance: −395.0
Other goods, services & income +: 897.7
Other goods, services & income −: −931.3
Other goods, services & income net: 33.6
Private unrequited transfers: 435.6
Official unrequited transfers: 69.1
Capital other than reserves: −4
Net errors & omissions: −100.7
Counterpart items: 33.4
Liabilities constituting foreign authorities reserves: 4.8
Total change in reserves: 167.7

GROSS DOMESTIC PRODUCT

GDP nominal (J. $ billions): 17.472 (1988)
GDP per capita ($): 1,529 (1989)
Average annual growth rate of GDP (%, 1980–88): 0.6
GDP by type of expenditure (%) 1987
  Consumption
    Private: 62
    Government: 15
  Gross domestic investment: 23
  Gross domestic saving: 19 (1988)
  Foreign trade
    Exports: 55
    Imports: −55
Cost components of GDP (%) 1986
  Net indirect taxes: 14
  Consumption of fixed capital: 8
  Compensation of employees: 43
  Net operating surplus: 34
Sectoral origin of GDP (%) 1987
  Primary
    Agriculture: 6
    Mining: 7
  Secondary
    Manufacturing: 22
    Construction: 8
    Public utilities: 3
  Tertiary
    Transportation & communications: 8
    Trade: 22
    Finance, other services, government: 28
Average annual sectoral growth rates (%, 1980–88)
  Agriculture: 0.9
  Industry: 0.0
  Manufacturing: 1.6
  Services: 0.9

The early years of the Seaga administration were spent in efforts to meet IMF conditions for a $650 million loan. In 1983, after the IMF had suspended further disbursements for lack of economic progress, the government announced a new agreement, for $180 million, that entailed the abolition of the parallel rate and a 43% devaluation. This along with the withdrawal of food subsidies provoked widespread riots. The government then backtracked by extending is program of food stamps to more than half the population.

The Jamaican economy faces several other long-term and short-term problems that hamper growth prospects.

Jamaica has suffered a serious problem of emigration of managerial, technical and entrepreneurial personnel. Although Jamaica always has had a high level of emigration during this century, the present phenomenon is different in that it represents a movement of individuals with higher education and income levels rather than those with limited prospects in Jamaica. Key personnel in many fields are leaving faster than replacements can be trained. This has resulted in a serious deterioration of the economy's ability to produce goods and services and to adjust to changing circumstances.

Crime has seriously affected the Jamaican economy. It has frightened tourists, raised business costs, hastened the emigration of skilled people and inhibited foreign specialists from accepting assignments in Jamaica. Nevertheless, since 1986 the economy has begun to improve. World prices for bauxite and alumina improved in 1987, manufacturing began to diversify and tourism achieved remarkable growth. Over one million tourists arrived in 1987 and in 1989.

Jamaica has one of the most highly developed labor movements in the Third World. Labor unrest has mounted as inflation and devaluation have eroded wages and living standards of the workers. Strikes in such key areas as electricity, railroads and ports have hampered production in a number of other sectors.

Jamaica has received significant foreign aid since independence. During 1979–81, for example, Jamaica received $166.2 million in aid from all sources, or $76.60 per capita.

PUBLIC FINANCE

The Jamaican fiscal year runs from April 1 through March 31. Recent budgets have shown chronic deficits. Although the government has projected a surplus in the 1990 budget, the projections seem unrealistic. Current expenditure forecasts total three times the surplus predicted.

Revenues are generated primarily from income tax, consumption, customs and stamp duties and a levy on bauxite. Approximately one-third of expenditures go to education, housing, health and social services and almost one-fourth to economic services.

Jamaica has one of the highest debts per capita in the Western Hemisphere. Total public debt was $4.5 billion in 1989. The debt-service ratio in 1986 was 31.7%.

CENTRAL GOVERNMENT EXPENDITURES, 1984

% of total expenditures
- Goods and Services: 49.4
- Interest: 33.5
- Subsidies & transfers: 2.5
- Capital expenditures: 14.6
- Total expenditures as % of GDP: 37.5 (1983)
- Overall surplus or deficit as % of GDP: −18.5 (1983)

CENTRAL GOVERNMENT REVENUES, 1984

% of total current revenues
- Taxes on income, profit & capital gain: 27.9
- Social Security contributions: 2.1
- Domestic taxes on goods & services: 36.4
- Taxes on international trade & transactions: 5.2
- Other taxes: 9.3
- Current nontax revenue: 19.1
- Total current revenue as % of GDP: 24 (1983)

General government consumption as % of GDP: 15
Annual growth rate of general government consumption: −1.5% (1980–87)

FOREIGN AID, 1989

Total foreign aid, (U.S. $ millions): 542.6
- Bilateral: 331.2
- Multilateral: 211.5

From 1970–88 Jamaica received $1.1 billion in aid from the United States. It received $1.2 billion from other Western nations during 1970–87. Communist aid totalled $349 million from 1974–88.

CURRENCY & BANKING

The Jamaican unit of currency is the Jamaican dollar, divided into 100 cents. Coins are issued in denominations of 1, 5, 10, 20 and 25 cents; notes are issued in denominations of 50 cents and 1, 2, 5 and 10 dollars.

The Jamaican dollar was introduced in 1969, replacing the Jamaican pound at the rate of 1 Jamaican pound = 2 Jamaican dollars. The Jamaican pound was at par with the pound sterling, so that the initial value of the Jamaican dollar was $1.20 ($1 = J. $0.83). In January 1973, the currency was devalued by 15.6%, when the rate became J. $1 = $1.10. This rate was sustained until August 1985, when the rate became $1 = J. $5.760. In June 1991 the dollar exchange rate was $1 = J. $10.15.

The central bank is the Bank of Jamaica, which also administers foreign reserves, issues and redeems currency and determines the volume and conditions of the money supply and credit.

Of the nine commercial banks, five are foreign. In 1977 the two U.S. banks reported that they were pulling out of Jamaica because of unfavorable conditions. The largest foreign bank is Barclays Bank, with 55 branches. Savings accounts are available through the Workers' Savings and Loans Bank, successor to the Government Savings Bank. Development finance is available through the Jamaican Development Bank and the Jamaica Mortgage Bank. Loans to small farmers are made by People's Cooperative Banks.

FINANCIAL INDICATORS, 1988

Total reserves minus gold (SDR's millions): 82
SDR's (millions): 0.0
Reserve position in IMF (SDR's milions): 0.0
Foreign exchange (SDR's millions): 82
Gold (fine troy oz. millions): 0.0
Ratio of external debt to total reserves: 23.9 (1988)
Central bank, 1989
  Assets %
    Foreign assets: 16.6
    Claims on government: 80.3
    Claims on banks: 3.1
    Claims on private sector: 0.0
  Liabilities %
    Reserve money: 110.6
    Government deposits: 107.0
    Foreign liabilities: 140.9
    Capital accounts: 8.4
Money supply, 1989
Stock (J. $ billions): 3.153
M[1] per capita: 1,320
Private banks, 1989
  Assets %
    Loans to government: 11.7
    Loans to private sector: 54.0
    Reserves: 28.4
    Foreign assets: 5.9
  Liabilities
    deposits (J. $ billions): 13.493
    of which %
      Demand deposits: 13.2
      Savings deposits: 55.3
      Government deposits: 2.7
      Foreign liabilities: 7.8
External debt 1987
  Total (U.S. $ billions): 4.446
    of which public (U.S. $ billions): 3,511
    of which private (U.S. $ millions): 58
  Debt service
    total (U.S. $ millions): 430.6 (1986)
    Repayment
      Principal (%): 50.1 (1986)
      Interest (%); 49.9 (1986)
  Debt service ratio (%): 31.7 (1986)
  External public debt as % of GNP: 138.9
  Debt service as % of GNP: 17.3
  Debt service as % of exports: 26.6
  Terms of public borrowing
    Commitments ($ U.S. millions): 369
    Average interest rate (%): 6.8
    Average maturity (years): 15
  Net flow of publicly guaranteed external capital (U.S. $ millions): 101
  Receipt of workers' remittances (U.S. $ millions): 44
  Net direct private investment (U.S. $ millions): −5

GROWTH PROFILE
(Annual Growth Rates, %)

Projected population (1988–2000): 0.5
Projected crude birth rate (/1,000): 1990–95: 22.7
Projected crude death rate (/1,000) 1990–95): 5.1
Urban population (1980–88): 2.6
Labor force (1985–2000): 2.4
GNP (1980–88): −0.4
GNP per capita (1986–88): 1.8
GDP (1980–88): 0.6
Inflation (1980–88): 18.7
Agriculture (1980–88): 0.9
Industry (1980–88): 0.0
Manufacturing (1980–88): 1.6
Services (1980–88): 0.9
Money holdings (1980–88): 25.9
Energy production (1980–88): 5.1
Energy consumption (1980–88): 2.8
Exports (1980–88): −4.5
Imports (1980–88): −0.5
General government consumption (1980–87): −1.5
Private consumption (1980–87): 2.4
Gross domestic investment (1980–87): −1.2

AGRICULTURE

Agriculture employed 23% of the total labor force in 1989 and contributed 6% to the GDP in 1988. Primary cash crops are sugar, bananas, coffee and cocoa. The government is encouraging cultivation of vegetables, fruit and rice in order to diversify agricultural exports and promote self-sufficiency in food.

Jamaican agriculture is divided into a modern sector, consisting of plantations (now in decline), and the traditional sector, consisting of smallholders. In 1972 the government introduced a project called GROW (Growing and Reaping Our Wealth), whose main elements were land lease (the leasing of state land to smallholders for a renewable period of five years); food farms, by which government properties are converted into farms; and self-help, a program of loan assistance to small farmers. Land redistribution is undertaken by the Land Settlement Scheme of 1938. By 1970 a total of 253 land settlements had been established with a total area of 88,356 ha. (218,325 ac.), and 33,180 allotments had been made to peasants covering 91,766 ha. (226,751 ac.). Mechanization is common only on plantations.

Between 1980 and 1988, agricultural production increased at an average annual rate of 1.3%. Agriculture was severely affected by Hurricane Gilbert in 1988. The entire poultry industry was wiped out, exports declined and subsistance farmers were forced to rely on government social programs for support.

Cultivation of marijuana is becoming widespread, and annual exports to the United States of this illegal crop were estimated at $560 million in 1988, making it the country's largest export earner. The government has attempted to curb drug production, and foreign earnings from marijuana dropped over $100 million from the mid-1980s.

In the livestock sector, government efforts are concentrated on development of new dairy breeds, such as Jamaica Hope, Jamaica Red Poll and Jamaica Brahman.

There are approximately 267,102 ha. (660,000 ac.) of forests, mainly in the upland regions. State forests, including 92 forest reserves, cover 42% of this area. There is an active 30-year reforestation program.

The island has considerable resources of freshwater and marine fish. The chief varieties of saltwater fish are kingfish, snapper, jack, mackerel, whiting, bonito and tuna; the chief varieties of freshwater fish are tarpon, snook, African perch and mullet.

Agricultural credit is provided by the Agricultural Credit Board either directly or through People's Cooperative Banks. The Agricultural Marketing Corpora-

AGRICULTURAL INDICATORS

Agriculture's share of GDP (%): 6 (latest)
Average annual growth rate (%, 1980–88): 0.9
Value added in agriculture (U.S. $ millions): 180 (1988)
Cereal imports (000 metric tons): 418 (1988)
Index of Agricultural Production (1979–81 = 100): 108 (1986)
Index of Food Production (1979–81 = 100): 108 (1986)
Index of Food Production per capita (1979–81 = 100): 101 (1986–88)
Number of tractors: 3,000 (1986)
Total fertilizer consumption: 11.8 (000 metric tons) (1985–86)
Fertilizer consumption (g./ha., hundreds): 914 (1987–88)
Number of farms (000): 184 (1979)
Average size of holding, ha.: 2.9 (1979)
Size class (%) (1979)
  Below 1 ha. (below 2.47 ac.): 32.5
  1–5 ha. (2.47–12.35 ac.): 60.7
  5–10 ha. (12.35–24.7 ac.): 4.8
  10–20 ha. (24.7–49.4 ac.): 0.9
  20–50 ha. (49.4–123.5 ac.): 0.4
  50–200 ha. (123.5–494 ac.): 0.3
  Over 200 ha. (over 494 ac.): 0.4
Tenure (%) 1969
  Owner-operated: 99.5
  Rented: 0.0
  Other: 0.3
Farms as % of total land area: 54.8 (1969)
Land use (%) 1969
  Permanent crops: 22.2
  Temporary crops: 72.2
    Fallow: 5.6
    Meadows & pastures: 21.6
    Woodland: 13.5
    Other: 23.6
Yields (kg./ha.) 1989
  Grains: 1,296
  Roots & tubers: 12,702
  Legumes: 905
  Fruits (000 metric tons): 374
  Vegetables (000 metric tons): 106
  Milk (kg./animal): 1,000
Livestock (000) 1989
  Cattle: 290
  Horses: 4 (1986)
  Sheep: 3
  Pigs: 250
Forestry 1988
  Production of roundwood (000 cu. m.): 220
    of which industrial roundwood (%): 94.1
  Value of exports (U.S. $ millions): 51
Fishing 1986
  Total catch (000 metric tons): 10.0
    of which marine (%): 85.0
  Value of exports (U.S. $ millions): 2,217

tion operates a network of facilities for collection, transportation, storage, grading and processing of agricultural produce.

MANUFACTURING

In the 1980s manufacturing and industry have grown from the processing of a few agricultural products into the largest economic sector, contributing 21% to the GDP in 1988. Industry has diversified and now produces a wide range of goods, such as clothing, footwear, textiles, glass, machinery and tools, paper and paperboard, paints, fertilizers, steel, cement and sports equipment. Manufacturing is concentrated in and around Kingston.

Several laws have been enacted to encourage and facilitate industrial development, including the Industrial Incentives Law, the Export Industry Encouragement Law and the Pioneer Industries (Encouragement) Law. By 1974 a total of 210 industries had been established under these laws. The major incentives are tax relief and liberal profit and capital repatriation provisions. Furthermore, the Jamaica Industrial Development Corporation, a statutory body, offers a wide range of services to the manufacturer. In the mid-1980s there were 120 U.S. firms on the island with a total investment of $1 billion.

Free zones have been set up in Kingston and Montego Bay for manufacturing and assembly industries. Although 250 companies have started production since 1980, average investment is small, and the promised benefits of the Caribbean Basin Initiative have proved disappointing. Lingering uncertainty stemming from the government's rhetoric and philosophy as well as general uncertainties concerning the political and economic future have delayed any significant new investment. There are some particular problems involved in doing business in an atmosphere marked by government regulations and tight exchange controls. Government policy allows for remittances of profits and dividends, repatriation of capital and payment of fees, etc.

MANUFACTURING INDICATORS, 1987

Average annual growth rate (%, 1980–88): 1.6
Share of GDP (%): 21 (1988)
Labor force in manufacturing (%): 13.2 (1989)
Value added in manufacturing (U.S. $ millions): 639
  Food and agriculture (%): 46 (1970)
  Textiles (%): 7 (1990)
  Chemicals (%): 10 (1970)
Earnings per employee in manufacturing, 1986
  Growth rate (%, 1970–80): −0.2
Total earnings as % of value added: 43 (1970)

MINING

With reserves of 500 to 600 million tons, Jamaica is one of the largest bauxite producers in the world. Bauxite is mined by five large companies: Alcan Jamaica, Alumina Partners of Jamaica, Kaiser Bauxite Company, Reynolds Jamaica Mines and Alcoa Minerals of Jamaica. Canada and Norway are the major importers of Jamaican alumina, taking in 46% and 28%, respectively. In 1988 bauxite and alumina accounted for over half of all export earnings.

Jamaica's other mineral resources, such as gypsum, marble and silica sand, are negligible in value.

ENERGY

Most of Jamaica's energy comes from petroleum imported from Venezuela and Mexico under the San Jose

ENERGY INDICATORS

Average annual energy production growth rate (%, 1980–88): 5.1
Energy consumption per capita (000 kg. oil equivalent): 855 (1988)
Energy imports as % of merchandise exports: 22 (1988)
Average annual growth rate of energy consumption (%, 1980–88): 2.8
Electricity, 1988
  Installed capacity (000 kw.): 740
  Production (billion kw.-hr.): 6.4
    % fossil fuel: 95.0
    % hydro: 5.0
    % nuclear: 0.0
  Consumption per capita (000 kw.-hr.): 973
Petroleum
  Production (million bbl.): 0.0 (1987)
  Consumption (million bbl.): 5 (1988)
  Refining capacity (000 bbl./day): 34 (1990)

Agreement, which offers favorable terms to nations in the Caribbean.

LABOR

Wages and working conditions are governed by legislation. The industrial workweek is 5.5 days of eight hours each for a total of 44 hours, the legal maximum.

Jamaica has one of the highest unemployment rates in the Western Hemisphere, estimated at 16% in 1989, according to official figures. Actual unemployment may run much higher.

About 25% of the labor force is unionized. In view of the close association between labor unions and the nation's two main political parties, organized labor wields great influence in national life. The three main labor unions are the Bustamante Industrial Trade Union (affiliated with the ULP), the National Workers' Union (affiliated with the PNP) and the Trades Union Congress of Jamaica.

LABOR INDICATORS, 1989

Total economically active population (million): 1.063
  % working-age population (15–64): 69.0
  % female: 46.4
Activity rate (%)
  Total: 44.8
  Male: 48.2
  Female: 41.4
Employment status (%)
  Employers & self-employed: 34.3 (1987)
  Employees: 41.7 (1987)
  Unpaid family workers: 3.2 (1987)
  Other: 20.9 (1987)
Sectoral employment (%)
  Agriculture, forestry, fishing: 23.3
  Construction: 5.2
  Manufacturing; mining, quarrying: 13.9
  Trade, hotels, restaurants: 12.9
  Transport, communications, public utilities: 4.0
  Finance, real estate, services: 16.3
Average annual growth rate of labor force, 1980–2000 (%): 2.4
Unemployment (000): 250 (1987)
Labor under 20 years (%): 23.0 (1986)

FOREIGN COMMERCE

Jamaica's primary exports are bauxite, alumina, sugar and bananas, 33% of which go to the United States. The United Kingdom, Canada, Trinidad and Tobago, and Norway are other major markets. Principal imports are petroleum (about 15% of total imports in 1989), machinery, food, consumer goods and construction materials. The United States provides almost 43% of all imports. Other major suppliers are the United Kingdom, Venezuela, Canada, Japan and Trinidad and Tobago.

Jamaica is a member of the free-trade Caribbean Common Market (CARICOM).

FOREIGN TRADE INDICATORS, 1989

Exports (U.S. $ millions): 948
Imports (U.S. $ billions): 1.6
Balance of trade (U.S. $ millions): −652
Annual growth rate, (1980–88), exports (%): −4.5
Annual growth rate, (1980–88), imports (%): −0.5
International reserves in terms of months of imports: 0.8
Terms of trade (1980 = 100): 97
Import Price Index (1980 = 100): 85.7 (1986)
Export Price Index (1980 = 100): 93.6 (1986)

Direction of Trade (%), 1989

	Imports	Exports
European Community	11.3	27.0
United States	43.3	33.1
U.S.S.R. &East European economies	0.9	2.0
Japan	3.7	0.8

Composition of Trade (%), 1989

	Imports	Exports
Food and agricultural raw materials	18.7	17.7
Fuels and other energy	15.2	1.6
Mineral ores and concentrates	0.2	60.6
Manufactured goods	66.0	20.1
of which chemicals	11.5	2.4
of which machinery	21.6	3.1

TRANSPORTATION & COMMUNICATIONS

The state-owned Jamaica Railway Corporation (JRC) operates a 339-km. (211-mi.) rail line running diagonally across the island to Montego Bay from Kingston, with branch lines to Port Antonio, Frankfield and Ewarton. The JRC also operates and maintains a 69-km. (43-mi.) private line for Alcoa.

There is a small refined petroleum products pipeline 10 km. (6 mi.) long.

The three major ports are Kingston, Montego Bay and Montego Freeport. Kingston is the main port, handling most of the imports and about 30% of the exports. The remaining exports are shipped through 18 minor ports, some of which specialize in commodities, such as bananas (Montego Bay and Port Antonio) and bauxite (Ocho Rios and Port Esquivel). The national shipping line is Jamaica Merchant Marine. Jamaica also has an interest in two multinational shipping lines, Naviera Multinacional del Caribe and the West Indies Shipping Corporation.

Jamaica's road system consists of 14,994 km. (9,317 mi.) of roads, of which about 24% are paved. The main roads encircle the island, running close to the coast in the northern and eastern ends and passing through all the main ports and towns. Regular mass transit is available on 44 routes outside the corporate area of Kingston and St. Andrew. Within the corporate area, passenger services are provided by Jamaica Omnibus Services.

The national airline is Air Jamaica, with a fleet of six aircraft serving domestic routes and foreign routes to the United States, Canada, the United Kingdom. West Germany and the Bahamas. The government owns a controlling interest in Trans Jamaica Airline, a domestic carrier. There are two major international airports, Norman Manley Airport at Kingston and Donald Sangster Airport at Montego Bay, both with runways over 2,500 m. (8,000 ft.). There are 40 other airports, of which 27 are usable and 14 have permanent-surface runways. There also are three seaplane stations.

Tourism is a major source of foreign exchange. In 1988 it made up two-thirds of the value of total commodity exports. During the 1970s it suffered a serious decline as a result of the U.S. recession, bad publicity and rising crime in Jamaica, but in 1978 that trend reversed as the number of visitors increased sharply. The trend continued through the 1980s.

TRANSPORTATION INDICATORS

Roads (latest)
  Length, km. (mi.): 14,994 (9,317)
  Paved (%): 24
Motor vehicles (latest)
  Automobiles: 92,841
  Trucks and buses: 14,279
  Persons per vehicle: 22
Railroads (latest)
  Track, km. (mi.): 339 (211)
  Passenger-km. (passenger-mi.) (millions): 36.1 (22.5)
  Freight, ton-km. (ton-mi.) (millions): 104.4 (48.9)
Merchant marine
  Vessels: 12 (1989)
  Total deadweight tonnage (000): 21.3 (1989)
Ports (pre-1986)
  Cargo loaded (million metric tons): 5.485
  Cargo unloaded (million metric tons): 3.672
Air (latest)
  Km. (mi.) flown (millions): 11.9 (7.4) (1985)
  Passenger-km. (passenger-mi.) (billions): 1.973 (1.226)
  Freight, ton-km. (ton-mi.) (millions): 17.8 (8.4)
  Mail, ton-km. (ton-mi.) (millions): 0.2 (0.1) (1985)
  Airports with scheduled flights: 6 (1990)
Pipelines 1990
  Refined, km. (mi.): 10 (6)

COMMUNICATION INDICATORS, 1986

Telephones
  Total (000): 168
    persons per telephone: 14
Phone traffic (million calls)
  International: 6.109
Post office
  Number of post offices: 788 (1985)
Telegraph
  Total traffic (000 calls): 273 (1984)
  National: 195 (1984)
  International: 78 (1984)
Telex
  Subscriber lines: 578
Telecommunications, 1990
  2 satellite stations, 3 coaxial submarine cables

TOURISM & TRAVEL INDICATORS, 1986

Total tourist receipts (U.S. $ millions): 525 (1988)
Expenditures by nationals abroad (U.S. $ millions): 45 (1988)
Number of hotel beds (000): 26
Average length of stay: 10 nights
Tourist nights (000): 6,780
Number of tourists (000): 571.7 (1985)
  of whom from U.S.: 433.1
    Canada: 82.3
    United Kingdom: 22.0
    Germany, Fed. Rep.: 3.4

DEFENSE

Although the queen is the titular head of the defense forces, the prime minister in his role as minister of defense acts as the political and operational head. There is a British training mission for the three services.

Military manpower is provided by voluntary enlistment.

The total strength of the armed forces is 2,850. There are also reserves of 870.

Army

Personnel: 2,500

Organization: 2 infantry battalions and 1 reserve infantry battalion

Equipment: 10 armored personnel carriers; 12 mortars

Coast Guard

Personnel: 200

Equipment: 4 patrol craft based in Kingston

Air Force

Personnel: 150

Equipment: 4 light aircraft and 6 helicopters based in Kingston

The Jamaican defense forces have no offensive capability and are designed solely for internal peacekeeping.

A British military training mission is retained, but there are no other British arms transfers or aid programs.

EDUCATION

Education is free, universal and compulsory for 10 years, from ages six to 15. Schooling lasts for 13 years, divided into six years of primary school, three years of lower secondary school and four years of upper secondary school. Females constitute 50% of primary-school enrollment. 53% of the secondary-school enrollment and 47.5% of postsecondary enrollment. The

EDUCATION INDICATORS, 1989

Literacy (over age 14)
  Total (%): 88.6
  Males (%): 88.2
  Females (%): 89.1
First level
  Schools: 791
  Students: 390,095
  Net enrollment ratio: 94 (1983)
Second level
  Schools: 127
  Students: 150,075
  Teachers: 7,598
  Student/teacher ratio: 19.8:1
  Net enrollment ratio: 57 (1980)
Vocational
  Schools: 15
  Students: 14,212
  Teachers: 757
  Student/teacher ratio: 18.8:1
Third level
  Institutions: 19
  Students: 19,473
  Gross enrollment ratio: 4.2 (1986)
  Students (/100,000 pop.): 508
  % of population over 24 with postsecondary education: 2.0
Foreign study
  Foreign students in national universities: 94 (1985)
  Students abroad: 2,388
    of whom in
      United States: 2,101 (1988)
      France: 40 (1988)
      Federal Republic of Germany: 12 (1988)
      United Kingdom: 66 (1987)
Public expenditures, 1987
  Total (J. $): 1,104,406,000
  % of GNP: 7.2
  % of national budget: 11.0 (1987)
  % of current expenditure: 79.2

GRADUATES, 1986

Total: 3,537
Education: 783
Humanities & religion: 544
Fine & applied arts: 190
Law: 199
Social & Behavioral sciences: 447
Commerce & business: 400
Mass communication: 17
Home economics: 133
Natural sciences: 315
Mathematics & computer science: 46
Medicine: 124
Engineering: 199
Architecture: 109
Agriculture, forestry, fisheries: 27
Other: 4

high female enrollments reflect the numerical dominance of females in the population.

The academic year runs from September to July. The medium of instruction is English throughout.

The shortage of trained teachers is the most serious educational problem. Many primary-school teachers lack any kind of formal teacher training.

The National Literacy Board, set up in 1972 and reorganized in 1974 as the Jamaica Movement for the Advancement of Literacy Foundation, is the principal body concerned with adult education. Despite continuing emphasis on vocational education, only about 3.3% of secondary-school enrollment is in the vocational stream. Private schools account for 5% of primary enrollment and 9% of secondary enrollment.

Both public and private education is ultimately controlled by the Ministry of Education.

Higher education is provided at the University of the West Indies, whose students are drawn from all countries of the West Indies.

LEGAL SYSTEM

The legal system is based on English common law. The highest courts of the land are the Supreme Court, comprising a chief justice, one senior puisne judge and 15 puisne judges; and the Court of Appeal, with a president and six judges. The chief justice of the Supreme Court and the president of the Court of Appeal are appointed by the governor-general on the recommendation of the prime minister after consultation with the leader of the opposition, while other judges are appointed by the governor-general on the advice of the Judicial Service Commission. Subordinate courts are resident magistrates' courts, petty sessions courts, traffic courts and juvenile courts.

Penal administration is the responsibility of the Department of Prisons. There are five prisons on the island.

LAW ENFORCEMENT

The law enforcement agency is the Constabulary Force, under the Ministry of Justice and with a strength of 3,879 officers, subofficers and constables. In addition, there are district constables and special constables. Per capita police strength is one policeman for every 540 inhabitants.

Although Jamaica's crime rate is lower than that of many major U.S. cities, and crime is largely concentrated in the capital city of Kingston, two factors increased its economic and psychological impact in the 1970s and early 1980s: the dramatic increase during the 1970s and the relatively high percentage of middle-class victims. The overall rate of violent crimes began to drop in the mid 1980s, but in 1987 drug-related violence soared.

HEALTH

Each parish operates a public health department, but national health programs are conducted by the Ministry of Health. The principal health problems are tuberculosis, hookworms and venereal disease.

FOOD & NUTRITION

The staple foods are corn and rice, supplemented by cassava, potatoes and yams. The per capita daily food intake is 2,489 calories (111% of requirements).

HEALTH INDICATORS

Health personnel, 1989
- Physicians: 415
  - Persons per: 5,723
- Dentists: 51
- Nurses: 2,223
- Pharmacists: 62
- Midwives: 423

Hospitals 1987
- Number: 36
- Number of beds (/10,000): 25
- Admissions/discharges (/10,000): 627
- Bed occupancy rate (%): 77.0
- Average length of stay (days): 7

Type of hospitals (%) 1987
- Government: 80.6

Public health expenditures (latest)
- As % of national budget: 7.8
- Per capita (U.S. $): 44.40

Vital statistics
- Crude death rate (/1,000): 5 (1990)
- Life expectancy at birth (1990)
  - Males: 75
  - Females: 79
- Infant mortality rate (/1,000 live births): 16 (1990)
- Child mortality rate under 5 yrs. (/1,000) (1985–90): 23
- Maternal mortality rate (/100,000 live births) (1980–84): 102.0

Population with access to safe water (%): 96 (latest)

MEDIA & CULTURE

In 1989 two daily newspapers were published in the country. Most of the media are government-owned. All newspapers are published in Kingston, except for two weeklies published in Montego Bay and a biweekly in Spanish Town. The dailies are the *Star* (44,000) and the privately owned *Daily Gleaner* (42,100).

The press is noted for its vigor and freedom from political restraints.

The national news agency is Jampress, founded in 1984. Reuters, AP and CANA (Caribbean News Agency) have bureaus in Kingston.

Although title output is negligible, there are five active book publishers in Kingston. Jamaica does not adhere to any copyright convention.

There are four broadcasting organizations: the Jamaica Broadcasting Corporation, a publicly owned statutory corporation run on semicommercial lines; Radio Jamaica, a commercial organization owned by Radiodiffusion; Educational Broadcasting Service, which operates during the school term; and Island Broadcasting System, a commercial organization.

Jamaica Broadcasting Corporation began television broadcasting in 1963, and it now covers 80% of the population through its main station at Kingston and seven relay stations. It is on the air for 40 hours a week.

The Jamaica Public Library Service has a total book stock of over a million volumes. The largest library is that on the Mona Campus of the University of the West Indies.

There are five museums, reporting an aggregate annual attendance of over 44,000.

MEDIA INDICATORS

Newspapers
- Number of dailies: 2 (latest)
- Circulation (000): 89 (latest)
- Per 000 pop.: 38 (latest)
- Newsprint consumption: (1988)
- Total metric tons: 5,400
- Per 1,000 pop. (kg.): 2,208

Book publishing
- Number of titles: 23 (pre-1986)

Radio
- Number of transmitters: 26 (latest)
- Number of persons per radio receiver: 2.6 (1989)

Television
- Television transmitters: 8 (latest)
- Number of persons per TV receiver: 5.9 (1989)

CULTURAL & ENVIRONMENTAL INDICATORS (latest)

Libraries
- Number: 14
- Volumes (millions): 1.17
- Registered borrowers (000): 656
- Loans (/1,000 pop.): 980

Museums
- Annual attendance (000): 44
- Attendance (/1,000 pop.): 22

Performing arts
- Number of performances: 868
- Annual attendance (millions): 1.143
- Attendance (1,000 pop.): 540

Nature reserves
- Number of facilities: 2

There are four theaters, all in the capital, serving three professional companies and 12 amateur groups. In 1977 these groups performed in 580 dramas, 126 operas and ballets, 28 traditional dance presentations and 105 other forms of entertainment.

SOCIAL WELFARE

The compulsory National Insurance Scheme covers workers. The program, administered by the Ministry of Social Security, provides a number of benefits, including old-age pensions, workers' compensation, widows' and widowers' pensions and grants, orphans' pensions and grants, employment injury and disablement pensions, and death benefits and funeral grants.

Social welfare programs are administered by official and voluntary agencies. The Jamaica Social Welfare Commission is the most important voluntary agency, active in over 500 communities. The National Youth Service has pioneered in social work among youth. The Council of Voluntary Social Services is a coordinating body of 35 voluntary social welfare organizations.

GLOSSARY

custos rotulorum: the chief magistrate of a parish.
parish: The basic unit of local government.

CHRONOLOGY (from 1962)

1962— Following national referendum in which Jamaicans reject the Federation of the West Indies, Jamaica becomes an independent dominion within the Commonwealth, with Sir William Alexander Bustamante as prime minister.

1967— Jamaican Labor Party (JLP) retains majority in the House of Representatives in national elections; Sir Donald Burns Sangster is sworn in as prime minister. . . . Sangster dies within a few months and is succeeded in office by Hugh Shearer.

1969— The Jamaican dollar is introduced as the national currency, replacing the Jamaican pound.

1972— The JLP is routed in elections by the People's National Party (PNP); Michael Manley forms new government.

1974— International Bauxite Association is formed in Kingston.

1976— The PNP improves its majority in the House of Representatives in national elections. . . . Violence flares in Kingston, leading to the proclamation of an emergency.

1977— Fidel Castro visits Jamaica as Manley draws closer to Cuba. . . . The government acquires controlling interests in the American-owned Kaiser Bauxite Company and Reynolds Jamaica Mines and the British-owned Barclays Bank.

1978— The Jamaican dollar is davalued on the advice of IMF, as Jamaica faces its worst economic crisis.

1979— The IMF economic recovery and austerity plan fails; the IMF grants new credit under strict conditions.

1980— In elections to the House of Representatives the JLP sweeps the polls, gaining 51 of the 60 seats; Edward Seaga is named prime minister.

1983— Seaga announces surprise elections before the election rolls are revised. . . . Manley protests and boycotts the elections. . . . The JLP wins all 60 seats in the House of Representatives.

1984— Jamaica joins other Caribbean nations in the United States-led invasion of Grenada.

1985— Demonstrations and riots mark the withdrawal of food subsidies and the steep rise in food prices.

1989— Michael Manley returns to power as prime minister.

1990— The People's National Party wins 60% of the vote in local elections, gaining control of 12 of the 13 municipal councils.

BIBLIOGRAPHY

BOOKS

Ayub, Mahmood. *Made in Jamaica: Development of the Manufacturing Sector.* Baltimore, 1981.

Beckford, George, and Michael Witter. *Small Gardens, Bitter Weeds: Struggle and Change in Jamaica.* London, 1982.

Boot, Adrian, and Michael Thomas. *Jamaica: Babylon on a Thin Wire.* New York, 1977.

Braithwaite, Edward. *The Development of Creole Society in Jamaica, 1770–1820.* New York, 1971.

Brown, Aggray. *Color, Class and Politics in Jamaica.* New Brunswick, N.J., 1979.

Cassidy, F. G. *Jamaican Talk.* New York, 1971.

Clarke, Colin G. *Kingston, Jamaica: Urban Growth and Social Change.* Berkeley Calif., 1975.

——— and Alan G. Hodgkiss. *Jamaica in Maps.* New York, 1974.

Curtin, Philip D. *Two Jamaicas.* New York, 1970.

Dawes, Hugh N. *Public Finance and Economic Development: Spotlight on Jamaica.* Lapham, Md., 1982.

Edquist, Charles. *Capitalism, Socialism and Technology: A Comparative Study of Cuba and Jamaica.* London, 1985.

Feuer, Carl Henry. *Jamaica and the Sugar Worker Cooperatives: The Politics of Reform.* Boulder, Colo., 1984.

Floyd, Barry. *Jamaica: An Island Microcosm.* New York, 1979.

Hurwitz, Samuel J., and Edith F. Hurwitz. *A Historical Portrait.* New York, 1971.

Ingram, K. E. *Jamaica* (World Bibliographical Series). Boulder, Colo., 1984.

Jefferson, O. *The Postwar Economic Development of Jamaica.* Kingston, 1972.

Kuper, Adam. *Changing Jamaica.* New York, 1975.

Lacey, Terrence J. *Violence and Politics in Jamaica, 1960–70.* Totowa, N.J., 1977.

Manley, Michael. *Jamaica: Struggle in the Periphery.* New York, 1982.

———. *The Politics of Change: A Jamaican Testament.* London, 1974.

———. *Up the Down Escalator.* Washington, D.C., 1985.

Nettleford, Rex. *Caribbean Cultural Identity: The Case of Jamaica.* Los Angeles, 1980.

———. *Identity, Race and Protest in Jamaica.* New York, 1972.

———. *Jamaica in Independence: Essays on the Early Years.* Kingston, Jamaica, 1989.

———. *Manley and the New Jamaica.* New York, 1972.

Payne, Anthony. *Politics in Jamaica.* New York, 1988.

Senior, Olive. *A–Z of Jamaica Heritage.* London, 1983.

Stone, C. *Class, Race and Political Behavior in Urban Jamaica.* Kingston, 1973.

———. *Democracy and Clientelism in Jamaica.* New Brunswick, N.J., 1980.

UNESCO, *Cultural Policy in Jamaica.* Paris, 1978.

Williams, Gary J. *Jamaica: The Importance of Its Bauxite to the United States.* Maxwell AFB, Ala., 1971.

OFFICIAL PUBLICATIONS

Finance Ministry. *Appropriation and Other Accounts* (unpublished).

———. *Estimates of Expenditure.*

———. *Financial Statements and Revenue Estimates.*

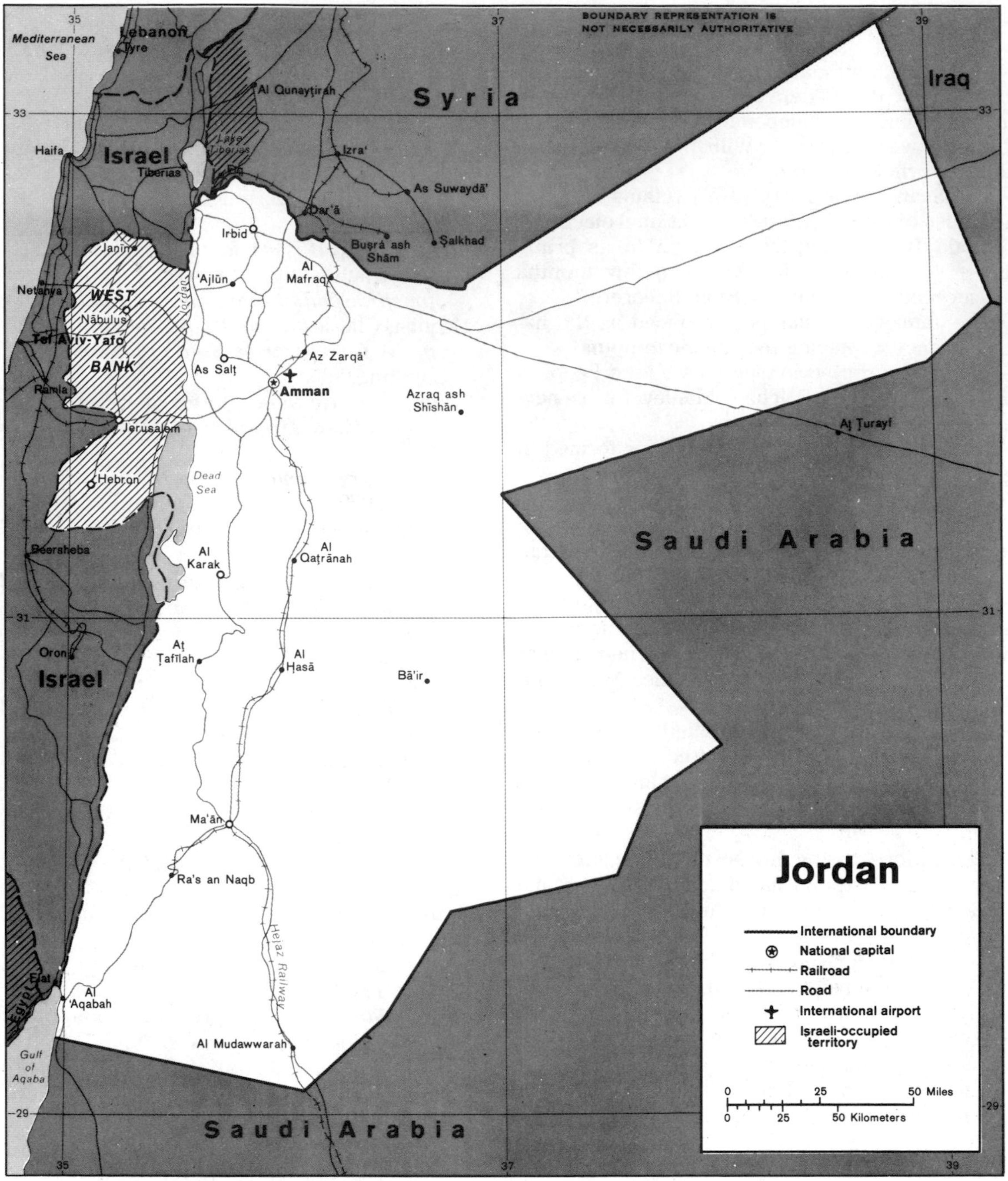

BOUNDARY REPRESENTATION IS NOT NECESSARILY AUTHORITATIVE

Mediterranean Sea
Lebanon
Tyre
Syria
Iraq
Al Qunayţirah
Lake Tiberias
Haifa
Israel
Tiberias
Izra'
As Suwaydā'
Dar'ā
Irbid
Buşrá ash Shām
Şalkhad
Janīn
'Ajlūn
Al Mafraq
Netanya
WEST BANK
Nābulus
Jordan
Tel Aviv-Yafo
Az Zarqā'
As Salţ
Amman
Ramla
Azraq ash Shīshān
Jerusalem
Aţ Ţurayf
Hebron
Dead Sea
Saudi Arabia
Beersheba
Al Karak
Al Qaţrānah
Oron
Aţ Ţafīlah
Al Ḩasā
Israel
Bā'ir
Ma'ān
Ra's an Naqb
Hejaz Railway
Elat
Egypt
Al 'Aqabah
Al Mudawwarah
Gulf of Aqaba
Saudi Arabia
35
37
39
33
31
29

Jordan

International boundary
National capital
Railroad
Road
International airport
Israeli-occupied territory

0 25 50 Miles
0 25 50 Kilometers

JORDAN

BASIC FACT SHEET

OFFICIAL NAME: The Hashemite Kingdom of Jordan (al-Mamlaka al-Urduniya al-Hashemiyah)

ABBREVIATION: JO

CAPITAL: Amman

HEAD OF STATE: King Hussein (from 1952)

HEAD OF GOVERNMENT: Prime Minister Mudar Badran (from 1990)

NATURE OF GOVERNMENT: Absolute monarchy

POPULATION: 3,064,508 (1990) (excluding the West Bank and East Jerusalem)

AREA: 92,290 sq. km. (35,536 sq. mi.) (excluding the West Bank)

ETHNIC MAJORITY: Arab

LANGUAGE: Arabic

RELIGION: Sunni Muslim

UNIT OF CURRENCY: Jordan dinar

NATIONAL FLAG: Three horizontal stripes of black, white and green are joined at the hoist by a red triangle with a seven-pointed white star at its center.

NATIONAL EMBLEM: The emblem is displayed against a canopy on the top of which rests a gold and red crown. A brown eagle with outstretched wings stands on a gold globe that is partially obscured by a round gold ceremonial shield. On the globe and shield are planted black, white, green and red flags, three to a side, and pairs of gold-hilted swords and gold bows with fixed arrows. Beneath the design three ears of wheat and a palm branch are placed over a badge of the Muslim Order of Resurrection and a green ribbon carrying the king's name and his prayer that "Allah may bring happiness and help."

NATIONAL ANTHEM: "The Royal Salute" (or "Long Live the King")

NATIONAL HOLIDAYS: May 25 (National Day, Independence Day), January 15 (Tree Day), March 22 (Arab League Day), June 10 (Arab Revolt and Army Day), May 1 (Labor Day), August 11 (King Hussein's Accession), November 14 (King's Birthday).

NATIONAL CALENDAR: Islamic (dating from the Hegira, A.D. 622)

PHYSICAL QUALITY OF LIFE INDEX: 77

DATE OF INDEPENDENCE: May 25, 1946

DATE OF CONSTITUTION: January 8, 1952

WEIGHTS & MEASURES: The metric system is in force, but certain traditional units, such as the dunum = 1 sq. km. (0.386 sq. mi.) still are used.

GEOGRAPHICAL FEATURES

Jordan is in southwestern Asia and occupies an area of 92,290 sq. km. (35,536 sq. mi.), excluding the West Bank, which has been under Israeli occupation since 1967. Jordan extends 562 km. (349 mi.) northeast to southwest and 349 km. (217 mi.) southeast to northwest.

Jordan shares its total international land boundary of 1,727 km. (1,070 mi.) with four countries: Syria (356 km.; 221 mi.), Iraq (147 km.; 91 mi.), Saudi Arabia (744 km.; 462 mi.) and Israel (480 km.; 298 mi.). Israel is a hostile nation and the common border is a cease-fire line that never has been accepted by Jordan. The border with Saudi Arabia was redefined in 1965, resulting in an exchange of territory. There are no other current border disputes.

Amman is the capital, with a 1983 population of 744,000. The other major urban centers are Zarqa (255,500) and Irbid (131,200).

Jordan consists of a tilted plateau region in the northwestern corner of the Great Arabian Plateau. To the west, the edge of the plateau is abruptly marked by the major rift system of the Dead Sea lowlands, which includes the lowest point on earth, more than 400 m. (1,312 ft.) below sea level. Relatively featureless desert plains occupy the East and the South. The country is landlocked except at its southern extremity, where about 26 km. (16 mi.) of coastline along the Gulf of Aqaba provide access to the sea. There are no natural borders with Syria, Iraq or Saudi Arabia. The average elevation is 500 m. (1,650 ft.), with occasional summits reaching 1,200 m. (4,000 ft.) in the North and 1,500 m. (5,000 ft.) in the South.

The principal river is the Jordan, which flows through Jordanian territory for 156 km. (97 mi.). It empties into the Dead Sea at 396 m. (1,300 ft.) below sea level. The Dead Sea is 65 km. (40 mi.) long and 15 km. (10 mi.) wide, with a surface salinity seven times that of the oceans'.

CLIMATE & WEATHER

Jordan has a modified Mediterranean type of climate with hot, dry summers and cool, damp winters. August is the hottest month and January the coolest. Daytime temperatures reach 38°C (100°F) in the summer and fall to 4°C (25°F) in the winter. The climate is modified by the hot *khamsin*, a siroccolike wind accompanied by dust clouds, and the dry *shamal*, which blows for days at a time. Average rainfall is 300 mm. (12 in.) a year. Rainfall is variable, and sudden cloudbursts are often followed by protracted dry periods.

POPULATION

The population of Jordan in 1990 was 3,064,508 (excluding the West Bank and East Jerusalem). The last official census was held in 1979.

The population density varies from 105 per sq. km. (273 per sq. mi.) in settled areas to 1.1 per sq. km. (3 per sq. mi.) in the desert.

A total of 6% of the population is seminomadic, while 13.3% live in cities of over 100,000. Of the population of Amman, 17% live in slums or squatter settlements; the number of slum dwellers is growing by 19.1% per year.

About half of the population consists of refugees from territories that presently constitute Israel. This gain in population is offset by emigration to other, oil-rich Arab states. It is estimated that about 320,000 Jordanians now live abroad. Nomads always have moved freely across the Syrian, Iraqi and Saudi Arabian borders. Since 1976 Jordan also has imported at least 150,000 mostly unskilled foreign laborers.

Women in Jordan, as in other Islamic states of the region, are traditionally disfavored economically and, to a lesser extent, educationally. The status of women is heavily influenced by traditional social values, which fix women in the role of housewife and mother. For example, women still are required to have the written permission of the family's eldest male to travel. This pattern, however, is changing. The government encourages more female participation in the labor force. Women work in managerial, professional and clerical positions in the public sector, the military and the police, albeit in much lower numbers and at a generally lower level than men. Women are steadily increasing their numbers in the workplace. Women have the right to initiate divorce under limited circumstances; they have the right to own and inherit property; and they have priority "rule of first right" for the custody of minor children.

King Hussein is one of the signatories of the World Leaders' Declaration on Population. Abortion is illegal, but the use of contraceptives is not prohibited by law. The Jordan Family Planning and Protection Association was founded in 1963 and operates 19 clinics.

STATUS OF WOMEN INDICATORS

Number of women (millions): 1.908 (1985)
Women of childbearing age (15–49) (% of pop.): 43 (1988)
Married women of childbearing age (15–49) using contraception (%): 26 (1985)
Women's literacy rate (%): 66.9 (1989)
Women in labor force (%): 9.9 (1988)
Total fertility rate (/woman): 6.2 (1990)
Women in national legislatures (%): 0.0 (1984)

DEMOGRAPHIC INDICATORS

Population (millions): 3.064 (1990)
Year of last census: 1979
Sex distribution (% at last census): males, 52.3; females, 57.7
Population estimates and projections (millions)

1950: 1.095	1980: 2.181	2000: 4.549
1960: 1.384	1990: 3.169	2010: 6.531
1970: 1.795		

Age profile (% at last census)

0–14: 51.6	30–44: 13.4	60–74: 3.1
15–29: 23.4	45–59: 7.4	75 and over: 1.1

Median age (yrs.): 15.8 (1985)
Youth population (% age 15–24): 21.1 (1985); 18.7 (2000)
Total dependency ratio: 103.3 (1985)
Annual growth rate (%)

1950–55: 3.14	1975–1980: 2.34	2000–2005: 3.62
1955–60: 3.16	1980–1985: 3.64	2005–2010: 3.29
1960–65: 2.93	1985–1990: 3.94	2010–2015: 2.87
1965–70: 3.17	1990–1995: 4.01	2015–2020: 2.55
1970–75: 2.47	1995–2000: 3.36	2020–2025: 2.26

Hypothetical size of stationary population (millions): 22
Assumed year of reaching net reproduction rate of 1: 2035
Urban population (millions): 2257 (1985)
Urban population (%): 67 (1988); 46 (1965)
Annual urban population growth rate (%, 1985–90): 5.08
Annual rural population growth rate (%, 1985–90): 1.72
Percentage of urban population in largest city: 37 (1980)
Percentage of urban population in cities of population over 500,000: 37 (1980)
Number of cities of population over 500,000: 1 (1980)
Population density per sq. km. (per sq. mi.): 35.6 (92.3) (latest)

VITAL STATISTICS

Crude birth rate (/1,000): 42 (1990); 53 (1965)
Crude death rate (/1,000): 5 (1990); 21 (1965)
Infant mortality rate (/1,000 live births): 55 (1990)
Life expectancy (yrs.) at birth: males, 68; females, 71 (1990)
Gross reproduction rate (/woman) (1980–85): 3.55
Total fertility rate (/woman): 6.2 (1990)
Rate of natural increase (/1,000): 28.9 (1986)
Marriage rate (/1,000): 6.1 (1987)
Average household size: 6.9 (latest)

ETHNIC COMPOSITION

The original Emirate of Transjordan was dominated by Arab Bedouin tribal groups, but as a result of the acquisition of Palestine (the West Bank) in 1948, Palestinian Arabs became a large and relatively unassimilated element in the population. Palestinians constituted 40% of the nation in 1973, but their economic and cultural influence far surpassed their numbers. Bedouins form 5% of the population and are looked after by the Office of Tribal Affairs. There is a long-standing cultural hostility between Bedouins and non-Bedouins.

Members of the minority ethnic groups, both non-Arab and non-Muslim, live in the cities and towns, where they occupy a disproportionate share of posts in government, business and the professions. Arab Christians dominate banking and commerce, but their numbers are diminishing through emigration. The Circassians, non-Arab Muslims from the Caucasus, number about 12,000 and are prominent in landowning, commerce and industry. They are concentrated in Amman, where their loyalty to the royal family ensures their invariable representation in the cabinet.

Western communities are concentrated in Amman.

LANGUAGE

The official language is Arabic, which is, like Islam, a unifying force in the country. Jordanians speak a dialect of Arabic that is common to Syria, Lebanon and parts of Iraq. It is even spoken by the ethnic minorities who maintain their own languages in their everyday lives. There are differences between the languages of the towns and of the countryside, and between those of the East and West banks. English is taught in the schools as a second language.

RELIGION

The official religion of Jordan is Islam of the Sunni sect. King Hussein himself is honored as a direct descendant of Prophet Muhammad. Sunnis constitute 93% of the population. The Druzes form the largest Muslim minority sect.

The largest religious minority group, the Christians, numbered 180,000 in 1965, divided into Greek Orthodox, Greek Catholic, Roman Catholic, Protestant and Armenian churches. Instances of religious persecution or intolerance are rare. Nevertheless, Jordanian Christians have been emigrating in large numbers.

HISTORICAL BACKGROUND

Jordan, then known as Transjordan, was placed under British mandate in 1921. In the same year Abdullah, son of Sharyf Husayn, was installed by the British as the emir of Transjordan. In 1923 the kingdom became independent under British tutelage. British control was partially relaxed in 1928, and cabinet government was introduced in 1939. British penetration was never deep, and Britain's only legacy was the legendary Arab Legion. Transjordan achieved full independence in 1946, and in May the Amir Abdullah was proclaimed King of the Hashemite Kingdom of Transjordan. Following the Arab-Israeli war of 1948, King Abdullah annexed the West Bank, an area of Palestine bordering Jordan which contained many Arab refugees from Israeli-held areas. In 1950 an act of union joined the West Bank and Transjordan to form the Hashemite Kingdom of Jordan. King Abdullah was assassinated in Jerusalem in July 1951 by a Palestinian Arab, and his eldest son, Talal, was proclaimed king. Because of mental illness, however, King Talal was declared unfit to rule, and succession passed to his son Hussein, then 16 years of age. King Hussein was formally enthroned in May 1953.

In an effort to ensure the survival of the state Hussein attempted to steer a middle course in international affairs. Despite internal and foreign opposition, the king maintained close relations with Great Britain, whose troops and military subsidies helped protect the regime. Hussein was forced to negotiate an end to Jordan's treaty with Britain following Anglo-French intervention at Suez in 1956. The king then formed a federation with Iraq, in 1958, which lasted until the assassination of his cousin, King Faisal of Iraq, a few months later. Hussein again turned to the West for support.

The early 1960s were a period of relative calm. Hussein steadied relations with other Arab states while retaining Western ties and establishing relations with the Soviet Union. Jordan lost the West Bank and East Jerusalem in the 1967 Arab-Israeli war and received still further Palestinian refugees. Efforts to encorporate the Palestinians into the Jordanian political system failed and the refugee camps became a center of Palestinian nationalism. By 1970 organized Palestinian groups had become a threat to the Jordanian government, and, over the course of a year, the Jordanian military was used to expell the Palestinian guerrilla groups.

Jordan played only a minor role in the 1973 Arab-Israeli war. Hussein reluctantly endorsed the Arab League's declaration in 1974 that the Palestine Liberation Organization (PLO) was the sole legitimate representative of the Palestinians. Jordan joined other Arab states in condemning the 1979 Egyptian-Israeli Peace Treaty but resumed relations in 1984 to form a moderate Arab block against Syria and Libya.

During the 1980s Jordan played a key role in attempts to deal with the Palestinian question. Initially, Jordan and the PLO agreed to work with each other towards settling the question, but in 1987 the agreement to do so was scrapped. In 1988, following the outbreak of the intifada on the West Bank, Hussein declared unconditional support for the intifada and insisted that the PLO was the sole representative of the Palestinians. In accordance with agreements reached during a summit of Arab leaders, he severed all legal and administrative links with the West Bank in preparation for turning administration over to the PLO. The PLO proclaimed the establishment of an independent state of Palestine in November 1988.

From the mid-1980s onward Jordan faced severe economic difficulties with riots occurring in response to austerity measures. The most serious rioting disturbances occurred in 1989 following government imposed price rises on basic goods and services. Elections were held in November, in which opposition groups won the majority of seats in the House of Representatives.

Jordan was deeply affected by the Gulf crisis of 1990–91. Although King Hussein condemned the invasion of Kuwait, he was slow to do so and spent the fall of 1990 attempting to negotiate an "Arab solution" to the crisis. He criticized what he called the Allies' "total war" and urged a cease-fire. The crisis crippled the Jordanian economy; Iraq was Jordan's chief trading partner and the source of most of its petroleum. Following the Allied victory over Iraq, Jordan was politically ostracized by coalition members.

CONSTITUTION & GOVERNMENT

The kingdom is a limited constitutional monarchy in name and an absolute monarchy in fact. The basis of

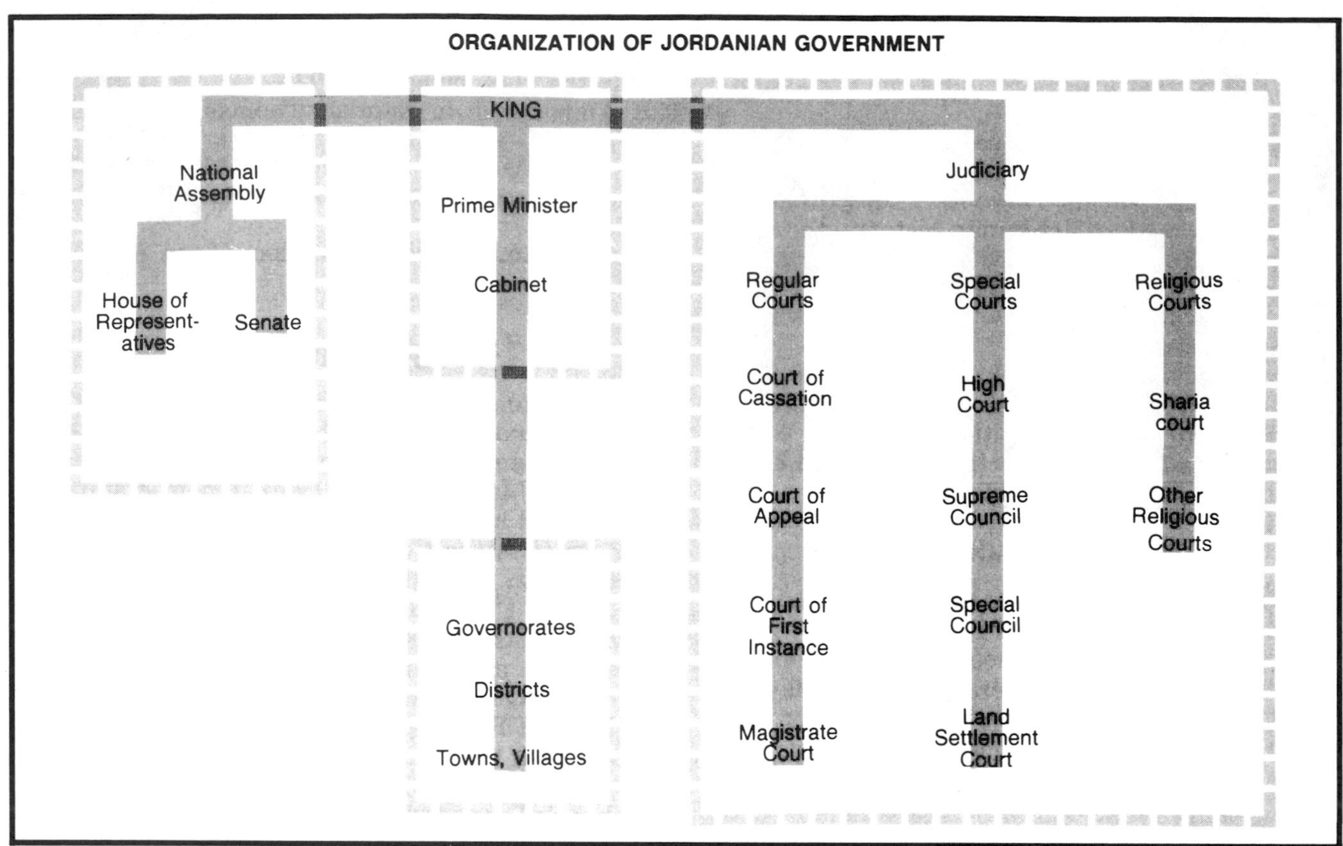

government is the Constitution of 1952, which provides for a royal executive and a bicameral legislature. Executive power is vested in the king and cabinet, but the monarch, the head of state, has the power to appoint and dismiss the prime minister and cabinet ministers. His power over the legislature is reinforced by his right to appoint senators, dissolve the House of Representatives, veto bills passed by the legislature, and issue royal decrees with the consent of the prime minister and at least four members of the cabinet. He also is the commander in chief of the army and head of the judicial system. The throne devolves by inheritance in the dynasty of ibn al-Hussein by direct line through male heirs. The present crown prince is Hasan.

Legislative power is vested in a bicameral National Assembly with a 30-member Senate appointed by the king and an 80-member House of Representatives elected by universal suffrage. The Assembly, in joint session, can override the king's veto of legislation. Since 1968 King Hussein has wielded nearly absolute power. He dissolved the Assembly in 1974. It met briefly in 1976, but Hussein did not reconvene it again until 1984.

Only three free elections have been held in Jordan, in 1956, 1984 and 1989. All political parties were banned in 1957. The country is divided into 17 electoral districts, of which three are reserved for Bedouins. Seats are apportioned not only according to population but also ethnic and religious factors. Under the Constitution, suffrage is universal over age 20.

The Jordanian cabinet is headed by Fld. Mar. Sharif Zeid bin Shaker, Hussein's 25th prime minister, who was appointed to that office in 1989. The cabinet

GOVERNMENT LIST
(July/August 1991)

King	Hussein I
Prime Minister	Masri, Tahir al-
Deputy Prime Minister	Suhaymat, 'Ali
Deputy Prime Minister	Masa'dah, Salim
Minister of Agriculture	Qasim, Subhi al-
Minister of Defense	Masri, Tahir al-
Minister of Education	Duhayyat, 'Id
Minister of Energy & Mineral Resources	Tahir, Thabit
Minister of Finance & Customs	Jardanah, Basil
Minister of Foreign Affairs	Nusur, 'Abdallah al-
Minister of Health	'Abbadi, Mamduh al-
Minister of Higher Education	Hammuri, Muhammad al-
Minister of Information & Culture	Karaki, Khalid al-
Minister of Interior	Subul, Jawdat al-
Minister of Islamic Affairs, Holy Places & Religious Trusts	Najm, Ra'if
Minister of Justice	Kan'an, Taysir
Minister of Labor and Cabinet Affairs	Dughmi, 'Abd al-Karim al-
Minister of Municipal, Rural & Environmental Affairs	Zu'bi, Salim al-
Minister of Planning	Fariz, Ziad
Minister of Public Works & Housing	Surur, Sa'd Hayil al-
Minister of Social Development	Bashir, 'Awni al-
Minister of Tourism & Antiquities	Kabariti, 'Abd al-Karim al-
Minister of Trade, Industry, & Supply	Abu al-Raghib, Ali
Minister of Transport & Communications	Suhaymat, 'Ali
Minister of Water Resources & Irrigation	Qa'war, Samir
Minister of Youth	Irshidat, Salih
Minister of State for Cabinet Affairs	Tarawinah, Muhammad Faris al-
Minister of State for Parliamentary Affairs	Furayhat, Abd al-Salam
Minister of State	Khurayshah, Jamal Hadithah al-
Governor, Central Bank	Nabulsi, Muhammad Said

RULERS OF JORDAN
Monarchs (from 1921)

March 1921–July 1951: Emir Abdullah; king from 1946
July 1951–August 1952: King Talal I
August 1952– : King Hussein I

members usually are chosen from among members of the royal family; the palace staff; former army officers; and representatives of noble tribes, such as the Majali. The cabinet always includes one Circassian and one Christian. King Hussein has taken steps to increase the participation of women in the political process, appointing the first female cabinet minister in Jordan's history in 1979.

There have been three assassinations in modern Jordanian history—those of King Abdullah in 1951, Prime Minister Hazza al-Majali in 1960 and Prime Minister Wasfi al-Tal in 1971. Hussein himself has survived seven known attempted assassinations.

FREEDOM & HUMAN RIGHTS

In terms of civil and political rights Jordan is classified as a not-free country.

Jordan has been under martial law since 1970. The general instability of the region and the tensions between Palestinians and Jordanians are cited as the reasons for the continuing denial of popular participation in government. Political issues have become less important as Jordan has begun to share in the general increase in Arab wealth spurred by the repatriated earnings of Jordanians working abroad and the growing commercial role of Amman replacing Beirut as the regional base of operations for many foreign banks and businesses. Despite the fact that Jordan is an absolute monarchy, there has been no systematic incursion into the rights of its citizens; torture as well as other cruel, inhuman and degrading forms of punishment are rare, and summary executions have not been reported. Under martial law the executive authority has the power to detain persons indefinitely without trial. This power has been used in a limited number of cases. Both civil and military courts operate, with the martial law court responsible for crimes such as espionage, bribery, trafficking in narcotics and weapons, black marketeering and security offenses. Although the martial law court is not bound to observe normal rules of evidence or procedure, they are observed in practice. Further, defendants may be represented by legal counsel and may cross-examine witnesses. Although sentences may not be appealed, they must be ratified by the prime minister in his capacity as martial law governor. Judges are independent and insulated from political pressures. They are selected by a board consisting of the members of the High Court of Justice, a representative of the attorney general's office and the senior civil servant in the Ministry of Justice, and may be removed only on grounds of specific transgressions and after a hearing before a disciplinary board.

Freedoms of the press and speech are limited. Electronic media are state-controlled, while private newspaper and periodicals practice a form of self-censorship. The result is that the media generally follow government positions on major national and foreign issues, with no attempt at critical analysis. Newspapers have been closed down for varying periods in the past for transgressing officially set bounds. Foreign publications are widely available but may be subject to occasional censorship, more on moral grounds than on political ones. Professional associations require government license, but these are routinely granted for nonpolitical groups. Toleration of non-Islamic minorities has been remarkable by Middle Eastern standards.

The king does not share political power with any other person or group; political parties remain banned.

CIVIL SERVICE

The Jordanian civil service is based on the British model. Selection is by competitive examination, and training is provided by the School of Public Administration at Amman. However, promotion is influenced by political and ethnic factors. After the civil war in 1971 a large number of Palestinian civil servants were forced to resign.

LOCAL GOVERNMENT

For purposes of local administration Jordan is divided into five *alwiya* (singular: *liwa*): Amman, Irbid, Balqa, Karak and Ma'an. The *alwiya* are further subdivided into *aqdiya* (singular: *qada*), or districts, and *nawahin*, or subdistricts. The West Bank is divided into three governorates—Nabulus, Jerusalem and Hebron—which function despite Israeli administration. The smaller villages are governed by the traditional headman or *mukhtar*. The councils of most cities and towns are elected by popular vote.

FOREIGN POLICY

Jordan's foreign policy has been marked by frequent periods of isolation from the rest of the Arab world. Relations with other Arab countries reached a nadir after Jordan's conflict with the Palestinian Liberation Organization (PLO) in 1971. Relations steadily improved after that date through the mediation of Saudi Arabian king Faisal. Jordan had returned to the mainstream of Arab politics by 1973, and diplomatic relations were restored with Egypt and Syria. Jordan also took an active part in Islamic summit conferences.

Resisting contrary pressures from without and within the country, King Hussein has followed a consistent pro-Western policy since 1952. Jordan had a special treaty relationship with Great Britain until 1957. The United States first established diplomatic relations in 1949. U.S. assistance began in 1951, and after 1957 the United States replaced Britain as the principal donor of aid. Diplomatic relations with the USSR, first established in 1963, have never been more than formally correct. Jordan is one of the charter members of the Arab League.

The Camp David Accords and the Egyptian-Israeli Peace Treaty proved to be watersheds in Jordanian foreign relations. Despite U.S. pressures, Jordan assumed a leading role in coordinating Arab opposition to the settlement, maintaining that the treaty did not guarantee with any degree of precision Arab rights to the Israeli-occupied territories, the status of Jerusalem and Israeli withdrawal from the West Bank.

After the Israeli invasion of Lebanon in June 1982, Hussein found himself with a key role in a plan for peace in the Middle East proposed by President Ronald Reagan. The plan involved the creation of an autonomous Palestinian authority on the West Bank, in association with Jordan. However, following talks with Hussein, Arafat rejected the plan. Jordan subsequently gave diplomatic support to Arafat when a Syrian-backed revolt erupted in May 1983 against his leadership of the Palestine National Liberation Movement (Fatah), the major guerrilla group within the PLO. During the last three months of 1983, Jordanian diplomats in several European countries, and targets in Amman, came under attack from terrorists who were thought to be members of a radical Syrian-backed Arab group that was angered by Jordan's backing for Arafat, by its call for Egypt to be readmitted to the community of Arab states and by the possibility of a revival of the Reagan plan.

With a view to recovering something from the West Bank before Jewish settlement there produces a *de facto* extension of Israel, Hussein dissolved the National Consultative Council in January 1984 and recalled the National Assembly for its first session since 1967. He thereby created the kind of Palestinian forum (60% of Jordan's population of 2.4 million are Palestinian, and there are 1.3 million Palestinians living on the West Bank) that was called for in the Reagan plan and effectively infringed on the Rabat Resolution of 1974, which recognized the PLO as the sole representative of the Palestinian people. Israel allowed the surviving West Bank deputies to attend the Assembly, which approved constitutional amendments enabling elections to be held on the East Bank alone, and West Bank deputies to be chosen by the Assembly itself. Also in January, the Jordanian Council of Ministers resigned, and a new one, containing a higher proportion of Palestinians took office.

King Hussein embarked on a series of talks with Yasser Arafat in January 1984, hoping to arrive at an agreed policy on the issue of Palestinian autonomy. In September 1984, to the anger of radical Arab states, Jordan decided to reestablish diplomatic relations with Egypt, five years after breaking them off in protest at the Egypt-Israel peace treaty of 1979. President Mubarak of Egypt has since given his support to King Hussein's proposals for peace negotiations between the Arabs and the Israelis. Hussein rejected the Israeli offer of direct negotiations, excluding the PLO, in October, calling instead for a conference of all concerned parties in the Middle East, including the PLO on an equal footing with nation-states in the region. He required Israel to accept the principle of "land for peace"—i.e., talks leading to the restoration of occupied territories (including East Jerusalem) to Jordan in return for a comprehensive Arab-Israeli peace treaty. Negotiations, according to Hussein, should proceed on the basis of the U.N. Security Council's Resolution 242 of November 1967. This last point has been the impediment to Jordanian and PLO agreement to a program for peace talks. Resolution 242 is not acceptable to the PLO, as it refers to the Palestinian Arabs as refugees, implicitly denying the existence of a Palestinian nation and Palestinians' right to self-determination.

In February 1984 the Jordanian embassy in Tripoli, Libya was burned down during a demonstration, and Jordan responded by severing diplomatic relations with Libya. Attacks by militant Arab groups on Jordanian diplomats around the world took place at irregular intervals throughout 1984. In February 1985 King Hussein and Yasser Arafat announced the terms of a joint Jordanian-Palestinian agreement, proposing a confederated state of Jordon and Palestine. This agreement foundered on Israel's refusal to negotiate with the PLO and Israel's rejection of proposals for an international peace conference.

Further progress was hampered, and frustrated by the lack of cooperation from Yasser Arafat in advancing the aims of the Jordanian-PLO peace initiative, King Hussein publicly severed political links with the PLO in February 1986. Following his announcement, Arafat was ordered to close his main PLO offices in Jordan. King Hussein urged the PLO either to change its policies or its leadership. In 1987 the Jordan-PLO accord of 1985 was formally abrogated.

In 1987 King Hussein pursued his efforts to reconcile Syria and Iraq, with the aim of securing Arab unity. He was instrumental in arranging the first full summit meeting of the Arab League in eight years. In September Jordon had restored diplomatic relations with Libya, which had modified its support for Iran in the Gulf War and urged a cease-fire. The resumption of cooperation between Jordan and the PLO was announced.

In June 1988 King Hussein gave his unconditional support to the violent Palestinian uprising and disclaimed any ambition to restore Jordanian rule in the West Bank. He also stressed the PLO's status as "the sole legitimate representative of the Palestinian people." At the end of July 1988 King Hussein severed Jordan's legal and administrative links with the region. In November 1988 the PLO proclaimed the establishment of an independent state of Palestine and, for the first time, endorsed the U.N. Security Council's Resolution 242 as a basis for a Middle East peace settlement. Jordan and 60 other countries recognized the new state.

Traditionally, Jordan, with close economic ties to Iraq, has been one of that nation's principal supporters in the Arab camp, often acting as Iraq's spokesman. It supported Iraq in its war with Iran and refused to enter the allied coalition that went to war with Iraq over its invasion of Kuwait. Jordan was slow in condemning the August 1990 invasion and worked for an Arab solution to the problem. It denounced what it called the "total" war against Iraq in 1991 and urged both sides to come to a cease-fire. As a result of its stand, Jordan was ostracized by members of the allied coalition following its victory.

Jordan and the United States are parties to 16 agreements and treaties, covering agricultural commodities, aviation, defense, economic and technical cooperation, investment guarantees, relief supplies and packages, taxation and telecommunications.

Jordan is a member of the United Nations; 13 related U.N. organizations; and nine other international organizations, including the Arab League. It joined the United Nations in 1955.

PARLIAMENT

Under the Constitution, the National Assembly is a bicameral body consisting of two chambers. The upper house is the Senate, with a membership of 30 appointed by the king for four-year terms. The lower house is the House of Representatives, with a membership of 80 elected for four-year terms. Under a proportional-representation system 10 of the seats in the House of Representatives are allotted to Christians.

Legislative proposals are placed before the House of Representatives and then referred to the Senate. If both chambers accept a bill it is sent to the king for confirmation. If it is rejected by one chamber and accepted by the other, a joint session is held, where decisions are made by two-thirds majority. If the king withholds approval from a law he returns it to the House within six months, and if a session passes it again it is promulgated. In practice the House has very little power because the Senate is packed with the king's supporters, and the king also wields the threat of dissolution.

The National Assembly was dissolved in 1974 after having become moribund in the wake of the 1967 war with Israel. From 1978 to 1984 the king ruled with the advice of the National Consultative Council, a 60-member appointive body he established for the purpose. In an effort to strengthen his hand in dealing with the Palestinian issue, King Hussein, in 1984, reconvened the House of Representatives. By-elections were held at that time for eight vacant seats.

The latest elections took place in 1989 during which 647 candidates contested for 80 seats. Although political parties were banned, opponents of the government made a surprisingly strong showing, winning over 40 seats.

POLITICAL PARTIES

All political parties were banned in 1957. In 1971 Hussein announced formation of the Jordanian National Union as Jordan's sole political party. In 1972 the party was renamed the Arab National Union. Hussein was its president and Hasan, the crown prince, its vice president. In 1976 the Union was abolished, leaving Jordan without any legal political party or group. The major illegal political parties or groups are the Muslim Brotherhood; smaller Fedayeen groups; and the Communist Party, estimated at 500 members.

ECONOMY

Jordan is one of the least-endowed countries of the world in natural resources and is one of 39-lower-middle-income countries of the world. Jordan has a free-market economy in which the dominant sector is private.

Jordan was a secondary beneficiary of the oil boom of the late 1970s and early 1980s, when its GNP growth averaged 10%–12%. Recent years, however, have witnessed a sharp reduction in cash aid from Arab oil-producing countries and worker remittances, with growth averaging 1%–2%. Imports have been outstripping exports by roughly $2 billion annually, the difference being made up by aid, remittances and borrowing. In 1989 the government pursued policies to encourage private investment, curb imports of luxury goods, promote exports, reduce the budget deficit and, in general, reinvigorate economic growth. U.N. sanctions against Iraq in 1990–91 had an extremely adverse effect on Jordan's economy. Iraq, Jordan's principal trading partner, takes approximately one-fourth of Jordan's total exports and supplies more than half of the nation's petroleum imports at subsidized prices. Initially Saudi Arabia compensated for the loss of Iraqi petroleum, but angered at Jordan's pro-Iraq stand in the crisis, it stopped supplies in September 1990. Yemen and Syria agreed to ship oil in February 1991, by which point the fuel shortage had had a serious effect on the economy.

PRINCIPAL ECONOMIC INDICATORS

Gross National Product (U.S. $ billions): 5.291 (1989)
GNP per capita (U.S. $): 1,730 (1989)
GNP average annual growth rate (%, 1980–89): 0.6
GNP per capita average annual growth rate (%, 1987–89): −6.2
Average annual rate of inflation (%, 1980–88): 2.2
Consumer price index (1980 = 100) 1986
  All items: 130
  Food: 123
Average annual growth rate (%, 1980–88)
  General government consumption: 4.7
  Private consumption: 6.6
  Gross domestic investment: −5.5

BALANCE OF PAYMENTS, 1987
(U.S. $ millions)

Current account balance: −351.8
Merchandise exports: 933.1
Merchandise imports: −2,400.1
Trade balance: −1,467.0
Other goods, services & income +: 1,350.0
Other goods, services & income −: −1,576.9
Other goods, services & income net: −226.9
Private unrequited transfers: 742.9
Official unrequited transfers: 599.1
Capital other than reserves: 493
Net errors & omissions: 27.9
Counterpart items: 120.1
Total change in reserves: −248.9

GROSS DOMESTIC PRODUCT

GDP nominal (J.D. billions): 2.556 (1989)
GDP per capita (U.S. $): 1,730 (1989)
Average annual growth rate of GDP (%, 1980–88): 4.2
GDP by type of expenditure (%) 1987
  Consumption
    Private: 76
    Government: 27
  Gross domestic investment: 26
  Gross domestic saving: −3 (1988)
  Foreign trade
    Exports: 45
    Imports: −74
Cost components of GDP (%) 1987
    Net indirect taxes: 14
    Consumption of fixed capital: 8
    Compensation of employees: 47
    Net operating surplus: 31
Sectoral origin of GDP (%) 1987
  Primary
    Agriculture: 7
    Mining: 4
  Secondary
    Manufacturing: 15
    Construction: 6
    Public utilities: 3
  Tertiary
    Transportation & communications: 11
    Trade: 16
    Finance, government and other services: 38
Average annual sectoral growth rates (%, 1980–88)
    Agriculture: 6.0
    Industry: 3.6
    Manufacturing: 3.4
    Services: 4.4

As a result of the crisis the unemployment rate rose to 30%, with refugees and returning migrant workers compounding the problem. It is estimated that the Gulf crisis cost Jordan $1.5 billion in lost trade and tourism. The figure is expected to reach over $3 billion in 1991.

PUBLIC FINANCE

The Jordanian fiscal year is the calendar year. The central fact about Jordan's public finance is the large part played by foreign aid, subsidies and subventions—about 51% in 1983.

Of total current revenues in 1990, 76% came from direct and indirect taxes, primarily taxes on international trade and transactions, and the remainder from foreign grants and loans. Of total current expenditures in 1988 42.9% went to administration, 26.5% to defense and security, 15.7% to economic development, 9.5% to social welfare and 2.8% to communications and transport.

Overall responsibility for development planning rests with the National Planning Council, which took over the functions of the Jordan Development Board in 1971. Owing to lack of funds, many large projects were abandoned after 1984, and development expenditures were cut by 16.4%.

Jordan is heavily dependent on foreign aid, the bulk of which comes from oil-rich Arab states. As a front-line state in the Arab-Israeli conflict, Jordan was pledged annual aid of $1.25 billion over 10 years by the Arab League at its 1978 summit meeting in Baghdad. This figure has never been achieved. Jordan's stance on the split within the PLO, relations with Egypt and the search for a settlement of the Palestinian question are, undoubtedly, largely responsible for the failure of certain Arab countries to make their aid payments.

CENTRAL GOVERNMENT EXPENDITURES (latest)

% of total expenditures
  Defense: 26.5
  Education: 13.0
  Health: 5.4
  Housing, social security, welfare: 9.5
  Economic services: 15.7
  Other: 30.0
Total expenditures as % of GNP: 49.9
Overall surplus or deficit as % of GNP: −15.7

CENTRAL GOVERNMENT REVENUES (latest)

% of total current revenues
  Taxes on income, profit & capital gain: 9.8
  Social security contributions: 0.0
  Domestic taxes on goods & services: 14.9
  Taxes on international trade & transactions: 31.1
  Other taxes: 7.4
  Current nontax revenue: 36.8
Total current revenue as % of GNP: 29.2
General government consumption as % of GDP: 27 (1988)
Average annual growth rate
  of general government consumption (%, 1980–88): 4.7

The amount of aid that Jordan receives also is dependent on the condition of the Middle East's petroleum industry. The falling price of petroleum meant that less money has been available for the oil-based economies to give aid.

As a front-line nation during the 1990–91 Persian Gulf crisis, Jordan received $1 billion in aid from the European Community, Germany and Japan.

FOREIGN AID

Total foreign aid (U.S. $ millions): 109.1 (1984)
  Bilateral: 63.7 (1984)
  Multilateral: 45.4 (1984)
Aid from international organizations, total (U.S. $ millions) 50.749 (1985)
  of which World Bank (U.S. $ millions) 43.100 (1985)
Per capita aid (U.S. $) 32.3 (1984)

During the period 1979 to 1989, Jordan received $95 billion in aid from OPEC. The nation was given $1.7 billion in aid from the United States from 1970 to 1988 and $1.2 billion in assistance from other Western nations from 1970 to 1987.

CURRENCY & BANKING

The Jordanian unit of currency is the dinar, divided into 1,000 fils. Coins are issued in denominations of 1, 5, 10, 20, 25, 50, 100 and 250 fils; notes are issued in denominations of 500 fils and 1, 5 and 10 dinars. In 1991 dollar exchange rate was $1 = JD 0.6800.

The Jordanian banking system consists of the Central Bank, established in 1964; eight national banks; and seven foreign banks. There also are eight specialized credit institutions, including the Agricultural Credit Corporation, the Industrial Development Bank, the Municipalities and Villages Loan Board, the Housing Corporation and the Jordan Cooperative Organization.

To further Amman's role as a financial center, since 1977 the government has been encouraging establishment of merchant (medium- and long-term loans) and investment banks.

FINANCIAL INDICATORS, 1989

Total reserves minus gold (SDRs millions): 358
SDRs (millions): 8
Reserve position in IMF (SDRs millions): 0
Foreign exchange (SDRs millions): 350
Gold (fine troy oz. millions): .75
Ratio of external debt to total reserves: 27.5 (1988)
Central bank 1989
- Assets (%)
  - Foreign assets: 45.1
  - Claims on government: 54.9
  - Claims on banks: 0.0
  - Claims on private sector: 0.0
- Liabilities (%)
  - Reserve money: 85.1
  - Government deposits: 1.6
  - Foreign liabilities: 0.0
  - Capital accounts: 0.0
- Money supply 1987
  - Stock (J.D. billions): 1.306
  - M1 per capita: 420

Private banks 1989
- Assets (%)
  - Loans to government: 12.2
  - Loans to private sector: 51.8
  - Reserves: 15.1
  - Foreign assets: 20.9
- Liabilities
  - Deposits (J.D. billions): 3.023
  - of which %
    - Demand deposits: 14.1
    - Savings deposits: 21.1
    - Government deposits: 5.3
    - Foreign liabilities: 16.7

External debt 1988
- Total (U.S. $ billions): 5.532
  - of which public (U.S. $ billions): 3.955
  - of which private (U.S. $ millions): 0.0
- Debt service (long-term)
  - Total (U.S. $ millions): 825
  - Repayment
    - Principal (%): 71.0
    - Interest (%): 29.0
- Debt service ratio (%): 243
- External public debt as % of GNP: 94.0
- Debt service as % of GNP: 19.6
- Debt service as % of exports: 31.9
- Terms of public borrowing
  - Commitment (U.S. $ millions): 999
  - Average interest rate (%): 7.5
  - Average maturity (yrs.): 11
- Net flow of publicly guaranteed external capital (U.S. $ millions): 0.0
- Receipt of workers' remittances (U.S. $ millions): 813 (1988 est.)
- Net direct private investment (U.S. $ millions): 0.0 (1988 est.)

GROWTH PROFILE
(Annual Growth Rates, %)

Projected population (1988–2000): 3.6
Projected crude birth rate (/1,000) (1990–95): 45.4
Projected crude death rate (/1,000) (1990–95): 5.5
Urban population (1980–88): 5.1
Labor force (1985–2000): 4.2
GNP (1980–89): 0.6
GNP per capita (1987–89): −6.2
GDP (1980–88): 4.2
Inflation (1980–88): 2.2
Agriculture (1980–88): 6.0
Industry (1980–88): 3.6
Manufacturing (1980–88): 3.4
Services (1980–88): 4.4
Money holdings (1980–88): 12.8
Manufacturing earnings per employee (1980–87): −1.1
Energy production (1980–88): 7.5
Energy consumption (1980–88): 6.9
Exports (1980–88): 6.5
Imports (1980–88): 0.3
General government consumption (1980–88): 4.7
Private consumption (1980–88): 6.6
Gross domestic investment (1980–88): −5.5

AGRICULTURE

Of Jordan's total land area of 9,229,000 ha. (22,804,859 ac.), 88% is desert and only 11%, or 1,015,190 ha. (2,508,534 ac.), are arable. Of this area, only 45% is under actual cultivation. Farming is mostly of a subsistence kind and contributes only 7% to the GDP.

The Ghor Valley, in the Northwest, is well-irrigated and suitable for agriculture. Jordan's other agricultural areas, less rich but far more extensive than the Ghor, are on the series of plateaus bordered by the Yarmuk River in the North, Wadi Musa in the South, the Ghor in the Northwest, Wadi Arab in the West and the desert in the East.

Development of the country's agricultural sector depends largely on irrigation, since 91% of Jordan's surface is arid; yet only 8.3% of arable land is irrigated. Exploitation of available water resources in the Jordan River Valley through modern farming techniques involving sprinkler and drip irrigation, the latter in combination with plastic greenhouses, shows striking increases in production of cashcrops. Plans for further expansion include a major earthfill dam, canal extension and associated irrigation equipment.

Most agricultural holdings are owner-operated dry farms. The principal system of land tenure are *mulk* (land held in absolute ownership), *miri* (state land granted in perpetuity), *waqf* (religious lands held in mortmain), *matruk* (public land), *mudawwara* (crown lands held in tenancy) and *niwat* (land over 1.6 km.; 1.0 mi. from a town or settlement).

Livestock is raised on land unsuitable for cultivation but that receives an average of 200 mm. (8. in.) of rain a year. In the winter the herds are moved to the Ghor. Livestock production is particularly sensitive to variations in climate, and a bad season may force the herders to slaughter the animals at a young age.

Fishing resources are limited to the Gulf of Aqaba.

AGRICULTURAL INDICATORS

Agriculture's share of GDP (%): 6 (1989)
Average annual growth rate (%, 1980–88): 6.0
Value added in agriculture (U.S. $ millions): 377 (1988)
Cereal imports (000 metric tons): 874 (1988)
Index of agricultural production (1979–81 = 100): 124 (1986)
Index of food production (1979–81 = 100): 125 (1986)
Index of food production per capita (1979–81 = 100): 111 (1986–88)
Number of tractors: 4,840 (1986)
Number of harvester-threshers: 340 (1986)
Total fertilizer consumption (000 metric tons): 15.4 (1985–86)
Fertilizer consumption (g./ha., hundreds) 362 (1987–88)
Number of farms (000): 57 (1983)
Average size of holding (ha.): 6.3 (1983)
Size class (%) 1983
  Below 1 ha. (below 2.47 ac.): 25.3
  1–5 ha. (2.47–12.35 ac.): 44.6
  5–10 ha. (12.35–24.7 ac.): 15.6
  10–20 ha. (24.7–49.4 ac.): 8.6
  20–50 ha. (49.4–123.5 ac.): 4.5
  50–200 ha. (123.5–494 ac.): 1.3
  Over 200 ha. (over 494 ac.): 0.1
Tenure (%) 1983
  Owner-operated: 80.5
  Rented: 13.1
  Other: 6.4
Activity (%) 1975
  Mainly crops: 58.2
  Mainly livestock: 14.9
  Mixed: 26.9
Farms as % of total land area: 4.1 (1983)
Land use (%) 1985–87
  Cropland: 3
  Pasture: 4
  Forest: 89
  Other: 4
Yields (kg./ha.) 1989
  Grains: 366
  Roots & tubers: 20,000
  Legumes: 629
  Milk (kg./animal): 1,886
Production 1989
  Fruits (000 metric tons): 162
  Vegetables (000 metric tons): 603
Livestock (000) 1989
  Cattle: 29
  Horses: 3 (1986)
  Sheep: 1,225
Forestry 1988
  Production of roundwood (000 cubic meters): 8
    of which industrial roundwood (%): 50.0
  Value of exports (U.S. $ million): 9.267
Fishing 1988
  Total catch (000 metric tons): 0.1
    of which marine (%): 100.0
  Value of exports (U.S. $ 000): 132

Agricultural credit is provided by over 200 cooperative societies, belonging to the Jordan Cooperative Organization or the Agricultural Credit Corporation.

MANUFACTURING

Five heavy industries—phosphates, cement, textiles, chemicals and oil refining—account for the bulk of the income from this sector. The vast majority of manufacturing establishments are small, employing less than 200 people.

MANUFACTURING INDICATORS, 1987

Average annual growth rate (%, 1980–88): 3.4
Share of GDP (%): 12 (1988)
Labor force economically active in manufacturing (% est.): 7.7
Value added in manufacturing (U.S. $ millions): 552
  Food & tobacco (%): 22
  Textiles & clothing (%): 3
  Machinery & transport equipment (%): 1
  Chemicals (%): 7
Earnings per employee in manufacturing 1986
  Growth rate (%, 1980–87): 1.1
  Index (1980 = 100): 101
Total earnings as % of value added: 22
Gross output per employee (1980 = 100): 161

Due to the paucity of private entrepreneurial capital, the government holds equity in over 25 firms in marketing, tourism, transportation, power and finance. State participation varies from 3% to 86%.

There was little foreign investment in Jordan until 1972, when the Foreign Investments Act was passed. The bulk of foreign investment in recent years has been from oil-rich Arab states.

Jordan's economy is essentially a free-enterprise system, although the government holds important equity positions in many of the country's larger enterprises. Foreign investment is welcome, and 100% foreign ownership of local enterprises is permitted. Jordan's investment law provides attractive tax holidays (six years for industries established in Amman and nine years for industries established outside the capital) and other incentives for investments that accord with the country's plans for development. Legislation also provides for repatriation of capital and dividends. Industrial free zones where manufacturers may take advantage of Arab Common Market regulations have been established.

In 1975 Jordan passed legislation to encourage establishment of regional business headquarters offices in Jordan. The law provides for all expatriate employees, and duty-free entry for office equipment and private vehicles of expatriate employees. By 1980 more than 50 American firms had established modest regional offices in Amman. Among Jordan's attractions are: the relative efficiency of the Jordanian government and the country's infrastructure, the Western orientation of business practices and the high degree to which English is a commercial language.

MINING

The country's only mineral wealth, phosphate, is mined by the Jordan Phosphate Mine Company. This firm, which is 64% owned by the government, is the country's largest employer. Phosphate reserves are estimated at 3 billion tons. Phosphate production in 1985 was 4,745,900 tons. Mining contributes 4% to the GDP.

ENERGY

Prior to the establishment of U.S. sanctions against Iraq in 1990, Jordan received a large portion of its

ENERGY INDICATORS

Average annual energy production growth rate (%, 1980–88): 7.5
Energy consumption per capita (kg. oil equivalent): 723 (1988)
Energy imports as % of merchandise exports: 42 (1988)
Average annual growth rate of energy consumption (%, 1980–88): 6.9
Electricity 1988
 Installed capacity (000 kw.): 991
 Production (billion kw.-hr.): 3.262
  % fossil fuel: 99.2
  % hydro: 0.8
 Consumption per capita (kw.-hr.): 827
Natural gas
 Proved reserves (billion cu. m.): 11 (1990)
 Production (million cu. m.): 110 (1989)
 Consumption (million cu. m.): 0 (1988)
Petroleum
 Proved reserves (million bbl.): 5 (1990)
 Years to exhaust proved reserves: 50 (1990)
 Production (million bbl.): 0.1 (1989)
 Consumption (million bbl.): 17 (1988)
 Refining capacity (000 bbl./day): 100 (1990)
Coal
 Reserves (million metric tons): 0 (latest)
 Production (000 metric tons): 0 (1988)
 Consumption (000 metric tons): 0 (1988)

petroleum from Iraq at subsidized prices. Attempts are being made currently to find alternatives to fossil fuels, including wind and solar power.

LABOR

During the mid and late 1980s, a large portion of the labor force worked outside the country. Consequently labor assumed increasing importance among factors of production. New plans and institutions, such as the Social Security Administration, were developed to deal with the unusual labor situation. The participation rate in Jordan's labor force is low, due primarily to the limited, although significantly expanding, role of women in the economy and the fact that almost half of the population is under 14.

The Gulf crisis of 1990–91 had an extremely adverse effect on Jordanian labor. U.N. trade sanctions against Iraq, Jordan's principal market, crippled the economy. Unemployment reached 30%,. exacerbated by the large number of migrant workers returning from other areas of the Gulf.

The General Federation of Jordanian Trade Unions is the principal labor organization. Jordanians may join labor unions and professional organizations. Such associations require a government license, but this is granted routinely. Unions and associations are permitted to defend the interests of their members, and their officers are elected by the membership. Strikes are legal; however, the Labor Ministry must be notified in advance (14 days for small firms, 28 days for large firms). During this period, the ministry attempts to arbitrate. If these efforts fail, employees may strike and have done so.

Only 20% of Jordanian labor is unionized; the low proportion is due primarily to the population's lack of familiarity with unions rather than government or business efforts to suppress unions. The unions maintain that the proportion of the work force they represent is growing. Unions have virtually no political role.

LABOR INDICATORS, 1986

Total economically active population (000): 524
 % working-age (15–64): 39.0
 % female: 10.9
Activity rate (%)
  Total: 19.6
  Male: 33.6
  Female: 4.5
Employment status (%) 1979
 Employers & self-employed: 22.8
 Employees: 67.2
 Unpaid family workers: 0.8
 Other: 9.2
Sectoral employment of economically active (%)
 Agriculture, forestry, fishing: 6.2
 Construction: 10.7
 Manufacturing, mining, quarrying, public utilities: 7.7
 Trade, hotels, restaurants: 10.5
 Transportation, communications: 8.6
 Finance, real estate: 3.3
 Services: 53.1
Average annual growth rate of labor force (%, 1985–2000): 4.2
Labor under 20 years (%): 10.9 (1979)

FOREIGN COMMERCE

Jordan imports mainly machinery and transportation equipment, food and live animals, chemicals and petroleum products, and textiles and clothing. The nation's main exports are fertilizers, fruits and vegetables, chemicals and wood products.

The major import sources are Saudi Arabia, the United States, Germany, Japan and Italy. Until the Gulf crisis of 1990–91, Jordan's primary export destination

FOREIGN TRADE INDICATORS, 1988

Exports (U.S. $ millions): 910
Imports (U.S. $ billions): 1.700
Balance of trade (U.S. $ millions): −790
Annual growth rate (1980–88), exports (%): 6.5
Annual growth rate (1980–88), imports (%): 0.3
International reserves in terms of months of imports covered: 1.2
Terms of trade (1980 = 100): 102
Import price index (1980 = 100): 94.1 (1986)
Export price index (1980 = 100): 94.3 (1986)

Direction of Trade (%), 1986

	Imports	Exports
European Community	23.9	9.7
United States	12.6	1.0
U.S.S.R. & eastern European economies	5.9	3.8
Japan	5.3	1.9

Composition of Trade (%), 1986

	Imports	Exports
Food & agricultural raw materials	20.9	9.7
Fuels & other energy	15.5	0.1
Mineral ores & concentrates	1.5	39.5
Manufactured goods	62.1	50.8
of which chemicals	9.9	24.8
of which machinery	22.6	5.8

was Iraq. Other important markets were Saudi Arabia, Syria, India and Kuwait.

TRANSPORTATION & COMMUNICATIONS

The Jordanian rail system consists of two sections: the Hedjaz Railway, which runs from the Syrian border to Naqb Ishtar, passing through Amman and Ma'an, and from Ma'an to the Saudi Arabian border (503 km.; 312 mi.); and a new extension, from Ma'an to Aqaba (115 km.; 71 mi.).

Aqaba is the only Jordanian port and outlet to the sea. It handled 11,268,000 metric tons of cargo pre-1986.

All cities and most towns are connected by a two-lane paved road system. Amman is linked by road with all parts of the kingdom and with neighboring countries.

The international flag carrier of Jordan is Alia Royal Jordanian Airlines, which flies to airports in the Middle East, Europe and the Far East with 20 aircraft. The country's two major international airports are at Amman and Aqaba. Prior to the 1967 war tourism was an important source of revenue because of the large number of pilgrims and tourists visiting religious sites on the West Bank. The loss of the West Bank in that war resulted in a sharp drop in tourism. Yet tourists still are attracted to Jordan by the ancient cities of Jerash and Petra and by the country's proximity to biblical sites. The Gulf crisis of 1990–91 virtually put a halt to tourism during that period.

TRANSPORTATION INDICATORS

Roads (latest)
- Length, km. (mi.): 5,625 (3,495)
- Paved (%): 100

Motor vehicles (latest)
- Automobiles: 164,864
- Trucks and buses: 58,437
- Persons per vehicle: 13
- Road freight, metric ton-km. (short ton-mi.) (billions): 27.934 (19.133) (pre-1986)

Railroads (latest)
- Track, km. (mi.): 788 (490)
- Passenger-km. (passenger-mi.) (millions): 6.0 (3.7)
- Freight, metric ton-km. (short ton-mi.) (millions): 1,262 (864)

Merchant marine
- Vessels (over 100 tons): 4 (1989)
- Total deadweight tonnage (000): 47.7 (1989)

Ports (latest) (pre-1986)
- Cargo loaded (million metric tons): 11.268
- Cargo unloaded (million metric tons): 8.748

Air
- Km. (mi.) flown (millions): 26.0 (16.2) (1985)
- Passenger-km. (passenger-mi.) (billions): 3.678 (2.285) (pre-1986)
- Freight, metric ton-km. (short ton-mi.) (millions): 206.5 (141.1) (pre-1986)
- Mail, metric ton-km. (short ton-mi.) (millions): 1.7 (1.2) (1985)
- Airports with scheduled flights: 3 (1990)

Inland waterways (pre-1986)
- Freight, metric ton-km. (short ton-mi.) (billions): 28.035 (19.202)

COMMUNICATIONS INDICATORS, 1988

Telephones
- Total (000): 212 (1987)
- Persons per telephone: 14 (1987)

Phone traffic (million minutes)
- Local: 2,294.477
- Long distance: 244.156
- Combined national: 2,538.633
- International: 30,877

Post office
- Number of post offices: 809
- Pieces of mail handled (millions): 106.521

Telegraph
- Total traffic (000 calls):
  - International: 3,197 (words)

Telex
- Subscriber lines: 2,429

Telecommunications 1990
- Satellite stations: 3

TOURISM & TRAVEL INDICATORS, 1986

Total tourist receipts (U.S. $ millions): 621 (1988)
Expenditures by nationals abroad (U.S. $ millions): 480 (1988)
Number of hotel beds (000): 14
Number of tourists (millions): 1.889.9 (1985)
- of whom from United States: 54.7
  - Egypt: 717.5
  - Saudi Arabia: 286.3
  - Turkey: 111.2

DEFENSE

The defense structure is headed by the king, who exercises his command in a personal and direct manner. The king is the supreme commander of the armed forces with the constitutional right to declare war, conclude peace and sign treaties. The senior officer is the commander in chief, who is answerable to the minister of defense and the prime minister. The commander in chief also is the army commander and, in times of martial law, the military governor-general. Under him is the chief of staff, who heads the general staff. The royal influence is felt on all aspects of armed forces operations; a Sandhurst-trained soldier and qualified test pilot, Hussein devotes most of his time to army matters and personally approves all promotions and transfers. Military service is for three years. Volunteers provide the bulk of the manpower. The Bedouins are the most numerous element in the armed forces and constitute the most loyal units. The main army base areas are the complexes at Amman and Az-Zarqa, with installations in the North around Irbid al-Mafraq and in the South at Maan and al-Aqaba.

The strength of the armed forces in 1990 was 84,250.

Army

Personnel: 74,000

Organization: 3 armored brigades; 6 mechanized brigades; 2 independent infantry brigades; 1 independent royal guards brigade; 1 special forces brigade; 15 artillery battalions; 4 AA brigades

Equipment: 795 tanks; 850 armored personnel carriers; 17 guns; 222 howitzers; 300 rocket launchers; 300 antitank guided weapons; 366 air defense guns; SAM

Navy

Personnel: 250
Equipment: 9 patrol craft
Naval base: Aqaba

Air Force

Personnel: 10,000

Organization and Equipment: 121 combat aircraft; 3 fighter squadrons; 2 interceptor squadrons; 1 operational conversion unit squadron; 1 transportation squadron; 1 VIP squadron; 2 helicopter squadrons; 1 training squadron; AAM; 14 air defense batteries

Air bases: Amman; Aqaba; al-Mafraq

The country has not experienced serious civil disturbances since 1971 when the PLO was expelled. Jordan is very much an army-run state, and the loyalty of the troops to the Hashemite dynasty makes any probability of international coup or subversion remote. Hussein also has proved himself an expert in the art of survival and has made himself acceptable, or at least tolerable, to most of the protagonists in the Middle East struggle.

Jordan has received substantial military aid from Great Britain, the United States and friendly Arab countries.

EDUCATION

Schooling is free and compulsory, in principle, for nine years, from ages six to 15. The educational ladder consists of six years of primary schooling and six years of junior and senior secondary schooling.

The academic year runs from September to June. The medium of instruction is Arabic, but English is taught from the fifth grade on.

Education is financed and administered by the Ministry of Education, while the National Council for Planning Human Resources makes broad policy decisions.

The nation's four universities are the University of Jordan, at Jubaiha, near Amman; Yarmuk University at Irbid; Mut'ah University, in Karak governorate in southern Jordan; and the University of Jordan for Science and Technology. During the 1970s, several polytechnical and community colleges were established.

EDUCATION INDICATORS, 1989

Literacy
- Total (%): 77.2
- Male (%): 87.5
- Female (%): 66.9

First level
- Schools: 2,983
- Students: 843,961
- Teachers: 34,861
- Student/teacher ratio: 24.2
- Net enrollment ratio: 88 (1983)

Second level
- Schools: 622
- Students: 118,462
- Teachers: 10,264
- Student/teacher ratio: 11.5
- Net enrollment ratio: 71 (1982)

Vocational
- Schools: 30
- Students: 24,859
- Teachers: 2,288
- Student/teacher ratio: 10.9

Third level (postsecondary)
- Institutions: 55
- Students: 62,633
- Teachers: 19,037
- Student/teacher ratio: 3.3
- Gross enrollment ratio: 37.4
- Students (/100,000 pop.): 1,992
- % of population age 25 and over with postsecondary education: 0.8

Foreign study
- Foreign students in national universities: 1,128 (1987)
- Students abroad: 17,497
  - of whom in
    - United States: 4,285 (1988)
    - France: 299 (1988)
    - Federal Republic of Germany: 974 (1988)
    - United Kingdom: 451 (1987)

Public expenditure
- Total (J.D. million): 95.306
- % of GNP: 6.1
- % of national budget: 7.6 (1987)
- % of current expenditure: 93.8

GRADUATES, 1985

Total: 15,186
Education: 4,714
Humanities & religion: 1,772
Fine & applied arts: 0
Law: 89
Social & behavioral sciences: 326
Commerce & business: 3,587
Mass communication: 0
Home economics: 0
Service trades: 44
Natural sciences: 1,568
Mathematics & computer science: 0
Medicine: 848
Engineering: 1,794
Architecture: 0
Industrial programs: 0
Transportation & communications: 0
Agriculture, forestry, fisheries: 207
Other: 237

LEGAL SYSTEM

The Shari'a is the dominant legal system, but as a result of the British occupation of Palestine from 1917 to 1948 much of English common law has been adopted either by statute or by case law.

The civil court system has four tiers. At the apex is the Court of Cassation, with seven judges; it is both the supreme court of appeal and the high court in matters of habeas corpus, mandamus and certiori. Below it are the two courts of appeal and seven courts of first instance. At the bottom are 14 magistrates' courts. Special courts include the Supreme Council, which interprets the Constitution; the Special Council, which interprets the constitutionality of laws; three special civil courts; tribal courts; and land settlement courts. There are two types of religious courts whose jurisdiction extends to all personal matters: the Shari'a courts for Muslims and ecclesiastical courts for Christians of each denomination: Melkite, Catholic and Armenian.

Under the civilian court system, cases must be reviewed by the public prosecutor's office within 24 hours of an arrest. The prosecutor must determine that sufficient evidence exist to warrant prosecution. The prosecutor then turns the case over to the attorney general's office, which prepares a bill of indictment if satisfied that enough evidence exists to warrant prosecution. The accused is entitled to be represented by legal counsel. However, many defendants are unaware of this right and fail to exercise it. The Law of Criminal Procedure specifies court appointment of lawyers for defendants who cannot obtain their own lawyers if the potential sentence is execution or life imprisonment. Judges are selected by a board composed of the chief prosecutor, two members of the courts of Amman, Jerusalem and Irbid; the inspector-general of the Royal Courts; and the under secretary of justice.

The corrections system includes 25 prisons under the Public Security Directorate, with a central prison at Amman.

HEALTH INDICATORS

Health personnel 1987
- Physicians: 4,500
  - persons per: 632
- Dentists: 1,041
- Nurses and midwives: 2,596
- Pharmacists: 800

Hospitals 1987
- Number: 56
- Number of beds (/10,000): 20
- Admissions/discharges (/10,000): 1,061
- Bed occupancy rate (%): 61.8
- Average length of stay (days): 4

Type of hospital (%) 1987
- Government: 39.0
- Private nonprofit and private profit: 61.0

Public health expenditures (latest)
- As % of national budget: 5.4
- Per capita (U.S. $): 41.10

Vital statistics
- Crude death rate (/1,000): 5 (1990)
- Life expectancy at birth 1990
  - Males: 68
  - Females: 71
- Infant mortality rate (/1,000 live births): 55 (1990)
- Child mortality rate under 5 yrs. (/1,000 births) (1985–90): 57
- Population with access to safe water (%): 96 (latest)

LAW ENFORCEMENT

Jordan has a national police force divided into metropolitan, rural (horse-mounted) and desert (camel-mounted). The head of law enforcement is the director-general of public security.

The most common crimes are those against property rather than persons. In remote areas crimes are often settled privately without the intervention of the criminal justice system.

Countersubversion is the most important activity of internal security forces and is considered vital to the survival of the regime.

HEALTH

Although medical services are located mainly in cities and large towns, the government has attempted to bring modern medical care to rural areas. The major health problems are trachoma, intestinal parasites and skin inflammations. The incidence of malaria and tuberculosis has been greatly reduced.

FOOD & NUTRITION

The staple Jordanian diet consists of bread, leben or yogurt, olives, cheese and fruits. Olive oil and samin, or clarified butter, are used with almost all kinds of food. Tea is the favorite drink. Per capita food intake is 2,882 calories (117% of requirements).

MEDIA & CULTURE

Jordan has five daily newspapers and four nondailies. Only one newspaper is independent, and *The Jordan Times* is the only English-language daily. Periodicals include 41 titles with a combined circulation of 211,000 copies.

Under the Press Law of 1967 official control was established over the press. All newspapers have to apply for licensing. There is no prepublication censorship, but most papers have been suspended at times for printing stories considered objectionable by the

MEDIA INDICATORS

Newspapers
- Number of dailies: 5 (latest)
- Circulation (000): 85 (latest)
- Per 1,000 pop.: 65 (latest)
- Number of nondailies: 4 (1984)
- Circulation (000): 2 (1984)
- Per 1,000 pop.: 1 (1984)
- Number of periodicals: 41 (1984)

Circulation (millions): 211 (1984)
- Newsprint consumption 1988
  - Total metric tons: 8,900
  - Per million pop. (kg.): 2.255

Radio
- Number of transmitters: 15 (1989)
- Number of persons per radio receiver: 4.4 (1989)

Television
- Television transmitters: 8 (1989)
- Number of persons per T.V. receiver: 12 (1989)

Cinema
- Number of fixed cinemas: 41 (pre-1986)
- Seating capacity (000): 20 (pre-1986)
- Annual attendance (millions): 15.0 (pre-1986)

Films
- Number of long films produced: 31 (latest)
- Number of long films imported: 438 (1983)
  - % from United States: 30.8
  - % from Italy: 19.4
  - % from India: 11.4
  - % from Hong Kong: 6.8

CULTURAL & ENVIRONMENTAL INDICATORS

Libraries (latest)
- Number: 65
- Volumes (000): 140
- Registered borrowers (000): 7
- Loans (/1,000 pop.): 16

Museums (pre-1986)
- Annual attendance (000): 147
- Attendance (/1,000 pop.): 58

Performing arts (pre-1986)
- Number of performances: 64
- Annual attendance (000): 180
- Attendance (/1,000 pop.): 84

Nature reserves (latest)
- Number of facilities: 2

government. The government has the right to confiscate all publications that attack religion, offend national dignity or public morality, or disturb public order. In 1973 the government launched an official newspaper, *al-Rai*, as a government mouthpiece. Jordan ranks 64th in the world in press freedom; it is scaled at −.51 (on an index with +4 as the maximum and −4 as the minimum).

The national news agency is the state-owned Jordan News Agency, founded in 1965.

The principal distributor of foreign and domestic books is the Jordanian Press and Publishing Company, in which the government has a 25% interest. Jordan does not adhere to any copyright convention.

The government-owned Jordan Radio and Television Corporation broadcasts for 90 hours weekly in Arabic and English.

The largest library in Jordan is the University of Jordan Library, with 100,000 volumes.

SOCIAL WELFARE

Public welfare in Jordan traditionally has been provided, as in most Muslim countries, by family, tribe or religious institution and not by the state. The Islamic alms tax, the *zakat*, has been converted, however, into a social welfare tax, and part of its proceeds is used to finance family welfare and rehabilitation of the handicapped. The principal state agency connected with social welfare is the Department of Social Affairs. Its work is supplemented by over 140 philanthropic agencies, including UNRWA. The social security legislation of 1978 provides pensions and distributes payments and medical treatment for job-related illness or injury.

GLOSSARY

diwan khas: Special Council which interprets the constitutionality of laws.

hadar: urban or sedentary Arabs, as distinguished from nomads.

hamula: clan or lineage consisting of a number of extended families.

harah: an urban quarter inhabited exclusively by one type of ethnic group.

iradah: royal decree.

kuttab: traditional village school, usually attached to a mosque.

Majlis al-Ayaan: Council of Notables, upper house of the Legislature.

Majlis al-Nuwwab: Council of Deputies, lower house of the Legislature.

Majlis al-Ummah: national parliament.

mukhtar: village headman.

nawahin: subdistrict.

qada: division of a province.

raiyyah: partly sedentary Arabs who are nomadic only during winter.

ruhhal: nomadic Arabs, especially as distinguished from the urban or settled Arabs.

CHRONOLOGY (from 1946)

1946— Kingdom of Transjordan is established, with Abdullah as king.

1948— Jordan invades Palestine in Arab-Israeli war and captures Old Jerusalem and the West Bank; a truce with Israel is reached under auspices of U.N. Truce Supervisory Organization—Palestine (UNTSOP); Jordan annexes West Bank.

1949— Transjordan is renamed Jordan. . . . United States recognizes government. . . . U.N. admission is vetoed by USSR.

1950— Administration headed by Prime Minister Tewfik Abul Huda yields to Prime Minister Said Pasha el-Mufti who later is succeeded by Samir Pasha Rifai.

1951— Abdullah is assassinated; his son Talal is named king. . . . Abul Huda is appointed prime minister; new elections are held.

1952— Talal is deposed in favor of his son Hussein, who is declared king.

1953— Hussein is crowned; Fawzi el-Mulki is named the new prime minister.

1954— El-Mulki government falls; Abul Huda forms cabinet.

1955— El-Mufti forms a government for a few months; other brief governments follow, headed by Hazza al-Majali and Ibrahim Hashim. . . . Jordan is admitted to the United Nations.

1956— Samir Rifai and Suleiman Nabulsi are prime ministers. . . . Glubb Pasha is ousted as Arab Legion commander; Arab Legion becomes Jordan Arab Army. . . . British ties are loosened. . . . Elections are held; leftist gains are reflected in Nabulsi cabinet.

1957— Nabulsi, after a conflict with the king over radical and pro-Soviet policies, is ousted and replaced by Hussein el-Khalidi; nationalists and Communists organize a general strike; Army Chief Abu Nuwar attempts a coup and is ousted and exiled; Hussein rides out the crisis with the help of a loyal army. . . . All political parties are banned. . . . Abdul Halim el-Nimr and Hashim head new cabinets.

1958— Rifai is named prime minister. . . . Relations with the United Arab Republic (UAR) are broken.

1959— Majali replaced Rifai as prime minister. . . . UAR ties are resumed.

1960— Majali is assassinated; Bahjat al-Talhouni becomes prime minister.
1962— Wasfi al-Tal becomes prime minister.
1963— Tal resigns and is replaced by Samir Rifai, who is later succeeded by Sherif Hussein ben Nasser. . . . Relations with the UAR, Iraq, Syria and other radical Arab nations worsen.
1964— Talhouni replaces Nasser as prime minister.
1965— Hasan is named crown prince.
1966— Nasser becomes prime minister.
1967— Arab-Israeli war results in loss of the West Bank to Israel; Hussein takes personal control of the army. . . . New Council of Representatives is elected. . . . Saad Jumaa and Talhouni serve as prime ministers.
1969— Talhouni quits; Abdel Moneim Rifai becomes prime minister.
1970— Civil war with the Palestinian guerrillas erupts; guerrillas are suppressed as fighting ends following Hussein-Yasser Arafat truce.
1971— Fighting with Palestinian commandos resumes; Jordanian forces crush the Palestinians after days of heavy fighting; Prime Minister Tal is assassinated in Cairo and is replaced by Ahmed al-Lowzi. . . . Jordanian National Union is founded as the country's sole political party.
1972— Jordanian National Union is renamed Arab National Union.
1973— Lowzi quits and is succeeded by Zaid al-Rifai. . . . Palestinian commandos receive amnesty.
1974— National Assembly is dissolved. . . . Hussein relinquishes right to the West Bank at Rabat Conference.
1976— Arab National Union is dissolved. . . . Rifai resigns and is succeeded briefly by Mudar Badran.
1977— Queen Alia and Health Minister Muhammad al-Bashir die in helicopter crash after inspecting hospital at Tafileh.
1978— Hussein creates National Consultative Council of 60 appointed members; Jordan rejects Egyptian-Israeli peace initiatives; Hussein meets with Arafat to demonstrate solid front against Egypt.
1979— Prime minister Mudar Badran resigns and is replaced by Sharif Abd al-Hamid Sharaf; Sharaf cabinet includes six West Bank Palestinians and, for the first time in Jordanian history, a woman; Egypt breaks diplomatic relations with Jordan; Hussein accuses the Carter Administration of "arm-twisting" to gain Jordan's support for the Egyptian-Israeli Peace Treaty.
1980— Prime Minister Sharaf dies of a heart attack; Hussein names Kassem al-Rimawi as interim prime minister, and on the latter's resignation brings back Mudar Badran, a former prime minister, to head the cabinet. . . . Jordan lends active aid to Iraq in Iran-Iraq war; Jordan and Syria come to the brink of armed conflict but are restrained by Saudi Arabia.
1983— Jordan backs Yasser Arafat faction against Syria.
1984— National Consultative Council is dissolved and National Assembly is reconvened. . . . Diplomatic ties are reestablished with Egypt and broken with Libya. . . . Jordanian embassy in Tripoli, Libya burned down. Hussein holds talks with Arafat.
1985— Prime Minister Badran is replaced by Zaid al-Rifai.
1986— King Hussein servers political links with the PLO.
1987— King Hussein arranges the first summit meeting of the Arab League in eight years.
1988— King Hussein declares unconditional support for the intifada and insists that the PLO is the sole representative of the Palestinians. Jordan severs all legal and administrative links with the West Bank and recognizes the independent state of Palestine.
1989— Serious rioting follows government imposed price rises on basic goods and services. Opposition groups win the majority of seats in the House of Representatives.
1990— King Hussein is slow in condemning the Iraqi invasion of Kuwait and works through the fall for an "Arab solution" to the problem. Jordan is overwhelmed by refugees fleeing occupied Kuwait. Frequent public demonstrations occur in support of Iraq.
1991— King Hussein condemns the ground offensive to liberate Kuwait and appeals for a cease-fire.

BIBLIOGRAPHY

BOOKS

American University. *Area Handbook for the Hashemite Kingdom of Jordan.* Washington, D.C., 1974.

Antoun, Richard, *Arab Village.* Bloomington, IN. 1972.

———. *Low-Key Politics: A Case Study of Local-Level Leadership and Change in the Middle East.* Albany, NY, 1979.

Aresvik, Oddvar. *The Agricultural Development of Jordan.* New York, 1976.

Bailey, Clinton. *Jordan's Palestinian Challenge, 1948–83.* Boulder, CO, 1985.

Bull, Vivian A. *The West Bank—Is It Viable?* Lexington, MA, 1975.

Cordesman, Anthony H. *Jordanian Arms and the Middle East Balance.* Washington, D.C., 1983.

Dann, Uriel. *Studies in the History of Transjordan.* Boulder, CO, 1984.

Faddah, M. I. *The Middle East in Transition: A Study of Jordan's Foreign Policy.* New York, 1974.

Gubser, Peter. *Jordan.* Boulder, CO, 1982.

Johnston, Charles. *The Brink of Jordan.* London, 1972.

Kanovsky, Eliahu. *The Economic Development of Jordan.* New Brunswick, NJ, 1976.

Lunt, James. *Hussein of Jordan: a Political Biography.* London, 1989.

Lustick, Ian. *Israel and Jordan: Implications of an Adversarial Partnership.* Berkeley, CA, 1978.

Mazur, Michael P. *Economic Growth and Development in Jordan.* Boulder, Co, 1979.

Middle East Economic Digest. *Jordan.* Boulder, CO, 1983.

Mishal, Shaul. *West Bank, East Bank: The Palestinians in Jordan, 1949–67.* New Haven, CT, 1978.

Plascov, A. O. *The Palestinian Refugees in Jordan, 1948–57.* London, 1981.

Seccombe, Ian J. *Jordan* (World Bibliographical Series). Boulder, CO, 1985.

Sinai, Anne, and Allen Pollack. *The Hashemite Kingdom of Jordan and the West Bank.* New York, 1977.

Snow, Peter. *Hussein: A Biography.* London, 1972.

OFFICIAL PUBLICATIONS

Central Bank. *Annual Report* (Arabic and English).

———. *Monthly Statistical Bulletin* (Arabic and English).

Finance Ministry. *Annual Report of Revenue and Expenditure. Budget Law* (Arabic and English).

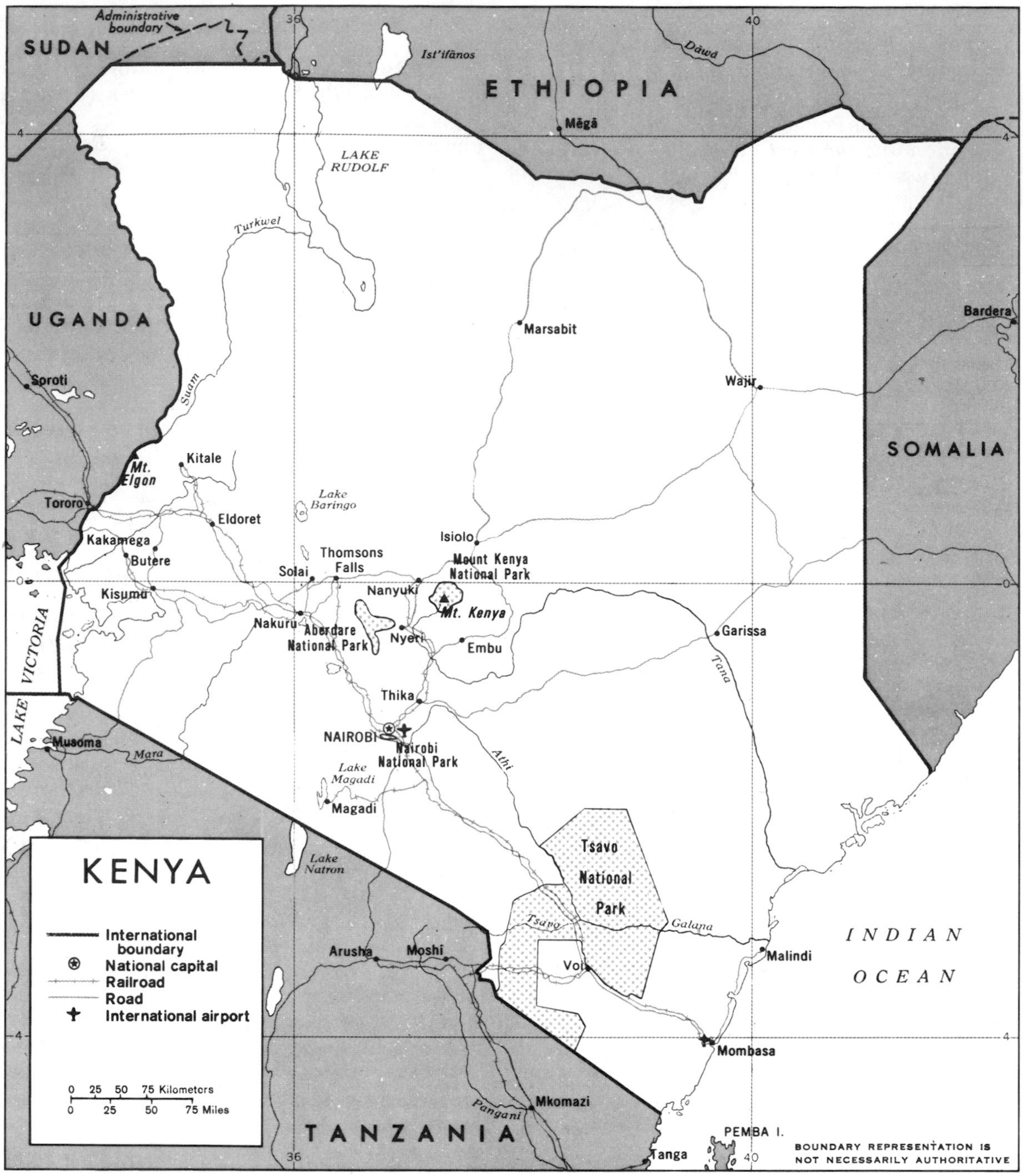

KENYA

International boundary
National capital
Railroad
Road
International airport

0 25 50 75 Kilometers
0 25 50 75 Miles

SUDAN
ETHIOPIA
UGANDA
SOMALIA
TANZANIA
INDIAN OCEAN
Administrative boundary
Ist'ifānos
Dawa
Mēgā
LAKE RUDOLF
Turkwel
Marsabit
Bardera
Wajir
Soroti
Suam
Kitale
Mt. Elgon
Tororo
Lake Baringo
Eldoret
Isiolo
Kakamega
Butere
Thomsons Falls
Solai
Mount Kenya National Park
Kisumu
Nanyuki
Mt. Kenya
Nakuru
Aberdare National Park
Nyeri
Embu
Garissa
LAKE VICTORIA
Tana
Thika
Musoma
NAIROBI
Nairobi National Park
Mara
Athi
Lake Magadi
Magadi
Tsavo National Park
Lake Natron
Tsavo
Galana
Arusha
Moshi
Voi
Malindi
Mombasa
Mkomazi
Pangani
PEMBA I.
Tanga
36
40
4
0
BOUNDARY REPRESENTATION IS NOT NECESSARILY AUTHORITATIVE

KENYA

BASIC FACT SHEET

OFFICIAL NAME: Republic of Kenya
ABBREVIATION: KE
CAPITAL: Nairobi
HEAD OF STATE & HEAD OF GOVERNMENT: President Daniel Teroitich arap Moi (from 1978)
NATURE OF GOVERNMENT: One-party modified democracy
POPULATION: 24,639,261 (1990)
AREA: 582,646 sq. km. (224,960 sq. mi.)
ETHNIC MAJORITY: Kikuyu, Luo, Luhya, Kamba and Kalenjin
LANGUAGES: English and Swahili
RELIGIONS: Christianity, animism and Muslim
UNIT OF CURRENCY: Kenya shilling; the Kenya pound is only a unit of account
NATIONAL FLAG: Black, red and green horizontal stripes in descending order separated by narrow white bands. In the center are a warrior's shield and crossed spears.
NATIONAL EMBLEM: The principal elements of the national coat of arms are two gold lions holding two crossed spears; an oval shield with the colors of the national flag; a white cockerel holding an ax, and the national motto, *Harambee* (Let Us Pull Together), at the bottom.
NATIONAL ANTHEM: "O God of All Creation"
NATIONAL HOLIDAYS: December 12 (National Day, Independence Day); January 1 (New Year's Day): May 1 (Labor Day): June 1 (Madaraka [Self-Government] Day); October 20 (Kenyatta Day); December 25 (Christmas); December 26 (Boxing Day). Also, variable Christian festivals such as Good Friday and Easter.
NATIONAL CALENDAR: Gregorian
PHYSICAL QUALITY OF LIFE INDEX: 58
DATE OF INDEPENDENCE: December 12, 1963
DATE OF CONSTITUTION: 1963 (amended in 1964 and 1967)
WEIGHTS & MEASURE: Imperial and metric

GEOGRAPHICAL FEATURES

Kenya lies astride the equator in eastern Africa between the Indian Ocean and Lake Victoria and has a total area of 582,646 sq. km. (224,960 sq. mi.), including 13,393 sq. km. (5,171 sq. mi.) of Lake Turkona (Lake Rudolf) and Lake Victoria. Kenya's maximum length south-southwest to north-northwest is 1,131 km. (703 mi.) and its maximum width east-northeast to west-southwest is 1,025 km. (637 mi.). The total length of the Indian Ocean coastline is 523 km. (325 mi.).

The length of Kenya's international land borders is 3,446 km. (2,142 mi.), shared with five neighbors: Sudan (306 km.; 190 mi.); Ethiopia (779 km., 484 mi.); Somalia (682 km.; 424 mi.) Tanzania (769 km.; 478 mi.); and Uganda (772 km.; 480 mi.). The border between Kenya and Sudan dates back to 1926, when part of the northeastern Uganda Protectorate was transferred to Kenya Colony. In 1931 an administrative line known as the Red Line was delineated between Sudan and Kenya following the northern limit of the Turkana grazing land. The border with Ethiopia, long disputed, was settled in 1970 when a border treaty was signed by the heads of the two states. The border with Somalia was established under the secret Anglo-Italian Treaty of 1924, which transferred 95,052 sq. km. (36,700 sq. mi.) to the Italian protectorate but still left sizable Somali tribal territories within Kenya. The border with Tanzania was fixed by the Anglo-German treaties of 1886 and 1914. The western border was fixed as an inter-territorial boundary in 1926 and incorporates territories within Uganda until then. This border was the subject of a dispute with Uganda in the early 1970s. The only current border dispute is with Somalia, which has pressed irredentist claims over Northeastern Province.

The capital is Nariobi, with a 1983 population of 1,103,600. Mombasa, the chief seaport, has a population of 425,606. The other major urban centers are Machakos (92,300), Kisumu (167,100) and Nakuru (101,700).

Topographically the country may be divided into seven regions. The coastal strip, or Temborari, is 3 to 16 km. (2 to 10 mi.) wide except in the valleys of the main rivers. The shoreline is broken by bays and branching creeks that separate the mainland from the islands Lamu, Manda and Patta (the Lami Archipelago). Beyond the coastal plain the country rises in well-defined steps to an altitude of over 300 m. (1,000 ft.) and a relatively featureless plain known as Nyika, a bushland of mostly thornscrub; and the Tana Plains, whose main feature is the Lorian Swamp. About 480 km. (300 mi.) inland the plains give way in the southwest to the Eastern Plateau region, with an average elevation of 300 m. (1,000 ft.) to 900 m. (3,000 ft.). This region includes the Amboseli, Serengeti and Aruba plains, and the Chyulu Range and Taita Hills, which rise to over 2,100 m. (7,000 ft.).

The vast Northern Plains lands region, forming three-fifths of the country, stretches from Somalia in the East to Uganda in the West. This region is a series of arid plains and includes Kenya's only true desert, Chalbi Desert. To the east of Lake Turkana rise Mounts Kulal (2,381 m.; 7,812 ft.) and Marsabit (1,695 m.; 5,561 ft.), with the Rendile Plains to the south. The Kenya Highlands region in the west-central part consists of two major divisions east and west of the Rift Valley. It also is known as the White Highlands because of the former concentration of European-owned estates in the area. This regions includes Mount Kenya (5,199 m.; 17,058 ft.); Mount Niandarawa (3,906 m.; 12,816 ft.); Mount Elgon (4,321 m.; 14,178 ft.); and the Aberdare Range, with the Kinangop Plateau to the south. The Rift Valley, which extends from Lake Turkana in the North into Tanzania, varies in width from 50 to 65 km. (30 to 40 mi.). Its floor is 450 m. (1,500 ft.) above sea level in the North, 1,900 m. (6,200 ft.) in the center and 610 m. (2,000 ft.) in the South. The eastern wall of the rift is marked by steep escarpments, while the western wall rises more gradually, to the Mau Range (3,002 m.; 9,848 ft.), the Elgeyo Escarpment and the Cherangani Hills (over 2,743 m.; 9,000 ft.). To the west of Elgeyo is the treeless plain of Uasin Gishu and the Kericho Highlands (1,800 to 2,300m.; 6,000 to 7,500 ft.). The basin of the Rift Valley consists of a series of extinct volcanoes and a chain of lakes with no outlets: Naivasha, Elementeita, Nakuri, Hannington (renamed Bogoria) and Magadi.

The Western Plateau region descends in a gentle slope to Lake Victoria and is cut in half by Winam Bay (formerly Kavirondo Gulf). South of the bay are the Kano Plain and the Gwasi and Homa mountains.

Kenya's principal rivers rise in the highlands and radiate eastward to the Indian Ocean, westward to Lake Victoria, or northward to Lake Turkana. The two largest rivers, Tana and Galana (also known as Athi or Sabaki), flow into the Indian Ocean. The Tana River is navigable for about 325 km. (200 mi.) and the Galana for about 160 km. (100 mi.). South of the Galana is the Goshi River (also called Voi), which is perennial for only about 80 km. (50 mi.). Of the rivers that empty into Lake Victoria the largest are the Nzoia (257 km.; 160 mi.), the Yala (177 km.; 110 mi.) and the Mara (160 km.; 100 mi).

CLIMATE & WEATHER

Although Kenya is on the equator, it has a varied climate. Seasons are distinguished by duration of rainfall rather than changes in temperature. In the Western Plateau and in the highlands rain falls in one long season, while east of the Rift Valley there are two distinct seasons: the long rains from March to May and the short rains from September to October. Rainfall is greatest in the highlands and on the coast, but over 70% of the country is arid or semi-arid, receiving less than 51 cm. (20 in.) a year. The rainfall also is erratic in the dry areas. The coast and the highlands receive an average of 101 cm. (40 in.) annually, while the Western Plateau receives over 178 cm. (70 in.).

Altitude is the major factor in variations in temperature changes among different parts of the country. The highlands generally have a cool and bracing climate, with a mean annual maximum of 26.1°C (79°F) and a mean annual minimum of 10°C (50°F). Nairobi, with an elevation of 1,670 m. (5,500 ft.), has a mean annual temperature of 19°C (67°F). The highest temperatures prevail in the Northern Plains, where the mean maximum is 34°C (93°F) and the absolute maximum often reaches 43.3°C (110°F). The temperature varies between 14°C (57°F) and 29°C (84°F) in the Eastern Plateau, between 34°C (93°F) and 17.8°C (64°F) in the lower plateau and between 27.8°C (82°F) and 21.1°C (70°F) in the coastal areas. The hottest months are January through March; June and July are the coldest months.

POPULATION

The population of Kenya in 1990 was estimated at 24,639,261, the basis of the last official census, in 1979, when the population was 15,327,061. The annual growth rate in population during 1989 was 4.2%, the highest in the world.

The southwestern quadrant, containing 10% of the land area, contains over 75% of the population. The main areas of concentration of population are Central Province in the eastern Kenya Highlands, the Lake Victoria area in Western and Nyanza provinces and the coastal zone around Mombasa. In the cultivated districts of these provinces density is over 386 per sq. km. (1,000 per sq. mi.). In the northern half of the country the density is less than 4 per sq. km. (10 per sq. mi.). The nationwide population density is 35 per sq. km. (90.6 sq. mi.), and the density in arable areas is 275.8 per sq. km. (714 per sq. mi.).

DEMOGRAPHIC INDICATORS

Population (millions): 24.639 (1990)
Year of last census: 1979
Sex distribution (% at last census): males, 49.7; females, 50.3
Population estimates and projections (millions)

1940: 4.470	1970: 11.225	2000: 37.505
1950: 6.018	1980: 16.667	2010: 56.629
1960: 8.115	1990: 24.872	

Age profile (% at last census)

0–14: 51.4	30–44: 13.2	60–74: 3.0
15–29: 24.8	45–59: 7.0	75 and over: 0.6

Median age (yrs.): 14.5 (1985)
Youth population (% age 15–24): 18.5 (1985); 19.6 (2000)
Total dependency ratio: 118.6 (1985)
Annual growth rate (%)

1950–55: 2.75	1975–80: 3.82	2000–2005: 3.70
1955–60: 2.95	1980–85: 4.04	2005–2010: 3.35
1960–65: 3.14	1985–90: 4.22	2010–2015: 2.85
1965–70: 3.30	1990–1995: 4.10	2015–2020: 2.43
1970–75: 3.56	1995–2000: 3.95	2020–2025: 2.17

Hypothetical size of stationary population (millions): 113
Assumed year of reaching net reproduction rate of 1: 2035
Urban population (millions): 4.002 (1985)
Urban population (%): 22 (1988); 9 (1965)
Annual urban population growth rate (%, 1985–90): 7.84
Annual rural population growth rate (%, 1985–90): 3.22
Percentage of urban population in largest city: 57
Percentage of urban population in cities of population over 500,000: 57 (1980)
Number of cities of population over 500,000: 1 (1980)
Population density per sq. km. (per sq. mi.): 42.7 (110.6) (latest)

VITAL STATISTICS

Crude birth rate (/1,000): 45 (1990); 52 (1965)
Crude death rate (/1,000): 7 (1990); 20 (1965)
Infant mortality rate (/1,000 live births): 60 (1990)
Maternal mortality rate (/100,000 live births): 168 (1986–87 est.)
Life expectancy (yrs.) at birth: males, 62; females, 67 (1990)
Gross reproduction rate (/woman) (1980–85): 4.00
Total fertility rate (/woman): 42.0 (1989–90)
Average household size: 6.2

There are 47 urban centers in Kenya with a population of over 2,000. There are only two cities—Nairobi and Mombasa—with populations of over 100,000. Nairobi itself accounts for 57% of the urban population. There are two other cities with populations between 20,000 and 100,000, seven cities with populations between 10,000 and 19,999, a total of 11 cities with populations between 5,000 and 9,999 and 25 cities with populations between 2,000 and 4,999. Asian, Arab and European minorities are overwhelmingly urban, but only 16.6% of the African population is urban. Through a relatively recent phenomenon, urbanization has resulted in significant shifts in population. The rate of urban growth is 7.84% compared to the national growth rate of 4.12%. Nairobi and Mombasa absorb most of the rural migrants seeking employment. A vast majority (67% in Mombasa and 70% in Nairobi) of urban residents live in slums and squatter settlements. Nairobi's slum population has grown to 70% from just 19% in 1965.

Until independence Kenya had a net gain in population through immigration. The position was reversed from 1964 as Europeans left Kenya. By 1967 approximately 70,000 Kenyan residents had opted for British citizenship, but the majority of them were Asians who had been denied physical entry into the United Kingdom. Kenya's 70,000-member Asian community directly accounts for approximately one-fourth of Kenya's total economic output. African resentment of Asians, primarily because of their extensive business holdings, has intensified in direct proportion to Kenya's economic decline. Kenya's Africanization campaign to encourage black African participation in commercial interests has resulted in some Asian emigration and disinvestment and has prompted concern within the community for the security of Asian ownership. The largest Kenyan expatriate community is in neighboring Uganda.

STATUS OF WOMEN INDICATORS

Number of women (millions): 1.708 (1985)
Women of childbearing age (15–49) (% of pop.): 41 (1988)
Married women of childbearing age (15–49) using contraception (%): 17 (1986)
Women's literacy rate (%): 49.2 (1988)
Women in labor force (%): 40.3 (1988)
Total fertility rate (/woman): 6.5 (1990)

Kenya's National Family Planning Program, announced in 1967, was the first such effort in Africa south of the Sahara. Since then the government and the private Family Planning Association have pursued vigorous policies designed to reduce population growth through voluntary means. Family planning services are provided on a daily basis at 400 rural centers and 17 mobile clinics under the auspices of the National Family Welfare Center. The clinics provide information, oral contraceptives and IUDs (supplied by the Swedish International Development Authority) free of charge. By 1984 the government had reduced maternal mortality by 46% and infant mortality by 30% through rural health programs and rural-urban balance.

Women constitute an essential factor in Kenya's labor equation. They still provide about three-quarters of Kenya's farm labor while carrying out their traditional familial responsibilities. Because of an accelerating rural outmigration of males to the cities in search of difficult-to-find but higher-paying jobs, female farm labor is likely to maintain its prominent position. Several of Kenya's tribes still practice female circumcision. The Kenyan government, however, has made a major effort to eliminate the practice. President Moi has publicly and repeatedly condemned female circumcision, and the Ministry of Health has forbidden such operations to be performed in government facilities.

ETHNIC COMPOSITION

No ethnic group is numerically dominant in Kenya. The largest, the Kikuyu, constitutes only 20% of the population, while the five largest—Kikuyu, Luo, Luhya, Kamba and Kalenjin—constitute 70%. The 32 major indigenous African groups constitute 97.58% of the population. The African population also may be divided into three broad linguistic and cultural groups: Bantu, Paranilotic and Cushitic.

Of these groups, the Kikuyu, who were most actively involved in the independence and Mau Mau movements, are represented disproportionately in all areas of public life, government, business and the professions. The Luo are mainly traders and artisans. The Kamba are overrepresented in the defense services and law enforcement forces. The Kalenjin are mainly farmers.

The principle ethnic minorities are the Asians and the Arabs. The Asians are descendants of Indian and Pakistani settlers; 70% are from Gujarat, 20% from the Punjab and 10% from Goa. Indians form a closed and cohesive community but are divided by religion into Muslims, Hindus, Sikhs and Roman Catholics. Before independence Asians constituted a prosperous middle class composed of merchants, artisans and professionals. After 1963 their future became uncertain. Of the 139,037 Asians, over 60,000 opted for Kenyan citizenship, while the rest were granted British passports but not British citizenship. Thus the Asian community itself became divided into Kenyan Asians and non-Kenyan Asians. The Indian community also faced considerable African hostility; they were attacked for controlling most of the small-scale trade and competing with the native Africans for middle-level positions, putting the government under pressure to expel the Asians for economic reasons. The government pursued a policy

ETHNIC GROUPS OF KENYA

Group	%	Language Group	Area or Province
Kikuyu	20.12	Bantu	Central
Luo	13.91	Nilotic	Nyanza
Luhya	13.28	Bantu	Western
Kamba	10.95	Bantu	Eastern
Kalenjin	10.88	Paranilotic	Rift Valley
Kisii	6.41	Bantu	Nyanza
Meru	5.07	Bantu	Eastern
Mijikenda	4.76	Bantu	Coast
Somali	2.29	Cushitic	North-eastern
Turkana	1.86	Paranilotic	Rift Valley
Masai	1.42	Paranilotic	Rift Valley
Embu	1.08	Bantu	Eastern
Taita	1.00	Bantu	Coast
Iteso	0.78	Paranilotic	Western
Kuria	0.54	Bantu	Nyanza
Samburu	0.50	Paranilotic	Rift Valley
Tharaka	0.45	Bantu	Eastern
Mbere	0.45	Bantu	Eastern
Pokomo	0.32	Bantu	Coast
Boran	0.31	Cushitic	Eastern
Bajun	0.22	Bantu	Coast
Nderobo	0.19	Paranilotic	Rift Valley
Rendille	0.17	Cushitic	Eastern
Orma	0.15	Cushitic	Coast
Gabbra	0.15	Cushitic	Eastern
Swahili-Shirazi	0.09	Bantu	Coast
Njemps	0.06	Paranilotic	Rift Valley
Taveta	0.06	Bantu	Coast
Sakuya	0.04	Cushitic	Eastern
Boni and Sanye	0.07	Cushitic	Coast

of moderation and gradualism motivated by a general desire to maintain economic stability and a realization that Asian skills and assets were needed in Kenya until alternatives could be found. The expulsion of 80,000 Asians from Uganda in 1972 intensified the pressure to speed the departure of non-Kenyan Asians. Under the Trade Licensing Act noncitizens were denied special permits to own or manage commercial establishments. Under British immigration laws about 3,000 Asians from East Africa are being admitted to the United Kingdom every year.

Over 99% of the 27,886 Arab residents have Kenyan citizenship, speak Swahili rather than Arabic and generally identify themselves with Africans. Almost all the Kenyan Arabs live in Coast Province, more than half of them in Mombasa. Non-Kenyan Arabs are called Shirini and mainly are petty traders from Yemen.

Kenya has one of the largest European communities in present-day Africa. Nearly 23% of the Americans there are missionaries, and the rest either worked with the official family planning programs or the Peace Corps or served in U.S. firms operating in the country. Europeans are still employed by the government and effectively control the industries, banks and the media. At the time of the 1969 census, 10% of Europeans had adopted Kenyan citizenship.

Kenyan attitudes toward Westerners have evolved over the years from resentment to respect based on interdependence and common interests. Kenya remains one of the staunchest pro-Western nations in Africa and actively fosters cultural, social and economic contacts with the West.

Interethnic rivalries among Kenya's numerous groups have obstructed national integration. The main ethnic problems are Kikuyu dominance in politics and commerce, Somali separatism and the conflict between the inland cultures and the Swahili cultures of the coast.

LANGUAGES

The official languages of Kenya are English and Swahili. Swahili, which was declared the co-official language in 1974, is the mother tongue of only a small group of people, notably the Swahili-Shirazi, Kenyan Arabs, some Mijikenda and the Pokomo. It is a Bantu language modified by contact with Arabic and incorporates words from Arabic, Hindi, Persian and English. Seven dialects and three subdialects of Swahili are spoken in Kenya, but the preferred standard for spoken Swahili is Kiunguja, the dialect of Mombasa. Written Swahili uses a Latin alphabet and is known as East African Standard. Europeans speak a form of kitchen Swahili known as Kisettla, while Asians use a form known as Kihindi. Swahili is almost universally used in small-scale trade, the media and secondary schools.

Over 30 distinct languages and dialect clusters are spoken in Kenya. They are broadly grouped into three categories: Bantu, Cushitic, and Paranilotic. Linguistic differences reinforce ethnic boundaries, and none of the African languages is used for intergroup communications. Bantu is spoken by 65% of the population, Cushitic by 4%, and Paranilotic by 31%. Each of these groups subsumes a number of dialect clusters.

Asians speak any of a number of Indian languages—depending on the state or origin—including Punjabi, Gujarati and Konkani. Hindustani is used as a lingua franca.

Asians speak any of a number of Indian languages—depending on the state of origin—including Punjabi, Gujarati and Konkani. Hindustani is used as a lingua franca.

English is the language of big business, higher education and government, with most bills being drafted in English in the National Assembly. The mass media consists of a mix of African dialects and English. Radio service is in Swahili, English and various African dialects. Television broadcasts and print materials are in Swahili and English.

RELIGION

As of 1989, almost 70% of the population was Christian (38% Protestant, 28% Catholic), about a quarter was of indigenous faiths and 6% was Muslim. Islam is practiced by both the Arab and Indian communities with some Hindu worship practiced by the latter group. Also important for East Africa is the Bahá'í faith. Numbers, however, fail to reflect the persistence and pervasiveness of indigenous and traditional beliefs even among those professing Christianity or Islam.

Christian missionary activity, which began in the late 19th century, achieved great successes among the major tribes—the Kikuyu, Luo, Luhya, Embu, Meru and Kisii. Missions not only took an active role in developing health, education and agriculture but also helped to breach the structure and values of indigenous African societies. However, the association of missionaries with colonialism led to some opposition in the form of anti-European messianic cults, such as the Mumbo cult among the Luo and the Watu Wa Mungu (People of God) among the Kikuyu.

Most recently, President Moi threatened religious restrictions because of Kenyan church opposition to his government during the growth of the underground Mwakenya group in the mid-1980s and also because of Anglican Church officials' opposition to Moi's human rights abuses.

The Roman Catholic Church, with about 3.5 million adherents, is organized in 12 dioceses under the archbishop of Nairobi. The Protestant churches are linked together by the National Christian Council of Kenya.

Of the Kenyan Muslims, more than half are Somalis, while the rest belong to the Swahili, Bajun or Wajun groups. Some Mijikendas, Gallas and Pokomos also are Muslims. Some 25% of the Asians belong to four Muslim sects: the Khoja Ismaili sect headed by the Aga Khan, the Bohra, the Ithna Ashariyya and the Ahmadiyya. The Muslims are heavily represented in coastal areas and in cities but are relatively scarce in interior regions.

Hinduism is represented by Indian adherents from Gujarat and Punjab.

HISTORICAL BACKGROUND

Kenya's contacts with the West began with an exploratory visit to East Africa in 1948 by Vasco da Gama, who initiated 200 years of Portuguese rule. The Portuguese showed no particular interest in colonization, and their presence was virtually eliminated after Fort Jesus fell to Omani forces in 1699. European influence was renewed in 1888 when the privately financed Imperial British East Africa Company was granted a royal charter to administer the territories of Uganda and Kenya, assigned to Britain under the Anglo-German Agreement of 1886. The British crown took over the company in 1895 and established the East Africa Protectorate under the charge of a commissioner. Except for a revolt in 1895, the British were never seriously challenged for the next 57 years. British rule was intense and led to far-reaching social and economic changes. As one of the few colonies to attract British immigrants, Kenya had a substantial British community until independence; the White Highlands were largely owned by British farmers.

Continuing resentment among the Kikuyu to European appropriation of land led to the emergence in 1952 of the secret society known as Mau Mau. As the Mau Mau movement spread, a state of emergency was declared in 1952. By the time the emergency was lifted in 1959 over 79,000 Africans, including Jomo Kenyatta, had been detained and nearly 3,000 civilians had been killed. Meanwhile, significant constitutional progress had been made in introducing black majority rule in the country. The Lyttleton Constitution of 1954, the Lennox-Boyd Constitution of 1957 and the MacLeod Constitution of 1960 brought the Kenyans to the verge of self-government. The final step toward independence was a constitutional conference in London in 1962, under which a national government was formed, including representatives of all political parties. Power was transferred in 1963 to a largely pro-British elite who have helped to preserve the chief legacies of British rule: the legal, administrative and educational systems and the English language.

In June 1963, Kenyatta was appointed prime minister, and in December 1964, Kenya became an independent republic with Kenyatta as its first president. Breaking with Great Britain proved difficult for early attempts to buy-back European owned land for relocation of African peasants required British assistance. Repayment problems forced many into debt and the canceling of resettlement projects. But with the entrenchment of power by the political elite, land acquisition was given less importance.

In an attempt to keep the land reform issue alive, a socialist opposition group emerged in 1966, the Kenya People's Union (KPU), under leftist Ajuma Oginga Odinga. Fearing this opposition, Kenyatta used newly instituted security laws against KPU supporters; and in December 1966, in order to strengthen his parliamentary position, he merged the legislature into the single-chamber National Assembly. Nevertheless, KPU won limited seats in that year's parliamentary elections.

Unrest was also fomented by intra-ethnic rivalries which led to an uneven disbursement of lands, along with those outside of the Kikuyu tribe being given lesser government positions. Conflict within the KANU between Kikuyus and non-Kikuyus is believed to be the primary cause for the assassination in July 1969 of Tom Mboya, an opposition leader of the Luo clan. This led to the banning of KPU prior to the 1970 elections and a solidifying of Kenyatta's power base. At this point, the National Assembly was, to a great extent, under Kenyatta's private control. Corruption amongst those in power was criticized by the unofficial leader of the parliamentary opposition, Josiah Mwangi Kariuki, and was probably the cause for his assassination in March 1975.

President Kenyatta died in August 1978, and was replaced by Vice President Daniel arap Moi. In the November 1979 elections Moi was the only candidate. Odinga was allowed back into KANU, but his outspoken positions on Kenyatta's rule and corruption in the government disallowed his taking part in parliamentary elections and precipitated his expulsion from the party in early 1982. In June of that year, the National Assembly declared KANU to be the only legal party.

An increase in press censorship and political detentions were the immediate causes of an attempted coup in August 1982, by the Kenyan Air Force. The University of Nairobi was closed and Moi disbanded the Air Force which had consisted of some 2100 people. Of these about 650 were convicted of mutiny. Odinga was connected with the coup and put under house arrest.

Tensions continued into the following year as a cabinet member, Charles Njono (Minister for Constitutional Affairs), was accused by Moi of seeking leadership via foreign intervention. Njono was forced to resign his seat in June 1983. In September, with only 48% of the electorate in attendance, Moi was re-elected for a second term, unopposed. The country then entered a period of relative stability with Moi attempting, in 1984, to cut inefficiency and root out corruption in the government.

The following several years were accented by dissent; student unrest and pamphleteering led to the closing of the University of Nairobi. And great concern was evident in the government over the rise of the left-wing opposition group, Mwakenya (Swahili for Union of Nationalists to Liberate Kenya). Starting in March 1986 and continuing for 18 months, many were arrested, and accused of being connected with Mwakenya. Included in these arrests were university teachers, students and journalists. Many were given prison terms and accusations were made that some were tortured.

The secret ballot was replaced in 1986 by a sort of line-up voting for the preliminary stage of general election. The National Christian Council (NCCK) protested the new system on the grounds that voting would discourage those connected to government who required impartiality. Presidential power was further strengthened in December 1986 with a constitutional amendment which increased the president's influence over the civil service and the judiciary and included the power to dismiss the Attorney General without recourse.

Following mass arrests of so-called illegal aliens in March of 1987 and continued detention of dissidents, Kenya was accused of human rights violations by Amnesty International and the U.S. Police officers said to be responsible for brutality were dismissed, and Elijah Mwangale, Minister of Foreign Affairs, was forced out of office for not being strong enough in defending Kenya's record on human rights. Soon afterwards, it was announced that only members of KANU could vote. Former Vice President Oginga Odinga denounced the government and called for a multi-party system. In October, riots amongst Muslims and student arrests led to a re-closing of the University of Nairobi.

Discovery was made in 1987 that the country had suffered enormous foreign exchange loses due to illegal bank transactions and smuggling. This was followed by two banks being cut-off from foreign exchange dealing, and the accusation that members of the political elite had amassed huge fortunes despite the growing national poverty.

Anticipating the national elections in March 1988, Moi dissolved the National Assembly in February, and 10 political prisoners were released (one, Raila Odinga, son of the former Vice President was re-arrested in August 1988). In February 1988, Moi dismissed the formality of a public election and was summarily re-elected president. These elections were contested by Mwakenya and NCCK, which was met by a banning of a NCCK publication and its editor jailed for nine months. Criticism of the elections by the Minister of Transportation and Communication was soon followed by his resignation and expulsion from the KANU.

Constitutional amendments in July 1988 made it possible for the president to dismiss senior judges. In addition, detention without trial was allowed to be increased to 14 days from a previous 24 hours. The Church's criticism of the government's human rights record increased; threats were made to restrict religious freedoms and "roaming" foreigners were arrested for helping the Church to undermine the government.

Opposition to Moi's one-party rule grew during 1990. At the beginning of the year a loose coalition of politicians, churchmen, lawyers and human-rights activists—citing the examples of Eastern Europe and growing pro-democracy activism in other African nations—called for political pluralism and accused the Moi government of repression, corruption and election-rigging. In the months that followed, Moi allowed some public debate on the multiparty issue, but in June he announced that the debate was over and that the Kenyan people had unanimously backed KANU as the country's sole party. Security police cracked down on the opposition in July and supressed the rioting that followed. In December a national counference of KANU was held to show that Moi was responsive to political demands. It rejected a multiparty political system but restored the use of secret ballots for voting in primary elections. The conference did not address complaints about one-party rule.

CONSTITUTION & GOVERNMENT

The basis of the government of Kenya is the Constitution of 1963 as amended in 1964 and 1967. The amendment of 1964, called the republican Constitution, established a republican form of government with a strong executive and a strong central government. Thirteen sections of the Constitution, known as the bill of rights, protect the fundamental rights and freedoms of the individual, including property rights. Some of these freedoms were abridged in 1966 under a preventive detention law. The National Assembly is the supreme state organ in theory, as the president has no powers of veto.

The president is the head of state, the head of government (as prime minister) and commander in chief of the armed forces. He must command a majority vote in the National Assembly, and if he loses a vote of confidence must either resign or dissolve the Assembly and call for new elections. The president is elected by popular vote at general elections for a term of five years. He also must be an elected member of the National Assembly and is entitled to attend its meetings and vote on bills. The vice president is the president's principal assistant and also his successor if the office of the presidency becomes vacant in midterm. The vice president is appointed by the president from among members of the National Assembly and may be removed by the president.

The cabinet consists of the president, the vice president and other ministers, who are collectively responsible to the National Assembly. As members of the

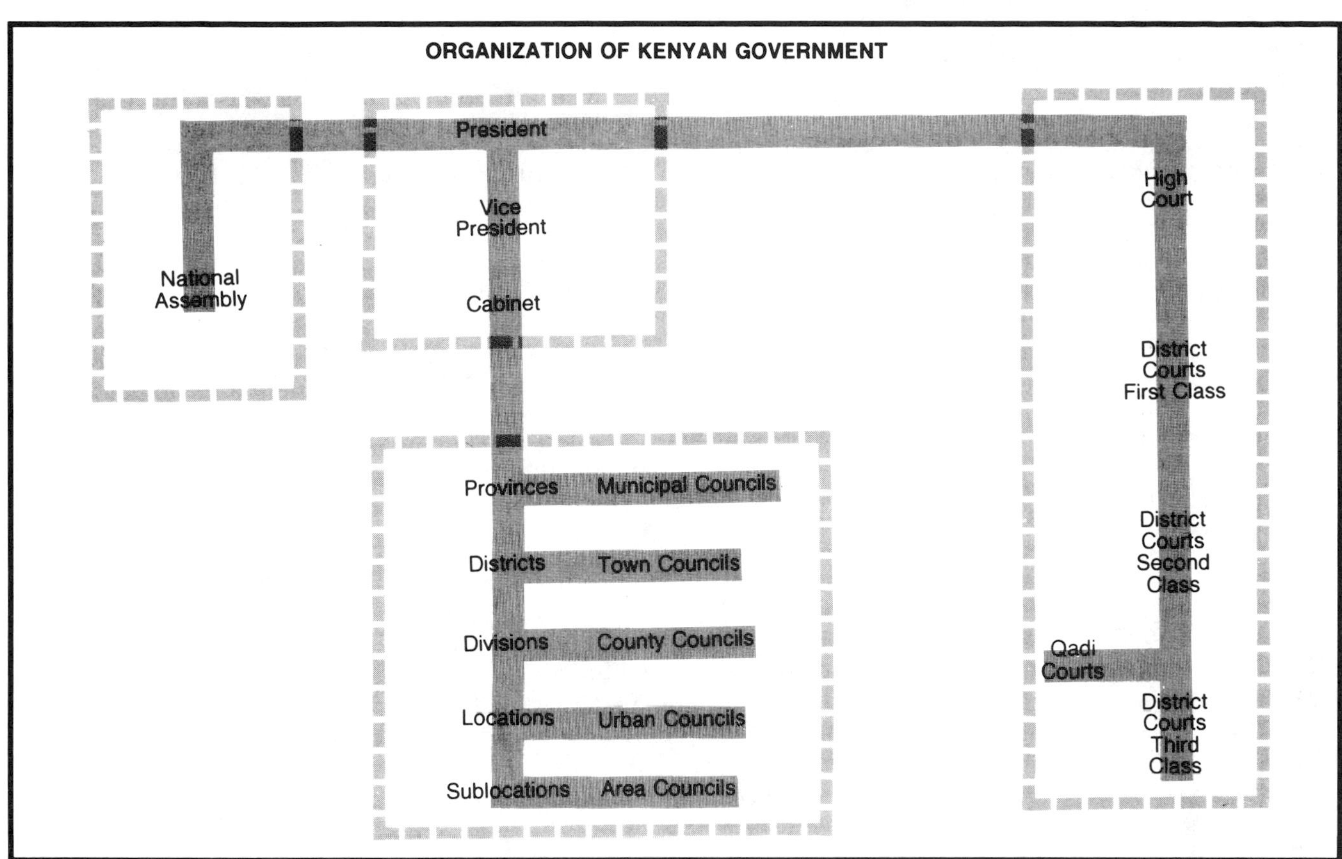

National Assembly, they also play a direct role in drafting legislation and in legislative deliberations. The only member of the cabinet not required to be selected from the National Assembly is the attorney general. Although not members of the cabinet, the assistant ministers also are appointed by the president, and their major responsibility is to work with the National Assembly and guide government measures through it. The National Assembly can force the resignation of the entire cabinet by a simple vote of no confidence in one or more of its members. The president also periodically reshuffles the cabinet, although there have been few radical changes in membership or structure since independence.

President Moi, supported by a small group of advisers, controls all aspects of policy-making and has increasingly consolidated political power, especially since the attempted coup of August 1, 1982. Kenya became a de jure one-party state on June 9, 1982, and, even though a wide range of candidates and views generally is permitted, elections have not been immune to government manipulation. However, within the one-party system, campaigns and balloting ordinarily are conducted in a generally free, fair and peaceful manner. The number of candidates for a particular public office frequently is a half dozen or more, and in the September 16, 1983, general elections, for example, up to 15 candidates ran for a single parliamentary seat. Of the 995 persons who applied for KANU Party clearance to run for the National Assembly, 992 were permitted to do so. Of these, roughly 700 ultimately had their names placed on the ballot.

The Kenyan government encourages but does not coerce the electorate to vote. Turnout generally has averaged between 60% and 70% of the eligible electorate, but it fell to just 42% in 1983.

Incumbents frequently are voted out of office in Kenya. Since Kenya's independence in 1963, as many as 50% of the country's sitting members of the National Assembly have been defeated during a single election. In 1988 legislative elections, the electorate rejected approximately 65% of the incumbents. In should be noted, however, that in Kenya's postindependence history neither the president nor the vice president ever has faced an opposing candidate.

President Moi has expanded tribal representation in the government and legislature. Members of all ethnic groups are permitted to contest for office, and Kenya has had one white member of the National Assembly who was reelected in a constituency that is 99% black African, despite the presence of several black African candidates on the ballot. Ten different tribes hold cabinet portfolios in the government, including the first ethnic Somali ever appointed to ministerial rank in Kenya. Twenty tribes are represented among the 43 assistant ministers in the government. The largest tribe, the Kikuyu (21%), however, now claims it is underrepresented in the political process.

RULERS OF KENYA (from 1963)

Presidents

June 1963–August 1978: Jomo Kenyatta
August 1978– : Daniel Teroitich arap Moi

GOVERNMENT LIST
(July/August 1991)

President	Moi, Daniel T. arap
Vice President	Saitoti, George
Minister for Agriculture	Mwangale, Elijah
Minister for Applied Technology	Ongeri, Samson K.
Minister for Commerce	Magugu, Arthur
Minister for Cooperative Development	Cheruiyot, John
Minister for Culture & Social Services	Njiru, James
Minister for Education	Aringo, Peter Oloo
Minister for Energy	Biwott, Nicholas Kiprono
Minister for Environment & Natural Resources	Njoroge, Mungai
Minister for Finance	Saitoti, George
Minister for Foreign Affairs & International Cooperation	Ayah, Wilson Ndolo
Minister for Health	Kibaki, Mwai
Minister for Home Affairs & National Heritage	Kuguru, Davidson
Minister for Industry	Kyalo, John
Minister for Information & Broadcasting	Waithana, Nahashon Kanyi
Minister for Labor	Masinde, Philip J. W.
Minister for Lands & Housing	Mbela, Darius
Minister for Livestock Development	Nyagah, Jeremiah
Minister for Local Government & Physical Planning	Ntimama, William ole
Minister for Manpower Development	Anyango, Dalmas Otieno
Minister for Planning & National Development	Onyonka, Zachary
Minister for Public Works	Mibei, Timothy
Minister for Reclamation & Development of Arid & Semi-Arid Wasteland	Ndotto, George
Minister for Regional Development	Onyango Midika, Mathews
Minister for Research, Science & Technology	Muhoho, George
Minister for Supplies & Marketing	Mudavadi, Wycliff Muslia
Minister for Tourism & Wildlife	Ngala, Noah Katana
Minister for Transportation & Communications	Kamotho, Joseph
Minister for Water Development	Okwanyo, John H.
Minister of State in the Office of the President	Angaine, Jackson Harvester
Minister of State in the Office of the President	Nabwera, Burudi
Minister of State in the Office of the President	Ngutu, J. K.
Attorney General	Wako, Amos
Governor, Central Bank	Kotut, Eric

FREEDOM & HUMAN RIGHTS

In terms of civil and political rights Kenya is ranked as a partially free country.

Kenya has attempted to combine both authoritarian and democratic features in the Constitution as well as in the administration. On the one hand, although a one-party state, there is broad tolerance of dissenting political activity, including multiple candidacies, which resulted in the defeat of 65% of incumbents in the recent elections. The judicial system is independent and, for the most part, impartial. The transfer of power from Kenyatta to Daniel arap Moi was smooth and in the best constitutional traditions. Elections are held regularly and in an orderly fashion. Candidates can challenge the election results successfully. On the negative side, it should be noted that in 1988 a controversial constitutional amendment confirmed President Moi's right to dismiss highly placed judges and the attorney general. Civil servants must be members of KANU.

The Public Security Act, renewed by President Moi, provides for the detention of political prisoners. Such prisoners are denied both written and face-to-face contact with family members and held in isolation and in degrading conditions. In 1979 paramilitary police units brutalized certain ethnic elements in northwestern Kenya, killing several people in a sweep for weapons. The Public Security Act, although restricted to five broad categories (Northwest Province and contiguous districts, armed forces, control of movement, Meru and detained persons) nullifies constitutional safeguards. However, the act provides certain precedural protections: Detainees must be informed of the reason for their detention within five days of their arrest, and they have the right to have their cases reviewed every six months by a special tribunal. The right to a fair trial is respected except in cases under the Public Security Act.

Incidences of politically motivated arrests have risen since student unrest in the mid-1980s. Suppression of the underground opposition group, Mwakenya, led to the arrest of 100 teachers, students and journalists in 1986. The mass arrests of reputed illegal aliens during 1987 were followed by international accusations of human rights violations. In 1988, what had been a maximum 24 hour detention prior to trial for capital offenses was extended to 14 days. In 1990, security police cracked down on dissidents and broke up pro-democracy protests. The U.S. ambassador strongly condemned the action as did Kenya's Roman Catholic heirarchy.

Freedom of speech and press are accepted in principle but are restricted under various sections of the Penal Code. The existence and past use of detention laws inhibit public exchange of views on sensitive political subjects. Because of past violations of members' immunity, National Assembly debates on public issues usually are noncontroversial and uncritical. The government, in fact, discourages political activism, especially in the academic sector. The press is active and assertive in reporting and commenting on internal and external developments. However, government guidelines generally are observed. There is no formal precensorship of published words and, in some cases, offending works remain on sale. Films are subject to the scrutiny of a 30-member film censorship board and television to a 10-member television censorship board. Freedom of association and of assembly are limited by the Public Order and Police Act, which gives local authorities wide powers. It is an offense to convene an unlicensed public meeting and, under the Societies Act, the government can, on grounds of national security, refuse to register any society or deregister any society that is already functioning. Although the trade union movement is relatively free, strikes always are illegal, and trade unions may be deregistered if they attempt to pursue a strike against government advice.

The government has substantial powers to regulate and restrict political activity. Opposition leaders sometimes are banned from running for the National Assembly. Those who wish to run for public office must be life members of KANU, and such membership usually is denied to individuals believed to hold dissenting opinions. Within the KANU framework, however, political activity is vigorous both in terms of the number of contestants and in the number of election upsets.

Kenya has been grudging in its efforts to cooperate with international human rights organizations such as Amnesty International

CIVIL SERVICE

The civil service of Kenya constitutes one of the most prestigious and powerful institutions in the country. Civil servants wield considerably more power than local government councillors, members of the cabinet or members of the National Assembly in the execution of government policies. Civil servants also are relatively better trained and less corrupt than those elected. The independence of the civil service is guaranteed by the Public Service Commission, whose chairman, deputy chairman and five members are not, according to the Constitution, "subject to the direction or control of any other person or authority." There is keen competition for civil service positions at all levels. Although Kenyanization has proceeded rapidly since independence, many technical and administrative positions still are held by noncitizens, especially Britons. A disproportionately large number of posts—estimated at 50% to 70%—are held by Kikuyus despite government efforts to achieve an ethnic balance.

Grades and salaries are fixed by the Public Service Commission. The civil service is divided into a number of functional classes, of which the top two echelons are the administrative officer class and the executive officer class. There are four training institutes for middle- and high-level personnel, of which the Kenya Institute of Administration is the largest.

LOCAL GOVERNMENT

Kenya is divided for administrative purposes into seven provinces and one area. The provinces are Coast, Northeastern, Eastern, Central, Rift Valley, Nyanza and Western. The area is Nairobi. Provinces are governed by provincial commissioners who are directly responsible to the president. The next level is the district, headed by the district commissioner. Each district contains a varying number of divisions, each headed by a district officer. The smallest units are called locations or sublocations, in which the government is represented by chiefs or subchiefs.

Outside of the regional administrative structure are local councils, which raise their own revenues by taxes, construct and maintain roads, administer public health programs, supervise education, construct housing and provide agricultural and social services.

The entire country falls under the jurisdiction of five levels of local authorities: municipal councils, town councils, county councils, urban councils and area councils. There are 11 municipal councils, including Nairobi City Council; six town councils; 38 county councils; 18 urban councils; and 54 area councils. Councillors and aldermen in the municipalities are elected directly by the people. In addition, the central government appoints members to each council. The functions and powers of these bodies vary according to their class, but all of them operate under the close supervision of the central government and the provincial administration. Further, provincial, district and division heads frequently serve as members and as chairmen of the local councils within their jurisdiction. With growing centralization of power, many of the functions and powers of the local councils are being transferred to the central ministries and regional administrations. Apart from the councils, the only means of participation for the people in rural areas in the governmental process is through meetings, called *barazas*, convened by chiefs, subchiefs or districts officers.

FOREIGN POLICY

The principal features of Kenya's foreign policy are moderation, pragmatism and a continuing reliance on the Western world. Kenya's three most significant international affiliations represent the three main areas of interest in its foreign policy: the East African Community, the Organization of African Unity and the Commonwealth of Nations.

Kenya, Uganda and Tanzania have made two attempts since the three countries became independent in the early 1960s to form a regional organization that would function as a loose federation and economic common market. In 1961 the East African Common Services Organization (EACSO) was created to provide the three countries with a number of services under a centralized administration. These services included transportation, communication, tax collection, scientific research, social services and university education. The EACSO charter also provided for a common currency, a common appellate court, and a common market in which goods and labor could move freely, under a central legislative assembly. By 1965 the EACSO had begun to disintegrate under the pressure of growing nationalism, competing economies and differing political policies. Therefore it was replaced in 1967 by the East African Community (EAC), which was created under the Treaty for East African Cooperation. Under the arrangement, cooperation in economic matters, trade, transport and education increased. However, tensions grew between the three countries as a result of ideological disputes with socialist Tanzania and differences with the brutal regime of Idi Amin in Uganda. The Community was defunct by 1977 and a final agreement on distribution of its assets was reached in 1983. Relations with Tanzania, strained during the late 1970s and early 1980s, improved in the wake of the agreement. Kenya's relations with Uganda traditionally have been stormy. The two nations have had disputes over Ugandan use of Kenyan transport routes and Kenyan purchase of power from Uganda. Although relations improved following the agreement on the distribution of EAC assets, new tensions arose in 1986 and 1987 as

Uganda accused Kenya of supporting rebels and Kenya accused Uganda of incursions into its territory.

Somali irredentism posed the most serious threat to Kenya at the time of independence. For four years the Somali guerrillas known as *shiftas*, inspired by the Voice of Somalia radio in Mogadishu, waged a campaign against the Kenyan police and army. The state of near-hostilities was eased after a change of government in Somalia in 1967, but Kenya was faced with the threat again in 1977 as Somali-Ethiopian warfare brought the issue to the foreground. Kenya threw its support behind Ethiopia in the Ogaden war. In early 1978 Kenya seized an Egyptian plane carrying arms to the Somali forces. This action brought it into conflict with Arab nations and with Iran. In 1984 President Moi paid his first visit to Mogadishu, during the course of which agreement was concluded on border claims and trade cooperation. In the same year, Somali members of an exile group, the Northern Frontier District Liberation Front, responded to a government amnesty and returned to Kenya. And though relations improved for a while, antagonisms between the two countries were rekindled in 1986. In 1987 accusations were made that 500 Ugandan nationals in Kenya had been abused and one had been killed. Ugandan troops then crossed Kenyan borders in search of anti-government rebels. The borders were closed and shots were exchanged between the two militaries. Early in 1988 agreements were reached though strained relations continue. The two countries also concluded a border security agreement designed to facilitate free movement for nationals of both countries across their common boundary.

Kenya's major ally in the West is Great Britain, with whom it has maintained unbroken friendly relations since independence. Britain still is the principal trading partner, chief source of economic and military aid and major provider of private investment capital. Relations with the United States, which faltered during Oginga Odinga's ascendancy, have been warm and friendly since Odinga's fall in 1966. In 1980, Kenya and the United States agreed to permit the latter to use Kenyan sea and air bases in exchange for economic and military aid. The U.S. presence in Kenya includes over 5,000 American citizens. The United States has an active U.S. AID and Peace Corps program in Kenya. In addition over 125 U.S. firms are represented in Kenya, with an investment of over $200 million. Relations with the Soviet Union and China, on the other hand, have been cool and cautious and marked by a number of diplomatic incidents.

Kenya joined the United Nations in 1963. It is a member of 15 U.N. organizations and 22 other international organizations. Kenya and the United States are parties to 10 treaties and agreements covering agricultural commodities, defense, economic and technical cooperation, extradition, investment guarantees, the Peace Corps and Social Security.

PARLIAMENT

The national legislature is the unicameral National Assembly. It consists of 188 elected members and 12 members nominated by the president. Since 1969 all members of the National Assembly have been members of the sole political party, the Kenya African National Union (KANU). Nevertheless, elections generally are free, as illustrated by the fact that in the 1988 general elections, only 65 members regained their seats unopposed, while the remaining 123 positions were contested. However, in the preliminary elections held in 1988, a line-up voting system was used that effectively eliminated the secret ballot in the primary.

Although the National Assembly is the supreme state organ under the Constitution, it has been dominated since independence by the executive. One reason for its subordinate role is that many of its 188 elected members hold either ministerial posts or sinecures on boards of government commissions and state-owned corporations. Thus the government always can command a substantial majority in the National Assembly. Almost all bills are drafted and presented by the government; in some years only one or two private bills may be passed. Members are not consulted when legislation is drafted by the ministries concerned in advance of its presentation on the floor of the National Assembly. The government has never suffered an outright defeat on any major legislative measure, although it often changes or withdraws a bill in the face of legislative criticism.

The real opposition in the National Assembly consists of junior members who use their right of interpellation to question ministers or voice complaints of their constituents. Debates in the National Assembly are subdued, although they reflect the degree of public concern over major issues.

POLITICAL PARTIES

Although political parties are not banned, Kenya has evolved into a one-party state, with the Kenya African National Union (KANU) as the sole party. Originally a Kikuyu organization, it has broadened its base of support by absorbing the Kenyan African Democratic Union and the African People's Party. Because it attempts to be a party of all Kenyans, KANU has never developed an effective political ideology. At the same time, it has not become a mass party or enlisted widespread popular support. It plays the limited role of an electoral party, functioning only in times of stress or elections. Its party institutions also are weak. National congresses of the party rarely are held, and the national officials of the party invariably are appointed by its leader. At the local levels the party units function only intermittently.

ECONOMY

Kenya is one of the low-income countries of the world. It has a free-market economy in which the private sector dominates. Agriculture is the mainstay of the economy, employing four-fifths of the population and accounting for one-third of GDP. The main export commodities are coffee, tea, fruit, vegetables and cotton. The pattern of agricultural exports and industrial

PRINCIPAL ECONOMIC INDICATORS

Gross National Product (U.S. $ billions): 8.785 (1989)
GNP per capita (U.S. $): 380 (1989)
GNP average annual growth rate (%, 1980–89): 4.2
GNP per capita average annual growth rate (%, 1987–89): 1.5
Average annual rate of inflation (%, 1980–88): 9.6
Consumer price index (1980 = 100) 1986
  All items: 215
  Food: 187
Average annual growth rate (%, 1980–88)
  General government consumption: 1.1
  Private consumption: 5.1
  Gross domestic investment: −1.1

BALANCE OF PAYMENTS, 1989
(U.S. $ millions)

Current account balance: −587.5
Merchandise exports: 926.1
Merchandise imports: −1,963.4
Trade balance: −1,037.3
Other goods, services & income + :1,008.5
Other goods, services & income − : −941.2
Other goods, services & income net: 67.3
Private unrequited transfers: 101.5
Official unrequited transfers: 280.9
Capital other than reserves: 709
Net errors & omissions: 67.6
Counterpart items: −61.2
Total change in reserves: −60.9

GROSS DOMESTIC PRODUCT

GDP nominal (K. Sh. billions): 152.679 (1988)
GDP per capita (U.S. $): 360 (1989)
Average annual growth rate of GDP (%, 1980–88): 4.2
GDP by type of expenditure (%) 1987
  Consumption
    Private: 62
    Government: 19
  Gross domestic investment: 25
  Gross domestic saving: 22 (1988)
  Foreign trade
    Exports: 21
    Imports: −26
Cost components of GDP (%) 1987
    Net indirect taxes: 14
    Consumption of fixed capital and net operating surplus: 50
    Compensation of employees: 36
Sectoral origin of GDP (%) 1987
  Primary
    Agriculture: 31 (1989)
    Mining: 0.0
  Secondary
    Manufacturing: 10
    Construction: 5
    Public utilities: 2
  Tertiary
    Transportation & communications: 5
    Trade: 12
    Finance: 12
    Other services: 3
    Government: 13
Average annual sectoral growth rates (%, 1980–88)
    Agriculture: 3.3
    Industry: 2.8
    Manufacturing: 4.6
    Services: 5.5

imports, common in Africa, make the economy vulnerable to undependable weather conditions. A shortage of arable land also hampers long-term agricultural growth.

One of Kenya's most serious underlying problems is its annual population growth rate—one of the highest in the world. GDP in the near term has been able to keep slightly ahead of population growth, but the outcome for the long term is uncertain.

PUBLIC FINANCE

The Kenyan fiscal year runs from July 1 through June 30. The central government's budget is divided into a recurrent budget for revenue and operating expenditures and a development budget for capital expenditures. Also included in the budget are over 150 autonomous state agencies, of which 14 are statutory marketing boards. These organizations account for 5% of government revenues and 33% of government expenditures for investments.

Of current revenues in 1989–90, almost two-thirds came from indirect taxes, principally sales taxes and custom and excise duties. Of current expenditures, approximately one-quarter goes to economic services, another quarter to education and health and approximately 10% to defense.

CENTRAL GOVERNMENT EXPENDITURES, 1988

% of total expenditures
  Defense: 9.2
  Education: 21.5
  Health: 6.1
  Housing, social security, welfare: 3.5
  Economic services: 19.8
  Other: 39.3
Total expenditures as % of GNP: 28.6
Overall surplus or deficit as % of GNP: −6.6

CENTRAL GOVERNMENT REVENUES, 1988

% of total current revenues
  Taxes on income, profit & capital gain: 28.5
  Social security contributions: 0.0
  Domestic taxes on goods & services: 41.2
  Taxes on international trade & transactions: 18.9
  Other taxes: 1.4
  Current nontax revenue: 10.1
Total current revenue as % of GNP: 21.5
General government consumption as % of GDP: 19
Average annual growth rate of general government consumption (%, 1980–88): 1.1

Development planning emphasizes a mixed economy in which the role of the public sector is limited to a few industries, such as oil refining, and the principal impetus is provided by the private sector.

Since independence, Kenya has received substantial development aid, as well as recurrent budgetary aid. The sources of aid have been diversified. The United Kingdom's share has fallen while those of the World Bank, European Development Fund, Japan, Germany, Sweden, the Netherlands, France and Norway have risen. Kenya is now among the largest recipients of U.S. aid per capita.

During the period 1970–88, the United States committed $771 million in aid, while other Western nations committed $6 billion from 1970–87. OPEC granted $74 million in bilateral assistance from 1979–89 and Communist countries sent $83 million from 1970–88.

FOREIGN AID, 1989

Total foreign aid (U.S. $ millions): 1385.0
- Bilateral: 823.1
- Multilateral: 561.9

CURRENCY & BANKING

The Kenyan unit of currency is the shilling, divided into 100 cents. The Kenyan pound is not a bank note but only a term of account equal to Sh20. Coins are issued in denominations of 5, 10 and 50 cents, and 1 and 2 shillings; notes are issued in denominations of 5, 10, 20, 50 and 100 shillings.

The Kenya shilling was introduced in 1966 and was tied to the U.S. dollar until 1975, when its value was fixed at 9.66 per SDR. The Kenya shilling was devalued twice in 1981 (by 4.8% in February and by a further 15.1% in September), and again in December 1982, by 15%, in an attempt to reduce the trade deficit and to meet the terms required by the IMF for continued assistance. The dollar exchange rate in March 1991 was $1 = KSh27.74.

The banking system consists of a bank of issue, the Central Bank of Kenya, which took over the functions of the former East African Currency Board in 1966; 12 commercial banks, of which three are Kenyan-owned and two are American; and a number of specialized credit and development institutions, including the Industrial and Commercial Development Corporation, the Development Finance Company, the Agricultural Finance Corporation, the Agricultural Development Corporation, the Housing Finance Company and the Industrial Development Bank. Nonbanking savings institutions include the Post Office Savings Bank.

FINANCIAL INDICATORS, 1989

Total reserves minus gold (SDRs millions): 217
SDRs (millions): 9
Reserve position in IMF (SDRs millions): 12
Foreign exchange (SDRs millions): 196
Gold (fine troy oz. millions): .08
Ratio of external debt to total reserves: 15.8 (1988)
Central Bank 1989
- Assets (%)
  - Foreign assets: 26.9
  - Claims on government: 73.1
  - Claims on banks: 0.0
  - Claims on private sector: 0.0
- Liabilities (%)
  - Reserve money: 59.8
  - Government deposits: 0.0
  - Foreign liabilities: 41.3
  - Capital accounts: 5.1

Money supply 1989
- Stock (K. Sh. billions): 19.160
- M1 per capita: 820

Private banks 1989
- Assets (%)
  - Loans to government: 14.2
  - Loans to private sector: 75.3
  - Reserves: 8.4
  - Foreign assets: 2.1
- Liabilities
  - Deposits (K. Sh. billions): 40.789
- of which %
    - Demand deposits: 28.3
    - Savings deposits: 58.1
    - Government deposits: 5.1
    - Foreign liabilities: 3.8

External debt 1988
- Total (U.S. $ billions): 5.888
  - of which public (U.S. $ billions): 4.241
  - of which private (U.S. $ millions): 627
- Debt service (long-term)
  - Total (U.S. $ millions): 365
  - Repayment
    - Principal (%): 59.2
    - Interest (%): 40.8
- Debt service ratio (%): 19.4
- External public debt as % of GNP: 51.0
- Debt service as % of GNP: 4.4
- Debt service as % of exports: 19.4
- Terms of public borrowing
  - Commitments (U.S. $ millions): 679
  - Average interest rate (%): 1.9
  - Average maturing (yrs.): 22
- Net flow of publicly guaranteed external capital (U.S. $ millions): 75
- Receipt of workers' remittances (U.S. $ millions): −3
- Net direct private investment (U.S. $ millions): 7

AGRICULTURE

Agriculture dominates Kenya's economy. Of the total land area of 58,264,600 ha. (143,971,820 ac.) 10% is considered as agricultural land.

Since independence the agricultural sector has undergone many changes. Reservation of land for white settlers had been legally ended in 1959; more than one-third of the former white-owned lands had been transferred to Africans by 1971. By 1970 a total of 2,250 of the 2,750 large white-owned farms were in African hands. About 647,500 ha. (1.6 million ac.) had been transferred intact as large estates, and about 52,609 ha. (1.3 million ac.) had been subdivided into smaller units. About 129,000 ha. (319,000 ac.) had been converted into cooperative farms and ranches. Some 35,000 families had been settled on the subdivided smallholdings and 3,400 families in cooperative settlements. These efforts have continued, so that for example, in 1981, small farms accounted for half the coffee growing area, and in 1987, 45% of the tea crop came out of these small farms. Resettlement programs, however, favored the relatively well-to-do, especially KANU party leaders and members of the dominant Kikuyu tribe.

Most of the cropland of high or medium potential is in the Western Highlands, around Lake Victoria and Mount Kenya and along the coast. Intensive cultivation is carried on in five districts of Central Province, Kisii District in Nyanza Province and the Embu and Meru districts in Eastern Province. On traditional smallholdings, called *shamba*, production continues to use ancient methods at subsistence levels. Irrigation is limited to about 11,735 ha. (29,000 ac.), chiefly in the Yala

GROWTH PROFILE
(Annual Growth Rates, %)

Projected population (1988–2000): 3.4
Projected crude birth rate (/1,000) (1990–95): 50.8
Projected crude death rate (/1,000) (1990–95): 9.9
Urban population (1980–88): 8.2
Labor force (1985–2000): 3.7
GNP (1980–89): 4.2
GNP per capita (1987–89): 1.5
GDP (1980–88): 4.2
Inflation (1980–88): 9.6
Agriculture (1980–88): 3.3
Industry (1980–88): 2.8
Manufacturing (1980–88): 4.6
Services (1980–88): 5.5
Money holdings (1980–88): 14.9
Manufacturing earnings per employee (1980–87): −2.3
Energy production (1980–88): 8.3
Energy consumption (1980–88): 0.2
Exports (1980–88): 0.1
Imports (1980–88): −0.6
General government consumption (1980–88): 1.1
Private consumption (1980–88): 5.1
Gross domestic investment (1980–88): −1.1

Swamp and Kano Plain in West Kenya and the upper and lower Tana River basins. Crop failures due to severe drought created a decline in agricultural output in 1984, but production increased with favorable weather the next year. However, adverse weather conditions in 1987 caused a repeated decline in growth.

There are three broad types of land tenure: government land, trust land and private or freehold land. Trust land, or land held in trust for various ethnic groups, comprises 73% of the total land area. Rights to use trust land are held by individual families but disposal rights are held by the tribe, and inheritance must be approved by the tribe elders. However, under an adjudication and registration program introduced in 1956, trust lands are gradually being converted into freehold lands.

More than half the smallholders have freehold titles to their lands. Of the 1.2 million smallholdings, about half are smaller than 2.02 ha. (5 ac.) and one-fourth less than 1.1 ha. (2.5 ac.). On the other end of the scale, there are 2,750 holdings over 20 ha. (50 ac.). The number of landless peasants is estimated at 300,000.

Kenya produces a variety of cash crops and nearly all its basic agricultural foodstuffs. Nonetheless the nation was forced to import cereals during 1983–85 because of severe drought. A total of 60% of the cultivated area is planted with corn, sorghum and millet. Corn is the leading crop in planted area. The principal export crops are coffee, tea, sisal and pyrethrum.

Kenyan farmers place a high value on ownership of cattle as a status symbol and as a store of wealth. More than 90% of the cattle are of the zebu indigenous breeds with low milk and meat yields; the Boran breed, which constitute 8% of the cattle, are dairy-grade. Milk production meets domestic demands, and some milk is exported. Cooperative ranching was introduced under the first livestock development project (1968–74). Under the second livestock development project (1974–78), 60 group ranches, 100 commercial ranches and 21

AGRICULTURAL INDICATORS

Agriculture's share of GDP (%): 31 (1989)
Average annual growth rate (%, 1980–88): 3.3
Value added in agriculture (U.S. $ billions): 2.265 (1988)
Cereal imports (000 metric tons): 86 (1988)
Index of agricultural production (1979–81 = 100): 127 (1986)
Index of food production (1979–81 = 100): 119 (1986)
Index of food production per capita (1979–81 = 100): 89 (1986–88)
Number of tractors: 8,530 (1986)
Number of harvester-threshers: 520 (1986)
Total fertilizer consumption (000 metric tons): 109 (1985–86)
Fertilizer consumption (g./ha., hundreds): 421 (1987–88)
Number of farms (millions:) 2.750 (1976–79)
Average size of holding (ha.): 2.5 (1976–79)
Size class (%) 1976–79
  Below 1 ha. (below 2.47 ac.): 65.5
  1–5 ha. (2.47–12.35 ac.): 27.3
  5–8 ha. (12.35–19.76 ac.): 2.7
  8–50 ha. (19.76–123.5 ac.): }
  50–200 ha. (123.5–494 ac.): }4.4
  Over 200 ha. (over 494 ac.): }
Farms as % of total land area: 11.9 (1976–79)
Land use (%) 1985–87
  Cropland: 4
  Pasture: 7
  Forest: 6
  Other: 83
Yields (kg./ha.) 1989
  Grains: 1,746
  Roots & tubers: 8,547
  Legumes: 667
  Milk (kg./animal): 450
Production 1989
  Fruits (000 metric tons): 764
  Vegetables (000 metric tons): 491
Livestock (000) 1989
  Cattle: 13,457
  Horses: 2 (1986)
  Sheep: 6,325
  Pigs: 100
Forestry 1988
  Production of roundwood (million cubic meters): 36.214
  of which industrial roundwood (%): 4.6
  Value of exports (U.S. $ millions): 22.255
Fishing 1988
  Total catch (000 metric tons): 137.4
  of which marine (%): 5.3
  Value of exports (U.S. $ millions): 10.119

cooperative ranches were opened and 4 million ha. (10 million ac.) of new rangeland were developed.

Forests cover 1,946,026 ha. (4,808,566 ac.) of land, or 3% of the total land area. Almost all the forests are publicly owned, including 135,200 ha. (333,944 ac.) of plantations. Forestry and forest industries contribute 2% of the GDP and employ 3% of the labor force. Kenya's chief hardwoods are musheragi, muiri, mukeo, camphor and musaise; the chief softwoods are podo, cypress and cedar. In 1983 there were 43 nature preservation sites and national parks, of which the giant Tsavo National Park is the largest. In addition, a number of game reserves have been established to protect wildlife.

Over 31,000 fishermen are engaged in commercial fishing in Lakes Victoria, Naivasha, Baringo and Turkana and in deepwater offshore fishing in the Indian Ocean. Over 1,500 vessels, of which 300 are motorized, are engaged in inshore fisheries. A number of fish farms also have been established.

Agricultural credit is provided by the Agricultural Finance Corporation and the Agricultural Development Corporation. In addition, there are 1,060 cooperatives, 6000 agricultural marketing cooperatives and 107 credit societies.

MANUFACTURING

In 1985 manufacturing employed 13.5% of the labor force and in 1987 contributed 10% to the GDP. Output in this sector had increased through the first three quarters of the 1980s, but industrial growth declined in the later part of the decade due to a lessening of exports and the need to import such items as spare parts, crude oil and other raw materials. The most important industries are: agro-based products, textiles and clothing, machinery and transportation equipment, and chemicals. More than 50% of manufacturing plants are in Nairobi, but the government is prompting location of new industries away from the capital.

At the time of independence Kenya had a more developed and diversified industrial base than most African countries. In the first decade of its existence the new nation experienced rapid growth stimulated by foreign investment and a favorable climate for private enterprise. But the manufacturing sector still is predominantly concentrated on the processing of domestic agricultural, forestry and livestock products. The food, drink and tobacco subsector is the largest, followed by machinery and vehicle assembly, chemicals and petroleum, textiles and building materials. Large-scale industries include a paper mill at Webuye, a fertilizer plant at Mombasa and three vehicle assembly plants.

The number of foreign investors and the total money invested have steadily risen, stimulated by the government's investment policy, which permits liberal repatriation of profits and extends other concessions and benefits. The United Kingdom and the United States remain the leading sources of foreign investment, but recently they have been joined by Germany, Japan, Norway, Sweden, Poland, Italy and Yugoslavia.

MANUFACTURING INDICATORS, 1987

Average annual growth rate (%, 1980–88): 4.6
Share of GDP (%): 12 (1988)
Labor force economically active in manufacturing (% est.): 7.1
Value added in manufacturing (U.S. $ millions): 839
  Food & tobacco (%): 38
  Textile & clothing (%): 11
  Machinery & transport equipment (%): 13
  Chemicals (%): 11
Earnings per employee in manufacturing 1987
  Growth rate (%, 1980–87): −2.3
  Index (1980 = 100): 87
Total earnings as % of value added: 48
Gross output per employee (1980 = 100): 108

Investment in the manufacturing industry has centered on factory expansion and construction and has continued in spite of unfavorable economic conditions, due largely to the activities of the various parastatal investment financing agencies.

Kenya is one of the few countries where the private sector has increased its share of the economy since independence; it also is one of the few African countries to espouse an economic philosophy based on private enterprise. In 1988, in order to stimulate investment and export of manufactured goods, major industrial reforms were generated by the government with the support of $102 million from the World Bank.

Industrial credit is provided by the Industrial Development Bank, the Industrial and Commercial Development Corporation and the Development Finance Company.

MINING

Kenya's known mineral resources include lead, silver, zinc, fluorspar, copper, ruby, nickel and gold. Of these, lead, silver, fluorspar and ruby deposits are believed to be extensive.

ENERGY

Kenya is heavily dependent on imported petroleum products to meet its energy needs. The government has made efforts to reduce the role of petroleum products in the domestic energy picture and has earned some success. Nevertheless, oil still constitutes four-fifths of the total primary energy consumption in the country, with hydroelectricity and coal accounting for only 17% and 1%, respectively. Although oil consumption can be expected to rise more slowly in the future, the prospects for substantially reducing the dominance of oil remain poor. Kenya has been generating 85% of its electricity from hydroelectric sources. Both hydroelectric and geothermal projects have been started, including the construction of two hydroelectrical plants with a total additional generating capacity of 245 MW.

ENERGY INDICATORS

Average annual energy production growth rate (%, 1980–88): 8.3
Energy consumption per capita (kg. oil equivalent): 94 (1988)
Energy imports as % of merchandise exports: 41 (1988)
Average annual growth rate of energy consumption (%, 1980–88): 0.2
Electricity 1988
  Installed capacity (000 kw.): 575
  Production (billion kw.−hr.): 2.844
    % of fossil fuel: 7.0
    % hydro: 81.7
    % geothermal: 11.3
  Consumption per capita (kw.−hr.): 128
Natural gas
  Proved reserves (billion cu. m.): 0 (1990)
  Production (million cu. m.): 0 (1989)
  Consumption (million cu. m.): 0 (1988)
Petroleum
  Production (million bbl.): 0 (1989)
  Consumption (million bbl.): 15 (1988)
  Refining capacity (000 bbl./day): 90 (1990)
Coal
  Production (000 metric tons): 0 (1988)
  Consumption (000 metric tons): 113 (1988)

One began operation in January 1988 and the other is scheduled for completion in 1991. Savings, however, would equal only about 2% of total oil consumption. Additionally, the continued lack of alternatives in the industrial and transportation sectors puts a real limit on how far the economy can be moved away from petroleum as the primary source of energy. Therefore, Kenya will continue to be vulnerable to oil supply disruptions. Similarly, purchases of petroleum will continue to place a heavy burden on the balance of payments, absorbing more than the total export earnings from coffee.

The East African Oil Refinery at Mombasa has an annual output of 79,000 bbl. per day. Offshore oil exploration is conducted by two Shell subsidiaries and Adobe International of Texas. The discovery of traces of oil and gas in 1988 creates the possibility of a domestic supply.

LABOR

There are more than one million wage earners in the formal sector of the economy. The informal sector includes the self-employed, unpaid family workers and others not earning established wages. Most of the remaining persons in the economically active population are considered to be involved in subsistence agriculture. Of those in the wage-earning group, 50% work in public jobs.

The agriculture and forestry industries are the leading employers, followed by trade, manufacturing, and public administration and defense.

Industrial relations are governed by the Trade Disputes Act of 1965. The government, mainly through the Ministry of Labor, dominates labor-management relations, beginning with the authority to register trade unions. To engage in collective bargaining a union must first gain recognition from an employer and then register with the registrar of trade unions. Union representation elections are supervised by the Ministry of Labor, and the results must be certified by the government before the winners can officially sit down at the bargaining tables. Labor-management disputes, both actual and potential, must be reported to the Ministry of Labor, which has several options for resolving differences.

LABOR INDICATORS

Total economically active population (millions): 8.389
- % working-age (15–64): 76.2
- % female: 40.9

Activity rate (%)
- Total: 40.7
- Male: 48.4
- Female: 33.2

Sectoral employment of economically active (%)
- Agriculture, forestry, fishing: 79.1
- Construction, manufacturing, mining, quarrying, public utilities: 7.1
- Trade, hotels, restaurants, transportation, communications, finance, real estate, services: 13.8

Average annual growth rate of labor force (%, 1985–2000): 3.7
Earnings in manufacturing (per/worker) (/mo.) (K. Sh.): 1,928.7

The Industrial Court passes on all new agreements dealing with wages and conditions of employment according to government guidelines. Employers can be fined for implementing an agreement before the court has approved it.

Two basic forms of labor-management negotiations are employed: the machinery of tripartite industry wage councils, and the more traditional collective bargaining between committees representing employers and employees. The wage councils fix wages and conditions of employment for specific trades, industries and occupations. Wage guidelines established by the government limit the councils' discretion. The collective bargaining process is used to establish conditions of employment that exceed minimums established by law and regulation. When unresolved differences arise between labor and management, the Trade Disputes Act of 1965 sets forth procedures for dealing with them. The minister of labor, after consulting with a tripartite committee, has various options: Use conciliation; appoint an investigator or committee of investigation to review the dispute, report and, if desired, propose a settlement; refer the dispute to a board of inquiry; or refer the dispute to the Industrial Court. The Industrial Court consists of a president appointed by the president of Kenya and other members appointed by the minister of labor. The court has two vice presidents, one representing employers and another employees.

The act permits the minister of labor to prohibit strikes and lockouts if he feels that a possibility of settlement remains. Strikes and lockouts may be banned by presidential decree. Between 600 and 700 labor management disputes are referred anually to the Ministry of Labor. About 14% of the disputes are passed on to the Industrial Court.

In 1964 the government adopted Kenyanization—the replacement of noncitizens by citizens in key jobs—as its official policy, but in its actual implementation Kenya has been more cautious and pragmatic than other African states. The rate of Kenyanization has varied from sector to sector, but in general considerable progress had been achieved by the mid-1980s. Of high- and middle-level jobs, 83% in the public sector and 68% in private enterprise were held by Kenyans, but more than 35% of management and 65% of professional positions still were held by non-Kenyans.

The conditions of safety, health and welfare of workers are regulated by the Employment Act of 1976.

A statutory minimum wage was established in 1975. It applies equally to women and men. The monthly minimums include modest housing allowances.

The Employment Act of 1976 contains provisions for a six-day workweek. The act prohibits women and children from working between 6:30 P.M. and 6:30 A.M., with women excepted from this provision in emergency situations. The act recognizes 10 public holidays annually and provides leaves of 21 working days with full pay after workers have completed 12 consecutive months of service. Within each 12-month period, sick leave with full pay is granted for seven working days, followed by seven days at half pay if a worker has completed two months of consecutive service. Women get two months of paid maternity leave, but the annual leave is forfeited.

Working conditions and wages are governed by legislation. There is no social insurance system for workers, but the National Social Security Fund provides a form of provident fund for covered workers. There is also a fairly comprehensive workmen's compensation system.

Unemployment figures are unavailable, but both unemployment and underemployment are known to be high. Unemployment presents a particularly intractable problem because of the high rate of population growth. There are 400,000 new job seekers for the approximately 20,000 new jobs every year.

Approximately 390,000 workers are members of the 31 major unions in the country. The organized workers represent about 43% of the wage earners. The major unions are organized on an industrywide basis. Although the lines of jurisdiction are not always clear, the trade union movement has been relatively free of interunion struggles for members and bargaining rights.

Kenya has a relatively free trade union movement. Its single trade union confederation, the Central Organization of Trade Unions, is affiliated with the Ghana-based, continentwide Organization of African Trade Union Unity. Complex labor legislation renders virtually all strikes illegal. Strikes are permitted only if the Ministry of Labor has not taken action within 21 days after the formal declaration of a dispute to have it resolved. The only major strike in the past decade occured in February 1984, when Nairobi's 8,000 woodworkers went on a one-week strike, which was quickly mediated by the Ministry of Labor. Wildcat strikes of no more than a day or two are quite common. Most disputes, however, are settled by the parties concerned. Kenya's dispute mechanism is centered in the Industrial Court, founded in 1964. All Kenyan wage earners are subject to government regulations limiting wage increases. Nevertheless, some unions have had notable success in obtaining salary adjustments for union members by filing litigation before the Industrial Court. Some unions also have obtained significant additional worker benefits, such as expanded health insurance coverage and increased housing allowances, in this way. All collective agreements must be approved by the Industrial Court before they can take effect. The court has become the model for several other such labor courts in Africa. Although the court's caseload has risen significantly over the years, it still dispenses justice quickly and fairly.

All permanent workers in a private enterprise of at least seven persons may be organized into a trade union. Approximately three-quarters of all such enterprise employees are unionized, and about half (300,000) pay voluntary union dues. Unions actually represent a greater number in collective bargaining because non-union workers are covered by collective agreements negotiated for their enterprise. Agreements usually are of two years' duration.

In August 1980 the government formally disbanded the Kenyan Civil Servants' Union (at that time Kenya's largest union) because of its alleged political activities. The Public Service International has continued to press for a genuine civil servants' union, given Kenya's membership in the International Labor Organization and its having signed the Convention on the Right to Organize and Collective Bargaining. In December 1984 President Moi announced that a civil servants' association could be formed, but under government guidelines.

FOREIGN COMMERCE

Kenya's primary exports are coffee, tea, manufactures and petroleum products. Its principal imports are machinery and transportation equipment, raw materials, fuels and lubricants and food and consumer goods. Major import sources are the United Kingdom, Saudi Arabia, Germany and France; major export destinations are the United Kingdom, Germany, and Uganda.

FOREIGN TRADE INDICATORS, 1988

Exports (U.S. $ billions): 1.0
Imports (U.S. $ billions); 1.8
Balance of trade (U.S. $ billions): −0.8
Annual growth rate (1980–88), exports (%): 0.1
Annual growth rate (1980–88), imports (%):−0.6
International reserves in terms of months of imports covered: 1.3
Terms of trade (1980 = 100): 91
Import price index (1980 = 100): 83.9 (1986)
Export price index (1980 = 100): 93.7 (1986)

Direction of Trade (%), 1987

	Imports	Exports
European Community	43.5	42.4
United States	7.1	5.4
U.S.S.R & eastern European economies	0.5	0.9
Japan	10.9	0.9

Composition of Trade (%), 1986

	Imports	Exports
Food & agricultural raw materials	9.5	70.1
Fuels and other energy	20.1	13.1
Mineral ores & concentrates	0.5	2.5
Manufactured goods	70.0	14.4
of which chemicals	17.8	4.1
of which machinery	34.3	2.5

By 1977 the East African Community, established in 1967 as a customs union of Kenya, Uganda and Tanzania, was dissolved and after some disputes, its assets and liabilities were distributed among its three former members. In 1984 Kenya was accepted into the Preferential Trade Area (PTA) which was expected to provide additional trading partners.

TRANSPORTATION & COMMUNICATIONS

With the suspension of the East African Railways and Harbors (EARH) Administration, Kenya took over its own track. The railroad system is meter-gauge and virtually all single-track. The main line runs from Mombasa to Uganda. A modernization program was begun in 1987 and is expected to be completed in the early 1990s at a projected cost of $45.4 million.

The country's main port is Mombasa, which also is the port of entry for Uganda.

Kenya's main road artery is from Nairobi to Mombasa. The Kenyan section of the highway from Nairobi to Addis Ababa was completed in 1974. Road haulage is the monoploy of the state-owned Kenya National Transport Company. Bus services are provided from Nairobi to all other population centers by East African Road Services.

In 1977 Kenya withdrew from the East African Airways Corporation and formed its own Kenya Airways, which has 12 planes. Major international airports are at Nairobi and Mombasa; Kisumu and Malindi also serve scheduled flights. Nairobi has a second airport, Wilson Field, which handles safaris and tourist flights.

TRANSPORTATION INDICATORS

Roads (latest)
  Length, km. (mi.): 54,700 (34,000)
  Paved (%): 15
Motor vehicles (latest)
  Automobiles: 133,335
  Trucks and buses: 110,806
  Persons per vehicle: 89
  Road freight, metric ton-km. (short ton-mi.) (millions): 196 (134) (pre-1986)
Railroads (latest)
  Track, km. (mi.): 2,733 (1,698)
  Passenger-km (passenger-mi.) (millions:) 848 (526.9)
  Freight, metric ton-km. (short ton-mi.) (billions): 1.740 (1.192)
Merchant marine
  Vessels (over 100 tons): 27 (1989)
  Total deadweight tonnage (000): 4.8 (1989)
Ports (pre-1986)
  Cargo loaded (million metric tons): 1.878
  Cargo unloaded (million metric tons): 4.437
Air
  Km. (mi.) flown (millions): 13.2 (8.2) (1985)
  Passenger-km. (passenger-mi.) (millions): 754.0 (468.5) (latest)
  Freight, metric ton-km. (short ton-mi.) (millions): 99.9 (68.4) (latest)
  Mail, metric ton-km. (short ton-mi.) (millions): 1.9 (1.3) (1985)
  Airports with scheduled flights: 16 (1990)
Pipelines 1990
  Refined, km. (mi.): 483
Telephones
  Total (000): 337
  Persons per telephone: 69
Phone traffic (million calls)
  Local: 5,737
  Long distance: 6,799
  Combined national: 12,536
  International: 15,776
Post office
  Number of post offices: 853 (1987)
  Pieces of mail handled (millions): 210.639 (1986)
Telegraph
  Total traffic (million words): 3.079
    National: 1.596
    International: 1.483
Telex
  Subscriber lines: 2,531
  Traffic (million minutes): 4.826
Telecommunications 1990
  Satellite stations: 2

Tourism is Kenya's fastest growing industry. Its attractions center on its wildlife—the nation has 15 national parks and 23 game reserves.

TOURISM & TRAVEL INDICATORS, 1986

Total tourist receipts (U.S. $ millions): 410 (1988)
Expenditures by nationals abroad (U.S. $ millions): 25 (1988)
Number of hotel beds (000): 26
Average length of stay (nights): 16
Tourist nights (000): 3,963
Number of tourists (000): 541.2 (1985)
  of whom from United States: 54.3
  Federal Republic of Germany: 100.3
  United Kingdom: 65.6
  Switzerland: 44.6

The major national parks are Nairobi, Tsavo, Meru, Aberdare, Mount Kenya, Lake Nakuru, Mount Elgon, Deny Sabuk and Marine. The three major reserves are Marsabit, Shimba Hills and Marine. Mount Kenya probably has the best scenery, and Lake Nakuru is best known for its huge flocks of flamingos. There are two official bodies concerned with tourism: the Ministry of Tourism and Wildlife and the Kenya Tourist Development Corporation.

DEFENSE

The defense structure is headed by the president as commander in chief of the armed forces. The minister of defense presides over the Defense Council, while the Defense Headquarters is headed by the chief of defense staff, who also is the commander of the army. The right to declare war is vested in the National Assembly.

Military manpower is provided by voluntary enlistment for nine years. A major problem is the preservation of an ethnic balance both within a command and among officers.

Total strength of the armed forces is 13,650.

Army

Personnel: 13,000

Organization: 1 armed brigade; 2 infantry brigades; 1 engineer brigade; 1 armored reconnaissance battalion; 2 artillery battalions; 2 engineer battalions; 1 independent air cavalry battalion; 5 infantry battalions; 1 parachute battalion; air wing with 15 armored helicopters

Equipment: 76 Vickers Mark 3 tanks; 76 armored reconnaissance vehicles, 62 armored personnel carriers, 56 105mm. guns, 12 155mm. howitzers, 30 mortars, 50 recoilless rifles and a number of antitank guided weapons.

Army aviation: 28 combat aircraft; 22 transports; 14 trainers; 44 helicopters.

Since the 1982 attempted coup by the air force, the air force is no longer an independent wing of the armed forces but a unit of the army.

Navy

Personnel: 650
Units: 3 patrol boats; 4 fast attack craft
Naval base: Mombasa

Air bases: Eastleigh (Nairobi), Nanyuki, Embakasi, Nyeri, Mombasa and Kisumu

Kenya has a small military force with no capacity for projecting power beyond its borders. It is relatively nonpoliticized (despite the attempted air force coup of 1982) and exerts little influence on national affairs. Its combat-worthiness and deterrent capability have never been tested in the field since independence. Its possible effectiveness against the highly trained Somali or Uganda forces in the event of a future conflict is therefore a matter of concern.

Over 300 British military officers continue on duty with the Kenyan armed forces, and joint training exercises of Kenyan and British units are held annually. Agreements between the United States and Kenya in the early 1980s allowed U.S. forces access to Kenyan air and naval facilities in exchange for increased military and economic aid.

EDUCATION

Kenya has not introduced universal and compulsory education though primary education is provided free of charge. Schooling consists of seven years of primary school, three years of lower secondary school and three years of upper secondary school, for a total of 13 years. Primary grades—called standards—teach language, mathematics, history, geography, science, arts and crafts and religions. Secondary grades—called forms—emphasize academic subjects, but science and vocational subjects are emphasized at the upper secondary level. In an effort to expand educational facilities, a number of *harambee* schools were built after independence and now account for 45% of total school enrollment. (*Harambee* [Let Us Pull Together] is the national motto, in Swahili.)

The academic year runs from January through December. The medium of instruction is English throughout the school system, although in some areas instruction is provided in the mother tongue in the first three grades.

The school system includes a number of private schools, some of them run by the Asian and European communities.

Primary-school teachers are trained in about 17 primary-teacher colleges, which graduate about 7,000 teachers annually. Secondary-school teachers are trained at Kenyatta College and Kenya Technical Teachers College. Despite considerable progress in the Kenyanization of the teaching staff, non-Kenyans still constitute about one-third of the teachers at the secondary level.

Technical and vocational education is provided by eight secondary schools and four technical high schools. The technical high schools and five of the secondary vocational schools offer four-year programs. More advanced training is provided at Kenya Polytechnic Institute at Nairobi and Mombasa Polytechnic Institute. In addition, *harambee* institutes of technology are being established with partial state sponsorship. The Village Polytechnic Program, begun by the National Christian Council of Kenya, offers technical training to rural primary-school leavers.

EDUCATION INDICATORS, 1988

Literacy
- Total (%): 59.2
- Male (%): 69.6
- Female (%): 49.2

First level
- Schools: 13,849
- Students: 5,031,340
- Teachers: 149,151
- Student/teacher ratio: 33.7
- Net enrollment ratio: 91 (1980)

Second level
- Schools: 2,592
- Students: 522,261
- Teachers: 24,251
- Student/teacher ratio: 21.5
- Net enrollment ratio: 11 (1975)

Vocational
- Schools: 22
- Students: 17,817
- Teachers: 1,332
- Student/teacher ratio: 13.4

Third level (postsecondary)
- Institutions: 4
- Students: 9,888
- Gross enrollment ratio: 1.3 (1985)
- Students (/100,000 pop.): 107

Foreign study
- Foreign students in national universities: 209 (1987)
- Students abroad: 5,503
  - of whom in
    - United states: 1,841 (1988)
    - France: 36 (1988)
    - Federal Republic of Germany: 85 (1988)
    - United Kingdom: 974 (1987)

Public expenditure
- Total (K. Sh. billion): 8.935
- % of GNP: 7 (1988)
- % of national budget: 22.7
- % of current expenditure: 92.6

GRADUATES, 1983

Total: 2,386
Education: 838
Humanities & religion: 0
Fine & applied arts: 1
Law: 88
Social & behavioral sciences: 357
Commerce & business: 160
Mass communication: 0
Home economics: 0
Service trades: 0
Natural sciences: 282
Mathematics & computer science: 0
Medicine: 278
Engineering: 167
Architecture: 48
Industrial programs: 0
Transportation & communications: 0
Agriculture, forestry, fisheries: 111
Other: 56

Adult education and literacy programs are coordinated by the Board of Adult Education. The Institute of Adult Studies at the University of Nairobi offers courses on a regular basis. There are adult studies centers in all major towns. Correspondence courses are offered by the Adult Education Division of the Ministry of Education.

All public schools except municipal primary schools are under the direct control of the Ministry of Education. Aided and maintained private schools are supervised by district education boards. Curriculum development is the responsibility of the Kenya Institute of Education.

Kenya has three state universities: Nairobi University, Kenyatta University and the most recently formed Moi University at Eldoret.

LEGAL SYSTEM

The main sources of Kenyan jurisprudence are English common law; African customary law; legislative acts of the National Assembly after independence and the British Parliament before independence; and judicial precedent as reported in *East African Law Reports.*

Before the East African Community was dissolved, the highest court in the land was the Court of Appeal for East Africa. Now that role is filled by the High Court, with a chief justice and 11 *puisne* judges sitting continuously in Nairobi, Mombasa, Nakuru and Kisumu. The subordinate district magistrate's courts are divided into three classes. At the third-class level are the six *qadi* courts, which have jurisdiction over Muslims in cases relating to personal status. At the village level bodies of elders settle disputes relating to African traditional law.

Aside from the unprecedented circumstances created by the attempted coup in August 1982, however, habeas corpus generally has been available in Kenya. Kenyan law requires that persons charged with crimes be brought biweekly before judicial authorities in public court to ensure that investigations are carried out in timely manner and that prisoners are not mistreated.

The Kenyan judiciary is noted for its independence and integrity. The courts can review acts of the government and legislation and declare laws and acts null and void. The state may be sued for damages caused by its illegal acts. Constitutional guarantees are enforced in practice. The chief justice is appointed by the president, but all other judicial appointments are made on the advice of the Judicial Service Commission. Appointments are permanent but with mandatory retirement at 65. Until 1988 senior judges could only be removed by a special tribunal, but constitutional amendments passed in July of that year gave the president the power to dismiss these judges. The majority of the judiciary still is composed of foreigners because of the continuing shortage of law school graduates. The chief justice and seven *puisne* judges of the High Court and 27 professional magistrates are non-Kenyans.

Kenya's correctional facilities are administered by the Kenya Prisons Service. Penal institutions include regular prisons as well as detention camps, work camps and prison farms. The treatment of prisoners conforms to modern principles and civilized standards and emphasizes rehabilitation, teaching new skills, literacy and education courses, remission of sentence for good conduct, a probation service program and halfway houses as alternatives to prolonged incarceration. The Prisoners Aid Society helps prisoners to return to civil life. Prison personnel are trained at the Prisons Training School at Nairobi.

LAW ENFORCEMENT

The national police force is headed by a commissioner, who is responsible to the Police Service Commission and the Ministry of Home Affairs. Operational control is centralized at national headquarters at Nairobi, which is the hub of an advanced nationwide police communications system. All police vehicles throughout the country are linked by a VHF network to the control center in police headquarters. The chain of command runs through eight provincial commands and 40 divisional or district commands (both under commissioners) to 200 stations and posts in cities, towns and other locations.

Besides the general-duty police there are six operations wings of the national headquarters. The best known is the paramilitary General Service Unit (GSU), a 1,800-man mobile combat force armed with rifles, Bren guns and mortars. The GSU is a highly trained internal security force. The other divisions are the Railways and Harbors Police; the Criminal Investigations Directorate (CID), which is the Kenyan secret police concerned with intelligence-gathering and countersubversion; the Police Air wing, with 10 aircraft; the Police Dog Section; and the Inspection Department. The Administrative Police, formerly known as the Tribal Police, enforce law and order in rural and tribal areas under the administrative control of district commissioners and the operational control of tribal chiefs. Administrative policemen usually are members of the local tribe or ethnic group. The Police Reserve is an auxiliary force activated during times of emergency.

The force has been completely Kenyanized, except in the intelligence and communications areas, and is ethnically balanced. Police training is provided at the Kenya Police College and the CID Training School in Nairobi.

Kenya, like many other developing nations, experienced an upswing in crime rates over the past two decades. The chief contributory causes for the rising crime rates are the breakdown of traditional social values and high unemployment. Urban crime is associated with *kondoism*, armed robbery by organized gangs using guns and long-bladed bush knives, with automobiles for fast getaways. Nairobi's crime and delinquency rates are the highest in the country. Prostitution and trafficking in *bhang*, a narcotic, are other major law-enforcement problems.

HEALTH

Kenya has a comprehensive health-care delivery system and infrastructure under the Ministry of Health. The famous Flying Doctor Service, a private organization founded in 1961 by a British physician, provides a mobile medical service. The main health problems are infectious respiratory diseases, malaria, leprosy and schistosomiasis. AIDS has been a growing medical problem in Kenya. There have been no reliable government figures due to the fear such information might hurt the lucrative tourist trade. The Minister of Health admitted to only eight cases and seven deaths up to 1986. Health problems are complicated by malnutrition and sanitation.

HEALTH INDICATORS

Health personnel 1987
- Physicians: 3,071
  - persons per: 7,174
- Dentists: 492
- Nurses: 23,064
- Pharmacists: 231 (1985)

Hospitals 1987
- Number: 536
- Number of beds (/10,000): 14 (1987)

Public health expenditures (latest)
- As % of national budget: 6.1
- Per capita (U.S. $): 6.10

Vital statistics
- Crude death rate (/1,000): 7 (1990)
- Life expectancy at birth 1990
  - Males: 62
  - Females: 67
- Infant mortality rate (/1,000 live births): 60 (1990)
- Child mortality rate under 5 yrs. (/1,000 live births) (1985–90): 113
- Maternal mortality rate (/100,000 live births) (1986–87): 168 (est.)
- Population with access to safe water (%): 30 (latest)

FOOD & NUTRITION

The staple food of Kenya is corn, which is ground and eaten in the form of a porridge called *posho*. Meat and fish are only occasionally eaten. There also are a number of traditional food taboos that militate against a balanced diet. Beer is the most popular drink except among the pastoralists, who drink tea, milk or milk mixed with animal blood. In general the Kenyan diet is deficient in proteins, vitamins and fats.

In 1983 the consumption of food per capita was 2,056 calories (88% of requirements).

MEDIA & CULTURE

Five daily newspapers are published in Nairobi—three in English and two in Swahili—with a circulation of approximately 280,000. Three newspapers are under private management and two are published by KANU. The principal dailies are the *Daily Nation* (165,000) *The Standard* (49,000), *Kenya Times* (36,000) and *Taifa Leo* (57,047). The *Taifa Leo* and the *Kenya Times* are the KANU party newspapers. The latter is a joint venture of a British group and KANU. Formed in 1986, it was to become the leading newspaper in East Africa. In addition, there are two nondailies with a total circulation in mid 1980s of 281,200 (16 per 1,000 inhabitants), 12 weeklies and over 40 monthlies and other periodicals.

There is no official censorship, although all newspapers are required by law to register and secure a publishing license. Under an unwritten and informal set of rules, harsh criticism of the government and direct attacks on the president are barred. Dissidence is permitted within bounds, and some freedom coexists paradoxically with an increasing degree of repression. Press-government relations generally have not been happy despite the restraint exercised by journalists on sensitive issues. Foreign newsmen often are threatened with expulsion if they file stories that elicit official displeasure.

The national news agency is Kenya News Agency (KNA). Foreign news agencies with bureaus in Nairobi include AFT, AP, Tass, CTK, Novosti, DPA, ANSA, Reuters, UPI and Ghana News Agency.

MEDIA INDICATORS

- Number of dailies: 5 (latest)
- Circulation (000): 280 (latest)
- Per 1,000 pop.: 13
- Newsprint consumption (1988)
  - Total metric tons: 12,000
  - Per 1,000 pop. (kg.): 520

Book publishing

Number of titles: 933 (first editions) (latest)

Radio
- Number of transmitters: 30 (1989)
- Number of persons per radio receiver: 13 (1989)

Television
- Television transmitters: 6 (1989)
- Number of persons per T.V. receiver: 119 (1989)

Cinema
- Number of fixed cinemas: 40 (pre-1986)
- Seating capacity (000): 20 (pre-1986)
- Annual attendance (millions): 9.2 (pre-1986)

CULTURAL & ENVIRONMENTAL INDICATORS

Libraries (pre-1986)
- Number: 2
- Volumes (000): 511
- Registered borrowers (000): 98
- Loans (/1,000 pop.): 34

Museums (pre-1986)
- Annual attendance (000): 531
- Attendance (/1,000 pop.): 27

Nature reserves (latest)
- Number of facilities: 35

Kenya has one of the largest book publishing industries in East Africa, with over 20 major publishers. Much of the annual output comes from the East African Publishing House and the East African Literature Bureau. Kenya adheres to the Universal Copyright Convention.

Broadcasting was operated by the state run Voice of Kenya (VOK), until it was replaced in 1989 by the Kenya Broadcasting Corporation (KBC), also a state corporation. KBC radio division has three services: the national service in Swahili from three medium-wave and four shortwave transmitters in Nairobi, Mombasa and Kisuma for 17 hours a day; the general service in English from one medium-wave, two shortwave and one FM transmitter in Nairobi for 17 hours a day; and a vernacular service in 18 languages from one medium-wave and two shortwave transmitters in Nairobi, one medium-wave and two shortwave transmitters in Kisumu and one medium-wave transmitter in Mombasa. Aggregate broadcasting time is 330 hours a week.

The KBC television service, begun in 1962 as Voice of Kenya operates a main station in Nairobi, a regional station in Mombasa and two relay stations. The Nairobi station is on the air for about seven hours a day beginning in the late afternoon, broadcasting over half of the programs in Swahili and the rest in English and Hindustani.

Kenya's two largest libraries are the McMillan Memorial Library at Nairobi and the Library of the University of Nairobi, with holdings of 110,000 volumes and 95,000 volumes, respectively.

SOCIAL WELFARE

Kenya has no comprehensive state-sponsored Social Security system or welfare services, although there are some voluntary programs sponsored by the national Social Security Fund. Much of social welfare work is in the hands of private organizations and mutual aid societies run by and for ethnic groups.

GLOSSARY

baraza: a public meeting or meetingplace in rural areas.

harambee: literally, pull together. National motto of Kenya, calling Kenyans to cooperate in building the nation. Schools constructed through voluntary community help are called harambee schools.

kondoism: armed robbery by organized gangs using guns and knives.

mzee: old man or elder; title of respect used in addressing Jomo Kenyatta.

shamba: agricultural plot or smallholding.

shifta: bandit, especially, Somali guerrilla engaged in secessionist movement.

wananchi: the common people (of Kenya).

CHRONOLOGY (from 1963)

1963— On June 1 Kenya becomes a self-governing nation with Jomo Kenyatta as prime minister under the Independence (Majimbo) Constitution. Army mutiny is suppressed with British help. . . . In national elections KANU wins 105 seats and KADU 22 in the National Assembly. Kenya becomes an independent nation within the Commonwealth.

1964— Kenya becomes a republic with Kenyatta as president. KANU becomes sole political party as KADU dissolves itself and merges with KANU.

1966— KANU congress ousts leftists from key positions; pro-Soviet Vice President Oginga Odinga resigns and founds new leftist party, Kenya People's Union (KPU), which suffers severe reverses in elections.

1967— Kenya, Tanzania and Uganda sign Treaty for East African Cooperation, establishing East African Community. . . . Under an amendment to the Constitution the National Assembly becomes a unicameral body. . . . Trade Licensing Act is passed restricting the economic rights of noncitizens, especially Asians.

1969— Tom Mboya, the popular Luo leader and minister of economic planning, is assassinated; the assassination touches off a wave of Luo riots and Kikuyu oathtaking. (Kikuyu oaths are famous. They are something like the pledge of allegiance ceremonies.) . . . The KPU is banned and Odinga is jailed.

1974— In new elections Kenyatta is reelected for a third term, but a number of cabinet ministers and KANU members of the National Assembly lose their seats.

1975— Josiah M. Kariuki, unofficial leader of the opposition, is assassinated; the opposition accuses the government of complicity in the murder.

1977— Kenya-Tanzania and Kenya-Uganda borders are closed as relations among the three EAC members worsen; Kenya withdraws from East African Airways and the East African Railways and Harbors Administration.

1978— Kenyatta dies; Daniel arap Moi is proclaimed president.

1979— In national elections, Daniel arap Moi is elected president. In a dramatic drive against official corruption, the commissioner of police and five of eight provincial police commissioners are ousted.

1980— Kenya and United States sign agreement allowing the latter to use Kenyan air and naval bases.

1982— Attempted coup by air force against President Moi is foiled. . . . Air force is disbanded and over 1,000 airmen are arrested.

1983— Kikuyu leader and cabinet minister Charles Njonjo is dismissed on unnamed charges. President Moi is reelected to office.

1984— Moi visits Somalia and signs agreements. . . . Violence in Wajr District leads to intervention by security forces and alleged massacre of 300 persons. Moi tries to stem internal corruption in KANU and the civil service; all civil servants must be members of KANU.

1986— Student unrest and pamphleteering lead to the closing of the university of Nairobi; Mwakenya is suppressed. A line-up system of voting in primary elections replaces the secret ballot; the NCCK protest this system. A constitutional amendment increases the president's influence over the civil service and the judiciary with the power to dismiss the attorney general without recourse.

1987— Kenya is accused of human rights violations by Amnesty International. It is announced that only members of KANU will be allowed to vote. Odinga denounces the government and calls for a multiparty system.

1988— Moi announces his re-election prior to a vote. A constitutional amendment makes it possible for the president to dismiss senior judges and extends the time for detention without trial to 14 days. Accusations of election fraud is shortly followed by the resignation of the Minister of Transportation and Communication.

1989— Kenya comes out in favor of an ivory ban.

Kenya threatens to retaliate for Somali incursion in pursuit of rebels.

1990— A loose coalition of politicians, churchmen, lawyers and human-rights activists call for political pluralism. Government forces crush pro-democracy rallies, leading to general rioting. KANU rejects the creation of a multiparty political system.

1991— Former Vice President Oginga Odinga launches an opposition group, the National Democratic Party.

BIBLIOGRAPHY

BOOKS AND FILMS

African Odyssey: The Red Bicycle. Color film, 14 min. Albert Waller.

African Odyssey: The Two Worlds of Musembe. Color film, 15 min. Albert Waller.

Amsden, Alice H. *International Firms and Labor in Kenya, 1945–1971.* New York, 1971.

Arnold, Guy. *Kenyatta and the Politics of Kenya.* London, 1974.

———. *Modern Kenya.* London, 1981.

Azania: A Changing Corner of Africa. Color film, 11 min. International Film Bureau.

Baldwin, Harriet, and Bruce Ross-Larson. *Economic Summary: Kenya.* Washington, D.C., 1981.

Barkan, Joel D., and John J. Okumu. *Politics and Public Policy in Kenya and Tanzania.* New York, 1979.

Berg-Schlosser, Dirk. *The Distribution of Income and Education in Kenya.* New York, 1970.

Bienen, H. *Kenya: The Politics of Participation and Control.* Princeton, NJ, 1974.

Bolton, Kenneth. Harambee *Country: A Guide to Kenya.* London, 1970.

Brett, E. A. *Colonialism and Underdevelopment in East Africa, 1919–39* New York, 1973.

Brown, Jeremy M. *Kenyatta.* London, 1973.

Collier, Paul, and Deepak Lal. *Poverty and Growth in Kenya.* Washington, D.C., 1980.

Collins, Robert L. *Kenya* (World Bibliographical Series). Santa Barbara, CA, 1982.

Cone, L. Winston, and J. F. Lipscomb. *The History of Kenyan Agriculture.* New York, 1972.

Court, David, and Dharam Ghai. *Education, Society and Development: Perspectives from Kenya.* New York, 1975.

East Africa. Color film, 23 min. Paul Hoefler.

East Africa: Ends and Beginnings. Black-and-white film, 48 min. National Educational Television.

East Africa: Kenya, Tanganyika, Uganda. Color film, 21 min. *Encyclopaedia Britannica* Films.

Fadiman, Jeffrey A. *The Moment of Conquest: Meru, Kenya, 1907.* Athens, OH, 1979.

Family of the Bush: Son of Warriors. Color film, 12 min. Contemporary Films.

Family of the City: Adventure in Nairobi. Color film, 11 min. Contemporary Films.

Faruqee, Rashid. *Kenya: Population and Development.* Washington, D.C., 1980.

Fedders, Andrew, and Cynthia Salvadori. *Peoples and Cultures of Kenya.* London, 1980.

Frost, Richard. *Race Against Time: Human Relations and Politics in Kenya Before Independence.* Totowa, NJ, 1978.

Gertzel, Cherry. *Politics of Independent Kenya.* Evanston, IL, 1970.

Ghai, Yash P., and J. P. McAuslan. *Public Law and Political Change in Kenya.* New York, 1970.

———. *Planning for Basic Needs in Kenya: Performance, Policies and Prospects.* Geneva, 1975.

Gordon, David F. *The State and Decolonization in Kenya.* Boulder, CO, 1985.

Gregory, Robert G. *India and East Africa: A History of Race Relations Within the British Empire, 1890–1939.* New York, 1972.

Harambee: *Pull Together.* Color film, 19 min. American University Field Service.

Harbeson, J. W. *Nation-Building in Kenya: The Role of Land Reform.* Evanston, IL, 1973.

Harris, Joseph E. *Repatriates and Refugees in a Colonial Society: The Case of Kenya.* Washington, D.C., 1986.

Hazelwood, Arthur. *The Economy of Kenya: The Kenyatta Era.* New York, 1979.

Heyer, Judith, and Dunstan Ireri. *Rural Development in Kenya.* New York, 1973.

———. *Agricultural Development in Kenya: An Economic Assessment.* New York, 1977.

Holm, John D. *A Comparative Study of Political Involvement in Three African States: Botswana, Ghana and Kenya.* Syracuse, NY, 1979.

Holtham, Gerald, and Arthur Hazelwood. *Aid and Inequality in Kenya: British Development Assistance to Kenya.* New York, 1976.

Hoyle, B. S. *Seaports and Development: The Experience of Kenya and Tanzania.* New York, 1983.

Hunt, Diana. *The Impending Crisis in Kenya: The Case for Land Reform.* London, 1984.

Kaplinsky, Rafael. *Readings on the Multinational Corporation in Kenya.* New York, 1978.

Kariuki, Josiah M. *Mau Mau Detainee.* New York, 1975.

Kenya Boran. Color film, 33 min. American University Field Service.

Kenya into the Second Decade: World Bank Country Economic Report. Baltimore, MD, 1975.

Kenya: Mombasa. Color film, 20 min. BBC.

Kenya: The Multiracial Experiment. Color film, 19 min. ABC.

Kenyatta. Color film, 28 min. Films, Inc.

Kenyatta. Color film, 51 min. Anthony David Productions.

Kenyatta, Jomo. *The Challenge of Uhuru: The Progress of Kenya, 1968–70.* New York, 1971.

Killick, Tony. *Papers on the Kenya Economy.* London, 1981.

King, John R. *Stabilization Policy in an African Setting, 1963–73.* London, 1979.

Kitching, Gavin. *Class and Economic Change in Kenya: The Making of an African Petite Bourgeoisie.* New Haven, CT, 1980.

Langdon, Steven W. *Multinational Corporations in the Political Economy of Kenya.* New York, 1981.

Leys, Colin. *Underdevelopment in Kenya: The Political Economy of Neocolonialism, 1964–71.* Berkeley, CA, 1975.

Livingstone, Ian. *Rural Development, Employment and Income in Kenya.* London, 1985.

Marris, Peter, and Anthony Somerset. *The African Businessman: A Study of Entrepreneurship and Development in Kenya.* New York, 1971.

Mbithi, Philip M., and Rasmus Rasmusson. *Self-Reliance in Kenya: The Case of Harambee.* New York, 1978.

Mboya, Tom. *The Challenge of Nationhood.* New York, 1970.

Meck, Margarete. *Problems and Prospects of Social Services in Kenya.* New York, 1971.

Miller, Norman. *Kenya: The Quest for Prosperity.* Boulder, CO, 1984.

Nicholls, C. S. *The Swahili Coast.* London, 1972.

Norcliffe, Glen. *Planning African Development: The Kenya Experience.* Boulder, CO, 1981.

Obudho, R. A. *Urbanization in Kenya.* Lanham, MD, 1983.

Ogot, Bethwell A. *Historical Dictionary of Kenya.* Metuchen, NJ, 1981.

Ominde, S. H. *Population and Development in Kenya.* London, 1984.

Oyugi, Walter O. *Rural Development Administration: A Kenyan Experience.* Bombay, 1980.

Potholm, Christian, and Richard A. Fredland. *Integration and Disintegration in East Africa.* Lanham, MD, 1980.

Rempel, Henry, and William H. Hourse. *The Kenyan Employment Problem.* New York, 1978.

Rothchild, Ronald R. *Racial Bargaining in Independent Kenya: A Study of Minorities and Decolonization.* New York, 1973.

Sandbrook, R. *Proletarians and African Capitalism: The Kenyan Case, 1960–72.* New York, 1975.

Slater, Charles C. *Kensim: A Systems Simulation of the Developing Kenyan Economy.* Boulder, CO, 1977.

Spear, T. *Kenya's Past: An Introduction to Historical Methods in Africa.* London, 1981.

Spencer, John. *The Kenya African Union.* London, 1985.

Stichter, Sharon. *Migrant Labor in Kenya: Capitalism and African Response.* London, 1982.

Strayer, R. *Inquiry into World Cultures: Kenya.* Englewood Cliffs, NJ, 1974.

Swainson, Nicola. *The Development of Corporate Capitalism in Kenya.* Berkeley, CA, 1980.

Thomas, Barbara P. *Politics, Participation and Poverty: Development through Self-Help in Kenya.* Boulder, CO, 1985.

Tignor, R. *Colonial Transformation in Kenya.* Princeton, NJ, 1975.

Umoja. *Struggle for Democracy in Kenya: Special Report on the 1988 General Elections in Kenya.* London, 1988.

Wasserman, G. B. *Politics of Decolonization.* New York, 1976.

Werlin, H. W. *Governing an African City: A Study in Nairobi.* New York, 1974.

Wolff, Richard D. *The Economics of Colonialism: Britain and Kenya, 1870–1930.* New Haven, CT, 1974.

Zwanenberg, R. M. van, and Anne King. *An Economic History of Kenya and Uganda, 1800–1970.* New York, 1975.

OFFICIAL PUBLICATIONS

Central Kenya Bank. *Economic and Financial Review.*

Central Statistics Bureau. *Economic Survey.*

———. *Statistical Abstract.*

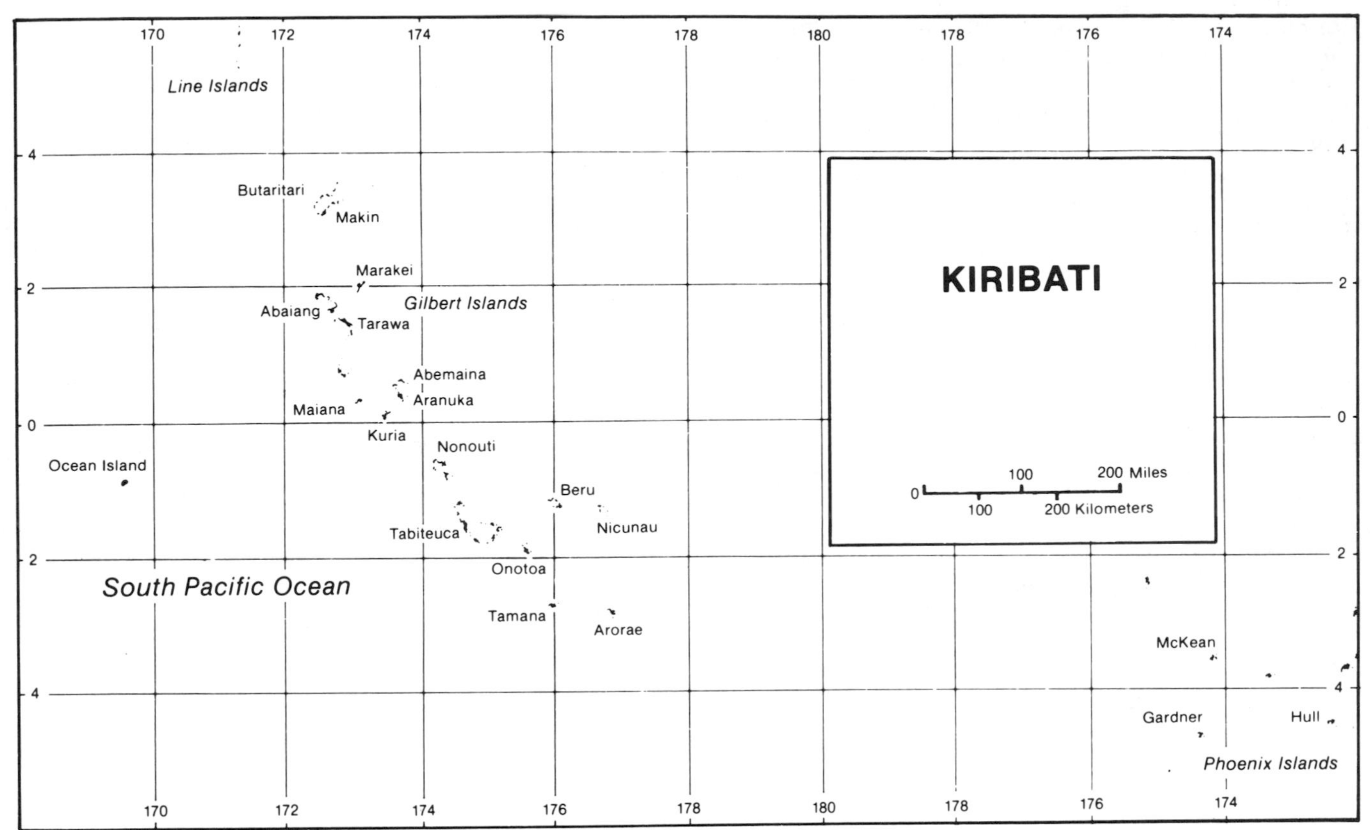

Source: American Geographical Society

Emblem not available

KIRIBATI

BASIC FACT SHEET

OFFICIAL NAME: Republic of Kiribati (formerly the Gilbert Islands)
ABBREVIATION: KI
CAPITAL: Bairiki
HEAD OF STATE & HEAD OF GOVERNMENT: President Teatao Teannaki
NATURE OF GOVERNMENT: Republic
POPULATION: 71,012 (1990)
AREA: 684 sq. km. (264 sq. mi.)
ETHNIC MAJORITY: Micronesian
LANGUAGES: English (official), I-Kiribati
RELIGIONS: Protestantism, Roman Catholicism
UNIT OF CURRENCY: Australian dollar
NATIONAL FLAG: A frigate bird in flight on a red background, above a rising sun, and alternating wavy lines of blue and white.
NATIONAL EMBLEM: A sun rising out of wavy lines of blue and white, with a frigate bird in flight above, on a red background, as on the national flag; at the bottom, in black lettering on a gold and red scroll, is the motto *Te Mauri Te Raoi Ao Te Tabomoa* (Health, Peace, Prosperity).
NATIONAL HOLIDAYS: New Year's Day, Independence Day, Youth Day (August 4), Christmas, Boxing Day, Good Friday, Easter Monday, Queen's Birthday, Bank Holiday (August), and Prince of Wales' Birthday
NATIONAL CALENDAR: Gregorian
DATE OF INDEPENDENCE: July 12, 1979
DATE OF CONSTITUTION: July 12, 1979
WEIGHTS & MEASURES: Metric

GEOGRAPHICAL FEATURES

Kiribati comprises three island groups of 32 low atolls and Ocean Island or Banaba, a raised atoll to the west. The total land area is 684 sq. km. (264 sq. mi.). The three island groups are dispersed over an area of 3 million sq. km. (1.1 million sq. mi.) in the mid-Pacific: the Gilbert Islands on the equator, the Phoenix Islands to the east, and the Line Islands to the north and south of the equator. The country extends 3,870 km. (2,400 mi.) from east to west and 2,050 km. (1,275 mi.) from north to south. The total coastline is 1,143 km. (778 mi.).

The Gilbert group consists of Abaiang, Abemama, Aranuka, Arorae, Beru, Butaritari, Kuria, Maiana, Makin, Marakei, Nicunau, Nonouti, Onotoa, Tabiteuca, Tamana and Tarawa. The Phoenix group comprises Birnie, Canton, Enderbury, Gardner, Hull, McKean, Phoenix and Sydney. The Line Group encompasses Kiritimati (Christmas), Tabuaeran (Fanning), Malden, Starbuck, Vostock, Teraina (Washington), Caroline and Flint, the last two leased to commercial interests on Tahiti. Only some of the islands are inhabited.

The capital is Bairiki, on Tarawa, with a population of 21,393 in 1985. There are few other settlements that can be even remotely considered as towns.

CLIMATE & WEATHER

Because Kiribati lies wholly within the tropics, the climate is uniformly hot and humid, tempered by continuous breezes from the sea. There are no true seasonal changes in the conventional sense of the term. Rather, the year is divided into periods of greater or lesser rainfall, with a season of northwesterly trade winds from March to October and a season of gales and rains from October to March. Average annual rainfall varies from 3,000 mm. (118 in.) in the northern islands to 1,500 mm. (59 in.) at Tarawa and 700 mm. (28 in.) in the southern Line Islands. Daytime temperatures vary between 28°C (79°F) and 32°C (90°F). Drought conditions are common on many atolls.

POPULATION

The population of Kiribati was estimated in 1990 at 71,012, on the basis of the last census, in 1985. The pressure on land is great, but population density is a moderate 83.7 per sq. km. (216.8 per sq. mi.) because many of the islands do not support any inhabitants at all.

The 1973–76 development plan gave high priority to control of population growth. A Committee on Population Policy has been set up to coordinate programs

DEMOGRAPHIC INDICATORS

Population (000): 71 (1990)
Year of last census: 1985
Sex distribution (% at last census): males, 49.6; females, 50.4
Population estimates and projections (000)

1930: 27	1960: 41	2000: 88
1940: 29	1970: 49	
1950: 33	1980: 57	

Age profile (% at last census)

0–14: 38.9	30–44: 16.1	60–74: 4.9
15–29: 29.9	45–59: 9.3	75 and over: 0.9

Number of cities of population over 500,000: 0 (1980)
Population density per sq. km. (per sq. mile): 83.7 (216.8) (1990)

VITAL STATISTICS

Crude birth rate (/1,000): 34 (1990)
Crude death rate (/1,000): 13 (1990)
Infant mortality rate (/1,000 live births): 65 (1990)
Life expectancy (yrs.) at birth: males, 53; females, 57 (1990)
Total fertility rate (/woman): 4.3 (1990)
Rate of natural increase (/1,000): 23.2 (1988)
Marriage rate (/1,000): 5.2 (1988)
Average household size: 6.1 (latest)

STATUS OF WOMEN INDICATORS

Number of women (000): 28 (1978)
% women in labor force: 36.1 (1985)
Total fertility rate (/woman): 4.3 (1990)

designed to bring about a permanent reduction in family size. In an attempt to reduce overcrowding due to the high population growth rate, the government announced plans in 1988 to relocate 4,700 people to outlying atolls. The government also is encouraging immigration to other countries in the Pacific region.

ETHNIC COMPOSITION

The population is overwhelmingly Micronesian. They are a people of moderate stature and straight or wavy black hair, and some Mongoloid features. In appearance they bear a striking resemblance to Indonesians. There is some evidence of intermingling with Polynesians, who constitute the largest minority. A scattering of Europeans and Chinese complete the ethnic mosaic.

LANGUAGES

English is the official language, but the language of the people is I-Kiribati (formerly Gilbertese), a Micronesian language derived from the Austronesian linguistic family.

RELIGIONS

Virtually all Kiribatians are Christians, but some traditional beliefs and practices have survived. The conversion of the islands is credited to Harry Bingham, of the American Board of Foreign Missions, and John S. Whitmee, of the London Missionary Society. Roman Catholics comprise 48% and Protestants 45% of the population.

HISTORICAL BACKGROUND

The islands were officially discovered by the British navy between 1764 and 1824. In 1892 they became a British protectorate under the name Gilbert and Ellice Islands, and remained so until they became a colony in 1915. They were under the jurisdiction of the British high commissioner for the western Pacific until 1972, when they were placed under a governor directly appointed from London. In 1978 the Ellice Islands became the independent nation of Tuvalu. Despite demands by the people of Ocean Island (Banaba) for separation and independence, the Gilbert Islands were granted internal self-government in 1977. In 1979 the islands became an independent republic within the commonwealth under the name Kiribati.

Upon independence in 1979 Ieremia T. Tabai, the former chief minister, assumed the presidency. He was returned to office in 1982. Later that year his government fell following a dispute over salary raises for several public officials. As provided by the Constitution, the Council of State assumed interim administration. Tabai was reelected in 1983 and again in 1987 following assertions that he would be in violation of a constitutional provision limiting the president to three terms. Tabai contended that he had not served three full terms, since his second government has been in power for less than a year.

CONSTITUTION & GOVERNMENT

Kiribati is a sovereign democratic republic under the Constitution that came into force on independence in 1979. The president, known as *beretitenti*, is both head of state and head of government and presides over the cabinet, which consists of the *beretitenti, the kauo-man-ni-beretitenti* or vice president, the attorney general and not more than eight ministers. Legislative power resides with the unicameral Maneaba ni Maungatabu, consisting of 39 elected members, one nominated member from Banaba and the attorney general as ex officio member.

The Constitution makes special provision for Banaba, guaranteeing the Banabans' inalienable right to enter and reside in Banaba (from which they had been evacuated because of the adverse effects of open-cast mining of phosphates), and their right to the land on completion of phosphate extraction. The Constitution also provides for a Banaba Island Council.

GOVERNMENT LIST
(July/August 1991)

President	Teannaki, Teatao
Vice President	Iuta, Teatao
Minister of Commerce, Industry & Employment	Tateraka, Remuera
Minister of Education, Science & Technology	Kaitaake, Anterea
Minister of the Environment & Natural Resources	Tabai, Ieremia
Minister of Finance & Economic Planning	Iuta, Taomati
Minister of Foreign Affairs & International Trade	Teannaki, Teatao
Minister of Health, Family Planning & Social Welfare	Toum, Baitika
Minister of Home Affairs & Rural Development	Tetaeka, Binata
Minister of Line & Phoenix Development	Boanereko, Boanereke
Minister of Transport, Communications & Tourism	Tebania, Inatao
Minister of Works & Energy	Tenieu, Teaiwa
Speaker of the House	Neeti, Beretitari
Attorney General	Takabwebwe, Michael N.

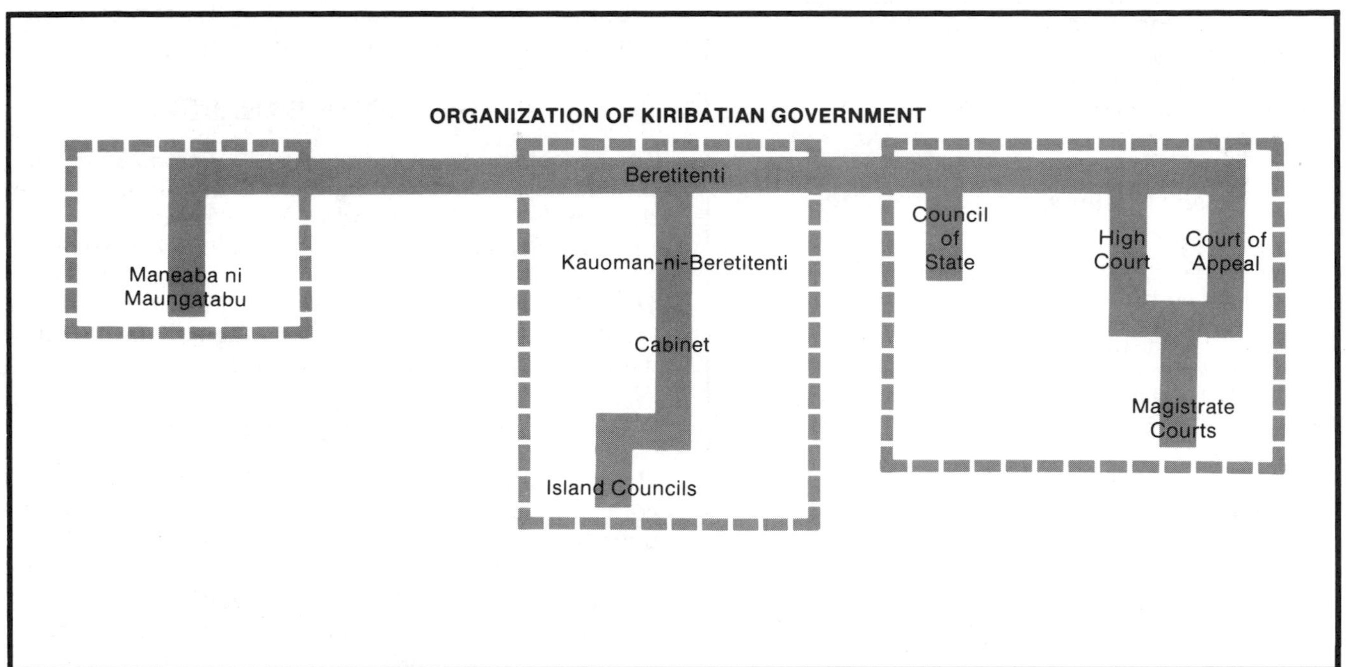

Elections are held on the basis of universal adult suffrage. The Constitution provides for a judicial system composed of the High Court, the Court of Appeals and local magistrates' courts.

FREEDOM & HUMAN RIGHTS

No violations of human rights have been reported in Kiribati.

CIVIL SERVICE

No information is available on the civil service in Kiribati.

LOCAL GOVERNMENT

Under the Local Government Ordinance of 1966, elected councils function in each of the inhabited islands with authority to enact local bylaws and oversee social services. Administrative government is divided into six districts: Tarawa, North Gilbert, South Gilbert, Central Gilbert, Banaba and the Line islands. The districts have retained much autonomy due to the geographic layout of the nation. Council powers include taxation and independent budget planning.

FOREIGN POLICY

Although Kiribati participates in certain U.N. agencies, it has not applied for membership. Its international contacts are limited mainly to the Commonwealth, of which it is a member. In 1979 it signed a friendship treaty with the United States under which the latter relinquished all claims to Canton, Enderbury and Hull islands in the Phoenix and Line island groups. It has seven other treaties and agreements with the United States, covering aviation, consuls, extradition, the Peace Corps, telecommunications, trademarks, visas, and tuna fishing. Kiribati does not have an embassy in Washington, D.C., although it does have a representative to cover a number of countries, one of which is the United States. The U.S. ambassador to Kiribati resides in Fiji.

PARLIAMENT

The national legislature is the Maneaba ni Maungatabu (House of Assembly), comprising 39 members elected for four-year terms, one nominated member from Banaba and the attorney general as ex officio member. The cabinet is directly responsible to the Maneaba ni Maungatabu.

The Constitution also provides for a Council of State composed of the chairman of the Public Services Commission, the chief justice and the speaker of the Maneaba ni Maungatabu. The council serves as an interim government when the president no longer enjoys the confidence of the legislature.

Elections are held on the basis of universal adult suffrage.

POLITICAL PARTIES

There are no organized political parties in Kiribati other than the Christian Democratic Party, formed in 1985 to oppose a fishing agreement with the Soviet Union. The party is headed by Dr. Harry Tong.

ECONOMY

The economy of Kiribati was based, until 1979, on the production of phosphates on the island of Banaba. Production ended in 1979, and the nation has been looking for alternate sources of revenue. The end of

GROSS DOMESTIC PRODUCT

GDP nominal (A. $ billions): 0.032 (1986)
GDP per capita (U.S. $): 500 (1989)
GDP by type of expenditure (%), 1986
- Consumption
  - Private: 85
  - Government: 56
- Gross domestic investment: 31
- Foreign trade
  - Exports: 23
  - Imports: −94

Cost components of GDP (%), 1986
- Net indirect taxes: 12
- Consumption of fixed capital: 12
- Compensation of employees: 52
- Net operating surplus: 25

Sectoral origin of GDP (%), 1988
- Primary
  - Agriculture: 30
- Secondary
  - Manufacturing: 2
  - Construction: 5
  - Public utilities: 2
- Tertiary
  - Transportation & communications: 14
  - Trade: 12
  - Finance: 7
  - Other services: 3
  - Government: 22

production had a devastating impact on the economy because receipts from that industry accounted for about 80% of total export earnings. The per capita GDP fell from $750 in 1979 to $370 in 1987. The economy is currently dependent on tuna fish and copra exports as well as foreign aid from international organizations as well as the United Kingdom and Australia. The nation has very few resources, and poor soil limits production of agricultural commodities.

Kiritati's GNP was $40 million in 1988, when its GNP per capita was $650. Its capital other than reserves had a deficit of $5 million in 1986.

PUBLIC FINANCE

The fiscal year is the calendar year. The fiscal year is the calendar year. Until 1979 the main source of tax revenues was the phosphate industry. Other sources of revenue are taxes on copra exports and income as well as a flat 25% tax companies pay on chargeable income. Revenues derived from these sources are minimal. The government also derives income from import duties, philately and agreements licensing foreign vessels to fish in Kiribati's exclusive fishing zone.

The current development plan is aimed at achieving economic self-sufficiency. It stresses support for fishing and agriculture as well as infrastructure development.

FOREIGN AID, 1989

Total foreign aid, ($ millions): 16.9
- Bilateral: 15.8
- Multilateral: 1.1

During 1970–87 Kiribati received $245 million in aid from Western (non-US) countries.

CURRENCY & BANKING

The Kiribatian unit of currency is the Australian dollar, divided into 100 cents. Coins are issued in denominations of 1, 2, 5, 10, 20 and 50 cents, while notes are issued in denominations 1, 2, 5, 10, 20 and 50 dollars.

The dollar exchange rate in June 1991 was $1 = A$1.312. The Bank of Kiribati in Tarawa is the primary banking establishment in the nation. The Kiribati Development Bank opened in 1987.

AGRICULTURE

Most of Kiribati, other than Banaba, is composed of coral atolls with poor-quality soil. As a result, much of the island's 64,000 ha. (158,144 ac.) is not suited for cultivation. Coconut palms provide the only agricultural export, in the form of copra. A government-owned company operates a coconut plantation in Kiritimati, and there are commercial plantations in two other atolls, in the Line Islands. Food crops include bananas, pandanus, breadfruit and papaw.

AGRICULTURAL INDICATORS

Agriculture's share of GDP (%): 30 (latest)
Number of tractors: 18 (1986)
Yields: kg./ha. 1989
- Roots & tubers: 8,634
- Fruits (000 metric tons): 6
- Vegetables (000 metric tons): 5

Livestock (000) 1989
- Pigs: 10

Fishing, 1988
- Total catch (000 metric tons): 37.7
  - of which marine (%): 100
- Value of exports (U.S. $ 000): 1,490

Nearly all land is owned by indigenous people in small individual proprietorships. Local customary law does not include the unrestricted right of disposal by the owner, who has only a lifetime interest and must pass the land on to his next of kin at his death. The land of an issueless person is divided among all of his next of kin. As a result, land ownership is characterized by excessive fragmentation and smallness of size.

No timber of commercial value grows on the islands. No cattle exist, and pigs and poultry are largely uncared for. Fishing has grown tremendously with the help of Japanese aid. The United States is permitted to catch tuna within Kiribatian waters.

MANUFACTURING

The processing of copra is the most important industry, and its quality is considered first class in world markets. The only other types of manufacture are the making of furniture and handicrafts. The labor force in manufacturing was 1.4% in 1985.

MINING

The phosphate mines of Banaba are completely exhausted. Currently there is no mining activity.

ENERGY

Kiribati does not produce any nonelectric form of energy. The government maintains electricity generating plants on Tarawa and Christmas Island. Private plants are on Banaba and several other islands.

ENERGY INDICATORS

Electricity 1988
- Installed capacity (000 kw.): 2
- Production (million kw.-hr.): 7
  - % fossil fuel: 100.0
  - % hydro: 0.0
  - % nuclear: 0.0
- Consumption per capita (kw.-hr.): 104

LABOR

There are few opportunities for paid employment for the inhabitants. The depletion of phosphate mines has meant the loss of over 500 jobs in Banaba, leaving the coconut plantations and the government as the major employers.

Conditions of employment are governed by the Employment Ordinance, and workmen's compensation is governed by the Workmen's Compensation Ordinance of 1952, as amended in 1966.

Only one trade union is registered under the Trade Union Ordinance: the Kiribati Trades Union Congress.

LABOR INDICATORS, 1985

Total economically active population (000): 25
As % of working-age population (15 and above): 67.8
% female: 36.1
Activity rate (%)
- Total: 41.2
- Male: 53.1
- Female: 29.5

Employment status (%)
- Employers & self-employed: 71.0
- Employees: 26.5
- Other: 2.5

Sectoral employment (%)
- Agriculture, forestry, fishing: 72.9
- Manufacturing, mining, quarrying, public utilities: 1.4

Unemployment (000): 2 (1977)
Labor under 20 years (%): 17.3 (1978)

FOREIGN COMMERCE

Kiribati's major imports are food, machinery and transportation equipment, manufactured goods, fuel and chemicals. Copra and fish are its primary exports. Its major suppliers are Australia, Japan, the United States, the United Kingdom, New Zealand and Fiji. The United Kingdom is its major market.

FOREIGN TRADE INDICATORS, 1988

Exports (U.S. $ millions): 5.1
Imports (U.S. $ millions): 21.5
Balance of trade (U.S. $ millions): 16.4

Direction of Trade (%), 1985

	Imports	Exports
European Community	1.7	38.2
United States	4.3	11.6
Japan	11.9	1.8

Composition of Trade (%), 1985

	Imports	Exports
Food and agricultural raw materials	38.1	71.5
Fuels and other energy	10.6	0.0
Mineral ores and concentrates	0.1	1.5
Manufactured goods	51.1	27.0
of which chemicals	5.0	0.0
of which machinery	20.8	0.0

TRANSPORTATION & COMMUNICATIONS

The principal mode of transportation is by sea. There are wharves at Kanton and Tarawa and ports of entry at Banaba, Tabuaeran (Fanning) and Kiritimati. Government boats call at each inhabited atoll at least once a month. Cargo ships call at Tarawa every two or three months and at Kiritimati, Tabuaeran (Fanning) and Teraina (Washington) twice a year. There is an irregular service from Tarawa to Suva, capital of Fiji, and a container service to New Zealand and Australia. The Kiribati Shipping Corporation, owned by the government, maintains a fleet of seven passenger/freight vessels.

There are 640 km. (398 mi.) of motorable roads on the major atolls. The northern Line Islands also have a small network of canals, totaling 5 km. (3 mi.).

The national airline is Air Tungaru, which operates a fleet of four aircraft out of Bonriki International Airport. There are 22 airfields and airstrips on various atolls, of which 21 are usable, and four have perma-

TRANSPORTATION INDICATORS

Roads (latest)
- Length, km. (mi.): 640 (398)

Motor vehicles (latest)
- Automobiles: 307
- Trucks and buses: 130
- Persons per vehicle: 147

Merchant marine
- Vessels: 7 (1989)
- Total dead weight tonnage (000): 2.7 (1989)

Ports (latest)
- Cargo loaded (000 metric tons): 10
- Cargo unloaded (000 metric tons): 25

Air (latest)
- Passenger-km. (passenger-mi.) (millions): 10.0 (6.2)
- Freight-km. (freight-mi.) (millions): 0.04 (0.03)
- Airports with scheduled flights: 17 (1990)

Inland waterways (latest)
- Length, km. (mi.): 5 (3)

COMMUNICATION INDICATORS, 1988

Telephones:
- Total (000): 13
- Persons per telephone: 53

Phone traffic (000 calls)
- Local: 6 (1982)
- Long distance: 60 (minutes)
- International: 122 (minutes)

Post office
- Number of post offices: 5 (1978)
- Pieces of mail handled (000): 374 (1971)

Telegraph
- Total traffic (000 calls): 796 (words)
- National: 759 (words)
- International: 37 (words)

Telex
- Subscriber lines: 32
- Traffic (000 minutes): 107 (1984)

Telecommunications 1990
- 1 satellite ground station

nent-surface runways. Kiribati also is served by Air Nauru and Air Pacific.

Tourism is undeveloped because of poor transportation.

DEFENSE

No information is available on defense.

EDUCATION

Every atoll has at least one primary school. Traditionally primary education was dominated by mission schools, but in the 1980s the government began to take control of it.

Schooling is free, universal and compulsory for nine years between ages six and 16. Schooling lasts 12 years, divided into six years of primary school, three years of middle school and three years of secondary school.

EDUCATION INDICATORS, 1988

Literacy
- Total (%): 90.0

First level
- Schools: 112
- Students: 13,868
- Teachers: 458
- Student/teacher ratio: 30.3:1

Second level
- Schools: 8
- Students: 2,437
- Teachers: 140
- Student/teacher ratio: 17.4:1

Vocational
- Schools: 6
- Students: 568
- Teachers: 52
- Student/teacher ratio: 10.9:1

Public expenditures, 1987
- Total (A.$): 3,157
- % of national budget: 18.9
- % of current expenditure: 100

There are no higher education facilities on the islands, but Kiribati participates in the University of South Pacific's Kiribati Extension Center, based in Fiji.

LEGAL SYSTEM

The judiciary comprises the High Court and the Court of Appeals as superior courts of record, presided over by the chief justice, who is appointed by the *beretitenti;* and local magistrates' courts, representing a consolidation of former land and other subordinate courts.

The only prison, on Tarawa, accommodates all prisoners sentenced to terms of two months or more; those given shorter terms are not confined, but serve their sentences in their homes. Prison conditions are generous, the diet is good and the discipline is not onerous or harsh. Prisoners generally must work on public projects. Prison officials may reduce sentences of more than a month by as much as one-third for good behavior. Imprisonment rarely carries any social stigma.

LAW ENFORCEMENT

The police force is the Constabulary, with a strength of 168 men under the command of a commissioner of police assisted by superintendents and inspectors. A second police organization, called the District Police, supports the work of the regular Constabulary in certain areas. The District Police is a decentralized group of part-time policemen operating under the administrative officer of each inhabited atoll rather than the chief police officer of the Constabulary. The strength of individual units of the District Police varies from one to as many as 24. The headquarters of the constabulary is in the capital; below the headquarters level the force operates through four police districts, serving Banaba and the Gilbert, Phoenix and Line groups of islands. Banaba has a single station, Gilbert 18; the Line Island group has three stations.

There is no widespread lawlessness, but the incidence of crime has increased. Most statutory cases involve offenses against property, followed by offenses against the person. The greatest number of violations against local regulations are traffic offenses and drunkenness. Juvenile delinquency appears to be increasing in South Tarawa as the population pressure increases.

HEALTH

All health services are free. Each inhabited atoll has a dispensary. Tuberculosis is the nation's most serious health problem. Dysentery, filariasis and leprosy are endemic.

FOOD & NUTRITION

Taro, bananas and sometimes breadfruit are the staple starches and are eaten with seafood and coconuts. Daily protein is gained only from seafood and, on rare occasions, fowl and small game. Fresh meat is invari-

HEALTH INDICATORS
Health personnel, 1986
Physicians: 16
persons per: 4,094
Dentists: 1 (1985)
Nurses: 125 (1985)
Pharmacists: 3 (1985)
Hospitals, 1982
Number: 34
Number of beds (/10,000): 43 (1986)
Admissions/discharges (/10,000): 633
Bed occupancy rate (%): 58
Average length of stay (days): 15
Type of hospitals (%), 1982
Government: 100.0
Private nonprofit: 0.0
Private profit: 0.0
Vital statistics
Crude death rate (/1000 pop.): 13 (1990)
Life expectancy at birth, 1990
Males: 52
Females: 57
Infant mortality rate (/1000 live births): 65 (1990)
Child mortality rate (1985–90) under 5 yrs. (/1,000): 36
Population with access to safe water (%): 44 (latest)

ably limited to feasts. The traditional beverage is the toddy, fermented from coconut flowers.

The daily per capita consumption of food in 1982 was 2,305 calories.

MEDIA & CULTURE

The Kiribatian press consists of two weeklies: *Te Uekern* and *Atoll Pioneer.* There are two monthlies; one is published by the Catholic Church, and the other is a Protestant publication. There are no news agencies or bureaus, and book publishing is nonexistent.

The government-owned Radio Kiribati broadcasts on medium-wave and shortwave transmitters. The programs are in English and I-Kiribati. There is no television service.

MEDIA INDICATORS
Newspapers
Number of nondailies: 4 (latest)
Radio
Number of transmitters: 2 (1989)
Number of persons per radio receiver: 7.0 (1989)

CULTURAL & ENVIRONMENTAL INDICATORS (latest)
Libraries
Number: 1
Volumes (000): 40
Nature reserves
Number of facilities: 4

The National Library and Archives has a collection of 40,000 volumes.

SOCIAL WELFARE

The government maintains a free medical service. The Provident Fund System provides an old-age benefit as well as workers' compensation and a survivor fund.

GLOSSARY

Beretitenti: title of president
Kauoman-ni-Beretitenti: title of vice president
Maneaba ni Maungatabu: House of Assembly

CHRONOLOGY (from 1979)

1979— Kiribati becomes an independent republic within the Commonwealth, with Ieremia T. Tabai as president. . . . Kiribati and the United States sign agreement under which the United States relinquishes all claims to territory in the Phoenix and Line island groups, including Canton, Enderbury and Hull.

1982— President Tabai is defeated in a vote of confidence in the Maneapa ni Maungatabu and resigns.

1983— President Tabai is reelected in legislative balloting and resumes office as president.

1987— Tabai is reelected after a constitutional debate over the legitimacy of a fourth term in office.

1990— Kiribati's economy suffers; the value of exports is little more than one-quarter of imports; Britain provides economic assistance to small-scale industries in an effort to help Kiribati reduce its imports.

BIBLIOGRAPHY

BOOKS

Sabatier, Ernest. *Astride the Equator.* New York, 1978.
University of South Pacific. *Kiribati: Aspects of History.* Suva, 1979.

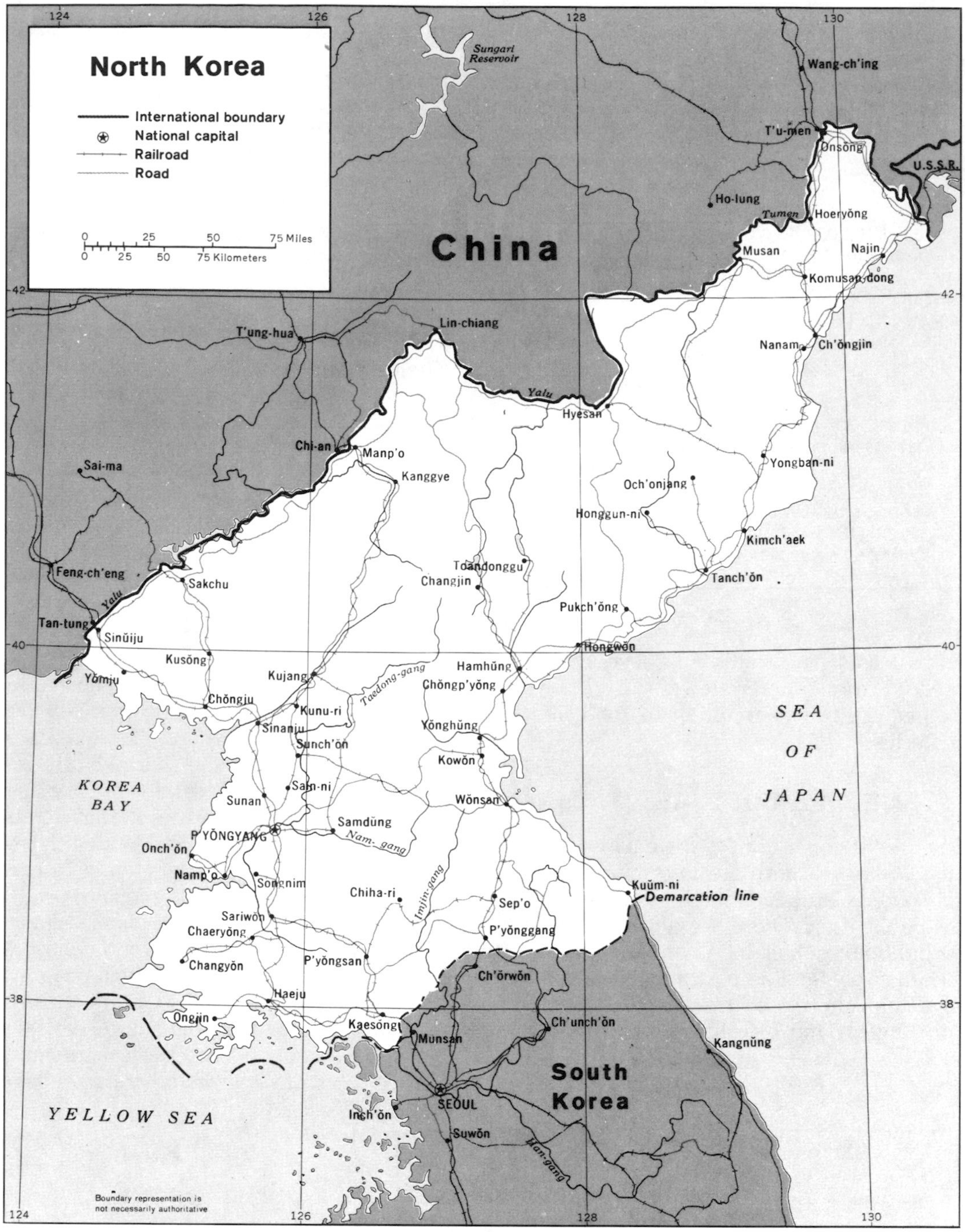
North Korea
International boundary
National capital
Railroad
Road
0 25 50 75 Miles
0 25 50 75 Kilometers
124
126
128
130
42
40
38
China
Sungari Reservoir
Wang-ch'ing
T'u-men
Onsŏng
U.S.S.R.
Ho-lung
Tumen
Hoeryŏng
Musan
Najin
Komusan-dong
Lin-chiang
T'ung-hua
Nanam
Ch'ŏngjin
Yalu
Hyesan
Chi-an
Manp'o
Kanggye
Yongban-ni
Sai-ma
Och'onjang
Hongggun-ni
Kimch'aek
Toandonggu
Changjin
Tanch'ŏn
Feng-ch'eng
Sakchu
Pukch'ŏng
Tan-tung
Sinŭiju
Hongwŏn
Kusŏng
Hamhŭng
Yŏmju
Kujang
Taedong-gang
Chŏngp'yŏng
Chŏngju
Kunu-ri
Sinanju
Yŏnghŭng
Sunch'ŏn
SEA OF JAPAN
Kowŏn
KOREA BAY
Sam-ni
Sunan
Wŏnsan
P'YŎNGYANG
Samdŭng
Nam-gang
Onch'ŏn
Namp'o
Songnim
Chiha-ri
Imjin-gang
Kuŭm-ni
Demarcation line
Sep'o
Sariwŏn
Chaeryŏng
P'yŏnggang
Changyŏn
P'yŏngsan
Ch'ŏrwŏn
Haeju
Ongjin
Kaesŏng
Munsan
Ch'unch'ŏn
Kangnŭng
South Korea
YELLOW SEA
Inch'ŏn
SEOUL
Suwŏn
Han-gang
Boundary representation is not necessarily authoritative

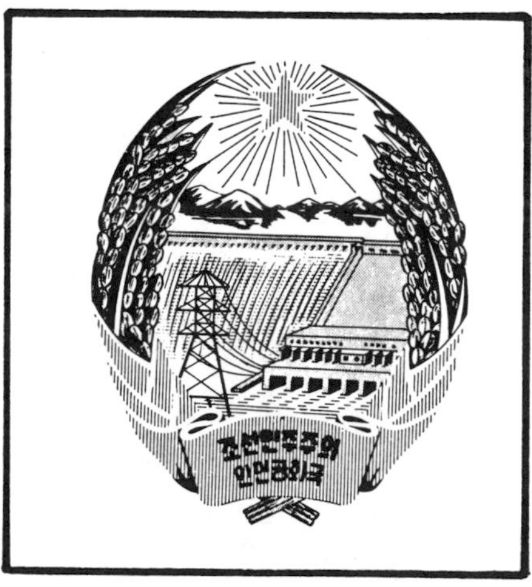

KOREA, NORTH

BASIC FACT SHEET

OFFICIAL NAME: Democratic People's Republic of Korea (Chosun Minchu-chui Inmin Konghwa-guk)

ABBREVIATION: KN

CAPITAL: Pyongyang

HEAD OF STATE: President Marshal Kim Il-sung (from 1972)

HEAD OF GOVERNMENT: Prime Minister Yong Hyong Muk (from 1988)

NATURE OF GOVERNMENT: One-party civilian dictatorship

POPULATION: 21,292,649 (1990)

AREA: 120,538 sq. km. (46,540 sq. mi.)

ETHNIC MAJORITY: Korean

LANGUAGE: Korean

RELIGIONS: Confucianism, Buddhism and Chondogyo

UNIT OF CURRENCY: Won

NATIONAL FLAG: Two blue horizontal stripes in the top and bottom separated from a broad, red center band by two white narrow stripes. The left half of the red stripe contains a red, five-pointed star within a white, circular field.

NATIONAL EMBLEM: The principal elements of the national coat of arms are two sheaves of rice, a five-pointed star, Mount Paektu, a dam, an electric power station and line and a factory. Under the device is the name of the country in Korean, "Democratic People's Republic of Korea."

NATIONAL ANTHEM: "Morning Sun, Shine over the Rivers and Mountains"

NATIONAL HOLIDAYS: September 9 (Founding of the Democratic People's Republic, National Day); January 1 (New Year's Day); August 15 (Liberation Day); May 1 (May Day).

NATIONAL CALENDAR: Gregorian

PHYSICAL QUALITY OF LIFE INDEX: 85

DATE OF INDEPENDENCE: August 15, 1945

DATE OF CONSTITUTION: December 17, 1972

WEIGHTS & MEASURES: Both metric and traditional systems are used. Traditional weights and measures include the *chongho* (1 ha.; 2.471 ac.) and the *ri* (3,927 m.; 12,884 ft.).

GEOGRAPHICAL FEATURES

North Korea is in the northern part of the Korean Peninsula in East Asia and occupies a total land area of 120,538 sq. km. (46, 540 sq. mi.), extending 719 km. (447 mi.) north-northeast to south-southeast and 371 km. (231 mi.) east-southeast to west-northwest. Its coastline on the Sea of Japan and the Yellow Sea runs 1,028 km. (639 mi.).

North Korea shares its total international boundary of 2,702 km. (1,679 mi.) with three countries: China (1,416 km.; 880 mi.); USSR (18 km.; 11 mi.); and South Korea (240 km.; 149 mi.). The northern border with China follows the Yalu River for part of its course, according to an agreement of 1875, and the Tumen River for part of its course, according to an agreement of 1909. An old dispute concerning control of Mount Paektu was settled in 1963. The border with South Korea is the Military Demarcation Line of 1953. It has not been formally accepted by either North or South Korea. The capital is Pyongyang, with a 1981 population of 1,283,000. Other major urban centers are Hamhung (775,000), Chongjin (490,000), Wonsan (240,000) and Kaesong (240,000).

Mountains cover four-fifths of the Korean Peninsula. The major mountain ranges crisscross the country in northwest-to-southeast and northeast-to-southwest patterns. Almost the whole of northern-central Korea is dominated by six mountain ranges: Machol-lyong, Hamgyong, Pujol-lyong, Nangnim, Myohyang and Choguryong. Crowning these ranges are a number of peaks celebrated for their natural beauty: Mount Paektu (2,744 m.; 9,003 ft.), Mount Kwanmo (2,541 m.; 8,337 ft.) and Mount Myohyang (1,908 m.; 6,263 ft.). Mount Kumgang, or the Diamond Mountain (1,637 m.; 5,374 ft.), is in the Taebaek Range, which rises south of Wonsan and extends down the eastern side of the peninsula. The land east of the Taebaek, Hamgyong and Pujol-lyong ranges consists of short, parallel ridges that extend to the sea.

The plains constitute only one-fifth of the land area but contain most of the farmlands and human settlements. The largest plains are Pyongyang, Unjon, Anju, Chaeryong, Yonbaek, Hamhung, Yongchon, Kilchu, Yonghung and Susong.

North Korea's major river is the Yalu, which flows from Mount Paektu to the Yellow Sea. It is navigable for part of its distance from its mouth to Hyesan, and oceangoing vessels can dock at Sinuiju. The Taedong is the most important waterway for internal commerce. Three major cities—Pyongyang, Nampo and Songnim—are on its banks. The Tumen, whose length of 519 km. (323 mi.) is second only to the Yalu's 804 km. (500 mi.), has little value as an inland waterway because of its narrowness. Other major rivers are the Songchon on the eastern coast, Chongchon to the northwest and Imjin to the south.

CLIMATE & WEATHER

Though North Korea is at the same latitude as the United States from New England to South Carolina, it is subject to more severe winters because it is exposed to cold winds from Siberia. Winter temperatures, however, are subject to great variations, from far below freezing in five of the winter months in the northern provinces to −3.9°C (25°F) at Wonsan, to the south. Summer temperatures are more uniform throughout the North, with average temperatures ranging from 24.4°C (76°F) in Pyongyang to 21°C (70°F) on the relatively cool northeastern coast. Recent government reports suggest climatic changes, including longer winters on the peninsula.

Annual rainfall ranges from 560 to 1,520 mm. (22 to 60 in.), with the Tumen and lower Taedong River valleys receiving the least and the Imjin River Basin and the upper Chongchon River Valley receiving the most. Up to 85% of the rainfall is concentrated in the summer months, especially from June to early August. Heavy downpours during the rainy season can cause floods and widespread damage to crops.

In contrast to South Korea and Japan, typhoons are uncommon.

POPULATION

The population of North Korea was estimated at 21,292,649 in 1990. No official census has been held in the country since 1944, and population figures are treated as strategic information and therefore confidential.

The population is concentrated in the coastal lowlands, particularly Pyongyang, the coastal northwestern area and the Hamhung-Hungnam area. The most populous provinces are South Pyongan, North Pyongan and South Hamgyong; the least populous provinces are Changang and Yanggang. Overall population density is 167 per sq. km. (438 per sq. mi.).

DEMOGRAPHIC INDICATORS

Population (millions): 21.292 (1990)
Sex distribution (% at last census): Males, 49.6; females, 50.4 (1985 est)
Population estimates and projections (millions)

1950: 9.740	1980: 18.025	2010: 33.115
1960: 10.526	1990: 22.937	
1970: 13.892	2000: 28.165	

Age profile (1985 est)

0–14: 38.7	30–44: 16.6	60–74: 4.7
15–29: 29.2	45–59: 9.8	75 and over: 1.0

Median age (yrs.): 20.3 (1985)
Youth population (% age 15–24): 20.2; 19.3 (2000)
Total dependency ratio: 73.2 (1985)
Annual growth rate (%)

1950–55: 1.36	1975–80: 2.57	2000–2005: 1.71
1955–60: 2.91	1980–85: 2.46	2005–2010: 1.53
1960–65: 2.79	1985–90: 2.36	2010–2015: 1.34
1965–70: 2.76	1990–1995: 2.16	2015–2020: 1.20
1970–75: 2.64	1995–2000: 1.95	2020–2025: 1.04

Urban population (millions): 13.009 (1985)
Annual urban population growth rate (%, 1985–90): 3.45
Annual rural population growth rate (%, 1985–90): 0.28
Population density per sq. km. (per sq. mi.): 187.4 (485.4) (latest)

VITAL STATISTICS

Crude birth rate (/1,000): 29 (1989)
Crude death rate (/1,000): 5 (1989)
Infant mortality rate (/1,000 live births): 27 (1990)
Maternal mortality rate (/100,000 live births): 41 (1986–87)
Life expectancy (yrs.) at birth: males, 69; females, 75 (1990)
Gross reproduction rate (/woman) (1980–85): 1.95
Total fertility rate (/woman): 2.1 (1990)
Rate of natural increase (1980–85) (/1,000): 23.5
Average household size: 5.7 (latest)

Since the Korean War there always has been an imbalance in the population in favor of females. This imbalance is reflected in the increasing employment of women in occupations traditionally restricted to men.

Though the rural population has remained fairly stable over the years, the urban population has been increasing dramatically and has absorbed virtually all the population growth. Close to 64% of the population is considered urban, compared to 33.1% in 1965.

Historically the northern half of the Korean Peninsula was less populated than the southern half. It was only during the Japanese occupation that a significant shift in population from the South to the North began, and even by 1944 only one-third of the Korean population lived north of the 38th parallel as permanent inhabitants. The partition of Korea in 1945 reversed this northward flow. It is estimated that 500,000 Koreans crossed into the South between 1945 and 1950, and another 4.5 million fled to the South during or immediately after the Korean War. Large-scale emigration of Koreans dates from the first decade of the 20th century and is attributed to the pressures of Japanese occupation. The main destinations were Japan, China, Manchuria, Siberia and the United States. Current estimates of the Korean diaspora include 1.1 million in China, 620,000 in Japan, 800,000 in Siberia and the island of Sakhalin and several thousand in the United States. Between 1959 and 1974 the only external gain in population resulted from the repatriation of 91,000 North Koreans from Japan.

To make up for the population losses of the Korean War and mass migration to South Korea, the North Korean government has pursued a pronatalist policy designed to increase population. Women are encouraged to bear more children through awards, maternity bonuses and up to 75 days of paid vacation. Working mothers also are granted reduction of working hours and provided with an extensive system of day-care centers. Since 1959 the government also has made sustained efforts to repatriate Koreans living abroad, particularly in Japan. Since then, however, reports of the harsh treatment given repatriates reached overseas Koreans, reducing the flow to North Korea to a trickle. (Because of their "corruption" by exposure to foreign influences, repatriates are isolated from North Korean society after their arrival until they can be indoctrinated and their ideological reliability gauged.) The only element in official policy that favors limited families is the regulation prohibiting marriage until men have completed military service, generally by age 24.

The Constitution states that "women hold equal social status and rights with men." Despite this provision, few women reach high levels of the ruling Korean Workers' Party (KWP) or the government. Women are represented proportionally in the labor force, and personnel in small factories are predominately women. Reportedly women often are paid less than men for similar work.

STATUS OF WOMEN INDICATORS

Number of women (millions): 10.125 (1985)
Women in labor force (%): 69 (1985)
Total fertility rate (/woman): 2.1 (1990)
Women in national legislatures (%): 20 (1984)

ETHNIC COMPOSITION

North Korea along with South Korea ranks first in the world in ethnic homogeneity, with 100% homogeneity. There are no racial or linguistic minorities. The total non-Korean resident population is probably about 50,000, nearly all of them Chinese.

The racial origins of Koreans are obscure, but the primary stock is believed to be Tungusic—i.e., related to the Mongols with some Chinese admixture.

LANGUAGES

The national language is Korean (officially known as Chosun Muntcha), using the *hangul* script. Korean is generally considered to be a member of the Altaic family. The alphabet consist of 14 basic consonants and 10 simple vowels. The letters are combined into syllables by clustering, as in Chinese. Chinese loanwords form roughly half the vocabulary.

English is the principal second language and is taught in all secondary schools.

RELIGIONS

North Koreans subscribe to a variety of religious beliefs, none of which wield any significant national influence. Historically, Buddhism and Confucianism, both tempered by persistent shamanist and animist beliefs, have filled the role of a national religion. Chondogyo (Religion of the Heavenly Way), a native eclectic sect, was introduced in the latter half of the 19th century. Christianity, the last of the major religions to penetrate North Korea, has the least number of adherents. In any case, the practice of religion is actively discouraged by the Communist government and has ceased to be a major factor in national life.

HISTORICAL BACKGROUND

From 1910 until 1945 Korea was under Japanese occupation as a colony administered by a governor-general from Seoul. The colonial experience is remembered with bitterness by Koreans. All civil liberties were revoked, the use of the Korean language was prohibited, Korean private schools were closed and Korean nationals were barred from important positions of authority. What improvements were made in industry, agriculture and transportation were designed to serve Japanese businessmen and landowners. Large tracts of land were appropriated and sold to Japanese immigrants, and much of the annual production was sold to Japan at artificially low rates. Though industries were developed, they were monopolized by Japanese migrants and were directed to supplementing the industrial capacity of Japan and to meeting Japan's growing military requirements. Korean workers were conscripted to serve in Japanese mines and factories. To deprive the Koreans of their cultural identity, the Japanese rulers banned the study of Korean history, forced Japanese surnames upon the people and introduced Shintoism in schools.

Japanese control of Korea ended with its defeat in World War II. The desire of the Allies at the Cairo Conference in 1943 was to restore an independent Korea, but a need to accomplish a prompt arrangement of the Japanese surrender led to a division of the country. The Soviets occupied the northern section whose industry had been developed by the Japanese, and the southern, more agrarian sector of the country was occupied by U.S. forces. In 1947 the problem of unifying Korea was referred to the U.N. General Assembly on U.S. initiative. A U.N.-observed election was held only in the southern part of Korea in May 1948, soon followed by the establishment of that half as the Republic of Koroea (ROK). The northern half, controlled by a communist government, established itself as the Democratic People's Republic of Korea (DPRK) on September 9th. The United Nations recognized only the Republic of Korea as the legitimate government of Korea. U.S. and Soviet troops withdrew from the area but on June 25, 1950 Democratic People's Republic of Korea troops invaded the Republic of Korea in an attempt to unify the Koreas. U.S. military forces immediately aided South Korea. Subsequently, 16 U.N. countries, along with the United States, made up the U.N. Unified Command, headed initially by Gen. Douglas MacArthur. In late 1950 some 300,000 Chinese troops fell in on the North Korean side causing a stalemate. An armistice agreement was eventually signed on July 27, 1953 at Panmunjom. A four-kilometer wide demiliterized zone was established bisecting Korea at the 38th parallel.

In 1949 a merger of communists in the north and south created the Korean Workers' Party (KWP) led by Kim Il-sung who has been the head of the Democratic People's Republic of Korea ever since. Kim gradually consolidated his power, liquidating rival factions within the KWP, until by 1958 his power was absolute. Kim's long period of rule has been characterized by the development of an extraordinary personality cult linked to his personal interpretation of Marxist-Leninism. His ideology, known as *Juche*, rests on the principles of the primacy of the party, self-sufficiency and self defense.

Kim has groomed his son, Kim Chong Il, as his successor and in 1984 Radio Pyongyang referred to Kim Chong Il as the "sole successor" to his father. Yet there is still a question of whether he has the support within the party and the army to continue his father's rule.

Reports of a November 1986 coup and the assassination of Kim Il-sung were proven untrue. In the same month elections were held to the North Korean legislature, the Supreme People's Assembly, in which all candidates ran unopposed and Kim Il-sung was re-elected president.

CONSTITUTION & GOVERNMENT

The constitutional basis of the North Korean government is the Constitution of 1972, which replaced the Constitution of 1948. The Constitution of 1972 defined North Korea as an "independent, socialist state that represents the interests of all the Korean peoples." The Constitution has 11 chapters and 149 articles. The first three chapters set forth the directive principles of the state. The ideological basis of the state is defined as the *Juche*, or *chuche sasang*, the ideology of self-reliance, which, along with Marxism-Leninism, furnish the doctrinal framework of the North Korean state. This ideology is also known as Kim Il-sungism, *hyongmyong sasang* (revolutionary ideology) and *yuil sasang* (the one and only ideology). The state is described as being under the dictatorship of the proletariat, where sovereignty emanates from four classes: workers, peasants, soldiers and working intellectuals. The Constitution also recognizes the Chollima Work Unit Movement (an intensive mass-production drive named after the legendary Chinese flying horse capable of galloping phenomenal distances in a single day); and the *chongsan-ni* method, formulated by Kim Il-sung and under which party and government functionaries must, instead of issuing orders and directives, mingle with the peasants and workers and provide them with personalized, on-the-spot ideological and practical guidance. The Constitution reaffirms the national desire to achieve unification of the Korean Peninsula and to protect the legitimate rights of overseas Koreans. The means of production are to be owned by the state as well as by cooperative organizations. The latter are to phased out eventually in favor of total communal ownership. Private property is restricted to property for immediate personal consumption, such as produce from home plots and enterprises. The state is committed to the development of a socialist culture; compulsory, free and universal education for 10 years; universal free medical service; freedom of religious belief; freedom of antireligious propaganda; the rights to work and to vote; and abolition of taxation.

Under the Constitution real decision-making power rests with the Korean Workers' Party and its Political Committee. Government agencies are only the executors of party policies and the administrative links between the party and the people. Through its extensive network of cadres within the organs of power, the party oversees administration and ensures compliance with party directives. Key positions in the central and local governments are assigned only to those party officials who are unquestioningly loyal to the party line or—more precisely—to Kim Il-sung.

The underlying principle of government is defined as "democratic centralism," which means that all representative or democratic bodies are elected by lower-level bodies and that they in turn elect the executives at their level. The highest legislative body and the highest organ of power is the Supreme People's Assembly (SPA) and, when the SPA is not in session, its Standing Committee.

The Standing Committee, also known as the Presidium, and the SPA function, despite the language of the Constitution, as rubber stamps, ratifying the decisions of the party leadership. The real focus of power is the president *(chusok)*, who is head of state and head of government. Although in theory he is elected every four years by the Supreme People's Assembly, there is

GOVERNMENT LIST
(July/August 1991)

President	Kim Il-sung
Vice President	Pak Song-ch'ol
Vice President	Yi Chong-ok
Premier	Yon Hyong-muk
Vice Premier	Ch'oe Yong-nim
Vice Premier	Chang Chol
Vice Premier	Hong Si-hak
Vice Premier	Hong Song-nam
Vice Premier	Kang Hui-won
Vice Premier	Kim Ch'ang-chu
Vice Premier	Kim Hwan
Vice Premier	Kim Pok-sin
Vice Premier	Kim Tal-Hyon
Vice Premier	Kim Yong-nam
Vice Premier	Kim Yun-hyok
Minister of Building Materials Industry	Chu Yong-hun
Minister of Chemical Industry	Kim Hwan
Minister of City Management	Yi Chol-pong, *Maj. Gen.*
Minister of Coal Industry	Kim Ki-Kyong
Minister of Commerce	Han Chang-kun
Minister of Construction	Cho Ch'ol-chun
Minister of Culture & Art	Chang Chol
Minister of External Economic Affairs	Chong Song-nam
Minister of Finance	Yun Ki-chong
Minister of Foreign Affairs	Kim Yong-nam
Minister of Foreign Trade	Kim Tal-Hyon
Minister of Forestry	Kim Chae-yul
Minister of Joint Venture Industry	Chae Hui-chong
Minister of Labor Administration	Yi Chae-yun
Minister of Local Industry	Kim Song-ku
Minister of Machine-Building Industry	Kye Hyong-sun
Minister of Marine Transportation	O Song-yol
Minister of Metal Industry	Pak Yong-to
Minister of Mining Industry	Kim Pil-hwan
Minister of Natural Resources Development	Kim Se-yong
Minister of Nuclear Energy	Choe Hak-kun
Minister of Post and Tele-Communications	Kim Hak-sop
Minister of Public Health	Yi Chong-yul
Minister of Public Security	Paek Hak-nim, *Gen.*
Minister of Railways	Pak Yong-sok

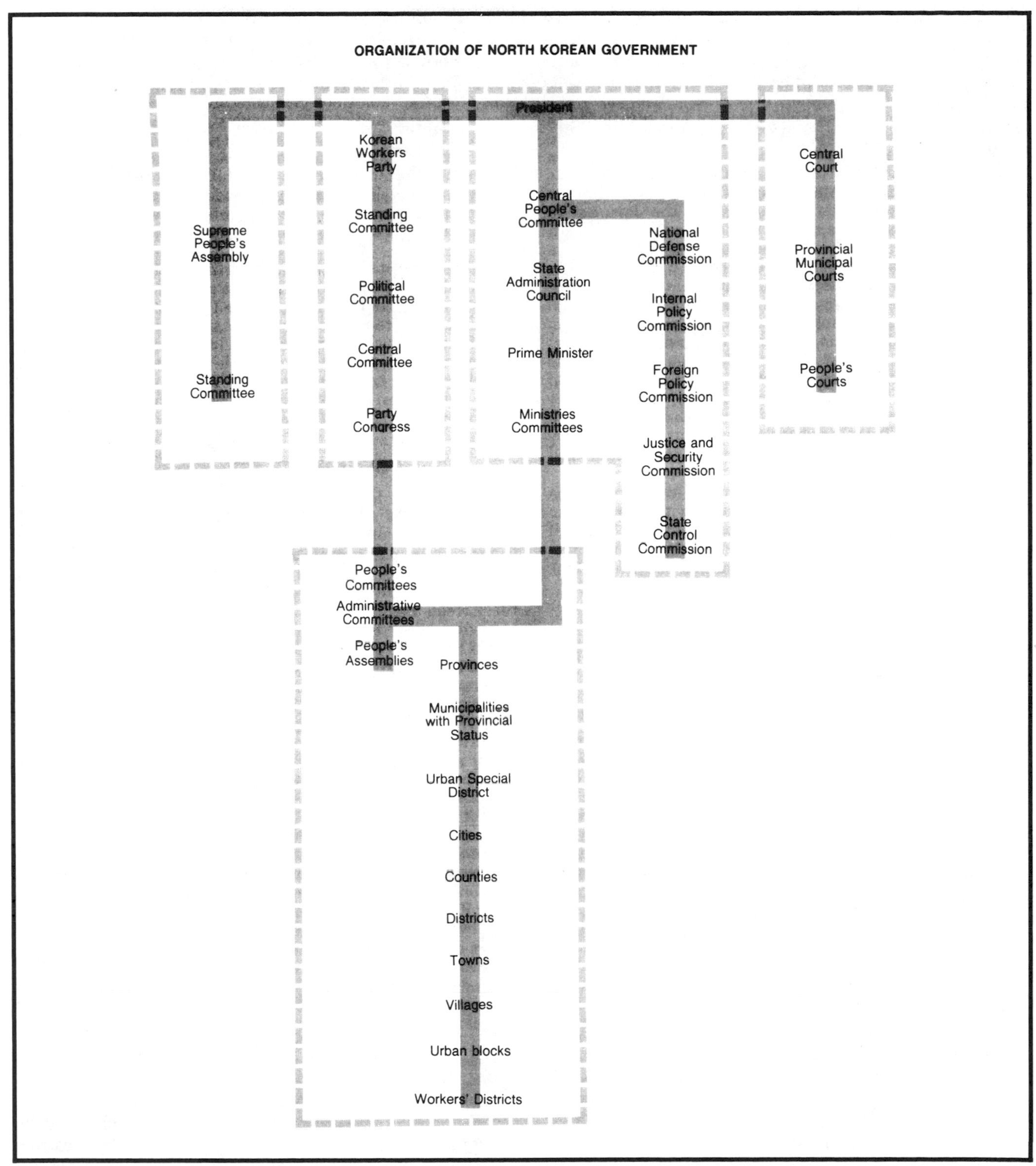

no constitutional limitation on his tenure or power, and he is not, in practice, accountable to any other branch of government. He presides over the Administrative Council and is the chairman of the National Defense Commission as supreme commander of the armed forces. The president directly "guides" the Central People's Committee, whose 24 members are named by him. Kim Il-sung is personally involved and active in every aspect of the government and is the object of an intense and widespread personality cult.

The Central People's Committee is, next to the presidency, the highest policy-making body within the government. It is chaired by the president and includes three vice presidents, a secretary and 20 other members elected, in theory, by the SPA but named, in practice, by the president. Its chief functions are supervision of the State Administrative Council, the local People's Assemblies and the local People's Committees; supervision of the work of the judiciary; appointment and removal of cabinet members and other high-ranking officers; establishment or abolition of ministries and state agencies; and declaration of a state of war. The committee is assisted by at least five commissions: the Internal Policy Commission, the Foreign Policy Commission, the National Defense Commission, the Justice and Security Commission and the State Control Commission.

The State Administration Council is the equivalent of a cabinet. The council is headed by the premier and includes vice premiers and ministers. It holds two kinds of meetings: a plenary session attended by all members, and a permanent or executive session. In addition to ministries there are ministry-level committees whose jurisdictions cut across several ministries.

The Constitution provides for national elections every four years. Suffrage is universal, direct and equal over age 17, and voting is by secret ballot. Despite the assertion of this democratic right, electoral procedures conform to Communist practices. Candidates always are selected by the party and invariably are chosen for their demonstrated loyalty to party leadership. Electoral campaigns take place only under official sponsorship and generally are combined with mass indoctrination and propaganda. Voters in the 541 electoral districts are presented with a single slate of party-approved candidates who may be, theoretically, accepted or rejected by them. But a negative vote may be potentially dangerous because a ballot can be crossed out only in full view of authorities. Every election since 1962 has therefore resulted in a 100% voter turnout and a 100% affirmative vote for the official slate. At the national level elections are conducted by the Standing Committee of the Supreme People's Assembly and at the provincial and county levels by the local People's Committees.

Two elements contributing to the impressive record of stability in North Korea are the solidarity, discipline and all-pervasive reach of the Korean Workers' Party and the total and absolute power enjoyed by President Kim Il-sung. The Korean Workers' Party has an estimated membership of 3 million, or 14% of the population, one of the highest of any Communist country. The party also is one of the most organized in the world, with basic cells in every factory, farm, school, office and military unit. The party is the sole channel for anyone to advance himself, and there is no room for dissent or opposition. The party's dual ideologies of Marxism-Leninism and *chuche sasang* are relentlessly applied to all areas of public and personal conduct. The second element is the exaltation of Kim Il-sung as the source of all legitimacy. North Korea is conceived in official propaganda as a giant family under the leadership of its *oboi* (father), Kim Il-sung. The party, the state and the national ideologies are personified in Kim, who is projected in party rhetoric as an infallible leader whose decisions must be accepted on faith. Nine of North Korea's 10 top leaders belong to the so-called Manchurian faction—a group that fought with Kim Il-sung against the Japanese in northeastern China during World War II. Though Kim Il-sung is an unassailable figure and the subject of a ritualized personality cult, he is past his political prime. Speculation now centers on a successor who can provide continuity and stability. Kim Il-sung's own apparent choice for this post is his son Kim Chong Il, a marshall in the Politburo. Kim Chung Il has reportedly assumed effective control of government economic and military affairs. In 1983 his visit to Beijing was seen as a tacit approval by China of his succession. In the October 1985 congress of the Korean Workers' Party the son inherited the father's title of general secretary. Because of the possible opposition of older men to the sudden rise to Kim Chong Il, he still is not being named openly in party or government communiqués and is simply being referred to as the "party center." Through July 1984, radio Pyongyang referred to Kim Chong Il as the only candidate to succeed his father. He is known to be an extreme hardliner, more rigid than his father. The succession, although well planned in advance, will be a gradual one.

FREEDOM & HUMAN RIGHTS

In terms of political and civil rights North Korea is ranked as a not-free country.

North Korea is perhaps the most highly regimented and controlled society in the world today. These controls are enforced by two security organizations. Persons who fail to cooperate with the regime face imprisonment, confiscation of property or enforced removal to remote villages. Observation by informers is so prevalent that suspicion has become a national characteristic. Movement from one area to another requires documentary permission. Not only are freedoms of assembly and expression denied, but also the government attempts to shape the citizens' consciousness, with both children and adults required to participate in daily indoctrination sessions and to recite party maxims by rote. Virtually no outside information, other than that approved and disseminated by North Korean authorities, is allowed to reach the public. Despite claims to a socialist and classless society, ideological considerations and control mechanisms have come to differentiate North Koreans into highly stratified classes, with the governing minority perched clearly on the top and having privileges associated in the past with royalty. Security ratings are awarded to each citizen, and these ratings determine access to better schools, positions and stores. Individuals with relatives or close family associates in South Korea are regarded as suspect.

According to the accounts by crew members of the USS *Pueblo* and Venezuelan poet Ali Lameda, prisoners are beaten and tortured, deprived of food, placed in solitary confinement and forced to undergo enforced walking periods and continuous interrogation. There are many reported attempts to kidnap individuals in North Korea and remove them by force to undisclosed destinations within the country. Lameda estimated that there are approximately 150,000 prisoners in North Korean camps. Lameda himself was detained for a year without charges and without trial. His requests for a lawyer of his choice and an open trial were ridiculed as "bourgeois." The judiciary is subordinate to the executive. Judges merely serve to announce the terms of imprisonment, which have already been determined by the Provincial Safety Bureaus. Often one person serves as both judge and prosecutor. Lameda states that he was denied the right to defend himself. His defense counsel "represented" him by making a lengthy speech praising Kim il-sung and then "requesting" a 20-year sentence, which the tribunal gladly imposed after a five-minute deliberation.

North Koreans do not enjoy any of the freedoms of speech, press or assembly. The Constitution requires citizens to follow the socialist norms of life and to have a collective spirit. Censorship of the media is strictly enforced. Listening to foreign broadcasts is prohibited, and violators are subject to severe punishment. The primary function of movies, plays, operas and books is to adulate "the great leader, Kim il-sung, and his son, the beloved leader Kim Chong Il." The government has developed a pervasive network of spies and informers to enforce these laws. Internal travel is strictly controlled. To monitor internal travel more effectively, the government discourages travel by automobiles and even bicycles, thus forcing travelers to depend on the more easily controlled buses.

Not only is the average citizen denied participation in the political processes, but even the lower levels of the KWP have no voice and serve only to carry out the fiats and decrees of Kim il-sung. The legislature and the so-called minority parties are facades that are never even consulted. Individuals with "bad social backgrounds" (those with former bourgeois or religious connections, those who have relatives who fled South during the Korean War and those who have relatives who are political prisoners) are totally excluded from politics.

CIVIL SERVICE

No current information is available on the North Korean civil service.

LOCAL GOVERNMENT

North Korea has a relatively elaborate system of local government, consisting of nine levels of administration. Of these, five are recognized in the Constitution, but the four bottom tiers have no constitutional status. The five principal divisions are provinces, cities with provincial status, ordinary cities, urban districts and counties. The provinces number nine as of 1977: North Pyongan, South Pyongan, South Hwanghae, North Hwanghae, Chagang, North Hamgyong, South Hamgyong, Yanggang and Kangwon. There are four municipalities with provincial status (Pyongyang, Hamhung, Chongjin and Najin) and one urban special district (Kaesong). The provinces are subdivided into 18 ordinary cities *(si)*, 156 countries *(kun)* and 36 districts *(kuyok)*. The four bottom tiers include 156 towns *(up)* serving as administrative headquarters for the counties, 3,403 villages *(ri)*, 684 urban blocks *(tong)* and 205 worders' districts and industrial settlements *(nondongjaku)*. Workers' districts are established in any industrial suburb with more than 400 workers, miners or fisherman.

Local People's Assemblies are established at the provincial and county levels. These bodies are responsible, in Kim Il-sung's words, "for the living conditions of the people," such as food, clothing, public buildings, housing, education and public health. The provincial Assembly members are elected for four-year terms and county Assembly members for two-year terms. The functions of the assemblies include approval of the local budgets and election of the People's Committees and Administrative Committees at each level, as well as judges of courts within their jurisdictions. The assemblies meet once or twice a year in sessions lasting no more than a few days.

The permanent executives and administrative organs at the local level are the People's Committees and Administrative Committees. The functions of the People's Committees, elected by the People's Assemblies, include supervision of local elections, implementation of decisions of People's Assemblies and higher state organs, and general control over all state institutions. The Administrative Committees are concerned with day-to-day affairs.

FOREIGN POLICY

North Korea's foreign policy is an extension, in a broader field, of the national ideology known as *chuche sasang*, or self-reliance. But its ideological framework remains proletarian internationalism and Marxism-Leninism, and its principal goal is the isolation of South Korea. Territorial unification of the Korean Peninsula has been abandoned as an immediate and feasible goal. The government's efforts have been directed to enhancing its stature in the Third World, diversifying its foreign contacts and supporting revolutionary movements throughout the world. North Korea is now recognized by 90 countries in the world—a gain of 49 since 1972—reflecting the success of its new strategy in international affairs. It also is the second communist country to become a member of the League of Nonaligned Nations. At the same time, North Korea has been careful not to offend either Beijing or Moscow because of its dependence on both of them for security and economic needs. Kim has described North Korea as the easternmost outpost of the socialist camp and has forsworn national communism. On the other hand, Kim has shown extreme sensitivity to interference by either Beijing or Moscow in the internal affairs of the country and, in general, has shown a marked distrust—shared by all North Koreans—of foreigners and major powers. North Korea's relations with the Soviet Union and China are the most crucial aspects of its foreign policy. North Korea has gone through both pro-Soviet and pro-Chinese phases, the first lasting until 1964 and the second until the Cultural Revolution. Since 1966 it has pursued a more evenhanded policy. In 1961 North Korea entered into treaties of friendship, mutual assistance and cooperation with both China and the Soviet Union, and these treaties remained in force and defined their mutual relations in the late 1970s. Relations with the Soviet Union ebbed to their lowest point between 1962 and 1964 following the Soviet retreat in the confrontation with the United States over Cuba. North Korea accused the Soviet Union of political interference, economic pressure, arrogance, big-power chauvinism and exploitation of North Korean natural resources. Relations improved after Khrushchev's fall in 1964, and by the mid-1970s the Soviet Union resumed its role as North Korea's principal source of arms and foremost trading partner. Relations between China and North Korea have been described as "blood-sealed militant friendship," in reference to the Chinese military intervention that saved the country from extinction in 1951. Although North Korea at first charted a neutral course in the Sino-Soviet dispute, it adopted a more openly pro-Chinese stand because of disenchantment with Soviet policies. When relations with the Soviet Union improved after 1964, the Chinese reaction was predictably hostile. During the Cultural Revolution Kim Il-sung was attacked as a revisionist. Relations were mended in 1969 and have returned to the pre-1966 levels of cordiality. It is clear, however, that neither the Soviet Union nor China would like to see a resumption of hostilities on the Korean Peninsula. Pyongyang therefore appears to have withdrawn from a policy of confrontation and brinksmanship, in line with the climate of détente favored by its two major allies. Since 1978 North Korea has learned to walk a neutral tightrope even more boldly without falling into either the Soviet or Chinese camp. On three key issues it supported the Chinese: It sided with China in the Vietnam-Cambodia conflict; it refused to condemn China's invasion of Vietnam; and it offered asylum to Norodom Sihanouk, a long-time friend of Beijing. Despite their unfriendly acts, Moscow went ahead with increased economic and military aid to North Korea; providing technical assistance for the production to T-62 tanks; inviting North Koreans to attend a COMECON conference as observers; shipping over 900,000 tons of plant facilities, crude oil, cotton and cement in 1978 alone; and sending 100 North Korean pilots to be trained on MiG-23's.

Despite heavy debts to the U.S.S.R., the two countries have signed trade protocols in which the Soviets are offering even more trade and aid to the Democratic People's Republic of Korea. In 1986 the Democratic People's Republic of Korea gave the U.S.S.R. use of its naval port at Nampo. A visit to Soviet Premier Gorbachev in October seemed to indicate a Sino-North Korea split, but in May 1987 Kim Il-sung met with China's General Secretary Zhao Ziyang. It is believed he sought, among other things, Chinese support for North Korea's new national development plan.

South Korea is critical to North Korea's foreign policy, and hostility toward its southern neighbor is one constant in the conduct of North Korean diplomacy. Unification of the Korean Peninsula remains a long-range goal of Pyongyang, though the tactics are changed from time to time. These tactics have included war, subversion, propaganda, underground struggle and peace talks. Increasing militancy by North Korea—encouraged by the Communist victory in Vietnam—was evidenced by the murder of two U.S. servicemen at Panmunjom in 1976. There also has been a new element of economic and diplomatic competition between the two Koreas.

The main hurdle has been the North Korean refusal to grant any form of de facto recognition to the South Korean government, and rejection of any meeting attended by South Koreans acting as government officials. At the 1979 preliminary talks, North Korea was represented not by government officials but by members of the Democratic Front for the Reunification of the Fatherland, who called for the convening of a "whole nation" congress comprising representatives of political and social organization from both North and South. Further, North Korea had rejected U.S. proposals for trilateral talks, insisting on prior American withdrawals followed by bilateral negotiations between Washington and Pyongyang in which South Korea would participate only as an observer. Pursuing the same logic, North Korea turned down all proposals whereby the North and the South would recognize each other and be simultaneously admitted to the United Nations, in effect legitimizing the division of the peninsula. With President Carter's freeze on further U.S. withdrawals from South Korea, North-South relations were back to square one. While the rhetorical emphasis was on "peaceful reunification," the North did not abjure the use of massive force or of covert operations aimed at exploiting the considerable domestic tension in the South to achieve its goal.

Working-level discussions were held in 1983 on a number of social and economic issues though little substantive progress was made. Economic cooperation talks were also held from 1984 to 1986 but were inconclusive. Nevertheless, in 1984 these talks resulted in certain agreements. Inter-parliamentary talks would be held regularly alternating between Pyongyang and Seoul. Additionally, families separated by the Korean split would be reunited during a brief exchange visit to the two capitals.

This movement toward unification was followed with some backsliding. North Korea suspended all talks following the scheduled U.S.–South Korean military maneuvers in February 1986. Also, Pyongyang insisted that it co-host the 1988 Olympic Games in Seoul. South Korea denounced the building of a dam by North Korea near the demilitarized zone saying that a sudden release of its accumulated waters threatened South Korean troops stationed nearby on the border.

In late 1986–early 1987, discussions proposed by Kim Il-sung on the possibility of a bilateral reduction of armed forces were deemed acceptable by both countries. In July, the Democratic Peoples Republic of Korea proposed that its armed forces be gradually reduced along with a withdrawal of U.S. troops and the establishment of a neutral force in the demilitarized zone. South Korea proposed that a meeting be held between the two countries' ministers of foreign affairs, but North Korea refused to participate unless the United States was also represented. Though willingness to discuss re-unification and reduction of armed forces were expressed by North Korean leaders, relations deteriorated rapidly when a South Korean civilian airliner exploded during a flight over Southeast Asia on November 29, 1987. Despite evidence of Kim Il-sung's complicity with the attack and threats of reprisal, formal talks resumed in August 1988 at Panmunjom. Discussions centered on the creation of a joint parliamentary meeting but were inconclusive though there was agreement to resume talks after the 1988 Olympic Games. In November the United States, in support of South Korean efforts to ease tensions, agreed to resume informal contacts with North Korean diplomats, as well as ease certain trade sanctions and travel restrictions that had been imposed on the Democratic People's Republic of Korea.

In 1990 the premiers of North and South Korea held an unprecedented series of three meetings in an effort to forward relations. Nevertheless, talks broke down because of South Korea's refusal to sign a North-proposed nonaggression pact. North Korea called off talks scheduled in early 1991, citing U.S.–South Korean military exercises as the reason for the cancellation.

North Korea's relations with Japan are shaped by a mixture of historical resentments and economic needs. Both Japan and North Korea are interested in promoting trade under the slogan "Separation of Trade from Politics." North Korea is now one of Japan's largest Communist trading partners. However, although there are many cultural and economic contacts, the two countries do not have any formal diplomatic relations. North Korean interests are effectively served in Japan through the General Association of Korean Residents in Japan. Following the November 1987 attack on the South Korean airliner, Japan suspended official visits and flights between North Korea and Japan. Trade was expected to continue. In September 1988 Japan removed its sanctions.

The United States has been the main target of North Korean propaganda, and "hate America" has been the major theme of its ideological campaigns. However, the United States supports the initiation of talks between the two Koreas, and there were signs that North Korea was responding by softening its anti-American posture in the early 1970s. But with the fall of Saigon and the murder of the two U.S. servicemen at Panmunjom in 1976, both countries returned to their old positions.

North Korea is not a member of the United Nations, but it maintains an observer group at U.N. headquarters and also is a member of a number of U.N. agencies. North Korea has no diplomatic relations with either the United States or the United Kingdom.

PARLIAMENT

The national legislature is the unicameral Supreme People's Assembly (SPA), consisting of 655 members, all of whom belong to the Korean Workers' Party. The SPA is described in the Constitution as the highest organ of state power. Its chief functions are the adoption and amendment of constitutional enactments; election of the president of the country and the members of the Central People's Committee; election of members of the Standing Committee, the premier, the president of the Central Court and other legal officials; approval of the state plan and budget; and declarations of war and peace. Though its normal term is four years, the 1982 election was the first since 1972. The SPA meets twice a year in sessions that last only a few days. The spring session meets in March or April and the fall session in November or December. Extraordinary sessions may be held at the request of at least one-third of the deputies. Bills may be introduced by the deputies or by the president.

When the SPA is not in session its functions are carried out by the Standing Committee, or Presidium, of 19 members elected by SPA members from among themselves. Many of the powers assigned to the Standing Committee and the SPA were transferred by the Constitution of 1972 to the president and the Central People's Committee.

POLITICAL PARTIES

The ruling party of North Korea since 1949 has been the Korean Workers' Party (KWP), founded through the merger of the Communist Party and the New People's Party. The Korean Workers' Party is a Marxist-Leninist party with an estimated membership of 3 million, representing a cross section of the population and divided into four categories: peasants, intellectuals, workers and military personnel. The party is a well-disciplined organization that controls every aspect of national life, including the army.

The highest organ of the party is the Party Congress, which is convened every four years and consists of over 2,000 delegates elected by members of provincial party assemblies. Major party congresses are used to weed out anti-Kim Il-sung factions and to intensify his hold on the party organs. To guide the party between sessions, the congress elects the Central Committee and the Central Auditing Commission. The Central Committee consists of 116 regular members and 57 candidate members. Only regular members are entitled to vote and hold offices in the party. Committee members also are assigned key posts in the government and army and serve in the Supreme People's Assembly. The committee is required to meet at least once every six months. Its principal function is the election of the party's general secretary; 13 secretaries; the Central Inspection Committee; and the Political Committee, the nerve center of the party. The Political Committee consists of 14 regular members and eight candidates. The Political Committee itself has a Standing Committee of six members. There are a number of other inner bodies within the Political Committee, such as the Secretariat, the Organization and Guidance Department and the Military Committee.

There are parallel party organizations at the provincial, municipal, county, city, urban district and village levels. The basic organizational units are the party cells, which range in size from three to 49 members in the countryside and to 99 members in urban areas. The pivotal role in political work is played by the party cadres, who are full-time party workers or ideological specialists. Party cadres are classified into three grades. The cadres are subject to constant indoctrination, and they are expected to mingle with the masses and provide them with on-the-spot guidance. They constitute an elite group in an otherwise egalitarian society. There are a number of specialized schools for cadre training.

The average citizen is completely excluded from any real participation in the political process. To achieve even a semblance of real participation, one must become a member of the KWP. The selection process for entrance to the party is long and rigorous. Individuals from "bad social backgrounds" (those who have relatives who fled South during the Korean War, those whose families had strong religious involvement or were once property owners or members of the bourgeoisie, and those who have relatives who are political prisoners) are effectively denied entry into the party and are discriminated against. Most levels of the party have no voice, serving only to carry out the decrees and "on-the-spot guidance" promulgated by party leader Kim Il-sung and his top subordinates.

In ideological terms the KWP stands between the Soviet and Chinese Communist parties. Its ideological basis, known as *chuche sasang* (self-reliance), also known as Kim Il-sungism or *hyongmyong sasang* (revolutionary ideology) or *yuil sasang* (the one and only ideology), is Kim Il-Sung's own contribution to international communism and represents an application of the broad principles of Marxism-Leninism to the Korean situation. Essentially it involves the solving of national problems independently without depending on foreign powers. Elevated to the status of a formal doctrine in 1972, *juche sasang* was used to combat pro-Soviet and pro-Chinese factions within the party.

Political activity also is carried out through a number of front organizations, some of which are used solely for propaganda, while others are designed to mobilize special-interest groups. These include the Socialist Working Youth League, the General Federation of Korean Trade Unions, the Korean Democratic Party, the Korean Democratic Women's Union, the Friends (or Chongu) Party and the Democratic Front for the Reunification of the Fatherland.

ECONOMY

North Korea is a lower-middle-income country, with an economy based on heavy and light industry. It has a centrally planned socialist economy in which the dominant and only sector is public.

State control of economic affairs is unusually tight even for a Communist country because of the small size and homogeneity of the society and the strict one-man rule of Kim.

GROSS DOMESTIC PRODUCT

GDP nominal (W. billions): 11.8 (1986)
GDP per capita (U.S. $): 1,240 (1989)
Average annual growth rate of net material product: (%, 1980–84): 8.5

North Korea has abundant natural resources and hydroelectric power, which have formed the basis of large scale industrial development first begun during the Japanese occupation. Manufacturing emphasizes heavy industry with light industry lagging far behind. Agriculture plays a far smaller role in the economy. However, North Korea is largely self-sufficient in food production.

All types of economic data are classified as strategic information and are not released to the public. Some figures are occasionally cited by Kim Il-sung in his speeches, but these are essentially self-serving and extremely unreliable.

Since 1973 North Korea has run huge trade deficits. By 1979 Pyongyang had accumulated a trade deficit of $1.3 billion with non-Communist countries and $700 million with Communist countries. By 1976 North Korea began defaulting on its debt payments. The debt problem was most serious with Japan, where by 1979 obligations approached $400 million. In 1979 an agreement was reached with Japan for rescheduling of a Y83 billion debt on a 1981–90 timetable.

When North Korea failed to re-schedule its foreign debts, Western bank creditors moved in August 1987 to seize its gold assets in London. A re-scheduling agreement was signed in September and in June 1988 the Democratic Peoples Republic of Korea paid its Western bank creditors $5 million under an agreement whereby 30% of the country's $900 million loans would be repaid by 1990 and the rest would be canceled.

PUBLIC FINANCE

The North Korean fiscal year is the calendar year. All direct taxes were abolished in 1974, and 100% of state revenues are derived from the public sector. The 1988 national budget was balanced, with revenues and expenditures of W30,308 billion. Of the expenditures, 63.3% went to economic functions, 20% to cultural functions, 14.6% to defense and 2.1% to other areas.

North Korea's planning history began in 1947 with two consecutive one-year plans (1947, 1948) followed by a two-year plan (1949–50); a three-year plan (1954–56); a five-year plan (1957–61); a seven-year plan (1961–68), which was extended until 1970; a six-year plan (1971–76) and a seven year plan (1978–84). It has been reported that virtually all the targets of the 1971–76 six-year plan were met 16 months ahead of schedule. The 1978–84 plan results were reported in 1987. Increases were reported in industrial production along with successful expansions in the production of steel, coal, non-ferrous metals, chemical fertilizers, synthetic fibers, industrial machinery, cement and textiles. During the two year period between 1984–86 annual grain production had increased. Economic planning is coordinated and plans are drawn up and implemented by the State Planning Committee, which is dominated by technocrats rather than ideologues. Despite the existence of Regional Planning Commissions and Provincial and County Planning Committees, the planning system is highly centralized. Little is known about planning techniques, but they are believed to be handicapped by the limited availability of statistics. The 1986–93 seven-year plan looked forward to a 10% annual increase in industrial production of electricity and increases in output of coal, steel, non-ferrous metals, machine tools, building materials, industrial robots and computers, as well as improvements in grain production.

No information is available on the industrial origin of the Gross Domestic Product.

In accordance with its policy of total self-reliance, North Korea does not permit any foreign investments. However, it is believed that both China and the Soviet Union have financed some of the development plans through loans and grants.

CURRENCY & BANKING

The North Korean unit of currency is the won, divided into 100 chon or jun. Coins are issued in denominations of 1, 5 and 10 chon and notes are issued in denominations of 50 chon and 1, 5, 10, 50 and 100 won.

The new won was introduced in 1959, replacing the old won at 1 new won = 100 old won. There are three types of exchange rates: a basic rate, which is linked to the Soviet ruble; a commercial or trade rate, introduced in 1961; and a tourist rate, introduced in 1973. The January 1989 dollar exchange rate was $1 = W2.3.

The central bank is the Korean Central Bank, established in 1946 as the bank of issue and administrative organ of the State Planning Committee. It also supervises the other two banking institutions: the Foreign Trade Bank and Korean Industrial Bank. Industrial enterprises, agricultural cooperatives and the post office maintain savings facilities.

FINANCIAL INDICATORS, 1988

External debt 1987
- Total (U.S. $ millions): 610
- Debt service (long term): 97
- Repayment
  - Principal (%): 70.1
  - Interest (%): 29.9

GROWTH PROFILE
(Annual Growth Rates, %)

Projected crude birth rate (/1000) (1990–95): 24.3
Projected crude death rate (/1,000) (1990–95): 5.0

AGRICULTURE

Of the total land area of 12,053,800 ha. (29,784,939 ac.), 17.4% is arable land or land under cultivation. Although agriculture is the highest employment sector of the economy, percentages have been dropping from 57% in 1965 to 32% in 1986.

Two-thirds of the arable land is found in four western provinces (North Pyongan, South Pyongan, North Hwanghae and South Hwanghae). The three provinces fronting the Yellow Sea also contain 60% of the nation's paddy fields. One-fourth of the arable land is contained in the three provinces of the eastern region (North Hamgyong, South Hamgyong and Kangwon). The interior region, comprising the provinces of Chagang and Yanggang, are mountainous, dry and cold but rich in forest resources. Though the relative share of agriculture in the GDP has been steadily declining, the sector has shown overall growth in absolute terms in area, crop yields and production. Much of the increase in area is directly attributable to reclamation projects and expansion of paddy fields into dry, upland fields. Reclamation programs brought 100,000 ha. (247,000 ac.) on the western coast into cultivation by the early 1980s. The increase in yield is attributable to introduction of "miracle" strains, intensive application of fertilizers and mechanization. Paddy lands under irrigation now account for one-third of all paddies, and observers agree that irrigation probably has been the most successful aspect of North Korea's agrarian policy. Progress in irrigation has been accompanied by equally impressive progress in mechanization and chemicalization. Use of tractors increased 400% from 1970 to 1982. It is claimed that 92% of the rice-transplanting process is now mechanized.

As a result of these upward trends, North Korea is now an exporter of food. Because of severe winters and short growing seasons, North Korea has only one rice harvest per year. Since the upper limit in arable land has been reached, agricultural development is concentrated on land reclamation projects. Irrigated rice also is being replaced by less productive crops such as corn, grain, sorghum, millet and rye, which are better suited to the country's short cropping period. Double-cropping of grains other than rice has been increased through such techniques as cold-bed seeding to an estimated half of the total cultivated land.

One of the first acts of the North Korean government after being set up in 1946 was the Land Reform Act, under which nearly 54% of cultivated land was confiscated from various classes: Japanese landowners; Korean landowners who had collaborated with the Japanese; absentee landlords; and religious organizations. All lands in continuous tenancy and lands over 5 ha. (12.3 ac.) also were confiscated. After the Korean War the country's farmlands were collectivized in three stages. The first was the labor cooperative stage, in which private ownership of land was retained; next came the land cooperative stage; and the third and last stage was the socialist cooperative stage. All private ownership of land was abolished by 1959. Initially there were more than 50,000 collective farms, but soon they were consolidated and reduced to 4,000, each farm geographically identical with the *ri* or village. An average farm covers 466 ha. (1,151 ac.) and consists of 80 to 300 farm families. Cooperatives account for 90% of cultivated land and agricultural production. The balance is accounted for by state farms, which are model farms run as industrial enterprises. State farms are, on average, larger and more mechanized than collectives and also are managed more efficiently. The management of collective farms is vested in county

AGRICULTURAL INDICATORS

Index of agricultural production (1979–81 = 100): 123 (1986)
Index of food production (1979–81 = 100): 123 (1986)
Number of tractors: 73,000 (1986)
Total fertilizer consumption (000 metric tons): 808 (1985–86)
Land use (%)
  Cropland: 24
  Pasture: 1
  Forest: 64
  Other: 11
Yields (kg./ha.) 1989
  Grains: 4,681
  Roots & tubers: 13,421
  Legumes: 914
  Milk (kg./animal): 2,441
Production 1989
  Fruits (million metric tons): 1.278
  Vegetables (million metric tons): 3.45
Livestock (000) 1989
  Cattle: 1,280
  Horses: 41 (1986)
  Sheep: 380
  Pigs: 3,145
Forestry 1988
  Production of roundwood (million cubic meters): 4.705
    of which industrial roundwood (%): 12.8
Fishing 1988
  Total catch (million metric tons): 1.7000
    of which marine (%): 94.1
  Value of exports (U.S. $ 000): 70.890

management committees composed of agricultural and technical experts. The committees set production quotas; allocate resources; determine and disburse wages; monitor credit; and direct use of seeds, tractors and fertilizers. The collective farms also have developed the *chongsan-ni* method of management, a personalized, on-the-spot guidance method that requires party functionaries to refrain from issuing orders and help the peasants to improve production through incentives and indoctrination. Rural reforms similar to those instituted in the People's Republic of China have been introduced since 1985. These reforms have permitted peasants to farm small plots for their own profit.

The livestock population has increased in all areas.

Forests and woodlands cover nearly 9 million ha. (22 million ac.), including rough grazing land, or three-fourths of the total land area. Over 60% of the forests are in the northern provinces of North Hamgyong and South Hamgyong, Yanggang and Changang. Forests are administered by the General Bureau of Forestry. The most valuable commercial stands include oak, alder, larch, pine, spruce and fir.

Fishing is a major economic activity and is concentrated in the Sea of Japan. The fishing fleet is estimated at 35,000 vessels, of which 10% are fully automated factory ships. The industry is totally nationalized and is administered by the Ministry of Fisheries and by Provincial Fisheries Administration committees. Fishing is undertaken by maritime cooperatives, and fish processing is done in marine industry plants.

MANUFACTURING

In the two decades following the end of the Korean War, the government adopted an economic policy of rapid industrialization. The metal processing and machine-building industries benefitted most from state investments. About 90% of all industry is state-owned, and 10% is owned by cooperatives. The government does not release any figures on industrial production, but the major industrial products are textiles, chemical fertilizers, glass, paper, machine tools, internal-combustion engines, electric motors, tractors, trucks, marine products, bicycles and sewing machines. Crude-steel production reached 3.5 million tons in 1981. A boost was given to cement production in 1978 with the completion at Sunchon of a new cement plant built with Danish and Japanese technology. By the mid-1970s manufacturing expanded into consumer-oriented products. The largest industrial subsectors are metal fabrication, textiles and food processing, accounting for 33%, 18.6% and 13.7%, respectively.

Industrial plants are concentrated in a few regions. The chemicals industry is clustered in the Hamhung, Sinuiju, Pyongyang and Nampo areas, iron and steel in the lower Taedong River area and Chongjin, textile industries in Pyongyang and Sinuiju, machine industries in Sinuiju and Pyongyang, electronics industries in Pyongyang and Nampo, shipbuilding in Haeju and Nampo, the cement industry in Haeju and the pulp industry in Chongjin. An expansion program was begun in late 1986 at North Korea's largest ironworks at Kimchaek. This Soviet-aided project is to double annual steelmaking output. Under the last seven-year plan, steel production is to increase to 10 million tons annually.

Corresponding to the *chongsan-ni* method in agricultural cooperatives, there is the *taean* system of industrial management in central and local state enterprises. Under this system workers are allowed to participate in the management decisions of the plant. Guidelines and goals are discussed in conferences in which both managers and workers take part.

MINING

North Korea's mineral resources are ranked third in Asia, after those of China and Japan, but the mining sector's performance has been erratic and productivity has been low. North Korea has significant deposits of coal, iron, copper, zinc, tin, silver and gold. It supplies about 57% of the world's tungsten.

ENERGY

The country has two petroleum refineries, with a total of 42,000 bd. capacity. One, built with Soviet aid, is at Unggi; the other, built with Chinese aid, is near the Chinese border. Although both plants are operating at less than capacity because of a shortage of crude, they have largely ended North Korea's large imports of refined petroleum products.

North Korean industry relies predominantly on hydroelectric power. In 1986 a hydroelectric power plant built as a joint venture between North Korea and China began operation. The government is currently building the nation's largest hydroelectric power station at Tae-

ENERGY INDICATORS

Electricity 1988
Installed capacity (million kw.): 9.500
Production (million kw.-hr.): 53.00
% fossil fuel: 40.6
% hydro: 59.4
% nuclear: 0.0
Consumption per capita (000 kw.-hr.): 2.420
Petroleum
Consumption (million bbl.): 18 (1988)
Refining capacity (000 bbl./day): 42 (1990)
Coal
Reserves (million metric tons): 600 (latest)
Production (million metric tons): 52.500 (1988)
Consumption (million metric tons): 54.950 (1988)

chon. The Soviet Union is helping to construct the nation's first nuclear power plant.

LABOR

The most significant fact about North Korea's labor force is a constant labor shortage in virtually all sectors, including agriculture. Various methods are being tried to compensate for this shortage, including employment of women in industries normally reserved for men, repatriation of North Koreans from abroad, use of volunteer labor drafts and team labor, and increasing productivity through technical training. The armed forces constitute a major drain on available labor resources.

One of the methods used to increase labor productivity is known as the Chollima Work Unit Movement, named after the flying horse of Chinese mythology that could cover enormous distances in a single day. Workers are organized into work teams that compete with one another, and wages are dependent on the output of the team rather than of the individual. Incentives and awards are given to teams that reach or surpass their production quotas. Wage schedules are drawn up by industrial sectors and are classified on a scale from 3 to 8. Fringe benefits include food allowances, subsidized housing and other amenities. An average worker receives about $45 monthly.

Organized labor is represented by the General Federation of Korean Trade Unions, which is completely subordinate to the Korean Workers' Party.

LABOR INDICATORS, 1985

Total economically active population (millions): 9.084
% working-age (15–64): 75.3
% female: 46.0
Activity rate (%)
Total: 44.6
Male: 48.6
Female: 40.6
Sectoral employment of economically active (%) (1980)
Agriculture, forestry, fishing: 42.8
Manufacturing, mining, quarrying, construction, public utilities: 30.3
Trade hotels, restaurants; transportation, communications; finance, real estate; services: 26.9
Labor under 20 years (%): 11.8 (1985)

FOREIGN COMMERCE

The principal exports are rice, fish, iron ore, pig iron, rolled steel and cement. Principal imports include petroleum, coal, rubber, wheat, cotton, machinery and transportation equipment. There never have been any trade relations between North Korea and the United States.

The U.S.S.R. as well as other Communist countries have been responsible for a large share of North Korea's trade, while Japan has consistently been its most important non-communist trade partner. North Korea's major import sources were the U.S.S.R., China, Japan, Western Europe and Hong Kong. Its major export destinations were the U.S.S.R., Japan, China, Western Europe, Australia, and Hong Kong.

Foreign trade is conducted soley through 15 state trading organizations, each of which specializes in one or more commodities. All foreign trade transactions are under the jurisdiction of the Ministry of Foreign Trade, the Ministry of External Economic Affairs and the Foreign Trade Bank.

FOREIGN TRADE INDICATORS, 1988

Exports (U.S. $ billions): 2.4 (1988)
Imports (U.S. $ billions): 3.1 (1988)
Balance of trade (U.S. $ billions): −0.7

Direction of Trade (%), 1988 (est)

	Imports	Exports
European Community	3.7	3.0
United States	0.0	0.0
U.S.S.R. & eastern European economies	63.0	50.0
Japan	8.8	14.8

TRANSPORTATION & COMMUNICATIONS

The principal means of transportation is the rail system, which hauls over 90% of freight and carries over 70% of the passenger traffic. There are 59 operating lines, of which the major ones link Kaesong on the southern border with Sunuiju on the northern border through Pyongyang; Wonsan and Najin; Pyongyang and Chongjin through Hamhung; and Pyongyang with Wonsan. Five rail lines connect North Korea with China. There also are direct international services between Pyongyang and Moscow and Beijing.

Regular commercial services are maintained on the navigable rivers that open onto the western coast. The total length of inland waterways is 2,253 km. (1,400 mi.) on the Yalu, Taedong and Chaeryong rivers.

Major ports are Wonsan, Chongjin and Najin in the East and Nampo, Haeju and Tasado in the West. There are 26 minor ports serving coastal traffic. North Korea had a small mercantile marine with a gross registered tonnage of 528,800 in 1989.

Road transportation is relatively undeveloped. There is an estimated 22,000 km. (13,670 mi.) of roads, only 2% of which are paved. Though the number of motor vehicles in the country is not known, private road travel is believed to be limited because of the lack of domestic fuel supplies. Bus services have been ex-

TRANSPORTATION INDICATORS

Roads (latest)
- Length, km. (mi.): 22,000 (13,670)
- Paved (%): 2

Railroads (latest)
- Track, km. (mi.): 8,533 (5,302)

Merchant marine
- Vessels (over 100 tons): 82 (1989)
- Total deadweight tonnage (000): 528.8 (1989)
- Oil tankers (000 GRT): 171 (1985)

Ports (pre 1986)
- Cargo loaded (000 metric tons): 609
- Cargo unloaded (million metric tons): 4.640

Air
- Passenger-km. (passenger-mi.) (millions): 84 (52) (latest)
- Freight, metric ton-km. (short ton-mi.) (millions): 2.0 (1.4) (latest)
- Airports with scheduled flights: 3 (1990)

Inland waterways (latest)
- Length, km. (mi.): 2,253 (1,400)

Telephones
- Total (000): 10 (1983)
- Persons per telephone: 2,000 (1983)

Telecommunications 1990
- Satellite ground stations: 1

panded to cover over 2,400—or over 50%—of the country's villages.

Civil air service between the major cities is provided by the Civil Aviation Administration. International services are provided by CAA and Aeroflot. Sunan Airport, north of Pyongyang, serves as the main international airport. Other civilian airports are at Pyongyang, Hamhung, Chongjin and Wonsan. Tourism is allowed with official permission. In 1986 there were about 85,000 visitors, mostly in Pyongyang.

DEFENSE

The defense structure is headed by the president, who also is the supreme commander of the armed forces and chairman of the National Defense Commission. Ultimate political control is vested in the Military Committee of the Korean Workers' Party. Operational control is under the Ministry of People's Armed Forces, with three principal divisions: the General Staff, the General Political Bureau and the General Bureau of Rear Services. Intelligence and secret police services are conducted by the Bureau of Political Security and the Reconnaissance Bureau. The line of command runs through the chief of the General Staff, who holds the rank of deputy minister, to the service commanders, who hold the rank of vice minister. The Capital Defense Command is a separate unit under the General Staff.

Political control over the army is enforced by a system of political commissars and a party structure paralleling the military structure at all levels of command. All soldiers are either members of the Korean Workers' Party or are enrolled in the Socialist Working Youth League.

Military manpower is provided through a system of conscription. The age of conscription is 20 to 25 for all able-bodied males. The term of service is three years in the army and four years in the navy and air force.

The total strength of the armed forces is estimated as of June 1988 at 842,000, which makes the North Korean armed forces one of the largest in the world. With 3.7% of its population under arms, North Korea ranks fifth in the world in per capita military strength. It also is the most militarized Communist state in the world. In addition, there are a paramilitary force of 38,000 security forces, border guards and a civilian militia of 3 million. The latter, known as the Worker and Peasant Red Guard, was originally conceived of as a territorial militia but is being converted into an auxiliary military force. Red Guard membership and training are compulsory for all able-bodied men between 18 and 45 and all unmarried women between 18 and 30. It is organized in over 5,000 units corresponding to territorial units, with institutions forming smaller units. As with the armed forces, the militia is under the political and operational control of the Military Affairs Committee of the Korean Workers' Party, and all command positions are held by party officials and cadres.

The Military Affairs Committee controls the Ministry of National Defense, under whom are three vice commissars, including the chief of the General Staff and the chief of the Politburo. The primacy of the party is built into the structure of the defense organization. There is a political vice commander in each army, division, regiment, battalion and company, along with a party committee at each of these levels. The nuclear party unit is the cell in each company. About 20% of platoon members are believed to be party members; the proportion is greater for the higher ranks. An interesting feature of the North Korean army is the importance placed on the construction of tunnels under the Demilitarized Zone. Eighteen such tunnels are believed to have been built; 5 km. (3 mi.) long, they would have permitted thousands of troops to enter the rear of the South Korean positions. Only two tunnels have been countermined by the South Koreans so far.

Army

Personnel: 750,000

Organization: headquarters: 3 mechanized divisions; 8 all-armored corps; 2 armored divisions; 5 motorized and mechanized divisions; 24 infantry divisions; 7 independent armored brigades; 9 independent infantry brigades; 27 operations brigades, including 3 commando, 4 reconnaissance and 1 river crossing regiments; 3 amphibious and 5 airborne battalions; Artillery Command; 2 heavy artillery, 2 motorized regiments; 6 SSM battalions

Air defense: 2 AA divisions; 7 AA regiments

Reserve: 23 infantry divisions Forces abroad in Iran, Angola, Madagascar, Seychelles and Uganda

Equipment: 3,475 tanks; 150 light tanks; 140 reconnaissance vehicles; 1,100 armored personnel carriers; 4,650 guns and howitzers; 2,000 rocket launchers; 11,000 mortars; 54 surface-to-surface missiles; antitank: 1,500 recoilless launchers; 800 guns. Air defense: 8,000 guns.

Navy

Personnel: 39,000

Units: 2 fleet headquarters; 20 submarines; 4 frigates; 30 fast attack craft with guns; 163 fast attack craft; 32 patrol craft; 6 landing ships; 114 landing craft

Coastal defense: 2 missile regiments

Naval bases: Four naval base commands, at Nampo and Haeju on the western coast and Wonsan and at Kimchaek on the eastern coast

Air Force

Personnel: 53,000

Organization and equipment: 800 combat aircraft; 3 light bomber squadrons; 10 fighter squadrons; 12 interceptor squadrons; 25 transportation squadrons; 170 helicopters; 254 trainers; 4 SAM brigades

Air bases: Pyongyang, Pyongyang East, Taechon, Wonsan, Pyong-ni, Viji, Sunan, Sinuiju and Saamcham

Though Korea has no military traditions (unlike Japan and China), the quality of military manpower is good. Koreans are tough fighters who adjust readily to military discipline and are noted for their loyalty; endurance; obedience; and ability to handle equipment when properly trained. The military personnel also have been heavily indoctrinated in Marxist ideology and personal loyalty to Kim Il-sung. However, North Korea no longer possesses the overwhelming military superiority it had in 1950. Its most serious strategic problems are the vulnerability of its transportation system, hydroelectric plants and population centers to air strikes from South Korea and Japan, and its continuing dependence on China and the Soviet Union for military supplies.

The major sources of military aid are China and the Soviet Union. Arms purchases abroad during 1973–80 totaled $1.590 billion, of which $210 million was supplied by the Soviet Union and $250 million by China.

EDUCATION

The national literacy rate is 90%. (Virtually no information has been available on the North Korean educational system since the early 1970s.)

Since 1975 education has been free, universal and compulsory for eleven years, from ages 4 to 15. Schooling divided into five years of primary school, four years of middle school and two years of high school. The curriculum emphasizes the ideology of Marxism-Leninism, and *chuche sasang* and party teachings are built into the content of every course. Adulation of Kim Il-sung is taught from nursery school on. All students are encouraged to acquire some technical skills, and practical knowledge is stressed over general knowledge. As part of the ideological orientation, students are instilled in the virtues of conformity, socialist patriotism, loyalty to "Father" Kim, love of labor, self-sacrifice for the collective good and respect for public property. Conversely, traditional religious values, innovativeness and deviance are condemned. All students also must undergo military training.

In addition, there is a special category of schools known as revolutionary schools for children destined to become national leaders. Enrollment in these schools favors children of party cadres.

The academic year runs from September to August. The medium of instruction in Korean. Both English and Russian are taught as second languages from the middle grades on.

Technical training is provided by two-year vocational schools and three-year higher technical schools. Students who wish to continue their technical education may go on to one of 15 technical colleges; seven medical colleges; one pharmaceutical college; or 40 "factory colleges," where work and training are combined. Adult education programs are designed not only to reduce illiteracy but also to provide ideological orientation and technical training. With the introduction of compulsory education and annual anti-illiteracy campaigns, illiteracy has largely been wiped out. Propaganda and literacy centers have been established in every collective farm, factory, mine, and village by the Scientific Knowledge Dissemination Federation. Adult education also is provided through correspondence schools and the media.

Paralleling the national education system is the party school system. Units of the party school system are the County Party Schools, Provincial Communist Colleges and the Kim Il-sung Higher Party School. In addition to regular training, instruction is provided in ideology, party history and organization.

Primary and middle education are the responsibility of the Ministry of Common Education; higher education is the responsibility of the Ministry of Higher Education. At the local levels teacher training, technical high schools, high schools and special schools are administered by the Education Bureau of the Provincial Administrative Committees, while kindergarten, primary, middle and technical education are under the control of County Administrative Committees. Educational policy is laid down at the national level by the KWP Central Committee and at the local levels by the school chapter of the county-level party committees.

EDUCATION INDICATORS, 1986

Literacy
- Total (%): 90.0

First level and second level
- Schools: 4,319
- Students: 4,308,000

General and Vocational
- Schools: 473
- Students: 215,000

Third level (postsecondary)
- Institutions: 281
- Students: 417,300
- Teachers: 9,244 (1982)

Foreign study
- Students aboard: 1,227
  - of whom in
    - United States: 28 (1988)
    - France: 15 (1988)
    - Federal Republic of Germany: 36 (1988)
    - United Kingdom: 15 (1987)

Figures on national educational expenditures are not released by the government.

There are about 280 institutions of higher education, including the national university, Kim Il-sung University; Kim Chaek Technical University; and seven medical colleges. College admissions are based less on scholastic record than on the student's political record, social origin and "trend of thought." In August 1988 the government announced the development of several new educational facilities: a university, eight colleges, three factory colleges, two farmers colleges and five special schools.

LEGAL SYSTEM

The judiciary is a three-tiered system consisting of the Central Court at the apex; provincial courts in each province and municipal courts in each municipality at the intermediate level; and people's courts in cities, counties and urban districts. Trials in the subordinate courts are held with one to three judges and two people's assessors. The judges and people's assessors of the Central Court are elected every four years by the Standing Committee of the Supreme People's Assembly, while at the local levels they are elected by the People's Assemblies for a term of four years in the provincial and municipal courts and a term of two years for the county and city people's courts. The terms of the Central Court judges are concurrent with those of SPA members.

The judiciary is subordinate to the party, and all judicial activities are guided and controlled by party committees. The courts and the prosecuting authorities are defined as "powerful weapons for proletarian dictatorship." The penal system also has been combined with political reeducation and indoctrination. Most judges usually are party members, and judicial decisions are subject to scrutiny for their conformity with party policies and directives. The nation's chief law enforcement officer is the central procurator general, who is appointed by the SPA. As the government's most powerful watchdog, he maintains constant vigilance over all citizens and public activities, directs all investigations, prosecutes crimes and oversees court proceedings. There are special courts outside the regular court system. In a 1979 interview with American journalist John Wallach, North Korean Supreme Court justice Li Chun-uk noted that the defense counsel's job is "to give the suspect due punishment." Open court appears to consist of an announcement of the term of imprisonment, which already has been determined by the Provincial Safety Bureau.

Prisons are administered by the Reform Bureau of the Ministry of Public Security. There are at least two prison camps for political prisoners.

LAW ENFORCEMENT

The national police force is the Protection and Security Bureau, under the Ministry of Public Security. There are public security bureaus in each province, city and county and a number of substations in cities. A resident policeman or constable is assigned to each village. All police personnel hold military ranks; county police are headed by a lieutenant colonel, and city police are headed by a colonel. An important police function is control over all types of movement, and examination of credentials of persons leaving or entering any area. Every North Korean is required to carry an identification card and to secure a travel permit before making a trip. Changes in place of residence and employment also require official sanction.

The Central Domestic Intelligence Agency is a second bureau within the Ministry of Public Security.

HEALTH

The major health problems are tuberculosis, leprosy, Japanese B encephalitis, typhoid, diphtheria, typhus and smallpox. All medical services have been nationalized, and a national health insurance system has been established. Though health services are available throughout the country through people's clinics, production of medicines and medical equipment does not meet national needs. Government encouragement also is extended to the traditional Korean system of medicine known as *tonguihak*.

HEALTH INDICATORS

Health personnel 1987
- Physicians: 57,800
  - persons per: 370

Hospitals 1982
- Number: 7,924
- Number of beds (/10,000): 130

Public health expenditures (latest)
- Per capita (U.S. $): 10.1

Vital statistics
- Crude death rate (/1,000): 5 (1990)
- Life expectancy at birth (1990)
  - Males: 69
  - Females: 75
- Infant mortality rate (/1,000 live births): 27 (1990)
- Child mortality rate under 5 yrs. (/1,000 live births) (1985–90): 31
- Maternal mortality rate (/100,000 live births) (1986–87): 41.0
- Population with access to safe water (%): 100 (latest)

FOOD & NUTRITION

The staple food is rice supplemented by fish, vegetables and fruit. The national dish is *kimchi*, a highly spiced pickle of cabbage. Meat, milk and eggs are consumed only occasionally.

The daily per capita consumption of food is estimated at 2,972 calories (113% of requirements).

MEDIA & CULTURE

Sixteen dailies are published in the country. Fourteen major periodicals are published in Korean and nine in foreign languages, all under state auspices. The largest daily is *Rodong Sinmun* (Labor Daily), the organ of the Central Committee of the KWP, which claims a circulation of close to 1 million copies. The official government organ is *Minju Chosun*.

MEDIA INDICATORS

Newspapers
  Number of dailies: 16 (latest)
Newsprint consumption (1988)
  Total metric tons: 3,200
  Per 1,000 pop. (kg.): 146
Radio
  Number of transmitters: 32 (1989)
  Number of persons per radio receiver: 6 (1989)
Television
  Television transmitters: 11 (latest)
  Number of persons per T.V. receiver: 90 (1989)
Cinema
  Number of fixed cinemas: 1,178 (latest)
  Seating capacity (000): 653 (latest)
  Seats (/1,000 pop.): 32.0 (1985)
  Annual attendance (millions): 187
  Gross box office receipts (millions): 48.5 (1985)
Films
  Number of long films produced: 37 (latest)
  Number of long films imported: 68 (1985)
    % from U.S.S.R. 45.6
    % from U.S. 0

The principal agency concerned with the media is the Propaganda and Agitation Department of the KWP. Its control is exercised through a number of state organs, such as the General Publications Bureau, the Publications and Press Bureau of the Ministry of Foreign Affairs, and the Ministry of Culture and Art. All newspaper companies and publishing houses are under the control of the Ministry of Public Security.

The national news agency is the Korean Central News Agency (KCNA), which is run by the State Administration Council. It publishes daily news bulletins, periodical bulletins in Russian and English, and a yearbook. Tass is the only foreign news bureau represented in Pyongyang.

There are 12 state-owned book publishing houses, of which the largest are the Foreign Languages Publishing House, the Publishing House of the General Federation of Literary and Art Unions and the Academy of Sciences Publishing House. North Korea does not adhere to any copyright convention.

The official Korean Central Broadcasting Committee operates seven medium-wave and 12 shortwave stations. It broadcasts two programs on the domestic service for 19 and 21 hours a day, respectively. The foreign program is broadcast in English (six hours a day); Chinese (three hours a day); French, Russian, Japanese and Spanish (two hours each daily); Arabic (one hour a day); and Korean (three hours a day).

Television, introduced in 1969, is estimated to cover 76% of inhabited areas.

The film industry produces about 100 full-length feature films annually, some of them in wide-screen color. In addition, films are imported from China and the Soviet Union. The film industry is controlled by the Films Bureau of the Ministry of Culture.

There are over 200 public libraries, of which the largest is the State Central Library in Pyongyang, with 1.5 million volumes.

SOCIAL WELFARE

Public welfare is one of the principal functions of the government under the Constitution. All citizens are entitled to free medical care, disability benefits and retirement allowances. The program is financed by a fund to which all workers contribute 1% of their wages. The state runs about 400 rest centers and resorts providing free vacations for workers. In addition, the government maintains special facilities for the aged, disabled and hanidcapped.

GLOSSARY

Choe Ko In Min Hoe Ui: Supreme People's Assembly

Chollima: a work unit and productivity movement, named after the legendary Chinese Flying Horse, in which workers are paid on the basis of team performance.

chongbo: a Korean unit of measurement equal to approximately one hectare.

chongmuwon: State Administration Council, the North Korean cabinet.

chongni: prime minister.

Chongsan-ni: personalized, on-the-spot guidance method devised by Kim Il-sung by which party and state officials are required to mingle with the peasants and help them solve their problems through counseling.

Chosun No-Dong Dang: Korean Workers' Party.

chuche sasang: ideology of self-reliance in politics, economics, and defense. Also, Kim Il-sungism, hyongmyong sasang (revolutionary ideology), yuil sasang (the one and only ideology), and tang sasang (party ideology).

chusok: president.

kun: county, as a unit of local administration.

kuyok: district, as a unit of local administration.

nodong chokwidae: Workers' and Peasants' Red Guard.

nodongjaku: workers' district, as a unit of local administration.

pu: ministry.

ri: village, as a unit of local administration.

sadaejuui: literally, flunkyism or "serve-the-great-ism;" servile attitude toward the great powers condemned by Kim Il-sung as a cardinal error.

si: city, as a unit of local administration.

taean: work system which permits worker participation in the management of factories.

Tang-Chungang: Literally, the center of the Party, unofficial title of Kim Il-sung's son, Kim Chong Il.

to: province, as a unit of local administration.

tong: urban block, as a unit of local administration.

tonguihak: Korean system of medicine stressing herbs and acupuncture.

up: town, as unit of local administration.

CHRONOLOGY (from 1945)

1945— Following Japanese surrender, Soviet occupation forces reach Pyongyang. . . . Power is transferred to a Communist-dominated coalition named the People's Political Committee and later to the

North Korean Five-Province Administrative Bureau. . . . North Korean Communist Party is founded.

1946— The Five-Province Administrative Bureau is reorganized as the North Korean Provisional People's Committee. . . . Sweeping social and economic reforms are introduced, including expropriation of farms over 5 ha. (12.25 ac.) and nationalization of basic industries, banks and transportation. . . . North Korean Democratic National United Front is formed, composed of 13 parties, including the Communist Party.

1947— Convention of the People's Committee elects the North Korean People's Assembly which in turn elects the North Korean People's Committee, headed by Kim Il-sung.

1948— North Korea declines to participate in elections under U.N. auspices. . . . Constituent Committee of the People's Assembly promulgates new Constitution, establishing Democratic People's Republic of Korea, with Kim Il-sung as prime minister. . . . Soviet occupation forces withdraw from North Korea.

1949— Korean Workers' Party (KWP) is founded through merger of Communist Party and New Democratic Party. Kim Il-sung is named chairman.

1950— North Korea launches full-scale invasion of the South; U.N. Security Council brands North Korea an aggressor; President Truman orders U.S. forces into battle under a multinational U.N. command. . . . North Korean forces are pushed back to the 38th parallel; U.N. forces cross the border, take Pyongyang and reach several points on the Yalu River; Chinese "volunteers" enter the fighting and force U.N. troops into a pell-mell retreat; North Korea is regained by combined Communist forces.

1951— Seoul is retaken by Communists and is regained by U.N. forces. . . . Battle lines are stabilized along the 38th parallel.

1953— Armistice is signed at Panmunjom, providing for military demarcation line, Demilitarized Zone, Military Armistice Commission and neutral nations Supervisory Commission.

1956— KWP holds Third Party Congress; Kim Il-sung faces and survives challenges from the Yenan and Soviet factions in the party. . . . Relations with the Soviet Union cool following Khrushchev's denunciation of Stalin.

1959— The new won is introduced, replacing the old won.

1961— Mutual Defense Assistance treaties are signed with Moscow and Beijing.

1964— Following Premier Kosygin's visit to North Korea, relations between North Korea and the Soviet Union are renormalized.

1967— Kim Il-sung is denounced by the Red Guards during the Chinese Cultural Revolution.

1968— North Korea seizes USS *Pueblo* off Wonsan. . . . North Korean guerrilla teams land in South Korea.

1969— North Korea downs a U.S. reconnaissance aircraft over international waters.

1970— KWP holds Fifth Party Congress.

1972— Kim Il-sung promulgates new Constitution under which he becomes president.

1976— Park Sung Chul is named prime minister. . . . North Korea apologizes for the killing of two U.S. servicemen at Panmunjom. . . . North Korea defaults on its international debt payments.

1977— Kim appoints Li Jong-ok as prime minister, replacing Park Sung Chul. . . . Kim announces new seven-year plan, 1978–84.

1979— Reunification talks are deadlocked despite mediation of U.N. Secretary General Kurt Waldheim.

1980— KWP Congress elevates Kim Chong Il as general secretary in place of his father, Kim Il-sung.

1983— North Korea is implicated in terrorist attack on South Korean delegation in Rangoon. . . . Burma suspends diplomatic ties with North Korea.

1984— Kim Il-sung visits the Soviet Union, Eastern Europe and China to gather support for his son's succession to the North Korean leadership. . . . Radio Pyongyang refers to Kim Chong Il as the successor to his father's rule.

1985— Negotiations between North and South Korea are held to discuss economic cooperation, reuniting divided families, cooperation between the two legislatures, sporting links and reductions of fortifications at Panmunjom, in the demilitarized zone. All negotiations between the two countries later are suspended due to the annual South Korean-U.S. military maneuvers.

1986— False reports are made of Kim Il-sung's assassination. Stability is quickly restored. Kim Il-sung is re-elected president; Li Gun Mo becomes premier.

1987— The DPRK Government proposes discussions begin immediately over establishing a "zone of peace" between the two countries, but friction continues over South Korea's hosting of the 1988 Olympic Games. . . . The United States reduces restrictions on informal contacts between diplomats of the United States and North Korea, and begins lifting its trade embargo. . . . Speculations of weakened relations with China are proven false when Kim Il-sung visits Beijing. . . . A South Korean aircraft is destroyed and blame is placed on North Korean agents.

1988— Japan imposes economic and diplomatic sanctions on North Korea following the South Korean airliner attack. North Korea announces it will not participate in the Olympic Games. Legislators from North and South Korea meet in Panmunjom but nothing substantive is agreed to. . . . Premier Li Gun Mo resigns due to reports of ill-health and is replaced by Yong Hyong Muk. . . . Yong Hyong Muk is named prime minister.

1989— Preliminary meetings are held to prepare a meeting between the North and South heads of government.

1990— The premiers of North and South Korea meet in a series of three conferences to try to improve relations. The meetings reach no agreement on the issues dividing the two nations.

1991— North Korea calls off talks with the South because of U.S.-South Korean military exercises.

BIBLIOGRAPHY

Books

An, Tai Sung. *North Korea: A Political Handbook.* Wilmington, Del., 1983.

Armbrister, Trevor. *A Matter of Accountability: The True Story of the* Pueblo *Affair.* New York, 1970.

Bernds, Williams J. *The Two Koreas in East Asian Affairs.* New York, 1976.

Brun, Ellen. *Socialist Korea: A Case Study in the Strategy of Economic Development.* New York, 1977.

———, and Jacques Hersh. *Socialist Korea.* Washington, D.C., 1976.

Chung, Chin O. *Pyongyang Between Peking and Moscow: North Korea's Involvement in the Sino-Soviet Dispute, 1958–75.* University, Ala. 1978.

Chung, J. S. *The North Korean Economy: Structure and Development.* Stamford, Conn., 1974.

Kim, I. J. *Communist Policies in North Korea.* New York, 1975.

Kim, Youn-soo. *The Economy of the Korean Democratic People's Republic.* New York, 1979.

Kiyosaki, Wayne S. *North Korea's Foreign Relations.* New York, 1976.

Koh, B. C. *The Foreign Policy of North Korea.* New York, 1969.

Kawak, Tae Hwan. *The Two Koreas in World Politics.* Boulder, Colo., 1984.

Macdonald, Donald Stone. *The Koreans: Contemporary Politics and Society.* London, 1988.

Merrill, John. *Democratic People's Republic of Korea: Politics, Economics and Society.* Boulder, Colo., 1986.

Nam, Koon Woo. *The North Korean Communist Leadership,* 1945–65. University, Ala., 1974.

Paige, Glenn D. *Korean People's Democratic Republic.* Stanford, Calif, 1966.

Scalapino, Robert A., and Chong-Sik Lee. *Communism in Korea.* Berkeley, Calif., 1972.

U.S. Department of the Army. *Communist North Korea: A Bibliographic Survey.* Washington, D.C., 1971.

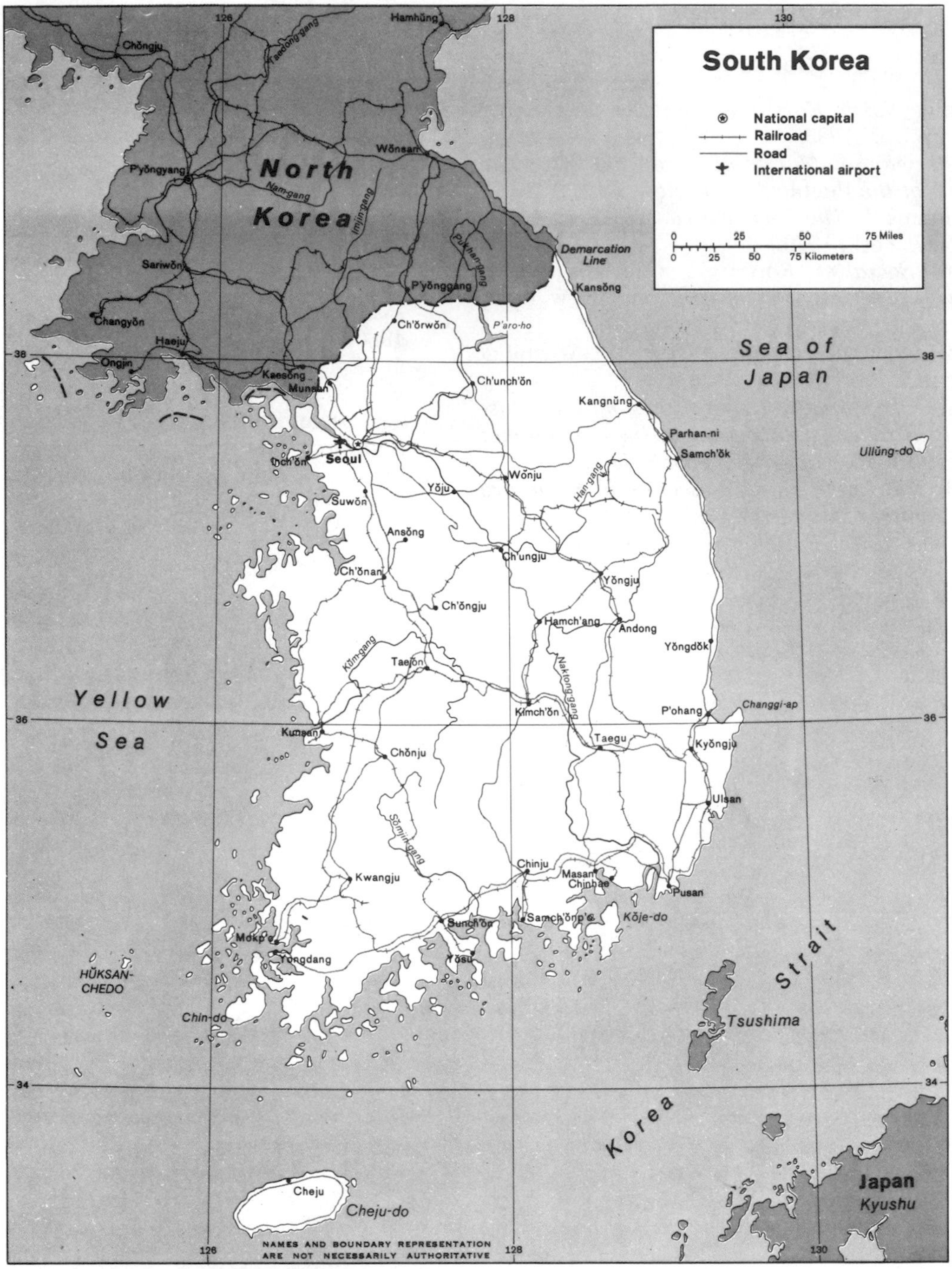

South Korea

- ⊛ National capital
- Railroad
- Road
- ✝ International airport

0 25 50 75 Miles
0 25 50 75 Kilometers

North Korea
Ch'ŏngju
Hamhŭng
Taedong-gang
Wŏnsan
P'yŏngyang
Nam-gang
Imjin-gang
Pukhan-gang
Sariwŏn
P'yŏnggang
Changyŏn
Haeju
Ongjin
Kaesŏng
Munsan
Demarcation Line
Kansŏng
Ch'ŏrwŏn
P'aro-ho
Ch'unch'ŏn
Sea of Japan
Kangnŭng
Parhan-ni
Samch'ŏk
Ullŭng-do
Inch'ŏn
Seoul
Wŏnju
Yŏju
Han-gang
Suwŏn
Ansŏng
Ch'ungju
Ch'ŏnan
Yŏngju
Ch'ŏngju
Hamch'ang
Andong
Yŏngdŏk
Kŭm-gang
Taejŏn
Naktong-gang
Yellow Sea
Kimch'ŏn
P'ohang
Changgi-ap
Kunsan
Taegu
Kyŏngju
Chŏnju
Ulsan
Sŏmjin-gang
Chinju
Kwangju
Masan
Chinhae
Pusan
Sunch'ŏn
Samch'ŏnp'o
Kŏje-do
Mokp'o
Yŏngdang
Yŏsu
HŬKSAN-CHEDO
Chin-do
Tsushima
Korea Strait
Cheju
Cheju-do
Japan
Kyushu

126 128 130
38 36 34

NAMES AND BOUNDARY REPRESENTATION ARE NOT NECESSARILY AUTHORITATIVE

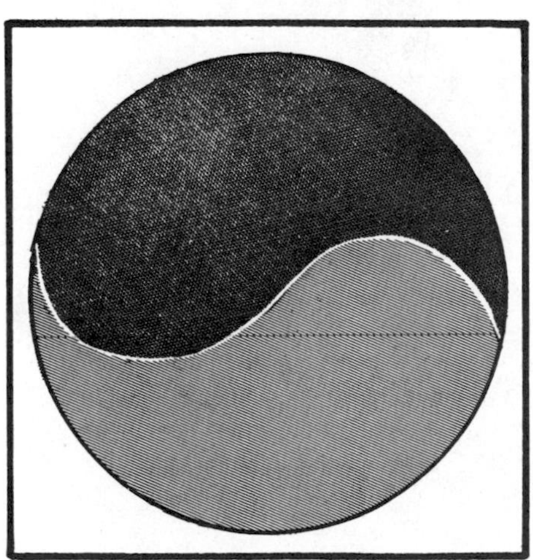

KOREA, SOUTH

BASIC FACT SHEET

OFFICIAL NAME: Republic of Korea (Taehan Min'guk)

ABBREVIATION: KO

CAPITAL: Seoul

HEAD OF STATE: President Roh Tae Woo (from 1988)

HEAD OF GOVERNMENT: Premier Kang Young Hoon (from 1988)

NATURE OF GOVERNMENT: Civilian dictatorship

POPULATION: 43,045,098 (1990)

AREA: 98,485 sq. km. (38,025 sq. mi.)

ETHNIC MAJORITY: Korean

LANGUAGE: Korean

RELIGIONS: Buddhism, Confucianism and Christianity

UNIT OF CURRENCY: Won

NATIONAL FLAG: The *taegukki,* consisting of a disc divided in the shape of the yin and yang symbols with red above and deep blue below in the center of the white field. In the four corners of the flag are black divination bars from the *I Ching,* in sets of three, representing heaven (in the upper hoist), water (in the upper fly), fire (in the lower hoist) and earth (in the lower fly). All three bars are unbroken in the upper hoist and are broken in two in the lower fly. Two bars are broken in the upper fly and one bar is broken in the bottom hoist.

NATIONAL EMBLEM: The yin and yang symbol is centered within a lotus with the name of the country beneath, on a scroll.

NATIONAL ANTHEM: "Till Paektu Mountain Wears Away, Until the Eastern Sea Is Drained"

NATIONAL HOLIDAYS: August 15 (Independence Day, National Day); January 1 (New Year's Day); March 1 (Sam Il Chul, Independence Movement Day); May 5 (Children's Day); June 6 (Memorial Day); July 17 (Constitution Day); September 27 (Choo Suk, Thanksgiving Day); October 1 (Armed Forces Day); October 3 (National Foundation Day); October 9 (Hangul Nal, Anniversary of the Proclamation of the Korean Alphabet); December 25 (Christmas); also variable Buddhist and Confucian festivals

NATIONAL CALENDAR: Gregorian

PHYSICAL QUALITY OF LIFE INDEX: 86

DATE OF INDEPENDENCE: August 15, 1948

DATE OF CONSTITUTION: October 27, 1987

WEIGHTS & MEASURES: Both metric and traditional units are used.

GEOGRAPHICAL FEATURES

South Korea, on the southern part of the Korean Peninsula in East Asia, has a total land area of 98,485 sq. km. (38,025 sq. mi.), excluding the demilitarized zone of 1,262 sq. km. (487 sq. mi.). The greatest distance north-northeast to south-southeast is 642 km. (399 mi.) and that east-southeast to west-northwest is 436 km. (271 mi.). The coastline on the Sea of Japan and the Yellow Sea runs for 1,318 km. (819 mi.).

South Korea shares its total international land boundary of 1,558 km. (968 mi.) with the Democratic People's Republic of Korea (North Korea). The border, the armistic line drawn more or less along the 38th parallel in 1953, has never been accepted by either North or South Korea.

The capital is Seoul, with a 1985 population of 9,645,824, making it the ninth-largest city in the world. There are 18 other cities with populations over 100,000: Pusan (3,516,768), Taegu (2,030,649), Inchon (1,387,475), Kwangju (905,896), Taejon (866, 303), Ulsan (551,219); Puch'on (456,311), Masan (449,236), Chonchu (426,490), Seongnam (447,832), Suweon (430,827), Mokpo (236,085), Cheongju (350,256), Jinju (227,309), Cheju (202,911), Gunsan (185,649), Chuncheon (162,988), and Yeosu (171,933).

South Korea is a rugged and mountainous country, though only one peak, Paektu Mountain, in the extreme North, exceeds 2,750 m. (9,000 ft.) in elevation. Only 15% of the land is classified as plains, and these are mostly along the coast. The dominant topographical feature is a chain of mountains with the Taebaek Range at its core, running parallel to the eastern coast. Midway, the lesser Sobaek Range branches off to the southwest, ending in Mount Chii (1,915 mi.; 6,283 ft.). Based on this mountainous configuration, the country has been divided into five major topographical regions: the Central Region to the west of the Taebaek Mountains and the Eastern Littoral to the east of it; the Naktong River Basin to the southeast of the Sobaek Mountains and the Southern Littoral to its south; and the Southern Mountain and Valley region, separating the Northwest from the Southeast. South Korea is divided from North Korea by a transpeninsular depression. The Imjin River Basin, bordering on this depression, sometimes is considered a separate region.

The four largest rivers entirely within South Korea are the Han (514 km.; 320 mi.), the Kum (400 km.; 249 mi.), the Naktong (524 km.; 326 mi.) and Somjin (212 km.; 132 mi.). The Yongsan and the Tongjin are used for irrigation. All these rivers are subject to floods in the summer.

CLIMATE & WEATHER

South Korea has a continental climate with dry, cold winters and hot, humid summers. Even though the winters are less severe than in North Korea, snowfalls are not uncommon in the South in winter. However, there is great climatic range even within the country in the winter. The average January temperature varies from −20.5°C (−5°F) at Chunggang to −5°C (23°F) at Seoul, −2°C (28.4°F) at Pusan and 4.4°C (40°F) on Cheju Island. Summer temperatures are more uniform, and average temperatures range from 25°C (77°F) to 27°C (80°F) in the South to 21°C (70°F) along the northeastern coast.

Though serious droughts occur periodically, especially in the Southwest, no region receives less than 762 mm. (30 in.) of rainfall annually. In most areas yearly rainfall is over 1,016 mm. (40 in.), with the Somjin River estuary receiving more than 1,524 mm. (60 in.) annually. Rainfall is concentrated in the April to September rainy season, causing damaging floods.

Typhoons occur at least once or twice a year, damaging crops and bringing torrential rains.

POPULATION

The population of South Korea was estimated at 43,045,098 in 1990, based on the last official census, in 1985, when the population was 37,436,315. The majority of the people live in the southern and southwestern coastal areas. Seoul is the most populous region, with 17.6% of the population, followed by North Kyongsang Province (14.5%), South Cholla Province (12.7%), Kyonggi Province (10.7%), South Kyongsang Province (9.9%) and South Chungchong Province (9.1%). The least populated region is Cheju Island Province, with only 1.2% of the population.

Since the 1960s the median age has been rising. Those below age 14 constituted only 30% of the population in 1984 as against 40.0% in 1970, while the age group between 15 and 64 made up 63% of the population in 1984 as against 56.0% in 1970. Those over 65 constituted almost 7% in 1984 and 3.0% in 1970. Females had the numerical advantage in urban areas, particularly Seoul.

South Korea is rapidly becoming a predominantly urban nation. In 1988 a total of 69% of the population lived in towns and cities as against 18.4% in 1950, representing an annual urban growth rate of 3.14%. There are seven cities with over 500,000 inhabitants with 77% of the urban population; there are 18 cities with over 100,000 inhabitants containing 46.8% of the national population and 139 cities with over 20,000 inhabitants containing 58.1% of the national population. Nearly 29% of the population of Seoul and 31% of the population of Pusan live in slums or squatter settlements. The number of these slum-dwellers is growing at the rate of 56.6% per year in Seoul and 32.2% in Pusan. Nationwide nearly 14% are believed to live in substandard conditions. The pace of urbanization has been highest in the large metropolitan cities, such as Seoul and Pusan, which averaged 9% annually between 1960 and 1970. Seoul itself contains one in every six South Koreans. The rural population lives in 35,000 farm villages. Government efforts to stem the flow of population from these villages to the towns include the New Community Movement, launched in 1971. This program is designed to stimulate the rural environment by channeling state development funds to rural areas. Government plans also call for dispersion of industries and educational and social services, and a residency tax on urbanites based on the size of their communities.

DEMOGRAPHIC INDICATORS

Population (millions): 43.045 (1990)
Year of last census: 1985
Sex distribution (% at last census): males, 50.0; females 50.0
Population estimates and projections (millions)

1950: 21.147	1980: 38.124	2010: 48.481
1960: 25.142	1990: 42.793	
1970: 32.976	2000: 48.828	

Age profile (% at last census)

0–14: 29.9	30–44: 19.5	60–74: 5.5
15–29: 31.3	45–59: 12.5	75 and over: 1.3

Median age (yrs.): 24.5 (1985)
Youth population (% age 15–24): 21.1 (1985); 15.9 (2000)
Total dependency ratio: 52.1 (1985)
Annual growth rate (%)

1950–55: 1.02	1975–80: 1.55	2000–2005: 0.81
1955–60: 3.09	1980–85: 1.48	2005–2010: 0.63
1960–65: 2.64	1985–90: 1.19	2010–2015: 0.49
1965–70: 2.25	1990–1995: 1.00	2015–2020: 0.38
1970–75: 2.00	1995–2000: 0.94	2020–2025: 0.27

Hypothetical size of stationary population (millions): 56
Assumed year of reaching net reproduction rate of 1: 2030
Urban population (millions): 26.829 (1985)
Urban population (%): 69 (1988); 32 (1965)
Annual urban population growth rate (%, 1985–90): 3.14
Annual rural population growth rate (%, 1985–90): −3.10
Percentage of urban population in largest city: 41 (1980)
Percentage of urban population in cities of population over 500,000: 77 (1980)
Number of cities of population over 500,000: 7 (1980)
Population density per sq. km. (per sq. mi.): 431.2 (1.116.8) (latest)

VITAL STATISTICS

Crude birth rate (/1,000): 20 (1990); 35 (1965)
Crude death rate (/1,000): 6 (1990); 11 (1965)
Infant mortality rate (/1,000 live births): 23 (1990)
Maternal mortality rate (/100,000 live virths): 9.7 (1986–87)
Life expectancy (yrs.) at birth: males, 66; females, 73 (1990)
Gross reproduction rate (/woman (1980–85): 1.17
Total fertility rate (/woman): 1.6 (1990)
Rate of natural increase (1988) (/1,000): 12.4
Marriage rate (/1,000): 8.6 (1986)
Average family size: 4.8 (latest)
Legitimate births (%): 99.5 (latest)

As in many other developing countries, there is substantial internal migration, and the population is becoming highly mobile. Between 60% and 80% of the residents of major cities are of rural origin. Until 1945 emigration was mainly in response to the Japanese occupation (1910–45), when some 3 million Koreans emigrated to Manchuria and other parts of China; an equal number of Japan; some 700,000 to Siberia; and 7,000 to the United States, especially Hawaii. Though the great majority of these emigrants returned to their homeland at the end of World War II, the pace of permanent emigration resumed at an accelerated pace after the passage of an overseas emigration law in 1965. The government encourages emigration to the United States, Brazil, West Germany and the Middle East. Some 87% of South Koreans residing abroad permanently are believed to be in Japan. Annual emigration to the United States has exceeded 20,000 since 1970. Over 10,000 South Koreans also are employed in Middle Eastern countries in various construction projects. Offsetting this outflow are the estimated 3 million to 4 million North Koreans who have crossed the 38th parallel since 1945.

STATUS OF WOMEN INDICATORS

Number of women (millions): 20.711 (1985)
Women of childbearing age (15–49) (% of pop.): 56 (1988)
Married women of childbearing age (15–49) using contraception (%): 70 (1986)
Women's literacy rate (%): 90 (1985)
Women in labor force (%): 33.9 (1988)
Total fertility rate (/woman): 1.6 (1990)
Women in national legislatures (%): 3 (1984)

Discrimination against women is declining, although, as in most traditional Asian societies, men still tend to be the primary income earners and property owners. A series of major revisions to the Legal Code in recent years has given women rights in inheritance, child custody, family headship and other areas that law and Confucian tradition had long denied them. Women enjoy full access to educational opportunities at all levels. They are increasingly represented, though still largely at entry levels, in the military, the police, the civil service, the professions and private industry. They are not legally protected against discrimination in hiring, pay or advancement, and these remain problem areas. For example, according to the Korea Employers' Federation, the average wage of female workers is 46.8% that of male workers. Korea has not developed a politically powerful feminist movement, but consciousness of women's issues has been increasing. During 1984 women's groups organized a federation to campaign for revision of the Family Law, including provisions concerning the head-of-family system, and in favor of equal property rights in case of divorce and equal rights in child custody. Traditional Confucian influence remains strong, however. The government announced that it would ask the National Assembly to ratify the U.N. Convention on the Prevention of Discrimination Against Women with a reservation on Articles 9 and 16, which conflict with present domestic Korean law.

Family planning was adopted as an official policy in the early 1960s with the establishment of the Planned Parenthood Federation of Korea, the Korean Institute of Family Planning and the Family Planning section of the Bureau of Maternal and Child Health. The government programs are carried out by 1,700 physicians, 75 hospitals, four clinics, 60 urban health centers and 138 rural health centers. Loops, condoms and vasectomies are offered free of charge, while contraceptive pills are subsidized. Abortion was legalized in 1973, and 26% of all married women of childbearing age are believed to have had one or more abortions. In 1976 the Population Policy Deliberation Committee chaired by the deputy prime minister was set up and charged with development of a comprehensive policy. In 1986 a total of 70% of married women of childbearing age were practicing some form of contraception.

ETHNIC COMPOSITION

Along with North Korea, South Korea is the world's most ethnically and linguistically homogeneous nation. Virtually the entire population is of Korean origin, and there is no evidence of non-Mongoloid admixture. There is no national ethnic minority. The total resident, non-Korean population is estimated at no more than 50,000, of whom the majority are Nationalist Chinese. There are no widespread anti-Western feelings among the indigenous population.

LANGUAGES

The national and official language is Korean, a member of the Altaic family of languages. Korean is written in a largely phonetic alphabet called *hangul*, consisting of 14 basic consonants and 10 simple vowels. The American presence in South Korea since the 1950s has stimulated the growth of English as the most important second language. English is taught in all secondary schools, and two English-language newspapers are published in Seoul.

RELIGIONS

South Korea has no state religion, and freedom of worship and conscience are guaranteed in the constitution. Buddhism claims the most adherents, but Christianity is the most influential organized religion.

RELIGIOUS MEMBERSHIP IN KOREA (1984)

Religion	Adherents
Buddhism	5,804,000
Confucianism	4,980,000
Protestantism	4,455,800
Roman Catholicism	1,460,300
Other Christian sects	5,317,000
New Religionists	5,317,000

South Korean Buddhism has 18 denominations, of which the Chogye-Jong is the largest order, accounting for almost half the number of believers. Wonbulgyo (Round Buddhism) is a variant of Buddhism that has acquired a syncretic flavor by incorporating some non-Buddhist elements. Confucianism, though less a religion than a moral and political philosophy, displaced Buddhism as the dominant intellectual force in the middle of the 14th century. Chondogyo, founded in 1860 by Choe Cheu, later martyred for his beliefs, is an eclectic faith borrowing heavily from Christianity, Buddhism and Confucianism. It is identified with the Korean nationalist movement known as Tonghak and inspired the Tonghak Rebellion of 1894. Shamanism survives in rural areas. Until it was banned in 1973, the Japanese Nichiren Buddhist sect known as Sakka Gokkai had spread rapidly, gaining nearly 300,000 adherents.

Christianity, introduced into South Korea in the late 16th century, was a persecuted religion until 1882 when, by a treaty of friendship signed with the United States, the country was opened to missionary work. Christian missionaries were generally more successful in Korea than in most other Asian countries. Christianity became acceptable to Koreans as a harbinger of Western learning, or *sohak.* Church schools were also responsible for the popularization of the *hangul* alphabet. Under the Park regime the church spearheaded resistance to the government's attempts at regimentation. Since 1974 the government has cracked down a number of times against Christian social activists pressing for economic and political reforms. As a counterblast to Christian influence, the government also is believed to have funded the Unification Church movement, a pseudo-Christian cult led by a self-styled messiah, the Rev. Sun Myung Moon.

HISTORICAL BACKGROUND

Korea was under Japanese occupation from 1910, when the Yi dynasty was abolished, to 1945, when the country was liberated by U.S. and Soviet forces. Japanese rule was entirely negative and oppressive. Although Japanese rule was accompanied by some economic development, the process represented a systematic national humiliation. The Japanese aimed openly to eradicate the Korean national identity, and to this end even the use of the Korean language was banned. Few Japanese legacies have survived the liberation, though relations between the two countries were normalized in 1965. South Korea became the independent Republic of Korea on August 15, 1948. Between 1948 and 1960 the nation was ruled by Dr. Syngman Rhee, head of the Liberal Party. Increasingly authoritarian and corrupt and unable to deal with economic problems, Rhee was forced to resign in May 1960 following student-led demonstrations against ballot tampering. He was succeeded by Chang Myon of the Democratic Party who was forced out of office by a military coup in May 1961 led by Gen. Park Chun-Hee. Park dissolved the National Assembly, suspended the Constitution and banned all political parties. The junta ruled by decree until 1963. That year Park created the Democratic Republican Party (DRP) as a step in the transition to civilian government. Following the adoption of a new Constitution in the fall, Park easily won election as president. Park won presidential elections in 1967 and 1971, but with only narrow margins against the New Democratic Party candidates. Park had the Constitution amended in 1969 to allow himself a third term in 1971.

The decade of the 1970s saw Park establish dictatorial, one-man rule. In October 1972 he proclaimed martial law and dissolved the National Assembly. A month later, he held a national referendum on a new constitution that vastly increased the power of the president. Political institutions as defined by the 1972 *yushin,* or "revitalization" Constitution were tailored to fit Park's preference for centralized rule. The National Assembly had little power because the Constitution denied it the previously guaranteed right to investigate the activities of the executive branch. The power of the president to declare martial law during "emergencies" and dissolve the Assembly at will also curtailed its powers.

Continued popular opposition caused Park to enact emergency measures in 1975, which made it a crime to criticize the *yushin* system or advocate its revision. The Korean Central Intelligence Agency (KCIA), which was under executive control, became increasingly powerful and feared as it used harsh methods to silence opposition, even among Koreans overseas.

Park was assassinated in October 1979 by the head of the KCIA, apparently for personal reasons. The assassination led to the collapse of the *yushin* system and the brief restoration of civilian rule under acting president Choi Kyu Ha. Factional struggles within the political parties, strikes by workers demanding higher wages and better working conditions, and a wave of student unrest, however, provided the military with yet another opportunity to establish its dominance over the political system during 1980. In May 1980 Gen. Chun Doo-Hwan, head of the Defense Security Command, proclaimed martial law. His decree banned all forms of political activity, closed the headquarters of political parties, outlawed strikes and muzzled journalists. An insurrection in Kwangju was suppressed with utmost brutality, resulting in the death of up to 2,000 persons.

Soon after his accession to power, Chun Doo-Hwan initiated a new constitutional referendum that was overwhelmingly approved by the electorate in October 1980. The new charter contained a number of new provisions, including a reduction of presidential powers. Human rights and habeas corpus were guaranteed, and forcible extraction of confessions from political prisoners was banned. Finally, all political parties were dissolved. Chun also launched one of the most drastic purification drives against corruption and inefficiency in South Korean history. Thousands of public servants, journalists, teachers and politicians were dismissed in these purges. The opposition leader Kim Dae Jung and 23 of his supporters were indicted on charges of violating national security laws and plotting insurrection.

President Choi Kyu Ha resigned in August and Chun retired from the military to run for the presidency. With the support of the military he was approved as interim president. Martial law was lifted in January 1981, and new political parties were formed. In February Chun was elected president, and in March, with his inauguration, the Fifth Korean Republic emerged. Elections were held for a new National Assembly, and Chun's Democratic Justice Party (DJP) became the majority party.

Stability and continuity at the price of civil and political rights were the watchwords of the Chun regime. The Chun regime successfully used "economic priorityism" and the Communist threat from North Korea as arguments for the maintenance of a garrison state marked by economic austerity, political regimentation, unresponsiveness to dissent and suppression of free expression. Chun also maintained one of the most ruthless secret services in the world, whose surveillance and subversive activities extended beyond Korea's borders.

A new opposition party, the New Korea Democratic Party (NKDP), was formed in January 1985 and won impressively in February elections, though the DJP retained its majority. The NKDP gained more power in the National Assembly in 1985 when several opposition members joined them.

Attempts by the NKDP to establish a new constitution limiting the president's powers made little progress. Student protests became so violent that the NKDP sought to distance itself from their demands.

In mid-1987 riots fomented over President Chun's announcement that reforms would cease until after the 1988 Olympic Games, which were to be held in Seoul. Further violent clashes led President Chun to meet in June with Kim Young-Sam, the head of the Reunification Democratic Party (RDP)—a newly formed NKDP splinter group. Demands for immediate constitutional reform were met by nation-wide peace marches. By July President Chun had stepped down from power and a bi-partisan committee was organized to draft a new constitution. The new Constitution was promulgated on October 29th.

Following the December presidential elections, the DJP retained power because of the failure of the opposition parties to agree on a single candidate. The newly elected president, Roh Tae-Woo, former chairman of the DJP, immediately began talks with the opposition parties over new electoral laws to be used in the April 1988 general elections. The leaders of the two opposition parties resigned in hope of unification but failed to agree on joint candidates. In the general elections held in April 1988, the DJP won fewer seats then the combined opposition, but because it was the largest single party it was awarded 38 of the 75 additional seats.

Students demonstrated throughout 1988 over, among other issues, the corrupt practices of Chun and his Fifth Republic. Fears of the Olympic Games being disrupted were unfounded. Chun responded to demands for his trial and execution with a televised apology and promises of repaying misappropriated monies. Subsequentally, he retired to a Buddhist monastery in the mountains east of Seoul. In December many high ranking and former members of the Fifth Republic were replaced.

The end of the decade was rife with peaceful and violent demands for reunification with North Korea and the removal of U.S. troops from South Korea. In student riots at Dongeui University seven policemen were killed and shortly afterward more than 70 students received prison terms. In October 1989 several students took over the U.S. ambassador's residence in Seoul. In mid-1989 there were major reshufflings and replacements in several ministries.

In a dramatic move in February 1990, the DJP merged with two of the opposition parties to create the Democratic Liberal Party (DLP). This move gave the DLP control of more than two thirds of the National Assembly. Students demonstrated against this merging of power in a single political party.

CONSTITUTION & GOVERNMENT

The Constitution of the Sixth Republic, approved in October 1987, rescinded many of the presidential powers allowed by the former *yushin* or revitalizing Constitution of 1972. This earlier Constitution had represented a break with previous South Korean Constitutions in its authoritarian and anti-democratic provisions. Where previously the president was elected indirectly via an electoral college for an undetermined number of terms, the 1987 Constitution calls for direct elections

GOVERNMENT LIST
(July/August 1991)

President	Roh Tae Woo
Prime Minister	Chung Won Shik
Deputy Prime Minister	Choi Ho Joong
Deputy Prime Minister	Choi Kak Kyu
Minister, Economic Planning Board	Choi Kak Kyu
Minister of Agriculture & Fisheries	Cho Kyong-shick
Minister of Communications	Song Eon Jong
Minister of Culture	Lee O Young
Minister of Education	Yoon Hyoung Sup
Minister of Energy & Resources	Chin Nyum
Minister of Environment	Kwon I hyock
Minister of Finance	Lee Yong Man
Minister of Foreign Affairs	Lee Sang Ock
Minister of Government Administration	Lee Yun Taek
Minister of Health & Social Affairs	Ahn Pil Joon
Minister of Information	Choi Chang Yoon
Minister of Interior	Lee Sahng Yeon
Minister of Justice	Kim Ki Choon
Minister of Labor Affairs	Choi Byung Yul
Minister of National Construction	Lee Jin Seol
Minister of National Defense	Lee Jong Ku
Minister of Natl. Unification	Choi Ho Joong
Minister of Science & Technology	Kim Jin Hyun
Minister of Sports	Park Chul Un
Minister of Trade & Industry	Lee Bong Suh
Minister of Transportation	Lim In Taik
Minister of State for Political Affairs	Kim Yun Hwan
Minister of State for Women & Youth	Lee Kye Soon
Director, National Security Planning Agency	Suh Dong Kwon
Governor, Central Bank	Kim Kun

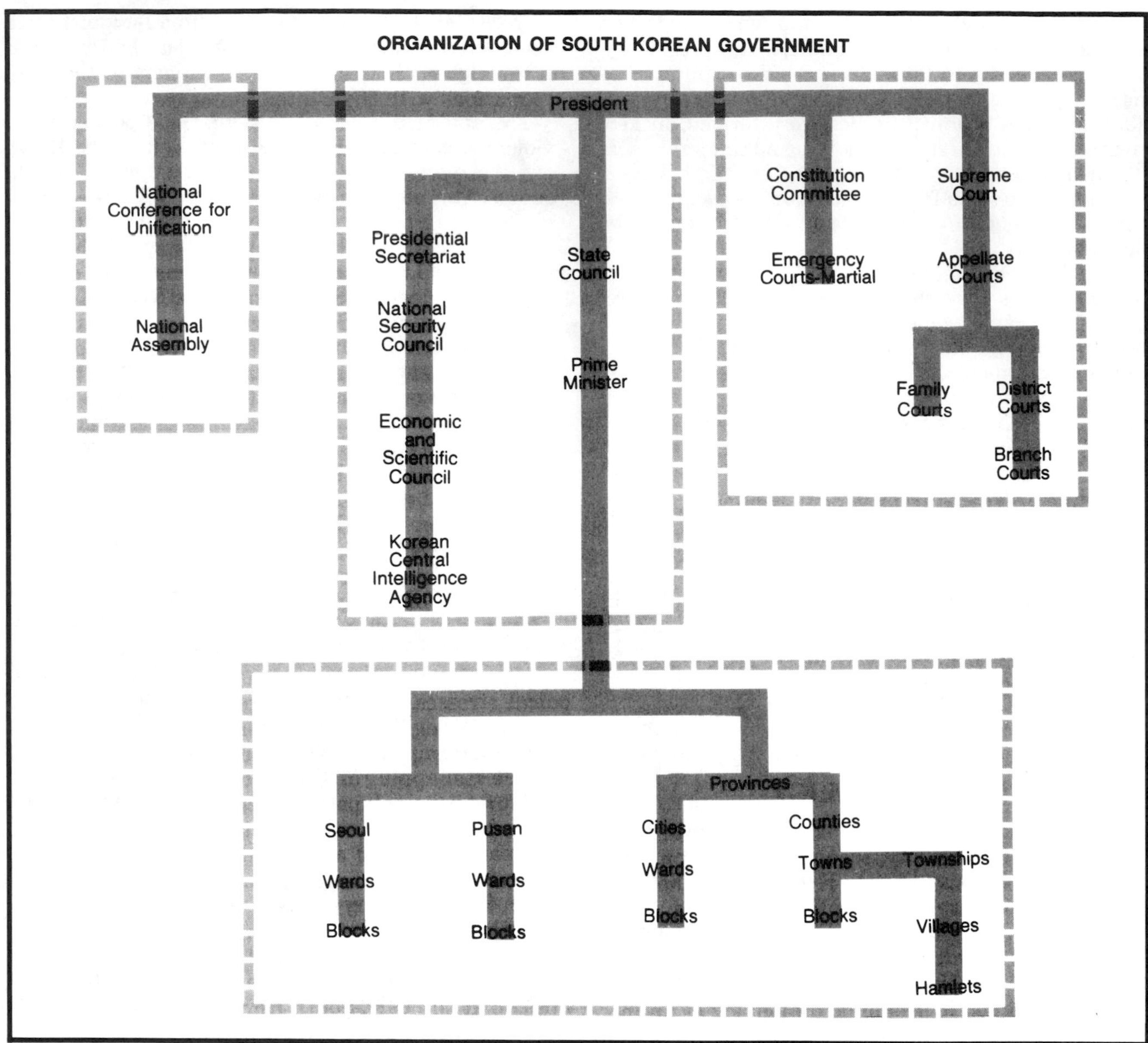

by universal suffrage to a five-year, non-renewable term. The president's emergency powers are reduced and the National Assembly is given power to end martial law. The president no longer has the power to dissolve the National Assembly but, as under the former Constitution, he may, for important issues, bypass the National Assembly by calling for a national referendum.

The State Council, which functions as the cabinet, is made up of the president, the prime minister and from 15 to 30 others appointed by the president. No active members of the military may be a member of the Council.

Legislative power is vested in the unicameral National Assembly, popularly elected for a four-year term. The judiciary is headed by a Supreme Court whose chief justice is appointed for a five-year term with the concurrence of the Assembly.

RULERS OF SOUTH KOREA

Presidents

August 1948–April 1960: Syngman Rhee
April–August 1960: Huh Chung
August 1960–May 1961: Yun Po-san
May 1961: Chang Do Yung
May 1961–March 1962: Yun Po-san
March 1962–October 1979: Park Chung Hee
October 1979–August 1980: Choi Kyu-hah
August 1980–February 1988: Chun Doo-Hwan
February 1988– : Roh Tae Woo

National elections and referenda are held and supervised by the Central Election Management Committee, an independent and nonpartisan body with nine members, of whom three are appointed by the president, three are nominated by the National Assembly and three are nominated by the Supreme Court. Election of members of the National Assembly is by universal, direct and secret vote. The age of suffrage is 20.

FREEDOM & HUMAN RIGHTS

In terms of political and civil rights South Korea is classified as a partly free country.

After some improvement in the early part of 1980, the human rights picture deteriorated sharply in South Korea. The first four months of 1980 witnessed the relaxation of press censorship, the resumption of political activity, the restoration of political rights to Kim Dae Jung and many others and the convening of a bipartisan National Assembly. But following student riots in Seoul and Kwanju and the heavy-handed military response that claimed hundreds of lives, the government retreated by declaring full martial law, dissolving the National Assembly, imposing strict press censorship and banning all political activity. The government rearrested Kim, who received the death sentence, while 23 of his codefendants received prison sentences. In a separate trial of persons accused in Kwangju, five people received death sentences, seven were sentenced to life imprisonment and 163 others received prison sentences ranging from five to 20 years. A sweeping process of purification was launched in June, coinciding with the appointment of Chun Doo-Hwan as president.

Amnesty International stated that its main concern in South Korea was torture. Kim charged that he was questioned for up to 12 hours without respite and sometimes questioned while naked, while his codefendants charged that they were beaten. As part of the purification campaign, some 30,000 "holligans" were arrested, and some of them were forced to undergo "reeducation." Habeas corpus was not granted under the old Constitution and did not exist under martial law. It was usual for police to detain suspects for several days without informing even their families. While open trials were the norm, court-martial trials usually were conducted in camera. Although all defendants were guaranteed the right to counsel, this right were abridged in cases involving political charges. However, the court system was considered relatively independent in nonpolitical trials.

Freedoms of the press, speech and assembly were circumscribed severely. Advance censorship by military officers, in effect since President Park's assassination in 1979, became tighter under emergency martial law. Editors were pressured to give space to government-inspired articles extolling the "new era." Several Japanese news agencies' Seoul bureaus were ordered closed in 1980. All domestic and foreign books required government approval before distribution. In August 1980 the press was subjected to purification by which 172 publications were shut down and hundreds of journalists were fired. Nine journalists, including the president of the Korean Journalists' Association, were arrested, and four were sentenced to prison terms. In January 1981 the government merged the two privately owned news services into one government-controlled agency. Retired military officers were installed in all newspaper offices and broadcasting stations as "building and safety inspectors," but in fact served to monitor compliance with government directives. All meetings of more than four persons required a permit.

Following the imposition of full martial law, a new Constitution was approved on October 22, 1980, that allowed the dissolution of any political party if its purposes and activities are contrary to the basic "democratic" order. The provisional assembly also banned over 500 persons from public life.

During 1984 the government took several significant positive steps in the human rights field. More than 220 students jailed for campus demonstrations were released from prison during the year in three separate amnesties, and about 1,400 students previously expelled for political activism were allowed to reenroll at their old campuses. About half this number had actually returned by the fall term. Some 86 dissident professors, banned from teaching since 1980, also were permitted to teach again at their original campuses. In early 1984 the government initiated a policy of "campus autonomy" under which it withdrew security forces from university campuses, a major student demand; allowed peaceful demonstrations on campuses; and stated that henceforth universities would bear the primary responsibility for enforcing campus discipline.

In another amnesty move, the government restored civil rights to more than 700 former political prisoners, including some prominent intellectuals and human rights activists, and many convicted under emergency decrees of the Park Chung Hee government. The government also announced that journalists who had been banned from employment since 1980 could be reemployed at the discretion of their former employers, and some have gone back to work.

Early in 1987 the revelation that a student protester had died following torture led to dismissals of several high level officials.

Following the promulgation of a new Constitution and Roh's inauguration in February 1988, about 100 political prisoners were released, though hundreds remained in detention. Further autonomy was given to universities in 1988 and restrictions on the press were lessened. Although several thousand political prisoners were released, Amnesty International reported that political arrests continued, with estimates of upwards of 800 political detainees. South Korean is not active in any international or regional human rights organizations.

CIVIL SERVICE

The South Korean civil service was first established in 1949, under the Civil Service Law. The system was reorganized under the National Civil Service Law of 1963. Civil servants are divided into two classes: special and general. Special civil servants include all heads and deputy chiefs of agencies, mayors, governors, ambassadors, judges, prosecutors, professors and police officers. The general class consists of employees of central government agencies, divided into five grades. Local government employees are classified separately. Recruitment is based on an open, competitive examination held every year. Training is provided by the Central Officials' Training Institute. There were over 500,000 civil servants in the mid-1970s and, despite government austerity measures, their number still was growing.

LOCAL GOVERNMENT

For purpose of local administration, South Korea is divided into an elaborate hierarchy of territorial units. These are, in descending order of size and importance:

Units	Korean Name	Number	Administrator
Provinces	*Do or to*	9	*Tojisa*
Cities of Seoul and Pusan		2	Mayor
Cities over 50,000	*Si*	30	*Sijang*
Counties	*Kun*	139	*Kunsu*
Towns (20,000–50,000)	*Up*	91	*Upchang*
Townships	*Myon*	1,376	*Myon jung*
Villages	*I or ri*	18,430	*Ri jang*
Hamlets	*Purak*		

The nine provinces are: Kyonggi, Kangwon, North Chungchong, South Chungchong, North Cholla, South Cholla, North Kyongsang, South Kyongsang and Cheju Island.

The cities of Seoul and Pusan are divided into wards or *ku*, each headed to a *kuchong jang;* the wards are further divided into blocks or *dong.*

There are no representative institutions at the local level.

FOREIGN POLICY

South Korea's foreign policy is geared to four major goals: national security, economic expansion, the unification of North and South Korea and enhancement of the country's international stature. The most important consideration in South Korean diplomacy is the maintenance of mutual defense commitments with the United States. The next highest priority is assigned to economic diplomacy as an instrument of transforming the country into a trading nation through development of friendly relations with as many countries as possible. In this area Japan has emerged as a key factor in South Korean strategy. The third function of foreign policy is to bolster South Korea's image vis-à-vis North Korea. The two halves of Korea have competed against each other vigorously whenever and wherever possible. In this respect, South Korea gained from the disastrous diplomatic performance of North Korea in many parts of the world, exemplified by the expulsion of North Korean diplomats from the Scandinavian countries.

Under President Park's "foreign policy of peace" there had been a shift from a markedly ideological and anti-Communist posture in foreign affairs to a more pragmatic and flexible effort to cultivate economic and political ties with all Communist nations, including the Soviet Union and Communist China. This departure was in tune with the new mood of détente among the major powers, but it also reflected South Korea's need to reduce its dependence on the United States.

Relations with the United States were clouded in the mid-1980s by a number of adverse factors. Among them was the mounting criticism within the United States of the suppression of human rights by the Chun regime. Ties with the United States were further hurt by congressional hearings on alleged bribes paid to U.S. congressmen by lobbyists for the Seoul regime.

South Korea still is technically at war with North Korea, and relations between the two countries are locked in cold-war patterns. Efforts to initiate a dialogue between them usually have degenerated into recriminations. Unification continues to be regarded as a desirable goal but is no longer an overriding determinant of foreign policy.

In October 1983 relations between the two Korean states deteriorated dangerously after four South Korean State Council ministers, including Foreign Minister Lee Bum Suk, were among the victims of a bomb explosion during a state visit to Rangoon, Burma. President Chun immediately blamed North Korea for the attack, which deprived him of his most influential political aides. In February 1984 he rejected the North's proposal for tripartite talks on reunification (involving the United States as well as North and South Korea), insisting instead on direct bilateral negotiations between the Korean states.

In 1985 economic and humanitarian issues were briefly discussed by representatives of the two countries. Talks were suspended when the North Korean leader, Kim Il-sung, protested "Team Spirit" military games jointly held by the United States and South Korea. The November mid-air bombing by North Korean agents of a South Korean airliner re-established verbal hostility. Nevertheless, continued efforts led to limited trade between the two countries in October 1988. Discussions in Panmunjom in early 1989 were disrupted because of the "Team Spirit" military exercises planned for the following month. In early 1990 proposals by Kim to eliminate travel restrictions between the two countries were warmly met, and Roh announced a reduction of the upcoming "Team Spirit" military exercises.

In September 1983 a Boeing 747 airliner of Korean Air Lines (KAL) of South Korea, having apparently strayed into USSR airspace, was shot down by a Soviet fighter aircraft, and the 269 people on board the airliner were presumed killed. The incident aroused widespread condemnation of the USSR and precipitated severe tension between East and West.

But by 1988 relations with the U.S.S.R. and other communist countries had improved. Full diplomatic relations were established with Hungary, Poland and Yugoslavia. Diplomatic relations with other Communist countries, including the U.S.S.R., were expected in 1990.

Japan is in many respects supplanting the United States as South Korea's political ally and economic partner. These relations have been subject to periodic stresses, such as the so called "silk war" in 1976 (resulting from the imposition of surcharges on silk fabrics imported from South Korea into Japan) and the kidnapping of Korean opposition leader Kim Dae Jung from a Japanese hotel in 1973. Japan was accused of being involved in the conspiracy that led to an attempted assassination of Park in 1974. However, relations were patched up after Japan issued a formal apology. Relations between South Korea and Japan, which had long been overshadowed by the memory of Japan's colonial treatment of Korea, improved following a visit to Tokyo by President Chun (the first ever state visit to Japan by a Korean head of state) in September 1984. In 1988 Japan's Prime Minster Takeshita praised President Roh for his efforts to end disputes with North Korea.

South Korea and the United States are parties to 63 agreements and treaties covering agricultural commodities, atomic energy, aviation, claims, consuls, defense, economic and technical cooperation, education, finance, fisheries, health, informational media guarantees, investment guarantees, military missions, mutual security, patents, the Peace Corps, petroleum, postal matters, publications, relief supplies and packages, scientific cooperation, surplus property, taxation, trade and commerce, and visas.

President Chun visited the United States in 1985 reestablishing a weakening military link between the two countries. The United States, however, continued to express reservations about President Chun's commitment to continued democratic reform. Discussions were held in 1990 about total withdrawal of U.S. troops from South Korea by 1994.

South Korea's many attempts to join the United Nations since 1949 have been rebuffed by Soviet vetoes, but the nation is represented by a permanent observer mission at the United Nations. South Korea is a member of 13 U.N. organizations and 17 other international organizations.

PARLIAMENT

The national legislature is the unicameral National Assembly (Kuk Hoe), consisting of 299 members elected for four-year terms. According to amendments made to the Constitution in 1988, all but 75 seats are directly elected. Of these appointed seats, 38 are awarded to the party receiving the most votes with the rest given out proportionally to the other parties. The Assembly remains in session for a maximum of 130 days a year, including regular and special sessions. The maximum length of a regular session is 100 days; that of each special session, 30 days. Much of the Assembly's legislative work is done in 13 standing committees, which examine all bills introduced by members or by the government. The Assembly can override a presidential veto with the concurrence of two-thirds of the members present.

Party make up in the National Assembly went through drastic changes in 1990 when the ruling DJP consolidated its power by merging with two independent parties to form the Democratic Liberal Party (DLP), gaining control of two-thirds of the legislative seats. This left the Peace and Democratic Party as the only effective opposition with 70 seats. Smaller independent parties control 10 seats.

Traditionally, the South Korean voting system was weighted in favor of the ruling party, making it all but impossible for the DJP to lose its majority in the Assembly. With the promulgation of the new Constitution in October 1987, the abolition of an electoral college in favor of direct popular voting eliminated the ruling party's advantage. Nevertheless, the newly formed DLP, under Roh Tae Woo, continues to rule as a result of splintering among the opposition.

POLITICAL PARTIES

The Constitution guarantees the free establishment of political parties. However, a political party whose aims or activities are contrary to accepted democratic order may be dissolved by the Constitution Committee.

The traditional role of the political parties as an integral part of the political system was undermined by the Revitalizing Constitution of 1972. Since 1987 opposition parties have been allowed to exist in a more open democratic environment.

The governing party is the Democratic Liberal Party formed in 1990 as a merger of the Democratic Justice Party, the New Democratic Republican Party and the Reunification Democratic Party. The party that dominated politics prior to 1990 was the Democratic Justice Party (DJP), formed in 1981 by President Chun to lend civilian legitimacy to the military junta. Historically, it had little or no ideological content beyond uncritical support for government policies, but has most recently been forced to partake in a democratic process.

ECONOMY

South Korea is one of the upper-middle-income countries of the world, with one of the most impressive records of economic growth in Asia since the early 1950s. This growth has transformed South Korea into

PRINCIPAL ECONOMIC INDICATORS

Gross National Product (U.S. $ billions): 186.467 (1989)
GNP per capita (U.S. $): 4,400 (1989)
GNP average annual growth rate (%, 1980–89): 10.1
GNP per capita average annual growth rate (%, 1987–89): 8.6
Income distribution (% household income)
  Lowest 20%: 5.7
  Highest 10%: 27.5
Average annual rate of inflation (%, 1980–88): 5.0
Consumer price index (1980 = 100) 1986
  All items: 144
  Food: 141
Wholesale price index (1980 = 100): 128 (1985)
Average annual growth rate (%, 1980–88)
  General government consumption: 5.3
  Private consumption: 7.5
  Gross domestic investment: 10.5

BALANCE OF PAYMENTS, 1989
(U.S. $ millions)

Current account balance: 14,161
Merchandise exports: 59,648
Merchandise imports: −48,203
Trade balance: 11,445
Other goods, services & income + : 11,252
Other goods, services & income − : 9,984
Other goods, services & income net: 1,268
Private unrequited transfers: 1,404
Official unrequited transfers: 44
Capital other than reserves: −4,845
Net errors & omissions: −591
Counterpart items: −5,633
Liabilities constituting foreign authorities reserves: 0.0
Total change in reserves: − 3,684

GROSS DOMESTIC PRODUCT

GDP nominal (W billions): 142.267
GDP per capita (U.S. $): 4,600 (1989)
Average annual growth rate of GDP (%, 1980–88): 9.9
GDP by type of expenditure (%) 1987
  Consumption
    Private: 53
    Government: 10
  Gross domestic investment: 29
  Gross domestic saving: 38 (1988)
  Foreign trade
    Exports: 42
    Imports: −34
Cost components of GDP (%) 1987
    Net indirect taxes: 12
    Consumption of fixed capital: 9
    Compensation of employees: 41
    Net operating surplus: 37
Sectoral origin of GDP (%) 1987
  Primary
    Agriculture: 11
    Mining: 1
  Secondary
    Manufacturing: 30
    Construction: 8
    Public utilities: 3
  Tertiary
    Transportation & communications: 8
    Trade: 13
    Finance: 11
    Other services: 3
    Government: 4
Average annual sectoral growth rates (%, 1980–88)
    Agriculture: 3.7
    Industry: 12.6
    Manufacturing: 13.5
    Services: 8.9

a semi-industrialized nation, though, because of its limited natural resources base, it still is far from becoming a major economic power. From the period 1976 through 1978 South Korea experienced very high real economic growth: 15.1% in 1976, 10.3% in 1977 and 11.6% in 1978. From 1980–89 South Korea's average annual GNP growth rate was 10.1%, one of highest in the world. All sectors of the economy shared in the expansion, with industrial production, exports, investment and real wages reaching new highs each year. The rapid increase in income, fueled by large increases in the money supply, led to an explosion in demand pressures. Although government policies have helped to cool the economy, the battle against inflation is far from won. But the continuing growth in consumer prices is due to the increased cost of imported raw materials, rather than domestic demand pressures. Both monetary and fiscal policies remained restrictive throughout the early 1980s.

South Korea has a free-market economy in which the dominant sector is private.

PUBLIC FINANCE

The South Korea fiscal year is the calendar year. The national budget is prepared by the Economic Planning Board. The government also prepares about 20 non-budgetary special accounts every year. Budgetary policies are characterized by controlled fiscal austerity, and expenditures are carefully monitored.

Of total central government revenues in 1988, approximately 70% came from internal taxes, 14% from customs duties, and 12% from a defense surtax. The remainder comes from profits on monopolies, an education surtax, and monies from governmental enterprises. Of total central government expenditures, 27% goes to defense, approximately 30% to education, health, social security and welfare.

CENTRAL GOVERNMENT EXPENDITURES, 1988

% of total expenditures
  Defense: 27.1
  Education: 19
  Health: 2.2
  Housing, social security, welfare: 8.5
  Economic services: 17.1
  Other: 26
Total expenditures as % of GNP: 15.7
Overall surplus or deficit as % of GNP: 1.6

CENTRAL GOVERNMENT REVENUES, 1988

% of total current revenues
  Taxes on income, profit & capital gain: 30.3
  Social security contributions: 3.8
  Domestic taxes on goods & services: 37.3
  Taxes on international trade & transactions: 14
  Other taxes: 4.9
  Current nontax revenue: 9.6
Total current revenue as % of GNP: 18.3
General government consumption as % of GDP: 10
Average annual growth rate of general government consumption (%, 1980–88): 5.3

Development planning began in 1962. During the late 1970s and early 1980s development strategy concentrated on engineering and metalworking industries and deemphasized capital and energy-intensive industries. The plan's financing underlined the government's determination to move away from reliance on foreign capital. More recent planning has been designed for another economic "takeoff." It called for a rise in tax revenues and a curtailment of preference loans at subsidized interest rates along with short-term export credit. More credit was to be made available to finance export sales on deferred terms. Government intervention in banking was to be reduced. The plan also liberalized imports, lowered tariffs, increased incentives for foreign investment and removed obstacles to competition.

Economic aid from the United States, estimated at $6.041 billion from 1946 through 1983, has been crucial for development. Assistance from international organizations was estimated at over $6.415 billion (of which the World Bank share was $4.5 billion) from 1946 to 1983. Japan is the next most important source of aid, providing $1.8 billion from 1965 through 1975. During the period 1979–81 South Korea received $531.8 million in bilateral and multilateral assistance, or $14 per capita.

FOREIGN AID, 1989

Total foreign aid (U.S. $ millions): 385.4
- Bilateral: 138.7
- Multilateral: 246.7

CURRENCY & BANKING

The South Korean unit of currency is the won, divided into 10 hwan, each hwan being divided into 10 chun (jeon). Coins are issued in denominations of 1, 5, 10, 50, 100 and 500 won; notes are issued in denominations of 500, 1,000, 5,000 and 10,000 won.

The new won was introduced in 1962 to replace the hwan at the rate of 1 won = 10 hwan. The hwan had been introduced in 1953, replacing the old won at the rate of 1 hwan = 100 old won. The won was devalued in 1971, and an official dollar exchange rate of $1 = W484/W1 = $0.00206, introduced in 1974, remained in effect through 1978 but slipped to $1 = W876.3 by August 1985. In June 1991 the rate of exchange was $1 = W725.0. In 1980 the Korean government undertook several adjustment policies to improve its balance of payments. By far the most dramatic was the won devaluation of nearly 20% on January 12, 1980, followed by pegging the local currency from the dollar to the SDR and a basket of trade-weighted currencies in late February.

The central bank is the Bank of Korea, with 13 domestic branches and seven overseas branches. The Bank of Korea is the only bank authorized to handle foreign exchange transactions. In 1985 there were 15 commercial banks and seven foreign banks. As of 1984, bank reserves totaled W856 billion; demand deposits W3.777 trillion; foreign assets W4.705 trillion; and time, savings and foreign currency deposits W17.885 trillion.

Authority over the banking community technically lies with the Bank of Korea, but it is virtually subordinate to the Ministry of Finance. The government normally imposes its monetary policy by detailed instruction on lending rather than by intervention in the money market. The government thus exerts tight control of the monetary sector. Banks, of which the majority are owned by the government, are divided into (1) commercial and special banks and (2) investment institutions. Commercial banks make just over one-half of all loans in the banking system; special banks—for lending to small companies, farmers and so on—about one-third; and the Korea Development Bank just under one-fifth. The banks follow a list of instructions drawn up each year on how much to lend to each type of borrower—small companies, manufacturers and those in a number of other categories.

In April 1984 the effort to decontrol the banking system was taken a significant step farther with the announcement of a two-year program of reforms that effectively aimed to remove most of the discriminatory

FINANCIAL INDICATORS, 1989

Total reserves minus gold (SDRs billions): 11.577
SDRs (millions): 1
Reserve position in IMF (SDRs millions): 178
Foreign exchange (SDRs millions): 11.397
Gold (fine troy oz. millions): 0.32
Ratio of external debt to total reserves: 8.7 (1988)
Central bank 1989
- Assets (%)
  - Foreign assets: 34.6
  - Claims on government: 11.3
  - Claims on banks: 54
  - Claims on private sector: 0.0
- Liabilities (%)
  - Reserve money: 42.9
  - Government desposits: 24.4
  - Foreign liabilities: 0.1
  - Capital accounts: 0.0

Money supply 1989
- Stock (trillions): 14.328.0
- M1 per capita: 336,000

Private banks 1989
- Assets (%)
  - Loans to government: 5.2
  - Loans to private sector: 78.8
  - Reserves: 10.4
  - Foreign assets: 5.7
- Liabilities
  - Deposits (W trillions): 95.354.0
- of which %
  - Demand deposits: 8.8
  - Savings deposits: 46.5
  - Government deposits: 4.8
  - Foreign liabilities: 7.0

External debt 1988
- Total (U.S. $ billions): 37.156
  - of which public (U.S. $ billions): 21.349
  - of which private (U.S. $ billions): 6.027
- Debt service (long term)
  - Total (U.S. $ millions): 21.349
  - Repayment
    - Principal (%): 75.8
    - Interest (%): 24.2
- Debt service ratio (%): 9.1
- External public debt as % of GNP: 12.66
- Debt service as % of GNP: 3.8
- Debt service as % of exports: 9.1
- Terms of public borrowing
  - Commitments (U.S. $ billions): 1.071
  - Average interest rate (%): 7.6
  - Average maturity (yrs.): 20
- Net flow of publicly guaranteed external capital (U.S. $ billions): −2.168
- Net direct private investment (U.S. $ millions): 720

restrictions hitherto imposed on foreign banks. They would then operate on an equal footing with the local banks, thus forcing the latter, it was hoped, to become better managed and more efficient.

Specialized credit and development finance institutions include the Citizen's National Bank, the Korea Development Bank, the Korea Exchange Bank, the Korea Housing Bank and the Medium Industry Bank. The Korea Development Finance Corporation assists in the development of private enterprise by medium- and long-term financing, including guarantees and purchase of equities. The money market in Korea is characterized by its dual structure: an organized market and an unorganized one, commonly known as the "curb" market. The former covers official financial institutions regulated and controlled by the government and still is limited in its operations. The lack of an intermediary link between investors having short-term idle funds and enterprises in need of short-term financing created the market for unlisted securities, or the "curb" market, which is essentially a short-term money market, since the majority of loans mature in less than three months. Because of their anonymous and discreet nature, the magnitude of "curb" market operations has never been accurately quantified, but it could be worth more than $5 billion per year; if so, it would account for about 40% of funds available for loan in the country. It is particularly active on urban housing estates; its existence reflects the absence of a well-organized finance company network. This market probably provides about 10% of available credit, at a cost normally twice that of bank finance.

GROWTH PROFILE
(Annual Growth Rates, %)

Projected population (1988–2000): 0.9
Projected crude birth rate (/1,000) (1990–95): 16.6
Projected crude death rate (/1,000) (1990–95): 6.1
Urban population (1985–90): 3.14
Labor force (1985–2000): 1.9
GNP (1980–89): 10.1
GNP per capita (1987–89): 8.6
GDP (1980–88): 9.9
Inflation (1980–88): 5.0
Agriculture (1980–88): 3.7
Industry (1980–88): 12.6
Manufacturing (1980–88): 13.5
Services (1980–88): 8.9
Money holdings (1980–88): 19.5
Manufacturing earnings per employee (1980–87): 5.6
Energy production (1980–88): 9.7
Energy consumption (1980–88): 5.5
Exports (1980–88): 14.7
Imports (1980–88): 9.9
General government consumption (1980–88): 5.3
Private consumption (1980–88): 7.5
Gross domestic investment (1980–88): 10.5

AGRICULTURE

Of the total land area of 9,848,500 ha. (24,325,579 ac.), 21.7% is considered agricultural area. Nearly all of the land area is actually under cultivation.

Agriculture sustained a reasonable growth rate during the 1960s and early 1970s, made possible by expansion of double-cropping, extensive use of pesticides and fertilizers, conversion of land to more profitable crops and a slight increase in the actual land under cultivation. However, almost all farm labor still is done by hand or draft animals.

Cropland is of two types: paddy fields that can be flooded with water, and upland fields used for growing a variety of grains, vegetables and fruits. Double-cropping paddy fields is common in the Southeast, and two-fifths of the upland fields are double-cropped. In some areas three or even four crops are grown in a single year. Irrigation facilities generally are primitive, utilizing tanks, weirs and pumping plants. In 1975 a total of 759,000 ha. (1,875,489 ac.) were under irrigation.

The South Korean land tenure system is based partly on land reforms instituted since 1945 and partly on traditional patterns. In 1945 the U.S. military government vested all lands formerly owned by Japanese landlords in the New Korea Company pending land reform legislation. In 1948 the New Korea Company was dissolved, and these lands were distributed to former tenants, with a 2-ha. (5-ac.) ceiling. Under the Farmland Reform Law passed in 1950, the government took the first concerted steps to reduce disparities in land ownership. Arable land ownership was limited to 3 ha. (7.4 ac.) per household, and all lands in excess of this limit were purchased by the government for distribution to peasants with little or no land. Two effects of the land reform were a reduction in tenancy and a reduction in the average farm size. Nearly 83% of farm families are full owners of the farms they work. In 1945 a total of 48.9% of farmers were tenants. However, disguised forms of tenancy may have returned in some areas. The average farm size is only 1.1 ha. (2.2 ac.), compared with 1.21 ha. (3 ac.) 50 years ago. Roughly two-thirds of the farms are smaller than this average. Moreover, the landholdings are physically fragmented and usually consist of a number of small plots at different locations. The most far-reaching effect of the land reforms was the diffusion of land ownership. In 1945 a total of 4% of the farmers owned half of all cropland, while 72% owned only 10%. Since 1953 a total of 65.3% of farmers have owned 38.7% of the cropland, while the top 6.3% have owned 20.2%.

Rice is the principal food crop, accounting for one-third of the planted area and 40% of all farm production in value. More than 50 different varieties of rice are grown, but the per-hectare yield is only 17 bu. (6.9 bu. per acre). South Korea is not self-sufficient in food.

Wheat, barley, potatoes, cereals and pulses also are grown. The fastest-growing sector of agriculture has been fruits and vegetables. The orchards in the Taegu area are famous for their apples. Pears, peaches, persimmons and melons also are grown in abundance. About two-thirds of the vegetable production consists of *mu* (a large white radish) and Chinese cabbage, the main ingredients of the Korean pickle known as *kimchi.* Cotton, hemp, silk and tobacco are the leading nonfood crops.

During the period of the fifth five-year plan (1982–86), the country's land was divided into 10 major farming areas in consideration of weather conditions and geographical features, to establish an effective crop planting system that would encourage growth of crops suitable for each farming area. To develop new sources for additional income, the plan selected malting barely, groundnuts, garlic, sesame seed and six other crops as 10 major strategic crops to be raised intensively during the plan period. It also called for breeding 50,000 head of cattle and importing 20,000 cattle per year to meet the growing meat demand and stabilize beef prices. Other highlights of the plan included modernization of the distribution channels of farm and marine products, introduction of an insurance system to reduce flood and drought damage, and diversification of import sources for feed grains.

AGRICULTURAL INDICATORS

Agriculture's share of GDP (%): 26 (1989)
Average annual growth rate (%, 1980–88): 3.7 (1980–88)
Value added in agriculture (U.S. $ millions): 18.561 (1988)
Cereal imports (million metric tons): 9.369 (1988)
Index of agricultural production (1979–81 = 100): 116 (1986)
Index of food production (1979–81 = 100): 117 (1986)
Index of food production per capita (1979–81 = 100): 98 (1986–88)
Number of tractors: 16,167 (1986)
Number of harvester-threshers: 15,502 (1986)
Total fertilizer consumption (000 metric tons): 807.1 (1985–86)
Fertilizer consumption (g./ha., hundreds) 3.920 (1987–88)
Number of farms (millions): 1.974 (1984)
Average size of holding (ha.): 1.1 (1984)
Size class (%) 1984
- Below 1 ha. (below 2.47 ac.): 66.6
- 1–5 ha. (2.47–12.35 ac.): 33.4
- 5–10 ha. (12.35–24.7 ac.): 33.4
- 10–20 ha. (24.7–49.4 ac.): 33.4
- 20–50 ha. (49.4–123.5 ac.): 0.0
- 50–200 ha. (123.5–494 ac.): 0.0
- Over 200 ha. (over 494 ac.): 0.0

Tenure (%) 1970
- Owner-operated: 82.5
- Rented: 17.4
- Other: 0.1

Activity (%) 1969
- Mainly crops: 94.0
- Mainly livestock: 0.4
- Mixed: 5.6

Farms as % of total land area: 21.7 (1984)
Land use (%)
- Cropland: 55
- Pasture: 3
- Forest: 0
- Other: 42

Yields (kg./ha.) 1989
- Grains: 5,984
- Roots & tubers: 18,353
- Legumes: 1,162
- Milk (kg./animal): 5,000

Production 1989
- Fruits (000 metric tons): 1.955
- Vegetables (million metric tons): 8.374

Livestock (000) 1989
- Cattle: 2,039
- Horses: 3 (1986)
- Sheep: 3
- Pigs: 4,852

Forestry 1988
- Production of roundwood (million cubic meters): 6.803
  - of which industrial roundwood (%): 34.0
- Value of exports (U.S. $ millions): 396.047

Fishing 1988
- Total catch (million metric tons): 2,727.1
  - of which marine (%): 98.7
- Value of exports (U.S. $ millions): 1,784,068

Although most farmers raise some livestock, especially draft animals and poultry, livestock contributes only 10% of the value of agricultural production, and commercial livestock breeding is limited to about 1% of the farmholdings.

Although 67% of the land area is officially classified as forests, commercially exploitable stands cover only 6.63 million ha. (16.4 million ac.). About three-fourths of the forestland is privately owned, managed by village mutual interest groups. The small forest industry has contributed 2% of the GDP, mostly through exports of plywood.

In the late 1980s South Korea emerged as one of the world's leading exporters of fish. By the mid-1970s South Korean deep-sea trawlers had extended their operations as far away as the Canary Islands in the Atlantic Ocean. The tuna fleet of 400 vessels serves as the backbone of the fishing fleet. Coastal fishing also remains important, and the domestic market consumes two-thirds of the industry's production. The Korean coastal fishing grounds support an enormous variety of tropical and cold-water fish.

Agricultural credit is provided by moneylenders. Institutional credit is available from the National Agricultural Cooperative Federation, which also is the principal government agency for marketing agricultural produce.

MANUFACTURING

South Korea, emulating its neighbor Japan, became an industrial nation in the 1960s, adopting a successful strategy to develop a substantial manufacturing capacity for export using imported materials. There is a conspicuous concentration on light industry with low capital requirements. The domestic market is highly protected, and exports are subsidized by a system of special incentives.

In 1988 manufacturing contributed 32% to the GDP, more than any other sector, including agriculture. Dur-

MANUFACTURING INDICATORS, 1987

Average annual growth rate (%, 1980–88): 13.5
Share of GDP (%): 32 (1988)
Labor force economically active in manufacturing (% est.): 27.8 (1989)
Value added in manufacturing (U.S. $ millions): 42.286
- Food & tobacco (%): 12
- Textiles & clothing (%): 17
- Machinery & transport equipment (%): 28
- Chemicals (%): 8

Earnings per employee in manufacturing 1987
- Growth rate (%, 1980–87): 5.6
- Index (1980 = 100): 145

Total earnings as % of value added: 27
Gross output per employee (1980 = 100): 165
Index of manufacturing production: 284 (1989)

ing the period 1980–88 manufacturing achieved a phenomenal growth rate of 13.5%. Manufacturing contributes at least one-half of current governmental revenues and 37% of total exports.

The economic stabilization plan introduced in 1979 marked a watershed in industrial growth, with its intention to increase the relative importance of domestic market-oriented light industry. Unfortunately, the economic crisis later in the same year forced a change of priority on the government. Less than a year after the heralding of the country's "second industrial revolution," both the domestic market emphasis and high-technology industrial growth strategy were drastically revamped to allow for the soaring cost of energy, the need to curb capital investment, export market sales difficulties and inflationary pressures. Projects already in the pipeline escaped the economy drive, but the moratorium imposed on new projects means that consolidation rather than expansion is to be the keynote. While large-scale industry faces a less buoyant future, small- and medium-scale operators will benefit from a one-third increase, to W400 billion, in the special support funds available to this sector. Such operators have tended to be overlooked in the past, but it is estimated that companies employing 300 people or less account for almost one-half of manufacturing employment. As a result of these developments, exports from the heavy industries did not perform as well as planned. In 1980, for example, 52.4% of exports came from light industries, with 29% emanating from the textile industry alone. In contrast, the leading product of heavy industry, electronic goods, contributed only 12%; many such industries, notably motor vehicles, were operating well below capacity.

Manufacturing is almost entirely concentrated in the Seoul region. The government has undertaken a plan of dispersing industries to achieve a more balanced development and to eliminate regional disparities. Privately owned small- and medium-scale manufacturing establishments, having under 200 regular employees, predominate, constituting 98% of all industrial units. But this category provides only 54% of employment and accounts for only 36% of value added in manufacturing. Most industries are family-owned. Light manufactures such as food, textiles and footwear account for 72% of industrial production; heavy manufactures such as chemicals, machinery and transportation equipment account for 25%

The government takes an active and decisive role in industry, although official policy supports private enterprise over public enterprise. Industrial development strategy is formulated and coordinated by the government through five-year plans. Government measures also include vigorous programs to promote the flow of foreign capital into the country, to assist the formation of domestic capital, and to fine-tune the product mix to achieve a well-balanced manufacturing base. In 1973 the government launched a program designed to force the full industrialization of the country by 1981. The core of this program was the expansion of heavy industry, iron and steel, nonferrous metals, machinery, shipbuilding, chemicals and electronics.

Beginning in the 1960s there has been a steady flow of foreign capital for direct investment in South Korean industry. The United States and Japan were the main sources of foreign investment during 1962–71, with $98.9 million (57.3% of the total) and $50.5 million (29.3% of the total), respectively. During 1972–74 the situation was reversed, with Japanese investors contributing $301 million (85% of the total) and U.S. investors $34 million (11% of the total). Private foreign investment totaled $124.1 million in 1974, $61.2 million in 1975 and $61 million in 1978.

The public sector is limited to transportation and communications systems; power; and projects requiring extraordinary capital investment, such as steel. However, the government does not consider the private sector competitive and, in many cases, new public-sector ventures are transferred to private ownership as soon as they are firmly established.

The major industries are textiles, food processing and beverages, chemicals and petrochemicals, iron and steel, nonferrous metals, industrial machinery and equipment, transportation equipment and electrical machinery.

In 1980 President Chun Doo-Hwan announced measures that sharply altered South Korea's corporate structure. The changes were intended in part to halt the development of diversified conglomerates built around trading companies. The reforms followed the collapse of the Yulsan Group, which was the country's largest general trading company. Under the new laws, a conglomerate is required to identify its main business activity and concentrate investments in that company. Subsidiaries whose activities are not related to that company must be sold. Businesses must report and get rid of unused real estate belonging to the company or its major shareholders. Companies also must separate ownership from management and be subject to external audit.

MINING

Mining is the smallest economic sector, employing less than 1% of the labor force and contributing less than 1% to the GNP.

Coal, iron ore, gold, copper, tungsten, lead and zinc are the most important and most actively exploited minerals. Since the oil crisis of 1973, priority has been given to the production of coal. The major coal deposits are near the eastern coast, in Kangwon Province, and on the southwestern coast, in South Cholla Province. Known reserves are estimated at 500 million tons. In 1983 production from 94 mines was 18.9 million tons. Iron ore reserves are estimated at 40 million tons and tungsten reserves at 7.5 million tons.

ENERGY

South Korea is heavily dependent on petroleum for energy needs and the government has taken measures to reduce dependency. It raised petroleum prices by 60% twice since July 1979.

ENERGY INDICATORS

Average annual energy production growth rate (%, 1980–88): 9.7
Energy consumption per capita (kg. oil equivalent): 1.515 (1988)
Energy imports as % of merchandise exports: 10 (1988)
Average annual growth rate of energy consumption (%, 1980–88): 5.5
Electricity 1988
  Installed capacity (million kw.): 22.173
  Production (million kw.-hr.): 85.462
    % fossil fuel: 48.9
    % hydro: 4.2
    % nuclear: 46.9
  Consumption per capita (kw.-hr.): 2.005
Natural gas
  Proved reserves (billion cu. m.): 0.0 (1990)
  Production (million cu. m.): 0.0 (1989)
  Consumption (million cu. m.): 2.920 (1988)
Petroleum
  Production (million bbl.): 0.0 (1989)
  Consumption (million bbl): 257 (1988)
  Refining capacity (000 bbl./day): 867 (1990)
Coal
  Reserves (million metric tons): 158 (latest)
  Production (million metric tons): 24.295 (1988)
  Consumption (million metric tons): 45.906 (1988)

Conservation efforts also have helped reduce the growth in demand, previously rising at a nearly 12% average per annum. Work is under way to modify or convert combustion facilities at thermal power plants to coal or combined bunker-C and liquified natural gas. The growth of coal combustion facilities was expected to increase, with coal accounting for 33% of energy supply by 1991. The role of petroleum was expected to fall to 51% by that year.

Just under half of South Korea's electric power production is derived from nuclear energy.

South Korea's first atomic power plant went on stream in 1978, at Kori, with a generating capacity of 587 mw. A second plant, also at Kori, with a capacity of 650 mw., and a third, at Wolsung, with a capacity of 678 mw., became operational in 1983, bringing total atomic power generation to 1,900 mw., or 13.5% of total power as of May 1984. A fourth plant, also at Kori and with a capacity of 900 mw., commenced operation in June 1985, and a fifth plant went on line in April 1986 with a capacity of 950 mw. By the end of the decade four more atomic power plants, each with 950 mw capacity, were in operation in Young Kwang-Gun and Uljin. All of this represents a growth of atomic energy in South Korea from less than a tenth of total electric output in 1980, to over half by 1987. The Atomic Energy Bureau is in charge of planning, research and development, international co-operation and radiation safety. The Atomic Energy Commission is responsible for fundamental plans and policies, coordinating activities and training personnel.

LABOR

South Korea's economically active population was estimated in 1989 at 17.975 million, of whom women account for 40.4%. The annual growth rate of the labor force during 1980–2000 is estimated at 1.9%. The most striking trend in employment is the decline in the percentage of the labor force employed in agriculture, from 63% in 1963 to 19% in 1989.

LABOR INDICATORS, 1989

Total economically active population (millions): 17.975
  % working-age (15–64): 62.2
  % female: 40.4
Activity rate (%)
  Total: 42.4
  Male: 50.2
  Female: 34.5
Employment status (%)
  Employers & self-employed: 28.1
  Employees: 57.6
  Unpaid family workers: 11.7
  Other: 2.6
Sectoral employment of economically active (%)
  Agriculture, forestry, fishing: 19.0
  Construction: 6.3
  Manufacturing, mining, quarrying, public utilities: 27.8
  Trade, hotels, restaurants: 20.9
  Transportation, communications: 4.8
  Finance, real estate: 4.8
  Services: 13.8
Average annual growth rate of labor force (%, 1980–2000): 1.9
Unemployment (000): 519 (1987)
Labor under 20 years (%): 4.4 (1987)
Earnings in manufacturing per worker (/mo) (W/worker): 269,652 (1985)
Hours of work per worker 1983
  Manufacturing (/wk.): 54.4
  Non-agricultural (/wk.): 52.5

Under an overseas work program established in 1963, the government encourages the emigration of workers. In 1978 there were 122,000 South Koreans employed abroad, of whom 40% were employed in West Germany and another 30% on foreign ships. Nearly 10,000 South Koreans are employed in various construction projects in the Middle East.

Working conditions are governed by legislation. The standard workweek is 48 hours, eight hours a day for six days. Working hours may be extended to 60 hours per week by mutual agreement, a practice that has become common in manufacturing and export industries. Further extension of overtime hours requires prior approval of the Office of Labor Affairs. Anything above the standard workweek is considered overtime and is subject to compensation at 150% of the standard hourly rate. Minors aged 13 to 16 are permitted to work 42 hours a week (seven hours a day). There are 14 legal holidays per year in Korea. In addition, employees are entitled by law to eight paid holidays a year if their attendance is at least 90% perfect.

Wages in the cities are notable for the extreme variation in rates paid for the same kind of work in the same industry. Wage rates in the different industries also vary widely. In 1982 the average monthly cash earnings of all employees in manufacturing was W202.117. Korea has no legal minimum wage system, although the Labor Standards Act authorizes the director-general of the Office of Labor Affairs to set a minimum wage according to industry. Base wages make up only part of a worker's income. Fringe benefits make up 50% to 60% of a wage earner's salary and in some cases may amount to 80% of total compensation. In 1978, average monthly earnings for all workers were about $197. The highest average monthly earnings were paid by the petroleum refining industry ($597) and the lowest by the wearing apparel industry ($126). In addition to an employee's base salary, bonuses of 100% or higher of monthly salary are paid several times a year. Many companies provide meals at lunch, and commuter services. One month's average salary for every year of employment is given as severance pay by employers with more than 16 workers. The average men's pay is 2.2 times that of women, although women work 5% longer hours.

Strikes are forbidden. In those cases where management and labor negotiate, differences are resolved by arbitration through the Administration of Labor Affairs (ALA) or through municipal or provincial arbitration committees. The ALA estimates that only about 5% of labor-management negotiations reach an impasse and get referred to binding arbitration.

Negotiations are carried on plant-by-plant rather than by industry; therefore, there are variations among firms involved in similar operations. The number of companies with a labor union chapter is over 5,000, most of which have concluded collective bargaining agreements. Agreements that have been concluded voluntarily need not necessarily be registered with the Office of Labor Affairs.

There are three basic laws concerning labor: the Labor Standards Law, the Labor Union Law and the Labor Dispute Settlement Law. In addition, a temporary special law dealing with foreign-invested enterprises has been appended to the latter law. This special law provides for establishment of the Foreign-Invested Enterprises Labor Dispute Settlement Committee in the Ministry of Health and Social Affairs. In case of a suspension of operations or the closing of a foreign enterprise, the Korean government must adjust labor disputes within 20 days. Foreign investors may be given up to five years' exemption from having to recognize a union. Child labor, although illegal, is winked at.

The government's principal goal in industrial relations is to keep wage rates below the growth of industrial productivity. The government's wage restraint policy is effectively enforced, and real wages have risen significantly slower than the growth in productivity. Unemployment is officially estimated at 4.1%, but unofficial estimates place it as high as 10%

Collective bargaining is recognized under the Constitution but has been restricted since the declaration of national emergency in 1971. About 10% of the nonagricultural labor force are unionized in the single national labor federation, the Federation of Korean Trade Unions (FKTU), and its 16 national affiliate unions. Their freedom of action however, is severely circumscribed by law. Labor organizations are forbidden to support politicians or political parties, though the FKTU does lobby national assemblymen and assemblymen often attend labor-organized gatherings. All local unions must be organized within individual enterprises, creating a structure of thousands of individual unions, most of them small and weak. Direct participation in local unions' bargaining activities by outside agencies such as the Asian-American Free Labor Institute, which maintains an office in Korea, is forbidden. The FKTU and its constituent national unions can and sometimes do bargain on behalf of the locals and conduct education programs, but only with government and employer approval. Collective actions and strikes, though technically legal, are to all intents and purposes forbidden. Religious labor ministries such as the Catholic Young Christian Workers and the Protestant Urban Industrial Mission also are severely limited in the assistance they can provide the unions. Under these circumstances, government and employer influence has greatly exceeded that of unions in setting wages and resolving other major labor issues. According to FKTU figures, dues-paying union membership in 1984 increased by 4%, after four years of decline. International contacts by the unions increased, with the FKTU and its member unions hosting three regional conferences, including the Asian meeting of the International Confederation of Free Trade Unions (ICFTU).

The checkoff system of collective dues is guaranteed by law and universally practiced in organized enterprises. A portion of the dues received by each union is allotted to the FKTU.

FOREIGN COMMERCE

Of the imports in 1988 just over one-third were machinery and transportation equipment, about a sixth were mineral fuels and just over a tenth were chemical related products. Of the exports more than 90% were manufactured goods, over a third were machinery and transport equipment with the rest made-up by food and live animals, and chemical related products.

FOREIGN TRADE INDICATORS, 1988

Exports (U.S. $ billions): 62.3 (1989)
Imports (U.S. $ billions): 61.3 (1989)
Balance of trade (U.S. $ millions): 1.0
Annual growth rate (1980–88), exports (%): 14.7
Annual growth rate (1980–88), imports (%): 9.9
International reserves in terms of months of imports covered: 2.6
Terms of trade (1980 = 100): 108
Import price index (1980 = 100): 82.5 (1986)
Export price index (1980 = 100): 91.9 (1986)

Direction of Trade (%), 1987

	Imports	Exports
European Community	11.2	14.0
United States	21.4	38.9
U.S.S.R & eastern European economies	0.0	0.0
Japan	33.3	17.8

Composition of Trade (%), 1987

	Imports	Exports
Food & agricultural raw materials	14.5	5.3
Fuels & other energy	14.7	1.6
Mineral ores & concentrates	4.3	0.3
Manufactured goods	66.5	92.8
of which chemicals	11.1	2.8
of which machinery	34.4	35.8

Major importers were Japan and the United States, together totaling about 55%. Others included, in descending order, Germany, Australia, Malaysia, Canada, France and Saudi Arabia.

The major export nation was the United States with almost two-fifths of the totals, followed by Japan with almost a fifth, followed in descending order by Hong Kong, Canada, Germany, the United Kingdom, Saudi Arabia and France.

Most of the country's foreign trade is conducted by the private sector, and the majority of the export-import firms are owned by Korean nationals. All firms desiring to engage in foreign trade are required to register with and obtain in a license from the Ministry of Commerce. The annual *Korean Trade Directory* lists over 1,000 such firms and 53 trade associations. The basic purpose of the government's's foreign trade policy is to expand the country's exports. To this end the government has established an elaborate system of export incentives and complex machinery to supervise and monitor it. However, this system clearly operates as a patronage machine, dispensing favors to political partisans and firms with the right connections. Government control over exports also extends to quality control. Most export commodities are required to pass official quality and quantity inspections before receiving customs clearance. Export regulations governing trade with Communist countries were liberalized in 1974. Government policy on imports is generally restrictive, with such controls as a negative list, advance deposit requirements, quotas and permits.

TRANSPORTATION & COMMUNICATIONS

The state-owned railroad system, operated by Korean National Railroads, consists of 6,456 km. (4,012 mi.) of track. The main trunk lines run from Seoul to Mokpo and from Seoul to Pusan. Seoul also has a 21-km (13-mi.) subway system operated by the Metropolitan Rapid Transit Bureau. South Korea has 13 major ports. The largest port is Pusan, one of South Korea's few natural harbors. Inchon, Ulsan, Mokpo and Pohang also are classified as first-class ports. Combined, these ports handled 104,505,000 tons of cargo in 1983. The rapid growth in foreign trade has required modernization of existing port facilities and creation of new ones. The port of Inchon has been expanded to include the largest dock in Asia. The ports and all branches of shipping are supervised by the Korea Maritime and Port Authority. South Korea has built up one of the largest merchant fleets in Asia, with 1,974 ships totaling 12,335,500 GRT.

The national highways include a four-lane superhighway linking Seoul and Pusan and Seoul and Inchon. The Namhae and Honam expressways link several cities in the West and South, while another national highway links Seoul with Kangnung and Mukho. The Olympic Expressway linking Taegu and Kwangju and the Chungpu Expressway linking Seoul and Cheongju opened in the mid-1980s.

The national airline is the privately owned Korean Air Lines (KAL), with 93 aircraft serving 10 domestic cities and 13 foreign cities, including Tokyo, Taipei, Hong Kong, Bangkok, Manila, Singapore, Honolulu, Los Angeles, Paris and Bahrain. Until 1988 KAL was the

TRANSPORTATION INDICATORS

Roads (latest)
- Length, km. (mi.): 55,778 (34,660)
- Paved (%): 61

Motor vehicles (latest)
- Automobiles: 1,117,999
- Trucks and buses: 895,045
- Persons per vehicle: 21
- Road freight, metric ton-km. (short ton-mi.) (billions): 8.645 (5.921)

Railroads (latest)
- Track, km. (mi.): 6,456 (4,012)
- Passenger-km. (passenger-mi.) (billions): 25.978 (16.142)
- Freight, metric ton-km. (short ton-mi.) (millions): 13.784 (9.441)

Merchant marine
- Vessels (over 100 tons): 1,974 (1989)
- Total deadweight tonnage (000): 12,335.5 (1989)
- Oil tankers (000 GRT): 1.0002 (1985)

Ports (pre-1986)
- Cargo loaded (000 metric tons): 54,300
- Cargo unloaded (000 metric tons): 144,192

Air
- Km. (mi.) flown (millions): 77.2 (48.0) (1985)
- Passenger-km. (passenger-mi.) (million): 18,168 (11,289) (latest)
- Freight, metric ton-km. (short ton-mi.) (millions): 2.413 (1.653) (latest)
- Airports with scheduled flights: 10 (1990)

Pipelines 1990
- Refined, km. (mi.): 294 (183)

Inland waterways (latest)
- Length, km. (mi.): 1,609 (994)
- Freight, metric ton-km. (short ton-mi.) (billions): 16.617 (11.381)

COMMUNICATION INDICATORS, 1988

Telephones
- Total (million): 12.415
- Persons per telephone: 3.4

Phone traffic (million calls)
- Local: 56,996,413 (pulses)
- Long distance: 13,791
- International: 33,163

Post office
- Number of post offices: 3,199 (1979)
- Pieces of mail handled (millions): 1,870,170

Telegraph
- Total traffic (million calls): 13,355
  - National: 13,292
  - International: .063

Telex
- Subscriber lines: 10,042
- Traffic (million calls): 9.692 (1987)

Telecommunications 1990
- Satellite ground stations: 3

TOURISM & TRAVEL INDICATORS, 1986

Total tourist receipts (U.S. $ billions): 3.265 (1988)
Expenditures by nationals abroad (U.S. $ billions): 1.354 (1988)
Number of hotel beds (000): 50
Average length of stay (nights): 6
Tourist nights (millions): 5.604
Number of tourists (millions): 1.426 (1985)
- of whom from United States: 239.4
  - Japan: 638.9
  - United Kingdom: 21.4
  - FRG: 18.6

nation's sole scheduled airline. That year Asiana Airlines, with a fleet of two aircraft was formed. It serves three major domestic cities and four cities in Japan. The largest international airports are at Chejo, near Pusan, and at Kimpo, near Seoul. Another is being built at Chongju.

In 1988 2.34 million tourists visited South Korea, creating receipts of about $3.265 billion. The influx of visitors for the 1988 Olympic Games in Seoul prompted construction on 19 new tourist hotels with an additional 1,687 rooms. At least 16% more tourists visited South Korea in 1988 than in the previous year.

DEFENSE

The defense structure is headed by the president, who also is commander in chief of the armed forces. In addition, the president heads the National Security Council (NSC), which includes the minister of national defense; the prime minister; the ministers of finance, home, economic planning and foreign affairs; and the director of the Agency for National Security Planning (ANSP) (formerly the Korean Central Intelligence Agency). The chairman of the Joint Chiefs of Staff also participates in NSC meetings. The JCS is made up of the army and air force chiefs of staff and the chief of naval operations. Operational command of the South Korean armed forces is vested in the commander in chief of the U.N. Command in the Republic of Korea, who also is concurrently the commanding general of the U.S,. Eighth Army in Korea and the commander of all U.S. forces in Korea.

The South Korean army has three numbered armies: The First Army of eight divisions is stationed on eastern sector; the Third Army of 10 divisions is garrisoned on the western sector which includes Seoul; and the Second Army, stationed in the interior, is divided into four commands. The islands are garrisoned by the marine corps.

Military manpower for the army and part of the marine corps is provided by conscription, while the air force and navy depend on voluntary enlistment. All male citizens are liable to compulsory military service upon reaching age 18. The minimum service period is 33 months for the army and the marine corps and three years for the navy and air force.

The Korean Peninsula is one of the world's most heavily armed regions. The combined North and South Korean armed forces total some 1.4 million fighting men. South Korean standing army forces account for 550,000. South Korea also has a 2-million-strong Homeland Defense Reserve.

Army

Personnel: 550,000

Organization: headquarters, 3 armies; 5 corps, each of 4 divisions; 2 mechanized infantry divisions (each of 3 brigades, 3 mechanized infantry battalions and 3 motorized battalions); 3 tank battalions; 1 reconnaissance battalion; 1 field artillery brigade; 19 infantry divisions (each of 3 infantry regiments, 1 reconnaissance battalion, 1 tank battalion, 1 engineer battalion and 1 artillery group); 7 special warfare brigades; 2 AA artillery brigades; 2 SSM battalions; 2 SAM brigades; 1 army aviation brigade

Reserves: 1 army headquarters; 23 infantry divisions

Equipment: 1,200 tanks; 600 armored personnel carriers; 3,000 artilley, including guns, howitzers, mortars, rocket launchers and surface-to-surface missiles; antitank guns; 580 air defense guns; 210 SAM's

Army aviation 14 planes; 250 helicopters

Navy

Personnel: 29,000 (navy); 25,000 (marine corps)

Organization and equipment: 5 command headquarters; 11 destroyers; 7 frigates; 7 corvettes; 11 fast attack craft; 84 patrol craft; 1 minesweeper; 32 amphibious craft; 2 supply ships; 6 tankers; 2 antisubmarine squadrons

Marine corps: 2 divisions; 1 brigade; 40 tanks

Naval bases: Chinhae; Pusan; Inchon

Air Force

Personnel: 40,000

Organization and equipment: 451 combat aircraft; 7 combat wings; 2 transportation wings; 18 fighter squadrons; 4 air defense squadrons; 1 counterinsurgency squadron; 1 reconnaissance squadron; 1 search and rescue squadron; 210 trainers; Sidewinder and Sparrow missiles

Air bases: Saechon; Chinhae; Osan; Chongju; Taegu; Suwon

The fighting qualities of the South Korean armed forces have been enhanced by the combat experience gained by some 250,000 men who served in Vietnam for varying periods. The South Korean soldier is noted for his toughness and hardiness. He also is backed up by some of the most sophisticated U.S. weapons and equipment. Because of South Korea's strategic vulnerability, the bulk of the armed forces is deployed in an east–west zone stretching from coast to coast south of the DMZ. They operate under the state of constant preparedness.

The South Korean army is virtually the creation of the post-World War II U.S. military government in Korea. The special strategic and military relationship of the United States and Korea is embedded in the Mutual Defense Treaty of 1954, by which the United States guaranteed South Korea's territorial integrity and committed itself to a program of maintaining South Korea's combat-readiness and deterrent capability. The scale of U.S. assistance, estimated at $8.159 billion from 1946 through 1983, ranges from direct budget support to grant assistance under the Military Assistance Program and supplies of hardware, fuels and munitions. Arms purchases from abroad from 1973 through 1983 totaled $3.750 billion. Though U.S. ground troops are being phased out, South Korea will remain for some time to come heavily dependent on U.S. logistical support, air cover and training programs. In addition, the U.S. Seventh Fleet has a carrier task force periodically patrolling Korean waters.

In 1978 the U.S. secretary of defense, Harold Brown, stated that the United States intended to carry out its treaty obligations to South Korea, and that South Korea would remain under the U.S. nuclear umbrella. The United States also pledged that it would not enter into unilateral negotiations with North Korea without South Korean participation. Further, the U.S. Senate approved a $275 million arms credit for South Korea and also the transfer of $800 million in advanced military equipment. In 1979 U.S. and South Korean troops launched their biggest joint exercise since 1953, with 42,000 U.S. personnel and 65,000 South Koreans. The U.S. air presence over South Korea has been strengthened with an additional squadron of 12 F-4 phantom jets as well as new F-15 and F-16 fighters.

However, South Korea has been looking to its own defenses. In 1978 the first nuclear power plant went on stream and the army successfully test-fired its ground-to-ground missiles and antitank projectiles.

South Korea has been included in various experts' lists of countries capable of producing their own atomic weapons within the next 10 years.

EDUCATION

The national literacy rate is 92.7% (97.5% for males and 87.9% for females).

Education is, in principle, compulsory, free and universal for six years, from ages six to 12.

Schooling consists of 12 years, divided into six years of primary school, three years of middle school and three years of secondary school. The curricula were standardized in 1954 but have undergone many modifications since then, including one in 1973 to reflect the national revitalization movement. A new curriculum was introduced in 1973 for the first three grades of the elementary school. Since 1970 all high-school students have been required to take military training.

The academic year runs from September through June. The medium of instruction is Korean, but English is taught as a compulsory subject from the secondary grades on.

Elementary-school teachers are trained at two-year teacher training colleges. Secondary-school teachers are trained at three national and nine private colleges of education. Qualified teachers constitute only a little over 50% of the national teaching staff.

Private schools function as an integral part of the national school system. Enrollment in private elementary schools is 1.2% at the first level but rises to 45% at the second level. Standards and facilities in private schools are generally better than those in public schools. Since 1973 the Ministry of Education has sought to increase its control over private schools. Appointments of new teachers in private schools are subject to approval by the ministry.

Vocational training is offered by technical schools at the middle-school level and by higher technical schools and junior technical colleges at the high-school level. About 18% of secondary-school enrollment is in the vocational stream, but it still is not large enough to meet projected manpower needs.

EDUCATION INDICATORS, 1989

Literacy
- Total (%): 92.7
- Male (%): 97.5
- Female (%): 87.9

First level
- Schools: 6,463
- Students: 4,819,857
- Teachers: 132,527
- Student/teacher ratio: 36.4
- Net enrollment ratio: 100 (1988)

Second level
- Schools: 3,492
- Students: 3,981,132
- Teachers: 127,423
- Student/teacher ratio: 31.2
- Net enrollment ratio: 76 (1982)

Vocational
- Schools: 620
- Students: 866,602
- Teachers: 31,835
- Student/teacher ratio: 27.2

Third level (postsecondary)
- Institutions: 485
- Students: 1,364,374
- Teachers: 35,753
- Student/teacher ratio: 37.5 (1988)
- Gross enrollment ratio: 36.5 (1988)
- Students (/100,000 pop.): 3,671
- % of population age 25 and over with postsecondary education: 8.9

Foreign study
- Foreign students in national universities: 1,598 (1988)
- Students abroad: 27,856
  - of whom in
    - United States: 17,874 (1988)
    - France: 1,343 (1988)
    - Federal Republic of Germany: 3,557 (1988)
    - United Kingdom: 314 (1987)

Public expenditure
- Total (w 000): 4,141,872
- % of GNP: 3.9
- % of national budget: 26.6
- % of current: 86.4

GRADUATES, 1987

Total: 260,720
Education: 37,346
Humanities & religion: 31,046
Fine & applied arts: 15,178
Law: 5,021
Social & behavioral sciences: 10,231
Commerce & business: 39,409
Mass communication: 1,863
Home economics: 9,657
Service trades: 2,081
Natural sciences: 8,965
Mathematics & computer science: 3,485
Medicine: 20,600
Engineering: 40,061
Architecture: 12,261
Industrial programs: 6,387
Transportation & communications: 1,551
Agriculture, forestry, fisheries: 12,753
Other: 2,825

Overall control of education is vested in the Ministry of Education, but the public-school system is under the administrative direction of city, county or provincial school boards. Only the higher educational institutions are directly under the Ministry of Education.

In 1989 there were 485 colleges and universities in South Korea, including four-year and two-year colleges. Of these, 67 institutions were privately run.

Major Universities of South Korea

University	City
Chonnam National University	Kwang Joo
Chosun University	Kwang Joo
Chungang University	Seoul
Chungnam University	Taijon
Chunpuk National University	Chun-Joo
Dan Kook University	Seoul
Dong A University	Pusan
Dongguk University	Seoul
Ewha Women's University	Seoul
Hankuk University of Foreign Studies	Seoul
Hanyang University	Seoul
Jeon Buk National University	Jeon Buk
Kon-Kuk University	Seoul
Korea University	Seoul
Kyung Hee University	Seoul
Kyung Puk National University	Taegu
Myong Ji University	Seoul
Pusan National University	Pusan
Seoul National University	Seoul
Sogang University	Mapoku, Seoul
Sookmyung Women's University	Seoul
Sung Jun University	Seoul
Sung Kyun Kwan University	Seoul
Woo Sok University	Seoul
Yeungnam University	Taegu
Yonsei University	Seoul

LEGAL SYSTEM

The judicial system is headed by the Supreme Court, consisting of a chief justice and no more than 14 justices. The chief justice is appointed by the president with the consent of the National Assembly for a term of six years, while other justices also are appointed for six-year terms by the president on the recommendation of the chief justice, and requires the consent of the National Assembly. The chief justice cannot be reappointed. The Supreme Court hears appeals from the Appellate Courts and also has jurisdiction over military tribunals. Constitutionality of laws is decided by the Constitution Court consisting of nine members appointed by the president. Three of the members are selected by the National Assembly and three by the Chief Justice. The term of office is six years.

The lower courts are described under the Court Organization Law of 1948 as appellate courts, district courts and family courts. Three appellate courts, sitting in Seoul, Taegu and Kwangju, hear appeals in civil and criminal cases. Each appellate court is composed of a presiding judge and three associate judges. District courts with original jurisdiction over civil and criminal cases are in Seoul and each provincial capital. Thirty-six branch courts are in other principal cities and towns. The Seoul district court is divided into a civil district court and a criminal district court. District courts sit as either single-judge or three-judge collegiate courts. There also is a family court sitting at Seoul. There has been increasing use, since 1972, of a new category of military courts, known as emergency courts-martial, to try civilians for violations of martial law.

The Constitution guarantees many rights of defendants: the right to presumption of innocence; the right against self-incrimination, ex post facto laws and double jeopardy; the right to a speedy trial; and the right to legal counsel. These rights generally are observed, although there have been cases in the past in which defendants in politically sensitive trials have not been able to obtain lawyers, reportedly because of lawyers' reluctance to accept such cases in the face of actual or potential government pressure. Trials usually are open to the public, but trial documents are not part of the public record. Charges against defendants in the courts are clearly stated, with the exception that in lengthy and complex indictments the relationship between specific acts alleged and violations of specific sections of the Penal Code may not always be clearly drawn.

Korean law requires that within 40 days after making an arrest the police notify an arrested person's family of his detention and whereabouts. The police normally wait at least several days, and occasionally more than 40 days, before making notification. The Constitution guarantees the right of prompt legal assistance and the right to request court review in case of arrest. For persons deemed "socially dangerous" the law allows preventive detention under provisions of the Social Protection and Social Stability laws. Preventive detention is for a fixed term, which, however, a judicial panel may extend for periods of up to 10 years.

Habeas corpus, not traditional in Korean law, was introduced after World War II, abolished in the 1970s and reintroduced in 1980. It does not apply to those charged with violations of the National Security Act or laws punishable by at least five years' imprisonment, which include most political offenses.

Penal institutions include two detention facilities, 21 regular prisons, two juvenile prisons and one branch prison. The average prison population in any one month is estimated at 30,000, of whom 10% are juveniles and 4% are women.

LAW ENFORCEMENT

The national law enforcement force is headed by the director-general of the Office of National Police Affairs, who holds the rank of vice minister. Below the headquarters the force is organized into 12 divisions with four auxiliary organs. At the regional levels there are police bureaus in the two cities of Seoul and Pusan and in each of the provincial capitals. At the base of the pyramid are 175 first- and second-class police stations, 1,344 substations and nearly 1,000 police boxes and other small posts throughout the country. In addition to the general police there are special units such as the special combat police, who are organized into 24 combat companies and charged with countersubversive operations. The maritime police function as a coast guard and are equipped with patrol ships and boats and light aircraft. Total strength of the national police is estimated at 44,000, or one policeman per 807 inhabitants.

Korean police practice requires police commanders to know a good deal about the personal and business affairs of all residents in their jurisdictions. This system is effective in crime control, and urban residents generally credit it with keeping their streets safe. By contrast, the presence of police informer networks on college campuses with the primary purpose of keeping track of political activities there has been a key issue among students, including those who are not politically active. Students have accused the government of maintaining police informers on-campus even after uniformed forces were withdrawn in accordance with the "campus autonomy" policy. Koreans who meet with foreigners, particularly with journalists and embassy officials, are often questioned afterward. While the Constitution requires a warrant issued by a judge upon request of a prosecutor for search and seizure in a residence, the police have at times forced their way into private homes without warrants.

Patterns and incidence of crime reflect the growing urbanization of the country. The largest categories of crime are larceny, robbery, theft and embezzlement. The most significant criminal trends are the growing number of victimless crimes (such as prostitution), juvenile delinquency and crimes committed by women.

The most feared institution in South Korea is the Agency for National Security Planning (ANSP), formerly the Korean Central Intelligence Agency, established in 1961 "to counter indirect aggression of the Communist forces and to remove obstacles to the execution of revolutionary tasks." It also was charged with the responsibility to supervise and coordinate national security-related intelligence and criminal investigation matters, both domestic and foreign. Virtually unlimited powers of investigation, arrest, detention and interrogation (without review by courts or prosecutors) were conferred on the agency. Along with the growth of authoritarianism in the country's political life, the ANSP became an all-pervasive institution, intruding on every aspect of national life. Ostensibly acting to counter Communist subversion, the ANSP wielded its enormous inquisitorial powers to wipe out all forms of dissent, particularly from opponents of former President Chun, including churchmen, journalists, intellectuals and students. The sixth bureau of the ANSP, known as the "dirty tricks" bureau, frequently employed torture, kidnaping and similar methods to harass, ferret out and intimidate President Chun's enemies. The ANSP's role in influence-peddling in the U.S. Congress was indicative of the long reach of this agency. The ANSP operates under the direct command of the president, and its strength is estimated at 7,000 to 8,000, not including informers.

HEALTH

Major health problems include tuberculosis, cholera, typhoid, dysentery, leprosy and diphtheria. About 77% of the population have access to safe water.

HEALTH INDICATORS

Health personnel 1988
- Physicians: 36,845
  - persons per: 1,139
- Dentists: 7,657
- Nurses: 76,143
- Pharmacists: 34,344
- Midwives: 7,167

Hospitals 1988
- Number: 997
- Number of beds (/10,000): 28
- Admissions/discharges (/10,000): 423
- Bed occupancy rate (%): 71.1
- Average length of stay (days): 13

Public health expenditures (latest)
- As % of national budget: 2.3
- Per capita (U.S. $): 17.90

Vital statistics
- Crude death rate (/1,000): 6 (1990)
- Life expectancy at birth 1990
  - Males: 66
  - Females: 73
- Infant mortality rate (/1,000 live births): 23 (1990)
- Child mortality rate under 5 yrs. (/1,000 live births) (1985–90): 31

Maternal mortality rate (/100,000 live births) (1986–87): 9.7
- Population with access to safe water (%): 77 (latest)

FOOD & NUTRITION

Rice is the staple food. Fruits and vegetables are consumed in large quantities. *Kimchi*, a highly spiced dish of vegetables, fruits, nuts and fish, is served with virtually every meal. The bulk of the protein is supplied by fish, which is eaten by all classes; meat and eggs are expensive items eaten only on special occasions. The national beverage is *sungyong*, a hot rice tea.

The per capita daily intake of food is 2,936 calories (125% of requirements).

MEDIA & CULTURE

Twenty-six daily newspapers are published, two of which were in English. *Hankook Ilbo*, a national daily, claims a circulation of two million. *Chosun Ilbo* and *Joong-ang Ilbo* have circulations of 1.8 million and 1.65 million respectively. Seven other national dailies claim circulations of over 400,000.

The periodicals press consists of 1,293 titles with a total circulation of 2,717,000, or 81 per 1,000 inhabitants. Of these, 20 are published in English and one in Chinese.

The most influential newspapers and periodicals are privately owned by wealthy individuals or families with direct or indirect ties to the government. Overt censorship was therefore not considered necessary until 1972, and the government contented itself with applying indirect pressures on those papers that strayed too

MEDIA INDICATORS

Newspapers
- Number of dailies: 26 (latest)
- Circulation (millions): 11,000 (latest)
- Per 1,000 pop.: 265 (latest)
- Newsprint consumption 1988
  - Total metric tons: 351,500
  - Per million pop. (kg.): 8,239

Book publishing
- Number of titles: 40,046 (latest)

Broadcasting
- Annual expenditures (W millions): 481,162.0

Radio
- Number of transmitters: 262 (latest)
- Number of persons per radio receiver: 1.0 (1989)
- Total program hours (/yr.): 74,761 (1987)

Television
- Television transmitters: 783 (latest)
- Number of persons per T.V. receiver: 4.9 (1989)
- Total program hours (/yr.): 17,804 (1987)

Cinema
- Number of fixed cinemas: 673 (latest)
- Annual attendance (millions): 48.6 (latest)
- Gross box office receipts (W millions): 79,566 (1987)

Films
- Number of long films produced: 89 (latest)
- Number of long imported films: 84 (1987)
  - % from U.S. 67.9
  - % from Hong Kong 20.2
  - % from France 4.8
  - % from U.K. 1.2

far from the official line. The declaration of national emergency in 1971 brought to an end the government's adherence to the concept of a free press. The discussion of national security issues was banned, and KCIA agents were assigned to press rooms to serve as censors. Many independent newspapers have been forced to close, and others have been muzzled.

Journalists were the final victims of the "social purification" campaign launched by Chun in 1980. Martial law authorities arrested over 65 journalists, including five working for foreign news agencies. All journalists and broadcasters who had resisted censorship or who had sought freedom of the press were fired, and their replacements were forced to attend "reeducation" classes. At the same time, the government banned 172 periodicals on charges of being lewd and having "low taste."

Until 1981 there were three privately owned news agencies in the country: the Hapdong News Agency, with six domestic bureaus and two foreign bureaus; the Orient Press, with 10 domestic bureaus and three foreign bureaus; and the Donghwa News Agency, with 21 domestic bureaus and three foreign bureaus. In January 1981 these news agencies were merged into one state-owned agency, Yonhap. AP, UPI, AFP and Reuters are represented in Seoul.

South Korea has a large book publishing industry, with over 75 major publishers. Since South Korea does not adhere to any copyright convention, there are no legal restrictions on the pirating of books (publication without payment of royalties to copyright owners). South Korea competes with Taiwan in catering to the large market for pirated books in Asia.

Although the electronic media are under government regulation and are licensed by the Ministry of Communications, there is no government monopoly. The government-owned Korean Broadcasting System (KBS) broadcasts on two national networks with 22 medium-wave transmitters, for a total of 266 hours a week. The foreign service consists of three stations at Seoul, Sewon and Taegu broadcasting for 19 hours a day with four shortwave transmitters. Private networks include the two Christian evangelical stations, the Christian Broadcasting System and radio station HLKX, two commercial networks, the Munhwa Broadcasting Corporation, radio station HLAZ, and the American Forces Korea Network.

Television also is shared by government and private networks. KBS has a television station in Seoul, operating a main transmitter with 11 low-power repeaters. It is on the air for 36 hours a week. In addition to the American Forces Korea Network, the Munhwa Broadcasting Corporation operates commercially out of Seoul.

South Korea has a vigorous film production industry, with a production of 89 feature films and an equal number of short films. The output declined from a high of 224 films in 1970. Government efforts to stimulate the film industry are channeled through the official Movie Promotion Corporation and the National Film Center. Every year a few coproductions are made with producers in Japan and Hong Kong. Films are subject to regulations set by the Ministry of Culture and Information and to censorship standards imposed by an advisory council.

CULTURAL & ENVIRONMENTAL INDICATORS

Libraries (latest)
- Number: 168
- Volumes (millions): 3.184
- Registered borrowers (millions): 17.949
- Loans (/1,000 pop.): 235

Museums (latest)
- Annual attendance (000): 665 (pre-1986)
- Attendance (/1,000 pop.): 16 (pre-1986)

Performing arts (latest)
- Number of performances: 3,449
- Annual attendance (000): 402
- Attendance (/1,000 pop.): 10

Nature reserves (latest)
- Number of facilities: 17

The largest libraries are the Seoul National University Library, with 882,000 volumes, and the National Central Library, with 400,000 volumes.

SOCIAL WELFARE

The national insurance program provides medical and industrial accident insurance for approximately one quarter of the total population. The government provides relief services for the handicapped, former servicemen and war widows. Christian agencies play an active role in caring for the handicapped, the orphaned and the destitute.

GLOSSARY

chongbo: traditional Korean measure of land area roughly equal to 1 hectare (2.45 acres).
Choson: an alternate name for Korea derived from the name of an ancient tribe.
chungin: traditional middle class of Korea, ranked next to the nobility.
dong: an urban neighborhood or block, a unit of a ward.
hangul: a largely phonetic alphabet, created under King Sejong, in which Korean is written. It consists of 14 basic consonants and 10 simple vowels.
ku: an urban ward headed by a kuchong jang.
kuk hoe: the national assembly.
kun: a county, as a subdivision of a province, headed by a kunsu.
kye: a mutual assistance group undertaking unpaid group labor in rural areas.
myon: a township, as a unit of local administration, headed by a myon jang.
purak: a hamlet, as a subdivision of a village.
ri: a village, as a unit of local administration, headed by a ri jang.
Saemaul Undong: the New Community Movement, an official program launched in 1970 to improve the rural environment.
sangmin: commoners, as a class of Korean society.
si: a city, as a unit of local administration, headed by a sijang.
Siwol Yusin: the Revitalizing Constitution of 1972.
Sohak: Western learning, the name given to Christianity in the 18th and 19th centuries.
Taegukki: the flag of South Korea with the ancient symbols of yin and yang and divination bars in the corners.
to: a province headed by a governor, or tojisa.
Tonghak: Eastern learning, as distinguished from Sohak.
up: a town, as a unit of local administration, headed by an upchang.

CHRONOLOGY (from 1948)

1948— The Republic of Korea is proclaimed and the first national elections are held; Syngman Rhee is elected speaker of the National Assembly and later president. . . . New Constitution is promulgated, establishing a strong presidential form of government.
1949— American forces leave Korea. . . . Land Reform Act is passed by the National Assembly.
1950— North Korea launches full-scale invasion of the South; U.N. Security Council brands North Korea an aggressor; President Truman orders U.S. ground, air and naval units into combat; multinational U.N. command is created to throw back the invaders. . . . U.N. forces turn back the tide with an amphibious landing at Inchon. . . . Gen. Douglas MacArthur, commanding U.N. forces, crosses the 38th parallel and takes Pyongyang; volunteers from the Chinese Liberation Army join the fighting and push the U.N. forces back to the south of the peninsula.
1951— Seoul is lost and regained again. . . . Battle lines are stabilized at the 38th parallel, and truce negotiations are begun.
1952— Syngman Rhee is reelected president.
1953— Armistice is signed at Panmunjom. . . . The hwan is introduced as the national currency, replacing the old won.
1954— United States and South Korea sign Mutual Defense Treaty.
1956— Rhee is reelected for a third term.
1960— Rhee is reelected president for a fourth term in a rigged election; he is forced to step down from the presidency and to go into exile following a student uprising. . . . New national elections are held. . . . Second Republic is established, with parliamentary form of government. . . . Yun Po-san is elected president and Chang Myon prime minister.
1961— Chang Myon government runs into heavy weather and is deposed in a military coup; power passes to the Supreme Council for National Reconstruction, headed by Gen. Park Chung Hee.
1962— The hwan is replaced by the new won as the national currency. . . . New constitutional amendments are adopted, providing for a civilian government. . . . The junta organizes a political party, the Democratic Republican Party, as a vehicle for their entry into politics.
1963— Park is elected president by a narrow margin over Yun Po-san.
1965— South Korea sends troops to South Vietnam. . . . Peace treaty is signed wth Japan.
1967— Park is elected to a second term.
1971— Park is elected to a third term, over Kim Dae Jung. . . . President proclaims a state of national emergency; National Assembly grants him sweeping emergency powers.
1972— President Park proclaims martial law. . . . The Fourth Korean Republic is established when the Yushin (Revitalizing) Constitution is endorsed by a popular referendum. . . . President Park is elected for a six-year term by a new electoral body, the National Conference for Unification.
1973— KCIA provokes international controversy by kidnapping opposition leader Kim Dae Jung from a hotel room in Tokyo.
1974— President Park survives an assassination attempt.
1975— Prime Minister Kim Jong Pil steps down and is replaced by Choi Kyu-hah. . . . New curbs are imposed on the media and opposition. . . . South Korea purchases nuclear generating plant from Canada.
1976— KCIA director Shin Jik Soo is fired as KCIA agents in Washington, D.C., and New York defect; "Koreagate" investigations intensify in Washington.
1977— Total of 2,123 prisoners are freed, including 17 political dissidents. . . . U.S. government announces decision to withdraw U.S. ground forces from South Korea within four or five years. . . . President Carter stresses deep concern over human rights problem in South Korea.
1978— President Park is reelected for a fourth six-

year term; running unopposed, he receives 2,577 votes in the National Conference for Unification, the country's electoral college.

1979— President Park is assassinated by a group led by Kim Jae Kyu, head of the Korean Central Intelligence Agency; Prime Minister Choi Kyu-hah is named interim president; Choi is elevated as South Korea's sixth president, with Shin Hyon Hwack as prime minister. The new government releases political detainees and promises social and political reforms. . . . The United States opts for a slow pullout from South Korea and halts further troop withdrawals. . . . Army rebels led by Chun Doo-Hwan, head of the Army Security Command, arrest Gen. Chung Seung Hwa and 16 other senior officers, including seven generals, for their alleged role in the assassination of President Park.

1980— Prime Minister Shin is replaced by Park Choon Hoon; President Choi steps down and Chun Doo Hwan is elected president; Chun orders mass purges in which over 8,000 public servants, politicians and journalists are dismissed. . . . The won is devalued to avert impending collapse of the economy. . . . A new Constitution is approved in national referendum, some of its basic provisions limiting presidential powers and abolishing existing political parties. . . . Opposition leader Kim Dae Jung is sentenced to death despite international pleas for leniency.

1981— Chun is elected president and the ruling Democratic Justice Party wins majority in National Assembly. . . . Martial law is lifted. . . . Korean Central Intelligence Agency is renamed Agency for National Security Planning (ANSP). . . . Amnesty is granted to 1,000 dissidents.

1982— Korea protests Japanese textbooks that ignore Japanese oppressive rule in Korea before 1945. . . . United States and Korea celebrate 100th anniversary of signing of first accord between them.

1983— South Korean airliner is shot down over Soviet territory after its intrusion into Soviet airspace. . . . Several cabinet members are killed during bomb blast in Rangoon during state visit by Chun. . . . North Korea is implicated in this act of terrorism. . . . Pope John Paul II visits Korea and pleads for human rights. . . . President Reagan visits Korea.

1984— Chun visits Japan and receives apology from Emperor Hirohito for Japan's harsh rule on the Korean Peninsula before the end of World War II.

1985— In National Assembly elections the official Democratic Justice Party (DJP) gains 148 seats, but the opposition New Korea Democratic Party is runner-up and the Democratic Korea Party is third, with 67 and 35 seats, respectively. . . . Opposition leader Kim returns from exile. . . . In reorganization, hardliners are named to the DJP leadership.

1985— Several of the opposition defect from the ruling party and join the NKDP whose parlimentary seats grew to 102. The NKDP ranks are diminished as 12 of its deputies form their own party—the People's Democratic Party.

1986— Violent student demonstrations on several university campuses lead to arrests of over 1,000 in Seoul. . . . Moves are made to create direct presidential elections.

1987— A new opposition party is formed—the Reunification Democratic Party (RDP)—under the leadership of Kim Young-Sam; its main agenda was reunification with North Korea. . . . Pres. Chong collapses to pressures from the opposition, student protest and members of his own party to begin work on a new constitution. A new Constitution is promulgated. Presidential elections are won by Roh Tae-Woo of the DJP and he is inaugurated in February.

1988— The Olympic Games are held in Seoul without serious incident despite large-scale student protests. . . . The DJP fails in general elections to win a majority of parliamentary seats.

1989— Large-scale student protests continue over the slow pace of reunification talks. Seven policemen are killed during student riots at Dongeui University.

1990— The ruling DJP merges with the RDP and the NDRP forming the new Democratic Liberal Party (DLP) gaining two thirds of the National Assembly.

BIBLIOGRAPHY

BOOKS & FILMS

Adleman, Irma, and Sherman Robinson. *Income Distribution Policies in Developing Countries: A Case Study of Korea.* Stanford, Calif., 1976.

Bahl, Roy. *Public Finance During the Korean Modernization Process.* Cambridge, Mass., 1985.

Baldwin, Frank. *Without Parallel: The American-Korean Relationship Since 1945.* New York, 1974.

Barnds, William J. *The Two Koreas in East Asian Affairs.* New York, 1976.

Bartz, Patricia M. *South Korea: A Descriptive Geography.* New York, 1972.

Bird, Isabella L. *Korea and Her Neighbors.* Rutland, Vt., 1985.

Boettcher, Robert, and Gordon L. Freedman. *Gifts of Deceit: Sun Myung Moon, Tongsun Park and the Korean Scandal.* New York, 1980.

Brandt, Vincent S. *A Korean Village Between Farm and Sea.* Cambridge, Mass., 1971.

Buss, Claude A. *The United States and the Republic of Korea.* Stanford, Calif., 1982.

Center for Korean Studies. *Korean Studies.* Honolulu, Hawaii, 1977.

Choi, Bong-youn. *A History of the Korean Reunification Movement.* Berkeley, Calif., 1984.

Choi, Woonsang. *Korea: A Chronology and Factbook.* Dobbs Ferry, N.Y., 1983.

———. *Korea: A History.* Tokyo, 1971.

Chung, Kyung Cho. *Korea: The Third Republic.* New York, 1971.

Cole, David C., and Princeton N. Lyman. *Korean Development: The Interplay of Politics and Economics.* Cambridge, Mass., 1971.

———. *The Korean Economy: Issues of Development.* Berkeley, Calif., 1979.

——— and Yung C. Park. *Financial Development in Korea, 1945–78.* Cambridge, Mass., 1983.

Covell, Jon C. *Korea's Cultural Roots.* Union City, Calif., 1984.

Cumings, Bruce. *Child of Conflict: The Korean American Relationship, 1945–53.* Seattle, Wash., 1983.

———. *The Two Koreas.* New York, 1984.

Curtis, Gerald L., and Han Sung-joo. *The U.S.-South Korean Alliance.* Lexington, Mass., 1983.

DeBary, Theodore, and Jahyun K. Haboush. *The Rise of Neo-Confucianism in Korea.* New York, 1985.

Euh, Yoon-Dae. *The Korean Banking System and Foreign Influence.* New York, 1990.

Fukuda, Tsuneari. *Future of Japan and the Korean Peninsula.* Elizabeth, N.J., 1979.

Gittings, John, and Mark Selden. *Korea, North and South: The Deepening Crisis.* New York, 1978.

Goulden, Joseph C. *Korea: The Untold Story.* New York, 1982.

Griffin, Trenholme J. *Korea: the Tiger Economy.* London, 1988.

Hamilton, Clive. *Capital Industrialization in Korea.* Boulder, Colo., 1985.

Han, Sung-joo. *The Failure of Democracy in South Korea.* Berkeley, Calif., 1974.

——— and Abraham M. Halpern. *The Future of the Korean Peninsula.* New York, 1977.

Han, Woo Keun. *The History of Korea.* Honolulu, Hawaii, 1972.

Hansen, Eric O. *Catholic Politics in China and Korea.* Maryknoll, N.Y., 1980.

Hasan, Parvez. *Korea: Policy Issues for Long-Term Development.* Baltimore, 1979.

Henderson, Gregory. *Korea: The Politics of the Vortex.* Cambridge, Mass., 1968.

Henthorn, William E. *A History of Korea.* New York, 1971.

Hinton, Harold C. *Korea Under New Leadership: The Fifth Republic.* New York, 1983.

Hong, Wontack. *Trade, Growth and Income Distribution: The Experience of the Republic of Korea.* Washington, D.C., 1981.

Hwang, In K. *The Neutralized Unification of Korea in Perspective.* Cambridge, Mass., 1980.

Jones, Leroy, and Il Sakong. *Government, Business and Entrepreneurship in Economic Development: The Korean Case.* Cambridge, Mass., 1979.

Kim, Chong Lim. *Political Participation in Korea: Democracy, Mobilization and Stability.* Santa Barbara, Calif., 1980.

——— and Seong-Tong Pai. *The Legislative Process in Korea.* Honolulu, Hawaii, 1981.

Kim, Chuk Kyo. *Industrial and Social Development Issues: Essays on the Korean Economy.* Honolulu, Hawaii, 1977.

———. *Planning Model and Macroeconomic Policy Issues: Essays on the Korean Economy.* Honolulu, Hawaii, 1977.

Kim, Jai-hyup. *Garrison State in Prewar Japan and Postwar Korea: A Comparative Analysis of Military Politics.* Washington, D.C., 1978.

Kim, Joungwon A. *Divided Korea: The Politics of Development.* Cambridge, Mass., 1975.

Kim, Se Jin. *The Politics of Military Revolution in Korea.* Chapel Hill, N.C., 1971.

——— and Cho Chang-hyun. *Government and Politics of Korea.* Silver Spring, Md., 1972.

Kim, Youn Soo. *Korea and Germany: The Status and Future Prospects of Divided Nations.* New York, 1979.

———. *Korean Annual.* New York, annual.

———. *Korean Directory.* New York, annual.

Kim, Young C. *Major Powers and Korea.* Silver Spring, Md., 1974.

Kim, Younok, and Han Sung-loo. *The Foreign Policy of the Republic of Korea.* New York, 1984.

Koh, Byung C. *The Foreign Policy Systems of North and South Korea.* Berkeley, Calif., 1984.

Korea. Color film, 25 min. Canadian Broadcasting Corp.

Korea: The First Twenty Years. Color film, 20 min. Producer: N.A.

Korea: The Long Road to Peace. B&W film, 27 min. March of Time.

Korea Story. B&W film, 20 min. Producer: N.A.

Korea: 38th Parallel. B&W film, 20 min. Films, Inc.

Korean Backgrounds. B&W film, 17 min. International Film Bureau.

Korean Development Institute. *Long-Term Prospects for Economic and Social Development, 1977–91.* Honolulu, Hawaii, 1979.

Korean People. Color film, 11 min. International Film Bureau.

Kuznets, Paul W. *Economic Growth and Structure in Republic of Korea.* Cambridge, Mass., 1980.

Kwak, Tae-hwan. *The Two Koreas in World Politics.* Boulder, Colo., 1984.

——— and John Chay. *The U.S.-Korean Relations. 1882–1982.* Boulder, Colo., 1983.

Lee, Chong-sik. *Japan and Korea: The Political Dimension.* Stanford, Calif., 1985.

Lee, Ki-baik. *A New History of Korea.* Cambridge, Mass., 1984.

Lim, Youngil. *Government Policy and Private Enterprise: Korean Experience in Industrialization.* Berkeley, Calif., 1981.

McCann, David R. *Studies on Korea in Transition.* Manoa, Hawaii, 1979.

Mason, Edward S. *The Economic and Social Modernization of the Republic of Korea.* Cambridge, Mass., 1980.

Matray, James I. *The Reluctant Crusade: American Foreign Policy in Korea, 1941–50.* Honolulu, Hawaii, 1985.

Moscowitz, Carl. *From Patron to Partner: The Development of U.S.-Korean Business and Trade Relations.* Lexington, Mass., 1984.

Nahm, Andrew C. *A Panorama of Five Thousand Years of Korean History.* Union City, Calif., 1984.

Paige, Glenn D. *The Korean Decision.* New York, 1974.

Pak, Chi-young. *Political Opposition in Korea, 1945–60.* Honolulu, Hawaii, 1980.

Palais, James B. *Policies and Politics in Traditional Korea.* Cambridge, Mass., 1975.

Park, Jae Kyu, and Jusuf Wanandi. *Korea and Indonesia in the Year 2000.* Boulder, Colo., 1985.

Park, Sung-jo. *Economic Development and Social Change in Korea.* New York, 1982.

Park, W. H., and J. L. Enos. *The Adoption and Diffusion of Imported Technology: The Case of Korea.* London, 1985.

Pearson, Roger. *Korea in the World Today.* Washington, D.C., 1976.

Reconstruction of Korea. B&W film, 25 min. National Film Production Center.

Sang, Chul Suhgro. *Growth and Structural Changes in the Korean Economy, 1910–40.* Cambridge, Mass., 1978.

Sohn, Hak-Kyu. *Authoritarianism and Opposition in South Korea.* New York, 1989.

Steinberg, David I. *South Korea Profile.* Boulder, Colo., 1981.

Stuek, William W., Jr. *The Road to Confrontation: American Policy Toward China and Korea, 1947–68.* Durham, N.C., 1981.

Suh, Dae-sook, and Chae Jin-lee. *Political Leadership in Korea.* Seattle, Wash., 1975.

Sunoo, Harold H. *America's Dilemma in Asia: The Case of South Korea.* Chicago, 1979.

UNESCO. *Cultural Policy in the Republic of Korea.* Paris, 1977.

Wade, L. L., and B. S. Kim. *The Economic Development of South Korea: The Political Economy of Success.* New York, 1978.

Weinstein, Franklin B., and Fuji Kamiya. *The Security of Korea: U.S. and Japanese Perspectives on the 1980s.* Boulder, Colo., 1980.

Westphal, Larry E., and Young W. Rice. *Korean Industrial Competence: Where It Came From.* Washington, D.C., 1981.

Wilson Center. *Reflections on a Century of United States-Korean Relations.* Washington, D.C., 1983.

World Bank. *Korea: Problems and Issues in a Rapidly Growing Economy.* Baltimore, 1976.

Woronoff, Jon. *Korea's Economy: Man-made Miracle.* Seoul, 1984.

Wright, Edward R. *Korean Politics in Transition.* Seattle, Wash., 1975.

Yi, Kyu-tae. *Modern Transformation of Korea.* New York, 1970.

Young, Whan Kihl. *Policies and Politics in Divided Korea: Regimes in Contest, 1945–83.* Boulder, Colo., 1983.

Yung, Whee Rhee. *Korea's Competitive Edge: Managing Entry into World Markets.* Baltimore, 1984.

Yusuf, Shahid, and Kyle Peters. *Capital Accumulation and Economic Growth: The Korean Paradigm.* Washington, D.C., 1985.

OFFICIAL PUBLICATIONS

Bank of Korea. *Economic Statistics Yearbook.*

———. *Monthly Economic Statistics.*

Economic Planning Board. *Monthly Statistics of Korea.*

Finance Ministry. *Monthly Treasury Bulletin* (Korean).

———. *Settlement of Government Accounts on Revenues and Expenditures* (Korean).

———. *Settlement of Government Debt* (Korean).

———. *Settlement of Government Funds* (Korean).

———. *Summary of Financial Statistics.*

Home Affairs Ministry. *Financial Abstract of Local Government.*

KUWAIT

BASIC FACT SHEET

OFFICIAL NAME: State of Kuwait (Dawlat al-Kuwayt)

ABBREVIATION: KU

CAPITAL: Kuwait City

HEAD OF STATE: Sovereign (Emir) Sheikh Jabir al-Ahmad Al Sabah (from 1978)

HEAD OF GOVERNMENT: Prime Minister Saad al-Abdallah al-Salim Al Sabah (from 1978)

NATURE OF GOVERNMENT: Constitutional hereditary emirate

POPULATION: 2,123,711 (1990)

AREA: 17,818 sq. km. (6,880 sq. mi.)

ETHNIC MAJORITY: Arab

LANGUAGE: Arabic

RELIGION: Sunni Islam

UNIT OF CURRENCY: Kuwaiti dinar

NATIONAL FLAG: Three horizontal green, red and white stripes with a black trapezium based on the hoist. The trapezium's shorter base is equal to the width of the white stripe.

NATIONAL EMBLEM: A circular badge on which a dhow, a white-sailed craft, appears on a blue-and-white sea against a blue sky and white clouds. At the crest appears the name "Dawlat al-Kuwayt" in Arabic and at the base appears a brown falcon, under which the Kuwaiti shield is shown in black, red, white and green.

NATIONAL ANTHEM: Unnamed melody only; no words

NATIONAL HOLIDAYS: February 25 (National Day); January 1 (New Year's Day); also variable Islamic festivals and Muslim New Year's Day

NATIONAL CALENDAR: Islamic calendar based on the Hegira

PHYSICAL QUALITY OF LIFE INDEX: 84

DATE OF INDEPENDENCE: June 19, 1961

DATE OF CONSTITUTION: November 12, 1962

WEIGHTS & MEASURES: Metric

GEOGRAPHICAL FEATURES

Kuwait, in the northeastern corner of the Arabian Peninsula at the western head of the Persian Gulf, is roughly rectangular in shape, extending 205 km. (127 mi.) southeast to northwest and 176 km. (109 mi.) northeast to southwest. Outlying islands include Bubiyan, Maskan, Auha, al-Warbah, al-Kubr, Umm al-Maradim, Umm al-Nami, Qaru, al-Sagirah and Failaka, of which only the last is inhabited. The total land area, estimated at 17,818 sq. km. (6,880 sq. mi.), includes the Kuwaiti section of the Neutral Zone (5,700 sq. km.; 2,201 sq. mi.) jointly owned by Kuwait and Saudi Arabia from 1922 to 1966. The length of the coastline excluding the islands is 212 km. (132 mi.).

The borders of Kuwait have never been precisely surveyed, but their length is estimated at 420 km. (261 mi.), of which the border with Saudi Arabia is 163 km. (101 mi.) long and the border with Iraq 257 km. (160 mi.) long.

The Neutral Zone was established with Saudi Arabia in the Treaty of Uqair in 1922. The zone was officially demarcated in 1969, although the two countries share oil revenues from the zone. Kuwait has had border disputes with Iraq since independence. In 1990 Iraq invaded and annexed Kuwait, which it claims is Iraqi territory. Kuwait was liberated following the Persian Gulf War in 1991.

The capital is Kuwait City, with a 1985 population of 44,335 and a suburban population greater than that of the city itself. The other principal urban centers are: Hawalli (145,126), Salmiya (153,369), Abraq Kheetan (45,120) and Farawiya (45,120). The town of Ahmadi is the headquarters of the Kuwait Oil Company. The old city of Kuwait has been demolished; only its main gate survives.

The terrain is an almost flat desert except for the Jal az Zor scarp to the west of Kuwait Bay. The central part of the country is separated from the narrow coastal plain by the 120-m. (394-ft.)-high Ahmadi Ridge, which runs north to south.

There are no streams or rivers in the country.

CLIMATE & WEATHER

Kuwait has an arid, subtropical climate. Summer, which lasts from May to October, is extremely hot, with temperatures ranging from 43°C (113°F) to 54°C (130°F). Winter, lasting from November to April, is generally pleasant, with night temperatures in December and January occasionally touching the freezing point. Annual rainfall varies between 30 mm. (1 in.) and 220 mm. (9 in.), mainly between November and April. Sand- and duststorms are frequent in the summer, when the *shamal*, a strong northeasterly wind, blows from the Gulf.

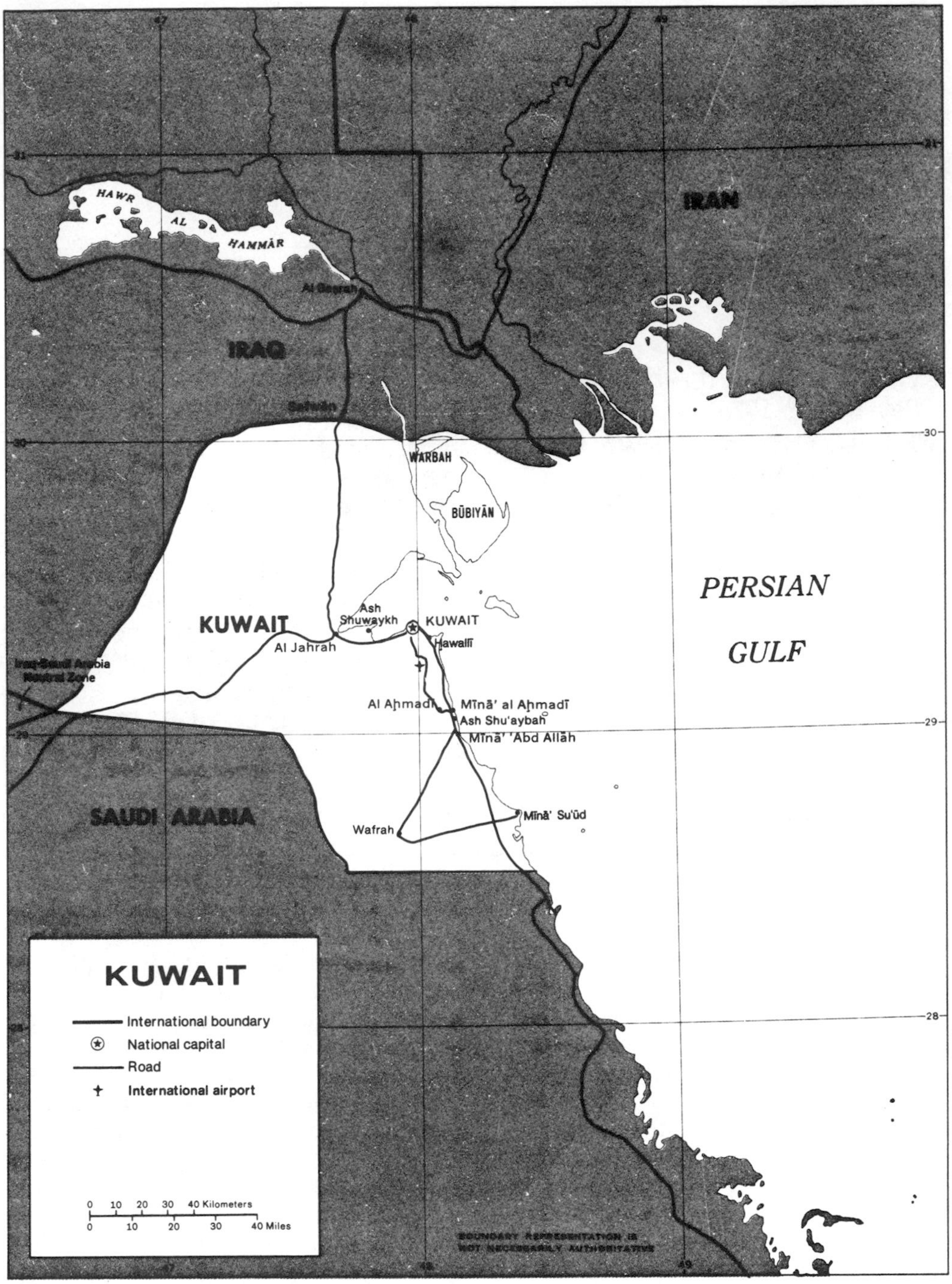

IRAN

HAWR AL HAMMĀR

Al Basrah

IRAQ

Safwān

WARBAH

BŪBIYĀN

PERSIAN GULF

KUWAIT

Ash Shuwaykh

KUWAIT

Al Jahrah

Hawallī

Iraq-Saudi Arabia Neutral Zone

Al Aḥmadī

Mīnā' al Aḥmadī

Ash Shu'aybah

Mīnā' 'Abd Allāh

SAUDI ARABIA

Wafrah

Mīnā' Su'ūd

30

29

28

BOUNDARY REPRESENTATION IS NOT NECESSARILY AUTHORITATIVE

KUWAIT

- International boundary
- ⊛ National capital
- Road
- ✝ International airport

0 10 20 30 40 Kilometers

0 10 20 30 40 Miles

POPULATION

The population of Kuwait in July 1990 was 2,123,711, but only 28% were ethnic Kuwaitis. Kuwait's population has increased very rapidly in recent years. Between 1950 and 1985 the population increased by more than 1,230%. Much of this growth is the result of immigration, but the country also has one of the highest natural increase rates in the world.

DEMOGRAPHIC INDICATORS

Population (million): 2.123 (1990)
Year of last census: 1985
Sex distribution (% at last census): males, 56.9; females, 43.1
Population estimates and projections (000)

1950: 145	1980: 1,370	2000: 2,841
1960: 292	1990: 2,123	2010: 3,516
1970: 748		

Age profile (% at last census)

0–14: 36.8	30–44: 24.1	60–74: 1.8
15–29: 28.3	45–59: 8.6	75 and over: 0.4

Median age (yrs.): 20.7 (1985)
Youth population (% age 15–24): 17.9 (1985); 18.6 (2000)
Total dependency ratio: 70.4 (1985)
Annual growth rate (%)

1950–55: 5.37	1975–80: 6.24	2000–2005: 2.30
1955–60: 6.67	1980–85: 4.36	2005–2010: 2.01
1960–65: 10.53	1985–90: 4.02	2010–2015: 1.76
1965–70: 9.17	1990–1995: 3.08	2015–2020: 1.55
1970–75: 6.04	1995–2000: 2.64	2020–2025: 1.32

Hypothetical size of stationary population (millions): 5
Assumed year of reaching net reproduction rate of 1: 2010
Urban population (000): 1,602 (1985)
Urban population (%): 95 (1988); 78 (1965)
Annual urban population growth rate (%, 1985–90): 4.42
Annual rural population growth rate (%, 1985–90): −3.18
Percentage of urban population in largest city: 30 (1980)
Number of cities of population over 500,000: 0 (1980)
Population density per sq. km. (per sq. mi.): 120.3 (311.5) (latest)

VITAL STATISTICS

Crude birth rate (/1,000): 33 (1990); 47 (1965)
Crude death rate (/1,000): 21 (1990); 8 (1965)
Infant mortality rate (/1,000 live births): 15 (1990)
Maternal mortality rate (/100,000 live births): 2.0 (1986–87)
Life expectancy (yrs.) at birth: males, 72; females, 76 (1990)
Gross reproduction rate (/woman) (1980–85): 2.55
Total fertility rate (/woman): 3.7 (1990)
Rate of natural increase (/1,000): 24.8 (1988)
Marriage rate (/1,000): 5.3 (1985)
Average household size: 7.4 (latest)

About 400,000 people fled during the Iraqi occupation of 1990–91. During the exile, the government paid refugee families an average monthly stipend of $1,700. The payments were ended in May 1991 to encourage return. But non-Kuwaiti refugees, including about 150,000 Palestinians, were barred from re-entry.

The distribution of the sexes is unequal as a result of the high preponderance of males among the immigrant population. The high proportion of immigrants drives up the median age of the populace.

The population is overwhelmingly urban, as areas outside towns and cities are virtually uninhabitable. The urban component of the population is estimated at 94%; the annual rate of urban growth during 1985–90 was 4.42%. There are five urban centers with over 44,000 population.

Since the 1950s, the economic growth of Kuwait has been paralleled by an explosive growth in the immigrant population, in response to the demand for skilled and unskilled labor. Kuwait is perhaps the only country in the world where immigrants and resident aliens form the majority of the population. In 1985 non-Kuwaitis constituted 60% of the population, but they formed 80% of the labor force. The large expatriate population has caused concern about social stability. In recent years the government expelled thousands of non-Kuwaitis annually and tightened restrictions on new and existing work permits. Following the Iraqi occupation of 1990–91, the government instituted harsh measures for Palestinians accused of collaborating with the invaders.

STATUS OF WOMEN INDICATORS

Number of women (000): 873 (1985)
Women of childbearing age (15–49) (% of pop.): 50 (1988)
Women's literacy rate (%): 69.6 (1988)
Women in labor force (%): 14.2 (1988)
Total fertility rate (/woman): 3.7 (1990)
Women in national legislatures (%): 0 (1984)

Kuwaiti women are allotted a subordinate role by statute and practice. Denied the vote, women also are limited by tradition from freely choosing their place in society, though less so than in some other Islamic countries. Nevertheless, some Kuwaiti women are outspoken in their demands for a broader role in society. In contrast to the practice in some neighboring countries, a Kuwaiti woman is permitted to drive a car, may wear Western dress in public and has legal access to higher education inside and outside the country. Although women have yet to join the work force in large numbers, they are able to compete for government and corporate employment and have the right to litigate against men (for example, in child custody suits). Women have occupied positions primarily in health care, education and domestic service. Many women have accumulated substantial personal wealth. However, the government has restricted women from being assigned abroad in Kuwait's diplomatic service. Some prominent, educated women also are wary of current fundamentalist trends, which they fear may lead the government to restrict their freedoms as a price for fundamentalist restraint on other issues.

Kuwait has no official birth control policy or programs, and large families are encouraged.

ETHNIC COMPOSITION

The majority of indigenous Kuwaitis are descendants of Arabs of the Anaiza tribe, who had immigrated from Nejd in Saudi Arabia in the 18th century. Among the early settlers was the al-Sabah family, which became the ruling dynasty.

The traditional Kuwaiti minorities are blacks, descendants of slaves; and Iranians, who have their own quarter in Kuwait City.

The oil boom of the 1950s and 1960s brought waves of new immigrants into the country. By 1970 resident aliens constituted more than half of the population. In the wake of the Iraqi invasion of Kuwait in August 1990, hundreds of thousands of expatriate workers fled the country. Prior to the war, the major ethnic groups among the aliens were: Jordanians, Palestinians, Iranians, Iraqis, Egyptians, Syrians, Lebanese, Indians, Pakistanis, Omanis and Saudi Arabians. Over 79% of aliens were economically active, and they dominated certain professions. Palestinians and Egyptians were prominent in medicine and education and Syrians and Lebanese in industry and trade. Iraqis, Omanis and Iranians were mostly unskilled laborers. South Asians were often employed as domestics. The major social distinction in Kuwait is between Kuwaiti nationals, who comprise only 40% of the population, and expatriates. Ownership of commercial establishments (above 49%), real estate and shares on the local stock market (the principal sources of private wealth in this capitalist economy) are open to Kuwaitis only. The rise in deportations and the tightening of regulations governing work permits in the 1980s made many immigrants insecure, and they began looking for employment outside Kuwait. Expatriate workers often earned the same base pay as Kuwaitis but received fewer fringe benefits. Benefits restricted to Kuwaiti citizens included higher government salaries; additional government stipends and social allowances; and, in general, retirement pensions. Resident expatriates were entitled to some medical benefits and to elementary and secondary schooling (but not kindergarten) for their children in the public schools. Kuwaitis were given preference for admission to Kuwait University. Many temporary "guest workers" came to Kuwait without their families and lived in camps or crowded apartments. All non-Kuwaitis working in Kuwait must have the sponsorship of a Kuwaiti citizen. Kuwait does not extend permanent residence to its expatriate population. Thus employers have the power to restrict job mobility and the continued residence in Kuwait of their expatriate employees. Because Kuwaiti sponsors are legally responsible for their employees' actions, many expatriates (including some government employees, such as teachers) are coerced by their employers into surrendering their travel documents, thus preventing them from leaving the country without the employer's consent. Those employed by government agencies are given residence visas that require an exit permit or "no objection" letter to leave the country. Non-Kuwaitis convicted of crimes are routinely deported after serving their sentences. Illegal entrants to Kuwait normally are returned to their home countries; exceptions have been made for those, mostly Iranians and Afghans, who are considered by the government to be legitimate refugees and have been permitted to remain in Kuwait or sent to third countries. Most of Kuwait's Palestinian population has Lebanese or Jordanian travel documents. Non-Kuwaitis are regarded as transients and are not encouraged to acquire citizenship. Under the naturalization decrees of 1959 and 1960, citizenship is limited to residents in Kuwait prior to 1920 and their descendants in the male line. Citizenship may be acquired by Arabs after eight years of continuous residence and by others after 30 years of continuous residence. Aliens may not join unions for the first five years.

The foreign community includes a dwindling number of British subjects in administrative positions in government and industry. Prejudice against foreigners was less pronounced in Kuwait than in neighboring Iraq or Saudi Arabia.

Much of that changed with the war of 1990–91. The estimated 400,000 Palestinians living in Kuwait before the Iraqi invasion became particular targets of vengeful citizens. Although probably only a small number of unemployed Palestinian youths worked with the Iraqis, the Palestianian Liberation Organization's support of Saddam Hussein created the impression of general Palestinian support for the invaders. After liberation in late February 1991, troops or gangs of Kuwaitis swept through Palestinian neighborhoods in the capital, beating, torturing and shooting suspected collaborators. As many as 40 people were killed in such raids.

LANGUAGES

Arabic is the official language of the country. English is the second language taught in the schools and is the medium of commercial communication.

RELIGIONS

Islam is the official religion of the emirate. Muslims, both Shi'a and Sunni, make up 85% of the population and Christians, Hindus, Parsis and other creeds constitute the other 15%. The exact proportions of Shi'as and Sunnis have not been determined, but Sunnis predominate.

The al-Sabah dynasty has been relatively tolerant of other faiths. Public Christian worship is permitted. The small Jewish community, numbering about 300 in the 1950s, has almost vanished. The construction of Hindu, Sikh, or Buddhist temples is prohibited. Proselytizing of Muslims by non-Muslims is prohibited. In 1986, the National Assembly approved legislation barring citizenship to non-Muslim applicants.

HISTORICAL BACKGROUND

Kuwait has never been under formal colonial rule. But from 1899 until 1961 it was a British protectorate.

Sheikh Amed, who ruled Kuwait from 1921 to 1950, was responsible for the development of the Kuwaiti oil industry. He was succeeded by his cousin, Sheikh Abdallah al-Salim al-Sabah, who, using petroleum revenues, developed an extensive welfare system for his people.

Kuwait achieved full independence in June 1961, when the United Kingdom terminated the 1899 treaty. The ruler assumed the title of emir. A National Assembly replaced the Constituent Assembly upon inauguration of the Constitution in 1962. The emir died in 1965 and was succeeded by the prime minister and heir apparent Sheikh Sabah al-Salem Al Sabah. His cousin, Sheikh Jaber al-Ahmed Al Sabah, was named prime minister and heir apparent.

The emir dissolved the National Assembly in 1976 on the grounds that it was acting against the state's interest by criticizing the government. He also suspended the constitutional provision that elections be held within two months and instituted severe restrictions on the press. Constitutional government returned in 1981 with elections for the National Assembly. However, following a series of confrontations over fiscal and internal security issues, Emir Saad al-Abdallah al-Salim Al Sabah, who had succeeded in 1978, dissolved the Assembly in 1986. As had his predecessor, the emir postponed elections and imposed strict press controls. The emir has since ruled by decree.

The war with Iraq of 1990–91 was an important juncture in Kuwait's modern history in several ways. It demonstrated the nation's military weakness and drew it into a close alliance with major Western powers, especially the United States. Iraq's destruction of Kuwait's petroleum industry could significantly impair the economy for years. Finally, in the aftermath of liberation, the emirate confronted serious questions about democracy and the presence of large numbers of non-Kuwaitis.

In late July 1990, before a meeting of the Organization of Petroleum Exporting Countries, Iraq made several demands of and threats against Kuwait. Iraq called for a waiver of the large debt to Kuwait accumulated during the Iranian war and accused the emirate of violating the common border to steal Iraqi oil reserves. Saddam Hussein also threatened to take military action against countries that ignored OPEC quotas and placed two armored divisions on the border with Kuwait. An OPEC meeting on July 25 appeared to calm the situation. Prices were raised $3 a barrel to $21, and Kuwait agreed to limit production. The two nations were also talking about disputed territory, mostly the islands of Bubiyan and Warbah.

But the border negotiations broke off August 1, and the next day Iraq invaded and easily conquered the emirate. Kuwait's army of 20,000 troops and 275 tanks was no match for Iraq's invading force of 100,000. Defending soldiers offered some resistance at the emir's palace, after the ruler had fled to Saudi Arabia by helicopter. Fighting also occurred around military barracks outside the capital. Perhaps 200 Kuwaitis were killed in the assault. Little evidence supported Hussein's claim that Iraq invaded to support domestic anti-emir insurgents.

On August 8, Hussein announced the annexation of Kuwait as Iraq's 19th province, and soon renamed the capital Kadhima, the city's name under the Ottoman Empire. The Iraqi occupation was brutal, especially after Ali Hassan Majid, cousin of Hussein, was made military governor in mid-September. Majid had organized the repression of Kurdistan in 1988. He gave orders to crush all Kuwaiti resistance, partly due to frustration over the refusal of the conquered to return to work and join a revolutionary government under Iraq.

The occupier's policy of killing six Kuwaitis for each Iraqi slain led to diminished resistance. But defiant groups continued sporadic night hit-and-run raids against Iraqi installations. These groups received weapons smuggled from Saudi Arabia. They also probably got help from the American Central Intelligence Agency. The Iraqis engaged in looting, torture and summary executions, and, for instance, killed and ate edible animals at the national zoo. About 7,000 Kuwaitis were killed and 17,000 detained during the occupation.

The Kuwaiti government-in-exile operated from a hotel in the western Saudi city of Taif. Although the emir was present, most affairs were handled by Crown Prince, Premier Sheik Saad al-Abdallah al-Sabah. The ruler was reportedly emotionally distraught over the invasion and occupation. The government in September 1990 pledged $5 billion to aid U.S. military operations and nations affected economically by the crisis. Kuwait's ambassador to the United States, Saud Masir Al Sabah, who had called for American help on the day of the invasion, was a key figure throughout the ordeal.

Led by the United States, under the aegis of the United Nations, the international community responded vigorously to the Iraqi invasion. U.N. sanctions declared the annexation of Kuwait null and void, demanded Iraqi withdrawal and eventually authorized the use of force to evict the occupiers. By January 1991, the U.S.-led alliance had more than 500,000 troops in the region.

In a two-stage campaign from mid-January to late February 1991, the Allies defeated and forced the Iraqis to leave the emirate. The first part was a massive air war against installations and troops in Kuwait and southern Iraq. Some Kuwaiti pilots participated in these bombing missions. The second stage was a ground campaign of February 24–28. As part of the Allied invasion force, Kuwaiti soldiers led the march into the capital February 27, although resistance forces claimed to control the city a day earlier.

Liberation, though, was a mixed blessing. Early estimates of the cost of reconstructing the emirate were $100 billion. Much of Kuwait City was in ruins, with many large buildings set afire just before the Iraqi retreat. Damage to the nation's petroleum industry was extensive. Of 1,080 oil wells, Iraq rendered more than 800 completely inoperable, including 535 fractured or set ablaze with explosives. Hundreds of wells were still burning months after the Iraqi departure. Also destroyed were half of the petroleum gathering centers and all above-ground oil storage facilities.

Internally, the major post-liberation questions confronting Kuwait were how to handle the expatriate issue and to what degree the nation's political system might be democratized. Tensions existed between resistance fighters and those who had taken refuge abroad during occupation. The energized opposition demanded elections for a new Parliament and a free press, but as of June 1991 the ruling Sabah family seemed to be moving slowly, if at all, on these fronts.

Many Kuwaitis accused foreigners, especially Palestinians, of siding with the occupying Iraqis. Vigilantes tortured and killed suspected collaborators, and in May–June special martial law courts convicted and sentenced many more. Among other things, these developments raised questions about the emirate's heavy reliance on non-nationals in its labor pool.

CONSTITUTION & GOVERNMENT

The Constitution of 1962 established a constitutional monarchy based on Arab traditions. Islam is declared to be the religion of the state and Islamic law the source of legislation. The Constitution also contains a bill of rights.

Executive power is vested in the emir, the head of state who also is the supreme commander of the armed forces, with enabling powers to declare "defensive war" ("offensive war" is prohibited by the Constitution). Succession to the emirate is confined to the heirs of Sheikh Mubarak al-Sabah. The emir exercises his executive powers through the Council of Ministers, headed by the prime minister, the chief of the government who is appointed by the emir after traditional consultations. Ministers, appointed on the recommendations of the prime minister, need not be members of the National Assembly, although all ministers assume ex officio membership in the Assembly for the duration of the office. The Assembly may pass a vote of no confidence in a minister, in which case he must resign, but a vote of no confidence in the prime minister is not permitted.

Many members of the cabinet, including the prime minister and deputy prime minister, are princes of the al-Sabah royal family.

The country is divided into 25 electoral districts. Voters must be literate, over 21, and may not be members of the armed forces. In 1981, the voting community comprised only 6.4% of the total population. Women are not allowed to vote or hold office.

Kuwait has a very stable government. Power is closely held in the Sabah family, and little or no opposition has been allowed to develop.

The upheaval of the war with Iraq severely tested Kuwait's system of government and politics, but by June 1991 the Sabah family and the traditional structure had both proven durable. During the occupation of 1990-91, the government conducted affairs at a hotel in Taif, a city in western Saudi Arabia. Emotionally affected by the invasion, the emir was largely overshadowed in this period by Crown Prince Saad. Exiled Kuwaiti opposition leaders won a pledge from Saad in late 1990 to abide by the 1962 Constitution, including an independent Parliament, once the occupation was ended.

On February 26, 1991, the day resistance leaders claimed control of Kuwait City, the emir declared martial law for three months, and named the crown prince as military governor. Saad returned to the capital on March 4, and the cabinet reassembled for its first post-occupation meeting. Saad pledged reforms, including internal democracy and possible recognition of Israel. On March 20, the crown prince and the entire cabinet resigned, partly because of public outrage over the government's inability to restore basic services.

Opposition leader Hamed al-Jouan was injured in an apparent assassination attempt February 28, fueling rumors that the Sabah family had a "hit list" of enemies. Nevertheless, a coalition of opposition leaders issued a set of demanded reforms on April 1. This cooperation among 100 top political and business figures was unprecedented in the weak history of the Kuwaiti opposition. The major points were a firm date for parliamentary elections, a free press, legalization of political parties and an independent judiciary.

In April the emir promised elections in 1992, and said he would consider giving the vote to women and naturalized Kuwaitis. But other officials ruled out political parties. A new 20-member cabinet named on April 20 included no opposition members. But there were 11 new faces. The al-Sabah family held five posts, down from seven in the prior cabinet, although the royal clan still held most important portfolios. Again, the crown prince was prime minister.

One of the key shifts was appointing Sheikh Ahmed Hamoud al-Jabir al-Sabah as interior minister. He replaced Sheikh Salim al-Sabah, who had been denounced for harsh responses to pro-democracy rallies. Salim was made deputy premier/defense minister, taking over from Sheikh Nawaf al-Ahmad al-Sabah, who was charged with incompetence for his handling of

GOVERNMENT LIST
(July/August 1991)

Emir	Sabah, JABIR al-Ahmad al-Jabir al-
Prime Minister	Sabah, Saad al-'Abdallah al-Salim al-
Deputy Prime Minister	Sabah, SALIM al-Sabah al-Salim al-
Minister of Awqaf & Islamic Affairs	Ma'ushurji, Muhammad Saqr al-
Minister of Commerce & Industry	Jarallah, 'Abdallah Hasan al-
Minister of Communications	Hayat, Habib Hasan Jawhar al-
Minister of Defense	Sabah, 'ALI al-Sabah al-Salim al-
Minister of Education	Badir, Sulayman Sa'dun al-
Minister of Electricity & Water	'Adasani, Ahmad Muhammad al-
Minister of Finance	Rudan, Nasir 'Abdallah al-
Minister of Foreign Affairs	Sabah, SALIM al-Sabah al-Salim al-
Minister of Higher Education	Shamlan, 'Ali 'Abdallah al-
Minister of Information (Acting)	Ya'qub, Badir Jasim al-
Minister of Interior	Sabah, AHMAD al-Hamud al-Jabir al-
Minister of Justice & Legal Affairs	Sammar, Ghazi Ubayd al-
Minister of Oil	Ruqba, Hamud 'Abdallah al-
Minister of Planning	Jasir, Ahmad 'Ali al-
Minister of Public Health	Fawzan, 'Abd al-Wahab Sulayman al-
Minister of Public Works	Qitami, 'Abdallah Yusif al-
Minister of Social Affairs & Labor	Sabah, NAWWAF al-Ahmad al-Jabir al-
Minister of State for Cabinet Affairs	'Uthman, Dhari 'Abdallah al-
Minister of State for Housing Affairs	'Asfur, Muhammad 'Abd al-Muhsin al-
Minister of State for Municipal Affairs	Shahin, Ibrahim Majid al-
Governor, Central Bank	Sabah, SALIM al'ABD AL-AZIZ al-

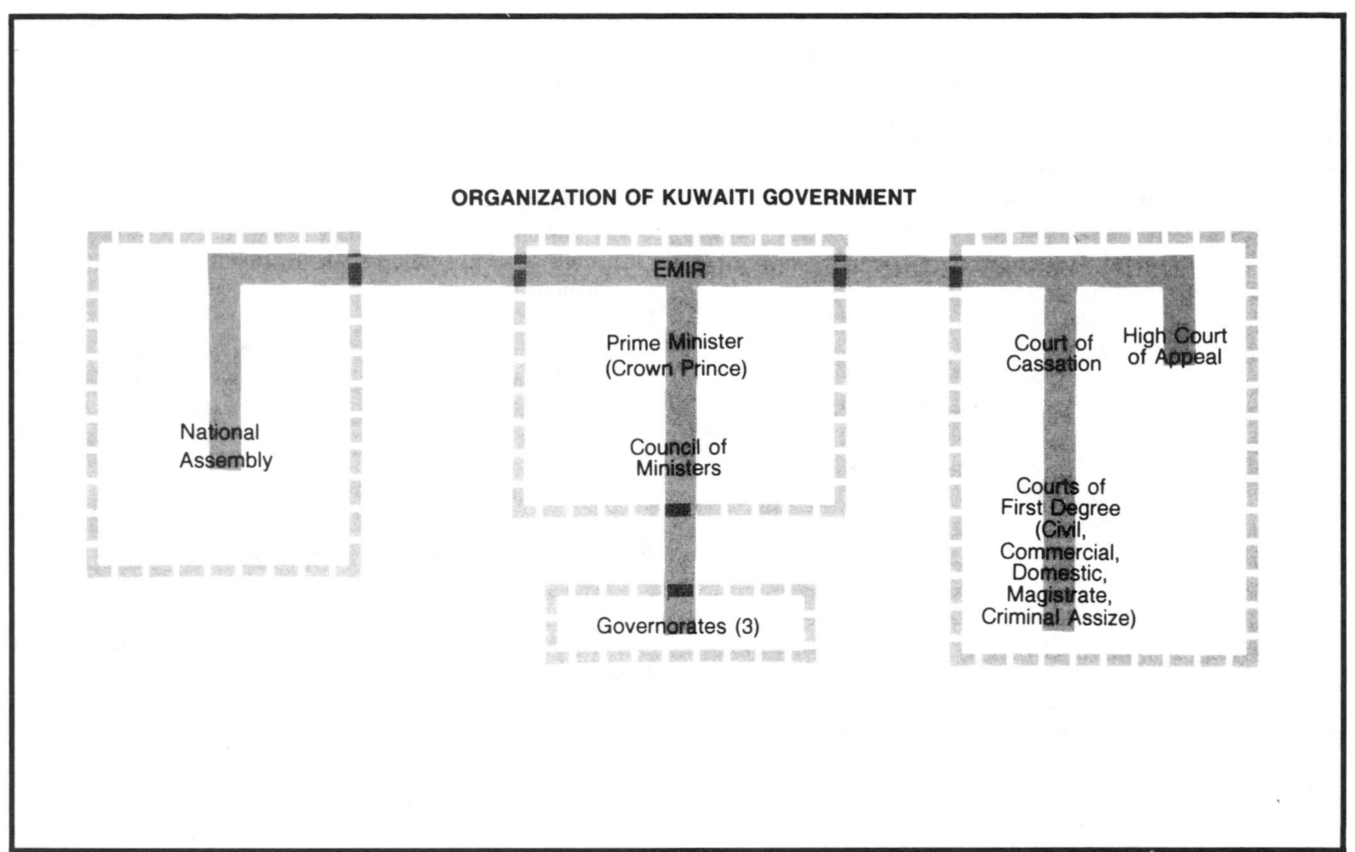

the prelude to the Iraqi invasion. The opposition denounced the new cabinet for leaving too much power in the hands of the Sabah clan.

In mid-May, the government began a series of trials of suspected collaborators. By appointing attorneys for defendants and opening the trials to the press and foreign observers, Kuwait tried to make the process seem fair. The emirate was criticized by human rights groups and foreign countries because the tribunals produced no evidence and refused to hear defense witnesses. Most of those tried were Palestinians, Jordanians and Iraqis.

In late June, the crown prince announced the commutation to life imprisonment of all 29 death sentences returned in the trials. The move seemed to reflect the government's sensitivity to widespread criticism abroad over the nature of the trials and other domestic developments since the end of the occupation.

FREEDOM & HUMAN RIGHTS

Until the 1990–91 Iraqi occupation, Kuwait's human rights situation had been stable. As a traditional emirate, it could afford to ignore political civil rights because of a number of unusual considerations: The oil wealth acted as a cushion against dissent, blunting tensions and rivalries; the majority of the population was expatriate, excluded from political power and depending on the good will of the government for continued residence; and the patriarchal system of Bedouin social life not merely assented to but also demanded an authoritarian government.

Although the government does not encourage torture, third-degree methods are employed by the police on occasion to extract confessions. Capital punishment by hanging is rarely sanctioned. Flogging is used, but with decreasing frequency. Arbitrary arrest most commonly occurs during spot checks or roadblocks of outdoor gatherings of expatriates to locate illegal immigrants. Expatriate troublemakers may be summarily expelled. Legally, a person may be held without charges for no more than four days. Thereafter, the suspect must either be released or turned over to a public prosecutor, who may authorize detention for up to an additional 21 days. Further detention may be authorized by a judge pending trial.

Kuwait's legal system is independent and provides for public trials, the right of appeal and representation by an attorney of one's choice. Secret trials are carried out by the State Security Court. There is no appeal of the court's decisions. Thirty-three people were convicted by the court in 1989 of plotting to overthrow the government. Warrants are required for searches unless the police are in actual pursuit of a suspect fleeing the scene of a crime or when the police are raiding a place where illegal liquor or narcotics are believed to be produced or sold.

Since 1986, the press has been subject to pre-publication censorship. All printed material must be approved by the government or rewritten, if not excised altogether. Under the Press Law, newspapers may be closed or suspended for violations of public morality or criticism of the ruling family or for any but the mildest comments on government policies and high-level officials. The most common grounds for suspensions are "spreading dissension" and "contradicting the national interest." Editors are criminally liable for attacking leaders of friendly Arab states and for inciting sectarian strife. Although foreign publications are available freely, they are subject to censorship and cannot clear customs without permission from the Ministry of the Interior. Censorship has become rigid since 1986. The State Security Court has sentenced citizens to prison for illegally printing politically oriented literature. Academic freedom is restricted by the same measures used to censor the press.

Any group of more than three people desiring to meet for public discussion (or to meet privately but issue a public statement) must receive explicit and prior permission from the Ministry of the Interior. *Diwaniyyas* (traditional gatherings) are exempt from this rule. The establishment of trade unions is officially permitted, but non-Kuwaitis are barred from membership for five years and may not hold union office.

Although the government restricted the political and civil rights of all residents, and particularly those of women and expatriates in the 1980s, it did not interfere drastically with the integrity of the individual. Kuwait's security apparatus was used primarily to maintain internal order. The role of Kuwait's security organizations increased substantially in 1984, particularly with regard to the noncitizen community. Conscious of being a minority in their own country, the Kuwaitis' sense of vulnerability was heightened by increased political turbulence in the region. Foreign-inspired terrorism (such as the December 1983 bombings of Kuwaiti installations and the American and French embassies and the hijacking of a Kuwaiti Airways flight to Iran in December 1984) and attempts by agents of foreign governments and organizations to subvert elements of the population led to tightened security measures and legal restrictions on public gatherings and dissemination of "subversive" literature. Increased attention to law and order also was viewed by some Kuwaitis as a means to protect their society against the threat they perceive to Kuwaiti moral and social values from the large foreign population. Since the December 1983 bombings, security organizations assiduously applied regulations governing the expatriate presence in Kuwait. Consequently, larger numbers of non-Kuwaitis were deported than in past years.

The long-term trends for human rights are subjects of much speculation in Kuwait. Internal socioeconomic changes brought on by sudden oil-related wealth, coupled in recent years with violent revolution in Iran, the Iran-Iraq War and the perceived failure of wealth to solve local and regional political problems have led to a growing demand by well-organized groups for stricter controls over public morality and political expression. A resurgent Islamic fundamentalist movement advocates adoption of a more stringent legal code based on Islamic Shari'a law.

Political participation is mainly through *diwaniyyas*, presided over by tribal leaders to whom any clan member may speak his mind freely, as well as through *wastas* (use of influential family connections to obtain favors or a more favorable hearing of a petition). Expatriates, who in 1980 outnumbered indigenous Kuwaitis by 67% to 33%, have no political rights of any kind.

In the aftermath of the Iraqi occupation of 1990–91, there was a period of repression. Aimed mostly at Palestinians accused of siding with the invaders, these actions in part reflected the confirmation of Kuwait's fears about the dangers of a large foreign element. Palestinian neighborhoods in the capital were the site of searches for suspected collaborators, many of whom were beaten and detained. Perhaps 40 were executed. Probably only a small minority of unemployed youths worked with the Iraqis, although the PLO's backing of Saddam Hussein created the impression of general Palestinian collaboration.

Kuwait's trials in May–June of collaborators drew considerable criticism from human rights groups and foreign governments. Despite efforts to make the proceedings seem fair, the trials, which produced 29 death sentences, forbade defense witnesses and prohibited defendants from meeting their attorneys before the hearings. Sensitive to the criticism, Crown Prince Saad later commuted the death sentences to terms of life in prison.

CIVIL SERVICE

No information is available on the codes, structure, entrance requirements or size of the Kuwaiti civil service.

LOCAL GOVERNMENT

For purposes of local govenment, Kuwait is divided into three governorates—Capital (Kuwait City), Ahmadi and Hawalli—each under a governor.

FOREIGN POLICY

The central problem in Kuwaiti foreign policy has been to balance its vital economic and political links with the West against a strong impulse toward identifying itself with Arab causes. With a large Palestinian population, Kuwait has demonstrated consistent hostility toward Israel. Influential Kuwaitis have led periodic anti-Western incidents. In 1977 Kuwait became the second Arab state, after Iraq, to conclude an arms agreement with the Soviet Union. Kuwait's economic clout, exercised through the Kuwait Fund for Arab Economic Development, has been used to advance Arab solidarity. Since 1967 Kuwait has paid an annual subsidy of $154 million to Egypt and Jordan and large sums (not made public) directly to Palestinian guerrillas. Although ruled by a conservative regime, Kuwait generally adopts a radical foreign-policy line. In some measure this policy reflects Kuwait's vulnerability to pressures from larger Arab neighbors.

Since 1973, terrorist acts by extremist groups (not benefiting from Kuwait's donations to individual war efforts) have resulted in sporadic incidents, causing embarrassment to the government. The most serious of these occurred in December 1983, when six bombs exploded, killing five people and injuring more than 60 at the U.S. and French embassies and at other strategic sites. Responsibility was claimed by the al-Jihad al-Islami (Islamic Holy War) organization, a group of militant Shiite Muslims with widely acknowledged connections in Iran. In December 1984, a Kuwaiti airliner traveling from Dubai to Karachi was forced to land in Iran by terrorists who demanded the release of some of those imprisoned, or condemned to death, for their part in the bombings. Increased concern for Kuwait's security was revealed in the arrest or expulsion of numerous Iranian Muslims throughout 1984, and new legal measures were introduced restricting free passage through the country. The same organizations attempted to assassinate Sheikh Jabir in 1985. In 1988, a plane carrying three members of the royal family was hijacked by Lebanese Shiites. After killing two passengers, all hostages were released in exchange for the hijackers' freedom.

Concern for regional security was a major factor in Kuwait's decision to join other Gulf states in setting up the Gulf Cooperation Council (GCC) in May 1981. The GCC has established a system of defense for the region, independent of any superpower. An indication of Kuwait's desire to remain independent of any superpower was its decision, in mid-1984, to purchase armaments from both the United States and the U.S.S.R.

Since independence, Kuwait's relations with Iraq have been strained by Iraq's claim to the emirate. Although Iraq recognized Kuwait's independence in 1963, it has maintained that Kuwait is part of Iraq on the historic grounds that it was part of the Basra province in Ottoman times. In 1964 Iraq pursued territorial claims to the Kuwaiti islands of Warbah and Bubiyan and in 1973 it occupied the Kuwaiti border post of Samitah. Iraq withdrew the following year.

Throughout the Iran–Iraq War, Kuwait, concerned about the spread of Muslim fundamentalism, gave substantial aid to Iraq. Relations with Iran were maintained despite Iran's bombing of Kuwaiti oil installations at Umm al-Aish in September 1981 and attacks against oil tankers. In 1987, after numerous attacks against oil tankers and facilities by Iranian forces and terrorists, Kuwait accepted offers from Liberia, the United States, the United Kingdom and the Soviet Union to reflag Kuwaiti tankers. The countries also assisted Kuwait in sweeping mines in its waters and provided escorts. After Iran attacked a Kuwaiti vessel under U.S. protection, U.S. forces retaliated by destroying an Iranian offshore oil rig in 1987.

Kuwait's relations with other Arab states and the West were affected in many ways by the 1990–91 war with Iraq. The war drew the emirate into closer alliance with Saudi Arabia and other Arab nations, and produced a remarkable multi-national coalition, led by the United States, which came to the rescue of the emirate.

Ties with Iraq began to unravel in the first half of 1990. Much of this was attributable to Saddam Hussein's demand that Kuwait forgive the massive debt run up during the Iranian war. He also made unsubstantiated claims that Kuwait was stealing Iraqi oil, and accused the emirate of violating OPEC quotas and conspiring to keep petroleum prices down. Kuwait agreed to cut oil production and was negotiating with Baghdad over the disputed islands of Bubiyan and Warbah when Hussein's troops invaded and quickly subdued the tiny emirate on August 2, 1990. Kuwait's military weakness in the one-day conflict was painfully evident. The emir set up a government-in-exile in Saudi Arabia.

But the world community came to Kuwait's defense swiftly and decisively. The Arab League condemned the invasion and called for Iraqi withdrawal. Only Iraq, Jordan, Yemen and the PLO dissented. Twelve of 20 Arab heads of state meeting in Cairo August 10 agreed to send troops to join the anti-Baghdad military effort.

Kuwait's envoy to the United States, Saud Masir Al Sabah, immediately sought American military help. The United States had viewed the emirate as a regional ally for some time, and the reflagging of Kuwaiti tankers in 1987 provided recent precedent for American military action in support of the emirate. The initial U.S. commitment of forces was designed to prevent an Iraqi invasion of Saudi Arabia. The eventual Allied offensive to liberate was motivated by several concerns, including responding to Iraqi aggression, a desire to destroy Baghdad's war machine, and the need to have Kuwait's petroleum on the world market.

Under the sponsorship of the United States, the United Nations also moved to reverse the occupation of the emirate. The world body passed resolutions condemning the invasion, voiding the annexation of Kuwait and authorizing member states to use force to evict the occupying Iraqi army. These motions received near unanimous support. During the war the alliance rejected an Iraqi proposal to comply with U.N. demands if several conditions were met, including the abdication of the Sabah family.

Kuwaiti forces played a symbolic role in the military operations of mid-January through late February, which defeated Iraq's forces and liberated the emirate. Most of the campaign was carried out by U.S. servicemen. Yet, Kuwaiti personnel were afforded the distinction of being the first to enter and formally liberate the capital on February 27, 1991.

Aside from damaged relations with Iraq, it was difficult to tell whether the war would significantly change Kuwait's foreign policy. Crown Prince Saad mentioned in March 1991 the possibility of recognizing Israel if the Jewish state withdrew from the occupied territories. Reliance on the Western-led alliance for liberation has made the emirate more sensitive to foreign opinion. Widespread criticism, for example, of trials of suspected collaborators in the spring of 1991 prompted the government to commute the death sentences handed down.

Kuwait and the United States are parties to eight treaties and agreements, covering consuls, defense, judicial assistance, postal matters, telecommunications and visas.

Kuwait joined the United Nations in 1963. It is a member of 16 U.N. organizations and six other international organizations including OPEC, the Arab League and OAPEC.

PARLIAMENT

Under the Constitution of 1962 the Majlis al-Umma, or National Assembly, is a unicameral legislature with a total membership of 66, of whom 50 are elected for four-year terms by native-born, literate males over 21. There are 25 electoral districts, each of which returns two members. The 16 appointed members served ex officio as cabinet ministers. The total electorate is believed to number less than 40,000 voters. A "grandfather clause" effectively limits suffrage to adult males who resided in Kuwait before 1920 and who maintained a residence there until 1959, and their descendants. Women's suffrage was considered and rejected by the National Assembly in 1982. A Kuwait women's organization was unsuccessful in 1984 both in its attempts to register women to vote and to take the issue to court.

The Assembly sits for at least eight months in a year. When in session it meets once or twice a week in four-hour sessions. Most of the legislative work, however, is done in committees.

Legislation may be initiated by a minister or by any member of the Assembly. If a law is passed by a two-thirds majority the emir signs it and promulgates it as law; if the law is passed by a simple majority vote the emir can withhold his signature until the next session if he so chooses. The emir also may issue decrees with the force of law when the Assembly is not in session, but the decrees must be submitted to the Assembly for approval when it convenes again.

The emir has the right to dissolve the Assembly. This right was exercised for the first time in 1976 in the wake of alleged "unjust attacks and denunciations against ministers" by members of the Assembly. The National Assembly was dissolved again in 1986, when the emir announced that he would henceforth rule by decree. He also suspended the constitutional provision requiring elections within two months. In the aftermath of the Persian Gulf War, the emir promised elections for 1992.

POLITICAL PARTIES

All candidates for election to the National Assembly run as independents. Although political parties are illegal, sympathizers exist for transnational organizations such as the Ba'ath, the Arab Nationalist Movement and various Islamic fundamentalist movements.

The opposition had a resurgence in the wake of the liberation following the Iraqi war. Crown Prince Saad, in exile in late 1990, pledged to opposition figures to abide by the 1962 Constitution, including an independent Parliament, once the occupation was over. A coalition of 100 political and business leaders seeking changes issued post-liberation demands, which included a free press and political parties.

But an open political process seemed elusive once the Iraqis were forced to withdraw. Opposition leader Hamed al-Jouan was wounded in a probable assassination attempt, fueling rumors that the Sabah family had a "hit list" of foes. The emir announced in April that assembly elections would be held in 1992, but that parties would not be permitted. No opposition figures were given portfolios in a new cabinet named in late April.

ECONOMY

Kuwait is a high-income country, with a private-enterprise economy based almost entirely on oil.

With oil reserves second only to Saudi Arabia, the oil sector dominates Kuwait's economy. Earnings from hydrocarbons generate more than 90% of both export and government revenues and contribute about 40% to GDP. Most of the nonoil sector is dependent upon oil-derived government revenues to provide infrastructure development and to promote limited industrial diversification.

Compared to the boom years in the mid-1970s, the 1980s were years of consolidation, if not slight recession in the Kuwaiti economy. The early years of the Iran-Iraq war pushed Kuwait's GDP well below its 1980 peak, and the Souk al Manakh, the unofficial stock exchange, crashed in 1982, contributing to the economic recession of the early 1980s. With the recovery of oil prices during the late 1980s, GDP increased annually.

Concerned by the inflationary effects of the somewhat overheated expansion of 1974–76 and by the

PRINCIPAL ECONOMIC INDICATORS

Gross National Product (U.S. $ billions): 33.082 (1989)
GNP per capita (U.S. $): 16,380 (1989)
GNP average annual growth rate (%, 1980–89): 2.2
GNP per capita average annual growth rate (%, 1987–89): 6.3
Average annual rate of inflation (%, 1980–88): −3.9
Consumer price index (1980=100) 1986
  All items: 126
  Food: 112
Average annual growth rate (%, 1980–88)
  General government consumption: 3.9
  Private consumption: 0.8
  Gross domestic investment: −2.3

BALANCE OF PAYMENTS, 1989
(U.S. $ millions)

Current account balance: 9,323
Merchandise exports: 11,383
Merchandise imports: −5,746
Trade balance: 5,637
Other goods, services & income+: 10,167
Other goods, services & income−: −4,983
Other goods, services & income net: 5,184
Private unrequited transfers: −1,287
Official unrequited transfers: −211
Capital other than reserves: −8,068
Net errors & omissions: −372
Counterpart items: 1,178
Liabilities constituting foreign authorities reserves: 0
Total change in reserves: −1,178

GROSS DOMESTIC PRODUCT

GDP nominal (K.D. billions): 6.779 (1989)
GDP per capita (U.S. $): 10,500 (1988)
Average annual growth rate of GDP (%, 1980–88): −1.1
GDP by type of expenditure (%) 1987
- Consumption
  - Private: 46
  - Government: 22
- Gross domestic investment: 16
- Gross domestic saving: 15 (1988)
- Foreign trade
  - Exports: 53
  - Imports: −38

Cost components of GDP (%) 1985
- Net indirect taxes: 0.0
- Consumption of fixed capital: 7
- Compensation of employees: 31
- Net operating surplus: 62

Sectoral origin of GDP (%) 1987
- Primary
  - Agriculture: 1
  - Mining: 41
- Secondary
  - Manufacturing: 14
  - Construction: 3
  - Public utilities: −1
- Tertiary
  - Transportation & communications: 5
  - Trade: 7
  - Finance: 8
  - Other services: 13
  - Government: 9

Average annual sectoral growth rates (%, 1980–88)
- Agricultural: 23.6
- Industry: −2.3
- Manufacturing: 1.4

Services: −0.9

possibility that the oil revenue surplus would decline, the government set up a "Fund for Future Generations" to prepare for the distant but still inevitable time when the oil runs out. Deposits into this fund—10% of all government oil revenue—may not be used for current expenditures and must be invested.

CENTRAL GOVERNMENT EXPENDITURES, 1988

% of total expenditures
- Defense: 13.9
- Education: 14.2
- Health: 7.7
- Housing, social security, welfare: 20.1
- Economic services: 18.1
- Other: 26.1

Total expenditures as % of GNP: 35.7
Overall surplus or deficit as % of GNP: 23.5

CENTRAL GOVERNMENT REVENUES, 1988

% of total current revenues
- Taxes on income, profit & capital gain: 0.9
- Social security contributions: 0.0
- Domestic taxes on goods & services: 0.7
- Taxes on international trade & transactions: 1.6
- Other taxes: 0.1
- Current nontax revenue: 96.7

Total current revenue as % of GNP: 51.9
General government consumption as % of GDP: 25
Average annual growth rate of general government consumption (%, 1980–88): 3.9

Because of inadequate opportunities for domestic investment, a sizable proportion of public and private Kuwaiti funds is invested in foreign assets. State external investments are coordinated by the Kuwait Foreign Trading and Investment Company.

The Kuwaiti economic infrastructure, especially the petroleum industry, was heavily damaged in the 1990–91 war with Iraq. Most damage resulted from intentional destruction by retreating Iraqi forces. Early estimates put the cost of reconstruction at $100 billion.

Of 1,080 oil wells, for instance, Iraq rendered more than 800 completely inoperable, with 535 fractured or set ablaze with explosives. By late March, the wells were still burning about six million barrels of oil per day, at a loss of $100–200 million daily. Additional damage included destruction of half of Kuwait's petroleum gathering centers and all above-ground oil storage facilities. The invaders also destroyed, damaged or stole $80 million worth of spare parts and support facilities.

One bright spot in economic reconstruction was the relatively swift clearing of marine mines off Kuwait's Gulf coast. By late June 1991 an international flotilla of minesweepers had removed an estimated 1,200 mines off the shore, permitting the resumption of commercial shipping.

PUBLIC FINANCE

The fiscal year runs from July 1 through June 30. Royalties from oil companies and income taxes from oil companies constitute over 95% of government revenues.

Development expenditures are included under the Finance Ministry Public Accounts, which alone account for approximately two-thirds of total expenditures.

Annexed budgets consist of the budgets of the various Kuwaiti institutions. These include the Kuwait National Petroleum Company, the Kuwait Oil Company, the General Housing Authority, Kuwait Airways, the Social Insurance Organization, the Central Bank of Kuwait and Kuwait University.

The Kuwait Planning Board, an autonomous organization created in 1962, has introduced the concept of central planning. The five-year development plans started in 1950 are designed to broaden the base of the economy and to maintain the annual rate of growth. Transportation and construction lead the sectoral allocations.

Kuwait has no external public debt.

During the 1990–91 war with Iraq, the Kuwaiti government spent considerable money on the civilian population and the military campaign that led to liberation. In September 1990, the emir, in exile, pledged $5 billion

FOREIGN AID

Total foreign aid (U.S. $ millions): 4.5 (1984)
- Bilateral: 3.4
- Multilateral: 1.1

to aid U.S. military operations and his nation. Kuwaiti refugees received a monthly average stipend of $1,700 per family. The reconstruction of the nation is expected to cost at least $100 billion.

During the 1980s Kuwait emerged as a major aid donor, and its economic assistance to other countries—bilaterally or through multilateral agencies—reached $5.4 billion, or 10% of its GNP in the mid 1980s. The principal instrument of this assistance has been the Kuwait Fund for Arab Economic Development (KFAED), established in 1961; by the mid 1980s the Fund disbursed more than $464 million in extended loans to: Egypt, Tunisia, Sudan, Jordan, Algeria, Morocco, Syria, Bahrain, Iraq, Yemen and Lebanon. Kuwait also has subscribed to the Arab Fund for Economic and Social Development, the Islamic Development Bank, the Arab-African Oil Assistance Fund, and the Arab Bank for African Industrial and Agricultural Development. Economic assistance is channeled to the Trucial States and Yemen through the General Organization for Assistance to Southern Arabia and the Gulf. In addition, direct government-to-government assistance is made available from state reserves with interest below 4% and terms of maturity ranging up to 25 years. Farther afield, Kuwait is a regular contributor to the UNRWA budget and the IMF Oil Facility.

CURRENCY & BANKING

The Kuwaiti unit of currency is the Kuwaiti dinar, divided into 10 dirhams and 1,000 fils. Coins are issued in denominations of 1, 5, 10, 20, 50 and 100 fils and notes in denominations of 250 and 500 fils and 1, 5 and 10 dinars.

The Kuwaiti dinar, introduced in 1961 and replacing the Persian Gulf Indian rupee, was at par with the pound sterling until 1967. Since 1975 the dinar's value has been determined in relation to a weighted group of currencies of the country's main trading partners. The dinar's market value in 1985 was $1 = KD .300. The 1984 sterling exchange rate was £1 = KD .353.

The banking system consists of the Central Bank of Kuwait, established in 1969 to take over the functions of the former Currency Board, eight commercial banks and three specialized banks. Kuwait's only foreign bank was nationalized when the British Bank of the Middle East was taken over by the government in 1971. The largest commercial bank is the National Bank of Kuwait, with total assets of KD 3.868 billion in 1989.

Since 1979 Kuwait has made significant strides as an international financial and lending center. Kuwait has pioneered the lending of funds to European and Third World borrowers in Arab, specifically Kuwaiti, currency. The total amount of Kuwaiti dinar bond-denominated issues outstanding exceeds $1 billion and includes issues made to the World Bank and a number of triple-A-rated institutions. The Kuwaiti dinar bond market was strengthened by the development of a local secondary bond market.

Besides participating in Kuwaiti dinar-denominated financing, Kuwait's 18 active investment houses have participated in billions of dollars of financing, primarily

FINANCIAL INDICATORS, 1989

Total reserves minus gold (SDRs billions): 2.360
SDRs (millions): 98
Reserve position in IMF (SDRs millions): 158
Foreign exchange (SDRs billions): 2.104
Gold (fine troy oz. millions): 2.54
Ratio of external debt to total reserves: 0.1 (1987)
Central bank 1989
- Assets (%)
  - Foreign assets: 100.0
  - Claims on government: 0.0
  - Claims on banks: 0.0
  - Claims on private sector: 0.0
- Liabilities (%)
  - Reserve money: 45.7
  - Foreign liabilities: 0.0
  - Capital accounts: 27.5

Money supply 1989
- Stock (KD millions): 939
- M1 per capita: 450

Private banks 1989
- Assets (%)
  - Loans to government: 0.0
  - Loans to private sector: 66.5
  - Reserves: 0.4
  - Foreign assets: 33.1
- Liabilities
  - Deposits (KD billions): 8.582
  - of which %
    - Demand deposits: 7.0
    - Savings deposits: 50.5
    - Government deposits: 1.3
    - Foreign liabilities: 17.2

External debt 1988
- Debt service (long-term)
  - Total (U.S. $ millions): 932 (1987)
  - Repayment
    - Principal (%): 96.9 (1987)
    - Interest (%): 3.1 (1987)

Debt service ratio (%): 4.9 (1987)
- Receipt of workers' remittances (U.S. $ billions): −1.179
- Net direct private investment (U.S. $ millions): −262

GROWTH PROFILE
(Annual Growth Rates, %)

Projected population (1988–2000): 2.8
Projected crude birth rate (/1,000) (1990–95): 28.2
Projected crude death rate (/1,000) (1990–95): 2.7
Urban population (1985–90): 4.42
Labor force (1985–2000): 3.5
GNP (1980–89): 2.2
GNP per capita (1987–89): 6.3
GDP (1980–88): −1.1
Inflation (1980–88): −3.9
Agriculture (1980–88): 23.6
Industry (1980–88): −2.3
Manufacturing (1980–88): 1.4
Services (1980–88): −0.9
Money holdings (1980–88): 5.3
Manufacturing earnings per employee (1980–87): 3.7
Energy production (1980–88): 0.0
Energy consumption (1980–88): 3.7
Exports (1980–88): −2.9
Imports (1980–88): −5.5
General government consumption (1980–88): 3.9
Private consumption (1980–88): 0.8
Gross domestic investment (1980–88): −2.3

in Eurodollars. Their activity and that of Kuwait's eight commercial banks is an important development, since it indicates the entry of Arab banks as channels employed by the oil nations for depositing their funds in Western financial markets.

In 1982 the Souk al-Manakh, the country's unofficial stock exchange, where investors had been permitted to use postdated checks in expectation that share appreciation would more than cover high initial premiums, collapsed. The government created a trust fund that took over, at discount, the assets of some 70 major debtors and issued promissory notes to smaller investors.

AGRICULTURE

Agriculture is the smallest economic sector, employing less than 2% of labor and contributing 1% to the GDP. The total cultivable area, estimated at 0.2% of the land area, is 8,500 ha. (21,003 ac.) divided into 524 holdings. Little grain is grown, and most food is imported. An experimental hydroponic farm is owned by the government. The government provides farmers with long-term loans and low cost irrigation as well as extension services and demonstration centers.

The Bedouin still raise camels, sheep and goats as they did before the oil industry was developed.

Kuwait has no natural forests. Afforestation projects cover 25,000 acres.

Fishing is dominated by the Kuwait United Fisheries, which is engaged in medium-scale fishing for shrimp and prawns on the Persian Gulf. The industry was severely affected by the 1990–91 war.

AGRICULTURAL INDICATORS

Agriculture's share of GDP (%): 1 (1989)
Average annual growth rate (%, 1980–88): 23.6
Value added in agriculture (U.S. $ millions): 176 (1987)
Cereal imports (000 metric tons): 417 (1988)
Number of tractors: 102 (1986)
Nitrogeneous fertilizer consumption (000 metric tons): 0.7 (1985–86)
Fertilizer consumption (g./ha., hundreds) 750 (1987–88)
Number of farms (000): 1.9 (1985–86)
Average size of holding (ha.): 2.4 (1985–86)
Size class (%) 1970
- Below 1 ha. (below 2.47 ac.): 48.6
- 1–5 ha. (2.47–12.35 ac.): 25.4
- 5–10 ha. (12.35–24.7 ac.): 10.2
- 10–20 ha. (24.7–49.4 ac.): 8.7
- 20–50 ha. (49.4–123.5 ac.): 4.0
- 50–200 ha. (123.5–494 ac.): 3.1
- Over 200 ha. (over 494 ac.): 0.0

Tenure (%) 1985–86
- Owner-operated: 95.3
- Other: 4.7

Activity (%) 1985–86
- Mainly crops: 36.7
- Mainly livestock: 61.8
- Mixed: 1.5

Yields (kg./ha.) 1989
- Grains: 5,499
- Roots & tubers: 17,791
- Milk (kg./animal): 3,338

Production 1989
- Fruits (000 metric tons): 2
- Vegetables (000 metric tons): 124

Livestock (000) 1989
- Cattle: 29
- Sheep: 320

Forestry 1988
- Production of roundwood (000 cubic meters): 0
  - of which industrial roundwood (%): 0
- Value of exports (U.S. $ 000): 20,152

Fishing 1988
- Total catch (000 metric tons): 10.8
  - of which marine (%): 100.0
- Value of exports (U.S. $ 000): 1,784,068

MANUFACTURING

Industrial development is limited by the relative absence of raw materials (other than crude petroleum and natural gas), high labor costs, lack of technical manpower and a small domestic market. To diversify and stimulate industrial growth, the government has established a number of institutions, including the Board of Construction and Economic Development and the Industrial Development Committee. The Shuaiba Industrial Board was established in 1964 to develop the Shuaiba Industrial Region between Kuwait City and Ahmadi. This region is the center of the giant petrochemical complex operated by Kuwait Chemical Fertilizer Company. Other light industries either serve the local construction market or produce consumer and food products.

Kuwait's industrial sector features a few large state-owned enterprises alongside numerous small and medium-size private concerns. Jobs are concentrated in large firms. The workforce is predominantly foreign; only 19% are Kuwaiti nationals.

Although the oil industry dwarfs other manufacturing and industrial activities, the value added in industrial production more than doubled between 1970 and 1982, from $368 million to $894 million; by 1987 manufacturing was contributing 14% to the GDP, compared with 3.8% in 1982.

Desalination, in which Kuwait's production capacity has become the highest in the world, is an important industry.

Kuwaiti industrial policy has not been fully defined but is based on the need to establish a viable industrial base that will outlast the oil era. The policy strikes a middle ground between diversification (the goal of the

MANUFACTURING INDICATORS, 1987

Average annual growth rate (%, 1980–88): 1.4
Share of GDP (%): 10 (1988)
Labor force economically active in manufacturing (% est.): 9.0
Value added in manufacturing (U.S. $ millions): 1,902
- Food & tobacco (%): 10
- Textiles & clothing (%): 7
- Machinery & transport equipment (%): 4
- Chemicals (%): 6

Earnings per employee in manufacturing 1987
- Growth rate (%, 1980–87): 3.7
- Index (1980 = 100): 142 (1986)

Total earnings as % of value added: 43 (1985)
Gross output per employee (1980 = 100): 153 (1985)

1967–71 five-year program) and capital-intensive industrialization (the goal of the 1977–81 five-year program). At the same time, Kuwait is investing in industrial enterprises in other Gulf countries.

Because the government remains committed to the principle of private enterprise, the initiative rests with the private sector. However, private investors prefer to place their funds in local financial markets of Eurocurrency deposits, which are considered more profitable than industrial projects. The government has therefore been compelled to step in to promote industrial development.

The cornerstone of the government's industrial policy is the Industry Act of 1965, which grants all licensed industrial concerns: a 10-year exemption from all existing or future income taxes, export taxes and import taxes; a 10-year tariff protection; a 50-year lease on building sites at nominal rents; and government financial and technical assistance. The Industry Act is implemented by the Committee for Industrial Development, chaired by the minister of commerce and industry.

The government's investment regulations require 51% Kuwaiti participation and 25% Kuwaiti employment in all industrial enterprises. All firms doing business must also be licensed. New industries receive some privileges, including exemption from customs duties, taxes and export duties and protection from import competition.

In 1974 the government established the Industrial Bank of Kuwait to finance the industrial sector. The bank has financed wholly or in part 114 projects at a total cost of $324 million. However, the rate of growth of the bank's commitments has eased, reflecting the feeling that the market may not have much more room for such projects. A firm desire not to make Kuwaitis even more of a minority in their own country has dampened interest in many industrial projects that would require foreign labor. Initial enthusiasm for industrial projects has waned as many of them have been beset by sharp import competition in Kuwait's virtually tariff-free economy, leading to calls for tariff protection for some "infant" industries. In any case, nonhydrocarbon-based projects amounted to only $1.5 billion of $4.4 billion projected for industrialization for the 1977–81 five-year plan. Many influential Kuwaiti officials oppose large-scale investments in petroleum-related industries because of environmental considerations, possible future shortage of feed stock, economic viability (given the number of similar projects being built or contemplated by Kuwait's neighbors) and concern over the amount of additional non-Kuwaiti manpower these highly capital-intensive projects might bring into Kuwait.

MINING

Kuwait is not known to have any mineral resources other than petroleum and natural gas.

ENERGY

Kuwait is the third-largest oil producer in the Middle East and the seventh-largest in the world. It also is the fifth-largest oil exporter in the world. Oil reserves are estimated at 98.4 billion bbl. At current production rates these reserves should last for 139 years. About 75% of energy output is exported. Kuwait's natural-gas reserves are estimated at 1.37 trillion cu.m. Kuwait has the additional advantage of having the lowest oil production costs in the world. Kuwait's vast pools of oil lie fairly close to the surface; the porosity and permeability of Kuwaiti sands and the flatness of the surface contribute to the ease of extraction. Most of the oil rises to the ground under its own pressure and flows down a natural gradient to the dockside without pumping. The producing fields, moreover, are close to shipping points.

ENERGY INDICATORS

Average annual energy production growth rate (%, 1980–88): 0.0
Energy consumption per capita (kg. oil equivalent): 4,637 (1988)
Energy imports as % of merchandise exports: 0 (1988)
Average annual growth rate of energy consumption (%, 1980–88): 3.7
Electricity 1988
- Installed capacity (million kw.): 6.580
- Production (billion kw.-hr.): 19.998
  - % fossil fuel: 100
  - % hydro: 0
  - % nuclear: 0
- Consumption per capita (kw.-hr.): 19,998

Natural gas
- Proved reserves (trillion cu. m.): 1.370 (1990)
- Production (billion cu. m.): 8.160 (1989)
- Consumption (billion cu. m.): 8.126 (1988)

Petroleum
- Proved reserves (billion bbl.): 98.444 (1990)
- Years to exhaust proved reserves: 139 (1990)
- Production (million bbl.): 661 (1989)
- Consumption (million bbl.): 239 (1988)
- Refining capacity (million bbl./day): 819 (1990)

The heart of the oil reserves is the Great Burgan field, considered the largest single deposit yet discovered. Great Burgan includes Burgan, Magwa and Ahmadi and the smaller fields of Umm Gudair and Minagish to the west. There are three smaller fields to the north—Raudhatain, Sabriyah and Bahrah—and one to the west—Wafra, in the Neutral Zone.

A total of 90% of the oil is produced within Kuwait proper, by the Kuwait Oil Company (KOC) formerly owned by British Petroleum Company and Gulf Oil Corporation and completely state-owned since 1975. Kuwait Oil Company has 576 producing wells. Kuwait National Petroleum Company, founded in 1960 with 60% state participation, holds exploration rights in certain onshore areas. It also has a monopoly on all petroleum sold domestically and, since 1968, has operated the refinery at Shuaiba. Crude oil is piped to Mina al-Ahmadi, a large tanker port capable of handling ships up to 500,000 tons at the Sea Island terminal.

In 1981 Kuwait began to expand the petroleum sector by investing overseas, partly to ensure retail outlets for its crude petroleum. The acquisition of a 22.5% interest in Elf Aquitaine's Morocco concession, and of Santa Fe International Corporation in the United States in 1981, provided important "upstream" facilities for energy exploration and oil field services, and by 1984 Kuwait had interests in concessions in Australia, Bahrain, the People's Republic of China, Egypt, Oman, the North Sea and the United States. Facilities for the distribution, marketing and retailing of refined products also have been expanded. Kuwait Petroleum Corporation (KPC) has interests in distribution outlets in Hawaii and the Federal Republic of Germany, and in 1983 purchased Gulf Oil's network of about 750 retail gasoline stations in Belgium, Denmark, Luxembourg, the Netherlands and Sweden. A British gasoline distributor, Pace Petroleum, also was acquired. This was followed in 1984 by acquisition of about 1,400 of Gulf Oil's gasoline stations in Italy, together with three aviation centers, and a 75% interest in a refinery near Milan. Occidental Petroleum Corporation also sold some of its operations to Sante Fe International Corporation.

Petroleum refining is the country's predominant industry. There are five refineries, of which the largest are the KOC's Mina al-Ahmadi complex and AMINOIL's Mina al-Abdullah. The retreating Iraqis devastated the nation's petroleum capacity in 1991. Of 1,080 oil wells, they rendered more than 800 unusable; explosives fractured or set afire 535 of those. Also destroyed were half of the emirate's petroleum gathering centers and all above-ground oil storage facilities. In addition, Iraq destroyed, damaged or stole spare parts and storage facilities valued at $80 million.

LABOR

The extent of foreign participation in Kuwaiti economic life is reflected in the fact that prior to the 1990–91 Iraqi occupation, more than four-fifths of the labor force were of non-Kuwaiti origin. Government is the largest single employer.

Compared to neighboring countries, wage rates and working conditions are very generous. The work week is 48 hours, and wages are fixed for skilled, professional and unskilled workers. The conditions of foreign worker entry and employment are regulated by work permits and restrictive labor laws. In 1979 Kuwait adopted a new immigration policy restricting the entry of foreign workers. As a result, the number of new work permits issued fell for the first time in 1979 (to 174,229, compared to 187,000 in 1978). There is virtually no unemployment.

Labor unions were legalized in 1964, but non-Kuwaitis are barred from membership for five years and also are barred from holding union office. The state-controlled General Confederation of Kuwaiti Workers is the central organization of which all unions are affiliates.

LABOR INDICATORS, 1988

Total economically active population (000): 699
- % working-age (15–64): 63.5 (1986)
- % female: 20.6 (1986)

Activity rate (%)
- Total: 39.0 (1986)
- Male: 54.8 (1986)
- Female: 18.5 (1986)

Employment status (%, age 15–59)
- Employers & self-employed: 5.9
- Employees: 92.4
- Unpaid family workers: 0.1
- Other: 1.5

Sectoral employment of economically active (%)
- Agriculture, forestry, fishing: 1.3
- Construction: 15.4
- Manufacturing, mining, quarrying, public utilities: 9.0
- Trade, hotels, restaurants: 11.4
- Transportation, communications: 5.3
- Finance, real estate: 3.2
- Services: 53.0

Average annual growth rate of labor force (%, 1980–2000): 3.5
Labor under 20 years (%): 2.2 (1985)

FOREIGN COMMERCE

Kuwait's primary imports are machinery and transportation equipment, manufactured goods, food and live animals, chemicals and raw materials. These products come from Japan, the United States, Germany, the United Kingdom and Italy. The main exports are mineral fuels, machinery and transportation equipment, and manufactured goods. These exports are purchased by Japan, Taiwan, South Korea, and Netherlands.

Kuwait has a liberal trade policy. There are no import taxes, and few goods are controlled or prohibited. However, imports are restricted to holders of an open general license, which is issued to Kuwaiti nationals only. During the Iraqi occupation of 1990–91, Kuwait's foreign commerce came to a halt. After the liberation, an international flotilla of minesweepers cleared most of the estimated 1,200 marine mines Iraq had laid off the emirate's coast. By late June 1991, commercial shipping resumed.

FOREIGN TRADE INDICATORS, 1988

Exports (U.S. $ billions): 7.1
Imports (U.S. $ billions): 5.2
Balance of trade (U.S. $ billions): 1.9
Annual growth rate (1980–88), exports (%): −2.9
Annual growth rate (1980–88), imports (%): −5.5
International reserves in terms of months of imports covered: 3.6
Terms of trade (1980 = 100): 54
Import price index (1980 = 100): 105.0
Export price index (1980 = 100): 48.9

Direction of Trade (%), 1986

	Imports	Exports (est.)
European Community	31.3	26.6
United States	12.3	3.6
U.S.S.R. & eastern European economies	1.0	0.2
Japan	23.6	13.8

Composition of Trade (%), 1986

	Imports	Exports
Food & agricultural raw materials	18.6	1.3
Fuels & other energy	0.6	84.4
Mineral ores & concentrates	0.5	0.2
Manufactured goods	80.3	14.1
of which chemicals	6.0	2.1
of which machinery	38.9	6.6

TRANSPORTATION & COMMUNICATIONS

Kuwait has no railways.

The main port of Kuwait is Shuwaikh in Kuwait Bay, enlarged in recent years to an annual rated capacity of 2 million tons. A secondary port has been built at Shuaib, with five berths. The oil port at Mina al-Ahmadi is considered one of the largest in the world. Its loading platform, 16 km. (10 mi.) out in the Gulf, can accommodate eight large tankers simultaneously, including supertankers of 326,000 deadweight tons. In 1983 these three ports handled 39,800,000 metric tons of cargo.

TRANSPORTATION INDICATORS

Roads (latest)
- Length, km. (mi.): 4,273 (2,655)
- Paved (%): 100

Motor vehicles (latest)
- Automobiles: 454,022
- Trucks and buses: 110,492
- Persons per vehicle: 3.6

Railroads (latest)
- Track, km. (mi.): 0
- Passenger-km. (passenger-mi.) (millions): 0
- Freight, metric ton-km. (short ton-mi.) (millions): 0

Merchant marine
- Vessels (over 100 tons): 220 (1989)
- Total deadweight tonnage (000): 2,886.8 (1989)
- Oil tankers (000 GRT): 1,395 (1985)

Ports (pre-1986)
- Cargo loaded (000 metric tons): 43,973
- Cargo unloaded (000 metric tons): 7,253

Air
- Km. (mi.) flown (millions): 26.0 (16.1) (1985)
- Passenger-km. (passenger-mi.) (millions): 3,893 (2,419) (latest)
- Freight, metric ton-km. (short ton-mi.) (millions): 233.4 (159.9) (latest)
- Mail, metric ton-km. (short ton-mi.) (millions): 4.4 (3.0) (1985)
- Airports with scheduled flights: 1 (1990)

Pipelines 1990
- Refined, km. (mi.): 40 (24.8)
- Natural gas, km. (mi.): 165 (102.5)

COMMUNICATION INDICATORS, 1988

Telephones
- Total (000): 362
- Persons per telephone: 5.5

Phone traffic (000 calls)
- International: 13,090

Post office
- Number of post offices: 54
- Pieces of mail handled (000): 115,215

Telegraph
- Total traffic (000 calls): 471 (1987)
  - National: 113
  - International: 350 (1987)

Telex
- Subscriber lines: 3,034
- Traffic (000 minutes): 8,338 (1987)

Telecommunications 1990
- Satellite stations: 5

TOURISM & TRAVEL INDICATORS, 1986

Total tourist receipts (U.S. $ millions): 118 (1988)
Expenditures by nationals abroad (U.S. $ millions): 2,358 (1988)
Tourist nights (000): 323
Number of tourists (000): 493.1 (1984)
- % of whom from:
- Saudi Arabia: 35.6
- Egypt: 6.8
- India: 4.1

The Kuwait oil tanker fleet is the largest of the OAPEC countries. In 1985 there were eight carriers for crude oil, four for liquid petroleum gas and three for oil products. In 1982 Kuwait acquired another 12 ships and carried 50% of its oil production under the Kuwaiti flag. There are two private shipping companies: Kuwait Oil Tanker Company, with 31 vessels and Kuwait Shipping Company (part of United Arab Shipping Company), with 60 vessels.

Kuwait has a modern highway network, with 4,273 km. (2,655 mi.) of highways. A tricountry highway system is being developed with Jordan and Saudi Arabia. In 1989, plans were made to construct a 30 km. (19 mi.) causeway across the Bay of Kuwait. Kuwait Transport Company operates a transportation system employing over 200 buses.

The national airline is Kuwait Airways, which operates a fleet of 15 aircraft flying to 28 cities out of the main international airport in Kuwait City. Like most other elements of the Kuwaiti infrastructure, transportation and communications facilities were extensively damaged in the Persian Gulf War of 1991.

DEFENSE

The defense structure is headed by the emir, who also is the commander in chief. The line of command runs through the army chief of staff and the deputy chief of staff, both of whom are princes of the Al Sabah royal family.

A national service was introduced in 1975. All males between 21 and 30 are required to enlist for military service of 18 months. Total strength of the armed forces before the Persian Gulf War of 1990–91 was 13,100.

Army

Personnel: 10,000

Organization: 2 armored brigades; 1 mechanized infantry brigade; 1 SSM battalion

Equipment: 330 tanks; 160 combat vehicles; 275 armored personnel carriers; 38 howitzers; 4 surface-to-surface missiles; mortars

Navy

Personnel: 1,100

Equipment: 12 fast attack craft: 48 patrol craft; 3 support ships; 9 landing craft

Air Force

Personnel: 2,000

Organization and equipment: 76 combat aircraft; 2 fighter squadrons; 1 interceptor squadron; 1 counter insurgency squadron; 2 transportation squadrons; 3 helicopter squadrons; 9 trainers; 1 air defense battalion

Although Kuwait has traditionally relied on Britain for most of its military equipment, it negotiated a large arms deal with the Soviet Union in 1977. Arms purchases abroad during 1973–83 totaled $1.190 billion.

The inability of the Kuwaiti military to defend the emirate against a serious assault was made painfully obvious in the Iraqi invasion of August 2, 1990. While it only utilized one-tenth of its army, Iraq's invading force of 100,000 overwhelmed Kuwait's army. Saddam Hussein's divisions also had a potential of 5,500 tanks, compared with Kuwait's 275.

The initial Iraqi advance was so fast and simple that some invading troops traveled down from the border in buses. Kuwait's army offered limited resistance around the emir's palace after he had fled by helicopter. By nightfall of August 2, Kuwaiti troops were still fighting only near military barracks outside the capital. Perhaps 200 emirate soldiers were killed in the one-day struggle.

The Kuwaiti military regained some symbolic prestige by participating in the American-led ground assault to liberate the emirate in late February 1991. Kuwaiti troops were the first Allied forces to enter the capital on February 27. After the war, Sheikh Nawaf al-Ahmad Al Sabah was deposed as defense minister, charged with incompetence in handling the Iraqi invasion. Sheikh Salim Al Sabah, former interior minister, was made deputy premier/defense minister.

EDUCATION

Kuwait has one of the most developed educational systems in the world. Education is free, universal and compulsory, in theory, between ages six and 14 and free from kindergarten (for Kuwaitis; from first grade for non-Kuwaitis) to the university level. Students also are offered free food, books, stationery, clothing and transportation. Enrollment at the secondary level includes a substantial proportion of foreign students attracted by Kuwait's subsidized and free education.

The academic year runs from September to May. The medium of instruction is Arabic. English is taught as a second language. Schooling consists of 12 years, divided into primary (four years), intermediate (four years) and secondary (four years) cycles. School curricula are based on Arab League standards. Schools are segregated by sex until the university level.

A high proportion of Kuwaiti teachers are foreigners, mostly Egyptians and Jordanians. Indigenous Kuwaitis constitute less than 2% of the teaching staff.

Private schools include a variety of institutions, such as the International School run by the U.S. community; English schools run by missionaries; and Indo-Pakistani schools. Private-school enrollment is 40% at the kindergarten level and 20% at the primary level.

In 1986, the government began a campaign to wipe out illiteracy.

Educational administration is centralized in the Ministry of Education.

Kuwait University founded in 1966, has become a major institution of higher learning in the Middle East. Almost one quarter of its students are non-Kuwaitis. New petroleum, engineering and medical colleges were opened in 1977.

Kuwaiti students who complete their secondary-school science courses in the upper 80% and arts courses in the upper 70% are eligible to study abroad

EDUCATION INDICATORS, 1988

Literacy
- Total (%): 75.1
- Male (%): 78.7
- Female (%): 69.6

First level
- Schools: 295
- Students: 181,844
- Teachers: 10,125
- Student/teacher ratio: 18.0
- Net enrollment ratio: 79 (1987)

Second level
- Schools: 431
- Students: 255,566
- Teachers: 19,996
- Student/teacher ratio: 12.8
- Net enrollment ratio: 74 (1982)

Vocational
- Schools: 6 (1987)
- Students: 11,388
- Teachers: 586
- Student/teacher ratio: 19.4

Third level (post-secondary)
- Institutions: 1
- Students: 15,751
- Teachers: 863
- Student/teacher ratio: 18.2
- Gross enrollment ratio: 16.6 (1987)
- Students (/100,000 pop.): 1,390
- % of population age 25 and over with postsecondary education: 12.7

Foreign study
- Foreign students in national universities: 5,253 (1988)
- Students abroad: 3,568
  - of whom in
    - United States: 2,367 (1988)
    - France: 72 (1988)
    - Federal Republic of Germany: 15 (1988)
    - United Kingdom: 276 (1987)

Public expenditure
- Total (K.D. 000): 382,869
- % of GNP: 5.5
- % of current: 955

GRADUATES, 1986

Total: 4,736
Education: 1,498
Humanities & religion: 392
Fine & applied arts:
Law: 135
Social & behavioral sciences: 566
Commerce & business: 1,031
Mass communication: 0
Home economics: 0
Service trades: 0
Natural sciences: 174
Mathematics & computer science: 168
Medicine: 298
Engineering: 203
Architecture: 0
Industrial programs: 271
Transportation & communications: 0
Agriculture, forestry, fisheries: 0
Other: 0

at government expense provided they pursue courses not offered at Kuwait University.

LEGAL SYSTEM

The judicial system, revised in 1959, is based on the Egyptian model. Its family, land and inheritance laws are derived from the Shari'a, but the Law of Commerce incorporates Western legal concepts.

The courts of first degree include criminal, assizes, magistrate, civil, domestic and commercial courts as well as the Misdemeanors Court of Appeal. The Domestic Court is subdivided into separate chambers for Shiites, Sunnis and non-Muslims. Civil appeal is to the High Court of Appeal and, in matters concerning personal status, to the Court of Cassation.

Kuwait's judicial system is independent and provides for public trial, the right of appeal and representation by an attorney of one's choice. Failure of the police to respect a suspect's rights may provide a defense in the courts. Trials in absentia have occurred. In such cases the defendant is allowed an additional right of appeal. There are no reports of secret or unfair trials or of discrimination against defense counsel. However, the court-appointed attorney of a defendant unable to engage his own lawyer is not always given adequate time to prepare a defense. Interpretation of court proceedings to ensure their understanding by non-Arabic-speaking defendants is sometimes inadequate. A special State Security Court was established by decree in December 1983 to try those charged in terrorist bombings. In the subsequent two-month trial, the government strictly applied procedures established for regular criminal courts, including the provision of a defense attorney for each of the accused. Except for the opening and closing sessions of the tribunal, however, all hearings were conducted in camera. Six of the accused were sentenced to death, including three tried in absentia. A number of others received prison sentences of varying lengths, and five were acquitted. The death sentences were referred to the emir, as required by law, but no decree has been issued to carry out the sentences. (Such delays are not unusual.) According to the Constitution, military courts have jurisdiction only over offenses committed by members of the armed or security forces, except during periods of martial law. The emir can pardon or commute sentences passed by civilian or military courts and occasionally has done so. Non-Kuwaitis convicted of crimes are routinely deported after serving their sentences.

Following the Iraqi war, martial law existed from February 26 to June 26, 1991. The emir appointed Crown Prince Saad as military governor for that period. Scores of suspected collaborators, mostly Palestinians, Jordanians and Iraqis, were arrested. There were reports of torture and execution of those charged with helping the Iraqis.

The government began a series of trials of alleged collaborators in mid-May. They were conducted by tribunals of military and civil judges. By appointing attorneys and opening the proceedings to the press and foreign observers, Kuwait sought to give the trials a semblance of fairness. But human rights groups and Western nations, including those that helped to liberate the emirate, denounced the process as unfair. Defendants were not permitted to meet lawyers before the trials; the tribunals produced no evidence; and they refused to hear defense witnesses.

Crown Prince Saad announced in late June that all 29 death sentences returned in five weeks of martial law trials would by commuted to life in prison. This was an apparent response to international criticism of the proceedings.

LAW ENFORCEMENT

The principal law enforcement force is the national constabulary of 2,500 men, which provides internal and border security.

HEALTH

Kuwait has a highly developed public health service. All medical facilities are provided free of charge to citizens and noncitizens.

HEALTH INDICATORS

Health personnel 1988
- Physicians: 2,900
  - persons per: 675
- Dentists: 355
- Nurses: 9,764
- Pharmacists: 873
- Midwives: 137

Hospitals 1988
- Number: 24
- Number of beds (/10,000): 35
- Admissions/discharges (/10,000): 1,235
- Bed occupancy rate (%): 71.7 (1982)
- Average length of stay (days): 8 (1982)

Type of hospitals (%) 1985
- Government: 66.7
- Private nonprofit: 33.3
- Private profit: 33.3

Public health expenditures (latest)
- As % of national budget: 7.7
- Per capita (U.S. $): 378.90

Vital statistics
- Crude death rate (/1,000): 2 (1990)
- Life expectancy at birth 1990
  - Males: 72
  - Females: 76
- Infant mortality rate (/1,000 live births): 15 (1990)
- Child mortality rate under 5 yrs. (/1,000 live births) (1985–90): 23
- Maternal mortality rate (/100,000 live births) (1986–87): 2.0
- Population with access to safe water (%): 100 (latest)

The principal health problems are trachoma, tuberculosis, measles and dysentery.

FOOD & NUTRITION

Kuwait is totally dependent on imports for food, but the urban diet is generally adequate. No information is available on food intake.

MEDIA & CULTURE

The daily press consists of five Arabic papers and two English-language newspapers; their combined circulation is 418,000. There are three nondailies, with a combined circulation of 475,000. The periodicals press consists of 73 titles (including a weekly official gazette published by the Ministry of Information) with a total circulation of 257,000.

The principal dailies are: *al-Anbaa*, *al-Qabas*, *al-Rai al-Amm*, *al-Siyasa*, *al-Watan*, *Arab Times* and *Kuwait Times* (English).

Constitutional guarantees of freedom of the press were suspended by the emir in 1976 following the dissolution of the National Assembly. Kuwait has an active Censorship Department that reviews all books, films, videotapes, periodicals and other material entering Kuwait in bulk or for commercial purposes. In practice, references to the state of Israel often are excised from educational materials, reference works and maps. Items arriving by mail for individuals or institutional use usually are not opened before delivery unless the contents are suspected of being pornographic. Printed and visual materials produced within Kuwait are not subject to precensorship but are liable to government action after publication or release. Radio and television are government-owned and -controlled.

The Kuwaiti press is not precensored. Articles and editorials critical of government action or of individuals appear infrequently. The press law sets down several categories that are restricted. These include criticism of the emir and the ruling family; official confidential communications or treaties and agreements with other states; material that might disturb relations with Arab or other friendly states or that might prove embarrassing to their heads of state; and a general category of stories that "might incite people to commit crimes, create hatred, or spread dissension among the people." In practice the list is interpreted selectively, and violators usually are issued only warnings. Editors and publishers are liable to imprisonment and fines for violations, but to date there have been no known imprisonments. Editors generallly are careful not to offend the government.

In 1986 the emir again suspended press freedom following the dissolution of the National Assembly. He announced that any publication printing material "against the national interest" would be punished. The government also deported 40 expatriate journalists in an attempt to Kuwaitize the media. In the aftermath of the Persian Gulf War of 1991, despite more calls by the opposition for loosening of restraints, the government seemed unwilling to permit a free press.

The national news agency is Kuwait News Agency (KUNA). Foreign news bureaus in Kuwait include MENA, AFP, Hsinhua, Reuters and Tass.

There is a small but active book publishing industry, with a recent output of 222 titles. Kuwait does not adhere to any copyright convention.

The state-owned Kuwait Broadcasting Service has 20 transmitters and broadcasts programs in Arabic, Farsi English, and Urdu.

The Television of Kuwait, a state-owned corporation, operates five main and two auxiliary transmitters and one experimental transmitter. It is on the air for 114 hours a week. Over 60% of the programs are of local origin.

Local film production is limited to documentaries.

The National Library of Kuwait has over 40,000 volumes.

MEDIA INDICATORS

Newspapers
- Number of dailies: 7
- Circulation (000): 418
- Per 1,000 pop.: 223
- Number of periodicals: 73 (1986)
- Circulation (000): 257 (1986)
- Newsprint consumption 1988
  - Total metric tons: 20,000
  - Per 1,000 pop. (kg.): 10,444

Book publishing
- Number of titles: 222 (latest)

Radio
- Number of transmitters: 20 (1989)
- Number of persons per radio receiver: 1.9 (1989)
- Total program hours (/yr.): 21,640 (1985)

Television
- Television transmitters: 6 (1989)
- Number of persons per T.V. receiver: 2.6 (1989)
- Total program hours (/yr.): 5,935 (1985)

Cinema
- Number of fixed cinemas: 14 (latest)
- Seating capacity (000): 15 (latest)
  - Seats (/1,000 pop.): 9.4 (1987)
- Annual attendance (millions): 0.9 (latest)
- Gross box office receipts (K.D. millions): 0.5 (1987)

Films
- Number of long films imported: 319 (1987)

% from
- India: 60.2
- United States: 21.3
- Italy: 2.2
- Japan: 0.9

CULTURAL & ENVIRONMENTAL INDICATORS

Libraries (latest)
- Number: 25
- Volumes (000): 738
- Registered borrowers (000): 585
- Loans (/1,000 pop.): 50

Museums (latest)
- Annual attendance (000): 326
- Attendance (/1,000 pop.): 174

Performing arts (latest)
- Annual attendance (000): 95
- Attendance (/1,000 pop.): 66

SOCIAL WELFARE

Kuwait has one of the most comprehensive social welfare systems in the world, financed by its vast oil revenues. The Public Assistance Law of 1962 provides assistance to widows, orphans, disabled and sick persons and low-income families.

GLOSSARY

akhdam: servile class of Kuwaiti society of mixed Negro descent.
emir: prince. Title of the rulers of Kuwait.
majlis al-Umma: National Assembly of Kuwait.
shamal: strong summer wind from the north.
shiat: political party or group.

CHRONOLOGY (from 1961)

1961— Kuwait becomes a fully independent state on the termination of the 1899 agreement with the United Kingdom under which Kuwait was a British military protectorate; Sheikh Abdallah takes the title of emir. . . . Kuwait is admitted to the Arab League. Iraq claims sovereignty over Kuwait and threatens invasion; British troops land in Kuwait in response to the emir's appeal for assistance; the Arab League intervenes in the dispute; an Arab League contingent replaces British troops as a guarantee of Kuwait's independence. . . . The Kuwaiti dinar replaces the Persian Gulf Indian rupee as the unit of currency. . . . Kuwait founds the Kuwait Fund for Arab Economic Development. . . . Elections are held for the National Assembly.
1962— New Constitution is promulgated.
1963— First session of the National Assembly is held; Sheikh Sabah al-Salim al-Sabah is named prime minister. . . . Iraq recognizes the Kuwaiti government and renounces territorial claims; a new trade and economic agreement with Iraq is concluded. . . . Kuwait is admitted to the United Nations.
1965— Emir Abdallah dies; Sheikh Sabah is named new emir, and Sheikh Jabir al-Ahmed becomes prime minister.
1966— Kuwait University is founded.
1969— The Neutral Zone is partitioned between Saudi Arabia and Kuwait.
1971— British withdraw all troops from the Gulf region . . . in new national elections, radicals register some gains.
1973— Iraqi troops occupy the Kuwaiti outpost at Samtah.
1975— Kuwait nationalizes Kuwait Oil Company. . . . The Kuwaiti dinar is floated.
1976— Emir Sabah dissolves the National Assembly in the wake of a constitutional crisis; a constitutional provision calling for new elections within two months of the dissolution is suspended; censorship is imposed on the media.
1977— Kuwait agrees to buy sophisticated military equipment from the Soviet Union. . . . Kuwait mediates Egypt–Libya dispute.
1979— Kuwait expels Ayatollah Khomeini's envoy amid Shiite protests.
1981— Gulf Cooperation Council is formed with six founding members, including Kuwait.
1983— U.S. and French embassies in Kuwait City are bombed by Arab terrorists. . . . Government retaliates with mass arrests of Shiite extremists.
1984— Kuwait Airways airliner is hijacked to Iran. . . . Kuwait concludes an arms purchase agreement with the Soviet Union.
1985— Terrorists attempt to assassinate the emir.
1986— The emir dissolves the National Assembly and imposes new restrictions on the press.
1990— Iraq invades and overruns the emirate, forcing the emir and most of the royal family to flee to Saudi Arabia, beginning a six-month Iraqi occupation of Kuwait, which includes considerable destruction of property and hostility toward natives. . . . About 400,000 Kuwaitis take refuge in other countries during the occupation. A resistance force continues to harass the Iraqis. . . . President Saddam Hussein annexes Kuwait as Iraq's 19th province, and later renames the capital Kadhima, Kuwait City's name under the Ottoman Empire. United Nations passes resolutions demanding Iraqi withdrawal from Kuwait, and authorizing use of force to evict Iraqi troops. . . . Mulit-national force, led by United States, assembles in region with intent to liberate Kuwait. Force includes troops of Syria, Egypt, Saudi Arabia and Kuwait, as well as most Western nations.
1991— From mid-January to the end of February, Allied forces stage air, sea and ground campaign that defeats Iraqi forces and liberates Kuwait. . . . al-Sabah family rulers return and retain firm hold on power. . . . New cabinet in April retains Crown Prince Saad as premier. Emir promises Parliamentary elections for 1992. . . . Government and Kuwaiti citizens crack down on Palestinians accused of siding with Iraq during occupation. Emirate begins massive reconstruction effort estimated to cost $100 billion. . . . Devastation to petroleum industry caused by retreating Iraqis expected to take years to return Kuwait's oil-based economy to pre-war levels.

BIBLIOGRAPHY

BOOKS

Al-Moosa, Abdulrasool, and Keith McLachlan, *Immigrant Labour in Kuwait.* London, 1985.
Al Sabah, Y. S. F. *The Oil Economy of Kuwait.* London, 1981.
Clements, Frank A. *Kuwait* (World Bibliographical Series). Santa Barbara, Calif., 1985.
Daniels, John. *Kuwait Journey.* Luton, Eng., 1972.
Demir, Soliman. *The Kuwait Fund and the Political Economy of Arab Regional Development.* New York, 1976.
El Mallakh, Ragaei. *Kuwait: Trade and Investment.* Boulder, Colo., 1979.
———, and Jacob K. Atta. *The Absorptive Capacity of Kuwait.* Lexington, Mass., 1981.
Freeth, Zahra. *A New Look at Kuwait.* New York, 1972.
Ismael, J. S. *Kuwait: Social Change in Historical Perspective.* Syracuse, N.Y., 1982.
Middle East Economic Digest. *Kuwait.* Boulder, Colo., 1985.
Winstone, H. V. F., and Zahra Freeth. *Kuwait: Prospects and Reality.* London, 1972.

OFFICIAL PUBLICATIONS

Finance Ministry. *Public Accounts and Accounts of the Funds* (annual).

Information Ministry. *Government Gazette* (weekly).

Kuwait Central Bank. *Annual Report* (Arabic and English).

———. *Quarterly Statistical Bulletin* (Arabic and English).

Kuwait Government Press. *Education in Kuwait, 1969–70.* Kuwait, 1971.

———. *Kuwait Economy, 1968–69.* Kuwait, 1970.

———. *The Oil of Kuwait: Facts and Figures.* Kuwait, 1970.

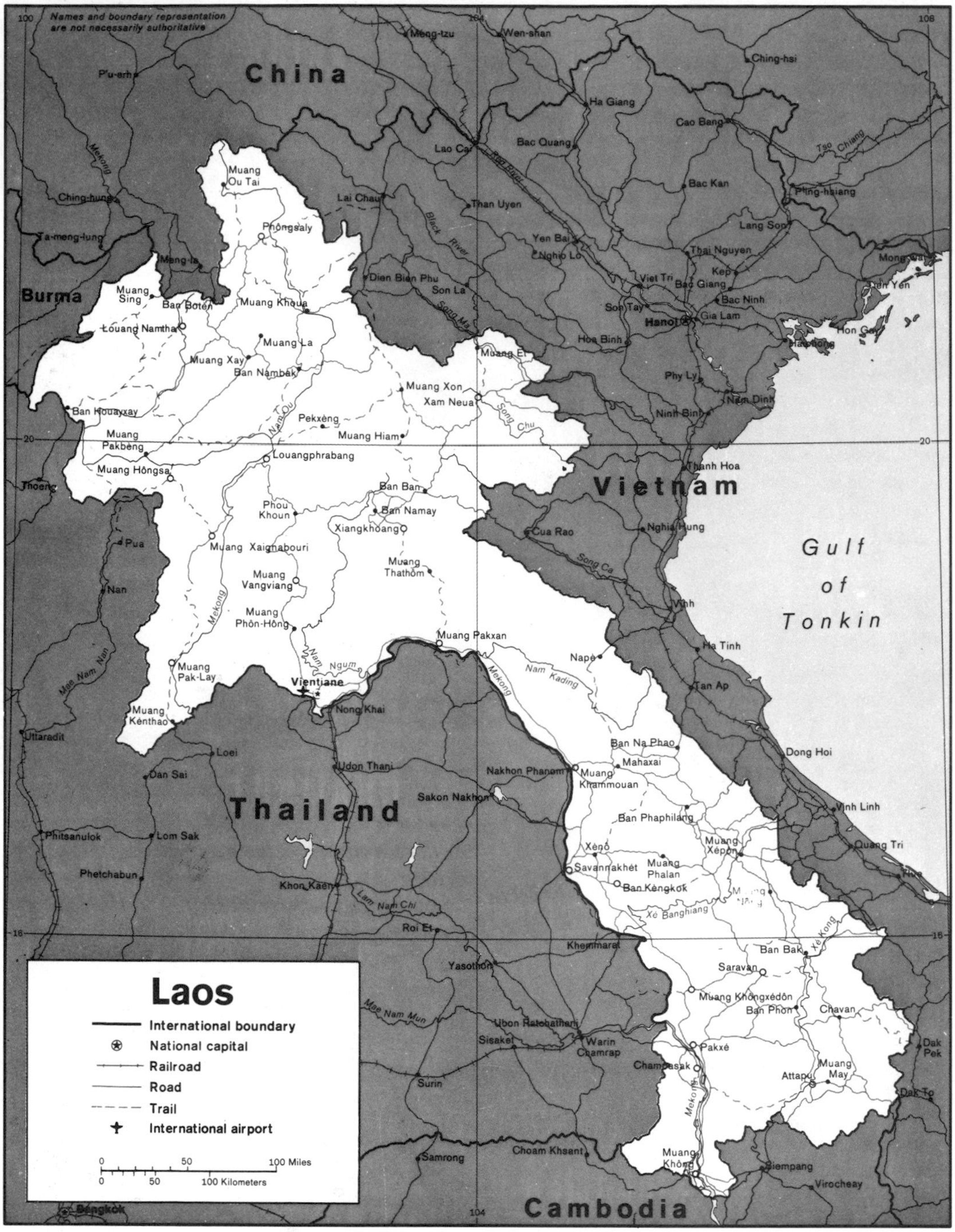

Names and boundary representation are not necessarily authoritative
China
Burma
Vietnam
Thailand
Cambodia
Gulf of Tonkin
Laos
International boundary
National capital
Railroad
Road
Trail
International airport
0 50 100 Miles
0 50 100 Kilometers
Mong-tzu
Wen-shan
Ching-hsi
P'u-erh
Ha Giang
Cao Bang
Bac Quang
Lao Cai
Red River
Tso Chiang
Muang Ou Tai
Lai Chau
Bac Kan
Ching-hung
P'ing-hsiang
Phôngsaly
Than Uyen
Lang Son
Black River
Ta-meng-lung
Yen Bai
Nghia Lo
Thai Nguyen
Meng-la
Kep
Dien Bien Phu
Son La
Viet Tri
Bac Giang
Muang Sing
Ban Boten
Muang Khoua
Bac Ninh
Son Tay
Hanoi
Gia Lam
Louang Namtha
Song Ma
Hoa Binh
Hon Gai
Muang La
Muang Xay
Muang Et
Ban Nambak
Phy Ly
Muang Xon
Xam Neua
Ninh Binh
Nam Dinh
Ban Houayxay
Pekxeng
Song Chu
Nam Ou
Muang Hiam
Muang Pakbeng
Louangphrabang
Thanh Hoa
Muang Hôngsa
Ban Ban
Ban Namay
Phou Khoun
Xiangkhoang
Cua Rao
Nghia Hung
Pua
Muang Xaignabouri
Muang Thathom
Song Ca
Muang Vangviang
Nan
Vinh
Mekong
Muang Phôn-Hông
Muang Pakxan
Ha Tinh
Nam Ngum
Napé
Mae Nam Nan
Muang Pak-Lay
Nam Kading
Vientiane
Tan Ap
Muang Kenthao
Nong Khai
Uttaradit
Loei
Ban Na Phao
Dong Hoi
Udon Thani
Mahaxai
Dan Sai
Nakhon Phanom
Muang Khammouan
Sakon Nakhon
Ban Phaphilang
Vinh Linh
Phitsanulok
Lom Sak
Muang Xepon
Quang Tri
Xénô
Savannakhét
Muang Phalan
Phetchabun
Ban Kengkok
Khon Kaen
Lam Nam Chi
Xé Banghiang
Roi Et
Ban Bak
Xé Kong
Khemmarat
Saravan
Yasothon
Muang Khôngxédôn
Ban Phon
Chavan
Mae Nam Mun
Ubon Ratchathani
Warin Chamrap
Sisaket
Pakxé
Dak Pek
Champasak
Muang May
Attapu
Surin
Dak To
Samrong
Choam Khsant
Muang Không
Siempang
Virocheay
Bangkok

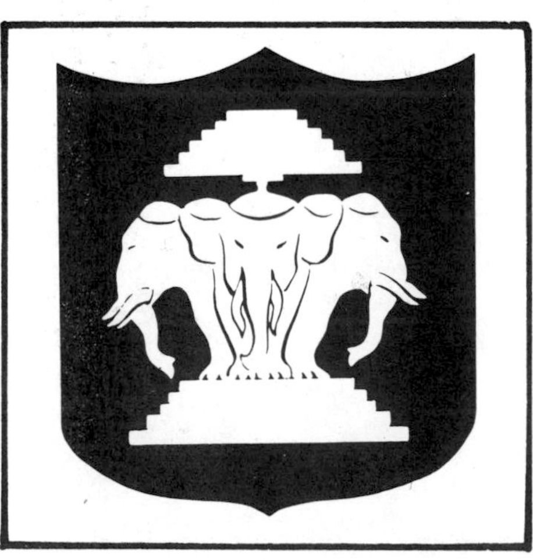

LAOS

BASIC FACT SHEET

OFFICIAL NAME: People's Democratic Republic of Laos (Saathiaranagroat Prachhathippatay Prachhachhon Lao)

ABBREVIATION: LS

CAPITAL: Vientiane

HEAD OF STATE: Acting President Phoumi Vongvichit (from 1986)

HEAD OF GOVERNMENT: Chairman of the Council of Ministers Kaysone Phomvihan (from 1975)

NATURE OF GOVERNMENT: Communist civilian dictatorship

POPULATION: 4,023,726 (1990)

AREA: 236,800 sq. km. (91,428 sq. mi.)

ETHNIC MAJORITY: Lao

LANGUAGE: Lao

RELIGION: Hinayana Buddhism

UNIT OF CURRENCY: New kip

NATIONAL FLAG: Three horizontal stripes of red, dark blue and red, with a white disc representing the full moon in the center

NATIONAL EMBLEM: The main elements of the national coat of arms are two sheaves of grain enclosing a star, a hammer and a sickle, a cogwheel and a farmstead.

NATIONAL ANTHEM: "Hymn of the Lao People"

NATIONAL HOLIDAYS: July 19 (Independence Day, National Day); May 1 (Labor Day); also variable Buddhist festivals

NATIONAL CALENDAR: Gregorian

PHYSICAL QUALITY OF LIFE INDEX: 52

DATE OF INDEPENDENCE: July 19, 1949

DATE OF CONSTITUTION: A new constitution is being drafted; the Constitution of 1947 (as amended in 1952 and 1956) was abrogated in 1975

WEIGHTS & MEASURES: Metric

GEOGRAPHICAL FEATURES

Laos, a landlocked nation located in the heart of the Indochinese peninsula, has an area of 236,800 sq. km. (91,428 sq. mi.), extending 1,162 km. (722 mi.) south-southeast to north-northeast and 478 km. (297 km.) east-northeast to west-southwest.

Laos's total international border of 4,513 km. (2,804 mi.) is shared with five countries: China (425 km.; 264 mi.); Vietnam (1,555 km.; 966 mi.); Cambodia (541 km.; 336 mi.); Thailand (1,754 km.; 1,090 mi.) and Myanmar (238 km.; 148 mi.). The border with Myanmar was delimited in the 1800s by the British and French powers and follows the Mekong River throughout. The border with China is based on treaties and conventions between France and China in the 19th century and confirmed by the Chinese Nationalist government in 1935. The border with Thailand is based on Franco-Siamese conventions and follows the Mekong River for 965 km. (600 mi.). The border with Cambodia was formerly an internal administrative boundary of French Indochina. The border with Vietnam was the subject of a border dispute well into the 1970s.

The capital is Vientiane, with a 1975 population of 210,000. Other large urban centers are Savannakhet (53,000), Pakse (47,000), Luang Prabang (46,000), Sayabouri (14,000), Khammouane (13,000) and Houei Sai (10,000).

Laos is divided topographically into the northern mountains, comprising two-fifths of the country, and the southern panhandle. The mountains of the Northwest are characterized by steep slopes and sharp crests, with a number of peaks over 1,800 m. (6,000 ft.). Laos's highest mountain, Phou Bia (2,819 m. 9,249 ft.), is in this region in Xieng Khouang Province. Another major feature is the Plain of Jars, on the Tran Ninh Plateau, between about 1,014 and 1,219 m. (3,330 and 4,000 ft.) above sea level, so named from the prehistoric stone jars found in the area. The panhandle is bounded on the east by the Annam Cordillera, a continuous range with peaks rising to 2,350 m. (8,000 ft.), effectively cutting off Laos from Vietnam. West of the divide the range is buttressed by a series of plateaus, such as the Khammouane Plateau and the Boloven Plateau.

The Mekong River is the lifeline of Laos. It is the major transportation artery and the major source of irrigation; its waters supply fish, a staple of the diet. All the larger towns are on or near its banks. The Mekong borders on or flows through Laos for more than 1,600 km. (1,000 mi.). It is navigable from Vientiane to Savannakhet, but rapids, some impassable, are numerous over most of its length north of Vietiane and south of Savannakhet. The Mekong's tributaries in the North are Nam Tha, Nam Ou and Nam Ngum; its tributaries in the South are Nam Kading, Se Bang Fai, Se Bang Hieng, Se Done and Se Kong.

CLIMATE & WEATHER

Laos has two seasons: a wet season during the Southwest Monsoons, from May to October, and a dry season during the Northeast Monsoons, from November to

April. July and August are the months of maximum precipitation, while November is almost dry.

The annual mean rainfall over all of Laos ranges from 1,270 mm. (50 ins.) to 2,290 mm. (90 in.). The lowest average rainfall is recorded in the region around Luang Prabang in northern Laos, while the highest rainfall—over 4,060 mm. (160 in.)—is recorded in the Boloven Plateau. Rainfall occurs at least 100 days a year throughout the country and in some areas on as many as 150 days a year.

Temperatures are never extreme but vary from tropical to subtropical with altitude, latitude and the monsoons. The hottest months are March and April just before the monsoon rains, when temperatures climb into the midthirties (C) or the midnineties (F). Absolute highs of well over 37.8°C (100°F) have been recorded. During the rainy season the temperatures fall to an average of 26.7°C (80°F). During the cooler part of the dry season, from December to February, the temperatures hover between 14°C and 28.4°C (57°F and 83°F). Below-freezing temperatures have been recorded occasionally in Xieng Khouang.

POPULATION

The population of Laos was 4,023,726 in 1990, based on C.I.A. estimates. No true census has ever been held in the country.

The densest settlement is in the Mekong River lowlands. The highlands are sparsely inhabited, and the northern and eastern borders are virtually uninhabited.

Fifty-four cities and towns are officially classified as urban areas. Nearly 50% of the urban population lives in the five largest cities: Vientiane, Luang Prabang, Khammouane, Savannakhet and Pakse. The rural population is scattered among 9,000 villages, almost wholly engaged in subsistence agriculture.

The Laos civil war, which ended in 1975, produced a massive movement of refugees westward. Most of these refugees had been displaced by the periodic Pathet Lao offensives and the battles in the Plain of Jars. Thousands crossed into Thailand, and by the time the Thai government closed the border in 1975 over 54,821 refugees from Laos had found asylum there. This number included Thai nationals who had lived in Laos under the monarchy. By the late 1980s the number of refugees had risen to an estimated 90,000. During 1985 Thailand instituted policies designed to repatriate those Laotians it termed economic refugees. In 1986 over 2,500 refugees returned to Laos voluntarily and the following year Thailand began forced repatriation.

Since 1975 more than 8% of the population has fled Laos. After dropping for several years, the rate of departures rose dramatically in 1984, primarily in response to perceived renewed resettlement opportunities in other countries and as a reflection of greater frustration with continuing economic hardship and lack of opportunity to improve one's lot in Laos. The departure of a significant portion of the skilled middle class has held back economic progress, as have the government's preoccupation with political and military security and its mistrust of the few well-educated persons who have remained.

VITAL STATISTICS

Crude birth rate (/1,000): 37 (1990); 45 (1965)
Crude death rate (/1,000): 15 (1990); 23 (1965)
Infant mortality rate (/1,000 live births): 126 (1990)
Life expectancy (yrs.) at birth: males, 48; females, 51 (1990)
Gross reproduction rate (/woman) (1980–85): 3.00
Total fertility rate (/woman): 5.1 (1990)
Rate of natural increase (/1,000): 24.8 (1988)
Average household size: 5.3 (latest)

DEMOGRAPHIC INDICATORS

Population (millions): 4.024 (1990)
Year of last census: 1985
Sex distribution (% at last census): males, 49.0; females, 51.0 (1985 est.)
Population estimates and projections (millions)

1940: 1.075	1970: 2.962	2000: 4.964
1950: 1.949	1980: 3.292	2010: 6.016
1960: 2.382	1990: 4.024	

Age profile (% at last census) 1985 est.

0–14: 42.5	30–44: 16.2	60–74: 4.3
15–29: 26.6	45–59: 9.7	75 and over: 0.7

Median age (yrs.): 18.6 (1985)
Youth population (% age 15–24): 19.0 (1985); 20.1 (2000)
Total dependency ratio: 83.6 (1985)
Annual growth rate (%)

1950–55: 2.05	1975–1980: 1.16	2000–2005: 2.06
1955–60: 2.26	1980–1985: 2.29	2005–2010: 1.82
1960–65: 2.22	1985–1990: 2.49	2010–2015: 1.61
1965–70: 2.18	1990–1995: 2.37	2015–2020: 1.44
1970–75: 2.18	1995–2000: 2.27	2020–2025: 1.27

Hypothetical size of stationary population (millions): 19
Assumed year of reaching net reproduction rate of 1: 2035
Urban population (000): 570 (1985)
Urban population (%): 18 (1988); 8 (1965)
Annual urban population growth rate (%, 1980–88): 6.1
Annual rural population growth rate (%, 1985–90): 1.82
Percentage of urban population in largest city: 48 (1980)
Number of cities of population over 500,000: 0.0 (1980)
Population density per sq. km. (per sq. mi.): 17 (44) (latest)

STATUS OF WOMEN INDICATORS

Number of women (millions): 2.080 (1985)
Women of childbearing age (15–49) (% of pop.): 46 (1988)
Women's literacy rate (%): 75.8 (1986)
Women in labor force (%): 71 (1985)
Total fertility rate (/woman): 5.1 (1990)

The role of women in Lao society has traditionally been subservient to that of men, but discrimination is not highly pronounced. The government-controlled Lao Women's Federation has as one of its stated goals achievement of rights for women "equal" to those of men. Lao women are currently being encouraged to take an increasing part in economic and state-controlled political activity.

In 1976 the Laotian government banned birth control. The ban was based on the government's decision to promote population growth to make up for the losses suffered during the civil war. The government declared that there was much empty land in Laos and that people were needed to develop it.

ETHNIC COMPOSITION

The ethnic configuration of Laos is characterized by diversity. Four main ethnic groups are officially listed: Lao Lum, Lao Theung, Lao Tai and Lao Soung. All groups are ethnically related to the Tai, or Thai, people.

The Lao Lum (the valley Lao, commonly referred to as the Lao) are the dominant ethnic group, constituting between one-third and one-half of the population. Historically the Lao have imposed their social values, religion, language and political system on the non-Lao peoples. The Lao, in fact, are the national ethnic group, while the non-Lao communities are limited to regions and localities.

Differing in many ways from the Lao but sharing their cultural origins are the Lao Tai, or Tribal Tai, who live in river valleys of the upland areas and make up about 16% of the population. Within this group are numerous subgroups, the Lu, Tai Nua, Tai Yuan, Tai Dam (Black Tai) and Tai Daeng (Red Tai). The Lao Tai are for the most part non-Buddhists.

About a fourth of the population is made up of the Lao Theung (Mountain Laos), who were, until recently, also known as *kha* (slave). The Lao Theung are believed to be the original inhabitants of the land and are distinguished by a darker skin, kinky hair and broader noses, suggesting a possible ancestral connection with Negrito races. The Khmu are the largest ethnic subgroup of the Lao Theung, but there are a number of smaller subgroups, such as the Tin, Lamet and Loven.

The name Lao Soung (Mountain Lao) is applied to two groups: the Meo and the Man (Yao). They are believed to be the most recent migrants from China, appearing in Laos as recently as 1850. The Meo are a proud people with a reputation as valiant fighters. They have been generally successful in maintaining their identity, owing partly to their more highly developed social organization. The Lao Soung groups make up 10% of the population.

In northern Laos there are a number of groups of Chinese origin, locally called Ho and Kho. There also are smaller groups of Tibeto-Burman speakers, such as the Akha, Lolo and Lisa, who are informally classified as Kha-Ko.

Until 1975 Laos had sizable communities of foreigners, including Americans, Frenchmen, Vietnamese, Chinese, Indians, Pakistanis, Filipinos and Cambodians. At one time Vietnamese constituted 7% of the population and Chinese 2%. The status and numbers of these foreign communities are not clear. Because of the anti-Western orientation of the Laotian government, no Westerners are believed currently resident in the country.

In terms of ethnic and linguistic homogeneity, Laos is ranked 44th in the world, with 40% homogeneity on an ascending scale (on which North and South Korea are ranked 135th with 100% homogeneity and Tanzania first with 7% homogeneity).

LANGUAGE

The official language of Laos is Lao, the language of the Lao ethnic group. However, French still is used as a logical and convenient language for diplomatic communication, and most of the Lao elite speak French. Most official publications continue to be issued in French. The American presence in Laos during the 1960s led to the adoption of English by many educated Laotians, but with the growing isolation of Laos since 1975 the status of English is in doubt.

Lao is a Sino-Tibetan language with a considerable literature of its own. Its alphabet is identical to that used in Thailand, but the spelling is not standardized, and there are many regional variations. There also is a literary form, known as Nang Xu Tham, derived from Pali and Sanskrit, used by priests. During the French period Lao assimilated French loanwords, and later a few English words. Though each ethnic subgroup has its own dialect, these dialects are mutually intelligible and have a generally common vocabulary.

The minority languages of Laos are for the most part unwritten and used only locally. The more important of these are the Mon-Khmer languages spoken by the Lao Theung people, the Tibeto-Burman languages spoken by the Lolo, Akha, and Lahu and the Miao-Yao languages spoken by the Meo and the Man.

RELIGION

Until a secular state was established in 1975, Theravada or Hinayana Buddhism was the official faith of Laos. The pervasive influence of Buddhism is attested to by the thousands of pagodas that dot the towns and the countryside—Vientiane and Luang Prabang have been called cities of a thousand temples. Most of the Lao and a smaller number of the non-Lao regard themselves as Buddhists. However, coexisting with orthodox Buddhism is a cult of Phi or spirit worship, which regulates a large part of the daily activities of the average Lao. Most non-Lao adhere to tribal religions in which spirit worship is the major element, modified in some cases by Buddhist or Confucian beliefs.

Christian missionary activity in Laos has not been rewarded with many converts, and in the 1960s there were only 50,000 Christians in the country. There are three Roman Catholic vicars apostolic—in Vientiane, Pakse and Khammouane.

After 1975 the government took over some Buddhist and Christian places of worship for use as political indoctrination centers or warehouses. This practice appears to have ceased, however, and construction of Buddhist temples can be observed. In general, Buddhist temples have become more active in the past few years, and the number of monks has increased. In official statements the government has recognized the right of the people to religious belief as well as the contributions religion can make to the development of the country. Many Lao, however, believe that the government has begun a long-term effort to subvert the role of religion—in part because it considers the maintenance of temples and the activities of monks non-productive. This effort includes carefully controlling the education of young monks and compelling the Buddhist clergy to propagate some elements of Marxist-Leninist doctrine. Monks, however, are the only remaining social group still entitled to special honorific terms of address, and even high party and government officials continue to use them. Religious festivals are permitted without hindrance. Young people regularly enter into religious orders for short periods. Links may be maintained with coreligionists and religious associations only in countries approved by the government, usually other Communist countries. Traditional links to Thai Buddhists are no longer permitted. In theory, missionaries are not banned from entering Laos to proselytize, but in most cases they have been denied permission. Many top party officials still participate in religious ceremonies, but the military are forbidden even to have Buddhist funerals.

Roman Catholics and Protestants are permitted to worship without harassment, but the activities of their churches are closely observed. Since 1975 they have not been permitted to operate schools, seminaries or associations. A new Roman Catholic bishop coadjutor of Vientiane was consecrated and several Protestants were released from "reeducation," but in 1984 a few church leaders remained under detention, allegedly for antigovernment activity. Catholic Church officials visited Laos to meet with local Catholic Church leaders in 1984. The bishops of Laos, however, did not go to nearby Bangkok to meet the pope during the latter's visit there in May 1984. The government tries to persuade hill tribe minority groups to abandon their "old-fashioned" animist beliefs.

HISTORICAL BACKGROUND

Laos was under French rule from 1893 to 1953, except for a five-year Japanese occupation from 1940 to 1945. On the whole, French rule rested lightly.

Patterns of local government under the French were not greatly changed, and local customs and traditions were respected when they were not incompatible with larger French objectives. The French *résident supérieur* exercised only indirect rule over Luang Prabang, though administration of the eight provinces outside that kingdom was more direct.

The Japanese pressured King Sisavang Vong to declare Laos independent in 1945, but following the Japanese surrender, he reaffirmed France's protectorate role. Free Lao forces deposed the king shortly thereafter. However, France regained Laos in early 1946 and reinstated the monarch. In 1949 Laos was granted limited self-government as an Associated State within the French Union. The royalist government was led by Prince Souvanna Phouma, who served as prime minister from 1951 to 1954. Anti-French forces coalesced in 1950 to form the Pathet Lao, led by pro-communist Prince Souphanouvong, Souvanna Phouma's half brother. Laos was granted full independence from France in 1953. Except for a short period in 1957–58, when Souvanna Phouma and Souphanouvong formed a coalition government, Laos was ruled by a series of pro-western, conservative regimes from 1954 to 1960. During the 1950s the Pathet Lao gradually gained control of the northern portion of the country with the assistance of Vietnamese communist forces. Attempts to end the guerrilla warfare and establish a unified state failed, and by 1965 the country was de facto partitioned into a communist north and "neutralist" government under Souvanna Phouma in the south. The two sides signed a ceasefire agreement in 1973 and the following year a coalition government led by Souvanna Phouma and Souphanouvong was formed. In the wake of the Communist victory in Vietnam, the Pathet Lao gradually established control of administration.

In December 1975 the monarchy was abolished, the coalition government dissolved and the People's Democratic Republic of Laos was declared. Within two years, the new regime had consolidated its power and given the country its first stable government since 1953. With a disciplined army and party as its power base, the government liquidated all opposition and began a process of national "reeducation" or indoctrination. Private industry was nationalized and agriculture collectivized. Faced with an economy near collapse and strong resistance to collectivization, the government during the 1980s slowed the pace of socialization and announced a limited return to free enterprise and private landownership.

In March 1989 Laos held its first national elections since the communists came to power in 1975. A total of 121 candidates vied for 79 seats in the Laos Supreme People's Assembly. Western news reports said that only 47% of the electorate participated in the voting.

CONSTITUTION AND GOVERNMENT

With the establishment of the People's Democratic Republic of Laos in December 1975, the Constitution of 1947 (as amended in 1952 and 1956) was abrogated. King Savang Vatthana abdicated in the same year, and

RULERS OF LAOS

Kings (from 1904)

March 1904–August 1959: Sisavang Vong
November 1959–December 1975: Savang Vatthana

President (from 1975)

December 1975–October 1986: Prince Souphanouvong

Prime Ministers (from 1945)

October 1945–April 1946: Prince Khammao
April 1946–1951: Prince Savang Vatthana
1951–1954: Prince Souvanna Phouma
1954–December 1955: Katay Don Sasorith
March 1956–July 1958: Prince Souvanna Phouma
August 1958–January 1959: Phoui Sananikone
January 1959–December 1959: Sunthone Patthamavong
January 1960–May 1960: Kou Masith Abhay
May 1960–August 1960: Prince Tiami Somsanith
August 1960–December 1960: Prince Souvanna Phouma
December 1960: Sunthone Patthamavong
December 1960: Quinim Pholsena
December 1960–June 1962: Prince Boun Oum na Champassac
June 1962–December 1975: Prince Souvanna Phouma
December 1975–October 1986: Kaysone Phomvihan
October 1986: Phoumi Vongvichit

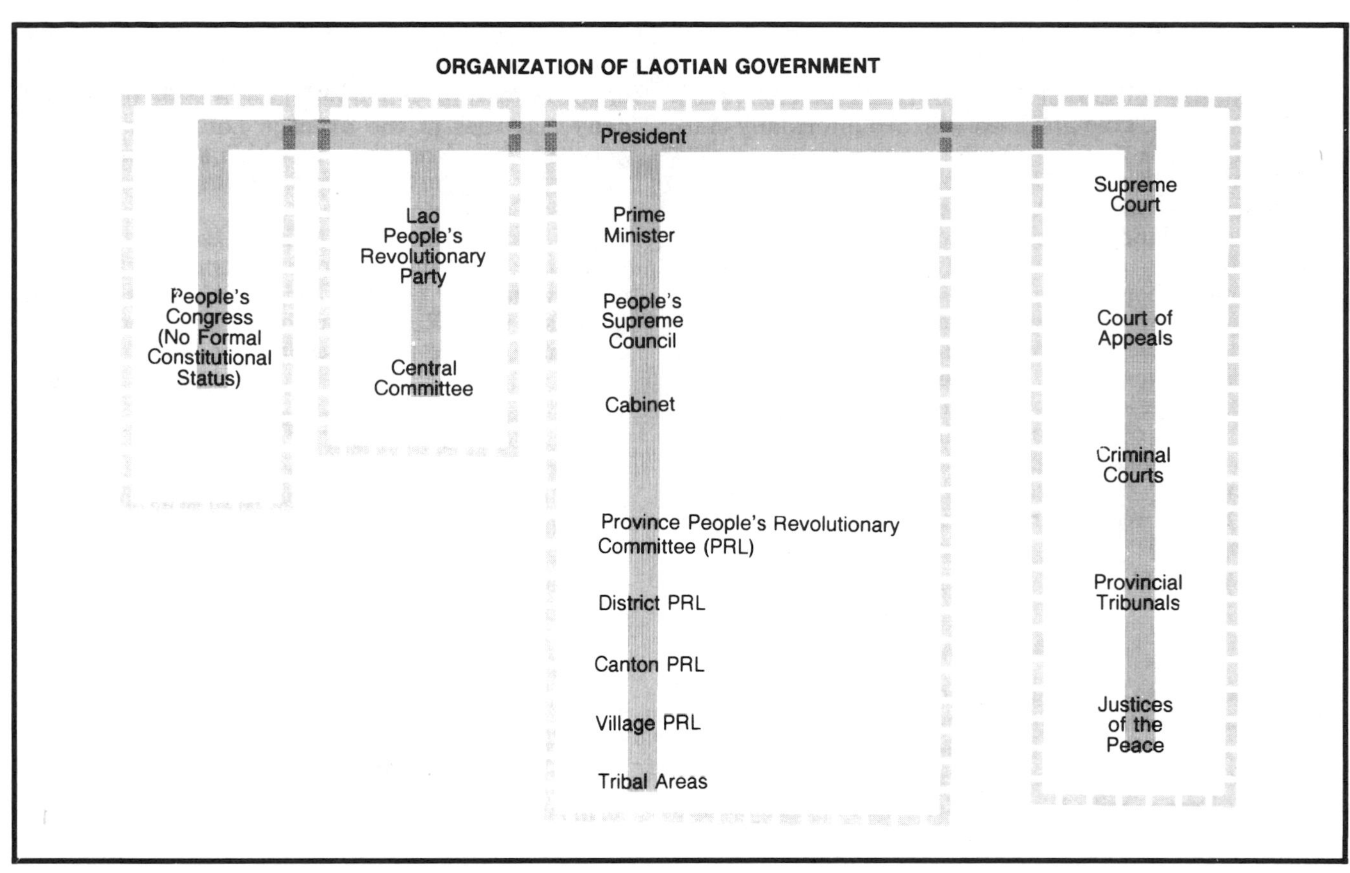

GOVERNMENT LIST
(July/August 1991)

President	Souphanouvong
Acting President	Phoumi Vongvichit
Chairman of the Council of Ministers	Kaysone Phomvihan
Vice Chairman	Nouhak Phoumsavan
ViceChairman	Khamtai Siphandon, *Gen.*
Vice Chairman	Phoun Sipaseut
Vice Chairman	
Minister of Agriculture & Forestry	Inkong Mahavong, *Brig. Gen.*
Minister of Commerce & Tourism	Khamphoui Keoboualapha
Minister of Communications, Transport, Posts & Construction	Bouathong
Minister of Economy, Planning & Finance (Acting)	Khamsai Souphanouvong
Minister of Education & Sports	Saman Vignaket, *Lt. Gen.*
Minister of Foreign Affairs	Phoun Sipaseut
Minister of Foreign Economic Relations	Phao Bounnaphon, *Col.*
Minister of Industry & Handicrafts (Acting)	Soulivong Daravong
Minister of Information & Culture	Son Khamvanvongsa
Minister of Interior	Asang Laoli, *Maj. Gen.*
Minister of Justice	Kou Souvannamethi
Minister of National Defense	Khamtai Siphandon, *Gen.*
Minister of Public Health	Khambou Sounisai
Minister of Science & Technology	Souli Nanthavong
Minister of Social Welfare & Veterans Affairs	Khamlieng Pholsena, *M.D.*
Minister in the Office of the Council of Ministers	Maisouk Saisompheng
Governor, National Bank	Pani Yathotou

supreme power passed to a National Congress of People's Representatives, consisting of 264 delegates elected by Pathet Lao-appointed local authorities. The National Congress in turn chose a 45-member Supreme Council to draw up a new constitution. The present government is headed by a president who also serves as chairman of the Supreme People's Council. However, real power is believed to lie with the secretary general of the Lao People's Revolutionary Party.

There also are four ministers attached to the prime minister's office, and 19 vice ministers. In 1975 ex-king Savang Vatthana was given the title of supreme counsellor to the president (until his arrest in 1977), and ex-prime minister Souvanna Phouma that of counsellor to the government (until his death in 1984).

FREEDOM & HUMAN RIGHTS

In terms of civil and political rights, Laos is classified as a not-free country.

Laos is virtually a protectorate of Vietnam and is constantly beset by fears of domestic insurgency and Chinese invasion. The resulting siege mentality expresses itself in constant hostility to all forms of human rights. Because the government distrusts the educated and the trained, it has entrusted its administration to loyal but inefficient party underlings.

The continuing human rights concern is with the "reeducation camps," where an estimated 10,000 to

15,000 people are held under varying conditions of coercion and isolation. These detainees are not necessarily charged with specific crimes but often simply with hostility to the regime or with socially undesirable habits and thought patterns, and include those suspected of collaboration with the former regime or with the United States, and professionals. According to information obtained from refugees, in 1980 there were at least 20 "reeducation camps." The camps are concentrated in the Viengsai area and Houa Phan Province near the Vietnamese border, in the Plain of Jars, near Ban Ban in Xieng Khouang Province, and in Saravane and Attopeu Provinces in southern Laos. Information collected on 4,182 inmates indicated that 3,134 were former soldiers (of whom 982 held the rank of major or above), 564 were former policemen and 350 were former government officials. In 1984 government officials claimed, as they had in 1983, that nearly all soldiers and officials sent to "reeducation camps" in 1975–76 had been "released" and that "only a few" people remained under detention. Some government officials contend that all the camps have been closed. It has not been possible to verify the accuracy of such statements. Those accused of hostility to the regime or of what the government calls "socially undesirable habits," such as prostitution, drug abuse, idleness or "wrong thought," are sent to "rehabilitation" centers, usually without trial. Most of these persons have been allowed to return to their homes after periods ranging from a few months to several years of hard labor, political indoctrination and admission of guilt. In 1984 there were reports that some unemployed and idle youths in Vientiane and other urban areas were rounded up and sent against their will to the countryside to work on public works projects, in some cases to join "patriotic youth" groups also working on such projects.

Searches of homes are authorized by the law-enforcement authorities themselves. The basic freedoms of speech, press and assembly as well as religion exist only in a rudimentary form or not at all. Some concessions to the Buddhist clergy continue, but some places of worship have been seized and converted into political indoctrination centers or warehouses.

The Pathet Lao have been particularly hostile to minorities such as the Hmong (Meo), the Chinese and the lowland Lao groups, using coercion to destroy their separate identities. The Hmong particularly have been suppressed brutally.

CIVIL SERVICE

Prior to the Communist takeover, the civil service was the most prestigious career in the country and offered the most direct avenue of acquiring wealth and power. Appointment to the civil service was open to any Laotian national. Though categories of civil service varied from ministry to ministry, there were four grades with nine pay scales. The top grade was the *maha amat*, followed by *amat* (superior), *long amat* (secondary) and *naikong* (special). The last category comprised those who were assigned to the tribal areas. A university degree was required only for the *maha amat* grades. Promotions were made on the basis of competitive examinations, held every two years for the lower grades and every three years for the higher grades.

LOCAL GOVERNMENT

For purpose of regional administration Laos is divided into 16 provinces and one municipality: Attapu, Bokeo, Bolikhamsai, Champaasak, Houaphan, Khammouan, Louang Namtha, Louangphrabang, Oudomzai, Phongsali, Saravan, Savannakhet, Sekong, Vientiane (province), Vientiane (municipality), Xaignabouri, and Xiangkhoang.

The provinces *(khoueng)* are subdivided into districts *(muong)*, districts into cantons *(tasseng)* and cantons into villages *(ban)*. Each province is headed by a governor *(chao khoueng);* each district is headed by a *chao muong;* and each village is headed by a chief, called *pho ban* in the South and *nai ban* in the tribal areas and in the North. The Meo and Kha tribes have chieftains who occupy administrative posts called *naikong lao theung*, corresponding to the office of *chao muong*. Vientiane and a few other cities and towns are administered as *muong* by a *chao muong*. All units of local administration are subject to close central government control. Although the governor is granted executive independence, he has no taxing or spending authority of his own. The district officer also is appointed by the central government and represents the last link between the central government and the people. The *nai tasseng* (canton chief) and the *nai ban* and the *pho ban* usually are elected, the former by the village headmen and the latter by heads of village households.

Since 1975 the representative institutions at the local level have been restructured: Elected people's committees in the villages serve as the base units. Similarly, people's revolutionary committees have been set up at the provincial, district and cantonal levels. Elections are held every three years for provincial and city councils, every two years for provincial capital councils and annually for district capital councils. The first nationwide local elections under the new system were held in 1975.

FOREIGN POLICY

In its first two years, the new regime brought Laos firmly into the Communist bloc. Relations with Western nations have been downgraded and those with the United States remain cool. Despite this, during the 1980s the Laotian government assisted the United States in its search for remains of troops lost during the Vietnam War.

As one of the smallest Communist nations, Laos took considerable care to remain neutral in the Sino-Soviet dispute but took the Soviet line on Angola, Japan, Israel, South Africa and Chile. Moscow also is the source of the greater part of Laos's vital foreign aid: foodstuffs, fuel, machinery, military equipment and credits.

In 1977 a high-level Vietnamese delegation led by Le Duan, Communist Party general secretary, visited Vientiane to sign a 25-year treaty of friendship and cooperation. The treaty made clear that Laos was closer to the Soviet Union and Vietnam in the Indochina power struggle.

In 1979 Laos finally shed its carefully designed neutralist image and became a Vietnamese ally. The Cambodian conflict faced Laos to choose sides, and there was no doubt where its sympathies lay. The ouster of the Pol Pot regime received quick support from Vientiane, which then made its own accusations against the Khmer Rouge. Three battalions of Laotian troops were sent to Cambodia on the Vietnamese side. When the Chinese attacked Vietnam, Laos completely abandoned its pretense of neutrality and condemned Peking by name. Finally, Laos issued a statement (apparently drafted in Hanoi) accusing China of massing many divisions on the Laotian border and asking for the withdrawal of Chinese road-building units in northern Laos. China promptly complied with this demand and later closed its embassy in Vientiane, thus finally ending Chinese presence in Indochina. Subsequently President Souphanouvong visited Phnom Penh and issued a communiqué calling for a common defense front against "aggression and interference by the imperialists and the Peking reactionaries." Hanoi's military presence in Laos was estimated in 1987 at 40,000 to 50,000 troops. In 1988 Vietnam withdrew 25,000 troops. Currently, the Laotian government alleges that there are no Vietnamese troops on its soil since its national security is no longer threatened.

Although China was very restrained in its response to Laotian moves, the Laotian government became extremely nervous about Chinese involvement in Meo guerrilla activities. The party daily, *Vientiane May*, accused China of sending "traitorous lackeys to sow discord among the people of various nationalities residing in northern border areas." According to Bangkok reports, China dispatched the "Lanna division" of 4,000 men to northern Laos.

Relations with China improved during the last half of the 1980s. In 1986 a Chinese delegation visited Laos, the first visit since 1978. The Chinese agreed not to fund Laotian guerrilla movements, and the two nations reestablished diplomatic relations on the ambassadorial level.

Despite a reputation for pragmatism, Laos's international voice has been uncompromisingly radical. Its relations with Thailand have illustrated its tendency to place ideology over practical needs. The exodus of Laotian refugees into Thailand added to the many problems between the two countries. The Laotian rulers also have cited Thailand for aiding rebels within Laos, and the border between the two countries was closed in 1977.

Relations improved markedly after the visit of Thai prime minister Kriangsak Chomanan, the first visit to Laos by a Thai leader. The visit was later returned by Laotian prime minister Kaysone Phomvihan, and in their communiqué the two agreed to cooperate to prevent terrorist activity. Thailand also offered Laos B100 million to buy food, clothing and other consumer goods. Relations between Thailand and Laos deteriorated in 1984 following a border dispute that led to military clashes in which there were hundreds of casualties. The two sides agreed to a ceasefire in 1988 and to the formation of a joint committee for border demarcation.

French influence has all but disappeared in the country. The French-owned tin mines were nationalized in 1977; diplomatic relations with Paris were broken in 1978 but restored in 1982.

Laos joined the United Nations in 1955.

PARLIAMENT

A 264-member National Congress of People's Representatives was convened in 1975 to establish a people's republic. Its principal function was to appoint a 46-member People's Supreme Council, charged with the drafting of a constitution. The powers of the Council were unclear in the absence of the constitution. It approved appointments made by the Lao People's Revolutionary Party and ratified laws it was asked to approve. The first national elections since the communists came to power in 1975 were held in 1989. A total of 121 candidates vied for 79 seats in the Laos Supreme People's Assembly. Only 47% of the electorate reportedly participated in the voting.

POLITICAL PARTIES

The sole legal political party in the country is the Lao People's Revolutionary Party (Phak Pasason Pativat Lao, PPPL), formerly the People's Party of Laos (Phak Pasason Lao, PPL). The PPPL is the Marxist core of the Lao Patriotic Front (Neo Lao Hak Xat, NLHX), the political wing of the former Pathet Lao, later the Lao People's Liberation Army. The secretary general and guiding genius of the PPPL is Kaysone Phomvihan.

The Laotian Patriotic Front was replaced in 1979 by the Lao Front for National Reconstruction. The new front is headed by Souphanouvong, as president; a seven-member Politburo; and a Central Committee of 23 members and four alternates. The Central Committee includes two Meo minority representatives.

ECONOMY

Laos is one of the poorest and least developed countries in Asia and the world. It has a centrally planned economy in which the public sector is absolute and monolithic.

The country is overwhelmingly agricultural with subsistence agriculture involving approximately 85% of the workforce and accounting for more than 60% of the GDP. The predominant crop is rice. Laos is a landlocked country with a primitive infrastructure. It has no railroads, few roads, limited external and internal telecommunications and electrical power available in only limited areas.

Following its assumption of power in 1975, the Lao People's Revolutionary Party debated the pace of socialist transformation. Hardliners demanded a rapid transition to a centralized economy while the more pragmatic favored a mixed state/private economy as a step in a gradual transition. During 1976–78 the government pursued a policy of rapid agricultural collectivization, but the policy failed dismally, and a more gradual approach was adopted. Recently, the government has been decentralizing control and encouraging private enterprise.

PRINCIPAL ECONOMIC INDICATORS

Gross National Product (U.S. $ millions): 693 (1989)
GNP per capita (U.S. $): 170 (1989)
GNP average annual growth rate (%, 1980–89): 3.0
GNP per capita average annual growth rate (%, 1987–89): 2.5
Average annual rate of inflation (%, 1980–87): 46.5

GROSS DOMESTIC PRODUCT

GDP nominal (K. millions): 585 (1989)
GDP per capita (U.S. $): 150 (1989)
Average annual growth rate of GDP (%, 1980–87): 5.3
GDP by type of expenditure (%) 1986
  Gross domestic saving: 21
Sectoral origin of GDP (%) 1987
  Primary
    Agriculture: 68
  Secondary
    Manufacturing, mining, public utilities: 5
    Construction: 4
  Tertiary
    Transportation & communications: 2
    Trade: 9
    Finance, government, other services: 7

PUBLIC FINANCE

The Laotian fiscal year runs from July 1 through June 30. More than 60% of the wartime budgets until 1975 was devoted to military operations. During the civil war years normal budgetary procedures were abandoned, and budgetary deficits were covered by foreign aid.

Most government revenue is derived from customs duties and other indirect taxation, but an agricultural tax and revenue from state-run shops augment government funds. Efforts to collect government revenue are often frustrated, however. The government has sought to increase taxation levied on the private sector, but collection of taxes from industry was reportedly 60%–70% short of expectations, and it was claimed that food aid received from abroad was being diverted to feed Vietnamese soldiers. To tap alternative sources of funds, a complex agricultural tax has been introduced, and efforts have been made to boost savings, but targets are unlikely to be attained: The population has little confidence that money secured by the government in this way will be properly used. Similarly, the government's determination to hold salary increases in the state sector below the rate of inflation has merely prompted civil servants to neglect their duties and seek secondary employment.

Since 1956 a number of development plans were prepared by the government and then abandoned because of internal strife. The first five-year plan following the communist takeover (1981–85) looked toward self-sufficiency in food and a doubling of industrial activity. The latest plan (1986–90) has similar objectives. In addition it calls for the development of economic zones to spur integrated growth and better monitoring of the environment.

FOREIGN AID, 1989

Total foreign aid (U.S. $ millions): 207.3
  Bilateral: 58.0
  Multilateral: 149.3

Until 1975 Laos received substantial foreign aid from the United States, France, the United Kingdom, Australia, West Germany, Thailand, Canada, India and the United Nations. The largest donor was the United States, whose economic assistance alone totaled $800 million through 1972. During the period 1970–88 Laos received $895 million in aid from Communist countries.

CURRENCY & BANKING

The Laotian unit of currency is the kip (officially known as the new kip), divided into 100 ats. Coins are issued in denominations of 10, 20 and 50 ats; notes are issued in denominations of 10, 20, 50, 100, 200 and 500 new kips.

The kip was introduced in 1955, replacing the Indochinese piastre with an initial dollar exchange rate of $1 = 35 kips. The currency was devalued in 1958, 1964 and 1971, when the official free rate was fixed at $1 = 600 kips. The currency was devalued again in 1975, when the rates were fixed at $1 = 750 kips (buying) and 1,200 kips (selling). In June 1976 the new kip was introduced, replacing the former currency at the rate of 1 new kip = 20 old kips. The currency was devalued by 70% so that the exchange rate became $1 = K200. This rate remained in force until 1978, when a new rate of $1 = K400 was introduced. In 1979 a revised version of the new kip was introduced, worth 100 of the former kips. At the same time the currency was devalued by 75%, and the exchange rate was set at $1 = 16 new kips. The currency was devalued by 67% in 1981, in 1982, and again in 1987 when it was devalued by 90%. The dollar exchange rate in June 1991 was $1 = NK699.

The Lao monetary system is composed of two institutions, the Banque d'État de la RDP Lao, the central bank; and the Banque du Commerce Extérieur Lao (BCEL), a subsidiary of the central bank. The central bank concerns itself mostly with domestic banking activities. Since 1980 the central bank has been the sole issuer of the national currency, the new kip. It is the major source of credit and also holds all government accounts in new kips.

FINANCIAL INDICATORS, 1989

Total reserves minus gold (SDRs millions): 12
SDRs (millions): 0
Reserve position in IMF (SDRs millions): 0
Foreign exchange (SDRs millions): 12
External debt 1988
Total (U.S. $ millions): 824
of which public (U.S. $ millions): 816
of which private (U.S. $ millions): 0
Debt service (long-term)
Total (U.S. $ millions): 816
Repayment
Principal (%): 77.8
Interest (%): 22.2
Debt service ratio (%): 128.6
External public debt as % of GNP: 153.5
Debt service as % of GNP: 1.8
Debt service as % of exports: 143.5
Terms of public borrowing
Commitment (U.S. $ millions): 86
Average interest rate (%): 0.3
Average maturity (yrs.): 46
Net flow of publicly guaranteed external capital (U.S. $ millions): 112

GROWTH PROFILE
(Annual Growth Rates, %)

Projected population (1988–2000): 2.9
Projected crude birth rate (/1,000) (1990–95): 38.1
Projected crude death rate (/1,000) 1990–95): 14.4
Urban population (1980–88): 6.1
Labor force (1985–2000): 2.2
GNP (1980–89): 3.0
GNP per capita (1987–89): 2.5
GDP (1980–88): 5.3
Inflation (1980–88): 46.5
Energy production (1980–88): −0.2
Energy consumption (1980–88): 2.0

The BCEL, as the holder of official reserves, is involved mostly in international transactions. It contracts foreign loans, and it registers most official foreign debt in its balance sheet as well as residents' foreign currency loans and deposits. Since 1980, to improve financial management, financial policies and priorities have been set within the framework of a cash plan that identifies areas in which action can be taken to influence the money demands of holders of private cash.

Vientiane's five commercial banks were shut down in 1975 in a government effort to stem the outflow of foreign currency.

AGRICULTURE

Of the total land area of 23,680,000 ha. (58,513,280 ac.), only 8% is considered suitable for agriculture. However, only 692,200 ha. (1,710,426 ac.) are actually under cultivation.

Land tenure rests on tradition and custom rather than on law. Generally, anyone who clears free land and cultivates it is considered to be its owner. Similarly, property abandoned for more than three years reverts to the state. There is very little absentee ownership, and more than 80% of rural families own their own ricefields. The average farm size is 2 ha. (5 ac.).

The right of land ownership has been retained by the Pathet Lao government, but larger holdings have been expropriated and redistributed to peasant farmers.

The two major farming methods are primitive and have remained relatively unchanged for centuries: wet rice cultivation in paddy fields utilizing irrigation canals, dikes and terraces; and dry rice cultivation employing swidden, or slash-and-burn agriculture, which soon exhausts the fertility of the soil. Yields may be as high as 1.5 tons of rice per hectare (0.6 ton of rice per acre) in the first year but fall to about 0.5 ton of rice per hectare (0.2 ton of rice per acre) after the second harvest. Less than 30,000 ha. (74,130 ac.) are under some form of irrigation. Though the government encourages mechanized farming, there were only 800 tractors in the country in 1986.

During 1978–80, the government attempted to collectivize agriculture. Although Kaysone Phomvihan acknowledged the difficulties and even the unwisdom of forcing cooperatives on unwilling peasants, overzealous party cadres made no efforts to slow the forced march to socialism. In the first six months of 1979 the number of cooperatives went up from 1,600 to 2,600. In terms of productivity, the program was a disaster because peasants either refused to hand over their land or fled to Thailand. To compensate for the loss of manpower, the government transferred thousands of civil servants to farms, but they, too, joined the exodus to Thailand.

In 1988 the government introduced legislation that permitted the assignment of cooperative rice fields to individuals. Families were no longer forced to farm collectively and were permitted to dispose of their crops as they liked rather than sell a proportion to the government at artificially low prices.

Considerable emphasis has been placed on land reclamation to expand ricefields. Emphasis also has been given to improving irrigation, but the most significant boost to rice production is likely to come from double-cropping through growing winter-spring rice.

One positive development was the increase in production of subsidiary crops such as tobacco and coffee.

The main crop is rice, almost entirely of the glutinous variety. The total area under rice is estimated at 680,000 ha. (1,680,280 ac.). In 1985 Laos, for the first time, produced enough rice to meet its own needs. Other major crops are corn, wheat, cotton, coffee, tobacco, vegetables and fruit. The most important cash crop is opium, although its sale is illegal.

Livestock breeding is an important activity in the southern plains. Before the civil war Laos was a net exporter of livestock, but the war has decimated the national herd.

Fish are abundant in the Mekong River and its tributaries, but fishing remains a supplementary occupation. Fish constitutes an important article of the Laotian diet, but since supplies from the Mekong River are inadequate to meet the demand, fresh fish and fish products are imported.

AGRICULTURAL INDICATORS

Agriculture's share of GDP (%): 59 (1988)
Value added in agriculture (U.S. $ millions): 297 (1988)
Cereal imports (000 metric tons): 115 (1988)
Index of agricultural production (1979–81 = 100): 146 (1986)
Index of food production (1979–81 = 100): 147 (1986)
Index of food production per capita (1979–81 = 100): 123 (1985–88)
Number of tractors: 800 (1986)
Total fertilizer consumption (000 metric tons): 1.4 (1985–86)
Fertilizer consumption (g./ha., hundreds): 6 (1987–88)
Farms as % of total land area: 7.1 (1983)
Land use (%) 1985–87
  Cropland: 4
  Pasture: 3
  Forest: 57
  Other: 36
Yields (kg./ha.) 1989
  Grains: 2,291
  Roots & tubers: 8,272
  Legumes: 2,133
  Milk (kg./animal): 200
Production 1989
  Fruits (000 metric tons): 186
  Vegetables (000 metric tons): 258
Livestock (000) 1989
  Cattle: 805
  Horses: 42 (1986)
  Pigs: 1,300
Forestry 1988
  Production of roundwood (million cubic meters): 3.878
    of which industrial roundwood (%): 8.0
  Value of exports (U.S. $ millions): 10.251
Fishing 1988
  Total catch (000 metric tons): 20.0
    of which marine (%): 0.0
  Value of exports (U.S. $ 000): 0.0

Forests cover two-thirds of the country, and half this area is economically exploitable. Lumbering is carried out in all regions, and the Mekong River and its tributaries provide a natural means of transporting logs. Teak is the most important wood, particularly in the Syaboury region. Other forest products include charcoal, benzoin, bamboo, rattan, stick lac and other resins.

MANUFACTURING

Laos has only rudimentary industry, employing 7.1% (1985) of the work force and contributing 7% (1988) to the GDP; the conditions favoring the introduction of modern manufacturing facilities are completely lacking. The country has few natural resources, few skilled workers, few experienced managers and a limited domestic market. Its sawmills and rice mills employ only a handful of workers each. Other industrial establishments include brick factories; distilleries; and plants manufacturing cigarettes, matches, plastic bags, shoes, candles, soft drinks, plastics, detergents, barbed wire and nails. Most of the 600 manufacturing plants are concentrated in Vientiane. The Pathet Lao government discourages foreign investment.

State ownership is not universal: Factories whose management is willing to follow government production guidelines have been allowed to continue. In these mixed ventures the state and the private sector share profits in accordance with the size of their shareholding.

Inadequate financial incentives, lack of entrepreneurial skills and shortages of raw materials have combined to stunt industrial development. The flight of technicians has made it impossible to operate even existing plants. The former French-owned Phon Tiou tin mine in southern Laos is now run with Soviet assistance. Compounding these problems is a persistent transportation bottleneck, which has resulted in large stocks of goods piling up at border points.

MANUFACTURING INDICATORS, 1987

Share of GDP (%): 7 (1988)
Labor force economically active in manufacturing (% est.): 7.1 (1985)
Value added in manufacturing (U.S. $ millions): 47

MINING

The only mineral commercially exploited by the state, is tin, the second most valuable export commodity. The tin deposits at Phontiou and Nangsun, now run with Soviet assistance, produced 352 tons in 1984. A survey of the mineral potential of the country yielded the discovery in 1974 of a potash-rich sylvite field covering 30 sq. km. (12 sq. mi.), and iron deposits with reserves of 68% pure ore estimated at 1 billion tons in the Plain of Jars. A major coal deposit was found at Saravane.

ENERGY

Electricity, which Laos sells to Thailand, is Laos's principal earner of foreign exchange. It contributed $32 million to export revenue in 1986. With the completion of the second phase of the Japanese-aided Nam Ngum hydroelectric project, installed capacity will be raised to 110,000 kw.-hr., of which over 100,000 kw.-hr. will be exported to Thailand. Laos is heavily dependent on petroleum from Thailand. This dependency

ENERGY INDICATORS

Average annual energy production growth rate (%, 1980–88): −0.2
Energy consumption per capita (kg. oil equivalent): 37 (1988)
Average annual growth rate of energy consumption (%, 1980–88): 2.0
Electricity 1988
  Installed capacity (000 kw.): 225
  Production (billion kw.-hr.): 1.100
    % fossil fuel: 4.5
    % hydro: 95.5
  Consumption per capita (kw.-hr.): 94
Petroleum
  Production (million bbl.): 0 (1989)
  Consumption (million bbl.): 0 (1988)
  Refining capacity (000 bbl./day): 0 (1990)

is expected to diminish following the completion of a 395-km. (246 mi.) pipeline from Vietnam.

LABOR

The economically active population of Laos in 1982 was estimated at 1.8 million, of whom 75% were employed in agriculture, 6% in industry and 19% in services. There was a high rate of participation by women and children in the rural work force.

Two major characteristics of Laotian labor are the serious shortage of skilled labor and the low level of occupational mobility. Until 1975 ethnic aliens made up a high proportion of skilled labor. Voluntary migration to the towns to seek permanent employment is rare. The result is a highly stratified labor force with few incentives or competitive pressures.

LABOR INDICATORS, 1985

Total economically active population (millions): 2.014
- % working-age (15–64): 84.2
- % female: 45.3

Activity rate (%)
- Total: 48.9
- Male: 53.1
- Female: 44.6

Sectoral employment of economically active (%) 1980
- Agriculture, forestry, fishing: 75.7
- Construction, manufacturing, mining, quarrying, public utilities: 7.1
- Trade, hotels, restaurants, transportation, communications, finance, real estate, services: 17.2

Average annual growth rate of labor force (%, 1985–2000): 2.2
Labor under 20 years (%): 20.8 (1985)

Working conditions and wages are governed by the Labor Code of 1967, as modified by decrees, orders and regulations that came into force after 1975. This code prohibited forced labor; prescribed conditions of work contracts and dismissal; regulated collective bargaining agreements; and determined working hours, holidays and overtime wages. It also established a system of workmen's compensation covering occupational diseases and industrial accidents. However, the code has been poorly enforced and as a result has been largely ignored by employers.

In 1975 the labor unions in the country were consolidated into the Labor Federation, under the auspices of the Lao People's Revolutionary Party. No strikes have been reported in the country since 1975.

FOREIGN COMMERCE

Major export products are electric power, timber, tin concentrates, coffee, and undeclared opium and tobacco. Major import products are rice, petroleum products, machinery and transportation equipment. Major import sources are Thailand, the Soviet Union, Japan, France and Vietnam. Major export destinations are Thailand and Malaysia.

The United States suspended trade with Laos in 1975.

FOREIGN TRADE INDICATORS, 1988

Exports (U.S. $ millions): 57.5
Imports (U.S. $ millions): 219.0
Balance of trade (U.S. $ millions): −161.5
International reserves in terms of months of imports covered: 0.9

Direction of Trade (%), 1980

	Imports	Exports
European Community	3.1	1.4
United States	0.3	3.3
Japan	9.1	7.2

Composition of Trade (%)

	Imports (1974)	Exports (1985)
Food and agricultural raw materials	32.1	46.5
Fuels & other energy	11.2	50.1
Mineral ores & concentrates	0.2	3.4
Manufactured goods	56.4	0.0
of which chemicals	6.1	0.0
of which machinery	25.7	0.0

TRANSPORTATION & COMMUNICATIONS

Laos has no rail system. The inland waterways provide the cheapest and most extensive means of transportation within the country. The length of inland waterways totals 4,587 km. (2,850 mi.). In addition, there are 2,897 km. (1,799 mi.) of rivers navigable by small craft. The Mekong is the largest transportation artery, but numerous rapids north of Vientiane and south of Savannakhet make necessary the transshipment of cargo. Five major river ports and four minor ones serve the river traffic.

There are 21,300 km. (13,227 mi.) of roads, of which 1,300 km. (807 mi.) are bitumen-surfaced. The main routes link Vientiane and Luang Prabang with Ho Chi Minh City, Vientiane with Savannakhet and Khammaouane with Ha Tink in northern Vietnam. China assisted in the construction of a road from Luang Prabang to Pak Bang as part of a network that will lead into China through Vietnam.

TRANSPORTATION INDICATORS

Roads (latest)
- Length, km. (mi.): 27,527 (17,105)
- Paved (%): 31

Motor vehicles (latest)
- Automobiles: 15,800
- Trucks and buses: 3,000
- Persons per vehicle: 200

Air
- Passenger-km. (passenger-mi.) (millions): 18 (11) (latest)
- Freight, metric ton-km. (short ton-mi.) (millions): 2.0 (1.4) (latest)
- Airports with scheduled flights: 4 (1990)

Pipelines 1990
- Refined, km. (mi.): 136 (84.5)

Inland waterways (latest)
- Length, km. (mi.): 4,587 (2,850)

The national airline is Lao Aviation, which operates services to Vietnam, Cambodia, Hong Kong and Thailand. Wattay Airport, at Vientiane, is the international airport.

COMMUNICATIONS INDICATORS, 1988

Telephones
- Total (000): 8.1 (1985)
- Persons per telephone: 450 (1985)

Phone traffic (000 minutes)
- Local: 128
- Long distance: 4,109
- Combined national: 4,237
- International: 785

Post office
- Number of post offices: 105 (1987)
- Pieces of mail handled (millions): 37.100 (1987)

Telegraph
- Total traffic (million words): 4.223
  - National: 4.044
  - International: .179

Telex
- Subscriber lines: 52

Telecommunications 1990
- Satellite ground station: 1

In 1982 a total of 29,000 tourists visited the country, mostly from Vietnam. Since 1975 very few Western tourists have been allowed into the country.

DEFENSE

Since 1975 the Pathet Lao, or the Lao People's Liberation Army, has been transformed into the national army, and the former royalist forces have been disbanded. The Pathet Lao was a wing of the PPPL, and its present command structure is not clear. The army is, however, subordinate to the party, and operational command rests with the minister of defense, who also is the supreme commander.

Until 1975 military manpower was provided by compulsory enlistment of all able-bodied males between 19 and 45. Currently, military service is compulsory for 18 months.

Army

Personnel: 52,000

Organization: 4 military regions; 4 infantry divisions; 1 artillery division; 7 independent infantry regiments; 1 engineer regiment; 2 construction regiments; 5 artillery and 9 AA artillery battalions; 65 independent infantry companies

Equipment: 30 heavy tanks; 25 light tanks; 48 armored personnel carriers; 80 guns and howitzers; mortars; rocket launchers; air defense guns

Navy

Personnel: 1,650

Patrol craft: 20

Air Force

Personnel: 2,000

Equipment: 20 combat aircraft; 1 fighter squadron; 1 transport squadron; 1 helicopter squadron; trainers; AAM

The Laotian armed forces consist of tough, seasoned men exposed to warfare for most of their adult lives. Though rated as inferior to the Vietnamese in fighting quality, their combat-worthiness is estimated by most military observers as higher than that of comparable Asian troops. The cutting edge of the armed forces is the irregular force, which can conduct independent and unorthodox operations even in unfamiliar terrain. The air force has also received praise for its combat performance, and its pilots are said to be skillful and courageous.

At the end of the civil war the Pathet Lao seized the armaments of the royalist forces, supplied over the years by the United States. Much of the equipment thus obtained is not operational now because of lack of spare parts. The Laotian armed forces continue to receive direct military assistance from the Soviet Union and Vietnam. Between 40,000 and 50,000 Vietnamese troops are stationed on Laotian soil in addition to 1,000 Soviets.

EDUCATION

The national literacy rate is 83.9% (males 92% and females 75.8%).

Education is in principal universal, compulsory and free for five years for children between ages seven and 12. Schooling consists of 11 years, divided into five years of primary education and six years of secondary education. Primary education is divided into two cycles of three and two years each. There are four types of schools at this level: district group elementary schools, which offer the full five-year course; village primary schools; elementary schools; and rural centers of community education, the last three offering shorter courses lasting less than five years. The elementary and secondary curricula have been reformed on the Vietnamese model to incorporate Marxist ideological courses. The educational system has two primary functions: to indoctrinate the student in the new values of a radical society, and to meet the manpower needs of the state.

The academic year runs from September to May. The medium of instruction is Lao, but French is taught as a second language from the primary grades on. English and Vietnamese are taught as additional languages in secondary schools.

Most teachers are poorly paid and ill-qualified. Primary-school teachers are required to hold a lower-cycle secondary school certificate and to attend a teacher-training school. Secondary-school teachers must be licentiates in education.

Since 1975 the government has nationalized and secularized the private educational institutions. Technical education is provided in technical colleges and crafts schools. Nearly 2.2% of the secondary-school enrollment is in the vocational stream.

Elementary schooling is traditionally the responsibility of the local communities. The national government supports all other aspects of the public education system, including construction and maintenance of

EDUCATION INDICATORS, 1986

Literacy
- Total (%): 83.9
- Male (%): 92.0
- Female (%): 75.8

First level
- Schools: 8,011
- Students: 523,347
- Teachers: 21,033
- Student–teacher ratio: 24.9

Second level
- Schools: 563 (1985)
- Students: 97,197
- Teachers: 8,032
- Student–teacher ratio: 12.1

Vocational
- Schools: 117 (1985)
- Students: 16,433
- Teachers: 2,114
- Student–Teacher ratio: 7.8

Third level (postsecondary)
- Institutions: 6
- Students: 4,950
- Teachers: 534
- Student–teacher ratio: 9.3
- Gross enrollment ratio: 1.7 (1985)
- Students (/100,000 pop.): 141

Foreign study
- Foreign students in national universities: 103 (1987)
- Students abroad: 680
  - of whom in
    - United States: 263 (1988)
    - France: 208 (1988)
    - Federal Republic of Germany: 16 (1988)
    - United Kingdom: 1 (1987)

Public expenditure 1987
- Total (K. 000): 4,141,872
- % of GNP: 4.2
- % of national budget: 26.6
- % of current expenditure: 86.4

GRADUATES, 1985

Total: 1,231
Education: 817
Humanities & religion: 0
Fine & applied arts: 0
Law: 0
Social & behavioral sciences: 0
Commerce & business: 0
Mass communication: 0
Home economics: 0
Service trades: 0
Natural sciences: 0
Mathematics & computer science: 0
Medicine: 162
Engineering: 0
Architecture: 94
Industrial programs: 0
Transportation & communications: 99
Agriculture, forestry, fisheries: 0
Other: 59

schools, teachers' salaries and textbooks. No information has been available since 1975 on educational expenditures.

Sisavong Vong University in Vientiane, is the country's only university.

LEGAL SYSTEM

Until a new constitution is ratified, the highest court of the land is the Central Supreme Court in Vientiane. Under its jurisdiction are a court of appeals, in Vientiane; three criminal courts, at Vientiane, Pakse and Luang Prabang; one provincial tribunal for each provincial capital; and 37 district justices of the peace. At the village level justice usually is dispensed by village headmen in the presence of village elders.

No code of law exists in Laos, and there is no guaranteed due process. The government still is revising the pre-1975 law code and rehabilitating the court system. It is expected to publish a constitution shortly. In the meantime, it has promulgated interim rules and regulations for the arrest and trial of those accused of specific crimes, including armed resistance to the government. These regulations were disseminated to local authorities in October 1978, primarily to correct the haphazard way in which they were carrying out their duties. Although the regulations allow the accused to make a statement presenting his side of the case, they provide no real opportunity for the accused to defend himself and do not permit bail or use of an attorney. Rather, the government has issued instructions on how to investigate, prosecute and punish wrongdoers. These instructions are applied capriciously and inconsistently. People can be arrested on the accusation of others and detained while the accusations are investigated. Those arrested are not always informed of the charges against them, and investigations often take a long time unless family members and friends take a strong interest in the cases. Influential government officials and their families can easily influence the judgments reached. There is some provision for appeal, except that important political cases tried by "people's courts" are without appeal.

No information is available on the penal system and corrections facilities in Laos.

LAW ENFORCEMENT

The national law enforcement force, the Tamrouat Lao, is organized regionally into the metropolitan police of Vientiane and the territorial police of the provinces, both centrally controlled by a director general. The total police strength is estimated at 6,000. In addition to regular uniformed police, there are three special units: security police, immigration police and judicial police. The territorial police are divided into four commands, each staffed by one police legion, further divided into provincial and district-level units. Where the road system is inadequate, regular policemen are supplemented by river and mounted police. The provincial police commissioners report both to the central headquarters and to their respective provincial governors.

No information is available on the incidence and nature of crime in Laos.

HEALTH

The major health problems are malaria, trachoma, dysentery, tuberculosis, pneumonia, typhoid, yaws and hepatitis. Twenty-one percent of the population has access to safe water.

Health services are free, but patients are charged for Western medicine when it is available. Most medicines are supplied by U.N. organizations or humanitarian agencies. The government emphasizes preventive medicine to improve public health.

HEALTH INDICATORS

Health personnel 1985
- Physicians: 558
  - persons per: 6,495
- Dentists: 15 (1976)
- Nurses and midwives: 6,753
- Pharmacists: 16 (1976)

Hospitals 1985
- Number: 38 (1975)
- Number of beds (/10,000): 31
- Admissions/discharges (/10,000): 96
- Bed occupancy rate (%): 19.7
- Average length of stay (days): 7

Vital statistics
- Crude death rate (/1,000): 17 (1990)
- Life expectancy at birth 1990
  - Males: 48
  - Females: 51
- Infant mortality rate (/1,000 live births): 126 (1990)
- Child mortality rate under 5 yrs. (/1,000 births) (1985–90): 160
- Population with access to safe water (%): 21 (latest)

FOOD & NUTRITION

Rice is the staple food of the average Laotian, making up nearly 90% of the daily diet. Other mainstays are fish and fish sauce, eggs, fruits and vegetables. Milk and meat are consumed only by the well-to-do. Corn is eaten as a supplementary food in hill tribe areas. Though the diet is deficient, few people go hungry even in times of crop failures. The daily intake of food per capita is 1,992 calories (90% of requirements).

MEDIA & CULTURE

All existing newspapers were suspended upon establishment of the People's Republic and replaced by a daily, *Vientiane May*, the organ of the Party Committee. About seven other periodicals are published in French and Lao, with a total circulation of about 10,000 copies. In 1977 the last permanent Western press correspondent in Vientiane was forced to leave Laos. Western journalists are, however, still allowed, but for them, as for the Western diplomats, most of the country is off limits.

The national news agency is Khao San Pathet Lao, which publishes a government organ of the same name in French and Lao. Novosti and Vietnam News Agency maintain bureaus in Vientiane.

There were at least three book publishers in Vientiane until 1975, when book publishing was nationalized by the new regime. Because of the low literacy rate, many publications are largely pictorial. Laos does not adhere to any copyright convention.

The official broadcasting organization, Lao National Radio, operates one shortwave and three medium-wave transmitters, which are on the air for 94 hours a week, broadcasting in Lao, French and Vietnamese. The Voice of Peaceful Laos and the Voice of Pathet Lao also are broadcast on medium-wave and short wave, to both domestic and foreign listeners.

MEDIA INDICATORS

Newspapers
- Number of dailies: 3 (latest)
- Circulation (000): 13 (latest)
- Per 1,000 pop.: 4 (latest)
- Newsprint consumption
  - Total metric tons: 200 (1980)
  - Per 1,000 pop. (kg.): 62 (1980)

Radio
- Number of transmitters: 19 (1989)
- Number of persons per radio receiver: 9.3 (1989)

Television
- Television transmitters: 2 (1989)
- Number of persons per T.V. receiver: 123 (1989)

Television was introduced in 1983 and is run by Lao National Television.

Though there were only 19 cinemas in 1971, motion pictures are very popular. There is no indigenous film production.

The largest library is the National Library at Vientiane, with a collection of over 9,000 volumes presented by the Rockefeller Foundation.

SOCIAL WELFARE

Laos has no Social Security or official social welfare programs. There is a limited provident fund system with optional membership covering all employees except unskilled workers. Public employees receive some old-age and death benefits.

GLOSSARY

amat: middle grade of the civil service.
ban: village, as a unit of local administration.
chao khoueng: governor of a province.
chao muong: chief of a district.
kha: literally, slave; term applied to the Lao Theung, or mountain Lao.
khoueng: province, as a unit of local administration.
maha amat: superior grade of the civil service.
muong: district, as a unit of local administration.
nai bon: a village headman in the north.
nai kong: special category of civil servants assigned to tribal areas.
nai tasseng: head of a canton.
Nang Xu Tham: liturgical language of the Buddhist clergy, derived from Sanskrit and Pali.
pho bon: a village headman in the south.
Tamrouat Lao: national police force of Laos.
tasseng: canton, as a unit of local administration.
tripartism: the Provisional Government of National

Union, a coalition of leftist, rightist and neutralist groups, which ruled Laos intermittently from 1962.

CHRONOLOGY (from 1949)

1949— Laos becomes a nominally independent state within the French Union, with Prince Boun Oum as prime minister.

1950— Phoui Sananikone replaces Boun Oum as prime minister. The Lao Patriotic Front (Neo Lao Hak Xat, NLHX) is founded, with Prince Souphanouvong as leader.

1951— Prince Souvanna Phouma forms his first ministry.

1953— Viet Minh troops with support from Pathet Lao troops cross into northern Laos and establish a resistance government in the province of Houa Phan. . . . Laos is granted complete independence by France.

1954— Souvanna Phouma yields post of prime minister to Katay Don Sasorith. . . . Geneva Conference reaches a settlement for Laos under which the two northern provinces, Phong Saly and Houa Phan, are granted to the Pathet Lao, and an International Commission for Supervision and Control (ICC) is set up with India, Canada and Poland as members.

1955— General elections are held.

1956— Souvanna Phouma resumes office of prime minister.

1957— Under the Vientiane Agreement a coalition government is formed, with the Pathet Lao as one group, as a first step toward their reintegration into the kingdom.

1958— The NLHX and its allies win 13 of the 21 seats in supplementary national elections; the United States suspends aid; the Government of National Union falls, and its successor, headed by Phoui Sananikone, excludes the Pathet Lao from the government. . . . Committee for the Defense of National Interests gains upper hand in the leadership; Prince Souphanouvong is jailed but manages to escape and renews revolt.

1959— Prince Savang Vatthana ascends the throne as king.

1960— Kouprasith Abhay and Prince Tiami Somsanith hold office of prime minister briefly. . . . Young paratroop commander Kong Le seizes Vientiane in a coup and installs new government with Souvanna Phouma as prime minister; rightist general Phoumi Nosovan leads countercoup, retakes the capital and expels Kong Le and Souvanna Phouma. . . . Neutralists and Pathet Lao join forces.

1961— Combined leftist and neutralist forces win back initiative. . . . Two governments prevail in Laos: Prince Boun Oum's royalist government in the capital and Souvanna Phouma's neutralist government at Khang Khay. . . . Boun Oum calls for a cease-fire. . . . International conference at Geneva guarantees cease-fire and signs agreement on the neutrality and independence of Laos and the evacuation of all foreign forces. . . . Government of National Union is formed with Souvanna Phouma as prime minister and General Phoumi Nosovan and Prince Souphanouvong as deputy prime ministers.

1963— Kong Le's forces and the Pathet Lao split. . . . The NLHX withdraws from the government, although the fiction of a coalition is maintained.

1964— Souvanna Phouma is briefly overthrown by a rightist coup but is almost immediately reinstated. . . . Pathet Lao resume fighting.

1965— Rightist general Phoumi Nosovan leads an abortive coup and is forced to flee to Thailand, where he is granted asylum. . . . The NLHX boycotts elections.

1967— National elections are again boycotted by the NLHX.

1974— In the aftermath of U.S. withdrawal from Vietnam, a third coalition government is formed, with the NLHX as the dominant partner. . . . The Pathet Lao is believed to control three-fourths of the national territory.

1975— The Pathet Lao launch final drive to achieve complete political and military supremacy; United States closes AID mission in capital; rightists flee country in thousands; United States ends two decades of military presence in Laos. . . . People's Democratic Republic of Laos is proclaimed; King Savang Vatthana abdicates throne. . . . People's Congress is convened, which, in turn, appoints 45-member People's Supreme Council; a new government is named, with Prince Souphanouvong as president and Kaysone Phomvihan as prime minister. Thai border is closed to stem flight of refugees.

1976— As the exchange value of the kip plummets to $1 = K14,000, the government introduces the new kip as the national currency.

1977— Border clashes with Cambodia are reported. . . . Ex-king Vatthana is arrested. . . . Laos and Vietnam conclude 25-year Treaty of Friendship and Cooperation.

1978— Diplomatic relations with France are broken over French support for Moe rebels.

1979— The Lao Patriotic Front is replaced by the Lao Front for National Construction; Laos backs Vietnam in conflict with Cambodia; Cambodian troops are deployed against the Khmer Rouge; Souphanouvong visits Phnom Penh and joins the Heng Samrin government and Vietnam in a call for mutual defense of Indochina. . . . Laos accuses China of massing troops on the Laotian border and orders withdrawal of Chinese road-builders in northern Laos; China complies with Laotian demand and closes embassy in Vientiane; Thai prime minister Kriangsak visits Vientiane, and Kaysone Phomvihan returns the visit as the two nations make an effort to reduce tensions. . . . The new kip is replaced by a revised version of the new kip and devalued by 75%.

1982— Diplomatic relations with France are restored.

1983— Third Congress of the Lao People's Revolutionary Party is held.

1984— Border dispute erupts with Thailand over three villages.

1986— Souphanouvong suffers a stroke in September and is replaced by Phoumi Vongvichit.

BIBLIOGRAPHY

BOOKS

Adams, Nina S., and Alfred W. McCoy. *Laos: War and Revolution.* New York, 1971.

Branfman, Frederic. *Voices from the Plain of Jars.* New York, 1972.

Brown, MacAlister, and Joseph Zasloff. *Apprentice Revolutionaries: The Communist Movement in Laos, 1930–45.* Stanford, CA, 1986.

Dommen, Arthur J. *Conflict in Laos.* New York, 1971.

———. *Laos: The Keystone of Indochina.* Boulder, CO, 1985.

Fall, Bernard. *Anatomy of a Crisis: The Laotian Crisis of 1960–61.* New York, 1969.

Goldstein, Martin. *American Policy Toward Laos.* Teaneck, NJ, 1973.

Halpern, Joel M. *Economy and Society of Laos.* New Haven, CT, 1964.

———. *Government, Politics and Social Structure in Laos.* New Haven, CT, 1964.

———. *Some Reflections on the War in Laos.* Brussels, 1970.

Langer, P. F., and J. J. Zasloff. *North Vietnam and the Pathet Lao.* Cambridge, MA, 1970.

Language and Orientation Resource Center. *The Peoples and Cultures of Cambodia, Laos and Vietnam.* Washington, D.C., 1981.

Le Bar, Frank M., and Adrienne Suddard. *Laos: Its People, Its Society, Its Culture.* New Haven, CT, 1960.

na Champassak, Sisouk. *Storm over Laos.* New York, 1961.

Ratnam, Perala. *Laos and the Superpowers.* Bombay, 1985.

Smith, Bardwell L. *Religion and Legitimation of Power in Thailand, Laos and Burma.* Chambersburg, PA, 1978.

Stuart-Fox, Martin. *Contemporary Laos: Studies in the Politics and Society of the Lao People's Republic.* New York, 1982.

Stuart-Fox, Martin. *Laos: Politics, Economics, and Society.* Boulder, CO., 1986.

Thee, Marek. *Notes of a Witness: Laos and the Second Indochinese War.* New York, 1973.

Toye, Hugh. *Laos: Buffer State or Battleground.* London, 1968.

Zasloff, J. J. *The Pathet Lao.* Lexington, MA, 1973.

LEBANON

BASIC FACT SHEET

OFFICIAL NAME: Republic of Lebanon (al-Jumhouriya al-Lubnaniya

ABBREVIATION: LE

CAPITAL: Beirut

HEAD OF STATE: President Elias Hrawi (from 1989)

HEAD OF GOVERNMENT: Prime Minister Omar Karami (from 1990)

NATURE OF GOVERNMENT: Multiparty republic

POPULATION: 3,339,331 (1990).

AREA: 10,400 sq. km. (4,015 sq. mi.)

ETHNIC MAJORITY: Arab

LANGUAGE: Arabic

RELIGIONS: Christianity and Islam

UNIT OF CURRENCY: Lebanese Pound

NATIONAL FLAG: A green and brown cedar tree in the center of a white stripe flanked by two red stripes each of which is half as wide as the white stripe

NATIONAL EMBLEM: A heraldic shield with a white stripe running diagonally from the bottom left to the upper right with a cedar tree in the center. The legend "Republic of Lebanon" appears on a scroll beneath in Arabic and English

NATIONAL ANTHEM: "All of Us for the Country, Glory, Flag."

NATIONAL HOLIDAYS: November 22 (Independence Day); December 31 (Evacuation Day); January 1 (New Year's Day); March 22 (Arab League Anniversary). Also variable Christian festivals observed according to the Gregorian and Julian calendars and variable Muslim festivals

NATIONAL CALENDAR: Gregorian and Islamic

PHYSICAL QUALITY OF LIFE INDEX: 79

DATE OF INDEPENDENCE: November 22, 1941 (Proclaimed) (Independence granted by France: January 1, 1944)

DATE OF CONSTITUTION: May 23, 1926

WEIGHTS & MEASURES: The metric system is offlclally used. Traditional weights and measures are still used in rural areas. They include the *okiya* (0.21 kg, 0.47 lb); *oke* (1.28 kg, 2.82 lb); *rottol* (2.55 kg, 5.64 lb); and the *kantar* (255 kg, 564 lb).

GEOGRAPHICAL FEATURES

Lebanon is located on the eastern coast of the Mediterranean Sea with a total land area of 10,400 sq. km. (4,015 sq. mi.) extending 217 km. (135 mi.) northeast to southwest and 56 km. (35 mi.) southeast to northwest. Its Mediterıanean coastline stretches 225 km. (140 mi.).

Lebanon's total international land boundary of 454 km. (282 mi.) is shared with two countries: Syria (375 km.; 233 mi.) and Israel (79 km.; 49 mi.). The border with Syria was determined by the French mandate in 1920. The border with Israel is the Armistice Line of 1949 and is in dispute.

The capital is Beirut, which is also the chief city with a 1990 population of 1.5 million. The second largest town is Tripoli (Tarabulus al-Sham) with a population of 160,000. Other major urban centers include Saida, Sur and Zahlah.

Topographically, Lebanon is divided into four regions: the coastal plain, the coastal mountain range, the central plateau and the eastern mountain range. The plain, a narrow strip about 12 km. (8 mi.) wide in the north, sometimes disappears where the mountains reach the sea. The mountain range, called the Lebanon Mountains, is a series of imposing crests and ridges, the highest peaks of which are the Qurnat as Sawda (3,083 m.; 10,115 ft.) and Jabal Sannin (2,608 m.; 8,557 ft.). To the east the land drops to a broad, troughlike valley known as the Biqa, which opens into the Syrian Plain at Homs. The Biqa Valley, which is about 900 m. (3,000 ft.) above sea level, is 8 to 13 km. (5 to 8 mi.) wide. To the east of the Biqa Valley rise the Anti-Lebanon Mountains (Jabal ash Sharqi) and their southern extension, Mount Hermon (Jabal ash Shaikh), which form the eastern boundary with Syria. With its superb mountain scenery, Lebanon is perhaps the most attractive region in the Middle East.

Two rivers rise in the Biqa: the Orontes, which flows northward into Syria and Turkey, and the Litani, or Leontes, which flows southward and, at a short distance from the Israeli border, bends westward to reach the Mediterranean through a deep gorge.

CLIMATE & WEATHER

Lebanon has, in general, a Mediterranean climate but with a wide variety in climatic conditions. The coastal lowlands are moderately hot in summer and warm in winter. In the coastal mountains about 16 km. (10 mi.) away there is a heavy winter snowfall, and the higher peaks are covered from December to May with snow. The Biqa has a moderately cold winter and a distinctly hot summer as it is cut off from sea winds.

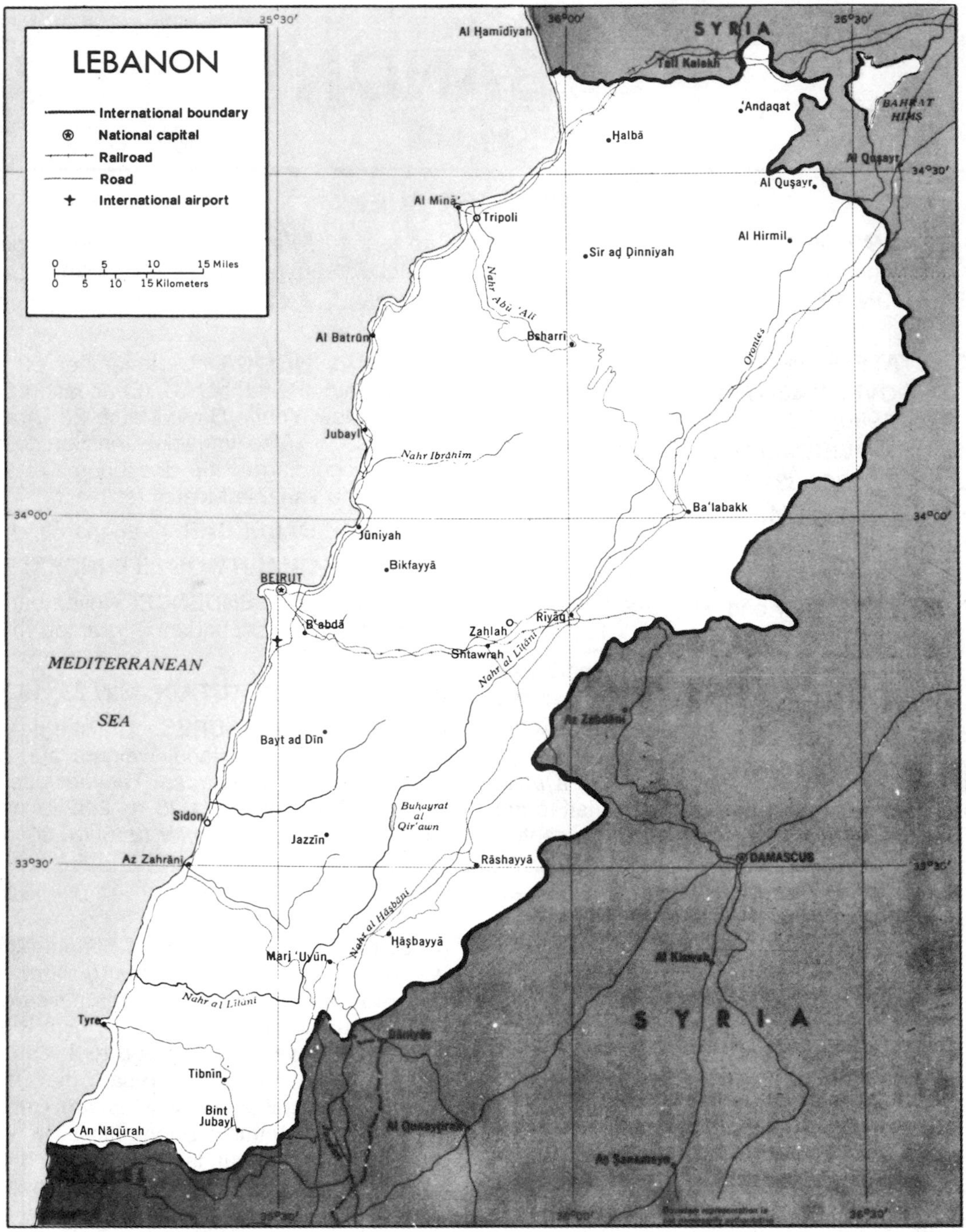

LEBANON

International boundary
National capital
Railroad
Road
International airport

0 5 10 15 Miles
0 5 10 15 Kilometers

35°30′ 36°00′ 36°30′

SYRIA

Al Ḩamīdīyah
Tall Kalakh
'Andaqat
BAHRAT HIMS
Ḩalbā
Al Quşayr
34°30′
Al Mīnā'
Tripoli
Sīr aḑ Ḑinnīyah
Al Hirmil
Nahr Abū 'Alī
Al Batrūn
Bsharrī
Orontes
Jubayl
Nahr Ibrāhīm
34°00′
Ba'labakk
34°00′
Jūniyah
Bikfayyā
BEIRUT
B'abdā
Zaḩlah
Riyāq
Shtawrah
Nahr al Līţānī
MEDITERRANEAN SEA
Az Zabdānī
Bayt ad Dīn
Buḩayrat al Qir'awn
Sidon
Jazzīn
33°30′
Az Zahrānī
Rāshayyā
DAMASCUS
33°30′
Nahr al Ḩāşbānī
Ḩāşbayyā
Marj 'Uyūn
Al Kiswah
Nahr al Līţānī
SYRIA
Tyre
Bāniyās
Tibnīn
Bint Jubayl
An Nāqūrah
Al Qunayţirah
Aş Şanamayn
35°30′ 36°00′ 36°30′

Rainfall, abundant on the whole, decreases rapidly toward the east so that the Biqa and the Anti-Lebanon are drier than the west. Annual rainfall on the coast is between 760 and 1,010 mm. (30 and 40 in.) with up to 1,270 mm. (50 in.) in the mountains but only 380 mm. (15 in.) in the Biqa. Almost all the rain falls between October and April, and the three summer months are completely dry. Average mean temperature in Beirut is 20.5° C (69° F). Average temperatures in the winter range from 13° C (55° F) on the coast to 10° C (50° F) inland while temperatures in the summer range from 29° C (84° F) on the coast to 30° C (86°F) inland.

The prevailing winds are the khamsin, a hot wind blowing from the Egyptian desert, and the severely cold north winter wind.

POPULATION

The population of Lebanon was estimated in 1990 as 3,339,331, based on the last true census held in 1970. Although the government has not taken an official census since 1932, it has maintained a population register in which Lebanese residing abroad are included as citizens. The total population figures excludes registered Palestinian refugees. A later census has never been held for fear of disturbing the supposed proportions of religious communities on which the nation's political balance is precariously based, but it is now generally recognized that the Muslims greatly outnumber the Christians.

It has been estimated that the population of Lebanon has actually been declining as a result of three factors: the deaths due to the civil war, decline in birthrate and emigration. Estimates of casualties in the civil war vary widely; estimates place them at well over 100,000. The decline in birthrate is higher among the Christians than among the Muslims. Finally, the civil war has accelerated a process of emigration that began in the 1920s. According to the Union Libanaise Culturelle Mondiale, over half a million Lebanese left the country during 1975–80 alone. Migration has most seriously affected the work force with the building and the industrial sectors alone losing between 32% and 30% of their employees.

Since the latter part of the 19th century, migration has been a significant factor affecting demographic patterns as well as social, cultural and political developments. Emigration of Lebanese Christians began around the 1860s in response to Ottoman oppression and armed clashes between the Maronites and Druzes. The earliest migrants left for Egypt, then under British rule. From a trickle, emigration became a flood between 1900 and 1914 when 15,000 Lebanese, almost all of them Christians, left each year for the United States, Brazil, or West Africa. It fell sharply during World War I and World War II, but between 1921 and 1939 and since 1945 migrants have averaged 3,000 annually. In the 1960s the establishment of immigration barriers in the United States and increasing hostility toward Lebanese merchants in the newly independent African countries tended to inhibit emigration. Since the mid-1960s emigration has been mostly to other Arab countries. The flow of emigration rose again during the civil war when over 200,000 displaced persons fled to Europe, Syria, Jordan, Egypt and the Persian Gulf countries. The total Lebanese diaspora is estimated at 1,000,000.

The number of aliens residing in Lebanon—most of them Muslims—has been estimated at 50% of the population. These include Syrians and Palestinians. They are excluded from Lebanese citizenship in order to preserve the present religious equilibrium.

Women enjoy equality of civil rights and attend institutions of higher learning in large numbers. Religion and custom still limit women, however. The prevailing atmosphere of insecurity and economic hardship makes it difficult for women to expand their participation in society. The women's organizations

VITAL STATISTICS

Crude birth rate (/1,000): 28 (1990); 40 (1965)
Crude death rate (/1,000): 7 (1990); 12 (1965)
Infant mortality rate (/1,000 live births): 49 (1990)
Life expectancy (yrs.) at birth: males, 66; females, 70 (1990)
Gross reproduction rate (/woman) (1980–85): 1.85
Total fertility rate (/woman): 3.7 (1990)
Rate of natural increase (/1,000): 21.0 (1989)
Marriage rate (/1,000): 7.0 (1973)
Average household size: 5.3 (latest)

DEMOGRAPHIC INDICATORS

Population (millions): 3.339 (1990)
Year of last census: 1970
Sex distribution (% at last census): males, 50.8; females, 49.2
Population estimates and projections (millions)

1940: .965	1970: 2.469	2000: 3.603
1950: 1.443	1980: 2.669	2010: 4.170
1960: 1.857	1990: 2.965	

Age profile (% at last census)

0–14: 42.6	30–44: 16.7	60 and over: 7.7
15–29: 23.8	45–59: 9.1	

Median age (yrs.): 20.2 (1985)
Youth population (% age 15–24): 21.8 (1985); 18.1 (2000)
Total dependency ratio: 74.2 (1985)
Annual growth rate (%)

1950–55: 2.23	1975–1980: −0.72	2000–2005: 1.56
1955–60: 2.82	1980–1985: −0.01	2005–2010: 1.36
1960–65: 2.94	1985–1990: 2.11	2010–2015: 1.22
1965–70: 2.75	1990–1995: 2.05	2015–2020: 1.14
1970–75: 2.28	1995–2000: 1.84	2020–2025: 1.07

Urban population (000): 2146 (1985)
Urban population (%): 60.1 (1970)
Annual urban population growth rate (%, 1985–90): 2.92 (est.)
Annual rural population growth rate (%, 1985–90): −1.58
Percentage of urban population in largest city: 79 (1980)
Percentage of urban population in cities of population over 500,000: 79 (1980)
Number of cities of population over 500,000: 1 (1980)
Population density per sq. km. (per sq. mi.): 289.8 (750.6) (latest)

STATUS OF WOMEN INDICATORS

Number of women (millions): 1.503 (1985)
Women's literacy rate (%): 68.9 (1985)
Women in labor force (%): 18 (1985)
Total fertility rate (/woman): 3.7 (1990)

which do exist are for the most part subordinate arms of one or another of the political parties and work to advance the interests of the parent party rather than of women in general. Moreover, the continuing turbulence has spawned Islamic religious movements which advocate confining women to traditional roles and "modest dress" (e.g., *chadors* and veils).

Though there is no official policy on family planning, there is a growing awareness of its importance and urgency among educated urban families.

ETHNIC COMPOSITION

Arabs constitute the dominant ethnic group in the country with 93% of the population. Armenians are the largest ethnic minority group, followed by Assyrians and Kurds. The few thousand Jews are officially regarded as a separate religious community and not as an ethnic group.

Broadly speaking the term Arab is applied in the Middle East to any one who speaks Arabic as his mother tongue and shares Arab culture. However, in common usage Muslim and Arab are used interchangeably and therefore Christian Lebanese are not always eager to identify themselves as Arabs. The Armenians who constitute roughly 6% of the population are the largest unassimilated group in the country. They inhabit separate quarters in the cities and proudly regard themselves as sojourners waiting for the day when Turkish Armenia will become independent. The Assyrians, who constitute less than 1% of the population, are properly Nestorian Christians (whose relationship to the ancient Assyrians is disputed). They fled from Iraq after World War I and from Syria in the 1950s, and some of them still are stateless. The Muslim Kurds, who also constitute less than 1% of the population, have been almost completely absorbed into the Arab mainstream. None of these minorities pose any threat to the Arab majority and interethnic relations are therefore harmonious.

Nationals of other countries constitute well over 50% of the population. Aliens include Syrians, Palestinians, Egyptians and other Africans. It has never been determined how many of these aliens are permanent residents.

Lebanon's relationship with its Palestinian community has been difficult. Most Palestinians have not been able to obtain citizenship. Their involvement in the internal fighting from 1975 until the evacuation of Palestinian fighters from Beirut in the Israeli invasion of 1982 brought them the bitter enmity of many other groups. Many Palestinians have encountered difficulty in renewing residence permits and travel documents. The delay may stem partly from a tremendous backlog of work at the Surete Generale, but several Palestinians have had their documents renewed with the provision that they not be used to return to Lebanon.

LANGUAGE

The official language is Arabic, which is used in both the classical and Modern Standard forms. (The coexistence of the classical and the colloquial forms of the same language is called *diglossia* by linguists). A third language is used in mass communications, incorporating elements from both classical and colloquial Arabic. In the central plateau and eastern mountain ranges a number of arabic dialects are spoken but few of these dialects have a written form and they also vary from place to place and from group to group.

Minority languages include Armenian, Kurdish, Assyrian and Syriac, the last a purely liturgical language.

Though French has no official status, government publications appear in French as well as Arabic and nearly all Lebanese have some knowledge of French. The Lebanese dialect of Beirut is heavily interlarded with French words, and modern Arabic literary style has been influenced by French authors. English has made considerable headway since World War II and now competes with French as a working language in education and business. English is believed to be spoken by about 15% of the population as compared to the 40% who reportedly speak French.

RELIGION

Religious affiliations in Lebanon transcend purely personal beliefs. They form the basis of the state itself. Every Lebanese adult carries an identity card that shows his religious community, regardless of his personal convictions. Each religious community also has its own hierarchical structure with its own *zaim* (or professional political leader), schools, hospitals, charitable institutions and newspapers. The relative proportion of communities within a district determines the composition of electoral slates for public office. Every Lebanese is primarily a member of his own *millet* (a term used in Ottoman law for religious communities) to which his loyalty is due in both a religious and political sense.

Seventeen different religious communities are officially recognized in Lebanon: 11 Christian sects, five Muslim ones, and the Jews. The 11 Christian sects are: Maronite, Greek Orthodox, Greek Catholic, Armenian Orthodox, Armenian Catholic, Protestant, Syrian Orthodox, Syrian Catholic, Roman Catholic, Chaldean, Nestorian. The 5 Muslim sects are: Shi'a, Sunni, Druze, Alawite, Ismailian.

The religious balance in the Lebanese state is based on the census of 1932, which established a Christian majority with six Christians to five Muslims. Christians then formed 53% of the population and Muslims 39%. The subsequent agreement known as the National Covenant reflected the strength of the competing religious groups on this basis. Though a later census has been avoided, it is believed that the Christian majority has been eroded and now Christians number less than 30% of the population. They are easily outnumbered by the combined numbers of Shi'as, Sunnis and Druzes. But the government clings to the fiction that the 1932 ratios still hold true and insists on the continued distribution of seats in the National Assembly and in the cabinet on the basis of the first census. This issue lies at the root of the conflicts that led to the civil war in 1975.

The age-old friction between Christians and Muslims has been further intensified by the intrusion of the Palestinian question, pressures from Islamic fanatics, such as President Muammar Qaddhafi of Libya, and the impact of growing Pan-Islamism.

Christian churches in Lebanon are broadly divided into Uniates, or those in communion with Rome, and Eastern Churches belonging to the Orthodox, or Melkite, rite and the Monophysite and Nestorian rites. The Maronites, headed by the Patriarch of Antioch and all the East, are the largest of the Uniate groups. They have been united with Rome continuously since the 16th century. The second largest Uniate community is Greek Catholic, which broke away from the Greek Orthodox Church in the 18th century although they still follow the Byzantine rite. Other Uniate groups include Catholics of the Syrian rite, Armenian Catholics and Catholics of the Chaldean, or Assyrian, rite. Eastern churches include the Greek Orthodox Church; the Armenian, or Gregorian Church under the Catholicos of Cilicia; the Syrian Jacobite Church under the Patriarch of Antioch at Homs, Syria; and the Assyrian, or Nestorian Church, whose patriarch, Mar Shimun, resides in Chicago.

Lebanese Muslims are divided almost evenly between the two branches of Islam: Shi'as and Sunnis. The Druzes do not regard themselves as Muslims and reject the prophethood of Muhammad. However, the Druze religion bears similarities to the Shi'a sect.

The population ratio has shifted in favor of the Muslims. Furthermore, the proportion of Shi'ites within the Muslim community has been increasing at the expense of the Sunnis. Unofficial estimates now indicate that Muslims constitute nearly 70% of the population, and Christians (predominantly Maronite Roman Catholic) less than 30%.

The socio-economic structure of the religious communities reveal much of their strengths and weaknesses. The Druze are the most rural and the Sunnis are the most urban but the Shi'ites are becoming increasingly urbanized as a result of the situation in south Lebanon. Christians are the most affluent group. There are relatively more Christians in the liberal professions and in the employer and manager categories than there are Muslims. Illiteracy is also more prevalent among Muslims than among Christians, although the Druzes are exceptions to this pattern. There are more university graduates among Christians than among Muslims.

Lebanon's small Jewish community completes the religious mosaic of the country. Though there is no overt persecution, they make themselves as inconspicuous as possible so as not to attract the attention of Muslims.

HISTORICAL BACKGROUND

Lebanon, together with Syria, was under French mandate from 1920, but it achieved independence early in 1944. French penetration of Lebanon was facilitated by the pro-Western attitudes of the dominant Christian community. Lebanon owes its position as the most culturally, educationally and economically advanced nation in the Middle East to its acceptance of French legacies and progressive assimilation of Western ideas.

At independence the various Christian and Muslim groups agreed on a delicate balance of power in order to avoid hostility. The so-called National Pact of 1943 allocated executive and legislative functions throughout government among religious groups. The country survived a revolt by Moslem leftists in 1958, when the government called in United States Marines to restore state authority, but the delicate balance between groups was disturbed by an influx of Palestinian Arabs fleeing Arab-Israeli wars. Tensions increased in the early 1970s when the Palestine Liberation Organization, expelled from Jordan, moved to Lebanon and became the target of Israeli retaliatory raids. An alliance between the PLO and Lebanese Muslim leftists alarmed the Lebanese Christians further. A series of clashes between the PLO and Christian militia, the Phalange, led to civil war in 1975.

The civil war was not so much a breakdown of the constitutional system but rather the renewal of the age-old hostility between Christians and Muslims that has existed since the time of the Crusades, fueled this time by new elements. The Christian community has a disproportionate share of the wealth and important positions in the civil service and armed forces. It is generally more conservative by Arab standards and takes a more moderate position toward Israel. The less privileged Arab majority is in favor of both domestic reform and a more militant posture toward Israel. In the Palestinians the Muslims found a useful ally with the appropriate ideological stance and military resources.

The political situation became more confused in 1978 when Israeli forces invaded southern Lebanon in an effort to root out terrorist bases. A month later, the U.N. authorized the dispatch of an Interim Force in Lebanon (UNIFIL). During the deployment of UNIFIL troops, fighting again broke out between Christian militiamen and the Arab Deterrent Force (ADF) troops in the north. The 30,000 strong ADF, heavily Syrian in composition, had become pro-Muslim and pro-PLO for all intents and purposes and was deterred from wiping out the Christian forces only because of a fear of Israeli retaliation. Backed up by Israel, the Christians were in no mood to make deals either with the ADF or with the Lebanese government, and were in the process of carving out a Christian enclave in the south. However, the situation was quite different in the north where a series of clashes between Christians and Syrian troops had escalated into open warfare using tanks, mortars, heavy artillery and rockets. While the Syrians suffered over 1,000 casualties in the period of a year the Christian losses were negligible. A French plan for ending the conflict was rejected by both parties and France withdrew its 800-strong contingent from the UNIFIL force. However, a cease-fire was arranged by the Saudis at a conference held at Beit Eddine under terms of which Saudi troops replaced the Syrians in East Beirut and took the heat out of the situation. Meanwhile, intrarightist conflict erupted at Beirut during which supporters of former president, Suleiman Frajiyah, were eliminated.

In 1982, the National Assembly chose a successor to President Elias Sarkis. The election, boycotted by most of the Assembly's Muslim members, was won by Bachir Gemayel, the youngest son of Pierre Gemayel, leader of the Phalangist Party. The president-elect was assassinated on September 14. His brother, Amin, was then elected in his place. Chafiq al-Wazzan continued as prime minister with a cabinet of 10 ministers drawn from outside the Assembly.

In the spring of 1982, infringements of the cease-fire imposed on the previous July became more frequent, and in June 1982 Israeli forces moved into Lebanon on "Operation Peace for Galilee." Its initial limited objective was enlarged into an effort to crush the PLO. Israeli forces surrounded West Beirut, trapping more than 6,000 Palestinian fighters. In late August, Philip Habib, President Ronald Reagan's special envoy, secured an agreement which brought about the dispersal of PLO fighters from Beirut to various Arab countries and the arrival of a multinational peacekeeping force. In September, the inhabitants of Shatila and Sabra Palestinian refugee camps were massacred by the right-wing Phalangists. The de facto complicity of Israel's authorities in this massacre generated widespread condemnation from abroad.

During late 1982 and early 1983, the presence of the 5,700-strong multinational force (2,000 French, 2,000 Italians, 1,600 Americans and 100 Britons) helped to stabilize the situation, although it came under increasing attack from Muslim militia men. In two grisly incidents, 241 U.S. and 58 French marines were killed in suicide bombings carried out by Muslim fanatics on October 23, 1983.

From September 1983, the fight for control of Fatah between the forces of Yassir Arafat and those of the Syrian-backed rebels under Abu Musa and Abu Saleh was concentrated in Arafat's last stronghold, the northern Lebanese port of Tripoli. After months of fighting, a truce allowed Arafat to leave Tripoli in December with about 4,000 of his supporters. Aboard five Greek ships, and under U.N. protection, they dispersed to Algeria, Tunisia and the Yemen Arab Republic.

Talks between Israel and Lebanon, begun in December 1982, culminated in the signing on May 17, 1983 of a 12-article agreement, formulated by U.S. Secretary of State George Shultz, declaring an end to hostilities and calling for a withdrawal of all foreign forces from Lebanon within three months. Syria refused to recognize the agreement (which was never ratified by President Gemayel), and kept 40,000 of its troops and 7,000 PLO men encamped in the Beka'a Valley and northern Lebanon. Israel consequently refused to withdraw its own forces from the south but deployed its 30,000 troops (reduced to 10,000 men by the end of the year) south of Beirut, along the Awali River. Members of Maj. Saad Haddad's South Lebanon Army (SLA) policed the Israeli-controlled south, thus effectively partitioning the country. Soon a full-scale war flared up between the Druze and Phalangist militias in the Chuf Mountains. Within months, the Druzes forced the Christians out of the region, establishing a Druze mini-state with its own local administration and executive council.

In Beirut, interfactional fighting continued, punctuated by numerous ceasefires. A Conference of National Reconciliation was held in Geneva from October 31 to November 4, 1983, attended by the Shi'ite Amal militia led by Nabih Berri; the Syrian-backed National Salvation Front, led by the Druze leader, Walid Joumblatt; and former prime minister, Rashid Karami. The conference foundered on President Gemayel's refusal to abrogate the May 1983 pact. By February 1984, fighting flared up again, on a more intense level, as the Muslim members of the army defected en masse to the militias, the Druzes and Shi'ites joined forces, and the multinational force was withdrawn. In March 1984, bowing to Assad's pressures, Amin Gemayel abrogated the May 17 agreement with Israel in return for Syrian guarantees. A week later the National Reconciliation Conference was reconvened in Geneva. It failed to produce a compromise and witnessed the disintegration of the National Salvation Front. Ex-president Sulaiman Franjiya vetoed Syrian plans which called for a diminution of presidential powers.

In April 1984, President Gemayel formed a government of national unity, with Rashid Karami as prime minister heading a cabinet of five Christians and five Muslims. Franjiya boycotted the government and his Greek Orthodox son-in-law, Abdullah al-Rassi, the interior minister, refused to attend cabinet meetings. The goals of the new government were to end Israeli occupation of the south, reorganize the army and disengage rival militias, and reform the constitution to provide more equitable representation for the Muslims. A Syrian-backed security plan was put into operation in July 1984, leading to the reopening of the port and seaport of Beirut and the clearing of the Green Line separating Christian and Muslim sectors in Beirut.

In 1984, Israel pledged itself to a withdrawal from Lebanon and entered into talks with the Lebanese government on the conditions of such a move. When the talks failed, Israel elected to vacate the territory unilaterally in three phases.

By mid-1985 the Israeli forces had withdrawn completely, although they remained in effective control of the border area and watchful of both the Syrian ADF forces and the resumed presence in Lebanon of the PLO. Thereafter, the fundamental Christian-Muslim divide became overlaid by more immediate conflicts between rival factions within the two broad camps. On the Christian side, a Syrian-sponsored peace plan proposed in 1985 was backed by one Phalangist faction but opposed by President Gemayel and his followers. On the Muslim side, the pro-Syrian Amal movement and the Iranian-backed Hezbollah vied for support within the Shi'ite community, and both came into conflict with the Druzes, Sunni militia and the PLO from 1986 to 1988. Moreover, militant Muslim groups resorted to the kidnapping of Western nationals, amid a total breakdown of government authority and inexorable destruction of the economic infrastructure.

On the expiry of Gemayel's six-year term in September 1988 it proved impossible to elect a successor, with the result that his final presidential act was to appoint a transitional military government headed by General Michel Aoun, the Maronite army commander. However, the Muslim nominees refused to serve under General Aoun and declared their support for the government of Selim al-Hoss (appointed Prime Minister in June 1987), from which Christian support had been withdrawn earlier. Aoun launched a "war of liberation" against Syria in March 1989, thereby initiating a new round in Lebanon's bloody conflict. Intervention by the Arab League to halt the ensuing fighting resulted in the drawing up of an "accord for national reconciliation," which was approved on October 22 by a majority of Lebanese MPs meeting in Taif, Saudi Arabia. Aoun vehemently rejected the accord on the grounds that it failed to provide for an immediate Syrian withdrawal. Under the terms of the Taif accord the MPs elected a new President, Rene Mouawad, on November 5. Mouawad was brutally assassinated 17 days later and was replaced on November 24 by Elias Hrawi.

Aoun condemned Hrawi as a Syrian puppet and considered himself the country's rightful ruler, refusing to vacate the bunker he occupied beneath the presidential palace in Baabda, an east Beirut suburb. As a result, Hrawi's government controlled only those areas occupied by Syrian soldiers. A decisive event occurred on April 3, 1990, when Lebanese Forces (LF) and Phalange military leader Samir Geagea declared his allegiance to Hrawi. The Lebanese parliament met on August 21 in Beirut and approved constitutional changes called for in the Taif peace accord that gave the Muslim majority greater political power. The amendments expanded the National Assembly to 108 seats from 99 and divided them equally between Christians and Muslims. It allowed for the Christians to retain their traditional hold on the presidency, but diluted the powers of that office by giving more authority to the Muslim prime minister and his cabinet. The next day Aoun reiterated his opposition to the Taif accord. Nevertheless, Hrawi signed the constitutional changes into law on September 21, 1990, and warned Aoun to join the peace process.

The violent eviction of General Aoun from the presidential palace at Baabda finally occurred on October 13, removing the biggest single obstacle to the reunification of Lebanon and fostering an immediate improvement of confidence both at home and abroad. After having lived through 750 days of Aoun's occupation of the palace, President Hrawi and his ministers were faced with the task of rebuilding the country.

On December 19, 1990 Prime Minister Selim al-Hoss resigned to make way for a government of national unity and was succeeded by Omar Karami, brother of the late prime minister Rashid Karami and, like Hoss, a Sunni Muslim. The new Cabinet, apparently formed with Syrian backing, included the leaders of seven militias, among them Geagea, Hobeika, Druze leader Walid Jumblatt and Nabih Berri of the Shi'ite Amal. The pro-Iranian Hezbollah rejected the new government.

CONSTITUTION & GOVERNMENT

The constitutional basis of the Lebanese government is a largely unwritten and unique system of compromise and adjustment known as the National Covenant (al-Mithaq al-Watani) superimposed on the constitution of 1926. The 1926 constitution, as amended in 1927, 1929, 1944 and 1947, established a centralized parliamentary republic in which executive power was shared by a strong president and a prime minister who headed a cabinet. Legislative functions are performed by a unicameral Chamber of Deputies which was renamed the National Assembly in March 1979. The constitution is predominantly French in character, but it is the National Covenant rather than the constitution that determines the specific political organization of the country. The National Covenant is based on Article 95 of the constitution, which provides for a distribution of all political and legislative positions according to a confessional system in proportion to the numerical strength of religious communities at the time of the 1932 census. The president, ministers and deputies act as members and representatives of their respective religious groups rather than as national or regional leaders. By custom, the president of the republic is a Maronite Christian; the prime minister, a Sunni Muslim; the foreign minister a Greek Orthodox; and so on. This system of government, known as confessionalism, worked satisfactorily until the civil war of 1975.

Under the terms of the Taif peace accord ratified by the National Assembly in 1990, executive powers have been transferred from the presidency to a cabinet, with portfolios divided equally amongst Muslims and Christians. The President appoints the prime minister in consultation with the members and president of the National Assembly and requires the approval of the cabinet before dismissing a minister or ratifying an international treaty. The number of seats in the National Assembly has increased from 99 to 108 and is divided equally amongst Christian and Muslim deputies. Constitutional provisions which remain un-

RULERS OF LEBANON

Presidents

May 1926–January 1934: Charles Dabbas
January 1934–January 1936: Habib Bacha as-Saad
January 1936–April 1941: Emile Edde
April 1942–March 1943: Alfred Naccache
March 1943–July 1943: Ayoub Tabet
July 1943–September: Petro Trad
September 1943–September 1952: Bisharra al-Khoury
September 1952: Fouad Chehab
September 1952–September 1958: Camille Chamoun
September 1958–September 1964: Fouad Chehab
September 1964–September 1970: Charles Helou
September 1970–September 1976: Suleiman Franjieh
September 1976–September 1982: Elias Sarkis
September 1982: Bachir Gemayel (assassinated)
September 1982–September 1988: Amin Gemayel
[September 1988: Outgoing President Gemayel appointed an interim military government, headed by General Michel Aoun]
November 5, 1989–November 22, 1989: Rene Mouawad
November 24, 1989– : Elias Hrawi

GOVERNMENT LIST
(July/August 1991)

President	Harawi, Ilyas
Prime Minister	Karami, Omar
Deputy Prime Minister	Murr, Michel al-
Minister of Agriculture	Dallul, Muhsin
Minister of Education	Harb, Boutros
Minister of Finance	Khalil, 'Ali Yusif al-
Minister of Foreign Affairs	Bouez, Faris
Minister of Housing & Cooperatives	Baydoun, Muhammad
Minister of Hydroelectric Resources	Baydoun, Muhammad
Minister of Industry & Petroleum	Jaroudi, Muhammad
Minister of Information	Mansur, Albert
Minister of Interior	Khatib, Sami al-
Minister of Justice	Babikian, Khatchig
Minister of Labor	Sassin, Michel
Minister of National Defense	Murr, Michel al-
Minister of National Economy & Trade	Hamadi, Marwan
Minister of Public Health	Kibbi, Jamil
Minister of Public Works & Transportation	Salem, Nadim
Minister of Telecommunications & Posts	Saadah, George
Minister of Tourism	Arslan, Talal
Minister of State for Administration Reform	Khatib, Zaher al-
Minister of State for Environment	Jokhadarian, Hagop
Minister of State for Transportation	Fakhoury, Shawki
Minister of State	Amin, Abdallah al-
Minister of State	Barri, Nabih
Minister of State	Bizri, Nazih al-
Minister of State	Franjieh, Suleiman Tony
Minister of State	Hardan, Asa'ad
Minister of State	Hobeika, Elie
Minister of State	Dib, Roger
Minister of State	Junblatt, Walid
Minister of State	Khoury, Nicholas
Governor, Central Bank	Khoury, Michel

changed are as follows: The president of the republic is elected for a term of six years and is not immediately re-eligible. The president of the republic must be a Maronite Christian and the prime minister a Sunni Muslim. Legislative power is exercised by one house, the National Assembly. A quorum of two-thirds and a majority vote is required in the Assembly for constitutional issues.

Suffrage is compulsory for all Lebanese males over 21 and authorized for all females over 21 with an elementary education. The country is divided into 5 governates which are subdivided into 26 electoral districts, in each of which seats are allocated to the different religious communities in proportion to their numerical strength. Although candidates are chosen on the basis of confessionalism, they are elected by voters of all communities by direct and secret ballot and thus represent the district as a whole.

The stability of Lebanon has been shattered by the civil war and the return to normalcy will be a long and slow process. The fragile system of compromise and accommodation on which the Lebanese state was based was the first casualty of the civil war. The survival of Lebanon as a nation now depends on the ability of its leaders to administer effectively the constitutional reforms which are designed to accommodate the different religious factions.

FREEDOM & HUMAN RIGHTS

In terms of civil and political rights, Lebanon ranks as a partly free country.

The major violations of human rights in Lebanon are committed not by the government, but by the armed groups and by the Syrian and Palestine Liberation Organization troops. These include torture, mutilation, murder, abductions, mass executions, arbitrary arrests and imprisonment, and wanton destruction of private and public property. Because of the collapse of the public security system judges are unwilling to pass sentences for fear of personal reprisal.

Civil strife since 1975 has rendered government institutions largely irrelevant to most Lebanese. Unofficial militias have seized control of many parts of the country, where they levy taxes and enforce their own version of justice without regard to the central government or legal norms.

Sixteen years of violence have severely weakened the Lebanese tradition of respect for the rights of others. Not only have civilians been endangered unintentionally by opposing groups which have fought major battles in densely populated areas, but noncomba-

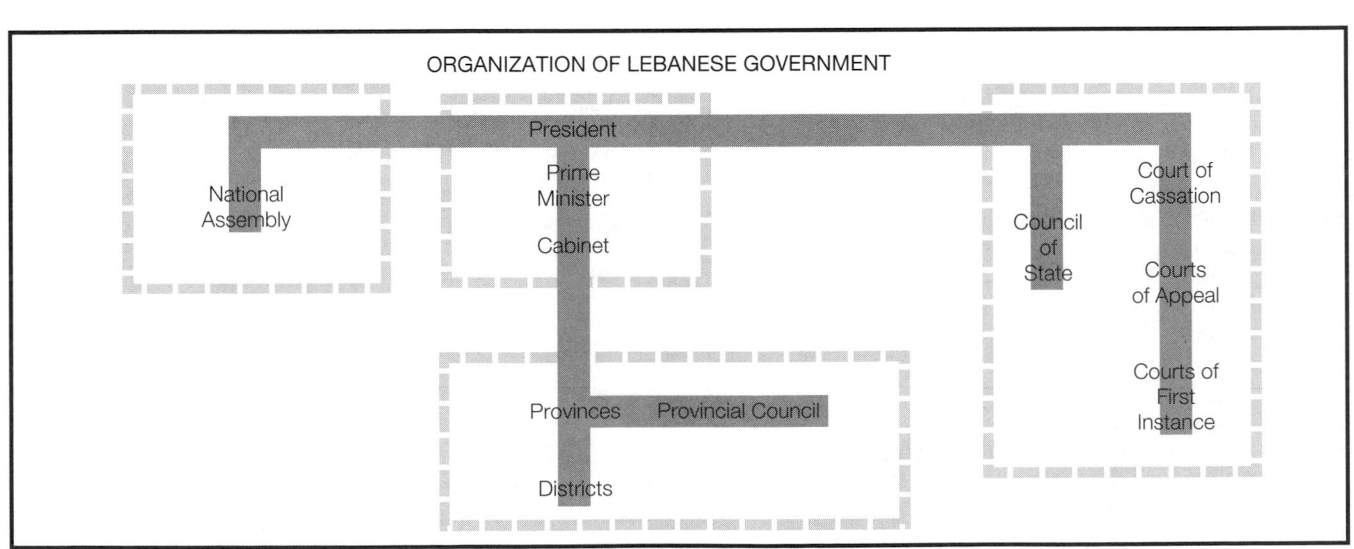

tants far removed from battlefronts also have been the deliberate target of indiscriminate violence (terrorist bombings, random shellings, abductions, etc.). On many occasions artillery fire has appeared to be deliberate. Civilians have also been the target of indiscriminate terrorist violence. On several occasions car bombs have exploded in crowded streets, killing and wounding large numbers of passersby. In most instances these explosions have occurred in neighborhoods in which one confessional group predominates and have thus appeared to be an attack against that group's members. In 1982, right-wing Phalangists, with Israeli complicity, massacred thousands of Palestinians in refugee camps.

No militia observes the legal safeguards which the government is committed to apply in arrest cases. Instead, members of the various groups frequently detain individuals arbitrarily for indefinite periods. The detainees are frequently held as hostages to be exchanged for persons held by rival militias. Some militias presume to enforce law and order in regions under their control, arresting and imprisoning individuals on purely criminal charges. The Progressive Socialist Party (PSP) and Tripoli-based Arab Democratic Party have executed individuals for criminal offenses.

Attacks on foreign diplomats stationed in Beirut assumed disturbing proportions in 1984. In addition to the September 20 car bomb attack on the U.S. embassy which left two U.S. personnel dead, diplomats from several other embassies were killed or wounded. Other diplomats, including representatives of France, Egypt and the United States, narrowly survived assassination attempts.

During the past 16 years many residents of Lebanon have disappeared. Estimates vary but all sources agree that the number runs into the thousands. Most seem to have been kidnapped by the militias at roadblocks or captured during the major battles of the civil war. It is probable that most of the disappeared are dead—summarily executed shortly after their capture. Although there are no official estimates, it is believed that well over 100,000 civilians in Lebanon have been killed during the 16 years of fighting. Many were slain in Beirut, caught in the crossfire between rival Christian militias as well as in fighting between Muslims and Christians. General Aoun's 1989 "war of liberation" alone killed nearly 1,000 people, mostly civilians.

Over 18,000 civilians were also killed when Israel invaded Beirut in 1982. In addition, the PLO and Israeli troops continue to trade blows, killing and injuring civilians living in Palestinian camps near Lebanon's border with Israel.

The violence has had a devastating effect on a once prosperous economy. The division of the country into zones controlled by militias and foreign armies has disrupted trade and led to serious economic hardship in some areas. Business confidence has evaporated; new investment has dried up; and remittances from overseas Lebanese (a major source of foreign exchange) have dropped sharply.

In October 1990, President Hrawi began consolidating control over Beirut by ordering the departure of rival militias from the previously divided capital. As the various militias withdrew from greater Beirut, their positions were gradually taken over by up to 16,000 regular soldiers from mixed Christians and Muslim brigades, contingents that made up about half of the previously fragmented national army. The government troops began dismantling the barricades along the green line that had long split the city.

CIVIL SERVICE

The civil service is supervised by the Civil Service Board and State Inspection Department, both founded by President Fuad Shihab. Training is provided by the National Public Administration School. A high prestige is attached to civil service jobs, and civil servants receive a number of benefits such as allowances for travel, disability, housing and retirement.

LOCAL GOVERNMENT

For purpose of regional administration Lebanon is divided into five provinces, or *muhafazaa:* Beirut, North Lebanon (or Ash Shamal), Mount Lebanon (or Jabal Lubnan), South Lebanon (or Al Janub) and Al Biqa. All are divided further into districts, or *aqdiyat,* of which there are 26 in number. The province is headed by a governor, or *muhafez,* and the district by a district chief, or *qaim maqam.*

The governor is assisted by the provincial council, or *Majlis al-Muhafazat,* whose members include the district chiefs, and two nominated representatives from each district. There are no organs of self-government at the district level.

Some towns have municipal councils, but only in Beirut do the councils and the mayor run the local government. Membership in the council is based on the size of the urban population, but the minimum number is eight.

FOREIGN POLICY

Until the mid-1970s Lebanon took pride in its role as the Switzerland of the Middle East and adopted a detached position on the Arab-Israeli conflict as well as on inter-Arab conflicts. The Christian half of the country traditionally looks westward. However, the National Covenant of 1943 bars the Christians from seeking foreign protection or attempting to bring Lebanon under a foreign sphere of influence. At the same time, the covenant forbids Muslims from attempting to bring Lebanon into any form of Arab federation.

Two further considerations influence the formulation of Lebanese foreign policy. As a small nation dependent on trade and services for its economic survival, Lebanon must maintain friendly relations with as many countries as possible. Secondly, with Lebanese emigrants in many countries of Africa, North and South America, and Asia, Lebanese foreign policy is an instrument in the promotion of their interests. Lebanon has a greater stake in those countries with large numbers of Lebanese than in those with few or none.

The most crucial area of Lebanese foreign relations is its relations with Syria. Fear of Syrian domination or annexation has always loomed large, particularly because Lebanon and Syria espouse differing economic philosophies. Another problem causing tension between the two countries is the presence of Syrian political refugees. Since 1949 Syria has experienced a number of coups and, in each case, displaced leaders have found asylum in Lebanon, causing friction with the group in power in Syria. Lebanon's moderate foreign policy has also alienated radical Arab states, who suspect it of being pro-Israeli and pro-American.

Although France and Lebanon are no longer as closely identified as before, French influence is considerable and pervasive. But relations are even closer with the United States, because it is both a country with a large Lebanese emigre population and a major trading partner and military protector.

The continuing civil war has greatly reduced Lebanon's freedom of action in foreign policy. Its leaders are, however, concerned with the fate of Western hostages in Lebanon, a situation which continues to preoccupy foreign diplomats in the country. A period of intense activity began in April 1990 with the freeing of a succession of Westerners, although over one dozen remain in captivity.

Lebanon joined the U.N. in 1945. It is also a member of the Arab League, NAM and ICO.

PARLIAMENT

The national legislature is the National Assembly, formerly the Chamber of Deputies, a unicameral body of 108 members elected by universal direct suffrage for four-year terms. The number of seats in the National Assembly are divided equally amongst Christian and Muslim Deputies.

Deputies are considered as representatives of the whole nation and are not bound to follow directives from their constituencies. The Assembly holds two sessions annually: from March to May and from October to December. Membership in the Assembly is open to all Lebanese citizens 25 years of age or older. The president of the Assembly is, by custom, a Shi'a Muslim.

The Assembly's substantial powers include controlling the national budget, interrogating cabinet members and voting no-confidence in the cabinet, and recommending constitutional amendments. The Assembly can also transform itself into a judicial body in order to arraign the president or members of the cabinet in cases of high treason or violation of the constitution.

POLITICAL PARTIES

Lebanese political parties are special interest groups rather than disciplined political organizations in the Western sense. Despite the existence of numerous parties, the country still lacks a fully developed and effective party system. Existing parties may be broadly divided into the Chehabist, which are pro-Muslim, pro-Arab and left-of-center, and Chamounist, which are pro-Christian, pro-Western and right-of-center. But ideology plays only a minor role in the evolution of these parties, which revolve around issues and personalities. The following is a list of the political parties operating in Lebanon.

- Armenian Revolutionary Federation (ARF): principal Armenian party; socialist ideology; collective leadership; 5 members in National Assembly (March 1990).
- Al-Baath: secular pro-Syrian party with policy of Arab union, 2 members in National Assembly (March 1990).
- Al-Baath: pro-Iraqi wing of Al-Baath party.
- Bloc National: right-wing Maronite party with policy of power-sharing between Christians and Muslims, and the exclusion of the military from politics; 5 members in the National Assembly (March 1990).
- Ad-Dustur (Constitutional Party): led struggle against French mandate, established 1943 Constitution; party of the political and business elite.
- Al-Harakiyines al-Arab: Arab nationalist party, with Marxist tendencies.
- Al-Hizb ad-Damuqratiya al-Ishtiraqi al-masihi (Christian Social Democratic Party); formerly Christian Social Democratic Union.
- Al-Jabha al-Damuqratiya al-Barlamaniya (Parliamentary Democratic Front): advocates maintenance of traditional power-sharing between Christians and Muslims; mainly Sunni Muslim support.
- Al-Kata'eb (Phalangist Party): nationalist, reformist, democratic social party; largest Maronite party; 7 members in National Assembly (March 1990); merged with Parti National Liberal in May 1979.
- An-Najjade (The Helpers): Arab socialist unionist party.
- Parti Communiste Libanais (Lebanese Communist Party): Marxist, with much support among intellectuals; 1 member in National Assembly (March 1990).
- Parti Democrate: supports a secular, democratic policy, private enterprise and social justice.
- Parti National Liberal (Al-Wataniyin al-Hhrar): liberal reformist party; 9 members in National Assembly (March 1990); merged with Phalangist Party in May 1979.
- Parti Socialiste Nationaliste Syrien: advocates a "Greater Syria," composed of Lebanon, Syria, Iraq, Jordan, Palestine and Cyprus; 1 member in National Assembly (March 1990).
- Parti Socialiste Progressiste (At-Takadumi al-Ishteraki): progressive party, advocates constitutional road to socialism; 10 members in National Assembly (March 1990).
- The Lebanese Front is a grouping of right-wing parties (mainly Christian).
- The National Front is a grouping of left-wing parties (mainly Muslim).
- Other parties include: Al-Hayat al-Wataniya; Mouvement de l'Action Nationale; An-Nida' al-Kawmi; Parti Socialiste Revolutionnaire; Independent Nasser-

ite Movement; Union of Working People's Forces; Nasserite Popular Organization; Arab Socialist Union; Amal; Islamic Amal; Islamic Jihad; Hezbollah; Popular Liberation Army; Tawheed Islami; and the Arab Democratic Party.

ECONOMY

Lebanon has a free-market economy in which the dominant sector is private. Because of its commercial tradition, Lebanon's living standard was high in comparison to most other Middle Eastern countries until the mid-1970s. The leading contributor to national income was the service sector, encompassing banking, insurance, tourism, transit trade, income from petroleum pipelines and shipping. Industrial development, though largely limited to small firms, was also important, the principal components being food processing, textiles, building materials, footwear, glass and chemical products. However, the 1975–76 civil war severely damaged the economy, with the 1976 GNP showing a 60% loss compared to 1974. In addition, casualties and dislocations among the civilian population yielded an estimated loss of two-thirds of skilled industrial workers. While nearly half of the GNP loss was regained by 1978, renewed turmoil contributed to further decline prior to the full-scale Israeli invasion of mid-1982.

Lebanon's economy continues to deteriorate under the impact of domestic turmoil. By 1985 some 70% of the country's productive capacity had come to a halt, 35% of all factories had been destroyed, 80% of industrial workers had been laid off and the national debt had grown by 700% in four years to $30.4 billion. The budget deficit grew from U.S. $1 billion in 1981 to U.S. $10 billion in 1984, absorbing one-third of the GNP. The agricultural sector in Lebanon declined by 36% in 1984 alone, while most government income from customs duties disappeared and the once-stable Lebanese pound lost approximately 99% of its 1982 value by March 1988.

At the end of 1987 it was estimated that the annual rate of inflation had reached 200%. In 1990 it was estimated that the rate of unemployment was as high as 50%.

The reconstruction of the Lebanese economy, the potential cost of which has been estimated at U.S. $9 billion, depends on a durable solution to the country's civil conflict. The most urgent task of any such reconstruction is the restoration of confidence in the Lebanese pound. Other urgent tasks include reducing very high rates of inflation and unemployment, and repairing infrastructural damage.

GROSS DOMESTIC PRODUCT

GDP nominal (L£ billions): 12.599 (1982)
GDP per capita (U.S. $): 700 (1989)
Average annual growth rate of GDP (%, 1965–80): −1.2
GDP by type of expenditure (%) 1984
- Consumption
  - Private: 12
  - Government: 38
- Gross domestic investment: 5
- Foreign trade
  - Exports: 41
  - Imports: −109

Cost components of GDP (%) 1984
- Net indirect taxes: 2
- Consumption of fixed capital, compensation of employees, net operating surplus: 98

Sectoral origin of GDP (%) 1984
- Primary
  - Agriculture: 8
  - Mining: 0.0
- Secondary
  - Manufacturing: 13
  - Construction: 3
  - Public utilities: 5
- Tertiary
  - Transportation & communications: 8
  - Trade: 28
  - Finance: 13
  - Other services: 11
  - Government: 11

PUBLIC FINANCE

The Lebanese fiscal year is the calendar year. The national budget consists of three parts: a general budget; an attached budget covering the Telephone Administration, the National Lottery, the Wheat Office and the Lebanese University; and the budgets of 24 independent agencies. Municipalities have independent budgets.

A 1990 budget estimate lists Lebanon as having a total revenue of L£ 210 billion and a total expenditure of L£ 597 billion. Lebanon's revenue is derived primarily from income taxes and customs; its expenditures include debt service, defense and education.

Lebanon's total external, outstanding public debt was estimated in 1989 at U.S. $235 million.

In the Lebanese climate of laissez-faire state planning has been hesitant and half-hearted. The first Five-Year Plan was interrupted by political trouble, the second was delayed and the third died quietly.

From 1970 to 1988 the United States committed $356 million in aid. Other Western nations gave $509 from 1970–87. OPEC was the largest source of aid, committing $962 million.

FOREIGN AID, 1989

Total foreign aid (U.S. $ millions): 114.7
- Bilateral: 76.3
- Multilateral: 38.4

CURRENCY & BANKING

The Lebanese unit of currency is the Lebanese pound divided into 100 piastres. Coins are issued in denominations of 1, 2½, 5, 10, 25 and 50 piastres; notes are issued in denominations of 1, 5, 10, 25, 50, 100, 250, 500 and 1,000 pounds.

The basic official rate of exchange is based on an effective rate whose parity is adjustable from month to month. Commercial transactions take place on the basis of a fluctuating free market rate. The 1991 dollar exchange rate was $1 = L£912.814.

Until 1964 the banking sector was totally unregulated. There was no special banking law, no central bank, no minimum reserve ratio, and no requirement to submit regular balance sheets. The result was the proliferation of banks, making Lebanon the financial capital of the Middle East with more banks per capita than any other country in the world.

The situation changed with the adoption of the Currency and Credit Code of 1963 and the creation of the Bank of Lebanon as the central bank in 1964. With the collapse of the Intra Bank, the largest Lebanese-owned bank, in 1968 the government intensified its efforts to place the banking sector on a sounder footing. The government encouraged the merger of smaller banks, tightened credit requirements and sanctions, began monitoring liquidity ratios and reserves, and authorized state takeover of unsound banks. As a result of these efforts the number of commercial banks operating in Lebanon was reduced from 93 to 74. Financing of foreign trade and discounting of trade bills make up most banking transactions. To encourage the movement of foreign capital into Lebanon, a bank secrecy law forbids banks to disclose details of a client's business even to judicial authorities. At the end of 1990, there were 70 banks in the country including 53 Lebanese banks, two development banks, Lebanese banks under foreign control, and 15 foreign banks. Other foreign banks have representative offices in Beirut. Foreign-currency deposits of nonresidents are exempt from domestic taxes.

Lebanese banking institutions, however, have shown remarkable resilience. Even during the Israeli invasion of 1982, Lebanese banks did good business, registering a record inflow of deposits. Up to $1 billion was entering the country from Arab and other backers of the various factions in the civil conflict. The resiliency of the Lebanese currency is attributable to the absence of restriction on withdrawals or foreign exchange transactions; to the inflow of foreign currency; to the 1.4 (U.S. $) billion central bank reserves; and to the remittances sent home by Lebanese workers.

During the first year of the civil war in 1975 more than L£2.5 billion was withdrawn from Lebanese banks and more than a dozen foreign banks moved their headquarters in the Middle East to Athens, Bahrain and Cairo. It is doubtful whether Beirut will ever regain its financial eminence.

GROWTH PROFILE
(Annual Growth Rates, %)

Projected crude birth rate (/1,000) (1990–95): 27.6
Projected crude death rate (/1,000) (1990–95): 7.1
Urban population (1965–80): 4.5
GDP (1965–80): −1.2
Inflation (1965–80): 9.3
Money holdings (1980–88): 42.3
Energy production (1980–88): −4.0
Energy consumption (1980–88): 3.4

FINANCIAL INDICATORS, 1989

Total reserves minus gold (SDRs millions): 938.2
SDRs (millions): 7.1
Reserve position in IMF (SDRs millions): 24.7
Foreign exchange (SDRs millions): 906.3
Gold (fine troy oz. millions): 9.22
Ratio of external debt to total reserves: 0.2 (1988)
Central bank 1988
- Assets (%)
  - Foreign assets: 96.2
  - Claims on government: 3.7
  - Claims on banks: 0.1
  - Claims on private sector: 0.0
- Liabilities (%)
  - Reserve money: 7.5
  - Government deposits: 7.1
  - Foreign liabilities: 0.0
  - Capital accounts: 0.0
- Money supply 1989
  - Stock (L. £. billions): 182.9
  - M1 per capita: 63,900

Private banks 1988
- Assets (%)
  - Loans to government: 10.8
  - Loans to private sector: 26.3
  - Reserves: 2.6
  - Foreign assets: 60.4
- Liabilities
  - Deposits (L. £. billions): 2.809
  - of which %
    - Demand deposits: 2.3
    - Savings deposits: 70.9
    - Government deposits: 0.2
    - Foreign liabilities: 17.8

External debt 1988
- Total (U.S. $ millions): 499
  - of which public (U.S. $ millions): 229
  - of which private (U.S. $ millions): 0
- Debt service (long-term)
  - Total (U.S. $ millions): 37.7
  - Repayment
    - Principal (%): 57.3
    - Interest (%): 42.7
- Debt service ratio (%): 1.9
- External public debt as % of GNP: 4.2 (1970)
- Terms of public borrowing
  - Commitment (U.S. $ millions): 40
  - Average interest rate (%): 7.5
  - Average maturity (yrs.): 27
- Net flow of publicly guaranteed external capital (U.S. $ millions): 5

AGRICULTURE

Since the major disruption caused to industry by the war agriculture has played an increasingly important part in Lebanon's economy, although the country is not self-sufficient in food. Of the total land area of 1,040,000 ha. (2,569,840 ac.) 30% is classified as agricultural land, 270,000 ha. (667,170 ac.) of which is actually cultivated.

Much of agricultural land consist of manmade terraces on mountain slopes. About half the acreage is in the Biqa Valley where the proportion of arable land to the total land area is 83%. This proportion decreases to 70% in South Lebanon, 56% in North Lebanon and 34% in Mount Lebanon. Because of Lebanon's favorable topography and climate, a wide variety of crops can be grown. The most intensely farmed area in the country is the narrow coastal strip between Tripoli and Tyre. The Biqa Valley is less intensively farmed, and because of light rainfall most of the land is dry farmed. Grain is grown primarily in the coastal Akar plain and in the Biqa Valley, while tree crops are grown on the coast and at the higher elevations of Mount Lebanon.

Because of the long dry summer season, intensive cultivation is dependent on irrigation. Some 720,000 ha. (178,000 ac.) were reported under irrigation in 1973, and irrigation was available to 45% of all farms in the country. Over 75% of irrigation water is supplied by ditches and 5% by pumps.

Mechanization is increasing but is still limited to the modern agricultural sector, which covers only 2% of the farmland. More than 78% of farms rely on animal power alone and 13% on human labor alone. Modern cropping techniques, such as crop rotation, are rarely practiced, and over 25% of the land is left fallow each year. Intercropping is common in the fruit orchards. Fertilizers, pesticides and fungicides are used only by the larger farms.

The majority of farms are small plots owned by the cultivators but half of all farms and three-fourths of the small farms are operated by persons who combine farming with other professions. Small farms, defined as holdings of less than 2 ha. (5 ac.), predominate in numbers but cover only 20% of cultivated area. At the other end of the spectrum, large holdings of between 50 ha. (125 ac.) and 253 ha. (625 ac.) make up only a small percentage of the number of farms but account for 17% of the farmland. The average farm size is 5 ha. (12.5 ac.) in the Biqa Valley, 2.63 ha. (6.5 ac.) in South Lebanon, 1.61 ha. (4.0 ac.) in North Lebanon and 1.3 ha. (3.25 ac.) in Mount Lebanon. Most of the farms are highly fragmented and divided into plots in different areas. The smallest holdings contain an average of three plots, while the largest contain as many as 26. Over 80% of all agricultural land and 97% of small farms up to 0.5 hectares (1.25 acres) are owned by cultivators. Tenancy is prevalent only on the larger farms and in Biqa and South Lebanon. Even in these provinces tenants cultivate less than one-fourth of the farms. Of the rented farms, 57% are sharecropped and 28% are leased for cash rents.

A 10-year agricultural development plan, known as the Green Plan, was launched in 1963 and was in operation until 1973. Its priorities were reclamation of marginal land, conservation and improvement of the soil, provision of farm equipment to small farmers, and extension of financial aid to farmers. The plan also promoted the introduction of new crops and of improved varieties. It established produce marketing agencies and cooperatives and initiated a crop insurance program to protect farmers against weather-related crop failures.

Despite these programs Lebanon is not self-sufficient in grains. Fruit growing, on the other hand, has increased, substantially over the last two decades. With only 18% of the acreage fruits contribute more than half of the total farm output and the bulk of the agricultural export earnings. Over 15 varieties of fruits are being grown, of which citrus, apples and bananas are the most important. Vegetables, olives, oilseeds, cereals and pulses, and industrial crops are the other major agricultural products.

AGRICULTURAL INDICATORS

Agriculture's share of GDP (%): 9 (1989)
Value added in agriculture (U.S. $ millions): 136 (1970)
Cereal imports (000 metric tons): 537 (1988)
Index of agricultural production (1979–81 = 100): 128 (1986)
Index of food production (1979–81 = 100): 129 (1986)
Number of tractors: 3,000 (1986)
Number of harvester-threshers: 90 (1986)
Total fertilizer consumption (000 metric tons): 35.7 (1985–86)
Fertilizer consumption (g./ha., hundreds): 671 (1987–88)
Number of farms (000): 143 (1970)
Average size of holding (ha.): 4.3 (1970)
Size class (%) 1970
- Below 1 ha. (below 2.47 ac.): 47.7
- 1–5 ha. (2.47–12.35 ac.): } 44.5
- 5–10 ha. (12.35–24.7 ac.): }
- 10–20 ha. (24.7–49.4 ac.): } 6.5
- 20–50 ha. (49.4–123.5 ac.): }
- 50–200 ha. (123.5–494 ac.): 1.2
- Over 200 ha. (over 494 ac.): 0.1

Activity (%) 1970
- Mainly crops: 77.0
- Mainly livestock: 8.1
- Mixed: 14.9

Farms as % of total land area: 27.0 (1980)
Land use (%) 1985–87
- Cropland: 29
- Pasture: 1
- Forest: 8
- Other: 62

Yields (kg./ha.) 1989
- Grains: 2,046
- Roots & tubers: 24,975
- Legumes: 1,027
- Milk (kg./animal): 2,593

Production 1989
- Fruits (000 metric tons): 649
- Vegetables (000 metric tons): 420

Livestock (000) 1989
- Cattle: 55
- Horses: 2 (1986)
- Sheep: 145
- Pigs: 22

Forestry 1988
- Production of roundwood (000 cubic meters): 488
  - of which industrial roundwood (%): 4.3
- Value of exports (U.S. $ millions): 2.451

Fishing 1988
- Total catch (000 metric tons): 1.8
  - of which marine (%): 94.4

Cattle are raised primarily as draft animals, and quality breeds have been introduced only on modern farms. Livestock production is inadequate to meet domestic needs; cattle, sheep, frozen meat and powdered milk are imported from abroad. Poultry production, on the other hand, is large enough to yield a surplus for export.

Fishing is a marginal industry with a total catch of 1,800 tons in 1988.

The country's forests, covering 134,000 ha. (331,114 ac.) have been greatly thinned by the ravages of the goat. Only a few of the celebrated cedars of Lebanon survive in the central part of the country.

Agricultural credit is provided by the Agricultural, Industrial and Real Estate Credit Bank. Because of its stringent collateral requirements, most small farmers can obtain credit only from the private moneylenders.

MANUFACTURING

Industry in Lebanon has been badly affected by the war and has not recovered. Production figures are not available, although major areas of activity are food processing, banking, textiles, cement, oil refining and chemicals. Main trading partners are Italy, the U.S., France, Saudi Arabia, Switzerland, Jordan, Kuwait and Turkey.

Most of the industrial plants are concentrated in Mount Lebanon Province and Beirut and its immediate vicinity. Other industrial establishments are located in Tripoli. Most industries have been traditionally small-scale operations. Before the civil war of 1975 the number of limited liability corporations was growing and had reached 44 in 1974. Major constraints on industrial production are the small size of the domestic market, lack of protective tariffs, lack of reliable credit information, and a dearth of industrial capital. Despite efforts to expand foreign outlets in the Middle East, access to these markets has continued to be uncertain and erratic.

MANUFACTURING INDICATORS, 1987

Labor force economically active in manufacturing (% est.): 17.8 (1986)
Value added in manufacturing (U.S. $ millions): 1970
- Food & tobacco (%): 27
- Textiles & clothing (%): 19
- Machinery & transport equipment (%): 1
- Chemicals (%): 3

The industrial sector has suffered most in the civil war. Several industrial areas became the sites of violent battles, especially, the Mkalles region, situated near the Palestinian camp of Tall al-Zaatar. A substantial recovery took place in 1977 when production climbed back to 80% of the 1974 level. However, clashes in the summer of 1978 between the Arab Deterrent Force and the Christian Militias once again paralyzed industry perhaps permanently. Estimates of the damage vary: the Ministry of Industry places the losses at L£12 billion including L£3 billion in direct losses in plants and equipment and L£9 billion in indirect losses in production. Over 250 of the 500 factories were destroyed and the industrial manpower was reduced by 85%.

In an effort to rebuild industry, the government has further liberalized its investment code and added fresh incentives. Industries credited between 1971 and 1976 were exempted from income tax for six years. An industrial free port has been created at Beirut and a new bank has been set up to provide long-term financial aid for the reconstruction of war-damaged property.

Government intervention in the industrial sector is minimal in conformity with the country's traditional free-trade and free-enterprise policies. The only industries specifically limited to the public sector are electric power, telephones and water. However, establishment of new industrial plants and expansion of existing ones are subject to government approval.

Foreign investments are principally from oil-rich Arab countries, Syria, France, the United Kingdom and the United States.

MINING

Iron ore exists but is difficult to work. Other minerals known to exist are iron pyrites, copper, bituminous shales, asphalt, phosphates, ceramic clays and glass sand; but the available information is of doubtful values.

ENERGY

Lebanon has two large oil refineries at Zahrani and Tripoli. The Zahrani refinery is run by the Mediterranean Refining Company (MEDRECO), jointly owned by Caltex and Mobil, and is the terminal of the Trans-Arabian Pipeline (TAP) bringing oil from Saudi Arabia. The Tripoli refinery handles oil piped from Iraq. The assets and installations of the latter pipline were taken over by the Lebanese government after the Iraq Petroleum Company was nationalized in 1972. Both refineries suspended operations in 1975, but Zahrani subsequently resumed under a revised agreement with TAP. Plans are being made for a third oil refinery with a throughput of seven million tons annually.

ENERGY INDICATORS

Average annual energy production growth rate (%, 1980–88): −4.0
Energy consumption per capita (kg. oil equivalent): 871 (1988)
Energy imports as % of merchandise exports: 51 (1965)
Average annual growth rate of energy consumption (%, 1980–88): 3.4
Electricity 1988
- Installed capacity (000 kw.): 819
- Production (billion kw.-hr.): 4.505
  - % fossil fuel: 86.7
  - % hydro: 13.3
- Consumption per capita (kw.-hr.): 1,605

Natural gas
- Proved reserves (billion cu. m.): 0 (1990)
- Production (million cu. m.): 0 (1989)

Petroleum
- Production (million bbl.): 0 (1989)
- Consumption (million bbl.): 9 (1988)
- Refining capacity (000 bbl./day): 37 (1990)

Coal
- Production (000 metric tons): 0 (1988)
- Consumption (000 metric tons): 0 (1988)

Electric power is derived primarily from thermal power stations, using imported petroleum.

LABOR

The composition of the labor force is affected by the inflow and outflow of migrants. Nearly 125,000 Lebanese are believed to be working in the oil states, while unskilled labor is drawn to Lebanon from Syria.

Many Palestinian refugees are also employed in various sectors of the economy.

As in other areas of national life, certain occupations are virtually monopolized by specific religious groups. Christians dominate banking, the media, the hotel and tourist industry, small business and the professions. Shipping and the wholesale and retail trade are in the hands of Sunni Muslims; arts and crafts are the preserve of Armenians. Kurds are mostly unskilled workers, while half the agricultural workers are Shi'a Muslims. Syrian migrants are employed in construction and agriculture.

Skills are in short supply because of a general prejudice against manual and factory work. Westerners hold a substantial number of managerial and administrative positions in business and industry. However, employers are required by law to give preference to Lebanese nationals with the appropriate qualifications and to train Lebanese nationals to replace foreigners. Foreigners are also required to obtain work permits before employment.

Working conditions are governed by the Labor Code of 1946, which covers all nonagricultural workers in shops and factories employing more than 15 persons. The code regulates work contracts, dismissal and severance pay. Every worker is required to carry a workbook issued by the Ministry of Labor and Social Affairs containing a record of his employment. The maximum workweek is 48 hours with time and a half for overtime. Workers also receive paid annual leave, sick leave, 12 official holidays a year and maternity leave for women workers. Minimum wages are fixed by legislative decrees and are revised from time to time on the basis of cost of living indices. Wages are supplemented by bonus payments. The larger establishments also provide free transportation, medical services, free cafeterias and educational assistance.

Social Security legislation, passed in 1965, provides for compulsory family allowances, sickness and maternity insurance, and severance and compensation benefits for industrial accidents and occupational diseases. The cost of some of these benefits is paid for by the employers exclusively, while that of others is financed by contributions from workers and employers.

LABOR INDICATORS, 1986

Total economically active population (000): 694
- % working-age (15+): 39.9
- % female: 21.7

Activity rate (%)
- Total: 25.1
- Male: 40.7
- Female: 10.6

Sectoral employment of economically active (%)
- Agriculture, forestry, fishing: 19.1
- Construction: 6.2
- Manufacturing, mining, quarrying, public utilities: 18.9
- Trade, hotels, restaurants: 16.5
- Transportation, communications: 7.0
- Finance, real estate: 3.5
- Services: 28.8

Labor under 20 years (%): 13.7 (1975)

Unofficial estimates of unemployment are as high as 50%. The civil war has intensified both the unemployment problem and the labor shortage in the country.

All labor unions are required to be registered with the Ministry of Labor and Social Affairs, and they are prohibited from engaging in political activities. The government not only supervises but also supports labor unions through financial subsidies. Organized workers number nearly 65,000, but the rate of unionization varies from 95% in the oil industry to less than 5% in the agricultural sector. Membership is divided among 100 labor unions affiliated with federations and 15 unaffiliated unions. The five major anti-Communist labor federations are the League of Trade Unions of Workers and Employees in the Lebanese Republic, United Unions for Employees and Workers, Federation of Independent Trade Unions, Federation of Unions of Workers and Employees of North Lebanon, and the Federation of Petroleum Employees and Workers Unions in Lebanon. The first four federations are consolidated in the General Labor Confederation of Lebanon. The Communist labor union is the Federation of Labor Unions.

Labor relations are regulated by the National Labor Council. The government encourages collective bargaining and collective agreements are in force in larger establishments. The machinery for the settlement of industrial disputes includes conciliation boards and provincial labor courts. The right to strike is acknowledged, but the Penal Code outlaws strikes that are politically motivated and strikes against public utilities and the government.

FOREIGN COMMERCE

Lebanon's principal exports are agricultural products, chemicals, textiles, and metals and metal products. Its major imports are consumer goods, machinery and transport equipment, and petroleum products. Saudi Arabia, Switzerland, Jordan and Kuwait are its major markets; Italy, France, the United States and Turkey are the main source of imports.

FOREIGN TRADE INDICATORS, 1988

Exports (U.S. $ billions): 1.0 (1987)
Imports (U.S. $ billions): 1.5 (1987)
Balance of trade (U.S. $ billions): −0.5 (1987)

Direction of Trade (%), 1988 est.

	Imports	Exports
European Community	41.0	14.1
United States	5.0	4.4
U.S.S.R. & eastern European economies	12.2	5.4
Japan	3.2	0.3

Composition of Trade (%), 1983

	Imports	Exports
Food and agricultural raw materials & mineral ores, & concentrates	17.3	14.3
Fuels & other energy	3.6	0.0
Manufactured goods	79.1	85.6
of which chemicals	7.8	1.1
of which machinery	29.3	18.2

Foreign trade is generally free of restrictions and there are few controls over trade remittances. Protective tariffs are relatively low. Import and export licensing is restricted to a few items and is designed only to maintain supplies or ensure a better balance of commodity trade. Export subsidies are extended for some commodities such as apples, textiles and some industrial products. Except for the Grains and Sugar Beets Office and the Fruit Office, foreign trade is entirely in the hands of the private sector.

TRANSPORTATION & COMMUNICATIONS

The Lebanese rail system, run by the Office des Chemins de Fer de l'Etat Libanais et du Transport en Commun de Beyrouth et de sa Banlieue, consists of a 82-km. (51-mi.) narrow-gauge track running from Beirut to Damascus in Syria and a 383-km. (203-mi.) standard-gage track running along the coast from Beirut to Tripoli and then inland to Homs in Syria, eventually linking up with the Syrian, Turkish and European networks.

Since 1947, when Haifa became a strictly Israeli port, Beirut has been the principal port of call for all of the Arab Levant. The port of Beirut includes a free zone where goods in transit are free of import taxes. Tripoli, the terminal for the Iraqi pipeline, is the major port for North Lebanon while Saida, the terminal of TAP, is growing in importance. There are also five other relatively underdeveloped ports.

There are two international highways, one leading eastward from Beirut to Damascus and the other southward from the Syrian border to the Israeli border via Tripoli and Beirut. Even remote villages are reachable by road.

There are two Lebanese owned airlines—Middle East Airlines, or Air Liban, and Trans-Mediterranean Airways. The largest international airport is Beirut (Khaldah), which is also the hub of the Middle Eastern airway system, and the second largest is Riyaq. Over the past few years, Beirut airport was closed several times.

Once the mainstay of the Lebanese economy, tourism has suffered badly as a result of the war. Most of the tourists are transit passengers to and from other Arab countries.

TRANSPORTATION INDICATORS

Roads (latest)
- Length, km. (mi.): 7,370 (4,580)
- Paved (%): 85

Motor vehicles (latest) (pre-1986)
- Automobiles: 473,372
- Trucks and buses: 49,560
- Persons per vehicle: 50

Railroads
- Track, km. (mi.): 222 (138) (latest)
- Passenger-km. (passenger-mi.) (millions): 8.6 (5.3) (pre-1986)
- Freight, metric ton-km. (short ton-mi.) (millions): 42 (29) (pre-1986)

Merchant marine
- Vessels (over 100 tons): 191 (1989)
- Total deadweight tonnage (000): 593.1 (1989)

Ports (pre-1986)
- Cargo loaded (million metric tons): 143
- Cargo unloaded (million metric tons): 2.311

Air
- Km. (mi.) flown (millions): 19.5 (12.1) (1985)
- Passenger-km. (passenger-mi.) (millions): 891.9 (554.2) (latest)
- Freight, metric ton-km. (short ton-mi.) (millions): 24.7 (16.9) (latest)
- Airports with scheduled flights: 1 (1990)

COMMUNICATION INDICATORS, 1988

Telephones
- Total (000): 150
- Persons per telephone: 18

Telegraph
- Total traffic (000 calls): 65
  - National: 39
  - International: 26

Telecommunications 1990
- Inactive satellite stations: 3
- Submarine cables: 3

DEFENSE

The defense structure is headed by the president of the republic. Since the start of the civil war little information is available on the structure and organization of the armed forces. The armed forces have been broken up along religious lines with the Christian officers fighting on the Phalangist side and the Muslim ranks on the leftist and Palestinian side. The situation is further complicated by the presence of Syrian and other Arab forces.

The total strength of the armed forces in 1989 was approximately 16,300. Both the air force and the navy are subordinate elements of the army rather than separate forces. Military manpower is provided by a selective 12-month service.

Army

Personnel: 15,000

Organization: 9 infantry brigades

Equipment: 90 main battle tanks; 50 light tanks; combat vehicles; armored personnel carriers; howitzers; mortars; antitank guided weapons

Navy

Personnel: 500

Naval Base: Beirut.

Units: Patrol Craft: 12; Landing craft: 2

Air Force

Personnel: 800

Organization: 50 aircraft, although their operational status is doubtful. Aircraft include: combat aircraft; armored helicopters; fighter squadron; trainers; and transport.

Air Bases: Beirut, Riyaq and Tripoli

Private Militias:

Maronite: 1,000 active; 6,000 all told.
Lebanese Forces Militia: 5,000 active; 15,000 all told.
South Lebanon Army: n/a
Druzes: Progressive Socialist Party 5,000 active, 12,000 all told.
Sunni: Islamic Unity Movement n/a; Al Mourabitoun n/a; October/24 Movement
Shi'a: Amal 5,000 regulars, 15,000 all told; Al Amal al Islam n/a; Hizbollah 3,500 active.

The Lebanese armed forces have always been subject to great internal stresses generated by the religious cleavage of the country. It remained politically neutral until 1975 when it split along religious lines with the Christians supported by Israel on the one side and the Muslims and Palestinians supported by the Soviet Union on the other. It emerged from the civil war as virtually two armies, both decimated in numbers and depleted in equipment.

Lebanon has traditionally received military aid from France, the United States and the United Kingdom. It received arms from the Soviet Union for the first time in 1971.

EDUCATION

Though free, universal and compulsory education has not been introduced, primary education is free. Schooling consists of five years of primary school and four years of primary-complementary school or seven years of secondary school for a total of nine or 12 years. During the fifth and sixth years of secondary school, students may elect to follow a general humanistic or a technical program. At the end of the sixth year students take a comprehensive public examination known as Baccalaureat I, and at the end of the seventh year they complete their schooling with a stiffer examination known as Baccalaureate II.

EDUCATION INDICATORS, 1985

Literacy
- Total (%): 77.0
- Male (%): 85.7
- Female (%): 68.9

First level
- Schools: 2,130 (1982)
- Students: 329,340
- Teachers: 22,810 (1982)

Second level
- Schools: 1,405 (1982)
- Students: 230,934
- Teachers: 21,344 (1981)
- Student/teacher ratio: 15.7

Vocational
- Schools: 181 (1982)
- Students: 37,036
- Teachers: 3,506
- Student/teacher ratio: 10.6

Third level (postsecondary)
- Institutions: 18 (1982)
- Students: 70,510
- Teachers: 7,460
- Student/teacher ratio: 9.5
- Gross enrollment ratio: 27.4
- Students (/100,000 pop.): 2,634
- % of population age 25 and over with postsecondary education: 3.1

Foreign study
- Foreign students in national universities: 25,515 (1985)
- Students abroad: 13,464
  - of whom in
    - United States: 4,448 (1988)
    - France: 4,706 (1988)
    - Federal Republic of Germany: 324 (1988)
    - United Kingdom: 265 (1987)

Public expenditure 1985
- Total (L.£.000): 1,639,467
- % of national budget: 16.8

GRADUATES, 1984

Total: 6,005

- Education: 47
- Humanities & religion: 1,339
- Fine & applied arts: 143
- Law: 581
- Social & behavioral sciences: 935
- Commerce & business: 1,105
- Mass communications: 126
- Home economics: 0
- Service trades: 0
- Natural sciences: 404
- Mathematics & computer science: 115
- Medicine: 430
- Engineering: 476
- Architecture: 157
- Industrial programs: 0
- Transportation & communications: 0
- Agriculture, forestry, fisheries: 144
- Other: 3

The academic year runs from October to June. The medium of instruction is French in private schools and Arabic and French in public schools. However, English is stressed from the primary grades on. The school system is characterized by the predominance of private schools both at the primary and secondary levels.

The administration of public education, formulation and implementation of educational policies, and budget planning are the responsibility of the director general of education.

Lebanon has 12 institutions of higher learning including five universities.

LEGAL SYSTEM

Lebanon follows French jurisprudence and judicial system. The court hierarchy consists of three tiers. At the bottom are 56 courts of first instance presided over by single judges who deal with both civil and criminal cases. Appeals from these courts go to 11 courts of appeal, each presided over by three judges. At the apex are four courts of cassation, three of which deal with civil and commercial cases and the fourth with criminal cases. In addition, there are two special courts: the Council of State, which serves as an administrative court of last resort, and the High Court, which may meet only to try the president of the republic upon indictment by the National Assembly for high treason or violation of the Constitution. Matters of personal status are handled by religious courts. Under the Constitution there is complete separation between the judiciary and the executive. Judges are appointed by the president but they may be transferred only with the approval of the Higher Council of the Magistracy, which functions as a watchdog of judicial integrity.

No information is available on the corrections system.

LAW ENFORCEMENT

The national police force is divided into the gendarmerie, with a pre-civil war strength of 2,500, and the national surete, with a strength of 750. No information is available on their current structure and organization. Information is also lacking on the incidence and nature of non-political crime in the country. The death penalty is in force. The number of judicial executions between 1975 and 1990 is not known.

HEALTH

Health care is mostly in private hands. Lebanon is a net exporter of doctors.

HEALTH INDICATORS

Health personnel 1979
- Physicians: 3,509 (1986)
  - persons per: 771 (1986)
- Dentists: 730
- Nurses: 3,681
- Pharmacists: 1,002
- Midwives: 614

Hospitals 1982
- Number: 130 (1973)
- Number of beds (/10,000): 38

Public health expenditures (latest)
- Per capita (U.S. $): 28.00

Vital statistics
- Crude death rate (/1,000): 7 (1990)
- Life expectancy at birth 1990
  - Males: 66
  - Females: 70
- Infant mortality rate (/1,000 live births): 49 (1990)
- Child mortality rate under 5 yrs. (/1,000 births) (1985–90): 49
- Population with access to safe water (%): 93 (latest)

Major health problems are tuberculosis, polio and eye infections. Heart diseases account for nearly one-third of reported deaths.

FOOD & NUTRITION

The staple item in the Lebanese diet is bread baked in the form of a thick pizza. Most popular is "fingered bread," made with unleavened dough and covered with olive oil, sugar and sesame seeds. Yogurt, fruits and vegetables are served with all meals. Meat is sometimes eaten raw, as in *kibbi*, the national dish. Fish is also consumed in large amounts. The national drink is *arrack*, a distilled grape liquor flavored with anise.

The daily intake of food per capita is 3,000 calories (120% of requirements).

MEDIA & CULTURE

Lebanon leads Middle Eastern countries in newspapers per capita with 39 daily newspapers. Other publications include political weeklies, nonpolitical weeklies and monthlies, nearly all of them published in Beirut. Most of the dailies are printed in Arabic; a few are printed in Armenian and French. Lebanese newspapers and periodicals are sold in substantial numbers in other Arab countries. The principal dailies are: *An-Nahar*, *Al-Anwar*, *Al-Amal*, *Al-Hayat*, *Lissan ul-Hal*, *L'Orient Le Jour*, *Al Liwa'* and *At-Tayyar*.

MEDIA INDICATORS

Newspapers
- Number of dailies: 39 (latest)
- Circulation (000): 573 (latest)
- Per 1,000 pop.: 212 (latest)
- Newsprint consumption 1988
  - Total metric tons: 3,900
  - Per 1,000 pop. (kg.): 1,371

Radio
- Number of transmitters: 55 (latest)
- Number of persons per radio receiver: 1.3 (1989)

Television
- Television transmitters: 23 (latest)
- Number of persons per T.V. receiver: 3.5 (1989)

CULTURAL & ENVIRONMENTAL INDICATORS

Libraries (latest)
- Number: 6
- Volumes (000): 94

Nature reserves (latest)
- Number of facilities: 1

Until the civil war Lebanese traditionally has been free from political controls. The freedom of the press is guaranteed by the Constitution subject to the restrictions imposed by the Press Laws of 1948 and 1962. Under these laws all newspapers and periodicals have to be licensed by the Ministry of Interior and are required to furnish a security deposit. Lebanese editors and publishers must be nationals of good standing, must possess university degrees, must not pursue any other profession and must not run more than one newspaper. The laws also prohibit publication of news that threatens national unity or security, that defames the president, prime minister or president of the National Assembly, or that incites criminal behavior. Newspapers may be suspended if their circulation drops below 1,500. Intimidation of journalists by militias and foreign intelligence services constitutes the most serious threat to press freedom. In 1984, the offices of the conservative newspaper *L'Orient Le Jour* were rocketed and the headquarters of the leading leftist daily *As-Safir* was bombed twice. The *As-Safir* publisher and editor-in-chief narrowly escaped death when a gunman shot him as he entered his apartment building. Foreign journalists were subjected to similar treatment. A U.S. journalist was kidnapped in March

1984 and has not been released. In September a Western wire service correspondent escaped from kidnappers who had held him for weeks.

The national news agency is the National News Agency (NNA), or Wakalat al-Anbaa al-Wataniyah, with two foreign bureaus in Paris and Cairo. Foreign news bureaus in Beirut include UPI, AP, AFP, Reuters, Tass, ADP and MENA. Beirut is also the most important base in the Middle East for foreign correspondents.

Along with Cairo, Beirut is the book publishing capital of the Middle East with over 20 large publishers. The majority of the titles are in Arabic, but a number of books are also published in French. Lebanese books are sold throughout the Middle East. Lebanon adheres to the Universal Copyright and Berne Conventions.

The official Lebanese Broadcasting Service broadcasts two home service programs, the first in Arabic and the second in English, French and Armenian on medium-wave and short wave. An FM station transmits mainly music. Domestic programs are all of domestic origin. The foreign service broadcasts in Arabic and European languages, with the signature Voice of Lebanon.

Television, introduced in 1959, is operated by two commercial enterprises. Compagnie Libanaise de Television (CLT), the older company, has two transmitters in Beirut and two relay transmitters, one in the mountains south of Beirut and the other near Tripoli. Tele-Liban, the second company, has two transmitters and is 50% government-owned. About 40% of the programs are of national origin and some programs are in color.

Lebanon has five film studios, although most feature films are imported. All films are subject to official censorship.

The largest libraries are the Library of the American University, Bibliotheque Orientale and the National Library. There are five museums.

SOCIAL WELFARE

Social security is administered by the National Social Security Fund. About 50% of the labor force receives social security benefits including sickness and maternity insurance, accident and disability insurance, sickness benefit payments up to 26 weeks and family allowances.

GLOSSARY

arrack: national beverage of Lebanon, a distilled grape liquor flavored with anise.

confessional: relating to the distribution of public offices proportionate to the supposed numerical strength of religious denominations.

khamsin: elliptic form of rih al-khamsin, wind of 50 days. A hot wind blowing from the Sahara desert in the fall and winter.

kibbi: national dish made of raw meat and cracked wheat ground together.

mahsub: follower of a national or communal leader.

majlis: council, as in Majlis al-Nuwwab, the Chamber of Deputies, or Majlis al-Muhafazat, provincial council.

marsum jamhouri: a presidential decree.

millet: (in Ottoman law) a non-Muslim community organized under a religious head who also exercised certain civil functions.

Mithaq al-Watani: the National Covenant of 1943, an unwritten accord under which all important political positions were assigned to religious denominations on the basis of their numerical strength at the time of the 1932 census.

muhafazat (plural: muhafazaa): province, as a unit of local administration.

muhafez: governor of a province.

qada (plural: aqdiyat): a subdivision of a province as an administrative district.

qaim maqam: chief of a qada.

qaim maqamiyyah (pl. qaim maqamiyyatan): a district.

zaim (pl. zuama): a professional politician in his role as the leader of his ethnic or religious community.

CHRONOLOGY (from 1945)

1945— British and French troops withdraw from Lebanon; Lebanon joins the Arab League.

1946— Lebanon achieves full independence with Bisharra al-Khoury as president.

1947— Riyad al-Sulh is named premier.

1948— Israeli troops capture Maroun er Rass in Lebanon, but later withdraw. Palestinian refugees flee to southern Lebanon.

1949— Khoury is reelected president.

1952— Khoury is forced to step down in the face of mounting unrest; Camille Chamoun is elected president with Khalid Chihab as premier.

1953— Saeeb Salam is named premier but is later replaced by Abdallah Yafi.

1956— Rashid Karami and Abdallah Yafi form brief governments. . . . Sami es-Solh forms cabinet.

1958— U.S. Marines land in Lebanon in response to President Chamoun's appeal to avert possible takeover by radical elements. . . . Chamoun leaves the presidency at end of term: Fuad Chihab, former commander in chief and a compromise candidate acceptable to the Muslims, is elected president; Rashid Karami is named premier. . . . Strength of the Chamber of Deputies is raised to 99.

1959— Television is introduced.

1961— Saeeb Salam is premier briefly but is replaced later by Rashid Karami.

1964— Charles Hilu is elected president with Hussein Oweini as premier.

1966— Rashid Karami is premier; he resigns and is succeeded in office by Abdallah Yafi but returns to office when Yafi cabinet falls. . . . The failure of the Intra Bank, largest Lebanese bank, sends shock waves through the Beirut financial community.

1968— Karami resigns and Yafi assumes the premiership.

1969— Syria closes Lebanese border. . . . Yafi resigns and Karami heads cabinet. . . . Lebanese army moves against Palestinian guerrillas. . . . Truce is arranged in Cairo between Emile Bustani, commander in chief of Lebanese Army, and Yassir Arafat, the PLO leader.

1970— Suleiman Franjieh is elected president with rightist and center support; Saeeb Salem is named premier.

1972— National elections are held. . . . Five-year preferential trade agreement is signed with EEC.

1973— Syria again closes border. . . . Amin Hafiz, Takeddin Sulh and Rashid Sulh form brief governments. . . . Lebanon plays virtually no role in October War against Israel.

1974— Israel begins retaliatory strikes against Lebanon for guerrilla incursions and terrorism.

1975— Civil war erupts between Christians and Muslims; Prime Ministers Noureddin Rifai and Rashid Karami fail in efforts to arrange cease-fire.

1976— Fighting escalates into civil war; Tal Zataar, guerrilla stronghold, falls to Christian Phalangists; Syria intervenes in force, initially in support of moderate Christian forces; Arab League sends 30,000-man peace-keeping force; Elias Sarkis, a moderate, is elected president with Syrian support; Salim Ahmad Hoss is named prime minister.

1977— Kamal Jumblatt, the Druze leader, is slain. . . . Israeli aid to Phalangists is reported. . . . Banks reopen as fighting subsides.

1978— Israel attacks PLO bases in South Lebanon; United Nations Interim Force in Lebanon is dispatched to enforce truce in the disputed area. . . . Maj. Saad Haddad's Lebanese forces in the south carve out an autonomous Christian enclave near the Israeli border, the pro-Syrian Suleiman Franjiyah quits the National Front of Christian right-wing groups.

1979— The Chamber of Deputies changes its name to National Assembly.

1980— Prime Minister Salim Ahmed al-Hoss, in office since 1976, (despite resigning several times) finally steps down and is succeeded in office by Shafiq al-Wazzan.

1982— Bachir Gemayel, youngest son of Pierre Gemayel, the Phalangist leader, is elected president but is assassinated before assuming office. . . . Bachir's older brother, Amin, is elected in his place and sworn in. . . . Prime Minister Chafiq al-Wazzan continues as head of government. . . . Israeli forces move into Lebanon on "Operation Peace for Galilee," and surround Beirut, trapping more than 6,000 Palestinian fighters. . . . Philip Habib, the U.S. special envoy, secures agreement under which PLO fighters are dispersed to various Arab countries. . . . Multinational peacekeeping force arrives in Beirut. . . . Rightwing Phalangists, with Israeli complicity, massacre refugees in Chatila and Sabra camps.

1983— Muslim kamikaze terrorists bomb U.S. and French military headquarters killing 241 U.S. and 58 French marines. . . . Fighting breaks out in Tripoli between PLO factions in which Yassir Arafat group is beaten. . . . Arafat and his followers leave Tripoli for Algeria, Tunisia and Yemen Arab Republic under U.N. protection. . . . Israel and Lebanon sign peace agreement calling for withdrawal of all foreign forces from Lebanon within three months. . . . Syria condemns agreement and takes over the Beka'a Valley and northern Lebanon while Israel continues to occupy southern Lebanon. . . . Full-scale war flares up between Druze and Phalangist forces in the Chouf Mountains. . . . The Druzes push Christians out of the region. . . . A Conference of National Reconciliation is held in Geneva but founders.

1984— The multinational forces are withdrawn from Beirut. . . . Bowing to Syrian pressures, President Gemayel abrogates the Israeli peace treaty. A second conference at Geneva fails to produce compromise and results in the disintegration of the National Salvation Front. . . . President Gemayel forms a government of national unity. . . . Syrian backed Security Plan leads to the reopening of the port and airport of Beirut and the clearing of the Green Line separating Christian and Muslim Beirut. . . . Israel announces unilateral withdrawal from southern Lebanon in three phases.

1985— Israeli troops withdraw completely, except for a 10 km.-deep security zone north of its boarder with Lebanon. A peace agreement is signed by leaders of the Druze, Amal and (Christian) Lebanese Forces to end the civil war, although clashes erupted again in Beirut later that year.

1986— Fighting erupts between Palestinian guerrillas and Shi'ite Amal militiamen for control of refugee camps in the south of Beirut; Lebanese and Syrian troops are deployed to impose cease-fire.

1987— Amal forces besiege Palestinian refugee camps near Beirut, Tyre and Sidon, in-fighting between Muslims erupts in Beirut; Syrian troops are again called in to restore peace. Israeli air attacks on Palestinian targets in southern Lebanon resume and continue in 1988, 1989 and 1990. Prime Minister Rashid Karami is assassinated; President Gemayel appoints Dr. Selim al-Hoss in his place.

1988— Nabih Berri, the leader of Amal, announces the ending of the siege of Palestinian refugee camps in Beirut and southern Lebanon. As no successor is elected, outgoing President Gemayel appoints a transitional military government headed by General Michel Aoun; Prime Minister Selim al-Hoss refuses to recognize this government; Christians and Muslims renew fighting in Beirut for control.

1989— General Aoun launches a "war of liberation" against Syria, killing thousands; Aoun later consents to an internationally sponsored cease-fire. A charter of national reconciliation is proposed by the Lebanese National Assembly meeting in Taif, Saudi Arabia, providing for expansion of the Assembly from 99 to 108 seats to be divided equally among Christians and Muslims. Rene Mouawad is elected President in November and is assassinated 17 days later. Elias Hrawi is elected President on November 24. General Aoun refuses to vacate the presidential palace.

1990— Geagea, leader of the Phalangist militia, pledges his allegiance to President Hrawi. The Lebanese National Assembly approves constitutional changes which it drafted in the Taif peace accord; Hrawi signs the constitutional changes into law. General Aoun is violently evicted from the palace, but escapes. President Hrawi begins to consolidate control over Beirut by ordering the departure of rival militias from the city. Prime Minister Selim al-Hoss resigns to make way for a government of national unity and is succeeded by Omar Karami.

1991— PLO guerrillas trade military blows with Israeli forces in southern Lebanon; clashes end with Lebanese government troops moving into the area.

BIBLIOGRAPHY (from 1970)

BOOKS

Abraham, A. J. *Lebanon: A State of Siege.* Bristol, IN, 1985.

Azar, Edward E. *The Emergence of a New Lebanon: Fantasy or Reality.* New York, 1984.

Baaklini, Adbo L. *Cultural Resources in Lebanon.* Mystic, CT, 1972.

———. *Legislatures and Political Development in Lebanon, 1842–1972.* Durham, NC, 1976.

Barakat, Halim. *Lebanon in Strife: Student Preludes to the Civil War.* Austin, TX, 1977.

Bavly, Dan and Eliahu Salpeter. *Fire in Beirut. Israel's War in Lebanon with the PLO: Prelude to Aftermath.* Briarcliff Manor, NY, 1984.

Browne, Walter L. *Lebanon's Struggle for Independence.* Salisbury, NC, 1980.

Chami, Joseph G. *Days of Wrath: Lebanon 1975–1982.* New Brunswick, NJ, 1982.

Cobban, Helena. *The Making of Modern Lebanon.* Boulder, CO, 1985.

Deeb, Marius. *The Lebanese Civil War.* New York, NY, 1980.

Dupuy, Trevor and Paul Martell. *Flawed Victory: The 1982 War in Lebanon.* Fairfax, VA, 1985.

Evans, Louella M. *Lebanon: Portrait of a People.* New York, 1973.

Feldman, Shai & Heda Rechnitz-Kijner. *Deception, Consensus and War: Israel in Lebanon.* Boulder, CO, 1985.

Fisk, Robert G. *Pity the Nation: Lebanon at War.* London, 1990.

Freyha, Annie. *Dictionary of the Names of Towns and Villages in Lebanon.* New York, 1972.

Friedman, Thomas L. *From Beirut to Jerusalem.* New York, 1989.

Gale, Jack. *The Lebanon Time Bomb.* London, 1982.

Gilmour, David. *Lebanon: The Fractured Country.* New York, 1984.

Gordon, David G. *Lebanon: The Fragmented Nation.* Stanford, CA, 1980.

———. *The Republic of Lebanon: A Nation in Jeopardy.* Boulder, CO, 1983.

Gabriel, L. *In the Ashes: The Story of Lebanon.* Ardmore, PA, 1978.

Haddad, Wedi D. *Lebanon: The Politics of Revolving Doors.* New York, 1985.

Haley P. Edward & Lewis W. Snider. *Lebanon in Crisis: Participants & Issues.* Syracuse, NY, 1979.

Hitti, Philip I. *Short History of Lebanon.* New York, 1965.

Hof, Frederic C. *Galilee Divided: The Israel-Lebanon Frontier, 1916–1984.* Boulder, CO, 1985.

Hourani, A. H. *Syria and Lebanon: A Political Essay.* Mystic, CT, 1972.

Hudson, Michael C. *The Precarious Republic: Modernization in Lebanon.* Boulder, CO, 1985.

Joumblatt, Kamal. *I Speak for Lebanon.* London, 1982.

Khairallah, Shereen. *Lebanon.* (World Bibliographical Series). Santa Barbara, CA, 1979.

Khalaf, Roseanne. *Once Upon a Time in Lebanon.* Delmar, NY, 1982.

Khalaf, Samir. *Persistence and Chance in 19th Century Lebanon.* Syracuse, NY, 1979.

Khalidi, Walid. *Conflict & Violence in Lebanon: Confrontation in the Middle East.* Cambridge, MA, 1980.

Ksirwani, Marum. *Patron-Client Politics & Bureaucratic Corruption: The Case of Lebanon.* Bloomington, IN, 1975.

Longrigg, Stephen H. *Syria and Lebanon Under French Mandate.* New York, 1972.

MacBridge, Sean. *Israel in Lebanon.* London, 1983.

Mahfoud, Peter. *Lebanon and the Turmoil of the Middle East.* New York, 1979.

Makdisi, Samir A. *Financial Policy and Economic Growth in Lebanon.* New York, 1979.

Meo, Leila. *Lebanon: The Improbable Nation.* Westport, CT, 1976.

Mikdadi, Lina. *Surviving the Siege of Beirut: A Personal Account.* Washington, D.C., 1983.

Murray, G. L. *Lebanon: The New Future.* London, 1974.

Norton, Augustus R. *External Intervention and the Politics of Lebanon.* New York, 1984.

Odeh, J. B. *Lebanon: Dynamics of Conflict: A Modern Political History.* London, 1985.

Petran, Tabitha. *The Struggle over Lebanon.* New York, 1985.

Rabin, Yitzhak and Uri Lubrani. *Israel's Lebanon Policy: Where to?* Boulder, CO, 1984.

Rabinovich, Itamar. *The War for Lebanon: 1970-1985.* Ithaca, NY, 1985.

Randal, Jonathan C. *Going All the Way: Christian Warlords, Israeli Adventurers and the War in Lebanon.* New York, 1984.

Sakada, Linda and Nawaf Salam. *The Civil War in Lebanon: A Bibliographical Guide.* Syracuse, NY, 1983.

Salem, Elie Abid. *Modernization Without Revolution: Lebanon's Experience.* Bloomington, IN, 1973.

Salibi, Kamal S. *Crossroads to Civil War in Lebanon, 1958–1976.* Portland, OR, 1976.

———. *The Modern History of Lebanon.* Westport, CT, 1976.

Schiff, Ze'ev and Ehud Ya'ari. *Israel's Lebanon War.* New York, 1984.

Shaker, Fouad E. *Fire Over Lebanon: Country in Crisis.* New York, 1976.

Smock, David R. and Audrey C. Smock. *The Politics of Pluralism: A Comparative Study of Lebanon and Ghana.* New York, 1975.

Suleiman, Michael W. *Political Parties in Lebanon.* Ithaca, NY, 1967.
Timerman, Jacobo. *The Longest War: Israel in Lebanon.* New York, 1982.
Vocke, Harold. *The Lebanese Civil War.* New York, 1978.
Witty, Cathie J. *Mediation and Society: Conflict Management in Lebanon.* New York, 1980.
Zamir, Meir. *The Formation of Modern Lebanon.* London, 1985.

OFFICIAL PUBLICATIONS

Bank of Lebanon. *Annual Reports.*
Central Statistical Office. *Monthly Statistical Bulletin.*

LESOTHO

BASIC FACT SHEET

OFFICIAL NAME: Kingdom of Lesotho (Muso oa Lesotho) (formerly Basutoland)

ABBREVIATION: LO

CAPITAL: Maseru

HEAD OF STATE: King Letsie III (from 1990)

HEAD OF GOVERNMENT: Prime Minister Col. Elias P. Ramaema (from 1991)

NATURE OF GOVERNMENT: Constitutional monarchy

POPULATION: 1,760,000 (1990)

AREA: 30,355 sq. km. (11,720 sq. mi.)

ETHNIC MAJORITY: Basotho

LANGUAGES: English and Sesotho

RELIGIONS: Christianity and animism

UNIT OF CURRENCY: Maloti

NATIONAL FLAG: Two narrow stripes of green and red at the hoist and on the right a blue field with a traditional Basuto hat (a conical straw hat) in white in the center

NATIONAL EMBLEM: The principal element of the coat of arms is a yellow native warrior's shield displaying a crocodile flanked by two heraldic horses with the legend *Khotso, Pula, Nala* (Peace, Rain, Abundance) beneath them. Behind the shield are an ostrich plume, a crossed spear *(assegai)* and a club *(knobkerrie).*

NATIONAL ANTHEM: "Lesotho, the Country of Our Fathers"

NATIONAL HOLIDAYS: October 4 (Independence Day, National Day); January 1 (New Year's Day); March 12 (Moshoeshoe's Day); May 3 (King's Birthday); June 13 (Commonwealth Day); August 5 (Arbor Day); October 1 (National Sports Day); Christian festivals, including Good Friday, Easter Monday, Ascension Day, Christmas and Boxing Day

NATIONAL CALENDAR: Gregorian

PHYSICAL QUALITY OF LIFE INDEX: 52

DATE OF INDEPENDENCE: October 4, 1966

DATE OF CONSTITUTION: October 4, 1966 (Constitution suspended since 1970)

WEIGHTS & MEASURES: Imperial

GEOGRAPHICAL FEATURES

Lesotho is an enclave within the east-central part of South Africa. It is the only county in the world entirely surrounded by another. It occupies an area of 30,355 sq. km. (11,720 sq. mi.), extending 248 km. (154 mi.) north-northeast to south-southwest and 181 km. (112 mi.) east-southeast to west-northwest.

Lesotho shares its entire international boundary of 909 km. (565 mi.) with South Africa. The borders of the country were finally delimited at the Convention of Aliwal North in 1869. This border has not been accepted by independent Lesotho, which has pressed claims before the United Nations for the return of Basothan territories added to Orange Free State after wars between the Boers and the Basotho more than 100 years ago.

The capital is Maseru, with a 1987 population of 75,000. Other major towns are Teyateyaneng (7,000) and Leribe (5,500).

Lesotho has three distinct geographical regions extending longitudinally across the country. The Western Lowlands cover approximately a quarter of the country's land area between the Caledon River and the Cave Sandstone foothills. They consist of undulating basins and plains ranging in width from 10 km. (6 mi.) to 64 km. (40 mi.), with altitudes averaging between 1,520 and 1,820 m. (5,000 and 6,000 ft.). The Cave Sandstone Terrace is an intermediate region between the highlands and the lowlands, with an average altitude of more than 1,820 m. (6,000 ft.). The Maluti Mountains, spurs of the main Drakensberg, with some peaks over 3,000 m. (10,000 ft.) high, mark the western edge of the Eastern Highlands, which are South Africa's main watershed. In this high plateau is Lesotho's highest point, Thabana Ntlenyana (3,482 m.; 11,425 ft.).

Lesotho is drained by tributaries of the Orange and Caledon rivers and the Tugela River.

CLIMATE & WEATHER

Lesotho's climate is dry and rigorous, with extremes of heat and cold. Mean annual temperatures in the lowlands range from 32°C (90°F) in the summer to −6.6°C (20°F) in the winter. Mean temperatures in the highlands range from 15.5°C (60°F) to as low as −18°C (0°F). Hail and snow are frequent in the mountains, while the lowlands may have snow occasionally in winter. Most areas have an average annual rainfall of 635 mm. (25 in.), with the highest precipitation in the highlands and the lowest in the Western Lowlands and the Orange River Valley. Rainfall is concentrated in October and April, and showers generally tend to be short and heavy. Thunderstorms are common in the rainy season.

LESOTHO

Names and boundary representation are not necessarily authoritative

International boundary
National capital
Railroad
Road

0 10 20 30 Miles
0 10 20 30 Kilometers

SOUTH AFRICA
Winburg
Marquard
Fouriesburg
Ficksburg
Butha Buthe
Leribe
Bergville
Tugela
Ladybrand
Teyateyaneng
MASERU
Mokhotlong
Madibamatso
ORANGE
Sinqunyane
Caledon
Mafeteng
Kornetspruit
Qachas Nek
Mohales Hoek
Zastron
Quthing
Matatiele
ORANGE
SOUTH AFRICA
Maclear

ANGOLA
ZAMBIA
SOUTH-WEST AFRICA (INT. TERR.)
SOUTHERN RHODESIA (U.K.)
BOTSWANA
MOZAMBIQUE
WALVIS BAY (S. AF.)
SWAZILAND
SOUTH AFRICA
LESOTHO
Atlantic Ocean
Indian Ocean

27
28
29
29
30
31
27
28
29

POPULATION

The population of Lesotho was estimated at 1,760,000 in 1990, on the basis of the last official census, in 1986.

Most of the population is concentrated in the Western Lowlands (the name Lesotho is a Sesotho word for lowlands).

Only 6% of the population live in urban settlements, and there is only one population center of over 30,000 inhabitants. However, the annual urban growth rate is 6.67%, or 2.34 times the national growth rate.

The median age is rising, reflecting a declining birth rate.

The male/female ratio is disproportionately in favor of females. This imbalance is explained by the steady immigration of males to work in South Africa. At any given time close to 200,000 Basotho workers are absent in South Africa. Nearly 50% of the male labor force is estimated to leave the country each year to seek work in South Africa. Many of them are recruited by the National Recruiting Corporation on behalf of South African employers.

Lesotho adopted an official family planning policy on recommendation of a national population commission in 1974. Under this policy the government supports family planning in the context of maternal and child health and coordinates its activities with those of the International Planned Parenthood Federation.

All Basotho have fairly equal opportunity within the confines imposed by political reality, although in the areas of property and contracts, married women's rights, independent of their husbands, are limited by custom and law. For example, married women cannot apply for loans without their husband's written consent. Women in Basotho society have traditionally been a stabilizing force, due to the absence of hundreds of thousands of men working in South Africa. Fuller use of women's abilities will depend on the progress Lesotho makes in providing education, health and other social services to the rural areas where the overwhelming majority of those women live.

DEMOGRAPHIC INDICATORS

Population (millions): 1.76 (1990)
Year of last census: 1986
Sex distribution (% at last census): males, 48.2; females, 51.8
Population estimates and projections (millions)

1930: .537	1960: .885	1990: 1.760
1940: .566	1970: 1.043	2000: 2.958
1950: .766	1980: 1.358	

Age profile (%, 1976 census)

0–14: 39.1	30–44: 15.5	60–74: 5.2
15–29: 25.5	45–59: 10.4	75 and over: 2.3

Median age (yrs.): 18.7 (1985)
Youth population (% aged 15–24): (1985), 18.4 (2000) 19.1
Total dependency ratio, 1985: 86.1
Annual growth rate (%)

1950–55: 1.57	1975–80:	2.41	2000–2005:	2.78
1955–60: 1.84	1980–85:	2.78	2005–10:	2.76
1960–65: 2.01	1985–90:	2.85	2010–15:	2.50
1965–70: 2.01	1990–95:	2.84	2015–20:	2.14
1970–75: 2.19	1995–2000:	2.82	2020–25:	1.80

Hypothetical size of stationary population (millions): 6
Assumed year of reaching net reproduction rate of 1: 2030
Urban population (000): 257 (1985)
Urban population (%): (1988) 19; (1965) 6
Annual urban population growth rate (%, 1985–90): 6.67
Annual rural population growth rate (%, 1985–90): 1.98
Number of cities of population over 500,000: 0 (1980)
Population density per sq. km. (per sq. mi.): 58 (150.2) (1990)

VITAL STATISTICS

Crude birth rate (/1,000): 37 (1990); 42 (1965)
Crude death rate (/1,000): 10 (1990); 18 (1965)
Infant mortality rate (/1,000 live births): 80 (1990)
Life expectancy (yrs.) at birth: males, 59; females, 62 (1990)
Gross reproduction rate (/woman) (1980–85): 2.85
Total fertility rate (/woman): 4.9 (1990)
Rate of natural increase (/1,000) (1980–85): 28.4
Average household size: 4.8 (latest)

STATUS OF WOMEN INDICATORS

Number of women (000): 763 (1985)
% women of childbearing age 15–49: 46 (1988)
% women literate: 84.5 (1987)
% women in labor force: 43.8 (1988)
Total fertility rate (/woman): 4.9 (1990)

ETHNIC COMPOSITION

Apart from a few thousand Europeans and a few hundred Asians, the population is entirely of Basotho stock. The Zulu-speaking Nguni, who comprise about 15% of the population, sometimes are classified as a separate group. Historically the Basotho and the Nguni consist of a number of groups, each with its own chief and totem. Belonging to the Nguni family are the Bathepu (Fengo, Pondo and Thembu), Ama Vundle, Baphetla (or Zizi), Baphuthi, Maphetla and Baroa. The principal divisions of the Basotho are the Bafokeng, Basia, Bataung and Batlokoa.

The number of Europeans in the country is estimated at 2,000 and the number of Asians and coloreds (those of mixed race) at a few hundred.

LANGUAGES

The official languages of Lesotho are English and Sesotho. Sesotho is spoken by virtually all Basotho. Also called Sotho and Suto, it is a member of the Bantu family of languages.

RELIGIONS

Christianity is the religion of the majority of the Basotho and is followed by over 70% of the population. The Catholic Church, under the archbishop of Maseru, is the dominant religious force in the country, with some 410,000 adherents. The Catholic Church operates four teacher-training colleges, eight high schools, 18 secondary schools and three vocational schools besides hospitals, seminaries, convents and the famous Mazenod Institute. The largest Protestant denomination is the Church of Lesotho, founded by the Paris Evangelical Missionary Society, which claims 22% of the population as followers. The smaller Anglican Church is administratively under the Province of South Africa. Nearly 30% of the population follows traditional African religions and cults.

HISTORICAL BACKGROUND

Lesotho, known until independence as Basutoland, was under British rule as a crown protectorate from 1868 to 1871 and from 1884 to 1966. British colonial policy toward Basutoland was characterized by parsimony and indifference. Actual governance was left to the numerous chieftains, who opposed all attempts to centralize and modernize the administration. The only condition of the protectorate agreement that was strictly observed by the British was the proviso that no white would be allowed to acquire land in Basutoland and that the land tenure system would remain unchanged. Much of the social and educational modernization of Lesotho is due to the work of Christian missionaries rather than the British Colonial Office. Britain guided the country to independence in 1966, and the British departure was peaceful.

At independence Lesotho became a constitutional monarchy. Moshoeshoe II, the paramount chief, became king, and Leabua Jonathan became prime minister. Jonathan was head of the Basutoland National Party (BNP), which had won a parliamentary majority in the pre-independence elections. Through alliances with powerful chieftains, Jonathan gradually consolidated his power at the expense of the king, who was left with primarily ceremonial duties.

In 1970, when the opposition Basotho Congress Party (BCP) seemed likely to win the parliamentary elections, Jonathan declared a state of emergency, suspended the Constitution and had opposition leaders arrested. The leaders were released the following year but forbidden to take part in politics. The state of emergency eventually was lifted in 1973. Clashes between the police and guerrilla groups allegedly aligned with the BCP prompted Jonathan to impose strict security measures in 1974. Outside funding of political groups was forbidden, and the government was permitted to detain individuals for two months without legal aid. He also established a BNP militia, which harassed political opponents.

Dissatisfaction with Jonathan's rule grew, and in 1984 a general meeting of the BNP ordered him to call legislative elections. After opposition parties refused to participate because of registration irregularities, Jonathan declared all BNP candidates elected. In 1986 Jonathan was toppled in a coup led by the commander in chief of the army, Gen. Justin Lekhanya. Government was established under the king, who was given legislative and executive powers. He ruled with a six-man Military Council, led by Lekhanya, which effectively exercised power. Although it stated its commitment to democracy, the Military Council banned all political activity pending a new constitution, but no movement was made toward drafting the document.

In 1990 Lekhanya stripped King Moshoeshoe II of his executive power, sending him into exile. Moshoeshoe's son, Prince Mohato, was then sworn in as King Letsie III. Leaders of all seven registered political parties appealed to Lekhanya to repeal an order banning political activity and urged him to halt plans to make the National Assembly only an advisory body to the Military Council. On April 30, 1991, Lekhanya was ousted by rebel army officers in a bloodless coup triggered by dissatisfaction in the army over pay. Col. Elias P. Ramaema, a member of Lesotho's ruling Military Council, was chosen to replace Lekhanya.

CONSTITUTION & GOVERNMENT

Lesotho currently has no constitution, the independence Constitution of 1966 having been suspended in 1970. However, pending the drafting of a new constitution, most of the provisions of the Constitution of 1966 continue to provide the legal basis for the structure and operations of government. Under the independence Constitution the paramount chief, or *motlotlehi,* is the sovereign, but his powers are subject to the constitutional guarantees of human rights and freedoms and to the legislative authority of the National Assembly and Senate. Executive authority is exercised by the king, the head of state, through a cabinet con-

GOVERNMENT LIST
(July/August 1991)

King	Letsie III
Chairman, Military Council, Head of Government	Ramaema, Elias Phisoana, *Col.*
Minister of Agriculture, Cooperatives & Marketing (Acting)	Dingiswayo, J. L., *Maj. Gen.*
Minister of Defense & Internal Security	Ramaema, Elias Phisoana, *Col.*
Minister of Education	Machobane, Lehlohonolo B. B. J.
Minister of Employment, Social Security & Pensions	Mothakathi, Leonard Paepae, *Col.*
Minister of Finance	Thoahlane, Abel Leshele
Minister of Foreign Affairs	Molapo, Tanki Pius, *Lt.*
Minister of Health	Khuele, William Molefi, *Col.*
Minister of Highlands Water & Energy	Habi, Reentseng, *Maj.*
Minister of Information & Broadcasting	Molapo, Tanki Pius, *Lt.*
Minister of Interior, Chieftainship Affairs & Rural Development	Matete, Mphosi
Minister of Justice, Prisons, Law, Constitutional & Parliamentary Affairs	Maope, Kelebone Albert, *Lt. Col.*
Minister of Planning, Economic & Manpower Development	Sekhonyana, Evaristus Retselisitsoe
Minister of Tourism, Sports & Culture	Mathealira, Lechesa
Minister of Trade & Industry	Mokoroane, Moletsane
Minister of Water, Energy & Mining	Jane, Alexander Lesole, *Col.*
Minister of Works, Transport & Communications	Mokone, Matsosa Valentius, *Lt. Col.*
Assistant Minister for Education	Mabathoana, Phillip Makalo
Assistant Minister for Youth & Women's Affairs	Hlalele, Anna Matlelima
Minister of State to the Military Council	Molapo, Patrick Jonathan
Governor, Central Bank	Maruping, Anthony Mothae

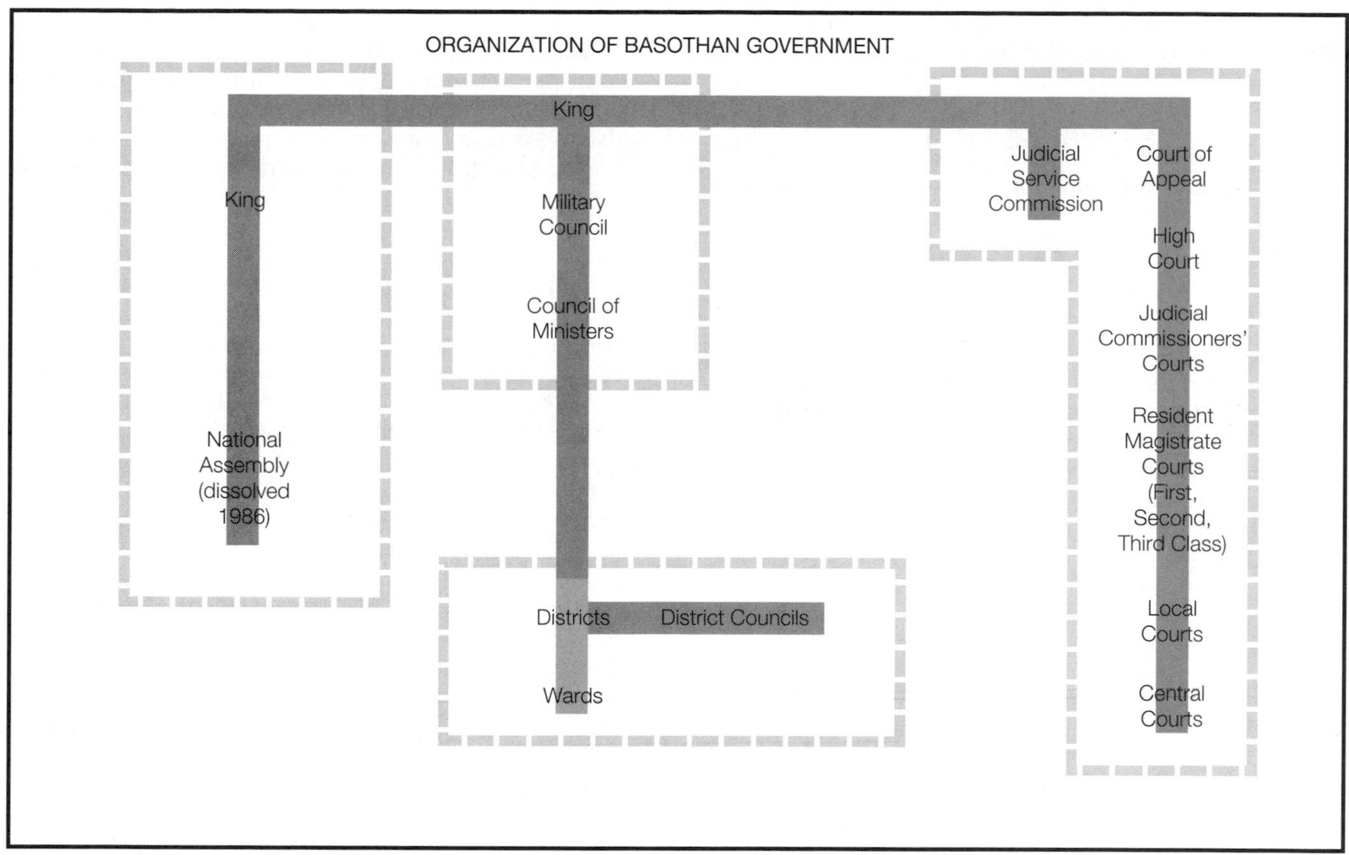

sisting of a prime minister, who is the head of government, and not less than seven other ministers, who together are known as the king's government. The king will act only on ministerial advice except in some minor matters where he has absolute discretion. He is advised by the Privy Council, consisting of the prime minister and two other members. The Constitution specifically provides that all land in Lesotho is owned by the nation and is administered in trust for the nation by the king. The Constitution also makes proviso for an impartial four-member Public Service Commission.

With the suspension of the Constitution of 1966 in 1970, Prime Minister Leabua Jonathan ruled by decree. In 1974 Jonathan said that the parliamentary system of government was unsuitable for Lesotho and that in the proposed new constitution there would be no room for political parties. In 1986 he was overthrown in a South-Africa-backed military coup led by Gen. Justin Lekhanya.

Under the Constitution of 1966 suffrage is universal for all adults. The last national elections were held in 1985, but opposition parties did not participate. The legislature was dissolved after the 1986 coup.

Following the coup of 1986, the Military Council announced that all executive and legislative power was in the hands of the king and that the Parliament Act of 1983 was repealed. The Military Council effectively exercises power.

The High Court, the Court of Appeals and subordinate courts comprise the judicial system. Members of the High and Appeals courts are appointed by the king on advice of the government. Sixty-three Lesotho courts administer customary law for Africans.

FREEDOM & HUMAN RIGHTS

In terms of political and civil rights Lesotho is classified as a partly free country.

The government of Lesotho suspended written guarantees of human rights in 1970 when it suspended the Constitution, but the existence of an independent and impartial judiciary has mitigated actual violations of human rights.

Under the provisions of the Internal Security Act of 1984, detainees may be held incommunicado for up to 60 days and are not accorded trials, and their detention may not be challenged in courts. But nonpolitical criminals receive fair trials under British-based law.

The Human Rights Act of 1983, technically guaranteeing many fundamental human rights, came into force in July 1984. However, this act is "subject to the provisions of existing law," which includes temporary detention without trial and other restrictions on human rights. The Internal Security Act codifies existing security laws, removes bail in cases of armed robbery, increases sentences for certain security offenses and allows for the detention of witnesses in security cases. Although the courts have not hesitated to rule against the government in security cases, potential for mistreatment of prisoners prior to trial remains high, as it also is for those detained for purely criminal offenses.

Free assembly is not guaranteed, and freedom of speech is restricted by the Internal Security Act.

CIVIL SERVICE

No information is available on the civil service in Lesotho.

LOCAL GOVERNMENT

For purpose of local government Lesotho is divided into 11 districts: Maseru, Qacha's Nek, Mokhotlong, Leribe, Butha-Buthe, Teyateyaneng, Mafeteng, Mohale's Hoek, Quthing and Thaba-Tseka.

Since 1970 each district has been administered by a commissioner appointed by the central government. The districts are divided into a total of 22 wards headed by ward chiefs.

FOREIGN POLICY

Lesotho's foreign policy is determined, on the one hand, by its status as an economic satellite of South Africa, and on the other by its desire to maintain cordial relations with independent black nations to the north. Lesotho's image suffered badly as a result of the 1970 coup. Prime Minister Jonathan bitterly resented African and Western criticism of his suppression of political and civil rights with South African aid. For a number of years thereafter Lesotho's foreign policy was marked by awkward and defensive efforts to resume its role in African councils. It has been partially successful in this respect, and relations with independent African states, especially Tanzania and Zambia, have been strengthened. Lesotho also has participated increasingly in OAU activities.

In the equally crucial area of relations with South Africa, Lesotho's foreign policy has been characterized by continuing ambivalence. Prime Minister Jonathan owed some of his initial successes to South African support. Lesotho and Malawi were the only countries to abstain from voting on an OAU resolution calling on Western powers not to supply arms to South Africa. Jonathan publicly proclaimed his adherence to the concept of a dialogue with South Africa. A new monetary agreement was signed among South Africa, Lesotho and Swaziland in 1974, and the South African-led customs union, which also includes Botswana, continues to sustain Lesotho's economy.

However, beginning in 1974 there was a gradual shift toward a more critical posture in relation to South Africa. In 1973 Prime Minister Jonathan made a number of sharp attacks on the Vorster government. Lesotho declared a temporary embargo on the recruitment of migrant labor for South African mines after five Basotho laborers were killed by South African police. In 1974 Lesotho raised its claim to conquered territory in Orange Free State and placed the issue before the U.N. General Assembly in 1975. Further tensions have resulted from the formation of the Transkei "homeland" and South African attempts to force Lesotho to recognize Transkei as an independent nation. In pursuit of a more open foreign policy, Lesotho also has established diplomatic and economic links with Yugoslavia, Mozambique and China. Relations between Lesotho and South Africa worsened in 1985 following a South African raid on Maseru that killed nine people, including six African National Congress (ANC) rebels. On January 1, 1986, South Africa imposed sanctions on Lesotho, allowing only migrant workers traveling to South African mines to cross the border. Following three weeks of tension, Prime Minister Jonathan was overthrown in a bloodless coup led by Gen. Justin Lekhanya. The new military rulers agreed to expel ANC rebels in return for lifting the blockade. Jonathan's ouster pleased Pretoria, which had been angered by his support for ANC rebels and by his allowing Soviet-bloc nations to open embassies in Maseru.

Lesotho's relations with Botswana received a considerable setback in 1975 when Lesotho unilaterally nationalized the Roma Campus of the joint University of Botswana, Lesotho and Swaziland.

Lesotho and the United States are parties to eight treaties and agreements covering extradition, investment guarantees, the Peace Corps, property, trademarks and visas.

PARLIAMENT

Under the Independence Constitution of 1966 that was suspended in 1970, the national legislature was the bicameral Parliament, consisting of the Senate and the National Assembly. The National Assembly consisted of 60 members elected for three-year terms by universal adult suffrage from single-member constituencies. The Senate consisted of 33 members, of whom 22 are chiefs and 11 are appointed by the chief of state.

The 1970 elections to the National Assembly were declared void, and an emergency was proclaimed by Prime Minister Jonathan. In 1973, in response to pressures from members of his own party as well as those of the opposition, Jonathan established 93-member Interim National Assembly to draw up a new constitution "compatible with traditional institutions." Contrary to the government's promise, the 1984 session of the interim Parliament adjourned without a date being set for elections. The interim Parliament did pass three electoral amendment acts that, inter alia, call for staggered voting, a significantly large deposit for each parliamentary candidate, and more voter signatures on a petition required for each candidate to be placed on the ballot. The opposition parties charged that these new measures could be used to intimidate voters and discourage opposition candidates from running.

Opposition parties boycotted the 1985 elections, and Jonathan announced that all his BNP candidates were elected unopposed. Following the 1986 coup, Parliament was dissolved and legislative power was vested in the king. However, actual legislative authority resides with the Military Council.

POLITICAL PARTIES

Before Prime Minister Jonathan's ouster in 1986 the ruling party was the Basotho National Party (BNP), a conservative party that drew its main support from Catholics and traditional chiefs. It favored free enterprise, retention of Commonwealth ties and economic cooperation with South Africa.

The principal opposition party was the Basotho Congress Party, a vigorous pan-Africanist group that consistently opposed Jonathan's autocratic regime. The party split into two factions: a parliamentary wing led by Gerard Ramoreboli, which accepted Jonathan's call for national reapprochement; and an exile group led by Ntsu Mokhehle and consisting of implacable foes of Jonathan. The former group entered an interim National Assembly under the name of the Progress Party. The next most important opposition party was the Marema Tloe Freedom Party, a royalist party that sought to enlarge the king's authority. The United Democratic Party was another splinter group of the Basotho Congress Party. In 1984 two new parties were formed: the Basotho Democratic Alliance, a conservative, pro-South Africa group; and the National Independence Party. There also is a small Communist Party, which, despite its proscribed status, claims a few supporters.

In 1986 the Military Council banned all political activity.

ECONOMY

Lesotho is one of the 49 low-income countries of the world, one of the 29 least-developed countries of the world and one of the 45 countries considered by the United Nations to be most seriously affected by the adverse economic conditions of the 1980s. Lesotho has few natural resources, and its economy is based on agriculture, light manufacturing and the export of labor.

The Lesothan economy is a free-market economy in which the dominant sector is private.

Subsistence farming employs 86% of the domestic labor force and accounts for 16% of the GDP. The land is generally poor. Overgrazing, overpopulation, drought and erosion have compounded the problem, resulting in generally poor yields. Manufacturing is a small but growing element of the economy. Its total share of the GDP rose from 6% in 1982 to 11% in recent years. Industry centers around food processing; other manufacturing includes textiles, clothing and light engineering. Until 1982 diamond mining was an important source of revenue, but unfavorable world prices forced the closing of the country's only mine that year.

Lesotho is heavily dependent on remittances from workers in South Africa. Because of lack of jobs, nearly one-third of the male work force finds employment in South Africa. Their remittances contributed 40% of the GNP during the mid-1980s.

PRINCIPAL ECONOMIC INDICATORS

Gross National Product (U.S. $ millions): 816 (1989)
GNP per capita (U.S. $): 470 (1989)
GNP average annual growth rate (%, 1980–89): 2.2
GNP per capita average annual growth rate (%, 1987–89): 3.5
Average annual rate of inflation (%, 1980–88): 12.2
Consumer Price Index (1980=100) 1986
- All items: 129
- Food: 219

BALANCE OF PAYMENTS, 1988 (U.S. $ millions)

Current account balance: −73
Merchandise exports: 64
Merchandise imports: −486
Trade balance: −422
Other goods, services & income +: 368
Other goods, services & income −: −80
Other goods, services & income net: 288
Private unrequited transfers: 4
Official unrequited transfers: 57
Capital other than reserves: 65
Net errors & omissions: 15
Total: −7
Counterpart items: −7
Total: −14
Total change in reserves: 14

GROSS DOMESTIC PRODUCT

GDP nominal (R. billions): 0.970 (1988)
GDP per capita (U.S. $): 245 (1989)
Average annual growth rate of GDP (%, 1980–88): 2.9
GDP by type of expenditure (%), 1987
- Consumption
  - Private: 150
  - Government: 28
- Gross domestic investment: 36
- Gross domestic saving: −73 (1988)
- Foreign trade
  - Exports: 16
  - Imports: −130

Cost components of GDP (%), 1986
- Net indirect taxes: 20
- Consumption of fixed capital compensation of employees and net operating surplus: 30

Sectoral origin of GDP (%), 1987
- Primary
  - Agriculture: 16 (1988)
- Secondary
  - Manufacturing: 11
  - Construction: 9
  - Public utilities: 1
- Tertiary
  - Transportation & communications: 2
  - Trade: 15
  - Finance: 11
  - Other services: 8
  - Government: 11

Average annual sectoral growth rates (%, 1980–88)
- Agriculture: 1.8
- Industry: 1.6
- Manufacturing: 12.4
- Services: 4.1

PUBLIC FINANCE

The Lesothan fiscal year runs from April 1 through March 1. Until 1973 both the capital and recurrent

CENTRAL GOVERNMENT EXPENDITURES, 1986

% of total expenditures
- Defense: 0.0
- Education: 22.4
- Health: 7.4
- Housing, Social Security, welfare: 6.0
- Economic services: 21.6
- Other: 42.7

CENTRAL GOVERNMENT REVENUES, 1986

% of total current revenues
- Taxes on income, profit & capital gain: 11.1
- Social Security contributions: 0.0
- Domestic taxes on goods & services: 10.3
- Taxes on international trade & transactions: 67.8
- Other taxes: 0.1
- Current nontax revenue: 10.5
- Total current revenue as % of GNP: 21.7

General government consumption as % of GDP: 28 (1988)

FOREIGN AID

Total foreign aid (U.S. $ millions): 135.7
- Bilateral: 90.1
- Multilateral: 45.6

budgets were dependent on British grants-in-aid. The grants-in-aid were terminated in 1973, but grants and loans from abroad still cover about 20% of government expenditures.

Lesotho has aimed at self-sufficiency through its development plans. High priority has been given to irrigation and rural development, financed through international loans. Development grants and loans made up 31% of government revenues in 1987. However, these loans have been offset by cutbacks in budget allocations for development.

Lesotho received $252 million in U.S. aid during 1970–88. Other Western nations contributed $714 million during 1970–87. Communist governments contributed $14 million during 1970–88.

CURRENCY & BANKING

The Lesothan unit of currency is the loti (plural: maloti), divided into 100 lisenti. Coins are issued in denominations of 1, 2, 5, 10, 25 and 50 lisenti; notes are issued in denominations of 2, 5, and 10 maloti.

The June 1991 dollar exchange rate was $1 = R2.794.

Under the revised monetary agreement among the governments of Lesotho, Swaziland and South Africa in 1974, Lesotho will receive interest on rand currency circulating in Lesotho retroactive in 1972. This agreement gives Lesotho an additional incentive to stay in the Rand Monetary Area.

The central bank for the Rand Monetary Area is the South African Reserve Bank, which manages the currency, controls international reserves and also functions as a lender of last resort. The commercial banking system consists of two British-owned banks. Development financing is provided by the Lesotho National Development Corporation (NDC) and the Basotho Enterprises Development Corporation (BEDCO).

FINANCIAL INDICATORS, 1989

International reserves minus gold (SDR's millions): 37
SDR's (millions): 1
Reserve position in IMF (SDR's millions): 1
Foreign exchange (SDR's millions): 35
Ratio of external debt to total reserves (1988): 4.8
Central bank 1989
- Assets %
  - Foreign assets: 30.6
  - Claims on government: 69.4
  - Claims on banks: 0.0
  - Claims on private sector: 0.0
- Liabilities %
  - Reserve money: 52.4
  - Government deposits: 36.8
  - Foreign liabilities: 0.7
  - Capital accounts: 10.5

Money supply 1989
Stock (R. billions): 0.245
M^1 per capita: 140
Private banks 1989
- Assets %
  - Loans to government: 32.2
  - Loans to private sector: 25.5
  - Reserves: 26.8
  - Foreign assets: 15.4
- Liabilities
  - Deposits (R. billions): 0.443
  - of which %
    - Demand deposits: 29.2
    - Savings deposits: 47.3
    - Government deposits: 3.5
    - Foreign liabilities: 6.3

External debt, 1988
- Total (U.S. $ millions): 282
  - of which public (U.S. $ millions): 237
  - of which private (U.S. $ millions): 0
- Debt service (long-term) total (U.S. $ millions): 22
- Repayment
  - Principal (%): 72.7
  - Interest (%): 27.3
- Debt service ratio (%): 5.1
- External public debt as % of GNP: 36.5
- Debt service as % of GNP: 3.0
- Debt service as % of exports: 5.2
- Terms of public borrowing
  - Commitments (U.S. $ millions): 191
  - Average interest rate (%): 4.6
  - Average maturity (yrs.): 24
- Net flow of publicly guaranteed external capital (U.S. $ million): 36
- Net direct private investment (U.S. $ million): 21 (1988)

GROWTH PROFILE
(Annual Growth Rates, %)

Projected population, (1988–2000): 2.6
Projected crude birth rate, (/1000) (1990–95): 39.9
Projected crude death rate, (/1000) (1990–95): 11.1
Urban population, (1980–88): 7.2
Labor force, (1985–2000): 2.1
GNP, (1980–89): 2.2
GNP per capita, (1986–88): 0.4
GDP, (1980–88): 2.9
Inflation, (1980–88): 12.2
Agriculture, (1980–88): 1.8
Industry, (1980–88): 1.6
Manufacturing, (1980–88): 12.4
Services, (1980–88): 4.1
Money holdings, (1980–88): 18.8

AGRICULTURE

Agriculture's contribution to the GDP fell from nearly 50% in the 1970s to less than 20% in the mid-1980s.

Agriculture is concentrated in the Western Lowlands. The principal food crop is corn, over 60% of which is marketed despite the predominance of subsistence farming. Overall Lesotho is a food-deficit area.

Under the traditional land tenure system all land is held in trust by the king for the nation and cannot be alienated. Historically this system has helped to keep the lands in African hands and to exclude white settlers. At the same time the system does not guarantee security of tenure, provides little incentive to fence or improve land and reduces the use of land as security for agricultural credit.

Lesotho has an advanced soil conservation and terracing program. Grass stripping and construction of irrigation canals also are used widely to combat erosion. Mechanization is common in the lowlands. Despite these efforts, yields are low and variable. The government has initiated five pilot rural development projects with help from the United States, the United Kingdom, Sweden and the IDA.

The effects of the drought on plans to upgrade production from arable land have been equally severe. Both 1983 and 1984 were declared to be years of "national food emergency," with crop production down by about 80% overall. Total cereal losses in late 1983 were calculated at $35 million by the FAO. Total cereal import requirements for 1983–84 were almost 40% above the usual level, at 180,000 tons. Requirements for 1984–85 were calculated at about 200,000 tons.

Animal husbandry accounts for about 40% of the agricultural sector's contribution to the GDP. Despite a large national herd, the quality of the livestock is poor, yields are low and overgrazing has become a serious problem. Lesotho's first abattoir (financed by Danishaid) opened in Maseru in 1983. The main livestock products are wool and mohair, but recorded exports in these products have been declining since 1970 because of smuggling. The Livestock Marketing Corporation functions as a monopoly organization for the marketing of all livestock and livestock products.

Lesotho has no natural forests. There is no commercial fishing, although the Malutsenyane River is stocked with fine trout. Agricultural credit is provided through 193 cooperative societies.

AGRICULTURAL INDICATORS

Agriculture's share of GDP (%): 24 (latest)
Average annual growth rate (%, 1980–88): 1.8
Value added in agriculture (U.S. $ millions): 67 (1988)
Cereal imports (000 metric tons): 107 (1988)
Index of Agricultural Production (1979–81 = 100): 94 (1986)
Index of Food Production (1979–81 = 100): 93 (1986)
Index of Food Production per Capita (1974–81 = 100): 80 (1986–88)
Number of tractors: 1,650 (1986)
Number of harvester-threshers: 30 (1986)
Total fertilizer consumption: 3.5 (000 metric tons) (1985–86)
Fertilizer consumption (g./ha., hundreds) 125 (1987–88)
Number of farms (000): 207 (1986)
Average size of holding, ha. (ac.): 2.0 (4.9) (1970)
Size class (%) (1970)
- Below 1 ha. (below 2.47 ac.): 27.0
- 1–5 ha. (2.47–12.35 ac.): 67.5
- 5–10 ha. (12.35–24.7 ac.): } 5.5
- 10–20 ha. (24.7–49.4 ac.): }
- 20–50 ha. (49.4–123.5 ac.): 0.0
- 50–200 ha. (123.5–494 ac.): 0.0
- Over 200 ha. (over 494 ac.): 0.0
- Mainly crops: 37.3 (1986)
- Mainly livestock: 0.0 (1986)
- Mixed: 62.7 (1986)

Farms as % of total land area: 12.3 (1970)
Land use (%): (1970)
- Temporary crops: 89.6
- Fallow: 10.4
- Other: 1.2

Yields: kg./ha. 1989
- Grains: 679
- Roots & tubers: 14,000
- Legumes: 305
- Fruits (000 metric tons): 15
- Vegetables (000 metric tons): 26
- Milk, kg. (lb.)/animal: 290

Livestock (000) 1989
- Cattle: 530
- Horses: 108 (1986)
- Sheep: 1,450
- Pigs: 73

Forestry 1988
- Production of roundwood, 000 cu. m.: 579
  - of which industrial roundwood (%): 0.0

MANUFACTURING

Manufacturing contributes 13% to the GDP. There were virtually no modern industrial plants in Lesotho until 1967, when the Lesotho National Development Corporation (LNDC) was set up in informal collaboration with Anton Rupert's Rembrandt Tobacco empire. The LNDC has vigorously assisted in the creation of various enterprises, including textile manufacture; motor, radio and electric lamp assembly; candlemaking; ceramic production; diamond cutting and polishing; and umbrella manufacture. The Basotho Enterprise Development Corporation also has been established to help indigenous entrepreneurs. Most of the enterprises in the modern sector are financed and controlled by the state. Lesotho's principal industrial advantages are duty-free access to the South African market and cheap and abundant labor. For the same reasons, South Africa has discouraged the establishment of competing industries in Lesotho.

To attract new firms and investments to Lesotho, the LNDC and the Lesothan government offer the

MANUFACTURING INDICATORS, 1987

Average annual growth rate (%, 1980–88): 12.4
Share of GDP (%): 13 (1988)
Value added in manufacturing (U.S. $ millions): 37
- Food and agriculture (%): 12 (1986)
- Textiles (%): 20 (1988)
- Machinery (%): 0.0
- Chemicals (%): 0.0

Total earnings as % of value added: 48 (1986)

following incentives: a six-year tax holiday under the Pioneer Industries Program; a nonnationalization policy; assurance of profit repatriation; industrial sites, buildings and utilities; equity or loan participation; and feasibility studies.

MINING

Kimberlite was first discovered in the country in 1947 but, until recently, diamond mining was limited to primitive diggings. A R23 million modern mine developed by De Beers at Latseng-La-Terai in the Maluti Mountains was closed in 1982. The government had a 25% equity in this operation and received 50% to 60% of the profits through dividends, taxes and export levies.

ENERGY

Lesotho does not produce any form of mineral energy. Its consumption of energy has not been determined. All electric power is imported from South Africa. Energy consumption per capita was 10,000 kg. (22,046 lb.) of oil equivalent in 1987.

LABOR

The most significant fact about Lesothan labor is that at any given time nearly 200,000 Basotho are working in South Africa in the coal or gold mines or as domestic servants. In 1981 wages paid to these mine workers in South Africa reached M47.2 million, or 40% of the GNP. This situation has created a high degree of political and economic dependence on South Africa, and its impact is felt in other fields as well. Wages and salaries in Lesotho are well behind comparable scales in South Africa. According to government regulations 60% of workers' earnings have to be remitted to the Lesotho Bank, and only half of this amount can be drawn immediately by the workers' families.

LABOR INDICATORS, 1976

Total economically active population (000): 424
As % of working-age population (15–64): 56.1
Activity rate (%)
- Total: 34.8
- Male: 48.9
- Female: 21.7

Employment status (%)
- Employers & self-employed: 76.5
- Employees: 49.9
- Unpaid family workers: 36.8
- Other: 5.8

Sectoral employment (%)
- Agriculture, forestry, fishing: 23.3
- Construction: 2.9
- Manufacturing, mining, quarrying, public utilities: 33.2
- Trade, hotels, restaurants: 2.0
- Transport, communications: 1.1
- Finance, real estate: 0.1
- Services: 17.6

Average annual growth rate of labor force, 1985–2000 (%): 2.1
Labor under 20 years (%): 13.4

There are seven active labor unions in Lesotho, of which the largest are the Lesotho General Workers' Union and the Lesotho Labor Organization. Organized Labor does not wield significant power.

FOREIGN COMMERCE

Lesotho's major exports are wool, mohair, wheat, cattle, peas, beans, corn, hides, skins and baskets. Over 80% of its goods are sold to South Africa. South Africa also is its major source of imports, mainly corn, building materials, clothing, vehicles, machinery, medicines, petroleum, oil and lubricants.

Lesotho, together with Botswana and Swaziland, is a member of a common customs union with South Africa, and no tariffs are levied on goods moving across their borders. South Africa levies and collects the customs, sales and excise duties for the four countries, paying a share determined by an established formula to the other three. Imports from outside the customs union are subject to the same tariff rates regardless of ultimate destination. Botswana, Lesotho and Swaziland substantially increased their share of the customs revenue when the customs agreement was renegotiated in 1969.

FOREIGN TRADE INDICATORS, 1989

Exports (U.S. $ millions): 55
Imports (U.S. $ millions): 526
Balance of trade (U.S. $ millions): −471
International reserves in terms of months of imports: 1.2
Import Price Index (1980 = 100): 112.8 (1986)
Export Price Index (1980 = 100): 103.0 (1986)

Direction of Trade (%), 1981

	Imports	Exports
East European economies	1.5	10.3
United States	0.2	0.1

Composition of Trade (%), 1981

	Imports	Exports
Food, agricultural raw materials, mineral ores and concentrates	25.9	35.2
Fuels and other energy	9.6	0.0
Manufactured goods	64.5	64.8
of which chemicals	6.4	1.5
of which machinery	17.0	0.9

TRANSPORTATION & COMMUNICATIONS

Lesotho is linked with the rail system of South Africa by a 2-km. (1-mi.) line from Maseru to Marseilles on the Bloemfontein–Natal main line.

Since Lesotho is completely landlocked, all roads radiate into South Africa. Of the total length of 4,194 km. (2,606 mi.), 15% are paved. The main road runs from Leribe in the North to Mafeteng past Maseru.

The national airline is Lesotho Airways Corporation, which operates a fleet of six aircraft (including four light planes) on scheduled flights between Maseru and Johannesburg. There are 28 airfields in the country, of

TRANSPORTATION INDICATORS

Roads (latest)
  Length, km. (mi.): 4,194 (2,606)
  Paved (%): 15
Motor vehicles (latest)
  Automobiles: 6,363
  Trucks and buses: 15,379
  Persons per vehicle: 73
Railroads (latest)
  Track, km. (mi.): 2 (1)
  Freight, ton-km. (ton-mi.): 3,145 (1,475)
Air (latest)
  Passenger-km. (passenger-mi.) (millions): 28.0 (7.4)
  Freight-km. (freight-mi.) (millions): 0.7 (0.5)
  Airports with scheduled flights: 7 (1990)

COMMUNICATION INDICATORS, 1988

Telephones
  Total (000): 19
  Persons per telephone: 88
Post office
  Number of post offices: 144
  Pieces of mail handled (000): 30,085
Telegraph
  Total traffic (000 calls): 57
  National: 14
  International: 43
Telex
  Subscriber lines: 286
  Traffic (000 minutes): 287 (1984)
Telecommunications (1990)
  1 satellite station

TOURISM & TRAVEL INDICATORS, 1986

Total tourist receipts (U.S. $ millions): 12 (1988)
Expenditures by nationals abroad (U.S. $ millions): 8 (1988)
Number of hotel beds (000): 2
Average length of stay: 2 nights
Number of tourists (000): 184.4 (1984)
  of whom from U.S.: 1.0
  United Kingdom: 1.0
  Germany, Fed. Rep.: 0.6
  Canada: 0.3

which all are usable, two with permanent-surface runways. An international airport at Thoteng-za-Moli, near Maseru, began operation in 1985.

Tourism is one of the major developmental priorities. Although lacking in game, Lesotho has spectacular natural attractions, such as the Malutsenyane Falls. A total of 95% of all tourists come from South Africa. The Lesotho National Development Corporation has a minority interest in the Maseru Holiday Inn and Casino, and a new Hilton Hotel and Casino are being built in Maseru.

DEFENSE

Lesotho has no official armed forces. Prior to 1986 it had a paramilitary force of about 1,000 in addition to the BNP militia of 4,000. Following the 1986 coup the paramilitary forces were reorganized as the Royal Lesotho Defense Force. The nation has no navy, and its air units consist of support craft. It has received military assistance from Great Britain, South Africa and Israel.

The prime minister also holds the title of minister of defense and internal security.

EDUCATION

Education is free, universal and compulsory for seven years, from ages six to 13. Schooling consists of 12 years, divided into seven years of primary school, three years of middle school and two years of secondary school. The final two-year course leads to the Cambridge Overseas School Certificate. Until the early 1970s primary and secondary education was almost entirely in the hands of Evangelical, Roman Catholic and Anglican missions, but the public-school system is gradually gaining. Private schools still account for 100% of primary-school enrollment and 89% of secondary-level enrollment.

The academic year runs from January to December. The medium of instruction is English, but Sesotho is taught as the vernacular from primary grades on.

Teacher training is provided in seven institutions. Vocational training is provided at nine vocational

EDUCATION INDICATORS, 1987

Literacy
  Total (%): 73.6
  Males (%): 62.4
  Females (%): 84.5
First Level
  Schools: 1,174
  Students: 331,858
  Teachers: 5,880
  Student/teacher ratio: 56.4:1
  Net enrollment rate: 71% (1984)
Second level
  Schools: 164
  Students: 41,138
  Teachers: 1,891
  Student/teacher ratio: 21.8:1
  Net enrollment ratio: 13 (1984)
Vocational
  Schools: 10
  Students: 2,567
  Teachers: 183
  Student/teacher ratio: 14.0:1
Third level
  Institutions: 1
  Students: 1,081
  Teachers: 132
  Student/teacher ratio: 8.2
  Gross enrollment ratio: 1.8 (1984)
  Students (/100,000 pop.): 158
  % of population over 24 with post secondary education: 0.1
Foreign study
  Foreign students in national universities: 210 (1988)
  Students abroad: 276
    of whom in
      U.S.: 91 (1988)
      France: 2 (1988)
      U.K.: 108 (1987)
Public expenditures, 1988
  Total (R.): 66,329
  % of GNP: 4.0
  % of current expenditure: 91.5

GRADUATES, 1983

Total: 730
Education: 492
Humanities & religion: 51
Fine & applied arts: 3
Law: 58
Social & behavioral sciences: 69
Commerce & business: 27
Mathematics & computer science: 4
Medicine: 7
Agriculture, forestry, fisheries: 19

schools. Adult education is provided at an adult education center at Maseru.

The National University of Lesotho was founded in 1975 with the former Roma campus of the University of Lesotho, Botswana and Swaziland as its nucleus.

LEGAL SYSTEM

The High Court, headed by the chief justice, is the superior court of record, with unlimited original jurisdiction and appellate jurisdiction to hear appeals and reviews from subordinate courts. There also is a Court of Appeals of five judges. The subordinate courts consist of judicial commissioners' courts; first-, second- and third-class resident magistrates' courts in each of the nine districts; 58 local courts; and 13 central courts. Customary laws are administered by paramount chiefs within their own tribal jurisdictions.

The judiciary in Lesotho is independent and has acted to limit police or military infringements of law and procedure on a number of occasions. Court decisions and rulings are respected and obeyed by the authorities. Civil suits alleging maltreatment are accepted and adjudicated. Verdicts of civil courts may be appealed to the High Court. In military cases, decisions may be appealed to officers of higher rank, including the Lesotho paramilitary force commander, but not to civilian courts. Under the system of Roman-Dutch law applied in Lesotho, there is no trial by jury. Habeas corpus applies to ordinary arrests, and few prisoners are held outside legal norms. Habeas corpus does not apply to those detained under the Internal Security (General) Act of 1984. This act provides for preventive detention under an interim custody order of an initial period of 14 days, after which a detention order must be issued or the individual released. The detention order is valid for 14 days and may be extended for an additional 14 days, after which the detainee must be charged or released. If released, the individual may be redetained for a different cause only.

The Judicial Service Commission is the statutory body concerned with the selection and discipline of judicial personnel. All judges of the High Court and the Court of Appeal are appointed by the chief of state acting on the advice of the Judicial Service Commission. The president of the Court of Appeal and the chief justice of the High Court are appointed by the chief of state on the advice of the prime minister.

No information is available on the correctional facilities and penal system in Lesotho.

LAW ENFORCEMENT

The national police force, the Lesotho Mounted Police, consists of 1,200 men, including 111 officers. The force also includes a cavalry unit of 350 horses used in combating theft of livestock. Until the mid-1970s the police force was commanded by an Englishman and equipped with South African arms.

In addition to the regular police there are special divisions, such as the Police Mobile Unit.

No information is available on the incidence and nature of crime in Lesotho.

HEALTH

The major health problems are tuberculosis, venereal diseases, pellagra and kwashiorkor. Only 36% of the population have access to safe drinking water. Delivery of health services is hampered by the location of clinics in lowland areas, where only a minority of the population lives.

HEALTH INDICATORS

Health personnel, 1982
  Physicians: 114
    Persons per: 12,265
  Dentists: 6
  Nurses: 452
  Pharmacists: 7
Hospitals 1985
  Number: 136
  Number of beds (/10,000): 16
  Admissions/discharges (/10,000): 410 (1977)
  Bed occupancy rate %: 79.6 (1977)
  Average length of stay (days): 10 (1977)
Type of hospitals (%)
  Government: 40.9 (1977)
  Private Nonprofit: 59.1 (1977)
  Private profit: 0.0
Public health expenditures (latest)
  As % of national budget: 7.8
  Per capita (U.S. $): 6.30
Vital statistics
  Crude death rate (/1,000 pop.): 10 (1990)
  Life expectancy at birth 1990
    Males: 59
    Females: 62
  Infant mortality rate (/1,000 live births): 80 (1990)
  Child mortality rate (1985–90) under 5 yrs. (/1,000): 135
Population with access to safe water (%): 36 (latest)

FOOD & NUTRITION

The staple articles of the Lesothan diet are corn and sorghum. The national drink is a beer made with sorghum and known as leting or joala.

Daily per capita availability of energy, proteins, fats and carbohydrates is 100% of WHO minimum requirements.

MEDIA & CULTURE

Lesotho has three dailies and four nondaily newspapers, including the official weekly publication *Mochochonono*, with a reported circulation of 3,000. South African daily newspapers circulate within the country. The other weeklies include one owned by a Catholic mission and one by the Basotho National Party. The press is subject only to nominal government regulations, although there is no opposition press within the country. The national news agency is LENA, founded in 1983 with UNESCO aid. Reuters maintains a bureau in Maseru.

Lesotho has a modest book publishing industry. The two major publishing houses are owned by the Catholic Mazenod Institute and the Evangelical Church. Lesotho does not adhere to any copyright convention.

The official broadcasting organization, Radio Lesotho, operates one medium-wave, one shortwave and one FM transmitter and is on the air for 115 hours a week, broadcasting in English and Sesotho. Radio Lesotho is under the administrative control of the Lesotho National Broadcasting Service. The Catholic School Secretariat operates radio station 7PA22, which broadcasts educational programs with a shortwave transmitter. Lesotho has three television transmitters and 1,085 persons per TV receiver.

The only library is the library of the National University of Lesotho, with 80,000 volumes.

There is only one museum in the country.

MEDIA INDICATORS

Newspapers
- Number of dailies: 3
- Circulation (000): 44
- Per 000 persons: 28
- Number of nondailies: 4
- Circulation (000): 44
- Per 1,000 pop.: 28

Radio
- Number of transmitters: 3 (latest)
- Number of persons per radio receiver: 34 (1989)

Television
- Television transmitters: 3 (latest)
- Number of persons per TV receiver: 34 (1989)

CULTURAL & ENVIRONMENTAL INDICATORS (latest)

Libraries
- Number: 1 (pre-1986)
- Registered borrowers per (000): 3 (pre-1986)
- Loans (/1,000 pop.): 14 (pre-1986)

Nature reserves
- Number of facilities: 1

SOCIAL WELFARE

Social welfare programs are coordinated by the Social Welfare Department, which sends community development teams into the countryside. The Oxford Committee for Famine Relief (Oxfam) is active in Lesotho.

GLOSSARY

Basotho hat: a shallow-cone hat, ornamented with circles, now used as the national symbol.

letsema (pl. matsema): obligatory feudal labor performed by men for the tribal chiefs, abolished in the 1940s.

khotla: village meeting place where the chief heard disputes and gave judgment.

motlotlehi: chief of state, title of the king of Lesotho.

pitso: general assembly of a tribe to listen to the chief. A national pitso was held regularly before independence to discuss the affairs of the Basothan people.

CHRONOLOGY (from 1966)

1966— Lesotho is granted independence under the independence Constitution; Moshoeshoe II is proclaimed king. . . . In a trial of strength between the king and Prime Minister Leabua Jonathan, the king is forced to yield.

1967— Lesotho National Development Corporation is founded.

1969— Lesotho, Botswana and Swaziland renegotiate customs union agreement with South Africa.

1970— Lesotho holds first national elections; when the electoral defeat of his Basotho National Party appears imminent, Prime Minister Jonathan proclaims an emergency and suspends the Constitution; opposition leaders are arrested; the king is placed under house arrest and later is exiled for nine months.

1971— All political prisoners are released under a general amnesty.

1973— An interim National Assembly is constituted with nominated members.

1974— Alleging an attempted coup by the opposition, Prime Minister Jonathan launches brutal reprisals against his enemies. . . . Lesotho claims the return of Basothan territories conquered by South Africa in the 19th century.

1975— National University of Lesotho is established by nationalizing the Roma campus of the University of Botswana, Lesotho and Swaziland.

1976— In a move toward political reconciliation, Prime Minister Jonathan appoints two members of the opposition to his cabinet. . . . Lesotho requests a special Security Council meeting to consider its charges of South African aggression for closing the Transkei border.

1979— Chief Jonathan announces the imminent establishment of a regular army drawn from paramilitary police units.

1980— Lesotho introduces a new currency called the loti to replace the South African rand; however, Lesotho remains within the Rand Monetary Area.

1982— South African forces raid Maseru in pursuit of African National Congress (ANC) dissidents.

1983— South Africa blockades Lesotho to punish Prime Minister Jonathan's regime for granting asylum to ANC dissidents.

1986— Jonathan is ousted in a pro-South Africa coup

led by Gen. Justin Lenkhanya, who is then sworn in as head of government.

1987— Charles Mofeli, leader of the opposition United Democratic Party (UDP), is detained for a week after petitioning the king for a return to parliamentary democracy.

1988— Five opposition parties appeal to the Organization of African Unity and the Commonwealth to use their influence to restore civilian government.

1990— Lekhanya strips King Moshoeshoe II of his power and sends him into exile; Moshoeshoe's son, Prince Mohato, sworn in as King Letsie III.

1991— Lekhanya ousted by rebel army officers in bloodless coup and replaced by Col. Elias P. Ramaema.

BIBLIOGRAPHY

BOOKS

Ashton, H. *The Basuto.* London, 1967.
Bardill, John E., and James H. Cobbe. *Lesotho Profiles.* Boulder, Colo., 1985.
Burman, Sandra. *Chiefdom Politics and Alien Law.* New York, 1980.
Coates, Austin. *Basutoland.* London, 1966.
Ferguson, James. *The Anti-Politics Machine: "Development," Depoliticization, and Bureaucratic Power in Lesotho.* New York, 1990.
Hailey, William Malcolm. *The Republic of South Africa and the High Commission Territories.* London, 1963.
Haliburton, Gordon. *Historical Dictionary of Lesotho.* Metuchen, N.J., 1977.
Halpern, Jack. *South Africa's Hostages: Basutoland, Bechuanaland and Swaziland.* Baltimore, Md., 1965.
Khaketla, B. M. *Lesotho, 1970: An African Coup Under the Microscope.* London, 1970.
Leistner, G. M. E. *Lesotho: Economic Structure and Growth.* Pretoria, 1966.
Maane, Willen. *Lesotho: A Development Challenge.* Baltimore, Md., 1975.
Schwager, Coleen, and Dirk Schwager. *Lesotho.* Mystic, Conn., 1975.
Selwyn, Percy. *Industries in Southern African Periphery.* Boulder, Colo., 1975.
Spence, John. *Lesotho.* New York, 1968.
Stevens, Richard P. *Botswana, Lesotho and Swaziland.* New York, 1967.
Strom, Gabriele W. *Development and Dependence in Lesotho.* New York, 1978.
Thompson, Leonard. *Survival in Two Worlds: Moshoeshoe of Lesotho.* New York, 1975.
Weisfelder, Richard F. *Defining National Purpose in Lesotho.* Athens, Ohio, 1969.
Willet, Shelagh M., and David P. Ambrose. *Lesotho: A Contemporary Bibliography.* Santa Barbara, Calif., 1980.
World Bank. *Lesotho: A Development Challenge.* Baltimore, Md., 1975.

OFFICIAL PUBLICATIONS

Finance Ministry. *Appropriation Accounts, Revenue Statements and Other Public Accounts* (annual).
———. *Estimates of the Revenue and Expenditure of the Kingdom of Lesotho* (annual).

LIBERIA

BASIC FACT SHEET

OFFICIAL NAME: Republic of Liberia

ABBREVIATION: LB

CAPITAL: Monrovia

HEAD OF STATE & HEAD OF GOVERNMENT: Amos Sawyer (since August 1990)

NATURE OF GOVERNMENT: Republic

POPULATION: 2,595,000 (1990)

AREA: 111,370 sq. km. (43,000 sq. mi.)

ETHNIC MAJORITY: Kpelle, Bassa, Gio, Kru, Grebo, Mano, Krahn and Gola.

LANGUAGE: English (official) spoken by 20%; more than 20 local languages of the Niger-Congo are also spoken.

RELIGIONS: Animism, Islam and Christianity

UNIT OF CURRENCY: Liberian dollar

NATIONAL FLAG: A variation of the U.S. flag with 11 horizontal strips alternately red (six) and white (five) and a five-pointed white star in a blue square five stripes deep in the upper left corner nearest the staff.

NATIONAL EMBLEM: A heraldic shield with a dove of peace carrying an open scroll; on the crest is the national motto, "The Love of Liberty Brought Us Here." Below is the sun rising over the sea on which there is a ship under full sail. In the foreground is land with a palm tree, a plow and a spade.

NATIONAL ANTHEM: "All Hail, Liberia, Hail"

NATIONAL HOLIDAYS: January 1 (New Year's Day); February 11 (Armed Forces Day); second Wednesday in March (Decoration Day); March 15 (Birthday of J. J. Roberts, first president); May 14 (Unification Day); July 26 (Independence Day); August 24 (Flag Day); first Thursday in November (Thanksgiving Day); November 12 (National Memorial Day); November 29 (President Tubman's Birthday); also various Christian holidays.

NATIONAL CALENDAR: Gregorian

PHYSICAL QUALITY OF LIFE INDEX: 43

DATE OF INDEPENDENCE: July 26, 1847

DATE OF CONSTITUTION: July 3, 1984

WEIGHTS & MEASURES: Imperial weights and measures, modified by U.S. usage.

GEOGRAPHICAL FEATURES

Liberia is a few degrees north of the equator on the southern coast of the western bulge of Africa. It extends 548 km. (341 mi.) east-southeast to west-northwest and 274 km. (170 mi.) north-northeast to south-southwest, with a total area of 111,370 sq. km. (43,000 sq. mi.). Its Atlantic Ocean coastline is 538 km. (334 mi.) long.

Liberia's international land boundary of 1,585 km. (945 mi.) is shared with three countries as follows: Guinea (563 km.; 350 mi.), Ivory Coast (716 km.; 445 mi.) and Sierra Leone (306 km.; 190 mi.). The border with Sierra Leone is determined by the Anglo-Liberian Agreement of 1885, and the borders with Guinea and Ivory Coast are determined by the Franco-Liberian Agreement of 1892 and 1907–10. There are no current border disputes.

The capital is Monrovia, named after U.S. President James Monroe, with a 1984 population of 421,058, up from 10,000 in 1940. Other major urban centers are Buchanan (23,999), Congo Town (21,495), Yekepa (14,189) and Tubmanburg (14,089).

Topographically, Liberia is divided into three regioins. The coastal region is a belt of gently rolling plains 30 to 55 km. (19 to 31 mi.) wide with tidal creeks, shallow lagoons and swamps. The plains rise slowly to a plateau, with elevations varying from 183 to 610 m. (600 to 2,000 ft.). The eastern section of the country is rugged and covered with forest, while the far northern region has densely forested, mountainous terrain culminating in Mount Wutivi (1,380 m.; 4,528 ft.). Other prominent features are the Nimbo Mountains (1,752 m.; 5,748 ft.) and the Wologisi Range (1,381 m.; 4,530 ft.).

The country's seven major rivers all flow perpendicular to the coast and are spaced at regular intervals. From the west they are the Mano, Loffa, Saint Paul, Farmington, Saint John, Cess or Cestos and Cavalla or Cavally. Except for the Cavalla, none of these rivers is navigable for more than short distances because of rapids. Sandbars obstruct the mouths of all rivers, making their entrances hazardous. Floods are common in the rainy season.

CLIMATE & WEATHER

Liberia has two rainy seasons in the Southeast and one rainy season, from May to October, in the rest of the country. From Monrovia, with an annual average of 4,650 mm. (183 in.), the rainfall decreases toward the southeast and north, falling to 2,240 mm. (88 in.) at Ganta. Although there are wide variations in precipitation patterns, most of the rainfall comes as heavy downpours that may last several hours or several days.

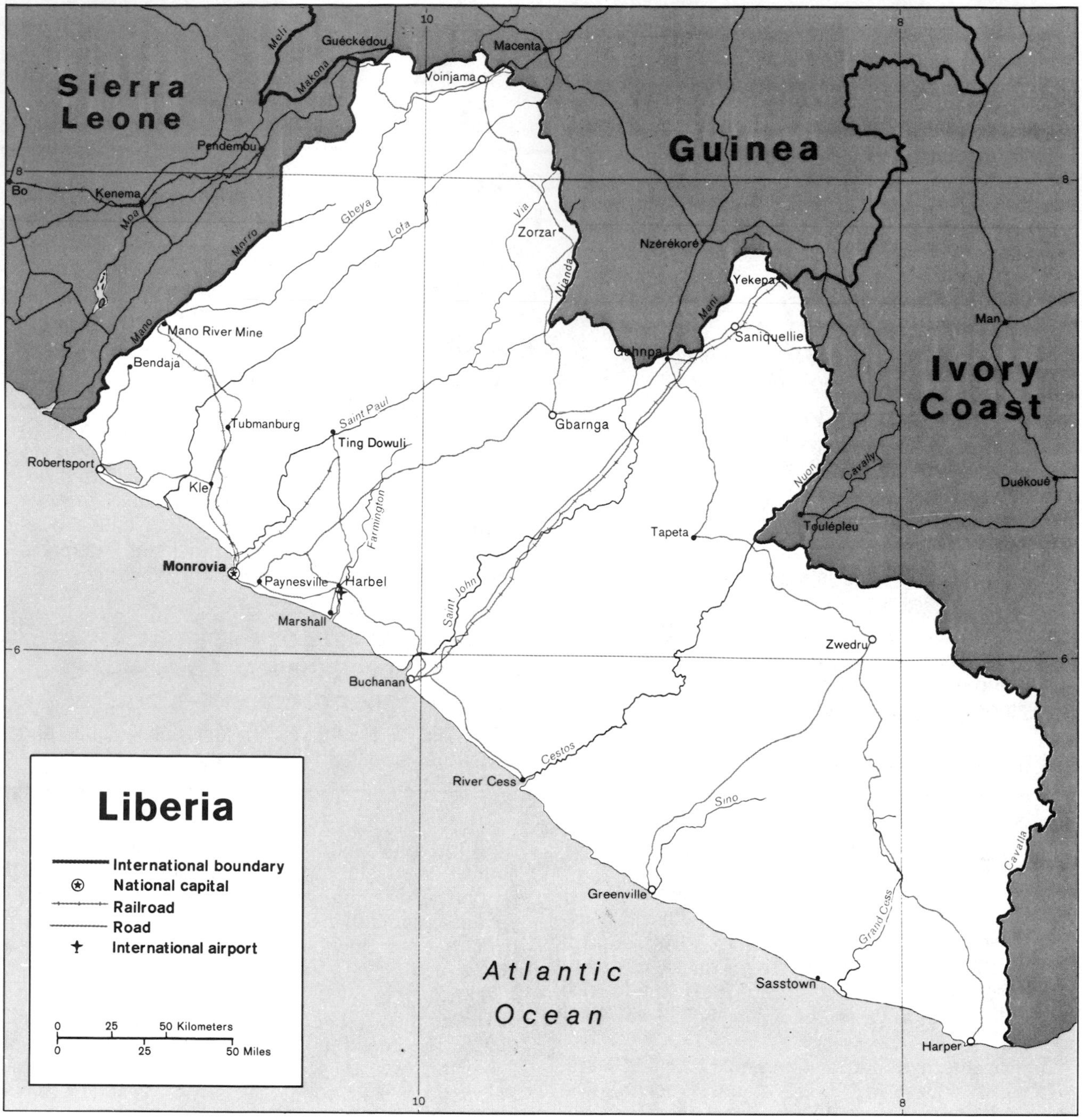

Liberia

Sierra Leone
Guinea
Ivory Coast
Atlantic Ocean

Guéckédou
Macenta
Voinjama
Pendembu
Kenema
Bo
Zorzar
Nzérékoré
Yekepa
Saniquellie
Gahnpa
Man
Mano River Mine
Bendaja
Tubmanburg
Ting Dowuli
Gbarnga
Robertsport
Kle
Monrovia
Paynesville
Harbel
Marshall
Buchanan
Tapeta
Toulépleu
Duékoué
Zwedru
River Cess
Greenville
Sasstown
Harper

Meli
Makona
Moa
Morro
Mano
Gbeya
Lofa
Via
Nianda
Mani
Saint Paul
Farmington
Saint John
Nuon
Cavally
Cestos
Sino
Grand Cess
Cavalla

10
8
6

International boundary
National capital
Railroad
Road
International airport

0 25 50 Kilometers
0 25 50 Miles

Temperatures are uniformly warm throughout the country, with only small daily variations. The average mean temperature is about 28°C (82°F), and the maximum rarely exceeds 38°C (100°F). In the North temperatures may rise to 44°C (111°F) in March and fall to 9°C (48°F) in December or January.

The prevailing wind systems are the northeastern and southwestern monsoons and the *harmattan*, a scorching wind from the Sahara. Destructive tornadoes are common at the beginning and end of the rainy season.

POPULATION

The population of Liberia in 1990 was 2,595,000, although it was estimated that by February 1991, nearly 1.3 million Liberian refugees had fled the country during the 13-month old civil war.

The population is unevenly distributed. Large areas in southeastern forests and in Loffa County in the West are virtually uninhabited. The population is concentrated in the area surrounding Monrovia and in a broad belt extending from Montserrado County northeast to the Guinea border.

DEMOGRAPHIC INDICATORS

Population (millions): 2.595 (1990)
Year of last census: 1984
Sex distribution (% at last census): males, 50.6; females, 49.4
Population estimates and projections (millions)

1950: .758	1980: 1.864	2000: 3.581
1960: 1.004	1990: 2.595	2010: 4.912
1970: 1.393		

Age profile (% at last census)

0–14: 43.2	30–44: 14.7	60–74: 4.4
15–29: 28.2	45–59: 7.7	75 and over: 1.8

Median age (yrs.): 17.5 (1985)
Youth population (% age 15–24): 18.3 (1985); 18.9 (2000)
Total dependency ratio: 93.2 (1985)
Annual growth rate (%)

1950–55: 2.02	1975–80: 3.09	2000–2005: 3.26
1955–60: 2.57	1980–85: 3.21	2005–2010: 3.16
1960–65: 2.72	1985–90: 3.18	2010–2015: 2.96
1965–70: 2.85	1990–95: 3.26	2015–2020: 2.65
1970–75: 2.99	1995–2000: 3.29	2020–2025: 2.26

Hypothetical size of stationary population (millions): 11 (1988)
Assumed year of reaching net reproduction rate of 1: 2035 (1988)
Urban population (000): 861 (1985)
Urban population (%): 42 (1988); 22 (1965)
Annual urban population growth rate (%, 1985–90): 5.33
Annual rural population growth rate (%, 1985–90): 1.64
Number of cities of population over 500,000: 0 (1980)
Population density per sq. km. (per sq. mi.): 26.2 (67.8) (latest)

VITAL STATISTICS

Crude birth rate (/1,000): 45 (1990); 46 (1965)
Crude death rate (/1,000): 14 (1990); 20 (1965)
Infant mortality rate (/1,000 live births): 126 (1990)
Maternal mortality rate (/100,000 live births): 173 (1980)
Life expectancy (yrs.) at birth: males, 54; females, 58 (1990)
Gross reproduction rate (/woman) (1980–85): 3.20
Total fertility rate (/woman): 6.6 (1990)
Rate of natural increase (/1,000): 1.7 (1985–90)
Average household size: 5.0

The urban population has been swollen by internal migration. However, the bulk of the rural people are deeply attached to their villages and only move to the cities temporarily or under economic pressure.

Immigration and emigration are not significant demographic factors. Few Liberians have settled permanently outside the country, and few tribesmen from neighboring countries have sought or been granted Liberian nationality.

In urban areas and along the seacoast, where settler dominance was strongest, a modern sector has evolved with a free-enterprise economy; substantial political and economic equality for men and women; and Anglo-American judicial procedures based on English common law, as transmitted and modified by the American experience. Here land is plotted, deeded and held in fee simple, and women can inherit equally. There is no formal discrimination in property ownership, educational opportunity or participation in economic and political processes. Women in Liberia have held ministerial and ambassadorial positions and are represented in the professions and throughout the modern economy.

In rural areas, the inhabitants practice subsistence agriculture and follow a traditional culture in which men's and women's roles are more strictly defined. Here, most land is held communally among the related families of a clan, and women provide most of the labor in food production and distribution, both for household consumption and market sale. As opposed to statutory marriage, seen as a contract between individuals, customary marriage is an agreement between families. With payment of dowry under the customary marriage system, a woman is considered the property of her husband and family. Upon the husband's death, the marital contract continues with the family, which has certain obligations and responsibilities to the widow, or more commonly widows, if they remain with the family as wives to other relatives. In the traditional sector, women usually are not entitled to inherit from their husbands or to administer their estates. In addition, women are informally excluded in many indigenous ethnic groups from chieftaincies or membership in the councils of elders that direct the affairs of the community. In practice, expecially in newly urban areas, many women use both the customary and statutory legal systems.

Birth control is not encouraged as an official policy.

STATUS OF WOMEN INDICATORS

Number of women (millions): 1.175 (1985)
Women of childbearing age (15–49) (% of pop.): 44 (1988)
Married women of childbearing age (15–49) using contraception (%): 6 (1986)
Women's literacy rate (%): 18.4
Women in labor force (%): 30.6 (1988)
Total fertility rate (/woman): 6.6 (1990)

ETHNIC COMPOSITION

The principal ethnic cleavage is between Americo-Liberians, described as the descendants of the early settlers, and the tribal and indigenous peoples, described as aborigines. Few of those classified as Americo-Liberians are the actual descendants of original settlers. Their ranks include over 4,000 Congos, whose ancestors were freed from captured slave ships, and detribalized people of indigenous origin. Therefore the group members usually are called "civilized" or "lettered" people. The tribals, who make up the bulk of the population, are themselves divided into nearly 28 tribes, though only 16 are recognized as major tribes by the government.

MAJOR TRIBAL AND OTHER GROUPS IN LIBERIA

Group	% of population
Bassa	16.3
Kru	8.0
Belle	0.5
Loma	5.3
Dei	0.5
Mandingo	2.9
Gbandi	2.8
Mano	7.1
Gio	8.2
Mende	0.5
Gola	4.7
Vai	2.8
Grebo	7.6
Other tribes	0.2
Kissi	3.4
Americo-Liberians	1.5
Kpelle	20.8
Non-Liberian tribes	0.9
Krahn	5.2
Non-Africans	0.8

Only three tribes—Bassa, Dei and Belle—are found solely in Liberia. The others are in greater numbers in neighboring countries. All tribes except the Mandingo are found in clearly defined localities. Intertribal relations are governed by membership in secret societies, known as *poro* for men and *sande* for women.

Since 1944, unification of tribal and nontribal peoples and their cultural and political integration have been important goals of the government. The policy deemphasizes social and cultural differences between the tribals and the Americo-Liberians and progressively assimilates the former into the mainstream of national life.

The Constitution does not permit non-blacks to become citizens. The non-Liberian resident population is estimated at 30,000 of whom five alien groups are numerically significant: Ghanaians, Lebanese, Americans, Spaniards, and Dutch. Ghanaians and Lebanese generally are permanent residents who regard Liberia as their home country. Most Ghanaians are Fanti fishermen, while most Lebanese are merchants and can be found in almost every town. Most of the Europeans and Americans are engaged in private or government-sponsored enterprises, and they remain in the country for limited periods only. Germans, Swedes, British and Italians also are represented in the country.

Liberia is one of the most Westernized nations in Africa, and the political, social and cultural attitudes of the Liberian elite are very close to those of their Western counterparts. Western cultural and economic penetration of the country has been reinforced and facilitated by government policies. Association with the United States and Europe is regarded as in no way conflicting with an African identity and pride in African heritage.

LANGUAGE

The official language is English, although only 30% of the population can speak it and less than 20% can read and write it.

The native languages of Liberia fall into three subgroups of the Niger-Congo family of languages: the western and eastern branches of Mande, the southern branch of the West Atlantic and the Kru branch of Kwa. Multilingualism is common, and intertribal communications usually are carried on in Pidgin English or through the more prestigious of the lingua francas, such as Vai and Mandingo.

RELIGION

Liberia often is referred to in official documents as a Christian state, but Christians form a small minority, outnumbered by both Muslims and animists, who make up at least 90% of the population. Although precise statistics are not available, some 70% of Liberians are believed to be animist, 20% Muslim and 10% Christian. The Constitution provides for the free exercise of religion and stipulates that no denomination be given preference by the state and that no religious tests be laid down for entry into the civil office or for the exercise of civil rights.

Despite their minority status, the Protestants—particularly the Methodists, Baptists and Episcopalians—constitute the social and political elite; they have formed virtually a ruling class since 1847. Almost all Protestant denominations are represented in the country, some by more than one missionary organization. The Roman Catholic Church is organized under the vicar-apostolic of Monrovia.

Until the early 1960s the Liberian churches were not self-supporting and were under the administrative control of sponsoring churches in Europe and the United States. Most of the local ministers were lay preachers, generally untrained, who devoted only part of their time to their vocations. Since 1963 there has been a gradual transfer of control to the Liberians and the achievement of some finanacial and administrative autonomy. This process has been encouraged by the state, which maintains close links with the church. Bible study is part of the school curriculum, and children are encouraged to attend church services. The ministry has provided many of the country's leaders.

Although both Christian and Muslim missionaries have been active among the tribes of the interior for more than a century, neither group has made much headway. On the other hand, traditional beliefs persist even among those who call themselves Christians or Muslims. There are a few groups who have tried, with varying degrees of success, to mix Christian and pagan practices. Islam is strongest among the Vai and Mandingo peoples and along the Guinea and Sierra Leone borders.

HISTORICAL BACKGROUND

Liberia was settled in 1822 by freed black slaves from the United States repatriated to Africa under the auspices of the American Colonization Society and six other philanthropic organizations. Black emigration from the United States continued until 1892, and these settlers were augmented by Africans freed from slaving vessels by the British and American navies. Each society established its own independent territory, such as Mississippi in Africa at Greenville and Maryland in Liberia around Harper. The first governors were agents appointed by the Colonization Society and it was only in 1847 that the independent Republic of Liberia was established, with a United States-type constitution. Liberia never was a colony of the United States, and relations between the two countries were not very close until the mid-1920s. Liberia received annual subsidies from the colonization societies until 1847, but after the establishment of the republic American assistance was suspended. To avert a financial breakdown, Liberia—whose budget in 1847 was only $8,000—turned to Europe. The period from 1871 until 1925 is known as the "European period" of Liberian history, and it was Europe, rather than the United States, that helped the new republic establish itself as a viable nation. Links with the United States were renewed in 1926 with the arrival of the Firestone Tire and Rubber Company in Liberia.

During the presidency of William Tubman after World War II, other foreign interests were encouraged and the influence of the U.S. gradually diminished. On his death in 1971, Tubman was succeeded by his vice-president, William Tolbert. Tolbert maintained Liberia's ties with the West but developed relations with the Eastern bloc and with Liberia's neighbors as well. Tolbert's domestic performance was less distinguished, with a series of lackluster campaigns to galvanize Liberians economically and politically.

On April 12, 1980, Tolbert was assassinated in a military coup led by Sgt. Samuel K. Doe, who took over power as Chairman of the People's Redemption Council (PRC), suspending the Constitution and banning all political parties. Opposition to and divisions within the PRC gave rise to a series of upheavals, alleged coup attempts and resignations by or dismissals of military and civilian members of the government in the early 1980s.

At the end of 1981 Doe undertook to return the country to civilian rule by April 1985. A new Constitution, similar to the precoup one, was drafted and was approved in July 1984 by a national referendum. The ban on political activity was lifted and a period of intense political turbulence followed. Elections were held in October 1985 and, amid widespread allegations of flagrant irregularities, Doe was elected president.

In November 1985 another coup was attempted and failed. On January 6, 1986 Doe was sworn in as elected president. The cabinet was reshuffled several times in 1987 and Liberia went through another period of political turbulence early in 1988. A coup plot was discovered in March and another was attempted and put down in July.

On December 24, 1989, an armed insurrection began, led by Charles Taylor of the rebel National Patriotic Force (NPF). For a time it seemed no more than a regional revolt in the northeast, but by June 1990 rebels were in the outskirts of Monrovia and President Doe and his supporters became besieged in the presidential mansion. The conflict was fueled by tribal differences. Doe's followers were mostly Krahn or Mandingo tribesmen while Taylor's were mostly members of the Gio and Mano tribes. Doe's army slaughtered thousands of Gio and Mano noncombatants for which the NPF retaliated by killing Krahn and Mandingo civilians. The army abuses angered many Liberians who then joined Taylor's original force of about 150 men, bringing the total number to more than 4,000 well-motivated fighters. By contrast, Doe's army of some 5,000 men, many of them forcibly conscripted, had shrunk by mass desertions.

By July 1990, the NPF had split into two rival factions, one led by Taylor and the other led by Prince Johnson (whose first name is a common one in Liberia and not an indication of royalty). In August, the Economic Community of West African States (ECOWAS) landed a peace keeping force in Monrovia and set up an interim government headed by Amos Sawyer.

On September 9, 1990, when Doe went to the ECOWAS headquarters to plan his escape, he and his men were intercepted by Johnson. By the next day Doe had been mutilated and killed.

On September 21, Taylor announced a cease-fire which lasted less than a week. Later, the ECOWAS sponsored a peace agreement which was signed on November 28, 1990 by Taylor, Johnson and Maj. Wilmott Diggs (who then represented the remaining followers of Doe). However, even though he signed the truce, Taylor refused to accept the interim government of Amos Sawyer (who had been sworn in as President on November 22), and a stalemate followed.

A final cease-fire was signed on February 13, 1991, ending the stalemate and an agreement was made by all three parties to take steps to form an interim government. The cease-fire was signed by Taylor, Johnson and Gen. Hezekiah Bowen (the commander of the remnants of Doe's army). The accord stated that until a new government was chosen, the provisioinal administration headed by Amos Sawyer would remain in power.

CONSTITUTION & GOVERNMENT

Until 1980, the constitutional basis of the Liberian government was the Constitution of 1847, which was framed by the original settlers and drafted by Professor

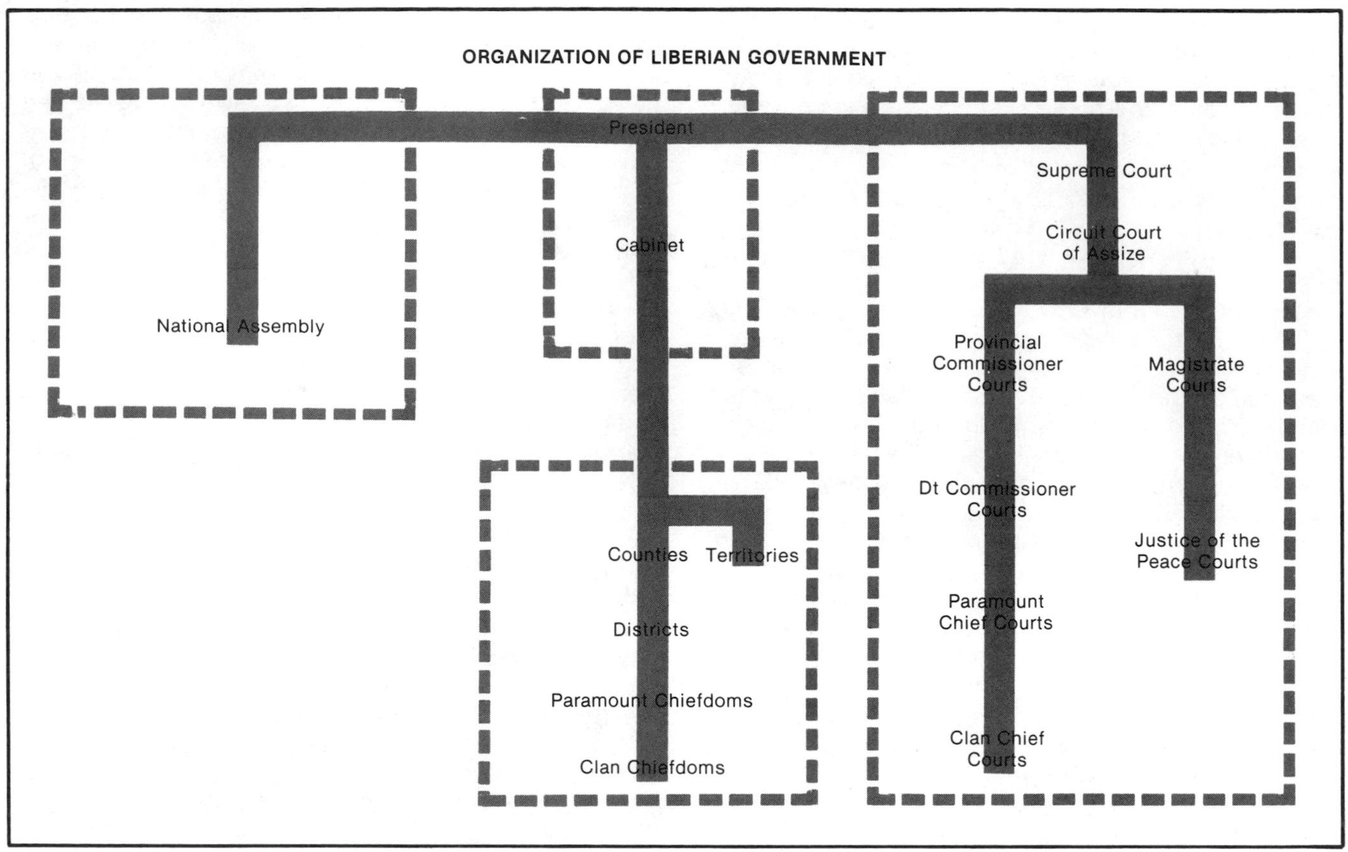

Simon Greenleaf of Harvard University on the model of the U.S. Constitution. It established a presidential and republican form of government with a strong executive, a subordinate legislature and a judiciary headed by a supreme court. Though the Constitution originally provided for the separation and balance of powers, power had become increasingly centralized in the person of the president. With the growing subordination of the legislature, the executive had found it easy to amend the Constitution. Further, despite a bill of rights providing ample guarantees of individual rights and liberties and religious freedom, the franchise was based on property qualifications and was being extended only gradually to the tribals, who constituted the bulk of the population. The phrase "We, the people" in the Constitution was, until recently, interpreted to mean only Americo-Liberians.

In 1980, following the overthrow and assassination of President William Tolbert, the coup leaders abolished the Constitution and set up the People's Redemption Council (PRC) of 17 noncommissioned officers as the country's supreme legislative and executive body. Despite these changes, there was a sense of continuity in government. In most government departments career staff remained in place, and the ministries enjoyed substantial autonomy, although the PRC decided matters of key national importance.

Most of President Samuel K. Doe's soldiers (who were described by the former vice president, Bishop Warner, as a bunch of high-school dropouts and juvenile delinquents) came from the rural areas of Liberia.

GOVERNMENT LIST
(July/August 1991)

President	Sawyer, Amos
Vice President	Naigow, Peter
Minister of Commerce & Industry	Holder, James
Minister of Defense	Kesselly, Edward Benyah
Minister of Finance	Tarr, S. Byron
Minister of Foreign Affairs	Matthews, Gabriel Baccus
Minister of Information, Culture & Tourism	Waritay, Lamini
Minister of Justice	Banks, Philips
Minister of Land, Mines & Energy	Mason, Jonathon
Minister of Planning & Economic Affairs	Ward, Amelia
Minister of Public Works	Nganana, Togba
Minister of State for Presidential Affairs	Guanna, Joseph Saye
Minister of State Without Portfolio	Zangai, Levi
Governor, Central Bank	Vinton, David

Few had experience outside the military, and none had traveled outside Liberia. The PRC itself had a diverse mixture of ideologies, levels of sophisitication, political ambitions and tribal identification. It was more concerned about economic, social and political inequities than the Tolbert government (which had become extremely corrupt and indifferent to the welfare of the common people), but it was decidedly not radical.

In 1984 a new Constitution was drafted by the Constitutional Commission, approved by the PRC, submitted to a national referendum and approved by 78.3% of the registered voters.

The new Constitution does not differ significantly from its predecessor, providing for a division of government into executive, legislature and judiciary. Executive powers are vested in the president, elected for a six-year term by universal adult suffrage; he is head of state, head of government and commander in chief of the armed forces. A two-chamber National Assembly is the seat of the legislature, comprising a Senate (26 members) and a House of Representatives (64 members), both directly elected. The Constitution provides for a multiparty system; the formation of a one-party state, dissolution of the legislature or suspension of the judiciary are prohibited under it. A two-thirds majority in both houses of the National Assembly is required to amend the Constitution.

The Constitution provides for the establishment of a Supreme Court, consisting of a chief justice and four associate justices, to be appointed by the president from a panel recommended by a Judicial Service Commission; the consent of the Senate is required for these appointments and for the confirmation of lower court judges, to which a similar procedure applies.

In August 1984 President Doe announced his formation of the National Democratic Party and his intention to run as its presidential candidate.

In the 1985 elections, President Doe was elected as the nation's first head of state under the new Constitution, with 50.9% of the registered vote. The election results were described as a "mockery" by the opposition who complained of widespread fraud in favor of the ruling party.

After the civil war began in December 1989, Doe remained in power until his assassination in September 1990. Meanwhile, the ECOWAS had appointed an interim government in August 1990 headed by Amos Sawyer, who has since been the country's president. Following the cease-fire at the end of the civil war in February 1991, the warring factions agreed to work together in planning an interim government until new elections could take place. However, there is no current information about plans for amending the Constitution.

RULERS OF LIBERIA (from 1943)

Presidents

May 1943–July 1971: William Tubman
July 1971–April 1980: William Richard Tolbert
April 1980–September 10, 1990: Samuel K. Doe
November 22, 1990–: Amos Sawyer

FREEDOM & HUMAN RIGHTS

In terms of political and civil rights Liberia is classified as a not-free country.

Following the coup of 1980 and the overthrow of President Tolbert's government, the human rights situation in Liberia deteriorated considerably. The "backward-looking stage" of the 1980 coup in which the army tried to correct historic abuses of power by the True Whigs led to many excesses. But within a few years pragmatism prevailed, and many of the True Whigs were restored to their rights and offices. However, in two areas the government continued to violate the exercise of basic rights granted by the old as well as the new constitutions. The first area was in the quick suppression of all threats to the Doe regime, and the second was in the muzzling of free speech through Decree 88A.

Reports of abuses by police and soldiers were frequent, although they declined somewhat in response to disciplinary efforts. Reports of harassment were common. Civilians reportedly were arrested or threatened with arrest by soldiers and police, who then required payment of a "fine." In other cases, members of the former PRC arrogated to themselves informal authority to arrest, detain and try persons involved in civil and labor disputes. Fines and short prison sentences sometimes were imposed without reference to due process or to relevant statutes and decrees. The government condemned these practices and regularly made statements calling for their eradication. However, once the civil war started in December 1989, abuses became so widespread that they were impossible to conceal. Civilians were frequently the target of government as well as rebel troops.

So brutal were the attacks by Doe's army during the course of the war that much of the civilian population became alienated and in turn joined the ranks of the rebels. As the violence mounted, the fighting degenerated in tribal warfare, with both sides indiscriminately slaughtering civilians of rival ethnic groups. Doe's soldiers, most of them from the Krahn tribe, turned their fury on members of the Gio and Mano tribes, from which the rebels drew most of their support. The rebels in turn killed Krahn and Mandingo (a tribe allied to the Krahn) noncombatants.

The July 1990 massacre by Doe's troops of 600 Gio and Mano civilians who had taken refuge in St. Peter's Lutheran Church in Monrovia was well-attested, though the government denied it. Survivors said the soldiers butchered men, women, children and babies with automatic gunfire, knives and cutlasses. A Doe spokesman claimed that the killers were rebels dressed up as government troops, but U.S. officials backed up the contention of the witnesses that the attackers were Krahn soldiers.

Rebel troops on many occasions shot down civilians in full view of foreign journalists, claiming that the victims were Doe supporters. Government soldiers did the same to alleged "subversives." There are no official estimates, but it is believed that tens of thousands of civilians were slain during the course of the thirteen month civil war.

The situation was so dangerous that by the end of the civil war in February 1991, about half of Liberia's population had fled to neighboring countries.

CIVIL SERVICE

The Liberian civil service is controlled by the Civil Service Bureau. Entry into the service is based on competitive examination in theory but in practice is influenced by patronage. Some effort is made to apportion appointments among the counties so that some regional balance is maintained. Civil servants may be removed from office by impeachment.

LOCAL GOVERNMENT

For purposes of regional administration, Liberia is divided into 13 counties and 2 territories, and the federal district of Monrovia as follows:

Counties: Grand Cape Mount, Sino, Grand Bassa, Grand Gedeh, Lofa, Nimba, Bong, Maryland, Montserrado, Rivercess, Bomi, Grand Kru and Margibi.

Territories: Marshal and Gibi.

The chief administrative official in each county is a county superintendent. Monrovia, the national capital, is governed directly by the central government. The territories are headed by territorial superintendents appointed by the president.

Counties are variously subdivided into districts, subdistricts, commonwealth districts and townships. Territories are divided into territorial districts. Each district is divided into several chiefdoms, headed by paramount chiefs. A paramount chief usually is elected by lower chiefs and elders but approved by the president. He receives no salary but is granted a percentage of the tax collected within his territory. He also presides over the tribal court, which enforces customary law. Under the paramount chief are a number of clan chiefs, and below them are town chiefs. Each clan chief and town chief is entitled to a percentage of the tax collected. All these chiefs serve as long as they command the confidence of the tribe and the president.

There are no representative institutions at the local level. Regional administration is completely centralized, and many county superintendents report directly to the president.

FOREIGN POLICY

Since Liberia never was subjected to colonial rule, its foreign policy has been characterized by the absence of the military and stridency of its neighbors. Until the end of World War II Liberia's positions on external issues were largely passive and defensive. Since World War II Liberian policy has become more pragmatic and positive, and there also has been a greater awareness of the key role of African unity in the formulation of foreign policies. President William Tubman was one of the founding fathers of the Organization of African Unity (OAU); its charter incorporates many of the ideas and guiding principles he had set forth in the charter of the Monrovia Group in 1961. Through his vigorous diplomatic activities Tubman ended Liberia's isolation from the rest of Africa. President William Tolbert was similarly respected in international forums, with the result that the April 1980 coup and his assassination were widely condemned. Liberian representatives were therefore barred from the 1980 summits of the OAU and the ECOWAS; however, with the help of a four-member watchdog committee established by ECOWAS in May, normal relations were established with most regional states by the end of the summer.

In the wake of the November 1985 coup attempt all Liberian borders were sealed, Gen. Quiwonkpa (the coup's leader) allegedly having reentered the country via Sierra Leone. The borders with Guinea and the Ivory Coast were quickly reopened to facilitate trade, and relations with Sierra Leone were normalized upon the conclusion of a tripartite security agreement that included Guinea in September 1986.

Doe resumed diplomatic relations with Israel in 1983 after a 10-year diplomatic boycott. This move was followed by a renewal of Israeli development aid, collaboration on matters of security and the purchase of Israeli weapons. In the same year, the Soviet Ambassador was expelled for alleged involvement in an anti-government conspiracy; relations with the Soviet Union were formally suspended in 1985. However, in May 1987 the Soviet embassy was permitted to reopen in the context of an overture to the eastern bloc that included the purchase from Romania of a battery of rocket launchers and anti-tank guns.

Liberia has had close and extensive ties with most European countries, including Great Britain, France, Sweden, Italy, West Germany, Switzerland, the Netherlands and the Vatican. Other non-African countries with significant programs in Liberia are the United States, Israel and Taiwan. However, diplomatic ties to almost all countries became strained during the civil war as well as the years leading up to it.

For many years, Liberia's traditional friendship with the U.S. was reflected both in the extent of U.S. private investment and in the existence of a bilateral defense agreement. Despite initial U.S. criticism of Doe's takeover in 1980, neither was seriously threatened during most of his regime. By May 1984 Liberia was receiving more U.S. economic and military aid per capita than any other African nation, such aid constituting over one-third of the nation's budget. However, after supporting the Doe regime throughout most of the 1980s, the U.S. had cut back aid substantially by 1989 in response to alleged corruption and human rights abuses. (In 1986, the U.S. had given nearly $54 million to Liberia in military and economic aid. In 1989, it provided only $10 million in humanitarian assistance and no military aid.)

In July 1990, ambassadors of five European Community nations in Liberia—Britain, West Germany, France, Italy and Spain—twice issued joint statements expressing their horror over the tribal killings of innocent civilians by both sides in the civil war. The U.S. urged peace negotiations between warring factions. In June a U.S. marine task force was sent to Liberia to evacuate Americans and other foreign nationals, but it did not intervene in the war.

Over one million refugees fled Liberia, most to the neighboring states of Guinea and the Ivory Coast. Others fled to Ghana, Nigeria, Mali, Gambia and Sierra Leone.

In August 1990, the ECOWAS sent a peace-keeping force to Liberia to intervene in its civil war. This marked the first time in modern history that African nations had organized a cooperative military intervention into the affairs of another African state. The

ECOWAS set up an interim government headed by Amos Sawyer and arranged peace negotiations between the warring factions in November 1990 and in February 1991.

Liberia joined the United Nations in 1945. It is a member of 14 U.N. organizations and nine other international organizations, including ECOWAS and OAU.

PARLIAMENT

Under the 1847 Constitution the Liberian Congress was a bicameral body consisting of the Senate and the House of Representatives. The Senate consisted of 18 members, two from each county, elected for six-year staggered terms. The House of Representatives consisted of 74 members elected for four-year terms. Though there were property qualifications for both members and electors, there was no literacy qualification for members, with the result that some members were illiterate. Much of the legislative work was conducted by 33 House committees and 17 Senate committees. The legislature met once a year, beginning in October. All members of the House belonged to the True Whig Party. At least half the Senate also belonged to the True Whig Party.

Over the years the Congress, shorn of much of its substantive powers, served as a purely deliberative body in which legislative initiative belonged to the president rather than to the members.

The National Assembly established by the 1984 Constitution was a bicameral body consisting of a Senate and a House of Representatives, both elected by universal adult suffrage. The Senate had 26 members serving six-year terms. At the election of October 15, 1985, the NDPL was awarded 22 seats; the LAP, 2; and the LUP and UP, one each. The House consisted of 64 members serving two-year terms. The allocation of seats following the 1985 balloting was NDPL, 51; LAP, 8; LUP, 3; and UP, 2.

After the February 1991 peace accord was signed, plans were made to organize a conference of all Liberians to discuss the new state of affairs regarding the government. Little is known about the developments at this date.

POLITICAL PARTIES

Until 1980 the sole political party was the True Whig Party, which had been in power continuously since 1878, longer than any other political party in the world. Its supremacy was, however, not enshrined in the Constitution, and other political parties operated legally, though for short periods.

Despite being a sole party, the True Whig Party managed to keep alive the semblance of a popular, grass-roots organization more American than African in its ideology and style. True to its form, the party also was known as the Grand Old Party, and its symbol was the elephant. Power was closely held in the hands of a small group of elite Americo-Liberians known as the "Honorables." The main channel of communication between the party faithful and the officeholders was a periodic nominating convention, which nominated the presidential candidate. The drama accompanying the conventions helped to disguise the fact that the candidate always was the incumbent or one chosen in smoke-filled rooms. County conventions were held every four years to choose candidates for the legislature. Business interests contributed liberally to the party, and "voluntary" contributions were deducted from civil service payrolls.

All political parties were banned following the 1980 coup, but they were reallowed in 1984 under the new Constitution. Thirteen parties were allowed to register, but smaller parties were discouraged by the requirement of a $150,000 fee for registration. Parties are prohibited from canvassing for members until they have met the $150,000 registration requirement.

In August 1984 President Doe founded the National Democratic Party of Liberia (NDPL) which then became the official ruling party. The principal opposition parties were:

- United People's Party (UPP), an outgrowth of the precoup People's Progressive Party and led by former foreign minister Gabriel Maccus Matthews; the UPP was banned before the 1985 elections
- Liberian Action Party (LAP) led by Tuan Wreh, a former aide to President Doe
- Convention Democratic Party (CDP) led by former True Whig leader Wasde Appleton
- Liberian People's Party (LPP), organized by members of the former Movement for Justice in Africa (MOJA), led by Amos Sawyer, who was arrested for plotting against the regime in 1984; the LPP was banned before the 1985 elections
- Unity Party
- Liberian Unification Party (LUP)
- National Integration Party (NIP)

Two additional parties are likely to arise, each having its origin in one of the two factions that split the National Patriotic Front. One leader is likely to be Charles Taylor, the other Prince Johnson.

ECONOMY

The civil war has practically destroyed Liberia's economy. A lower middle-income country with an economy based on agriculture and exports of iron ore and rubber, Liberia has a free-market in which the private sector dominates. Consequently, the destruction of iron-ore and rubber production sites together with the mass exodus of half the country's populatioin has left Liberia in a state of financial ruin.

In May 1990 the rebels seized Yekepa, site of an iron-ore mine that was Liberia's biggest industrial facility. Later in the month rebels attacked Buchanan, the country's second-largest city and the chief port for the export of iron ore, which consistently earns 55%–70% of Liberia's foreign exchange.

At the end of the civil war (February 1991), Liberia's agricultural system had been almost totally disrupted by fighting in the countryside. The nation was in desperate need of emergency food supplies. By the end

PRINCIPAL ECONOMIC INDICATORS

Gross National Product (U.S. $ billions): 1.051 (1987)
GNP per capita (U.S. $): 450 (1987)
Average annual rate of inflation (%, 1980–87): 1.5
Consumer price index (1980 = 100) 1986
 All Items: 123
 Food: 108
Average annual growth rate (latest)
 General government consumption: 1.3
 Private consumption: 0.8
 Gross domestic investment: −16.7

BALANCE OF PAYMENTS, 1987 (U.S. $ millions)

Current account balance: −118
Merchandise exports: 375
Merchandise imports: −312
Trade balance: 63
Other goods, services & income +: 58
Other goods, services & income −: −263
Other goods, services & income net: −205
Private unrequited transfers: −21
Official unrequited transfers: 45
Capital other than reserves: −155
Net errors & omissions: 30
Counterpart items: −47
Total change in reserves: 47

GROSS DOMESTIC PRODUCT

GDP nominal (L. $ billions): 1.035 (1986)
GDP per capita (U.S. $): 395 (1988)
Average annual growth rate of GDP (%, 1980–88): −1.3 (latest)
 Consumption
  Private: 66
  Government: 13
 Gross domestic investment: 12
 Gross domestic saving: 18 (latest)
 Foreign trade
  Exports: 45
  Imports: −37
Cost components of GDP (%) 1986
  Net indirect taxes: 8
  Consumption of fixed capital, compensation of employees, net operating surplus: 92
Sectoral origin of GDP (%) 1986
 Primary
  Agriculture: 21
  Mining: 10
 Secondary
  Manufacturing: 9
  Construction: 4
  Public utilities: 3
 Tertiary
  Transportation & communications: 7
  Trade: 20
  Finance and other services: 4
  Government: 22
Average annual sectoral growth rates (%, 1980–88)
  Agriculture: 1.2
  Industry: −6.0
  Manufacturing: −5.0
  Services: −0.8

of December 1990, hundreds of Liberians had died of starvation and doctors predicted that thousands more would succumb unless a huge relief program were launched. (Monrovia had been cut off from regular supplies of food and drinking water—as well as electricity—since June 1990. Several previous relief attempts had been hampered by Doe troops pilfering the shipments. In addition, Liberia's main ports, Monrovia and Buchanan, had been damaged by fighting, temporarily halting relief efforts.)

By the end of the 13-month-old civil war, almost 1.3 million Liberian refugees had fled the country. The U.S. had donated $127.2 million in relief, while foreign contributors had donated $44.1 million. Nevertheless, Liberia will need many more millions of dollars in aid if it is to rebuild its economy, which even before the war was heavily dependent on foreign aid.

PUBLIC FINANCE

The Liberian fiscal year runs from January 1 to December 31.

CENTRAL GOVERNMENT EXPENDITURES, 1988

% of total expenditures
 Defense: 8.9
 Education: 8.8
 Health: 1.5
 Housing, social security, welfare: 1.7
 Economic services: 23.5
 Other: 55.9

 Total expenditures as % of GNP: 24.0
 Overall surplus or deficit as % of GNP: −0.9

CENTRAL GOVERNMENT REVENUES, 1988

% of total current revenues
 Taxes on income, profit & capital gain: 33.9
 Social security contributions: 0.0
 Domestic taxes on goods & services: 25.1
 Taxes on international trade & transactions: 34.6
 Other taxes: 2.3
 Current nontax revenue: 4.2

 Total current revenue as % of GNP: 17.0 (latest)
 General government consumption as % of GDP: 17 (latest)
 Average annual growth rate
 of general government consumption: 1.3 (latest)

Of current revenues in 1988, approximately one third came from import duties and consular fees. Almost 30% came from income and profits taxes and the remainder from excises taxes and nontax revenue. Of current expenditures that year, approximately one third went to wages and salaries, 13% to interest on public debt and almost nine percent to development expenditure.

Government planning has not been concerned with providing an overall direction for the economy but rather with handling government expenditures. In 1962 the National Planning Agency was established to co-

FOREIGN AID, 1989

Total foreign aid (U.S. $ millions): 71.0
 Bilateral: 53.6
 Multilateral: 17.4

ordinate all projects and proposals relating to economic development.

During the period 1977–88 Liberia received $634 million in aid from the United States and $77 million from Communist countries. It received $793 million in assistance from other Western nations from 1970–87 and $25 million in bilateral aid from OPEC during 1979–89.

CURRENCY AND BANKING

The Liberian unit of currency is the Liberian dollar, divided into 100 cents. Coins are issued in demonimations of 1, 5, 10, 25 and 50 cents and 1 dollar; notes are issued in denominations of 1, 5, 10 and 20 dollars.

FINANCIAL INDICATORS, 1989

Total reserves minus gold (SDRs millions): 61
SDRs (millions): 0
Reserve position in IMD (SDRs millions): 0
Foreign exchange (SDRs millions): 6
Ratio of external debt to total reserves: 2,621.4 (1988)
Central bank 1989
  Assets (%)
    Foreign assets: 1.1
    Claims on government: 98.0
    Claims on banks: 0.8
    Claims on private sector: 0.1
  Liabilities (%)
    Reserve money: 36.8
    Government deposits: 33.9
    Foreign liabilities: 40.1
    Capital accounts: 10.8
Money supply 1989
  Stock (L. $ billions): 0.227
  M1 per capita: 90
Private banks 1989
  Assets (%)
    Loans to government: 7.5
    Loans to private sector: 5.9
    Reserves: 27.7
    Foreign assets: 58.8
  Liabilities
    Deposits (L. $ billions): 0.261
    of which %
      Demand deposits: 23.0
      Savings deposits: 28.3
      Government deposits: 10.0
      Foreign liabilities: 16.5
External debt 1988
  Total (U.S. $ billions): 1.632
    of which public (U.S. $ billions): 1.101
    of which private (U.S. $ millions): 0
  Debt service (long-term)
    Total (U.S. $ millions): 14
    Repayment
      Principal (%): 57.1
      Interest (%): 42.9
  Debt service ratio (%): 2.6
  External public debt as % of GNP: 62.6 (1987)
  Debt service as % of GNP: 8.2 (1987)
  Debt service as % of exports: 27.8 (1987)
  Terms of public borrowing
    Commitments (U.S. $ billions): 5.262 (1987)
    Average interest rate (%): 6.1 (1987)
    Average maturity (yrs.): 20 (1987)
  Net flow of publicly guaranteed external capital (U.S. $ millions): 26
Receipt of workers' remittances (U.S. $ millions): −51 (latest)
  Net direct private investment (U.S. $ millions): 39 (latest)

Since 1940 the Liberian dollar has been at par with the U.S. dollar, and U.S. currency is legal tender in the country.

The central bank is the National Bank of Liberia, established in 1974. Liberia's seven commercial banks are all located in Monrovia. Five of these banks are owned, wholly or partially, by U.S. banks. The two developmental banks are the Liberian Bank for Development and Investment and the Liberian Trading and Development Bank Ltd.

GROWTH PROFILE
(Annual Growth Rates, %)

Projected population (1988–2000): 2.8
Projected crude birth rate (/1,000) (1990–95): 44.5
Projected crude death rate (/1,000) (1990–95): 12.0
Urban population (1980–88): 5.8
Labor force (1985–2000): 2.7
GDP (1980–88): −1.3 (latest)
Inflation (1980–87): 1.5
Agriculture (1980–88): 1.2 (latest)
Industry (1980–88): −6.0 (latest)
Manufacturing (1980–88): −5.0 (latest)
Services (1980–88): −0.8 (latest)
Manufacturing earnings per employee (1980–87): 1.6
Energy production (1980–88): −0.9
Energy consumption (1980–88): −8.4
Exports (1980–88): −3.2
Imports (1980–88): −9.8
General government consumption: 1.3 (latest)
Private consumption: 0.8 (latest)
Gross domestic investment: −16.7 (latest)

AGRICULTURE

Of the total land area of 11,137,000 ha. (27,519,527 ac.), roughly 20% is considered agricultural land.

Liberia has two distinct systems of land tenure. The tribal people, officially known as aborigines, hold land under the traditonal principle of collective ownership, by which the tribal chief or headman administers the land but assigns the right to use it to members of the community. The "civilized" people hold individual titles to land or lease it from people who hold such title. The prevailing farming technique is known as bush rotation, involving burning and clearing, rotation of fields and periodic fallow periods. Mechanization is practiced only on large plantations.

The principal food crops are rice, cassava, palm oil and coffee. Since the 1970s the government has placed greater emphasis on self-sufficiency in rice production. Under the Special Rice Projects and the Expanded Rice Programs the Agricultural Land Development and Mechanization Corporation has developed over 4,451 ha. (11,000 ac.) in Foya, and specialists from Taiwan have been invited to introduce new strains.

Liberia's principal cash crops are rubber, timber, coffee and cocoa. Rubber outranks all other agricultural products in its contribution to export earnings, which was 28% in 1988. The 36,421-ha. (90,000-ac.) Firestone Tire and Rubber Company plantation is the largest rubber producer in the country.

Animal husbandry is relatively underdeveloped because of the absence of traditional herders, the prevalence of the tsetse fly and the lack of grazing land.

AGRICULTURAL INDICATORS

Agriculture's share of GDP (%): 37 (latest)
Average annual growth rate (%, 1980–88): 1.2 (latest)
Value added in agriculture (U.S. $ millions): 368 (1988)
Cereal imports (000 metric tons): 103 (1988)
Index of agricultural production (1979–81 = 100): 116 (1986)
Index of food production (1979–81 = 100): 118 (1986)
Index of food production per capita (1979–81 = 100): 92 (1986–88)
Number of tractors: 318 (1986)
Total fertilizer consumption (000 metric tons): 1.5 (1985–86)
Fertilizer consumption (g./ha., hundreds): 94 (1987–88)
Number of farms (000): 122 (1971)
Average size of holding (ha.): 3.0 (1971)
Size class (%) 1971
  Below 1 ha. (below 2.47 ac.): 52.8
  1–5 ha. (2.47–12.35 ac.): 31.0
  5–10 ha. (12.35–24.7 ac.): 12.0
  10–20 ha (24.7–49.4 ac.): 3.7
  20–50 ha. (49.4–123.5 ac.): 3.7
  50–200 ha. (123.5–494 ac.): 0.5
  Over 200 ha. (over 494 ac.): 0.5
Tenure (%) 1971
  Owner-operated: 40.0
  Rented: 0.0
  Other: 16.7
Farms as % of total land area: 3.8 (1971)
Land use (%) 1985–87
  Cropland: 4
  Pasture: 2
  Forest: 22
  Other: 72
Yields (kg./ha.) 1989
  Grains: 1,234
  Roots & tubers: 8,113
  Legumes: 550
  Milk (kg./animal): 100
Production 1989
  Fruits (000 metric tons): 130
  Vegetables (000 metric tons): 77
Livestock (000) 1989
  Cattle: 42
  Sheep: 240
  Pigs: 140
Forestry 1988
  Production of roundwood (million cubic meters): 5.889
    of which industrial roundwood (%): 19.6
  Value of exports (U.S. $ millions): 93.729
Fishing 1988
  Total catch (000 metric tons): 16.1
    of which marine (%): 75.1
  Value of exports (U.S. $ millions): 1.300

Forests and woodlands cover 2,500,000 ha. (6,177,630 ac). Over 225 species of hardwoods have been identified, of which at least 60 are in commercially exploitable stands. Under a forest conservation law passed in 1953, a total of 1.5 million ha. (3.8 million ac.) have been set apart as national forests.

The Liberian coast is a rich fishing zone, with over 32 species of fish for commercial use. Commercial fishing is carried on mainly by Kru and Fanti fishermen, the latter from Ghana. Large-scale, deep-sea fishing is dominated by the Mesurado Fishing Company.

Agricultural credit is provided by the Agricultural Credit Corporation.

MANUFACTURING

There is virtually no heavy industry in Liberia, and manufacturing is limited to food processing. Though rich in iron ore, Liberia has no secondary industries based on this mineral. Most of the small plants date from the Investment Incentives Code of 1966, under which more than 34 manufacturing industries were established. An industrial park was built near Paynesville. The main constraints on industrial development are the small size of the domestic market, the absence of an entrepreneurial class, and excessive concentration of manufacturing plants in the Monrovia region.

MANUFACTURING INDICATORS, 1987

Average annual growth rate (%, 1980–88): −5.0
Share of GDP (%): 5 (1988)
Labor force economically active in manufacturing (% est.): 1.6 (1984)
Value added in manufacturing (U.S. $ millions): 47
Earnings per employee in manufacturing
  Growth rate (%, 1980–87): 1.6
  Index (1980 = 100): 99 (1986)

Liberia's generous industrial investments policy, known as the Open Door Policy, is reflected in the dominance of private foreign enterprise in the Liberian economy. The rubber and mining industries, the banking system, construction and the railways are almost entirely in the hands of foreign investors, particularly American businesses. Practically all trade is in the hands of non-Liberians. Most of the foreign companies operate under special concession agreements. Of these, the Firestone Tire and Rubber Company and a dozen other concessions are the most productive segments of the monetary economy. As large employers and producers, these foreign concessions have become powerful forces. Their policies and decisions affect national life at all levels. Although none of them function as a monopoly, there is growing criticism in the country of their excessive profits and discriminatory employment policies.

MINING

Liberia is one of the largest iron ore exporters in the world. Iron ore production in 1988 accounted for 55% of export earnings. Iron is mined on the Mano River by the National Iron Ore Company, a Liberian corporation; at Mount Nimba by the Liberian American Mineral Company; in the Bong Mountains by the German-owned Bong Mining Company; and at Wologisi by the Japanese-owned Liberian Iron and Steel Corporation. Of these, the largest is the Liberian American Mineral Company, which accounts for 44% of the total output. Liberia's proven iron ore reserves are estimated at 1 billion tons of high-grade ore with an iron content of 35% to 67%.

Diamonds, mined in the lower Loffa River area, are the next most important mineral. In 1988 diamonds accounted for 2.17% of export earnings. Small deposits of gold also are mined. Other mineral discoveries include bauxite, copper, columbite-tantalite, lead, manganese, tin, barite, kyanite and zinc.

ENERGY

Energy imports accounted for 22.7% of all merchandise imports in 1988. A petroleum refinery with an annual capacity of 15,000 bbl. per day is operated at Paynesville by the Liberia Refinery Company.

ENERGY INDICATORS

Average annual energy production growth rate (%, 1980–88): −0.9
Energy consumption per capita (kg. oil equivalent): 164 (1988)
Energy imports as % of merchandise exports: 12 (1988)
Average annual growth rate of energy consumption (%, 1980–88): −8.4
Electricity 1988
- Installed capacity (000 kw.): 325
- Production (million kw.-hr.): 834
  - % fossil fuel: 61.2
  - % hydro: 38.8
- Consumption per capita (kw.-hr.): 348

Natural gas
- Proved reserves (billion cu. m.): 0 (1990)
- Production (milllon cu. m.): 0 (1989)
- Consumption (million cu. m.): 0 (1988)

Petroleum
- Production (million bbl.): 0 (1989)
- Consumption (million bbl.): 0 (1988)
- Refining capacity (000 bbl./day): 15 (1990)

LABOR

The bulk of the labor force is unskilled; only one-third of the labor force is classified as skilled to some degree. About 90% of skilled Liberians are employed by the government, while 95% of positions of responsibility in private enterprises are held by expatriates. Like many other African countries, Liberia suffers from both unemployment and serious shortages of skilled manpower.

Working conditions are governed by the Labor Practices Law of 1961. The maximum workweek is 48 hours for mine workers and agricultural workers, with time and a half for overtime on regular working days and double time for overtime on holidays. The law also provides for paid holidays and annual leave. Minimum wages are set by the Minimum Wage Board for all classes of employees covered by labor legislation. In addition to cash wages, workers receive free housing, free or subsidized rice, medical care, scholarships for their children and incentive bonuses.

The unemployment rate is not known at this time, as nearly half the population fled the country during its civil war; it is not yet clear how many have returned since the war ended in February 1991.

Although labor unions have existed in the country since 1949, the government has viewed their task as one of increasing productivity in cooperation with the government rather than making demands for higher pay and benefits. Organized labor represented only 2% of the labor force in 1990. Liberia has one national labor federation, the Liberian Federation of Trade Unions (LFTU), which includes eight member unions and approximately 2,000 dues-paying members. There are several significant unions not affiliated with the LFTU, such as the National Agricultural and Allied Workers of Liberia (NAAWL), which represents the 17,000 workers of the Firestone Rubber and Tire Company and the LAMCO Mine Workers' Union.

Unions are prohibited from strike action, but brief strikes have occurred despite the ban. In most cases, workers were persuaded to return peacefully to their jobs and the government took no punitive action. In considering the case of an agricultural union suspended in 1982, the International Labor Organization noted that the prohibition against strikes "constitutes in itself a serious violation of trade union rights." The suspension, based on allegations of embezzlement against the union's secretary general, came shortly after illegal strikes he had allegedly instigated. The suspension was lifted in October 1984 shortly after embezzlement charges were brought against the secretary general and two other officials. In 1983 and again in 1984, the Liberian government was cited by the ILO for violations of ILO Convention 87, regarding freedom of association (because Liberian legislation does not recognize the right of workers in the public service or in government enterprises to form unions), and Convention 29, regarding forced labor. The Liberian government drafted a new labor code that eliminated the objectionable legislation cited by the ILO but has not yet passed it into law; thus the legislation for which the government was cited by the ILO remains on the books.

Under the Constitution and the election laws, unions and business are prohibited from forming political parties or canvassing for or contributing to political parties.

LABOR INDICATORS, 1984

Total economically active population (000): 704
- % working-age (15–64): 56.3
- % female: 41.0

Activity rate (%)
- Total: 33.5
- Male: 39.1
- Female: 27.8

Employment status (%)
- Employers & self-employed: 59.1
- Employees: 21.6
- Unpaid family workers: 14.4
- Other: 5.0

Sectoral employment of economically active (%)
- Agriculture, forestry, fishing: 68.3
- Construction: 0.6
- Manufacturing, mining, quarrying, public utilities: 4.4
- Trade, hotels, restaurants: 6.7
- Transportation, communications: 2.0
- Finance, real estate and services: 9.0

Average annual growth rate of labor force (%, 1985–2000): 2.7
Labor under 20 years (%): 7.4 (1974)

FOREIGN COMMERCE

In 1988 and 1989, Liberia posted its best two years in a decade, thanks to a resurgence of the rubber industry and rapid growth in exports of forest products. Richly endowed with water, mineral resources, forests and a climate favorable to agriculture, Liberia is a producer and exporter of basic products.

Liberia's major exports in 1988 were iron ore, rubber, logs and timber, diamonds, gold and coffee. Major export destinations were West Germany, the U.S., Italy, France, Belgium-Luxembourg, the Netherlands and Spain.

Its major imports were machinery and transport equipment, petroleum and petroleum products, basic manufactures, food and live animals, and chemicals. Major import sources were the U.S., West Germany, Japan, and U.K., the Netherlands, Spain and Belgium-Luxembourg.

The civil war has taken its toll on both the iron-ore and rubber production facilities as well as on the agricultural sector. Ports were also damaged in the fighting, including Liberia's two major ports at Monrovia and Buchanan. After two of its most successful years in exporting, Liberia now faces an uncertain future in that realm until it can rebuild its economy.

Foreign trade is almost entirely in the hands of private enterprises. There are no controls on foreign exchange and no quotas on imports. Liberia is a member of two trade groups: the Economic Community of West African States (ECOWAS) and the Mano River Union.

FOREIGN TRADE INDICATORS, 1988

Exports (U.S. $ millions): 550 (1989)
Imports (U.S. $ millions): 335 (1989)
Balance of trade (U.S. $ millions): 215 (1989)
Annual growth rate (1980–88), exports (%): −3.2 (latest)
Annual growth rate (1980–88), imports (%): −9.8 (latest)
International reserves in terms of months of imports covered: 0.0
Terms of trade (1980 = 100): 103 (latest)
Import price index (1980 = 100): 81.0 (1986)
Export price index (1980 = 100): 77.5 (1986)

Direction of Trade (%), 1984

	Imports	Exports
European Community	40.0	70.5
United States	22.3	20.2
U.S.S.R. & Eastern European economies	1.1	1.9
Japan	8.1	1.3

Composition of Trade (%), 1986

	Imports	Exports
Food and agricultural raw materials	25.5	34.1
Fuels and other energy	19.8	0.0
Mineral ores & concentrates	0.9	64.8
Manufactured goods	53.9	1.1
of which chemicals	6.7	0.1
of which machinery	26.8	0.3

TRANSPORTATION & COMMUNICATIONS

Liberia's 490 km. (204 mi.) rail system is controlled and operated by foreign steel and financial interests. Passenger service is limited to the Liberian American Mineral Company's line between Mount Nimba and Buchanan.

The Liberian flag is ranked first on the seas, with over 2,000 vessels, with a gross registered tonnage of 51.2 m. in 1987. The Liberian flag is a flag of convenience, and only a small percentage of the fleet is owned by Liberian interests. Nevertheless, registration charges provide an important source of revenue. The Liberian flag has been regarded since the end of World War II as a flag of convenience because of lenient labor laws, low registration fees and minimal safety regulations. Spurred by a number of accidents involving Liberian-registered ships since 1976, the Liberian Shipping Council announced plans in 1977 to tighten safety standards for ships, especially tankers. The new regulations require inspections every nine months for ships over 20 years old and for vessels with poor safety records. The principal ports are Monrovia, Buchanan, Harper, Greenville and Robertsport. Monrovia is operated as a free port. Buchanan is used primarily for iron ore exports. The total length of navigable rivers is 370 km. (230 mi.). The most important of the inland waterways is the Cavalla River.

The road system consists of 8,064 km. (5,011 mi.). The main trunk road is the Monrovia–Sanniquellie road, running northeast from the capital to the Guinean border.

The national airline is Air Liberia.

Air Taxi Company of Liberia services internal routes. Robertsfield International Airport, 56 km. (35 mi.), from Monrovia, is the principal international airport, while James Spriggs Payne Airfield handles internal traffic. There are more than 100 airfields and airstrips in the country.

TRANSPORTATION INDICATORS

Roads (latest)
- Length, km. (mi.): 8,064 (5,011)
- Paved (%): 9

Motor vehicles (latest)
- Automobiles: 7,148
- Trucks and buses: 4,031
- Persons per vehicle: 210

Railroads (latest)
- Track (route length), km. (mi.): 490 (304)
- Freight, metric ton-km. (short ton-mi.) (billions): 2.549 (1.746)

Merchant marine
- Vessels (over 100 tons): 1,455 (1989)
- Total deadweight tonnage (millions): 89.501 (1989)
- Oil tankers (million GRT): 31.585 (1985)

Ports (pre-1986)
- Cargo loaded (million metric tons): 14.640
- Cargo unloaded (million metric tons): 1.729

Air
- Passenger-km. (passenger-mi.) (millions): 17 (11) (pre-1986)
- Freight, metric ton-km. (short ton-mi.) (millions): 0.10 (0.1) (pre-1986)
- Airports with scheduled flights: 1 (1990)

Inland waterways (latest)
- Length, km. (mi.): 370 (230)

The Liberian tourist industry is negligible. No statistics are available on the number of tourists visiting the country. Total tourist receipts in 1986 were U.S. $6 million.

COMMUNICATION INDICATORS, 1988

Telephones
- Total (000): 28
- Persons per telephone: 86

Phone traffic (000) calls)
- Local: 1,100 (pulses)
- International: 336

Post office
- Number of post offices: 44
- Pieces of mail handled (millions): 23.786

Telecommunications 1990
- Satellite stations: 2

DEFENSE

The defense structure is headed by the president, who also is the commander in chief. The president heads the Liberian Joint Security Commission, the supreme policy-making body in defense affairs. The line of command runs through the minister of national defense to the General Staff, headed by the chief of staff of the armed forces. The U.S. Military Mission is designated as a component of the Defense Department. American personnel also are represented on the Liberian Joint Security Commission.

Military manpower is provided by voluntary enlistment. However, a law establishing conscription of male citizens between 16 and 45 is on the statute books and is used to maintain the 20,000-strong militia.

The total strength of the armed forces in 1989 under Doe was approximately 5,000, although the number diminished greatly due to mass desertions during the civil war.

Doe's army was set up as follows:

Organization: six infantry battalions, one artillery battalion, one guard battalion, one engineer battalion, one service battalion, one armored reconnaissance battalion, one air reconnaissance battalion.

Equipment: 12 scout cars; howitzers; rocket launchers; mortars

Since Liberia has no air force, a small aviation unit consisting of two transports and 13 light aircraft was attached to the army.

Organization of the navy was as follows:

Units: five patrol boats, one motor gunboat

Bases: Monrovia, Bassa, Sinoe, Cape Palmas

Under the terms of the mutual defense treaty with the United States, the defense of Liberia against external aggression is guaranteed by the United States. Therefore the Liberian armed forces were maintained at a low level of combat-effectiveness and perform a largely ceremonial role. With the country in such disarray, it is difficult to tell how many troops are currently serving under the interim government, how many of Doe's troops are left, how many soldiers are loyal to Taylor and how many to Johnson. Ostensibly, once the official interim government can be agreed upon, all the troops will unite under government control.

EDUCATION

Education is free, universal and compulsory, in principle, for 10 years from ages six to 16. Nevertheless, gross school enrollment ratios are very low.

Schooling consists of 12 years divided into six years of primary school, three years of junior high school and three years of senior high school. There is a high dropout rate at the primary level, and only about 15% of those who enter primary school complete it. Fewer attend secondary schools because of commuting difficulties. Many well-to-do students attend secondary schools in Europe; the United States; or nearer home, in Ghana or Nigeria.

The academic year is from March to December. The medium of instruction is English in all schools, although tribal languages are used in the lower grades in rural schools. Textbooks are prescribed by the government. Most textbooks originate in the United States and are priced beyond the reach of most children. The resulting textbook shortage has acted as a brake on the expansion of education.

In principle teachers have to be certified annually by the Department of Education, but this requirement is rarely enforced. Some 85% of teachers lack minimum

EDUCATION INDICATORS, 1980

Literacy
- Total (%): 22.4
- Male (%): 27.4
- Female (%): 18.4

First level
- Schools: 1,651
- Students: 227,431
- Teachers: 9,099
- Student/teacher ratio: 25.0

Second level
- Schools: 419
- Students: 51,666
- Teachers: 1,129
- Student/teacher ratio: 45.8

Vocational
- Schools: 6
- Students: 2,322
- Teachers: 63
- Student/teacher ratio: 36.9

Third level (postsecondary)
- Institutions: 3
- Students: 3,955 (1985)
- Teachers: 190
- Gross enrollment ratio: 2.5 (1979)
- Students (/100,000 pop.): 220
- % of population age 25 and over with postsecondary education: 1.5

Foreign study
- Foreign students in national universities: 147 (1987)
- Students abroad: 796
  - of whom in
    - United States: 622 (1988)
    - France: 53 (1988)
    - Federal Republic of Germany: 16 (1988)
    - United Kingdom: 30 (1987)

Public expenditure
- Total (L. $ million): 61.778
- % of GNP: 5.7
- % of national budget: 24.3
- % of current expenditure: 85.9

GRADUATES, 1989

Total: 730
Education: 492
Humanities & religion: 51
Fine & applied arts: 3
Law: 58
Social & behavioral sciences: 69
Commerce & business: 27
Mass communication: 0
Home economics: 0
Service trades: 0
Natural sciences: 0
Mathematics & computer science: 4
Medicine: 7
Engineering: 0
Architecture: 0
Industrial programs: 0
Transportation & communications: 0
Agriculture, forestry, fisheries: 19
Other: 0

professional qualifications. A serious shortage of teachers is compounded by poor salaries and consequent loss of prestige. The school system therefore relies heavily on foreign, particularly U.S. Peace Corps, teachers. Teacher training is provided through a number of institutions, of which the best known are the Tubman Teachers'College and Our Lady of Fatima College.

Private schools, run by Christian missions and foreign concessions, account for almost 35% of primary enrollment and 43% of secondary enrollment. Some schools are run by tribal authorities, where the training for boys is known as *poro* and the training for girls is known as *sande*.

The earliest adult education programs in Liberia were launched with the help of distinguished American missionary and literacy expert Frank Laubach. In the 1950s the government established the Klay Fundamental Education Center. Official programs are supplemented by private efforts, such as those by the YMCA and YWCA.

A number of high schools offer exclusively vocational secondary educational programs. Of these, the best known is the Booker Washington Agricultural and Industrial Institute at Kakata. Other schools offer a limited number of vocational courses.

The school system is under the direct control of the Department of Education. Foreign aid for educational programs and projects is received from the United States, Germany and Sweden.

The principal institution of higher learning is the University of Liberia in Monrovia. There are two smaller denominational colleges: Episcopalian Cuttington College and the Roman Catholic Our Lady of Fatima College. There are also a number of scientific, vocational and technical training institutions.

LEGAL SYSTEM

The judicial system is headed by the People's Supreme Court, consisting of a chief justice and four associate justices, all appointed by the President from a panel recommended by a Judicial Service Commission; the consent of the Senate is required for these appointments. Immediately below it are the circuit courts of assize, one in each county and two in Monrovia. Inferior courts include magistrate courts and justice of the peace courts. A parallel tribal court system dispenses justice according to tribal law. The key court under this system is the court of the paramount chief, which is superior to the court of the clan chief. Appeals from these courts are heard by the court of the district commissioner and the court of the provincial commissioner. The district commissioner and the paramount chief sometimes hold a joint court to settle disputes falling within their dual competence. Trial by ordeal is an accepted procedure in tribal courts.

Historically, the judiciary in Liberia has been very weak and vulnerable to influence exerted by the executive branch. However, in 1984 the courts showed considerable independence and integrity in two major cases of interest to the government. Traditional courts presided over by tribal chiefs are not bound by Anglo-American common law or judicial principles but apply customary unwritten law to domestic and land disputes and petty theft. Customary court decisions may be reviewed in the statutory court system or may be appealed through a hierarchy of chiefs, followed by administrative review by the Ministry of Internal Affairs, and in some instances a final review by the head of state. Allegations of corruption and incompetence involving the traditional courts are often heard.

The penal system includes over 20 institutions, of which the Central Prison in Monrovia is the largest. The average prison population in these correctional facilities is about 500. Prisoners are not segregated by type of sentence, crime, sex or age but are bunched together indiscriminately. Few records are maintained. Though the treatment of prisoners has become more humane in recent years, there are no rehabilitation or vocational programs.

LAW ENFORCEMENT

The national police force is commanded by a director under the direct jurisdiction of the attorney general and the president. All police officials hold military rank, the highest being that of colonel, held by the director. The Monrovia Police and the County Police are under the Operations Office of the Central Headquarters. The Monrovia Police, the military police of the capital and each regional (county) post are headed by a deputy inspector.

Although precise statistics are lacking, crime, particularly juvenile delinquency, has been on the rise since the 1960s. Organized gangs, common in many other African countries, have not become a major law enforcement problem. Crimes of violence are comparatively rare.

There are two official secret service organizations. The first is the National Bureau of Investigation, which is charged with criminal investigation. The other is the Executive Action Bureau, which coordinates the security functions of government agencies and undertakes counterintelligence and antisubversion operations.

HEALTH

Before the civil war, Liberia's principal health problems were malaria, tuberculosis, leprosy, bilharziasis, trypanosomiasis, intestinal parasites, skin diseases and tropical ulcers. Roughly 50% of the population had access to safe water. Due to the war even fewer people now have access to safe water, and widespread starvation and malnutrition are predicted.

HEALTH INDICATORS

Health personnel 1985
  Physicians: 89
    persons per: 24,600
  Dentists: 5
  Nurses: 908
  Pharmacists: 4 (1980)
  Midwives: 443
Hospitals 1981
  Number: 85 (1980)
  Number of beds (/10,000): 15
Type of hospitals (%) 1980
  Government: 60.0
  Private nonprofit and private profit: 40.0
Public health expenditures (latest)
  As % of national budget: 5.7
  Per capita (U.S. $): 7.00
Vital statistics
  Crude death rate (/1,000): 14 (1990)
  Life expectancy at birth 1990
    Males: 54
    Females: 58
Infant mortality rate (/1,000 live births): 126 (1990)
Child mortality rate under yrs. (/1,000 live births) (1985–90): 206
Maternal mortality rate (/1,000 live births) (1980): 173
Population with access to safe water (%): 55 (latest)

FOOD & NUTRITION

The staple Liberian diet consists of rice or manioc. Meat, dairy products and eggs are scarce. Fish is popular, but the fish catch is not enough to meet needs. The per capita daily intake of food in 1988 was 2,344 calories (less than the 2,600 recommended by the WHO).

MEDIA & CULTURE

Liberia's official newspaper is *The New Liberian.* Independent newspapers include the *Daily Observer* and the *Mirror* which produce five editions a week. There are also about six independent monthlies. However, publication has often been irregular or at times has ceased altogether because of government intervention.

Freedom of the press is guaranteed by the Constitution in sweeping terms reminiscent of the U.S. Bill of Rights, but the laws of sedition, libel and slander are so strictly enforced that criticism of public officials is virtually impossible and often entails suspension of the offending newspaper and jailing of its editor. Where criticism appears, it is more often than not officially inspired as a prelude to the dismissal of the person under attack. Furthermore, one newspaper is government-inspired, and most other periodicals receive government subsidies. These economic constraints are more powerful than open censorship. However, prepublication censorship is practiced only in broadcasting and the movies.

In 1980 Council Decree 2-A was passed, outlawing efforts to "Control, influence, oppose, castigate or deride [government] actions or policies." The law mandates death by firing squad for offenders. Only two prosecutions have been brought under Decree 2-A, both prior to 1983, and in both the convicted defendants were pardoned by the head of state. But in 1984 the government increased its restrictions on freedom of speech and the press. In August the government announced Decree 88A, which makes it a felony to accuse any government official or other individual of any crime if the purpose of the accuser is to injure the person's reputation, create disharmony, spread rumors, undermine the security of the state or impede the electoral process. In April 1989 the official accreditation of journalists was made compulsory. In September 1989 a government commission was established to regulate the media; the Press Union of Liberia (PUL) refused to participate in the project, on the grounds that it restricted press freedom.

A result of the government's actions to restrict free speech and press has been to introduce an unspecified degree of self censorship to avoid confrontation. The independent press usually avoids direct criticism of government policies. In analyzing public issues, finding fault with the status quo and suggesting remedies, however, editorials regularly express criticism indirectly. In some instances the government has forbidden reports on specific events, such as labor unrest or school disturbances, when disclosure could prove embarrassing.

The national news agency is the Liberian News Agency (LINA). Foreign news agencies represented in Monrovia include UPI.

Local book publishing is almost nonexistent at present, but a few publishing houses have been established recently. Liberia adheres to the Universal Copyright Convention.

MEDIA INDICATORS

Newspapers
  Number of dailies: 7 (latest)
  Newsprint comsumption 1988
    Total metric tons: 100
    Per 1,000 pop. (kg.): 42
Radio
  Number of transmitters: 15 (latest)
  Number of persons per radio receiver: 4.2 (1989)
Television
  Television transmitters: 5 (1989)
  Number of persons per T.V. receiver: 56 (1989)
Cinema
  Number of fixed cinemas: 13 (pre-1986)
  Seating capacity (000): 9 (pre-1986)
  Annual attendance (millions): 1.5 (pre-1986)

The official Liberian Broadcasting Corporation (call letters ELBC) operates one medium-wave and two shortwave transmitters at Monrovia and one medium-wave transmitter at Harper. These stations are on the air for 125 hours a week, broadcasting in English and nine vernaculars. A second broadcasting service is the private ELWA, operated by the Sudan Interior Mission. ELWA has one medium-wave transmitter and four shortwave transmitters with a home service and a foreign service. ELWA programs are broadcast in English, French, Arabic and 42 west African vernaculars. The Voice of America's shortwave relay station in Monrovia with six 250-kw. and two 50-kw. transmitters, is the most powerful on the continent. Another private station is owned by a mining company at Nimba.

CULTURAL & ENVIRONMENTAL INDICATORS

Libraries (pre-1986)
- Number: 3
- Volumes (000): 78

Nature reserves (latest)
- Number of facilities: 1

The Liberian Broadcasting Corporation's television service (ELTV) covers 20% of the country, with a transmitter at Monrovia and relays at Buchanan and Bomi Hills. Broadcasting time is 5½ hours daily Monday through Friday; 9½ hours daily on Saturday and Sunday.

Only documentary films are produced within the country.

The largest libraries in the country are the Cuttington College Library, with 60,000 volumes, and the University of Liberia Library, with 50,000 volumes.

SOCIAL WELFARE

Basic health services are limited, and there is no adequate state welfare system. The publicly-owned National Social Security and Welfare Corporation was established in 1976 to administer pensions, sickness benefits and welfare funds. In 1987 it launched an Employment Injury Scheme, to provide compensation for workplace injuries, and a National Pension Scheme. Medical care is provided free of charge to children less than two years old. Other welfare activities are carried out by private agencies, including Christian missions.

GLOSSARY

bush school: school run by tribal authorities in the interior.

civilized: term designating Americo-Liberians and other Westernized peoples as distinguished from tribal peoples.

harmattan: hot, scorching wind from the Sahara, blowing over Liberia in the summer.

hinterland: term used in the Liberian laws to designate interior areas outside of the coastal counties.

honorable: title applied to a member of the Americo-Liberians elite, who constitute the ruling class.

lettered: as applied to the Americo-Liberians, a synonym for civilized.

palaver house: the central building in a tribal town or village serving as a town hall or community center.

poro: a tribal secret society for males.

sande: a tribal society for females.

CHRONOLOGY (from 1947)

1947— By the seventh amendment to the Constitution, representation in Congress is given to the tribals of the hinterland provinces; by the eighth amendment, suffrage is extended to all Liberians, including women.

1952— Liberia pays off the notorious Firestone Loan 15 years before maturity; a monument is erected in Monrovia to commemorate this event.

1961— Monrovia Group is formed by Liberia and seven other African countries to counter the Casablanca Group lead by Ghana.

1962— Liberia holds its first national census.

1963— Hinterland provinces are abolished in extensive reorganization of local administration; Liberia is divided into nine counties and six territories. . . . President Tubman launches "Operation Production."

1968— Henry Fahnbullah is arrested and convicted in the so-called Red China Plot.

1971— President Tubman dies; Vice President William Tolbert succeeds to the presidency.

1972— Tolbert establishes first Liberian mission in Moscow.

1973— Liberia joins the Mano River Union (with Sierra Leone) and the Economic Community of West African States.

1975— Constitution is amended to restrict presidential term to eight years. . . . Liberia signs the Lome Convention.

1976— Tolbert is elected unopposed to an eight-year term.

1977— Liberia establishes diplomatic links with China.

1978— U.S. President Jimmy Carter receives warm welcome on brief visit.

1979— The main opposition group, Progressive Alliance of Liberia, holds first conference. . . . A proposal to increase the price of rice is followed by riots, bloodshed and looting.

1980— A group of disgruntled non-commissioned officers led by Sergeant Samuel Doe leads successful coup in which President Tolbert is killed; Doe sets up a People's Redemption Council with full legislative and executive powers; the national constitution is suspended along with parliament; 13 prominent officials of the former regime are arrested and executed.

1981— Five members of the PRC, including Thomas Weh Syen, are executed for plotting against Doe. . . . Government adopts strong measures to put down dock strike in Monrovia.

1983— Brigadier General Thomas Quiwonkpa, the strong-man of the regime, is dismissed and forced to flee the country. . . . Diplomatic relations with Libya are suspended.

1984— Doe submits draft constitution, formulated by

the constitutional commission, to the electorate who approve it in a national referendum.

1985— Political parties are legitimized and 13 new parties announce their intention to contest the elections. . . . Doe announces the formation of the Liberian Democratic Party with himself as leader. . . . In national elections, Doe is elected president and his LDP wins strong majority with over 50% of the vote. . . . Diplomatic relations with Soviet Union are suspended.

1986— Doe is sworn in as elected President. . . . Teachers' strikes and student demonstrations are brutally suppressed by the army. . . . The Liberian Unification Party, the Liberian Action party and the Unity Party form a united front as the Liberia Grand Coalition led by William Kpolleh. The three parties of the Grand Coalition boycott by-elections.

1988— Kpolleh is among 10 people arrested in March on charges of plotting to overthrow the government. He is later sentenced to 10 years' imprisonment for treason. . . . Another attempted coup, led by Nichola Podier, is put down in July.

1989— Armed insurrection, led by Charles Taylor of the National Patriotic Force (NPF), begins in the northeast.

1990— Fighting degenerates into a civil war between Doe's ethnic group, the Krahn, and the local Gio and Mano tribes. . . . The NPF divides into two rival factions, one led by Taylor and the other led by Prince Johnson. . . . The Economic Community of West African States sends in a peace keeping force and sets up an interim government headed by Amos Sawyer. . . . Doe is killed by followers of Johnson.

1991— A cease-fire is signed in February.

BIBLIOGRAPHY (from 1970)

Best, Kenneth Y. *Cultural Policy in Liberia.* New York, 1974.

Boley, G. E. *Liberia: The Rise and Fall of the First Republic.* New York, 1985.

Clapham, C. *Liberia and Sierra Leone.* New York, 1976.

Clifford, Mary Louise. *The Land and People of Liberia.* Philadelphia, 1971.

Dennis, Benjamin G. *The Gbandes: A People of the Liberian Hinterland.* Chicago, 1973.

Dunn, D. Elwood. *Liberia: A National Polity In Transition.* Metuchen, N.J. 1988.

Gnielinski, Stefan Von. *Liberia in Maps.* New York, 1972.

Hlope, Stephen S. *Class, Ethnicity & Politics in Liberia: Analysis of Power Struggles in the Tubman and Tolbert Administrations from 1944 to 1975.* Washington, D.C., 1979.

Liebenow, J. Gus. *Liberia: The Quest for Democracy.* Bloomington, Ind. 1987.

Lowenkopf, Martin. *Political and Economic Development in Liberia.* Stanford, Calif., 1977.

———. *Politics in Liberia: The Conservative Road to Development.* Stanford, Calif., 1976.

Nimley, Anthony. *The Liberian Bureaucracy: An Analysis & Evaluation of the Environment, Structures, and Functions.* Washington, D.C., 1979.

Schulz, Willi. *A New Geography of Liberia.* London, 1973.

Siegmann, William C. and Cynthia E. Schmidt. *Rock of the Ancestors.* Newark, Del., 1977.

Storette, Ronald F. *The Politics of Integrated Social Investment: An American Study of Swedish LAMCO Project in Liberia.* Stockholm, 1971.

Sundita, I. K. *Black Scandal: America and the Liberian Labor Crisis 1929–36.* Philadelphia, Pa., 1980.

Wilson, Charles Morrow. *Liberia: Black Africa in Microcosm.* New York, 1971.

Wonkeryor, Edward L. *Liberia: Military Dictatorship.* Chicago, Ill., 1985.

Wreh, Tuan. *The Love of Liberty: The Rule of President William V. S. Tubman in Liberia.* New York, 1976.

OFFICIAL PUBLICATIONS

Budget Bureau, *Budget of the Government of Liberia.*

———, *Development Budget.*

Finance Ministry, *Annual Report Covering Operations of the Ministry of Finance.*

———, *Expenditure Report.*

———, *Revenue Report.*

———, *Summary of Estimated and Actual Revenue Collected* (monthly unpublished).

Liberian National Bank, *Annual Report.*

Planning and Economic Affairs Ministry, *Economic Survey of Liberia.*

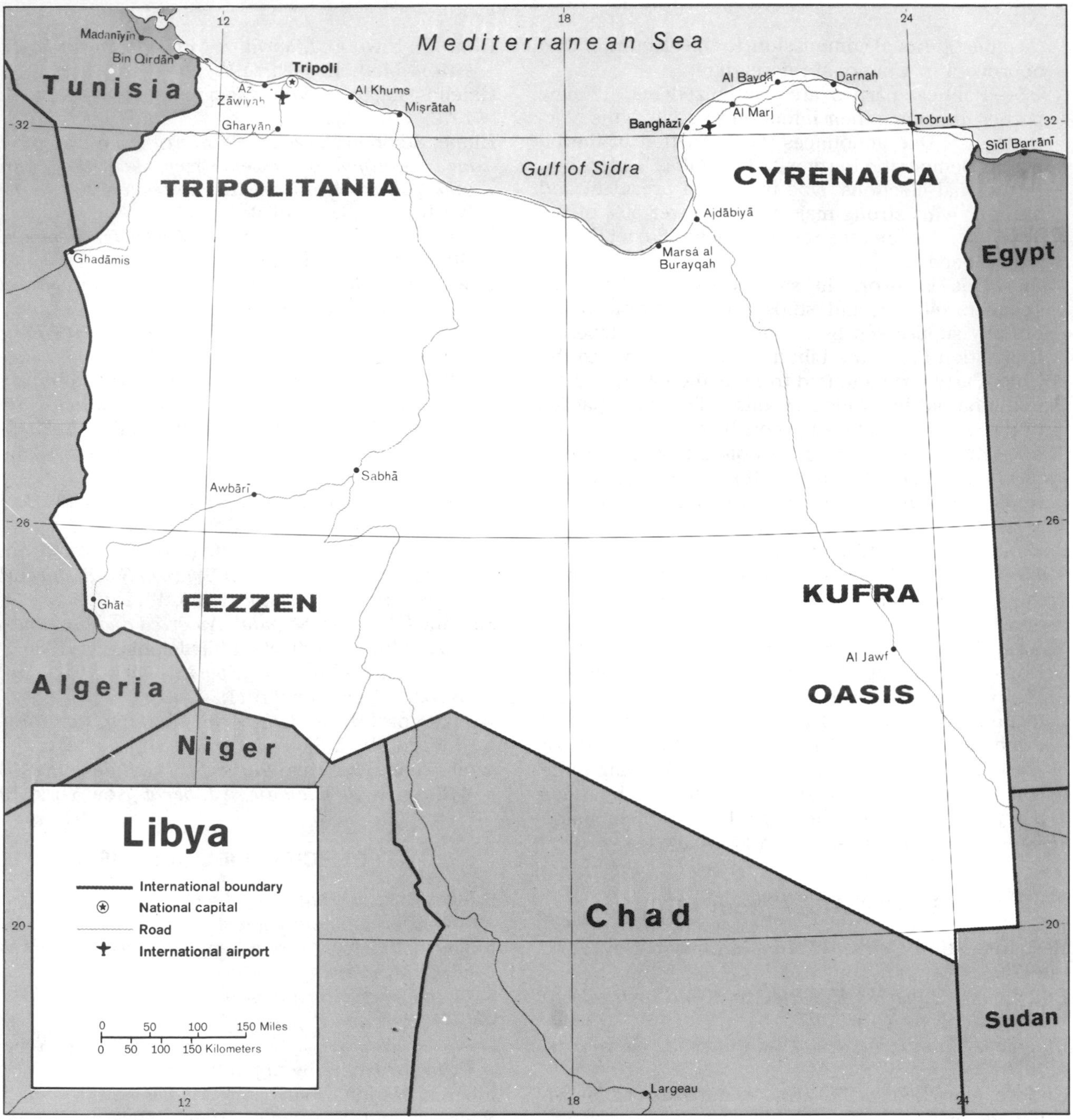

Mediterranean Sea

Madanīyīn
Bin Qirdān
Tunisia
Tripoli
Az Zāwiyah
Al Khums
Mişrātah
Gharyān
Al Bayḑā
Darnah
Al Marj
Banghāzī
Tobruk
Sīdī Barrānī
Gulf of Sidra
TRIPOLITANIA
CYRENAICA
Ajdābiyā
Marsá al Burayqah
Ghadāmis
Egypt
Awbārī
Sabhā
Ghāt
FEZZEN
KUFRA
Al Jawf
OASIS
Algeria
Niger
Chad
Sudan
Largeau

12 18 24
32 26 20

Libya

International boundary
National capital
Road
International airport

0 50 100 150 Miles
0 50 100 150 Kilometers

LIBYA

BASIC FACT SHEET

OFFICIAL NAME: The Great Socialist People's Libyan Arab Jamahiriya (al-Jamahiriya al-Arabiya al-Libiya al-Shabiya) al-Ishtirakiyu; formerly Socialist People's Libyan Arab Jamahiriya

NOTE: *Jamahiriya* is an Arabic neologism made up of the words "republic" and "masses" and may best be translated as "peopledom."

ABBREVIATION: LY

CAPITAL: Tripoli

HEAD OF STATE: Col. Mu'ammar al-Qaddafi (from 1969)

HEAD OF GOVERNMENT: Secretary-General of the General People's Committee Abu Zayd Umar Durda (from 1990)

NATURE OF GOVERNMENT: Military dictatorship

POPULATION: 4,221,141 (1990)

AREA: 1,759,540 sq. km. (679,360 sq. mi.)

ETHNIC MAJORITY: Arab

LANGUAGE: Arabic

RELIGION: Sunni Islam

UNIT OF CURRENCY: Libyan dinar

NATIONAL FLAG: A solid green field, green being the traditional color of Islam

NATIONAL EMBLEM: A green eagle with a green shield on its breast. In the base is the nation's name in Arabic.

NATIONAL ANTHEM: "Almighty God"

NATIONAL HOLIDAYS: September 1 (National Day; Revolution Day); March 28 (Evacuation Day); June 11 (Evacuation Day); October 7 (Evacuation Day); December 24 (Independence Day); also variable Islamic festivals

NATIONAL CALENDAR: The Islamic Hegira calendar is official and mandatory. It is a lunar calendar beginning in 622.

PHYSICAL QUALITY OF LIFE INDEX: 57

DATE OF INDEPENDENCE: December 24, 1951

DATE OF CONSTITUTION: December 11, 1969, amended March 2, 1977

WEIGHTS & MEASURES: Metric

GEOGRAPHICAL FEATURES

Libya is on the central Mediterranean coast of North Africa and extends 1,502 km. (933 mi.) from the coast to the north-central highlands of the Sahara and 1,989 km. (1,236 mi.) from the Egyptian border to the east to the Algerian border to the west. Libya's total area of 1,759,540 sq. km. (679,360 sq. mi.) makes it the fourth-largest country in Africa and as large as France, Italy, Spain and West Germany combined.

The total length of Libya's land boundaries and coastline is 6,032 km. (3,748 mi.). The land borders, with six nations, are as follows: Egypt (1,115 km.; 693 mi.); Sudan (383 km.; 238 mi.); Chad (1,054 km.; 655 mi.); Niger (354 km.; 220 mi.); Algeria (982 km.; 610 mi.); and Tunisia (459 km.; 285 mi.). The borders with Algeria and Chad were delimited by the Franco-Libyan Treaty of 1955 as amended in 1956. There is an active border dispute with Chad. The total length of the coastline is 1,685 km. (1,047 mi.).

The capital of Libya is Tripoli, but in September 1988 it was announced that all but two of the secretariats of the General People's Committee were to be relocated from Tripoli mostly to Sirte, 400 km. (249 mi.) east of Tripoli. The population of Tripoli in 1984 was 990,697 and that of Benghazi 485,386. The other major urban centers are: Zuwarah (181,584), noted for camel breeding; Al Baydah (120,662); Al Khums (149,642), a tourist center; Misurata (178,295), noted for its carpet industry; Darnah (105,031); Al Marj (102,763), almost completely rebuilt after a disastrous earthquake in 1963; Sabhah (76,171), an oasis town in the interior; and Tobruk (94,006), the site of a crucial World War II battle.

The major topographical areas are Tripolitania (Western Muqataa), Cyrenaica (Eastern Muqataa) and Fezzan (Southern Muqataa). Tripolitania consists of a series of terraces of different levels rising in the main toward the South like a flight of steps. A low-lying coastal plain known as the Jafara terminates in a line of hills, Jabal Nafusah, 322 km. (200 mi.) long; it is a plateau ranging from 600 m. to 900 m. (2,000 to 3,000 ft.). South of this jabal lies a rocky and barren plateau region known as Hamada el-Homra, or red, stony desert. This plateau features a number of depressions, or playas, such as Sabkhat Ghuzayyil and Sabkhat al-Qanayyin. Cyrenaica consists of al-Marj Plain, which rises in two narrow steps to an upland plateau called Jabal al-Akhdar, or Green Mountain. This plateau, rising to 600 m. (2,000 ft.) in elevation, gives the region a rugged coastline. The western side of the jabal falls steeply to the Gulf of Sirta, while the eastern side, known as Marmarica, falls more gradually, in a series of ridges. South of Jabal al-Akhdar is a lowland desert with a few oases, Jalo and Jaghbub in the North, and Jawf, Zighen al-Kufra, the largest of all, in the South. In the far South of Cyrenaica lie the Central Saharan Mountains, known as the Tibesti Ranges, whose highest peak is 3,150 m. (10,335 ft.) high. The Fezzan region is a series of depressions with a few oases. The main highlands of Fezzan are Jabal al-Sawda and Haruj al-Aswad in the central portion and Jabal bin Ghunaymah in the Southwest. The rest of the country consists of the Libyan Desert; the pebble plain of Sarir Calanscio; and the huge sand seas of Marzuq, Awbari and Raby-anah.

There are no permanently flowing rivers but only watercourses known as wadis that are dry in summer but are flooded during rains. The most notable of these are Wadi Lebda, Wadi Sawfajjin, Wadi Zamzam, Wadi Majinin, Wadi Etlah, Wadi Qattarah, Wadi Tilal, Wadi al-Glass, Wadi Darnah, Wadi Marqas and Wadi al-Maal-legh.

CLIMATE & SEASONS

The climate of Libya is influenced by both the Sahara and the Mediterranean Sea. The northern area is typically Mediterranean, generally warm and dry. Winter is fairly cold in the North with sleet and snow on the hills. Weather transitions are abrupt, and there are wide variations in temperature.

The country has five climate zones: the coastal strip in Tripolitania and Cyrenaica, with hot, humid summers and rainfall ranging from 200 to 400 mm. (8 to 16 in.); the maritime and continental steppe in Tripolitania and Cyrenaica, with a higher range of diurnal temperatures and rainfall ranging from 300 to 350 mm. (12 to 14 in.); the northern highlands, with lower summer temperatures and colder winters and rainfall ranging from 50 to 610 mm. (2 to 24 in.); and the predesert and the desert, with temperatures rising to 43.3°C (110°F) and irregular and infrequent rainfall. Average mean summer temperatures are 40.6°C to 46°C (105°F to 115°F) along the Tripolitanian coast, 26.7°C to 32°C (80°F to 90°F) in northern Cyrenaica and 26°C (79°F) in Tobruk.

The winds blow from the north and east between May and October and from the west and north between November and April. The strongest and hottest of these winds are the *ghibli* and the *gadamsi*. The *ghibli* is a dry, sand-laden wind from the South that can raise temperatures by 17 to 22° (30 to 40°F) within a few hours; damage growing crops; and scorch human beings. The *ghibli* is most frequent in the spring and autumn but may blow during any season of the year.

POPULATION

The population of Libya was estimated in 1990 at 4,221,141. The projection is based on the last official census, in 1984, when the population was 3,637,488. Nomads and seminomads are estimated to constitute about one-sixth of the population. They have been declining as a segment of the population since the 1970s, when the government attempted to convert them into villagers. The confiscation of unclaimed land and the upheaval of long-standing but officially unprofitable villages was common. Modernization of viable villages included electrification and provision of water, radio and even television. The numbers of seminomads are expected to decline still further in the future.

The population is heavily concentrated in the northern fringes of Cyrenaica and Tripolitania. Nearly 90% of the population live on 10% of the land area, and 75% live within 10 km. (6 mi.) of the sea. Tripolitania accounts for 66% of the population, Cyrenaica for 29% and Fezzan for 5%. Nearly 25% of the population live in the governorate of Tarabulus, which has less than 1% of the land area.

As with most Muslim countries, Libya reports a high percentage of males in the population. In the 1984 census there was a ratio of 53.61 males to 46.39 females. The population is young, with 44.7% under 15 years of age.

The urban population constituted 64.5% of the total population in 1984, as compared to 22% in 1954 and 27% in 1964. Urbanization was most obvious in the growth of the cities of Tripoli and Benghazi, which

DEMOGRAPHIC INDICATORS

Population (millions): 4.21 (1990)
Year of last census: 1984
Sex distribution (%, 1973 census): males, 53.61; females, 46.39
Population estimates and projections (millions)

1930: .800	1960: 1.349	1990: 4.206
1940: .900	1970: 1.982	2000: 5.559
1950: 1.029	1980: 3.034	2010: 6.990

Age profile (%, 1973 census)

0–14: 44.7	30–44: 15.7	60–74: 3.2
15–29: 25.3	45–59: 7.4	75 and over: 0.6

Median age (yrs.): 16.8 (1985)
Youth population (% aged 15–24): (1985) 18.0; (2000) 19.1
Total dependency ratio, 1985: 95.0
Annual growth rate (%)

1950–55: 1.80	1975–80: 4.37	2000–2005: 3.38
1955–60: 3.61	1980–85: 4.37	2005–10: 3.08
1960–65: 3.70	1985–90: 3.65	2010–15: 2.71
1965–70: 4.04	1990–95: 3.62	2015–20: 2.37
1970–75: 4.17	1995–2000: 3.54	2020–25: 2.09

Hypothetical size of stationary population (millions): 35
Assumed year of reaching net reproduction rate of 1: 2050
Urban population (000): 2,440 (1985)
Urban population (%): (1988) 67; (1965) 26
Annual urban population growth rate (%, 1985–90): 5.35
Annual rural population growth rate (%, 1985–90): 0.16
Percentage of urban population in largest city: 64 (1980)
Percentage of urban population in cities of population over 500,000: 64.5 (1980)
Number of cities of population over 500,000: 1 (1980)
Population density per sq. km. (per sq. mi.): 2.4 (6.2) (1990)

VITAL STATISTICS

Crude birth rate (/1,000): 37 (1990); 49 (1965)
Crude death rate (/1,000): 7 (1990); 18 (1965)
Infant mortality rate (/1,000 live births): 82 (1987)
Maternal mortality rate (/100,000 live births): 64 (1990)
Life expectancy (yrs.) at birth (1980–85): males, 65; females, 70 (1990)
Gross reproduction rate (/woman) (1980–85): 3.50
Total fertility rate (/woman): 5.2 (1990)
Rate of natural increase (/1,000) (1980–85): 34.5
Marriage rate (/1,000): 6 (1979)
Average family size: 5.4 (latest)

STATUS OF WOMEN INDICATORS
Number of women (000): 1,708 (1985)
% Women of childbearing age 15–49: 44 (1988)
% women literate: 62 (1985)
% women in labor force: 8.7 (1988)
Total fertility rate (/woman): 5.2 (1990)

grew at an annual rate of 8.2% during the 1960s and early 1970s. Migration from rural to urban areas has resulted in a significant shift of population, much of it permanent and is expected to result in a deterioration of urban living and the emergence of shantytowns. There are more than 24 towns with populations over 50,000.

The country's need for skilled workers and professional and technical experts has encouraged a steady flow of immigrants into the country. The number of foreigners is estimated to exceed 200,000, among whom are included Greeks, Maltese, Italians, Egyptians, Pakistanis, Turks, Indians and Tunisians. Offsetting this immigration was the exodus of over 100,000 Italians since 1939, including 25,000 who left after the expropriation of their farms in 1970, and 38,000 Jews, most of whom immigrated to Israel under pressure of persecution after the establishment of Israel as a Jewish homeland. More than 3,000 Egyptians and 5,000 Tunisians were ordered to leave Libya in 1976 as a retaliatory measure against their home countries. Because emigration of Libyans to other countries is slight, Libya has had a net gain in population through immigration equal to 6% to 10% since 1970.

The traditional, conservative cultural attitudes of Libya's Islamic society serve to restrict the rights of certain groups, most notably women. Within the confines of Islamic beliefs, Qaddafi has taken a leadership role in efforts to change the status of women and expand their access to educational and employment opportunities. Although his proposal that women along with men be subject to military conscription was originally defeated, Qaddafi succeeded in having the decision reversed, and women currently receive basic military training and are subject to a draft. Women make up 8.1% of the official labor force, with one-third of this number involved in unpaid agricultural work and the rest in civil service, health and education. There is minimal female representation in government.

The Libyan government favors a policy of population expansion for demographic and economic reasons. Birth control programs are therefore discouraged. Population policies have concentrated on stabilizing the rural population and stemming the flow of migration to the cities from rural areas. These programs have included resettlement of urban workers on farms and improvement of the standard of living in the countryside.

ETHNIC COMPOSITION

Libya has a highly homogeneous population, with Arab Muslims of mixed Arab-Berber ancestry constituting 90% of the population. Libya has been described as the most Arab of the Arab states outside of Saudi Arabia. However, because of considerable intermarriage between Arab invaders and indigenous people over the centuries, few Libyans can claim pure Arabian ancestry. Berber descent outweighs Arab in the population at large.

The principal ethnic minorities are Berbers, Touaregs, Tebus and black Africans. Berbers, defined as native speakers of a Berber dialect, account for about 4% of the population. There are Berber enclaves in coastal towns and oases, but the Berbers live primarily in small, secluded villages in inaccessible mountain areas. Berbers are generally light-skinned and tall. They farm or herd in single-family households. Although Berber men assume Arabic dress and language, they conceal their women and thus maintain Berber language and customs in the family. Berbers belong to the Kharidjite sect of Islam. The Touaregs, black Africans and Tebus are small ethnic groups that are extensions of larger communities outside Libya. Together they constitute about 1% of the population. Arabic-speaking black Africans are known as Harratins.

Egyptians have replaced Italians as the most numerous alien residents and are estimated to number over 100,000.

There is a small urban community of Westerners from Europe and the United States, mainly petroleum personnel and technical advisers. The number of Americans in the country declined following the closure of Wheelus (now Uqba bin Nafi) Air Base. In 1985 Washington warned that Americans living in Libya were doing so at their own risk.

Hostility toward all foreigners, particularly Westerners, is a significant element of Libya's revolutionary ideology. Non-Arabs and non-Muslims work under severe restrictions. This hostility extends to all expressions of Western culture, including books, films, magazines, language and Christian institutions. Libraries and cultural centers run by foreign governments in the country were ordered closed in 1971.

LANGUAGES

Arabic has been the official language of Libya since 1969. Its use in official communications, street signs, private letterheads, and even passports of visiting foreigners is mandatory. The spoken dialects of Tripolitania and Fezzan belong to the Maghrebi group used in the Maghreb countries, while the dialects of Cyrenaica are related to those used in Egypt and the central Middle East.

Minority languages include Berber, a Semitic language distantly related to Arabic but with a limited written form and literary tradition; and the Tamahek dialect of Berber used by the Tuaregs, with a script known as Tifinagh.

The use of foreign languages such as English and Italian is discouraged.

RELIGION

Sunni Islam is the religion of almost all Libyans. Identification with religion traditionally has been strong in

Libya. Since 1969 the military regime has converted religion into a keystone of state domestic and foreign policy by reaffirming Islamic values and establishing literal Koranic practice in national life at home and propagating Islam abroad. The Constitutional Declaration of 1969, while guaranteeing freedom of practicing religious rites to all religious groups, declared Islam to be the state religion. The Qaddafi regime, however, has opposed the Sanusi movement, which constituted the mainstream of religious life in Libya until 1969.

In an effort to restore the cultural and religious values of Islam to a central place in Libyan society, the Qaddafi regime has enacted laws in accordance with orthodox Muslim practice. These have included a ban on alcohol, bars, nightclubs and miniskirts. Two early acts of the regime were the appointment of a grand mufti for the country to supervise religious affairs, and conversion of Sacred Heart of Jesus Cathedral in Tripoli to Gamal Abdel Nasser Mosque.

Propagation of Islam abroad has been accepted as a state duty by the Qaddafi regime. Much of Libya's new oil wealth is being expended on extending financial aid to Muslim institutions and movements throughout the world, while the Jihad Fund, supported by a payroll tax, subsidizes Muslim guerrilla movements opposing Israel, the Philippines, Ethiopia and other countries. The University of Libya is charged with spearheading a revival of Arabic civilization, training Muslim missionaries, preserving Islamic legacy "and working to present the truth of Islaam and its affect on the glory of Man." Further, the Islamic Missionary Organization (Daawa al Islamiya) has been founded with the object of furthering the spread of Islam throughout the world.

The number of Christians in Libya is estimated at 38,000. Services are permitted in Christian churches, which are exclusively attended by the foreign community. The Roman Catholic Church in Libya has three apostolic vicariates, at Tripoli, Benghazi and Darna, and there is one apostolic prefecture. The Episcopal Church in Jerusalem and the Middle East and the Coptic Orthodox Church also are represented.

Nearly all of the formerly sizable Jewish community has emigrated, and no information is available on the status of any Jews who may remain. Qaddafi has stated that he is opposed to Zionism, not Judaism, and that Arab nations should welcome Arab Jews who wish to return to their countries of origin. But in a speech in June 1985 he cited the prophet Muhammad as stating that Judaism and Islam cannot coexist in the land of the Arabs, and in September 1985, in virulently anti-Jewish broadcasts on Libyan radio, he called for anti-Jewish violence in areas of Tunisia within broadcast range.

HISTORICAL BACKGROUND

Libya was under Italian rule from 1912 until 1942, when British and French troops occupied the country. The United Kingdom governed Cyrenaica and Tripolitania, while France administered Fezzan from that time until independence.

A U.N. resolution in 1949 led to Libyan independence as the United Kingdom of Libya in 1951. The postindependence period can be divided into two distinct phases. The first, under King Idris, was a time of internal political stability and economic growth that, as a result of oil discoveries, permitted the nation to end its dependence on Western funds. Idris's reign also was a period of good relations with the Arab world and with the West, although by the mid-1960s Libya had become an outspoken critic of Israel and South Africa.

A bloodless revolution in 1969 brought about a complete change in government and the establishment of the Libyan Arab Republic, with Col. Muammar al-Qaddafi as chairman of the Revolution Command Council (RCC), which functioned as the executive. Qaddafi dissolved the legislature and declared the Socialist People's Libyan Arab Jamahiriya. Over the next five years he began a series of reforms that transformed every aspect of society. He nationalized banks and forced oil companies to sell 51% of their holdings to the Libyan government. In foreign affairs he moved to the left, supporting the Palestine Liberation Organization (PLO) and Syria. In 1973 he initiated his "cultural revolution" as set forth in his *Green Book*. It was an attempt to eliminate all foreign ideologies and to blend Arab socialism and Islamic fundamentalism in the administration of the country.

In 1975 the General National Congress of the Arab Socialist Union became the nation's legislative body. The following year its name was changed to the General People's Congress (GPC). The body had minimal legislative power; real power remained in Qaddafi's hands. The Constitution was amended in 1977 to declare the nation's adherence to socialism and Arab unity. Direct people's authority was set forth as the basis of Libyan political order in the form of People's Congresses and Popular Committees. The Koran was declared the social code of the country.

During the 1970s and 1980s Qaddafi indiscriminately backed terrorism, providing arms, money and asylum for any revolutionary cause he supported without regard for the issues behind the movements. Libyan funds went to Ulster, Chad, Sudan, Morocco, Uganda and Zimbabwe as well as the more extreme wings of the PLO.

In foreign affairs Qaddafi attempted to forge alliances with other Arab states, many of whom were deterred by his volatile leadership style. Libya's support of terrorism and repression of dissent angered many Western nations. In 1984 Great Britain severed diplomatic relations following a series of bomb attacks in Britain aimed at Libyan dissidents. Conflict with the United States came to a head in 1986, when the United States bombed Tripoli and Benghazi in response to Libyan missile attacks on U.S. planes and terrorist attacks on U.S. personnel in Europe.

In the mid-1970s Libya annexed the Aozou Strip in Chad and became an active participant in that nation's civil war, generally opposing the forces of President Hissein Habre. Qaddafi was humiliated in 1987 when his militarily superior forces were resoundingly de-

RULERS OF LIBYA

Kingdom

December 1951–September 1969: Idris a-Sanusi

Republic

September 1969– : Mu'ammar al-Qaddafi

feated by those of the Chadian government. This defeat came during a period of economic decline as a result in the drop of world oil prices. Many observers saw conditions ready for a coup, but Qaddafi emerged unscathed.

In response to the events of the mid-1980s Qaddafi modified his political and diplomatic programs. In 1987 he appointed the pragmatic Omar Muntasir as prime minister and outlined a series of reforms designed to privatize business and curb public investment programs. He offered amnesty to many political prisoners and endorsed a charter of human rights. In 1988 he restored diplomatic relations with Chad. The following year all state institutions were abolished. Also in 1989, Qaddafi restored full diplomatic relations with Egypt.

Libya's international posture during the Persian Gulf war in 1990 and 1991 was non-confrontational. Although Qaddafi disapproved of the occupation of Kuwait by Iraq, he could not support the U.S. leadership role of the U.N. force that assembled in Saudi Arabia. However, the need for improved relations with the United States underlay Libyan policy in 1990 and 1991. In January 1991, Libya supported a French proposal for peace in the Persian Gulf. Moreover, it was later reported that during the Persian Gulf war, Libya had reined in terrorist groups under its sponsorship.

CONSTITUTION & GOVERNMENT

The present Constitution was ratified by the General People's Congress (GPC) in 1977. It declared the nation's adherence to socialism, commitment to Arab unity and readiness to defend freedom at home and abroad. It stated that direct people's authority was the basis for political order and that the Koran formed the social code of the nation.

Executive power is assigned to Muammar al-Qaddafi as revolutionary leader. He is head of state and commander in chief of the armed forces, although he periodically renounces these titles to devote himself to "ideological study." The daily administration of the country is in the hands of the General People's Committee, led by the prime minister. In the past Qaddafi was able to override Committee decisions. But his influence weakened in the late 1980s.

The 1,112-member General Party Congress (GPC) acts as the legislative body. Members are elected by people's committees, trade unions and professional organizations. All are members of the Arab Socialist Union, the only legal political party. The GPC has little real power.

The judiciary consists of the Supreme Court, courts of appeal and courts of first instance and summary courts. The Supreme Court is the highest court in the land.

ORGANIZATION OF LIBYAN GOVERNMENT

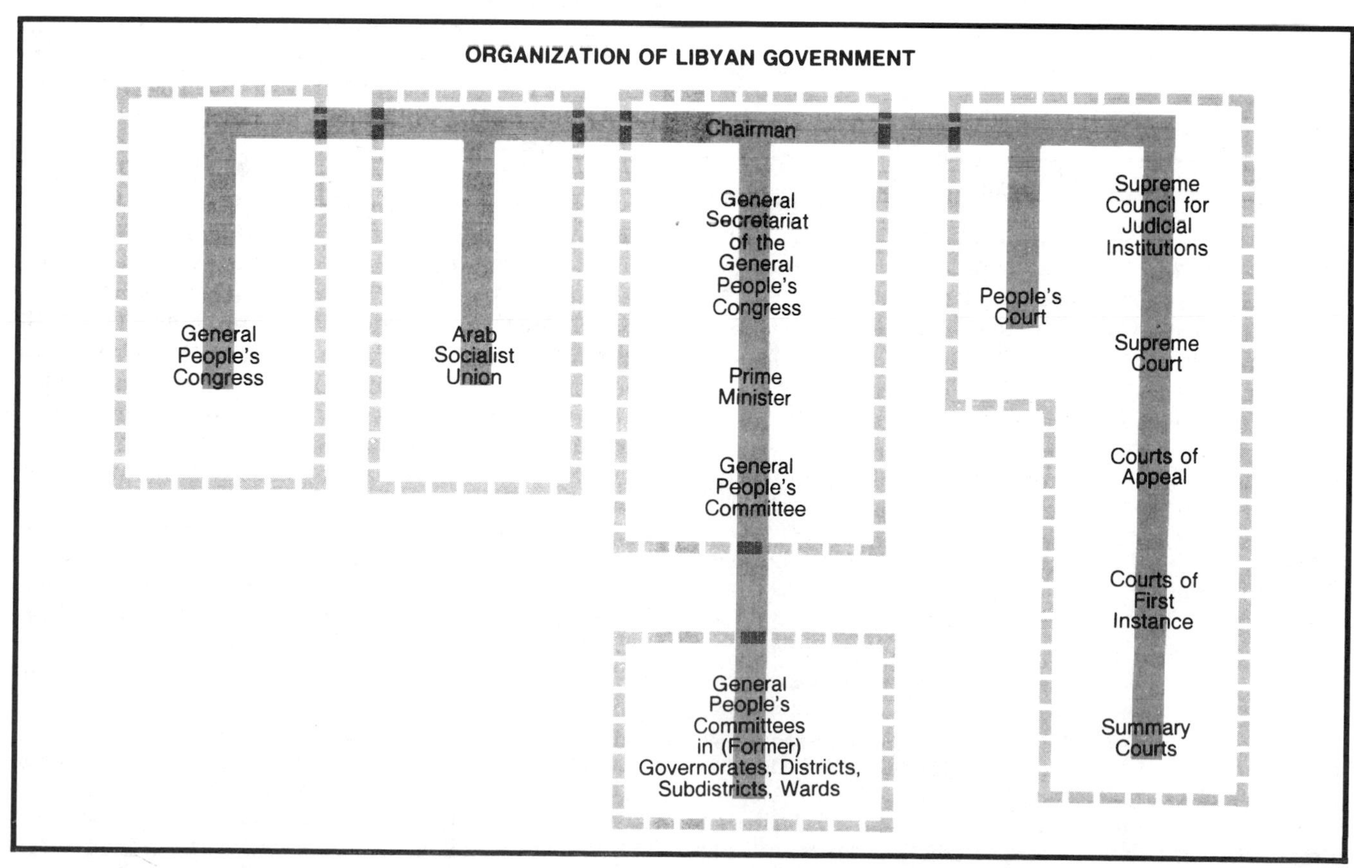

GOVERNMENT LIST
(July/August 1991)

Leader	Qaddafi, Mu'ammar Abu Minyar al-, *Col.*
Secretary, General People's Congress	Sawsa, Abd al-Raziq al-
Secretary, General People's Committee	Durda, Abu Zayd Umar
Secretary of Agrarian Reform & Land Reclamation	Qu'ud, Abd al-Majid al-
Secretary of Arab Maghrev Union Affairs	Rajab, Muhammad Zarruq
Secretary of Communications & Transport	Hinshari, Izz al-Din al-
Secretary of Economy & Planning	Muntasir, Umar Mustafa al-
Secretary of Education	Abu Tuwayrat, Madani Ramadhan
Secretary of Electricity	Arbash, Juma Salim al-
Secretary of Health	Zaydan, Badr Zaydan
Secretary of Heavy Industry	Shatwan, Fathi Ahmad
Secretary of Higher Education	Abu Bukhzam, Ibrahim Misbah
Secretary of Information & Culture	Abu Jaziya, Ali Milud
Secretary of Justice	Bakkar, Ibrahim Muhammad
Secretary of Light Industry	Shatwan, Fathi Ahmad
Secretary of Marine Resources	Kuaybah, Miftah Muhammad
Secretary of People's Committee's Affairs	Shuhumi, Sulayman Sasi al-
Secretary of the People's Congress's Affairs	Ishkal, Umar
Secretary of the People's External Liaison & International Cooperation Bureau	Bishari, Ibrahim Muhammad
Secretary of Petroleum	Badri, Abdallah Salim al-
Secretary of Religious Affairs	Sharif, Ahmad
Secretary of Scientific Research	Madani, Nuri al-Fayturi al-
Secretary of Services & Public Works	Funayr, Salim Ahmad
Secretary of Social Security	Sharadah, Ismail Miftah
Secretary of Strategic Industries	Talhi, Jadallah Azzuz al-
Secretary of Supervision and Follow-up	Litayf, Ammar Mabruk
Secretary of Treasury	Bukhari, Muhammad al-Madani al-
Secretary of Vocational Congress's Affairs	Huwaydi, Bashir Huwayj
Secretary of Vocational Training	Matuq, Matuq Muhammad
Secretary of Youth & Sports	Hawdah, Bukari Salim
Governor, Central Bank	Zilitni, Abd al-Hafidh

As of the end of 1989 power remained securely in the hands of Qaddafi and the General People's Committee. It appears that the collective military leadership continues to receive the support and loyalty of the armed forces and the approval or passive endorsement of the general populace. That there is internal dissent is indicated by at least five coup attempts since 1969: one led by Adam Said Hawwaz and Musa Ahmad in 1969, a tribal uprising in 1970, a coup led by Omar Miheishi in 1975, a coup attempt in 1978 and a series of commando attacks in 1984 by members of the National Front for the Salvation of Libya.

The 1975 coup (whose leaders, Maj. Omar Abdallah al-Meheishi and Maj. Abdul Moneim al-Huni, later fled to Egypt) was followed by the execution of at least 22 officers accused of involvement, the first death sentences carried out in the country since 1954. An opposition movement of Libyan exiles in Europe known as al-Tajammu al-Watani began to smuggle anti-Qaddafi literature into the country. In 1978 the fourth coup was uncovered, leading to the arrest of the head of Libya's Security and Intelligence Service, Capt. Muhammad Idris al-Sharif. In the ensuing investigation about 100 officers and men of the 7th Armored Brigade at Benghazi were arrested.

In 1980 Qaddafi launched a drive against both domestic and foreign opposition, warning exiles to return to Libya or be "liquidated." Within Libya over 2,000 persons were reported to be under arrest, while anti-Qaddafi exiles were shot and killed by hit squads in London, Paris and Rome. The original 12 members of the old RCC have been reduced to four by death or defection.

FREEDOM & HUMAN RIGHTS

In terms of civil and political rights Libya is classified as a not-free country.

Variously described as a socialist or an Islamic country, Libya has established a reputation as patron of a wide variety of terrorist groups in every area of the globe. At the same time, it has established a not-so-well-known reign of terror at home that has become increasingly brutal and intolerant. International press reports have alleged that over 2,000 enemies of Qaddafi have been arrested and that hundreds have been tortured to death. Detainees are frequently beaten during interrogation, a practice that is condoned by government officials. Amnesty International bulletins are full of accounts of deaths during custody. Qaddafi also pursued his enemies abroad. The Third Conference of Revolutionary Councils in 1980 declared: "Physical liquidation [is] the final stage in the revolutionary struggle." In the months following this declaration, at least 11 expatriate Libyan dissidents were assassinated by Qaddafi's hit squads, including a Libyan graduate student in Colorado. Amnesty International further reports that a number of former businessmen, government officials and political activists have simply disappeared after being summoned by the police for questioning.

On March 10, 1983, Amnesty International warned that Libyans abroad were under threat following a February 17 decision by the General People's Congress that all Libyans considered "hostile" would be liquidated. In early 1984 the government directed resumption of assassinations of Libyan exiles, and in May it announced formation of "suicide squads" to hunt down and kill Libyan dissidents abroad. There have since been assassinations of Libyans in Greece, England, Italy, Germany and Spain. Qaddafi subsequently called on pilgrims to Islamic holy places to attack their fellow Libyans who opposed the "revolution." In November there was a much-publicized claim by the government radio that Libyan agents had assassinated former Libyan prime minister Abdel Hamid al-Bakoush in Cairo, but the Egyptian government revealed that it had intercepted the assassination team, prevented the killing and duped Qaddafi into believing Bakoush had been killed. When Libya claimed credit for the "death," Bakoush was presented alive and well to the press.

Libya's security apparatus operates at various levels, involving not only Qaddafi's personal bodyguards and the official countrywide police/interior establishment but also the Revolutionary Committees and Basic People's Committees, which act independently of other authorities when encouraged by Qaddafi. The result is a complex of multilayered tight controls, not necessarily explicitly dictated, over individual activities and freedoms. The conservative attitudes of a strict Islamic society produce further restrictions on the individual freedoms and rights of certain groups, such as businesspersons.

Under Libyan law, detainees may be held incommunicado for unlimited periods. Many allegedly are held without charge or trial, apparently as an example to would-be opponents of the regime. Qaddafi has justified imprisonment on political as opposed to criminal charges. In a 1981 speech he stated, "Those who are put into prisons are there because they are enemies of the people. There is no shame and there is nothing wrong in putting these persons in prison or in treading on them with your feet." In March 1985, in addressing the General People's Congress, Qaddafi again encouraged Revolutionary Committees to investigate and arrest persons guilty of treason whose cases, for whatever reason, the police could not handle. Although he also opposed secret arrests, there is no evidence that this exhortation has resulted in any improvement in practice. Foreigners are not immune from arbitrary arrest. Four British citizens were arrested in 1984 and held for 10 months in apparent retaliation for the United Kingdom's arrest of Libyans responsible for bombings and assassinations in the United Kingdom. While Qaddafi disclaimed personal responsibility, stating that these arrests resulted from the action of "the people," he did acknowledge that the issues was "basically political." The four eventually were released following negotiations conducted on their behalf by Terry Waite, an aide to the archbishop of Canterbury.

Basic freedoms of speech and expression are increasingly restricted. Token criticism is permitted, but only at party meetings. The media are controlled rigorously, and newspapers do not even print editorials. There are a number of restrictions on traveling abroad.

CIVIL SERVICE

In 1969 the RCC established the General Administration of the Civil Service under the office of the prime minister, with the function of reorganizing the civil service and purging it of foreign elements. The Central Directorate of Administrative Surveillance was set up in 1970, and the Ministry of Civil Service was added to the cabinet in 1972; however, that post was later eliminated.

Civil servants are governed by the Civil Service Law of 1964. Entry into the service is on the basis of competitive examinations. Positions are classified into a sequence of grades, each with a salary schedule.

LOCAL GOVERNMENT

From 1951 to 1963 Libya was divided into three semi-autonomous divisions—Cyrenaica, Tripolitania and Fezzan—corresponding to historical and topographical regions. In 1963 the kingdom was divided into 10 *mohafadas*, or governorates, each under a *mohaafiz*, or governor. The governorates were divided into *mutasarrifiyaat*, or districts, each under a *mutasarrif*, or district chief. The districts, in turn, were subdivided into *mudiriyat*, each headed by a *mudir*, or chief. Municipalities such as Tripoli and Benghazi were divided into *aqsam*, or wards, each with a *mukhtar*, or headman, who was invariably a tribal sheikh.

This form of local government was retained by the RCC when it assumed power in 1969. All local government officials were appointed by the RCC, and at least half the number of governors were members of the police or armed forces. Municipal and local councils, where they functioned, had only nominal and advisory powers. In 1974 all *mohafadas* were abolished and the administrative structures and departments of the local governments were transferred to the central ministries. Control offices were established in the major municipalities. The towns themselves were subdivided into quarters, each quarter having its own Basic People's Committee.

The country is now divided into three provinces and 10 governorates: Al-Bayda, Al-Khums, Awbari, Az-Zawiyah, Benghazi, Darnah, Gharyan, Misratha, Sabhah and Tarabulus. Administration based on "direct people's authority" takes place through local People's Congresses, People's Committees, trade unions and vocational syndicates.

FOREIGN POLICY

The foreign policy of Libya is an extension of its domestic revolutionary and Islamic ideology. Central to this ideology are the themes of Arab unity, Islamic supremacy and unrelenting hostility to Israel and the West. The keen edge of this ideology is the visionary dream or mystique of Arab unity, and its driving force is Islamic puritanism. In his public pronouncements Qaddafi often assumes the role of a latter-day Nassar and a spokesman not merely for Libya but also for the "Arab nation," the "Arab masses" and the "Arab homeland." By 1972 Qaddafi had emerged as the *enfant terrible* of the Arab world, busily exporting his own brand of revolution to such distant and unrelated countries as Malta, the Philippines, Uganda, Ireland and Chad. Nearer home he employed his oil wealth to organize a vast network of terrorism and subversion in Tunisia, Egypt, Morocco, Jordan and Sudan. But his main success has been south of the Sahara, where Libyan men and money have been responsible for Libyan-inspired civil war in Chad throughout the 1980s. In October 1988 Libya resumed diplomatic relations with Chad, but the issue of sovereignty of the Aozou Strip, along the border shared by the two countries, remained unresolved.

In 1984 President Reagan declared Libya to be the foremost terrorist state in the world and a major exporter of terrorism. Among the many terrorist groups that Qaddafi supports are Colombia's M19 group, the Kanak Socialist National Liberation Front of New Caledonia and the anti-Turkish Armenians. In March 1986 Qaddafi played host to the Congress of the World

Center for Struggle Against Imperialism and Zionism, which included representatives of the Basque ETA, the Irish Republican Army and Black Muslims from the United States. According to Israeli sources, Libya maintains 20 terrorist training camps, where 7,000 guerrillas are being taught the basics of guerrilla warfare.

In April 1984 members of the "Libyan People's Bureau," or embassy, in London fired on a crowd of demonstrators from within the embassy, killing a British policewoman. This incident followed a series of bombings in London attributed to Libyan terrorists and resulted in the severing of diplomatic relations between Britain and Libya.

Qaddafi's attitude toward Israel has been a source of discord between Libya and other Arab states. He has been strongly opposed to any negotiated settlement and has consistently taken the position that the Arab-Israeli conflict can be resolved only by a *jihad*, or holy war, to exterminate Israel. Qaddafi was not informed of the Egyptian and Syrian plan to attack Israel in 1973, was critical of the Arab battle plan and refused to attend the Algiers meeting after the war. However, he took part enthusiastically in the Arab oil embargo. Endorsing the concept of a guerrilla war of national liberation against Israel, Qaddafi has funneled large funds to the Palestine Liberation Organization (PLO) and applauded every act of their terrorism. He also has recruited Libyan volunteers to serve with Al Fatah and used Uqba bin Nafi (formerly Wheelus) Air Base to equip and train guerrillas from all over the world. Later Quaddafi turned against Yasser Arafat and supported the Syrian-backed faction against him. In 1987 he reconciled himself with Yasser Arafat and actively began to encourage reunification of opposing groups within the PLO. Qaddafi also sided with Syria in its support of Iran against Iraq in the Gulf War.

Libya's relations with neighboring states have been shaped by efforts to translate the slogan of Arab unity into a reality. Between 1971 and 1974 Libya was involved in three abortive attempts at union: with Egypt and Syria (1971), with Egypt (1972) and with Tunisia (1974). In fact, Libya has conducted a love-hate relationship with Egypt since Qaddafi's rise to power, and the attempts at merger have been followed by steadily worsening relations, leading to open border conflict in 1977. Relations are strained with all conservative regimes on the Arabian Peninsula except Saudi Arabia. In August 1984 Libya and Morocco unexpectedly signed a treaty of union in Oujda, Morocco. The proposed Arab-African Federation of the two countries was approved by the GPC in Libya and by referendum in Morocco. Later, in December 1984, Libya and Malta signed a five-year security and military cooperation treaty, which requires Libya to defend Malta if it is requested to do so by the Maltese government.

Three of the earliest acts of the Qaddafi regime set the tone for Libya's worsening relationship with the West: the expropriation of British Petroleum's assets, the expulsion of the Italian community and the forced closure of the U.S. Wheelus Air Base. The United States has been the target of special criticism, although American technology still is respected, Libyan students continue to enroll in American universities and American firms continue to do business in Libya. Trade with Britain and Italy continues to be substantial, and large numbers of Italians reportedly have returned to Libya. Although opposition to communism is one of the main strands of Libyan foreign policy, Libya has entered into various trade and arms agreements with the Soviet Union and East European countries.

Relations with the United States deteriorated in 1981. The Reagan administration had made plain that it objected to Libya's presence in Chad, and in August 1981 relations became even more strained when U.S. fighter aircraft shot down two Libyan jets that had intercepted them over the Gulf of Sirte (or Sidra). In November the U.S. oil company Exxon announced that it was closing down its Libyan operation (as, shortly afterward, did Mobil), and in December President Reagan alleged that a Libyan hit squad had been sent to assassinate him. The discovery in February 1983 of an alleged Libyan coup plot against the Sudanese government further soured relations.

In 1986 Libya and the United States moved closer to a showdown as a result of U.S. naval maneuvers in the Gulf of Sirte. The exercises were designed to test Quaddafi's claim that the entire gulf was Libyan territorial waters, instead of the 19-km. (12-mi.) limit recognized by most nations. The real intention of the operation, however, was to punish Qaddafi for his backing of international terrorism, particularly the bomb attacks in December 1985 on Rome and Vienna airports. Libya had drawn an imaginary "line of death" running approximately from Misurata in the west to Benghazi in the east. The U.S. confrontation with Libya provoked lukewarm support from the United States' closest allies but sharp criticism from Arab nations and the southern flank NATO nations of Italy, Greece and Spain.

In April 1986 further hostilities between the two nations commenced with the bombing of terrorist camps in Libya by U.S. planes.

Libya spends millions every year on supporting not only anti-Israeli terrorist groups but also Muslim revolutionary groups around the world. These subsidies are not shown in the budget but come from separate funds, such as the Jihad Fund and the Defense and Arab Cooperation Fund. Subsidies to more sensitive groups come from secret funds and front organizations, such as the Africa Trading Company in Tripoli, which receives a 5% commission on arms purchases.

Of Qaddafi's many African adventures, only Chad remains as a trophy. (See the chapter on Chad for a history of Libyan involvement in the civil war.) Northern Chad has been virtually annexed by Libya, which maintains an army of 3,000 troops on Chadian territory despite a Franco-Libyan agreement to withdraw all foreign forces.

In 1973 Qaddafi presented a new ideology for international consumption called the "Third Theory," as an alternative to capitalist materialism and communist atheism. The Third Theory called for a return to Muslim fundamentalism as a panacea for the world's ills.

PARLIAMENT

The Senate and the House of Representatives were dissolved after the coup of 1969, and the Constitution of 1969 made no mention of a return to an elected legislature. In 1975 a 1,112-member General National Congress was established, consisting of the members of the Revolutionary Command Council, leaders of the existing people's congresses, trade unions and professional organizations. The Congress held its first session in 1976. In late 1976 the Congress renamed itself the General People's Congress. Although it ratified the Constitution of 1977, it has minimal legislative power.

In prerevolutionary Libya seven elections were held between 1952 and 1968. Universal suffrage was introduced in 1963, and women were permitted to vote, though by social convention they often did not. The age of suffrage is 18. Since 1972 Libya has held at least one referendum and a number of local and federal elections and elections to the regional committees of the Arab Socialist Union (ASU). There are 20 electoral districts and 85 ASU precincts based on population density. Voting is compulsory, and failure to vote is a punishable crime. Military and police personnel are excluded from voting. Electoral committees and judges are provided at each level, and there are procedures for challenging candidates or results. Voting is by written, secret ballot, and all ballot boxes are marked with an identifying symbol for the help of the illiterate. Elections are supervised by the Central Committee for Elections Administration. All candidates must be members of the ASU, over 30 years of age and secondary-school graduates. Multiple candidacies are prohibited, but residence within the district is not required for candidates. Elections are determined by a simple plurality. Participation in elections is mandatory, and the candidates are cleared by the revolutionary committees from among persons who are not "merchants, contractors, tribal advocates, elections brokers, officials of the former [pre-1969] government or people who have been attacked by the power of the revolution." Political parties and tribal or local political groupings are prohibited, and involvement in such activities remains punishable by death.

POLITICAL PARTIES

All political parties were banned under the monarchy, and the ban was continued under the Constitution of 1969. One of the tasks of the Revolutionary Command Council was to create an organization for mass mobilization without legalizing political parties. The answer was the Arab Socialist Union (ASU), which was founded in 1971 and which held its first National Congress in 1972. The ASU is not described as a party in government circles but as a "popular revolutionary alliance of the working forces." Its function is not so much to provide a means of popular participation in government or politics as to generate popular enthusiasm for the regime's policies, politicize the masses, serve as a transmission belt to implement government decisions at local levels and channel local concerns upward, and supply a pervasive network of spies and observers capable of reporting on antigovernment activities.

In terms of its structure, the ASU is a copy of the Egyptian party of the same name and is organized at three levels: basic, governorate and national. At each level the membership cuts across the functional and geographical sectors. Each unit consists of two organs: the Conference, including the whole membership, and the Committee, or the leadership. The Basic Unit Committee consists of 10 members elected for two years, the Governorate Committee of 20 members elected for four years, while the National Committee is the General Secretariat (formerly the RCC) itself. The National Congress consists of delegates from each governorate conference. The number of basic units is fixed at 366.

The actual power of the ASU is slight. During the 1973 cultural revolution it nearly disappeared. When it was reconstituted in 1974 all Libyan citizens over 18 years of age were required to join it.

It is reported that both Baath and Communist parties may be operating clandestinely in the country. The National Front for the Salvation of Libya (NFSL) is the major opposition group. It was established in 1981 in Khartoum, Sudan, and its goal is to "find a democratic alternative."

ECONOMY

Libya has a socialist-oriented economy with state intervention and participation in banking, insurance, public transportation and the petroleum industry. The discovery of oil in 1959 and its development through the 1960s and on into the 1980s transformed the country, which once relied on esparto grass as its chief export, into a major oil producer. Oil accounts for up to 99.9% of export revenues. However, a drastic drop in world oil prices since 1980 resulted in a decrease in revenues and a general weakening of the economy. Despite lowered oil revenues, Libya was, in 1987, the African nation with the highest per capita GNP.

The drive by Qaddafi to transform Libya into a socialist society was accelerated beginning in 1977. With manufacturing, transportation and communications, utilities and banking already fully nationalized, emphasis was placed on replacement of private importers by state trading monopolies and the replacement of small, private shops with state-owned supermarkets. As a result, shortages developed in local markets. Currently more licenses for private shops are being issued, in a move away from universal public control, a move that implies the failure of state-sponsored supermarkets. The nationalization of the services sector was extended to lawyers in private practice, who theoretically work for a national syndicate, and to consultants, architects, engineers and accountants.

A major event in 1978 was the publication of the *Green Book*, Part II, which outlined Qaddafi's economic philosophy. It declared that workers should be partners in their enterprises, not hired hands; that there should be no landlords; and that the accumulation of wealth should be prohibited. Implementation of the *Green Book* philosophy began three months later, when

PRINCIPAL ECONOMIC INDICATORS

Gross National Product (U.S. $ millions): 22,976 (1988)
GNP per capita (U.S. $): 5,410 (1988)
GNP average annual growth rate (%, 1980–89): −6
GNP per capita average annual growth rate (%, 1980–89): −9.9
Average annual rate of inflation (%, 1980–88): 0.1 (latest)

the government seized all landlords' properties (with exceptions for a landlord's own dwelling and with certain provisions for his sons). Col. Qaddafi urgently renewed his earlier demands that workers seize control of their enterprises. They did so throughout the country, and most enterprises were placed under control of worker committees. The third major feature of the *Green Book*, Part II—elimination of holdings of wealth "surplus to need" and progression toward a society where money is unnecessary has never been implemented. Bank accounts are under withdrawal controls. With exchange controls; elimination of rental houses; seizure of private businesses; and an absence from the market of valuables such as gold, fine furniture and Persian carpets, there is no longer an outlet for investment by Libyans with surplus dinars, and large amounts apparently are being held as cash.

Libya's proven oil reserves are able to maintain output for 55 years; production at the country's first offshore oil field, Bouri, was initiated in August 1988. It is thought to be the largest oil field in the Mediterranean. However, lowered demand between 1979 and 1984 resulted in declining average daily production during that period and a concurrent drop in revenues from petroleum. In 1985, to gain a "fair" share of the world market, Libya consistently ignored the production quota of 990,000 bd. that OPEC had imposed. In December 1986 OPEC members further reduced Libya's quota to 948,000 bd.; however, Libya continued to violate quota restrictions. Libya's production quota was later raised by OPEC to 1.037 million bd., but this has not prevented the economic crisis that lowered oil prices have wrought on the Qaddafi government.

Agriculture is a minimal contributor to the GDP, although it employs 18% of the labor force. Unfavorable weather and poor soil have limited production, necessitating importation of 75% of food supplies.

BALANCE OF PAYMENTS, 1988
(U.S. $ millions)

Current account balance: −1,823
Merchandise exports: 5,644
Merchandise imports: −5,753
Trade balance: −109
Other goods, services & income +: 889
Other goods, services & income −: −2,071
Other goods, services & income net: −1,182
Private unrequited transfers: −496
Official unrequited transfers: −37
Capital other than reserves: 433
Net errors & omissions: 270
Total: −1,390
Counterpart items: −126
Total: −1,516
Liabilities constituting foreign authorities reserves: −8 (1983)
Total change in reserves: 1,516

GROSS DOMESTIC PRODUCT

GDP nominal (LD. billions): 6.473 (1986)
GDP by type of expenditure (%), 1986
- Consumption
  - Private: 39
  - Government: 33
- Gross domestic investment: 24
- Foreign trade
  - Exports: 35
  - Imports: −31

Cost components of GDP (%), 1982
- Net indirect taxes: 4
- Consumption of fixed capital: 5
- Compensation of employees: 30
- Net operating surplus: 61

Sectoral origin of GDP (%), 1986
- Primary
  - Agriculture: 4
  - Mining: 38
- Secondary
  - Manufacturing: 5
  - Construction, public utilities: 12
- Tertiary
  - Transportation & communications, trade, finance, other services, government: 40

Average annual sectoral growth rates (%, 1965–80)
- Agriculture: 10.7
- Industry: 1.2
- Manufacturing: 13.7
- Services: 15.5

PUBLIC FINANCE

The Libyan fiscal year is the calendar year. By law, 15% of state revenues from oil are set apart as reserves, and 70% of the remainder is earmarked for development. Progressive taxes are levied on individual incomes and incomes of limited companies. In addition, there is a levy on agricultural income and foreign income, and there is a 4% war tax. There also is a high tariff on luxury items. Government consumption was 33% of the GDP in 1986.

Libya's development plans have attempted to attack all perceived needs simultaneously—agriculture, industry, utilities, transportation and communications, as well as housing and education. The 1981–85 plan also called for a reduction in dependence on oil. No further plans were announced during the 1980s.

Though Libya joined the ranks of donor nations in the early 1970s, there is no organization comparable to those of Kuwait or Abu Dhabi for distributing economic development aid. Foreign aid is extended in an

FOREIGN AID

Total foreign aid (U.S. $ millions): 4.0 (1984)
- Bilateral: 2.2 (1984)
- Multilateral: 1.8 (1984)

Aid from international organizations, total (U.S. $ 000): 2,176 (1985)
- for which World Bank (U.S. $ 000): 0 (1985)

Per capita aid (USA $): 1.1 (1984)

erratic and capricious manner and mostly as a reward for support of Libyan policies. Recipients of Libyan aid have included Malta, Chad, Uganda, Somalia and Zaire.

From 1970–87, Libya received $242 million in aid from Western (non-US) countries.

CURRENCY & BANKING

The Libyan unit of currency is the Libyan dinar, divided into 1,000 dirhams. Coins are issued in denominations of 1, 5, 10, 20, 50 and 100 dirhams; notes are issued in denominations of 250 and 500 dirhams and 1, 5 and 10 dinars.

The dinar replaced the Libyan pound, which was the national currency from 1952 to 1971. It was at par with the pound sterling until 1967. The January 1990 dollar exchange rate was $1 = LD0.2896.

The central bank and the bank of issue is the Central Bank of Libya, which supervises the banking system, regulates the currency and administers exchange control. During the period 1969–70 the military regime nationalized and socialized all commercial banks and by a process of merger reduced their number to five.

FINANCIAL INDICATORS, 1989

Total reserves minus gold (SDRs millions): 3,297
SDRs (millions): 249
Reserve position in IMF (SDRs millions): 244
Foreign exchange (SDRs millions): 2,804
Gold (fine troy oz. millions): 3.60
Ratio of external debt to total reserves (1981): 0.1
Central bank 1989
- Assets %
  - Foreign assets: 26.7
  - Claims on government: 72.2
  - Claims on banks: none
  - Claims on private sector: 1.0
- Liabilities %
  - Reserve money: 45.9
  - Government deposits: 15.0
  - Foreign liabilities: 0.0
  - Capital accounts: 0.0

Money supply 1988
Stock (£.L. billions): 3.012
M^1 per capita: 750
Private banks, 1989
- Assets
  - Loans to government: 0.0
  - Loans to private sector: 70.9
  - Reserves: 25.8
  - Foreign assets: 3.3
- Liabilities
  - Deposits (£.L. billions): 3.280
  - Of which %
    - Demand deposits: 60.4
    - Savings deposits: 34.1
    - Government deposits: 4.2
    - Foreign liabilities: 4.7

External debt 1987
- Debt service (long-term), total millions U.S. $: 249
  - Repayment
    - Principal (%): 96.8
    - Interest (%): 3.2

Debt service ratio: (%) 5.9 (1985)
Receipts of workers' remittances (U.S. $ millions): −496 (latest)
Net direct private investment (U.S. $ millions): 43 (1988)

GROWTH PROFILE
(Annual Growth Rates, %)

Projected population, (1988–2000): 3.6
Projected crude birth rate (/1000) (1990–95): 43.4
Projected crude death rate (/1000) (1990–95): 8.1
Urban population, (1980–88): 6.7
Labor force, ((1985–2000): 3.5
GNP, (1980–89): −6.0
GNP per capita, (1986–88): −5.0
Inflation, (1980–88): 0.1
Manufacturing, (1965–80): 13.7
Money holdings, (1980–88): 2.1
Energy production, (1980–88): −5.0
Energy consumption, (1980–88): 4.8
Exports, (1980–88): −5.4 (latest)
Imports, (1980–88): −14.8

In addition to the commercial banks there are three specialized credit institutions: the Libyan Arab Foreign Bank, the National Industrial and Real-Estate Bank and the National Agricultural Bank.

AGRICULTURE

The agricultural sector has suffered a steep decline in employment and production since the 1960s. Of the total land area, only about 5% is considered agriculturally productive, and of this only 25% is considered arable; 144,000 ha. (356,000 ac.) are under permanent cultivation. Agriculture employed 18% of the labor force in 1988, as against 70% in 1960. Agriculture's contribution to the GDP in 1986 was 4%. Libya's major agricultural crops are barley, wheat, olives, potatoes and tomatoes.

Oil exploration and its rapid development have resulted in a flood of migration from farms to the towns, leaving farmlands deserted. Although Libya exported some foodstuffs under Italian rule, it now has to import 75% of its food requirements. There are serious shortages of flour, rice and fruit. After the expulsion of Tunisian bakers in 1985, there were long bread lines.

Agricultural progress is hampered by a combination of natural and social factors. As a result of government efforts, mechanization has made considerable headway. Yield per acre is the lowest among all the countries of North Africa. Irrigation is limited to 107,000 ha. (264,000 ac.) and depends almost exclusively on groundwater, underground reservoirs and aquifers, whose levels have been falling for nearly half a century. Further, Islamic laws of inheritance have resulted in fragmentation of holdings. Under tribal ownership of land, tenants and sharecroppers have little incentive to invest in soil conservation or productive improvements to land.

The main agricultural areas are the oases along the coast, the steppe and Jebel districts in Tripolitania and the Barce Plain in Cyrenica. The most productive agricultural property includes 36,420 ha. (90,000 ac.) of irrigated farmlands in Tripolitania confiscated from their Italian owners in 1970 and owned by the General Agricultural Company, a state corporation. Other expropriated lands include those belonging to the deposed royal family.

Agricultural development is one of the top priorities of the government. A 10-year plan for agriculture (1974–83) aimed to increase the land under irrigation in the Jafara Plain, Jabal Akhdar and the oases of Kufra and Sarir. The desert is being reclaimed in the Fezzan to grow irrigated fodder crops. Agriculture received the largest sectoral allotment (LD1.226 billion) in the 1976–80 five-year plan. Included in the plan were projects to reclaim 350,000 ha. (864,850 ac.) of cropland and 650,000 ha. (1.6 million ac.) of pastures. In the early 1970s the government also established a number of state corporations under the Ministry of Agriculture and Agrarian Reform. These include the General Organization for Agrarian Reform and Land Reclamation, the General Land Reclamation Company, the General Company for Drilling Water Wells, the Agricultural Cooperative Society, the al-Kufra Agricultural Company, the National Food Commodities Institute and the General Tobacco Corporation.

Given the state of the country's finances, dwindling oil revenues and the reluctance of foreign banks to provide loans, there are doubts as to how the government will pay for what is reputedly the largest contract ever awarded in the Middle East, worth $3.3 billion but expected to cost perhaps twice that amount, which Libya signed with the South Korean construction firm Dong Ah in late 1983. Scheduled for completion in 1990, the contract is for the manufacturing and laying of 2,000 km. (1,243 mi.) of pipe, ultimately to carry 5 million cu. m. (177 million cu. ft.) of water per day from the Southeast, beneath the Sahara, to agricultural projects and towns on the Mediterranean coast. The second stage of what has come to be known as "the great man-made river project" will pipe water from Sawknah to Tripoli, a distance of 600 km. (373 mi.) Three additional phases are expected to link the first and second stages by means of pipes along the coast.

Herding and livestock breeding are almost entirely a nomadic or seminomadic occupation.

Although 63,000 ha. (156,000 ac.) are officially designated as forests, the country has no commercially exploitable forests, and its lumber needs are met by imports. Government efforts at reafforestation include experimental planting of eucalyptus seedlings in soil treated with synthetic rubber spray to prevent the seedlings from being blown away, and planting of windbreakers for dune stabilization.

Libya's fishing grounds abound in tuna, sardines and other fish, but most of the fishing is done by Maltese, Greeks and Italians. There also are rich spongebeds along the continental shelf, which are monopolized by Greek fishermen. The local fish catch, estimated at 7,800 tons in 1986, is insufficient to meet domestic demand, and nearly 9,000 tons of fish are imported annually. There are tuna and sardine canning factories and storage facilities in the principal ports.

Agricultural credit is provided by the Agricultural Bank.

AGRICULTURAL INDICATORS

Agriculture's share of GDP (%): 4 (1986)
Cereal imports (000 metric tons): 1,435 (1988)
Index of Agricultural Production (1979–81 = 100): 177 (1986)
Index of Food Production (1979–81 = 100): 178 (1986)
Index of Food Production per Capita (1979–81 = 100): 119 (1986–88)
Number of tractors: 29,500 (1986)
Total fertilizer consumption (000 metric tons) (1985–86): 56.3
Fertilizer consumption (g./ha., hundreds): 416 (1987–88)
Number of farms (000): 170 (1977)
Farms as % of total land area: 5.1 (1981)
Land use (%): (1977)
  Permanent crops, temporary crops: 33.3 (1981)
  Fallow: 66.7 (1981)
  Meadows & pastures: 79.5 (1981)
Yields: kg./ha. (lb./ac.) 1989
  Grains: 702
  Roots & tubers: 7,030
  Legumes: 1,193
  Fruits (000 metric tons): 291
  Vegetables (000 metric tons): 618
  Milk, kg. (lb.)/animal: 1,560
Livestock (000) 1989
  Cattle: 240
  Horses: 25 (1986)
  Sheep: 5,800
Forestry, 1988
  Production of roundwood, 000 cu. m.: 640
    of which industrial roundwood (%): 16.2
Fishing 1986
  Total catch (000 metric tons): 8.6
    of which marine (%): 100.0

MANUFACTURING

Libya has few natural resources other than oil on which to build industry. Manufacturing contributes 5% to the GDP and employs 15% of the labor force. Tripoli accounts for 56% of the industrial establishments and Benghazi for 14%.

Manufacturing has expanded beyond processing local agricultural products. Industrial products now include petrochemicals, iron, steel and aluminum.

Despite increasing state intervention, the majority of the industrial units are privately owned. In 1969 the RCC issued a decree defining its industrial policy and the roles of the private and public sectors. The decree classified industrial projects as major, intermediate and minor and permitted foreign investment in major and intermediate projects. New industrial enterprises receive tax exemptions, exemptions from customs duties on machinery and raw materials, and state assistance in acquisition of sites. Under a 1970 law companies engaged in foreign trade must be wholly owned by Libyans, while a minimum of 51% of the capital of joint

MANUFACTURING INDICATORS, 1987

Average annual growth rate (%, 1965–80): 13.7
Share of GDP (%): 5 (1986)
Labor force in manufacturing (%): 15.2 (1985)
Value added in manufacturing (U.S. $ millions): 81 (1970)
Total earnings as % of value added: 37 (1970)
Gross output per employee (1980 = 100): 45 (1970)

stock companies must be held by Libyans, and the chairman of the board must be a Libyan national.

MINING

Libya has few mineral resources other than oil. Iron ore reserves estimated at 700 million tons were discovered at Wadi Shatti in 1974. Natron deposits occur in Fezzan, and potash deposits in the Sidra Desert near Maradah.

ENERGY

Libya is the fourth-largest oil producer in the Middle East and the second-largest in Africa. Reserves are estimated at 21.270 billion metric tons—enough to last for 55 years at present rates of production. Natural gas reserves are estimated at 1,218 billion cu. m. In December 1984 the government reported a 25% increase in its oil reserves following the discovery of oil fields believed to contain 2,849 billion bbl. of oil. In 1983 Libya replaced the United Kingdom as the largest supplier of oil to the European Economic Community after Saudi Arabia. One of the cardinal elements of the Libyan government's oil policy is conservation, or controlled production of petroleum, maintaining a proper balance between output and reserves. The main oil-producing fields are at Zliten, where oil was first discovered by Esso in 1959, Gialo, Amal, Waha, Ragouba, Mafoora, Sarir, Dahra, Beida and Idris. The number of producing wells is over 1,600. New discoveries continue to be made. The Libyan National Oil Company struck oil in 1975 in western Libya; Occidental discovered oil in the Sirte Basin; and Aquitaine announced discovery of an offshore field, believed to be Libya's largest. The main terminals are at Marsa Brega, Marsa Hariga (formerly Tobruk), Zuetina, Es-Sidra and Ras Lanuf.

The Ministry of Petroleum coordinates and supervises all petroleum-related activities. Under the ministry are five national companies. The National Oil Corporation (LINOCO), successor to the Libyan General Petroleum Corporation (LIPETCO), undertakes joint ventures with foreign companies; builds and operates refineries, storage facilities, pipelines and tankers, and markets crude and refined petroleum products in Libya. LINOCO includes the nationalized foreign-owned companies Esso, Libya Shell, ENI marketing subsidiaries and Petro Libya. The other national companies are Arabian Gulf Exploration Company, formerly BP; Brega Oil Marketing Company; Umm al-Jawaby Petroleum Company; and National Drilling Company.

By 1973 over 51 foreign oil companies had been nationalized, but the government had not taken a 100% interest in all of them by 1975. Of these, the Oasis Group remained the largest, followed by Occidental, Esso Libya and Esso Sirte, Agip, Mobil, Aquitaine and Amoco. Those that have been completely nationalized include Amoseas, BP/Bunker Hunt, Shell, Texaco, California Asiatic and Atlantic Richfield. Under concessions granted in 1974 the government is to receive 81% to 85% of oil found, with the companies receiving the rest free of taxes or royalties. Some agreements also call for supply of military and industrial equipment to Libya and training of Libyan personnel.

ENERGY INDICATORS

Average annual energy production growth rate (%, 1980–88): −5.0
Energy consumption per capita (000 kg. oil equivalent): 2,719 (1988)
Average annual growth rate of energy consumption (%, 1980–88): 4.8
Electricity 1988
  Installed capacity (million kw.): 2.900
  Production (million kw.-hr.): 16
    % fossil fuel: 100.0
    % hydro: 0.0
    % nuclear: 0.0
  Consumption per capita (kw.-hr.): 3,780
Natural gas
  Proved reserves (billion cu. m.): 1,218 (1990)
  Production (billion cu. m.): 6.000 (1989)
  Consumption (billion cu. m.): 6.125 (1988)
Petroleum
  Proved reserves (million bbl.): 22,800 (1990)
  Years to exhaust proved reserves: 55 (1990)
  Production (million bbl.): 407 (1989)
  Consumption (million bbl.): 58 (1988)
  Refining capacity (bbl./day): 329,000 (1990)
Coal
  Consumption (metric tons): 2,000 (1988)

Libyan crude is the highest-priced in the Middle East and therefore is sensitive to fluctuations in world demand. Libya has been in the forefront of OPEC and OAPEC members demanding controlling interest in or full ownership of oil companies and also higher posted prices and royalties. The Libyan government also favors barter agreements involving the exchange of crude oil for goods and services. Such agreements have been concluded with France, Italy, Yugoslavia, Poland and the Union of Soviet Socialist Republics.

Libya is expanding its downstream facilities in common with other large oil producers. In addition to the 60,000-bpd. refinery at Zawai and two other small, privately owned plants, three more refineries are planned: at Tobruk (220,000 bpd), Misurata (220,000 bpd) and Zuetina (400,000 bpd). A petrochemical complex and a gas liquefaction plant are being built at Marsa Brega. The oil tanker fleet is being enlarged, with three tankers from Japan, two from Yugoslavia and two from Sweden.

LABOR

The economically active population in 1988 numbered 1.062 million, of whom more than 25% were resident foreigners. The labor force is largely unskilled or semiskilled. In 1988 a total of 18% were employed in agriculture, 15% in manufacturing, 27% in services and 24% in government. Projections call for major gains in employment in the manufacturing sector and a sharp decline in agricultural employment.

Because of continuing shortages of skilled manpower, the economy relies on migrant workers, pro-

LABOR INDICATORS, 1985

Total economically active population (000): 1,062
As % of working-age population (15–64): 47.6
% female: 8.1
Activity rate (%) 1973
  Total: 24.1
  Male: 42.3
  Female: 3.5
Employment status (%) 1973
  Employers & self-employed: 23.7
  Employees: 69.6
  Unpaid family workers: 4.2
  Other: 2.6
Average annual growth rate of labor force, 1980–2000 (%): 3.5
Labor under 20 years (%): 5.7 (1973)

fessionals and managers. The number of foreign workers was estimated in 1983 at 550,000, or 37% of the total labor force. More than 68% of professional and managerial positions, 22% of intermediate-level technical jobs and about 1.5% of unskilled jobs were held by foreigners. Over 85% of foreign workers were from Arab countries, with Egyptians constituting the largest single community. In an effort to increase the Libyan share of the work force, the government has permitted foreigners to be employed only if there are no Libyans available with comparable qualifications. Further, all companies must offer training programs under government supervision. The government also requires that preference be shown to Arab nationals over non-Arabs. In 1985, as oil revenues began to plummet, 65,000 foreign workers were summarily expelled, many under humiliating circumstances.

Conditions of labor are governed by the Labor Law of 1970, which provides for a 48-hour workweek and paid annual holidays.

The Labor Law of 1970 also provides for one labor union per trade and establishes procedures for conciliation and arbitration. The largest labor unions are the National Trade Union Federation and the General Union for Oil and Petrochemicals.

FOREIGN COMMERCE

Libya's primary export is petroleum, with peanuts and hides also sources of foreign exchange. Principal imports are machinery, transportation equipment, food and manufactured goods. Most imports come from Italy, the Soviet Union, Germany, the United Kingdom and Japan. The country's main markets are Italy, the Soviet Union, Germany, Spain, France, Belgium, Luxembourg and Turkey.

TRANSPORTATION & COMMUNICATIONS

Since the closure of the Benghazi–Barce line in 1964, Libya has had no railways. However, in 1983 Libya signed an agreement with the People's Republic of China to build a 170-km. (106-mi.) standard-gauge line from Tripoli to Ras Jedir on the Tunisian border. This was to be the first phase of a network that is eventually expected to total 3,000 km. (1,865 mi.).

FOREIGN TRADE INDICATORS, 1987

Exports (U.S. $ billions): 6.1
Imports (U.S. $ billions): 5.0
Balance of trade (U.S. $ billions): 1.1
Annual growth rate, (1980–88), exports (%): −5.4 (latest)
Annual growth rate, (1980–88), imports (%): −14.8 (latest)
International reserves in terms of months of imports: 9.0 (latest)
Terms of trade (1980=100): .47 (latest)
Import Price Index (1980=100): 104.0 (1986)
Export Price Index (1980=100): 40.7 (1986)

Direction of Trade (%), 1982

	Imports	Exports
EEC	51.6	60.6
U.S.	0.9	0.0
U.S.S.R. & East European economies	17.3	20.9
Japan	4.0	0.1

Composition of Trade (%), 1982

	Imports	Exports
Food and agricultural raw materials	17.1	0.0
Fuels and other energy	1.4	99.9
Mineral ores and concentrates	0.4	0.0
Manufactured goods	81.1	0.1
of which chemicals	3.9	N.A.
of which machinery	36.8	N.A.

The main deepwater ports are Tripoli, Benghazi, Tobruk and Misurata. In addition, there are five crude-oil terminals, at Marsa Brega, Marsa Hariga, Zuetina, Es-Sidra and Ras Lanuf. Darna is under development as a port. Both Benghazi and Tripoli are undergoing large-scale expansion. Maritime trade is handled by the state-owned General National Maritime Transport Company.

There are 19,300 km. (11,992 mi.) of roads, including the coastal highway, which runs the whole length of the country from the Egyptian to the Tunisian border and passes through both Tripoli and Benghazi. Another runs from a point south of Misurata through Waddan and Hun to Sadhah and then to Sardalas and Ghat, near the Algerian border. In 1973 Nalut and Ghadames

TRANSPORTATION INDICATORS

Roads (latest)
  Length, km. (mi.): 19,300 (11,992)
  Paved (%): 56
Motor vehicles (latest)
  Automobiles: 428,000
  Trucks and buses: 216,000
  Persons per vehicle: 5.9
Merchant marine
  Vessels: 109 (1989)
  Total deadweight tonnage (000): 1,462.5 (1989)
Ports (pre-1986)
  Cargo loaded (000 metric tons): 47,172
  Cargo unloaded (000 metric tons): 6,975
Air (latest)
  Km. (mi.) flown (millions): 9.5 (5.9) (1985)
  Passenger-km. (passenger-mi.) (millions): 1,447 (900)
  Freight-km. (freight-mi.) (millions): 3.5 (2.4)
  Mail ton-km. (mail ton-mi.): 0.4 (0.1) (1985)
  Airports with scheduled flights: 11 (1990)
Pipelines 1990
  Refined, km. (mi.): 443 (275) (includes 265 km.; 165 mi. liquid petroleum gas)
  Natural gas, km. (mi.): 1,947 (1,210)

COMMUNICATION INDICATORS, 1986

Telephones
  Total (000): 500 (1987)
  Persons per telephone: 7.8 (1987)
Post office
  Number of post offices: 317
  Pieces of mail handled (000): 78,758
Telecommunications (1990)
  16 satellite stations

TOURISM & TRAVEL INDICATORS, 1988

Total tourist receipts (U.S. $ millions): 3
Expenditures by nationals abroad (U.S. $ millions): 210

were linked by a 350-km. (217-mi.) road. A 690-km. (429-mi.) road connecting Tripoli and Sebha, and one 626 km. (389 mi.) long, from Agedabia in the North to Kufra in the Southeast, were opened in 1983. The Tripoli–Ghat section (941 km.; 585 mi.) of the 1,352-km. (840-mi.) national road was opened in September 1984. There is a road crossing the desert from Sebha to the frontiers of Chad and Niger.

There are five pipelines connecting the crude oil terminals with the producing fields. A pipeline connects the Zliten oil fields with Marsa Brega. Another pipeline joins the Sarir oil field with Marsa Hariga, the port of Tobruk. A pipeline from the Sarir field to Zuetina was opened in 1968.

The national airline is Libyan Arab Airlines, which operates a fleet of 62 aircraft flying to more than 25 foreign cities. There are four civil airports: Tripoli International Airport at Ben Gashir; Benina, near Benghazi; Sebha; and Misurata. A new $90-million international airport is being built at Benghazi, and a new airport is being built at Ghat. Of the total of 115 airfields, 105 are usable, 35 have permanent-surface runways and 23 have runways over 2,500 m. (8,000 ft.). There are two seaplane stations.

There is little tourism. In 1972 Qaddafi declared that he did not favor government investment to encourage foreigners to visit Libya.

DEFENSE

The defense structure is headed by Qaddafi as commander in chief of the armed forces and as defense minister. The highest rank in the armed forces is colonel.

Compulsory military service was introduced in 1975. The conscription service period is two years.

The total strength of the armed forces is 73,000, or 19.4 armed personnel per 1,000 inhabitants.

Army

Personnel: 55,000

Organization: headquarters, 1 tank and 1 mechanized infantry division; 20 tank battalions; 30 mechanized infantry battalions; 1 National Guard brigade; 10 artillery and 2 AA artillery battalions; 2 special forces groups (10 battalions); 3 air defense regiments; 2 SSM brigades; 3 air defense regiments; 9 SAM battalions.

Equipment: 2,800 tanks; 700 mechanized infantry combat vehicles; 500 reconnaissance combat vehicles; 1,160 armored personnel carriers; 420 guns; 734 howitzers; 600 rocket launchers; 450 mortars; 48 surface-to-surface missiles; 200 antitank rocket launchers; 3,000 antitank guided weapons; 450 air defense guns; 350 SAM's

Navy

Personnel: 6,500 (including Coast Guard)

Units: 6 submarines; 5 frigates; 9 corvettes; 37 fast attack craft; 5 patrol craft; 7 mine-countermeasures vessels; 6 amphibious vessels; 1 transport

Naval bases: Tripoli, Benghazi, Darnah, Tobruk, Burayqah

Air Force

Personnel: 10,000

Organization and equipment: 535 combat aircraft; 42 armored helicopters; 1 bomber squadron; 3 interceptor squadrons; 5 fighter squadrons; 1 counterinsurgency squadron; 1 reconnaissance squadron; 2 transportation squadrons; 8 helicopter squadrons; 4 training squadrons; SAM's: 3 brigades, 2 battalions; air-to-air missiles; air-to-surface missiles; of the combat aircraft, 110 are Mirages

Air bases: Uqba bin Nafi (formerly Wheelus), Idris (Tripoli), Benina (Benghazi), el Adem, el Awai, Lutiyyah

Since the termination of the U.S. Military Aid Program in 1971, France, Egypt, the Union of Soviet Socialist Republics and Czechoslovakia have been the principal suppliers of military hardware. Imports of armaments totaled $712 million for 1970–74. In 1975 Libya signed a $2-billion agreement with the Soviet Union providing for delivery of 1,100 tanks, 800 armored personnel carriers and 50 batteries of antiaircraft missiles. Libya's greatest coup was obtaining Mirage jet fighters from France in 1972. Pilots and naval cadets are trained in Greece, Egypt and Pakistan. Arms purchases abroad during 1979–83 totaled $12.095 billion, of which $5.8 billion came from the Soviet Union and $850 million from France.

Despite the growing hardware support, the Libyan army performed badly in all its engagements in recent times; against Egypt, in which it lost its entire 9th Armored Batallion; in Uganda, where it was badly routed; in Tunisia; and in Chad.

EDUCATION

Schooling has been, in principle, free, universal and compulsory since 1975, for nine years, from ages six to 15. Schooling consists of six years of primary school, three years of preparatory school, and three years of secondary school.

The academic year runs from October to June. The medium of instruction is Arabic. The study of foreign languages is discouraged at the primary and preparatory levels. Curricula and textbooks are designed to reflect the Arab-Libyan spirit. Islamic heritage is vigorously stressed, and Western traditions are either ignored or derided.

Private schools operated by foreign communities (Italian, French, German and Greek) serve the children of resident aliens. Some wealthy Libyan children also attend these schools. Only 1% of primary-school children attend private schools. Koranic primary, preprimary and preparatory schools, although outside the public-school system, are financed by state subsidies and increasingly encouraged.

Because of an acute teacher shortage, the educational system continues to rely heavily on foreign teachers, especially at the preparatory and secondary levels. Egypt is the main source of foreign teachers. Teachers are trained at 84 teacher-training institutions, of which the most prestigious is the Faculty of Teacher Training of the University of Libya.

Literacy drives and adult education courses have helped to decrease illiteracy dramatically since independence. Adult illiterates are enrolled in evening classes. Vocational training is officially encouraged because of the critical need for technical personnel. Vocational preparatory schools offer a four-year program. Graduates of this program are admitted to senior vocational schools that offer further three- or four-year programs in commercial, industrial or agricultural subjects. Vocational training centers operate in the major cities under the General Vocational Training Administration. These include the Petroleum Affairs Institute, the Higher Petroleum Institute and the Intermediate Petroleum Institute to train skilled workers, technicians and managers for the oil industry.

Educational administration is centralized in the Ministry of Education.

In 1958 the University of Libya was opened, in Benghazi. It was divided in 1973 into two units, to form the University of Benghazi and the University of Tripoli, later renamed the Ghar Yunis University of Benghazi and the al-Fateh University at Tripoli, respectively. Women account for about 24% of the student body. The Faculty of Arabic Language and Islamic Studies was created in 1970 in place of the former Islamic University. The universities are heavily dependent on foreign faculty members.

EDUCATION INDICATORS, 1988

Literacy (over age 10)
- Total (%): 74.4
- Males (%): 85.0
- Females (%): 62.0

First level
- Schools: 2,744 (1983)
- Students: 788,780
- Teachers: 41,515
- Student/teacher ratio: 19.0

Second level
- Schools: 1,555 (1983)
- Students: 373,374
- Teachers: 30,524
- Student/teacher ratio: 12.2

Vocational
- Schools: 195 (1983)
- Students: 57,511
- Teachers: 5,301
- Student/teacher ratio: 10.8

Third level
- Institutions: 8 (1982)
- Students: 30,000
- Teachers: 1,340 (1980)
- Student/teacher ratio: 19 (1983)
- Gross enrollment ratio: 10.1
- Students (/100,000 pop.): 792
- % of population over 24 with post-secondary education: 1.0

Foreign study
- Foreign students in national universities: 1,262 (1975)
- Students abroad: 1,555
  - of whom in
    - U.S.: 254 (1988)
    - France: 72 (1988)
    - Federal Republic of Germany: 35 (1988)
    - United Kingdom: 455 (1987)

Public expenditures, 1986
- Total (£L.): 636,260,000
- % of GNP: 10.1
- % of national budget: 20.8
- % of current expenditure: 79.6

LEGAL SYSTEM

The Libyan legal system still is evolving, with basic codes being modified and changed to conform more closely to the Shari'a. In a resolution in 1972 the RCC affirmed the spiritual values of the Islamic Shari'a as the chief source of legislation. In 1973 all laws formulated before the 1969 revolution were suspended, and a committee of jurists was formed to draft a new secular statute of personal status based on the Shari'a. Control of the legal system also was changed when the RCC abolished the old Supreme Judicial Council and replaced it with the Supreme Council for Judicial Institutions, which supervises and coordinates judicial institutions at all levels. The secular judicial system is headed by the Supreme Court, with 10 justices and a chief justice. Below the Supreme Court are the Courts of Appeal, at Tripoli, Benghazi and Misurata, with a president, vice president and three judges. There also are courts of first instance in each province and summary courts in varying numbers in the jurisdiction of each court of first instance, which deal in low-penalty cases. Outside this pyramid is the People's Courts program, set up in 1969 to deal with political crimes and administrative corruption.

The normal court structure in Libya has been bypassed to a significant extent by the People's Courts program; these courts conduct show trials and executions. This parallel legal system provides fewer safeguards, and trials frequently are held in camera or in absentia. A 1981 law prohibits the practice of law and makes all attorneys employees of the Secretariat of Justice. The Union of Arab Lawyers, in France, has expressed concern for the ability and freedom of attorneys simultaneously to provide legal defense for political prisoners and to serve as government employees. Libya claims it "guarantees prisoners all necessary means of defense and safeguards of justice adequate to the principles contained in the Declaration of Human Rights" and provides for legal assistance "as soon as possible with respect to the exigencies of interrogation," but there are numerous reports that these rights frequently are denied. In security cases in particular there are many reports of prisoners being held without trial for long periods. While undergoing interrogation, sometimes for several months, they are given no access to legal representation. Alleged political offenses are increasingly tried before ad hoc "revolutionary courts" rather than under the normal judicial procedure, with the opportunities for defense severely restricted. Moreover a number of these "trials" have been held in secret. Ther is no precise estimate of the number of political prisoners in Libya.

No information is available on the penal system.

LAW ENFORCEMENT

The Libyan police, or Shurtah, was completely reorganized after the 1969 revolution. Under a new police law in 1970, regional police forces were integrated into a unified command under a Directorate General of Public Investigations. The force also was renamed Police at the Service of the People and the Revolution. Individual police units are placed under the direct jurisdiction of the security directorate of each governorate. A police affairs council was created within the Ministry of the Interior to coordinate the activities of the various police branches. The structure of the police force follows closely that of the regular armed forces.

No criminal statistics have been published.

HEALTH

Under the Constitution of 1969 medical care is a right guaranteed by the state.

A number of serious diseases are endemic in the country. These include typhoid, leishmaniasis, schistosomiasis, venereal disease and leprosy. Other scourges include tuberculosis, trachoma, nutritional deficiency diseases and infectious hepatitis. Intestinal parasites pose a common threat to health. Only malaria, once a major problem, has been completely eradicated, with the help of WHO.

HEALTH INDICATORS

Health personnel, 1984
- Physicians: 5,272
- Persons per: 690
- Dentists: 400 (1983)
- Nurses & midwives: 5,924 (1983)
- Pharmacists: 618 (1983)

Hospitals, 1982
- Number: 64
- Number of beds (/10,000): 48
- Admissions/discharges (/10,000): 719
- Bed occupancy rate %: 52.7
- Average length of stay (days): 13

Type of hospitals (%) 1982
- Government: 100.0
- Private Nonprofit: 0.0
- Private profit: 0.0

Public health expenditures (latest)
- Per capita (U.S. $): 165.60

Vital statistics
- Crude death rate (/1,000 pop.): 7 (1990)
- Life Expectancy at birth (1990)
  - Males: 65
  - Females: 70
- Infant mortality rate (/1,000 live births): 64 (1990)
- Child mortality rate (1985–90) under 5 yrs (/1,000): 118
- Maternal mortality rate (/100,000 live births) (1980–1984): 80.0

Population with access to safe water (%): 97 (latest)

FOOD & NUTRITION

The average Libyan diet is reported to be inadequate and nutritionally deficient. The staple foods are barley and wheat flour (in the form of couscous), olive oil, onions, tomatoes, potatoes, sugar and tea. Libyans are believed to drink more tea per capita than any other people in the world. Eggs, milk, meat, fish and fresh fruits are only rarely eaten.

MEDIA & CULTURE

In 1973 all private newspapers in the country were nationalized, and the Public Press Organization was created to publish newspapers and journals. One daily newspaper is published in Arabic in Tripoli. *Al-Fajr al-Jadid* is published by the national news agency, Jamahiriya (JANA). The nondaily press consists of numerous weekly, biweekly or monthly periodicals published by JANA, government secretariats, the Press Service or by trade unions. All are published in Tripoli.

Freedom of the press is guaranteed by the Constitution of 1969 "within the principles of the revolution." There is no prepublication censorship, but journals are not permitted to challenge or criticize principles of the revolution, spread rumors, or publish material offensive to religion. The Press Prosecution Department is within the Ministry of Information and Culture to enforce compliance with the law. Foreign journalists who publish material derogatory to the regime are refused entry into the country, and foreign newspapers often are censored or banned on the same score.

The national news agency, Jamahiriya (JANA), was founded in 1965. DPA, Tass, Reuters and MENA have bureaus in the country.

MEDIA INDICATORS

Newspapers
- Number of dailies: 1 (latest)
- Circulation (000): 40 (latest)
- Per 1,000 pop. 10 (latest)
- Newsprint consumption (1988)
- Total metric tons: 2,000
  - Per 1000 pop. (kg.): 474

Book publishing
- Number of titles: 481 (pre-1986)

Radio
- Number of transmitters: 31 (latest)
- Number of persons per radio receiver: 4.1 (1989)

Television
- Television transmitters: 13 (latest)
- Number of persons per TV receiver: 8.2 (1989)

Cinema
- Number of fixed cinemas: 49 (pre-1986)
- Seating capacity (000): 22 (pre-1986)
- Annual attendance (million): 10.2 (pre-1986)

Films
- Production of long films: 2 (latest)

CULTURAL & ENVIRONMENTAL INDICATORS (latest)

Libraries
  Number: 5
  Volumes (000): 100
Museums (pre-1986)
  Annual attendance (000): 50
  Attendance (/1,000 pop.): 16
Performing arts (pre-1986)
  Number of performances: 439
  Annual attendance (000): 160
  Attendance (/1,000 pop.): 50
Nature reserves
  Number of facilities: 3

Libya has a modest book publishing industry, which produced 481 titles in 1982. Libya has not signed any copyright conventions.

Radio and television are controlled by the Great Socialist People's Libyan Arab Jamahiriya Broadcasting Corporation. Since 1973 all radio and TV stations have been operated by People's Committees. The radio service broadcasts in Arabic and English from Tripoli and Benghazi.

The television service has two transmitters, at Tripoli and Benghazi, and seven repeater stations connected by microwave links. Broadcasting is done primarily in Arabic, but recently limited hours in English, Italian and French have been added. Most of the programs are imported.

There are five public libraries, with a total of 100,000 volumes. The largest library in the country is the University of Libya's, whose three centers have a combined holding of over one million volumes, including a valuable collection on Islamic religious history.

There are 26 museums in the country, with total annual attendance of 50,000.

SOCIAL WELFARE

Social welfare is administered by the National Social Insurance Institute, founded in 1957. Under the Institute's Social Security program all employees, other than domestics and agricultural workers, are covered and provided with unemployment insurance, old-age disability pensions, maternity and sickness benefits, workmen's compensation and orphans' and widows' benefits. Free medical care also is extended to covered workers through the Institute's own hospitals and pharmacies.

The Ministry of Social Affairs operates a number of social welfare institutions and supports private welfare organizations, such as the Red Crescent Society.

GLOSSARY

aqsam: ward or quarter of a town.
gadamsi: strong southwesterly wind, blowing from the direction of Ghadamis.
ghibli: hot, scorching wind that blows across Libya from the south.
jihad: holy war or struggle, enjoined in the Koran, for establishing the supremacy of Islam and annihilating its enemies.
mohaafiz: governor.
mohafada: governorate, major unit of Libyan local administration until recently.
mudir: chief of a subdistrict.
mudiriyat: subdistrict.
mukhtar: headman of a village or town quarter.
mutasarrif: chief of a district.
mutasarrifiyat: district, secondary unit of local administration in Libya.
qadi (pl. qadaa): chief judge of a Shari'a court dispensing justice according to Muslim traditions and religious injunctions.
Senusi: Sunni religious fraternal organization founded near Mecca in 1837 by Sayid Muhammad bin Ali al Senusi al Idrisi al Hasani. The mother lodge of this order was set up in Cyrenaica in 1843. It grew into a powerful religio-political movement and helped to win independence for Libya in 1951. The Senusi influence disappeared from Libya with the overthrow of the Senusi monarchy in 1969.
shurtah: Libyan police.
tifinagh: script of the Tamahek dialect of Berber, used by the Tuaregs.
zawiya (pl. zawaaya): lodge of the Senusi brotherhood.

CHRONOLOGY (from 1951)

1951— Libya gains independence under U.N. auspices, with Muhammad Idris al-Mahdi al-Senusi as king. . . . Mahmoud Ben Muntasser is named prime minister.
1952— In the first national elections to the federal parliament held under the Constitution of 1951 the Party of Independence wins control. . . . The Libyan pound is introduced as the national currency.
1953— Libya joins the Arab League. . . . Libya concludes a 20-year treaty with United Kingdom, granting the latter military bases in return for an annual subsidy.
1954— Libya concludes treaty with the United States granting the latter military bases in return for an annual subsidy. . . . Sayid Muhammad Saghlisi is appointed prime minister.
1955— Libya is admitted to the United Nations. . . . New elections are held to the legislature. . . . The Central Bank of Libya is established.
1956— Mustafa Halim succeeds Saghlisi as prime minister.
1957— Radio service is introduced in Libya. . . . Abd al-Majid Kubar is new prime minister.
1958— The University of Libya is founded.
1959— Esso strikes oil at Zliten.
1960— New elections are held; Muhammad Ben Othman is appointed prime minister.
1963— Mohieddin Fekini takes over as prime minister. . . . Libya is transformed from a federal into a unitary state as the three provinces of Fezzan, Tripolitania and Cyrenaica are abolished and are replaced

by 10 governorates. . . . Provincial administrative councils are abolished.

1964— New elections are held; Mahmoud Ben Muntasser is elected prime minister.

1965— Husayn Maziq becomes prime minister; new elections are held.

1967— Anti-Jewish riots break out following the Arab-Israeli War. . . . Maziq is replaced by Abdul Qadir Badri as prime minister briefly and later by Abdul Hamid Bakkush.

1968— Warris al-Qaddafi is named prime minister; new elections are held.

1969— In swift and bloodless coup the monarchy is overthrown and a republic is set up by a group of army officers, known as Free Unionist officers, led by a young captain, Muammar al-Qaddafi; the Revolutionary Command Council is named the supreme state organ; a new civilian cabinet is appointed under Mahmud Sulayman al-Maghrabi; Constitution is promulgated. . . . Qaddafi, President Nasser of Egypt and President Jaffar al-Numayri of Sudan issue the Tripoli Charter announcing their intention to work toward unity of their countries. . . . New regime survives attempted coup led by defense and interior ministers.

1970— Mahgrabi resigns as prime minister. . . . Under Libyan pressure United States abandons air base at Wheelus; all Italian-owned properties are confiscated; foreign and domestic banks are nationalized. . . . Qaddafi takes over as prime minister.

1971— The Libyan dinar replaces the Libyan pound as the national currency. . . . The Arab Socialist Union (ASU) is founded as Libya's sole political party. . . . Libya joins Egypt and Syria in forming the Federation of Arab Republics.

1972— The ASU meets in its first National Congress. . . . Qaddafi and President Anwar Sadat of Egypt issue the Benghazi Declaration, announcing de facto unification of their two countries. . . . Maj. Abdul Salam Jalloud takes over as prime minister. . . . Relations with the United Kingdom deteriorate following nationalization of British Petroleum interests in Libya.

1973— Libya launches cultural revolution; People's Committees are appointed at all levels as catalysts of the revolution. . . . Al-Fateh University is founded. . . . Libya takes no part in October War with Israel but participates in oil embargo.

1974— Abortive union with Tunisia leads to strained relations between the two countries.

1975— Attempted coup by Maj. Abdalla al-Meheishi is crushed.

1977— Dispute with Egypt escalates into border skirmish. . . . Thousands of Egyptians and Tunisians are expelled from Libya. . . . The People's Congress of the ASU renames Libya the Socialist People's Libyan Arab Jamahiriya; the Revolutionary Command Council is renamed the General Secretariat of the General People's Congress; and the Council of Ministers is renamed the General People's Committee.

1978— U.S. sources report that an assassination attempt on Qaddafi in early March resulted in the deaths of at least two prominent East German officials visiting Libya, in a helicopter explosion and crash; Qaddafi was not aboard the aircraft.

1979— Qaddafi resigns from post of secretary-general of the General Secretariat of the General People's Congress to devote more time to "preserving the revolution"; Abd al-Ati Ubaydi is designated in Qaddafi's place as secretary-general. . . . Libya breaks with al-Fatah. . . . Tunisia breaks diplomatic relations with Libya over attack on the border town of Gafsa. . . . Qaddafi's opponents in exile are shot down by hit squads in London, Paris and Rome as the government vows to silence all opposition.

1980— Libya, having installed pro-Libyans in power in Chad, moves in with armed force and announces merger of the two countries, despite protests from France and African nations.

1981— Mauritania and Niger expel Libyan diplomats. . . . Somalia and Sudan cut diplomatic ties. . . . Diplomatic relations with Morocco are resumed. . . . Libya boycotts Islamic Conference. Soviet-made jets are downed by U.S. planes over Gulf of Sirte. . . . Libyan troops exit Chad. . . . Exxon ends oil operations in Libya.

1982— Qaddafi reportedly wounded in assassination attempt. . . . Ghana diplomatic ties are restored following pro-Libyan coup led by Jerry Rawlings. . . . In an effort to end Libya's diplomatic isolation, Qaddafi visits Malta, Austria, Tunisia and other countries.

1983— Mobil ends oil operations in Libya. . . . Pro-Libya coup in Upper Volta (now Burkina Faso) is successful. . . . Diplomatic ties with Saudi Arabia are restored. . . . Libya again intervenes in Chad.

1984— Libya is tied to mining of Red Sea that damages shipping, and a plot to disrupt the *hajj* pilgrims at Mecca. . . . Jordan cuts diplomatic ties following blast at its embassy in Tripoli. . . . Libya sides with anti-Arafat faction of PLO led by Abu Nidal. . . . Pact is reached with Morocco under which Libya cuts aid to Polisario. . . . Libya reaches agreement with France for a joint pullout of troops from Chad but reneges by maintaining a clandestine force of 3,000 in northern Chad. . . . In incident at Libyan embassy in London, Libyan terrorists kill a British policewoman.

1985— As oil prices plummet, Libya expels 65,000 foreign workers. . . . Iraq breaks diplomatic ties. . . . Libya is suspected of masterminding terrorist attacks in Rome and Vienna airports.

1986— United States imposes severe economic sanctions against Libya. . . . U.S. naval maneuvers in Gulf of Sirte are held to foil Libyan claim to sovereignty over the gulf south of the "line of death." Libya fires missiles at U.S. fighter aircraft. . . . United States retaliates against Libya by attacking radar and missile facilities in town of Sirte and firing on four Libyan patrol boats in gulf.

1987— Qaddafi is reconciled with Yasser Arafat's section of the Palestine Liberation Organization and actively encourages reunification of opposing factions within the PLO.

1988— Meeting of leaders of the five nations of the Maghreb (Algeria, Morocco, Tunisia, Libya and Mauritania) takes place in Algeria, resulting in establishment of a Maghreb commission to investigate possibilities for regional integration.

1989— Summit meeting in Morocco results in a treaty declaring a "Union of the Arab Maghreb" composed of Algeria, Libya, Mauritania, Morocco and Tunisia. Treaty goals include eventual free movement of people, goods, services and capital among the five member nations. . . . Libya restores full diplomatic relations with Egypt.

1990— Abu Zayd Umar Durda named prime minister; Libya criticizes Iraq's invasion of Kuwait as well as the U.S.-led U.N. force in Saudi Arabia.

1991— During Persian Gulf War, Libya remains nonconfrontational.

BIBLIOGRAPHY

BOOKS

Allan, J. A. *Libya: Agriculture and Economic Development.* London, 1972.

———. *Libya Since Independence: Economic and Social Development.* New York, 1982.

Ansell, M. O., and I. M. al-Arif. *The Libyan Revolution.* London, 1972.

Arif, T. M., and M. O. Ansell. *The Libyan Revolution: A Sourcebook of Legal and Historical Documents.* New York, 1981.

Bates, Oric. *Eastern Libyans.* London, 1970.

Blundy, David. *Qaddafi and the Libyan Revolution.* London, 1987.

Buru, Mukhtar. *Planning and Development in Modern Libya.* Boulder, Colo., 1985.

Carvely, A. *Institutionalizing Revolution: Egypt and Libya.* Washington, D.C., 1977.

Cooley, John K. *Libyan Sandstorm: The Complete Account of Qaddafi's Revolution.* New York, 1982.

Deeb, Marius K., and Mary J. Deeb. *Libya Since the Revolution.* New York, 1982.

Farley, Rowle. *Planning for Development in Libya.* London, 1971.

Fathaly, Omar I. *Political Change and Bureaucracy in Libya.* Lexington, Mass., 1977.

———. *Political Development and Social Change in Libya.* Lexington, Mass., 1980.

First, Ruth. *Libya: The Elusive Revolution.* London, 1974.

Hahn, Lorna. *Historical Dictionary of Libya.* Metuchen, N.J., 1981.

Haley, P. Edward. *Qaddafi and the United States Since 1969.* New York, 1984.

Harris, Lillian Craig. *Libya: Qadhafi's Revolution and the Modern State.* Boulder, Col., 1986.

Joffe, E., and D. McLachlan. *Social and Economic Development of Libya.* Boulder, Colo., 1983.

Lemarchand, Rene (editor). *The Green and the Black: Qadhafi's Policies in Africa.* Bloomington, Ind., 1988.

Neuberger, Benyamin. *Involvement, Invasion and Withdrawal: Qaddafi's Libya and Chad, 1969–81.* Syracuse, N.Y., 1982.

Pasha, Aftab K. *Libya and the United States: Qaddafi's Response to Reagan's Challenge.* Columbia, Mo., 1985.

Pelt, Adrian. *Libyan Independence and the United Nations: A Case of Planned Decolonization.* New Haven, Conn., 1970.

Reynolds, Joyce. *Libyan Studies.* Lawrence, Mass., 1975.

Sabki, Hisham M. *The United Nations and the Pacific Settlement of Disputes: A Case Study of Libya.* London, 1973.

St. John, Ronald Bruce. *Qaddafi's Worst Design: Libyan Foreign Policy, 1969–1987.* Atlantic Highlands, NJ, 1987.

Schleuter, Hans. *Index Libycus.* Boston, 1972.

Segre, Claudio. *Fourth Shore: The Italian Colonization of Libya.* Chicago, 1975.

Waddams, Frank C. *The Libyan Oil Industry.* Baltimore, 1980.

Wright, John. *Libya: A Modern History.* Baltimore, 1982.

———. *Libya, Chad and the Central Sahara.* London, 1989.

OFFICIAL PUBLICATION

Central Bank of Libya. *Economic Bulletin.*

MADAGASCAR

BASIC FACT SHEET

OFFICIAL NAME: Democratic Republic of Madagascar (République Démocratique de Madagascar; Repoblika Demokratika Malagasy) Note: From 1960 to 1975, Madagascar was officially known as the Malagasy Republic. Both names have long been treated as interchangeable. However, Malagasy properly denotes, as a noun form, only the people of Madagascar and their language. In any other context it may be used only as an adjective. Some of the confusion was removed when the Constitution of 1975 officially adopted the name Madagascar in both English and French.

ABBREVIATION: MG

CAPITAL: Antananarivo (formerly Tananarive)

HEAD OF STATE: President Didier Ratsiraka (from 1975)

HEAD OF GOVERNMENT: Prime Minister Victor Ramahatra (from 1988)

NATURE OF GOVERNMENT: One-party dictatorship

POPULATION: 11,800,524 (1990)

AREA: 587,041 sq. km. (226,657 sq. mi.)

ETHNIC MAJORITY: Merina, Betsimisaraka, Betsileo and Tsimihety

LANGUAGES: French and Malagasy

RELIGIONS: Animism, Christianity and Islam

UNIT OF CURRENCY: Malagasy franc

NATIONAL FLAG: A white vertical stripe at the hoist with two stripes extending horizontally across the remaining area, red on the upper half and green on the lower half

NATIONAL EMBLEM: A white badge within a black-rimmed circle displays a black-and-white stylized head of a zebu bull between green rice plants; above its head, fronds of the ranivala palm tree sprout in stylized curves.

NATIONAL ANTHEM: "O Our Dear Native Land"

NATIONAL HOLIDAYS: June 26 (National Day, Independence Day); January 1 (New Year's Day); March 29 (Commemoration of 1947 Rebellion); May 1 (Labor Day); December 30 (Anniversary of the Republic); also Christian festivals including Assumption, Ascension, All Saints' Day, Easter Monday, Pentecost Monday and Christmas

NATIONAL CALENDAR: Gregorian

PHYSICAL QUALITY OF LIFE INDEX: 51

DATE OF INDEPENDENCE: June 26, 1960

DATE OF CONSTITUTION: December 21, 1975

WEIGHTS & MEASURES: Metric

GEOGRAPHICAL FEATURES

Madagascar is in the southwestern Indian Ocean, about 400 km. (250 mi.) off the coast of Africa, from which it is separated by the Mozambique Channel. Madagascar is the fourth-largest island in the world, after Greenland, New Guinea and Borneo. Madagascar's land area of 587,041 sq. km. (226,657 sq. mi.) extends 1,570 km. (976 mi.) north-northeast to south-southwest and 569 km. (354 mi.) east-southeast to west-northwest. The coastline stretches 3,991 km. (2,480 mi.).

The capital is Antananarivo (formerly Tananarive), with a 1980 population of 547,139. The other major urban centers (with former name in parentheses) are Mahajunga or (Majunga) (80,801), Toamasina (Tamatave) (79,505), Fianarantsoa (83,250), Antseranana (Diégo-Suzarez) (45,487), Toliary (Tuléar) (38,978) and Antsirabe (33,287).

Topographically, Madagascar consists of a central highland region rising abruptly from a narrow eastern coastal strip and descending gradually to the broad plains on the western coast. On the basis of a more detailed analysis, there are six topographical regions: the Diégo-Suarez region in the North; the northwestern region converging on the port of Majunga; the southwestern coastal plains; the southernmost province; the densely populated eastern coast; and the mountainous hinterland. There are three main groups of mountains of volcanic origin, the highest of which is the Tsaratana (2,880 m.; 9,449 ft.). The others are the Ankaratra and the Andringingtra (both over 2,590 m.; 8,500 ft.).

Madagascar has numerous rivers, since the central highlands act as a powerful watershed. The rivers flowing west include the Sambirano, the Betsiboka, the Tsiribihina, the Mangoky, the Onilahy and the Menarandra, while those flowing east into the Indian Ocean include the Mandrare, the Mananara, the Mananjary, the Mangoro and the Maningory. Behind the coral beaches on the eastern coast is a series of lagoons, some of which are connected by the Pangalanes Canal.

There are 19 major lakes, of which the largest are Lake Alaotra, Lake Ihotry and Lake Itasy.

The country also includes a number of small coastal reefs and islands, of which only five have more than a handful of inhabitants: Île Sainte-Marie, Île Nossi-Mitsio, Île Nossi-Bé, Île Nossi-Fali and Îles Barren.

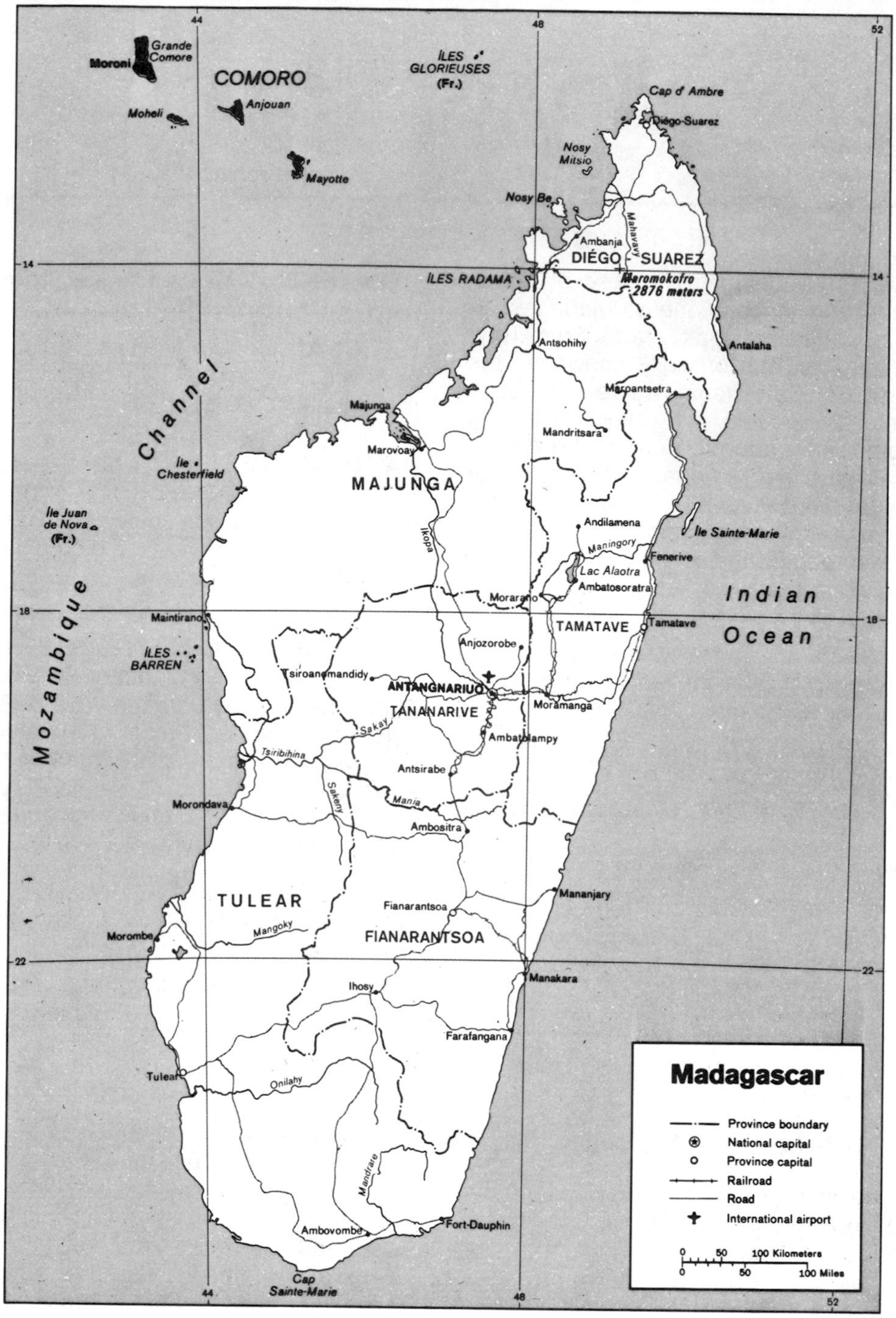

Madagascar

Province boundary
National capital
Province capital
Railroad
Road
International airport

0 50 100 Kilometers
0 50 100 Miles

COMORO
Grande Comore
Moroni
Moheli
Anjouan
Mayotte
ÎLES GLORIEUSES (Fr.)
Cap d' Ambre
Diégo-Suarez
Nosy Mitsio
Nosy Be
Ambanja
Mahavavy
DIÉGO SUAREZ
ÎLES RADAMA
Maromokotro 2876 meters
Antsohihy
Antalaha
Maroantsetra
Mandritsara
Majunga
Marovoay
Île Chesterfield
MAJUNGA
Ikopa
Île Juan de Nova (Fr.)
Mozambique Channel
Andilamena
Maningory
Île Sainte-Marie
Fenerive
Lac Alaotra
Ambatosoratra
Moramanga
Morarano
Indian Ocean
Maintirano
TAMATAVE
Tamatave
ÎLES BARREN
Anjozorobe
Tsiroanomandidy
ANTANANARIVO
TANANARIVE
Sakay
Ambatolampy
Tsiribihina
Antsirabe
Sakeny
Mania
Morondava
Ambositra
TULEAR
Fianarantsoa
Mananjary
Mangoky
FIANARANTSOA
Morombe
Manakara
Ihosy
Farafangana
Tulear
Onilahy
Mandrare
Ambovombe
Fort-Dauphin
Cap Sainte-Marie
44
48
52
14
18
22

CLIMATE & WEATHER

Madagascar has a tropical marine climate in which the main influences are altitude, monsoons and proximity to the sea. Although the external climatic influences are well defined, it is not accurate to speak of one single climate in Madagascar. The central highlands divide the island into two main climatic zones: a windward zone facing the Indian Ocean and a leeward zone facing the Mozambique Channel. A wet, tropical climate with no completely dry season prevails on the eastern coastal plain and the northern peninsula. The western slope region, which has a larger land area, receives its rainfall from a different wind system and has distinct wet (summer) and dry (winter) seasons. The central highlands constitute a transition zone influenced by both climates. In the extreme South, long dry periods occur between irregular rainstorms; droughts are not uncommon. Among these major zones are at least four ecological subregions and many more microclimates based on altitude and contour. In general, the most healthful and comfortable climate is in the central highlands.

The eastern and northwestern coasts receive their heaviest rainfall during the austral winter (May to September), while the central highlands and the West receive rains from the monsoon winds that blow during the austral summer (October to April). In an average year, the eastern coast receives 2,030 to 3,250 mm. (80 to 120 in.), the maximum being recorded at Toamasina; the northern peninsula receives 1,010 to 1,270 mm. (40 to 50 in.); the Northwest and the central highlands, 1,010 to 2,030 mm. (40 to 80 in.). Antananarivo, the capital, receives 1,340 mm. (53 in.), while Toliary, in the Southwest, receives only 510 mm. (20 in.).

Temperatures are also moderated by altitude, with the coastal regions being hotter than the plateau. The mean temperatures in the former regions range from 21°C to 26.6°C (70°F to 80°F) and in the latter region from 13°C to 19.4°C (55°F to 67°F). Temperatures over 37.8°C (100°F) are uncommon; so also are freezing temperatures and snow.

Because of the frequent and violent clashes of air masses over the island, lightning is a permanent hazard—more than 60 people are killed every year by it. The most dramatic feature of the island's weather is the frequency of tropical storms and cyclones, generally lasting from December to March. These cyclones consist of winds blowing over 177 to 241 km. (110 to 150 mi.) per hour, accompanied by torrential rains. In some years there are as many as five cyclones, but other years may pass without any. The most catastrophic of these cyclones was that recorded in 1927, which left Toamasina in ruins.

POPULATION

The population of Madgascar was estimated in 1990 at 11,800,524, on the basis of the last official census, in 1974–75, when the population was 7,603,790.

The population density is highest in the eastern lowlands, the central highlands, the northern coast in Antseranana Province, the offshore island of Nossi-Bé and in river deltas such as the Majunga area of the northwestern coast. In 1970 Fianarantsoa had the highest population of all provinces, while Antseranana had the lowest. Toamasina had the highest annual growth rate (11%) and Fianarantsoa the lowest (6.1%).

About 66% of the population is rural. Although the urban annual growth rate of 5.97% is significantly higher than the national growth rate, migration from rural areas accounts for only a small proportion of this increase. There are five cities with over 50,000 inhabitants, 47 intermediate towns with 5,000 to 50,000 inhabitants and 340 towns with 1,000 to 5,000 inhabitants. Antananarivo accounts for 36% of the urban population.

There is little emigration or immigration. Even internal migration is not significant. The population of Antananarivo, the capital, for example, is 99% locally born. The relative immobility has caused some concern because lands with good agricultural potential in less densely populated areas remain undeveloped from lack of workers.

Madagascar has what is essentially a matriarchal society, and a highly visible role for women has long been a recognized and integral part of the country's sociological framework. There are no restrictions concerning activities in which women may engage. Women have a lengthy tradition of involvement in high-level political activity, and there are women members of the cabinet, Supreme Revolutionary Council and the People's National Assembly. Women also are active and play major roles in the various political parties. Women have prominent positions in the business and eco-

DEMOGRAPHIC INDICATORS

Population (millions): 11.8 (1990)
Years of last census: 1974–75
Sex distribution (% of last census): males, 50.0; females, 50.0
Population estimates and projections (millions)

1930: 3.722	1960: 5.390	1990: 11.980
1940: 4.034	1970: 6.742	2000: 15.562
1950: 4.330	1980: 8.777	2010: 22.594

Age profile (% of last census)

0–14: 44.4	30–44: 14.2	60–74: 4.6
15–29: 25.7	45–59: 10.0	75 and over: 1.1

Median age (yrs.): 17.7 (1985)
Youth population (% aged 15–24): (1985); 19.2 (2000) 19.0
Total dependency ratio, 1985: 90.3
Annual growth rate (%)

1950–55: 2.18	1975–80: 2.90	2000–2005: 3.17
1955–60: 2.36	1980–85: 3.05	2005–10: 3.04
1960–65: 2.50	1985–90: 3.18	2010–15: 2.86
1965–70: 2.28	1990–95: 3.22	2015–20: 2.54
1970–75: 2.38	1995–2000: 3.26	2020–25: 2.17

Hypothetical size of stationary population (millions): 42
Assumed year of reaching net reproduction rate of 1: 2030
Urban population (000): 2,225 (1985)
Urban population (%): (1988); 24 (1965) 12
Annual urban population growth rate (%, 1985–90): 5.97
Annual rural population growth rate (%, 1985–90): 2.32
Percentage of urban population in largest city: 36 (1980)
Percentage of urban population in cities of population over 500,000: 36 (1980)
Number of cities of population over 500,000: 1 (1980)
Population density per sq. km. (per sq. mi.): 20.4 (52.9) (1990)

VITAL STATISTICS

Crude birth rate (/1,000): 47 (1990); 47 (1965)
Crude death rate (/1,000): 15 (1990); 22 (1965)
Infant mortality rate (/1,000 live births): 97 (1990)
Maternal mortality rate (/100,000 live births): 300 (1980)
Life expectancy (yrs.) at birth: males, 50; females, 54 (1990)
Gross reproduction rate (/woman) (1980–85): 3.25
Total fertility rate (/woman): 6.9 (1990)
Rate of natural increase (/1,000) (1985–90): 31.7
Marriage rate (/1,000): 2.6 (1975)
Average household size: 4.7 (latest)

STATUS OF WOMEN INDICATORS

Number of women (000): 5,094 (1985)
% Women of childbearing age 15–49: 44 (1988)
% women literate: 61.6 (1988)
% women in labor force: 39.7 (1990)
Total fertility rate (/woman): 6.9 (1990)

nomic life of the country, with many of them managing or owning businesses or filling management positions in state industries. Education at all levels is open to women. However, women in rural areas and among the poor face a greater degree of hardship. In addition to the responsibilities associated with childrearing and household management, economic necessity forces these women to engage in long hours of farm labor or similar activities. These conditions stem more from socioeconomic factors than from any discrimination against women in Madagascar society.

Official policy is pronatalist despite the high birth rate. However, the National Council on Population has been created, and limited family planning services are offered as part of the maternal and child health services.

ETHNIC COMPOSITION

The population of Madagascar may be described as homogeneous because all ethnic groups speak the same language, share the same culture and also claim the same Afro-Asian origins, although the proportion in which the elements are mixed varies from group to group. In general, it is more accurate to term the ethnic groups clans rather than tribes, because tribes in the true African sense of peoples of differing origin speaking mutually unintelligible tongues and practicing different social customs do not exist on the island.

The ethnic affiliations and origins of the Malagasy have not been precisely determined and still are subject to considerable speculation. The most commonly accepted theory is that proto-Malagasy were Malayo-Polynesian immigrants who came to the island in successive waves by sailing across the Indian Ocean in primitive craft in much the same way as Polynesians are supposed to have sailed across the Pacific to South America. To this basic stock were added later arrivals from Africa, resulting in a remarkable blending of Indonesian and African cultures.

There are 18 clans in Madagascar, each with its own territorial niche.

The largest of the clans is the Merina, the ascendant group since the 18th century and therefore resented by other groups. They divide themselves into the *fotsy* (white) descendants of the free Merina and the *mainty* (black) descendants of slaves. Well educated, relatively prosperous and urbanized, they are represented heavily in commerce, administration and the professions. The Betsileo are noted as skilled craftsmen, model cultivators, herders and merchants and are well represented in government. The Betsimisaraka are predominantly cultivators and are the main inhabitants of Île Sainte-Marie. The Tsimihety are one of the most dynamic, mobile and independent of all Malagasy groups. Philibert Tsiranana, the first president of the republic, from 1960 to 1972, was a Tsimihety. Of the other groups, the Makoa are the most Africanized, and the Anatambahoaka and the Antaimoro are the most Arabized.

Despite a common ethnic heritage, interclan attitudes are colored by historical rivalries and controversies. The main rivalry is between the highlanders and the people of the plains, known as *côtiers.* This rivalry underlines much of the civil turbulence of recent times. There also is bad blood between the Merina and other clans and between the Northerners and the people of the South, called collectively Tatsimo.

The principal ethnic alien groups include the Comorans, the Chinese and the Indians. Because Comorans are Muslims speaking a different language, they tend to live apart, and many return to Comoros after a few years. Nevertheless, widespread anti-Comoran riots in 1977 led the Comoros government to call for their repatriation. Most of the Chinese came from South China in the early 1930s and most of the Indians in about 1901 to work on the railroads. Both Chinese and Indians are small merchants.

Of permanent Western residents, the French are the most numerous. Also counted as French are the Creoles from Réunion. There also are Greeks scattered among the foreign population.

LANGUAGES

French and Malagasy are the official languages of the republic. Malagasy belongs to the Malayo-Polynesian family, but its vocabulary has an overlay of African, Sanskrit, Arabic and European words. Of the many mutually intelligible dialects, Merina, also called Hova, is considered the standard. Malagasy makes use of a Latin Script first devised by Christian missionaries in the early 1800s.

RELIGIONS

Nearly 52% of the population follow traditional African religions; 41% are Christians, evenly divided between Catholic and Protestant churches; and 7% are Muslims. However, Christianity is the dominant religious force in the country and is particularly associated with the elite ruling groups.

Traditional Malagasy religion had no dogma or clergy, but its central concept is belief in the soul and its immortality. Besides the creator of the universe (Zanahary or Andrianahary), secondary divinities are worshiped, especially ancestors and legendary queens and kings. For this reason burial places have special significance and are in themselves objects of veneration. Often tombs are more splendid structures than the houses of the living. Funerals are elaborate, accompanied by ritual feasting for which oxen often are sacrificed. Divination is widely practice.

Christianity was introduced in the early 19th century, and its progress was helped by the conversion of the Merino and their royalty. The earliest missionaries were Anglicans; Protestantism has traditionally been the faith of the upper-class Merinos and Catholicism that of the slaves and the *côtiers.* The Roman Catholic Church claims 1.5 million members, divided into three archidioceses based in Antseranana, Antananarivo and Fianarantsoa. About a third of the clergy are Malagasy, including the archbishop of Antananarivo. Six Protestant denominations belonging to the Protestant Federation are represented in the country. Most of the Protestant pastors also are Malagasy.

In the mid-1970s some 500,000 people, concentrated mainly on the northwestern coast, were adherents of Islam. Most of the Comoran immigrants also are Muslim.

HISTORICAL BACKGROUND

French influence was introduced in Madagascar piecemeal, beginning with a treaty in 1840 with the Merino monarchy. The French later claimed a protectorate over parts of the kingdom; when this claim was disputed, they launched a war, which ended in 1885 with the French gaining control over the kingdom's foreign policy. The Anglo-French Agreement of 1890, which acknowledged Madagascar as a French zone of influence, paved the way for the final annexation of the country in 1896. However, resistance, especially in the South, was not overcome until 1904. In 1946 Madagascar became an overseas territory of France, and the Malagasy became French citizens, although the franchise was extended to a few only. A Territorial Assembly was established with some control over the budget. In 1947 a rebellion broke out, which was suppressed only after a loss of life estimated as high as 80,000. In 1958 Madagascar voted overwhelmingly for the new French Constitution and thus became an autonomous member of the new French Community. Full independence was achieved in 1960.

Since independence Madagascar has had a history of political upheaval. No leader has come to power in accordance with the constitutional process. At independence the government was led by President Philibert Tsiranana, who ruled with the support of the Social Democratic Party. His tenure was characterized by general social unrest. Ethnic conflict stemmed from Merine opposition to the government's pro-French stance. Economic problems led to a revolt by peasants in Tulear Province in 1971, and lack of job prospects precipitated a student insurrection in 1972. Unable to govern, Tsiranana resigned, and a military government was formed under the leadership of Gen. Gabriel Ramanantsoa in May 1972. The general was confirmed as leader in a popular referendum that year.

Following a coup attempt by dissident *côtier* officers in 1975, Col. Richard Ratsimandrava replaced Ramanantsoa. Ratsimandrava was assassinated after six days in office. Gen. Gilles Andriamahazo assumed leadership. He, in turn, was succeeded in June 1975 by Cdr. Didier Ratsiraka. A referendum in that same year endorsed the Charter of Socialist Revolution, which committed the government to the nationalization of foreign companies, banks and agriculture. State corporations were set up to coordinate food production. Free health care and education were introduced.

In 1975 Ratsiraka was designated president under a new constitution in which the chief executive had extensive powers. He was returned to office in 1982 with 80% of the vote in an election widely criticized as fraudulent.

During the late 1970s and 1980s Madagascar's economy declined dramatically. A massive program of public investment in industry and conversely a neglect of agriculture resulted in growing foreign debt. French aid declined in the face of the government's leftist programs. Madagascar received aid from the Eastern bloc, but this was primarily in the form of equipment, not desperately needed foreign currency. In 1982 the government signed a restructuring agreement with the IMF that led to the introduction of a free market and a rollback of Ratsiraka's socialist programs.

The austerity measures dictated by the IMF had a disastrous impact on the quality of life and generated civil unrest. Nevertheless, Ratsiraka was returned to office in 1989 with over 60% of the vote.

Civil unrest continued, however, and in March 1990 Ratsiraka lifted a ban on political parties that had been in effect since 1975. Three new parties immediately registered. In May a group of armed rebels briefly seized control of the national radio headquarters in Antananarivo but were soon put down by security forces. It was estimated that up to 50 people died in the failed coup attempt.

CONSTITUTION & GOVERNMENT

The Constitution of 1975 provides for a strong presidential form of government. The president is elected by direct universal suffrage for a seven-year term and may seek reelection. He is assisted by a Supreme Revolutionary Council, described in the Constitution as "the guardian of the Malagasy socialist revolution." The president presides over this council and also names eight of its 12 members. The other four members are chosen by him from a list presented by the People's National Assembly. The Constitution assigns the president, who is the head of state, extensive and diverse powers, including that of declaring a state of national emergency, under which he may suspend the Constitution. The executive consists of, in addition to the president and the Supreme Revolutionary Council, the

Council of Ministers, called a cabinet when presided over by the prime minister instead of the president. The council includes ministers of state, ministers and secretaries of state, in that order. The size of the council is not fixed by law. Within this administrative structure are two bodies that wield considerable power. One is the General Secretariat of the Government, which includes the inspector general of the state. The other is the Military Development Committee, a consultative organ whose endorsement is essential for any program relating to national defense as well as for social and economic programs that may impinge on national welfare.

In 1977 six advisory commissions were created within the Supreme Revolutionary Council, covering production and finance, supply and commerce, social affairs, juridical and administrative affairs, defense, and infrastructure and development. There also is a plenary commission covering the development plan, foreign affairs and ideology.

President Didier Ratsiraka has broad constitutional powers, and his position is further strengthened by the influential role played by AREMA, his "revolutionary association" within the ruling FNDR. AREMA holds an overwhelming majority in the People's National Assembly and has a broad base of popular support. Also contributing to the president's power are his close ties to the state security apparatus. The president's role has evolved in recent years toward one of a power broker among various competing interests. He must contend with opposition not only from other groups in the FNDR but also, behind the scenes, from elements within the Supreme Revolutionary Council and his own political group.

The Supreme Revolutionary Council is an advisory group broadly representative of Madagascar's regional and social structure. The leaders of all seven parties sit on the council. The council approves basic policy guidelines, convenes and adjourns the National Assembly, and passes laws when the Assembly is not sitting. Its members have broad patronage power through their control of scholarships and influence on government assignments.

The Malagasy political temperament generally avoids excess and violence and seems to prefer orderly processes. However, there were numerous instances since World War II of armed uprisings and organized rioting. The 1947 rebellion against the French was evidence of this subsurface aggressiveness. The nation enjoyed over two decades of political stability between 1950 and 1970, but in 1972 thousands of strikers and demonstrators took to the streets for two bloody months and forced President Philibert Tsiranana to step down. The nation's second president, Gabriel Ramanantsoa, a Merina, revived the *côtiers'* fears of Merina domination and was unable to reconcile the opposing ideologies of the moderates and radicals in his cabinet. In 1975 he yielded office to the leader of the radical faction, Col. Richard Ratsimandrava, who was assassinated within six days of being sworn in. A provisional 18-man military directorate was invested with supreme power until Didier Ratsiraka was chosen president.

GOVERNMENT LIST
(July/August 1991)

President	Ratsiraka, Didier, *Adm.*
Prime Minister	Ramahatra, Victor, *Col.*
Minister of Agricultural Production, Agrarian Reform & Landed Heritage	Andriamanohisoa, Nelson
Minister of Animal Husbandry, Fisheries, Forest & Water Resources	Zafera, Maxime
Minister of Civil Service, Labor & Social Law	Ruphin, Georges
Minister of Commerce	Solofson, Georges
Minister of Defense	Razafitombo, Leon Evariste, *Gen.*
Minister of Finance	Rajaobelina, Leon
Minister of Foreign Affairs	Bemananjara, Adrianaribone Jean
Minister of Health	Seraphin, Jean-Jacques, *M.D.*
Minister of Higher Education	Rakoto, Ignace
Minister of Industry, Energy & Mining	Radanielson, Vincent
Minister of Information & Ideological Orientation	Rahaga, Jean Claude
Minister of Interior	Ampy Portos, Augustin
Minister of Justice & Keeper of the Seals	Bedo, Joseph
Minister of Planning & Economy	Robiarvony, Jean
Minister of Planning, Social Condition & Youth	Badhroudine
Minister of Posts & Telecommunications	Pierre, Simon
Minister of Public Works	Tsaranazy, Jean Emile
Minister of Revolutionary Art & Culture	Rabesahala, Gisele
Minister of Scientific Research & Development of Technology	Zafers, Antoine Rabesa
Minister of Secondary & Primary Education	Velompanahy, Aristide
Minister of Transportation, Meteorology & Tourism	Zasy, Lucien
Special Counselor to the President for Financial Affairs	Andriamanerasoa, Nirina
Governor, Central Bank	Razafimanjato, Blandin

RULERS OF MADAGASCAR
Presidents

June 1960–October 1972: Philibert Tsiranana
October 1972–February 1975: Gabriel Ramanantsoa
February 1975: Richard Ratsimandrava
February 1975–June 1975: Gilles Andriamahazo
June 1975– : Didier Ratsiraka

Soon after taking office, Ratsiraka made a long series of broadcasts detailing his policy, which were later collected and published as the *Charter of the Malagasy Socialist Revolution* (popularly known as the Little Red Book). In it he promised to continue the policy of closer relations with Communist, Arab and Third World nations; to nationalize banks, oil, shipping and foreign enterprises; and to carry out agrarian reforms. The stabilty of the Second Republic (as the Ratsiraka regime describes itself) depends on the success of these policies.

The legislative branch consists of the unicameral 137-seat People's National Assembly. It is elected for a five-year term by universal suffrage.

The judiciary is headed by the Supreme Court. Below that court is the Court of Appeals, which has highest appellate jurisdiction, and the High Court, whose sole function is to try the president or members of the Council of Ministers.

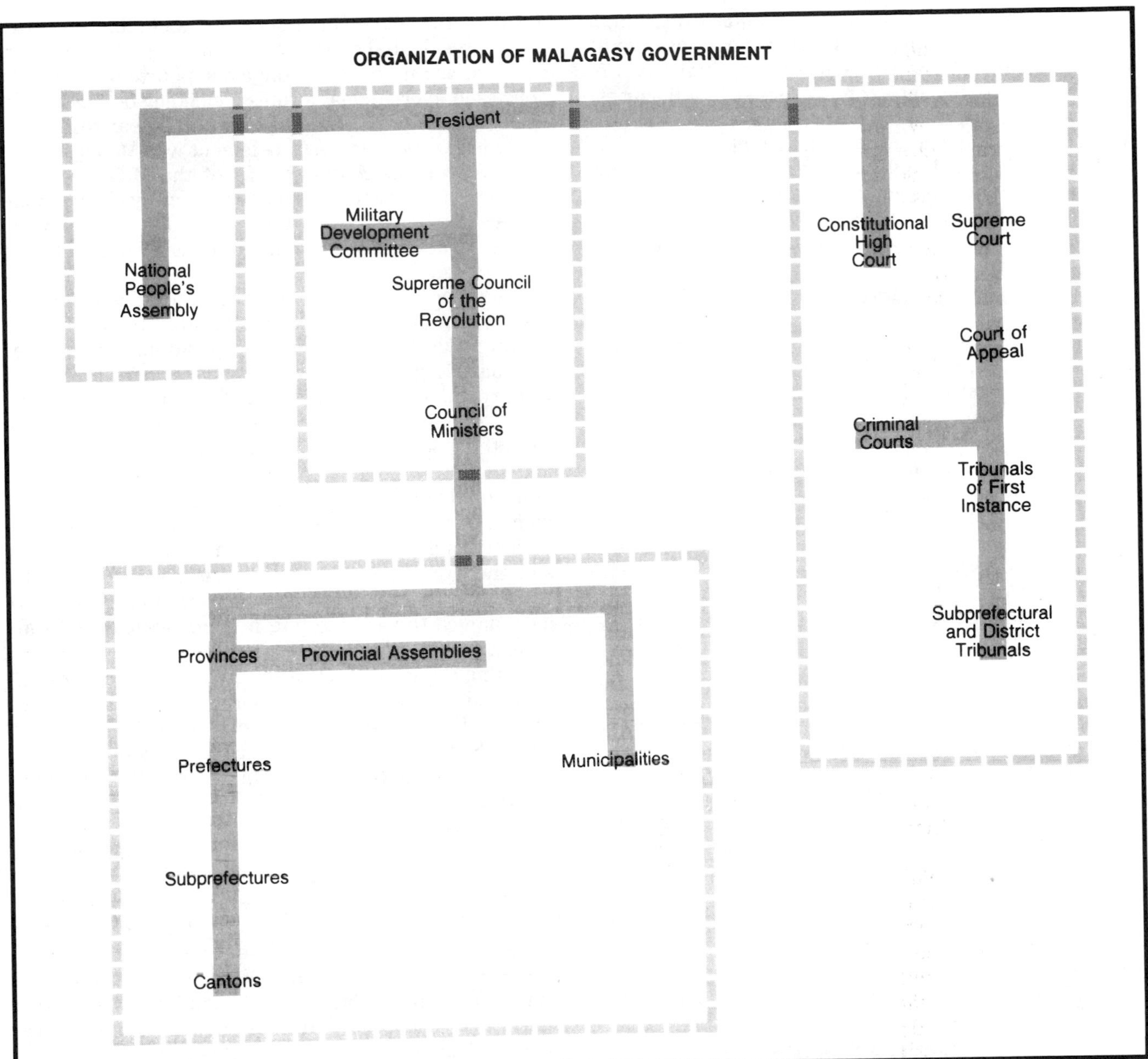

FREEDOM & HUMAN RIGHTS

In terms of political and civil rights, Madagascar is classified as a not-free country.

Although Madagascar is a radical and one-party state, human rights have not fared too badly under its revolutionary government. The government periodically blames its difficulties on supporters of the old regime but has not systematically acted against them. Madagascar's Penal Code is patterned after the French code, with the result that the concept of habeas corpus does not exist. Individuals suspected of activity against the state can be held incommunicado for up to 15 days, and this period may be extended at the discretion of the government.

Freedoms of assembly and expression are limited, but they do find a place in political life. Anyone arguing openly against the government's policies or advocating what the government calls "tribalism" risks contravening Article 16 of the Constitution, which authorizes the suspension of the rights and liberties of individuals impeding the advent of the socialist state. Permits to hold meetings can be withheld under the same article. There is prepublication censorship of the press, with the result that criticism tends to be subtle, indirect and carefully worded. Books and works of art are not censored. All political activities must be within the framework of the National Front for the Defense of the Revolution. The large majority of the electorate is politically apathetic. There are no resident human rights groups in the country.

CIVIL SERVICE

The civil service is under the control of the secretary of state for the civil service, who establishes recruitment policies, sets pay scales and handles discipline. In major policy decisions he is required to consult with the Higher Council for the Civil Service. Civil servants are divided broadly into three classes: functionaries, those with full tenure; auxiliaries, those without tenure but who may participate in pension plans; and contractual employees. In the last class are a few thousand French personnel assigned to various ministries as specialists. All three classes are further divided into five grades from A to E, with grade A being the highest.

LOCAL GOVERNMENT

For purpose of local government, Madagascar is divided into six provinces, 18 prefectures, 92 subprefectures and 705 cantons. The provinces are Toliary, Fianarantsoa, Antananarivo, Toamasina, Mahajunga and Antseranana. Each province is headed by a secretary of state delegate. Each prefecture is under a prefect, each subprefecture under a subprefect and each canton under a cantonal chief. Forty-three of the larger subprefectures have been split into administrative districts *(arrondissements administratifs)*. Some cantons are divided into villages or wards *(quartiers)*. The capital city of Antananarivo constitutes a prefecture by itself and is divided into urban communes.

The only representative institutions at the local level are the provincial assemblies, also called general councils, and the communal councils in the communes, which are territorially identical in most cases with cantons. These communal councils were transformed under the Ramanantsoa regime into the traditional *fokonolonas*. A *fokonolona* is an organization or council composed of the heads of all households of a village or hamlet, in many cases members of the same kinship group. *Fokonolonas* have been assigned a major role in the Constitution of 1975 as catalysts in the transformation of rural Malagasy society.

Forty-one urban municipalities have governments headed by mayors. There are 735 rural municipalities.

FOREIGN POLICY

Malagasy foreign policy since independence has been marked by two phases. The main determinants of foreign policy under President Philibert Tsiranana's 12-year regime were alignment with the West; close economic, cultural and defense ties with France; fear of Communist infiltration and subversion; admiration for Israel; and diplomatic and trade contacts with South Africa. On all these issues Tsiranana went counter to the prevailing trends in newly independent countries in Asia and Africa. The dominant influence in foreign relations during these 12 years appears to have been Madagascar's ties with France, which were institutionalized through a multiplicity of agreements covering defense, raw materials, aviation, the merchant marine, communications, justice and higher education. The Malagasy currency was linked to the franc; France was the leading trade partner; French interests monopolized various sectors of the economy; the Malagasy administration relied on French technicians; about two-thirds of the higher civil servants, including one-fifth of the presidential staff, were Frenchmen. Madagascar emerged as one of the strongest supporters of French policies in international forums, defending both France's use of force in Algeria and French nuclear testing in the Sahara. Another related element was Madagascar's emphasis on the Asian origins of the Malagasy race and the concomitant reluctance to identify closely with pan-African movements. What relations existed with African countries were oriented toward French-speaking nations.

The reversal of this policy, which took place on the assumption of power by Gabriel Ramanantsoa, was in part a reaction to the extreme positions adopted by Tsiranana. Agreements with France and South Africa were repudiated; diplomatic relations were established with Communist-bloc nations; Madagascar withdrew from the Common African and Malagasy Organization and the franc zone; and pro-Arab policies were announced. Madagascar's turn to the left also coincided with a general reaffirmation of common links with radical black African nations. French military bases and the U.S. space tracking station were forced to close down. But although Madagascar is considered to have moved toward the left, it is not within the Communist sphere of influence.

During the latter part of the 1970s Madagascar consolidated its relations with Communist and Arab nations at the expense of relations with the West and Israel. Significantly two friendship agreements were concluded with the Soviet Union, and the Palestine Liberation Organization was invited to function in the former Israeli embassy. North Korea has helped to build a "Pioneer Children's Palace" at Taomasina to train "young revolutionaries."

In the 1980s Madagascar reestablished ties with the West while continuing trade and diplomatic talks with the Soviet Union and China. It has signed aid agreements with the United States, France, Japan and Scandinavian nations. Madagascar joined with Mauritius and the Seychelles to form the Indian Ocean Commission in 1982.

PARLIAMENT

The People's National Assembly is a 137-member unicameral body elected for five-year terms. The first elections to this body were held in 1977. It replaced the People's National Development Council, which was set up in 1973.

The People's National Assembly holds two sessions each year, beginning in May and October. The October session is concerned primarily with approval of the national budget, which must be passed within 65 days of the opening; otherwise the budget becomes law without parliamentary approval. New legislation may be introduced either by the government or by members of the People's National Assembly. In the latter case, the draft must be approved first by the ministry concerned before being presented on the floor. Each bill is later considered by a commission of deputies specializing in the field to which the bill relates. Special commissions of inquiry may be appointed to handle complex bills. Although parliamentary approval is required for major legislation, the People's National Assembly may authorize the executive through enabling legislation to regulate routine matters. Basic legislation called organic laws are considered supplements to the Constitution, and acts that do not conform to the Constitution or organic laws may be declared unconstitutional by the Supreme Court. When the People's National Assembly is not in session, a permanent commission or bureau is elected to discharge its constitutional functions.

Suffrage is universal over 18. Each province and the capital district form an electoral district, in each of which political parties present a single list of candidates to fill the seats allotted to that district. The voters cast ballots for the list they prefer. If any party's list receives 55% or more of the total number of votes cast, it is awarded all the seats in the district. If no party receives the required majority, the seats are awarded to the competing parties in proportion to the percentage of the vote each receives, excluding, however, parties that receive less than 5% of the votes cast.

In the post-1983 People's National Assembly, the ruling FNDR held all 137 seats. Among the "revolutionary associations" comprising the FNDR's membership, the breakdown was as follows: AREMA, 117 seats; Congress Party for the Malagasy Revolution, nine seats; Popular Impulse for National Unity, six seats; Movement for Proletarian Power, three seats; and National Movement for the Independence of Madagascar, two seats.

POLITICAL PARTIES

From 1975 to 1990, the country's sole political party was the National Front for the Defense of the Malagasy Socialist Revolution (Front National pour la Défense de la Révolution Socialiste Malgache, FNDR). It was an umbrella organization that comprised the following "revolutionary associations" or parties:

- Vanguard of the Malagasy Revolution (Avante-garde de la Révolution Malgache, AREMA), headed by President Didier Ratsiraka
- Congress Party for the Malagasy Revolution (Antokon'ny Kongresy Ho An'ny Fahaleovantenan'i Madagasikara, AKFM), a leftist alliance including pro-Soviet Communists
- Popular Impulse for National Unity, a moderate group mostly made up of followers of former president Tsiranana
- Movement for Proletarian Power, an extreme left-wing party
- National Movement for the Independence of Madagascar (Mouvement National pour l'Indépendance de Madagascar, MONIMA), a left-wing nationalist party based in the South
- Malagasy Christian Democratic Union, formerly known as Rassemblement National Malgachy
- Socialist Monima, a pro-Beijing group

All opposition political parties were banned in 1975. Faced with increasing political pressure, Ratsiraka lifted the ban in March 1990. The result was the appearance of three new political groups: the relaunched Social Democratic Party (PSD), whose predecessor had held power from 1960–72; the AMF/3FM, which generally supported the government; and the right-wing Christian Democratic Movement.

ECONOMY

Madagascar is one of the 49 low-income countries of the world and also is one of the 45 countries classified by the United Nations as most seriously affected by the adverse economic conditions of the 1980s. It has a free-market economy in which the private sector is dominant.

During the first half of the 1980s Madagascar had an annual population growth of 3%, while the GDP declined annually.

Agriculture, including fishing and forestry, is the mainstay of the economy, accounting for 43% of the GDP, employing about 80% of the labor force and contributing about 85% to export earnings. Coffee, the principal crop, suffered from low yields and declining world prices in the 1980s. Demand for vanilla and cloves, also important crops, declined as other sources, principally Indonesia, developed.

Attempts at agricultural diversification have met with mixed results. Production of cotton, sugarcane and tobacco increased rapidly in the mid-1980s. However, most of the output was domestically consumed. Development of the cattle industry has met with little success because of poor hygiene, but earnings from fishing have improved.

Industry contributed only 14% to the GDP in 1985 and employed about 6% of the work force. It is confined to textile manufacturing and the processing of agricultural products. Development has been hampered by government policies that have restricted imports of equipment and spare parts and put strict controls on foreign-owned enterprises.

The island has extensive mineral deposits—chromite, graphite, mica, quartz, phosphates, bauxite, uranium and iron—but commercial exploitation is minimal.

In response to a growing trade deficit and increasing external debt, Madagascar was obliged to seek assis-

PRINCIPAL ECONOMIC INDICATORS

Gross National product (U.S. $ billions): 2,543 (1989)
GNP per capita (U.S. $): 230 (1989)
GNP average annual growth rate (%, 1980–89): 0.1
GNP per capita average annual growth rate (%, 1987–89): 1.0
Average annual rate of inflation (%, 1980–88): 17.3
Consumer Price Index (1980 = 100) 1986
All items: 285
Food: 297
Average annual growth rate (%, 1980–88)
General government consumption: −0.8
Private consumption: −0.4
Gross domestic investment: −0.7

BALANCE OF PAYMENTS, 1987
(U.S. $ millions)

Current account balance: −143
Merchandise exports: 314
Merchandise imports: −302
Trade balance: 12
Other goods, services & income +: 108
Other goods, services & income −: −416
Other goods, services & Income net: 308
Private unrequited transfers: 35
Official unrequited transfers: 117
Capital other than reserves: 60
Net errors & omissions: 73
Total: −83
Counterpart items: −100
Total: −183
Liabilities constituting foreign authorities reserves: 1
Total change in reserves: −36

GROSS DOMESTIC PRODUCT

GDP nominal (M.F. billions): 1,806.9 (1986)
GDP per capita (U.S. $): 155 (1988)
Average annual growth rate of GDP (%, 1980–88): 0.6
GDP by type of expenditure (%), 1986
- Consumption
  - Private: 79
  - Government: 14
- Gross domestic investment: 14
- Gross domestic saving: 8 (1988)
- Foreign trade
  - Exports: 13
  - Imports: −20

Cost components of GDP (%), 1986
- Net indirect taxes: 12
- Consumption of fixed capital, Compensation of employees, net operating surplus: 88

Sectoral origin of GDP (%) 1986
- Primary
  - Agriculture: 43
- Secondary
  - Industry: 10
- Tertiary
  - Transportation & communications, trade, finance, other services, government: 41

Average annual sectoral growth rates (%, 1980–88)
- Agriculture: 2.2
- Industry: −1.0
- Services: −0.1

tance from the IMF in 1982. In return for assistance, it agreed to a structural adjustment program that called for import controls, price increases, currency devaluations and layoffs. The government has met most of its annual targets and qualified for additional loans. However, economic growth has been minimal, and the nation has met its obligations by reducing its import bill. This in turn restricts the import-dependent industrial sector. With no effective economic growth, Madagascar faces a continuing cycle of IMF loans followed by stringent economic measures that weigh heavily on an increasingly restive population.

PUBLIC FINANCE

The Malagasy fiscal year is the calendar year. The national budget is published in two parts: current and capital. It also includes the annexed budgets of seven autonomous public agencies: the National Railroad, the National Radio and Television System, the Post Office, the National Printing Office, the Government Garage, the Public Works Department Workshop and the Harbor Authority. The Treasury accounts in the budget also include the National Lottery and the tobacco and match monopoly. The six provincial governments have separate budgets, as have the 41 urban municipalities and the 735 rural municipalities. Control over public expenditures is monitored by a branch of the Supreme Court. A special budgetary fund, the National Development and Investment Fund, acts as the channeling agency for capital expenditures.

FOREIGN AID, 1989

Total foreign aid (U.S. $ millions): 417.6
- Bilateral: 301.7
- Multilateral: 115.9

Madagascar's development plans have reflected the government's determination to restructure the economy by substituting national for foreign interests and state-financed or state-controlled companies for private capital. Initially, public and private domestic funds were expected to provide most of the money needed, but shrinkage in domestic revenues led to a reliance on foreign sources. Emphasis was put on infrastructure and agriculture, with one of the main objectives to establish the basic conditions for expansion of production. The program quickly exhausted foreign reserves and increased public debt. By the end of the 1970s the economy was in serious trouble, and the government was forced to seek IMF assistance. The assistance had a dramatic effect on government policy. Madagascar accepted a program of structural readjustment that included a reduction in public spending; the abolition of food subsidies; and restrictions on wage increases. The Malagasy franc was devalued by 15% in 1982 and 1984 and by 20% in 1986. The following year it was devalued by 41%.

The government's five-year development plan for 1986–90 emphasized self-sufficiency in food, a rise in export products, improvement in living standards and reduction in energy imports. A total of 40% of the plan's financing was to come from external sources and 30% from private investment.

Despite implementation of adjustment programs, economic growth has been minimal—only 2% in 1988. The programs have fanned inflation, which exceeded 20% in 1987, and generated widespread domestic criticism.

During 1970–88 Madagascar received $118 million in aid from the United States. Other Western aid totalled $2.6 billion from 1970–87. Assistance from Communist countries totalled $491 million from 1970–88.

CURRENCY & BANKING

The Malagasy unit of currency is the Malagasy franc, divided into 100 centimes. Coins are issued in denominations of 1, 2, 5, 10 and 20 francs; notes are issued in denominations of 50, 100, 500, 1,000 and 5,000 francs.

In 1969 the Malagasy franc was devalued in line with the French franc. Since 1973 the French monetary authorities have ceased to maintain the franc-dollar rate within previously agreed margins. As a result, the value of the Malagasy franc has fluctuated on foreign exchange markets. In June 1991 the dollar exchange rate was $1 = MF1,443.864. In response to IMF demands, the franc was devalued by 15% in 1982 and 1984, by 20% in 1986 and by 41% in 1987.

On leaving the franc zone in 1973, the government established the Banque Centrale de la République Malgache as the central bank and the bank of issue. All commercial banks and insurance companies were nationalized in 1975, but in 1988 the government announced that the banks would become limited liability companies open to private and foreign investment. The banking sector consists of four banks, of which the Banque Centrale de la République Malagache is the bank of issue.

FINANCIAL INDICATORS, 1988

Total reserves minus gold (SDR's millions): 187
SDR's (millions): 0.0
Reserve position in IMF (SDR's millions): 0.0
Foreign exchange (SDR's millions): 187
Ratio of external debt to total reserves (1986): 14.8 (1988)
Central bank, 1989
- Assets %
  - Foreign assets: 21.9
  - Claims on government: 77.4
  - Claims on banks: 0.7
  - Claims on private sector: 0.0
- Liabilities %
  - Reserve money: 19.0
  - Government deposits: 43.4
  - Foreign liabilities: 142.7
  - Capital accounts: 0.5

Money supply 1986
Stock (M.F. billions): 598.4
M[1] per capita: 50,700
Private banks, 1989
- Assets %
  - Loans to government: 8.8
  - Loans to private sector: 65.2
  - Reserves: 12.4
  - Foreign asssets: 13.6
- Liabilities
  - Deposits (M.F. billions): 893.5
  - of which %
    - Demand deposits: 42.7
    - Savings deposits: 12.7
    - Government deposits: 10.0
    - Foreign liabilities: 3.6

External debt 1988
- Total (U.S. $ millions): 3,602
  - of which public (U.S. $ millions): 3,317
  - of which private (U.S. $ millions): 0
- Debt service, (long-term) total (U.S. $ millions): 161
  - Repayment
    - Principal (%): 49.7
    - Interest (%): 50.3
- Debt service ratio: (%) 39.1
- External public debt as % of GNP: 192.7
- Debt service as % of GNP: 9.3
- Debt service as % of exports: 39.0
- Terms of public borrowing
  - Commitments (million U.S. $): 352
  - Average interest rate (%): 2.4
  - Average maturity (yrs.): 31
- Net flow of publicly guaranteed external capital (U.S. $ millions): 150

GROWTH PROFILE
(Annual Growth Rates, %)

Projected population, (1988–2000): 2.6
Projected crude birth rate, (/1000) (1990–95): 44.8
Projected crude death rate, (/1000) (1990–95): 12.6
Urban population, (1980–88): 5.9
Labor force, (1985–2000): 2.3
GNP, (1980–88): 0.1
GNP per capita, (1986–88): −2.4
GDP, (1980–88): 0.6
Inflation, (1980–88): 17.3
Agriculture, (1980–88): 2.2
Industry, (1980–88): −1.0
Services, (1980–88): −0.1
Money holdings, (1980–87): 16.3
Manufacturing earnings per employee, (1980–88): −10.3
Energy production, (1980–88): 9.3
Energy consumption, (1980–88): 1.5
Exports, (1980–87): −3.5
Imports, (1980–87): −1.8
General government consumption, (1980–88): −0.8
Private consumption, (1980–87): −0.4
Gross domestic investment, (1980–87): −0.7

AGRICULTURE

Agriculture accounts for 43% of the GDP and employs 79.6% of the labor force. It contributes almost 85% to export earnings.

Much of the land is unsuitable for cultivation because of inadequate rainfall, laterization or mountainous terrain, and only 3.5% of the land area is under some form of cultivation. About 25% of the land under cultivation is fallow, 10% is under irrigated crops, 10% under tree crops and 30% under dryland crops such as sisal, tobacco, cassava, corn or peanuts. The tree crops are grown primarily in the East and North, the irrigated crops in the central highlands and the West, and the dryland crops throughout the island. Crops growing in the northern and eastern regions are subject to periodic devastation by cyclones.

The majority of the farms are small-scale subsistence units. Plantations formerly owned by the French and Réunionnais are small both in number and in their share of the total cultivated area. But they dominate the production of sisal, sugar, tobacco, bananas and cotton. The total number of farms is estimated at 940,000. The average holding is about 1 ha. (2.4 ac.); only 3% of all holdings exceed 4 ha. (10 ac.); 35% are less than 0.5 ha. (1.2 ac.); 30% are 0.5 ha. (1.2 ac.) to 1 ha. (2.4 ac.); 15% are 1 ha. (2.4 ac.) to 1.5 ha. (3.7 ac.); 17% are 1.5 ha. (3.7 ac.) to 4 ha. (10 ac.). Almost all holdings are heavily fragmented. About 5% of the farms are cultivated by sharecroppers. Landless agricultural workers constitute only 0.7% of the agricultural labor force.

Agricultural techniques vary from one ethnic group to another and also in accordance with terrain, climate and water supply. The most intensive form of cultiva-

AGRICULTURAL INDICATORS, 1984–85

Agriculture's share of GDP (%): 31 (1989)
Average annual growth rate (%, 1980–88): 2.2
Value added in agriculture (U.S. $ millions): 775 (1988)
Cereal imports (000 metric tons): 217 (1988)
Index of Agricultural Production (1979–81 = 100): 113 (1986)
Index of Food Production (1979–81 = 100): 114 (1986)
Index of Food Production per Capita (1979–81 = 100): 97 (1986–88)
Number of tractors: 2,800 (1986)
Number of harvester-threshers: 138 (1986)
Total fertilizer consumption: 34 (000 metric tons) (1985–86)
Fertilizer consumption (g./ha., hundreds) (per ac., 3.5 oz.): 21 (8.5) (1987–88)
Number of farms (000): 1,544
Average size of holding, ha. (ac.): 1.3 (3.2)
Size class (%)
  Below 1 ha. (below 2.47 ac.): 65.0
  1–5 ha. (2.47–12.35 ac.): 35.0
  5–10 ha. (12.35–24.7 ac.): 0.0
  10–20 ha. (24.7–49.4 ac.): 0.0
  20–50 ha. (49.4–123.5 ac.): 0.0
  50–200 ha. (123.5–494 ac.): 0.0
  Over 200 ha. (over 494 ac.): 0.0
Farms as % of total land area: 3.5
Land use (%):
  Permanent crops: 15.4
  Temporary crops: 84.6
Yields: kg./ha. (lb./ac.) 1989
  Grains: 1,857
  Roots & tubers: 6,369
  Legumes: 826
  Fruits (000 metric tons): 824
  Vegetables (000 metric tons): 303
  Milk, kg. animal: 700
Livestock (000) 1989
  Cattle: 10,250
  Horses: 1 (1986)
  Sheep: 800
  Pigs: 1,420
Forestry, 1988
  Production of roundwood, 000 cu. m.: 7,634
    of which industrial roundwood (%): 10.6
Fishing, 1988
  Total catch (000 metric tons): 80.0
    of which marine (%): 32.5
  Value of exports (U.S. $ 000): 32,960

tion is practiced among the Merina and the Betsileo of the central highlands. The Betsileo are noted for their terrace cultivation and intricate irrigation systems. In the central highlands, two crops may be grown in a year. Plowing usually is done with a long-handled spade or hoe, and sometimes trampling the field replaces plowing. On the eastern coast, the prevalent form of cultivation is known as *tavy,* or the slash-and-burn method. Under this method, trees are felled and burned just before the rainy season. After two or three years of cultivation, the clearing is left fallow and is replanted only after an interval of 10 to 20 years. Because of its destructive effects on the soil and vegetation, *tavy* is banned by the government, but nevertheless it continues to practiced widely because of the shorter crop cycle for *tavy* rice. A similar system, known as *tetikala,* is practiced in the arid South and Southwest. On the western coast and in the Southwest, empty streambeds are cultivated in the dry season, a practice known as *baiboho.* The cultivation of marginally productive land on the hillsides is known as *tanety.* The small size of the average plot, the mountainous nature of the terrain and the poverty of the farmers inhibit both mechanization and the application of chemical fertilizers.

Agricultural development programs have emphasized fokonolona types of cooperatives and regional land development projects: There are 12 special rural development areas initiated originally by private French ventures. They were, until the nationalization measures of the mid-1970s, operated by companies of mixed economy and directed by French experts. These programs have included the Lake Alaotra Rice Growing Project, the Mangoky Delta Cotton-Growing Project, the Marovoay Basin Rice-Growing Project and the Morondava Region Project.

The island's diverse soils and climate permit cultivation of a wide range of agricultural products, including over 15 export crops. The country is basically self-sufficient in its staple food products, especially rice, which is grown by an estimated 80% of the country's farmers, occupies up to one-third of the cultivated land area and accounts for 40% to 50% of the annual value of agricultural production. Nevertheless, 24,000 tons of cereals were imported in 1983. The central highlands is considered as the granary of the country, accounting for nearly half of the irrigated rice production. Cassava (manioc) is the second food crop in terms of area, grown throughout the island, especially in the South. The principal export crops are coffee, sugarcane, vanilla, cloves, pepper, sisal and tobacco.

The main livestock-producing areas are the province of Toliary in the South and West, the prefectures of Alaotra in the central highlands and Vohemar, all of which account for two-thirds of the national herd. The annual takeoff rate is high because all the available animals are slaughterd, and the per capita consumption of meat also is high. In addition, cattle are used to trample the rice fields and to draw plows. Other factors favoring an expansion of the sector are the absence of major cattle diseases, extensive pastures covering about 34 million ha. (84 million ac.) and a suitable climate. The national cattle herd consists largely of zebu, but improved breeds are being introduced. Livestock censuses usually suffer from underenumeration because of the liability of the cattle tax.

Forests cover about 12 million ha. (29.6 million ac.), or about 12% of the land area, but only 500,000 ha. (1.2 million ac.) are publicly owned.

Despite a long coastline and 19 major lakes, fishing is largely unorganized and contributes less than 1% to the GDP. The strong winds and currents off the eastern coast discourage fishing. Most of the sea catch is exported, while the freshwater fish are consumed domestically. A large commercial fishing port is being built at Mahajunga.

MANUFACTURING

Industry contributed 10% of the GDP in 1986, compared to 5% at the time of independence, although from 1973–

85 industry had a negative growth rate. It employs about 6% of the economically active population. Agro-based products account for 95% of manufacturing output. Of the 365 manufacturing establishments, about 100 are rice mills, of which only 20 can be classiifed as large-scale. A large proportion is owned by French, Asian or other nationals. There is very little concentration of industrial capacity in any one geographical area. There are major plants at Toamasina, Antsirabe, Antseranana and Mahajunga, but smaller plants are in almost every regional center. However, dispersion of plants has resulted in higher unit costs and transportation bottlenecks. There also is a serious shortage of entrepreneurs and managerial personnel.

MANUFACTURING INDICATORS, 1987

Share of GDP (%): 10 (1986)
Value added in manufacturing (U.S. $ millions): 118 (1970)
  Food and agriculture (%): 49 (latest)
  Textiles (%): 25 (latest)
  Machinery (%): 5 (latest)
  Chemicals (%): 9 (1970)
Earnings per employee in manufacturing (latest)
  Growth rate (%, 1980–87): −10.3
  Index (1980=100): 66 (1985)
Total earnings as % of value added: 40 (1985)

The largest industrial subsector is the processing of agricultural products, which accounts for 50% of the value added in manufacturing. Another 25% is accounted for by textiles. Under the second and third economic plans, the largest investments went to textiles, leather, wood and paper, petroleum refining and food processing—all of which made satisfactory gains in output, averaging more than 10% a year.

The government's radical orientation was reflected in the many restrictions on private foreign investment. Under the Investment Code of 1973, investments are restricted to nonvital sectors. Foreign investors are required to be minority stockholders, accept stringent currency controls, transfer their company headquarters to Madagascar, Malagasize their personnel and reinvest 10% of their profits and reserves locally.

Nationalization of key industries, which began in 1975, slowed down in 1978 and 1979. In several cases, notably insurance, banking, import-export, and oil refining and distribution, industries were nationalized completely, while in other cases the government has taken majority but not complete control of former private companies. Just as the percentage of nationalization has varied, so have the tactics. In some cases the private investors, mostly foreign, have been given no choice in the matter, and some have received little or no compensation. In other cases the government and private investors have reached negotiated settlements and compensation has been agreed to. In May 1979 the prime minister announced that the government controlled more than 70% of the national economy, as opposed to 13% when it came to power in June 1975.

In response to the IMF restructuring programs of the 1980s, the government announced that unprofitable state enterprises would be closed.

MINING

The only minerals currently exploited are chromite and graphite. Madagascar is the seventh-largest graphite producer in the world. Recoverable deposits of nickel (70,000 tons), bauxite (500 million tons) and coal (60 million tons) have been located but remain unexploited because of technical problems.

ENERGY

Madagascar is not self-sufficient in energy and imports fuel, mainly from the Soviet Union. Crude petroleum accounted for 10% of the cost of imports in 1987.

Despite extensive exploration, no oil deposits have been discovered. The Toamasina oil refinery has a potential throughput of 16,000 bbl. per day.

ENERGY INDICATORS

Average annual energy production growth rate (%, 1980–88): 9.3
Energy consumption per capita (000 kg. oil equivalent): 39 (1988)
Energy imports as % of merchandise exports: 45 (1988)
Average annual growth rate of energy consumption (%, 1980–88): 1.5
Electricity 1986
  Installed capacity (000 kw.): 219
  Production (million kw.-hr.): 516
    % fossil fuel: 41.3
    % hydro: 58.7
    % nuclear: 0.0
  Consumption per capita (kw.-hr.): 46
Petroleum
  Consumption (million bbl.): 3
  Refining capacity (bbl./day): 16,000 (1990)
Coal
  Reserves (billion metric tons): 1.075 (1989)
  Consumption (metric tons): 12,000

LABOR

Only 10% of the total economically active population is wage-earning; the remainder are either self-employed or unpaid agricultural help.

Wages and working conditions are governed by the Labor Code of 1960, which guarantees minimum wages. Each province is divided into three zones each for minimum-wage regulations, which are periodically revised by advisory committees. The law also grants workers accident insurance, maternity benefits, family allowances, medical care and retirement pensions.

Unemployment has been estimated at over 20% since the 1970s and has led to serious riots against the Comorans (who were believed to be competing with the Malagasy for available jobs).

Only 4% of the labor force is unionized. Of the 36 labor unions, some 32 are affiliated with the African Federation of Free Trade Unions. The four largest

LABOR INDICATORS, 1985

Totally economically active population (000): 3,929
% working-age population (15–64): 74.9
% female: 44.2
Activity rate (%)
  Total: 39.2
  Male: 48.8
  Female: 31.6
Sectoral employment (%)
  Agriculture, forestry, fishing: 79.6
  Manufacturing, mining, quarrying, public utilities, construction: 6.3
  Trade, hotels, restaurants, transport, communications, finance, real estate, services: 14.1
Average annual growth rate of labor force, 1980–2000 (%): 2.3
Unemployment (000): 29 (1984)
Labor under 20 years (%): 24.0 (1975)

unions are the Christian Confederation of Malagasy Trade Unions, with 158 affiliated unions and 41,670 members; the Union des Syndicats Autonomes de Madagascar, with 46 affiliated unions and 29,445 members; the Confédération des Travailleurs Malgaches, with 30,000 members; and the Union des Syndicats des Travailleurs de Madagascar, with 30,000 members.

FOREIGN COMMERCE

In 1987 coffee made up 45% of exports, vanilla 15% and cloves 11%. Madagascar also exported sugar and petroleum products. Its principal markets were France, Japan, Italy, West Germany and the United States. Intermediate manufactures comprised 30%, capital goods 28%, petroleum 15%, consumer goods 14% and food 13% of imports in 1987. Most goods came from France, West Germany, the United Kingdom and other members of the European Community as well as the United States.

FOREIGN TRADE INDICATORS, 1987

Exports (U.S. $ millions): 284
Imports (U.S. $ millions): 319
Balance of trade (U.S. $ millions): −35
Annual growth rate, (1980–87, exports %): −3.5
Annual growth rate, (1980–87, imports %): −1.8
Ratio of international reserves in terms of months of imports: 3.7
Terms of trade (1980 = 100): 95
Import Price Index (1980 = 100): 77.8 (1986)
Export Price Index (1980 = 100): 107.7 (1986)

Direction of Trade (%), 1986

	Imports	Exports
EC	48.6	58.2
U.S.	10.7	14.8
U.S.S.R. & East European economies	10.3	3.6
Japan	6.5	10.9

Composition of Trade (%), 1986

	Imports	Exports
Food and agricultural raw materials	17.0	84.6
Fuels and other energy	23.1	2.2
Mineral ores and concentrates	0.4	5.7
Manufactured goods	59.5	7.5
of which chemicals	11.7	1.3
of which machinery	28.8	1.9

TRANSPORTATION & COMMUNICATIONS

The state-operated rail system consists of 883 km. (549 mi.) of meter-gauge track. The main lines run from Antananarivo to Toamasina, with a branch from Moramanga to Lake Alaotra; from Antananarivo to Antsirabe; and from Fianarantsoa to Manakara.

The main inland waterway is the Pangalanes Canal, which runs for 700 km. (434 mi.) from Toamasina to Farafangana. Most rivers in the West are navigable.

TRANSPORTATION INDICATORS

Roads (latest)
  Length, km. (mi.): 49,555 (30,792)
  Paved (%): 11
Motor vehicles (latest)
  Automobiles: 27,317
  Trucks and buses: 20,519
  Persons per vehicle: 228
Railroads (latest)
  Track, km. (mi.): 883 (549)
  Passenger-km. (passenger-mi.) (millions): 205 (127)
  Freight, ton-km. (ton-mi.) (millions): 201 (94.5)
Merchant marine
  Vessels: 76 (1989)
  Total deadweight tonnage (000): 87.8 (1989)
Ports (latest)
  Cargo loaded (000 metric tons): 468
  Cargo unloaded (000 metric tons): 1,596
Air (latest)
  Km. flown (millions): 2.0 (1985)
  Passenger-km. (passenger-mi.) (millions): 435.8 (270.8)
  Freight-km. (freight-mi.) (millions): 65.2 (30.5)
  Mail-ton-km. (mail ton-mi.) (millions): 1.2 (0.5) (1985)
  Airports with scheduled flights: 40 (1990)
Inland waterways (latest)
  Length, km. (mi.): 1,170 (727)

COMMUNICATION INDICATORS, 1986

Telephones
  Total (000): 46 (1987)
  Persons per telephone: 239 (1987)
Phone traffic (000 calls)
  Local: 23,540
  Long distance: 4,890
  Combined national: 28,430
  International: 318
Post office
  Number of post offices: 9,106 (1988)
  Pieces of mail handled (000): 47,897 (1988)
Telegraph
  Total traffic (000 calls): 183
  National: 172
  International: 11
Telex
  Subscriber lines: 387
  Traffic (000 minutes): 988
Telecommunications 1990
  Satellite stations: 2

TOURISM & TRAVEL INDICATORS, 1986

Total tourist receipts (U.S. $ millions): 11 (1988)
Expenditures by nationals abroad (U.S. $ millions): 32 (1988)
Number of hotel beds (000): 4
Average length of stay: 13 nights
Tourist nights (000): 169

The road system comprises national highways, provincial roads and local roads, with a total length of 49,555 km. (30,792 mi.), of which 11% are paved. The main national highways radiate from Antananarivo to Mahajunga, Antseranana, Toamasina, Fianarantsoa, Ihosy and Toliary. There are five moderate-size trucking companies in addition to a number of truckers' cooperatives.

The national airline is the Société Malgache des Transports Aériens, which operates a fleet of six aircraft on internal services as well as external routes to France, Comoros, Djibouti, Kenya, Mauritius, Réunion and Tanzania. The principal airport is at Ivato, near Antananarivo. There are 149 airfields in the country, of which 119 are usable and 30 have permanent-surface runways. Three have runways over 2,500 m. (8,000 ft.).

Tourism has received low priority in development programs and is hindered by a lack of facilities. The government approved a tourism investment program in 1989.

DEFENSE

The defense structure is headed by the president, who exercises his operational authority through the Military Development Committee.

Military manpower is ensured by conscription of all males from 20 to 50 for 18-month periods. However, it has not been necessary to enforce conscription law because of a surplus of voluntary enlistees.

Army

Personnel: 20,000

Organization: 1 battalion group; 1 engineer regiment; 1 signals regiment; 1 service regiment; 7 construction regiments

Equipment: 12 tanks; 38 combat vehicles; 30 half-tracks; 12 guns; 12 howitzers; rocket launchers; 50 air defense guns

Navy

Personnel: 500 (including 100 marines)

Units: 1 marine company; 1 patrol craft; 2 landing craft

Naval bases: Antseranana, Toamasina, Mahajunga, Toliary, Nossi-Bé, Fort-Dauphin and Manakara

Air Force

Personnel: 500

Organization: 12 combat aircraft; 1 fighter squadron; 1 transportation squadron; 1 helicopter squadron

Air bases: Arivoniamamo (Antananarivo), Ivato, Antseranana, Fort-Dauphin, Toamasina, Mahajunga and Toliary.

The army has no offensive capability.

Until 1972 France maintained military bases in Madagascar and also provided military training and equipment for the Malagasy security forces. Sources of military supplies have diversified since President Ratsiraka assumed power.

EDUCATION

Education is in principle free, universal and compulsory from ages six to 13 in some areas and from seven to 14 in other areas.

Schooling lasts for 13 years, divided into six years of primary school and seven years of secondary school. The primary course is itself divided into three cycles of two years each: a preparatory course, an elementary course and a middle course. Upon completion of primary education, the student is awarded a *certificat d'études primaires élémentaires.* Secondary schools offer two cycles: the short cycle *(enseignement court)* lasts four years and the long cycle *(enseignement long)* lasts three years. Upon completion of secondary education, the student receives a *baccalauréat.*

The school year runs from February to October. The languages of instruction are Malagasy in primary schools and French in secondary schools and higher institutions.

Teacher shortages exist at every level. Secondary-school teachers are trained at the National Institute of Advanced Research and Teacher Training.

Vocational training programs in more than 40 specializations are available to Malagasy students with primary education. Four-year programs are offered in

EDUCATION INDICATORS, 1988

Literacy
- Total (%): 67.5
- Males (%): 73.7
- Females (%): 61.6

First level
- Schools: 13,404
- Students: 1,487,726
- Teachers: 38,361
- Student/teacher ratio: 38:8

Second level
- Schools: 1,367
- Students: 350,024
- Teachers: 12,473
- Student/teacher ratio: 28.1

Vocational
- Schools: 61
- Students: 15,526
- Teachers: 1,172
- Student/teacher ratio: 13.2

Third level
- Institutions: 5
- Students: 27,294
- Teachers: 613
- Student/teacher ratio: 44.5
- Gross enrollment rate: 3.2% (1987)
- Students (/100,000 pop.): 333

Foreign study
- Foreign students in national universities: 147 (1988)
- Students abroad: 3,983
  - of whom in
    - U.S.: 74 (1988)
    - France: 3,420 (1988)
    - Federal Republic of Germany: 58 (1988)
    - U.K.: 13 (1988)

Public expenditures, 1988
- Total (M.F.): 59,842,000,000
- % of GNP: 2.5
- % of current expenditure: 97.8

GRADUATES, 1987

Total: 2,587
Education: 172
Humanities & religion: 552
Law: 292
Social & behavioral sciences: 45
Commerce & business: 580
Natural sciences: 410
Mathematics & computer science: 35
Medicine: 231
Engineering: 210
Agriculture, forestry, fisheries: 60

technical colleges and seven-year programs in technical institutes. Private schools account for a major share of the educational enrollment: 2.3% at the first level and 49% at the second level.

The responsibility for both private and public education is vested in the Ministry of Cultural Affairs. However, primary education is also partly financed by local funds.

Higher education is provided by the University of Madagascar.

LEGAL SYSTEM

The legal system is based on French civil law and customary Malagasy law. The judicature is headed by the Supreme Court, with three chambers: the Chamber of Cassation, with five justices; the Chamber of Administrative Law, with three justices; and the Chamber of Accounts, also with three justices. Below the Supreme Court are the Court of Appeals and the High Court. The Court of Appeals is the highest appellate court; it also hears disciplinary cases against magistrates and advocates. The court has six chambers of three judges each: civil, commercial, land registration, labor law, minor criminal and chamber of accusations. The High Court is composed of the first president of the Court of Appeals, two presidents of the chambers of the Court of Appeals, five other judges of the court drawn by lot; and eight members of the People's National Assembly; the High Court's sole function is to try the president or members of the Council of Ministers.

All criminal cases are tried by one of 10 criminal courts without permanent location. The court comprises a magistrate and four assessors (or laymen picked from a list of 18 at the beginning of each court term). The subordinate courts are the tribunals of first instance, located in 25 urban centers; and subprefectural and district courts. Tribunals of first instance have complete jurisdiction over civil cases but only limited jurisdiction over criminal cases. Each generally has five chambers, of which the first three deal with civil, commercial and labor law. The fourth chamber, also known as the police court or the court of petty sessions, deals with criminal charges involving minor crimes. The fifth chamber deals with land registration. All cases are heard by at least two judges assisted by an investigating magistrate, an officer peculiar to the French judicial system. At the base of the judicial system are 105 subprefectural and district tribunals, which hear minor cases.

There is no concept of habeas corpus in the Malagasy legal system. In criminal cases the accused must be charged within three days or be released. However, persons suspected of activity against the state may be legally detained incommunicado for 15 days, subject to indefinite extension if considered necessary by the government. Defendants are generally charged formally within the specified time frame and, on being charged, are entitled to the assistance of counsel. Counsel is readily available, and in cases of indigence, court-appointed counsel is provided. Arbitrary arrest or detention generally occurs, however, in cases that involve an alleged threat to the state.

Each province and subprefecture has a central prison for prisoners serving sentences of less than five years. In addition, there are 25 lesser prisons at the seats of various courts housing prisoners serving terms of less than two years or who are awaiting trial. Prisoners serving terms of over five years are sent to maximum-security jails on the smaller coastal islands.

LAW ENFORCEMENT

The three principal law enforcement agencies are the National Gendarmerie, the Republican Security Force and the Civil Police. The National Gendarmerie is the principal agency concerned with public order. It is controlled directly by the Ministry of the Interior. The Republican Security Force is an elite force with antiriot capability. The Civil Police maintains order in small towns and villages.

No information is available on the nature and incidence of crime in Madagascar.

HEALTH

The government's austerity program has entailed severe cutbacks in health services. The Ministry of Health provides only 25% of drug requirements, and prices of drugs at private dispensaries have doubled since 1987. Malnutrition is high, particularly in the Antsirabe region, where 61% of the children suffer from stunted growth.

The most serious health problems are malaria, schistosomiasis, tuberculosis, leprosy and bubonic plague. On the other hand, the island is free from many common tropical diseases, such as sleeping sickness and smallpox. Only 32% of the population have access to safe drinking water.

FOOD & NUTRITION

The staple food is rice, which is consumed in prodigious quantities. The Malagasy rank fifth in the world in per capita consumption of rice: 136 kg. (300 lb.) per year. The national dish is *romazava*, made of boiled rice, and the national drink is *ranopango*, or water in which rice has been boiled. No sauces and very little

HEALTH INDICATORS

Health personnel, 1982
- Physicians: 1,283
  - Persons per: 7,451
- Dentists: 94 (1981)
- Nurses: 3,813
- Pharmacists: 87 (1981)
- Midwives: 1,232

Hospitals, 1978
- Number: 749
- Number of beds (/10,000): 23 (1982)
- Admissions/discharges (/10,000): 699
- Bed occupancy rate: 57.9%
- Average length of stay (days): 2

Type of hospitals (%), 1978
- Government: 100.0
- Private nonprofit: 0.0
- Private profit: 0.0

Public health expenditures, (latest)
- Per capita (U.S. $): 1.90

Vital statistics
- Crude death rate (/1,000 pop.): 15 (1990)
- Life Expectancy at birth (1990)
  - Males: 50
  - Females: 54
- Infant mortality rate (/1,000 live births): 97 (1990)
- Child mortality rate (1985–90) under 5 yrs. (/1,000): 90

Population with access to safe water (%): 32 (latest)

MEDIA INDICATORS

Newspapers
- Number of dailies: 5 (latest)
- Circulation (000): 138 (latest)
- Per 1,000 pop.: 12 (latest)
- Number of periodicals: 24 (latest)
- Newsprint consumption: (1988)
- Total metric tons: 240
- Per 1,000 pop. (kg.): 21

Book publishing
- Number of titles: 441 (latest)

Broadcasting
- Annual expenditures (millions M.F.): 56.0 (1985)

Radio
- Number of transmitters: 24 (latest)
- Number of persons per radio receiver: 5.4 (1989)

Television
- Television transmitters: 41 (latest)
- Number of persons per TV receiver: 89 (1989)

Cinema
- Number of fixed cinemas: 37 (latest)
- Seating capacity (000): 12 (latest)
  - Seats (/1,000) pop: 1.1 (1987)
- Gross box office receipts (millions M.F.): 441 (1987)

Films
- Import of long films: 68 (1987)
  - % from U.S.: 73.5
  - % from USSR: 16.2
  - % from France: 1.5
  - % from Italy: 1.5

fat, salt or spices are used. Consumption of meat is limited to festive occasions.

Government austerity measures have had a severe impact on everyday life. A total of 80% of households cannot afford minimum calorie requirements, and malnutrition is the chief cause of infant death.

MEDIA & CULTURE

In 1987 five daily newspapers were published in the country, with total circulation of 138,000. Only one daily is published in both French and Malagasy. The largest-selling daily is *Midi Madagascar* (French, 28,000). The periodicals press consists of 24 titles.

After more than a decade of relative freedom under President Tsiranana, when there was a vigorous opposition press, the press experienced rigid controls and politically oriented guidelines under Ratsiraka. The Constitution of 1975 guarantees freedom of the press only if it advances "the strengthening of the new democracy for the advent of the socialist state." In 1989 Ratsiraka announced the end of restrictions on press freedom and the permanent abolition of press censorship.

The national news agency is Agence Nationale d'Information Taratra (ANTA), which replaced Agence Madagascar Presse in 1977. AFP, Reuters and UPI maintain bureaus in Antananarivo.

In terms of the number of books published annually, Madagascar ranks among the top African countries. Madagascar adheres to the Berne and Florence conventions.

The official broadcasting service, Radiodiffusion Nationale Malgache, operates 24 transmitters (in addition to a relay station at Fenoarivo with eight transmitters) broadcasting two home-service networks: Network I, broadcasting in Malagasy for 18½ hours daily; and Network II, broadcasting in French for 20 hours daily. All programs are of national origin. Network III is an international shortwave service, broadcasting in French and English for seven hours per week.

Television, introduced in 1967, covers about 10% of the population and is on the air for about 16 hours a week. Of the 2,300 annual television broadcasting hours, 552 hours are dedicated to information, 529 hours to education, 483 hours to culture and 736 hours to entertainment.

There is no local film production.

CULTURAL & ENVIRONMENTAL INDICATORS (latest)

Libraries (pre-1986)
- Number: 56
- Volumes (000): 76
- Registered borrowers (000): 69
- Loans (/1,000 pop.): 2

Museums
- Annual attendance (000): 21
- Attendance (/1,000 pop.): 2

Performing arts (pre-1986)
- Number of performances: 140
- Annual attendance (000): 60
- Attendance (/1,000 pop.): 7

Nature reserves:
- Number of facilities: 31

SOCIAL WELFARE

The National Social Insurance Fund administers a limited Social Security program. Among benefits provided are family allowances for children under 14 years of age (21 if they are students), old age, disability and death allowances and half wages for employed pregnant women. In addition, there are a number of private social welfare agencies and mutual assistance societies. Social welfare spending has been affected by the government austerity program.

GLOSSARY

baiboho: cultivation of empty streambeds in the dry season.

côtier: an inhabitant of the coastal region, as distinguished from the Merinas who inhabit the highlands of the interior.

fokonolona: a council composed of the heads of all households in a village or hamlet, serving as the basic unit of local government.

tanety: cultivation of marginally productive land on the hillsides.

tavy: slash-and-burn cultivation, now illegal.

CHRONOLOGY (from 1960)

1960— Madagascar becomes a sovereign independent republic within the French Community under the name the Malagasy Republic, with Philibert Tsiranana as president.

1971— The Antandroy, an ethnic group in the South, revolts in protest against northern domination; the government takes drastic action to suppress the revolt. . . . Vice President André Resempa is dismissed.

1972— In national elections, Tsiranana is reelected with 99.72% of the votes. . . . A strike by students at the medical school escalates into nationwide riots; amid the clamor for his resignation, Tsiranana hands over all his powers to Gen. Gabriel Ramanantsoa, who forms a government of national unity. . . . Voters approve a constitutional referendum to abolish all existing parliamentary institutions until 1977 and replace them with the High Council of Institutions (Conseil Supérieur des Institutions).

1973— Madagascar leaves the franc zone and the Common African and Malagasy Organization.

1975— In a surprise move, Ramanantsoa yields office to Col. Richard Ratsimandrava, who is assassinated within six days; power is assumed by an 18-man military directorate headed by Gen. Gilles Andriamahazo; the directorate is superseded by the Supreme Revolutionary Council, headed by Commander Didier Ratsiraka. The Second Republic is inaugurated as the electorate approves a new constitution; Ratsiraka issues the *Charter of the Malagasy Socialist Revolution* (populary known as the Little Red Book). . . . The republic's official designation is changed from the Malagasy Republic to Madagascar.

1976— Ratsiraka is sworn in as president for a seven-year term. . . . The name of the capital is changed from Tananarive to Antananarivo. . . . Prime Minister Joel Rakotomalala is killed in a plane crash and is replaced by Justin Rakotoniaina. . . . Hundreds of Comorans are killed in anti-Comoran riots.

1977— In a major cabinet reshuffle, Desire Rakotoarijaona is named prime minister.

1982— President Ratsiraka is reelected.

1983— AREMA "revolutionary association" of the ruling FNDR wins decisively in national legislative elections.

1986— Violent demonstrations take place in Toamasina in response to food shortages and the government austerity program. Student protests erupt at the University of Madagascar in Antananarivo.

1987— Rioting breaks out. Indian and Pakistani traders are attacked because of resentment at their comparative wealth during a period of increased poverty.

1988— Prime Minister Desire Rakotoarijaona resigns and is replaced by Victor Ramahatra.

1989— President Ratsiraka is reelected with over 60% of the vote.

1990— Ratsiraka lifts a 15-year-old ban on political parties; the PSD, AMF/3FM and CDM immediately register; a coup attempt is ended by security forces.

1991— Madagascar defies the OAU ban on South Africa by restoring trade and transportation ties with that country.

BIBLIOGRAPHY

BOOKS

Covell, Maureen Ann. *Madagascar: Politics, Economics and Society.* New York, 1987.

Gow, Bonar A. *Madagascar and the Protestant Impact.* New York, 1979.

Halverson, Alton, C. O. *Madagascar: Footprint at the End of the World.* Minneapolis, Minn., 1973.

Heseltine, Nigel. *Madagascar.* New York, 1971.

Joshi, P. C. *Madagascar: Recent Economic Development and Future Prospects.* World Bank, 1980.

Kottak, Conrad P. *Madagascar: Society and History.* Durham, N.C., 1985.

Thompson, Virginia, and Richard Adloff. *The Malagasy Republic.* Stanford, Calif., 1965.

OFFICIAL PUBLICATIONS

Finance Ministry. *Loi de Finances* (Approved Budget).

———. *Loi de Finances de Règlement* (Supplementary Budget).

———. *Situation Résumée des Opérations du Trésor* (monthly).

MALAWI

BASIC FACT SHEET

OFFICIAL NAME: Republic of Malawi

ABBREVIATION: MW

CAPITAL: Lilongwe

HEAD OF STATE & HEAD OF GOVERNMENT: President for Life Ngwazi (chief) Hastings Kamuzu Banda (prime minister from 1964; president from 1966; president for life from 1971)

NATURE OF GOVERNMENT: Partial democracy

POPULATION: 9,157,528 (1990)

AREA: 118,485 sq. km. (45,747 sq. mi.)

ETHNIC MAJORITY: Bantu tribes such as the Chewa, Nyanja, Yao, Lomwe, Ngoni, and Tumbuka

LANGUAGES: Chichewa or Chinyanja (national) and English (official)

RELIGIONS: Animism, Christianity and Islam

UNIT OF CURRENCY: Kwacha (M.K.)

NATIONAL FLAG: Tricolor of black, red, and green horizontal stripes with a red rising sun in the center of the black stripe

NATIONAL EMBLEM: A central shield divided into three horizontal parts. The top part contains wavy blue and white lines, the center part a gold lion on a red background and the bottom part a golden rising sun on a black field. The shield is flanked by a golden lion and tiger standing on the ranges of Mount Mlanje. Cresting the design is a silver helmet mantled in red and gold, on top of which a fish eagle in gold, brown and white is outlined against a rising sun. At the bottom appears the national motto, "Unity and Freedom."

NATIONAL ANTHEM: "O God Bless Our Land of Malawi"

NATIONAL HOLIDAYS: July 6 (National Day, Republic Day); January 1 (New Year's Day); March 3 (Martyrs' Day); May 14 (Kamuzu Day); August 1 (bank holiday); October 17 (Mothers' Day); also Christmas, Boxing Day, Good Friday, Holy Saturday and Easter Monday

NATIONAL CALENDAR: Gregorian

PHYSICAL QUALITY OF LIFE INDEX: 29

DATE OF INDEPENDENCE: July 6, 1964

DATE OF CONSTITUTION: July 6, 1966

WEIGHTS & MEASURES: Imperial

GEOGRAPHICAL FEATURES

Malawi, a landlocked country in southeastern Africa, has an area of 118,485 sq. km. (45,747 sq. mi.), of which the land area is 94,916 sq. km. (36,647 sq. mi.). The country extends 853 km. (530 mi.) north to south and 257 km. (160 mi.) east to west.

Malawi shares its total international boundary of 2,768 km. (1,720 mi.) with three neighbors: Tanzania (451 km.; 280 mi.), Mozambique (1,497 km.; 930 mi.) and Zambia (820 km.; 510 mi.). In 1968 President Hastings Banda made claims to territories in all three neighboring countries, specifically to 160 km. (100 mi.) north of the Songwe River in Tanzania, to the Zambezi River in Mozambique, to the Luangwa River in Zambia and to the Indian Ocean to the east. The claims were never pressed.

The capital is Lilongwe, which replaced Zomba as the capital in the mid-1970s. In 1977 the populations of the three main urban centers were Blantyre, 219,011; Lilongwe, 98,718; and Zomba, 24,234.

Three-fourths of the land area is covered by plateaus. The best-known of these, in the southern region, is the Shire plateau, covering 7,251 sq. km. (2,800 sq. mi.). A much broader plateau in the central region is the Lilongwe Plain. The highest plateau, the Nyika Plateau, in the northern region, covers 23,310 sq. km. (9,000 sq. mi.), at an average elevation of 2,100 to 2,500 m. (6,900 to 8,200 ft.). There are six other plateaus, some of which are known locally as hills or plains. A few mountains or mountain ranges rise above the level of the highest of these plateaus: Dedza Mountain (2,250 m. 7,400 ft.), in the central region; Zomba Mountain (2,100 m. 6,900 ft.); and the Mulanje Mountains, whose highest peak, Sapitwa, rises to 3,000 m. (9,840 ft.).

The most prominent physical feature of the country is Lake Malawi (formerly Lake Nyasa), which extends north to south for more than 563 km. (359 mi.), representing an extension of the East African Rift Valley system. The lake's surface is about 472 m. (1,550 ft.) above sea level, while its bottom lies 213 m. (699 ft.) below sea level. The shoreline of the lake is a flat littoral plain marked by many swamps.

The shallow section of the Rift Valley, continuing southward from the shoreline of the lake to the southern border, is known as the Shire Valley. Floodplains and riverine swamps cover this area, the largest of which is known as the Elephant March. Two other major valleys join the lower Shire Valley: the Mwanza and the Ruo.

Malawi is part of the Zambezi River basin. Lake Malawi is drained through Lake Malombe by the Shire River, which flows through the Shire Valley before joining the Zambezi in Mozambique. Eight rivers and

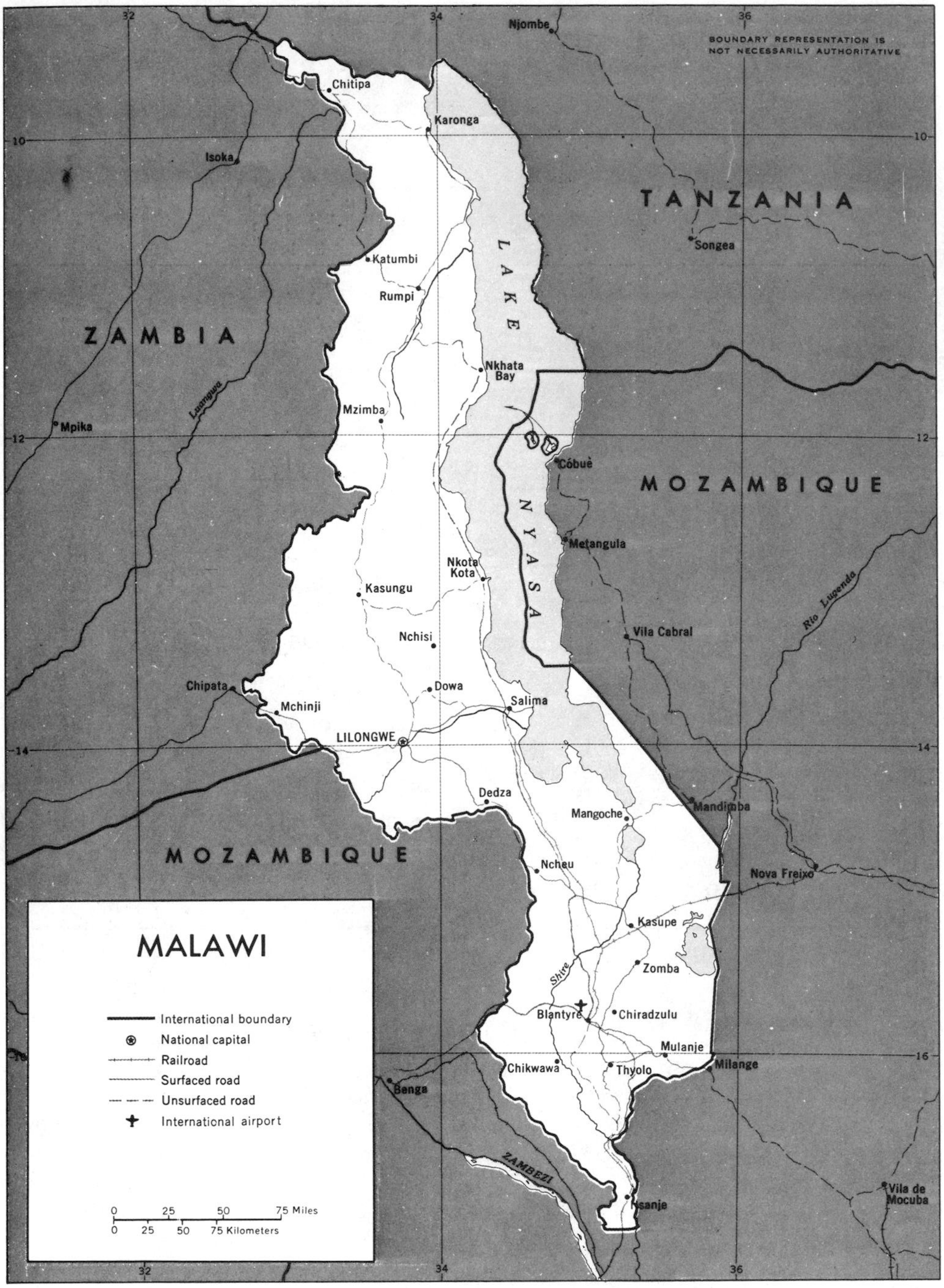
MALAWI
BOUNDARY REPRESENTATION IS NOT NECESSARILY AUTHORITATIVE
International boundary
National capital
Railroad
Surfaced road
Unsurfaced road
International airport
0 25 50 75 Miles
0 25 50 75 Kilometers
TANZANIA
ZAMBIA
MOZAMBIQUE
MOZAMBIQUE
LAKE NYASA
Njombe
Chitipa
Karonga
Isoka
Songea
Katumbi
Rumpi
Nkhata Bay
Mzimba
Mpika
Luangwa
Cóbuè
Metangula
Nkota Kota
Kasungu
Vila Cabral
Rio Lugenda
Nchisi
Chipata
Dowa
Mchinji
Salima
LILONGWE
Dedza
Mandimba
Mangoche
Ncheu
Nova Freixo
Kasupe
Zomba
Shire
Blantyre
Chiradzulu
Mulanje
Milange
Chikwawa
Thyolo
Benga
ZAMBEZI
Nsanje
Vila de Mocuba
32
34
36
10
12
14
16

UNITY AND FREEDOM

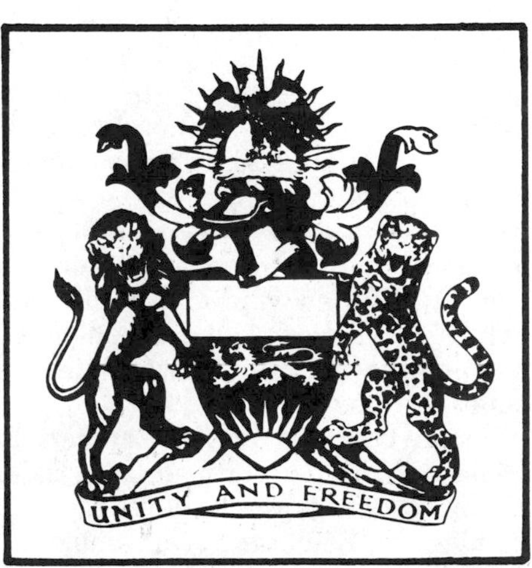

hundreds of streams carry surface runoff from the plateaus and hills into Lake Malawi, but a few streams in the southeast drain into Lake Chilwa.

CLIMATE & WEATHER

The country's latitudinal extent and great variations in altitude produce a wide range of climatic conditions. In general, the seasons may be divided into cool (May to mid-August), hot (mid-August to November), rainy (November to April) and post-rainy (April to May). The broad contrasts are between the cooler and wetter highlands and the hot and humid low-lying Rift Valley region.

The temperatures range between 35°C (95°F) and 7°C (45°F) at Zomba, between 36°C (97°F) and −3.1°C (26°F) at Lilongwe, between a July mean of 21°C (70°F) and an October mean of 29°C (84°F) at Nsanje, between a July mean of 14°C (57°F) and an October mean of 21°C (70°F) at Dedze, between 15.6°C (60°F) and 24.4°C (76°F) on the plateaus and between 20°C (68°F) and 30°C (86°F) in the Rift Valley. Most of Malawi receives 760 to 1,010 mm. (30 to 40 in.) of precipitation; some areas in the northern region receive 1,520 to 2,540 mm. (60 to 100 in.), and lower elevations of the Shire Valley receive less than the national average.

The country is subject to occasional cyclones from the Indian Ocean, some of which prove destructive.

DEMOGRAPHIC INDICATORS

Population (000): 9,157 (1990)
Year of last census: 1987
Sex distribution (% at last census): males, 48.6; females, 51.4
Population estimates and projections (000)

1940: 1,696	1970: 4,511	2000: 12,201
1950: 3,033	1980: 6,137	2010: 16,573
1960: 3,481	1990: 9,157	

Age profile (% at 1977 census)

0–14: 44.6	30–44: 14.2	60–74: 4.3
15–29: 25.7	45–59: 9.0	75 and over: 2.0

Median age (yrs.): 16.9
Youth population (% age 15-24): 19.3 (1985); 18.4 (2000)
Total dependency ratio: 94.5 (1985)
Annual Growth rate (%)

1950–55: 1.91	1975–80: 3.00	2000–2005: 3.20
1955–60: 2.15	1980–85: 3.18	2005–2010: 3.02
1960–65: 2.38	1985–90: 3.31	2010–2015: 2.73
1965–70: 2.56	1990–1995: 3.32	2015–2020: 2.37
1970–75: 2.98	1995–2000: 3.25	2020–2025: 2.03

Hypothetical size of stationary population (millions): 79
Assumed year of reaching net reproduction rate of 1: 2055
Urban population (000): 860 (1985)
Urban population (%): 14 (1988); 5 (1965)
Annual urban population growth rate (%, 1985–90): 7.38
Annual rural population growth rate (%, 1985–90): 2.69
Percentage of urban population in largest city: 19 (1980)
Percentage of urban population in cities of population over 500,000: 0.0 (1980)
Number of cities of population over 500,000: 0 (1980)
Population density per sq. km. (per sq. mi.): 74.5 (193.0) (latest)

VITAL STATISTICS

Crude birth rate (/1,000): 54 (1988); 56 (1965)
Crude death rate (/1,000): 20 (1988); 26 (1965)
Infant mortality rate (/1,000 live births): 130 (1990)
Maternal mortality rate (/100,000 live births): 250 (1980)
Life expectancy (yrs.) at birth: males, 48; females, 50 (1990)
Gross reproduction rate (/woman) (1980–85): 3.45
Total fertility rate (/woman): 7.7 (1990)
Rate of natural increase (/1,000) (1985–90): 33.0
Marriage rate (/1,000): 7.8 (1977)
Average household size: 4.5 (latest)

POPULATION

The population of Malawi was estimated in 1990 at 9,157,528, on the basis of the last official census, in 1987, when the population was 5,547,460.

The overall density of population is higher than that of Malawi's three neighbors and is exceeded only by Rwanda, Burundi and Nigeria in Africa. The density is highest in the southern region and lowest in the northern region.

Only 14% of the population may be described as truly urbanized, but another 1% live within designated urban areas while farming in rural areas. Another 2% live in commercial agricultural estates, which have some urban characteristics. Of the four population centers with over 10,000 inhabitants, Blantyre and Zomba were developed by Europeans. The urban growth rate of over 7% is expected to reduce the rural population significantly.

The median age is falling as a result of a higher birth rate. The female predominance in the male/female ratio reflects the substantial migration of males to South Africa, Zimbabwe and Zambia.

Because population movements across national borders are free and unrestricted, there is no record of the number of Malawians in neighboring countries; some sources place their number at close to 300,000. Of these, nearly one-third work in South Africa on contract. An equal number are believed to be working in Zimbabwe. In certain communities, about 60% of the men had worked outside the country at some time in their lives. During Mozambique's independence struggle there was an influx of Mozambicans into the country, resulting in a net gain in population in some areas. As a result of its open-door policy toward refugees fleeing the brutal civil war in Mozambique, one in 10 people were Mozambican by 1990.

As mothers, women have enjoyed a high degree of access to the traditional health services and to extension programs geared toward improving women's homemaking abilities. Such programs, while beneficial, have failed to recognize the importance of women as agricultural producers in the rural sector (roughly 70% of all smallholder farming and over 50% of subsistence holdings are headed by women) and the potential role women can have in the modern sector. Although males still have a comparative advantage in terms of educational and employment opportunities, the government has initiated sufficiency broad-scale programs to begin to rectify the discrimination that exists. A third of the positions in the public education system are reserved for women. Within Malawi's traditional and primarily matrilineal tribal leadership structures there are several small ethnic groups wherein women possess fewer rights and privileges and where female circumcision is occasionally practiced.

STATUS OF WOMEN INDICATORS

Number of women (millions): 3.689 (1985)
Women of childbearing age (15–49) (% of pop.): 45 (1988)
Women's literacy rate (%): 31 (1985)
Women in labor force (%): 41.7 (1988)
Total fertility rate (/woman): 7.7 (1990)
Women in national legislatures (%): 13 (1984)

The official policy is pronatalist and strongly opposed to birth control, population planning and sex education. The president has personally commended the prospect of continued rapid population growth. However, limited family-planning facilities are available under the auspices of the International Planned Parenthood Federation and are reluctantly tolerated by the government.

ETHNIC COMPOSITION

Africans constitute 99.5% of Malawi's population, but they are divided ethnically into numerous groups. The closely related Chewa and Nyanja together constitute about half of the population. They are descendants of a Bantu group called the Maravi (from which Malawi derives its name), who crossed Zambia from the southern Congo and entered Malawi centuries ago. On reaching the area north of Lake Malawi, the tribe split; the ancestors of the present-day Chewa moved south to the western bank, and the forebears of the Nyanjas moved down the eastern bank. Today the Chewas are numerically dominant in the central region and the Nyanjas in the southern region, around Lake Chilwa and in the districts of Zomba and Blantyre.

The Lomwe, who make up about a fifth of the population, are concentrated in the eastern part of the southern region. Also called Nguru, they are found in great numbers across the border in Mozambique. The Yao, former allies of the Arabs and, like the Arabs, slave traders, do not form a homogeneous entity in any locality but are intermingled with the Nyanja and the Lomwe in the districts of Mangoche and Ncheu. The Ngoni, who account for about 9% of the population, are descendants of conquerors who moved into Malawi in the early 19th century and assimilated the local inhabitants by marrying their women and rearing their children as Ngoni. They live in the Mzimba district in the northern region and the districts of Ncheu, Dedza, Lilongwe and Dowa of the central region. The Tumbuka, who make up 9% of Malawians, are actually a cluster of different groups, such as the Henga and the Kananga. They live between the Dwanga and North Rukuru rivers in the northern region. The Sena are an admixture of Tonga and Nyanja and live along the Zambezi, Shire and Luangwe rivers. The Tonga (not to be confused with people of the same name in Zambia) are closely related to the Tumbuka and live in the northern region. The Ngonde live in the extreme north of Malawi between the Songwe River and the lower reaches of the north Rukuru River. They are part of a larger group whose main strength is in Tanzania. Also in the north are smaller numbers of the Nyakusa, Lambya and Sukwa, all of whom are related to the Ngonde. Among other small tribes are the Kunda and the Khokola.

Ethnicity has declined in importance, and interethnic relations are characterized by tolerance and flexibility. Intermarriages are common, and many chieftaincies are of heterogeneous origin. The new national alignments are regional, political or religious rather than ethnic in character.

All whites are classified as Europeans, but they are mostly of British origin. They constitute only 0.05% of the population, and very few have become Malawian citizens. Nearly 65% of the Europeans live in the urban centers of Blantyre, Zomba and Lilongwe. They continue to exercise a disproportionate influence on the administration and economy.

Asians, nearly all of them Indians, constitute a still smaller minority. As in other parts of Africa, they play an important role in the economy as small traders, craftsmen and professionals. Asian residents and citizens are free to travel within the country but must reside and work in one of three urban areas (Lilongwe, Zomba or Blantyre/Limbe). Within some of these urban centers, strict rules governing where Asians may own property result in limitations on where they may reside. Asian residents, whether Malawian citizens or not, have been compelled to transfer ownership of rural shops and trucking businesses to ethnic African Malawian citizens. Asians are free to expand into other areas of business, however, and industrial licenses for new Asian businesses are routinely granted. Nevertheless, Asians are not subjected to official harassment; President Banda was one of the few African leaders who condemned Idi Amin's expulsion of Asians from Uganda, and he offered to accept 1,000 of those so expelled as permanent settlers in Malawi.

LANGUAGES

Chichewa or Chinyanja, the mother tongue of the Chewa and the Nyanja (the prefix *chi-* is used before the name of the tribe to mean "the language of"), was declared the national language in 1968. A standardized form of Chichewa is used in the administration, schools and the media. Chichewa is spoken by over 50% of the population as their mother tongue. The rest speak a number of African languages, of which the leading ones are Chilomwe, Chiyao, Chitumbuka and Chisena. Because the Chewa and Nyanja tribes are concentrated in the central and southern regions, Chichewa is understood by only 2.5% of the population in the north. Many Africans are bilingual by necessity.

English, the official language of the country, is spoken by at least 6% of the population and is used as a lingua franca by educated Africans.

RELIGIONS

Religious affiliations have not been included in the census; furthermore, religious loyalties are fluid. However, according to unofficial sources, an estimated 35% of the population are Christian, 12% are Muslim and 53% are animist.

Traditional African religions share a belief in the life force that permeates everything, a concept generally equated with God or a Supreme Being (called *mulungu* in Chichewa), but most religious activities revolve around intermediary spirits, of whom there are two types: ancestral spirits called *mizimu*, and nature spirits. Sorcery, witchcraft and other practices are closely related to efforts to win the good favor of these spirits.

Christianity was introduced in the Shire Highlands in 1861 by Anglican missionaries and in 1889 by the Roman Catholic White Fathers. In the 1970s there were three Protestants to every two Roman Catholics. There are a number of independent African churches, which broke away from the established churches in protest against white control and racial discrimination. These churches are characterized by their millenarianism, emphasis on rituals and incorporation of typical African religious beliefs. One of these African-controlled churches was the Watch Tower Bible and Tract Society (commonly known as Jehovah's Witnesses), an American sect introduced into Malawi in the 1920s. The refusal of Witnesses to join the Malawi Congress Party brought them into conflict with the government; the sect was banned in 1967, and its members were expelled from the country.

Most Muslims belong to the Yao tribe, which derives its faith from Arab slave traders in the 19th century. Because the Yao are largely illiterate, Islam exerts little or no influence on national affairs.

HISTORICAL BACKGROUND

The first white man to explore the territory now known as Malawi was David Livingstone, who discovered Lake Nyasa (now Lake Malawi) in 1859. Livingstone was instrumental in establishing a series of mission stations in Nyasaland in the 1870s, two named Livingstonia and a third named Blantyre. In 1878 the African Lakes Company was formed by Scottish businessmen to open up the interior and to supply the needs of the missions. By the 1890s over 100 coffee plantations had been established. The expansion of British commercial interests brought them into conflict with both the Arabs and the Portuguese. By the 1890s the boundaries of the British sphere of influence had been defined through Anglo-German and Anglo-Portuguese agreements. in 1891 the British Foreign Office announced the establishment of the Nyasaland Districts Protectorate (renamed two years later as the British Central Africa Protectorate), under a commissioner. In 1907 the territory was again renamed, as Nyasaland Protectorate, under a governor. From the beginning, Nyasaland had been viewed by the imperial government as a dependency rather than as a settlers' colony. Missionaries and civil servants outnumbered planters in the British community, and British-owned plantations did not dominate agriculture, as they did in Rhodesia. Administration was based on the concept of indirect rule, which permitted African headmen a significant role in the lower echelons of government. Under these circumstances, nationalism developed early in Nyasaland; it was not the inflamed or rebellious type, but one that sought to expand existing African opportunities in government. For this reason there was considerable native opposition to union with Northern and Southern Rhodesia (now Zambia and Zimbabwe) in the Central African Federation in 1953. The Malawi Congress Party under Dr. Banda led a successful fight against the federation, and in 1962 the British government accepted Nyasaland's right to secede from the federation. Nyasaland became an independent dominion in 1964 under the name of Malawi. Two years later it became a republic with Dr. Banda as president.

During the first years of independence, Banda consolidated power under a strong presidency. A strict conservative, he made early policies that included the retention of Europeans in the civil service, espousal of free-enterprise capitalism and maintenance of good relations with Rhodesia and South Africa.

Banda has maintained his power through patronage and frequent cabinet reshuffles that prevent opponents from establishing power bases. In the 1960s two minor insurrections took place, led by radicals from Banda's own party. He easily subdued them, and by 1971, when he had himself sworn in as president for life, he was fully entrenched as the national leader.

Political controversy has surrounded Banda's possible successors. During the 1980s two of the three leading candidates died; one, Dick Tennjeyson Matenje in what the government termed an automobile accident, and the other, Dr. Attati Mpakati by assassination. The third opposition leader, Orton Chirwa, was tried for treason and condemned to death. International pressure forced the commutation of his sentence in 1984.

Banda, nearly 90, still runs the country as a personal fiefdom with the support of the police and his party.

CONSTITUTION & GOVERNMENT

The legal basis of government is the Constitution of 1966, which established a one-party state, a parliamentary form of government and a strong presidency. The Constitution reflects the great personal authority of President Banda and endows the office of the presidency with unchallengeable prerogatives. The president may act at his own discretion in the discharge of his duties and is not obliged to follow the advice of any other person or body. He functions as both head of state and head of government. The president may select and appoint any persons he chooses as ministers, and they function more or less as his personal staff. Not only is he the supreme commander of the armed forces, but also he can deploy them at will. Significantly, although requiring "unity, discipline, obedience and loyalty" from all citizens, the Constitution does not guarantee or specify civil rights or liberties.

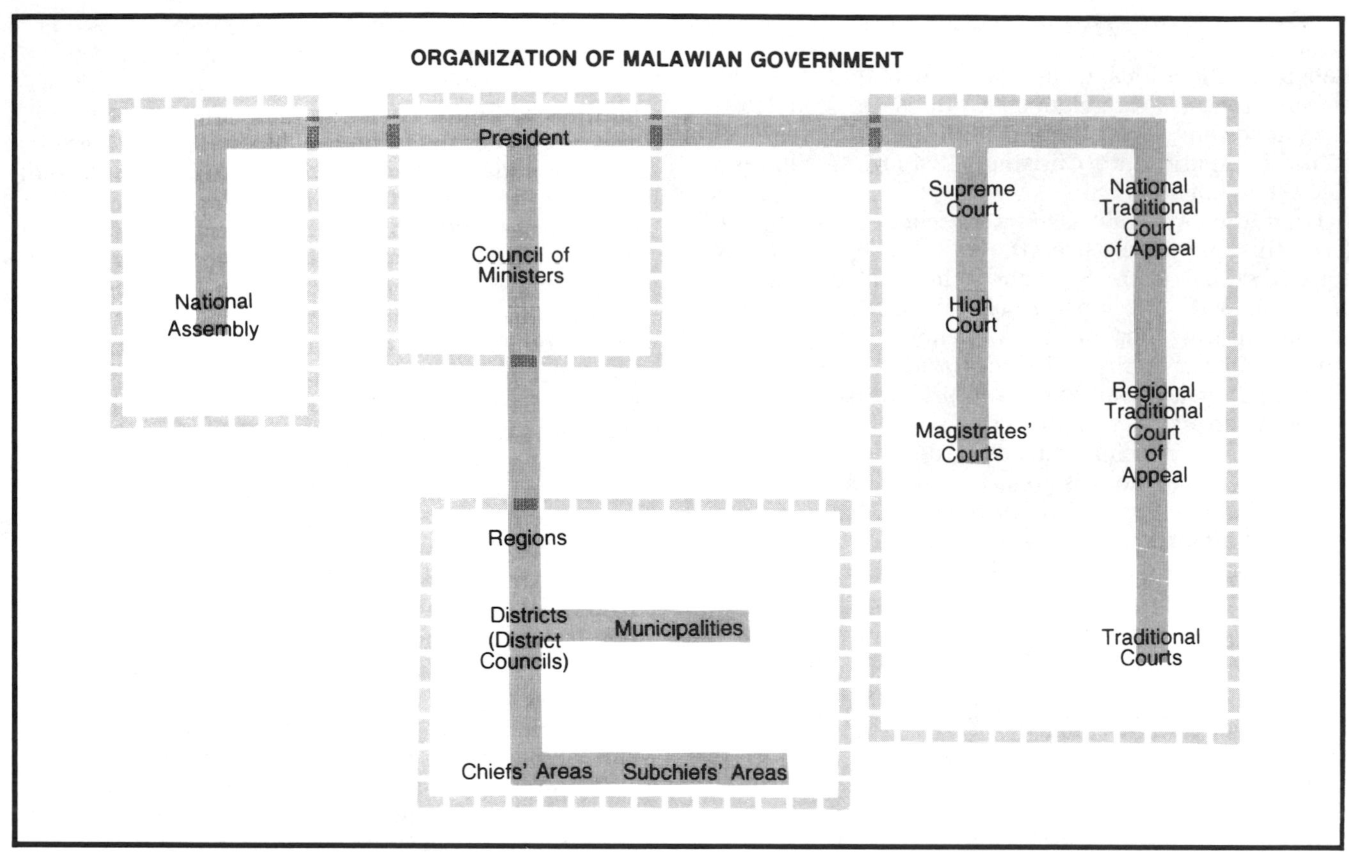

GOVERNMENT LIST
(July/August 1991)

President	Banda, H. Kamuzu, *M.D.*
Minister of Agriculture	Banda, H. Kamuzu, *M.D.*
Minister of Community Services	Mwakikunga, Mfunjo
Minister of Education & Culture	Mlambala, Michael
Minister of External Affairs	Banda, H. Kamuzu, *M.D.*
Minister of Finance	Chimango, Louis
Minister of Forestry & Natural Resources	Ntaba, Heatherwick M., *M.D.*
Minister of Health	Phiri, Eliya Katola
Minister of Justice	Banda, H. Kamuzu, *M.D.*
Minister of Labor	Deleza, Wadson B.
Minister of Local Government	Phiri, Eliya Katola
Minister of Trade, Industry & Tourism	Chirwa, Robson
Minister of Transport & Communications	Katopola, Dalton S.
Minister of Works & Supplies	Banda, H. Kamuzu, *M.D.*
Minister Without Portfolio	Pashane, Maxwell
Governor, Central Bank	Lesshaft, Hans Joachim

Thus the Constitution is fully in accord with African political traditions, under which unquestioning obedience is due to the chieftain of a tribe, who is not, however, constrained by reciprocal obligations. In 1971 Dr. Banda was made president for life by a unanimous resolution of the Malawi Congress Party (MCP) convention and subsequent constitutional amendment. The president presides over a cabinet of ministers whose membership is unlimited. Members are generally chosen from Parliament.

A unicameral Parliament, elected for up to a five-year term, serves as the legislature. Members are chosen by universal sufferage from a list offered by the MCP and approved by the president.

The judiciary includes both Western and traditional courts. The High Court has unlimited criminal and civil jurisdication. The Supreme Court is the highest appellate court.

The country is divided into 60 single-member constituencies. National Assembly elections are held every five years. In the 1976 elections, all Malawi Congress Party candidates were unopposed; therefore, polling did not take place.

In the 1979 elections, President Banda reversed his policy and permitted two or three candidates to run in each constituency, but only members of the MCP were allowed to run, and all candidates were vetted by the president. Dr. Banda also launched a hesitant policy of liberalization with the release of nearly all political detainees.

FREEDOM & HUMAN RIGHTS

In terms of political and civil rights, Malawi is classified as a not-free country.

Malawi has achieved a unique record of steady economic growth, and its foreign relations have been characterized by a certain courage and realism, but its political growth has been in the direction of a one-party monolithic state. Civil and human rights have been readily abridged when perceived as threats or challenges to established authority. Such opposition as exists does not enjoy widespread popular support. However, a general trend toward liberalization that began in 1977 with the release of 2,000 political detainees has continued. Although arbitrary detentions still occur, such powers are exercised with greater restraint and an increased observance of legal provisions. The modern court system, following British procedures, is believed to be reasonably fair, and occasional irregularities are more often administrative than political in nature.

The exercise of freedoms of speech and press is restricted in practice, as all media are under direct or indirect government control. Although strikes are legally permitted, none has occurred. Malawi's political processes do not permit the existence of organized dissent, not essentially because it is authoritarian in the Western sense but because of ingrained social values favoring hierarchical relationships, respect for authority and a desire to work through consensus and avoid conflict.

POLITICAL SUBDIVISIONS

Region	District	Municipality
Southern	Nsanje, Thyolo, Zamba, Blantyre, Chikwawa, Kasupe, Mangoche, Mwanza, Chiradzulu, Mulanje	Blantyre, Zomba, Mangoche, Balaka
Central	Ncheu, Dedza, Lilongwe, Dowa, Mchinji, Salima, Ntchisi, Nkhota Kota, Kasungu	Lilongwe, Salima, Dedze
Northern	Chitipa, Karonga, Rumphi, Nkhata Bay, Mzimba	Mzuzu

CIVIL SERVICE

All civil servants are appointed (or dismissed) by the president, but administratively the service is controlled by the Civil Service Commission (CSC), consisting of a chairman and three to five other members. However, the commission has no authority over the armed forces, the foreign service, the judiciary or the police. Also excluded from the CSC's authority are the highest civil service positions, such as the secretary to the cabinet and the permanent secretaries. Despite pressures from nationalists, President Banda has proceeded very cautiously in Africanizing the civil service, in line with his announced policy of placing efficiency above political considerations. Nevertheless, considerable progress has been achieved since independence, when there were only 104 Malawian civil servants of nearly 2,000 in the senior grades. In 1971 there were 133 Malawians in the top positions (compared with 900 British nationals). But all these Malawians were academically qualified and trained either overseas or at the Institute of Public Administration. Efforts are being made to increase the percentage of Africans at the higher levels without reducing qualifications or performance levels.

LOCAL GOVERNMENT

For purposes of local government Malawi is divided into three regions, 24 districts and eight municipalities.

Although the district is the lowest unit of local government directly administered by the national government, there are 134 chiefs' areas and 60 subchiefs' areas into which districts are divided on the basis of tribal territoriality. Each region is under a cabinet minister, and each district is under a district commissioner.

Popular representative institutions exist at two levels: the district councils and the town councils. The size of the district councils varies from as few as 13 to as many as 39. District councillors are elected by universal franchise, and they in turn elect their own chairmen annually. District councils serve as local primary-education authorities, provide markets and postal agencies, maintain roads and water supplies, run public health clinics and control the brewing and sale of beer. They are required to meet quarterly, but most meet more frequently. District councils receive funds from the national budget as grants-in-aid and also generate revenues through license and service fees, head taxes and some forms of property tax.

The town councils also vary in size, with 10 as the average. All town councillors are appointed rather than elected; they usually are chosen by the local party executive. All urban councils are required to meet bimonthly, but most meet more frequently. The councils elect their own chairmen, who function as mayors, though not in name. The powers of the town councils are similar to those of the district councils except for responsibility for primary education. The primary source of funds is the property tax.

FOREIGN POLICY

In foreign relations, Malawi is one of the most conservative of the newly independent nations of Africa. Unlike most other black African countries, Malawi does not believe that isolation, embargo or violence will succeed in promoting racial equality in South Africa. Malawi therefore maintains full diplomatic relations with Pretoria. In 1971 President Banda paid an official visit to South Africa, the first head of state of a black African nation to do so. The South African prime minister returned the visit in 1972. Malawi was granted £4.7 million by South Africa to finance the first stage of the new capital at Lilongwe. Malawi's relations with Rhodesia were, at least until it became Zimbabwe, ostentatiously cordial. Prior to Mozambique's independence, Banda maintained close links with Portugal and was even accused of supporting a settler breakaway movement led by Jorge Jardim. The prowhite bias in Malawian foreign policy is explained partly by economic determinants and partly by the personal philosophy of President Banda, who alone has decided the direction of external relations. As a landlocked country, Malawi needs transportation routes through Mozambique, which provides its only outlet to the sea. Second, the Malawian economy is so totally dependent on that of South Africa that any break would result in irreparable economic damage. Migrant workers' remittances from South Africa and Zimbabwe finance 13% of the country's imports and provide an equal percentage of cash income of rural households.

Despite ethnic ties and common economic interests, relations between Malawi on the one hand and Tanzania and Zambia on the other deteriorated rapidly after independence, a result of Malawi's willingness to maintain full relations with the white minority regimes in South Africa and preindependent Mozambique. The Zambian government retaliated by expelling a large number of Malawians, and the Tanzanian government did so by providing a refuge to dissident Malawians, permitting them to organize to overthrow Banda. Diplomatic relations between Tanzania and Malawi were broken in 1968. Since 1971 a partial rapprochement has taken place between Malawi and its black neighbors, reflecting the new balance of power in southern Africa following the independence of Mozambique. Zambia opened a high commission in Malawi in 1971, and Presidents Kenneth Kaunda and Banda have exchanged state visits.

During the 1980s, Malawi took steps to improve relations with neighboring states. In part the change in policy was a result of pressure by Zambia and Tanzania. In part it was prompted by the need to find alternate trade routes because the civil war in Mozambique had closed its traditional routes to the Indian Ocean.

In 1980 Malawi joined the Southern African Development Coordination Conference. Five years later it reestablished ties with Tanzania, despite suspicions that Tanzania supported opponents of the Banda regime.

Malawi did not support the independence struggle in Mozambique and did not develop close ties with the independence government. There is evidence that Malawi initially backed the South African rebels, but in 1986 changed its policy and, with Mozambique, formed a joint security commission to fight the insurgents.

Malawi's closest ties are with the United Kingdom. British civil servants occupy many key positions in government, and British business interests continue to dominate the modern sector of the Malawian economy. The United Kingdom also provides a large proportion of foreign economic assistance, particularly direct grants. President Banda was prompted by these considerations to accept 1,000 Asian British citizens expelled from Uganda. Relations with the United States have been influenced by Banda's admiration for the American system, of which he had firsthand experience as a resident in the United States from 1926 to 1937. Malawi has consistently supported U.S. positions on African and world issues. Nevertheless, Malawi terminated the U.S. Peace Corps program in 1970 because of Banda's personal disapproval of the appearance and attitudes of many Peace Corps volunteers. Malawi maintains no relations with any Communist government.

Malawi and the United States are parties to nine treaties and agreements covering economic and technical cooperation, extradition, investment guarantees, and taxation.

PARLIAMENT

The unicameral National Assembly is an 112-member body "elected" for five-year terms. An unlimited number of additional members can be nominated by the president. The Constitution assigns broad powers to the Assembly, covering all classes of legislation, the national budget and constitutional amendments. Theoretically it can override a presidential veto, and the Assembly may not be dissolved without at the same time requiring a new presidential election. All members of the Assembly belong to the Malawi Congress Party (MCP).

Suffrage is universal over 21. Candidates represent single-member constituencies—there are 60 such constituencies—but candidates are grouped as representatives of a district and are not required to reside in their titular constituencies. Each district's nominating conference forwards the names of at least five nominees for each seat to the president, who vets them. During the early years after independence, few seats were contested, but since 1978, all have been, although all candidates must still be members of the MCP.

The Assembly's weakness in relation to the executive is emphasized by the presidential right to take an active part in its debates, to deprive a member of his seat by detaining him under security laws and to expel a member from both the party and the Assembly.

POLITICAL PARTIES

The sole legal party in the country is the Malawi Congress Party (MCP), founded in 1959 by Dr. Banda as the Nyasaland African Congress. The MCP is one of the most conservative political parties in Africa. Since 1964 it has been completely dominated by Dr. Banda, its president for life.

No opposition parties are based in Malawi. Three exist in exile; the Malawi Freedom Movement, The Socialist League of Malawi and the Congress for the Second Republic.

ECONOMY

Malawi is one of the low-income countries of the world; it is also among the least developed in the world. It has a free-market economy in which the dominant sector is private.

Malawi's economy is predominantly agricultural. Agriculture accounts for 36% of the GDP and 95% of export revenues. Subsistance farming dominates the north and large estates and cash-crop agriculture are dominant in the south. Tobacco, tea and sugar are the principal cash crops. Malawi's dependence on agriculture makes it extremely vulnerable to changes in world demand and world prices. The decline in cash-crop prices during the early 1980s contributed significantly to the country's increasing external debt.

PRINCIPAL ECONOMIC INDICATORS

Gross National Product (U.S. $ billions): 1.475 (1989)
GNP per capita (U.S. $): 180 (1989)
GNP average annual growth rate (%, 1980–89): 3.3
GNP per capita average annual growth rate (%, 1987–89): 1.1
Average annual rate of inflation (%, 1980–88): 12.6
Consumer price index (1980 = 100) 1986
  All items: 211
  Food: 193
Average annual growth rate (%, 1980–88)
  General government consumption: 3.8
  Private consumption: 3.1
  Gross domestic investment: −8.3

BALANCE OF PAYMENTS, 1988 (U.S. $ millions)

Current account balance: −53.1
Merchandise exports: 297.0
Merchandise imports: −253.0
Trade balance: 44
Other goods, services & income +: 37.8
Other goods, services & income −: −230.3
Other goods, services & income net: −192.5
Private unrequited transfers: 15.1
Official unrequited transfers: 80.4
Capital other than reserves: 113
Net errors & omissions: −18.0
Counterpart items: −2.6
Total change in reserves: −105.0

GROSS DOMESTIC PRODUCT

GDP nominal (M.K. billions): 2.162
GDP per capita (U.S. $): 180
Average annual growth rate of GDP (%, 1980–88): 2.6
GDP by type of expenditure (%) 1987
  Consumption
    Private: 70
    Government: 18
  Gross domestic investment: 15
  Gross domestic saving: 8
  Foreign trade
    Exports: 24
    Imports: −27
Cost components of GDP (%) 1987
    Net indirect taxes: 10
    Consumption of fixed capital, compensation of employees, net operating surplus: 90
Sectoral origin of GDP (%) 1987
  Primary
    Agriculture: 36
    Mining: 0.0
  Secondary
    Manufacturing: 12
    Construction: 4
    Public utilities: 2
  Tertiary
    Transportation & communications: 6
    Trade: 13
    Finance: 11
    Other services: 4
    Government: 13
Average annual sectoral growth rates (%, 1980-88)
    Agriculture: 2.7
    Industry: 3.0
    Services: 2.4

Industry is not highly developed, and manufacturing contributes only about 12% of GDP. The country must import most of its industrial goods. Consequently the government has focused on developing import substitution. The nation has no known mineral deposits suitable for economic development.

During the last half of the 1980s, the economy declined as a result of a drop in prices for cash crops and an increase in the cost of imports. Higher transportation expenses also contributed to a growing deficit. Since 1980, the country has faced a problem of chronic unemployment and an inflation rate of about 12%.

Malawi relies heavily on foreign investment and aid, primarily from the World Bank, the European Economic Community, the United Kingdom and South Africa. Debt service has become an increasing problem. In 1988 external debt service was the equivalent of 17.2% of export revenues.

PUBLIC FINANCE

The Malawian fiscal year runs from April 1 to March 31. The national budget is divided into two parts: a current budget and a development budget. Not included in the central government budget are the finances of local authorities and state corporations.

Foreign aid finances the greatest portion of the development program. Generally the government uses the largest proportion of domestic revenues to provide matching funds for foreign-financed programs. The balance of finances go for domestic programs for which no foreign aid can be found.

CENTRAL GOVERNMENT EXPENDITURES (latest)

% of total expenditures
  Defense: 5.6
  Education: 10.0
  Health: 5.9
  Housing, social security, welfare: 2.0
  Economic services: 27.0
  Other: 49.4
Total expenditures as % of GNP: 32.0 (1988)
Overall surplus or deficit as % of GNP: −8.6 (1988)

CENTRAL GOVERNMENT REVENUES (latest)

% of total current revenues
  Taxes on income, profit & capital gain: 33.7
  Social security contributions: 0
  Domestic taxes on goods & services: 33.0
  Taxes on international trade & transactions: 16.0
  Other taxes: 0.4
  Current nontax revenue: 16.8
Total current revenue as % of GNP: 20.6
General government consumption as % of GDP: 14 (1988)
Average annual growth rate of general government consumption (%, 1980–88): 3.8

Development programs in the late 1980s emphasized transportation, agriculture and import substitution. The goal was to achieve 3% real GDP growth annually, reduce inflation to 5% annually and reach a supportable balance-of-payments position.

Malawi received $182 million in aid from the United States from 1970 to 1988 and $1.8 billion from other Western nations during the period 1970–87.

FOREIGN AID, 1989

Total foreign aid (U.S. $ millions): 478.0
  Bilateral: 217.0
  Multilateral: 261.0

CURRENCY & BANKING

The Malawian unit of currency is the kwacha, divided into 100 tambala. Coins are issued in denominations of 1, 2, 5, 10 and 20 tambala; notes are issued in denominations of 50 tambala and 1, 5 and 10 kwacha.

FINANCIAL INDICATORS, 1989

Total reserves minus gold (SDRs millions): 76
Reserve position in IMF (SDRs millions): 2
Foreign exchange (SDRs millions): 74
Gold (fine troy oz. millions): .01
Ratio of external debt to total reserves: 8.1 (1988)
Central bank 1989
  Assets (%)
    Foreign Assets: 32.4
    Claims on government: 67.6
    Claims on banks: 0.0
    Claims on private sector: 0.0
  Liabilities (%)
    Reserve money: 52.3
    Government deposits: 26.1
    Foreign liabilities: 31.6
    Capital accounts: 0.0
Money supply 1989
    Stock (M.K. billions): 427
    M1 per capita: 50
Private banks 1989
  Assets (%)
    Loans to government: 15.2
    Loans to private sector: 51.5
    Reserves: 30.3
    Foreign assets: 3.0
  Liabilities
    Deposits (M.K. millions): 744
    of which %
      Demand deposits: 31.0
      Savings deposits: 54.9
      Government deposits: 0.0
      Foreign liabilities: 6.7
External debt, 1988
  Total (U.S. $ billions): 1.349
    of which public (U.S. $ billions): 1.190
    of which private (U.S. $ millions): 3
  Debt service (long term)
    Total (U.S. $ millions): 58
    Repayment
      Principal (%): 51.7
      Interest (%): 48.3
  Debt service ratio (%): 18.0
  External Public Debt as % of GNP: 85.7
  Debt service as % of GNP: 4.1
  Debt service as % of exports: 17.2
  Terms of public borrowing
    Commitments (U.S. $ millions): 123
    Average interest rate (%): 0.9
    Average maturity (yrs.): 41
  Net flow of publicly guaranteed
    external capital (U.S. $ millions): 86
  Net direct private investment (U.S. $ millions): 0

GROWTH PROFILE
(Annual Growth Rates, %)

Projected population (1988–2000): 3.5
Projected crude birth rate (/1,000) (1990–95): 51.5
Projected crude death rate (/1,000) (1990–95): 18.3
Urban population (1980–88): 7.9
Labor force (1985–2000): 2.6
GNP (1980–89): 3.3
GNP per capita (1987–89): 1.1
GDP (1980–88): 2.6
Inflation (1980–88): 12.6
Agriculture (1980–88): 2.7
Industry (1980–88): 3.0
Services (1980–88): 2.4
Money holdings (1980–87): 17.7
Manufacturing earnings per employee (1980–87): 1.6
Energy production (1980–88): 4.3
Energy consumption (1980–88): 0.2
Exports (1980–88): 3.3
Imports (1980–88): −3.4
General government consumption (1980–88): 3.8
Private consumption (1980–88): 3.1
Gross domestic investment (1980–88): −8.3

The kwacha was introduced in 1971 to replace the Malawi pound at the rate of M.£1 = M.K. 2. From 1972 the kwacha began floating with the pound sterling. From 1973 to 1975 the value of the kwacha was determined independently on the basis of movements of sterling and the U.S. dollar in exchange markets. Since 1975 the kwacha has been valued in terms of the IMF Special Drawing Right, based on a weighted basket of 16 national currencies with a relationship to the SDR of 1 SDR = M.K. 1.054. The exchange value against the U.S. dollar is adjusted from month to month. In June 1991 it was $1 = M.K. 2.789.

The banking sector consists of a central bank, the Reserve Bank of Malawi; two commercial banks; the Post Office Savings Bank; one savings and loan society; and a development bank, the Investment and Development Bank of Malawi.

AGRICULTURE

Of the total land area of 11,848,500 ha. (29,265,795 ac.), 14.1% is classified as agricultural area.

The agricultural sector consists of three subsectors: estates, small holders and subsistence farms. By contribution to the GDP, subsistence farms account for 64.1%, smallholders 25.2% and estates 10.7%. By number of persons employed, 96.4% were employed on smallholdings and subsistence farms and only 2.9% on estates. Smallholdings account for 88% for the country's production and over 50% of the agricultural exports. Smallholdings also constitute the most dynamic subsector; nevertheless, cash incomes of smallholders are among the lowest in Africa.

More than 45% of the arable land is in five districts: Mzimba in the northern region, Kasungu and Lilongwe in the central region and Mangoche and Kasupe in the southern region. The central region leads in percentage of arable land as well as in production of tobacco, peanuts and pulses. Rice is grown around Lake Malawi; tea, tung and coffee on mountain slopes; and cotton in the lower Shire Valley. Corn is grown almost universally, while millet and sorghum are grown in the South and cassava in the North. Intercropping (growing two crops in alternate rows) appears to be the general rule.

Because of the high density of population, there is increasing pressure on available land. Land hunger is evident in the more populated areas, but countrywide there is no shortage as yet of cultivable arable land. On the basis of aerial photographs, there are 505,000 ha. (1,248,400 ac.) of good-quality land, 1,046,000 ha. (2,583,600 ac.) of moderate-quality land and 1,747,000 ha. (4,315,100 ac.) of poor-quality land still available for cultivation, most of it in the central region. Efforts to resettle farmers in these areas are impeded by kinship ties and a general preference for the Southern Region.

The traditional shifting-cultivation system, involving slash-and-burn clearing, virtually disappeared by the 1970s, but the bush-fallow system, characterized by rotation of fields instead of crops, still is prevalent in many areas. Permanent cultivation is common in the central and southern regions, although it often is combined with bush fallow. The most intensive cultivation takes place in the periodically flooded lowlands. Levels of mechanization and fertilizer application are low.

There are three official categories of land tenure: public, private and customary. Only 2.5% of the land area is private, and about 2% is in the hands of non-Africans, consisting almost entirely of large estates. Public land makes up 12.5% of the land area, including government estates. On the whole, there are 95 large estates, including 28 owned by the Malawi Congress Party. The remaining 85% is customary land held under traditional African tenure systems, under which cultivation and usufructary rights are held by individuals and disposal rights are held by the group. The inalienability of land protects the territorial integrity of the community: promotes communal cohesiveness; discourages interregional mobility; and foils acquisitive, unscrupulous creditors and land exploiters. At the same time, it offers no incentives to farmers to improve the land and inhibits the redistribution of land and resettlement of farmers. There are an estimated 885,000 holdings under customary tenure, covering 1,427,012 ha. (3,524,700 ac.) and employing 1,028,300 farmers. Fragmentation of holdings is common in areas of population pressure. The average size of a holding is under 1.6 ha. (4 ac.); about 10% of the holdings exceed 4 ha. (10 ac.), making up one-third of the cultivated acreage. There are few holdings over 40 ha. (100 ac.).

In an effort to raise agricultural productivity, the government has initiated a number of integrated rural development projects, each of which is designed to serve as a catalyst in a strategically located area. These projects vary in size and scope, but the four largest are the Shire Valley Agricultural Development Project in the South; the Lilongwe Land Development Program and the Central Region Lakeshore Development Project, both in the central region; and the Karonga Rural Development Project in the north. Marketing and price stabilization programs are handled by the Agricultural Development and Marketing Corporation, the main purchaser for export and domestic resale of all important cash crops such as tobacco, corn, peanuts, cotton, pulses, wheat and coffee. Estate crops have their own marketing organizations.

As Malawi has almost no exploitable mineral resources and a limited manufacturing base, the performance of the agricultural sector is the key to continued development. In 1977 estate production, principally tobacco, tea and sugar, increased almost 15% in value, while the growth rate of the sector as a whole was about 6%. The estates provide over half of Malawi's total exports and have been the most dynamic element of the economy in recent years. Results from the smallholder farmers, who produce about 85% of the total agricultural output, have been less encouraging, but hard statistics are not available. The Agricultural

AGRICULTURAL INDICATORS

Agriculture's share of GDP (%): 35 (1989)
Average annual growth rate (%, 1980–88): 2.7 (1988)
Value added in agriculture (U.S. $ millions): 402 (1988)
Cereal imports (000 metric tons): 44 (1988)
Index of agricultural production (1979–81 = 100): 112 (1986)
Index of food production (1979–81 = 100): 106 (1986)
Index of food production per capita (1979–81 = 100): 85 (1986–88)
Number of tractors: 1,350 (1986)
Total fertilizer consumption (000 metric tons): 34 (1985–86)
Fertilizer consumption (g./ha., hundreds) 203 (1987–88)
Number of farms (000): 1,136 (1980–81)
Average size of holdings (ha.): 1.2 (1980–81)
Size class (%) 1980–81
- Below 1 ha. (below 2.47 ac.): 54.9
- 1–3 ha. (2.47–7.41 ac.): 40.1
- 3–10 ha. (12.35–24.7 ac.):
- 10–20 ha. (24.7–49.4 ac.):
- 20–50 ha. (49.4–123.5 ac.): 5.0
- 50–200 ha. (123.5–494 ac.):
- Over 200 ha. (over 494 ac.):

Activity (%) 1980–81
- Mainly crops: 22.1
- Mixed: 77.9

Land use % 1985–87
- Cropland: 25
- Pasture: 20
- Forest: 47
- Other: 8

Yields (kg./ha.) 1989
- Grains: 1,179
- Roots & tubers: 3,072
- Legumes: 602
- Milk (kg./animal): 460

Production 1989
- Fruits (000 metric tons): 411
- Vegetables (000 metric tons): 228

Livestock (000) 1989
- Cattle: 1,100
- Horses: 0 (1986)
- Sheep: 220
- Pigs: 220

Forestry 1988
- Production of roundwood (million cubic meters): 7.407
  - of which industrial roundwood (%): 4.5
- Value of exports (U.S. $ 000): 600 (1984)

Fishing 1988
- Total catch (000 metric tons): 88.6
  - of which marine (%): 0.0
- Value of exports (U.S. $ 000): 485

Development and Marketing Corporation (ADMARC), a statutory organization, is the residual buyer of smallholder produce that is neither consumed by the grower nor sold privately.

Since independence in 1964, the principal focus of the government's development strategy has been on raising agricultural production. As Malawi now is virtually self-sufficient in food production, greater emphasis is being placed on increasing and diversifying agricultural exports. Sugar, peanuts and rice have been targeted as crops with additional export potential. With the aim of improving crop yields, the government instituted the National Rural Development Program (NRDP) in 1977. Under the NRDP, a 20-year project, selected packages of inputs will be provided to smallholders, and additional instruction from agricultural extension workers will be made available.

The three major export crops are, in order of export earnings, tobacco, tea and peanuts. Other export crops include corn, cotton and sugar. In good crop years the country is self-sufficient in essential foodstuffs and there are no serious food shortages.

Because Malawi has no pastoral tribes specializing in herding, the livestock population is low in relation to the population. The country, however, produces 99% of the beef consumed there. Because of pressure on land for cultivation and the prevalence of the tsetse fly, the outlook for cattle development is poor.

Forests cover 47% of the land area, of which 68% are protected forests. Most of the areas classified as forests are actually bush-covered woodlands of little economic value. There are few commercially valuable hardwood stands. The newly established plantations are of pine, cypress or cedar.

The country's four main fishing areas—Lakes Malawi, Malombe and Chilwe, and the Shire River—possess substantial fishing potential and employ over 3,000 full-time and 3,000 part-time fishermen. Some 14% of the fish catch is accounted for by other swamps, marshes and rivers. About 225 fish species are in Lake Malawi alone, of which the five most commercially valuable are tilapia, utaka, chisawasawa, usipa, and catfish. Limbe, the main distribution center for the fish trade, has adequate cold-storage facilities.

MANUFACTURING

Manufacturing accounts for about 12% of the GDP. The principal manufacturing activity is processing of agricultural products such as tea, tobacco and cotton, but new capacity introduced after independence includes cement, transistor radio assembly, bicycle frames, agricultural implements, whiskey and beer. Manufacturing is heavily concentrated in the Blantyre-Limbe area, but decentralization is an important priority in the government's industrial policy.

The manufacturing sector is dominated by foreign capital. Private foreign investors are attracted to Malawi because of its political stability. A wide range of incentives—some of them among the most generous offered by any country—reflects Malawi's desire to accelerate the pace of development. Industrial sites are offered at low cost; market studies and feasibility surveys are financed by the government; exclusive production licenses are granted for a specified period; and adequate guarantees are provided against nationalization. The most effective inducements are liberal provisions for the repatriation of profits and capital, tariff protection and generous depreciation allowances.

The government participates directly in industry through the Malawi Development Corporation, founded in 1964. The MDC has equity participation in more than 30 industrial and financial enterprises; its profits are reinvested. The Investment and Development Bank of Malawi concentrates on strictly commercial ventures.

MANUFACTURING INDICATORS, 1987

Share of GDP (%): 12 (1988)
Labor force economically active in manufacturing (% est.): 3.2
Value added in manufacturing (U.S. $ millions) latest
  Food & tobacco (%): 33
  Textiles & clothing (%): 21
  Machinery & transport equipment (%): 3
  Chemicals (%): 17
Earnings per employee in manufacturing 1985
  Growth rate (%, 1980–87): 1.6 (latest)
  Index (1980 = 100): 115
Total earnings as % of value added: 39
Gross output per employee (1980 = 100): 139
Index of manufacturing production: 98 (1988)

MINING

Malawi has no known reserves of commercially valuable minerals.

ENERGY

In 1982 Malawi produced 49,000 metric tons of coal equivalent of energy and consumed 325,000 metric tons of coal equivalent of energy, or 51 kg. (112 lb.) per capita. The annual growth rates during 1973–83 were 8.3% for energy production and 4.3% for energy con-

ENERGY INDICATORS

Average annual energy production growth rate (%, 1980–88): 4.3
Energy consumption per capita (kg. oil equivalent): 42 (1988)
Energy imports as % of merchandise exports: 9 (1988)
Average annual growth rate of energy consumption (%, 1980–88): 0.2
Electricity 1986
  Installed capacity (000 kw.): 185
  Production (million kw.-hr.): 583
    % fossil fuel: 2.4
    % hydro: 97.6
  Consumption per capita (kw.-hr.): 74
Petroleum
  Production (million bbl.): 0 (1989)
  Consumption (million bbl.): 0 (1988)
  Refining capacity (000 bbl./day): 0 (1990)
Coal
  Reserves (million metric tons): 12 (latest)
  Consumption (000 metric tons): 66 (1988)

sumption. Energy imports, 287,000 tons in 1982, constitute 15% of all merchandise imports. Apparent per capita consumption of gasoline is 7 gal. per year.

LABOR

The most significant characteristic of the Malawian labor force is the employment of about 250,000 Malawians—equal to the total domestic wage-earning labor force—outside the country. Labor is characterized as Malawi's third-largest export. Foreign exchange remittances from migrant workers account for 13% of the total cash income of all rural families. South Africa admits foreign workers on two-year contracts only. These workers are recruited by a South African organization known as Wenela, after the initials of its former name, the Witwatersrand Native Labor Association. The corresponding organization in Zimbabwe is called Mthandizi. Under agreement with these organizations, part of the wages of Malawian workers is deferred and paid into the Reserve Bank of Malawi, which invests the funds until the worker returns.

Malawi has proceeded more slowly in Africanization than other black African countries. Nevertheless, there has been significant progress in localization (as the replacement of foreign personnel by Africans is called in Malawi). In the early 1980s a total of 83.2% of all salaried jobs were filled by black Malawians; in the private sector the percentage was 69%, and in the public sector it was 95.4%. The largest proportion of non-Malawians is in the professional cadres and in the superscale grades. President Banda is known to be interested personally in localizing the higher cadres.

Official policy favors wage restraints; therefore, wage levels are depressed. The minimum wage is set by law at M.K.25 per day in all areas outside the population centers of Zomba, Lilongwe, and Mzuzu and in the urban center of Blantyre/Limbe.

LABOR INDICATORS, 1987

Total economically active population (million): 3.300
- % working-age (15–64): 89.4
- % female: 51.5

Activity rate (%)
- Total: 41.3
- Male: 41.2
- Female: 41.5

Employment status (%)
- Employers & self-employed: 69.9
- Employees: 13.4
- Unpaid family workers: 11.3
- Other: 5.4

Sectoral employment of economically active (%)
- Agriculture, forestry, fishing: 81.8
- Construction: 1.6
- Manufacturing, mining, quarrying, public utilities: 3.2
- Trade, hotels, restaurants: 3.1
- Transportation, communications: 0.5
- Finance, real estate: 0.2
- Services: 4.2

Average annual growth rate of labor force (%, 1980–2000): 2.6
Labor under 20 years (%): 22.6 (1983)
Earnings in manufacturing per worker (/mo) (M.K.): 72.46 (1984)

The minimum working age is 14, though this applies only to the relatively small urban sector. Less than 14% of the work force is employed in the formal wage sector. For those fortunate enough to hold paid jobs, wages and working conditions generally are adequate, and paid holidays and safety standards in the workplace are required by law. However, wage levels are low, reflecting the abundance of unskilled labor and the government's desire to limit the rural-urban income gap and hence the rate of internal migration. During the 1980s inflation and unemployment became significant problems as a result of a general decline in the economy.

There are 15 labor unions affiliated with the Trades Union Congress of Malawi, which claims 6,500 members.

FOREIGN COMMERCE

Malawi's major exports are tobacco, tea, sugar, coffee and peanuts; its main imports are food, petroleum, semimanufactures, consumer goods and transportation equipment. Its principal export destinations are the United States, the United Kingdom, Zambia, South Africa and Germany. Major import sources are South Africa, Japan, the United States, the United Kingdom and Zimbabwe.

Malawi suffers from a serious trade imbalance as a result of declining world prices for its cash crops and the rising cost of imports. Trade has also become costly because of the closing of traditional transportation routes through Mozambique as a result of that nation's civil war.

FOREIGN TRADE INDICATORS, 1988

Exports (U.S. $ millions): 292
Imports (U.S. $ millions): 402
Balance of trade (U.S. $ millions): −110
Annual growth rate (1980–88), exports (%): 3.3
Annual growth rate (1980–88), imports (%): −3.4
International reserves in terms of months of imports covered: 3.7
Terms of trade (1980 = 100): 72
Import price index (1980 = 100): 99.9 (1986)
Export price index (1980 = 100): 75.4 (1986)

Direction of Trade (%)

	Imports	Exports
European Community	23.8	57.2
United States	4.2	8.6
U.S.S.R. & eastern European economies	0.0	0.0
Japan	8.2	3.0

Composition of Trade (%)

	Imports	Exports
Food & agricultural raw materials & mineral ores and concentrates	10.8	95.1
Fuels & other energy	16.5	0.0
Manufactured goods	72.7	4.9
of which chemicals	22.0	0.5
of which machinery	23.3	1.7

TRANSPORTATION & COMMUNICATIONS

Malawi Railways and its wholly owned subsidiary Central Africa Railway Company operate between Nsanje and Salima and between Nkaya and Nayuci on the eastern border with Mozambique, with total trackage of 789 km. (490 mi.). The link between Malawi and the Indian Ocean port of Nacala was completed in 1970. In 1978 construction was completed on an extension of the line through Lilongwe to Mchinji on the Zambian border. At Chipoka, south of Salima, the railway connects with the steamer service, consisting of two vessels, also operated by Malawi Railways.

Inland waterways include Lake Malawi (1,290 km.; 801 mi.) and the Shire River (144 km.; 89 mi.). There are three lake ports: Chipoka, Bandawe and Karonga.

The total length of the road system is 12,693 km. (7,887 mi.), of which 2,364 km. (1,429 mi.) are paved. The main road runs from Salisbury to Blantyre and then north through Lilongwe and Mzimba to join Tanzania and Zambia at Tunduma. Feeder roads link this north–south artery with Lake Malawi and Mozambique. The Kamuzu Highway, 186 km. (300 mi.) long, runs along the edge of Lake Malawi. About 60% of road freight is handled by Road Motor Service. The Malawi Road Transport Authority, with about 150 members, is engaged in introducing operating efficiency through pooling resources and eliminating competition. Bus services are provided by United Transport.

The national airline is Air Malawi, which flies to five countries (including South Africa) with a fleet of six civil aircraft; there are two smaller, private airlines. In 1982 the Kamuzu International Airport was opened at Lilongwe. It handles all international traffic. There are 50 airfields in the country, of which 47 are usable and one has a permanent-surface runway. There are no airfields over 2,500 m. (8,200 ft.).

Tourism is Malawi's fourth largest source of foreign exchange. The country's scenery, beautiful lake beaches and wildlife make tourism an increasingly important potential source of revenue, but it still remains undeveloped.

TRANSPORTATION INDICATORS

Roads (latest)
  Length, km. (mi.): 12,693 (7,887)
  Paved (%): 22
Motor vehicles (latest)
  Automobiles: 14,911
  Trucks and buses: 16,698
  Persons per vehicle: 242
Railroads (latest)
  Track, km. (mi.): 789 (490)
  Passenger-km. (passenger-mi.) (millions): 114.2 (71.0)
Freight, metric ton-km. (short ton-mi.) (millions): 95.2 (65.2)
Merchant marine
  Vessels (over 100 tons): 1 (1989)
  Total deadweight tonnage (000): 0.3 (1989)
Air
  Km. (mi.) flown (millions): 1.3 (0.8)
  Passenger-km. (passenger-mi.) (millions): 86.9 (54.0) (latest)
  Freight, metric ton-km. (short ton-mi.) (millions): 9.7 (6.6) (latest)
  Mail, metric ton-km. (short ton-mi.) (millions): 0.1 (0.07) (1985)
  Airports with scheduled flights: 4 (1990)
Inland waterways (latest)
  Length, km. (mi.): 1,434 (891)
  Freight, metric ton-km. (short ton-mi.) (millions): 9.8 (6.7)

COMMUNICATION INDICATORS, 1988

Telephones
  Total (000): 47 (1987)
  Persons per telephone: 172 (1987)
Phone traffic
  Combined national (pulses): 134.7 (1978)
  International (minutes): 2,348
Post office 1985
  Number of post offices: 263
  Pieces of mail handled (million): 113.9
Telegraph 1987
  Total traffic (000 calls): 182
    National: 146
    International: 36
Telex 1987
  Subscriber lines: 592
Telecommunications 1990
  Satellite stations: 2

TOURISM & TRAVEL INDICATORS, 1986

Total tourist receipts (U.S. $ millions): 6 (1988)
Expenditures by nationals abroad (U.S. $ millions): 3 (1988)
Average length of stay (nights): 8
Tourist nights (000): 573

DEFENSE

The defense structure is headed by the president. The armed forces are partially commanded by British officers. Military manpower is provided by voluntary enlistment for a period of four years.

The total strength of the armed forces is 5,250, or 0.9 military man for every 1,000 civilians.

Army

Personnel: 5,000

Organization: 3 infantry battalions; 1 special battalion, including 1 reconnaissance squadron

Equipment: 20 scout cars; 9 guns; mortars; rocket launchers; SAM

Navy

Personnel: 100

Units: 5 patrol craft based on Lake Malawi

Air Force

Personnel: 150

Organization: no combat aircraft; 1 transportation squadron; 1 helicopter squadron

Air bases: Blantyre-Limbe, Lilongwe, Mzimba, Mzuzu and Karonga

The Malawian armed forces, known as the Malawi Rifles, have no offensive capability. If faced with an invasion by any of the forces of surrounding states or well-equipped guerrilla forces, the army may not be able to defend more than a few key points or survive for more than a few days. However, there are no probable threats against Malawi from its neighbors.

Military training assistance and equipment are received exclusively from the United Kingdom.

EDUCATION

Malawi has not introduced universal, compulsory, free education.

Schooling lasts for 12 years, divided into eight years of primary school, two years of junior secondary school and two years of upper secondary school. On completion of secondary school, students receive the Malawi Certificate of Education.

The school year runs from October to August. The languages of instruction are Chichewa in primary schools and English in secondary schools.

Primary-school teachers are trained in 13 two-year teacher-training colleges, and secondary-school teachers at the University of Malawi. Nearly three-quarters of secondary-school teachers are expatriates. Teachers with diplomas or degrees are members of the civil service and enjoy great prestige.

Vocational and technical education is provided by technical schools at Soche, Lilongwe, Nasawa and Blantyre and at specialized schools administered by departments other than the Ministry of Education. Outside the school system, vocational programs are conducted at 20 or more training centers of the Malawi Young Pioneers. Adult education programs are limited in scope and enrollment and do not seem to be emphasized.

Control of the school system is vested in the Ministry of Education.

Higher education is provided by the University of Malawi, with three constituent colleges.

EDUCATION INDICATORS, 1988

Literacy
  Total (%): 41.2
First level
  Schools: 2,660
  Students: 1,066,642
  Teachers: 16,885
  Student/teacher ratio: 63.1
  Net enrollment ratio: 49 (1987)
Second level
  Schools: 79
  Students: 26,396
  Teachers: 1,258
  Student/teacher ratio: 21.0
Vocational
  Schools: 12
  Students: 3,634
  Teachers: 234
  Student/teacher ratio: 15.5
Third level (postsecondary)
  Institutions: 4
  Students: 2,330
  Teachers: 306
  Student/teacher ratio: 7.6
  Gross enrollment ratio: 0.6 (1986)
  Students (/100,000 pop.): 54
  % of population age 25 and over with postsecondary education: 0.2
Foreign study
  Foreign students in national universities: 5 (1980)
  Students abroad: 682
    of whom in
      United States: 213 (1988)
      France: 15 (1988)
      Federal Republic of Germany: 3 (1988)
      United Kingdom: 382 (1987)
Public expenditure 1988
  Total (M.K. 000): 114,254
  % of GNP: 3.2
  % of national budget: 9.9 (1986)
  % of current: 72.9

GRADUATES, 1986

Total: 639
Education: 157
Humanities & religion: 10
Fine & applied arts: 0
Law: 9
Social & behavioral sciences: 66
Commerce & business: 92
Mass communications: 0
Home economics: 0
Service trades: 0
Natural sciences: 40
Mathematics & computer science: 0.0
Medicine: 61
Engineering: 45
Architecture: 0
Industrial programs: 0
Transportation & communications: 0
Agriculture, forestry, fisheries: 159
Other: 0

LEGAL SYSTEM

The legal system is based on English common law and African custom.

The judicature consists of two parallel court systems: the traditional and the modern. At the apex of the modern system is the Supreme Court of Appeal, presided over by the chief justice. Cases are heard by three or five judges, all drawn from the High Court. The High Court is composed of the chief justice and four other judges. The lower courts are known as magistrates' courts and are divided into four levels: resident, and first-, second- and third-grade. There are 23 magistrates' courts scattered throughout the country.

The traditional court structure was established in 1969, and it parallels the modern sector. At the base are the 176 traditional courts, divided into four levels. Appeals from these courts lie to the regional traditional court of appeal and finally to the National Traditional Court of Appeal. The traditional courts are supervised by the traditional Courts commissioner, who functions under the minister of justice. The commissioner may alter or set aside sentences or transfer cases to another court.

Those charged with criminal offenses are tried in either the traditional or the modern court system, depending on the nature of the charge. Those charged under the Codes of Military Justice are tried in military courts. The defendant has the right of access to counsel before and during the judicial proceedings in the modern courts. In practice, government and party exert little control over the trial system in cases tried before the High Court or magistrate courts; hence the modern judiciary is almost totally independent of the executive branch, notwithstanding the fact that the president appoints the chief justice of the High Court who, in turn, appoints other modern court justices. These courts are open to the public, and defendants are charged publicly. Traditional court justices are appointed directly by the president. The right of appeal exists in both the modern and tradition court systems. It is generally believed that there is little executive interference in traditional court cases dealing in matters of customary law, and there is no evidence of indirect executive pressure on traditional courts adjudicating cases of a political nature. Although the decision is that of the director of public prosecution or the attorney general, the recent trend indicates that political prisoner cases are likely to be tried before a traditional court, as in the Chirwa case. Amnesty international, in its 1985 report, noted that Orton and Vera Chirwa, by being tried in a traditional court rather than the High Court, were placed at a disadvantage: They were denied the right to legal representation, and the rules of evidence observed in the High Court did not apply.

Both modern and traditional courts utilize the same legal system and employ the same procedures, such as the Code of Criminal Procedure and Evidence. However, traditional courts do not deal with cases that arise in the Westernized sectors of society or the economy. Furthermore, in traditional courts the rules of evidence are less strict, the accused need not be represented by a lawyer and cases may be tried in secret. The creation of the traditional court system was in part politically motivated and was an effort to bring the judiciary under party control. Traditional judges owe their positions to the party, and the minister of justice has the freedom to assign cases to the judge who, in his opinion, is most likely to favor the government. The Judicial Service Commission has no role in the traditional system.

There exists in Malawi a form of unusual punishment called forfeiture. The Forfeiture Act permits the government to revoke the property rights of those suspected of economic crimes without recourse to appeal. It is an executive fiat with no judicial review. When the Forfeiture Act is invoked, the individual loses all his or her worldly possessions in Malawi, including business, financial holdings and personal possessions.

There are about 20 prisons. The central prison is in Zomba; the other main prisons are in Lilongwe, Kanjedza and Mzuzu. There is an open prison farm for first offenders. The average prison population is 3,000.

LAW ENFORCEMENT

The Malawi Police is a 3,000-member force under the Ministry of Justice. Promotions, recruitment and other matters are supervised by the Police Service Commission. Under the national headquarters, there are regional police headquarters in each of the three regional capitals, police stations in each of the 24 districts, and 37 substations and posts elsewhere. The ordinary members of the force are called constables. All police operations are centrally directed. Of the nearly 300 officers and inspectors, the majority were until the mid-1970s British nationals. The first native Malawian police commissioner was appointed only in 1971.

There is a special elite unit, known as the Police Mobile Force, whose members are stationed at the headquarters and at each of the three regional capitals. Police Mobile Force personnel are equipped with rifles, light machine guns and riot gear and can react quickly to riots and disorders.

The level of crime is relatively low, and the crime growth rate is moderate. Burglaries are perhaps the most common crime. Few statistical criminal records are maintained or published.

HEALTH

Primary health services are provided free of charge. Unfortunately, Malawi's health services are among the poorest in Africa. The infant mortality rate is the highest in East Africa. The major health problems are malaria, tuberculosis, bilharzia, relapsing fever and gastrointestinal diseases.

HEALTH INDICATORS

Health personnel 1984
- Physicians: 262
  - persons per: 27,094
- Dentists: 12 (1983)
- Nurses and midwives: 2,002
- Pharmicists: 12 (1983)

Hospitals 1987
- Number: 395
- Number of beds (/10,000): 16
- Admissions/discharges (/10,000): 436 (1985)
- Bed occupancy rate (%): 90.6 (1985)
- Average length of stay (days): 8 (1985)

Type of hospitals (%) 1987
- Government: 59.2
- Private nonprofit and profit: 40.8

Public health expenditures (latest)
- As % of national budget: 5.9
- Per capita (U.S. $): 2.80

Vital statistics
- Crude death rate (/1,000): 18 (1990)
- Life expectancy at birth 1990
  - Males: 48
  - Females: 50
- Infant mortality rate (/1,000 live births): 130 (1990)
- Child mortality rate under 5 yrs. (/1,000) (1985–90): 263
- Maternal mortality rate (/1000,000 live births) (1980–84): 250
- Population with access to safe water (%): 56 (latest)

FOOD AND NUTRITION

The Malawian diet varies from tribe to tribe, but the common ingredient is a stiff porridge made from corn, millet or rice. The porridge is invariably eaten with a relish made from vegetables or fish. Other foods include peanuts and sweet potatoes. Meat is used only during religious ceremonies. The national drink is beer, usually made from finger millet.

MEDIA & CULTURE

The two daily newspapers are the *Daily Times*, published in English, and the *Malawi News*, with a combined circulation of 32,000. Five weekly papers are published in English and Chichewa. Forty-three periodicals are published in Malawi. With the exception of the *Daily Times* and the *Malawi News*, which are owned by Banda's Press Holdings, most newspapers are privately owned and run by Europeans.

There is no official censorship, but the government does not tolerate any form of criticism. The Prohibited Publications Act permits the government to ban any publication that prints information considered false, distorted or critical. A list of books, periodicals and films whose import is prohibited is published periodically by the government. Included in this list is *Awake*, the organ of the Watch Tower Bible and Tract Society (Jehovah's Witnesses). Restrictions on the media have become more numerous since President Banda personally assumed responsibility for media relations and media policies in 1973. Dr. Banda is particularly sensitive to criticism by foreign correspondents and usually reacts by deporting the offending journalist.

The national news agency is the Malawi News Agency (MANA). Reuters maintains a permanent bureau in Lilongwe.

Malawi does not adhere to any copyright convention.

MEDIA INDICATORS

Newspapers (latest)
- Number of dailies: 2
- Circulation (000): 32
- Per 1,000 pop.: 5
- Number of nondailies: 5 (1986)
- Circulation (000): 121 (1986)
- Per 1,000 pop.: 16 (1986)
- Number of periodicals: 43 (1986)
- Circulation (000): 166 (1986)
- Newsprint consumption 1988
  - Total metric tons: 500
  - Per 1,000 pop. (kg.): 63

Book publishing
- Number of titles: 99 (latest)

Broadcasting
- Annual expenditures (M.K. millions): 3.5

Radio
- Number of transmitters: 13 (latest)
- Number of persons per radio receiver: 4.4 (1989)
- Total program hours (/yr.): 6,976 (1987)

Cinema (pre-1986)
- Number of fixed cinemas: 4
- Seating capacity (000): 2
- Annual attendance (millions): 1.5

The state-controlled Malawi Broadcasting Corporation (MBC) operates one medium-wave and three shortwave transmitters in Blantyre and six regional medium-wave transmitters and three FM transmitters at Chichiri, Dedza and Limbe. MBC broadcasts a home service in Chichewa and English for 127 hours a week. There is no television service.

There is no local film production.

The largest library in the country is the University of Malawi Library, with 140,000 volumes. The depository library is the National Archives at Lilongwe. The national Library Service, with 80,000 volumes, operates a countrywide lending service.

CULTURAL & ENVIRONMENTAL INDICATORS

Libraries (latest)
- Number: 2
- Volumes (000): 305
- Registered borrowers (000): 55
- Loans (/1,000 pop.): 83

Museums (pre-1986)
- Annual attendance (000): 80
- Attendance (/1,000 pop.): 12

Nature reserves
- Number of facilities: 9

SOCIAL WELFARE

Malawi has no Social Security program. Workers receiving less than M.K. 1,000 annually are entitled to work injury benefits. Social welfare services are provided by a number of voluntary and official organizations and are coordinated by the Ministry of Community Development and Social Welfare.

GLOSSARY

dambo: a small, grassy floodplain

ngwazi: literally, chief or provider, the title of Dr. Hastings Banda, the president.

CHRONOLOGY (from 1964)

1964— Nyasaland becomes a fully independent dominion within the Commonwealth under the name of Malawi, with Hastings Banda as prime minister. . . . Six cabinet ministers, including Kanyama Chiyumi, Henry B. M. Chipembere and Yatuta Chisiza, are dismissed because of their opposition to Banda's domestic and foreign policies, particularly his pro-Western stance and tardiness in Africanization of the civil service.

1965— Banda's opposition takes up arms; Chipembere attacks Fort Johnston but is repulsed at Liwonde ferry; the revolt is crushed, and the dissidents flee into exile.

1966— Malawi is declared a republic, with Banda as president; a republican constitution is promulgated.

1967— A group of 25 rebels led by Chisiza attack Malawi; Chisiza is killed and 13 other infiltrators are captured, of whom five are sentenced to death. . . . Jehovah's Witnesses are banned as a subversive organization.

1968— Tanzania breaks diplomatic ties with Malawi; Malawians are expelled from Zambia; Banda makes territorial claims on Tanzania and Zambia.

1970— Banda is made for president for life. . . . Peace Corps volunteers are expelled from Malawi.

1971— Banda visits South Africa, the first black African head of state to do so. . . . The kwacha is introduced as the national currency.

1972— Prime Minister Johannes Vorster of South Africa visits Malawi.

1974— The capital is moved from Zomba to Lilongwe. . . . Banda visits Zambia in an attempt to improve relations.

1975— Recruitment of Malawian workers for South African mines is temporarily banned following crash of plane carrying 75 Malawians from South Africa.

1976— The Goan community, comprising immigrants from Goa, a former Portuguese colony in India, is expelled from Malawi.

1979— In National assembly elections more than one official candidate is allowed to contest. . . . Foreign reporters are banned following unfavorable comments on Banda by foreign press.

1983— New elections are held for the National Assembly.

1987— Malawi stations troops in Mozambique to protect the strategic rail line to the sea.

1988— Malawi and Mozambique sign an agreement on the repatriation of Mozambican refugees in Malawi.

1990— Malawi exempts itself from a global ban on ivory trading.

BIBLIOGRAPHY

BOOKS

Agnew, Sanzie, and Michael Stubbs. *Malawi in Maps.* New York, 1972.

Boeder, Robert B. *Malawi* (World Bibliographical Series). Santa Barbara, Calif., 1979.

———. *Malawi* (Nations of Contemporary Africa Series). Boulder, Colo., 1986.

Carter, Judy. *Malawi: Wildlife, Parks and Reserves.* London, 1987.

Chanock, Martin. *Law, Custom and Social Order: The Colonial Experience in Malawi and Zambia.* New York, 1985.

Crosby, Cynthia A. *Historical Dictionary of Malawi.* Metuchen, N.J., 1980.

Gann, Lewis H. *Central Africa: The Former British State.* Englewood Cliffs, N.J., 1971.

Heyneman, Stephen P. *The Evaluation of Human Capital in Malawi.* Washington, D.C., 1980.

Macdonald, Roderick J. *From Nyasaland to Malawi: Studies in Colonial History.* Nairobi, 1975.

Madu, Oliver V. *Models of Class Domination in Plural Societies of Central Africa.* Washington, D.C., 1978.

McCracken, J. *Politics and Christianity in Malawi.* New York, 1977.

McMaster, Carolyn. *Malawi: Foreign Policy and Development.* New York, 1974.

Mtewa, Mekki. *Malawi: Democratic Theory and Public Policy.* Cambridge, Mass., 1986.

Pachai, Bridglal. *Land and Politics in Malawi (1875–1975).* Vestal, N.Y., 1978.

———. *Malawi.* London, 1973.

Pike, John. *Malawi.* New York, 1968.

Rafael, B. R. *A Short History of Malawi.* Washington, D.C., 1980.

Short, Philip. *Banda.* London, 1974.

Williams, T. David. *Malawi: The Politics of Despair.* Ithaca, N.Y., 1978.

OFFICIAL PUBLICATIONS

Finance Ministry. *Estimates of Expenditure on Development Account.*

———. *Estimates of Expenditure on Revenue Account.*

———. *Public Sector Financial Statistics.*

Malawi Reserve Bank. *Annual Report and Statement of Accounts.*

MALAYSIA

BASIC FACT SHEET

OFFICIAL NAME: Malaysia

ABBREVIATION: MY

CAPITAL: Kuala Lumpur

HEAD OF STATE: Yang di-Pertuan Agong Paduka Seri Sultan Azlan Muhibbuddin Shah ibni Al-Marhum Sultan Yusuf Ghafarullahu-Lahu Shah (Sultan of Perak) (from 1989)

HEAD OF GOVERNMENT: Prime Minister Datuk Seri Mahathir bin Mohamad (from 1981)

NATURE OF GOVERNMENT: Constitutional monarchy

POPULATION: 17,510,546 (1990)

AREA: 329,749 sq. km. (127,316 sq. mi.)

ETHNIC MAJORITY: Malay

LANGUAGE: Bahasa Malaysia

RELIGION: Islam

UNIT OF CURRENCY: Ringgit

NATIONAL FLAG: Fourteen red and white stripes of equal width with a yellow, 14-point star and a yellow crescent in the upper right-hand quarter on a dark blue field. The 14 points of the star and the 14 stripes originally represented the 14 states of the federation, including Singapore. Each individual state also has its own state flag. Seven of the state flags display the Islamic crescent. The flag of Sabah contains four horizontal stripes of red, white, yellow and blue, with a green quarter bearing an outline of Mount Kinabalu in brown. The flag of Sarawak is a red and black cross on a golden-yellow background with a crown in the center.

NATIONAL EMBLEM: A shield supported by two tigers. The crest is a 14-point star and a crescent, both yellow. On the red, upper one-third of the shield are superimposed five gold *kris* (swords). The center of the shield has four equal panels of red, black, silver and yellow. The outer quarters of the lower third of the shield portray, on the left, three blue feathers on a sky of yellow over blue and white waves and, on the right, a Malacca tree. The lower portion of the shield contains three panels representing Sabah and Sarawak, with the national flower, *bungaraya* or *Hibiscus rosa sinensis,* in the middle. The motto below the shield in black lettering on yellow reads "Unity is Strength," in Romanized script on the left and in Jawi script on the right. Most states have their own emblems.

NATIONAL ANTHEM: "Negara Ku" (My Country). The national anthem has three official versions: a full royal version, an abridged royal version and a short version to be played at the end of public performances. Most states have their own state anthems. That of Sarawak is "Fair Land Sarawak."

NATIONAL HOLIDAYS: August 31 (National Day; Independence Day); Chinese New Year (movable); May 1 (Labor Day); Wesak Day (May 2); Deepavali (movable); Hari Raya Pu Haji (movable); Christmas; also variable Islamic festivals

NATIONAL CALENDAR: Gregorian; Chinese, Hindu and Islamic calendars also are used

PHYSICAL QUALITY OF LIFE INDEX: 81

DATE OF INDEPENDENCE: August 31, 1957

DATE OF CONSTITUTION: September 16, 1963

WEIGHTS & MEASURES: The metric system was introduced in 1972, but the following traditional weights and measures also are used:

Weight: 1 tahil = 37 ml. (1.3 oz.); 16 tahils = 1 kati; 100 katis = 1 pikul; 40 pikuls = 1 koyan = 2,419 kg. (5,333 lb.)

Linear: 1 pole or perch = 5 m. (5.5 yd.); 40 poles or perches = 1 fur.; 8 fur. = 1.6 km. (1 mi.)

Long measure: 2 jengkal = 1 hasta; 2 hasta = 1 ela; 2 ela = 1 depa = 182 cm. (6 ft.).

Land measure: 12 in. = 1 kaki = 30.48 cm. (1 ft.); 6 kaki = 1 depa; 4 sq. depa = 1 jemba = 13.4 sq. m. (144 sq. ft.); 100 jemba = 1 penjuru; 4 penjuru = 1 relong; 24 relong = 0.5 ha. (1.3 ac.).

GEOGRAPHICAL FEATURES

Malaysia consists of two geographical and political segments: West Malaysia occupies the southern third of the Malay Peninsula in Southeast Asia, while East Malaysia, separated from it by 644 km. (400 mi.) of the South China Sea, occupies most of the northern quarter of the island of Borneo. West Malaysia consists of 11 states: Johore, Kedah, Kelantan, Pahang, Perak, Perlis, Selangor, Trengganu, Negri Sembilan, Melaka and Pulau Pinang. East Malaysia consists of two states: Sabah and Sarawak. There are two federal territories: Kuala Lumpur and Labuan. The total area is 329,749 sq. km. (127,316 sq. mi.), encompassing West Malaysia (131,588 sq. km.; 50,806 sq. mi.), Sabah (73,711 sq. km.; 28,460 sq. mi.) and Sarawak (124,450 sq. km.; 48,050 sq. mi.). The greatest distances in West Malaysia are 748 km. (465 mi.) south-southeast to north-northwest and 322 km. (200 mi.) east-northeast to west-southwest, while the greatest distances in East Malaysia are 1,126 km.

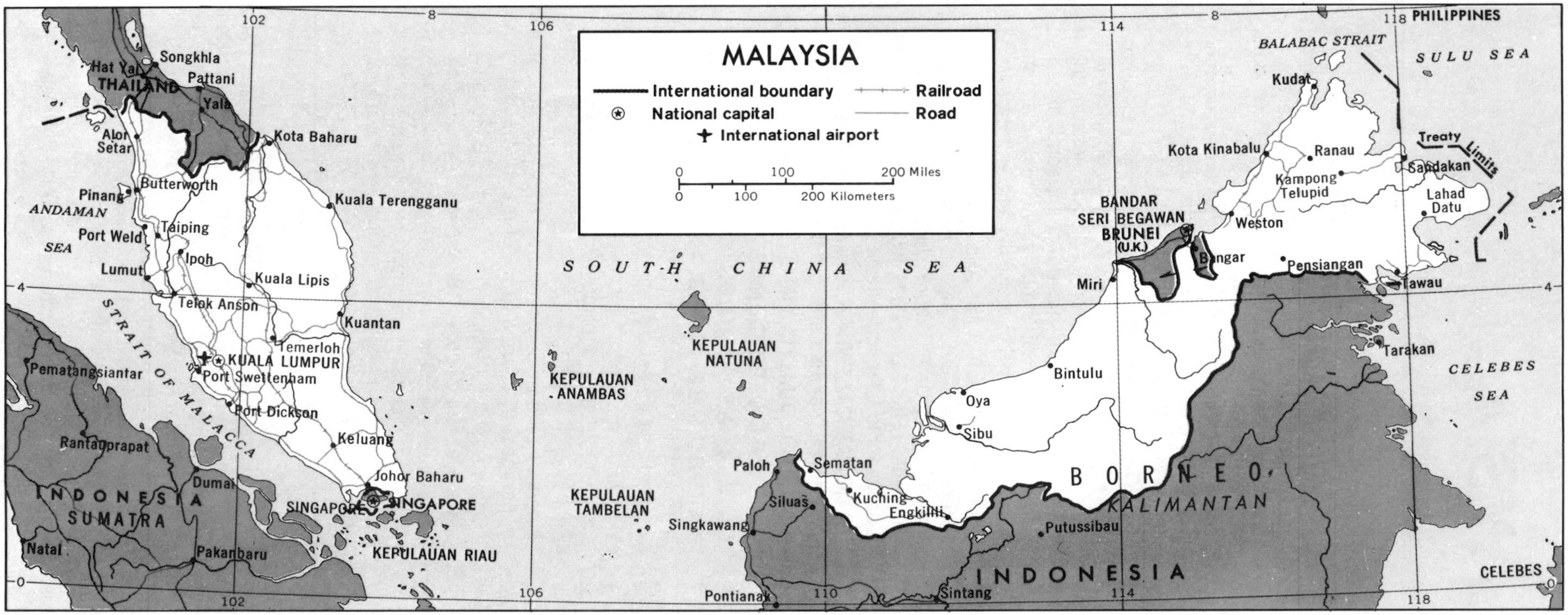
MALAYSIA
International boundary
National capital
International airport
Railroad
Road
0 100 200 Miles
0 100 200 Kilometers
PHILIPPINES
BALABAC STRAIT
SULU SEA
Kudat
Kota Kinabalu
Ranau
Treaty Limits
Sandakan
Kampong Telupid
Lahad Datu
Weston
BANDAR SERI BEGAWAN
BRUNEI (U.K.)
Bangar
Pensiangan
Tawau
Miri
Tarakan
CELEBES SEA
Bintulu
Oya
Sibu
Sematan
Paloh
Kuching
Engkilili
Siluas
Singkawang
BORNEO
KALIMANTAN
Putussibau
INDONESIA
CELEBES
Pontianak
Sintang
SOUTH CHINA SEA
KEPULAUAN NATUNA
KEPULAUAN ANAMBAS
KEPULAUAN TAMBELAN
Hat Yai
Songkhla
Pattani
THAILAND
Yala
Kota Baharu
Alor Setar
Pinang
Butterworth
ANDAMAN SEA
Port Weld
Taiping
Ipoh
Lumut
Kuala Terengganu
Kuala Lipis
Telok Anson
Kuantan
STRAIT OF MALACCA
Temerloh
KUALA LUMPUR
Port Swettenham
Pematangsiantar
Port Dickson
Keluang
Rantauprapat
Johor Baharu
Dumai
SINGAPORE
INDONESIA
SUMATRA
Natal
Pakanbaru
KEPULAUAN RIAU
102
106
110
114
118
8
4
0

BERSEKUTU
BERTAMBAH MUTU

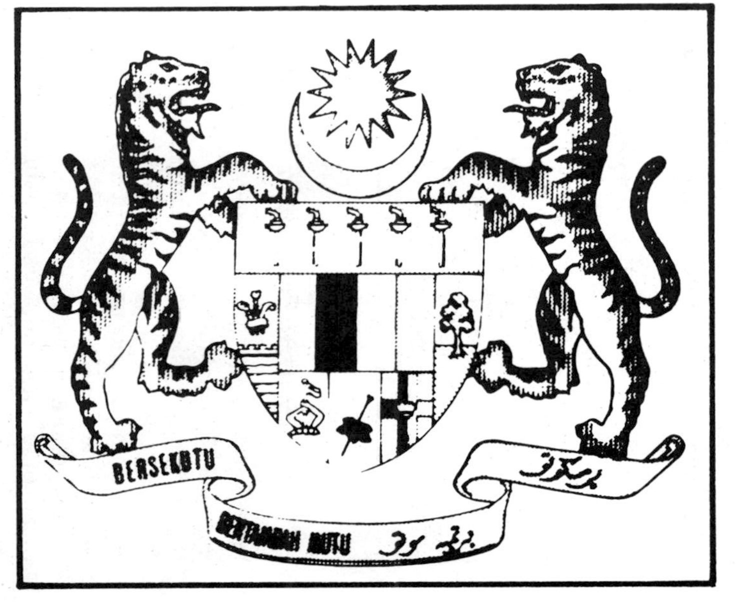

(700 mi.) north to south and 241 km. (150 mi.) east to west. The length of the coastline in West Malaysia is 1,931 km. (1,200 mi.) and that in East Malaysia 1,558 km. (968 mi.). Malaysia has a land boundary with Thailand (576 km.; 358 mi.) another, largely unexplored border with Brunei of 553 km. (343 mi.) and a border with Indonesia's Kalimantan province of 1,496 km. (930 mi.). The border with Indonesia was a subject of dispute during the Sukarno era.

The national capital is Kuala Lumpur, which became a federal territory in 1974. Its population in 1987 was 1,158,200. The state capitals are as follows:

State	Capital	Population
Johore	Johore Bahru	1,963,600
Kedah	Alor Setar	1,325,700
Kelantan	Kota Bahru	1,116,400
Melaka	Melaka	548,800
Negri Sembilan	Seremban	679,000
Pahang	Pahang	978,100
Pulau Pinang	Pinang	1,087,000
Perak	Ipoh	2,107,800
Perlis	Kangar	175,600
Sabah	Kota Kinabalu	1,322,900
Sarawak	Kuching	1,550,000
Selangor Darul Ehsan	Shah Alam	1,830,800
Trengganu	Kuala Trengganu	683,900

West Malaysia is a range of steep, forest-covered mountains running north to south along the center of the peninsula, flanked on the east and west by coastal plains. The western coastal lowland is 16 to 80 km. (10 to 50 mi.) wide, and the eastern coastal lowland, more irregular and less densely populated, is 8 to 64 km. (5 to 40 mi.) in width. Sarawak is a broad, coastal plain, frequently swampy, that merges into jungle-covered hills in the interior. Sabah's narrow coastal plain, 16 to 32 km. (10 to 20 mi.) in width, gives way to a complex series of parallel ranges culminating in Mount Kinabalu, the highest peak in Malaysia at 4,101 m. (13,455 ft.) and extending to the Sulu Sea.

The Pahang is the principal river in West Malaysia and the longest 458 km. (285 mi.). The other rivers are the Perak, the Kelantan, the Trengganu and the Endau, which flow into the South China Sea, and the Muar and the Muda, flowing into the Strait of Malacca. Both Sarawak and Sabah have extensive river systems. Major rivers of Sarawak include the 56-km.- (35-mi.)-long Rajang, the 402-km.- (250-mi.)-long Baram, the 228-km.- (142-mi.)-long Lupar and the 196-km.- (122-mi.)-long Limbang. The Rajang is navigable by small ocean vessels for 96 km. (60 mi.). The 563-km.- (350-mi.)-long Kinabatangan is the longest river in Sabah and is navigable by launches for 193 km. (120 mi.). The Padas River, which cuts across the Crocker Range, drains the interior lowland.

CLIMATE & WEATHER

Both West and East Malaysia lie in the same latitudes and have almost identical climates. The year is divided into two monsoon periods. The northwesterly monsoons prevail from October to the end of February. The southwesterly monsoons blow from mid-April to October but are milder and less predictable. The latter monsoon period also is one of sudden squalls and thunderstorms.

The mean temperature in the coastal area is 21.1° C to 32.2° C (70° F to 90° F) and in the mountains 12.8° C to 26.7° C (55° F to 80° F). Temperatures rarely rise above 35° C (95° F) or drop below 20° C (68° F.). Humidity is high throughout the year.

The annual mean rainfall in West Malaysia is just over 2,540 mm. (100 in.), with maximum precipitation during the southwesterly monsoon period. In East Malaysia the annual mean rainfall is 4,420 mm. (150 in.), most of which occurs during the northwesterly monsoon season. There are local variations even within these zones, from a low of 1,620 mm. (64 in.) in Jelebu in Negri Sembilan to over 5,080 mm. (200 in.) in the Larut Hills in Perak. The wettest place in Malaysia is Long Akah in Sarawak, with an annual rainfall of 6,000 mm. (236 in.).

POPULATION

The population of Malaysia in 1990 was 17,510,546, on the basis of the last official census, in 1980, when the population was 13,745,241.

West Malaysia contains 85% of the population, with 40% of the land area. Three-fourths of the population are concentrated in the western portion of the Malay Peninsula. In both Sabah and Sarawak the population is concentrated in the coastal regions, and the interiors are virtually uninhabited.

DEMOGRAPHIC INDICATORS

Population (millions): 17.510 (1990)
Year of last census: 1980
Sex distribution (% at last census): males, 50.2; females, 49.8
Population estimates and projections (millions)

1950: 6.187	1980: 13.764	2000: 21.485
1960: 7.908	1990: 17.886	2010: 24.363
1970: 10.466		

Age profile (% at last census)

0–14: 39.5	30–44: 16.5	60–74: 4.6
15–29: 29.1	45–59: 9.2	75 and over: 1.1

Median age (yrs.): 20.7 (1985)
Youth population (% age 15–24): 20.9 (1985); 19.0 (2000)
Total dependency ratio: 71.1 (1985)
Annual growth rate (%)

1950–55: 2.72	1975–1980: 2.32	2000–2005: 1.34
1955–60: 3.02	1980–1985: 2.31	2005–2010: 1.19
1960–65: 3.09	1985–1990: 2.31	2010–2015: 1.18
1965–70: 2.66	1990–1995: 2.02	2015–2020: 1.10
1970–75: 2.44	1995–2000: 1.68	2020–2025: 0.98

Hypothetical size of stationary population (millions): 40
Assumed year of reaching net reproduction rate of 1: 2010
Urban population (millions): 5.905 (1985)
Urban population (%): 41 (1988); 26 (1965)
Annual urban population growth rate (%, 1985–90): 4.34
Annual rural population growth rate (%, 1985–90): 0.94
Percentage of urban population in largest city: 27 (1980)
Percentage of urban population in cities of population over 500,000: 27 (1980)
Number of cities of population over 500,000: 1 (1980)
Population density per sq. km. (per sq. mi.): 54.1 (140.2) (latest)

VITAL STATISTICS

Crude birth rate (/1,000): 46 (1990); 40 (1965)
Crude death rate (/1,000): 9 (1990); 12 (1965)
Infant mortality rate (/1,000 live births): 30 (1990)
Maternal mortality rate (/100,000 live births): 59 (1986–87)
Life expectancy (yrs.) at birth: males, 65; females, 71 (1990)
Gross reproduction rate (/woman) (1980–85): 1.90
Total fertility rate (/woman): 3.5 (1990)
Rate of natural increase (/1,000): 24.4 (1988)
Average household size: 5.2

There are striking differences in the ethnic composition of urban dwellers. The Chinese are predominantly urban, while the Malay are in the vast majority in rural settlements. With the exception of Kuching in Sarawak, all the major towns are in West Malaysia. Over 37% of the population of Kuala Lumpur live in slums or squatter settlements.

Immigration has been restricted since 1939 under the Aliens Ordinance Act. It was further limited by subsequent legislation in 1946 and 1953 and currently is almost nonexistent, except as noted below. The only significant migration is from West to East Malaysia.

Until 1989 Malaysia provided first asylum to many Vietnamese refugees since 1975. It cooperated closely with international organizations and resettlement countries in facilitating the eventual movement of the refugees to those countries. Malaysia itself resettled over 7,000 Khmer Muslim refugees but did not accept non-Muslim refugees for permanent settlement. About 40,000 Philippine Muslims have permanently settled in Sabah since 1975.

Malaysia announced, in 1988, that beginning in 1989 it would treat newly arriving Indo-Chinese refugees as illegal immigrants and would deport them. The change of policy was due to the continuing influx of refugees and the growing reluctance of other nations to resettle them.

There are no restrictions on the political rights of Malaysian women. Government policy supports their full and equal participation in government, education and the work force. The position of women in society is conditioned by the cultural and religious traditions of the country's major ethnic groups. With a general resurgence of Islamic piety among Malays, Malay women have in recent years tended toward close conformity with Koranic stipulations on women's roles.

Concerned about the effect of rapid population growth, the government adopted a national family planning program in 1964. This was followed by the National Family Act of 1966, which established the National Family Planning Board as a statutory body under the Prime Minister's Department.

STATUS OF WOMEN INDICATORS

Number of women (millions): 7.855 (1985)
Women of childbearing age (15–49) (% of pop.): 51 (1988)
Married women of childbearing age (15–49) using contraception (%): 51 (latest)
Women's literacy rate (%): 63.2 (1988)
Women in labor force (%): 35.0 (1988)
Total fertility rate (/woman): 3.5 (1990)
Women in national legislatures (%): 5 (1984)

ETHNIC COMPOSITION

The ethnic composition of the population is now fairly well stabilized and falls into four broad categories. The first consists of numerous native tribal groups in East and West Malaysia whose members, descended from the earliest inhabitants of their areas, share some physical characteristics and maintain their own cultural identities. These include the Negrito tribes—Semang, Senoi and Jakun (in West Malaysia), the Ibans or Sea Dayaks—the original headhunters of Borneo—the Land Dayaks, Melanaus, Kayans, Kenyahs, Kajangs, Muruts and Kelabits (of Sarawak) and the Kadazans, Muruts and Bajans (of Sabah). The Ibans form the largest group in Sarawak, with 32% of the population; the Kadazans form the largest group in Sabah, with the same percentage of population.

The second category comprises the Malays. The ethnic identity of the Malays is elusive, and the term is applied arbitrarily to any Muslim for whom Malay is the mother tongue. They form 50% of the population in West Malaysia but constitute only the third ethnic group in size in East Malaysia. The primacy of the Malays in the nation has been built into the Constitution in a number of provisions and has been further reinforced by the establishment of Islam as the official religion and Malay as the national language. The offices of the *yang di pertuan agong* (the Malaysia head of state) and the prime minister are open only to Malays, and the structure of the federal parliament also favors Malay membership. Vast areas of state lands are reserved for Malays, and public service is virtually a Malay preserve by virtue of their position as *bumiputras* (sons of the soil). Despite government efforts to urbanize the Malays, nearly 85% of them live in rural areas as peasants or in coastal regions as fishermen.

The third group consists of the Chinese, who not only constitute the second-largest ethnic group but also dominate the economy, monopolize commerce and trade and provide a large part of the professional and general labor force. The Chinese remain isolated from Malay society and maintain a closely knit structure based on clans and voluntary benevolent associations. Until recently they were indifferent to politics and were excluded from government. Over 75% of the Chinese are urban dwellers. In terms of cultural and linguistic orientation they fall into three distinct types: the traditional, ethnocentric Chinese who speak Mandarin or any of a number of other Chinese dialects; the assimilated or Bala Chinese, who speak Mandarin and Malay; and the British-educated Chinese, who speak only English.

The fourth major ethnic group consists of Indians, a term loosely used to cover Pakistanis and Sri Lankans as well as Indians proper. Among Indians the Tamils are the most numerous, followed by Malayalees, Andhras and Punjabis. Indians form 10% of the population and work mostly on plantations and as merchants, moneylenders and white-collar workers. They are less resented than the Chinese by the Malays because Indians do not aspire to political power and their attachment to India is much weaker than that of the Chinese to China.

Ethnic aliens such as Indonesians and Thais also are strongly represented in the population. British and Australians are most numerous among Western communities.

LANGUAGE

Bahasa Malaysia is the official language of the country.

Bahasa Malaysia may be written in *Jawi* or Rumi (Roman) script. It has an extensive vocabulary of loanwords from Sanskrit, Arabic and English. Five different styles or modes or speech are used: standard, trade or bazaar, court, traditional literary and modern literary. The Dewan Bahasa dan Pustaka (State Office for Language and Books) was established in 1959 to develop and enrich the language. In 1967 an agreement was reached with Indonesia to coordinate the spelling systems of Bahasa Malaysia and Bahasa Indonesia and to increase their mutual intelligibility. Along with the exclusive use of Bahasa Malaysia in all state offices, street and city names have been Malaysianized.

The Chinese speak nine distinct, mutually unintelligible languages: Hakka, Foochow, Cantonese, Hokkien, Tiechiu, Hailam, Henghua, Luichow and Kwangsi; the Indians speak one of seven languages.

Despite government efforts, English is the language of the educated elite and is almost exclusively used in courts and commerce. English is a compulsory second language in all schools, beginning with the primary grades. English-language newspapers have a total daily circulation of over 350,000.

RELIGION

Islam is the official religion of Malaysia, and Muslims form 53% of the population of the nation as a whole. The interlocking relationship of mosque and state is strengthened by a number of constitutional provisions, especially those that designate the *yang di pertuan agong* as the religious head and rulers in each state as the heads of Islam in that state. Sabah and Sarawak are exempt from many of the strictly religious provisions of the Constitution, under which only Muslims are considered Malays. Instruction in Islam is provided in all government-assisted schools. Muslims have special obligations as well as special rights under law; they have a separate system of courts and pay special taxes. Each state has a religious affairs department. The National Council of Islamic Affairs coordinates the activities of these religious departments and also administers the National Mosque.

Conversion is permitted, but proselytizing of Muslims is strongly discouraged. Although an Islamic religious establishment is supported by government funds and it is government policy to infuse "Islamic values" into the administration of Malaysia, the government has refused to accede to demands for the imposition of Islamic religious law in cases involving non-Muslims. Non-Muslims are excused from public-school instruction in the Muslim religion.

Most of the Chinese follow Confucianism, Buddhism or Taoism, while most of the Indians are Hindus. The high correlation between race and religion has been a potentially divisive factor in national life. The number of Christians is estimated at over 300,000. The indigenous tribes of Sarawak and Sabah are mostly animist, but substantial numbers have been converted to Christianity.

HISTORICAL BACKGROUND

West Malaysia was under Portuguese rule from 1511 to 1641, under Dutch rule from 1641 to 1795 and under British rule from 1795. Sabah became a British territory in 1881 and Sarawak in 1888. British colonial rule was relatively brief, largely indirect and produced less social cleavage than previous colonial regimes. Malaysia was established as an independent nation within the Commonwealth on September 16, 1963. It was created through the merger of the 11-state Federation of Malaya, which had achieved independence in August 1957; the internally self-governing state of Singapore; and the former British Crown Colonies of Sarawak and Sabah. Singapore because of its largely Chinese population was seen as a threat to Malay dominance in the country. It left the federation in August 1965. Tunku Abdul Rahman, as head of the United Malays National Organization (UMNO) served as prime minister from independence until 1970 when serious rioting resulting from Malay/Chinese tensions over electoral returns led to his resignation.

Tun Abdul Razak, after assuming the prime ministership broadened the UMNO-dominated government coalition to establish the National Front which absorbed most former opposition parties. Abdul Razak died in office in 1976 and was succeeded by Deputy Prime Minister Datuk Hussein bin Onn. Datuk Hussein assumed leadership of the National Front as well. In early federal and state elections in July 1978 the National Front firmly established control of the House of Representatives.

Datuk Hussein chose not to run for re-election in 1981, and he was succeeded as UMNO president in June by Datuk Seri Dr. Mahathir bin Mohamad. Dr. Mahathir was designated prime minister on July 16 and called for an early election on April 22–26. In both that election and the succeeding election held August 2–3, 1986, the National Front won impressive victories.

However, issues which had been raised during the 1986 electoral campaign resurfaced in early 1987 and provoked a major crisis in the prime minister's party. Deputy Prime Minister Musa bin Hital accused Dr. Mahathir of tolerating corruption, mismanagement and overspending and supported Trade and Industry Minister Razaleigh Hamzah's candidacy for the party presidency. Although Mahathir managed to defeat Razaleigh by a slim margin, and Encik Abdul Ghaffar by an even narrower one, the party split into two factions. Soon after that Mahathir announced Razaleigh's resignation and the dismissal of several other ministers who had supported him.

Late in the year racial tensions between Chinese and Malays arose over sensitive political issues. In order to prevent riots, the government ordered the detention of more than 100 prominent members of both the National Front and opposition parties. Additionally the publishing licenses of three major newspapers were revoked. New Legislation which took effect in December gave the Minister of Information power to monitor television and radio broadcasts as well as to revoke the license of any private broadcasting company not adhering to "Malaysian values." By late January 1989 nearly all detainees had been released. Lim Kit Siang and his son, both prominent members of the opposition DAP, remained in detention.

In June 1987 dissension within UMNO led to a suit claiming that since some delegations participating in the UMNO party elections of April 1987 had not been officially registered, the elections should be declared null and void. In February 1988, the High Court of Peninsular Malaysia ruled that in fact there had been no election. Mahathir claimed that the ruling did not affect the legal status of the Government or of the Head of State. Former Prime Ministers Tunku Abdul Rahman and Hussein Onn attempted to assume control of UMNO by forming a new party, UMNO Malaysia. They were prevented from doing so by Mahathir, who in his role as Minister of Home Affairs controlled the office of Registrar of Societies. Instead Mahathir himself formed a new party, UMNO (Baru) and transferred the assets of UMNO to his new party. At the same time he excluded Razaleigh and Hussein Onn from UMNO (Baru) membership.

Additionally already existing tension between the executive and the judiciary was exacerbated by new constitutional amendments which restricted the judiciary's power to interpret laws. When Tun Mohammed Salleh, the Lord President of the Supreme Court, wrote to the Head of State to protest government's attempts to limit the independence of the Judiciary, he was suspended from office. A tribunal set up to investigate the matter rejected Salleh's claims, and he was dismissed from office in August. In November Tan Sri Abdul Hamid Omar who had chaired the tribunal was confirmed as President of the Supreme Court.

Mahathir's leadership continued to be contested in two separate by-elections held in Johore Bahru and in Parit Raja. Razaleigh, Musa and 13 MPs left the National Front coalition to form UMNO '46 (the year UMNO was founded). In a conciliatory move, Mahathir invited his opponents to join UMNO (Baru). In December these opponents led by Musa drew up the Johore Declaration stating their terms for joining UMNO (Baru) among them automatic admission of former UMNO members to the new party. UMNO (Baru) accepted the terms while declaring that they were valid only for the state of Johore. By January 1989 Musa had declared his membership in UMNO (Baru).

Mahathir won reelection to a third term in 1990. His ruling National Front captured 127 seats, enough to maintain the majority needed to pass constitutional amendments. The election was the toughest ever faced by the UMNO. Mahathir was challenged for the first time by a fellow ethnic Malay, Razaleigh Hamzah, a former ally of the prime minister who had quit UMNO in 1987 to found his own party, Spirit of '46, named after the year in which UMNO was founded. The new party allied itself with ethnic Chinese and Moslem parties to form a powerful opposition coalition that campaigned on a platform of reforms that included an end to detention without trial and more aggressive probes of alleged government corruption. The opposition also criticized the government program of privatization. The ruling coalition campaigned on the strength of an economy that had been increasing at a rate of 9% after inflation.

CONSTITUTION & GOVERNMENT

The government of Malaysia is based on the Constitution of 1957 as amended to accommodate the special interests of Sabah and Sarawak, which joined the federation in 1963. It established a federal system of government under a constitutional monarchy. The head of state is the paramount ruler, the *yang di pertuan agong*, who is chosen by and from among the Confer-

GOVERNMENT LIST
(July/August 1991)

Paramount Ruler	AZLAN Muhibbuddin Shah ibni Sultan Yusof Izzudin
Deputy Paramount Ruler	JA'AFAR ibni Abdul Rahman
Prime Minister	MAHATHIR bin Mohamad
Deputy Prime Minister	Abdul GHAFAR bin Baba
Minister of Agriculture	SANUSI bin Junid
Minister of Culture, Arts & Tourism	SABARUDDIN bin Chik
Minister of Defense	Mohamed NAJIB bin Tun Haji Abdul Razak
Minister of Domestic Trade & Consumer Affairs	Abu HASSAN bin Haji Omar
Minister of Education	SULAIMAN bin Daud
Minister of Energy, Telecommunications & Posts	VELLU, Samy
Minister of Finance	ANWAR bin Ibrahim
Minister of Foreign Affairs	ABDULLAH bin Haji Ahmad Badawi
Minister of Health	LEE Kim Sai
Minister of Home Affairs	MAHATHIR bin Mohamad
Minister of Housing & Local Government	TING Chew Peh
Minister of Human Resources	LIM Ah Lek
Minister of Information	MOHAMED bin Rahmat
Minister of International Trade & Industry	RAFIDAH binti Aziz
Minister of Justice	Syed HAMID bin Syed Jaafar Albar
Minister of Land & Cooperative Development	Haji SAKARAN bin Dandai
Minister of National Unity & Community Development	NAPSIAH binti Haji Omar
Minister of Primary Industries	LIM Keng Yaik
Minister of Public Enterprises	Mohamed YUSOF bin Haji Mohamed Nor
Minister of Public Works	Leo MOGGIE Anak Irok
Minister of Rural Development	Abdul GHAFAR bin Baba
Minister of Sciences, Technology & Environment	LOW Hian Ding
Minister of Transport	LING Liong Sik
Minister of Youth & Sports	Haji ANUAR bin Musa
Minister in the Department of the Prime Minister	Abang ABU BAKAR bin Abang Haji Mustafa
Minister in the Department of the Prime Minister	Syed HAMID bin Syed Jaafar Albar

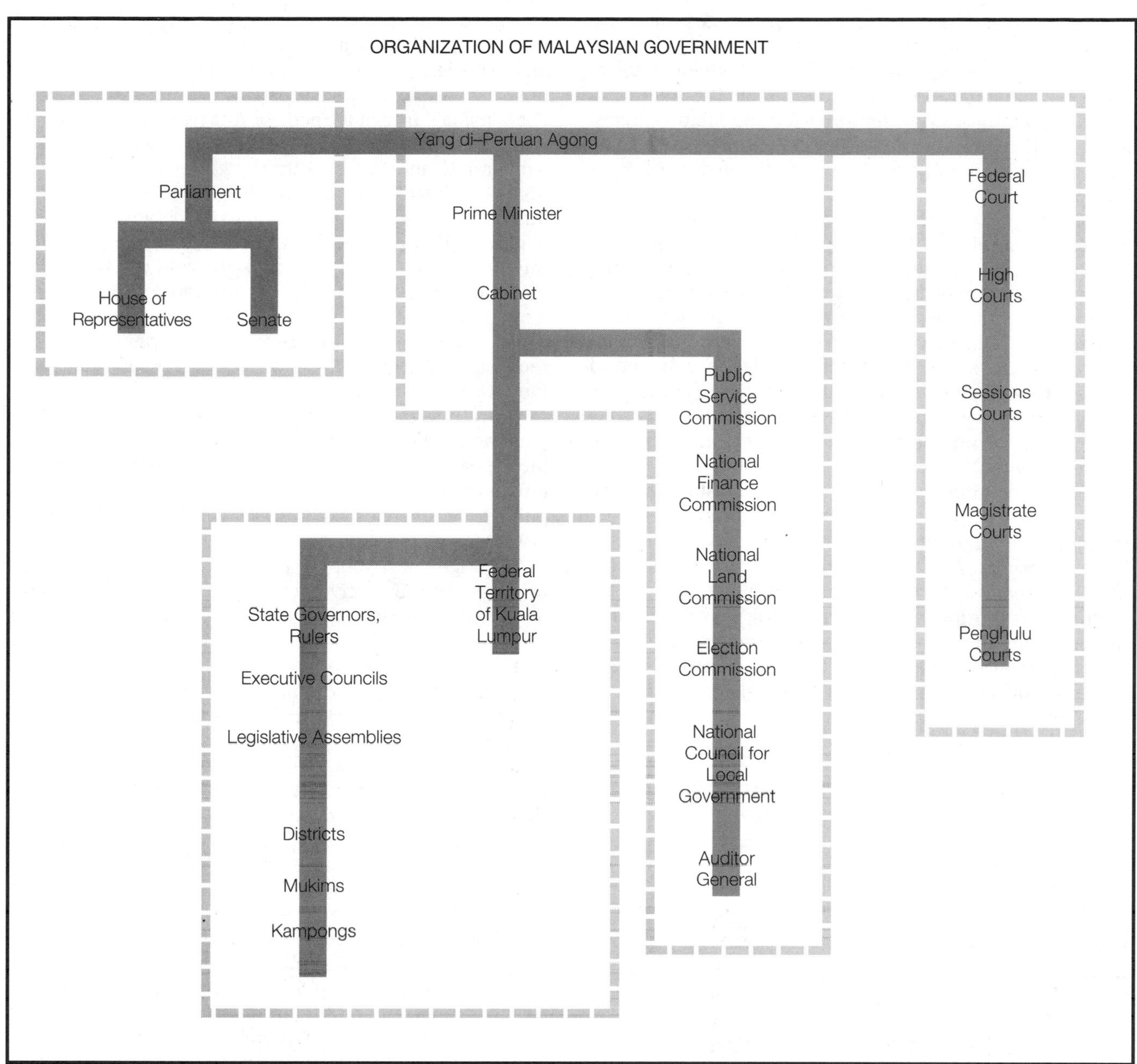

ence of Rulers, the Majlis Raja Raja, for a period five years. He performs the duties of a constitutional monarch and also is the supreme head of Islam in Pinang, Melaka and his own state. Mostly he acts on the advice of the prime minister and has limited veto power but may refuse to dissolve parliament even against the wishes of the prime minister.

Executive power is vested in the prime minister (the head of government) and cabinet responsible to the federal parliament. The administration is strongly centralized. The federal parliament has sole authority to legislate in the fields of external affairs, defense and internal security, justice (except Islamic law or *adat*), citizenship (except in Sabah and Sarawak), industry, commerce, finance, communications, transportation and education. In all cases federal legislation takes precedence over state law where a conflict exists. Sabah and Sarawak were granted special provisions and safeguards in the Constitution in matters of land law, local government, finances, official language and official religion.

The Constitution also grants to Malays as *bumiputras* (sons of the soil) a special favored position, with quotas in education and public service (and reservations of land) out of proportion to their actual numbers. Another feature of the Constitution is the right of parliament (and when parliament is not in session, of the paramount ruler) to declare a state of emergency permitting the federal government to deal with national crises with absolute powers.

The conference of rulers, the *majlis raja raja*, consists of nine hereditary rulers of the Malay states and governors of the states of Malacca, Penang, Sabah and Sarawak. The primary duty of the inner conference of hereditary rulers is to elect or remove the *yang di pertuan agong* and to decide matters concerning the preservation of Malay and Muslim privileges and their own dignities. The conference must be consulted on the appointment of judges and other high officials. It must be consulted and must concur in the alteration of state boundaries, legislation affecting Islam, amendments to the Constitution and regulations affecting the special position of the Malays and natives of East Malaysia.

The cabinet *(juma'ah mentri)* is a council of ministers appointed by the *yang di pertuan agong* to advise him in the administration. It is headed by the prime minister, who must always command the confidence of the majority of the House of Representatives. The powers and privileges of the prime minister and cabinet conform to the British model. A number of assistant ministers and parliamentary secretaries are appointed from among members of parliament. In 1989 there were 24 ministers in the cabinet, including the prime minister.

In 1983 the Mahathir administration pushed through the federal parliament a constitutional amendment that restricted the paramount ruler's power to veto money bills. In other cases, the veto could not be invoked after the second reading and a month's delay.

The Constitution also provides for certain autonomous bodies under cabinet control: the National Land Council, the National Finance Council, the Election Commission and the National Council for Local Government.

RULERS OF MALAYSIA

Prime Ministers (from 1963)

September 1963–September 1970: Tunku Abdul Rahman Putra bin Abdul Hamid Halim Shah
September 1970–January 1976: Tun Abdul Razak bin Datuk Hussein
January 1976–July 1981: Datuk Hussein bin Onn
July 1981– : Datuk Seri Mahathir bin Mohamad

FREEDOM & HUMAN RIGHTS

In terms of civil and political rights, Malaysia is ranked as a partially free country. Malaysia is and prides itself as a multiethnic and democratic society, but both these characteristics have been under severe strains and pressures, and the potential for violence and social conflict is ever present in the country. Citing security reasons, including the threat of Communist insurgents and the possibility of renewed communal violence, the Malaysian government maintains legislation that makes legal the arrest and detention without trial of persons suspected of subversive activity. Cruel and inhuman treatment of prisoners is barred even in times of national emergency; summary executions are not carried out, and convictions that carry the death penalty are automatically subject to appeal to the Federal Court or the Pardons Board. The government also uses the Emergency (Essential Powers) Ordinance to deal with terrorists. These regulations substantially abridge the rights of the accused by allowing in camera trials, anonymous witnesses and presumption of guilt. Modeled on the British judiciary, Malaysian courts generally are regarded as committed to the rule of law and not susceptible to pressures from the executive.

Malaysia's Internal Security Act (ISA) permits arrest and detention without trial of persons suspected of subversive activity or other actions contributing to domestic instability. It provides for initial preventive detention for up to two years, extendable indefinitely. A person detained under the emergency laws has no recourse to the courts but must be told the reason for his or her detention and given an opportunity to challenge the detention order as soon as possible after arrest. The government reserves the right to refuse requests for information on specific individuals detained under security legislation.

The media are constrained under the Constitution (Amendment) Act of 1971 from discussing certain ethnically sensitive topics in order not to inflame racial tensions. Mindful of the need for annual renewal of publishing licenses, the press is circumspect in its criticisms of the government.

Although non-Malays consider the government's practices of affirmative action on behalf of the Malays as discriminatory against other races, the Chinese and the Indian minorities receive better treatment in Malaysia than they do in some other Southeast Asian countries, such as Myanmar and Indonesia. While the state religion is Islam, the government has regularly resisted Muslim extremists' demands for replacing common law with Islamic law and for wider enforcement of Islamic practices. Although the rights to freedom and peaceable assembly exist and are guaranteed by the Constitution, these rights have been restricted by legislation in the interests of security and public order. All societies and associations are required to be registered and thus are subject to close scrutiny.

In the realm of politics, British traditions continue to have great impact. Elections are held regularly. While the ruling National front takes full advantage of its incumbency, even the opposition concedes that the votes are cast freely and recorded accurately.

Although union activity is circumscribed by existing legislation, its power was demonstrated in 1980 when union leaders pressured the Ministry of Labor into withdrawing certain antilabor provisions in an amended labor relations statute. The freedom to strike exists and is used often.

CIVIL SERVICE

The Malaysian civil service conforms to the British model and retains British structure and designations. The Constitution grants a virtual monopoly in the civil service to Malays, and recruitment is heavily weighted to preserve this. Civil servants are classified into four grades. They are prohibited from participating in politics.

All cadres of public servants are governed by one general and four specialized commissions: the Public Services Commission, the Judicial and Legal Services Commission, the Railway Service Commission, the

Armed Forces Council and the Police Force Commission. Each state has its own civil service under a separate state public service commission.

LOCAL GOVERNMENT

The administration of the states (11 in West Malaysia and two in East Malaysia) is carried out by rulers or governors acting on the advice of state executive councils. Each state has its own constitution, flag, anthem and a unicameral legislative assembly that shares legislative powers with the federal parliament.

Each of the 13 states is governed by a written Constitution and has its own state executive and legislative assembly. States in West Malaysia are more closely linked to the federal government than those in East Malaysia, which enjoy a certain autonomy to protect their special interests. The chief executive of each state is the ruler or governor. The heads of the nine dynastic states of West Malaysia are their hereditary rulers, seven of whom are called sultans. The title of the ruler of Perlis is *raja* and that of Negri Sembilan is *yang di pertuan besar.* All of them hold office for life. The head of the states of Melaka and Pinang are governors and that of Sabah is *yang di pertuan negara.* The governors are chosen by the *yang di pertuan agong* and usually are appointed for a four-year term. They may be removed only by a two-thirds vote of the state legislative assembly.

Every state has an executive council or cabinet (known in Sarawak as the Supreme Council) headed by a chief minister (in Melaka, Pinang, Sabah and Sarawak) or a *mentri besar* (in other states). The cabinet is collectively responsible to the state legislature. Cabinet advice is binding on the rulers or governors, but the nine rulers have a wider field of discretionary powers than the governors.

The basic unit of local government is the district, headed by a district officer, usually a civil servant, who also may hold the office of magistrate. Within the districts are *mukims,* of which there were over 900 in West Malaysia, administered by *penghulus,* assisted by *naibs* or *sidangs. A mukim* usually is a collection of *kampongs* (villages), each with an elected *ketua kampong.*

Sabah and Sarawak have their own systems of local government. Sabah is divided into four residencies: West Coast, Interior, Sandakan and Tawau. The island of Labuan is administered separately under a district officer. Sarawak is divided into five divisions, each in charge of a resident. The divisional headquarters are Kuching, Simanggang, Sibu, Miri and Limbang.

FOREIGN POLICY

Malaysian foreign policy was shaped largely by the nation's first prime minister, Tunku Abdul Rahman, who directed its primary orientation to the West. Despite its Western ties, Malaysia considers itself nonaligned and is a member of the nonaligned Afro-Asian group at the United Nations. Malaysia has moved away from its earlier special relationship with Great Britain. With the departure of British military forces east of Suez, Malaysia has been developing alternative sources of security. Close relations with Great Britain continue but are declining in importance. They were weakened in the early 1980s as a result of Malaysia's "buy British last" policy on official contracts. Though this restriction was relaxed somewhat in 1983, Malaysia continued to develop its commercial ties to Japan and Korea at the expense of the West.

Relations with Singapore, which were cool following the latter's withdrawal from the Malaysian Federation in 1965, have improved considerably in recent years. The most dramatic improvement in relations has been with Indonesia. Since the end of the confrontation in 1966, the two countries have moved closer in a number of fields, guided by ethnic ties and compatible political ideologies. An agreement was signed in 1969 delimiting the continental shelf in the Straits of Malacca. The two countries also have adopted a common spelling for their related languages.

Relations with the Philippines have been strained since 1962 by the Philippine claim to Sabah and over Malaysian assistance to Moro rebels in Mindanao. Diplomatic relations between the two countries were broken between 1963 and 1966 and between 1968 and 1969. There also is an unresolved territorial dispute with Thailand over Thai claims to the Malaysian provinces of Kedah, Trengganu, Perlis and Kelantan, and Malaysian claims to the four southern Thai provinces with a predominantly Muslim and ethnic Malay population. Outside Southeast Asia, Malaysia has strongest ties with India, which it has consistently supported in disputes with Pakistan and China. Despite bonds of Islam, relations with Pakistan have been uneven, with a break in diplomatic relations from 1965 to 1966 over Malaysian support for India during the Indo-Pakistani conflict.

In a determined effort to widen diplomatic contacts, ties were established with the Soviet Union, East European countries, North Korea and Vietnam. Relations with the People's Republic of China were normalized in 1974. Malaysia also enhanced its role within the Muslim world by acting as the host of the Fifth Islamic Conference, at Kuala Lumpur in 1974, and by officially supporting the Palestine Liberation Front (PLO) against Israel.

For Malaysia, as for other nations in Southeast Asia, 1979 was the year of the refugee. Seen as the most critical event in 1979 and early 1980, the flood of refugees, principally ethnic Chinese from Vietnam, became an international issue. Initially, official policy was friendly, accepting all arrivals and placing them in camps pending their resettlement elsewhere. But when the number of refugees reached 75,000, the influx began to cause widespread resentment among coastal Malays, mostly for religious and racial reasons. Numerous boat people were forced to return to the sea after being stoned by local residents. In November 1978 the government announced that it would no longer permit refugees in seaworthy vessels to disembark. After failing to convince Vietnam to stem the flow, the then deputy prime minister, Mahathir bin Mohamed, announced in 1979 that Vietnamese refugees coming into Malaysian waters would be shot on sight. In the resulting international uproar, a number of countries, the United States among them, promised to increase their intake of refugees. Developments in Indochina, particularly the danger posed to Thailand by Vietnam, have brought Malaysia closer to other ASEAN members as well as China while drawing it away from the Soviet Union. Relations with Thailand have improved beyond all expectations. Malaysia has promised to go to Thailand's aid in case of foreign attack.

In 1980 Malaysia proclaimed an Exclusive Economic Zone (EEZ) extending for up to 322 km. (200 mi.) from the country's territorial sea limits. These limits are recognized only by Indonesia.

Regional cooperation is one of the central concepts of Malaysian foreign policy, and Malaysia has played an active role in the Association of Southeast Asian Nations (ASEAN) since its inception in 1967. Malaysia also is a member of a five-power defense pact (with Britain, Australia, New Zealand and Singapore), under which Commonwealth forces are stationed in Malaysia. In recent years Malaysia has advocated creation of a zone of "peace, freedom and neutrality" in Southeast Asia under guarantees by the superpowers.

The United States has maintained unbroken diplomatic relations with Malaysia since 1963 and supported its efforts to achieve stability and combat Communist insurgency. Malaysia and the United States are parties to 21 treaties and agreements covering aviation, consuls, defense, economic and technical cooperation, education, extradition, investment guarantees, narcotics, the Peace Corps, postal matters, property, trademarks, trade and commerce, and visas.

Malaysia joined the United Nations in 1957. It is a member of 14 U.N. organizations and 19 other international organizations, including the Commonwealth.

PARLIAMENT

The federal parliament is a bicameral body consisting of the Senate and the House of Representatives. The Senate (Dewan Negara) is made up of 26 elected members (two from each state) and 42 members appointed by the *yang di pertuan agong.* The elected members are elected by the state legislatures; the appointed senators have achieved distinction in public service or the professions or are representatives of minorities. The Senate is never dissolved, new elections being held by the appropriate state legislative assembly as often as there are vacancies. A senator's term of office is six years.

The House of Representatives (Dewan Rakyat) has 177 members. It is composed of 132 members from Peninsular Malaysia (including seven members from the federal territory), 24 from Sarawak and 21 from Sabah. Representatives from Sabah and Sarawak are selected by the state legislative assemblies, while those from West Malaysia are popularly elected. The term of the House is five years, subject to dissolution. Voting is weighted in favor of Malay rural areas, with Chinese urban constituencies having three to four times as many voters as their rural counterparts. National elections are held every five years on the basis of universal adult suffrage over 21. The election Commission reviews delimitation of constituencies, conducts elections and keeps electoral rolls.

Parliament must be summoned at least once every six months. If a parliament is dissolved, a general election must be held within 60 days, and the newly elected parliament must meet within 90 days.

Each state has its own unicameral legislative assembly, which shares legislative powers with the federal parliament and bears the same relation to the state executive as the federal parliament does to the federal executive. All members are directly elected from single-member constituencies. The term of assembly is five years. Most state legislatures meet only four or five times a year, and the sessions are short except for budget debates. Every state legislature has the right to legislate on matters not reserved for the federal parliament or included in the joint list. The most important of the state subjects is land regulation. A member of parliament may be simultaneously a member of a state legislature.

The Sarawak legislative assembly has 48 members, while the Sabah legislative assembly has 48 elected members and six nominated members.

POLITICAL PARTIES

Political parties in Malaysia represent fragmented ethnic, religious and linguistic constituencies rather than secular ideologies. They function not so much as links between government and the people as means of identifying government patronage and safeguarding the vested interests of each community.

The ruling Barisan National Front, a multiracial coalition of 13 parties, founded as the Alliance Party in 1972, has been in power since 1957. The constituent members of this alliance are: United Malays National Organization (UMNO); Berjasa; Malaysian Chinese Association; Malaysian Indian Congress; Parti Gerakan Rakyat Malaysia; People's Progressive Party of Malaysia; Parti Pesaka Bumiputra Bersatu; Sarawak United People's Party; Sarawak National Party; United Sabah National Organization; Hizbul Muslimin; Parti Bansa Dayak Sarawak; and Parti Bersatu Sabah.

After a bitter interparty struggle in 1987, Razaleigh Hamzah, a former ally of Prime Minister Mahathir Mohamad, quit UMNO and founded his own party, Spirit of '46, named after the year in which UMNO was founded. The new party allied itself with ethnic Chinese and Moslem parties to form a powerful opposition coalition.

In the 1990 elections, the National Front captured 127 seats, down from the 133 in the previous parliament. The opposition coalition won 49 seats, up from 40. Independents held even at four seats. Political observers called the election the toughest test ever for the dominant faction of the National Front, the UMNO.

The major illegal opposition is the Communist Party of Malaysia, banned since 1948. From its headquarters in southern Thailand its agents have made persistent efforts to infiltrate left-wing organizations, and its paramilitary operations were resumed in the mid-1970s.

ECONOMY

Malaysia has one of the most impressive economies in Asia after Japan and Singapore. The economy is export-based and is therefore vulnerable to changes in world prices for its principal raw materials: rubber, palm oil and tin.

Malaysia is one of the upper-middle-income countries of the world, with a free-market economy in which the private sector is dominant.

Agriculture which includes forestry, hunting and fishing has traditionally been the most important sector of the Malaysian economy. Rubber and palm oil are the chief agricultural products, and Malaysia is the world's leading producer of those two crops. However, by 1988 manufacturing had surpassed agriculture in importance so that it was contributing 25% of GDP compared to agriculture's 21%. The processing of the raw rubber and palm oil are the major industries. A steady demand and strong prices for Malaysia's major commodities—rubber and palm oil—have boosted export earnings and led to a very favorable balance of trade in 1988 of $20 billion in exports and $14.9 billion in imports. Major imports are food, crude oil and consumer goods with Japan, Singapore and the United States being the primary trade partners. Malaysia is not self-sufficient in food even though a large percentage of the labor force is employed in agriculture. Rice is the principal food crop, and although high-yielding varieties have been introduced and drainage and irrigation have both been improved the country is still heavily reliant on food imports. Conservation measures which were put into effect in the late 1980s to slow the depletion of the country's forest resources resulted in a significant decline in timber exports for 1988. A crisis in the world tin market beginning in October 1985 adversely affected the country's mining sector and resulted in the closing of some 260 of the country's 450 tin mines. Tin prices improved in 1987 and 1988 and 40 of the mines reopened.

The Malaysian Industrial Development Authority has used tax and export allowances to encourage investment and to aid the growth of manufacturing. While the processing of locally produced raw materials continues to predominate, expansion and diversification are being encouraged. In mid-1985 a 10-year Industrial Master Plan was introduced to promote long-range development in the manufacturing sector. Exploitation of newly discovered offshore oil deposits made petroleum a leading source of government revenue by the late 1980s. Copper production is also gaining in importance.

PRINCIPAL ECONOMIC INDICATORS

Gross National Product (U.S. $ billions): 37.005 (1989)
GNP per capita (U.S. $): 2,130 (1989)
GNP average annual growth rate (%, 1980–89): 4.6
GNP per capita average annual growth rate (%, 1987–89): 6.8
Income distribution (% household income)
  Lowest 20%: 4.6
  Highest 10%: 34.8
Average annual rate of inflation (%, 1980–88): 1.3
Consumer price index (1980 = 100) 1986
  All items: 126
  Food: 123
Average annual growth rate (%, 1980–88)
  General government consumption: 2.2
  Private consumption: 0.9
  Gross domestic investment: 0.0

BALANCE OF PAYMENTS, 1989
(U.S. $ millions)

Current account balance: −145
Merchandise exports: 24,831
Merchandise imports: −21,051
Trade balance: 3,779
Other goods, services & income +: 3,985
Other goods, services & income −: 7,978
Other goods, services & income net: −3,993
Private unrequited transfers: −25
Official unrequited transfers: 94
Capital other than reserves: 1,376
Net errors & omissions: 247
Counterpart items: 15
Liabilities constituting foreign authorities reserves: 5
Total change in reserves: −1,250

GROSS DOMESTIC PRODUCT

GDP nominal (M.$ billions): 97.522
GDP per capita (U.S. $): 2,270 (1989 est.)
Average annual growth rate of GDP (%, 1980–88): 4.6
GDP by type of expenditure (%) 1987
  Consumption
    Private: 47
    Government: 15
  Gross domestic investment: 24
  Gross domestic saving: 36 (1988)
  Foreign trade
    Exports: 63
    Imports: −49
Cost components of GDP (%) 1983
  Net indirect taxes: 16
  Consumption of fixed capital and net operating surplus: 51
  Compensation of employees: 34
Sectoral origin of GDP (%) 1987
  Primary
    Agriculture: 21
    Mining: 11
  Secondary
    Manufacturing: 22
    Construction: 4
    Public utilities: 2
  Tertiary
    Transportation & Communications: 7
    Trade: 11
    Finance: 9
    Other services: 2
    Government: 12
Average annual sectoral growth rates (%, 1980–88)
  Agriculture: 3.7
  Industry: 6.1
  Manufacturing: 7.3
  Services: 3.6

PUBLIC FINANCE

The Malaysian fiscal year is the calendar year. Under the Constitution annual budgets are prepared by both the central government and the 13 state governments. Certain fields of taxation are reserved for the states, and they also receive an annual capitation grant from the central government along with a share of export duties on minerals produced within their borders. Resource allocations are determined by the National Finance Council. In 1969 a new budget format known as the program and performance budget was introduced.

CENTRAL GOVERNMENT EXPENDITURES, 1988

% of total expenditures
- Defense: 14.4
- Education: 20.0
- Health: 4.8
- Housing, social security, welfare: 4.0
- Economic services: 18.1
- Other: 38.7

Total expenditures as % of GNP: 31.3 (1988)
Overall surplus or deficit as % of GNP: −8.0 (1988)

CENTRAL GOVERNMENT REVENUES, 1988

% of total current revenues
- Taxes on income, profit & capital gain: 32.2
- Social security contributions: 0.7
- Domestic taxes on goods & services: 18.0
- Taxes on international trade & transactions: 17.3
- Other taxes: 2.0
- Current nontax revenue: 29.8

Total current revenue as % of GNP: 25.1
General government consumption as % of GDP: 14 (1988)
Average annual growth rate of general government consumption (%, 1980–88): 2.2

In 1988 approximately 30% of government revenues came from nontax sources. Income taxes contributed 30%, import duties slightly over 10% and excise taxes 7%. Twenty-eight percent of expenditures went to debt service and another 28% to social services. Security and administration accounted for just over one-quarter of total expenditures.

Planning has been a key factor in the steady growth and continued strength of the Malaysian economy. The New Economic Policy (NEP) was introduced in 1970 and intended to last until 1990. Its goal was to boost ownership of the economy by the *bumiputra* (ethnic Malay) to 30% by 1990 with 40% owned by other ethnic groups and 30% by foreigners. Expectations were later revised and it was thought that by 1990 only 22% would be owned by the *bumiputra*. The NEP had the adverse effect of leading to capital flight during the period 1976–85 so that it almost doubled during that period from $1.2 billion per year to $2.3 billion. Anxieties on the part of ethnic Chinese were the major reason for the capital flight. Drafting of a new plan to replace the NEP was begun in December 1988 with the creation of a non-partisan National Economic Consultative Council.

Centralized economic planning began in 1966 with the First Malaysia Plan and has continued to the present with each plan covering a five-year period. The Fifth Malaysia Plan 1986–90 is intended to continue policies initiated by the Fourth Plan aimed at increasing private-sector investment. By 1988 a significant increase in foreign investment had been achieved with Japan being the largest investor. The Malaysian Industrial Development Authority deals with all foreign investment proposals.

Malaysia is not a major recipient of aid; foreign economic aid has been mostly in the form of technical assistance, equity participation, project loans and export credits. From 1970–84 the United States committed $170 million aid; from 1970–87 other Western nations committed $3.8 billion. Malaysia also received $42 million in OPEC bilateral aid from 1979–89.

FOREIGN AID

Total foreign aid (U.S. $ millions): 377.5 (1984)
- Bilateral: 299.3 (1984)
- Multilateral: 78.2 (1984)

Aid from international organizations, total (U.S. $ millions): −37.603 (1985)
- of which World Bank (U.S. $ millions): −51.494 (1985)

Per capita aid (U.S. $): 24.8 (1984)

CURRENCY & BANKING

The Malaysian unit of currency is the ringgit, or the Malaysian dollar, divided into 100 sen. Coins are issued in denominations of 1, 5, 10, 20 and 50 sen; notes are issued in denominations of 1, 5, 10, 50, 100 and 1,000 ringgits.

Until June 1973 the Malaysian dollar was valued at 39.407 U.S. cents. Since June 1973 the Malaysian dollar has been allowed to float. In 1975 its link with the U.S. dollar was ended, and its value was determined on the basis of a weighted basket of the currencies of its principal trading partners. In 1976 the Malaysian dollar

GROWTH PROFILE
(Annual Growth Rates, %)

Projected population (1988–2000): 2.2
Projected crude birth rate (/1,000) (1990–95): 25.4
Projected crude death rate (/1,000) (1990–95): 5.2
Urban population (1980–88): 4.9
Labor force (1985–2000): 2.6
GNP (1980–89): 4.6
GNP per capita (1987–89): 6.8
GDP (1980–88): 4.6
Inflation (1980–88): 1.3
Agriculture (1980–88): 3.7
Industry (1980–88): 6.1
Manufacturing (1980–88): 7.3
Services (1980–88): 3.6
Money holdings (1980–88): 13.0
Manufacturing earnings per employee (1980–87): 5.2
Energy production (1980–88): 15.6
Energy consumption (1980–88): 5.9
Exports (1980–88): 9.4
Imports (1980–88): 0.4
General government consumption (1980–88): 2.2
Private consumption (1980–88): 0.9
Gross domestic investment (1980–88): 0.0

was renamed the ringgit. The exchange rate in June 1991 was $1 = R 2.756.

The Malaysian banking system consists of the central bank, Bank Negara Malaysia; 36 commercial banks, with 396 branches at the end of 1975; and a number of specialized financial institutions. Of the commercial banks, only 18 are domestic banks. Specialized financial institutions include the National Savings Bank; the Muslim Pilgrims Savings Corporation; the Agricultural Bank of Malaysia; Bank Rakyat (formerly known as the Cooperative Bank); Sabah Credit Corporation; Malaysian Industrial Development Finance Berhad; Borneo Development Corporation; and MARA, the Council of Trust for Indigenous People. Malaysia also has a stock exchange that is the source of a small volume of long-term investment funds.

FINANCIAL INDICATORS, 1989

Total reserves minus gold (SDRs billions): 5.922
SDRs (millions): 127
Reserve position in IMF (SDRs millions): 170
Foreign exchange (SDRs billions): 5.626
Gold (fine troy oz. millions): 2.37
Ratio of external debt to total reserves: 2.4 (1988)
Central bank 1989
  Assets (%)
    Foreign assets: 93.4
    Claims on government: 6.6
    Claims on banks: 0.0
    Claims on private sector: 0.0
  Liabilities (%)
    Reserve money: 63.7
    Government deposits: 4.6
    Foreign liabilities: 0.1
    Capital accounts: 0.0
Money supply 1989
  Stock (R billions): 21.978
  M1 per capita: 1,240
Private banks 1989
  Assets (%)
    Loans to government: 12.5
    Loans to private sector: 75.8
    Reserves: 4.4
    Foreign assets: 7.3
  Liabilities
    Deposits (R.$ billions): 94.534
    of which %
      Demand deposits: 12.7
      Savings deposits: 50.0
      Government deposits: 8.0
      Foreign liabilities: 6.7
External debt 1988
  Total (U.S. $ billions): 20.541
    of which public (U.S. $ billions): 16.101
    of which private (U.S. $ billions): 2.340
  Debt service (long-term)
    Total (U.S. $ billions): 4.243
    Repayment
      Principal (%): 71.2
      Interest (%): 28.8
  Debt service ratio (%): 17.5
  External public debt as % of GNP: 49.1
  Debt service as % of GNP: 13.0
  Debt service as % of exports: 17.5
  Terms of public borrowing
    Commitments (U.S. $ billions): 2.259
    Average interest rate (%): 6.1
    Average maturity (yrs.): 15
  Net flow of publicly guaranteed external capital (U.S. $ billions): −1.336
  Receipt of workers' remittances (U.S. $ millions): 0
  Net direct private investment (U.S. $ millions): 649

AGRICULTURE

Until the late 1980s agriculture was the dominant sector of the economy. Of the total land area of 32,974,900 ha. (81,480,977 ac.), 10% is classified as arable land. About 80% of the total area cultivated in Malaysia is devoted to either rubber or rice and another 14% to coconut and oil palm production. West Malaysia accounts for 90% of the land under rubber trees, 85.4% of land under oil palms and 70.8% of land under rice.

Land utilization programs are coordinated by the National Land Council, which has developed a uniform code. Landowners are bound to follow certain state-imposed conditions regarding cropping, acreage and soil conservation. Land development programs are undertaken by four major state agencies to open unused or undeveloped land to settlement for landless families. Of these, the largest is the Federal Land Development Authority, which developed 129,000 ha. (319,253 ac.) between 1971 and 1974. The National Land Consolidation and Rehabilitation Authority, the Sabah Land Development Board and the Sarawak Land Development Board are charged with replanting, diversification and other programs in special sectors.

The largest irrigation projects are the Muda River and Kembu projects, which brought 11,600 ha. (28,663 ac.) under rice and nearly tripled rice production in the regions. Mechanized equipment was not introduced until after World War II, and progress has been slow.

Land tenure patterns vary considerably among regions. There are five basic types of tenure in West Malaysia: *sewa*, or fixed rent; *pajak*, or long-term tenure with the tenant paying a lump sum of the cash in advance; *pawai*, or sharecropping; *gadai*, or temporary transfer of *usufruct* in return for money loans; and *jual janji*, or transfer of proprietary rights as security for a loan. The land tenure systems of Sabah and Sarawak are designed to protect the native population by setting apart zones exclusively for the use of natives under customary tenure. In addition, certain areas in West Malaysia are reserved for ethnic Malays.

About 75% of the farms in West Malaysia are owner-cultivated, and about 20% are cultivated by tenants. The rate of owner-operated units is 90% in export-crop estates but only 50% in rice holdings.

In terms of size of holdings, 27% of the rubber area is comprised of large estates and 73% is run by smallholders. The average size of rubber estates is 323 ha. (800 ac.), and about 10% have more than 809 ha. (2,000 ac.). Coconut estates average 404 ha. (1,000 ac.) and oil palm estates 809 ha. (2,000 ac.). On the other hand, the average rice holding is only about 1.6 ha. (4.0 ac.).

Natural rubber is the most important agricultural product in Malaysia. It contributes 12% of the GDP, or about 43% of agriculture's contribution to the GDP. About 2.010 million ha. (4.966 million ac.) are under rubber, of which 84.7% is in West Malaysia. The average yield per acre is nearly 453 kg. (1,000 lb.). In 1965 the government introduced a new classification called

AGRICULTURAL INDICATORS

Agriculture's share of GDP (%): 21 (1987)
Average annual growth rate (%, 1980–88): 3.7
Cereal imports (million metric tons): 2.387 (1988)
Index of agricultural production (1979–81 = 100): 122 (1986)
Index of food production (1979–81 = 100): 130 (1986)
Index of food production per capita (1979–81 = 100): 106 (1986–88)
Number of tractors: 11,600 (1986)
Total fertilizer consumption (000 metric tons): 611.4 (1985–86)
Fertilizer consumption (g./ha., hundreds): 1,596 (1987–88)
Number of farms (000): 920 (1980)
Average size of holding (ha.): 2.2 (1980)
Tenure (%) 1970
  Owner-operated: 53.2
  Rented: 19.6
  Other: 9.0
Farms as % of total land area: 31.2 (1982)
Land use (%) 1982
  Cropland: 9
  Pasture: 25
  Forest: 31
  Other: 34
Yields (kg./ha.) 1989
  Grains: 2,645
  Roots & tubers: 9,354
  Milk (kg./animal): 550
Production 1989
  Fruits (million metric tons): 1.185
  Vegetables (000 metric tons): 509
Livestock (000) 1989
  Cattle: 532
  Horses: 5 (1986)
  Sheep: 100
  Pigs: 2,350
Forestry 1988
  Production of roundwood (million cubic meters): 44.431
    of which industrial roundwood (%): 81.8
  Value of exports (U.S. $ million): 2,571.735
Fishing 1988
  Total catch (000 metric tons): 604.1
    of which marine (%): 97.3
  Value of exports (U.S. $ million): 190.277

Standard Malaysian Rubber (SMR), designed to enable natural rubber to compete with synthetic rubber in quality and uniformity. Malaysia now is the world's largest producer of rubber, supplying 38% of the non-Communist world's needs.

Palm oil is Malaysia's second-largest export earner. Total area under oil palm in 1983 was 1.266 million ha. (3.128 million ac.), of which 89% was in West Malaysia, 9% in Sabah and 2% in Sarawak. Malaysia is the world's largest exporter of palm oil, with 75% of global exports. Malaysia also supplies 35% of the world's pepper.

Rice is the staple food and the second-largest crop after rubber. West Malaysia produces about 80% of the country's crop. Efforts to increase domestic production include double cropping, use of new hybrid varieties of paddy rice and more extensive use of fertilizers. A large part of paddy production in Sarawak and Sebah is hill, or dry, paddy.

The Malaysian rice bowl, under the Muda Agricultural Development Authority, is in northwestern Malaya and consists of the states of Perlis, Kedah, Pinang and Perak. The rice bowl accounts for 55% of production, while the states of Kelantan and Trengganu produce another 25%.

The country's environment is ill suited to animal husbandry. The National Livestock Development Corporation administers development projects in animal husbandry.

Malaysia's nearly 230,510 sq. km. (89,000 sq. mi.) of forest land represent 62% of the total land area. Government reserves constitute 43%, or 15,621 ha. (38,600 ac.). Malaysia is the world's largest producer and exporter of tropical hardwoods. To ensure a continuous supply of domestic timber resources, a national forestry policy was introduced in 1978. Its aims include establishment of a permanent forest estate, forest rehabilitation, reduction in the rate of forest harvesting, effective forest management and optimum utilization of forest resources. In accordance with the national forestry policy, 64,747 ha. (160,000 ac.) of forested land per year were harvested during 1982–85, compared with about 97,124 ha. (240,000 ac.) harvested in 1981. These measures were needed following rapid rates of exploitation and export of sawn logs in past years. The wood products industry has suffered a shortage of logs since 1972. All exports of logs were banned from West Malaysia in 1985.

Fish are relatively abundant in Malaysian waters and are staples of the diet. The total fish catch declined during the 1980s. Fisheries development is coordinated by the Fisheries Development Authority.

The Agricultural Bank of Malaysia is the central government agency for the provision of agricultural credit. The Bank Rakyat, formerly called the Cooperative Bank, and the Farmers' Organization Authority are other major sources of institutional credit in the agricultural sector. The Farmers' Organization Authority coordinates the activities of 1,684 agro-based cooperative societies and 251 farmers' associations with a total of 293,603 members. Private sources of credit in rural areas include Chinese and Indian moneylenders. The Federal Agricultural Marketing Authority coordinates and supervises marketing and warehousing.

MANUFACTURING

Manufacturing is the dominant sector of the Malaysian economy. Agro-based were the most important industrial products, followed by textiles and clothing and cement.

Although, like most developing countries, Malaysia at independence had only a rudimentary manufacturing industrial sector, Chinese entrepreneurship and a vigorous encouragement of foreign private investment led to a rapid growth of the sector during the 1960s and early 1970s, so that by 1975 the sector contributed 14.4% of the GDP, with the value of manufactured exports reaching M$2.1 billion.

Manufacturing is concentrated in West Malaysia, which accounts for 87% of the units. The largest industrial concentration is in and around Kuala Lumpur. Large units dominate the output: The 82% of the establishments employing less than 10 workers each accounted for only 14% of production, while the 4% of the establishments employing over 50 workers ac-

MANUFACTURING INDICATORS, 1987

Average annual growth rate (%, 1980–88): 7.3
Share of GDP (%): 21 (1987)
Labor force economically active in manufacturing (% est.): 13.2 (1980)
Value added in manufacturing (U.S. $ millions): 500 (1970)
  Food & tobacco (%): 21
  Textiles & clothing (%): 6
  Machinery & transport equipment (%): 22
  Chemicals (%): 15
Earnings per employee in manufacturing 1987
  Growth rate (%, 1980–87): 5.2
  Index (1980 = 100): 138
Total earnings as % of value added: 29
Index of manufacturing production: 197 (1989)

counted for 60% of the production. Ten products accounted for the bulk of the value of manufacturing production: processed agricultural products, tobacco, chemicals, wood products, rubber products, basic metals, nonmetallic mineral products, machinery, beverages and transportation equipment.

The government's industrial policy in general is based on cooperation with private enterprise, with only a minimum of state participation. However, government influences the location, ownership and employment makeup of manufacturing and specifically requires 51% Malaysia ownership and Malaysianization of employees in industries claiming special status under the Investment Incentives Act of 1968. The Industrial Coordination Act of 1975 required all manufacturing companies to obtain a license.

Foreign investment, originally restricted to British firms engaged in rubber plantations and tin mining, diversified by the 1970s into manufacturing and services and involved 19 countries. Ranked on the basis of paid-up capital, the leading foreign investors are the United States, the United Kingdom, Hong Kong, Japan and Canada, which together account for 93% of the total. Through 1979, U.S. firms had invested over $1 billion in Malaysia. By far the major portion is in the petroleum industry. There also are significant U.S. investments in the electronics industry and the banking sector.

While government guidelines generally require the formation of joint ventures, with the foreign investor limited to a minority equity interest, under certain circumstances a foreign company engaged entirely in manufacturing goods for export from Malaysia can receive approval for 100% foreign ownership. In all cases involving new foreign investment, the government is prepared to take a flexible position with the foreign investors.

Industrial credit is provided by Industrial Development Finance Berhad. The Council of Trust for Indigenous People (MARA) extends technical and financial aid to ethnic Malays. The Sino-Malay Economic Cooperation Board is an advisory unit that promotes cooperation among ethnic economic sectors. The Capital Investment Committee undertakes marketing and feasibility studies. The Malaysian Industrial Development Authority coordinates industrial development work of various agencies. Perbadanan Nasional (PERNAS) is a state-owned conglomerate with interests in mining, industry, transportation and construction.

MINING

Major minerals under exploitation are bauxite, copper, gold, iron, tin, manganese, china clay lime and rare earths. The most important of these is tin, which ranks fifth among Malaysian exports by value. Malaysia is the world's largest exporter of tin and is a member of the International Tin Council. Because known deposits of tin are declining, prospecting is an important activity. Tin mining is dominated by Chinese capital and entrepreneurship. All of the country's mines and smelters are in West Malaysia.

ENERGY

Malaysia's known petroleum reserves are estimated at 3.675 billion bbl. With the discovery of offshore petroleum reserves, Malaysia's production of crude petroleum rose by an average annual rate of more than 30% during the 1970s. Since 1980, petroleum has been Malaysia's largest single source of government revenue. It accounted for 24% of total export earnings in 1983, but by 1987 had dropped to 13.9% of total exports. The first shipment of liquefied natural gas (LNG) was exported to Japan in January 1983. All Malaysia's LNG output is exported. Natural gas reserves are estimated at 1.485 trillion cu. m. (48 trillion cu. ft.). Three domestic oil refineries processed about 205,000 bbl. of crude oil per day in 1982. The national oil company, Petronas, was established in 1975 to coordinate oil exploration and production.

ENERGY INDICATORS

Average annual energy production growth rate (%, 1980–88): 15.6
Energy consumption per capita (kg. oil equivalent): 784 (1988)
Energy imports as % of merchandise exports: 5 (1988)
Average annual growth rate of energy consumption (%, 1980–88): 5.9
Electricity 1988
  Installed capacity (million kw.): 4.902
  Production (billion kw.-hr.): 19.287
    % fossil fuel: 70.9
    % hydro: 29.1
  Consumption per capita (kw.-hr.): 1,164
Natural gas
  Proved reserves (trillion cu. m.): 1.485 (1990)
  Production (billion cu. m.): 17.160 (1989)
  Consumption (billion cu. m.): 4.785 (1988)
Petroleum
  Proved reserves (billion bbl.): 3.675 (1990)
  Years to exhaust proved reserves: 16 (1990)
  Production (million bbl.): 214 (1989)
  Consumption (million bbl.): 52 (1988)
  Refining capacity (000 bbl./day): 209 (1990)
Coal
  Reserves (million metric tons): 4 (latest)
  Production (000 metric tons): 22 (1988)
  Consumption (000 metric tons): 386 (1988)

LABOR

There is a high correlation between race and occupation in Malaysia. Malays dominate agriculture and public services; Chinese virtually monopolize retail trade and mining; Indians form the majority on plantations.

Malaysian labor legislation and conditions of employment are among the most advanced in Asia.

Wages and salaries are lower than in developed countries and vary considerably between rural and urban areas, and from firm to firm for the same occupations. Wages in East Malaysia are generally higher than in West Malaysia. No national minimum wage exists. However, the government can set minimum wage levels and has done so in a few limited cases. The minimum wage rates vary according to age and the size of the town, ranging from a low in a "Class B" town to a high in a "Class A" town. Class A towns include most state capitals; Class B towns are smaller.

Benefits include a cost-of-living allowance and a yearly bonus equivalent to one month's basic wages.

LABOR INDICATORS, 1980

Total economically active population (millions): 4.924
- % working-age (15–64): 62.1
- % female: 33.7

Activity rate (%)
- Total: 37.5
- Male: 49.6
- Female: 25.3

Employment status (%)
- Employers & self-employed: 28.7
- Employees: 54.3
- Unpaid family workers: 10.2
- Other: 6.7

Sectoral employment of economically active (%)
- Agriculture, forestry, fishing: 37.7
- Construction: 4.2
- Manufacturing, mining, quarrying, public utilities: 13.2
- Trade, hotels, restaurants: 11.4
- Transportation, communications: 3.3
- Finance, real estate: 1.6
- Services: 13.5

Average annual growth rate of labor force (%, 1985–2000): 2.6
Unemployment (000): 79 (1987)
Labor under 20 years (%): 12.9 (1980)
Hours of work (/worker) (1984)
- Manufacturing (/wk.): 45.6
- Non-agricultural (/wk.): 44.8

Of primary importance to workers is the Employment Ordinance of 1955. It governs contracts of service, including provisions for minimum periods of notice in case of termination; working hours (generally 48 per week); overtime (not more than 32 hours per month, and paid at the rate of time and a half); rest days (each employee must have one per week); paid holidays (seven per year for workers with five years' employment or less, 14 for those with five or more years); sick leave (14 days per year if no hospitalization is required, up to 60 if it is); and protection of women (maternity pay and leave and no night work except in special cases).

Working conditions on plantations and in mines are generally good by Asian standards. Free housing, medical care and education are provided for all plantation workers and most mine workers. All workers are covered by Provident Fund programs, and there are pension programs for government employees and those in certain other categories. A comprehensive Social Security program was introduced in 1969.

The Industrial Relations Act of 1967, passed in May 1980, contains prohibitive and oppressive antiunion provisions that erode the basic rights of workers, restrict union activities and result in government and employer interference in the internal administration of trade unions. In 1983 the ILO urged the Malaysian government to amend these laws further to bring them into conformity with the convention of the right to organize and to bargain collectively. In 1985 the MTUC and the Malaysian Employers' Federation conducted a joint seminar on Malaysia's labor laws in which Ministry of Labor personnel participated. As a result of this seminar, Malaysia's labor laws may eventually be amended to expand the right to organize and bargain collectively.

The organized labor union movement is entirely the creation of Indian and Chinese groups. The government is wary of strong labor movements, and nationwide labor organizations are prohibited. Trade unions in Malaysia have about 612,000 members. Of the labor force, 10.6% are organized into 392 registered trade unions, most of them small and poor. The largest is the National Union of Plantation Workers (NUPW), with 82,000 members, most of them Indian and about half women. Of the remaining 391, only a dozen or so have more than 10,000 members, and the largest of these only 18,000. Indians, though numbering only 10% of the population, make up a substantially higher percentage of the union membership. An unusually high percentage of unions is in the public sector—40% of the total.

Among labor federations, the most important is the Malaysian Trades Union Congress (MTUC). Its 137 affiliates have 75% of the trade union membership. However, its legal status under the Societies Ordinance Act does not allow it to bargain for its members. Although unions do not engage in political activity, individual trade union leaders have served in the parliament, and individual union members may belong to political parties.

Another trade union federation is the Congress of Unions of Employees in the Public Administrative and Civil Services (CUEPACS), with 53 affiliated unions and membership of 115,000. It has been actively involved in mostly unsuccessful attempts to improve salaries and wages of government employees.

In 1975 the Congress of Unions in the Private Sector (CUPS) was set up, in part over frustration and lack of confidence in the MTUC leadership. It claims 25 unions as members.

FOREIGN COMMERCE

Malaysia's major exports are natural rubber, palm oil, tin, timber, petroleum, electronics and light manufactures. Its principal imports are food, crude oil, consumer goods, intermediate goods, capital equipment and chemicals. Singapore, Japan, Australia, the United States and the Soviet Union are major trading partners.

FOREIGN TRADE INDICATORS, 1988

Exports (U.S. $ billions): 24 (1989)
Imports (U.S. $ billions): 20 (1989)
Balance of trade (U.S. $ billions): 4 (1989)
Annual growth rate (1980–88), exports (%): 9.4
Annual growth rate (1980–88), imports (%): 0.4
International reserves in terms of months of imports covered: 4.0
Terms of trade (1980 = 100): 74
Import price index (1980 = 100): 98.4 (1986)
Export price index (1980 = 100): 63.8 (1986)

Direction of Trade (%), 1989

	Imports	Exports
European Community	14.0	15.4
United States	16.9	18.7
U.S.S.R. & eastern European economies	0.6	1.2
Japan	24.2	16.1

Composition of Trade (%), 1989

	Imports	Exports
Food & agricultural raw materials	10.5	31.8
Fuels & other energy	4.8	16.2
Mineral ores & concentrates	2.3	0.9
Manufactured goods	82.4	51.0
of which chemicals	8.9	1.8
of which machinery	47.9	32.4

TRANSPORTATION & COMMUNICATIONS

The Malaysian rail system consists of 2,222 km (1,381 mi.) of track in West Malaysia and Sabah. There are no railways in Sarawak. In West Malaysia a western coast line runs from Singapore to Butterworth near Pinang, and an eastern coast line from Gemas to Tumpat, besides branch lines.

There is an extensive inland waterways system consisting of 3,209 km. (1,993 mi.) in West Malaysia and 4,200 km. (2,608 mi.) in East Malaysia.

Maritime transport is controlled by the Malaysian International Shipping Corporation and the Kris Shipping Company of Malaysia, which together operate a fleet of 376 vessels with a registered tonnage of 2,075,400. The principal ports are Pinang, Port Klang, Dungun, Telow, Anson, Melaka and Port Dickson in West Malaysia; Labuan, Sandakan, Kota Kinabalu, Kudat, Tawau, Sempoma and Lahad Datu in Sabah; and Miri and Kuching in Sarawak.

The pipelines carrying crude oil and natural gas are 707 km. (439 mi.) and 379 km. (235 mi.) long, respectively.

The road network in Malaysia consists of 39,340 km. (24,445 mi.). Over 80% of all roads are paved. The east–west highway linking Jeli in Kelantan with Grik in Perak was opened in 1982. Work commenced in 1982 on a 928-km. (1,493-mi.) interurban toll expressway, including the 14-km. (22-mi.) Penang Bridge linking Penang Island and peninsular Malaysia and forming the last link of the east–west highway. There are over 800 bus routes, a large number of which are operated by the Council of Trust for Indigenous People (MARA).

TRANSPORTATION INDICATORS

Roads (latest)
  Length, km. (mi.): 39,340 (24,445)
  Paved (%): 65
Motor vehicles (latest)
  Automobiles: 1,504,208
  Trucks and buses: 338,980
  Persons per vehicle: 9.0
Railroads (latest)
  Track, km. (mi.): 2,222 (1,381)
  Passenger-km. (passenger-mi.) (millions): 1,524 (947)
  Freight, metric ton-km. (short ton-mi.) (millions): 1,332 (912)
Merchant marine
  Vessels (over 100 tons): 491 (1989)
  Total deadweight tonnage (000): 2,364.2 (1989)
  Oil tankers (000 GRT): 216 (1985)
Ports (pre-1986)
  Cargo loaded (million metric tons): 15.876
  Cargo unloaded (million metric tons): 24.468
Air
  Km. (mi.) flown (millions): 45.5 (28.2) (1985)
  Passenger-km. (passenger-mi.) (millions): 10,105 (6,279) (latest)
  Freight, metric ton-km. (short ton-mi.) (millions): 403.7 (276.5) (latest)
  Mail, metric ton-km. (short ton-mi.) (millions): 8.1 (5.5) (1985)
  Airports with scheduled flights: 39 (1990)
Pipelines 1990
  Natural gas, km. (mi.): 379 (235)
Inland waterways (latest)
  Length, km. (mi.): 7,409 (4,594)

COMMUNICATION INDICATORS, 1988

Telephones
  Total (millions): 1.646
  Persons per telephone: 10
Phone traffic (millions)
  Combined national: 8,490.642 (pulses) (1986)
  International: 45.720 (minutes)
Post office
  Number of post offices: 5,791
  Pieces of mail handled (millions): 708.804
Telegraph
  Total traffic (000 calls): 839
    National: 746
    International: 93
Telex
  Subscriber lines: 9,930
  Traffic (000 minutes): 23,895
Telecommunications 1990
  Satellite stations: 4
  Submarine cables: 4

TOURISM & TRAVEL INDICATORS, 1986

Total tourist receipts (U.S. $ millions): 766 (1988)
Expenditures by nationals abroad (U.S. $ millions): 1,324 (1988)
Number of hotel beds (000): 57
Average length of stay (nights): 5
Tourist nights (000): 2,389
Number of tourists (000): 2,906.3 (1985)
  of whom from United States: 42.7
  Japan: 120.0
  Australia: 77.8
  United Kingdom: 64.2

The national airline is the Malaysian Airline System (MAS), which operates a fleet of 37 aircraft on domestic and international service. Malaysia has five international airports, at Kuala Lumpur, Kota Kinabalu, Pinang, Johore Bahru and Kuching.

Malaysia has a rapidly growing tourist industry. In 1987 the number of tourists exceeded five million, compared to the 1.7 million in 1981.

DEFENSE

The defense structure is headed by the *yang di pertuan agong*, though only the parliament has the right to declare war. Actual operational control is exercised by the Armed Forces Council under the chairmanship of the minister of defense.

Manpower is provided by voluntary enlistment, although a system of conscription is available if needed. Malaysian soldiers are noted for their discipline and sustained performance under adverse conditions. They are acknowledged as extremely skillful in jungle warfare, and the Ibans of Sarawak are without equals in knowledge of jungle conditions. The total strength of the armed forces in 1989 totaled 114,500.

Army

Personnel: 90,000 (reserves: 46,000)

Organization: 5 regional commands—3 in West Malaysia, at Sungei Besi, Ipoh and Temerloh, and 2 in East Malaysia; 1 corps; 4 division headquarters; 9 infantry brigades, consisting of 36 infantry battalions, 4 cavalry, 4 field artillery, 1 AA artillery, 5 signals and 5 engineer regiments; 1 Special Services regiment with 3 battalions

Equipment: 26 tanks; 264 armored fighting vehicles; 685 armored personnel carriers; 170 howitzers; 150 rocket launchers; 70 air defense guns

Navy

Personnel: 12,500

Units: 3 frigates; 30 fast attack craft; 40 patrol craft; 6 minesweepers; 29 small vessels; 3 support vessels

Air Force

Personnel: 12,000

Organization and equipment: 42 combat aircraft; 2 air regions; 1 support command; 3 fighter squadrons; 1 maritime reconnaissance squadron; 5 transport squadrons; 4 liaison squadrons; 3 training squadrons; air-to-air missiles

Air bases: Kuala Lumpur, Ipoh, Paya Lebar, Labuar, Kuantan, Alor Star, Gong and Kedak

The annual military budget in 1985 was $1.624 billion, or 11.8% of the national budget.

Malaysian armed forces are noted for their antiguerrilla capability. Since there are no hostile border areas, the army is deployed mainly in the peninsular region. Malaysia has received $174.3 million in U.S. military assistance credit sales through 1983. Great Britain has now phased out its substantial military assistance program, but a five-power Asian defense pact (with Britain, Australia, New Zealand and Singapore) has to some extent replaced Britain's role. Both Britain and Australia have small ground forces stationed in Malaysia under this pact. Arms purchases abroad during 1973–83 totaled $1,070 billion, of which $180 million was supplied by the United States and $60 million by the United Kingdom.

Military service is voluntary.

EDUCATION

In theory, the state provides free but not universal and compulsory education for seven years, from ages six to 13. The academic year runs from January to November. The medium of instruction is Malay in state schools. There also are 525 English-language schools, which enjoy the greatest prestige; 1,052 Chinese-language schools, using Kuo Yu or Mandarin; and 617 Tamil-language schools.

Schooling consists of six grades of primary school; three grades of lower secondary school; two grades of upper secondary school; and two years of pre-university classes, consisting of a lower sixth form and an upper sixth form in the British fashion.

There are significant differences in the educational systems of East Malaysia. Sarawak is moving toward a full English-language education, while Sabah has adopted the West Malaysian plan of converting to Bahasa Malaysia. The first six years of school are free but not compulsory. Secondary schools are divided

EDUCATION INDICATORS, 1988

Literacy
- Total (%): 72.6
- Male (%): 82.2
- Female (%): 63.2

First level
- Schools: 6,754
- Students: 2,328,400
- Teachers: 108,387
- Student/teacher ratio: 21.5

Second level
- Schools: 1,198
- Students: 1,320,636
- Teachers: 62,434
- Student/teacher ratio: 21.1

Vocational
- Schools: 65
- Students: 33,178
- Teachers: 3,115
- Student/teacher ratio: 10.7

Third level (postsecondary) (1987)
- Institutions: 42
- Students: 110,918
- Teachers: 11,181
- Student/teacher ratio: 9.9
- Gross enrollment ratio: 6.8
- Students (/100,000 pop.): 680

Foreign study
- Foreign students in national universities: 326
- Students abroad: 36,278
  - of whom in
    - United States: 14,021
    - France: 164
    - Federal Republic of Germany: 49
    - United Kingdom: 6,310 (1987)

Public expenditure 1987
- Total (M.$ 000): 5,146,946
- % of GNP: 6.9
- % of current expenditure: 87.5

GRADUATES, 1987

Total: 15,163
Education: 2,169
Humanities & religion: 660
Fine & applied arts: 174
Law: 271
Social & behavioral sciences: 880
Commerce & business: 4,422
Mass communication: 514
Home economics: 79
Service trades: 0
Natural sciences: 72
Mathematics & computer science: 749
Medicine: 564
Engineering: 1,938
Architecture: 515
Industrial programs: 87
Transportation & communications: 0
Agriculture, forestry, fisheries: 602
Other: 1,467

into lower secondary (three years) and upper secondary, consisting of fourth and fifth forms leading to the sixth form, a two-year college preparatory program at the end of which students take the Cambridge University (Britain) Higher Schools/Certificate Examination. There are no universities in East Malaysia.

There is a critical shortage of trained Malaysian teachers, which is partially made up by employing Indonesians and Commonwealth and Peace Corps volunteers.

There is a shortage of vocational and professional training in East Malaysia, which has only four such institutions, compared to 82 in West Malaysia. Only 1.5% of secondary-school students are enrolled in the vocational stream. Compulsory religious instruction in Islam is provided in all schools receiving government funds (except in East Malaysia) during regular school hours. Adult education is furnished by the Ministry of National and Rural Development.

The education system is centralized in the federal Ministry of Education, although both Sabah and Sarawak operate their school systems autonomously.

There are nine universities in Malaysia. English is being gradually replaced at the university level by Bahasa Malaysia.

LEGAL SYSTEM

The judiciary is an entirely federal service, while the Muslim religious courts are under the states' jurisdictions. The Constitution provides for an independent judiciary consisting of a federal court with original jurisdiction in constitutional cases and appellate and original jurisdiction in civil and criminal cases; there also are two high courts, one for West Malaysia and other other for East Malaysia, with unlimited jurisdiction in civil and criminal cases. The federal court consists of a lord president together with the two chief justices of the high courts and four federal judges. There is a limited right of appeal from the federal court to the *yang di pertuan agong*, who may refer such appeals to the judicial committee of the Privy Council in the United Kingdom. The lord president and judges of the federal court and the chief justices and judges of the high courts are appointed by the *yang di pertuan agong* on the advice of the prime minister and the Conference of Rulers. The high court in East Malaysia sits alternately in Kota Kinabalu (Sabah) and Kuching (Sarawak).

Lower courts include sessions courts, magistrate courts and *penghulu* (district) courts in each *mukim* (subdistrict). Civil cases usually are heard without a jury. The Muslim *kadi* courts are state courts with civil jurisdiction over Muslims.

The Malaysian judiciary is generally regarded by the public and the legal community as committed to the rule of law. Although the courts have rarely challenged legislation, they have not hesitated to rule against government prosecutors in specific cases, both civil and criminal. With the exception of security cases not brought to trial, defendants have the right to counsel, and lawyers are able to represent clients without penalty to themselves. Most civil and criminal cases are tried under the regular judicial system, derived from British jurisprudence, and thus public trials and fair hearings occur in all but security-related cases. In all other cases, the courts apply criminal law and procedures, including strict rules of evidence. Charges must be levied against a defendant within 24 hours of arrest, and police must decide within 14 days whether to bring the case to court. Defendants may appeal lower court decisions to the federal courts and, in criminal cases, also may appeal for clemency to the king or to local state rulers, as appropriate.

Persons detained for security reasons and for certain classes of crimes, however, may be held and given hearing under special procedures outside the ordinary court system. These procedures allow suspects to be detained without charge for a period that may, in practice, be extended indefinitely. If the accused is brought to trial under the internal security regulations and does not receive a statement of the evidence, trial is by a single judge without a jury, and witnesses may be examined in the absence of the accused. Admissible evidence includes hearsay and secondary evidence, testimony of children and spouses, self-incriminating statements to police and information from seized records or communications. If the accused is found guilty, the judge must impose the maximum penalty. For certain internal security crimes, including the possession of firearms, the mandatory sentence is death. In 1985 at least three persons were executed after conviction under the ISA for illegal possession of firearms.

Prisons are administered by the Royal Malaysian Police and range from maximum-security stone cells to open farms and detention camps. Prison practices conform to the U.N. Standard Minimum Rules for the Treatment of Prisoners. Prisons include the Central Prison at Taiping for prisoners serving long-term sentences, the Central Prison at Seremban for political prisoners, four regional prisons, five penal institutions for women, three reform schools and two custody centers, all in West Malaysia. There are five penal institutions in Sabah and six in Sarawak.

LAW ENFORCEMENT

The principal law enforcement agency is the Royal Malaysian Police, with a strength of 38,000 in its regular force and 10,000 in its paramilitary public order units. Some 4.6 persons per 1,000 working population are employed in law enforcement, and Malaysia ranks 33rd in the world in this respect.

The Royal Malaysian Police is headed by an inspector general. Operational divisions are called contingents in West Malaysia and components in East Malaysia. The 10 contingents in West Malaysia correspond to the states except for Kedah and Perlis, which share one unit. East Malaysia has two components for its two states. Each contingent is headed by a chief police officer and each component by a commissioner. At the base of the structure are precinct-type stations, a number of which, their number depending on population, make up a police division. Specialized units include border scouts in Sabah and Sarawak, the police field force, federal reserve units, the police volunteer reserve and the marine branch.

The Royal Malaysia Police Annual Reports contain detailed statistics showing the incidence of crime by region and category. Most crime in Malaysia is organized rather than casual or individual. Criminal gangs, especially in West Malaysian towns, engage in robbery, extortion, smuggling, gambling and narcotics traffic. Police records list 204 criminal societies and gangs.

The Malaysian Secret Service is known as Department E.

HEALTH INDICATORS

Health personnel 1987
- Physicians: 5,794
  - per person: 2,853
- Dentists: 1,220
- Nurses: 33,545
- Pharmacists: 815 (1984)
- Midwives: 14,525 (1983)

Hospitals 1987
- Number: 254
- Number of beds (/10,000): 24
- Admissions/discharges (/10,000): 635 (1981)

Type of hospitals (%) 1981
- Government: 39.9
- Private nonprofit: 0.0
- Private profit: 60.1

Public health expenditures (latest)
- As % of national budget: 4.6
- Per capita (U.S. $): 26.30

Vital statistics
- Crude death rate (/1,000): 9 (1990)
- Life expectancy at birth 1990
  - Males: 65
  - Females: 71
- Infant mortality rate (/1,000 live births): 30 (1990)
- Child mortality rate under 5 yrs. (/1,000 live births) (1985–90): 35
- Maternal mortality rate (/100,000 live births) (1986–87): 59
- Population with access to safe water (%): 84 (latest)

HEALTH

Malaysia has had notable success in specialized campaigns against major diseases formerly widespread: malaria, tuberculosis and leprosy. The major causes of death are organic and degenerative diseases, led by heart ailments.

FOOD & NUTRITION

Food preferences vary among communities and regions. In West Malaysia the staple food is rice supplemented by fish, curries and some meat, while in East Malaysia tapioca, yams, corn and sweet potatoes supplement rice. In East Malaysia the favorite drinks are *tuak* and *borak*, both rice liquors. In all regions the standard diet is deficient in protein.

The daily per capita food intake is 2,723 calories (over 120% of requirements).

MEDIA & CULTURE

The West Malaysian newspaper press consists of 42 dailies, 14 of which are published in the capital. Five of them are in English, seven in Chinese, five in Malay, three in Tamil and two in Punjabi. The most widely distributed and respected daily is the *New Straits Times*, with a circulation of about 200,000 on weekdays and 242,000 on Sundays. Another English-language daily, the *Malay Mail*, also enjoys a good reputation but a far smaller circulation: 70,000. Other principal dailies are *Utusan Malaysia* (240,000), in Malay; *Nanyang Siang Pao* (145,000), in Chinese; *Shin Min Daily News* (67,000), in Chinese; *Berita Harian* (250,000), in Malay; and *Thung Pao* (62,000), in Chinese. Sabah has seven dailies, one in English, four in Chinese, and the remainder in a combination of English, Malay and Kadazan. Sarawak has 9 dailies, two in English and seven in Chinese.

Control of the press is indirect; outright censorship is rarely imposed. All newspapers and publications are required to register with the Ministry of Information and Broadcasting; they may not be published or distributed without a government permit, which may be revoked or suspended for the publication of material officially termed undesirable. News also is controlled at the source by the official programs of the Ministry of Information and Broadcasting. More stringent limitations are imposed in times of emergency under the provisions of the Internal Security Act of Malaya, as was done in 1969–71.

The media are further constrained by ownership and legislation. All radio stations and two of the three television stations are government-owned. The other television station, which began broadcasting in 1984, and most of the press are owned by groups close to the government. Government control over publishing licenses, reinforced in 1984 by the passage of the Printing and Publications Act, has moved the press toward considerable self-censorship. This act also allows the government to restrict importation of foreign publications. Although the government permits individuals and the media a relatively large degree of freedom of expression, a number of important restrictions exist. The statements and activities of domestic political figures are reported in some detail; opposition politicians get significantly less coverage. The government is particularly sensitive to criticism of the constitutionally guaranteed special position of Malays in society and, closely related to this, any statement that threatens public order by promoting ill feeling among races. Under the Sedition Act of 1948, strengthened by amendment after the 1969 rioting, such public criticism is considered seditious, as is criticism of the government's administration of justice and other matters.

The national news agency, Bernama, has one foreign bureau, in Djakarta, and four domestic bureaus. The major foreign new agencies are AP, UPI, AFP and Reuters.

Book publishing in Malaysia is largely in the hands of the Chinese. In East Malaysia the Borneo Literature Bureau, sponsored by the state governments of Sabah and Sarawak, is an active publisher of educational and children's books in English, Malay, Chinese and Iban. Total output in 1982 was 2,801 titles, of which 919 titles were in English. Malaysia adheres to the Florence Copyright Convention.

Broadcasting is a state monopoly operated by Radio Malaysia with three networks. The West Malaysian network consists of eight stations with 37 medium-wave and short wave transmitters totaling 955 kw. and broadcasts in Malay (168 hours a week), English (100 hours a week), Chinese (101 hours a week) and Indian languages (92 hours a week). The regional stations both relay national programs and originate their own. Educational broadcasting is conducted jointly with the Ministry of Education. Radio Malaysia Sabah, with short wave and medium-wave transmitters, is on the air for 126 hours a week and originates some programs in local languages. Radio Malaysia Sarawak, with 18 medium-wave and short wave transmitters, is on the air for 342 hours a week, broadcasting in seven languages. The Malay Forces and English Forces services are on the air for 14 hours and 1 hour, respectively, per week. The overseas service broadcasts 11 hours a day in Indonesian, Chinese and English under the signature Suara Malaysia (Voice of Malaysia). A private wire rediffusion service is available in Kuala Lumpur, Penang and Ipoh. A license fee is payable for radio receivers.

MEDIA INDICATORS

Newspapers
- Number of dailies: 42 (latest)
- Number of nondailies: 20 (1984)
- Circulation (millions): 4.292 (1984)
- Per 1,000 pop.: 284 (1984)
- Number of periodicals: 1,631 (1984)
- Circulation (millions): 1.689 (1984)
- Newsprint consumption 1988
  - Total metric tons: 117,700
  - Per million pop. (kg.): 7.111

Book publishing
- Number of titles: 1,984 (latest)

Broadcasting 1987
- Annual expenditures (M.$ millions): 256.5

Radio
- Number of transmitters: 83 (latest)
- Number of persons per radio receiver: 2.3 (1987)
- Total program hours: 23,222 (1987)

Television
- Television transmitters: 43 (latest)
- Number of persons per T.V. receiver: 7.2 (1987)
- Total program hours: 11,716 (1987)

Cinema
- Number of fixed cinemas: 138 (latest)
- Seating capacity (000): 82 (latest)
  - Seats (/1,000 pop.): 5.1 (1987)
- Annual attendance (millions): 20.0 (latest)
- Gross box office receipts (M.$ millions): 40 (1987)

Films
- Number of long films produced: 14 (latest)
- Number of long films imported: 558 (1987)
  - % from United States: 53.9
  - % from Hong Kong: 29.7
  - % from India: 4.3
  - % from Federal Republic of Germany: 0.5

CULTURAL & ENVIRONMENTAL INDICATORS

Libraries (latest)
- Number: 13
- Volumes (millions): 3.535
- Registered borrowers (000): 730
- Loans (/1,000 pop.): 310

Performing arts (pre-1986)
- Number of performances: 1,303
- Annual attendance (000): 312
- Attendance (/1,000 pop.): 25

Nature reserves (latest)
- Number of facilities: 41

A television service is operated by Television Malaysia and Sistem Televisyen Malaysia Bhd (STMB) Network I, with its main station at Kuala Lumpur and regional stations at Johore Bahru, Taiping, Pinang, Ipoh, Melaka, Batu Pahat and Kluang. It is on the air for nine hours a day, while Network II, with the same stations, broadcasts for four hours a day. Some 45% of the programs are imported or received in exchange through the Asian Broadcasting Union. Existing stations cover 15% of the population. A license fee is payable for television sets.

The largest library is the National Library, with 200,000 volumes.

SOCIAL WELFARE

Social welfare is coordinated by two government departments: the Ministry of Health and the Ministry of Welfare Services. The work of private organizations is integrated into government efforts by the Central Welfare Council. The Fifth Malaysia Plan (1986–90) provided for development of a new health investment program intended to improve staff training and administration and promote construction of new hospitals. In 1986 proposed government spending for health and social services was 8.4% of total spending.

The Social Security Law of 1969 expanded the coverage and benefits available to workers to include an injury plan and an invalidity plan, both providing for medical care and treatment. The law also extended Employment Fund coverage, providing unemployment benefits to all industrial units employing five or more workers.

GLOSSARY

adat: traditional custom having legal force in Islamic societies.

anak dagang: foreign Malays; later immigrants from Indonesia and Islamized natives who were assimilated into Malay society.

bala Chinese: assimilated Chinese who speak Malay and adopt Malay customs.

bumiputra: literally, sons of the soil. Ethnic Malays, especially as distinguished from Indian and Chinese immigrants.

component: a territorial division for law enforcement purposes in East Malaysia.

contingent: a territorial division for law enforcement purposes in West Malaysia.

dato: title of honor granted by the ruler of a Malaysian state.

dewan negara: the senate of Malaysia.

dewan ra'ayat: the house of representatives.

jawi: Arabic script in which Bahasa Malaysia is sometimes written.

kampong: village or hamlet.

kongri: Chinese clan or unit of social organization.

kris: Malaysian knife with wavy blade.

longhouse: bamboo or wooden rural dwelling in rural Malaysia inhabited by an extended family group. It consists of a number of compartments, or *bileks*, each assigned to a nuclear family.

majlis raja raja: the conference of rulers.

mentri besar: chief minister of a state.

Merdeka Day: Independence Day.

mukim: a subdivision of a district, usually a group of villages.

penghulu: administrator of a mukim.

pondok: a Muslim religious school set up in a temporary dwelling.

residency: a district in Sabah, as a unit of local government.

rumi: roman script in which Bahasa Malaysia is officially written.

sepak raga: Malaysian football played with a light ball made of plaited rattan.

tun: form of Malaysian address, equivalent to "Sir."

yang di-pertuan agong: paramount ruler, or Malaysian head of state.

yang di-pertuan besar: title of the ruler of Negri Sembilan.

yang di-pertuan negara: title of the governors of Sabah and Sarawak.

CHRONOLOGY (from 1957)

1957— Malaya becomes an independent nation within the Commonwealth, with Tunku Abdul Rahman as prime minister; Constitution prepared by the Reid Commission is adopted.

1959— First local elections are held in Sarawak. . . . Last Communist rebels surrender. . . . Central Bank of Malaya is founded.

1960— Emergency is ended.

1962— First elections are held in Sabah (known as British North Borneo).

1963— Malaya, Singapore, Sarawak and North Borneo joint together as the State of Malaysia. . . . Confrontation with Indonesia begins over the membership of Sarawak and North Borneo (Sabah) in Malaysia.

1965— Singapore leaves the Malaysian federation.

1966— Confrontation with Indonesia ends as Sukarno is toppled from power.

1967— Malaysia joins the Association of Southeast Asian Nations as a charter member.

1969— Ruling Alliance Party suffers reverses in national elections. . . . Race riots between Malays and Chinese break out in Kuala Lumpur; emergency is declared, the Constitution is suspended and a National Operations Council is set up to direct emergency rule.

1970— Emergency is ended. . . . Prime Minister Tunku Abdul Rahman steps down and is succeeded by Tun Abdul Razak.

1973— Malaysia establishes diplomatic relations with Hanoi. . . . The Malaysian dollar is allowed to float.

1974— Diplomatic relations are established with Communist China. . . . The ruling Alliance Party, renamed the Barisan National Front, gains a decisive majority in national elections to the federal parliament. . . . Islamic summit conference is held at Kuala Lumpur. . . . Kuala Lumpur becomes a federal territory.

1976— Datuk Hussein bin Onn becomes prime minister on death of Tun Abdul Razak. . . . The Malaysian dollar is renamed the ringgit.

1977— Federal government proclaims emergency in Kelantan State; four ministers quit in protest.

1978— The ruling Barisan National Front wins an absolute majority in parliamentary elections.

1979— Malaysia admits over 75,000 Vietnamese "boat people" but threatens to "shoot on sight" further arrivals.

1981— Prime Minister Datuk Hussein bin Onn steps down and is succeeded in office by Datuk Seri Mahathir bin Mohamad. In national elections, the Barisan National Front routs opposition parties and gains 132 of 154 seats in the House of Representatives. . . . Mahathir announces a "look East" economic policy stressing increased ties to Japan and Korea.

1983— The veto power of the paramount ruler in nonfinancial bills is curtailed. . . . Financial scandal involving loans made by Bank Bumiputra to Hong Kong's Carrion Group rocks the government.

1985— Joseph Pairin Kitingan, a Christian and ethnic Borneo Kadazan, is installed as chief minister in Sabah after his party, Party Bersatu Sabah (PBS), wins 25 of the 48 state assembly seats there.

1986— Malay nationalism gains victory in elections to House of Representatives when National Front wins 148 seats in the enlarged House consisting of 177 members. National Front also retains power in all state assemblies in Peninsular Malaysia.

1987— Datuk Seri Dr. Mahathir Mohamad, whose

leadership had been called into question since 1986, wins National Front party presidency by a narrow majority. Racial tensions between Chinese and Malays lead to government detention of numerous prominent members of National Front and opposition parties. Government revokes publishing licenses of three major newspapers including the English language daily, *The Star.*

1988— UMNO is reformed as UMNO (Baru) by means of much political, legislative and judicial maneuvering. President of the Supreme Court, Tun Mohammed Salleh is dismissed from office along with two Supreme Court judges as a result of tensions between executive and judiciary. In the face of a massive influx of Indo-Chinese refugees, Malaysia announces that they will be treated as illegal immigrants and be deported.

1990— Mahathir Mohamad wins reelection to a third term. The UMNO maintains control of parliament in its toughest test since formation.

BIBLIOGRAPHY

BOOKS & FILMS

Ahmad, Zakaria Haji. *Government and Politics of Malaysia.* New York, 1987.

Ali, S. Husein. *Malay Peasant Society and Leadership.* New York, 1975.

Andaya, Barbara W., and Leonard Y. Andaya. *A History of Malaysia.* New York, 1984.

Arasaratnam, Sinnappah. *Indians in Malaysia and Singapore.* New York, 1980.

Ariff, Mohamed. *Malaysia and Asian Economic Cooperation.* London, 1981.

Bailey, Conner. *Broker, Mediator, Patron and Kinsman: An Historical Analysis of Key Leadership Roles in a Rural Malaysian District.* Athens, OH, 1980.

Barber, Noe'l. *The War of the Running Dogs: The Malayan Emergency, 1948–60.* New York, 1962.

Bedlington, Stanley S. *Malaysia and Singapore: The Building of New States.* Ithaca, NY, 1978.

Bhanoji Rae, V. V. *Malaysia: Development Patterns and Policy, 1947 to 1971.* Athens, OH, 1980.

Chin, Kin Wah. *The Defense of Malaysia and Singapore: The Transformation of a Security System, 1957–71.* New York, 1983.

Clutterbuck, Richard. *Conflict and Violence in Singapore and Malaysia, 1945–83.* Boulder, CO, 1984.

Crouch, Harold. *Malaysia's 1982 General Elections.* London, 1982.

Datar, Kiran K. *Malaysia: Quest for Politics or Consensus.* New York, 1983.

De Silva, Judith. *Malaysia Official Year Book.* New York, annual.

Esman, Milton J. *Administration and Development in Malaysia.* Ithaca, NY, 1972.

Family Life in Malaysia: We Live in a Kampong. Color film, 14 min. Contemporary Films.

Fisk, E. K., and Osman Rani. *The Political Economy of Malaysia.* New York, 1982.

Fong, Chan O. *Technological Leap: Malaysian Industry in Transition.* New York, 1985.

Funston, John. *Malay Politics in Malaysia.* London, 1981.

Ghee, Lim T. *Peasants and Their Agricultural Economy in Colonial Malay (1874–1941).* New York, 1978.

Goh Cheng Teik. *The May 13th Incident and Democracy in Malaysia.* New York, 1971.

Grenfell, Newell. *Switch On, Switch Off: The Mass Media Audiences of Malaysia.* New York, 1979.

Gulick, John. *Malaysia: Economic Expansion and National Unity.* Boulder, CO, 1981.

Hai, Tan Soo, and Hamzah Sendut. *Public and Private Housing in Malaysia.* London, 1979.

Hashim, Wan. *Race Relations in Malaysia.* London, 1983.

Hills, Peter. *China and Malaysia: Social and Economic Effects of Petroleum Development.* Geneva, 1987.

Hirschman, C. *Malaysian Studies.* Detroit, 1979.

Hoffman, Lutz, and Tan S. Ee. *Industrial Growth, Employment and Foreign Investment in Peninsular Malaysia.* New York, 1980.

Hua Wu Yin. *Class and Communalism in Malaysia: Politics in a Dependent Capitalist State.* London, 1983.

Jackson, A. C., and M. Rudner. *Issues in Malaysian Development.* London, 1980.

Jain, R. K. *China and Malaysia, 1946–83.* Atlantic Highlands, NJ, 1984.

Kahin, George. *Government and Politics of Southeast Asia.* Ithaca, NY, 1976.

Kasper, Wolfgang. *Malaysia: A Study in Successful Economic Development.* Washington, D.C., 1974.

Kennedy, J. *History of Malaya.* New York, 1970.

Koentjaraningrat, R. M. *Introduction to the Peoples and Cultures of Indonesia and Malaysia.* Menlo Park, CA, 1975.

Kuchiba, Masuo. *Three Malay Villages.* Honolulu, HI, 1979.

Lee Soo, Ann. *Economic Growth and the Public Sector in Malaysia and Singapore.* New York, 1974.

Lim, David. *Economic Growth and Development in West Malaysia, 1947–70.* New York, 1973.

———. *Further Readings in Malaysian Economic Development.* New York, 1983.

Loong-Hoe, Tan. *The State and Economic Distribution in Malaysia.* London, 1982.

Mackie, J. A. *Konfrontasi: The Indonesia-Malaysia Dispute, 1963–66.* New York, 1974.

Malaya: Land of Tin and Rubber. Color/B&W film. Encyclopaedia Britannica.

Malay Peninsula: People and Products. Color/B&W film, 11 min. Coronet Films.

Malaysia: Building a Nation. Color film, 19 min. Contemporary Films.

Malaysian River Boy. Color film, 17 min. Producer N.A.

Means, Gordon. *Malaysian Politics.* New York, 1970.

Meerman, Jacob P. *Public Expenditure in Malaysia: Who Benefits and Why.* New York, 1979.

Milne, R. S., and K. J. Ratnam. *Malaysia: New States in a New Nation.* London, 1974.
———, and Diane Mauzy. *Malaysia Profile.* Boulder, CO, 1986.
———. *Malaysia: Tradition, Modernity, and Islam.* Boulder, CO, 1986.
Milner, A. C. Kerajaan. *Malay Political Culture on the Eve of Colonial Rule.* Tucson, AZ, 1983.
Musolf, Lloyd D., and J. Frederick Springer. *Malaysia's Parliamentary System: Representative Politics and Policymaking in a Divided Society.* Boulder, CO, 1979.
Naidu, Ratna. *The Communal Edge to Plural Societies: India and Malaysia.* New York, 1978.
New Star: Federation of Malaya. Color film, 12 min. Fleetwood Films.
Norris, M. W. *Local Government in Peninsular Malaysia.* London, 1980.
Ongkili, James P. *Nation-Building in Malaysia, 1946–74.* New York, 1984.
Puthucheary, Mavis. *Politics of Administration: The Malaysian Experience.* New York, 1978.
Rabushka, Alvin. *Race and Politics in Urban Malaysia.* Stanford, CA, 1973.
Rao, Chandria A. *Issues in Contemporary Malaysia.* London, 1977.
Rao, V. Bhanoji. *National Accounts in West Malaysia, 1947–71.* London, 1976.
Roff, William R. *Kelantan: Religion, Society and Politics in a Malay State.* New York, 1974.
Rubber from Malaya. B&W film, 15 min. British Information Services.
Ryan, N. J. *Cultural Heritage of Malaya.* New York, 1971.
Sandhu, K. S., and Paul Wheatley. *Melaka: The Transformation of a Malay Capital, 1400–1978.* New York, 1983.
Singapore and Malaya: New States in Southeast Asia. Color film, 17 min. Dudly.
Singh, Jaginder. *Credit and Security in West Malaysia.* Brisbane, Australia, 1980.
Snodgrass, Donald R. *Inequality and Economic Development in Malaysia.* New York, 1980.
Strauch, Judith. *Chinese Village Politics in the Malaysian State.* Cambridge, MA, 1981.
Suffian, Tun M. *The Malaysian Constitution: Its Development in 1957 to 1977.* New York, 1979.
Svensson, Thommy, and Per Sorensen. *Indonesia and Malaysia.* London, 1981.
Tee, Lim H. *Malaysia.* Santa Barbara, CA, 1980.
Three Families of Malaysia. Color film, 16 min. Coronet.
Turnbull, C. Mary. *A Short History of Malaysia.* Singapore, 1981.
Van Vorys, Karl. *Democracy Without Consensus: Communalism and Political Stability in Malaysia.* Princeton, NJ, 1975.
Vasil, R. K. *Politics in a Plural Society: A Study of Noncommunal Political Parties in West Malaysia.* New York, 1971.
———. *Malaysian General Elections of 1969.* New York, 1979.
———. *Ethnic Politics in Malaysia.* New York, 1980.
Voices of Malaya. B&W film, 35 min. British Information Services.
Wegelin, E. A. *Urban Low-Income Housing and Development: A Case Study in Peninsular Malaysia.* Boston, 1978.
Wiebe, Paul, and S. Mariappan. *Indian Malaysians: The View from the Plantations.* Durham, NC, 1979.
Young, Kevin. *Malaysia: Growth and Equity in a Multiracial Society.* Baltimore, 1980.

OFFICIAL PUBLICATIONS

Accountant General, Statistics Department. *Monthly Statistical Bulletin.*
———. *Economic and Functional Classification of Government Transactions.*
Bank Negara Malaysia. *Annual Report.*
———. *Central Bank Quarterly Economic Bulletin.*
Federal Land Development Authority (FELDA). *Annual Report.*
Majlis Amanah Rakyat (MARA) (Council for the Promotion of Malay Participation in Business). *Annual Report.*
National Fisheries Development Authority. *Annual Report.*
National Livestock Development Authority. *Annual Report.*
Rubber Industries Smallholders Development Authority (RISDA). *Annual Report.*
Social Security Organization. *Annual Report.*

MALDIVES

BASIC FACT SHEET

OFFICIAL NAME: Republic of Maldives (Divehi Jumhuriya)

ABBREVIATION: MD

CAPITAL: Malé

HEAD OF STATE & HEAD OF GOVERNMENT: President Maumoon Abdul Gayoom (from 1978)

NATURE OF GOVERNMENT: Partial democracy

POPULATION: 217,945 (1990)

AREA: 298 sq. kim. (115 sq. mi.)

ETHNIC MAJORITY: Mixed Sinhalese, Arab, Dravidian and Black

LANGUAGE: Divehi

RELIGION: Sunni Islam

UNIT OF CURRENCY: Maldivian rufiyaa (M.R.)

NATIONAL FLAG: Green rectangle bordered by red field; centered in the rectangle is a white crescent

NATIONAL EMBLEM: A black and white five-pointed star surrounded by a crescent with horns nearly touching each other. The device is flanked by crossed national flags with a white scroll at their base carrying the nation's name in Kufic script. Behind the device is a tall palm with green fronds.

NATIONAL ANTHEM: "National Anthem"

NATIONAL HOLIDAYS: July 26 (National Day); November 11 (Republic Day); also, variable Islamic festivals

NATIONAL CALENDAR: Gregorian and Islamic (dating from the Hegira)

PHYSICAL QUALITY OF LIFE INDEX: 57

DATE OF INDEPENDENCE: July 26, 1965

DATE OF CONSTITUTION: June 4, 1964

WEIGHTS & MEASURES: Metric

GEOGRAPHICAL FEATURES

The Maldives are an archipelago of tropical atolls in the north-central Indian Ocean about 670 km. (415 mi.) southwest of Sri Lanka and 600 km. (372 mi.) from the southern tip of India. The islands span an arc of 804 km. (498 mi.) north to south and 159 km. (99 mi.) east to west with a total land area of 298 sq. km. (115 sq. mi.). The country consists of 1,190 islands, comprising 26 natural atolls (itself a Divehi word), but for administrative purposes, they are divided into 19 atolls. The total coastline is 2,393 km. (1,484 mi.) and the country's area, including sea and land, is nearly 90,000 sq. km. (55,800 sq. mi.)

Malé, the capital, is only about 1.6 km. (1 mi.) long and 0.8 km. (0.5 mi.) wide; its population was estimated in 1989 at 58,000.

Of the 1,190 islands, only 202 are inhabited. The average size of the islands is 0.64 sq. km. (0.25 sq. mi.), and none is larger than 13 sq. km. (5 sq. mi.). The islands are low, rising only a few feet above the level of the sea, and many of the islands are just tiny banks washed by the ocean. Some disappear over time, and others are formed. Some atolls have encircling reefs, and others are made up of many small ring-shaped reefs. Many contain freshwater lagoons. The inner shores of the islands are frequently marshy. East–west passage through the island chain is facilitated by a number of clear navigable channels: Kardivia, or Five-Degree Channel (38.6 km.; 24 mi. wide); Veimandu, or Kolumadula Channel (24 km.; 15 mi. wide); One-and-a-Half-Degree Channel (80 km.; 50 mi. wide) and Equatorial Channel (74 km.; 46 mi.) wide.

WEATHER

The climate is hot and humid, with little daily variation. The mean temperature is 27°C (81°F). The temperature ranges from 26.6°C to 29°C (80°F to 84°F) in December to from 29.4°C to 32°C (85°F to 90°F) in March and April. The islands are subject to southwesterly monsoons from June to August and to northeasterly monsoons from November to March. Annual rainfall averages 2,540 mm. (100 in.) in the North and 3,810 mm. (150 in.) in the South.

Violent storms are common during the monsoons.

POPULATION

The population of Maldives was estimated at 217,945 in July 1990.

Only 20% of the islands are inhabited. About one-fourth of the population is concentrated in the capital. The overall density of population is 718.1 per sq. km. (1,860.9 per sq. mi.). There are few urban settlements apart from Malé, the capital. Males have outnumbered females every year since 1966. Neither emigration nor immigration has significantly affected population growth. The high rate of growth is acknowledged as a serious problem by the government, but birth control has not, as yet, been adopted as an official policy.

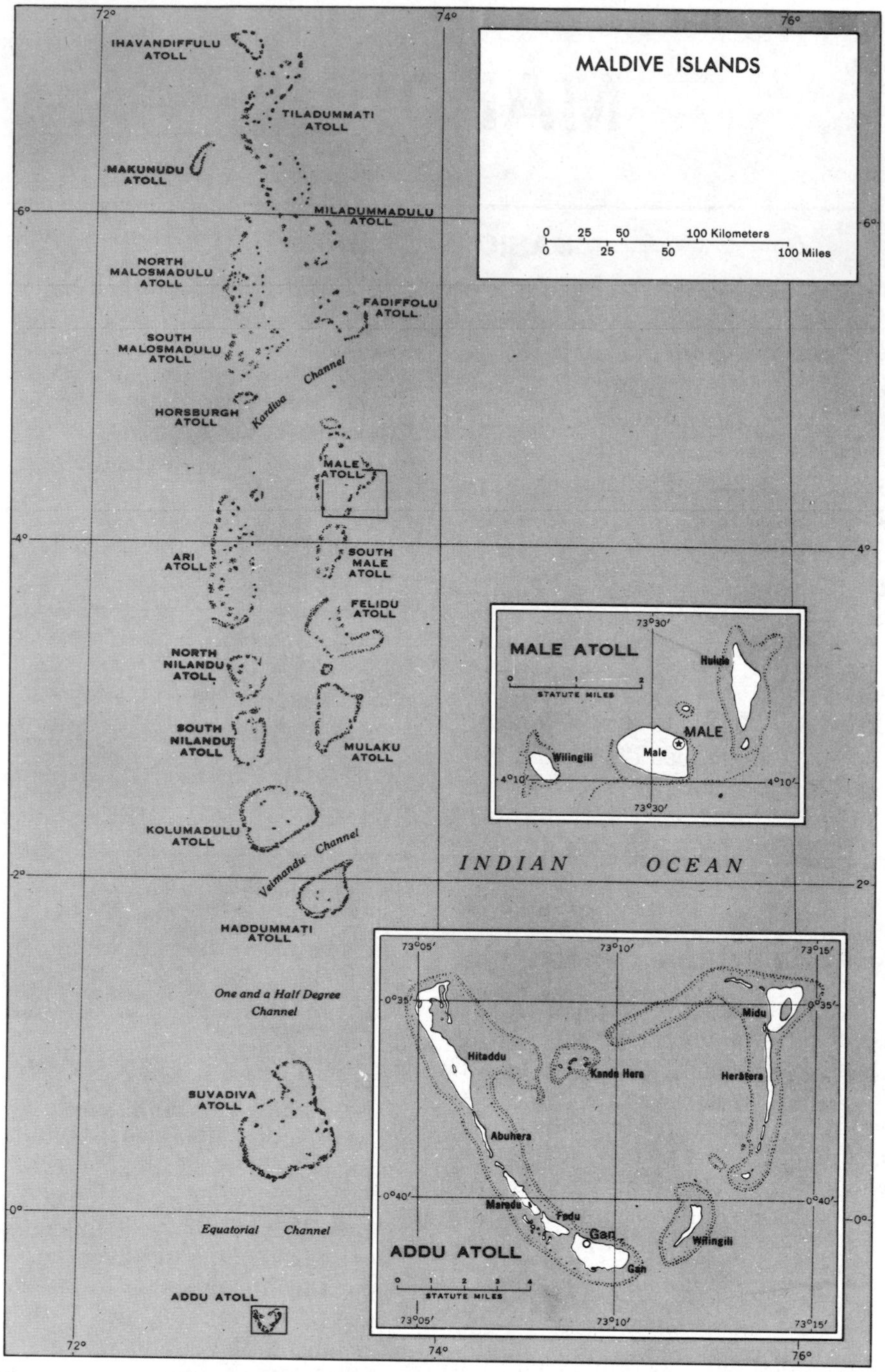

MALDIVE ISLANDS

0 25 50 100 Kilometers
0 25 50 100 Miles

72° 74° 76°
6° 4° 2° 0°

IHAVANDIFFULU ATOLL
TILADUMMATI ATOLL
MAKUNUDU ATOLL
MILADUMMADULU ATOLL
NORTH MALOSMADULU ATOLL
FADIFFOLU ATOLL
SOUTH MALOSMADULU ATOLL
Kardiva Channel
HORSBURGH ATOLL
MALE ATOLL
ARI ATOLL
SOUTH MALE ATOLL
FELIDU ATOLL
NORTH NILANDU ATOLL
SOUTH NILANDU ATOLL
MULAKU ATOLL
KOLUMADULU ATOLL
Veimandu Channel
HADDUMMATI ATOLL
INDIAN OCEAN
One and a Half Degree Channel
SUVADIVA ATOLL
Equatorial Channel
ADDU ATOLL

MALE ATOLL

0 1 2
STATUTE MILES
73°30′ 4°10′
Hulule
MALE
Male
Wilingili

ADDU ATOLL

0 1 2 3 4
STATUTE MILES
73°05′ 73°10′ 73°15′ 0°35′ 0°40′
Hitaddu
Kandu Hera
Midu
Herätera
Abuhera
Maradu
Fedu
Gan
Wilingili

DEMOGRAPHIC INDICATORS

Population (000): 218 (1990)
Year of last census: 1985
Sex distribution (% at last census), males: 51.7 females: 48.1
Population estimates and projections (000)

1930: 78	1960: 106	1990: 214
1940: 81	1970: 128	2000: 281
1950: 82	1980: 155	

Age profile (%, 1970 census)

0–14: 45.1	30–44: 12.3	60–74: 2.9
15–29: 28.3	45–59: 9.6	75 and over: 0.7

Population density per sq. km. (per sq. mi.): 718.1 (1,860.9) (latest)

VITAL STATISTICS

Crude birth rate (/1,000): 46 (1990)
Crude death rate (/1,000): 9 (1990)
Infant mortality rate (/1,000 live births): 76 (1990)
Life expectancy (yrs.) at birth: males, 60; females, 65 (1990)
Total fertility rate (/woman): 6.6 (1990)
Rate of natural increase (/1,000): 31.3 (1988)
Average household size: 6.1 (latest)

Although traditionally women and men have not equally benefited from political and economic opportunities of their country, Maldivian women have benefited from the current government's efforts to improve opportunities for them. Patterns of behavior and living conditions for women are less restrictive than in some other Islamic countries. For example, they are not required to wear the veil, and a growing number of women serve in responsible positions in the government and in the professions.

By Islamic and Maldivian tradition, women play a lesser role than men in public life. No women served as members of the Majlis elected in 1980; President Gayoom appointed one. In 1982 the president appointed a National Women's Committee, which is seeking ways to increase participation by women in the country's life.

ETHNIC COMPOSITION

The four main ethnic strains in the population are Sinhalese, Dravidian, Arab and Black. These elements each predominate within a specific geographical area. The northern islanders resemble the Dravidians; the middle islanders the Arabs; and the southern islanders the Sinhalese, the latter two being lighter-skinned and taller. Persons of Black origin form a separate endogamous subgroup called the Ravare. The original population of the islands is thought to have been Dravidian, but they were displaced in about the ninth century by the Arabs. Malayan and Portuguese influences also are noticeable in the population.

The only ethnic minority are the Indians, who have formed a colony in the Maldives since the 17th century. They also form a religious and linguistic minority.

LANGUAGES

The national language is Divehi, an Indo-European language closely related to Elu, an archaic form of Sinhalese. Divehi has numerous loanwords from Arabic, Hindi and Tamil. Until recently Divehi had two alphabets: one an adaptation of Arabic and the other called Thaana, derived from Sanskrit and Sinhalese scripts but written from right to left with diacritics. In 1977 the government announced that the Divehian script would be romanized, but in 1979 the country returned to the Thaana script. English, Sinhalese and Hindi are the principal foreign languages used in commerce.

RELIGION

Islam is the state religion. Almost all Maldivians belong to the Sunni sect, which was introduced into the islands in the 9th century. Religion is a dominant force in national life, and there are numerous mosques.

HISTORICAL BACKGROUND

The Maldive Islands were a British protectorate from 1887 to 1965. The country was granted internal self-government in 1960 and full independence five years later. The Maldives retained their ancient sultanate during their first three years of independence. After a November 1968 referendum, the country became a republic with a president as head of state and prime minister as head of government. Ibrahim Nasir became the first president. In a 1975 constitutional revision, the post of prime minister was abolished, and the president assumed all executive responsibilities.

Nasir did not run for reelection in 1978 and was succeeded by Maumoon Abdul Gayoom, his minister of transport. On taking office, Gayoom indicated that he would devote himself to the development of the country's impoverished rural areas and maintain the nation's foreign policy of nonalignment.

Nasir departed the Maldives following his resignation, but the government subsequently wanted him to return to the country to be tried on charges of misusing government moneys. In 1980 Nasir was implicated in an unsuccessful coup against Gayoom. Nasir denied any involvement, and government efforts to extradite the former Maldives president from Singapore, where he lived in exile, failed. Gayoom was reelected president in 1983 and again in 1988.

In 1983 and 1988, there were still other unsuccessful coup attempts against the government. The latter was crushed when Indian army commandos arrived to repel an amphibious attack force made up largely of ethnic Tamil mercenaries from Sir Lanka. The coup attempt was believed to have been organized by four prominent political opponents of Gayoom, including Nasir, although he denied having played any part in the incident. In 1989, 16 people were sentenced to death and another 59 received jail sentences for their involvement in the failed 1988 coup attempt.

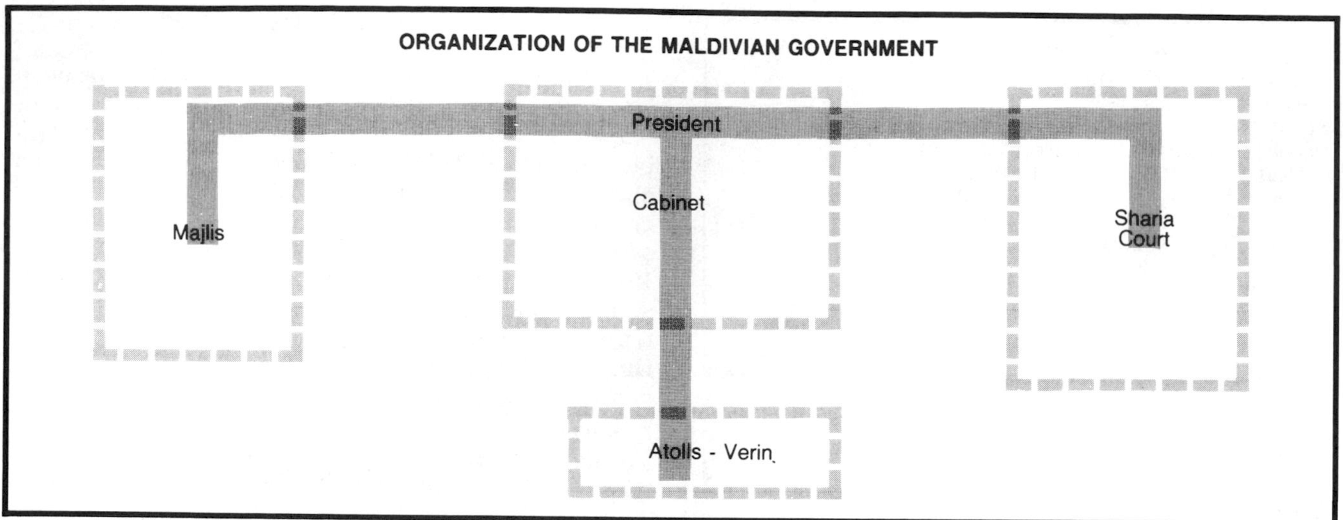

As of August 1990, Nasir remained in exile in Singapore.

Growing concern in Maldives in 1990 and 1991 focused not on internal dissent, but on how much longer the country would remain above sea level. In two separate international reports, scientists warned that global warming could cause ocean waters to rise and submerge the Maldives, which is only six feet above sea level, within 100 years.

CONSTITUTION & GOVERNMENT

The country is governed by an amended version of the Constitution of 1964, which was drawn up by the British jurist Sir Ivor Jennings. The Constitution was written for the short-lived republic of 1953 and was reactivated when the republican system was revived in 1968. Under its provisions the Majlis (the Legislature) chooses by secret ballot, from as many candidates as are proposed by members of the Majlis, a single nominee for president. The nomination then is confirmed or rejected in a nationwide referendum, also by secret ballot. In 1983 the Majlis voted 47 to 1 to nominate Gayoom to a second five-year term. Maldivians confirmed this nomination by giving Gayoom 95.6% of their votes. At the time of this nomination and reelection, President Gayoom was long established in office and there was no serious competitor for the position.

In 1988 he was reelected, again running unopposed, to a third five-year term, winning 96.4% of the popular vote. The president appoints and heads the cabinet, whose strength is fixed at nine members. The Constitution originally provided for a prime minister, but that post was abolished in a 1975 constitutional revision that permitted the president to appoint an unlimited number of vice-presidents. This provision was abolished in 1977. President Gayoom functions as both head of state and head of government.

The nation's parliament is a unicameral body known as the Majlis (Citizen's Assembly). The Maldivian judicial system is based on the Shari'a, which is Islamic law. Justice is administered through a presidentially appointed body, the Maldives High Court, which was initiated in 1980. There is also a Police Court, a Court of Summary Jurisdiction and eight additional courts in Malé, the capital. In addition, there are Island Courts on every populated island in the country. All of the nation's courts fall under the jurisdiction of the Ministry of Justice. The government of the islands is uncomplicated and simple; there is no Department of Defense, no Post Office Department (although stamps are issued) and no Social Security administration.

Following former president Ibrahim Nasir's retirement and the installation of Gayoom as president, the Majlis launched an investigation by a parliamentary commission into the official conduct of Nasir and his family. The commission examined over 346 cases and found Nasir guilty on three counts: embezzlement, collection of illegal taxes and violation of the Constitution in banishing former prime minister Ahmed Zaki. Efforts are being made to have Nasir extradited from his present home in Singapore.

GOVERNMENT LIST
(July/August 1991)

President	Gayoom, Maumoon Abdul
Minister of Atolls Administration	Jameel, Abdullah
Minister of Defense & National Security	Gayoom, Maumoon Abdul
Minister of Education	Hameed, Abdulla
Minister of Finance	Gayoom, Maumoon Abdul
Minister of Fisheries & Agriculture	Ibrahim, Abbis
Minister of Foreign Affairs	Jameel, Fathulla
Minister of Health & Welfare	Didi, Abdul Sattar Moosa
Minister of Home Affairs & Sports	Zahir, Umar
Minister of Justice	Ibrahim, Mohamed Rasheed
Minister of Planning & Environment	Jameel, Fathulla
Minister of Public Works & Labor	Kamaaludheen, Abdulla
Minister of Tourism	Shafeeu, Ismail
Minister of Trade & Industries	Mujuthaba, Ahmed
Minister of Transport & Shipping	
Minister Without Portfolio	Hussain, Mohamed Zahir
Minister of State for Finance	Fathy, Ismail
Minister of State for Presidential Affairs	Hussain, Abdul Rasheed
Iman of the Islamic Center	Shathir, Ahmed
Governor, Central Bank	Gayoom, Maumoon Abdul

The last major threat to the political unity of the Maldives was the so-called Suvadivan Rebellion in 1960, which established a short-lived United Suvadiva Republic. Political loyalties are determined by tradition and geography. Both favor the present regime, which has encountered no serious opposition.

FREEDOM & HUMAN RIGHTS

The Maldives is perhaps the only country in the world without prisons. There is, however, a detention center. Common forms of punishments are fines, house arrest and banishment to thinly inhabitated islands where the person is expected to earn his own living. Violent crimes occur very rarely. Statistics are not available, but a high government official said in 1980 that nine persons were in detention for misuse of power under a former regime; five were under house arrest; and one, the former president, was in exile. The legal system is based on the Shari'a, although the more draconian punishments provided for in the Shari'a are never administered. However, violators of the law may be subject to flogging. There is no prior press censorship, although all publications must be registered with the government, and journalists are subject to prosecution for contravening any number of laws, such as "arousing ill feelings against a lawfully formed government." There are no trade unions, and no strikes have taken place in Maldivian history. There are no organized political parties, and candidates run for election on the basis of their personal influence. Women's role is limited, as in all Islamic societies.

CIVIL SERVICE

No current information is available on Maldivian civil service.

LOCAL GOVERNMENT

The Maldives is divided, for purposes of local government, into 19 atolls, as follows: Haa-Alif, Haa-Dhalu, Shaviani, Nun, Raa, Baa, Miimu, Ga afu-Alif, Laviani, Faafu, Gaafu-Dhalu, Kaafu (Malé), Dhalu, Nya, Alif, Taa, Sinu (Addu), Waa and Lamu.

Each atoll is headed by a *verin*, or chief, who is assisted by an elected committee. On each inhabited island there is a *kateeb*, or headman. Both *kateebs* and *verins* are appointed by the president. All populated islands also have assistant headmen, and a mosque official called a *mudim*. The capital city of Malé is divided into four administrative wards.

FOREIGN POLICY

Maldivian foreign policy is oriented to the Islamic Middle East out of religious as well as economic considerations. The country has regularly attended Islamic summit conferences. In 1977 Libya opened an embassy in Malé (the capital's second embassy, the first having been opened in 1976 by India) and was followed by Pakistan. Libya also sponsored the Maldives for membership in the Nonaligned Conference at Colombo. In a related move, the Iranian navy visited the islands to demonstrate Iranian interest in Indian Ocean affairs. Similar friendly visits were paid by U.S., Indian, Sri Lankan and Soviet warships. Since the British pulled out of Gan in 1976, the government has placed the island on the auction block as open for lease for nonmilitary purposes. As of mid-1990, the military facility on Gan remained in Maldivian control. Both India and Sri Lanka have expressed fears that the United States might take over the air base. In 1982 the Commonwealth admitted the Maldives as its 47th member.

There are no direct diplomatic relations between the United States and the Maldives. The British high commissioner in Colombo also serves concurrently as ambassador to the Maldives.

PARLIAMENT

The Majlis, or the Citizen's Assembly, is a unicameral body of 48 members, eight of whom are appointed by the president, with the other 40 elected by universal suffrage, on the basis of two from each atoll, or territorial unit, and two from the capital, Malé. Elections to the Majlis are held individually; thus a Majlis representative elected in the middle of a term continues to hold office through the following session until he completes the regular parliamentary term of five years. Candidates for the Majlis must be over 25 years of age, Muslim, be able to read and write both Arabic and Maldivian script, not have been involved in a crime for the past five years and be in good mental and physical condition. Suffrage is universal over age 21. Despite the facade of free elections, the government is closely controlled by vested interests. Once elected, Majlis representatives are freely approached by citizens or groups with grievances or points of view on proposed legislation. The Majlis meets three times a year.

The Majlis under President Gayoom is a different institution compared with its rubber-stamp predecessor. The proceedings are characterized by spirited debates, which are reported freely. Members are now granted parliamentary immunity for their speeches in the Majlis.

Since there are no political parties, factions in the Majlis tend to coalesce around individuals or points of view and vary according to the issue. Any member may introduce legislation, which, if seconded, must be considered by the Majlis. All laws must be approved by the Majlis. The Majlis can question ministers and call for their removal. In practice, however, the Majlis generally supports the government after carefully discussing and sometimes amending its proposals.

POLITICAL PARTIES

No political parties are permitted to function. All candidates run for the Majlis as independents.

ECONOMY

The Maldives is one of the low-income countries of the world, and it also is one of the countries considered by the United Nations as least developed. The private sector predominates in the basically free-market economy of the Maldives.

The Maldivian economy's foundation rests primarily on fishing, with tourism, and to a far lesser degree, shipping also of importance. Agriculture makes up only a relatively small portion of the economy, since only a few subsistence crops such as coconuts, maize, yams and millet are grown. These domestic staple crops meet only 10% of the country's food requirements. The fishing industry employees about 80% of the work force and produces more than 70% of exports, as well as providing a significant contribution to government revenues. Tourism expanded considerably in the 1980s following the opening of an international airport in 1981 and the initiation of direct charter flights from Europe to Maldives. The shipping trade was severely damaged by the international shipping recession during the 1980s, although the industry was reorganized and managed to show a small profit in 1987 and 1988.

PRINCIPAL ECONOMIC INDICATORS

Gross National Product (U.S. $ millions): 87 (1989)
GNP per capita (U.S. $): 420 (1989)
GNP per capita average annual growth rate (%, 1987–89): 6.5

BALANCE OF PAYMENTS, 1988
(U.S. $ millions)

Current account balance: 2.3
Merchandise exports: 44.6
Merchandise imports: −94.9
Trade balance: −49.9
Other goods, services & income +: 76.9
Other goods, services & income −: −34.8
Other goods, services & income net: 42.1
Private unrequited transfers: −0.6
Official unrequited transfers: 10.7
Capital other than reserves: 8
Net errors & omissions: 10.9
Counterpart items: 2.8
Total change in reserves: −13.4

GROSS DOMESTIC PRODUCT

GDP nominal (M.R. millions): .537 (1984)
GDP per capita (U.S. $): 670 (1988)
Average annual growth rate of GDP (%, 1980–84): 9.5
GDP by type of expenditure (%) 1985
- Consumption
  - Private: 59
  - Government: 18
- Gross domestic investment: 33
- Foreign trade
  - Exports: 68
  - Imports: −78

Sectoral origin of GDP (%) 1988
- Primary
  - Agriculture: 10
  - Mining: 2
- Secondary
  - Manufacturing & public utilities: 6
  - Construction: 8
- Tertiary
  - Transportation & communications: 5
  - Trade: 17
  - Finance, other services & government: 52

PUBLIC FINANCE

The Maldivian fiscal year is the calendar year. The fiscal system is extremely rudimentary. There is no income tax or any other direct tax. Revenues are derived from customs duties, rental of islands to individuals and institutions such as *Club Nature* and *Club Méditerranée*, sale of postage stamps and licensing fees on boats.

CENTRAL GOVERNMENT EXPENDITURES, 1988

% of total expenditures
- Defense: 0.0
- Education: 10.6
- Health: 5.1
- Housing, Social Security, welfare: 28.2
- Economic services: 21.2
- Other: 34.9
- Total expenditures as % of GDP: 33.1 (est.)
- Overall surplus or deficit as % of GDP: 2.2 (est.)

CENTRAL GOVERNMENT REVENUES, 1988

% of total current revenues
- Taxes on income, profit & capital gain: 1.8
- Social Security contributions: 0.0
- Domestic taxes on goods & services: 14.3
- Taxes on international trade & transactions: 46.8
- Current nontax revenue: 35.5
- Total current revenue as % of GDP: 27.6 (est.)

General government consumption as % of GDP: 18 (1985)

FOREIGN AID, 1989

Total foreign aid (U.S. $ millions): 662.0
- Bilateral: 443.5
- Multilateral: 20.8

In 1985 over 15% of government expenditures went to the main airport. In 1988, education, social services and health were allotted almost 44% of total expenditures.

There is no integrated development planning, but there is a series of projects to improve and expand fishing and related industries, food processing, communications, tourism and health services.

From 1970–88 the Maldives received $28 million in US aid. Other Western aid totalled $84 million during 1970–87. OPEC bilateral aid totalled $14 million during 1979–89.

FINANCIAL INDICATORS, 1989

Total reserves minus gold (SDRs millions): 19
SDRs (millions): 0.0
Reserve position in IMF (SDRs millions): 0.0
Foreign exchange (SDRs millions): 19
Gold (fine troy oz. millions): 0.0
Ratio of external debt to total reserves (1986): 2.8 (1988)
Central bank 1989
- Assets %
  - Foreign assets: 51.6
  - Claims on government: 48.4
  - Claims on banks: 0.1
  - Claims on private sector: 0.0
- Liabilities %
  - Reserve money: 80.7
  - Government deposits: 24.7
  - Foreign liabilities: 1.8
  - Capital accounts: 8.3

Money supply 1989
Stock (M.R. 000): 270,000
M^1 per capita: 1,270
Private banks 1989
- Assets %
  - Loans to government: 30.5
  - Loans to private sector: 31.3
  - Reserves: 25.7
  - Foreign assets: 12.6
- Liabilities
  - Deposits (M.R. millions): 631
  - of which %
    - Demand deposits: 11.7
    - Savings deposits: 36.6
    - Government deposits: 1.5
    - Foreign liabilities: 34.8

External debt 1988
- Debt service (long-term)
  - Total (U.S. $ millions): 8.6
  - Repayment
    - Principal (%): 80.2
    - Interest (%): 19.8
- Debt service ratio (%): 6.7

CURRENCY & BANKING

The Maldivian unit of currency is the rufiyaa, introduced in 1981 and divided into 100 larees (sing.: lari.). In July 1990 the dollar exchange rate was $1 = M.R. 9.5.

In 1980 the Maldivian Monetary Authority was set up to undertake the functions of a central bank. The first bank to be established in Malé was a branch of the State Bank of India in 1974. A branch of the Habib Bank (of Pakistan) was set up in 1976. In 1982 the country's first indigenous commercial bank, the Bank of Maldives, opened for business.

AGRICULTURE

Of the total land area of 29,800 ha. (73,606 ac.), about 63.5% is cultivated. The main agricultural products are millet, corn, sweet potatoes, pineapples, sugarcane, fruits and coconuts. Virtually all the rice, the staple food of the Maldivians, is imported. The northern, southern and eastern islands are more fertile than the central and the western. Agriculture contributes 10% of the GDP.

Because of the scarcity of fodder there are few cattle. There are no forests.

Fishing is the islands' most important industry providing more than 70% of the export earnings. The principal catches are tuna and bonito, which are cut in pieces, boiled and then smoked. The dried product, known as Maldive fish, is exported to India and Sri Lanka, where it is served as a delicacy.

There are several thousand fishing boats built in the country out of coconut wood, each boat holding about a dozen fishermen. In the mid-1980s, the fishing fleet comprised 2,000 pole and line fishing boats *(masdhoani)* and about 2,500 trawling boats *(vadhudhoani)*. Using sails, they go 24 to 32 km. (15 to 20 mi.) from the shores, depending on the prevailing winds and currents. Provided a good shoal is encountered, the daily catch per boat exceeds 500 and may be as much as 1,500.

Under a 50-year loan of $3.2 million from the IDA, the fishing fleet has been mechanized, diesel engines replacing sails, and five more maintenance and repair centers have been built. Although a long-term investment, this has had the unfortunate effect of increasing the country's oil bill to the equivalent of 30% of export earnings. A grant of $4.1 million was made to the Maldives by Norway in 1983 to finance construction of a refrigeration complex. This is part of a $12.6 million project, to be completed with the help of various international organizations, to improve productivity in the industry. In 1989 fishing involved 80% of the labor force and provided about 20% of the GDP.

Half of the fish purchase rights have been leased to a Japanese company and half to a South Korean company. In 1978 the government set up the Fisheries Corporation and a fish cannery and processing plant with Japanese aid. A joint venture has been launched with Iraq as a partner for exploiting deep-sea fishing grounds outside the reach of traditional boats. In 1988 the fish catch was 500 metric tons.

MANUFACTURING

The principal industries are fish processing, rope and coir matting and handicrafts, such as handmade pillow laces, woven mats and lacquerwork. Although the potential for modern industry is viewed as minimal, the past few years have seen the opening of three garment manufacturing facilities.

MINING

The Maldives has no mineral resources.

ENERGY

The only form of energy produced in the islands is electric power generated by diesel engines. Electric power production in 1988 was 5 million kw.-hr.

LABOR

About 30% of the labor force of Maldives is employed in fishing and agriculture, with smaller numbers of

ENERGY INDICATORS

Electricity 1988
- Installed capacity (000 kw.): 5
- Production (million kw.-hr.): 14
  - % fossil fuel: 100
- Consumption per capita (kw.-hr.): 69

people working in tourism, manufacturing, trade, construction, government service and finance.

There are no trade unions in the Maldives. Workers' rights to organize, bargain collectively and strike are not recognized or protected by statute. Until the 1970s most Maldivians were self-employed or held government jobs, and there was a relative lack of interest in workers' rights or organization. However, during the past few years three sizable garment manufacturing facilities opened, employing large numbers of workers. There were no special provisions regarding workers' rights or treatment in the agreements to establish these companies between the government and the foreign investors. However, a Department of Labor was formed in 1982, and it has been studying the labor situation in the Maldives and in other countries with a view eventually to developing appropriate labor regulations for the Maldives.

Very few labor standards are set by the government. Only government workers are entitled, by presidential directive, to free health care in the event of work-caused illness and to a paid annual vacation. There is no minimum age for the employment of young people. The government has set no restrictions on conditions under which young people may be employed, although most employers do not hire young people for work at night or in what are considered hazardous conditions. There is no national minimum wage, although the government has established wage floors for certain kinds of work. There is no restriction on the number of hours per week an employee can be required to work, and there is no requirement that private-sector employees receive an annual paid vacation.

LABOR INDICATORS, 1985

Total economically active population (000): 52
- As % of working-age population (15–64): 52.8
- % female: 21.7

Activity rate (%)
- Total: 29.0
- Male: 43.8
- Female: 13.1

Employment status (%) 1977
- Employers & self-employed: 49.4
- Employees: 39.1
- Other: 5.4

Sectoral employment (%)
- Agriculture, forestry, fishing: 29.5
- Construction: 4.9
- Manufacturing, mining, quarrying, public utilities: 24.3
- Trade, hotels, restaurants: 10.4
- Transport, communications: 6.4
- Finance, real estate, services: 20.8

FOREIGN TRADE INDICATORS, 1988

Exports (U.S. $ millions): 47
Imports (U.S. $ millions): 90
Balance of trade (U.S. $ millions): −43

Direction of Trade (%), 1988

	Imports (est.)	Exports
European Community	7.8	17.2
United States	0.0	23.1
U.S.S.R. & East European economies	0.0	0.0
Japan	9.4	1.4

Composition of Trade (%), 1988

	Imports	Exports
Food and agricultural raw materials	26.2	72.9
Fuels and other energy	11.9	0.0
Mineral ores and concentrates	1.7	0.1
Manufactured goods	60.2	27.0
of which chemicals	5.9	0.0
of which machinery	24.0	0.0

FOREIGN COMMERCE

Fish is the leading export, accounting for about 70% of all exports by value. Other exports are coconuts, copra, coir, shells and handicrafts.

Imports include manufactured goods, machinery and transportation equipment, petroleum, rice, sugar and chemicals. The major importers are India, Germany, Japan, Sri Lanka, Burma and Pakistan. Maldivian goods are exported to Thailand, the United States, Sri Lanka, Japan, Canada and Germany. Trade with Sri Lanka is carried by *buggalows*, which are wooden sailing craft similar to Arab dhows.

TRANSPORTATION & COMMUNICATIONS

The primary means of interisland transportation are sailing craft and a few motorized craft. Services are not regular but depend on cargo and need. Besides a fleet of wooden fishing boats, Maldives has a rapidly growing shipping line of 43 ships, of 148.5 total deadweight tonnage. Maldives Shipping Ltd. has branches in Singapore, Bombay and London. Malé, which is a free port, handled 51,000 tons of cargo in 1983.

Most of the islands have at least two streets, one stretching the length of the island and the other intersecting it at a right angle. The most common vehicle is the bicycle.

Air Maldives, founded in 1984 as Maldives Airway by the government-owned Maldives Aviation Co. Ltd. and foreign investors, provides domestic service. There are two usable airfields, both with permanent-surface runways and one, Hulule, across Malé Harbor, with a runway of over 2,500 m. (8,000 ft.).

The tourist industry brings considerable foreign exchange to Maldives, and receipts from tourism provided an estimated 17.4% of national revenues in 1983. The islands' attractions include white, sandy beaches and multicolored coral formations. Earnings from tourism are equivalent to four-fifths of visible export rev-

TRANSPORTATION INDICATORS

Motor vehicles (latest)
 Automobiles: 440
 Trucks and buses: 616
 Persons per vehicle: 190
Merchant marine
 Vessels: 43 (1989)
 Total deadweight tonnage (000): 148.5 (1989)
Ports (latest)
 Cargo loaded (000 metric tons): 20
 Cargo unloaded (000 metric tons): 70
Air (latest)
 Airports with scheduled flights: 1 (1990)

COMMUNICATION INDICATOR, 1985

Telephones
 Total (000): 2.5
 persons per telephone: 75
Phone traffic (000 calls)
 Local: 3,600
 Long distance: 68 (minutes)
 International: 260 (minutes)
Post office
 Number of post offices: 28 (1988)
 Pieces of mail handled (millions): 1.944 (1988)
Telegraph (000 calls)
 International: 5.6
Telex
 subscriber lines: 150
Telecommunications: 1 satellite station (1990)

TOURISM & TRAVEL INDICATORS, 1986

Total tourist receipts (U.S. $ millions): 63 (1988)
Expenditures by nationals abroad (U.S. $ millions): 5 (1988)
Number of hotel beds (000): 6
Average length of stay: 9 nights
Tourist nights (millions): 1.036
Number of tourists (000): 114.6 (1985)
 of whom from United States: 1.4
 Germany, Fed. Rep.: 29.1
 Italy: 17.5
 Japan: 14.1

enues and constitute more than one-seventh of the country's GDP. The tourism industry received a special boost in 1985 with the establishment of direct scheduled flights from Malé to Europe and Singapore.

DEFENSE

The internal security forces consist of the *lascoreen* (militia) and a sea patrol.

EDUCATION

Education is neither free nor compulsory. Schooling lasts 11 years, divided into five years of primary school and six years of secondary school. Secondary schooling consists of two cycles of three years each. Paralleling the modern school system is the traditional system consisting of *kuttabs* and *madrasahs,* in which children receive Islamic instruction.

The academic year runs from January to December. The medium of instruction is Divehi in secular schools

EDUCATION INDICATORS, 1986

Literacy
 Total (%): 90.4
 Males (%): 90.6
 Females (%): 90.1
First level
 Schools: 243
 Students: 41,812
 Teachers: 1,138
 Student/teacher ratio: 36.7
Second level
 Schools: 9
 Students: 3,581
 Teachers: 291
 Student/teacher ratio: 12.3
Vocational
 Schools: 10
 Students: 462
 Teachers: 52
 Student/teacher ratio: 8.9
 % of population over 24 with post secondary education: 0.4
Public expenditures 1987
 Total (M.R.): 33,400
 % of national budget: 8.5
 % of current expenditure: 88.3

and Arabic in Islamic schools. Government middle schools in Malé use English as the medium of instruction.

LEGAL SYSTEM

Maldivians follow Shari'a (Islamic) law, and occasionally violators are flogged. Usually punishment is confined to less physical means: fines; payment of compensation; house arrest; imprisonment; or banishment to a sparsely populated island, where the prisoner must earn his daily keep. During trial, the accused may defend himself and call witnesses. He also may be assisted by a lawyer, but there are few lawyers, and lawyers are not provided by the courts. The accused is sentenced by the judge; the length and type of sentence are established by law and custom.

There is a High Court and eight lesser courts in the capital at Malé, each dealing with specific types of cases (e.g., debt, theft, property claims). On other islands there are courts that deal with all types of cases. Judges are trained in Islamic law, are appointed by the president and serve at his pleasure and thus cannot be considered fully independent. Cases in island courts that present knotty legal points are referred to the appropriate specialized court at Malé, whose judge may in turn refer the legal point to four judges attached to the Ministry of Justice for assistance. The High Court acts as a court of appeal and handles political cases, such as the trials of the participants in an attempted coup d'état in 1980 and of four Majlis members found guilty of bribery in 1983.

LAW ENFORCEMENT

There is a small police force with a reported strength of 500.

HEALTH INDICATORS

Health personnel 1988
- Physicians: 26
  - persons per: 7,957
- Nurses: 121
- Pharmacists: 13 (1985)
- Midwives: 141 (1985)

Hospitals 1985
- Number: 4
- Number of beds per (/10,000): 7
- Admissions/discharges per 10,000: 291
- Bed occupancy rate (%): 57.5
- Average length of stay (days): 5

Type of hospitals (%) 1985
- Government: 100
- Private nonprofit: 0.0
- Private profit: 0.0

Public health expenditures (latest)
- As % of national budget: 3.6
- Per capita (U.S. $): 9.40

Vital statistics
- Crude death rate (/1,000): 9 (1990)
- Life expectancy at birth, 90
  - Males: 60
  - Females: 65
- Infant mortality rate (/1,000 live births): 76 (1990)

Population with access to safe water (%): 17 (latest)

HEALTH

Medical facilities generally are primitive. Major health problems include tuberculosis, leprosy, poliomyelitis, filariasis, venereal disease, eye infections and a form of malaria known as Maldivian fever.

FOOD & NUTRITION

The staple food is rice, usually served with seasoned sauces of meat, fish or vegetables. Pork is not eaten, and beef is too expensive. The diet is supplemented by tropical fruits and vegetables, such as mangoes, pineapples and coconuts. The daily per capita availability of energy, proteins, fats and carbohydrates is estimated at 1,781 calories.

MEDIA & CULTURE

Two daily newspapers are published in Malé in Divehi and in English. Twenty-three other nondaily newspapers also are published.

The national news agency is HANA (Haveeru News Agency). Book publishing activity is reflected in the average annual title output of three volumes.

The state-owned radio station, Voice of Maldives, operates one medium-wave transmitter and four shortwave transmitters. It broadcasts 4,288 hours annually in English and Divehi. Daily news bulletins from Radio Peking, the BBC and Radio Australia also are relayed. One of the first acts of the Gayoom government was to stop renting airtime to Christian evangelistic ministries.

A limited television service was begun in 1978. Annual movie attendance is 147,230. Malé has a public library and a public museum.

MEDIA INDICATORS

Newspapers
- Number of dailies: 2 (latest)
- Number of nondailies: 23 (1986)
- Circulation (000): 7 (1986)
- Per 1,000 pop.: 37 (1986)
- Number of periodicals: 64 (1986)
- Circulation (000): 70 (1986)

Book Publishing
- Number of titles: 3 (pre-1986)

Broadcasting (1985)
- Annual expenditures (M.R. millions): 1.5

Radio
- Number of transmitters: 2 (1989)
- Number of persons per radio receiver: 8.4 (1989)
- Total program hours: 5,024 (1987)

Television
- Television transmitters: 1 (1989)
- Number of persons per T.V. receiver: 44 (1989)
- Total program hours: 2,123 (1985)

Cinema
- Number of fixed cinemas: 7 (pre-1986)
- Seating capacity (000): 3 (pre-1986)
  - Seats (/1,000 pop.): 16.5 (1983)

Films
- Import of long films: 49 (1983)
  - % from India: 85.7
  - % from United States: 8.2
  - % from France: 2.0
  - % from United Soviet Socialist Republics: 2.0

CULTURAL & ENVIRONMENTAL INDICATORS (latest)

Libraries
- Number: 1
- Volumes (000): 8

Museums
- Annual attendance (000): 3
- Attendance (/1,000 pop.): 17

SOCIAL WELFARE

In addition to the assistance traditionally provided by the mosques to the indigent, the Maldivian government also has implemented programs to aid the disabled and the aged. In addition, the government provides free medical care for the poor at the country's main hospital in Malé.

GLOSSARY

buggalow: wooden sailing craft, similar to the dhow.
kateeb: headman of an inhabited village.
lascoreen: the militia, composed of lashkars, or foot-soldiers.
Majlis: parliament.
verin: chief of an atoll.

CHRONOLOGY (from 1965)

1965— The Maldives proclaims formal independence and joins the United Nations. Independence agreement provides for retention of a British air base in Gan.

1968— Following popular referendum the Maldives sultanate is replaced by a republican form of government with Ibrahim Nasir as president.

1972— Ahmed Zaki is named prime minister.

1975— Zaki is dismissed and placed under house arrest.

1976— United Kingdom withdraws from the Gan air base.

1977— Divehi script is romanized. . . . All five vice presidents are demoted to the rank of minister.

1978— President Nasir steps down for reasons of health, and Maumoon Abdul Gayoom is elected president.

1979— The Majlis launches an investigation into former president Nasir's administration; Nasir is charged with embezzlement, collection of illegal taxes other violation of the Constitution.

1980— The Maldivian Monetary Authority is set up as the nation's central bank.

1981— The national currency name is changed from rupee to rufiyaa.

1982— Maldives joins the Commonwealth as its 47th member. . . . The Bank of Maldives, the first indigenous commercial bank, is established.

1983— President Gayoom is reelected to a five-year term.

1986— Accord signed with India in which Delhi pledged to give Maldives about $17 million towards the building of a hospital at Malé as well as other projects.

1988— President Gayoom is reelected to another five-year term in September. In November, a coup attempt launched by an amphibious force composed mostly of ethnic Tamil mercenaries from Sri Lanka is quashed with the assistance of Indian Army commandos.

1989— Sixteen people are sentenced to death and another 59 are jailed for their involvement in the failed 1988 coup attempt.

1990— Two separate international reports warn that global warming could cause the ocean to submerge the Maldives within 100 years.

BIBLIOGRAPHY

BOOKS

Bernini, Francesco, and George Corbin. *Maldive.* Turin, Italy, 1973.

Lateef, K. S. *The Maldives: An Introductory Economic Report.* Washington, D.C., 1980.

Maloney, Clarence. *People of the Maldive Islands.* New Delhi, 1981.

Ministry of External Affairs. *The Maldive Islands.* Colombo, Sri Lanka, 1952.

REPUBLIQUE DU MALI
UN PEUPLE.UN BUT.UNE FOI

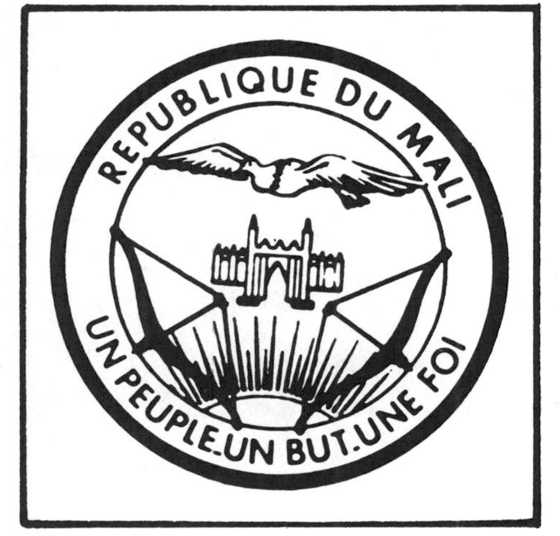

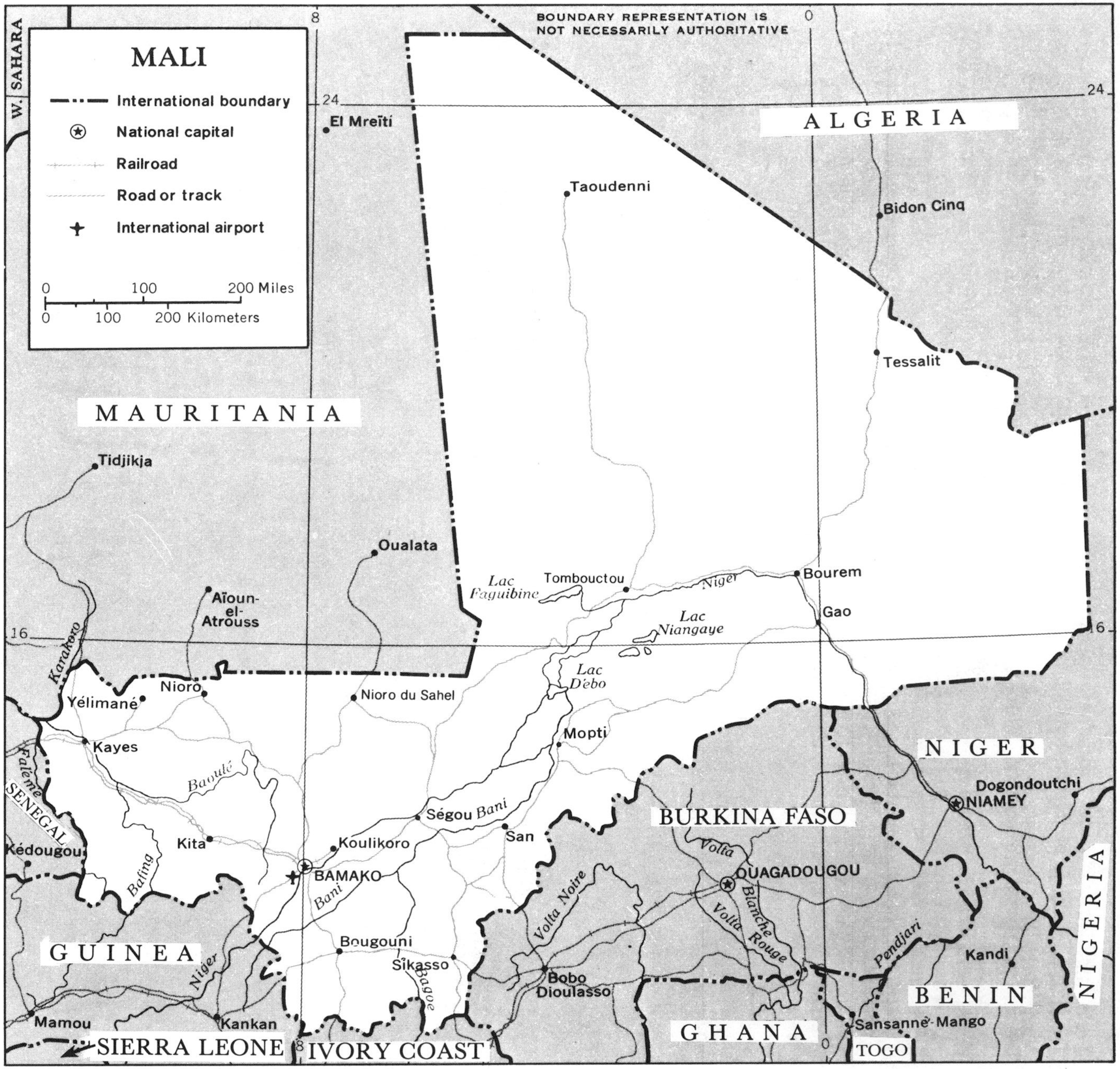
MALI
International boundary
National capital
Railroad
Road or track
International airport
0 100 200 Miles
0 100 200 Kilometers
BOUNDARY REPRESENTATION IS NOT NECESSARILY AUTHORITATIVE
W. SAHARA
ALGERIA
MAURITANIA
NIGER
BURKINA FASO
NIGERIA
BENIN
TOGO
GHANA
IVORY COAST
SIERRA LEONE
GUINEA
SENEGAL
El Mreïti
Taoudenni
Bidon Cinq
Tessalit
Tidjikja
Oualata
Aïoun-el-Atrouss
Lac Faguibine
Tombouctou
Niger
Bourem
Gao
Lac Niangaye
Lac Débo
Karakoro
Nioro
Yélimané
Nioro du Sahel
Kayes
Mopti
Falémé
Baoulé
Ségou
Bani
San
Kita
Koulikoro
Kédougou
Bafing
BAMAKO
Bougouni
Sikasso
Bagoe
Mamou
Kankan
Volta Noire
Bobo Dioulasso
OUAGADOUGOU
Volta Blanche
Volta Rouge
Pendjari
Sansanné-Mango
Kandi
Dogondoutchi
NIAMEY
24
16
8
0

MALI

BASIC FACT SHEET

OFFICIAL NAME: Republic of Mali (République du Mali)

ABBREVIATION: ML

CAPITAL: Bamako

HEAD OF STATE & HEAD OF GOVERNMENT: Lt. Col. Amadou Toumani Toure (from 1991)

NATURE OF GOVERNMENT: Military dictatorship

POPULATION: 8,142,373 (1990)

AREA: 1,204,021 sq. km. (464,874 sq. mi.)

ETHNIC MAJORITY: Bambara, Fulani, Marka, Songha, Malinke, Tuareg and Senufo

LANGUAGES: French (official) and Bambara (Bambara-ka) (lingua franca)

RELIGIONS: Islam, animism and Christianity

UNIT OF CURRENCY: Communauté Financière Africaine franc (C.F.A.F.)

NATIONAL FLAG: Tricolor of green, yellow and red vertical stripes

NATIONAL EMBLEM: A circular red badge in which a bird hovers above a mosquelike structure; golden bows with taut black strings and gold-tipped fixed arrows are poised outward, while a yellow sun illuminates the red background. Black letters on the green border carry the legend *République du Mali* on the top and the national motto. *Un Peuple, Un But, Une Foi* (One People, One Aim, One Faith), at the bottom

NATIONAL ANTHEM: "Praise to Soundiata"

NATIONAL HOLIDAYS: September 22 (National Day, Independence Day); January 1 (New Year's Day); May 1 (Labor Day); Christmas; also variable Islamic festivals

NATIONAL CALENDAR: Gregorian

PHYSICAL QUALITY OF LIFE INDEX: 27

DATE OF INDEPENDENCE: September 22, 1960

DATE OF CONSTITUTION: June 2, 1974 (became effective only in 1979); suspended March 26, 1991

WEIGHTS & MEASURES Metric

GEOGRAPHICAL FEATURES

Mali, a landlocked country located in West Africa, has an area of 1,204,021 sq. km. (464,874 sq. mi.), extending 1,852 km. (1,151 mi.) east-southeast to west-southwest and 1,258 km. (782 mi.) north-northwest to south-southeast.

Mali shares its international border of 7,501 km. (4,661 mi.) with seven neighbors: Algeria (1,376 km.; 855 mi.); Niger (821 km.; 510 mi.); Burkina Faso (1,202 km.; 747 mi.); Ivory Coast (515 km.; 320 mi.); Guinea (932 km.; 579 mi.): Senegal (418 km.; 260 mi.); and Mauritania (2,237 km.; 1,390 mi.). All these countries were formerly part of the French territories in Africa, and their current borders were internal French administrative divisions. There are no current border disputes, except with Burkina Faso over a 160-km. (100-mi.) stretch in the Agachar region.

The capital is Bamako, with a 1977 population of 440,000. Other important towns are Mopti (53,585), Kayes (44,736), Ségou (64,890), Sikasso (47,030), Gao (15,400), San (14,900) and the legendary town of Timbuktu (also spelled Tombouctou) (9,000).

Mali is generally flat, except in the South and the East. In the South the Futa Djallon Highlands and the Manding Mountains provide a barrier separating Mali from Guinea. The eastern region contains two spectacular mountain ranges: the Bandiagara Plateau and the Hombori Mountains, the highest point of which is the Hand of Fatima and Hombori Tondo (1,149 m.; 3,772 ft.). The Adrar des Iforas is an eroded sandstone plateau in northeastern Mali that forms part of the Ahaggar Mountains system. The central part of Mali is filled by the floodplains of the Niger Delta, covering a surface area of some 103,599 sq. km. (40,000 sq. mi.). Northern Mali lies within the Sahara. In the extreme north are vast plains known as the Tanezrouft and Taoudenni, covered in many areas by shifting sand dunes known as ergs.

Mali is traversed by the Senegal and the Niger (known in Mali as the Djoliba) rivers and their tributaries. The Senegal is formed at the small town of Bafoulabe through the confluence of the Bafing and Bakoye rivers. The Niger traverses Mali for 1,625 km. (1,010 mi.), nearly one-third of its total length. Beyond the town of Ségou the Niger forms a vast inland delta and then receives its main tributary, the Bani, at Mopti. Beyond Mopti it breaks up into two channels, the Bara Issa and the Issa Ber, which spread out to form a number of shallow seasonal lakes—Debo, Fati, Teli, Korientze, Tanda, Niangaye, Do, Garou, Aougoundou and others. Just above Dire the two main branches join again, changing to an eastern direction beyond Kabara and making the great bend toward the southeast at Bourem.

The Niger is navigable in Mali for large craft from Koulikoro and Garo during the high-water period (August to January).

CLIMATE & WEATHER

Mali has three climatic zones: Sudanic, Sahelian and Saharan. In general, the year is divided into three main seasons: a rainy season from June to October; a cool, dry season from November to February; and a hot, dry season from March to May. The average temperature in the Sahelian region is 30°C (86°F), but in the summer temperatures over 40°C (104°F) are common. The Saharan Zone, which comprises 40% of the national territory, receives little or no rain. The Sahelian Zone receives 20 to 40 cm. (8 to 16 in.) and the Sudanese Zone 70 to 100 cm. (28 to 39 in.) annually. Rains rarely last for more than a few hours in all regions.

From November through January, the alize blows cool air from the northeast. In February the dreaded harmattan begins to blow hot, scorching wind from the Sahara, causing temperatures to rise to 60°C (140°F).

POPULATION

The population of Mali was estimated in 1990 at 8,142,373 on the basis of the last official census, in 1987. The population is expected to reach 9.8 million by 2000. The annual growth rate is 3%.

The bulk of the population is concentrated in the South. The eight northern *cercles* and the *cercles* of Nara, Niono, Bafoulable and Kita have a density of less than the national average of 6.3 per sq. km. (16.2 per sq. mi.). The most densely populated region is the Dire *cercle*, with a density of over 25 per sq. km. (65 per sq. mi.).

By types of human settlements, 19% are urban and 81% are rural. The balance of the population is nomadic. There are eight towns with populations over 9,000. These towns account for 41% of the urban population, with Bamako itself accounting for 24%. Annual urban growth during 1985–90 was 4.2%.

Traditionally, all nomadic groups, such as the Fulani, Tuareg, Maure and others, move freely across national borders into neighboring countries. Almost all of these migrate only seasonally and return to their homes. The only permanent group of expatriate Malians lives in France, where they number over 25,000.

Women are free to participate in the Malian political process, and, while underrepresented, are present at all levels of government and the ruling UDPM, especially at the local level. A limited number of women occupy positions of responsibility in most ministries. In 1985 the first woman cabinet director was appointed, in the Ministry of Health. The Union of Malian Women is an active political organization under party auspices and a channel through which women can voice their concerns. The role of women is negatively affected in Mali more by social, cultural and general poverty factors than by political or economic determinants. Custom often restricts women to "women's issues" when they do participate in politics. The Union of Malian Women promotes health and education issues and has disseminated information on the disadvantages of female circumcision, but the practice still is widely followed, without government sanction, throughout Mali.

Mali was the first French-speaking country in Africa to adopt an official family planning program. Family planning activities are coordinated by the National Family and Public Health Service

DEMOGRAPHIC INDICATORS

Population (millions): 8.14 (1990)
Year of last census: 1987
Sex distribution (% at last census): males, 48.9; females, 51.1
Population estimates and projections (millions)

1930: 2.815	1960: 4.224	1990: 8.152
1940: 3.388	1970: 5.690	2000: 9.753
1950: 3.426	1980: 6.814	

Age profile (%, 1976 census)

0–14: 44.0	30–44: 16.1	60–74: 4.8
15–29: 24.9	45–59: 8.7	75 and over: 1.5

Median age (yrs.): 16.8 (1985)
Youth population (% aged 15–24): (1985) 18.9; (2000) 19.2
Total dependency ratio, 1985: 96.0
Annual growth rate (%)

1950–55: 1.72	1975–80: 2.19	2000–2005: 3.00
1955–60: 1.99	1980–85: 2.81	2005–10: 2.89
1960–65: 1.93	1985–90: 2.94	2010–15: 2.69
1965–70: 2.15	1990–95: 3.00	2015–20: 2.35
1970–75: 2.03	1995–2000: 3.03	2020–25: 1.99

Hypothetical size of stationary population (millions): 63
Assumed year of reaching net reproduction rate of 1: 2050
Urban population (000): 1453 (1985)
Urban population (%), 1988: 19; 1965: 13
Annual urban population growth rate (%, 1985–90): 4.20
Annual rural population growth rate (%, 1985–90): 2.65
Percentage of urban population in largest city: 24 (1980)
Number of cities of population over 500,000: 0 (1980)
Population density per sq. km. (per sq. mi.): 6.6 (17.0) (latest)

VITAL STATISTICS

Crude birth rate (/1,000): 51 (1990); 50 (1965)
Crude death rate (/1,000): 21 (1990); 27 (1965)
Infant mortality rate (/1,000 live births): 116 (1990)
Life expectancy (yrs.) at birth (1980–85): males, 45; females, 47 (1990)
Gross reproduction rate (/woman) (1980–85): 3.30
Total fertility rate (/woman): 7.1 (1990)
Rate of natural increase (/1,000): 29.0 (1989)
Marriage rate (/1,000): 2.8 (1989)
Average household size: 5.6 (latest)

STATUS OF WOMEN INDICATORS

Number of women (000): 4,061 (1985)
% women of childbearing age 15–49): 45 (1988)
% married women using contraception: 5 (1986)
% women literate: 1.8 (1986)
% women in labor force: 16.4 (1988)
Total fertility rate (/woman): 7.1 (1990)
% women in national legislature: 1 (1984)

ETHNIC COMPOSITION

Mali is ethnically a mosaic of tribes, each with its own language, dominant territory, occupation and social organization.

The vast majority of these tribes are Negroid. The Tuareg, however, are classified as Caucasoid and probably are of Berber origin. The Fulani are of mixed origin. The Fulani also are physically distinct from their neighbors, being thin, tall and light-skinned, with some Caucasian facial features. The Tuareg, Fulani and Maure are primarily shepherds; the Bozo and Somono are fishermen; the Sarakole and Dioula are merchants; the others are agriculturists. Because of inhospitable climatic conditions, Mali never had a large Western community, even as a French territory. The number of Frenchmen in the country is estimated at 4,000.

MAJOR TRIBES OF MALI

Tribe	Number	Geographic Area
Bambara Bamana	1,000,000	Central Mali from Nara to Ivory Coast
Bobo	100,000	Cercles of San and Tominian
Bozo	20,000	Middle Niger Valley
Diawara	80,000	*Cercles* of Nara and Nioro
Dioula	60,000	Southern Mali
Dogon (Habe, Cadau)	130,000	Bandiagara Plateau; *Cercles* of Koro, Bankass, Bandiagara and Douentza
Fulani (Peul, Fulbe, Fula)	450,000	Niger Delta and Mopti
Khassonke	80,000	*Cercles* of Kayes, Bafoulabe and Kita
Malinke (Maninka, nMandenka)	200,000	Western Mali
Marka	280,000	Ségou
Maure	60,000	*Cercles* of Nioro, Goundam, Timbuktu, Bourem, Gao, Ansongo and Menaka
Minianka	430,000	*Cercles* of Koutiala and Yorasso
Sarakole	420,000	Northwestern Mali; *cercles* of Kayes, Yelimané, Nioro and Nara
Senufo Siena	375,000	Southeastern Mali
Somono	20,000	Niger Valley
Songhai	230,000	Eastern Mali along the Niger
Tuareg	240,000	Northeastern Mali
Tukulor	10,000	Futa Tora
Wassalunke	12,000	*Cercles* of Yanfolila and Bougouni

LANGUAGES

The official language is French, but it is doubtful if more than 1% of the population can speak or write it. Bambara (properly Bambara-ka) qualifies as the lingua franca and, since a large proportion of the educated administrators belong to the Bambara tribe, it tends to replace French as the language of administration in certain situations. In the inland delta, Fulfulde, the vernacular of the Fulani, competes with Bambara as the lingua franca, while in eastern and northeastern Mali, Songhai is widely spoken. Most of these languages belong to the Niger-Congo group.

RELIGIONS

Islam, introduced in the 11th century, is the predominant religion of the land, claiming 65% of the population as adherents. Islam is the religion of the Sarakole, Maure, Tuareg, Songhai, Dioula and Tukulor tribes. The Bozo, Fulani and Somono are only partially Islamized. Animism still is strong in the South and the West among the Bambara, Malinke, Bobo and Senufo. Most Muslims belong to the Malekite School of the Sunni sect. Of the many brotherhoods found in West Africa, both Tijaniya and Qadiriya are represented in Mali. More recently, the Wahhabis, a fundamentalist group originating in Saudi Arabia, have gained many adherents. Djenne and Timbuktu are noted centers of Islamic learning.

Animists constitute about 30% of the population, but their numbers are being eroded by vigorous Islamic missionary activity, supported by petrodollars from Libya and Saudi Arabia.

Christians number approximately 50,000, of whom some 10% are Catholics. The first Catholic missions were established in the late 19th century by the White Fathers, and by 1895 Catholicism had penetrated the stronghold of Islam in Timbuktu. Among the tribes the Bobo are the most Christianized. The Catholic Church is organized in five dioceses—Kayes, Mopti, San, Ségou and Sikasso—and one archdiocese, at Bamako. The majority of the Protestant missionaries are from the United States.

HISTORICAL BACKGROUND

The French began the conquest of the territory now known as Mali in 1881; Col. Gustave Borgnis Debordes opened the campaign by seizing Kita and building a fort at Bamako. Later, Marabout Ahmadou and Al Mami Samory Toure, the leaders of the Muslim resistance, were compelled to accept a French protectorate; when they resisted further encroachments, Col. Louis Archinard led a military expedition from 1888 to 1893 that captured Ségou, put Ahmadou to flight and forced Toure to withdraw to the northern Ivory Coast. With the capture of Timbuktu in 1893 and Sikasso in 1899, the conquest of Mali was complete.

Mali remained part of French West Africa until 1958, when it became a part of the Soudan Federation (not to be confused with Sudan in East Africa, although both names are derived from the Arabic term *bilad es sudan*, the land of the black people), which also included Senegal, Dahomey (now Benin) and Upper Volta (now Burkina Faso). Dahomey and Upper Volta withdrew from the Soudan Federation in 1959, and the surviving union between Senegal and Mali, known as the Mali Federation, expired in 1960, when Senegal withdrew.

Unlike Senegal, Mali was not subjected to systematic Gallicization, and French influences on the administration, economy and education are slight. The major French legacy is the French language. Current relations with France are good, although Mali is no longer a member of the French Community.

At independence, Mali's government was headed by President Modibo Keita, leader of the Soudanese Union Party, which had won all seats in the 1959 legislative elections. Keita, a Marxist, gradually moved the country to a one-party socialist dictatorship, with all opposition banned. He nationalized major enterprises and attempted to free Mali of French economic domination by moving it out of the franc zone. His attempts at pursuing a socialist development policy failed as a result of rising inflation, poor government management and increased taxes. In 1968 Keita was overthrown in a bloodless coup organized by a group of junior officers who set up the Military Committee for National Liberation (Comité Militaire pour la Libération Nationale, CMLN), which installed Moussa Traore as president and Yoro Diakite as head of government.

The military regime abrogated the Constitution, banned political parties and reversed the economic collectivization of the previous regime. It pledged a quick return of political and civil rights, but instability within the regime led to further centralization of the military command. In 1969 a total of 20 officers were arrested in an attempted coup; Diakite was removed as prime minister, and Traore assumed the post. In 1972 Diakite was tried and convicted of plotting to overthrow the government the previous year. He died in prison in 1973.

To placate growing opposition to military rule, in 1974 the government submitted a Constitution providing for return to civilian rule by 1979. The document was approved by a vote of 99%. During the period of transition, Traore announced the formation of the Mali People's Democratic Union (UDPM) as the country's single party. This further exacerbated opposition to the regime by students and politicians barred from political activity. Army resistance to civilian rule led to an attempted coup in 1978.

Civilian rule was formally restored in 1979, with the UDPM as the country's sole political party. Traore was elected, unopposed, to a five-year term as president. The presidential term was increased to six years in 1982. Running without opposition, Traore won reflection in 1985, the same year as pro forma legislative balloting. The office of prime minisiter was re-created in 1986, with Mamadou Dembele assuming the post. Traore abolished the position two years later without any explanation.

Bending to prevailing political winds, Traore agreed in 1990 to allow opposition leaders to speak freely and gave permission for four new independent journals to be published. However, two months later a journalist was arrested for distributing antigovernment literature. Soon after, 175 prominent Malians published an open letter demanding multiparty democracy. In 1991, prodemocracy supporters protested from March 22–25, calling for Traore's resignation. Government troops opened fire on the crowds, killing as many as 150 citizens.

The protests culminated in a coup on March 26, when soldiers overthrew Traore and his government, promising to replace it with a multiparty democracy. The coup leaders formed the National Reconciliation Council, headed by Lt. Col. Amadou Toumani Toure, and dissolved the UDPM. Toure announced plans to establish "social justice and total democracy" for Mali "when the conditions are right."

CONSTITUTION & GOVERNMENT

The Military Committee for National Liberation (Comité Militaire pour la Libération Nationale, CMLN) which took power in 1968, abrogated the Constitution of 1960 and replaced it with a Fundamental Law, under which the Military Committee and the Supreme Court ruled by decree. A new Constitution, drafted in 1974 and approved by referendum, took effect in 1979. Under the provisions of this Constitution, Mali is to be a single-party state, with the newly formed Union Démocratique du Peuple Malien (UDPM) as the sole legal party. The president is both head of government and head of state. Under amendments in 1982 and 1985,

GOVERNMENT LIST
(July/August 1991)

Chief of State	Toure, Amadou Toumani
Prime Minister	Sako, Soumana
Minister of Communication & Culture & Spokesperson for the Government	Traore, Ousmane
Minister of Defense & Internal Security	Doumbia, Tiecoura, *Lt. Col.*
Minister of Economy & Finance	Toure, Bassary
Minister of Education	N'Diaye, Issa
Minister of Foreign Affairs	Sidibe, Souleymane Yacouba, *Col.*
Minister of Industry & Mines	Bamba, Kadary
Minister of Justice & Keeper of the Seals	Ouattara, Mamadou
Minister of Planning & International Cooperation	Mariko, Bakary
Minister of Public Employment	Diawarra, Damba
Minister of Public Health, Social Action & the Promotion of Women	Oldlbe, Sy Oumou Louise
Minister of Rural Development & Environment	Ba, Sy Maimouna
Minister of Territorial Administration	
Minister of Transport & Public Works	Diarra, Cheick Oumar, *Col.*
Ministerial Delegate Attached to the Prime Minister's Office	Diall, Amadou Mody
Ministerial Delegate Attached to the Prime Minister's Office	Keita, Salif
Ministerial Delegate Attached to the Minister of Economy & Finance in Charge of Budget	Kassogue, Mamadou
Ministerial Delegate Attached to the Minister of Economy & Finance in Charge of Tourism & Artisans	Fall, Mohamed
Ministerial Delegate of Foreign Affairs in Charge of Malians Overseas	Drame, Tiebile
Ministerial Delegate of Interior Security	Coulibaly, Bakary, *Lt. Col.*
Ministerial Delegate in Charge of Sports & Youth	Fany, Mamadou
State Controller General with the Rank & Perogatives of Minister	Maiga, Ousmane Issoufi
Manager, Central Bank	Toure, Younoussi

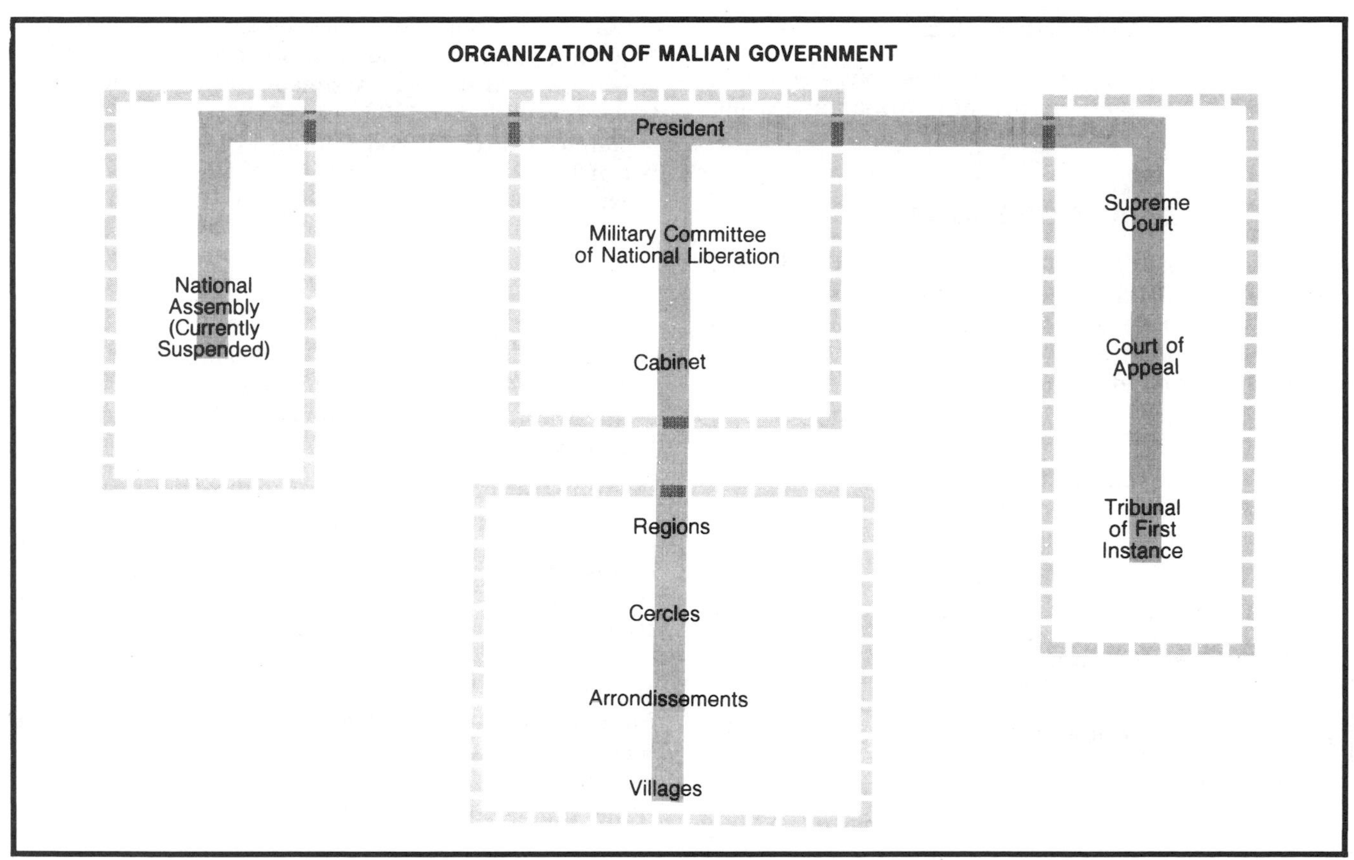

RULERS OF MALI

September 1960–November 1968: Modibo Keita
November 1968–March 1991: Moussa Traore
March 1991– : Amadou Toumani Toure

the president is elected by universal suffrage for an unlimited number of six-year terms.

The unicameral National Assembly, consisting of 82 members, is elected for three-year terms from a list of candidates drawn up by the UDPM.

The judiciary is headed by a Supreme Court and includes the Court of Appeal, magistrates courts and labor courts.

Following the 1979 elections the CMLN was dissolved and Moussa Traore was elected president for a five-year term. The first elections under the new Constitution were held in 1979.

Following the coup of March 26, 1991, the 1979 Constitution was suspended and the UDPM dissolved. The coup leaders, led by Lt. Col. Amadou Toumani Toure, formed the National Reconciliation Council (NRC). Upon taking power, the NRC promised to lead the country to multiparty democracy.

FREEDOM & HUMAN RIGHTS

In terms of political and civil rights, Mali is classified as a not-free country, with the maximum negative rating of 7 in political rights and 6 in civil rights (on a descending scale in which 1 is the highest and 7 the lowest in rights).

If 1979 was a year of considerable promise in the progress toward liberalization, 1980 saw a decline and even a reversal in efforts to broaden popular participation in government and politics. Disorder and student demonstrations supported by teachers stimulated the government to become increasingly repressive. One student leader was reported to have died in detention, and others were reported to have been subjected to cruel, inhuman and degrading treatment. The government, concerned about its own security, tended to overreact and characterize all forms of dissent as treason. Pretrial and trial proceedings conformed, for the most part, to French precedents, with pretrial proceedings lasting up to a month and even more.

Freedom of expression and of the press did not exist, as the state controlled all media. Private publications expressing divergent views on government policy always risked official displeasure. Missionaries reported that freedom of religion was more widespread under Traore than at any time in Malian history. The labor movement, on the other hand, was very weak and subject to close official monitoring.

Although Traore government avoided use of ethnic "quotas," in practice virtually all ethnic groups were represented at the highest state and party level. In local government, officials were assigned outside their native regions. Although some nomadic groups remained outside the economic and political mainstream, Mali was relatively free of ethnic tension.

CIVIL SERVICE

The number of civil servants in Mali has been estimated at 50,000. No other current information is available.

LOCAL GOVERNMENT

For purposes of regional government, Mali is divided into six regions and 42 *cercles* (counties).

There is no representative institution at the local level, and all units are administered by officials appointed by the national government.

STRUCTURE OF REGIONAL GOVERNMENT

Region	Arrondisements	Cercles	Villages
Kayes	Kayes, Bafoulabe, Kenieba, Kita, Nioro, Yelimané	51	1,917
Bamako	Bamako, Banamba, Dioila, Kangaba, Kolokani, Koulikoro, Nara	40	1,971
Ségou	Ségou, San, Macina, Niona, Tominian	37	1,869
Sikasso	Sikasso, Bougouni, Kadiolo, Kolondieba, Koutiala, Yanfolila, Yorosso	49	1,907
Mopti	Motpi, Bandiagara, Bankass, Djenne, Douentza, Koro, Niafunké, Tenenkou	62	2,260
Gao	Gao, Ansongo, Bourem, Dire, Goundam, Kidal, Gourma-Rharous, Timbuktu	47	766

FOREIGN POLICY

The 1968 revolution had its greatest impact in the field of foreign relations by transforming the country from a socialist, pro-Moscow enclave in West Africa into a less ideologically oriented country. Relations with the West, particularly the United States, have been reasonably correct, if not cordial. Mali also has emerged as a strong advocate of regional economic cooperation, a far cry from the early 1960s when, following the demise of the Mali Federation, it tended to isolate itself from its West African neighbors. Along with Senegal and Mauritania, it is a member of the Organization for the Development of the Senegal River Valley (Organization Pour la Mise en Valeur du Fleuve Sénégal, OMVS). Mali takes an active part in the Liptako-Gourma Authority, the Niger River Commission, the Permanent Interstate Committee for drought control in the Sahel, the West African Economic Community and the Economic Community of West African States. Links with the European Community are maintained through the Lomé Convention.

Mali had a continuing dispute with Burkina Faso during the 1970s and 1980s over ownership of the Agacher Strip, a border section 161 km. (100 mi.) long between the two countries. The dispute led to military action in 1985 but was settled by the World Court the following year, with the territory equally divided between the two nations. A similar dispute with Mauritania was settled in 1988.

Mali joined the United Nations in 1960. It is a member of 14 U.N. organizations and 16 other international organizations.

PARLIAMENT

Under the Constitution of 1979, the National Assembly was an 82-member unicameral body elected for a three-year term. All members belonged to the only legal political party at the time, the Union Démocratique du Peuple Malien.

POLITICAL PARTIES

Before the coup of March 1991, the Mali People's Democratic Union (Union Démocratique du Peuple Malien, UDPM), formally constituted in 1979, was the country's sole legal political party. It was governed by an 18-member Bureau Exécutif Central (BEC) selected from a 100-member National Council. The Council served as the party's executive body between Congress meetings.

The coup leaders have promised to return the country to a multiparty democracy.

ECONOMY

Mali is one of the poorest nations of the world, with about 80% of its land area desert or semidesert and few natural resources. The former Keita government's socialist policies, inefficiencies in nationalized industries and service, and recurring droughts contributed to economic decline throughout the 1980s. Real per capita GNP growth was zero between 1980 and 1987 and −2.5% between 1986 and 1988, but by 1987–89, that growth indicator had moved to a positive 1.3. As a result of its economic problems, Mali was forced to rely heavily on aid, and debt service is heavy.

The economy is primarily agricultural, engaging approximately 80% of the labor force and in 1989 contributing 50% of the GDP. Drought and locust infestation caused a decline in crop and livestock production during the 1980s. Between 40% and 80% of all livestock were destroyed by the drought of 1983–85, and a significant proportion of the nomadic herdsmen settled in towns. The country's chronic food shortages became more severe and were aggravated by crop smuggling to more lucrative markets in neighboring countries. Cotton, the country's chief cash crop, made a dramatic recovery from drought in 1986, but a decline in world cotton prices resulted in a reduction in government revenues from this product.

Mali's few resources are undeveloped. Salt, marble, phosphates, uranium and gold are mined in small quantities. Industry is a minor sector of the economy. Manufacturing is mainly based on processing farm commodities.

PRINCIPAL ECONOMIC INDICATORS

Gross National Product (U.S. $ billions): 2.109 (1989)
GNP per capita (U.S. $): 260 (1989)
GNP average annual growth rate (%, 1980–88): 3.5
GNP per capita average annual growth rate (%, 1987–89): 1.3
Average annual rate of inflation (%, 1980–88): 3.7
Consumer Price Index (1980 = 100) 1986
  Food: 147
Average annual growth rate, % (1980–88)
  General government consumption: 3.1
  Private consumption: 3.4
  Gross domestic investment: 2.8

BALANCE OF PAYMENTS, 1989 (U.S. $ millions)

Current account balance: −85.6
Merchandise exports: 274.3
Merchandise imports: −345.4
Trade balance: −71.2
Other goods, services & income +: 82.1
Other goods, services & income −: −363.9
Other goods, services & income net: −281.8
Private unrequited transfers: 36.0
Official unrequited transfers: 231.3
Capital other than reserves: 134
Net errors & omissions: −8.6
Counterpart items: 19.6
Total change in reserves: −98.6

GROSS DOMESTIC PRODUCT

GDP nominal (C.F.A.F. billions): 470.2 (1984)
GDP per capita (U.S. $): 220 (1988)
Average annual growth rate of GDP (%, 1980–88): 3.2
GDP by type of expenditure (%), 1986
  Consumption
    Private: 88
    Government: 11
  Gross domestic investment: 22
  Gross domestic saving: 0 (1987)
  Foreign trade
    Exports: 16
    Imports: −37
Cost components of GDP (%), 1984
  Net indirect taxes: 8
  Consumption of fixed capital: 7
  Compensation of employees: 25
  Net operating surplus: 60
Sectoral origin of GDP (%), 1986
  Primary
    Agriculture: 50 (1989)
    Mining: 2
  Secondary
    Manufacturing: 5
    Construction, public utilities: 5
  Tertiary
    Transportation & communications, trade, finance, other services, government: 28
Average annual sectoral growth rates (%, 1980–88)
  Agriculture: 0.3
  Industry: 8.1
  Services: 5.8

In an attempt to revitalize the economy, the Traore government in 1983 agreed to adopt a series of radical economic reforms in return for IMF aid. Private enterprises were encouraged, and unprofitable state-owned enterprises were closed. The state also gave up its monopoly on trade in essential commodities. It was hoped that the new emphasis on private enterprise would encourage foreign investment, but with few natural resources there has been little to interest investors.

Mali is heavily dependent on foreign aid, chiefly from France. In 1986 Mali signed an agreement with the Soviet Union to schedule almost one-third of its public external debt. On two occasions during the 1980s the IMF agreed to provide resources to back the Traore government's economic readjustment program. Mali was the first nation to benefit from a system of exceptional debt relief established by Western creditor nations in 1987.

Mali's long-term economic development is limited by its limited resources and its reliance on agricultural products that are impacted by climatic conditions.

PUBLIC FINANCE

The Malian fiscal year is the calendar year.

Mali's development plans emphasize stimulating agricultural production and increasing domestic savings. The government has established a fund to develop water resources, hydroelectric power and petroleum.

US aid commitments to Mali totalled $313 million during 1970–88. Other Western aid totalled $2.4 billion during 1970–87. OPEC gave $92 million in bilateral aid during 1979–89. Assistance from Communist countries totalled $190 million during 1970–88.

CENTRAL GOVERNMENT EXPENDITURES, 1988

% of total expenditures
  Defense: 8.4
  Education: 9.8
  Health: 2.6
  Housing, Social Security, welfare: 3.3
  Economic services: 18.4
  Other: 57.5
  Total expenditures as % of GNP: 28.2
  Overall surplus or deficit as % of GNP: −5.5

CENTRAL GOVERNMENT REVENUES, 1988

% of total current revenues
  Taxes on income, profit & capital gain: 8.1
  Social Security contributions: 4.5
  Domestic taxes on goods & services: 21.7
  Taxes on international trade & transactions: 27.5
  Other taxes: 29.2
  Current nontax revenue: 9.1
  Total current revenue as % of GNP: 16.0
General government consumption as % of GDP: 10 (1988)
Annual growth rate of general government consumption: 3.1% (1980–88)

FOREIGN AID, 1989

Total foreign aid (U.S. $ millions): 662.0
  Bilateral: 443.5
  Multilateral: 20.8

CURRENCY & BANKING

The Malian unit of currency is the CFA franc, divided into 100 centimes. Coins are issued in denominations of MF5, 10 and 25; notes are issued in denominations of MF50, 100, 1,000, 5,000 and 10,000.

The CFA franc, reintroduced in 1984, replaced the Mali franc at 2 Mali francs = 1 CFA franc. In June 1991 the dollar exchange rate was $1 = CFAF290.5.

In October 1983 the countries of West African Monetary Union (UMOA) finally decided to accept Mali as a full member. Mali's admission to the UMOA had been blocked since 1974 because of a veto by Upper Volta (now Burkina Faso), although Mali had been a *de facto* participant in the Franc Zone since 1967. Mali formally joined the UMOA in February 1984, and in August the Mali franc was replaced by the CFA franc (worth 2 Mali francs) as legal tender.

The banking system is headed by the Central Bank of Mali, with a paid-up capital of MF1 billion. Other state-owned banks include the Banque de Développement du Mali and the Banque Malienne de Crédit et de Dépôts. Two French banks also operate in the country.

FINANCIAL INDICATORS, 1989

Total reserves minus gold (SDR's millions): 88
SDRs (millions): 0.0
Reserve position in IMF (SDR's millions): 9
Foreign exchange (SDR's millions): 79
Gold (fine troy oz. millions): .02
Ratio of external debt to total reserves: 53.1 (1988)
Central bank 1987
- Assets %
  - Foreign assets: 25.2
  - Claims on government: 56.9
  - Claims on banks: 17.9
  - Claims on private sector: 0.0
- Liabilities %
  - Reserve money: 74.2
  - Government deposits: 0.0
  - Foreign liabilities: 13.9
  - Capital accounts: 0.0

Money supply 1989
Stock (C.F.A.F. billions): 110.4
M[1] per capita: 13,700
Private banks 1989
- Assets %
  - Loans to government: 1.6
  - Loans to private sector: 58.2
  - Reserves: 28.3
  - Foreign assets: 11.9
- Liabilities
  - Deposits (C.F.A.F. billions): 154.8
  - of which
    - Demand deposits: 30.9
    - Savings deposits: 20.4
    - Government deposits: 13.9
    - Foreign liabilities: 17.4

External debt 1987
- Total (U.S. $ millions): 2,067
  - of which public (U.S. $ millions): 1,928
  - of which private (U.S. $ millions): 0
- Debt service, (long-term) total (U.S. $ millions): 47 (1988)
  - Repayment
    - Principal (%): 68.1
    - Interest (%): 31.9
- Debt service rate (%): 14.2 (1986)
- External public debt as % of GNP: 100.8
- Debt service as % of GNP: 2.5
- Debt service as % of exports: 14.2
- Terms of public borrowing
  - Commitments (U.S. $ millions): 131
  - Average interest rate (%): 1.2
  - Average maturity (yrs.): 35
- Net flow of publicly guaranteed external capital (U.S. $ millions): 122
- Receipt of workers' remittances (U.S. $ millions): 49 (latest)
- Net direct private investment (U.S. $ millions): 1 (latest)

GROWTH PROFILE
(Annual Growth Rates, %)

Projected population, (1988–2000): 3.0
Projected crude birth rate, (/1000) (1990–95): 49.0
Projected crude death rate, (/1000) (1990–95): 19.0
Urban population, (1980–88): 3.5
Labor force, (1985–2000): 2.7
GNP, (1980–88): 3.5
GNP per capita, (1986–88): −2.5
GDP, (1980–88): 3.2
Inflation, (1980–88): 3.7
Agriculture, (1980–88): 0.3
Industry, (1980–88): 8.1
Services, (1980–88): 5.9
Money holdings, (1980–88): 12.3
Energy production, (1980–88): 9.3
Energy consumption, (1980–88): 2.9
Exports, (1980–88): 7.0
Imports, (1980–88): 3.7
General government consumption, (1980–88): 3.1
Private consumption, (1980–88): 3.4
Gross domestic investment, (1980–88): 2.8

AGRICULTURE

Of the total land area of 120,402,100 ha. (297,513,580 ac.), only about 20% is suitable for agriculture. Agriculture employs about 80% of the economically active population, and in 1989 its share of the GDP was 50%. Prior to the droughts of the 1970s and 1980s Mali normally was self-sufficient in the production of its major food crops, which are millet, sorghum, corn and rice. Except for rice, which is grown in irrigated areas, all other cereals are produced in areas dependent on the seasonal rains. Cotton, the nation's chief cash crop, is grown in southern Mali, and there are about 100,000 ha. (247,000 ac.) under cultivation.

Cultivation is limited to the southern part of Mali. Millet and sorghum are cultivated mainly in Ségou, Bandiagara and Nioro; rice is cultivated in Mopti, Ségou and Niafunké; and peanuts are grown in the Sudanese Zone. Commercial agriculture has been advanced by the state-controlled Office du Niger, a giant irrigation program in the inland delta covering 80,940 ha. (200,000 ac.). The infrastructure includes dams, canals, ditches and dikes as well as warehouses, mills, factories and schools.

Most of the holdings are subsistence farms with an average size of 4 ha. (9.9 ac.). In tribal areas in southern Mali, the traditional African systems of tenure prevail. Under these systems, land is held in mortmain by the community and may be farmed only by members of

AGRICULTURAL INDICATORS

Agriculture's share of GDP (%): 50 (1989)
Average annual growth rate (%, 1980–88): 0.3
Value added in agriculture (U.S. $ millions): 952 (1988)
Cereal imports (000 metric tons): 109 (1988)
Index of Agricultural Production (1979–81 = 100): 123 (1986)
Index of Food Production (1979–81 = 100): 122 (1986)
Index of Food Production per Capita (1979–81 = 100): 97 (1986–88)
Number of tractors: 835 (1986)
Number of harvester-threshers: 47 (1986)
Total fertilizer consumption: 26.7 (000 metric tons) (1985–86)
Fertilizer consumption (g./ha., hundreds) 59 (1987–88)
Number of farms (000): 562 (1983)
Average size of holding, ha. (ac.): 4.0 (9.9)
Size class (%) (1983)
  Below 1 ha. (below 2.47 ac.): 20.1
  1–5 ha. (2.47–12.35 ac.): 54.1
  5–10 ha. (12.35–24.7 ac.): 17.4
  10–20 ha. (24.7–49.4 ac.):
  20–50 ha. (49.4–123.5 ac.): } 8.4
  50–200 ha. (123.5–494 ac.):
  Over 200 ha. (over 494 ac.): 0.0
Tenure (%) (1983)
  Owner-operated: 96.8
Land use (%)
  Permanent crops: 0.0
  Temporary crops: 100.0
  Fallow: 0.0
Yields: kg./ha. 1989
  Grains: 1,096
  Roots & tubers: 8,400
  Fruits (000 metric tons): 15
  Vegetables (000 metric tons): 247
  Milk, kg./animal: 200
Livestock (000): 1989
  Cattle: 4,880
  Horses: 62 (1986)
  Sheep: 5,650
  Pigs: 60
Forestry 1988
  Production of roundwood, 000 cu. m. 5,358
    of which industrial roundwood (%): 6.4
Fishing 1988
  Total catch (000 metric tons): 55.7
    of which marine (%): 0.0
    Value of exports (U.S. $ 000): 950

the tribe. Individual farmers have no right to sell or dispose of the land but may inherit it. Registration of titles is common only outside tribal lands. Agricultural techniques are among the most primitive in Africa.

In June 1983 Mali joined other cotton-producing developing countries to form the International Cotton Producers' Association. Mali's food shortages have been aggravated by the long-standing problem of crop smuggling across the country's borders to the more lucrative markets of Burkina Faso, Ivory Coast and Senegal.

Mali is one of the largest livestock producers in West Africa. Before the great drought of 1972, there were 6 million cattle and 14 million goats and sheep in the country, but the national herd was reduced by about 30% in that catastrophic year. Virtually all cattle are owned by the nomads. Cattle-herding is concentrated in the Sahel and the central Niger Delta. There is an extensive but illegal export trade in live animals because of higher prices for cattle in Ivory Coast and Ghana and for sheep and goats in Ivory Coast and Algeria. There are two modern slaughterhouses in the country.

Some 7% of the total land area is covered by forests. Of these, over 8 million ha. (19.7 million ac.) are game forests.

Fishing is intensively practiced throughout the Niger Valley, particularly in the delta region and in the series of lakes inside the bend of the river. Since 1960 the fishermen have been organized into cooperatives, and the pirogue fleet is being motorized. The main fishing centers are Ségou, Mopti and Gap.

MANUFACTURING

Manufacturing, which contributes 5% to the GDP, is largely directed toward meeting local demand for food and consumer products. There is virtually no heavy industry. The present structure of industry is characterized by the dominance of a few large public enterprises, mostly processing local raw materials for domestic and export markets, and by a smaller private sector consisting of a number of small and mainly foreign-owned firms in miscellaneous activities. The cotton textile industry is Mali's largest single employer in the industrial sector and an important contributor to foreign earnings. Almost all the major industrial plants have been built with foreign aid: For example, an oil mill was built with West German aid, two textile plants with Chinese aid and a cement works with Soviet aid.

MANUFACTURING INDICATORS, 1987

Share of GDP (%): 5 (latest)
Value added in manufacturing (U.S. $ millions): 100 (latest)
  Food and agriculture (%): 36 (1970)
  Textiles (%): 40 (1970)
  Machinery (%): 4 (1970)
  Chemicals (%): 5 (1970)
Earnings per employee in manufacturing 1986
  Growth rate (%, 1970–80): −8.4
Total earnings as % of value added: 46 (1970)

MINING

Commercial mining is in initial stages of development. Phosphates, salt and uranium are mined, as is gold, with the help of the Soviet Union. At the end of the 1980s Mali announced the establishment of an iron mining industry and the commercial exploitation of marble. Reserves of diamonds, bauxite, manganese, copper and tin have been identified but not exploited.

ENERGY

Mali is heavily dependent on foreign petroleum, which represented almost 20% of total imports in 1983. Mali's hydroelectric industry generated about 80% of its needs

ENERGY INDICATORS

Average annual energy production growth rate (%, 1980–88): 9.4
Energy consumption per capita (000 kg. oil equivalent): 21 (1988)
Energy imports as % of merchandise exports: 31 (1988)
Average annual growth rate of energy consumption (%, 1980–88): 2.9
Electricity 1988
- Installed capacity (000 kw.): 87
- Production (million kw.-hr.): 205
  - % fossil fuel: 20.5
  - % hydro: 79.5
  - % nuclear: 0.0
- Consumption per capita (kw.-hr.): 23

in 1988. It has been enhanced by the completion of a dam at Manantali in 1988.

LABOR

The labor force was estimated in 1982 at 3.9 million, but nearly 89% of the economically active population is outside the modern wage sector. Women constitute 47% of the labor force. About 80% of the labor force is employed in agriculture.

Wages and working conditions are governed by legislation. The legal workweek is 48 hours, and the average workweek is 44.6 hours. Workers are entitled to 18 days of paid annual leave. Minimum wages known as SMAG *(salaire minimum agricole garanti)* and SMIG *(salaire minimum interprofessional garanti)* are regulated by the government. SMAG governs wages of workers in the large agricultural projects and SMIG in other sectors.

In 1960 all the labor unions in the country joined to form the Union Nationale des Travailleurs de Mali (UNTM), which continues to be the sole voice of organized labor in Mali. For some time in the 1970s, the UNTM tried to move into politics against the military regime but was sharply chastised; since then it has remained nonpolitical.

The cost of living rose steadily during the 1970s and 1980s. One source estimated that it rose 150% in 1980 alone. Frequently salaries are not sufficient for living expenses, and smuggling and corruption are serious problems in many sectors of the economy.

FOREIGN COMMERCE

Mali's lack of development and its reliance on agricultural products affected by climatic conditions have resulted in a large trade imbalance. For more than a decade the cost of imports has greatly exceeded exports. The nation's primary exports are raw cotton and cotton products, livestock, peanuts, dried fish and skins. Its major imports are textiles, vehicles, petroleum products, machinery, sugar and cereals. The major import sources and export destinations are the franc zone and Western Europe.

Mali is a member of the West African Economic Community and the Economic Community of West African States.

FOREIGN TRADE INDICATORS, 1988

Exports (U.S. $ millions): 260
Imports (U.S. $ millions): 493
Balance of trade (U.S. $ millions): −233
Annual growth rate, 1980–88, exports (%): 7.0
Annual growth rate, 1980–88, imports (%): 3.7
International reserves in terms of months of imports: 0.7
Terms of trade (1980 = 100): 88
Import Price Index (1980 = 100): 91.1
Export Price Index (1980 = 100): 68.1

Direction of Trade (%), 1982

	Imports	Exports
European Community	43.8	29.4
United States	2.4	0.0
U.S.S.R. & East European economies	0.9	0.0
Japan	1.3	1.6

Composition of Trade (%), 1982

	Imports	Exports
Food and agricultural raw materials	21.3	97.2
Fuels and other energy	27.5	0.0
Mineral ores and concentrates	0.7	0.0
Manufactured goods	50.4	2.8
of which chemicals	9.2	0.0
of which machinery	18.4	0.0

TRANSPORTATION & COMMUNICATIONS

Mali has 646 km. (401 mi.) of track, linking with the rail system of Senegal, which provides Mali with its only rail outlet to the sea. Plans have been drawn up with Soviet help to link Mali with the Guinean rail system.

The Niger River is navigable from Koulikoro to Gao from August to January and from Mopti to Gao from August through February. The upper Niger is navigable from Bamako to Guinea from August through January. The Senegal is navigable from Kayes downstream to Saint-Louis from July to October. Most river transportation is handled by Compagnie Malienne de Navigation.

The road system comprises 18,000 km. (11,185 mi.) of classified roads, of which 8% are paved. The main roads run between Bamako and Bougouni and between Bamako and Ségou.

TRANSPORTATION INDICATORS

Roads (latest)
- Length, km. (mi.): 18,000 (11,185)
- Paved (%): 8

Motor vehicles (latest)
- Automobiles: 29,436
- Trucks and buses: 7,556
- Persons per vehicle: 207

Railroads (latest)
- Track, km. (mi.): 646 (401)
- Passenger-km. (passenger-mi.) (millions): 772.8 (480.1)
- Freight, ton-km. (ton-mi.) (millions): 429.3 (146.1)

Air (latest)
- Passenger-km. (passenger-mi.) (millions): 110 (68) (pre-1986)
- Freight-km. (freight-mi.) (millions): 0.6 (0.3)
- Mail-ton-km: N.A.
- Airports with scheduled flights: 1 (1990)

Inland waterways (latest)
- Length, km. (mi.): 1,815 (1,128)
- Cargo, ton-km. (ton-mi.): 27 (12)

COMMUNICATION INDICATORS, 1988

Telephones
  Total (000): 13
  Persons per telephone: 628
  Phone traffic (per 000 calls)
    Long distance: 90 (1982)
    International: 4,040 (minutes)
Post office
  Number of post offices: 152 (1987)
  Pieces of mail handled (000): 4,638 (1987)
Telecommunications 1990
  2 satellite ground stations

TOURISM & TRAVEL INDICATORS, 1986

Total tourist receipts (U.S. $ millions): 37 (1988)
Expenditures by nationals abroad (U.S. $ millions): 53 (1988)
Number of hotel beds: N.A.
Average length of stay: 3 nights
Tourist nights (000): 176

The national airline is Air Mali, with a fleet of one Boeing 727, one DC-3 and four light planes serving domestic routes, with weekly service to Paris. Air Mali is operated by the Soviet Union. The international airport at Bamako and the nearby Sénou airport have runways over 2,500 m. (8,000 ft.). In addition, there are 38 airfields, of which 31 are usable and eight have permanent-surface runways.

DEFENSE

Before the coup of March 1991, the defense structure was headed by the president. The line of command ran through the minister of defense.

Military manpower is provided by voluntary enlistment. The total strength of the armed forces was 4,950.

Army

Personnel: 4,600

Organization: 1 tank battalion; 3 infantry battalions; 1 artillery battalion; 1 engineer battalion; 1 parachute battalion; 1 special force battalion; 2 AA artillery companies; 1 SAM battery

Equipment: 21 heavy and 12 light tanks; 20 reconnaissance vehicles; 50 armored personnel carriers; 20 guns; 2 rocket launchers; 30 mortars; 12 air defense guns; 6 SAM

Navy

Personnel: 50

Units: 3 river patrol craft

Air Force

Personnel: 300

Organization: 5 combat aircraft; 5 MiG-17's; 2 transports; 2 helicopters; 1 trainer

Air bases: Bamako, Gao, Mopti, Kayes, Nioro, Timbuktu and Yelimané

The Malian armed forces have never been tested in battle, and much of the equipment obtained by former President Keita from the Soviet Union is now obsolete. Military deployment is designed primarily not for protection against neighbors but rather to ensure the survival of the regime in any potential conflict with internal enemies. The air force is not an independent unit but operates within the army command structure.

Between 1961 and 1971, Mali received $20 million from the Soviet Union in arms transfers and technical and training assistance. Between 1946 and 1983 the United States provided $3.6 million in military assistance. Arms purchases abroad from 1973 to 1983 totaled $185 million, of which $40 million was from the Soviet Union.

EDUCATION

Mali is a nation with a large number of linguistically diverse ethnic groups and a significant nomad population. These factors have made development of a uniform educational system difficult. Illiteracy is a major problem; only 10.1% of the population is literate. In an effort to solve the linguistic difficulties, the country adopted French as the language of instruction. It also is using funds from the World Bank to make schooling more accessible in remote rural areas.

Education is technically universal, free and compulsory for nine years, between ages six and 15.

Schooling lasts for 12 years, divided into three cycles: a lower primary cycle of six years, an upper

EDUCATION INDICATORS, 1983

Literacy
  Total (%): 10.1
  Males (%): 18.6
  Females (%): 1.8
First level
  Schools: 1,348
  Students: 292,395
  Teachers: 8,597
  Student/teacher ratio: 34.0
Second level and vocational
  Schools: 277
  Students: 50,596
  Teachers: 4,024
  Student/teacher ratio: 12.3
Third level
  Institutions: 7
  Students: 5,792
  Teachers: 499
  Student/teacher ratio: 11.6
  Gross enrollment ratio: 0.8
  Students (/100,000 pop.): 67
  % of population over 24 with post secondary education: 0.2
Foreign study
  Foreign students in national universities: 274 (1986)
  Students abroad: 1,804
    of whom in
      U.S.: 112 (1988)
      France: 576 (1988)
      Federal Republic of Germany: 84 (1988)
      U.K.: 12 (1987)
Public expenditures, 1987
  Total (C.F.A.F.): 18,693,000,000
  % of GNP: 3.3
  % of national budget: 17.3
  % of current expenditure: 97.8

GRADUATES, 1984

Total: 1,195
Education: 339
Law: 82
Social & behavioral sciences: 73
Commerce & business: 255
Medicine: 57
Engineering: 45
Transportation & communications: 135
Agriculture, forestry, fisheries: 209

primary cycle of three years (these two cycles comprising what is known as basic education) and a secondary cycle of three years.

The school year lasts from October to July.

Primary-school teachers are trained in secondary-level normal schools, and secondary-school teachers in a teachers' college.

There is no university per se, but higher education is provided in five advanced-level schools, including a teachers' college, an administration school, an engineering school, a medical school and an agricultural institute.

LEGAL SYSTEM

The legal system is based on French civil law and customary law. The judiciary is headed by the Supreme Court, with 19 judges sitting in two sections: the judicial section, comprising three civil chambers and one criminal chamber; and the administrative section, consisting of a single chamber. The members of the Supreme Court are nominated for five-year terms.

The Malian judicial system is based on the French model, so the principle of habeas corpus does not exist. Bail is not legally available, but sometimes prisoners are released on their own recognizance. Usually prisoners are allowed access to a lawyer of their choosing. Administrative backlogs often cause delays in bringing people to trial.

The judiciary is part of the executive branch and therefore potentially subject to interference. Generally trials are short in duration. Although confessions are not coerced, defendants usually admit guilt, and defense lawyers tend to argue mitigating circumstances. The verdict and the sentence are rendered by a panel of three judges. The appeals process is limited to presidential pardon or a call for a new trial. The National Assembly can convene the High Court of Justice to hear cases against state ministers. This court did not meet during 1985. Amnesty International indicates that at least nine political prisoners were reportedly held in Taoudenit Prison in 1984 for involvement in a coup plot.

A separate Special Court of State Security sits in Bamako. It is composed of two magistrates and eight army officers.

The Court of Appeal also sits in Bamako. There are two *tribunaux de première instance* as well as courts for labor disputes.

No information is available on the number of correctional facilities or the nature of the penal system.

LAW ENFORCEMENT

There are two national law enforcement agencies: the Gendarmerie of 1,500 and the Civil Police of 1,000. Both agencies are under the Ministry of Defense, Interior and Security. There is one policeman for every 2,400 inhabitants.

HEALTH

Public medical services include a network of several hundred medical centers and dispensaries supplemented by a mobile service. The principal health problems are malaria, enteritis, cholera, pneumonia and parasitical diseases. Only 17% of the population have access to safe drinking water.

HEALTH INDICATORS

Health personnel, 1983
- Physicians: 349
  - Persons per: 20,602
- Dentists: 1.5
- Nurses: 2,058
- Pharmacists: 58
- Midwives: 305

Hospitals, 1983
- Number: 162
- Number of beds (/10,000): 6
- Admissions/discharges (/10,000): 178 (1977)
- Bed occupany rate: 58.8 % (1977)
- Average length of stay (days): 7 (1977)

Type of hospitals (%), 1983
- Government: 100.0
- Private nonprofit: 0.0
- Private profit: 0.0

Public health expenditures, (latest)
- As % of national budget: 2.6
- Per capita (U.S. $): 1.80

Vital statistics
- Crude death rate (/1,000 pop.): 21 (1990)
- Life Expectancy at birth (1987)
  - Males: 45
  - Females: 47
- Infant mortality rate (/1,000 live births): 116 (1990)
- Child mortality rate (1985–90) under 5 yrs. (/1,000): 291

Population with access to safe water (%): 17 (latest)

FOOD & NUTRITION

The staple foods are millet, sorghum, rice and corn. Many regions suffer from the *soudure*, a near-famine that prevails just before the harvest when the stocks of food are exhausted.

MEDIA & CULTURE

There are only two daily newspapers in the country: *L'Essor*, the daily UDPM party paper with a circulation of 40,000; and *Bulletin Quotidien de la Chambre de Commerce et d'Industrie du Mali*, issued by the Chamber of Commerce. Nondailies include two weeklies and five monthlies.

MEDIA INDICATORS

Newspapers
  Number of dailies: 2 (latest)
  Number of nondailies: 7 (latest)
Book publishing
  Number of titles: 160 (pre-1986)
Radio
  Number of transmitters: 9 (latest)
  Number of persons per radio receiver: 53 (1989)
  Total program hours: c. 100 hr. per wk. (latest)
Television
  Television transmitter: 1 (latest)
  Number of persons per TV receiver: 791 (1989)
  Total program hours (hr./wk.): 2 (latest)
Film
  Production of long films: 1 (latest)

CULTURAL & ENVIRONMENTAL INDICATORS (latest)

Libraries (pre-1986)
  Number: 46
  Volumes (000): 552
Museums
  Annual attendance (000): over 90,000
Nature reserves
  Number of facilities: 6

There is no independent or opposition press. The national news agency is the Agence Malienne de Presse et de Publicité (AMPP). Foreign news agencies represented in Bamako include CTK, Novosti, Tass and AFP. Édition Imprimerie du Mali, the only book publisher in the country, has an annual output of about five titles.

Radiodiffusion Nationale du Mali broadcasts a home service with two medium-wave transmitters at Bamako and Mopti and six shortwave transmitters in French and eight vernaculars, for about 100 hours a week. Mali has two hours weekly of color television service.

The largest library is the National Library at Bamako, with 5,000 volumes.

SOCIAL WELFARE

Social welfare is traditionally a function of the tribe. Official programs are limited to benefits under the Labor Code. Retirement benefits are provided by the Mali Retirement Bureau. Certain classes of wage earners receive family allowances, maternity allowances and children's allowances.

The increase in urban population as a result of drought has exacerbated the problem of homelessness in many urban areas.

GLOSSARY

alize: cool wind blowing from the northeast from November through January.

barani: migrant, seasonal agricultural workers who travel to any region or country where work is available.

cercle: a territorial unit, a subdivision of a region.

chef lieu: the headquarters of a cercle.

harmattan: scorching wind blowing out of the Sahara from February through June.

CHRONOLOGY (from 1958)

1958— Following a referendum in which the new Constitution of the Fifth French Republic is approved by the voters, the French Sudan (also Soudan) becomes the République Soudanaise within the French community.

1959— Mali Federation is established, with Senegal and the République Soudanaise as members; Modibo Keita is elected president of the Federation.

1960— Mali Federation breaks up as Senegal withdraws; Republic of Mali is proclaimed in Bamako; new Constitution is promulgated.

1962— At the Sixth Congress of the Union Soudanaise, the government affirms its socialist ideology. . . . Malian franc is introduced as the national currency.

1963— The Tuareg begin a two-year revolt against the national government.

1966— Comité National de Défense de la Révolution is established.

1967— Malian franc is devalued by 50%. . . . President Keita launches a cultural revolution on the Chinese model; the Popular Militia is reactivated with Chinese advisers.

1968— National Assembly dissolves itself. . . . President Keita is overthrown by a military coup; Comité Militaire de Libération Nationale is formed with Lt. Gen. Moussa Traore as president; provisional government is formed with Capt. Yoro Diakite as president; Fundamental Law replaces the Constitution of 1960.

1969— Attempted coup by Capt. Dilby Silas Diarra is suppressed. . . . Traore replaces Diakite as president.

1972— Diakite and Diallo are expelled from the CMLN and sentenced to hard labor. . . . A three-year catastrophic drought affects the Sahel; 80,000 refugees are housed in 33 camps.

1974— New Constitution is approved by an overwhelming majority in a national referendum.

1975— Border dispute erupts between Mali and Burkina Faso, followed by border skirmishes.

1976— Union Démocratique de Peuple Malien (UDPM) is formed as the nation's sole legal political party according to the Constitution.

1978— In a major cabinet reshuffle, four civilians are dismissed from the cabinet; Foreign Minister Charles Cissokho and Defense Minister Kissima Doukara are accused of complicity in an antistate plot and expelled from the CMLN and the government.

1979— First national elections under the Constitution of 1974 are held; the CMLN is disbanded; President Traore is elected to a five-year term; the National Assembly is reconvened and more civilians are included in the cabinet.

1981— The Constitution is amended to limit the term of the National Assembly to three years.

1982— Elections are held for the National Assembly.

1983— Border dispute with Algeria is settled, while that with Burkina Faso is submitted to the International Court of Justice. . . . President Traore visits Guinea and issues joint declaration on eventual unification of the two countries.

1985— Presidential and legislative elections are held; President Traore is reelected with 98% of the vote.

1986— The post of prime minister is re-created. Burkina Faso and Mali accept World Court settlement of dispute over Agacher Strip.

1988— The post of prime minister is abolished.

1990— 175 prominent Malians publish an open letter demanding multiparty democracy.

1991— Traore is ousted after four days of violent protests; Lt. Col. Amadou Toumani Toure, the coup's leader, becomes head of the National Reconciliation Council and promises to establish multiparty democracy in Mali.

BIBLIOGRAPHY

BOOKS

Ernst, Klaus. *Tradition and Progress in the African Village: Noncapitalist Reform of Rural Communities in Mali.* New York, 1977.

Foltz, William J. *From French West Africa to the Mali Federation.* New Haven, Conn., 1967.

Hargreaves, John D. *West Africa: The Former French States.* Englewood Cliffs, N.J., 1967.

Imperato, Pascal J. *Historical Dictionary of Mali.* Metuchen, N.J., 1986.

——— and Eleanor M. Imperato. *Mali: A Handbook of Historical Statistics.* Boston, Mass., 1982.

Jones, William. *Planning and Economic Policy: Socialist Mali and Her Neighbors.* New York, 1976.

Mandot-Bernard J., and M. Labonne. *Satisfaction of Food Requirements in Mali to 2000.* Paris, 1982.

Megahed, Horeya T. *Socialism and Nation-Building in Africa: The Case of Mali.* New York, 1974.

Snyder, Frank Gregory. *One-Party Government in Mali.* New Haven, Conn., 1965.

Zolberg, Aristide R. *Creating Political Order: The Party-States of West Africa.* Chicago, 1966.

OFFICIAL PUBLICATIONS

Treasury. *Balance Générale des Comptes du Trésor* (Statement of Treasury Accounts) (quarterly).

———. *Certificats de Recettes et de Dépenses* (Certificates of Receipts and Payments) (monthly).

———. *États Comparatifs et Bordereaux Sommaires* (Comparative Statements and Summary Lists) (quarterly).

———. *Situation de l'Exécution du Budget* (Statement on Budget Execution) (annual).

MAURITANIA

BASIC FACT SHEET

OFFICIAL NAME: Islamic Republic of Mauritania (République Islamique de Mauritanie, Jumhouriyya Mouritaniyya al Islamiyya)

ABBREVIATION: MU

CAPITAL: Nouakchott

HEAD OF STATE & HEAD OF GOVERNMENT: President Col. Maaouya Ould Sid' Ahmed Taya (from 1984)

NATURE OF GOVERNMENT: Military dictatorship

POPULATION: 1,934,549 (1990)

AREA: 1,030,700 sq. km. (397,950 sq. mi.)

ETHNIC MAJORITY: Moors (Maures)

LANGUAGES: Arabic and French

RELIGION: Islam

UNIT OF CURRENCY: Ouguiya (UM)

NATIONAL FLAG: A yellow star over a yellow crescent on a light green field

NATIONAL EMBLEM: A circular badge bearing an Islamic star and crescent, stalks of millet and a date palm with "Islamic Republic of Mauritania" in Arabic and French on the border

NATIONAL ANTHEM: "Mauritania"

NATIONAL HOLIDAYS: November 28 (Independence Day, National Day); January 1 (New Year's Day); May 1 (Labor Day); May 25 (African Liberation Day); also variable Islamic festivals

NATIONAL CALENDARS: Islamic and Gregorian

PHYSICAL QUALITY OF LIFE INDEX: 33

DATE OF INDEPENDENCE: November 28, 1960

DATE OF CONSTITUTION: May 23, 1961 (Constitution suspended)

WEIGHTS & MEASURES: Metric

GEOGRAPHICAL FEATURES

Mauritania, in northwestern Africa, extends 1,515 km. (941 mi.) northeast to southwest and 1,314 km. (816 mi.) southeast to northwest. It has a total land area of 1,030,700 sq. km. (397,950 sq. mi.). Mauritania's Atlantic coastline stretches 666 km. (414 mi.).

Mauritania has a total international land border of 4,726 km. (2,937 mi.), shared with four countries: Algeria (463 km.; 288 mi.); Mali (2,237 km.; 1,390 mi.); Senegal (813 km.; 505 mi.); Morocco (1,213 km.; 754 mi.); and the disputed territory of the Western Sahara (occupied by Morocco) to the north. The only natural boundary is that with Senegal, which follows the Senegal River. The frontier with Mali was defined by the Treaty of Kayes in 1963. The border with Morocco in Western Sahara was demarcated by mutual agreement in 1976. There are no current active border disputes, but Mauritania recognizes the rights of the Polisario group to the Western Sahara territories occupied by Morocco.

The capital, Nouakchott, had a 1987 population of 600,000. The other principal towns are Nouadhibou (30,000), F'Derik (18,000), Kaedi (32,000), Rosso (13,000) and Atar (10,000).

The country is a vast flat plain divided in the middle by a series of plateaus with elevations of over 457 m. (1,500 ft.). To the east of these plateaus lies the El Djouf, or empty quarter, and to the west clayey plains, or *regs*, and sandy dunes, or *ergs*. Topographically the country is divided into four zones: the Saharan; the Sahelian; the Senegal River Valley, or Chemama; and the coastal. The Saharan zone comprised two-thirds of the country. The Sahelian zone consists of grasslands and steppes. The Chemama, or Senegal River Valley zone, is a narrow belt of land extending 15 to 30 km. (10 to 20 mi.) north of the Senegal River. The coastal zone extends the length of the Atlantic coast in a relatively unindented arc from Cape Blanc to the Senegal River.

The only permanent river is the Senegal River, which flows for 813 km. (515 mi.) out of its total length of 4,023 km. (2,500 mi.) as the border between Senegal and Mauritania. The river is navigable as far as Kayes in Mali during the rainy season and as far as Podor in Senegal in the dry season. From September to October the river is normally in flood, covering the entire valley.

CLIMATE & WEATHER

Mauritania has four climatic zones: The Chemama zone has the highest rainfall in the country, with up to 660 mm. (26 in.) a year, beginning in May and lasting until September. Temperatures are less hot than the rest of the country, with a maximum of 34.4°C (94°F) and a minimum of 23.3°C (74°F).

The Sahelian zone has one rainy season, from July to October, with a maximum of 460 mm. (18 in.). Temperature extremes are less severe than in the Sahara.

The coastal zone has a humid but temperate climate modified by trade winds from the Canary Islands. Rainfall is less than 25 mm. (1 in.) annually. Temperatures are moderate, ranging from maximum of 26°C (79°F) in January and 32°C (90°F) in October to minimum of 13°C (56°F) in January and 19°C (66°F) in July.

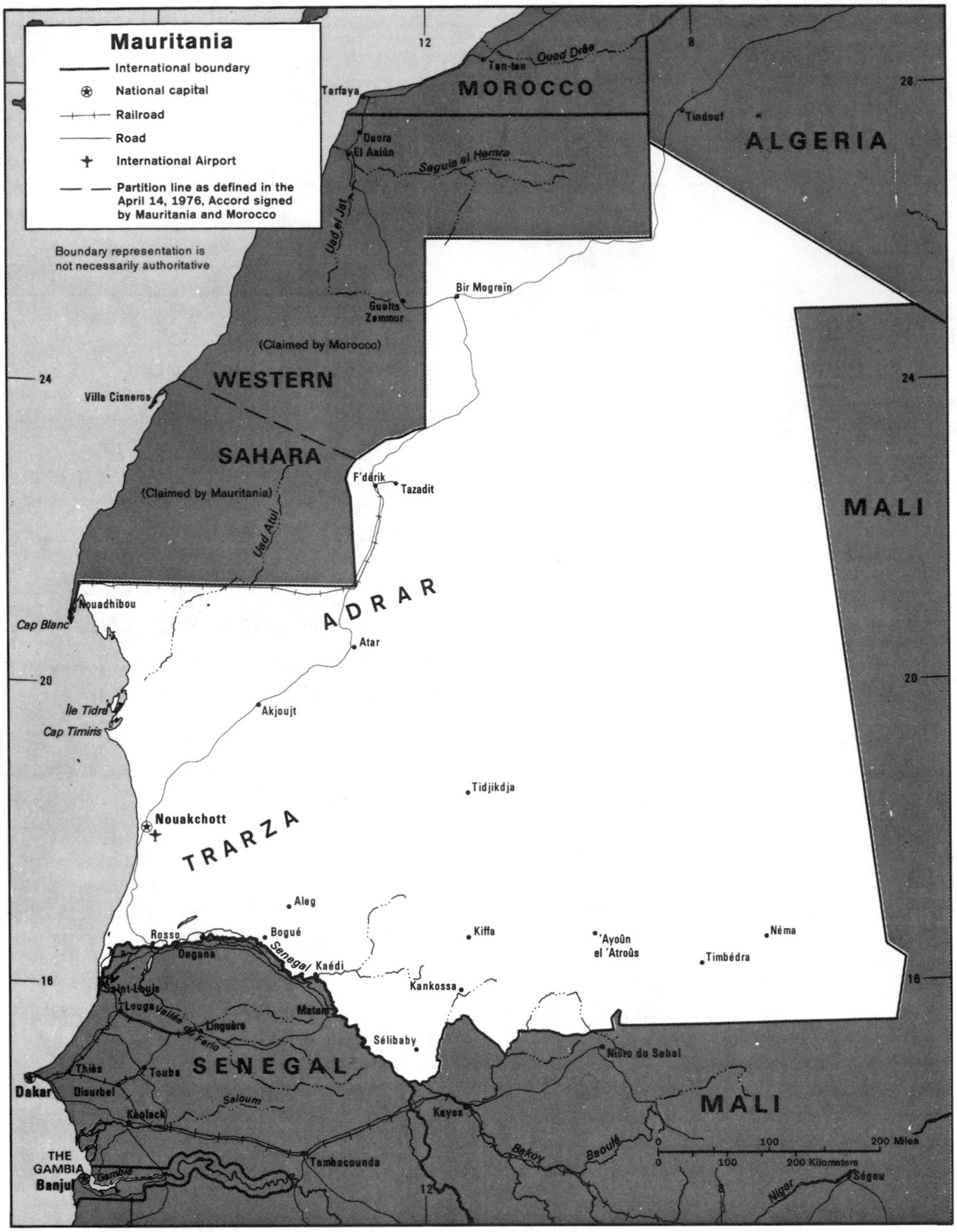
Mauritania
International boundary
National capital
Railroad
Road
International Airport
Partition line as defined in the April 14, 1976, Accord signed by Mauritania and Morocco
Boundary representation is not necessarily authoritative
MOROCCO
ALGERIA
WESTERN
SAHARA
(Claimed by Morocco)
(Claimed by Mauritania)
MALI
ADRAR
TRARZA
SENEGAL
THE GAMBIA
Oued Drâa
Tan-tan
Tarfaya
Tindouf
Daora
El Aaiún
Seguia el Hamra
Ued el Jat
Guelta Zemmur
Bir Mogreïn
Villa Cisneros
Ued Atui
F'dérik
Tazadit
Nouadhibou
Cap Blanc
Atar
Akjoujt
Île Tidra
Cap Timiris
Tidjikdja
Nouakchott
Aleg
Rosso
Bogué
Dagana
Senegal
Kaédi
Kiffa
'Ayoûn el 'Atroûs
Néma
Timbédra
Kankossa
Saint-Louis
Louga
Vallée du Ferlo
Linguère
Matam
Sélibaby
Nioro du Sahel
Thiès
Touba
Dakar
Diourbel
Saloum
Kaolack
Kayes
Bakoy
Baoulé
Banjul
Gambia
Tambacounda
Niger
Ségou
0 100 200 Miles
0 100 200 Kilometers
12
8
28
24
20
16

الجمهورية الإسلامية الموريتانية
RÉPUBLIQUE ISLAMIQUE DE MAURITANIE

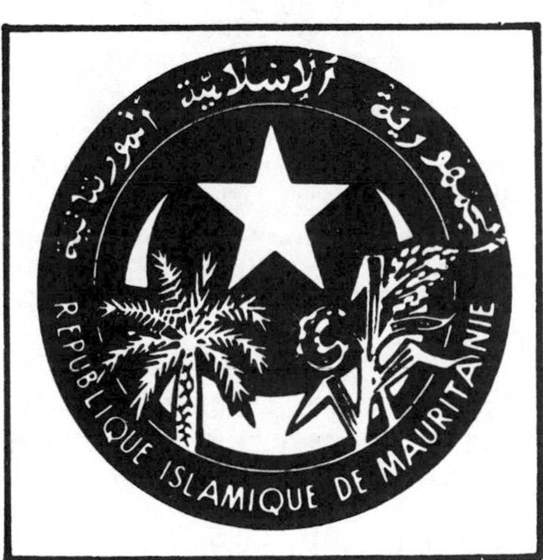

The Saharan zone receives 25 to 127 mm (1 to 5 in.) of rain annually during the rainy season, called *hivernage*, from July to September. Temperature extremes are more pronounced. Winter temperatures range from 0°C (32°F) at night to 37.8°C (100°F) at midday, while summer temperatures range from 15.6°C (60°F) at night to over 48.9°C (120°F) at midday. The hottest months are May, June and July.

The desert conditions of the country are intensified by hot, dry and blinding sandstorms known as *harmattan.*

POPULATION

The population of Mauritania in 1990 was 1,934,549, on the basis of the last census, in 1976–77, when the population was 1,419,939.

Over 90% of the population lives in the southern quarter of the country, and over 80% lives in the southern seventh of the country. Even along the Senegal River, the country's most densely populated area, the density never rises above 8 per sq. km. (22 per sq. mi.).

DEMOGRAPHIC INDICATORS

Population (millions): 1.934 (1990)
Year of last census: 1976–77
Sex distribution (% at last census): males, 50.1; females, 49.9
Population estimates and projections (millions)

1940: .666	1970: 1.245	2000: 2.673
1950: .781	1980: 1.548	2010: 3.616
1960: .970	1990: 1.999	

Age profile (% 1980 est.)

0–14: 45.7	30–44: 14.8	60–74: 4.0
15–29: 26.1	45–59: 8.7	75 and over: 0.6

Median age (yrs.): 17.9 (1985)
Youth population (% age 15–24): 18.6 (1985); 19.0 (2000)
Total dependency ratio: 89.6 (1985)
Annual growth rate (%)

1950–55: 1.76	1975–80: 2.46	2000–2005: 2.85
1955–50: 1.90	1980–85: 2.60	2005–2010: 2.71
1960–65: 2.02	1985–90: 2.73	2010–2015: 2.55
1965–70: 2.17	1990–1995: 2.80	2015–2020: 2.26
1970–75: 2.32	1995–2000: 2.85	2020–2025: 1.92

Hypothetical size of stationary population (millions): 13 (1988)
Assumed year of reaching net reproduction rate of 1: 2050 (1988)
Urban population (000): 612 (1985)
Urban population (%): 480 (1988); 10 (1965)
Annual urban population growth rate (%, 1985–90): 6.62 (est.)
Annual rural population growth rate (%, 1985–90): 0.32 (est.)
Percentage of urban population in largest city: 39 (1980)
Number of cities of population over 500,000: 0 (1980)
Population density per sq. km. (per sq. mi.): 1.9 (5.0) (latest)

VITAL STATISTICS

Crude birth rate (/1,000): 49 (1990); 47 (1965)
Crude death rate (/1,000): 18 (1990); 26 (1965)
Infant mortality rate (/1,000 live births): 96 (1990)
Maternal mortality rate (/100,000 live births): 119 (1980)
Life expectancy (yrs.) at birth: males, 44; females, 49 (1990)
Gross reproduction rate (/woman): 3.20
Total fertility rate (/woman): 7.3 (1990)
Rate of natural increase (/1,000): 27.2 (1985–90)
Average household size: 5.0 (latest)

STATUS OF WOMEN INDICATORS

Number of women (000): 955 (1985)
Women of childbearing age (15–49) (% of pop.): 45 (1988)
Married women of childbearing age (15–49) using contraception (%): 1 (1985)
Women's literacy rate (%): 17.0 (1987)
Women in labor force (%): 21.8 (1988)
Total fertility rate (/woman): 7.3 (1990)

Mauritania is one of the few Islamic countries where females have numerical parity with males.

Mauritania has one of the largest nomadic populations in the world. In the early 1970s, nomads made up 80% of the population, but due to severe drought resulting in pasture land loss, nomads now comprise only 25% of the population. The urban to rural population ratio was 36.1:63.9 in 1986. This represents a movement towards urbanization and a more sedentary life style. The wars in the Western Sahara had been an important casual factor, but now the continuing lack of rain contributes to this shift.

Nouakchott, a new city built to accommodate 30,000 inhabitants, now contains a population estimated at over 600,000. The government has encouraged this trend by inducing nomads to form permanent settlements. Temporary or seasonal migration is universal among nomads. Most of the permanent emigrants are black laborers seeking work in Senegal and Mali. Some 2,000 to 3,000 Mauritanians, mostly blacks, work in France.

Although Mauritanian women are legally free to participate fully in governmental affairs and private business, traditional values and practices limit their scope of activities. A number of women have risen to important positions in the fields of health and education or hold midlevel government positions; however, their number is small, and the possibilities for advancement are slight.

The government has not acknowledged the population problem, and it has no official family planning programs or policies.

ETHNIC COMPOSITION

The largest ethnic group is the Moor, or Maure, who constitute about 82% of the population. The remaining 18% are blacks belonging to the Fulbe, Toucouleur, Soninke, Wolof or Bambara groups. In the early 1960s the ethnic compositon was: Moors (Maures), 81%; Toucouleur (Tukulor, Takruri, Halphoolaren), 9%; Fulbe (Peuls, Peulh, Fulani, Foulah), 5%; Soninke (Sarakole, Marka), 4%; Wolof (Ouolof), 0.5%; and Bambara (Bamba), 0.5%.

The Moors are of Arab-Berber stock and are divided into subgroups based on the degree of Negro admixture and social status. The white Moors, or *bidan*, are predominantly Arab-Berber. The noble white Moors, both the warrior class, or *hassan*, and the religious elite, the *zwaya*, lay claim to pure Arab ancestry. The common white Moors, or the *zenaga*, are clearly Berber. The black Moors also are Berber in origin, but they have a greater admixture of Negro blood. The black Moors are essentially a slave class, though they are officially called *harratin* (freedmen). Moor society is characterized by a rigid hierarchical caste system and tribal divisions within the context of an Islamic society, with the *zwaya* and the *hassan* at the top and the *harratin* at the bottom.

Of the five black ethnic minority groups, the largest is the Toucouleur. The other four—the Fulbe, the Soninke, the Wolof and the Bambara—are representative of widely dispersed peoples who are found in greater numbers in neighboring countries. The Fulbe, like the Moors, are nomadic, while other minorities are sedentary farmers concentrated in the fertile Senegal River Valley.

Social and political relations between the Moorish North and the black South have been characterized by considerable tension. Moors look upon the blacks as socially inferior former slaves, while the blacks regard the Moors as slaveholders with a vested interest in keeping the blacks in subjugation and out of the mainstream of political life. By the time of independence the blacks had achieved, as a result of their closer contacts with the French, a disproportionate share of economic and political power. Much of this influence was dissipated in the 1960s and early 1970s.

The black population is represented at all levels of government, but in numbers far less than its proportion of the total population. Many blacks claim that the Moors are substantially overrepresented in the government and religious institutions, since blacks believe they constitute a majority of the population. The government insists, however, that a substantial majority of Mauritanians are Moors. A sizable segment of the black population (blacks whose mother tongue is Hassaniyya Arabic) is considered by the government, and considers itself, to be Moors.

The European presence in the country consists of nearly 2,000 Frenchmen and Canary Islanders.

Mauritanians are not Western-oriented and are uncomfortable when confronted with traditions and ways of life alien to their own. Whatever degree of receptivity to the West exists is limited entirely to the blacks.

LANGUAGES

The Constitution of 1961 designates Arabic as the national language and French and Arabic as the official languages. The Moors speak various dialects of Arabic, grouped together as Hassaniya. The Moor elite classes speak a purer form of Arabic, while the white Moor commoners and the black Moors speak a form of Arabic mixed with Berber.

All the black groups speak languages belonging to the West Atlantic, or Mande, subgroups, of the Niger-Congo group of the Congo-Kordofanian family. Nearly all these languages have some Arabic elements introduced as a result of contacts with the Northerners. The Fulbe speak Fulfulde, or Poular, and the Toucouleur speak a dialect of Fulfulde. Soninke and Bambara are Mande languages, while the Wolof have absorbed more Arabic words than others.

Language is a sensitive issue that has served to widen the ethnic division between the Moorish North and the black South. The introduction of Arabic as the medium of instruction in primary schools touched off riots in 1966. The compulsory use of Arabic in all schools was postponed in 1979 but reintroduced in 1988.

RELIGIONS

Islam is the official religion of Mauritania and is adhered to by virtually all Mauritanians. The centers of religious orthodoxy in the country are the two major brotherhoods, called *tariqa* (ways), the Qadiriya and the Tijaniya, both of which are organized hierarchically. Mauritania subscribes to the Malikite rite of the Sunni branch of Islam. Chinguetti, in the district of Adrar, is considered the seventh holy place in Islam.

Most of the 6,500 Christians in the country are Roman Catholics, under the jurisdiction of the bishop of Nouakchott. Proselytism and the construction of churches and other non-Islamic houses of worship are prohibited without express government permission, which has been granted in several instances, however, to Mauritania's small Roman Catholic community. Several Catholic churches operate freely. There are no restrictions on personal religious expression, but in 1982 some members of the Bahai faith were threatened with expulsion.

HISTORICAL BACKGROUND

French influence in Mauritania dates from the turn of the century, when Xavier Coppolani, delegate general of the government of Mauritanian Sahara, initiated the idea of a separate territory of Mauritania. By 1904 Coppolani had established French military posts in southern Mauritania. His work was continued by Gen. Henri Gouraud, who, as the commissioner of the Civil Territory of Mauritania, captured Atar in 1904. By 1912 all resistance in Adrar and southern Mauritania had been put down. Except for minor raids by Moor warriors, the French dominance was never challenged until 1961.

The French policy of assimilation and direct rule was never applied vigorously in Mauritania. Rather, the French relied on existing political structures to maintain their power. Further, no attempt was made to develop the economic resources of the country. French rule was summed up by former president Moktar Ould Daddah when he said, "Mauritania has hardly known colonization and has, therefore, neither suffered its ill effects nor realized its benefits."

In 1958, Mauritania became a self-governing member of the French community and gained full independence on November 28, 1960 with Moktar Ould Daddah as both head of state and government. By 1964, Daddah had established a one party state under the rule of the Parti du Peuple Mauritanien (PPM). From late 1976 to mid-1979 many of Mauritania's political and economic problems stemmed from disputes over the Western Sahara territories which had been ceded by Spain to Mauritania and Morocco in November 1975 with the agreement to take effect in March 1976. On July 10, 1978, a bloodless coup replaced Ould Daddah with Lt-Col. Mustapha Ould Salek. The Constitution was suspended and the Government, the National Assembly and the PPM were dissolved. The newly formed Military Committee for National Recovery (CMRN) would exercise executive authority. Salek's continued desire to end hostilities over the disputed Western Sahara led him to replace the CMRN with the Military Committee for National Salvation (CMSN) in April 1979. At the same time he gave over the prime ministry to Lt-Col. Ahmed Ould Bouceif who was killed in a plane crash the following month. Lt-Col. Mohamed Khouna Ould Haidalla, formerly the Minister of Defense, was then appointed by the CMSN as a replacement. Salek resigned in June and the presidency was filled by Lt-Col. Mohamed Mahmoud Ould Ahmed Louly. On August 5, after talks in Algiers, Mauritania formally renounced all claims to the Western Sahara regions called Tiris El-Gharbia and subsequently withdrew troops from the territory which was quickly occupied by Morocco. At the same time Algiers and Mauritania re-established diplomatic relations.

In 1980, Haidalla consolidated his position by taking over the presidency from Louly, and moved towards introducing civilian rule and a multi-party system with the Government to be headed by Sid Ahmed Ould Bneijara. But civilian participation in the Government ended following an attempted coup by a group of officers in March 1981 in which Morocco was accused of involvement. Prime Minister Bneijara was replaced by Col. Maaouiya Ould Sid Ahmed Taya on April 26th. A coup was discovered early in 1982 and resulted in the arrest and imprisonment of ex-President Salek and former Prime Minister Bneijara.

Student unrest in 1984 led Haidalla to take over the prime minister's office. But in December, while Haidalla was out of the country, Taya effected a bloodless coup and assumed both head of state and government. An amnesty for all political prisoners was announced. In the next several years Taya restructured the administrative system and began a major program of economic recovery.

In the mid-1980s, civil disturbances broke out with black Mauritanians claiming oppression by Moorish ethnic groups. In late 1987, a discovered coup attempt led to the arrest 51 people reported to be of the black Toucouleur ethnic group. Secret trials in December sentenced three officers who were executed and 41 who were imprisoned. Internal problems in 1988 were followed with the arrest of several hundred people who were linked to the Pro-Iraqi Ba'athist movement. At the same time Amnesty International and the black African opposition group Forces de libération africaine de Mauritanie (FLAM) accused the Government of inhuman treatment of prisoners in the desert Walata prison. Promises were made by the Government to improve conditions.

CONSTITUTION & GOVERNMENT

Until 1978 the constitutional basis of the Mauritanian government was the Constitution of 1961, which established an Islamic republic and a presidential form of government. It provided for a government composed of three branches—executive, legislative and judicial—whose respective powers were modeled on that of the French Fifth Republic.

The president functioned as head of state and head of government and was elected for five-year terms by direct and universal suffrage. He appointed and dismissed the Council of Ministers, whose members were responsible solely to him. The president was required by law to be a Muslim and to be nominated by the sole political party, the Mauritanian People's Party (Parti du Peuple Mauritanien, PPM). The president had no right to dissolve the National Assembly, but he had a suspensive veto over legislation, the right of initiating legislation and the right to call upon the Supreme Court for an advisory opinion on the constitutionality of a law or a bill. He also had extraconstitutional powers in national emergencies. The National Assembly could pass a vote of no confidence in his government but could not force his resignation.

The Constitution provided for universal, direct and secret suffrage for all Mauritanian citizens of both

GOVERNMENT LIST
(July/August 1991)

President, Military Committee for National Salvation (CMSN); Chief of State	Taya, Maaouya Ould Sid'Ahmed, *Col.*
Minister of Civil Service, Administrative Training, Youth & Sports	Moine, Mohamed Abdrahmane Ould
Minister of Commerce, Handicrafts & Tourism	Oumar, Soumare
Minister of Culture & Islamic Orientation	Bounama, Didi Ould
Minister of Defense	Taya, Masouya Ould Sid'Ahmed, *Col.*
Minister of Equipment & Transportation	Harouna, Dieng Oumar, *Lt. Col.*
Minister of Finance	Boubaker, Sidi Mohamed Ould
Minister of Fisheries & Maritime Economy	Ahmed, Mohamed Lemine Ould
Minister of Foreign Affairs & Cooperation	Didi, Hasni Ould
Minister of Information	Jiddou, Ahmed Ould Khalifa Ould
Minister of Interior, Post & Telecommunications	Baba, Cheikh Sid'Ahmed Ould, *Maj.*
Minister of Justice	Bohoum, Sow Adama Samba
Minister of Mines & Industry	Mogueya, Boullah Ould
Minister of National Education	Haye, Moctar Ould
Minister of Planning	Michel, Mohamed Ould
Minister of Public Health & Social Affairs	Haimer, Mohamed Ould
Minister of Rural Development	Lekhal, Mohamed Ould Sid'Ahmed, *Lt. Col.*
Minister of State Audits	Yessa, Ethmane Sid'Ahmed
Minister of Water Supply & Energy	Abeiderrahmane, Moustapha Ould
Secretary of State for Literacy & Traditional Education	Saleh, Rachid Ould
Secretary of State for Maghreb Union (UMA) Affairs	Sid'Ahmed, Ahmed Ould
Governor, Central Bank	Zein, Ahmed Ould

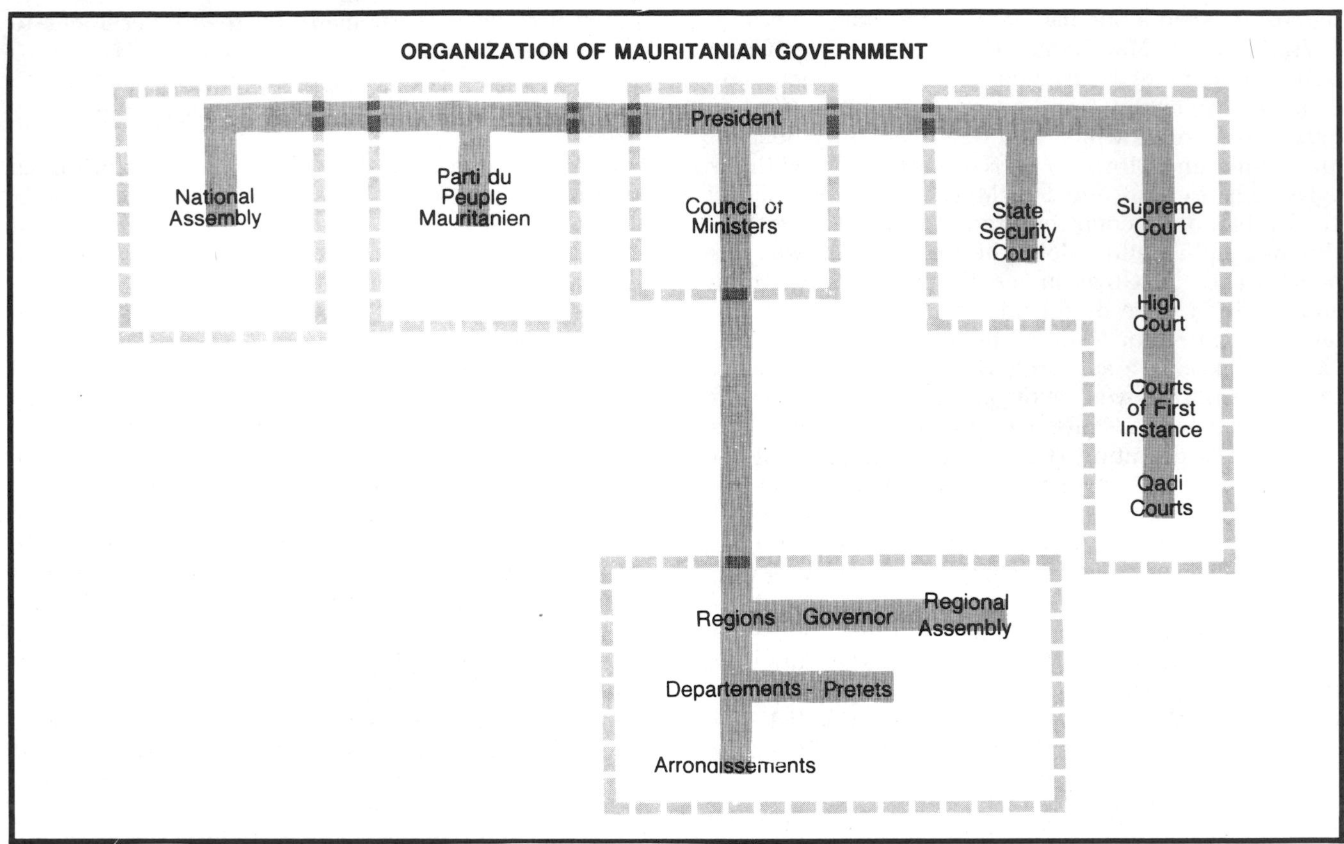

sexes. In the 1975 elections to the National Assembly the turnout was over 94%, or about 500,000 voters, and the single list presented by the PPM received 99.99% of the votes cast.

In July 1978 President Ould Daddah was overthrown in a coup led by army chief of staff Col. Mustapha Ould Mohamed Salek. The new government, headed by the Military Committee for National Rectification (CMRN), suspended the Constitution of 1961 and dissolved the National Assembly and the PPM. The CMRN was composed of 16 officers, and the cabinet of eight civilians and eight military officers. In 1979 the CMRN was replaced by the 27-member Military Committee for National Salvation (CMSN). The composition of this committee underwent another change after the coup that ousted Mohamed Louly and brought Mohamed Haidalla as president.

RULERS OF MAURITANIA (from 1958)

Presidents

November 1958–July 1978: Moktar Ould Daddah
July 1978–June 1979: Mustapha Ould Mohamed Salek
June 1979–January 1980: Mohamed Mahmed Ould Ahmed Louly
January 1980–December 1984: Mohamed Khouna Ould Haidalla
December 1984– : Col. Maaouiya Ould Sid Ahmed Taya

FREEDOM & HUMAN RIGHTS

In terms of civil and political rights, Mauritania is classified as a not-free country.

Since the coup of 1980 the Mauritanian political scene has been marked by extraordinary instability. The peace treaty with the Polisario added the hostility of Morocco to the problems facing the Military Committee for National Salvation. Under these circumstances, the government has taken measures to restrict political activity severely. It has banned all assemblies organized for political discussion, whether in public or in private dwellings. The ban generally has been strictly enforced, and suspected dissidents have been regularly detained, although normally for short periods only. Movement in major cities has been restricted by a midnight-to-morning curfew. Some prominent citizens also have been refused permission to leave the country.

Though mass arrests are not the rule, in mid-1988, 600 people, including members of the armed services, were reported arrested following protests against the December 1987 executions of officers involved in the October coup. Accusations of torture and inhumanity towards prisoners has been levied against the Government by the ethnic opposition group, FLAM and Amnesty International. The Government admitted its blame for four deaths. Taya announced an amnesty for all political prisoners, exiles and former leaders late in 1984. The administration of law continues to acknowledge both the French and the Universal declarations on human rights. Some negative human rights features are:

• The government can hold in detention anyone it considers a threat to national security, without trial and outside normal prison quarters. The term of detention is for six months, renewable for another six months. Under this law, members of former governments have been held several times, although most of them were subsequently released.

• An exit visa is required for foreign travel. Opponents of the regime are denied permission to leave the country, and in some cases their passports have been confiscated.

• The suspension of democratic institutions following the 1978 coup has not been lifted, and no timetable has been set for this.

Some positive features are:

• The government has abandoned its long-standing Arabization policy and now permits its non-Arab citizens to be educated in French, although a plan was reintroduced in mid-1988 to make Arabic the compulsory first language.

• There are no restrictions on religious expression or practice, and both freedom of religious conscience and the right to practice one's religion are enjoyed by all citizens.

• Foreign magazines and newspapers are freely sold on the streets, and foreign broadcasts are heard without interference.

Although the government remains opposed to slavery and has established a commission to implement abolition decrees, vestiges of the practice still exist. In the spring of 1985, the U.N. Subcommission on Human Rights released a report on slavery in Mauritania, based on a 1984 visit by a commission representative. The report criticized the continued existence of slavery, especially in rural areas, but acknowledged the government's intent to stamp it out. Efforts to implement Mauritania's 1980 Declaration of the Abolition of Slavery have been limited and only partially effective. Some government-sponsored resettlement programs for former slaves have been implemented. Estimates of the number of persons remaining in a slave status run as high as 100,000, although such figures are impossible to verify. The institution persists largely in southern Mauritania, where it originated in historic conflicts between nomadic Moors and sedentary blacks. The drought has had a tremendous impact on slavery, causing many Moors to release their slaves as, under deteriorating economic conditions, they could no longer meet the costs of slaveholding. Slavery in Mauritania is not identifiable with the chattel servitude of the American historical experience. There is no commercial market for slaves, and the large class of freed slaves and their descendants are regulated by complex social obligations.

CIVIL SERVICE

No current information is available on the Mauritanian civil service.

LOCAL GOVERNMENT

For purpose of regional administration Mauritania is divided into 10 numbered regions plus the capital district of Nouakchott.

REGIONS

Number	Region	Chief Town
I	Hodh-Oriental	Nema
II	Hodh Occidental	Ayoun el Atrous
III	Assaba and Guidimaka	Kiffa
IV	Gorgol	Kaedi
V	Brakna and Tagant	Aleg
VI	Trarza and Inchiri	Rosso
VII	Adrar and Tiris-Zemmour	Atar
VIII	Baie du Levrier	Nouadhibou
IX	Tiris al Gharbia (Western Saharan annexed territory)	
X	Guera (Western Saharan annexed territory)	

Each region is headed by a governor. The regions are divided into departments, each headed by a prefect, and subdivided into *arrondissements.* Each region has a regional assembly of 20 to 30 members named by the president. However, these assemblies enjoy little or no substantive powers. Elections to local councils were held in urban areas in late 1986, in Mauritania's 32 departments in early 1988, and in 164 rural communities in early 1989.

FOREIGN POLICY

As a partly Arab and partly black nation, Mauritania's principal goal in foreign affairs is to serve as a link between the Arab world and black Africa. However, the pull of Islam has been stronger than its sense of identity with sub-Saharan countries and, since 1973, Mauritania has been actively aligning itself with Arab causes. Although ties with France always have remained strong, they have been refashioned from time to time on the basis of cooperation agreements, last renegotiated in 1973. The agreement called for cultural, technical and economic cooperation but excluded military and monetary collaboration. But when Mauritania withdrew from the Western Sahara in 1979, France supplied some military support to ensure territorial integrity. To offset the country's nearly total economic dependence on France, relations have been established with the Soviet Union, East European countries and the People's Republic of China, from all of whom Mauritania receives aid. As a further departure from its earlier conservative foreign policy, Mauritania broke diplomatic relations with the United States in 1967, in line with Arab policy after the June war, but reestablished them in 1969.

The most important issues in Mauritania's diplomatic history have been the nonrecognition of Mauritanian independence by Morocco until 1970; the border conflict with Mali, settled by the Treaty of Kayes in 1963; and the annexation of the southern third of the former Spanish Sahara (the northern two-thirds going to Morocco), in defiance of U.N. resolutions and in opposition to the Algerian-backed Polisario Front, in 1976. By 1977 Mauritania was spending over two-thirds of its national budget on the defense of its half of the disputed territory (which has no particular economic benefits to offer), and this, combined with the effects of a long drought, brought the country to near bankruptcy. In 1979 Mauritania announced a peace treaty with the Polisario Front under which Mauritania renounced all claims to Tiris el Gharbia, the former Spanish Sahara. At once, Morocco removed its troops in Mauritania and occupied the Mauritanian sector, now renamed Oued Eddahab. Mauritania's links with the sub-Saharan states are symbolized by its active membership in the Senegal River States Organization (Organisation des États-Riverains de Sénégal—OERS), replaced in 1972 by the Organization for the Development of the Senegal River (Organisation pour la Mise en Valeur du Fleuve Sénégale, OMVS).

Mauritania and the United States are parties to four agreements and treaties, covering development assistance, economic and technical cooperation, investment guarantees and the Peace Corps.

During 1983 Mauritania played an active part in attempting to improve relations among the Maghreb countries (Algeria, Morocco, Mauritania, Tunisia and Libya). In December 1983 Mauritania signed the Maghreb Fraternity and Cooperation Treaty, which originally had been drawn up between Algeria and Tunisia in March. The treaty had been left open for other Maghreb states to sign, in the hope that it would eventually form the basis of a Greater Maghreb Union. However, relations with Morocco deteriorated further in February 1984, when Mauritania announced its recognition of the Sahrawi Arab Democratic Republic, the Western Saharan state that was proclaimed in 1976 by the Polisario Front. In August 1984 President Haidalla again denied Morocco's renewed claims that Mauritania was providing bases for Polisario Front guerrilla attacks across the border with Western Sahara. But in April 1985, diplomatic relations with Morocco were restored. In February 1989, an agreement between five north African countries, including Morocco, formed the Arab Maghreb Union (UMA) which created a common market for the region. Racial and economic tensions between Senegal and Mauritania erupted in April 1989 with 450 people killed. An international airlift repatriated over 50,000 people from both countries.

Mauritania joined the United Nations in 1961.

PARLIAMENT

Until 1978 the national legislature was the National Assembly (Al-Majlis al-Watani). Of its 77 members, 70 were elected for five-year terms by universal, direct suffrage from a single list presented to the electorate by the PPM. The other seven deputies were named by the president to represent the newly annexed Western Sahara territory. The legislative powers of the National Assembly were defined in the Constitution and included defense, administration, labor, education and taxation. The president could not dissolve the National Assembly. The Assembly also could override a president's veto, pass a no-confidence motion in the government and deny budgetary allocations. However, with the development of a single party controlled by the president, the National Assembly's powers had become largely academic. The Assembly held two ordinary sessions a year and special sessions at the request of the president. Sometimes the president bypassed the National Assembly altogether by submitting bills to referendum. But since the military coup of 1978 the Military Committee for National Recovery (CMRN) assumed all powers pending the establishment of "democratic institutions."

POLITICAL PARTIES

All political parties and opposition groups are banned. In the absence of any formalized means of communication between the government and the people, the Structure for the Education of the Masses was created in 1982 on a nationwide basis. Organized down to the village and neighborhood level, it is used to explain government policy, mobilize manpower for self-help projects, and air grievances. The exercise of state power is tempered by traditions of informal consensual decision making and the historical fragmentation of authority among various tribes, families and regions.

Until 1978 the sole political party in the country was the Mauritanian People's Party (Parti du Peuple Mauritanien, PPM), formed in 1961 as a coalition of four existing parties: Parti du Régroupement Mauritanien; Union Nationale Mauritanienne; Nahda; and Union des Socialistes Musulmans Mauritaniens. It was elevated to the status of supreme political organ of the state and declared the sole political party by legislation passed in 1964. Effective decision-making within the party was done by a small permanent committee headed by the party's secretary general, President Moktar Ould Daddah, although the party was governed, theoretically, by the National Political Bureau (BPN). Although opposition parties were illegal, dissent and criticism were permitted within the party on issues on which no decision had been made.

Although opposition parties have been proscribed, at least six continue to function in exile: the Paris-based Alliance for a Democratic Mauritania; the Senegal-based Movement of Free Officers; the Rabat-based Islamic Party and Movement of National Unity; the Senegal-based Mauritanian Democratic Union and the Free Man Movement, both comprised of black dissidents; and the Organization of Mauritanian Nationalists.

ECONOMY

Mauritania is one of the 49 low-income countries in the world. Mauritania also is a classic example of a dual economy in which the traditional and modern sectors coexist with little interaction. The private sector predominates within a free-market economy.

A majority of the population still depends on agriculture and livestock for a livelihood, even though most of the nomads and many subsistence farmers were forced into the cities by recurrent drought in 1983. Mauritania has extensive deposits of iron ore that account for almost 50% of total exports. The

PRINCIPAL ECONOMIC INDICATORS

Gross National Product (U.S. $ millions): 953 (1989)
GNP per capita (U.S. $): 490 (1989)
GNP average annual growth rate (%, 1980–89): 0.4
GNP per capita average annual growth rate (%, 1987–89): 0.8
Average annual rate of inflation (%, 1980–88): 9.4
Average annual growth rate (%, 1980–88)
General government consumption: −4.3
Private consumption: 4.3
Gross domestic investment: −5.3

BALANCE OF PAYMENTS, 1988 (U.S. $ millions)

Current account balance: −96.0
Merchandise exports: 437.6
Merchandise imports: −348.9
Trade balance: 88.8
Other goods, services & income + : 39.4
Other goods, services & income − : −306.7
Other goods, services & income net: −267.3
Private unrequited transfers: −22.1
Official unrequited transfers: 104.6
Capital other than reserves: 81
Net errors & omissions: −18.5
Counterpart items: 4.3
Liabilities constituting foreign authorities reserves: 19.5 (1984)
Total change in reserves: 10.2

GROSS DOMESTIC PRODUCT

GDP nominal (C.F.A.F. billions): 44.500 (1984)
GDP per capita (U.S. $): 520 (1988)
Average annual growth rate of GDP (%, 1980–88): 1.6
GDP by type of expenditure (%) 1986
Consumption
Private: 74
Government: 22
Gross domestic investment: 22
Gross domestic saving: 10 (1988)
Foreign trade
Exports: 58
Imports: −77
Cost components of GDP (%) 1985
Net indirect taxes: 9
Consumption of fixed capital: 6
Compensation of employees: 27
Net operating surplus: 58
Sectoral origin of GDP (%) 1986
Primary
Agriculture: 35
Mining: 15
Secondary
Manufacturing: 4
Construction and public utilities: 7
Tertiary
Transportation & communications: 9
Trade, finance, other services: 18
Government: 12
Average annual sectoral growth rates (%, 1980–88)
Agriculture: 1.5
Industry: 4.9
Services: −0.5

decline in world demand for this ore, however, has led to cutbacks in production in recent years. The nation's coastal waters are among the richest fishing areas in the world, but overexploitation by foreigners threatens this key source of revenue.

In a period from the mid-1970s to mid-1980s, Mauritania's economy had stagnated and its external debt had grown excessively. By 1984, the World Bank estimated Mauritania's external debt to be $1.171 billion. This along with a persistent budget deficit and a declining GDP led to the Economic and Financial Recovery Program for 1985–88 which was put together in conjunction with the World Bank. Economic gains under this program were consolidated by the 1989–91 Economic-Support and Revival Program. Loans and credits also were supplied to Mauritania through the World Bank through the rest of the decade to aid in restructuring public enterprises and the iron ore industry, and the financing of essential imports. In 1988, general government consumption consitituted 14% of the GDP, while the annual growth rate of general government consumption from 1980–88 was −4.3%.

PUBLIC FINANCE

The Mauritanian fiscal year is the calendar year. The central government budget consists of two parts: a current budget and a capital budget. The capital budget is drawn up by the Ministry of Planning and the current budget by the Ministry of Finance. The budget also covers over 20 special funds, including regional administrations, and semipublic and public agencies such as the Social Security Fund and the Post Office and Telegraph Department.

Of the 1989 revenues well over half came from tax revenues. Of the expenditures in the same year two-fifths went to rural development, one-quarter to industrial and fishing development and over one-fifth to improvement to the infrastructure.

By mid-1988, Mauritania's external debt was estimated at $2.0 billion. This was up from 1984 totals of $1.17 billion. Plans devised in conjunction with the World Bank and the IMF have worked towards improving this debt imbalance as well as towards balancing the trade deficits and budgetary inequities and raising the GDP and GNP levels.

Development planning began with the first four-year plan (1963–67). A second four-year plan (1970–74) was based on an assessment of the results of the first plan and on recommendations of the World Bank. The priorities were shifted from capital-intensive modern-sector projects to rural development, and the Ministry of Planning was created. The third four-year develop-

FOREIGN AID, 1989

Total foreign aid (U.S. $ millions): 280.9
Bilateral: 169.7
Multilateral: 111.2

ment plan (1975–79) focused on development of the rural sector in an integrated economy. For 1980–85, total planned investment expenditures amounted to UM50 billion, of which about half was realized by public enterprises, mainly the Société Nationale Industriel et Minière (SNIM), and the other half by the government. More than half of these investments were allocated to productive sectors, with primary emphasis on mining (30%), transportation (25%) and agriculture (13%). The remaining investments were distributed among housing and social infrastructure.

A plan implemented in 1986 by the SNIM-SEM (-Société d'Economie Mixte), involved measures to improve the productivity of iron ore deposits in the Guelbs region along with improvements on railway links and port handling facilities. In early 1989 SNIM-SEM studied the viability of the commercial exploitation of deposits at M'Haoudat.

Mauritania's potentially rich fishing industry was helped by the 1985–88 Economic and Financial Recovery Program which envisaged extensive modernization of the fishing fleet. A new deep-water port was opened at Nouakchott in 1986.

France continues to be the largest source of international assistance through Fonds d'Aide et de Cooperation (FAC) and Caisse Centrale de Cooperation Économique (CCCE). Aid from the EEC is channeled through Fonds Européens de Développement (FED). More recent donors have included the Kuwait Fund for Arab Economic Development, Saudi Arabia and the Canadian Development Agency. By 1974 an estimated 35% of foreign aid was derived from oil-producing Arab states. Aid from the United States has been relatively small, although U.S. grants accounted for more than 40% of emergency assistance made available to Mauritania during the severe drought of 1969–74. From 1970 to 1988 the United States committed $160 million in aid, communist nations $277 million and other Western countries and international agencies $1.1 billion.

FINANCIAL, INDICATORS 1989

Total reserves minus gold (SDRs millions): 63
SDRs (millions): 0
Reserve position in IMF (SDRs millions): 0
Foreign exchange (SDRs millions): 63
Gold (fine troy oz. millions): 0.1
Ratio of external debt to total reserves: 25.9 (1987)
Central bank 1989
- Assets (%)
  - Foreign assets: 37.6
  - Claims on government: 49.9
  - Claims on banks: 12.5
  - Claims on private sector: 0.0
- Liabilities (%)
  - Reserve money: 47.5
  - Government deposits: 2.7
  - Foreign liabilities: 75.6
  - Capital accounts: 19.8

Money supply 1989
- Stock (C.F.A.F. billions): 15.062
- M1 per capita: 7,640

Private banks 1989
- Assets (%)
  - Loans to government: 0.6
  - Loans to private sector: 84.2
  - Reserves: 9.2
  - Foreign assets: 6.0
- Liabilities
  - Deposits (C.F.A.F. billions): 27.148
  - of which %
    - Demand deposits: 32.5
    - Savings deposits: 13.1
    - Government deposits: 0.4
    - Foreign liabilities: 22.0

External debt 1988
- Total (U.S. $ billions): 2.076
  - of which public (U.S. $ billions): 1.823
  - of which private (U.S. $): 0
- Debt service (long-term)
  - Total (U.S. $ millions): 111
  - Repayment
    - Principal (%): 70.3
    - Interest (%): 29.7
- Debt service ratio (%): 21.7
- External public debt as % of GNP: 192.6
- Debt service as % of GNP: 11.9
- Debt service as % of exports: 21.6
- Terms of public borrowing
  - Commitments (U.S. $ millions): 111
  - Average interest rate (%): 1.1
  - Average maturity (yrs.): 38
- Net flow of publicly guaranteed external capital (U.S. $ millions): 51
- Receipt of workers' remittances (U.S. $ millions): −26
- Net direct private investment (U.S. $ millions): 2

CURRENCY & BANKING

The Mauritanian unit of currency is the ouguiya, divided into five khoums. Coins are issued in denominations of 1 khoum and 1, 5, 10 and 20 ouguiyas; notes are issued in denominations of 100, 200 and 1,000 ouguiyas.

The ouguiya was introduced in June 1973, replacing the CFA franc, but Mauritania remained within the franc zone until December 1973. The dollar exchange rate in June 1991 was ouguiya per U.S. $1 = 81.73.

The banking system consists of a central bank, Banque Centrale de Mauritanie, established in 1973 when Mauritania withdrew from the Communauté Financière Africaine (CFA); five commercial banks, including the International Bank for Mauritania, in which the state holds a 51% interest; and one development bank, Société d'Équipement de la Mauritanie. In 1984 the commercial banks had reserves of UM627 million, demand deposits of UM5.891 billion and time deposits of UM1.682 billion.

AGRICULTURE

Of the total land area only 0.2% is used for agriculture, about two-fifths are grazing lands, 15% is forested and almost half is desert. Permanent agriculture is restricted to the strip of land along the Senegal River, and nearly all food production is for family consumption or local distribution. Based on 1975–76 = 100, the Index of Agricultural Production was 126, the Index of Food Production was 126 and the per capita Index of Food Production was 102.

Agriculture employed 66% of the labor force in 1987 compared with 89% in 1965. Agriculture, including fish-

GROWTH PROFILE
(Annual Growth Rates, %)

Projected population (1988–2000): 2.7
Projected crude birth rate (/1,000) (1990–95): 45.4
Projected crude death rate (/1,000) (1990–95): 17.4
Urban population (1980–88): 7.8
Labor force (1985–2000): 3.1
GNP (1980–89): 0.4
GNP per capita (1987–89): 0.8
GDP (1980–88): 1.6
Inflation (1980–88): 9.4
Agriculture (1980–88): 1.5
Industry (1980–88): 4.9
Services (1980–88): −0.5
Money holdings (1980–88): 12.1
Energy consumption (1980–88): 0.3
Exports (1980–88): 9.7
Imports (1980–88): 2.4
General government consumption (1980–88): −4.3
Private consumption (1980–88): 4.3
Gross domestic investment (1980–88): −5.3

ing, contributes one-third to the GDP and is the largest economic sector in terms of its share of the GDP.

The construction of two major dams on the Senegal River under the Mauritanian-Senegalese-Malian development agency Organization for the Development of the Senegal River (Organisation pour la Mise en Valeur du Fleuve Sénégal, OMVS) were completed in 1985, at an estimated cost of $186 million. The two dams are to bring 215,000 ha. (531,265 ac.) under irrigation in Mauritania. Even with these projects Mauritania may not achieve agricultural self-sufficiency because of the continuing impact of the Sahelian drought, official neglect and increasing desertification. Output of grain has declined since the 1960s and is projected to take care of only 47% of the country's needs.

Land tenure systems vary from tribe to tribe, but in general personal or family ownership is the dominant pattern. Among the Toucouleur, who are the major farming community, cultivation rights are in many cases allocated by the local lineage or village chief, who is the traditional master of the land.

In 1975 the government inaugurated a $560 million hydroagricultural program at Kaédi to open up 7,000 ha. (17,500 ac.) of new farming land along the Gorgol River, a tributary of the Senegal River. This project was designed to make Mauritania self-sufficient in rice and sugar and meet much of its cereal requirements. Mechanization is nonexistent apart from 300 tractors on the largest farms.

Millet and sorghum are the most important crops, mostly grown on the floodplains. The yields are quite low because the soil normally is not tilled, and little fertilizer is used. Dates are the most important products in the North, where there are an estimated 1 million date palms. Rice was introduced in the mid-1960s and now is grown as part of a number of experimental projects.

Livestock-breeding is the principal activity in the traditional agricultural sector, generating 75% of total primary production. Seven of every 10 Mauritanians are herdsmen, and there are more than five animals

AGRICULTURAL INDICATORS

Agriculture's share of GDP (%): 37 (1989)
Average annual growth rate (%, 1980–88): 1.5
Value added in agriculture (U.S. $ millions): 339 (1988)
Cereal imports (000 metric tons): 219 (1988)
Index of agricultural production (1979–81 = 100): 110 (1986)
Index of food production (1979–81 = 100): 110 (1986)
Index of food production per capita (1979–81 = 100): 89 (1986–88)
Number of tractors: 314 (1986)
Total fertilizer consumption (000 metric tons): 2 (1985–86)
Fertilizer consumption (g./ha., hundreds): 55 (1987–88)
Farms as % of total land area: 0.2 (1985)
Land use (%), 1985–87
- Cropland: 0
- Pasture: 38
- Forest: 15
- Other: 47

Yields (kg./ha.) 1989
- Grains: 750
- Roots & tubers: 1,845
- Legumes: 390
- Milk (kg./animal): 350

Production 1989
- Fruits (000 metric tons): 15
- Vegetables (000 metric tons): 9

Livestock (000) 1989
- Cattle: 1,260
- Horses: 16 (1986)
- Sheep: 4,200

Forestry 1988
- Production of roundwood (000 cubic meters): 12
  - of which industrial roundwood (%): 41.7

Fishing 1988
- Total catch (000 metric tons): 97.5
  - of which marine (%): 93.8
- Value of exports (U.S. $ millions): 194.979

for every person. The livestock population was decimated in the drought years of 1969–74. From 1970 to 1985 the number of cattle declined from a high of 2 million in 1970 to 1.35 million in 1985. Much livestock is exported, primarily to markets in Senegal. The government has launched efforts to integrate livestock-raising into the modern sector by building a refrigerated slaughterhouse at Kaédi and tanneries at Kaedi and Nouakchott.

The country's only forests are in the southern savanna regions. The principal forest product is gum arabic, in which Mauritania ranks as the world's second-largest producer, after Sudan. Production has dropped almost fourfold in recent years.

Mauritania's coastal waters are rich in various types of fish but, until recently, they had been exploited mainly by foreign fishermen. Of the 37,000 tons of fish caught off the coast in 1982, only 30,000 tons were handled by Mauritanian fishermen, who carry on traditional fishing along the Senegal River and the coastal waters near Nouadhibou. The government has placed considerable emphasis in development plans on development of fishing. The fishing fleet was enlarged by the addition of 14 industrial fishing boats, two of them refrigerated. Nouadhibou, with a new deep-water port opened in 1986, has a refrigerated warehouse, freezing plants and fishmeal factories.

MANUFACTURING

Manufacturing is the smallest economic sector, contributing only 4% to the GDP and employing less than 10% of the labor force. For 1970, the value added in manufacturing was U.S. $10 million. Most of the existing industrial units are limited to fish processing. During the late 1960s a match factory was established at Kaédi and an acetylene and liquid oxygen factory at Nouadhibou.

Despite recent large-scale investments in the manufacturing sector, real growth is estimated to have been low. An oil refinery, completed in 1977, was unable to operate because it lacked a supply of crude oil and had no markets for excess production, no administrative structure and no trained manpower. An electric iron furnace, which was expected to produce 10,000 tons of steel a year from scrap metal (worn rails from SNIM), did not start operation as scheduled in early 1979 because of technical difficulties. After these unfortunate experiences, the government shifted emphasis from large-scale projects to small-scale and medium-scale industries with greater potential for employment. To that effect, in March 1979 the government replaced the Investment Code of 1976 and established a research center, the Centre d'Étude et de Promotion Industrielle (CEPI), to identify, appraise and supervise viable small-scale projects and to provide management assistance to small and medium-size firms.

Private investment in industry exceeded public investment in absolute terms until 1972, but since then state policy has favored state participation in existing enterprises as well as establishment of large-scale industries under state rather than private auspices.

MINING

Mauritania's modern economic sector consists entirely of three mining operations: Complex Minier du Nord (COMINOR), formerly Société Anonyme des Mines de fer de Mauritanie (MIFERMA); Société Minière de Mauritania (SOMIMA); and Société Nationale Industriale et Minière (SNIM).

The largest of these companies is COMINOR, so named when MIFERMA was nationalized in 1974 and that exploits the vast iron ore deposits at F'Derik, Rouissat and Tazadit. Reserves are estimated at 150 million to 250 million tons of relatively pure ore of 60% iron content. COMINOR's production constitutes 30% of the Mauritanian GDP and 78% of its exports.

SOMIMA, nationalized in 1975, was formed in 1967 to exploit the copper reserves of Akjoujt, estimated at 7 million tons of oxidized copper ore with a copper content of 2.6%, and about 20 million tons of sulphuric ore with a copper content of 1.8%. Production of copper was suspended in 1978 and extraction was expected to be resumed in the early 1990s.

SNIM was formed in 1972 by the state to exploit sulphur, rare earths and phosphates. Of the rare earths, the most valuable is yttrium, which is found in quantities in Bou Naga, east of Nouakchott. Yttrium mining is conducted by Mauritanian Mining Research and Exploitation Company (SOMIREMA).

One of the bright spots in the economic situation has been the rapid recovery of iron ore operations, which followed the end of Saharan hostilities in July 1978. Polisario Front harassment had been extremely effective in disrupting ore shipments from the mines to the port at Nouadhibou. As a result, exports totaled little more than 3 million tons during the first half of 1978, while stocks slipped to levels barely sufficient to cover one week's exports. Total production of 6.5 million tons was the lowest in the mines' history and well below the break-even point of 8 million tons.

The discovery of phosphate deposits in the Aleg–Kaédi region was announced in 1984; reserves are estimated at 95 million tons of ore, with a 20% phosphate content. Mauritania has considerable reserves of gypsum, estimated at 4 billion tons, and in November 1984 a gypsum quarry and plaster works were inaugurated.

Production in El Rhein in the Guelbs region began in 1984. A multi-state loan package of $320 million is to be spent in this region to produce an eventual output of 6 million tons of iron ore. Additionally, this area is to improve its production via programs instituted by SNIM-SEM between 1986 to 1988. Also, SNIM-SEM, early in 1989, conducted studies concerning the commercial viability of deposits at M'Haoudat.

ENERGY

Mauritania does not produce any form of energy other than electric power, which is all generated from thermal energy. Offshore exploration currently is being carried out by six foreign forms.

Mauritania, Mali and Senegal have cooperated as members of the Organization for the Development of the Senegal River. One project which was to be completed in 1988, involves the construction and operation of dams at Djama, Senegal to provide hydroelectricity to member states.

ENERGY INDICATORS

Energy consumption per capita (kg. oil equivalent): 111 (1988)
Energy imports as % of merchandise exports: 6 (1988)
Average annual growth rate of energy consumption (%, 1980–88): 0.3
Electricity 1988
  Installed capacity (000 kw.): 114
  Production (million kw.-hr.): 121
    % fossil fuel: 79.3
    % hydro: 20.7
  Consumption per capita (kw.-hr.): 63
Petroleum
  Production (million bbl.): 0 (1989)
  Consumption (million bbl.): 8 (1988)
  Refining capacity (000 bbl./day): 0 (1990)
Coal
  Production (000 metric tons): 0 (1988)
  Consumption (000 metric tons): 6 (1988)

LABOR

Mauritania's labor force is estimated at about 600,000. Only 45,000 were wage earners in 1980. Over one-fifth of those participating in the economy are women. Though agriculture employed about 66% of the labor force in 1987 this number is still below 1965 levels. One-tenth of those employable were in industry, and one-fifth were in service industries. There are no unemployment rates available. Lack of employment opportunities in the towns has forced many black workers to emigrate either to France or to neighboring Senegal or Mali.

There is a guaranteed minimum wage, established in 1985 for unskilled workers and for agricultural workers and in 1984 for skilled workers. Information on actual wage levels is scanty and often unreliable. The standard nonagricultural workweek in Mauritania is not to exceed 40 hours, nor six days per week. Enforcement of labor laws is the responsibility of the Labor Inspectorate, Ministry of Labor. Disputes over labor issues are heard before special three-person labor courts, which are jointly overseen by the Ministries of Justice and Labor. The leadership of the Mauritanian Workers' Union indicates that the courts are unbiased and effective.

Labor unions were the only nationwide organizations with any political import that were not dissolved following the 1978 coup. Labor unions are grouped in a national organization called the Mauritanian Workers' Union (UTM). In 1984 the government arrested the secretary general of the UTM, as well as the secretary general of the politically active (since 1981) National Student Union, for allegedly possessing material indicating active Libyan involvement in their activities. The government then installed an entirely new leadership at the UTM, and student union activities were "frozen." Later in 1984, former president Haidalla released these two leaders, who shortly thereafter resumed their former positions. In the case of the UTM, this led to an acrimonious split within union ranks, which continues to paralyze the organization.

The UTM is allowed a large measure of freedom in its organizational efforts. The union is associated with a number of regional and international labor organizations, and its officials are permitted to travel abroad to attend international labor meetings. Within the confines of Mauritania's basic foreign policies, union officials are free to take positions on international labor matters. Unions are recognized only when they register with the official body and accept an appointed director general. Local union officials claim that their membership has reached 30,000 members. Union membership is not universal; workers must pay an annual membership fee of $4, but the government indirectly finances most union activities. The right to strike exists in theory, but an extended strike probably would be strongly opposed by the government. There have been two brief strikes in recent years.

LABOR INDICATORS, 1985

Total economically active population (000): 590
- % working-age (15–64): 55.7
- % female: 21.0

Activity rate (%)
- Total: 31.2
- Male: 49.8
- Female: 13.0

Sectoral employment of economically active (%)
- Agriculture, forestry, fishing: 66.0
- Construction, manufacturing, mining, quarrying, public utilities: 10.0
- Trade, hotels, restaurants, transportation, communications, finance, real estate, and services: 24.0

Average annual growth rate of labor force (%, 1985–2000): 3.1

FOREIGN COMMERCE

Mauritania's major exports are iron ore, processed fish, and small amounts of gum arabic and gypsum. There are significant cattle exports to Senegal although numbers are not recorded. Its main imports are foodstuffs, consumer goods, petroleum products and capital goods. The European Community, the United States and Japan are its primary trading partners.

Wholesale trade in rice, tea, sugar and textiles is a government monopoly handled by the Société National Import-Export (SONIMEX).

FOREIGN TRADE INDICATORS, 1988

Exports (U.S. $ millions): 424
Imports (U.S. $ millions): 365
Balance of trade (U.S. $ millions): 59.0
Annual growth rate (1980–88), exports (%): 9.7
Annual growth rate (1980–88), imports (%): 2.4
International reserves in terms of months of imports covered: 1.4 (latest
Terms of trade (1980 = 100): 104
Import price index (1980 = 100): 88.1 (1986)
Export price index (1980 = 100): 64.4 (1986)

Direction of Trade (%), 1987 est.

	Imports	Exports
European Community	64.3	51.4
United States	3.4	1.4
U.S.S.R. & Eastern European economies	0.0	0.0
Japan	1.5	31.3

Composition of Trade (%)

	Imports (1980)	Exports (1984)
Food & agricultural raw materials	30.3	50.2
Fuels & other energy	14.0	0.0
Mineral ores & concentrates	4.5	49.1
Manufactured goods	51.2	0.7
of which chemicals	4.3	0.0
of which machinery	27.0	0.0

TRANSPORTATION & COMMUNICATIONS

The rail system consists of a 690-km. (429-mi.) track between Nouadhibou and Tazadit and the new iron ore fields at F'Derik.

The Senegal River serves as an important inland waterway for 800 km. (497 mi.), with the towns of Kaédi, Rosso and Boghe as the major ports. A steamship service is operated on the Senegal River by a Senegalese company.

There are three major ports on the Atlantic: Nouakchott, and two facilities in Nouadhibou—Port Central, which is the iron ore port for MIFERMA; and the port of Nouadhibou itself, which is a commercial port for general shipping and fishing fleets.

The main road in Mauritania runs from Saint Louis in Senegal to Nouakchott. There also are two so-called national highways, one connecting F'Derik with Nouakchott and Rosso and the other linking Rosso and Nema.

The national airline is Air Mauritanie, which operates a fleet of two aircraft. Mauritania also holds a 7% interest in Air Afrique.

TRANSPORTATION INDICATORS

Roads (latest)
  Length, km. (mi.): 8,150 (5,064)
  Paved (%): 17
Motor vehicles (pre-1986)
  Automobiles: 15,017
  Trucks and buses: 2,188
  Persons per vehicle: 96
Railroads
  Track, km. (mi.): 690 (429) (latest)
  Passenger-km. (passenger-mi.) (millions): 7.0 (4.3) (pre-1986)
  Freight, metric ton-km. (short ton-mi.) (billions): 6.142 (4.207) (pre-1986)
Merchant marine
  Vessels (over 100 tons): 119 (1989)
  Total deadweight tonnage (000): 22.2 (1989)
Ports (pre-1986)
  Cargo loaded (million metric tons): 9.956
  Cargo unloaded (000 metric tons): 486
Air
  Km. (mi.) flown (millions): 3.1 (1.9) (1985)
  Passenger-km. (passenger-mi.) (millions): 208.6 (129.6) (latest)
  Freight, metric ton-km. (short ton-mi.) (millions): 35.2 (24.1) (latest)
  Mail, metric ton-km. (short ton-mi.) (millions): 46 (31.5) (1985)
  Airports with scheduled flights: 10 (1990)
Inland waterways (latest)
  Length, km. (mi.): 800 (497)

COMMUNICATION INDICATORS, 1988

Telephones
  Total (000): 4.8 (1983)
  Persons per telephone: 350 (1983)
Phone traffic (000 calls)
  Local: 7,712 (pulses) (1983)
  Long distance: 131 (minutes)
  International: 2,470 (minutes)
Post office
  Pieces of mail handled (millions): 3.035 (1978)
Telegraph
  Total traffic (000 calls): 31
    National: 20
    International: 11
Telex
  Subscriber lines: 254
  Traffic (000 minutes): 618
Telecommunications 1990
  Satellite stations: 3

Tourism is an insignificant part of the economy. There are only 1,000 hotel beds in the country, mostly in Nouakchott. Total tourist receipts in 1988 were U.S. $14 million. Expenditures by nationals abroad in that same year were U.S. $27 million.

DEFENSE

The defense structure is headed by the president, who also is the commander in chief of the armed forces. The line of command runs through the minister of national defense to the chief of the national staff of the armed forces. The country is divided into three military regions.

Military manpower is provided by voluntary enlistment, although mandatory conscription for two-year periods of service was introduced in 1962. After service periods veterans are subject to recall in the event of a threat to national security.

The strength of the armed forces is 11,000.

Army

Personnel: 10,400

Organization: 1 infantry battalion; 1 artillery battalion; 1 camel corps; 3 armored reconnaissance squadrons; 1 AA battery; 1 engineer company; 1 parachute company

Equipment: 80 armored reconnaissance vehicles; 40 armored personnel carriers; mortars; antitank rocket launchers, air defense guns; SAM

Navy

Personnel: 350

Units: 8 patrol boats

Naval base: Nouadhibou

Air Force

Personnel: 250

Organization: 9 combat aircraft, including 5 counterinsurgency and 4 maritime reconnaissance craft; 6 transports

Air bases: Atar, Nouakchott, Nouadhibou, Kaédi, Rosso, Kiffa, F'Derik, Akjoujt and Aioun-el-Atrous

In size and equipment the armed forces of Mauritania are not geared to an external offensive role but only for internal peacekeeping operations. In terms of combat-worthiness and capability of sustained operations, the armed forces have a poor track record and repeatedly had to pull back when faced with the better-disciplined Polisario Front forces. In fact, the army's poor performance in the field persuaded the Mauritanian government to seek a nonmilitary solution to the Western Saharan problem and finally abandon its claim to Tiris el-Gharbia and seek its own peace settlement with the Polisario Front in the face of Moroccan pressures. However, martial traditions are strong in the country, and the armed forces have an influence on national life that is not limited to defense needs. The armed forces provide a pool of technical and administrative skills and function as the engine of the modernization processes.

Until French military aid was withdrawn in 1973, France was the major supplier of equipment and training programs to the Mauritanian army. French aid was received at the rate of $1.2 million annually.

EDUCATION

Mauritania has introduced free, universal and compulsory education for six years, from ages six to 12. The enrollment rates are low: 46% in the primary age group (six to 11) and 15% in the secondary age group (12 to 17).

Schooling consists of 12 years, divided into six years of primary school, three years of middle school and three years of secondary school.

The academic year runs from October to June. The media of instruction are Arabic and French in primary grades and Arabic, French and English in secondary grades.

Strong racial tensions, present throughout the society, have been consistently reflected in the schools. An attempt to enforce the use of Arabic in all schools was abandoned due to strong opposition by blacks, who traditionally prefer the use of French and their tribal tongues. Nevertheless, a plan was introduced in 1988 to make Arabic the compulsory first language in all schools.

One of the reasons for the poor educational attainments of Mauritanians is the continuing emphasis on a purely Islamic education at all levels. Traditional Islamic schools are found in both nomadic communities and settled villages. The best-known of these Islamic schools is the Institute of Islamic Studies at Boutilimit.

The majority of the teachers in the school system are black because of the greater educational attainments among blacks and the opposition of Islamic marabouts to secular education. Teaching personnel and curricula have been completely Mauritanianized.

Mauritania has 10 technical schools. Both COMINOR and SOMIMA, the mining companies, run their own vocational schools. Vocational enrollment represents 12.5% of secondary-school pupils.

Public education is administered by the Ministry of National Education and the Ministry of Primary Education.

Students in post-secondary studies numbered 4,380 in 1986. The Ecole Nationale d'Administration and the Ecole Naturale des Sciences in Nouakchott began degree courses in 1982. The University of Nouakchott opened in 1983 and by 1986 had an enrollment of 2,850.

EDUCATION INDICATORS, 1987

- Literacy
  - Total (%): 28.0
  - Male (%): 38.0
  - Female (%): 17.0
- First level
  - Schools: 1,035
  - Students: 157,216
  - Teachers: 3,158
  - Student/teacher ratio: 49.8
  - Net enrollment ratio: 33 (1984)
- Second level
  - Schools: 44 (1986)
  - Students: 37,308
  - Teachers: 1,729
  - Student/teacher ratio: 21.6
- Vocational
  - Schools: 6
  - Students: 13,606
  - Teachers: 1,138
  - Student/teacher ratio: 12.0
- Third level (postsecondary)
  - Institutions: 7 (1984)
  - Students: 5,407
  - Teachers: 268
  - Student/teacher ratio: 20.2
  - Gross enrollment ratio: 3.4
  - Students (/100,000 pop.): 290
- Foreign study
  - Students abroad: 1,859
    - of whom in
      - United States: 62 (1988)
      - France: 404 (1988)
      - Federal Republic of Germany: 10 (1988)
      - United Kingdom: 3 (1987)
- Public expenditure (1976)
  - Total (C.F.A.F. millions): 847,400
  - % of GNP: 4.9 (1987)
  - % of national budget: 14.3
  - % of current expenditure: 98.7

LEGAL SYSTEM

Although the Mauritanian legal system was shaped in modern times by French juridicial concepts, the Malikite school of Islamic law is the law of the land in all civil matters. Criminal law, on the other hand, is largely based on French sources.

At the apex of the judicial system are the Supreme Court, the State Security Court and the High Court of Justice. The Supreme Court, with six members, has a modern jurist as president and an Islamic judge as vice president. It has four functions under the Constitution: constitutional, appellate, administrative and financial. The State Security Court consists of nonprofessionals appointed by the president. The High Court of Justice consists of a president and 11 other judges, six of whom are elected by the National Assembly from among its own members and five of whom are elected by the National Assembly from a list of Islamic jurists.

Below these courts are courts of first instance at Nouakchott, Ayoun el Atrous, Atar, Kiffa, Kaédi and Nouadhibou. Each of these courts has two judges, one modern and the other Islamic. At the base of the judicial structure are *qadi* courts presided over by traditional Islamic judges, or *qadis*.

Under the Constitution the judiciary is independent of the executive in principle, and the judiciary's integrity is ensured by the Superior Council of Magistrates. In practice, however, the judiciary is only an appendage of the government and rarely acts contrary to the known policies of the president.

An inadequate and under financed judicial system results in suspects being held for long periods before trial. The Shari'a Islamic code, as instituted in Mauritania in 1980, covers adultery, personal theft and murder. A Muslim judge presides over a jury chosen by the governor of the region. The defendant has a right to counsel and can appeal a guilty verdict to the Supreme Islamic Court within 15 days. Circumstantial evidence cannot be admitted as proof of guilt. Admission of guilt sometimes is obtained in the context of a promised reduction in punishment. An inability to convince the sitting magistrate that the government's charges are in error in itself is considered by the courts as a legal admission of guilt, as is convincing testimony of a firsthand witness or codefendant. Extended confinement sometimes is used to encourage self-incrimination. All sentences must be approved by the president. Opposition to the Shari'a code has been expressed by certain blacks and women, who believe that the Shari'a code favors the Moor way of life and limits the role of women. Although a strict interpretation of the Shari'a code in earlier years produced communal tension, the issue has largely passed from public debate due to a more moderate government implementation.

No information is available on the nature of the penal system.

LAW ENFORCEMENT

The principal law-enforcement agencies are the National Civil Police and the Gendarmerie. The National Civil Police are unified under a single command within the Ministry of Interior, but operational control is normally exercised by the governors of the regions and the prefects of the departments. The strength of the National Civil Police is estimated at 1,000.

The Gendarmerie is organized on military lines and equipped with military weapons. Its 300 men form two companies in the capital and brigades of a few members in each department.

No information is available on the incidence and nature of crimes.

HEALTH

Medical conditions are poor and life expectancies are among the lowest in the world. Major health problems include malaria, tuberculosis, measles and influenza.

HEALTH INDICATORS

Health personnel 1984
- Physicians: 170
  - persons per: 9,547
- Dentists: 8
- Nurses: 582
- Pharmacists: 16
- Midwives: 129

Hospitals 1984
- Number: 13
- Number of beds (/100,000): 8
- Admissions/discharges (/10,000): 115 (1977)
- Bed occupancy rate (%): 97.8
- Average length of stay (days): 5

Type of hospitals (%) 1984
- Government: 100.0
- Private nonprofit: 0.0
- Private profit: 0.0

Public health expenditures (latest)
- As % of national budget: 2.8
- Per capita (U.S. $): 4.50

Vital statistics
- Crude death rate (/1,000): 18 (1990)
- Life expectancy at birth 1990
- Males: 44
- Females: 49

Infant mortality rate (/1,000 live births): 96 (1990)
Child mortality rate under 5 yrs. (/1,000 live births) (1985–90): 214
Maternal mortality rate (/100,000 live births): 119 (1980)
Population with access to safe water (%): 37 (latest)

FOOD & NUTRITION

The staple diet of the average nomad consists of milk and millet. The per capita intake of food per day has been estimated at 2,228 calories (97% of requirements).

MEDIA & CULTURE

Mauritania's first daily newspaper, *El Chaab*, was founded in 1975. Its current circulation is no more than 300, or 0.2 per 1,000 inhabitants. All media are owned and controlled by the government.

A national news agency, *Agence Mauritanienne de Presse*, was founded in 1975. AFP maintains a bureau in Nouakchott.

Mauritania, a signatory of the Berne Copyright Convention, has a moderately active book publishing industry.

The official broadcasting organization is *Radiodiffusion Nationale de Mauritanie*, which operates four transmitters, two of 100 kw., and broadcasts in Arabic, French, Toucouleur, Sarakole and Wolof for 61 hours a week. A limited television service was inaugurated in 1984. Mauritania is one of the largest importers of films, with most films coming from France, the United States and India.

The largest library is the National Library at Nouakchott, with 10,000 volumes.

MEDIA INDICATORS

Newspapers
- Number of dailies: 1 (latest)

Book publishing
- Number of titles: 21 (pre-1986)

Radio
- Number of transmitters: 4 (1989)
- Number of persons per radio receiver: 7.8 (1989)

Television
- Television transmitters: 2 (1989)
- Number of persons per T.V. receiver: 1,769 (1989)

Cinema
- Number of fixed cinemas: 19 (pre-1986)
- Seating capacity (000): 8 (pre-1986)

Films
- Number of long films imported:
  - % from United States: 51.0
  - % from France: 25.0
  - % from India: 24.0

CULTURAL & ENVIRONMENTAL INDICATORS

Libraries (latest)
 Number: 1
 Volumes (000): 26
Performing arts (pre-1986)
 Number of performances: 136
 Annual attendance (000): 36
 Attendance (/1,000 pop.): 38
Nature reserves (latest)
 Number of facilities: 3

SOCIAL WELFARE

Family allowances, accident benefits and old-age benefits are administered by the National Social Insurance Fund.

GLOSSARY

arrondissement: subdivision of a department.
bidan: White Moors.
departement: a unit of regional administration and a subdivision of a region.
djemaa: traditional council of notables among Moors.
harmattan: hot and dry sandstorm blowing from the desert in the summer.
harratin: freedmen, used to denote the black Moors.
hassan: the Moor warrior class.
hivernage: the rainy season in desert areas.
marabout: chief of an Islamic religious order or brotherhood.
qadi: traditional Islamic judge.
tariqa: literally, the way. Islamic religious orders which serve as centers of religious orthodoxy in Mauritania.
zenaga: White Moorish commoners from whom tributes were exacted by the Moorish nobility until French rule.
zwaya: the religious elite who constitute the top class of the White Moorish nobility.

CHRONOLOGY (from 1960)

1960— Mauritania gains independence as a member of the French Community, with Moktar Ould Daddah as prime minister.

1961— New Constitution is promulgated, establishing a presidential form of government; Ould Daddah assumes the presidency. . . . Mauritanian People's Party (Parti du Peuple Mauritanien, PPM) is founded through a coalition of four existing parties.

1963— Treaty of Kayes is concluded with Mali, defining the border between Mali and Mauritania.

1964— PPM is declared the sole political party and the supreme state organ.

1966— Mauritania withdraws from the French Community.

1967— Diplomatic relations with the United States are broken following the Arab-Israeli War.

1968— Government efforts to abandon French and introduce Arabic as the official language and medium of instruction in schools lead to riots in the black South. . . . The great Sahelian drought disrupts the economy, brings famine to thousands and decimates the livestock population.

1969— Diplomatic relations with the United States are resumed.

1970— Morocco recognizes the independence of Mauritania and abandons its irredentist claims.

1971— Ould Daddah is reelected president. . . . Riots mark President Pompidou's state visit to the country. . . . Mauritania joins Organization for the Development of the Senegal River (Organisation pour la Mise en Valeur des Fleuve Sénégal, OMUS)

1973— Revised agreement of cooperation is concluded with France, excluding monetary and military programs; French military advisers are withdrawn; Mauritania withdraws from the franc zone and introduces new national currency, the ouguiya. . . . Mauritania joins the Arab League.

1974— MIFERMA, the iron-mining company, is nationalized.

1975— SOMIMA, the copper-mining company, is nationalized.

1976— In a joint operation with Morocco, Mauritania annexes the southern third of Spanish Sahara. . . . Ould Daddah is reelected for a fourth term.

1977— In a major cabinet reshuffle, 11 ministries are abolished. . . . The Polisario Front rebels in Western Sahara gain initial successes but are repulsed with French help.

1978— Ould Daddah is ousted in a bloodless coup led by army chief of staff Mustapha Ould Mohamed Salek; the Constitution of 1961 is suspended and the National Assembly and the PPM are dissolved; the Military Committee for National Rectification (CMRN) is set up as supreme executive and legislative authority.

1979— Following internal power struggles, Ahmed Bouceif is named prime minister; following Bouceif's death in an air accident, Mohamed Khouna Ould Haidalla succeeds as head of government; President Salek resigns office and is replaced by Mohamed Mahmed Ould Ahmed Louly; OAU summit conference calls for referendum in former Spanish Sahara; Mauritania renounces territorial claims on Tiris el-Gharbia and signs peacy treaty with Polisario Front.

1980— Mohamed Haidalla takes over as president as Louly steps down; the nation experiences an economic upturn as iron ore production edges upward. Haidalla resigns posts of prime minister and minister of defense. . . . An entirely civilian cabinet is named, with Sidi Ahmed Ould Bneijara as prime minister. . . . A draft Constitution is drawn up.

1981— An attempted coup, believed to be backed by Morocco, is foiled. . . . Civilian rule ends. . . . A new military-dominated cabinet is named, with Col. Maaouiya Ould Sid Ahmed Taya as prime minister and minister of defense. . . . Draft Constitution is abandoned. . . . Coup led by former president Salek and former prime minister Bneijara is foiled.

1984— Mauritania signs Maghreb Fraternity and Cooperation Treaty with Algeria and Tunisia. . . . Haidalla assumes post of prime minister and minister of defense and reverts Taya to his old post as chief of staff. . . . Taya ousts Haidalla in bloodless coup and installs himself as president, prime minister and minister of defense. . . . Mauritania recognizes the Polisario Front-backed Sahrawi Arab Democratic Republic.

1985— Relations with Morocco are restored.

1986— Opposition to the oppression of black Mauritanians Moorish ethnic groups leads to arson attacks and arrests. Elections are held to local councils in urban areas.

1987— High Government officials, along with the former Governor of the Central Bank, are arrested in connection with a financial scandal. A coup attempt by members of the black Toucouleur ethnic group opposed to ethnic inequality is thwarted. In secret trials held by the Special Court of Justices, 41 are found guilty and sent to prison and three officers were sentenced to death and executed.

1988— Following the executions it is reported that some 500 black officers are dismissed from the armed forces. Some 600 people arrested in connection with the pro-Iraqi Ba'athist movement and 13 allegedly connected to the movement are imprisoned. FLAM and Amnesty International accuse the state of inhuman conditions at its desert prison in Walata. Haidalla and five associates are released on the anniversary of Taya's take-over. Students at the University of Nouakchott boycott classes protesting for improved education and welfare facilities and for a better distribution of grants.

1989— Mauritania signs a treaty with Algeria, Libya, Morocco and Tunisia to establish the Union of the Arab Maghreb.

1990— Arab militants hold pro-Iraq, anti-American protests during the Persian Gulf crisis.

BIBLIOGRAPHY

BOOKS

Economist Intelligence Unit, The. *Country Profile. Guinea, Mali, Mauritania.* London, 1986.

Economist Intelligence Unit, The. *Country Report. Guinea, Mali, Mauritania.* London, 1986.

Gerteiny, Alfred G. *Historical Dictionary of Mauritania.* Metuchen, NJ, 1980.

———. *Mauritania.* New York, 1967.

Handloff, Robert E. ed. *Mauritania, a Country Study.* 2nd ed. Washington, D.C., 1990.

Stewart, C. C., and E. K. Stewart. *Islam and Social Order in Mauritania.* New York, 1970.

Westebbe, Richard M. *The Economy of Mauritania.* New York, 1971.

OFFICIAL PUBLICATIONS

Treasury. *Balance Générale des Comptes du Grand Livre* (General Balance Sheet) (monthly, quarterly and annual, unpublished).

———. *Borderaux Sommaires des Paiements Effectués sur Mandats de l'Ordonnateur du 1 Janvier au 31 Mars Année Suivante.* (Summary Lists of Payments Issued Against the Treasurer's Orders from January 1 to March 31 of the Following Year) (annual, unpublished).

———. *États Comparatifs des Recettes de l'Exercice au 31 Mars.* (Comparative Statement of Receipts to March 31) (monthly, unpublished).

MAURITIUS

BASIC FACT SHEET

OFFICIAL NAME: Mauritius
ABBREVIATION: MF
CAPITAL: Port Louis
HEAD OF STATE: Queen Elizabeth II, represented by Governor-General Sir Veerasamy Ringadoo (from 1986)
HEAD OF GOVERNMENT: Prime Minister Sir Anerood Jugnauth (from 1982)
NATURE OF GOVERNMENT: Parliamentary democracy
POPULATION: 1,070,005 (1990)
AREA: 1,974 sq. km. (762 sq. mi.)
ETHNIC MAJORITY: Indian
LANGUAGE: English (official), Creole (lingua franca)
RELIGIONS: Hinduism, Christianity and Islam
UNIT OF CURRENCY: Mauritian rupee
NATIONAL FLAG: Four equal horizontal stripes of red (top), blue, yellow and green
NATIONAL EMBLEM: A shield of alternate blue and yellow quarters in which are displayed a golden sailing vessel with crossed masts and rowing oars, three palm trees, a red key and a triangle capped by a white star. The latter two symbols are based on the national motto, which appears on a white ribbon at the base: *Stella Clavisque Maris Indici* (Star and Key of the Indian Ocean). The device is flanked by a dodo on one side and a sambur (native deer) on the other, each holding a stalk of sugarcane.
NATIONAL ANTHEM: "Glory to Thee, Motherland, O Motherland of Mine"
NATIONAL HOLIDAYS: March 12 (National Day, Independence Day); January 1 and 2 (New Year's Days); October 24 (United Nations Day); Christian festivals include Assumption, Easter, Good Friday, Holy Saturday, All Saints' Day, Christmas and Boxing Day; also nine Hindu festivals, three Islamic festivals and one Chinese festival
NATIONAL CALENDAR: Gregorian
PHYSICAL QUALITY OF LIFE INDEX: 81
DATE OF INDEPENDENCE: March 12, 1968
DATE OF CONSTITUTION: March 12, 1968
WEIGHTS & MEASURES: Metric

GEOGRAPHICAL FEATURES

The island of Mauritius is in the southern Indian Ocean about 800 km. (500 mi.) east of Madagascar. Mauritius is a roughly semicircular island 61 km. (38 mi.) north to south and 47 km. (29 mi.) east to west. The country also includes the island of Rodrigues, about 560 km. (350 mi.) east of Mauritius; the Agalega Islands, a group of small islands 869 km. (540 mi.) east-northeast of Madagascar; and the St. Brandon Group (formerly Cargados Carajos Archipelago), 402 km. (250 mi.) northeast of Mauritius. The combined area of Mauritius and the lesser islands is 1,974 sq. km. (762 sq. mi.), of which Rodrigues accounts for 103.6 sq. km. (40 sq. mi.). The island of Mauritius has a coastline of 217 km. (135 mi.).

The capital is Port Louis, with a 1985 population of 136,323. Most of the other major urban centers are along a line stretching across the island from Port Louis to Mahebourg and Plaisance Airport. These include Curepipe (63,181), Beau Bassin-Rose Hill (91,786), Vacoas-Phoenix (54,430) and Quatre Bornes (64,506).

Both Mauritius and Rodrigues are of volcanic origin. The surface of Mauritius consists of a broad plateau sloping toward a northern coastal plain, with elevations of up to 826 m. (2,710 ft.) near the southern coastline. Three ranges of mountains, the Moka Range, the Grand Port Range and the Black River Range, follow in sequence from north to southwest. The island has a jagged coastline with many natural harbors and is nearly encircled by a coral reef. Rodrigues is composed of basalt and is mountainous throughout, with very little flat land. A central ridge 400 m. (1,300 ft.) high divides the island from the southeast to the northwest for most of its length, with spurs extending from the northern and southern coasts.

The main river is the Grande-Rivière Sud-Est, which flows for 16 km. (10 mi.) through a large gorge. Some of the volcanic craters contain lakes, and there are impressive falls.

CLIMATE & WEATHER

Mauritius has a tropical maritime climate. The southeasterly trade winds blow from April to October, during which months the climate is mild on the plain and cold on the plateau. The hot and wet season lasts from November to March. The temperature varies from 16.6°C (62°F) to 30°C (86°F) at sea level to 13°C (55°F) to 26°C (79°F) in the highlands.

The rains are heaviest in summer and autumn, from December to May, but there is no dry season as such except in the northwestern and western lowlands. The southeastern and central regions receive 1,520 to 5,080 mm. (60 to 200 in.) of rain annually. The relatively dry western coast, where the capital is located, receives

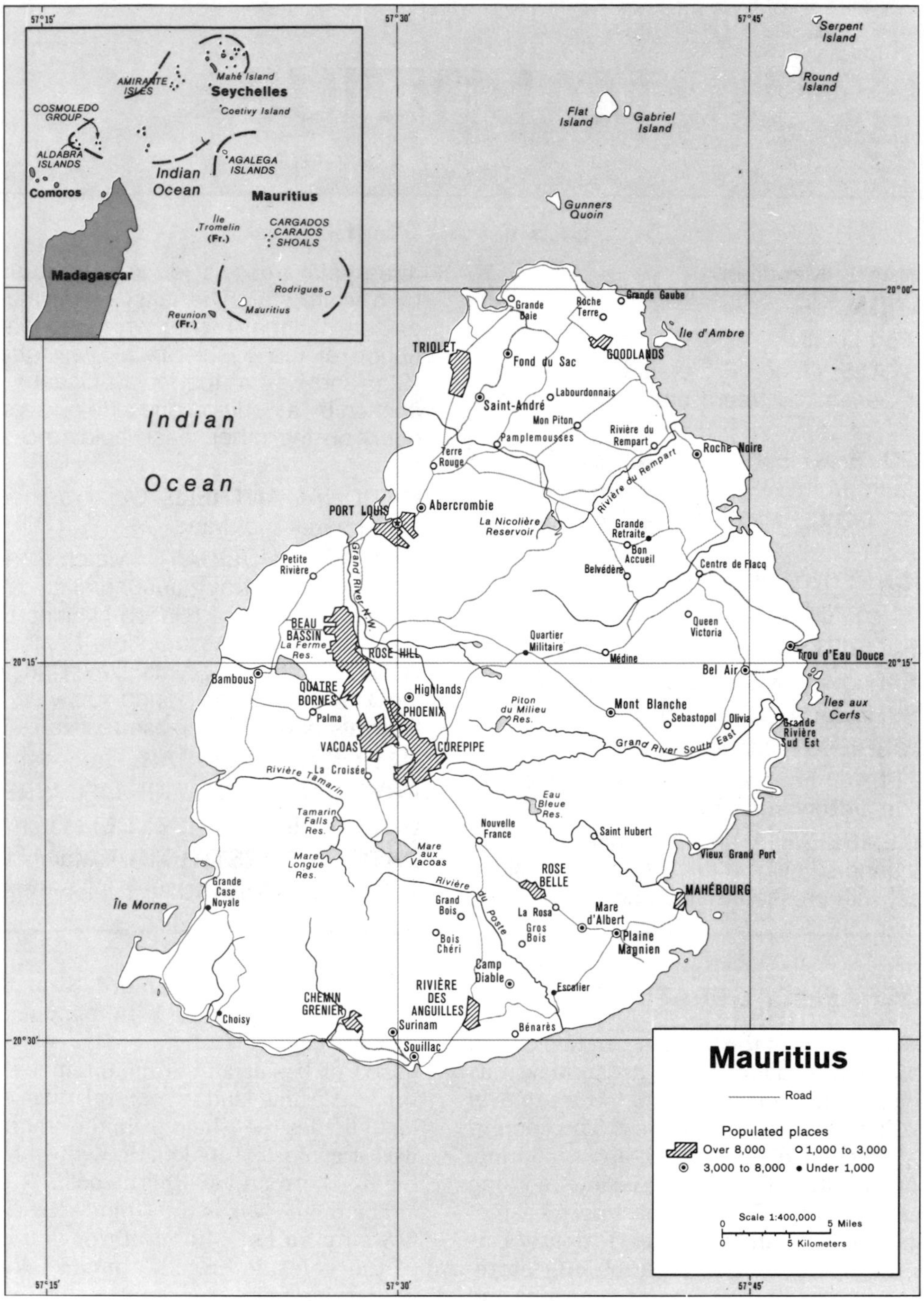

Mauritius
Road
Populated places
Over 8,000
1,000 to 3,000
3,000 to 8,000
Under 1,000
Scale 1:400,000
0
5 Miles
0
5 Kilometers
57°15'
57°30'
57°45'
20°00'
20°15'
20°30'
AMIRANTE ISLES
Mahé Island
Seychelles
Coetivy Island
COSMOLEDO GROUP
ALDABRA ISLANDS
AGALEGA ISLANDS
Comoros
Indian Ocean
Mauritius
Île Tromelin (Fr.)
CARGADOS CARAJOS SHOALS
Madagascar
Rodrigues
Reunion (Fr.)
Mauritius
Serpent Island
Round Island
Flat Island
Gabriel Island
Gunners Quoin
Indian
Ocean
Grande Gaube
Roche Terre
Grande Baie
Île d'Ambre
TRIOLET
Fond du Sac
GOODLANDS
Labourdonnais
Saint-André
Mon Piton
Pamplemousses
Rivière du Rempart
Terre Rouge
Roche Noire
Rivière du Rempart
PORT LOUIS
Abercrombie
La Nicolière Reservoir
Grande Retraite
Bon Accueil
Belvédère
Centre de Flacq
Petite Rivière
Grand River N.W.
Queen Victoria
BEAU BASSIN
La Ferme Res.
ROSE HILL
Quartier Militaire
Médine
Trou d'Eau Douce
Bambous
QUATRE BORNES
Highlands
Bel Air
Palma
PHOENIX
Piton du Milieu Res.
Mont Blanche
Sebastopol
Olivia
Îles aux Cerfs
Grande Rivière Sud Est
VACOAS
CUREPIPE
Grand River South East
La Croisée
Rivière Tamarin
Eau Bleue Res.
Tamarin Falls Res.
Nouvelle France
Saint Hubert
Mare aux Vacoas
Mare Longue Res.
Vieux Grand Port
ROSE BELLE
Grande Case Noyale
MAHÉBOURG
Rivière du Poste
Île Morne
Grand Bois
La Rosa
Mare d'Albert
Gros Bois
Bois Chéri
Plaine Magnien
Camp Diable
Escalier
CHEMIN GRENIER
RIVIÈRE DES ANGUILLES
Choisy
Surinam
Bénarès
Souillac

STELLA CLAVISQVE MARIS INDICI

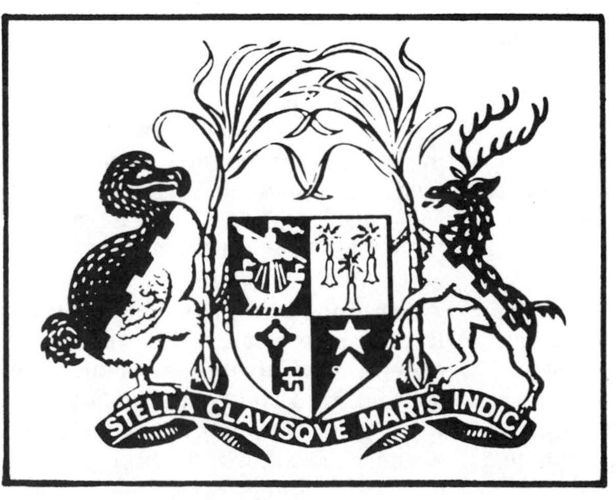

less than 1,010 mm. (40 in.) of rain a year. The annual rainfall in Rodrigues is 1,250 to 1,750 mm. (49 to 69 in.), most of it between November and March.

Devastating tropical cyclones occur from November to March.

POPULATION

The population of Mauritius was estimated in 1990 at 1,070,005, on the basis of the last official census, in 1983, when the population was 993,700.

Mauritius has one of the highest density rates in the world. Densities vary somewhat among different sections, but pressures on land remain intense throughout the country.

Historically, Mauritius has had an unbalanced sex ratio as a result of a consistent excess of males over females because of the importation of male laborers from India. This imbalance has been corrected over the years, and in the 1983 census the male–female ratio reached 49.8:50.2.

Emigration is encouraged by the government as a solution to the island's massive overpopulation problem. The annual emigration rate has been estimated at about 4.5 per 1,000, but it is slowing because potential destinations such as Australia, Canada and Great Britain have severe restrictions as to color, occupation and numbers of immigrants.

The Mauritian government is on record as seeking to improve the status of women. Recent amendments to laws ranging from emigration to inheritance have removed sexually discriminatory sections. The emphasis on mother-child health care has encouraged food supplements for pregnant women, greater prenatal care and female education. There is a Ministry of Women's Rights and Family Affairs, headed by a woman. Nonetheless, despite a sixfold increase in the 1984–85 budget, this ministry receives only $300,000. The literacy rate in 1988 for women was 74.8%, compared to 89% for men. Women tend to occupy the less-skilled and lower-paid jobs in the economy, such as operators in the textile plants. They are particularly susceptible to layoffs during economic downturns. The average industrial salary for women is about 30% less than that of men. Women in Mauritius are free to participate in all types of political, business and social activities, and a few hold high positions. Nonetheless, conservative religious and ethnic attitudes do inhibit women, and in the mid-1980s only 8.6% of the 70 Legislative Assembly members and one of 19 ministers were women. Some inequality remains, including a prohibition against women serving on juries.

Overpopulation is a matter of serious national concern, and family planning had significantly reduced the birth rate to 1.25% in 1985–90. In addition to government programs, family planning is promoted by the private Family Planning Association and the Catholic Church-supported Action Familiale. A total of 78% of married women of childbearing age are believed to practice some form of contraception.

DEMOGRAPHIC INDICATORS

Population (millions) 1.070 (1990)
Year of last census: 1983
Sex distribution (% at last census): males, 49.8; females, 50.2
Population estimates and projections (000)

1930: 413	1960: 662	2000: 1,210
1940: 428	1970: 824	
1950: 479	1980: 957	

Age profile (% at last census)

0–14: 32.6	30–44: 17.8	60–74: 5.7
15–29: 31.7	45–59: 10.9	75 and over: 1.3

Median age (yrs.): 23.8 (1985)
Youth population (% aged 15–24): (1985) 23.2; (2000) 17.5
Total dependency ratio, 1985: 51.8
Annual growth rate (%)

1950–55: 2.92	1975–80: 1.91	2000–2005: 0.99
1955–60: 3.17	1980–85: 1.60	2005–10: 0.83
1960–65: 3.18	1985–90: 1.25	2010–15: 0.69
1965–70: 1.83	1990–95: 1.21	2015–20: 0.57
1970–75: 0.49	1995–2000: 1.13	2020–25: 0.45

Hypothetical size of stationary population (millions): 2
Assumed year of reaching net reproduction rate of 1: 2030
Urban population (000): 437 (1985)
Urban population (%): 42 (1988); 37 (1965)
Annual urban population growth rate (%, 1985–90): 1.34
Annual rural population growth rate (%, 1985–90): 1.18
Percentage of urban population in largest city: 13.5 (1985)
Number of cities of population over 500,000: 0 (1985)
Population density per sq. km. (per sq. mi.): 529.4 (1,370.6) (latest)

VITAL STATISTICS

Crude birth rate (/1,000): 21 (1990); 36 (1965)
Crude death rate (/1,000): 6 (1990); 8 (1965)
Infant mortality rate (/1,000 live births): 20 (1990)
Maternal mortality rate (/100,000 live births): 99 (1980)
Life expectancy (yrs.) at birth (1980–85): males, 66; females, 73 (1990)
Gross reproduction rate (/woman) (1980–85): 1.18
Total fertility rate (/woman): 2.0 (1990)
Rate of natural increase (/1,000): 11.4 (1986)
Marriage rate (/1,000): 11.6 (1987)
Average family size: 5.3 (latest)
Legitimate births (%): 72.8 (latest)

STATUS OF WOMEN INDICATORS

Number of women (000): 526 (1985)
% women of childbearing age 15–49: 56 (1988)
% married women using contraception: 78 (1985)
% women literate: 74.8 (1988)
% women in labor force: 25.9 (1988)
Total fertility rate (/woman): 2.0 (1990)
% women in national legislature: 8.6 (1984)

ETHNIC COMPOSITION

When the Dutch discovered Mauritius in the late 16th century, there was no indigenous population on the island. None of the Dutch remained on the island. The earliest permanent inhabitants were the French and African blacks. Later immigrants to the island included Indians, Chinese and mulattoes. A large majority of current inhabitants of the island are the Indo-Mauritians. The next-largest group are the Creoles. Minority groups are the Sino-Mauritians and Franco-Mauritians.

Interethnic relations are characterized by intense economic and political rivalry. None of these communities shares common values or institutions, and each community has its own sector of the economy in which it has a virtual monopoly. Because ethnic identity usually is reinforced by religious and linguistic heritage, ethnic barriers tend to be fixed and inflexible. Only the Creoles permit some degree of assimilation. In Rodrigues the ethnic ratio is reversed, with Europeans and Creoles forming a large majority of the population.

LANGUAGES

English is the official language. However, the lingua franca is Creole. Creole is a language (not a dialect, as commonly described) derived from French but with its syntax, pronunciation and vocabulary modified through borrowings from African languages. It was originally a slave language, but it has managed to coexist with and even displace French over the years. Six Indian languages are spoken in Mauritius. Three are spoken by sizable numbers: Hindi, Urdu and Tamil. Hindi is an Indo-European language derived from Sanskrit and Pali and written in the ancient Devanagiri script, while Urdu, spoken almost exclusively by Muslims, is a related language with loanwords from Arabic, Turkish and Persian and is written in a modified Arabic script. The other Indian languages are Marathi, Gujarati and Telugu, of which Marathi and Gujarati are Indo-European languages and Telugu, like Tamil, is a Dravidian language. Chinese is a minor language.

French enjoys more prestige than English and is spoken by over 60,000 persons, although the quality of spoken French varies according to the educational level of the speaker.

RELIGIONS

The religious configuration closely follows the ethnic and linguistic divisions. Nearly 51% of the population is Hindu, 33% Christian and 16% Muslim. Religious minorities include Buddhists, Confucians, Bahais and Ahmadiyyahs; the latter two are heterodox sects related to Islam. Of the orthodox Muslims, the vast majority belong to the Sunni sect.

Christianity, the oldest religion on the island, also has the greatest ethnic diversity among its adherents, with membership among all races. The largest single religious institution is the Roman Catholic Church, which also maintains the most extensive educational system on the islands. The entire island of Mauritius is one diocese, with 38 parishes. The Vatican is represented by an apostolic delegate without formal diplomatic status. The Church of England is headed by a bishop in Phoenix. Nearly all of Rodrigues' inhabitants are Christians.

HISTORICAL BACKGROUND

Mauritius was discovered and named by the Dutch (after their stadtholder Prince Maurice of Nassau) in 1598. It was abandoned by them in 1710. The French took possession of the island in 1715. It was governed by the French East India Company until 1767 and by the French government until 1810, when British forces seized control during the Napoleonic Wars. The most important events during British rule were the abolition of slavery in 1835 and the importation of indentured laborers from India. Since 1948, when property qualifications were abolished and the franchise was made universal, the Indian community has dominated the legislature.

The political history of Mauritius has been marked by the development of political parties based on ethnic rather than ideological divisions and by the formation of coalition governments.

The Mauritian Labor Party (MLP), founded and led by Sir Seewoosagur Ramgoolam and representing the Hindu majority, was the dominant political party prior to independence. Fearful of Indian domination, Europeans and creoles, under the leadership of Sir Gaetan Duval, united to form the Parti Mauricien Social-Democrate (PMSD), which opposed independence. In the island's first elections, held in 1957, the MLP won a narrow majority. Ramgoolam invited the PMSD to join forces with the MLP, establishing the precedent of government through coalition. The coalition won the August 1967 legislative elections, and Ramgoolam took office as prime minister at independence in March 1968.

Opposition to Ramgoolam's coalition government centered around the Mouvement Militant Mauricien (MMM), a leftist party led by Paul Berenger. The growth of the MMM resulted in political unrest as the party mobilized the island's trade unions in a series of strikes. In 1971, in response to a wave of strikes, the government imposed a state of emergency and suspended the elections due to be held in 1972. The PMSD and the MLP alliance collapsed in 1974, but the parties realigned following the MMM's victory in the 1976 elections to form a second coalition government.

During the late 1970s a collapse in world sugar prices severely affected the Mauritian single-crop economy. Drastic measures were taken to compensate for the 30% devaluation of the Mauritian rupee and the halt to economic growth. Wages were frozen, and taxes were increased. As a result, the MMM won a massive victory in the 1982 elections. MMM president Aneerood Jugnauth became prime minister, and Berenger was named minister of finance. In 1983 the party split and Berenger left the government, expelling Jugnauth from the MMM. Jugnauth formed a new party, the Mouvement Socialiste Mauricien (MSM). Through shrewd maneuvering he allied his party with the MLP and PMSD, an alliance that continued in power through the 1980s. Under Jugnauth's leadership Mauritius was economically transformed from a single-crop economy dependent on world sugar prices to a mixed economy in which manufacturing was the largest sector.

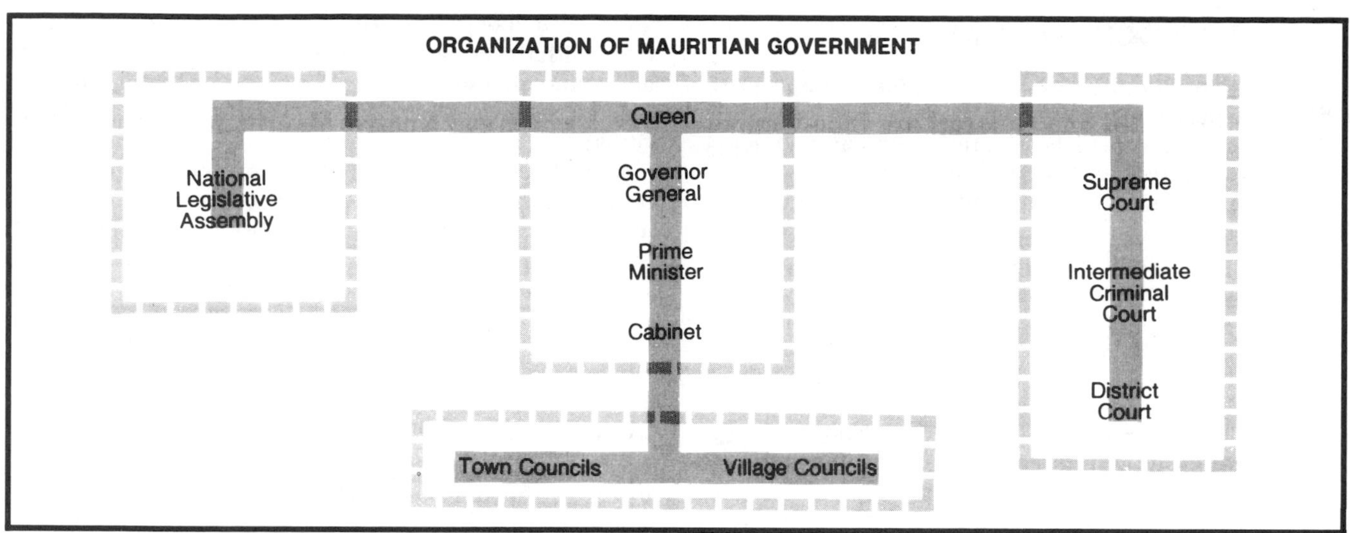

A drug-running scandal in 1985, involving high-ranking government officials, created a crisis for Jugnauth that lasted until November 1986, when he suspended the Legislative Assembly. In elections held in August 1987 the MSM aligned with the PMSD and the MLP against the MMM. Both groups had almost identical campaign platforms, and the drug scandal surfaced as the major campaign issue. In an effort to broaden support for the MMM, Berenger stepped down as party chief and was replaced by Prem Nababsingh. Despite this move, the government alliance won a majority of the seats but with less than half the popular vote.

During the summer of 1990, the MSM and the MMM formed an alliance again led by Berenger. The alliance involved an understanding that Mauritius would become a republic with Berenger as president. However, opposition to the arrangement in business circles and the Indian community made it doubtful that the two-thirds majority needed to change the Constitution could be mustered in Parliament. The vote was never called, and in August Parliament was dissolved. In late September the MMM entered the government.

CONSTITUTION & GOVERNMENT

The Mauritius Independence Order of 1968 was amended by the Constitution of Mauritius (Amendment) Act 39 of 1969. It established Mauritius as an independent parliamentary democracy within the Commonwealth. The British monarch is recognized by Mauritius as head of state and is represented by an appointed governor-general. The governor-general appoints the prime minister and the Council of Ministers based on the latter's recommendations. The Council of Ministers (which may consist of up to 20 ministers) is responsible to the unicameral Legislative Assembly, which consists of the speaker and 62 members elected by universal adult suffrage for a five-year term. An additional eight members are added to the Assembly based on the "best loser" system to provide balanced representation of all ethnic groups.

The judiciary is composed of the Supreme Court of nine judges, who also are judges of the Court of Criminal Appeal and the Court of Civil Appeal. Final appeal is to the Privy Council in the United Kingdom.

GOVERNMENT LIST
(July/August 1991)

Prime Minister	Jugnauth, Anerood, *Sir*
Deputy Prime Minister	Nababsing, Prem
Governor General	Ringadoo, Veerasamy, *Sir*
Minister of Agriculture, Fisheries & Natural Resources	Dulloo, Murlidas
Minister of Civil Service & Employment	Ruhee, Kailash
Minister of Cooperatives	Goburdhun, Jagdish
Minister of Defense & Internal Security	Jugnauth, Anerood, *Sir*
Minister of Economic Planning & Development	Ghurburrun, Beergoonath
Minister of Education, Arts & Culture	Parsooramen, Armoogum
Minister of Energy & Internal Communications	Utchanah, Mahyendra
Minister of Environment & Land	Kasenally, Swaley
Minister of External Affairs & Emigration	de l'Estrac, Jean-Claude
Minister of External Communications	Jugnauth, Anerood, *Sir*
Minister of Finance	Jugnauth, Anerood, *Sir*
Minister of Health	Goburdhun, Jagdish
Minister of Housing	Cuttaree, Jayen
Minister of Industry	Uteem, Cassam
Minister of Information	Jugnauth, Anerood, *Sir*
Minister of Interior	Jugnauth, Anerood, *Sir*
Minister of Justice	Cuttaree, Jayen
Minister of Labor & Industrial Relations	Bappoo, Sheila
Minister of Local Government	Finette, Regis
Minister of Outer Islands	Jugnauth, Anerood, *Sir*
Minister of Regional Administration	Finette, Regis
Minister of Rodrigues	Clair, Louis Serge
Minister of Social Security, National Solidarity & Reform Institutions	Sajadah, Vishwanath
Minister of Trade & Navigation	Gungah, Dwarkanath
Minister of Women's Rights & Family Affairs	Bappoo, Sheila
Minister of Works	Jaddoo, Ramduthsing
Minister of Youth, Sports & Tourism	Glover, Michaël James Kevin
Attorney General	
Governor, Central Bank	Ramphul, Induruth

FREEDOM & HUMAN RIGHTS

In terms of political and civil rights, Mauritius is classified as a partly free country.

Because of its British-oriented political and legal system, Mauritius has successfully adhered to the accepted standards of human rights. There are no political prisoners, although members of the opposition party are occasionally arrested and held for brief periods. Trials are conducted in conformity with the Constitution, and no instances of cruel, inhuman or degrading treatment or torture have been reported. The sanctity of the home is guaranteed under law and respected in practice, as are the basic freedoms of the press, assembly, speech and religion. There are no restrictions on movement within the country, foreign travel and emigration. Political participation is open to every adult citizen. Labor unions are free to organize, bargain collectively and strike.

CIVIL SERVICE

The civil service is headed by the chief secretary, who also is an ex officio member of the Legislative Assembly and a member of the Council of Ministers. Recruitment is based on competitive examinations. Recruitment, promotion and discipline are regulated by the Public Service Commission. The total strength of the civil service is estimated at 35,000.

LOCAL GOVERNMENT

For purposes of local government Mauritius is divided into nine administrative districts, with separate councils for urban and rural areas. There are five municipal and town councils in urban areas: Port Louis, Curepipe, Beau Bassin-Rose Hill, Quatre Bornes and Vocoas-Phoenix. Both urban and village councils have elected and nominated members. They raise their own taxes; make their own bylaws; regulate property rights; and handle road building, sanitation and water and food supply.

Of the dependencies, Rodrigues has considerable autonomy under a resident commissioner and five parish councils. The island sends two elected representatives to the Legislative Assembly and has a minister in the cabinet.

FOREIGN POLICY

For historical reasons Mauritian ties are closest to the United Kingdom, France and India, in that order. There are no major issues in foreign policy, although the Jugnauth government remains committed to the closure of U.S. military facilities on Diego Garcia (in July 1982 the MMM/PSM government had introduced legislation to declare the Chagos Archipelago part of Mauritius). In January 1983 Mauritius, Madagascar and Seychelles reached agreement on the terms of a constitution for the Indian Ocean Commission (IOC), formed to promote regional cooperation. In January 1984 the three countries signed the IOC's first regional cooperation agreement. Mauritius maintains diplomatic relations with the Soviet Union and China and also sustains active memberships in the OAU and OCAM (Common Organization of African and Malagasy States and Mauritius).

Mauritius and the United States are parties to 11 treaties and agreements, covering agricultural commodities, aviation, consuls, economic and technical cooperation, extradition, investment guarantees, the Peace Corps, property and trademarks.

PARLIAMENT

The Legislative Assembly is a unicameral body with 70 members, of whom 62 are elected (including two from Rodrigues) and eight are appointed from among the unsuccessful candidates who received the most votes. These usually represent communities underrepresented in the Legislative Assembly. The legislative term is five years.

The 1987 Legislative Assembly elections resulted in the following distribution of seats: Mouvement Socialiste Mauricien (MSM), 26; Mouvement Militant Mauricien (MMM), 21; Mauritian Labor Party (MLP), nine; Parti Mauricien Social-Democrate (PMSD), four; and Organisation du Peuple Rodrigais (OPR), two. The eight "best losers" were appointed as follows: MSM/PMSD/MLP, five; MMM, three.

POLITICAL PARTIES

A wide range of political parties has emerged through Mauritius' tradition of government by coalition. Most have grown out of ethnic rather than ideological alliances. The Mauritian Labor Party (MLP) was founded in 1936 under the leadership of Sir Seewoosagur Ramgoolam, who later was the first prime minister of independent Mauritius. It was the party of the Indian majority and initiated the drive for independence.

Fearing Indian domination, Europeans and creoles united to form the Parti Mauricien Social Democrate (PMSD), under the leadership of Sir Gaetan Duval. It is antisocialist, anti-Communist and Francophile. A third major political party is the Mouvement Militant Mauricien (MMM), a Marxist party strongly supported by the trade unions. Its membership cuts across ethnic lines. It is led by Paul Berenger, its founder, and has been active since the 1970s. A new political party was formed in April 1983 by Aneerood Jugnauth following his expulsion from the MMM by Berenger. It is the Mouvement Socialiste Militant (MSM), later renamed the Mouvement Socialiste Mauricien.

In the most recent elections for the Legislative Assembly, held August 30, 1987, the MSM allied itself with the PMSD and the MLP and gained 39 of the 62 elective seats. The MMM remains the major opposition party.

Minor political parties include the Muslim Action Committee; the Independent Forward Bloc, supported by Hindu workers and small planters; the Mauritian Democratic Union, formed by PMSD dissidents; the left-wing Mauritius People's Progressive Party; and the

Maoist Mauritian Social Progressive Militant Movement.

ECONOMY

During the 1980s Mauritius moved from a single-crop agricultural economy based on sugar to a mixed economy. The Export Processing Zone (EPZ), established in 1971, has attracted foreign investment in manufacturing and has shown remarkable growth in terms of number of enterprises and increases in both employment and earnings. The vast majority of EPZ exports are textiles, primarily knitwear. Since 1986 the government has encouraged diversification into other industries, such as offset printing and the manufacture of electronic equipment.

Agriculture follows manufacturing in importance to the economy and is dominated by sugar production. A five-year plan initiated by the government in 1985 was intended to restructure the sugar industry. Increases in efficiency and productivity and reduction of production costs were the main goals. The plan was supported by a World Bank loan in 1986. An acute labor shortage in the industry by 1988 hindered reaching proposed goals.

Because of concentration of most agricultural land on a single crop, subsistence agriculture is minimal. Food imports account for a significant segment of total imports. The government is endeavoring to increase food production on the island through its national policy goal of reducing by 1% each year the acreage devoted to sugar production.

Tourism ranks third in importance as a source of foreign exchange and has expanded rapidly since 1967. The main markets are Réunion, France and South Africa. Arrivals from Great Britain and other European countries are steadily increasing. Australia and Singapore are potential markets due to new Air Mauritius flights. Acceptance of the Indian rupee as convertible currency is expected to produce increased arrivals from India.

Plans are under way to develop Mauritius as an offshore financial center for the Indian Ocean. Investment capital is expected to come from European as well as South African and Hong Kong sources.

PRINCIPAL ECONOMIC INDICATORS

Gross national product (U.S. $ billions): 2,068 (1989)
GNP per capita (U.S. $) 1,950 (1989)
GNP average annual growth rate (%, 1980–89): 6.4
GNP per capita average annual growth rate (%, 1987–89): 4.8
Income distribution (%, household income)
  Lowest 20%: 40.0
  Highest 10%: 46.7
Average annual rate of inflation (%, 1980–88): 7.8
Consumer Price Index (1980 = 100), 1986
  All items: 123
  Food: 128
Average annual growth rate (%, 1980–88)
  General government consumption: 2.2
  Private consumption: 3.6
  Gross domestic investment: 14.0

BALANCE OF PAYMENTS, 1989
(U.S. $ millions)

Current account balance: −71.1
Merchandise exports: 989.7
Merchandise imports: −1,170.4
Trade balance: −180.6
Other goods, services & income +: −465.0
Other goods, services & income −: −432.2
Other goods, services & income net: 32.8
Private unrequited transfers: 68.2
Official unrequited transfers: 8.5
Capital other than reserves: −207 (1988)
Net errors & omissions: 169.7
Counterpart items: −29.0
Total change in reserves: −116.1

GROSS DOMESTIC PRODUCT

GDP nominal (R. billions): 43.559 (1987)
GDP per capita (U.S. $): 1,910 (1988)
Average annual growth rate of GDP, % (1980–88): 5.7
GDP by type of expenditure (%), 1987
  Consumption
    Private: 59
    Government: 11
  Gross domestic investment: 27
  Gross domestic saving: 25 (1988)
  Foreign trade
    Exports: 64
    Imports: −61
Cost components of GDP (%), 1987
  Net indirect taxes: 17
  Compensation of employees: 38
  Net operating surplus and consumption of fixed capital: 45
Sectoral origin of GDP (%), 1986
  Primary
    Agriculture: 13 (1988)
  Secondary
    Manufacturing: 24 (1987)
    Construction: 5
    Public utilities: 2
  Tertiary
    Transportation & communications: 11
    Trade: 15
    Finance: 13
    Other services: 4
    Government: 10
Average annual sectoral growth rates (%, 1980–88)
  Agriculture: 4.0
  Industry: 9.0
  Manufacturing: 11.4
  Services: 4.6

PUBLIC FINANCE

The Mauritian fiscal year runs from July 1 through June 30.

The government's development policy has focused on the transformation of the single-crop agricultural economy into a mixed economy with emphasis on exports. The focus has been on the creation of the Export Processing Zone (EPZ), which currently is the main generator of economic growth. Fiscal and other incentives in the budget have attracted over 200 companies to the zone, while government policies have reduced inflation and turned a negative growth rate of 5.9% in 1980 to a positive growth rate of 6.4% in 1989.

CENTRAL GOVERNMENT EXPENDITURES, 1988

% of total expenditures
- Defense: 0.8
- Education: 12.7
- Health: 7.6
- Housing, Social Security, welfare: 16.6
- Economic services: 23.8
- Other: 38.6
- Total expenditures as % of GNP: 24.8
- Overall surplus or deficit as % of GNP: 0.3

CENTRAL GOVERNMENT REVENUES, 1987

% of total current revenues
- Taxes on income, profit & capital gain: 10.9
- Social Security contributions: 4.0
- Domestic taxes on goods & services: 18.6
- Taxes on international trade & transactions: 50.8
- Other taxes: 5.2
- Current nontax revenue: 10.5
- Total current revenue as % of GNP: 25.1

General government consumption as % of GDP: 11 (1988)
Annual growth rate of general government consumption: 2.4% (1980–88)

FOREIGN AID, 1989

Total foreign aid (U.S. $ millions): 131.2
- Bilateral: 95.6
- Multilateral: 35.7

The government is attempting to diversify the economy further by making Mauritius an international financial center. It has relaxed exchange controls and plans to waive travel allowance, restructure banking regulations and open a stock exchange.

The government receives over half its revenues from taxes on international trade and transactions, with taxes on income, profit and capital gain and domestic taxes on goods and services contributing another 29.5%. Over half its expenditures go to social and general public services.

During 1970–88 Mauritius received $72 million in US aid. From 1970–87 it received $538 million in assistance from other Western countries. Communist countries contributed $54 million during 1970–88.

FINANCIAL INDICATORS, 1988

Total reserves minus gold (SDR's millions): 394
SDR's (millions): 5
Reserve position in IMF (SDR's millions): 0.0
Foreign exchange (SDR's millions): 389
Gold (fine troy oz. millions): .06
Ratio of external debt to total reserves (1986): 1.5 (1983)
Central bank, 1989
- Assets %
  - Foreign assets: 84.9
  - Claims on government: 13.3
  - Claims on banks: 1.8
  - Claims on private sector: 0.0
- Liabilities %
  - Reserve money: 43.5
  - Government deposits: 16.8
  - Foreign liabilities: 10.2
  - Capital accounts: 3.7

Money supply, 1987
Stock (R. billions): 4.383
M^1 per capital: 4,110
Private banks, 1989
- Assets %
  - Loans to government: 29.5
  - Loans to private sector: 54.7
  - Reserves: 3.1
  - Foreign assets: 7.7
- Liabilities
  - Deposits (R. billions): 19.832
  - of which %
    - Demand deposits: 9.9
    - Savings deposits: 78.9
    - Government deposits: 0.0
    - Foreign liabilities: 0.7

External debt, 1987
- Total (U.S. $ millions): 861
  - of which public (U.S. $ millions): 652
  - of which private (U.S. $ millions): 57
- Debt service, (long term) total (U.S. $ millions): 142
  - Repayment
    - Principal (%): 71.1
    - Interest (%): 38.9
- Debt service ratio (%): 10.1 (1986)
- External public debt as % of GNP: 34.1
- Debt service as % of GNP: 7.4
- Debt service as % of exports: 10.1
- Terms of public borrowing
  - Commitments (U.S. $ millions): 176
  - Average interest rate (%): 7.7
  - Average maturity (yrs.): 15
- Net flow of publicly guaranteed external capital (U.S. $ millions): 111
- Net direct private investment (U.S. $ millions): 31

CURRENCY & BANKING

The Mauritian unit of currency is the Mauritian rupee, divided into 100 cents. Coins are issued in denominations of 1, 2, 5, 10, 25 and 50 cents and 1 rupee; notes are issued in denominations of 5, 10, 25 and 50 rupees.

Before 1976 the Mauritian rupee was tied to the pound sterling; In 1976 the rupee's link with sterling was broken, and the currency was pegged to the SDR (Special Drawing Rights), based on a weighted basket of 16 national currencies. In June 1991 the dollar exchange rate was $1 = R 15.97.

The banking system is headed by the central bank, the Bank of Mauritius, with a paid-up capital of R10 million. Other domestic banks include the Development Bank of Mauritius, the Mauritius Cooperative Central Bank, the Mauritius Commercial Bank Ltd. and the State Commercial Bank. Several branches of overseas commercial banks operate in the country.

AGRICULTURE

Sugarcane is the principal crop; subsistence farming is minimal.

There are 21 large estates, covering 48,039 ha. (118,656 ac.), each with a factory for processing the estate sugar and the cane grown by planters in the surrounding areas. The other land under sugarcane, producing 40% of the total crop, is owned by 452 "big" planters and at least 30,000 "small" planters. Many of the latter, who

GROWTH PROFILE
(Annual Growth Rates, %)

Projected population, (1988–2000): 0.8
Projected crude birth rate, (/1,000) 1990–95: 18.0
Projected crude death rate, (/1,000) 1990–95: 5.6
Urban population, (1980–88): 0.8
Labor force, (1985–2000): 2.1
GNP, (1980–89): 6.4
GNP per capita, (1986–88): 9.3
GDP, (1980–88); 5.7
Inflation, (1980–88): 7.8
Agriculture, (1980–88): 4.0
Industry, (1980–88): 9.0
Manufacturing, (1980–89): 11.4
Services, (1980–88): 4.6
Money holdings, (1980–88): 20.2
Manufacturing earnings per employee, (1980–87): −1.8
Energy production, (1980–88): 6.7
Energy consumption, (1980–88): 2.8
Exports, (1980–88): 12.1
Imports, (1980–88): 8.7
General government consumption, (1980–88): 2.4
Private consumption, (1980–88): 3.6
Gross domestic investment, (1980–88): 14.0

are mostly Indo-Mauritian and who cultivate about a quarter of the total land under cane, have grouped themselves into cooperatives to facilitate consignment of cane to factories on the estates. Progress has been made in improving yields through introduction of irrigation and new strains of sugarcane. The large-scale Northern Plains irrigation program is expected to increase yields from 62 to 104 metric tons per hectare (25 to 42 metric tons per acre). Most of the island's sugar was at one time sold to the United Kingdom at a guaranteed price under the Commonwealth Sugar Agreement, but in the mid-1970s this arrangement was replaced by a protocol of the first Lomé Convention, which was signed that year by the EEC and 46 developing countries, including Mauritius. Under this protocol and its successor, Mauritius is given an annual quota of 500,000 metric tons of raw cane sugar. In practice, most of this goes to the United Kingdom, which takes about 70% of Mauritius' total sugar exports. Other important customers are the United States, Canada and New Zealand. Local consumption in 1983 was 36,546 metric tons. Tea is grown in the humid highlands, which are unsuitable for sugar, but since 1959 the government has been expanding the area and distributing it to smallholders grouped into cooperatives. The area under tea is now over 4,971 ha. (12,278 ac.), and the number of tea smallholders is 1,500. The Tea Development Authority (TDA) was created by the government in 1971. There are nine tea factories.

Since other agricultural production is limited by the scarcity of cultivable land not already planted in sugar, Mauritius must import most of its food. The authorities are actively promoting greater self-sufficiency in food production. Owners of sugar estates, for example, are being encouraged to raise vegetables between rows of cane.

The land area in forest is owned equally by state and private interests.

AGRICULTURAL INDICATORS, 1980

Agriculture's share of GDP (%): 13 (1989)
Average annual growth rate (%, 1980–88): 4.0
Value added in agriculture (U.S. $ millions): 211 (1988)
Cereal imports (000 metric tons): 177 (1988)
Index of Agricultural Production (1979–81 = 100): 121 (1986)
Index of Food Production (1979–81 = 100) 120 (1986)
Index of Food Production per Capita (1979–81 = 100): 103 (1985–87)
Number of tractors: 344 (1986)
Total fertilizer consumption: 28 (000 metric tons) (1985–86)
Fertilizer consumption (g./ha., hundreds): 3,075 (1987–88)
Number of farms (000): 32.5
Average size of holding (ac.): 1.1 (2.7)
Size class (%)
- Below 1 ha. (below 2.47 ac.): 61.3
- 1–5 ha. (2.47–12.35 ac.): 36.2
- 5–10 ha. (12.35–24.7 ac.): 1.9
- 10–20 ha. (24.7–49.4 ac.): 0.3
- 20–50 ha. (49.4–123.5 ac.): 0.2
- 50–200 ha. (123.5–494 ac.): } 0.1
- Over 200 ha. (over 494 ac.): }

Tenure (%)
- Owner-operated: 95.8
- Rented: 4.2

Farms as % of total land area: 91.5
Land use (%)
- Permanent crops: 5.9
- Temporary crops: 94.1
- Meadows & pastures: 4.4
- Woodland: 33.4

Yields kg./ha. (lb./ac.) 1989
- Grains: 4,000
- Roots & tubers: 19,588
- Legumes: 675
- Fruits (000 metric tons): 10
- Vegetables (000 metric tons): 34
- Milk, kg./animal: 2,500

Livestock (000) 1989
- Cattle: 33
- Horses: 0 (1986)
- Sheep: 7
- Pigs: 10

Forestry 1988
- Production of roundwood, (000 cu. m.): 34
  - of which industrial roundwood (%): 38.2

Fishing 1988
- Total catch (000 metric tons): 17.2
  - of which marine (%): 99.7
- Value of exports (U.S. $ 000): 16,186

MANUFACTURING

Manufacturing, the largest sector of Mauritius' GDP, grew considerably during the 1980s. Substantial investment in the industrial sector in the first development plan has resulted in the establishment of more sophisticated industries, making use of the island's relatively cheap but skilled labor. Among these, textiles, diamonds and electronics are the fastest-growing subsectors. However, the potential for further industrial development appears limited.

Given the limited domestic market, the high level of unemployment and the need to lessen dependence on the sugar sector, the government adopted a policy of export promotion by developing the Export Processing Zone (EPZ), a sector that concentrates on labor-intensive processing of imported goods for the export market. Within the EPZ, the government offers both local

MANUFACTURING INDICATORS, 1987

Average annual growth rate (%, 1980–88): 11.4
Share of GDP (%): 25 (1989)
Labor force in manufacturing (%): 30.7 (1989)
Value added in manufacturing (U.S. $ millions): 358
- Food and agriculture (%): 27
- Textiles (%): 52
- Machinery (%): 2
- Chemicals (%): 4

Earnings per employee in manufacturing 1987
- Growth rate (%, 1980–87): −1.8
- Index (1980 = 100): 94

Total earnings as % of value added: 43
Gross output per employee (1980 = 100): 74

and foreign investors attractive packages of incentives, including tax "holidays", exemption from import duties on most raw materials and capital goods; free repatriation of capital, profits and dividends; and cheap electricity. More than half of the industries are locally owned, the remainder being mainly Hong Kong, Pakistani, Indian, French, West German and British. The fastest-growing EPZ sectors have been textiles and clothing (more than half of the firms, employing 85% of all EPZ labor and accounting for about 60% of EPZ exports), electronics components and diamonds, and emphasis has been put on the development of precision engineering (electronics, watch and instrument making, etc.) and skilled crafts (diamond cutting and polishing, furniture, quality goods, etc.). Other products include toys, razor blades, nails, industrial chemicals, detergents, rattan furniture, plastic goods, tires and assembly of recording cassettes. During the early 1980s many of the EPZ industries experienced difficulties, and several closed down, partly because of stagnant European markets but also because of huge rises in costs, both of labor and of imported raw materials. In addition, import quotas imposed by the major textiles customers, France and the United Kingdom, were damaging. Nevertheless, Mauritius is the world's third-largest exporter of items bearing the International Wool Secretariat's "pure new wool" symbol. In terms of the Lomé Convention, most of the output of the EPZ is eligible for duty-free entry to the EC.

MINING

There are no known mineral deposits in Mauritius.

ENERGY

Mauritius is not self-sufficient in energy and must import petroleum. The cost of these imports was 13.6% of total imports in 1985 but fell to 7.5% in 1987 as a result of the decline in world oil prices. Hydroelectric power provides about 16% of electricity and recycled sugar byproducts (bagasse) 12%. The government plans the expansion of both hydroelectric and bagasse facilities.

ENERGY INDICATORS

Average annual energy production growth rate (%, 1980–88): 6.7
Energy consumption per capita (000 kg. oil equivalent): 402 (1988)
Energy imports as % of merchandise exports: 9 (1988)
Average annual growth rate of energy consumption (%, 1980–88): 2.8
Electricity 1988
- Installed capacity (000 kw.): 302
- Production (million kw.-hr.): 639
  - % fossil fuel: 84.4
  - % hydro: 15.6
  - % nuclear: 0.0
- Consumption per capita (kw.-hr.): 593

Coal
- Consumption (metric tons): 40,000

LABOR

The breakdown of the labor force changed during the 1980s. At the beginning of the decade the largest portion of the labor force, almost 30%, was employed in the sugar industry. By the end of the decade almost one-third of the labor force was employed in the EPZ. Unemployment, traditionally a serious problem, fell from 18% at the beginning of the decade to 11% in 1987. Rates differ dramatically between men and women. Since two of three jobs in the EPZ are held by women, unemployment is three times higher for men. Inducements to attract men to the EPZ have resulted in a labor shortage in the sugar industry.

Ethnic background is an important consideration in determining occupations. Thus, an overwhelming majority of cane workers are Hindus. Muslims tend to be urban landholders and traders. The Chinese are small shopkeepers and Creoles monopolize white-collar jobs.

Conditions of employment in Mauritius, including wage and leave conditions, are generally sufficient to afford an acceptable standard of living for workers in the agricultural, service and manufacturing sectors. A maximum workweek of 45 hours is allowed, and children below age 14 cannot be legally employed, although scattered cases of child labor have been reported. The government mandates minimum wage increases each year based on inflation. It also operates an unemployment insurance program and a Social Security fund, although an effective social safety net does not yet exist. Mauritius has stringent health and safety legislation that requires, inter alia, that a full-time health and safety inspector be present at all major industrial and agricultural workplaces.

There are over 270 labor unions, representing 35% of the work force and organized in four large confederations: the General Workers' Federation, with 43 affiliated unions; the Fédération des Syndicats du Service Civil, with 18 affiliated unions; the Mauritius Labor Congress, with 19 affiliated unions; and the Mauritius Federated Trade Unions. Unions are free to organize workers in all sectors, including the Export Processing Zone (EPZ). Unions can press wage demands, establish ties to domestic political parties and international organizations and address political issues. One leading

LABOR INDICATORS, 1989

Total economically active population (000): 440
% working-age population (15–64): 67.1
% female: 34.8
Activity rate (%)
 Total: 42.7
 Male: 56.2
 Female: 29.5
Employment status (%) 1983
 Employers & self-employed: 9.0
 Employees: 60.8
 Unpaid family workers: 0.6
 Other: 29.6
Sectoral employment (%)
 Agriculture, forestry, fishing: 18.4
 Construction: 5.2
 Manufacturing, mining, quarrying, public utilities: 17.1
 Trade, hotels, restaurants: 12.8
 Transport, communications: 6.5
 Finance, real estate: 20
 Services: 20
Average annual growth rate of labor force, 1985–2000 (%): 2.1
Unemployment (000): 47 (1987)
Labor under 20 years (%): 9.8 (1987)
Earnings in manufacturing (/day): R35,17 (1985)

federation actively supports the main opposition party. The largest confederation, the Mauritius Labor Congress, is a member of the International Confederation of Free Trade Unions. Union in theory have the right to strike. Nonetheless, in labor disputes the Industrial Relations Act requires a prestrike 21-day cooling-off period followed by binding arbitration, which has the effect of circumventing most strikes. Some labor leaders have expressed concern over the elimination in January 1985 of minimum wage rates for male workers in the EPZ, and the unwillingness of some new EPZ investors to recognize their unions fully.

FOREIGN COMMERCE

Mauritius' major exports are textiles, sugar and light manufactures. Its major imports are manufactured goods, capital equipment, foodstuffs, petroleum products and chemicals. Its primary markets are the European Community and the United States, both of which have preferential treatment. Most imports come from the European Community, the United States, South Africa and Japan.

Mauritius is a member of OCAM, which it joined in 1971. In 1972 Mauritius became an associate member of the EEC. Following the expiration of the Commonwealth Sugar Agreement in the mid-1970s Mauritius was allotted an annual quota of 500,000 tons of sugar in EEC markets.

FOREIGN TRADE INDICATORS, 1988

Exports (U.S. $ billions): 1
Imports (U.S. $ billions): 1.3
Balance of trade (U.S. $ millions): −300
Annual growth rate 1980–87, exports (%): 12.1
Annual growth rate, 1980–87, imports (%): 8.7
International reserves in terms of months of imports: 3.5
Terms of trade (1980 = 100): 117
Import Price Index (1980 = 100): 93.4 (1986)
Export Price Index (1980 = 100): 35.3 (1986)

Direction of Trade (%), 1987

	Imports	Exports
European Communities	31.3	76.8
United States	12.8	13.3
East European economies	0.1	0.0
Japan	7.6	0.2

Composition of Trade (%), 1987

	Imports	Exports
Food and agricultural raw materials	15.7	40.9
Fuels and other energy	7.5	
Mineral ores and concentrates	1.5	
Manufactured goods	75.3	59.1
of which chemicals	6.4	0.6
of which machinery	22.1	0.6

TRANSPORTATION & COMMUNICATIONS

Mauritius has no railways or inland waterways. The principal port, Port Louis, handled 1,658,000 metric tons of cargo in 1982. The islands lie on one of the main shipping lanes from the Cape of Good Hope to Singapore. The national merchant marine consists of 35 vessels with total deadweight tonnage of 215.7.

Of the 1,783 km. (1,108 mi.) of roads, 92% are paved.

The national airline, Air Mauritius, provides service to the Comoros, Madagascar, Réunion, Rodrigues, Kenya, South Africa, India, Italy, France, Singapore, Switzerland, the Federal Republic of Germany and the United Kingdom. Sir Seewoosagur Ramgoolam International Airport is at Plaisance. Upgrading of the airport, begun in 1984, was completed in 1987, enabling it to serve one million passengers annually.

Tourism is the third-largest industry in Mauritius. The industry declined during the worldwide recession of the late 1970s and early 1980s but has increased steadily since. Most tourists come from Réunion, France and South Africa, but arrivals from Great Britain, West Germany, Italy and Switzerland have increased steadily.

TRANSPORTATION INDICATORS

Roads (latest)
 Length, km. (mi.): 1,783 (1,108)
 Paved (%): 92
Motor vehicles (latest)
 Automobiles: 26,160
 Trucks and buses: 1,775
 Persons per vehicle: 38
Merchant marine
 Vessels: 35 (1989)
 Total deadweight tonnage (000): 215.7 (1989)
Ports (pre-1976)
 Cargo loaded (000 metric tons): 876
 Cargo unloaded (000 metric tons): 1,236
Air (latest)
 Km. (mi.) flown (millions): 6.2 (3.9) (1985)
 Passenger-km. (passenger-mi.) (millions): 542.2 (336.9)
 Freight ton-km. (freight ton-mi.) (millions): 65.7 (45.0)
 Mail ton-km. (millions): 0.8 (mail ton-mi.): 0.8 (0.3)
 Airports with scheduled flights: 1 (1990)

COMMUNICATION INDICATORS, 1988

Telephones
  Total (000): 72
  Persons per telephone: 15
Phone traffic (per 000 calls)
  National: 83,851
  International: 7,985 (minutes)
Post office
  Number of post offices: 112
  Pieces of mail handled (000): 32,370
Telegraph
  International: 12,000 calls
Telex
  Subscriber lines: 784
  Traffic (000 minutes): 2,537
Telecommunications 1990
  1 satellite station

TOURISM & TRAVEL INDICATORS, 1986

Total tourist receipts (U.S. $ millions): 172 (1988)
Expenditures by nationals abroad (U.S. $ millions): 50 (1988)
Number of hotel beds (000): 6
Average length of stay: 12 nights
Tourist nights (000): 1,900
Number of tourists (000): 160.8 (1985)
  of whom from U.S.: 1.5
    France: 27.5
    Germany, Fed. Rep.: 8.9
    U.K.: 7.1

DEFENSE

Although there is a formal Ministry of National Defense and Internal Security, Mauritius has no defense forces, and the United Kingdom is bound by treaty to defend the island against external attack. Internal security is covered by a special 800-man police mobile unit.

EDUCATION

Educational standards are high. Almost all (98%) eligible attend primary and secondary schools.

Primary education is free and compulsory for seven years, between ages five and 12. Schooling lasts for 13 years, divided into six years of primary school and seven years of secondary school, which in turn is divided into three years of lower secondary and four years of upper secondary. Most secondary schools are operated by religious orders or other private groups. Private schools are regulated by the Private Secondary School Authority.

The school year is the calendar year. The language of instruction is English, but French also is stressed. The curriculum follows the British model.

Mauritius has a surplus of teachers.

Higher education is provided at the University of Mauritius. The Mauritius College of the Air was established in 1972 to provide TV seminars, radio and cassette instruction and correspondence courses.

EDUCATION INDICATORS, 1988

Literacy
  Total (%): 81.8
  Male (%): 89.0
  Female (%): 74.8
First level
  Schools: 273
  Students: 134,136
  Teachers: 6,504
  Student/teacher ratio: 23:1 (1986)
  Net enrollment ratio: 94 (1987)
Second level
  Schools: 125
  Students: 72,389
  Teachers: 3,683 (1987)
  Student/teacher ratio: 19:1 (1986)
  Net enrollment rate: 34% (1975)
Vocational
  Schools: 7
  Students: 518
  Teachers: 69
  Student/teacher ratio: 7:1
Third level
  Institutions: 2 (1984)
  Students: 344 (1982)
  Teachers: 184 (1982)
  Student/teacher ratio: 2:1 (1986)
  Gross enrollment rate: 1.3 (1987)
  Students (/100,000 pop.): 149
  % of population over 24 with post secondary education: 3.6
Foreign study
  Foreign students in national universities: 23 (1988)
  Students abroad: 2,406
    of whom in
      U.S.: 114 (1988)
      France: 1,397 (1988)
      Federal Republic of Germany: 22 (1988)
      U.K.: 270 (1989)
Public expenditure 1988
  Total: R1,046,800,000
  % of GNP: 4.1
  % of national budget: 10.6
  % of current expenditures: 94.7

GRADUATES, 1987

Total: 475
Education: 212
Social & behavioral sciences: 16
Commerce & business: 77
Mathematics & computer science: 65
Medicine: 28
Engineering: 7
Industrial programs: 47
Agriculture, forestry, fisheries: 23

LEGAL SYSTEM

The Mauritian legal system is a blend of English common law and French civil law.

Mauritius' judicial system, modeled on that of Great Britain, consists of a Supreme Court with appellate powers and a series of lower courts. The Supreme Court consists of a chief justice and eight junior judges, who also preside over the courts of civil and criminal appeal. Final appeal to the Queen's Privy Council in the United Kingdom is provided for by the Constitution. There are no political or military courts. The courts have a very good record of assuring fair, public trials to those charged with crimes. Defendants have the right to private or court-appointed legal counsel.

There have been no allegations by political parties, human rights groups or the media of political bias in the judiciary. In the past the judiciary has made several politically unpopular decisions, such as finding a prominent minister guilty of corruption. An intermediate criminal court with three senior magistrates can try criminal cases without juries. The subordinate courts are the district courts, with both civil and criminal jurisdiction, and the industrial court, with jurisdiction over labor disputes.

The correctional system consists of four facilities: one prison, one rehabilitation center, one youth institution and one industrial school, with a daily average prison population of about 700.

LAW ENFORCEMENT

The national law enforcement agency comprises a regular armed police, a special constabulary and a special mobile force. The regular police, with an authorized strength of 2,071, are deployed in outstations. At the headquarters the force is divided into a number of units, such as criminal investigation, riot control, traffic control, immigration and water police.

No information is available on the nature and incidence of crime in Mauritius.

There are no secret or political police in Mauritius.

HEALTH

Mauritius was once notorious as a very unhealthy place. Until World War II the population of the island was decimated periodically by various epidemics: cholera in the 1850s, malaria in 1867, bubonic plague in 1899, influenza in 1919 and poliomyelitis in 1945. Although malaria has almost been eradicated, other serious health problems remain, such as tuberculosis and bilharzia, or schistosomiasis.

Mauritius has a well-developed public health care system. Health services are free to all citizens.

HEALTH INDICATORS

Health personnel, 1987
- Physicians: 801
  - Persons per: 1,298
- Dentists: 120
- Nurses, midwives: 2,258
- Pharmacists: 100 (1986)

Hospitals, 1986
- Number: 19
- Number of beds (/10,000): 28
- Admissions/discharges (/10,000); 1,139 (1985)
- Bed occupancy rate (%): 84.5 (1980)
- Average length of stay (days): 8 (1980)

Type of hospitals (%), 1986
- Government: 89.5
- Private non-profit, private profit: 10.5

Public health expenditures, (latest)
- As % of national budget: 8.9
- per capita (U.S. $): 39.70

Vital statistics
- Crude death rate (/1,000 pop.): 6 (1990)
- Life expectancy at birth, 1990
  - Males: 66
  - Females: 73
- Infant mortality rate (/1,000 live births): 20 (1990)
- Child mortality rate (1985–90) under 5 yrs. (/1,000): 28
- Maternal mortality rate (/100,000 live births) (1980–84): 99.2

Population with access to safe water (%): 100 (latest)

FOOD & NUTRITION

The various ethnic groups in Mauritius have their own dietary habits and taboos. Rice is the staple for the Indians, both Hindus and Muslims, as well as the Creoles, but it is generally accompanied by stewed greens among the Creoles, meat and vegetable curries among the Indians, and Chinese dishes among the Chinese. French cuisine survives only among upper-class Creoles.

The per capita daily intake exceeds the WHO-recommended minimum.

MEDIA & CULTURE

Eight daily newspapers are published in the country, in English and French. *Le Mauricien*, *The Sun* and *L'Express* are those with the highest circulations. There are two Chinese daily newspapers, *Chinese Daily News* and *China Times*. There are numerous weekly and biweekly publications also. Most are written in English and French, although there is one each in Creole, Hindi and Chinese.

Mauritius has a long tradition of a free press, broken only during the emergency from 1971 to 1976. There

MEDIA INDICATORS

Newspapers
- Number of dailies: 8 (latest)
- Circulation (000): 90 (latest)
- Per 1,000 pop.: 86 (latest)
- Number of nondailies: 18 (1988)
- Circulation (000): 45 (1988)
- Per 1,000 pop.: 42 (1988)
- Number of periodicals: 58 (1988)
- Newsprint consumption: (1988)
- Total metric tons: 2,600
- Per 1,000 pop. (kg.): 2,407

Book Publishing
- Number of titles: 85 (latest)

Radio
- Number of transmitters: 5 (latest)
- Number of persons per radio receiver: 4.2 (1989)
- Total program hours: 116 per wk. (latest)

Television
- Television transmitters: 4 (latest)
- Number of persons per TV receiver: 8.3 (1989)
- Total program hours: 2,694 per yr. (latest)

Cinema
- Number of fixed cinemas: 37 (latest)
- Seating capacity (000): 34 (latest)
  - Seats (/1,000 pop.): 31.9 (1987)
- Annual attendance (million): 7.5 (latest)
- Gross box office receipts (millions R.): 18 (1987)

Films
- Import of long films: 273 (1987)
  - % from U.S. and France: 73.3
  - % from India: 26.7

CULTURAL & ENVIRONMENTAL INDICATORS (latest)

Libraries
- Number: 2
- Volumes (000): 260

Museums (pre-1986)
- Annual attendance (000): 237
- Attendance (/1,000 pop.): 236

Performing arts (pre-1986)
- Number of performances: 136
- Annual attendance (000): 36
- Attendance (/1,000 pop.): 38

Nature reserves
- Number of facilities: 1

is no national news agency. Both Reuters and AFP maintain bureaus in Port Louis.

Mauritius has a fairly active book publishing industry. It does not adhere to any copyright convention.

The government-controlled Mauritius Broadcasting Corporation operates one medium-wave transmitter and two shortwave transmitters, which are on the air for 116 hours a week broadcasting in French, English, Indian languages and Chinese. Television, introduced in 1965, is broadcast over five main stations and one auxiliary station for 50 hours a week. Of the 2,694 program hours a year, 810 are nationally produced.

All feature films exhibited are imported, and box office receipts indicate that cinema is a major form of entertainment. Films come from France, the United States and India.

Of the two public libraries, the larger is the Mauritius Institute Library.

There are three museums, reporting aggregate annual attendance of 237,000. There is one nature reserve.

SOCIAL WELFARE

Mauritius has a well-developed social welfare structure. Unemployed heads of families are able to obtain relief under the Unemployment Hardship Relief Program. A means-tested benefit and monthly allowance are provided for families through the Social Aid Program. In 1978 a national pension program was initiated. Health and social security were allotted 16% of current expenditures in the 1987–88 budget.

GLOSSARY

brede creole: stewed greens, a popular Creole dish.

CHRONOLOGY (from 1968)

1968— Following a popular referendum, Mauritius is granted full independence within the Commonwealth; riots between Muslims and Creoles force declaration of a state of emergency and the airlifting of British troops from Singapore to restore order; emergency is imposed.

1970— Emergency is lifted.

1971— Emergency is reimposed following nationwide unrest led by the Mauritian Militant Movement.

1972— Governor General Sir Arthur Williams dies and is replaced by Sir Rahman Osman.

1973— Resettlement that began in 1965 of indigenous population of Diego Garcia to Mauritius is completed.

1976— In first national elections since independence, leftists register impressive gains, capturing 30 seats in the Legislative Assembly.

1980— United States announces plans to make Diego Garcia the chief air and naval base in the Indian Ocean.

1982— The left-wing Mouvement Militant Mauricien (MMM), in alliance with the Parti Socialiste Mauricien (PSM), wins all 60 elective seats in the Legislative Assembly. . . . Aneerood Jugnauth is installed as prime minister and Paul Berenger of the MMM as finance minister. . . . Government introduces legislation making Chagos Archipelago part of Mauritius.

1983— Paul Berenger resigns as finance minister in clash with Jugnauth over economic and language issues. . . . Jugnauth is expelled from the MMM and forms his own party, Mouvement Socialiste Mauricien (MSM). . . . The Legislative Assembly is dissolved and early elections are called in August 1983. . . . A coalition of the MSM, the Labor Party and the Parti Mauricien Social-Democrate (PMSD) wins 41 of 60 elective seats. . . . Jugnauth retains his position as prime minister, and Sir Gaetan Duval of the PMSD is named deputy prime minister. . . . Strained relations between the Labor Party and the MSM result in the dismissal of Labor Party leader Sir Satcam Boolell from the cabinet. . . . However, 11 members of the Labor Party supported the government. . . . Draft constitutional amendment to make Mauritius a republic fails to get the required three-quarters majority in the Legislative Assembly. . . . Mauritius, Madagascar and Seychelles form the Indian Ocean Commission (IOC). . . . Sir Seewoosagur Ramgoolam is named governor general, succeeding Sir Dayendranath Burrenchobay.

1986— Sir Veerasamy Ringadoo succeeds Sir Seewoosagur Ramgoolam as governor-general.

1987— Election for the Legislative Assembly are held August 30. Berenger fails to win a seat and is replaced by Prem Nababsingh as Assembly opposition leader. Jugnauth coalition retains power.

1988— Mauritius renews attempts to regain sovereignty over Diego Garcia. Attempt is made on Jugnauth's life.

1989— Opposition demands Jugnauth's resignation because of his support of Soo Soobiah, former high commissioner to the United Kingdom prior to Soobiah's arrest on drug-smuggling charges. Second attempt is made on Jugnauth's life.

1990— An alliance formed between the MSM and the MMM, once again led by Berenger; Parliament is dissolved; the MMM enters the government.

BIBLIOGRAPHY

BOOKS

Baker, Philip. *Kreol: A Description of Mauritian Creole.* New York, 1973.

Benedict, Burton. *Mauritius: Problems of a Plural Society.* New York, 1965.

Meade, J. E. *The Economic and Social Structure of Mauritius.* London, 1961.

Ramdin, T. *Mauritius: A Geographical Survey.* London, 1973.

Rivere, Lindsay. *Historical Dictionary of Mauritius.* Metuchen, N.J., 1982.

Simmons, Adele S. *Modern Mauritius: The Politics of Decolonization.* Bloomington, Ind., 1982.

Titmuss, R. M., and B. Abel-Smith. *Social Policies and Population Growth in Mauritius.* London, 1961.

Wright, Carol. *Mauritius.* Harrisburg, Pa., 1974.

OFFICIAL PUBLICATIONS

Central Statistical Office. *Population Census of Mauritius and Its Dependencies.* Port Louis, Mauritius, 1972.

Finance Ministry. *Accountant General's Financial Statements in Government Gazette* (monthly).

———. *Capital Budget Estimates.*

———. *Financial Report.*

———. *Recurrent Budget Estimates with Memorandum.*

Mauritius Bank. *Annual Report.*

———. *Quarterly Review.*

Ministry of Information and Broadcasting. *Mauritius at a Glance.* Port Louis, Mauritius, 1967.

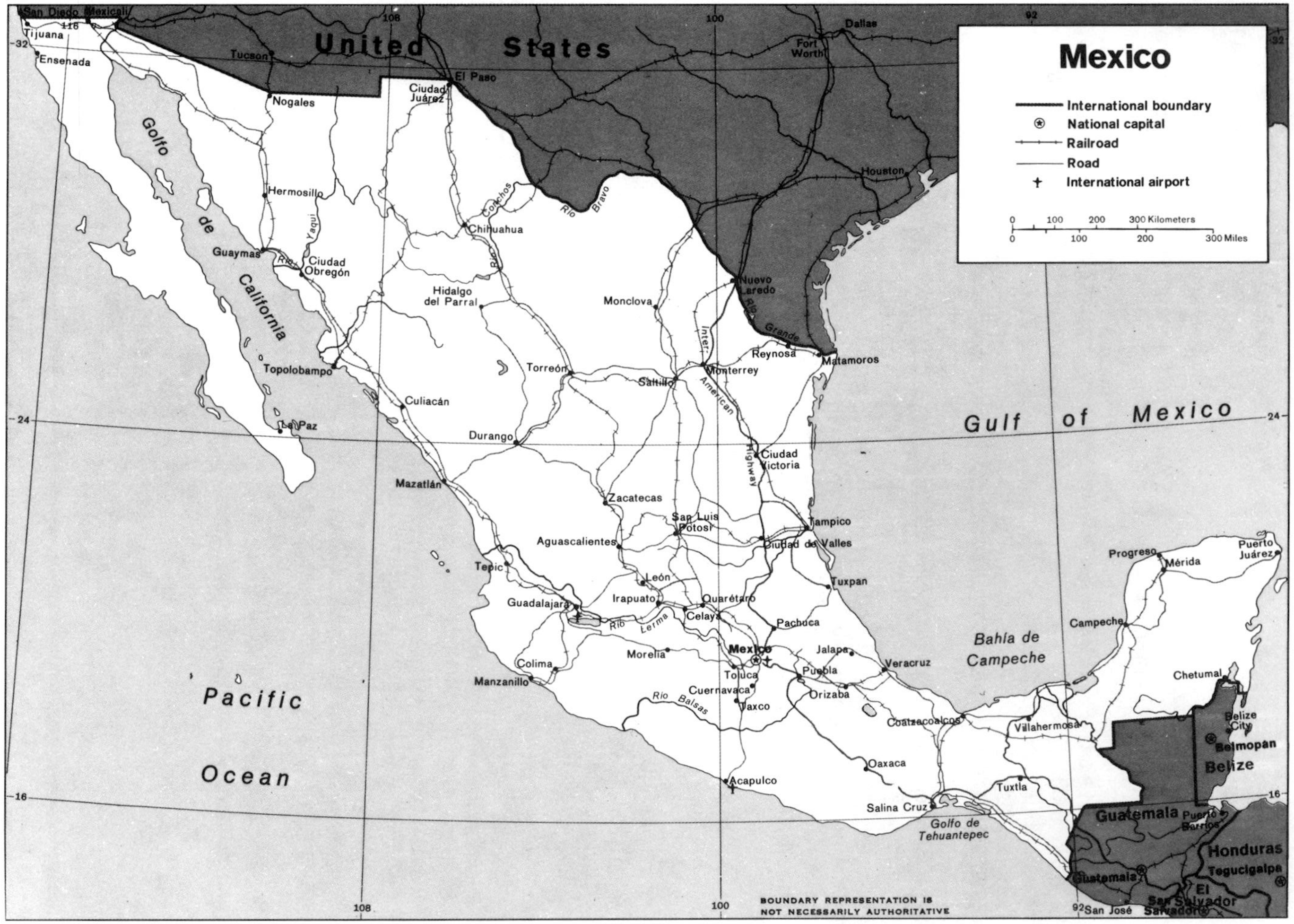

Mexico

International boundary
National capital
Railroad
Road
International airport

0 100 200 300 Kilometers
0 100 200 300 Miles

United States
Gulf of Mexico
Pacific Ocean
Golfo de California
Bahía de Campeche
Golfo de Tehuantepec
Guatemala
Belize
Honduras
El Salvador

San Diego
Mexicali
Tijuana
Ensenada
Tucson
Nogales
El Paso
Ciudad Juárez
Dallas
Fort Worth
Houston
Hermosillo
Guaymas
Ciudad Obregón
Topolobampo
La Paz
Chihuahua
Hidalgo del Parral
Culiacán
Mazatlán
Durango
Torreón
Monclova
Nuevo Laredo
Reynosa
Matamoros
Monterrey
Saltillo
Ciudad Victoria
Zacatecas
San Luis Potosí
Aguascalientes
Tampico
Ciudad de Valles
Tepic
Guadalajara
León
Irapuato
Querétaro
Celaya
Tuxpan
Pachuca
Colima
Manzanillo
Morelia
Mexico
Toluca
Cuernavaca
Taxco
Jalapa
Puebla
Orizaba
Veracruz
Acapulco
Oaxaca
Coatzacoalcos
Salina Cruz
Villahermosa
Tuxtla
Campeche
Progreso
Mérida
Puerto Juárez
Chetumal
Belize City
Belmopan
Puerto Barrios
Guatemala
Tegucigalpa
San Salvador
San José

Río Bravo
Río Grande
Río Conchos
Río Yaqui
Río Lerma
Río Balsas
Inter-American Highway

32
24
16
116
108
100
92

BOUNDARY REPRESENTATION IS NOT NECESSARILY AUTHORITATIVE

MEXICO

BASIC FACT SHEET

OFFICIAL NAME: United States of Mexico (Estados Unidos Mexicanos)

ABBREVIATION: MX

CAPITAL: Mexico City

HEAD OF STATE & HEAD OF GOVERNMENT: President Carlos Salinas de Gortari (from 1988)

NATURE OF GOVERNMENT: Partial democracy

POPULATION: 87,870,154 (1990)

AREA: 1,972,547 sq. km. (761,602 sq. mi.)

ETHNIC MAJORITY: Mestizos

LANGUAGE: Spanish

RELIGION: Roman Catholicism

UNIT OF CURRENCY: Peso ($1 = P2,641.0, December 1989)

NATIONAL FLAG: A tricolor of green, white and red vertical stripes with the national emblem at the center of the white stripe

NATIONAL EMBLEM: A brown eagle perched on a green *nopal* (cactus) holding a green serpent in its beak, recalling an omen associated with the founding of Tenochtitlán, the Aztec predecessor of Mexico City.

NATIONAL ANTHEM: "Mexicans, to the Cry of War"

NATIONAL HOLIDAYS: September 16 (National Day, Independence Day); January 1 (New Year's Day); February 5 (Constitution Day); March 18 (Anniversary of Oil Expropriation of 1938); March 21 (Benito Juárez's Birthday); May 1 (Labor Day); May 5 (Anniversary of the Battle of Puebla); September 1 (Opening of Congress); October 12 (Columbus Day); November 20 (Anniversary of the Revolution of 1910). Christian festivals include Christmas, Holy Thursday, Good Friday, Holy Saturday, All Souls' Day and festival of Our Lady of Guadalupe

NATIONAL CALENDAR: Gregorian

PHYSICAL QUALITY OF LIFE INDEX: 84

DATE OF INDEPENDENCE: September 16, 1810

DATE OF CONSTITUTION: February 5, 1917

WEIGHTS & MEASURES: The metric system is in force.

GEOGRAPHICAL FEATURES

Mexico is in the South of the North American continent, with an area of 1,972,547 sq. km. (761,602 sq. mi.), including uninhabited offshore islands. Mainland Mexico extends 3,220 km. (2,001 mi.) south-southeast to north-northwest and 1,060 km. (659 mi.) east-northeast to west-southwest. Mexico's coastline on the Gulf of Mexico and the Caribbean Sea extends 2,749 km. (1,708 mi.) and that on the Pacific Ocean 7,148 km. (4,441 mi.).

Mexico shares its international border of 4,346 km. (2,701 mi.) with three neighbors: the United States of America (3,125 km.; 1,942 mi.), Belize (259 km.; 161 mi.) and Guatemala (962 km.; 598 mi.). All these borders have been fully demarcated, and there are no current border disputes. There is a dormant Mexican claim to Belize north of 17 degrees north latitude, according to a treaty signed with Guatemala in 1882. Earlier minor disputes with the United States related to the frequent shifts of the Río Grande (Rio Bravo to Mexicans) and the Colorado River and were settled in 1971; the former El Chamizal district of El Paso, Texas was returned to Mexico. The border with the United States is perhaps the world's most frequently crossed international frontier. At San Ysidro, the California town opposite Tijuana, annual recorded authorized crossings number over 24.5 million.

The capital is Mexico City, the former capital of the Aztecs and the oldest continuously inhabited urban settlement in the Americas. Its population, including the entire Federal District, was estimated in 1980 at 12,932,116.

MAJOR CITIES OF MEXICO
(1980 population)

City	Population	City	Population
México	(12,932,116)	Morelia	(353,055)
Guadalajara	(2,244,715)	Hermosillo	(340,779)
Monterrey	(1,916,472)	Saltillo	(321,758)
Puebla de Zaragoza	(835,759)	rrVictoria de Durango	(321,148)
Leon de los Aldamas	(655,809)	Veracruz Llave	(305,456)
Ciudad Juarez	(567,365)	Querétaro	(293,586)
Culiacan Rosales	(560,011)	Tampico	(267,957)
Mexicali	(510,554)	Villa Hermosa	(250,903)
Tijuana	(461,257)	Mazatlán	(249,988)
Merida	(424,529)	Irapuato	(246,308)
Acapulco de Juarez	(409,335)	Matamoros	(238,840)
Chihuahua	(406,830)	Cuernavaca	(232,355)
San Luis Potosi	(406,630)	Celaya	(219,010)
Torreón	(363,886)	Jalapa Enriquez	(212,769)
Aguascalientes	(359,454)	Reynosa	(211,412)
Toluca de Lerdo	(357,071)	Reynosa	(211,412)

Two-thirds of Mexico is mountainous; the topography of the country was compared by Hernán Cortés, the 16th-century conqueror of Mexico, to a crumpled piece of paper. For official purposes the country is divided into five natural regions: the North Pacific, The North, Central Mexico, the Gulf Coast and the South Pacific.

The North Pacific region lies to the west of the Sierra Madre Occidental and includes the peninsula of Baja California. Most of this region is the Sonoran Desert, which continues south into Sinaloa. A narrow coastal plain extends inland for 15 to 25 km. (10 to 15 mi.). Baja California is a desert on which block mountains of up to 2,750 m. (9,000 ft.) in elevation drop precipitously into the Gulf of California (called Mar de Cortés by Mexicans). The North extends eastward from the crests of the Sierra Madre Occidental to the Gulf of Mexico. Apart from a small coastal area, this region comprises the Northern Plateau of Mexico, narrowing somewhat from north to south as it increases in elevation. Known also as the Central Meseta, this region contains great desert basins called *bolsons*. Central Mexico is the heartland of the country, consisting of rolling hills and the dissected cones of old volcanoes and interspersed by broad basins and valleys with floors at elevations of 1,500 to 2,500 m. (5,000 to 8,000 ft.). The seven largest of these valleys are Puebla, Toluca, Guanajuato, Jalisco, Morelos, Aguascalientes and (the Valley of) Mexico. The Gulf Coast is made up of the fairly broad plain of Vera Cruz, Tabasco and the Yucatán Peninsula, the northeastern tip of which is a desert. The South Pacific is a mountainous enclave in the region of Central Mexico.

The principal mountain systems of Mexico are the Sierra Madre Occidental and the Sierra Madre Oriental, a series of north-to-south ranges with an average elevation of 3,000 m. (10,000 ft.), with three volcanic peaks reaching 5,200 m. (17,000 ft.): Pica De Orizabo or Citlaltepetl (5,699 m., 18,700 ft.); Popocatepetl (5,452 m., 17,887 ft.); and Ixtaccihuatl (5,286 m., 17,343 ft.). Most of the volcanoes are extinct; Ixtaccihuatl last erupted in the 18th century, but its top is hidden by plumes of smoke even now. South of the Isthmus of Tehuantepec, the Sierra Madre de Chiapas extends to the Guatemalan border; the Chiapas Highlands occupy most of the interior to the east and south.

There are few large rivers, but there are a number of short rivers in the North Pacific, Central Mexico and the South Pacific, including the Sonora, the Yaqui, the Fuerte, the Sinaloa, the Culiacán, the Lerma, the Santiago, the Grijalva, the Usumacinta, the Balsas, the Panuco, the Soto la Marina, and the Papaloapán.

The country's largest lake is Lake Chapala, on the outskirts of Guadalajara.

CLIMATE & WEATHER

Mexico is half inside and half outside the tropics, but the climate is modified by a number of factors, such as altitude, winds and cool Pacific currents. On the basis of natural terrain, there are three climatic zones: the tropical and subtropical zone *(tierra caliente)*, rising up to 900 m. (3,000 ft.) in elevation; the temperate zone *(tierra templada)*, at elevations of between 900 m. and 1,800 m. (3,000 ft. and 6,000 ft.); and the cool zone *(tierra fría)*, at over 1,800 m. (6,000 ft.). The *tierra caliente*, which includes the coastal plains, the Yucatán Peninsula and the lower areas of southern Mexico, has a mean temperature of 25°C to 27°C (77°F to 80.6°F), with a minimum of 15.6°C (60°F) and a maximum of 49°C (120°F). The *tierra templada* has a mean temperature of 15.5°C (59.9°F). The *tierra fría*, where Mexico City is located, has a mean annual temperature of 17°C (63°F).

Most of Mexico is dry; only about 15% of the national territory receives adequate rainfall in all seasons. Densely populated Central Mexico lies in the rain shadow of the Sierra Madre Oriental, but the two coastal belts on the Gulf of Mexico and the Pacific Ocean receive an average of from 100 cm. (39 in.) to 360 cm. (118 in.). The highest precipitation is recorded in Chiapas and Tabasco (502 cm., 200 in.), and the lowest in Baja California, where no rain at all may fall in some years.

During summer and autumn, both coastal areas are subject to hurricanes. Extratropical hurricanes from the Rocky Mountains sometimes blow across the northern deserts.

POPULATION

The population of Mexico was estimated in 1990 at 87,870,154 the basis of the last official census, held in 1980, when the population was 67,382,581.

Nearly half the population lives in Central Mexico, which comprises 14% of the national territory; 19% in the North, which comprises 40% of the national territory; 8% in the North Pacific, which comprises 21% of the national territory; and 12% each in the Gulf Coast and South Pacific, with 12% each of the national territory. The North Pacific and the Gulf Coast are experiencing greater increases in population than Central Mexico.

Nearly 70% of the population live in urban areas, defined as localities with populations of over 2,500. The progressive decline in the rural population began in the 1950s, when the urban component was only 43%. Although birth rates are higher in the countryside, the rural sector gained only 15.3% in population during 1960–70 while the urban sector gained 52.5%. There are eight cities with populations of over 500,000; they have an aggregate population of 28 million, representing nearly half the total urban population. The highest growth rates were experienced by Tijuana (82.2%), León (73.8%), Chihuahua (71.3%), Guadalajara (62%) and Cuidad Juarez (55.3%). Mexico City itself (with 32% of the urban population) ranked low, with a growth rate of 29.1% during the same base period of 1960–70. Nearly 42% of the urban population in Mexico City live in slums and squatter settlements, and this inner city has an annual growth rate of 12%. The Mexican government is deeply concerned over the continuing migration and the resulting depopulation of the countryside and has made a number of efforts to stanch this

DEMOGRAPHIC INDICATORS

Population (millions): 87.870 (1990)
Year of last census: 1990
Sex distribution (% at last census): males, 49.1; females, 50.9
Population estimates and projections (millions)

1940: 19.815	1970: 48.934	2000: 95.490
1950: 25.828	1980: 69.655	2010: 111.360
1960: 34.993	1990: 81.883	

Age profile (% 1988)

0–14: 43.0	30–44: 14.9	60–74: 4.0
15–29: 27.8	45–59: 8.4	75 and over: 1.8

Median age (yrs.): 18.9 (1985)
Youth population (% age 15–24): 21.5 (1985); 19.5 (2000)
Total dependency ratio: 80.2 (1985)
Annual growth rate (%)

1950–55: 2.92	1975–80: 2.57	2000–2005: 1.62
1955–60: 3.19	1980–85: 2.40	2005–2010: 1.47
1960–65: 3.26	1985–90: 2.20	2010–2015: 1.33
1965–70: 3.30	1990–1995: 2.01	2015–2020: 1.21
1970–75: 3.20	1995–2000: 1.81	2020–2025: 1.08

Hypothetical size of stationary population (millions): 184 (1988)
Assumed year of reaching net reproduction rate of 1: 2005 (1988)
Urban population (000): 55,276 (1985)
Urban population (%): 71 (1988); 55 (1965)
Annual urban population growth rate (%, 1985–90): 3.03
Annual rural population growth rate (%, 1985–90): 0.16
Percentage of urban population in largest city: 32 (1980)
Percentage of urban population in cities of population over 500,000: 48 (1980)
Number of cities of population over 500,000: 8 (1980)
Population density per sq. km. (per sq. mi.): 41.8 (108.3) (latest)

VITAL STATISTICS

Crude birth rate (/1,000): 29 (1990); 45 (1965)
Crude death rate (/1,000): 5 (1990); 11 (1965)
Infant mortality rate (/1,000 live births): 33 (1990)
Maternal mortality rate (/100,000 live births): 81.8 (1983)
Life expectancy (yrs.) at birth: males, 68; females, 76 (1990)
Gross reproduction rate (/woman) (1980–85): 2.05
Total fertility rate (/woman): 3.4 (1990)
Rate of natural increase (/1,000): 29.2 (1987)
Marriage rate (/1,000): 7.1 (1985)
Average household size: 5.1 (latest)
Legitimate births (%): 72.5 (latest)

flow by decentralizing industry and opening up new farmlands through irrigation and land reform.

As a result of the high birth rate, the median age has been falling.

Mexican immigration into the United States has assumed serious proportions as a bilateral issue. In 1951 the United States and Mexico agreed to control the seasonal migration of *braceros* (field workers). The agreement expired in 1964; since that time millions of migrants, called wetbacks (so known because many enter the United States illegally by crossing the Río Grande), have illegally settled in the United States; according to some accounts, nearly 1 million illegal crossings take place each year. Many of these "wetbacks" are recruited by contractors known in the trade as "chicken herders." Illegal Mexican laborers hold 20% of all farm jobs in California and make up all of the potato harvest teams in Idaho. Mexico, in turn, receives illegal migrants from the poorer countries to the south, Belize and Guatemala. Legal emigration and immigration are only the tip of the iceberg and do not reflect the size of population movements across borders; nevertheless, in the mid-1980s there was a net population loss through migration, according to the official figures.

STATUS OF WOMEN INDICATORS

Number of women (millions): 40.057 (1985)
Women of childbearing age (15–49) (% of pop.): 50 (1988)
Married women of childbearing age (15–49) using contraception (%): 53 (1986)
Women's literacy rate (%): 88.3 (1990)
Women in labor force (%): 27.1 (1988)
Total fertility rate (/woman): 3.4 (1990)
Women in national legislatures (%): 33 (1984)

Mexico's annual population growth rate is one of the highest in the world and is one of the major problems confronting the Mexican government. Historically, the national policy has been described as *poblacionista* (pronatalist). The first steps in reversing this policy were taken by President Luis Echeverria, himself the father of eight children, after the census of 1970 alarmed the government by revealing the runaway population growth. The population policy law of 1974 established the National Population Council to provide family planning services in the public sector and to monitor and coordinate private sector efforts consistent with the manpower needs of the country as well as the dignity of the family.

The government that took office in late 1976 indicated its strong commitment to reducing the population growth rate by means of programs of family planning, sex education and other development activities. To ensure the efficient coordination of family planning programs, the government established the National Coordination of Family Planning. The National Family Planning Plan was approved in October 1977. The plan aims to stabilize demographic growth at about 1% by the beginning of the next century.

Men and women are equal in principle under law. Mexican women have the right to file for divorce and separation. There are no travel restrictions on women, and they can own property in their own name. Over the past 10 years, women have increased their presence in nontraditional occupations. Although the concept of women as mothers and homemakers continues to dominate, the number of women's action groups is increasing, and it appears that the objectives of women are becoming more diversified. Women comprise approximately 26% of the work force in urban areas but continue to work predominantly in nonsupervisory jobs, with few at the executive level.

ETHNIC COMPOSITION

Mestizos constitute the ethnic majority in Mexico, making up 60% of the population. Indians constitute the largest minority, with 30% of the population. The rest of the population is divided between whites (9%) and scattered groups of blacks.

The mestizos of Mexico are the guardians of Hispanic culture, although most of them are predominantly of Indian extraction. Individual Indians may also join mestizo society by a process of acculturation known as "passing" (i.e., passing off as a mestizo) by adopting a Spanish surname, speaking Spanish and adopting Western dress. The proportion of mestizos in the population is bound to increase because of the incentives offered by the government to Indians who integrate with the national culture.

Although racially pure, few Mexican Indians have retained their pre-Hispanic cultural traits intact. Indians are distinguished from their mestizo neighbors not so much by racial differences (because Spanish genetic influences on the racial stock are slight) as through social organization. There are six primary distinguishing factors that provide the basis of Indianhood: language, community type, village government, economic organization, family and kinship, and religion. Furthermore, most Indians are rural dwellers who have an umbilical attachment to the land, from which they draw their economic as well as social and religious sustenance. An Indian loses his ethnic identity when separated from his land, community, family or village. It is at the family or village level that Indian life has been least affected by the Spanish value systems.

Indians are not evenly distributed throughout the country. Nearly 34% live on the Central Plateau, 35% in the South Pacific and 23% on the Gulf Coast. According to the *Handbook of Middle American Indians*, there are five major Indian groupings: the Maya-speaking peoples of Chiapas and Yucatán; Indians of the Southern Mexico Highlands of Oaxaca, Guerrero and parts of Puebla, Veracruz and nearby coastal regions; Indians of the Central Mexican Highlands; Indians of Western Mexico, including Tarascan Indians; and Indians of Northwest Mexico.

Indian groups live outside the mainstream of mestizo and white society; relations between the two groups are characterized by exploitation of the Indians on the one hand and attempts to integrate them on the other. Inequality of status between the two groups is reflected in the use of the term "Indio" in a pejorative way, implying inferiority, whereas mestizos are called *gente de razón* (reasonable people). The integration of Indians into the national society is directed by the National Indian Institute through education, health and agricultural programs. At the same time there is increasing recognition of the need to preserve the cultural heritage of the Indians.

Other ethnic minorities include blacks, mulattoes and Chinese. Among the European communities the largest is Spanish, numbering close to half a million, followed by French and Italians. Europeans occupy a number of important economic and political positions. The North American community includes descendants of Southerners who fled the United States after its Civil War, preferring to live in an alien land rather than under Reconstruction. Jews are more recent arrivals, but although they play an important role in the economy, there have been evidences of anti-Semitism along with instances of overt repression in recent history.

LANGUAGE

Mexico is the world's largest Spanish-speaking country, with more Spanish-speakers than Spain. Monolingual Indians constitute 7% of the population and speak one of several Indian languages, the largest of which are Maya and Nahuatl. Maya is actually a cluster of mutually unintelligible languages spoken in Yucatán and Chiapas. The two largest linguistic groups in the Southern Mexican Highlands are the Macro-Mixtecan, comprising Zapotec, Mixtec, Popolocán and Macro-Mayance, including Zoqueán and Mixe. Other groups in this region are Chontol, Tlapanec, Cuitlatec and Nahua, all related to Nahuatl. There are three linguistic families in the Central Mexican Highlands: Uto-Aztecán, Otomián and Totonacán. Nahuatl, the most important Uto-Aztecán language, is the most widely spoken language after Spanish and is spoken primarily in Puebla, the heart of what was once the Aztec Empire. Modern Nahuatl contains a large number of Spanish loanwords, and Mexican Spanish contains many Nahuatl words. Otomián includes two major subgroups: Otomi and Mazahua. The Totonacán group comprises Totonac and Tepehua. The major language in Western Mexico is Tarascán. There are three language families in Northwest Mexico: Taracahitán (together with its three subfamilies, Cahitán, Tarahumara and Opatán); Pimán (including Tepehuán); and Aztecoidán (together with the subfamilies Cora and Huichol). All these languages belong to the Uto-Aztecán group.

RELIGION

Despite Mexico's long history of conflict between church and state, nearly 92.6% of the population were Roman Catholic, according to the 1980 census. Just over three-percent were Protestant; 0.1% Jewish, 0.9% other and 3.1% were atheist. Indeed, the bitter anticlericalist era of Benito Juárez (1867–72) and of the Revolution of 1910 seems to be over, and there has been a significant resurgence of Catholicism in national life.

However, the anticlerical period of Mexican history is reflected in the Constitution, which devotes many provisions to restrict the influence and privileges of the church. Ecclesiastical corporations have no legal rights and theoretically cannot acquire property. Religious ceremonies cannot be held in public, and all church buildings are considered national property. The establishment of monastic orders is prohibited. Ministers of religion must have Mexican nationality; they have no political rights and may not criticize the fundamental laws of the country in either public or private meetings. In November 1991 Pres. Salinas revealed plans to ease restrictions on church activities.

In a paradoxical reversal of roles, the church has emerged in recent times as the defender of social justice, and the more progressive clergy have allied themselves with underprivileged groups to work for economic and social reform. Yet this trend contains the potential for a new rift, not only between church and state but also between conservative and liberal wings within the church.

For ecclesiastical purposes, Mexico comprises 14 archdioceses, 55 dioceses, seven territorial prelatures and one Apostolic Vicariate.

Many Indians practice a form of folk Catholicism, but they participate in rituals more fervently than others. For the Indian, spiritual practices and beliefs impinge on temporal affairs almost constantly. Particularly significant is the Indian veneration of the Virgin of Guadalupe, the patron of Mexico, who appeared in a vision to a poor Indian named Juan Diego during the early days of the Conquest. The shrine of the Virgin is considered the holiest in Mexico. There is a very small group of Jewish Indians who speak Hebrew and attend synagogues.

Protestant Evangelists, especially from outside Mexico, are active and especially successful in certain rural, largely indigenous communities. In July 1984, state authorities in Chihuahua announced the expulsion of 52 such missionaries over a 98-day period in that state. The government reportedly charged them with violating Article 130 of the Constitution, which limits the holding of religious services to inside church buildings and homes. Some critics of the action have charged that the government is selectively enforcing the anticlerical laws in favor of the predominant Roman Catholic Church. Other critics state that in some outlying areas the laws are not being enforced against the Evangelists so as to reduce the influence of the Catholic Church.

HISTORICAL BACKGROUND

Conquered by Hernán Cortés in the 16th century, Mexico was ruled by Spain until the wars of independence (1810–21). Spain formally recognized Mexican independence in 1836. The mid-19th century was a period of political instability and strained relations with the United States, which went to war with Mexico in 1844. Under the Treaty of Guadalupe Hidalgo of 1848, Mexico ceded one-half of its territory to the United States. Attempts at political and social reform culminated in the War of Reform of 1858–61. In 1861 French troops invaded Mexico, ostensibly because the nation had not paid its foreign debts, and installed Archduke Maximilian of Austria as emperor. He was overthrown by Benito Juárez and the republic was restored in 1867. Porfirio Díaz seized power in 1876 and, with the exception of the period 1880–84, was president continuously until 1911. Under Díaz Mexico modernized, opening its doors to foreign investors. Díaz strengthened the central government and formed an alliance with the landed interests. Dissent was suppressed while the problems of the peasants were ignored. Díaz was overthrown in 1911, in a nationalist, reformist revolt that lasted until 1917. That year a Constitution was proclaimed that embodied the aims of the revolution. It curtailed the power of the Catholic church, established state education, declared mineral and subsoil rights the property of the nation, ensured basic labor rights and limited the president to one term in order to prevent the recurrence of a long period of dictatorship.

Since 1929 the country has been dominated by the Partido Revolucionario Institucional until 1946 known as Partido Nacional Revolucionario in an effective one-party system, while maintaining a democratic form of election.

The 1940s was a period of dramatic economic development, an "economic miracle," that ensured political stability and laid the foundation for economic expansion and the rise of the middle classes in the postwar years. In the 1970s, however, the economy began to decline in the face of the rapidly rising population, an end to agricultural self-sufficiency and an international slump in petroleum prices. The country reached a crisis in 1982 when it was forced to acknowledge that it could not make payments on its foreign debt. The financial crisis coincided with a change in government that revealed discontent with the PRI. The incoming president, Miguel de la Madrid Hurtado received only 74% of the vote while his predecessor had received 95% in 1976. De la Madrid was unable to deal with the increasingly severe economic problems and his personal choice of successor, Carlos Salinas de Gortari, won the presidency with little more than 50% of the vote in 1988.

CONSTITUTION & GOVERNMENT

The legal basis of the Mexican government is the Constitution of 1917, which established a federal republic with 31 states and the Federal District. Although Mexico has been subject to at least 40 forms of government since independence, it has had only three constitutions (1824, 1857 and 1917). The Constitution of 1917 provides for a strong government in which the executive overshadows all other branches of government and one political party overshadows all other institutions but, at the same time, retains the forms of parliamentary democracy: a relatively active National Congress, a token opposition and considerable local autonomy. The distribution of powers is asymmetrical but not sufficient to make the government a dictatorship. For this reason it defies normal categorization.

The Constitution contains many radical sections. It affirms the collective ownership of land, waters, seas, natural resources and sources of power and fuel. There

RULERS OF MEXICO (from 1940)

Presidents

December 1940–December 1946: Manuel Avila Camacho
December 1946–December 1952: Miguel Alemán Valdés
December 1952–December 1958: Adolfo Ruiz Cortines
December 1958–December 1964: Adolfo López Mateos
December 1964–December 1970: Gustavo Díaz Ordaz
December 1970–December 1976: Luis Echeverría Alvarez
December 1976–December 1982: José López Portillo y Pacheco
December 1982–December 1988: Miguel de la Madrid Hurtado
December 1988– : Carlos Salinas de Gortari

are elaborate provisions on the rights of labor. The concept of *amparo*—a wider form of habeas corpus that the individual Mexican may invoke in protection of his rights—is enshrined in the first 29 articles of the Constitution. The right of *amparo* also safeguards personal equity and property rights.

Executive authority is vested in the president—the head of state as well as the head of government—who is elected for a nonrenewable term of six years. There is no vice president; should the president die or resign, a provisional president is elected by the Senate. The presidency is the most important institution in the state, and the extent of the president's power is limited only by his capacity to use it. In addition to broad appointive powers, he controls foreign relations, defense, the budget and other vital economic and financial areas. The president orders the introduction of laws in Congress, which has no power to override his veto. In fact, the Mexican presidency has often been characterized as a six-year dictatorship.

The president is assisted by a cabinet of 20 ministers, or, properly, secretaries of departments, the most powerful of which is the Ministry of Government, which combines the portfolios of Justice and Interior.

Suffrage is universal over age 18. Voting is compulsory according to the Constitution, but this provision is rarely enforced. The Electoral Reform Act of 1977 resulted in the registration of three new political parties.

Even after nearly 80 years, the Partido Revolucionario Institucional (PRI) that led the revolution of 1910, faces no serious internal challenge. Its confidence is reflected in the decision to permit a token opposition in the Chamber of Deputies, even when opposition parties are unable to obtain seats. Organized violence had stemmed from two groups—students and guerril-

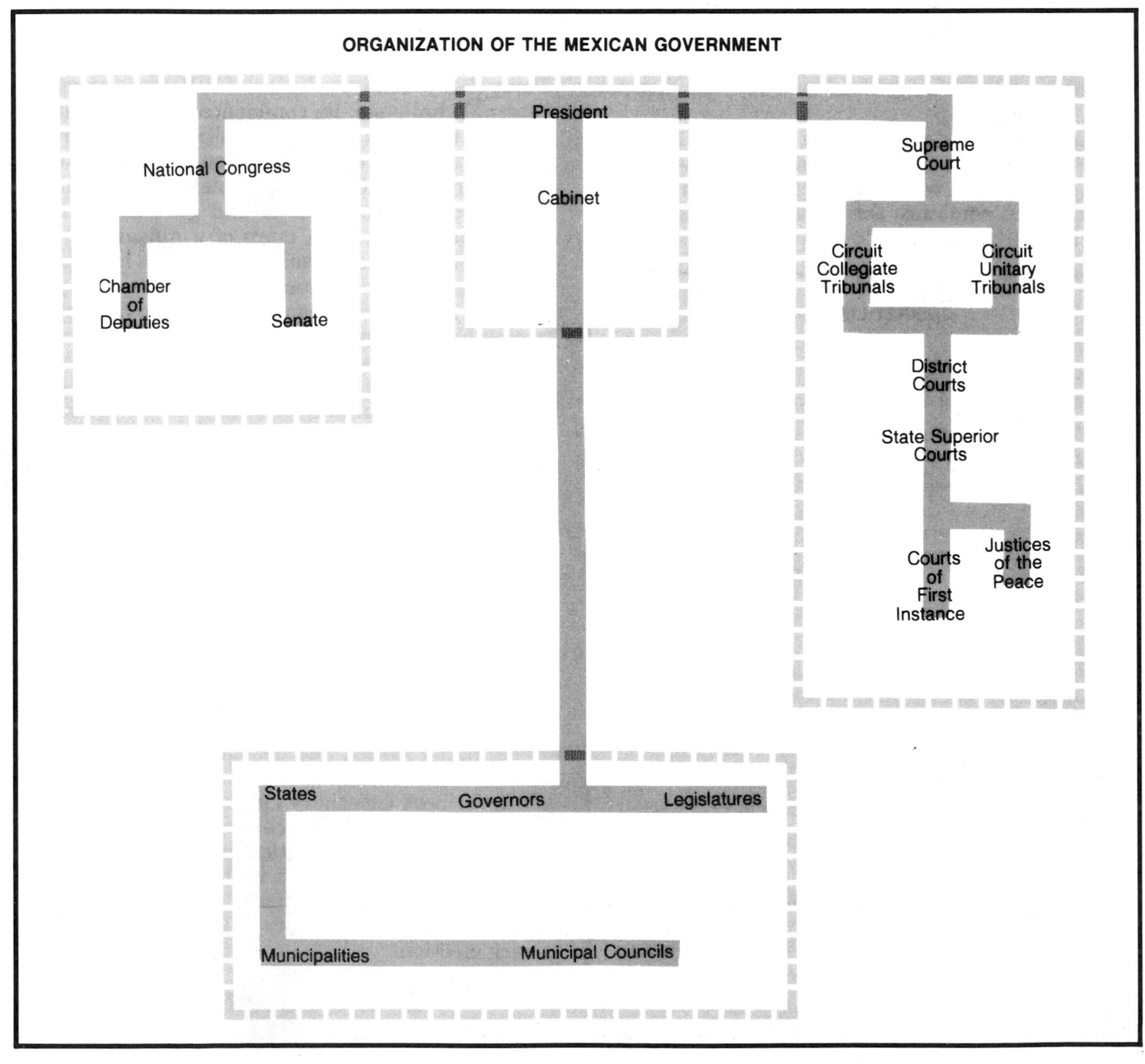

las—and in both cases it has been more of a nuisance than a threat. Most of these groups have only a local following and exploit local issues. Furthermore, the opposition has no leaders, no specific goals, no finances and no compelling ideology. At the same time, there has been a general loosening of the formerly close relations between the armed forces and the government. The last time a ranking general held the presidency was in 1946, and the number of senior military officers in the cabinet, legislatures and state houses has declined.

GOVERNMENT LIST
(July/August 1991)

President	Salinas de Gortari, Carlos
Secretary of Agrarian Reform	Cervera Pacheco, Victor
Secretary of Agriculture & Hydraulic Resources	Hank González, Carlos
Secretary of Commerce & Industrial Development	Serra Puche, Jaime José
Secretary of Communications & Transport	Caso Lombardo, Andrés
Secretary of Comptroller General	Vázquez Nava, María Elena
Secretary of Education	Bartlett Díaz, Manuel
Secretary of Energy, Mines & Parastatal Industry	Hiriart Balderrama, Fernando
Secretary of Finance & Public Credit	Aspe Armella, Pedro
Secretary of Fisheries	Jimenez Morales, Guillermo
Secretary of Foreign Relations	Solana Morales, Fernando
Secretary of Government	Gutiérrez Barrios, Fernando
Secretary of Health	Kumate Rodríguez, Jesús, *M.D.*
Secretary of Labor & Social Welfare	Farell Cubillas, Arsenio
Secretary of National Defense	Riviello Bazán, Antonio, *Gen.*
Secretary of Navy	Ruano Angulo, Luis Carlos, *Adm.*
Secretary of Programing & Budget	Zedillo Ponce de Léon, Ernesto
Secretary of Tourism	Joaquin Coldwell, Pedro
Secretary of Urban Development & Ecology	Chirinos Calero, Patricio
Attorney General	Morales Lechuga, Ignacio
Chief, Department of the Federal District	Camacho Solís, Manuel Victor
Attorney General, Federal District	Montes García, Miguel
Director General, Bank of Mexico	Mancera Aguayo, Miguel

FREEDOM & HUMAN RIGHTS

In terms of political and civil rights, Mexico is classified as a partly free country.

The Mexican Constitution consistently affirms social justice and equality as the basic ideals of the revolution. Individual rights, guaranteed by the Constitution, are generally respected in practice, except where terrorism is involved. Further, Mexico actively participates in promoting human rights in other parts of the world.

In February 1985 U.S. Drug Enforcement Administration agent Enrique Camarena and his Mexican pilot were kidnapped in Guadalajara and subsequently killed. The crime involved a gang of narcotics traffickers as well as local and state police, some of whom were arrested during the investigation of the killings. Two major drug traffickers, Rafael Caro Quintero and Ernesto Fonseca Carrillo were sentenced in Guadalajara in December 1989 for masterminding the slaying of Camarena and his pilot. Twenty-three other people were also convicted in the murders. Caro Quintero was sentenced to 40 years in prison, and a further 76 years, to be served concurrently, for convictions on kidnapping and drug trafficking charges. Fonseca was sentenced to a 40-year prison term, and another 104 years also to be served concurrently.

In January 1985 an American citizen doing research for a book on drug trafficking in Mexico disappeared with a friend in Guadalajara. Their bodies were discovered months later. It appears that at least some of the individuals implicated in the Camarena case were involved in these murders as well.

Although official Mexican policy condemns the use of torture, mistreatment of suspects often follows the period following arrest, especially during interrogation. Reports from U.S. citizens indicate that suspected narcotics traffickers are physically abused during interrogation. Such abuse takes the form of beating, electric shocks, submersion in water or forcing water up the nostrils. The police also resort to unconstitutional means to obtain a confession from a suspect. These violations, however, occur most frequently only in connection with guerrillas, demonstrators, terrorists, students and drug pushers.

Prisoners, especially women, sometimes are subjected to extortion, sexual advances and other types of mistreatment. Cruel and degrading treatment of U.S. tourists arrested on various charges has declined because of its negative impact on tourism.

Although Mexican citizens are guaranteed the right of *amparo* against coercive and abusive acts of authority, there are credible charges by human rights groups, opposition parties and the press that arrest without warrant, incommunicado detention and disappearance of suspects often occur.

Although fair trials are the norm, the Mexican legal system does not grant the accused the same rights as the Anglo-Saxon system. Further, the law permits the detention of individuals whom the authorities have reason to suspect of planning a crime. Many U.S. citizen prisoners have been held for over 12 months without being formally arraigned. Some reports indicate that a clandestine military-civilian task force, known as the White Brigade, operates as an extralegal law enforcement agency, with official encouragement. An International League for Human Rights Mission concluded that many of Mexico's political prisoners were denied a fair trial, due process of law and adequate legal counsel.

The Constitution guarantees freedom of speech and press, and while this guarantee is generally respected in practice, the government still exercises significant indirect influence over the media through its monopoly of newsprint and selective grant of government advertising. The media generally avoid direct criticism of an incumbent president. On issues affecting sensitive areas of government the press provides only minimal coverage.

CIVIL SERVICE

The civil service is generally acknowledged to be highly skilled and dedicated. Nevertheless, it suffers from two drawbacks: the prevalence of *mordidas* (bribes), especially among the lower levels of employees; and the absence of a competitive merit system of examination. Political patronage in the classic spoils-system tradition is the accepted rule, and most appointments are based on family ties. As a rule there is a high turnover of appointive posts with every election.

LOCAL GOVERNMENT

For purposes of local administration, Mexico is divided into 31 states and a Federal District (the Distrito Federal). Each state has a Constitution and a unicameral legislature. An ordinary session of the legislature is held annually, and bills may be introduced by the legislators, by the state governor, by the state supreme court or by municipalities.

STATES OF MEXICO

State	Capital
Aguascalientes	Aguascalientes
Baja California Norte	Mexicali
Baja California Sur	La Paz
Campeche	Campeche
Chiapas	Tuxtla Gutierrez
Chihuahua	Chihuahua
Coahuila	Saltillo
Distrito Federal	Mexico City
Durango	Durango
Colima	Colima
Guanajuato	Guanajuato
Guerrero	Chilpancingo
Hidalgo	Pachuca
Jalisco	Guadalajara
Mexico	Toluca
Michoacán	Morelia
Morelos	Cuernavaca
Nayarit	Tepic
Nuevo León	Monterrey
Oaxaca	Oaxaca
Puebla	Puebla
Queretaro	Queretaro
Quintana Roo	Chetuma
San Luis Potosi	San Luis Potosi
Sinaloa	Culiacan
Sonora	Hermosillo
Tabasco	Villa Hermosa
Tamaulipas	Ciudad Victoria
Tlaxcala	Tlaxcala
Veracruz	Jalapa
Yucatán	Mérida
Zacatecas	Zacatecas

The principal units of the states are the municipalities, of which there are 2,300. Municipal councils are elected by direct popular vote but have no powers of taxation.

FOREIGN POLICY

Since the revolution of 1910, which was partly sparked by resentment of U.S. influence in the country, foreign policy has been an instrument for the vigorous assertion of national independence and identity. Two factors have helped Mexico to recover from the series of foreign onslaughts and national humiliations at the hands of France and the United States in the 19th century. The first was the emergence of a stable government through the so-called institutionalization of the revolution, and the other has been the increasing preoccupation of the United States with its own foreign policy problems since 1940: with the Axis powers until 1945 and with the Soviet Union, Cuba and Vietnam in the 1950s and 1960s. Mexico has defied the United States on a number of crucial hemispheric issues: Mexico refused to participate in the military assistance programs established by the Mutual Security Act, and it has consistently opposed U.S. attempts to fashion the Organization of American States (OAS) as an anti-Communist alliance. Under the so-called Estrada Doctrine (which holds that a nation does not have the right to withhold recognition of a foreign regime based on a de jure consideration), Mexico has maintained diplomatic relations with Cuba, even though the OAS ostracized Castro's Cuba in 1964. However, Mexican opposition to U.S. policies generally has been legalistic rather than ideological and therefore has not affected the larger relations between the two countries.

Mexico and the United States have settled a number of bilateral issues and have cooperated in a number of areas of mutual concern. Examples of such settlements include the 1977 agreement on the transfer of U.S. prisoners held in Mexican jails (mostly on drug charges) to U.S. jurisdiction, agreement on reducing the salinity of the Colorado River, a treaty on stolen archaeological properties, settlement of the Chamizal border dispute under which the disputed area was returned to Mexico and joint efforts to stem the flow of narcotics from Mexico into the United States.

Mexico's relations with other states in Central America and in South America are generally cordial. Relations with Western Europe are also strong. However, in two instances Mexico has violated her own Estrada Doctrine, by refusing to recognize the Spanish government under Francisco Franco and the Chilean government under Gen. Augusto Pinochet. Mexico was one of the most outspoken critics of the Pinochet regime and welcomed refugees from Chile.

During President Echeverria's term (1970–76), Mexico took on the role of spokesman for the Third World. In 1972 Mexico proposed the idea of a Charter of Economic Rights and Duties of States that would define the relationship between developed and developing countries in the fields of aid, trade and investment. Included in this charter, which was approved by the U.N. General Assembly in 1974, were such provisions as reparations for colonialism, nationalization of industries and indexation of raw materials (linking the prices of raw materials to the cost of finished goods from developed countries), all of which were totally unacceptable to the United States. President Echeverria also called for a common front of all Third World countries to obtain better raw materials prices.

The rapid expansion of petroleum production since the mid-1970s gave Mexico a new independence, and under President Lopez Portillo the country assumed the role of a Third World leader and hosted the North-South summit of 1981. In Latin American foreign policy, Mexico has favored the left-wing regimes in Cuba and Nicaragua and in 1981 called for negotiations with the left-wing factions in El Salvador. Relations with the United States deteriorated in 1982 after the U.S. government rejected Lopez Portillo's peace plan, which offered Mexican mediation among the United States, Cuba and Nicaragua. As a member of the Contadora group (with Colombia, Panama and Venezuela), Mexico advocated a negotiated settlement to the conflicts in Central America and called for the withdrawal of all foreign advisers in the region. The United States continued to oppose these recommendations. The visit of President de la Madrid to the United States in May 1984 ended in discord after the Mexican president was strongly critical of U.S. policy in Central America.

In February 1985, relations between Mexico and the U.S. deteriorated, following the murder of Enrique Camarena, an agent of the U.S. Drug Enforcement Administration by Mexican drug traffickers. Throughout 1986, relations between Mexico and the U.S. remained tense, largely because of disagreement over the problem of illegal immigration from Mexico to the U.S. and Mexico's failure to take effective action against the illegal drugs trade. In February 1989, Mexico and the United States signed a co-operation agreement on combating the illegal drugs trade, and the arrest of Mexico's most notorious drugs-trafficker, Miguel Angel Rico, in April further improved relations. In October, Mexico signed a comprehensive trade pact and environmental agreement with the U.S., establishing an improved negotiating process to increase bilateral trade.

Mexico has in the past traditionally followed a liberal asylum policy, and its borders have been open to Central Americans fleeing from their countries. Recently there has been some attempt to control these entries without closing the southern border. Early in 1984, the government began to relocate all the refugee camps in the South to the Yucatán Peninsula, stating that this was necessary to protect the refugees from border incursions from Guatemala and to improve their living conditions. Critics of the relocations, however, say that their purpose was to discourage the influx of additional refugees. Government spokesmen have stated that there is no plan to encourage the refugees to leave Mexico; however, Mexican authorities have assisted Guatemalans who have voluntarily returned to Guatemala. Estimates of Salvadoran refugees in Mexico continue to be unavailable from the government, and Mexico does not consider them to be refugees.

Mexico and the United States are parties to 123 treaties and agreements covering agricultural commodities, agriculture, aviation, boundaries, boundary waters, claims, consuls, cultural property, cultural relations, customs, defense, desertification, disaster assistance, economic and technical cooperation, education, energy, environmental cooperation, extradition, fisheries, health, housing, judicial assistance, mapping, maritime matters, migratory birds and game mammals, migratory workers, narcotic drugs, peace treaties, police equipment, prisoner transfer, publications, scientific cooperation, Social Security, space, stolen property, taxation, telecommunications, tourism, trade and commerce, transportation, visas and weather stations.

Mexico joined the United Nations in 1945. It is a member of 15 U.N. organizations and 46 other international organizations.

PARLIAMENT

The National Congress (Congreso de la Unión) is a bicameral body consisting of a Senate (Cámara de Senadores) and a Chamber of Deputies (Cámara de Diputados).

The Senate consists of 64 members elected for six-year terms. Each state as well as the Federal District is entitled to two seats.

The Chamber of Deputies consists of 300 members elected for three-year terms on the basis of one deputy and one alternate for every 250,000 people or for every fraction above 125,000, with a minimum of two deputies from each state. Under the 1977 law on electoral procedure, 200 deputies are elected (in addition to the 300 elected by majority vote by single-member electoral districts) by a system of proportional representation from regional lists within multimember constituencies. Minority parties receiving a minimum of 1.5% of the national vote in a federal election are entitled, in addition to seats won outright, to five at-large seats in the Chamber of Deputies plus one seat for each additional 0.5% of the votes polled, up to a maximum of 25 seats for each party. Members of Congress are barred from reelection.

Regular sessions of Congress begin on September 1 and may not continue beyond December 31 of the same year. For the rest of the year a permanent committee consisting of 14 senators and 15 deputies attends to legislative business. Legislation may be introduced by the president, senators, deputies or by acts of state legislatures. Each house has a number of committees or commissions to study and recommend bills. When the two houses disagree, a joint committee is charged with drafting a compromise version. There is no provision for overriding a presidential veto.

The powers of Congress include ratifications of treaties and conventions made with foreign powers, approval of judicial appointments of members of the Supreme Court and the superior courts, approval of the national budget, declaration of war and the establishment of schools.

Following the 1988 legislative elections, the Partido Revolucionario Institucional (PRI) won 60 seats in the Senate; the Frente Democratico Nacional won four seats. The PRI garnered 260 seats in the Chamber of Deputies while the Frente Democratico Nacional won 139 and the Partido Accion Nacional won 101.

POLITICAL PARTIES

The ruling party is the Partido Revolucionario Institucional (PRI), a moderately left-wing party founded in 1929 as the National Revolutionary Party and redesignated in 1938 as the Mexican Revolutionary Party. Strongly rooted in the revolution of 1910, the party gradually broadened its base over the years until it became a genuinely mass party. Three large pressure groups, embracing all shades of political opinions, operate within the PRI: labor, the peasantry and the popular sector (comprising bureaucrats, businessmen and teachers).

The party's organization is pyramidal. Below the president of the republic (who also is the president of the PRI) is the National Executive Council. Next in the hierarchy is the Grand Commission, or the National Council. At the base is the National Assembly, which meets only once every six years to lay down party policies and nominate the party's candidate for the presidency.

The most significant opposition groups in the 1988 elections were the Frente Democrático Nacional (FDN) and the Partido Acción Nacional (PAN). The FDN was an electoral alliance formed in 1988 to contest the presidential and congressional elections. It was composed of the Corriente Democrática, Movimiento al Socialismo, Partido Autentico de la Revolución Mexicana, Partido Mexicano Socialista and Partido Popular Socialista. The coalition's candidate, Cuauhtemoc Cardenas Solorzano, made a surprisingly strong showing in the 1988 presidential race, garnering 31% of the vote. The coalition ran second in the 1988 legislative elections. It was dissolved in 1989 and elements of the coalition formed a new party, the Partido de la Revolucion Democrática, under the leadership of Cardenas. The Partido Acción Nacional (PAN) is a pro-Catholic, conservative party. Since its founding in 1939, the PAN has always offered presidential and congressional candidates (except in 1946, when it did not contest the presidency). The party ran third in both the presidential and legislative balloting of 1988.

There is one party without legal registration to permit it to appear on the electoral ballots: the Partido Social Democrata.

The principal illegal revolutionary movements within the country are:

- Ejercito de los Pobres
- Frente Democrático Oriental de Mexico Emiliano Zapata
- Los Tecos
- Partido Revolucionario Obrerista y Clandestino de Union Popular

There has been a marked decrease in political violence in Mexico in recent years. Rural guerrilla activity has virtually died out. At the same time, there has been an unchecked growth in the ordinary type of violent crimes in the slums.

ECONOMY

Mexico is one of the 35 upper middle-income countries of the world with a free-market economy in which the private sector is dominant. Since the mid-1970s, the expansion of Mexico's petroleum industry has provided the main stimulus to the country's economic development, but the fall in world petroleum prices in the mid-1980s seriously reduced income from this source. Industrialization has been rapid since World War II, but its benefits have been unevenly distributed and much of the rural population remains substantially unaffected. The gross national product grew by a yearly average of 16% during 1972–75, with the growth rate declining to a still-respectable 8% in 1978–81. Subsequently, the economy fell into deep recession, with an unserviceable foreign debt, massive capital flight, widespread unemployment and rampant inflation. Successive IMF interventions slowed the decline in 1983–84, but by mid-1986, in the wake of a disastrous earthquake at Mexico City the preceding September and a further collapse in oil prices, crisis conditions had returned, with inflation surging to more than 140% in 1987. The government responded late in the year with a number of initiatives, including its participation in an innovative buy-back plan for foreign debt and an Economic Solidarity Pact (Pacto de Solidaridad Económica) among government, management and labor to hold down prices and wages. This succeeded in reducing the monthly inflation rate from 15.5% in January 1988 to a remarkable 0.6% in September before a marginal upswing to 2.1% in December.

Negotiations to reduce Mexico's vast foreign debt were given priority by the new Government in 1989. In January 1989, a pact for Economic Stability and Growth was implemented, with the agreement of em-

PRINCIPAL ECONOMIC INDICATORS

Gross National Product (U.S. $ billions): 170.053 (1989)
GNP per capita (U.S. $): 1,990 (1989)
GNP average growth rate (%, 1980–89): 0.6
GNP per capita average annual growth rate (%, 1987–89): 0.4
Income distribution (% household income)
  Lowest 20%: 2.9
  Highest 10%: 40.6
Average annual rate of inflation (%, 1980–88): 73.8
Consumer price index (1980 = 100) 1986
  All items: 1.995
  Food: 1,921
Wholesale price index (1980 = 100): 1,054 (1985)
Average annual growth rate (%, 1980–88)
  General government consumption: 2.7
  Private consumption: 0.3
  Gross domestic investment: −6.9

BALANCE OF PAYMENTS, 1988
(U.S. $ millions)

Current account balance: −2,905
Merchandise exports: 20,657
Merchandise imports: −18,905
Trade balance: 1,752
Other goods, services & income +: 11,172
Other goods, services & income −: −16,444
Other goods, services & income net: −5,272
Private unrequited transfers: 452
Official unrequited transfers: 163
Capital other than reserves: −7,158
Net errors & omissions: −467
Counterpart items: −171
Liabilities constituting foreign authorities reserves: 1,217 (1983)
Total change in reserves: 6,789

GROSS DOMESTIC PRODUCT

GDP nominal (Mex. P. trillions): 192.935 (1987)
GDP per capita (U.S. $): 2,165 (1989)
Average annual growth rate of GDP (%, 1980–88): 0.5
GDP by type of expenditure (%) 1987
- Consumption
  - Private: 66
  - Government: 9
- Gross domestic investment: 19
- Gross domestic saving: 23 (1988)
- Foreign trade
  - Exports: 20
  - Imports: −13

Cost components of GDP (%) 1987
- Net indirect taxes: 10
- Consumption of fixed capital: 14
- Compensation of employees: 26
- Net operating surplus: 50

Sectoral origin of GDP (% 1988)
- Primary
  - Agriculture: 9
  - Mining: 4
- Secondary
  - Manufacturing: 26
  - Construction: 4
  - Public utilities: 1
- Tertiary
  - Transportation & communications: 8
  - Trade: 27
  - Finance: 4
  - Other services: } 15
  - Government: }

Average annual sectoral growth rates (%, 1980–88)
- Agriculture: 1.2
- Industry: −0.1
- Manufacturing: 0.2
- Services: 0.7

ployers' organizations and trade unions, which aimed to control inflation and public expenditure. (The Pact was later extended to March 1990 and then to August 1990.)

An ambitious debt-reduction program incorporating the "Brady Plan" for debt relief, proposed by the U.S. Government and supported by the World Bank and the IMF, was finalized in 1990 and was expected to allow the economy to expand.

PUBLIC FINANCE

The Mexican fiscal year is the calendar year. The national budget includes the finances of the federal government; some autonomous government bodies; some state enterprises; and local governments, including states, the federal district and municipalities. Only 16 of the largest government enterprises and autonomous agencies have been brought under central budgetary control, but their combined share of the annual federal budget normally exceeds the budget of the federal government. The budgets of agencies and enterprises not under the Ministry of Finance are reviewed and approved by the Ministry of National Properties. The budgets of state financial organizations are approved by the Ministry of Finance and Public Credit. The fiscal policy of the government is generally conservative, and the current account shows a surplus in most years. As much as 40% of the federal government's current budget is transferred as subsidies to states and other agencies such as the National Railways to help make up their operating deficits. The average tax burden is considered moderate for a developing country. The Ministry of Education and Culture generally receives the largest budgetary allotment, followed by the Ministry of Hydraulic Resources. Constitutionally, power over expenditures rests solely with the Chamber of Deputies, and power over revenues is shared between the Senate and the Chamber of Deputies.

CENTRAL GOVERNMENT EXPENDITURES, 1988

% of total expenditures
- Defense: 1.4
- Education: 7.4
- Health: 1.1
- Housing, social security, welfare: 9.3
- Economic services: 11.4
- Other: 69.3

Total expenditures as % of GNP: 27.9
Overall surplus or deficit as % of GNP: −10.0

CENTRAL GOVERNMENT REVENUES, 1988

% of total current revenues
- Taxes on income, profit & capital gain: 26.8
- Social security contributions: 11.8
- Domestic taxes on goods & services: 68.5
- Taxes on international trade & transactions: 3.4
- Other taxes: −18.1
- Current nontax revenue: 7.5

Total current revenue as % of GNP: 18.0
General government consumption as % of GDP: 10
Average annual growth rate of general government consumption (%, 1980–88): 2.7

Although the government is directly involved in setting the goals and thrust of economic development, there is no formal national planning system as such. Centralized planning is limited to regional and sectoral development. In May 1989 President Salinas announced a National Development Plan that identified political and economic objectives for 1989–94 as the defense of Mexican interests and sovereignty, the strengthening of democratic life, the recovery of economic growth and price stability, and improvement in the standard of living.

Mexico is a major recipient of foreign aid. In the last two decades it received $3 billion from the United States, $6.8 billion from other Western sources and $110 million from Communist nations.

FOREIGN AID, 1989

Total foreign aid (U.S. $ millions): 6,313.7
- Bilateral: 3321.3
- Multilateral: 2992.4

CURRENCY & BANKING

The Mexican unit of currency is the peso, divided into 100 centavos. Coins are issued in denominations of 1,

5, 10, 20 and 50 centavos and 1, 5, 10, 20, 50, 100 and 200 pesos; notes are issued in denominations of 500, 1,000, 5,000, 10,000, 20,000 and 50,000 pesos.

The par value of the peso was fixed at $0.8 ($1 = P12.50) in 1954; this rate remained in effect until 1976. From 1976 the peso was allowed to float. In June 1991 the dollar exchange rate was $1 = P3,008.0. A dual exchange rate system is in effect. The exchange rates given above refer to the controlled market rate, applicable to payments for virtually all imports and to receipts on most merchandise exports. There is also a "parallel" free market rate (which may be above or below the controlled rate), determined by market forces.

FINANCIAL INDICATORS, 1989

Total reserves minus gold (SDRs billions): 4.816
SDRs (millions): 292
Reserve position in IMF (SDRs millions): 0
Foreign exchange (SDRs billions): 4.525
Gold (fine troy oz. millions): 1.03
Ratio of external debt to total reserves: 15.0 (1988)
Central bank 1989
- Assets (%)
  - Foreign assets: 31.7
  - Claims on government: 67.8
  - Claims on banks: 0.3
  - Claims on private sector: 0.2
- Liabilities (%)
  - Reserve money: 40.3
  - Government deposits: 0.0
  - Foreign liabilities: 24.7
  - Capital accounts: 1.8

Money supply 1989
Stock (Mex. P. trillions): 28.742
M1 per capita: 338,000
Private banks 1989
- Assets (%)
  - Loans to government: 31.1
  - Loans to private sector: 60.5
  - Reserves: 3.5
  - Foreign assets: 5.0
- Liabilities
  - Deposits (Mex. P. trillions): 140.314
  - of which %
    - Demand deposits: 7.1
    - Savings deposits: 45.8
    - Government deposits: 7.2
    - Foreign liabilities: 17.5

External debt 1988
- Total (U.S. $ billions): 88.665
  - of which public (U.S. $ billions): 81.207
  - of which private (U.S. $ billions): 7.458
- Debt service (long-term)
  - Total (U.S. $ billions): 9.641
  - Repayment
    - Principal (%): 32.0
    - Interest (%): 68.0
- Debt service ratio (%): 30.0
- External public debt as % of GNP: 48.0
- Debt service as % of GNP: 5.7
- Debt service as % of exports: 23.6
- Terms of public borrowing
  - Commitments (U.S. $ billions): 2.579
  - Average interest rate (%): 8.2
  - Average maturity (yrs.): 15
- Net flow of publicly guaranteed external capital (U.S. $ billions): 1.619

Receipt of workers' remittances (U.S. $ millions): 264
- Net direct private investment (U.S. $ billions): 2.594

The banking system of Mexico is one of the most developed in Latin America. This sector comprises a central bank and six types of banking institutions: public development banks, public credit institutions, private commercial banks, private investment banks, savings and loan associations, and mortgage banks. The central bank is the Bank of Mexico, with 10 branches; its monetary and credit policies exert a powerful influence on the economy. It also serves as a reserve bank, the fiscal agent of the federal government, the bank of issue for the peso, the regulator of the foreign exchange market and the money supply and as a discount house for private deposit banks. Through the National Banking Commission it supervises the private banking sector.

Of the more than 24 state financial institutions other than the central bank, the largest is the Nacional Financiera (NAFINSA). NAFINSA promotes investment companies, purchases equities in private companies, oversees issuance of public securities, directs the operations of stock exchanges and serves as the legal depository of government securities. The second-largest state development bank is the National Bank of Public Works and Services. Three state banks serve the agricultural sector.

The private banking sector consists of more than 200 banks with over 2,500 branches. The large number of institutions is accounted for by the regulation prohibiting banks from combining more than two banking functions. The largest private banks is the Commerce Bank of Mexico, comprising 35 affiliated banks with over 500 branches. The second-largest is the National Bank of Mexico.

Development banks, called *financieras*, organized by commercial banks in association with major industrial enterprises, provide most development financing in the private sector. Mexico is closed to foreign banks. The one exception is Citibank, which established its

GROWTH PROFILE
(Annual Growth Rates, %)

Projected population (1988–2000): 1.9
Projected crude birth rate (/1,000) (1990–95): 26.6
Projected crude death rate (/1,000) (1990–95): 5.4
Urban population (1980–88): 3.1
Labor force (1985–2000): 3.0
GNP (1980–89): 0.6
GNP per capita (1987–89): 0.4
GDP (1980–88): 0.5
Inflation (1980–88): 73.8
Agriculture (1980–88): 1.2
Industry (1980–88): −0.1
Manufacturing (1980–88): 0.2
Services (1980–88): 0.7
Money holdings (1980–88): 62.6
Manufacturing earnings per employee (1980–87): −3.5
Energy production (1980–88): 2.4
Energy consumption (1980–88): 0.7
Exports (1980–88): 5.5
Imports (1980–88): −4.9
General government consumption (1980–88): 2.7
Private consumption (1980–88): 0.3
Gross domestic investment (1980–88): −6.9

resident branch in Mexico before a law, providing for representative offices only, was promulgated.

All private banks were nationalized in September 1982. In August 1983 the government authorized up to 34% of shares to be returned to the private sector. In a move to streamline the banking system, the government merged 50 banks into 29 national credit institutions and eliminated 11 other banks. One bank, Banco Obrero, is allowed to operate as a private bank. In March 1985 the government announced a further reduction in the number of commercial banks, from 29 to 19. In November 1986 the government announced that, from January 1987, 34% of the stock in 19 government-owned commercial banks would be made available to private investors by public auction. In 1989 it was announced that from 1990, 34% of non-voting shares in state-owned commercial banks would be made available to foreign investors.

AGRICULTURE

Of the total land area, 48% is classified as agricultural land. Agriculture employs 23% of the labor force.

Only 12% of Mexico's land area is under cultivation; of this, 80% requires regular irrigation. The government built 153 storage dams by 1972. Irrigation and flood control programs are administered by numerous river basin commissions, such as the Papaloapán Basin Commission, the Tepalcatepec Commission, the Fuerte River Commission, the Lerma-Chapala-Santiago Commission and the Tehuantepec Isthmus Commission.

There are three types of tenure: private, communal and public. Private and communal landholdings are worked by owners, sharecroppers, landless peasants and *colonos* (colonists), or members of *ejidos*, known as *ejidatarios*. *Ejidos* are communal landholdings predating the Spanish Conquest. They have juridical status as corporations and are administered by elected officials. An *ejidatario* may assign his share of an *ejido* to a successor. The maximum area of land an *ejidatario* can work is 10 ha. (25 ac.) of irrigated land and 20 ha. (50 ac.) of dry land, but the average is about 6.4 ha. (16 ac.). An *ejidatario* may lose his farming rights if the allotted land is not cultivated for two consecutive years. Although there are limits on the size of private holdings (varying from crop to crop and between irrigated and dry land, but generally 100 ha., or 247 ac.), there are over 40,000 farms of over 101 ha. (250 ac.) and 500 farms of over 50,000 ha. (124,000 ac.).

More than 70 years after the Constitution of 1917 made land reform a national obligation, serious inequalities of land ownership persist. Of the total number of farms, 4% account for 50% of agricultural production, about 1% produce all of the agricultural exports and about 15% produce most of the food for urban areas.

In some areas the primitive shifting system of cultivation is still practiced. The use of machinery, fertilizers and soil conservation techniques is spreading, helped by government extension programs.

Almost half the crop land is devoted to corn, the staple food. Other major crops include wheat, coffee, sorghum, cotton and sugarcane. Henequen, from which sisal fiber is made, is grown in Yucatán. Mescal plants, from the leaves of which the popular drink tequila is made, are grown in Jalisco, Nayarit and Michoacán. Mexico became a net grain importer in the 1970s.

Nearly one-third of the land area is classified as pasture. The national herd of cattle is concentrated in two general areas: the northern states, where Hereford and other breeds are raised for export to the United States; and the southern, central and southeastern states, where native beef cattle are raised. Mexico is among the major beef-producing and beef-exporting

AGRICULTURAL INDICATORS

Agriculture's share of GDP (%): 9 (1989)
Average annual growth rate (%, 1980–88): 1.2
Value added in agriculture (U.S. $ billions): 15.958 (1988)
Cereal imports (million metric tons): 5.650 (1988)
Index of agricultural production (1979–81 = 100): 111 (1986)
Index of food production (1979–81 = 100): 113 (1986)
Index of food production per capita (1979–81 = 100): 93 (1986–88)
Number of tractors: 160,000 (1986)
Number of harvester-threshers: 17,800 (1986)
Total fertilizer consumption (000 metric tons): 2,332.4 (1985–86)
Fertilizer consumption (g./ha., hundreds): 753 (1987–88)
Number of farms (000): 2,848 (1970)
Average size of holding (ha.): 49 (1970)
Size class (%) 1970
- Below 1 ha. (below 2.47 ac.): 23.5
- 1–5 ha. (2.47–12.35 ac.): 39.4
- 5–10 ha. (12.35–24.7 ac.): 21.1
- 10–20 ha. (24.7–49.4 ac.): 8.8
- 20–50 ha. (49.4–123.5 ac.): 2.7
- 50–200 ha. (123.5–494 ac.): 2.9
- Over 200 ha. (over 494 ac.): 1.5

Tenure (%) 1970
- Owner-operated: 97.6
- Rented: 1.0
- Other: 1.5

Activity (%) 1970
- Mainly crops: 88.8
- Mainly livestock: 8.3
- Mixed: 2.9

Land use (%)
- Cropland: 13
- Pasture: 39
- Forest: 23
- Other: 25

Yields (kg./ha.) 1989
- Grains: 2,138
- Roots & tubers: 13,655
- Legumes: 661
- Milk (kg./animal): 1,424

Production 1989
- Fruits (million metric tons): 9.009
- Vegetables (million metric tons): 4.873

Livestock (million) 1989
- Cattle: 34.999
- Horses: 6.135 (1986)
- Sheep: 6.000
- Pigs: 14.080

Forestry 1988
- Production of roundwood (million cubic meters): 22.302
  - of which industrial roundwood (%): 33.3
- Value of exports (U.S. $ millions): 13.884

Fishing 1988
- Total catch (million metric tons): 1.363
  - of which marine (%): 87.0
- Value of exports (U.S. $ millions): 439.194

nations. The cattle industry also supports tanning and leather goods production.

About 9% of the land area is covered by forests, of which 59% are in the tropics, 15% in the subtropical zone and 26% in the temperate and cool zones. About 9% of the forests are on state or federal lands, 19% on *ejido* lands and 72% on private and municipal lands. About two-thirds of the forests are hardwoods; the remainder are softwoods. The major timber stands are of mahogany, cedar, primavera, sapote, oak, copal and pine. Because of the destructive effects of indiscriminate cutting since colonial times, the government has made special efforts to rationalize the exploitation of forest resources. The National Forestry Plan was issued in 1965, and the Forestry Fund was set up to finance reforestation and conservation from logging and concession fees. The states of Hidalgo, Pueblo and Morelos have been placed off limits to loggers.

Mexico's coastal fishing grounds are rich in a variety of fish and other seafood: lobster, shrimp, croaker, albacore, skipjack and anchovies from the Pacific and shrimp, jewfish, croaker, snapper, mackerel, snook and mullet from the Gulf of Mexico and the Caribbean. Certain species such as shrimp, lobster, abalone, clam, croaker, grouper and sea turtle are reserved for fishing cooperatives. There are more than 284 such cooperatives, with over 39,070 members. A state-owned holding concern, the Mexican Fishing Products Company, markets about 15% of the fish production.

Agricultural credit is provided by the National Agricultural and Livestock Bank.

MANUFACTURING

The manufacturing sector employs 10.6% of the labor force.

There is a heavy concentration of industrial plants in and around the Federal District, Monterrey and Guadalajara, overloading the housing, medical and social facilities in these areas. In an effort to attract industry to other areas, the government has built 110 industrial parks and offered fiscal benefits to companies locating their plants in these designated zones. The In-Bond Industry Program (formerly the Border Industry Program) permits foreign companies to import component parts free of duty if the assembled product is reexported. This program has attracted over 530 U.S. firms.

By number of units, the largest subsectors are food processing and apparel, accounting for 54% and 12%, respectively. In value of production, food, beverages and tobacco form the leading subsector, followed by machinery and transportation equipment, textile and clothing, and chemicals. The heavy industry field is led by petroleum and petroleum refining (also the largest industry in sales and the largest employer), followed by iron and steel, auto assembly, paper and paper products, manufacturing, and chemicals. The Mexican iron and steel industry is one of the oldest in Latin America, comprising 10 large steel producers and numerous smaller firms. There are seven automobile companies, led by Volkswagen. The state-owned Petroleos Mexicanos (Pemex) dominates the more than 200 petrochemical companies. Some 56 firms control three-fourths of the production of pharmaceuticals. The textile industry has been plagued by antiquated, inefficient equipment and high labor costs.

Foreign investments are regulated by the National Commission on Foreign Investment in accordance with the Law to Promote Mexican Investment and to Regulate Foreign Investment of 1973. Foreign investments are welcomed under certain conditions, such as when they complement domestic investment, introduce new technology, help to increase exports and import-substitution, use a high percentage of local components, are labor-intensive and are in a depressed area of the country. There are no restrictions on the expatriation of profits and the convertibility of foreign exchange. Foreign investment is not permitted in sectors controlled by the state such as petroleum, railroads, telecommunications, radio, television and forestry. Foreign companies may not control more than 49% of the equity, although some flexibility is allowed. All companies must register technology contracts with the National Registry of Technology Transfer. The inflow of foreign funds is also encouraged by enabling foreign depositors to "launder" their money by making bank deposits without revealing their identity.

Mexico's border industries program, favored by Mexican investment laws and U.S. tax law provisions, capitalizes on Mexico's lower wage levels. Started in 1965, it now numbers 470 border plants *(maquiladoras)* and 60 newer in-bond plants (permitted since 1972) in Mexico's interior. The plants in this program, wholly or partly foreign-owned, are licensed to manufacture but not to sell products in Mexico.

Most plants operate in the 12 principal cities along Mexico's northern border. Some have counterparts across the border, but others draw components from other parts of the United States or from other countries for assembly in Mexico. Virtually all the products are exported to the United States, and those that are only assembled in Mexico from components made elsewhere enjoy preferential duty status under Items 807 and 806.30 of the U.S. tariff schedule.

At least 80 Mexican companies operate abroad, three-fourths of them in Central American countries.

MANUFACTURING INDICATORS, 1987

Average annual growth rate (%, 1980–88): 0.2
Share of GDP (%): 26 (1988)
Labor force economically active in manufacturing (% est.): 10.6 (1984)
Value added in manufacturing (U.S. $ millions): 36.381 (1987)
- Food & tobacco (%): 24
- Textiles & clothing (%): 12
- Machinery & transport equipment (%): 14
- Chemicals (%): 12

Earnings per employee in manufacturing 1986
- Growth rate (%, 1980–87): −3.5
- Index (1980 = 100): 87

Total earnings as % of value added: 26
Gross output per employee (1980 = 100): 107
Index of manufacturing production: 112 (1988)

Although the Mexican economy is described as mixed, the state has a primary or dominant role in at least eight subsectors: petroleum, railroads, electricity, communications, irrigation, steel manufacture, aviation and petrochemicals. The government runs the largest agricultural marketing and retailing organization and dominates finance through its development finance institutions.

MINING

Mexico is rich in minerals and hydrocarbons. It is one of the world's leading producers of silver and fluorite, ranks fourth in the production of mercury and lead, sixth in the production of antimony and seventh in the production of cadmium, manganese and zinc. In 1978 important deposits of phosphates were discovered in Baja California, and it is hoped that Mexico's proven uranium reserves will make Mexico the world's third-largest producer.

The Mexicanization of the mining industry has been a major national issue since the revolution of 1910, and as a result the mining sector is the most completely Mexicanized in the economy. The government has also decreed that minerals such as iron, coal and tin may not be exported. Refined metals account for almost 20% of all nonpetroleum exports. Mexico's output of silver was expected to increase after 1983, following the opening of the world's largest silver mine at Real de Angeles in Zacatecas. Mexico's first phosphate mine, at San Juan de la Costa, began production in 1980.

ENERGY

With the announcements in 1974 of new discoveries of petroleum in Veracruz, Baja California and Chiapas-Tabasco, Mexico's petroleum reserves were revised upward, to 52 billion barrels. Under a constitutional amendment, the government holds a monopoly in the exploration, production, refining and distribution of petroleum and natural gas and in the manufacture and sale of basic petrochemicals. These activities are conducted by Pemex. Mexico has not yet been admitted to membership in OPEC.

Mexico was the world's leading petroleum producer in 1921 but by 1938, when the industry was nationalized, production had fallen dramatically. The discovery of extensive petroleum reserves in Tabasco and Chiapas enabled output to increase significantly in the 1970s. The state oil agency, Petroleos Mexicanos (Pemex), has declared that the Bay of Campeche is the richest offshore oilfield in the world. In 1984 a total of 26 new oil and gas fields were discovered. Pemex is the largest single employer and the largest single industrial investor in Mexico. Oil and gas account for 70% of electricity production. Mexico has the 11th-largest refining capacity in the world.

ENERGY INDICATORS

Average annual energy production growth rate (%, 1980–88): 2.4
Energy consumption per capita (kg. oil equivalent): 1,305 (1988)
Energy imports as % of merchandise exports: 1 (1988)
Average annual growth rate of energy consumption (%, 1980–88): 0.7
Electricity 1988
- Installed capacity (million kw.): 27.698
- Production (billion kw.-hr.): 110.876
  - % fossil fuel: 78.3
  - % hydro: 17.6
  - % geothermal: 4.1
- Consumption per capita (kw.-hr.): 1,285

Natural gas
- Proved reserves (trillion cu. m.): 2,060 (1990)
- Production (million cu. m.): 24.9 (1989)
- Consumption (billion cu. m.): 22.791 (1988)

Petroleum
- Proved reserves (billion bbl.): 51.983 (1990)
- Years to exhaust proved reserves: 57 (1990)
- Production (million bbl.): 946 (1989)
- Consumption (million bbl.): 437 (1988)
- Refining capacity (million bbl./day): 1.514 (1990)

Coal
- Reserves (billion metric tons): 1.886 (latest)
- Production (000 metric tons): 11,275 (1988)
- Consumption (000 metric tons): 11,000 (1988)

LABOR

Historically, Mexican women have had few opportunities for paid employment. This excludes the many women who work as domestic servants and on family farms. An estimated 500,000 persons enter the labor market each year. Unemployment is widespread, affecting nearly 19% of the labor force.

LABOR INDICATORS, 1988

Total economically active population (millions): 31.806
- % working-age (15–64): 60.6
- % female: 30.0

Activity rate (%)
- Total: 38.4
- Male: 53.7
- Female: 23.1

Employment status (%)
- Employers & self-employed: 27.7
- Employees: 55.0
- Unpaid family workers: 14.1
- Other: 3.3

Sectoral employment of economically active (%)
- Agriculture, forestry, fishing: 22.9
- Construction: 5.3
- Manufacturing, mining, quarrying, public utilities: 20.6
- Trade, hotels, restaurants: 18.8
- Transportation, communications: 3.7
- Finance, real estate: 5.1
- Services: 21.1

Average annual growth rate of labor force (%, 1985–2000): 3.0
Unemployment (000): 472 (1977)
Labor under 20 years (%): 17.9 (1980)
Earnings in manufacturing (/worker) (/mo.) (Mex. P.): 70,068 (1985)
Hours of work (/worker) 1985
- Manufacturing (/wk.): 46.0

Minimum wages are set for over 111 separate labor market areas by a tripartite national commission. They are revised annually. Mexican law sets the minimum age for the employment of children at 14 years; children over 14 but under 16 years of age may work but are subject to special legal protections and shorter working hours than adults and cannot be employed in certain jobs. The law also provides for a minimum wage, which is revised semi-annually; a maximum legal workweek of 48 hours; and a maximum workday of eight hours. Extensive regulations pertaining to occupational health and safety also exist. Child labor laws in Mexico are observed fairly strictly in medium-size and large manufacturing and commercial establishments, but less so in small shops and in occupations such as that of street vendor, where occurrence of child labor is hard to control. Industrial safety laws are less frequently observed in practice, particularly in the heavy industrial sector and in the construction industry.

In recent years, the commissions have begun to set minimum wages for an expanding number of semiskilled, skilled and office jobs. The commission for the Federal District established rates for 82 different skills in 1978.

Many employers fail to pay the minimum wage. Estimates of noncompliance range from 30% to 50% among employers of urban workers, to as high as 80% in the rural areas. The best record of compliance is in Mexico City. In addition, workers receive a percentage of the employers' annual profits. The statutory workday is either six eight-hour day shifts, six seven-hour night shifts or a seven and one-half-hour day if a mixed shift is worked. The 48-hour week is prevalent in industry. In offices, a 40-hour or 44-hour week is often the practice. Overtime of up to three hours per day (not more than three times in one week) must be paid at a double-time rate. Each employee also is entitled to one weekly day of rest, five paid holidays every year and six to eight days of vacation during each full year of employment.

Mexico loses thousands of workers yearly through immigration to the United States. Although precise statistics are lacking, it is generally believed that Mexicans constitute the largest alien work force in the United States.

In the industrialized sector, probably more than 90% of the production workers in establishments of over 25 workers are organized. Few white-collar employees join unions. Considering that almost half the work force is either unemployed or underemployed, and therefore not organizable, Mexico must be considered highly organized.

In practice, the basic unit of Mexican labor organization is the plant or work-site union. There are few craft unions. Local units *(secciónes)* are federated either into national unions *(sindicatos)* or into local, regional (intrastate) or state federations, which may then form confederations.

The Confederation of Mexican Workers is the country's largest labor organization. Its women's division is the Workers' Federation of Women's Organizations. Other prominent union federations include the Regional Confederation of Mexican Workers, the Revolutionary Confederation of Mexican Workers and Farmers, the Federation of Independent Trade Unions and the Federation of Unions of Government Workers. Most of these unions are affiliated with the Congress of Labor, which encompasses 85% of all organized workers.

Mexico's first comprehensive labor law, promulgated in 1931, was based on principles enunciated in the Constitution. The present labor law is the Federal Labor Act of 1970. The law requires an employer to negotiate a collective contract if requested by a union. Collective bargaining has been the practice in Mexican industry for many years. Agreements customarily augment the minimum legally required benefits, and may include additional holidays, higher wages, schools, health clinics, recreational facilities and retirement benefits. Collective contracts usually include detailed provisions for grievance procedures, seniority and job security. Most contracts call for a union shop or a closed shop.

Industrywide bargaining is practiced in the textile, sugar and petroleum industries.

Labor laws are enforced by state as well as federal authorities. Certain areas of jurisdiction are, however, reserved to the federal government. The Mexican Constitution asserts the authority of the federal government over industrywide bargaining in the textile, electric, motion picture, rubber, sugar, mineral and mining, hydrocarbon, railway, petrochemical, cement and steel industries.

All industrial disputes are required to be submitted to boards of conciliation and arbitration, consisting of an equal number of workers and employers and one government representative.

The right to strike is guaranteed by the Constitution and affirmed in the Federal Labor Act. The union must file a notice of strike with the employer and with the conciliation board, after a decision by a majority of workers involved. An attempt must first be made to settle the dispute through conciliation. If this fails, the government may or may not declare the strike legal. There are relatively few strikes in Mexico. Most are in the smaller or newly organized enterprises and rarely last more than 10 days. In 1989 trade union disputes and demands for pay increases led to strikes by teachers, bus drivers, steel workers and motor-industry workers. A further cause of labor unrest was the comprehensive divestment program, initiated by the Government in 1989.

FOREIGN COMMERCE

In 1988 Mexico recorded a visible trade surplus of U.S. $1.752 billion but there was a deficit of $2.905 billion on the current account of the balance of payments. Mexico's principal trading partner is the U.S., both in exports as well as in imports. Other major trading partners are Japan, Spain, France, Germany and Canada. Principal exports are crude petroleum, engines and spare parts for road vehicles, coffee and seafoods. Principal imports are foods, iron and steel, vehicles and machinery.

President Salinas signed an agreement on October 3, 1989, intended to expand bilateral trade and investment with the U.S. It was reported to be the

FOREIGN TRADE INDICATORS, 1988

Exports (U.S. $ billions): 23.1 (1989)
Imports (U.S. $ billions): 23.3 (1989)
Balance of trade (U.S. $ billions): −.2
Annual growth rate (1980–88), exports (%): 5.5
Annual growth rate (1980–88): imports (%): −4.9
International reserves in terms of months of imports covered: 2.1
Terms of trade (1980=100): 67
Import price index (1980=100): 101.7 (1986)
Export price index (1980=100): 67.4 (1986)

Direction of Trade (%), 1988

	Imports	Exports
European Community	14.7	13.0
United States	66.7	66.0
U.S.S.R. & eastern European economies	0.3	0.7
Japan	6.0	6.0

Composition of Trade (%), 1985

	Imports	Exports
Food & agricultural raw materials	16.6	8.9
Fuels & other energy	4.4	60.1
Mineral ores & concentrates	2.6	2.1
Manufactured goods	76.5	28.9
of which chemicals	13.9	3.1
of which machinery	43.5	15.9

broadest economic agreement ever between the two countries. The pact expanded a 1987 accord that had set up consultative talks on trade disputes. In addition, an agreement on steel limited Mexican shipments to the U.S. over the next two and a half years and eliminated trade-distorting practices in the steel sector. Salinas also urged the U.S. to lower trade barriers.

TRANSPORTATION & COMMUNICATIONS

The Mexican rail system is an integrated network of six lines. Five of the six lines are owned by the government. The largest, National Railways, operates about 70% of the total trackage and carries about 80% of the total traffic. The second largest is the Pacific Railroad, linking Nogales with Guadalajara. Both these railways are autonomous government agencies. The three other government lines are the Chihuahua to Pacific Railroad, the Sonora–Baja California Railroad and the United Railroads of the Southeast. The rail system links with the United States at several points, such as at Ciudad Juarez, Laredo, Piedras Negras, Reynosa, Matamoros, Nogales, Naco and Agua Prieta, and with Central America through Guatemala. A short stretch of 102 km. (63 mi.) is electrified. An underground railway system was opened in Mexico City in 1969. Inland waterways play only a minor role in the country's transportation system.

Five of Mexico's 49 ocean ports—Tampico, Veracruz, Guayamas, Mazatlán and Manzanillo—handle 80% of the nation's ocean freight. Veracruz, on the Gulf of Mexico, is the major general cargo port, especially for goods to and from Mexico City. Tampico handles petroleum and petroleum products and is the outlet for the nearby petroleum refinery. Other seaports include Coatzacoalcos, on the Gulf coast, and Acapulco, on the Pacific. The Mexican merchant marine has 642 vessels including an oil tanker fleet of 540 tankers owned and operated by Pemex. Most of the other ships are operated by the state-owned Maritime Transport of Mexico. Coastal shipping carries as much cargo as ocean shipping and more passengers. Ferries operate between the Yucatán Peninsula and the offshore islands between the peninsula of Baja California and the mainland.

Mexico has one of the most modern road networks in Latin America. Roads reach 40% of the national territory. The highway system consists of federal roads, state roads and local roads. The federal government bears 50% of the cost of building state roads and one-third of the cost of building local roads. The three major federal highways are: the Baja California Dorsal Highway, from Tijuana on the U.S. border to Cabo San Lucas at the tip of the peninsula; the Trans-Mexico Highway, paralleling the U.S. border from Tijuana to Matamoros of the Gulf of Mexico; and the Pacific Coast Highway, from Tijuana to Tapachula on the Guatemalan border. Trolleys operate in Mexico City, Veracruz and some other cities. Mexico City also has an unusual kind of taxi called the *pesero*, which plies between fixed points like a bus.

There are 77 domestic airlines, but only two of them have international stature: Aeromexico (Aeronaves de Mexico) and Compania Mexicana de Aviación (Mexicana). The government stake in aviation includes a 100% interest in Aeromexico and a 58% interest in Mexicana. The Mexico City airport is the hub of the air traffic.

Tourism is Mexico's second largest net earner of foreign exchange. The relics of the Mayan and Aztec

TRANSPORTATION INDICATORS

Roads (latest)
- Length, km. (mi.): 235,431 (146,290)
- Paved (%): 45

Motor vehicles (latest)
- Automobiles: 537,635
- Trucks and buses: 502,421
- Persons per vehicle: 9.9

Railroads (latest)
- Track (route length), km. (mi.): 26,299 (16,341)
- Passenger-km. (passenger-mi.) (billions): 5.900 (3.666)
- Freight, metric ton-km. (short ton-mi.) (billions): 41.700 (28.262)

Merchant marine
- Vessels (over 100 tons): 642 (1989)
- Total deadweight tonnage (millions): 1.883 (1989)
- Oil tankers (000 GRT): 540 (1985)

Ports (pre-1986)
- Cargo loaded (million metric tons): 89.580
- Cargo unloaded (million metric tons): 11.244

Air
- Km. (mi.) flown (millions): 185.9 (115.5)
- Passenger-km. (passenger-mi.) (billions): 12.252 (7.613) (latest)
- Freight, metric ton-km. (short ton-mi.) (millions): 78.3 (53.6) (latest)
- Mail, metric ton-km. (short ton-mi.) (millions): 4.2 (2.8) (1985)
- Airports with scheduled flights: 78 (1990)

Pipelines 1990
- Refined, km. (mi.): 8,345 (5,185)
- Natural gas, km. (mi.): 13,254

Inland waterways (latest)
- Length, km. (mi.): 2,900 (1,802)

COMMUNICATION INDICATORS, 1987

Telephones
 Total (millions): 8.696 (1988)
 Persons per telephone: 9.2 (1988)
Phone traffic (million calls)
 Local: 2,978.969
 Long distance: 724.668
 Combined national: 3,703.637
 International: 30.348
Post office
 Number of post offices: 6,082
 Pieces of mail handled (millions): 742.093
Telegraph
 Total traffic (million calls): 25.142
  National: 24.902
  International: 240
Telex
 Subscriber lines, 24,526
 Traffic (million minutes): 77.858
Telecommunications 1990
 Domestic satellite ground terminals: 120
 Satellite ground antennas: 2

TOURISM & TRAVEL INDICATORS, 1986

Total tourist receipts (U.S. $ billions): 3.994 (1988)
Expenditures by nationals abroad (U.S. $ billions): 3.197 (1988)
Number of hotel beds (000): 551
Average length of stay (nights): 10
Tourist nights (000): 42,077

civilization as well as Mexico's colonial historic sites remain the main attractions.

DEFENSE

The defense structure is headed by the president, who exercises control through the minister of national defense, customarily a professional military officer. Mexico is divided for military purposes into 35 zones, corresponding with the 31 states, except that Oaxaca, Veracruz and Guerrero have two zones each and the Federal District has one zone.

Military manpower is obtained through voluntary enlistment, but under the universal military training program all males over 18 are required to undergo one year of basic army or marine training.

The total strength of the armed forces is 141,500.

Army

Personnel: 105,500

Organization: 1 infantry brigade (presidential guard of 3 battalions); 2 infantry brigades; 3 armored regiments; 36 zonal garrisons, including 21 independent cavalry, 3 artillery regiments and 70 independent battalions; AA engineer and support units

Equipment: 45 tanks; 55 combat vehicles; 43 personnel carriers; 108 howitzers; 1,660 mortars; 35 antitank guns; 40 air defense guns

Navy

Personnel: 28,000 (including marines)

Units: 2 areas (Gulf and Pacific) of 5 and 12 zones, respectively.

Equipment: 2 destroyers; 6 frigates; 6 corvettes; 35 patrol ships; 31 patrol craft; 10 amphibious vehicles; 1 repair ship; 1 transport; 2 harbor tankers

Naval air force: 8 combat aircraft; 1 maritime reconnaissance squadron; 1 liaison squadron; 1 helicopter squadron

Marines: 3 HQ battalions; 19 security companies

Air Force

Personnel: 8,000

Organization: 85 combat aircraft; 1 interceptor squadron; 6 counterinsurgency squadrons; 1 reconnaissance photo squadron; 2 search and rescue squadrons; 1 presidential transport squadron; 4 transport squadrons; 94 trainers; 1 airborne brigade

Mexico's last foreign war was in 1846, which means that the nation has been at peace for over 140 years. The army has been considerably depoliticized, although some 20 to 30 officers are elected to the National Congress every session.

The Mexican armed forces are smaller in relation to the national population, and military expenditures are smaller in relation to the GNP and the national budget than those of nearly every other country in Latin America. The logic behind this low profile is that the great size of Mexico's northern neighbor, the United States, makes resistance to armed invasion useless, and the small size of her southern neighbors makes a large army unnecessary. The only possibility that remains is infiltration by guerrillas, and the military establishment is therefore trained to counter terrorist, subversive and other such activities. The air force is not considered a separate establishment but a part of the army. However, there has been a noticeable increase in professionalism in the armed forces as well as an improvement in conditions of service.

There is significant internal defense production, mainly of small arms and ammunition.

EDUCATION

Education is free, universal and compulsory for six years, from ages six to 11. Schooling lasts for 12 years, divided into six years of primary school, three years of lower secondary school and three years of upper secondary school. The government maintains a free textbook program for primary schools. Article 3 of the Constitution and Article 9 of the new Federal Education Law of 1973 forbid religious organizations from participating in institutions providing elementary, secondary or teacher education, or education for laborers. All private schools must be licensed by the state and must use state-authorized curricular materials. However, these articles have never been fully enforced.

The school year runs from September to June. The language of instruction is Spanish, but the study of at least one foreign language, usually English, is compulsory in secondary schools.

Primary-school teachers are trained at normal schools. Rural normal-school graduates have to undergo additional courses of study to teach in urban schools.

Secondary-school teachers are trained in teacher-training schools.

Technical schools offer terminal middle-level training in practical skills or preparation for further study.

EDUCATION INDICATORS, 1990

Literacy
- Total (%): 90.3
- Male (%): 92.3
- Female (%): 88.3

First level
- Schools: 82,137
- Students: 14,675,300
- Teachers: 471,033
- Student teacher ratio: 31.2
- Net enrollment ratio: 100 (1987)

Second level
- Schools: 19,098
- Students: 4,000,400
- Teachers: 234,600
- Student/teacher ratio: 18.8
- Net enrollment ratio: 44 (1987)

Vocational
- Schools: 6,507
- Students: 167,000
- Teachers: 176,232
- Student/teacher ratio: 12.3

Third level (post secondary)
- Institutions: 1,347 (1986)
- Students: 1,786,200
- Teachers: 121,896
- Student/teacher ratio: 14.7
- Gross enrollment ratio: 15.7 (1987)
- Students (/100,000 pop.): 1,578
- % of population age 25 and over with postsecondary education: 5.3

Foreign study
- Students abroad: 7,055
  - of whom in
    - United States: 5,014 (1988)
    - France: 573 (1988)
    - Federal Republic of Germany: 245 (1988)
    - United Kingdom: 240 (1987)

Public expenditure 1988
- Total (Mex. P.: 000): 7,968,125
- % of GNP: 3.4 (1990)
- % of current: 93.8

GRADUATES, 1987

Total: 153,131
Education: 33,586
Humanities & religion: 978
Fine & applied arts: 500
Law: 11,926
Social & behavioral sciences: 10,309
Commerce & business: 27,857
Mass communication: 3,099
Home economies: 0
Service trades: 0
Natural sciences: 4,858
Mathematics & computer science: 1,747
Medicine: 17,842
Engineering: 30,891
Architecture: 4,984
Industrial programs: 0
Transportation & communications: 0
Agriculture, forestry, fisheries: 2,939
Other: 1,615

There are nearly 11,000 adult literacy centers in addition to literacy programs on radio and television.

The basic responsibility for public education rests with the Secretaria de Educación Pública (SEP), but day-to-day responsibility for maintenance and operations rests with state and municipal governments. Private schools are required to be entirely secular and to conform to standards set by the government.

Higher education is provided in various universities and institutes. The largest universities are the Universidad Nacional Autónoma de México, the Universidad Autonoma del Estado de Mexico, the Universidad de Coahuila, the Universidad de Guadalajara, the Universidad Autonoma de Guadalajara, the Universidad Michoacana de San Nicolas de Hidalgo, the Universidad Autonoma de Nuevo León, the Universidad Autonoma de Puebla, the Universidad Autonoma de Tamaulipas and the Universidad Veracruzana.

LEGAL SYSTEM

The legal system is based on Spanish civil law with an admixture of U.S. elements.

The judiciary is divided into federal and state systems, but both are headed by the Supreme Court. The Supreme Court is composed of 21 justices called ministers and five auxiliary judges, organized into four general chambers (salas)—penal, administrative, criminal and labor—each with five justices. The position of chief justice rotates among the justices annually, but a chief justice may be reelected. A fifth chamber, the auxiliary chamber, takes the overload from the other chambers.

Below the Supreme Court are three levels of courts: five circuit collegiate tribunals, each with three magistrates; six circuit unitary tribunals, each with six magistrates; and 46 one-magistrate district courts.

Each state has its own judiciary, generally following the federal pattern. The highest state courts are known as the state superior courts, whose judges are appointed by the governors with the consent of the state legislatures. They in turn appoint members of subordinate courts, such as courts of first instance and justices of the peace, also called police judges.

The system of trial by jury exists but is not commonly employed. The most powerful judicial instrument is the writ of *amparo*, similar to habeas corpus. The death penalty was abolished in 1930.

Under the Constitution, trial and sentencing must be completed within 12 months of arrest for crimes that would carry at least a two-year sentence. Nevertheless, trial delays are often caused by cumbersome court procedures and by the defendants' inability or unwillingness to pay bribes in the form of "gratuities" to bring the case to trial. State authorities in some localities are attempting to correct such abuses. In February 1984 the governor of the state of Yucatán announced that he had discovered "grave irregularities" in the office of the attorney general, centering mainly on the solicitation of bribes. The governor stated that basic changes have been implemented. Defendants have a right to counsel, and public defenders are available.

Although certain sections of the criminal code provide for convoking tribunals with juries, in practice this almost never takes place. In most cases, a judge, generally acting alone, examines written statements, expert opinion and, less commonly, oral testimony and then renders his verdict.

The penal system has both federal and state correctional facilities. The largest federal prison is the penitentiary for those sentenced in the Federal District. The notorious Lucumberri Penitentiary now serves as a preventive jail. The Federal District also has four detention centers, a women's jail and 16 smaller jails. Hardened criminals serving long sentences are sent to one of two penal colonies. The penal colony in the Maria Islands in the Pacific Ocean has an average prison population of about 1,000. Married prisoners are permitted to bring their families with them and are provided thatched huts. All prisoners move freely on the island but are required to answer roll calls daily and to participate in some useful activity.

Each state has its own state penitentiary; in addition, there are 2,350 municipal jails. Most state and municipal jails are old and overcrowded.

Federal jails are run by military officers under military discipline. U.S. prisoners who have served in Mexican jails have reported harsh conditions, but in general prison life is less brutalized and more informal than in many other developing countries.

LAW ENFORCEMENT

There are three levels of law enforcement agencies: federal, state and municipal. There are two federal police forces: the General Directorate of Police and Traffic under the Ministry of Government, and the Judicial Police under the Public Ministry. The former includes the Secret Service Division. Other government ministries and agencies, such as Highways, Railways and Public Health, maintain their own police forces. Both state and municipal police forces are commanded by the state governors. Larger cities have special units known as foreign-language police to assist tourists with problems. Most of the policemen operate from precincts, called delegations, commanded by a *comandante*, an officer with the rank of first captain and assisted by first sergeants, second sergeants and corporals. Each delegation has an average of 200 policemen, most of whom are stationed at the headquarters, called *comandancias*, and others at two-man kiosks. There are frequent allegations in the Mexican press of police brutality, corruption, immorality and incompetence.

Over 72% of reported crimes belong to one of three kinds: assault and battery (32%), robbery (25%) and homicide (15%). Other categories are sex-related crimes (6%), property damage (3%) and fraud (2%). However, the most alarming growth rate is noted in three areas: juvenile crime, kidnapping, and narcotics traffic and drug abuse. Mexico City and other urban areas have numerous youth gangs that specialize in terrorizing other youths. Most of the kidnappings are believed to be the work of political dissidents. The use of drugs in Mexico in the mid-1970s was reported to have increased by 300% to 500% in a five-year period. According to a 1973 survey, nearly 15% of secondary-school students admitted taking drugs, while 3% are regular users. Another dimension of this problem is the flow of narcotics across the border into the United States.

Out of every 100 people charged with crimes, 92 are men and only eight are women. The low female rate compared to other countries is explained by the fact that prostitution is not a crime in Mexico, although soliciting and nonregistration for medical examination are punishable offenses.

HEALTH

Mexico has the oldest hospital in the Americas, the Jesus Nazareno Hospital in Mexico City, founded by Hernán Cortés in the early 16th century and maintained by an endowment in his will. In 1974 a 10-year national health plan was launched integrating the health-care facilities of all government agencies. Diarrhea, pneumonia and heart disease are the major health problems, while malaria, poliomyelitis, tuberculosis, leprosy and onchoceriasis remain serious threats. A total of 77% of the population have access to safe water. Damage caused by the severe earthquake in September 1985 resulted in the loss of 6,000 hospital beds in Mexico City.

HEALTH INDICATORS

Health personnel 1984
- Physicians: 74,640 (1983)
  - persons per: 980 (1983)
- Dentists: 3,207
- Nurses: 36,443
- Pharmacists: 112 (1974)
- Midwives: 634 (1974)

Hospitals 1974
- Number: 1,575
- Number of beds (/10,000): 9 (1984)

Public health expenditures (latest)
- As % of national budget: 1.1
- Per capita (U.S. $): 6.20

Vital statistics
- Crude death rate (/1,000): 5 (1990)
- Life expectancy at birth 1990
  - Males: 68
  - Females: 76
- Infant mortality rate (/1,000 live births): 33 (1990)
- Child mortality rate under 5 yrs. (/1,000 live births) (1985–90): 68
- Maternal mortality rate (/100,000 live births): 81.8 (1983)
- Population with access to safe water (%): 77 (latest)

FOOD & NUTRITION

The staple foods are corn and beans, particularly corn, which constitutes three-fourths of all grain consumed. Beef is consumed only on special occasions, and fish is unpopular. The consumption rates of eggs and milk also are low. On the other hand, Mexicans are known to have a sweet tooth and consume nearly 36 kg. (80 lb.) of sugar per capita annually.

Mexican cuisine is a blend of Indian and Spanish cookery. Its best-known contribution to the world of food is the tortilla, made of corn kernel paste and eaten like a bread or in variant forms, such as the taco, tamale or enchilada. The national drinks are *pulque*, a beer made from the juice of the maguey cactus; and *atole*, made from cornmeal.

The daily per capita intake of food is 2,976 calories (above the 2,600 minimum recommended by the WHO).

MEDIA & CULTURE

Mexico City's dailies account for half of the national circulation. Over 80 other towns and cities have daily newspapers, the larger ones having up to six each. The largest circulation is claimed by the independent morning *Esto* (450,000), and there are eight newspapers in Mexico City with circulations of over 100,000. All the papers are in Spanish, except for three that appear in English.

The one Mexican daily that finds a place in most lists of the world's elite newspapers is *The Excelsior* (200,000). Other principal dailies include *La Prensa* (300,000), *Ovaciónes* (220,000), *El Heraldo de Mexico* (209,600), *Novedades* (210,000), *El Universal* (181,375), *El Sol de Mexico* (morning 90,000, midday 92,250) and *La Afición* (98,500).

Freedom of the press is specifically granted in the Constitution, and Article 7 forbids prior censorship. However, it is acknowledged that this freedom is conditioned by the needs of public order, and its limits often vary with the sensitivities of the president in office.

Press sources report that the administration influences the press by giving financial supplements to individual reporters for favorable articles; by withholding newsprint and ink (government monopolies) from critical papers; and, more significantly, by selectively placing government advertising, an important source of income for the press. Some payments to journalists reportedly were reinstituted by the de la Madrid administration, after having been suspended following the administration's entry into office. In some cases the payments are indirect, as when a journalist receives a percentage of the advertising sold to the entities he covers. Opposition parties and some journalists have publicly accused the PRI's Office of Information of making large payments directly to other journalists. They say that this explains the reduction in direct government subsidies to journalists.

The national news agencies are Informex, Notimex and Agencia Mexicana, of which the largest is Informex, with 85 domestic offices and 17 overseas correspondents. Foreign news bureaus represented in Mexico City include AFP, UPI, AP, Kyodo, DPA, PRELA, Reuters, Efe, CTK, ANSA and Tass.

Mexico has one of the largest book industries in Latin America, with over 120 publishers, of whom at least 70 are active. Book publishing is partly subsidized by the state, as publishers do not pay taxes other than an excess profits tax. Textbooks are distributed free to children in primary schools. Mexico adheres to the Universal Copyright and Buenos Aires Copyright conventions and the Florence Agreement, but nevertheless there is a flourishing business in producing and selling pirated books.

MEDIA INDICATORS

Newspapers
- Number of dailies: 392 (latest)
- Circulation (millions): 11.256 (latest)
- Per 1,000 pop.: 142 (latest)
- Number of nondailies: 30 (1988)
- Circulation (000): 889 (1988)
- Per 1,000 pop.: 10 (1988)
- Number of periodicals: 203 (1988)
- Circulation (millions): 27,203 (1988)
- Newsprint consumption 1988
- Total metric tons: 446,000
- Per million pop. (kg.): 5,253

Book publishing
- Number of titles: 7,725 (latest)

Broadcasting 1987
- Annual expenditures (Mex. P. billions): 13.9575

Radio
- Number of transmitters: 790 (1989)
- Number of persons per radio receiver: 5.2 (1989)
- Total program hours: 5,503,835 (1985)

Television
- Television transmitters: 430 (1989)
- Number of persons per T.V. receiver: 8.9 (1989)
- Total program hours: 2,903,575 (1985)

Cinema
- Number of fixed cinemas: 2,226 (latest)
- Annual attendance (millions): 212.5 (latest)

Films
- Number of long films produced: 83 (latest)
- Number of long films imported: 258 (1987)
- % from United States: 60.5
- % from Italy: 7.0
- % from France: 5.0
- % from United Kingdom: 4.3

Broadcasting stations are divided into two types—commercial and cultural. The commercial stations, numbering over 800, operate 558 low- and medium-frequency transmitters, 28 high-frequency transmitters and 82 very-high- and super-high-frequency transmitters. There are a number of large networks, such as Radio Programas de Mexico and Radio Cadena Nacional. All stations are financed by commercial advertising but are required to make available up to 12.5% of their available broadcasting time to the government. Cultural stations are operated either by government agencies or by educational institutions. External services are operated by Radio Mexico, an official station with two 100-kw. transmitters.

Television, introduced in 1950, reaches 70% of the population through 126 stations, of which 118 are commercial and eight are cultural. Over half of these are affiliated with one private corporation, Telesistema Mexicano, which operates three commercial networks in Mexico and four stations in the United States. The main network is on the air for 24 hours a day and the others for 12 to 18 hours a day, with a number of programs in color. It also exports 20,000 program-hours to other Latin American countries. Another network, Televisión Independiente, operates seven stations; there are also some 20 independent stations and two government-owned stations: Telecadena Mexicana and Instituto Politécnico.

The Mexican film industry is only slowly recovering from the long doldrums that began in the 1950s. Of the six film studios that existed in 1946, only one—Churubusco—survives.

CULTURAL & ENVIRONMENTAL INDICATORS

Libraries (pre-1986)
- Number: 557
- Volumes (millions): 3.720
- Registered borrowers (millions): 8.492
- Loans (/1,000 pop.): 174

Museums (latest)
- Annual attendance (000): 160
- Attendance (million pop.): 12.388

Performing arts (pre-1986)
- Number of performances: 17,069
- Annual attendance (millions): 6.549
- Attendance (/1,000 pop.): 97

Nature reserves (latest)
- Number of facilities: 47

The National Library, affiliated with the National University, has over 1 million volumes.

The National Museum of Anthropology is one of the finest in the world. Other important museums include the Colonial Museum of Tepozotlán, Chapultepec Castle, and the Museum of La Venta at Villahermosa.

SOCIAL WELFARE

The principal social welfare agencies are the Mexican Institute of Social Security and the Institutes of Social Security and Services for Government Employees. The programs offer three types of benefits: medical, economic and social. Medical benefits include illness and maternity allowances and workmen's compensation for occupational illnesses. Economic benefits include sick pay, marriage expenses, old-age and disability pensions, funeral expenses, and pensions for widows and orphans. Social benefits include housing loans, vacation centers and training programs.

Official social security programs are supplemented by institutions known as civil associations. Mexican families retain many of the welfare characteristics of traditional extended families, and destitute children or senior citizens are readily cared for by their immediate relatives.

GLOSSARY

amparo: a class of legal actions safeguarding individual civil liberties.

ciudad perdidas: literally, lost city. An urban or suburban slum.

colono: a colonist settled on public land.

comandancia: the headquarters of a police precinct headed by a comandante.

delegacion: a police precinct.

ejidatrio: a peasant who holds usufructary rights to *ejido* land.

ejido: a communal corporation in which the land rights of a community are vested.

financiera: a private development finance company.

mestizo: a person of Spanish and Indian descent.

mordidas: bribes, considered as perquisites of office by Mexican civil servants.

passing: assimilation of Indians into the mestizo community, a process involving acquisition of Spanish speech, manners and dress.

pesero: a taxi that plies between regular points, like a bus.

CHRONOLOGY (from 1946)

1946— Partido de la Revolución Mexicana, the ruling party, is renamed Partido Revolucionario Institucional (PRI); Miguel Aleman Valdés is elected president.

1947— Suffrage is extended to women.

1951— Baja California Norte is granted statehood as the 29th state.

1952— Adolfo Ruiz Cortines is elected president.

1958— Adolfo López Mateos is elected president.

1961— The National Consultative Committee, composed of the living ex-presidents, is formed.

1962— The electoral law is reformed by giving national opposition parties additional seats in proportion to their overall vote.

1964— Gustavo Díaz Ordaz is elected president. . . . Mexico opposes OAS sanctions against Cuba and decides to maintain diplomatic relations with it.

1967— Mexico and the United States settle the Chamizal border dispute through the return of disputed territory to Mexico.

1968— Olympic Games are held in Mexico City; the Games are marred by bloody student riots; troops occupy the National Autonomous University and arrest thousands of students and professors; in an incident popularly known as the Tlatelolco Massacre, troops fire into a crowd of demonstrators, killing and wounding hundreds.

1970— Luis Echeverría Alvarez is elected president.

1973— President Echeverria embarks on world tour to demonstrate Mexico's solidarity with the Third World.

1974— Baja California Sur and Quintana Roo are admitted as states.

1976— José López Portillo y Pacheco is elected president.

1977— Agreement is concluded with the United States transferring U.S. citizens in Mexican jails to the United States.

1978— Four former ministers in the Echeverria cabinet are arrested on charges of corruption. . . . Under a new electoral law, the Communist Party and two other opposition parties are legalized and the opposition is guaranteed at least 25% of the membership in the Chamber of Deputies.

1979— The ruling PRI wins an absolute majority in national elections to the Chamber of Deputies. . . . Pope John Paul II visits Mexico. . . . The former shah of Iran is granted asylum in the country.

1981— Mexico hosts the Cancún North-South Conference.

1982— In general elections the PRI retains control of the Assembly, but the PAN makes gains. . . . The peso is devalued twice in a year, and an austerity program gets under way under IMF monitoring. . . . President Lopez steps down at the end of his six-year term and Miguel de la Madrid is installed as president. . . . All private banks are nationalized. . . . Foreign creditors assemble a bail-out package as Mexico is unable to meet its debt repayment schedules.

1983— Sixty police chiefs are dismissed as widespread bribery scandals break open.

1985— Earthquake hits Mexico City, killing over 4,000 and destroying many buildings. . . . In general elections opposition parties generally lose while the PRI retains its massive control of the Assembly and the municipalities.

1988— PRI candidate Carlos Salinas de Gortari is elected president in a bitterly contested election.

1989— Mexico reaches agreement with the "Paris Club" on rescheduling its foreign debt. Mexico begins a comprehensive divestment program. Opposition parties make significant gains in gubernatorial and municipal elections. . . . Earthquake strikes Mexico City, killing one person, injuring 350 others and damaging several buildings. Two major drug traffickers are arrested for the 1985 slaying of a U.S. drug agent and his Mexican pilot.

1990— An official Mexican research institute publishes a report stating that human rights abuses among the police are widespread. Three Mexicans and a Honduran are convicted in connection with the 1985 slaying of Enrique Camarena Salazar, an American drug agent. President Salinas visits Washington on a three-day visit June 10–12. Pope John Paul II visits Mexico.

BIBLIOGRAPHY (from 1970)

BOOKS & FILMS

A Portrait of Mexico. Color film, 14 min. International Film Bureau.

Ackstein, Susan, *The Poverty of Revolution: The State and the Urban Poor in Mexico.* Princeton, NJ, 1977.

Adobe Village. B&W film, 20 min. Universal.

Archer, Jules. *Mexico and the United States.* New York, 1973.

Atkins, Ronald. *Revolution Mexico, 1910–1920* New York, 1970.

Banco Nacional de Comercio Exterior. *Mexico: Facts, Figures & Trends.* Mexico City, annual.

Barchfield, J. W. *Peasants, Politics & Development in Mexico.* New Brunswick, NJ, 1980.

Berlow, Lawrence H. *Mexico in the 1980s.* Munroe, NY, 1983.

Briggs, Donald C., and Marvin Alisky, *Historical Dictionary of Mexico.* Metuchen, NJ, 1981.

Buzaglo, Jorge. *Planning the Mexican Economy: Alternative Development Strategies.* New York, 1984.

Calvert, Peter. *Mexico* Boulder, CO, 1977.

———. *Mexicans: How They Live and Work.* New York, 1973.

Camp, Roderic, *Mexico's Leaders: Education & Recruitment.* Tucson, AZ, 1980.

——. *The Making of a Government: Political Leaders in Modern Mexico.* Tucson, AZ, 1984.

Carlos, Manuel L. *Politics and Development in Rural Mexico.* New York, 1974.

Cheetam, Nicholas. *Mexico: A Short History.* New York, 1971.

Cypher, James M. *State and Capital in Mexico: Development Policy Since 1940.* Boulder, CO, 1990.

Climate & Resources. B&W film, 11 min. Progressive Pictures.

De Rouffignac, Ann E. Lucas. *The Contemporary Peasantry in Mexico: A Class Analysis.* New York, 1985.

De Walt, B. R. *Modernization in a Mexican Ejido.* New York, 1979.

Eckstein, S. *The Poverty of Revolution: The State & the Urban Poor in Mexico.* Princeton, NJ, 1977.

Fernandez, Raul A. *The United States-Mexico Border: A Politico-Economic Profile.* Notre Dame, IN, 1977.

Festival in Mexico. Color film, 29 min. Ray Manley.

Friedrich, Paul. *Agrarian Revolt in a Mexican Village.* Chicago, IL, 1978.

Gonzales Casanova, Pablo. *Democracy in Mexico.* New York, 1970.

Goulet, Denis. *Mexico: Development Strategies for the Future.* Notre Dame, IN, 1982.

Graham, Lawrence. *Mexican State Government.* Austin, TX, 1971.

Greenberg, Martin Harry. *Bureaucracy and Development: A Mexican Case Study.* Lexington, MA, 1970.

Grindle, Merilee S. *Bureaucrats, Politicians and Peasants in Mexico.* Berkeley, CA, 1977.

Guzman, Martin Luis. *The Eagle and the Serpent.* London, 1970.

Haas, Antonio. *Mexico.* New York, 1982.

Hansen, Roger. *The Politics of Mexican Development.* Baltimore, MD, 1971.

Heart of Mexico. B&W film, 10 min. 20th Century-Fox.

Heath, Shirley Price. *Telling Tongues: Language Policies in Mexico.* New York, 1972.

Hellman, Judith Adler. *Mexico in Crisis.* New York, 1983.

Hewlett, Sylvia A., and Richard Weinert. *Brazil and Mexico: Patterns in Late Development.* Philadelphia, PA, 1984.

Hofstadter, Dan. *Mexico, 1946–73.* New York, 1974.

Intermatrix Ltd. *Stockton International Business Reports: Mexico.* London, 1985.

Johnson, Kenneth. *Mexican Democracy: A Critical View.* New York, 1984.

Kibble, Pauline R. *A Guide to Mexican History.* Claremont, CA, 1983.

Krieger, Ronald A. *Mexico: An Economic Survey.* New York, 1971.

Land of Mexico. B&W film, 10 min. Encyclopaedia Britannica.

Levy, Daniel, and Gabriel Szekely. *Mexico: Profile of Stable Development.* Boulder, CO, 1982.

Lewis, Paul H. *The Governments of Argentina, Brazil and Mexico.* New York, 1975.

Looney, Robert E. *Mexico's Economy: A Policy Analysis with Forecasts to 1990.* Boulder, CO, 1978.

———. *Development Alternatives of Mexico: Beyond the 1980s.* New York, 1982.

———. *Economic Policymaking in Mexico.* Durham, NC, 1984.

Mancke, Richard B. *Mexican Oil & Natural Gas: Political, Strategic & Economic Implications.* New York, 1979.

Markiewicz, Dana. *Ejido Organization in Mexico.* Los Angeles, 1980.

Mexican Village Life. Color film, 14 min. Coronet.

Mexico. Color film, 15 min. Neubacher Vetter.

Mexico. Color film, 10 min. University of Minnesota.

Mexico: A Changing Land. Color film, 21 min. Alfred Higgins.

Mexico: An Economy in Transition. Color film, 13 min. Doubleday.

Mexico at Work. Color film, 16 min. CBS.

Mexico Builds a Democracy. B&W film, 20 min. Producer not available.

Mexico: Central and Gulf Coast Regions. Color film, 18 min. Contemporary.

Mexico City. Color film, 11 min. U.S. Department of State.

Mexico City: Patterns for Progress. Color film, 17 min. Paul Hoeffler.

Mexico: Four Views. Color film, 15 min. Robert Flaxman.

Mexico: Geography of the Americas. Color/B&W film, 11 min. Coronet.

Mexico: Giant of Latin America. Color film, 23 min. Lemont Films.

Mexico's Heritage. Color film, 17 min. Paul Hoeffler.

Mexico's History. Color film, 16 min. Coronet.

Mexico: History and Government. B&W film, 11 min. Progressive Pictures.

Mexico in the 70s: Heritage and Progress. Color film, 12 min. Frank Gardony.

Mexico: Land of Color and Contrast. Color film, 16 min. Neubacher-Vetter.

Mexico: Northern and Southern Regions. Color film, 17 min. Contemporary Films.

Mexico: The Frozen Revolution. Color film, 16 min. Raymundo Gleyzer.

Mexico: The Land and the People. Color/B&W film, 20 min. Encyclopaedia Britannica.

Mexico: The Workers of Mexico. B&W film, 11 min. Progressive Pictures.

Mexico: The World Parade. B&W film, 10 min. Producer not available.

Mexico: 12,000 Years of History. Color film, 24 min. Black Star.

Meyer, Michael C., and William L. Sherman. *The Course of Mexican History.* New York, 1983.

Mills, Robert E. *Mexico: A History.* Norman, OK, 1985.

Modern Mexicans. Color film, 22 min. Scorpio Productions.

Montgomery, Tommy Sue. *Mexico Today.* Philadelphia, PA, 1982.

Needler, Martin C. *Mexican Politics: The Containment of Conflict.* New York, 1982.

———. *Politics and Society in Mexico.* Albuquerque, NM, 1971.

Newell, Robert, and Luis Rubio. *Mexico's Dilemma: The Political Origins of Economic Crisis.* Boulder, CO, 1985.

Ortiz-Martinez, Guillermo. *Capital Accumulation and Economic Growth: A Financial Perspective on Mexico.* New York, 1984.

Pacific Coast of Mexico. Color film, 11 min. Johnson-Hunt.

Padgett, Vincent L. *The Mexican Political System.* Boston, 1976.

People of Mexico. B&W film, 11 min. Encyclopaedia Britannica.

Philip, George. *Politics in Mexico.* London, 1985.

Quirk, Robert E. *The Mexican Revolution and the Catholic Church, 1910–1929.* Bloomington, IN, 1973.

Randall, Laura. *The Political Economy of Mexican Oil.* New York, 1989.

Reyna, José L., and Richard S. Weinert. *Authoritarianism in Mexico.* Philadelphia, 1977.

Reynolds, Clark W. *Mexican Economy.* New Haven, CT, 1970.

Rodman, Selden. *A Short History of Mexico.* Briarcliff Manor, NY, 1982.

Ronfeldt, D. *Atencingo: The Politics of Agrarian Struggle in a Mexican Ejido.* Stanford, CA, 1973.

Ross, John B. *The Economic System of Mexico.* Stanford, CA, 1971.

Schmitt, Karl M. *Mexico and the United States, 1821–1973.* New York, 1974.

Schoonover, Thomas D. *Dollars over Dominion: The Triumph of Liberalism in Mexican–United States Relations 1861–67.* Baton Rouge, LA, 1976.

Serron, Luis A. *Scarcity, Exploitation & Poverty: Malthus & Marx in Mexico.* Norman, OK, 1980.

Shafer, Robert Jones. *Mexican Business: Organization, History and Analysis.* Syracuse, NY, 1973.

Shapira, Yoram. *Mexican Foreign Policy: Echeverria's Influence.* Beverly Hills, CA, 1978.

Sinkin, Richard N. *The Mexican Reform: 1855–1876.* Austin, TX, 1979.

Smith, Peter H. *Labyrinths of Power: Political Recruitment in Twentieth-Century Mexico.* Princeton, NJ, 1979.

———. *Mexico: The Quest for a U.S. Policy.* New York, 1980.

Smith, Robert F. *The United States and Revolutionary Nationalism in Mexico, 1916–1932.* Chicago, 1972.

Soils, Leopoldo. *Economic Policy Reform in Mexico: A Case Study for Developing Countries.* Elmsford, NY, 1981.

Steven, Evelyn P. *Protest and Response in Mexico.* Cambridge, MA, 1974.

Tenkate, Robert, and Robert B. Wallace. Protection and Development in Mexico. New York, 1981.

The Many Faces of Mexico. Color film, 16 min. Film, Inc.

Thompson, John K. *Financial Policy, Inflation, &*

Economic Development: The Mexican Experience. Greenwich, CT, 1979.
Turner, Frederick C. *The Dynamics of Mexican Nationalism.* Chapel Hill, NC, 1970.
Van Ginneken, Wouter. *Socio-Economic Groups & Income Distribution in Mexico.* New York, 1980.
Vasquez, Carlos, and Manuel Garcia y Griego. *Mexican–U.S. Relations: Conflict and Convergence.* Los Angeles, CA, 1983.
Vasquez, Josefina Z., and Lorenzo Meyer. *The United States and Mexico.* Chicago, IL, 1985.
Weintraub, Sidney. *A Marriage of Convenience: Relations Between Mexico and the United States.* New York, 1990.
Wilkie, James W. *The Mexican Revolution: Federal Expenditure and Social Change Since 1910.* Berkeley, CA, 1970.
William, Edward J. *The Rebirth of the Mexican Petroleum Industry.* Lexington, MA, 1979.

OFFICIAL PUBLICATIONS

Mexican Bank. Annual report.
———. *Economic indicators.*
Finance Ministry. *Cuenta de la Hacienda Pública Federal* (Federal Public Accounts). Contaduria de la Frederación (Federal Accountant General).
———. *Cuenta Pública del Departamento del Distrito Federal* (Public Accounts of the Department of the Federal District). Contaduria de la Federación (Federal Accountant General).
———. *Estados de la Recaudación por Ejecución de la Ley de Ingreso de la Federación y Desglose por Renglones* (Detailed Revenue Statements for the Execution of the Federal Revenue Law). *Dirección General de Estudios Hacendarios.* (Finance Research Directorate) (monthly).
———. *Informe de la Tresoreria* (Treasury Report) (monthly).
Industry & Commerce Department. *Cuentas de los Gobiernos Estatales* (State Government Accounts). Dirección Nacional de Estadistica de la Secretaria de Industria y Comercio (National Statistical Office).

MOROCCO

- International boundary
- Partition line as defined in the April 14, 1976, Accord signed by Mauritania and Morocco
- National capital
- Road or track
- Railroad
- International airport

0 50 100 150 Miles
0 50 100 150 Kilometers

PORTUGAL
SPAIN
Cádiz
Algeciras
Gibraltar (U.K.)
Tangier
Ceuta (Sp.)
Tétouan
Mediterranean Sea
Oran
Al Hoceima
Melilla (Sp.)
Larache
Souk el Arba du Rharb
Oued Sebou
Oujda
Tlemcen
Rabat
Kenitra
Fès
Taza
Meknès
Al Aricha
Casablanca
Azrou
El Jadida (Mazagan)
Settat
Khouribga
Oued Moulouya
Midelt
Bou Arfa
Safi
Benguerir
Beni Mellal
Ksar es Souk
Béchar
Essaouira (Mogador)
Marrakech
Erfoud
Atlantic Ocean
Ouarzazate
Oued Dades
Agadir
Zagora
Tiznit
Sidi Ifni
Bou Izakarn
Oued Drâa
Canary Islands (Sp.)
Tan-Tan
Tarfaya
ALGERIA
Tindouf
Daora
El Aaiún
Hagunia
Semara
Lemsid
Bu Craa
Cabo Bojador
Guelta Zemmur
Bir Mogrein
(Claimed by Morocco)
Villa Cisneros
Taguersimst
WESTERN SAHARA
(Claimed by Mauritania)
Tazadit
F'dérik
MAURITANIA
MALI
Bir Gandus
Nouadhibou
Güera
Atar
Akjoujt
Nouakchott

MOROCCO

BASIC FACT SHEET

OFFICIAL NAME: Kingdom of Morocco (al-Mamlaka al-Maghrebiya)

ABBREVIATION: MR

CAPITAL: Rabat

HEAD OF STATE: King Hassan (from 1961)

HEAD OF GOVERNMENT: Prime Minister Dr. Azzedine Laraki (from 1986)

NATURE OF GOVERNMENT: Constitutional monarchy

POPULATION: 25,113,241 (1990)

AREA: 624,550 sq. km. (241,139 sq. mi), including Western Sahara, whose area is 178,000 sq. km. (68,726 sq. mi); Western Sahara's incorporation in the kingdom has not been accepted by the United Nations

ETHNIC MAJORITY: Berber and Arab

LANGUAGES: Arabic (official), French, Berber

RELIGION: Sunni Islam

UNIT OF CURRENCY: Dirham

NATIONAL FLAG: A red field with a green five-pointed star in the center

NATIONAL EMBLEM: Two golden lions, one facing outward, flank a central device crested by the royal red, gold and green crown. Within the device appears a sun rising over the snow-capped Atlas Mountains and a blazing desert depicted in red. In the foreground is the five-pointed star known as Solomon's (or Suleyman's) star. Beneath the device a golden scrollwork carries in Arabic script a verse from the Koran: "If You Aid God He Will Aid You."

NATIONAL ANTHEM: "Hymne Cherifien," a composition without words

NATIONAL HOLIDAYS: March 3 (National Day, Feast of the Throne, Anniversary of the Accession of Hassan II); May 1 (Labor Day); August 14 (Anniversary of 1979 annexation); November 6 (Anniversary of the Green March); November 12 (Independence Day); also variable Islamic festivals

NATIONAL CALENDAR: Islamic (Hegira) and Gregorian

PHYSICAL QUALITY OF LIFE INDEX: 54

DATE OF INDEPENDENCE: March 2, 1956

DATE OF CONSTITUTION: March 10, 1972

WEIGHTS & MEASURES: Metric

GEOGRAPHICAL FEATURES

Morocco is in the northwestern corner of Africa and is separated from Europe by the 12 km. (7 mi.) Strait of Gibraltar. Geographically it is part of a larger region called the Maghreb, and in Arabic the kingdom is called al-Maghreb al-Aqsa (the Far West), meaning to the far west of the Arab world. It extends 1,809 km. (1,124 mi.) northeast to southwest and 525 km. (326 mi.) southeast to northwest and covers an area of 624,550 sq. km. (241,139 sq. mi.), including 178,000 sq. km. (68,726 sq. mi.) of Western Sahara, whose incorporation into Morocco proper is disputed. The total length of the Mediterranean and Atlantic coastlines is 2,177 km. (1,355 mi.).

The total length of the international borders is 2,820 km. (1,759 mi.). The border with Algeria runs 1,617 km. (1,005 mi.) and that with Mauritania 1,213 km. (754 mi.). Both borders are the subject of recurrent controversies. Territorial claims against Mauritania were abandoned in 1969 and are not currently active. The border between Algeria and Morocco, fixed by the Treaty of Lalla Marhnia in 1845, has been contested by both countries, resulting in border clashes in 1963 and 1966. A commission appointed to delineate the border in 1970 left the disputed region in the possession of Algeria.

The capital is Rabat, with a 1987 population of 1,287,000. The largest city is Casablanca (2,904,000). Other major urban centers are Tangier (509,000), Marrakesh (1,425,000), Fez, the religious capital, (933,000), Meknès (704,000), Oujda (895,000), Tétouan (800,000), Kenitra (833,000) and Safi (793,000).

Topographically, Morocco is divided into an open, agriculturally rich and populous area in the Northwest and mountains and plateaus in the eastern and southern areas. The coastal plains of western Morocco stretch from Tangier south to Essaouira and comprise the fertile plains of Gharb, Chaouia, Doukkala, Meseta, Abda, Djebilet and Rehmana. Between the mountains and the western plains is a transitional region composed of the highlands of Zaer and Zaiiane and the inland plains of Tadla and Haouz. The area around Khouribga is known as the "phosphates plateau."

The plains are enclosed in the North by a complex, rugged arc of mountains known as the Rif, which run parallel to the Mediterranean coast from the Strait of Gibraltar to south of Al Hoceima and which vary in elevation from 1,800 m. (5,900 ft.) in the east to 2,450 m. (8,000 ft.) in the center. The snow-clad High Atlas, 800 km. (497 mi.) in length and 65 km. (40 mi.) in depth, divides the country into two climatic zones. Its highest point rises to 4,164 m. (13,664 ft.) at Djebel Toubkal. East of Tichka Pass it continues as the Eastern High Atlas, with elevations up to 4,070 m. (13,353 ft.), and the Ayachi Mountains. The High Atlas declines to the east and breaks up into isolated, small chains (Djellabib, Ourak and Bou Arfa), which join the Saharan Atlas in Algeria. To the south of the Rif and the Taza Pass is the Middle Atlas, which comprises the whole of central Morocco, with elevations up to 3,890 m. (12,762 ft.). It is bordered on the west by the Tadla Plain and on the east by the Moulouya Valley. South of the High Atlas is a high platform known as the Anti-Atlas, connected with the High Atlas by the Siroua Massif (3,300 m.; 10,827 ft.). Its average elevation is 2,530 m. (8,300 ft.). To the east it merges into the Sarho Mountains and drops gradually to the pre-Saharan *hamaidiya*, or rocky desert areas. Eastern Morocco is a series of arid, rolling plateaus characterized by the high Dhara Plateau.

Morocco has an extensive river system. The Moulouya (563 km.; 350 mi.) is the major river, emptying into the Mediterranean. The principal rivers flowing into the Atlantic are the Oumer Rebia, the Sebou, the Bou Regreg, the Tensift, the Draa and the Sous. Of these, the Sebou and its tributaries account for 45% of the country's water resources. The rivers flowing into the Sahara are known as *oueds*, or rivers that disappear completely in the dry season and contain water only intermittently in the winter. Of these, the main rivers are the Ziz and the Guir.

CLIMATE & WEATHER

Morocco has two climatic zones: a Mediterranean climate with warm, wet winters and hot, dry summers in northern and central Morocco, and a semiarid climate in the pre-Saharan South. The coast in general has a more stable and fresher climate than the interior. The Atlantic coast is cooled by winds blowing off the sea. The mean temperature is 16.4° to 23° C (62° F to 73° F) on the western coast and 10° C to 27° C (50° F to 81° F) in the interior. January is the coldest month and August is the hottest.

The rainy seasons are from April to May and from October to November. Summer rain occurs only in the mountains. The amount of rainfall varies considerably among regions, from 254 mm. (10 in.) at Marrakash to 1,090 mm. (43 in.) at Ifrane, 800 to 1016 mm. (32 to 40 in.) on the Atlantic coast, 200 to 300 mm. (8 to 12 in.) in Haouz, 100 to 200 mm. (4 to 8 in.) in eastern Morocco and 100 mm. (4 in.) in the pre-Saharan region.

During the summer intensely hot winds from the Sahara, known as the sirocco or *chergui*, sweep across the lowlands. The winds from the northwest are known as the levant. Storms are common in the winter, especially in the mountains.

POPULATION

The population of Morocco in 1990 was estimated at 25,113,241, on the basis of the last census, in 1982, when the population was 20,419,555.

In comparison with other North African countries, the population is spread over a large area of the nation.

DEMOGRAPHIC INDICATORS

Population (millions): 25.113 (1990)
Year of last census: 1982
Sex distribution (% at last census): males, 50.1; females, 49.9
Population estimates and projections (millions)

1940: 7.750	1970: 15.126	2000: 31.264
1950: 8.953	1980: 19.082	2010: 36.805
1960: 11,640	1990: 25.113	

Age profile (% at last census)

0–14: 42.2	30–44: 14.1	60–74: 4.8
15–29: 28.3	45–59: 9.2	75 and over: 1.5

Median age (yrs): 18.6
Youth population (% age 15–24): 20.0 (1985); 20.3 (2000)
Total dependency ratio: 85.4 (1985)
Annual growth rate (%)

1950–55: 2.48	1975–80: 2.27	2000–2005: 1.76
1955–60: 2.75	1980–85: 2.64	2005–2010: 1.53
1960–65: 2.73	1985–90: 2.56	2010–2015: 1.35
1965–70: 2.78	1990–1995: 2.35	2015–2020: 1.17
1970–75: 2.45	1995–2000: 2.07	2020–2025: 1.12

Hypothetical size of stationary population (millions): 69
Assumed year of reaching net reproduction rate of 1: 2020
Urban population (millions): 9.910 (1985)
Urban population (%): 47 (1988); 32 (1965)
Annual urban population growth rate (%, 1985–90): 4.12
Annual rural population growth rate (%, 1985–90): 1.19
Percentage of urban population in largest city: 26
Percentage of urban population in cities of population over 500,000: 50
Number of cities of population over 500,000: 4
Population density per sq. km. (per sq. mi.): 54.7 (141.8) (latest)

VITAL STATISTICS

Crude birth rate (/1,000): 31 (1990); 49 (1965)
Crude death rate (/1,000): 8 (1990); 18 (1965)
Infant mortality rate (/1,000 live births): 78 (1990)
Maternal mortality rate (/100,000 live births): 327 (1980)
Life expectancy (yrs.) at birth: males, 63; females, 66 (1990)
Gross reproduction rate (/woman) (1980–85): 2.65
Total fertility rate (/woman): 4.0 (1990)
Rate of natural increase (/1,000): 25.6 (1985–90)
Average household size: 5.8 (latest)

STATUS OF WOMEN INDICATORS

Number of women (millions): 11.921 (1985)
Women of childbearing age (15–49) (% of pop.): 48 (1988)
Married women of childbearing age (15–49) using contraception (%): 36 (1986)
Women's literacy rate (%): 58.7 (1989)
Women in labor force (%): 20.3 (1988)
Total fertility rate (/woman): 4.0 (1990)

The main population concentrations are in the Atlantic lowlands and the foothills of the Atlas Mountains. The overall density in 1988 was 52.0 per sq. km. (134 per sq. mi.), and 99.8 per sq. km. (258 per sq. mi.) in agricultural areas, although it reached 390 per sq. km. (1,000 per sq. mi.) in the coastal strip around Casablanca.

Rural-to-urban migration has rapidly increased since independence, and over 100,000 people are estimated to migrate every year from the villages to the cities;

32% of urban dwellers were born in the countryside. Most of the poor migrants cluster in *bidonvilles*, slums of makeshift shacks built of flattened oil drums. The favorite destinations of migrants are Casablanca, Marrakesh and Fez, including their metropolitan areas. Nationwide 48% of the urban population live in slums or squatter settlements; the percentage is 60% in Rabat and 70% in Casablanca.

The population is being reduced, although not significantly, by two types of outmigration: exodus of resident Jews and Europeans, and emigration of Moroccan workers to Europe or other Maghrebian countries. The workers' emigration is officially encouraged because of its beneficial effects on balance of payments. The largest European communities of Moroccan workers are in France (250,000), and Belgium (16,000). There are smaller groups in the United Kingdom, West Germany, the Netherlands, Switzerland and Spain.

The Constitution reaffirms the legal equality of all Moroccans and provides that "men and women enjoy equal political rights." Women occupy responsible government positions, including at the ministerial staff level, as well as in law, medicine and teaching. Two women pilots fly regular routes for Royal Air Maroc. However, progress in professional fields has not always been matched in society at large. There are areas where traditional standards prevail, especially in private law. Divorce is permitted, but a husband can repudiate his wife, while she cannot repudiate him. A man is permitted four wives according to Islamic tradition, although multiple marriages are increasingly rare. Segregation of sexes is common, especially in social settings. However, in urban areas and among the urban poor, as well as increasingly among middle- and upper-class families, women are employed outside the home and contribute to family income.

Women's role in public life remains restricted. No women hold seats in the 306-member Chamber of Representatives, although women have run for positions there. Women serve on the executive committees of several of the major political parties and on the Saharan Consultative Council, a body created in 1981 to advise the king on Western Saharan issues. The government actively supports labor and family planning projects designed to improve the condition of women and has organized employment programs for them. However, religious and social resistance to such efforts remains strong.

The government has officially adopted birth control as a population policy. In 1966 the High Commission on Population was established and a birth control program launched with the aid of the Ford Foundation. Despite opposition from conservative Islamic leaders, the sale of contraceptives was legalized in 1968. The National Family Planning Center was founded in 1975 to carry forward birth control programs.

ETHNIC COMPOSITION

Moroccans are generally descendants of the indigenous Berbers, and Morocco is considered one of the least Arabized regions of the Maghreb. However, distinctions between the Hamitic Berber and the Semitic Arab have ceased to have social and political significance because of the common bond of religion. Though Berbers predominate in numbers, they have been yielding through the centuries to the strong assimilationist tendencies of the Arabs and moving across the permeable ethnic boundary to become "total" Arabs. Berbers and Arabs together constitute 99.1% of the population.

In the past, Jews constituted Morocco's only true minority. In 1948, numbering over 227,000, they lived in predominantly Jewish rural villages or in *mallahs* (urban quarters set apart for them). Although the government has always disavowed anti-Jewish sentiments and although the Jews provided a valuable source of scarce technical, legal and administrative skills, their community was steadily depleted by emigration to Israel and in 1978 numbered no more than 31,000. There are now virtually no Jews left in the countryside, and the remaining Jews, numbering about 30,000, are mostly in the older age groups.

There are small groups of Harratins, Berber-speaking black nomads, in the South.

The European presence consists primarily of Frenchmen and Spaniards. The European population is concentrated in the coastal cities. Until the Moroccanization programs of the early 1970s, Europeans controlled 80% of the industrial and commercial enterprises, owned 7% of the farmland, accounted for 85% of agricultural production and monopolized the technical and medical professions.

Although intensely Arab in outlook, Moroccans are capable of forming warm personal friendships with foreigners. Exposure to the French *mission civilisatrice* (civilizing mission) also has made Moroccans more tolerant of foreign modes and more willing to accept biculturalism.

LANGUAGE

The official language of Morocco is Arabic, although only 60% of the population are native speakers. The others speak it as a second language. About 40% can speak both Arabic and French. As in other parts of the Arab world, Arabic is used in two modes: the classical, employed by religious leaders, and the spoken Maghribi dialects, referred to as Moroccan Arabic, which is neither written nor used in literature or in the media. Moroccan Arabic is so different from classical Arabic that it is unintelligible to a Syrian or Iraqi Arab.

The principal minority language is Berber, spoken by at least 40% of Moroccans as a mother tongue. Also, half the Berber-speakers are bilingual, knowing Arabic also, while some are trilingual, knowing Arabic and French. The Berber dialects are divided into three main groups: the Rifi or the Rif, the Tamazight of the central High Atlas and the Sahara, and the Tashilhit of the High Atlas and the Anti-Atlas. The dialects perhaps correspond to the three main Berber groups distinguished by Ibn Khaldun: the Sanhaja, the Masmuda and the Zanata.

Bilingualism is one of the major legacies of French rule and one of the central concerns of the Moroccan government. French has been the language of the modern bureaucratic, commercial and intellectual sectors of society, while Arabic has been identified with the backward-looking, old-fashioned religious authorities, not offering prestige, jobs or cultural mobility. This has resulted in a social cleavage between the 6% of the population who are educated in French, therefore considered the elite class, and the 94% who speak only Arabic and therefore are excluded from the most desirable jobs in government, industry and the media. A Moroccanization and Arabization policy was initiated in the 1960s but never made much headway because of the lack of trained Arabic-speaking staff. As a concession to nationalist sentiments, the government maintains a Bureau of Arabization in Rabat.

RELIGION

The Constitution establishes Islam as the official religion of Morocco and the king as the *amir al-muaminin* (commander of the faithful). Almost all Moroccans are Muslims of the Maliki rite of the Sunni sect. The government actively supports orthodox Islam through the *habus* (religious foundations) and the Islamic Affairs Ministry, construction of new mosques at state expense, establishment of Koranic schools, Islamic broadcasts on radio and television and royal participation in religious activities. The center of religious life in the country is Fez, the site of a 1,000-year-old Qarawiyin University which draws Islamic students from all over the world. Construction of the world's second largest mosque began in Casablanca in the mid-1980s. It was paid for by public subscription.

The Constitution provides guarantees for freedom of worship, but proselytizing is forbidden. Conversion to another faith from Islam is not banned in the Civil Code, but the Islamic faith strongly discourages it. There are two non-Islamic religions with organized communities in Morocco: Judaism and Christianity. There are some 30,000 Jews, living mainly in Casablanca and several other major cities. The Jewish community operates schools and social institutions as well as 20 major synagogues. Publications in Hebrew are permitted, and rabbis serving the Jewish community are trained in Morocco. Moroccan Jews serve in leading positions in the business community. The president of the Administrative Chamber of the Supreme Court is Jewish, as is one member of the Chamber of Representatives. In September 1985 King Hassan, in a gesture designed to show his continued support for the Jewish community, sent one of his sons to the Jewish community's Yom Kippur ceremony. The Jewish community has close ties to Jewish communities in other countries, including Israel. In October 1985 the Congress of Jewish Communities of Moroccan Origin was held in Montreal with the Moroccan government's endorsement.

There are approximately 30,000 Roman Catholics in Morocco forming two archdioceses. There also are institutional links between the Moroccan government and the Roman Catholic Church. In August 1985 Pope John Paul II visited Morocco at the invitation of King Hassan, at which time the pope met with Morocco's Islamic leaders and delivered an address to 80,000 Muslim youths. In 1983 King Hassan pledged, in a letter to the pope, to guarantee the Catholic Church's right to conduct both religious and charitable work. The letter also formally recognized the work of the Catholic clergy, who come exclusively from abroad, to minister to some 100,000 foreign residents, with parishes in most cities.

There were few incidents affecting the Protestant community in 1985. Prior to the visit of Pope John Paul, a few Moroccan Christians were questioned by police, but the practice was quickly stopped. In October 1985 the Supreme Court overturned earlier administrative rulings that had closed a bookstore in Fez owned by a Protestant minister and that carried a limited number of Bibles and other Christian literature. The Moroccan Protestant community is small, numbering less than 100. There also are several thousand expatriate Christians. Morocco forms part of the diocese of Gibraltar in Europe within the Church of England. Anglican churches are located in Tangier and Casablanca.

Throughout 1984 the government moved to counteract the growth of Islamic fundamentalism, especially after reports of fundamentalist involvement in the January disturbances. In December 1983 leading Moroccan fundamentalist scholar Abdeslam Yassine was arrested for printing an illegal newspaper and for trying to form an Islamic fundamentalist political party. He was sentenced to two years in prison. King Hassan announced a program under the Ministry of the Interior to oversee teaching in the mosques. Ministry of the Interior personnel are to monitor and report teachings that deviate from orthodox Islam. Government spokesmen and the king also have counseled the population against extremist religious philosophies and admonished religious scholars to hew to orthodoxy.

HISTORICAL BACKGROUND

Morocco was a French Protectorate from 1912 until 1956 when it was declared independent as the Sultanate of Morocco. In August 1957 Sultan Mohammed V became king. King Mohammed V assumed the role of prime minister in May 1960, but he died soon after in February 1961.

He was succeeded by his son, Moulay Hassan, who took the title King Hassan II. During his nearly three decades in power Hassan has overridden the relative instability of his early years as monarch. Despite coup and assassination attempts, demonstrations and riots he has managed to consolidate power in the throne while at the same time allowing for a measure of political freedom in the form of the democratically elected Chamber of Representatives. Successive constitutions were drawn up during the period between 1962 and March 1972 when the current constitution was approved. A constitution promulgated in December 1962 had provision for a bicameral legislature and in May 1963 Morocco's first House of Representatives was elected. In November Hassan gave up the role of prime minister. Students and workers rioted because of unfavorable economic conditions in 1965, and in June Hassan declared a "state of exception" taking on full executive and legislative powers. Emergency conditions remained in effect until July 1970 when a new constitution was approved. It served to strengthen monarchical power while at the same time providing for a modest return to parliamentary government through the creation of the Chamber of Representatives elected in August.

Dissatisfaction with economic conditions and the king's programs resulted in abortive military coups in 1971 and 1972, the former proportedly supported by Muammar Qaddhafi of Libya and the latter by Gen. Muhammad Oufkir, Hassan's minister of defense.

In 1972 the current constitution was approved by popular referendum, but the king delayed elections until 1977 when parliamentary democracy was restored. A Government of National Unity was established, led by Ahmed Osman. The government was composed of members of the two most powerful political parties, Istiqlal and the Mouvement Populaire as well as pro-monarchist independents. Osman resigned his post in 1979, reportedly over his handling of the dispute over the Western Sahara. He was replaced by Maati Bouabid.

During the 1980s there were several occasions of serious internal unrest—in 1981 and in 1984—as a result of rises in staple food prices and rumors of rises in the cost of education. Using a mixture of ruthless suppression and encouragement of some democratic participation, the King managed to consolidate and retain his power. Discontent was never channeled into effective political opposition.

In November 1983 the existing Cabinet, which had reached the end of its constitutional six-year term, was replaced by an interim Government of National Unity headed by Muhammad Karim Lamrani. Elections for the Chamber of Representatives resulted in Lamrani again being named prime minister in 1985. Lamrani resigned for health reasons in 1986, and Hassan appointed Azzedine Laraki to replace him.

In 1985 Islamic fundamentalists were allegedly involved in a plot to overthrow the monarchy; 30 were arrested. Domestic opposition groups and Amnesty International charged the government with human rights abuses and suppression of dissents throughout the 1980s. In response, Hassan issued amnesties for political and non-political detainees in 1986 and 1987. A human rights group, Organisation des Droits de l'Homme, was created in 1988 and granted official status that same year. In 1989, on the anniversary of Hassan's enthronement, he issued a royal pardon for 1,200 prisoners.

CONSTITUTION & GOVERNMENT

The operating basis of the government of Morocco is the Constitution of 1972, itself based on the King's Charter of Public Liberties of 1968, the Fundamental Law of 1961, the Constitution of 1962 and the Constitution of 1970. The Constitution proclaims Morocco as a sovereign Islamic state, part of the Great Maghreb and an African state seeking realization of African unity. The monarchy is described as constitutional, democratic and social. Its authoritarian and traditionalist powers are legitimatized, and its role as the source of all power and patronage is reaffirmed. The person of the king—the head of state—is declared sacred and inviolable as commander of the faithful, and he is described as the guardian of the Constitution, symbol of national unity and protector of the rights and liberties of citizens. His powers include the authority to appoint or dismiss the prime minister and Council of Ministers, to preside over the Council of Ministers, to dissolve the Chamber of Representatives by a decree *(dahir)*, to bypass the legislature by submitting a referendum to the people on any major issue, to make all civil and military appointments and to declare a state of emergency when the integrity of national ter-

GOVERNMENT LIST
(July/August 1991)

King	Hassan II
Prime Minister	Laraki, Azzedine
Minister of State	Alaoui, Moulay Ahmed
Minister of State for Foreign Affairs & Cooperation	Filali, Abdellatif
Minister of State for Maghreb Union (UMA) Affairs	Barakat, Abdesslam
Minister of Agriculture & Agrarian Reform	Demnati, Othman
Minister of Commerce & Industry	Azmani, Abdallah
Minister of Cultural Affairs	Benaissa, Mohamed
Minister of Energy & Mines	M'Daghri, Moulay Driss Alaoui
Minister of Equipment & Cadre Training	Kabbaj, Mohamed
Minister of External Trade	Abouyoub, Hassan
Minister of Finance	Berrada, Mohamed
Minister of Foreign Investments	Alaoui, Mohamed M'Daghri
Minister of Handicraft & Social Affairs	Labied, Mohamed
Minister of Housing & Land Management	Boufettas, Abderrahmane
Minister of Interior & Information	Basri, Driss
Minister of Islamic Affairs	Alaoui M'Dghari, Abdelkebir
Minister of Justice	Alaoui, Moulay Mustapha Belarbi
Minister of Labor	Abbadi, Hassan
Minister of National Education	Chkilli, Taieb
Minister of Ocean Fisheries & Merchant Marine	Smili, Bensalem
Minister of Posts & Telecommunications	Laensar, Mohamed
Minister of Public Health	Bencheikh, Tayeb
Minister of Tourism	Benslimane, Abdelkader
Minister of Transportation	Bouamound, Mohamed
Minister of Youth & Sports	Semlali, Abdellatif
Secretary General of the Government	Kaissi, Abbes el
Secretary of State for Foreign Affairs	Cherkaoui, Moulay Ahmed
Minister Delegated for Administrative Affairs	Ben Abdeljalil, Abderrahim
Minister Delegated for the Development of the Saharan Province	Errachid, Khali Hanna Ould
Minister Delegated for Economic Affairs, Privatization	Zahidi, Moulay Zine
Minister Delegated for Moroccan Communities Abroad	Hadaoui, Rafik
Minister Delegated for Planning	Ghazouani, Rachid
Minister Delegated for Relations with the European Community	Guessous, Azzedine
Governor, Bank of Morocco	Seqat, Mohamed

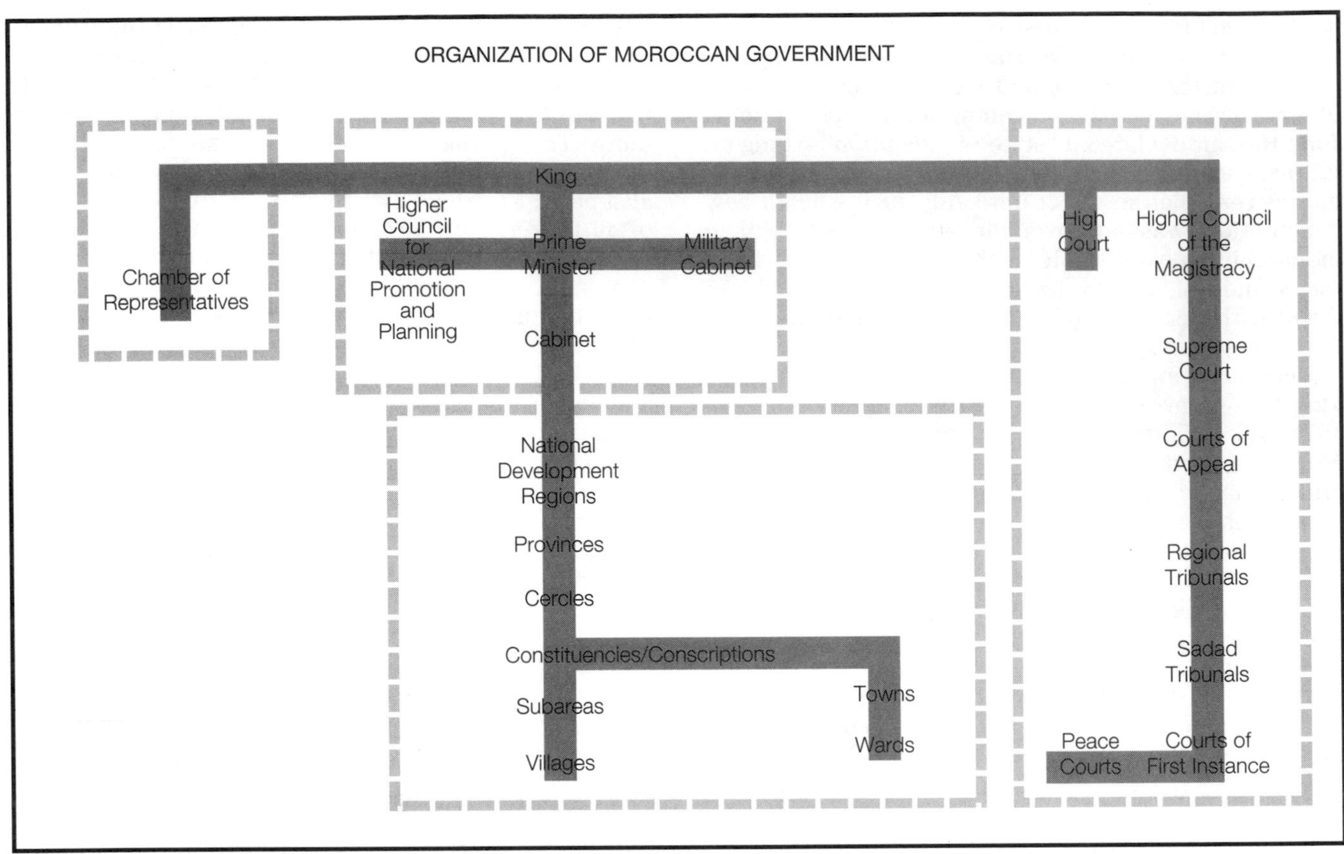

RULERS OF MOROCCO

(Members of the House of Sad; sultan from 1927 to 1953 and kings from 1953)
November 1927–August 1953: Sidi Muhammad V
August 1953–October 1955: Muhammad VI Ben Arafa
October 1955–February 1961: Sidi Muhammad V
February 1961– : Hassan II

ritory is menaced or when events threaten to jeopardize the functioning of national institutions. The Constitution also defines succession to the throne as hereditary by male primogeniture in the line of Hassan except if the king, during his lifetime, designates a successor other than his eldest son.

The government is headed by the prime minister in council. The cabinet is appointed by and is responsible to the king. The composition of the cabinet is a royal prerogative. The prime minister countersigns laws, except those reserved to the monarch's sole power. In practice, however, the cabinet functions more as a body of royal advisers (or *wazara*, under the old regimes). Executive changes have been frequent, and the average length of cabinet tenure has been less than two years.

The legislature is the 306-member unicameral Chamber of Representatives. Its members are elected for six-year terms, two-thirds of them by direct universal suffrage and one-third by an electoral college made up of local government councillors and employers' and employees' representatives. It has power to approve legislation proposed by its members or the prime minister, to authorize any declaration of war, and to approve the extension of any state of emergency beyond 30 days.

The judiciary is independent of the other branches of government. Judges are appointed based on recommendation of the Supreme Council of the Judiciary, over which the king presides.

The position of the monarch in the political system is the most crucial element determining the stability of the Moroccan government. On the positive side, the king commands widespread allegiance as commander of the faithful and as a descendant of the Prophet Muhammad. Although not invulnerable, the monarchy has established itself as the focal point of national loyalty and identity and thus indispensable to institutional continuity. On the negative side, the army's loyalty is uncertain, power is becoming entrenched in a small and exclusive privileged class and the urban proletariat is increasingly alienated from the political system.

FREEDOM & HUMAN RIGHTS

In terms of civil and political rights Morocco is classified as a partially free country.

Morocco is an authoritarian state where human rights are enjoyed by the subjects at the suffrance of the government.

Amnesty International often has charged that the government permits or endorses torture and that it is not confined to political prisoners. However, the frequency of such charges has declined in recent years. Although no one has been executed for high treason since 1974, those arrested for disturbances or coup attempts are held for prolonged periods without trial. Most prisons are old and overcrowded, and there are frequent reports of hunger strikes by prisoners over prison conditions. Although most prisoners are tried in open court and given a fair trial, there are numerous instances where the rights of prisoners to counsel as well as the right of the defendant to testify were not respected. There are scattered reports also of invasion of private homes by police officials without legal authorization, but there is no evidence of any widespread abuse in this regard.

Although criticism of the monarch is not permitted, criticism of the administration and government officials is commonplace. Morocco is also notable for religious tolerance and is one of the few Arab countries that encourages Jews to return. Whereas the role of women remains restricted, as in all Islamic societies, discrimination against them is prohibited by law. The Constitution guarantees the right to join trade unions and to strike, although strikes in the public sector are illegal. There is a fair semblance of political opposition, and the right of all Moroccans to participate in the political process is maintained, at least in theory.

There are frequent charges of prisoner abuse in Moroccan prisons. Lawyers, observers and even government officials assert that prisoners are exposed to cold, damp and crowded conditions, and some prisoners allegedly are subjected to cruel treatment at the hands of prison officials. On January 12, 1985, the local press reported the suicides of two prisoners in Kenitra Prison, allegedly in part because of systematic beatings by prison guards. Human rights groups reported the deaths of four prisoners in November and December 1985 allegedly due to cold and damp jails. On November 12 the government confirmed earlier reports from human rights groups that a detainee, Amine Tahani, had died on November 6 in a Casablanca prison. Although there were charges by human rights activists in France that Tahani died as the result of torture, the government rejected the charges and said his death resulted from asthmatic seizures.

In 1985 and 1986 the government dealt harshly with groups thought to threaten internal stability. Thirty members of the Islamic fundamentalist gourp Jeauness Islamique (Islamic youth) were convicted of attempting to overthrow the monarchy in 1985. The following year 26 left-wing activists were sentenced to prison terms for alleged subversion. Hassan granted amnesty for political and non-political detainees in late 1986 and 1987.

CIVIL SERVICE

The civil service is patterned after the French model established during the protectorate, but it was completely Moroccanized by 1970. In each department the civil service is headed by *chefs de service*, among whom there is considerable mobility. The civil service is characterized by the press as corrupt and venal. There are seven state institutes for administrative training, of which the Moroccan School of Administration is the most prestigious.

LOCAL GOVERNMENT

Morocco is divided into 36 provinces and two urban prefectures. The provinces are: Agadir, Al-Hocima, Azilal, Beni Mellal, Ben Slimane, Boulemane, Chaouen, El-Jadida, El-Kellaa des Srarhna, Er-Rachidia, Essaouira, Fez, Figuig, Guelmim, Ifrane, Kenitra, Khemisset, Khenifra, Khouribga, Laayoune, Marrakesh, Meknes, Nador, Ouarzazate, Oujda, Safi, Settat, Sidi Kacem, Tangier, Tan-Tan, Tauounati, Taroundant, Tata, Taza, Tetouan and Tiznit. The urban prefectures are Casablanca and Rabat-Sale. Morocco administers the annexed territory of the Western Sahara based on a division into four provinces: Boujdour, Es-Smara, El-Aainun and Oued Ed-Dahab.

The basic regional units of the pyramidal structure of local government are the constituency, or *circonscription;* the *cercle;* and the province. The constituency is the traditional unit of administration (or the *caidat*, headed by an executive called the *caid*). Constituencies are of two types: rural and urban. Rural constituencies are further subdivided into communes, each administered by a sheikh. Small villages within each commune are under the traditional authority of the *muqaddams*, or headmen. The urban constituencies are headed by officials known as *pashas*, while each municipal ward in an urban constituency is under a *khalif*. Each ward is the equivalent of a French *arrondissement*.

The *cercle*, headed by a *supercaid*, is an intermediate administrative unit. The provincial governor is one of the most important and pivotal officials in the administration and is directly responsible to the king.

Representative institutions at the local government level include provincial and prefectural councils, or assemblies, and urban and rural communal councils. Urban and rural councillors are elected for six-year terms by direct universal suffrage. Each council is composed of nine to 51 members, depending on the size of the commune. Public two-week-long sessions are held four times a year. Provincial councils have wider legislative powers, and their members are chosen by communal councillors from among their own members. Provincial assemblies and communal councils possess little political power; political discussion is prohibited by law. All council and assembly decisions are subject to approval by appointed officials of the central government.

Western Sahara

Moroccan administration includes portions of Western Sahara, now divided into four provinces. Morocco assumed administration of the northern three provinces after the withdrawal of Spanish forces in 1975, and it asserted control over the southernmost portion in 1979, when Mauritania renounced its claim to the area and ceased administering the region, over which its authority had been vested by the Madrid accords of 1975. Since 1977 the northern provinces of El Aaiún, Es-Smara and Boujdour have participated in elections held throughout Morocco. Communal elections were held in the southernmost province of Oued Ed-Dahab in May 1981. The four Saharan provinces participated in 1983 elections and all votes in 1984, including the August 31 referendum on the Moroccan-Libyan Treaty of Union, the September 14 direct elections to the Majlis and the October 2 indirect elections. Participation in the first two votes of 1984 tended to run higher than in most of the rest of Morocco, with some areas in Western Sahara registering as high as 100% participation, according to official figures, in the August 31 referendum.

Moroccan Western Saharan incumbents fill all 10 Majlis seats from the Western Saharan provinces, and politicians of Western Sahara origin also fill seats from other provinces.

Governors of the Western Saharan provinces, appointed by the king, are all native Western Saharans. In consultation with elected municipal and provincial councils, the four governors administer their provinces in the same manner as provinces and prefectures of Morocco proper. Most village and civil servants also are locally recruited Western Saharans. The governors are concerned primarily with accelerating development and delivery of social services. Large-scale public works projects, expansion of public services and upgrading of long-impoverished areas continue.

A consultative council on Western Sahara was elected in 1981. The council, some of whose 80 members are women, first met in late 1981 and continued to function in 1985.

FOREIGN POLICY

The chief architect of Moroccan foreign policy is the king, who also determines the priorities of foreign relations and serves as the chief negotiator. Unity of the Maghrebian countries of Tunisia, Algeria, Libya and Morocco was one of the early goals of Moroccan policy, and in February 1989 a treaty creating the Union of the Arab Maghreb was signed in Marrakesh by Algeria, Libya, Mauritania, Morocco and Tunisia. Its goal is to promote trade and free movement of goods, people and services among the member nations. Relations with Algeria were strained after the latter achieved independence in 1962. Border disputes over the Colomb-Bechar and Tindouf-Djebilet areas escalated into armed conflict in 1963. The dispute was patched up by the Tlemcen accord of 1970 but continued to surface in other forms until 1973. Another source of discord was introduced in 1976, when Morocco annexed the northern part of Western Sahara while Algeria and Libya actively supported the Polisario Front in its declaration of independence for the territory. In May 1988 Algeria resumed diplomatic relations with Morocco severed since 1976. Relations with Libya were strained from 1971 to 1983 because of alleged Libyan involvement in attempts to overthrow the Moroccan monarchy. Relations with Morocco's southern neighbor Mauritania, long soured by Moroccan territorial claims, were normalized in 1970. In 1976 Morocco and Mauritania joined in an uneasy alliance to divide up Western Sahara, but the alliance broke up in 1978 when Mauritania signed a unilateral peace treaty with Polisario and withdrew from its zone in Western Sahara. Morocco immediately occupied this zone, renaming it Oued Ed-Dahab. However, despite the fact that the annexation of Western Sahara is popular at home, Rabat has become increasingly isolated internationally over the issue. Polisario forces have succeeded in staging a number of spectacular raids inside the Moroccan border. Heavy defense spending also has adversely affected the economy.

In early 1989, in a reversal of longstanding policy, King Hassan met with officials of Polisario and SADR in Marrakesh. This was the first direct contact between the monarch and leaders of the national liberation movement in 13 years. In response Polisario declared a unilateral cease-fire, but when no further overtures from Hassan were forthcoming, Polisario resumed hostilities.

On August 15, 1984, King Hassan and Col. Qaddhafi of Libya signed the Arab-African Federation Treaty, the first step toward a Maghreb union. The treaty provided for close economic and political cooperation between Morocco and Libya, and for mutual defense in the event of attack. The treaty was to take effect only after being approved by the people of each country. A referendum was therefore held in Morocco on August 31, and the treaty was approved by 99.97% of voters. Libya's General People's Congress backed the agreement unanimously. With the alliance of Algeria, Tunisia and Mauritania through the Maghreb Fraternity and Cooperation Treaty and Mauritania's recognition of the SADR in July 1984, Morocco found itself isolated in the Maghreb. By signing the treaty on union with Libya, Morocco not only provided itself with an ally but also persuaded Col. Qaddhafi to cut off Libyan aid to the Polisario Front. Polisario responded in October by launching the Greater Maghreb Offensive, a major military effort involving widespread fighting in southern Morocco. At the same time, Muhammad Abdelaziz, president of the SADR, undertook an extensive African tour to gather support prior to the November summit of the OAU in Addis Ababa. This proved fruitful, as the SADR delegation was seated at the summit with little protest from other states. However, Morocco resigned from the OAU in protest, thus becoming the first state to leave the organization.

Morocco has actively participated in the affairs of African nations south of the Sahara. It sent a contingent of Moroccan troops to Zaire in 1970 and again in 1976 and 1978. It provided political support to revolutionary groups in Angola and Mozambique before their independence and to Zimbabwean rebels. Morocco was charged in 1977 by the OAU with fomenting a coup in Benin.

In an effort to defuse political opposition at home, King Hassan adopted a more visible pro-Arab policy in the Arab-Israeli conflict. In 1974 Moroccan troops were sent to the Syrian front, and during the 1973 October War detachments were sent to Egypt. These efforts helped to produce a rapprochement between Morocco and the radical hard-line Arab states. Hassan also demonstrated ultra-Islamic sympathies by hosting both the Islamic and Arab summit conferences of 1969.

Relations with France, Morocco's principal Western ally, were stabilized after periods of strain, including suspensions of diplomatic ties, in 1956, 1960 and 1965. Morocco also settled all outstanding territorial problems with Spain. Although nonaligned in principle, Morocco has not concealed its ties with the United States, based on a treaty of friendship signed between the two countries in 1787—the longest unbroken treaty relationship in United States history. Morocco and the United States also are parties to 18 agreements and treaties covering agricultural commodities, aviation, cultural relations, economic and technical cooperation, education, investment guarantees, the Peace Corps, peace treaties, postal matters and visas.

Morocco joined the United Nations in 1956. It is a member of 15 U.N. organizations and 30 other international organizations.

PARLIAMENT

The Moroccan national legislature is the unicameral 306-member Chamber of Representatives, or Majlis al Nuwab which is elected for six years. Two-thirds of the members are elected by direct universal suffrage and one-third by an electoral college composed of councillors in local government and employers' and employees' representatives.

The Chamber of Representatives holds two sessions annually, each lasting more than two months, the first in October and the second in April. Draft bills may be introduced by the king, the prime minister or any member of the legislature. The government is answerable to the Chamber of Representatives, and the passage of a no-confidence motion or vote of censure by an absolute majority results in the collective resignation of the prime minister and his ministers.

The Chamber of Representatives participates in the formulation of overall policy, including the review of the annual budget and other major legislation. However, many measures of lesser importance are promulgated as government decrees or occasionally by royal proclamation. Several layers of directly or indirectly elected officials participate in formulating decisions, including members of the legislature, provincial assemblies and municipal councils. More than a dozen political parties, representing a spectrum of political philosophies from far left to conservative, competed in the 1983 municipal elections and elections to the Chamber of Representatives in 1984. Local government and the Chamber of Representatives are generally considered representative, although a number of election results have been challenged. There is frequently lively debate on all subjects and often split votes. While government proposals in the Chamber of Representatives rarely are rejected outright, specific measures often are modified. Political pressure on occasion has persuaded the government to delay or withdraw legislation.

Election procedures are spelled out in detail in a royal decree of 1970. Suffrage is universal over age 20. Certain categories of people such as soldiers are not eligible to vote or run for office. The machinery for the management and observation of elections is highly organized and is administered by the Ministry of the Interior and supervised by a commission composed of the president of the constitutional chamber, a judge of the administrative chamber and the minister of the interior.

The government occasionally uses a direct referendum on major questions affecting the Constitution and the state structure. There were no such cases in 1985. In 1984 the voters were asked to approve the Moroccan-Libyan Treaty of Union. The government announced that 97% of those casting ballots voted for the union.

In direct elections on September 14, 1984, a total of 12 parties participated, with an average of six to seven candidates for each of 306 seats. All parties were offered free time on government television and radio. In the election, 67% of eligible voters cast ballots, according to official figures. The vote was followed by some charges of fraud and government interference, and the 67% participation rate is widely questioned. Nevertheless, the vote was considered to be among the fairest in modern Moroccan history. Thus far, few if any results have been challenged in court.

POLITICAL PARTIES

Despite their exclusion from political life for extended periods, political parties in Morocco are more numerous and have broader constituencies than in other North African countries. The main national parties are:

- Istiqlal (Independence Party), founded in 1943, spearheaded the nation's independence movement. It split in 1959 and has been out of government since 1963. Once monarchical, Istiqlal now follows a reformist attitude, supporting the king on selected foreign policy issues only. Its leader is Muhammad Boucetta.
- Constitutional Union, founded in 1983 by former prime minister Maati Bouabid, is a moderate party that is believed to enjoy royal support.
- National Assembly of Independents was launched at the Constitutive Congress in 1978. Although branded as the "king's party" by left-wingers, it was designated as the official opposition in 1981.
- National Union of Popular Forces (NUPF) was founded in 1959 by Istiqlal dissidents as a coalition of left-wing nationalists, trade unionists and urban leaders. The bulwark of its strength was, until 1963, the Moroccan Labor Union. Weakened by internal factionalism and infighting, it split again in 1972, with its suspended Political Bureau forming the Socialist Union of Popular Forces. The leader of NUPF is Abdullah Ibrahim.

• Socialist Union of Popular Forces, formed in 1972, has a radical program calling for total nationalization. Its leader is Abderrahim Bouabid.

• Popular Movement is a monarchical party with a predominantly Berber membership.

• Constitutional and Democratic Popular Movement is a splinter party of Popular Movement.

• Party of Action was formed in 1974 by a group of Berber intellectuals. Its leader is Abdullah Senhaji.

• Party of Progress and Socialism is the Communist Party of Morocco under a different title. Its leader is Ali Yata.

• Organization for Democratic and Popular Action was founded in 1983.

• Other groups include the Social Center Party, the Democratic Party of Independence and the Party of National Union and Solidarity.

ECONOMY

The Moroccan economy has a resilience based on diversification. Agriculture which includes forestry and fishing is the strongest segment of the economy contributing 30% of export revenues and employing 40–50% of the labor force. It provides food for domestic consumption and citrus fruits for export. However, Morocco is not self-sufficient in cereal, sugar and other food products. Agricultural production showed slow growth during the early 1980s, but in 1987–88 there was a record harvest of cereals due to success in fighting locusts.

Although Morocco has no known expolitable oil reserves, it does have 75% of known world phosphate deposits, and high international prices for phosphates during the 1970s promoted significant expansion of this segment of the economy at that time. The mining sector also benefits from such byproducts as phosphoric acid and superphosphates. During the 1980s fertilizer consumption declined and world prices for phosphates decreased resulting in depressed revenues from this sector. "Moroccanization" of manufacturing and trading enterprises formerly owned and administered by foreign concerns increased substantially in the years following independence and phosphate mining is a major area of the economy which remains under state control.

Moroccan workers living abroad in France, Spain, the Netherlands and Germany contribute substantially to Morocco's economy.

Tourism is the fourth important sector of the economy. Revenues from this sector have been on the rise since the mid-1980s when a 30% devaluation of the dirham gave it a boost. Additionally a $1 billion foreign investment primarily from Kuwait, Abu Dhabi and Saudi Arabia for construction of a 15,000-room tourist com-

PRINCIPAL ECONOMIC INDICATORS

Gross National Product (U.S. $ billions): 22.069 (1989)
GNP per capita (U.S. $): 900 (1989)
GNP average annual growth rate (%, 1980–89): 4.1
GNP per capita average annual growth rate (%, 1987–89): 3.7
Income distribution (% household income)
  Lowest 20%: 9.8
  Highest 10%: 25.4
Average annual rate of inflation (%, 1980–88): 7.7
Consumer price index (1980 = 100) 1986
  All items: 174
  Food: 181
Average annual growth rate (%, 1980–88)
  General government consumption: 4.7
  Private consumption: 2.7
  Gross domestic investment: 3.7

BALANCE OF PAYMENTS, 1988

(U.S. $ millions)
Current account balance: 467
Merchandise exports: 3.608
Merchandise imports: −4.360
Trade balance: −752
Other goods, services & income + : 1.798
Other goods, services & income − : −2.185
Other goods, services & income net: −387
Private unrequited transfers: 1.303
Official unrequited transfers: 303
Capital other than reserves: −207
Net errors & omissions: −20
Counterpart items: 35
Liabilities constituting foreign authorities reserves: 4
Total change in reserves: −299

GROSS DOMESTIC PRODUCT

GDP nominal (D.H. billions): 150.92 (1988)
GDP per capita (U.S. $): 740 (1987)
Average annual growth rate of GDP (%, 1980–88): 4.2
GDP by type of expenditure (%) 1987
  Consumption
    Private: 70
    Government: 16
  Gross domestic investment: 24 (1988)
  Gross domestic saving: 23 (1988)
  Foreign trade
    Exports: 17
    Imports: −26
Cost components of GDP (%) 1980
    Net indirect taxes: 14
    Consumption of fixed capital and net operating surplus: 53
    Compensation of employees: 33
Sectoral origin of GDP (%) 1987
  Primary
    Agriculture: 16
    Mining: 3
  Secondary
    Manufacturing: 25
    Construction: 5
    Public utilities: 3
  Tertiary
    Transportation & communications: 7
    Trade: 17
    Finance: 3
    Other services: 11
    Government: 12
Average annual sectoral growth rates (%, 1980–88)
    Agriculture: 6.6
    Industry: 2.8
    Manufacturing: 4.2
    Services: 4.2

plex in Tangier has further assisted the expansion of tourism.

King Hassan declared 1988 the "Year of the Economy," and recovery is the key word to describe what took place at that time. The budget deficit declined by 9.5%, there was a record grain harvest, and the tourist industry was booming.

Morocco continues to face some serious economic problems, primarily servicing the foreign debt which in 1988 was $19.8 billion. Rescheduling of debt repayments took place in 1987 and in 1988. Additional rescheduling was not expected for 1989. Other problems are high unemployment estimated at 15% in 1988 and a high dependence on imported energy.

PUBLIC FINANCE

The Moroccan fiscal year is the calendar year. The central government budget is divided into three parts: the general state budget, a series of separate agency budgets and a series of special Treasury accounts. The general budget includes the current budget, the investment budget and public debt expenditures.

The government derives revenue primarily from loans and indirect taxes. Debt service consumes a major portion of expenditures even after the rescheduling agreement with the Paris Club in 1987. Morocco received substantial assistance from the IMF during the 1980s in return for curbing public spending, encouraging exports and reducing the balance-of-payments deficit.

CENTRAL GOVERNMENT EXPENDITURES (latest)

% of total expenditures
- Defense: 15.1
- Education: 17.0
- Health: 3.0
- Housing, social security, welfare: 7.3
- Economic services: 21.4
- Other: 38.0

Total expenditures as % of GNP: 29.2 (1988)
Overall surplus or deficit as % of GNP: −4.6 (1988)

CENTRAL GOVERNMENT REVENUES (latest)

% of total current revenues
- Taxes on income, profit & capital gain: 19.0
- Social security contributions: 5.0
- Domestic taxes on goods & services: 46.1
- Taxes on international trade & transactions: 12.7
- Other taxes: 7.0
- Current nontax revenue: 10.2

Total current revenue as % of GNP: 24.4 (1988)
General government consumption as % of GDP: 15 (1988)
Average annual growth rate of general government consumption (%, 1980–88): 4.7

Under the 1988–92 development plan, economic decision making was to be made by the local rather than the central government, private enterprise was to be encouraged, most government-owned industries were to be privatized and restrictions on foreign investment lifted. The introduction of a value-added tax and other tax reforms increased revenues and lowered the overall deficit.

Over the years Morocco has been the recipient of economic assistance from both the IMF and the World Bank. During 1983–88 the IMF assisted Morocco with the implementation of its economic reform policies in three specific areas: reducing public spending, encouragement of exports and reduction of its balance of payments deficit. The World Bank has made a series of loans to Morocco in recent years. In 1987 it loaned $225 million for assistance with the 1987–88 agricultural recovery program designed to increase agricultural production. In the same year it also loaned $240 million to assist in increasing the efficiency of public sector enterprises and in 1988 it loaned $200 million to support liberalized trade and tax reforms.

Morocco is to receive $85 million annually from the EEC to pay for fishing rights in Moroccan waters according to a protocol signed in March 1989.

From 1970 to 1988 Morocco received $1.2 billion in aid from the United States, $6.3 billion from other Western nations, $4.8 billion from OPEC and $2.3 billion from communist countries.

FOREIGN AID

Total foreign aid (U.S. $ millions): 490.5 (1984)
- Bilateral: 227.7 (1984)
- Multilateral: 242.8 (1984)

Aid from international organizations, total (U.S. $ millions) 156.592 (1985)
- of which World Bank (U.S. $ millions): 139.663 (1985)

Per capita aid (U.S. $): 22.9 (1984)

CURRENCY & BANKING

The Moroccan unit of currency is the dirham, divided into 100 francs. Coins are issued in denominations of 10, 20 and 50 francs and 1 dirham; notes are issued in denominations of 5, 10 and 50 dirhams. The dollar exchange rate of the dirham in June 1991 was $1 = D8.830 The dirham was introduced in 1959, replacing the Moroccan franc. Morocco maintained the dirham's link with the French franc until 1973. Since 1973 the market exchange rate has fluctuated widely.

The banking system consists of Banque al-Maghrib, the central bank; 18 commercial banks, including a number of major foreign banks nationalized in 1975; seven people's cooperative banks; and six special-purpose credit institutions: The National Bank of Economic Development, the Deposit and Investment Fund, the National Agricultural Credit Bank, the Construction and Hotel Credit Organization, the Bureau of Industrial Research and Participation and the Bureau of Mineral Exploration and Participation.

The central bank, Banque al-Maghrib, founded in 1959, as Banque du Maroc, acts as the sole issuer of currency, administrator of foreign exchange reserves and agency for the control of national credit policies. It functions under the Ministry of Finance and the Committee of Money and Credit.

FINANCIAL INDICATORS, 1989

Total reserves minus gold (SDRs millions): 372
SDRs (millions): 0
Reserve position in IMF (SDRs millions): 0
Foreign exchange (SDRs millions): 371
Gold (fine troy oz. millions): .70
Ratio of external debt to total reserves: 32.0 (1988)
Central bank 1989
- Assets (%)
  - Foreign assets: 10.9
  - Claims on government: 36.5
  - Claims on banks: 33.3
  - Claims on private sector: 19.3
- Liabilities (%)
  - Reserve money: 82.1
  - Government deposits: 1.1
  - Foreign liabilities: 19.3
  - Capital accounts: 0.0
- Money supply 1989
- Stock (D. billions): 68.395
- M1 per capita: 2.760

Private banks 1985
- Assets (%)
  - Loans to government: 38.6
  - Loans to private sector: 52.7
  - Reserves: 1.6
  - Foreign assets: 7.1
- Liabilities
  - Deposits (D. billions): 43.934
  - of which %
    - Demand deposits: 54.4
    - Savings deposits: 37.8
    - Government deposits: 0.0
    - Foreign liabilities: 1.1

External debt 1988
- Total (U.S. $ billions): 19.923
  - of which public (U.S. $ billions): 18.567
  - of which private (U.S. $ millions): 200
- Debt service (long-term)
  - Total (U.S. $ billions): 1.341
  - Repayment
    - Principal (%): 39.7
    - Interest (%): 60.3
- Debt service ratio (%): 20.0
- External public debt as % of GNP: 88.8
- Debt service as % of GNP: 6.4
- Debt service as % of exports: 24.8
- Terms of public borrowing
  - Commitments (U.S. $ billions): 1.156
  - Average interest rate (%): 6.9
  - Average maturity (yrs.): 18
- Net flow of publicly guaranteed external capital (U.S. $ millions): 476
- Receipt of workers' remittances (U.S. $ billions): 1.289
- Net direct private investment (U.S. $ millions): 85

AGRICULTURE

Agriculture is the key economic sector, employing 40–50% of the labor force and contributing 30% of the exports.

The agricultural sector is characterized by a marked contrast between the traditional and the modern. A total of 90% of all arable land (including 70% of irrigated land) is under traditional cultivation. Traditional methods are used on 800,000 to 1 million holdings, covering approximately 4 million hectares (9.884 million acres) and averaging 3.62 ha. (8.7 ac.) per holding.

GROWTH PROFILE
(Annual Growth Rates, %)

Projected population (1988–200): 2.4
Projected crude birth rate (/1,000) (1990–95): 31.7
Projected crude death rate (/1,000) (1990–95): 8.2
Urban population (1980–88): 4.4
Labor force (1985–2000): 3.1
GNP (1980–89): 4.1
GNP per capita (1987–89): 3.7
GDP (1980–88): 4.2
Inflation (1980–88): 7.7
Agriculture (1980–88): 6.6
Industry (1980–88): 2.8
Manufacturing (1980–88): 4.2
Services (1980–88): 4.2
Money holdings (1980–88): 14.5
Energy production (1980–88): −0.1
Energy consumption (1980–88): 2.4
Exports (1980–88): 5.0
Imports (1980–88): 1.8
General government consumption (1980–88): 4.7
Private consumption (1980–88): 2.7
Gross domestic investment (1980–88): 3.7

The traditional sector's main characteristics are the small size of holdings, primitive agricultural techniques, complex tenure systems, low productivity and the predominance of subsistence crops. The average employment is 1.2 workers per hectare (0.5 worker per acre), and the per-hectare (per acre) and per-worker contribution to the GDP are $209 ($85) and $174, respectively. On the other hand, the modern sector, with 10% of the land, produces 85% of the output. To encourage modernization, the Agricultural Investment Code of 1969 sets minimum standards of efficiency.

The main agricultural areas are the plains and the uplands of Morocco between the Atlas ranges and the Atlantic Ocean, together with the valleys of the Middle Atlas range. The country is 90% self-sufficient in food in good years (except for sugar and edible oils), while cereals have to be imported in poor years.

In the traditional sector there are five principal types of land tenure. *Makhzan* land is owned by the state or the king, *jaysh* land is owned by the tribe and *habus* land is owned by Islamic religious foundations. *Makhzan, jaysh* and *habus* lands constitute 1.9% of all arable lands. About 54% of the holdings are privately owned, or milk, lands. Much of milk lands are worked under a number of forms of sharecropping. Individual ownership based on registered titles is a recent phenomenon, dating back only to the French protectorate. Water rights, even those within individual properties, are separate from land rights and are governed by a different set of rules. Generally they are owned by a group. Finally, there are collective lands, which constitute over 40% of agricultural lands.

Some 671,000 ha. (1,658,041 ac.) are under some form of irrigation. Of these, 70% are in the traditional sector, where irrigation is by springs and wells; diversions from streams; and modern dams, tunnels and reservoirs. In 1975 there were 24 major dams, with a reservoir capacity of 6 billion cu. m. (212 billion cu. ft.) of water. These include the Ait Aidel Dam, the

AGRICULTURAL INDICATORS

Agriculture's share of GDP (%): 16 (1989)
Average annual growth rate (%, 1980–88): 6.6 (1989)
Value added in agriculture (U.S. $ billions): 3.770 (1988)
Cereal imports (million metric tons): 1.643 (1988)
Index of food production (1979–81 = 100): 137 (1986)
Index of food production per capita (1979–81 = 100): 106 (1986–88)
Number of tractors: 32,000 (1986)
Number of harvester-threshers: 3,190 (1986)
Total fertilizer consumption (000 metric tons): 299 (1985–86)
Fertilizer consumption (g./ha., hundreds): 376 (1987–88)
Number of farms (millions): 1.900 (1978)
Average size of holding (ha.): 3.9 (1978)
Size class (%) 1978
- Below 1 ha. (below 2.47 ac.): } 75.0
- 1–5 ha. (2.47–12.35 ac.): }
- 5–10 ha. (12.35–24.7 ac.): } 25.0
- 10–20 ha. (24.7–49.4 ac.): }
- 20–50 ha. (49.4–123.5 ac.): }
- 50–200 ha. (123.5–494 ac.): }
- Over 200 ha. (over 494 ac.): }

Farms as % of total land area: 17.6 (1985–86)
Land use (%) 1985–87
- Cropland: 19
- Pasture: 47
- Forest: 12
- Other: 23

Yields (kg./ha.) 1989
- Grains: 1.342
- Roots and tubers: 20.002
- Legumes: 703
- Milk (kg./animal): 543

Production 1989
- Fruits (million metric tons): 2.329
- Vegetables (million metric tons): 1.588

Livestock (000) 1989
- Cattle: 3.500
- Horses: 170 (1986)
- Sheep: 17.500
- Pigs: 9

Forestry 1988
- Production of roundwood (million cubic meters): 2.074
- of which industrial roundwood (%): 35.2

Value of exports (U.S. $ millions): 63.462
Fishing 1988
- Total catch (000 metric tons): 551.4
  - of which marine (%): 99.8
- Value of exports (U.S. $ millions): 415.703

Mansour Eddahbi Dam, the Hassan Eddakil Dam, the Timinoutine Dam, the Sidi Cheho Dam and the Tleta Dam.

The government's land reform and Moroccanization programs began a few months after independence. Between 1956 and 1971 a total of 90,000 ha. (222,394 ac.) were "recuperated," or reacquired from French colons. The remaining lands, 260,000 ha. (642,474 ac.) in 1,800 holdings, were taken over in 1973 from their French owners by a *dahir*, or government decree. Under a redistribution program, 18,000 small farmers received land, and 538 cooperatives were established by the Société de Développement Agricole and the Société de Gestion des Terres Agricoles.

The government's land policy is defined in the Agricultural Investment Code of 1969, under which farmers are expected to irrigate the land according to government recommendations, accept government guidance in land use and crop rotation, agree not to subdivide land below viable limits and plant only with high-yield strains supplied by government. The holdings of inefficient farmers may be expropriated. The programs are reinforced by guaranteed prices, incentives and subsidies.

Livestock-raising contributes 30% to 40% of agricultural income and is carried on in 10 million to 14 million ha. (25 million to 35 million ac.) of pastureland by some 100,000 nomads and seminomads. Overgrazed pasture and periods of drought limit the quality of livestock. Beef, goat meat and milk production have declined during recent years.

Forests cover about 8 million ha. (19,768,000 ac.) and provide employment for about 40,000 families. The principal forest product is cork, which is grown on 300,000 ha. (741,316 ac.) of state-owned forests. Cedar forests cover 152,000 ha. (375,000 ac.); eucalyptus forests 48,000 ha. (120,000 ac.); and argan, a tropical evergreen tree, 688,000 ha. (1.7 million ac.). Other forest resources include Tizra wood (used for tanning); thuja; esparto grass; and vegetable horsehair, obtained from the leaves of the dwarf Mediterranean palm.

Fishing is an important activity in its own right and employs 20,000 persons. The coastal waters, extending to 112 km. (70 mi.), abound in sardines, tuna, mackerel and anchovies. Although some fish is consumed locally, most is exported. Agadir is the main fishing port, but Safi, Casablanca and Essaouira also are important fishing centers. In 1974 a joint Moroccan-Spanish fishing company, Maropeche, was set up to operate an ocean-going fishing fleet.

Agricultural credit is provided by the National Agricultural Credit Bank.

MANUFACTURING

Some 70% of the industrial activity is concentrated in the Casablanca-Muhammadia region. Industrial growth is paced by light industry, particularly food processing, fish canning and sugar refining. Heavy industry consists of the Safi chemicals complex, which processes mineral phosphate; seven car-assembly plants, and fertilizer complexes. A metals product industry also is well established. An iron and steel mill is planned at Nador.

MANUFACTURING INDICATORS, 1987

Average annual growth rate (%, 1980–88): 4.2
Share of GDP (%): 18 (1988)
Labor force economically active in manufacturing (% est.): 16.9 (1982)
Value added in manufacturing (U.S. $ billions): 3.398
- Food & tobacco (%): 26 (1986)
- Textiles & clothing (%): 16 (1986)
- Machinery & transport equipment (%): 10 (1986)
- Chemicals (%): 11 (1986)

Total earnings as % of value added: 51 (1986)
Index of manufacturing production: 135 (1988)

Traditional handicrafts employ over 200,000 persons.

The manufacturing sector is largely private, but there is state participation. The phosphate and chemical fertilizer industry is wholly state-owned, while the sugar and car-assembly industries have major state participation. The principal state enterprises are Office Cherifien des Phosphates, Complexe Textile de Fès and Société Nationale de Siderurgie.

The government launched a policy of Moroccanization in 1971. By a 1973 decree the chairman, the managing director, a majority of the board and at least half the shareholders of all companies in Morocco are required to be Moroccan nationals. Wholesale and retail businesses, import agencies and industrial concerns had to be Moroccanized by 1974 and banking and insurance companies by 1975. This policy led to a decline in foreign investment and investor confidence, and the government therefore passed a new Investment Code in 1973 offering substantial concessions to foreign private investors and guarantees against expropriation. The Investment Commission and the Investment Promotion Center were established to administer the code and to provide information, feasibility studies and documentation to overseas investors. Basic incentives include: rights to repatriate capital, profits and salaries; total or partial exemption from customs duties on imported capital goods; a 10-year stabilization guarantee on local taxes; and liberal depreciation scales. Morocco also has signed a number of investment guarantee agreements with investor countries.

The Moroccan Investment Code offered inducements to firms prepared to accord local partners at least half ownership plus board chairmanship. In such priority sectors as mining, tourism and export industries, 100% foreign ownership was authorized. To encourage the eventual decentralization of Moroccan industry, even more favorable investment terms were available to firms willing to locate their operations in urban centers outside the dominant Casablanca-Rabat industrial area (e.g., Tangier, Tétouan, Fez, Meknès, Oujda). Moreover, for any new investments over D30 million (approximately $7.7 million), advantages in addition to those specified in the code could be negotiated with the Moroccan government. The "50% Moroccan" requirement was revoked in the 1980s and an investment code offering tax and duty exemptions put in its place.

MINING

Mining is an important sector of the Moroccan economy. Morocco is the world's largest exporter of phosphates and, with the acquisition of the Bu Craa mines in Western Sahara, it also has become the world's largest producer of phosphates. Phosphate mining is a state monopoly operated by the Office Cherifien des Phosphates. The phosphate deposits are in the center of the country in the so-called phosphates plateau. In addition to the older mines at Khouribga and Youssoufia, new mines have been opened at Ben Guerir and Sidi Majaj as well as at Maskalas. The Bu Craa and Izic mines in Western Sahara are believed to contain 1.5 billions tons of phosphates. Total reserves of phosphate rock have been estimated at over 40 billion tons, or 45% of total world reserves. Some of the phosphates are processed for domestic use at the Safi chemicals complex.

Morocco is the world's fourth-largest producer of cobalt, the eighth-largest producer of lead and the tenth-largest producer of manganese. Cobalt is mined at Bou Azzar; lead and zinc at Boukber, Touissit, Aouli and Mikbladen; and manganese at Bou Arfa and Siroua. There also are iron ore reserves at Nador, Uixan and Ait Amar (estimated at 25 million tons) and coal reserves at Jerada (estimated at over 100 million tons).

ENERGY

Morocco has exhausted its petroleum reserves and must import a large portion of its domestic energy requirement. In 1988 it signed an agreement with Algeria for construction of a natural gas pipeline to be completed in 1995. Morocco has begun the exploitation of natural gas, shale oil and hydroelectric power to reduce dependency on foreign sources.

ENERGY INDICATORS

Average annual energy production growth rate (%, 1980–88): −0.1
Energy consumption per capita (kg. oil equivalent): 239 (1988)
Energy imports as % of merchandise exports: 17 (1988)
Average annual growth rate of energy consumption (%, 1980–88): 2.4
Electricity 1988
  Installed capacity (million kw.): 2.327
  Production (billion kw.-hr.): 8.834
    % fossil fuel: 89.4
    % hydro: 10.6
  Consumption per capita (kw.-hr.): 369
Natural gas
  Proved reserves (billion cu. m.): 3 (1990)
  Production (million cu. m.): 60 (1989)
  Consumption (million cu. m.): 74 (1988)
Petroleum
  Proved reserves (million bbl.): 2 (1990)
  Years to exhaust proved reserves: 26 (1990)
  Production (000 bbl.): 100 (1989)
  Consumption (million bbl.): 37 (1988)
  Refining capacity (000 bbl./day): 155 (1990)
Coal
  Reserves (million metric tons): 45 (latest)
  Production (000 metric tons): 637 (1988)
  Consumption (million metric tons): 1.628 (1988)

LABOR

The great majority of workers are unskilled. Only one-third of industrial workers are classified as skilled or semiskilled. Despite government efforts at complete Moroccanization of the economy, skilled personnel are not available to replace foreigners in many areas. The present labor force participation rate for the working-age population is estimated at 40% to 50%.

Morocco has one of the highest unemployment rates in the world, estimated at 15% in 1988. The government therefore adopted a policy of encouraging emigration of Moroccan workers to foreign countries, especially to France and other Western European countries. Agreements for employment of Moroccan workers are in effect with France, Belgium, the United Kingdom, Germany, the Netherlands, Switzerland, Spain, Algeria and Libya. Because Moroccan workers are among the least skilled of "guest workers," Belgium, France, West Germany and the Netherlands no longer admit Moroccan workers.

Working conditions are governed by extensive legislation covering all factories employing over 10 workers, although labor laws are enforced only irregularly and haphazardly. The principal bodies concerned with labor legislation and administration are the Ministry of Labor and Social Affairs and the Manpower Council.

Children may not be employed or apprenticed before age 12, and there are special regulations governing employment of children between 12 and 16. Minimum-wage legislation also exists, and minimum wages were raised twice in 1985 to take account of rises in the cost of living. In the traditional sectors of the economy, children often are apprenticed earlier than age 12, especially where school places are not available. Safety and health conditions in many enterprises are substandard. Labor inspectors do not have adequate resources to monitor compliance with the law, and occupational health inspectors, although mandated by legislation, do not exist because the government never has allocated the resources to hire or train them.

LABOR INDICATORS, 1982

Total economically active population (millions): 5.999
- % working-age (15–64): 48.9
- % female: 19.7

Activity rate (%)
- Total: 29.3
- Male: 47.1
- Female: 11.6

Employment status (%)
- Employers & self-employed: 27.1
- Employees: 40.5
- Unpaid family workers: 17.6
- Other: 14.8

Sectoral employment of economically active (%)
- Agriculture, forestry, fishing: 39.2
- Construction: 7.3
- Manufacturing, mining, quarrying, public utilities: 16.9
- Trade, hotels, restaurants: 8.3
- Transportation, communications: 2.3
- Finance, real estate, services: 7.9

Average annual growth rate of labor force (%, 1985–2000): 3.1
Unemployment (000): 36.1 (1985)
Labor under 20 years (%): 20.8 (1982)

Apart from negotiated pay increases, an indexing system enables the government to raise by decree all wages and salaries when the Central Commission for Prices and Wages records an increase in the cost of living of at least 5%. Wage rates for comparable work tend to vary from one industry to another and according to areas. However, fixed differentials in minimum wages according to geographic area were discontinued in 1971. A 1972 law established length-of-service wage increases as 5% after two years of work; 10% after five years; 15% after 12 years; and 20% after 20 years.

Although annual bonuses are not required by law, most employers pay employees a *gratification de fin d'année* in the form of an additional month's salary at the end of the calendar year. In addition, wage earners also are due a *prime d'ancienneté* of 5% if they have worked for two years in the same establishment and 10% after five years in the same firm or under the same employer.

Workers must be paid at least twice a month, at a maximum interval of 16 days. The overtime rate is set at 125% of the hourly wage for work between 5 A.M. and 10 P.M. and at 150% between 10 P.M. and 5 A.M. These increases rise to 50% and 200%, respectively, if overtime occurs on the weekly rest day.

The workweek is limited to 48 hours, the working day to 10 hours. Every worker has the right to a weekly 24-hour day of rest and to seven paid holidays a year. Recruitment and dismissal also are regulated by law. Social Security covers about 15% of the labor force and provides pensions and compensation for victims of industrial accidents or occupational diseases.

It is required by law that worker delegates be elected in all industrial, commercial and agricultural enterprises; in professional offices; and in other organizations that employ at least 10 persons. The work force in each enterprise is divided into two groups for the purpose of electing delegates: one for technical personnel, office chiefs and foremen; the other for workers. Delegates form a single committee. Their function is to present to management any collective or individual demands regarding wages, job classification and the application of labor legislation. If the delegates do not obtain satisfaction, the matter may be appealed to a labor inspector. This committee of worker delegates, not the union or unions, forms labor's bargaining agent with management.

Morocco's Constitution and laws provide full protection to labor. These guarantees, including the right to be represented in the settlement of disputes and the right to protection against interference, are widely applied in the modern sector of the economy but are less well observed, and sometimes totally ignored, in the informal and underground economy. The right to strike is guaranteed by Article 14 of the Constitution, but the detailed law defining this right, promised in Article 14, never has been drafted. Legislation governing settlement of labor disputes was enacted in 1946, but the mandated procedures, which are lengthy and complicated as well as in conflict with later constitutional guarantees of the right to strike, are customarily ignored, as each dispute is handled on an ad hoc basis by the government. The August–September 1985 strike at the Jerada coal mine, for example, was settled after three weeks of police intimidation; the arrest and sentencing to prison terms of some two dozen strikers; and protracted negotiations involving worker representatives, the management of the government-owned mine and local and regional officials. In this case as in many others involving strikes and work protests, workers were prosecuted and convicted under criminal law statutes that outlaw picketing and damage to employers' property. Criminal law dating from the eve of World War II also outlaws strikes in sectors deemed to affect national security. This law is ill-defined and has been used in recent years to stop teachers' strikes, among others. Moroccan trade unions complain that workers frequently are dismissed or suspended for union activity and that the legal system too rarely punishes such illegal actions. The UMT has several complaints pending with the ILO on these and other alleged infractions of the ILO conventions on freedom of association and collective bargaining. Despite the fact that these cases have not been resolved to the unions' satisfaction, employers often are prosecuted and punished by the courts for labor law violations. A recent case involved an employer sanctioned for an illegal plant shutdown.

The Constitution also guarantees representation of workers in the Chamber of Representatives. Of 10 seats reserved for trade union organizations in the 306-member Chamber of Representatives, the UMT elected five members, the CDT three and the UGTM two in the 1984 elections. Although industrial relations still are characterized by employer paternalism, the practice of collective bargaining and negotiated contracts is spreading. There are committees at each unit level for the settlement of disputes. If not settled at this level, disputes usually are taken before one of the 12 labor courts, which have both conciliation and judicial committees. Strikes have become commonplace in recent years. Most settlements fall short of worker demands. The pressures that unions can exert are limited, considering that they lack strike funds and face a government that tolerates dismissals of workers for prolonged strikes and that lacks sufficient labor inspectors to enforce Morocco's labor laws. Work slowdowns and short walkouts are the rule.

Collective and individual grievances not settled at the enterprise level, either by direct negotiation or with the help of a labor inspector, may be taken to labor courts, which are under the joint jurisdiction of the Ministries of Justice and of Labor and Social Affairs. There is a conciliation committee and an appeals committee. Employers and workers are represented on both.

Labor is a powerful pressure group in Morocco, and unions are heavily politicized. The three most important unions are Union Marocaine du Travail (UMT), until 1963 affiliated with Istiqlal but now aligned with Union National des Forces Populaire; Confédération Démocratique de Travail (CDT); and Union Générale des Travailleurs du Maroc (UGTM), the organized-labor wing of Istiqlal. UMT is in the front line of Moroccan politics and frequently is consulted by the king and represented on government agencies. Both UMT and UGTM have affiliates for farmers, women and youth.

FOREIGN COMMERCE

Morocco's principal exports are food and beverages, semiprocessed goods, metals, minerals and ores, tobacco, chemicals and textiles. Its major imports are petroleum, industrial machinery and equipment, food and beverages and iron and steel. The European Community, the United States, Canada, Iraq, the Soviet Union and Japan are its major sources of imports while the European Community, India, Japan, the Soviet Union and the United States are its primary markets.

FOREIGN TRADE INDICATORS, 1988

Exports (U.S. $ billions): 3.1 (1989)
Imports (U.S. $ billions): 5.1 (1989)
Balance of trade (U.S. $ billions): −2.0 (1989)
Annual growth rate (1980–88), exports (%): 5.0
Annual growth rate (1980–88), imports (%): 1.8
International reserves in terms of months of imports covered: 1.5
Terms of trade (1980 = 100): 103
Import price index (1980 = 100): 80.6 (1986)
Export price index (1980 = 100): 82.5 (1986)

Direction of Trade (%), 1988

	Imports	Exports
European Community	52.4	58.6
United States	7.0	1.4
U.S.S.R. & Eastern European economies	5.5	7.8
Japan	1.6	4.3

Composition of Trade (%), 1985

	Imports	Exports
Food & agricultural raw materials	19.6	29.1
Fuels & other energy	13.2	2.1
Mineral ores & concentrates	7.4	17.3
Manufactured goods	58.9	51.6
of which chemicals	11.9	25.6
of which machinery	24.0	1.6

The government has a monopoly over the export of phosphates, fruits and vegetables, fish, wine and cotton and over the importation of tobacco, sugar and tea. Import regulations generally are liberal, and export controls are minimal. Export taxes were completely abolished in 1971.

In 1969 Morocco concluded a five-year treaty of association with the EEC. This was amended in 1974 when Britain, Ireland and Denmark joined the Community. A new form of association was signed in 1976 under which the EEC was to drop most of its barriers to the free importation of most agricultural products from Morocco but retain tariffs on olive oil, citrus fruits and refined petroleum. Morocco also was to receive $100 million in aid for agricultural and industrial development.

The Foire International de Casablanca (International Fair of Casablanca) is held biennially during April and May.

TRANSPORTATION AND COMMUNICATIONS

The rail system, administered by the state-owned Office National des Chemins de Fer du Maroc, consists of 1,893 km. (1,176 mi.) of track, of which 974 km. (440 mi.) are electrified. The main line runs from Marrakesh to Casablanca, Rabat and Sidi Kasem, with an eastern branch line to Meknès and a northern branch line to Tangier.

The country has four major ports: Tangier, the passenger and tourist port and free zone; Casablanca, which carries about 75% of the country's freight traffic; Safi, the fish and phosphates export port; and Muhammadia, the oil port. There also are three regional ports—

TRANSPORTATION INDICATORS

Roads (latest)
  Length, km. (mi.): 59,176 (36,767)
  Paved (%): 47
Motor vehicles (latest)
  Automobiles: 554,059
  Trucks and buses: 255,149
  Persons per vehicle: 29
  Road freight, metric ton-km. (short ton-mi.) (millions): 1,212 (830)
Railroads (latest)
  Track, km. (mi.): 1,893 (1,176)
  Passenger-km. (passenger-mi.) (billions): 2.069 (1.286)
  Freight, metric ton-km. (short ton-mi.) (billions): 4.613 (3.160)
Merchant marine
  Vessels: 359 (1989)
  Total deadweight tonnage (000): 594.1 (1989)
  Oil tankers (000 GRT): 62 (1985)
Ports (pre-1986)
  Cargo loaded (million metric tons): 19.632
  Cargo unloaded (million metric tons): 14.460
Air
Km. (mi.) flown (millions): 22.9 (14.2) (1985)
  Passenger-km. (passenger-mi.) (billions): 2.436 (1.514) (latest)
  Freight, metric ton-km. (short ton-mi.) (millions): 50.1 (34.3) (latest)
  Mail, metric ton-km. (short ton-mi.) (millions): 0.7 (0.5) (1985)
  Airports with scheduled flights: 15 (1990)
Pipelines 1990
  Refined, km. (mi.): 49 (30.5)
  Natural gas, km. (mi.): 241 (150)
Inland waterways (latest)
  Length, km. (mi.): 1,000 (621)
  Freight, metric ton-km. (short ton-mi.) (millions): 3.828 (2.622) (pre-1986)

COMMUNICATIONS INDICATORS, 1988

Telephones
  Total (000): 362
  Persons per telephone: 67
Phone traffic (million calls)
  Combined national: 1.043,900 (pulses)
  International: 2,151.169 (pulses)
Post office
  Number of post offices: 1,199
  Pieces of mail handled (millions): 195.904
Telegraph
  Total traffic (million calls): 1.312
    National: 1.207
    International: 105
Telex
  Subscriber lines: 7,319
  Traffic (million calls): 4.025
Telecommunications 1990
  Satellite stations: 5
  Submarine cables: 3

TOURISM & TRAVEL INDICATORS, 1986

Total tourist receipts (U.S. $ billions): 1.102 (1988)
Expenditures by nationals abroad (U.S. $ millions): 132 (1988)
Number of hotel beds (000): 70
Tourist nights (000): 16,630
Number of tourists (000): 2,180.1 (1985)
  of whom from United States: 100.7
  France: 401.4
  Spain: 198.1
  Federal Republic of Germany: 162.8

Kenitra, Agadir and Al Hoceima—and 10 minor ports, including Larache and Jebha. Three new ports are being constructed, at Nador, Tan-Tan and Tarfaya. The Compagnie Marocaine de Navigation, the largest shipping company, is 96% government-owned. The national fleet of 359 vessels has a gross registered tonnage of 594,100.

Morocco has a well-developed road system, with 59,176 km. (36,767 mi.) of roads, of which 46% are paved. Road transportation is under the jurisdiction of the Compagnie de Transports au Maroc 'Lignes Nationales'.

The national airline is Royal Air Maroc, an autonomous corporation in which the government has a 93% interest. It provides domestic and international air service. Nine airports are open to international traffic: Casablanca-Nouasseur, Tangier-Boukhalf, Agadir, Marrakesh, Oujda, Al Hoceima, Casablanca-Anfa, Rabat-Salé and Fez-Sais. There also are four seaplane stations.

Tourism is Morocco's fastest-growing industry, generating revenues of $800 million in 1986. The annual growth rate of tourism is estimated at 20%, well over the world average of 11%. Hotel construction is a government priority. Tourist development and information activities are coordinated by the National Tourist Office, the Moroccan Company for the Development of Tourism (Morocco-Tourism) and the Construction and Hotel Credit Organization. In 1986 2,186,444 tourists visited Morocco, the largest group represented Moroccans living abroad. Other important sources of tourists were France, Spain, the United Kingdom and the Federal Republic of Germany. Expenditures by nationals abroad totaled $94 million in 1981.

DEFENSE

The defense structure is headed by the king as supreme commander and as chief of the general staff. The line of command runs through the military cabinet on the one hand and the Ministry of Defense and chief of staff on the other. The Royal Guard is directly under the king's personal command. Manpower is provided by national conscription, established in 1966. An estimated 4,000 conscripts are inducted each year. The age of military service is 18, and the duration of military service is 18 months.

The total strength of the armed forces is 191,500.

Army

Personnel: 170,000

Organization: 3 mechanized infantry divisions; 1 light security brigade; 1 parachute brigade; 1 AA group; 9 mechanized infantry regiments; 9 artillery groups; 7 armored battalions; 1 royal guard battalion; 4 camel corps battalions; 2 desert cavalry battalions; 1 mountain battalion; 4 commando battalions; 4 engineer battalions; 4 armored car squadrons

Equipment: 120 heavy tanks; 70 light tanks; 612 combat reconnaissance vehicles; 806 armored personnel carriers; 98 guns; 138 howitzers; 20 rocket launchers; 1,290 mortars; antitank guided weapons; rocket launchers; guns; 140 air defense guns; 30 SAM's

Navy

Personnel: 6,500, including 600 Marines

Units: 1 frigate; 2 fast attack craft; 17 patrol craft; 4 amphibious vehicles; 1 naval infantry battalion

Naval bases: Casablanca, Safi, Agadir, Kenitra, Tangier

Air force

Personnel: 15,000

Organization and Equipment: 105 combat aircraft; 5 fighter squadrons; 1 counterinsurgency squadron; 1 transport squadron; 18 attack helicopters; 90 transport helicopters; 74 trainers; air-to-air missiles

Forces abroad: 300 in Equatorial Guinea

Air bases: Rabat-Salé, Meknès, Marrakesh, Nouasseur

Berbers constitute 80% of the troops in the Royal Moroccan Army and over half of the officers. Berbers are known as fierce and tenacious fighters, conditioned to hardship, capable of great endurance and very loyal to the king. The only foreign armed intervention in the history of modern Morocco came during the brief border war with Algeria in 1963, during which Moroccan troops fought skillfully and successfully. Moroccan soldiers also performed well against the Polisario Front forces in the former Spanish Sahara, and in Zaire during the 1978 military conflict. However, the armed forces must depend on irregular foreign sources of supply for weapons and equipment and therefore are burdened with disparate types of arms and artillery.

At independence the newly created Royal Moroccan Army received $40 million worth of military equipment from France and some equipment from Spain. French military aid continued until 1966. In 1977 French forces were flown from Senegal to aid Moroccan troops against the Algeria-backed Polisario forces. Soviet aid began in 1960, and tanks were obtained from Czechoslovakia in 1968. From 1949 through 1983 U.S. aid amounted to $483 million, including F-5 jet fighters and antitank weapons. Over 2,000 Moroccan army officers have been trained in the United States under the Military Assistance Program (MAP). Arms purchases abroad during 1973–83 totaled $2.805 billion, including $950 million from France and $430 million from the United States.

EDUCATION

In 1963 education was made compulsory for children between 7 and 13, but this decree is not strictly enforced. Schooling consists of five years of primary school, four years of the first secondary-school cycle and three years of the university-preparatory secondary-school cycle, for a total of 12 years. Attendance at Koranic schools is compulsory for children between 5 and 7 years of age. Completion of a two-year program in these schools is accepted as the equivalent of the first primary grade. The curriculum includes learning the Koran by rote, Islamic history and Islamic reading and writing.

The academic year runs from October to June. The medium of instruction is Arabic in the first two years

EDUCATION INDICATORS, 1989

Literacy
- Total (%): 70.7
- Male (%): 82.4
- Female (%): 58.7

First level
- Schools: 3,749
- Students: 2,110,719
- Teachers: 82,082
- Student/teacher ratio: 26.0
- Net enrollment ratio: 57 (1987)

Second level
- Schools: 1,241 (1988)
- Students: 1,347,517
- Teachers: 68,986
- Student–teacher ratio: 18.7
- Net enrollment ratio: 29 (1987)

Vocational
- Schools: 696 (1988)
- Students: 70,075 (1988)
- Teachers: 5,705 (1988)
- Student–teacher ratio: 12.3 (1988)

Third level (postsecondary)
- Institutions: 30
- Students: 205,873
- Teachers: 7,088
- Student–teacher ratio: 29.0
- Gross enrollment ratio: 9.8 (1987)
- Students (/100,000 pop.): 911

Foreign study
- Foreign students in national universities: 3,621 (1987)
- Students abroad: 30,325
  - of whom in
    - United States: 884 (1988)
    - France: 23,975 (1988)
    - Federal Republic of Germany: 422 (1988)
    - United Kingdom: 42 (1987)

Public expenditure
- Total (D.H. 000): 11,103,134
- % of GNP: 7.3
- % of national budget: 25.5
- % of current expenditures: 72.9

GRADUATES, 1987

Total: 16,344
Education: 198
Humanities & religion: 6,446
Fine & applied arts: 0
Law: 1,786
Social & behavioral sciences: 867
Commerce & business: 670
Mass communication: 148
Home economics: 0
Service trades: 226
Natural sciences: 2,610
Mathematics & computer science: 0
Medicine: 1,176
Engineering: 360
Architecture: 45
Industrial programs: 84
Transportation & communications: 377
Agriculture, forestry, fisheries: 593
Other: 758

and Arabic and French in the final three years of primary school. French is the language of instruction in secondary schools and colleges. English is taught as a modern language from the first year of the lower secondary cycle.

Besides Koranic schools, private schools are permitted to operate. Private schools include French Cultural Mission schools and Jewish schools.

About two-thirds of the teachers are Moroccan; the rest are French. The proportion of French teachers is greater in private schools and secondary schools. Most Moroccan teachers are poorly paid, and only 25% of teachers in the lower secondary cycle are fully qualified.

Adult education is handled through the radio. A special newspaper using simplified type is published for the newly literate. About 3% of secondary-school students are enrolled in the vocational stream. Three-year industrial programs offer a baccalaureat degree in technology. There also are one-year courses in technical and commercial occupations and four-year courses in agriculture.

Public education is administered by the Ministry of Primary Education and the Ministry of Higher, Secondary and Technical Education. The two ministries are assisted by 12 field offices and the Higher Board of Education.

Higher education is provided by the 1,000-year-old Islamic University of Al Quarawiyin located in Fez, and Muhammad V University at Rabat. There also are institutes of administration, industry, mining, agriculture and statistics.

LEGAL SYSTEM

Until independence the legal system was a mixture of the Islamic Shari'a code, Berber customary law, rabbinical law and French and Spanish legal codes. The work of creating a unified legal structure and court system was undertaken between 1956 and 1959. A new Code of Personal Status was compiled in 1958, and a reformed Penal Code was published in 1959.

All courts established under the French protectorate were terminated in 1964. In 1965 Arabic was made the court language and the judicial system was completely Moroccanized. The revised court system is headed by the Higher Council of the Magistracy, the Supreme Court and the High Court. The Higher Council of the Magistracy consists of 10 members, of whom six are elected by the judiciary and four are appointed by the king, who also is its president. It regulates the judiciary and guarantees its freedom. The Supreme Court, or Majlis al-Aala, is divided into four chambers: civil, criminal, administrative and social. The High Court adjudicates cases involving appeal at Fez, Marrakesh and Casablanca. Under the courts of appeal there are 16 regional tribunals; 27 Sadad tribunals, or traditional conciliation courts for rural areas and older cities; and courts of peace and courts of first instance in modern cities.

The Moroccan judicial system generally is considered fair and is in most respects independent of political control. Cases are brought before an initial review court, which can call for a hearing. The detainee is informed of charges and questioned by the judge to decide if they have merit. If not, or if the infraction is minor, the judge can release the detainee or impose a light sentence. If a lengthy investigation is required, the judge can release detainees on their own recognizance. In cases involving serious crimes, courts generally move quickly to bring cases to trial. If convicted by a court of first instance, a defendant has the right to appeal.

Although most cases are handled by civilian/secular courts based in part on French legal tradition, Morocco has a parallel judicial system using Islamic law principles to deal with marriage, divorce, child custody and inheritance for Muslim Moroccans. Although Western legal norms are not applicable in the Islamic courts, Koranic principles and the limited kinds of the cases heard reduce the possibility of abuse.

There have been allegations of growing judicial corruption. In October 1985, four court officials (including one judge) in the northern city of Al Hoceima were tried and found guilty of illegal practices.

The penal system operates under the Penitentiary Administrative Division of the Ministry of Justice. There are some 35 prisons in the country, including three maximum-security prisons. Detention facilities are attached to most police stations.

LAW ENFORCEMENT

The national police is the Sûreté National, commanded by a director-general who invariably is an army officer. The force is divided into 10 operational regions (or *sûretés*) and five administrative subdirectorates. There also are four broad internal divisions: the Urban Corps, which constitutes two-thirds of the force; the Judiciary Police; the Mobile Intervention Companies; and the Internal Security Service. In each region the Sûreté National unit functions under a commissioner. The Royal Gendarmerie also performs police functions and is organized as a police unit. There is an auxiliary police with a reported strength of 20,000 men, commanded by an inspector-general. This force, known as Maghzani, is divided into an administrative division and a mobile division.

The kingdom's secret service and counterespionage and countersubversion agency is the Internal Security Service. No information is released about the size and operations of this organization.

HEALTH

Medical care is free, but availability of services varies depending on location. It is best in urban areas. Infant mortality is high in rural regions.

Health standards are relatively low. Gastrointestinal infections, tuberculosis, trachoma, typhoid and malaria are widespread. Major contagious diseases have been controlled.

HEALTH INDICATORS

Health personnel 1988
- Physicians: 4,946
  - persons per: 4,873
- Dentists: 261 (1987)
- Nurses: 22,430
- Pharmacists: 1,351 (1987)

Hospitals 1988
- Number: 186
- Number of beds (/10,000): 11
- Admissions/discharges (/10,000): 233
- Bed occupancy rate (%): 59.8
- Average length of stay (days): 10

Type of hospital (%) 1988
- Government: 100.0
- Private nonprofit: 0.0
- Private profit: 0.0

Public health expenditures (latest)
- As % of national budget: 3.0
- Per capita (U.S. $): 6.90

Vital statistics
- Crude death rate (/1,000): 8 (1990)
- Life expectancy at birth 1990
  - Males: 63
  - Females: 66
- Infant mortality rate (/1,000 live births): 78 (1990)
- Child mortality rate under 5 yrs. (/1,000 births) (1985–90): 118
- Maternal mortality rate (/100,000 live births): 327.0 (1980)
- Population with access to safe water (%): 60 (latest)

MEDIA INDICATORS

Newspapers
- Number of dailies: 11 (latest)
- Circulation (000): 305 (latest)
- Per 1,000 pop.: 13 (latest)
- Newsprint consumption 1988
  - Total metric tons: 11,500
  - Per 1,000 pop. (kg.): 482

Radio
- Number of transmitters: 35 (latest)
- Number of persons per radio receiver: 5.6 (1989)

Television
- Television transmitters: 77 (1989)
- Number of persons per T.V. receiver: 20 (1989)

Cinema
- Number of fixed cinemas: 267 (latest)
- Seating capacity (000): 162 (latest)
  - Seats (/1,000 pop.): 7.7 (1983)
- Annual attendance (millions): 39.0 (pre-1986)
- Gross box office receipts (D. H. millions): 115 (1983)

Films
- Production of long films: 12 (latest)
- Import of long films: 302 (1983)
  - from United States: 21.2
  - India: 18.9
  - France: 17.2
  - Hong Kong: 15.9

CULTURAL & ENVIRONMENTAL INDICATORS

Libraries (latest)
- Number: 8
- Volumes (000): 448

Museums (latest)
- Annual attendance (millions): 1.580
- Attendance (/1,000 pop.): 74

Performing arts (pre-1986)
- Attendance (/1,000 pop.): 12

Nature reserves (latest)
- Number of facilities: 10

FOOD & NUTRITION

The Moroccan diet is based on cereals—barley, wheat and corn—supplemented by vegetables and fruits. Consumption of meat and milk is low.

The daily intake of food per capita exceeds WHO minimum requirements.

MEDIA & CULTURE

The Moroccan press consists of 11 daily newspapers and over 35 nondailies. Six newspapers are published in Rabat and five in Casablanca; six are published in Arabic and three in French. Two are published in Arabic and French. The principal dailies are: *Le Matin du Sahara* (100,000), *al-Alam* (45,000), *L'Opinion* (60,000) and *Maroc Soir* (50,000).

Although freedom of the press is guaranteed in the Constitution, the basic Press Code of 1958 empowers the government to adopt severe measures to limit that freedom, including suspension of newspapers and seizure of copies. This right was exercised by the king a number of times during the political crises of the 1960s and 1970s.

Many foreign journals are available in Morocco; seven have local editions there. All publications, whether printed in Morocco or imported from abroad, require government approval before they can be sold. Foreign publications usually are seized when they refer negatively to Morocco. Some Spanish papers—in particular, *Cambio 16*—have been unavailable following alleged sensationalist reporting of the January 1984 disturbances.

The national news agency is the government-owned Wikalat al-Maghreb al-Arabi, with headquarters in Rabat. Nine foreign news agencies including Agence France-Presse, Reuters and TASS maintain offices in Morocco.

Morocco's small book publishing industry comprises about a dozen publishers. Morocco adheres to the Berne and Universal copyright conventions.

Most broadcasting is operated by Radiodiffusion Télévision Marocaine (RTM), also known as Radio Maroc, an agency of the Ministry of Information. With a powerful long-wave transmitter (400 kw.) at Azilal, 22 medium-wave transmitters and six FM transmitters, RTM broadcasts three separate domestic-service programs: Network A in Arabic; Network B in French, and Network C in English, Spanish and Berber. These three programs are on the air for 400 hours a week. The former Radio Tangier operates a separate network known as the Voice of Morocco.

Television, introduced in 1962, now covers all densely populated areas with a network of nine main transmitters and five low-power repeaters. The network is linked through Spain with Eurovision. Programs are on the air 45 hours weekly in Arabic and French. Most of the programs are imported. A private television company, 2M International was created in 1988 and began broadcasting in French and Arabic in 1989. It is jointly owned by Omnium Nord Africain and Moroccan financial organizations and by foreign investors.

SOCIAL WELFARE

Social and welfare services are administered by a number of ministries, of which the Ministry of Labor and Social Affairs is concerned with Social Security and the operation of orphanages, day-care centers and nursing homes for the aged. Social Security, run by the Social Security Bank, covers about 15% of the labor force and offers family allowances, old-age, sickness, accident, maternity and death allowances and other benefits. All employees must contribute to the Social Welfare Fund.

The major private voluntary social welfare organizations include the National Mutual Aid, which distributes food and clothing to the needy; the Moroccan League for the Protection of Children; and the Red Crescent.

GLOSSARY

amir al muaminin: Commander of the Faithful; title of the King of Morocco in his religious role as head of Muslim religious establishment.
bidonville: shantytown consisting of makeshift shacks built of flattened oil drums.
bilad al makhzan: land in which the authority of the central government is acknowledged and firmly established, i.e. the Berber highlands.
caid: the executive head of a rural constituency.
casbah: the central, and exclusively Arab, quarters of a city; literally, the citadel.
cercle: intermediate unit of local administration.
chergui: intensely hot wind blowing from the Sahara in the summer.
circonscription: variant name of a rural constituency.
colon: a French colonial settler.
constituency: basic regional unit of local government.
dahir: royal decree having the force of law.
habus (also, habous): Muslim religious endowment, Moroccan equivalent of a wakf.
jaysh: military tribes; by extension, land owned by such tribes which are exempt from taxation.
khalif: executive of municipal ward.
khalifa: the governor or viceroy of a province in the Spanish Protectorate.
Levante: wind blowing from the northeast in the summer.
maghzani: the auxiliary police force.
majlis al Aala: Supreme Court.
majlis al Nuwab: House of Representatives.
makhzan: central government.
mallah: traditional Jewish quarter in a town.
milk: private freehold (land).
muqaddam: headman of a village.
oued: wadi, or riverbed, usually dry in winter; French transliteration of wadi.
pasha: mayor of a municipal area.
shaykh: executive of a rural subdivision of a constituency.
supercaid: executive of a cercle.
wakf: a Muslim religious endowment in the Middle East.
wazara: cabinet.
wazir: a minister or royal adviser.

CHRONOLOGY (from 1956)

1956— Morocco gains independence, with Muhammad V as king. Relations with France are broken over French hijacking of a plane carrying Algerian leader Ben Bella. . . . Spanish Tangier is restored to Morocco.
1958— The king's Charter of Public Liberties is issued. . . . Spain relinquishes the southern zone of its Spanish protectorate. . . . M'barek Bekkai and Ahmed Belafrej serve briefly as prime ministers. . . . Abdullah Ibrahim is named prime minister, succeeding Balafrej.
1959— The dirham is introduced as the unit of currency, replacing the Moroccan franc.
1960— Agadir is destroyed in an earthquake; 4,500 persons are killed. . . . Ibrahim is ousted as prime minister; the king takes over the prime ministership. . . . Diplomatic relations with France are broken over French nuclear testing in the Sahara.
1961— King Muhammad dies; Crown Prince Hassan succeeds to the throne as Hassan II; Hassan also heads the cabinet as prime minister.
1962— New Constitution is promulgated; it is ratified in a referendum.
1963— Border conflict erupts with Algeria. . . . U.S. air bases in Morocco are returned to the Moroccan government. . . . The king yields the prime ministership to Ahmed Bahnin.
1965— In the wake of nationwide riots, Hassan proclaims a state of emergency or "exception." . . . The king takes over the prime ministership again. . . . Diplomatic relations with France are suspended over the murder of Ben Barka in Paris by the king's agents.
1967— Muhammad Benhima is named to head the cabinet.
1969— Morocco hosts Islamic and Arab Summit conferences at Rabat. . . . Ahmed Laraki heads new government. . . . Spain relinquishes Ifni to Morocco.
1970— National state of "exception" is lifted; New Constitution is promulgated; it is approved in a referendum.
1971— Hassan survives an assassination attempt and an army coup. . . . Muhammad Karim Lamrani heads a new cabinet.
1972— Hassan survives a second assassination attempt as his plane is shot at in midair; Muhammad Oufkir, the powerful defense minister, is implicated in plot and commits suicide. . . . New Constitution is promulgated; it is approved in a referendum. . . . Ahmed Osman takes over the prime ministership.
1973— Morocco accelerates Moroccanization and Ar-

abization programs. . . . All French-owned farms are taken over by the state. . . . Morocco reaches accord with Algeria over disputed border.

1975— Hassan leads "Green March" to Spanish Sahara to demonstrate Moroccan claims to the region.

1976— Morocco and Mauritania divided Spanish Sahara between themselves, while Algeria supports Western Sahara's claim to independence; Morocco and Algeria reach the brink of war once again.

1977— In nationwide elections independents and royalists gain absolute majority in the Chamber of Representatives.

1978— As Mauritania signs a unilateral peace treaty with the Polisario forces, Morocco claims the whole of Western Sahara and occupies Tiris el-Gharbia.

1979— Prime Minister Ahmad Osman steps down and is replaced by Maati Bouabid.

1981— Consultative Council of Western Sahara meets. Riots break out in major cities following hike in food prices and implementation of IMF austerity program.

1983— Muhammad Karim Lamrani is named prime minister, replacing Maati Bouabid.

1984— Arab-African Federation Treaty signed by King Hassan and Colonel Qaddhafi of Libya is approved in referendum. Morocco leaves the OAU over the Western Sahara issue. New elections are held for the Chamber of Representatives.

1985— Thirty Islamic fundamentalists are convicted of a plot to overthrow the monarchy. Morocco declares unilateral cease-fire in Western Sahara. UN General Assembly upholds Polisario's resolution that direct negotiations with Morocco must precede referendum on self-determination in Western Sahara.

1986— Morocco severs diplomatic relations with Syria. Twenty-six left-wing activists are sentenced to prison terms for subversion. Later in year King Hassan declares a series of amnesties for political and nonpolitical prisoners. Morocco announces boycott of all UN talks on Western Sahara.

1987— Royal pardon is granted to Muhammad Basri, who had allegedly been involved in plots against King Hassan. Little progress is made in UN/OAU sponsored indirect talks between Morocco and Polisario. Intense fighting involving Moroccan and Polisario forces breaks out on Mauritanian border.

1988— By mid-year 71 countries have granted diplomatic recognition to SADR. Morocco and Polisario provisionally accept a peace plan proposed by UN Secretary General.

1989— For the first time in 13 years direct contact takes place between King Hassan and officials of Polisario and SADR in Marrakesh in January. Polisario announces cease-fire which lasts six weeks. Polisario resumes hostilities in mid-March. Diplomatic relations with Syria are resumed.

1990— Morocco condemns the Iraq invasion of Kuwait and provides troops to defend Saudi Arabia.

1991— In response to pro-Iraqi demonstrations, the government supports a one-day general strike to express solidarity with the Iraqi people.

BIBLIOGRAPHY

BOOKS AND FILMS

Abu-Laghod, Janet L. *Rabat: Urban Apartheid in Morocco.* Princeton NJ, 1980.

Amin, Samir. *The Maghreb in the Modern World.* Harmondsworth, England, 1971.

Bennett, Norman Robert. *A Study Guide for Morocco.* Boston, 1970.

Bidwell, Robin. *Morocco Under Colonial Rule.* London, 1973.

Blue Men of Morocco. Color film, 27 min. Disney.

Country of Islam. Color/B&W film, 16 min. Churchill Films.

Entelis, John P. *Culture and Counterculture in Moroccan Politics.* Boulder, CO, 1988.

Findlay, Ann M. *Morocco* (World Bibliographical Series). Santa Barbara, CA, 1984.

Hall, Luella J. *United States and Morocco, 1776–1976.* Metuchen, NJ, 1971.

Hassan II. *Le Defi.* Paris, 1976.

Julien, Charles. *History of North Africa: Tunisia, Algeria, Morocco.* New York, 1970.

Kinross, Lord, and D. Hales-Gary. *Morocco.* London, 1971.

Life in Morocco. Color film, 11 min. Pat Dowling Pictures.

Ling, Dwight L. *Morocco & Tunisia: A Comparative History.* Washington, D.C., 1979.

Merat, Christian. *Morocco: Economic and Social Development Report.* Washington, D.C., 1981.

Moore, Clement H. *Politics in North Africa: Algeria, Morocco, Tunisia.* Boston, 1970.

Morocco—Chaoui Faces His Future. Color film, 20 min. Universal.

Morocco Today. B&W film, 27 min. Contemporary.

Morocco: Two Arab Boys of Tangier. Color film, 18 min. Frith Films.

Moulay Idriss. B&W film, 11 min. Les Actualités Françaises.

Our State in Troubled Morocco. B&W film, 37 min. March of Time.

Rabinow, Paul. *Symbolic Dominations: Cultural Symbols and Historic Change in Morocco.* Chicago, 1975.

Spencer, William. *Historical Dictionary of Morocco.* Metuchen, NJ, 1980.

Waterbury, John. *Commander of the Faithful: Moroccan Political Elite.* New York, 1970.

Willcox, Mellon. *In Morocco.* New York, 1971.

OFFICIAL PUBLICATIONS

Moroccan Bank. *Rapport Annuel.*

Morrocan Treasury. *Balance Générale des Comptes du Grand Livre et Tableaux Statistiques Annexes* (General Balance Sheet and Additional Statistical Tables) (monthly).

———. *Situation Annuelle des Finances Locales* (Annual Statement of Local Finances).

MOZAMBIQUE

BASIC FACT SHEET

OFFICIAL NAME: Republic of Mozambique (República de Moçambique)

ABBREVIATION: MZ

CAPITAL: Maputo (formerly Lourenço Marques)

HEAD OF STATE: Joaquim Alberto Chissano (from 1986)

HEAD OF GOVERNMENT: Prime Minister Mario da Graca Machungo (from 1986)

NATURE OF GOVERNMENT: Civilian dictatorship

POPULATION: 14,565,656 (1990)

AREA: 783,030 sq. km. (302,329 sq. mi.)

ETHNIC MAJORITY: Maku-Lomue-Neto in the North; Tsonga in the South

LANGUAGE: Portuguese (official)

RELIGIONS: Animism, Christianity and Islam

UNIT OF CURRENCY: Metical

NATIONAL FLAG: Four triangles radiating from a common apex at the upper hoist corner. The stripes, separated by white slivers are, from top to bottom, green, red, black and yellow. Elements of the national emblem are superimposed in the upper left.

NATIONAL EMBLEM: The main elements of the national emblem are a cogwheel of 24 cogs, a white book outlined in black, and black silhouettes of a hoe and an AK-47 rifle placed on a relief of Mozambique with the Indian Ocean in the foreground. The emblem appears within a wreath with a red star on the top and the legend "República Popular de Moçambique" at the bottom.

NATIONAL ANTHEM: "Viva Viva FRELIMO"

NATIONAL HOLIDAYS: June 25 (National Day, Independence Day); also all principal Catholic festivals

NATIONAL CALENDAR: Gregorian

PHYSICAL QUALITY OF LIFE INDEX: 40

DATE OF INDEPENDENCE: June 25, 1975

DATE OF CONSTITUTION: November 30, 1990

WEIGHTS & MEASURES: Metric in general use

GEOGRAPHICAL FEATURES

Mozambique, on the southeastern coast of Africa opposite the island of Madagascar, has an area of 783,030 sq. km. (302,329 sq. mi.) extending 2,016 km. (1,253 mi.) north-northeast to south-southwest and 772 km. (480 mi.) east-southeast to west-northwest. Its coastline on the Indian Ocean stretches 2,504 km. (1,556 mi.).

Mozambique shares its international border of 4,499 km. (2703 mi.) with six neighbors: South Africa (491 km.; 305 mi.); Swaziland (108 km.; 67 mi.); Zimbabwe (1,223 km.; 760 mi.); Zambia (424 km.; 263 mi.); Malawi (1,497 km.; 930 mi.); and Tanzania (756 km.; 470 mi.). The borders generally coincide with natural features but do not define ethnic boundaries. There are no current border disputes.

The capital is Maputo, with a population of 882,814 (1986). Beira is the next-largest city, with a population of 269,700 (1986). The names of almost all major cities have been Africanized, as follows:

Old Name	New Name	Old Name	New Name
Lourenço Marques	Maputo	Malvernia	Chicualacuala
Beira	Sofala	Aldeia da Madragoa	Chilembene
Vila Pery	Manica	Trigo da Morais	Chokwe
Moçambique	Nampula	Novo Freixo	Cuamba
Joao Belo	Xai-Xai	Vila Alferes Chamusca	Guija
Vila Cabral	Lichinga	Olivenca	Lupichili
Porto Amelia	Pemba	Miranda	Macaloge
Vila Pery (provincial capital)	Chimoio	Santa Comba	Mahlazene
Antonio Enes	Angoche	Vila Salazar	Matola
Vilo Gouveia	Catandica	Muchopes	Manjacaze

Topographically, the country is divided by the Zambezi River into two halves. North of the Zambezi the narrow coastline yields to hills and low plateaus and farther west to rugged highlands, of which the three most prominent are the Livingstone-Nyasa Highlands, the Shire or Namuli Highlands, the Angonia Highlands, the Tete Highlands and the Maconde Plateau. South of the Zambezi the littoral is broader, extending in places almost the entire width of the country. In the South are the Gorongosa Highlands, an extension of the Mashonaland Plateau, and the Lebombo Mountains in the deep South. Only 44% of Mozambique is littoral lowlands and marshes; another 17% is low plateaus and hills, 26% is high plateaus, and 13% is mountainous area. The highest points in the country are the mountain peaks of Namuli (2,418 m.; 7,936 ft.), Binga (2,436 m.; 7,992 ft.) and Serra Zuira (2,227 m.; 7,306 ft.).

Mozambique is drained by five major river systems and several smaller ones, all of which flow into the

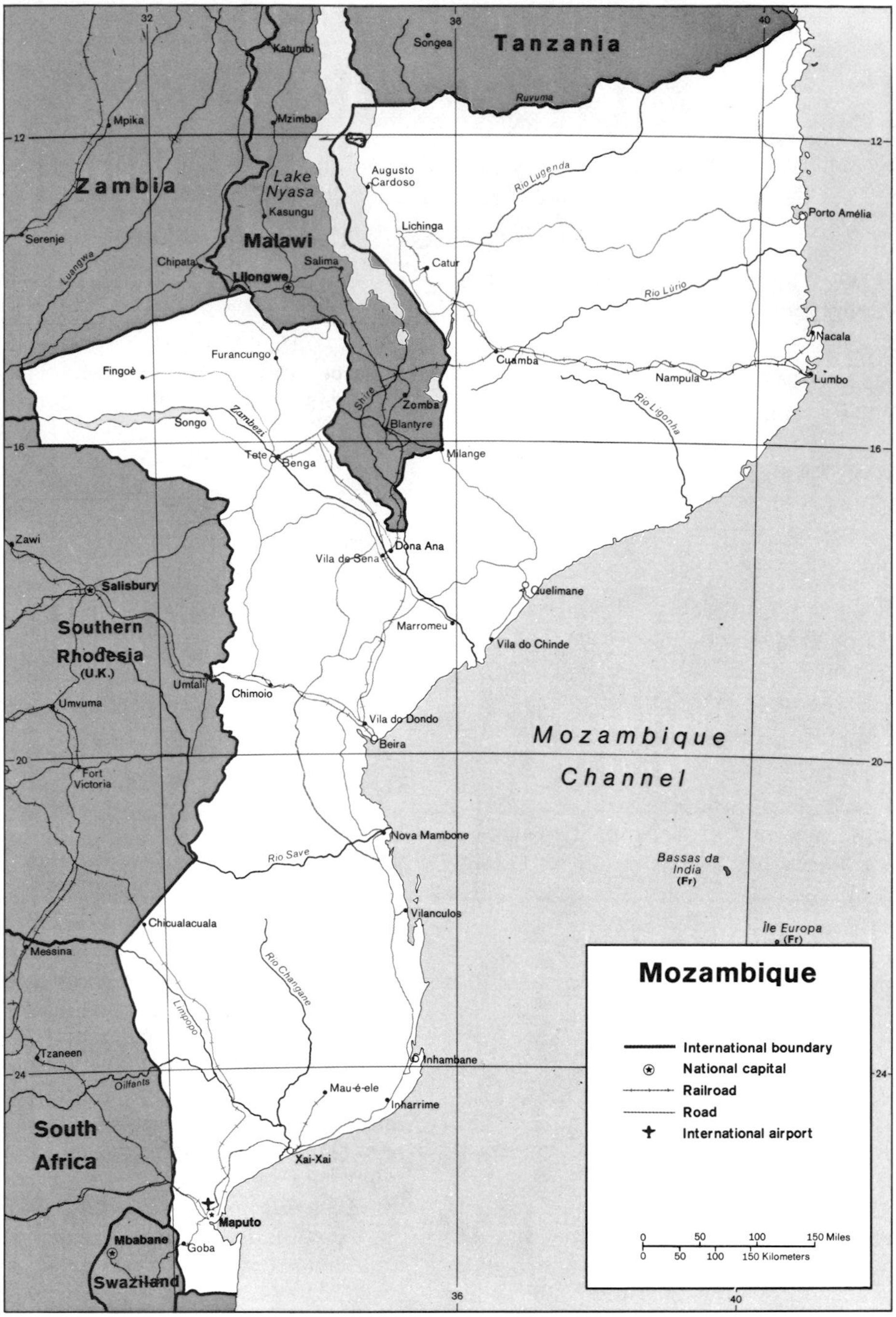

Mozambique

International boundary
National capital
Railroad
Road
International airport

0 50 100 150 Miles
0 50 100 150 Kilometers

Tanzania
Zambia
Malawi
Lake Nyasa
Southern Rhodesia (U.K.)
South Africa
Swaziland
Mozambique Channel
Bassas da India (Fr)
Île Europa (Fr)

Songea
Ruvuma
Katumbi
Mpika
Mzimba
Kasungu
Serenje
Luangwa
Chipata
Lilongwe
Salima
Augusto Cardoso
Rio Lugenda
Porto Amélia
Lichinga
Catur
Rio Lúrio
Nacala
Cuamba
Nampula
Lumbo
Rio Ligonha
Furancungo
Fingoè
Shire
Zomba
Blantyre
Songo
Zambezi
Tete
Benga
Milange
Zawi
Salisbury
Dona Ana
Vila de Sena
Quelimane
Marromeu
Vila do Chinde
Umtali
Chimoio
Umvuma
Vila do Dondo
Beira
Fort Victoria
Nova Mambone
Rio Save
Vilanculos
Chicualacuala
Messina
Rio Changane
Limpopo
Tzaneen
Olifants
Inhambane
Mau-é-ele
Inharrime
Xai-Xai
Maputo
Mbabane
Goba

12
16
20
24
32
36
40

Indian Ocean. The largest and historically the most important is the Zambezi, which flows through Mozambique for 820 km. (509 mi.), of which 460 km. (285 mi.) are navigable. At Songo the river is the site of the Cabora Bassa Dam, one of the largest in the world and the last monumental legacy of Portuguese rule. Other major river basins from north to south include the Ruvuma, fed by the Messinge, Luchulingo, Chiulezi and Lugenda rivers; the Lurio, comprising the Lurio and its tributaries; the Maracoleta, Luleio, Macequesse, Nirongene, Nualo, Malema and Lalana rivers; the Save Basin; and the Limpopo and its tributaries. There are three lakes in the northern region: Lakes Malawi, Chiuta and Shirwa.

CLIMATE & WEATHER

Mozambique has a tropical climate with two seasons: wet, lasting from October to March; and dry, lasting from April to September. During the wet season monthly temperatures average 26.6°C to 29.4°C (80°F to 85°F); during the dry season the June and July temperatures average 18.4°C to 20°C (65°F to 68°F).

Within this general framework there is considerable variation in climate, influenced by differences in elevation, the presence of Lake Malawi in the West and the warm Mozambique Current along the coast. Rainfall is particularly heavy along the central coast but decreases to the north and south of this region. Sofala (formerly Beira) receives over 1,420 mm. (56 in.), while the southern coast receives 760 to 1,010 mm. (30 to 40 in.); the northern coast 610 to 1,220 mm. (24 to 48 in.) and the Zambezi lowlands 400 to 800 mm. (16 to 32 in.). Rainfall is irregular; the southern districts are subject to both droughts and floods. Cyclones are common in the wet season.

POPULATION

The population of Mozambique was estimated in 1990 at 14,565,656 on the basis of the last official census, in 1980, when the population was 12,130,000.

The highest population densities are recorded in the provinces of Maputo (48.8 per sq. km.; 126 per sq. mi.) and Nampula (21.9 per sq. km.; 57 per sq. mi.); the lowest densities are recorded in Niassa (2.4 per sq. km.; 6.2 per sq. mi.) and Tete (4.9 per sq. km.; 12.7 per sq. mi.).

The urban component of the population was estimated at 24% in 1988, although it is not clear how the departure of the Portuguese in 1975 and 1976 affected this percentage. The urban growth rate, 1985–90, is 9.03%. There is evidence of a steady shift in population from rural to urban areas. There are at least four cities of over 50,000 inhabitants, of which both Maputo and Beira may be described as modern. Maputo itself accounts for 83% of the urban population.

Since 1930, when an incredible sex ratio of 86.8 men for every 100 women was reported (reflecting high male emigration rates), the ratio has been moving toward greater equilibrium. At the time of the 1980 census there were 48.7 men for every 51.3 women.

DEMOGRAPHIC INDICATORS

Population (millions): 15.70 (1990)
Year of last census: 1980
Sex distribution (% at last census): males, 48.7; females, 51.3
Population estimates and projections (millions)

1930: 3,890	1960: 7,584	1990: 15,696
1940: 5,086	1970: 9,318	2000: 20,463
1950: 6,458	1980: 12,103	

Age profile (% at last census)

0–14: 44.4	30–44: 15.9	60–74: 3.6
15–29: 26.7	45–59: 8.7	75 and over: 0.7

Median age (yrs.): 18.1 (1985)
Youth population (% aged 15–24): (1985) 19.0; (2000) 19.2
Total dependency ratio, 1985: 88.2
Annual growth rate (%)

1950–55: 1.69	1975–80: 2.83	2000–2005: 2.56
1955–60: 2.02	1980–85: 2.51	2005–10: 2.40
1960–65: 2.23	1985–90: 2.65	2010–15: 2.12
1965–70: 2.39	1990–95: 2.69	2015–20: 1.79
1970–75: 2.22	1995–2000: 2.64	2020–25: 1.52

Hypothetical size of stationary population (millions): 93
Assumed year of reaching net reproduction rate of 1: 2045
Urban population (000): 2,667 (1985)
Urban population (%): 24 (1988); (1965) 5
Annual urban population growth rate (%, 1985–90): 9.03
Annual rural population growth rate (%, 1985–90): 0.75
Percentage of urban population in largest city: 83 (1980)
Percentage of urban population in cities of population over 500,000: 83 (1980)
Number of cities of population over 500,000: 1 (1980)
Population density per sq. km. (per sq. mi.): 19.1 (50.9) (latest)

VITAL STATISTICS

Crude birth rate (/1,000): 47 (1990); 49 (1965)
Crude death rate (/1,000): 18 (1990); 77 (1965)
Infant mortality rate (/1,000 live births): 138 (1990)
Maternal mortality rate (/100,000 live births): 479 (1980)
Life expectancy (yrs.) at birth (1980–85): males, 45; females, 49 (1990)
Gross reproduction rate (/woman) (1980–85): 320
Total fertility rate (/woman): 6.5 (1990)
Rate of natural increase (/1,000) (1985–90): 26.5
Marriage rate (/1,000) (1985–90): 0.7
Average family size: 4.4 (latest)
Legitimate births (%): 73.1 (latest)

STATUS OF WOMEN INDICATORS

Number of women (000): 6,093 (1985)
% women of childbearing age 15–49: 45 (1988)
% women literate: 13.3 (1988)
% women in labor force: 47.9 (1988)
Total fertility rate (/woman): 6.5 (1990)

On the eve of independence in 1975 there were an estimated 250,000 permanent European residents in Mozambique. Of these, only a few thousand remain, remnants of one of the most massive flights of whites in African history. The loss in population that this exodus entailed was only partially offset by the repatriation of some 100,000 Mozambicans who had fled to Tanzania and Malawi during the struggle for independence. Independence has affected only marginally the steady flow of Mozambican workers to South Africa.

Because the government does not maintain records of movements of workers across borders, no information is available on the number of Mozambican workers in neighboring countries.

The status of women in Mozambique has not altered appreciably since independence. The Constitution of 1975 provided that there should be no discrimination on the basis of sex. In fact, however, two societies exist: (a) the contemporary society of the larger urban areas; and (b) the more traditional society of the rural areas. Women play a prominent role in the urban society. They have equal access to education. There is a surprisingly large number of women in the professions, the military and within the bureaucracy, and many hold policy positions. They also engage in a wide range of economic activity, including commerce. Few women hold important political posts. There is a new organization devoted to women's affairs. In the rural areas, traditional practices reinforce discrimination against women. Specific customs vary according to ethnic grouping, but generally women do much of the manual labor in agriculture as well as care for the home and family. In certain ethnic groups women may retain the earnings from cash crops they cultivate, but in most instances economic and political decisions are made by men.

In February 1977 the Third Congress of FRELIMO, the ruling party, announced its commitment to reducing the population growth rate by family planning programs and health care services involving educational materials and contraceptives.

ETHNIC COMPOSITION

Unlike other African countries, the ethnic composition and groups of Mozambique have not been studied and analyzed in detail by ethnographers, and there are gaps in available data. Most scholars identify 10 ethnic clusters with certain common characteristics. However, few of these tribes have the social organization or cohesiveness usually associated with such groups; there are in fact few common bonds that transcend a single village or groups of villages. Social organization, while essentially tribal, is too fragmented to be described in general terms.

In terms of territoriality, the Makua-Lomue cluster and the Neto subgroup dominate the region north of the Zambezi, while the Tsonga cluster dominates the region south of the Zambezi.

The number of Portuguese permanently resident in Mozambique has been variously estimated, but the generally cited figure is 15,000. The country's economic and political troubles and its growing Marxist orientation have been responsible for the steady exodus of even non-Portuguese Western residents.

LANGUAGES

Portuguese is the official language and the medium of administration, education and commerce. Numerous African languages, including Ronga, Shangaan and Muchope, are widely spoken, but none predominates enough to be a lingua franca.

MAJOR ETHNIC GROUPS OF MOZAMBIQUE

Cluster	Subgroups	Number	%
Makua-Lomue	Makua	3,000,000	38.4
	Lomue		
	Neto		
	Lolo		
	Xirima		
Tsonga	Ronga	1,850,000	23.7
	Shangana		
	Tswa		
	Hlengwe		
Lower Zambezi	Sena	800,000	10.2
	Podzo		
	Tonga		
	Nhungwe		
	Chicunda		
	Chuabo		
Shona-Karanga	Karanga	765,000	9.8
	Tawara		
	Bargue		
	Xanga		
	Teve		
	Manika		
	Ndau		
	Tombodji		
	Danda		
Islamic Coastal	Swahili	500,000	6.4
	Maca		
	Mwani		
Chopi		350,000	4.5
Maravi	Senga	250,000	3.2
	Zimba		
	Chewa		
	Pimbe		
	Nyanja		
Yao		170,000	2.2
Maconde		100,000	1.3
Nguni	Chipeta	35,000	0.4
	Atjumba		
	Amba		
	Zwagendaba		
	Ngwana		
	Shoshangane		

RELIGIONS

The great majority of Mozambicans—estimated at 65.6%—adhere to traditional African religions. Perhaps 20% are Roman Catholics and 5% are Protestants. Muslims, found chiefly along the northern littoral, account for the balance.

Roman Catholicism was the dominant religion of Mozambique during Portuguese rule. Catholic missionary efforts began with the arrival of the Jesuits in 1560 and the Dominicans in 1577. Catholics are widely distributed among the population, while Protestants are mainly in the South. The Niassa Nguni are perhaps the most completely Christianized of all tribes.

The Constitution of 1975 established a secular state. The FRELIMO leadership is explicitly atheist and particularly hostile to the Catholic Church. Most foreign-born priests and missionaries were expelled in 1976.

Although the Constitution of 1975 guaranteed freedom of religion, in the past the government placed restrictions on the activities of religious groups. It reserved the right to decide whether individual church buildings could operate and whether individual clergy could visit outlying areas. It also nationalized church schools and hospitals. Over the past few years, however, there was an improvement in church/state relations. Organized religions operated with relative freedom, and some churches were effective in social work activities and in acting as channels for distribution of emergency food donations to the poorest regions of the country. Pastoral letters issued in 1985 by the Catholic bishops that were critical of governmental policies circulated widely without reprisals by the authorities. Muslims were allowed to establish a national organization, to resume religious training and to reopen mosques. Attendance at religious rites was thought generally to be on the rise, and party members were no longer specifically prohibited from membership in a church or mosque. Critical comments by the government regarding religious beliefs were almost always general in nature and not directed against specific individuals or churches. Membership in a religious group did not appear to affect, either favorably or unfavorably, a person's secular standing.

HISTORICAL BACKGROUND

Mozambique was one of the first African territories to be colonized by a Western power and among the last to gain independence. The earliest Portuguese settlements were established in the 16th century. The territory was ruled as part of Goa, a Portuguese territory in India, until 1752, when it was given its own administration. After losing Brazil in 1822 Portugal made a conscientious effort to build up its African territories. Mozambique was given a governor general in place of a captain general. The government also took over the task of providing formal education for the indigenes. By 1890 the borders of the colony were officially demarcated. At the end of the 19th century, when the Portuguese Treasury was overburdened by the administrative costs of maintaining its African colonies, the territories were farmed out to chartered companies that were granted virtual monopoly rights and even some measure of sovereignty. The three largest of these companies were the Zambezia Company, the Mozambique Company and the Nyassa Company. The two latter companies came under the control of the British and Germans, respectively, thus effectively reducing Portuguese influence in the region. Portugal's general apathy about its African possessions and the rapacity of the private companies combined to inspire at least 16 African revolts between 1890 and 1905, including the Zambezi rebellion of 1917.

The next landmark in Portuguese rule was the rise of Antonio Salazar as finance minister from 1928 to 1932 and as dictator from 1932. Salazar introduced a radical change in Portugal's approach to its colonies. He broke up the special commercial interests and passed the Colonial Act of 1930, under which the colony was to be administered by a governor general. Salazar envisioned a romantic and spiritual unity of Portugal and its African possessions. He encouraged Portuguese to emigrate to Mozambique and Africans to identify themselves as Portuguese. The government also expanded the economic base of Mozambique through the development of agriculture, industry and transportation. Beginning in 1927, Africans who were able to speak Portuguese, who earned incomes from occupations in commerce or industry and who became "civilized" by accepting Portuguese values and standards were legally defined as *assimilados* and freed from the humiliating restrictions imposed on other Africans, known as *indígenas*. Throughout the 1950s and 1960s Portugal made a number of cosmetic changes in colonial administration in response to external pressures. In 1951 Mozambique became an overseas province; in 1955 the Organic Law gave African areas their own local councils. The forced cultivation of commercial crops was ended; expenditures on education, health and welfare were increased; and the legal distinction between *assimilados* and *indígenas* was abolished.

However, these efforts were too little and too late. In 1962 three African resistance groups coalesced to form the Frente de Libertação de Moçambique (FRELIMO). Under the leadership of Dr. Eduardo Mondlane, FRELIMO initiated armed resistance to Portuguese rule beginning in 1964, and by 1966 much of the North was under FRELIMO control. In 1969 Mondlane was assassinated, and after a brief power struggle Samora Machel succeeded him as FRELIMO leader. FRELIMO then adopted a more radical, prosocialist ideology. A coup in Portugal in 1974 made possible negotiations between FRELIMO and the new Portuguese government. These led to a period of transitional government until full independence in 1975.

Machel assumed the presidency of the independent "people's republic." Elections were held from September to December 1977 for FRELIMO-sponsored candidates to local, district, provincial and national assemblies, and at its third congress FRELIMO declared itself a Marxist-Leninist party, with its goals being social, economic and political transformation of the country.

Following independence there was a mass exodus of some 235,000 of the 250,000 resident Portuguese settlers. The Portuguese had been the educated, professional and skilled segment of the population. In abandoning what they saw as their territory they angrily destroyed many buildings and much machinery. The economy has not completely recovered from this devastating loss of property and trained manpower.

Government policymakers envisioned nationalization of abandoned enterprises but generally were hindered in achieving their goals due to lack of experienced personnel. Collective farms were formed, but without skilled management there was a precipitous decline in agricultural production. Floods in 1977 and drought during the early 1980s further lowered agricultural production.

Perhaps the most significant hindrance to Mozambican development, however, was the presence of the subversive guerrilla force Movimento Nacional de Resistência de Moçambique (Mozambican National Resistance, MNR) (RENAMO). RENAMO was founded in

1976 and came into being through the workings of the Rhodesian Central Intelligence Organization. Its aim was to harass FRELIMO and to monitor Zimbabwean guerrilla forces within Mozambique. Following Zimbabwe's independence in 1980, RENAMO activities were fostered by South Africa. RENAMO was in armed conflict with the Mozambican government, disrupting and sabotaging government initiatives. While South Africa actively supported RENAMO, Mozambique harbored South African opposition forces of the African National Congress (ANC). In March 1984 Mozambique and South Africa signed the Nkomati Accord. Each government agreed to prevent opposition forces from attacking the other from bases located in the other's territory. When in 1985 the terms of the agreement appeared not to be met by South Africa, Mozambique called on foreign powers for increased military assistance.

The Council of Ministers was divided into three sections in March 1986 to strengthen FRELIMO's control of the country. The post of prime minister was created in July and assumed by Mario Machungo, who had been minister of planning. Legislative elections that were to have been held in 1982 but that were postponed in October because of security problems finally began in 1986. However, they were delayed by internal conflict, and they were again postponed, in October, due to President Machel's death in an airplane crash. In November 1986 Joaquim Chissano, who had been minister of foreign affairs and who was a longtime associate of Machel, was appointed president by the Central Committee of FRELIMO. Elections were resumed, but unlike the 1977 election, voters had a choice of candidates. A total of 299 FRELIMO candidates were nominated for the 250 legislative seats. However, when elections were completed in December, all government and party leaders had been reelected. Reshuffling of the Council of Ministers took place in January 1987 and again in May 1988 and January 1989. Bowing to political pressure, FRELIMO adopted a new platform in December 1989 that abandoned Marxism-Leninism as the party's official ideology and expressed support for a free-market economy. In December 1990 representatives of the Mozambican government and RENAMO signed a partial cease-fire, the first ever in their 14-year-old civil war. One month earlier, the Mozambique legislature had adopted a new Constitution designed to establish a Western-style democracy. Under the new Constitution, the country's name was changed from the People's Republic of Mozambique to the Republic of Mozambique. Multiparty elections were scheduled to take place some time in 1991.

GOVERNMENT LIST
(July/August 1991)

President	Chissano, Joaquím Alberto
Prime Minister	Machungo, Mário de Graça
Minister of Agriculture	Zandamela, Alexandre Jose
Minister of Construction & Water	Salomao, Jo a Mario
Minister of Cooperation	Veloso, Jacinto
Minister of Culture	Catupa, Jose Mateus Muaria
Minister of Defense	Chipande, Alberto, *Gen.*
Minister of Education	Dos Muchangos, Aniceto
Minister of Finance	Osman, Abdul Magid
Minister of Foreign Affairs	Mocumbi, Pascoal Manuel
Minister of Health	Simao, Leonardo
Minister of Industry & Power	Mutemba, Octavio
Minister of Information	Maguni, Rafael
Minister of Interior	Antonio, Manuel Jorge
Minister of Justice	Dauto, Ossumane Ali
Minister of Labor	Hunguana, Teodato
Minister of Mineral Resources	Kachamilla, John
Minister of Security	Matsinhe, Mariano, *Maj. Gen.*
Minister of Trade	Tembe, Daniel Filipe Gabriel
Minister of Transport & Telecommunications	Guebuza, Armando, *Lt. Gen.*
Minister in the Presidency	Gundana, Feliciano
Minister in the Presidency for State Administration	Mazula, Aguiar
Governor, Central Bank	Comiche, Eneas

CONSTITUTION & GOVERNMENT

The Mozambique legislature in November 1990 adopted a new Constitution designed to establish a Western-style democracy. The document contains a bill of rights that affirms such rights as habeas corpus, freedom of speech and of the press as well as the right to strike. However, many of these rights can be restricted depending on circumstances. Citizens have the right to form political parties, although the legislature may enact laws discouraging splinter groups. The Constitution promises strict separation of the executive, judicial and legislative branches.

Under the new Constitution executive power is vested in a president who is directly elected for a five-year term. There are no limits on reelection. The president heads the military forces and has the power to declare war. With the support of a legislative majority, he can declare martial law. He has the exclusive power to negotiate internationally and appoints all officers of the national government, except those in Congress, with the advice and consent of the Senate.

Legislative power is vested in a bicameral Congress. Members of the lower house serve five-year terms; senators eight year terms. The judiciary is headed by a Supreme Court whose members are appointed for life by the president on the advice of the Senate.

The new Constitution effectively ended 15 years of one-party rule by FRELIMO. Free, multiparty elections were scheduled to take place at some time in 1991.

FREEDOM & HUMAN RIGHTS

Before 1991, Mozambique was a one-party Marxist-Leninist state controlled by FRELIMO. As in other Marxist-Leninist states, the citizens were directed to serve the party and the state, and there were no freedoms outside of party activities. In most rural areas "people's courts" (with party members as judges) tried persons suspected as deviants. In some cases state officials functioned as both judges and prosecutors in private trials. All legal counsel was provided by the state, the private practice of law having been abolished in 1975. Public criticism of officials, the party or its

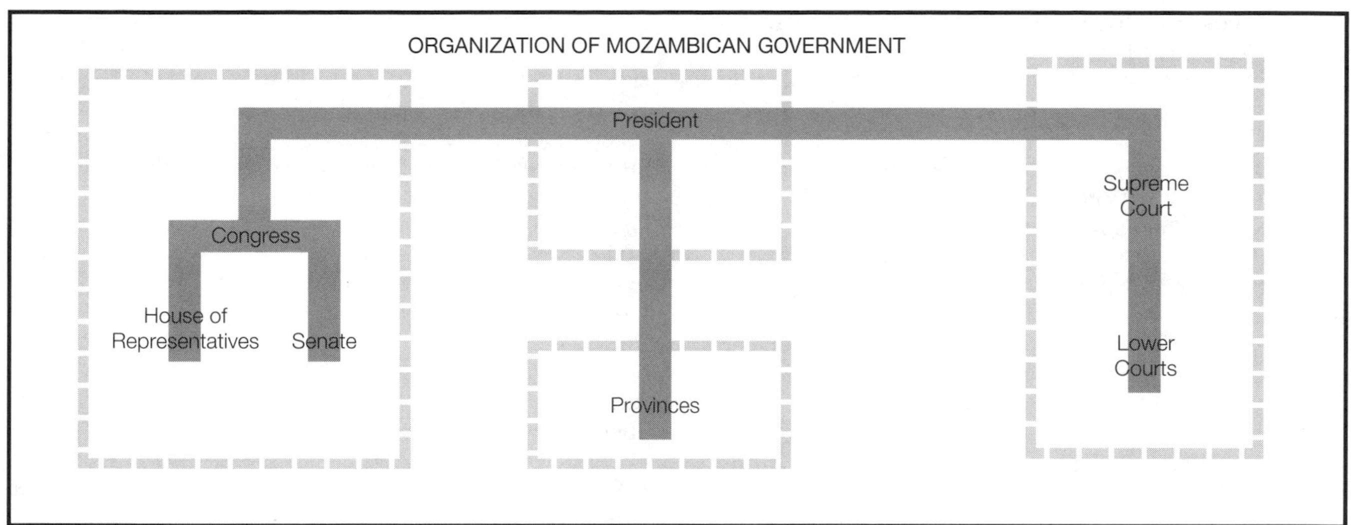

policies was almost never allowed. Persons who showed critical tendencies were sent to "reeducation" camps. Religion was tolerated as a rather inconvenient evil; party publications published long diatribes against the Catholic Church because of its association with the former Portuguese rulers. Priests were expelled from the country; church buildings were closed in the more populous areas; the clergy were required to seek permission to publish tracts or travel outside their parishes; and churches were not permitted to operate schools, hospitals or social centers. Although there was freedom of travel within the country, foreign travel was discouraged. Opposition political movements were not permitted at any level, although there were spirited contests for elective office within the party itself. Trade unions were not allowed to function, and the rights to strike, organize freely and bargain collectively were not recognized.

Torture was widely practiced in Mozambique. In the early years of independence, according to numerous reports, prisoners at remote government-organized "reeducation camps" were brutally bound, beaten and often killed. These camps were used to intern political prisoners and "antisocial elements." Starting in 1979, however, the government promulgated laws that established a formal judicial system in Mozambique, and in 1981 President Machel declared that henceforth no one would be sent to a reeducation camp without due process. In the same year the president also launched an "offensive for legality," and in the following months a number of security and defense force members were fired for abusing prisoners. Amnesty International, in its report on torture in Mozambique, characterized the campaign as the government's "most important effort to end the practice of torture and to control other abuses which had come to be committed by the security and defense forces." Despite changes, including closing of some camps, reports indicated that prisoners had extremely Spartan living conditions. The situation with regard to torture in 1985 represented a significant improvement in comparison with previous years, but reports continued to be received alleging capricious and cruel treatment by some members of the security and defense forces.

A few of the most blatant abuses were corrected as some people were allowed back to their former dwelling places. People were not forced to belong to FRELIMO. However, the party attempted to establish local chapters in most functioning government and business organizations. There was a notable correlation of professional advancement and party membership, although it was not total.

It was widely assumed that surveillance devices were employed in local and international telecommunications systems. There also were instances of tampering with mail, especially international mail.

Prisoners charged with crimes against the state were tried by the Revolutionary Military Tribunal. These trials were held in camera, and there was no appeal. However, this court apparently had not been called into session since 1983. The Constitution of 1990 guarantees freedom of religion as well as freedom of speech and press, although legal restraints are permitted on speech in wartime or "comparable national security emergencies." Political parties are permitted, but laws can be passed discouraging splinter parties. The Constitution bans security or secret police forces and guarantees due process. Torture and other cruel punishments are prohibited, although the death penalty for "grave crimes" is permitted.

CIVIL SERVICE

No current information is available on the Mozambican civil service.

LOCAL GOVERNMENT

For purposes of local government, Mozambique is divided into 10 provinces: the city of Maputo, Gaza, Inhambane, Manica, Sofala, Tete, Zambézia, Nampula, Cabo Delgado and Niassa. The Constitution of 1990 provides directly elected local assemblies in each province.

Provinces are divided into districts (formerly *concelhos*), each headed by a district administrator.

FOREIGN POLICY

Before 1991, foreign relations were an extension of FRELIMO's revolutionary ideology and were conceived in Marxist terms as a struggle against imperialism and colonialism.

Relations with South Africa involved complicated, long-established economic ties inherited by the FRELIMO regime. These included transportation links from the interior to Mozambique's ports; Mozambican migrant labor in South Africa's gold mines; and the great hydroelectric complex at the Cabora Bassa Dam on the Zambei, financed by South Africa in return for a contract for 80% of its electrical power output. Thus, while formal relations with South Africa were suspended on independence in 1975, complete disengagement was viewed as economically unrealistic, and a South African trade mission was permitted to remain in Maputo. In fact, South African technicians performed a critical function in Mozambique's economy. However, a full break with South Africa was part of FRELIMO's long-range plans.

In March 1984 the government of Mozambique and the South African government signed the Nkomati Accord, by which each side agreed not to let its territory be used as a staging area for insurgent attacks on the other. Later in 1984, negotiations began under the auspices of the South African government to attempt to achieve a cease-fire in Mozambique. In October 1986 South Africa claimed that because of increased ANC guerrilla activities in the Mozambican border region it was banning recruitment of Mozambican miners and repatriating 60,000 Mozambicans employed in South African mines. However, in Janaury 1987 South African backed down and allowed 30,000 Mozambicans to continue working in its mines.

Economic relations with Zimbabwe were close because Mozambique provided a haven for the Zimbabwe People's Army during the struggle against white rule in Rhodesia.

Mozambique's closest relations were with Tanzania, which provided FRELIMO not only with a haven during the struggle for independence but also with training bases, supply routes and men and matériel. Although the two countries differed in ideological orientation, there were efforts to link them closely. In 1975 a joint committee was set up to coordinate economic development efforts and also to integrate their diplomatic personnel. This was followed in 1976 with a loose joint defense organization that also included Zambia, Angola and Botswana. Similarly, relations with Zambia were warm. On the other hand, President Kamuzu Banda of Malawi was the object of disfavor for his open pro-Portuguese and pro-Western stance.

Mozambique maintained special relations with the other two Portuguese-speaking countries in Africa, Angola and Guinea-Bissau, which were linked by a common colonial experience. President Agostinho Neto of Angola was particularly admired as a true Marxist-Leninist and an ideological comrade. All three countries belonged to the Congress of Nationalist Organizations of the Portuguese Colonies, founded in 1961.

Relations with Portugal steadily deteriorated after independence. The underlying animosity was generated by remembered injustices of colonial rule, but there were a number of specific issues, such as responsibility for colonial external debts, expropriation of Portuguese-owned properties, and the jailing and expulsion of Portuguese nationals. There also was an ideological gap between the socialist government of Portugal and the Marxist-Leninist FRELIMO.

Links with Communnist countries, described as "natural allies" in the Constitution of 1975, were strengthened over the years. Both Cuba and the Soviet Union expanded their scale of assistance, and a treaty of friendship and cooperation was signed with the Soviet Union in 1977. Nevertheless, there was speculation that FRELIMO was disillusioned with the high price and low quality of Soviet aid and with attempts to turn Mozambique against China. Among Western nations only Sweden was well regarded. In the mid-1980s relations between the United States and Mozambique improved. At the same time Mozambique also strengthened its ties to the United Kingdom and other members of the European Community. In 1987 Mozambique was given observer status at a meeting of Commonwealth heads of state. Mozambique and the United States were parties to a treaty covering agricultural commodities.

PARLIAMENT

Under the Constitution of 1990, legislative power is vested in a bicameral Congress consisting of a Senate and a House of Representatives. Members of the House are directly elected for five-year terms. Two senators are elected from each province for eight-year terms. Free multiparty elections were scheduled to take place during 1991.

POLITICAL PARTIES

Before 1991, the sole legal party was the Frente de Libertação de Moçambique (FRELIMO), a Marxist-Leninist party formed in 1962 through the merger of three existing nationalist parties: the União Democrática Nacional de Moçambique, the Mozambique African Nationalist Union and the União Africana de Moçambique Independente.

FRELIMO's ideology was uncomprisingly Marxist-Leninist. This ideology was defined in 1977 at the Third National Congress of the party, which also restricted membership to those described as "the vanguard of the proletariat." The supreme organ of the party was the National Congress, which was required to meet every four years. Between meetings of the Congress the party was directed by the Central Committee, whose membership was increased in 1983 to 130 members. The Central Committee met infrequently. Most of its duties were carried out by two smaller bodies: political-military committees at the provincial level and the 10-member Political Bureau at the national level.

The Political Bureau was the true center of political power in the country.

Both during the independence struggle and after independence, FRELIMO has had to deal with a number of rival parties, collectively referred to by FRELIMO as phantom parties. Before independence, the most serious threat came from the Partido de Coligação Nacional (PCN), led by the Rev. Uria Simango. Organized settler opposition took shape in the Frente Independente de Continuidade Ocidental (FICO, an acronym that means "I stay" in Portuguese). The most serious postindependence threat came from the Frente de Unidade Democratica de Moçambique (FUMO), led by a black socialist, Domingos Arouca. In 1976 FUMO set up a government-in-exile and in 1977 claimed control of northern Cabo Delgado Province.

Since the early 1980s the major guerrilla movement was Mozambique National Resistance Movement (Movimento Nacional de Resistência de Moçambique, RENAMO). Also known as the André Group, after its late founder, André Matade Matsangai, RENAMO operates from bases in the country's western mountains, near the Zimbabwean border.

In late 1987 RENAMO activity intensified. Starvation and food shortages affected 6 million people, and 3 million people were displaced. Outside major cities security was minimal and health and educational facilities virtually nonexistent. In April 1988 the U.S. State Department declared RENAMO responsible for a "holocaust" resulting in the deaths of over 100,000 civilians in the two previous years. International donors volunteered $270 million in emergency aid when urged by the United Nations. The Constitution of 1990 provides for the existence of political parties, including RENAMO. In December 1990, the Mozambique government and RENAMO signed a partial cease-fire.

ECONOMY

Mozambique is one of the lower-middle-income countries of the world and also is one of the 45 countries most seriously affected by adverse economic conditions during the 1980s.

Mozambique has failed to achieve the objective of "building of an independent economy" set forth in its Constitution. The combination of drought, guerrilla insurgency and underdevelopment of known mineral resources has hindered economic progress.

The economy is predominantly agricultural and employs about 84% of the population mostly in subsistence farming. Major cash crops include cashew nuts, coffee, tea, sugarcane, cotton and sisal. The main subsistence crop is cassava. Production of both cash export crops and domestic food crops is currently below 1974 levels, resulting in overwhelming dependence on imported food.

The manufacturing sector contributes 26% to the GDP. Prior to independence, manufacturing was dominated by the white population and was limited to agricultural-processing industries serving local white needs. Sugar refining, cashew- and wheat-processing are current agricultural industries. During the 1980s textile production and brewing grew in importance. Manufacture of cement, fertilizers and agricultural implements are other industries. During the 1980–86 period industrial output declined, but it recovered somewhat in 1986 and rose by approximately 20% in 1987. Frequent sabotage of power lines by RENAMO has severely hindered further industrial development in the country.

Substantial mineral deposits of coal, diamonds and bauxite are known to exist in the country, although only coal is currently being exploited. Internal unrest and variations in world mineral prices have acted to disrupt the mining sector seriously. Other known mineral resources include high-grade iron ore deposits, copper, titanium, tantalite, graphite, gold, emeralds and semiprecious stones.

The country's negative trade balance has been an ongoing economic problem and is exacerbated by massive defense spending (projected to be as high as 40% of expenditures in the 1989 budget). Guerrilla insurgency and troublesome weather have reduced export volumes. The 1986 order by the South African government forcing the repatriation of Mozambican miners further reduced earnings from foreign exchange. The situation improved somewhat when South Africa announced in January 1987 that 30,000 miners were al-

PRINCIPAL ECONOMIC INDICATORS

Gross National Product (U.S. $ billions): 1,193 (1989)
GNP per capita (U.S. $): 80 (1989)
GNP average annual growth rate (%, 1980–89): −3.5
GNP per capita average annual growth rate (%, 1987–89): −3.0
Average annual rate of inflation (%, 1980–87): 33.6
Average annual growth rate (%), 1980–88
- General government consumption: −4.6 (latest)
- Private consumption: −1.0 (latest)
- Gross domestic investment: −6.6 (latest)

GROSS DOMESTIC PRODUCT

GDP nominal (M. billions): 88.5 (1986)
Average annual growth rate of GDP (%, 1980–88): −2.8
GDP by type of expenditure (%), 1986
- Consumption
  - Private: 84
  - Government: 21
- Gross domestic investment: 12
- Gross domestic saving: −15 (1988)
- Foreign trade
  - Exports: 5
  - Imports: −16

Sectoral origin of GDP (%), 1986
- Primary
  - Agriculture: 57 (1988)
- Secondary
  - Manufacturing, mining: 26
  - Construction: 11
- Tertiary
  - Transportation & communications: 8
  - Trade, finance, other services, government: 10

Average annual sectoral growth rates (%, 1980–88)
- Agriculture: −0.8 (latest)
- Industry: −7.1 (latest)
- Services: −3.1 (latest)

lowed to remain, and in late 1988 restrictions on recruitment of Mozambican miners were lifted.

Mozambique suffers from a massive external debt, which grew considerably between 1983 and 1988 despite rescheduling of repayment and arrears in 1984 and 1987. Debt service payments in 1988 amounted to approximately 60% of the country's exports of goods and services. After a meeting in Paris organized by the World Bank in November 1989, nearly $1.2 billion in aid was offered to Mozambique in the form of debt relief and grants and loans to finance imports.

FINANCIAL INDICATORS

External debt, 1988
- Total (U.S. $ millions): 4,406
- Debt service (long-term) total (U.S. $ millions): 20
  - Repayment
    - Principal (%): 40.0
    - Interest (%): 60.0
- Debt service ratio: (%) 7.7
- Debt service as % of exports: 2.0 (1988)
- Receipt of workers' remittances (U.S. $ millions): 33 (1987 est.)

PUBLIC FINANCE

The Mozambican fiscal year is the calendar year.

Mozambique's fiscal outlook has rapidly deteriorated over the past decade. Direct and indirect taxes, which account for the major sources of revenue, have declined considerably since 1981 and in 1987 were estimated at $122 million. Meanwhile, expenditures have continued to increase and in 1987 were estimated at $321 million, approximately three times revenues. Government consumption was 18% of the GDP in 1987.

The total outstanding debt is massive; between 1983 and 1988, it rose from $583 million to $4.4 billion.

Mozambique's budget priorities reflect the government's ideological perspectives and its geopolitical/military preoccupations.

During 1970–88 Mozambique received $887 million in aid from Communist countries and $282 million from the United States. Other Western nations committed $3.1 billion during 1970–87. OPEC bilateral aid totalled $37 million from 1979 to 1989.

GROWTH PROFILE
(Annual Growth Rates, %)

Projected population (1988–2000): 3.1
Projected crude birth rate (/1,000) 1990–95: 43.7
Projected death rate (/1,000) 1990–95: 16.9
Urban population (1980–88): 11.0
GNP (1980–88): −3.5
GNP per capita (1986–88): −5.9
GDP (1980–87): −2.8
Inflation (1980–88): 33.6
Agriculture (1980–88): −0.8
Industry (1980–88): −7.1
Services (1980–88): −3.1
Energy production (1980–88): −39.0
Energy consumption (1980–89): 2.0
General government consumption (1980–87): −4.6 (latest)
Private consumption (1980–88): −1.0 (latest)
Gross domestic investment (1980–88): −6.6 (latest)

FOREIGN AID, 1989

Total foreign aid (U.S. $ millions): 1,157.8
- Bilateral: 721.4
- Multilateral: 436.4

CURRENCY & BANKING

The Mozambican unit of currency is the metical (plural: meticais), divided into 100 centavos. Coins are issued in denominations of 10, 20 and 50 centavos and 1, 2½, 5, 10 and 20 meticais; notes are issued in denominations of 50, 100, 500 and 1,000 meticais. One thousand meticais make one conto. The metical was introduced in 1980, replacing the former escudo at par.

In 1988 the dollar exchange rate of the Mozambique metical was $1 = M626.25. The sterling exchange rate on this basis was £1 = M1,158.88.

In 1975 the government nationalized the Portuguese National Overseas Bank and reconstituted it as the Bank of Mozambique. The Bank of Mozambique, with 36 branches throughout the country, functions as the central bank and the bank of issue. The governor of the central bank is a member of the cabinet. All private domestic and foreign banks were nationalized in 1978 following government charges of economic sabotage against them. The principal source of development finance is the Banco de Fomento Nacional, with paid-up capital of M2.393.2 billion and deposits of M6.913 billion.

AGRICULTURE

Of the total land area of 78,303,000 ha. (193,486,000 ac.), 60% is classified as agricultural land, or 5.2 ha. (13 ac.) per capita; however, only 17.6% is farmed. Agricultural products account for almost 80% of export earnings.

At the time of independence only 6.4% of the land area was under actual cultivation. About 1% of the farm population was employed on large-scale mechanized farms occupying 2,487,554 ha. (6,146,746 ac.) divided into 4,626 farming units and representing about 50% of all farmlands. These farmers were nearly all white expatriates growing cash crops. Subsistence farmers, constituting 99% of the population, cultivated 2,493,504 ha. (6,161,144 ac.), divided into 1,647,702 family plots.

After independence, the new government proclaimed that all land belonged to the state and encouraged peasants to form collectives. Farms abandoned by former Portuguese settlers were the first to be formed into such collectives. By 1979 the government controlled 130,000 ha. (325,000 ac.) of agricultural land. Despite the emphasis on food production, Mozambique has had to import foodstuffs.

The prevalent form of cultivation is the slash-and-burn system, in which fields are cleared, the trees felled and burned, and their ashes scattered before planting. Such fields are cultivated for a few years and then left fallow. Cultivation and harvesting are traditionally women's jobs. Mechanization has been introduced on the large estates. The main irrigation projects are the Limpopo Basin Development Program, the Cabora Bassa Project and the Massingire Dam.

A prolonged and severe drought during 1981–84 compounded by floods and cyclones in 1984 led to a decline in agricultural production estimated at 70% to 80%. The crops most affected were cassava, corn, cashew nuts and sugar. Tea remained relatively stable. Mozambique received considerable food aid during the drought, including 153,000 tons in 1981, 235,000 tons in 1982 and 227,000 tons in 1983.

Nearly 70% of Mozambique lies within the tsetse zone, especially areas north of the Save River. Cattle are raised mainly south of the Save in the districts of Maputo, Gaza, Inhambane and the Angonia Highlands north of the river. Goats, sheep and swine are not affected by the tsetse fly and therefore are raised on farms throughout the country. Among tribes such as the Tsonga and the Nguni, the religious and social significance of cattle exceed their economic value.

The major timber-producing area is in the hinterland of Sofala, where commercial exploitation is confined to a few hardwoods. Most of the former forestry concessions were terminated and taken over by the state.

Mozambique's fishing potential includes the longest coastline along the Indian Ocean among African states and a portion of Lake Malawi. Nevertheless, fishing is a neglected industry. Shortly after independence the government nationalized two of the largest fishing companies and began organizing fishery cooperatives.

AGRICULTURAL INDICATORS, 1973

Agriculture's share of GDP (%): 64 (1989)
Average annual growth rate (%, 1980–88): 0.8
Value added in agriculture (U.S. $ millions): 679 (1988)
Cereal imports (000 metric tons): 527 (1988)
Index of Agricultural Production (1979–81 = 100): 100 (1986)
Index of Food Production (1979–81 = 100): 101 (1986)
Index of Food Production per Capita (1979–81 = 100): 83 (1986–88)
Number of tractors: 5,750 (1986)
Total fertilizer consumption: 3.8 (000 metric tons) (1985–86)
Fertilizer consumption (g./ha., hundreds): 21 (1987–88)
Number of farms (000): 1,605
Average size of holding, ha. (ac.): 3.1 (7.7)
Size class (%)
  Below 1 ha. (below 2.47 ac.): } 89.7
  1–5 ha. (2.47–12.35 ac.): }
  5–10 ha. (12.35–24.7 ac.): }
  10–20 ha. (24.7–49.4 ac.): } 10.0
  20–50 ha. (49.4–123.5 ac.): }
  50–200 ha. (123.5–494 ac.): } 0.3
  Over 200 ha. (over 494 ac.): }
Farms as % of total land area: 17.8
Land use (%):
  Permanent crops, temporary crops: 44.9
  Fallow: 55.1
  Meadows & pastures: 45.0
Yields, kg./ha. 1989
  Grains: 642
  Roots & tubers: 5,919
  Legumes: 480 (496)
  Fruits (000 metric tons): 370
  Vegetables (000 metric tons): 199
  Milk, kg.(lb.)/animal: 170
Livestock (000) 1989
  Cattle: 1,370
  Sheep: 120
  Pigs: 165
Forestry, 1988
  Production of roundwood, 000 cu. m.: 16,002
    of which industrial roundwood (%): 6.1
  Value of exports (U.S. $ 000): 3,118
Fishing, 1986
  Total catch (000 metric tons): 33.5
    of which marine (%): 99.3
  Value of exports (U.S. $ 000): 65,000

MANUFACTURING

On the eve of independence there were nearly 4,000 manufacturing establishments in the country, employing 18% of the work force and generating 8.5% of the GDP. The near-anarchy that followed independence reduced this sector to confusion. Many factories were damaged or destroyed during the final fighting; many industrialists fled the country, abandoning the factories; some closed down because there was no market for their goods after the departure of the Portuguese. By 1976 about 50 abandoned plants had been nationalized and their management turned over to workers' committees. As production declined in the absence of managerial skill, the government invited Soviet-bloc technicians to assist it, but these did not speak Portuguese and were unfamiliar with African conditions.

Manufacturing activity is concentrated in Maputo, which accounts for 47% of industrial production, and to a lesser extent in Beira, Nampula and Chimoio. Food processing accounts for one-fifth of output by value; other important subsectors are beverages, textiles, chemicals, and bicycle and automotive assembly.

Decree Law 18/77 of April 1977, the centerpiece of Mozambique's investment policy, guarantees investors the rights of profit repatriation and protection from nationalization and outlines the terms of foreign participation. Joint ventures are preferred, and possession of or access to financing is a prime consideration.

During 1984 Mozambique took further steps to revitalize the economy. It was hoped that new laws relating to foreign exchange and investment, introduced in May and September, would act as incentives to increased industrial production and greater foreign investment. These measures were accompanied by increasingly close economic links with the West. Follow-

MANUFACTURING INDICATORS, 1970

Labor force in manufacturing (%): 6.1 (1980)
  Food and agriculture (%): 51
  Textiles (%): 13
  Machinery (%): 5
  Chemicals (%): 3
Total earnings as % of value added: 29

ing the signing of the Nkomati Accord in March 1984 the United States announced in June that its congressional ban on direct bilateral aid to Mozambique had been lifted. In July Mozambique signed an agreement with the U.S. Overseas Private Investment Corporation, providing for bilateral investment guarantees to U.S. investors, and in September the United States approved an $8 million aid program for Mozambique.

MINING

Coal, bauxite and diamonds are the only mineral resources currently being exploited, and internal unrest has prevented their being fully developed. Variations of world mineral prices during the 1980s also adversely affected the mining sector, driving down export revenues from M200 million in 1981 to M10 million in 1986. Reserves of coal in the Tete region are estimated at 1 billion tons; however, security and technical problems have resulted in a production output at Moatize in Tete Province of 40,000 metric tons, compared to a capacity of 600,000 metric tons. Other important mineral reserves include high-grade iron ore deposits, copper, titanium, tantalite, graphite, gold, emeralds and semiprecious stones.

Reserves of 32 billion cu. m. (1.13 trillion cu. ft.) of natural gas were discovered during the 1960s, but they have not yet been developed. Proved reserves in 1988 were 62 billion cu. m. (2.19 trillion cu. ft.).

ENERGY

Energy imports account for approximately one-quarter of all merchandise imports. There is no production of crude petroleum, but a number of companies are engaged in both offshore and onshore exploration. A refinery at Maputo handles 17,000 bl. per day. Mozambique's electrical needs were met by the generation of hydroelectric power at Cahora Bassa Dam. Surplus power was sold to South Africa under an agreement with South Africa and Portugal (which owns the dam) signed in 1984. However, sabotage subsequently halted power supply at that facility.

ENERGY INDICATORS

Average annual energy production growth rate (%, 1980–88): −39.0
Energy consumption per capita (000 kg. oil equivalent): 86 (1988)
Average annual growth rate of energy consumption (%, 1980–88): 2.0
Electricity, 1986
  Installed capacity (million kw.): 2.358
  Production (million kw.-hr.): 475
    % fossil fuel: 89.5
    % hydro: 10.5
    % nuclear: 0.0
  Consumption per capita (kw.-hr.): 54
Natural gas
  Proved reserves (billion cu. m.): 65 (1990)
Coal
  Reserves (million metric tons): 240 (latest)
  Production (metric tons): 45,000
  Consumption (metric tons): 65,000

LABOR

The number of Mozambican workers in South Africa is conservatively estimated at 45,000, down from a pre-independence peak of 118,000. However, after an improvement in relations between the two countries during 1984, South Africa agreed to allow a further 8,000 Mozambican miners to work in South Africa in 1985. These workers earn a fixed income of £270 annually per person. Because of the beneficial impact of these workers' remittances on the economy, the FRELIMO regime is unwilling to terminate the arrangement. Work contracts are governed by the so-called Mozambique Convention and are limited to a period of 18 months, although subsequent contracts may be signed after a short waiting period. There also is a fairly large number of South African technicians working in Mozambique, particularly in the port complex at Maputo.

Wages and working conditions are regulated by law. The unemployment rate in 1974 was estimated at 2.1%, but it is believed to have increased dramatically since independence.

In June 1983 the government introduced "Operation Production," comprising measures to expel an estimated 100,000 unemployed people from the cities and to resettle them in rural areas to work on agricultural programs. The program was ended in 1984.

Labor unions, known as syndicates, are organized for every sector. In 1983 the government established the Mozambique Workers' Organization, intended to function as a national labor union that remains affiliated to the FRELIMO ruling party. However, an organized union movement has yet to develop, and labor has little influence on economic policy or politics. There are occasional exchanges of delegations in the labor field with other countries, especially with those of Eastern Europe. Existing labor law is generally very favorable to the employee, but in practice it is difficult to enforce because of the fragility of the institutions associated with labor. The Mozambique Workers' Organization is a member of the continentwide, Ghana-based Organization of African Trade Union Unity.

LABOR INDICATORS, 1980

Total economically active population (000): 5,671
  % working-age population (15–64): 87.3
  % female: 52.4
Activity rate (%)
  Total: 48.6
  Male: 47.6
  Female: 49.5
Employment status (%) 1970
  Employers & self-employed: 44.4
  Employees: 40.0
  Unpaid family workers: 14.5
  Other: 1.1
Sectoral employment (%)
  Agriculture, forestry, fishing: 83.8
  Construction: 0.7
  Manufacturing; mining, quarrying, public utilities: 6.1
  Trade, hotels, restaurants: 2.0
  Transportation & communications: 1.4
  Finance, real estate, services: 4.3
Labor under 20 years (%): 4.0 (1980)

FOREIGN TRADE INDICATORS, 1988		
Exports (U.S. $ millions): 100		
Imports (U.S. $ millions): 764		
Balance of trade (U.S. $ millions): −664		
Direction of Trade (%), 1984		
	Imports	Exports
European Community	32.1	26.9
United States	5.8	14.6
U.S.S.R. & Eastern European economies	25.7	15.4
Japan	3.2	11.9
Composition of Trade (%), 1984		
	Imports	Exports
Food and agricultural raw materials	25.0	79.3
Fuels and other energy	18.7	6.3
Mineral ores and concentrates		1.4
Manufactured goods	56.4	13.0
of which chemicals	4.6	0.0
of which machinery	17.3	0.0

FOREIGN COMMERCE

The foreign commerce of Mozambique consisted in 1988 of exports of $100 million and imports of $764 million, meaning that Mozambique's already unfavorable trade balance had worsened during the period 1984–88.

Food is the major import, accounting for more than one-fourth of total imports, followed by capital equipment, machinery and spare parts, crude petroleum and derivatives, chemicals and metals. Major import sources are the United States, the U.S.S.R., South Africa, Italy, France and Portugal.

Shrimp is the major export commodity and represents nearly half of Mozambique's export revenues. Cashews and sugar are the other major exports, followed by petroleum products, citrus fruits and copra. Major export destinations are Japan, the United States, Spain, Germany and Portugal.

TRANSPORTATION & COMMUNICATIONS

Although highly developed, Mozambique's transportation system has been severely disrupted by guerrilla attacks and sabotage. Rail and road links along with a petroleum pipeline form the "Beira Corridor" and provide an important outlet for landlocked countries of southern Africa, including Malawi, Zambia, Swaziland and especially Zimbabwe. The Southern African Development Coordination Conference (SADCC) has made development of this corridor a major priority. The Beira Corridor is seen as an alternative to trade routes through South Africa, and it was announced in May 1987 that a project to rehabilitate the corridor was to be undertaken at an estimated cost of $589 million.

All Mozambican railways are state-owned, and the five main systems form links between Mozambican ports and South Africa, Malawi and Zimbabwe.

The total length of inland waterways is 3,750 km. (2,330 mi.). The principal ports are Maputo, Beira, Nacala and Quelimane. In 1986 the government unveiled a 10-year plan to modernize and expand the port of Beira and increase its cargo-handling capacity. By 1988 rehabilitation of the port of Nacala had been completed and work on the port of Maputo had begun.

The road system consists of 26,095 km. (16,215 mi.) of roads, of which 20% are paved. The only all-weather national highway runs from Maputo to Beira.

The national airline is Linhas Aereas de Moçambique (LAM), which operates a fleet of seven aircraft serving domestic routes as well as international destinations in South Africa, Zimbabwe, Tanzania, Denmark, France, West Germany and Portugal. A second airline, Empresa Nacional de Transportes e Trabalho Nereo, schedules services to 35 destinations. Aeroporto Internacional de Maputo is the principal airport. There are 214 airports in the country, of which 171 are usable. Twenty-seven have permanent-surface runways; six have runways over 2,500 m. (8,000 ft.).

TRANSPORTATION INDICATORS

Roads (latest)
  Length, km. (mi.): 26,095 (16,215)
  Paved (%): 20
Motor vehicles (latest)
  Automobiles: 87,000
  Trucks and buses: 24,000
  Persons per vehicle: 127
Railroads (latest)
  Track, km. (mi.): 3,512 (2,182)
  Passenger-km. (passenger-mi.) (millions): 75.3 (46.8)
  Freight, ton-km. (ton-mi.) (millions): 231.8 (158.8)
Merchant marine
  Vessels: 109 (1989)
  Total deadweight tonnage (000): 27.1 (1989)
Ports (pre-1986)
  Cargo loaded (000 metric tons): 2,110
  Cargo unloaded (000 metric tons): 2,427
Air (latest)
  Km. flown (millions): 3.8 (1985)
  Passenger-km. (passenger-mi.) (millions): 156 (97)
  Freight ton-km. (freight-mi.) (millions): 3.7 (2.5)
  Mail ton-km. (mail ton-mi.) (millions): 0.9 (0.4)
  Airports with scheduled flights: 2 (1990)
Pipelines, 1989
  Refined km. (mi.): 289 (180)
Inland waterways (latest)
  Length, km. (mi.): 3,750 (2,330)

COMMUNICATION INDICATORS, 1988

Telephones
  Total (000): 63
  Persons per telephone: 238
Phone traffic (000 calls)
  Local & long distance: 84,000
  International: 2,961 (minutes)
Post office
  Number of post offices: 268
  Pieces of mail handled (000): 26,187
Telegraph
  Total traffic (000 calls): 15
  National: 2
  International: 13
Telex
  Subscriber lines: 824
Telecommunications, 1990
  4 satellite stations

DEFENSE

The defense structure is headed by the president. Before 1991, the armed forces, officially called Forças Populares da Libertação de Moçambique (FPLM), were under the control of the FRELIMO Political Committee. There were no ranks within the defense forces. A people's organization, Serviço Nacional de Segurança Popular, was established to assist the armed forces in matters relating to national security. Boats left behind by the Portuguese were used for coastal patrol work.

The total strength of the armed forces in 1989 was reported to be 36,700. Two years of military service was compulsory; however, recruitment was selective. The army served mainly as a counterinsurgency force whose goal was the defeat of RENAMO.

Army

Personnel: 35,000

Organization: 1 tank brigade; 7 infantry brigades (each 1 tank, 3 infantry, 2 motorized, 2 artillery, 1 air defense battalions); 2 independent mechanized battalions; 7 AA artillery battalions

Equipment: 290 tanks; 30 combat reconnaissance vehicles; 200 armored personnel carriers; 348 guns; 30 rocket launchers; howitzers; 325 mortars; antitank guided weapons; 300 air defense guns; 10 SAM

Navy

Personnel: 700

Units: 26 patrol craft; 3 amphibious craft

Naval bases: Maputo, Beira Nacala, Pemba, Metangula

Air Force

Personnel: 1,000

Units: 18 combat aircraft; 3 fighter squadrons; 1 helicopter squadron; 1 transportation squadron; 10 trainers

Opposition Forces: 18,000 to 20,000 guerrilla fighters with RENAMO

The leadership has placed greater emphasis on political training than on military capability. There is no evidence that the FPLM will be capable of defending the country against determined aggression by a capable enemy.

Military aid has been received from China, the Soviet Union, Cuba and Eastern Europe. The extensive range of weapons provided by these sources include Kalashnikov assault carbines, light machine guns, mortars, antitank rockets and recoilness rifles. FRELIMO combat leaders also were trained in the Soviet Union (at the Guerrilla Warfare Training School at Simferapol), China, North Korea and Cuba. In addition, nearly 800 military technicians were assigned to work with FRELIMO, including 350 from Cuba, 400 from the Soviet Union and 50 from East Germany. Arms purchases abroad since independence total $860 million.

EDUCATION

Literacy has improved considerably since independence, but it is still low: 16.6%.

Although children are required by law to attend school for seven years, only about 40% do.

Schooling lasts for nine years, divided into four years of primary school, three years of lower secondary school and two years of upper secondary school. There are approximately 8,500 primary schools and 138 secondary schools. All schools have been nationalized and secularized. Education is closely related to the needs of national development and emphasizes reading, vocational training and food production. Political indoctrination is part of the curriculum. Nearly 10% of secondary-level enrollment is in the vocational stream.

The school year runs from September to August. The language of instruction is Portuguese throughout.

EDUCATION INDICATORS, 1988

Literacy
- Total (%): 16.6
- Males (%): 20.0
- Females (%): 13.3

First level
- Schools: 3,647
- Students: 1,199,669
- Teachers: 21,410
- Student/teacher ratio: 56:0
- Net enrollment ratio: 45 (1987)

Second level
- Schools: 207
- Students: 107,080
- Teachers: 3,422
- Student/teacher ratio: 31.3
- Net enrollment ratio: 34

Vocational
- Schools: 32
- Students: 10,604
- Teachers: 968
- Student/teacher ratio: 10.9

Third level
- Institutions: 2
- Students: 2,562
- Teachers: 457
- Student/teacher ratio: 5.6
- Gross enrollment ratio: 0.2 (1987)
- Students (/100,000 pop.): 16

Foreign study
- Foreign students in national universities: 130 (1987)
- Students abroad: 648
  - of whom in
    - U.S.: 24 (1988)
    - France: 22 (1988)
    - Federal Republic of Germany: 8 (1988)
    - U.K.: 58 (1987)

GRADUATES, 1987

Total: 252
Education: 115
Medicine: 10
Engineering: 42
Agriculture, forestry, fisheries: 24

After independence, the school system suffered from the exodus of non-African teachers. Temporary replacements were brought in from Soviet bloc countries.

Higher education is provided by the Universidade Eduardo Mondlane, named after the first president of FRELIMO, who was assassinated in 1969.

LEGAL SYSTEM

The legal system is based on Portuguese civil law and African customary law. Under the 1990 Constitution, the judicial system is headed by the Supreme Court. From 1979 to 1990, two separate legal systems existed. The first was the civil/criminal system with a judicial service and a police force under the authority of the Ministry of the Interior. The second system, which was characterized in its initiating legislation as transitional, was the military-run State Security System, which incorporated the secret police, the Serviço National de Segurança Popular (SNASP, National Service of Popular Security). This latter system, established to deal with the growing armed insurgency, had jurisdiction over both political crimes against the state and economic sabotage. These two systems operated separately and were subject to separate controls.

Under the State Security System all investigations and arrests were carried out by the SNASP. The SNASP often held detainees indefinitely without formal charges. Although detainees held by SNASP were legally entitled to counsel, prisoners reportedly had been held incommunicado. Amnesty International recommended that the SNASP's power to detain persons be drastically reduced because it believed that this situation invited abuse and lead to prisoner mistreatment.

Under the civil/criminal court system, persons accused of the most serious crimes could be detained for up to 84 days without investigation. At the end of this period the police could request an additional period of up to 84 days. Trials conducted by the civil/criminal court system were public. At the local level they were often conducted in a public place in the village where the crime was allegedly committed, to encourage public attendance and participation. The proceedings were conducted by a trained representative of the Ministry of Justice, assisted by two or four popularly elected "judges." Since the legal knowledge of those involved was limited, they were instructed to exercise common sense and to apply locally accepted principles. These courts could handle only minor offenses; more serious crimes were judged in peoples' courts at the district and provincial levels. District and provincial trials also were open to the public, except in certain cases, such as rape, where the defendant could request a closed trial. Persons convicted of a serious crime had the automatic right of appeal to the next higher court.

The 1990 Constitution abolished secret or security police forces. The accused is guaranteed a speedy trial and timely notice of the prosecutor's accusations. Guarantees of due process are written into the Constitution.

LAW ENFORCEMENT

The principal law enforcement agencies are the Corpo Polícial de Moçambique (CPM, Mozambique Police Corps); the Serviço Nacional de Segurança Popular (SNASP, National Service of Popular Security), the secret police; and the Polícia de Investigação Criminal (PIC, Criminal Investigation Police). The CPM is headed by a commander in chief, the SNASP by a director and the PIC by a national director. The SNASP is directly under the control of the president.

The major law enforcement problems are alcoholism, prostitution, banditry and a special class of offenses classed as political crimes, such as vagrancy, religious belief and economic sabotage. Those arrested on these charges are sent for "reeducation" to mental decolonization centers.

HEALTH

All health care services are nationalized. Private medical practice is forbidden by the state. Measles and pulmonary tuberculosis are the major diseases.

Health services collapsed following the flight of non-African medical personnel and the abolition of private medical practice. Current health programs are staffed by East European and Tanzanian personnel. Only 16% of the population has access to safe water.

FOOD & NUTRITION

Staple foods are corn and cassava; the national drink is beer. The per capita daily consumption of food is 1,891 calories, (below the recommended minimum of 2,600 calories).

HEALTH INDICATORS

Health personnel, 1987
- Physicians: 327
  - Persons per: 44,392
- Dentists: 138
- Nurses: 2,871
- Pharmacists: 301
- Midwives: 1,112

Hospitals, 1986
- Number: 250
- Number of beds
  - Per (/10,000): 11
- Admissions/discharges (/10,000): 92 (1980)
- Bed occupancy rate %: 70.2 (1980)
- Average length of stay (days): 9 (1980)

Type of hospitals (%), 1986
- Government: 100.0
- Private nonprofit: 0.0
- Private profit: 0.0

Public health expenditures, (latest)
- Per capita (U.S. $): 3.20

Vital statistics
- Crude death rate (/1,000 pop.): 18 (1990)
- Life expectancy at birth, 1990
  - Males: 45
  - Females: 49
- Infant mortality rate (/1,000 live births): 138 (1990)
- Child mortality rate (1985–90) under 5 yrs. (/1,000): 241
- Maternal mortality rate (/100,000 live births) (1980–84): 300

Population with access to safe water (%): 16 (latest)

MEDIA & CULTURE

The two daily newspapers, *Diário de Moçambique*, published at Beira, and *Notícias*, at Maputo, are government-owned and in Portuguese. In addition, there are two weeklies, *Domingo* and *Tempo*, both also in Portuguese and published in Maputo.

The official news agency is AIM (Agência de Informação de Moçambique), which issues daily reports in Portuguese and English and a monthly bulletin in French and English. Numerous European and Soviet foreign bureaus also maintain offices in Maputo. About 29 books are published annually. Mozambique does not adhere to any copyright convention.

The Constitution of 1990 guarantees freedom of speech although restraints on speech are permitted in wartime or "comparable national security emergencies."

All radio stations were nationalized in 1975. The former Radio Clube de Moçambique was reconstituted as Radio Moçambique with one FM transmitter and 16 shortwave and six medium-wave transmitters broadcasting four home-service programs for 63½ hours a day. In addition, programs in local vernaculars such as Ronga, Shangane, Chissena, Chuabo, Chiningue and Macua as well as other African languages such as Nyanja, Swahili and Alaua are broadcast over regional stations at Sofala, Pemba, Quelimane and Nampula. The other two radio services, Radio Pax and Emissora do Aéro Clube, also broadcast in Portuguese and vernaculars.

A television service, Televisâo Experimentral (TVE) was introduced in 1981, covering the three cities of Maputo, Biera and Nampula and broadcasting on Wednesday, Thursday, Saturday and Sunday only.

MEDIA INDICATORS

Newspapers
- Number of dailies: 2 (latest)
- Circulation (000): 81 (latest)
- Per 1,000 pop.: 6 (latest)
- Newsprint consumption (1988)
- Total metric tons: 100
- Per 1,000 pop. (kg.): 7

Book publishing
- Number of titles: 29 (pre-1986)

Radio
- Number of transmitters: 31 (latest)
- Number of persons per radio receiver: 31 (1989)

Television
- Television transmitters: 1 (latest)
- Number of persons per TV receiver: 437 (1989)

Cinema
- Number of fixed cinemas: 60 (latest)
- Seating capacity (000): 30 (latest)
  - Seats (/1,000 pop.): 2.0 (1987)
- Annual attendance (million): 4.1 (latest)
- Gross box office receipts (millions M.): (post 1984) 406 (1987)

Films
- Import of long films: 53 (1987)
  - % from USSR: 37.7
  - % from Federal Republic of Germany: 30.2
  - % from U.S.: 9.4
  - % from Italy: 5.7

CULTURAL & ENVIRONMENTAL INDICATORS (latest)

Libraries
- Number: 6
- Volumes (000): 154

Museums
- Annual attendance (000): 350,000
- Attendance (/1,000 pop.): 25

Nature reserves
- Number of facilities: 6

There is no local film production. There are 70 fixed cinemas, with 27,000 seats.

The largest public library is the National Library at Maputo, with 95,000 volumes. There are 5 other libraries.

There are 10 museums, with a reported annual attendance of 350,000.

SOCIAL WELFARE

Social welfare programs are being restructured to conform to FRELIMO ideology, but their expansion is limited by the country's economic difficulties.

GLOSSARY

aldeamento: a nuclear village established for Africans by Portuguese, especially in the north. Africans from dispersed villages were forcibly resettled in aldeamentos in order to protect them from FRELIMO troops.

bairro: a ward in larger towns as a unit of local government.

circulo: a local FRELIMO party unit or cell controlling local government in liberated areas.

concelho: formerly, a district as a unit of local government.

grupo dinamizadores: literally, a dynamizing group; a local FRELIMO unit formed in villages, towns, wards, factories, and commercial farms to indoctrinate people in Marxist-Leninist ideology.

CHRONOLOGY (from 1975)

1975— Mozambique becomes an independent people's republic under FRELIMO auspices, with Samora Moises Machel as president; white settlers continue to flee the country as white-led FICO movement collapses; army coup led by northern malcontents is thwarted.

1976— Mozambique closes border with Rhodesia. . . . A joint cooperation committee is established with Tanzania. . . . All private homes and buildings are nationalized. . . . Lourenço Marques, the capital, is renamed Maputo, and other Portuguese geographical names are Africanized. . . . Resistência Nacional Moçambicana (RENAMO), also known as Movimento Nacional de Resistência (MNR), is formed.

1977— FRELIMO holds Third National Congress and defines its Marxist-Leninist ideology. . . . Treaty of friendship and cooperation is signed with the Soviet Union. . . . Portuguese nationals are expelled from the country as relations with Portugal deteriorate. . . . Rhodesian troops raid ZIPA bases in Mozambique.

1978— Banking is nationalized. . . . The cabinet is reshuffled in an effort to stem the country's mounting economic difficulties.

1979— Fifteen Catholic missions are ordered to be closed down as the Marxist government enters on a collision course with the church.

1980— President Machel announces a reorientation in economic policy, permitting a greater role for private enterprise. . . . The cabinet is reshuffled twice in a drive against corruption and inefficiency. Mozambique adopts metical as unit of currency in place of escudo. After Zimbabwean independence in April, South Africa assumes Rhodesia's former role as supporter of RENAMO.

1984— Mozambique joins the IMF and the World Bank and becomes a party to the Third Lomé Convention. The Nkomati Accord is reached with South Africa whereby the two countries agree not to offer asylum to rebels and guerrillas.

1985— Mozambique moves toward free enterprise in limited sectors of the economy. Major military offensive against RENAMO results in capture of rebel command center, "Casa Banana."

1986— RENAMO recaptures "Casa Banana." RENAMO declares war on Zimbabwe. President Machel dies in suspicious plane crash in South Africa. Joaquim Chissano is appointed president by Central Committee.

1987— Rebel activities, including massacre of 424 civilians in town of Hormoine and ambush of convoy from Maputo killing 270 people, lead to severe food shortages and increasing numbers of Mozambican refugees outside the country.

1988— Amnesty for RENAMO members who surrender weapons results in more than 3,000 rebel defections.

1989— Senior U.S. government official claims South Africa still is providing supplies to RENAMO. . . . FRELIMO abandons its Marxist-Leninist ideology; De Klerk meets with Chissano and claims that his government has cut off all aid to RENAMO.

1990— The Mozambique legislature adopts a new Constitution designed to establish a Western-style democracy; the country's name is changed to the Republic of Mozambique; the Mozambican government and RENAMO sign a partial cease-fire; free multiparty elections are scheduled to take place some time in 1991.

BIBLIOGRAPHY

BOOKS

Abshire, David M., and Michael A. Samuels. *Portuguese Africa.* New York, 1969.

Bloomfield, Richard J. *Regional Conflict and U.S. Policy: Angola and Mozambique.* Algonac, MI, 1988.

Chilcote, Ronald. *Portuguese Africa.* Englewood Cliffs, N.J., 1967.

Gibson, R. *African Liberation Movements.* New York, 1972.

Hanlon, Joseph. *Mozambique: The Revolution Under Fire.* London, 1984.

Hardy, Ronald. *Rivers of Darkness.* New York, 1979.

Henriksen, Thomas H. *Revolution and Counter Revolution: Mozambique's War of Independence, 1964–1974.* Westport, Conn., 1983.

Hoile, David. *Mozambique: A Nation in Crisis.* London, 1989.

Isaacman, Allen. *The Tradition of Resistance in Mozambique.* Berkeley, Calif., 1976.

——— and Barbara Isaacman. *Mozambique: Sowing the Seeds of Revolution.* Boulder, Colo., 1984.

Knight, Derrick. *Mozambique, Caught in the Trap.* London, 1988.

Lappe, Frances M., and Adele Beccar-Varela. *Mozambique and Tanzania: Asking the Big Question.* San Francisco, 1980.

Martins, Elisio. *Colonialism and Imperialism in Mozambique.* Gretna, La., 1974.

Minter, W. *Portuguese Africa and the West.* Baltimore, 1972.

Mittelman, James H. *Underdevelopment and the Transition to Socialism: Mozambique and Tanzania.* Orlando, Fla., 1981.

Mondlane, Eduardo C. *The Struggle for Mozambique.* Baltimore, 1969.

Munslow, Barry. *Mozambique: The Revolution and Its Origins.* White Plains, N.Y., 1983.

Newitt, M. D. *Portuguese Settlement on the Zambezi.* New York, 1973.

Potholm, Christian, and Richard Dale. *Southern Africa in Perspective.* Boston, 1972.

Searle, Chris. *We're Building a New School: Diary of a Teacher in Mozambique.* New York, 1981.

Serapiao, Luis B., and Mohamed El-Khawas. *Mozambique in the Twentieth Century.* Washington, D.C., 1979.

Vail, Leroy, and Landeg White. *Capitalism and Colonialism in Mozambique.* Minneapolis, Minn., 1981.

Walt, Gillian, and Angela Melamed. *Mozambique: Toward a People's Health Service.* London, 1983.

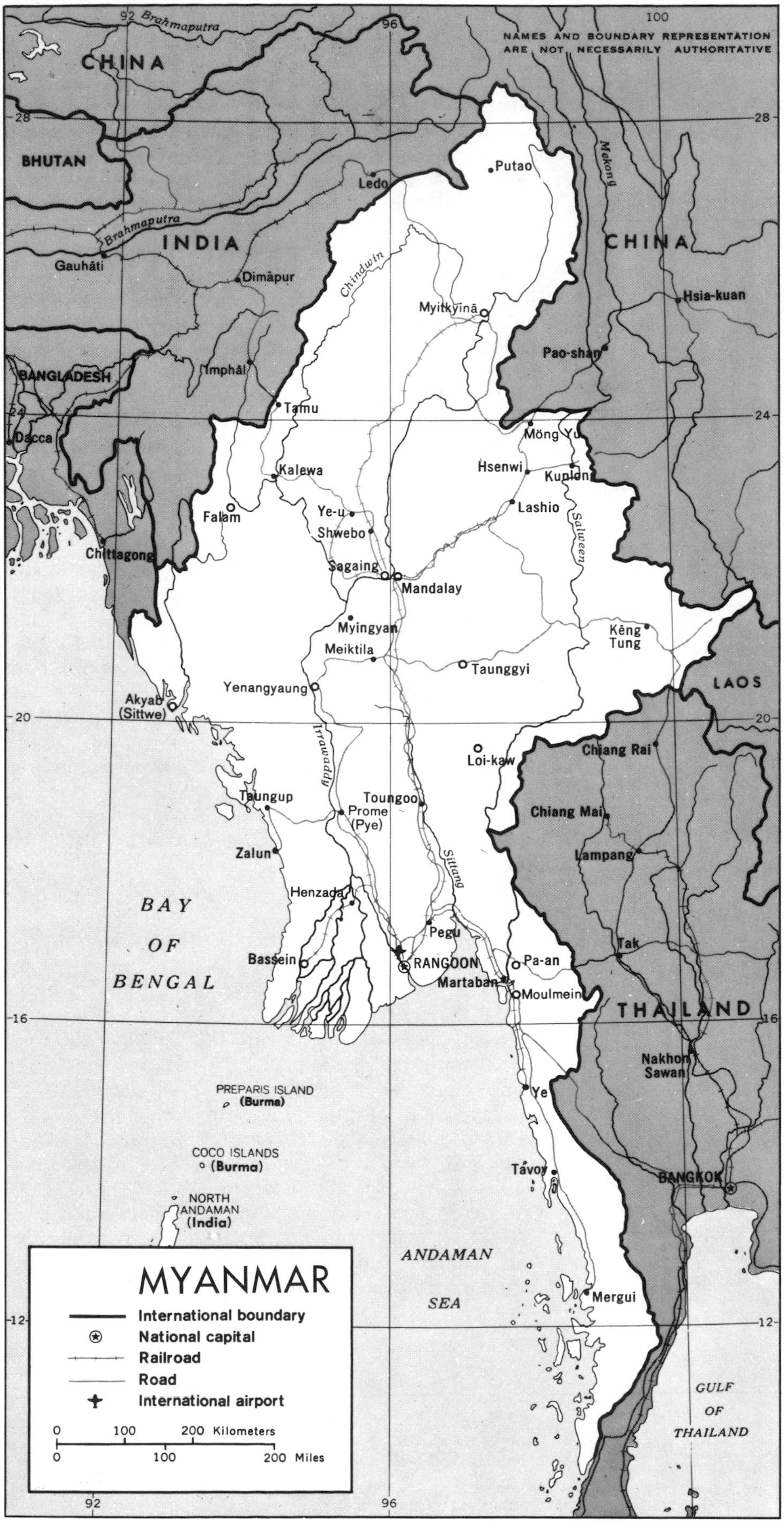
NAMES AND BOUNDARY REPRESENTATION
ARE NOT NECESSARILY AUTHORITATIVE
CHINA
BHUTAN
INDIA
BANGLADESH
CHINA
LAOS
THAILAND
Brahmaputra
Chindwin
Mekong
Salween
Irrawaddy
Sittang
Ledo
Putao
Gauhāti
Dimāpur
Myitkyinā
Hsia-kuan
Pao-shan
Imphāl
Tamu
Dacca
Möng Yu
Hsenwi
Kunlong
Kalewa
Lashio
Falam
Ye-u
Shwebo
Chittagong
Sagaing
Mandalay
Myingyan
Kēng Tung
Meiktila
Taunggyi
Yenangyaung
Akyab (Sittwe)
Loi-kaw
Chiang Rai
Taungup
Toungoo
Prome (Pye)
Chiang Mai
Zalun
Lampang
Henzada
BAY OF BENGAL
Pegu
Tak
Bassein
RANGOON
Pa-an
Martaban
Moulmein
Nakhon Sawan
PREPARIS ISLAND (Burma)
Ye
COCO ISLANDS (Burma)
Tavoy
BANGKOK
NORTH ANDAMAN (India)
ANDAMAN SEA
Mergui
GULF OF THAILAND
MYANMAR
International boundary
National capital
Railroad
Road
International airport
0 100 200 Kilometers
0 100 200 Miles
92
96
100
28
24
20
16
12

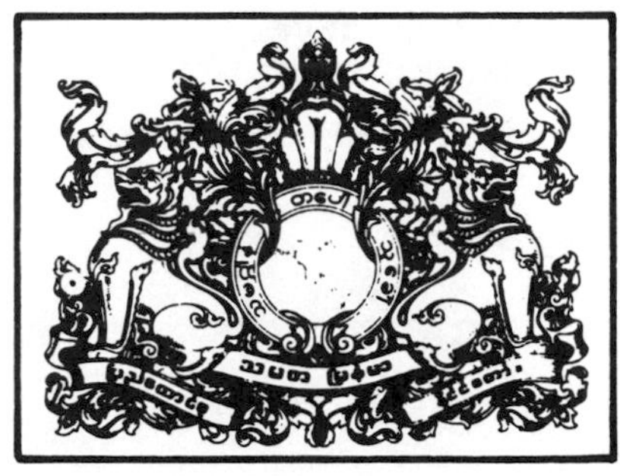

MYANMAR

BASIC FACT SHEET

OFFICIAL NAME: Union of Myanmar (Pyidaungzu Myanma Naingngandaw)

CAPITAL: Yangon (also known as Rangoon)

HEAD OF STATE AND HEAD OF GOVERNMENT Gen. Saw Maung (from September 1988)

NATURE OF GOVERNMENT: Military regime

POPULATION: 41,277,389 (1990)

AREA: 678,033 sq. km. (261,789 sq. mi.)

ETHNIC MAJORITY: Burman

LANGUAGE: Burmese

RELIGION: Buddhism

UNIT OF CURRENCY: Kyat

NATIONAL FLAG: Red with an upper left blue canton bearing two ears of rice within a cogwheel and a ring of 14 stars all in white

NATIONAL EMBLEM: A map of Myanmar in the center with a circular border with the motto "The Pursuit of Unity Is Happiness and Prosperity." A full-face heraldic cheetah of classic Burmese design is at the top with a heraldic cheetah at each side facing outward. The legend "Socialist Republic of the Union of Myanmar" is inscribed in scrollwork in Burmese at the base.

NATIONAL ANTHEM: "Our Free Homeland"

NATIONAL HOLIDAYS: January 4 (National Day, Independence Day); February 12 (Union Day); March 2 (Peasants' Day); March 27 (Armed Forces Day); May 1 (World Workers' Day); July 19 (Martyrs' Day); December 25 (Christmas); also variable Buddhist festivals, such as Full Moon of Tabaung, Thingyan or Water Festival, Full Moon of Kason, Waso or Beginning of Buddhist Lent, end of Buddhist Lent, Tazaungdaing and Burmese New Year's Day

NATIONAL CALENDAR: Gregorian

PHYSICAL QUALITY OF LIFE INDEX: 71

DATE OF INDEPENDENCE: January 4, 1948

DATE OF CONSTITUTION: January 3, 1974 (Suspended September 1988)

WEIGHTS & MEASURES: Imperial system.

GEOGRAPHICAL FEATURES

Myanmar (formerly known as Burma), the largest country on the mainland of Southeast Asia, has a total land area of 678,033 sq. km. (261,789 sq. mi.). It extends 1,931 km. (1,200 mi.) north to south and 925 km. (575 mi.) east to west. It has a total coastline of 2,276 km. (1,414 mi.) and total international land borders of 5,858 km. (3,641 mi.) with five countries, as follows: China (2,185 km.; 1,358 mi.), Laos (238 km.; 148 mi.), Thailand (1,799 km.; 1,118 mi.), Bangladesh (233 km.; 145 mi.) and India (1,403 km.; 872 mi.). Most of the land frontiers are defined by mountains.

The capital is Yangon, with a 1983 population of 2,513,023. The other major urban centers are Mandalay (532,895), Moulmein (219,991), Bassein (335,000), Akyab (143,000) and Taunggyi (100,000).

Myanmar is divided topographically into four regions. The eastern Shan Plateau is a highland region averaging 900 m. (3,000 ft.) in height and merging with the Dawna Range and the Tenasserim Yoma toward the Isthmus of Kra. The Central Belt spans the valleys of the Irrawaddy, Chindwin and Sittang rivers with a mountainous region in the North and a vast, low-lying delta in the South that covers an area of 25,900 sq. km. (10,000 sq. mi.). It produces almost all the nation's rice. The Western Mountain Belt, also known as the Arakan Mountains, is a series of ridges that originate in the northern mountain arc and extend southward to the southwestern corner. The Arakan Coastal Strip is a narrow, predominantly alluvial belt lying between the Arakan Mountains and the Bay of Bengal. In some places the strip disappears as the mountain spurs reach the sea. Offshore there are hundreds of islands, many of which are cultivated.

The Irrawaddy River is the lifeline of the country and provides a vast drainage and nagivation system. The river rises near the northernmost tip of Myanmar and flows the entire length of the country for about 2,173 km. (1,350 mi.). It receives the Chindwin, its principal tributary, just below Mandalay. The Irrawaddy enters its vast delta at Henzada. On one of its nine mouths is the port of Yangon. The Irrawaddy is navigable for 1,287 km. (800 mi.), while the Chindwin is navigable for another 160 km. (100 mi.). The Sittang River, which rises just south of Mandalay and parallels the Irrawaddy on the eastern flank, also is part of the Irrawaddy Basin. The Sittang suffers from excessive silting and is navigable for short distances only.

Another large river is the Salween, which rises in China and flows through the Shan Plateau to Moulmein on the Gulf of Martaban. During its 2,816-km. (1,750-mi.) course it flows through narrow gorges and is navigable in sections only. A number of other rivers flow in the Arakan Yoma into the Bay of Bengal and in Tenasserim into the Andaman Sea.

There are few lakes of significant size. The largest is Lake Inle, in a basin of the Shan Plateau.

CLIMATE & WEATHER

Myanmar has a tropical climate with three seasons: the monsoon or rainy season from May to October, the hot season in April and October/November and the cool season from December to March. The temperatures are high all year, and the cool season is cool only by comparison. The mean annual temperature is 26°C (80°F), with higher temperatures, reaching 37.8°C (100°F), in the lowlands and more moderate ones in the Shan Plateau.

Rainfall is regulated by the southwesterly and northeasterly monsoons, with considerable regional variations in the amount. Along the coastal regions rainfall is heavy, with a high of 5,080 mm. (200 in.). Lower Myanmar receives 2,540 mm. (100 in.), while central Myanmar, in the lee of the Arakan Mountains, receives only from 630 mm. (25 in.) to 1,140 mm. (45 in.).

POPULATION

The population of Myanmar was estimated in 1990 at 41,277,389. The last true census was held in 1983, when the population was 35,313,905. Over 62% of the population is concentrated in the lower delta region of the Irrawaddy Basin and the lowlands of the Sittang River. The Shan Plateau, the Western Mountain belt and the northern hills of the central belt acccount for 50% of the land area but contain only 15% of the population.

There is no significant disparity in the male/female ratio. The majority of the population lives in 14,000 villages, with an average population of 1,738. Most villages are clusters of houses surrounded by a stockade. There are only six cities with populations of over 100,000: Yangon, Mandalay, Moulmein, Bassein, Akyab, and Taungyyi.

Women in Myanmar have distinct social roles, which vary with their cultural traditions and ethnic backgrounds. In general, Burmese women enjoy most of the same rights as Burmese men. Burmese women keep their own names after marriage, are active in trade, often control family finances and enjoy the same legal rights as Burmese men. Buddhism, like many religions, limits the religious role of women and assigns them a theoretically inferior status to men. Women are greatly underrepresented in senior positions in the ruling SLORC.

Immigration is virtually nonexistent. Until 1948 immigration of Indians, Pakistanis and Chinese had created a sizable alien minority. This flow was reversed when a ban was placed on immigration soon after independence. The Enterprise Nationalization Law was passed in 1963, specifically designed to exclude aliens from all economic activities. Over 90% of registered Indians and Pakistanis left voluntarily, abandoning their properties and other possessions. The decline in the number of Indians and Chinese continued through the mid-1970s.

The government does not consider that the growth in population in relation to the country's area and resources poses a serious problem. Accordingly, official policy does not favor family planning. Family planning materials are not permitted to be imported or locally manufactured, and birth control assistance by the medical profession is punishable by law.

VITAL STATISTICS

Crude birth rate (/1,000): 33 (1990); 40 (1964)
Crude death rate (/1,000): 13 (1990); (1965)
Infant mortality rate (/1,000 live births): 97 (1990)
Maternal mortality rate (/100,000 live births): 140 (1980)
Life expectancy (yrs.) at birth: males, 53.1; females, 56.0 (1990)
Gross reproduction rate (/woman) (1980–85): 2.25
Total fertility rate (/woman): 4.2 (1990)
Rate of natural increase (1988) (/1,000): 20.5
Average household size: 5.2 (latest)

STATUS OF WOMEN INDICATORS

Number of women (millions): 20.028 (1985)
Women of childbearing age (15–49) (% of pop.): 49 (1988)
Women's literacy rate (%): 71.6 (1988)
Women in labor force (%): 46 (1985)
Total fertility rate (/woman): 4.2 (1990)

DEMOGRAPHIC INDICATORS

Population (million): 41.277 (1990)
Year of last census: 1983
Sex distribution (% at last census): males, 49.6; females, 50.4
Population estimates and projections (million)

1940: 16.119	1970: 26.997	2000: 51.129
1950: 18.489	1980: 33.821	2010: 60.567
1960: 22.063	1990: 41.675	

Age profile (% at last census)

0–14: 40.7	30–44: 15.0	60 and over: 6.1
15–29: 27.7	45–59: 10.5	

Median age (yrs.): 20.0
Youth population (% age 15–24): 20.4 (1985); 22.4 (2000)
Total dependency ratio: 75.5 (1985)
Annual growth rate (%)

1950–55: 1.85	1975–80: 2.10	2000–2005: 1.80
1955–60: 2.12	1980–85: 2.09	2005–2010: 1.54
1960–65: 2.11	1985–90: 2.09	2010–2015: 1.37
1965–70: 2.24	1990–1995: 2.09	2015–2020: 1.16
1970–75: 2.32	1995–2000: 2.00	2020–2025: 1.10

Hypothetical size of stationary population (millions): 94
Assumed year of reaching net reproduction rate of 1: 2010
Urban population (million): 8.973 (1985)
Urban population (%): 24 (1988); 21 (1965)
Annual urban population growth rate (%, 1985–90): 2.65
Annual rural population growth rate (%, 1985–90): 1.91
Percentage of urban population in cities of population over 500,000: 23 (1980)
Number of cities of population over 500,000: 2 (1980)
Population density per sq. km. (per sq. mi.): 61.6 (159.5) (latest)

ETHNIC COMPOSITION

There are over 100 indigenous ethnic groups and subgroups in the country; the most numerous are the Burmans, the Karens, the Kayahs, the Shans, the Kachins and the Chins. The Burmans constitute the ethnic majority, with 65% to 70% of the population. The Shans form the largest minority group, estimated to be 9% of the population. The Shans, calling themselves Tai and speaking a Tai dialect, live primarily in Shan State.

They are primarily a lowland people engaged in wet-rice agriculture. The Karens are the second largest minority group, estimated at 7%. The Karens are divided into the Hill Karens and the Plains Karens. Within this broad division there are further subdivisions, into Pwo Karens, Sgaw Karens and Bwe Karens. The other minorities are mostly hill tribes, such as the Chins, living in the Chin Special Division; the Kachins, living in Kachin State; and the Kayahs, also known as the Karennis or the Red Karens, living in Kayah State. The Burmans, who are ethnically related to the Tibetans, descended into the Irrawaddy Valley in historical times and intermarried with the Mon and Pyu peoples. The Karens, Shans, and others were later migrants.

No census figures or estimates are available for the Mons and the Arakanese, the former living on the Tenasserim coast and the latter in Arakan Division. Both groups are culturally related to the Burmans. Of interest to ethnographers are a number of lesser groups found scattered throughout the highlands: Palaungs, Paos, Ithas, Padaungs, Akhas, Lahus, Lisus, Kaws, Ekaws and Was.

The official policy of the Burmese government has been to deemphasize ethnic differences. Terms such as "racial minorities" and "nationalities" have disappeared from official usage. The government also has founded an Academy for the Development of National Groups at Ywathitgyi to train students of different ethnic backgrounds in the ideology of national unity.

The ethnic aliens of Myanmar, whose numbers have been in sharp decline in recent years, number about 520,000 and are divided among Chinese (400,000), Indians (100,000), and Pakistanis and Bangladeshis (20,000). Similarly, the number of Eurasians has been eroded through emigration. The European population, except for the diplomatic and U.N. community, is virtually nonexistent. The Ne Win regime raised xenophobia to the status of an official policy. In an effort to reduce foreign influence, the country cut itself off from all cultural and economic contacts with the outside, particularly Western, world. Western tourism was discouraged; when permitted to enter, Western tourists were not allowed to stay longer than a week. Western culture and dress were condemned, the teaching of English was discouraged and Western organizations such as the Rotary Club were disbanded. Beginning in the 1980s, however, there was a gradual restoration of English in the educational system. English is now taught in secondary schools and is the medium of instruction in universities. In addition, the government announced in 1988 that it would welcome foreign investment in Myanmar's economy.

LANGUAGES

Under the Constitution of 1974 the official language of Myanmar is Burmese. Spoken by 80% of the population, it is a Tibeto-Burman language with an alphabet derived from the Pahlavi script of South India. Burmese and to a lesser extent, Tai, the language of the Shans, also are used as lingua francas by the linguistic minorities who retain their own language. The most developed of these minority languages are Mon, Chin, Karen and Kachin. Mon (also called Talaing) is a member of the Mon-Khmer branch of the Austro-Asiatic family of languages. Kachin (also called Singh-Pho) is a member of the Bodo-Naga-Kachin group. Karen is a Sino-Tibetan language, a member of the Tai subfamily. According to the Constitution, minority languages may be used in areas where their speakers predominate.

English is now taught in schools as a second language from the fifth grade, and its use is permitted in some types of official communications. English is now the medium of instruction in the universities. Two major daily newspapers are published in English, and their combined circulation of 33,000 may provide a clue to the number of English-speakers in the country.

RELIGIONS

Buddhism is the religion of over 85% of the people. Under the U Nu regime Buddhism was made the state religion, but it was disestablished by Ne Win, and the Constitution of 1974 guarantees the "right of everyone to profess and practice his religion freely."

Relations between the Sangha, representing the traditional Buddhist clergy, and the Ne Win regime were strained periodically. Ne Win's efforts to reduce the political influence of the Buddhist clergy led to massive protest demonstrations by the monks. After 1965 Revolutionary Council moderated its secularization programs and, to broaden its base of support, began a campaign to prove that the "Burmese way to socialism" and Buddhism shared common principles. Buddhist monks and students stepped up protests against the Ne Win regime in the months preceding the September 1988 coup which Saw Maung came to power. Monks and students protested again in 1990 in response to Saw Maung's refusal to step down after the May 1990 elections in which the National League for Democracy (NLD) won 80% of parliamentary seats. Government troops killed protestors during a march in August. In October at least 40 monks were detained by military police.

An estimated 5% of the population is Christian, the majority belonging to the Karen group. Two other Christianized groups are the Kachin-Lisu and the Chin-Lushai. Christian missionaries have long been active in the delta and border areas; their greatest success was among the hill peoples. Another 4% of the population is Muslim, concentrated in the Arakan District. Animism and spirit worship have not been totally displaced among the hill peoples, and beliefs in spirits in some form or other persists even among Buddhists.

HISTORICAL BACKGROUND

All of Myanmar was a province of the British Indian Empire from 1886 to 1937, when it was separated from India and granted a constitution for limited self-government. During World War II the country was under Japanese occupation. Full independence was granted to Myanmar, then called the Union of Burma, on January 4, 1948.

The fledgling Union of Burma, led by U Nu, was almost immediately assailed by a widespread insurrection of communists and ethnic insurgents. By 1951 the unrest was brought under control by government forces. Differences within Burma's ruling party, the Anti-Fascist People's Freedom League (AFPFL), led to an intraparty split in 1958. In order to maintain law and order, the Government invited the army chief, Gen. Ne Win, to assume temporary control of the country until new elections could take place. After winning by an overwhelming majority in April 1960, U Nu resumed office.

U Nu was ousted from office in March 1962 when Ne Win staged a coup and regained control of the country. The Constitution and parliament were suspended. Free enterprise and private trade were abolished and privately owned companies were placed under military control. In July 1962 the Burma Socialist Program Party (BSPP) was formed. The BSPP was dominated by the military and was the only legal political party in the country.

The new Constitution, which was promulgated in January 1974, called for a one-party socialist government. Despite the new Constitution, power continued to be held by the military, with Ne Win as chairman of the council of state and president. Although Ne Win retired in 1981, he remained in charge of the BSPP, remaining the real source of political power in the country.

Economic problems and growing unrest among ethnic groups continued to plague the government. Student-led demonstrations in September 1987 marked the beginning of a 12-month period of turmoil. Massive demonstrations against Ne Win compelled him to resign his party post in August 1988. On September 18, 1988, Gen. Saw Maung, at the head of a military-dominated State Law and Order Restoration Council (SLORC), assumed power, ostensibly to maintain order until multi-party elections could be held.

The SLORC abolished all executive and legislative institutions (including the People's Assembly, the State Council and the Council of Ministers). Although Ne Win held no official position in the new regime, it was widely believed that he retained a controlling influence over its leaders, all of whom, including Gen. Saw Maung, were known to be his supporters.

In 1988 the law maintaining the BSPP as the sole party was abrogated; the BSPP registered under a new name, the National Unity Party (NUP). Although new parties were encouraged to register for upcoming elections, the military arrested and harassed opposition leaders throughout 1989.

A new constitution was scheduled to be promulgated after the May 1990 general elections. Of the 485 parliamentary seats contested in the elections, however, the government-backed NUP won only 10, whereas the National League for Democracy (NLD) won nearly 400. The NLD's triumph only brought more repression by the military, which refused to step down from power. By December 1990 the military had arrested 50 NLD leaders. More than one year after elections, military leaders continue to refuse the NLD its place in government. Gen. Saw Maung, still considered a puppet of Ne Win, continues to rule Myanmar.

CONSTITUTION & GOVERNMENT

The most recent constitution was promulgated in January 1974. This Constitution was suspended following the army coup of September 18, 1988.

On June 18, 1989, the country's name was officially changed to the Union of Myanmar (Pyidaungzu Myanma Naingngandaw). A new constitution was scheduled to be promulgated after the general elections of May 1990. However, the government has refused to allow the winning party to take its seats in parliament and continues to rule by decree.

The Constitution of 1974 defined the Socialist Republic of the Union of Burma as a unitary, socialist state with only one party, the Burma Socialist Program Party (BSPP). The Constitution replaced the Revolutionary Council by a State Council as the supreme state organ. Four subordinate bodies (Council of Ministers, Council of Attorneys, Council of Judges and Council of Inspectors) implemented policies set by the State Council. The State Council was headed by the president of the republic, who was the head of state; the Council of Ministers, by the prime minister, who was head of government. The supreme representative body at the national level was the People's Assembly; at the regional level, the People's Councils.

Though military ranks were dropped by Ne Win and members of the ruling military group in 1972, under the Constitution the military continued to be the dominant power. Members of the armed forces also retained key positions in the BSPP.

The president of republic was elected for a term of four years by the State Council from among its own members. The president's executive functions were exercised through the State Council, which was composed of 29 members (including one representative

GOVERNMENT LIST
(July/August 1991)

Chairman, State Law & Order Restoration Council (SLORC)	Saw Maung, *Sr.Gen.*
Secretary 1, SLORC	Khin Nyunt, *Maj. Gen.*
Secretary 2, SLORC	Tin Oo, *Maj. Gen.*
Minister of Agriculture & Forests	Chit Swe, *Lt. Gen.*
Minister of Construction	Aung Ye Kyaw, *Lt. Gen.*
Minister of Cooperatives	Aung Ye Kyaw, *Lt. Gen.*
Minister of Defense	Saw Maung, *Sr. Gen.*
Minister of Education	Pe Thein, *Col.*
Minister of Energy	Maung Maung Khin, *VAdm.*
Minister of Foreign Affairs	Saw Maung, *Sr. Gen.*
Minister of Health	Pe Thein, *Col.*
Minister of Home & Religious Affairs	Phone Myint, *Lt. Gen.*
Minister of Industry No. 1	Sein Aung, *Lt. Gen.*
Minister of Industry No. 2.	Sein Aung, *Lt. Gen.*
Minister of Information & Culture	Phone Myint, *Lt. Gen.*
Minister of Livestock Breeding & Fisheries	Chit Swe, *Lt. Gen.*
Minister of Mines	Maung Maung Khin, *VAdm.*
Minister of Planning & Finance	Abel, David Oliver, *Brig. Gen.*
Minister of Social Welfare & Labor	Tin Tun, *Lt. Gen.*
Minister of Trade	Abel, David Oliver, *Brig. Gen.*
Minister of Transport & Communications	Tin Tun, *Lt. Gen.*

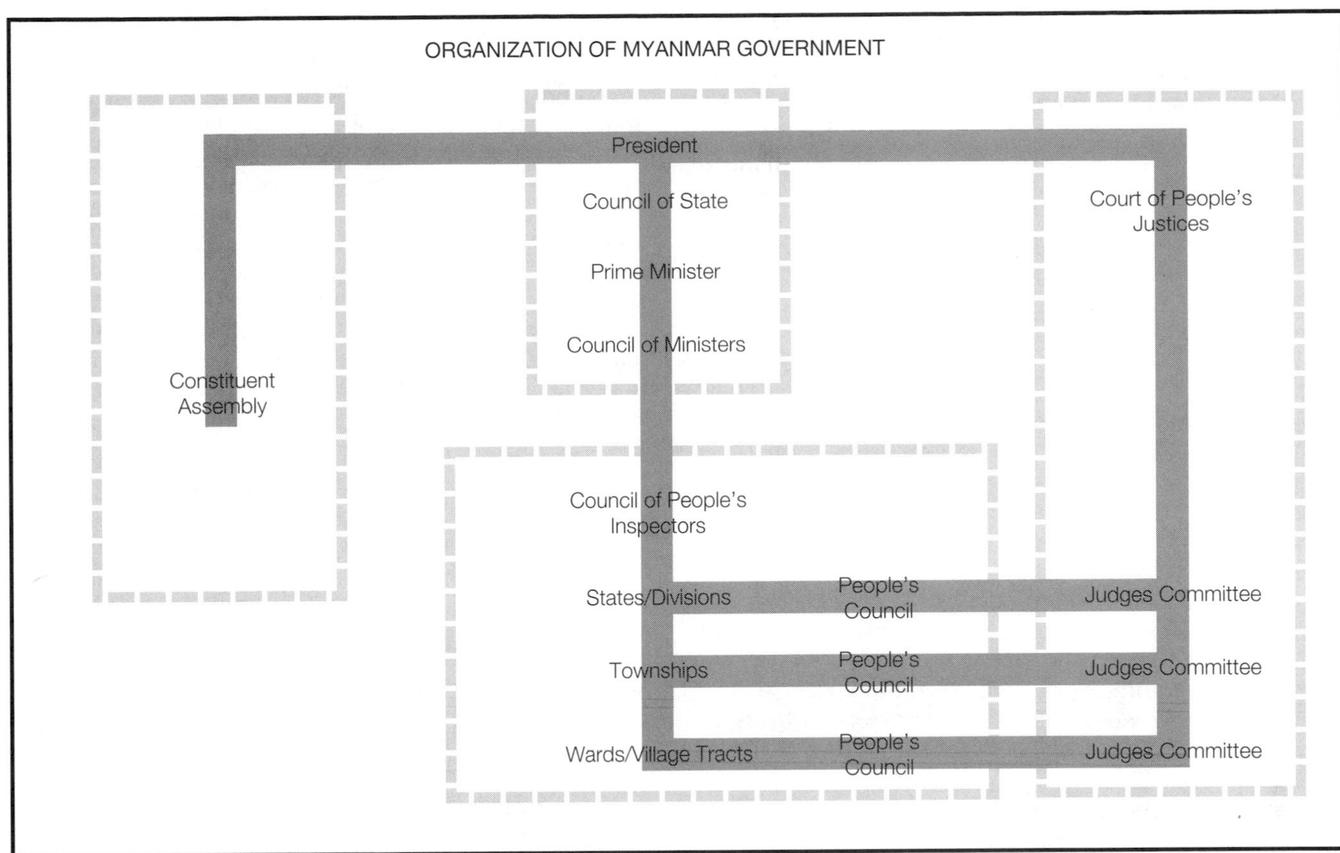

from each of the 14 states and divisions) elected by the People's Assembly from among its members for a term of four years. The State Council had plenary legislative and appointive powers and the right to grant amnesties and pardons. It could declare martial law during a state of emergency, subject to subsequent approval by the People's Assembly.

Half of the members of the State Council was elected by the People's Assembly from a list of candidates submitted by the State Council. The prime minister was elected by the Council of Ministers from among its members.

After the coup of September 1988, a State Law and Order Restoration Council (SLORC) was established. This body has unqualified executive, legislative and judicial authority. The executive and legislative institutions established under the Constitution of 1974 (notably the People's Assembly, the State Council and the Council of Ministers) was abolished.

The chairman of SLORC, Gen. Saw Maung, serves as head of state and head of government. Local government is administered by military officers appointed by SLORC. The judicial system is headed by a Supreme Court whose five members are appointed by SLORC.

In 1988 the government lifted the ban on political parties and in 1989 Gen. Saw Maung announced that free multi-party elections would take place in May 1990. Nonetheless, after the May elections, the government refused to honor the outcome and barred the winning party from taking its seats in parliament. Gen. Saw Maung and the SLORC continue to rule the country by decree.

RULERS OF MYANMAR (from 1948)

Presidents

January 1948–March 1952: Sao Shwe Thaik (Saopalong Yaung Hwe)
March 1952–March 1957: Agga Maha Thiri Thudhamma Ba U
March 1957–February 1962: U Wing Maung
February 1962–March 1962: Sama Duwa Sinwa Nawng
March 1962–November 1981: Ne Win
November 1981–July 1988: San Yu
July 1988–August 1988: Sein Lwin
August 1988–September 1988: Dr. Maung Maung
September 1988– : Gen Saw Maung

Prime Ministers (from 1946)

September 1946–July 1947: U Aung San
July 1947–June 1956: Thakin Nu (later known as U Nu)
June 1956–February 1957: U Ba Swe
February 1957–October 1958: U Nu
October 1958–March 1960: Ne Win
April 1960–March 1962: U Nu
March 1962–March 1974: Ne Win
March 1974–March 1977: U Sein Win
March 1977–March 1978: U Maung Maung Kha
March 1978–November 1981: Ne Win
November 1981–July 1988: Gen. San Yu
July 1988–August 1988: Sein Lwin
August 1988–September 1988: Dr. Maung Maung
September 1988– : Gen. Saw Maung

FREEDOM & HUMAN RIGHTS

In terms of political and civil rights Myanmar is ranked as a not-free country. Ne Win was officially in power for close to two decades—one of the longest tenures for any statesman in the world. According to Amnesty

International, torture and physical abuse of prisoners was common during his long regime. During this time, his political philosophy and his mode of operation did not change much, although he appeared to have mellowed in his approach to his opponents. His archenemy, U Nu, was permitted to return to Yangon in 1980 along with 2,200 other exiles and insurgents who accepted a general pardon. However, in December 1989 the SLORC disqualified U Nu, who had since formed the League for Democracy and Peace (LDP), from contesting the May 1990 elections. In January 1990 U Nu was placed under house arrest.

According to human rights organizations, the military government of Myanmar continues to be guilty of gross violations of human rights. In the first few days following the September 1988 coup, more than 1,000 demonstrators were killed. In July 1989, the government placed the two top leaders of the National League for Democracy (NLD) under house arrest: Aung San Suu Kyi (the daughter of Gen. Aung San, who helped lead his country to independence before his assassination in 1947) and Tin U (a former chief of staff and minister of defense). In December 1989 Tin U was sentenced by a military tribunal to three years' imprisonment at hard labor. Aung San Suu Kyi, still under house arrest, was barred from contesting the May 1990 elections.

During 1989 the government sought to consolidate its power by means of repression before the May 1990 elections. The military arrested leading opposition figures, tortured and executed dissident students and, in an effort to decrease antigovernment demonstrations, forcibly evicted 200,000 Myanma citizens from major cities, where the opposition had received much support. At least 400 members of the NLD were in prison at the time of the elections.

Nonetheless, the NLD won a sweeping victory in the May elections, winning 80% of the 485 parliamentary seats contested. Saw Maung and the State Law and Order Restoration Council (SLORC), whose National Unity Party (NUP) won only 10 seats, refused to step down, escalating its campaign of repression.

A 1990 report by U.S.-based Asia Watch cited cases of political dissidents dying in custody under suspicious circumstances and accused the government of torturing prisoners. A separate report by Amnesty International cited "serious torture" of political prisoners by the government as well as brutality and murder of civilians by the army.

The army opened fire on a crowd of 5,000 protestors in August 1990, killing two monks and two students. The monks reacted by later refusing to minister to government soldiers or to their families. The army responded by raiding dozens of monasteries in October and placing at least 40 monks under arrest. About 1,000 protestors battled with police again in September.

By the end of June 1991, at least 50 NLD leaders were in prison, including all but three of the original 16 members of the NLD's central executive committee. There has been no sign that Saw Maung and his military government will relinquish power to the NLD.

CIVIL SERVICE

Before the September 1988 coup, civil service was governed by the Public Service Commission, but all appointments were politicized by requiring that appointees be cleared by the Burma Socialist Program Party. The prestige and powers of the civil service were seriously eroded under military rule. Political indoctrination was provided in the "Burmese way to socialism" at the Central Services Training School. Pay scales, reduced in 1948, were never rescheduled despite inflation. Less than one-third of civil servants enjoyed constitutional guarantees of tenure. The more important administrative positions were been reserved for military personnel.

LOCAL GOVERNMENT

For purpose of local administration Myanmar is divided into 14 states and divisions. States are areas where a national ethnic minority is the local majority group. There are seven such states: Arakan, Chin, Kachin, Karen, Kayah, Mon and Shan. The districts, seven in number, are areas with a Burman majority: Irrawaddy, Magwe, Mandalay, Pegu, Sagaing, Yangon and Tenasserim. States and divisions are divided into townships, including village tracts and towns.

The Constitution of 1974 provided for People's Councils at all levels of local government. Their members were elected from a single slate of candidates nominated by the Burma Socialist Program Party (BSPP). Each of the People's Councils elected an executive committee with a chairman and a secretary. There were local councils of people's inspectors corresponding to the national Council of People's Inspectors, elected by the People's Assembly. In addition, a nationwide network of party cells and committees exercised policy control over local governments. After the September 1988 coup, the State Law and Order Restoration Council created new state and divisional administrative institutions composed mainly of military officers. Township groups now comprise a defense service officer as chairperson, the deputy head of the state or divisional general department, the deputy commander of the relevant police force and a secretary.

FOREIGN POLICY

Myanmar (formerly Burma) became independent at the height of the cold war, like many other Asian nations, and this fact has left an impression on its foreign policy, which has been dominated by three considerations: preservation of the nation's territorial integrity; achievement of internal unity; and reduction of dependence on foreign powers through a policy of strict nonalignment. Since 1949 Myanmar has sought the goodwill of its most important neighbor, the People's Republic of China, through a policy of accommodation. Myanmar was the first non-Communist nation to recognize the Peking regime in 1949. A Sino-Burmese border agreement was signed in 1960, followed by a Treaty of Friendship and Nonaggression.

However, relations deteriorated sharply after anti-Chinese riots in Yangon in 1967. China declared its support of an insurgent movement led by the White Flag Burma Communist Party and later suspended its technical and economic assistance program. Relations with China were normalized by 1970. Myanmar's relations with Thailand were complicated by the presence in Thailand of U Nu, the exiled head of an anti-Ne Win movement, and by Thai sympathies for Shan rebels.

Despite its policy of excluding foreign influence from national life, Myanmar has maintained generally friendly relations with both the United States and Great Britain, on the one hand, and the Soviet Union, on the other.

Myanmar's relations remain friendly with its neighbors India, Malaysia and Singapore and, farther afield, with Japan, the Philippines, Pakistan and South Korea. Diplomatic relations with North Korea were suspended following that nation's complicity in a Yangon bomb attack in October 1983 that left 17 South Koreans dead during an official visit by South Korean president Chun Do Hwan.

In 1976 Myanmar also strengthened its political and economic links with Hanoi. Measured by the consistency of its nonalignment policy and the friendliness of its relations with countries of all types of ideological orientation, Ne Win's regime achieved remarkable success in the foreign affairs field.

Following the Sixth Summit Conference of the Nonaligned Movement at Havana in 1979, Myanmar announced its withdrawal from the group. "The principles of the movement are not recognizable anymore," the leader of the Burmese delegation, Myint Maung, told the meeting. He charged that certain ideological groups were exploiting the movement for their own ends. "We cannot allow ourselves to be so exploited," he said. He called for the creation of a new movement comprising nations that were genuinely nonaligned.

Relations with Bangladesh, which had deteriorated following the exodus of thousands of Arakanese Muslims over the border into Bangladesh, were quickly repaired. An accord was reached under which Myanmar agreed to take back all the refugees.

Myanmar showed its continuing goodwill toward Britain by observing a three-day mourning for Earl Mountbatten of Burma, killed in a bomb explosion in 1978.

Despite its long-standing policy of non-alignment and rejection of foreign influence, by the end of the 1970s Myanmar had begun to modify its policy of refusing foreign economic aid and technical assistance. In 1980 Myanmar accepted aid from West Germany and Japan, OPEC and, for the first time since 1963, the United States. Most such aid was suspended following the military's seizure of power in September 1988 owing to widespread human rights abuses. Nonetheless, in an effort to encourage further foreign investment, the government announced in October 1988 that it would adopt a market-oriented economic policy and allow foreign investors to form wholly owned enterprises or joint ventures with local companies.

The 1990 U.S. State Department's report on human rights criticized Myanmar's "dismal human rights situation" which had "deteriorated even further in 1989." The report accused the Myanma government of arbitrarily arresting and detaining several thousand persons and repressing all forms of political opposition.

Myanmar's relations with several countries have deteriorated because of its government's escalating violation of human rights in the wake of the May 1990 elections (after which the ruling SLORC refused to relinquish power despite its defeat).

Late in 1990 the U.N. passed a resolution in censuring human rights violations in Myanmar.

Myanmar joined the United Nations in 1948. It is a member of 16 U.N. organizations and nine other international organizations.

PARLIAMENT

Before the September 1988 coup, the national legislature was the 485-member People's Assembly (Pyithu Hluttaw). It was directly elected by secret ballot for a term of four years. Regular sessions took place twice a year, the intervening period being no more than eight months. All members of the People's Assembly belonged to the sole political party, the Burma Socialist Program Party (BSPP).

The People's Assembly elected the Council of Ministers and half the membership of the State Council and from a list of candidates submitted by the State Council. It also selected a Council of People's Inspectors charged with the inspection of the organs of local government, ministries and public bodies. The People's Assembly, the Council of Ministers and the State Council were abolished after the 1988 coup. Gen. Saw Maung and his officers became the members of the State Law and Order Restoration Council, which now has unqualified executive, legislative and judicial authority.

Under the Constitution of 1974, suffrage was universal over age 18. The minimum age for running for election was 21.

POLITICAL PARTIES

After 1964, when all political parties were banned in Myanmar, the sole Burmese political organization was the Burma Socialist Program Party (BSPP), also known as the Lanzin Party. The BSPP was founded in 1962 by Ne Win. Its ideological basis was a blend of Marxism, Buddhism and humanism called the "Burmese way to socialism." This ideology was embodied in a document titled *The System of Correlation of Man and His Environment.* (The system rejects both parliamentary democracy and Marxism-Leninism but at the same time clothes Buddhist and Burmese concepts in Marxist terms.)

The BSPP was a cadre party until the First Party Congress in 1971, when it was transformed into a mass party and given theoretical control of the government. The party's constitution vested supreme authority in the Revolutionary Council, which, in reality, ran the government.

After the September 1988 coup when the government lifted the ban on political parties, the BSPP registered under a new name, the National Unity Party (NUP). Although the country had a new leader, Gen. Saw Maung, it was widely believed that Ne Win retained a controlling influence over Maung and other leaders, all of whom had been members of the BSPP.

By December 1989, 117 political parties had registered with the electoral commission. The major opposition parties are listed below.

National League for Democracy (NLD): The NLD is an outgrowth of an organization formed by a number of leading dissidents in 1988. Its founding president, Aung Gyi, withdrew to form the UNDP after having called, unsuccessfully, for the expulsion from the League of a number of alleged communists. President Tin U and General Secretary Aung San Suu Kyi have been in prison since July 1989. The NLD claims more than half a million members.

Union National Democratic Party (UNDP): The UNDP was launched in December 1988 by Aung Gyi, following his withdrawal from the NLD. In 1963, Aung Gyi broke with Ne Win and was imprisoned (at the time, he was a brigadier general and ranked number two in the ruling Ne Win hierarchy). Gyi had emerged as one of the country's leading dissidents because of a series of anti-regime open letters circulated in the wake of the March 1988 riots.

Democratic Party (DP): The DP is backed by Bohmu Aung, one of the legendary independence leaders of the 1940s, and former prime minister U Nu. Its leader is Thu Wai.

Anti-Fascist People's Freedom League (AFPFL): The AFPFL is a reincarnation of Myanmar's first ruling party, supported primarily by a faction of the earlier group that broke with U Nu in 1958.

People's Democratic Party (PDP): The PDP was launched in 1988 by Thakin Lwin, a prominent labor leader of the early 1950s.

Unity and Development Party (UDP): The UDP was organized by the former leader of the Communist Party of Burma, Thakin So.

There are many illegal opposition groups comprised of members of ethnic minorities including the Arakans, the Karens, the Shans, the Mons, the Lahns, the Palaungs, the Was, the Kachins and the Chins, most of which advocate the creation of their own independent states.

Of the 485 parliamentary seats contested in the May 1990 elections, the NLD won 397 and the NUP 10, with the remaining 78 seats being shared by other, smaller parties.

ECONOMY

Myanmar is considered a low-income country. With a per capita GNP of less than US $500, Myanmar is one of the poorest and least-developed countries in the world. Since 1962 it has had a socialist, centrally planned economy in which the dominant sector is public, although in the closing years of the 1980s it was clear that these statist policies were being dismantled.

After independence, the government pursued four principal economic objectives outlined in the policy document *The Burmese Way to Socialism.* These objectives were to eliminate foreign control of the economy, to reduce dependence on foreign markets, to reduce dependence on primary production and increase the importance of the industrial sector, and to centralize economic power and economic decision making in the hands of the state. The result was the creation of an essentially autarkic economy that severely neglected the primary exports of rice, teak and petroleum that had been the foundation of the preindependence economy. In addition, Myanmar excluded multinational investment, accepted only limited government and international agency aid, and shunned the development of a major tourism trade. It was an economy in which the state closely planned and minutely regulated, although major areas of production and domestic trade remained in private ownership.

Throughout the 1960s and 1970s, the economy's growth was hampered primarily by the government's failure to provide essential infrastructural and technical support for the dominant agricultural sector as well as by serious bureaucratic mismanagement of state enterprises and almost exclusive dependence on domestic sources for capital investment. Toward the late 1970s, the economy experienced more rapid growth as government policy objectives and economic administration underwent adjustment. Important here was a firm commitment to raising agricultural productivity, a partial return to the world trading community and an increased reliance on international aid.

In 1987 the government announced that the economy would in the future be more open to domestic and international market forces. In September of that year the government abandoned its long-established control

PRINCIPAL ECONOMIC INDICATORS

GNP per capita (U.S. $): <500 (1989 est.)
Consumer price index (1980=100) 1986
All items: 135
Food: 128

BALANCE OF PAYMENTS, 1986
(U.S. $ millions)

Current account balance: −294.0
Merchandise exports: 330.7
Merchandise imports: −620.9
Trade balance: −290.2
Other goods, services & income + : 70.6
Other goods, services & income − : −167.6
Other goods, services & income net: −97.0
Private unrequited transfers: 5.8
Official unrequited transfers: 87.5
Capital other than reserves: 343
Net errors & omissions: 81.1
Counterpart items: 32.9
Liabilities constituting foreign authorities reserves: 0
Total change in reserves: −32.9

GROSS DOMESTIC PRODUCT

GDP nominal (K. billions): 71.059 (1988)
GDP per capita (U.S. $): 280 (1988)
Average annual growth rate of GDP (%, 1985–88): 1.8
GDP by type of expenditure (%): 1987
- Consumption
  - Private, government: 92
- Gross domestic investment: 12
- Foreign trade
  - Exports: 2
  - Imports: −6

Cost components of GDP (%): 1987
- Net indirect taxes: 8
- Consumption of fixed capital: 9
- Compensation of employees: 38
- Net operating surplus: 44

Sectoral origin of GDP (%) 1985
- Primary
  - Agriculture: 51
  - Mining: 1
- Secondary
  - Manufacturing: 9
  - Construction: 2
  - Public utilities: 0
- Tertiary
  - Transportation & communications: 4
  - Trade: 22
  - Finance: 2
  - Other services, government: 9

of rice and other basic commodity prices. In October 1988 restraints on internal and external trade were abolished, but the government retained a monopoly on exports of teak, gems, pearls, natural gas and petroleum. In order to procure foreign exchange, the government began to sell licenses, mostly to Thailand, for extensive exploitation of the country's natural resources. In November 1988 a liberal law regulating foreign investment was promulgated, allowing foreign investors to form wholly owned enterprises or joint ventures with local companies.

Although the U.N. had granted Myanmar the status of a "least developed country" in December 1987, Japan and the principal Western donors suspended aid to Myanmar in September 1988, pending the introduction of political and economic reforms. Owing to the political turmoil, there were no official exports between July and December 1988, and Myanmar defaulted on foreign debt repayments coming due in 1988, while reserves of foreign exchange remained low. The main obstacles to foreign investment remain the country's political instability, poor infrastructure, inability to end drug trafficking, and the artificially high value of the kyat compared with other currencies.

Much of Myanmar's economic activity is illicit, notably the smuggling of gold and drugs. The government's efforts to control drug trafficking have been ineffective. Illegal trade was estimated to be equivalent to 50% of official trade in 1985. Large quantities of smuggled consumer goods are sold in Myanma cities, where the black market thrives. The black market, frequent shortages of basic consumer goods and sudden price jumps continue to cause hardships to the salaried class and the peasants.

PUBLIC FINANCE

The Myanma fiscal year is from April 1 through March 31. The national budget is a consolidated budget of the government sector and covers the central government, state enterprises and local bodies. The budget appears in three versions at three times during the fiscal year: an original estimate, a revised estimate in the middle of the year and an actual budget after the close of the fiscal year.

The major sources of government revenue are taxes on commodities and services, receipts from state economic enterprises and customs duties. Other sources of revenue are taxes on income and property, taxes on the use of state properties and interest income.

Major expenditures are allocated to manufacturing, transport and communications, agriculture and mining. Other expenses include power, administration and social services.

Despite its socialist ideology, Myanmar had no development plan until 1971, when the government announced its first four-year economic development plan. Early planning goals were to achieve a growth rate of over 8% in exports and to increase investment to 15% of GNP. Planning in the 1980s emphasized the development of agriculture rather than an increase in industrial capacity and envisaged average annual growth of over 6%.

CENTRAL GOVERNMENT EXPENDITURES, 1988

% of total expenditures
- Defense: 12.9
- Education: 13.4
- Health 4.9
- Housing, social security, welfare: 13.2
- Economic services: 38.6
- Other: 16.9

Total expenditures as % of GNP: 16.3 (1987)
Overall surplus or deficit as % of GNP: −0.8 (1987)

CENTRAL GOVERNMENT REVENUES, 1987

% of total current revenues
- Taxes on income, profit & capital gain: 6.7
- Social security contributions: 0.0
- Domestic taxes on goods & services: 39.8
- Taxes on international trade & transactions: 14.3
- Other taxes: 0.0
- Current nontax revenue: 39.2

Myanmar has received substantial foreign aid, from both the East and the West. Most of the aid has been reimbursable credits extended on a government-to-government basis with no political strings attached. Until the late 1980s the government opposed private investment by foreign entrepreneurs and joint ventures with foreign governments. From 1970–88 Myanmar

FOREIGN AID, 1989

Total foreign aid (U.S. $ millions): 35.9
- Bilateral: 17.3
- Multilateral: 18.7

received $158 million in aid. Other Western nations as well as ODA and OOF bilateral commitments totaled $3.8 billion from 1970–87. Communist countries contributed $424 million in aid from 1970–88.

CURRENCY & BANKING

The Myanma unit of currency is the kyat, divided into 100 pyas. Coins are issued in denominations of 1, 5, 10, 25, 50 and 100 pyas and notes in denominations of 1, 5, 10, 15, 45 and 90 kyats. The kyat was known as the Burmese rupee before 1952 and was part of the sterling area currency system until 1966. The currency was floated in 1974 and in 1975 was devalued by 23%. Subsequently the exchange rate against the U.S. dollar has been adjusted from month to month. The market rate in June 1991 was $1 = K6.57.

FINANCIAL INDICATORS, 1989

Total reserves minus gold (SDRs millions): 200
SDRs (millions): 0
Reserve position in IMF (SDRs millions): 0
Foreign exchange (SDRs millions): 200
Gold (fine troy oz. millions): .25
Ratio of external debt to total reserves: 47.5 (1988)
Central bank 1989
- Assets (%)
  - Foreign assets: 2.8
  - Claims on government: −45
  - Claims on banks: 142.3
  - Claims on private sector: 0.0
- Liabilities (%)
  - Reserve money: 64.8
  - Government deposits: 0.0
  - Foreign liabilities: 3.2
  - Capital accounts: 0.0

Money supply 1989
- Stock (K. billions): 15.668
- M1 per capita: 390

Private banks 1988
- Assets (%)
  - Loans to government: 93.8
  - Loans to private sector: 4.4
  - Reserves: 1.8
  - Foreign assets: 0.0
- Liabilities
  - Deposits (K. billions): 64.073
  - of which %
    - Demand deposits: 1.6
    - Savings deposits: 11.9
    - Government deposits: 8.5
    - Foreign liabilities: 15.7

External debt 1988
- Total (U.S. $ billions): 4.321
  - of which public (U.S. $ billions): 4.217
  - of which private (U.S. $ millions): 0
- Debt service (long term)
  - Total (U.S. $ millions): 1,061
  - Repayment
    - Principal (%): 63.2
    - Interest (%): 36.8
- Debt service ratio (%): 21.6
- Debt service as % of exports: 59.3 (1987)
- Terms of public borrowing
  - Commitments (U.S. $ millions): 0
  - Average interest rate (%): 0.0
  - Average maturity (yrs): 0
- Net flow of publicly guaranteed external capital (U.S. $ millions): 220

GROWTH PROFILE
(Annual Growth Rates, %)

Projected population (1988–2000): 2.0
Projected crude birth rate (/1,000) (1990–95): 29.7
Projected crude death rate (/1,000) (1990–95): 8.7
Urban population (1985–90): 2.65
Money holdings (1980–88): 10.3
Energy production (1980–88): 4.8
Energy consumption (1980–88): 5.1
Exports (1980–88): −7.0
Imports (1980–88): −8.0

The country has a monobank system, with the Union of Myanmar Bank serving as the central bank and the sole commercial bank. The Union of Myanmar Bank is the successor to the People's Bank of the Union of Burma, an amalgamation of all the country's banks and founded in 1976. All private commercial banks were nationalized in 1963.

There are three specialized state banks, established under law in 1975. These are the Myanma Economic Bank, the Myanma Foreign Trade Bank and the Myanma Agricultural Bank.

AGRICULTURE

Agriculture is the largest sector of the economy in terms of contribution to the GDP and share of the total labor force. In addition, at least two-thirds of the manufacturing sector is agro-based. Of the total land area of 67 million ha. (167 million ac.), about 19% is under cultivation. Almost 1,618,700 ha. (4 million ac.) of arable land are lost every year because of flooding of the Irrawaddy and Sittang rivers. Agriculture contributes over 60% of exports; its annual growth rate has been rising since 1976 after declining for a number of years.

The government holds formal title to all land. Under the land nationalization program of 1953–58, a total of 3,510,780 ha. (8.7 million ac.) were expropriated from landlords. In 1965 all tenanted lands were nationalized and allotted to peasants. Although during this period agriculture had come increasingly under state control, only a few collective farms had been organized and most farms still were privately owned. About 86% of farmowners and tenants owned 4.04 ha. (10 ac.) or less (55% of cultivable land), while 14% held from 4.04 to 20.23 ha (10 to 50 ac.) (43.5% of all cultivable land). Only 1% held more than 20.23 ha (50 ac.) (1.5% of cultivable land). The average holding was about 2 ha. (4.94 ac.).

Three types of cultivation are practiced, depending on the nature of the country, the soil and the rainfall. The first is the *le* cultivation in the delta area of the Irrawaddy and Sittang rivers and on the coasts of Arakan and Tenasserim, where the fields are annually flooded. Cultivation is limited to a single crop of rice. *Kaing* cultivation is practiced in the central regions, with less heavy rainfall. Two crops may be grown here annually, with the second crop planted in the dry season. The third type of cultivation, called *ye (shifting),* is practiced in the hilly areas, often with double

AGRICULTURAL INDICATORS

Value added in agriculture (U.S. $ millions): 4,707 (1987)
Index of agricultural production (1979–81 = 100): 141 (1986)
Index of food production (1979–81 = 100): 143 (1986)
Index of food production per capita (1979–81 = 100): 127 (1985–87)
Number of tractors: 10,204 (1986)
Number of harvester-threshers: 38 (1986)
Total fertilizer consumption (000 metric tons): 199 (1985–86)
Fertilizer consumption (g./ha., hundreds): 125 (1987–88)
Number of farms (000): 4,308 (1987–88)
Average size of holding (ha.): 2.3 (1987–88)
Size class (%) 1987–88
  Below 2 ha. (below 4.94 ac.): 61.2
  2–4 ha. (4.94–9.88 ac.) 24.7
  4–8 ha. (9.88–19.76 ac.): 11.5
  8–20 ha. (19.76–49.4 ac): 2.5
Over 20 ha. (over 49.4 ac.): 0.8
Farms as % of total land area: 18.6 (1987–88)
Land use (%)
  Cropland: 1
  Pasture: 38
  Forest: 14
  Other: 47
Yields (kg./ha.) 1989
  Grains: 2,697
  Roots & tubers: 8,109
  Legumes: 844
  Milk (kg./animal): 246
Production 1989
  Fruits (000 metric tons): 935
  Vegetables (000 metric tons): 2,223
Livestock (000) 1989
  Cattle: 10,000
  Horses: 119 (1986)
  Sheep: 295
  Pigs: 3,000
Forestry 1988
  Production of roundwood (000 cubic meters): 21,003
    of which industrial roundwood (%): 19.0
  Value of exports (U.S. $ 000): 87,442
Fishing 1988
  Total catch (000 metric tons): 704.5
    of which marine (%): 79.4
  Value of exports (U.S. $ 000): 17,420

cropping. Mechanization is not common, and government tractor stations are underutilized.

The total area under irrigation is 889,000 ha. (2 million ac.), or less than 10% of the land under cultivation. Irrigation is practiced principally in central Myanmar, where the annual rainfall is unevenly distributed, falling almost entirely during a five-month period. The largest of the irrigation projects are in the Mu Valley and the Sedawgyi Reservoir, the Kinywa Reservoir, the Nyaung-kyat Reservoir and Hanthawaddy on the Sittang River.

Rice represents half the value of all agricultural output and covers about 5 million ha. (12.5 million ac.) of land. Prior to World War II Myanmar was the world's leading exporter of rice. However, the war caused extensive damage to the rice fields, and prewar levels of acreage and output were not achieved until 1964. Minor crops include sugar, peanuts, beans, peas, corn, wheat, tobacco, sesame and jute.

Distribution of agricultural products is a state monopoly. The Agricultural Marketing Board handles rice, tapioca and tobacco, while the Agricultural and Rural Development Corporation controls jute, roselle and cotton. The Ministry of Supply and Cooperatives deals with wheat.

Most farms raise some form of livestock. Zebu cattle and water buffalo are valuable for draft, transportation, and, to a lesser extent, natural fertilizer provided by their dung.

Forests cover 55% of the country and contain many commercially valuable species of timber, of which teak is the most important. As the world's leading exporter of teak, Burma supplies about 75% of the world market. Timber resources were nationalized in 1963, and the State Timber Board has a monopoly over logging, milling and export of timber. However, extraction methods still are primitive, and transportation bottlenecks can delay logs in transit for up to three years.

Fishing is a major activity, and fish provide a major source of protein in the Burmese diet. The Burmese preference for freshwater fish has restricted deep-sea fishing. Coastal fishing still is undeveloped, but the government has embarked on an expansion of deep-sea fishing.

Agricultural credit is provided by the Myanma Agricultural Bank to individual farmers through cooperatives or other farmers' groups, who are collectively responsible for repayment.

MANUFACTURING

The major industrial area is Pegu District, particularly Yangon. The vast majority of manufacturing establishments are privately owned.

The government's industrial policy is based on an ideology of total socialization of all means of production. Where state ownership is impractical, state-controlled production cooperatives are set up under the Cooperative Council. In spite of their monopoly position, most state enterprises have suffered continuing losses since 1963. The state enterprises are not free to determine their prices, to recruit personnel or to fix their salary scales. Their performance is judged solely on the basis of their ability to meet production quotas without consideration of quality or service. They have little control over their income, and the surpluses of profitable enterprises are used to help meet the deficits of unprofitable ones.

Foreign investment in industry was entirely eliminated after the nationalization measures of 1963. Foreign companies were allowed to operate only if invited, and even then only under contract with the government. The investment ban was partially lifted in 1973. Foreign participation was permitted in mining, and some private businesses were allowed to reopen. In 1973 eight foreign firms were granted concessions for offshore oil explorations. Towards the end of the 1980s the government began to make serious efforts to attract foreign capital.

In 1984 the government announced formation of a joint venture company with a West German firm to produce heavy industrial equipment. The government invested K8.153 billion in the state sector in 1983–84.

Industrial credit is provided by the Myanma Industrial Bank and the Myanma Economic Development Corporation.

MINING

Myanmar was a major exporter of minerals prior to World War II, but the war and subsequent civil strife has disrupted mineral production. The country still is largely unexplored, and only 30% has been geologically surveyed. Known deposits include lead, silver, zinc, copper, nickel and tungsten. Jades, rubies, sapphires and gold also are mined. Coal deposits of 128 million tons have been discovered along with iron ore in the Taunggyi and Maymyo areas.

ENERGY

In 1963 the British-owned Burmah Oil Company was nationalized and renamed People's Oil Industry, later changed to Myanma Oil Corporation in 1970. Though an oil-exporting nation before World War II, Burma became a net importer by the early 1970s as a result of increased domestic requirements. New contracts for oil exploration were awarded to eight foreign companies in 1973. The older oil fields at Chauk and Yenangyaung continue to be active, with secondary methods of extraction being used. The fields at Mann and Prome are the most productive among the new ones. Total reserves are estimated at 30 million bbl. There are two oil refineries, at Syriam and Chauk, with a total capacity of 26,000 bbl. per day. Reserves of natural gas are estimated at 5 billion cu. m. (176 billion cu. ft.). Myanmar has excess crude that it cannot process. In 1979 the government contracted to sell 1 million bbl. to Japan. Myanmar also is an exporter of paraffin wax, petroleum coke and furnace oil; nearly 135,000 tons of these items are exported annually.

About 50% of electric power is produced by hydropower; the other 50% comes from fossil fuels.

ENERGY INDICATORS

Average annual energy production growth rate (%, 1980–88): 4.8
Energy consumption per capita (kg. oil equivalent): 74 (1988)
Energy imports as % of merchandise exports: 5 (1988)
Average annual growth rate of energy consumption (%, 1980–88): 5.1
Electricity 1988
- Installed capacity (million kw.): 1.009
- Production (million kw.-hr.): 2,272
  - % fossil fuel: 50.7
  - % hydro: 49.3
  - % nuclear: 0.0
- Consumption per capita (kw.-hr.): 57

Natural gas
- Proved reserves (billion cu. m.): 226 (1990)
- Production (billion cu. m.): 1.190 (1989)
- Consumption (billion cu. m.): 1.147 (1988)

Petroleum
- Proved reserves (million bbl.): 190 (1990)
- Years to exhaust proved reserves: 39 (1990)
- Production (million bbl.): 5 (1989)
- Consumption (million bbl.): 5 (1988)
- Refining capacity (000 bbl./day): 32 (1990)

Coal
- Reserves (million metric tons): 2 (latest)
- Production (000 metric tons): 65 (1988)
- Consumption (000 metric tons): 105 (1988)

LABOR

Myanmar's economically active population is estimated at 15,849,000.

Myanmar was one of the first Asian countries to enact comprehensive labor legislation covering minimum wages, Social Security, child labor and occupational safety. The normal workday is 7.7 hours, and the workweek is 45.6 hours in most factories. Agricultural labor may work longer, up to 12 hours every day. In addition, workers are entitled to up to 60 days off in annual vacation, casual leave, national holidays and sick leave. Wage levels are depressed.

Labor unions were dissolved in 1964 under the Law to Protect National Solidarity. In their place a network of workers' councils and peasants' councils was created under two central organizations, the Central People's Workers' Council and the Central Peasants' Council. The councils were not bargaining agents but political units of the Burma Socialist Program Party (BSPP). Strikes are not permitted. Labor disputes are submitted to local conciliation committees consisting of labor officers. The Central Labor Committee is the final authority in industrial disputes.

LABOR INDICATORS

Total economically active population (000): 15,847
- % working-age (15–64): 64.2 (1983)
- % female: 35.3 (1983)

Activity rate (% 1983)
- Total: 40.2
- Male: 52.4
- Female: 28.2

Sectoral employment of economically active (%)
- Agriculture, forestry, fishing: 63.9
- Construction: 1.6
- Manufacturing, mining, quarrying, public utilities: 9.2
- Trade, hotels, restaurants: 9.5
- Transportation, communications: 3.2
- Finance, real estate, and services: 6.3

Average annual growth rate of labor force (%, 1980–2000): 1.8
Unemployment (000): 331 (1987)
Earnings in manufacturing per worker (/mo) (K.): 505.51 (1983)
Hours of work per worker 1983
- Manufacturing (/wk.): 7.6

FOREIGN COMMERCE

Myanmar's major import sources from 1988 to 1989 were Japan, the European Economic Community, China, Southeast Asian countries, East European countries, and North America. Its major imports were industrial raw materials, machinery and equipment, construction materials, tools and spare parts, and consumer goods.

Myanmar's major export destinations from 1988 to 1989 were Southeast Asian countries, India, China, the European Economic Community, African countries and Japan. Its major exports were forest products (notably teak), agricultural products (notably rice, oilseed and rubber), minerals and gems, and animal and marine products.

FOREIGN TRADE INDICATORS, 1988

Exports (U.S. $ millions): 311
Imports (U.S. $ millions): 536
Balance of trade (U.S. $ millions): −225
Annual growth rate (1980–88), exports (%): −7.0
Annual growth rate (1980–88), imports (%): −8.0
International reserves in terms of months of imports covered: 2.7
Terms of trade (1980 = 100): 72

Direction of Trade (%), 1987

	Imports (est.)	Exports (est.)
European Community	23.1	5.9
United States	1.3	2.2
U.S.S.R. & eastern European economies	11.7	5.5
Japan	28.8	6.1

Composition of Trade (%), 1984

	Imports	Exports
Food & agricultural raw materials	33.2	69.9
Fuels & other energy	13.8	NA
Mineral ores & concentrates	1.0	6.2
Manufactured goods	82.1	23.9
of which chemicals	NA	0.3
of which machinery	49.9	1.4

TRANSPORTATION & COMMUNICATIONS

The state-owned rail system operates 3,137 km. (1,949 mi.) of meter-gauge, single-track railway. The main lines all run north to south, from Yangon to Mandalay and then to Myitkyina, and from Yangon to Moulmein. There also is another line, from Yangon to Prome and Bassein.

Inland waterways are the primary means of transportation in Myanmar. The Irrawaddy is navigable for 1,287 km. (800 mi.) throughout the year from the delta to Bhamo, and in the summer to Myitkyina. The Chindwin and the Salween also serve as major arteries parallel to the Irrawaddy. The Arakan coastal strip, which has no railroads and almost no roads, is almost entirely served by the Kaladan River and its tributaries. Some 500,000 small craft ply the Irrawaddy alone. The state Inland Waterways Transportation Board operates all routes, with a fleet of about 670 vessels.

The principal port is Yangon, which handles over 85% of seaborne traffic. Akyab, Bassein and Moulmein are secondary ports. The country's only shipping line is the Myanma Five Star Line, which operates a fleet of 102 vessels. All shipping agencies were nationalized in 1969.

Because of Myanmar's terrain, roads are only a secondary means of transportation. Road transportation is important for medium and short distances. The bullock and the buffalo are used as modes of transportation, along with passenger cars and commercial vehicles. The state-owned Road Transportation Corporation (RTC) operates 18% of trucks and 30% of bus transportation, with an eventual goal of full nationalization.

The national airline is Myanma Airways (MA), which acts as the agent for all foreign airlines. The airline flies to 15 cities with a fleet of 15 aircraft. The principal international airport is Mingaladon, outside Yangon. There are secondary airports at Akyab and Moulmein.

Tourism is undeveloped. Because of internal security problems tourism is limited to the major cultural cen-

TRANSPORTATION INDICATORS

Roads (latest)
- Length, km. (mi.): 23,200 (14,416)
- Paved (%): 17

Motor vehicles (latest)
- Automobiles: 35,000
- Trucks and buses: 45,000
- Persons per vehicle: 479
- Road freight, metric ton-km. (short ton-mi.) (millions): 103.7 (71)

Railroads (latest)
- Track, km. (mi.): 3,137 (1,949)
- Passenger-km. (passenger-mi.) (millions): 3,924 (2,438)
- Freight, metric ton-km. (short ton-mi.) (millions): 456 (312)

Merchant marine
- Vessels (over 100 tons): 117 (1989)
- Total deadweight tonnage (000): 363.3 (1989)

Ports (pre-1986)
- Cargo loaded (000 metric tons): 483
- Cargo unloaded (000 metric tons): 260

Air
- Passenger-km. (passenger-mi.) (millions): 133.3 (82.8) (latest)
- Freight, metric ton-km. (short ton-mi.) (millions): 2.1 (1.4) (latest)
- Airports with scheduled flights: 21 (1990)

Pipelines 1990
- Natural gas, km. (mi.): 330 (205)

Inland waterways (latest)
- Length, km. (mi.): 12,800 (7,954)
- Freight, metric ton-km. (short ton-mi.) (millions): 345.3 (236.5)

COMMUNICATION INDICATORS, 1988

Telephones
- Total (000): 81
- Persons per telephone: 501

Phone traffic (000 calls)
- Local and long distance: 460,400
- International: 149

Post office
- Number of post offices: 1,114 (1987)
- Pieces of mail handled (000): 67,040

Telegraph
- Total traffic (million calls): 1.028 (1987)

Telex
- Subscriber lines: 138

Telecommunications 1990
- Satellite ground station: 1

TOURISM & TRAVEL INDICATORS, 1986

Total tourist receipts (U.S. $ millions): 17 (1988)
Expenditures by nationals abroad (U.S. $ millions): 1 (1988)
Number of hotel beds (000): 2
Average length of stay (nights): 5
Tourist nights (000): 215
Number of tourists (000): 33.7 (1985)
- % of whom from United States: 5.2
- Germany: 4.6
- France: 3.5
- U.K.: 3.1

ters: Yangon, Mandalay, Pagan Pegu and Taunggyi. The maximum permitted length of stay is 14 days.

Telecommunication facilities include one ground satellite station.

DEFENSE

Before the September 1988 coup, the defense structure was headed by the president of the republic, who also was the commander in chief of the armed forces. The line of command ran through the Defense Services Staff, which included vice chiefs of staff for the army, navy and air force, to the five army area commands and three naval regions. The Defense Council Executive Committee was the policy-making body.

Units were deployed under nine regional commands, each consisting of one to three tactical operation commands (equivalent to a brigade). In addition, the Ministry of Defense had direct control over three divisions that were assigned to the regional commands for special purposes. After the 1988 coup all executive and legislative organs were abolished, placing the armed forces under the State Law and Order Restoration Council's command. It's leader, Gen. Saw Maung, also served as Minister of Defense. Reflecting its British origin, the army was until quite recently based on the regimental system, each regiment being composed of a distinct ethnic group. Official policy now discourages ethnicity in regimental composition and favors a racial mix that would inhibit local or ethnic loyalties.

Manpower is provided by voluntary enlistment for two years. The National Service Law of 1959 provides for universal military service, but it has never been enforced except in the case of physicians, engineers and technicians, who may be conscripted up to age 56. Yangon and Mandalay universities maintain a corps of student trainees, but there is no other organized reserve.

The total strength of the armed forces in 1989 was 200,000. The number of enlisted men is relatively small in terms of total available manpower.

The Myanma army has been engaged continuously since independence in anti-insurgency operations. Therefore the defense service is structured to meet internal security needs rather than to defend against external threats. The army consists largely of light, mobile infantry battalions, and the air force is designed for ground support.

Army

Personnel: 182,000

Organization: 8 regional and 1 garrison commands; 7 light infantry divisions under central control with 3 tactical operational commands; 16 tactical operational commands; 85 infantry battalions; 4 artillery battalions; 1 antiaircraft battery. In addition, there are 2 paramilitary units: People's Police Force (38,000) and People's Militia (35,000).

Equipment: 24 tanks; 85 reconnaissance armored vehicles

Artillery: 50 guns; 120 howitzers; 80 mortars; rocket launchers

Navy

Personnel: 9,000 (including 800 marines)

Units: 4 corvettes; 36 gunboats; 46 river craft; 1 support vessel; 12 landing craft

Marines: 1 battalion

Naval bases: Monkey Point, Seikyi, Sinmalaik, Sittwe, Moulmein, Mergui and Bassein

Air Force

Personnel: 9,000

Organization: 22 combat aircraft; 2 counterinsurgency squadrons; 3 transportation squadrons; 7 liaison aircraft; 4 helicopter squadrons

Major air bases: Mingaladon (near Yangon), Meiktila (2), Hmawbi, Mandalay, Myitkyina and Kentung

Myanmar has received military aid from a variety of sources: India, the United Kingdom, Israel, Italy, West Germany, Yugoslavia and the United States. Since the 1988 coup most such foreign aid has been cut off. Before 1988, the largest amount of military aid came from the United States. Through a military aid agreement concluded in 1958, Myanmar obtained $80 million worth of equipment from the United States, including jet fighters, helicopters and gunboats. Over 800 Burmese military officers were trained in the United States under the Military Assistance Program.

Myanmar has no defense production apart from a submachine gun factory established with Italian help and a rifle factory started with West German help.

EDUCATION

Primary education is free and universal but not compulsory. Schooling consists of 11 years, divided into primary (grades one through five), middle (grades six through nine), and secondary (grades 10 through 11). The primary-school curriculum includes Burmese, science, social studies and arithmetic. English is introduced from grade five. Vocational courses are introduced in the middle grades. There are specialized agricultural and technical schools at the secondary level.

Adult literacy courses are offered under the auspices of the Mass Education Council. Monastic schools *(kyaungs)* continue to provide traditional Buddhist education in rural areas. All private schools have been nationalized.

High-school teachers are trained at the Institute of Education at Yangon; middle-school teachers at teachers' colleges at Mandalay, Moulmein and Yangon; and primary-school teachers at seven teacher training institutes. Most schools are crowded. In June 1989 the government reopened primary schools, which had been closed in June 1988. Middle schools and high schools were reopened in August and September 1989, respectively.

The academic year runs from May to March. The medium of instruction is Burmese, but minorities are permitted to use their mother tongues.

Educational administration was centralized in the Ministry of Education; it is now administered by the State Law and Order Restoration Council. The country is divided into 13 educational zones, with an inspector in each for secondary education. For primary education each zone has three districts, with an education officer assisted by three or four inspectors. All public education is financed by the national government.

EDUCATION INDICATORS, 1988

Literacy
- Total (%): 78.5
- Male (%): 85.8
- Female (%): 71.6

First level
- Schools: 31,499
- Students: 5,369,641
- Teachers: 188,417
- Student/teacher ratio: 28.5
- Net enrollment ratio: 65 (1977)

Second level
- Schools: 2,429
- Students: 1,591,927
- Teachers: 61,556
- Student/teacher ratio: 25.9
- Net enrollment ratio: 16 (1977)

Vocational
- Schools: 146
- Students: 17,000
- Teachers: 1,536
- Student/teacher ratio: 11.1

Third level (postsecondary)
- Institutions: 35
- Students: 255,866
- Teachers: 7,191
- Student/teacher ratio: 35.6
- Gross enrollment ratio: 5.1 (1981)
- Students (/100,000 pop.): 489
- % of population age 25 and over with postsecondary education: 0.2

Foreign study
- Students abroad: 495
  - of whom in
    - United States: 236 (1988)
    - France: 12 (1988)
    - Federal Republic of Germany: 18 (1988)
    - United Kingdom: 40 (1987)

Public expenditure
- Total (K. 000): 1,290,519
- % of GNP: 1.6 (1977)
- % of national budget: 12.2 (1977)
- % of current: 83.7

Higher education is consolidated under two large universities, the Arts and Sciences University of Yangon and the Arts and Sciences University of Mandalay, each with independent degree-granting colleges. Ten colleges are affiliated with the University of Yangon and five are affiliated with the University of Mandalay.

LEGAL SYSTEM

The basis of the Myanma legal system is the Myanmar Code, which is derived from the Indian Penal Code of 1860 and the Indian Criminal Procedure Code of 1898.

The judiciary has been reorganized a number of times since independence. On September 26, 1988, the State Law and Order Restoration Council established by decree a new judicial structure under a Supreme Court of one chief judge and no more than five other judges. Subordinate state, divisional and township courts, manned by judicial officers, were established by the Supreme Court on September 29, 1988. Under the Constitution of 1974 the highest court was the Council of People's Justices, elected by the People's Assembly from a list submitted by the State Council. This court's term of office was the same as that of the People's Assembly. The People's Councils at lower levels similarly elected state and divisional judges' committees and township, village and ward judges' committees. The People's Assembly also elected a Council of People's Attorneys from a list submitted by the the State Council. The Council of People's Attorneys was responsible for directing state, township and divisional law officers, protecting the rights of the people and supervising the central and local organs of state power.

There was no provision in Myanma law for a person in detention to seek a judicial determination of the legality of the detention. In cases involving national security, persons sometimes were never formally charged but held in indefinite detention without trial. The government neither acknowledged holding political prisoners nor considered itself compelled to justify the detention or imprisonment of anyone. The number of political detainees was thought to have decreased in the 1980s, when there was a general amnesty. Some estimates place the current number in the hundreds, however, owing to widespread detention of dissidents and political opponents which has escalated since the May 1990 elections.

In common criminal cases, police often detained suspects up to 24 hours, after which a court order had to be sought from competent judicial authorities. These court orders, which were renewable, authorized extensions of the detention for 14-day periods until charges were formally brought before a court. Detainees frequently were held incommunicado during the period of investigation and interrogation but normally were allowed visitors thereafter. Refugees and other stateless persons were regarded as illegal immigrants subject to arrest. If they could not be repatriated after serving sentences for illegal entry, they could be detained indefinitely. The Myanma government is thought to have had under detention several hundred illegal immigrants from a number of Asian countries. Over 100 of these detainees were voluntarily repatriated in recent years, and the Myanma government reportedly was willing to release those remaining if they were accepted for permanent resettlement elsewhere.

Justice was administered by "judges' committees." These committees were elected from a single slate of candidates chosen by the BSPP. Almost all judges were BSPP members, and a large number were military officers, either active or retired. Although untrained in the law, they normally were advised by professional legal officers. The legal code was residually based on the British colonial system of law, with an overlay from the 1974 Constitution and other legal measures imposed by Ne Win's government. The judiciary was not independent of the government, which could influence both verdict and sentence, particularly in political/security cases. The 1974 Constitution provided for public trials in most cases, and this practice was followed in common criminal cases. In political/security cases, special judiciary committees could be named by the State Council. The public normally was not allowed to attend such trials.

When both common criminal and political/security cases came to trial, the burden of proof was on the prosecution, and the accused had the right to counsel. Legal counsel was provided for indigent defendants if they were faced with a possible sentence of seven years or more. Normally, defendants could consult freely and privately with their lawyers, and defendants and their lawyers were made aware of the charges and evidence and were permitted to submit their own evidence. The verdicts of civil, security and military courts could be appealed to the next higher court, up to the State Council.

The correctional system, administered by an inspector general of prisons, consisted of over 40 detention facilities, of which 10 were central prisons, 20 were district jails and 10 were subjails or guardhouses, the last for short-term prisoners convicted of minor offenses. The average prison population was estimated at 6,000 in a given month.

LAW ENFORCEMENT

The principal law enforcement agency is the People's Police Force, with a strength of about 38,000. It is divided into the Yangon City Police, with responsibility for law enforcement in the metropolitan area of the capital, and the Myanmar Civil Police, which operates in all other areas. The army dominates the higher echelons of the police force, including the post of director general. Since 1988 the State Law and Order Restoration Council has been in charge of all policymaking decisions and appointments.

The Myanmar Civil Police is organized into 14 units, corresponding to the administrative divisions. Each unit is headed by a director and is subdivided into districts, stations and outposts.

Crime statistics are incomplete and outdated. Political unrest, marked by violence and revolt, is the major law enforcement problem.

Before the 1988 coup, intelligence and surveillance activities were carried out by the National Intelligence Bureau, made up of the Special Intelligence Department of the National People's Police, the Military Intelligence Service and the Bureau of Special Investigations in the office of the president. The bureau was headed by the director of the Military Intelligence Service. All intelligence activities now are under control of the SLORC.

HEALTH

Malaria, respiratory diseases, leprosy, venereal diseases, intestinal disorders, cholera and plague are the most serious health problems in the country. Lack of preventive sanitation is the main environmental factor affecting public health. Only 27% of the population has access to safe water.

HEALTH INDICATORS

Health personnel 1982
- Physicians: 11,076 (1987–88)
  - persons per: 3,485 (1987–88)
- Dentists: 410
- Nurses: 6,978
- Pharmacists: 80
- Midwives: 15,543

Hospitals 1982
- Number: 614
- Number of beds (/10,000): 7 (1987–88)
- Admissions/discharges (/10,000): 289
- Bed occupancy rate (%): 78.1
- Average length of stay (days): 9

Public health expenditures (latest)
- As % of national budget: 4.9
- Per capita (U.S. $): 1.80

Vital statistics
- Crude death rate (/1,000): 13 (1990)
- Life expectancy at birth 1990
  - Males: 53.1
  - Females: 56
- Infant mortality rate (/1,000 live births): 97 (1990)
- Child mortality rate under 5 yrs. (/1,000 live births) (1985–90): 85
- Maternal mortality rate (/100,000 live births) (1986–87): 135 (est.)
- Population with access to safe water (%): 27 (latest)

FOOD & NUTRITION

The staple Burmese diet consists of rice; a bland curry sauce; and *ngapi*, a salted paste of fish or shrimp. Pork is the most common meat. Fish is the main source of protein.

MEDIA & CULTURE

Myanmar's media are wholly government-owned and all forms of communications are subject to government censorship. The government-controlled press consists of six daily newspapers with a combined circulation of 533,000. There are numerous non dailies and periodicals with a combined circulation of well over 1 million. Of the six daily newspapers, two are published in English. Newspapers in languages other than Burmese or English are not permitted. There is little or no advertising. All the daily newspapers have national circulation.

All controversial materials are censored, and discussions of national policy in the press that do not praise the "Myanma way to socialism" are banned.

In 1976 the Central Press Registration Board issued guidelines for publishers, film producers and musicians. The document set out the principles under which the government would censor materials. The statement

PRINCIPAL DAILIES	
Daily	Circulation
Kyemon (Mirror)	140,000
Botahtaung (Vanguard Daily)	140,000
Loketha Pyithu Neizin (Working People's Daily)	135,000
Myanma Alin (New Light of Burma)	50,000
Guardian	19,000
Working People's Daily	14,000

said, "Everyone has the freedom of literary expression so long as the freedom is used in the interests of the people." Among the do's was publication of literature that would "educate the people for active participation in socialist construction." Among the don'ts was publication of literature lauding capitalism or the "decadent" Western culture.

The 1974 Constitution guaranteed freedom of speech, expression and publication but stipulated that the exercise of such freedoms should not be "contrary to the interest of the working people and socialism." In practice, opposition viewpoints and public criticism of the government are not tolerated. Anyone criticizing the government's leadership in public or private is subject to arrest.

All mass media in Myanmar are government-owned and government-operated, including television, radio and the six daily newspapers. Newspaper editors are appointed by the SLORC. Editorials must be approved in advance. Journalists are subject to strict guidelines as to what can be broadcast or published, especially on domestic matters. Although subject to prior review, international news reporting generally is objective and balanced. All foreign publications must be cleared by the Press Scrutiny Board before they may be legally imported or distributed. Criticism of government officials is not permitted.

MEDIA INDICATORS

Newspapers
- Number of dailies: 6 (latest)
- Circulation (000): 533 (latest)
- Per 1,000 pop.: 14 (latest)
- Newsprint consumption (1988)
  - Total metric tons: 6,300
  - Per 1,000 pop. (kg.): 158

Book publishing
- Number of titles: 673 (pre-1986)

Radio
- Number of transmitters: 6 (1989)
- Number of persons per radio receiver: 13 (1989)

Television
- Television transmitters: 8 (1989)
- Number of persons per T.V. receiver: 41 (pre 1986)

Cinema
- Number of fixed cinemas: 175 (pre-1986)
- Seating capacity (000): 136 (pre-1986)

Films
- Number of long films produced: 28 (latest)
- Number of long films imported: 38 (1987)
  - % from India: 36.8
  - % from Japan: 26.3
  - % from U.K.: 13.2
  - % from U.S.: 10.5

The national news agency is the News Agency of Myanmar (NAM), which has no foreign correspondents but obtains its news from other news agencies. Foreign news bureaus in Yangon include Xinhua, TASS, ANSA, AFP, AP, Reuters and dpa.

The book publishing industry consists of eight publishing houses. The Myanmar Translations Society or Sarpay Beikman (Palace of Literature) is a state agency engaged in translations of Western writings into Burmese and in the publication of *Encyclopaedia Burmanica*. Myanmar does not adhere to any copyright convention.

The state-owned Myanmar Broadcasting Service operates one FM, nine shortwave and two medium-wave transmitters, broadcasting 111 hours a week in Burmese and English and 23 hours in minority languages. A color television service went on the air in 1980, broadcasting from Yangon for two hours daily.

Myanmar has a relatively well-developed motion picture industry. The Film Council directs government assistance to the film industry. The Motion Picture Agency Board has a monopoly over the importation of foreign films.

CULTURAL & ENVIRONMENTAL INDICATORS

Libraries (latest)
- Number: 6
- Volumes (000): 154

Nature reserves (latest)
- Number of facilities: 2

The largest library is the National Library at Yangon; there are five other libraries. Total number of volumes is 154,000. There are 12 museums, with an annual attendance of nearly 500,000.

SOCIAL WELFARE

Social Security was introduced in 1955 and is applicable to all establishments with 10 or more workers. The program covers sickness, maternity and work injuries. Work injury benefits include free medical care, disability payments, funeral grants and survivors' pensions. There are no unemployment benefits, and old-age pensions are available only to government employees. The program is administered by the Social Security Board, which maintains its own clinics and hospitals.

GLOSSARY

bogyoke: literally, great general. Title of Ne Win and Aung San.

kyaung: Buddhist monastery and, by extension, Buddhist religious school maintained by monks.

Lanzin: the Burma Socialist Program Party.

maung: title of address used toward a male of lesser status than the speaker.

Myanma: native term for Burma derived from Chinese, *mien;* also Myanma Pyi, land of the Burmans.

myo: town or township or a similar administrative unit. Thus, **myo-wun** (governor), **myo-ok** (township officer), **myo-thugyi** (headman of a village).
pongyi: Buddhist monk.
pyidawtha: literally, happy land. Burmese welfare state.
Pyithu Hluttaw: People's Assembly, the parliament of Myanmar.
Red Flag: Moscow-oriented Communist Party.
Sangha: the community of Buddhist monks, considered as the core of Buddhist church.
sawba: title of hereditary Shan chiefs.
Thakin: title of address used toward a superior, equivalent to sir.
triangle: name given to a territory in eastern Burma comprising Shan and Karenni states.
U: term of address used toward a man of great learning or piety.
White Flag: Peking-oriented Communist Party.

CHRONOLOGY (from 1948)

1948— Myanmar (at the time, Burma) becomes an independent republic, with U Nu as prime minister. . . . White Flag Communists and Karen secessionists launch rebellions.
1951— In national elections U Nu's Anti-Fascist People's Freedom League (AFPFL) gains absolute majority.
1952— Kyat is introduced as Burmese currency, replacing the Burmese rupee.
1953— Sixth Great Buddhist Synod is held in Yangon. . . . Eight-year development plan, also known as Pyidawtha Plan, is launched.
1956— In second national elections, AFPFL retains power but with a reduced majority. . . . Soon after elections U Nu steps down from power for eight months. . . . AFPFL is split into two factions: the Clean AFPFL, led by U Nu, and the Stable AFPFL, led by U Ba Swe.
1958— Faced with internal dissensions and threat from insurgents, U Nu yields power to a caretaker government led by Ne Win, the army chief of staff.
1960— U Nu returns to power in national elections at head of Clean AFPFL, later renamed Pyidaungsu Party. . . . Border pact with People's Republic of China is concluded, followed by a Treaty of Friendship and Nonaggression.
1961— Buddhism is made the state religion.
1962— In bloodless coup Gen. Ne Win seizes power; he sets up Revolutionary Council as supreme legislative and executive organ, promulgates manifesto titled *The Burmese Way to Socialism* and founds the Burma Socialist Program Party (BSPP). U Nu is placed in detention.
1963— All banks and major industries are nationalized. . . . Under the Enterprise Nationalization Law aliens, such as Indians and Chinese, are excluded from all types of economic activity.
1964— All political parties are banned except the BSPP, which becomes the sole political organization in the country.
1965— Government-controlled Buddha Sasana Sangha Organization is formed in an effort to reduce political power of the monks.
1966— Myanmar leaves the sterling area.
1967— Anti-Chinese riots erupt in Yangon; Sino-Burmese relations are strained.
1969— Former prime minister U Nu escapes and is granted asylum in Thailand.
1972— Ne Win and associates in the Revolutionary Council give up military ranks.
1974— New Constitution is promulgated. . . . The country's official name is changed to Socialist Republic of the Union of Burma. . . . Ne Win is elected president. . . . Buddhism is no longer the state religion.
1975— Kyat is devalued by 23%. . . . Students riot in Yangon over burial of U Thant, former secretary general of United Nations. . . . Five Kachin and Karen insurgent groups organize the Federal National Democratic Front to overthrow Ne Win.
1976— Plot to assassinate Ne Win is uncovered.
1977— U Maung Maung Kha is named new prime minister, replacing Sein Win.
1978— President Ne Win is reelected in national elections. . . . Arakanese Muslims flee across the border into Bangladesh, charging persecution and genocide; Myanmar reaches peaceful accord with Bangladesh over repatriation of Muslim refugees and their resettlement in Myanmar.
1979— Myanmar quits the nonaligned movement after the Havana summit of nonaligned nations.
1980— Following general amnesty, former prime minister U Nu returns to Myanmar from Thailand. . . . Government proposes two-tier citizenship in move to exclude naturalized Burmese of Chinese, Indian or Pakistani origin from political and economic life of the country.
1981— Ne Win steps down as president in favor of San Yu.
1983— Former key Ne Win aide Tin U is arrested for corruption, and his supporters are purged. . . . Bomb blast during visit of South Korean president kills 17 South Korean officials; North Korea is implicated in the terrorist attack; Myanmar cuts diplomatic relations with North Korea.
1985— Ne Win resumes BSPP chairmanship; San Yu becomes vice president of the BSPP.
1987— Students lead demonstrations against Ne Win; civil unrest continues to grow
1988— Anti-government riots are violently repressed; Ne Win resigns his post in the BSPP; Gen. Saw Maung, as head of the SLORC, assumes power in a military coup. . . . Western aid to Myanmar is halted as thousands are killed in riots; the Constitution is suspended, giving the SLORC unrestricted executive, legislative and judicial authority. . . . Maung's government lifts ban on political parties; the ruling BSPP changes its name to the National Unity Party (NUP). The military arrests and harasses opposition leaders.
1989— The country's name (formerly Burma) is officially changed to the Union of Myanmar (Pyidaungzu

Myanma Naingngandaw). . . . Maung announces upcoming free-multi-party elections and plans for a new constitution. . . . Maung disqualifies the NLD's two leading members from contesting the May 1990 elections. . . . the government forcibly evicts 200,000 citizens from their city homes.

1990— Elections are held in May: of the 485 parliamentary seats contested, the NLD wins 397, the NUP only 10; Saw Maung and the SLORC refuse to relinquish power. . . . U Nu is placed under house arrest; government troops kill thousands of protestors including monks and students; opposition leaders are arrested and tortured.

1991— Saw Maung continues to rule Myanmar; at least 50 NLD leaders are currently in prison; human rights abuses continue.

BIBLIOGRAPHY

BOOKS & FILMS

Adas, Michael. *The Burma Delta: Economic Development and Social Change on the Rice Frontier.* Madison, Wis., 1974.

Aung-Thwin, Michael. *Pagan: The Origins of Modern Burma.* Honolulu, Hawaii, 1985.

Bandhopadyaya, Kalyani. *Burma and Indonesia: Comparative Study of Political Economy and Foreign Policy.* Highland Park, N.J., 1983.

Bandyopadhyaya, Sekhara. *Burma To-day: Economic Development and Political Control Since 1962.* Calcutta, India, 1987.

Bixler, Norma. *Burma.* New York, 1971.

Burma: Buddhism and Neutralism. B&W film, 16 mm., 55 min. Contemporary Films.

Burma: People of the River. Color film, 16 mm., 14 min. *Encyclopaedia Britannica.*

Cady, John F. *The United States and Burma.* Cambridge, Mass., 1976.

Donnison, F. S. V. *Burma.* New York, 1970.

Dorn, F. W. *With Stilwell in Burma.* New York, 1973.

Gyi, Maung. *Burmese Political Values.* New York, 1983.

Keyes, Charles F. *Ethnic Adaptation and Identity: The Karen on the Thai Frontier with Burma.* Philadelphia, 1979.

Lissak, Moshe. *Military Roles in Modernization: Civil-Military Relations in Thailand and Burma.* Beverly Hills, Calif., 1976.

Maring, Joel M., and Ester G. Maring. *Historical and Cultural Dictionary of Burma.* Metuchen, N.J., 1973.

Nash, Manning. *Golden Road to Modernity.* Chicago, 1973.

Nu, U. *Saturday's Son.* New Haven, Conn., 1975.

Sein, Ma Mya. *The Administration of Burma.* New York, 1973.

Silverstein, Josef. *Burma: Military Rule and the Politics of an Asian State.* Ithaca, N.Y., 1977.

———. *Burmese Politics: The Dilemma of National Unity.* New Brunswick, N.J., 1980.

Singh, Kumar Badri Narain. *Freedom Struggle in Burma.* New Delhi, India, 1989

Smith, Bardwell. *Religion and Legitimation of Power in Thailand, Laos and Burma.* Chambersburg, Pa., 1978.

Smith, Eric D. *Battle for Burma.* New York, 1979.

Southeast Asia: Burma and Thailand. Color film, 16 mm., 13 min. Coronet Films.

Steinberg, David I. *Burma: A Socialist Nation.* Boulder, Colo., 1982.

———. *Burma's Road to Development: Growth and Ideology Under Military Rule.* Boulder, Colo., 1981.

Trager, Frank N., and Thomas T. Winant. *Burma: Japanese Military Administration: Selected Documents, 1941–45.* Philadelphia, 1971.

OFFICIAL PUBLICATIONS

Central Statistical Organization. *Economic Indicators* (English).

Planning and Finance Ministry. *Budget Estimates.* Books I–III for People's Congress and various councils, ministries and departments.

———. *Budget Estimates.* Book IV for boards and corporations.

———. *Budget Estimates.* Book V for local authorities.

———. *Budget Estimates.* Book VI for capital expenditures of above units.

———. *Report to the Council of People's Representatives* (Burmese and English).

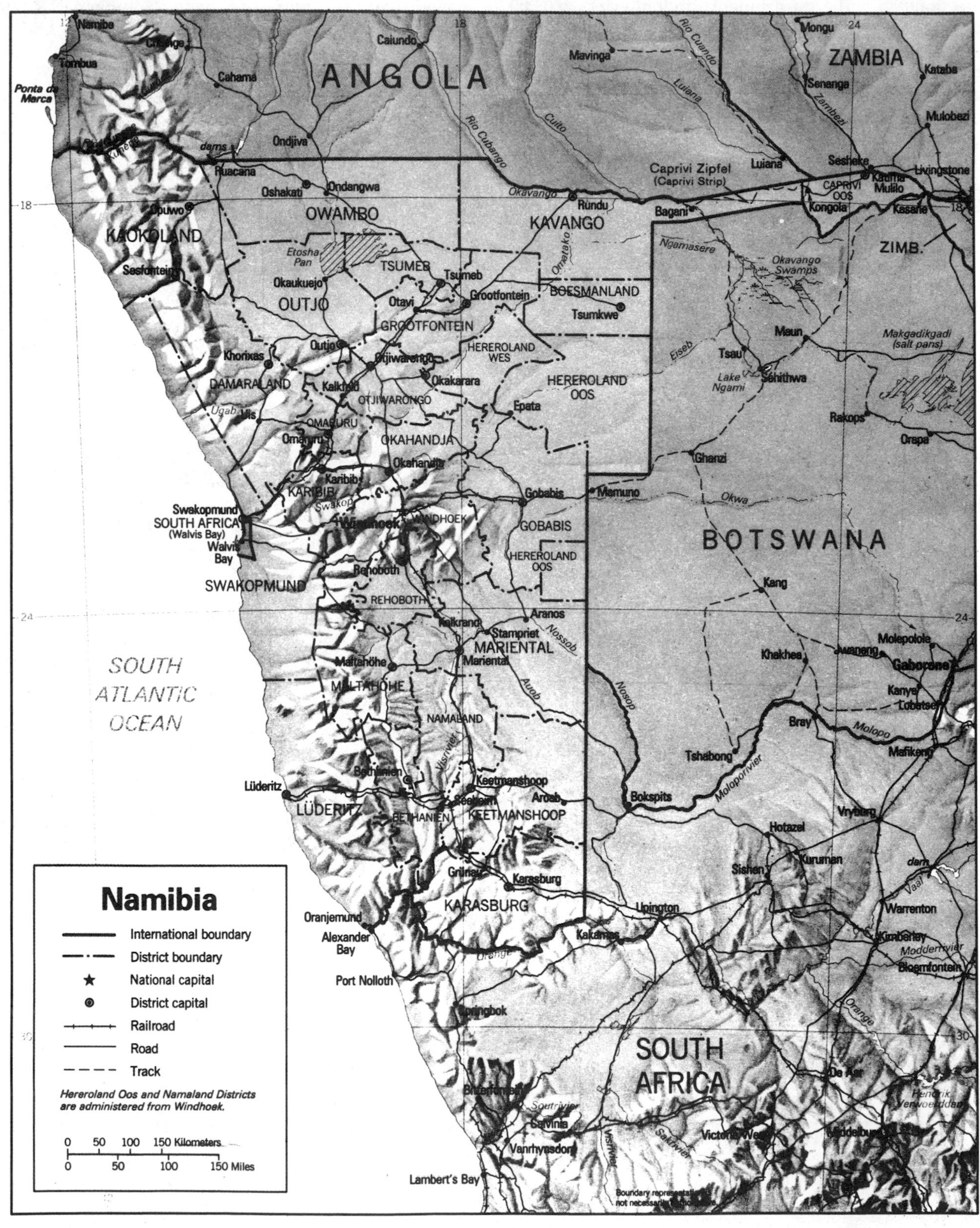

Namibia
International boundary
District boundary
National capital
District capital
Railroad
Road
Track
Hereroland Oos and Namaland Districts are administered from Windhoek.
0 50 100 150 Kilometers
0 50 100 150 Miles
ANGOLA
ZAMBIA
ZIMB.
BOTSWANA
SOUTH AFRICA
SOUTH ATLANTIC OCEAN
Caprivi Zipfel
(Caprivi Strip)
OWAMBO
KAOKOLAND
KAVANGO
TSUMEB
OUTJO
GROOTFONTEIN
BOESMANLAND
HEREROLAND WES
HEREROLAND OOS
DAMARALAND
OTJIWARONGO
OMARURU
OKAHANDJA
KARIBIB
WINDHOEK
GOBABIS
SWAKOPMUND
SOUTH AFRICA
(Walvis Bay)
REHOBOTH
MARIENTAL
MALTAHÖHE
NAMALAND
LÜDERITZ
BETHANIEN
KEETMANSHOOP
KARASBURG
CAPRIVI OOS
Namibe
Tombua
Ponta da Marca
Cahama
Caiundo
Mavinga
Ondjiva
Ruacana
Oshakati
Ondangwa
Opuwo
Sesfontein
Etosha Pan
Okaukuejo
Tsumeb
Grootfontein
Otavi
Tsumkwe
Rundu
Bagani
Outjo
Khorixas
Otjiwarongo
Okakarara
Kalkfeld
Epata
Omaruru
Okahandja
Karibib
Swakopmund
Walvis Bay
Windhoek
Gobabis
Mamuno
Rehoboth
Aranos
Kalkrand
Stampriet
Mariental
Maltahöhe
Bethanien
Keetmanshoop
Seeheim
Aroab
Lüderitz
Grünau
Karasburg
Oranjemund
Alexander Bay
Port Nolloth
Springbok
Lambert's Bay
Vanrhynsdorp
Calvinia
Upington
Kakamas
Bokspits
Tshabong
Hotazel
Kuruman
Sishen
Vryburg
Mafikeng
Warrenton
Kimberley
Bloemfontein
De Aar
Victoria West
Middelburg
Hendrik Verwoerddam
Ghanzi
Kang
Khakhea
Jwaneng
Molepolole
Gaborone
Kanye
Lobatse
Bray
Tsau
Sehithwa
Maun
Rakops
Orapa
Lake Ngami
Okavango Swamps
Makgadikgadi (salt pans)
Ngamasere
Mongu
Senanga
Kataba
Mulobezi
Sesheke
Livingstone
Katima Mulilo
Kongola
Kasane
Luiana
Rio Cuando
Luiana
Cuito
Rio Cubango
Okavango
Zambezi
Kunene
Omatako
Eiseb
Okwa
Nossob
Auob
Ugab
Swakop
Visrivier
Molopo
Moloporivier
Orange
Vaal
Modderrivier
Soutrivier
Sakrivier
Vis rivier
Boundary representation not necessarily authoritative
dams
dam
18
24
30

NAMIBIA

BASIC FACT SHEET

OFFICIAL NAME: Republic of Namibia

CAPITAL: Windhoek

HEAD OF STATE AND HEAD OF GOVERNMENT: Sam Nujoma

NATURE OF GOVERNMENT: multiparty republic

POPULATION: 1,302,000 (1990)

AREA: 824,295 sq. km. (317,827 sq. mi.)

ETHNIC MAJORITY: Ovambo

OFFICIAL LANGUAGE: English

OFFICIAL RELIGION: none; 90% of population is Christian

UNIT OF CURRENCY: 1 South African rand (R) = 100 cents

NATIONAL FLAG: A blue triangle (with its base at the hoist and its apex in the upper fly) and a green triangle (with its base in the fly and its apex at the lower hoist) separated by a broad, white-edged red stripe (running from the lower hoist to the upper fly); a gold sun with 12 triangular rays sits atop in the blue triangle.

NATIONAL ANTHEM: Namibia Land of the Brave

NATIONAL HOLIDAYS: January 1 (New Year's Day), March 21 (Independence Day), May 1 (Workers' Day), September 5 (Settlers' Day), December 10 (Human Rights Day), and various Christian holidays.

NATIONAL CALENDAR: Gregorian

PHYSICAL QUALITY OF LIFE INDEX: 47

DATE OF INDEPENDENCE: March 21, 1990

DATE OF CONSTITUTION: February 9, 1990

WEIGHTS AND MEASURES: metric

GEOGRAPHICAL FEATURES

Namibia is located on the southwest coast of Africa and bisected by the Tropic of Capricorn. It is bordered by South Africa to the south and southeast, by Botswana to the east and by Angola to the north. In the west Namibia has a long coastline on the Atlantic Ocean. The narrow Caprivi Strip, between Angola and Botswana in the northeast, extends Namibia to the Zambezi River, giving it a short border with Zambia as well.

Namibia covers a total area of 824,295 sq. km. (317,827 sq. mi.), including the enclave of Walvis Bay (900 sq. km./347 sq. mi.), over which South Africa maintains control, but which Namibia's 1990 independence Constitution declares to be part of Namibian territory.

The capital is Windhoek with an estimated population of 120,000 in 1990. The other principal urban centers are Swakopmund (15,500), Rehoboth (15,000) and Rundu (15,000).

The country is divided into three basic geographical zones: the Namib Desert along the west coast, the central plateau, and the Kalahari Desert in the east. The Namib Desert covers about one-sixth of Namibia's total area and is uninhabitable. Diamonds are the most valuable natural resource in the Namib Desert; they are found in the coastal dunes and in the sand on the seabed. The central plateau, an area of savanna and bush, covers just over half of the land area. Although it receives more rain than the desert areas, it is still dry and more suitable to raising livestock than to farming. The most fertile and best-watered areas of Namibia are in the north near the Kunene River and in the Caprivi Strip.

CLIMATE & WEATHER

Namibia's climate is the driest in Africa, with sunny, warm days and cooler nights. The mean January temperature at Windhoek is 23° C (73° F); in winter, the mean temperature is 13° C (55° F). The fertile northern strip is always warmer.

The rainy season lasts from December to March. In the Namib Desert it may be as short as one month, two to four months on the central plateau and five months in the Caprivi strip. The mean annual rainfall in the Namib Desert and southern central plateau is 0–250 mm. (0–10 in.); in the Kalahari Desert and central plateau 250–500 mm. (10–20 in.); in the Caprivi Strip and northern Ovamboland 500–1,000 mm. (20–40 in.).

POPULATION

The total population of Namibia is variously estimated at between 1,300,000 (internal government estimate before independence) and 1,700,000 (U.N. estimate) and is predominantly rural. Differences in population figures may result from different calculations of the number of refugees who fled Namibia to Angola, Botswana and Zambia. In addition, the South African internal government figure was widely believed to be inaccurate because of that country's desire to play down the low level of welfare spending per capita and to give an inflated picture of the proportion of whites in the population.

About 75% of the population lives in the northern part of the country.

DEMOGRAPHIC INDICATORS

Population (000): 1.302 (1990)
Year of last census: 1981
Sex distribution (% at last census): males, 49.2; females, 50.8
Population estimates and projections (000)

1940: 336	1970: 761	2000: 1,667
1950: 405	1980: 1,002	2010: 2,136
1960: 522	1990: 1,302	

Age profile (% 1980 est.)

0–14: 44.0	30–44: 15.5	60–74: 4.3
15–29: 26.0	45–59: 9.3	75 and over: 0.9

Population density per sq. km. (per sq. mi.): 1.6 (4.1) (latest)

VITAL STATISTICS

Crude birth rate (/1,000): 46 (1990)
Crude death rate (/1,000): 10 (1990)
Infant mortality rate (/1,000 live births): 71 (1990)
Life expectancy (yrs.) at birth: males, 57; females, 63 (1990)
Total fertility rate (/woman): 6.6 (1990)
Rate of natural increase (/1,000): 31.8 (1985–90)
Average household size: 4.8

STATUS OF WOMEN INDICATORS

Women's literacy rate (%): 7.8 (1987)
Total fertility rate (/woman): 6.6 (1990)

ETHNIC COMPOSITION

Approximately 86% of Namibians are black, 6.5% are white, and 7.5% are of mixed descent. About 45% of the population belongs to the Ovambo tribe and 9% to the Kavango tribe.

The black population has the following subdivisions: the Bantu-speaking Ovambo, Kavango, Herero and Himba; the non-Bantu Damara; the Khoi, known as Nama; the San, comprising the Khung, Heikum, Naron and Mbarakwengo subgroups; the Tswana; and various smaller groups related to communities in Angola, Botswana and Zambia.

The largest ethnic group is the Ovambo, who live mainly in the well-watered north and are made up of seven tribes: the KwaNjama, the Ndonga, KwaMbi, Ngandjera, Mbalantu, KwaLuthi and Nkolonkati. The second largest group, believed to be an offshoot of the Ovambo, is the Kavango, who reside along the Okavango River and consist of the KwaNgali, Mbunza, Sambju, Keiriku and Mbukushu. The Damara live east of the arid coast and to the south of the Ovambo. The Herero, a herding people, range north of Windhoek. The Nama, also herders, live in the deep south.

The mulatto community, consisting of people of mixed Caucasian and black ancestry, include the Rehoboth Basters and some Cape Mulattos who migrated from South Africa. The Basters are a farming community; the Cape Mulattos are primarily city dwellers.

The white community consists of descendants of the Germans who originally colonized Namibia, Afrikaners and a few English-speaking South Africans. Whites live predominantly in cities and in central and southern Namibia.

LANGUAGE

The official language is English, although Afrikaans and German are also widely used. Most of the African ethnic groups have their own languages.

Bantu-speaking groups in the northern regions include the Ovambo, the largest single group, and the Okavango, East Caprivian and Kaokolander ethnic groups. To the south, the major ethnolinguistic divisions are the Bantu-speaking Herero and Tswana and the Khoisan-speaking Bergdama, Nama and San peoples. The Rehoboth Basters represent a racial mix of Afrikaners and Nama.

Afrikaans is spoken by 60% of the white population, the rest speak German or English.

RELIGION

There is no official state religion, although about 90% of Namibians are Christian. Of the remaining 10%, a significant number follow traditional animist beliefs. The largest Christian denomination is Lutheran, with more than half of the Christian population; other denominations include Roman Catholic, Dutch Reformed, Anglican and Methodist.

HISTORICAL BACKGROUND

Prior to European contact, Namibia was occupied by the San, Ovambo, Nama, Damara and Herero peoples. In the late 1480s, Portuguese navigators first explored the country's coastal regions and were followed in the 17th, 18th and early 19th centuries by Dutch and British explorers. The German presence began in the 1840s with the arrival of the Rhenish Missionary Society. In 1878 Britain annexed Walvis Bay; an Anglo-German agreement in 1890 acknowledged German control of Namibia, with Britain retaining Walvis Bay. The Germans took the land and cattle from the indigenous population, creating a dispossessed African wage-labor force. In their effort to subdue the African inhabitants, the Germans fought extensive campaigns against the Hereros and Namas. A history of resistance to occupation, initiated by these two groups, ended in their near annihilation by the Germans. In 1904 the Herero again rose up against the German colonizers but were ruthlessly suppressed, their population being reduced from 80,000 to 16,000 starving refugees. German retaliation against the Nama and Damara uprisings wiped out about half of those groups.

German rule ended during World War I. In 1915, South African troops defeated the Germans and occupied Namibia. The territory was mandated to South Africa by the League of Nations in 1920, to be administered on behalf of Britain with the duty of preparing it for eventual self-determination. However, South Africa had no intention of giving up Namibia and governed it as though it were another province of the Union of South Africa. The first attempts to make

South Africa adhere to its mandate came in 1945 after formation of the United Nations as successor to the League of Nations. All other countries controlling mandated territories agreed to make them trusteeship territories under the United Nations. But South Africa refused, demanding full incorporation of Namibia into the Union, against the conditions of the original mandate. The United Nations refused to accept this demand. In 1950 the International Court of Justice (ICJ) ruled that the territory remain under an international mandate. In 1966 the U.N. General Assembly terminated South Africa's mandate over the territory, placing it under U.N. control, and from 1968 referred to it as Namibia. (Until that time the territory had been referred to as South West Africa.)

South Africa did not accept the United Nation's right to terminate its administration and in 1966 extended its apartheid laws to Namibia, retroactive to 1950. In an effort to marginalize Africans politically, South Africa divided the territory into homelands for different ethnic groups, with whites receiving the best farming and mining areas and the remainder being allocated to the African population. Mass removals of Africans were required to implement this policy.

The South West African People's Organization (SWAPO) was founded in 1958, under the leadership of Sam Nujoma. After having failed to persuade South Africa to negotiate independence for Namibia, SWAPO launched an armed struggle against the regime in 1966. Although the ICJ ruled in 1971 that South Africa's claims to Namibia and its occupation of the territory were invalid, South Africa ignored the rulings and tightened its grip on Namibia. In 1973 the U.N. General Assembly recognized SWAPO as the sole legitimate representative of the Namibian people and the United Nation's first commissioner for Namibia was appointed.

In 1974 as Angola prepared for independence from Portugal, South Africa grew fearful of what appeared to be the imminent installation of a socialist government there. Since SWAPO had strong links with the pro-socialist MPLA (Popular Movement for the Liberation of Angola) in Angola, South Africa built up links with the MPLA's rivals, UNITA (National Union for the Total Independence of Angola) and the FNLA (National Front for the Liberation of Angola). In 1975 South African troops invaded Angola in support of UNITA but were pushed out of the country in 1976 by the Cuban-backed MPLA forces. Consequently, the MPLA pledged its support for SWAPO's guerrilla war against South African occupation of Namibia, allowing SWAPO to establish training camps, refugee centers, schools, clinics and military bases in Angola. Fighting between the two countries continued throughout the 1970s and 1980s, with South Africa periodically invading Angola in alleged pursuit of SWAPO guerrillas.

Although the United Nations continued its efforts to bring about a negotiated solution for Namibia, South Africa refused to cooperate, pursuing its own plans for an internal settlement instead. A 1975 constitutional conference of internal groups was boycotted by SWAPO. The Democratic Turnhalle Alliance (DTA), consisting of pro-South African white groups and small Namibian parties willing to cooperate with the South Africans, emerged from the conference with a plan for a form of independence by 1978. Dirk Mudge, the DTA leader, announced that under the plan South African forces would remain in Namibia after independence. SWAPO rejected this and boycotted the 1978 elections, which were won by the DTA. After the elections, a South African–backed Constituent Assembly was set up, but it was not recognized internationally and had little internal standing.

In 1978 the U.N. Security Council adopted Resolution 435, which called for a cessation of hostilities, the complete withdrawal of South African troops and U.N.-supervised elections prior to Namibia's independence. However, the Pretoria government continued to attempt to consolidate the interim administration in Namibia and to reach a settlement on the independence issue outside the framework of Resolution 435. Nonetheless, the terms of Resolution 435 were finally set in motion as part of a tripartite agreement formally signed at the United Nations in December 1988 by Angola, Cuba (which was to withdraw its troops from Angola) and South Africa.

Implementation of the settlement began officially on April 1, 1989, marred initially by large-scale violence as SWAPO guerrillas sought to cross into Namibia and clashed with South African forces. A cease fire was negotiated to allow the transition process to proceed, and elections were held in November 1989 under the supervision of a U.N. Transition Assistance Group. SWAPO won 41 seats in a 72-member Constituent Assembly; the DTA won 21 seats. In December 1989 the parties that were represented in the Constituent Assembly introduced proposals for a draft constitution. The Constitution was formally adopted on February 9, 1990, to take effect at independence. In mid-February the Constituent Assembly elected Sam Nujoma to be the country's first president.

On March 21, 1990, Namibia became independent. The Constituent Assembly became the National Assembly, and the president assumed executive power.

CONSTITUTION & GOVERNMENT

The Constitution of the Republic of Namibia was formally adopted on February 9, 1990 and took effect at independence on March 21, 1990. Under the Constitution, the Republic of Namibia is a sovereign, secular, democratic and unitary state, and the Constitution is the supreme law. It guarantees the fundamental rights and freedoms of the individual regardless of sex, race, color, ethnic origin, religion, creed or social or economic status and gives all citizens the right to form and join political parties.

Executive power is vested in the president and the Cabinet. The president, who is head of state and of the government and the commander-in-chief of the defense force, is elected by direct, universal and equal suffrage and must receive more than 50% of the votes cast. The term of office is five years, and one person may not hold the office for more than two terms.

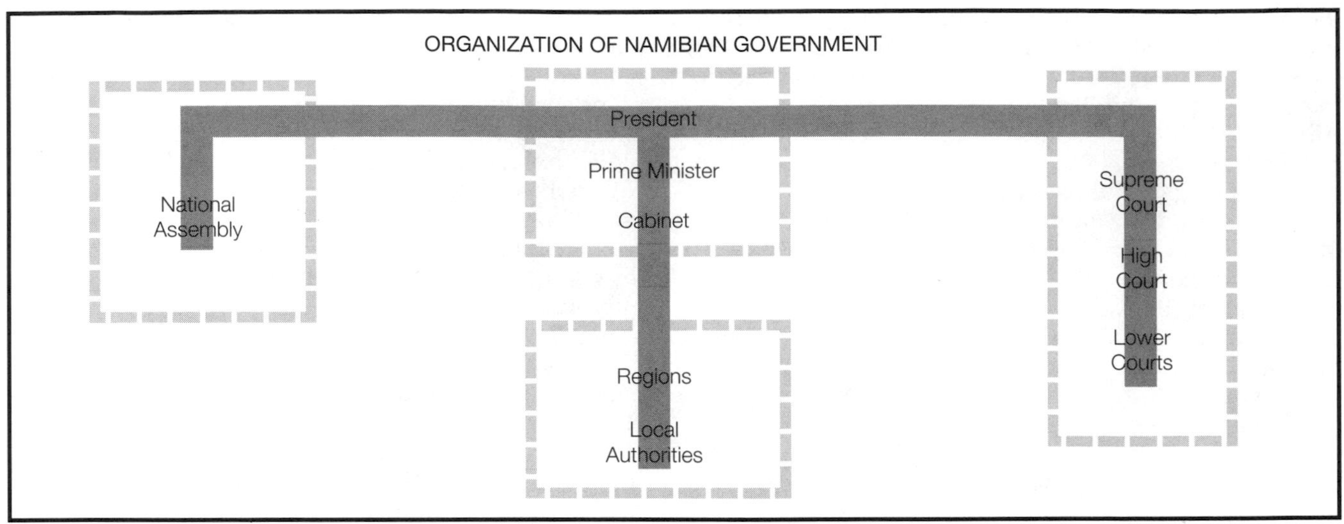

GOVERNMENT LIST
(July/August 1991)

President	Nujoma, Sam
Prime Minister	Geingob, Hage
Minister of Agriculture, Water & Rural Development	Hanekom, Gerhardt
Minister of Defense	Mueshihange, Peter
Minister of Education & Culture	Angula, Nahas
Minister of Finance	Herrigel, Otto
Minister of Fisheries & Marine Resources	Angula, Helmut
Minister of Foreign Affairs	Gurirab, Theo-Ben
Minister of Health & Social Services	Iyambo, Nicky, *M.D.*
Minister of Home Affairs	Pohamba, Hifikepunye
Minister of Information & Broadcasting	Hamutenya, Hidipo
Minister of Justice	Tjiriange, Ngarikutuke
Minister of Labor, Public Service & Manpower Development	Witbooi, Hendrik
Minister of Lands, Resettlement & Rehabilitation	Hausiku, Markus
Minister of Local Government & Housing	Amathila, Libertine, *M.D.*
Minister of Mines & Energy	Toiva ya Toiva, Andimba
Minister of Trade & Industry	Amathila, Ben
Minister of Wildlife, Conservation & Tourism	Bessinger, Nico
Minister of Works, Transport & Communications	Kapelwa, Richard
Minister of Youth & Sports	Ithana, Pendukeni
Governor, Central Bank	Benard, Wouter

The Cabinet consists of the president, the prime minister and other ministers whom the president appoints from members of the National Assembly. The Cabinet's functions include directing the activities of government departments, initiating bills for submission to the National Assembly, formulating the budget, and advising the president on matters of national defense.

Legislative authority lies with the Parliament. The former Constituent Assembly was converted upon independence into the lower house of a bicameral parliamentary structure, known as the National Assembly. An upper house, the National Council, will represent regional leaders and is to be created two years after independence. The repeal of, or amendments to, the Constitution require the approval of two-thirds of the members of the National Assembly and two-thirds of the members of the National Council; if the proposed repeal or amendment secures two-thirds of the members of the National Assembly, but not two-thirds of the members of the National Council, the president may make the proposals the subject of a national referendum, in which a two-thirds majority is needed for approval of the legislation.

The Constitution provides for an independent judiciary with a Supreme Court as its highest body.

FREEDOM & HUMAN RIGHTS

During its occupation and rule over Namibia, South Africa enforced many repressive laws, such as the Terrorism Act of 1967, which enabled security units to detain persons on suspicion; Proclamation AG26 of 1978, which allowed for indefinite detention for acts of sedition; and Proclamation AG50 of 1978, which provided for deportation for such acts. Torture and murder of prisoners were believed to be common practice.

Throughout the 1970s and 1980s, South African troops made many search and destroy raids into Angola in alleged pursuit of SWAPO guerrillas. During one of these raids in May 1978, South African troops attacked a SWAPO refugee camp inside Angola killing 600 refugees, many of them children, and wounding 1,000 more.

In the November 1989 elections, SWAPO won 41 of the 72 Constituent Assembly seats, failing to achieve the two-thirds majority that would have enabled the party to impose its own draft constitution on the emergent nation. It was widely held that SWAPO's popularity had been adversely affected by allegations that the organization had imprisoned and tortured some of its opponents; these allegations had been consolidated by a ruling of the Supreme Court in September 1989 that SWAPO was illegally detaining Namibian citizens abroad.

The independence Constitution guarantees the fundamental rights and freedoms of the individual regardless of sex, race, color, ethnic origin, religion, creed or social or economic status and gives all citizens the right to form and join political parties. It also makes apartheid a criminal offense, outlaws torture and formally bans the death penalty.

CIVIL SERVICE

No current information is available on the Namibian civil service.

LOCAL GOVERNMENT

Prior to independence, Namibia was divided into 26 districts. In an effort to marginalize Africans politically, South Africa had passed divisive laws creating homelands (Bantustans) for different ethnic groups. Elected bodies representing each of the 11 officially designated population groups (except the Bushmen) exercised semiautonomous authority in what were called "second-tier" assemblies. (Bushmen were governed by a commissioner and advisory council.) Municipal governments, village management boards and other "third-tier" entities provided local services.

Upon independence, the government announced plans to divide the country into new regions, with elected Regional Councils in charge of administering local government.

FOREIGN POLICY

Before independence, Namibia's foreign affairs were administered by South Africa. The South West Africa Constitutional Act passed in 1925 by the South African Parliament specified that the foreign affairs of South West Africa were the responsibility of the Republic of South Africa.

However, beginning in 1973, the United Nations recognized SWAPO as Namibia's only legitimate representative. During the Angolan civil war, SWAPO supported the prosocialist MPLA movement which, in turn, supported SWAPO's guerrilla war against the South African regime.

Already recognized as a member of the FAO, ILO, UNESCO and WHO, upon independence Namibia was to become a full member of the UN, NAM, Commonwealth, OAU and SADCC. It also planned to seek World Bank membership while remaining a part of the Southern African Customs Union for at least two years. Namibia also planned to join the Southern African Development Co-ordination Conference.

The independence government has stressed its support for a mixed economy, urging foreign investors to help Namibia escape from its almost complete economic dependence on South Africa. In 1990 President George Bush lifted all economic sanctions that had been imposed on Namibia while it was controlled by South Africa, and Canada announced that it would lift sanctions against Namibia and provide more than $4 million in aid to the new state.

Namibia's relations with South Africa are strained, due in part to their disagreement over the right of ownership to Walvis Bay. High-level talks concerning the port, which took place in March 1991, became deadlocked within a few hours and were broken off. The dispute poses a serious obstacle to normal relations between the two countries.

PARLIAMENT

Under the independence Constitution, legislative power is vested in the National Assembly, composed of 72 members elected by general, direct and secret ballots, and not more than six non-voting members appointed by the president. Every National Assembly may continue for a maximum period of five years, but may be dissolved by the president before the expiration of its term.

The National Council, planned to come into existence two years after independence, will have a term of six years and consist of two members from each region. Its functions will include considering all bills passed by the National Assembly, investigating any subordinate legislation referred to it by the National Assembly for advice and recommending legislation to the National Assembly on matters of regional concern.

In the November 1989 elections, SWAPO won 41 of the 72 seats contested in the National Assembly; the DTA won 21 seats; the United Democratic Front won 4; and the remaining 6 seats went to other parties.

POLITICAL PARTIES

Following is a partial list of political parties in Namibia:

Christian Democratic Action for Social Justice (CDA): supported by Ovambos and former members of the National Democratic Party, the CDA was established in 1982.

Democratic Turnhalle Alliance (DTA): A conservative and pro-South African party established in 1975, the DTA is a coalition of 11 ethnically based political groups.

Federal Convention of Namibia (FCN): The FCN is an alliance of 13 ethnically-based parties.

South West Africa People's Organization of Namibia (SWAPO): Founded in 1958 as the Ovamboland People's Organization, it was renamed South West Africa People's Organization in 1960 and adopted its present name in 1968. Although SWAPO has consistently maintained a leftist ideology, in 1989 it began to tone down its socialist rhetoric in favor of a more moderate stand on economic issues.

SWAPO-Democrats (SWAPO-D): A breakaway group, SWAPO-D was established in 1978 by a number of SWAPO dissidents.

United Democratic Front (UDF): The UDF is a coalition of eight parties.

Other parties include the Action Christian National, the Namibia National Democratic Party, the Namibia National Front and the National Patriotic Front.

ECONOMY

When Namibia became independent in 1990, SWAPO professed commitment to establishing a mixed economy and to attracting foreign investment. It made assurances that Namibia would apply to join the International Monetary Fund and also announced plans to redress the imbalance whereby more than half the land was owned by the country's white minority.

Namibia has the basis for a strong economy, despite its poor agricultural land and frequency of droughts. Its abundant mineral resources, including diamonds and metals, and rich fisheries are expected to form the basis of future economic prosperity.

However, after the devastation of war, and with an economy heavily dependent on ties with South Africa, the country faces severe problems. In 1990 it was estimated that as many as three in five Namibians were without formal employment. Walvis Bay, the only deep-water port, remained under the jurisdiction of South Africa. Moreover, shortly before independence, the South African government transferred an estimated $270 million from Namibia's state-controlled pension fund to major South African insurance companies, thus depriving the new government of a potential source of investment capital.

Nonetheless, Namibia decided to become a full member of the Southern African Customs Union and declared that the South African rand would remain the currency for at least two years. Namibia also planned to join the Southern African Development Co-ordination Conference, which seeks to reduce the dependence of southern African states on South Africa. In June 1990 foreign powers pledged some $160 million to $200 million in aid for 1990–91, against the $270 million requested by the government.

GROSS DOMESTIC PRODUCT

GDP per capita (U.S. $): 1,245 (1987)
GDP by type of expenditure (%): 1988
- Consumption
  - Private: 55
  - Government: 30
- Gross domestic investment: 20
- Foreign trade
  - Exports: 50
  - Imports: −56

Cost components of GDP (%) 1987
- Net indirect taxes: 13
- Consumption of fixed capital: 4
- Compensation of employees: 45
- Net operating surplus: 38

Sectoral origin of GDP (%) 1987
- Primary
  - Agriculture: 12
  - Mining: 25
- Secondary
  - Manufacturing: 5
  - Construction: 2
  - Public utilities: 2
- Tertiary
  - Transportation & communications: 7
  - Trade: 12
  - Finance: 8
  - Other services: 2
  - Government: 22

PUBLIC FINANCE

Namibia's budget for 1990–91 estimated revenues of R 2,366 billion and expenditures of R 2,516 billion.

Major sources of revenue come from income and profit taxes, nontax revenues, and customs and excise taxes.

The chief expenditure is for debt finance. Other expenditures include national defense, transportation, education, and health and welfare.

Namibia's fiscal year runs from April 1 to March 31.

From 1970–87 Namibia received $47.2 million in Western (non-U.S.), ODA and OOF bilateral aid.

CURRENCY & BANKING

The South African rand is divided into 100 cents. Upon independence, the government announced its continued use for a transitional period of at least two years.

The dollar exchange rate in June 1991 was $1 = R 2.566.

The South African Reserve Bank branch in Windhoek performs the functions of a central bank. In 1988 liabilities of R 1.458 trillion were on deposit in the country's banks.

AGRICULTURE

Namibia is essentially a stock-raising country, the scarcity of water and poor rainfall rendering crop-farming almost impossible. Less than 1% of Namibia is arable; that area stretches along the northern border.

Generally speaking, the southern half of the country is suited for the raising of small stock, while the central and northern parts are more suited for cattle. The principal agricultural activities are the production of karakul sheep pelts and raising beef cattle for export either as live animals or processed meat.

AGRICULTURAL INDICATORS

Farms as % of total land area: 0.8 (1983)
Land use % (1983)
- Permanent crops: 0.3
- Temporary and fallow crops: 99.7

Yields (kg./ha.) 1989
- Grains: 589
- Roots & tubers: 8,833
- Legumes: 1,046
- Milk (kg/animal): 412

Production 1989
- Fruits (000 metric tons): 35
- Vegetables (000 metric tons): 30

Livestock (000) 1989
- Cattle: 2,060
- Sheep: 6,500
- Pigs: 49

Fishing 1988
- Total catch (000 metric tons): 6.7
  - of which marine (%): 100.0

At independence, some 5,000 white ranchers owned about 80% of cultivable land and produced 95% of agricultural output (primarily cattle, sheep and karakul sheep pelts). The majority black population had a mere 5% of the land suitable for farming. A declared objective of the independence government is to implement land reform in co-operation with white landowners.

The waters off the Atlantic Coast are among the best fishing grounds in the world, giving Namibia the potential to be one of the richest fisheries in the world. However, Namibia's coastal waters were seriously overfished by foreign fleets during the 1980s, which severely depleted stocks and has since cut annual catches as well as overall output of fish products.

The main crops cultivated in Namibia are corn, millet and wheat. A large proportion of the indigenous population relies on subsistence farming for its livelihood. Namibia is not self-sufficient in food.

MANUFACTURING

Manufacturing is limited, concentrating on fish and meat processing for export, and brewing and baking for local consumption. No textile, construction materials or other industries have been developed. Namibia relies entirely on imports from South Africa. In 1980, 21.8% of the labor force was involved in manufacturing.

MINING

Mining is centered on diamonds, which account for almost half of the country's mineral exports. The diamond fields, a restricted area, run from the border with South Africa to an area just south of Walvis Bay. Uranium is the next most important source of mineral earnings. Most of Namibia's mines are situated in the center of the country, where lead and copper are among the base metals produced for export.

Before Namibia's independence, South African capital dominated the mining sector, even though other foreign companies had major shareholdings. The effect of this domination was that its mineral resources did not benefit Namibia, but South Africa's mining companies and their shareholders. South African government revenues from taxes and royalties were not put back into developing Namibia's infrastructure or economy, but into strengthening the South African military presence there and paying for Namibia's repressive government apparatus and white infrastructural facilities.

ENERGY

Namibia draws power from a hydroelectric facility on the Angola-Namibian border and from thermal plants near Walvis Bay and Windhoek. It also has a link to South Africa's power grid. All coal and petroleum products come from South Africa.

LABOR

Under South African rule Namibia developed an export-oriented economy owned by whites or by foreign multinational companies. The black population served purely as cheap labor for the whites and for the administration. A major role was played in exploitation by British, German and U.S. companies. Black workers, unable to gain employment or support themselves outside white businesses, supplied the export industries and the government with a convenient pool of cheap labor.

In July 1978 membership in trade unions was legalized for workers of all races. Fifteen trade unions, including groupings of unions and independent unions, exist. The largest is the mine worker's union, which has a sizeable black membership.

LABOR INDICATORS, 1985

Total economically active population (000): 477
- % working age (15–64): 55.4
- % female: 23.9

Activity rate (%)
- Total: 30.8
- Male: 47.3
- Female: 14.6

Sectoral employment of economically active (%) 1980

Sector	%
Agriculture, forestry, fishing:	43.4
Construction:	21.8 (combined)
Manufacturing, mining, quarrying, public utilities:	
Trade, hotels, restaurants:	34.7 (combined)
Transportation, communications:	
Finance, real estate:	
Services:	

In 1990, the unemployment rate was estimated to be as high as 69%. The majority of the economically active population was employed by the agricultural sector, which included subsistence farming. The rest of the labor force worked primarily in industry and commerce, services, government, and mining.

FOREIGN COMMERCE

About 90% of the goods produced in Namibia are exported. About 85%, including half of the country's food needs, are imported, chiefly from South Africa.

Minerals account for more than 72% of Namibia's exports. Almost half of the minerals exported are diamonds, but uranium, zinc and copper are also exported in large quantities. Agricultural products, primarily cattle, fish and karakul sheep pelts, account for the remainder of exports.

Namibia's major export destinations are South Africa, the United States and Japan.

FOREIGN TRADE INDICATORS, 1988

Exports (U.S. $ millions): 935
Imports (U.S. $ millions): 856
Balance of trade (U.S. $ millions): 79

Composition of Trade (%)

	Exports
Food & agricultural raw materials	16.4
Fuels & other energy	NA
Mineral ores & concentrates	72.6
Manufactured goods	11.0
of which chemicals	NA
of which machinery	NA

Food and machinery and manufactured consumer goods account for the majority of imports. Other principal imports include fuel, transport equipment and other capital goods.

Namibia's major import source is South Africa, although other import partners include Germany, the United Kingdom and the United States.

In an effort to encourage foreign investment in Namibia, the independence government issued liberal guidelines for foreign investment in June 1990.

TRANSPORTATION & COMMUNICATIONS

Railways in Namibia were administered by South African Transport Services (SATS) until May 1985, when the Namibian government assumed financial and operational control of all transport facilities associated with the railways. However, the service continued to be operated on a contractual basis by SATS until July 1988. The main railway line runs from the border with South Africa in the southeast to Windhoek, then northwest to Swakopmund, and south again to Walvis Bay.

The international airport is at Windhoek. There are some 150 other airports or airstrips in the country, of which 20 have permanently surfaced runways.

Walvis Bay, the only deep-water port, handles almost all of the country's shipping. The only other port is Luderitz. Although Namibia's independence Constitution declares Walvis Bay to be part of Namibian territory, South Africa continues to maintain control of it.

TRANSPORTATION INDICATORS

Roads (latest)
  Length, km. (mi.): 55,088 (34,232)
  Paved (%): 9
Motor vehicles (latest)
  Automobiles, trucks and buses: 103,715
  Persons per vehicle: 11
  Railroads (latest)
  Track, km. (mi.): 2,383 (1,481)
  Freight, metric ton-km. (short ton-mi.) (billions: 4.900 (3,356)
Ports (pre-1986)
  Cargo loaded (000 metric tons): 483
  Cargo unloaded (000 metric tons): 260
Air
  Airports with scheduled flights: 9 (1990)
Pipelines 1990
  Refined, km. (mi.): 289 (180)

COMMUNICATION INDICATORS, 1988

Telephones
  Total (000): 72
  Persons per telephone: 17
Phone traffic (millions)
  Long distance: 22.555 (1987) (minutes)
  International: 35.502 (1987) (minutes)
Post office
  Number of post offices: 81 (1978)
Telecommunications 1990
  Satellite stations: 4

TOURISM & TRAVEL INDICATORS

Total tourist receipts (U.S. $ millions): 46 (1981)

Namibia has a fairly active tourist trade. In the west, Swakopmund is the center for tours of the nearby Namib Desert dunes, and for visits to the wild Skeleton Coast to the north, so named because of the many vessels that were shipwrecked along the Atlantic shore. In the south, the Fish River Canyon ranks second in size to the Grand Canyon. There are also many guest and safari farms throughout the country.

DEFENSE

In accordance with the treaties signed by Angola, Cuba and South Africa on December 22, 1988, South Africa reduced its presence in Namibia from an estimated 50,000 troops to 1,500 by the beginning of July 1989, and completed the withdrawal of its forces immediately after the election held in November 1989. A military observer force, the U.N. Transition Assistance Group (UNTAG), was established to monitor the South African withdrawal, and an international police force helped to supervise the election. UNTAG was scheduled to withdraw from Namibia by April 1990, following the country's independence in March 1990.

In February 1990 recruitment for a Namibian defense force began. Former members of the disbanded South West Africa Territory Force, which had been controlled by South Africa, and former members of SWAPO's disbanded military wing, the People's Liberation Army of Namibia, were to be integrated into the new defense force. The first integrated units, comprising 500 men, began training in February under supervision by Kenyan members of UNTAG. Britain also sent military instructors to assist with the formation of a national defense force.

The total number of active-duty personnel reached 9,000 troops by the end of 1990. At present, the only military branch is the army.

EDUCATION

Prior to independence, education was administered by several ethnically based education authorities, the result being considerable discrepancies in the quality of education available to different ethnic groups. Budget allocations for education were paltry, with the majority allotted to white, rather than black, education. Education was compulsory for whites but not for blacks. About 68% of whites attended secondary school, but only 1% of blacks. Pupil/teacher ratios were better for whites than blacks, with one teacher for every 18 white children, compared with one to 45 for blacks.

The independence government has announced its intention to make education free and compulsory for all children up to 16 years of age. Higher education is provided by an academy and four teacher-training colleges. Various programs for informal adult education are also in operation in an effort to combat illiteracy. In 1985, according to estimates by UNESCO, the average rate of adult literacy was 72.5%. Other estimates have placed the literacy rate among blacks as low as 16%. The literacy rate among whites in Namibia is 100%.

EDUCATION INDICATORS, 1987

Literacy
- Total (%): 72.5
- Male (%): 74.2
- Female (%): 70.8

First and second level
- Schools: 1,122
- Students: 364,000
- Teachers: 11,945
- Student/teacher ratio: 30.5

Vocational
- Schools: 5
- Students: 1,200 (1982)
- Teachers: 81 (1982)
- Student/teacher ratio: 14.8 (1982)

Third level (post secondary)
- Institutions: 1
- Students: 4,200
- Teachers: 170
- Student/teacher ratio: 24.7

Public expenditure 1982
- Total (nat. currency): 34,781,000
- % of GNP: 1.9
- % of national budget: 4.1
- % of current expenditure: 89.3

LEGAL SYSTEM

Before independence, under South African administration, the system of justice was based on Roman-Dutch and Customary law.

The independence Constitution provides for an independent judiciary with a Supreme Court as its highest body. The Supreme Court consists of a Chief Justice and such additional judges as the President, acting on the recommendation of the Judicial Service Commission may determine. The Court hears appeals from the High Court, including those that involve constitutional matters. It also deals with matters referred to it by the Attorney General and other matters that may be authorized by act of Parliament.

The High Court, consisting of a Judge-President and additional judges as determined by the President acting on the recommendation of the Judicial Service Commission, has original jurisdiction in civil disputes and criminal prosecutions. It also hears appeals from lower courts. Lower courts are to be established by act of Parliament.

The independence constitution contains a bill of rights—including the right of freedom of speech, right to a fair trial and cultural and religious freedoms. It is entrenched against amendment.

LAW ENFORCEMENT

Before independence, law enforcement was imposed by the South African-controlled South West Africa Territorial Force and the South Africa Defence Force. Laws originated from the needs and security requirements of these occupying forces. The many repressive laws included the Terrorism Act of 1967, which enabled security units to detain persons on suspicion; Proclamation AG26 of 1978, which allowed for indefinite detention for acts of sedition; and Proclamation AG50 of 1978, which provided for deportation for such acts.

The independence Constitution reversed these and other acts. It also makes apartheid a criminal offense, outlaws torture and formally bans the death penalty.

HEALTH

Before independence, allocation of resources for health followed racial lines, with whites having greater access. Infant mortality rates reflected these priorities. In 1975, white infant mortality was 21 per 1,000 live births; the mulatto rate was 145, and the black rate 163. By 1990, infant mortality was 71 per 1,000 live births. Medical facilities exist primarily in towns, where most whites live, and are very scarce, often nonexistent, in rural areas.

HEALTH INDICATORS

Health personnel 1988
- Physicians: 281
  - persons per: 4,450
- Dentists: 41
- Nurses: 3,390
- Pharmacists: 70

Hospitals 1988
- Number: 61
- Number of beds (/10,000): 60

Vital statistics
- Crude death rate (/1,000): 10 (1990)
- Life expectancy at birth 1990
  - Males: 57
  - Females: 63
- Infant mortality rate (/1,000 live births): 71 (1990)
- Child mortality rate under 5 yrs. (/1,000 live births) (1985–90): 176

FOOD & NUTRITION

Vegetable products account for about 77% of the average caloric intake, animal products for about 23%. The average Namibian gets 96% of the FAO recommended minimum requirement.

MEDIA & CULTURE

Before independence, press freedom was heavily circumscribed by government controls. In 1987 the Namibian news agency Nampa was formed by SWAPO. Nampa operated with the continent-wide Pan-African News Agency. SWAPO also broadcast its own radio program, the Voice of Namibia, in English and vernacular languages, using facilities provided by Angola, Ethiopia, Tanzania, Zambia and Zimbabwe.

There are three daily and four weekly newspapers, all published in Windhoek. Foreign news bureaus in Namibia include the Inter Press Service and the South African Press Association.

The South West Africa Broadcasting Corporation, controlled by South Africa, had been responsible for domestic radio and television broadcasting. Renamed the Namibian Broadcasting Corporation, it now broadcasts on eight radio channels in 13 languages; television programs are broadcast in three languages.

Libraries serve most cities and towns. There is a national museum in Windhoek and local museums in Luderitz and Swakopmund.

MEDIA INDICATORS

Newspapers (latest)
- Number of dailies: 3
- Circulation (000): 9
- Per 1,000 pop.: 7

Radio
- Number of transmitters: c.40 (latest)
- Number of persons per radio receiver: 5.7 (1987)

Television
- Television transmitters: 13 (latest)
- Number of persons per T.V. receiver: 36

CULTURAL & ENVIRONMENTAL INDICATORS

Libraries (latest)
- Number: 8
- Volumes (000): 157

Nature reserves
- Number of facilities: 9 (latest)

SOCIAL WELFARE

By many economic and social indicators, Namibia is statistically better off than many black African countries. However, such figures are skewed by Namibia's white population. Such comparisons also mask the disparities between rural and urban Namibia.

Housing standards for black Africans are very low, although white residents' houses are better than satisfactory. The vast majority of rural dwellings are little more than hovels, and no government assistance is provided to upgrade them. Regional and local governments build and rent housing in the towns to migrant workers, but the supply of even such substandard accommodations is very small.

Before independence, only South African-based firms provided insurance coverage.

CHRONOLOGY

1915— South African troops defeat the Germans and occupy Namibia.

1920— Namibia is mandated to South Africa by the League of Nations.

1945— The United Nations calls for Namibia to become a U.N. trusteeship, but South Africa refuses to relinquish its rule.

1950— The ICJ rules that Namibia remain under an international mandate.

1958— SWAPO founded under the leadership of Sam Nujoma.

1966— The U.N. General Assembly terminates South Africa's mandate over Namibia, placing it under U.N. control. South Africa ignores this and extends its apartheid laws to Namibia. SWAPO launches an armed struggle against the South African regime in Namibia.

1968— The United Nations renames the country Namibia. (Until 1968 the country had been referred to as South West Africa.)

1971— The ICJ rules that South Africa's claims to Namibia are invalid.

1973— The U.N. General Assembly recognizes SWAPO as the sole legitimate representative of the Namibian people.

1974— Angola prepares for independence from Portugal; South Africa grows fearful of the likely installation of a socialist government there.

1975— South African troops invade Angola.

1976— South African troops pushed out of Angola by the Cuban-backed MPLA forces. The MPLA pledges its support for SWAPO.

1978— The DTA wins elections boycotted by SWAPO and a South African-backed internal government is established. The U.N. Security Council adopts Resolution 435, which calls for Namibia's independence.

1988— The terms of Resolution 435 are finally set in motion as part of a tripartite agreement formally signed by Angola, Cuba and South Africa.

1989— U.N.-supervised elections held in November. SWAPO wins 41 seats in a 72-member Constituent Assembly; the DTA wins 21 seats. In December the Constituent Assembly introduces proposals for a draft constitution.

1990— On February 9, the Constitution is formally adopted. Sam Nujoma is elected as the country's first president. On March 21, Namibia becomes independent. The Constituent Assembly becomes the National Assembly and the president assumes executive power.

BIBLIOGRAPHY

Dore, Isaak I. *The International Mandate System & Namibia.* Boulder, Colo., 1985.

Rocha, Maria. *In Search of Namibian Independence: The Limitations of the United Nations.* Boulder, Colo., 1984.

NAURU

BASIC FACT SHEET

OFFICIAL NAME: Republic of Nauru

ABBREVIATION: NU

CAPITAL: No formal capital. The seat of government is in the district of Uaboe,while government offices are in the district of Yaren.

HEAD OF STATE & HEAD OF GOVERNMENT: President Bernard Dowiyogo (from 1989)

NATURE OF GOVERNMENT: Parliamentary democracy

POPULATION: 9,202 (1990)

AREA: 21 sq. km. (8.2 sq. mi.)

ETHNIC MAJORITY: Nauruan

LANGUAGES: Nauruan (official), English

RELIGION: Christianity

UNIT OF CURRENCY: Australian dollar

NATIONAL FLAG: A blue field divided horizontally by a narrow gold band, symbolizing the equator. Below the band is a white 12-pointed star to the left.

NATIONAL EMBLEM: The principal elements of the national emblem are an oval wreathed by palm fronds, and ritual objects made of sharks' teeth and frigate bird feathers, with a 12-pointed star and the name Naoero on the top and the national motto. "God's Will First," at the bottom. Within the oval are a triangle surmounted by a cross, the alchemists' symbol for phosphorus; a frigate bird; and a sprig of *tomano,* a tropical plant.

NATIONAL ANTHEM: "Anibare Bay"

NATIONAL HOLIDAYS: January 31 (National Day, Independence Day); May 17 (Constitution Day); October 23 (Angam Day, commemorating the return of the population of Nauru to pre-World War II level); Christian festivals, including Christmas, Boxing Day and Good Friday

NATIONAL CALENDAR: Gregorian

PHYSICAL QUALITY OF LIFE INDEX: N.A.

DATE OF INDEPENDENCE: January 31, 1968

DATE OF CONSTITUTION: January 29, 1968

WEIGHTS & MEASURES: Imperial

GEOGRAPHICAL FEATURES

Nauru is an oval-shaped island in the western-central Pacific 53 km. (33 mi.) south of the equator, 3,539 km. (2,200 mi.) northeast of Sydney and 3,934 km. (2,445 mi.) southwest of Honolulu. Nauru is the smallest nation in Asia, with an area of 21 sq. km. (8.2 sq. mi.), extending 5.6 km. (3.5 mi.) north-northeast to south-southwest and 4 km. (2.5 mi.) east-southeast to west-northwest. Its coastline stretches 19 km. (12 mi.).

There is no formal capital; there are no urban centers. The Nauru Local Government Council meets in the Uaboe district.

The island is encircled by a sandy beach, which rises gradually, forming a fertile section no wider than 275 m. (300 yd.). A coral cliff rises from this belt to a central plateau about 60 m. (200 ft.) high. A brackish lagoon, known as Buada, covers some 121 ha. (300 ac.) at the southeastern end of the plateau.

CLIMATE & WEATHER

Nauru has a tropical climate, with a dry season from March to October and a wet season from November to February. The temperature in the shade ranges from 22.8° C (73° F) to 33.9° C (93° F). The average annual rainfall is only 45 mm (18 in.), but the range of annual variation is great; in some years the annual rainfall is 10 times normal, while in other years droughts are common.

POPULATION

The population of Nauru is not reported by the United Nations, but it was estimated at 9,202 in 1990, on the basis of the last official census, in 1983, when it numbered 8,042.

The overall density of population is 438.7 per sq. km. (1,134.1 per sq. mi.). Nauruans live in small settlements scattered throughout the island. The male/female ratio is 52.03:47.97. This predominance of males may be explained by the fact that the bulk of expatriates on

DEMOGRAPHIC INDICATORS

Population (000): 9.2 (1990)
Year of last census: 1983
Sex distribution (%, 1977 census): males, 52.1; females, 47.9
Population estimates (000)

1930: 3	1950: 4	1970: 7
1940: 3	1960: 5	1980: 8

Age profile (%, 1977 census)

0–14: 44.1	30–44: 11.4	60–74: 1.9
15–29: 33.1	45–59: 8.5	75 and over: 1.0

Number of cities of population over 500,000: 0 (1980)
Population density per sq. km. (per sq. mi.): 438.7 (1,134.1) (1990)

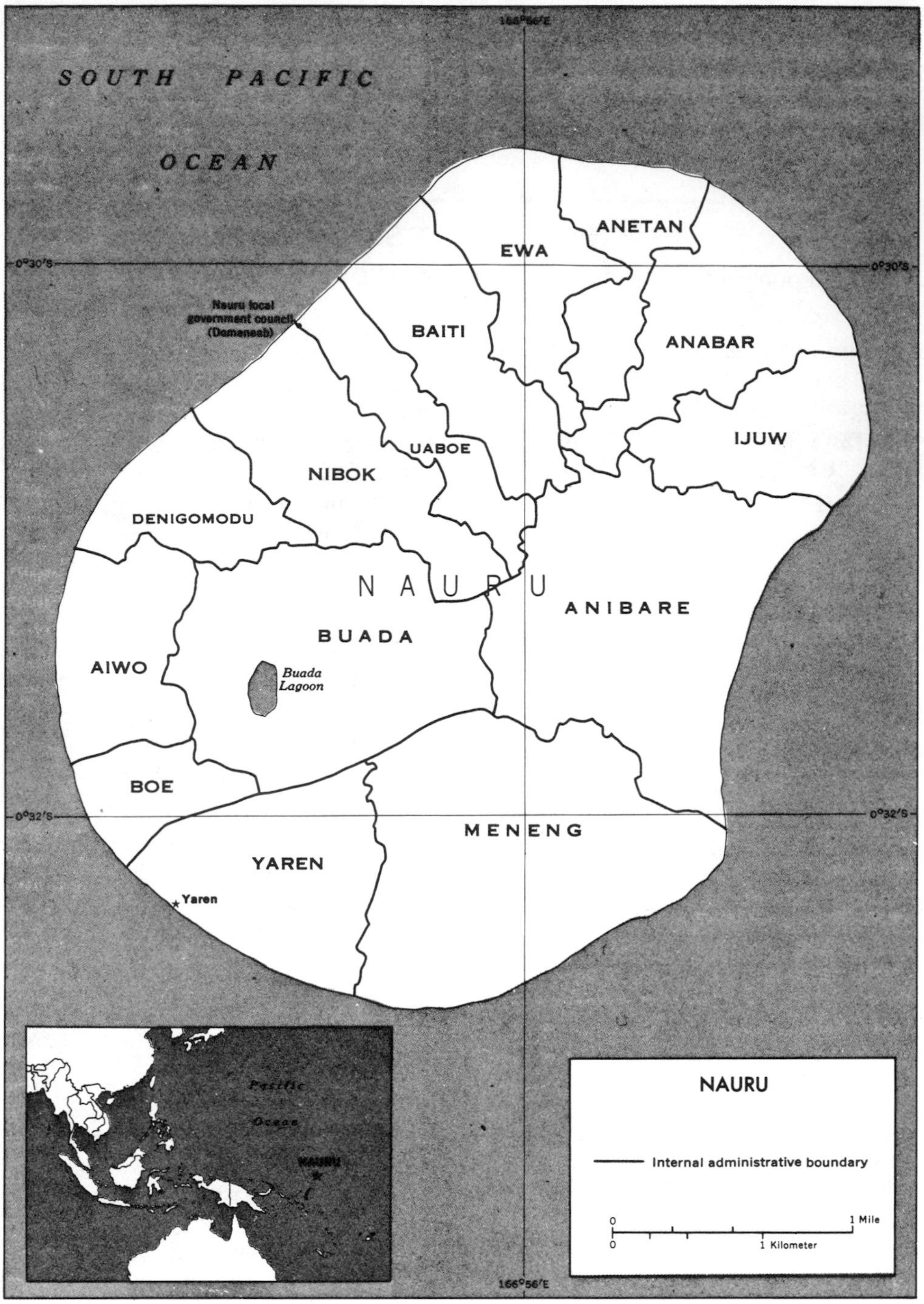

SOUTH PACIFIC OCEAN

166°56'E

0°30'S

0°32'S

Nauru local government council (Domaneab)

ANETAN

EWA

BAITI

ANABAR

IJUW

UABOE

NIBOK

DENIGOMODU

NAURU

ANIBARE

BUADA

AIWO

Buada Lagoon

BOE

MENENG

YAREN

Yaren

Pacific Ocean

NAURU

NAURU

Internal administrative boundary

0 1 Mile

0 1 Kilometer

VITAL STATISTICS

Crude birth rate (/1,000): 20 (1990)
Crude death rate (/1,000): 5 (1990)
Infant mortality rate (/1,000 live births): 41 (1990)
Life expectancy (yrs.) at birth: males, 64; females, 69 (1990)
Total fertility rate (/woman): 2.3 (1990)
Rate of natural increase (/1,000): 16 (1989)
Marriage rate (/1,000): 6.3 (1977)
Average household size: 8 (latest)

the island are males. Immigration to Nauru is strictly controlled by the government in an effort to preserve the Nauruan majority in the population. There are no birth control programs or policies. There were 2.3 children per woman in 1990. The labor force was 8.8% female in 1977.

ETHNIC COMPOSITION

In 1982 the population included 3,300 indigenous Nauruans, 1,800 Tuvaluans and Kiribatians, 1,100 Chinese and 500 Caucasians. Nauruans are a mixture of three Pacific racial groups: Micronesian, Melanes and Polynesian.

LANGUAGES

Nauruan is the official language, although English is used widely in government and the school system. The origin of Nauruan has not been determined by linguists. Nauruan syntax and vocabulary have no relationship to either Polynesian or Melanesian.

RELIGIONS

Nearly all Nauruans are professing Christians. About 60% are Protestant; the remainder are Roman Catholic.

HISTORICAL BACKGROUND

Nauru was discovered in 1798 by Capt. John Fearn of the whaling ship *Hunter*. From the 1830s to the 1880s Nauru was a haven for a succession of white beachcombers—runaways, convicts and deserters. Following the partition of the western Pacific into German and British zones of influence, Nauru came under German rule and remained so until occupied by an Australian expeditionary force in 1914. At the close of World War I Nauru became a League of Nations mandate, administered jointly by Australia, New Zealand and Great Britain under an Australian-appointed administrator. The Japanese occupied the island in 1942 and in the ensuing three years virtually devastated it. Two-thirds of the population was deported to Truk, a small atoll 1,609 km. (1,000 mi.) northwest of Nauru, and all mining facilities and houses were destroyed. Australian forces reoccupied Nauru in 1945, and the Nauruans in Truk were repatriated to their homeland. In 1947 the island became a trust territory of the United Nations administered by the former mandatory powers. A system of progressive self-government introduced in 1927 culminated in the establishment of a local governing council in 1951 and an elected legislature in 1966. Full political independence came in 1968, with the establishment of a republic, and economic independence in 1970 with the nationalization of the British Phosphate Commission, a three-man board that owned and operated Nauru's only natural resource, its vast phosphate mines.

Nauru's political life has been characterized by government instability. At independence, Parliament elected Hammer DeRoburt president. He had been head chief since 1956. He was reelected in 1971 and 1973. Dissatisfied by DeRoburt's increasingly personal rule, Parliament elected Bernard Dowiyogo president in 1976. Dowiyogo resigned in January 1978 because of a budgetary deadlock, only to be immediately reelected. He resigned again in April after the defeat of a bill dealing with phosphate royalties. His successor, Lagumot Harris, resigned three weeks later as a result of an impasse over an appropriations bill. Harris was replaced by former president DeRoburt, who won reelection in 1978, 1980 and 1983. He was forced to resign for 10 days in October 1986, during which Kennan Adeang served as president, and for four days following an election in December. DeRoburt was sworn in for a ninth term in 1987. Two years later he was removed by a vote of no confidence and replaced by his biological son Kenas Aroi. Aroi resigned on the grounds of ill health in December 1989. He was succeeded by Bernard Dowiyogo.

Current political issues center on what to do once the phosphate deposits are depleted and on demands for compensation from Australia, New Zealand and the United Kingdom for depletion of topsoil when they were participants in the British Phosphate Commission.

CONSTITUTION & GOVERNMENT

Nauru is the smallest independent republic in the world. The Constitution of 1968 provides for a parliamentary type of government. The Constitution restricts citizenship to those of Nauruan or other Pacific islander descent. This is a subject of special importance, because short-term migrants constitute over half the population. The Constitution also defines Nauru's relationship with the Commonwealth, which is that of a partial member attending all meetings except prime ministers' meetings. The president is the head of state, head of government and chief minister of the cabinet. He is elected by Parliament from among its members for a three-year term that corresponds to that of Parliament. Although he wields broad powers, the Constitution does not require his assent to parliamentary bills, which become law under the speaker's signature. The president is assisted by a five-member cabinet, which he appoints.

The Constitution provides for a Supreme Court, which has original and appellate jurisdiction. Cases may be appealed from it to the High Court of Australia.

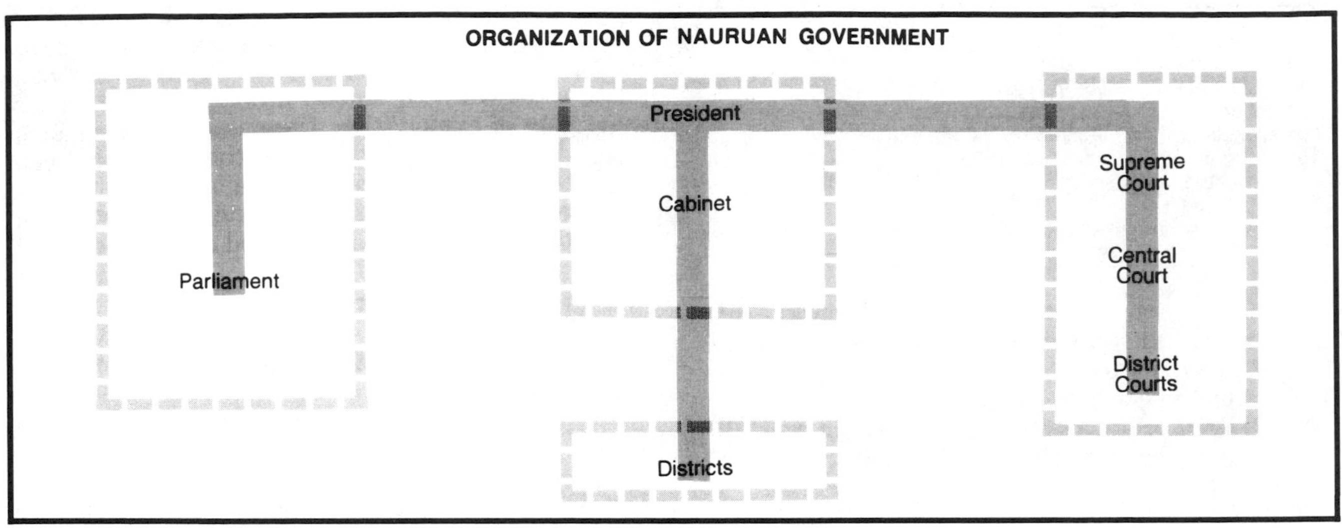

GOVERNMENT LIST (July/August 1991)	
President	Dowiyogo, Bernard
Minister of Civil Aviation	Dowiyogo, Bernard
Minister of External Affairs	Dowiyogo, Bernard
Minister of Finance	Clodumar, Kinza
Minister of Health & Education	Clodumar, Vinci
Minister of Internal Affairs	Dowiyogo, Bernard
Minister of Island Development & Industry	Dowiyogo, Bernard
Minister of Justice	Adeang, Kennan
Minister of Public Service	Dowiyogo, Bernard
Minister of Works & Community Services	Detenamo, Vincent
Minister Assistant to the President	Detenamo, Vincent
Speaker of the House	Gioura, Derog

FREEDOM & HUMAN RIGHTS

In terms of civil and political freedom Nauru is classified as a free country.

CIVIL SERVICE

The Constitution provides for a public service and a public service commissioner. Only Nauruans are eligible for appointment to the public service, although the commissioner may appoint a non-Nauruan if no qualified Nauruan is available for any position.

LOCAL GOVERNMENT

For purposes of local government Nauru is divided in 14 districts: Boe, Aiwo, Anabar, Ijuw, Anibare, Aetan, Ewa, Buada, Denigomodu, Nibok, Uaboe, Baiti, Meneng and Yaren.

Nauru's local government councils are elected from the same constituencies as is Parliament, except that seven constituencies return seven members to Parliament, while Ubenide (Denigomodu, Nibok, Uaboe and Baiti combined) returns two members to Parliament.

FOREIGN POLICY

Nauru maintains diplomatic relations with about a dozen nations, including the United States and the Soviet Union. In 1989 Nauru broke off diplomatic relations with Australia following a dispute over the safety of Air Nauru. The country has decided not to apply for membership in the United Nations, but it is a member of the U.N. Economic and Social Commission for Asia and the Pacific, the South Pacific Commission and the South Pacific Forum. The principal international tie is the Commonwealth, although Nauru is not represented at Commonwealth prime ministers' meetings. Nauru is within the consular district of the U.S. embassy at Canberra.

PARLIAMENT

The unicameral Nauruan Parliament consists of 18 members popularly elected for three-year terms. The speaker of Parliament has the right to certify bills into law.

Suffrage is universal for all citizens, and voting is compulsory for those over 20 years of age.

POLITICAL PARTIES

The only political party is the Democratic Party of Nauru, formed in 1987. It was established by Kennan Adeang to curb the power of the presidency following the reelection of Hammer DeRoburt.

ECONOMY

Nauru is one of the high-income countries of the world, with a free-market economy in which the dominant sector is private. The economy is based almost completely on phosphates, the reserves of which are estimated to be exhausted by 1995. There are few other resources and, because topsoil was depleted as a result of mining, almost no agriculture.

Phosphates have given Nauruans one of the highest standards of living in the world.

The government's economic policy is to invest the revenues from the phosphate exports in long-term trust funds and Australian real estate. About $4.50 of every $6.00 net that the government receives from every ton of phosphate is invested in these funds. The government also has diversified into shipping, fishing and tourism. Virtually the entire GDP is received from the phosphate mines.

Nauru has a strong and favorable balance of trade, and there are substantial investments abroad.

Nauru has neither sought nor received any foreign aid.

PUBLIC FINANCE

The Nauruan fiscal year runs from July 1 through June 30. There is no national debt.

CURRENCY & BANKING

Nauru uses the Australian currency in all monetary transactions. The Australian dollar is divided into 100 cents. Coins are issued in demoninations of 1, 2, 5, 10, 20 and 50 cents; notes are in denominations of 1, 2, 5, 10, 20 and 50 dollars.

In June 1991 the exchange rate of the Australian dollar was $1 = A$1.312.

The Bank of Nauru was founded in 1977 as the nation's first banking institution. The Commonwealth Bank of Australia and the Bank of New South Wales have branches in Nauru.

AGRICULTURE

There is little commercial agriculture on the island. The main crop is coconuts. There is no forestry or fishing. There were 22,000 pigs on the island in 1987.

MANUFACTURING

There are no manufacturing plants on the island.

MINING

Nauru's resources of phosphate rock were estimated at 40.5 million tons in 1985. At the present rate of exploitation, these reserves are expected to be exhausted by 1995. The phosphate mines are owned by the state and operated through Nauru Phosphate Corporation.

ENERGY

Nauru produces no form of mineral energy.

ENERGY INDICATORS

Electricity 1986
- Installed capacity (000 kw.): 10
- Production (million kw.-hr.): 29
  - % fossil fuel: 100.0
  - % hydro: 0.0
  - % nuclear: 0.0
- Consumption per capita (kw.-hr.): 3,222

LABOR

Of the work force of 2,473, a total of 1,408 were employed in the phosphate industry, 845 were employed by the government and 220 worked in other occupations. There are only two labor unions, the Nauruan Workers' Organization and the Phosphate Workers' Organization. Almost half the labor force consists of Chinese, Australian or other Pacific island migrants.

LABOR INDICATORS, 1977

Total economically active population (000): 2.2
% working-age population (15–64): 69.8
% female: 8.8
Activity rate (%)
- Total: 30.5

FOREIGN COMMERCE

Phosphates are the nation's only export. It must import all supplies, including drinking water, from Australia. Its major markets are Australia and New Zealand. Australia, New Zealand, the United Kingdom and Japan are its major suppliers.

FOREIGN TRADE INDICATORS

Exports (U.S. $ millions): 93 (1984)
Imports (U.S. $ millions): 73 (1984)
Balance of trade (U.S. $ millions): 20 (1984)

Composition of Trade (%), 1987

	Imports	Exports
Fuels and other energy	9.0	N.A.
Mineral ores and concentrates, food	36.0	100.0
Manufactured goods	55.0	0.0
of which chemicals	1.6	0.0
of which machinery	8.4	0.0

TRANSPORTATION & COMMUNICATIONS

The state-owned Nauru Pacific Line owns five ships and operates regular passenger and cargo services to Australia, the United States and other South Pacific islands.

There is only one major ring road on the island, 19 km. (12. mi.) long, all of which is paved.

The national airline is Air Nauru, which operates four Boeings on regular services to Australia, Hong Kong, Japan, Okinawa, Guam and other Pacific islands. Questions have been raised about the airline's safety standards, prompting Australia and New Zealand to withdraw certification of Air Nauru. Pilots went on

TRANSPORTATION INDICATORS

Roads (latest)
  Length, km. (mi.): 19 (12)
  Paves (%): 100
Motor vehicles (latest)
  Automobiles: } 1,788
  Trucks and buses: }
  Persons per vehicle: 4.0
Railroads (latest)
  Track, km. (mi.): 6 (4)
Merchant marine
  Vessels: 5 (1989)
  Total dead weight tonnage (000): 45.4 (1989)
Ports (latest)
  Cargo loaded (000 metric tons): 1,483
  Cargo unloaded (000 metric tons): 59
Air (latest)
  Passenger-km. (passenger-mi.) (millions): 238 (148)
  Freight-km. (freight-mi.) (millions): 1.6 (1.1)
  Airports with scheduled flights: 1 (1988)

EDUCATION INDICATORS, 1989

Literacy
  Total (%): 99.0
First level
  Schools: 3
  Students: 1,367
  Teachers: 61
  Student/teacher ratio: 22:4
Second level
  Schools: 2
  Students: 629
  Teachers: 34
  Student/teacher ratio: 18:5
Vocational
  Schools: 1
  Students: 30
  Teachers: 3
  Student/teacher ratio: 10.0
Third level
  Students: 88

COMMUNICATION INDICATORS, 1988

Telephones
  Total (000): 1.5
  Persons per telephone: 5.9
Phone traffic (000 calls)
  National: 960
  International: 350
Post office
  Number of post offices: 1 (1985)
  Pieces of mail handled (000): 168 (1985)
Telegraph (000 calls)
  International: 78 (words)
Telex
  Subscriber lines: 16
  Traffic (000 minutes): 54 (1986)
Telecommunications, 1990
  Satellite ground station: 1

strike in 1988, only to be fired by President DeRoburt. Air Nauru still is not fully operational.

The Nauru airport has a runway of 1,220 m. (4,000 ft.).

No information is available on the volume of mail traffic or on the number of tourist arrivals.

DEFENSE

Nauru has no standing army or other defense forces.

EDUCATION

Education is free, universal and compulsory for 10 years, from ages six to 16. Schooling lasts for 11 years, divided into seven years of primary school and four years of secondary school. The Roman Catholic Church runs a few mission schools.

The academic year runs from February to December. The language of instruction is English throughout.

Higher education overseas, mainly in Australia, is encouraged by the government in the form of scholarships.

LEGAL SYSTEM

The legal system is based on English common law. The judicial system consists of the Supreme Court as the highest court of the land, the Central Court as the superior court of record; and the District Court, presided over by the resident magistrate. The chief justice presides over the Supreme Court, which exercises both original and appellate jurisdiction. The resident magistrate also acts as coroner under the Inquests Act of 1977. The Supreme Court and district courts are courts of record. The Family Court consists of three members, one being the resident magistrate, as chairman; the two other members are drawn from a panel of Nauruans.

A small compound in the southwestern corner of the island serves as a local jail.

LAW ENFORCEMENT

One member of the local government council is responsible for maintenance of public order and is designated director of police; he supervises a force of 60 constables.

Crime is not a major problem on the island. The most common offenses are wife-beating as well as violations of local ordinances against drinking and brawling.

HEALTH

The principal health problems are tuberculosis, leprosy and vitamin deficiencies.

In 1988 the *Pacific Islands Monthly* reported that the islanders were "dying of wealth." The island had one of the lowest life expectancies and one of the highest rates of diabetes in the world as a result of the importation of alcohol, junk food and canned goods.

HEALTH INDICATORS

Health personnel, 1980
  Physicians: 11
    Persons per: 700
  Dentists: 2 (1971)
  Nurses, midwives: 61 (1971)
  Pharmacists: 1 (1971)
Hospitals, 1980
  Number: 2 (1971)
  Number of beds (/10,000): 250
  Admissions/discharges (/10,000): 2,660 (1971)
Type of hospitals (%), 1971
  Government: 50.0
  Private nonprofit: 50.0
  Private profit: 0.0
Public health expenditures (latest)
  As % of national budget: 14.2
  Per capita (U.S. $): 178.50
Vital statistics
  Crude death rate (/1,000 pop.): 5 (1990)
  Life expectancy at birth, 1990
    Males: 64 years
    Females: 69 years
  Infant mortality rate (/1,000 live births): 41 (1990)
  Child mortality rate under 5 yrs (/1,000) (1985–90): 36

MEDIA INDICATORS

Newspapers
  Number of nondailies: 1 (latest)
  Circulation (000): 0.75 (latest)
  Per 1,000 pop.: 82.85 (latest)
Radio
  Number of transmitters: 1 (1989)
  Number of persons per radio receiver: 2.0 (1989)
  Total program hours: 2,184 (latest)
Cinema
  Number of fixed cinemas: 2 (latest)
  Seating capacity (000): 0.8 (latest)

FOOD & NUTRITION

The major portion of the diet consists of foreign foods such as canned meat and fish, polished rice, bread made from refined flour, and sweetened and condensed milk. In general the diet is noted for its high starch and sugar content.

The per capita daily intake of food consists of 3,202 calories.

MEDIA & CULTURE

The only newspaper published on the island is a weekly official bulletin with a circulation of 750. There is no national news agency. No books are published locally.

The state-owned Nauru Broadcasting Service is on the air for 42 hours a week with one medium-wave transmitter. There is no television service. There are two fixed cinemas, with 800 seats.

There is a small lending library containing a few thousand books.

SOCIAL WELFARE

Like education, medical, dental and hospital treatment is free. Other benefits, such as old-age and invalids' pensions, widows' and sickness benefits and child endowment are provided for under the Social Services Ordinance of 1965. Furthermore, eyeglasses and newspapers are free, and patients are sent abroad for treatment if necessary at government expense.

GLOSSARY

Domaneab: a Nauruan meetinghouse, where the government offices are located.

CHRONOLOGY (from 1968)

1968— Nauru is granted full independence, with Hammer DeRoburt as president.

1970— Nauru takes over the British Phosphate Commission, owner of the island's phosphate mines.

1976— DeRoburt is replaced as president by Bernard Dowiyogo.

1978— President Dowiyogo is replaced by Lagumot Harris and later by Hammer DeRoburt.

1982— Nauru signs the South Pacific Regional Trade Agreement.

1983— DeRoburt is redesignated as president.

1986— DeRoburt resigns for 10 days, during which Kennan Adeang serves as president.

1987— DeRoburt is reelected president. Kennan Adeang forms the Democratic Party of Nauru.

1989— DeRoburt resigns as president and is replaced by Kenas Aroi. In December Aroi resigns and is succeeded by Bernard Dowiyogo.

1990— President Dowiyogo takes a high profile at the meeting of the South Pacific Forum, arguing strongly that chemical weapons should not be destroyed in the Pacific at Johnston Atoll because of the South Pacific Nuclear Free Zone Treaty.

BIBLIOGRAPHY

BOOKS

Packett, C. Neville. *Guide to the Republic of Nauru.* Bradford, Eng., 1971.

Petit-Skinner, Solange. *The Nauruans.* San Francisco, 1981.

Tudor, Judy. *Pacific Islands Yearbook.* Sydney, 1976.

Viviani, N. M. *Nauru—Phosphate and Political Progress.* Canberra, Austral., 1970.

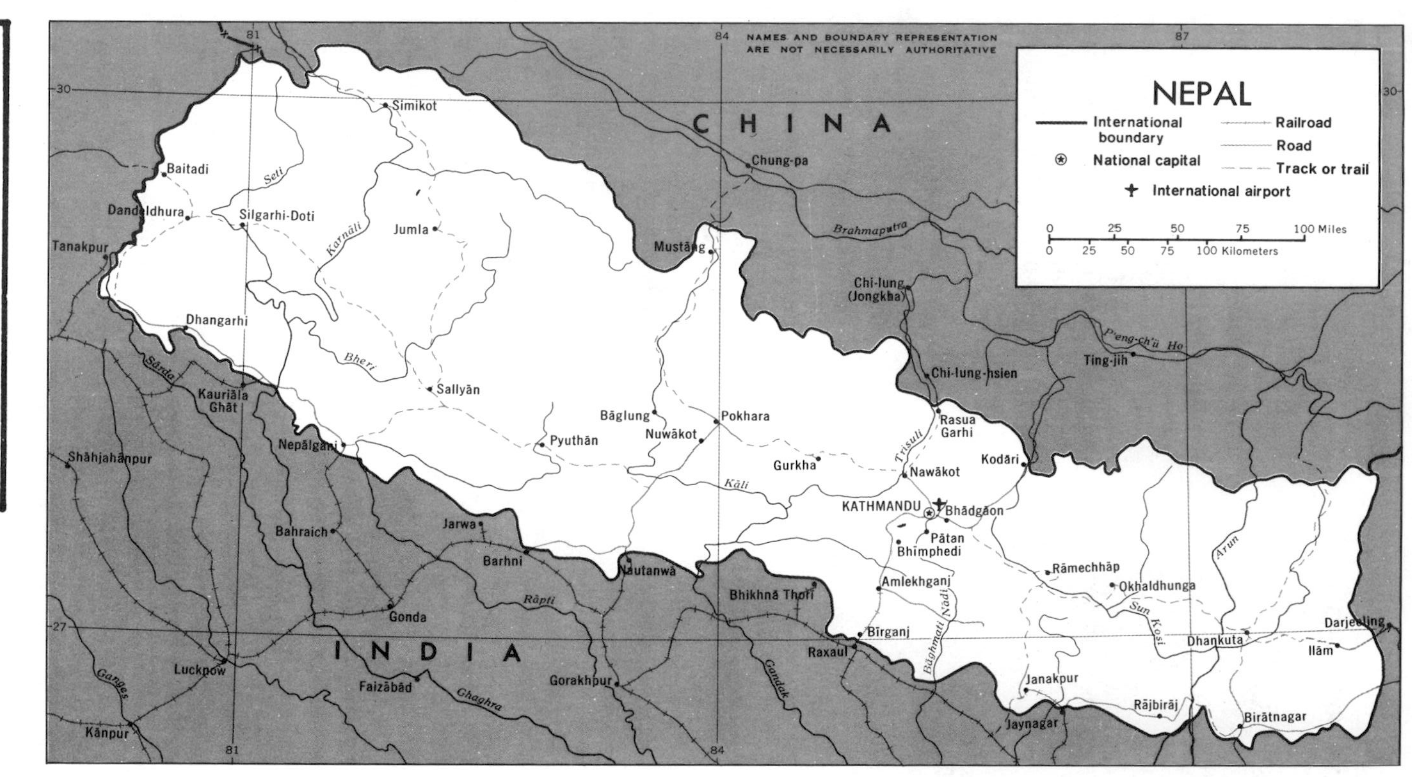
NEPAL
International boundary
National capital
International airport
Railroad
Road
Track or trail
0 25 50 75 100 Miles
0 25 50 75 100 Kilometers
NAMES AND BOUNDARY REPRESENTATION ARE NOT NECESSARILY AUTHORITATIVE
CHINA
INDIA
KATHMANDU
Simikot
Baitadi
Dandeldhura
Silgarhi-Doti
Tanakpur
Jumla
Dhangarhi
Sallyān
Kauriāla Ghāt
Nepālganj
Shāhjahānpur
Bahraich
Jarwa
Barhni
Gonda
Lucknow
Faizābād
Kānpur
Gorakhpur
Nautanwā
Pyuthān
Bāglung
Nuwākot
Pokhara
Mustāng
Chung-pa
Chi-lung (Jongkha)
Chi-lung-hsien
Rasua Garhi
Nawākot
Gurkha
Kodāri
Bhādgāon
Pātan
Bhimphedi
Amlekhganj
Bīrganj
Raxaul
Bhikhnā Thori
Rāmechhāp
Okhaldhunga
Janakpur
Jaynagar
Rājbirāj
Dhankuta
Ilām
Darjeeling
Birātnagar
Ting-jih
Seti
Karnāli
Bheri
Sārda
Rāpti
Ghāghra
Ganges
Gandak
Kāli
Trisuli
Bāghmati Nadi
Sun Kosi
Arun
Brahmaputra
P'eng-ch'ü Ho
30
27
81
84
87

NEPAL

BASIC FACT SHEET

OFFICIAL NAME: Kingdom of Nepal (Nepal Adhirajya)

ABBREVIATION: NP

CAPITAL: Katmandu

HEAD OF STATE: King Birendra Bir Bikram Shah Dev (from 1972)

HEAD OF GOVERNMENT: Prime Minister Girija Prasad Koirala (from 1991)

NATURE OF GOVERNMENT: Constitutional monarchy

POPULATION: 19,145,800 (1990)

AREA: 141,499 sq. km. (54,633 sq. mi.)

ETHNIC MAJORITY: Nepali

LANGUAGE: Nepali (official)

RELIGION: Hinduism and Buddhism

UNIT OF CURRENCY: Rupee

NATIONAL FLAG: Two red triangles edged with blue, with white emblems representing the moon and the sun

NATIONAL EMBLEM: The main elements of the national emblem are the national flower (the rhododendron); a white cow; a green pheasant; two Gurkha soldiers, one carrying a kukri and a bow and an arrow and the other a modern rifle; peaks of the Himilaya Mountains; the moon and the sun, both with faces showing Hindu caste marks, two crossed Nepali flags and kukris; the footprints of Gorakhnath, the guardian deity of the Gurkhas; and the royal headdress. At the base of the design a red scroll carries the national motto in Sanskrit: "The Fatherland Is Worth More Than the Kingdom of Heaven."

NATIONAL ANTHEM: "May Glory Crown Our Illustrious Sovereign"

NATIONAL HOLIDAYS: December 28 (National Day; Birthday of the King); January 11 (Prithvi Jayanti); February 18 (Independence Day); also Hindu and Buddhist festivals

NATIONAL CALENDAR: The Nepali year begins in mid-April and is divided into 12 months: Baisakh, Jestha, Asadh, Shrawan, Bhadra, Aswin, Kartik, Marga, Poush, Magh, Phalgun, Chaitra. Saturday is the official weekly holiday.

PHYSICAL QUALITY OF LIFE INDEX: 36

DATE OF INDEPENDENCE: 1775

DATE OF CONSTITUTION: November 9, 1990

WEIGHTS & MEASURES: Traditional measures are commonly used. The most important of these are *ropani* = 0.3 ha. (0.8 ac.); *bigha* = 0.67 ha. (1.67 ac.); *murhi* = 72 kg. (160 lb.).

GEOGRAPHICAL FEATURES

Nepal is in southern Asia, along the southern slopes of the Himalaya Mountains. A landlocked country about 885 km. (550 mi.) long and 201 km. (125 mi.) wide, it has two neighbors, India and China, the largest nations in Asia. The total length of international borders is 2,671 km. (1,660 mi.), of which the border with China is 1,078 km. (670 mi.) and that with India 1,593 km. (990 mi.). There are no current border disputes. The total land area is 141,499 sq. km. (54,633 sq. mi.).

Katmandu is the capital, with an estimated 1982 population of 393,494. Only eight other population centers have more than 10,000 residents: Patan (59,100), Biratnagar (93,544), Lalitpur (79,875), Bhaktapur (48,472), Polkhara (46,642), Bhagaon (84,250), Nepalganj (15,800) and Birganj (10,800).

Nepal has three main topographical regions: (1) the high mountains of the main Himilayan range, covering one-third of the country; (2) Katmandu Valley; and (3) the Tarai, a narrow belt that extends along the boundary with India in the South. The complex mountain mass in the North contains some of the world's highest peaks: Mount Everest (8,847 m.; 29,028 ft.), Mount Lhotse (8,500 m.; 27,890 ft.), Mount Makalu (8,480 m; 27,824 ft.), Mount Cho Oyu (8,189 m.; 26,867 ft.), Dhaulagiri (8,172 m.; 26,813 ft.) and Annapurna (8,077 m.; 26,502 ft.). To the south, less than 60 km. (37 mi.) from the icy heights, is a narrow, flat belt of alluvial land 45 to 182 m. (150 to 600 ft.) above sea level known as the Tarai. In some places the Tarai is less than 80 km. (50 mi.) wide. On the northern border of the Tarai are tertiary ranges known as the Siwalik Hills and secondary ranges known as Mahabharat Lekh. Katmandu Valley is a circular basin only 564 sq. km. (218 sq. mi.) north of the central Tarai.

The entire country is drained by three river systems: in the East by the Kosi and its seven tributaries, in the center by the Narayani or Gandak and in the West by the Karnali or Gogra. Most of the human settlements are on the banks of these rivers.

CLIMATE & WEATHER

Nepal's climate ranges from subtropical summers and mild winters in the South to cool summers and severe winters in the northern mountains. In the Tarai and Katmandu Valley there are three seasons: hot, rainy and cold. The hot season lasts from May to June, the rainy from July to September and the cold from October to April. In January, the coldest month, temperatures range between a daily average minimum of 2.2° C (36° F) and a maximum of 17.8° C (64° F), while in the hot months they range between 26.7° C (80° F) and 32.2° C (90° F). The average annual rainfall in Katmandu is about 1,520 mm. (60 in.). Violent thunderstorms are common.

POPULATION

The population of Nepal was estimated at 19,145,800 in 1990, based on the last official census, in 1981, when the population was 15,022,839.

The population is unevenly distributed: The barren highlands are virtually uninhabited, while Katmandu Valley is one of the most densely populated areas of the world. The average density is 117 per sq. km. (303 per sq. mi.). The density of population per sq. km. of cultivated area is considerably higher, at 355.7 (921 per sq. mi.).

DEMOGRAPHIC INDICATORS

Population (millions): 19.145 (1990)
Year of last census: 1981
Sex distribution (% at last census): males, 51.2; females, 48.8
Population estimates and projections (millions)

1940: 7.000	1970: 11.232	2000: 23.176
1950: 8.000	1980: 14.642	2010: 27.807
1960: 9.180	1990: 19.145	

Age profile (% at last census)

0–14: 41.4	30–44: 17.4	60–74: 4.7
15–29: 25.5	45–59: 10.0	75 and over: 1.0

Median age (yrs.): 19.0
Youth population (% age 15–24): 18.1 (1985); 20.1 (2000)
Total dependency ratio: 82.7 (1985)
Annual growth rate (%)

1950–55: 1.17	1975–1980: 2.67	2000–2005: 1.97
1955–60: 1.61	1980–1985: 2.59	2005–2010: 1.68
1960–65: 1.91	1985–1990: 2.48	2010–2015: 1.44
1965–70: 2.10	1990–1995: 2.34	2015–2020: 1.26
1970–75: 2.47	1995–2000: 2.25	2020–2025: 1.11

Hypothetical size of stationary population (millions): 61
Assumed year of reaching net reproduction rate of 1: 2030
Urban population (millions): 1.303 (1985)
Urban population (%): 9 (1988); 4 (1965)
Annual urban population growth rate (%, 1985–90): 6.86
Annual rural population growth rate (%, 1985–90): 2.06
Percentage of urban population in largest city: 27 (1980)
Number of cities of population over 500,000: 0 (1980)
Population density per sq. km. (per sq. mi.): 128.5 (332.8) (latest)

VITAL STATISTICS

Crude birth rate (/1,000): 39 (1990); 46 (1965)
Crude death rate (/1,000): 15 (1990); 24 (1965)
Infant mortality rate (/1,000 live births): 99 (1990)
Maternal mortality rate (/100,000 live births): 850 (1980)
Life expectancy (yrs.) at birth: males, 50; females, 50 (1990)
Gross reproduction rate (/woman) (1980–85): 3.05
Total fertility rate (/woman): 5.6 (1990)
Rate of natural increase (/1,000): 24.7 (1988)
Average family size: 5.8 (latest)

STATUS OF WOMEN INDICATORS

Number of women (millions): 7.794 (1985)
Women of childbearing age (15–49) (% of pop.): 47 (1988)
Married women of childbearing age (15–49) using contraception (%): 15 (1988)
Women's literacy rate (%): 9 (1985)
Women in labor force (%): 33.8 (1988)
Total fertility rate (/woman): 5.6 (1990)
Women in national legislatures (%): 5 (1984)

The urban component of the population is only 9%. Nepalese live in 29,120 villages with an average population of less than 350 inhabitants. There are nine population centers with over 10,000 inhabitants. The Indo-Nepali border has no guards or checkpoints, and there is free movement of people across the border. Because border crossings are unrestricted, no statistics are maintained on the number of Nepalese working in India, but they are believed to number over 100,000. Following the annexation of Tibet by China in 1959, nearly 7,000 Tibetans fled to Nepal, where they have settled near the border villages.

What legal rights women have, as a result of national legislation, are irrelevant to the vast majority of Nepal's women. Lack of education, formidable communications obstacles, and communal and tribal customs that dictate a secondary role for women combine to make it virtually impossible for women to achieve the equal status with men that is granted them under Nepalese law. As a result, rights are conferred on women—or denied them—on the basis of community and ethnic tradition. An AID/Nepal-financed study of eight rural villages showed that women in these areas have no personal right to landed property or inheritance but can gain access through marriage or male progeny. In Katmandu Valley, on the other hand, women can hold land in their own right.

A family planning program was established in 1966 with U.S. aid and has met with no serious opposition.

ETHNIC COMPOSITION

By historical origin, linguistic connections and religious affiliations Nepalese may be divided into two broad ethnic categories: Indo-Nepalese and Tibeto-Nepalese. The Indo-Nepalese group, which comprises nearly 80% of the population, includes the Pahari, the Newar, the Tharu and the Indians of the Tarai. The Pahari make up nearly half the total population. In social organization and physical appearance they resemble the inhabitants of northern India, though many of these features have been modified in the Nepali environment. The Newar, who make up half the population of Katmandu Valley, are distinctively Mongoloid in appearance but Hindu in social and religious organization. Their high educational level, economic prosperity and artistic skills have enabled them to play a dominant role in the country. The Tharu also are Hinduized as a result of long and intimate contact with the neighboring Biharese. The Tibeto-Nepalese category, which makes up 20% of the population, includes a number of ethnic islands without any real sense of common identity. These groups are clustered in the northern and eastern parts of the country, where they are subsistence farmers and stock raisers at higher altitudes. Though related culturally and racially to the Tibetans, they have developed regional distinctions and cultural variations. The more numerous of the Tibeto-Nepalese tribes are the Tamang, Rai, Limbu, Bhote, Sunwar, Magar and Gurung. These groups have supplied the bulk of the famous Gurkha contingents to British, and later Indian and Malaysian armies. Common to most of these groups is the acceptance of a patterned social relationship based on the caste system, though less elaborately graded and less rigid in its sanctions than the Indian caste system.

Ethnic aliens include Indians and Tibetans, mostly refugees from Tibet, but since Nepal was closed to foreigners until 1951, aliens form, at best, a floating community.

LANGUAGES

The census of 1952 listed 30 distinct languages spoken in the country, not counting dialects. Of these, 20 were spoken by less than 1,000 persons each. Nepali (also called Gurkhali, Khaskura or Parbatiya) is the official language, and its use in schools and offices is enabling it to displace the minor languages. It is an eastern dialect of Pahari and is distinguished from western and central Pahari. By percentage of speakers the main languages of Nepal are: Nepali (48.7%), Maithili Pradesh dialects (7.5%), Tamang (6.0%), eastern Tarai dialects (5.6%), Newari (4.7%), Tharuhati (4.4%), Maithili (3.7%), Magar (3.3%), midwestern Tarai dialects (3.1%), Rai (2.9%) and Gurung (2.0%), Khambu, Yakha, Hayu, Limbu and Thami belong to the Munda group of the Austroasiatic family; Gurung, Mahar, Newari, Sunwar and Murmi belong to the Tibeto-Burman family; Nepali belongs to the Indo-European group. Tibetan is spoken by the Bhotias in the North, and dialects of Hindi such as Bhojpuri, Kumaoni and Maithili, along the southern border. Newari and Pahari show strong Sanskrit influence. Only Pahari and Newari have any literature of their own.

English is the principal second language.

RELIGION

By the Constitution of 1962 Nepal was officially proclaimed a Hindu state. Nearly 89% of the population is Hindu, 9% Buddhist and 2% Muslim.

Religious tolerance is traditional, and the Constitution provides that "every person, having regard to the traditions, may profess and practice his own religion as handed down from ancient times." However, the Constitution also provides that "no person shall be entitled to convert another person from one religion to another." The legal code provides a maximum penalty of one year in prison for any Hindu who converts to another religion and three to six years in prison for any person who seeks to proselytize a Hindu. In 1985 nine new cases were registered in which 46 people were charged with conversion or proselytizing. In contrast to statements by official government spokesmen that any adult Nepali is free to change his religion, there were 18 convictions during 1985 for simple conversion from Hinduism to Christianity, with sentences from three months to one year. In addition, two Christian pastors were convicted of proselytizing for preaching within their own churches; each was sentenced to the maximum six years. Five other individuals convicted of proselytizing were each sentenced to three years.

HISTORICAL BACKGROUND

Nepal has never been under direct foreign rule in modern times, although it was bound by treaty obligations to Great Britain until 1947.

Initially composed of 46 sovereign principalities, modern Nepal was founded in 1769 by the Gurkha ruler Prithvinarayan Shah who consolidated political power through conquest and assimilation. From 1846 to 1951 the country was under the control of the Rana family, one of whose members always held the office of prime minister. Their autocratic rule ended in 1950 when a revolution, inspired by India's successful bid for independence, restored the power of the monarchy. The last of the Rana prime ministers resigned in 1951. A period of quasi-constitutional rule followed until a constitution was promulgated in 1959.

The constitution provided for a parliamentary government but left sovereignty in fact in the hands of the king who could dismiss the prime minister, prorogue parliament and veto all legislation. Under the direction of Prime Minister B. P. Koirala, head of the Nepali Congress Party, the government began a program of land reform designed to give tenants greater security and redistribute some of the large Rana estates. However, tension increased between the prime minister and King Mahendra, who made no pretense of his dislike of parliamentary government and political parties. In 1960 the king, charging the government with misuse of power, staged a coup and assumed control. He jailed government leaders, suspended the constitution, and banned political parties. In 1962 a new constitution established the panchayat, or assembly, system, a four-tiered administrative structure headed by the king who appointed the prime minister. Under the system, directly elected town and village assemblies elected members to bodies above them in the hierarchy.

The system encountered opposition from NCP supporters and university students. Increasing demands for political liberalization led to the resignation of two prime ministers during the 1970s and to prolonged demonstrations in 1979. That year King Birendra, who inherited the throne from his father in 1972, announced a referendum on the maintenance of the panchayat system or the institution of a multiparty system. The population voted down the latter, and in 1980 the king proclaimed several constitutional changes. A national assembly was to be chosen by direct election and the prime minister was to be designated by the assembly rather than by the king. In November 1990, Nepal adopted a new constitution which established a constitutional monarchy with executive power vested in a prime minister that was the leader of the majority party in the legislature. Legislative elections were scheduled for May 1991.

CONSTITUTION & GOVERNMENT

Under the 1990 constitution, Nepal is a constitutional monarchy with the king as head of state and a prime minister as head of government. Executive power is vested in a prime minister who is the leader of the majority party in the 205-member parliament. The prime minister forms a cabinet which is responsible to the legislature.

Since 1951 Nepal has been relatively free from violent changes of government.

GOVERNMENT LIST
(July/August 1991)

King	Birendra Bir Bikram Shah Dev
Prime Minister	Koirala, Girija Prasad
Minister of Agriculture	Acharya, Shailaja
Minister of Commerce	Shrestha, Gopal Man
Minister of Communications	Risal, Basu Dev
Minister of Defense	Koirala, Girija Prasad
Minister of Education & Culture	Joshi, Ram Hari
Minister of Finance	Koirala, Girija Prasad
Minister of Foreign Affairs	Koirala, Girija Prasad
Minister of Forest & Soil Conservation	Acharya, Shailaja
Minister of General Administration	Singh, Maheswor Prasad
Minister of Health	Koirala, Girija Prasad
Minister of Home Affairs	Deupa, Sher Bahadur
Minister of Housing & Physical Planning	Rai, Bal Bahadur
Minister of Industry	Shastri, Dhundi Raj
Minister of Labor & Social Welfare	Idris, Sheikh
Minister of Land Reform Management	Acharya, Jagan Nath
Minister of Law, Justice & Parlimanetary Affairs	Bhat, Tara
Minister of Local Development	Poudel, Ram Chandra
Minister of Royal Palace Affairs	Koirala, Girija Prasad
Minister of Supply	Wagle, Chiranjibi
Minister of Tourism	Joshi, Ram Hari
Minister of Transport	Khadka, Khum Bahadur
Minister of Water Resources	Risal, Basu Dev
Minister of Works	Khadka, Khum Bahadur
Governor, Central Bank	

FREEDOM & HUMAN RIGHTS

In terms of civil and political rights Nepal is classified as a partly free country.

The overwhelming approval of the partyless, panchayat form of government in the referendum of 1980 defused political tension in the country and enhanced the popularity of the monarch. At the same time, it set back hopes of an early adoption of a parliamentary form of government and democratic reforms in the system of administration. Nevertheless, there has been no serious diminution in the level of human rights or overt acts of repression. Some positive features are:

Torture and police brutality are legally prohibited and officially frowned upon. Although abuses occur, they are not widespread. Capital punishment is seldom imposed, and only in cases involving treason. Although there are occasional rumors of alleged disappearances, no cases have been confirmed. Political prisoners generally receive better treatment than common criminals. The law provides the right to a fair public trial, and this right generally is honored in practice. Defendants are entitled to counsel (though not always of their choice). However, judges are known to seek tacit government approval of their rulings in cases involving political considerations. The sanctity of the home is safeguarded by law and practice. Arrests and search warrants are required prior to search and seizure except in certain cases, such as those involving narcotic drugs. Religious tolerance is not a special problem because the nation is overwhelmingly Hindu, but conversion to other religions is prohibited. The royal family is considered above criticism, but otherwise the media report objectively on opposition activities and positions. Criticism of the bureaucracy is common. The ban on political parties continues, although a number of political exiles have returned without being arrested, and opposition groups hold mass rallies. The trade unions have few rights by law and are technically illegal. But trade union activity is on the increase, and strikes are common. The advocacy of women's rights is the responsibility of class organizations, which are notably ineffective. There are a number of restrictions on women's rights, both legal and traditional; women are seriously underrepresented in economic and political life.

Internal security is maintained in the first instance by the national police and as necessary by the army. Owing to Nepal's limited communications facilities, local officials have a large degree of autonomy and exercise wide discretion in dealing with law and order issues.

In 1985 the government demonstrated a growing tendency to respond with force to control or prevent the expression of opposition views. Riot police were used extensively to prevent public demonstrations by schoolteachers, students and banned political parties. Several thousand opposition political activists were kept in preventive detention for several months after attempting to stage a civil disobedience campaign in May 1985. Reportedly as many as 20 newspaper editors were arrested during the year, apparently for publishing articles critical of the king or the royal family. Allegations of police brutality were common.

CIVIL SERVICE

No current information is available on the Nepali civil service.

LOCAL GOVERNMENT

Nepal has a unitary system of government. The country is divided into 14 zones and 75 districts, with the district as the basic unit of administration. The 14 zones are: Bagmati, Bheri, Dhaulagiri, Gandaki, Janakpur, Karnali, Kosi, Lumbini, Mahakali, Mechi, Na-

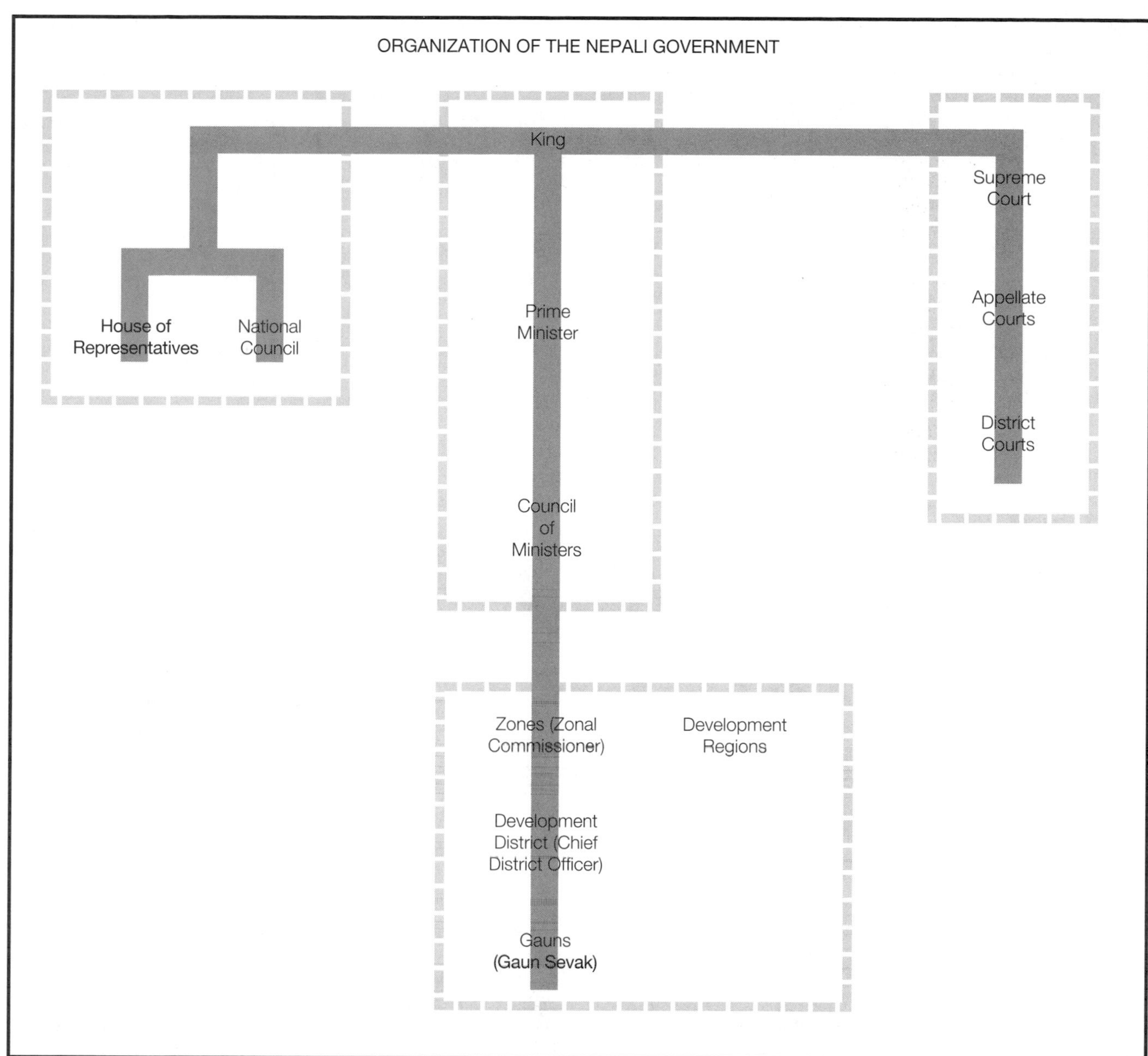

rayani, Rapti, Sagarmata and Seti. Each zone is administered by a commissioner and assistant zonal commissioners, all appointed by the central government. At the district level the principal administrative officer is the chief district officer, formerly known as the governor, or *bada hakim.* The chief district officer also serves as secretary to the panchayat of each development district. Certain former subdivisions, such as the *jilla* and *thum* or *parganna,* have been abolished as administrative units, but they retain some significance as tax or rent units. At the bottom of the hierarchy are the groups of villages *(gauns)* and towns *(nagars).* The ultimate point of contact between the villagers and the central government traditionally has been the headman, who is variously known as *mukhiya, talukdar, jimidar, zimiwal, patwari* or *subbha.* Overlapping this structure is another division, more recently introduced, of the country into four development regions: Dhankuta or Eastern Katmandu, Katmandu, Pokhara or Central, and Surkhet or Western.

FOREIGN POLICY

The central determinant of Nepali foreign policy is the nation's geographical position between two opposing giants, India and China. Nepal's relations with India are governed by the Treaty of Peace and Friendship and the Treaty of Trade and Commerce, both signed in 1950. The former acknowledged the independence, territorial integrity and sovereignty of Nepal. The latter recognized Nepal's right to import and export commodities through Indian territory and ports without payment of customs.

India, however, continues to exercise an advisory influence on Nepali politics, and Nepali leaders frequently visit New Delhi to seek counsel and even approval and support of policies and plans. Sometimes this has led to charges of undue interference and domination, and anti-Indian riots have been frequent. Relations with India were particularly strained between 1961 and 1963, when Nepali opposition leaders who had fled to India conducted armed raids across the border into Nepal. India has provided Nepal with substantial economic assistance, currently totaling more than $14 million annually. Since 1952 India has maintained an economic and technical aid mission and a military mission in Katmandu.

In June 1987, Nepal and India signed an agreement to establish a joint commission for the promotion of economic cooperation between the two countries.

Relations between the two countries deteriorated in December 1987 when the chief minister of the Indian state of West Bengal accused Nepal of providing sanctuary for activists campaigning for separate status within the state. This accusation was denied by the Nepalese government. Relations further deteriorated in 1989 when India decided not to renew the two treaties determining trade and transit, but instead insisted on a common treaty that covered both issues. Nepal insisted on keeping the issues separate, on the grounds that trade issues are negotiable, whereas the right of transit is a recognized right of land-locked countries. India responded by closing 13 of the 15 transit ports through which most of Nepal's trade is conducted. This resulted in severe shortages of food and fuel in Nepal. Relations remained strained in mid-1989, and trade was at a virtual standstill.

Diplomatic relations with the People's Republic of China were established in 1955, followed by a Treaty of Friendship in 1956. By this treaty Nepal recognized Chinese suzerainty over Tibet and surrendered all privileges and rights granted by the treaty of 1856, including annual tribute from Tibet. Nepal opened a consulate-general in Lhasa, with four trade agencies in Lhasa and regional centers, while China was permitted to open three trading centers in Nepal. The status of the undemarcated Sino-Nepalese boundary was settled by a treaty in 1961. A Treaty of Peace and Friendship was signed in Katmandu in 1960, placing Sino-Nepalese relations on a firm basis. The Chinese have contributed large amounts of economic aid to Nepal through specific projects, the most important of which is the highway linking Katmandu and Tibet. During the Sino-Indian border war in 1962 Nepal maintained an official posture of neutrality.

The Soviet Union opened an embassy in Nepal in 1958 and has provided some economic assistance. U.S.-Nepali relations were formally established in 1947, although a resident American embassy was opened in Katmandu only in 1959. The United States has provided approximately $200 million worth of economic assistance to Nepal since the aid program began in 1951. The U.S. Agency for International Development now provides an annual input of about $8 million through programs in agriculture, education, social welfare and communications. In addition, Nepal and the United States are parties to seven agreements and treaties covering economic and technical cooperation, education, highways, investment guarantees, judicial assistance, the Peace Corps, and trade and commerce.

Nepal joined the United Nations in 1955.

In international relations Nepal follows a nonaligned and neutralist policy, often voting with an Afro-Asian group in the U.N. It is a member of 13 U.N. organizations and six other international organizations.

PARLIAMENT

Under the 1990 constitution, legislative power is vested in a 205-seat unicameral legislature chosen by universal suffrage.

POLITICAL PARTIES

All political parties were banned from 1960–90 but operated more or less openly. The major party was the Nepali Congress Party, which originated in the 1940s as a movement against the Ranas. It won an absolute majority in the first general elections of 1959. Following the coup of 1960, the party was actively persecuted because it provided the strongest opposition to the panchayat system. Party leaders went underground or into exile, but the NCP emerged viable during the 1980s. Under the 1990 constitution, political parties were permitted to function, and over 40 were reported in early 1991.

ECONOMY

Nepal is one of the poorest and least developed countries in the world with a per capita income of only $170 in 1989. Subsistence agriculture is the primary economic activity. Industrial activity is limited, and what exists is involved in the processing of agricultural products. Although a large amount of foreign aid has been invested in agriculture, that sector's growth has not kept pace with population growth. Nepal's few exploitable natural resources include mica, hydroelectric power and tourism. Economic growth has been limited by the country's isolation, unskilled, largely illiterate workforce, and the lack of internal communications. Real economic growth slowed at the end of the 1980s and is expected to decrease considerably because of trade disputes with India.

PRINCIPAL ECONOMIC INDICATORS

Gross National Product (U.S. $ billions): 3.206 (1989)
GNP per capita (U.S. $): 170 (1989)
GNP average annual growth rate (%, 1980–89): 4.7
GNP per capita average annual growth rate (%, 1987–89): 3.2
Average annual rate of inflation (%, 1980–88): 8.7
Consumer price index (1980 = 100) 1986
All items: 185
Food: 187

BALANCE OF PAYMENTS, 1989
(U.S. $ millions)

Current account balance: −243.4
Merchandise exports: 156.2
Merchandise imports: −571.4
Trade balance: −415.2
Other goods, services & income +: 226.5
Other goods, services & income −: −154.6
Other goods, services & income net: 71.9
Private unrequited transfers: 52.0
Official unrequited transfers: 48.0
Capital other than reserves: 199
Net errors & omissions: 4.8
Counterpart items: 39.5
Total change in reserves: 4.7

GROSS DOMESTIC PRODUCT

GDP nominal (N.R.S. billions): 74.575 (1989)
GDP per capita (U.S. $): 170 (1990)
Average annual growth rate of GDP (%, 1980–88): 4.7
GDP by type of expenditure (%) 1987
- Consumption
  - Private: 80
  - Government: 10
- Gross domestic investment: 20
- Gross domestic saving: 10 (1988)
- Foreign trade
  - Exports: 13
  - Imports: −23

Cost components of GDP (%) 1987
- Net indirect taxes: 6
- Consumption of fixed capital: 4
- Compensation of employees and net operating surplus: 90

Sectoral origin of GDP (%) 1986
- Primary
  - Agriculture: 58
  - Mining: 0.0
- Secondary
  - Manufacturing: 4
  - Construction: 6
  - Public utilities: 0.0
- Tertiary
  - Transportation & communications: 6
  - Trade: 4
  - Finance, government, and other services: 21

Average annual sectoral growth rates (%, 1980–88)
- Agriculture: 4.4

PUBLIC FINANCE

The Nepali fiscal year runs from July 15 to July 14.

Published budgets are a relatively recent development in Nepal, dating back only to 1958.

The government's principal sources of revenue are taxes on goods and services and customs duties. Almost half of its expenditures are for economic services. Almost a quarter is for social services.

Initial development planning focused on the establishment of an infrastructure. During the early 1980s, plans emphasized agriculture and small-scale and cottage industries as well as increased irrigation and hydroelectric power generation. The most current plan is designed to move the nation away from subsistence agriculture.

CENTRAL GOVERNMENT EXPENDITURES, 1988

% of total expenditures
- Defense: 5.6
- Education: 10.9
- Health: 4.3
- Housing, social security, welfare: 3.3
- Economic services: 51.2
- Other: 24.7

Total expenditures as % of GNP: 19.7
Overall surplus or deficit as % of GNP: −6.2

CENTRAL GOVERNMENT REVENUES, 1988

% of total current revenues
- Taxes on income, profit & capital gain: 8.4
- Social security contributions: 0.0
- Domestic taxes on goods & services: 36.1
- Taxes on international trade & transactions: 31.1
- Other taxes: 5.4
- Current nontax revenue: 19.1

Total current revenue as % of GNP: 10.3
General government consumption as % of GDP: 10 (1988)

Nepal receives most of its foreign aid from India, the People's Republic of China, the European Community, Canada, the United States and Switzerland.

From 1970–88 Nepal received $285 million in aid from the United States. Other Western nations granted $1.8 billion from 1980–87. Communist countries contributed $273 million from 1970–88.

FOREIGN AID, 1989

Total foreign aid (U.S. $ millions): 633.2
- Bilateral: 244.9
- Multilateral: 388.3

CURRENCY & BANKING

The Nepali unit of currency is the rupee, divided into 100 pice. Coins are issued in denominations of 1, 2, 4, 5, 10, 20, 25 and 50 pice and 1 rupee; notes are issued in denominations of 1, 5, 10, 100, 500 and 1,000 rupees. The official rate of exchange in June 1991 was US$1 = R34.70.

The Nepali banking system consists of the central bank, the Nepal Rastra Bank, and two commercial banks, of which the Nepal Bank is partly government-owned. Specialized credit institutions include the Nepal Industrial Development Corporation and the Agricultural Development Bank. Until recently the main source of credit in rural areas was the ubiquitous moneylender.

AGRICULTURE

Subsistence farming is the principal economic activity in Nepal. Agricultural land constitutes 28% of the total land area or 0.3 ha. (0.8 ac.) per capita. Of the total land surface of 14,149,900 ha. (34,964,402 ac.), 3,885,120 ha. (9,600,000 ac.) are under crops. The country's breadbasket is the Tarai, in the South.

FINANCIAL INDICATORS, 1989

Total reserves minus gold (SDRs millions): 163
SDRs (millions): 0
Reserve position in IMF (SDRs millions): 6
Foreign exchange (SDRs millions): 157
Gold (fine troy oz. millions): .15
Ratio of external debt to total reserves: 4.8 (1988)
Central bank 1988
  Assets (%)
    Foreign assets: 34.1
    Claims on government: 58.6
    Claims on banks: 6.3
    Claims on private sector: 1.0
  Liabilities (%)
    Reserve money: 52.3
    Government deposits: 22.7
    Foreign liabilities: 6.1
    Capital accounts: 23.4
  Money supply 1988
    Stock (N.R.S. billions): 9.826
    M1 per capita: 540
Private banks 1988
  Assets (%)
    Loans to government: 31.1
    Loans to private sector: 48.3
    Reserves: 7.4
    Foreign assets: 13.2
  Liabilities
    Deposits (N.R.S. billions): 18.469
    of which %
      Demand deposits: 13.9
      Savings deposits: 72.5
      Government deposits: 0.0
      Foreign liabilities: 4.0
External debt 1988
  Total (U.S. $ billions): 1.164
    of which public (U.S. $ billions): 1.088
    of which private (U.S. $ millions): 0
  Debt service (long-term)
    Total (U.S. $ millions): 37
    Repayment
      Principal (%): 48.6
      Interest (%): 51.4
  Debt service ratio (%): 8.6
  External public debt as % of GNP: 34.6
  Debt service as % of GNP: 1.2
  Debt service as % of exports: 8.5
  Terms of public borrowing
    Commitments (U.S. $ millions): 217
    Average interest rate (%): 0.9
    Average maturity (yrs.): 39
  Net flow of publicly guaranteed external capital (U.S. $ millions): 184

In 1951 less than 32,376 ha. (80,000 ac.) were under irrigation, but over 21 irrigation projects undertaken during the plan periods have increased the irrigated area to over 404,700 ha. (1 million ac.).

Under the Land Reorganization Act of 1962, the zamindari system of land tenure was abolished and a ceiling was placed on land ownership at 17 ha. (42 ac.) in the Tarai, 5.09 ha. (12.6 ac.) in the mountains and 2.6 ha. (6.6 ac.) in Katmandu Valley. Ceilings also were placed on tenancy holdings. Security of tenancy rights was established, and a maximum rent of 50% of crops was set. The average farm size in the Tarai is 2 to 6 ha. (5 to 15 ac.), while in Katmandu Valley it is only 0.6 ha. (1.5 ac.). Besides proprietary holdings, three other systems of land tenure are prevalent: *raikar*, or

GROWTH PROFILE
(Annual Growth Rates, %)

Projected population (1988–2000): 2.5
Projected crude birth rate (/1,000) (1990–95): 36.3
Projected crude death rate (/1,000) (1990–95): 12.9
Urban population (1980–88): 7.4
Labor force (1985–2000): 2.3
GNP (1980–89): 4.7
GNP per capita (1987–89): 3.2
GDP (1980–88): 4.7
Inflation (1980–88): 8.7
Agriculture (1980–88): 4.4
Money holdings (1980–88): 19.3
Energy production (1980–88): 11.6
Energy consumption (1980–87): 9.4
Exports (1980–88): 5.5
Imports (1980–88): 7.0

AGRICULTURAL INDICATORS

Agriculture's share of GDP (%): 59 (1989)
Average annual growth rate (%, 1980–88): 4.4
Value added in agriculture (U.S. $ millions): 1.601 (1988)
Cereal imports (000 metric tons): 52 (1988)
Index of agricultural production (1979–81 = 100): 111 (1986)
Index of food production (1979–81 = 100): 112 (1986)
Index of food production per capita (1979–81 = 100): 100 (1986–88)
Number of tractors: 2,850 (1986)
Total fertilizer consumption (000 metric tons): 43.5 (1985–86)
Fertilizer consumption (g./ha., hundreds): 232 (1987–88)
Number of farms (million): 2.194 (1981–82)
Average size of holding (ha.): 1.1 (1981–82)
Size class (%) 1981–82
  Below 1 ha. (below 2.47 ac.): 66.7
  1–5 ha. (2.47–12.35 ac.): 29.9
  5–10 ha. (12.35–24.7 ac.): 2.7
  10–20 ha. (24.7–49.4 ac.): }
  20–50 ha. (49.4–123.5 ac.): } 0.7
  50–200 ha. (123.5–494 ac.): }
  Over 200 ha. (over 494 ac.): }
Tenure (%) 1981–82
  Owner-operated: 97.5
  Rented: 1.6
  Other: 0.9
Farms as % of total land area: 16.7 (1981–82)
Land use (%) 1985–87
  Cropland: 3
  Pasture: 7
  Forest: 2
  Other: 88
Yields (kg./ha.) 1989
  Grains: 1,848
  Roots & tubers: 7,065
  Legumes: 525
  Milk (kg./animal): 543
Production 1989
  Fruits (000 metric tons): 162
  Vegetables (000 metric tons): 280
Livestock (000) 1989
  Cattle: 6,343
  Sheep: 880
  Pigs: 515
Forestry 1988
  Production of roundwood (million cubic meters): 17.388
    of which industrial roundwood (%): 3.2
  Value of exports (U.S. $ millions): 12.000
Fishing 1988
  Total catch (000 metric tons): 12.5
    of which marine (%): 0.0

state land under tenure; *guthi*, or land granted to religious institutions; and *kipat*, or land granted to certain ethnic groups.

Forests cover about one-third of the country and are almost all government-owned. Alarming deforestation and poor land-use practices have resulted in reduction of forest acreage. The main commercial woods are sal and somal. Most of the timber is exported to India. The coarse sabai grass is harvested and sold to Indian paper and pulp factories.

MANUFACTURING

The modern industrial sector is small and located primarily in Katmandu Valley. The country's small industrial labor force is mostly illiterate and unskilled. The largest single employer is the Biratnagar Jute Mills, with over 3,000 workers on its payroll. Jute, cigarettes and sugar are the major industrial products. The Nepal Industrial Development Corporation grants loans, conducts feasibility studies and purchases stock.

Aside from a small investment in a tourist jungle-lodge complex, there is no U.S. investment in Nepal. This is due primarily to problems of geography, limited knowledge of conditions in Nepal, and the lack of obvious exploitable opportunities. Seeking to overcome these barriers and recognizing the country's need for foreign capital and management expertise, the government offers a liberal foreign investment policy. Up to 100% foreign ownership is permitted under certain conditions, and a variety of tax concession and other incentives are offered.

MANUFACTURING INDICATORS

Share of GDP (%): 6 (1988)
Labor force economically active in manufacturing (% est.): 0.5 (1981)
Value added in manufacturing (U.S. $ millions): 165 (1987)

MINING

Nepal has never been completely surveyed, but mineral deposits are known to exist in widely separated areas. They include coal, copper, cobalt, gold, iron, lignite, mica, zinc and limestone. None of them is commercially mined. The only mineral discovered in significant quantities is mica.

ENERGY

Nepal's per capita energy consumption of 23 kg. is the lowest in the world. Hydroelectric power is one of the major economic resources of Nepal—the other two being forestry and tourism—and the swift Himalayan rivers afford considerable potential for development of electric power.

The 1985–90 five-year plan called for the addition of 56,945 kw. to Nepal's generating capacity. Most of this will come from a series of major dams, although the installation of small generating plants large enough to supply a village also is getting under way. Nepal and India are negotiating a regional agreement for construction of a $1.5 billion dam on the Karnali River.

Two new hydroelectric plants were expected to be completed in the early 1990s, another is in the planning stage, and further development of existing plants is in progress. Foreign donors have promised U.S. $600m. in assistance for these projects. However, only a fraction of the country's energy requirements are met by electricity. Over 96% of the country's energy is supplied by traditional sources (fuelwood, agricultural waste products and animal waste).

ENERGY INDICATORS

Average annual energy production growth rate (%, 1980–88): 11.6
Energy consumption per capita (kg. oil equivalent): 23 (1988)
Energy imports as % of merchandise exports: 29 (1988)
Average annual growth rate of energy consumption (%, 1980–88): 9.4
Electricity 1988
 Installed capacity (000 kw.): 270
 Production (billion kw.-hr.): 589
  % fossil fuel: 4.4
  % hydro: 95.6
  % nuclear: 0.0
 Consumption per capita (kw.-hr.): 35
Natural gas
 Production (million cu. m.): 0 (1987)
 Consumption (million cu. m.): 0 (1986)
Petroleum
 Production (million bbl.): 0 (1989)
 Consumption (million bbl.): 0 (1988)
 Refining capacity (000 bbl./day): 0 (1990)
Coal
 Production (000 metric tons): 0 (1989)
 Consumption (000 metric tons): 0 (1988)

LABOR

The majority of the men and women are self-employed, and over 90% are engaged in subsistence farming. Nonagricultural sectors are undeveloped, and the technical, managerial and professional class includes only a few thousand persons.

Many men and women emigrate seasonally to India and Tibet, while over 50,000 Gurkhas serve in the Indian, British and Malaysian armies. This exodus reaches its peak in late fall, but most of the workers return to their farms by early spring.

Labor welfare is governed by the Nepal Factories and Factory Workers' Act of 1963, which provides for paid vacation, sick leave, overtime pay and accident compensation. The workweek consists of 54 hours, or six nine-hour workdays.

The Nepal Factories and Factory Workers' Act of 1959, as amended, sets minimum wage rates and working conditions, including special rules for women and a minimum working age of 14 years. Enforcement is spotty, however, and there have been reports of child labor being used in match and *bidi* (country cigarette) factories. The government banned trade unions in 1960. The Nepal Labor Organization, a creation of the government, is the only organization officially permitted

LABOR INDICATORS, 1986

Total economically active population (millions): 7.760
- % working-age (15–64): 82.5
- % female: 34.7

Activity rate (%)
- Total: 45.5
- Male: 57.8
- Female: 32.5

Employment status (%) 1981
- Employers & self-employed: 86.2
- Employees: 9.1
- Unpaid family workers: 2.5
- Other: 2.2

Sectoral employment of economically active (%) 1981
- Agriculture, forestry, fishing: 91.1
- Construction: 0.0
- Manufacturing, mining, quarrying, public utilities: 0.5
- Trade, hotels, restaurants: 1.6
- Transportation, communications: 0.1
- Finance, real estate: 0.1
- Services: 4.6

Average annual growth rate of labor force (%, 1985–2000): 2.3
Unemployment (000): 414.7 (1984)
Labor under 20 years (%): 26.0 (1981)

to perform trade union-like functions. There are some independent workers' associations, which are repressed by the government when they become too active. In early 1985 schoolteachers staged a determined strike, demanding pay parity with civil servants and recognition of their association. The government made concessions on pay but refused to grant official recognition to the teachers' association. Many teachers were placed under preventive detention, and their demonstrations were broken up.

FOREIGN COMMERCE

Nepal's primary imports are petroleum products, fertilizer, machinery and basic manufactured goods; primary exports are clothing, carpets, leather goods and grain. India is its primary trading partner. Other important markets are the United States and the United Kingdom. Trade with Tibet is hampered by lack of transportation and restrictions on free trade by the Chinese. Nepal, however, continues to maintain four trading posts in Tibet, to which it is entitled by the 1956 treaty.

FOREIGN TRADE INDICATORS, 1988

Exports (U.S. $ millions): 374
Imports (U.S. $ millions): −724
Balance of trade (U.S. $ millions): −350
Annual growth rate (1980–88), exports (%): 5.5
Annual growth rate (1980–88), imports (%): 7.0
International reserves in terms of months of imports covered: 4.5
Terms of trade (1980 = 100): 93
Import price index (1980 = 100): 93.4 (1986)
Export price index (1980 = 100): 92.1 (1986)

Direction of Trade (%)

	Imports	Exports
European Community	5.9	15.5
United States	1.7	28.5
U.S.S.R. & Eastern European economies	1.2	3.7
Japan	15.7	0.5

Composition of Trade (%)

	Imports	Exports
Food and agricultural raw materials	15.5	34.9
Fuels & other energy	12.0	0.0
Mineral ores & concentrates	0.6	0.2
Manufactured goods	71.9	64.9
of which chemicals	13.3	3.2
of which machinery	20.6	0.0

TRANSPORTATION & COMMUNICATIONS

The state-owned rail system consists of 53 km. (33 mi.) of track linking Jayanagar in India with Janakpurdham and Bijalpura. Another section, the Nepal Government Railway, links Raxaul to Amlekhganj. A 42-km. (26-mi.) ropeway links Hatauda and Katmandu. Both railways and ropeways are under the Transport Corporation of Nepal.

Though a landlocked nation, Nepal has two shipping companies, both based in Katmandu.

TRANSPORTATION INDICATORS

Roads (latest)
- Length, km. (mi.): 6,406 (3,980)
- Paved (%): 44

Motor vehicles (pre-1986)
- Automobiles: 14,201
- Trucks and buses: 9,988
- Persons per vehicle: 574
- Road freight, metric ton-km. (short ton-mi.) (millions): 1,437 (1984)

Railroads (latest)
- Track, km. (mi.): 53 (33)

Air
- Km. (mi.) flown (millions): 8.8 (5.5) (1985)
- Passenger-km. (passenger-mi.) (millions): 408 (254) (latest)
- Freight, metric ton-km. (short ton-mi.) (millions): 10.9 (7.5) (latest)
- Airports with scheduled flights: 5 (1990)

COMMUNICATION INDICATORS, 1987

Telephones
- Total (000): 26
- Persons per telephone: 686

Phone traffic (000 calls)
- Combined national: 4,479 (minutes)
- International: 1,583 (minutes)

Telegraph
- Total traffic (million calls): 1.203
  - National: 1.134
  - International: .069

Telex
- Subscriber lines: 230

Telecommunications 1990
- Satellite ground station: 1

TOURISM & TRAVEL INDICATORS, 1986

Total tourist receipts (U.S. $ millions): 64 (1988)
Expenditures by nationals abroad (U.S. $ millions): 35 (1988)
Number of hotel beds (000): 7
Number of tourists (000): 181.0
- of whom from United States: 18.5
- India: 54.6
- United Kingdom & Federal Republic of Germany: 12.1
- France: 10.9

The major highways are the Tribhuvan Rajpath between Katmandu and Raxaul on the Indian border; the Siddhartha Highway connecting Pokhara Valley with Sonauli on the Indian border; the Mahendra Highway, or the East–West Highway, which will extend the length of the country; and the Pokhara–Surkhet Road. All have been built with foreign assistance. Most goods are carried by porters, particularly the Sherpas, who transport up to 36 kg. (80 lb.) per man traveling in single file over mountain tracks and primitive suspension bridges.

The official flag carrier is Royal Nepal Airlines, which has a fleet of 21 aircraft. The international airport is at Guachar, near Katmandu.

Tourism has become increasingly important to the country's economy, generating $64 million in 1988. Among the most important attractions are the birthplace of Buddha and the Himalaya mountains, including Mt. Everest. The tourist industry was damaged in 1989 by trade disputes with India. In an effort to develop the industry, the government lifted travel restrictions in northern areas in 1989.

DEFENSE

The defense structure is headed by the king as the supreme commander of the armed forces. Manpower is provided by volunteers; there is no conscription system.

The strength of the armed forces is 35,000.

Nepal has neither an air force nor a navy. The army battle order consists of 2 divisions comprised of 5 infantry brigades, 1 parachute battalion; 1 palace guard brigade, including 1 cavalry squadron and 1 garrison battalion; 1 support brigade (1 artillery battalion, 1 engineer battalion and 1 signals battalion); 1 logistics brigade, including 1 transportation battalion; and 1 air squadron. The equipment consists of 16 light tanks, 25 combat vehicles, artillery, mortars and AA guns. Nine aircraft constitute the army's aviation wing. The Gurkhas of Nepal are among the most noted martial ethnic groups of the world, and the average soldier has been described as tough, fearless and intensely loyal. The Nepali army has not been engaged in military combat in modern times, but Gurkhas serve in the British, Indian and Malaysian armies. The country's best defense, however, is not the army but the terrain, which makes it difficult for any enemy to penetrate it, let alone subjugate it.

Until 1969 Nepal had a mutual security agreement with India under which it received arms and training. Britain and the United States also have provided military assistance; the latter gave $2.4 million through 1983 in military hardware and training programs.

EDUCATION INDICATORS, 1988

Literacy
- Total (%): 20.7
- Male (%): 31.9
- Female (%): 9.2

First level
- Schools: 12,491
- Students: 1,952,504
- Teachers: 55,207
- Student/teacher ratio: 35.4
- Net enrollment ratio: 59 (1984)

Second level
- Schools: 5,325
- Students: 579,517
- Teachers: 20,662
- Student–teacher ratio: 28.0
- Net enrollment ratio: 19 (1984)

Vocational 1986
- Schools: 5
- Students: 648
- Teachers: 117
- Student–teacher ratio: 5.5

Third level (postsecondary)
- Institutions: 116 (1986)
- Students: 67,555 (1986)
- Teachers: 4,165 (1986)
- Student–teacher ratio: 16.2
- Gross enrollment ratio: 4.9 (1985)
- Students (/100,000 pop.): 414
- % of population age 25 and over with postsecondary education: 6.8

Foreign study
- Students abroad: 2,209
  - of whom in
    - United States: 523 (1988)
    - France: 10 (1988)
    - Federal Republic of Germany: 23 (1988)
    - United Kingdom: 91 (1987)

Public expenditure 1985
- Total (N.R.S.): 1,240,717
- % of GNP: 2.8
- % of national budget: 10.8

GRADUATES, 1983

Total: 3,142
Education: 31
Humanities & religion: 1,696
Fine & applied arts: 0
Law: 243
Social & behavioral sciences: 0
Commerce & business: 488
Mass communication: 0
Home economics: 0
Service trades: 0
Natural sciences: 373
Mathematics & computer science: 0
Medicine: 127
Engineering: 64
Architecture: —
Industrial programs: 0
Transportation & communications: 0
Agriculture, forestry, fisheries: 101
Other: 19

EDUCATION

Schooling is, in principle, universal, free and compulsory for five years, from ages six through 11. It lasts for 10 years, divided into primary (five grades), middle (two grades) and secondary or high school (three grades). The attrition rate is high, attendance is irregular and facilities and equipment are inadequate.

The academic year runs from February to December. The medium of instruction is Nepali in the primary grades and English in the secondary grades. Private schools are autonomous, but in the Buddhist *gompas* and the Sanskrit schools the range of study is considerably narrower, often limited to sacred texts. There is an acute shortage of teachers, which is partly made up by hiring Indian teachers and retired Gurkha soldiers.

Responsibility for public education is centralized in the Ministry of Education, which exercises this function through seven zonal inspectorates and 32 subinspectorates.

Nepal has only one university, Tribhuvan University, at Katmandu, with an enrollment of 55,555 in 1984.

LEGAL SYSTEM

The present legal system is based on the Mulki Ain, the code of law promulgated in 1962. Among other things the code ended discrimination based on caste and sex, permitted divorce and abolished the death sentence except for treason.

The law provides for the right to a fair public trial in most cases (some security and customs cases excepted), and this right usually is honored. Except for those held in preventive detention, the constitution guarantees the right to counsel and protection from double jeopardy and ex post facto laws, but these rights are not always respected. There are separate military and civilian courts. Military courts generally deal only with military personnel, but civilians may be tried in these courts for crimes involving the military. Judges are appointed by the government, and decisions in political and security cases sometimes reflect the government's view. All lower-court decisions (including acquittals) are subject to appeal, and the Supreme Court is the court of last appeal. The king may grant pardons and set aside judgments.

The judicial system consists of the Supreme Court and 15 zonal and 75 district courts. The Supreme Court is composed of a chief justice and nine judges. The attorney general is assisted by three advocates, and the zonal and district courts are provided with public prosecutors and defense advocates.

LAW ENFORCEMENT

Nepal's modern National Police Force was established only in 1955, when the Nepal Police Act was promulgated by royal decree. It created the National Police headquarters at Katmandu under an inspector general and three zonal headquarters under deputy inspectors general. Each zone consists of four or five police districts under superintendents of police. At the bottom of the hierarchy are the police stations, headed by head constables, each of whom is responsible for three or four villages.

Nepal has one of the lowest crime rates in the world, primarily because of the respect for authority implicit in the caste system. Theft is the most frequent crime, and politically motivated disorders are not uncommon.

HEALTH

The major health problems are cholera, malaria, black fever (kala azar), dysentery, tuberculosis, typhoid and venereal diseases.

HEALTH INDICATORS

Health personnel 1988
- Physicians and dentists: 879
  - persons per: 20,234
- Nurses: 601
- Pharmacists: 427 (1986)
- Midwives: 2,062

Hospitals 1988
- Number: 96
- Number of beds (/10,000): 2
- Admissions/discharges (/10,000): 54
- Bed occupancy rate (%): 61.5 (1980)
- Average length of stay (days): 7 (1980)

Type of hospital (%) 1980
- Government: 82.4
- Private nonprofit: 17.6
- Private profit: 0.0

Public health expenditures (latest)
- As % of national budget: 5.7
- Per capita (U.S. $): 1.70

Vital statistics
- Crude death rate (/1,000): 15 (1990)
- Life expectancy at birth 1990
  - Males: 50
  - Females: 50
- Infant mortality rate (/1,000 live births): 99 (1990)
- Child mortality rate under 5 yrs. (/1,000 births) (1985–90): 196
- Maternal mortality rate (/100,000 live births): 850 (1980)
- Population with access to safe water (%): 29 (latest)

The lack of modern health service is partly offset by the existence of a vast group of shamans known as *bijuwas*, and Ayurvedic physicians known as *vaids*.

FOOD & NUTRITION

Rice is the staple food. Per capital daily food intake is 1,914 calories (as against the minimum daily requirement of 2,600 calories recommended by the World Health Organization).

MEDIA & CULTURE

Fifty-nine daily newspapers are published in the country. Just after the liberalization of licensing policies, the number of daily newspapers increased fourfold. Two of the more influential dailies are published in English: *The Rising Nepal* and *The Motherland.* All are published in the capital. Nondaily newspapers number 345. Some 94 periodicals also are published.

Under the Constitution, freedoms of speech and the press may not be exercised in support of a political party or to the detriment of the common good, the monarch or members of the royal family. In practice this rule is widely interpreted to permit criticism of the government but not the monarch or the royal family. The number of independent newspapers and journals continues to grow, and there is wide tolerance of frank criticism of the government in the press. Journals and newspapers that overstep the established guidelines may be suspended from publication. In 1986–87, the government banned 14 weeklies and suspended another 97. The two largest-circulation dailies are government organs, but they carry reports of opposition activities and criticism of the government. Following a 1982 liberalization of government policy governing the licensing of new newspapers, an estimated 150 papers began publishing. Although many of these papers have a very small circulation (less than 100 copies), this development demonstrates a growing government acceptance of a broader role for the press in Nepalese society.

Official censorship is exercised in two forms: By subsidizing publications that support the government and by suspending publications that criticize its programs. Official clearance is required for the publication of political material. Bans have occurred with relative frequency.

MEDIA INDICATORS

Newspapers
- Number of dailies: 59 (latest)
- Number of nondailies: 345
- Number of periodicals: 94
- Newsprint consumption 1988
  - Total metric tons: 1,300
  - Per 1,000 pop. (kg.): 71

Book publishing
- Number of titles: 117 (latest)

Radio
- Number of transmitters: 3 (latest)
- Number of persons per radio receiver: 31 (1989)
- Total program hours (/yr.): 6,252 (1987)

Television
- Television transmitters: 1 (latest)
- Number of persons per T.V. receiver: 683 (1989)

Films
- Number of long films produced: 1 (latest)

CULTURAL & ENVIRONMENTAL INDICATORS

Libraries (latest)
- Number: 400

Performing arts (pre-1986)
- Attendance (/1,000 pop.): 5

Nature reserves (latest)
- Number of facilities: 11

The official news agency is Rastriya Sambad Samiti, an autonomous company with 60% state participation.

Indigenous book publishing is negligible. The Royal Nepal Academy, a state-sponsored society is one of the few domestic publishers. There are six other publishers, whose output is very uneven. Nepal does not adhere to any copyright convention.

Radio Nepal, founded in 1951, broadcasts a domestic service for eight hours a day and an external service for two hours a week on two medium-wave (0.25- and 10-kw.) and two shortwave (50 and 100-kw.) transmitters. An annual license is payable for radio receivers. Nepal Television Corporation broadcasts for 23 hours a week. Feature films are imported, mostly from India.

Almost all the libraries are in Katmandu. The largest are the National Library and Tribhuvan University Library.

There are seven museums and ten nature preservation sites.

SOCIAL WELFARE

There are no organized official social welfare programs.

GLOSSARY

adalat amini: the judiciary.

anachal: zone; largest administrative unit of local government.

bada hakim: district governor; now replaced by the chief district officer.

bigha: unit of land equal to 0.67 ha. (1.67 ac.).

bijuwa: a shaman in the upland areas whose treatment consists of magical incantations.

birta: virtually tax free lands the revenues from which are assigned to individuals rather than the state.

Bon: a shamanistic religion with Buddhist elements prevalent in Tibet, Nepal, Bhutan and Sikkim.

chetri: Brahmin caste of Nepal to which the Ranas of Nepal belonged.

gaun: village.

gaun sevak: chief administrative officer of a gaun; also, gram sevak.

gompa: Buddhist temple; by extension, school attached to the Buddhist temple in which primary education is provided.

goswara: civil administration, as distinguished from law enforcement and revenue administration.

guthi: land providing income for the endowment of shrines and charitable institutions.

ilaka: district as a division of local administration.

jatiya: modified form of caste system, prevalent among the Indo-Nepalese.

jilla: district or development block.

kipat: an extended family; by extension, land held in common by such a family.

maharaja: title assumed by the ruling Rana prime ministers until 1951.

mal adda: district office for the collection of land taxes.

mukhiya: headman of a village.

nagar: town.

pancha: member of a panchayat.

panchayat: a representative assembly or council; (as used in Nepal) a form of partyless government consisting of hierarchically arranged parallel series of such assemblies and councils.

paraganna: county; also, thum.

pradhan pancha: chief of a panchayat.

raikar: state land held by tenants under perpetual lease.

rajya: land granted to vassals with certain privileges.

Rana: title of the hereditary prime ministers of Nepal from 1846 to 1951.

sabai grass: a coarse grass used for the manufacture of paper pulp.
sal: a hardwood grown in the Himalayas.
sissoo: a hardwood used for making furniture.
semal: a softwood used for making plywood.
talukdar: nonofficial tax agent in a village.
Thakuri: Brahmin caste to which the royal family of Nepal belongs.
thana: a police station.
thum: county.
vaid: an Ayurvedic physician.
varna: color, especially as the determinant of caste.

CHRONOLOGY (from 1945)

1945— Rana Padma Shamsher becomes prime minister.
1946— The Nepali Congress Party is founded.
1947— The United States establishes diplomatic relations with Nepal.
1948— The country's first constitution, the Government of Nepal Act, is promulgated; Padma resigns in the wake of opposition to the new constitution from conservative Ranas; Mohan Shamsher becomes prime minister; constitution is suspended.
1950— Ranas are in open conflict with the monarch, Tribhuvan. . . . Tribhuvan, implicated in Nepali Congress Party conspiracy against Rana power, seeks and is granted asylum in India; general rebellion is stamped out; second offensive by the rebels gains ground; government troops desert to the rebel side; over 140 Ranas join the dissidents. Treaty of Peace and Friendship and Treaty of Trade and Commerce are signed with India.
1951— Mohan capitulates; King Tribhuvan is restored to the throne; elections and the formation of a constituent assembly are promised; Rana power ends; Mohan Shamsher heads new coalition cabinet for 10 months; he is succeeded by Nepali Congress Party leader M. P. Koirala as prime minister; interim constitution, the Government of Nepal Act, is promulgated.
1952— Koirala resigns; king assumes direct rule.
1953— Koirala is recalled as prime minister.
1955— Tribhuvan dies and is succeeded by Mahendra as king. . . . Nepal joins the United Nations. . . . National Police Force is formed. . . . Koirala resigns; Mahendra takes over direct control.
1956— Tanka Prasad Acharya is named prime minister. . . . Border treaty with China is concluded.
1957— Acharya resigns; K. I. Singh becomes prime minister for a few months.
1958— USSR opens an embassy at Katmandu. . . . Subarna Shamsher is named new prime minister.
1959— The United States opens an embassy at Katmandu. . . . New constitution is promulgated, superseding Constitution of 1951. . . . First general elections are held; Nepali Congress Party wins absolute majority. . . . Tribhuvan University is founded.
1960— Koirala heads first popular government; Koirala's policies are opposed by the king, and Koirala is abruptly dismissed; all political parties are banned; the king takes over direct control of government. . . . Treaty of Peace and Friendship with China is concluded.
1961— King proclaims guided democracy. . . . Boundary treaty with China is renewed.
1962— New constitution, third since 1951, establishes panchayat form of government. . . . Land Reorganization Act and Mulki Ain, new legal code, are promulgated. . . . Anti-Indian riots erupt in Katmandu over Indian aid to dissidents.
1963— Emergency is ended. . . . Panchayat elections begin. . . . National Guidance Council is formed. . . . Tulsi Giri is named prime minister.
1965— Local government is reorganized. . . . Giri resigns; Surya Bahadur Thapar is appointed prime minister.
1969— Thapar yields office to Kirti Nidhi Bista. . . . Indian military mission is withdrawn.
1970— Bista resigns; Raj Bhandari becomes interim prime minister.
1971— Bista is recalled as prime minister. . . . New trade and transit treaty is negotiated with India.
1972— Mahendra dies and is succeeded as king by Birendra. . . . Tribhuvan University is closed. . . . Development regions are established under National Development Council.
1973— Nagendra Prasad Rijal is named prime minister. . . . Singha Durbar, the residence of the Ranas, is burned by rebels.
1974— Relations with India worsen.
1975— Rijal resigns; Tulsi Giri is appointed prime minister. . . . King Birendra is crowned. . . . "Go to the Village" national campaign is launched.
1976— Koirala returns from India and is arrested. . . . Treaty with India expires and is not renewed.
1977— Prime Minister Tulsi Giri resigns in the wake of corruption charges; former prime minister Kirti Nidhi Bista is reinstated as prime minister.
1979— Following nationwide demonstrations by students, Bista is replaced as prime minister by Surya Bahadur Thapa; king announces referendum on the panchayat form of government.
1980— In national referendum people vote for continuance of the panchayat form of government and against the reintroduction of political parties.
1983— Prime Minister Surya Bahadur Thapa is defeated in the Rashtriya Panchayat and is replaced by Lokendra Bahadur Chand.
1986— Marich Man Singh Shrestka becomes prime minister.
1990— Nepal adopts a new constitution providing for the king as head of state. Executive power is exercised by a prime minister who leads the majority party in the legislature.

BIBLIOGRAPHY

BOOKS

Agarwal, H. N. *Administrative System of Nepal.* New York, 1976.
Banister, Judith and Shyam Thapa. *The Population Dynamics of Nepal.* Honolulu, 1981.
Baral, Lok R. *Nepal's Policies of Referendum: A Study*

of Groups, Personalities and Trends. New York, 1984.

———. *Opposition Politics in Nepal.* Columbia, MO, 1977.

Beyer, Jon C. *Budget Innovations in Developing Countries: The Experience of Nepal.* New York, 1973.

Bhooshan, B. S. *The Development Experience of Nepal.* Atlantic Highlands, NJ, 1980.

Blaikie, M. P. *The Struggle for Basic Needs in Nepal.* Paris, 1980.

Caplan, Lionel. *Administration and Politics in a Nepalese Town.* New York, 1975.

Dharamdasani, M. D. *Political Participation and Change in South Asia in the Context of Nepal.* Bombay, 1985.

Gaige, Frederick H. *Regionalism and National Unity in Nepal.* Berkeley, CA, 1975.

Hagen, T. *Nepal: The Kingdom in the Himalayas.* New York, 1971.

Hendrick, Basil C. *A Bibliography of Nepal.* Metuchen, NJ, 1973.

——— and Anne K. Hendrick. *A Historical and Cultural Dictionary of Nepal.* Metuchen, NJ, 1972.

Kumar, D. P. *Nepal: Year of Decision.* New York, 1980.

Military History of Nepal, 2 vol. New Delhi, 1984.

Muni, S. D. *Foreign Policy of Nepal.* New York, 1974.

Nath, Tribhuban. *The Nepalese Dilemma.* Mystic, CT, 1975.

Pant, Y. P. *Population Growth and Employment Opportunities in Nepal.* New Delhi, 1985.

Poudyal, Madhab. *Public Administration and Nation-Building in Nepal.* Bombay, 1984.

Poudyal, Sriram. *Planned Development in Nepal.* New Delhi, 1982.

Ramakant. *Nepal, China and India.* Columbia, MO, 1976.

Rawat, P. C. *Indo-Nepal Economic Relations.* Mystic, CT, 1974.

Regmi, D. R. *Modern Nepal,* 2 vol. Columbia, MO, 1975.

Regmi, M. C. *Landownership in Nepal.* Berkeley, CA, 1976.

Rose, Leo E. *Nepal: Strategy for Survival.* Berkeley, CA, 1971.

——— and Margaret W. Fisher. *Politics of Nepal: Persistence and Change in an Asian Monarchy.* Ithaca, NY, 1970.

——— and John T. Scholz. *Nepal: Profile of a Himalayan Kingdom.* Boulder, CO, 1980.

Shaha, R. *Nepali Politics: Retrospect and Prospect.* New York, 1975.

Taylor, Daniel, and Hem B. Hamal. *Population Education for Nepal.* Chapel Hill, NC, 1974.

Thapa, Poonam. *Nepal: Socio-Economic Change and Rural Migration.* New Delhi, 1988.

Tuladhar, Jayanti M. *The Population of Nepal.* Detroit, MI, 1977.

OFFICIAL PUBLICATIONS

Central Statistics Bureau. *Statistical Bulletin.*

Finance Ministry. *His Majesty's Government Budget Document* (annual, Nepalese).

———. *His Majesty's Government Budget Speech* (annual).

Nepal Rastra Bank. *Quarterly Economic Bulletin.*

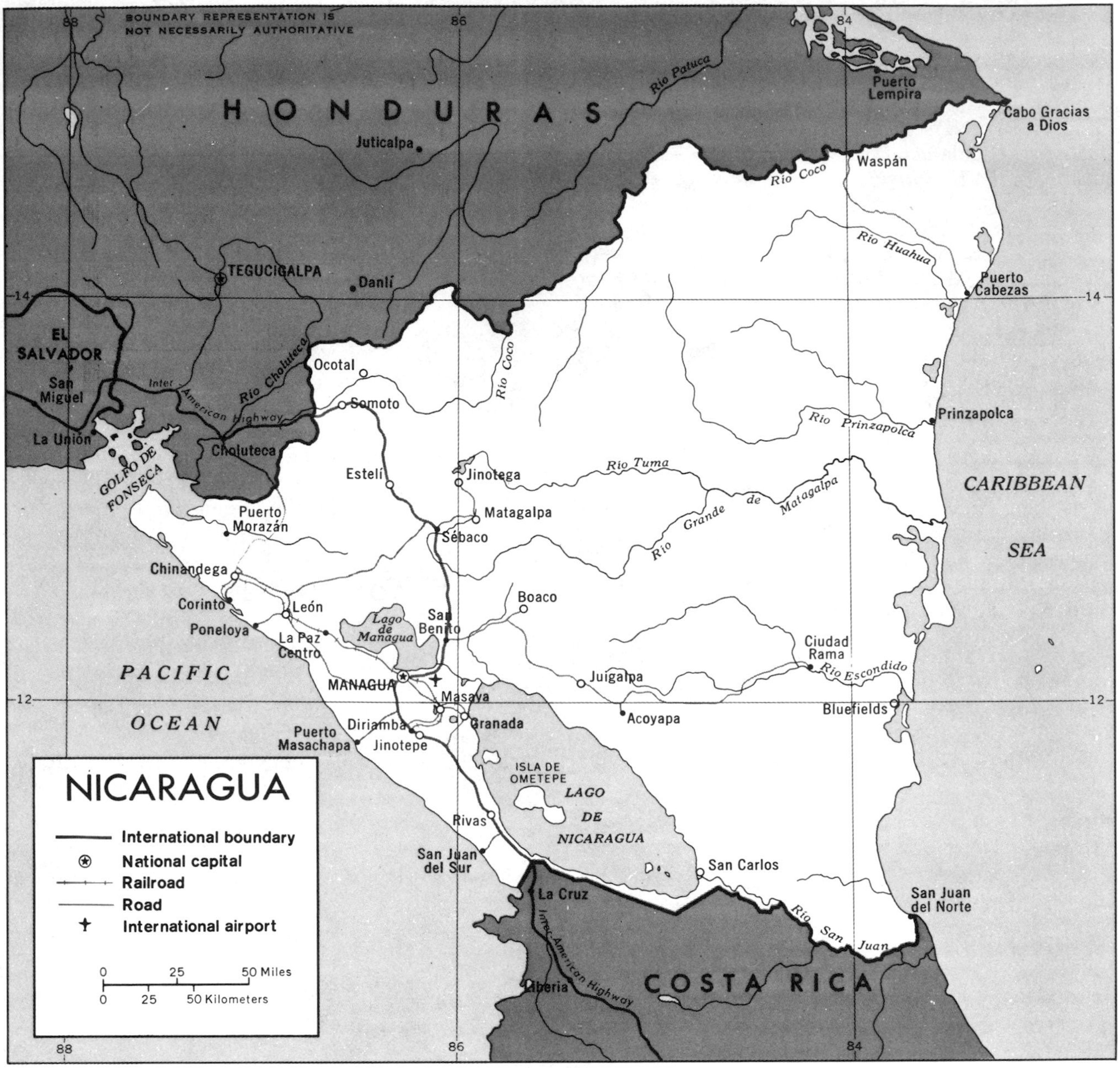

BOUNDARY REPRESENTATION IS NOT NECESSARILY AUTHORITATIVE

HONDURAS

Río Patuca
Puerto Lempira
Cabo Gracias a Dios
Juticalpa
Waspán
Río Coco
Río Huahua
TEGUCIGALPA
Danlí
Puerto Cabezas
EL SALVADOR
San Miguel
Ocotal
Somoto
Río Choluteca
Inter-American Highway
La Unión
Choluteca
GOLFO DE FONSECA
Río Coco
Prinzapolca
Río Prinzapolca
Río Tuma
Estelí
Jinotega
CARIBBEAN
Matagalpa
Río Grande de Matagalpa
Puerto Morazán
Sébaco
SEA
Chinandega
Boaco
Corinto
León
Lago de Managua
San Benito
Poneloya
La Paz Centro
Ciudad Rama
Río Escondido
PACIFIC
MANAGUA
Juigalpa
Masaya
Bluefields
OCEAN
Granada
Acoyapa
Diriamba
Puerto Masachapa
Jinotepe
ISLA DE OMETEPE
LAGO DE NICARAGUA
Rivas
San Juan del Sur
San Carlos
La Cruz
San Juan del Norte
Río San Juan
Liberia
Inter-American Highway
COSTA RICA

88
86
84
14
12

NICARAGUA

International boundary
National capital
Railroad
Road
International airport

0 25 50 Miles
0 25 50 Kilometers

NICARAGUA

BASIC FACT SHEET

OFFICIAL NAME: Republic of Nicaragua (República de Nicaragua)

ABBREVIATION: NQ

CAPITAL: Managua

HEAD OF STATE & HEAD OF GOVERNMENT: Violeta Barrios de Chamorro (from 1990)

NATURE OF GOVERNMENT: Republic

POPULATION: 3,722,683 (1990)

AREA: 129,494 sq. km. (50,191 sq. mi.)

ETHNIC MAJORITY: Mestizo

LANGUAGE: Spanish

RELIGION: Roman Catholicism

UNIT OF CURRENCY: Córdoba

NATIONAL FLAG: Two cobalt blue horizontal bands separated by a central white band with an encircled triangle, the national emblem, in the middle.

NATIONAL EMBLEM: An equilateral triangle encircled by gold letters, "República de Nicaragua" in the top and "America Central" in the bottom. Within the triangle five mountains rise from the ocean beneath a rainbow in the blue sky. From the middle of the mountain range rises a red Phrygian cap of liberty on a pole.

NATIONAL ANTHEM: "Beloved Homeland"

NATIONAL HOLIDAYS: September 15 (National Day, Independence Day); January 1 (New Year's Day); February 1 (Air Force Day); May 1 (Labor Day); May 27 (Army Day); July 14 (Abrogation of the Chamorro-Bryan Treaty Day); August 1 and 10 (Feast days of St. Domingo, Nicaragua's patron saint); September 14 (Battle of San Jacinto Day); October 12 (Columbus Day); also, all major Catholic festivals.

NATIONAL CALENDAR: Gregorian

PHYSICAL QUALITY OF LIFE INDEX: 74

DATE OF INDEPENDENCE: September 15, 1838

DATE OF CONSTITUTION: None

WEIGHTS & MEASURES: Metric

GEOGRAPHICAL FEATURES

Nicaragua has an area of 129,494 sq. km. (50,191 sq. mi.), of which the land area, excluding the two large lakes, Lake Managua and Lake Nicaragua, is 120,254 sq. km. (46,610 sq. mi.). The country extends 580 km. (360 mi.) northeast to southwest and 494 km. (307 mi.) northwest to southeast. The total length of the Caribbean coastline is 478 km. (297 mi.); that of the Pacific coastline is 346 km. (215 mi.)

Nicaragua shares its total international boundary of 1,292 km. (803 mi.) with two neighbors: Honduras (992 km., 616 mi.) and Costa Rica (300 km., 186 mi.). The Costa Rican border was settled in 1896. For much of its length it follows the southern shore of Lake Nicaragua and the San Juan River. The Honduran border was in dispute until 1960, when the International Court of Justice ruled in favor of Honduras. Nicaragua also maintains a claim, disputed by Colombia, to the Quita Sueno Bank, about 240 km. (150 mi.) off Nicaragua's Caribbean coast.

The capital is Managua, with a population in 1985 of 682,111. The city was destroyed twice in this century by major earthquakes, in 1931 and 1972. The 1972 earthquake killed 9,000 persons, injured another 25,000, displaced some 300,000 and destroyed about three-quarters of the buildings. The other major urban centers are León (100,982), Granada (88,636), Masaya (74,946), Chinandega (67,792), Matagalpa (36,982), Esteli (30,635), and Tipitapa (30,078).

On the basis of human settlements, the country is divided into four regions: the West, including the Pacific highlands and the lakes of the Great Rift Depression; the highland frontier; the Empty Lands, including the Caribbean coastal plains; and the East, comprising settlements at the mouths of the rivers on the Mosquito Coast.

Topographically, there are four main divisions: the coastal highlands, the Great Rift or the central lowlands, the central highlands and the Caribbean lowlands. The first region consists of the coastal or Diriamba Highlands, locally called sierras, that are structurally a continuation of the Costa Rican highlands. To the south, the highlands trail off into the low Rivas Isthmus. The Great Rift, or the central lowlands, is partially occupied by the country's two large freshwater lakes, Lake Managua (known locally as Xolotlán) and Lake Nicaragua (known locally as Cocibolca). Lake Nicaragua is about 161 km. (100 mi.) long and 72 km. (45 mi.) wide and occupies an area of 18,000 sq. km. (6,950 sq. mi.). Lake Managua is 56 km. (35 mi.) long and 24 km. (15 mi.) wide and occupies an area of 1,000 sq. km. (386 sq. mi.). The central highlands lie to the north and east of the Great Rift. Structurally, these highlands form part of the system of volcanic ranges that begins in the Aleutians and the Alaskan mountains and continues through western British Columbia, the Rocky Mountains, the islands of the West Indies and the Andes to Tierra del Fuego and Cape Horn. Within Nicaragua the system includes the Cordillera Dariense, the Montanas de Huapi and the Cordillera de Yolaina, terminating in the Punta del Mono (Monkey Point). The highest peak in this region is Zelaya (2,000 m., 6,560 ft.). Toward the east the highlands merge into the Caribbean lowlands, also known as La Mosquitia (the Mosquito or Miskito Coast), comprising alluvial plains and valleys with numerous shallow bays, lagoons and salt marshes.

There are two drainage systems, one flowing into the Pacific and the other into the Caribbean. The most important of the latter is the San Juan, which receives the runoff from Lake Nicaragua and—through the Tipitapa River (an underground channel for part of its course)—from Lake Managua. The San Juan Valley provides a nearly sea-level route from the Caribbean to Lake Nicaragua, the southwestern edge of which is only 19 km. (12 mi.) from the Pacific. With modern engineering capability, this route could provide an alternative to the Panama Canal. The other east-flowing rivers are the Escondido, the Río Grande (with its tributary the Río Tuma), the Prinzapolco and the Segovia or the Coco. The main west-flowing rivers are the Río Negro and the Viejo.

WEATHER

Nicaragua has a tropical climate with two seasons: wet from May to January and dry from January to mid-May. As in other Central American countries, there are three climatic zones: wet tropical, wet and dry tropical, and mild highland. The mean average temperature in the Pacific coastal region is 25.6°C (78°F), with extremes of 15.5°C (60°F) and 35°C (95°F). In the higher altitudes of the interior, the temperature varies between 15.5°C (60°F) and 27.5°C (80°F), and in the lower altitudes between 24°C (75.2°F) and 32°C (89.6°F). In Managua the monthly average temperatures range from 26°C (79°F) to 30°C (86°F). Annual average rainfall along the Mosquito Coast ranges from 254 to 635 cm. (100 to 250 in.). Managua receives an average of 114 cm. (45 in.) and the Pacific coast 203 cm. (80 in.) a year.

Neither the Caribbean hurricanes nor the Pacific storms known as *cordonazos* affect Nicaragua other than occasionally. In midwinter there are storms and cold winds locally known as *papagayo* (parrot storms).

POPULATION

The population of Nicaragua was estimated in 1990 at 3,722,683 on the basis of the last official census, held in 1971, when it was 1,877,952.

The population is heavily concentrated in the Pacific zone, which accounts for only one-quarter of the land area but roughly 60% of the population. The northern and central zones account for about 35% of the population and the Atlantic zone for about 5%. The highest urbanization trend has been experienced in the densely populated Pacific zone.

With the elimination of restrictions on member country migration among Central American Common Market countries, there has been considerable emigration from Nicaragua to Costa Rica. There is also some emigration to the United States and Mexico. The largest Nicaraguan expatriate colony is in Costa Rica and the second-largest in San Francisco. Because of limited employment opportunities, immigration has not been significant. The foreign-born population has never exceeded 20,000 at any one time during the past few decades.

Women are not subject to any special restrictive measures by the government and are active at all levels of society and government. Women serve as officials in the independent political parties. Participation of women in the military is voluntary.

DEMOGRAPHIC INDICATORS

Population (million): 3.722 (1990)
Year of last census: 1971
Sex distribution (% at last census): males, 48.3; females, 51.7
Population estimates and projections (million)

1940: .825	1970: 1.972	2000: 5.261
1950: 1.109	1980: 2.771	2010: 6.824
1960: 1.472	1990: 3.871	

Age profile (% at last census)

0–14: 48.1	30–44: 14.1	60–74: 3.8
15–29: 25.6	45–59: 7.4	75 and over: 1.1

Median age (yrs.): 16.5 (1985)
Youth population (% age 15–24): 20.0 (1985); 20.3 (2000)
Total dependency ratio: 97.1 (1985)
Annual growth rate (%)

1950–55: 3.03	1975–80: 2.81	2000–2005: 2.72
1955–60: 3.12	1980–85: 3.32	2005–2010: 2.48
1960–65: 3.19	1985–90: 3.36	2010–2015: 2.24
1965–70: 3.19	1990–1995: 3.19	2015–2020: 2.00
1970–75: 3.20	1995–2000: 2.95	2020–2025: 1.78

Hypothetical size of stationary population (millions): 14
Assumed year of reaching net reproduction rate of 1: 2025
Urban population (million): 1.851 (1985)
Urban population (%): 58 (1988); 43 (1965)
Annual urban population growth rate (%, 1985–90): 4.46
Annual rural population growth rate (%, 1985–90): 1.84
Percentage of urban population in largest city: 47 (1980)
Percentage of urban population in cities of population over 500,000: 47 (1980)
Number of cities of population over 500,000: 1 (1980)
Population density per sq. km. (per sq. mi.): 29.6 (76.7) (latest)

VITAL STATISTICS

Crude birth rate (/1,000): 41 (1990); 49 (1965)
Crude death rate (/1,000): 7 (1990); 16 (1965)
Infant mortality rate (/1,000 live births): 68 (1990)
Maternal mortality rate (/100,000 live births): 65 (1980)
Life expectancy (yrs.) at birth: males, 61; females, 62 (1990)
Gross reproduction rate (/woman) (1980–85): 2.90
Total fertility rate (/woman): 5.0 (1990)
Rate of natural increase (/1,000): 33.8 (1988)
Marriage rate (/1,000): 3.6 (1985)
Average household size: 6.9 (latest)

STATUS OF WOMEN INDICATORS

Number of women (million): 1.616 (1985)
Women of childbearing age (15–49) (% of pop.): 45 (1988)
Women's literacy rate (%): 88 (1985)
Women in labor force (%): 24.6 (1988)
Total fertility rate (/woman); 5.0 (1990)

There is no great official concern about overpopulation and little interest in family planning. Some private groups are involved in token family planning activities. These include the Demographic Association of Nicaragua, the National Social Security Institute and the Moravian Missionary Group.

In the mid-1980s the government began forced evacuation of thousands of peasants from the northern countryside. According to officials, the purpose of the program was twofold: to deprive resistance forces of local support and to create free-fire zones where the People's Army could operate freely. Another objective was to create a new dependence on the government on the part of the displaced people. In the town of Limay, houses were burned and animals killed by government troops to prevent the peasants from returning. Since 1980 over 200,000 Nicaraguans have fled to Costa Rica, Honduras and other neighboring countries and another 200,000 to 250,000 are in the United States, Mexico and elsewhere.

ETHNIC COMPOSITION

Nicaragua may be ethnically classified as mestizo country, in which the process called *mestizaje* (or the ethnic and cultural blending of Europeans and Indians) is more or less complete, especially in the central and western regions, where the Ladino (or Hispanicized) culture is shared by nearly 90% of the population and where Spanish is the principal language and Roman Catholicism is the dominant religion.

The term Ladino is a cultural rather than an ethnic label. Historically, the term was used to indicate Hispanicization apart from racial purity or color, although physical traits may influence social status within Ladino society. Even the Ladinized Indian thinks of himself as the bearer of Spanish heritage. (The use of Ladino in this context is distinguished from that used to denote the Spanish dialect of Jews of Spanish descent.)

Outside the mainstream of Nicaraguan society are the blacks who constitute roughly 10% of the population, and the Indians, who constitute about 5%. Both these groups are concentrated in the East, where they escaped Spanish assimilationist influences.

The blacks form the principal ethnic minority, and their separate identity has been reinforced by geographical isolation, their use of the English language, their Protestant affiliations and their British West Indian origins. Locally called Samboes (a pejorative term in the United States) or *costeños* (coast-dwellers), they call themselves creoles. The blacks are the descendants of slaves who escaped from slave ships, as well as slaves brought in from the West Indies to work on British-owned plantations. There also are a few French-speaking blacks from French West Indian colonies and Spanish-speaking blacks from the Central American interior.

The Indian population is concentrated in three major areas: the Miskito, Sumu, Rama and the black Carib on the Atlantic coast and in the eastern highlands; the Matagalpa in the central highlands; and the Subtiaba and the Monimbo in the Pacific lowlands. Of these, the Matagalpa, Subtiaba and Monimbo have been heavily Hispanicized, while the Miskito, Sumu, Rama and black Carib retain their traditional cultural traits and ways of life. The largest of these groups is the Miskito, who comprise about half of the Indian population. Many Miskito have intermarried with blacks, Chinese, Arabs or Spaniards; are mainly Protestant; and speak their own Chibcha language or English. The 10,000 Miskito Indians forcibly resettled from their Río Coco homelands in 1982 continue to be prohibited from returning there. In the mid-1980s there were credible reports that the security forces tortured and killed Miskito Indians and confiscated or destroyed their food supply and property. The second-largest Indian group is the Matagalpa, most of whom are found in the departments of Matagalpa and Jinotega.

Official ethnic policy is directed toward the assimilation of minority groups into the national culture. The process of Hispanicization may result in the complete absorption of Indians into the dominant Ladino culture within a few generations. The government's Indian programs are coordinated by the Indian National Institute.

There are a few other distinct ethnic groups, none of them numerically important. These include Chinese, Jews and Levantines. There are North American and European communities in all major cities.

LANGUAGES

The official language is Spanish, spoken by nearly 96% of the population. The percentage of non-Spanish speakers has been steadily decreasing, suggesting that the government's Spanish-language programs in the Atlantic provinces may be taking effect. Nearly 91% of the non-Spanish-speaking population is concentrated in the Department of Zelaya, on the eastern coast, the home of the Miskito and Sumu Indians and the English-speaking creoles. Some Indians may speak English, but most of them still use any of various Chibcha dialects. Even when Indians speak Spanish, their speech is marked by corruptions, Indian loanwords and the linguistic feature known as datism (the incorrect use of an acquired language by a nonnative speaker).

RELIGIONS

Roman Catholicism, the dominant religion of the country, is followed by nearly 90% of the population. Protestants constitute the only significant religious minority. Nicaragua was spared much of the violent church-state conflict that marred the history of other Latin American countries, and has anticlerical laws. Although there is no constitutional provision for an official religion, the government recognizes religion in practice and grants it certain privileges. Official diplomatic ties are maintained with the Vatican, and the upkeep of old churches is subsidized by the national treasury. Churches may own and acquire property, and the clergy are not banned from participating in politics. Ecclesiastically, the country is divided into one archbishopric, at Managua, and five dioceses, at León, Granada, Bluefields, Matagalpa and Estelí.

Relations between the government and the Catholic hierarchy and some Protestant churches have been strained for the past several years, but a new deterioration of relations between the Catholic Church and the government began in the early summer of 1985 with the elevation of Archbishop Miguel Obando y Bravo to cardinal. Hundreds of thousands of Nicaraguans poured into the streets to welcome the cardinal in June when he returned from Rome. Two events, involving police intervention, somewhat marred the ceremonies.

In 1985 the government also violated an informal agreement with the Catholic Church exempting seminarians from military service. Government pressure on evangelicals also was stepped up in the mid-1980s.

Protestantism, introduced in the 19th century, expanded as a result of missionary work by German and U.S. Moravians. Protestants, constituting only 5% of the population are largely settled in Zelaya and Cabo Gracias a Dios.

HISTORICAL BACKGROUND

Nicaragua was discovered by Christopher Columbus in 1502. During the next 300 years the country—which received its name from the Indian chief Nicarao—was ruled from Guatemala. In 1821 the independence of the five provinces of Central America, including Nicaragua, was proclaimed, and Nicaragua joined the United Provinces of Central America. In 1838 Nicaragua declared its independence from the United Provinces.

For more than a century after independence, Nicaraguan politics was dominated by a power struggle between the Liberal and Conservative Parties, punctuated by periods of United States intervention. Under the Knox–Castillo Treaty in 1911 Nicaragua, at that government's request, became a U.S. protectorate. The United States maintained troops in the nation from 1912 to 1933. For over 50 years (from 1938 to 1979) political power remained in the hands of the Somoza family, which used the National Guard and the National Liberal Party to maintain its dictatorship and domination of economic life. Although elections were held, the victors were always family members or their supporters.

During the 1970s the regime's repressive measures—its ban on political opposition, human rights abuses—and corruption alienated large segments of society. The Somoza regime was overthrown in July 1979 by the Sandinista National Liberation Front (FSLN), a leftist guerrilla organization that had pursued its struggle against the central government since 1961. The FSLN consolidated its dominant role in the revolutionary government within the first six months following Somoza's ouster. The Sandinista regime initiated a program of agrarian and industrial reform designed to improve the living standards of the lower classes, restore industry destroyed during the guerrilla war and pave the way toward socialism. The government nationalized 40% of the nation's industrial capacity. Although civil rights were formally restored in January 1980, intimidation and the restriction of basic human rights were significant factors in the consolidation of power. Promised elections were postponed and, in August 1980, the leader of the junta, Daniel Ortega Saavedra, announced that the FSLN would remain in power until 1985.

Opposition to the government, both within and outside the regime, increased during 1981 and many of the opponents fled to Costa Rica and Honduras where they formed guerrilla groups dubbed "contras." The contras initiated guerrilla warfare against the Sandinista regime in 1982. They were helped by significant amounts of aid from the United States, which saw the leftist Sandinista regime as a destabilizing influence in the region.

Elections were held in 1984 for both the executive and legislative branches. Important sectors of the political opposition declined to participate because of the government's failure to establish the conditions necessary for a fair and free campaign. Pro-government forces repeatedly harassed the opposition parties throughout the campaign and press censorship prohibited coverage of opposition rallies and statements. Ortega won the presidency while the FSLN won the majority of seats in the legislature. Real power nevertheless continued to be wielded by the National Directorate of the FSLN.

Nicaragua was a signatory to the regional peace plan drawn up by President Oscar Arias Sanchez of Costa Rica in 1987. Under the agreement, each government was to declare a ceasefire, open negotiations with unarmed internal opposition groups, restore civil rights and hold free elections. In 1989 Central American presidents agreed on a program of electoral reform for Nicaragua that would permit the free operation opposition parties. Elections were held in February 1990 in which Violeta Chamorro, the candidate of a 14-party coalition, defeated the favored Ortega. Before taking

RULERS OF NICARAGUA (from 1937)

Presidents

January 1937–May 1947: Anastasio Somoza Garcia
May 1947: Leonardo Arguello
May–August 1947: Benjamin Lacayo Sacasa
August 1947–May 1950: Victor Manuel Roman y Reyes
August 1950–September 1956: Anastasio Somoza Garcia
September 1956–May 1963: Luis Somoza Debayle
May 1963–August 1966: René Schick Gutiérrez
August 1966–May 1967: Lorenzo Guerrero Gutierrez
May 1967–May 1972: Anastasio Somoza Debayle
May 1972–December 1974: triumvirate consisting of Roberto Martinez Lacayo, Alfonso Lobo Cordero and Fernando Aguero Rocha
May 1974–July 1979: Anastasio Somoza Debayle
July 1979–January 1985: junta consisting of Daniel Ortega Saavedra, Moises Hassan Morales, Sergio Ramirez Mercado, Violeta Barrios de Chamarro (replaced in 1980 by Arturo J. Cruz) and Alfonso Robelo Callejas (replaced in 1980 by Rafael Cordoba Rivas)
January 1985–April 1990: Daniel Ortega Saavedra
April 1990– : Violeta Barrios de Chamorro

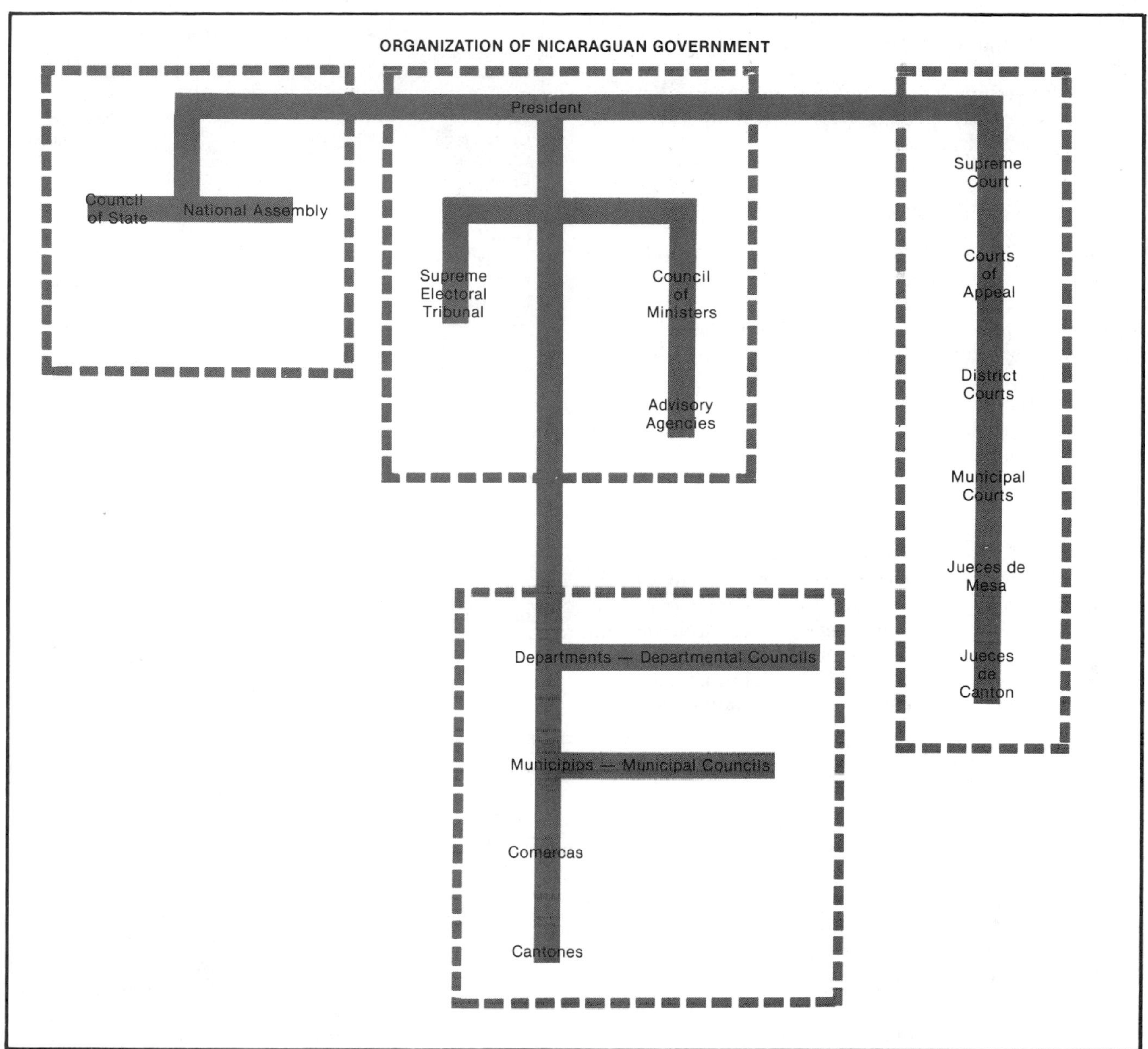

office, the Chamorro government negotiated an end to hostilities between the government and the contras.

CONSTITUTION & GOVERNMENT

Nicaragua has had ten written constitutions since independence from Spain in 1821, those of 1826, 1838, 1858, 1893, 1905, 1911, 1939, 1950, 1974, and 1986, each reflecting the ideology of the ruling party. On seizing power in 1979, the Sandinista-led Government of National Reconstruction abolished the 1974 Constitution and issued a Fundamental Statute (including a Bill of Rights) and a Program to guide its actions until a new Constitution was promulgated in 1986.

Under the 1986 Constitution, the president and vice president are directly elected by universal suffrage for six-year terms. The president, who is head of state and head of government, is assisted by an appointed Cab-

GOVERNMENT LIST
(July/August 1991)

President	Chamorro, Violeta
Vice President	Godoy Reyes, Virgilio
Minister of Agriculture & Livestock	Rondon Sacasa, Roberto
Minister of Construction & Transportation	Icabalceta Mayorga, Jaime
Minister of Defense	Chamorro, Violeta
Minister of Economy	de Franco, Silvio
Minister of Education	Belli Pereira, Humberto
Minister of Finance	Pereira Alegria, Emilio
Minister of Foreign Affairs	Dreyfus Morales, Enrique
Minister of Foreign Cooperation	Kruger, Erwin
Minister of Government	Hurtado Cabrera, Carlos
Minister of Health	Salmerón Bermúdez, Ernesto
Minister of Labor	Rosales Arguello, Francisco
Minister of Presidency	Lacayo Oyanguren, Antonio
Minister of Sports	Garcia, Carlos
Attorney General for Justice	Baltodano Mayorga, Duilio
President, Central Bank	Lacayo, Raul

inet. The president has the right to declare a state of emergency and suspend certain of the Constitution's civil rights provisions.

Legislative power is vested in a unicameral National Assembly directly elected by proportional representation.

FREEDOM & HUMAN RIGHTS

During the civil war, human rights organizations charged both sides with serious human rights abuses. Government security forces reportedly tortured and executed persons suspected of assisting the guerrillas, while the government accused the guerrillas of killing, torturing and kidnapping civilians. The Sandinista Army instigated military impressment, conducting sweeps of public facilities and forcibly removing youths as young as 12 years old.

Under government states of emergency, various legal guarantees and civil rights relating to judicial processes were suspended. These included the right to be informed of charges, to have a public trial before a competent judge, to participate personally in all proceedings from the start and to challenge evidence. There was no legal requirement for a search warrant and so police and state security officials regularly entered and searched private residences. Suspected opponents were arbitrarily arrested and subject to incommunicado detention.

With the ending of hostilities in 1990, many of the major sources of human rights abuses were removed. Laws regulating freedom of expression were lifted after Chamorro assumed the presidency. In an effort at national reconciliation, in March 1990 the Sandinista-controlled National Assembly, with the support of the opposition, passed an unconditional amnesty for those who committed crimes against public order and security. This prevented the prosecution of those accused of human rights abuses during the civil war.

CIVIL SERVICE

No current information is available on the Nicaraguan civil service.

LOCAL GOVERNMENT

There are four levels of local government: departments, *municipios*, *comarcas* and *cantones*. Each department is headed by a *jefe político* (political chief) and each *municipio* by an *alcalde* (mayor).

The departments are divided into 123 *municipios*. Article 181 of the Constitution provides for autonomous governments for the department of Zelaya to offer self-government for the Miskitos, Sumos, Ramos, Creoles, Gurifunas, and Mestizos Indians. The Managua National District is administered separately by a five-member commission appointed by the president.

Representative institutions at the local level include six-member district councils elected by direct popular vote for four-year terms, and five-member municipal councils, also elected by direct popular vote for four-year terms.

NICARAGUAN DEPARTMENTS

Department	Capital
Boaco	Boaco
Carazo	Jinotepe
Chinandega	Chinandega
Chontales	Juigalpa
Estelí	Estelí
Granada	Granada
Jinotega	Jinotega
León	León
Madriz	Samoto
Managua	Managua
Masaya	Masaya
Matagalpa	Matagalpa
Nueva Segovia	Ocotal
Río San Juan	San Carlos
Rivas	Rivas
Zelaya	Bluefields

FOREIGN POLICY

Since the settlement of boundary disputes with Honduras and Costa Rica, economic and political cooperation with Central American republics has become the keystone of Nicaraguan foreign policy. Nicaragua has been one of the proponents of closer union among the five member states of the Central American Common Market.

The Sandinista's war with the contras dominated Nicaragua's foreign policy in the 1980s. Although the Carter administration extended reconstruction aid to the new Sandinista government, the Reagan administration was opposed to the regime, citing its support for leftist guerrillas in El Salvador. During the decade it channeled large amounts of aid to the contras through the Central Intelligence Agency. In response, the Managua government asked the Communist bloc for assistance. Attempts to end the conflict in 1982 failed and relations between Nicaragua and the United States deteriorated during 1983–87. In 1984 Nicaragua filed a case against the United States in the International Court of Justice alleging that the United States had mined ports along the Atlantic coast. The Court ruled in 1986 that the United States had violated international law by intervening in Nicaraguan affairs.

During the late 1980s, efforts to end the war were led by Central American leaders. In 1987 Nicaragua signed the regional peace pact drawn up by Oscar Arias Sanchez of Costa Rica, in which each Central American government pledged to open negotiations with unarmed internal opposition groups, restore civil rights and hold free elections. In February 1989 the presidents of the five Central American countries agreed to the dismantling of Contra bases in Honduras in return for pledges of Nicaraguan elections in early 1990. During August 1989 the presidents signed the Tela agreement providing for the voluntary demobilization and relocation of the contras over a 90-day period. Following charges in November by Nicaraguan President Daniel Ortega that the Tela agreement was not being implemented, the presidents held a summit in December 1989 that resulted in the recommendation for immediate demobilization of contra forces.

Opposition candidate Violeta Chamorro overwhelmingly defeated Sandinista President Ortega in the February 1990 elections and the contras agreed to surrender their weapons by June. In response, the United States announced the abolition its five-year trade embargo and a resumption of aid.

Nicaragua joined the United Nations in 1945. It is a member of 15 U.N. organizations and some 30 other international organizations.

Nicaragua and the United States are parties to more than 30 treaties and agreements covering agricultural commodities, agriculture, aviation, customs, defense, economic and technical cooperation, extradition, highways, investment guarantees, air force missions, army missions, nationality, the Peace Corps, postal matters, privileges and immunities, publications, rules of warfare, telecommunications, trade and commerce, and visas.

PARLIAMENT

Under the Constitution of 1974 legislative power was vested in a bicameral Congress. Following the 1979 coup, the junta suspended the Constitution and issued the Fundamental Statute that provided for a Council of State to advise the junta on legislation. A new Constitution was written in 1986 and promulgated in 1987 under which legislative power is vested in a unicameral National Assembly. The chamber is composed of 90 members, directly elected by a system of proportional representation. Legislators serve six-year terms. The legislature also includes those unelected presidential and vice-presidential candidates (as representatives or alternates respectively) whose support exceeds a specified threshold. The legislature has the right to initiate legislation, elect judges to the Supreme Court and fill permanent vacancies for the presidency or vice presidency. The president may veto legislation within 15 days of passage by the Assembly.

In the February 1990 legislative elections, the Union Nacional Opositora won 51 seats, the Frente Sandinista de Liberacion Nacional won 39 seats, and the Moveimiento de Unidad Revolucionaria and the Partido Social Cristiano each won one seat.

POLITICAL PARTIES

The Union Nacional Opositora (UNO) and the Frente Sandinista de Liberación Nacional are the two dominant political groupings in Nicaragua. The ruling UNO is an electoral alliance of 14 parties of various philosophies formed in 1989 to present a united opposition to the Sandinistas in the 1990 elections. Its leader is Violeta Chamorro, the owner and director of the opposition daily newspaper La Prensa, who became president following the alliance's 1990 victory.

The former ruling party is the Frente Sandinista de Liberación Nacional (FSLN). (The Sandinistas are named after Agusto César Sandino, 1895–1934, one of Latin America's earliest authentic guerrilla heros. For six years (1926–32) he fought an unrelenting guerrilla war against the U.S. Marine Expeditionary Force and is credited with devising a guerrilla strategy that later was employed by Fidel Castro and Che Guevara.) The FSLN was organized in 1961 as a Castroite guerrilla group by Carlos Fonseca Amador who, along with Julio Tirado Lobez, was killed in a shoot-out with the National Guard in 1976. In 1975 the Sandinistas split into three "tendencies", of which the largest was the Third Party (Terceristas) or Insurrectionists (Insurreccionales), without any ideological label. The two smaller of the three "tendencies" were the Protracted Popular Warfare (Guerra Popular Prolongada) and the Proletarian Tendency (Tendencia Proletaria), both Marxist in orientation. The junta that took control of Nicaragua in 1979 was composed primarily of Terceristas, but the withdrawal of moderates in 1980 left the FSLN with a distinctly leftist thrust.

There are 11 minor parties.

Prior to the ending of the civil war in 1990, the primary guerrilla group was the Unidad Nicaraguense de Reconciliacion (UNIR).

Founded in 1984, UNIR was a coalition of guerrilla forces including the Democratic Revolutionary Alliance, led by Eden Pastora Gomez, the former FSLN "Commander Zero"; the Nicaraguan Revolutionary Armed Forces; and the Christian Democratic Solidarity Front Nicaraguan Democratic Forces (Fuerzas Democráticas Nicaraguenses, FDN) a Samocista group based in Honduras.

ECONOMY

Nicaragua is one of the lower-middle-income countries of the world, with a free-market economy in which the dominant sector is private.

Nicaragua's economy is primarily agricultural, with coffee and cotton the principal export crops. Economic mismanagement, trade difficulties and armed opposition activity all contributed to Nicaragua's serious economic decline in the 1980s. Although the private sector accounts for roughly 55% of the GDP, it is closely controlled by government regulations of all sales, distribution, prices, bank credits and foreign trade. The Ortega government responded to economic problems by increasing rather than decreasing its degree of control over production and marketing processes—a solution that further stifled private investment and initiative and perpetuated bureaucratic inefficiencies.

As a result of the war, private investment in the economy virtually ceased and government investment was restricted to projects related to the war effort. Trade sanctions imposed by the United States in May 1985 had a serious effect on private industry as well as on the flow of foreign aid and sugar revenue. Hard-currency shortages restricted imports, and the government relied on donations of insecticides, fertilizers and other vital imports. The effects of the civil war and the economic sabotage that accompanied it were compounded by severe floods that devastated the cotton and coffee crops.

PRINCIPAL ECONOMIC INDICATORS

Gross National Product (U.S. $ billions): 2.911 (1987)
GNP per capita (U.S. $): 830 (1987)
GNP average annual growth rate (%, 1980–89): 1.4
Average annual rate of inflation (%, 1980–88): 86.6
Average annual growth rate (%, latest)
  General government consumption: 16.0
  Private consumption: −8.1
  Gross domestic investment: 4.0

BALANCE OF PAYMENTS, 1988
(U.S. $ millions)

Current account balance: −715.2
Merchandise exports: 235.7
Merchandise imports: −718.3
Trade balance: −482.6
Other goods, services & income +: 39.7
Other goods, services & income −: −402.3
Other goods, services & income net: −362.6
Private unrequited transfers: 8.7 (1987)
Official unrequited transfers: 130.0
Capital other than reserves: 355
Net errors & omissions: 51.7
Counterpart items: −.1 (1985)
Liabilities constituting foreign authorities reserves: −60.5
Total change in reserves: −43.9

GROSS DOMESTIC PRODUCT

GDP nominal (nat. currency billions): 330.97
GDP per capita (U.S. $): 470 (1989)
Average annual growth rate of GDP (%, 1980–88): −0.3 (latest)
GDP by type of expenditure (%) 1987
  Consumption
    Private: 55
    Government: 36
  Gross domestic investment: 10
  Gross domestic savings: 18 (1965)
  Foreign trade
    Exports: 13
    Imports: −15
Cost components of GDP (%) 1985
    Net indirect taxes: 9
    Consumption of fixed capital: 4
    Compensation of employees: 56
    Net operating surplus: 31
Sectoral origin of GDP (%) 1989
  Primary
    Agriculture: 23
    Mining: 0.0
  Secondary
    Manufacturing: 21
    Construction: 4
    Public utilities: 2
  Tertiary
    Transportation & communications: 6
    Trade: 18
    Finance: 7
    Other services: 5
    Government: 13
Average annual sectoral growth rates (%, latest)
    Agriculture: −0.2
    Industry: 0.4
    Manufacturing: 0.6
    Services: −0.9

Nicaragua experienced a decrease in real per capita GDP throughout the 1980s. Agricultural production declined and industry operated below 1979 levels. Per capita external debt is one of the highest in the world. Inflation, which reached a record 35,000% in 1988 remains a serious problem. Shortages of basic consumer goods are widespread.

Prospects for an economic recovery improved following the 1990 elections. The Chamorro government ended the war and pledged to reduce government control of the economy. The United States ended its embargo and pledged emergency aid.

PUBLIC FINANCE

The Nicaraguan fiscal year is the calendar year. The national budget is prepared by the Directorate General of the Budget.

Revenues come primarily from taxes, principally excise and import duties. Almost half of current expenditures go to payments for goods and services.

Development planning is the responsibility of the Planning Office. Under the Samoza regime, development plans emphasized improvement in living conditions through greater employment, regional development and an increased role in the Central American Common Market. Following the Sandinista revolution, the government nationalized banking, insurance, mining, fishing and other key industrial facilities in an effort to redirect the economy.

CENTRAL GOVERNMENT EXPENDITURES, 1988

& of total expenditures
  Defense: 12.3
  Education: 16.6
  Health: 4.0
  Housing, social security, welfare: 16.4
  Economic services: 27.2
  Other: 23.4
Total expenditures as % of GNP: 58.0 (latest)
Overall surplus or deficit as % of GNP: −16.3 (latest)

CENTRAL GOVERNMENT REVENUES, 1988

% of total current revenues
  Taxes on income, profit & capital gain: 15.35
  Social security contributions: 7.31
  Domestic taxes on goods & services: 43.40
  Taxes on international trade & transactions: 16.87
  Other taxes: 4.05
  Current nontax revenue: 9.51
Total current revenue as % of GNP: 40.7 (latest)
General government consumption as % of GDP: 36 (1987)
Average annual growth rate of general government consumption (%, latest): 16.0

Between 1970 and 1982 the United States provided Nicaragua with approximately $290 million in development grants and loans. When the United States cut off aid in the wake of the Sandinista takeover, the government looked to the Eastern bloc and to a lesser degree to Western Europe for assistance. Cuba, Bulgaria, East Germany and the Soviet Union contributed aid as did Libya, Sweden and the Netherlands. The Communist bloc gave $3.3 billion in aid from 1970–88 while Western aid (excluding the United States), ODA and OOF bilateral commitments amounted to $981 million from 1970–88.

FOREIGN AID, 1989

Total foreign aid (U.S. $ millions): 684.5
- Bilateral: 639.7
- Multilateral: 44.8

CURRENCY & BANKING

The Nicaraguan unit of currency is the córdoba, divided into 100 centavos. Coins are issued in denominations of 5, 10, 25 and 50 centavos and 1 córdoba; notes are issued in denominations of 1, 5, 10, 20, 50, 100, 500 and 1,000 córdobas.

The market rate of the new córdoba in June 1991 was $1 = C5.00. The new córdoba, equivalent to 1,000 of the former units, was introduced in February 1988 as part of a massive currency devaluation. The currency was devalued 30 times in 1989; it had been fixed at 10 to the dollar in February 1989 but ended the year at 42,000 to the dollar. In July 1990 the government announced the gradual conversion to a new monetary unit, the gold córdoba, in an effort to control hyperinflation. The currency was introduced on par with the dollar. By the end of the year, however, the currency had been devalued over 40 times. The Chamorro government announced an economic stabilization plan in March 1991 that included still another devaluation of the currency. The exchange rate for the gold córdoba was five to the dollar, for the older córdoba, five million per gold córdoba. The value of the older córdoba had fallen in one day, March 1, 1991, to 12 million per U.S. dollar from seven million. The drastic fall and resulting price confusion virtually paralyzed the country's economy.

GROWTH PROFILE
(Annual Growth Rates, %)

Projected population (1988–2000): 3.0
Projected crude birth rate (/1,000) (1990–95): 38.7
Projected crude death rate (/1,000) (1990–95): 6.2
Urban population (1985–90): 4.46
Labor force (1985–2000): 3.9
GNP (1980–89): −1.4
GDP (1980–88): −0.3 (latest)
Inflation (1980–88): 86.6
Agriculture (1980–88): −0.2 (latest)
Industry (1980–88): 0.4 (latest)
Manufacturing (1980–88): 0.6 (latest)
Services (1980–88): −0.9 (latest)
Money holdings (1980–88): 15.0
Manufacturing earnings per employee (1980–87): −14.5
Energy production (1980–88): −0.2
Energy consumption (1980–88): 1.8
Exports (1980–88): −6.3
Imports (1980–88): 0.4
General government consumption (1980–88): 16.0 (latest)
Private consumption (1980–88): −8.1 (latest)
Gross domestic investment (1980–88): 4.0 (latest)

The monetary system is controlled by the superintendent of banks and is headed by the Banco Central de Nicaragua. The commercial banking sector is dominated by Banco Nacional, owned until 1940 by Chase National Bank. Other state financial institutions include the Bank of Popular Credit, the National Development Bank, the National Housing Bank and the National Pawn Shop. All Nicaraguan banks were nationalized in 1979. Foreign banks were no longer permitted to secure local deposits. A 1985 decree permitted the establishment of private exchange houses. Following the 1990 electoral defeat of the Sandinistas, the legislature enacted measures to establish a private banking system.

FINANCIAL INDICATORS, 1989

Total reserves minus gold (SDRs millions): 167
SDRs (millions): 0
Reserve position in IMF (SDRs millions): 0
Foreign exchange (SDRs millions): 167
Gold (fine troy oz. millions): .12
Central bank 1983
- Assets (%)
  - Foreign assets: 7.8
  - Claims on government: 74.3
  - Claims on banks: 17.9
  - Claims on private sector: 0.0
- Liabilities (%)
  - Reserve money: 34.9
  - Government deposits: −0.9
  - Foreign liabilities: 84.5
  - Capital accounts: 1.3

Money supply 1983
- Stock (nat. currency billions): 10.937
- M1 per capita: 3,520

Private banks 1983
- Assets (%)
  - Loans to government: 0.0
  - Loans to private sector: 84.4
  - Reserves: 13.8
  - Foreign assets: 1.8
- Liabilities
  - Deposits (nat. currency millions): 21
  - of which %
    - Demand deposits: 26.2
    - Savings deposits: 20.5
    - Government deposits: 21.6
    - Foreign liabilities: 6.4

External debt 1988
- Total (U.S. $ billions): 8.052
  - of which public (U.S. $ billions): 6.744
  - of which private (U.S. $ millions): 0
- Debt service (long term)
  - Total (U.S. $ millions): 155
  - Repayment
    - Principal (%): 52.9
    - Interest (%): 47.1
- Debt service ratio (%): 50.5
- External public debt as % of GNP: 207.8 (1987)
- Debt service as % of GNP: 1.2 (1987)
- Debt service as % of exports: 10.6 (1970)
- Terms of public borrowing
  - Commitments (U.S. $ millions): 563
  - Average interest rate (%): 5.1
  - Average maturity (yrs.): 19
- Net flow of publicly guaranteed external capital (U.S. $ millions): 497
- Receipt of workers' remittances (U.S. $ millions): 3 (1987)
- Net direct private investment (U.S. $ millions): 15 (1970)

AGRICULTURE

Of the total land area of 12,040,000 ha. (29,738,800 ac.), 44% is classified as agricultural and under permanent cultivation. Agriculture employs about one-third of the labor force. The principal cash crops are coffee (accounted for about 38% of export earnings in 1988), cotton, sugarcane and bananas. Corn, beans and rice are the major food crops. During 1980–87 agricultural production decreased by an annual average of 0.2%. In 1988 agricultural production was devastated by Hurricane Joan.

In terms of land use, Nicaragua is divided into three principal zones: the Pacific region, the bread basket of the country; the central highlands, with relatively inferior soils and yields; and the largely undeveloped eastern plains region. Corn, the staple of Nicaragua's subsistence agriculture, is grown throughout the country, while coffee is grown principally in the highlands and cotton in the Pacific lowlands.

AGRICULTURAL INDICATORS

Agriculture's share of GDP (%): 21 (1988)
Average annual growth rate (%, 1980–88): −0.2
Value added in agriculture (U.S. $ millions): 570 (1989)
Cereal imports (000 metric tons): 206 (1988)
Index of agricultural production (1979–81 = 100): 86 (1986)
Index of food production (1979–81 = 100): 91 (1986)
Index of food production per capita (1979–81 = 100): 71 (1986–88)
Number of tractors: 2,450 (1986)
Total fertilizer consumption (000 metric tons): 62.9 (1985–86)
Fertilizer consumption (g./ha., hundreds) 433 (1987–88)
Size class (%, 1984)
- below 1 ha. (below ac.):
- 1–5 ha. (2.47–12.35 ac.):
- 5–10 ha. (12.35–24.7 ac.):
- 10–20 ha. (24.7–49.4 ac.): } 26.2
- 20–50 ha. (49.4–123.5 ac.):
- 50–200 ha. (123.5–494 ac.): } 30.6
- Over 200 ha. (over 494 ac.): 43.3

Tenure (area) (%) 1984
- Owner-operated: 100.0
- Rented: 0.0
- Other: 0.0

Land use (%)
- Cropland: 11
- Pasture: 44
- Forest: 32
- Other: 13

Yields (kg./ha.) 1989
- Grains: 1,522
- Roots & tubers: 12,093
- Legumes: 550
- Milk (kg./animal): 621

Production 1989
- Fruits (000 metric tons): 355
- Vegetables (000 metric tons): 53

Livestock (000) 1989
- Cattle: 1,650
- Horses: 270 (1986)
- Sheep: 4
- Pigs: 680

Forestry 1988
- Production of roundwood (million cubic meters): 3.870
  - of which industrial roundwood (%): 22.7
- Value of exports (U.S. $ millions): 2.569

Fishing 1988
- Total catch (000 metric tons): 4.7
  - of which marine (%): 97.8
- Value of exports (U.S. $ 000): 9.575

On both subsistence farms and intermediate holdings, known as *fincas*, the prevalent mode of cultivation is heavily dependent on oxen, ox plows and hand tools, such as the digging stick. Many subsistence farmers still practice slash-and-burn agriculture. On the other hand, large-scale estates, especially in the Pacific lowlands, have become increasingly mechanized and use fertilizers and pesticides regularly.

The pattern of land ownership is unequal, with 50% of the farms occupying only 3.5% of the area under cultivation, while 2% of the farms account for more than 40% of the total. Nearly 30% of farm workers are tenants, sharecroppers or squatters. Most of the subsistence farms are less than 7 ha. (17.3 ac.) in size. About 26% of farmers own individual holdings of less than 20 ha. (49.4 ac.). The government's principal agency for land reform is the National Agrarian Institute, set up in 1964. The law that this institute administers provides for the nationalization of holdings that are (1) idle or underutilized, (2) over 500 ha. (1,235 ac.) and (3) not properly conserved according to regulations. The institute may grant clear title to tenants and squatters who have cultivated unappropriated state lands for more than one year: In the case of squatters, up to 100 ha. (247 ac.), and in the case of others, up to 50 ha. (123.5 ac.), without payment, and the rest at a reasonable price. The institute also is empowered to plan and administer agricultural settlements on either a private or a cooperative basis. The institute also supervises extension of credit to settlers and farmers. Although plagued by inadequate funds, the institute has made some progress in reducing the inequities of land ownership.

The Agrarian Reform Act of 1981 grants rights to use only to land distributed to landless peasants under the program. Holders cannot sell the land or divide it. Children may inherit it as an indivisible unit. Possession is contingent on participation in a cooperative and upon cultivation of a particular crop. State farms account for 20% of coffee output, 17% of cotton output and 43% of sugar output.

Nicaragua is the largest cattle-rising country in Central America, and in most years there is a surplus for export. Considerable assistance is given to this sector through the National Livestock Development Program. Exports on the hoof are at present minimal as the bulk of the production is now channeled through three large modern abattoirs.

Forests cover about one-third of the land area, and usable timber stands have been estimated at 4 million ha. (9.8 million ac.). The tropical rain forests in the eastern coastal areas contain a variety of hardwoods, but these are not in pure stands; therefore exploitation presents access and transportation problems. There are large stands of pine in the northern and northeastern parts of the eastern lowlands and balsa stands in the South. Present production is principally in mahogany and Spanish cedar. Although some 50% of forests are state-owned, commercial lumber concessions are operated mainly by U.S. and Canadian firms. An Israeli company is engaged in the production of plywood. Mahogany, cedar, rosewood and dyewoods are the chief commercial timber.

Fishing is a relatively new industry, although the inland lakes and the Atlantic and Pacific coastal fishing grounds have rich potential. Shrimp and other types of shellfish are the most important part of the catch.

MANUFACTURING

Manufacturing has received considerable stimulus from the Central American Common Market and now contributes about 24% to the GDP. The chief manufacturing sectors are food products, beverages, textiles, chemicals and petroleum refining. Nearly two-thirds of the 9,000 manufacturing establishments are in Managua, León, Chinandega and Masaya. Over 90% of the manufacturing output by value originates in the Pacific zone, 7% in the central highlands and only 2% in the eastern region. Managua itself accounts for almost two-fifths of the value of the nation's manufactures.

MANUFACTURING INDICATORS, 1987

Average annual growth rate (%, 1980–88): 0.6
Share of GDP (%): 24 (1988)
Labor force economically active in manufacturing (% est.): 8.0
Value added in manufacturing (U.S. $ millions): 759
  Food & tobacco (%): 54
  Textiles & clothing (%): 12
  Machinery & transport equipment (%): 2
  Chemicals (%): 10
Earnings per employee in manufacturing 1986
  Growth rate (%, 1980–87): −14.5
  Index (1980 = 100): 31
Total earnings as % of value added: 22
Gross output per employee (1980 = 100): 109

Ownership of industry is predominantly private. The role of government in manufacturing is mainly indirect. Domestic and foreign private investment is encouraged by the Law for the Protection and Stimulation of Industry Development of 1958. All plants are classified as (1) fundamental, (2) necessary or (3) advantageous, in descending order of their contribution to the national economy. The classification is based on a number of factors, such as the amount of foreign exchange the industry will save, the amount of investment, the quantity and value of domestic raw materials that the industry will consume, the number of workers it will employ and the proportion of the market it will supply. These categories are further broken down into new industries, new installations and existing industries. All these categories are entitled to a descending order of benefits. The highest categories enjoy exemption from customs duties for 10 years and exemption from specified taxes for five years. Foreign capital is especially encouraged under the Law on Foreign Investments of 1955. The law provides for repatriation of registered capital; transfer of profits, earnings and interest; and guarantees against all investment risks, including inconvertibility, expropriation and war.

Lack of foreign exchange forced several factories to close after December 1981, and in February 1982 the government introduced incentives for private manufacturers. During the 1980s, foreign countries such as France, Cuba, Libya and Mexico invested in agro-industrial processing complexes.

ENERGY

Energy is derived chiefly from imported petroleum, which accounts for almost half the nation's needs. Hydroelectric power is of increasing importance, and a hydroelectric plant on the Rio Grande is scheduled to begin operation in 1991.

ENERGY INDICATORS

Average annual energy production growth rate (%, 1980–88): −0.2
Energy consumption per capita (kg. oil equivalent): 252 (1988)
Energy imports as % of merchandise exports: 42 (1988)
Average annual growth rate of energy consumption (%, 1980–88): 1.8
Electricity 1988
  Installed capacity (000 kw.): 395
  Production (billion kw.-hr.): 1.068
    % fossil fuel: 46.8
    % hydro: 25.1
    % geothermal: 28.1
  Consumption per capita (kw.-hr.): 347
Natural gas.
  Proved reserves (billion cu. m.): 0 (1990)
  Production (million cu. m.): 0 (1989)
  Consumption (million cu. m.): 0 (1988)
Petroleum
  Production (million bbl.): 0 (1989)
  Consumption (million bbl.): 4 (1988)
  Refining capacity (000 bbl./day): 15 (1990)

LABOR

The labor force is characterized by a low level of skills, a high degree of geographical and occupational mobility and a traditional preference for independent occupations.

LABOR INDICATORS, 1989

Total economically active population (millions): 1.277
  % working-age (15–64): 61.9
  % female: 23.0
Activity rate (%)
  Total: 33.5
  Male: 46.3
  Female: 21.5
Sectoral employment of economically active (%), 1987
  Agriculture, forestry, fishing: 32.4
  Construction 1.5
  Manufacturing, mining, quarrying, public utilities: 9.0
  Trade, hotels, restaurants: 8.4
  Transportation, communications: 1.8
  Finance, real estate: 1.7
  Services: 13.2
Average annual growth rate of labor force (%, 1980–2000): 3.9
Unemployment (000): 864 (1980)
Labor under 20 years (%): 38.2 (1977)

Working conditions are governed by the Labor Code of 1945, modeled after Mexican labor legislation. The code contains specific provisions on the hiring of women and children, employment contracts and conciliation procedures. It establishes a maximum workweek of 48 hours, prohibits overtime for women and minors and permits only three hours' overtime no more than three times a week for males over 16. Workers are entitled to double pay for night work except on regular shifts, 15 days of paid vacation after six months of continuous service, and eight nationally observed paid holidays in addition to locally observed saints' days. Under the Nicaraguan Social Security program, initiated in 1957 and administered by the National Social Security Institute, workers receive a wide range of benefits, including compensation for work-related accidents and occupational illnesses, maternity benefits, nonoccupational medical care, pensions, and death and survivors' benefits. Amendments to the Labor Code in 1962 legalized sympathy strikes, provided penalties for employers who do not pay wages regularly, granted workers time off with pay to look for work after being given notice, and established the right to claim proportionate vacation pay on termination of employment. Minimum wages are set periodically by the National Minimum Wages Commission.

There is a general absence of hard-core unemployed. A more serious problem is underemployment, which is widespread in rural areas and contributes significantly to the low level of rural income. Rural employment also is highly seasonal, labor shortages alternating with unemployment, and many agricultural workers migrate almost continuously. There is only one employment exchange in the whole country, and in some cases unemployment reflects lack of information about existing employment opportunities.

Skilled laborers, technicians and professionals continue to leave Nicaragua, and in many cases there is no one to replace them. About 50% of unemployed are agricultural workers, many of whom leave the land to seek greater income in the national capital. At the same time, the agricultural sector experienced a serious labor shortage in the mid-1980s. Students, office workers and international volunteers were mobilized to pick coffee and cotton, both vital export crops.

Children under age 14 are not permitted to work legally. Ministry of Labor officials, however, admit that the prohibition on child labor is often disregarded in the countryside, where entire families often labor for wages, particularly at harvest time. Under the National Organizational System for Work and Salaries (SNOTS), minimum and maximum salaries have been established for all of Nicaragua's salaried employees working in the public and private sectors. Agricultural workers have not been incorporated into SNOTS, and most are paid on the basis of productivity (the amount of coffee or cotton picked). For those who labor in the fields daily, however, a minimum wage per task (a task is defined as a three- to four-hour period) plus a daily food allowance have been established. Farm laborers may elect to perform two tasks daily. Workers paid under the SNOTS system also receive an extra month's vacation per annum. Workers may elect, however, to take all or part of their vacation days as salary. As the SNOTS system established maximum as well as minimum wages, collective bargaining was eliminated. However, employers or workers can apply to the Ministry of Labor for permission to pay or receive either a one-time or annual bonus.

Nearly 6% of the labor force is believed to be unionized. Seven major labor confederations operate in Nicaragua. The two largest are linked directly to the FSLN: the Sandinista Workers Central (CST) and the Rural Workers Association (ATC). Three others are Marxist organizations with ties to Nicaragua's various Communist parties (the Independent General Confederation of Workers; the Confederation of Labor Action and Unity; and the Workers' Front, a marginal organization). Of the remaining two independent confederations, one is affiliated with the Christian Social Party (the Nicaraguan Workers' Central); the other, democratically oriented, has no party affiliation).

The CST is the FSLN's umbrella confederation for mostly nonagricultural workers and with over 45,000 members is the country's largest labor confederation. The ATC is the farm labor confederation, with over 35,000 members, not including 10,000 seasonal workers. The Sandinistas used to control most of the smaller unions representing various workers groups, such as teachers, health workers, journalists and government employees.

Despite these efforts, the worsening economic situation in the mid-1980s led to increasing labor dissatisfaction among both the FSLN-affiliated and independent labor organizations. This unrest most often was expressed in short-lived wildcat strikes, which in every instance were put down through the use of the police and generally brief arrests of activists and leaders.

FOREIGN COMMERCE

Nicaragua's chief exports are coffee, cotton, bananas, beef, seafood, chemicals and gold. Chief imports are

FOREIGN TRADE INDICATORS, 1988

Exports (U.S. $ millions): 250 (1989, est.)
Imports (U.S. $ millions): 550 (1989, est.)
Balance of trade (U.S. $ millions): −300 (1989, est.)
Annual growth rate (1980–88), exports (%): −6.3
Annual growth rate (1980–88), imports (%): 0.4
Terms of trade (1980 = 100): 84
Import price index (1980 = 100): 95.2 (1986)
Export price index (1980 = 100): 87.9 (1986)

Direction of Trade (%), 1984

	Imports	Exports
European Community	16.3	36.2
United States	16.2	12.6
U.S.S.R. & eastern European economies	21.3	3.0
Japan	2.9	24.7

Composition of Trade (%), 1984

	Imports	Exports
Food & agricultural raw materials	14.1	91.7
Fuels & other energy	17.7	0.0
Mineral ores & concentrates	0.2	0.0
Manufactured goods	68.0	8.3
of which chemicals	20.7	4.6
of which machinery	27.8	0.0

crude petroleum and petroleum products, food items, consumer goods and machinery. Historically, the United States has been one of the nation's chief trading partners. However, from 1985 to 1990, the United States imposed a trade embargo on Nicaragua and the nation turned to the Eastern bloc and Western Europe for trade. The embargo and civil war resulted in severe shortages of consumer goods.

Nicaragua is one of the most active members of the Central American Common Market but has so far derived few of the anticipated advantages of membership.

TRANSPORTATION & COMMUNICATIONS

The Pacific Railways of Nicaragua, with a total trackage of 331 km. (206 mi.), links Managua with Corinto via León and Chinandega, and Managua with Granada. During the early 1990s there were plans to link Corinta to Granada, Diriamba, and Port Sandino. All railways are government owned. There is a short pipeline of 56 km. (34 mi.) for carrying crude oil.

TRANSPORTATION INDICATORS

Roads (latest)
- Length, km. (mi.): 14,997 (9,319)
- Paved (%): 10

Motor vehicles (latest)
- Automobiles: 46,184
- Trucks and buses: 30,535
- Persons per vehicle: 44

Railroads (latest)
- Track, km. (mi.): 331 (206)
- Passenger-km. (passenger-mi.) (millions): 25.5 (15.8)
- Freight, metric ton-km. (short ton-mi.) (millions): 68 (47)

Merchant marine
- Vessels (over 100 tons): 21 (1989)

Total deadweight tonnage (000): 2.9 (1989)

Ports (pre-1986)
- Cargo loaded (000 metric tons): 333
- Cargo unloaded (000 metric tons): 1.453

Air
- Passenger-km. (passenger-mi.) (millions): 92 (57) (latest)
- Freight, metric ton-km. (short ton-mi.) (millions): 1.2 (0.8) (latest)
- Airports with scheduled flights: 1 (1990)

Inland waterways (latest)
- Length, km. (mi.): 2,220 (1,379)

Eastern Nicaragua has a number of navigable rivers, including the Río Coco, the Río San Juan, the Prinzapolka, the Escondido and the Río Grande. There are 25 lake ports on Lakes Nicaragua and Managua. However, lake transport has been declining in importance because of uncompetitive rates and the obsolescence of vessels and ports.

Corinto, Puerto Cabezas, Puerto Sandino and San Juan del Sur are the nation's four major coastal ports. Corinto handles about three-fifths of the traffic. A deep-water port is under development at El Bluff. NANICA (Naviera Nicaraguense) operates three vessels with regular service between Central America and Europe.

The Pan-American Highway runs for 485 km. (301 mi.) within Nicaragua and links Managua with Honduran and Costa Rican border towns, while the Atlantic and Pacific highways link Managua with coastal towns. Since the establishment of the Central American Common Market, expansion of trucking has been rapid. However, there are no uniform tariffs or freight rates.

AERONICA (Aerolineas Nicaraguenses) operates a fleet of seven planes on domestic and international routes to El Salvador, Honduras, Costa Rica, Panama, Mexico and United States. The largest international airport is Contiguo Aeropuerto Internacional Augusto C. Sandino, near Managua.

Nicaragua's civil war adversely affected the tourist industry and receipts from tourism declined during most of the 1980s. In 1988 a campaign to attract tourism and develop facilities was begun with a loan from Italian investors.

COMMUNICATION INDICATORS, 1984

Telephones
- Total (000): 50
- Persons per telephone: 64

Phone traffic (million calls)
- Combined national: 272.503
- International: 5.069

Post office
- Pieces of mail handled (million): 35.890

Telegraph
- Total traffic (000 calls): 770
  - National: 755
  - International: 15

Telex
- Subscriber lines: 391 (1981)
- Traffic (millions of minutes): 1.572

Telecommunications 1990
- Satellite stations: 2

TOURISM & TRAVEL INDICATORS, 1986

Total tourist receipts (U.S. $ millions): 5

Expenditures by nationals abroad (U.S. $ millions): 7 (1983)

MINING

Mining is a relatively insignificant sector in Nicaragua's economy. It experienced a negative growth during most of the 1980s. Gold production, once important, and copper production have been steadily declining. Nicaragua has workable deposits of gold, lead, copper, and zinc. There also are tungsten deposits in Nueva Segovia. No other known deposits of commercially valuable minerals exist in the country.

DEFENSE

The defense structure is headed by the president. The air force has a separate chief, but it is not an independent or separate service.

Under the Constitution, military service was obligatory, but the provision was never enforced until the civil war. Military personnel were recruited through voluntary enlistment. Compulsory military service was abolished in April 1990.

The total strength of the armed forces in 1989 was 80,000.

Army

Personnel: 73,500

Organization: 3 military zones with 6 militia; 1 special region; 1 motorized infantry brigade; 5 armored battalions; 10 infantry battalions; 10 counterinsurgency battalions; 1 field artillery brigade; 6 engineer battalions; 1 AA artillery group; 160 battalions of reserves

Equipment: 122 heavy tanks; 30 light tanks; 56 reconnaissance vehicles; 172 armored personnel carriers; 12 guns; 84 howitzers; 24 rocket launchers; 24 mortars; 98 antitank guns; 186 air defense guns; SAM

Navy

Personnel: 3,500

Units: 25 patrol craft; 6 mine countermeasure craft; 1 amphibious craft

Air Force

Personnel: 3,000

Organization: 17 combat aircraft; 8 helicopters; 1 counterinsurgency squadron; 1 transport squadron; 1 helicopter squadron; trainers; 3 radar installations

Opposition forces: Some 20,300, of which ARDE 2,000, FDN 15,000 and Misura 1,500.

EDUCATION

Education is free, universal and compulsory for six years, from ages seven to 12. Schooling lasts for 11 years and is divided into six years of primary school and two cycles of secondary school, one of three years and the other of two years.

The majority of the primary schools are rural; these generally offer only one or two grades. Attrition rates and grade repetition rates are high throughout the school system. There are severe shortages of pencils, notebooks and textbooks.

The school year runs from February to November. The language of instruction is Spanish, even in the eastern district, where a large minority is English-speaking.

The most serious educational problem is the shortage of teachers. Only one-third of primary-school teachers and roughly 5% of secondary-school teachers have teaching certificates.

Technical and vocational programs are offered in secondary school during the second cycle, in agricultural schools, in private and public commercial schools and in the Instituto Nacional Tecnico Vocaciónal.

Control of the school system is vested in the Ministry of Education, which establishes curricula, supervises examinations, regulates the teaching profession, appoints teachers and disburses their salaries, and builds and maintains schools.

Higher education is provided by the country's four universities. The National Independent University has nine faculties: medicine, law, and dentistry and pharmacy in León; economy, business, sciences, education and engineering in Managua; and pedagogy in Jinotepe. The University of Central America, is run by the Jesuits.

EDUCATION INDICATORS, 1988

Literacy
- Total (%): 74.0

First level
- Schools: 4,624
- Students: 678,937
- Teachers: 24,127
- Student/teacher ratio: 28.1
- Net enrollment ratio: 76 (1987)

Second level & Vocational
- Schools: 328
- Students: 172,108
- Teachers: 7,167
- Student/teacher ratio: 24.0
- Net enrollment ratio: 21 (1984)

Third level (postsecondary)
- Institutions: 13
- Students: 25,478
- Teachers: 1,484
- Student/teacher ratio: 17.2
- Gross enrollment ratio: 8.4 (1987)
- Students (/100,000 pop.): 768

Foreign study
- Foreign students in national universities: 167 (1987)
- Students abroad: 2,603
  - of whom in
    - United States: 1,927 (1988)
    - France: 55 (1988)
    - Federal Republic of Germany: 34 (1988)
    - United Kingdom: 4 (1987)

Public expenditure 1987
- Total (C billion): 144.275
- % of GNP: 6.2 (1988)
- % national budget: 12.0
- % of current: 97.2

GRADUATES, 1987

Total: 2,073
Education: 359
Humanities & religion: 43
Fine & applied arts: 26
Law: 39
Social & behavioral sciences: 57
Commerce & business: 283
Mass communication: 43
Home economics: 31
service trades: 0
Natural sciences: 91
Mathematics & computer science: 29
Medicine: 534
Engineering: 112
Architecture: 19
Industrial programs: 0
Transportation & communications: 0
Agriculture, forestry, fisheries: 407
Other: 0

LEGAL SYSTEM

The Nicaraguan legal system is based on Roman law and Spanish civil law.

The judiciary is headed by the Supreme Court, comprised of at least seven justices elected for six-year terms by the National Assembly. Three of these justices are required to belong to the principal opposition. The presidency of the court changes annually by election, and the chief justice is the head of the entire judicial branch of government. The court does not possess powers of judicial review of legislative acts, but it is the court of last resort in all other cases.

At the next level are five courts of appeal, at León, Masaya, Granada, Matagalpa and Bluefields. Those at Masaya, León and Granada have six judges each, and those at Matagalpa and Bluefields have five judges each. These magistrates are elected by Congress in plenary session for four-year terms. One of the judges is required to be from the principal opposition party.

At the third level are district courts and municipal courts. The number of magistrates in each district court depends on the population, and the magistrates are appointed by the Supreme Court for two-year terms. Municipal judges are appointed by the district judges and serve for one-year renewable terms. At the *comarca* (subdivision of a department) level the judges *(jueces de mesa)* are appointed by the mayor or *alcalde* of the respective municipality, with the approval of the political chief of the district. The *juez de mesa* in turn appoints the *jueces de canton* within his jurisdiction.

The death penalty was abolished in 1979.

No information is available on the number of prisons or the nature of the penal system.

LAW ENFORCEMENT

The police force is divided into three categories—rural, urban and judicial—all under the administrative control of the Ministry of the Interior. The judicial police are concerned with police administration, jails, apprehension of suspects and investigation of crimes. Each departmental political chief has the overall responsibility for law enforcement within his jurisdiction. The departmental police force is commanded by a police judge. Each department has at least one police judge; two departments, Río San Juan and Chinandega, have two each.

There also is an unknown number of intelligence personnel within the police corps.

Apart from politically motivated crimes (which rose dramatically in the 1970s), Nicaragua has a low crime rate. The majority of the reported crimes are drunken and disorderly behavior and crimes against property.

HEALTH

The Sandinista government gave high priority to health care and, during the 1980s, services improved substantially. Shortly after the 1990 elections, the Chamorro government announced plans to establish a unified health service.

The major health problems are gastritis, duodenitis, enteritis, colitis and cardiovascular and respiratory ailments.

HEALTH INDICATORS

Health personnel 1987
- Physicians: 2,086
  - persons per: 1,678
- Dentists: 277
- Nurses: 1,142

Hospitals, 1985
- Number: 52
- Number of beds (/10,000): 16
- Admission/discharges (/10,000): 634

Type of hospitals (%) 1976
- Government: 46.2
- Private nonprofit: 0.0
- Private profit: 53.8

Public health expenditures (latest)
- As % of national budget: 14.6
- Per capita (U.S. $): 33.10

Vital statistics
- Crude death rate (/1,000): 7 (1990)
- Life expectancy at birth 1990
  - Males: 61
  - Females: 62
- Infant mortality rate (/1,000 live births): 68 (1990)
- Child mortality rate under 5 years (/1,000 live births) (1985–90): 93
- Maternal mortality rate (/100,000 live births) (1980–84): 65.0 (est.)
- Population with access to safe water (%): 49 (latest)

FOOD

The staple food is corn, which is prepared and eaten in various ways, the most common form being tortillas. Masa or corn paste is prepared into tamales and nacatamales, the latter containing meat, potatoes, tomatoes, rice, chili and yuca. Most of the national drinks also are made from corn: atol from green corn; atolillo from dry corn; pinol from toasted corn; pinolillo from toasted corn and cacao; chica, fermented from corn; and cususa, distilled liquor made from chicha.

The daily per capita intake of food is 2,284 calories (compared to a daily recommended minimum of 2,600 calories).

MEDIA & CULTURE

Four daily newspapers are published in the country, all in Spanish. The most influential of the dailies is *La Prensa* with a daily circulation of 75,000.

In 1979 a new press law was announced under which all publications were required to display "a legitimate concern for the defense of the conquests of the revolution, the reconstruction process and the problems of the Nicaraguan people." Those who do not do so were often suspended, as was the leftist newspaper *El Pueblo* in 1979.

The government intensified its policy of prior censorship and practice of harassment of the private and electronic media during the mid-1980s. *La Prensa* suffered widespread censorship of news materials and editorials, while other newspapers, which supported the Sandinista government, at times published the same items that were censored from *La Prensa*. Many small publications not aligned directly with the Sandinista government were forced to cease publication because of their inability to obtain newsprint. Although a July 1984 decree proclaimed that censorship would affect only matters of national security, censorship in fact continued on internal political matters, economic problems, church affairs, human rights and many other nonsecurity issues. The Sandinista government also banned private and internal publications not for sale to the general public, and organizations that had not first received permission to publish nor agreed to submit to prior censorship.

In October 1985 the Ministry of the Interior issued a notice that all communications media and printing facilities must register with the Ministry. A literary magazine was confiscated prior to that date, and an opposition political party was told it could no longer print and distribute its monthly newsletter without prior censorship. *La Prensa* was closed by the government in 1986 but resumed publication in September 1987. The newspaper's reopening was part of government efforts to comply with the Arias peace plan, signed in August 1987. Under the plan, signatories were required to maintain complete freedom of press, radio and television. President Ortega, in March 1990, announced that his government would remove all restraints on freedom of expression.

Under the Sandinista regime, the government owned two-thirds of the radio stations in the country. During the 1980s a number of independent radio news programs went off the air because of excessive censorship. All radio programming, including commentary, names of music selections and sponsors had to be submitted to the censors in advance. In the case of two independent religious radio stations, the censors found verses from the Bible and messages from the pope and other religious leaders objectionable. Live transmisssions on radio or television of services were prohibited. The government closed down Radio Católica in January 1986 because it failed to join a national radio network in broadcasting President Ortega's end-of-year message. It reopened in October 1987 following the signing of the Arias peace plan. The Sandinista government, in March 1990, revoked the law banning private ownership of television stations.

MEDIA INDICATORS

Newspapers
- Number of dailies: 4 (latest)
- Circulation (000): 219 (latest)
- Per 1,000 pop.: 62 (latest)
- Newsprint consumption 1988
  - Total metric tons: 6,300
  - Per 1,000 pop. (kg.): 1,740

Book publishing
- Number of titles: 26 (latest)

Radio
- Number of transmitters: 46 (1989)
- Number of persons per radio receiver: 4.3 (1989)

Television
- Television transmitters: 7 (1989)
- Number of persons per T.V. receiver: 18 (1989)

Cinema (pre-1986)
- Number of fixed cinemas: 127
- Seating capacity (000): 74
- Annual attendance (millions): 5.2

Films (pre-1986)
- Number of long films produced: 1

The Agencia Nicaraguense de Noticias (ANN) is the official news agency.

CULTURAL & ENVIRONMENTAL INDICATORS

Libraries (pre-1986)
- Number: 41

Nature reserves (latest)
- Number of facilities: 6

The Nicaraguan book industry consists of 17 small publishers, most in Managua. Nicaragua adheres to the Universal Copyright, Buenos Aires and Florence conventions.

There is virtually no domestic film production.

The largest library is the National Library at Managua, with 70,000 volumes.

SOCIAL WELFARE

Social welfare is administered by two official agencies: the National Social Assistance Board and the National Social Security Institute. The 1956 Social Insurance Law covers employees in industry, commerce and public services and provides a wide range of benefits, such as sickness allowance, maternity allowance, occupational accident and disability compensation, old age pensions, and death and survivors' benefits. Participation in the program is mandatory for all employers.

GLOSSARY

acuerdo: an executive regulation having the force of law.

alcalde: mayor of a municipio or municipality.

arbitrio: a scheduled tax levied by local boards.

campesino: a peasant, usually of the Indian community.

cantones: administrative subdivisions of comarcas (q.v.).

comarcas: administrative subdivisions of a municipio.

designado: a provisional president elected by the Congress in the event of the death, resignation or incapacitation of an incumbent president.

finquero: rural farmer, owner of a finca.

hacendado: owner of a large hacienda or plantation.

jefe politico: literally political chief; the civil head of a department.

juzgado de distrito: a district court.

latifundio: a vast plantation, such as those originally granted by the kings of Spain

mestizaje: ethnic and cultural mixing of Europeans and Indians.

municipio: manicipality, a subdivision of a department.

mestizo: a person of mixed Spanish and Amerindian blood.

organismos asesores: advisory institutions attached to the Council of Ministers.

patronismo: paternalistic leadership.

procuradores judiciales: lawyers with limited functions.

CHRONOLOGY (from 1947)

1947— President Anastasio Somoza steps down in favor of Leonardo Arguello. . . . Arguello's efforts to eliminate military influence from the administration leads to his ouster and replacement by Benjamin Lacayo Sacasa; Somoza is named minister of war in Lacayo's cabinet; Constituent Assembly names Victor Roman y Reyes, an aged uncle of Somoza, as president; most of the other American republics refuse to recognize the new regime.

1949— San Juan created the nation's 16th department.

1950— President Roman y Reyes dies in office; Somoza named acting president.

1951— Somoza elected to a six-year term as president.

1953— The National Development Institute (Institut de Fomento Nacional) established.

1954— Costa Rica attempts invasion of Nicaragua but is stopped by OAS intervention.

1956— President Somoza assassinated while campaigning; Luis Somoza Debayle, a son of the president, succeeds to the presidency despite constitutional ban.

1957— Border dispute with Honduras flares into violence; both Honduras and Nicaragua accuse the other of armed invasion.

1960— International Court of Justice awards disputed Gracias de Dios to Honduras.

1962— Luis Somoza steps down, barred from succeeding himself; René Schick Gutiérrez named president.

1963— National Agrarian Institute established in first concerted effort at land reform.

1966— Schick dies; first vice president Lorenzo Guerrero sworn in as provisional president.

1967— In presidential elections Anastasio Somoza Debayle, younger son of the elder Somoza and brother of Luis, elected president.

1972— Somoza evades constitutional bar on succeeding himself by creating a puppet triumvirate consisting of two Liberals and one Conservative: Roberto Martinez Lacayo and Alfonso Lobo Cordero, both Liberals, and Fernando Aguero Rocha, a Conservative. . . . Managua devastated by earthquake, killing 9,000, injuring 25,000 and displacing 300,000.

1974— New Constitution is promulgated. . . . Somoza legally elected to a new term in office. . . . Terrorists kidnap several leading Nicaraguans, including members of Somoza family, who are released only after political prisoners are flown out of the country.

1978— Pedro Joaquin Chamorro, opposition leader, is assassinated; opposition calls general strike; Somoza under increasing pressure from the Carter administration to end repression. . . . The Sandinista guerrillas, led by the moderate Terceristas, launch all-out civil war; Somoza imposes martial law; nationwide strike cripples economy; guerrillas invade the national palace, kill six and take others hostage, and force Somoza to yield to their demands; opposition groups unite to oust Somoza while Costa Rica, Panama, Venezuela and the United States join in condemning Somoza.

1979— Rebels, gaining the upper hand in open conflict, seize the capital; Somoza resigns and leaves the country, handing over the office to Francisco Urcuyo Malianos, who attempts to perpetuate himself in office; Sandinista provisional junta accepts the unconditional surrender of National Guard. . . . New government, calling itself the Government of National Reconstruction, abolishes the Constitution and the legislature; under a series of governmental statutes, including the Fundamental Statute, a five-member ruling junta is designated, including Daniel Ortega Saavedra, Moises Hassan Morales, Sergio Ramirez Mercado, Violeta Barrios de Chamarro (widow of the assassinated Pedro Joaquin Chamorro) and Alfonso Robelo Callejas; banks, insurance companies, mining and fishing firms nationalized; the junta names the Provisional Government Council (cabinet) and six new Supreme Court justices.

1980— The Council of State, convened according to the Fundamental Statute, meets without the participation of the leftists. . . . Violeta Barrios de Chamarro and Alfonso Robelo Callejas resign from the junta and are replaced by Arturo J. Cruz and Rafael Córdoba Rivas, respectively, the latter an eminent jurist. The leftist paper *El Pueblo* is suspended following criticism of the "bourgeoise" tendencies of the junta. Anastasio Somoza Debayle is assassinated in Paraguay; Paraguay suspends diplomatic relations with Nicaragua.

1981— Land reforms distribute expropriated land to landless peasants. . . . Libya, Soviet Union and Mexico offer aid.

1982— Miskito Indians charge genocide. . . . Francisco Fiallos Navarro, Nicaraguan ambassador to the United States, defects, charging leftist dictatorship at home.

1983— Pope visits Nicaragua, urges church unity and scorns priests' involvement in politics.

1984— United States holds joint military maneuvers with Honduras. . . . Constitutional guarantees of civil liberties suspended. . . . In general elections, boycotted by most of the opposition, the FSLN wins an easy victory. . . . The World Bank suspends loans to Nicaragua, citing defaults. . . . Ortega elected president, winning 66% of the votes cast.

1985— Ortega sworn in as president, and the junta is dissolved. . . . Four-tier exchange system introduced. . . . U.S. Congress votes against aid to contras. . . . The World Court condemns U.S. mining of Nicaraguan harbors. . . . The United States imposes a trade embargo on Nicaragua. . . . Prior censorship is imposed on the media. . . . Anti-Sandinista cleric Miguel Obando y Bravo, is elevated as cardinal, and defies government by celebrating public Mass.

1986— Radio Católica suspended for failing to broadcast Ortega's year-end message. . . . Reagan calls Nicaragua "the Libya of the Western Hemisphere." . . . Ortega estimates the death toll in the civil war at 13,930.

1987— On January 9, new Constitution is promulgated. The same day a state of emergency is reimposed, suspending many of the liberties granted under the new Constitution. . . . In August Nicaragua signs a regional peace plan, drawn up by President Arias of Costa Rica.

1988— A currency reform implemented, and a new córdoba introduced in February. . . . In May the government signs a permanent ceasefire agreement with the Yatama group of Miskito Indian rebels. . . . Inflation reaches 35,000%. . . . The U.S. Senate in August approves the provision of $27 million in humanitarian aid for the contras.

1989— In November El Salvador suspends diplomatic relations with Nicaragua. . . . The U.N. Security Council establishes the U.N. Observer Group in Central America (ONUCA) to monitor and prevent cross-border incursions by rebel groups and to assist in the forthcoming Nicaraguan elections.

1990— In the February elections, Violeta Chamorro, the candidate of a 14-party coalition, defeats President Ortega. The Chamorro government negotiates an end to hostilities between the government and the contras. . . . The United States pledges $300 million in emergency aid and lifts its five-year trade embargo.

1991— Chamorro announces an economic stabilization plan that includes the devaluation of the new gold córdoba. . . . Former contra rebels begin to rearm.

BIBLIOGRAPHY (from 1970)

BOOKS

Berryman, Phillip. *Inside Central America.* New York, 1985.

Black, George. *Triumph of the People: The Sandinista Revolution in Nicaragua.* London, 1981.

Booth, John A. *The End & the Beginning: The Nicaraguan Revolution.* Boulder, Colo., 1985.

Camejo, Pedro, and Fred Murphy. *The Nicaraguan Revolution.* New York, 1979.

Collins, Joseph. *What Difference Could a Revolution Make? Food and Farming in the New Nicaragua.* San Francisco, 1982.

Crawley, Eduardo. *Dictators Never Die: Nicaragua and the Somoza Dynasty.* New York, 1979.

———. *Nicaragua in Perspective.* New York, 1984.

Dilling, Yvonne, and Philip Wheaton. *Nicaragua: A People's Revolution.* Washington, D.C., 1980.

McKuen, Gary E. *The Nicaraguan Revolution; Ideas in Conflict.* Hudson, Wis., 1985.

Meiselas, Susan. *Nicaragua: 1978–1979.* New York, 1981.

Meyer, Harvey K. *Historical Dictionary of Nicaragua.* Metuchen, N.J., 1972.

Millett, Richard. *Guardians of the Dynasty: A History of the U.S.-Created Guardia Nacional de Nicaragua and the Somoza Family.* Maryknoll, N.Y., 1977.

Selser, Gregorio. *Sandino.* New York, 1981.

Squier, E. G. *Nicaragua.* New York, 1973.

Tierney, John A., Jr. *Somozas and Sandinistas: The U.S. and Nicaragua in the 20th Century.* Washington, D.C. 1982.

Vandermeer, Jon, and Peter Rosset. *The Nicaraguan Reader: Documents of a Revolution Under Fire.* New York, 1983.

Walker, Thomas W. *The Christian Democratic Movement in Nicaragua.* Tuscon, Ariz., 1970.

———. *Nicaragua: Five Years Later*, New York, 1985.

———. *Nicaragua: The Land of Sandino.* Boulder, Colo., 1985.

———. *Nicaragua in Revolution.* New York, 1982.

Walker, William. *War in Nicaragua.* Lanham, Mass., 1985.

Weber, Henry. *The Sandinist Revolution.* New York, 1982.

Woodward, Ralph L., Jr. *Nicaragua.* (World Bibliographical Series.) Santa Barbara, Calif., 1983.

Zwerling, Phillip, and Connie Martin. *Nicaragua: A New Kind of Revolution.* Westport, Conn., 1985.

OFFICIAL PUBLICATIONS

Finance Ministry. *Estado de Ingresos y Egresos del Presupuesto General de la República* (Statement of National Budgetary Revenue and Expenditure of the Republic) (quarterly).

———. *Memoria* (Annual Report).

National Electrical Energy Institute. *Annual Report.*

NIGER

BASIC FACT SHEET

OFFICIAL NAME: Republic of the Niger (République du Niger)

ABBREVIATION: NG

CAPITAL: Niamey

HEAD OF STATE: Brig. Gen. Ali Saibou, chief of state and president of the Supreme Military Council (from 1987)

HEAD OF GOVERNMENT: Aliou Mahamidou (from 1990)

NATURE OF GOVERNMENT: Dictatorship moving toward multiparty system

POPULATION: 7,969,309 (1990)

AREA: 1,267,000 sq. km. (489,190 sq. mi.)

ETHNIC MAJORITY: Hausa in the center, Djerma-Songhai in the South

Note: In this section the French term "Nigerien" denotes the people of Niger to avoid possible confusion with the people of Nigeria.

LANGUAGES: French (official); Hausa and Djerma (lingua francas)

RELIGION: Islam

UNIT OF CURRENCY: Communauté Financière Africaine franc (CFAF)

NATIONAL FLAG: Tricolor of orange, white and green horizontal stripes with an orange orb in the center of the white

NATIONAL EMBLEM: A shield displaying crossed gold Tuareg swords and lances, crossed ears of millet, a native buffalo head and a blazing sun. Four national flags are crossed behind the shield, two on each side, and a white scroll at the base carries the legend "République du Niger"

NATIONAL ANTHEM: "Stand Up, Niger"

NATIONAL HOLIDAYS: December 18 (National Day, Republic Day); January 1 (New Year's Day); May 1 (Labor Day); August 3 (Independence Day); also all the major Christian and Islamic festivals

NATIONAL CALENDARS: Gregorian and Islamic

PHYSICAL QUALITY OF LIFE INDEX: 27

DATE OF INDEPENDENCE: August 3, 1960

DATE OF CONSTITUTION: September 24, 1989

WEIGHTS & MEASURES: Metric

GEOGRAPHICAL FEATURES

Landlocked Niger is the largest country in West Africa, with an area of 1,267,000 sq. km. (489,190 sq. mi.), extending 1,845 km. (1,146 mi.) east-northeast to west-southwest and 1,025 km. (637 mi.) north-northwest to south-southeast.

Niger shares its total international boundary of 5,621 km. (3,493 mi.) with seven neighbors: Algeria (956 km.; 594 mi.); Mali (821 km.; 510 mi.); Burkina Faso (628 km.; 390 mi.); Benin (190 km.; 118 mi.); Nigeria (1,497 km.; 930 mi.); Chad (1,175 km.; 730 mi.) and Libya (354 km.; 220 mi.).

The capital, on the Niger River, is Niamey, with a 1983 population of 399,100 permanent inhabitants, excluding nomads who constantly travel in and out of the city. The other major urban centers are Zinder (82,800), Maradi (65,100), Tahoua (49,100), Agadez (30,000), Arlit (15,000) and Dosso (25,000).

Four-fifths of Niger is an arid desert; the remaining fifth is savanna. Vast areas in the North are characterized by the same relief: sandy basins, low plateaus, isolated hills and peaks, and limestone or sandstone bluffs. The Tamgak Mountains in the Northwest rise 1,800 m. (5,900 ft.) above the Iferouane Valley. In the north-central region is the volcanic Air Massif pierced by deep valleys, called koris, where there is dense vegetation of acacias and doum palms. Farther east is the Tenere, a sandy and arid desert.

The lifeline of the country is the Niger River, which flows through the South for 300 km. (186 mi.). Niger also shares Lake Chad with Nigeria, Chad, and Cameroon.

CLIMATE & WEATHER

Niger is one of the hottest regions on the planet, with temperatures often rising to 50°C (122°F); the intense heat makes rain evaporate before it reaches the ground. From November to February the weather is dry and relatively cool, the temperature often dropping to 29.4°C (85°F). The rainy season lasts from June to October in the South, with maximum rainfall in August. Annual rainfall averages 50 cm. (29 in.) south of the 16th parallel; to the north it drops below 20 cm. (8 in.), and conditions become subdesert (Sahelian) and then desert (Saharan). At the town of Agadez rainfall is no more than 10 cm. (4 in.) in good years.

The prevailing wind is the harmattan, a scorching wind that parches all living things during the dry months.

RÉPUBLIQUE DU NIGER

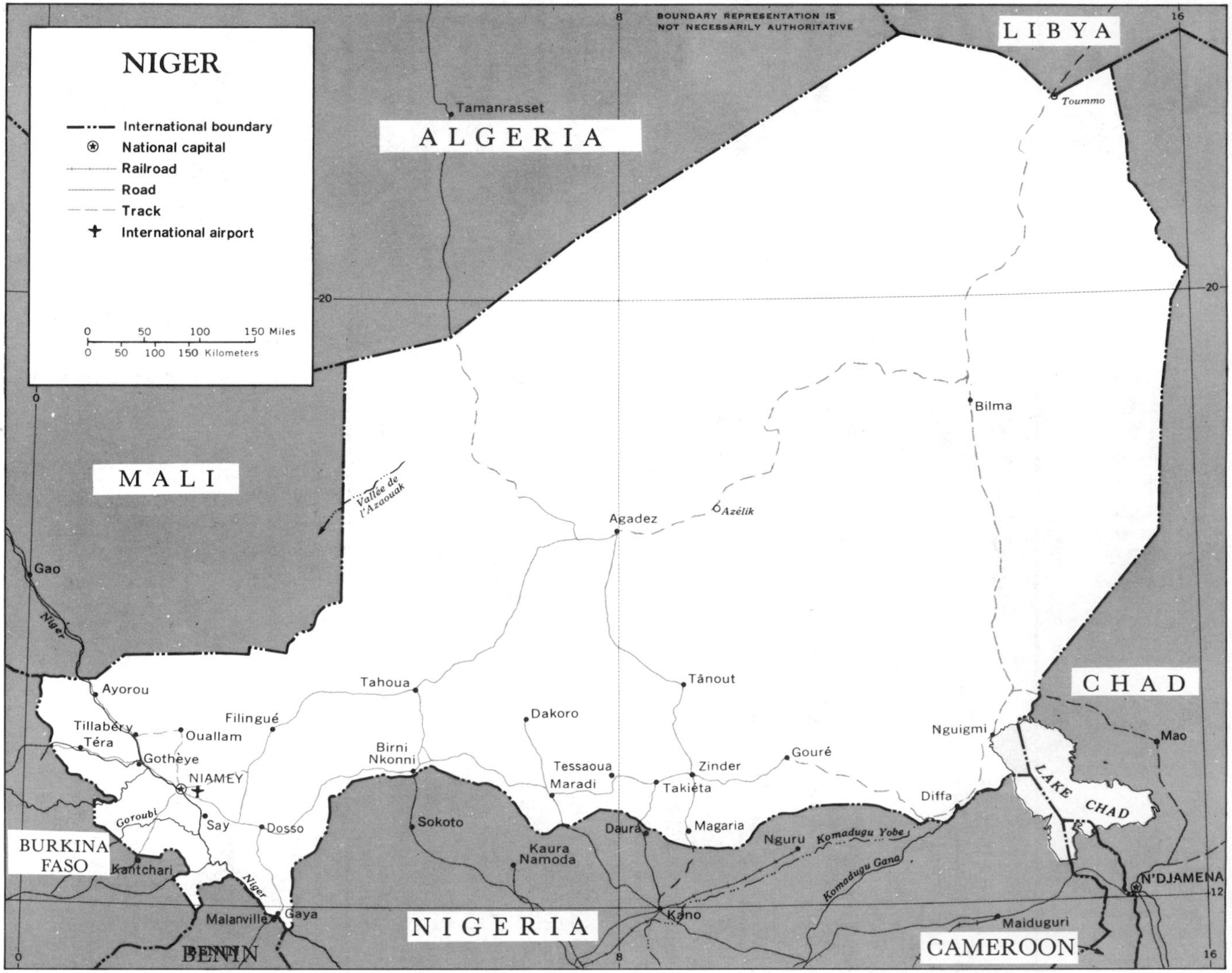

NIGER
International boundary
National capital
Railroad
Road
Track
International airport
0 50 100 150 Miles
0 50 100 150 Kilometers
BOUNDARY REPRESENTATION IS NOT NECESSARILY AUTHORITATIVE
LIBYA
ALGERIA
MALI
CHAD
NIGERIA
BURKINA FASO
BENIN
CAMEROON
LAKE CHAD
Toummo
Tamanrasset
Bilma
Agadez
Azélik
Vallée de l'Azaouak
Gao
Niger
Ayorou
Tillabéry
Téra
Ouallam
Filingué
Gothèye
NIAMEY
Say
Dosso
Goroubi
Kantchari
Malanville
Gaya
Tahoua
Birni Nkonni
Sokoto
Dakoro
Tessaoua
Maradi
Kaura Namoda
Daura
Kano
Tânout
Zinder
Takiéta
Magaria
Gouré
Nguru
Komadugu Yobe
Komadugu Gana
Nguigmi
Diffa
Maiduguri
Mao
N'DJAMENA
0
8
16
20
12

POPULATION

The population of Niger was estimated in 1990 at 7,969,309, on the basis of the last official census, in 1988.

Nearly 90% of the population is concentrated along the Niger River, where population density approaches 60 to 70 per sq. km. (155 to 181 per sq. mi.). The density falls to 15 per sq. km. (39 per sq. mi.) in the Southeast and to less than 1 per sq. km. (2.5 per sq. mi.) in the North. Overall the density is 6.6 per sq. km. (17.0 per sq. mi.).

Niger is among the least urbanized nations in the world, with 82% of its population living in either rural areas or as nomads. Other than Niamey there are no population centers with over 100,000 inhabitants, and only seven towns have over 15,000 inhabitants. The annual urban growth rate, 1985–90, was 6.74%.

The age profile shows 46.7% under 14, 50% between 15 and 64 and 3.3% over 65. The sex ratio is slightly tilted toward females, who are 50.4% of the population.

Migration is a way of life for all nomads, and borders are meaningless, artificial restrictions. However, by the same token, most nomads eventually return home and show no inclination to settle in other countries.

Males have considerable advantages in terms of education, employment and property rights. In case of divorce, custody of all children under eight years is given to the husband. Conscious of this situation, the government has made progress in improving the status of women by launching work on a new family code, by making better employment opportunities available to women, by giving them a significant role in the Development Society network of councils and by supporting the National Women's Association.

In 1985 the government undertook a major initiative to encourage Nigerians to use birth control.

STATUS OF WOMEN INDICATORS

Number of women (000): 3,127 (1985)
% woman of childbearing age 15–49: 44 (1988)
% woman literate: 5.8 (1985)
% woman in labor force: 47 (1988)
Total fertility rate (/woman): 7.4 (1990)

DEMOGRAPHIC INDICATORS

Population (millions): 7.969 (1990)
Year of last census: 1988
Sex distribution (% of last census): males, 49.6; females, 50.4
Population estimates and projections (millions)

1930: 1,490	1960: 2,913	2000: 10,656
1940: 1,700	1970: 4,016	
1950: 2,291	1980: 5,568	

Age profile (%, 1985 est.)

0–14: 46.7	30–44: 14.9	60–74: 3.9
15–29: 25.6	45–59: 8.0	75 and over: 0.9

Median age (yrs.): 16.6 (1985)
Youth population (% aged 15–24): (1985) 18.6; (2000) 19.1
Total dependency ratio, 1985: 99.9
Annual growth rate (%)

1950–55: 1.04	1975–80: 2.59	2000–2005: 3.15
1955–60: 1.36	1980–85: 2.82	2005–10: 3.00
1960–65: 2.89	1985–90: 3.01	2010–15: 2.72
1965–70: 2.08	1990–95: 3.13	2015–20: 2.37
1970–75: 2.36	1995–2000: 3.19	2020–25: 2.03

Hypothetical size of stationary population (millions): 82
Assumed year of reaching net reproduction rate of 1: 2060
Urban population (000): 989 (1985)
Urban population (%): (1987) 18; (1965) 7
Annual urban population growth rate (%, 1985–90): 6.74
Annual rural population growth rate (%, 1985–90): 2.21
Percentage of urban population in largest city: 31 (1980)
Number of cities of population over 500,000: 0 (1980)
Population density per sq. km. (per sq. mi.): 6.6 (17.0) (latest)

VITAL STATISTICS

Crude birth rate (/1,000): 52 (1990); 51 (1965)
Crude death rate (/1,000): 17 (1990); 29 (1965)
Infant mortality rate (/1,000 live births): 131 (1990)
Maternal mortality rate (/100,00 live births): 420 (1980)
Life expectancy (yrs.) at birth (1980–85): males, 48; females, 53 (1990)
Total fertility rate (/woman) (1980–85): 7.4 (1990)
Rate of natural increase (/1,000) (1985–90): 30.0
Average household size: 6.2 (latest)

ETHNIC COMPOSITION

Niger has a complex ethnic configuration, but three Negroid tribes make up nearly 79% of the population: the Hausa, inhabiting the center and South, with 50%; the Djerma-Songhai, in the Southwest, with 23%; and the Beriberi-Manga, in the East, with 6%. Nomadic herdsmen, some of whom are of Caucasian stock, live alongside the Negro tribes—the Fulani (or Peul) in the South, numbering 450,000; the Tuareg in the North, numbering 127,000; and the Tedara and Daza, branches of the Tebu (also called Tubu), in the East. Other important tribes include the Kanuri and the Tamachek.

The two primarily nomadic groups, Tuaregs and Fulani (Peul), have less access to government services, partly because their transient lifestyles make it difficult for the government to supply them with services and partly because of historical animosities between the nomads and the sedentary Djerma and Hausa ethnic groups, which dominate the government. Such animosities undoubtedly contributed to a slowness by some government officials in 1985 to guarantee that adequate quantities of food relief reached isolated Tuareg and Fulani populations.

There are small Western communities in Niamey and other major towns.

LANGUAGES

The official language is French, spoken, however, by only a tiny minority. All major ethnic groups have their own vernaculars, usually bearing the same name as the group except in the case of the Tuareg, whose language is known as Tomacheq. Arabic is the preferred language in literature. As the language of the dominant ethnic groups, Djerma and Hausa are used as lingua francas.

RELIGIONS

Niger has been almost completely Islamized, except for some 14% who are believed to practice some form of traditional religions, and 0.5% who are Catholics or Protestants. The dominant sect is Sunni but, as in other parts of North Africa, the most powerful religious organizations are the brotherhoods, of which the three most influential are the Tijaniyya, the Senoussi and the Hamallists.

Christian churches are allowed to operate freely. Conversion from one religion to another is not prohibited but occurs only rarely. Foreign missionaries are permitted to live, work and travel in Niger. There have been no reports of religious discrimination, but adherence to Islam tends to give an advantage in all sectors of life. The government, cautious because of the Islamic fundamentalist violence that erupts periodically in northern Nigeria, monitors religious activity through the Islamic Association, which is funded by the government. Local religious leaders are subject to an informal government screening process, and Islamic services that have gone beyond strictly religious subjects have been shut down by the government. Religious groups are allowed to maintain links with coreligionists in other countries.

HISTORICAL BACKGROUND

The earliest French military expeditions into the territory now called Niger met with fierce resistance from the Tuareg and other tribes, but the French steadily pushed forward and by 1900 succeeded in encircling Lake Chad with military outposts. In 1901 the military district of Niger was created as part of the province of Haut-Sénégal et Niger. Sporadic rebellions continued to bedevil the French until 1914, when a major German-inspired uprising took place, which was put down only with British assistance. It was only by 1922 that the country was fully pacified. Until 1932 the country was administered directly from Paris through the governor general in Dakar, Senegal. From 1932 to 1947 it was administered jointly with Upper Volta (now Burkina Faso). In 1958 Niger became an autonomous state and in 1960 proclaimed its independence. Niger, although no longer a member of the French Community, still maintains close economic and political ties with France.

Following independence the country became a one-party state led by Hamani Diori, president and head of the Niger Progressive Party. Opposition to the regime centered around the Marxist-oriented Sawaba Party, which continued its activities from abroad. Diori and his government won overwhelming reelection in 1965 and 1970, but their failure to deal with widespread political discontent and official corruption as well as the problems caused by severe drought resulted in their overthrow in a military coup in 1974. The coup was lead by Seyni Kountche and Sani Souna Sido, who installed themselves as president and vice president, respectively, of the Supreme Military Council (CMS). The following year Kountche had Sido arrested for attempting to organize another coup.

An initial period of liberalization followed the coup, and political prisoners were released. Economic conditions improved with the end of the drought in 1976 and the recovery of export commodity prices. However, sporadic opposition to the regime continued, culminating in an attempted coup in 1976. Student unrest increased in the early 1980s. In an attempt to win popular support, Kountche introduced more civilians into the government in 1980 and initiated procedures to develop a more representative form of government in 1982. Local elections were held for village councils, which in turn elected local councils. These bodies elected regional councils that elected the National Development Council (CND). The CND, initially established in 1974, was given quasi-leadership status in 1983 after the election of 150 delegates. The office of prime minister was created, and Kountche appointed Oumarou Mamane to the post. Mamane also assumed the post of president of the CND. Following a coup attempt in October 1983, Kountche replaced Mamane with Hamid Algabid as prime minister.

The following year Kountche announced creation of the National Charter Commission to draft a national constitution. Largely made up of members of the CND, it made slow progress, in part because its work was suspended for a time as the government made dealing with the recurring drought and economic problems priorities. It introduced a draft document in 1985 that was adopted by the government in 1986 and approved by referendum in 1987. Nevertheless, the military remained firmly in command.

Kountche died in 1987 and was succeeded by the armed forces chief of staff, Ali Saibou. The civilian Algabid remained prime minister, but Saibou strengthened the army's role in government by increasing army participation in the cabinet. In 1988 Saibou announced formation of another commission to draft guidelines for a constitution. He subsequently made it clear that the army would continue to play the dominant role in government following the adoption of a constitution. In the same year he announced the lifting of the ban on all political organizations and the formation of a political party, the National Movement for Social Development (NMSD), which was intended to form the core of a one-party state. Saibou restated his opposition to a multiparty system.

In September 1989 the nation adopted a new constitution providing for the direct election of the president and the legislature. In the December elections that followed, Saibou was confirmed as president with over 99% of the vote. A single list of candidates approved by the Conseil Supérieur d'Orientation Nationale, which replaced the CMS, won endorsement to the legislature with over 99% of the vote as well.

During 1990 the government, in an effort to calm continuing political unrest, continued to move toward democratization. In November Saibou announced a multiparty political system would be established with multiparty elections scheduled for the first quarter of 1992. Further reform continued in 1991 when Saibou

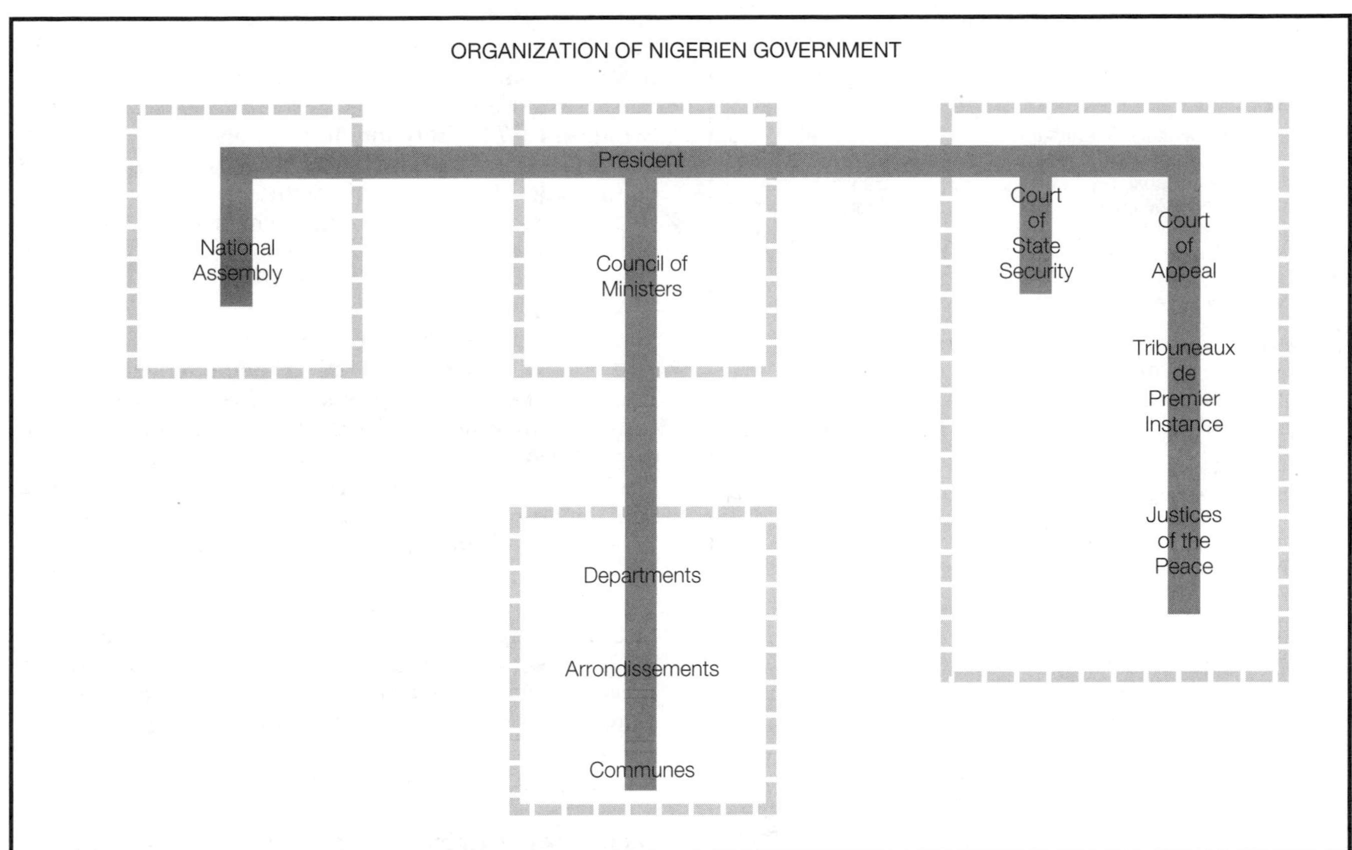

came to an agreement with the opposition over access to the media.

CONSTITUTION & GOVERNMENT

The Constitution of 1960 was suspended following the coup of 1974. All executive and legislative powers were taken over by the Supreme Military Council, headed by the president. Niger was ruled by an authoritarian military regime. Virtually all political power was concentrated in the hands of the president. He ruled in the name of the Supreme Military Council, a small group of military officers, most of whom participated in the 1974 coup that brought Kountche to power. The president ruled by decree, made all government appointments and decided the pace of all political change. The military remained the source of power. Government operations were conducted largely by civilian technocrats.

As an alternative to a party-based democracy, in 1979 the government began to create a structure it called the Development Society, a hierarchical network of councils at the village, subregional, regional and national levels. The councils, all of which were in place by late 1983, contained at each level a mixture of elected and appointed members, but only at the village level were some of the members elected directly by the people. At the higher levels, members were elected by the members at the next lower level. The precise role of the Development Society councils was not defined in practice. Theoretically their role was to involve the people in economic and social development. But even then their role was strictly advisory, and the councils have no financial support from the government. The National Development Council (NDC) assumed some of the aspects of a legislature in 1983 following the indirect election of 150 delegates.

RULERS OF NIGER (from 1960)

Presidents

November 1960–April 1974: Hamani Diori
April 1974–November 1987: Seyni Kountche
November 1987– : Ali Saibou

In 1989 the nation adopted a new constitution. Under the Constitution of the Second Republic, the president is elected by direct universal suffrage for a seven-year term. The 93-member National Assembly is directly elected from a single list of candidates approved by the Conseil Supérieur d'Orientation Nationale. A 1991 amendment to the constitution calls for a multiparty system with elections to a new legislative body in 1992.

FREEDOM & HUMAN RIGHTS

In terms of civil and political rights, Niger is classified as a not-free country.

In April 1984, on the 10th anniversary of the coup that brought Kountche to power, the government released about 20 political prisoners, including former president Diori. These political prisoners, connected with the 1974 coup or subsequent coup attempts, all had been detained without trial. After these releases,

GOVERNMENT LIST (July/August 1991)

President	Saibou, Ali, *Brig. Gen.*
Prime Minister	Mahamidou, Aliou
Minister of Agriculture & Animal Breeding	Souna, Adamou
Minister of Civil Service & Labor	Dagra, Mamadou
Minister of Communications	Abdoulaye, Khamed
Minister of Defense	Saibou, Ali, *Brig. Gen.*
Minister of Economic Promotions	Sabo, Nassirou
Minister of Equipment	Ousmane, Issaka, *Maj.*
Minister of Finance	Mahamane Badamassi, Malam Annou
Minister of Foreign Affairs & Cooperation	Sani Bako, Mahamane
Minister of Higher Education, Research, Technology & National Education	Adamou, Aboubakar
Minister of Interior	Djika, Abara
Minister of Justice & Keeper of the Seals	Bandiere, Ali
Minister of Mines & Energy	Insa, Abdou
Minister of Planning	Soumaila, Al Moustapha
Minister of Public Health	Gazere, Ousman, *Lt. Col.*
Minister of Social Affairs & Promotion of Women	Aissata, Moumouni
Minister of Transport & Tourism	Gros, Hamadou Moussa, *Maj.*
Minister of Water Resources & Environment	Ousmane, Issaka, *Maj.*
Minister of Youth, Sports & Culture	Seydou, Abdourahmane, *Capt.*
Minister of State & Counselor to the President	Oumarou, Ide, *Maj.*
Minister of State for Public Institutions & Parastatals	Abdoulaye, Mohamed
Secretary of State for Finance	Koussou, Ibrahim
Secretary of State for Interior	Ousmane, Boukar Elhadji
Secretary of State for National Education	Mariama, Maillele
Secretary of State for Planning	Moussa, Douramane
Secretary of State to Minister of Agriculture & Animal Breeding in Charge of Cooperation	Boulama, Mamane
Secretary of State to Minister of Foreign Affairs in Charge of Cooperation	Djambala, Issaka
Ministerial Delegate for the Interior	Darkoye, Atahere
Ministerial Delegate to the Presidency in Charge of Administrative Reforms	Boukary, Mamane
Special Counselor at the Presidency	Chardon, Amoki, *Lt. Col.*
High Commissioner for the Kandadji Dam	Mamadou, Amadou
Official in Charge of Special Duties at the Presidency with rank of Minister	Maiga, Amadou Fiti
Governor, Central Bank	Fadiga, Abdoulaye

the government acknowledged that 36 political prisoners still were being held, most of them associated with an October 1983 coup attempt. An increasing preoccupation with internal security led the government to tighten internal restrictions on travel and population movements in 1984.

The human rights situation in Niger did not improve in 1985. In response to an armed attack by Tuareg dissidents on an administrative post at Tchin-Taboradam in late May, during which one Tuareg and two soldiers were killed, the government arrested about 1,000 ethnic Tuaregs in Niamey. On June 6 the government expelled over 200 Malian and Mauritanian Tuaregs. Former president Diori was put back under the house arrest from which he had been released in April 1984, and restrictions were placed on nighttime travel in Niger as a result of the same incident. In July a state security court tried 11 Tuaregs arrested at Tchin-Taboradam and condemned at least eight of them to death. The death sentences are not believed to have been carried out.

In late 1987 Saibou announced amnesty for all political prisoners. The trial of those involved in the 1983 coup took place in 1988, with the Court of State Security sentencing four to death in absentia, imposing prison sentence on 16 and acquitting eight. Saibou announced another amnesty in 1989.

Although the government rules by decree and there is no operative constitution, both the judicial and legal systems (both based on the French model) remain intact. In the absence of specific institutional guarantees of human and civil rights, incidents of arrests of political opponents (especially those who belonged to the Sawaba Party or the previous governments) occasionally are reported, but there are no widespread abuses or indiscriminate brutality. Cases involving political prisoners are handled by military tribunals, but there have been only a handful of such cases in recent history. There is a tradition of social justice and fair play that serves to moderate the exercise of absolute power. However, dissent is rarely voiced openly. Because the country is overwhelmingly Muslim, religious rivalries are not sources of social tension. The news media are government-controlled, but the absence of a free press does not seem to be felt much by the people. Labor rights, including the right to strike, are respected but rarely exercised.

CIVIL SERVICE

No current information is available on the Nigerian civil service.

LOCAL GOVERNMENT

For purposes of local government, Niger is divided into seven departments, 32 *arrondissements* and 150 communes or rural districts.

The chief administrator in each department is the prefect, appointed by and responsible to the president.

DEPARTMENTS OF NIGER

Department	Capital	Number of Arrondissements
Naimey	Niamey	6
Dosso	Dosso	5
Tahoua	Tahoua	7
Maradi	Maradi	4
Zinder	Zinder	5
Diffa	Diffa	3
Agades	Agadez	2

FOREIGN POLICY

Prior to the 1974 coup Niger pursued a moderate but pro-Western foreign policy; it maintained cordial relations with all neighboring states except, briefly, with Benin (then Dahomey) as a result of conflicting territorial claims. Foreign policy has been one of the areas where the Kountche regime set out to demonstrate its break with the past. Its diplomatic relations with China, North Korea and East Germany have been the more immediate consequences of this change in policy.

After the Libyan army moved to occupy Chad in 1980, the Nigerian government became wary of the prospect of Libyan "destablization" in Niger and sought to forge closer relations with Tunisia, Algeria and Morocco as well as with conservative Arab states of the Persian Gulf, many of which Kountche has visited. Relations with Libya were particularly strained by Col. Qaddhafi's accusation in 1980 that the Niger government was persecuting the Tuareg population. The government also resented Libyan broadcasts aimed at Niger in the Hausa and Tamacheo languages. The problem was exacerbated when 12 Nigerien civil servants of Tuareg origins defected to Libya, including one individual who was said to have been close to President Kountche. During the Persian Gulf War in early 1991, Niger sent ground troops to support the U.S.-led U.N. forces amassed in Saudi Arabia.

Niger and the United States are parties to five treaties and agreements covering defense, economic and technical cooperation, investment guarantees, the Peace Corps and Social Security.

Niger joined the United Nations in 1960. It is a member of 13 U.N. organizations and 25 other international organizations.

PARLIAMENT

The 1989 Constitution provides for a directly elected National Assembly. Elections to that 93-member body held in December 1989 resulted in the approval of a single list of candidates put forth by the Conseil Supérieur d'Orientation Nationale. A multiparty system is scheduled to go into effect in 1992.

POLITICAL PARTIES

Until 1988 all political parties and activities were suspended by the military government.

Until then Niger knew only two political parties in its history as an independent nation. Until 1974, the only legal party was the Parti Progressiste Nigerien (PPN, Niger Progressive Party), a conservative and nationalist party founded in 1946 as the Niger branch of Rassemblement Démocratique Africaine. It was led by former president Hamani Diori.

The opposition party was the Sawaba (Freedom) Party, successor to the left-wing Union Démocratique Nigerienne, which was banned in 1959 but remained active in exile under the leadership of Djibo Bakary. In 1988 Saibou announced the formation of his party, the National Movement for Social Development, but reiterated his opposition to a multiparty system. However, in response to political pressure, the government legalized political pluralism and promised multiparty elections in 1992. By mid-1991 15 parties had registered with the government.

ECONOMY

Niger is one of the 49 low-income countries of the world, one of the 29 least-developed countries and one severely affected by periodic drought and price fluctuations in export commodities. Niger has a free-market economy in which the dominant sector is private.

Approximately 90% of Niger's population is engaged in either stock raising or subsistence farming, activities that generate more than a third of the national income. Droughts during the 1970s and early 1980s and locust plagues in the late 1980s severely affected farming, and on several occasions the country had to appeal for emergency food aid. The natural disasters helped contribute to the average 2.1% annual decline in per capita GNP from 1965 to 1985.

The economy also is heavily dependent on uranium production, which grew rapidly in the mid-1970s but declined in the 1980s because of the slump in world prices. Its contribution to export earnings dropped from 80% in 1980 to 30% in 1986. Cassiterite, phosphates, salt and coal also are mined. Deposits of iron ore, petroleum, diamonds, gold, copper, manganese, lithium, lead and tungsten have been discovered but have not yet been exploited.

Industry is not well developed; the manufacturing sector accounted for 4% of the GDP in 1987.

The need to import basic commodities and the fall in uranium prices led to a severe trade imbalance and a rapidly mounting external debt. Niger relies heavily on foreign aid, particularly from France, to cover de-

PRINCIPAL ECONOMIC INDICATORS

Gross National Product (U.S. $ billions): 2,195 (1989)
GNP per capita (U.S. $): 290 (1988)
GNP average annual growth rate (%, 1980–89): −1.7
GNP per capita average annual growth rate (%, 1987–88): −2.2
Average annual rate of inflation (%, 1980–88): 3.6
Consumer Price Index (1980 = 100) 1986
All items: 139
Food: 131
Average annual growth rate (%), 1980–88
General government consumption: 1.5
Private consumption: 1.7
Gross domestic investment: −10.2

BALANCE OF PAYMENTS, 1989
(U.S. $ millions)

Current account balance: −94.3
Merchandise exports: 369.0
Merchandise imports: −430.4
Trade balance: −61.4
Other goods, services & income +: 32.2
Other goods, services & income −: −173.9
Other goods, services & income net: 141.7
Private unrequited transfers: −45.5
Official unrequited transfers: 153.8
Capital other than reserves: 81
Net errors & omissions: 54.5
Counterpart items: −22.5
Total change in reserves: −11.5

GROSS DOMESTIC PRODUCT

GDP nominal (C.F.A.F. billions): 682.3 (1985)
GDP per capita (U.S. $): 330 (1988)
Average annual growth rate of GDP (%, 1980–88): −1.2
GDP by type of expenditure (%), 1986
  Consumption
    Private: 76
    Government: 11
  Gross domestic investment: 17
  Gross domestic saving: 4 (1988)
  Foreign trade
    Exports: 30
    Imports: −32
Cost components of GDP (%), 1983
  Net indirect taxes: 7
  Consumption of fixed capital: 9
  Compensation of employees: 18
  Net operating surplus: 66
Sectoral origin of GDP (%), 1987
  Primary
    Agriculture: 36 (1988)
    Mining: 7
  Secondary
    Manufacturing: 4
    Construction: 2
    Public utilities: 3
  Tertiary
    Transportation & communication: 4
    Trade, finance: 13
    Other services: 17
    Government: 8
Average annual sectoral growth rates (%, 1980–87)
  Agriculture: 2.8 (latest)
  Industry: −4.3 (latest)
  Services: −8.0 (latest)

velopment and debt service. It is thought that foreign debt increased sixfold between 1976 and 1983. Since 1983 Niger has received IMF support in return for implementation of a structural adjustment program designed to cut spending in the public sector and transfer state-owned companies to private ownership. Niger also received aid from the United States, West Germany, Japan, Italy, Libya and the European Community.

PUBLIC FINANCE

The Nigerien fiscal year runs from October 1 through September 30.

Niger depends heavily on external funding to support its budget deficit and its development plans.

With the fall in uranium prices in the early 1980s, Niger had difficulty repaying investment loans. Foreign debt increased sixfold between 1976 and 1985, and debt service accounted for about 21% of export earnings in 1988. Both its official and commercial creditors agreed to successive debt rescheduling throughout the decade. Since 1983 the country has received aid from the IMF in return for a program of structural adjustment designed to cut government spending and implement privatization of government enterprises.

Niger's latest five-year economic plan, adopted in 1987, called for total expenditures of CFAF580,000 million, almost three-fourths of which had to come from outside sources. The plan aimed at encouraging private investment, streamlining revenue procurement and reducing government spending. A total of 40% of the investment was directed at agriculture and rural development.

Government consumption was 10% of the GDP in 1987. The annual growth rate of government consumption, 1980–87, was 1.2%.

During 1970–88 Niger received $349 million in US

FOREIGN AID, 1989

Total foreign aid (U.S. $ millions): 311.1
  Bilateral: 236.0
  Multilateral: 75.2

FINANCIAL INDICATORS, 1989

Total reserves minus gold (SDR's millions): 162
SDRs (millions): 1
Reserve position in IMF (SDR's millions): 9
Foreign exchange (SDR's millions): 152
Gold (fine troy oz. millions): .01
Ratio of external debt to total reserves: 5.5 (1988)
Central bank, 1989
  Assets %
    Foreign assets: 49.1
    Claims on government: 30.3
    Claims on banks: 20.6
    Claims on private sector: 0.0
  Liabilities %
    Reserve money: 64.2
    Government deposits: 9.3
    Foreign liabilities: 20.5
    Capital accounts: 0.0
Money supply, 1989
  Stock (C.F.A.F. billions): 88.2
  M^1 per capita: 11,500
Private banks, 1989
  Assets %
    Loans to government: 14.2
    Loans to private sector: 49.7
    Reserves: 31.6
    Foreign assets: 4.5
  Liabilities
    deposits (C.F.A.F. billions): 120.8
    of which %
      Demand deposits: 36.9
      Savings deposits: 42.4
      Government deposits: 17.2
      Foreign liabilities: 30.2
External debt, 1988
  Total (U.S. $ millions): 1,742
    of which public (U.S. $ millions): 1,286
    of which private (U.S. $ millions): 256
  Debt service (long-term) total (U.S. $ millions): 84
    Repayment
      Principal (%): 36.9
      Interest (%): 63.1
  Debt service rate (%): 20.9
  External public debt as % of GNP: 55.1
  Debt service as % of GNP: 3.6
  Debt service as % of exports: 21.1
  Terms of public borrowing
    Commitments (U.S. $ millions): 159
    Average interest rate (%): 1.4
    Average maturity (yrs.): 31
  Net flow of publicly guaranteed external capital (U.S. $ millions): 119
  Receipt of workers' remittances (U.S. $ millions): −43

aid. From 1970–87 it received $2.8 billion in assistance from other Western countries. Communist countries contributed $61 million during 1970–88. OPEC bilateral aid totalled $504 million during 1979–89.

CURRENCY & BANKING

Niger's unit of currency is the CFA (Communauté Financière Africaine) franc, divided into 100 centimes. Coins are issued in denominations of 1, 2, 5, 10, 25, 50 and 100 francs; notes are issued in denominations of 50, 100, 500, 1,000 and 5,000 francs.

In June 1991 the CFA franc's dollar exchange rate was $1 = CFAF290.5. Because the CFA franc is a floating currency, its value fluctuates widely in foreign exchange markets.

The bank of issue of the CFAF is the Central Bank of the West African States (Banque Centrale des États de l'Afrique de l'Ouest, BCEAO). Niger has a monetary committee that reports to the BCEAO and works within its monetary framework but possesses a certain autonomy in internal credit matters. The other five banks include three banks in which the state has a controlling interest: the Development Bank of the Republic of the Niger, the Crédit du Niger and the Union Nigerienne de Crédit et de Cooperation.

GROWTH PROFILE
(Annual Growth Rates, %)

Projected population, (1987–2000): 3.3
Projected crude birth rate, (/1000) (1990–95): 50.2
Projected crude death rate, (/1000) (1990–95): 19.0
Urban population, (1980–88): 8.0
Labor force, (1985–2000): 2.6
GNP, (1980–89): −1.7
GNP per capita, (1986–88): −2.1
GDP, (1980–88): −1.2
Inflation, (1980–88): 3.6
Agriculture, (1980–87): 2.8
Industry, (1980–87): −4.3
Services, (1980–87): −8.0
Money holdings, (1980–87): 6.1
Energy production, (1980–87): 15.7
Energy consumption, (1980–88): 3.2
Exports, (1980–88): −4.9
Imports, (1980–88): −4.2
General government consumption, (1980–88): 1.5
Private consumption, (1980–88): 1.7
Gross domestic investment, (1980–88): −10.2

AGRICULTURE

Of the total land area of 126,700,000 ha. (313,075,700 ac.), 2.9% is classified as agricultural land.

Cultivation is limited to a narrow strip of land along the Niger River and the border with Nigeria. Most of the farms are subsistence units that provide a living for the owners only in years of adequate rainfall. Almost all the farms are cultivated by nonnomadic African tribes, such as the Hausa and the Djerma-Songhai, and land tenure is communal. Agricultural techniques are primitive, and mechanization and fertilizer application are virtually unknown.

Even before the droughts of the 1970s and 1980s, the population growth rate outpaced production, and Niger was not self-sufficient in foodstuffs. The Office des Produits Vivriers du Niger (Food Products Bureau) keeps reserves of cereals in an effort to ensure regular food supplies and to maintain standard prices across the country. However, the country's food stocks fell to 40,000 tons in 1984, compared with 200,000 tons in 1983, as a result of one of the worst harvests ever recorded in Niger. The severe drought affected both livestock and cereal production, and in November 1984 President Kountche launched an emergency appeal for food aid following a cereal shortfall of 477,000 tons at the end of the 1983–84 season. The country also suffered as a result of the closure of the border with Nigeria in April 1984, which prevented much food aid from entering Niger and destroyed traditional livestock markets. A government campaign to encourage production of out-of-season crops (such as potatoes, haricot beans and cassava) was launched in 1984 in an effort to offset the cereal deficit. Nevertheless, subsequent droughts, locust infestations, desertification and overgrazing have undermined the nation's attempts to become self-sufficient. The major food crops are millet,

AGRICULTURAL INDICATORS

Agriculture's share of GDP (%): 35 (1989)
Average annual growth rate (%, 1980–87): 2.8
Value added in agriculture (U.S. $ millions): 729 (1989)
Cereal imports (000 metric tons): 151 (1988)
Index of Agricultural Production (1979–81 = 100): 108 (1986)
Index of Food Production (1979–81 = 100): 108 (1986)
Index of Food Production Per Capita (1979–81 = 100): 83 (1986–88)
Number of tractors: 172 (1986)
Total fertilizer consumption: 3.5 (000 metric tons) (1985–86)
Fertilizer consumption (g./ha., hundreds) (per ac., 3.5 oz.): 8 (2.8) (1987–88)
Number of farms (000): 699
Average size of holdings, ha. (ac.): 4.9 (12.1)
Size class (%)
- Below 1 ha. (below 2.47 ac.): 3.8
- 1–5 ha. (2.47–12.35 ac.): 54.1
- 5–10 ha. (12.35–24.7 ac.): 37.8
- 10–20 ha. (24.7–49.4 ac.):
- 20–50 ha. (49.4–123.5 ac.):
- 50–200 ha. (123.5–494 ac.):
- Over 200 ha. (over 494 ac.): } 4.3

Farms as % of total land area: 2.9
Yields, kg./ha. (lb./ac.), 1989
- Grains: 368
- Roots & tubers: 7,465
- Legumes: 186
- Fruits (000 metric tons): 43
- Vegetables (000 metric tons): 167
- Milk, kg. (lb.)/animal: 200 (441)

Livestock (000), 1989
- Cattle: 3,600
- Horses: 292 (1986)
- Sheep: 3,500
- Pigs: 37

Forestry 1986
- Production of roundwood, 000 cu. m.: 4,285 (142,637)
  - of which industrial roundwood (%): 6.2

Fishing 1986
- Total catch (000 metric tons: 2.3
  - of which marine (%): 0.0

sorghum and rice. Peanuts, the main source of agricultural income, are grown mainly in the Zinder area.

In recent years a number of nations, including France, West Germany, Canada and Japan, as well as the World Bank, the European Community and OPEC, have funded agricultural development projects. Soil conservation efforts, irrigation projects and measures to stop desertification have been among those receiving aid.

Livestock suffered severely during the droughts of the 1970s and 1980s. Following the 1970 drought, the government initiated a program to reconstitute the herds, but the subsequent drought destroyed them again. Another rebuilding effort was begun in 1986. Livestock was an important source of foreign exchange earnings, and the destruction of the herds was a severe blow to the economy.

Forests cover only about 1% of the land area, and the principal stands are teak and eucalyptus.

There is very little commercial fishing except on the Niger River by the Sorko and on Lake Chad by the Boudouma. Over 80% of the annual catch is exported, mainly to Ghana, Nigeria and Togo.

MANUFACTURING

Manufacturing is limited to the processing of agricultural produce and generated 4% of the GDP in 1987. The value added in manufacturing was $142 million in 1986. Nonagricultural products include cement and textiles. As a partner, the government is directly involved in Niger's thirty-odd "mixed enterprises," in which it maintains equity participation. These include most of Niger's largest industrial concerns.

Constraints on industrial development in the past have included the small domestic market, inadequate infrastructure and the exorbitant cost of transportation to the coastal ports. These have tended to discourage foreign private capital despite the generous incentives offered by the Investment Code of 1968.

The Investment Code of 1974 provides for two major grace periods of tax relief and tariff protection (if necessary), allocated according to levels of investment in selected fields: energy production, mineral exploration, textiles, agriculture, fertilizers, consumer goods, forestry, husbandry, fishing and hotels. Although foreign investors have concentrated investments in the mining sector, the code seeks to encourage and attract private investment and participation, foreign and local, throughout the economy. Government participation in commercial ventures, while common in Niger, is not required by law.

A reform of the state and parastatal sector was begun in 1983, in conjunction with the World Bank. In accordance with IMF recommendations, the state-owned distribution network lost its monopoly on the import of basic commodities in October 1983, in a move toward a more open market economy. A general audit of 54 state and parastatal companies, carried out in early 1984, revealed widespread mismanagement and large deficits. By 1988 a total of 32 fully or partially state-owned companies were privatized.

MINING

Following the discovery of high-grade uranium ore in the Air mountain range in 1967, mining became the most promising sector in the economy. Deposits were conservatively estimated at 100,000 tons. The concession is being worked by SOMAÏR (Société des Mines de l'Aïr), in which the French Atomic Energy Commission holds 40% interest, private French interests hold another 27% and the Niger government holds 33%. Production of uranium ore reached 4,585 tons in 1981, making Niger the fifth-largest uranium producer in the non-Communist world. Additional estimated reserves of 30,000 tons have been located at Akouta, which is being worked by a concession held jointly by the French Atomic Energy Commission and a Japanese consortium. A West German company is exploring the Djado region for further deposits. Total investment in this field has reached CFAF11.293 billion.

Uranium provided about 75% of Niger's export earnings by 1980, but a drop in world prices led to a reduction in revenues and it contributed only 12% of government earnings in 1986. France remains Niger's principal customer, but the Nigerien government is actively seeking to diversify its markets, particularly toward North Africa and the Middle East; in December 1983 agreement was reached for Niger to supply uranium for Egypt's nuclear power program. Lack of transportation facilities hampers Niger's uranium development, but a "uranium road" between the mines and the capital was completed in 1981. However, the slump in world demand has led to delay in plans to open up new deposits.

Other known mineral resources include iron, tin, tungsten, coal and phosphates. Mining of phosphate deposits, estimated at 250 million tons, began in 1978. Cassiterite, a tin-bearing mineral, is mined in three locations. Production of tin in 1982 totaled 96,000 tons.

ENERGY

Niger is heavily dependent on imported fuel to meet its energy needs. In 1980 imported petroleum absorbed over one-quarter of the country's export income. Dur-

ENERGY INDICATORS

Average annual energy production growth rate (%, 1980–88): 15.7
Energy consumption per capita (000 kg. oil equivalent): 43 (1988)
Energy imports as % of merchandise exports: 15 (1988)
Average annual growth rate of energy consumption (%, 1980–87): 3.2
Electricity, 1988
  Installed capacity (000 kw.): 63
  Production (million kw.-hr.): 160
    % fossil fuel: 100.0
    % hydro: 0.0
    % nuclear: 0.0
  Consumption per capita (kw.-hr.): 44
Coal
  Reserves (million metric tons): 7.0 (latest)
  Production (metric tons): 67,000 (latest)
  Consumption (metric tons): 67,000 (latest)

ing the early 1980s Niger took measures to reduce this dependency. It opened an electricity-generating station fueled by local coal in 1981 and announced plans for development of a thermal power station in 1988. The nation also has plans to construct a power line that would enable Niger to utilize electricity generated in Nigeria. In addition, Niger has proposed construction of a dam at Kandadji to provide irrigation and to generate hydroelectric power.

LABOR

Because of the instability of agricultural employment and the presence of nomads, enumeration of the economically active population has presented statistical difficulties. But it is generally estimated that about 90% of the economically active population of 3,203,000 is employed in agriculture, including livestock-raising; 2% in industry; and 4% in government. Women make up 47.4% of the labor force.

Under the Nigerien labor code, workers receive benefits for on-the-job injury, leave for family emergencies and health benefits. Annual holidays and leave benefits are clearly spelled out. Children between 12 and 18 may be employed, but there are strict provisions concerning the hours and types of employment of this age group. All labor provisions, especially those concerning child labor, apply in practice only to urban areas. In the agricultural sector, which employs most Nigeriens, children work on family plots under conditions that exceed the provisions of the labor code.

The only active labor union is the Workers' Union of Niger.

LABOR INDICATORS, 1985

Total economically active population (000): 3,203
As % of working-age population (15–64): 89.7
% female: 47.4
Activity rate (%)
  Total: 52.4
  Male: 55.6
  Female: 49.2
Sectoral employment (%)
  Agriculture, forestry, fishing: 89.6
  Manufacturing, mining, quarrying, public utilities, construction: 2.0
  Trade, hotels, restaurants, transport, communications, finance, real estate, services: 8.4
Average annual growth rate of labor force, 1980–2000 (%): 2.6
Unemployment (000): 28 (1986)
Labor under 20 years (%): 19.2 (1977)

FOREIGN COMMERCE

Peanuts and livestock were Niger's main exports at the time of independence. During the 1970s uranium became the main export. By 1981 Niger was the fourth-largest uranium exporter in the non-Communist world. Revenues from uranium mining provided two-fifths of the government's income from 1973 to 1978. At the same time, spending on imports increased, resulting in an unfavorable trade balance. The trade deficit worsened following the decline in uranium prices after 1978.

Niger's primary trading partner is France, which purchases most of its uranium and gives it much aid. Other import sources are Nigeria, Algeria, Ivory Coast and Pakistan. The major export destinations are France, Japan, Nigeria, Libya and Spain.

FOREIGN TRADE INDICATORS, 1987

Exports (U.S. $ millions): 371 (1988)
Imports (U.S. $ millions): 441 (1988)
Balance of trade (U.S. $ millions): −70 (1988)
Annual growth rate, 1980–88, exports (%): −4.9
Annual growth rate, 1980–88, imports (%): −4.2
International reserves in terms of months of imports covered: 4.7
Terms of trade (1980 = 100): 83
Import Price Index (1980 = 100): 93.9 (1986)
Export Price Index (1980 = 100): 91.0 (1986)

Direction of Trade (%), 1985

	Imports	Exports
European Community	42.0	72.9
United States	11.4	0.1
U.S.S.R. East European economies	0.2	0.0
Japan	3.8	6.0

Composition of Trade (%), 1985

	Imports	Exports
Food and agricultural raw materials (1981)	24.8	17.1
Fuels and other energy	11.1	0.0
Minerals ores and concentrates (1981)	14.8	79.7
Manufactured goods	47.6	3.4
of which chemicals	8.1	0.3
of which machinery	20.5	1.4

TRANSPORTATION & COMMUNICATIONS

Niger has no railroads. The principal direct sea link is the River Niger, navigable from Gaya near the Nigerian border to Port Harcourt in Nigeria between August and April and from Niamey to Gaya for a shorter period of the year. River and sea transportation is handled by the Société Nigerienne de Transports Fluviaux et Maritimes.

The road transportation system serves only a small part of the country. The principal roads run from west to east, beginning at Ayorou, passing through Niamey,

TRANSPORTATION INDICATORS

Roads (latest)
  Length, km. (mi.): 39,970 (24,836)
  Paved (%): 8
Motor vehicles (latest)
  Automobiles: 27,254
  Trucks and buses: 25,248
  Persons per vehicle: 136
Air (latest):
  Km. (mi.) flown (millions): 1.9 (1.2) (1985)
  Passenger-km. (passenger-mi.) (millions): 237.6 (147.6)
  Freight-km. (freight-mi.) (millions): 38.5 (26.3)
  Mail-ton-km. (mail ton-mi.) (millions): 0.7 (0.4) (1985)
  Airports with scheduled flights: 1 (1990)
Inland waterways (latest)
  Length, km. (mi.): 300 (1986)

COMMUNICATION INDICATORS, 1988

Telephones
- Total (000): 12 (1985)
- Persons per telephone: 563 (1985)
- Phone traffic (per 000 calls)
  - National: 57,366 pulses (1982)
  - International: 2,231 minutes (1985)

Post office
- Number of post offices: 283
- Pieces of mail handled (000): 6,958

Telegraph
- Total traffic (000 calls): 621 (1985)
- National: 598 (1985)
- International: 23 (1985)

Telex
- Subscriber lines: 297 (1985)

Telecommunications 1990
- 6 satellite stations

TOURISM & TRAVEL INDICATORS, 1986

Total tourist receipts (U.S. $ millions): 7 (1988)
Expenditures by nationals abroad (U.S. $ millions): 7 (1989)
Number of hotel beds (000): 2
Average length of stay: 3 nights
Tourist nights (000): 79
Number of tourists (000): 29.0 (1984)
- of whom from U.S.: 1.4
  - France: 9.8
  - Belgium: 1.9
  - Germany, Fed. Rep.: 1.0

Dosso, Maradi and Zinder and terminating at N'guigmi. The main routes link with the road systems of Algeria, Nigeria, Burkina Faso and Benin. With 25 tons of chemical and other inputs required for production of a ton of uranium, expansion of the mining sector has required improvement in Niger's transportation infrastructure. A 648-km. (408-mi.) "uranium road," built at a cost of $191 million to link the mines in the North to the country's existing road network, was opened in 1981. Work on the Niger section of the Trans-Saharan Highway began in 1985. The national road hauler is the Société Nationale des Transports Nigeriens, which is 49% state-owned.

The national airline is Trans Niger, which operates four aircraft on domestic and international routes to Algeria and Libya. The main international airport is at Niamey. There are 32 airports in the country, of which 30 are usable, seven have permanent-surface runways and one has a runway over 2,500 m. (8,000 ft.).

In 1984 a total of 29,000 tourists visited Niger. Tourism generated revenues of $7 million in 1988. There are 2,000 hotel beds, and the average length of stay was three nights in 1986.

DEFENSE

The defense structure is headed by the president, who also is chairman of the Supreme Military Council. The line of command runs through the minister of defense to the army chief of staff. There is no navy, and the air force is a purely transportation arm.

Military manpower is obtained through conscription. The conscript service period is two years.

The total strength of the army in 1988 was 3,200; the air force consists of approximately 100 men. Paramilitary forces total 4,500 men.

Army

Personnel: 3,200

Organization: 3 military districts; 2 armored reconnaissance squadrons; 6 infantry companies; 1 engineer company; 1 parachute company; 1 logistics support company

Equipment: 56 combat vehicles; 14 armored personnel carriers; guns; mortars; antitank guns

Air Force

Personnel: 100

Organization: No combat aircraft or helicopter; 1 transport

Major air bases: Niamey, Zinder, Agadez, Tahoua and Maradi

The Nigerien armed forces have no offensive capability and have yet to be tested in field combat. The army has very little mobility and is deployed almost entirely in the South; northern areas are left defenseless.

Until 1974 French troops were stationed in the country under bilateral defense agreements. These troops were withdrawn at the request of the Kountche regime, but defense and military assistance agreements remain in force.

EDUCATION

The national literacy rate is 13.9% (males 19.4% and females 8.6%).

Education is free, universal and compulsory, in principle, for eight years, from ages seven to 15, but the number of schools is insufficient.

Schooling lasts for 13 years, divided into six years of primary school, four years of secondary school (lower cycle) and three years of secondary school (upper cycle). The curriculum, on the French model, is being Nigerienized with the help of UNESCO. There are relatively fewer Christian schools in Niger than in other countries of West Africa. Private schools account for 5% of primary-level enrollment and 14% of secondary-level enrollment.

The school year runs from October to June. The language of instruction is French.

GRADUATES, 1986

Total: 837
Education: 74
Humanities & religion: 316
Law: 81
Social & behavioral sciences; 183
Natural sciences: 64
Mathematics & computer science: 51
Medicine: 31
Agriculture, forestry, fisheries: 37

EDUCATION INDICATORS, 1986

Literacy
- Total (%): 13.9
- Males (%): 19.4
- Females (%): 8.6

First level
- Schools: 1,976
- Students: 293,512
- Teachers: 7,690
- Student/teacher ratio: 38.2

Second Level
- Schools: 64 (1981)
- Students: 51,448 (1985)
- Teachers; 1,963 (1985)
- Student/teacher ratio: 26.2 (1985)
- Net enrollment rate: 4% (1980)

Vocational
- Schools: 8 (1981)
- Students: 2,208 (1985)
- Teachers: 120 (1981)
- Student/teacher ratio: 19.6 (1980)

Third Level
- Institutions: 3
- Students: 4,101 (1988)
- Teachers: 310 (1988)
- Student/teacher ratio: 13.2 (1988)
- Gross enrollment rate: 0.6% (1984)
- Students (/100,000 pop.): 48

Foreign study
- Foreign students in national universities: 296 (1988)
- Students abroad: 877
  - of whom in
    - U.S.: 43 (1988)
    - France: 259 (1988)
    - Federal Republic of Germany: 9 (1987)
    - U.K.: 17 (1988)

Public expenditure, 1980
- Total (C.F.A.F.): 16,532,722
- % of GNP: 3.1
- % of national budget: 22.9
- % of current expenditure: 47.0

The school system is controlled by the Ministry of Education.

Higher education is provided at the Université de Niamey, with 4,101 students in 1988. The Islamic University of West Africa, at Say, opened in 1987.

LEGAL SYSTEM

One of the first acts of the Kountche regime was to abolish the Supreme Court, which until 1974 had headed the judiciary. The Supreme Court had comprised three chambers—constitutional, juridical and accounting—and the High Court of Justice. The High Court had been appointed by the National Assembly from among its own membership and was empowered to try the president and members of the government for offenses relating to their conduct in office.

The Supreme Court was replaced by the Court of State Security, a military court that deals with criminal offenses. Below this is the Court of Appeal. The Chambre d'Accusations hears appeals from assize courts in Niamey, Maradi and Zinder. Below these are district magistrates' courts and labor courts.

The police have the right to enter homes between 5:00 A.M. and 9:00 P.M. but will enter at other times if they believe they have sufficient cause. A court warrant is not required. There have been no reports of forced entry, but other violations of privacy, such as monitoring correspondence and the operation of an informer system, occur on a selective basis. A few cases of forced population resettlement are occurring as a government response to the drought.

No current information is available on the nature of the penal system or the number of correctional facilities.

LAW ENFORCEMENT

The National Gendarmerie is a force of 1,300 men under the Ministry of the Interior. The per capita strength of the force is one policeman for every 3,300 inhabitants. Niger ranks 115th in the world in this respect.

No information is available on incidence or types of crimes.

HEALTH

Life expectancy is low—48 years for men and 53 years for women in 1990—but had increased significantly in 25 years. In 1965 the figures were 35 years and 38 years, respectively.

The major health problems are malaria, trachoma, leprosy, plague and yellow fever. Only 47% of the population have access to safe water.

HEALTH INDICATORS

Health personnel, 1985
- Physicians: 160
  - Persons per: 38,500
- Dentists: 10 (1978)
- Nurses: 1,080 (1978)
- Pharmacists: 12 (1978)
- Midwives: 192

Hospitals, 1978
- Number: 212
- Number of beds (/10,000): 6 (1979)
- Admissions/discharges (/10,000): 83
- Bed occupancy rate %: 62.0
- Average length of stay (days): 9

Type of hospitals (%), 1978
- Government: 97.2
- Private Nonprofit: 2.8
- Private profit: 0.0

Public Health expenditures (latest)
- As % of national budget: 5.3
- Per capita (U.S. $): 4.80

Vital statistics
- Crude death rate (/1,000): 17 (1990)
- Life Expectancy at birth 1990
  - Males: 48
  - Females: 53
- Infant mortality rate (/1,000 live births): 131 (1990)
- Child mortality rate (1985–90) under 5 yrs (/1,000): 228
- Maternal mortality rate (/100,000 live births (1980–84): 420

Population with access to safe water (%): 47 (latest)

FOOD & NUTRITION

The staple food is millet. The per capita intake of food is 2,217 calories and 66.7 g. (2.4 oz.) of protein, 31 g. (1.1 oz.) of fats and 332 g. (11.7 oz.) of carbohydrates.

MEDIA & CULTURE

One daily newspaper and one weekly, *Le Sabel* and *Le Sabel Dimanche*, respectively, are published in French in the capital. Fifteen periodicals also are published. All newspapers are published by official agencies, with a total circulation of 5,000. Niger's official news agency is Agence Nigerienne de Presse, founded in 1987. AFP maintains a bureau at Niamey.

There is a solitary book publisher, in the capital, L'Imprimerie Nationale du Niger.

Broadcasting is a state monopoly operated by Office de Radiodiffusion-Télévision du Niger (ORTN), also known as La Voix du Sahel. ORTN operates 17 transmitters. In addition to French, ORTN broadcasts in five vernacular languages (Djerma, Hausa, Peulh, Tomacheq and Beri-Beri). There were 19 persons per radio receiver in 1989. The television service, run by Tele-Sahel, with 12 transmitters, covers 85% of the country and is on the air four days a week. All programs are imported from France.

There is a growing domestic film industry, with an annual production of three long and 10 short films.

MEDIA INDICATORS

Newspapers
- Number of dailies: 1 (latest)
- Circulation (000): 5 (latest)
- Number of periodicals: 15 (latest)
- Newsprint consumption (1988)
- Total metric tons; 500
- Per 1,000 pop. (kg.): 75

Radio
- Number of transmitters; 19 (1989)
- Number of persons per radio receiver: 19 (1989)
- Total program hours: N.A.

Television
- Television transmitters: 12 (1989)
- Number of persons per T.V. receiver: 301 (1989)
- Total program hours: N.A.

Cinema
- Number of fixed cinemas: 4 (latest)
- Seating capacity (000): 3,800 (latest)
- Annual attendance (million): 0.8 (latest)

Films
- Production of long films: 3 (latest)

CULTURAL & ENVIRONMENTAL INDICATORS (latest)

Libraries
- Number: n.a.

Museums (pre-1986)
- Annual attendance (000): 600
- Attendance (/1,000 pop.): 110

Nature reserves:
- Number of facilities: 3

SOCIAL WELFARE

There is no organized publicly funded social welfare program. A few Christian missions provide relief for the aged. The 1987–91 development plan allocated 20% of expenditures to development of social services, including housing, education, health and water supply.

GLOSSARY

arrondissement: a district, subdivision of a department.

CHRONOLOGY (from 1960)

1960— Niger proclaims its independence as a republic, with Hamani Diori as president.

1963— Eighty people are arrested and scores are executed for plotting against the regime.

1965— Hamani Diori escapes assassination.

1967— Uranium deposits, the largest in black Africa, are discovered in the Aïr mountain range.

1968— Following a dispute between the ruling Niger Progressive Party and the graft-ridden civil service, the party is given a larger role in the national administration.

1973— Drought of unprecedented severity ravages Niger, decimates the national herd and wrecks the economy.

1974— The chief of staff, Lt. Gen. Seyni Kountche, seizes power in a bloody coup, Diori is placed under house arrest, National Assembly is suspended and all political parties are banned.

1975— Vice President Sani Souna Sido is arrested for alleged conspiracy against the regime.

1976— Former minister of rural development Moussa Bayere leads abortive coup and is sentenced to death along with eight other conspirators.

1983— National Development Council is expanded to 150 delegates and given possible role of drafting a new constitution. . . . Ouamarou Mamane is named prime minister but later is replaced by Hamid Algabid. Kountche puts down coup and arrests hundreds of dissidents. . . . Former president Diori is released from prison.

1985— Tuareg dissidents attack Tchin-Taboradam but are crushed by government troops. . . . Diori is rearrested. External debt is rescheduled as Niger initiates austerity measures.

1986— Preparation of draft national charter is completed.

1987— The government adopts a national charter, which is approved by over 99% of voters in a referendum. Kountche dies and is succeeded by Ali Saibou. Diori is released from house arrest. Saibou announces a general amnesty for all political prisoners.

1988— The CND is given the task of drafting a new constitution. The ban on all political parties is repealed. Saibou announces formation of a new party, the National Movement for Social Development.

1990— Demonstrators killed by police; Saibou tries to calm the situation by announcing plans for democratization; Aliou Mahamidou named prime minister.

1991— A constitutional amendment allowing for a multiparty system is adopted in April. . . . Multiparty elections are promised for 1992.

BIBLIOGRAPHY

BOOKS

Bonardi, Pierre. *La République de Niger.* Paris, 1960.
Clair, André. *Le Niger Indépendant.* Paris, 1966.
Decalo, Samuel. *Historical Dictionary of Niger.* Metuchen, N.J., 1989.
Hartgreaves, John. *West Africa: The Former French States.* Englewood Cliffs, N.J., 1967.
Lancrenon, François, and Pierre Donaint. *Le Niger.* Paris, 1972.

OFFICIAL PUBLICATIONS

Directorate of Budget and Government Accounting Directorate. *Situations Mensuelles des Recettes et des Crédits* (Monthly Statements of Budgetary Revenues and Expenditures).
Bulletin des Statistiques (Bulletin of Statistics), Direction de la Statistique (quarterly).
General Government Secretariat. *Journal Officiel de la République du Niger* (Official Gazette of the Republic of Niger).
———. *Loi de Reglement du Budget et l'État* (Closing Government Financial Statement).
Treasury. *Situation des Comptes du Trésor* (Statement of Treasury Accounts).

Nigeria

International boundary
National capital
Railroad
Road

0 100 200 Miles
0 100 200 Kilometers

Niger
Chad
Nguigmi
Gouré
Zinder
Maradi
Niamey
Dosso
Gaya
Lake Chad
Nguru
Sokoto
Kaura Namoda
Kano
Maiduguri
Dahomey
Kainji Lake
Kainji Dam
Wawa
Kaduna
Bauchi
Jos
Minna
Parakou
Shendam
Baro
Ilorin
Oyo
Ibadan
Lokoja
Idogo
Porto-Novo
Lagos
Benin City
Enugu
Warri
Port Harcourt
Calabar
Mamfe
Douala
Victoria
Edéa
Malabo
Kribi
Bata
Equatorial Guinea
Gulf of Guinea
Cameroon
Garoua
Ngaoundéré
Tibati
Gabon
Congo
Sokoto
Kaduna
Niger
Gongola
Benue
Katsina Ala
Ogun
Osse
Cross
Wouri
12
4

NIGERIA

BASIC FACT SHEET

OFFICIAL NAME: Federal Republic of Nigeria
ABBREVIATION: NR
CAPITAL: Abuja
HEAD OF STATE & HEAD OF GOVERNMENT: President Maj. Gen. Ibrahim Babangida (from 1985)
NATURE OF GOVERNMENT: Military dictatorship
POPULATION: 118,819,377 (1990)
AREA: 923,768 sq. km. (356,668 sq. mi.)
ETHNIC MAJORITY: Hausa, Fulani, Yoruba and Ibo
LANGUAGES: English (official); Hausa, Yoruba and Ibo (regional lingua francas)
RELIGIONS: Islam, Christianity and animism
UNIT OF CURRENCY: Naira
NATIONAL FLAG: Three vertical stripes, the outer two green and the center white
NATIONAL EMBLEM: A black shield on which appears a silver pall or "Y" sign representing the confluence of the Benue and Niger rivers. The shield is flanked by rearing white horses standing on a green mound covered with *Coctus spectabilis,* the commonest wildflower in Nigeria. Above the design is a red eagle and below a yellow scroll carrying the national motto: "Unity and Faith"
NATIONAL ANTHEM: "Nigeria, We Hail Thee"
NATIONAL HOLIDAYS: October 1 (National Day, Independence Day); January 1 (New Year's Day); December 25–26 (Christmas); Good Friday, Good Saturday and Easter; also variable Islamic festivals
NATIONAL CALENDAR: Gregorian
PHYSICAL QUALITY OF LIFE INDEX: 47
DATE OF INDEPENDENCE: October 1, 1960.
DATE OF CONSTITUTION: October 1, 1979 (suspended in 1983)
WEIGHTS & MEASURES: Metric

GEOGRAPHICAL FEATURES

Nigeria is in West Africa and has a total land area of 923,768 sq. km. (356,668 sq. mi.), extending 1,127 km. (700 mi.) east to west and 1,046 km. (650 mi.) north to south. Its coastline, on the Gulf of Guinea, stretches 774 km. (480 mi.).

Nigeria shares its international border of 4,047 km. (2,513 mi.) with four neighbors: Chad (88 km.; 55 mi.); Cameroon (1,690 km.; 1,050 mi.); Benin (772 km.; 480 mi.); and Niger (1,497 km.; 930 mi.). In the East, Nigeria includes the former U.N. trust territory of the British Cameroons. The borders with Benin, Niger and Chad are based on the Anglo-French treaty of 1898. There Until 1989 are no current border disputes.

Until 1989 the capital was Lagos, with a population of about 1,200,000, but the government recently replaced Lagos as the capital with Abuja in Niger State.

In terms of vegetation, altitude and climate, there are four natural divisions from south to north: the coastal belt of mangrove swamps, about 15 to 95 km. (10 to 60 mi.) wide; the tropical rain forest of undulating plains and scattered hills, about 80 to 160 km. (50 to 100 mi.) wide; the high central plateau of open woodland and savanna, about 600 to 1,800 m. (2,000 to 6,000 ft.) in elevation; and the semidesert in the extreme North. Lowlands predominate except in the central Jos Plateau. The northern semidesert, known as the High Plains of Hausaland, is a broad expanse of

MAJOR CITIES OF NIGERIA*

City	Population
Lagos	1,097,000
Ibadan	1,060,000
Ogbomosho	527,400
Kano	487,100
Oshogbo	344,500
Ilorin	343,900
Abeokuta	308,800
Port Harcourt	296,200
Zaria	274,000
Ilesha	273,400
Onitsha	268,700
Ado-Ekiti	265,800
Iwo	261,600
Kaduna	247,100
Mushin	240,700
Maiduguri	230,900
Enugu	228,400
Ede	221,900
Aba	216,000
Ife	214,500
Ila	189,700
Oyo	185,300
Ikerre-Ekiti	176,800
Benin City	165,900
Iseyin	157,000
Katsina	149,300
Jos	149,000
Sokoto	148,000
Ilobu	143,800
Offa	142,300

*Based on 1983 estimates

sandy plains broken here and there by rocky dome outcrops.

The Niger River, which rises in the mountains to the northeast of Sierra Leone, enters Nigeria from the west and then runs in a southeasterly direction till it receives the waters of its principal tributary, the Benue, at Lokoja, about 547 km. (340 mi.) from the sea. From that point it flows due south to the delta, dividing into numerous interlacing channels to empty itself into the Gulf of Guinea. The Benue, which has its source in Cameroon, flows in a southwesterly direction to its junction with Niger, receiving on its course the waters of the Katsina Ala and Gongola rivers. The other main tributaries of the Niger within Nigeria are the Sokoto, the Kaduna and the Anambra. A second, relatively minor drainage system flows north and east from the central plateau into the Yobe River, which eventually flows into Lake Chad. There are numerous smaller rivers along the coast: the Ogun River in the West, flowing into the Lagos Lagoon; the Benin; the Escravos; the Forcados; the Sombreiro; the Bonny, the last providing an outlet to the sea at Port Harcourt; and the Cross River system, with the Opobo and the Kwa rivers.

The largest lake is the Kainji, in the Northwest.

CLIMATE & WEATHER

Nigeria lies entirely within the tropics, but there are wide climatic variations. In general, there are two seasons, dry and wet, throughout Nigeria, but near the coast the seasons are less sharply defined. Temperatures over 37.8°C (100°F) are common in the North, but coastal temperatures seldom climb over 32.2°C (90°F). The humidity at the coast, however, is higher than in the North. Inland there are two distinct seasons: a wet season from April to October and a dry season from November to March. Temperatures are highest from February to April in the South and from March to June in the North and lowest in July and August over most of the country.

The annual average rainfall varies from 1,700 mm. (70 in.) on the western end of the coast and 4,310 mm. (170 in.) along the eastern section of the coast to 1,270 mm. (50 in.) over most central areas and the Jos Plateau and 500 mm. (20 in.) in the extreme North. The length of the rainy season also shows a similar decrease, from 12 months in the South to under five months in the North. The rain starts in January in the South and progresses gradually inland, and by July, August and September there is rainfall throughout the country. In many parts in the South there is a slight break in the rains for two or three weeks in late July and early August, known as the little dry season. No such break is experienced in the North, where the rains continue uninterruptedly for three to six months. The beginning and the end of the rainy season are marked by thunder and lightning.

The prevailing wind systems are the rain-bearing southwesterlies and the hot and dry harmattan from the northeast.

POPULATION

The population of Nigeria was estimated in 1990 at 118,819,377 on the basis of the last official census, in 1963, when the population was 55,670,055.

The population is unevenly distributed, with the greatest concentrations in the South and the Southwest, followed by the East-Central region and the Kano region. The lowest densities were reported in the Northeast region, the Kwara region and the Northwest region.

DEMOGRAPHIC INDICATORS

Population (millions): 118,819 (1990)
Year of last census: 1963
Sex distribution (% at last census): males, 50.5; females, 49.5
Population estimates and projections (millions)

1950: 33.320	1980: 87.255	2010: 224.314
1960: 42.366	1990: 119.812	
1970: 56.346	2000: 166.012	

Age profile (% at last census)

0–14: 43.0	30–44: 16.5	60–74: 2.5
15–29: 31.9	45–59: 5.1	75 and over: 1.0

Median age (yrs.): 15.8 (1985)
Youth (% age 15–24): 19.0 (1985); 19.5 (2000)
Total dependency ratio: 102.8 (1985)
Annual growth rate (%)

1950–55: 2.38	1975–80: 3.49	2000–2005: 3.21
1955–60: 2.63	1980–85: 3.35	2005–2010: 2.92
1960–65: 2.80	1985–90: 3.43	2010–2015: 2.55
1965–70: 3.24	1990–1995: 3.46	2015–2020: 2.19
1970–75: 3.35	1995–2000: 3.39	2020–2025: 1.89

Hypothetical size of stationary population (millions): 617
Assumed year of reaching net reproduction rate of 1: 2040
Urban population (millions): 29.556 (1985)
Urban population (%): 33 (1988); 17 (1965)
Annual urban population growth rate (%, 1985–90): 5.92
Annual rural population growth rate (%, 1985–90): 2.20
Percentage of urban population in largest city: 17 (1980)
Percentage of urban population in cities of population over 500,000: 58 (1980)
Number of cities of population over 500,000: 3 (1980)
Population density per sq. km. (per sq. mi.): 129.7 (335.9) (latest)

VITAL STATISTICS

Crude birth rate (/1,000): 46 (1990); 51 (1965)
Crude death rate (/1,000): 17 (1990); 23 (1965)
Infant mortality rate (/1,000 live births): 119 (1990)
Maternal mortality rate (/100,000 live births): 1,500 (1980–84 est.)
Life expectancy (yrs.) at birth: males, 48; females, 49 (1990)
Gross reproduction rate (/woman) (1980–85): 3.50
Total fertility rate (/woman): 6.5 (1990)
Rate of natural increase (/1,000): 34.2 (1985–90)
Average household size: 5.0 (latest)

The rate of rural–urban migration has been steadily increasing, as reflected in the growth of the urban component of the population from 11% in 1952 to 16% in 1963, 20% in 1978 and 23% in 1984. The annual rate of urban growth is estimated at 8% to 10%. There are at least 43 cities with populations in excess of 100,000.

There is very little immigration. Emigration, mostly to other African countries, has been discouraged by the manpower policies of neighboring countries.

The status of women in Nigeria involves a complex of economic, legal and social factors. Women are regarded as inferior to men in virtually all fields. Discrimination in employment is common. Benefits and services—travel allowances for dependents, medical benefits and housing allowances, for example—sometimes are denied to women employees. There is no legal recourse to this discrimination because the principle of equal treatment is not enshrined in Nigerian law. Women do not receive equal pay for equal work. Male professionals receive fringe benefits not extended to their female counterparts. Female circumcision, which has never become a major public issue, still is practiced in many areas. Nevertheless, women are neither powerless nor without representation in government, business, the media and education. Women have economic power and exert influence either through women's councils or through their family connections. Women in southern Nigeria are the principal managers of the market economy in the villages. Women have their greatest impact on society in education, culture and youth affairs. Women faculty members are present in many university departments, and women fill many midlevel positions in federal and state ministries of education. There has been a dramatic increase in the number of women with university degrees and in the number who have become professionals, including teacher, lawyers, doctors, judges, senior civil servants, media figures and business executives. The new government has named the first woman vice chancellor of one of the country's universities.

STATUS OF WOMEN INDICATORS

Number of women (millions): 46.040 (1985)
Women of childbearing age (15–49) (% of pop.): 43 (1988)
Women's literacy rate (%): 31.5 (1988)
Women in labor force (%): 35.1 (1988)
Total fertility rate (/woman): 6.5 (1990)

Women are subject to a number of discriminatory legal provisions, which vary from state to state. Although a woman keeps and controls her own wealth after marriage, her husband still is head of the household. Husbands can, for example, prevent their wives from obtaining employment or passports in many states. A woman may be arrested for leaving her husband. Fathers have superior legal authority over children. For example, a woman cannot take her child out of the country without the father's consent, but a father does not require the consent of the mother to do this. In many states a widow is prohibited from inheriting her husband's property, which in the absence of children usually reverts to the husband's family. Property acquired jointly may be taken from the wife and passed to their children or to the husband's family. Husbands are not legally responsible for their wives' debts.

Some official support has been forthcoming for family planning activities, but for other than demographic reasons. A National Population Council was established in 1975 to formulate, implement and coordinate population policies and programs, to advise the government and to secure internal and external assistance for family planning. The Second National Development Plan, 1970–74, called for "opportunities for individual family planning on a voluntary basis."

ETHNIC COMPOSITION

Nigeria is a typical African country in the diversity and heterogeneity of its ethnic heritage. There are an estimated 250 ethnic groups in Nigeria. No group enjoys an absolute numerical majority, but the four dominant groups—the Hausa and Fulani in the North, the Yoruba in the West and the Ibos in the East—constitute 60% of the population. The Hausa comprise the largest single group in the Niger, Sokoto, Kaduna, Bauchi, Borno, Gongola, Kwara, Kano, Benue and Plateau states. The Yoruba predominate in Ogun, Ondo, Oyo and Bendel states. The Ibo, once spread throughout the country, have returned to their former home in the eastern region since the end of the civil war and now predominate in Anambra, Imo and Cross River states. Other important groups include the Kanuri in Bauchi and Borno states, the Edo in Bendel State, the Ibibio in Cross River State, the Ijaw in Rivers and Bendel states, the Tiv in Benue and Plateau states, the Nupe in Niger and Sokoto states, the Efiks in the Eastern region and the Benis in the Midwest. The major non-Negroid peoples are the Fulani, of Mediterranean extraction, who live in the six northern states; and the Shuwa Arabs, who are confined to the Lake Chad area in the extreme Northeast.

Relative to Nigeria's population, the size of the non-African community, estimated at 27,000, is small, but it is fairly diverse and includes Britons, Indians, Lebanese and Americans.

ETHNIC COMPOSITION*

Hausa	21.3%
Yoruba	21.3%
Igbo (Ibo)	18.0%
Fulani	11.2%
Ibibio	5.6%
Kanuri	4.2%
Edo	3.4%
Tiv	2.2%
Ijaw	1.8%
Bura	1.7%
Nupe	1.2%
Other	8.1%

*Based on an unofficial 1983 survey

There was a mass expulsion of foreign citizens in 1985. As in 1983, the government cited illegal employment of aliens and the high crime rate as reasons for the measure. An estimated 700,000 persons were affected, and, according to the Ministry of the Interior, more than half of this number actually left. Nigerian law and practice permit temporary refuge and asylum in Nigeria for political refugees from other countries. Nigeria supports and cooperates with the work of the

Lagos office of the U.N. high commissioner for refugees.

LANGUAGE

English is the official language, as well as that of administration, law, commerce and of education at all levels. It is spoken with varying degrees of fluency by nearly 50% of the population, making Nigeria the largest English-speaking country in black Africa.

Of the 250 vernaculars spoken in the country, Hausa is used most widely as a lingua franca in the north, Yoruba in the west and Igbo in the east. Locally dominant languages tend also to be used officially in the various states.

RELIGION

Nigeria represents the southernmost outpost of the sweep of Islam across the Sahara from the 10th to the 19th centuries, but the penetration was stopped before it reached southern Nigeria. On the other hand, Christianity established itself firmly in the South but made little impact in the North or West. The resulting religious composition of the population closely follows geographic and ethnic lines: the southern Ibo are predominantly Christian, while the northern Hausa are almost entirely Muslim and the western Yoruba are partly Christian and partly Muslim. The six northern states are about two-thirds Muslim; Lagos, Bendel, Ogun, Ondo and Oyo states are almost evenly divided among Christians, Muslims and animists; Imo, Anambra, Cross River and Rivers states are predominantly Christian. Overall, an estimated 45% of Nigerians are Muslim and 38% are Christian, while 11% practice indigenous animist faiths and 6% practice traditional African beliefs. Religious divisions run deep, threatening to destroy the fragile national unity achieved since the end of the civil war.

Of Nigeria's nearly 46 million Christians, 26% are of Protestant faiths and 12% are Roman Catholic, this being the largest single denomination. There are three Roman Catholic archdioceses, at Kaduna, Lagos and Onitsha. The Anglican church is under the archbishop of the Province of West Africa, whose seat is in Freetown, Sierra Leone.

Constitutional provisions of freedom of religion, religious practice and religious education are generally observed throughout the country. Places of worship are established freely. No restrictions are placed on the number of clergy trained in Nigeria. Links with coreligionists in other countries are maintained. Religious travel, including the hajj, is permitted and officially supported. Missionaries and foreign clergy are permitted to enter Nigeria but are not encouraged.

Interreligious marriages occur frequently. Polarization between Christianity and Islam most often occurs where a "religious difference" is associated with geographic or ethnic differences. Islam and Christianity compete for converts and influence throughout much of the country, especially in the belt of states between the predominantly Muslim North and the predominantly Christian South. Religious, economic and tribal differences between Nigeria's oil-rich, mostly Christian and animist southern regions and the poorer but politically dominant Muslim north have led to civil unrest in the past. Southerners have complained that the federal government is controlled by the northern peoples and that it has distributed the nation's wealth unfairly and is trying to make Nigeria into an Islamic state. In 1990, a failed coup attempt was launched by junior officers protesting the domination of Nigeria's Christian south by the Muslim north. Despite this conflict, most non-Muslim/non-Christian religious minority communities live throughout the country in generally peaceful conditions.

HISTORICAL BACKGROUND

The extension of British influence over Nigeria in the 19th century was gradual and, at least initially, unplanned. Official British interest in Nigeria dates from 1849, when John Beecroft was appointed consul and agent for the Bights of Benin and Biafra to gain access to the famous markets of the Sokoto Caliphate and Bornu. The trade routes through Yoruba country were secured through the conquest of Lagos in 1851 and its formal annexation in 1861. Lagos was administered from 1866 to 1874 from Freetown, Sierra Leone, and from 1874 to 1886 from Accra, Ghana (then the Gold Coast); in 1886 Lagos was made a separate territory and placed under a governor. Meanwhile, in 1879 the United African Company was formed by the four largest British firms operating on the Niger. By 1884 the company (renamed the National African Company in 1882) had signed more than 70 treaties with local rulers on both banks of the Niger up to Lokoja. The Berlin Conference of 1884–85, at which Africa was partitioned among European imperial rivals, accepted British claims to areas controlled by the company. In 1886 the company was chartered under the title Royal Niger Company, and its territory became known as the Oil Rivers Protectorate, renamed Niger Coast Protectorate in 1893.

Over the next decade the company met, and suppressed to some extent, strong resistance from local rulers such as the Jojo of Opopo and the Nana of Itshekiriland. In 1899, when it became obvious that the company was not able to bring the emirates under effective rule, the British government revoked its charter and took over the administration of all its territories. Areas south of Idah were constituted as the Protectorate of Southern Nigeria and those north of Idah as the Protectorate of Northern Nigeria, each under a high commissioner. In 1906 the Colony and Protectorate of Lagos was merged with the Protectorate of Southern Nigeria to form the Colony and Protectorate of Southern Nigeria under one governor.

The next step was the merger in 1914 of northern and southern Nigeria into the Colony and Protectorate of Nigeria, with Sir Frederick Lugard as governor general. This amalgamation was one of the most crucial events in Nigerian history, but it still was a limited union; North and South continued with their separate administrations. Lugard introduced throughout the country the system of indirect rule he had successfully begun in the North. Basically this system involved a division of power between the British government, which kept overall responsibility for law and order, and the traditional rulers, who were left to run the day-to-day affairs of the people in accordance with traditional laws and customs. It was a policy of expediency full of contradictions because it discouraged social and economic change where it was needed most. The activities of Christian missionaries were restricted in the North but promoted in the South. The result was to perpetuate the economic and educational disparity between the two regions.

After World War II increasing nationalist pressures resulted in a succession of short-lived constitutions, each bringing the country closer to self-government. As pressure for independence mounted, various nationalist parties competed for influence over the final form of the Constitution. The northern groups wanted a loose federal structure that would give them considerable regional autonomy, while the powerful parties in the southeast and southwest favored less autonomy for the north, although they did not oppose some measure of regional autonomy. In 1959 elections were held for a federal legislature prior to national independence. Not surprisingly, the legislature was split into these three regional blocs. Full independence was achieved on October 1, 1960 and in June 1961, part of British Cameroon was incorporated into Nigeria.

Within two years of independence regional, ethnic and religious tensions were already putting the new Constitution under strain. In January 1966 the army staged a coup, killing many leading politicians including the prime minister and the regional premiers of the north and west. The coup, led by General Ironsi, was seen as having been carried out in the selfish interests of the east where huge oil reserves had recently been discovered. This new military regime was short-lived. Ironsi was killed in a counter-coup in July. Those who carried out the coup named General Gowon, the army chief of staff, the new leader. Gowon had managed to stay out of the previous coup attempts.

General Gowon, a Christian from the middle belt of Nigeria, had succeeded in establishing his authority in the north and west but was rejected in the east where Nigerians followed the lead of Lieutenant Colonel Ojukwu in calling for greater autonomy. Attempts at reconciliation between the two sides failed and in May 1967 Ojukwu announced the formal secession of the east, under the new name "Biafra." From May 1967 until January 1970 Nigeria was plunged into civil war in which thousands perished before the federal forces defeated the Biafran army. Gowon revived constitutional plans for the creation of 12 states out of the three regions and initiated a policy of national reconciliation.

In July 1975 Gowon was toppled in a bloodless coup and replaced by Brigadier Muhammed who was murdered in an abortive coup in February 1976. The new head of the federal military government, General Obasanjo, continued Mohammed's plan for a return to civilian rule and established a further seven states bringing the total to 19.

In December 1983 the army staged a coup, and Major-General Buhari became head of a 19-member Supreme Military Council. He was replaced by Major-General Babangida in an internal military coup in August 1985. Babangida promised a return to civilian rule by 1992 and a civilian constitution which would satisfy the various ethnic, regional and religious demands. In May 1989 Babangida announced the creation of two entirely new parties (the only parties allowed by his government), the Social Democratic Party and the National Republican Convention, situated respectively on the left and on the right of the political spectrum.

In April 1990, a coup attempt led by Major Orkar failed; in July, Babangida ordered the execution of Orkar and 138 participating soldiers. Prior to their executions, the coup leaders publicly expressed their deep fears of north-south rivalries and domination of Christians by Muslims as well as economic discontent in a country where certain groups were seen to have profited while the majority suffered from depressed living standards.

CONSTITUTION & GOVERNMENT

Under the Constitution of 1978, which came into effect in October 1979, the Federal Republic of Nigeria is a federation of 19 states and the Federal Capital Territory. In 1987 two new states were created from existing territory, bringing the total number of states to 21. The executive power of the federation is vested in the president (who is directly elected for a period of four years) and may be exercised either directly or through the vice president, ministers of government or officers in the public service. The president is both head of state and head of government. Both the president and the vice president must obtain a majority of the electoral college votes, including at least one-quarter of the electoral votes in two-thirds of the 21 states. The executive power of a state is vested in its governor (who is directly elected for four years) and may be exercised either directly or through the deputy governor, commissioners of government of that state or officers in the public service; such powers are to be exercised so as not to impede the executive powers of the federation or endanger federal government. The appointment of federal ministers and state commissioners is subject to the approval of the Senate or the State House of Assembly, respectively, and any members of the federal or state legislatures so appointed must resign their seats. There must be at least one federal minister from each state. The president shall not declare war on another country without the consent of both houses of the National Assembly. Without prior approval by the Senate, no member of the armed forces is to take part in combat duty outside Nigeria.

The National Assembly may alter any of the provisions of the Constitution except for the sections regarding creation of new states, boundary alterations and fundamental rights, provided the proposal is sup-

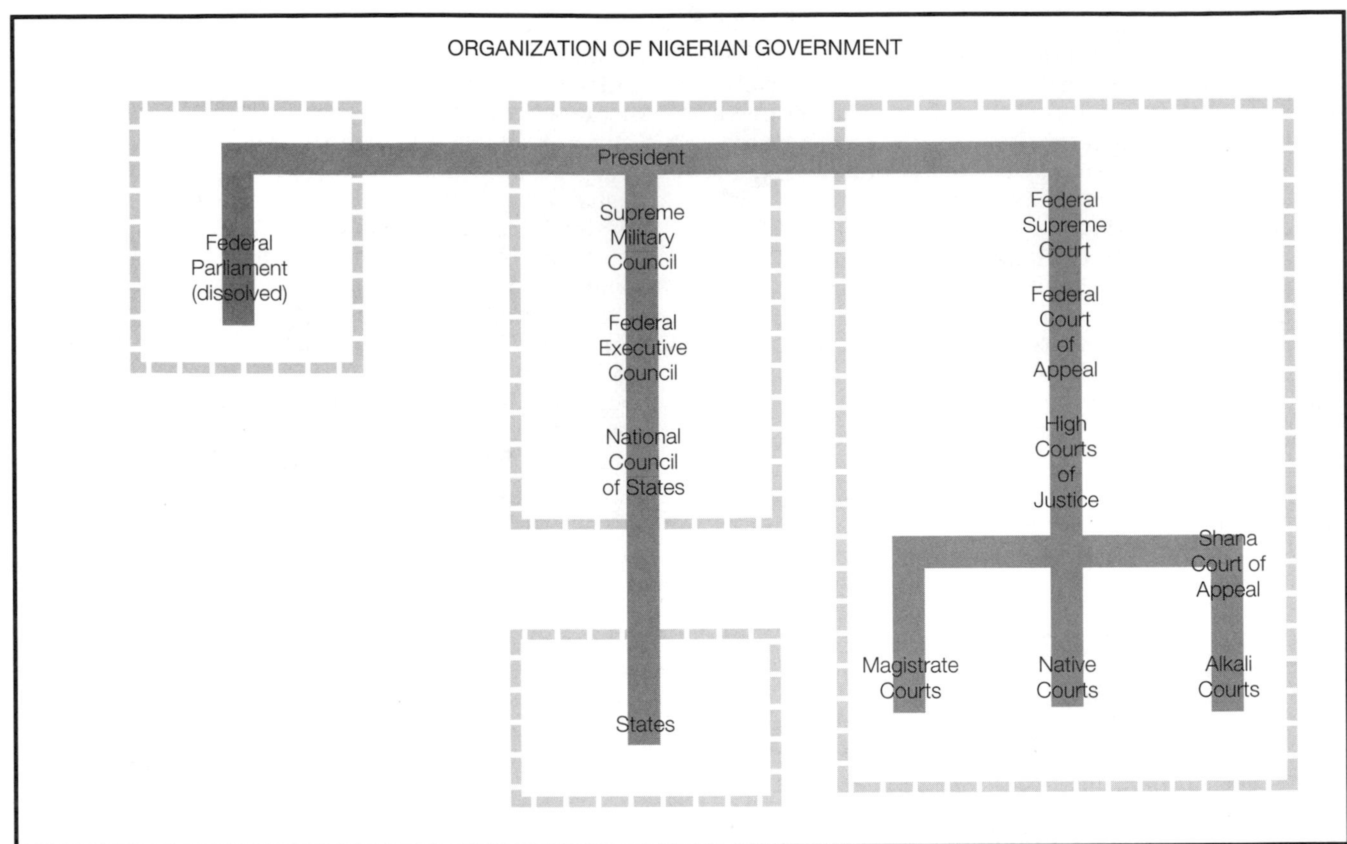

ported by a two-thirds majority in the houses of the National Assembly and by the Houses of Assembly of at least two-thirds of the states.

The government of the federation or of a state shall not adopt any religion as a state religion.

Legislation at both the federal and state levels continues to be promulgated by decrees issued by the AFRC. (The National Assembly was dissolved in 1983.) All decrees are exempt from challenge in the courts, and under the previous military government some decrees had ex post facto effect. The government enforces its authority through the federal security apparatus: the national police, the military and the Nigerian Security Organization (NSO). No separate law enforcement agencies exist at the state and local levels.

The current system of military rule is based on the Constitution (Suspension and Modification) Decree of 1984 and the Amendment Decree of 1985. However, in September 1987, Babangida announced a five-year agenda for a return to civilian government. The schedule calls for promulgation of a new Constitution and lifting of the ban on political parties, elections to unicameral state legislatures, and federal presidential and legislative elections.

Election of local governments was one of the early stages of the procedures decided by the federal government for reestablishing civilian rule in 1992. In 1989, elections for 301 local governments were the first stage in restoring competitive party-electoral processes in the system.

The judicial system operates at both federal and state levels. There is also a system of Muslim law and for limited purposes traditional courts still operate.

Since independence Nigeria has experienced one civil war, resulting in the deaths of nearly 1 million inhabitants; two assassinations of heads of state; two successful coups; and countless abortive coups. The fragility of Nigerian political institutions is directly attributable to the patchwork unity imposed on the country by the British for administrative convenience. However, more recently there has been a maturing of political attitudes, and many Nigerians are beginning to perceive the connection between stability and unity on the one hand and economic prosperity and enhanced international stature on the other. Nonetheless, there remains some unrest among segments of the Christian and Muslim population, as evidenced by a failed coup attempt in 1990. The coup leaders expressed concern over the domination of Christians by

RULERS OF NIGERIA

Presidents (from 1963)

October 1963–January 1966: Benjamin Namdi Azikwe
January–August 1966: Johnson Aguiyi-Ironsi
August 1966–August 1975: Yakubu Gowon
August 1975–July 1976: Murtala Ramat Muhammed
July 1976–October 1979: Olusegun Obasanjo
October 1979–December 1983: Shehu Shagari
January 1984–August 1985: Muhammadu Buhari
August 1985– : Ibrahim Babangida

Prime Ministers (from 1960)

October 1960–January 1966: Sir Alhaji Abu Bakar Tafawa Balewa
January–August 1966: Johnson Aguiye-Ironsi
The Prime ministry was abolished in 1966.

GOVERNMENT LIST
(July/August 1991)

President	Babangida, Ibrahim, *Gen.*
Vice President	Aikhomu, Augustus, *Adm. (Ret.)*
Minister for Special Duties	Abdullahi, Hamza, *Air VMar. (Ret.)*
Minister of Agriculture & Natural Resources	Mustapha, Shetima
Minister of Aviation	Graham-Douglas, Tonye
Minister of Budget & Planning	Okongwu, Chu S.P.O.
Minister of Communications	Ige, Olawele
Minister of Culture & Social Welfare	Gwom, Lamba Dung, *Comdr. (Ret.)*
Minister of Defense	Abacha, Sanni, *Gen.*
Minister of Education	Fafunwa, Oliyu Babatunde
Minister of Employment, Labor & Productivity	Musa, Bunu Sheriff
Minister of External Affairs	Nwachukwu, Ike, *Maj. Gen. (Ret.)*
Minister of Federal Capital Territory	Nasko, Muhammadu Gado, *Maj. Gen. (Ret.)*
Minister of Finance & Economic Development	Alhaji, Alhaji Abubakar
Minister of Health	Ransome-Kuti, Olikoye
Minister of Industries	Yahaya, Mohammed, *Air VMar. (Ret.)*
Minister of Information	Akinyele, Alex
Minister of Internal Affairs	Mamman, Abdulahi, *Maj. Gen. (Ret.)*
Minister of Justice	Ajibola, Bola
Minister of Mines, Power & Steel	Imam, Nura, *Air VMar. (Ret.)*
Minister of Petroleum Resources	Aminu, Jibril
Minister of Science & Technology	Ezekwe, Gordian
Minister of Trade	Ukpaneh, Senas John
Minister of Transport	Ikhazoboh, Anthony A., *Air Comdr. (Ret.)*
Minister of Water Resources	Hashidu, Alhaji Abubakar
Minister of Works & Housing	Kontagora, Mamman, *Maj. Gen. (Ret.)*
Minister of Youth & Sports	Kure, Yohanna, *Maj. Gen. (Ret.)*
Minister of State for External Affairs	Ibrahim, Zakari
Minister of State for Police Affairs	Gwarzo, Ismaila
Governor, Central Bank	Ahmed, Abdulkadir

Muslims, as well as economic disparity between the wealth of the few and the poverty of the masses.

FREEDOM & HUMAN RIGHTS

The 1979 Constitution contained broad human rights guarantees, comparable in scope to those in the most democratic constitutions in the world. The new government moved quickly to demonstrate its commitment to human rights. It repealed a controversial decree that inhibited press freedom; named a panel to review the remaining decrees of the previous government; formed a committee to review the cases of all current and former detainees as well as those previously sentenced by military tribunals; and named a prominent, outspoken human rights advocate as attorney general and minister of justice. Since the coup the government has released approximately 150 persons detained without charges and released or remanded to the criminal court system common criminals detained by the NSO. The once independent judiciary is severely limited by the existence of military and special tribunals created by decree in 1984. In fact, all judges are appointed by the Armed Forces Ruling Council under the current regime.

As many as 5,000 politicians and officeholders in the ousted government—at the federal, state and local levels—were ordered to surrender to the police in January 1985 for interrogation regarding alleged corruption and abuse of office. Most did so, but a few fled the country. No one was exiled. Most of those who reported to the authorities were admonished not to travel outside their home states. Others were held under house arrest, and about 500 were imprisoned. In October 1985 a total of 250 of these detainees were released after investigations failed to incriminate them. Some detainees' bank accounts were frozen, passports confiscated, houses searched and documents and currency seized. Arrests and detentions were covered extensively by the press. The detainees were originally permitted visits by family members but after two or three weeks were held incommunicado.

Special military tribunals have been set up to try persons suspected of corrupt practices or otherwise contributing to the country's economic adversity. Tribunals on corruption are chaired by military officers, with a justice of a federal or state high court as legal adviser. Tribunals established to try cases regarding other crimes, such as currency violations, accusations against public officials, arson, import and export of certain goods, destruction of public property and use or possession of drugs, are chaired by justices of the federal or state high courts but include military and police officers. The investigating police officer may not serve on the tribunal. All tribunal verdicts are subject to review by the Armed Forces Ruling Council, which may confirm, overturn or reduce the penalties. No appeal or other court challenge to the council's final decision is allowed.

Currently human rights are still under threat despite some positive actions by the government.

In 1989, Babangida lifted a ban on political party activity, but he rejected all ensuing applications. Instead he created two entirely new parties, the only two sanctioned by law.

In January 1990, Babangida declared a general amnesty that was expected to lead to the release of thousands of prisoners. The move followed charges by a Nigerian human rights group that scores of inmates had died in 1989 due to overcrowding and disease in the nation's jails. Ordered released were all prisoners who had served three-fourths of their sentences, all those jailed for minor crimes whose terms did not exceed one year, and those sentenced to life who had already served more than 10 years.

In July 1990, Babangida ordered the execution of 42 soldiers convicted by a military tribunal for participating in a failed coup attempt earlier in the year. Despite protests from the U.K. and other Western governments, executions continued into September. At least 138 soldiers in total were executed for involvement in the attempted coup.

CIVIL SERVICE

The civil service, organized on the British model, is under the control of the Public Service Commission, but all appointments to the higher posts are made directly by the Armed Forces Ruling Council. Following complaints of widespread corruption, the civil service was purged in 1975 of a number of key officials. Each department of the civil service is headed by a secretary; ranking next to him are directors of autonomous state boards, agencies and corporations.

LOCAL GOVERNMENT

In 1976 the federal government reorganized local administration by increasing the number of states from 12 to 19. In 1988 two new states were created by division of existing states, bringing the total number of states to 21.

STATES OF NIGERIA

States	Capital
Akwa Ibom	Uyo
Anambra	Enugu
Bauchi	Bauchi
Bendel	Benin City
Benue	Makurdi
Borno	Maiduguri
Cross River	Calabar
Gongola	Yola
Imo	Owerri
Kaduna	Kaduna
Kano	Kano
Katsina	Katsina
Kwara	Ilorin
Lagos	Ikeja
Niger	Minna
Ogun	Abeokuta
Ondo	Akure
Oyo	Ibadan
Plateau	Jos
Rivers	Port-Harcourt
Sokoto	Sokoto

Each military governor is assisted by a cabinet of civilian commissioners. Although governors have some local autonomy, the federal government retains strong administrative control. Election of local governments is an early stage in procedures decided by the federal government for re-establishing civilian rule in 1992. Elections for 301 local governments in 1989 were the first stage in restoring competitive party-electoral processes in the system.

FOREIGN POLICY

As the most populous and the richest nation in black Africa, Nigeria is naturally suited to the role of the continent's spokesman and bellwether. Since the end of the civil war, the country has been strongly asserting itself in both regional and continental affairs; President Jimmy Carter's visit to Lagos in 1978 was an acknowledgment of Nigeria's growing importance. One area of critical concern is South Africa, toward which President Olusegun Obasanjo, following his mentor and predecessor, President Murtala Ramat Muhammed, adopted an increasingly militant posture which has been continued by President Babangida. This militancy marks a significant departure from Nigeria's former policy of moderation and is directly related to its newfound economic independence. Nigeria's opposition to South Africa was a key factor in its support for the Communist-dominated MPLA (Popular Movement for the Liberation of Angola); this support, in turn, proved crucial in securing OAU backing for the MPLA.

On the regional level, Nigeria was the prime mover in negotiations leading to the establishment of the Economic Community of West African States (ECOWAS), which is bound to exert a positive influence on West Africa's economy. Relations are cordial with most neighboring states, even those that recognized Biafra during the civil war. Relations with Zaire have been strained since the expulsion of Nigerian citizens in 1971.

Relations with other neighboring countries were strained after the mass expulsion, in January and February 1983, of more than 2 million illegal immigrants, mostly Ghanaians, as part of austerity measures to protect the sagging Nigerian economy. In April 1983 a dispute over border demarcation led to fighting between Nigerian and Chadian troops stationed at Lake Chad. The border was closed between April and July, but the dispute was eventually settled peacefully by the two governments.

In July 1984 relations between Nigeria and the United Kingdom were adversely affected by the attempted kidnapping in London of Umaru Dikko, formerly minister of transport in the Shagari administration. Dikko, a political exile and outspoken critic of the Buhari regime, was wanted for trial in Nigeria on charges of corruption. The Nigerian High Commission in London was strongly implicated in the kidnapping attempt, and this resulted in the British government's expulsion of two Nigerian diplomats. However, full diplomatic relations with the United Kingdom were restored in 1986.

In June 1988, Nigeria requested the withdrawal of the Italian charge d'affaires after large amounts of toxic waste were dumped at the port of Koko by an Italian vessel using forged documentation. In 1990, Nigeria led a multi-national peacekeeping force into Liberia to intervene in its civil war. It was the first time in modern history that African nations had organized a cooperative military intervention into the affairs of another African state. In 1991, Nigeria was part of a Commonwealth committee that decided to maintain trade and financial sanctions against South Africa pending further steps by the government toward the abolition of apartheid.

Outside Africa, new ties have been established with the Soviet Union and China.

Nigeria and the United States are parties to 15 treaties and other agreements covering aviation, consuls, defense, economic and technical cooperation, extradition, investment guarantees, judicial assistance, mutual security, property, telecommunications, tracking stations and trademarks.

Nigeria joined the United Nations in 1960. It is a member of 16 U.N. organizations and 31 other international organizations.

PARLIAMENT

Until 1983 legislative powers were vested in a bicameral National Assembly for the federation, consisting of a Senate and House of Representatives. All these bodies were directly elected. The Senate contained five members for each state, a total of 95. The House of Representatives consisted of 449 members. The national and state legislatures each sat for not less than 181 days per year, and their maximum duration was four years. If a law enacted by the House of Assembly of a state was inconsistent with one enacted by the National Assembly, the latter prevailed. The exercise of legislative powers by the National Assembly or by the House of Assembly of a state was subject to the jurisdication of courts of law. However, since the suspension of the Constitution in 1983, all federal laws are made by decree of the Armed Forces Ruling Council. State laws are made by the Governor of the state by edict, although federal decrees prevail where there is a conflict.

POLITICAL PARTIES

All political parties were dissolved in 1983 when the military took over the government. In 1989 Babangida lifted the ban on political party activity. A number of parties applied for registration, but Babangida rejected all the applications and formed two new parties: the Social Democratic Party and the National Republican Convention.

These two parties, the only allowed to participate in elections, were created in an effort to reduce tensions between ethnic, regional and religious factions. However, it seems that Christians have been drawn primarily to the Social Democratic Party, which leans to the left, and Muslims to the National Republican Convention, which is more conservative.

ECONOMY

Nigeria is one of the 49 low-income countries of the world, with a free-market economy based on oil and dominated by the private sector.

Nigeria has enormous natural resources that could form the basis for significant development. It is rich in petroleum and natural gas, and hydroelectric power as well as tin, coal and columbite. The leading cash crops are cocoa, cotton, peanuts and palm products. Nevertheless its economic difficulties are similar in kind to those of other African countries: vast developmental needs, mishandled development, ill-managed agriculture and excessive food import dependency, reliance on a limited range of primary product exports the pricing of which is not controlled by the exporting state, chronic budget deficits, large-scale external debt accumulation, and unmanageable debt servicing and repayment.

Nigeria benefited from the oil boom of the 1970s, when oil revenue fueled rapid industrial expansion.

PRINCIPAL ECONOMIC INDICATORS

Gross National Product (U.S. $ billions): 28.314 (1989)
GNP per capita (U.S. $): 250 (1989)
GNP average annual growth rate (%, 1980–89): −0.3
GNP per capita average annual growth rate (%, 1987–89): 1.1
Average annual rate of inflation (%, 1980–88): 11.6
Consumer price index (1980 = 100) 1986
  All items: 249
  Food: 252
Average annual growth rate (%, 1980–88)
  General government consumption: −1.5
  Private consumption: −0.1
  Gross domestic investment: −14.5

BALANCE OF PAYMENTS, 1988
(U.S. $ millions)

Current account balance: −966
Merchandise exports: 7,297
Merchandise imports: −4,895
Trade balance: 2,402
Other goods, services & income +: 374
Other goods, services & income −: −3,731
Other goods, services & income net: −3,357
Private unrequited transfers: −33
Official unrequited transfers: 21
Capital other than reserves: −3,882
Net errors & omissions: −64
Counterpart items: −77
Total change in reserves: 514

GROSS DOMESTIC PRODUCT

GDP nominal (N billions): 158.271 (1989)
Average annual growth rate of GDP (%, 1980–88): −1.1
GDP by type of expenditure (%) 1987
  Consumption
    Private: 72
    Government: 6
  Gross domestic investment: 10
  Gross domestic savings: 15 (1988)
  Foreign trade
    Exports: 26
    Imports: −14
Cost components of GDP (%) 1983
    Net indirect taxes: 4
    Consumption of fixed capital: 2
    Compensation of employees: 29
    Net operating surplus: 65
Sectoral origin of GDP (%) 1985
  Primary
    Agriculture: 37
    Mining: 20
  Secondary
    Manufacturing: 6
    Construction: 3
    Public utilities: 1
  Tertiary
    Transportation & communications: 3
    Trade: 19
    Finance: 2
    Other services: 4
    Government: 4
Average annual sectoral growth rates (%, 1980–88)
    Agriculture: 1.0
    Industry: −3.2
    Manufacturing: −2.9
    Services: −0.4

However, the drop in oil prices during the early 1980s precipitated an economic decline. Industrial development slowed and the government was forced to cut back on spending and institute a stringent Structural Adjustment Program that focused on reviving exports other than petroleum, achieving a realistic exchange rate for the naira and discouraging the purchase of luxury goods.

PUBLIC FINANCE

The Nigerian fiscal year runs from January 1 to December 31. The federal government is responsible for the collection of taxes on income and property, as well as import and export taxes and excise duties. A fixed portion of these revenues is redistributed to the state governments. Revenue is derived primarily from petroleum profit taxation and import duties. Debt service and capital expenses comprise major expenditures; others include education, defense, police and health.

CENTRAL GOVERNMENT EXPENDITURES (latest)

% of total expenditures
- Defense: 2.8
- Education: 2.8
- Health: 0.8
- Housing, social security, welfare: 1.5
- Economic services: 35.9
- Other: 56.2

Total expenditures as % of GNP: 27.8 (1988)
Overall surplus or deficit as % of GNP: −10.3 (1988)

CENTRAL GOVERNMENT REVENUES (latest)

% of total current revenues
- Taxes on income, profit & capital gain: 39.9
- Social security contributions: 0.0
- Domestic taxes on goods & services: 5.1
- Taxes on international trade & transactions: 6.6
- Other taxes: −14.5
- Current nontax revenue: 62.9

Total current revenue as % of GNP: 18.5 (latest)
General government consumption as % of GDP: 12 (1988)
Average annual growth rate of general government consumption (%, 1980–88): −1.5

Economic planning began soon after World War II, under the auspices of the United Kingdom Colonial Development and Welfare Act. The impetus was continued after independence with a series of plans that aimed at developing each area of the country at a similar rate. Early plans emphasized improving industry, agriculture and education. The government launched two development plans in the late 1970s and early 1980s that aimed at creating the economic and social infrastructure for self-sustained growth. Priority was given to agriculture, housing, industry, health, energy and communications. Both plans were scaled down as a result of a sharp decline in earnings from petroleum exports. In the last half of the 1980s, Nigeria instituted austerity measures in return for international aid.

Nigeria received substantial amounts of foreign aid, particularly in the form of grants, until the early 1970s when oil revenues reduced the need for assistance. The country again became a recipient of aid following the steep decline in petroleum prices in the 1980s. From 1970–88 Nigeria received $662 million in U.S. commitments, including Ex-Im. Aid from other Western nations and ODA and OOF bilateral commitments totalled $1.9 billion from 1970–87. Communist countries committed $2.2 billion in assistance from 1970 to 1988.

FOREIGN AID, 1989

Total foreign aid (U.S. $ millions): 2,578.3
- Bilateral: 1,733.6
- Multilateral: 844.7

CURRENCY & BANKING

The Nigerian unit of currency is the naira, divided into 100 kobo. Coins are issued in denominations of ½, 1, 5, 10 and 25 kobo; notes are issued in denominations of 50 kobo and 1, 5, 10 and 20 naira.

The naira was introduced in 1973 to replace the Nigerian pound. In June 1991, the dollar rate was U.S. $1 = N12.61.

The banking system is headed by the Central Bank of Nigeria, which also is the bank of issue. The Central Bank regulates commercial domestic banking, but foreign banking is controlled by the Ministry of Finance. The principal source of development finance is the Nigerian Industrial Development Bank, with a paid-up capital of N198.5 million (1986). Under the indigenization decree of 1976, all foreign-owned banks are required to have 60% Nigerian ownership.

GROWTH PROFILE
(Annual Growth Rates, %)

Projected population (1988–2000): 3.1
Projected crude birth rate (/1,000) (1990–95): 48.7
Projected crude death rate (/1,000) (1990–95): 14.2
Urban population (1980–88): 6.3
Labor force (1985–2000): 2.6
GNP (1980–89): −0.3
GNP per capita (1987–89): 1.1
GDP (1980–88): −1.1
Inflation (1980–88): 11.6
Agriculture (1980–88): 1.0
Industry (1980–88): −3.2
Manufacturing (1980–88): −2.9
Services (1980–88): −0.4
Money holdings (1980–88): 11.9
Manufacturing earnings per employee: −9.6 (latest)
Energy production (1980–88): −1.4
Energy consumption (1980–88): 6.6
Exports (1980–88): −3.6
Imports (1980–88): −13.7
General government consumption (1980–88): −1.5
Private consumption (1980–88): −0.1
Gross domestic investment (1980–88): −14.5

FINANCIAL INDICATORS, 1989

Total reserves minus gold (SDRs billions): 1.344
SDRs (millions): 0
Reserve position in IMF (SDRs millions): 446 (1981)
Foreign exchange (SDRs billions): 1.343
Gold (fine troy oz. millions): .69
Ratio of external debt to total reserves: 41.9 (1988)
Central bank 1989
  Assets (%)
    Foreign assets: 23.3
    Claims on government: 61.6
    Claims on banks: 10.7
    Claims on private sector: 4.5
  Liabilities (%)
    Reserve money: 38.2
    Government deposits: 36.5
    Foreign liabilities: 0.1
    Capital accounts: 3.8
Money supply 1989
  Stock (£N billions): 21.446
  M1 per capita: 190
Private banks 1989
  Assets (%)
    Loans to government: 19.0
    Loans to private sector: 57.3
    Reserves: 6.4
    Foreign assets: 17.4
  Liabilities
    Deposits (£N. billions): 43.141
    of which %
      Demand deposits: 22.6
      Savings deposits: 38.7
      Government deposits: 1.7
      Foreign liabilities: 2.0
External debt 1988
  Total (U.S. $ billions): 30.718
    of which public (U.S. $ billions): 28.630
    of which private (U.S. $ millions): 337
  Debt service (long-term)
    Total (U.S. $ billions): 1.869
    Repayment
      Principal (%): 25.8
      Interest (%): 74.2
  Debt service ratio (%): 24.2
  External public debt as % of GNP: 101.3
  Debt service as % of GNP: 6.6
  Debt service as % of exports: 24.2
  Terms of public borrowing
    Commitments (U.S. $ billions): 1.461
    Average interest rate (%): 7.6
    Average maturity (yrs.): 16
  Net flow of publicly guaranteed external capital (U.S. $ millions): 209
  Receipt of workers' remittances (U.S. $ millions): −34
  Net direct private investment (U.S. $ millions): 836

AGRICULTURE

Of the total land area of 92,376,800 ha. (228,263,070 ac.), 51% is classified as agricultural land or 0.8 ha. (2 ac.) per capita. Agriculture employs nearly 60% of the labor force and contributes 34% of the GDP.

Agricultural holdings generally are small and scattered; the peasant mode of production is characterized by simple tools and shifting, or the bush fallow system of cultivation. Large-scale cultivation is primarily in the form of plantations owned by private native or expatriate interest and public authorities.

The area under actual cultivation, estimated at 17%, has shown only a small increase since 1970. Land use patterns vary; the main products are yams, cassava and plantains in the South and corn, sorghum, rice, millet and cowpeas in the North. The country is not self-sufficient in food. In 1976 the military government introduced an emergency program called "Operation Feed the Nation" to increase food production.

Perhaps the only thing common to all the peoples who inhabit Nigeria is communal ownership of land and the absence of any conception of individual property. Under this system, use of land is granted by the chiefs or elders of the tribe and can be taken from the grantee at any time if he fails to cultivate it. According to customary law, land is inalienable; the sale of land is considered a crime. Freehold land outside this system exists only in the case of large plantations and corporations.

Although successive governments have recognized the need to cut the substantial food imports and to revitalize agriculture, the farming sector is still underfunded. Major projects have been launched to increase wheat and rice production, but to no great effect. The

AGRICULTURAL INDICATORS

Agriculture's share of GDP (%): 34 (1988)
Average annual growth rate (%, 1980–88): 1.0
Value added in agriculture (U.S. $ billions): 10.105 (1988)
Cereal imports (000 metric tons): 333 (1988)
Index of food production (1979–81 = 100): 128 (1986)
Index of food production per capita (1979–81 = 100): 103 (1986–88)
Number of tractors: 10,500 (1986)
Total fertilizer consumption (000 metric tons): 316 (1985–86)
Fertilizer consumption (g./ha., hundreds): 94 (1987–88)
Size class (%) 1971
  Below 1 ha. (below 2.47 ac.): 92
  1–5 ha. (2.47–12.35 ac.): 7.8
  5–10 ha. (12.35–24.7 ac.): 0.2
  10–20 ha. (24.7–49.4 ac.): 0.0
  20–50 ha. (49.4–123.5 ac.): 0.0
  50–200 ha. (123.5–494 ac.): 0.0
  Over 200 ha. (over 494 ac.): 0.0
Farms as % of total land area: 37.1 (1971)
Land use (%)
  Cropland: 34
  Pasture: 23
  Forest: 16
  Other: 27
Yields (kg./ha.) 1989
  Grains: 1,132
  Roots & tubers: 10,905
  Legumes: 731
  Milk (kg./animal): 295
Production 1989
  Fruits (million metric tons): 3.200
  Vegetables (million metric tons): 3.946
Livestock (millions) 1989
  Cattle: 12.200
  Horses: .250 (1986)
  Sheep: 13.200
  Pigs: 1.300
Forestry 1988
  Production of roundwood (million cubic meters): 104.881
    of which industrial roundwood (%): 7.5
  Value of exports (U.S. $ millions): 6.091
Fishing 1988
  Total catch (000 metric tons): 261.1
    of which marine (%): 60.4
  Value of exports (U.S. $ millions): 13.100

major problem is a combination of the failure of the peasants to produce enough food for the rapidly growing urban population and the failure of economic planners to improve producer prices and distribution of crops.

Major irrigation projects have been launched to bring more land into use, but little headway has been made. Generally, government policies have favored large landowners and major agricultural companies over the important small farmers.

Livestock-raising is restricted primarily to the North because of the prevalence of the tsetse fly in other areas. Almost one-fourth of the national herd of 12 million cattle is owned by the nomadic Fulani and Hausa. Humped breeds predominate in the North and shorthorns in the South. An estimated 1 million cattle and 2 million goats are slaughtered annually under supervision of the Livestock and Meat Authority.

Nearly one-third of the national territory is classified as forest lands, mainly in Ogun, Ondo and Oyo states in the West. About 30 species are commercially exploited, of which the obeche is the most valuable.

Most fishing is carried on in Lake Chad and in the numerous creeks and lagoons.

Agricultural credit is provided by the Nigerian Agricultural Bank.

MANUFACTURING

The contribution of the manufacturing sector to the GDP is small, at 6%, but it has maintained a consistently high annual growth rate. This sector still is dominated by first-generation light industries of the import-substitution variety, but the third development plan, 1975–80, envisaged the country's entry into a rapid phase of industrialization, with an emphasis on heavy industries such as iron and steel and petrochemicals as well as on consumer durables such as automobiles. Major industrial projects in the plan included three new oil refineries, an iron and steel complex with a rated capacity of 1 million to 2 million tons annually, two liquified natural-gas plants, three sugar refineries, two pulp and paper mills and three new cement plants. The textile industry, currently the largest, plans to begin the manufacture of synthetic fiber textiles. Since 1978 Leyland, Peugeot, Volkswagen, Fiat and Daimler-Benz have established assembly plants in the country. A major iron and steel complex at Ajaokuta, built with assistance from the USSR and France, was due to become fully operational in 1991.

Apart from agriculture, the government sees manufacturing as offering the greatest prospects for rapid development and transformation of the economy and placed high priority on developing this sector during the fourth development plan period (1981–1985). A total of $15.2 billion was allocated to the public sector program in this area. Approximately $9.7 billion supported federal government participation in already identified areas such as the iron and steel industry, and the production of nitrogenous fertilizers. Approximately $1.2 billion was for the Nigerian Industrial Development Bank and the Nigerian Bank for Commerce and Industry to help make more financing available to private-sector enterprises. The remaining funds were allocated to state and local governments, some of which have substantial industrial programs. Among the important branches of industry are brewing, aluminum products, motor vehicles, textiles, cigarettes, footwear, pharmaceuticals, pulp and paper, and cement.

MANUFACTURING INDICATORS, 1970

Average annual growth rate (%): −2.9 (latest)
Share of GDP (%): 18 (1988)
Labor force economically active in manufacturing (% est.): 18.2 (1985)
Value added in manufacturing (U.S. $ billions): 5.196 (latest)
  Food & tobacco (%): 36 (1970)
  Textiles & clothing (%): 26
  Machinery & transport equipment (%): 1
  Chemicals (%): 6
Earnings per employee in manufacturing 1987
  Growth rate (%): −9.6 (latest)
Total earnings as % of value added: 18
Gross output per employee (1980 = 100): 105

A number of industrial estates have been established in various parts of the country. That at Lagos has more than 450 factories. Other estates are in Ikeja and Mushin, both suburbs of Lagos; Kano; Kaduna; Jos; and the Trans-Amadi Industrial Area, just outside Port Harcourt.

Both federal and state governments welcome foreign investment and provide a wide array of incentives, including help in locating sites, tax holidays, protection from imports, export rebates and duty-free raw materials.

The Nigerian Enterprises Promotion Decree of 1977 places limitations on the share of foreign equity permitted in Nigerian firms, bars alien participation in certain types of industries and makes "indigenization" mandatory. The decree has three schedules: Schedule I contains 40 categories of business reserved exclusively for Nigerians; Schedule II contains 56 categories of businesses that must have at least 60% participation by Nigerians, including banking, construction and mining; and Schedule III requires at least 40% ownership by Nigerian nationals and covers all industries not specified in the first two schedules. Strict penalties oppose the sale of ownership to a Nigerian "front man" to conceal continued alien control. Nigerian officials point out that at least 70% of vital economic sectors still are in the hands of foreigners, and the decree is designed to enable Nigerian nationals to recapture "the commanding heights of the economy."

MINING

Nigeria is well endowed with mineral resources, including gold in the West, tin in the North, coal in the East and lead and zinc in the Midwest. Nigeria also produces 90% of the world's supply of columbite. Reserves of iron ore estimated at 86–105 million tons have been discovered at Itakpe in Kwara State. Nigeria ranks sixth among the producers of tin and belongs to the International Tin Council. Almost all the tin ore is smelted locally by the Makeri Smelting Company at Jos.

ENERGY

With proved reserves of 16.700 billion bbl., enough to last for 27 years at current rates of extraction, Nigeria is one of the world's largest producers of oil. The production of crude petroleum, first discovered in 1956, has transformed the economy and now accounts for 95% of the total value of exports.

ENERGY INDICATORS

Average annual energy production growth rate (%, 1980–88): −1.4
Energy consumption per capita (kg. oil equivalent): 150 (1988)
Energy imports as % of merchandise exports: 2 (1988)
Average annual growth rate of energy consumption (%, 1980–88): 6.6
Electricity 1988
- Installed capacity (millions kw.): 4.040
- Production (billion kw.-hr.): 9.925
  - % fossil fuel: 77.7
  - % hydro: 22.3
  - % nuclear: 0.0
- Consumption per capita (kw.-hr.): 93

Natural gas
- Proved reserves (trillion cu. m.): 2.476 (1990)
- Production (billion cu. m.): 4.700 (1989)
- Consumption (billion cu. m.): 3.665 (1988)

Petroleum
- Proved reserves (billion bbl.): 16.700 (1990)
- Years to exhaust proved reserves: 27 (1990)
- Production (million bbl.): 586 (1989)
- Consumption (million bbl.): 50 (1988)
- Refining capacity (000 bbl./day): 408 (1990)

Coal
- Reserves (million metric tons): 190 (latest)
- Production (000 metric tons): 135 (1988)
- Consumption (000 metric tons): 95 (1988)

Exploration and production are carried out mainly in the southern part of the country, in Rivers, Cross River, Imo, Anambra and Bendel states. Offshore wells are near Port Harcourt. Shell-BP is responsible for two-thirds of the production, but 14 other companies are in the field, including Nigerian Gulf Oil, Mobil, Texaco, Agip-Phillips, Ashland, Occidental and Japan Petroleum. Negotiations in 1974 led to a government majority shareholding in Shell-BP, Agip-Phillips, Safrap, Mobil and Texaco. Compensation was granted through buy-back rights to 50% of production with an option of a further 25%. In 1977 the Nigerian National Oil Corporation and the Federal Ministry of Petroleum were merged to form the National Petroleum Corporation.

Production costs of Nigerian oil are from three to seven times higher than those in the Middle East, but Nigerian oil has an exceptionally low sulfur content. There was a sharp cutback in the production of oil beginning in 1975 as a result of world recession and slack demand. The United States takes more than 30% of Nigerian oil and is the largest customer. A petrochemicals plant, to be built at Alesa Eleme at a cost of $2 billion, was due for completion in the early 1990s. The plant should make Nigeria self-sufficient in raw plastic products.

There are plans to build two gas liquefaction plants, each with a rated daily capacity of 28.6 million cu. m. (1 billion cu. ft.).

There are oil refineries at Port Harcourt, Warri, Kaduna and Alesa Eleme.

LABOR

The 1974 Labor Decree forbids industrial and commercial employment of children under 15 and restricts other child labor to home-based agricultural or domestic work. The decree also provides a number of special health and safety provisions to protect young and female workers, in addition to general provisions with respect to hours of work and occupational health and safety. It allows the apprenticeship of youths 13 to 15 under specified conditions, including a written contract approved by a government labor officer.

LABOR INDICATORS, 1986

Total economically active population (millions): 29.974
- % working-age (15–64): 55.7
- % female: 32.2

Activity rate (%)
- Total: 30.3
- Male: 40.7
- Female: 19.7

Employment status (%)
- Employers & self-employed: 65.4
- Employees: 18.2
- Unpaid family workers: 10.0
- Other: 6.5

Sectoral employment of economically active (%)
- Agriculture, forestry, fishing: 44.6
- Construction: 1.7
- Manufacturing, mining, quarrying, public utilities: 4.5
- Trade, hotels, restaurants: 23.3
- Transportation, communications: 3.6
- Finance, real estate: 0.3
- Services: 14.3

Average annual growth rate of labor force (%, 1985–2000): 2.6
Unemployment (000): 57 (1987)
Labor under 20 years (%): 9.7 (1983)
Earnings in manufacturing (/worker) (/day) (£N.): 4.30 (1980)

Normal working hours in commerce and industry are 40 hours weekly, with two to four weeks' annual leave. Nigeria's minimum hourly wage for commerce and industry is one of the highest in Africa. Employers must compensate injured workers and dependent survivors of those fatally injured in industrial accidents. The 1974 Labor Decree and the Factories Act provide for government establishment and enforcement of occupational health and safety standards under the Ministry of Employment, Labor and Productivity.

There is no general minimum wage law, but the state governments have established uniform rates for general laborers, and the federal government can set minimum standards in any sector where prevailing rates are deemed particularly low.

Over and above the minimum wage, civil servants also are paid a minimum N25 per month housing and transportation allowance, a fringe benefit that most private employers also provide. Firms that do not have their own retirement plans are required to make modest monthly contributions to the National Provident Fund for their employees, and employers with more than 500 workers also are required to provide housing near the place of work.

There are 42 recognized trade unions, all of which come under a single national labor federation, the Nigerian Labor Congress. Although numerous and fairly active, labor unions wield very little political or economic influence. More than 3,500,000 wage earners belong to trade unions. All Nigerian workers 16 years or older may join trade unions, except members of the armed forces and designated employees of essential government services at the federal, state and local levels. Employers are obliged to recognize trade unions and, since 1978, must pay a dues checkoff for employees who are members of a registered trade union. The establishment of closed shops is prohibited.

Nigerian law and practice generally provide that the terms and conditions of labor will be determined by collective bargaining agreements between management and trade unions. However, in 1984 the government imposed a national wage freeze and virtually ordered the NLC trade unions to suspend collective bargaining.

The number of foreign workers in Nigeria is small. Due to the depressed economy and in an effort to end economic waste, the government expelled nearly 3 million illegal aliens—most of them from Ghana—between 1983 and 1985.

In 1976 the government promulgated the Labor Disputes Decree, setting forth procedures for settling labor disputes. Should these procedures fail, the next step is to report the dispute to the labor commissioner, who may appoint a conciliator to try to mediate the dispute. If this also fails, the dispute is then referred to the Industrial Arbitration Panel, which names an arbitration tribunal consisting of a single arbitrator, who may be assisted by assessors. If the dispute still is unresolved, it can be referred to the National Industrial Court (NIC), the highest body adjudicating labor disputes. Parties to a dispute may be represented by lawyers; an NIC decision is final and not subject to appeal.

Strikes and lockouts are forbidden while disputes are under consideration by these bodies. In theory this means that most strikes are illegal, but in practice government intervention has varied widely.

FOREIGN COMMERCE

Crude oil exports consistently provide well over 90% of Nigeria's earnings overseas. In 1989, these exports brought in 95% of earnings. Other exports included cocoa, palm kernels, rubber and cashew nuts. Major export destinations were the U.S., Spain, Germany, France and the Netherlands.

Major imports in 1989 included machinery and transport equipment, chemicals, manufactured goods and food. Major import sources were the U.K., Germany, France, the U.S., Japan and Italy. Although oil is an extremely rich resource for development, import and debt servicing requirements, it is one that is vulnerable to international market conditions. These have proved, both in terms of demand and price, to be volatile and not wholly protected against by Nigeria's participation in the supply and price control arrangements made by OPEC.

Foreign trade imbalances have been held down by progressive restraints on imports since the early 1980s, largely by import levies and exchange limitations.

FOREIGN TRADE INDICATORS, 1988

Exports (U.S. $ billions): 8.4 (1989)
Imports (U.S. $ billions): 5.7 (1989)
Balance of trade (U.S. $ millions): 2.7 (1989)
Annual growth rate (1980–88), exports (%): −3.6
Annual growth rate (1980–88), imports (%): −13.7
International reserves in terms of months of imports covered: 1.3
Terms of trade (1980 = 100): 40
Import price index (1980 = 100): 103.8 (1986)
Export price index (1980 = 100): 46.1 (1986)

Direction of Trade (%), 1987

	Imports	Exports
European community	56.4	41.4
United States	8.3	47.0
U.S.S.R. & eastern European economies	5.0	0.0
Japan	9.0	0.1

Composition of Trade (%), 1987

	Imports	Exports
Food & agricultural raw materials	12.8	3.7
Fuels & other energy	0.4	95.4
Mineral ores & concentrates	2.7	0.0
Manufactured goods	84.1	0.9
of which chemicals	16.9	0.2
of which machinery	38.2	0.0

Nigeria is a founding member of the Economic Community of West African States (ECOWAS), designed as an African answer to the European Economic Community. An international fair is held annually at Lagos.

TRANSPORTATION & COMMUNICATIONS

The Nigerian rail system, operated by the state-owned Nigerian Railway Corporation, consists of 3,505 km. (2,178 mi.) of single track to two north-to-south lines. The western line runs northeast from Lagos through Ibadan, Jebba and Kaduna to Kano, while the eastern line runs from Port Harcourt through Enugu and Makurdi to join the western line at Kaduna. A recent extension links Kafanchan to Maidugiri. Services are generally slow and inefficient.

Because the oil fields are relatively close to the coast, the pipelines are short: 1,207 km. (749 mi.) for crude oil, 97 km. (60 mi.) for natural gas and 5 km. (3 mi.) for refined products.

Navigable inland waterways total 8,575 km. (5,328 mi.), mainly the Niger and the Benue rivers, but river transportation is restricted by difficulties of access to the delta ports.

Nigeria's principal ports are Lagos-Apapa, Tin Can Island (near Lagos), the Delta Port complex (including Warri, Koko, Burutu and Sapele ports), Port Harcourt and Calabar. The main petroleum ports are Bonny and Burutu.

The merchant marine consists of 35 ships of 1,000 GRT or over.

The length of the road network is 124,000 km. (77,054 mi.). The Trans-Africa Highway links Lagos with Mombasa in Kenya.

TRANSPORTATION INDICATORS

Roads (pre-1986)
- Length, km. (mi.): 124,000 (77,054)
- Paved (%): 48

Motor vehicles (pre-1986)
- Automobiles: 262,550
- Trucks and buses: 90,731
- Persons per vehicle: 241

Railroads (latest)
- Track, km. (mi.): 3,505 (2,178)
- Passenger-km. (passenger-mi.) (billions): 3.808 (2.366)
- Freight, metric ton-km. (short ton-mi.) (millions): 827.4 (566.7)

Merchant marine
- Vessels (over 100 tons): 242 (1989)
- Total deadweight tonnage (000): 736.9 (1989)
- Oil tankers (000 GRT): 154 (1985)

Ports (pre-1986)
- Cargo loaded (million metric tons): 62.830
- Cargo unloaded (million metric tons): 11.490

Air
- Km. (mi.) flown (millions): 36.5 (22.7) (1985)
- Passenger-km. (passenger-mi.) (billions): 1.140 (0.708) (latest)
- Freight, metric ton-km. (short ton-mi.) (millions): 30.9 (21.2) (latest)
- Mail, metric ton-km. (short ton-mi.) (millions): 1.2 (0.8) (1985)
- Airports with scheduled flights: 13 (1990)

Pipelines 1990
- Refined, km. (mi.): 3,000 (1,864)
- Natural gas, km. (mi.): 500 (311)

Inland waterways (latest)
- Length, km. (mi.): 8,575 (5,328)

The national airline is the government-owned Nigerian Airways, which operates a fleet of 72 aircraft (including three Boeing 707s) on scheduled domestic services as well as international services to eight European cities, seven African cities, Beirut and New York. There are 87 airports and airfields in the country, of which 83 are usable, 29 have permanent-surface runways and 14 have runways over 2,500 m. (8,000 ft.) The largest international airport, at Lagos, is Murtala Muhammed International Airport (formerly Ikeja Airport, renamed in 1976). Nigeria has an above average telecommunications system although it is limited by poor maintenance. The federal government controls broadcasting through the Federal Radio Corporation of Nigeria and the Nigerian Television Authority. Nigeria has 2 Atlantic Ocean INTELSATs, 1 Indian Ocean INTELSAT and 1 coaxial submarine cable.

COMMUNICATION INDICATORS, 1988

Telephones 1986
- Total (000): 265
- Persons per telephone: 397

Phone traffic (million calls) 1985
- Local: 86.947 (pulses)
- Long distance: 1.140
- International: 25.257 (minutes)

Post office
- Number of post offices: 3,479
- Pieces of mail handled (millions): 476.971

Telegraph 1985
- Total traffic (000 calls): 484
  - National: 431
  - International: 53

Telex 1985
- Subscriber lines: 4,848

Telecommunications 1990
- Satellite stations: 22
- Coaxial submarine cables: 1

TOURISM & TRAVEL INDICATORS, 1986

Total tourist receipts (U.S. $ millions): 78 (1988)
Expenditures by nationals abroad (U.S. $ millions): 39 (1988)
Number of hotel beds: 45,000

DEFENSE

The defense structure is headed by the president in his capacity as chairman of the Armed Forces Ruling Council. The chiefs of staff of the three services are represented on the council. The chain of command runs through a general staff, after the British model. The army is organized into four numbered divisions, the first at Kaduna, the second at Ibadau, the third at Jos and the fourth at Lagos.

The armed forces consist entirely of volunteers; there is no conscription. Reserves have been planned but at present there are none organized.

Total strength of the armed forces is 94,500.

Army

Personnel: 80,050

Organization: 1 armored division; 1 composite division, including 1 airborne, 1 air portable and 1 amphibious brigade; 2 mechanized divisions; 4 artillery brigades; 4 engineer brigades, 4 reconnaissance brigades; 1 guards brigade

Equipment: 76 heavy tanks; 50 light tanks; 165 armored vehicles; 46 armored personnel carriers; 230 guns; 200 howitzers; 200 mortars; rocket launchers; 90 air defense guns; SAM

Navy

Personnel: 5,000

Units: 2 naval commands; 2 frigates; 4 corvettes; 6 fast attack craft; 9 patrol craft; 4 amphibious craft; 3 helicopters; 80 small patrol launches

Naval bases: Lagos and Calabar

Air Force

Personnel: 9,450

Organization: 49 combat aircraft; 3 fighter squadrons; 1 search and rescue squadron; 2 transport squadrons; 3 support squadrons; 22 helicopters; 43 trainers; antiaircraft missiles; 1 Boeing 727

Air bases: Lagos, Kaduna, Ikeja, Maiduguri and Kano

The Nigerian armed forces are the largest and the best-trained in West Africa. The army has been completely modernized, and military expenditures have risen sharply in recent years, reflecting substantial arms purchases. The navy is the weakest service, but the air force, with 17 MiG-15s and 14 MiG-17s, has adequate strike power. Since 1980 the federal military government has reduced the strength of the armed forces from 146,000 to 94,500.

Between independence and the civil war, Nigeria received military aid from the United Kingdom, the United States, France, West Germany and the Netherlands. The level of external military aid fell sharply during the civil war.

Nigeria has no internal defense production.

EDUCATION

The national literacy rate is 42.4%.

Nigeria introduced free, universal and compulsory education under the third development plan, 1975–80, for six years, from ages six to 12. Schooling lasts for 13 years, divided into six years of primary school, five years of lower secondary school and two years of upper secondary school.

The school year runs from September to June. In primary schools the language of instruction is the local vernacular for the first two years, but thereafter instruction is in English.

Next to the shortage of schools, the shortage of trained teachers is the most serious educational problem.

Technical education is provided in technical institutes, trade centers and handicraft centers; the most notable of technical education centers is Yaba Technical Institute, which provides training in a variety of vocational subjects.

Although primary education is free throughout the country, the commitment to universal free education has been modified, with almost all states imposing some fees on secondary students. In 1989, there were 23 federal and 9 state universities.

Primary and secondary education falls within the jurisdiction of the state governments, while the federal government controls the universities and is responsible for educational policy.

GRADUATES, 1981

Total: 17,215
Education: 4,495
Humanities & religion: 2,746
Fine & applied arts: 0
Law: 727
Social & behavioral sciences: 2,800
Commerce & business: 1,291
Mass communication: 0
Home economics: 0
Service trades: 0
Natural sciences: 1,889
Mathematics & computer science: 0
Medicine: 1,157
Engineering: 841
Architecture: 460
Industrial programs: 0
Transportation & communications: 0
Agriculture, forestry, fisheries: 809
Other: 0

EDUCATION INDICATORS, 1988

Literacy
- Total (%): 42.4
- Male (%): 53.8
- Female (%): 31.5

First level
- Schools: 34,240
- Students: 11,540,178
- Teachers: 307,034
- Student/teacher ratio: 37.3

Second level
- Schools: 5,594
- Students: 2,794,961
- Teachers: 122,207
- Student/teacher ratio: 22.9

Vocational
- Schools: 376
- Students: 310,278
- Teachers: 9,646
- Student/teacher ratio: 32.2

Third level (postsecondary)
- Institutions: 48
- Students: 55,068
- Teachers: 3,235
- Student/teacher ratio: 17.0
- Gross enrollment ratio: 2.9 (1984)
- Students (/100,000 pop.): 239

Foreign study
- Foreign students in national universities: 446 (1975)
- Students abroad: 14,063
  - of whom in
    - United States: 8,340 (1987)
    - France: 587 (1987)
    - Federal Republic of Germany: 263 (1986)
    - United Kingdom: 2,704 (1985)

Public expenditure (1986)
- Total (N. millions): 1,170
- % of GNP: 1.4
- % of national budget: 12.0
- % of current expenditure: 62.2

UNIVERSITIES OF NIGERIA

University	Location
Ahmadu Bello University	(Zaria)
University of Benin	(Benin City)
University of Calabar	(Calabar)
University of Ibadan	(Ibadan)
University of Ife	(Ile-Ife)
University of Ilorin	(Ilorin)
University of Jos	(Jos)
University of Lagos	(Lagos)
University of Maiduguri	(Maiduguri)
University of Nigeria	(Nsukka)
University of Port Harcourt	(Port Harcourt)
University of Sokoto	(Sokoto)

LEGAL SYSTEM

The legal system is an amalgam of English common law; African customary law; and Islamic law, or Sharia.

The judicature is headed by the Federal Supreme Court, comprising a chief justice and up to 15 justices appointed by the AFRC. The Federal Court of Appeal was established in 1976 as an intermediate appellate court. There are high courts of justice in each state as superior courts of record with unlimited jurisdiction, except in matters affecting disputes between states or between a state and the federal government.

The subordinate courts include magistrates' courts and native courts. Magistrate courts have original jurisdiction in civil and criminal cases, and some have the right to hear appeals from native courts. Native courts administer native law and custom prevailing within their jurisdiction. In northern states with a Muslim majority, the Sharia is administered through *alkali* courts, Sharia courts of appeal and courts of resolution.

The judiciary has no independence; its integrity is tempered by administrative and political control by the executive.

No information is available on the nature of the penal system or the number of penal institutions, although the death penalty is known to be in force. At least 439 executions took place in Nigeria between 1985 and mid-1988.

LAW ENFORCEMENT

The national law enforcement agency is the Nigeria Police Force, commanded by an inspector general with headquarters at Lagos. Administrative, as distinguished from the operational, control lies with the Police Council, on which both the federal and state governments are represented. The police are divided into regional commands, each under a commissioner. Below the commissioners are superintendents and inspectors, the bottom ranks of the officer corps. The regional commissioners maintain close relations with the regional military governors. Detachments assigned to local police stations vary from 200 or 300 men to a handful. The total strength of the police force is 40,000, or one policeman for every 1,675 inhabitants.

No information is available on the nature or incidence of crime in the country.

HEALTH

Nigeria is one of the most disease-ridden and unhealthy countries in the world, even by tropical standards. High among the list of diseases prevalent in the country are yellow fever, smallpox, malaria, pulmonary tuberculosis, bilharziasis, Guinea worm, trachoma, cerebrospinal meningitis, trachoma, river blindness, yaws, sleeping sickness (trypanosomiasis) and leprosy. The civil war and the resulting malnutrition and starvation are believed to have set back health conditions in the nation by a generation. Most rural areas are out of the reach of modern medicine.

HEALTH INDICATORS

Health personnel 1985
- Physicians: 14,757
  - persons per: 6,900
- Dentists: 899
- Nurses: 57,108
- Pharmacists: 3,567
- Midwives: 47,052

Hospitals 1985
- Number: 11,588
- Number of beds (/10,000): 9

Type of hospitals (%) 1985
- Government: 81.4
- Private nonprofit and profit: 18.6

Public health expenditures (latest)
- As % of national budget: 0.8
- Per capita (U.S. $): 0.50

Vital statistics
- Crude death rate (/1,000): 17 (1990)
- Life expectancy at birth 1990
  - Males: 48
  - Females: 49
- Infant mortality rate (/1,000 live births): 119 (1990)
- Child mortality rate under 5 yrs. (/1,000 live births) (1985–90): 173
- Maternal mortality rate (/100,000 live births) (1980–84 est.): 1,500
- Population with access to safe water (%): 46 (latest)

FOOD & NUTRITION

The staple foods are Guinea corn and millet in the North and yams and manioc in the South. Meat consumption is high among the livestock-breeding Hausa and Fulani.

Daily per capita consumption of food is 2,337 calories (compared to recommended minimum of 2,600 calories).

MEDIA & CULTURE

National and local (state) newspapers abound in Nigeria. Traditions of energetic and critical journalism go back to the colonial days. There are 26 daily newspapers, national and state, government and privately funded. Circulations range from 400,000 for the *Daily Times* (Lagos), 150,000 for the *Nigerian Observer* (Bendel) and *The Punch* (Lagos), and 100,000 to 80,000 for the *Herald* (Ilorin), *Tribune* (Ibadan) and *New Nigerian* (Kaduna). Several state papers have circulations around 20,000 to 30,000. Many papers have Sunday supplements. There are numerous ethnic, cultural, business and professional weeklies as well as periodicals. News magazines after the style of the American *Newsweek* have become a critical and much followed section of the press.

While the constitution modification decree left intact the provisions of the 1979 Constitution guaranteeing freedom of expression and the press, the federal military government issued a decree that tended to inhibit full expression of opinion. The decree makes it an offense for any person to "publish in any form, whether written or otherwise" a statement, rumor, message or report that is false or that "is calculated to bring the federal military government or the government of a state or a public officer to ridicule or disrepute." The print media include privately owned and state-owned publications. The federal government owns 100% of one large daily newspaper and 60% of another. Most state governments own a daily newspaper responsive to the military governor. There are several privately owned newspapers, with wide circulation. There are no restrictions on ownership of other forms of print media. The Constitution reserves the right to own and operate radio and television stations to the state and federal governments. There is no book censorship by the government, but book publishers are subject to the same laws that govern the print media.

MEDIA INDICATORS

Newspapers
- Number of dailies: 26 (latest)
- Number of periodicals: 92 (1988)
- Circulation (000): 15 (1988)
- Newsprint consumption (1988)
  - Total metric tons: 54,800
  - Per 1,000 pop. (kg.): 520

Book publishing
- Number of titles: 1,792 (latest)

Radio
- Number of transmitters: 81 (1989)
- Number of persons per radio receiver: 2.2 (1989)

Television
- Television transmitters: 61 (1989)
- Number of persons per T.V. receiver: 21 (1989)

Cinema
- Number of fixed cinemas: 240 (pre-1986)

Films
- Number of long films produced: 20 (pre-1986)

The national news agency is the News Agency of Nigeria (NAN), founded in 1976. Foreign news bureaus represented in Lagos include AFP, AP, Ghana News Agency, Novosti, Reuters, DPA, Jiji and Tass.

Nigeria has the most active book industry in English-speaking Africa. The bulk of the annual output is in the hands of British multinationals—Oxford University Press, Longman, Evans, Macmillan, Heinemann and Thomas Nelson—all of which also have local publishing programs in African vernaculars. In addition, there is a flourishing and diversified indigenous book industry, ranging from textbooks to African fiction. The country's four university presses produce a steady output of scholarly titles each year. Nigeria adheres to the Universal Copyright and Florence conventions.

Radio and television broadcasting is a state monopoly operated by the Federal Radio Corporation of Nigeria (FRCN). FRCN broadcasts national programming from Lagos and programming from six states—Ibadan, Benin City, Kaduna, Maiduguri, Enugu and Calabar—in English, Hausa and Ibo as well as in other vernaculars, such as Efik, Ijaw, Fulani, Kanuri, Tiv, Edo and Urhoho. Programming is on the air for 19 hours daily. NBC's external service, the Voice of Nigeria, operates five short wave transmitters at Ikorodu, broadcasting about nine hours a day in French, English and Arabic. Northern Nigeria is served by Radio-Television Kaduna, with two medium-wave and three shortwave transmitters broadcasting in English and Hausa about 18 hours daily. Western Nigeria is served by Western Nigeria Radiovision Service, with two medium-wave transmitters and one shortwave transmitter, located at Abafon adn Ibadan. Broadcasting is in English, Yoruba and Hausa for 18 hours daily.

Television is operated by both the federal and the state governments. The federal service, Nigerian Television Authority, is based in Lagos and is on the air about 37 hours a week, while the state-owned services in Ibadan, Kaduna and Benin City are each on the air about 35 hours a week. In 1976 the National Television Authority was established to operate all television stations.

CULTURAL & ENVIRONMENTAL INDICATORS

Libraries (latest)
- Number: 11
- Volumes (000): 729
- Registered borrowers (000): 41
- Loans (/1,000 pop.): 2

Performing arts (pre-1986)
- Number of performances: 23

Nature reserves (latest)
- Number of facilities: 4

Domestic feature film production began in 1970.

SOCIAL WELFARE

The National Provident Fund provides for sickness, retirement and old-age benefits. In 1974 the federal military government introduced a workers' welfare program and the National Emergency Relief Agency. Welfare, insurance and pension benefits have for many yeras been a principal attraction to public service employment. However, retrenchments in the services have made these less accessible. Welfare, insurance and pension benefits continue to feature in conditions of service available in the industrial and private company sectors.

GLOSSARY

alkali: a court administering Islamic law in northern Nigeria.

sardauna: spiritual head of the Muslim Hausa of northern Nigeria.

CHRONOLOGY (from 1960)

1960— Nigeria becomes an independent member of the Commonwealth with Sir Alhaji Abu Bakar Tafawa Balewa as prime minister.

1961— Northern Cameroons votes in plebiscite to join Nigeria. . . . Defense pact with the United Kingdom is terminated.

1963— Nigeria becomes a republic with Namdi Azikwe as first president. . . . A fourth region, the Midwestern, is carved out of the Western Region. . . . Nation holds census, the first after independence, but census figures are disputed by Eastern and Midwestern Region governments.

1966— Part of the army, led by Maj. Chukwuma Kaduna Nzeogwu, rises in revolt, killing Northern Region premier Alhaji Ahmadu Bello, Western Region primer S. L. Akintola and federal prime minister Sir Alhaji Abu Bakar Tafawa Balewa; troops loyal to the government foil the coup, but the Council of Ministers hands over the government to the armed forces; Maj. Gen. Johnson Aguiyi-Ironsi is invested as head of the federal military government; political parties and legislature are suspended; General Ironsi is kidnapped by Muslim soldiers at Ibadan and killed along with the military governor of the Western Province; Lt. Col. Yakubu Gowon assumes supreme power; in continuing unrest in the North, between 10,000 and 30,000 Ibos are massacred by the Muslims.

1967— The military governor of the Eastern Region, Colonel Odumegwu Ojukwu, and the Eastern Nigeria Consultative Assembly at Enugu declare the Eastern Region the independent Republic of Biafra; fighting breaks out between 40,000 federal troops and the 25,000-strong Biafran forces; Biafrans gain early successes and occupy Benin City; Biafran capital of Enugu falls to federal troops, followed by the port of Calabar.

1968— Biafran cities of Onitsha and Port Harcourt fall to federal troops; Aba, Umuahia and Owerri fall in quick succession to federal troops, thus making the blockade of Biafra total; Tanzania, Gabon, the Ivory Coast, Zambia and Haiti recognize Biafra; efforts to achieve a negotiated settlement fail.

1970— Biafran resistance collapses; Ojukwu hands over power to Maj. Gen. Philip Effiong and flees to the Ivory Coast; Effiong signs instrument of surrender at Lagos with the declaration, "Biafra ceases to exist."

1975— Gowon is ousted in a bloodless coup and replaced by Brig. Murtala Ramat Muhammed; new administration launches cleanup campaign.

1976— Government announces plans to transfer capital to Abuja. . . . The country is redivided into 19 states. . . . Muhammed is assassinated in the course of an abortive coup in which Gen. Gowon is suspected to have been involved; Lt. Gen. Olusegun Obasanjo is invested as the new head of state. . . . New draft Constitution, drafted by a committee headed by Rotimi Williams, is announced.

1977— Constituent Assembly is elected to discuss the draft Constitution.

1978— State military governments are abolished, and the ban on political parties is lifted; New Constitution is approved by the military government.

1979— New House of Representatives and Senate elections are held under the new Constitution, which came into effect in October; in a freely contested presidential election, Shehu Shagari is elected nation's first civilian president in 13 years.

1982— Over 2 million non-Nigerian Africans are expelled from the country.

1983— President Shagari is returned for a second term, and his party wins significant gains in gubernatorial and legislative elections. . . . Shagari is ousted in a bloodless coup led by Maj. Gen. Muhammadu Buhari, who sets up a Supreme Military Council.

1984— Buhari suspends sections of the Constitution dealing with civil government and liberties and curtails press freedoms; 500 politicians, including Shagari, are placed in detention. . . . Relations with the United Kingdom are strained over kidnapping of Buhari opponent in London.

1985— Buhari is toppled in a bloodless coup led by Ibrahim Babangida, who assumes title of president; a counter-coup by rival officers is attempted and fails; the Supreme Military Council is renamed the Armed Forces Ruling Council.

1986— Nigeria and Britain restore full diplomatic relations. Ten leading officers of the 1985 coup attempt are executed.

1987— Babangida announces a timetable providing for return to civilian rule by 1992; in one of the earliest steps in re-establishing civilian rule, local elections are held in 301 electoral areas. . . . Growing tension between Christians and Muslims lead to clashes which leave 25 dead.

1988— A constituent assembly is inaugurated to debate provisions for the new draft Constitution, to be modeled after the Constitution of 1979. Two new states are created by division of existing states bringing the total number of states to 21. . . . The appointment of a new Sultan of Sohoto sparks violence among Muslims.

1989— Babangida lifts ban on political parties, only to reject all ensuing applications and create two new parties, the Social Democratic Party and the National Republican Convention.

1990— Anti-government demonstrations are sparked by a Cabinet shakeup in which Babangida sacks Defense Minister Bali, assuming his portfolio himself. Another coup is attempted and fails; later in the year, 138 soldiers convicted of participating are executed. . . . In August, Nigeria leads a multi-national African peacekeeping force into Liberia to intervene in its civil war.

1991— Nigeria sends troops to Sierra Leone to help that country repulse rebels from neighboring Liberia.

BIBLIOGRAPHY

BOOKS & FILMS

Achebe, Chinua. *The Trouble with Nigeria.* London, 1984.

Adekson, J. Bayo. *Nigeria in Search of a Stable Civil-Military System.* Boulder, CO, 1982.

Adewoye, O. *The Judicial System in Southern Nigeria.* New york, 1977.

Africa Awakens: Modern Nigeria. Color and black-and-white film, 23 min. Atlantis Productions.

Africa Is my Home. Color film, 22 min. Atlantis Productions.

Aiyai, Simeon, and Oladeji O. Ojo. *Money and Banking Analysis and Policy in the Nigerian Context.* London, 1981.

Akinyemi, A. Bolaji. *Nigeria and the World: Readings in Nigerian Foreign Policy.* New York, 1979.

———. *Foreign Policy and Federalism.* Ibadan, 1974.

Akpan, Ntieyong U. *The Struggle for Secession, 1966–70.* London, 1970.

Aluko, Olajide. *Ghana and Nigeria, 1957–1970: A Study in Inter-Africa Discord.* New York, 1976.

Anamaleze, John. *The Nigerian Press.* New York, 1978.

Anifowose, F. O. *The Politics of Violence in Nigeria.* New York, 1980.

———. *Violence and Politics in Nigeria: A Case Study of the Tiv and Yoruba.* New York, 1982.

Arnold, Guy. *Modern Nigeria.* New York, 1977.

Ayaji, J. F. *Milestones in Nigerian History.* New York, 1980.

Ayandele, E. A. *The Educated Elite in Nigerian Society.* Ibadan, 1974.

Ayeni, Bola, and Akin L. Moboquunie. *Political Processes and Regional Development Planning in Nigeria.* Paris, 1982.

Balbkins, Nicholas. *Indigenization and Economic Development: The Nigerian Experience.* Westport, CT, 1981.

Bienen, Henry, and V. P. Diejomaoh. *The Political Economy of Income Distribution in Nigeria.* New York, 1981.

Cervenka, Zdenek. *The Nigerian Civil War, 1967–70.* Frankfurt, Germany, 1971.

Cohen, Robin. *Labor and Politics in Nigeria.* London, 1982.

Cole, Patrick. *Modern and Traditional Elites in the Politics of Lagos.* New York, 1975.

Collis, Robert. *Nigeria in Conflict.* London, 1970.

Cronje, Suzanne. *The World and Nigeria.* London, 1972.

Damachi, U. G. *Nigerian Modernization.* New York, 1972.

Davis, Morris. *Interpreters for Nigeria: The Third World and International Public Relations.* Carbondale, IL, 1977.

de St. Jorre, John. *Brothers' War.* Boston, 1972.

Dent, Martin. *Nigeria: The Politics of Military Rule.* London, 1985.

Dudley, Billy. *Introduction to Nigerian Government and Politics.* Bloomington, IN, 1985.

Dusgate, Richard H. *The Conquest of Northern Nigeria.* London, 1985.

Eicher, Carl K., and Carl Liedholm. *Growth and Development of the Nigerian Economy.* East Lansing, MI, 1970.

Falola, Toyin, and Julius Ihonvbere. *The Rise and Fall of Nigeria's Second Republic, 1979–84.* London, 1985.

Fasuyi, T. A. *Cultural Policy in Nigeria.* Paris, 1973.

Gailey, Harry A. *The Road to Aba: A Study of British Administrative Policy in Eastern Nigeria.* London, 1971.

Giehon, Noser. *To Build a Nigerian Nation.* Mystic, CT, 1976.

Hatch, John. *Nigeria: A History.* London, 1971.

Herskovits, Jean. *Nigeria: Power and Democracy in Africa.* New York, 1982.

Idang, Gordon J. *Nigeria: Internal Politics and Foreign Policy, 1960–66.* Ibadan, 1971.

Ikime, Obaro. *The Fall of Nigeria: The British Conquest.* New York, 1977.

Isichei, Elizabeth A. *Studies in the History of Plateau State, Nigeria.* New York, 1979.

———. *A History of Nigeria.* White Plains, NY 1983.

Kirk-Greene, A.H.M. *Crisis and Conflict in Nigeria: A Documentary Sourcebook, 1966–70.* London, 1971.

———. and Douglas Rimmer. *Nigeria Since 1970: A Political and Economic Outline.* New York, 1981.

Luckham, Robin A. *The Nigerian Military: A Sociological Analysis of Authority and Revolt, 1960–67.* New York, 1971.

Madunagu, Edwin. *Problems of Socialism: The Nigerian Challenge.* London, 1982.

Murray, D. J. *Studies in Nigerian Administration.* New York, 1978.

Nafziger, E. Wayne. *African Capitalism: A Case Study of Nigerian Entrepreneurship.* Stanford, CA, 1977.

———. *The Economics of Political Instability: The Nigerian-Biafran War.* Boulder, CO, 1982.

Nigeria: Africa in Miniature. Color film, 16 min. Associated Film Service.

Nigeria-Biafra. Color film, 30 min. CBS.

Nigeria: Giant in Africa. Black-and-white film, 52 min. National Film Board of Canada.

Nigeria: Its Art and Its People. Color film, 28 min. Mobil.

Nigeria-New Nation. Black-and-white film, 27 min. Coronet.

Nigeria: Problems of Nationbuilding. Color film, 22 min. Atlantis Productions.

Niven, Rex. *The War of Nigerian Unity.* Ibadan, 1970.

Nkemdirim, Bernard. *Social Change and Political Violence in Colonial Nigeria.* Mystic, CT, 1976.

Nnoli, Okwudiba. *Path to Nigerian Development.* London, 1981.

Nwabueze, B. O. *The Presidential Constitution of Nigeria.* New York, 1982.

Nwankwo, Arthur Agwuncha. *The Power Dynamics of the Nigerian Society: People, Politics, and Power.* Enugu, Nigeria, 1988.

Nwanko, G. O. *The Nigerian Financial System.* New York, 1980.

O'Connell, James, and Paul Beckett. *Education and Power in Nigeria.* New York, 1978.

Odetola, Theophilus. *Military Politics in Nigeria: Economic Development and Political Stability.* New Brunswick, NJ, 1978.

Ofiaja, Nicholas D. *Stability and Instability in Nigeria: The Case of Nigeria and Cameroon.* New York, 1979.

Ohiorhenuan, John F. E. *Capital and the State in Nigeria.* New York, 1989.

Okoli, Ekweume. *Institutional Structure and Conflict in Nigeria.* Lanham, MD, 1980.

Okonjo, I. M. *British Administration in Nigeria, 1900–50.* New York, 1974.

Okpaku, Joseph. *Nigeria: Dilemma of Nationhood.* Westport, CT, 1972.

Ola, R. O. *Public Administration in Nigeria.* London, 1984.

Olaloku, F. Akin. *The Structure of the Nigerian Economy.* New York, 1979.

Olaniyan, Richard. *Nigerian History and Culture.* London, 1984.

Olorunsola, Victor A. *Soldiers and Power: The Development Performance of the Nigerian Military Regime.* Standford, CA, 1977.

Omu, Fred I. *Press and Politics in Nigeria.* New York, 1978.

Onimode, Bade. *Imperialism and Underdevelopment in Nigeria.* London, 1982.

Onoh, J. K. *The Nigerian Oil Economy from Prosperity to Glut.* New York, 1981.

———. *The Foundations of Nigeria's Financial Infrastructure.* London, 1980.

Orimolya, S. A. *Biografia Nigerian: A Dictionary of Eminent Nigerians.* Boston, 1977.

Ostheimer, John M. *Nigerian Politics.* New York, 1973.

Osuagwu, Harold G. *Investment Demand in a Developing Country: The Nigerian Case.* Lanham, MD, 1982.

Oyediran, Oyeleye. *Survey of Nigerian Affairs.* New York, annual.

———. *Nigerian Government and Politics Under Military Rule.* New York, 1979.

Oyinbo, John. *Nigeria—Crisis and Beyond.* London, 1971.

Oyovbaire, S. Egite. *Federalism in Nigeria: A Study in the Development of the Nigerian State.* New York, 1985.

Panter-Brick, S. K. *Nigerian Politics and Military Rule: Prelude to the Civil War.* London, 1970.

———. *Soldiers and Oil: The Transformation of Nigeria.* Totowa, NJ, 1978.

Pearson, Scott R. *Petroleum and the Nigerian Economy.* Stanford, CA, 1970.

Post, Kenneth, and Michael Vickers. *Structure and Conflict in Nigeria.* Madison, WI, 1973.

Reed, William C. *The Role of Traditional Rulers in Elective Politics in Nigeria.* Bloomington, IN, 1982.

Schatz, Sayre P. *Nigerian Capitalism.* Berkeley, CA, 1978.

Schatzel, L. *Industrialization in Nigeria.* New York, 1974.

Schwartz, Sayre P. *African Capitalism: Development Policy in Nigeria.* Berkeley, CA, 1977.

Shaw, Timothy M., and Olajide Aluko. *Nigerian Foreign Policy.* New York, 1981.

Sklar, R. *Nigerian Political Parties: Power in an Emergent African Nation.* New York, 1983.

Smock, Audrey C. *Ibo Politics.* Cambridge, MA, 1971.

Stremlau, John J. *The International Politics of the Nigerian Civil War, 1967–1970.* Princeton, NJ, 1977.

Udo, Reuben K. *Geographical Regions of Nigeria.* Berkeley, CA, 1970.

Ukpong, Ignatius I. *The Charms and Perils of the Nigerian Presidential System: A Critical Review of Issues, Performances and Trends.* New York, 1984.

UNESCO. *Communication Policies in Nigeria.* Paris, 1979.

Uyanga, Joseph T. *A Geography of Rural Development in Nigeria.* Washington, D.C., 1980.

Wells, Jerome C. *Agricultural Policy and Economic Growth in Nigeria, 1962–1968.* New York, 1975.

West Africa: Nigeria. Color film, 22 min. *Encyclopaedia Britannica.*

Whitaker, C. S. *The Politics of Tradition: Continuity and Change in Northern Nigeria, 1945–66.* London, 1970.

White, Jeremy J. *Central Administration in Nigeria, 1914–1948: The Problem of Polarity.* Dublin, 1981.

Williams, *Nigeria: Economy and Society.* Totowa, NJ, 1976.

Williams, David. *President and Power in Nigeria: The Life of Shehu Shagari.* London, 1982.

Zartman, I. William. *The Political Economy of Nigeria.* New York, 1983.

OFFICIAL PUBLICATIONS

Central Nigerian Bank. *Annual Report and Statement of Accounts.*

———. *Monthly Report: Economic and Financial Review.*

Federal Statistics Office. *Digest of Statistics.*

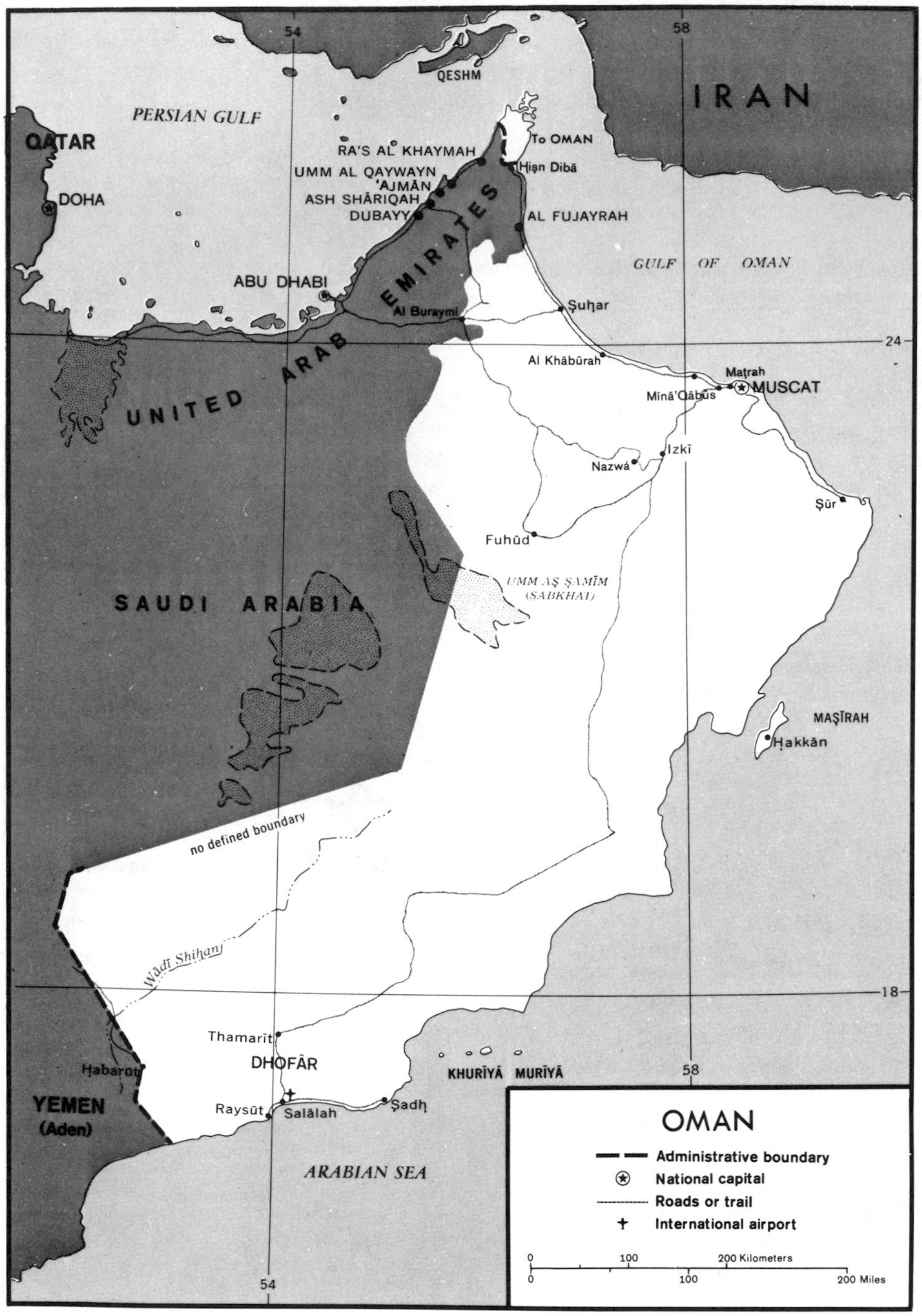

IRAN

QESHM

PERSIAN GULF

QATAR

DOHA

RA'S AL KHAYMAH

UMM AL QAYWAYN

'AJMĀN

ASH SHĀRIQAH

DUBAYY

To OMAN

Ḥiṣn Dibā

AL FUJAYRAH

GULF OF OMAN

ABU DHABI

UNITED ARAB EMIRATES

Al Buraymi

Ṣuḥar

Al Khābūrah

Maṭrah

Minā' Qābūs

MUSCAT

Izkī

Nazwá

Ṣūr

Fuhūd

UMM AŞ ŞAMĪM (SABKHAH)

SAUDI ARABIA

MAṢĪRAH

Ḥakkān

no defined boundary

Wādī Shiḥan

Thamarīt

DHOFĀR

Ḥabarūt

YEMEN (Aden)

Raysūt

Ṣalālah

Ṣadḥ

KHURĪYĀ MURĪYĀ

ARABIAN SEA

54

58

24

18

OMAN

Administrative boundary

National capital

Roads or trail

International airport

0 100 200 Kilometers

0 100 200 Miles

OMAN

BASIC FACT SHEET

OFFICIAL NAME: Sultanate of Oman (Sultanat 'Uman); formerly Muscat and Oman

ABBREVIATION: OM

CAPITAL: Muscat

HEAD OF STATE & HEAD OF GOVERNMENT: Sultan Qabus ibn Said al-Bu Said (from 1970)

NATURE OF GOVERNMENT: Absolute monarchy

POPULATION: 1,457,064 (1990)

AREA: 212,457 sq. km. (82,030 sq. mi.)

ETHNIC MAJORITY: Arab

LANGUAGE: Arabic

RELIGION: Ibadi sect of Islam

UNIT OF CURRENCY: Rial Omani

NATIONAL FLAG: Vertical red band at hoist side with national emblem at upper left in white; three horizontal stripes of white, red (one-fifth of the depth) and green

NATIONAL EMBLEM: A belt with silver scimitars crossed over a ceremonial curved dagger, known as gambia

NATIONAL ANTHEM: "God Save Our Sultan"

NATIONAL HOLIDAYS: November 18 (National Day); July 22–24 (Accession of the Sultan); November 19 (Birthday of the Sultan); also variable Islamic festivals

NATIONAL CALENDAR: Islamic

PHYSICAL QUALITY OF LIFE INDEX: 46

DATE OF INDEPENDENCE: 1650

DATE OF CONSTITUTION: None

WEIGHTS & MEASURES: Metric system adopted in 1974. Traditional measures still in use include the kiyas (1.55 kg.; 3.4 lb.), the maund (37.29 kg.; 82.2 lb.), the farasala (10 maunds) and the bahar (200 maunds).

GEOGRAPHICAL FEATURES

Oman, the second-largest country on the Arabian Peninsula, is at the southeastern corner of that peninsula, facing the Gulf of Oman and the Arabian Sea. Its area is estimated at 212,457 sq. km. (82,030 sq. mi.), including the island of Masirah and the tip of Musandam Peninsula, which juts into the Strait of Hormuz. Oman proper extends 972 km. (604 mi.) northeast to southwest and 513 km. (319 mi.) southeast to southwest.

Oman's boundaries are only partially surveyed and defined. The sultanate's border with Saudi Arabia has been the subject of intermittent and violent disputes. The focal point of this controversy has been Buraimi Oasis in northern Oman, which was forcibly occupied by the sultan's levies, aided by the British, in 1955. The status of the frontier has remained unresolved, for the Saudis have never withdrawn their claim. On the other hand, the sultans of Oman continue to regard their frontier with Saudi Arabia to be the so-called Riyadh Line. The total length of the international land borders is estimated at 1,374 km. (854 mi.), divided as follows: South Yemen, 288 km. (179 mi.); Saudi Arabia, 676 km. (420 mi.); and United Arab Emirates, 410 km. (255 mi.). The total length of the coastline is 1,860 km. (1,156 mi.).

The capital is Muscat, with a 1982 population of 53,000. The so-called Capital Region extends from Muscat to Sib and includes Mutrah, the commercial center; Ruwi, the administrative center; and Bawshar. The other major towns are Salalah, (17,000) in the South (the residence of the last sultan); Nizwah; Sohar; and Haima. Nizwa was once the capital of the imams of Oman.

The country is divided topographically into the following regions:

- The tip of the Musandam Peninsula, the Ras al-Jabal, which touches the strait of Hormuz and is separated from the rest of the sultanate by a belt of United Arab Emirates territory. It consists entirely of low mountains.
- The fertile and populous coastal plain known as Batinah, sloping gradually on the landward side to the foothills of the western Hajar.
- The Muscat Matrah coastal region, bounded almost throughout its length by cliffs.
- The high tableland of central Oman west of the coastal area. The tableland consists of two ranges: the Hajar al-Gharbi, or western Hajar, and the Hajar al-Sharqi, or eastern Hajar, divided by the Wadi Samail, which forms the traditional route between Muscat and the interior. The general elevation is 1,220 m. (4,000 ft.), but some peaks of a high ridge known as Jabal Akhdar rise to 3,050 m. (10,000 ft.). Beyond the Hajar Mountains are sandy inland districts that recede into a stony desert before merging with the wastes of Rub al-Khali.
- The barren and forbidding coastline south to Dhofar.
- The virtually uninhabited and inhospitable island of Masirah.

• Dhofar Province, with a coastal plain noted for rich vegetation and natural beauty. Sixteen km. (10 mi.) inland rise the Qara Mountains, which meet the Rub al-Khali 240 km. (150 mi.) to the north.

A small number of surface-flowing wadis are found in the Hajar Mountains but never reach the sea.

CLIMATE & WEATHER

Oman has an arid subtropical climate. The summer months run from May to October, with a maximum average temperature of 46°C (115°F) and humidity in excess of 90%. The summer climate is regarded as one of the hottest in the world, and temperatures as high as 54°C (130°F) have been recorded. A west wind known as the gharbi, blowing from the Rub al-Khali, makes the heat more oppressive. Mean average temperatures in Muscat for January and July, respectively, are 22°C (71.5°F) and 33°C (92°F).

Average rainfall is 50 to 100 mm. (2 to 4 in.), with wide regional variations. Some coastal areas receive no rain at all in the course of a year, while the Hajar Mountains region receives up to 250 mm. (10 in.) annually. An exception to the general climatic pattern is southwestern Dhofar, which receives abundant rain during the southwesterly monsoon season between June and September.

POPULATION

The population of Oman in 1990 was 1,457,064, according to C.I.A. estimates. Oman has never conducted an official census.

A third of the population live in the Batinah coastal plain, and nearly half live in small interior towns. The number of nomads is estimated at 100,000. Over 50,000 are believed to live in the southern province of Dhofar and 5,000 in Musandam Peninsula. Muscat and its environs have undergone a population explosion, increasing from 25,000 in 1970 to 53,000 in 1982.

The median age is not weighted as much in favor of the young as in most developing countries: 44.3% are below 14 years, 51.7% are between 15 and 59 and 4.1% are over 60.

The population is overwhelmingly rural. There are no towns with over 100,000 population. Unlike other countries in the Middle East, there has been comparatively little migration from the countryside to the towns, except for the growth of Muscat.

Though conservative, Oman has not been extreme in its attempts to impose strict adherence to Islamic precepts on women. For example, women have shared in the benefits of the social and economic growth of recent years, and schooling for girls is available to the same extent as for boys in urban areas, but less so in rural areas. However, for cultural reasons the educational level of girls still lags behind that of boys. Many urban Omani women drive. A few women have reached high levels in the public sector. One woman is presently an acting undersecretary in the government. By and large, however, occupational advances available to women are limited to the traditional spheres of teaching, secretarial work and nursing. Oman's labor laws are protective of women, guaranteeing maternity leave and working conditions. The gains achieved by a small minority of women are largely irrelevant to the great majority, both in the towns and in the rural areas, whose lives are carried out within the confines of the house and the local marketplace. The previous lack of adult education facilities means that all but the youngest females in rural areas are illiterate. This problem is being addressed via adult evening classes sponsored by the government; more than half the government's 402 literacy centers are exclusively for female participants. This general lack of education, combined with communal and tribal customs that dictate a subsidiary role for women, make it difficult for most adult women to participate fully in the modern sector. The expansion of educational facilities for girls (including the new university) will allow for some equalization of the position of women in the future, but communal and tribal customs will continue to militate against full participation by women in the foreseeable future.

Oman has no official birth control policy or programs.

DEMOGRAPHIC INDICATORS

Population (millions): 1.47 (1990)
Sex distribution (%, 1985 est.): males, 52.9; females, 47.1
Population estimates and projections (000)

1950: 413	1970: 654	1990: 1,468
1960: 505	1980: 984	2000: 2,057

Age profile (%, 1985 est.)

0–14: 44.3	30–44: 18.0	60–74: 3.5
15–29: 24.8	45–59: 8.9	75 and over: 0.6

Median age (yrs.): 18.2 (1985)
Youth population (% aged 15–24): (1985); 16.9 (2000) 19
Total dependency ratio, 1985: 87.9
Annual Growth Rate (%)

1950–55: 1.94	1975–80: 5.01	2000–2005: 3.43
1955–60: 2.08	1980–85: 4.67	2005–2010: 3.82
1960–65: 2.46	1985–90: 3.34	1010–2015: 3.05
1965–70: 2.71	1990–1995: 3.34	2015–2020: 2.67
1970–75: 3.16	1995–2000: 3.40	2020–2025: 2.33

Hypothetical size of stationary population (millions): 8
Assumed year of reaching net reproduction rate of 1:2045
Urban population (000): 110 (1985)
Annual urban population growth rate (%, 1985–90): 7.00
Annual rural population growth rate (%, 1985–90): 2.95
Population density per sq. km. (per sq. mi.): 4.9 (12.2) (latest)

VITAL STATISTICS

Crude birth rate (/1,000): 43 (1990); 5 (1965)
Crude death rate (/1,000): 12 (1990); 24 (1965)
Infant mortality rate (/1,000 live births): 105 (1990)
Life expectancy (yrs.) at birth: males, 56; females, 58 (1990)
Gross reproduction rate (/woman): (1980–85): 3.50
Total fertility rate (/woman): 6.81 (1990)
Rate of natural increase (/1,000): 31.2 (1986)
Average household size: 3.7 (latest)

ETHNIC COMPOSITION

The population is estimated to be seven-eighths Arab, divided into two principal groups: the first known as Yamaniyah, Azdi, Qatitani or Hinawi, and the second as Nizari, Adani or Ghafiri. The first predominate in the southeastern districts and the second in the northwestern ones, but members of both groups can be found in every village. This split has played an important part in Oman's civil wars and internal politics.

The small non-Arab population is concentrated in the coastal towns of Muscat and Matrah. The most significant minorities in numerical terms are Iranians, Baluchis, Indians, Pakistanis and East Africans, most of whom serve as soldiers, civil servants, merchants or laborers. The Baluchis were originally inhabitants of the sultan's former possession of Gwadur, which he ceded to Pakistan in 1958. The East African Blacks are reminders of the days not so long ago when Muscat was the most important center of the slave trade in the East. Two aboriginal tribes of uncertain origin are the Qara and the Shihuh, who probably are descendants of aboriginal inhabitants of southern Arabia.

Foreigners were banned from the interior of the country under the former sultan, Said bin Taimur, who was deposed in 1970. The Ibadi Omanis are among the most xenophobic of Arabs and, despite recent liberalization, prejudice against Westerners persists throughout the country except perhaps in the capital region.

LANGUAGE

The official language of Oman is Arabic. The main linguistic minorities are Iranians, who speak Farsi; Indian Khojas and Pakistanis, who speak Urdu; and Hindus, who speak a variety of Indian dialects. English is widely understood and even used to some extent in government.

While there is no government policy to discourage the use of other languages in speech or print, or in religious instruction in the home, the government has increasingly insisted that correspondence with it, and in public and legal documents, be in Arabic.

RELIGION

Ibadism, a strict and fanatical sect dating back to the Kharedjite schism in early Islam, is the national religion of Oman. The Ibadis, who are fundamentalists, follow Abdullah Ibn Ibad, an Iraqi Kharedjite theologian. They regard all contacts with infidels and non-Ibadi Muslims as sinful and are notorious for their puritanism and doctrinal rigidity. There are a number of Sunni Muslims of the Wahhabi, Hanbali and Shafai persuasion, particularly among the Ghafiri tribes.

Non-Muslim foreigners, both Christian and Hindu, are allowed to worship at designated locations. The government of Oman has donated land for building a Christian church and a new Hindu temple. Non-Muslims in Oman are prohibited from proselytizing. Conversely, conversion to Islam is encouraged and publicized.

HISTORICAL BACKGROUND

Oman was never under foreign rule in modern times. However, in 1798 Said bin Sultan of Muscat concluded a treaty with Britain that established a special relationship between the two countries. The relationship sometimes verged on dependence, but the British were careful not to interfere in the internal administration. Until 1975 Oman was in a state of civil war. The authority of the present al-Bu Said dynasty was frequently challenged, and the sultans were able to prevail only through British assistance, and more recently through the use of Iranian, Baluchi and Pakistani troops. On two occasions in this century (in 1913 and 1954), the imans of Oman have rebelled against the al-Bu Saids. But the gravest threat to the sultan's regime came from the People's Front for the Liberation of Oman and the Arabian Gulf, which conducted extensive guerrilla warfare with support from radical Arab countries. The end of this civil war in 1975 brought a measure of stability to the sultanate.

In 1970 Said bin Taimur, who had been in power since 1930, was brought down in a bloodless palace coup led by his son Qabus bin Said. Unlike his father, Qabus has been a modernist influence on a very tradition-bound country. Under his rule, the government has been liberalized, and spending on development and social services has increased. He also ended his father's policy of isolationism. Under his direction, Oman joined the Arab League, the International Monetary Fund, the Gulf Cooperation Council and the United Nations. In 1980 Oman signed a treaty with the United States permitting the U.S. use of ports and air bases in the Gulf in exchange for U.S. military and economic aid and a commitment of U.S. security. During the Persian Gulf Crisis in 1990 and the ensuing war in 1991, Oman opened its air bases to U.S.-led U.N. forces and sent ground troops to Saudi Arabia to assist in its defense.

CONSTITUTION & GOVERNMENT

Oman is politically among the least developed nations of the world. It has no constitution and has never had one. It has no political parties and never has held an election. The sultan has absolute power and legislates by decree with the assistance of an appointed Council of Ministries. Although Oman has no legislature, there is a Consultative Assembly of nominated members, which was created by Sultan Qabus in October 1981. The Assembly meets four times a year and can comment only on social and economic development and future policy. The present sultan, the head of state, also holds the offices of prime minister; the head of government; foreign minister; defense minister; supreme commander of the armed forces; and finance minister.

FREEDOM & HUMAN RIGHTS

In terms of civil and political rights the sultanate is classified as a not-free country.

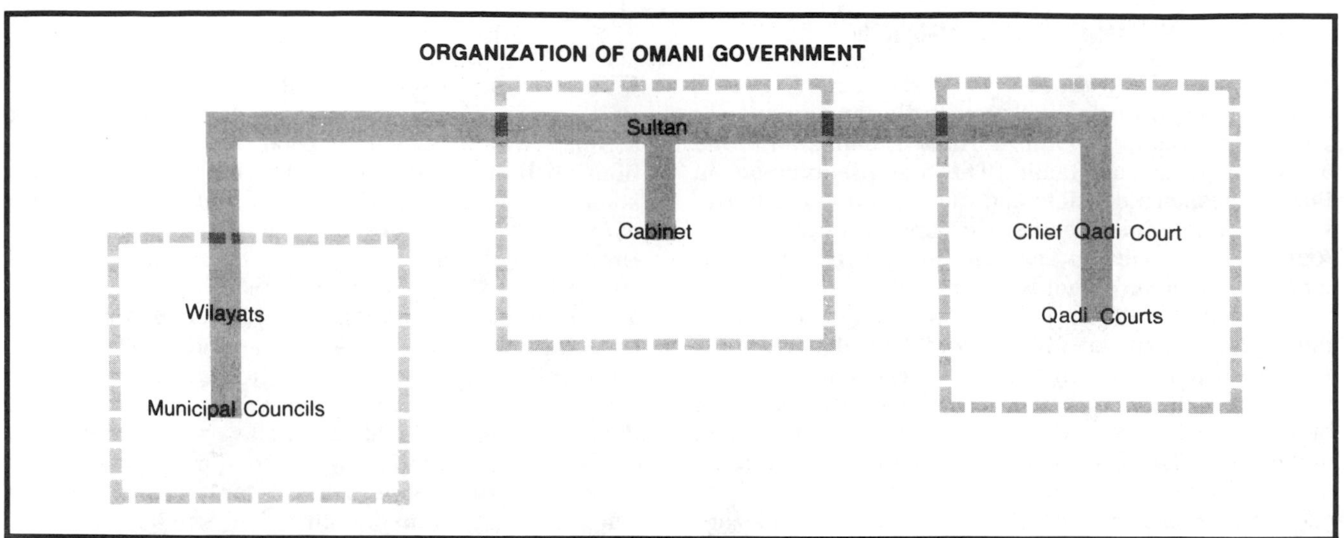

Oman is a traditional Islamic society with one foot in the 19th century and the other barely and cautiously in the 20th. Almost all types of freedom are circumscribed. Ethnic, tribal, family and religious ties are so strong that they exclude normal political processes. The Shari'a, which governs Omani law, does not recognize habeas corpus, but citizens can petition the sultan himself personally for remedies for violations of human rights. There are no widespread cases of repression, and instances of petty arbitrariness by local officials are no more frequent than in other similarly ruled countries. Warrants are not required for police searches of private homes. There are persistent allegations of bribery, but because most officials have good connections at the sultan's court, few such cases are brought out into the open. Publications are routinely censored and occasionally banned. Political parties do not exist, and elections have never been held. Because the population is almost entirely Muslim, the issue of religious tolerance is purely academic.

CIVIL SERVICE

No current information is available on the Omani civil service.

LOCAL GOVERNMENT

The sultanate is divided into 40 *wilayats*, each governed by a *wali*, or governor, appointed by the sultan. Dhofar Province and the Capital Region have comparatively more autonomy under governors. A system of rural municipalities is being gradually introduced with limited responsibilities for land use, public health and sanitation.

FOREIGN POLICY

Sultan Qabus's most dramatic shift from the traditionalist policies of his father was in foreign relations. Under the old sultan, only two consular offices—those of the United Kingdom and India—were maintained in Muscat, and the sultan had no representative abroad except a consul-general in London. Until 1971 Muscat was not a member of the United Nations or any other international organization.

Sultan Qabus has moved to establish diplomatic and trade relations with most Arab countries. Oman's closest relations are with the Kingdom of Jordan, because of common military and political traditions and a common outlook on Arab affairs, Until 1975 the Omani military forces were trained and led by Jordani officers. The Jordani military presence has been reduced since 1975, but political relations with Jordan were very close until 1991, when Oman announced that it would no longer provide financial aid to Jordan because of Jordan's support of Iraq during the Persian Gulf War. In 1974 the United States established its first embassy in Muscat, and the first Omani embassy was opened in Washington, D.C., in 1973. Relations were strained with South Yemen and with Communist countries until the early 1980s. Oman is a member of the Arab League but not of OPEC or OAPEC.

In February 1980 Sultan Qabus agreed, in principle to use by U.S. forces of Masirah Island, off the eastern coast of Oman, as a military base in an emergency. In June 1980 Oman and the United States signed a defense pact whereby, in exchange for U.S. military and economic aid and a U.S. commitment to Oman's security, Oman would grant use of port and air-base facilities in the Gulf to U.S. forces. The United States was to spend about $320 million on the construction and improvement of military bases from 1981. Oman's acceptance of U.S. assistance in defense aroused protests from South Yemen in 1981, but mediation by other Gulf states led to a "normalization" agreement in 1982, and diplomatic relations between Oman and South Yemen were resumed in October 1983. In May 1981 Oman joined with six other Middle Eastern countries to form the Gulf Cooperation Council (GCC), which, among other aims, planned to work toward a unified system of defense in the Gulf region. In October 1983 Oman was the site of the GCC's first joint military exercises, seen as the foundations of an independent rapid deployment force for Gulf countries.

GOVERNMENT LIST
(July/August 1991)

Sultan .... Said, QABUS ibn Said al-Bu
Prime Minister .... Said, QABUS ibn Said al-Bu
Deputy Prime Minister for Financial & Economic
Affairs .... Zawawi, Qais bin 'Abd al-Mun'im al-
Deputy Prime Minister for Legal
Affairs .... Sa'id, FAHD bin Mahmud Al
Deputy Prime Minister for Security &
Defense .... Sa'id, FAHAR bin Taymur Al
Minister of Agriculture &
Fisheries ..... Hina'i, Muhammad bin 'Abdallah bin Zahir al-
Minister of Civil Service .... Makki, Ahmad bin 'Abd al-Nabi al-
Minister of Commerce &
Industry ....Ghazali, Salim bin 'Abdallah al-, *Col.*
Minister of Communications .. Harthi, Hamud bin 'Abdallah al-
Minister of Defense .... Sa'id, QABUS bin Sa'id Al
Minister of Diwan of Royal
Court ....Busa'idi, SAIF bin Hamad al-
Minister of Education & Youth
Affairs .... Manthiri, Yahya bin Mahfud al-
Minister of Electricity &
Water .... Qutaybi, Muhammad bin 'Ali al-
Minister of Environment .... Sa'id, SHABIB bin Taymur Al
Minister of Finance .... Sa'id, QABUS bin Sa'id Al
Minister of Foreign Affairs .... Sa'id, QABUS bin Sa'id Al
Minister of Health .... Musa, 'Ali bin Muhammad al-
Minister of Housing .... Ma'mari, Malik Sulayman al-
Minister of
Information ....Ruwas, 'Abd al-'Aziz bin Muhammad al-
Minister of Interior ..... Busa'idi, BADR bin Saud bin Harib al-
Minister of Justice & Awqaf & Islamic
Affairs .... Busa'idi, HILAL bin Saud al-
Minister of Labor & Vocational
Training .... Busa'idi, MUTASIM bin Hamud bin Nasir al-
Minister of National Heritage &
Culture .... Sa'id, FAYSAL bin 'Ali Al
Minister of Palace Office Affairs .. Ma'mari, 'Ali bin Majid, *Gen.*
Minister of Petroleum &
Minerals .... Shanfari, Sa'id bin Ahmad al-
Minister of Posts, Telegraphs &
Telephones .... Baluchi, Ahmad bin Suwaydan al-
Minister of Regional Municipalities
Affairs .... Husni, Amr bin Shuwayn al-
Minister of Social Affairs ....Ma'shani, Mustahil bin Ahmad al-
Minister of State for Foreign
Affairs .... 'Abdallah, Yusuf bin 'Alawi bin
Minister of Water Resources .. Wahaybi, Khalfan bin Nasir al-
Personal Representative of His Majesty
the Sultan ....Sa'id, THUWAYNI bin Shihab Al
Secretary to the Council of
Ministers .... Sa'id, HAMUD bin Faysal Al
Special Adviser to His Majesty for Economic
Planning Affairs ....Zubayr, Muhammad al-
Governor of the Capital ..... Busa'idi, SULTAN bin Hamad al-
Wali of Dhofar & Minister of
State ....Busa'idi, MUSALLAM bin 'Ali al-
President, Central Bank .... Sangur, Hamud

Oman and the United States are parties to three treaties and agreements covering investment guarantees, the Peace Corps and trade and commerce.

Oman joined the United Nations in 1971. It also is a member of 13 other U.N. organizations.

PARLIAMENT

Oman has no legislature. All decrees of the sultan have the force of law.

In October 1981 the sultan established an appointive Consultative Assembly of 45 members, 17 members representing the central government, 17 representing regional authorities and 11 drawn from the private sector. This number was increased to 55 in October 1983. The Consultative Assembly's mandate is to give advice to the sultan through its president. It sits for two years.

POLITICAL PARTIES

Oman has no legal political parties. The main illegal opposition was, until 1975, the Popular Front for the Liberation of Oman and the Arabian Gulf (PFLOAG). The PFLOAG revolt was crushed in 1975, and most of its leaders surrendered in 1976. Some remnants of the Front continue to operate illegally at home and openly in radical Arab countries.

ECONOMY

Oman is an upper-middle-income country, with an economy based primarily on oil. The private sector is predominant in Oman's free-market economy. During the last three decades, the economy expanded dramatically. It is estimated that from 1980 through 1988 the GNP increased an average 10.3% annually. The collapse of oil prices in the mid-1980s adversely affected the economy, but increases at the end of the decade resulted in recovery. Despite Oman's dramatic economic growth, the nation was so underdeveloped and military expenditures during the civil war were so high that it had to borrow to develop. It has a tacit agreement of other Arab oil producers to produce at maximum.

Although petroleum provides most of the nation's revenue and GDP, a majority of the population is

PRINCIPAL ECONOMIC INDICATORS

Gross National Product (U.S. $ billions): 7.756 (1989)
GNP per capita (U.S. $): 5,220 (1989)
GNP average annual growth rate (%, 1980–88): 10.3
GNP per capita average annual growth rate (%), 1987–89: −4.0
Average annual rate of inflation (%, 1980–87): −6.5
Average annual growth rate (%, 1980–87) latest
General government consumption: } 13.6
Private consumption: }
Gross domestic investment: 18.4

BALANCE OF PAYMENTS, 1987
(U.S. $ millions)

Current account balance: 851
Merchandise exports: 3,805
Merchandise imports: −1,769
Trade balance: 2,036
Other goods, services & incomes +: 533
Other goods, services & income −: −1,044
Other goods, services & income net: −511
Private unrequited transfers: −681
Official unrequited transfers: 8
Capital other than reserves: −743
Net errors & omissions: −522
Counterpart items: 375
Total change in reserves: −483

GROSS DOMESTIC PRODUCT

GDP nominal (R.O. billions): 2.919 (1988)
GDP per capita (U.S. $): 6,110 (1987)
Average annual growth rate of GDP (%, 1980–87): 12.7
GDP by type of expenditure (%) 1987
- Consumption
  - Private: 31
  - Government: 30
- Gross domestic investment: 19
- Foreign trade
  - Exports: 49
  - Imports: −28

Cost components of GDP (%) 1981
- Net indirect taxes: 1
- Consumption of fixed capital: } 99
- Compensation of employees: } 99
- Net operating surplus: } 99

Sectoral origin of GDP (%) 1987
- Primary
  - Agriculture: 4
  - Mining: 47
- Secondary
  - Manufacturing: 4
  - Construction: 5
  - Public utilities: 1
- Tertiary
  - Transportation & communications: 3
  - Trade: 11
  - Finance: 9
  - Other services: 1
  - Government: 17

Average annual sectoral growth rates (%, 1980–87) (latest)
- Agricultural: 9.4
- Industry: 15.1
- Manufacturing: 37.9
- Services: 12.2

involved in agriculture, mainly at the subsistence level. Economic growth has been centered in the coastal cities, and the vast interior is largely undeveloped.

PUBLIC FINANCE

The fiscal year runs from January 1 through December 31. The only tax in the budget is a corporate income tax.

CENTRAL GOVERNMENT EXPENDITURES, 1988
(% of Total Expenditures)

- Defense: 38.2
- Education: 10.7
- Health: 4.8
- Housing, Social Security, welfare: 8.3
- Economic services: 12.9
- Other: 25.1
- Total expenditures as % of GNP: 49.3
- Overall surplus or deficit as % of GNP: −12.6

CENTRAL GOVERNMENT REVENUES, 1987
(% of Total Current Revenues)

- Taxes on income, profit & capital gain: 19.0
- Social Security contributions: 0.0
- Domestic taxes on goods & services: 0.8
- Taxes on international trade & transactions: 3.0
- Other taxes: 0.8
- Current nontax revenue: 76.4
- Total current revenue as % of GNP: 35.9

General government consumption as % of GDP: 25

The government derived over 75% of its revenue from oil and gas in 1988. Over 38% of government expenditures were on defense, almost 13% of economic services and approximately 23% on development, including education.

Three five-year development plans have been launched by the National Development Council, covering 1976–80, 1980–85 and 1986–90. The major targets for development have been industry, education, housing, roads, welfare, defense, tourism and agriculture. The last sector received special emphasis in the 1986–90 plan.

The plans were instituted to hedge against the eventual loss of petroleum reserves. With increased oil prices in 1978, projects not scheduled until the third five-year plan were implemented ahead of time. These projects included the completion of the national roads and the university. But with the fall of oil prices in 1985, Oman cut back drastically on these plans.

During 1970–88 Oman received $122 million in US aid. From 1970–87 it received $92 million in assistance from other Western countries. OPEC contributed $797 million in bilateral aid during 1979–89.

FOREIGN AID, 1989

Total foreign aid, U.S. $ millions: 265.5
- Bilateral: 222.9
- Multilateral: 42.5

CURRENCY & BANKING

The Omani unit of currency is the rial Omani (formerly the rial Saidi), divided into 1,000 baiza. Coins are issued in denominations of 2, 5, 10, 25, 50 and 100 baiza; notes are issued in denominations of 100, 250 and 500 baiza and 1, 5 and 10 rials.

The rial Omani, introduced in 1970, was at par with the pound sterling until 1972. Following the fall in oil prices in 1985, the Omani rial was devalued 11% against the U.S. dollar. The rate of exchange has been fixed since 1986 at $1 = R.O. 0.3845.

The banking system consists of the Central Bank of Oman, set up in 1975; eight domestic commercial banks; 13 foreign banks; and three development banks. In 1984 these banks had reserves of R.O. 104.6 million, demand deposits of R.O. 134.0 million and foreign assets of R.O. 311.8 million.

AGRICULTURE

Of the total land area of 21,245,700 ha. (52,498,124 ac.), only 0.3% is cultivated. And although the majority of the work force is engaged in agriculture, primarily subsistance agriculture, it contributed only 4% of the GDP in 1987.

Land use is determined by the availability of water. Cultivation is extensive along the Batinah and Shumailiyah coasts but in the interior is confined to areas near the wadis. The total area under actual cultivation is about 36,000 ha. (88,956 ac.), of which Batinah

FINANCIAL INDICATORS, 1988

Total reserves minus gold (SDRs millions): 1,031
SDRs (millions): 9
Reserve position in IMF (SDRs millions): 28
Foreign exchange (SDRs millions): 992
Gold (fine troy oz. millions): .29
Ratio of external debt to total reserves (1986): 2.3 (1988)
Central bank 1989
- Assets (%)
  - Foreign assets: 92.9
  - Claims on government: 7.1
  - Claims on banks: 0.0
  - Claims on private sector: 0.0
- Liabilities (%)
  - Reserve money: 40.8
  - Government deposits: 17.2
  - Foreign liabilities: 0.1
  - Capital accounts: 21.7

Money supply 1987
Stock (R.O. millions): 345
M^1 per capita: 240
Private banks 1989
- Assets (%)
  - Loans to government: 1.9
  - Loans to private sector: 66.0
  - Reserves: 8.9
  - Foreign assets: 23.3
- Liabilities
  - Deposits (R.O. trillions): 1.249
  - of which %
    - Demand deposits: 13.3
    - Savings deposits: 57.7
    - Government deposits: 7.9
    - Foreign liabilities: 8.2

External debt 1987
- Total (U.S. $ billions): 2.940
  - of which public (U.S. $ billions): 2.488
  - of which private (U.S. $ millions): 0
- Debt service (long-term)
  - Total (U.S. $ millions): 529
  - Repayment
    - Principal (%): 65.6
    - Interest (%): 34.4
- Debt service ratio (%): 14.0 (1987)
- External public debt as % of GNP: 34.7
- Debt service as % of GNP: 7.4
- Terms of public borrowing
  - Commitments (U.S. $ millions): 285
  - Average interest rate (%): 7.5
  - Average maturity (yrs.): 10
- Net flow of publicly guaranteed external capital (U.S. $ millions): −66
- Receipt of workers' remittances (U.S. $ millions): −681
- Net direct private investment (U.S. $ millions): 33

GROWTH PROFILE
(Annual Growth Rates, %)

Projected population (1987–2000): 3.9
Projected crude birth rate (/1,000) 1990–95: 44.1
Projected crude death rate (/1,000) 1990–95: 10.8
Urban population (1980–88): 8.7
Labor force (1985–2000): 2.7
GNP (1980–89): 10.3
GNP per capita (1986–88): −4.1
GDP (1980–87): 12.7
Inflation (1980–88): 6.4
Agriculture (1980–87): 9.4
Industry (1980–87): 15.1
Manufacturing (1980–87): 37.9
Services (1980–87): 12.2
Money holdings (1980–88): 17.7
Energy production (1980–88): 10.3
Energy consumption (1980–88): 7.7
Private consumption (1980–87): 13.6
Gross domestic investment (1980–87): 18.4

AGRICULTURAL INDICATORS

Agriculture's share of GDP (%): 3 (latest)
Average annual growth rate (%, 1980–88): 9.4
Value added in agriculture (U.S. $ millions): 293
Cereal imports (000 metric tons): 287 (1987)
Number of tractors: 125 (1986)
Number of harvester-threshers: 30 (1986)
Total fertilizer consumption: 4.8 (000 metric tons) (1985–86)
Fertilizer consumption (g./ha., hundreds) 417 (1987–88)
Number of farms (000): 65
Average size of holding, ha.: 1.3
Farms as % of total land area: 0.3
Land use (%)
- Permanent crops: 68.6
- Temporary crops: 31.4
- Fallow: 0.0
- Meadows & pastures, woodland, other: 50.8

Yields (kg./ha.) 1989
- Grains: 1,178
- Roots & tubers: 13,333
- Fruits (000 metric tons): 197
- Vegetables (000 metric tons): 237
- Milk (kg./animal): 420

Livestock (000)
- Cattle: 136
- Sheep: 220

Fishing 1986
- Total catch (000 metric tons): 166.1
  - of which marine (%): 100.0
- Value of exports (U.S. $ millions): 50.188

accounts for 13,800 ha. (34,099 ac.) and the interior for 19,920 ha. (49,222 ac.).

Qabus, in declaring 1988 to be "Agricultural Year," brought 405 ha. of additional land under wheat cultivation. Plans were made to increase land use for date cultivation by one-third. The second five-year plan (1981–85) saw some headway in its plan to modernize farm techniques. The third five-year plan was to focus primarily on agriculture, but the fall in oil prices in 1985 forced cutbacks in this plan. A concessionary loan agreement with Japan in 1987 supplied $200 million to Oman for, in part, agricultural development. As of 1988 about 2,500 government-owned research experimental farms had been organized.

Most farms in the interior are irrigated by a system of water channels. Farm holdings are typically less than 2 ha. (5 ac.) in size.

There are three types of land tenure: private ownership, long-term rental of state land for planting tree crops and short-term rental of state lands for planting of annual crops. The principal product is dates, grown along the Batinah coast and in the highlands of inner Oman. Limes, another export crop, are grown on the southwestern portion of the Dhofar coastal plain. Other crops include melons, bananas and plums. Some wheat is grown around Nizwah.

Omani camels are prized throughout Arabia for their hardiness.

Oman's rich maritime traditions survive in the local fishing industry. The inshore waters are rich in a variety of fish, of which the most plentiful are sardines. Fish is the principal source of animal protein in the Omani diet. Some of the catch is exported to India, Sri Lanka and the Gulf countries.

The Oman National Fisheries Company (ONFC) was organized in early 1980 by the government to act as the principal agent of fisheries development. The ONFC is owned 20% by the government, 20% by traditional fishermen and 60% by private Omani investors, and it commenced operations with a working capital of about $3 million.

The inner highlands contain forests of some size, but the wood is used principally for fuel.

MANUFACTURING

Most of the labor force engaged in manufacturing is in small-scale food processing. The development of large-scale industries began with the establishment of a cement plant with an initial capacity of 250,000 tons per annum and a grain mill at Matrah. Refined petroleum for domestic use is provided by the Mina al-Fahal refinery, which began operation in 1982. To encourage light industry, an industrial zone has been established at Rusayl.

Compared with other Middle Eastern countries, Oman's petroleum reserves and production levels are quite small. These limitations, together with the country's chronic shortage of skilled labor, did not favor the development of heavy industry on a large scale. One major project was the opening in July 1983 of a copper smelting and refining complex. Total output of refined copper in 1984 was estimated at 15,000 tons, and the complex accounted for 38% of total revenue from nonoil exports. In general, however, the Omani leadership has preferred to pursue development that catered for the country's own needs. Extensive investment in infrastructure and private industry after 1970 caused a boom in the construction industry, and two new cement plants began production in 1984. With a combined capacity of almost 750,000 tons per year, these plants were expected to provide about 60% of the country's needs. An industrial estate, the first phase of which was expected to provide 77 units for small industries, also opened in 1984. The government provided interest-free loans as an incentive to private investors. Other incentives offered to foreign investors include a five-year tax holiday. New foreign investors include a U.S. company developing commercial fishing in the Gulf of Oman and a British firm building 19 diesel power stations.

MANUFACTURING INDICATORS

Average annual growth rate (%, 1980–87): 37.9
Share of GDP (%): 6 (1987) (latest)
Labor force in manufacturing (%): 3.3 (1986)
Value added in manufacturing (U.S. $ millions): 464
  Food and agriculture (%): 29
  Textiles (%): 0.0
  Machinery (%): 0.0
  Chemicals (%): 0.0
Total earnings as % of value added: 61

MINING

Although oil has been the only mineral produced in Oman, movement has been made to exploit other reserves. In September 1988, a two-year study was started to evaluate the possibility of mining copper in the Sohar region, where reserves with a high silver and gold content were estimated at 4 million tons. In November, a contract was signed by the government and a French company to explore for copper, chromium and coal reserves. Early in 1989, chromium deposits were explored by a British company.

ENERGY

Oil production in 1988 was 226 million bbl., almost all exported. The main producing fields are Fahud, Ghaba, Yibal and Natih and al-Huwaisah, all connected by pipeline to a terminal at Mina al-Fahal, near Muscat. Oil reserves are estimated at about 4.291 billion bbl., which represent 18 years of production. The sole operating company is Petroleum Development (Oman) Ltd., 60% owned by the Oman government, 34% by Shell, 10% by Compagnie Française des Pétroles and 2% by Partex (C. S. Gulbenkian Foundation). Exploration is conducted by Sun Oil, Elf/Sumitome and the Wintershall Group. Nonassociated natural-gas reserves are estimated to be about 80 billion cu. m. (2.825 trillion cu. ft.), enough to last 80 years at the unpressurized pipeline delivery capacity of 4 million standard cu. m. (140 million standard cu. ft.) per day. As Oman is not a member of OPEC, it is free from controls on production, although it does tend to follow pricing policy in line with the organization. Oman's first petroleum refinery came into operation in June 1982; its capacity of 50,000 bd. was sufficient to meet domestic demand for gasoline.

ENERGY INDICATORS

Average annual energy production growth rate (%, 1980–88): 10.3
Energy consumption per capita (000 kg. oil equivalent): 2.01 (1988)
Energy imports as % of merchandise exports: 2 (1988)
Average annual growth rate of energy consumption (%, 1980–87): 9.4
Electricity 1988
  Installed capacity (million kw.): 1.429
  Production (billion kw.-hr.): 3.895
    % fossil fuel: 100
  Consumption per capita (000 kw.-hr.): 2.827
Natural gas
  Proved reserves (billion cu. m.): 283 (1990)
  Production (billion cu. m.): 2.790 (1989)
Petroleum
  Proved reserves (billion bbl.): 4.291 (1990)
  Years to exhaust proved reserves: 18 (1990)
  Production (million bbl.): 226 (1989)
  Consumption (million bbl.): 20 (1988)
  Refining capacity (000 bbl./day): 77 (1990)

LABOR INDICATORS, 1986

Total economically active population (000): 468
  % working-age population (15–64): 60.9
  % female: 7.5
Activity rate (%)
  Total: 35.7
  Male: 57.6
  Female: 6.2
Sectoral employment (%)
  Agriculture, forestry, fishing: 6.8
  Construction: 27.5
  Manufacturing, mining, quarrying, public utilities: 33
  Trade, hotels, restaurants: 26.4
  Transport, communications; 1.4
  Finance, real estate: 1.7
  Services: 16.5
Average annual growth rate of labor force (%), 1980–2000: 2.7

LABOR

The skilled local labor force is small and must be constantly augmented by expatriate workers, who are from India, Pakistan and other parts of Arabia. The proportion of Omanis in the skilled nonrural labor force is estimated at 35%.

There are no trade unions in Oman. Since the early days of the reigning sultan's rule, Oman has had a comprehensive labor law defining conditions of employment for both Omani and foreign workers, who constitute a large percentage of the work force. Reports are that the labor law is fairly enforced and that workers' grievances, which are handled within the Ministry of Labor and Social Affairs, are generally given the benefit of the doubt in hearings conducted by labor inspectors.

Employment of those under 13 is prohibited. Omani law regulates the employment of juveniles, defined as those between ages 13 and 16, prohibiting evening and nighttime work, strenuous occupations and overtime and holiday work. A special section deals with employment conditions for women, prohibiting evening and nighttime work, safeguarding health and morals and setting out their rights to maternity leave. Omani labor law is very specific on matters of occupational safety and access to medical treatment. Likewise, the workweek is set at 48 hours (36 hours for Muslims during Ramadan), and various categories of leave are set forth.

Labor unions and strikes are illegal, and there is no collective bargaining; although Oman's labor law specifically prohibits the right to strike, it does mention the concept of "collective grievance" and encourages conciliation of disputes through formation of joint consultative bodies of labor and management.

FOREIGN COMMERCE

Oman's primary export is petroleum. Other exports include processed copper, dates, nuts and fish. Japan, South Korea and Thailand are its principal markets. Its major imports are machinery, transportation equipment, manufactured goods, food, livestock and lubricants, which it receives from Japan, the United Kingdom, the United States, Germany and the United Arab Emirates.

FOREIGN TRADE INDICATORS, 1987

Exports (U.S. $ billions): 3.6 (1988)
Imports (U.S. $ billions): 1.9 (1988)
Balance of trade (U.S. $ billions): 1.7 (1988)
International reserves in terms of months of imports covered: 6.6 (latest)

Direction of Trade (%), 1988

	Imports	Exports (est.)
European Community	31.6	10.4
United States	8.8	3.0
U.S.S.R. & Eastern European economies	0.1	0.0
Japan	16.8	51.3

Composition of Trade (%), 1988

	Imports	Exports
Food and agricultural raw materials	20.4	3.0
Fuels and other energy	1.5	86.6
Mineral ores and concentrates	0.6	0.1
Manufactured goods	77.4	10.3
of which chemicals	6.1	0.2
of which machinery	33.4	6.0

TRANSPORTATION & COMMUNICATIONS

Oman has no railroads or inland waterways. The port of Mina Qaboos, completed in 1974, provides eight deep-water berths. A coastal harbor has been completed at Raysut with berths for five ships as an outlet for Salalah. The oil terminal at Mina al-Fahal can accommodate the largest supertankers. The deep-water port at Matrah can handle 1.5 million tons of cargo per year. There are facilities for smaller craft at Sohar, Khaboura, Sur and Marbat.

The total length of the road network is 20,749 km (12,893 mi.), compared with less than 400 km. (248 mi.) in 1970. All main towns are linked by graded roads. Nearly 3,330 km. (2,064 mi.) of tarmac roads

TRANSPORTATION INDICATORS

Roads (latest)
  Length, km. (mi.): 20,749 (12,893)
  Paved (%): 20
Motor vehicles (latest)
  Automobiles: 120,367
  Trucks and buses: 106,097
  Persons per vehicle: 5.9
Merchant marine
  Vessels: 31 (1989)
  Total deadweight tonnage (000): 16.4 (1987)
Ports (pre-1986)
  Cargo loaded (million metric tons): 22.143
  Cargo unloaded (million metric tons): 4.028
Air (latest)
  Km. (mi.) flown (millions): 9.3 (5.8) (1985)
  Passenger-km. (passenger-mi.) (millions): 1,522 (946)
  Freight, ton-km. (ton-mi.) (millions): 40.1 (27.4)
  Mail, ton-km. (ton-mi.) (millions): 1.7 (1) (1985)
  Airports with scheduled flights: 6 (1990)
Pipelines, 1990
  Natural gas, km. (mi.): 1,030 (640)

COMMUNICATION INDICATORS, 1988

Telephones
- Total (000): 110
- Persons per telephone: 13

Phone traffic (million calls)
- Combined national: 374.133 (1989) (pulses)
- International: 18.053 (minutes)

Post office
- Number of post offices: 70
- Pieces of mail handled (millions): 33,163

Telegraph
- Total traffic (000 calls): 140
- National: 11
- International: 124

Telex
- Subscriber lines: 1,319
- Traffic (million minutes): 2.880

Telecommunications 1990
- 11 satellite stations

TOURISM & TRAVEL INDICATORS, 1986

Expenditures by nationals abroad (U.S. $ millions): 46
Number of hotel beds (000): 3
Average length of stay: 16 nights

have been completed, with 800 km. (500 mi.) completed in northern Oman as part of a rapid road construction program begun in 1970. A main road has been built from Muscat to Suhar, a distance of 240 km. (92 mi.) A rural bus service began operation in 1975.

Oman has no national airline but is a partner in Gulf Air, together with United Arab Emirates, Bahrain and Qatar. The main international airport is at Sib, near Muscat.

Tourists are discouraged from visiting Oman. Muscat's first international hotel was completed only in 1975, and it represented a break with tradition. There are 3,000 hotel beds, and the average length of stay is 16 days.

DEFENSE

The defense structure is headed by the sultan, who also is the defense minister. The defense forces have been commanded by British officers, but the proportion of British officers has been steadily declining; it is estimated that by mid-1980 there will be less than 1,000. There are, in addition, several thousand Baluchi tribesmen in the armed forces. Also, Jebalis, or mountain dwellers, are organized into home-guard units, or *firqats*, in tribal areas. Maintenance and other technical work is contracted out to a British firm. Enlistment for the armed forces is voluntary. The total strength of the armed forces was 25,500 in 1989.

Army

Personnel: 20,000

Organization: 2 headquarters brigades; 1 royal guard brigade; 1 armored regiment of 2 tank squadrons and 1 self-propelled AA battery; 1 reconnaissance regiment of 2 armored car squadrons; 2 light field artillery regiments; 2 medical artillery batteries; 1 light AA battery; 8 infantry regiments; 1 special force regiment; 1 signals regiment; 1 field engineer regiment; 1 parachute regiment

Equipment: 33 heavy tanks; 30 light tanks; 6 armored vehicles; 21 armored personnel carriers; 51 guns; 52 howitzers; 24 mortars; 10 antitank guided weapons; 4 air defense guns; SAM

Navy

Personnel: 2,500

Units: 1 royal yacht; 4 fast attack craft; 4 patrol craft; 4 amphibious vehicles; 1 training ship

Naval bases: Muscat and Matrah

Air Force

Personnel: 3,000, mostly ex-British RAF pilots and technicians

Organization and equipment: 52 combat aircraft; 2 fighter squadrons; 1 reconnaissance fighter squadron; 1 counterinsurgency squadron; 3 transportation squadrons; 2 helicopter squadrons; 2 air defense squadrons; trainers; air-to-air missiles.

Air bases: Bait al-Falaj, Salalah and Azaiba

The 1985 annual military budget was $2.076 billion. This expenditure was 49.1% of the national budget, 27.9% of the GNP, a staggering $1,695 per capita, the highest in the world.

The Omani army and air force are almost entirely British-trained and -equipped. Since 1945 the Omani forces have been tried on the field against the Saudis and the Dhofar insurgents; in both conflicts the Omani forces were successful. But the preponderance of mercenary elements makes their viability as a national army questionable. Arms purchases abroad during 1973–83 totaled $960 million.

EDUCATION

Oman has not introduced free, universal and compulsory education in the elementary grades. Nevertheless, attendance has increased. Schooling consists of 12 years, divided into six years of primary school, three of preparatory school and three of secondary school.

The academic year runs from September to May. The medium of instruction is Arabic, but English is taught from the secondary grades on. Adult education at primary to secondary level has received increased attention. Adult evening classes are held in 181 centers, 71 of which are for females. Over 6,000 men and less than half that amount of women are enrolled in these programs. A study-at-home program provides students with books and materials.

Schooling is under the control of the Ministry of Education.

Until the opening of the Sultan Qabus University in late 1986 all of Oman's higher studies students had to go abroad. Of the over 2,000 students who studied abroad in 1984–85, about one-sixth were female. Only those students with the highest grades are sent to non-Arab countries. Of these students, most have been

EDUCATION INDICATORS, 1990

Literacy (over age 6)
- Total (%): 41.0
- Males (%): 58.0
- Females (%): 24.0

First level
- Schools: 671
- Students: 304,207
- Teachers: 12,344
- Student/teacher ratio: 24.6
- Net enrollment ratio: 80 (1987)

Second level
- Schools: 128
- Students: 36,617
- Teachers: 2,219
- Student/teacher ratio: 16.5
- Net enrollment ratio: 14 (1981)

Vocational
- Schools: 25
- Students: 5,595
- Teachers: 728
- Student/teacher ratio: 7.7

Third Level
- Institutions: 5
- Students: 3,925
- Teachers: 482
- Student/teacher ratio: 8.1
- Gross enrollment ratio: 2.1 (1988)
- Students (/100,000 pop.): 168

Foreign study
- Students abroad: 2,496
  - of whom in
    - United States: 593 (1988)
    - France: 9 (1988)
    - Federal Republic of Germany: 4 (1987)
    - United Kingdom: 409 (1988)

Public expenditures 1988
- Total (R.O.) 110,351,000
- % of GNP: 4.0
- % of national budget: 14.9
- % of current expenditure: 89.5

accepted in the United States. Egypt has been the Arab country with most Oman university students.

The Sultan Qabus University took in 520 students in its first year, but is expected to have places for 3,000 students. In 1987–88 there were over 200 teachers at the university.

LEGAL SYSTEM

The legal system of Oman is based entirely on the Islamic Shari'a and is interpreted by *qadis*, or religious judges. Tribal custom, or *urf*, still governs crime and punishment in the interior. The severity of penalties prescribed by the Shari'a has been tempered to some extent, and mutilations and decapitations are unknown. At the apex of the court system is the chief court of the *qadis*, which hears appeals, but the ultimate court of appeal is the sultan himself. A separate court deals with cases involving foreigners, and the United Kingdom retains limited jurisdiction over British subjects.

Islamic law prescribes a fair and speedy trial before experienced and impartial judges, and judicial practice in Oman conforms largely to these prescriptions. In fact, however, the majority of cases are settled by out-of-court negotiations. There is no right under law to a jury, counsel or public trial, but members of the public do attend trials and hearings. The defendant is formally charged, either before a magistrate of the police court in the capital area, or a local magistrate *(qadi)* in outlying areas. The defendant may call and question witnesses. If convicted, he may appeal his case to the chief magistrate of the police court system, and ultimately to the sultan in cases involving serious offenses. In 1984 the government announced the opening of several petty courts throughout the country to bring judicial services closer to the citizenry. The various judicial systems are technically subordinate to the sultan, but they operate independently in the vast majority of cases.

The principal jail, the Jalali, an old Portuguese fort on the coast near Muscat, has a reputation sufficient to inspire terror in most Omanis. Few who pass through its forbidding gates ever emerge alive.

LAW ENFORCEMENT

The national police consists of about 300 men, of whom 50 are stationed in Muscat and Matrah. Crimes of violence are rare. The major law enforcement problem is smuggling, a traditional Omani activity.

HEALTH

The two main health scourges in the country are tuberculosis and trachoma. Malaria also is common in the coastal lowlands. No inoculation is available against communicable diseases. The low level of health is attributed to nutritional deficiencies and improper sanitation.

HEALTH INDICATORS

Health personnel 1987
- Physicians: 1,243
  - persons per: 1,071
- Dentists: 83
- Nurses: 3,497
- Pharmacists: 227
- Midwives: 33 (1983)

Hospitals 1987
- Number: 174
- Number of beds (/10,000); 30
- Admissions/discharges (/10,000): 1,248
- Bed occupancy rate (%): 8.30
- Average length of stay (days): 5

Types of hospitals (%), 1986
- Government: 100
- Private nonprofit: 0.0
- Private profit: 0.0

Public health expenditures (latest)
- As % of national budget: 4.8
- Per capita (U.S. $): 126.90

Vital statistics
- Crude death rate (/1,000): 12 (1990)
- Life expectancy at birth 1990
  - Males: 56
  - Females: 58
- Infant mortality rate (/1,000 live births): 105 (1990)
- Child mortality rate under 5 yrs. (/1,000) (1985–90): 157

Population with access to safe water (%): 53 (latest)

FOOD & NUTRITION

Fish and fishmeal are the main sources of protein in the Omani diet. Generally the diet of the nomads is better balanced than that of townspeople and consists of dates, rice, flour, mutton and milk.

No information is available on the caloric and protein intake of Omanis.

MEDIA & CULTURE

Three daily newspapers are published in Muscat, two in Arabic and one in English. Five weeklies are published.

There are no guarantees in law that protect freedom of speech or freedom of press. Criticism of the sultan in any form or medium is prohibited by law. Criticism of individual officials, agencies and their programs is tolerated but is not given media coverage. The government controls all radio and television broadcasting. Government control of all printed matter, including newspapers and magazines, is specified in the Press and Publication Law issued in May 1984. The law imposes strict controls on, and a mechanism for prior censorship of, all information in printed form in both domestic and imported publications. The government owns two of the three daily newspapers, one in Arabic and one in English. Subsidies to the several privately owned weekly and biweekly publications provide an effective incentive to self-censorship, although there have been arrests and closure for offensive articles. Thus editorials and news coverage invariably reflect government views. Publications arriving in Oman from foreign countries are censored for politically or sexually offensive material and occasionally are banned. The censor's attention generally focuses on articles that directly attack or embarrass the Omani government. In 1985 the sultanate's only resident Western correspondent had his residence permit revoked and was forced to leave the country. Authorities are reported to have objected to his pursuit of news stories on sensitive matters. Such stories never appeared in the Omani media, but the authorities objected to their publication elsewhere.

The national news agency is Oman News Agency. No international news bureaus are in Muscat.

Oman has no book publishing houses of any size.

Radio Oman broadcasts 20 hours a day in Arabic, and English on FM 14 hours daily with radio transmitters at Bait al-Falaj, Sib and Salalah. Radio Salalah transmits programs in Arabic and the Dhafari languages daily. The BBC has an eastern relay station on the island of Masirah. A color television station, built at Qurm outside Muscat, began transmission in 1974. Another color television station, for Dhofar, was opened in 1975.

The major library in Muscat is run by the British Council.

MEDIA INDICATORS

Newspapers
- Number of dailies: 3 (latest)
- Circulation (000): 30 (latest)
- Per 000 persons: 22 (latest)
- Number of nondailies: 2 (1986)
- Circulation (000): 10 (1986)
- Per 1,000 pop.: 8 (1986)
- Number of periodicals: 19 (1986)
- Circulation (000): 117 (1986)
- Newsprint consumption (1988)
- Total metric tons: 600
- Per 1,000 pop. (kg.): 438

Radio
- Number of transmitters: 15 (1989)
- Number of persons per radio receiver: 1.6 (1989)
- Total program hours: 3,954 (1987)

Television
- Television transmitters: 57 (1989)
- Number of persons per television receiver: 1.4 (1989)

Total program hours: 3,979 (1987)

Cinema
- Number of fixed cinemas: 24 (post 1984)
- Annual attendance (millions): 0.9 (pre 1984)

CULTURAL & ENVIRONMENTAL INDICATORS (latest)

Libraries (pre-1986)
- Number: 1
- Volumes (000): 20

Performing arts
- Number of performances: 35
- Annual attendance (000): 5
- Attendance (/1,000 pop.): 5

Nature reserves
- Number of facilities: 2

SOCIAL WELFARE

There is no social or public welfare program in the sultanate.

GLOSSARY

aflaj: man-made underground channel used for irrigation.
fukudh: clan or unit of a tribal division.
gharbi: west wind that blows in summer across Muscat and Oman from Rub al-Khali.
qadi: Muslim religious judge.
shaykh: tribal chieftain.
tamimah: supreme chief of a tribe
wali: governor of a wilayat or province.

CHRONOLOGY (from 1955)

1955— The imam of Oman, Muhammad ibn Abdullah, dies; his successor, Iman Ghalib ibn Ali, rebels against the sultan of Muscat and Oman, Said bin Taimur.

1956— With the aid of the British-led Muscat and Oman Field Force, the sultan occupies the capital of the imamate, Nizwah; the imam's brother Talib ibn Ali escapes to Cairo and with Egyptian and Saudi help sets up an imamate-in-exile.

1957— The civil war intensifies as Talib returns to Oman.

1959— The civil war ends with the complete rout of the rebel imam.

1960— Muscat and Oman concludes treaty with the United States.

1964— Dhofar tribes revolt against the sultan; the revolt escalates into a civil war as the rebel group, known as the Popular Front for the Liberation of Oman and the Arabian Gulf, receives aid from the Soviet Union and neighboring South Yemen.

1970— Sultan Said bin Taimur is overthrown in a palace coup led by his son Qabus ibn Said; Tariq ibn Ali is named new prime minister.

1971— Tariq resigns, and the sultan assumes the post of prime minister.

1974— First U.S. embassy opens in Muscat.

1975— The 11-year civil war ends as the Dhofar insurgents are crushed and their leaders surrender.

1979— At Persian Gulf Security Conference Oman offers a new routing system for ships through the Strait of Hormuz. . . . Oman becomes the first Arab state to endorse the Israeli-Egyptian Peace Treaty.

1981— Oman becomes a founding member, along with six other Middle East states, of the Gulf Cooperation Council.

1983— Oman and South Yemen resume diplomatic relations.

1985— Oman establishes diplomatic relations with the Soviet Union.

1987— Oman establishes diplomatic relations with Syria.

1990— Oman opens its air bases to U.S.-led U.N. forces during the Persian Gulf crisis.

1991— Oman sends ground troops to Saudi Arabia to assist in its defense; Oman ends financial aid to Jordan because of that country's support of Iraq during the Persian Gulf War.

BIBLIOGRAPHY

BOOKS

Anthony, J. D. *Historical and Cultural Dictionary of the Sultanate of Oman and the Emirates of Eastern Arabia.* Metuchen, N.J., 1976.

Clements, F. A. *Oman* (World Bibliographical Series). Santa Barbara, Calif., 1981.

———. *Oman: The Reborn Land.* White Plains, N.Y., 1980.

Department of Information. *Muscat.* London, 1972.

Department of State. *U.S. Relations with Arabian Peninsula/Persian Gulf Countries.* Washington, D.C., 1974.

Duchess of St. Albans. *Where Time Stood Still: Portrait of Oman.* London, 1982.

Grazl, Liesl. *The Omanis: Sentinels of the Gulf.* White Plains, N.Y., 1982.

Hawley, D. F. *Oman.* London, 1984.

———. *The Trucial States.* London, 1971.

Hill, Ann, and Daryl Hill. *The Sultanate of Oman: A Heritage.* New York, 1977.

Hopwood, D. *The Arabian Peninsula: Society and Politics.* London, 1972.

Middle East Economic Digest. *Oman.* Boulder, Colo., 1984.

Narayan, B. K. *Oman and Gulf Security.* New York, 1979.

Peterson, John. *Oman in the 20th Century.* New York, 1978.

Pridham, B. R. ed. *Oman: Economic, Social, and Strategic Developments.* London: Croom Helm, 1987.

Risso, Patricia. *Oman and Muscat: An Early Modern History.* New York, 1986.

Searle, Pauline. *Dawn over Oman.* London, 1979.

Skeet, Ian. *Muscat and Oman Before 1970: The End of an Era.* London, 1985.

Townsend, John. *Oman: The Making of a Modern State.* New York, 1977.

Whelan, John ed. *Oman: A MEED Practical Guide.* 2nd edition. London: Croom Helm, 1984.

Wikan, Unni. *Behind the Veil in Arabia: Women in Oman.* Baltimore, 1982.

Wilkinson, John Craven. *The Inmate Tradition of Oman.* New York, 1987.

OFFICIAL PUBLICATIONS

Deputy Prime Minister for Legal Affairs Office. *Official Gazette* (regular publication of data on government transactions).

Development Council. *Statistical Yearbook.*

Finance General. *Government Final Accounts. Directorate* (Arabic and English).

Oman Central Bank. *Annual Report* (Arabic and English).

———. *Quarterly Bulletin* (Arabic and English).

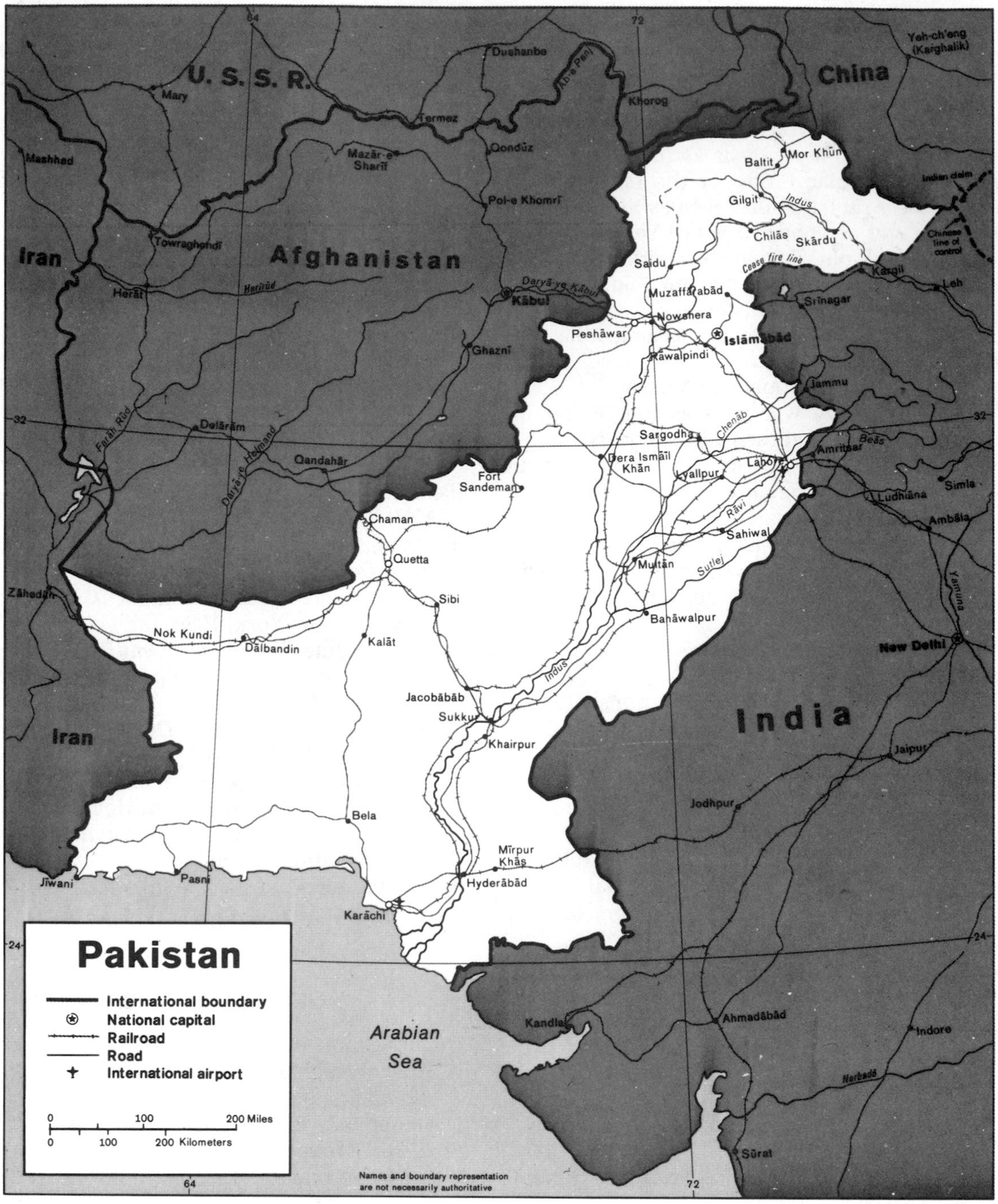

Pakistan

International boundary
National capital
Railroad
Road
International airport

0 100 200 Miles
0 100 200 Kilometers

Names and boundary representation are not necessarily authoritative

U. S. S. R.
China
Afghanistan
Iran
India
Arabian Sea
Mary
Dushanbe
Termez
Khorog
Mashhad
Mazār-e Sharīf
Qondūz
Pol-e Khomrī
Towraghondī
Herāt
Kābul
Ghaznī
Delārām
Qandahār
Zāhedān
Yeh-ch'eng (Karghalik)
Baltit
Mor Khūn
Gilgit
Chilās
Skārdu
Kargil
Leh
Indian claim
Chinese line of control
Cease fire line
Saidu
Muzaffarābād
Srīnagar
Peshāwar
Nowshera
Islāmābād
Rawalpindi
Jammu
Sargodha
Dera Ismāīl Khān
Lyallpur
Lahore
Amritsar
Fort Sandeman
Chaman
Quetta
Sahiwal
Ludhiāna
Simla
Ambāla
Multān
Sibi
Bahāwalpur
Nok Kundi
Dālbandin
Kalāt
New Delhi
Jacobābād
Sukkur
Khairpur
Jaipur
Jodhpur
Bela
Mīrpur Khās
Hyderābād
Jīwani
Pasni
Karāchi
Kandla
Ahmadābād
Indore
Sūrat
Indus
Chenāb
Rāvi
Sutlej
Beās
Yamuna
Narbada
Harīrūd
Daryā-ye Kābul
Farāh Rūd
Daryā-ye Helmand
Āb-e Panj
64
72
32
24

PAKISTAN

BASIC FACT SHEET

OFFICIAL NAME: Islamic Republic of Pakistan (Islami Jamhuria-e-Pakistan)

ABBREVIATION: PK

CAPITAL: Islamabad

HEAD OF STATE: President Ghulam Ishaq Khan (from 1988)

HEAD OF GOVERNMENT: Prime Minister Nawaz Sharif (from 1990)

NATURE OF GOVERNMENT: Federal republic

POPULATION: 114,649,406 (1990)

AREA; 803,943 sq. km. (310,403 sq. mi.)

ETHNIC MAJORITY: Punjabi

LANGUAGES: Urdu (official), English, Punjabi, Sindhi, Baluchi, Pushtu, Brahui, and Saraiki

RELIGION: Sunni Islam

UNIT OF CURRENCY: Rupee

NATIONAL FLAG: White crescent and a star centered on a field of dark green alongside a white stripe that runs the length of the post side

NATIONAL EMBELEM: A wreath of narcissus, a shield, a crescent, a star and a scroll. Surrounded by the wreath, the shield is divided into four sections, each showing a major product of the country: cotton, wheat, tea and jute. A crescent moon and star, the traditional Islamic symbols, are set above the shield between the open ends of the wreath. The scroll at the base of the emblem bears the national motto ("Faith, Unity, Discipline") in Urdu.

NATIONAL ANTHEM: "Blessed Be the Sacred Land"

NATIONAL HOLIDAYS: March 23 (Pakistan Day); May 1 (Labor Day): August 15 (Independence Day); September 6 (Defense of Pakistan Day); September 11 (Death Anniversary of Quaide-e-Azam, M. A. Jinnah); November 9 (Allama Iqlut Day); and December 25 (Birth Anniversary of Quaide-e-Azam); also variable Islamic and Christian festivals

NATIONAL CALENDAR: Gregorian

PHYSICAL QUALITY OF LIFE INDEX: 43

DATE OF INDEPENDENCE: August 15, 1947

DATE OF CONSTITUTION: August 14, 1973

WEIGHTS & MEASURES: In addition to the metric system, introduced in 1967, both imperial and traditional weights and measures are prevalent. The traditional units are:

- *Area:* 1 karam = 1.6 m. (5.5 ft.); 9 sq karams = 1 marla; 20 marlas = 1 kanal; 4 kanals = 1 bigha; 2 bighas = 1 ghumaon or 0.4047 ha. (1 ac.); 1 moraba = 10 ha. (25 ac.)
- *Length:* 1 girah = 3 unglies or 5.715 cm. (2.3 in.); 1 gaz = 16 girahs or 0.914 m. (3 ft.); 1 hath = 45.72 cm. (18 in.); 1 danda = 4 haths or 1.8 m. (2 yds.); 1,000 dandas = 1,828 m. (5,997 ft.)
- *Weight:* 1 ruttee = 8 chawals or 12.1 g. (0.427 oz.); 1 masha = 8 ruttees or 97 g. (3.4 oz.); 1 tola = 12 mashas or 1,164 g. (41 oz.); 1 chattak = 5 tolas or 58.32 gm. (2.05 oz.); 1 pao = 4 chattaks or 233.28 gm. (8.2 oz.); 1 seer = 4 paos or 933.1 gm. (32.9 oz.); 1 maund = 40 seers or 37.324 kg. (82.29 lb.)
- *Numerals:* 1 lakh = 100,000; 1 coror = 10 million; 1 arb = 1 billion

GEOGRAPHICAL FEATURES

Pakistan is in South Asia and extends from the Arabian Sea to the Hindu Kush mountain ranges. The total land area is 803,943 sq. km. (310,403 sq. mi.), excluding Azad or Pakistan-held Kashmir, Gilgit, Baltistan, Junagadh and Manavadar. The greatest distance is 1,875 km. (1,165 mi.) northeast to southwest and 1,006 km. (625 mi.) southeast to northwest. The total length of the coastline is 814 km. (506 mi.).

Pakistan shares its total international boundary of 5,847 km. (3,631 mi.) with four neighbors: Iran (830 km.; 516 mi.), Afghanistan (2,466 km.; 1,532 mi.), China (523 km.; 325 mi.) and India (2,028 km.; 1,260 mi.). Pakistan's boundary with Iran has been free of serious dispute. The border with the People's Republic of China was delimited in 1961–65. The boundary with Afghanistan, the Durand Line, had been the subject of dispute between the two countries since 1947. In the northeastern part of the country, Pakistan controls about 83,807 sq. km. (32,358 sq. mi.) of Jammu and Kashmir, and the Indo-Pakistan cease-fire line runs from Karakoram Pass to about 128 km. (80 mi.) northeast of Lahore. This line was arranged by the United Nations and runs for 772 km. (480 mi.). The rest of the Indo-Pakistan boundary, the 1,287 km. (800 mi.) Radcliffe Award line, includes 405 km. (252 mi.) delimited in the Rann of Kutch by the U.N. Indo-Pakistan Western Boundary Case Tribunal.

The federal capital is Islamabad (1981 population 204,364), which became a centrally administered area in 1970. The other major urban centers are Karachi (5,180,562), Lahore (2,952,689), Faisalabad (Lyallpur) (1,104,209), Hyderabad (751,529), Rawalpindi (794,843), Multan (722,070), Gujranwala (658,753), Peshawar (566,248), Sialkot (302,009), Sargodha (291,361), Quetta (285,719), Jhang (195,558) and Bahwalpur (180,263).

Pakistan is divided into three main geographic regions: the northern highlands, the Indus River Plain and the Baluchistan Plateau. The northern border and the western border with Afghanistan are enclosed in the convex arc of the Hindu Kush Mountains. Most of this area is over 2,500 m. (8,000 ft.), half over 4,500 m. (15,000 ft.), and there are 50 peaks over 6,700 m. (22,000 ft.), including K-2. South of the Khyber Pass are a series of mountain ranges; the Safed Koh Range, 4,761 m. (15,620 ft.); the Toba Kakar Range, 2,743 m. (9,000 ft.); and the Ras Koh Range, west of Quetta. The Baluchistan Plateau is an arid tableland of about 349,650 sq. km. (135,000 sq. mi.) with a number of smaller mountain ranges, such as the Central Brahui Range, the Kirthar Range, the Makran Range and the Sulaiman Range. The Indus River Plain corresponds roughly to the provinces of Punjab and Sind and contains some of the most fertile agricultural regions in the country. West of the Indus River Plain are the Thal and the Thar deserts.

The Indus is the principal river system, and it flows through Pakistan for 1,609 km. (1,000 mi.) of its total length of 2,413 km. (1,500 mi.). Its major tributaries are the Kabul River, the Gumal River and the Panjnad River, which is actually a confluence of five rivers: the Jhelum, the Chenab, the Ravi, the Beas and the Sutlej. The Indo-Pakistan boundary cuts across four of these rivers, but by the Indus Waters Treaty of 1960 Pakistan has been allocated the waters of the Indus, Jhelum and Chenab. The principal river of Baluchistan is the Zhob.

DEMOGRAPHIC INDICATORS

Population (millions): 114.649 (1990)
Year of last census: 1981
Sex distribution (% at last census): males, 52.5; females, 47.5
Population estimates and projections (millions)

1940: 28.300	1970: 65.706	2000: 162.467
1950: 39.513	1980: 85.299	2010: 205.472
1960: 49.955	1990: 122.666	

Age profile (% at last census)

0–14: 44.5	30–44: 15.4	60–74: 5.3
15–29: 23.9	45–59: 9.3	75 and over: 1.6

Median age (yrs.): 17.5 (1985)
Youth population (%, age 15–24): 20.2 (1985); 19.9 (2000)
Total dependency ratio: 90.1 (1985)
Annual growth rate (%)

1950–55: 2.24	1975–80: 2.64	2000–2005: 2.45
1955–60: 2.45	1980–85: 3.82	2005–2010: 2.25
1960–65: 2.69	1985–90: 3.45	2010–2015: 2.02
1965–70: 2.79	1990–1995: 2.87	2015–2020: 1.75
1970–75: 2.57	1995–2000: 2.75	2020–2025: 1.47

Hypothetical size of stationary population (millions): 556
Assumed year of reaching net reproduction rate of 1: 2040
Urban population (millions): 30.751 (1985)
Urban population (%): 31 (1988); 24 (1965)
Annual urban population growth rate (%, 1985–90): 4.87
Annual rural population growth rate (%, 1985–90): 2.81
Percentage of urban population in largest city: 21 (1980)
Percentage of urban population in cities of population over 500,000: 51 (1980)
Number of cities of population over 500,000: 8 (1980)
Population density per sq. km. (per sq. mi.): 139.4 (361.1) (latest)

CLIMATE & WEATHER

Pakistan is basically a dry country, and the general climatic character is one of aridity, although differences prevail between North and South. The country has four seasons: a dry, cool winter (December to February); a dry, hot summer (March to May); the southwesterly monsoon season (June through September); and northeasterly monsoon season (October and November). Average rainfall is less than 250 mm. (10 in.). Actual rainfall varies from region to region: 1,520 mm. (60 in.) or more in the northern highlands to 127 mm. (5 in.) or less in Baluchistan, the Thar and Thal deserts and the lower Indus River Plain. The northern mountains and Baluchistan have cool winters and moderate summer temperatures, while the upper and lower Indus River Plains have oppressive summers, with temperatures over 37.8°C (100°F). The highest maximum temperature on the Indian subcontinent was 52.2°C (126°F), recorded at Jacobabad in northern Sind. The heat is made intolerable by the dry wind called the *loo* that blows in summer.

VITAL STATISTICS

Crude birth rate (/1,000): 43 (1990); 48 (1965)
Crude death rate (/1,000): 14 (1990); 21 (1965)
Infant mortality rate (/1,000 live births): 110 (1990)
Maternal mortality rate (/100,000 live births): 600 (1980–84 est.)
Life expectancy (yrs.) at birth: males, 56; females, 57 (1990)
Gross reproduction rate (/woman) (1980–85): 3.42
Total fertility rate (/woman): 6.7 (1990)
Rate of natural increase (/1,000): 33.2 (1989)
Average household size: 6.5 (latest)

POPULATION

The population of Pakistan was 114,649,406 in 1990 on the basis of the last official census, in 1981, when the population was 84,253,644.

Punjab and Sind are the most populous provinces. Punjab and the North-West Frontier Province (NWFP) have the highest densities.

Despite growing urbanization, Pakistan is predominantly rural, with almost three-fourths of the population living outside cities. There are eight cities with over 500,000 inhabitants each. Nearly one fourth of the population of Karachi live in slums or squatter settlements.

According to official sources some 60,000 Pakistanis, mostly professionals, emigrate each year. Some 100,000 Pakistanis live in the United Kingdom, 50,000 in the United Arab Emirates and before the Iraqi invasion of Kuwait on August 2, 1990, 30,000 lived in Kuwait. After the formation of independent Bangladesh, Pakistan accepted a limited number of Biharis and repatriated Bangladeshis living in Pakistan. After the Soviet invasion of Afghanistan over 3 million Afghans moved to Pakistan. Pakistan has borne half the cost of their resettlement.

Pakistani society is traditional and Islamic. It assigns women a subordinate role in terms of civil, political and individual rights. Many Pakistani Muslims interpret the Koran's injunction on modesty to mean that women should remain in *purdah*, either at home or behind the veil. These attitudes have contributed to an adult female literacy rate approximately half that of men. Eight times as many men as women work outside the home, and those women who work or attend school usually do so in separate facilities. Few women hold political office, yet Benazir Bhutto was prime minister from 1988 to 1990.

Urban women were represented in the universities, but postgraduate employment opportunities remain largely limited to teaching, medical services and the law, with a small number of women entering the commercial and public sectors. The government's policy of "Islamization" has reversed some of the social and legal gains made by women in past years. The Benazir Bhutto government quietly halted the Islamization process but did not move to dismantle all of Zia's Islamic reforms.

STATUS OF WOMEN INDICATORS

Number of women (millions): 48.098
Women of childbearing age (15–49) (% of pop.): 46 (1988)
Married women of childbearing age (15–49) using contraception (%): 12 (latest)
Women's literacy rate (%): 15.2 (1990)
Women in labor force (%): 12.1 (1988)
Total fertility rate (/woman): 6.7 (1990)

Active birth control programs date only from 1965 and are coordinated by the Central Family Planning Council. A nationwide administrative apparatus has been created for physical implementation and motivation. Nearly 12% of women are believed to practice contraception. All these programs, however, had only a minimal effect on the rate of population growth.

ETHNIC COMPOSITION

Pakistan is a mosaic of ethnic groups held together only by a common religion. Each group has its own occupation and even dress, and also its own geographic, linguistic and social boundaries. The four dominant groups correspond roughly to the four provinces: Punjabis in the Punjab, Sindhis in Sind, Baluchis in Baluchistan and Pushtuns in the NWFP.

Punjabis, who form the numerical majority in Pakistan, comprise three major castes, or endogamous and functional groups: the Rajputs, the Jats and the Arains. There are a number of other smaller groups, such as Bilochs, Awans, Gujars, Lohars and Tarkhans. The Sindhis also are divided into scores of ethnic, linguistic, occupational and caste groupings. Baluchis form an important minority in Baluchistan and Sind; their main divisions are eastern Baluchis with seven tribes and western Baluchis with nine tribes. The Brahuis form 25% of the population of Baluchistan and are believed to be descendants of the original Dravidian inhabitants of the area. Minor groups in Baluchistan include the Jatts, who are unrelated to the Jats of the Punjab, and the Lassis. Pushtuns or Pathans constitute the dominant ethnic group in the NWFP and a sizable minority in Baluchistan. Fiercely independent, the Pathans lack a central organization, but each Pathan belongs to a tribe or descent group that determines his home territory and code of conduct. The more important of these tribes in Pakistan are Afridis, Yusufzais, Khattaks, Wazirs, Mohmands, Mahsuds and Orakzais.

Ethnic minorities include the *mujahirs* or Urdu-speaking refugees from India, the Makranis of Baluchistan and the Khos and Kafirs of Chitral. The Hindus, Parsis and some other smaller groups are properly considered as religious rather than ethnic minorities.

LANGUAGE

In the Constitution of 1973 Urdu is declared the official language, although English was to remain official medium of communication for 15 years. Urdu, however, is spoken by only 8% of the population and English by 2%. Over 30 distinct languages are spoken in Pakistan, besides a number of dialects. Of these, Punjabi is the most important in terms of the number of speakers, estimated at 63% of the population. Some of its dialects are classed as Western, or Lahnda, while others are called Eastern, or Majhi. Punjabi can be written in Urdu, Gurmukhi or Devanagiri scripts and shares a large vocabulary with Urdu. Sindhi is spoken by only 12% of the population, but it has fewer dialects and has important literary traditions of its own and a separate script. Opposition to the use of Urdu is strongest in Sindhi-speaking areas. Pushtu is the mother tongue of all Pushtuns or Pathans and has been strongly identified with the Pushtu separatist movement. Like Punjabi, Pushtu is not normally a written language, and the script and much of the vocabulary are borrowed from Urdu, Arabic and Persian. Baluchi, an Iranian language like Pushtu, and Brahui, a Dravidian language, are spoken by the Baluchis and Brahuis, respectively, in Baluchistan. Speakers of Pushtu, Brahui and Baluchi combine to form about 16% of the population.

English, spoken by about 1.5 million, is the language of the educated elite and the bureaucracy. Successive nationalist efforts to dislodge it from its primacy have failed partly because of regional opposition to Urdu.

RELIGION

As an Islamic republic, Pakistan is a theocratic state. Islam is the official religion and is followed by 96.7% of the population. In political terms religion forms the basis of national unity for diverse linguistic and ethnic groups, and the temporal Pakistani nation and the religious Muslim community or *umma* are inseparably one. The Constitution invokes Islamic principles and provides for the Advisory Council of Islamic Ideology to evaluate legislation in terms of its congruence with the Shari 'a. Both Sunnis and Shiites are represented in Pakistan, although Sunnis form the overwhelming majority. The government continues its efforts to make Pakistan into an Islamic society. It established a system of Nizam-e-Salaat in which "pious men" in every locality were appointed to encourage all Muslims to pray five times a day. Ordinances established Qazi (Islamic) courts and amended the military service acts to allow courts-martial to impose Islamic punishments.

Minority religious groups are protected, but Hindus, Christians and Parsis do not enjoy the same legal rights as Muslims. Reports of discrimination against minority groups in employment and education appear well founded. Seats in the national and provincial legislatures are reserved for members of minority religious groups, and under the reinstated Constitution of 1973 the president and the prime minister must be Muslims. In general, minority groups can practice their religion openly. Members of minority religious groups can maintain links with their coreligionists in other countries and undertake travel for religious purposes. Foreign clergy may enter the country to serve congregations. Although conversions are permitted, the government prohibits proselytizing among Muslims and has refused to renew the residence permits of some foreign missionaries who have ignored this ban.

The Ahmadi sect, which considers itself Muslim despite theological differences with traditional Islam, has historically been repressed. In 1974 the Zulfikar Ali Bhutto regime amended the Constitution to declare the Ahmadis a non-Muslim minority. In April 1984 the Zia government banned the use of Muslim terminology and proselytizing by the Ahmadis.

HISTORICAL BACKGROUND

Pakistan was part of the Indian Empire from 1857 to 1947. The territories that today constitute Pakistan were the last on the Indian subcontinent to come under British rule. Sind was conquered only in 1842 (15 years before the East India Company transferred its Indian territories to the Crown) by Sir Charles Napier, who wired the news of his conquest to London with a single cryptic word, *Peccavi* (I have Sin(ne)d). British rule over the North-West Frontier Province and Baluchistan always was tenuous and indirect.

Pakistan became independent in 1947 under the leadership of Jinnah.

The new nation received two serious blows to its political development during its first years of independence: Jinnah died in 1948 and his successor, Liaqat Ali Khan, was assassinated in 1951. It was only in 1956 that the nation adopted its first Constitution. The Constitution declared Pakistan to be an Islamic republic with a legislature composed of an equal number of representatives from East and West Pakistan. The Constitution did little to provide political stability and in 1958 President Iskander Mirza declared martial law, banned all political parties and abrogated the Constitution. Gen. Ayub Khan was initially appointed chief martial law administrator, but when Mirza was exiled, Ayub assumed the presidency.

A second Constitution was adopted in 1962 that established a presidential system based on indirect election. Parity between East and West Pakistan was preserved but Pakistan was no longer called an Islamic republic. Although Pakistan made considerable economic progress under Ayub, political discontent, particularly in East Pakistan, grew during 1968–69 and Ayub was forced to resign in March 1969. The nation was placed under martial law by Gen. Yahya Khan, head of the armed forces while preparations were made for the 1970 presidential elections. The 1970 elections precipitated a crisis. The East Pakistan Awami League won a clear majority, but the reluctance of West Pakistan to accept a government dominated by the East led to civil war and the creation of Bangladesh in 1971.

In December 1971 Yahya Khan relinquished the presidency to Zulfikar Ali Bhutto, leader of the Pakistan People's Party (PPP) which had won a majority in West Pakistan in the 1970 elections. Under Bhutto's guidance Pakistan adopted a new Constitution in 1973 and curtailed the power of the military. Committed to "Islamic socialism," Bhutto nationalized banking, heavy industry and educational institutions. He also improved relations with India, the United States and with the Muslim world. Bhutto's PPP won a victory in the 1977 elections amid charges of vote rigging. These allegations and other dissatisfactions led to rioting and in July 1977 Bhutto was overthrown by Gen. Zia ul-Haq, who established martial law. (Bhutto was eventually convicted of complicity in murder and hanged in 1979 despite international protests.)

Zia promised that his would be a caretaker regime leading to elections and the eventual return to civilian government. However elections were repeatedly postponed. Martial law continued in effect and all political parties were banned while he moved towards establishing a "truly Islamic order" in Pakistan. In 1984 he held a nationwide referendum on his Islamization program in which more than 60% of the voters were said to have favored his program. Zia used this as an excuse to continue in the presidency for another five years. Elections were held in 1985 which were boycotted by the Movement for the Restoration of Democracy, a coalition led by the former prime minister's daughter, Benazir Bhutto.

Following the elections Zia appointed Muhammad Khan Junejo prime minister and lifted martial law. Political parties were legalized in 1986. Zia abruptly dismissed the Junejo government because of alleged corruption in May 1988. He dissolved the assembly and announced elections within 90 days.

Zia was killed in a plane crash in August 1988. Elections took place in November in which Benazir Bhutto's PPP won a strong plurality. Bhutto became the first women premier of an Islamic state the following month. Faced with ethnic conflict and severe economic problems, Bhutto never established a solid base in the legislature and in late 1989 her government narrowly survived a vote of no confidence. Her party suffered a decisive defeat in the October 1990 elections and Nawaz Sharif, leader of the Islamic Democratic Alliance, was sworn in as prime minister in November.

CONSTITUTION & GOVERNMENT

Between independence in 1947 and 1973, Pakistan adopted three permanent and four interim constitutions. The Constitution promulgated on April 10, 1973 established Pakistan as an Islamic Republic, "where Muslims are enabled to live in accordance with the

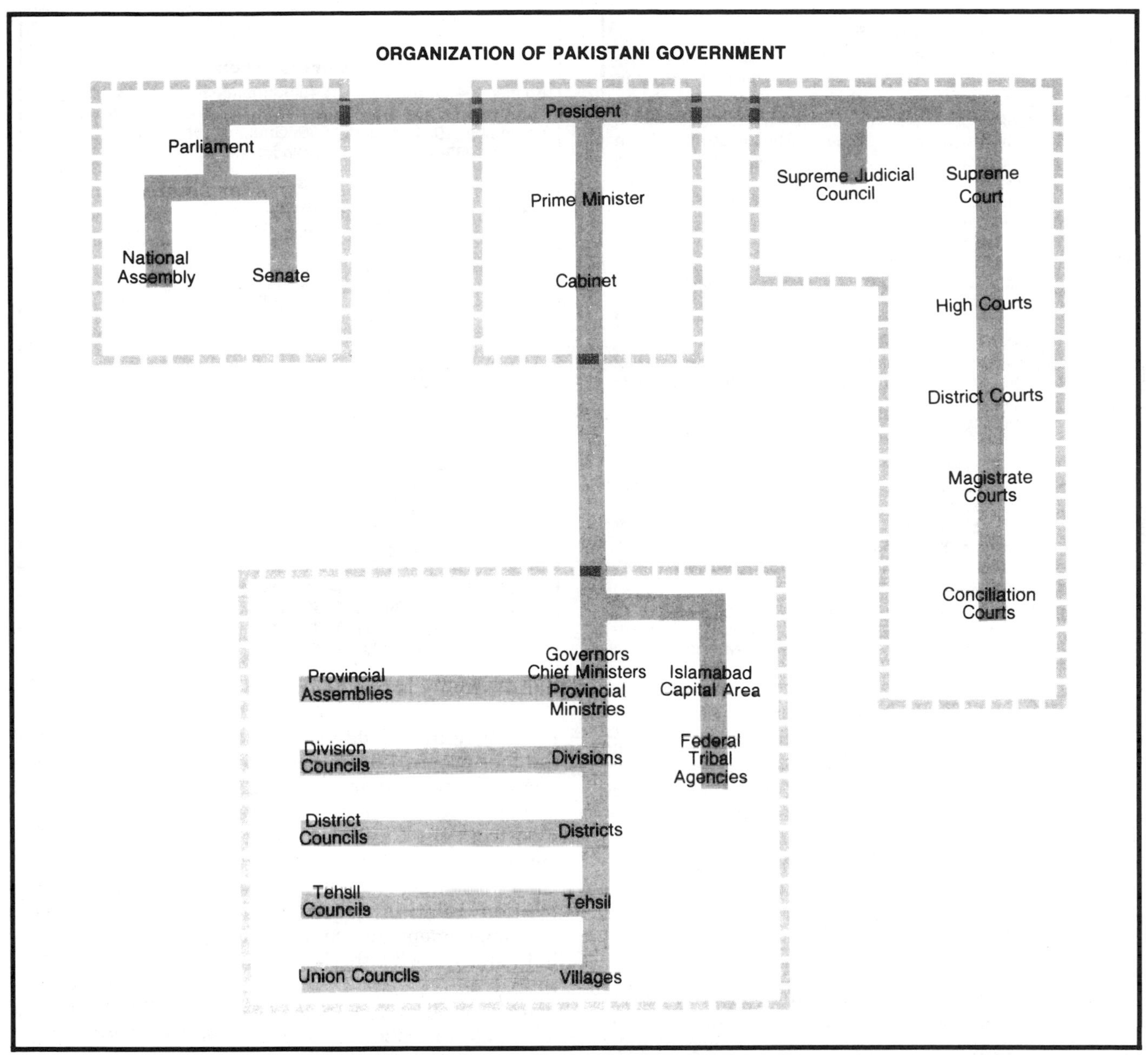

teachings and requirements of Islam." It provides for a parliamentary form of government, with the Majlis-i-Shura, the legislature, consisting of the National Assembly and the Senate, and the executive consisting of the president and the prime minister. The Eighth Amendment to the Constitution, added in 1985, strengthened the president vis-a-vis the prime minister. Benazir Bhutto attempted to have the Amendment repealed in 1989 but without success. All four provinces have their own legislatures elected on the same basis of adult franchise as the National Assembly, with chief ministers responsible to the provincial assemblies. The Constitution also outlines the relationship between the central government and the provinces and demarcates areas of legislation by means of a concurrent list, a federal list and a provincial list. Matters in the Federal list are subject to the exclusive authority of the Majlis-i-Shura, while both Majlis-i-Shura and Provincial Assemblies can legislate on matters in the Concurrent list. Defense, external affairs, currency, communications and foreign trade are under central jurisdiction. Education, labor, health, industry, law and order, agriculture, roads and social welfare are entrusted to provinces. The Council of Common Interests formulates and regulates central provincial and interprovincial policies. Among other institutions established by the Constitution are the National Economic Council, the National Finance Commission and the Council of Islamic Ideology.

The Constitution also enumerates and guarantees individual and communal fundamental rights and the independence of the judiciary. The state is directed to prevent the concentration of wealth and the means of production and distribution in the hands of a few and to eliminate all forms of exploitation. The Constitution also provides that the prime minister shall be elected

GOVERNMENT LIST
(July/August 1991)

President	Ghulam Ishaq Khan
Prime Minister	Sharif, Nawaz
Minister of Commerce	Khan, Malik Mohammad Naeem
Minister of Communications	Jatoi, Ghulam Murtaza Khan
Minister of Construction	Mahmud, Syed Tariq
Minister of Defense	Sharif, Nawaz
Minister of Education	Iman, Syed Fakhr
Minister of Environment & Urban Affairs	Naseer, Sardar Yaqub Khan
Minister of Finance & Economic Affairs	Aziz, Sartaj
Minister of Food & Agriculture	Malik, Abdul Majid, *Lt. Gen. (Ret.)*
Minister of Foreign Affairs	Sharif, Nawaz
Minister of Health	Gardezi, Syed Tasneem Nawaz
Minister of Industries	Hussain, Chaudhry Shujat
Minister of Interior	Hussain, Chaudhry Shujat
Minister of Labor, Manpower & Overseas Pakistanis	Haq, Mohammad Ejazul
Minister of Law, Justice & Parliamentary Affairs	Iman, Syed Fakhr
Minister of Local Government & Rural Development	....
Minister of Narcotics Control	Singh, Rana Chandar
Minister of Petroleum & Natural Resources	Khan, Chaudhry Nasir Ali
Minister of Planning & Development	Chatta, Chaudhry Hamid Nasir
Minister of Production	Nabi, Islam
Minister of Railways	Bijrani, Mir Hazar Khan
Minister of Science & Technology	Chatta, Chaudhry Hamid Nasir
Minister of Special Education & Social Welfare	....
Minister of Youth Affairs	Shah, Syed Ali Gohar
Special Adviser to the Prime Minister	Khan, Roedad
Special Adviser for Information & Public Affairs	Ahmed, Sheikh Rashid
Minister of State for Law & Parliamentary Affairs	Hussain, Chaudhry Amir
Minister of State for Sports	Khan, Ajmal
Attorney General	Munshi, Aziz A.
Governor, State Bank	Parekh, Qasim

RULERS OF PAKISTAN

Governors-General

August 1947–September 1948: Muhammad Ali Jinnah
September 1948–October 1951: Khwajah Nazimuddin
September 1951–August 1955: Ghulam Muhammad
August 1955–March 1956: Iskander Mirza

Presidents

March 1956–October 1958: Iskander Mirza
October 1958–March 1969: Muhammad Ayub Khan
March 1969–December 1971: Agha Muhammad Yahya Khan
December 1971–August 1973: Zulfikar Ali Bhutto
August 1973–September 1978: Fazal Elahi Chaudhry
September 1978–August 1988: Muhammad Zia ul-Haq
December 1988– : Ghulam Ishaq Khan

Prime Ministers

August 1947–October 1951: Liaquat Ali Khan
October 1951–April 1953: Khwajah Nazimuddin
April 1953–August 1955: Muhammad Ali Bogra
August 1955–September 1956: Chaudhry Muhammad Ali
September 1956–October 1957: Husain Shahid Suhrawardy
October 1957–December 1957: Ismail Ibrahim Chundrigar
December 1957–October 1958: Malik Firuz Khan Noon
Prime minister's post abolished until 1973
August 1973–September 1978: Zulfikar Ali Bhutto
Prime minister's post abolished again in 1978
March 1985–May 1988: Muhammad Khan Junejo
December 1988–August 1990: Benazir Bhutto
August 1990–November 1990: Ghulam Mustafa Jatoi
November 1990– : Nawaz Sharif.

by the National Assembly and along with the other ministers responsible to it. The government also can invoke emergency provisions of the Defense of Pakistan Rules in times of war, internal disorder and financial crisis. The emergency has to be approved by the Majlis-i-Shura at the end of the first two months and thereafter every six months. The prime minister can dismiss provincial governments.

The Constitution of 1973 provides for an election commission under a chief election commissioner whose duties include preparation and revision of electoral rolls. Suffrage is universal over age 21.

FREEDOM & HUMAN RIGHTS

In terms of civil and political rights Pakistan is classified as a partly-free country.

The human rights situation progressively deteriorated in Pakistan under President Zia. Combining Islamic puritanism with authoritarianism, Zia eliminated all vestiges of freedom in the country. According to Martial Law Order 72, inserted as an amendment to the Constitution, military courts were authorized to try virtually all criminal cases in Pakistan. The government endorsed the system of punishments outlined in the Islamic Code of Shari 'a, including public floggings. Amputation was recommended as a punishment for certain types of crimes. However, the judiciary, representing the only institution in the country with the authority to stand up to the government, showed considerable independence. Even after enactment of Marital Law Order 72, the Lahore High Court ordered the release of 47 political prisoners held under preventive detention. Strict censorship was reintroduced, and at least four opposition papers were forced to close down. According to Amnesty International there was a sharp increase after Zia's accession to power in the number of cruel, inhuman and degrading punishments handed down by the military courts. Most of the opposition leaders belonging to former president Zulfikar Ali Bhutto's Pakistan's People Party were placed under detention, and there were many travel and political restrictions on the others not in jail. Minority groups, including the Ahmadiyas, were denied rights enjoyed by Muslims but were permitted to participate in local elections in 1980. National elections were postponed for an indefinite period. Parties opposed to Islamic ideology or the integrity and security of Pakistan, as well as those believed to receive funds from abroad, were banned. A Human Rights Society was permitted to function, but its activities were pathetically feeble.

Religion dominated the political scene in the Zia regime. Prayers were compulsory in all government offices, and the inscription "In the name of the Almighty, the Beneficient and the Merciful" appeared on all letterheads. All courts had special religious benches, and they made sure that the most draconian penalties were imposed under Islamic law. Enactment of religious laws on drinking, adultery and theft did not reduce crime but significantly broadened opportunities for corruption. Smuggling, gambling, prostitution and bootlegging thrived under the protection of powerful functionaries. The government also ordered the imposition of traditional Islamic levies (2½% of all savings and 5% of agricultural production), ostensibly for charity. These levies were imposed even on the Shiites, whose doctrines do not call for such a tax. On campuses the fanatic Jamaat-e-Islami were encouraged to beat up students who demonstrated against the government.

During the 1980s the trend in human rights was toward improvement, although abuses continued. The government lifted martial law and held elections in 1985. However, the balloting was boycotted by the opposition coalition. Political parties were legalized in 1986. The nation held free elections in 1988, following Zia's death, and again in 1990. Press freedom increased markedly. Military courts, which had operated with scant regard for due process, were abolished in 1985. However, their decisions could not be appealed to civilian courts. On the negative side, there were continuing allegations of torture and traditionally harsh and abusive treatment of prisoners.

Some believe that corruption became more widespread during the 1980s as large sums of money entered the country from overseas workers and from narcotics trafficking. Socially prominent Pakistanis suffered less at the hands of officialdom than those less well off, partly because of the ability of the former to return favors or offer inducements to appropriate civil servants and partly because of the general deference still accorded social "betters." Although the original caste distinctions common to South Asian societies are disappearing in Pakistan, clan (Baradari) affiliations, which in some ways parallel the old system, still can help or hinder those seeking education, employment or justice.

CIVIL SERVICE

In 1973 Prime Minister Zulfikar Ali Bhutto established the All-Pakistan Unified Civil Service, with 22 pay grades, after abolishing the former prestigious Central Superior Services, which consisted of the Civil Service of Pakistan, the Pakistan Foreign Service, the Police Service of Pakistan and other services. Recruitment is made by the Central Public Service Commission, 20% on the basis of merit and 80% on the basis of merit and regional parity. Lateral entry is encouraged for scientists, specialists and professionals.

LOCAL GOVERNMENT

Pakistan is divided into four provinces and the Islamabad Capital Area, plus agencies, and tribal areas for purposes of regional administration. The governor of each province is appointed by the president, while the chief minister is elected by the provincial assembly. Provincial assemblies are unicameral bodies elected for five-year terms on the basis of universal suffrage. The size of the assembly is 40 in Baluchistan, 80 in the NWFP, 240 in Punjab and 100 in Sind. The provincial capitals are Karachi (Sind), Lahore (Punjab), Quetta (Baluchistan) and Peshawar (NWFP).

The provinces are divided into divisions headed by commissioners, and the divisions into districts headed by deputy commissioners. Punjab has five divisions, NWFP three, Sind three and Baluchistan two. The deputy commissioner remains the linchpin of the administration, as in the days of the British Raj, and is involved in all governmental activities at the district level. The bottom tiers of local government consist of *tehsils* and *talukas*, the last of which are revenue or tax units. Popular participation in local government is channeled through union councils in villages, town councils in towns, *tehsil* councils, district councils, divisional councils and municipal committees.

There are 12 provincially administered tribal areas and 10 federally administered ones, known as agencies, each under a political agent. Tribal areas are granted varying degrees of autonomy, especially in the administration of justice. The Northern Areas (72,520 sq. km.; 28,000 sq. mi.), consisting of the Diamir, Gilgit and Baltistan agencies, are governed by the Ministry of the Interior, States, Frontier Regions and Kashmir Affairs. Pakistan-held Jammu and Kashmir, known as Azad Kashmir (11,639 sq. km; 4,494 sq. mi.), consists of four districts under its own president and prime minister, with the seat of government at Muzaffarabad.

FOREIGN POLICY

The central determinant of Pakistani foreign policy is its hostility to India, based on centuries-old mutual suspicion between Hindus and Muslims. This rivalry finds its sharpest expression in the conflict over Kashmir. The conflict began in 1947, has led to three wars and still is far from a resolution. Indo-Pakistani relations reached their nadir in 1971 in the wake of India's military victory in East Pakistan, but the "Simla Process" of step-by-step normalization has produced some constructive results, especially the repatriation of over 91,000 Pakistani prisoners of war in Indian hands. Bangladesh was recognized by Pakistan in 1974, and in the same year trade and communications links with India were restored.

The two nations made several attempts to improve relations in the last two decades. In 1981 General Zia proposed a "no war" agreement which India rejected as a trick. When India later offered a similar proposal, Pakistan viewed it with suspicion. Nevertheless, the two nations were able to conclude agreements on technical cooperation and trade. Relations between the two countries were strained during the early 1980s when the Indian government accused Pakistan of aiding Sikh extremists and Pakistan accused India of supporting antigovernment demonstrations. A border dispute over the Siachen Glacier, which both countries claim, remains unresolved.

The most sensitive issue between the two nations has been nuclear proliferation. India exploded a nuclear device in 1974 and, in response, Pakistan vowed to achieve the capability. Pakistan later offered to enter an agreement for mutual abandonment of nuclear capacity, but India refused. Following Zia's death in 1988 India and Pakistan agreed to sign a treaty not to attack each other's nuclear facilities. Nevertheless, the two nations did not address the problem of border disputes.

In 1985 Pakistan joined India and other nations on the Indian subcontinent in forming the South Asian Association for Regional Cooperation (SAARC).

Relations with the United States have been cemented by Pakistani membership in U.S.-sponsored regional alliances. Following a low point in 1971 during the Indo-Pakistani War, U.S. military and economic aid was resumed. But relations remained low key because of Pakistan's desire to develop nuclear weapons. The United States strengthened ties following the Soviet invasion of Afghanistan. In an effort to maintain Pakistani opposition to the invasion and guarantee the nation's role as a conduit for arms to Afghan rebels, the United States increased aid to Pakistan tremendously. The Reagan administration negotiated an agreement providing for $3.2 billion in economic and military assistance over five years as well as $1.1 billion in direct sale of 40 F-16 aircraft.

Development of good relations with the Soviet Union has eluded Pakistan, but it remains an important concern.

Mutual hostility toward India brought Pakistan and the People's Republic of China close in the 1960s. This alliance has grown stronger over the years. China has been one of the most generous providers of loans to Pakistan. In 1971 the Chinese opened the Karakoram Highway, built by Chinese engineers, linking Sinkiang and Gilgit. In August 1984 the Khunjerab Pass on the Karakoram highway, linking China and Pakistan, was formally opened, and a joint Sino-Pakistani economic commission was established after President Zia's visit to Beijing in October.

Pakistan is required by its Constitution to preserve and strengthen relations with Muslim countries. Pakistan has faithfully adhered to this policy, but most Arab and Muslim states have remained neutral in Indo-Pakistani conflicts. With some Islamic countries, such as Iraq, relations have been erratic. Pakistan's staunchest friend has been Turkey, former comember in CENTO (Central Treaty Organization). Iran, an old ally, has become a hostile neighbor. In the face of such enmity, Pakistan relentlessly pursued its one and only goal in foreign relations: to draw closer to the powers of Islam. Islamic chauvinism was raised to the level of an ideology in Islamabad. The ties with Islamic countries such as Saudi Arabia also are lucrative in the economic sense, bringing in much-needed development funds. At the end of the 1980s, the number of Pakistani emigrants in Middle Eastern countries was estimated at over 1 million. Militarily, Pakistan is prepared to lend its men and matériel (more of the former because the latter is mostly aged and decrepit) to the defense of Islam anywhere in the world.

Pakistan and the United States are parties to 43 agreements and treaties, covering agricultural commodities, aviation, consuls, customs, defense, economic and technical cooperation, education, extradition, finance, informational media guarantees, investment guarantees, judicial assistance, lend-lease, maritime matters, the Peace Corps, postal matters, property, publications, relief supplies, taxation, trade and commerce, trademarks and visas.

Pakistan joined the United Nations in 1947. It is a member of 16 U.N. organizations and 33 other international organizations. Its membership in the Commonwealth was terminated in 1972 as a protest against Britain's alleged bias toward India.

PARLIAMENT

The federal parliament, the Majlis-i-Shura, is a bicameral body consisting of the Senate and the National Assembly. The National Assembly consists of 237 members, of whom 207 are elected directly by universal suffrage over age 21. Twenty seats are reserved for women and 10 for minorities. The term of the National Assembly is five years, and it holds sessions at least twice a year, with not more than 120 days between the end of one session and the beginning of the next. The Constitution (Tenth Amendment) Bill set the minimum number of working days of the National Assembly at 130 days reducing it from 160 days. The Senate consists of 87 members. Members are elected for six-year terms, one-third retiring every two years. The Senate performs an advisory role in matters relating to almost all subjects. Money bills and legislation relating to national defense, foreign affairs, the civil service and certain other areas can originate only in the National Assembly. The Senate has the right to send legislation back to the National Assembly for reconsideration only once. On certain subjects, a joint session is held to decide the matter by simple majority. In the 1990 legislative elections, the Islamic Democratic Alliance won 105 seats; the Pakistan Democratic Alliance 45 seats; the Muhajir National Movement 15 seats; the Assembly of Islamic Clergy and the Awami National Party each 6 seats; the Assembly of Pakistani Clergy 3 seats; and, the Jiway Pakistan Party and the Pakistan National Party each two seats. Independents won 22 seats.

POLITICAL PARTIES

Political parties have functioned only intermittently in Pakistan. They were banned from 1958 to 1962 and from 1979 to the end of 1985, when they were permitted to operate under highly controlled circumstances. The process for legalizing parties was simplified in 1988.

The Government party is the Islamic Democratic Alliance (IDA), formed in 1988 as an alliance of nine right-wing and Islamic parties to oppose the leftist Pakistan People's Party (PPP). It favors increased Islamization and support of the Afghan Mujaheddin.

The dominant opposition party is the Pakistan People's Party (PPP) formed by Zulfikar Ali Bhutto in 1967 as a moderate socialist party. Following Bhutto's execution, party leadership was assumed by his widow, Begum Nusrat Bhutto, and his daughter, Benazir Bhutto. In February 1981 the PPP joined eight other parties to form a joint Movement for the Restoration of Democracy (MRD) in opposition to General Zia. As a result of the disagreement over electoral strategy in 1988, the PPP campaigned separately in that year's election. The party won a plurality in parliament, and Benazir Bhutto was asked to form a government. The party campaigned in the 1990 election as part of an informal grouping composed of the PPP, the Tehrik-i-Istiqlal, the Pakistan Muslim League (Chatta Group) and the Tehrik Firqah Jafariya. It lost decisively to the IDA.

Other political parties include:

- the Muhajir National Movement, formed in 1986, representing the interests of Muslim migrants in Pakistan
- Assembly of Islamic Clergy, formed in 1950, advocating adoption of a constitution in accordance with Sunni Islamic teachings
- Assembly of Pakistani Clergy, formed in 1948, advocating progressive Sunni Islamic principles
- Pakistan National Party, a left-wing, pro-Soviet, Pro-Indian party
- Awami National Party, formed 1986, advocating federalism and socialism, supporting the Soviet government in Afghanistan.

ECONOMY

Pakistan is one of the low-income countries of the world. It has a free-market economy in which the dominant sector is private.

PRINCIPAL ECONOMIC INDICATORS

Gross National Product (U.S. $ billions): 40.134 (1989)
GNP per capita (U.S. $): 370 (1989)
GNP average annual growth rate (%, 1980–89): 6.3
GNP per capita average annual growth rate (%, 1987–89): 2.9
Income distribution (%, household income) (1984–85)
  Lowest 20%: 7.8
  Highest 10%: 31.3
Average annual rate of inflation (%, 1980–88): 6.5
Consumer price index (1980 = 100) 1986
  All items: 151
  Food: 150
Wholesale price index (1980 = 100): 133 (1985)
Average annual growth rate (%, 1980–88)
  General government consumption: 11.0
  Private consumption: 4.3
  Gross domestic investment: 6.5

Pakistan is primarily an agricultural country with serious problems including a rapidly increasing population, sizable government deficits and heavy dependence on foreign aid. In addition, the economy must support a large military establishment and provide for millions of Afghan refugees.

The nation enjoyed a period of strong economic growth in the late 1970s and early 1980s with a real growth rate of 5%–6% annually. This growth was based on large amounts of foreign aid as well as remittances from Pakistani workers abroad. With the end of the oil boom and the 1990 Iraqi invasion of Kuwait, remittances dropped sharply.

The Bhutto government nationalized much of the country's industry in the early 1970s, but more recent leaders have moved to privatize the economy. In 1980 the government announced plans to Islamize the economy. This affected mainly the financial sector, abolishing interest and limiting liability. The move also led to

BALANCE OF PAYMENTS, 1988 (U.S. $ millions)

Current account balance: −1,403
Merchandise exports: 4,405
Merchandise imports: −7,012
Trade balance: −2,607
Other goods, services & income +: 903
Other goods, services & income −: −2,397
Other goods, services & income net: −1,494
Private unrequited transfers: 2,084
Official unrequited transfers: 614
Capital other than reserves: 1,525
Net errors & omissions: 66
Counterpart items: 25
Total change In reserves: −281

GROSS DOMESTIC PRODUCT

GDP nominal (P.R.s billions): 772.34 (1989)
Average annual growth rate of GDP (%, 1980–88): 6.5
GDP by type of expenditure (%) 1987
  Consumption
    Private: 73
    Government: 14
  Gross domestic investment: 19
  Gross domestic saving: 13 (1988)
  Foreign trade
    Exports: 14
    Imports: −19
Cost components of GDP (%) 1987
    Net indirect taxes: 10
    Consumption of fixed capital: 6
    Compensation of employees & net operating surplus: 84
Sectoral origin of GDP (%) 1987
  Primary
    Agriculture: 22
    Mining: 2
  Secondary
    Manufacturing: 18
    Construction: 6
    Public utilities: 2
  Tertiary
    Transportation & communications: 8
    Trade: 16
    Finance: 7
    Other services: 9
    Government: 10
Average annual sectoral growth rates (%, 1980–88)
    Agriculture: 4.3
    Industry: 7.2
    Manufacturing: 8.1
    Services: 7.4

the introduction of religious taxes as specified in the Koran.

PUBLIC FINANCE

The Pakistani fiscal year runs from July 1 through June 30.

Public revenue collections and disbursements take place at three levels: central, provincial and local. The central government, which enjoys the bulk of the taxing power, is legally required to share part of the revenues with the provinces according to a formula revised periodically by the National Finance Commission. The annual budgets of both the central and the provincial governments include a revenue (current) and a capital (development) budget.

Of current revenues, 31% come from customs duties, 14% from excise taxes and 10% from income taxes. Approximately one-fourth of all current expenditures go to public debt service and another fourth to defense. Education and health account for less than 5% of expenditures.

CENTRAL GOVERNMENT EXPENDITURES (latest)

% of total expenditures
- Defense: 29.5
- Education: 2.6
- Health: 0.9
- Housing, social security, welfare: 8.7
- Economic services: 34.5
- Other: 23.8

Total expenditures as % of GNP: 21.7 (1988)
Overall surplus or deficit as % of GNP: −7.0 (1988)

CENTRAL GOVERNMENT REVENUES (latest)

% of total current revenues
- Taxes on income, profit & capital gain: 11.9
- Social security contributions: 0.0
- Domestic taxes on goods & services: 33.0
- Taxes on international trade & transactions: 31.0
- Other taxes: 0.3
- Current nontax revenue: 23.8

Total current revenue as % of GNP: 16.5
General government consumption as % of GDP: 14 (1988)
Average annual growth rate of general government consumption (%, 1980–88): 11.0

Central planning was introduced in the mid-1950s under the auspices of the Planning Commission, which determined both the direction and the pace of economic growth. The first three five-year plans emphasized the growth of the gross national product, especially industry, and functioned within the framework of a basically private-sector economy. With the intervention of the Indo-Pakistani War and the dismemberment of east Pakistan, the planning mechanism fell into disrepair. The Zulfikar Ali Bhutto regime changed the ideological orientation of development policy from industry to agriculture and from income growth per se to income growth coupled with income redistribution and from the private sector to the public sector. Development plans during the 1980s focused on the underfunded social sectors. The 1988–93 plan emphasized industry in the private sector.

During 1970–88 Pakistan, including Bangladesh before 1972, received $4.2 billion in U.S. aid. Commitments from other Western countries and ODA and OOF bilateral aid totaled $7.5 billion during 1980–87. OPEC contributed $2.3 billion in bilateral aid from 1979–89. Communist countries granted $2.9 billion from 1970–88.

FOREIGN AID, 1989

Total foreign aid (U.S. $ millions): 3,472.4
- Bilateral: 1,433.3
- Multilateral: 2,039.1

CURRENCY & BANKING

The Pakistani unit of currency is the rupee, divided into 100 paisa. Coins are issued in denominations of 1, 2, 5, 10, 25 and 50 paisa and 1 rupee and notes in denominations of 1, 5, 10, 50 and 100 rupees. In June 1991 the official rate of exchange was $1 = R 23.73.

The Pakistani banking system consists of the central bank, the State Bank of Pakistan; five state-owned commercial banks; and about 10 foreign banks. In 1974 all Pakistani banks were nationalized. Foreign banks were not affected but were not permitted to open any new branches in Pakistan. Specialized credit institutions include the Agricultural Development Bank of Pakistan, the Industrial Development Bank of Pakistan, the Investment Corporation of Pakistan, the National Investment (Unit/Trust) Limited, the Pakistan Industrial Credit and Investment Corporation, the People's Finance Corporation and the Life Insurance Corporation. In 1976 all existing cooperative banks were dissolved, and cooperative credit became a function of the Federal Bank for Cooperatives and the provincial cooperative banks.

GROWTH PROFILE
(Annual Growth Rates, %)

Projected population (1988–2000): 3.1
Projected crude birth rate (/1,000) (1990–95): 41.9
Projected crude death rate (/1,000) (1990–95): 10.6
Urban population (1980–88): 4.5
Labor force (1985–2000): 2.8
GNP (1980–89): 6.3
GNP per capita (1987–89): 2.9
GDP (1980–88): 6.5
Inflation (1980–88): 6.5
Agriculture (1980–88): 4.3
Industry (1980–88): 7.2
Manufacturing (1980–88): 8.1
Services (1980–88): 7.4
Money holdings (1980–88): 14.4
Manufacturing earnings per employee (latest): 6.2
Energy production (1980–88): 6.6
Energy consumption (1980–88): 6.2
Exports (1980–88): 8.4
Imports (1980–88): 3.8
General government consumption (1980–88): 11.0
Private consumption (1980–88): 4.3
Gross domestic investment (1980–88): 6.5

FINANCIAL INDICATORS, 1989

Total reserves minus gold (SDRs millions): 396
SDRs (millions): 1
Reserve position in IMF (SDRs millions): 0
Foreign exchange (SDRs millions): 395
Gold (fine troy oz. millions): 1.95
Ratio of external debt to total reserves: 28.7 (1988)
Central bank 1989
  Assets (%)
    Foreign assets: 13.9
    Claims on government: 61.1
    Claims on banks: 25.0
    Claims on private sector: 0.0
  Liabilities (%)
    Reserve money: 68.2
    Government deposits: 10.8
    Foreign liabilities: 14.8
    Capital accounts: 0.0
Money supply 1989
    Stock (P.R. billions): 217.027
    M1 per capita: 1,800
Private banks
  Assets (%)
    Loans to government: 24.1
    Loans to private sector: 60.4
    Reserves: 9.2
    Foreign assets: 6.2
  Liabilities
    Deposits (P.R. billions): 323.157
    of which %
      Demand deposits: 34.3
      Savings deposits: 25.7
      Government deposits: 0.3
      Foreign liabilities: 15.6
External debt 1988
  Total (U.S. $ billions): 17.010
    of which public (U.S. $ billions): 3.064
    of which private (U.S. $ billions): 13.944
  Debt service (long-term)
    Total (U.S. $ billions) (long term): 1.258
    Repayment
      Principal (%): 65.8
      Interest (%): 34.2
  Debt service ratio (%): 17.1
  External public debt as % of GNP: 37.4
  Debt service as % of GNP: 3.4
  Debt service as % of exports: 23.5
  Terms of public borrowing
    Commitments (U.S. $ billions): 2.020
    Average interest rate (%): 5.2
    Average maturity (yrs.): 23
  Net flow of publicly guaranteed external capital (U.S. $ millions): 794
  Receipt of workers' remittances (U.S. $ billions): 2.018
  Net direct private investment (U.S. $ millions): 23

In 1979 movement toward an "Islamic economy" was announced. In June 1980 the *zakat* (a poor tax at the rate of 2.5% annually on banks' deposits and savings accounts) was deducted from all savings accounts, and in 1983 the *ushr* (a tax on agricultural produce at the rate of 5%) also was implemented. In January 1981 Pakistan introduced interest-free banking, which became compulsory for all banks in July 1985.

AGRICULTURE

Of the total land area of 80,394,300 ha. (198 million ac.), forests constitute 2 million ha. (5 million ac.), other uncultivated land 31.5 million ha. (78 million ac.) and cultivated land 19 million ha. (48 million ac.).

Pakistan's most important natural resource is land, and agriculture accounts for more than one-fourth of GDP. Agricultural land constitutes 30% of the land area.

Small farms predominate in terms of units. Of the 4.8 million farms, over half are 2 ha. (5 ac.) or less, only 2% are over 20 ha. (50 ac.) and only 14,000 have as much as 60 ha. (150 ac.) or more. Four types of land tenure are prevalent: *zamindari*, or absolute ownership of large estates; peasant proprietorship of comparatively small holdings; *ryotwari*, or tenancy on state-owned land on a permanent basis; and *jagirdar*, or land held as a grant from the state. Zulfikar Ali Bhutto's land reforms of 1973, individual land owner-

AGRICULTURAL INDICATORS

Agriculture's share of GDP (%): 27 (1989)
Average annual growth rate (%, 1980–88): 4.3
Value added in agriculture (U.S. $ billions): 8.935 (1988)
Cereal imports (000 metric tons): 602 (1988)
Index of agricultural production (1979–81 = 100): 128 (1986)
Index of food production (1979–81 = 100): 124 (1986)
Index of food production per capita (1979–81 = 100): 107 (1986–88)
Number of tractors: 164,000 (1986)
Number of harvester-threshers: 680 (1986)
Total fertilizer consumption (million metric tons): 1.511 (1985–86)
Fertilizer consumption (g./ha., hundreds): 829 (1987–88)
Number of farms (millions): 4.070 (1980)
Average size of holding (ha.): 4.7 (1980)
Size class (%) 1980
  Below 1 ha. (below 2.47 ac.): 17.2
  1–5 ha. (2.47–12.35 ac.): 56.2
  5–10 ha. (12.35–24.7 ac.): 17.4
  10–20 ha. (24.7–49.4 ac.): 6.5
  20–50 ha. (49.4–123.5 ac.):
  50–200 ha. (123.5–494 ac.): } 2.7
  Over 200 ha. (over 494 ac.):
Tenure (area) (%) 1980
  Owner-operated: 64.1
  Rented: 35.6
  Other: 0.0
Farms as % of total land area: 24.0 (1980)
Land use (%)
  Cropland: 27
  Pasture: 6
  Forest: 4
  Other: 63
Yields (kg./ha.) 1989
  Grains: 1,767
  Roots & tubers: 10,197
  Legumes: 464
  Milk (kg./animal): 1,110
Production (1989)
  Fruits (million metric tons): 3.824
  Vegetables (million metric tons): 3.475
Livestock (000) 1989
  Cattle: 17,363
  Horses: 472 (1986)
  Sheep: 28,345
Forestry 1988
  Production of roundwood (million cubic meters): 23.928
    of which industrial roundwood (%): 6.1
Fishing 1988
  Total catch (000 metric tons): 445.4
    of which marine (%): 78.3
  Value of exports (U.S. $ millions): 121.803

ship was limited to 60 ha. (150 ac.) of irrigated land or 120 ha. (300 ac.) of nonirrigated land.

In view of the primacy of agriculture in the national economy, the government plays an active role in its development through price support programs, credit and extension work. Seeds and fertilizers are distributed to farmers at subsidized rates. The Pakistan Agricultural Development Corporation is the principal state agency concerned with procurement and distribution of agricultural crops. However, yields per acre of wheat in the Pakistani portion of the Punjab still are considerably lower than yields in the Indian portion; farmland that has been irrigated for years is being lost to salinity and waterlogging, and growth in consumption of fertilizer will slow down as a result of a government decision to raise fertilizer prices an average of 50%. Agricultural credit is provided by the Agricultural Development Bank of Pakistan. *Taccavi* or emergency credit is extended to farmers by provincial governments on a long-term basis.

The livestock sector has been declining on account of poor marketing, inadequate feed forage and genetic degeneration of breeds.

Most of the fish is exported, and it provides a significant source of foreign exchange.

MANUFACTURING

Pakistan's manufacturing activity is composed of a large private sector and a small public sector. Until 1969 a total of 22 families controlled 22% of the industrial capital, 80% of banking and 97% of insurance. This concentration of wealth was broken up in 1972 by the Economic Reforms Order, under which 10 basic industries were taken over by the state: iron and steel, metals, heavy engineering, heavy electricals, motor vehicles, tractors, chemicals, petrochemicals, cement and public utilities, comprising 32 industrial units. The government also controls industry through its licensing system and through its credit institutions, including the Industrial Development Bank of Pakistan, the Pakistan Industrial Credit and Investment Corporation and the Life Insurance Corporation. The managing agency system was dismantled in 1973. Official policy was committed under Zulfikar Ali Bhutto to a mixed economy, dispersal of industrial ownership and foreign investment. The military regime reversed this policy and introduced a number of measures to restore levels of private-sector investment. However, banking, utilities, insurance and shipping remained under state control. Pakistan's first steel mill was completed with Soviet aid in 1980 and began production in 1983.

Most government companies generally are plagued by inefficiency, old equipment and swollen payrolls. Eight government-owned corporations account for about 20% of Pakistan's industrial output, but most of them operate at less than 50% capacity and show a poor return on assets.

Pakistan's uncertain external financial situation; the unsettled political situation; and the labor laws, which make it difficult to fire excessive or unproductive employees, have deterred some large-scale private investment. Private-sector fears of nationalization subsided somewhat when government policies consistently offered guarantees and incentives to private investment while trying to reduce government involvement in industry. The Protection of Rights and Industrial Property Order was promulgated in February 1979 to safeguard private industrial firms from arbitrary nationalization. In 1978 private investment was permitted in three industries previously reserved for government-owned firms: cooking oil, basic chemicals and cement.

Small-scale industries have been much more successful than their larger counterparts, so much so that organizations such as the World Bank recommend that more encouragement be given to smaller-scale industries.

The government offers liberal incentives to overseas investors, including guarantees for the repatriation of capital, facilities for remittance of profits, and compensation in the event of nationalization. There is no requirement that overseas investors must accept a certain percentage of local capital or yield controlling interest to nationals.

MANUFACTURING INDICATORS, 1987

Average annual growth rate (%, 1980–88): 8.1
Share of GDP (%): 17 (1988)
Labor force economically active in manufacturing (% est.): 13.2 (1985)
Value added in manufacturing (U.S. $ billions): 5.001
  Food & tobacco (%): 34 (latest)
  Textiles & clothing (%): 19 (latest)
  Machinery & transport equipment (%): 9 (latest)
  Chemicals (%): 14 (latest)
Earnings per employee in manufacturing 1986
  Growth rate (%): 6.2 (latest)
  Index (1980 = 100): 138
Total earnings as % of value added: 20 (1986)
Gross output per employee (1980 = 100): 149 (1986)
Index of manufacturing production: 173 (1988)

MINING

Pakistan is poorly endowed with mineral wealth. There are known to be large reserves of at least 16 minerals, but only chromite is exported. The country's iron ore reserves are estimated at 560 million tons.

ENERGY

Energy is derived principally from petroleum and natural gas. Pakistan is not self-sufficient in energy and imports approximately one-third of its fuel. The nation has estimated crude oil reserves of 100 million barrels as well as extensive reserves of both coal and natural gas. Total deposits of coal have been estimated at 545 million tons, but it is of poor quality and its production has been limited by inefficient mining technology. Oil and gas exploration is undertaken by the state-owned Oil and Gas Development Corporation and by seven foreign concessionaires. Aggressive exploitation in the mid-1980s reduced Pakistan's oil imports and improved its trade balance. The country has three oil refineries—two at Karachi and one at Rawalpindi.

About two-thirds of Pakistan's electrical output comes from hydroelectric sources. Pakistan has a nuclear plant at Karachi which is being augmented by construction of an atomic power plant at Chasma.

ENERGY INDICATORS

Average annual energy production growth rate (%, 1980–88): 6.6
Energy consumption per capita (kg. oil equivalent): 210 (1988)
Energy imports as % of merchandise exports: 27 (1988)
Average annual growth rate of energy consumption (%, 1980–88): 6.2
Electricity (1988)
  Installed capacity (million kw.): 6.876
  Production (billion kw.-hr.): 36.940
    % fossil fuel: 53.0
    % hydro: 45.4
    % nuclear: 1.6
  Consumption per capita (kw.-hr.): 321
Natural gas
  Proved reserves (billion cu. m.): 650 (1990)
  Production (billion cu. m.): 13.450 (1989)
  Consumption (billion cu. m.): 10.772 (1988)
Petroleum
  Proved reserves (million bbl.): 305 (1990)
  Years to exhaust proved reserves: 9 (1990)
  Production (million bbl.): 17 (1989)
  Consumption (million bbl.): 44 (1988)
  Refining capacity (000 bbl./day): 121 (1990)
Coal
  Reserves (million metric tons): 102 (latest)
  Production (million metric tons): 2.723 (1988)
  Consumption (million metric tons): 3.574 (1988)

LABOR

Labor productivity is low because of the shortage of skills, a high rate of absenteeism, dietary deficiencies and generally poor living and working conditions. Although basic labor rates are low, overall labor costs are not as low as might first appear because of the low output and absenteeism mentioned above as well as liberal leave benefits. Other expenses include cost-of-living allowances or bonus payments plus housing, medical, retirement and other benefits. Representatives of the textile industry estimate that an unskilled worker's legislated minimum wage actually costs employers three times as much because of these fringe benefits and allowances. In addition, foreign enterprises are expected to pay higher wages and provide superior benefits to their employees. Besides the financial benefits, the Pakistani labor laws provide that (1) workers be given participation in management; (2) each shop or department in a large industrial unit have a shop steward who will represent the workers' interests and point of view in the management of that shop and will act as a link between the workers and management; and (3) every establishment employing 50 or more persons is to have a Works Council consisting of representatives of employers and employees. The Works Council promotes measures for securing and preserving good relations and particularly promotes settlement of differences through bilateral negotiations.

LABOR INDICATORS (1989–90)

Total economically active population (millions): 31.818
  % working-age (15–64): 50.3
  % female: 11.4
Activity rate (%)
    Total: 28.8
    Male: 49.4
    Female: 6.8
Employment status (%)
  Employers & self-employed: 48.2
  Employees: 24.7
  Unpaid family workers: 24.0
  Other: 3.1
Sectoral employment of economically active (%)
  Agriculture, forestry, fishing: 49.5
  Construction: 6.2
  Manufacturing, mining, quarrying, public utilities: 13.0
  Trade, hotels, restaurants: 11.5
  Transportation, communications: 4.7
  Finance, real estate: 0.7
  Services: 11.0
Average annual growth rate of labor force (%, 1985–2000): 2.8
Unemployment (millions): 1.074 (1985)
Labor under 20 years (%): 22.0 (1985)
Earnings in manufacturing (/worker) (/mo.) (P.R.): 627.2 (1982)

Pakistani law sets minimum wages for both skilled and unskilled labor. Comprehensive health and safety legislation provides for inspection of the workplace by government inspectors to ensure compliance with health, safety and workmen's compensation regulations. Although observed mainly in the breach, the law requires that no adult work more than nine hours without payment of overtime, that no worker work more than 10 hours of overtime per week and that no child under age 15 is to be employed. Children between 15 and 17 are not to work more than five hours a day.

The labor unions are heavily politicized because the unions are weak in relation to employers, and workers have to turn to outside politicians for redress of grievances. The major trade unions are the All-Pakistan Federation of Labor; the All-Pakistan Federation of Trade Unions; the Pakistan Central Federation of Trade Unions; the Pakistan National Federation of Trade Unions; the Pakistan Railway Employees Union; the Pakistan Trade Union Federation; the Pakistan Transport Workers Federation; and the United Workers Federation.

FOREIGN COMMERCE

Pakistan's primary exports are rice, cotton, textiles and clothing. Its principal imports are petroleum and petroleum products, machinery, transportation equipment and chemicals. The European Community, Japan and the United States are its main trading partners.

TRANSPORTATION & COMMUNICATIONS

Administration of the rail system is vested in the Railway Board, under the Ministry of Railways. The system also was the second-largest employer in the country, with 140,000 employees. The pipeline system

FOREIGN TRADE INDICATORS, 1988

Exports (U.S. $ billions): 4.5 (1989)
Imports (U.S. $ billions): 7.2 (1989)
Balance of trade (U.S. $ millions): −2.7 (1989)
Annual growth rate (1980–88), exports (%): 8.4
Annual growth rate (1980–88), imports (%): 3.8
International reserves in terms of months of imports covered: 1.5
Terms of trade (1980 = 100): 106
Import price index (1980 = 100): 83.9 (1986)
Export price index (1980 = 100): 79.8 (1986)

Direction of Trade (%), 1989

	Imports	Exports
European Community	23.1	26.9
United States	15.7	11.4
U.S.S.R. & eastern European economies	1.8	2.2
Japan	13.8	11.5

Composition of Trade (%), 1989

	Imports	Exports
Food and agricultural raw materials	22.0	33.9
Fuels & other energy	14.4	0.7
Mineral ores & concentrates	2.4	0.6
Manufactured goods	61.1	64.8
of which chemicals	15.7	0.4
of which machinery	29.4	0.8

had in 1987 250 km. (155 mi.) of crude-oil pipeline, 4,044 km. (2,513 mi.) of natural-gas pipeline and 885 km. (550 mi.) of refined-products pipeline.

The chief port is Karachi. A second port, Port Muhammad Bin Qasim, became operational in 1980. A third port, Port Gwadar is used for the ship-breaking industry while construction of Port Pasni on the Baluchistan coast began in 1988. The government took over the management of all shipping companies in 1974 and reorganized them into two corporations, the National Shipping Corporation and the Pakistan Shipping Corporation, which were merged in 1979 into the Pakistan National Shipping Corporation. The Pakistani shipping fleet consists of 87 ships, including 46 general cargo ships, one tanker, one bulk carrier and four passenger ships. Together they carry about 10% of the country's seaborne traffic.

Government assistance for road development comes from the Road Fund, financed from a share of the excise and customs duty on sales of petroleum and from development loans. In 1978 the 800-km. (497-mi.) Karakoram Highway, linking Xinjiang Province in China with Havelian, north of Islamabad, was completed after being under construction for 20 years. An ambitious project in the advanced planning stage is the Indus Superhighway, which, when completed at a cost of Rs3.1 billion, will link Peshawar and Karachi and reduce the distance by road between the two cities by 400 km. (248 mi.).

The international flag carrier is Pakistan International Airlines, which operates regular services to 24 cities abroad and 20 towns and cities in Pakistan. It has a fleet of 30 aircraft. The major international airports are at Karachi, Rawalpindi, Peshawar, Quelta, Islamabad and Lahore.

TRANSPORTATION INDICATORS

Roads (latest)
  Length, km. (mi.): 112,137 (69,682)
  Paved (%): 53
Motor vehicles (latest)
  Automobiles: 540,835
  Trucks and buses: 158,895
  Persons per vehicle: 159
Railroads (latest)
  Track, km. (mi.): 12,620 (7,842)
  Passenger-km. (passenger-mi.) (billions): 18.710 (11.626)
  Freight, metric ton-km. (short ton-mi.) (billions): 8.160 (5.589)
Merchant marine
  Vessels (over 100 tons): 72 (1989)
  Total deadweight tonnage (000): 525.7 (1989)
  Oil tankers (000 GRT): 44 (1985)
Ports (pre-1986)
  Cargo loaded (million metric tons): 4.308
  Cargo unloaded (million metric tons): 17.604
Air
  Km. (mi.) flown (millions): 49.3 (30.6) (1985)
  Passenger-km. (passenger-mi.) (billions): 8.743 (5.433) (latest)
  Freight, metric ton-km. (short ton-mi.) (millions): 388.8 (266.3) (latest)
  Mail, metric ton-km. (short ton-mi.) (millions): 6.6 (4.5) (1985)
  Airports with scheduled flights: 32 (1990)
Pipelines 1987
  Refined, km. (mi.): 885 (550)
  Natural gas, km. (mi.): 4,044 (2,513)

COMMUNICATION INDICATORS, 1988

Telephones
  Total (000): 740
  Persons per telephone: 158
Phone traffic (million calls)
  Local and long distance: 4,941.994 (pulses)
  International: 4.112
Post office
  Number of post offices: 12,736
  Pieces of mail handled (millions): 701.183
Telegraph
  Total traffic (million calls): 3.303
    National: 3.050
    International: .253
Telex
  Subscriber lines: 7,970
Telecommunications 1990
  Satellite stations: 3

TOURISM & TRAVEL INDICATORS, 1986

Total tourist receipts (U.S. $ millions): 142 (1988)
Expenditures by nationals abroad (U.S. $ millions): 366 (1988)
Number of hotel beds (000): 61
Tourist nights (millions): 1.608
Number of tourists (000): 440.5 (1985)
  of whom from United States: 23.9
  India: 191.3
  United Kingdom: 81.3
  Federal Republic of Germany: 9.9

DEFENSE

The defense structure is headed by the president, under whom are the commanders of the three separate armed services and the paramilitary forces.

Military service is voluntary and lasts for two years.

The strength of the armed forces is 482,800, including the Frontier Corps. Service personnel constitute 6.2 armed persons per 1,000 inhabitants.

Army

Personnel: 450,000, including 29,000 Azad Kashmir (Frontier Corps) troops

Organization: 7 headquarters corps; 1 field command; 2 armored divisions; 16 infantry divisions; 8 artillery brigades; 3 AA artillery brigades; 6 armored reconnaissance regiments; 4 independent armored brigades; 8 independent infantry brigades; 7 SAM batteries; 1 special services group

Equipment: 1,506 tanks; 545 armored personnel carriers; 1,000 guns; 175 howitzers; mortars; rocket launchers; antitank guided weapons; air defense guns; 112 SAM's

Army aviation: 1 liaison squadron; 4 helicopter squadrons; 95 observation aircraft; 89 helicopters

Navy

Personnel: 15,200

Naval bases: Karachi; Kaptai

Equipment: 11 submarines; 8 destroyers; 16 fast attack craft; 24 patrol craft; 3 mine countermeasures vessels; 2 tankers

Naval aviation: 3 combat aircraft; 6 helicopters; 1 antisubmarine maritime reconnaissance squadron; 2 helicopter search and rescue squadrons; antisubmarine missiles

Air Force

Personnel: 17,600

Organization: 375 combat aircraft; 8 fighter squadrons; 11 interceptor squadrons; 1 reconnaissance squadron; 2 transportation squadrons; 1 helicopter search and rescue squadron; 1 helicopter utility squadron; 1 training squadron; air-to-air missiles

Air bases: Peshawar; Kohat; Mauripur; Samundri; Deigh Road; Risalpur; Sargodha; Gilgit; Chitral; Malir; Miramshah

In terms of national willingness to employ force and the quality of manpower (itself an amalgam of morale, training and physical stamina), Pakistan's armed forces are among the best in South Asia. Their logistical range and effectiveness actually improved as a result of the dismemberment of the country in 1971, enabling them to be deployed intensively along the Indian border. In the three wars against India since independence in 1947 Pakistan has performed poorly only in the last, in 1971, when it had to fight on two fronts separated by thousands of kilometers. But in any future conflict with India it will be at a decided disadvantage because of the sheer physical and economic superiority of its opponent as well as the exposure of its bases to swift strikes by the Indian air force.

EDUCATION

Pakistan has a low literacy rate of 25.6% (36.0% for males and 15.2% for females). The principle of universal, free education was accepted as official policy by the Zulfikar Ali Bhutto government. When and if fully implemented, it will be extended to grade eight, or age 15.

The school year runs from July to June in the Karachi region and from April to March in other areas. The medium of instruction is English at all levels of private schools and from the secondary level in public schools. Adult education is an important concern, and a National Literacy Corps is planned to undertake a massive program in this field.

The educational ladder consists of 12 years of schooling: five years in primary school, three in middle school and four in high school. The tertiary level is of seven years' duration, including two-year intermediate, two-year undergraduate and three-year postgraduate courses. Passage between levels is controlled by standard government-controlled examinations.

EDUCATION INDICATORS, 1989

Literacy
- Total (%): 25.6
- Male (%): 36.0
- Female (%): 15.2

First level
- Schools: 87,545
- Students: 7,768,000
- Teachers: 189,200
- Student/teacher ratio: 41.1

Second level
- Schools: 11,743
- Students: 2,931,000
- Teachers: 150,100
- Student/teacher ratio: 19.5

Vocational
- Schools: 235
- Students: 64,000
- Teachers: 4,702
- Student/teacher ratio: 13.6

Third level (postsecondary)
- Institutions: 720
- Students: 588,677
- Teachers: 42,446
- Student/teacher ratio: 13.9
- Gross enrollment ratio: 5.0 (1986)
- Students (/100,000 pop.): 469
- % of population age 25 and over with postsecondary education: 1.9

Foreign study
- Foreign students in national universities: 1,109 (1985)
- Students abroad: 8,864
  - of whom in
    - United States: 6,114 (1988)
    - France: 42 (1988)
    - Federal Republic of Germany: 210 (1988)
    - United Kingdom: 946 (1987)

Public expenditure 1987
- Total (P.R.): 17,512,000
- % of GNP: 3.1
- % of national budget: 5.0 (1980)
- % of current: 75.8

Private and elite schools have played a significant role in Pakistan and enjoy greater prestige than public schools.

Pakistan has 12 universities. The universities are as follows: University of Baluchistan (Quetta), Gomal University (Dara Ismail Khan), Islamia University (Bahwalpur), University of Karachi (Karachi), Multan University (Multan), Open University (Islamabad), Pakistan Agricultural University (Lyallpur), Pakistan

University of Engineering and Technology (Lahore), University of Peshawar (Peshawar), University of the Punjab (Lahore), Quaid-e-Azam University (Islamabad) and University of Sind (Hyderabad).

LEGAL SYSTEM

The legal system is based on English common law.

The central judiciary consists of the Supreme Court of Pakistan, four provincial high courts for each of the four provinces, district and session courts at the district level and conciliation courts at the village level. The Supreme Court has original, appellate and advisory jurisdiction, including jurisdiction over disputes between the federal and provincial governments and between provincial governments. The constitution of 1973 provides for the separation of the judiciary and the executive from 1976. As the guardian of the independence and integrity of the judiciary, the Supreme Judicial Council can discipline judges and monitor the judicial system in general. The Council is composed of the chief justice, the two most senior justices of the Supreme Court and chief justices of the provincial high courts.

Until the lifting of martial law on December 30, 1985, there were three judicial systems: a civilian judiciary based on Anglo-Saxon law, Shari 'at benches operating under Islamic law and military courts functioning under various martial law regulations. According to a 1981 provisional constitutional order, the civilian judiciary could not review the actions of the martial law authorities and the military courts. Among the steps taken to pave the way for the lifting of martial law, the regime transferred to civilian courts all cases being tried in military courts under certain martial law orders.

Shari 'at benches try offenses under the Hadood Ordinances but otherwise operate similarly to ordinary civilian courts. Cases referred to the Shari 'at benches are heard by judges from the civilian court system who, in practice, apply ordinary criminal procedures in most cases. Defendants in the Shari 'at courts can obtain bail and lawyers of their choice; judges and attorneys must be familiar with Islamic law. The appellate benches also are staffed with ordinary judges from the provincial higher courts. The government's 1979 Hadood Ordinances prescribe traditional Islamic punishments for theft, adultery and consumption of alcohol; penalties include flogging, stoning and amputation. There are occasional floggings, but because of the strict Islamic rules of evidence and the reluctance of officials to carry penalties out, no stonings or amputations have been reported, except in tribal areas.

Under martial law, summary military courts customarily did not grant defendants the right to counsel and could dispose of cases in minutes. Although special military courts did not prohibit defense counsel, judges could impose secrecy on the proceedings and expel witnesses and defendants accused of acting in a "subversive" or "dilatory" manner. Normally at least two of the three judges of a special military court were military men with little training in law or familiarity with legal procedures and safeguards. Military court sentences could be appealed only to the deputy martial law administrators (i.e., the provincial governors) if the sentence was for less than 14 years' imprisonment, or to the chief martial law administrator if the sentence was either death or more than 14 years' imprisonment.

The corrections systems is headed by the inspector-general of prisons. Pakistani jails have low standards, and prison reform was one of the priorities of the Zulfikar Ali Bhutto administration.

LAW ENFORCEMENT

Except in federally administered areas and tribal territories, law enforcement is under provincial jurisdiction. But the police function as a common system in actual operation, and law enforcement policies are decided at the national level. Two national-level police agencies are the Special Police Establishment and the Federal Security Force. The former investigates corruption, black-marketeering, and misappropriation by public officials. There also is a paramilitary police known as the Frontier Corps, with headquarters at Peshawar. Its principal function is to keep peace in tribal areas and to combat smuggling. Provincial police are headed in each province by an inspector-general. The organizational structure corresponds to the administrative divisions of local government. At the precinct level are the *thanas* or station houses. Assisting the police in rural areas are part-time village constables called *chowkidars* or *dafadars*. Each province also has a Special Armed Police to deal with emergencies. At all levels the police officials are answerable to civil administrators. The abrupt increase in civil and political disturbances, riots and disorders is reflected in the rise in police expenditures from Rs171 million in 1970 to Rs349 million in 1974.

The Penal Code of Pakistan is the most important penal statute, and this has been supplemented over the years by a number of statutes directed against subversion, smuggling, espionage, corruption, public disturbances, publication of undesirable materials and violation of official secrecy.

The agency in charge of intelligence and internal espionage is the Intelligence Bureau.

HEALTH

Over half of the country's medical graduates emigrate to foreign countries, especially the United States, each year.

The major health problems are malaria, tuberculosis, intestinal diseases, venereal diseases and skin diseases.

Besides the Western system of medicine, both the Unani, the Arab or Muslim system, and the Ayurvedic, or Hindu system are officially recognized and their practitioners are licensed.

FOOD & NUTRITION

Chappatty, made from wheat flour, is the staple diet and lamb the main source of meat. The most popular

HEALTH INDICATORS

Health personnel 1988
- Physicians: 55,238
  - persons per: 2,081
- Dentists: 1,734
- Nurses: 17,731
- Pharmacists: 2,785 (1986)
- Midwives: 10,650 (1987)

Hospitals 1982
- Number: 895
- Number of beds (/10,000): 6

Type of hospital (%) 1982
- Government: 82.2
- Private nonprofit: 1.1
- Private profit: 16.7

Public health expenditures (latest)
- As % of national budget: 0.9
- Per capita (U.S. $): 0.60

Vital statistics
- Crude death rate (/1,000): 14 (1990)
- Life expectancy at birth 1990
  - Males: 56
  - Females: 57
- Infant mortality rate (/1,000 live births): 110 (1990)
- Child mortality rate under 5 yrs. (/1,000 births) (1985–90): 165
- Maternal mortality rate (/100,000 live births) (1980–84 est.): 600
- Population with access to safe water (%): 44 (latest)

dish is pilau, made from rice mixed with meat and vegetables. Per capita daily food intake is 2,300 calories (which falls below the minimum 2,600 calories recommended by the World Health Organization).

MEDIA & CULTURE

In 1988, there were 177 daily newspapers, 368 weeklies and biweeklies published in Pakistan. The dailies have an aggregate circulation of 1.689 million. Of the daily newspapers, 70 are published in Urdu and 22 in English. Karachi has 20 dailies and Lahore 17. Although the English language press reaches only 2% of the population, it is influential in political, academic and professional circles. A number of newspapers are controlled by or have close ties with political parties. The largest dailies are *Jang* (507,000), *Mashriq* (160,000), *Nawa-i-Waqt* (250,000), *Dawn* (70,000) and *Pakistan Times* (50,000). The periodicals press consisted of 282 titles in 1988.

The Constitution of 1973 ended censorship and provided guarantees for freedom of the press. But relations between the press and Zia were strained. Government reprisals against what it considered irresponsible journalism included closure of four opposition newspapers.

After the 1985 elections there was increasingly free discussion of government policies and criticisms of the government in the privately owned press. During the spring 1985 election campaign the press was barred from reporting any statements advocating a boycott of the polls. In addition to providing relatively unfettered reporting of statements made by the newly elected legislators, the press also extensively covered hostile remarks by the leadership of the extraparliamentary opposition.

MEDIA INDICATORS

Newspapers (latest)
- Number of dailies: 177
- Circulation (millions): 1.689
- Per 1,000 pop.: 12
- Number of nondailies: 264 (1988)
- Circulation (millions): 4.138 (1988)
- Per 1,000 pop.: 36 (1988)
- Number of periodicals: 282 (1988)
- Circulation (000): 7,674 (1988)
- Newsprint consumption 1988
  - Total metric tons: 43,600
  - Per 1,000 pop. (kg.): 382

Book publishing
- Number of titles: 1,600 (pre-1986)

Radio 1989
- Number of transmitters: 97
- Number of persons per radio receiver: 74
- Total program hours (/yr.): 116,098 (1987)

Television 1989
- Television transmitters: 28
- Number of persons per T.V. receiver: 74
- Total program hours (/yr.): 16,841 (1987)

Cinema (latest)
- Number of fixed cinemas: 444
- Seating capacity (000): 194
  - Seats (/1,000 pop.): 1.8 (1987)
- Annual attendance (millions): 25.3

Films
- Number of long films produced: 57 (latest)
- Number of long films imported: 50 (1987)
  - % from United States: 36.0
  - % from Hong Kong: 36.0
  - % from United Kingdom: 8.0
  - % from Japan: 6.0

The Associated Press of Pakistan is the official news agency. It has been government-controlled since 1961. It has seven regional but no foreign bureaus. Pakistan Press International and United Press of Pakistan are independent news agencies. Foreign news agencies like Agence France-Presse, Deutsche Presse-Agenterr, Xinhua and Tass also maintain offices in some large cities.

The National Book Foundation was established in 1974 to publish cheap reprints of foreign textbooks. To facilitate its work, the copyright ordinance of 1962 was amended. In addition to the Foundation, there are over 300 private publishers in Pakistan. Pakistan adheres to the Berne, Universal, Florence and Buenos Aires Copyright conventions. Many Pakistani publishers are taking advantage of the Stockholm Agreement (which legalized the reprinting of educational and related works by local publishers in developing countries even without the permission of the copyrightholders if such permission is refused or if the publishers ask for unreasonable royalties) to reprint expensive textbooks as well as other types of books not covered by the agreement. This activity has in recent years become a lucrative industry not very different from open piracy.

Radio broadcasting is a state monopoly. The Pakistan Broadcasting Corporation (PBC), set up in 1973, replaced the former Radio Pakistan. The PBC has seven stations, at Karachi, Islamabad/Rawalpindi, Lahore, Multan, Peshawar, Hyderabad and Quetta. It broadcasts domestic service programs for over 800 hours a week in addition to school broadcasts. External service under the call sign Radio Pakistan broadcasts 80 hours a week. Commercials were introduced in 1961.

Television was introduced in the country in 1964. The Pakistan Television Corporation, a public company in which the government is the majority shareholder, now operates five stations, at Rawalpindi/Islamabad, Karachi, Lahore, Quetta and Peshawar, broadcasting for 105 hours a week, of which 19 hours of programming are imported. A ground satellite station was completed in 1972. Television is financed by advertising revenues and receiver licenses of Rs50 a year.

CULTURAL & ENVIRONMENTAL INDICATORS

Libraries
- Number: 98
- Volumes (millions): 1.340
- Loans (/1,000 pop.): 6

Museums
- Annual attendance (millions): 2.052
- Attendance (/1,000 pop.): 21

Performing arts
- Number of performances: 18
- Annual attendance (000): 169
- Attendance (/1,000 pop.): 2

Nature reserves
- Number of facilities: 57

The National Library at Islamabad and the Liaquat Library in Karachi are the depository libraries under the copyright act. The largest libraries are the Punjab University Library (265,000 volumes), the University of Karachi Library (200,000 volumes) and the Punjab Public Library (200,000 volumes).

SOCIAL WELFARE

Social welfare services operate mainly through the Development Schemes and Urban Community Projects. The National Council of Social Welfare provides care for children, women, delinquents and handicapped people. The state-sponsored Social Security program under the Ministry of Social Welfare provides unemployment, health and funeral benefits to covered workers. Also, over 4,000 private volunteer agencies provide a wide range of welfare services.

GLOSSARY

chaudhary: the village landlord, serving as leader and arbiter of a rural community.

chowkidar: a semiofficial, part-time village constable; also, *dafadar.*

hakim: practitioner of *unani,* the Arab Muslim system of medicine.

jagirdar: holder of a *jagir* or estate granted by the state as reward for service.

jirga: council of *maliks* or elders of a tribe in NWFP.

lashkar: war party of *Pushtu* tribes conducting plundering raids.

maktab: Muslim primary school.

maulana: Muslim scholar learned in law and theology.

maulvi: itinerant preacher, learned in the Muslim scriptures.

mohalla: urban quarters assigned to an ethnic or occupational group.

mujahir: Urdu-speaking refugee from India and Bangladesh after the Indo-Pakistani War of 1971.

pir: a Sufi spiritual guide with large numbers of disciples and followers.

political agent: administrator of a tribal agency.

ryotwari: system of land tenure in Sind in which tenants enjoy permanent tenancy rights over state lands.

taccavi: emergency loans extended to farmers during periods of drought or flood.

taluka: a revenue or tax unit of local administration.

tehsil: subdivision of a district.

zamindari: system of land tenure in which large estates owned by individual landlords form the basic revenue units.

CHRONOLOGY (from 1947)

1947— Pakistan is established as an independent dominion consisting of the former provinces of Sind and NWFP, Baluchistan and parts of Punjab and Bengal; Muhammad Ali Jinnah becomes governor-general; Karachi is made the capital; Pakistan joins United Nations; Liaquat Ali Khan becomes prime minister.

1948— Jinnah dies and is succeeded as governor-general by Khwajah Nazimuddin. . . . Dispute with India breaks out over Kashmir.

1951— Military coup attempt by Gen. Muhammad Akbar Khan fails. . . . Liaquat Ali Khan is slain. . . . Khwajah Nazimuddin becomes prime minister and Ghulam Muhammad governor-general.

1953— Anti-Ahmadiya riots occur in Punjab and Sind. . . . Muhammad Ali Bogra becomes the new prime minister, replacing Nazimuddin.

1954— Chief Minister Khan Sahib is assassinated.

1955— Ghulam Muhammad dismisses the Majlis-i-Shura; second Majlis-i-Shura meets; Ghulam Muhammad leaves office. . . . Dominion status is ended. . . . Iskander Mirza becomes new governor-general. . . . Rupee is devalued.

1956— Sind, Punjab, Baluchistan and NWFP merge to form West Pakistan unit. . . . Husain Shahid Suhrawardy becomes prime minister. . . . Constitution is adopted; Pakistan is proclaimed an Islamic republic, with Mirza as first president; it remains in the Commonwealth.

1957— Ismail Ibrahim Chundrigar succeeds Suhrawardy as prime minister.

1958— Malik Firuz Khan Noon is elected prime minister. . . . The Majlis-i-Shura is dissolved and the cabinet is ousted in a military coup; Mirza heads the government briefly but later yields to Muhammad Ayub Khan as president.

1959— Military government decides to shift national capital from Karachi to Rawalpindi. . . . Basic democracies or tiered system of popular representation is introduced.
1960— Canal Waters Treaty is concluded with India.
1961— Ties with Afghanistan are cut over Afghan support for Pushtun separatist movement.
1962— Martial law is ended; new Constitution is adopted.
1963— Zulfikar Ali Bhutto becomes foreign minister and initiates new Rawalpindi-Beijing axis.
1964— Television is introduced.
1965— Muhammad Ayub Khan is elected president, defeating Fatima Jinnah.
1966— War with India ends without a clear victory for either nation; Tashkent peace accord ends the war.
1967— Metric system is introduced.
1968— Border agreement with India over disputed areas in the Rann of Kutch is concluded.
1969— Muhammad Ayub Khan steps down as president and hands power over to Agha Muhammad Yahya Khan.
1970— In national direct elections the Awami League of East Pakistan, led by Mujibur Rahman, wins a clear majority. . . . West Pakistan is redivided into four provinces. . . . Islamabad becomes the nation's new capital.
1971— In a disastrous effort to stem the tide of separatism in East Pakistan, the army jails Mujibur Rahman and unleashes a reign of terror; Indian intervention in East Pakistan leads to war; the Pakistani army in East Pakistan is overwhelmed and forced to surrender; East Pakistan proclaims itself the independent state of Bangladesh; Yahya Khan steps down in disgrace; Zulfikar Ali Bhutto forms a new government as president; Pakistan leaves the Commonwealth; Yahya Khan is jailed.
1972— Bhutto attends a summit meeting with Indira Gandhi at Simla. More than 90,000 prisoners of the 1971 war are returned under an accord reached by the two leaders. . . . Land and educational reforms are announced.
1973— New Constitution, Pakistan's second, is ratified by the National Assembly, establishing a federal republic with a largely ceremonial president, and with a strong prime minister as chief executive. . . . Zulfikar Ali Bhutto assumes offices as prime minister.
1974— Banks and heavy industries are nationalized. . . . Trade and communications links with India are resumed. Pakistan recognizes Bangladesh.
1977— In first elections under new Constitution, Bhutto's Pakistan People's Party wins a landslide victory; widespread disturbances occur in Baluchistan and the NWFP; martial law is imposed in three cities; Bhutto forms a new cabinet. . . . Bhutto is overthrown in a coup led by army commander in chief Muhammad Zia ul-Haq; new martial law is proclaimed. . . . Bhutto is arrested on murder charges; chief justice orders hearing on Bhutto arrest but is himself dismissed.
1978— Zia announces creation of an advisory council. . . . Opposition papers belonging to Bhutto's party are suspended. Lahore High Court sentences Zulfikar Ali Bhutto to death for conspiracy to murder a political opponent.
1979— Bhutto is executed despite appeals for clemency from many nations; Pakistan National Alliance (PNA) quits the government; U.S. embassy in Islamabad is stormed and burned by angry mobs heeding the call of Ayatollah Khomeini; Zia turns down U.S. offer of $200 million in military credits.
1980— Local elections are held, but national elections are postponed indefinitely; the government announces plans to Islamize the economy by abolishing interest, limited liability and incorporation.
1984— Khunjerab Pass on the Karakorum Highway is opened. . . . First U.S. F-16 fighters are delivered to Pakistan.
1985— In a cautious return to democracy, Zia relinquishes some authority to a civilian prime minister, Muhammad Khan Junejo, leader of the Muslim League.
1988— President Zia is killed in a plane explosion in August. After elections in November, Benazir Bhutto, daughter of Zulfikar Ali Bhutto, is named prime minister, the first female leader of a modern Muslim country. Ishaq Khan becomes president.
1990— Prime Minister Benazir Bhutto is dismissed August 6 by President Isaq Khan; Ghulam Mustafa Jatoi is named to head an interim government pending national elections scheduled for October 24, 1990. Nawaz Sharif is elected prime minister.
1991— Pakistan contributes 10,000 troops to the international coalition against Iraq in the Persian Gulf War. Opinion polls show an overwhelming support for Saddam Hussein. Prime Minister Nawaz Sharif submits to parliament legislation to adopt Islamic law in place of the current secular code.

BIBLIOGRAPHY

BOOKS & FILMS

Adams, John, and Sabiha Igbal. *Exports, Politics and Economic Development: Pakistan.* Boulder, CO, 1983.
Ahmed, Manzooruddin. *Contemporary Pakistan: Politics, Economics, Society.* Durham, NC, 1980.
Ahmed, Viqar, and Rashid Amjad. *The Management of Pakistan's Economy.* New York, 1985.
Ali, Tariq. *Can Pakistan Survive? The Death of a State.* New York, 1984.
Altaf, Zafar. *Pakistani Entrepreneurs: Their Development, Characteristics and Abilities.* London, 1983.
Amjad, Rashid. *Private Industrial Investment in Pakistan.* New York, 1983.
Bahadur, Kalim. *The Jammat-e-Islami of Pakistan: Political Thoughts and Political Action.* Columbia, MO, 1977.
Baxter, Craig. *Zia's Pakistan: Politics and Stability in a Frontline State.* Boulder, CO, 1985.
Bhatia, B. M. *Pakistan's Economic Development.* New York, 1979.

Breecher, Irving, and S. A. Abbas. *Foreign Aid and Industrial Aid in Pakistan.* New York, 1971.
Brown, W. Norman. *United States and India, Pakistan, Bangladesh.* Cambridge, MA, 1972.
Burani, D. H. *The Future of Pakistan.* Columbia, MO, 1985.
Burke, S. M. *Pakistan's Foreign Policy.* New York, 1973.
Burki, Shahid J., and Robert LaPorte, Jr. *Pakistan's Development Priorities: Choice for the Future.* New York, 1984.
Chaudhry, G. W. *The Last Days of United Pakistan.* Nedlands, Australia, 1975.
———. *Pakistan and the Great Powers.* Karachi, 1970.
Chopra, Pran. *Contemporary Pakistan: New Aims and Images.* New Delhi, 1983.
Cohen, Stephen P. *The Pakistan Army.* Berkeley, CA, 1984.
Duncan, Emma. *Breaking the Curfew: A Political Journey Through Pakistan.* New York, 1989.
Falcon, Walter P., and Gustav F. Papanek. *Development Policy: The Pakistan Experience.* Cambridge, MA, 1971.
Feldman, Herbert, *The End and the Beginning: Pakistan 1969–76.* New York, 1976.
———. *From Crisis to Crisis: Pakistan 1962–69.* New York, 1972.
Gardezi, Hassan, and Jamil Rashid. *The Roots of Dictatorship: The Political Economy of a Praetorian State.* London, 1983.
Gopinath. *Pakistan in Transition.* Columbia, MO, 1975.
Griffin, K., and A. R. Khan. *Growth and Inequality in Pakistan.* New York, 1972.
Hayes, Louis D. *Politics in Pakistan: The Struggle for Legitimacy.* Boulder, CO, 1984.
Hodson, H. V. *Pakistan.* London, 1984.
Hussain, Asah. *Elite Politics in an Ideological State: The Case of Pakistan.* Hamden, CT, 1979.
India and Pakistan: Lands and Peoples. Color film, 13 min. Coronet.
Indus Waters. Color film, 27 min. Interfilm.
Islam, Nurul. *Foreign Trade and Economic Controls in Development: The Case of United Pakistan.* New Haven, CT, 1981.
Jalal, Ayesha. *The Sole Spokesman: Jinnah, the Muslim League and the Demand for Pakistan.* New York, 1985.
Johan, Rounaq. *Pakistan: Failure in National Integration.* New York, 1972.
Johnson, B. L. *Pakistan.* London, 1980.
Keesing's Publications. *Pakistan: From 1947 to the Creation of Bangladesh.* New York, 1973.
Khan, Fazal M. *Pakistan's Crisis in Leadership.* Columbia, MO, 1973.
Khan, Muhammad A. *Generals in Politics: Pakistan, 1958–82.* New York, 1983.
Kochanek, Stanley A. *Interest Groups and Development: Business and Politics in Pakistan.* New York, 1983.
Kumar, Satish. *The New Pakistan.* Totowa, NJ, 1978.
Land Divided: India and Pakistan at War. B&W film, 15 min. Producer: N.A.
LaPorte, Robert. *Power and Privilege, Influence and Decisionmaking in Pakistan.* Berkeley, CA, 1976.
Maniruzzaman, Talukdar. *Group Interests and Political Changes: Studies of Pakistan and Bangladesh.* Columbia, MO, 1982.
Meenai, S. A. *Money and Banking in Pakistan.* New York, 1984.
Muttam, John. *United States, Pakistan and India: Role of United States in Indo-Pakistani Arms Race.* Columbia, MO, 1974.
Nagarkar. *Genesis of Pakistan.* Columbia, MO, 1975.
Nayak, P. *Pakistan Society and Politics.* Columbia, MO, 1985.
———. *Pakistan, Political Economy of a Developing State.* New Delhi, 1988.
Nazim. *Babus, Brahmans and Bureaucrats: A Critique of the Administrative System in Pakistan.* Columbia, MO, 1973.
Pakistan. Color film, 12 min. Encyclopaedia Britannica.
Pakistan Historical Society. *A History of the Freedom Movement,* 2 vol. New Delhi, 1984.
Pakistan—Its Land and People. Color film, 17 min. Edward Levonian.
Progress Report on Pakistan. B&W film, 28 min. Contemporary Films.
Promise of Pakistan. B&W film, 17 min. March of Time.
Querishi, S. Aleem. *Pakistan* (World Bibliographical Series). Santa Barbara, CA, 1985.
Rehman, Inamur. *Public Opinion and Political Development in Pakistan.* New York, 1982.
Rizvi, Hasan A. *The Military and Politics in Pakistan.* Columbia, MO, 1974.
Sahni, N. C. *Political Struggle in Pakistan.* Mystic, CT, 1971.
Satyaprakash. *Pakistan: A Bibliography, 1962–74.* Columbia, MO, 1974.
Sayeed, Khalid B. *Politics in Pakistan: The Nature and Direction of Change.* New York, 1980.
Shahid, A. Burki. *Pakistan: A Nation in the Making.* Boulder, CO, 1985.
Shahid, J. B. *Pakistan Under Bhutto.* New York, 1979.
Sharan, Parmatma. *Government of Pakistan.* New York, 1976.
Shukla, S. P. *India and Pakistan: The Origins of Armed Conflict.* New Delhi, 1984.
Siddiqui, Kalim. *Conflict, Crisis and War.* New York, 1972.
Singhal, Damodar P. *Pakistan.* Englewood Cliffs, NJ, 1972.
Sisson, Richard. *War and Secession: Pakistan, India, and the Creation of Bangladesh.* Berkeley, Calif, 1990.
Stanford, Richard A. *Rural Development in Pakistan.* Durham, NC, 1980.
Stern, Joseph, and Walter Falcon. *Growth and Development in Pakistan, 1959–69.* Lanham, MD, 1984.
Stevens, Robert D. *Rural Development in Bangladesh and Pakistan.* Honolulu, HI, 1976.

Syed, Anwar H. *Pakistan: Islam, Politics and National Solidarity.* New York, 1982.

Venkataramani, M. S. *The American Role in Pakistan.* Atlantic Highlands, NJ, 1982.

Verghese, George. *End to Confrontation: Bhutto's Pakistan.* Mystic, CT, 1972.

Wheeler, Richard S. *The Politics of Pakistan: A Constitutional Quest.* Ithaca, NY, 1970.

Wriggins, Howard. *Pakistan in Transition.* Columbia, MO, 1976.

Ziring, Lawrence. *The Ayub Era.* Syracuse, NY, 1971.

———. *Pakistan: The Enigma of Political Development* Boulder, CO, 1980.

———, Ralph Braibanti and W. Howard Wriggins. *Pakistan: The Long View.* Durham, NC, 1977.

OFFICIAL PUBLICATIONS

Finance, Planning and Provincial Ministry. *Annual Budget Statement of the Government of Pakistan.*

———. *Budget-Demand for Grants and Appropriations.*

———. *Economic Analysis of the Budgets.*

———. *Estimates of Foreign Assistance.*

———. *Explanatory Memorandum on the Budget of the Government of Pakistan.*

Pakistan Auditor General. *Appropriation Accounts.*

———. *Central Civil Accounts* (monthly).

———. *Combined Finance and Revenue Accounts of the Federal and Provincial Governments in Pakistan.*

———. *Finance Accounts.*